HIRO MASHIMA

2

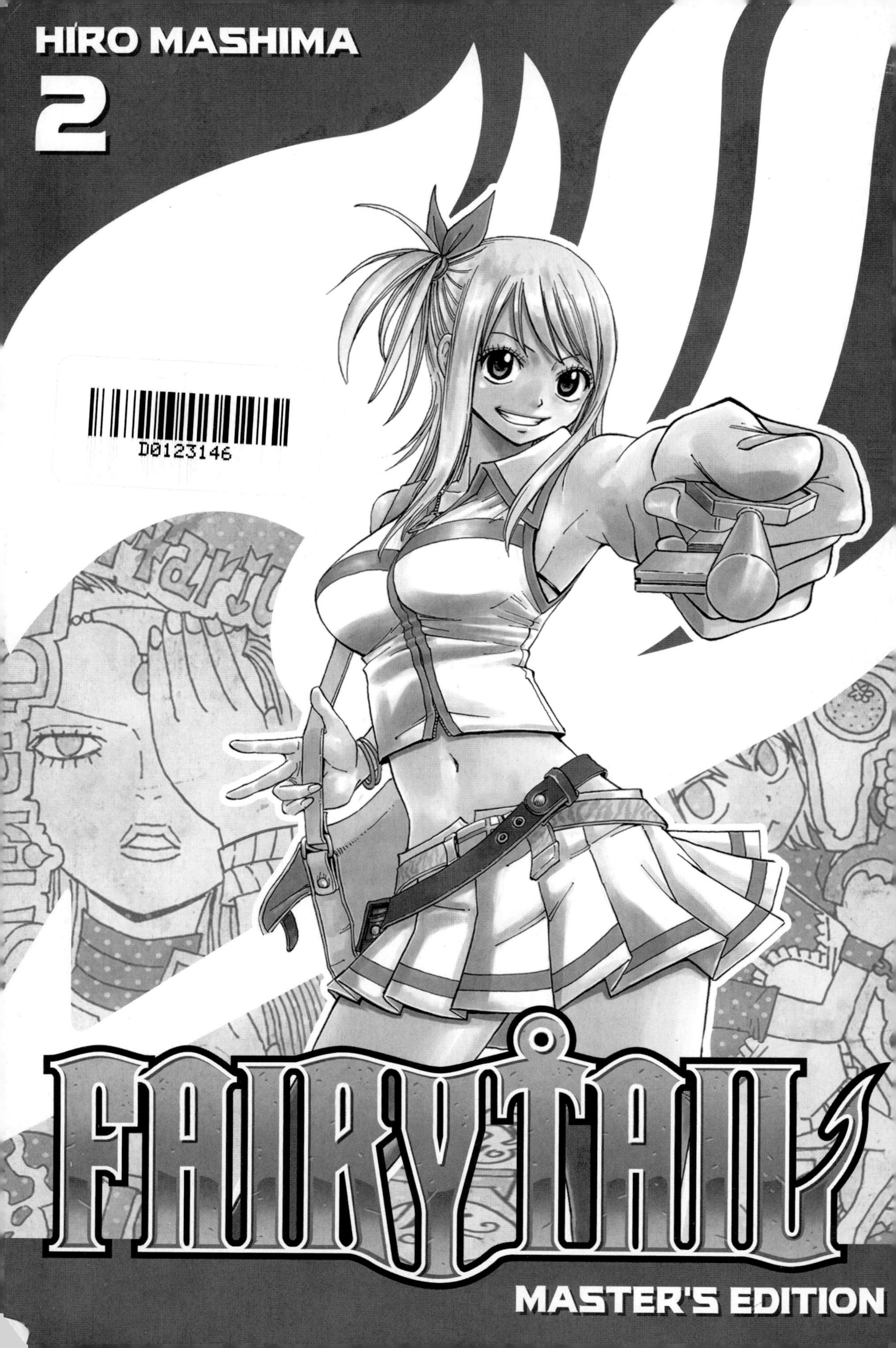

FAIRY TAIL

MASTER'S EDITION

Listen up, guys! This is the table of contents for *Fairy Tail* Master's Edition 2!

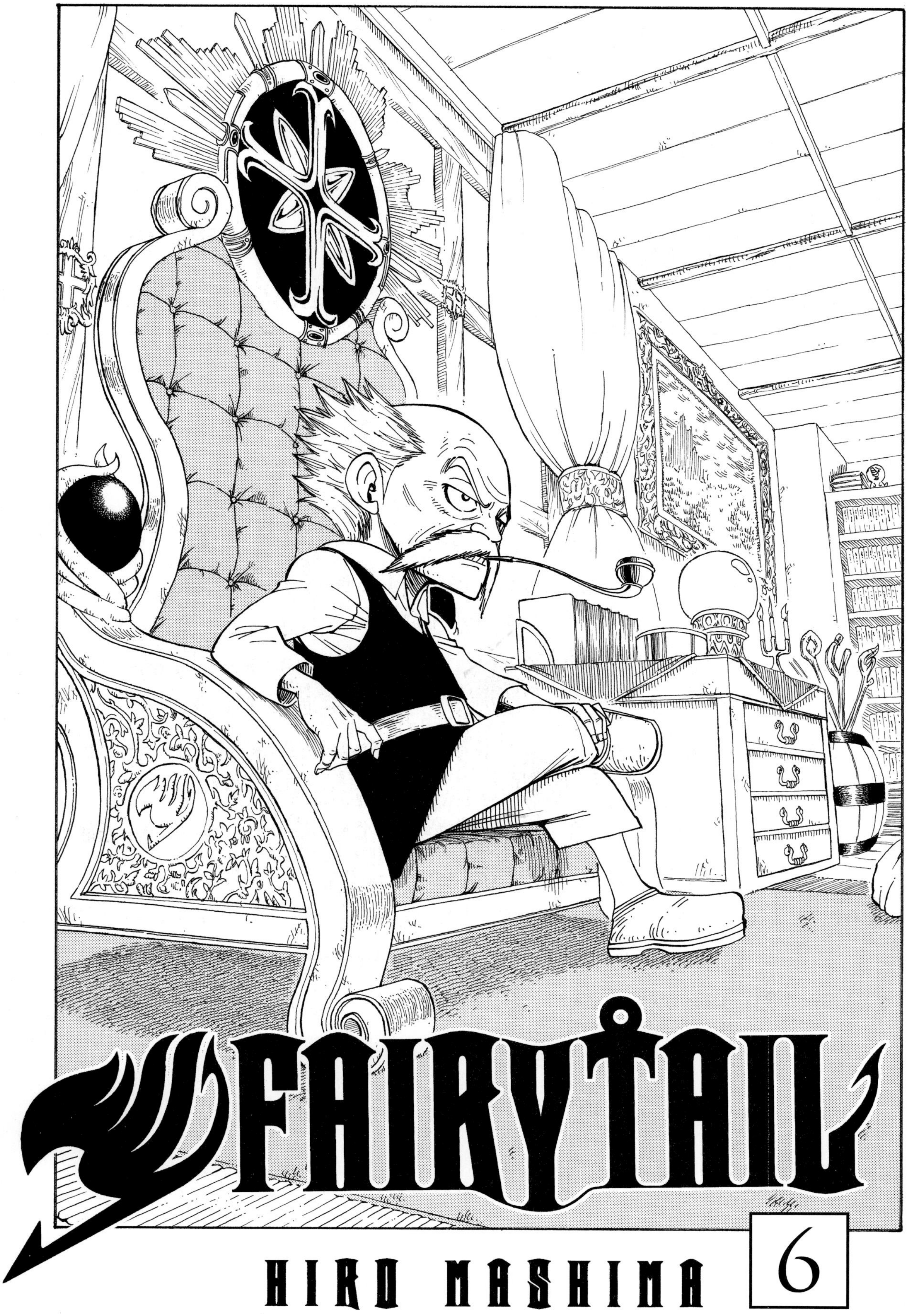

FAIRY TAIL

6

HIRO MASHIMA

Oohh!! I wasn't able to add a
Happy bonus manga this time!
And I really wanted to draw it
too…
You see, bonus pages are only
added when there are extra
unassigned pages in the book.
And since the number of pages
per book is preassigned, I can't
do anything about it.
So the next time I have a lot of
extra pages, I will definitely add
a Happy manga, so please look
forward to it.

—Hiro Mashima

FAIRY TAIL

Chapter 40:
Galuna Island: The Final Battle

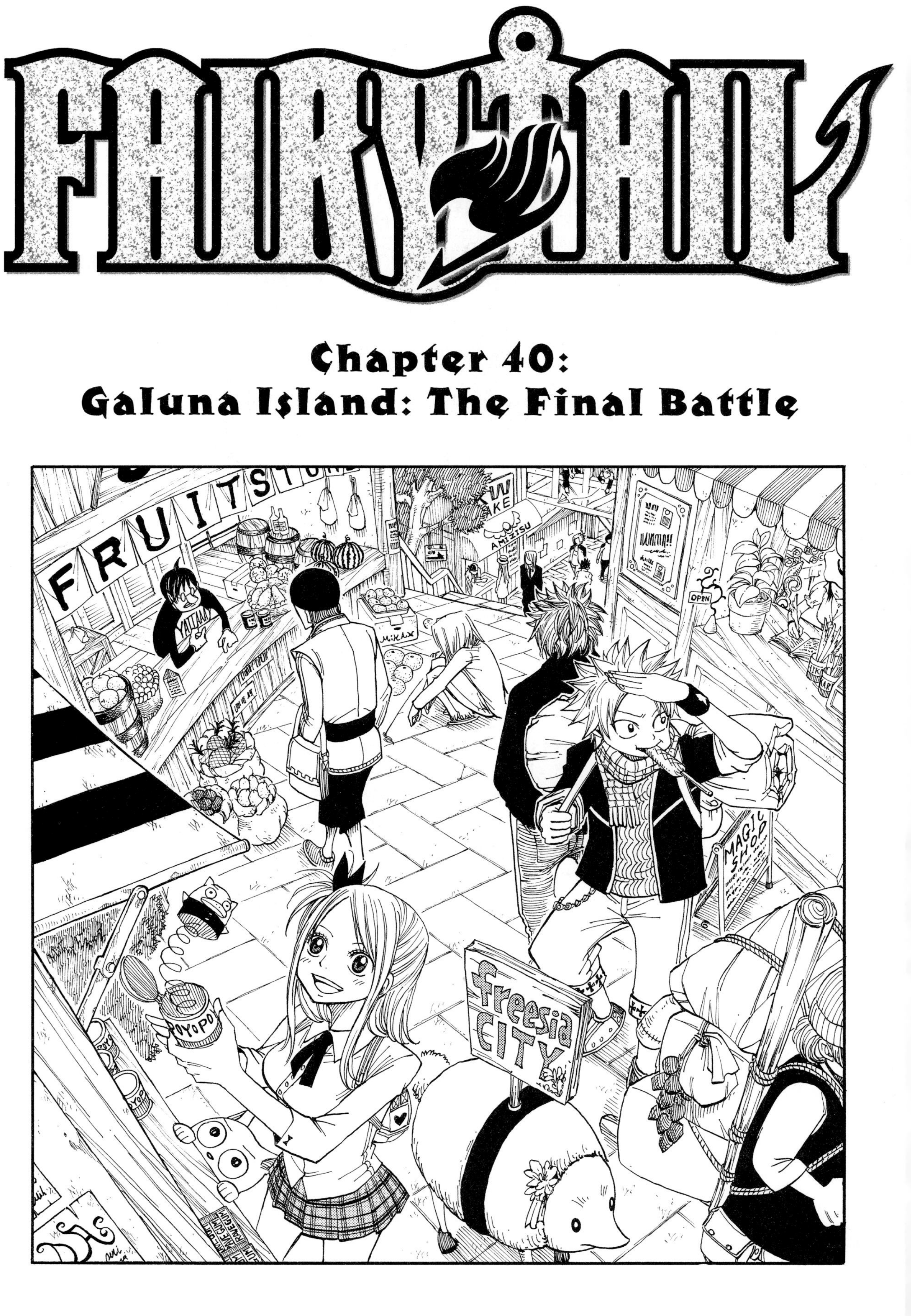
FRUITSTORE
YATTAAA
OPEN
MAGIC SHOP
Freesia CITY
POYOPO

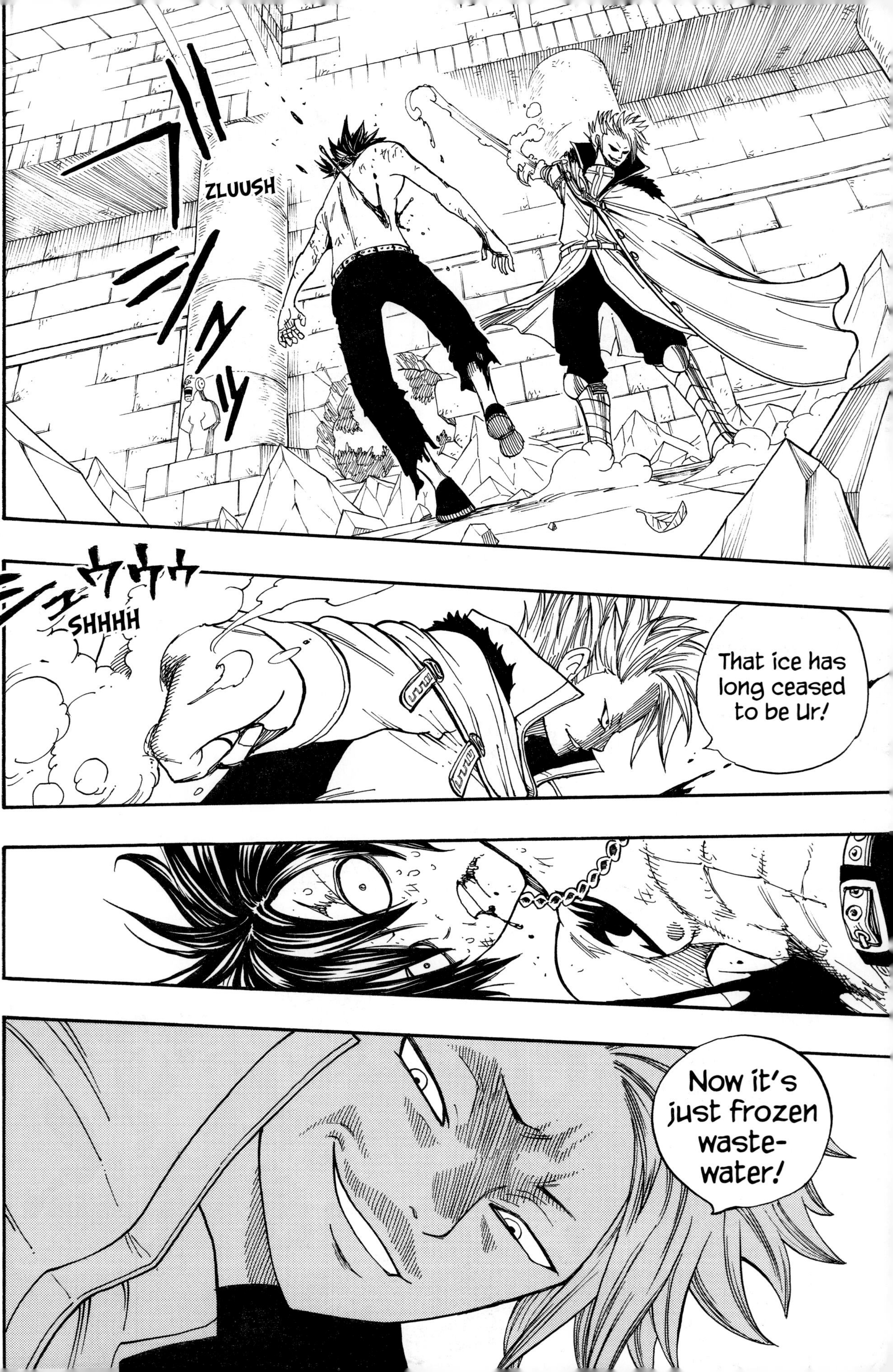
ZLUUSH
シュウウウ
SHHHH
That ice has long ceased to be Ur!
Now it's just frozen waste-water!

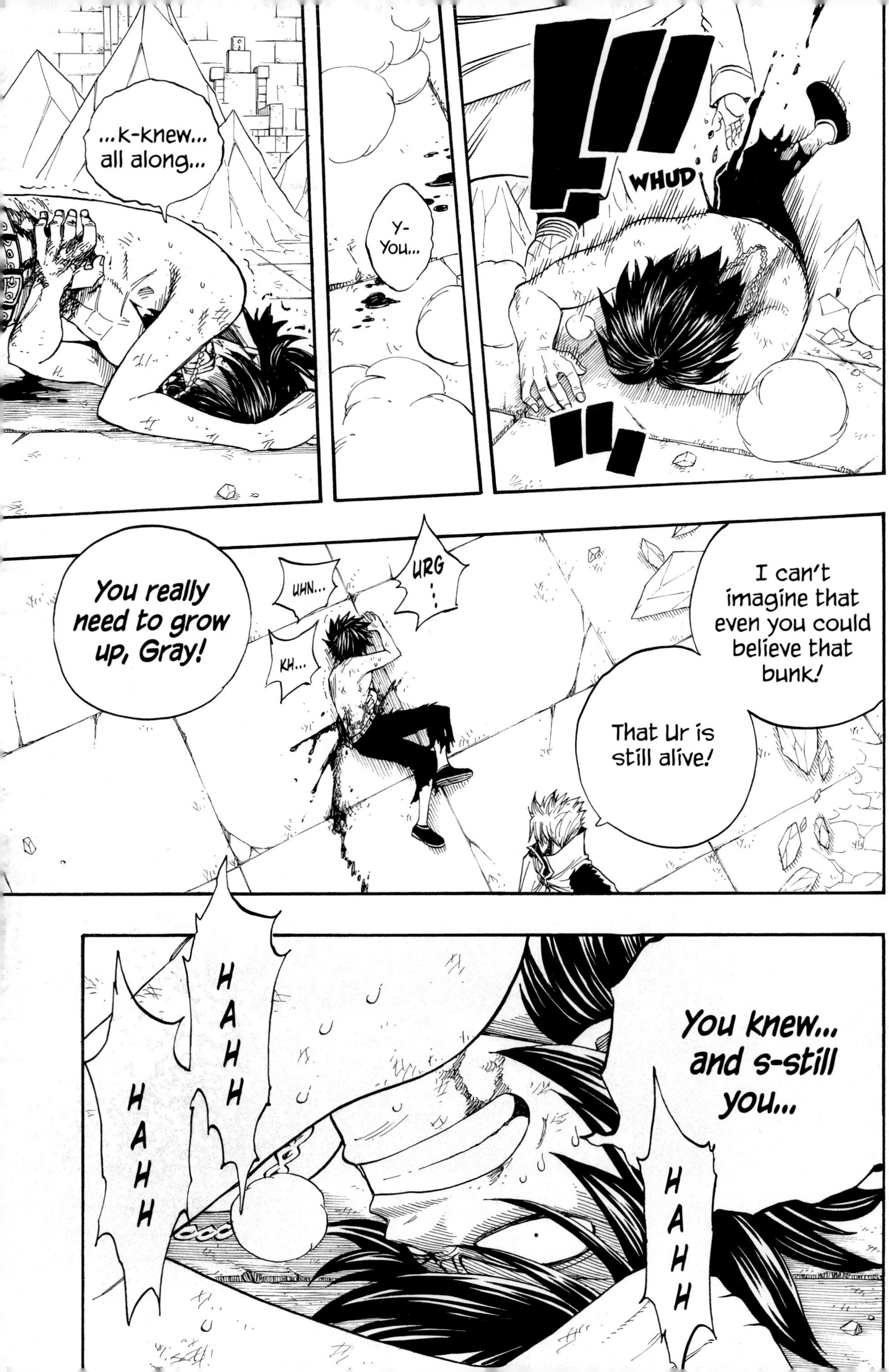
WHUD
Y- You...
...k-knew... all along...
I can't imagine that even you could believe that bunk!
That Ur is still alive!
URG ...
UHN...
KH...
You really need to grow up, Gray!
HAHH
You knew... and s-still you...
HAHH
HAHH

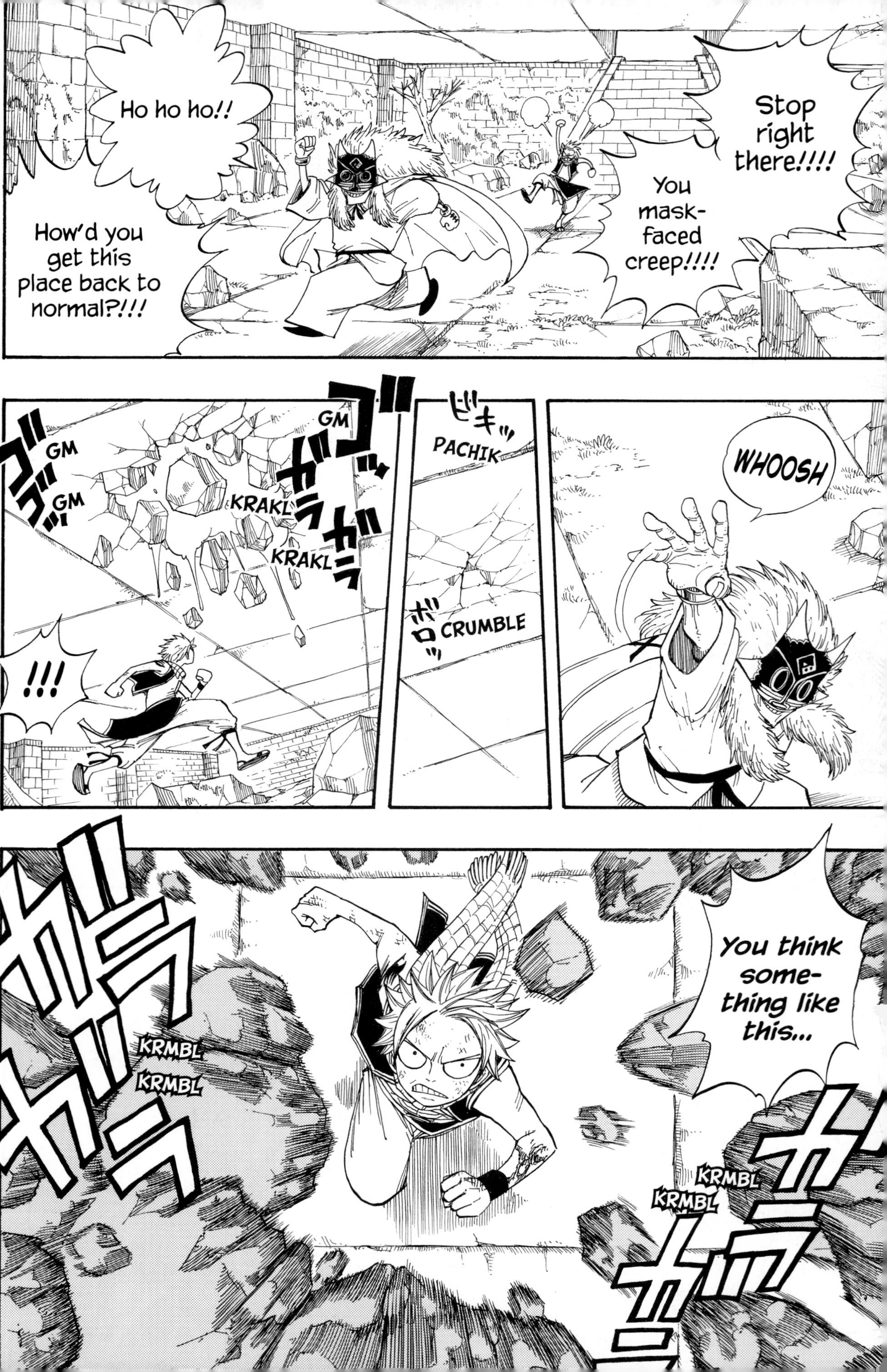
Stop right there!!!!
You mask-faced creep!!!!
Ho ho ho!!
How'd you get this place back to normal?!!!
WHOOSH
ビキッ
PACHIK
ボロッ
CRUMBLE
ゴッ
GM
ゴゴゴ
GM
GM
ガラガラ
KRAKL
KRAKL
!!!
You think some-thing like this...
KRMBL
KRMBL
ガラガラ
KRMBL
KRMBL
ガラガラ

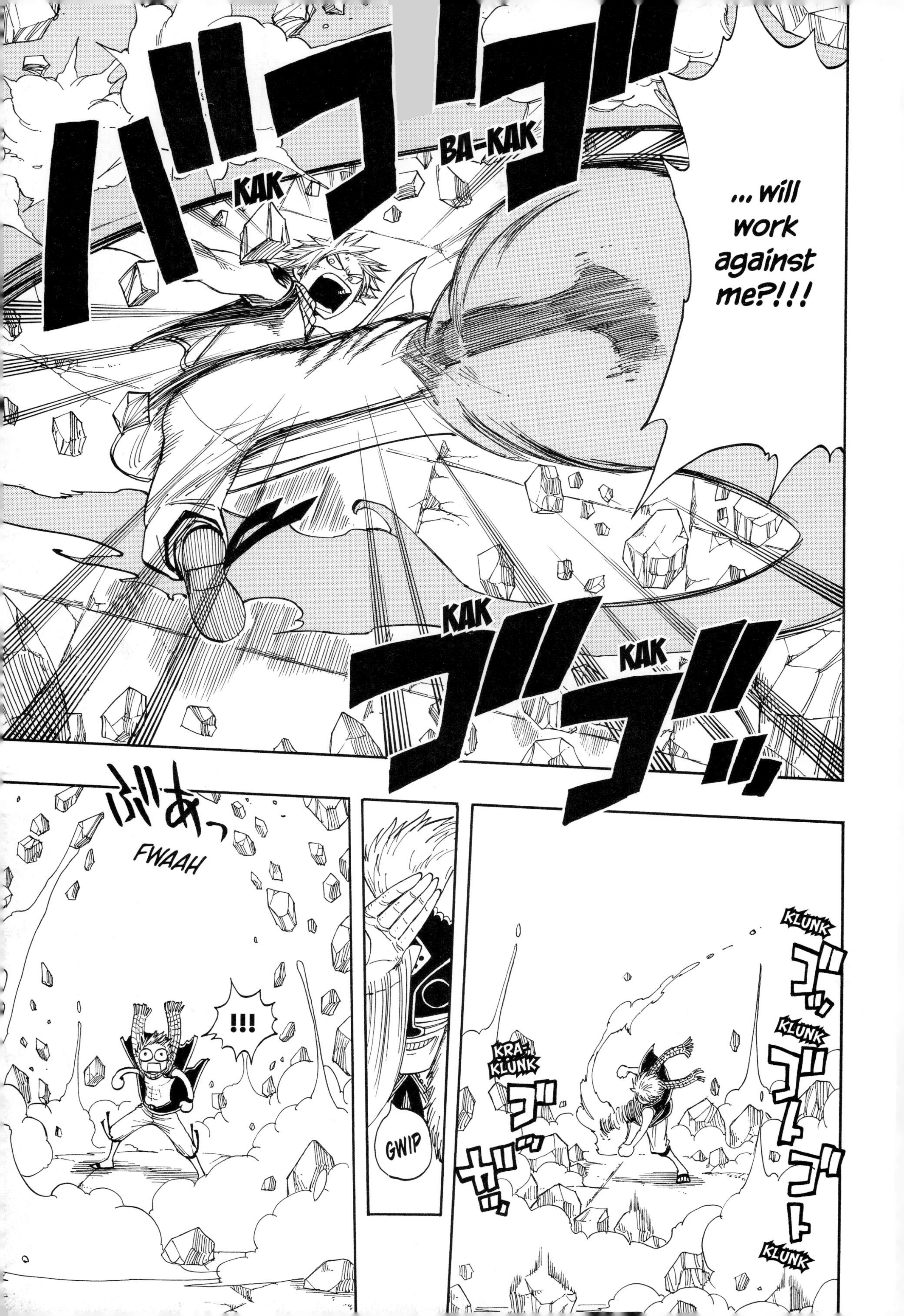
... will work against me?!!!
BA-KAK
KAK
KAK
KAK
KLUNK
KLUNK
KRA-KLUNK
KLUNK
GWIP
ぶあっ
FWAAH
!!!

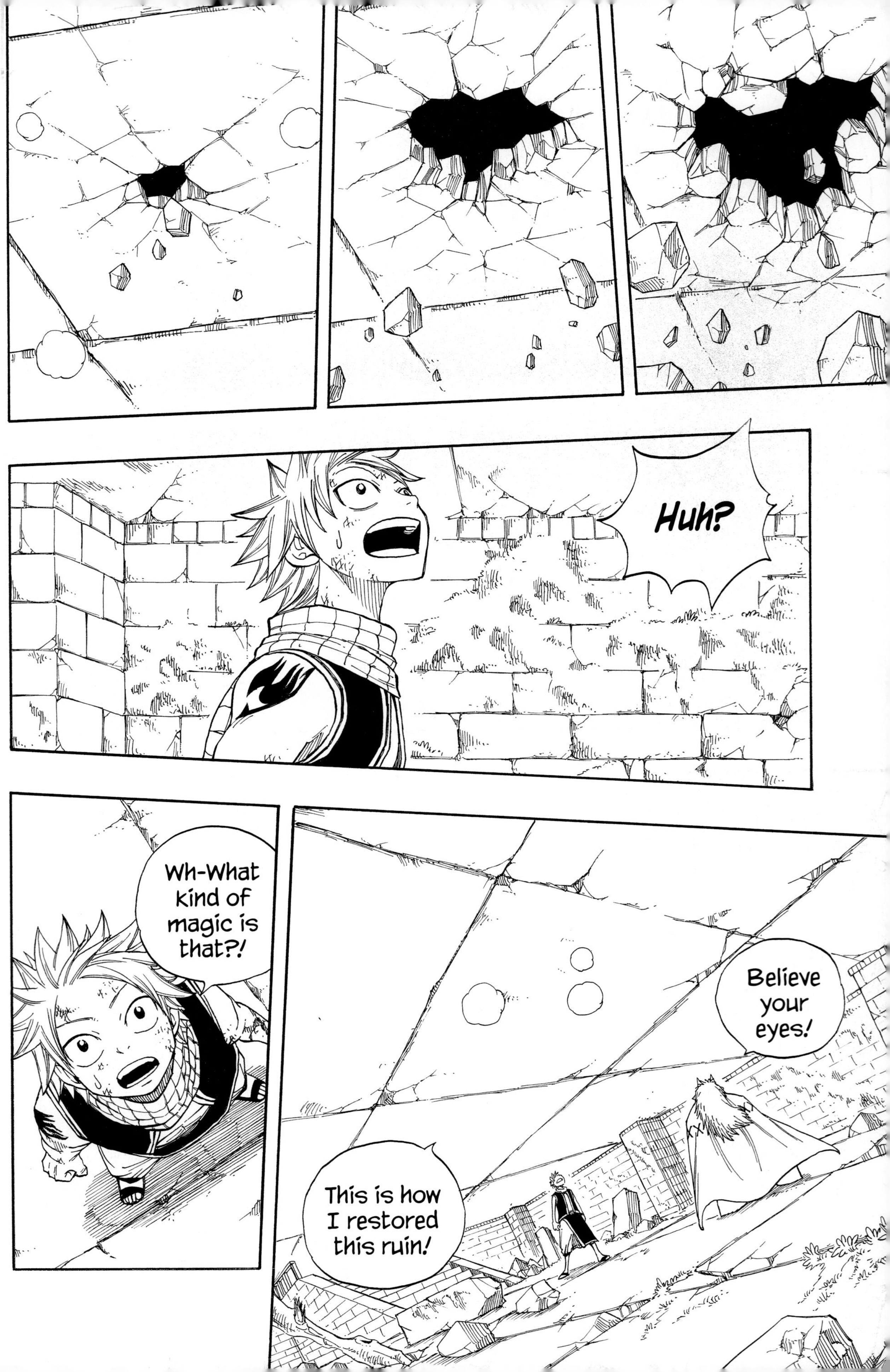
Huh?
Believe your eyes!
This is how I restored this ruin!
Wh-What kind of magic is that?!

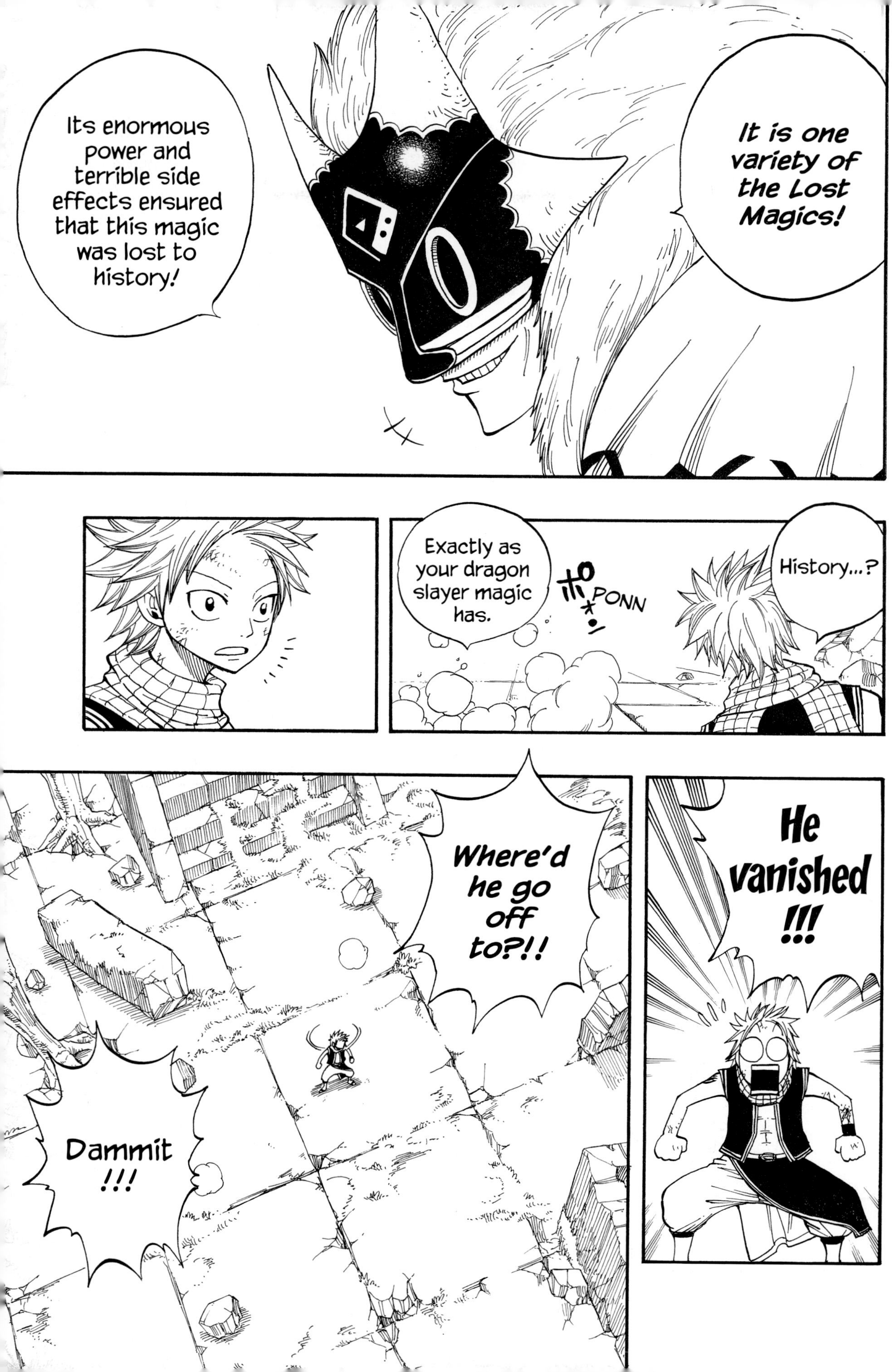
It is one variety of the Lost Magics!
Its enormous power and terrible side effects ensured that this magic was lost to history!
History...?
PONN
Exactly as your dragon slayer magic has.
He vanished!!!
Where'd he go off to?!!
Dammit!!!

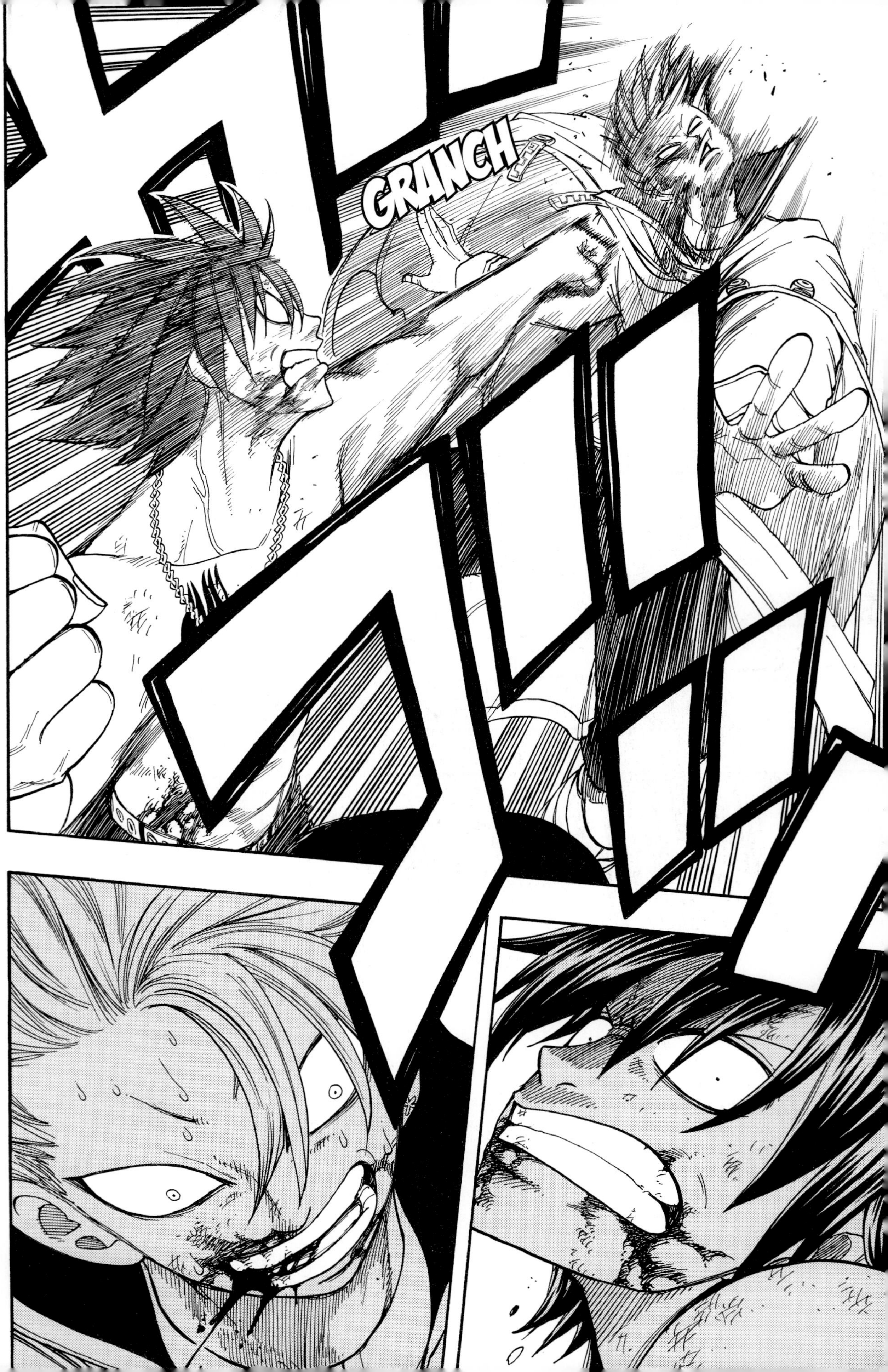
GRANCH

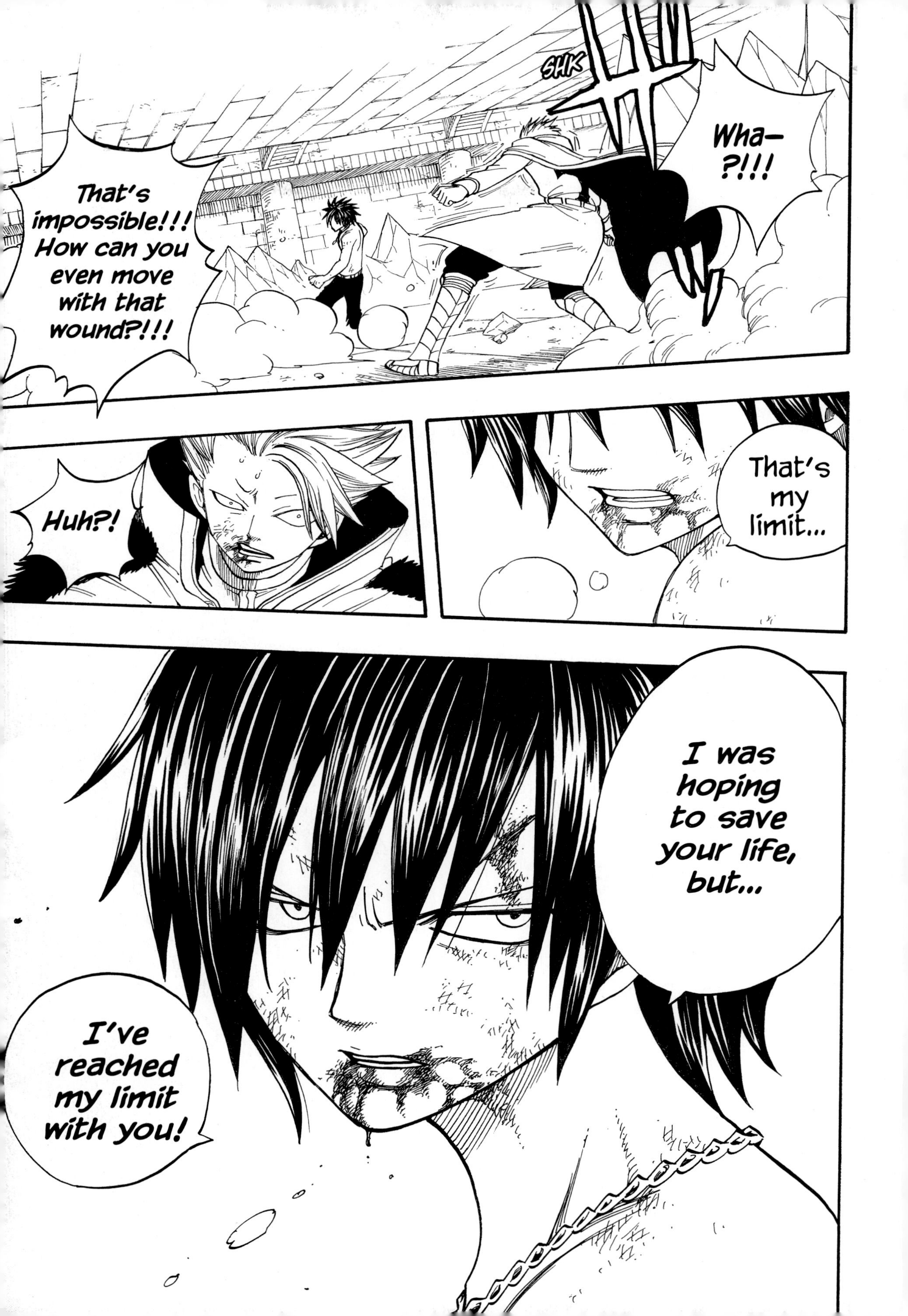
SHK
Wha-?!!!
That's impossible!!! How can you even move with that wound?!!!
That's my limit...
Huh?!
I was hoping to save your life, but...
I've reached my limit with you!

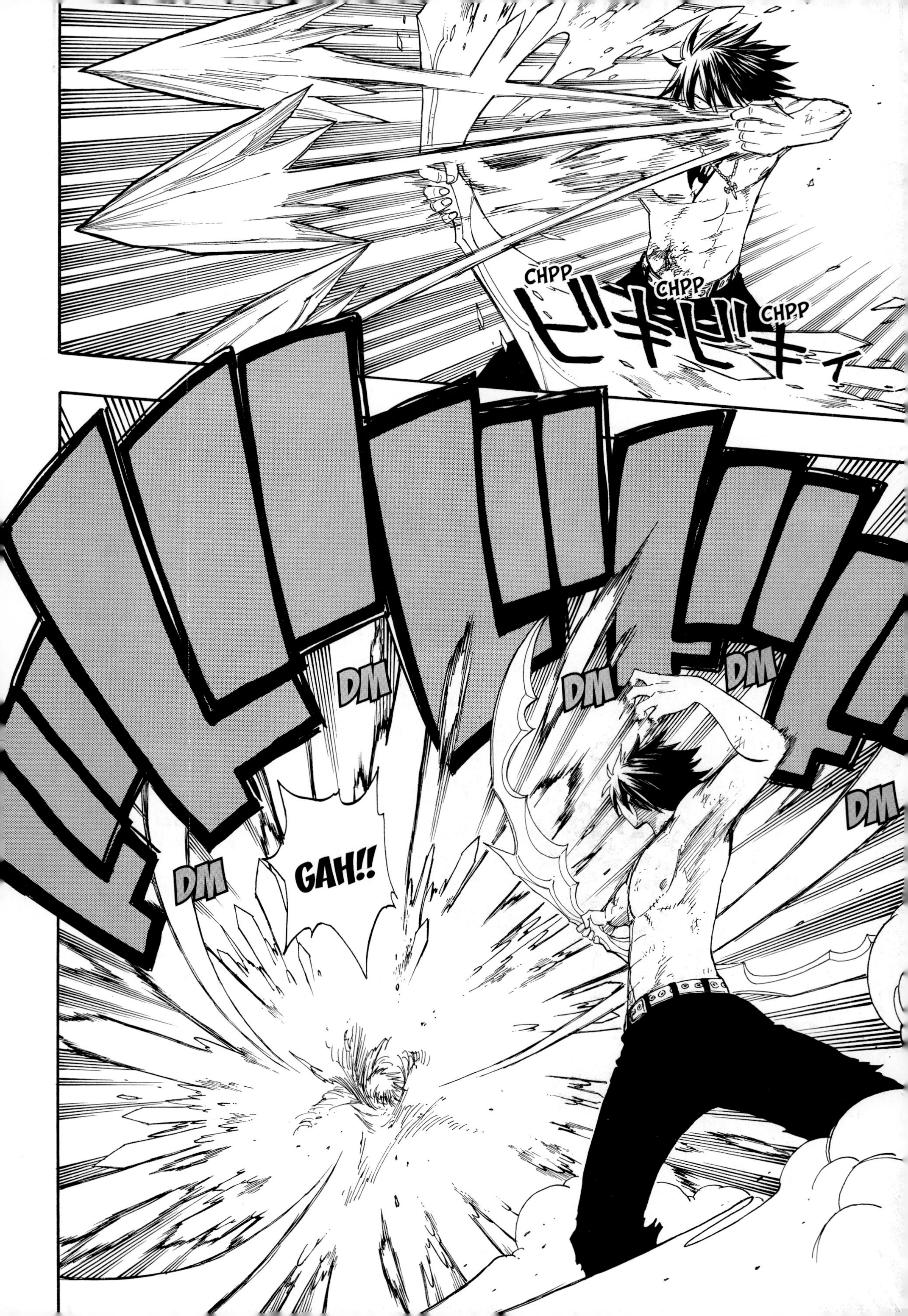
CHPP
CHPP
CHPP
ビキビキィ
DM
DM
DM
DM
GAH!!
DM

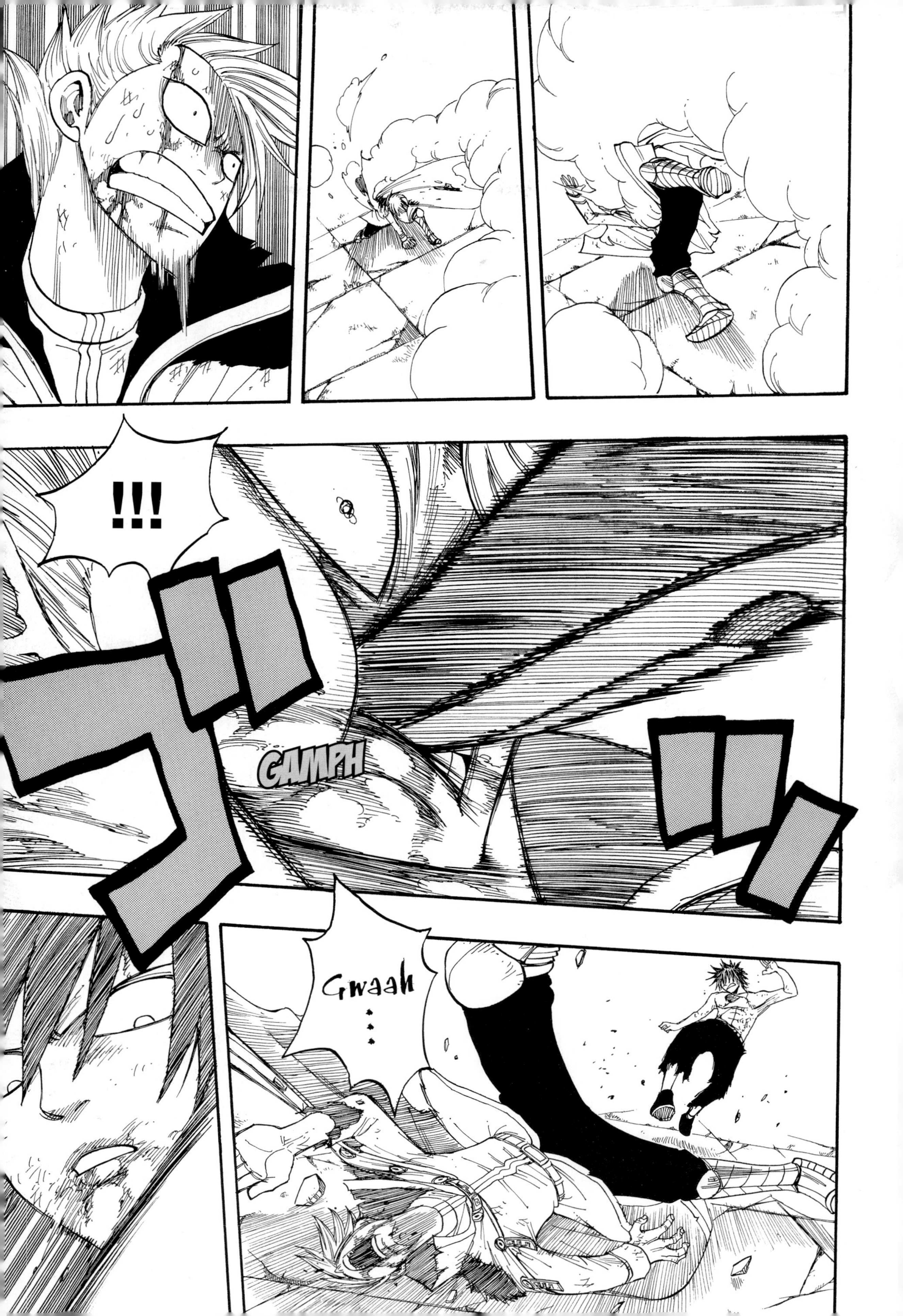
!!!
GAMPH
Gwaah...

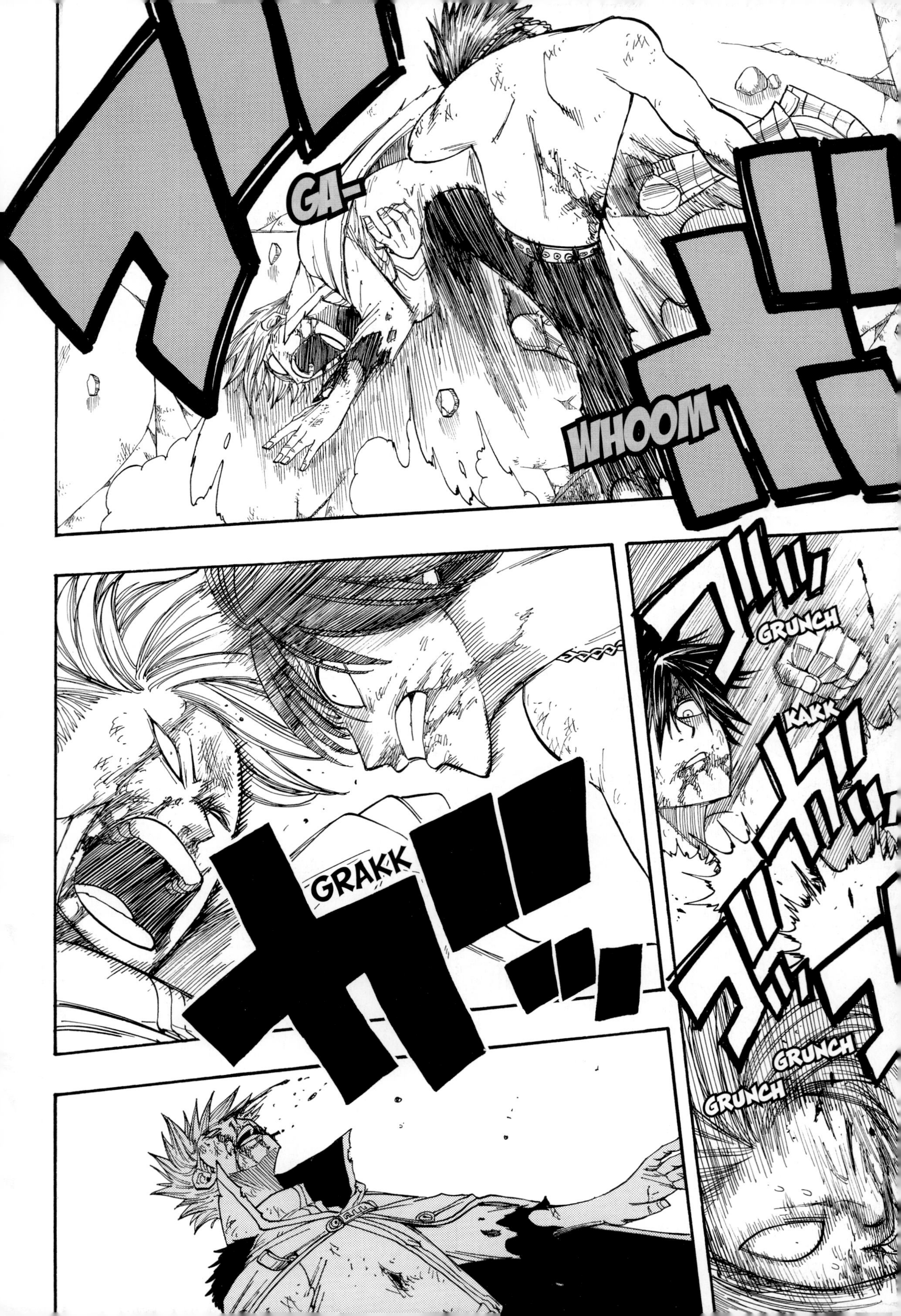
GA-
WHOOM
GRUNCH
KAKK
GRUNCH
GRUNCH
GRUNCH
GRAKK

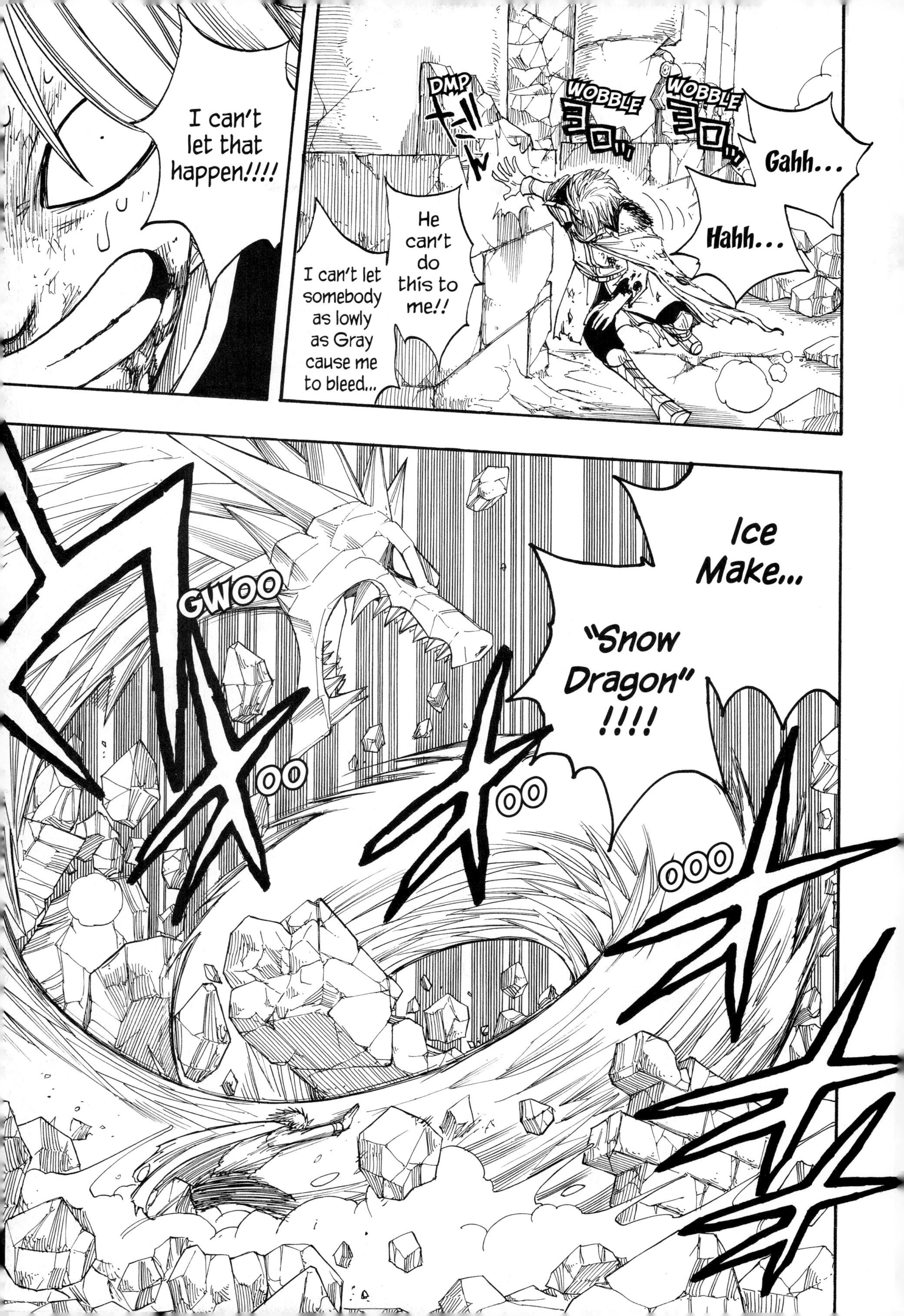
Gahh...
Hahh...
WOBBLE
WOBBLE
DMP
He can't do this to me!!
I can't let somebody as lowly as Gray cause me to bleed...
I can't let that happen!!!!
Ice Make...
"Snow Dragon"!!!!
GWOO
OO
OO
OOO

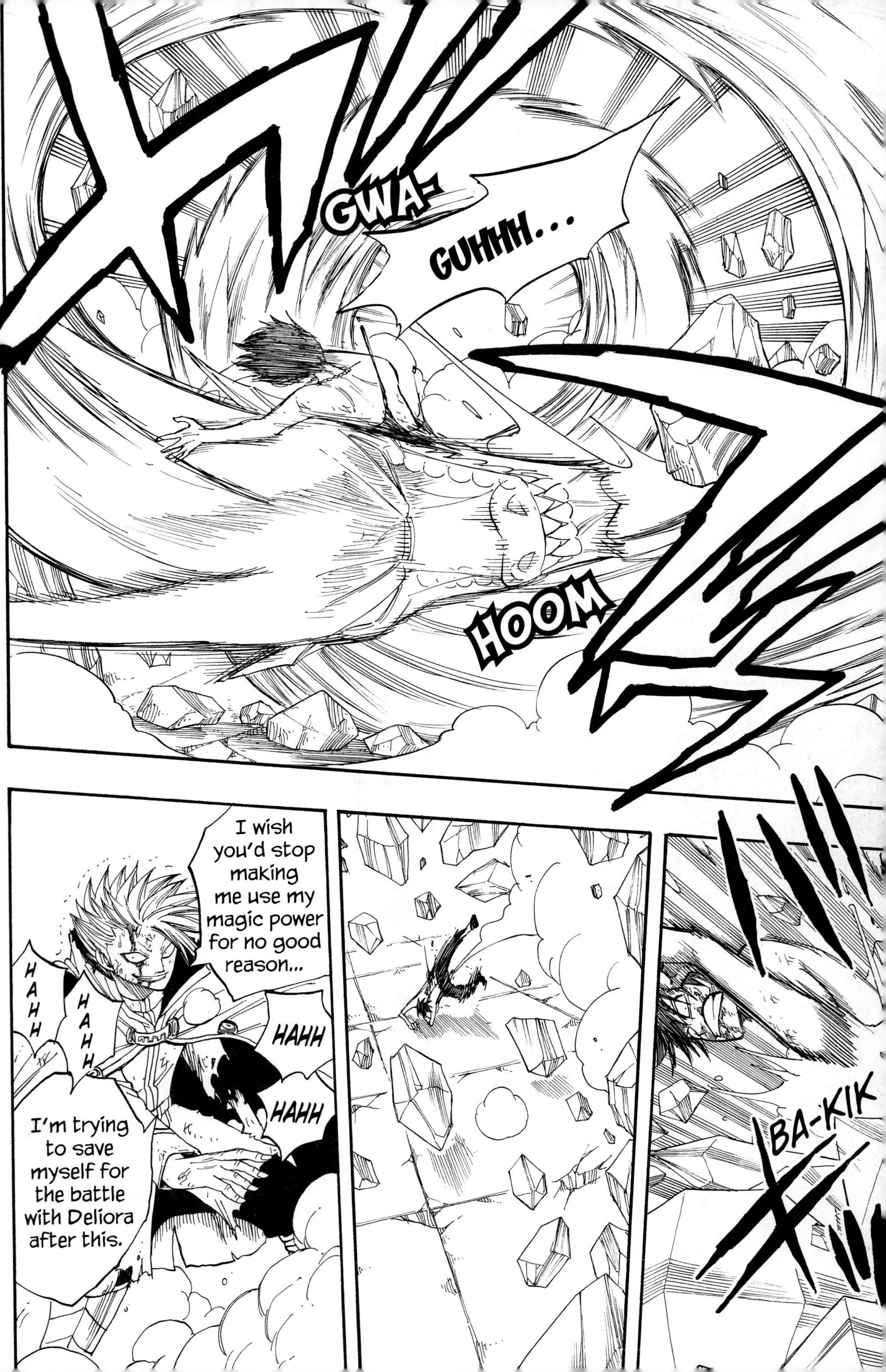
GWA-
GUHHH...
HOOM
BA-KIK
I wish you'd stop making me use my magic power for no good reason...
HAHH
HAHH
HAHH
HAHH
I'm trying to save myself for the battle with Deliora after this.

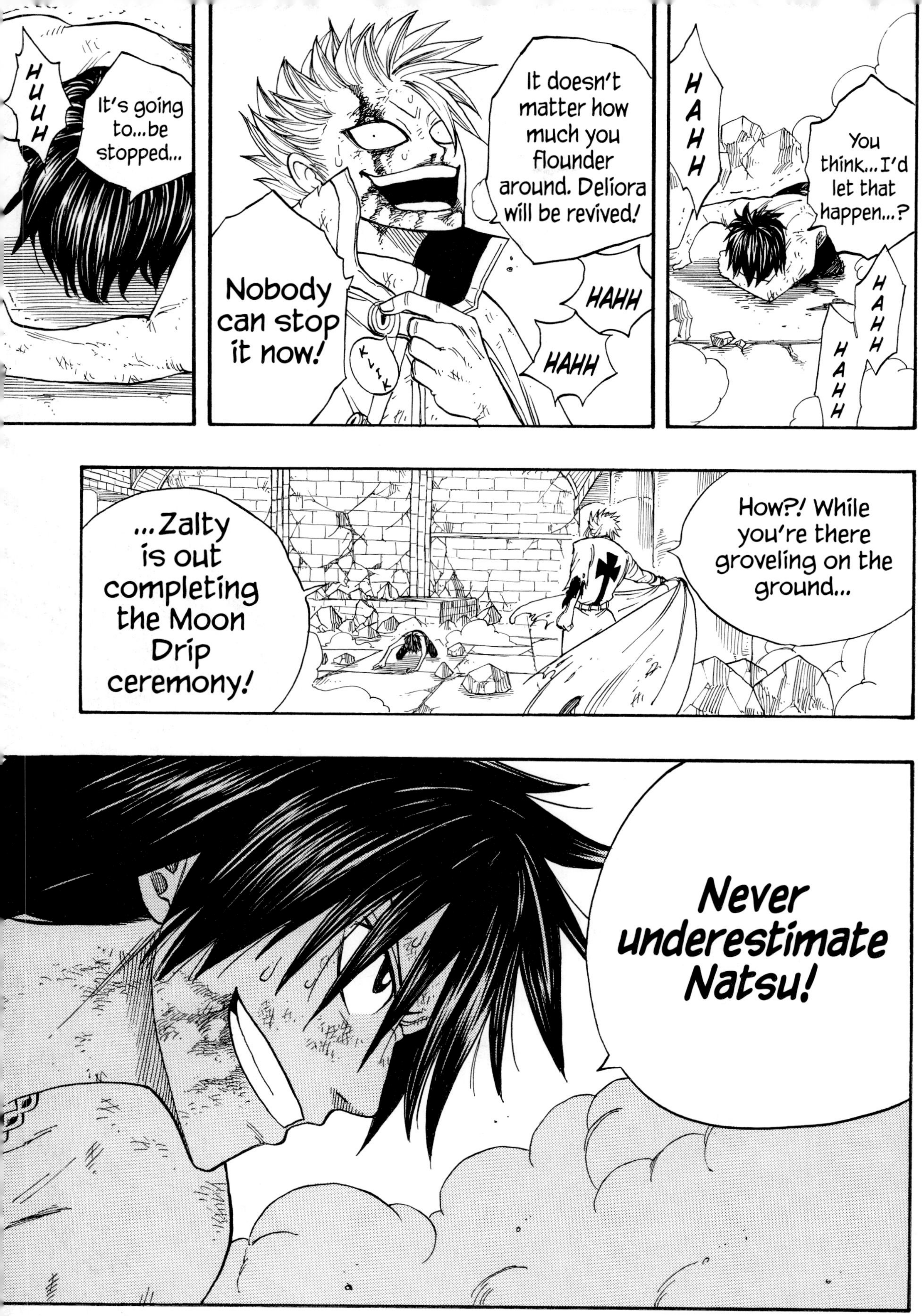
HAHH
You think...I'd let that happen...?
HAHH
HAHH
It doesn't matter how much you flounder around. Deliora will be revived!
HAHH
HAHH
Nobody can stop it now!
KLIK
HUUH
It's going to...be stopped...
How?! While you're there groveling on the ground...
...Zalty is out completing the Moon Drip ceremony!
Never underestimate Natsu!

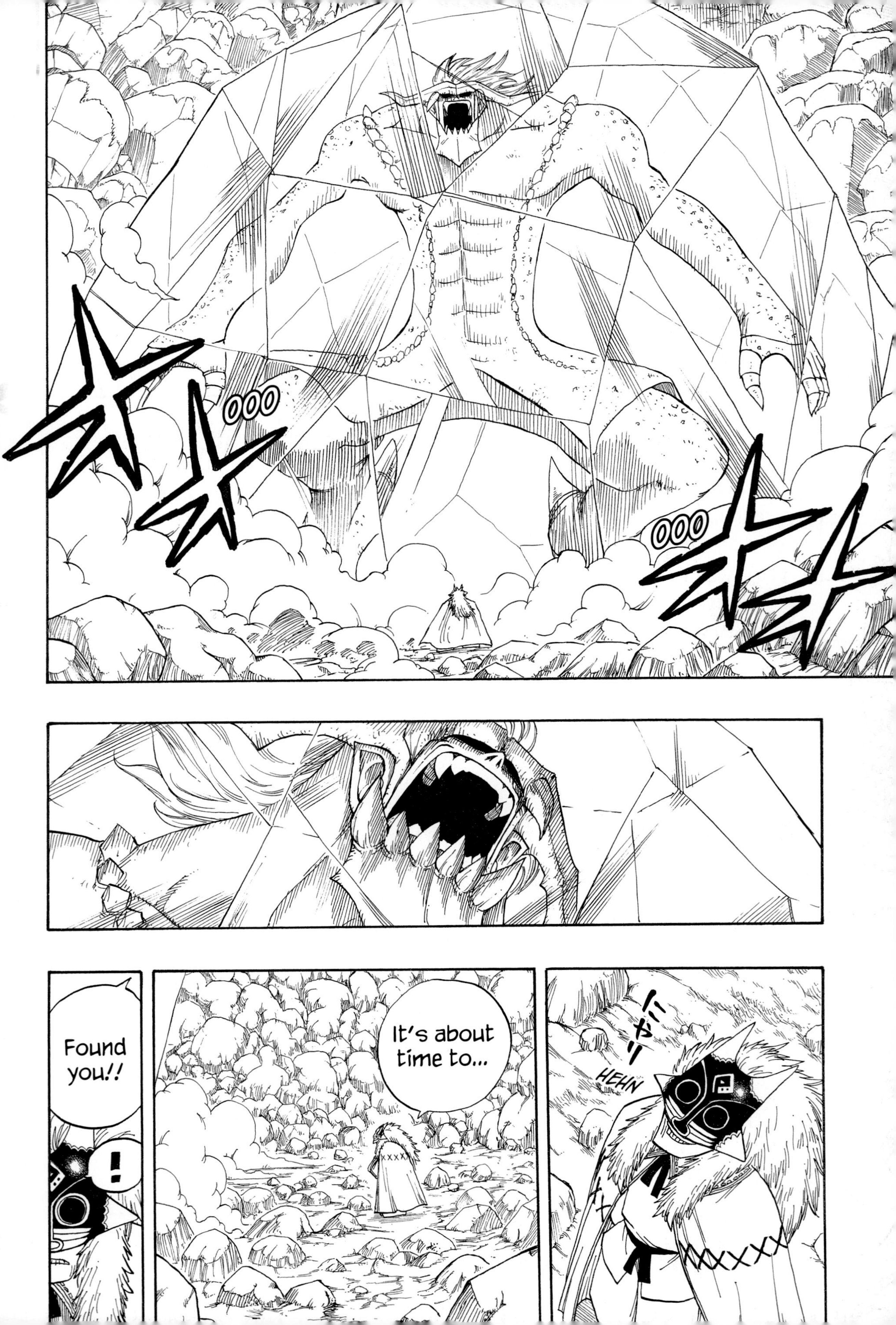
OOO
OOO
HEHN
It's about time to...
Found you!!
!

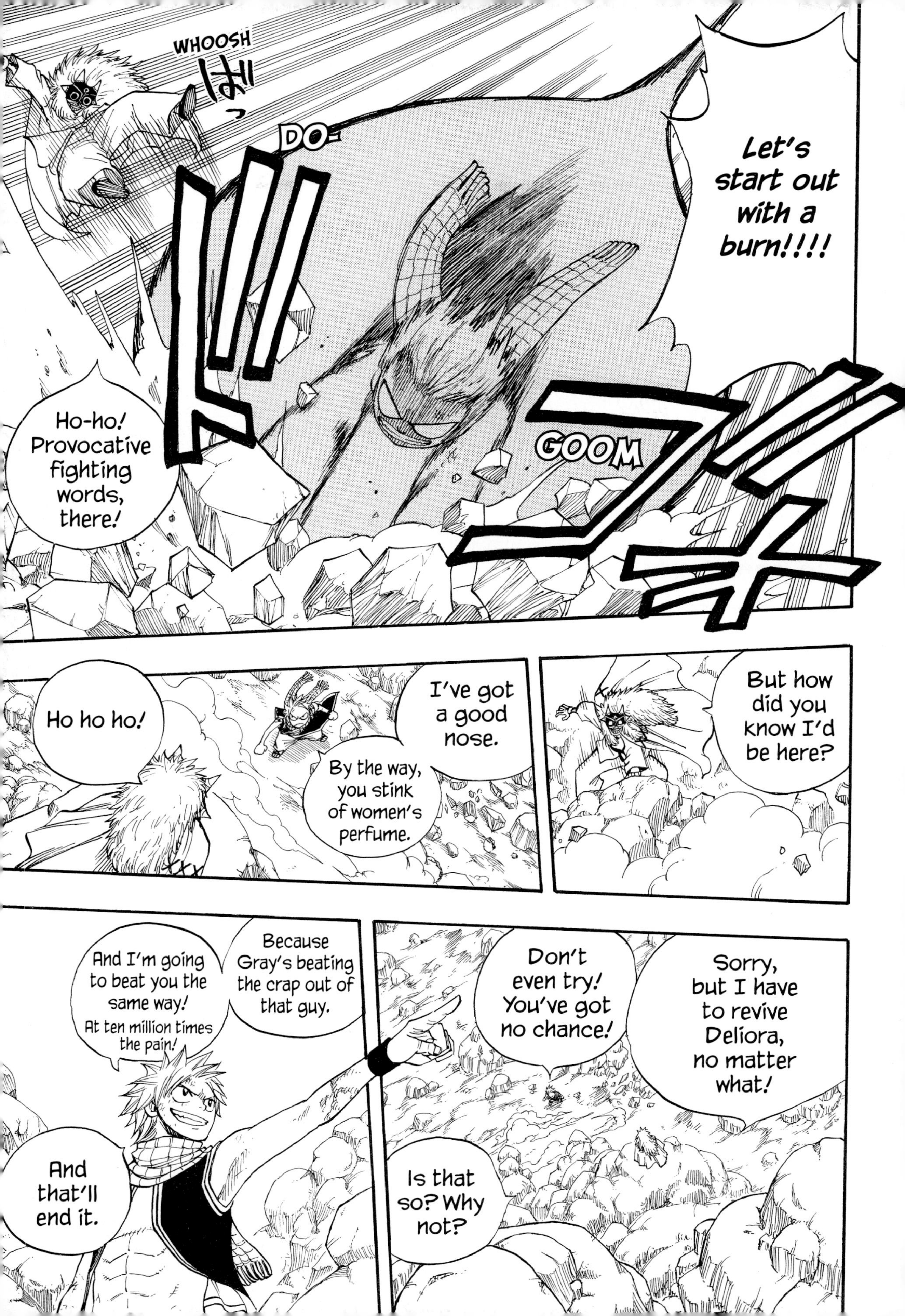
Let's start out with a burn!!!!
WHOOSH
DO-
GOOM
Ho-ho! Provocative fighting words, there!
But how did you know I'd be here?
I've got a good nose.
By the way, you stink of women's perfume.
Ho ho ho!
Sorry, but I have to revive Deliora, no matter what!
Don't even try! You've got no chance!
Is that so? Why not?
Because Gray's beating the crap out of that guy.
And I'm going to beat you the same way! At ten million times the pain!
And that'll end it.

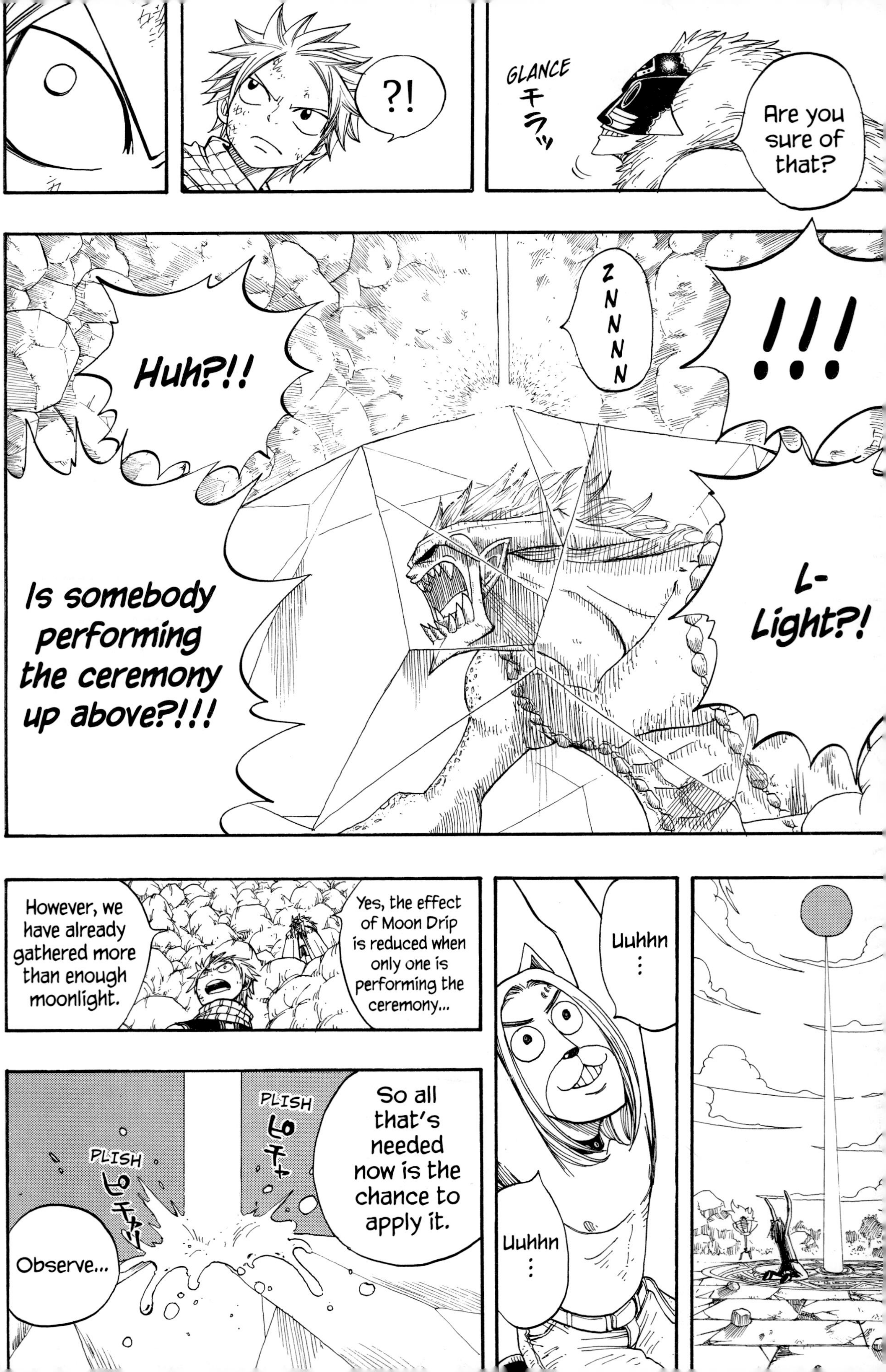

Are you sure of that?
GLANCE
キラッ
?!
!!!
ZNNNN
Huh?!!
L-Light?!
Is somebody performing the ceremony up above?!!!
Uuhhn…
Uuhhn…
Yes, the effect of Moon Drip is reduced when only one is performing the ceremony…
However, we have already gathered more than enough moonlight.
So all that's needed now is the chance to apply it.
PLISH
ピチャ
PLISH
ピチャッ
Observe…

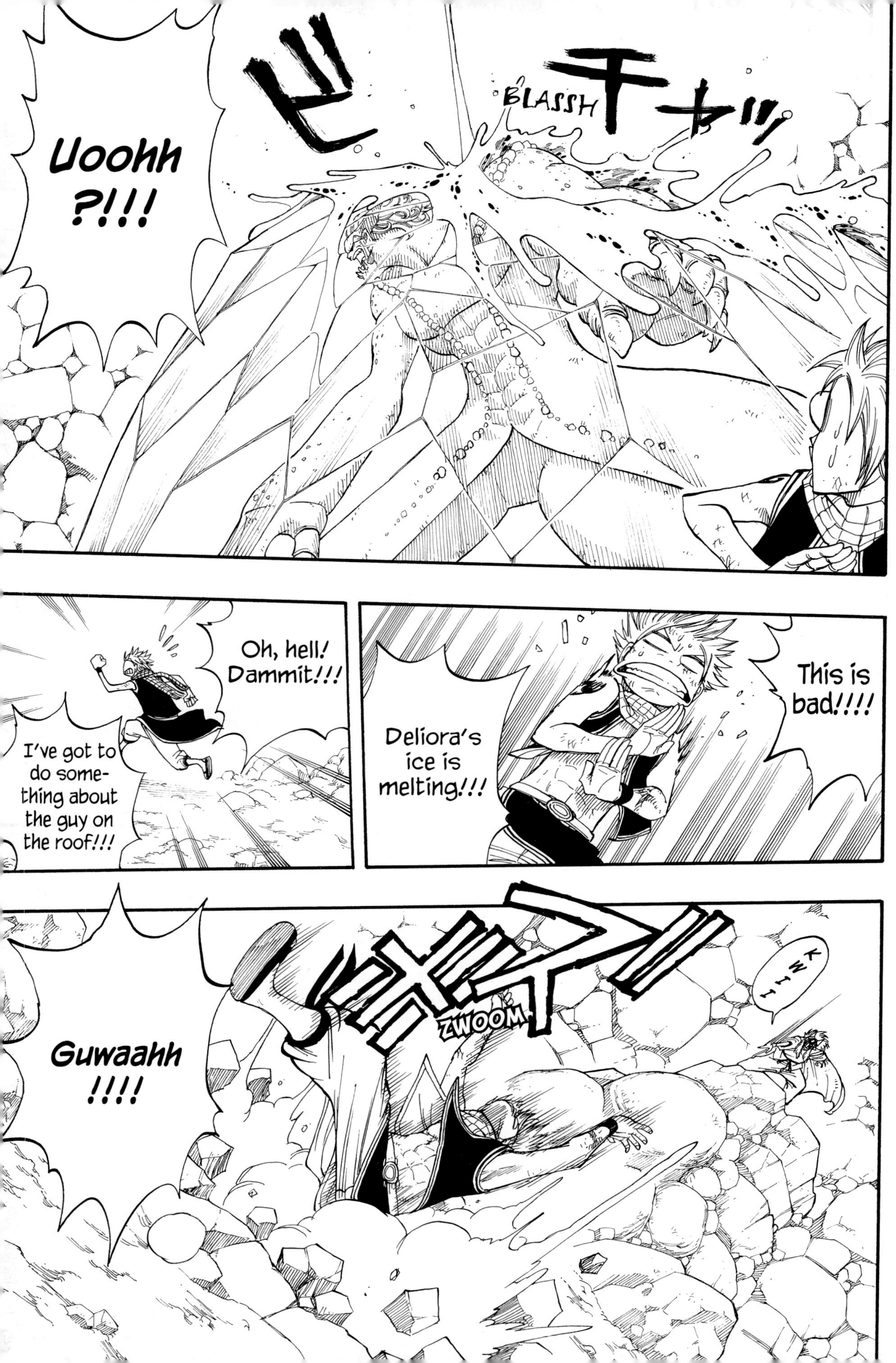
BLASSH
Uoohh ?!!!
This is bad!!!!
Deliora's ice is melting!!!
Oh, hell! Dammit!!!
I've got to do something about the guy on the roof!!!
KWII
ZWOOM
Guwaahh !!!!

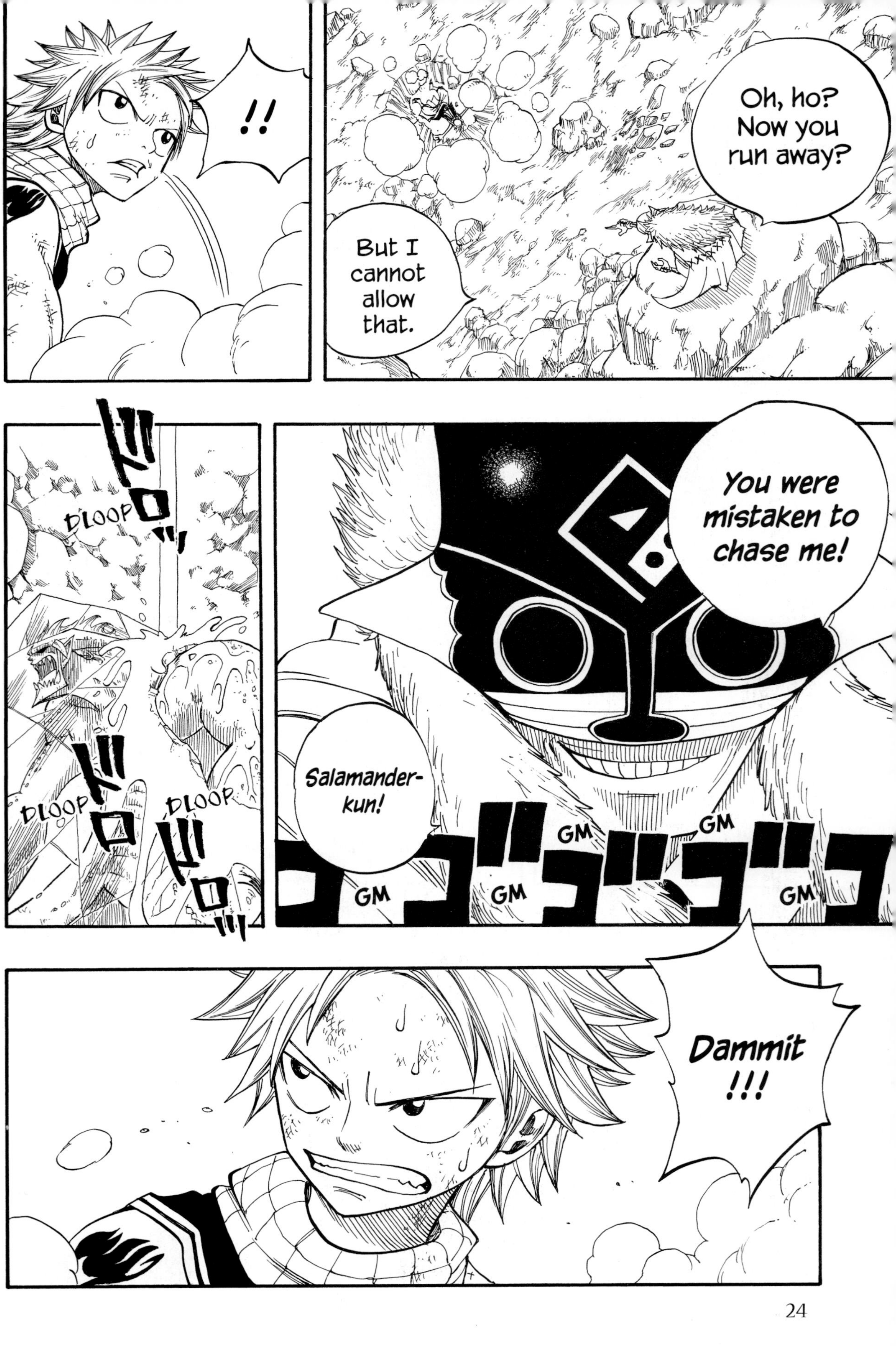
Oh, ho? Now you run away?
But I cannot allow that.
!!
You were mistaken to chase me!
Salamander-kun!
GM GM GM GM GM GM
DLOOP
DLOOP
DLOOP
Dammit!!!

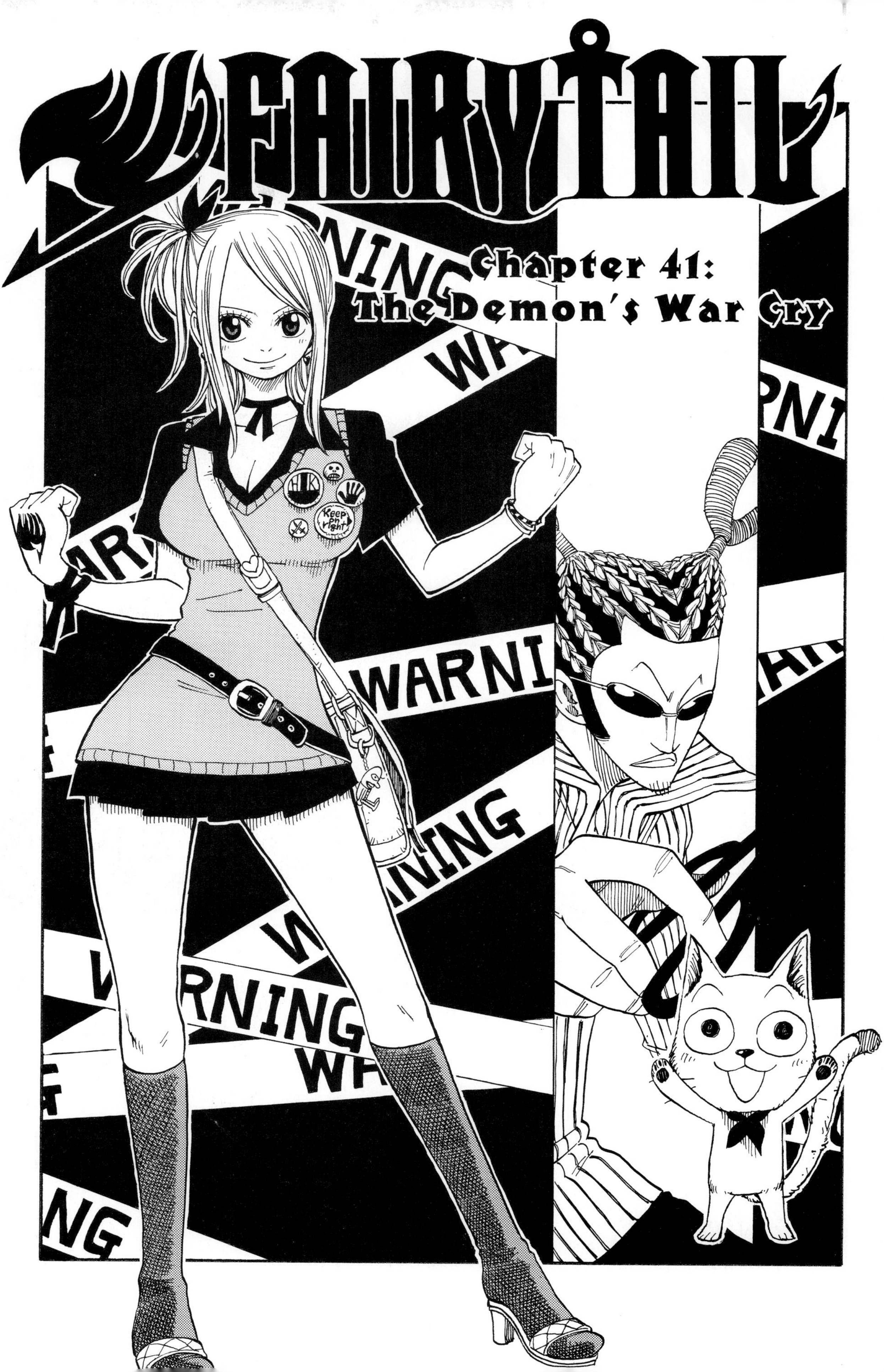
FAIRY TAIL
Chapter 41:
The Demon's War Cry
WARNING
Keep on Fight

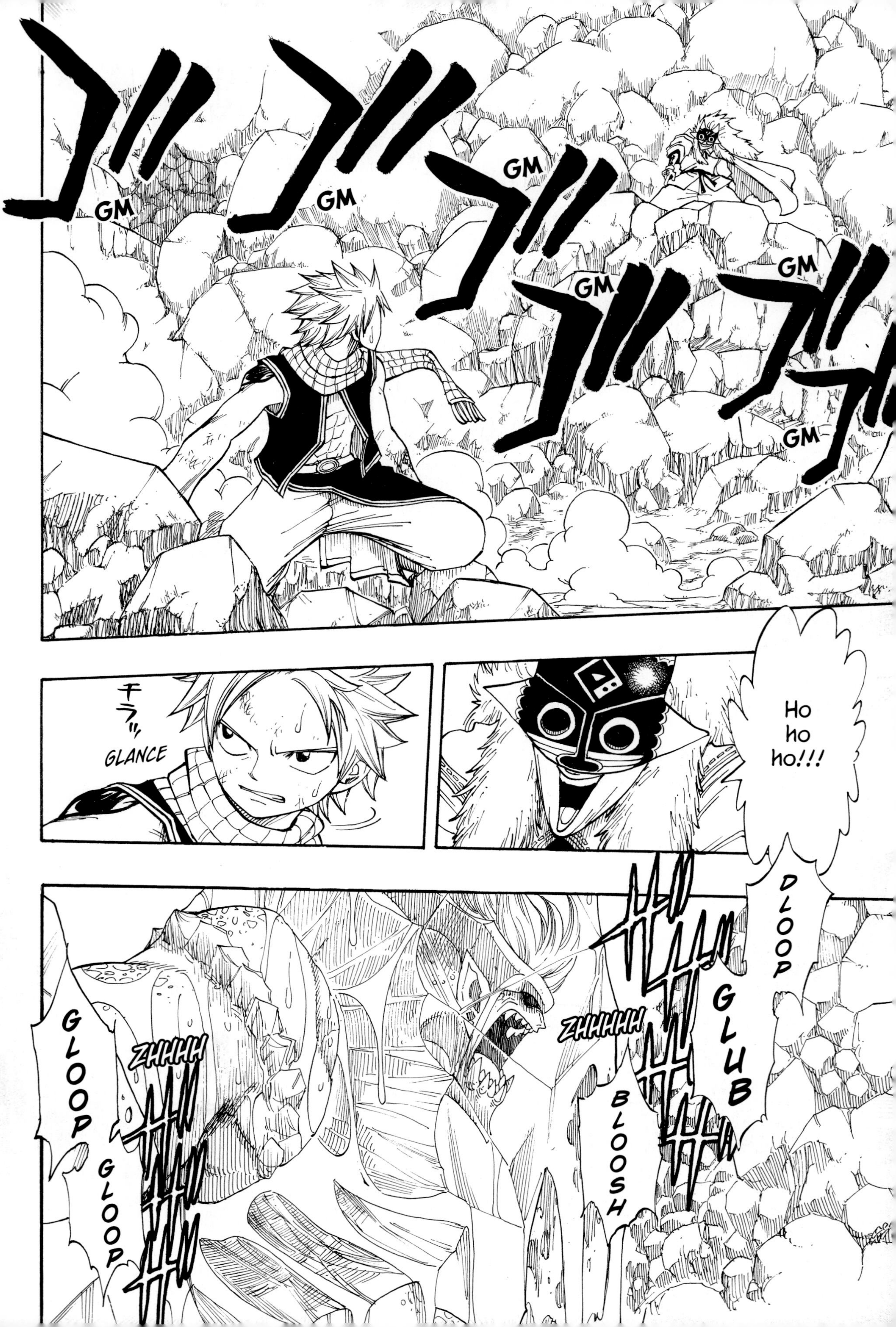
GM
GM
GM
GM
GM
GM
Ho ho ho!!!
チラッ
GLANCE
DLOOP
GLUB
ZHHHHH
BLOOSH
ZHHHH
GLOOP
GLOOP GLOOP

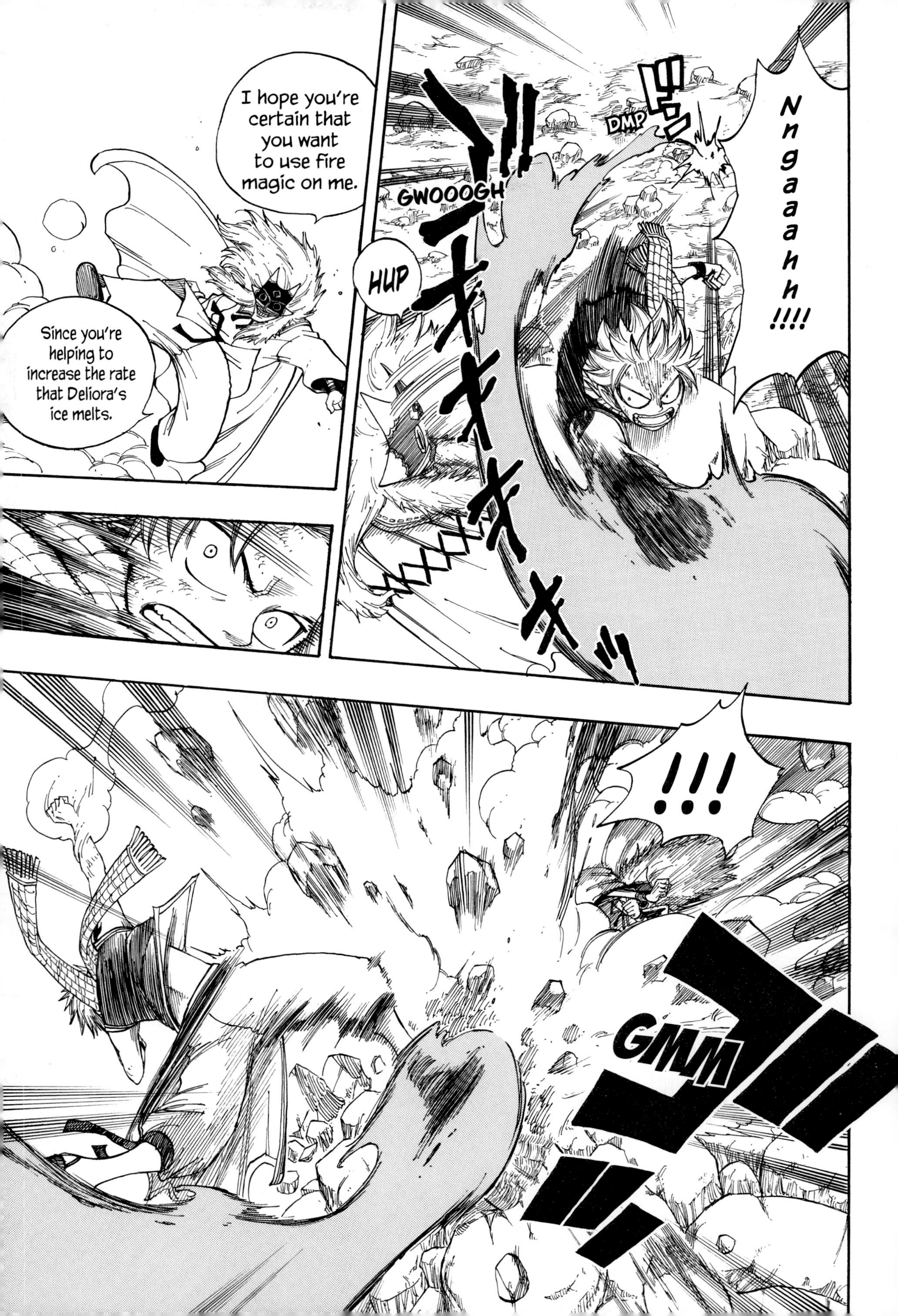
Nngaaaahh!!!!
DMP
GWOOOGH
HUP
I hope you're certain that you want to use fire magic on me.
Since you're helping to increase the rate that Deliora's ice melts.
!!!
GMM

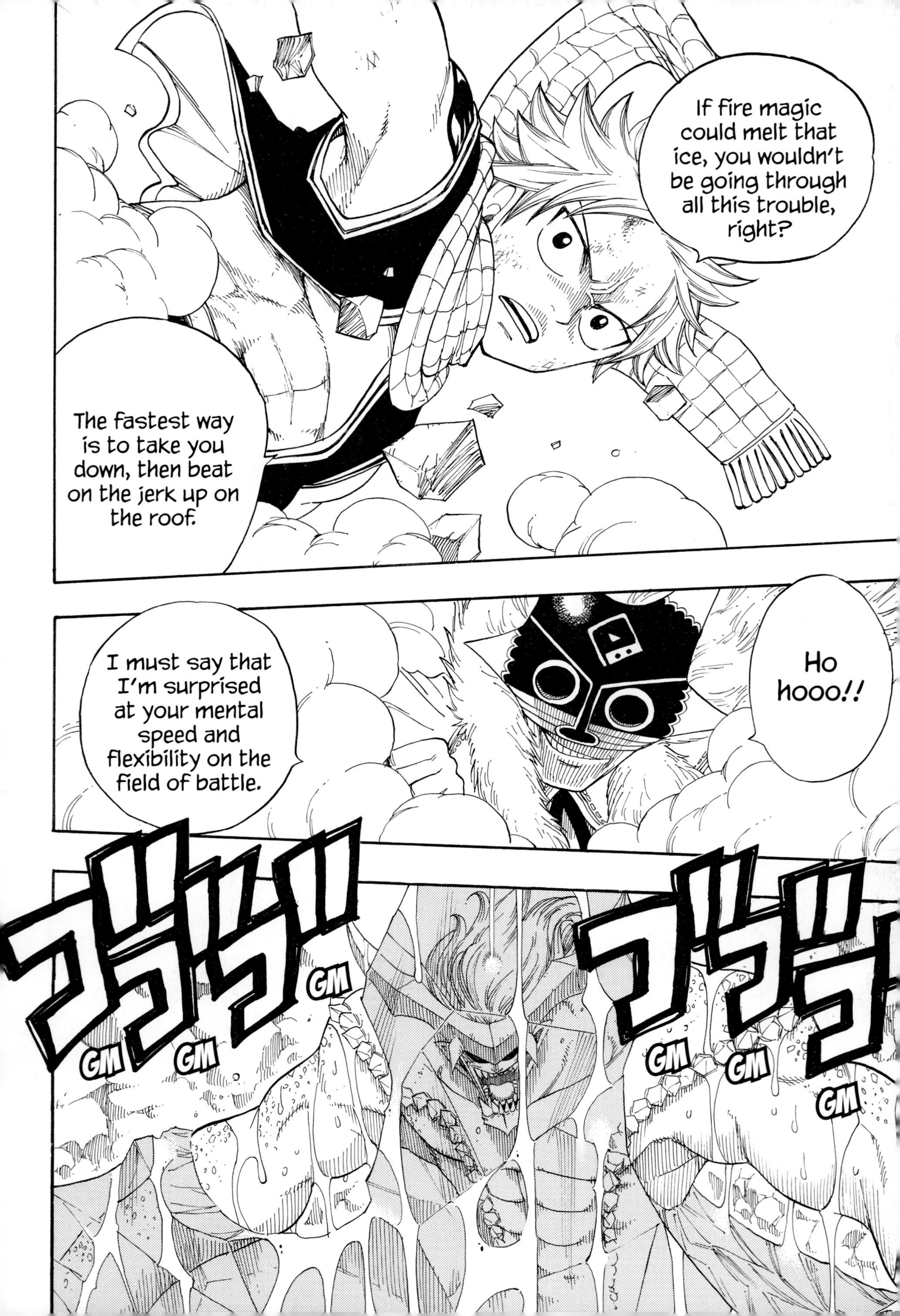
If fire magic could melt that ice, you wouldn't be going through all this trouble, right?
The fastest way is to take you down, then beat on the jerk up on the roof.
Ho hooo!!
I must say that I'm surprised at your mental speed and flexibility on the field of battle.
GM
GM
GM
GM
GM
GM

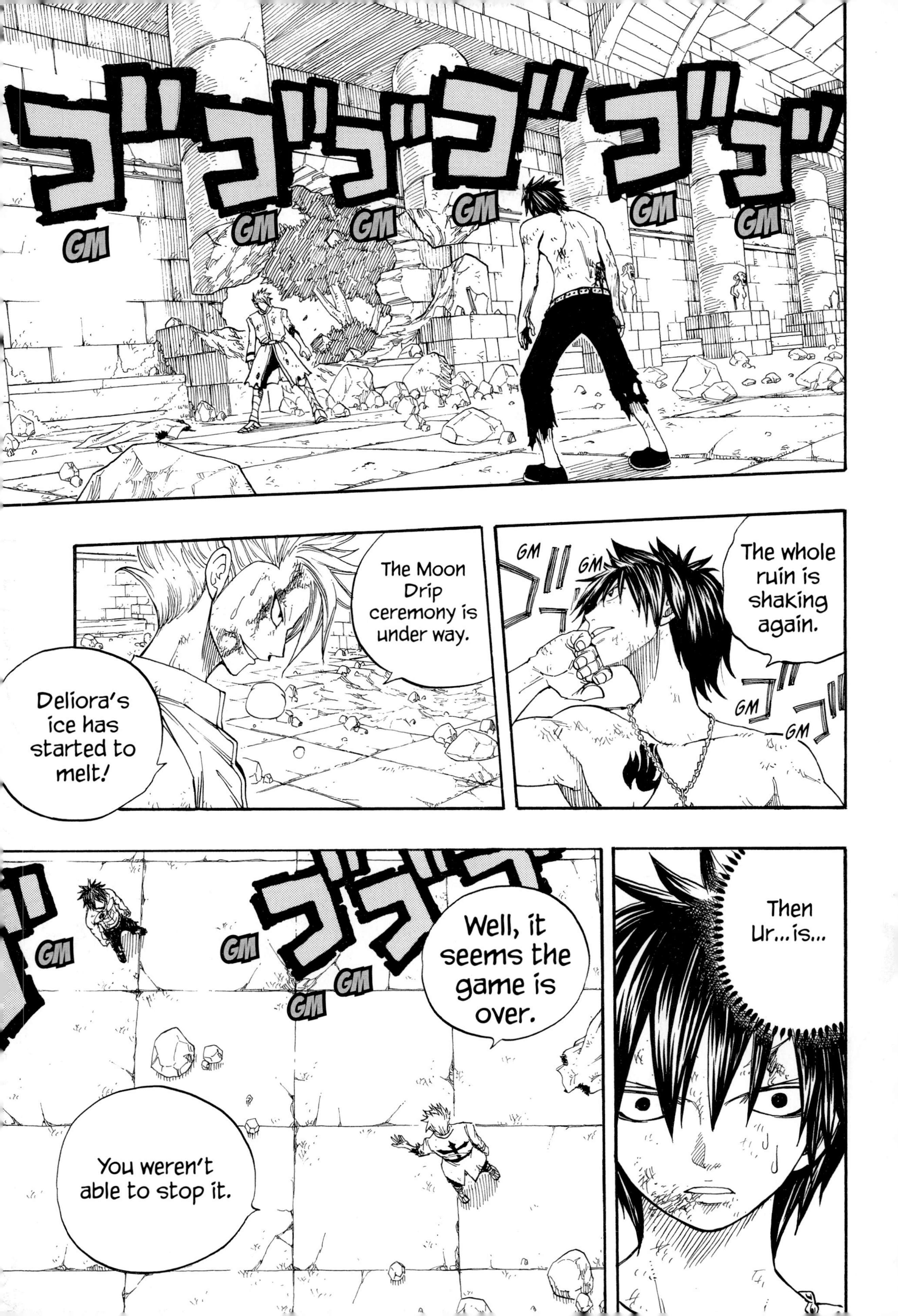
ゴゴゴゴゴゴ
GM GM GM GM GM GM
The whole ruin is shaking again.
GM GM GM GM
The Moon Drip ceremony is under way.
Deliora's ice has started to melt!
Then Ur...is...
GM GM GM GM
Well, it seems the game is over.
You weren't able to stop it.

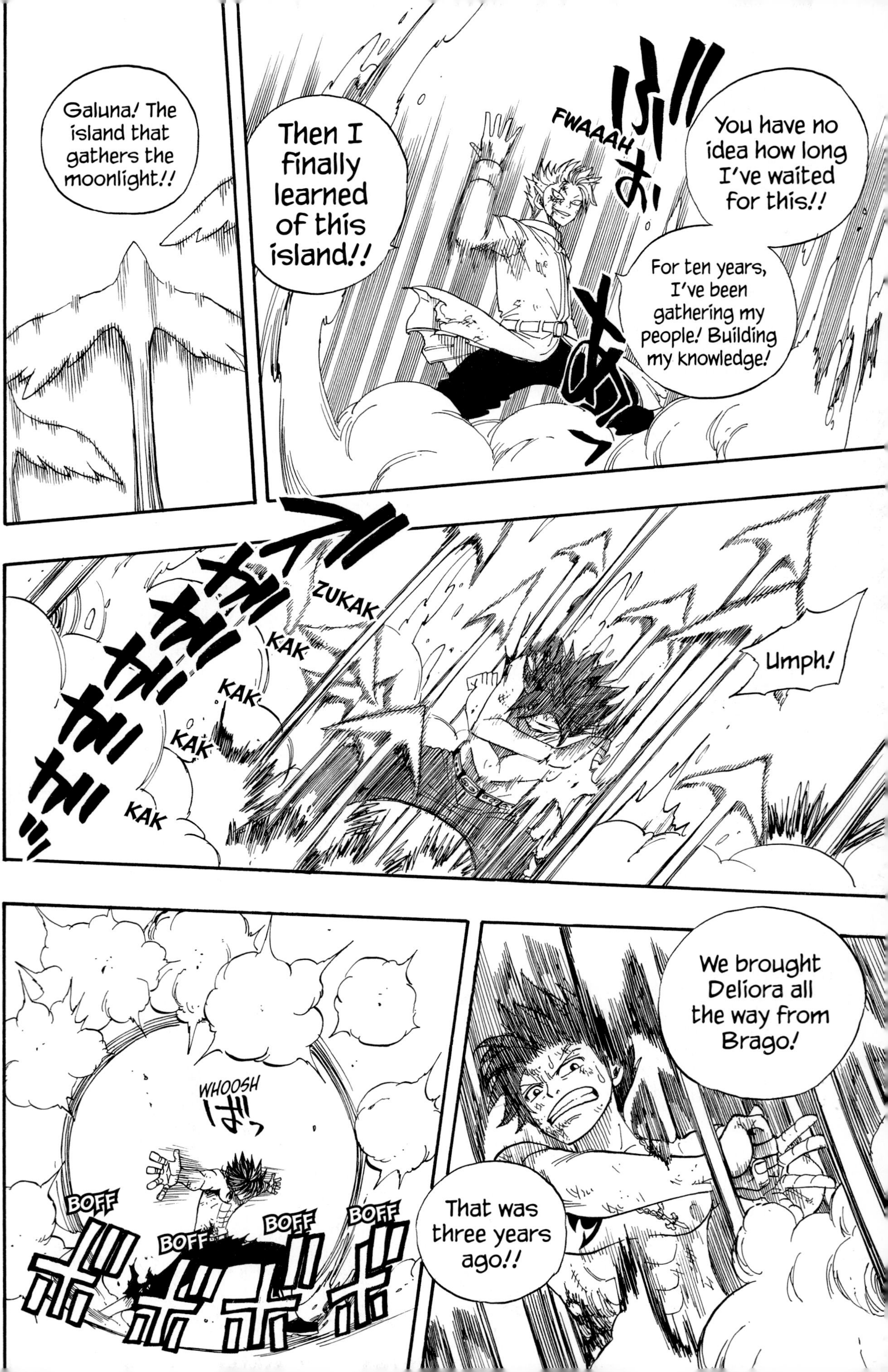
You have no idea how long I've waited for this!!
FWAAAH
For ten years, I've been gathering my people! Building my knowledge!
Then I finally learned of this island!!
Galuna! The island that gathers the moonlight!!
ZUKAK
KAK
KAK
KAK
KAK
Umph!
We brought Deliora all the way from Brago!
That was three years ago!!
WHOOSH
ばっ
BOFF
BOFF
BOFF
BOFF

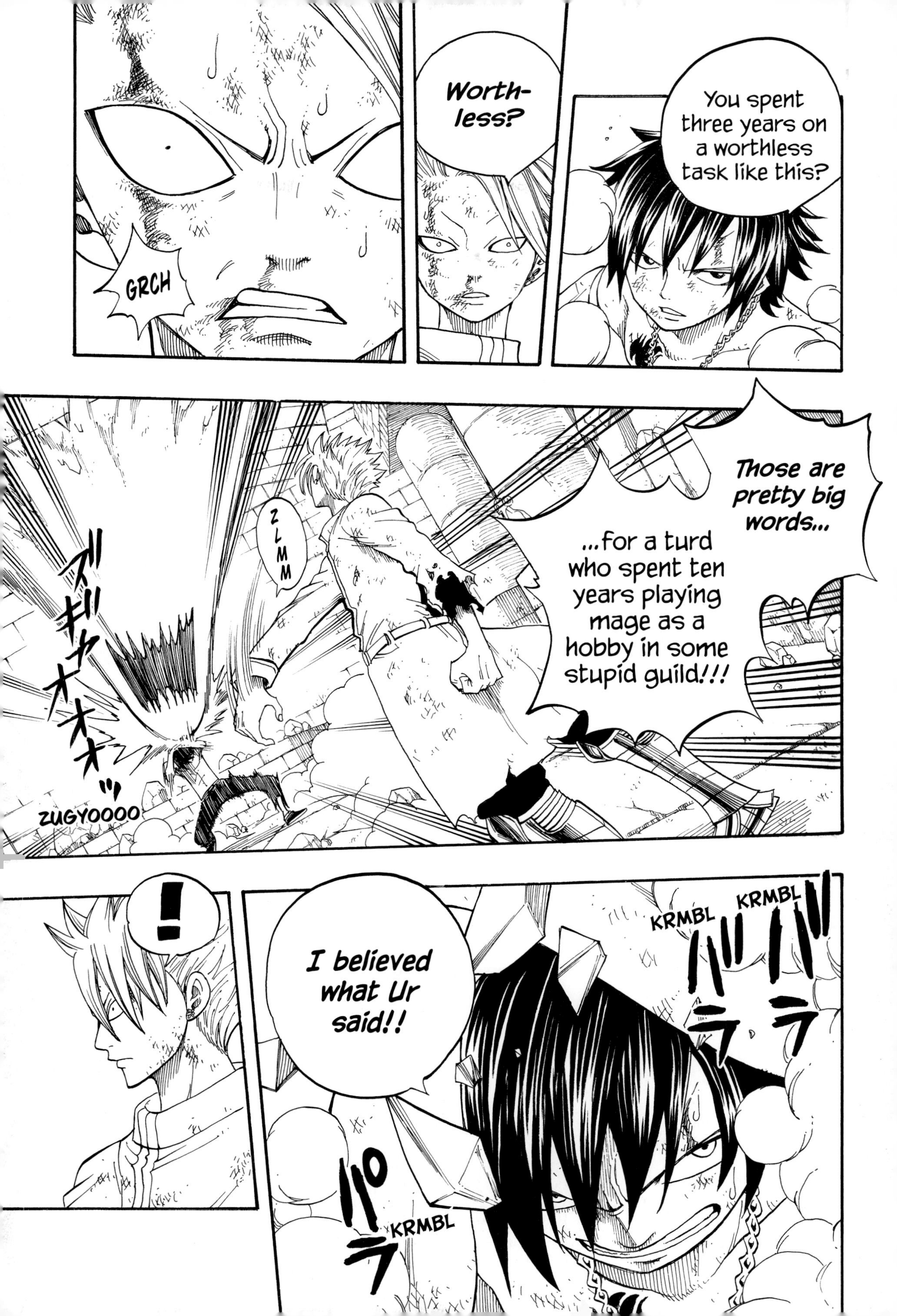
You spent three years on a worthless task like this?
Worth-less?
GRCH
Those are pretty big words...
...for a turd who spent ten years playing mage as a hobby in some stupid guild!!!
ZLMM
ZUGYOOOO
KRMBL
KRMBL
I believed what Ur said!!
KRMBL
!

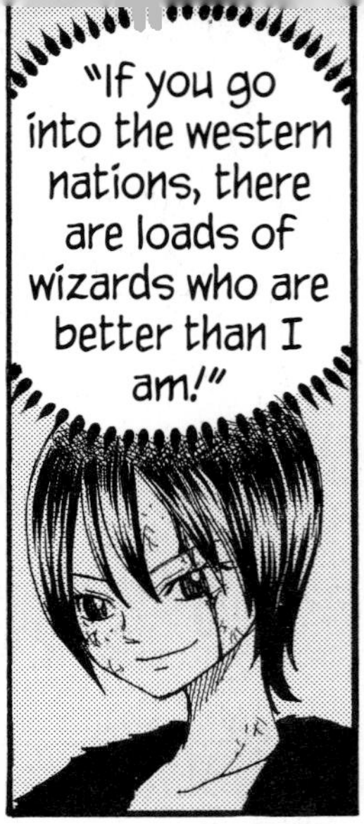
"If you go into the western nations, there are loads of wizards who are better than I am!"

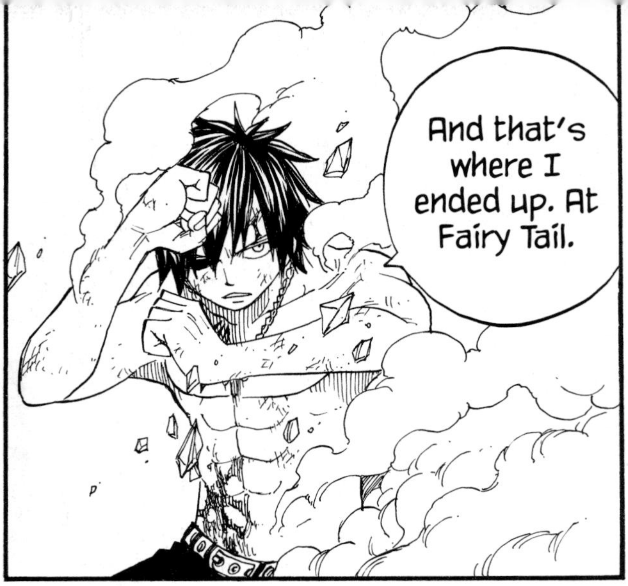
And that's where I ended up. At Fairy Tail.

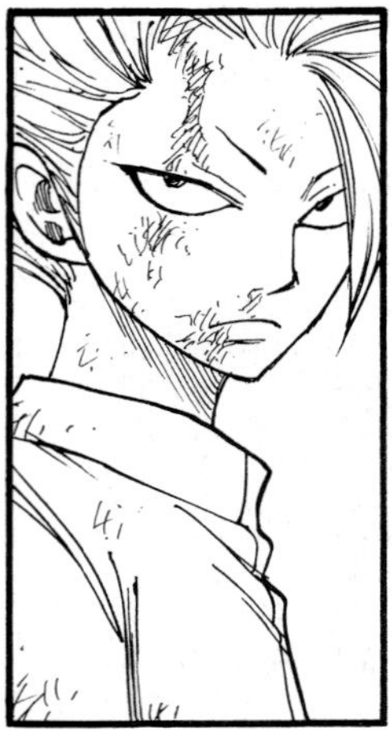

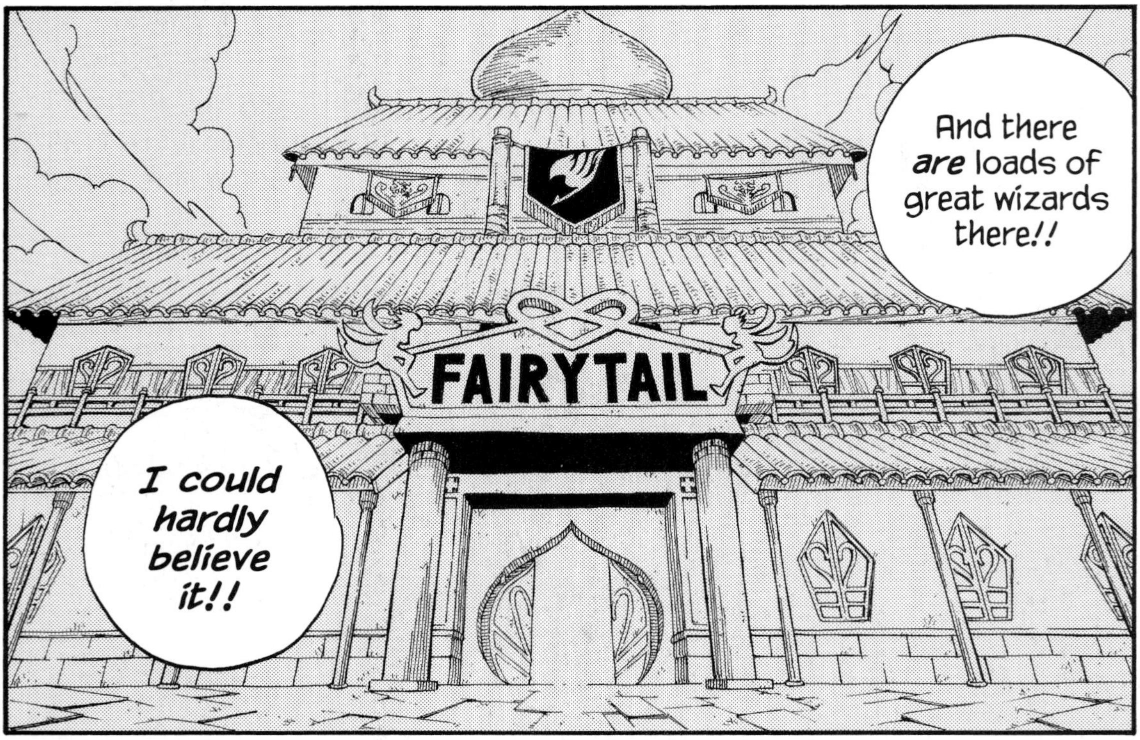
And there *are* loads of great wizards there!!
FAIRYTAIL
I could hardly believe it!!

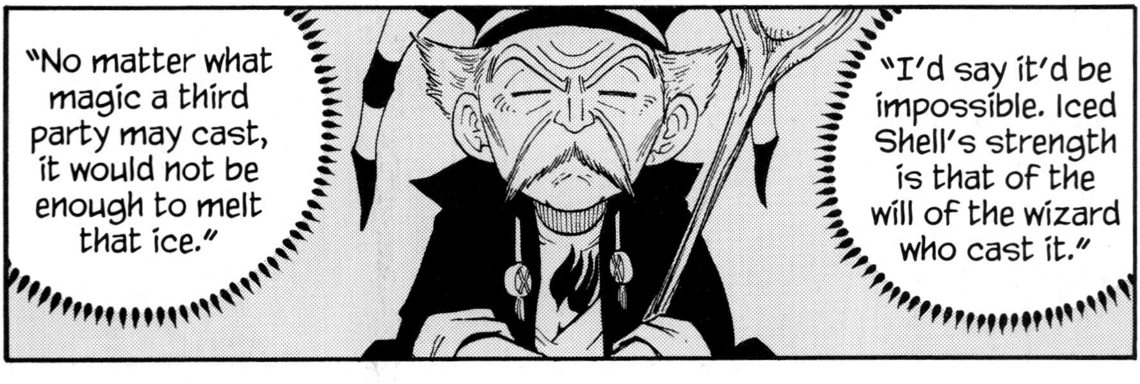
"I'd say it'd be impossible. Iced Shell's strength is that of the will of the wizard who cast it."
"No matter what magic a third party may cast, it would not be enough to melt that ice."

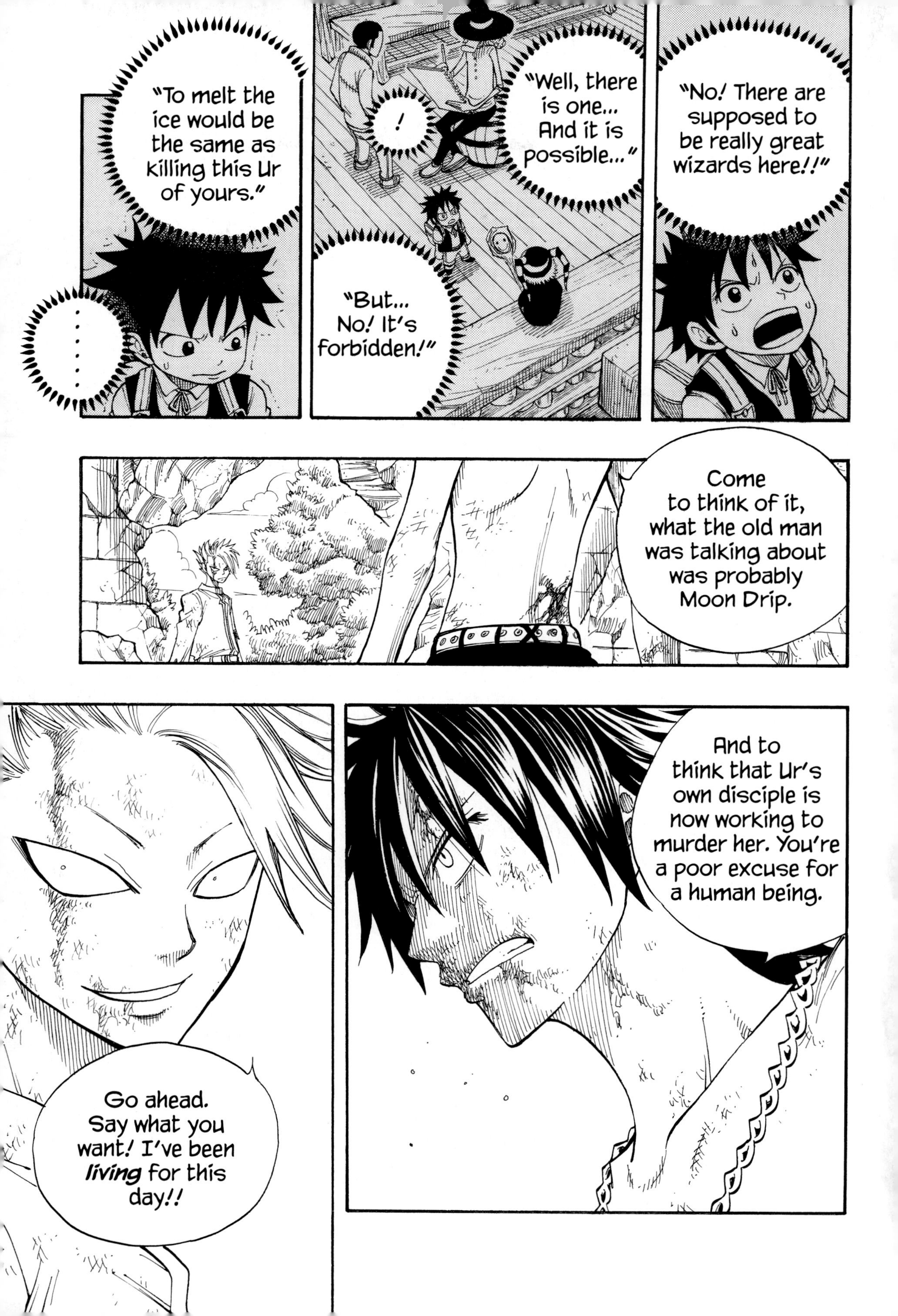
"No! There are supposed to be really great wizards here!!"
"Well, there is one... And it is possible..."
!
"But... No! It's forbidden!"
"To melt the ice would be the same as killing this Ur of yours."
......
Come to think of it, what the old man was talking about was probably Moon Drip.
And to think that Ur's own disciple is now working to murder her. You're a poor excuse for a human being.
Go ahead. Say what you want! I've been *living* for this day!!

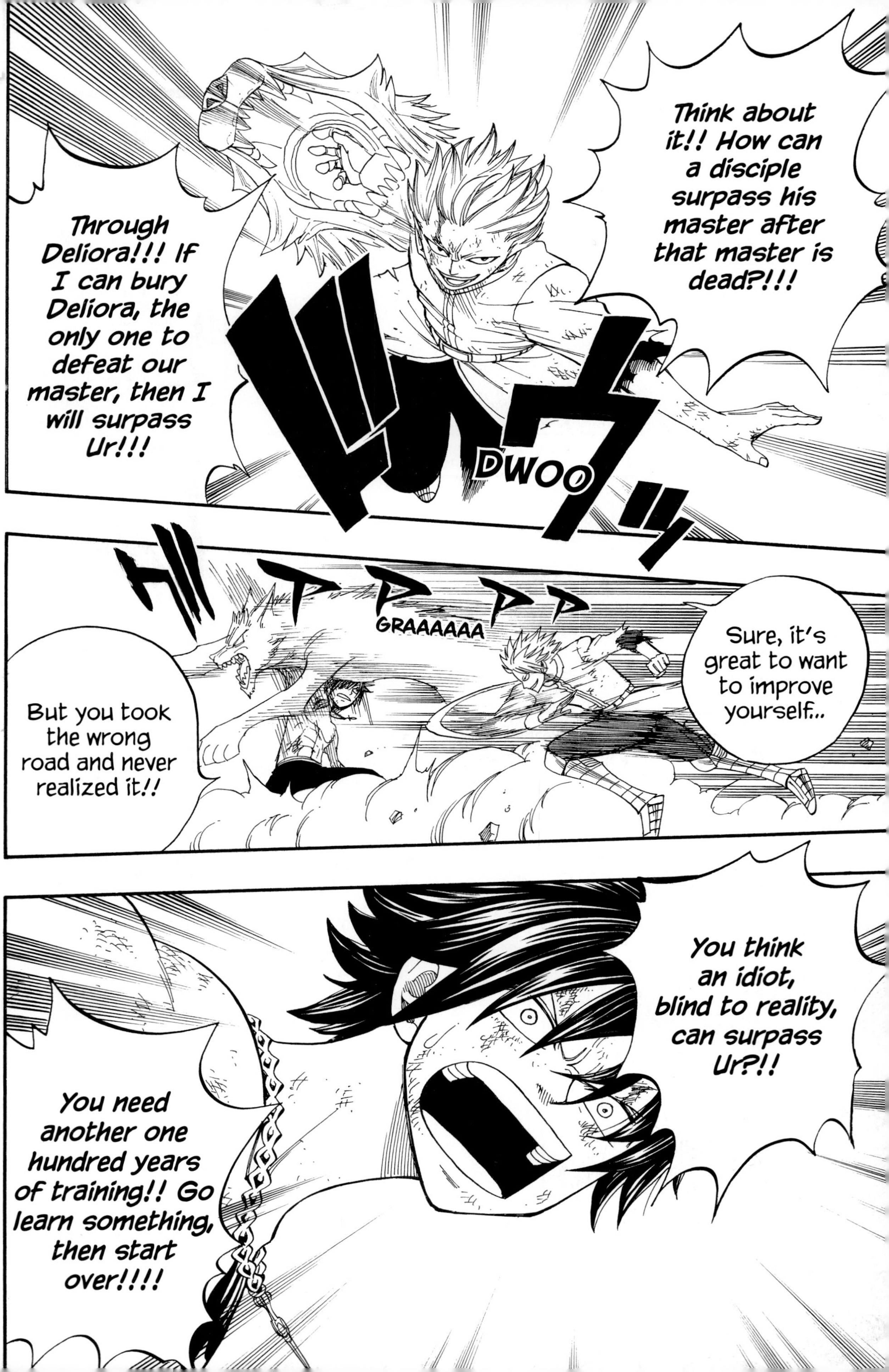
Think about it!! How can a disciple surpass his master after that master is dead?!!!
Through Deliora!!! If I can bury Deliora, the only one to defeat our master, then I will surpass Ur!!!
DWOO
GRAAAAAA
Sure, it's great to want to improve yourself...
But you took the wrong road and never realized it!!
You think an idiot, blind to reality, can surpass Ur?!!
You need another one hundred years of training!! Go learn something, then start over!!!!

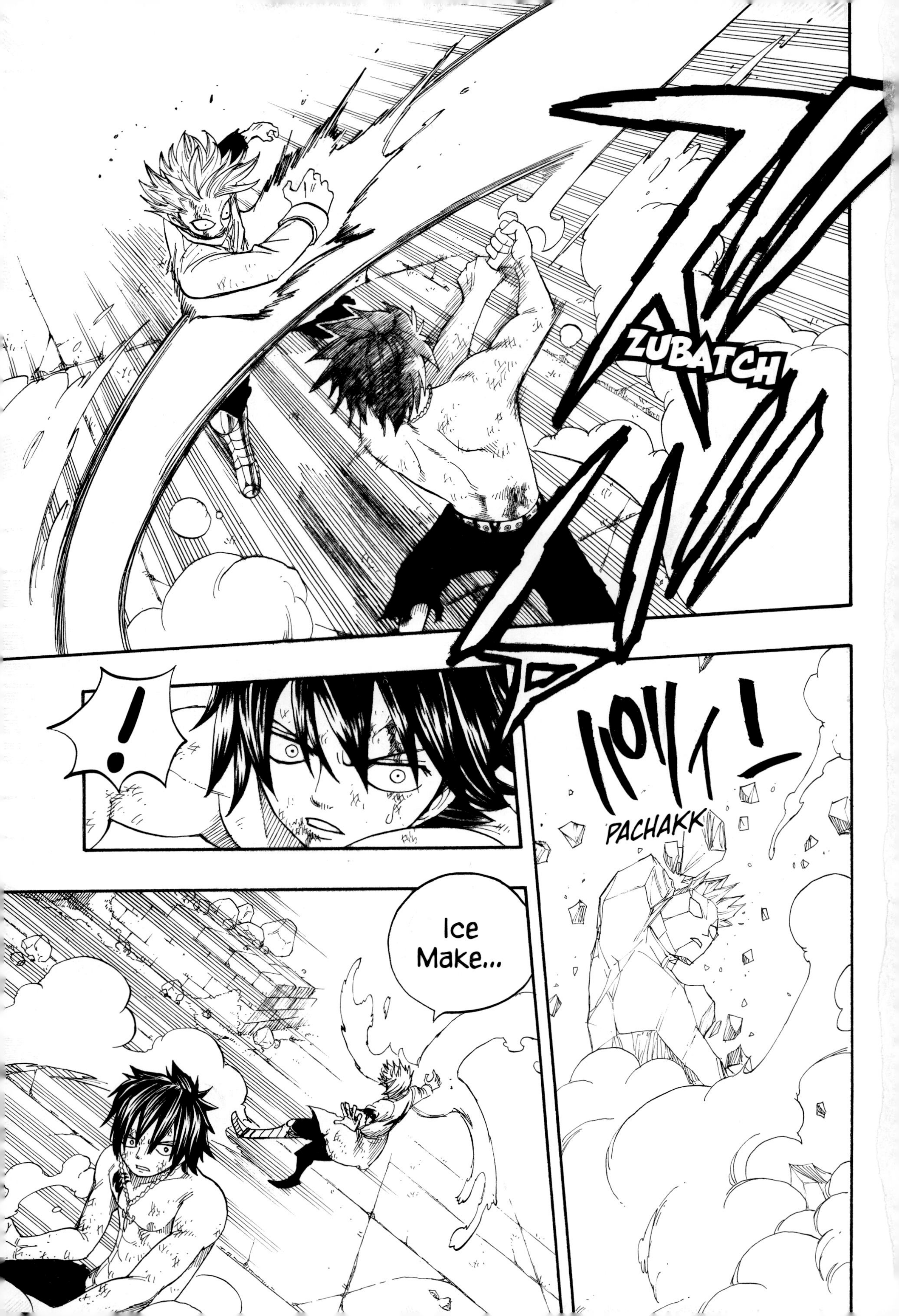
ZUBATCH
!
パキィ!
PACHAKK
Ice Make...

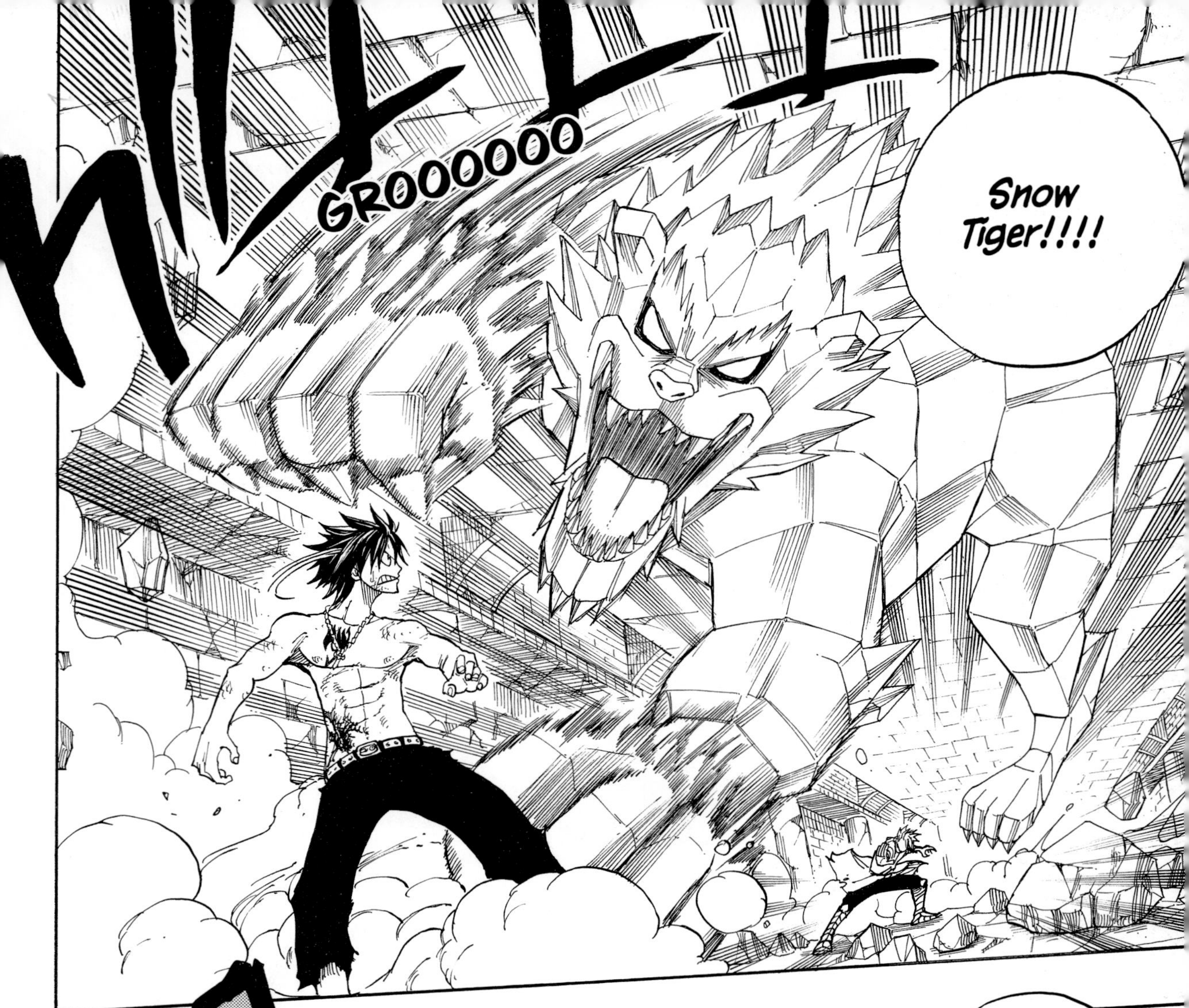
Snow Tiger!!!!
GROOOOOO
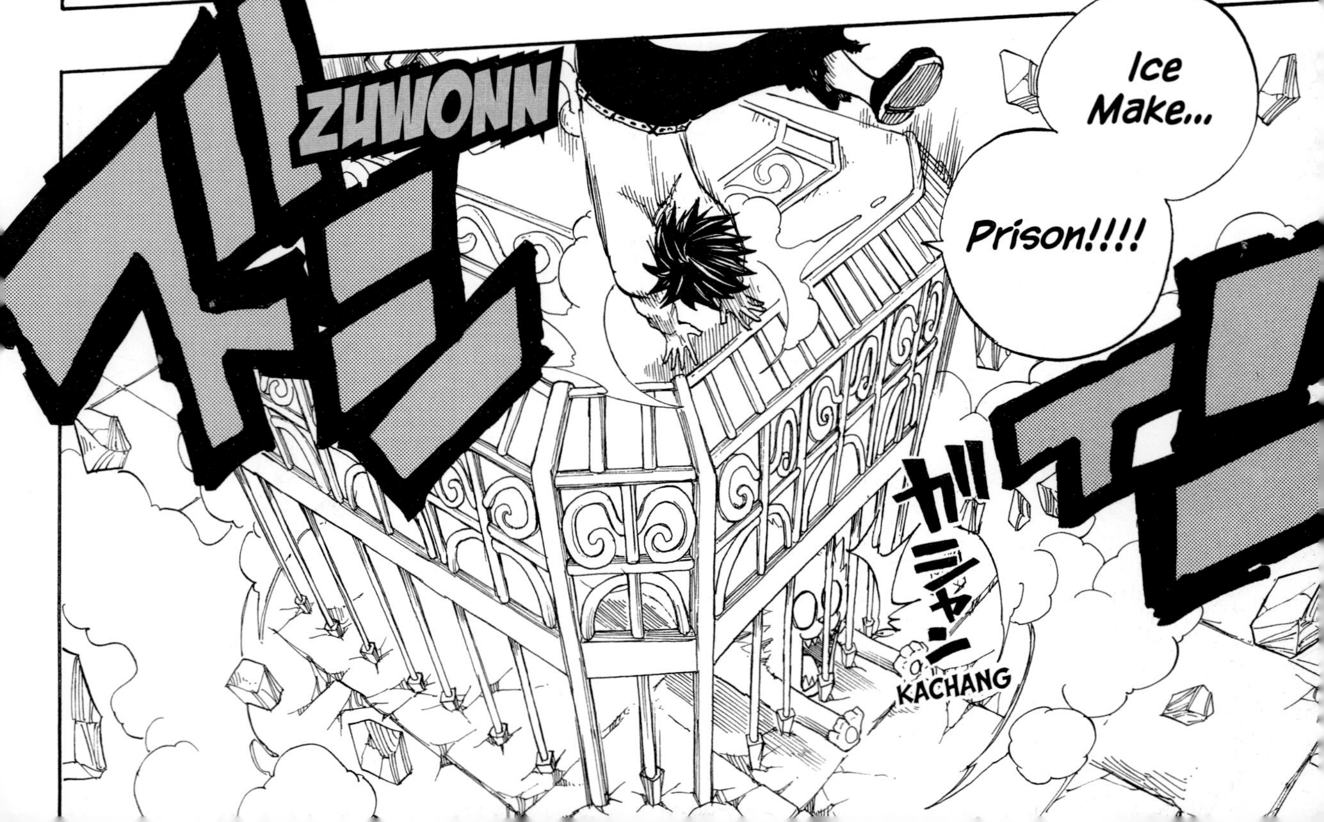
Ice Make...
Prison!!!!
ZUWONN
KACHANG

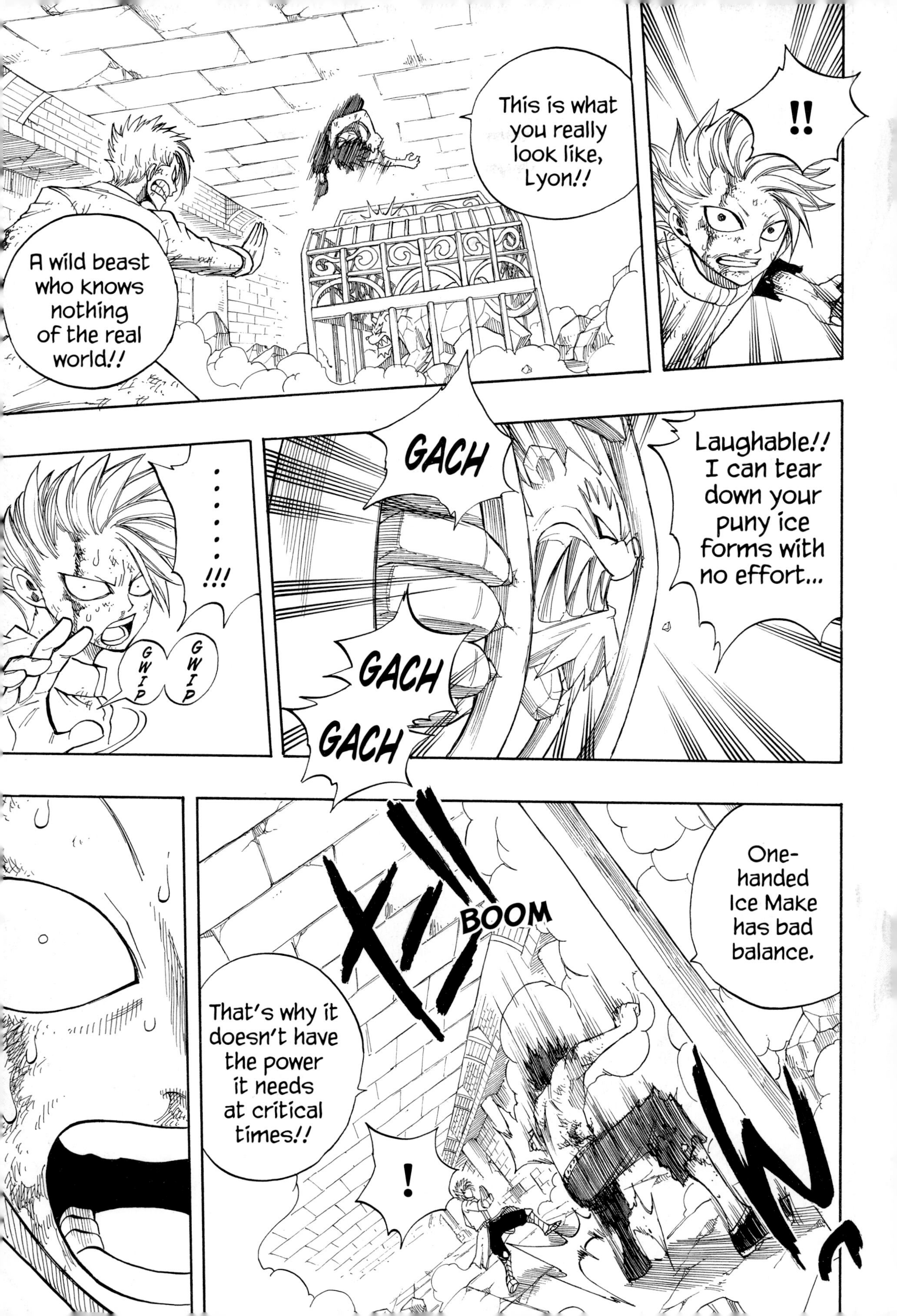
!!
This is what you really look like, Lyon!!
A wild beast who knows nothing of the real world!!
Laughable!! I can tear down your puny ice forms with no effort...
GACH
GACH
GACH
......!!!
GWIP
GWIP
One-handed Ice Make has bad balance.
BOOM
That's why it doesn't have the power it needs at critical times!!
!

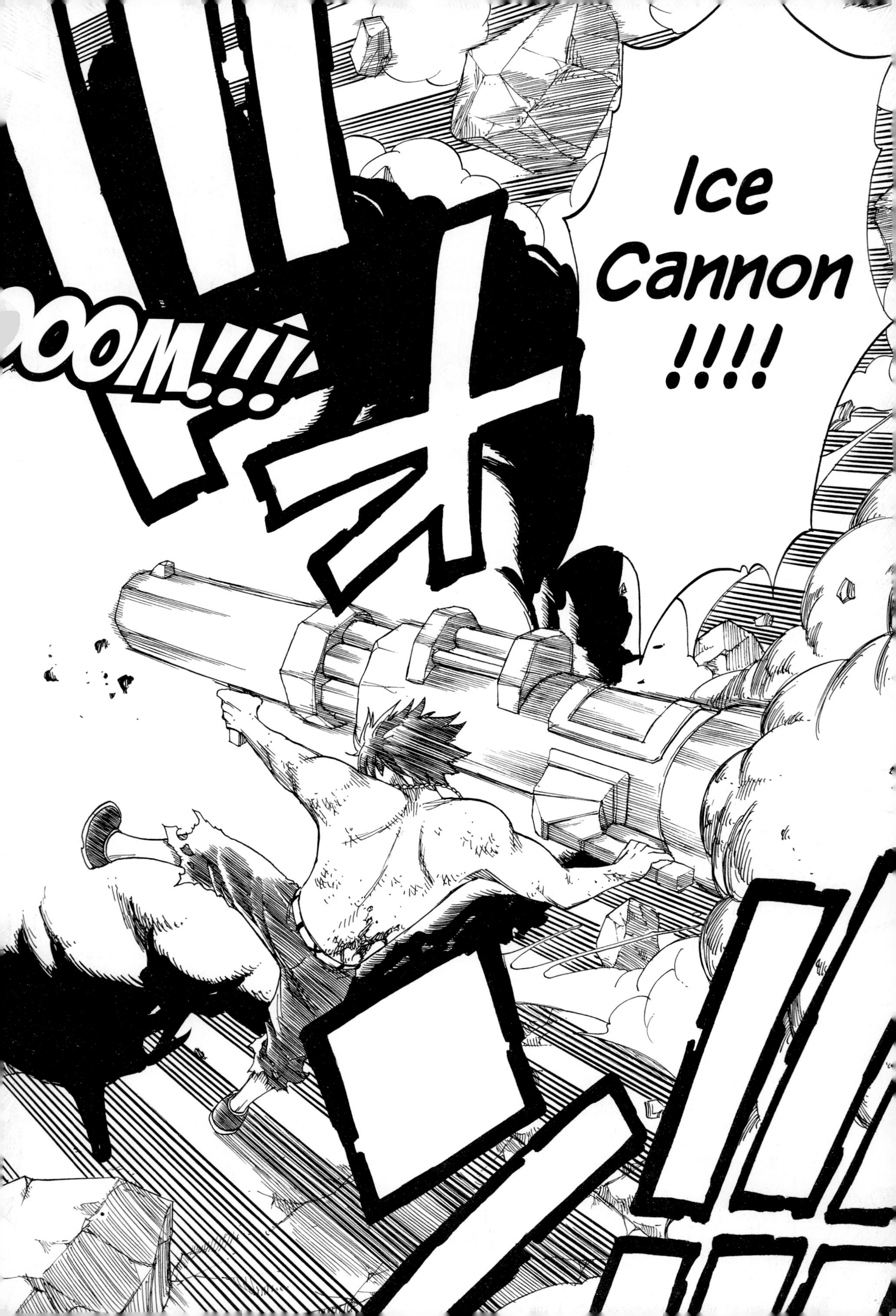
Ice Cannon !!!!
...OOM!!!

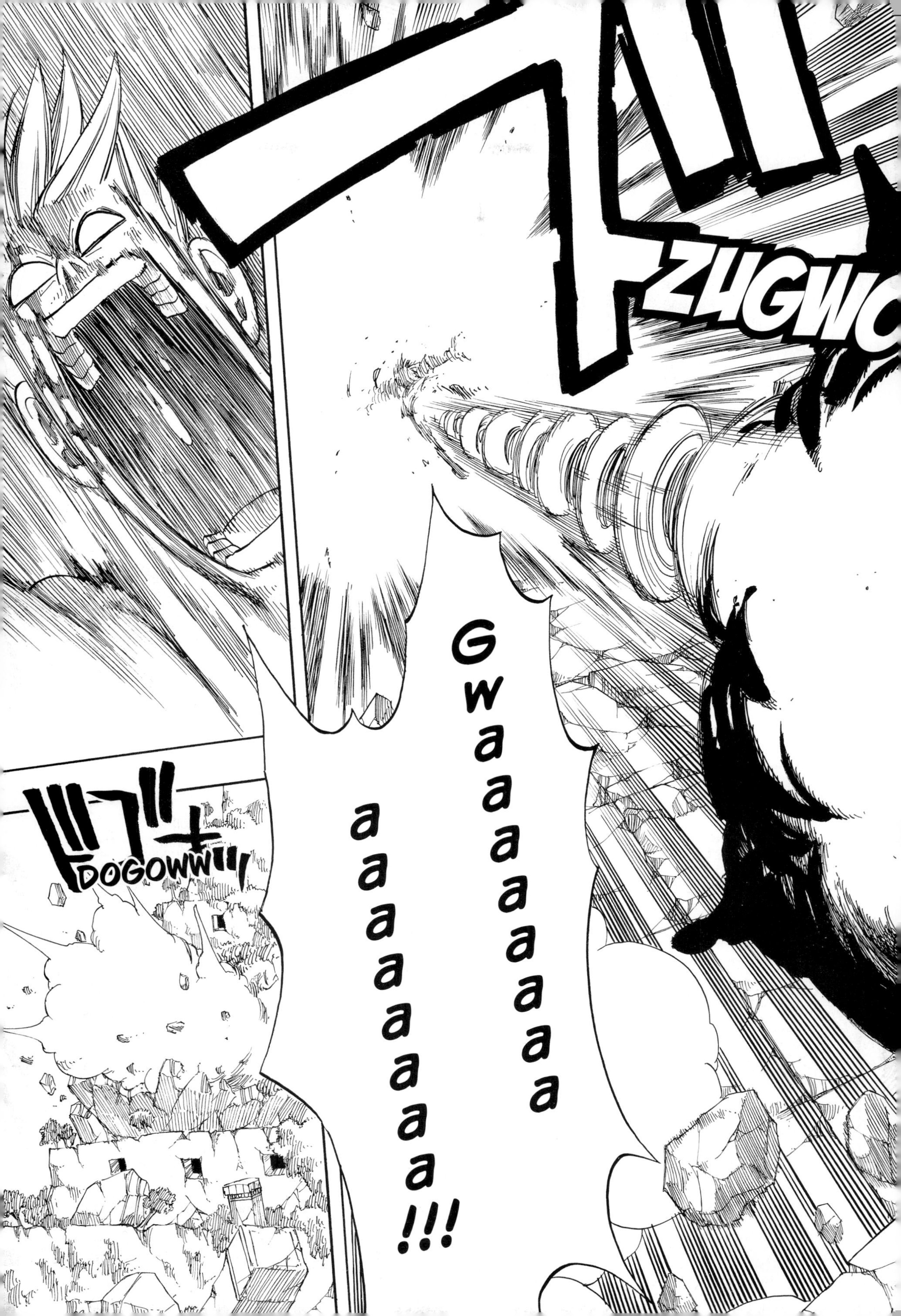
ZUGWO
Gwaaaaaaaaaaaaaaaaaaa!!!
DOGOWW

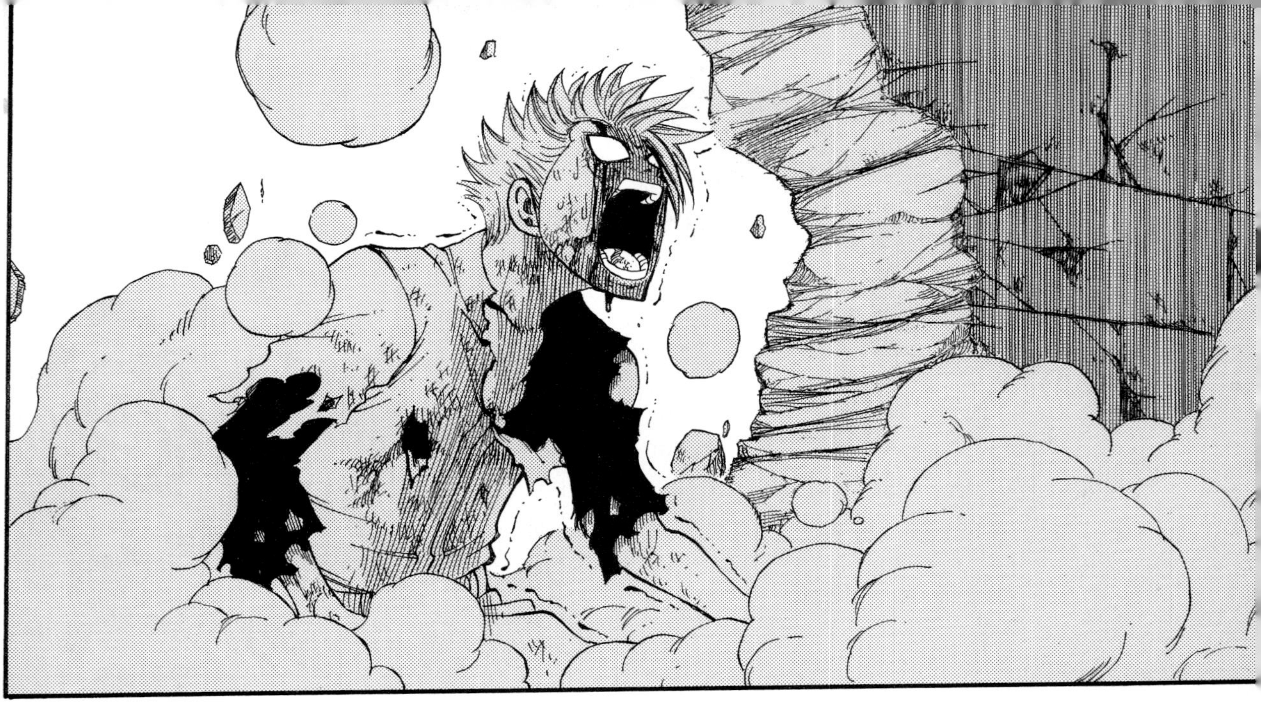

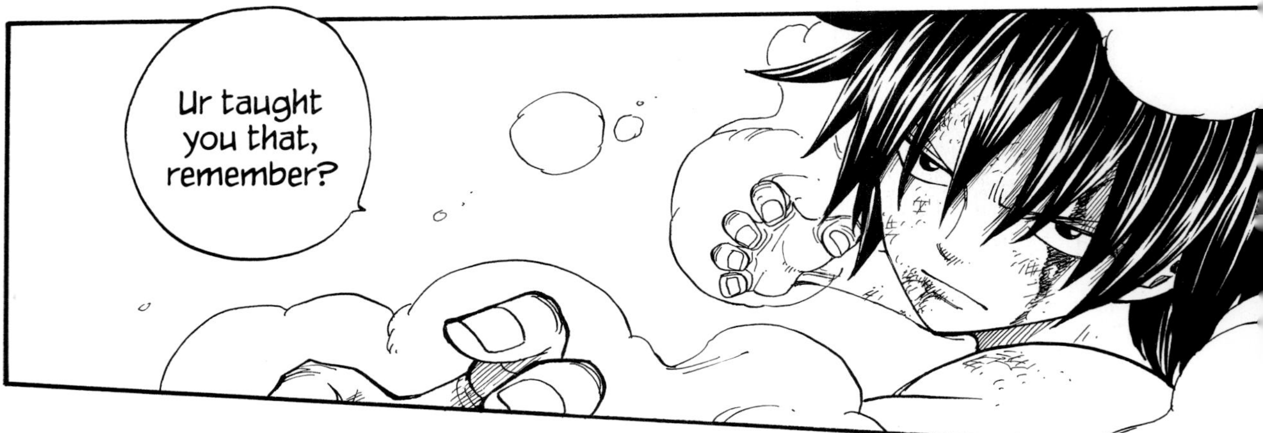
Ur taught you that, remember?

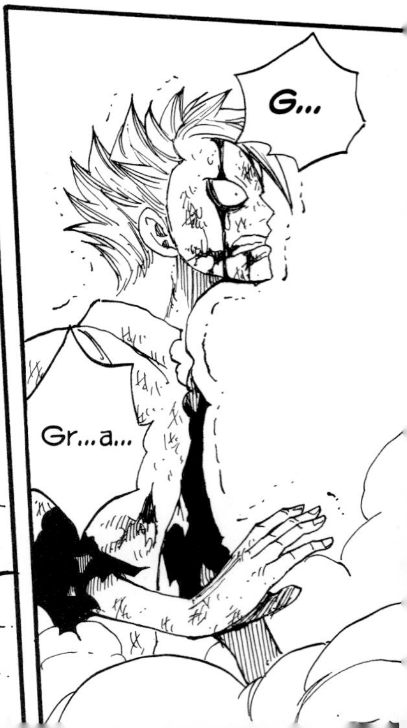
G...
Gr...a...

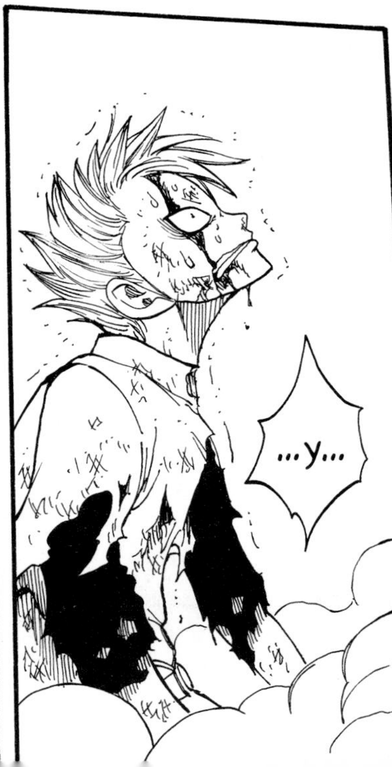
...y...

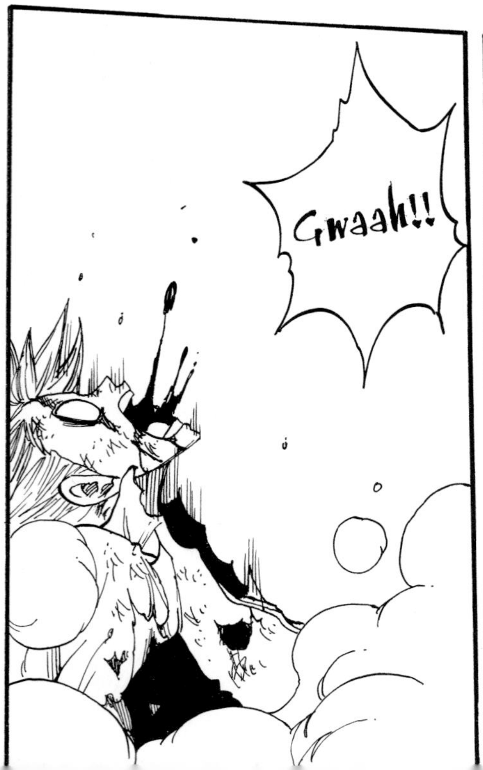
Gwaah!!

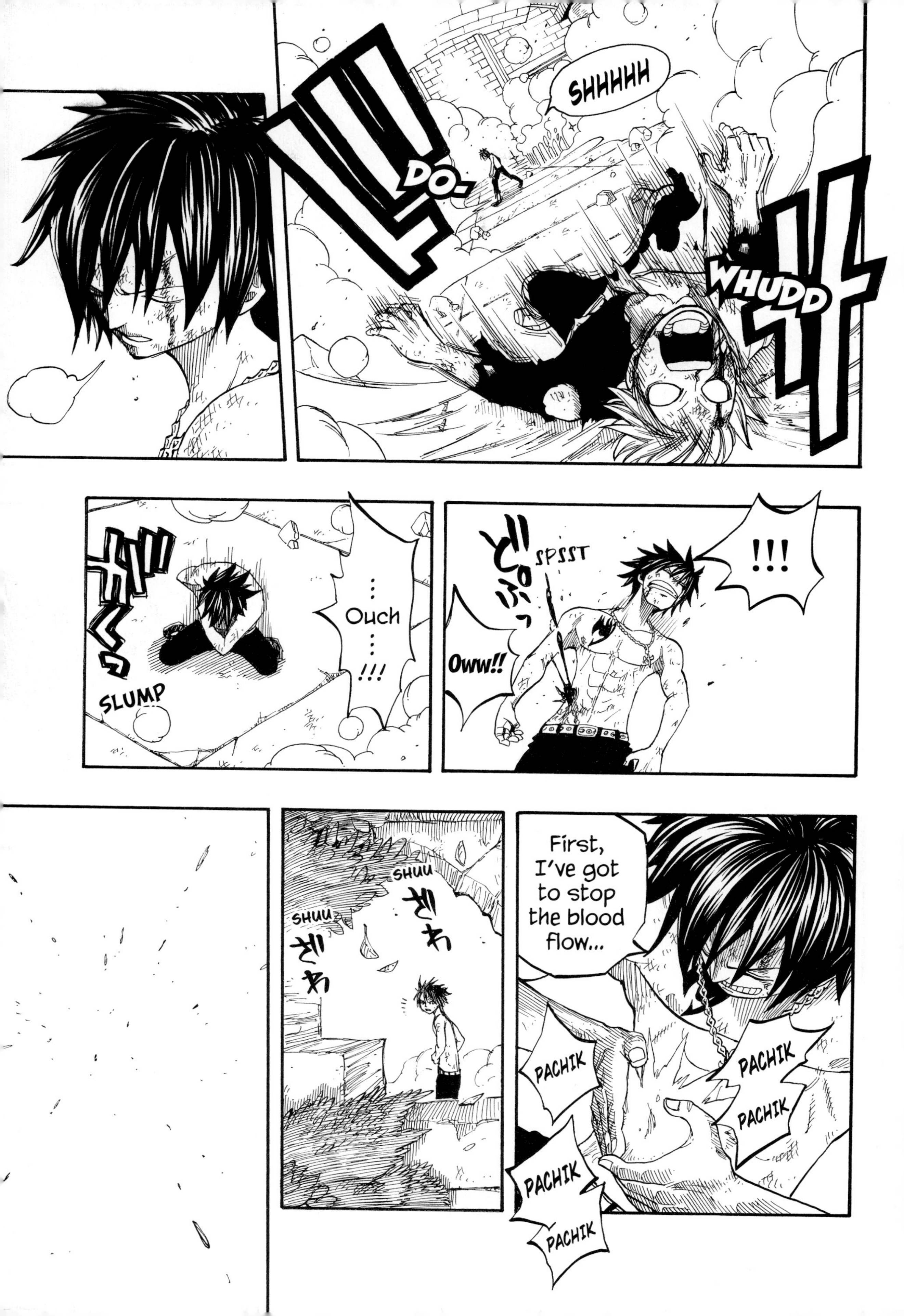
SHHHHH
DO-
WHUDD
!!!
SPSST
Oww!!
...Ouch...!!!
SLUMP
First, I've got to stop the blood flow...
PACHIK
PACHIK
PACHIK
PACHIK
PACHIK
SHUU
SHUU

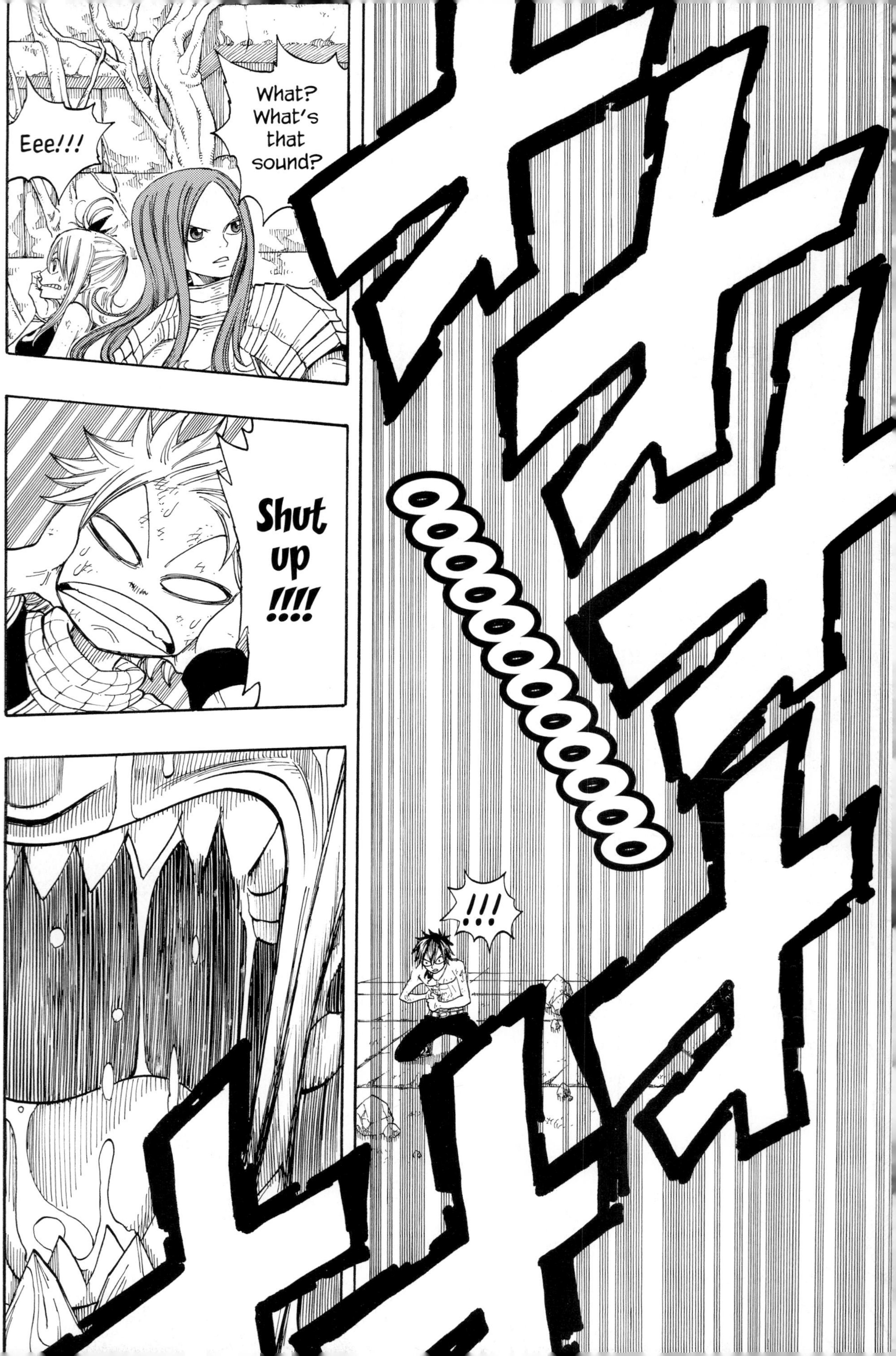
oooooooooooooo
!!!
What? What's that sound?
Eee!!!
Shut up!!!!

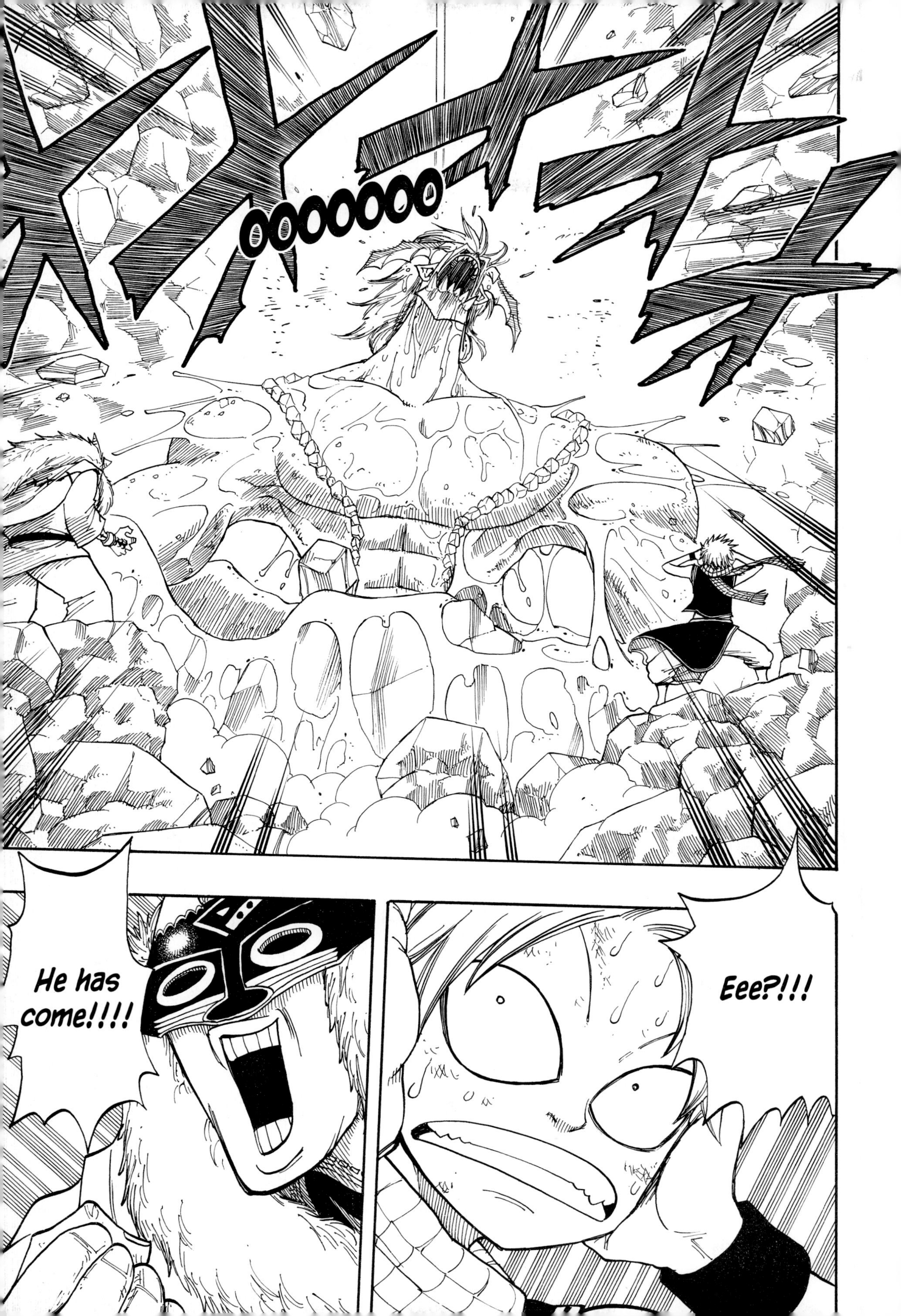
OOOOOOO
He has come!!!!
Eee?!!!

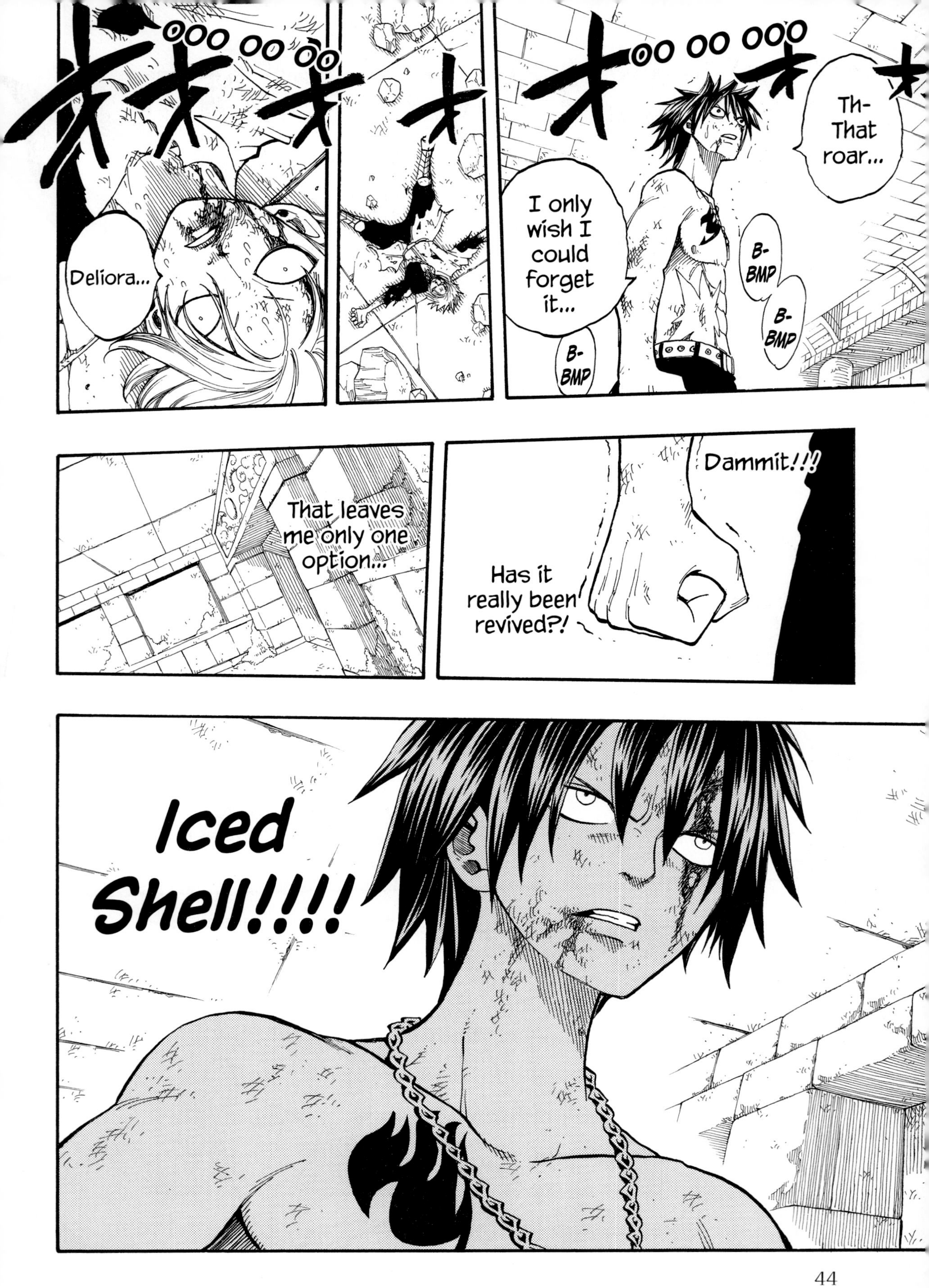
OOO OO OOO
Th- That roar...
B-BMP
B-BMP
I only wish I could forget it...
B-BMP
OOO OO OOO
Deliora...
Dammit!!!
Has it really been revived?!
That leaves me only one option...
Iced Shell!!!!

FAIRY TAIL

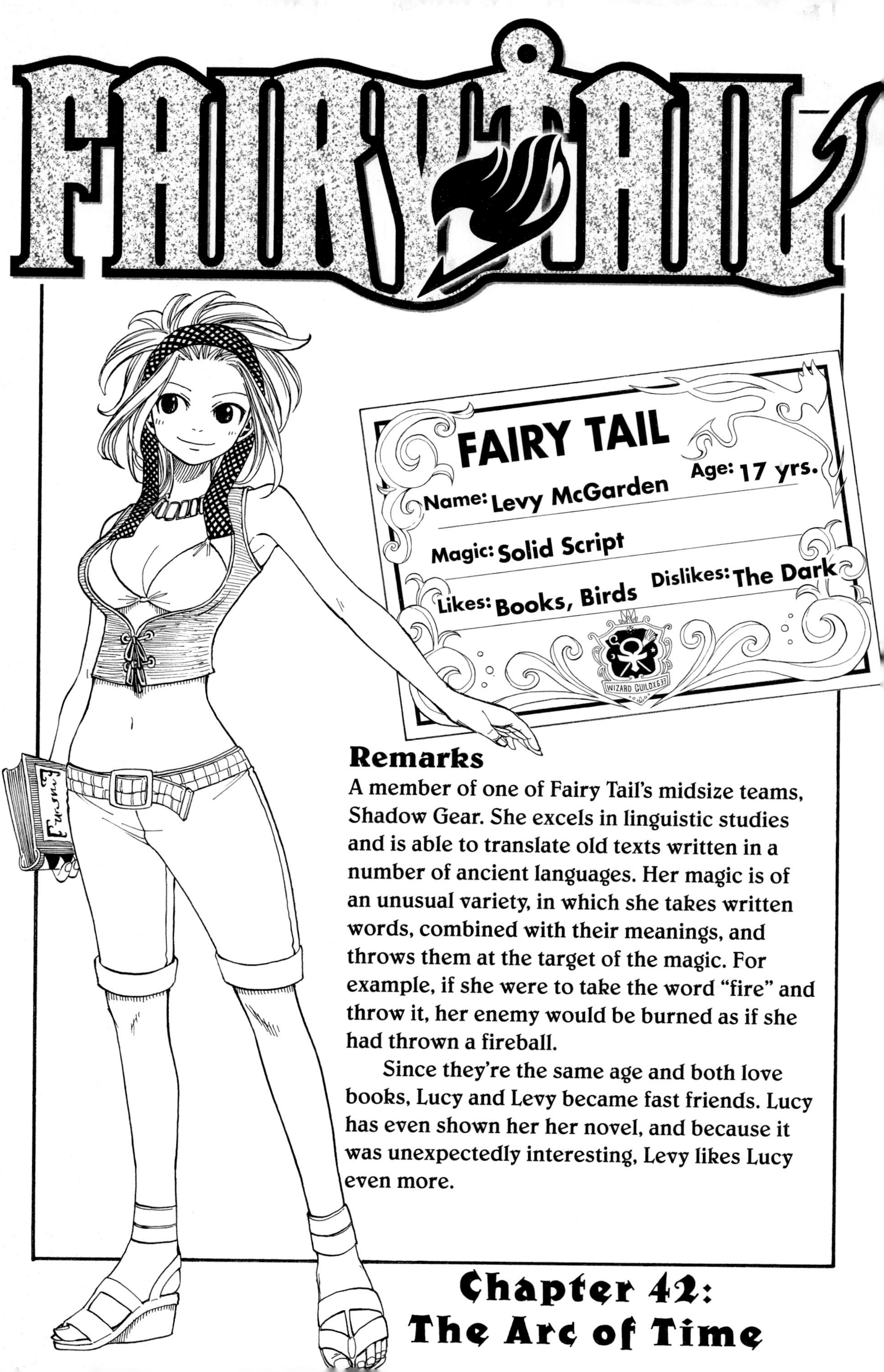

FAIRY TAIL

Name: Levy McGarden Age: 17 yrs.

Magic: Solid Script

Likes: Books, Birds Dislikes: The Dark

WIZARD GUILDX633

Remarks

A member of one of Fairy Tail's midsize teams, Shadow Gear. She excels in linguistic studies and is able to translate old texts written in a number of ancient languages. Her magic is of an unusual variety, in which she takes written words, combined with their meanings, and throws them at the target of the magic. For example, if she were to take the word "fire" and throw it, her enemy would be burned as if she had thrown a fireball.

Since they're the same age and both love books, Lucy and Levy became fast friends. Lucy has even shown her her novel, and because it was unexpectedly interesting, Levy likes Lucy even more.

Chapter 42: The Arc of Time

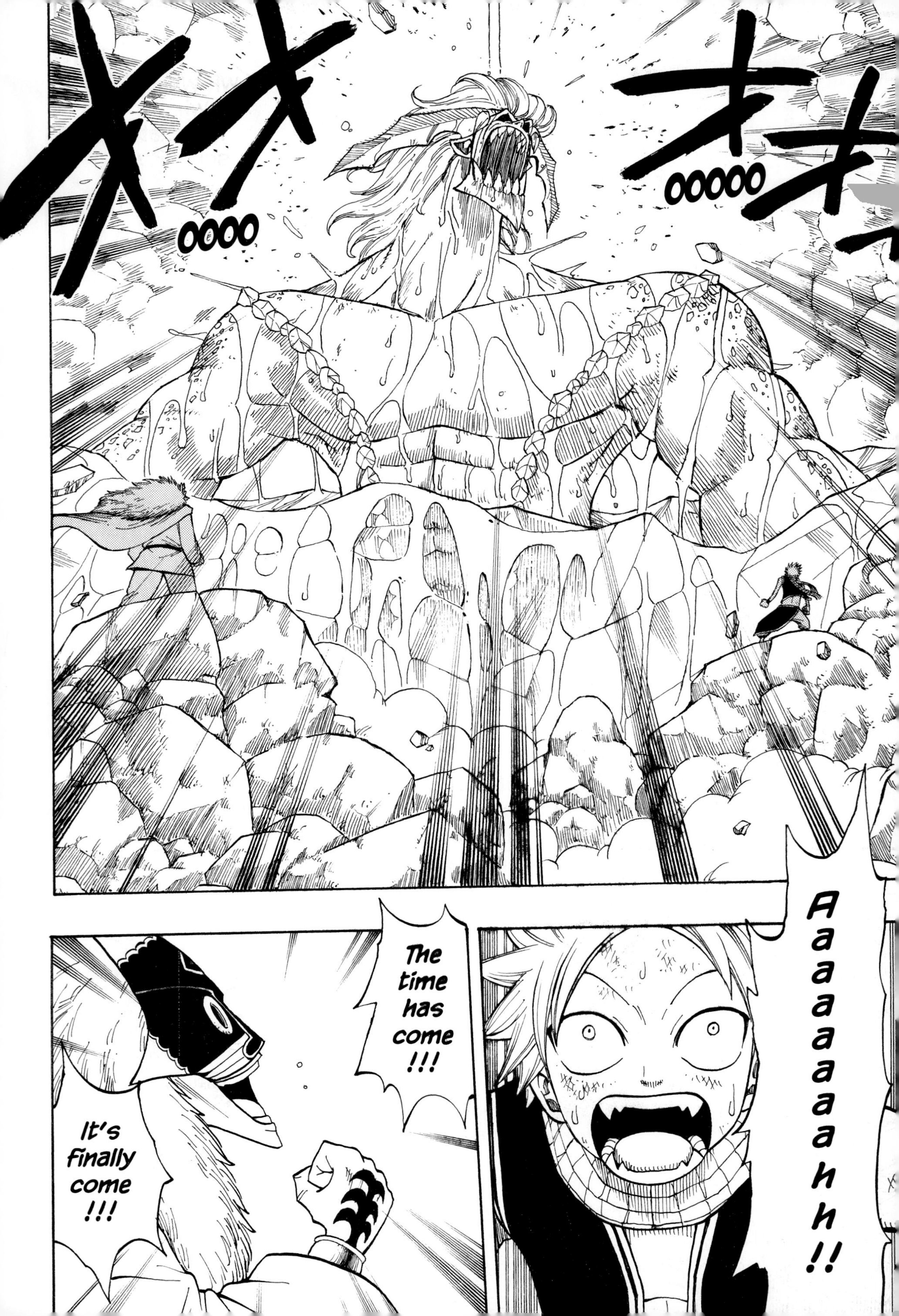
ooooo
oooo
Aaaaaaaaaahh!!
The time has come!!!
It's finally come!!!

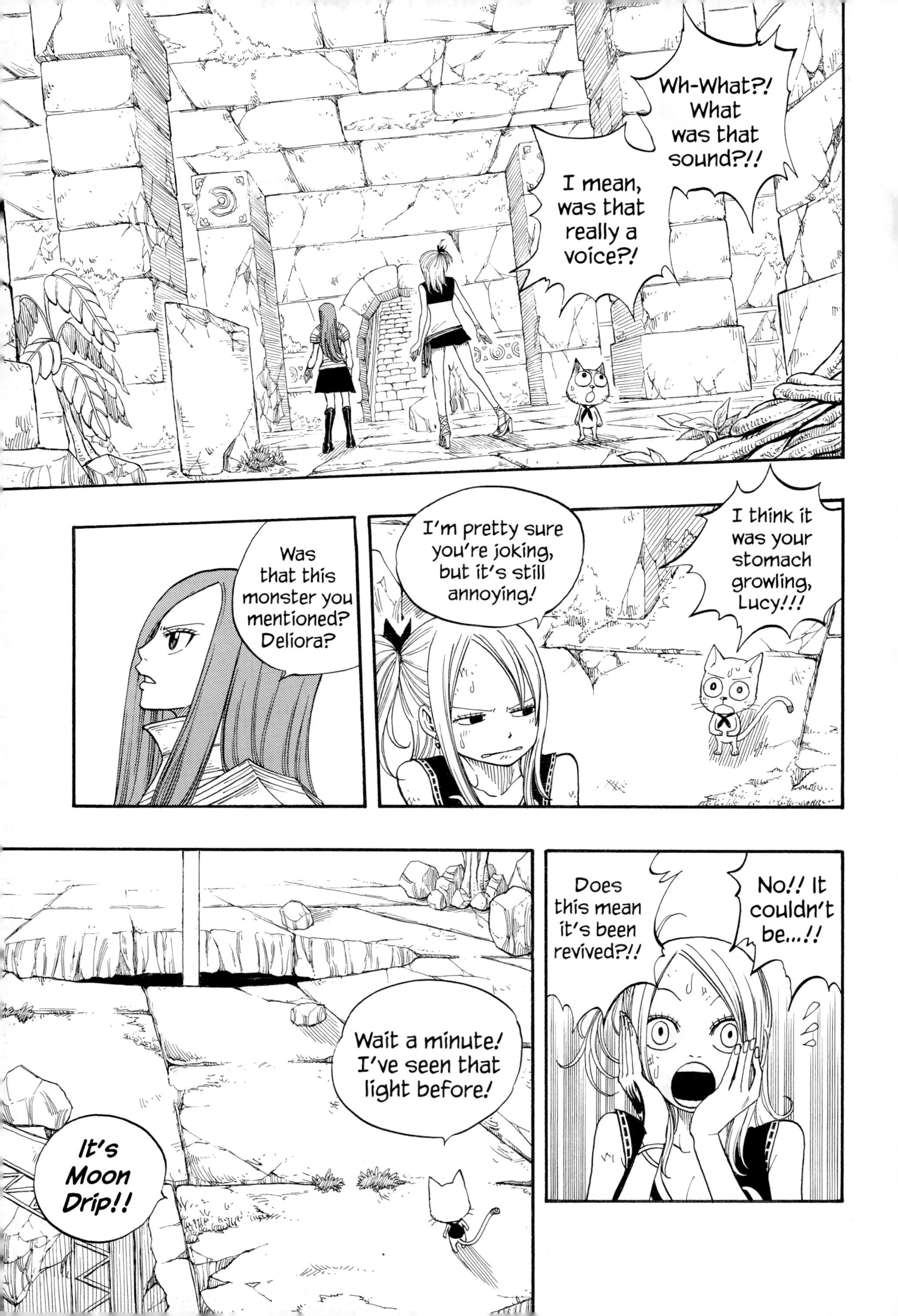
Wh-What?! What was that sound?!!
I mean, was that really a voice?!
I think it was your stomach growling, Lucy!!!
I'm pretty sure you're joking, but it's still annoying!
Was that this monster you mentioned? Deliora?
No!! It couldn't be...!!
Does this mean it's been revived?!!
Wait a minute! I've seen that light before!
It's Moon Drip!!

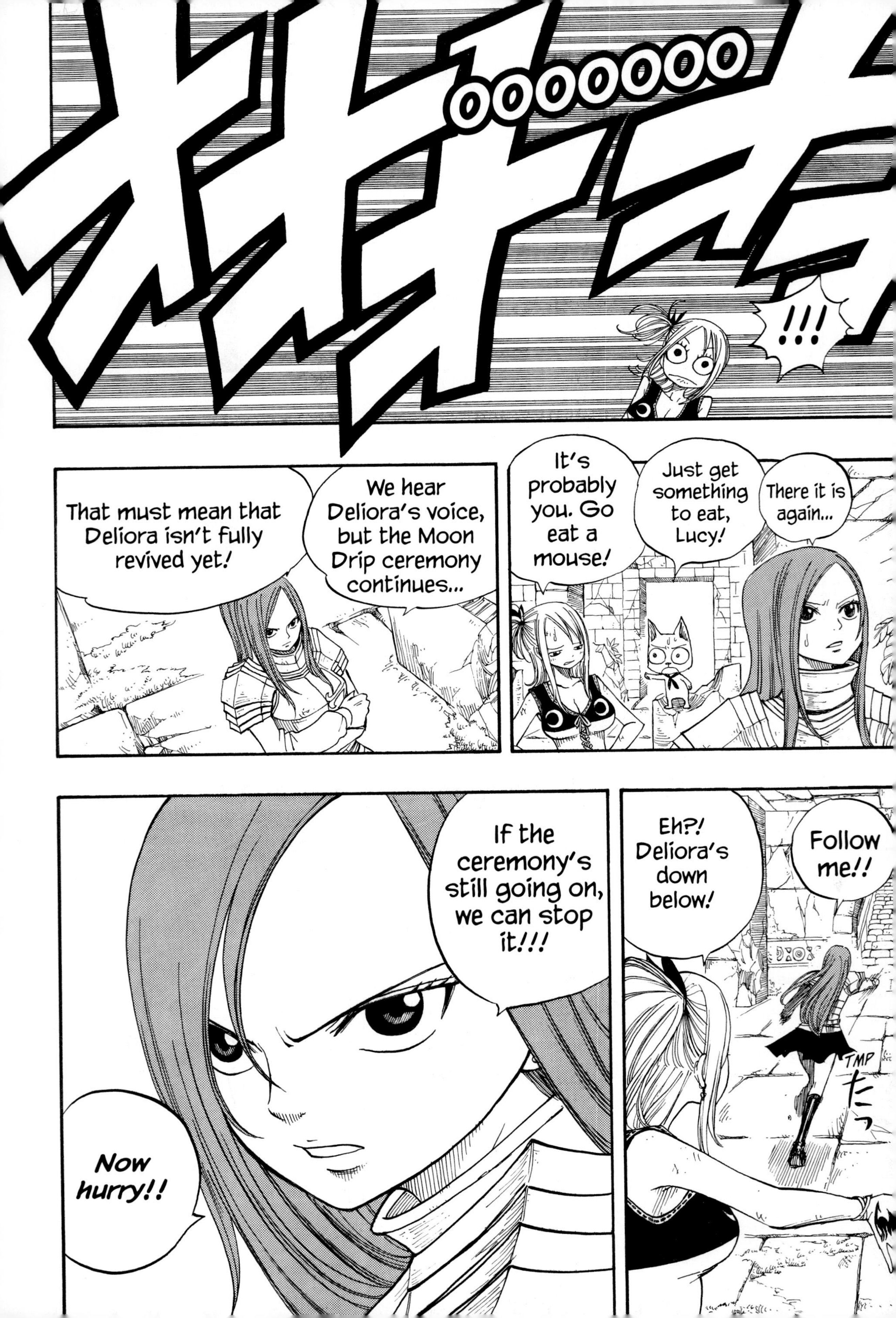
OOOOOOO
!!!
There it is again...
Just get something to eat, Lucy!
It's probably you. Go eat a mouse!
We hear Deliora's voice, but the Moon Drip ceremony continues...
That must mean that Deliora isn't fully revived yet!
Follow me!!
Eh?! Deliora's down below!
TMP
If the ceremony's still going on, we can stop it!!!
Now hurry!!

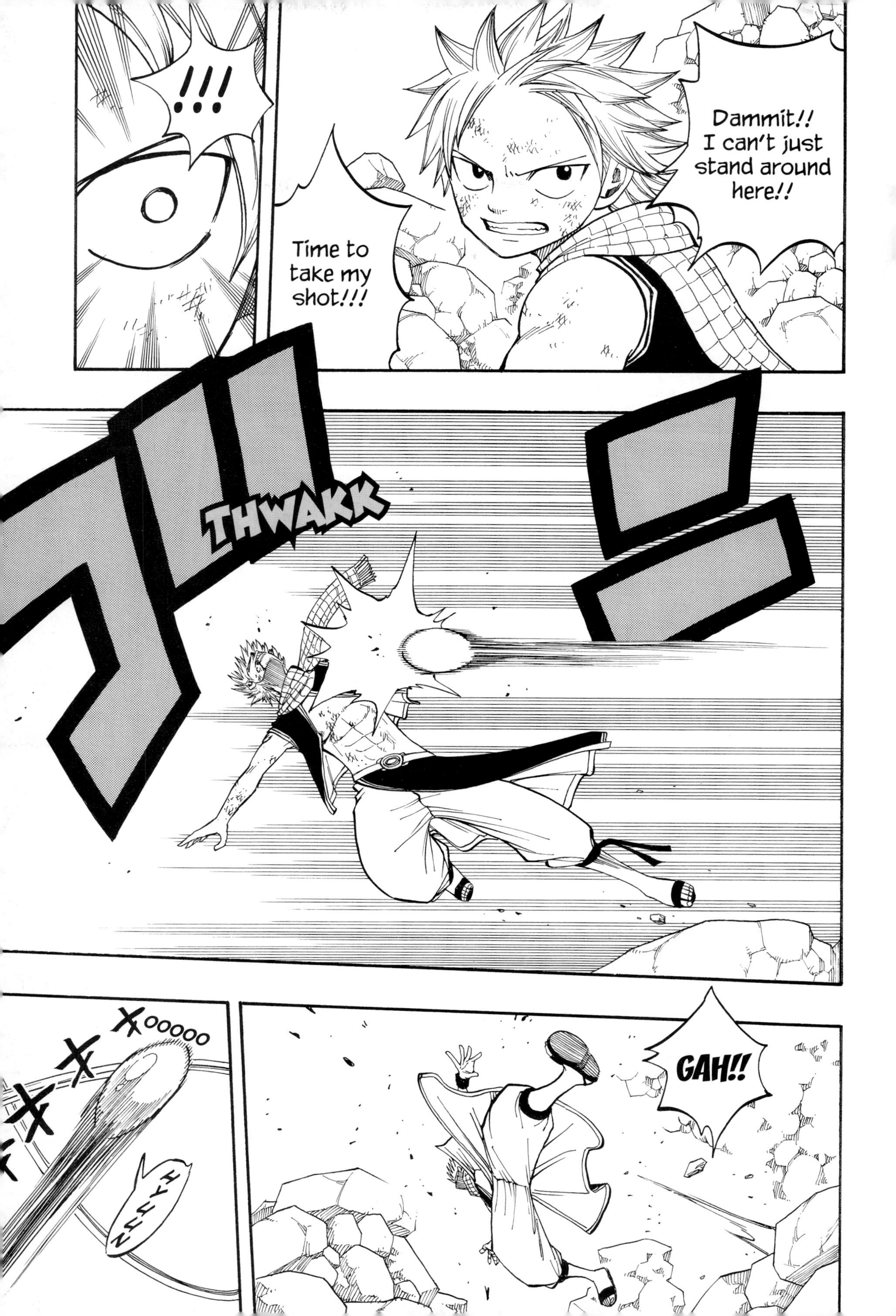
Dammit!! I can't just stand around here!!
Time to take my shot!!!
!!!
THWAKK
GAH!!
Xooooo
NNNYYH

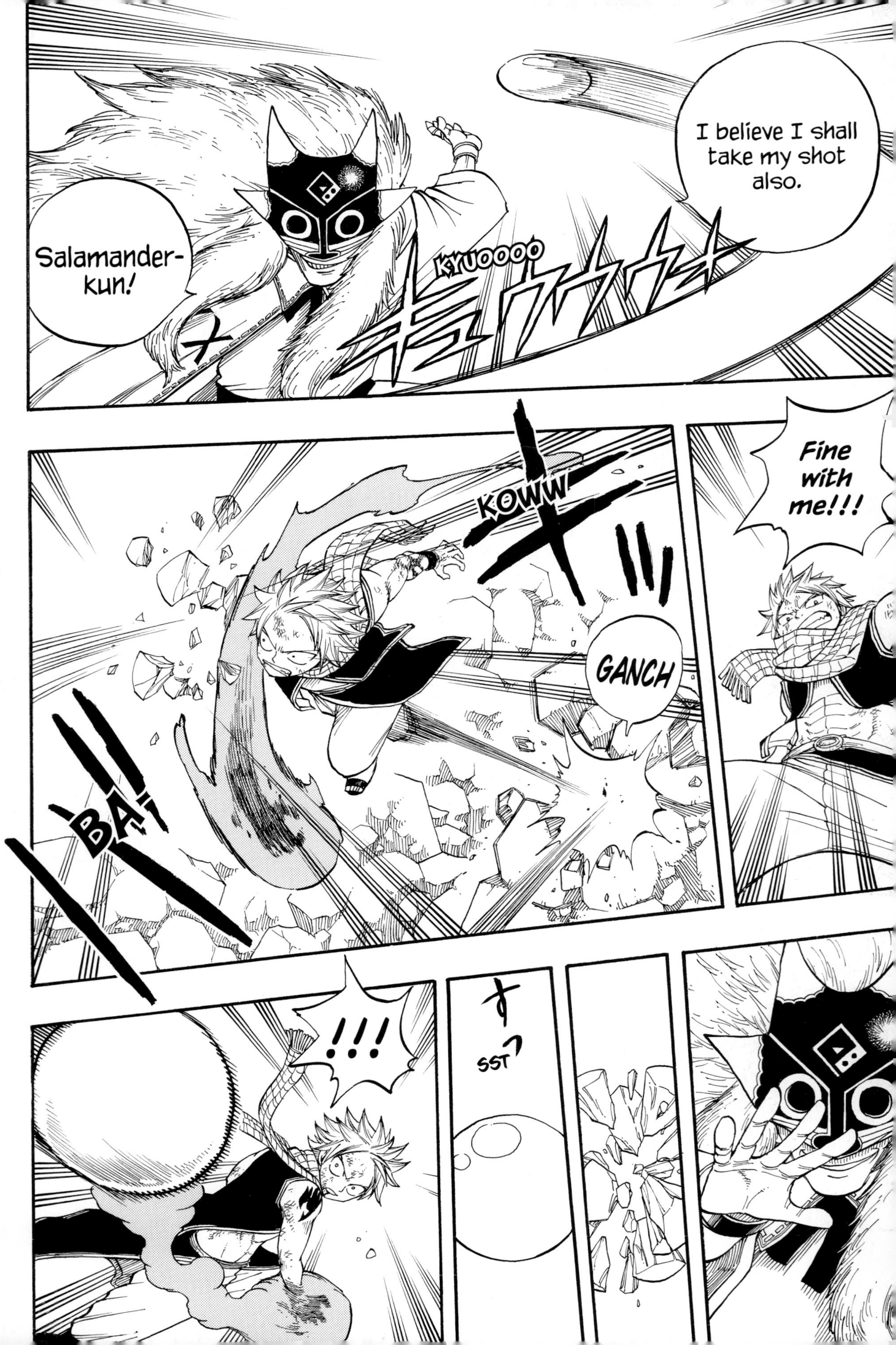
I believe I shall take my shot also.
Salamander-kun!
KYUOOOO
Fine with me!!!
KOWW
GANCH
BA
!!!
SST

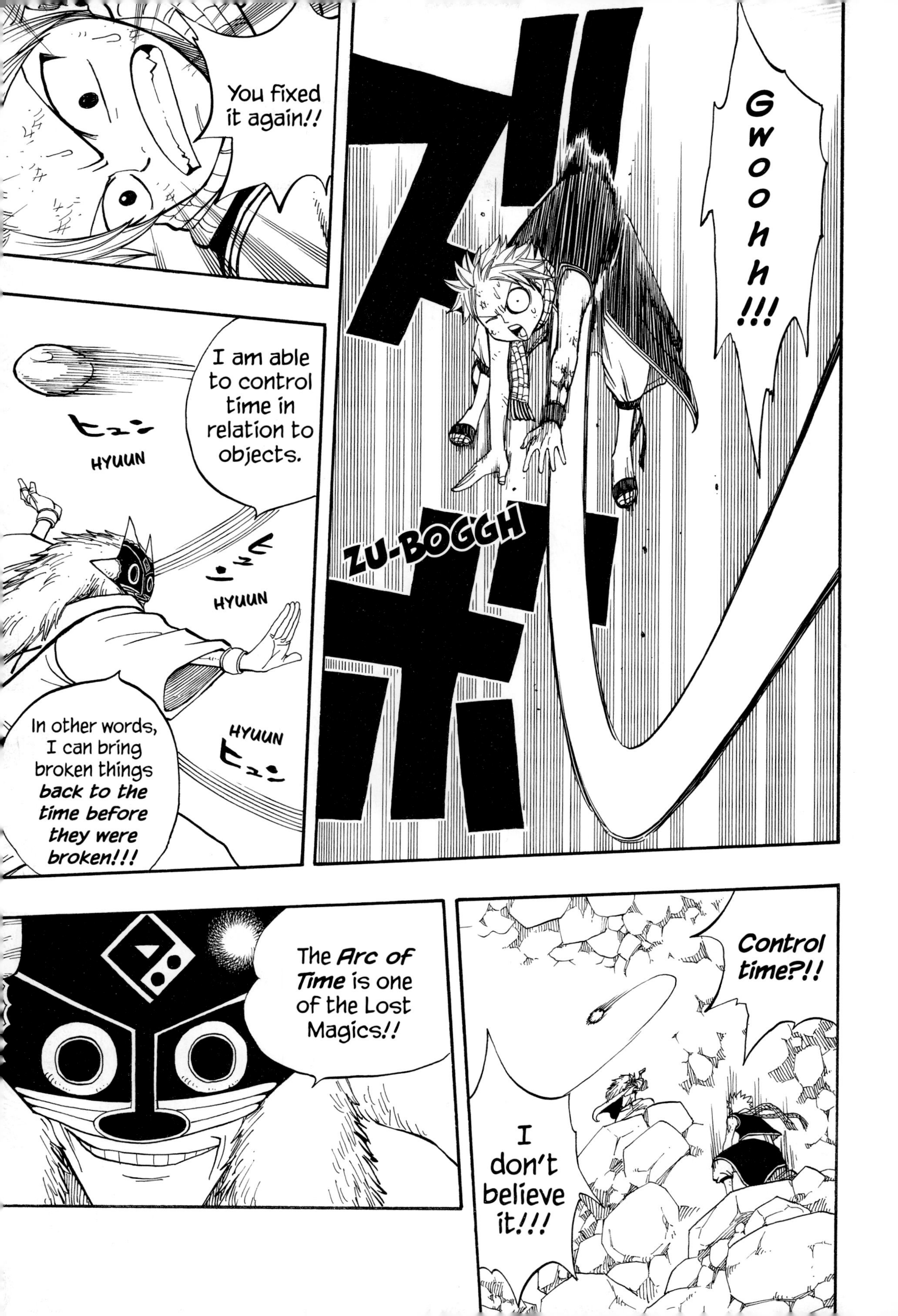
Gwooohh!!!
ZU-BOGGH
You fixed it again!!
I am able to control time in relation to objects.
HYUUN
HYUUN
In other words, I can bring broken things *back to the time before they were broken!!!*
HYUUN
Control time?!!
I don't believe it!!!
The *Arc of Time* is one of the Lost Magics!!

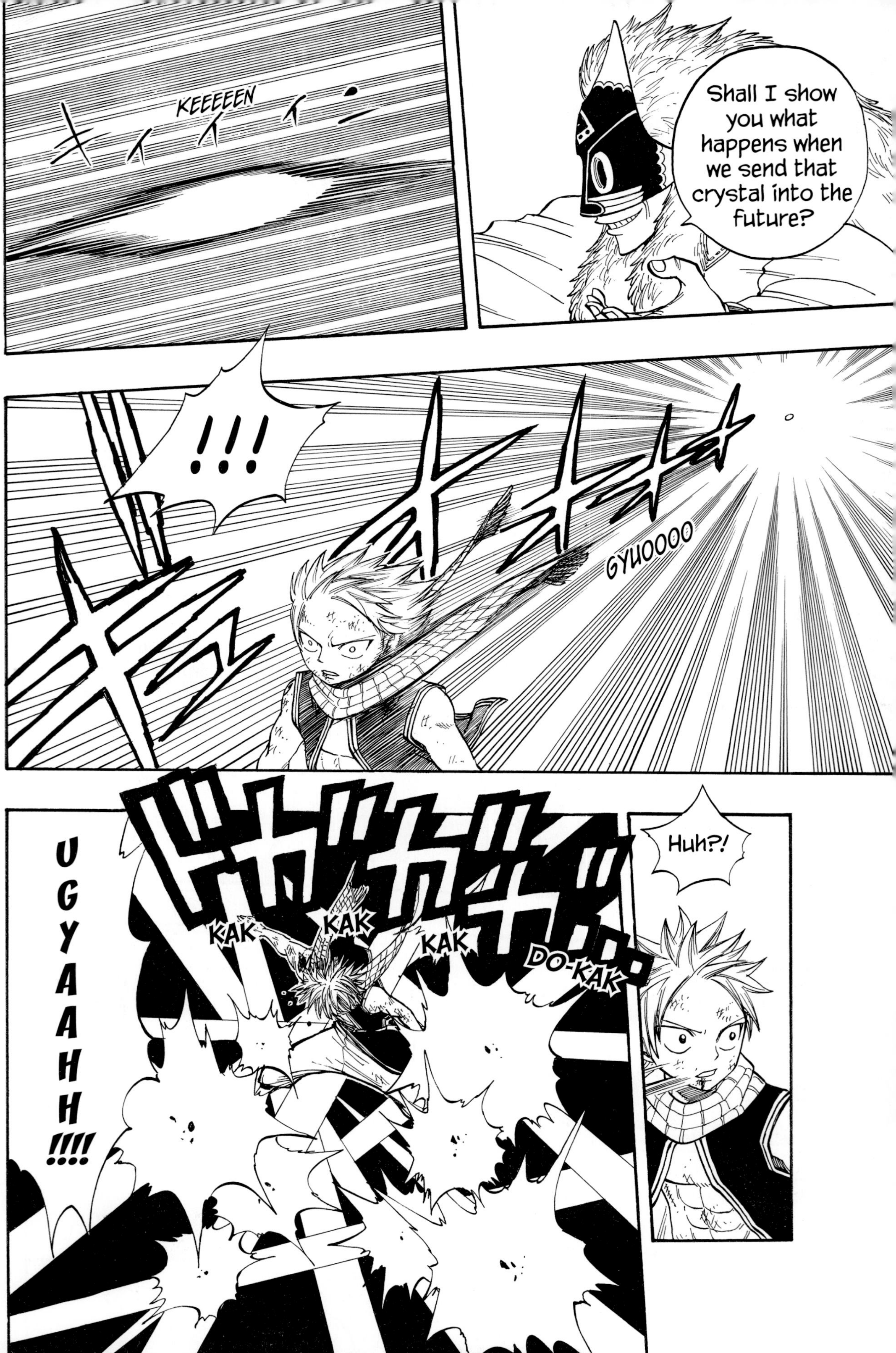
Shall I show you what happens when we send that crystal into the future?
KEEEEEN
!!!
GYUOOOO
Huh?!
UGYAAAHH!!!!
KAK
KAK
KAK
DO-KAK

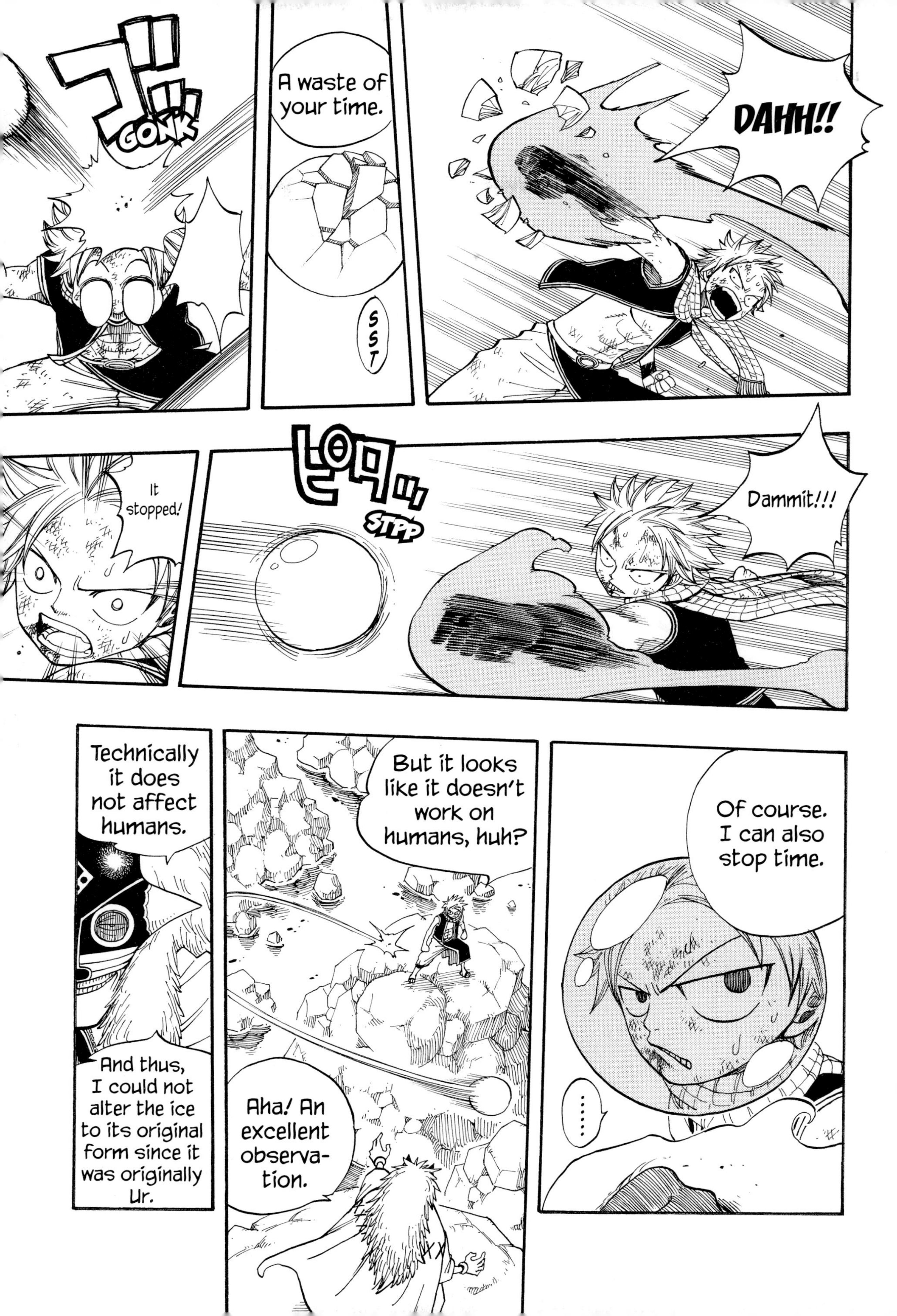
DAHH!!
A waste of your time.
SST
GONK
Dammit!!!
STPP
It stopped!
Of course. I can also stop time.
......
But it looks like it doesn't work on humans, huh?
Aha! An excellent observa-tion.
Technically it does not affect humans.
And thus, I could not alter the ice to its original form since it was originally Ur.

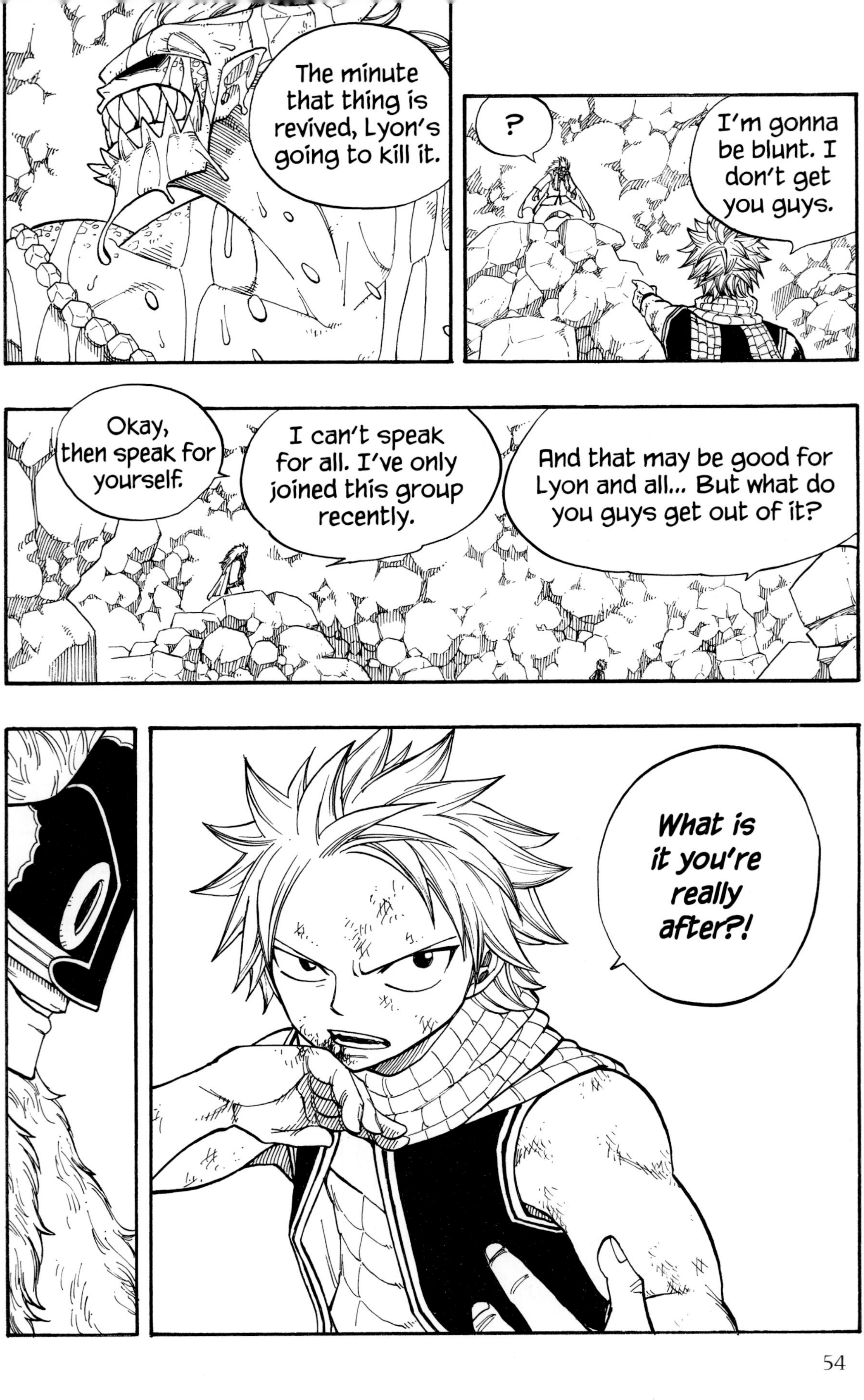
I'm gonna be blunt. I don't get you guys.
?
The minute that thing is revived, Lyon's going to kill it.
And that may be good for Lyon and all... But what do you guys get out of it?
I can't speak for all. I've only joined this group recently.
Okay, then speak for yourself.
What is it you're really after?!

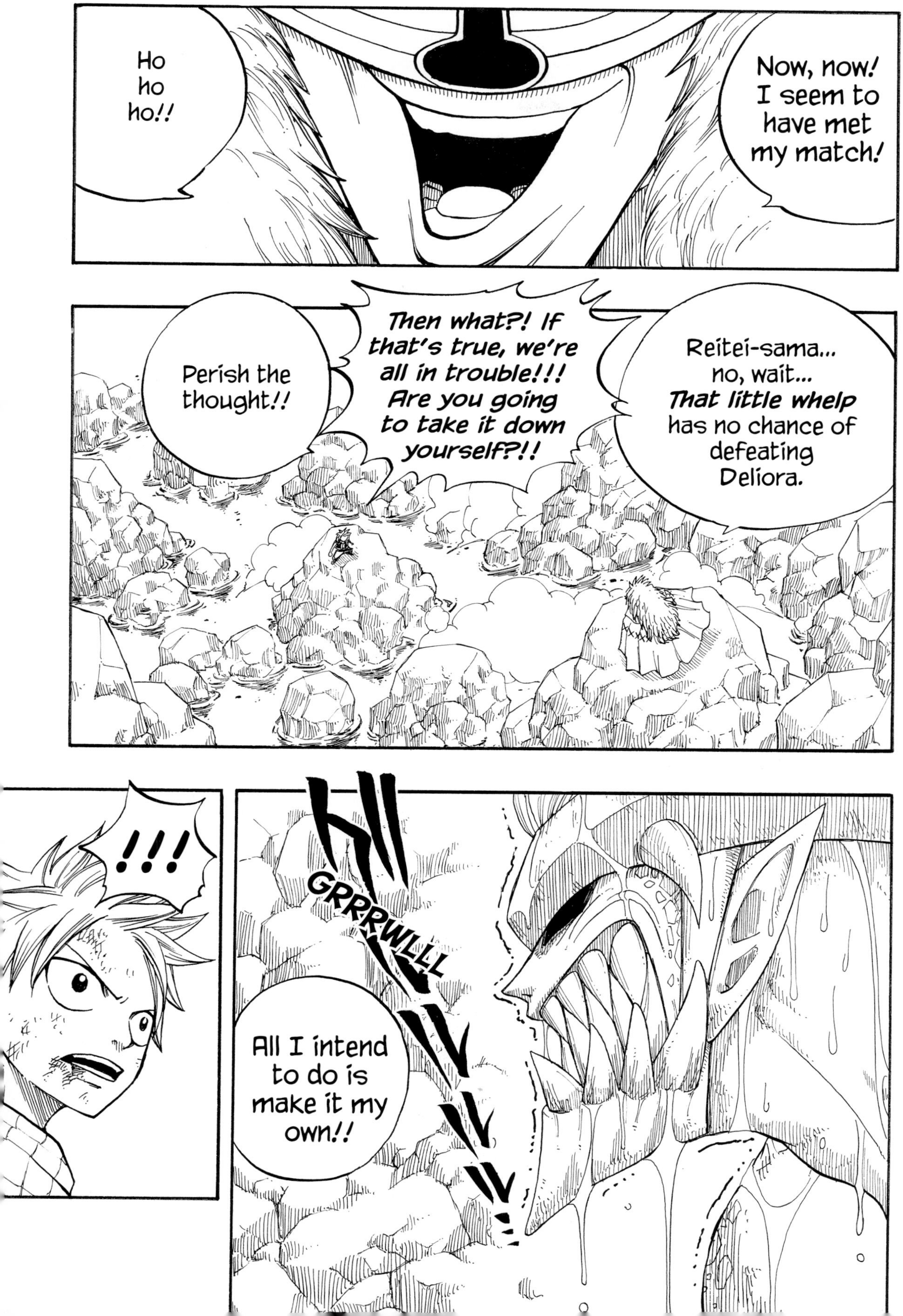
Now, now! I seem to have met my match!
Ho ho ho!!
Reitei-sama... no, wait... *That little whelp* has no chance of defeating Deliora.
Then what?! If that's true, we're all in trouble!!! Are you going to take it down yourself?!!
Perish the thought!!
GRRRWLLLL
All I intend to do is make it my own!!
!!!

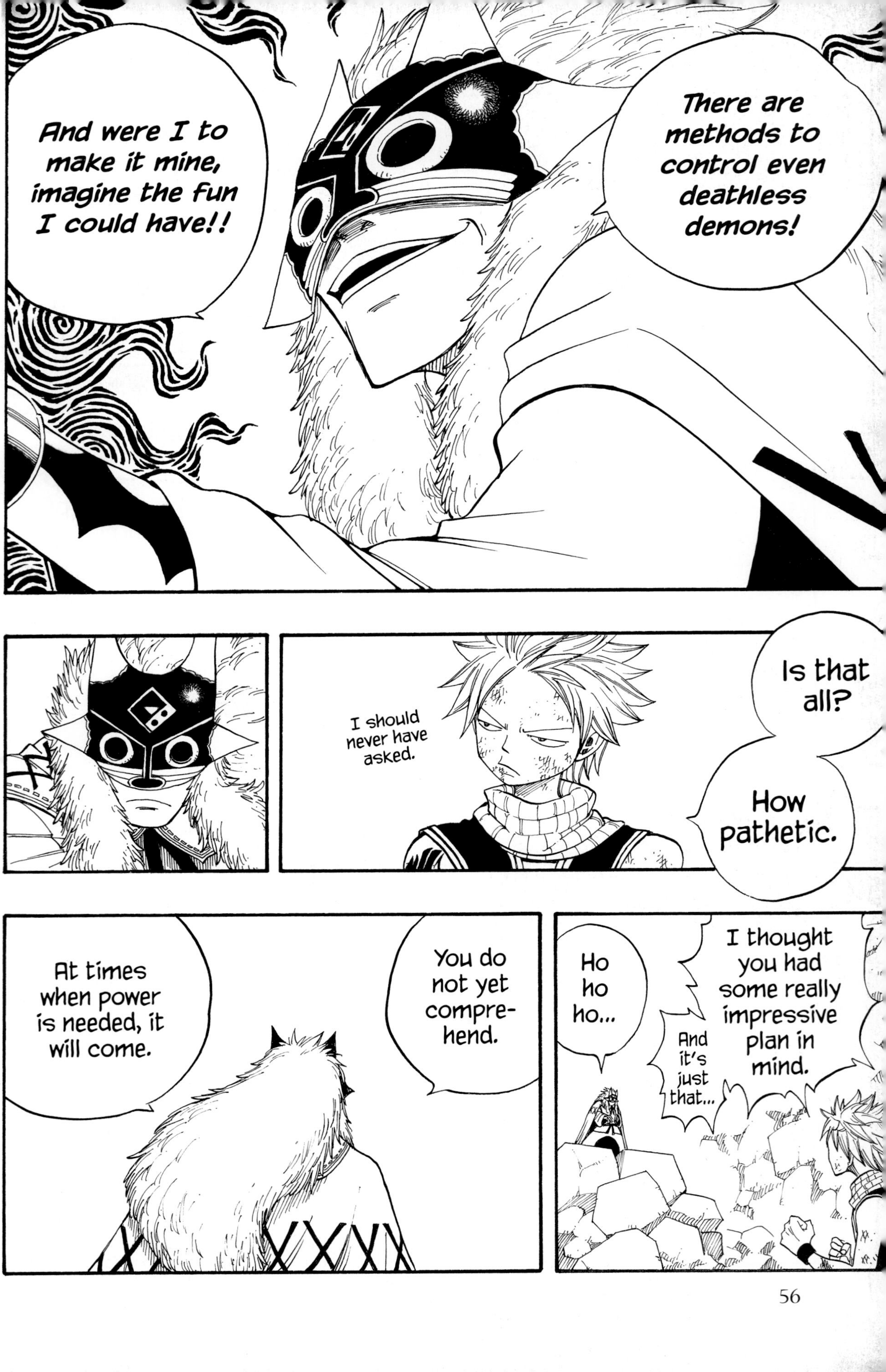
There are methods to control even deathless demons!
And were I to make it mine, imagine the fun I could have!!
Is that all?
How pathetic.
I should never have asked.
I thought you had some really impressive plan in mind.
And it's just that...
Ho ho ho...
You do not yet compre-hend.
At times when power is needed, it will come.

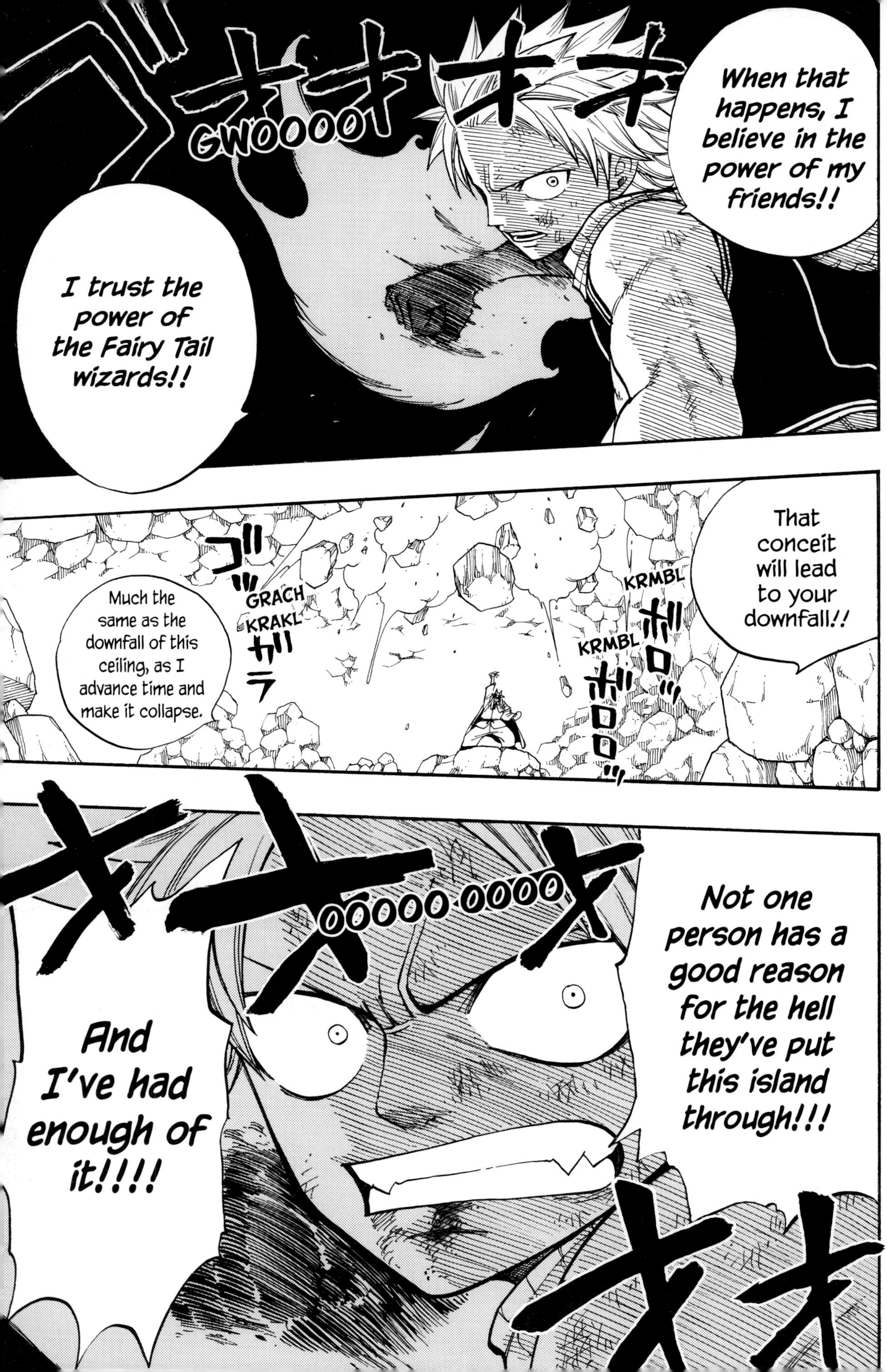

GWOOOO
When that happens, I believe in the power of my friends!!
I trust the power of the Fairy Tail wizards!!
That conceit will lead to your downfall!!
KRMBL
KRMBL
Much the same as the downfall of this ceiling, as I advance time and make it collapse.
GRACH
KRAKL
OOOOO OOOO
Not one person has a good reason for the hell they've put this island through!!!
And I've had enough of it!!!!

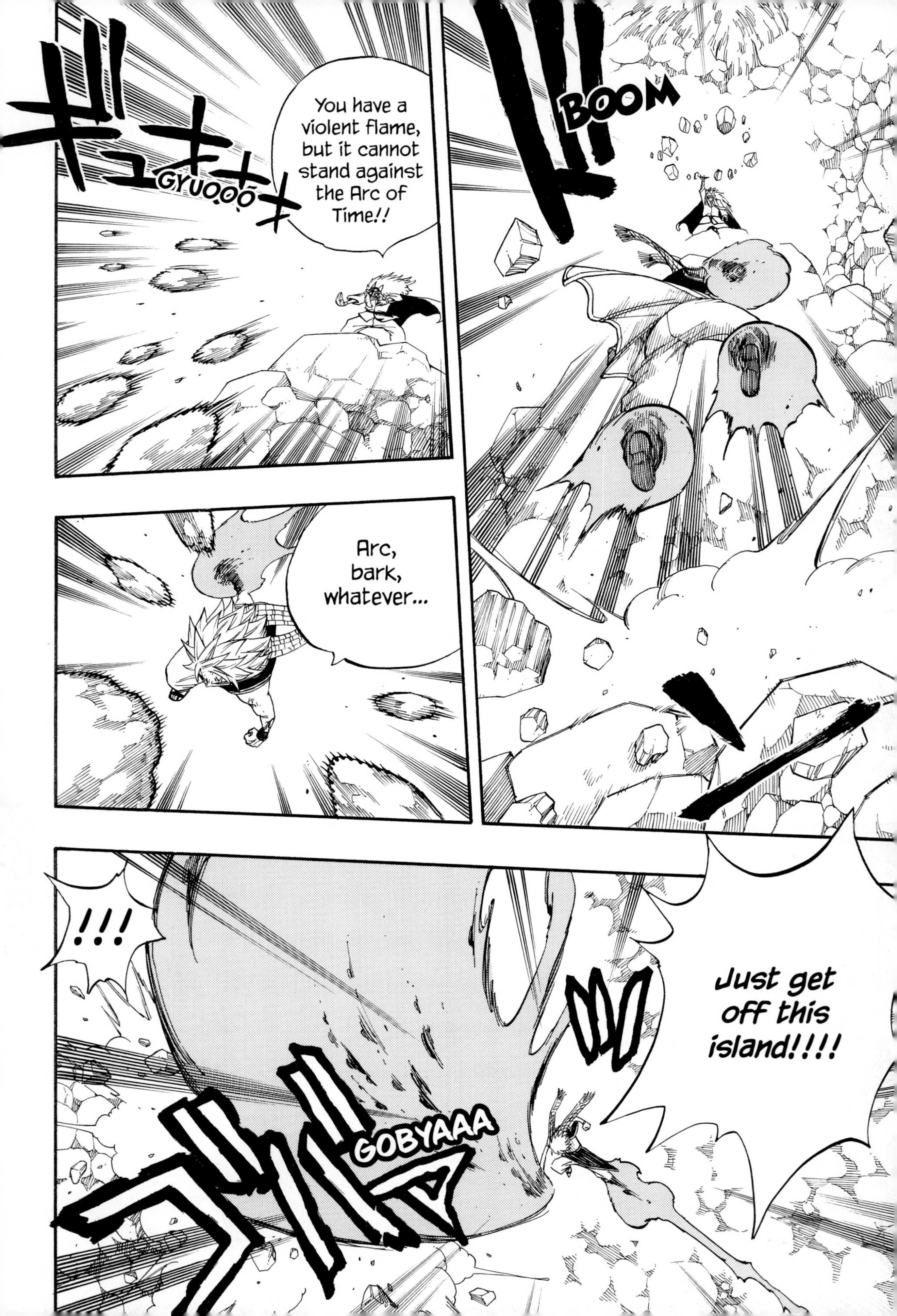
BOOM
GYUOOO
You have a violent flame, but it cannot stand against the Arc of Time!!
Arc, bark, whatever...
!!!
Just get off this island!!!!
GOBYAAA

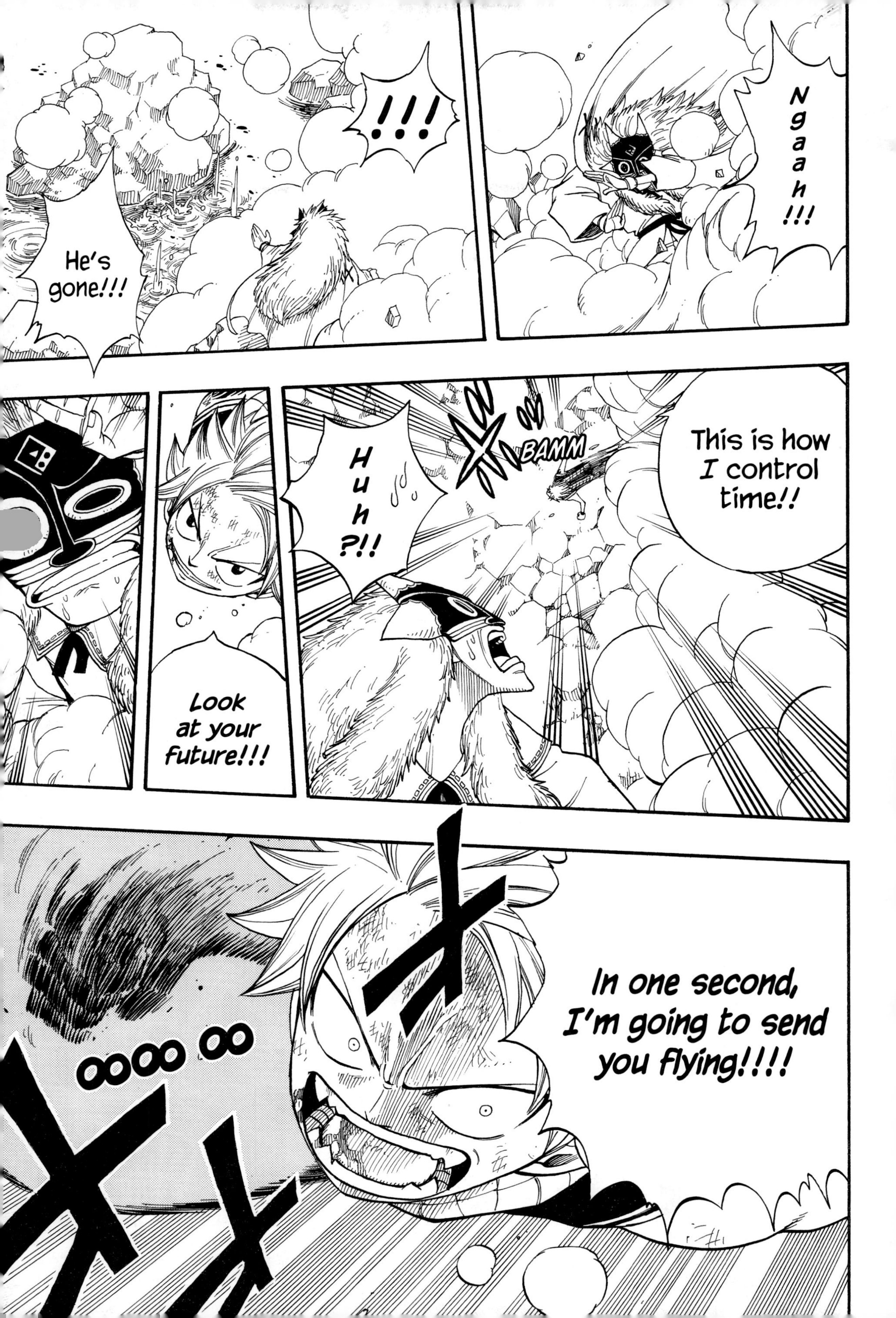

Ngaah!!!
!!!
He's gone!!!
This is how I control time!!
BAMM
Huh?!!
Look at your future!!!
In one second, I'm going to send you flying!!!!
oooo oo

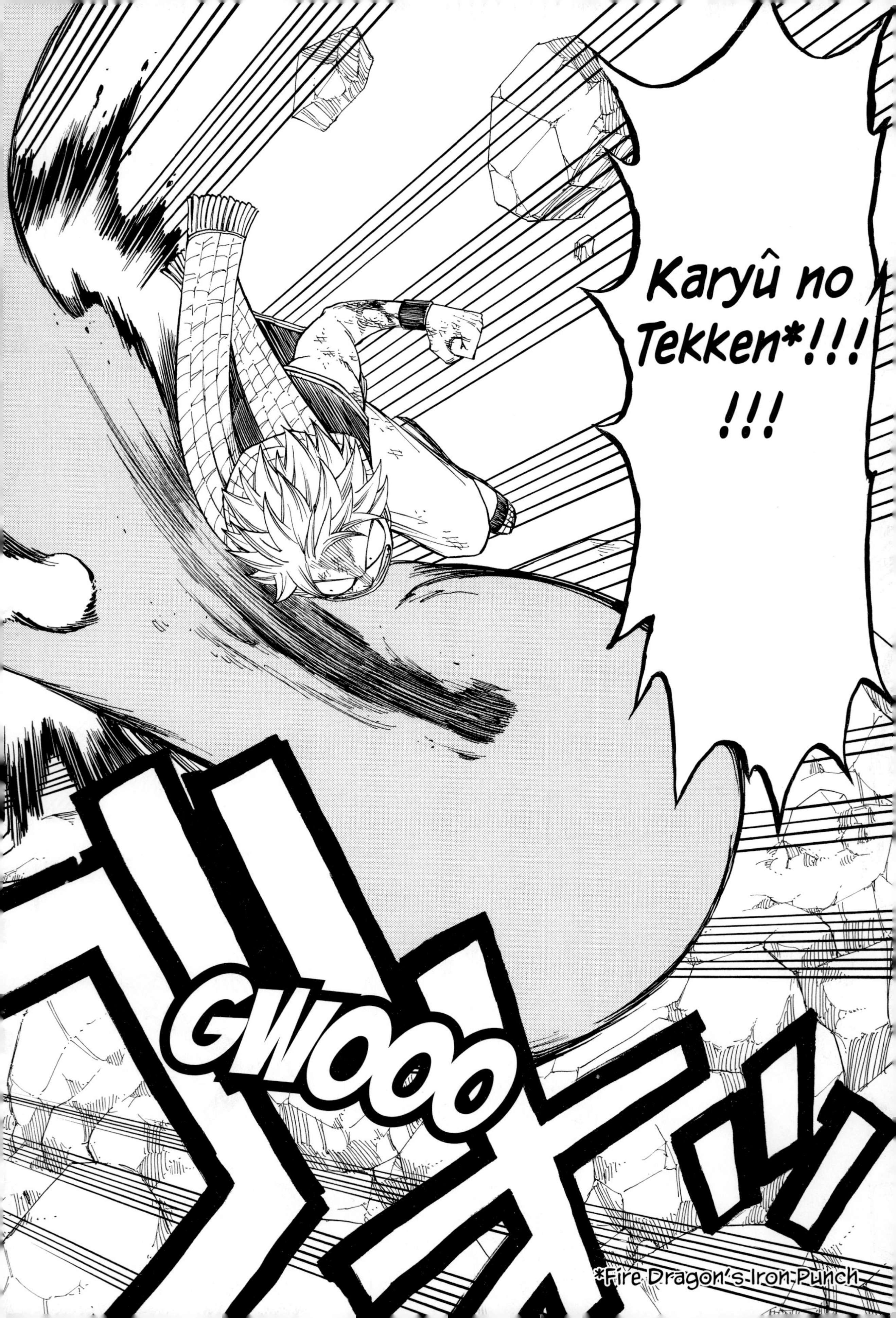
Karyû no Tekken*!!!! !!!
GWOOO
*Fire Dragon's Iron Punch

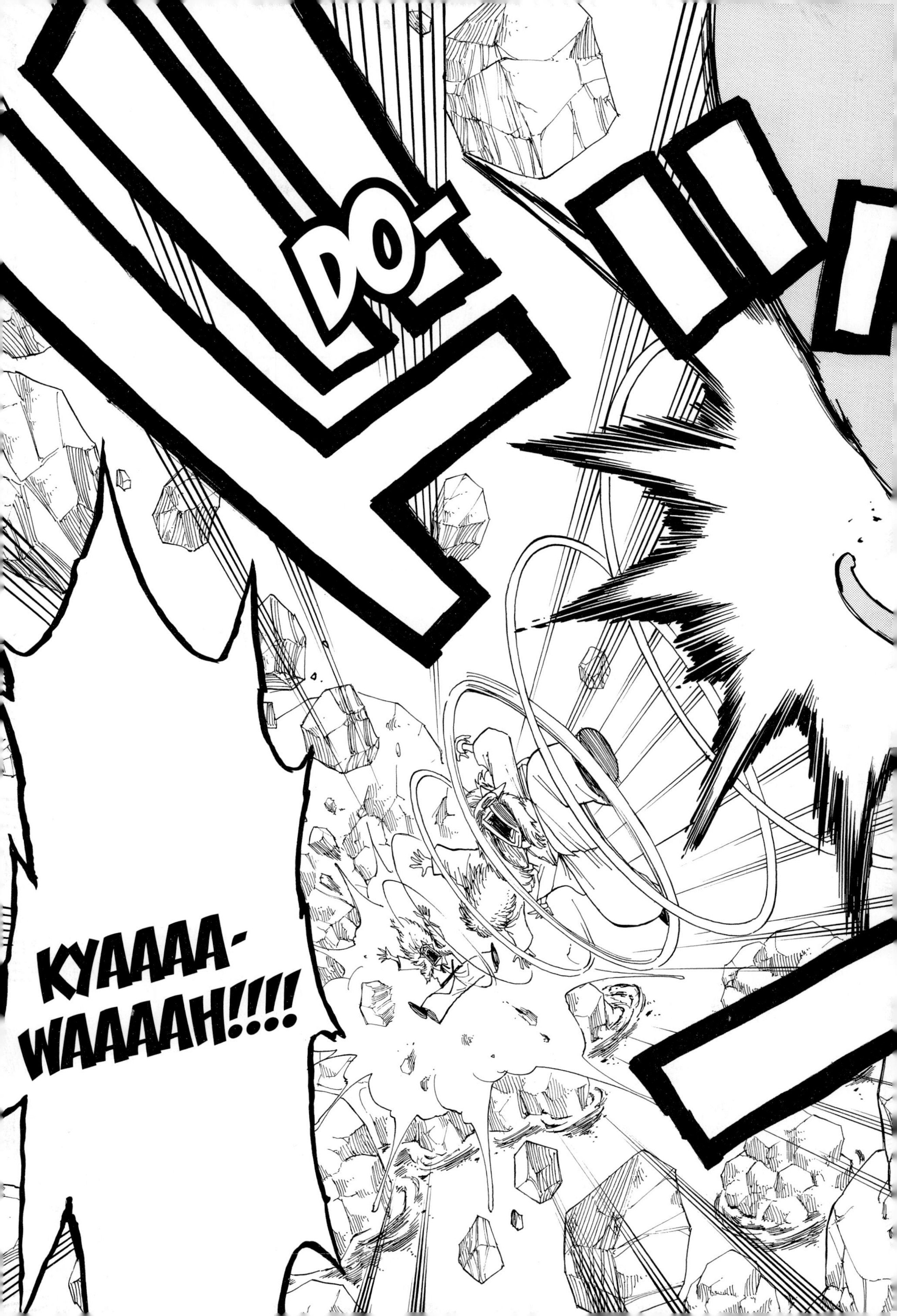
DO-
KYAAAA-
WAAAAH!!!!

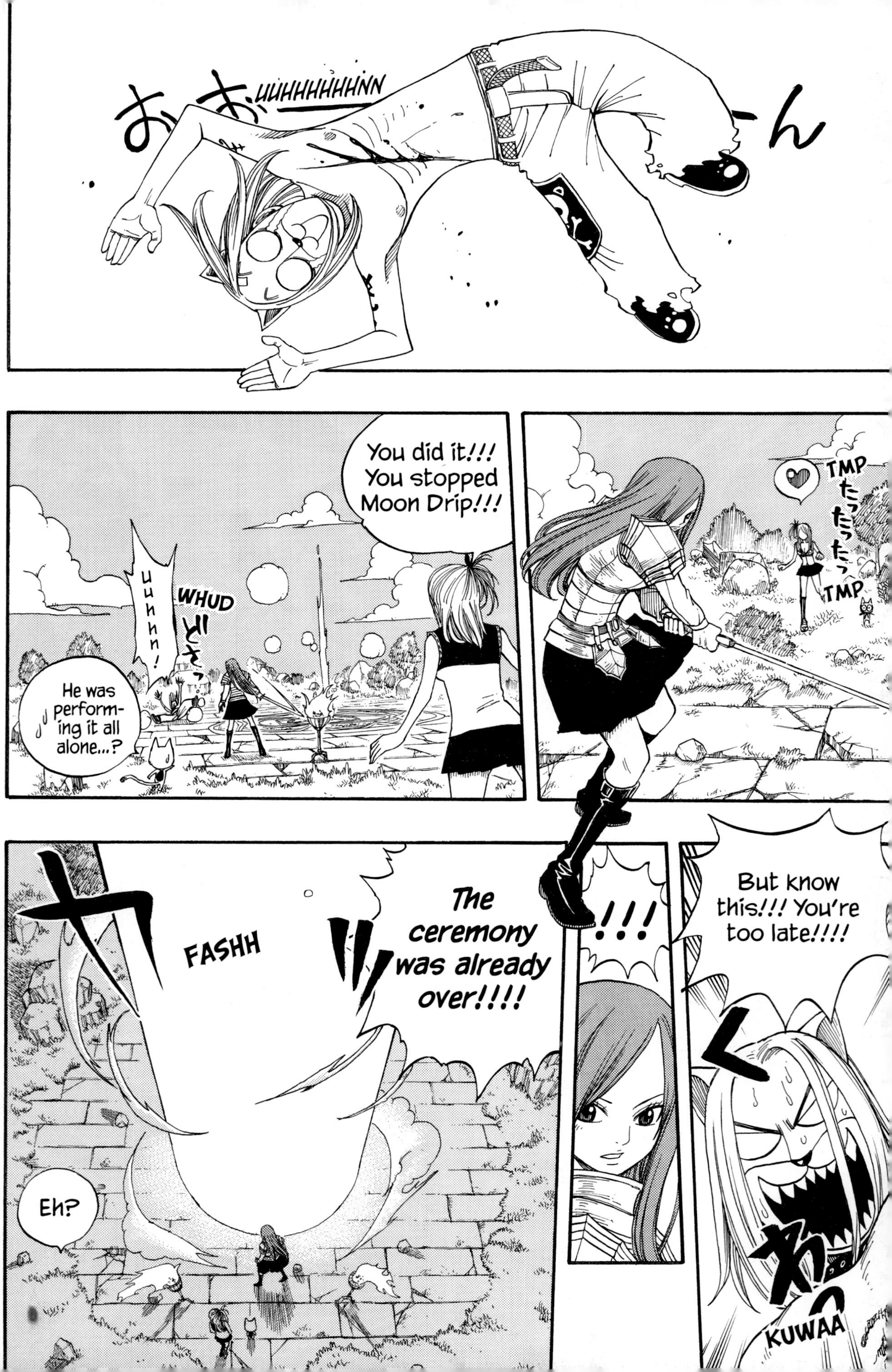
UUHHHHHHHNN
TMP
たったったっ
TMP
You did it!!! You stopped Moon Drip!!!
Uuhhnn!
WHUD
どさっ
He was performing it all alone...?
But know this!!! You're too late!!!!
KUWAA
!!!
The ceremony was already over!!!!
FASHH
Eh?

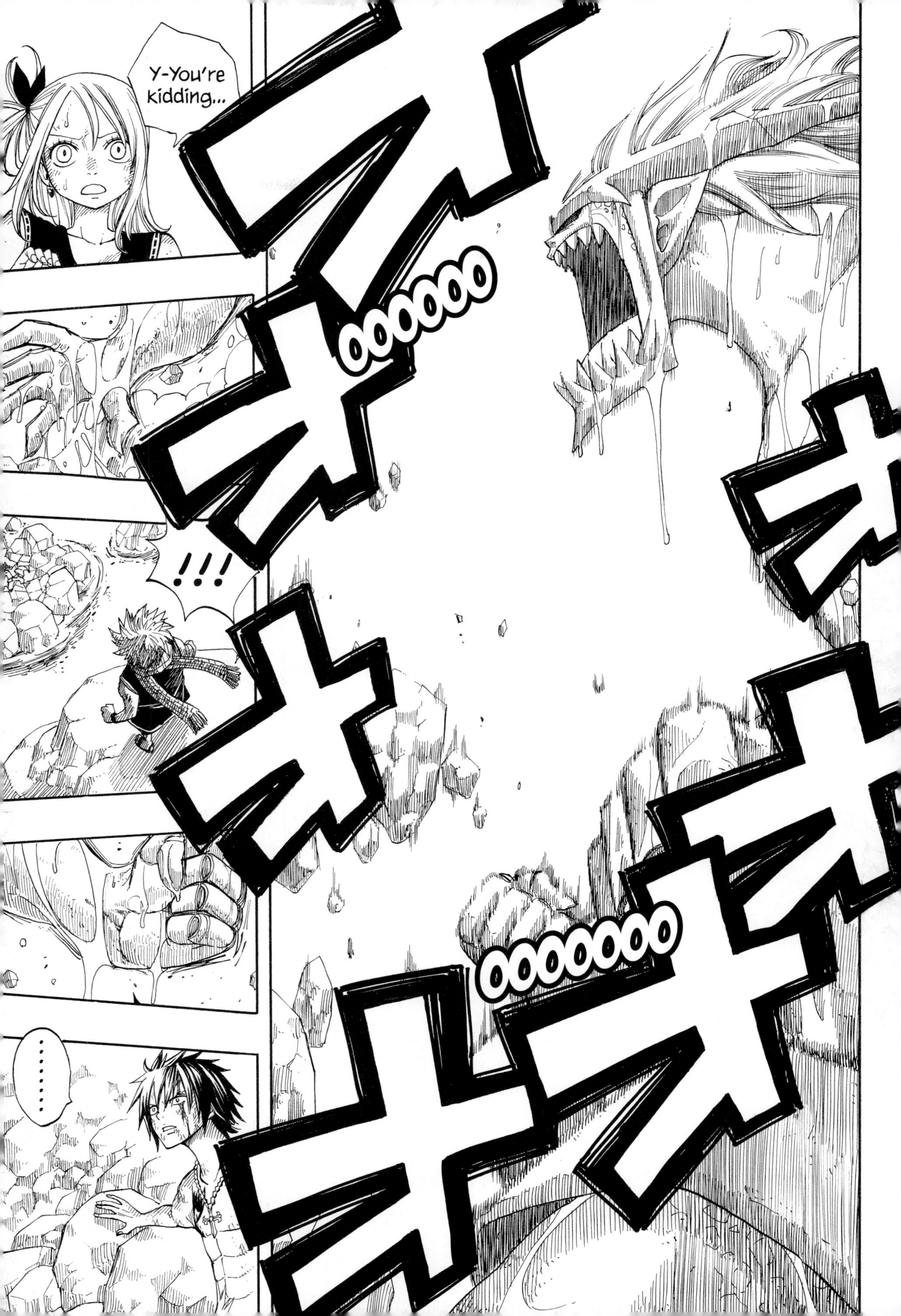
OOOOOO
OOOOOOO
Y-You're kidding...
!!!
....

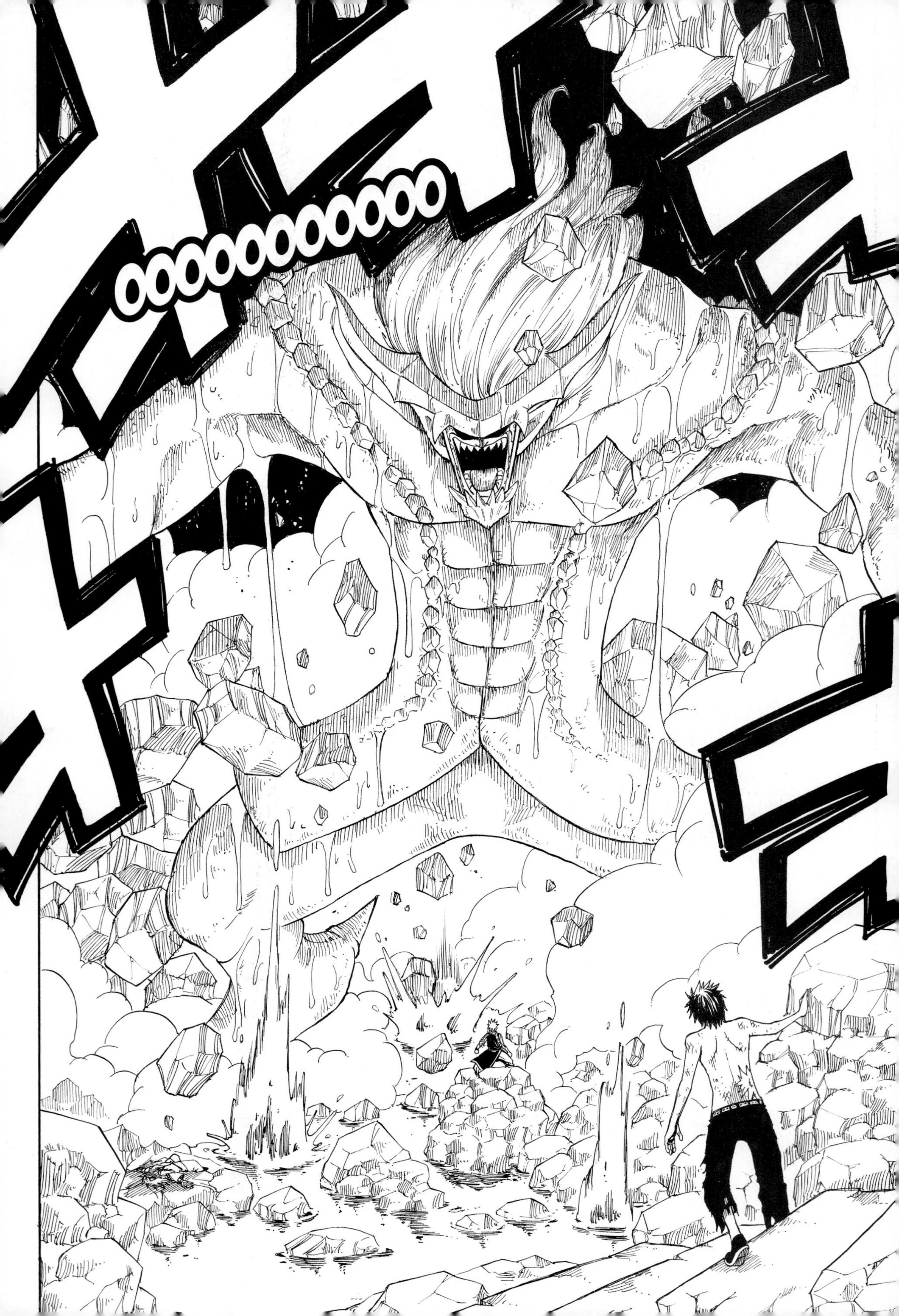
OOOOOOOOOOO

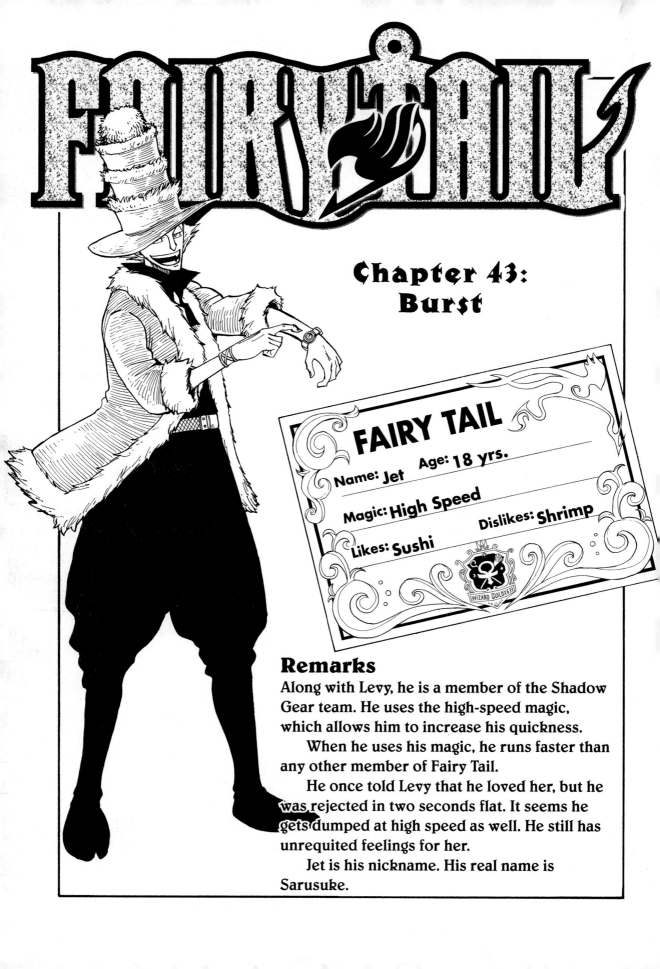

FAIRY TAIL

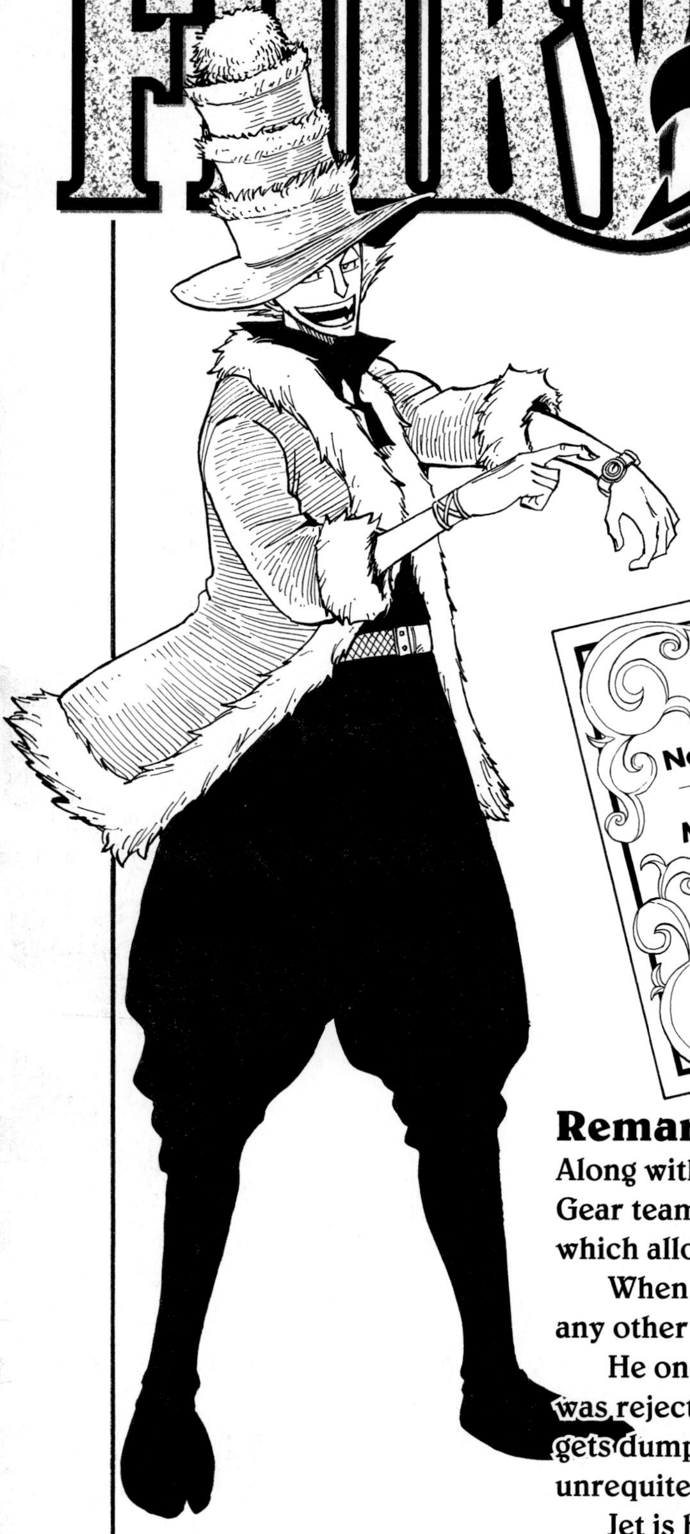

Chapter 43: Burst

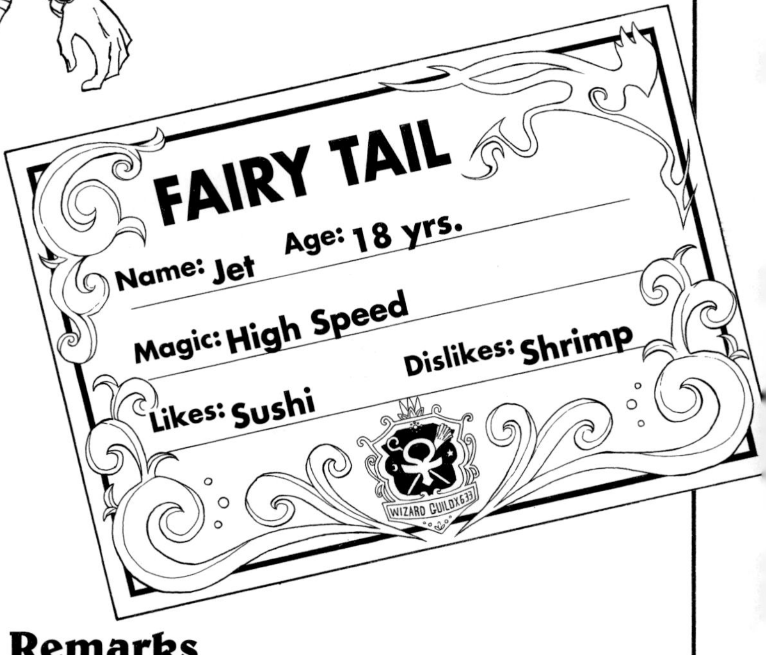
FAIRY TAIL
Name: Jet
Age: 18 yrs.
Magic: High Speed
Likes: Sushi
Dislikes: Shrimp
WIZARD GUILDX633

Remarks

Along with Levy, he is a member of the Shadow Gear team. He uses the high-speed magic, which allows him to increase his quickness.

When he uses his magic, he runs faster than any other member of Fairy Tail.

He once told Levy that he loved her, but he was rejected in two seconds flat. It seems he gets dumped at high speed as well. He still has unrequited feelings for her.

Jet is his nickname. His real name is Sarusuke.

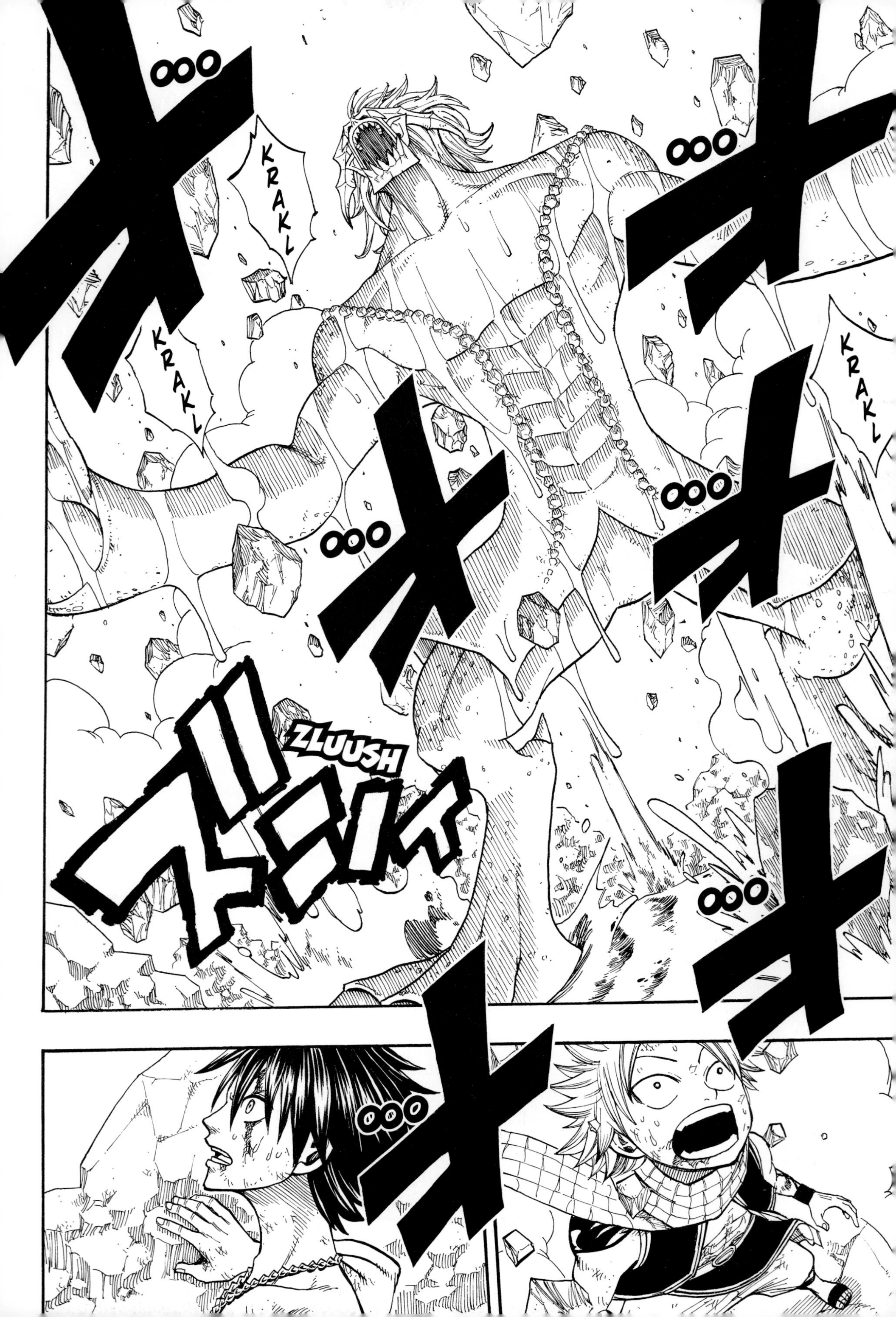
KRAKL
OOO
OOO
KRAKL
OOO
KRAKL
OOO
ZLUUSH
OOO
OOO

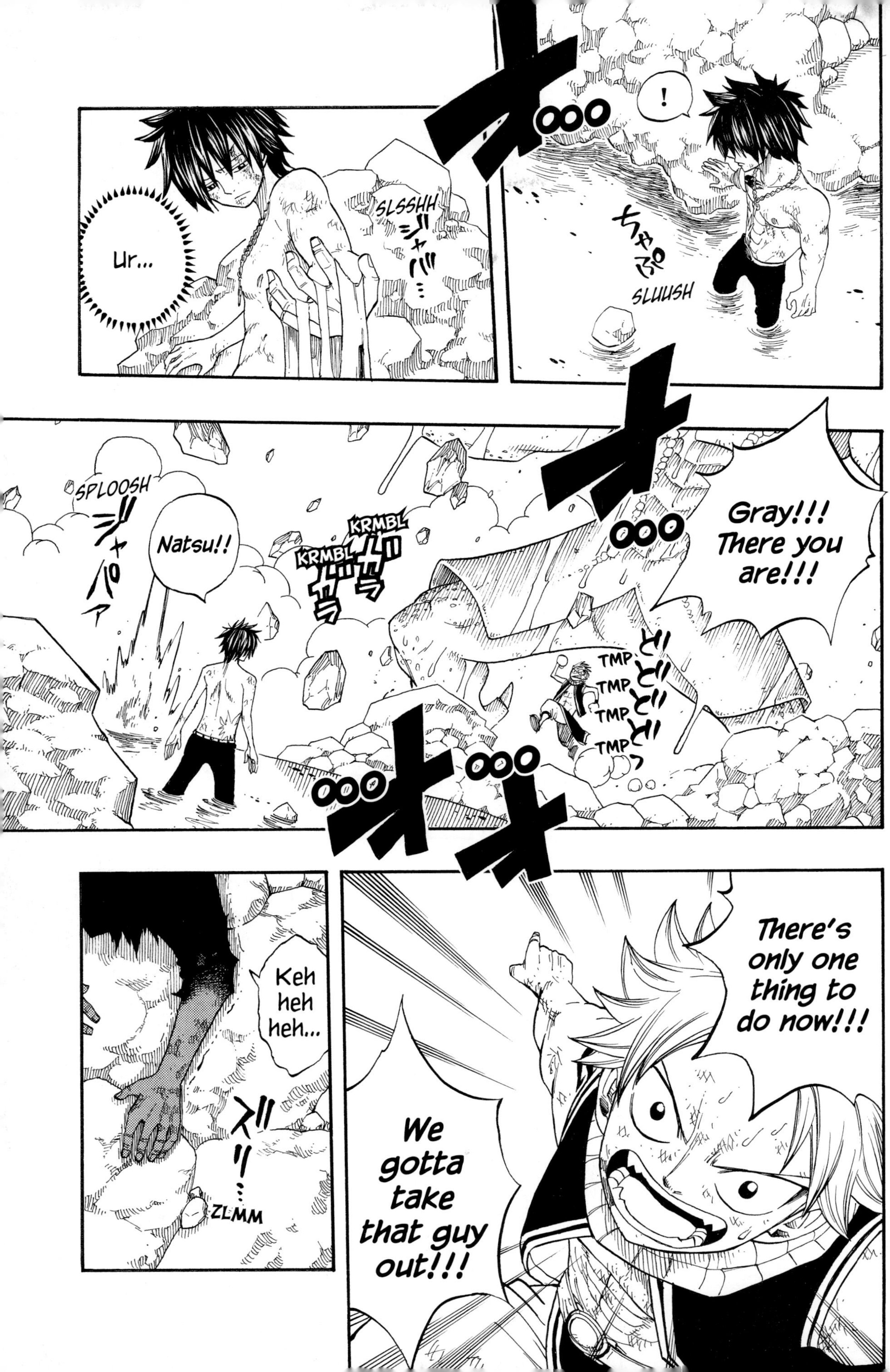
!
ちゃぷ
SLUUSH
SLSSHH
ジャバ…
Ur...
Gray!!! There you are!!!
どどどどっ
TMP
TMP
TMP
TMP
ガラガラ
KRMBL
KRMBL
Natsu!!
ジャパァ
SPLOOSH
There's only one thing to do now!!!
We gotta take that guy out!!!
Keh heh heh...
ズリ…
ZLMM

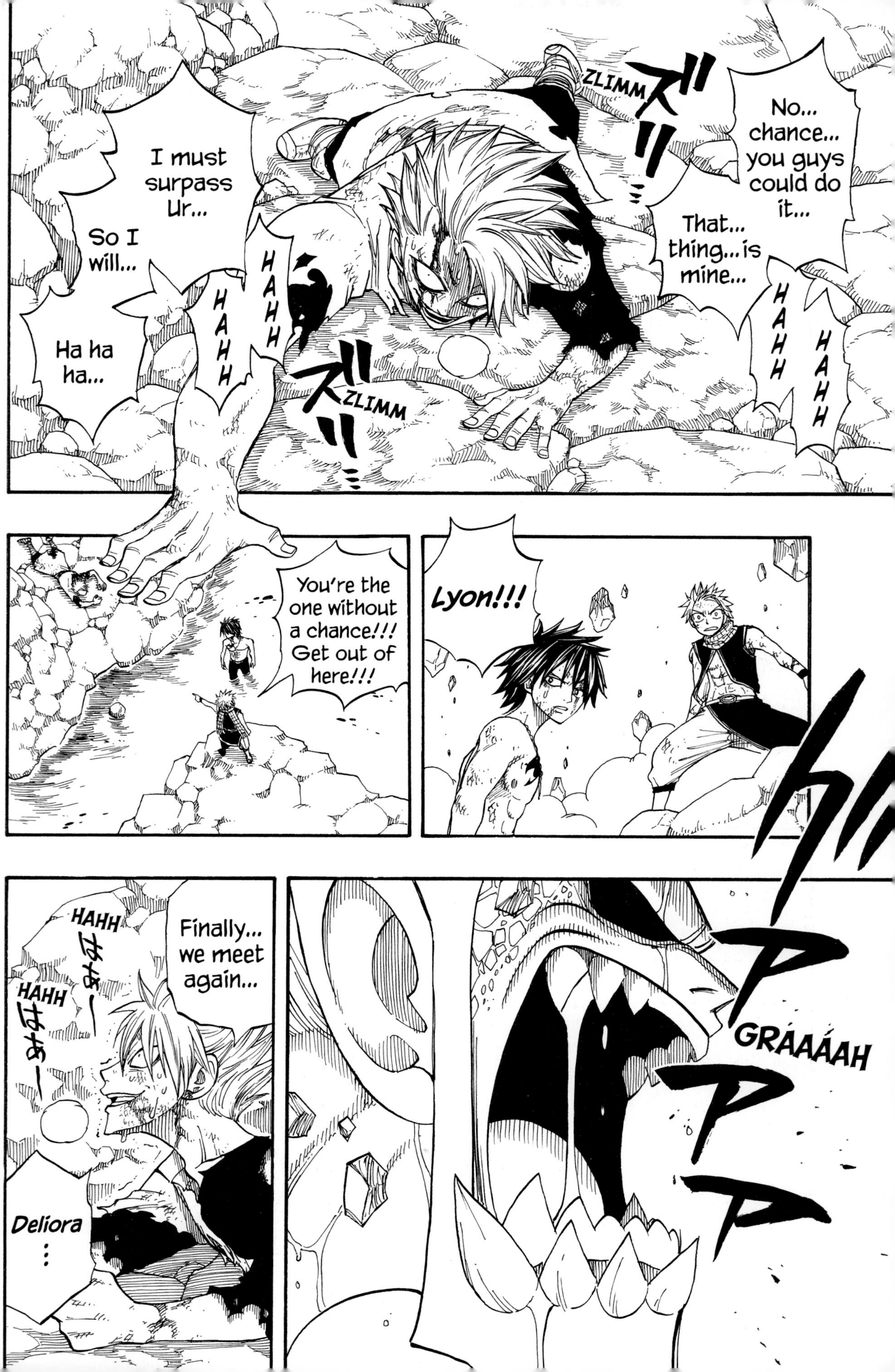
ZLIMM
No... chance... you guys could do it...
That... thing... is mine...
HAHH
HAHH
I must surpass Ur...
So I will...
Ha ha ha...
HAHH
HAHH
ZLIMM
Lyon!!!
You're the one without a chance!!! Get out of here!!!
GRAÁÁAH
Finally... we meet again...
HAHH
HAHH
Deliora...

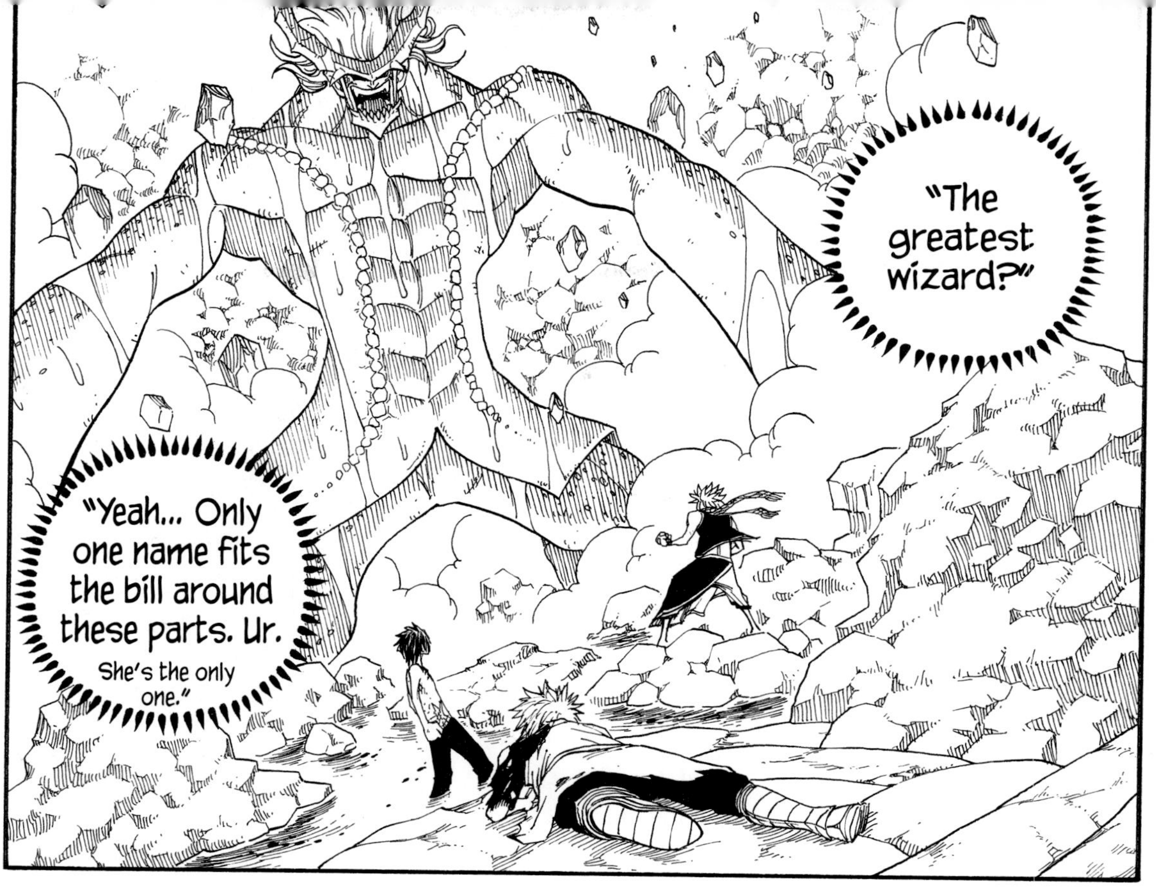
"The greatest wizard?"
"Yeah... Only one name fits the bill around these parts. Ur. She's the only one."
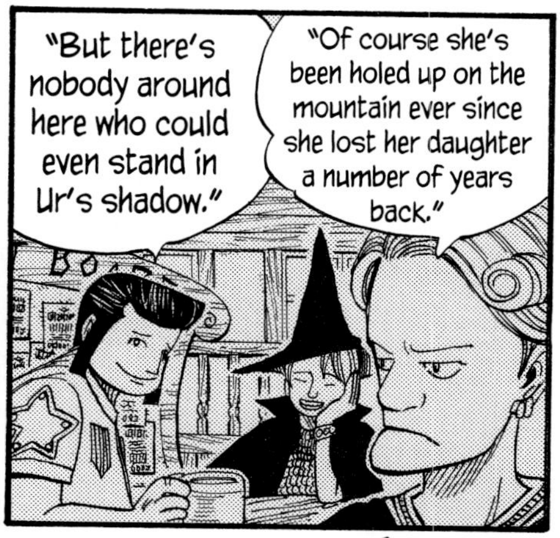
"But there's nobody around here who could even stand in Ur's shadow."
"Of course she's been holed up on the mountain ever since she lost her daughter a number of years back."
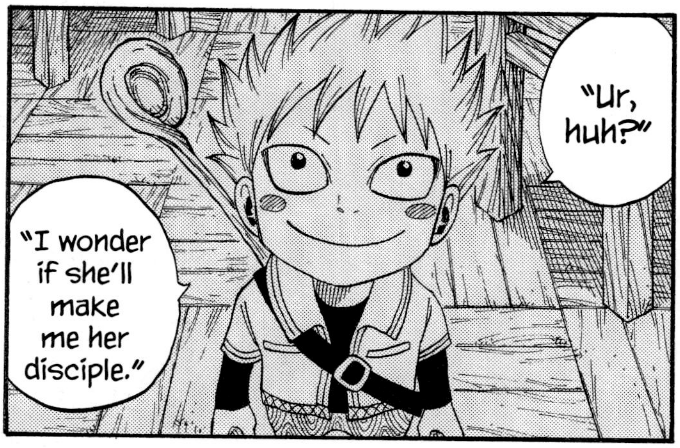
"Ur, huh?"
"I wonder if she'll make me her disciple."
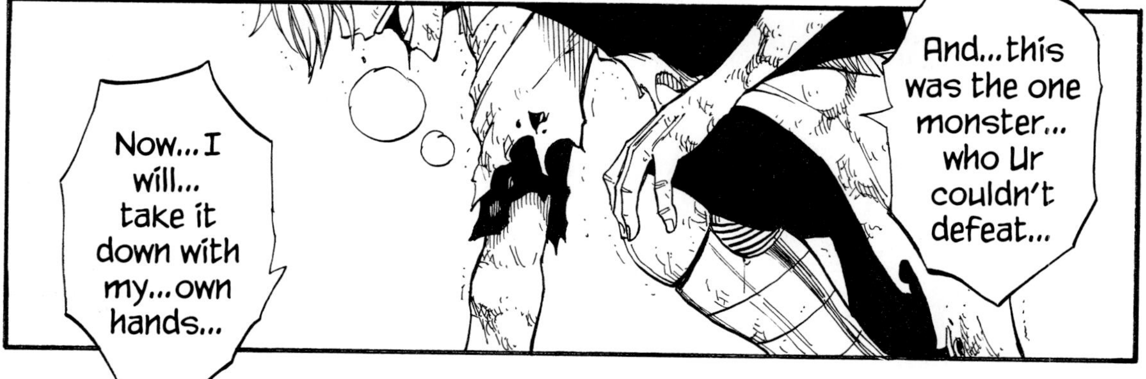
And...this was the one monster... who Ur couldn't defeat...
Now...I will... take it down with my...own hands...

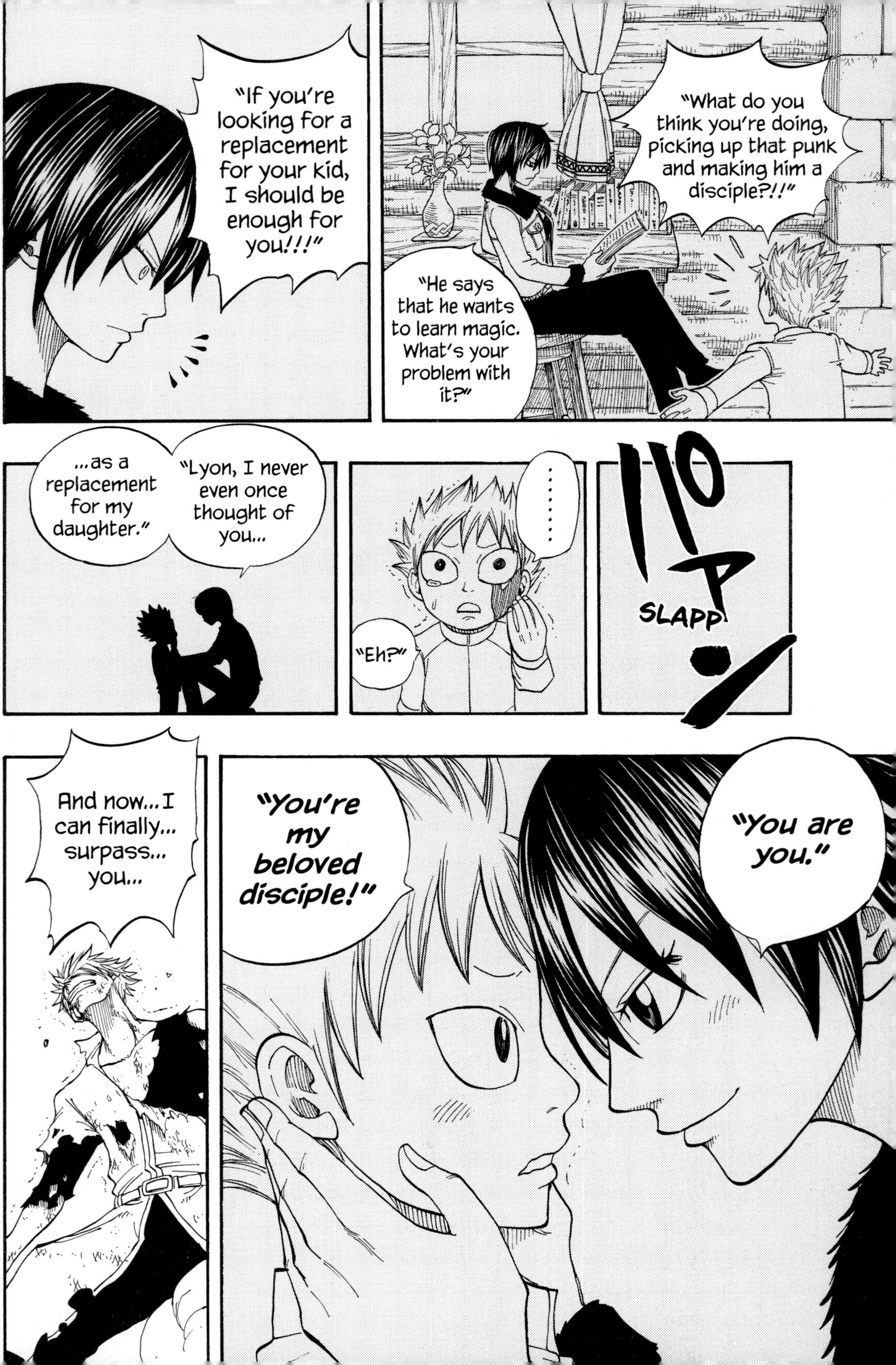
"What do you think you're doing, picking up that punk and making him a disciple?!!"
"He says that he wants to learn magic. What's your problem with it?"
"If you're looking for a replacement for your kid, I should be enough for you!!!"
SLAPP
......
"Eh?"
"Lyon, I never even once thought of you...
...as a replacement for my daughter."
"You are you."
"You're my beloved disciple!"
And now... I can finally... surpass... you...

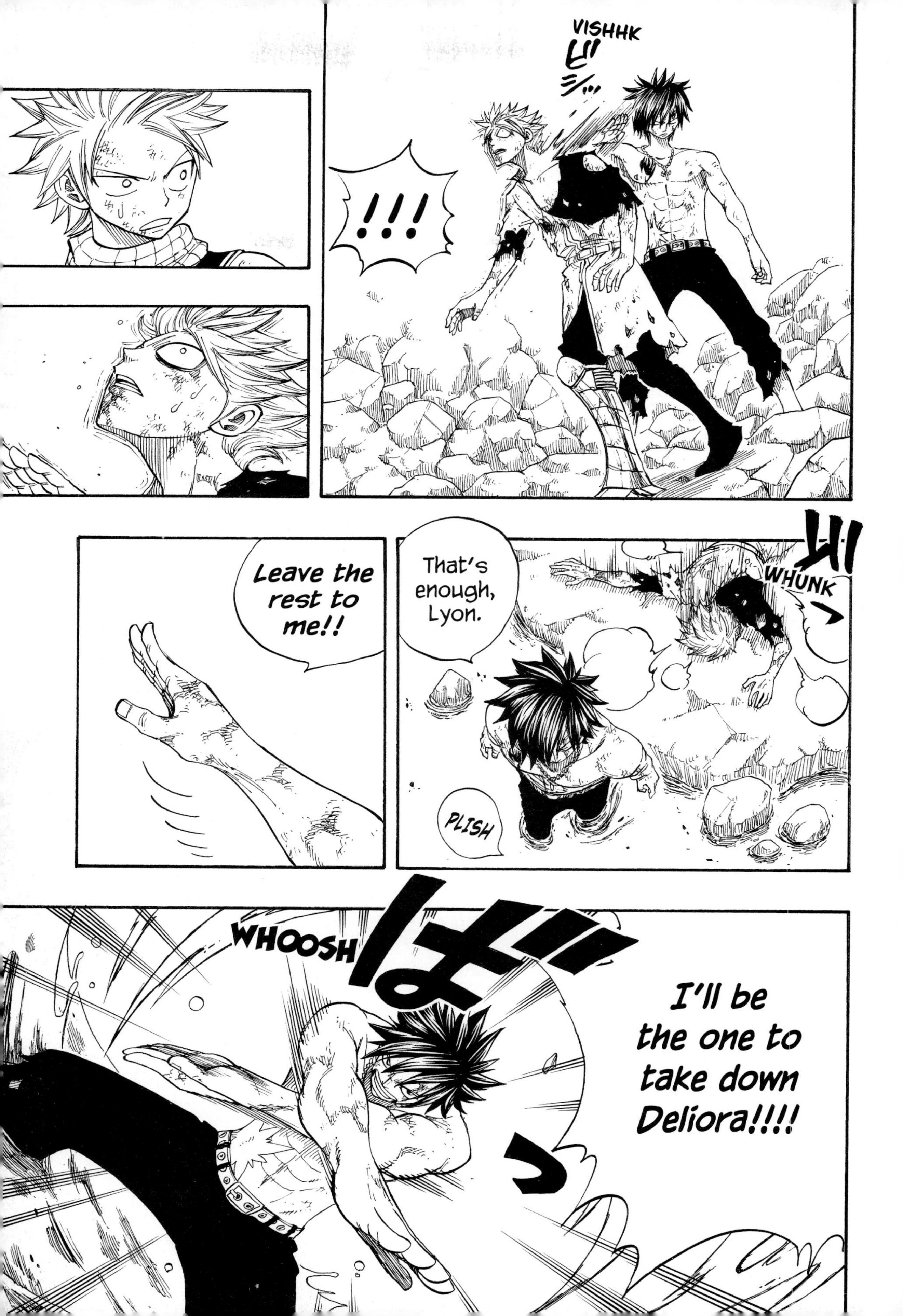

VISHHK
!!!
WHUNK
That's enough, Lyon.
PLISH
Leave the rest to me!!
WHOOSH
I'll be the one to take down Deliora!!!!

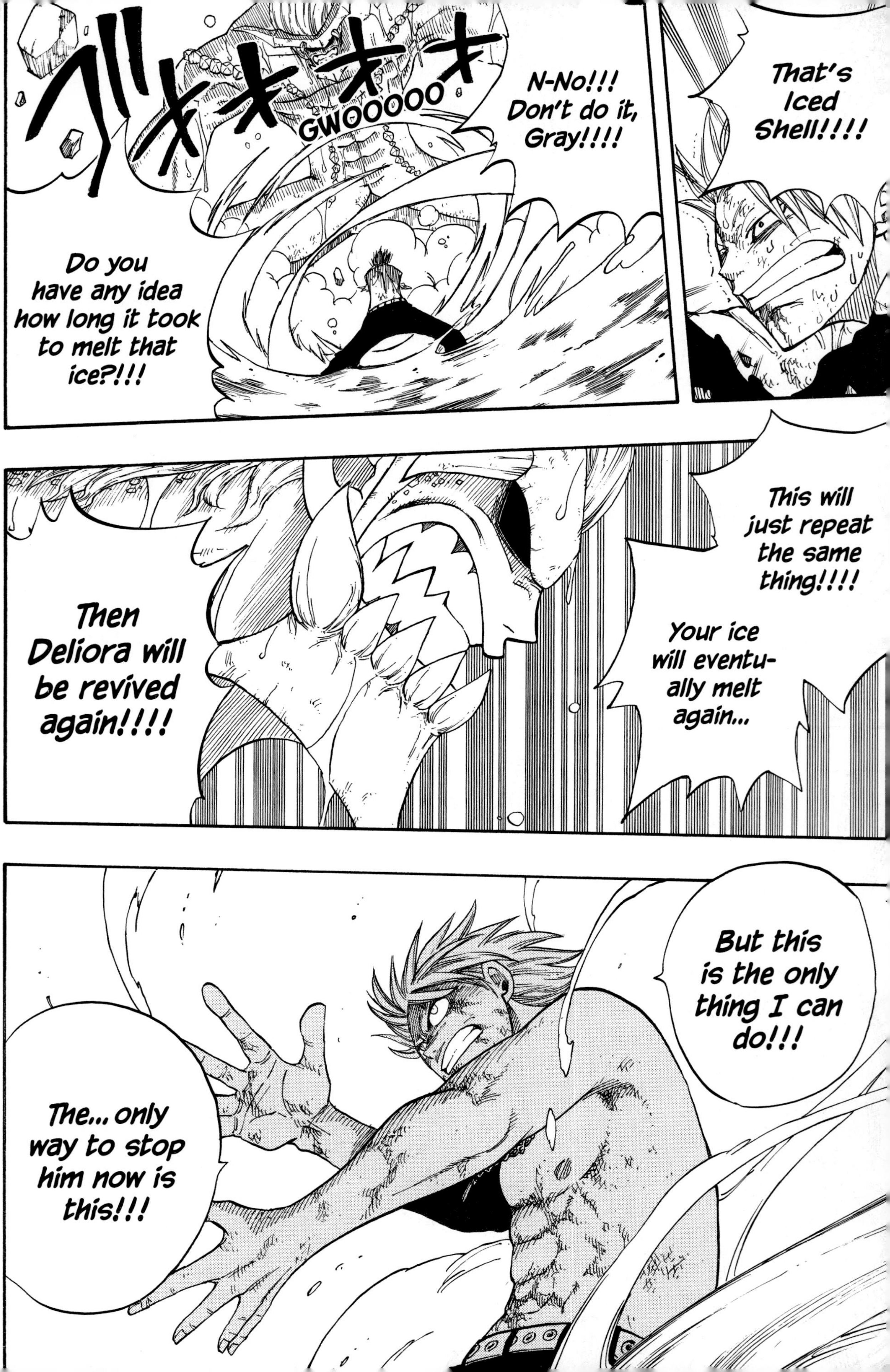
That's Iced Shell!!!!
N-No!!! Don't do it, Gray!!!!
GWOOOOO
Do you have any idea how long it took to melt that ice?!!!
This will just repeat the same thing!!!!
Your ice will eventu-ally melt again...
Then Deliora will be revived again!!!!
But this is the only thing I can do!!!
The... only way to stop him now is this!!!

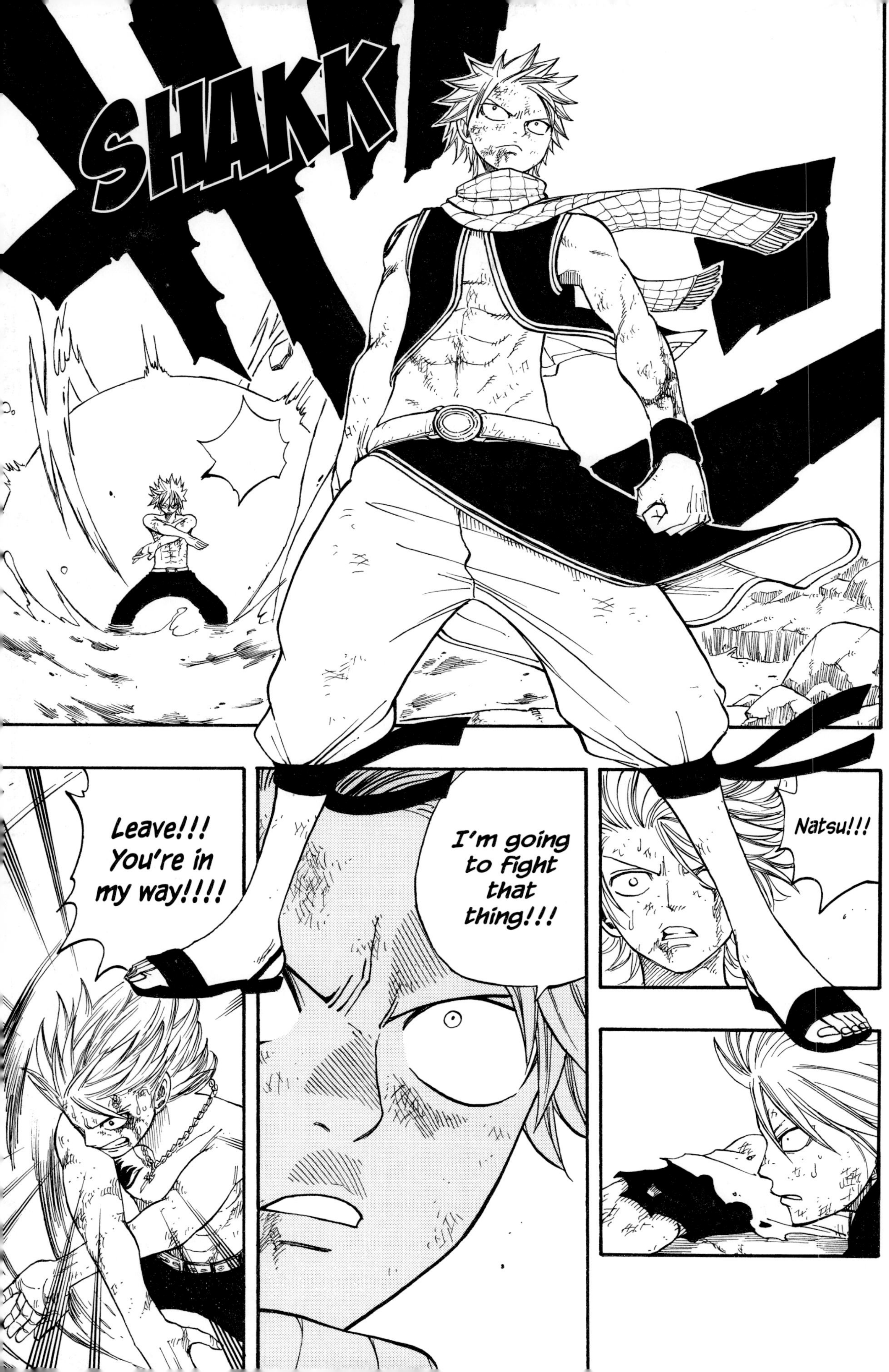
SHAKK
Natsu!!!
I'm going to fight that thing!!!
Leave!!! You're in my way!!!!

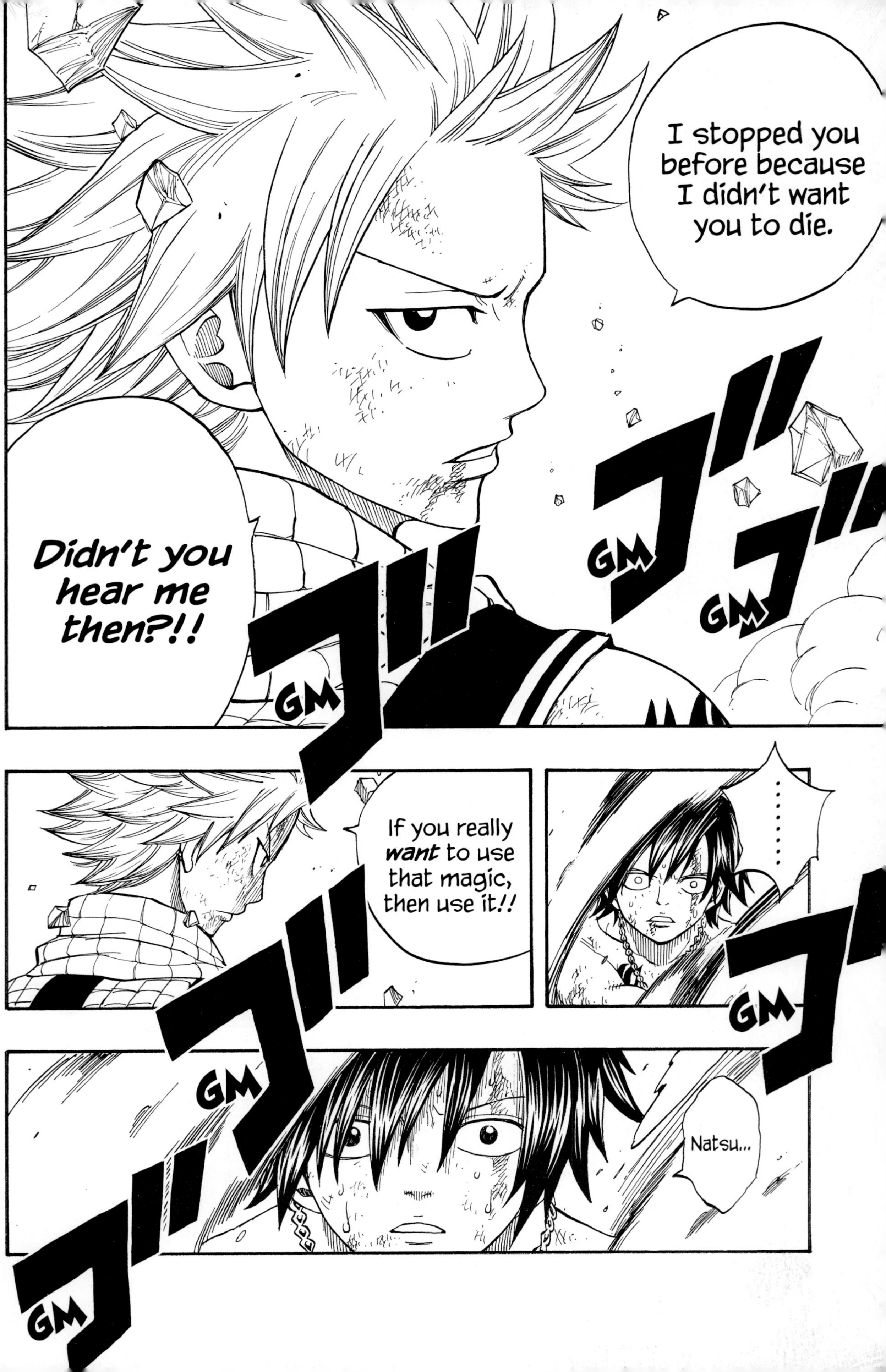
I stopped you before because I didn't want you to die.
GM
GM
Didn't you hear me then?!!
GM
......
If you really *want* to use that magic, then use it!!
GM
GM
Natsu...
GM

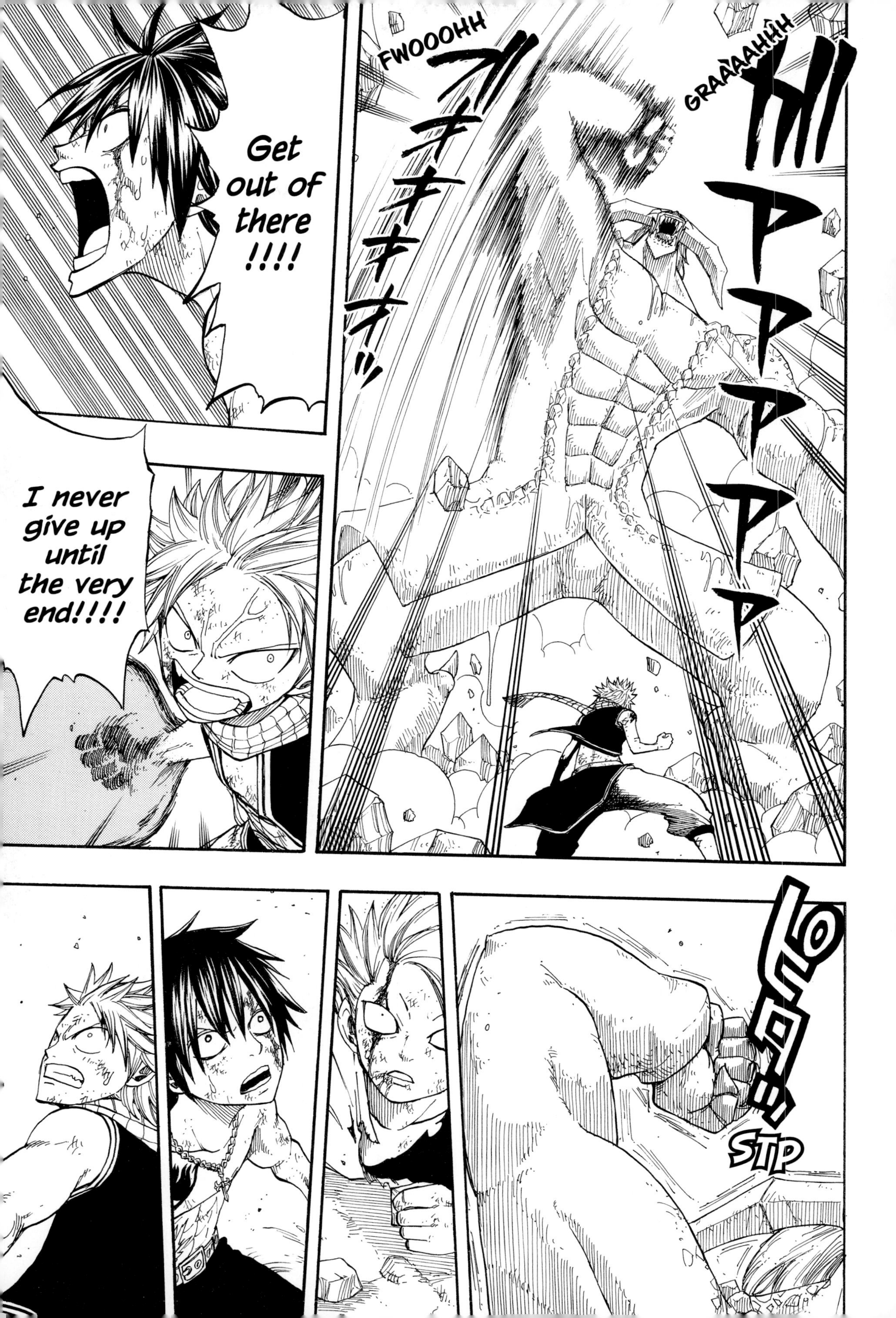
FWOOOHH
GRAÀÀAHHH
Get out of there !!!!
I never give up until the very end!!!!
STP

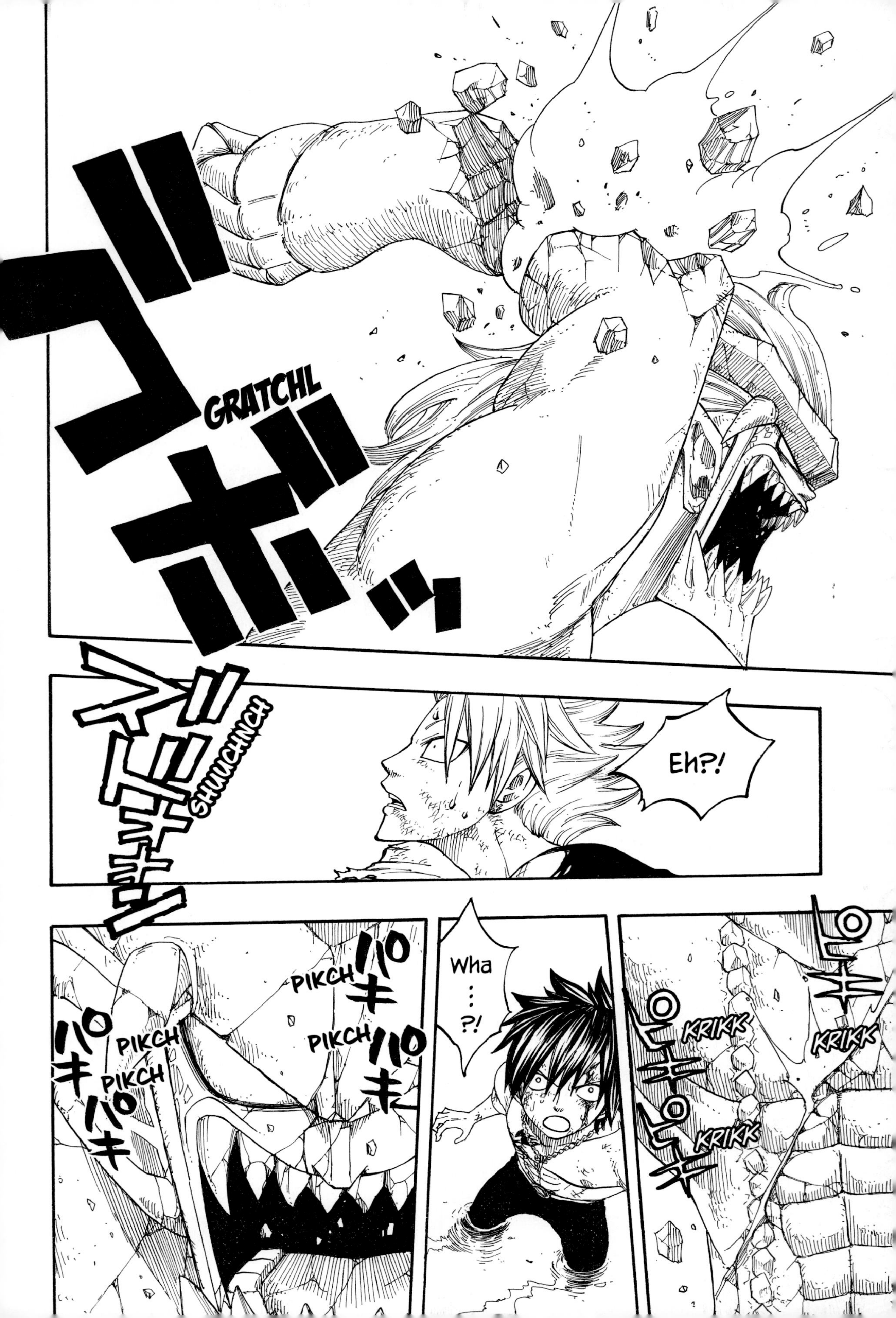
ゴボッ
GRATCHL
ズチィ
SHUUCHNCH
Eh?!
ピキ
KRIKK
ピキ
KRIKK
ピキ
KRIKK
Wha ... ?!
パキ
PIKCH
パキ
PIKCH
パキパキ
PIKCH
PIKCH

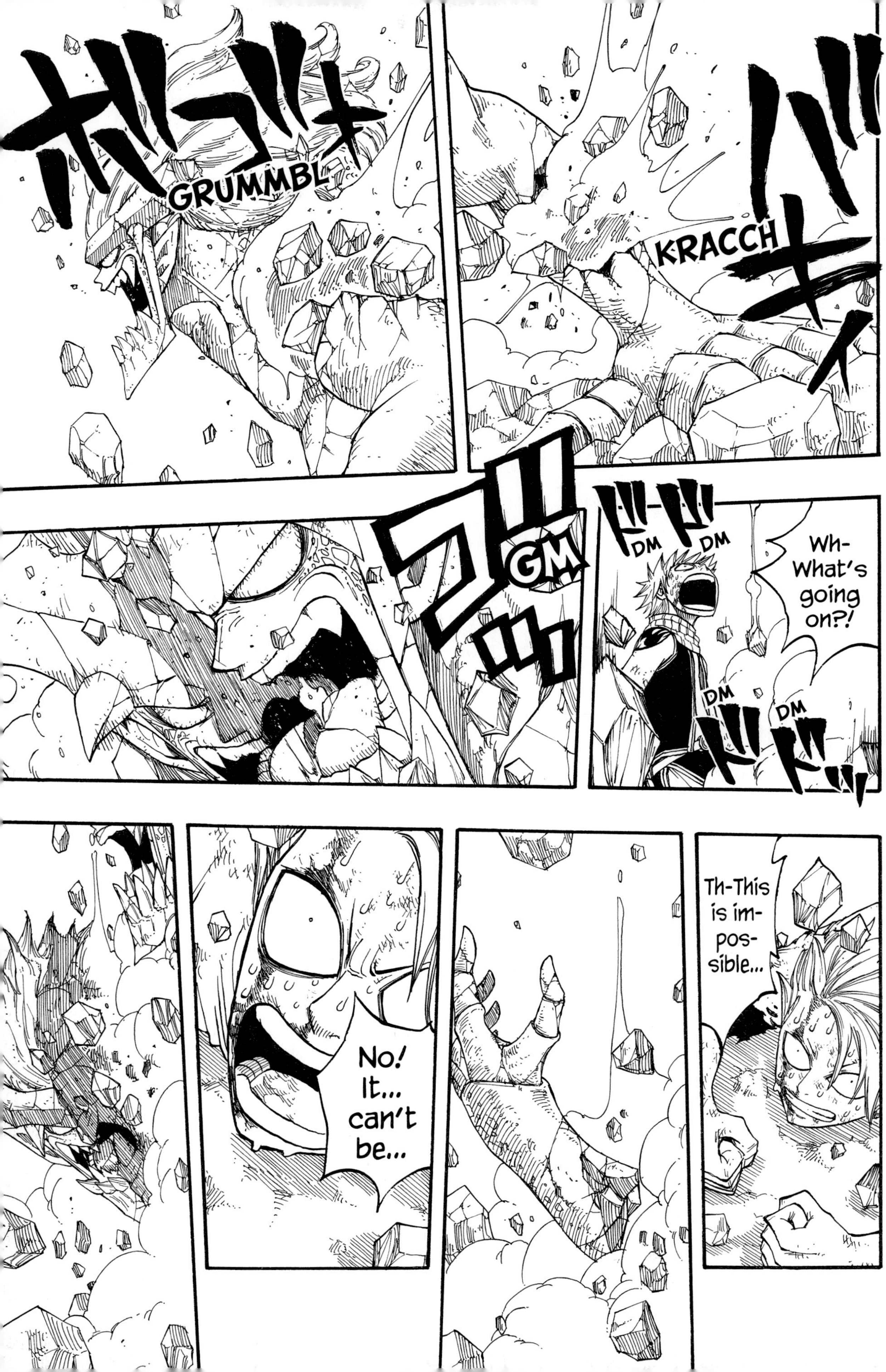
KRACCH
GRUMMBL
DM DM
Wh- What's going on?!
DM DM
GM
Th-This is im- pos- sible...
No! It... can't be...

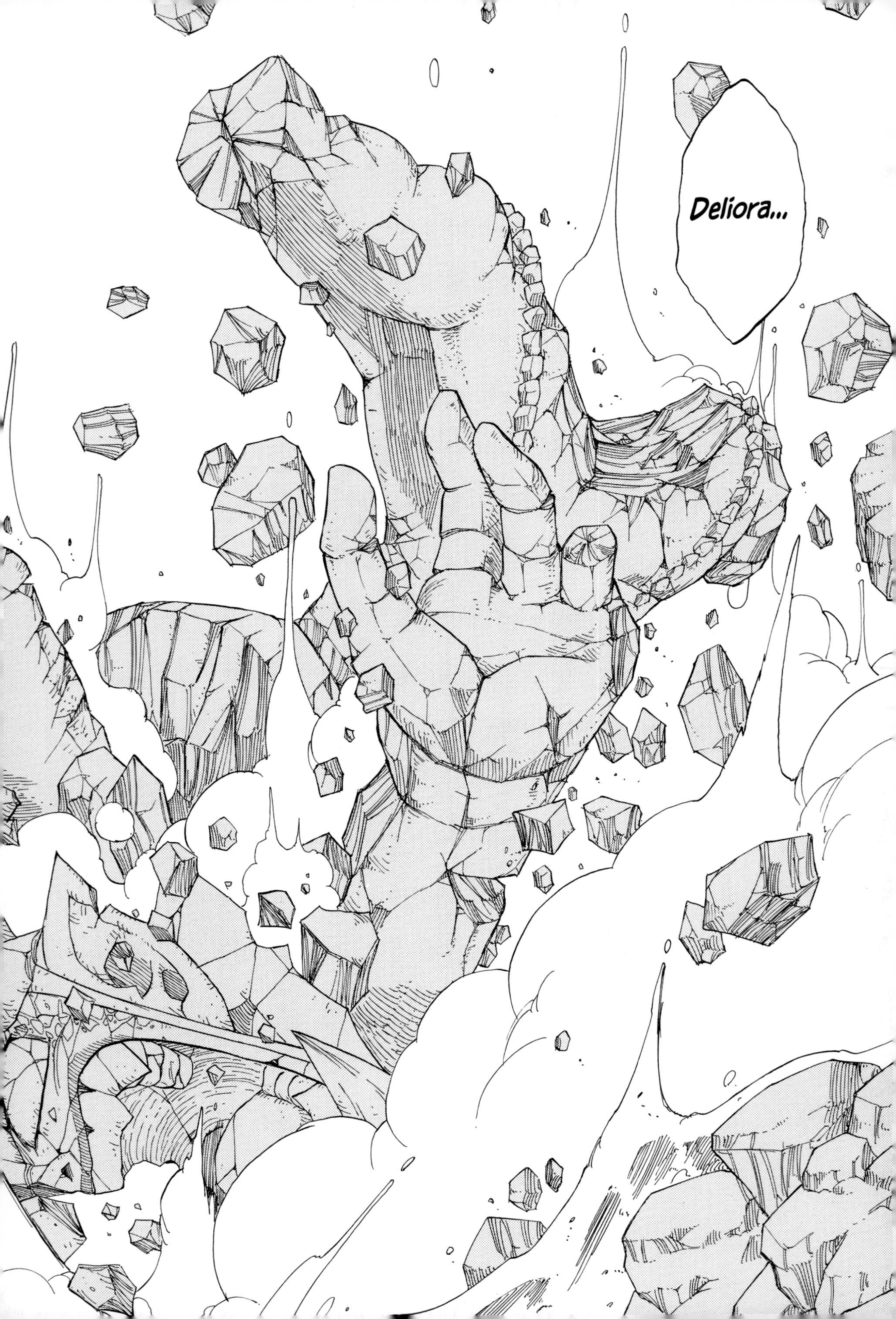
Deliora...

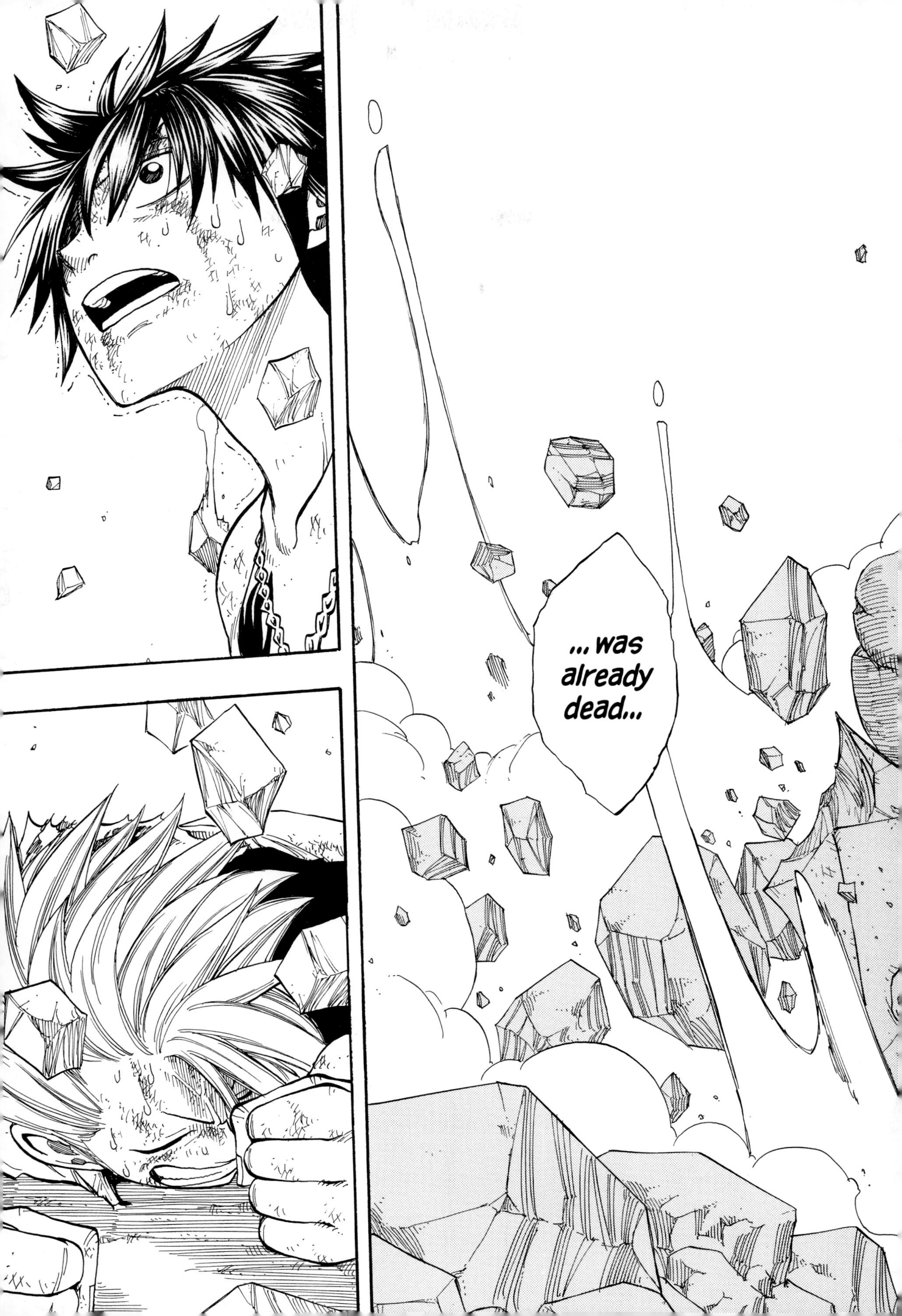
...was already dead...

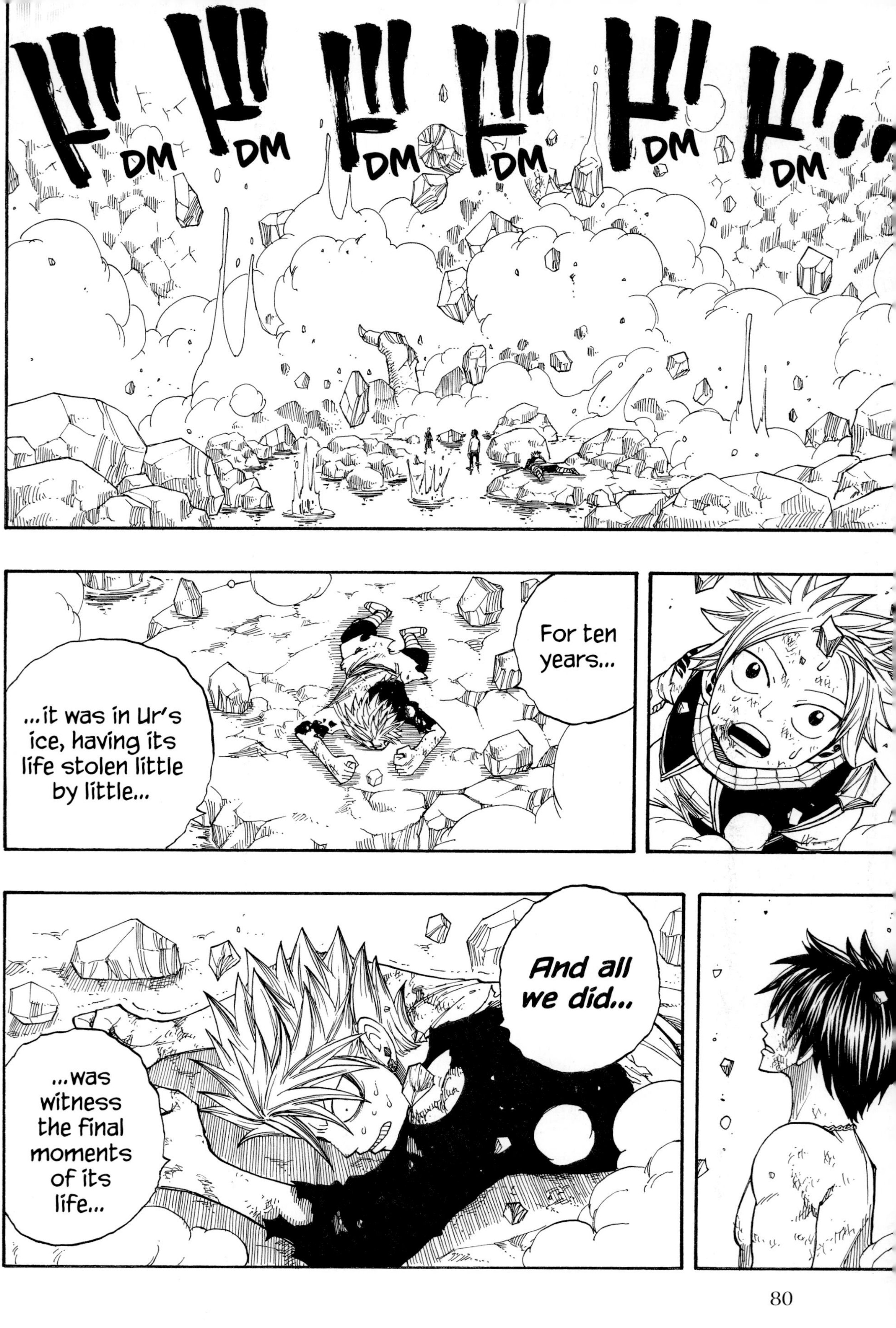
DM DM DM DM DM DM
For ten years...
...it was in Ur's ice, having its life stolen little by little...
And all we did...
...was witness the final moments of its life...

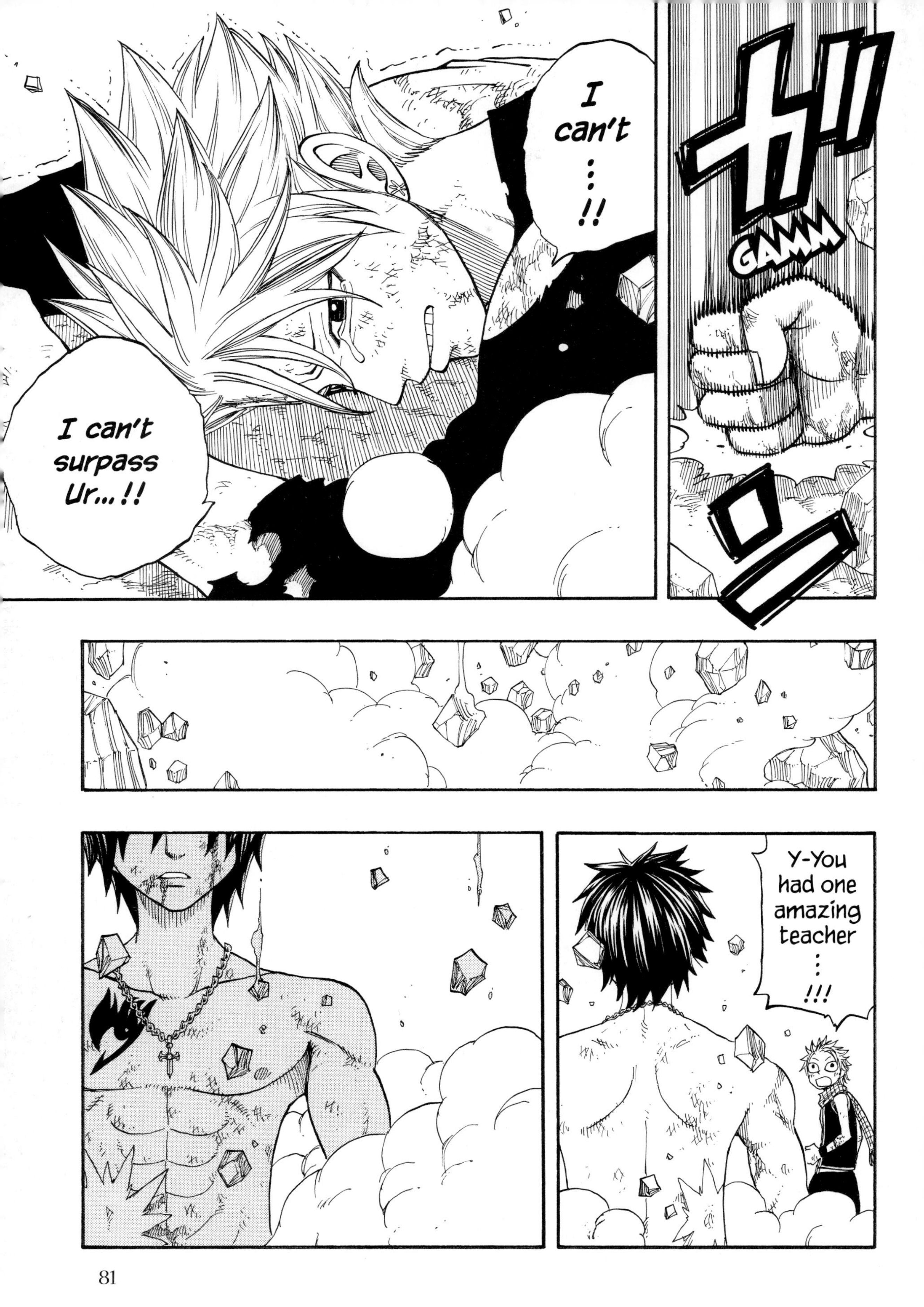
GAMM
I can't ...!!
I can't surpass Ur...!!
Y-You had one amazing teacher ...!!!

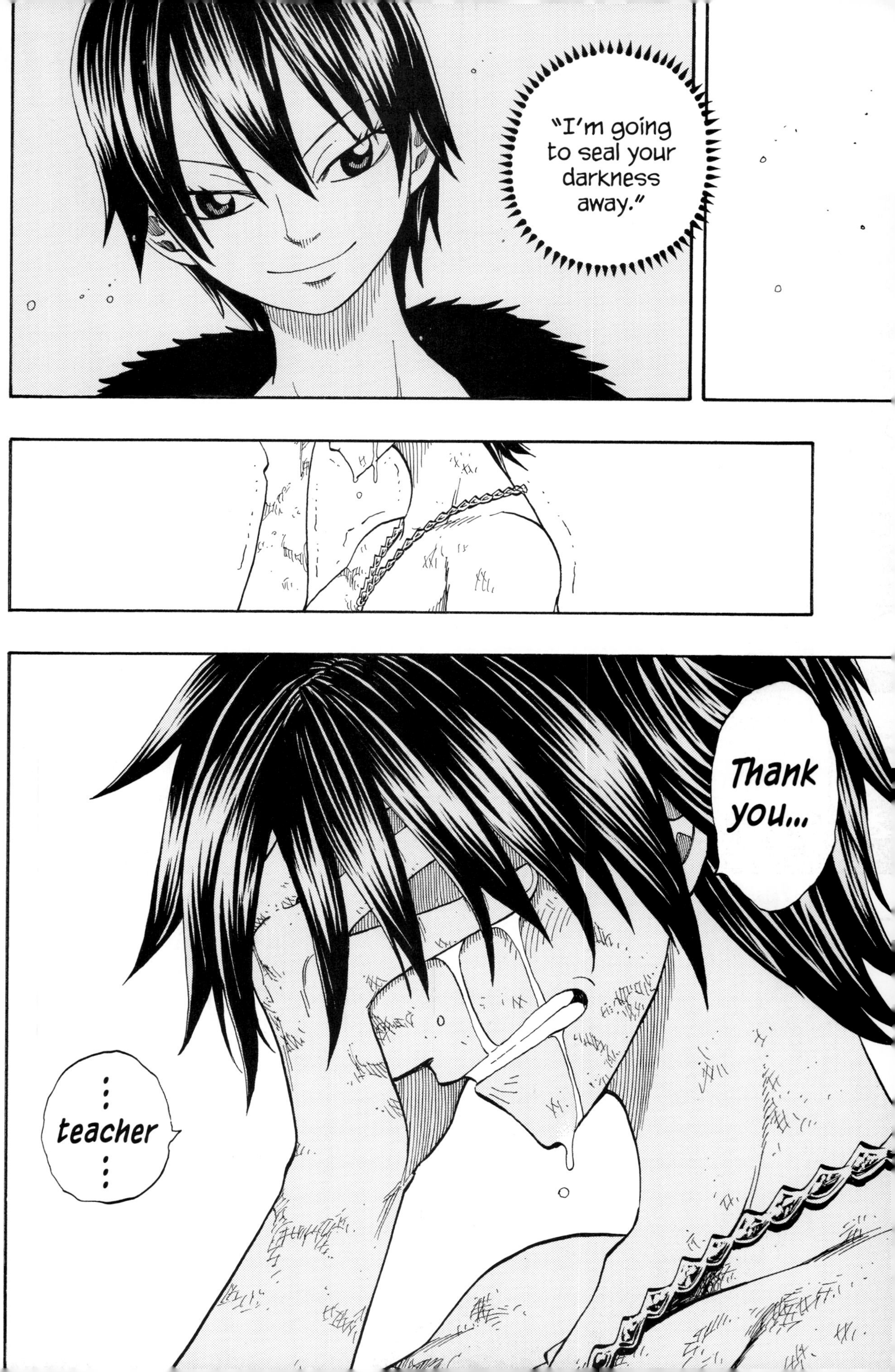
"I'm going to seal your darkness away."
Thank you...
...teacher...

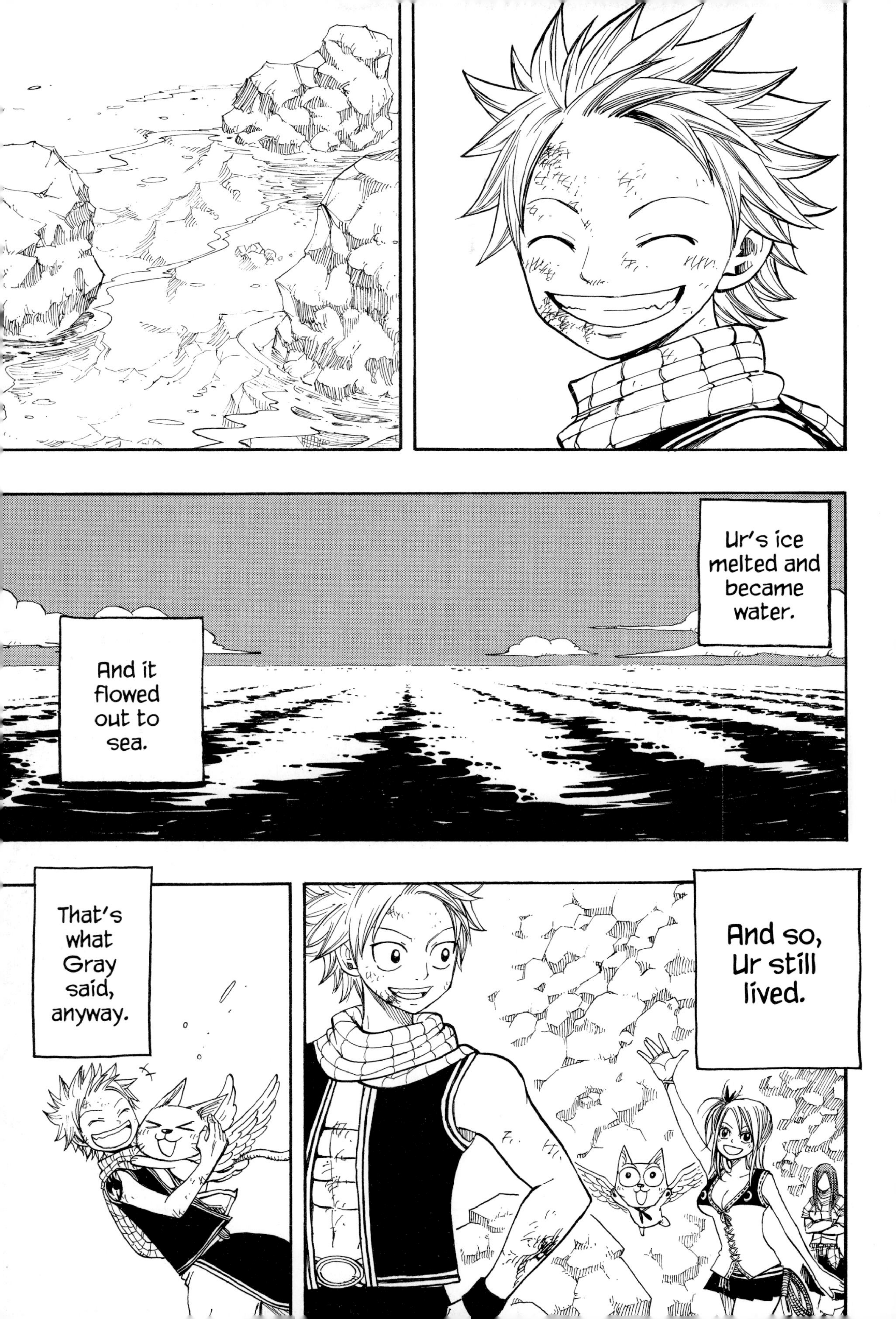
Ur's ice melted and became water.
And it flowed out to sea.
And so, Ur still lived.
That's what Gray said, anyway.

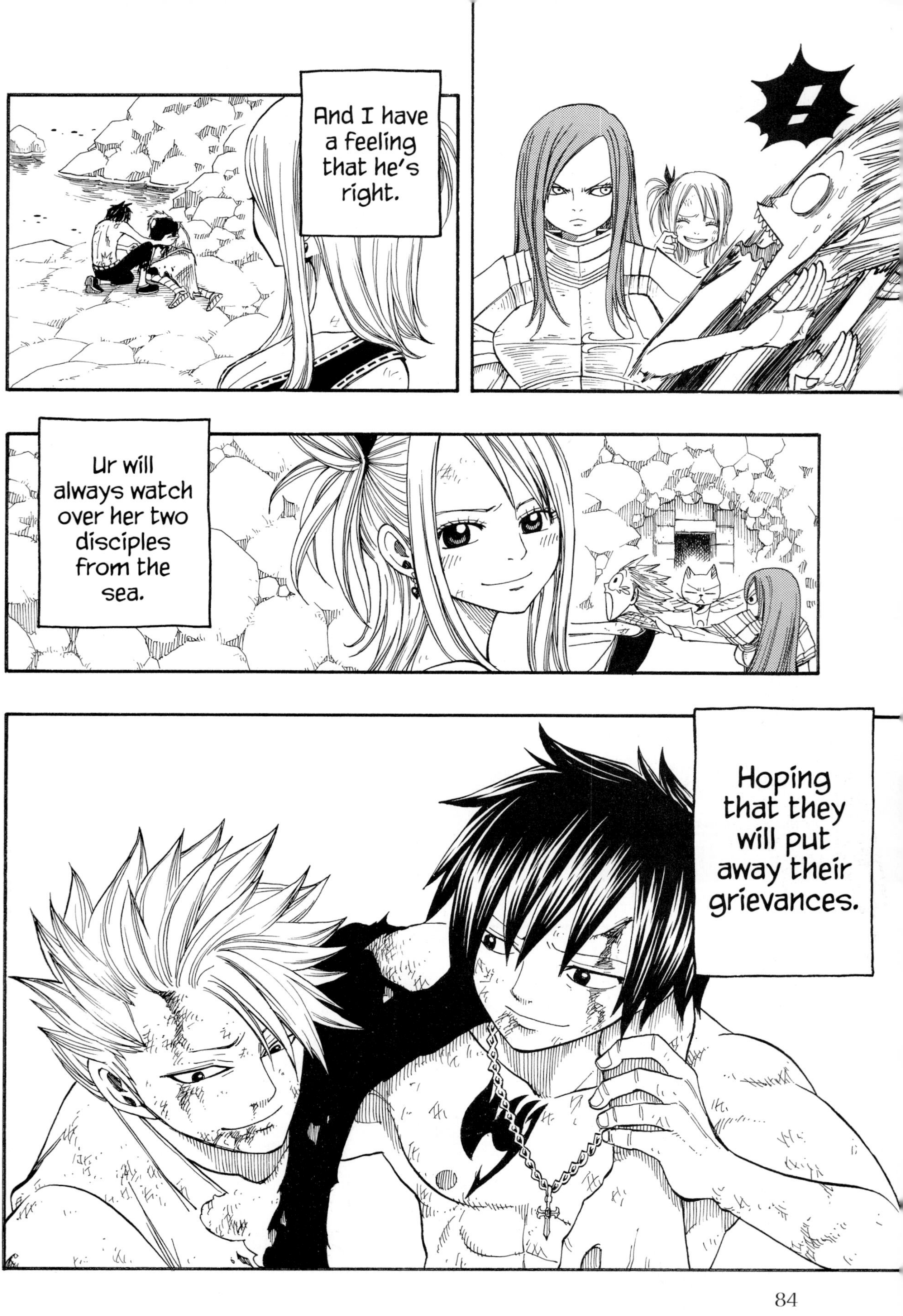
!
And I have a feeling that he's right.
Ur will always watch over her two disciples from the sea.
Hoping that they will put away their grievances.

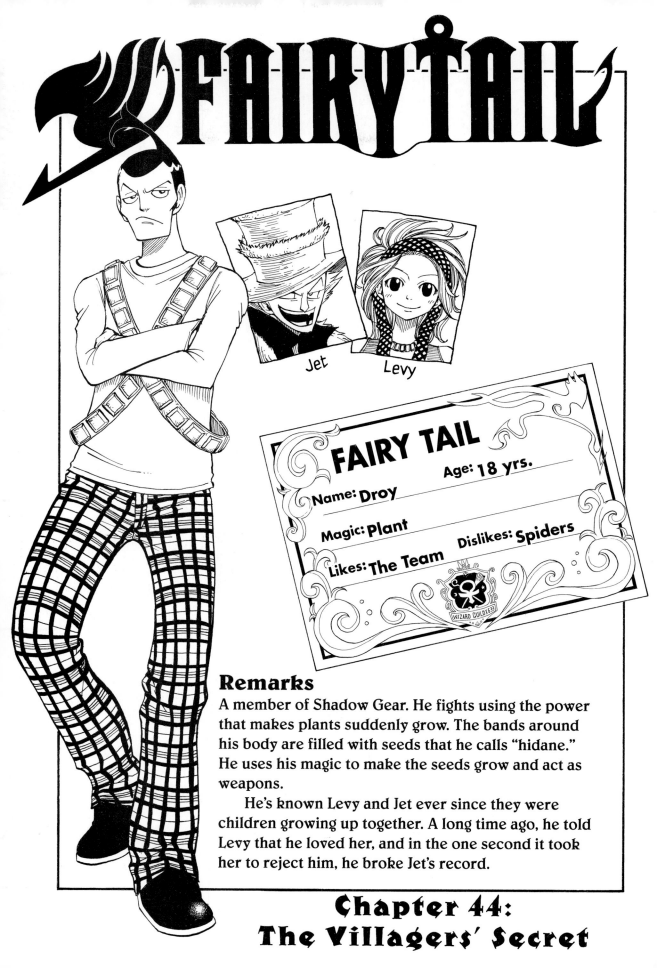

FAIRY TAIL

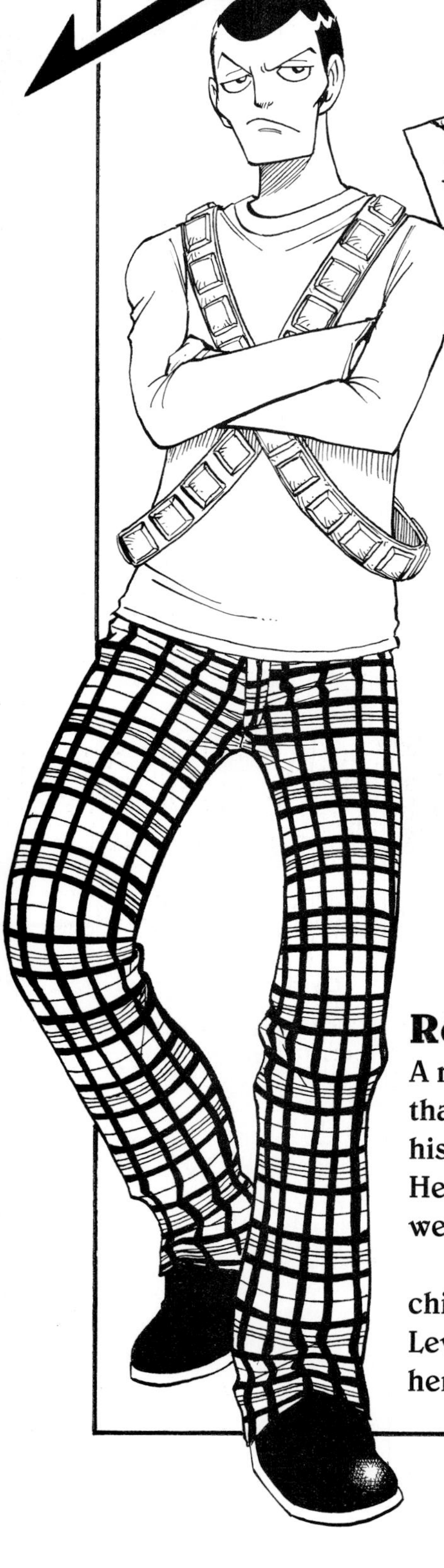

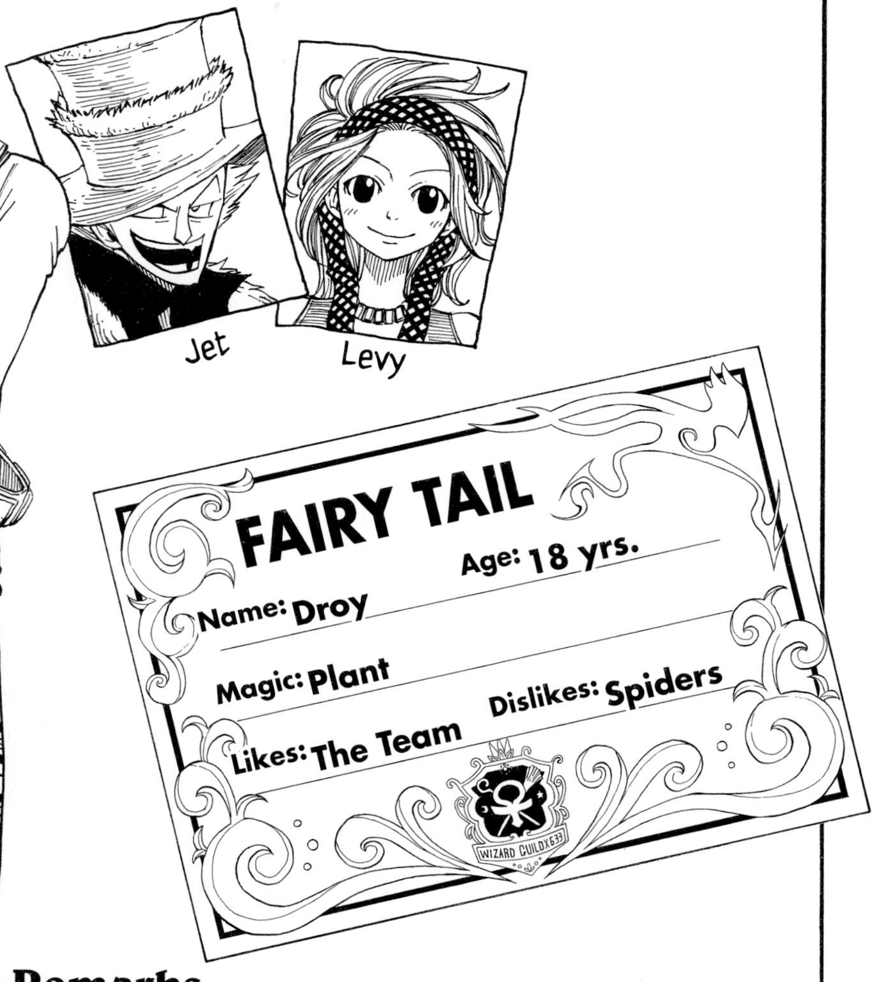
Jet
Levy
FAIRY TAIL
Age: 18 yrs.
Name: Droy
Magic: Plant
Dislikes: Spiders
Likes: The Team
WIZARD GUILD X633

Remarks

A member of Shadow Gear. He fights using the power that makes plants suddenly grow. The bands around his body are filled with seeds that he calls “hidane.” He uses his magic to make the seeds grow and act as weapons.

He’s known Levy and Jet ever since they were children growing up together. A long time ago, he told Levy that he loved her, and in the one second it took her to reject him, he broke Jet’s record.

Chapter 44: The Villagers’ Secret

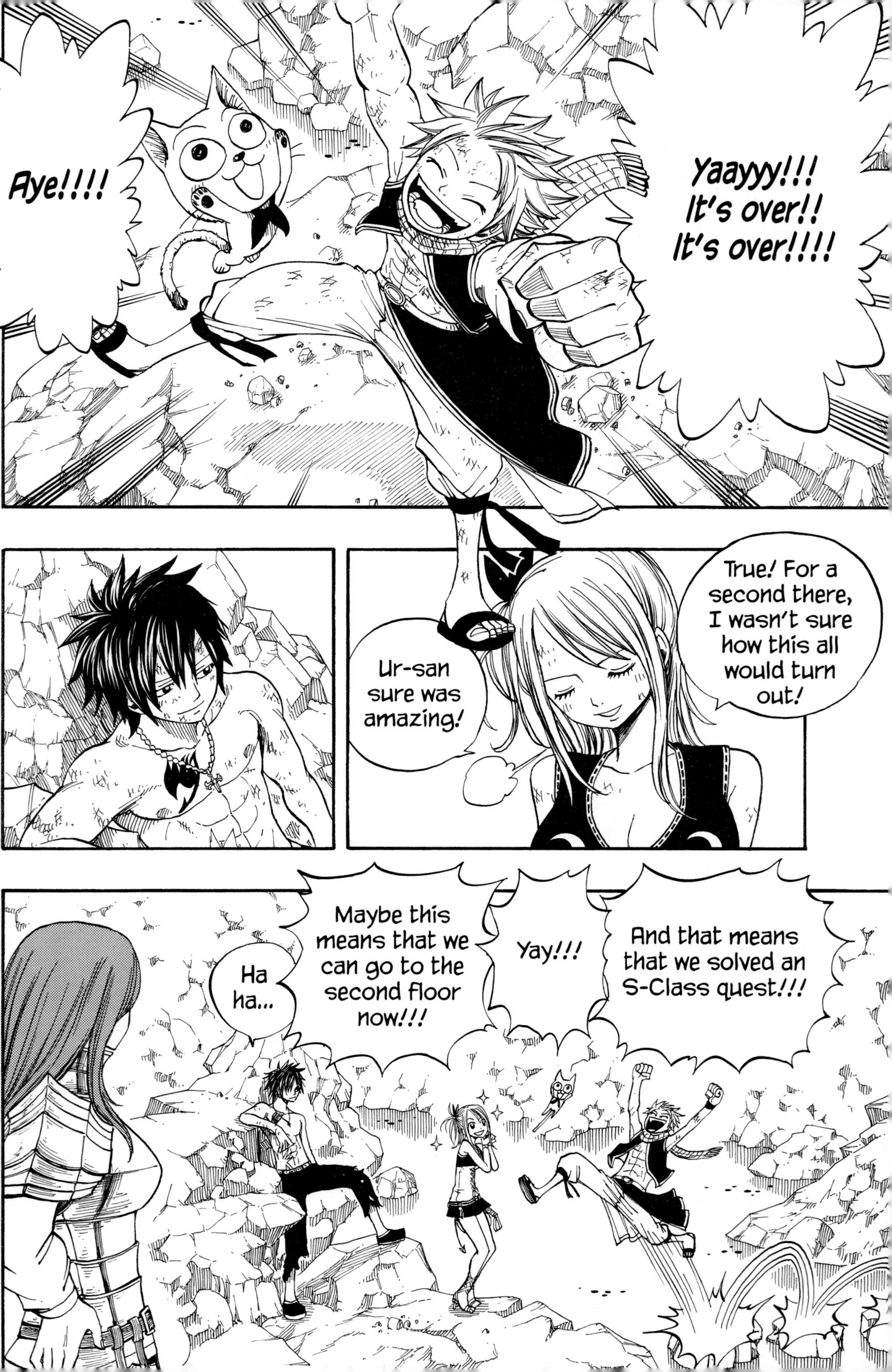
Yaayyy!!! It's over!! It's over!!!!
Aye!!!!
Ur-san sure was amazing!
True! For a second there, I wasn't sure how this all would turn out!
And that means that we solved an S-Class quest!!!
Yay!!!
Maybe this means that we can go to the second floor now!!!
Ha ha...

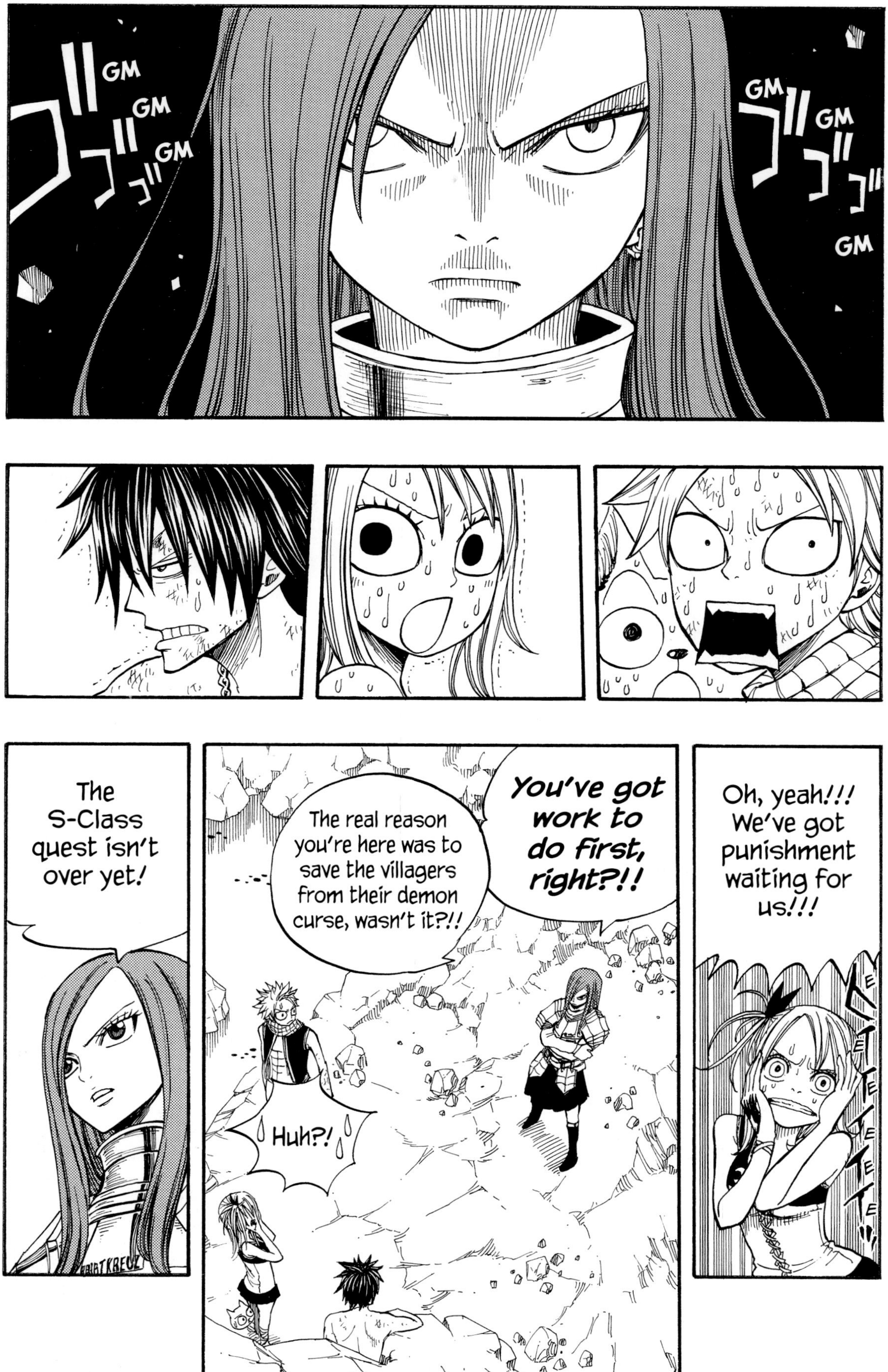
GM
GM
GM
GM
GM
GM
Oh, yeah!!! We've got punishment waiting for us!!!
You've got work to do first, right?!!
The real reason you're here was to save the villagers from their demon curse, wasn't it?!!
Huh?!
The S-Class quest isn't over yet!

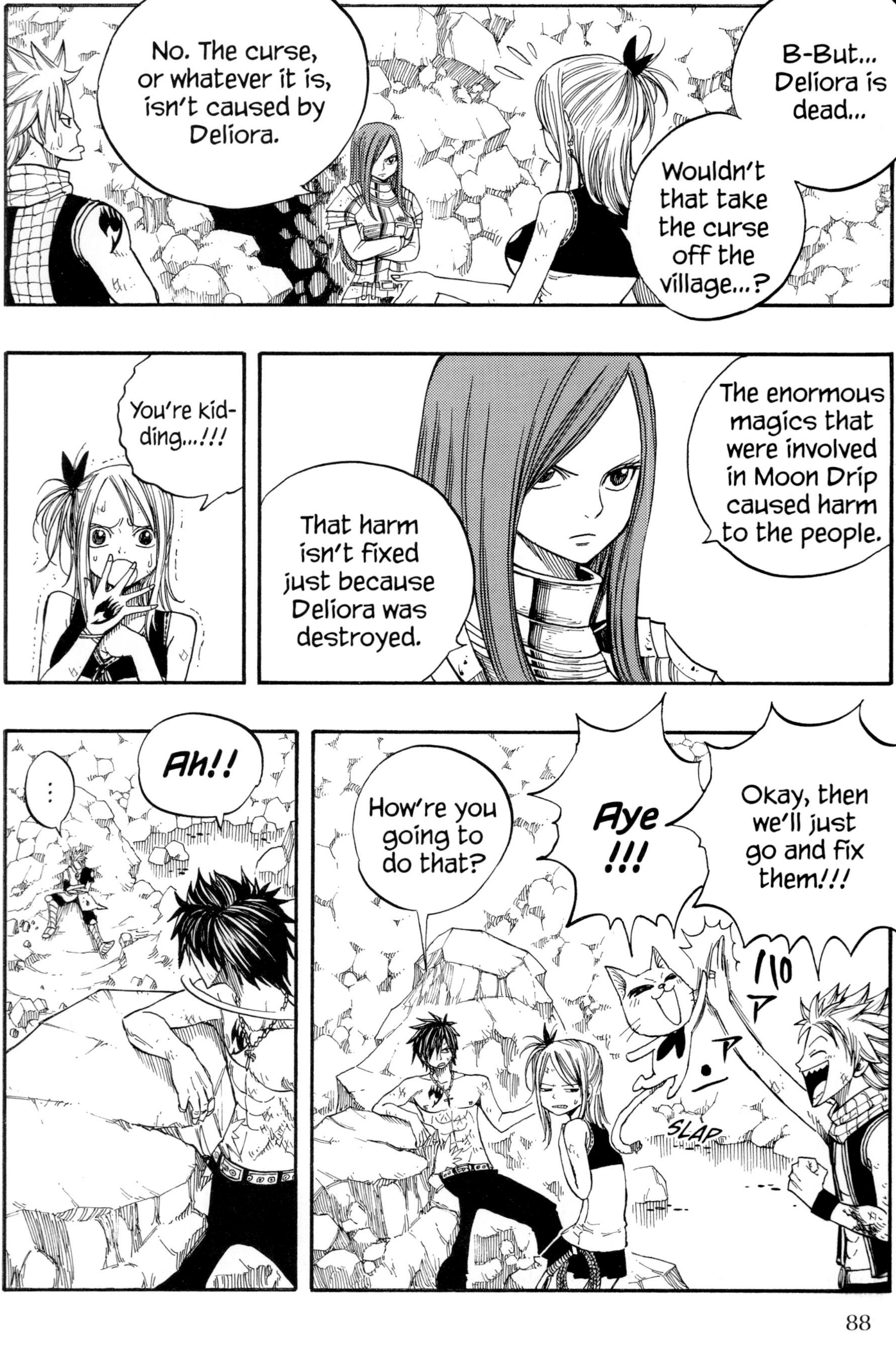
B-But... Deliora is dead...
Wouldn't that take the curse off the village...?
No. The curse, or whatever it is, isn't caused by Deliora.
The enormous magics that were involved in Moon Drip caused harm to the people.
That harm isn't fixed just because Deliora was destroyed.
You're kid-ding...!!!
Okay, then we'll just go and fix them!!!
Aye!!!
How're you going to do that?
SLAP
Ah!!
...

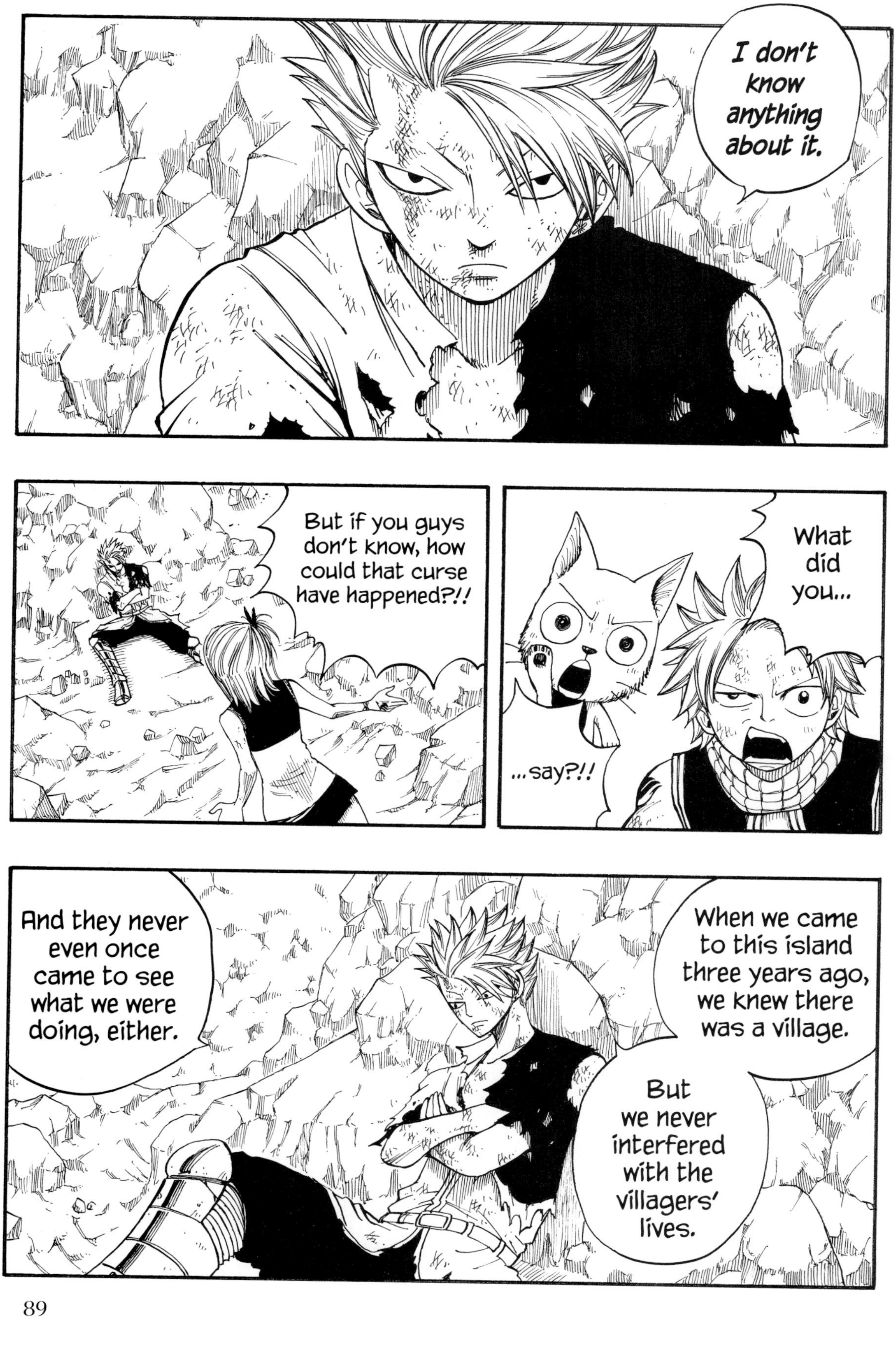
I don't know anything about it.
What did you...
...say?!!
But if you guys don't know, how could that curse have happened?!!
When we came to this island three years ago, we knew there was a village.
But we never interfered with the villagers' lives.
And they never even once came to see what we were doing, either.

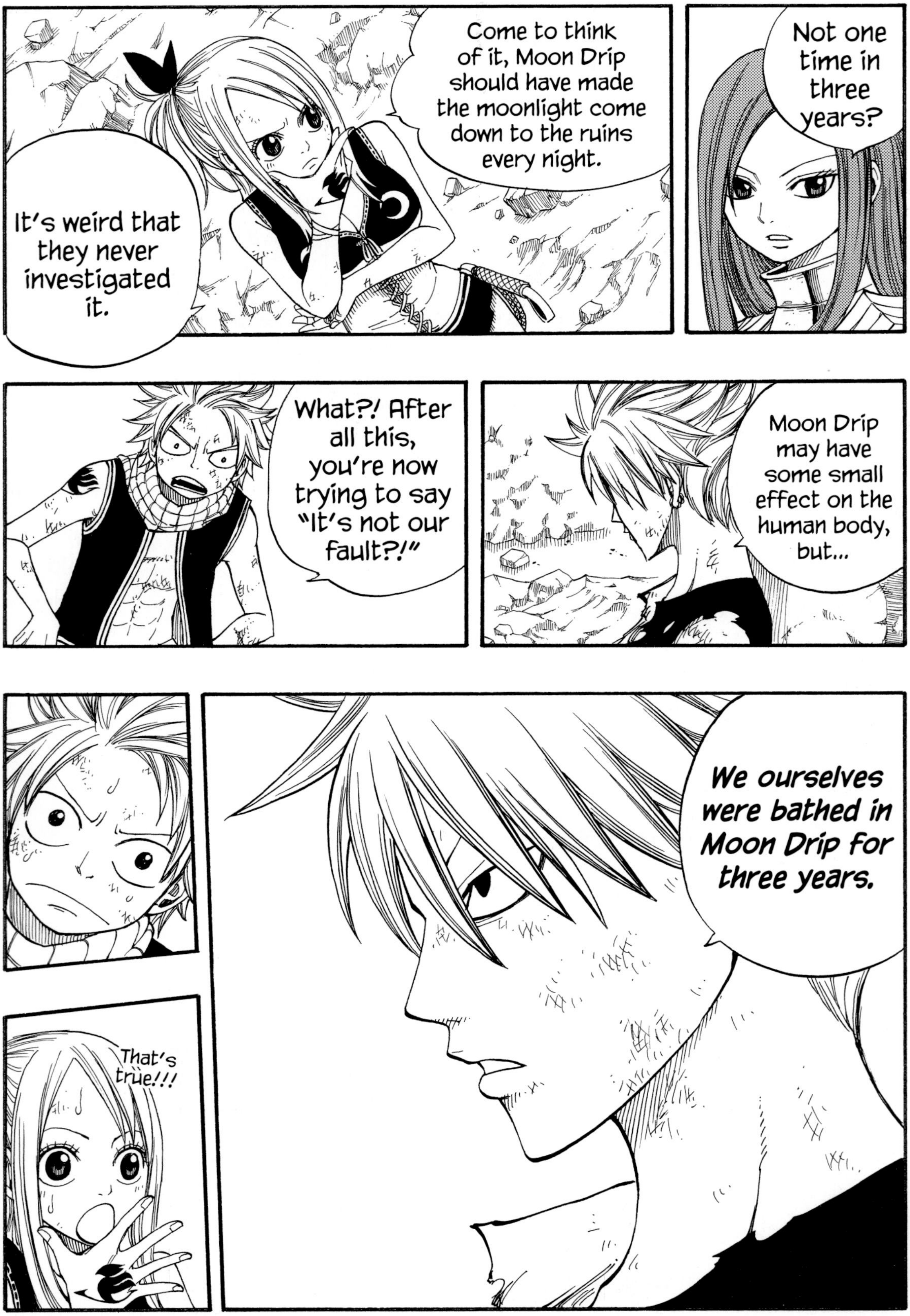
Not one time in three years?
Come to think of it, Moon Drip should have made the moonlight come down to the ruins every night.
It's weird that they never investigated it.
Moon Drip may have some small effect on the human body, but...
What?! After all this, you're now trying to say "It's not our fault?!"
We ourselves were bathed in Moon Drip for three years.
That's true!!!

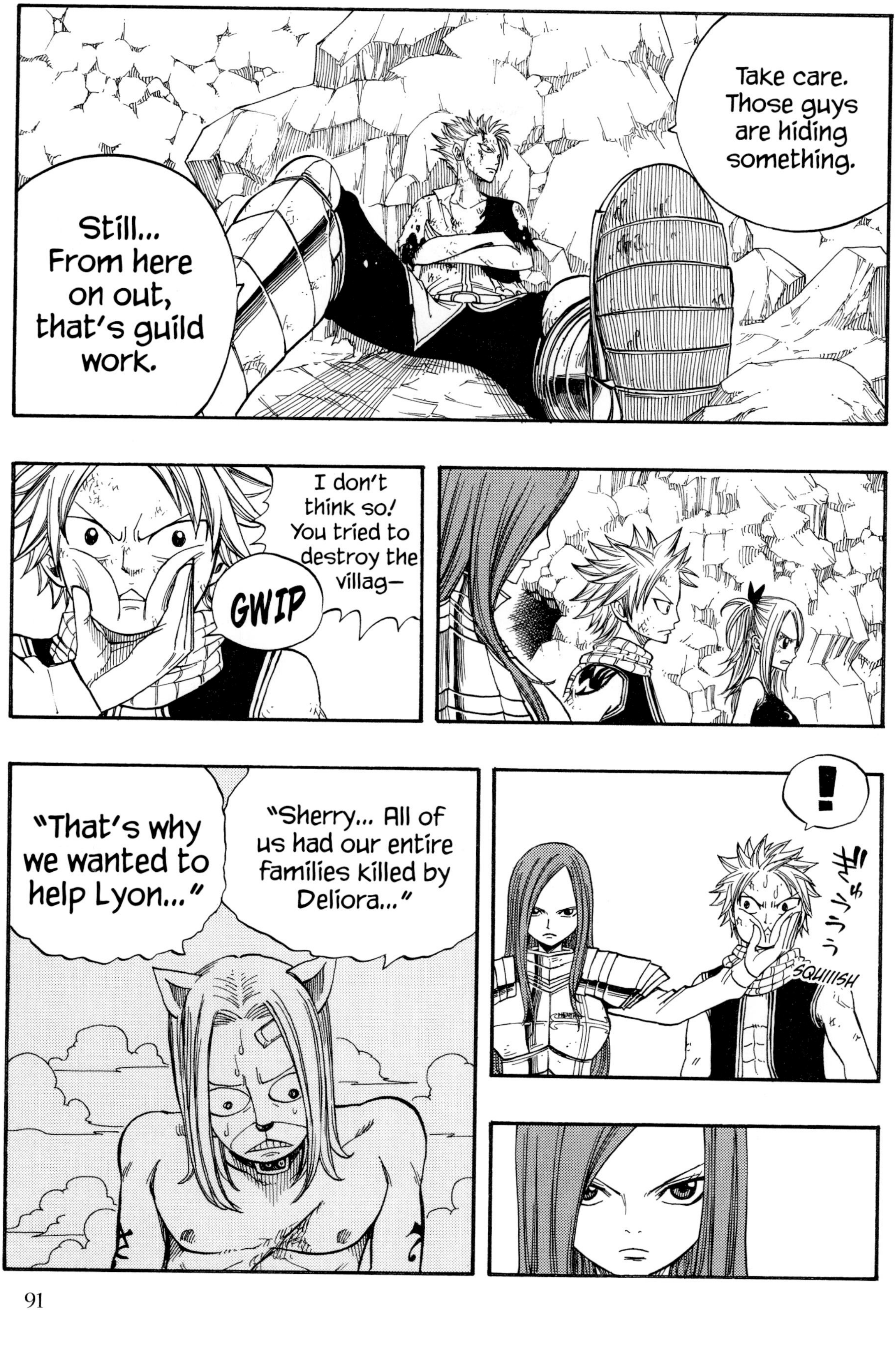
Take care. Those guys are hiding something.
Still... From here on out, that's guild work.
I don't think so! You tried to destroy the villag—
GWIP
!
SQUIIISH
"Sherry... All of us had our entire families killed by Deliora..."
"That's why we wanted to help Lyon..."

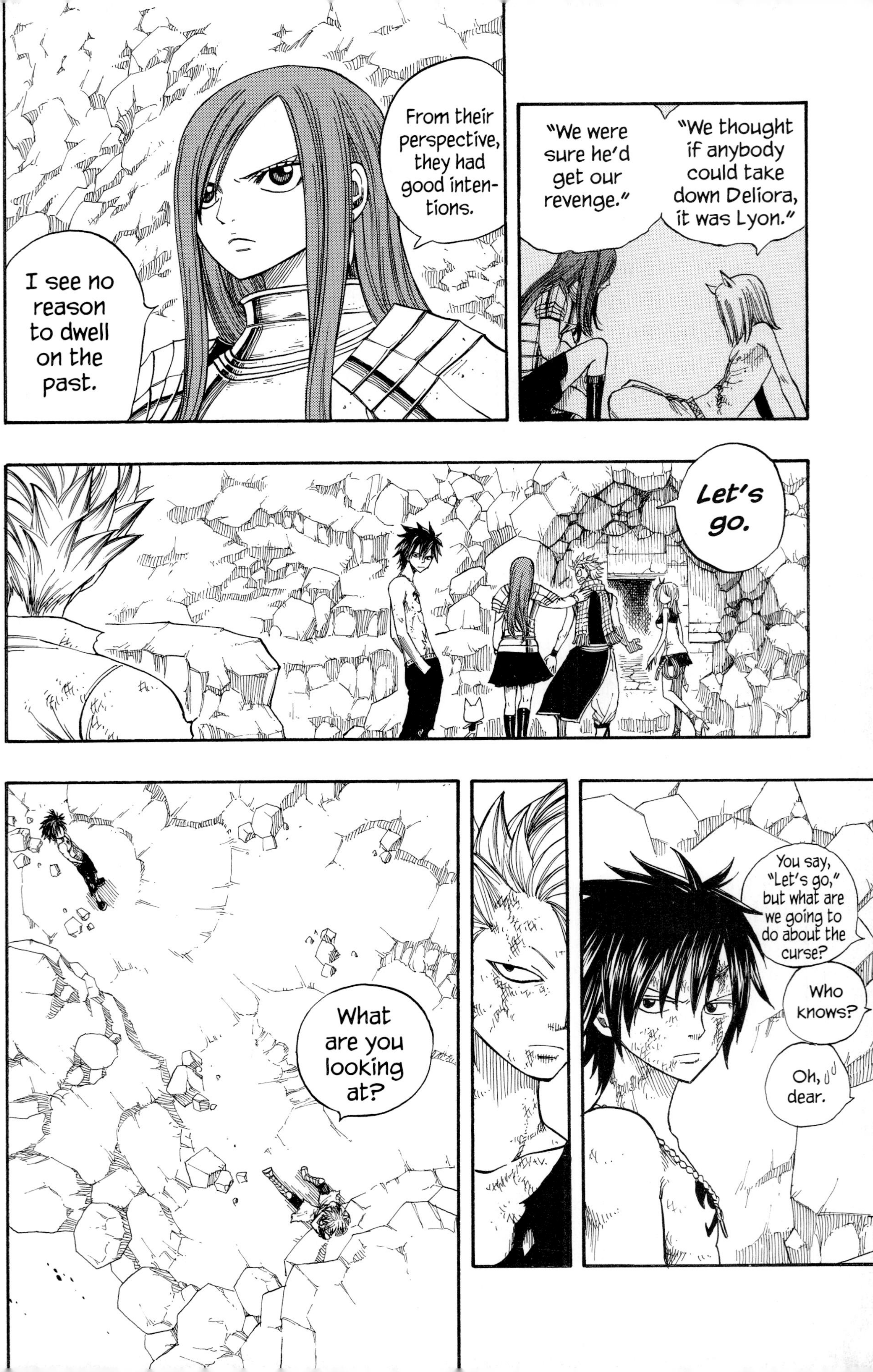
"We thought if anybody could take down Deliora, it was Lyon."
"We were sure he'd get our revenge."
From their perspective, they had good intentions.
I see no reason to dwell on the past.
Let's go.
You say, "Let's go," but what are we going to do about the curse?
Who knows?
Oh, dear.
What are you looking at?

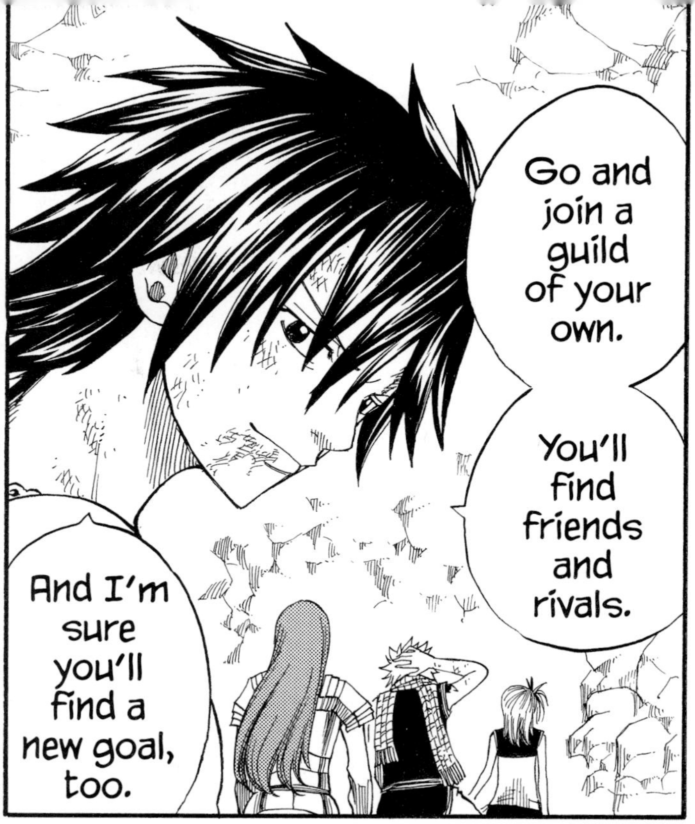
Go and join a guild of your own.
You'll find friends and rivals.
And I'm sure you'll find a new goal, too.
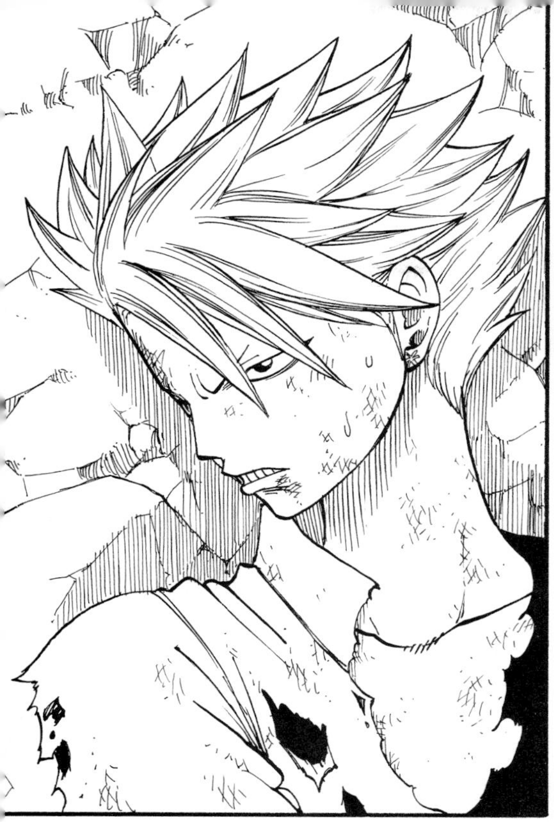
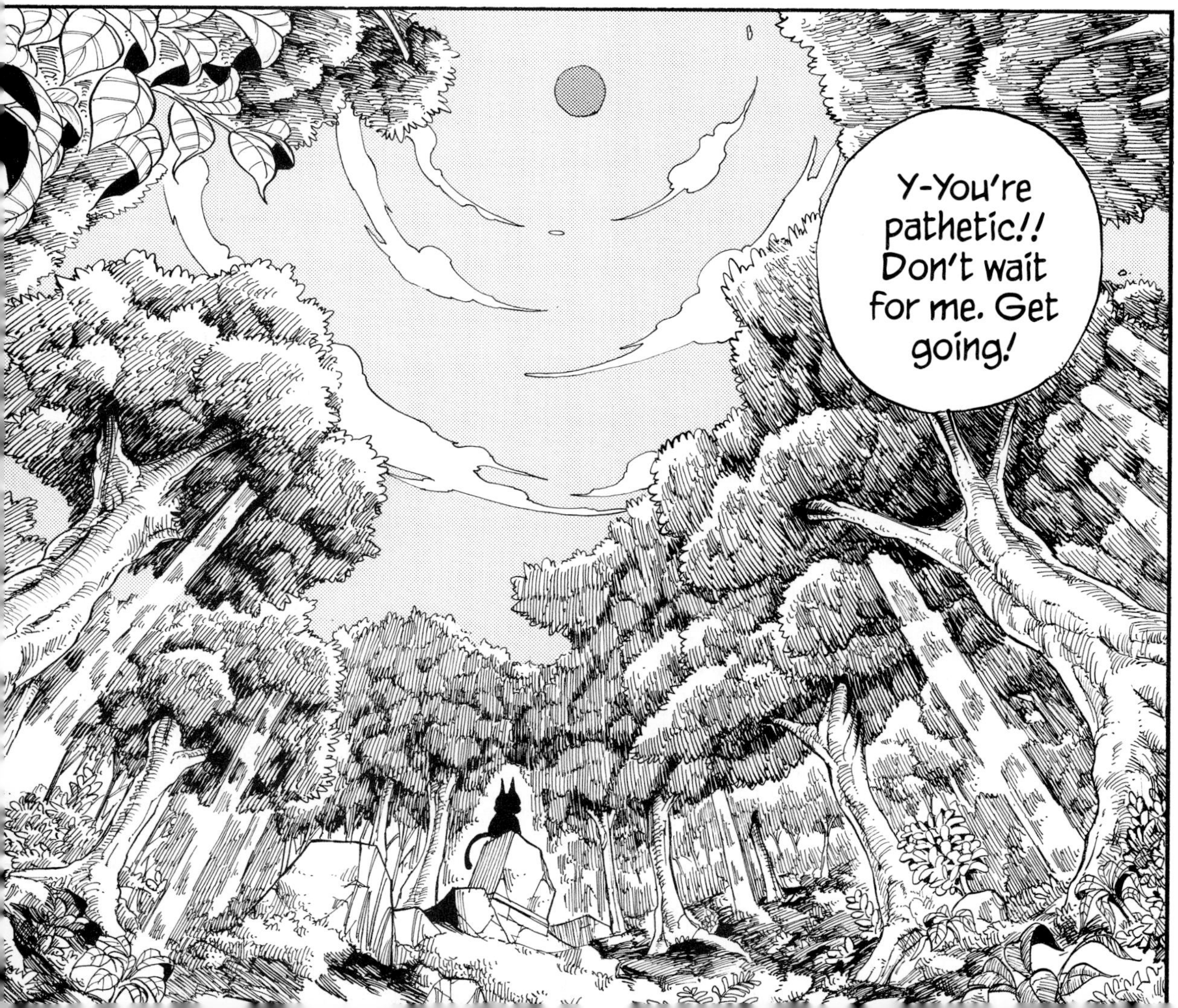
Y-You're pathetic!! Don't wait for me. Get going!

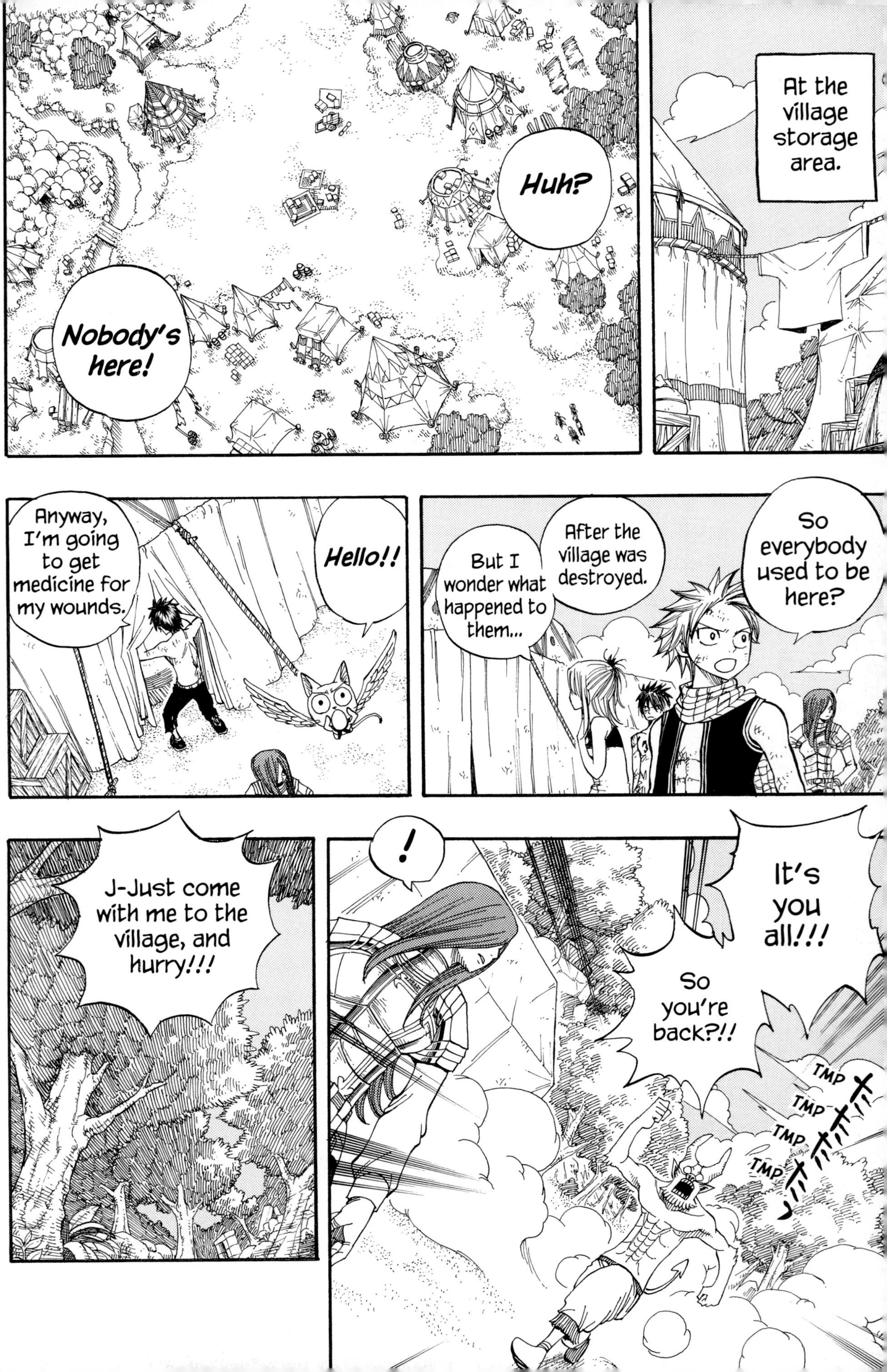
At the village storage area.
Huh?
Nobody's here!
So everybody used to be here?
After the village was destroyed.
But I wonder what happened to them...
Hello!!
Anyway, I'm going to get medicine for my wounds.
It's you all!!!
!
So you're back?!!
TMP
TMP
TMP
TMP
J-Just come with me to the village, and hurry!!!

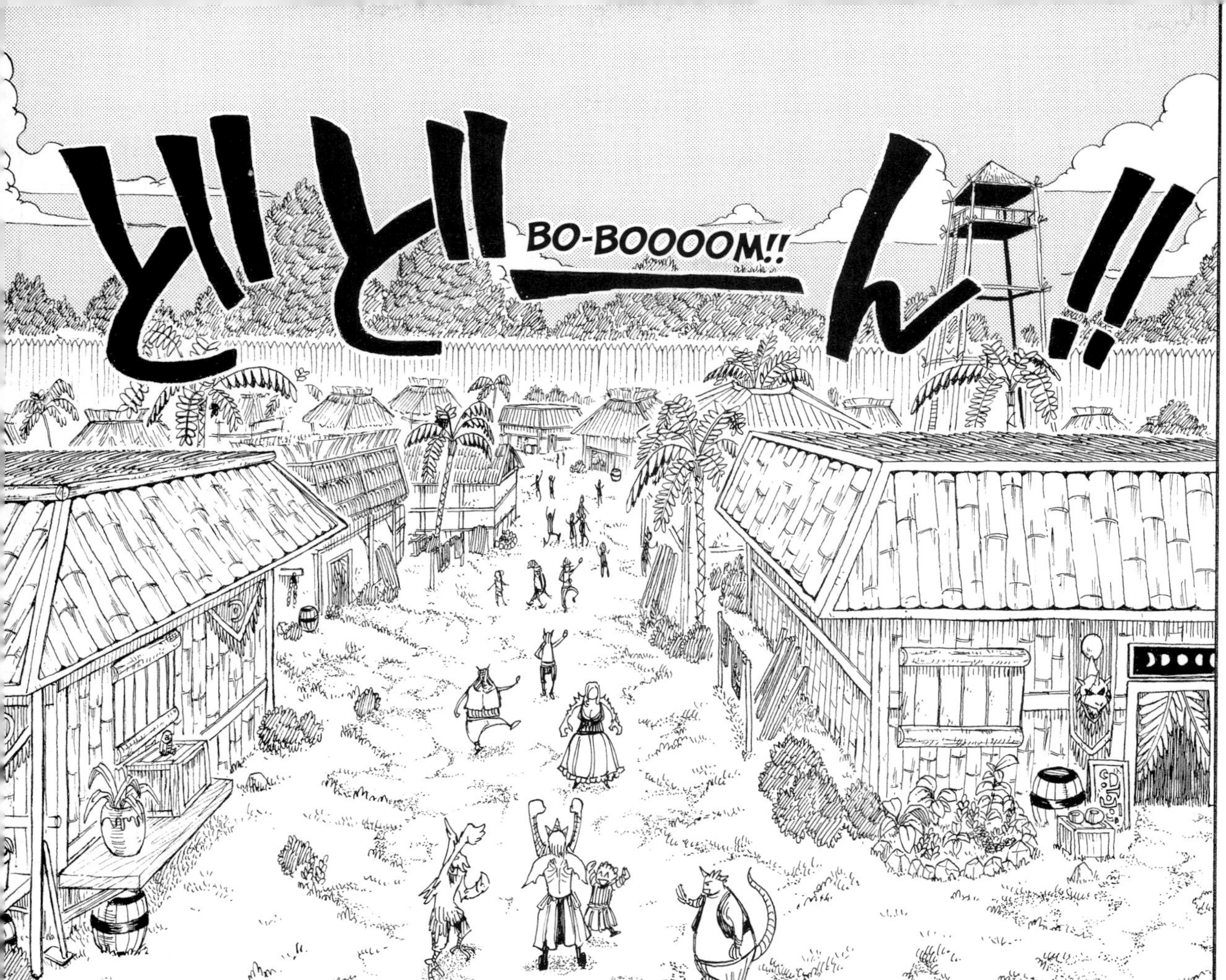
どどーん!!
BO-BOOOOM!!

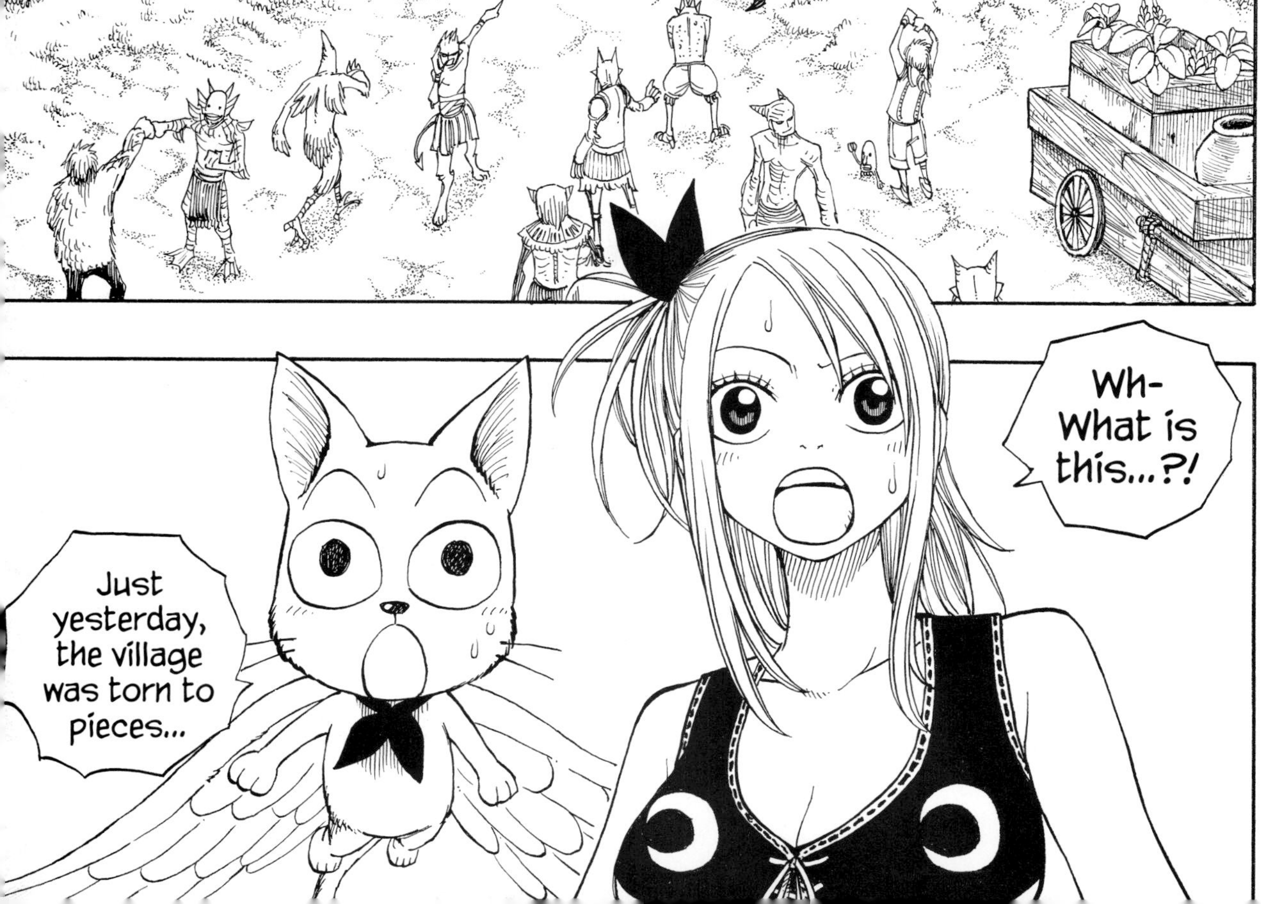
Wh- What is this...?!
Just yesterday, the village was torn to pieces...

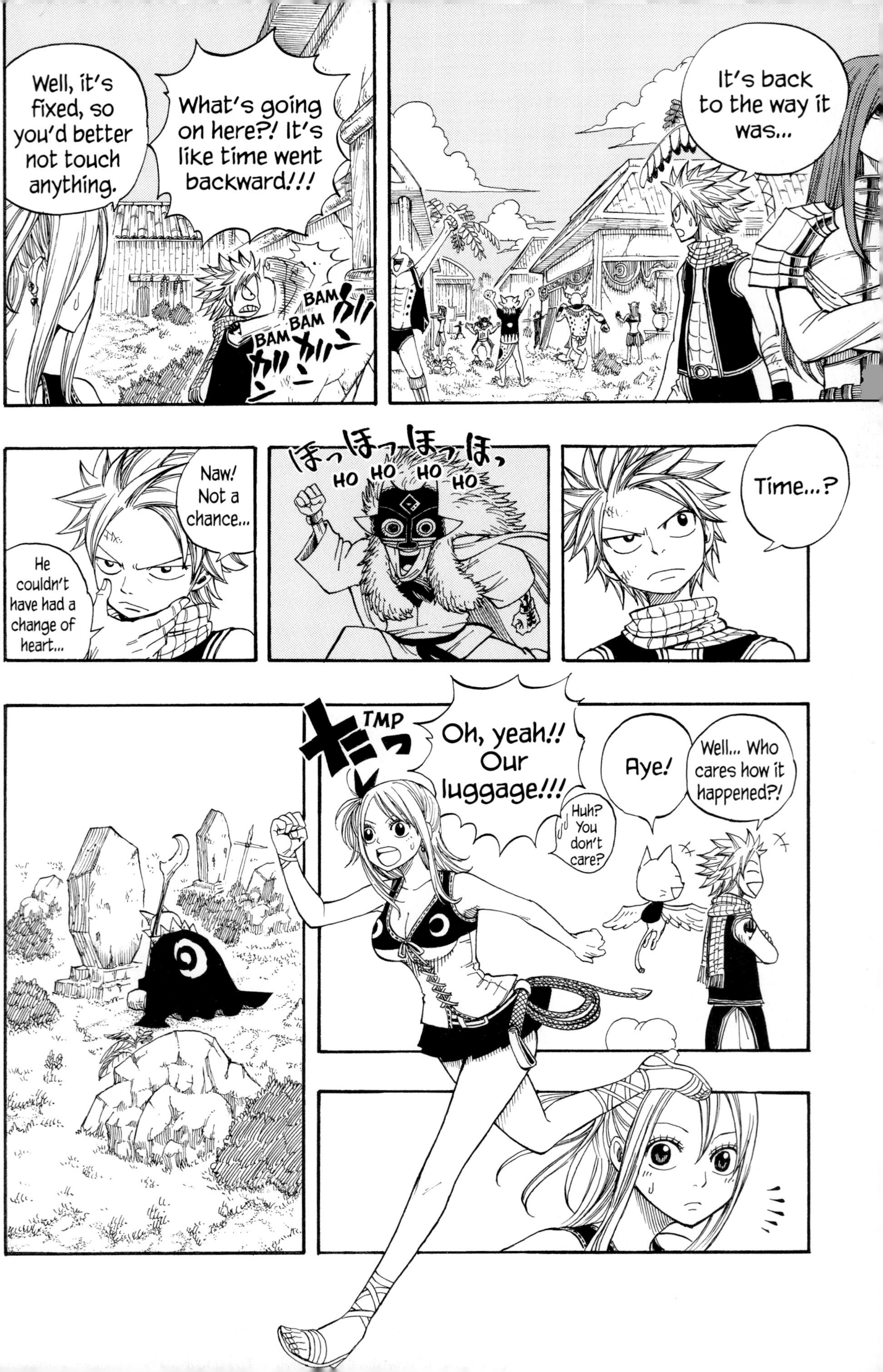
It's back to the way it was...
What's going on here?! It's like time went backward!!!
BAM BAM BAM
Well, it's fixed, so you'd better not touch anything.
Time...?
ほっほっほっほっ
HO HO HO HO
Naw! Not a chance...
He couldn't have had a change of heart...
Well... Who cares how it happened?!
Aye!
Huh? You don't care?
TMP
Oh, yeah!! Our luggage!!!

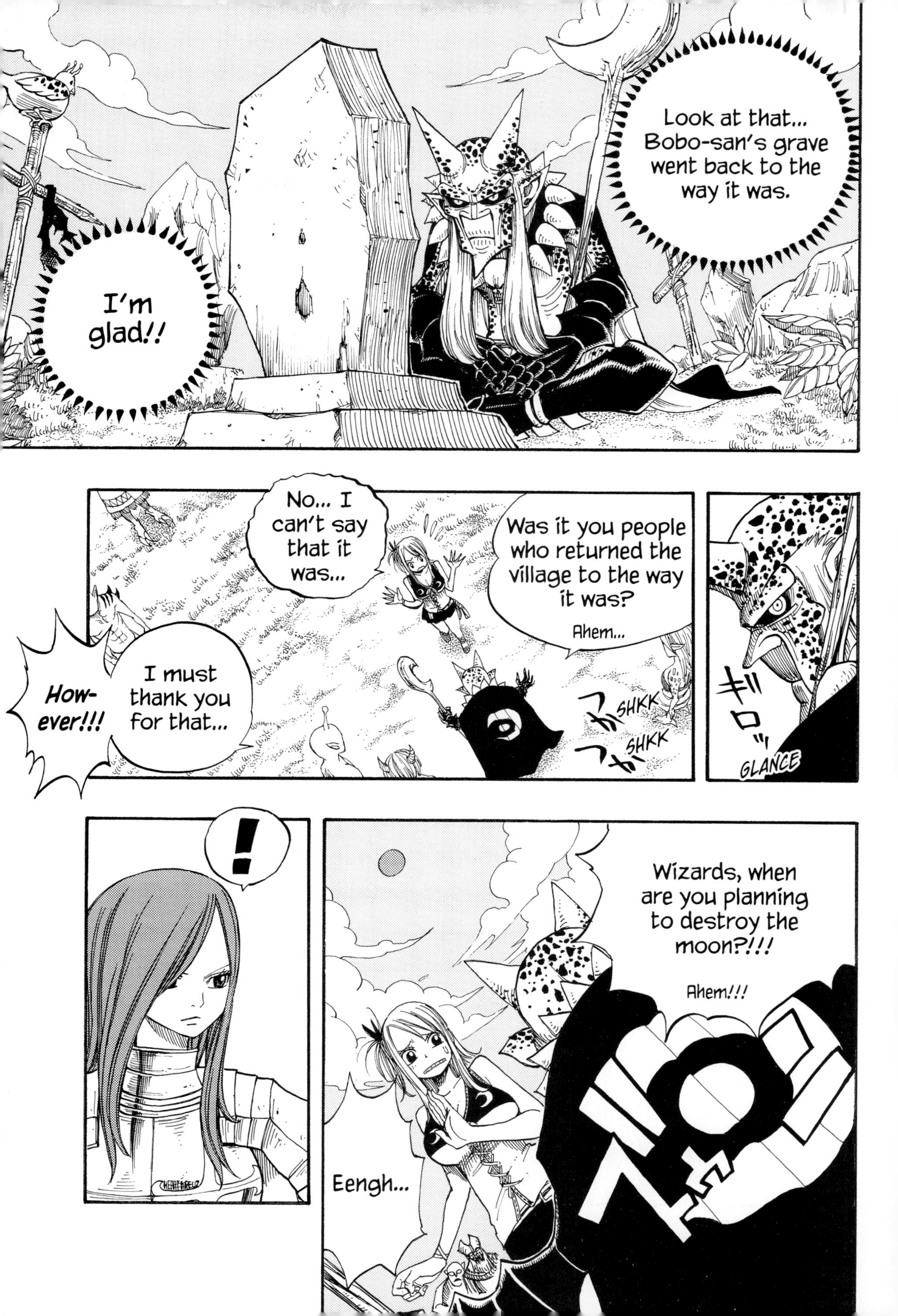
Look at that... Bobo-san's grave went back to the way it was.
I'm glad!!
GLANCE
Was it you people who returned the village to the way it was?
Ahem...
No... I can't say that it was...
SHKK
SHKK
I must thank you for that...
How-ever!!!
Wizards, when are you planning to destroy the moon?!!!
Ahem!!!
Eengh...
!

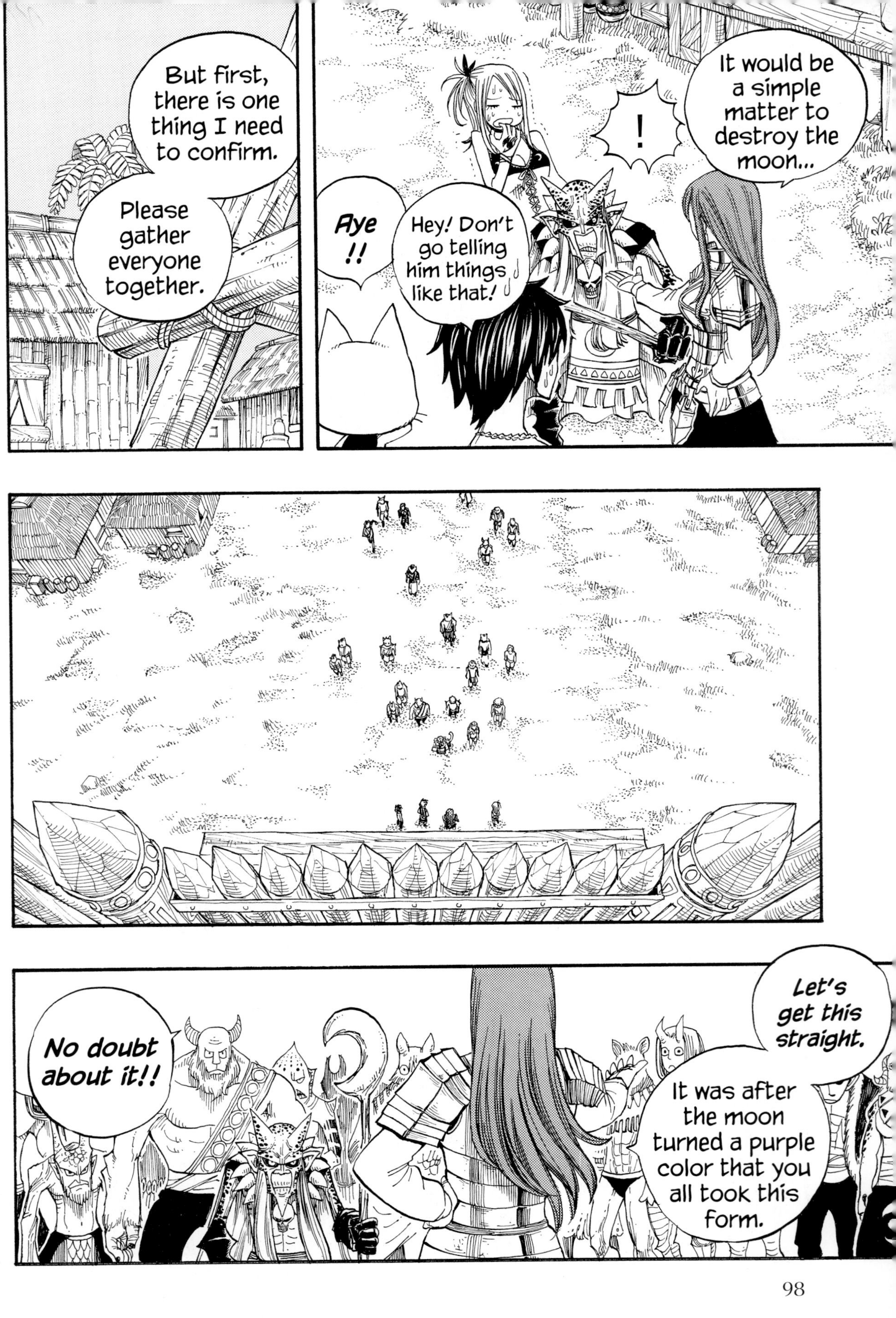
It would be a simple matter to destroy the moon...
!
Hey! Don't go telling him things like that!
Aye!!
But first, there is one thing I need to confirm.
Please gather everyone together.
Let's get this straight.
It was after the moon turned a purple color that you all took this form.
No doubt about it!!

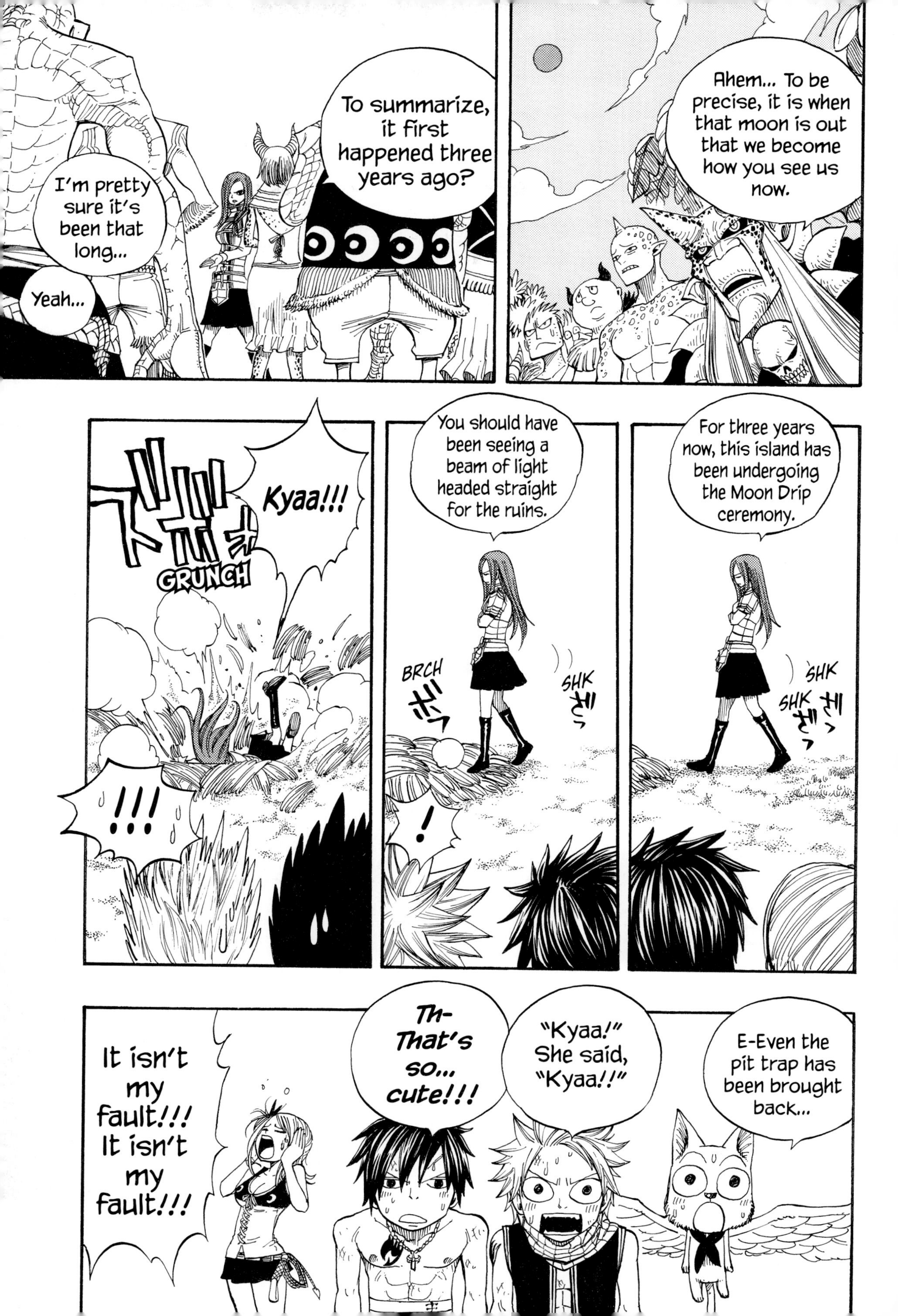
Ahem... To be precise, it is when that moon is out that we become how you see us now.
To summarize, it first happened three years ago?
I'm pretty sure it's been that long...
Yeah...
For three years now, this island has been undergoing the Moon Drip ceremony.
SHK
SHK
You should have been seeing a beam of light headed straight for the ruins.
SHK
BRCH
!
Kyaa!!!
GRUNCH
!!!
E-Even the pit trap has been brought back...
"Kyaa!" She said, "Kyaa!!"
Th-That's so... cute!!!
It isn't my fault!!! It isn't my fault!!!

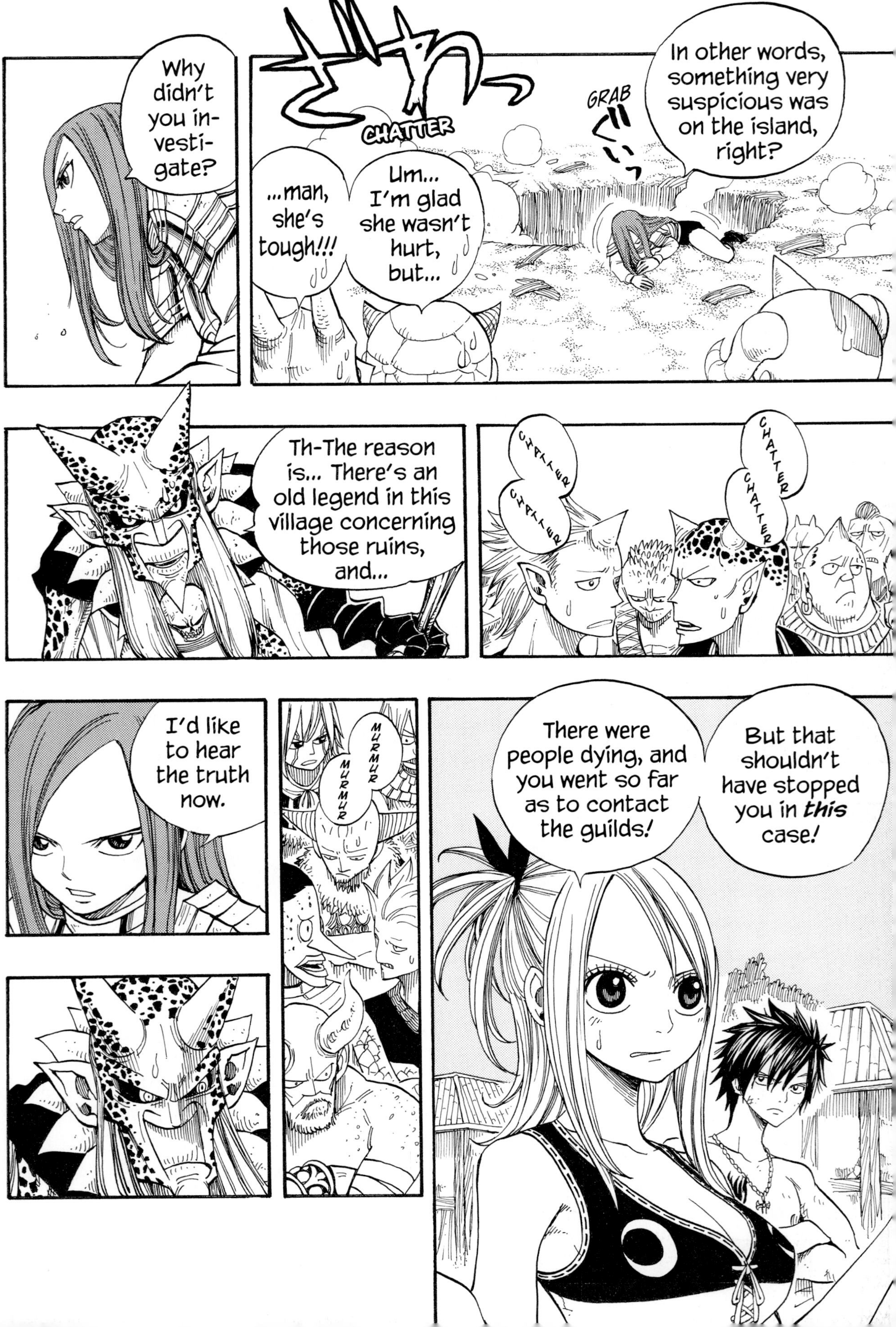
In other words, something very suspicious was on the island, right?
GRAB
CHATTER
Um... I'm glad she wasn't hurt, but...
...man, she's tough!!!
Why didn't you in-vesti-gate?
CHATTER CHATTER
CHATTER CHATTER
Th-The reason is... There's an old legend in this village concerning those ruins, and...
There were people dying, and you went so far as to contact the guilds!
But that shouldn't have stopped you in *this* case!
MURMUR MURMUR
I'd like to hear the truth now.

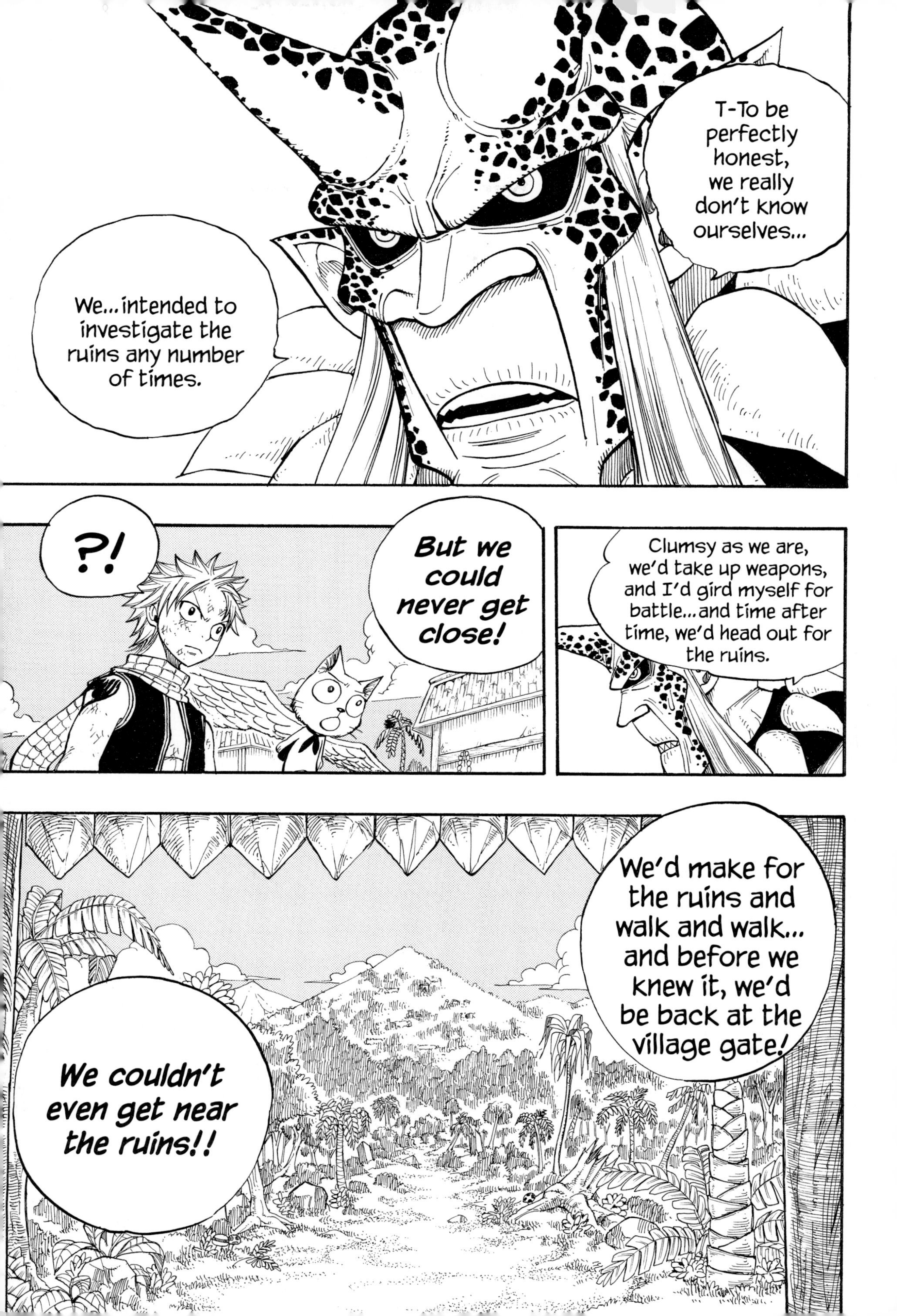
T-To be perfectly honest, we really don't know ourselves...
We...intended to investigate the ruins any number of times.
Clumsy as we are, we'd take up weapons, and I'd gird myself for battle...and time after time, we'd head out for the ruins.
But we could never get close!
?!
We'd make for the ruins and walk and walk... and before we knew it, we'd be back at the village gate!
We couldn't even get near the ruins!!

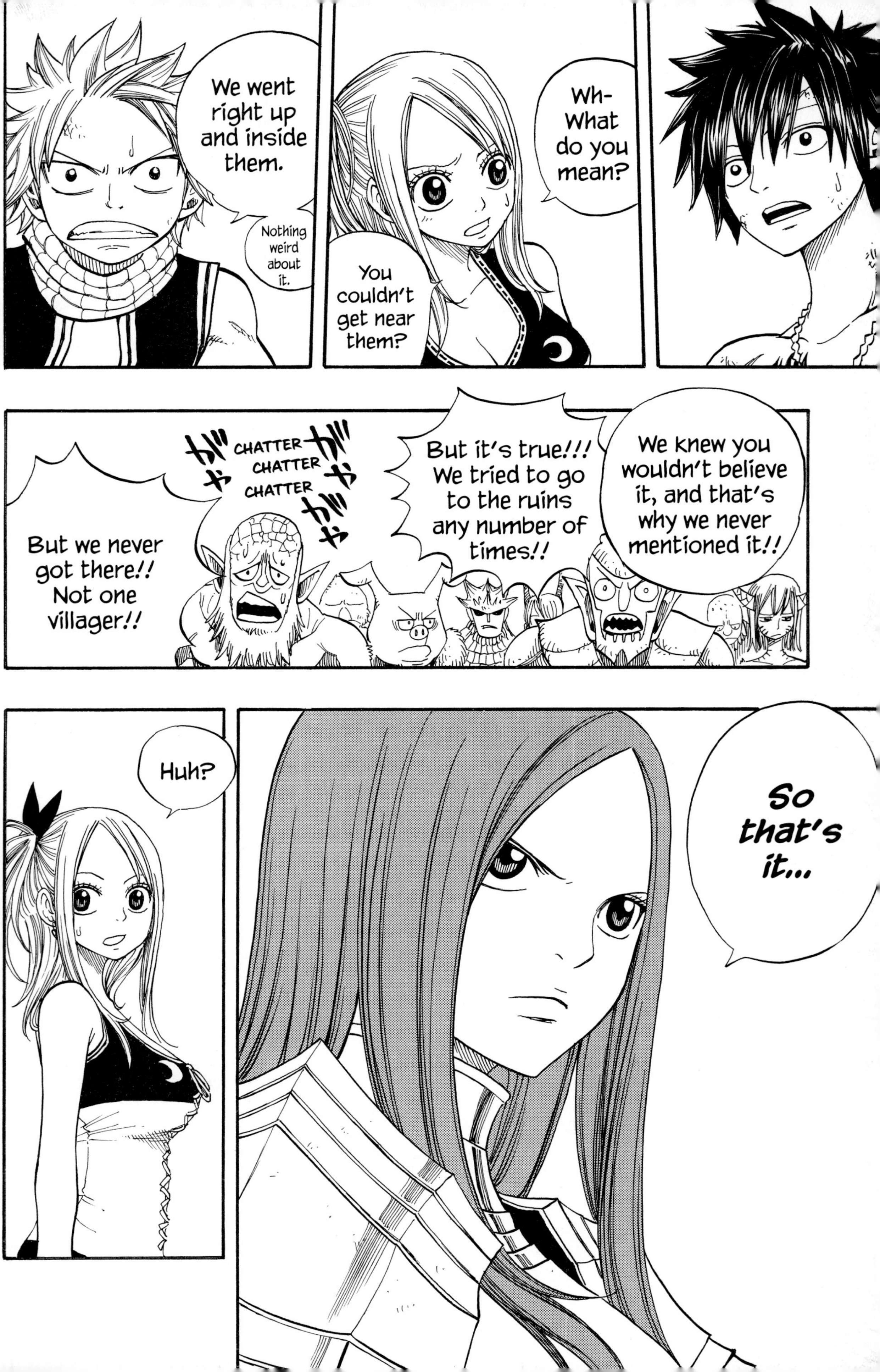
Wh- What do you mean?
You couldn't get near them?
We went right up and inside them.
Nothing weird about it.
We knew you wouldn't believe it, and that's why we never mentioned it!!
But it's true!!! We tried to go to the ruins any number of times!!
CHATTER CHATTER CHATTER
But we never got there!! Not one villager!!
So that's it...
Huh?

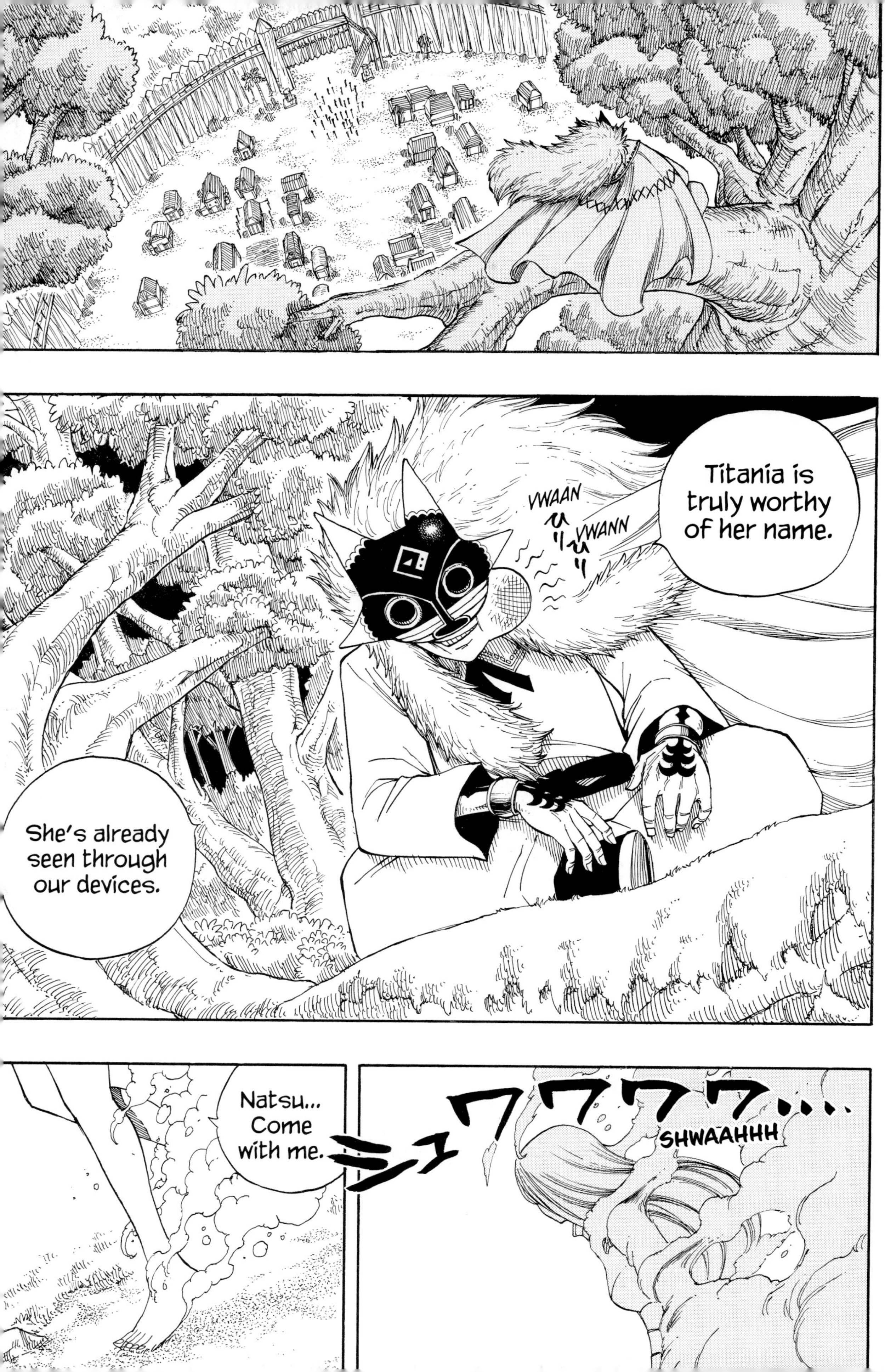
Titania is truly worthy of her name.
VWAAN
VWANN
She's already seen through our devices.
シュワワワ…
SHWAAHHH
Natsu... Come with me.

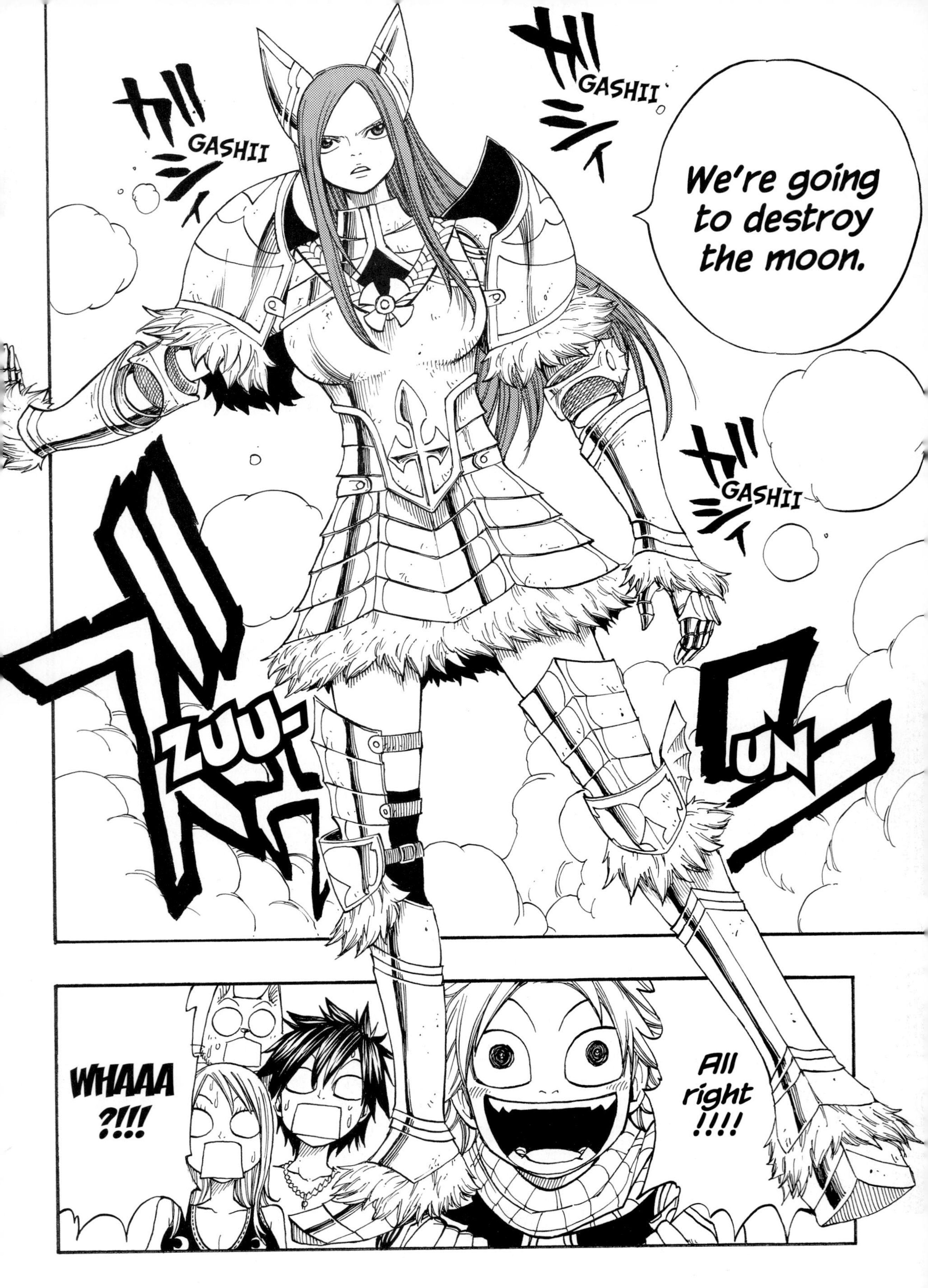
GASHII
We're going to destroy the moon.
GASHII
GASHII
ZUU-
UN
All right!!!!
WHAAA?!!!

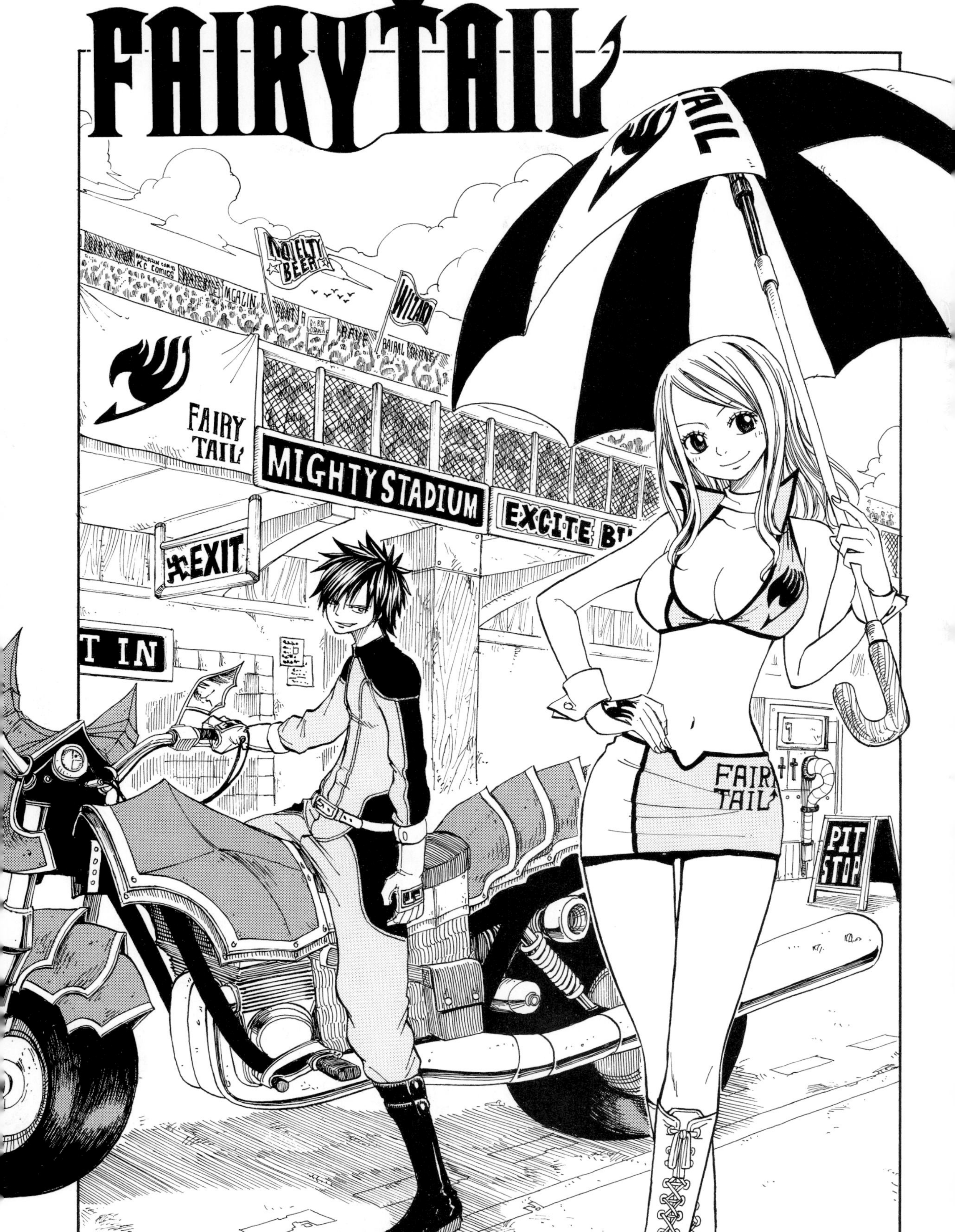
FAIRY TAIL
NOVELTY BEER
WIZARD
FAIRY TAIL
MIGHTY STADIUM
EXCITE B
EXIT
T IN
FAIRY TAIL
PIT STOP

Chapter 45: Make It There, to the Sky

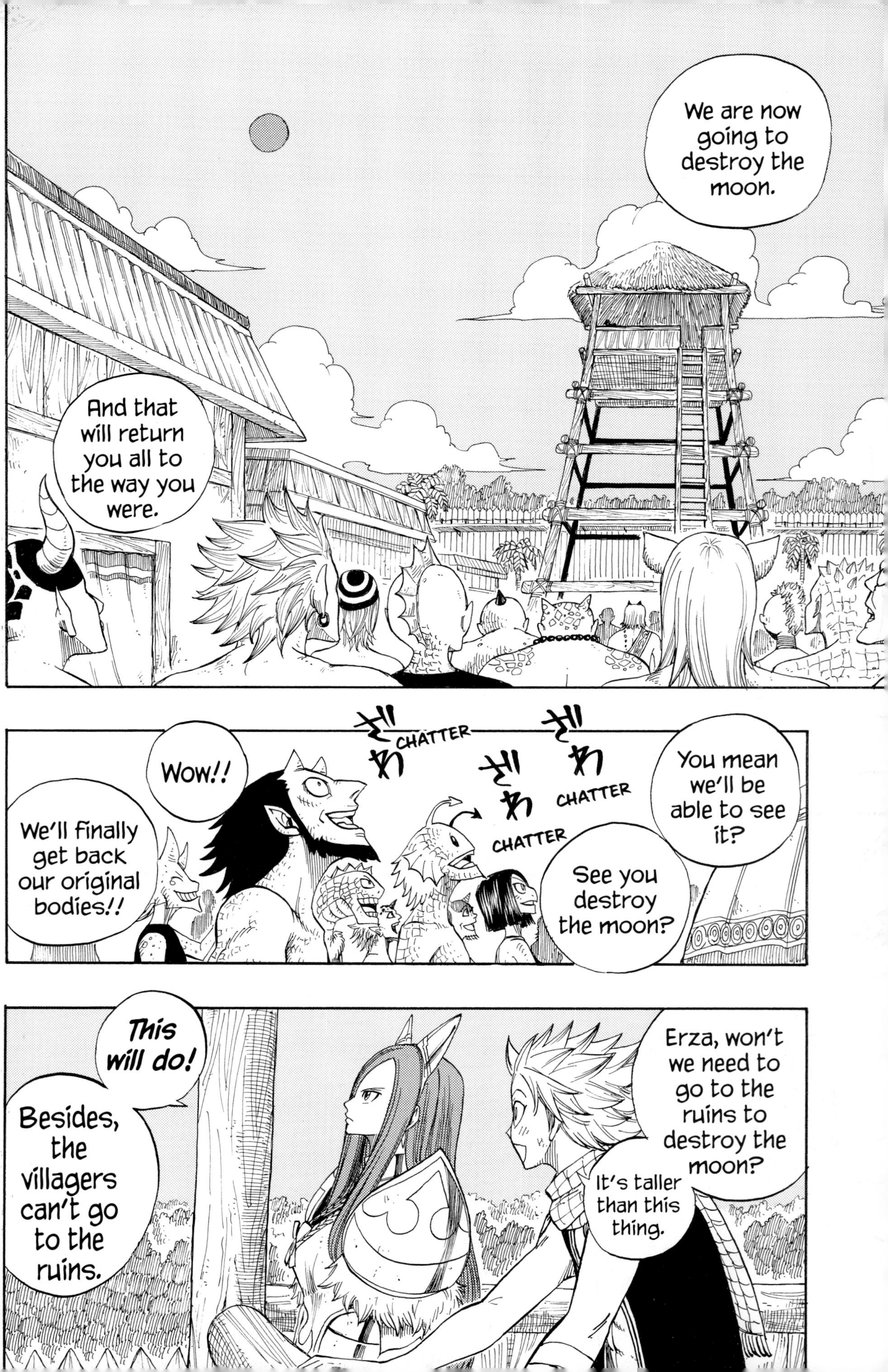
We are now going to destroy the moon.
And that will return you all to the way you were.
You mean we'll be able to see it?
See you destroy the moon?
ざわ CHATTER
ざわ CHATTER
ざわ CHATTER
ざわ
Wow!!
We'll finally get back our original bodies!!
Erza, won't we need to go to the ruins to destroy the moon?
It's taller than this thing.
This will do!
Besides, the villagers can't go to the ruins.

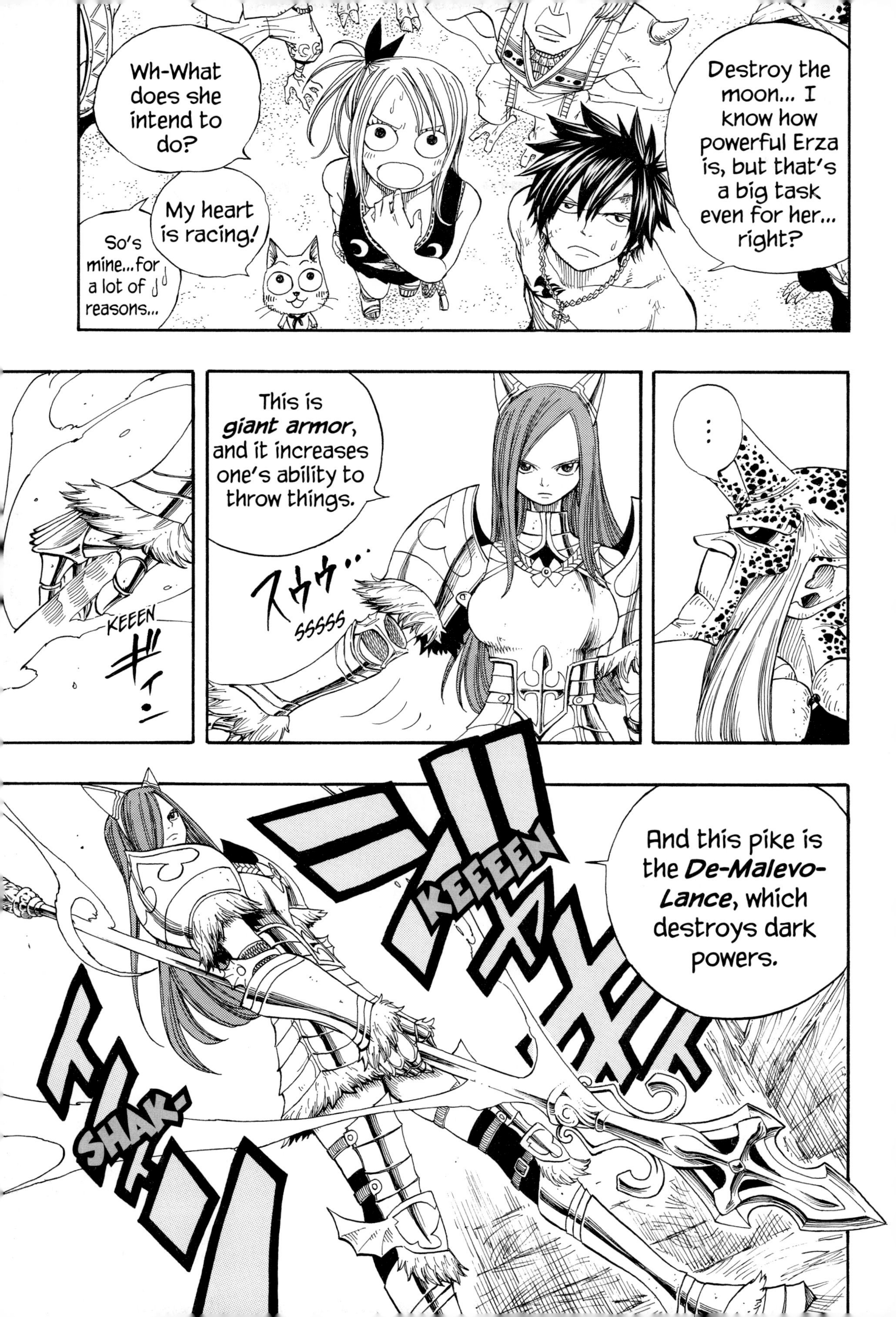
Destroy the moon... I know how powerful Erza is, but that's a big task even for her... right?
Wh-What does she intend to do?
My heart is racing!
So's mine...for a lot of reasons...
...
This is *giant armor*, and it increases one's ability to throw things.
SSSSS
KEEEN
And this pike is the *De-Malevo-Lance*, which destroys dark powers.
KEEEEN
SHAK-

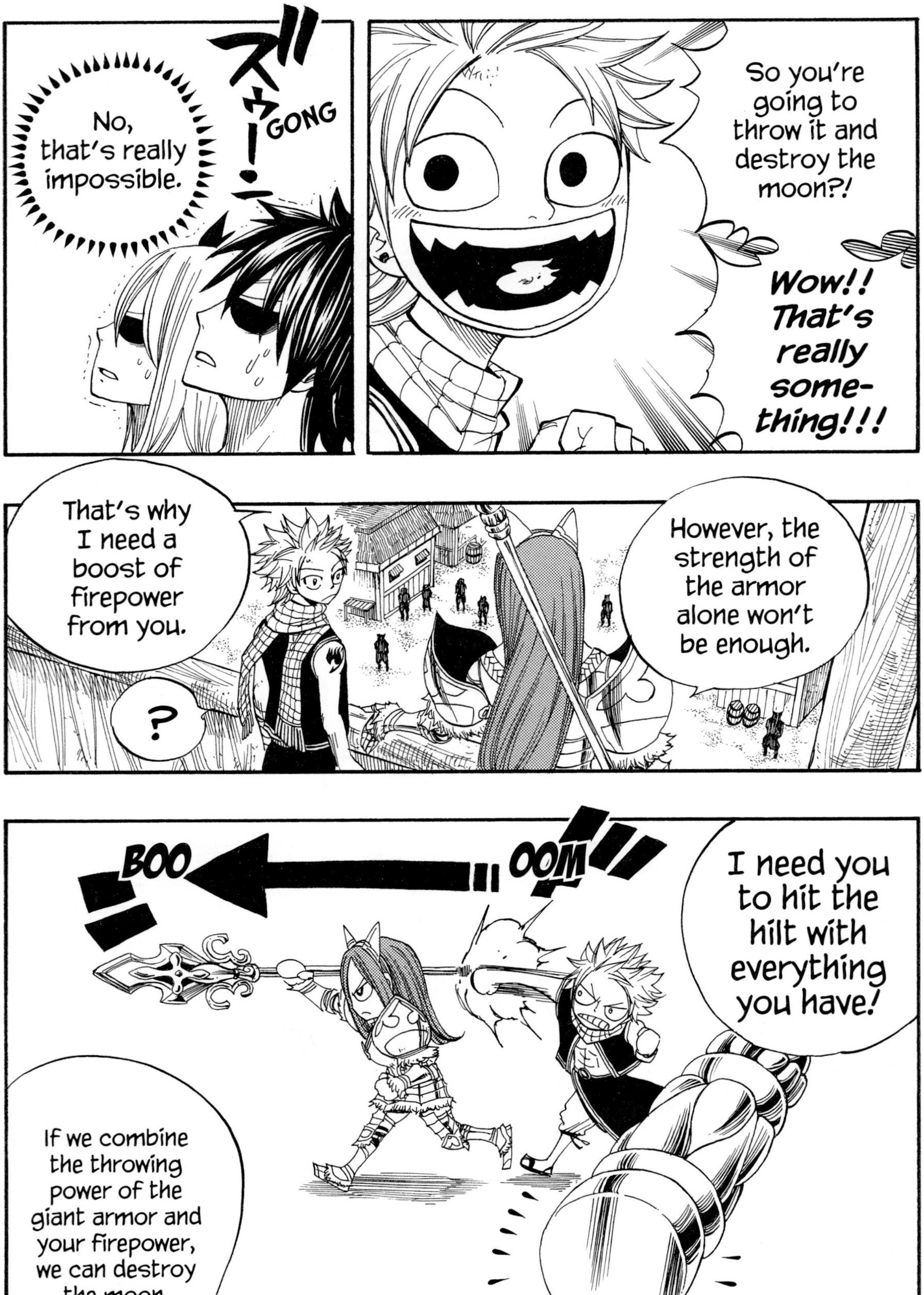
So you're going to throw it and destroy the moon?!
Wow!! That's really some-thing!!!
GONG
No, that's really impossible.
However, the strength of the armor alone won't be enough.
That's why I need a boost of firepower from you.
?
I need you to hit the hilt with everything you have!
BOO
OOM
If we combine the throwing power of the giant armor and your firepower, we can destroy the moon.

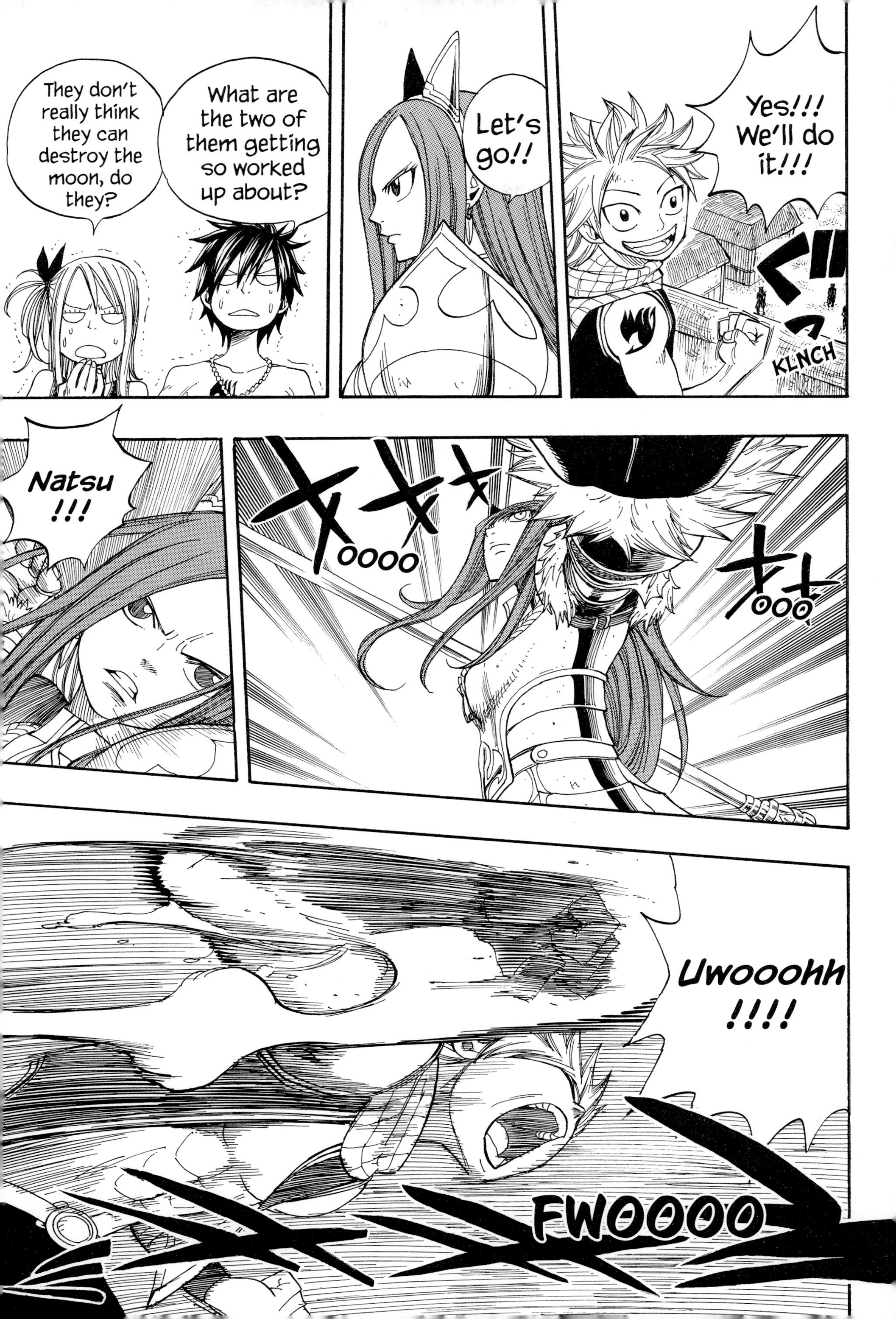
Yes!!! We'll do it!!!
KLNCH
Let's go!!
What are the two of them getting so worked up about?
They don't really think they can destroy the moon, do they?
ooo
oooo
Natsu!!!
Uwooohh!!!!
FWOOOO

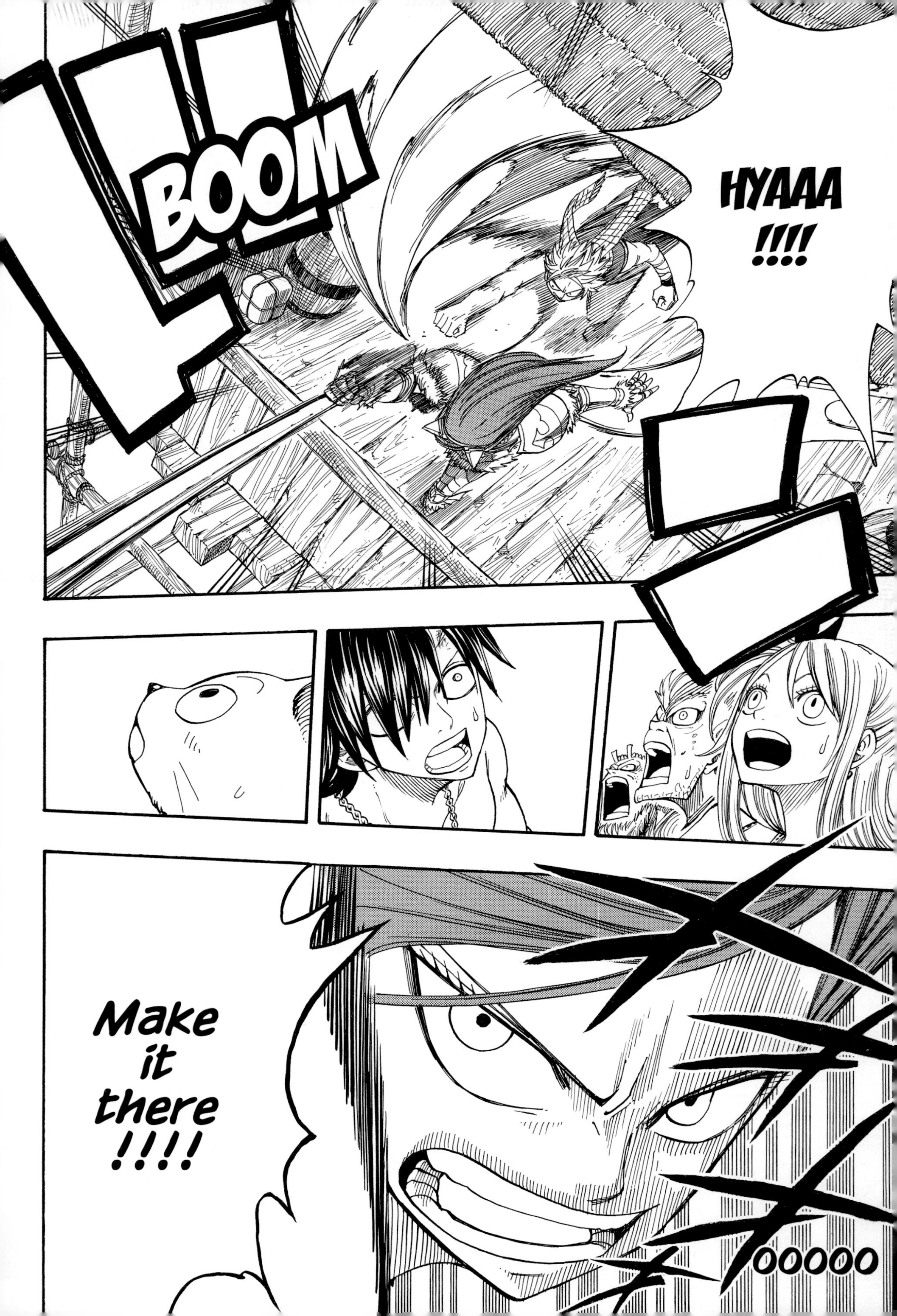
HYAAA !!!!
BOOM
Make it there !!!!
OOOOO

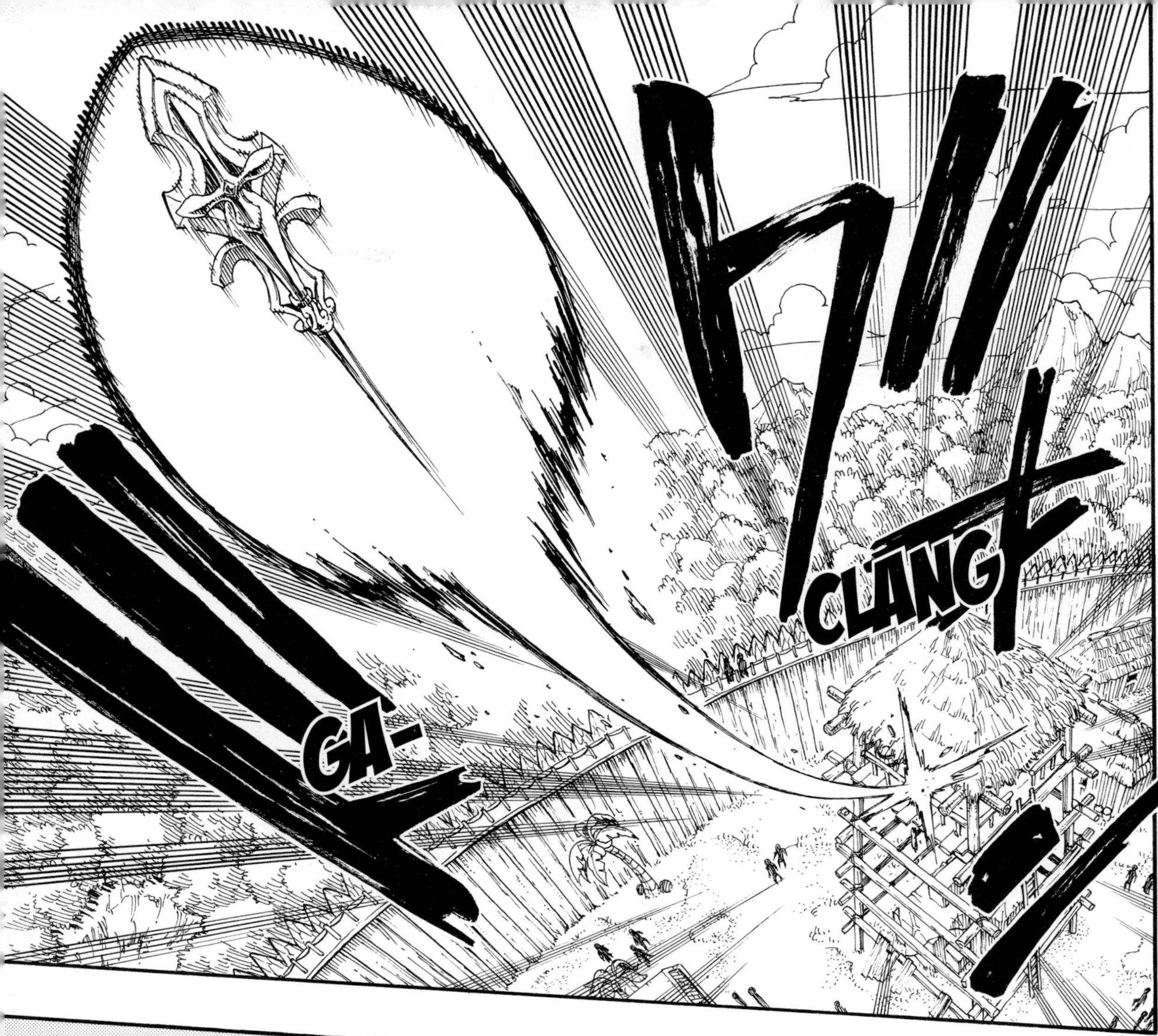
CLANG
GA-

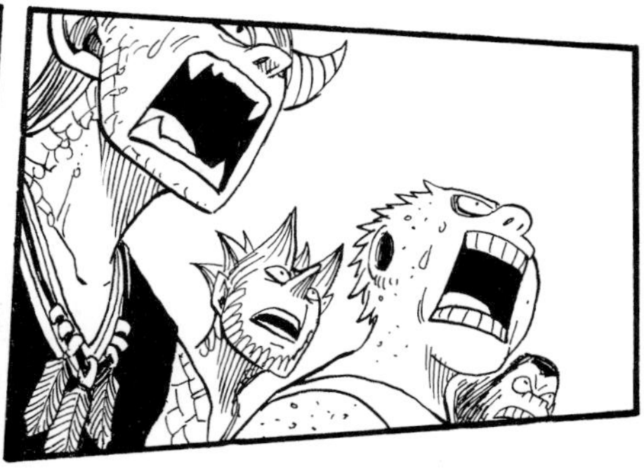

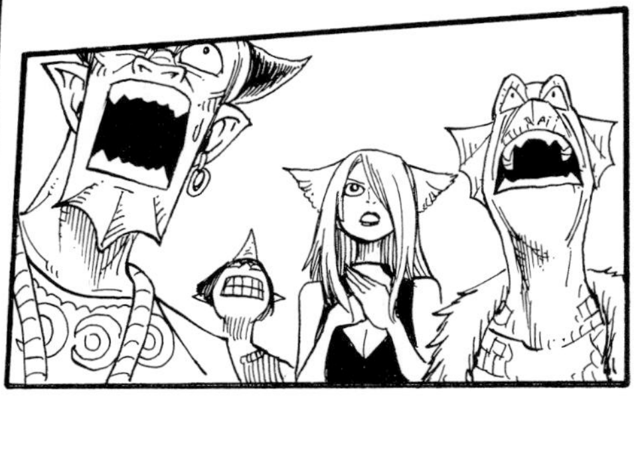

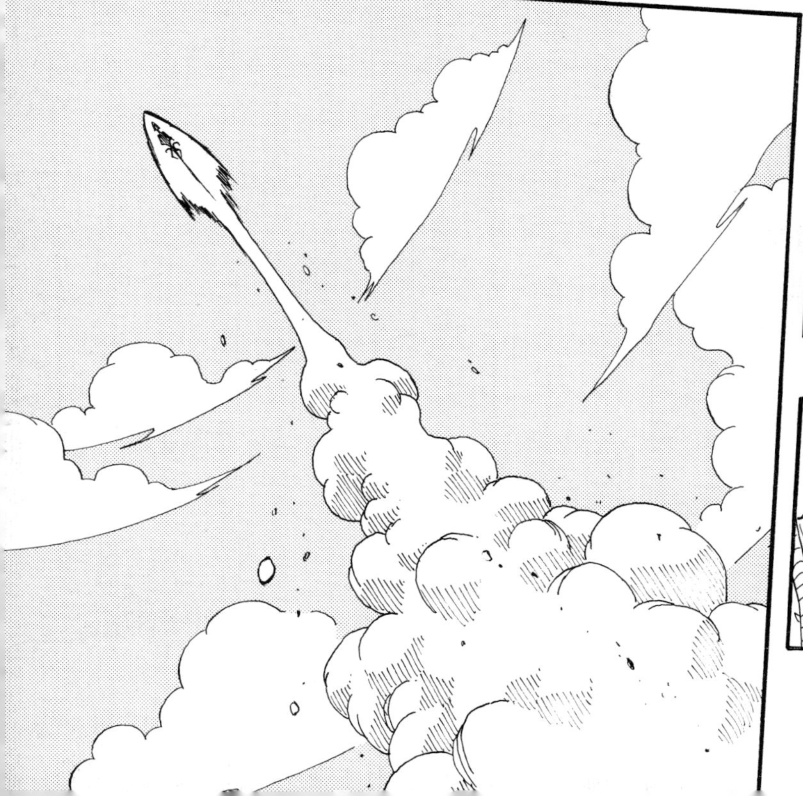

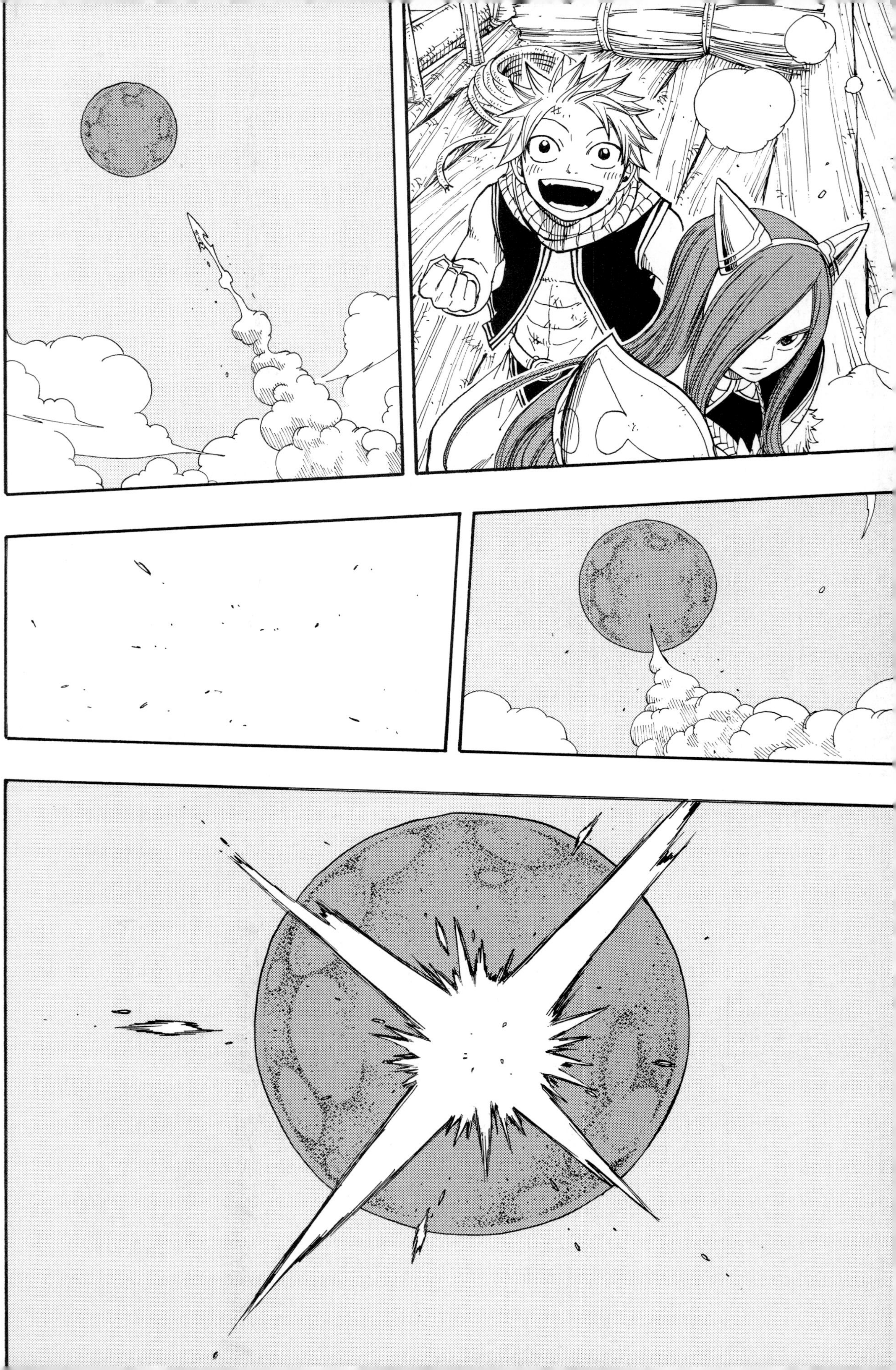

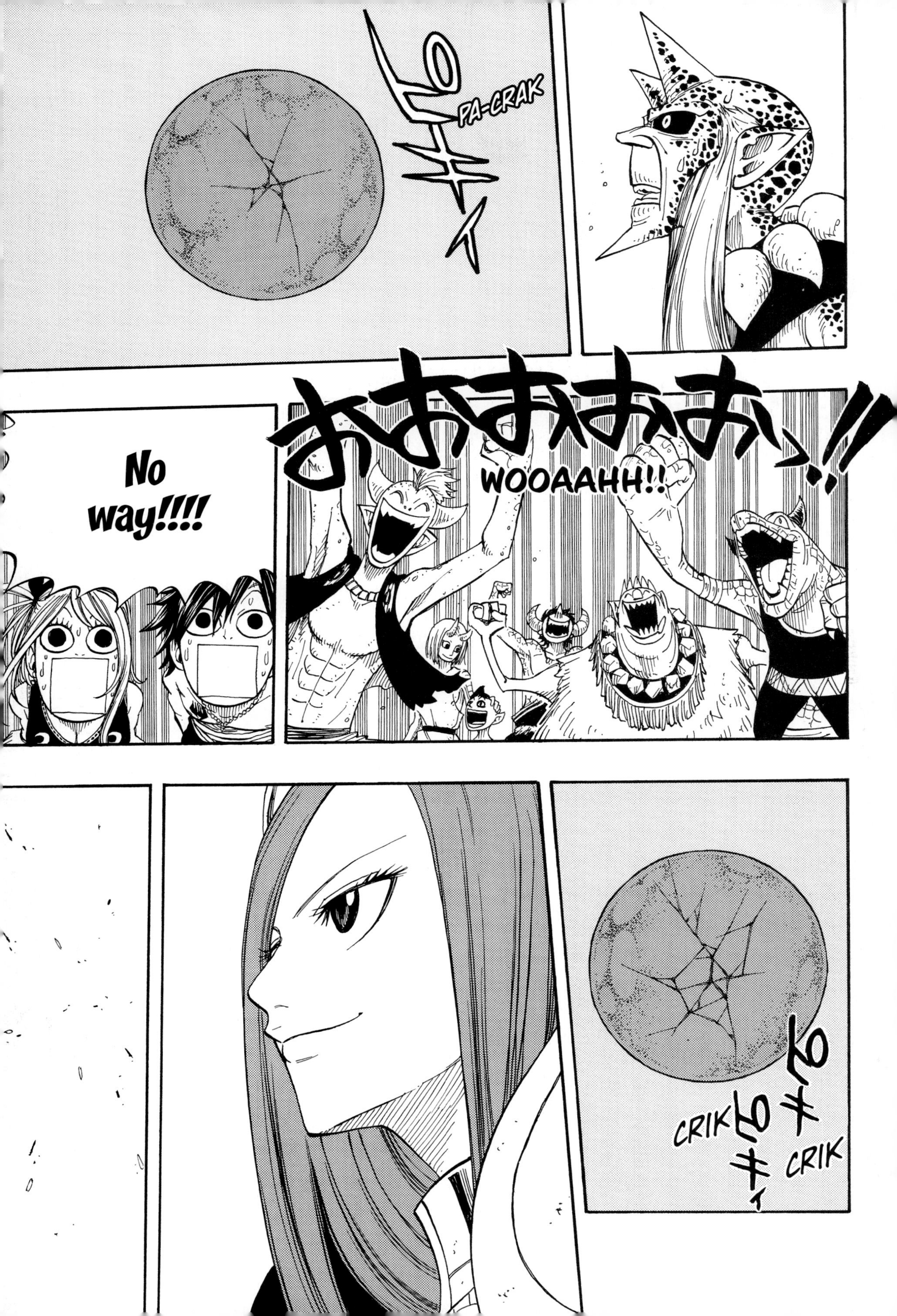
ピキィ
PA-CRAK
おおおおおっ!!
WOOAAHH!!
No way!!!!
ピキ ピキィ
CRIK CRIK

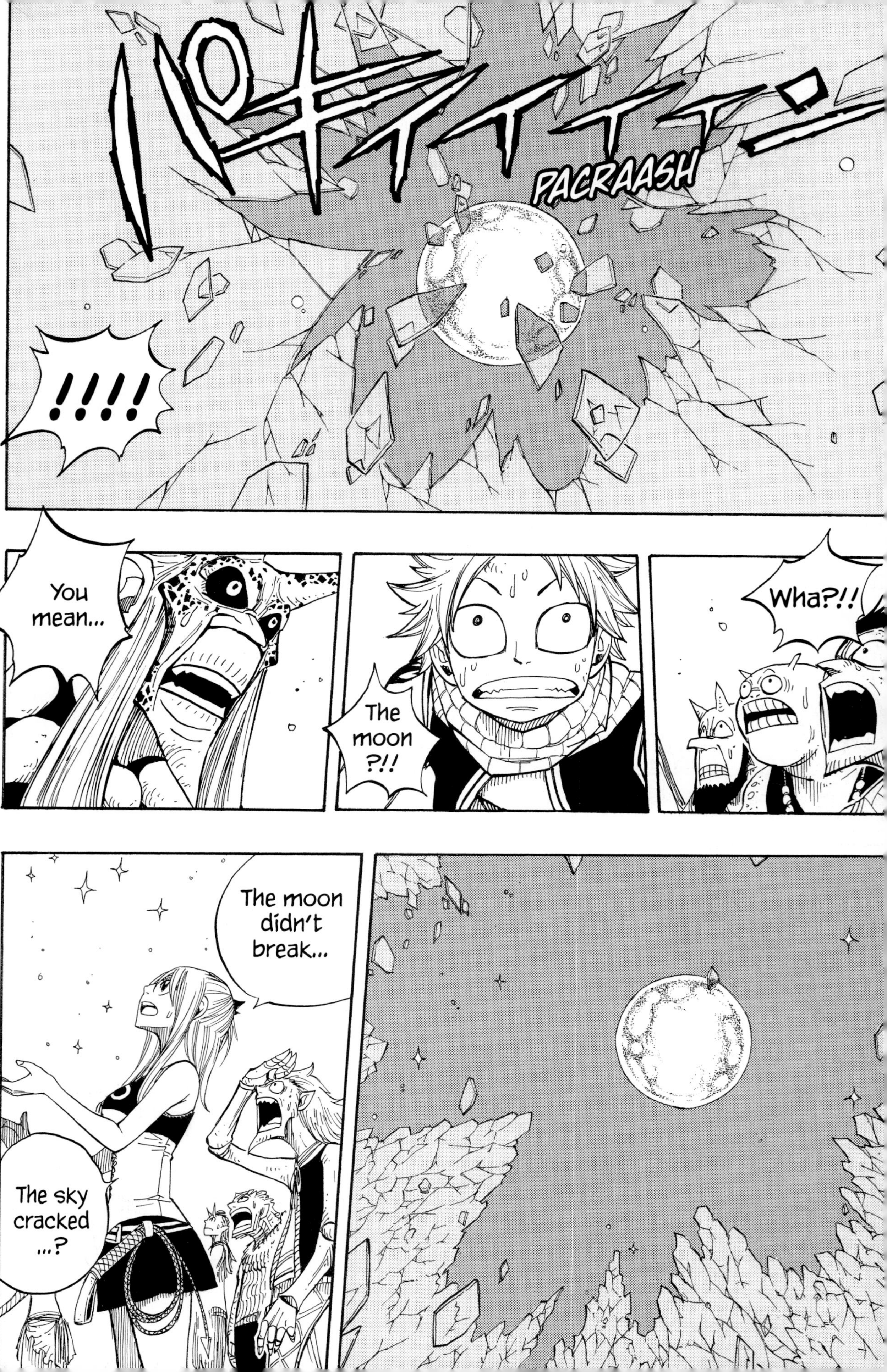
PACRAASH
!!!!
Wha?!!
The moon ?!!
You mean...
The moon didn't break...
The sky cracked ...?

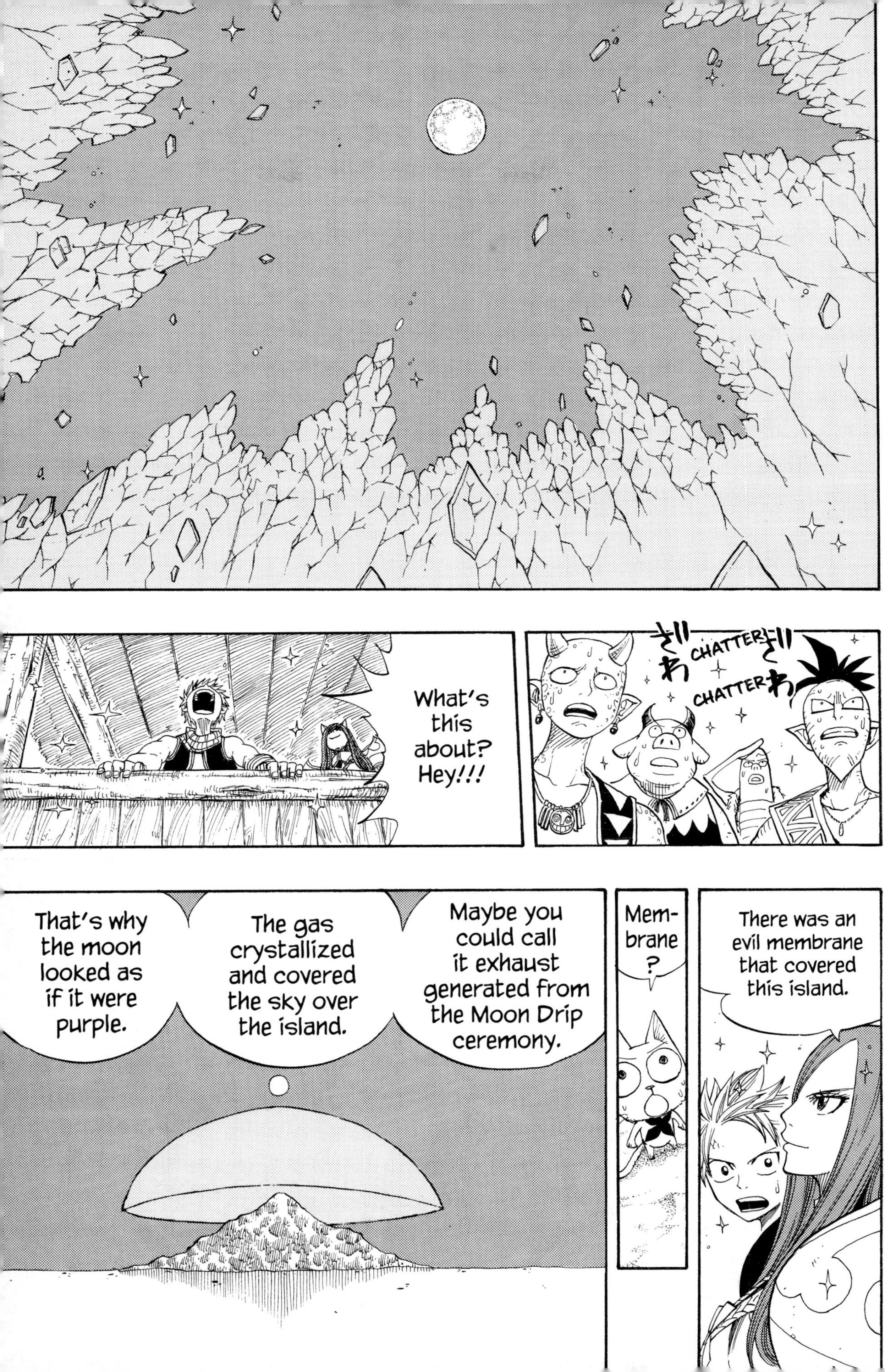
CHATTER
CHATTER
What's this about? Hey!!!
There was an evil membrane that covered this island.
Mem-brane?
Maybe you could call it exhaust generated from the Moon Drip ceremony.
The gas crystallized and covered the sky over the island.
That's why the moon looked as if it were purple.

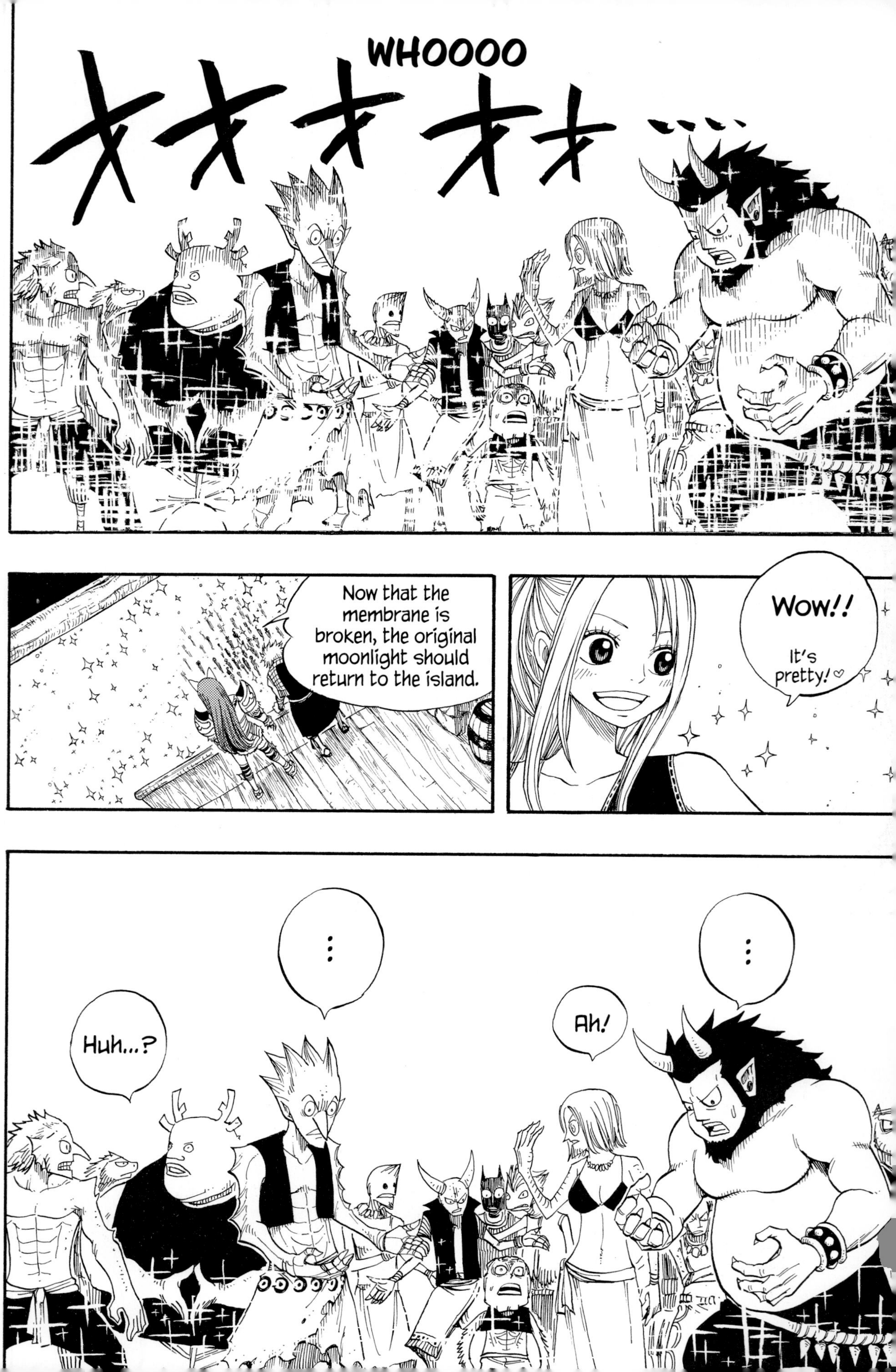
WHOOOO
Wow!!
It's pretty!♡
Now that the membrane is broken, the original moonlight should return to the island.
...
Ah!
...
Huh...?

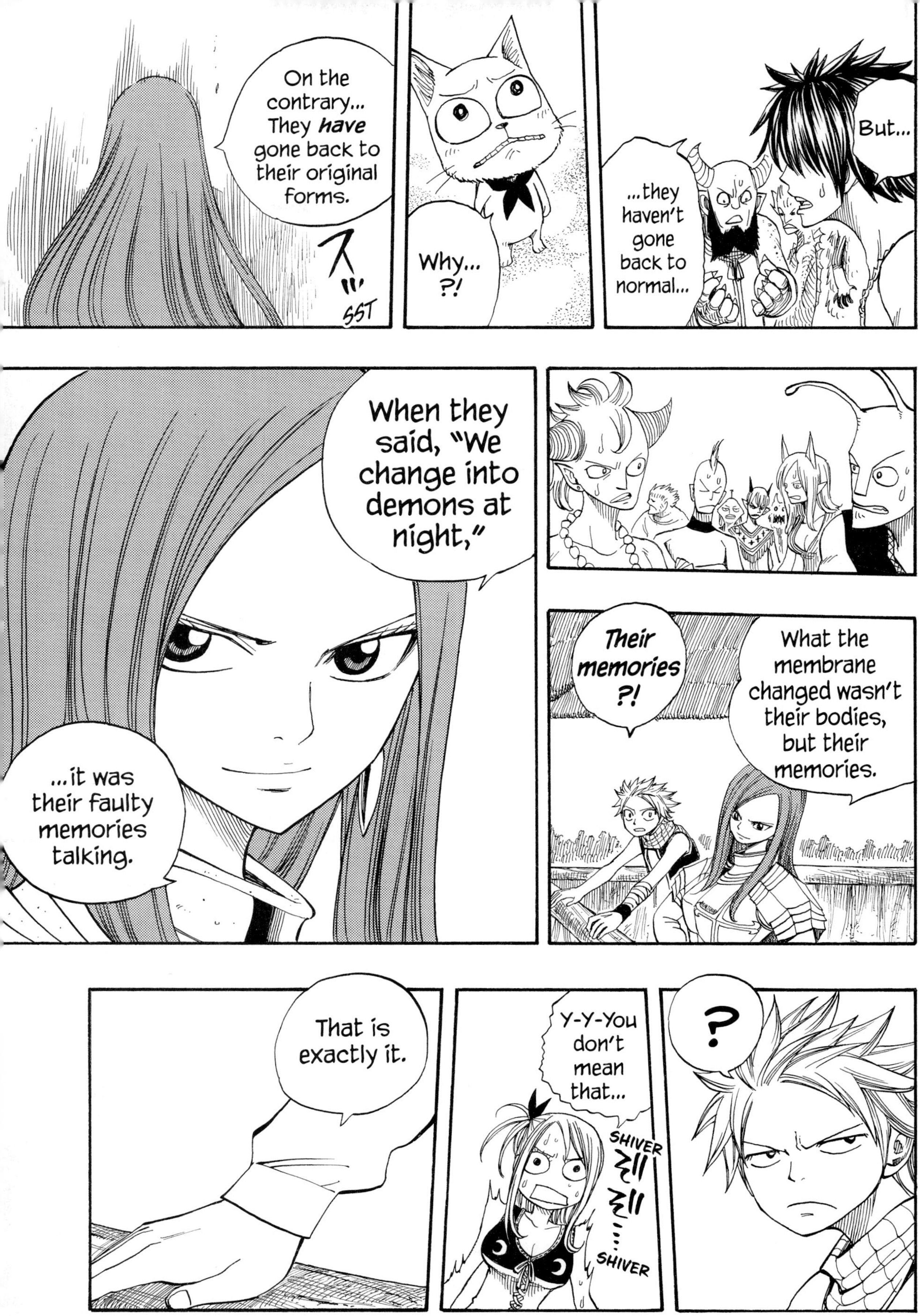
But...
...they haven't gone back to normal...
Why...?!
On the contrary... They *have* gone back to their original forms.
SST
What the membrane changed wasn't their bodies, but their memories.
Their memories?!
When they said, "We change into demons at night,"
...it was their faulty memories talking.
?
Y-Y-You don't mean that...
SHIVER
SHIVER
That is exactly it.

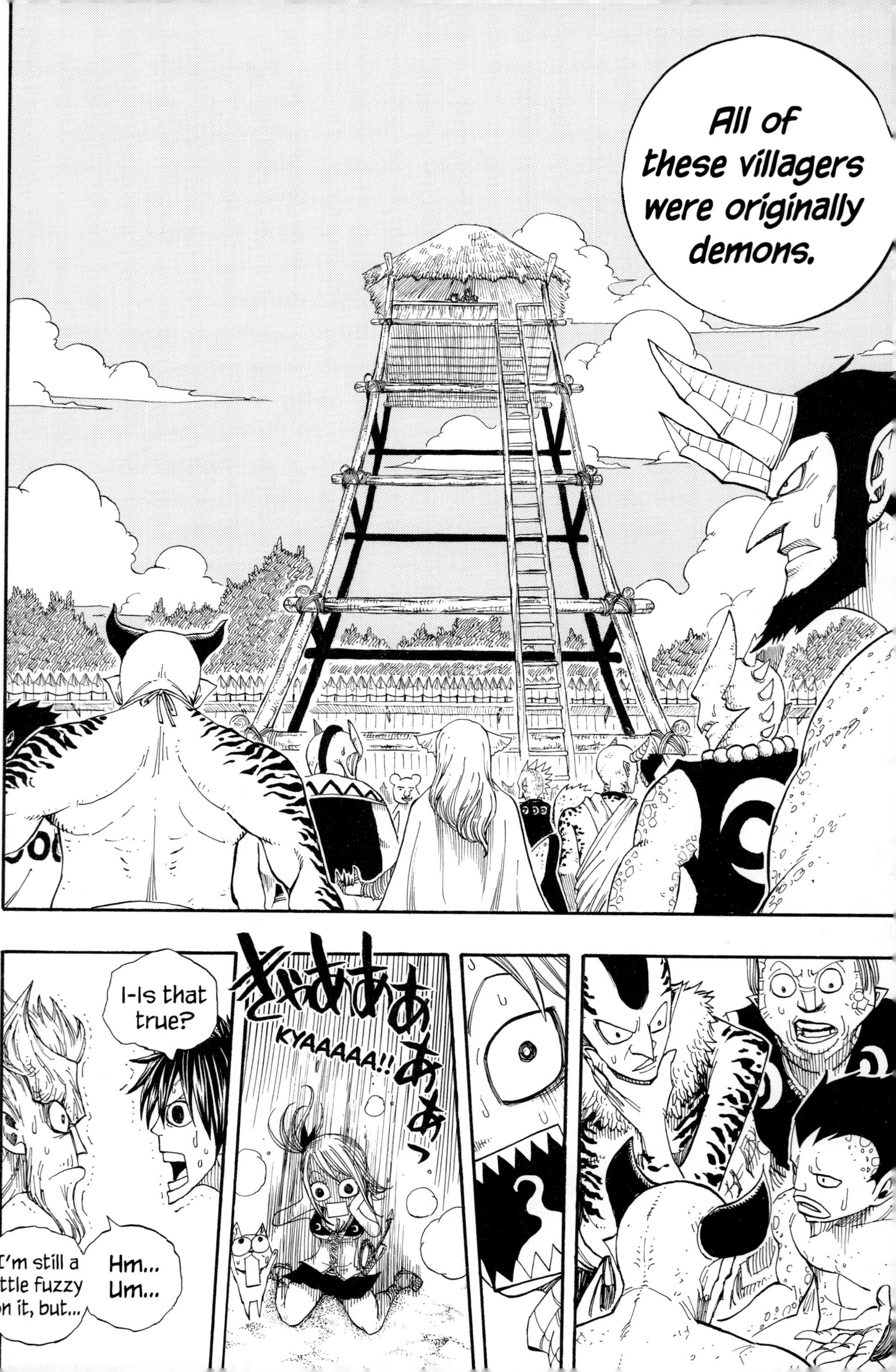
All of these villagers were originally demons.
きゃあああああっ
KYAAAAA!!
I-Is that true?
Hm... Um...
I'm still a little fuzzy on it, but...

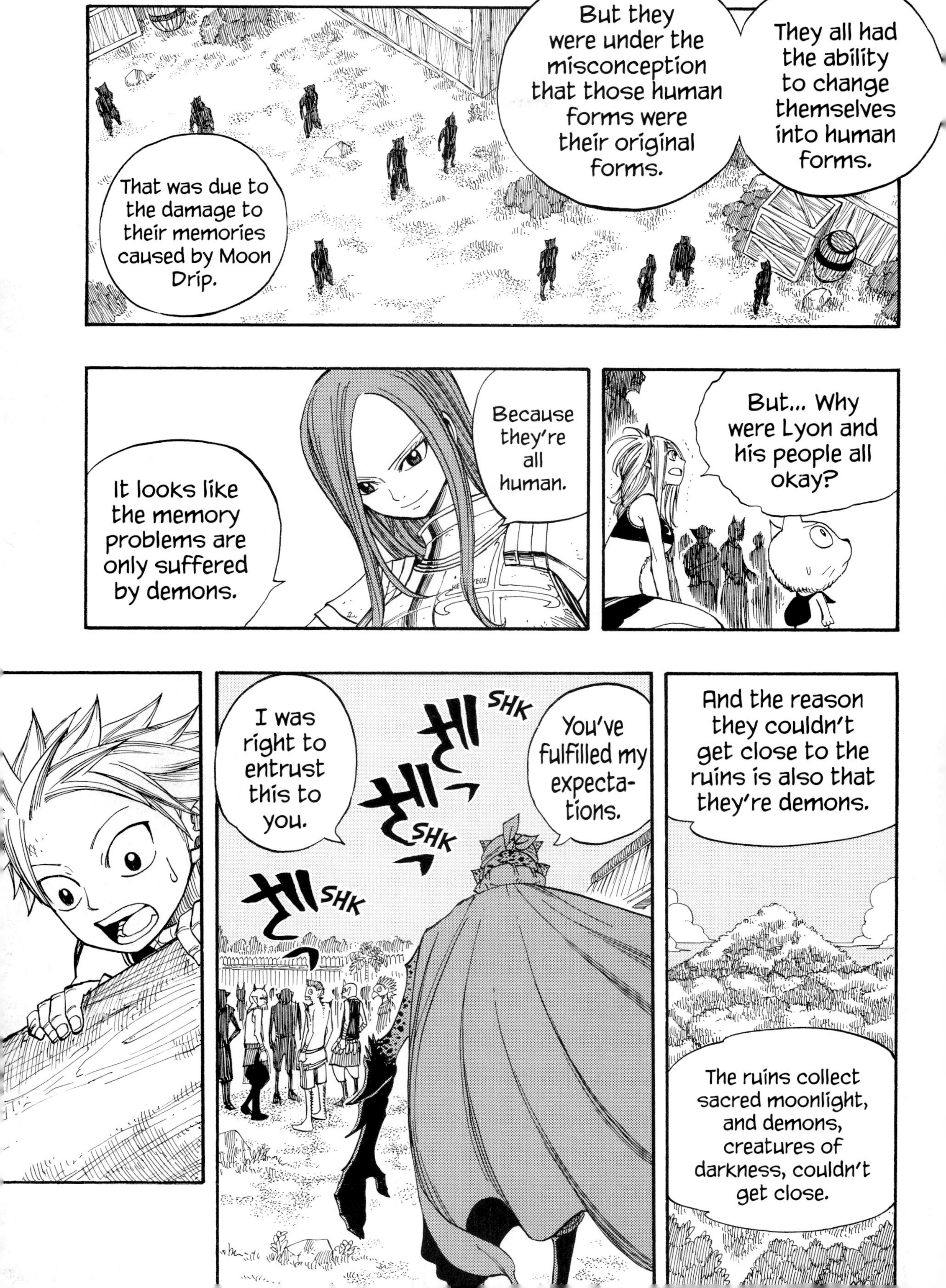
They all had the ability to change themselves into human forms.
But they were under the misconception that those human forms were their original forms.
That was due to the damage to their memories caused by Moon Drip.
But... Why were Lyon and his people all okay?
Because they're all human.
It looks like the memory problems are only suffered by demons.
And the reason they couldn't get close to the ruins is also that they're demons.
The ruins collect sacred moonlight, and demons, creatures of darkness, couldn't get close.
SHK
You've fulfilled my expectations.
SHK
I was right to entrust this to you.
SHK

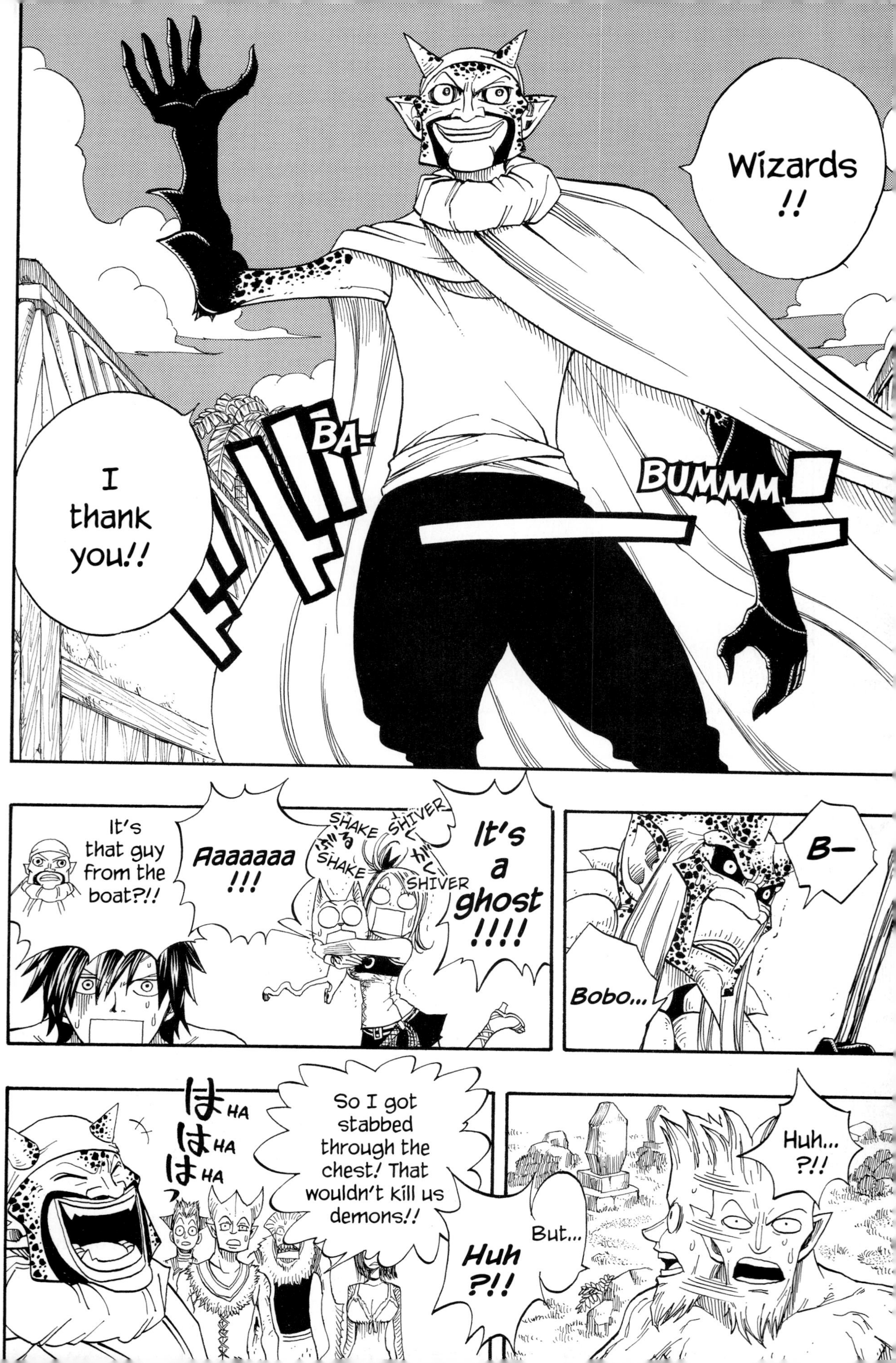
Wizards !!
BA- BUMMM!
I thank you!!
B—
Bobo...
It's a ghost !!!!
SHIVER SHIVER
SHAKE SHAKE
Aaaaaaa !!!
It's that guy from the boat?!!
Huh... ?!!
But...
Huh ?!!
So I got stabbed through the chest! That wouldn't kill us demons!!
ははは HA HA HA

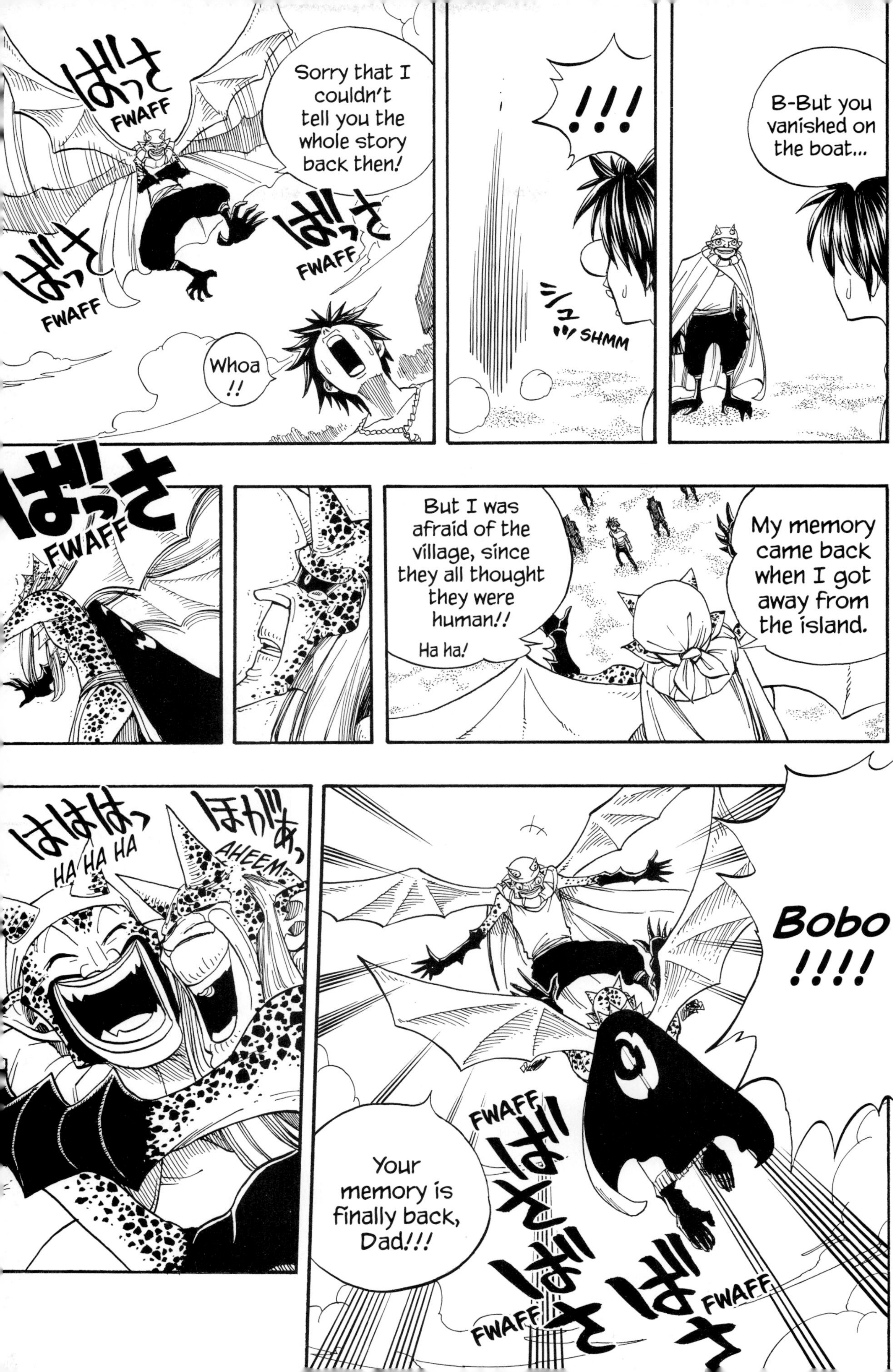

B-But you vanished on the boat...
!!!
SHMM
Sorry that I couldn't tell you the whole story back then!
ばっさ
FWAFF
ばっさ
FWAFF
ばっさ
FWAFF
Whoa !!
My memory came back when I got away from the island.
But I was afraid of the village, since they all thought they were human!!
Ha ha!
ばっさ
FWAFF
Bobo !!!!
Your memory is finally back, Dad!!!
FWAFF
FWAFF
FWAFF
ほがあっ
AHEEM
ははは
HA HA HA

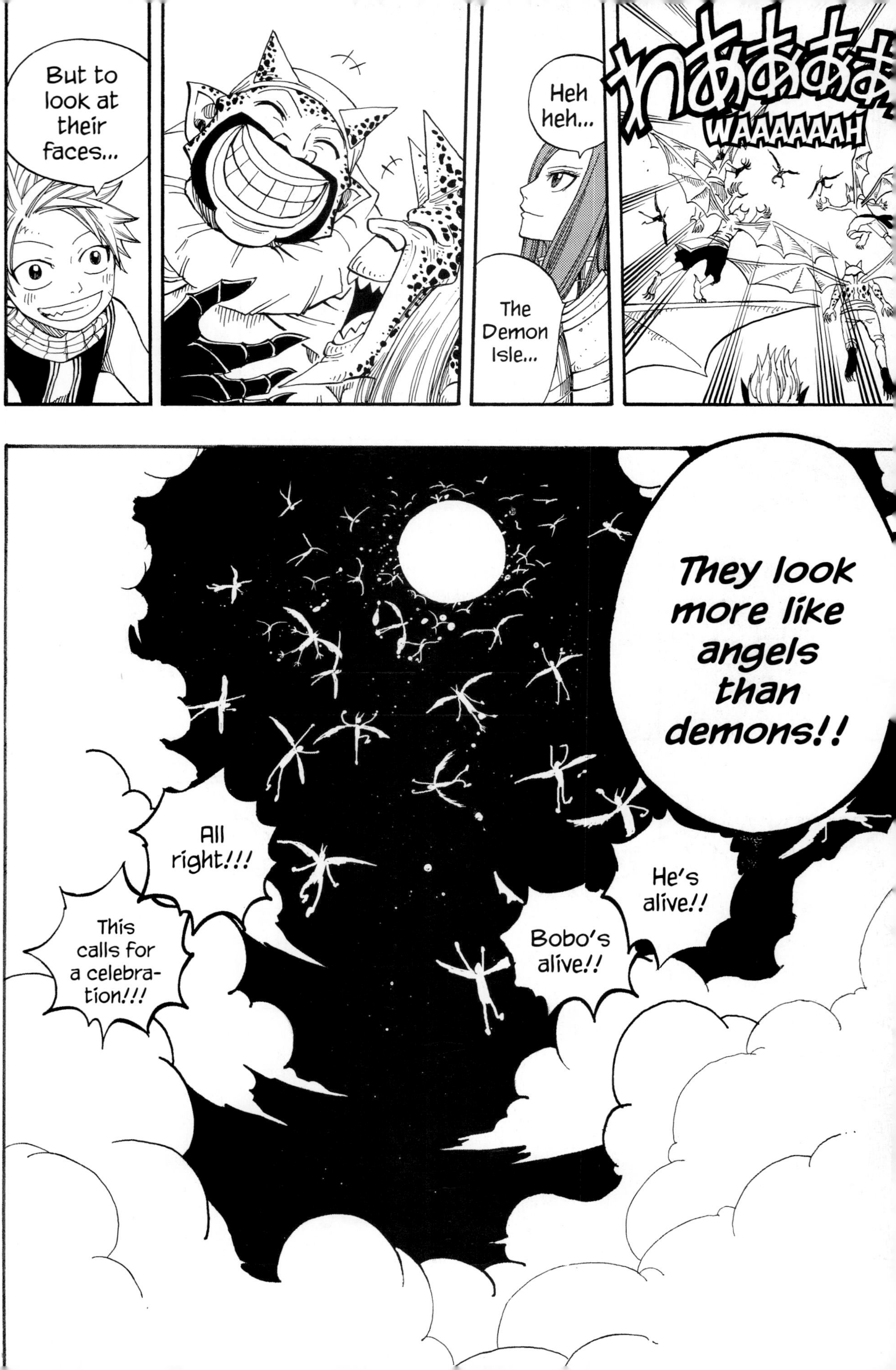
わあああああ
WAAAAAAH
Heh heh...
The Demon Isle...
But to look at their faces...
They look more like angels than demons!!
He's alive!!
Bobo's alive!!
All right!!!
This calls for a celebration!!!

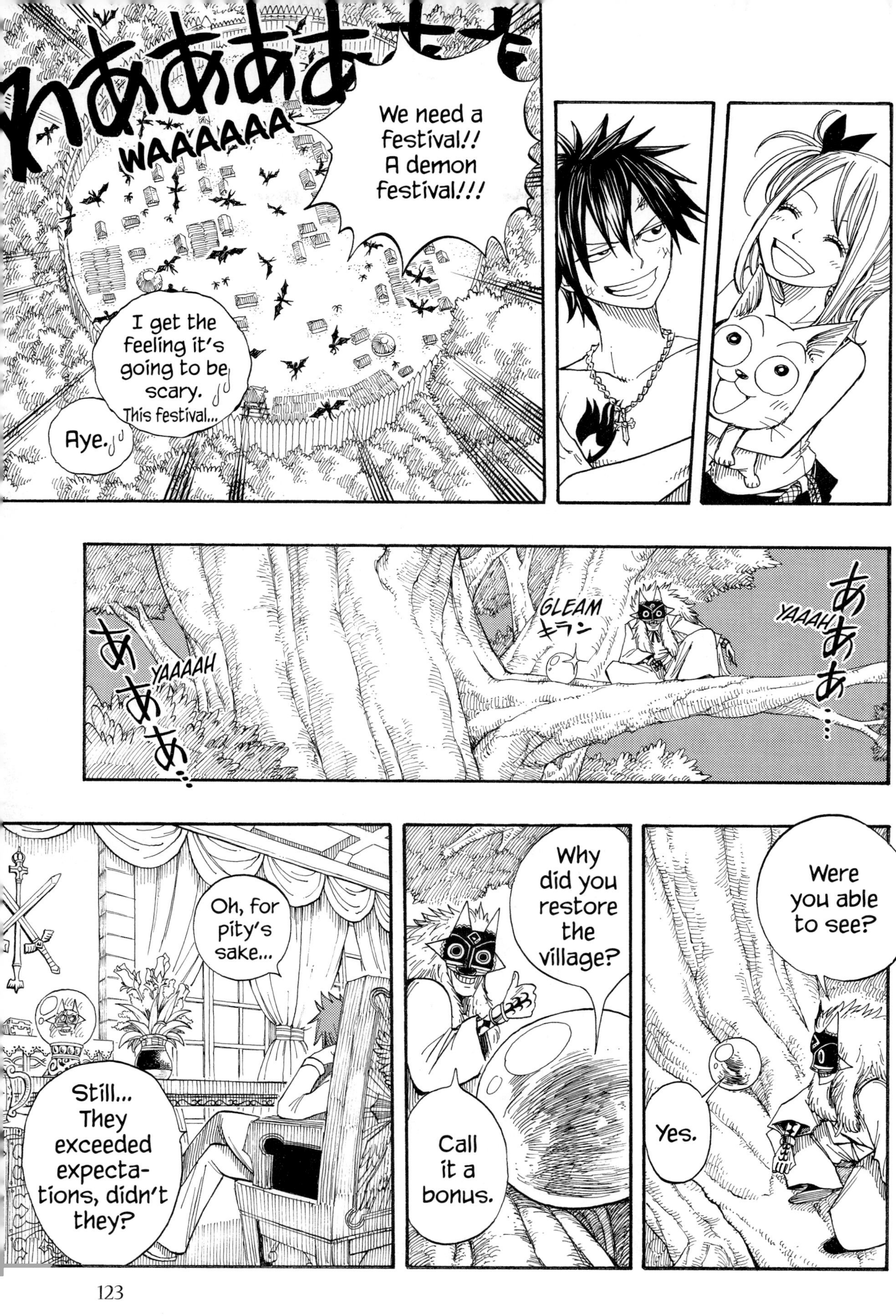
We need a festival!! A demon festival!!!
わあああぁーー
WAAAAAA
I get the feeling it's going to be scary. This festival...
Aye.
ああぁ…
YAAAH
GLEAM
キラン
あぁぁ…
YAAAAH
Were you able to see?
Yes.
Why did you restore the village?
Call it a bonus.
Oh, for pity's sake...
Still... They exceeded expectations, didn't they?

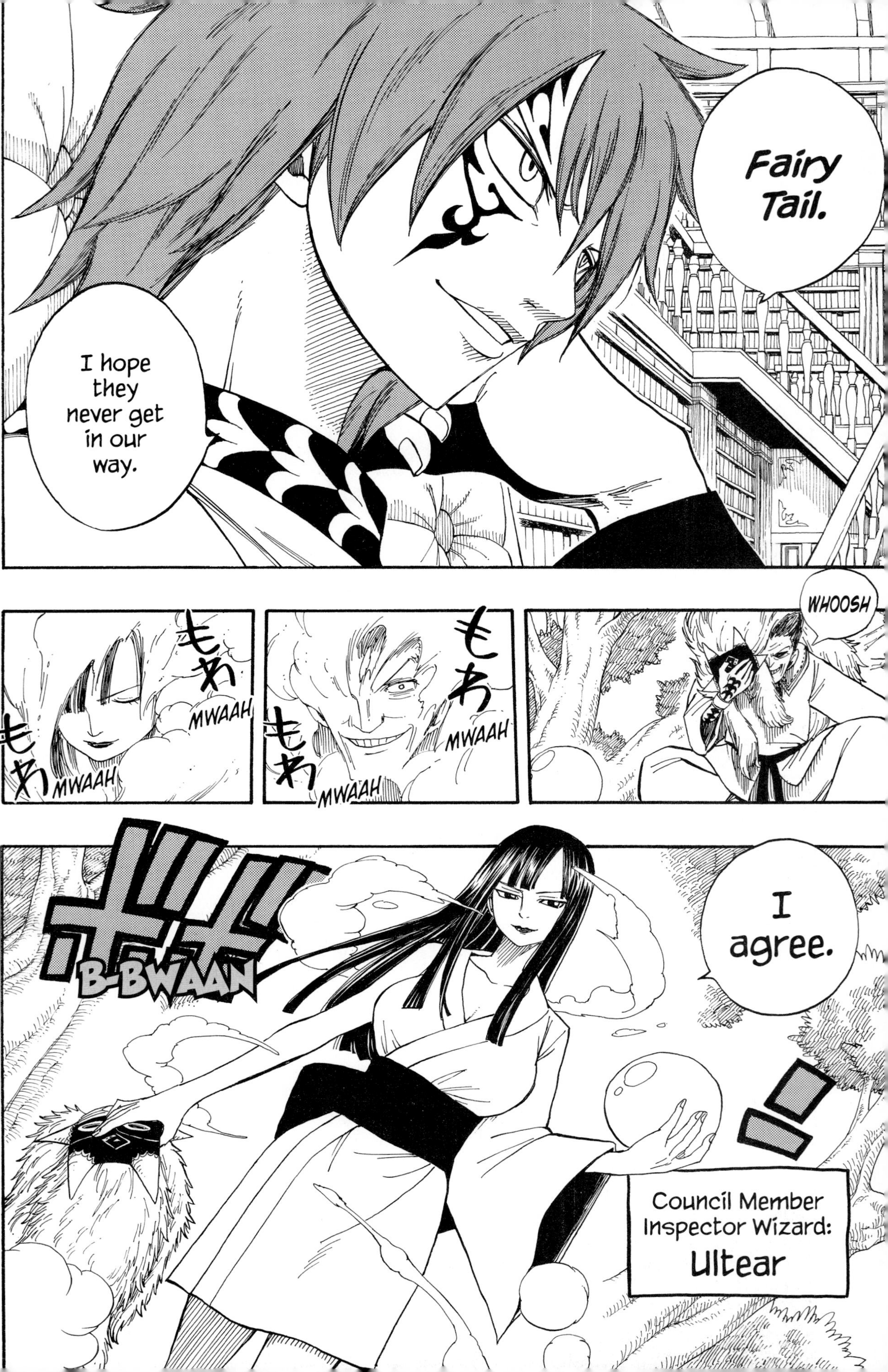
Fairy Tail.
I hope they never get in our way.
WHOOSH
もわ
MWAAH
もわ
MWAAH
もわ
MWAAH
もわ
MWAAH
I agree.
B-BWAAN
Council Member Inspector Wizard: Ultear

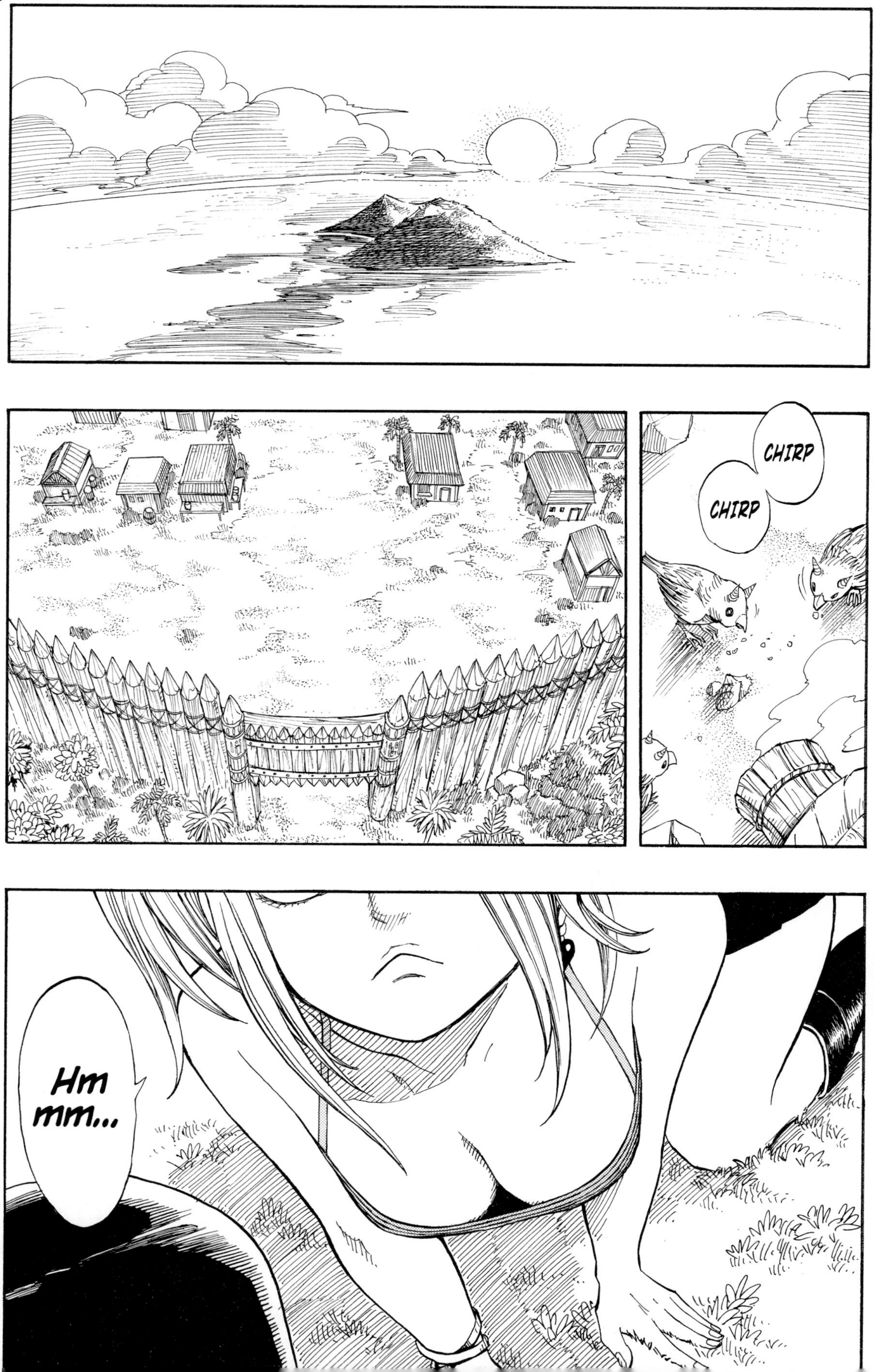
CHIRP
CHIRP
Hm mm...

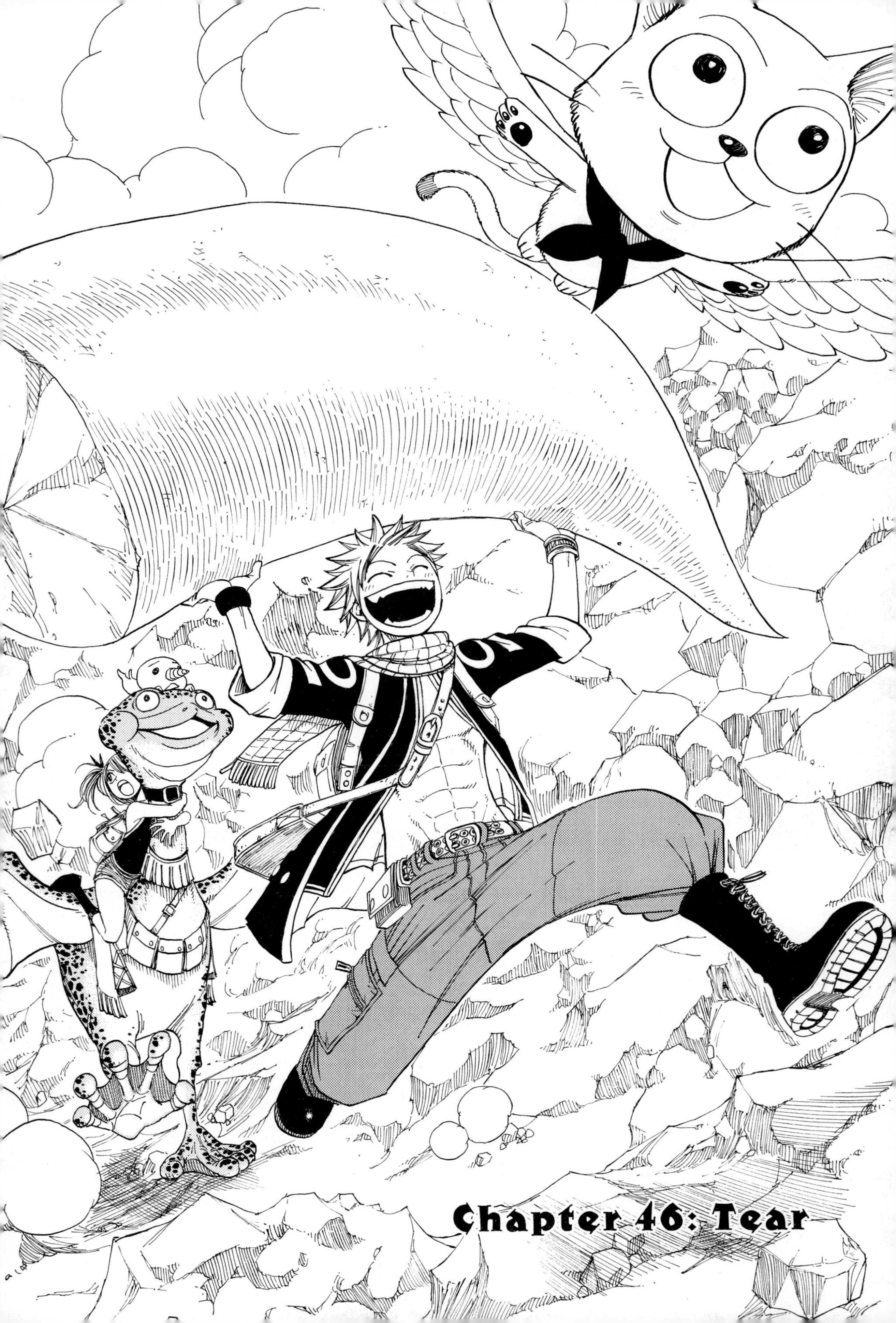
Chapter 46: Tear

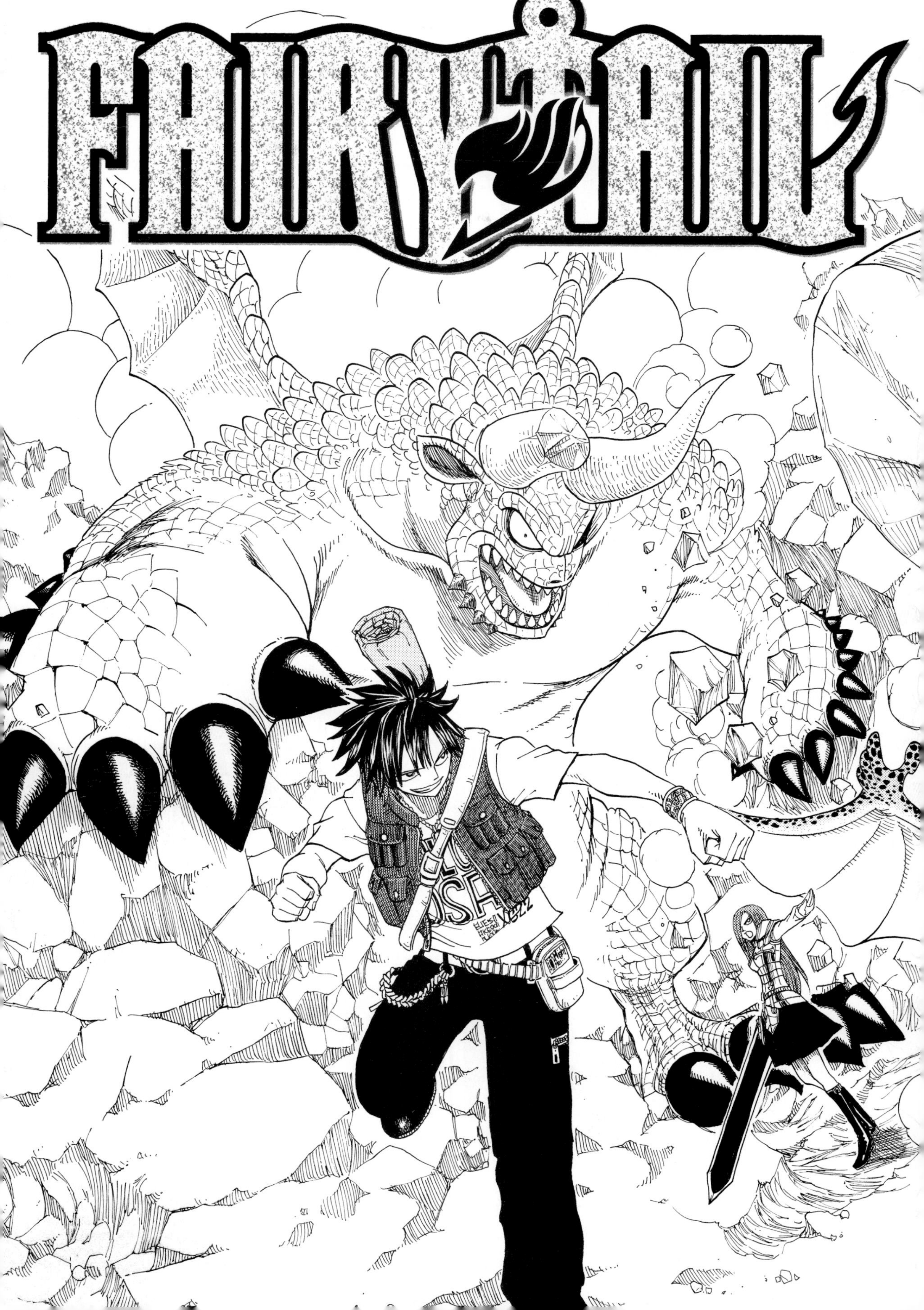
FAIRY TAIL

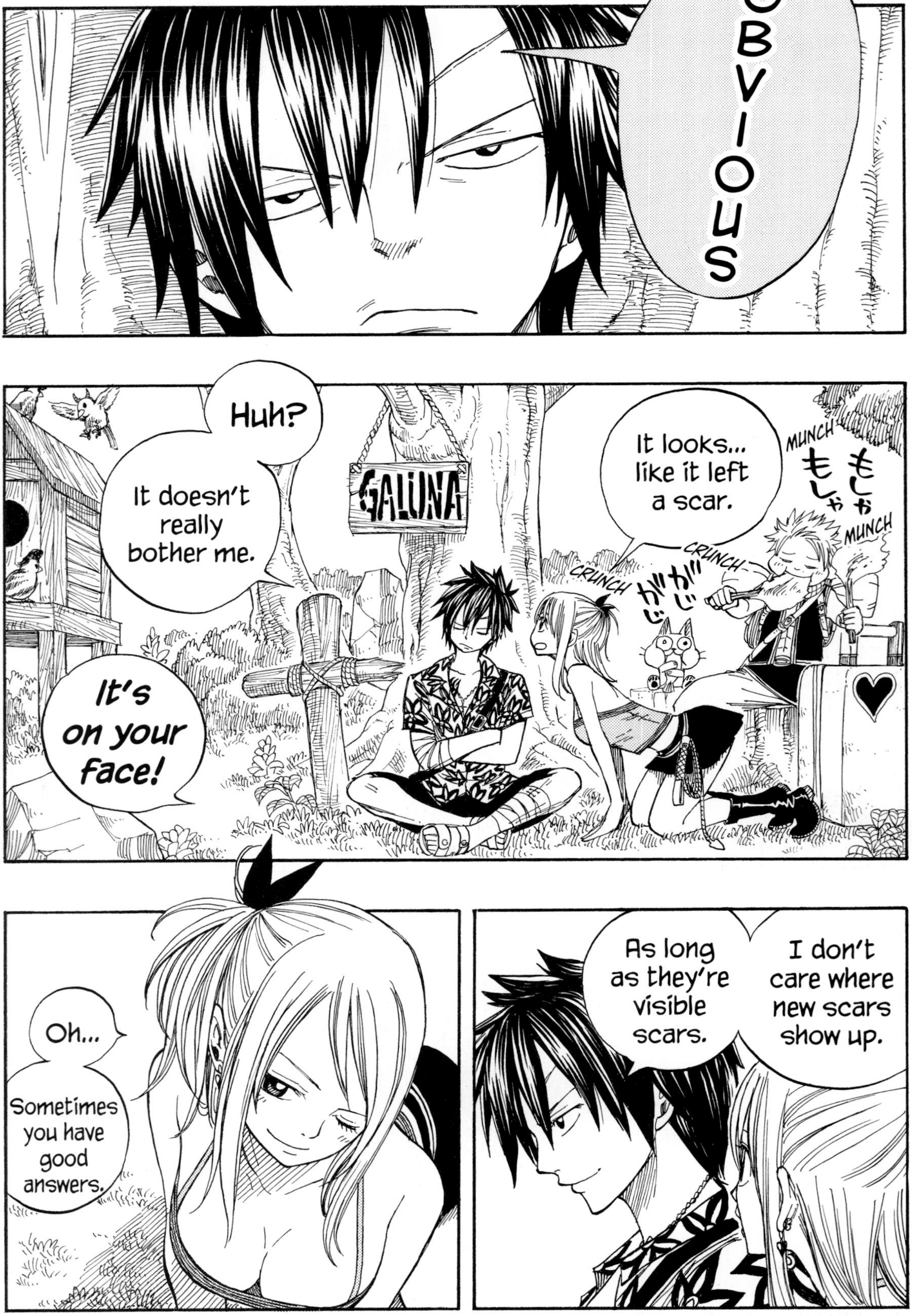
OBVIOUS
MUNCH
もしゃ もしゃ
MUNCH
GALUNA
It looks... like it left a scar.
CRUNCH
ガジ ガジ
CRUNCH
Huh?
It doesn't really bother me.
It's on your face!
I don't care where new scars show up.
As long as they're visible scars.
Oh...
Sometimes you have good answers.

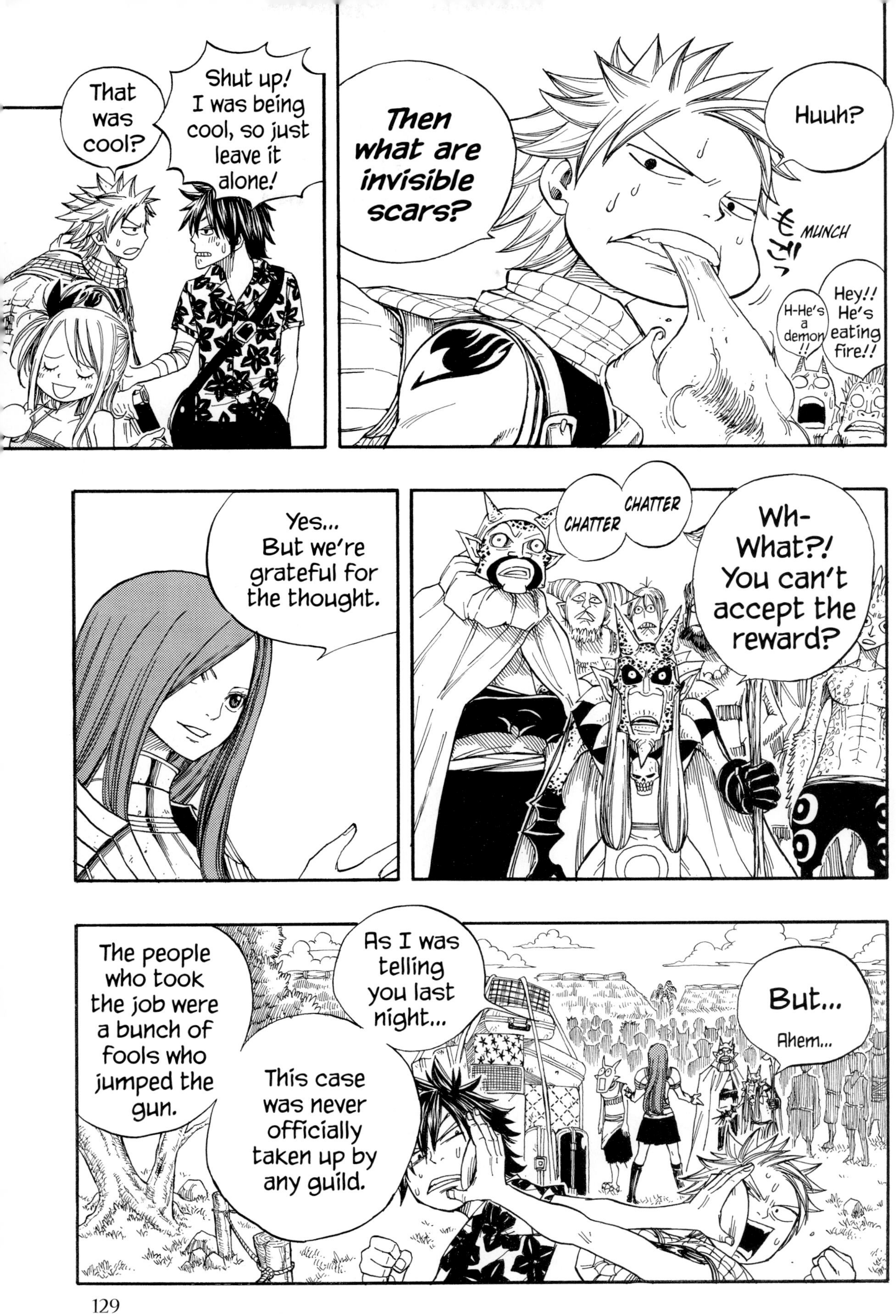

Huuh?
Then what are invisible scars?
MUNCH
Hey!! He's eating fire!!
H-He's a demon!!
That was cool?
Shut up! I was being cool, so just leave it alone!
Wh-What?! You can't accept the reward?
CHATTER CHATTER
Yes... But we're grateful for the thought.
But...
Ahem...
As I was telling you last night...
This case was never officially taken up by any guild.
The people who took the job were a bunch of fools who jumped the gun.

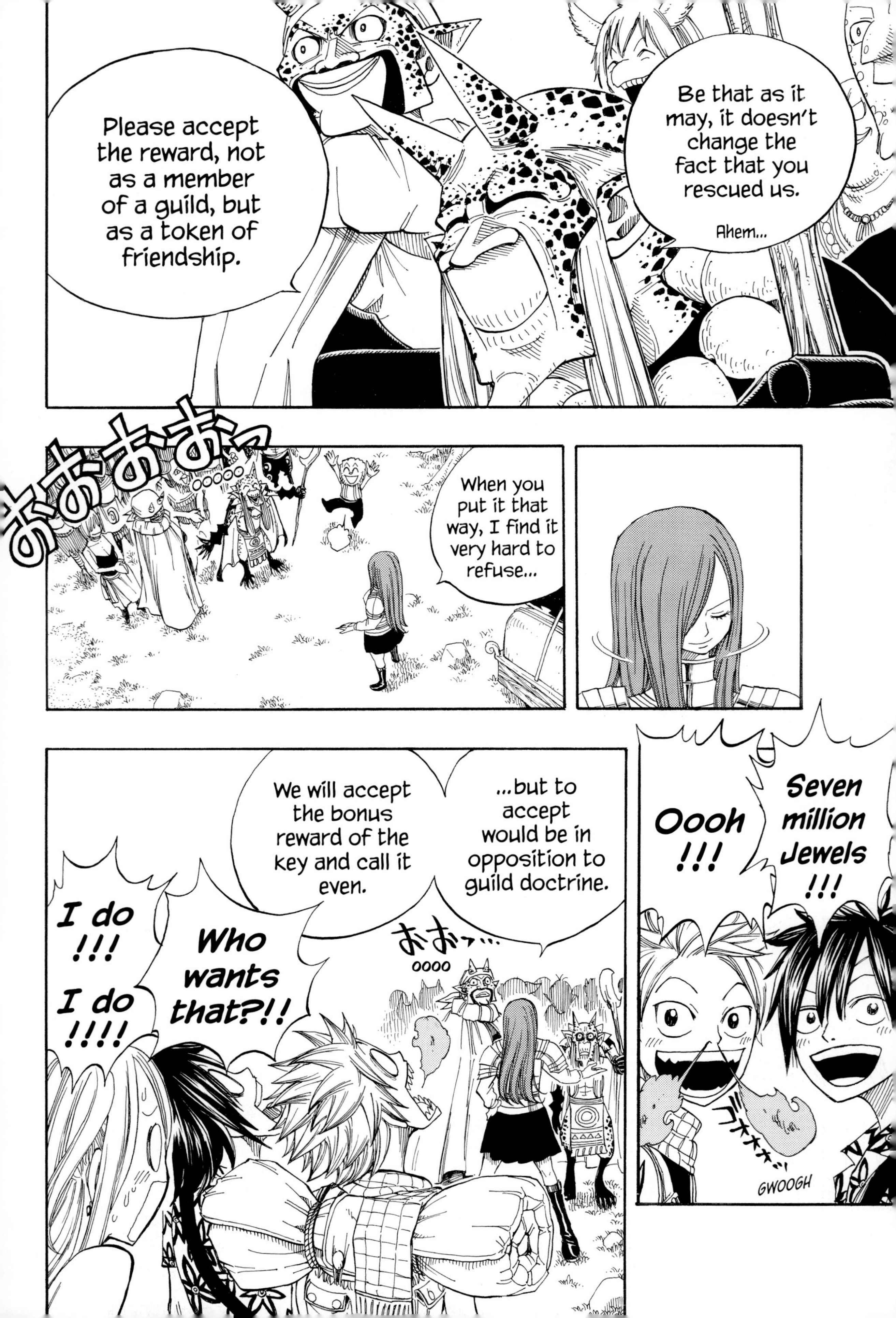
Be that as it may, it doesn't change the fact that you rescued us.
Ahem...
Please accept the reward, not as a member of a guild, but as a token of friendship.
When you put it that way, I find it very hard to refuse...
おおおおっ
OOOOO
Seven million Jewels!!!
Oooh!!!
ゴオオオッ
GWOOGH
...but to accept would be in opposition to guild doctrine.
We will accept the bonus reward of the key and call it even.
おおっ…
OOOO
Who wants that?!!
I do!!!
I do!!!!

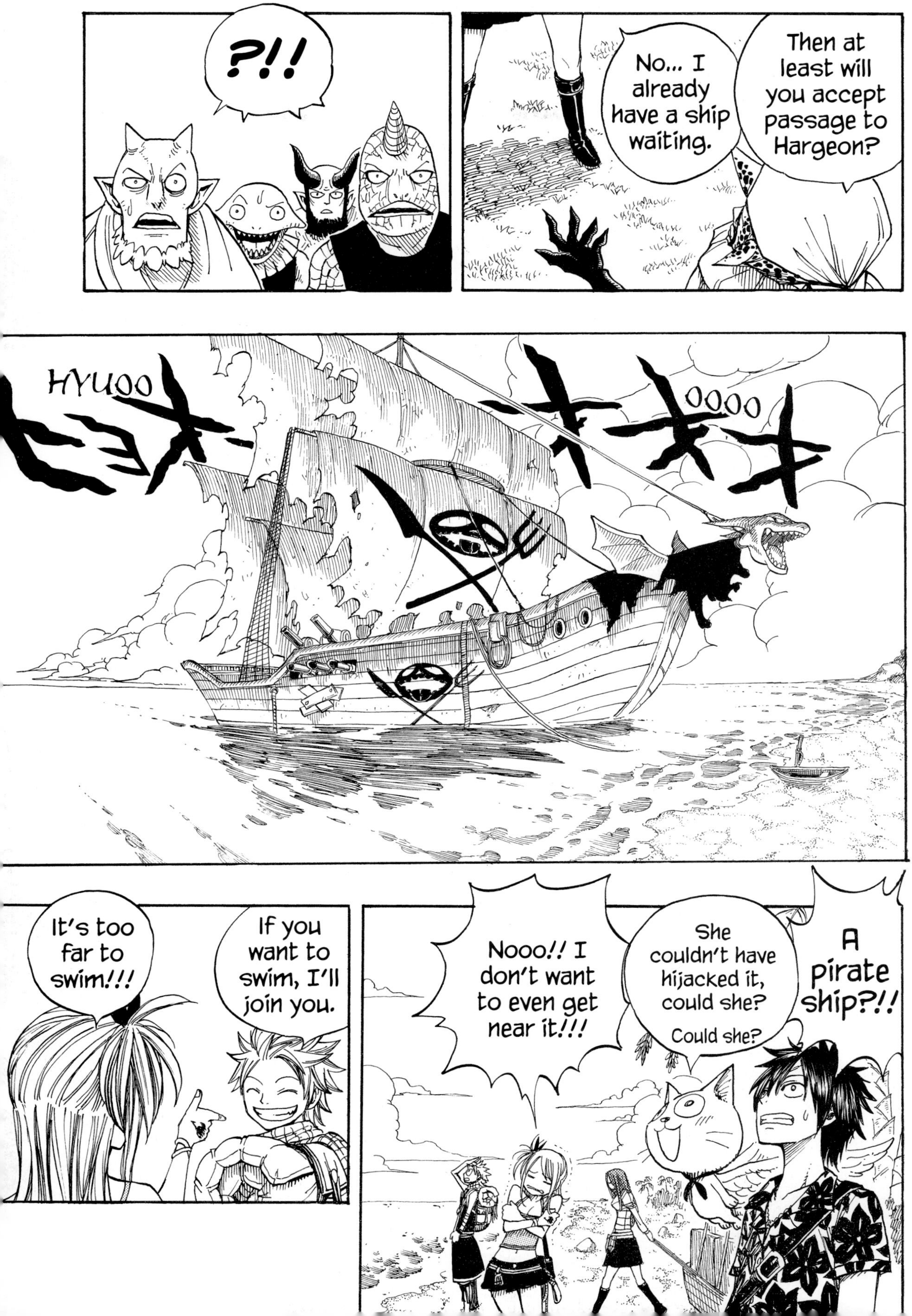
Then at least will you accept passage to Hargeon?
No... I already have a ship waiting.
?!!
HYUOO
OOOO
A pirate ship?!!
She couldn't have hijacked it, could she?
Could she?
Nooo!! I don't want to even get near it!!!
If you want to swim, I'll join you.
It's too far to swim!!!

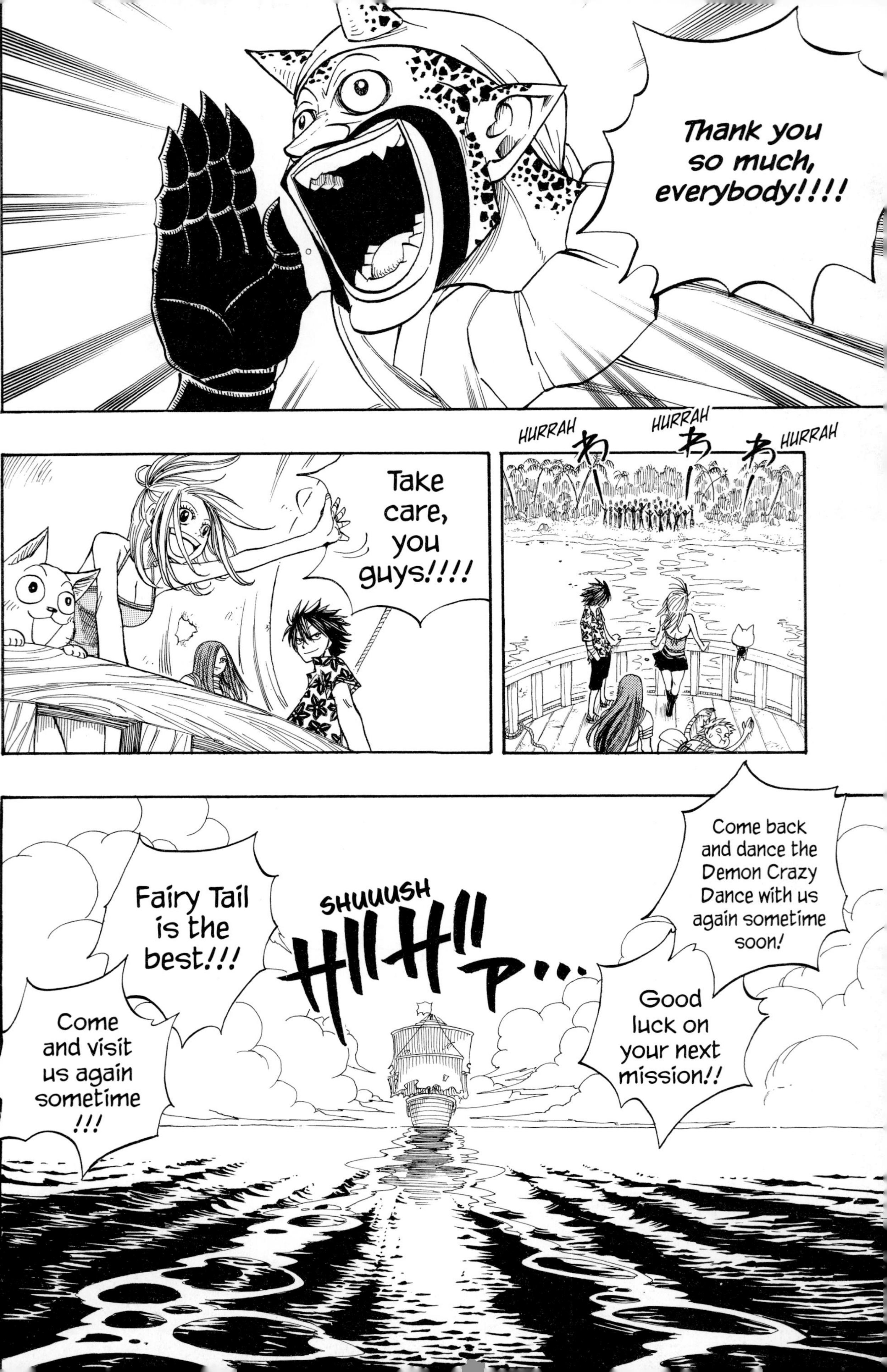
Thank you so much, everybody!!!!
HURRAH
HURRAH
HURRAH
Take care, you guys!!!!
Come back and dance the Demon Crazy Dance with us again sometime soon!
Good luck on your next mission!!
SHUUUSH
Fairy Tail is the best!!!
Come and visit us again sometime!!!

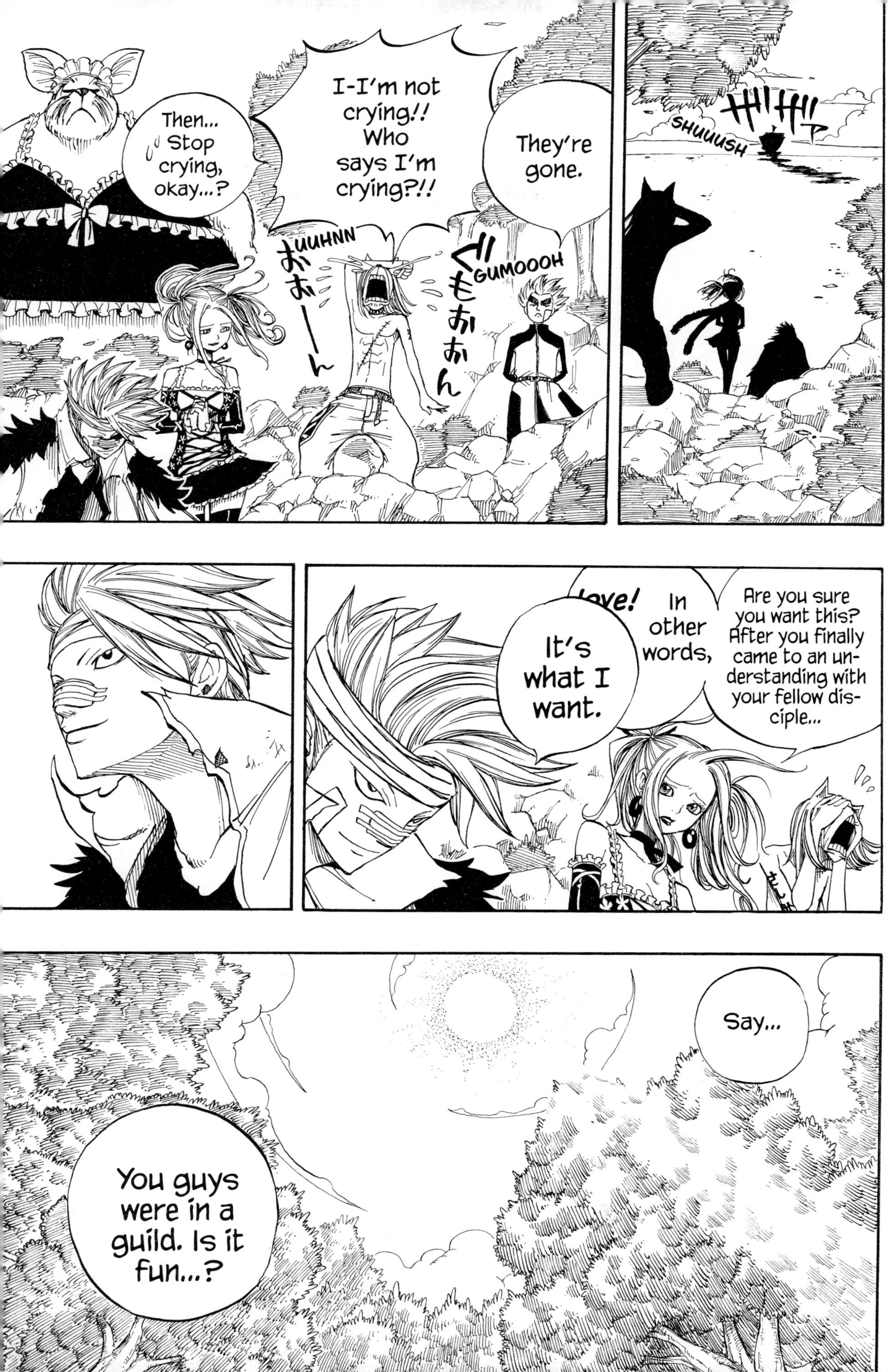
SHUUUSH
ザザザ
They're gone.
GUMOOOH
ぐもぉぉん
I-I'm not crying!! Who says I'm crying?!!
UUHNN
おぉーん
Then... Stop crying, okay...?
Are you sure you want this? After you finally came to an understanding with your fellow disciple...
In other words,
love!
It's what I want.
Say...
You guys were in a guild. Is it fun...?

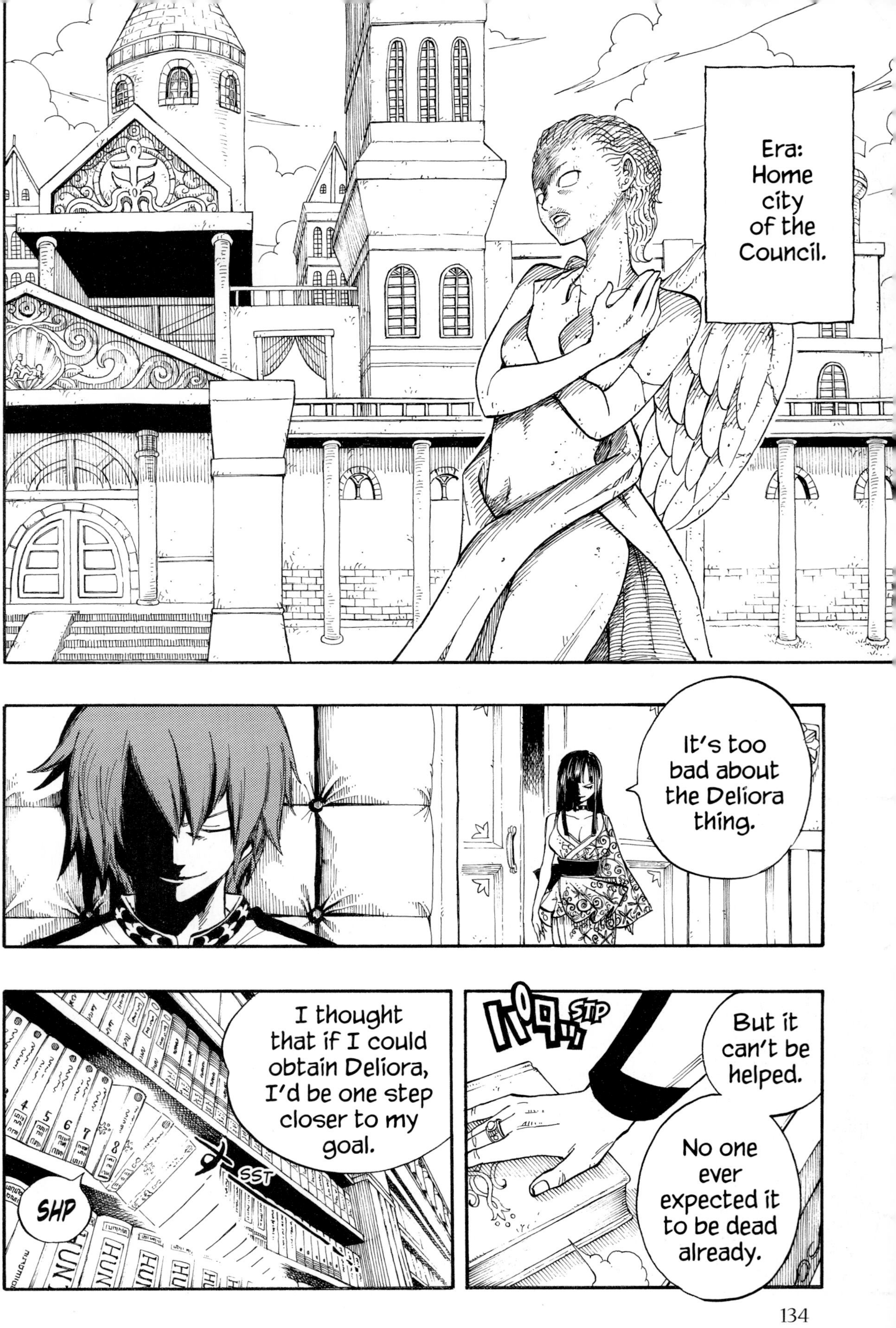
Era: Home city of the Council.
It's too bad about the Deliora thing.
I thought that if I could obtain Deliora, I'd be one step closer to my goal.
SST
SHP
STP
But it can't be helped.
No one ever expected it to be dead already.

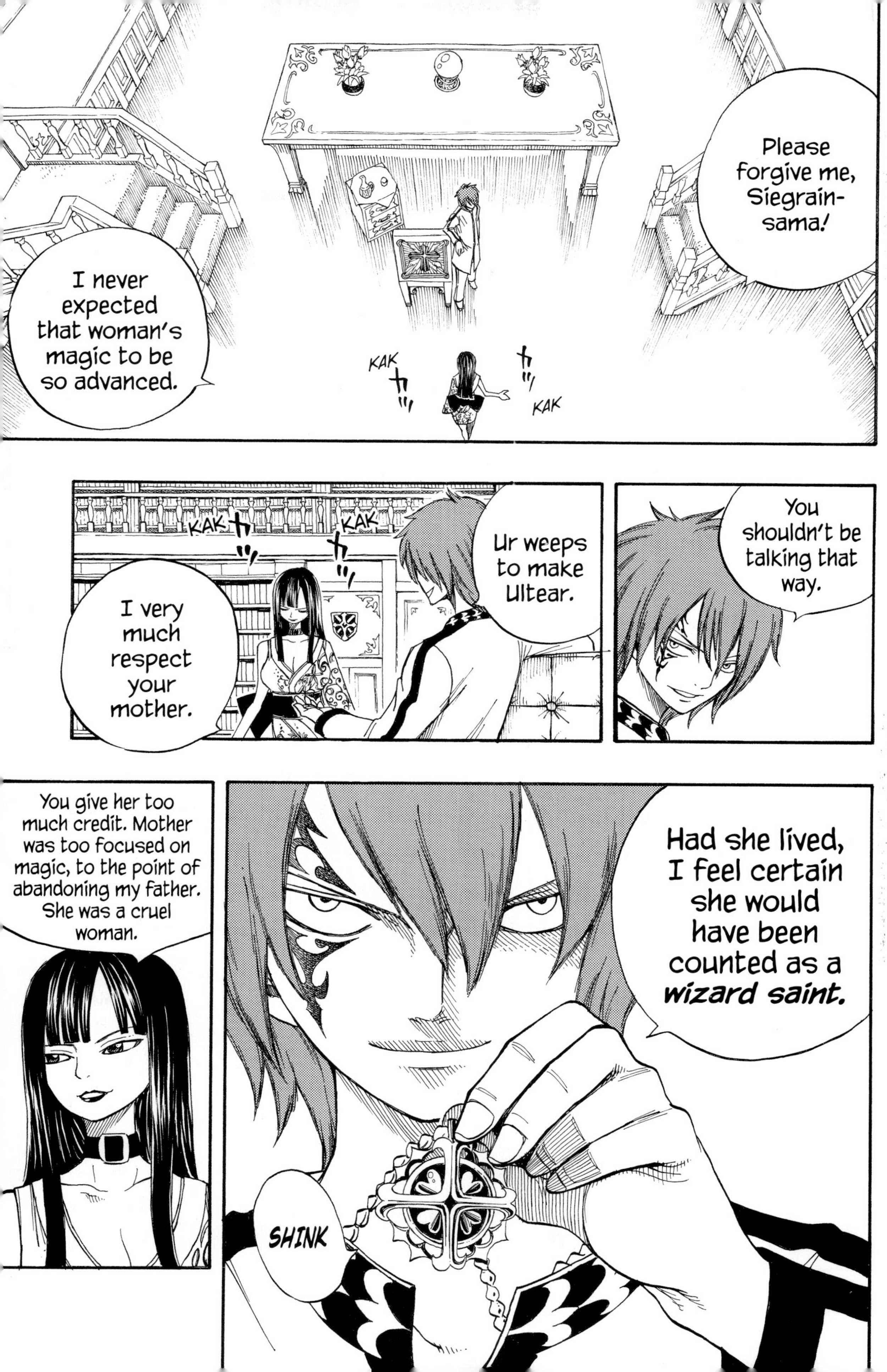
Please forgive me, Siegrain-sama!
KAK
KAK
I never expected that woman's magic to be so advanced.
You shouldn't be talking that way.
Ur weeps to make Ultear.
KAK
KAK
I very much respect your mother.
Had she lived, I feel certain she would have been counted as a *wizard saint.*
SHINK
You give her too much credit. Mother was too focused on magic, to the point of abandoning my father. She was a cruel woman.

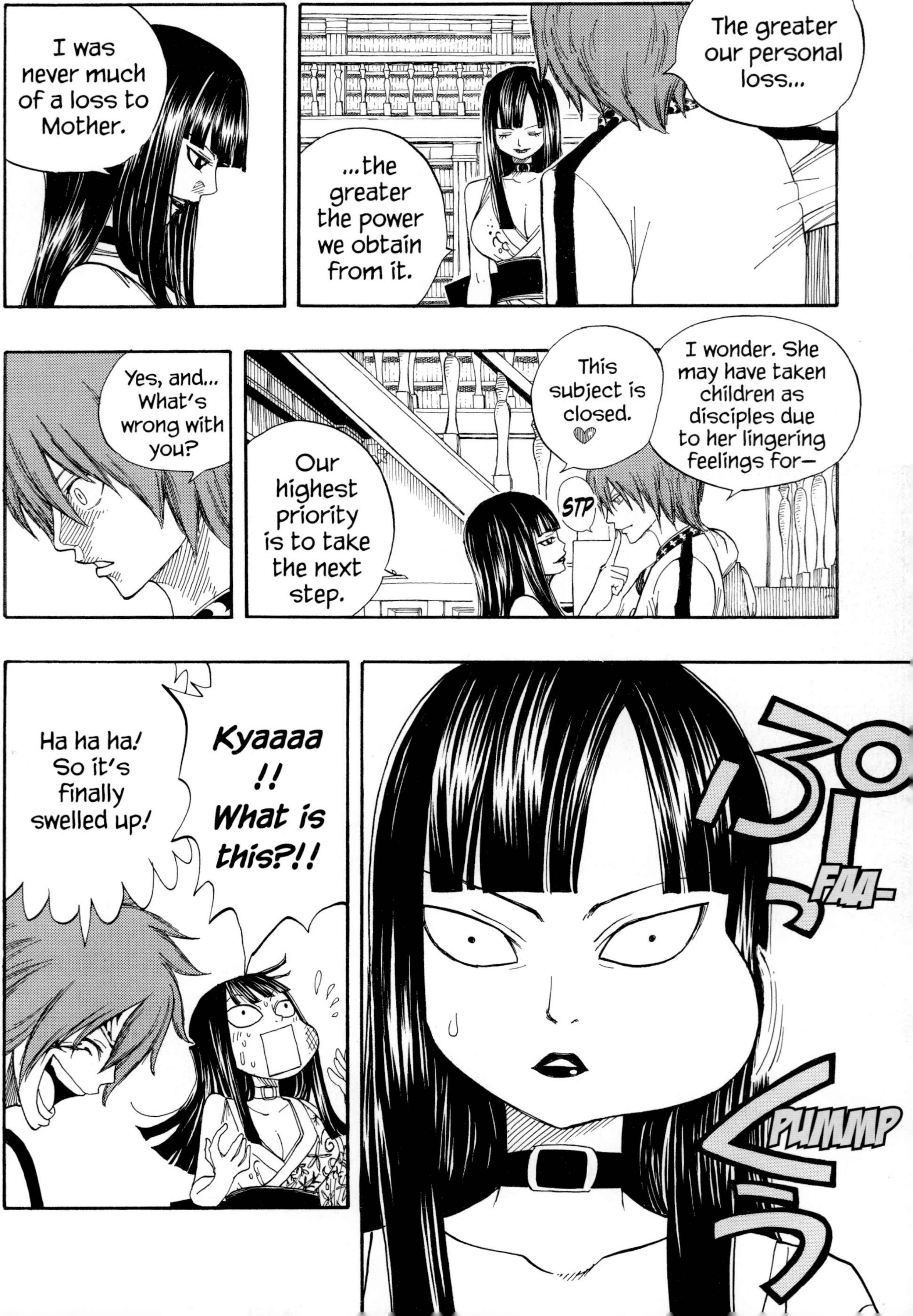
The greater our personal loss...
...the greater the power we obtain from it.
I was never much of a loss to Mother.
I wonder. She may have taken children as disciples due to her lingering feelings for—
STP
This subject is closed. ♥
Our highest priority is to take the next step.
Yes, and... What's wrong with you?
FAA-
PUMMP
Kyaaaa!! What is this?!!
Ha ha ha! So it's finally swelled up!

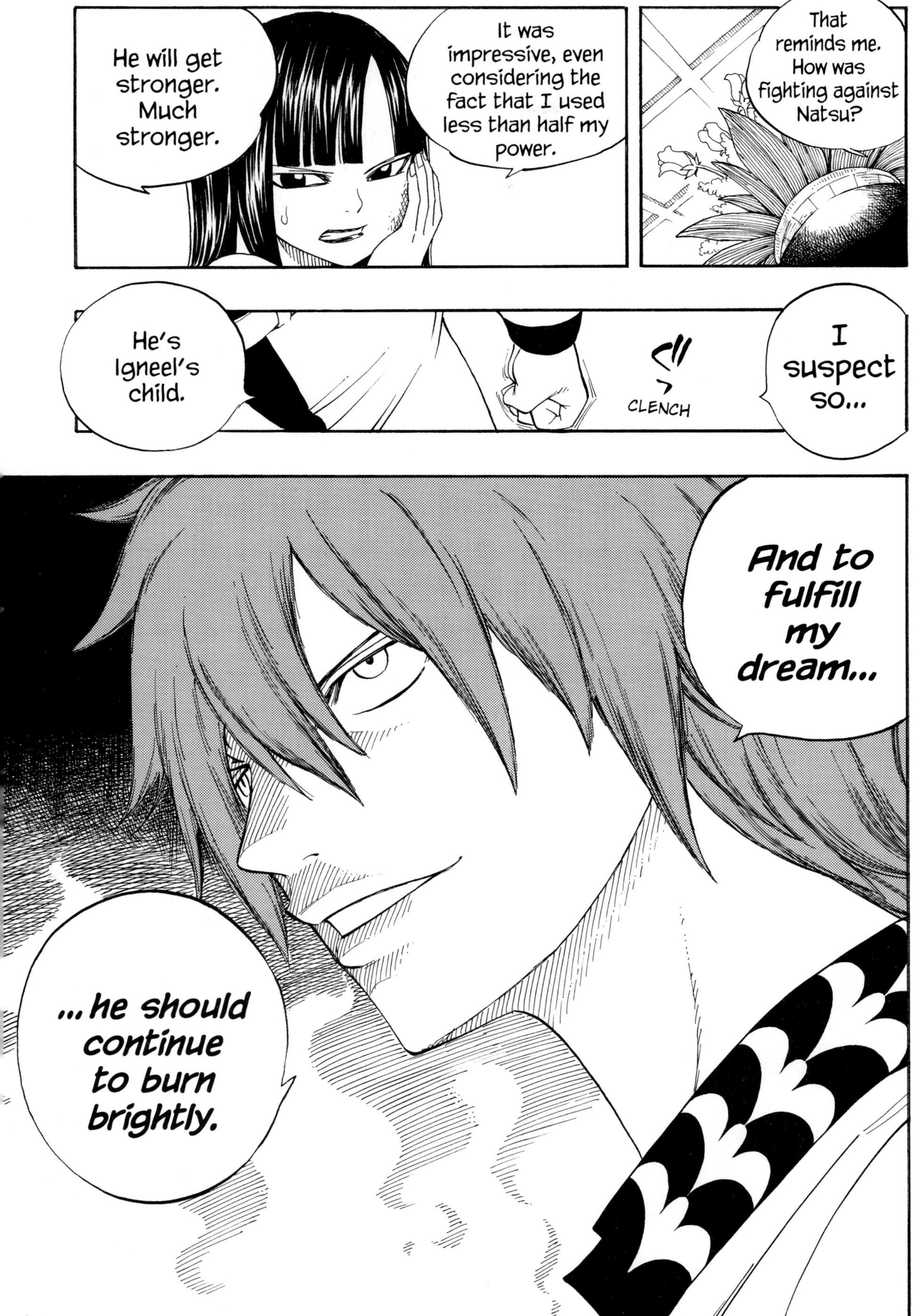
That reminds me. How was fighting against Natsu?
It was impressive, even considering the fact that I used less than half my power.
He will get stronger. Much stronger.
I suspect so...
CLENCH
He's Igneel's child.
And to fulfill my dream...
...he should continue to burn brightly.

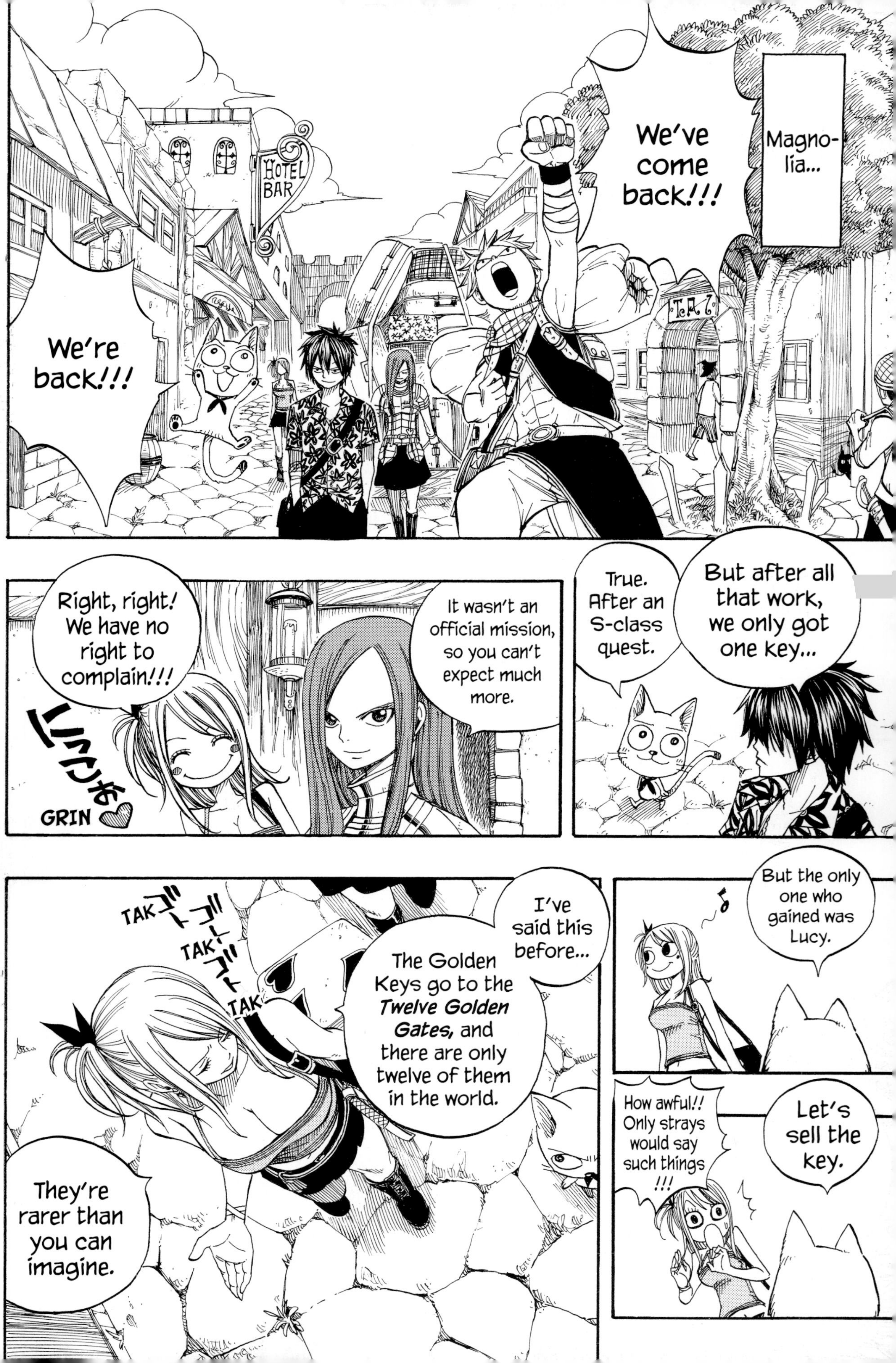
Magno-lia...
We've come back!!!
We're back!!!
But after all that work, we only got one key...
True. After an S-class quest.
It wasn't an official mission, so you can't expect much more.
Right, right! We have no right to complain!!!
GRIN
But the only one who gained was Lucy.
Let's sell the key.
How awful!! Only strays would say such things!!!
TAK TAK TAK
I've said this before...
The Golden Keys go to the *Twelve Golden Gates,* and there are only twelve of them in the world.
They're rarer than you can imagine.

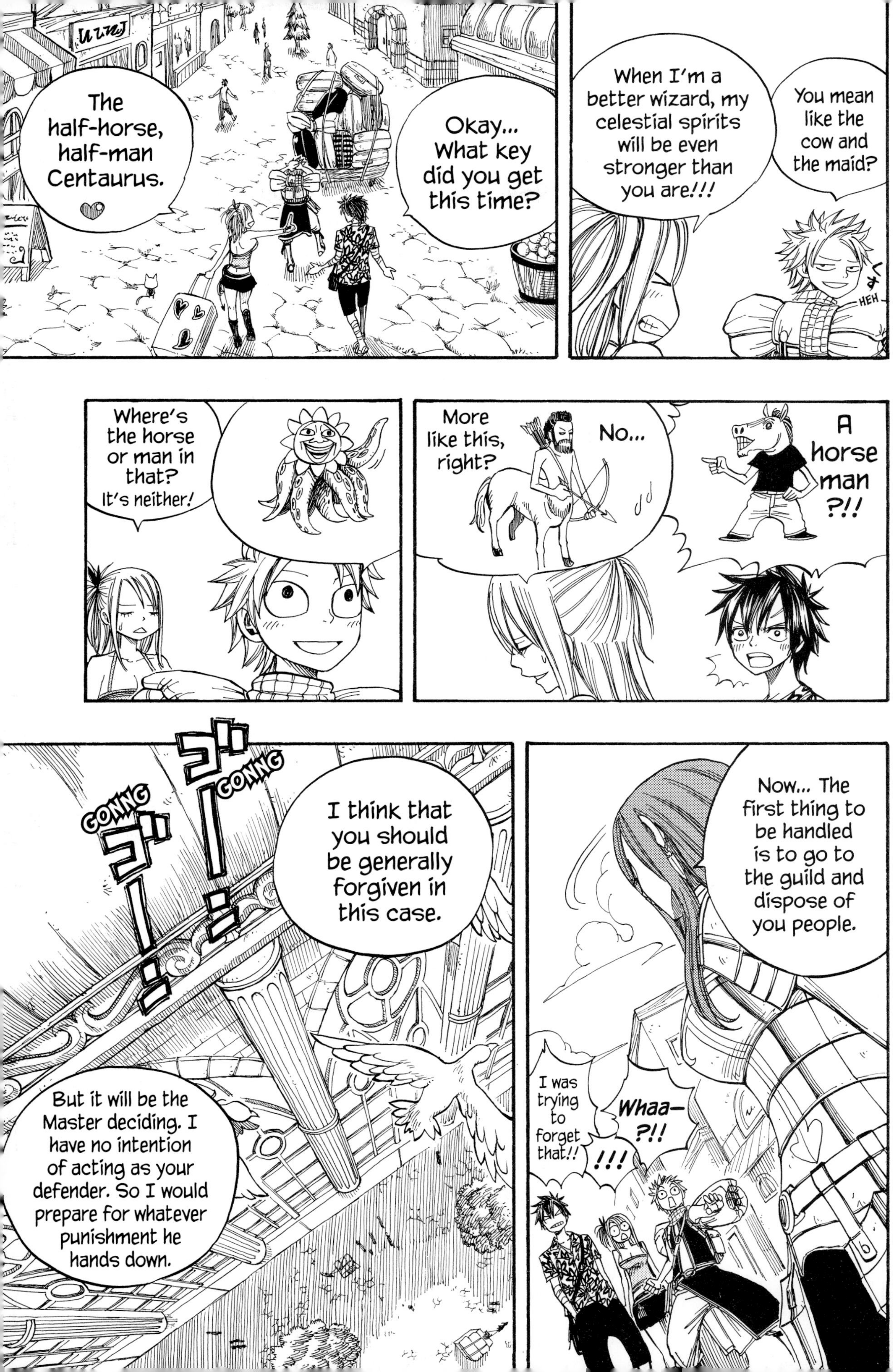
Okay... What key did you get this time?
The half-horse, half-man Centaurus.
When I'm a better wizard, my celestial spirits will be even stronger than you are!!!
You mean like the cow and the maid?
HEH
Where's the horse or man in that? It's neither!
More like this, right?
No...
A horse man ?!!
GONNG
GONNG
I think that you should be generally forgiven in this case.
But it will be the Master deciding. I have no intention of acting as your defender. So I would prepare for whatever punishment he hands down.
Now... The first thing to be handled is to go to the guild and dispose of you people.
Whaa- ?!!
!!!
I was trying to forget that!!

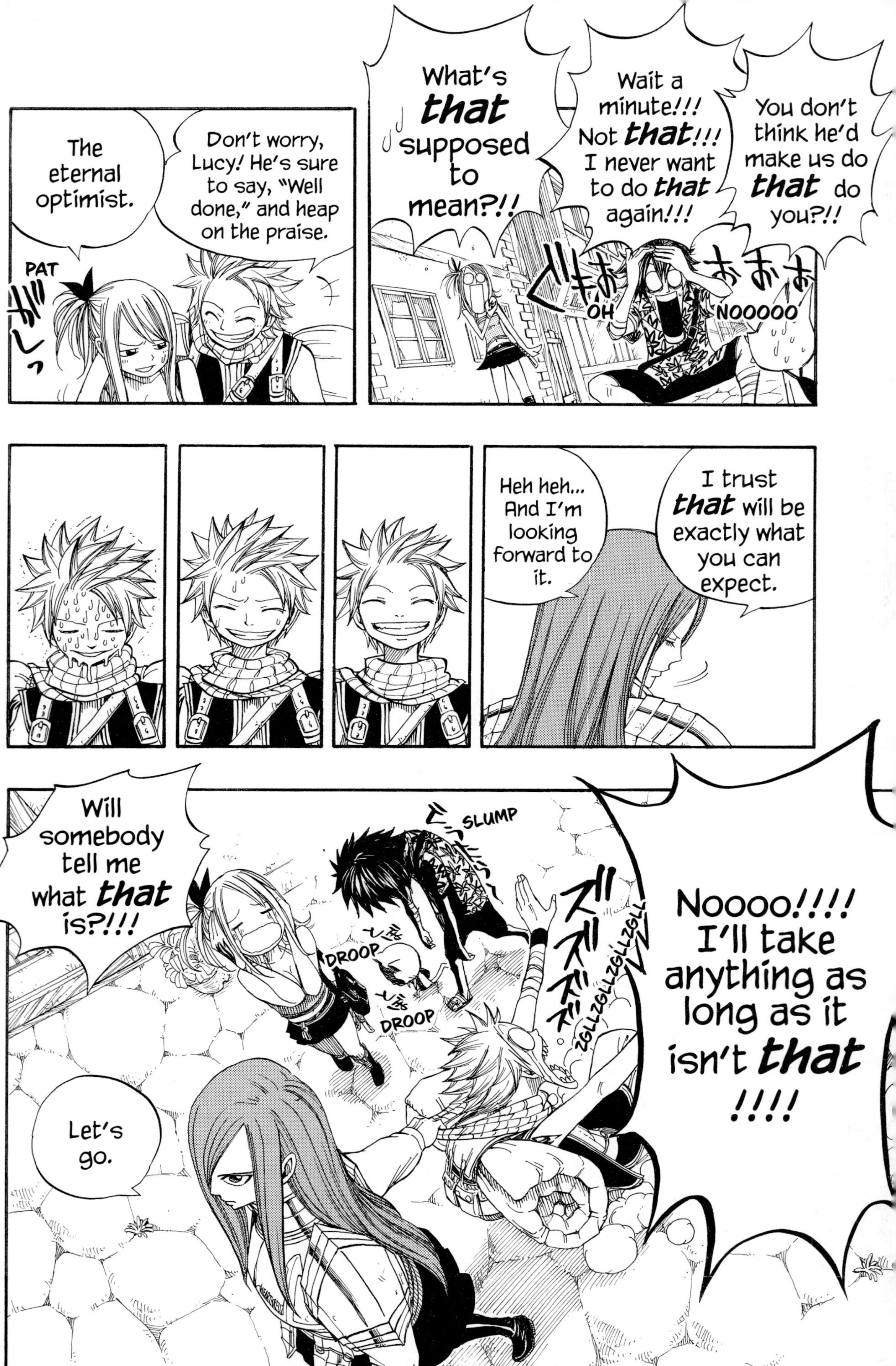

You don't think he'd make us do *that* do you?!!
Wait a minute!!! Not *that*!!! I never want to do *that* again!!!
What's *that* supposed to mean?!!
NOOOOO
OH
Don't worry, Lucy! He's sure to say, "Well done," and heap on the praise.
The eternal optimist.
PAT
I trust *that* will be exactly what you can expect.
Heh heh... And I'm looking forward to it.
Noooo!!!! I'll take anything as long as it isn't *that*!!!!
ZGLLZGLLZGLL
SLUMP
Will somebody tell me what *that* is?!!!
DROOP
DROOP
Let's go.

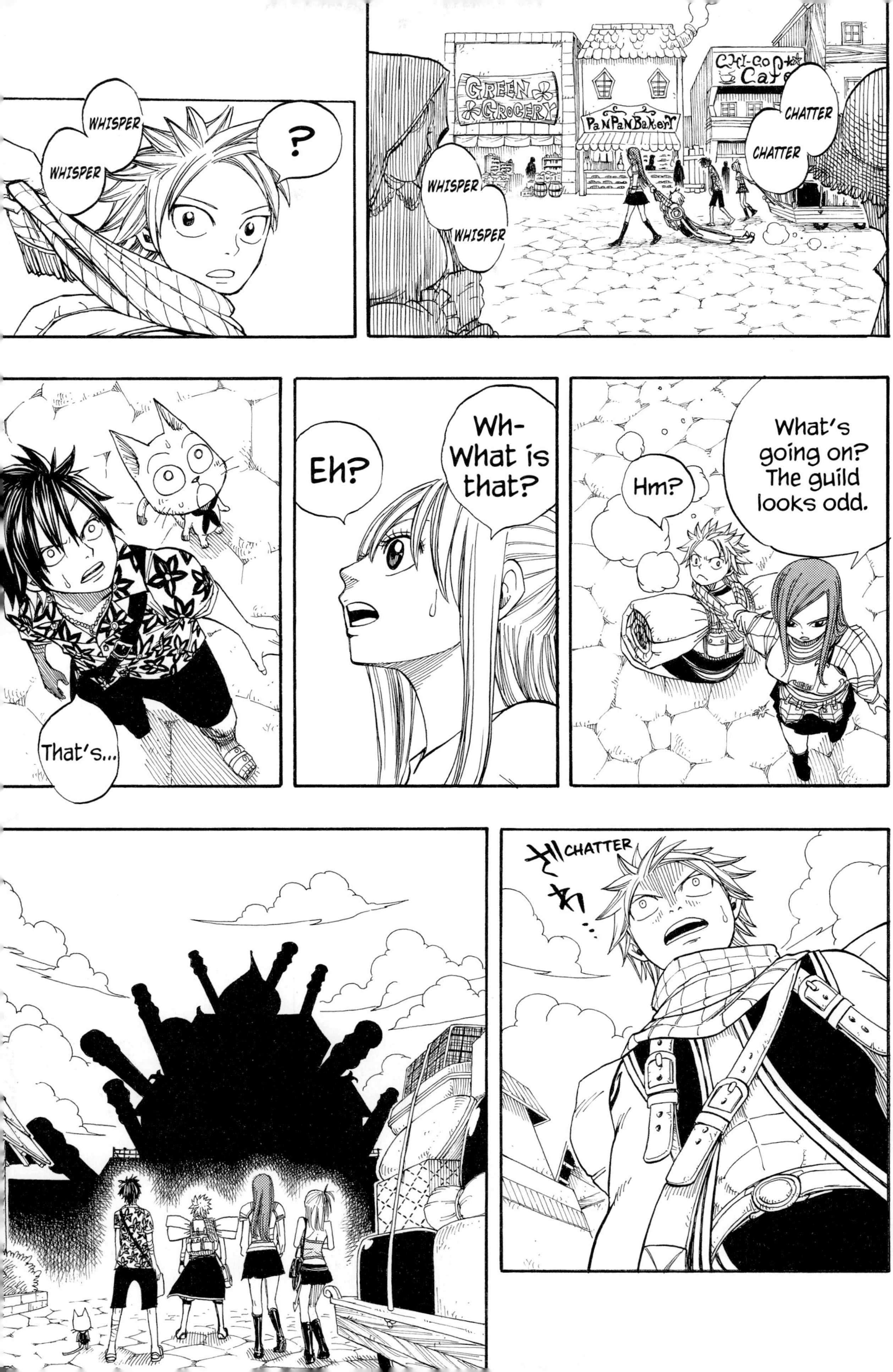
CHATTER
CHATTER
WHISPER
WHISPER
?
WHISPER
WHISPER
What's going on? The guild looks odd.
Hm?
Wh- What is that?
Eh?
That's...
CHATTER

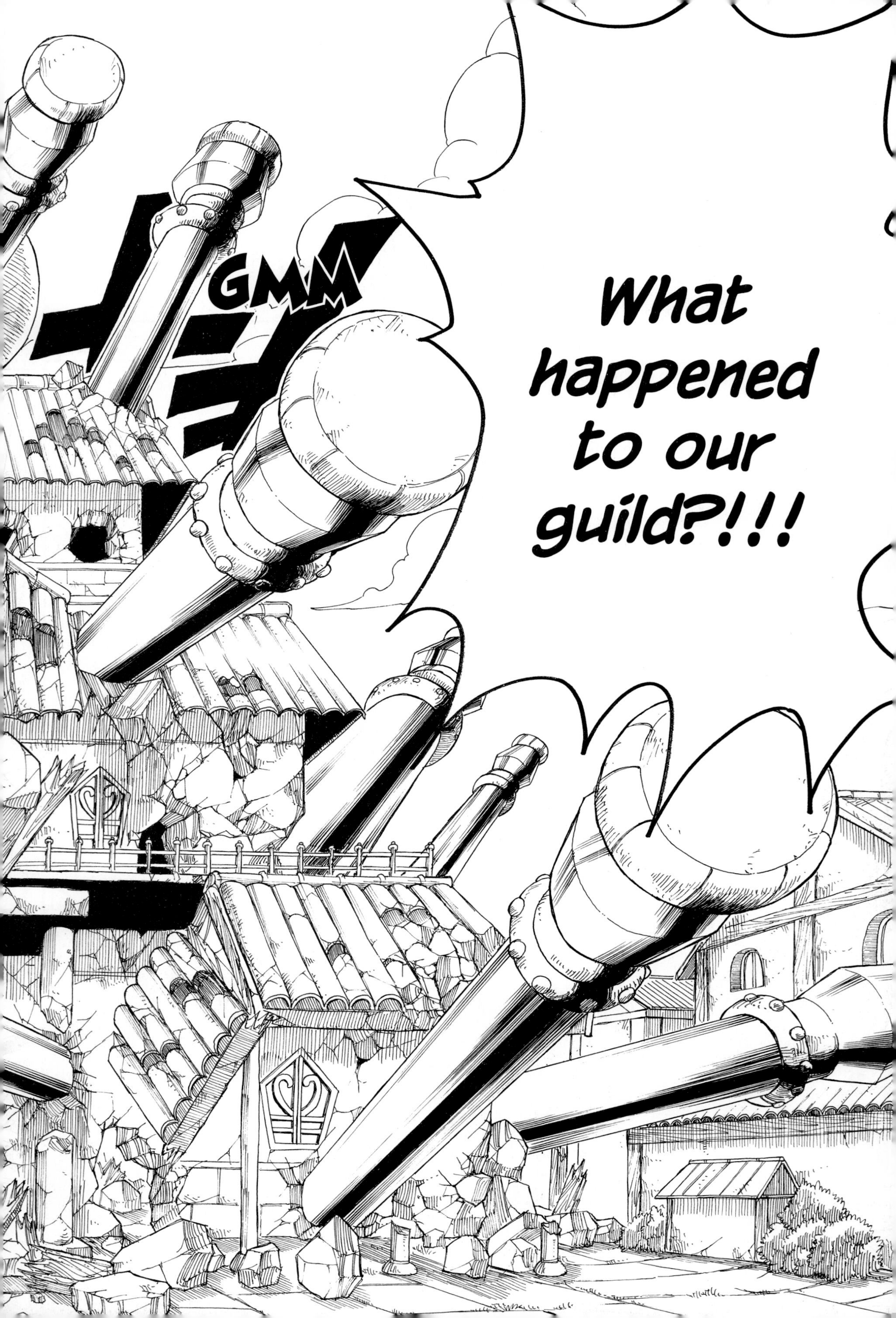
What happened to our guild?!!!
GMM

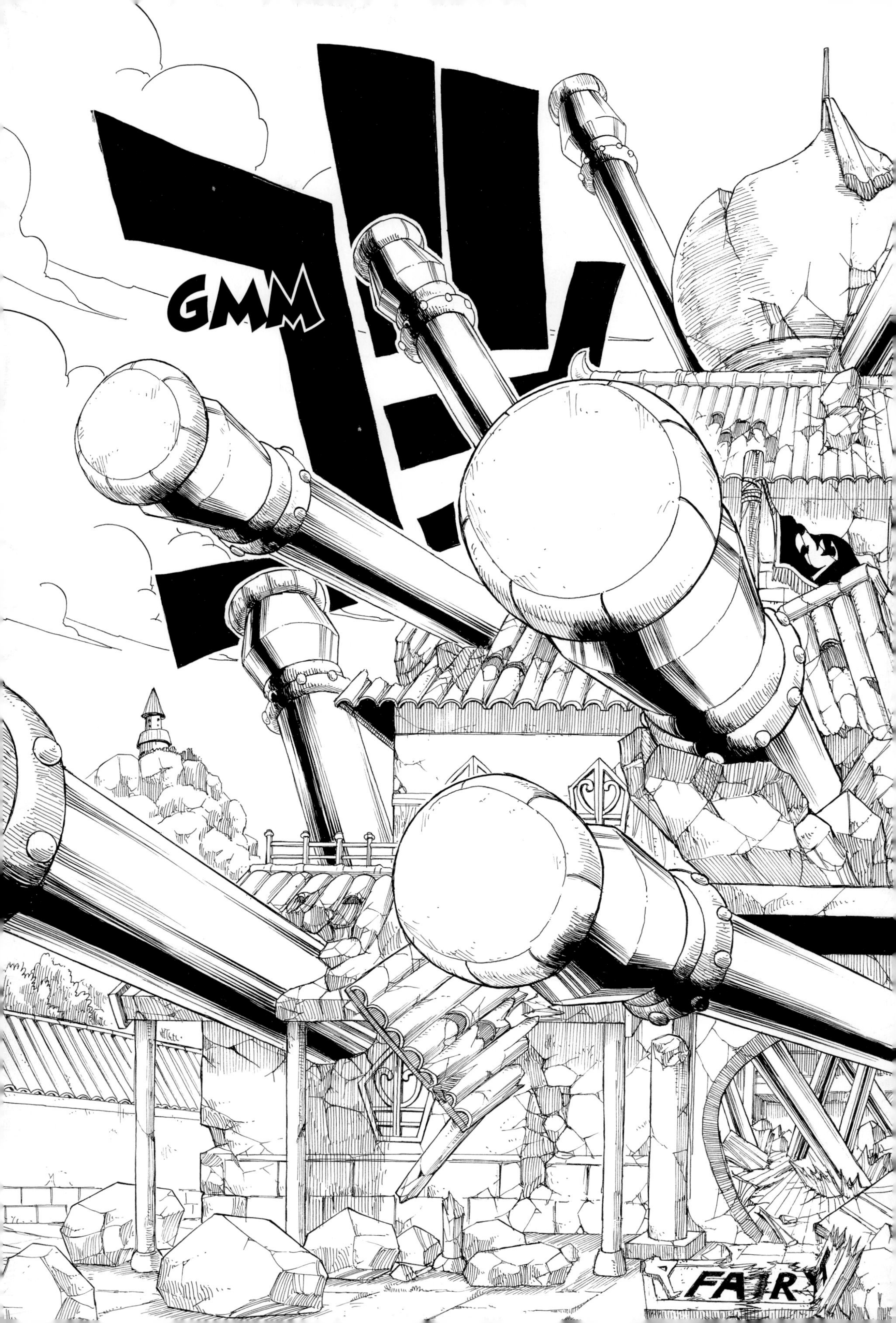
GMM
FAIRY

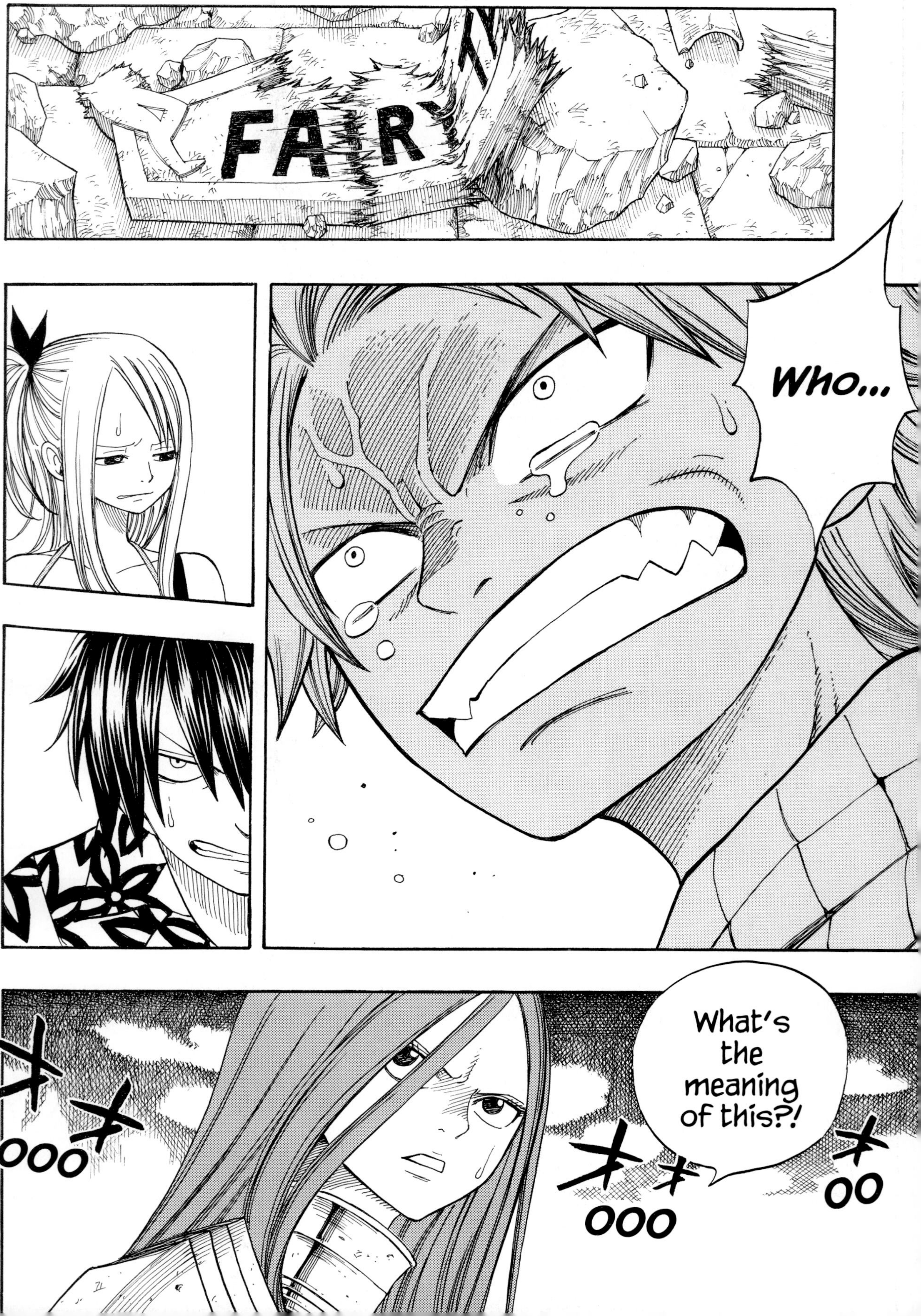
FAIRY
Who...
What's the meaning of this?!
OOO
OOO
OO

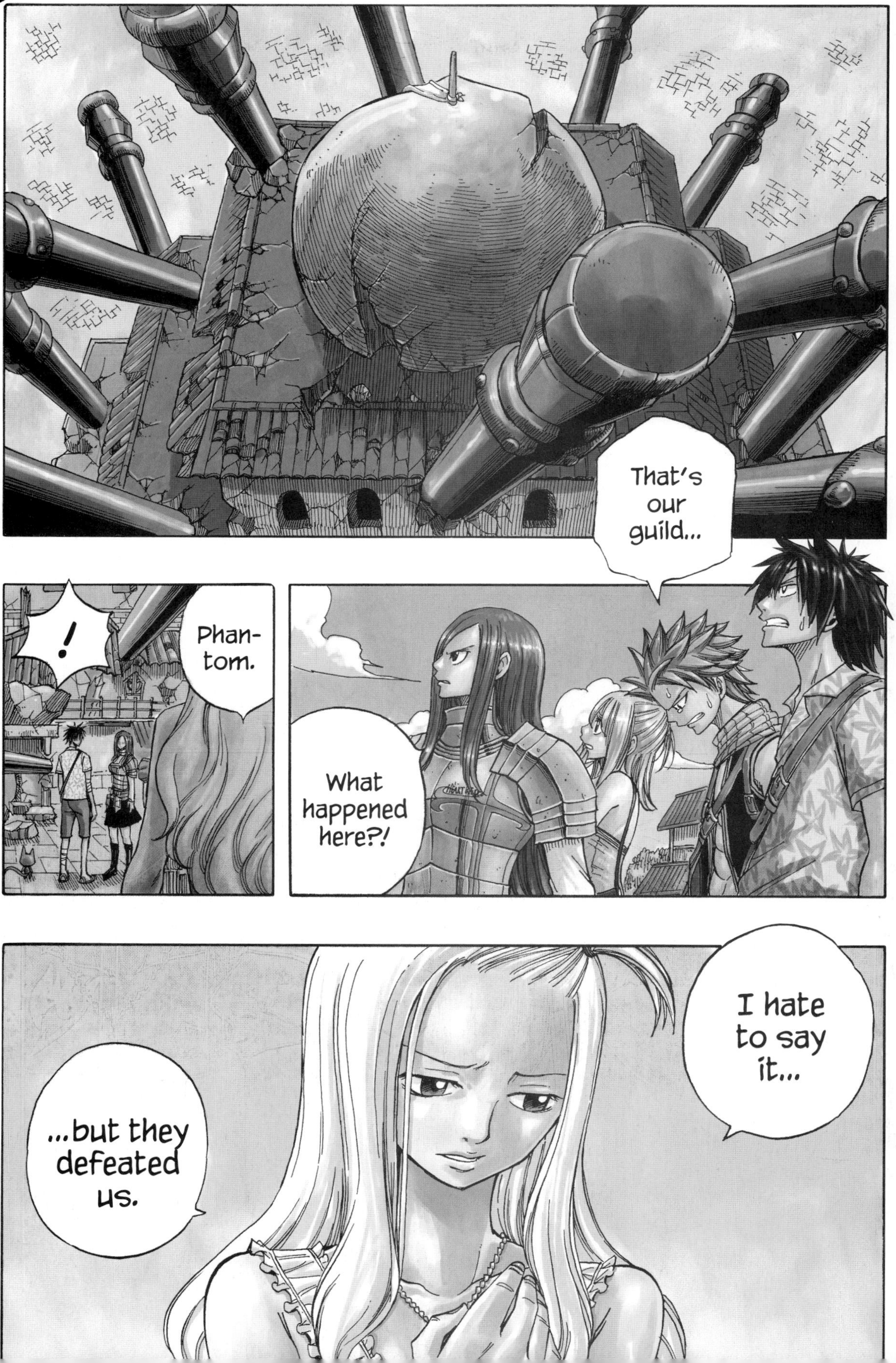
That's our guild...
What happened here?!
!
Phan-tom.
I hate to say it...
...but they defeated us.

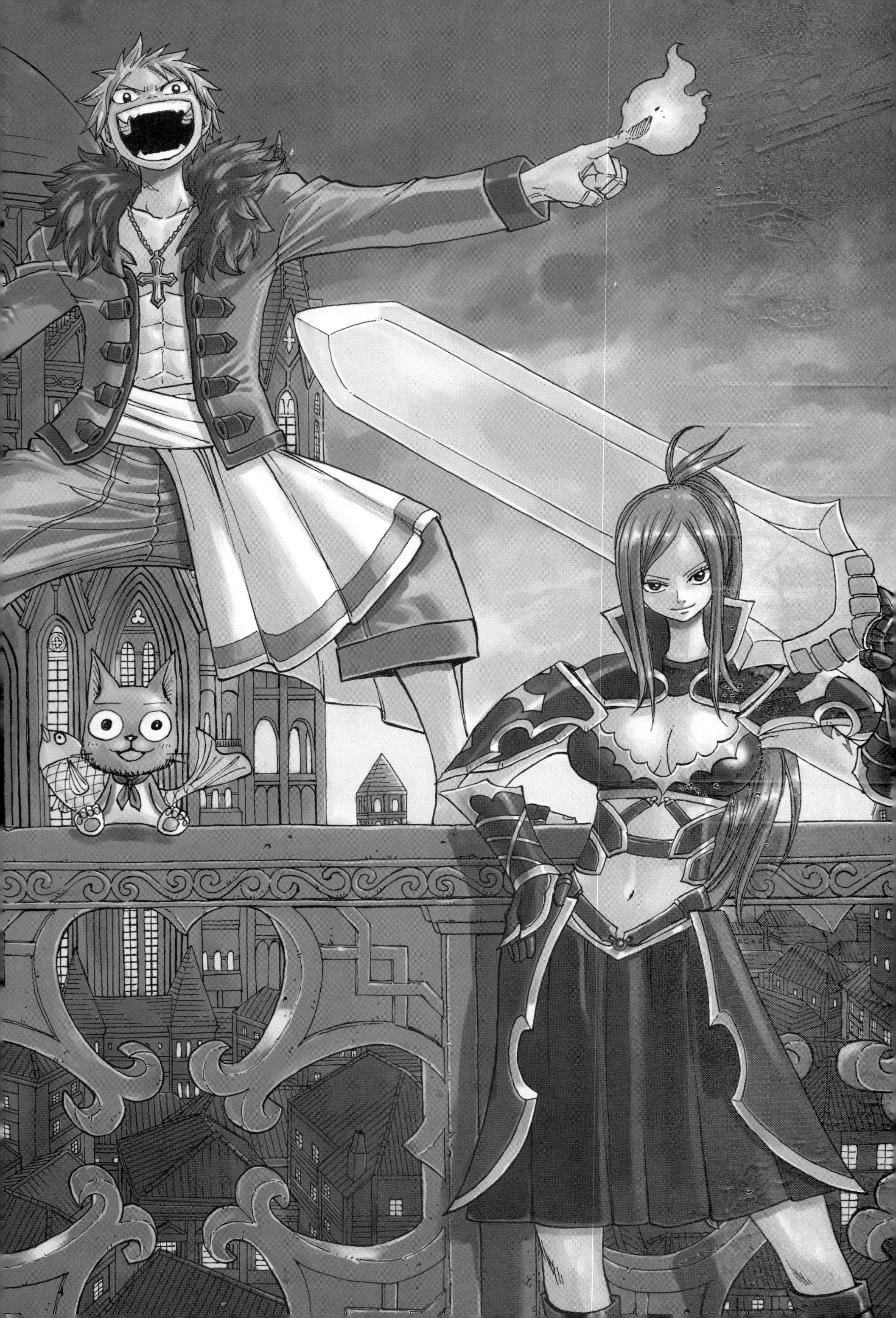

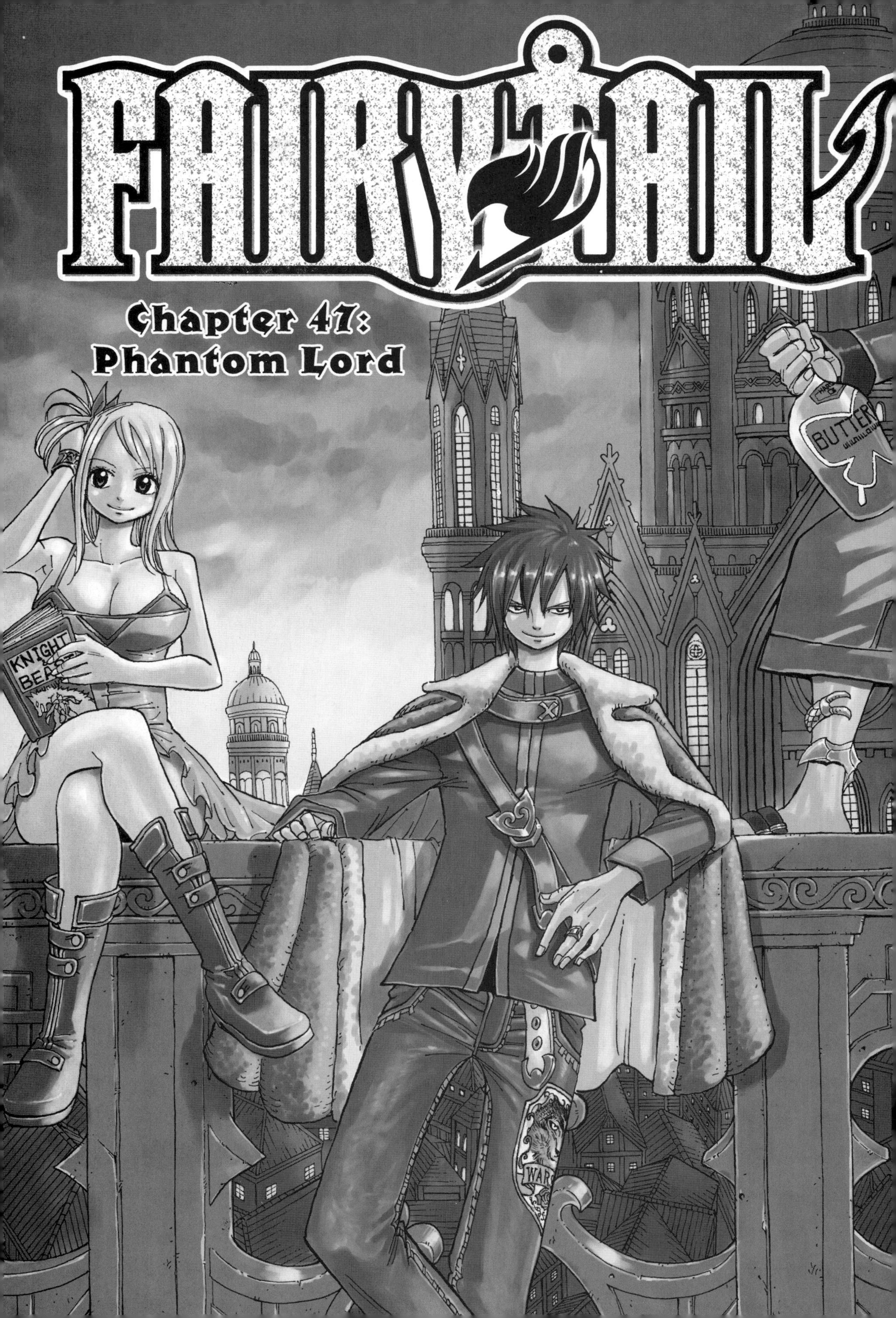
FAIRY TAIL
Chapter 47:
Phantom Lord
KNIGHT & BEA
BUTTER

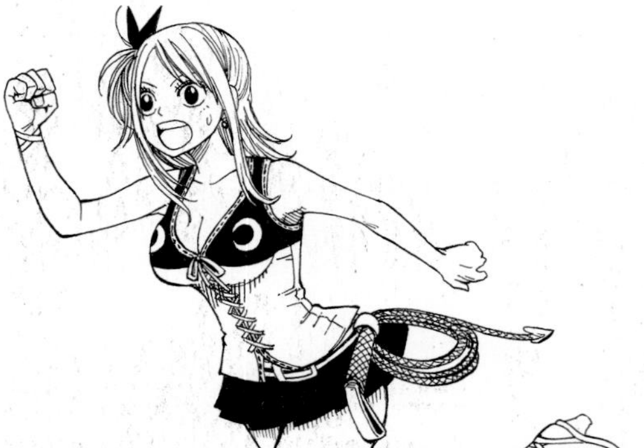

FAIRY TAIL

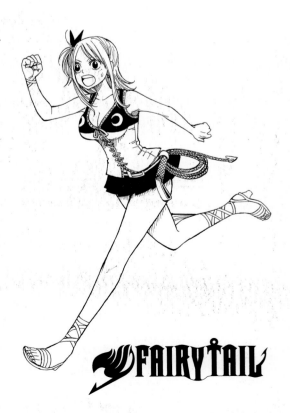

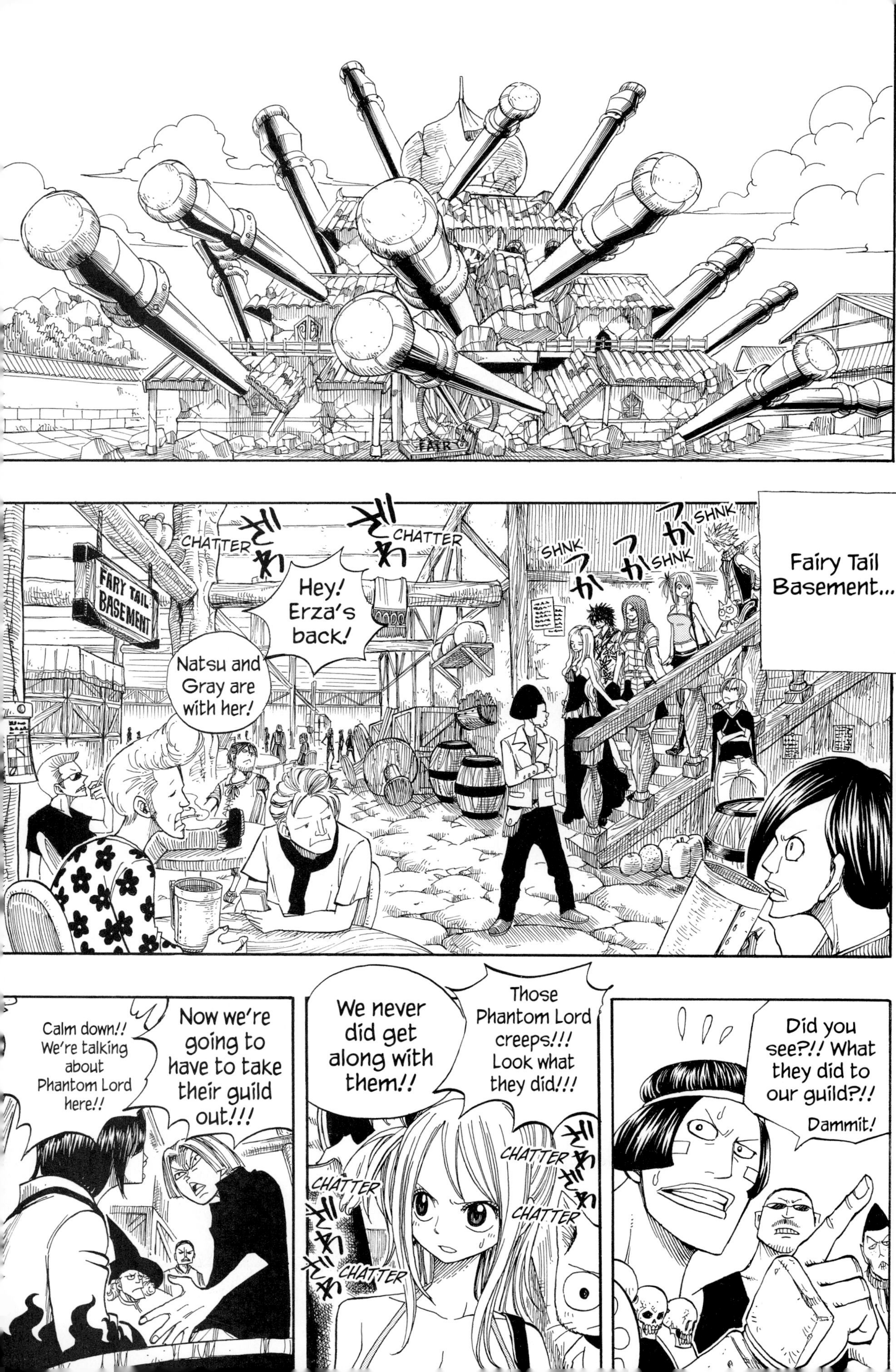
FAIR
Fairy Tail Basement...
SHNK
SHNK
SHNK
CHATTER
CHATTER
Hey! Erza's back!
Natsu and Gray are with her!
FAIRY TAIL BASEMENT
Did you see?!! What they did to our guild?!!
Dammit!
Those Phantom Lord creeps!!! Look what they did!!!
We never did get along with them!!
CHATTER
CHATTER
CHATTER
CHATTER
Now we're going to have to take their guild out!!!
Calm down!! We're talking about Phantom Lord here!!

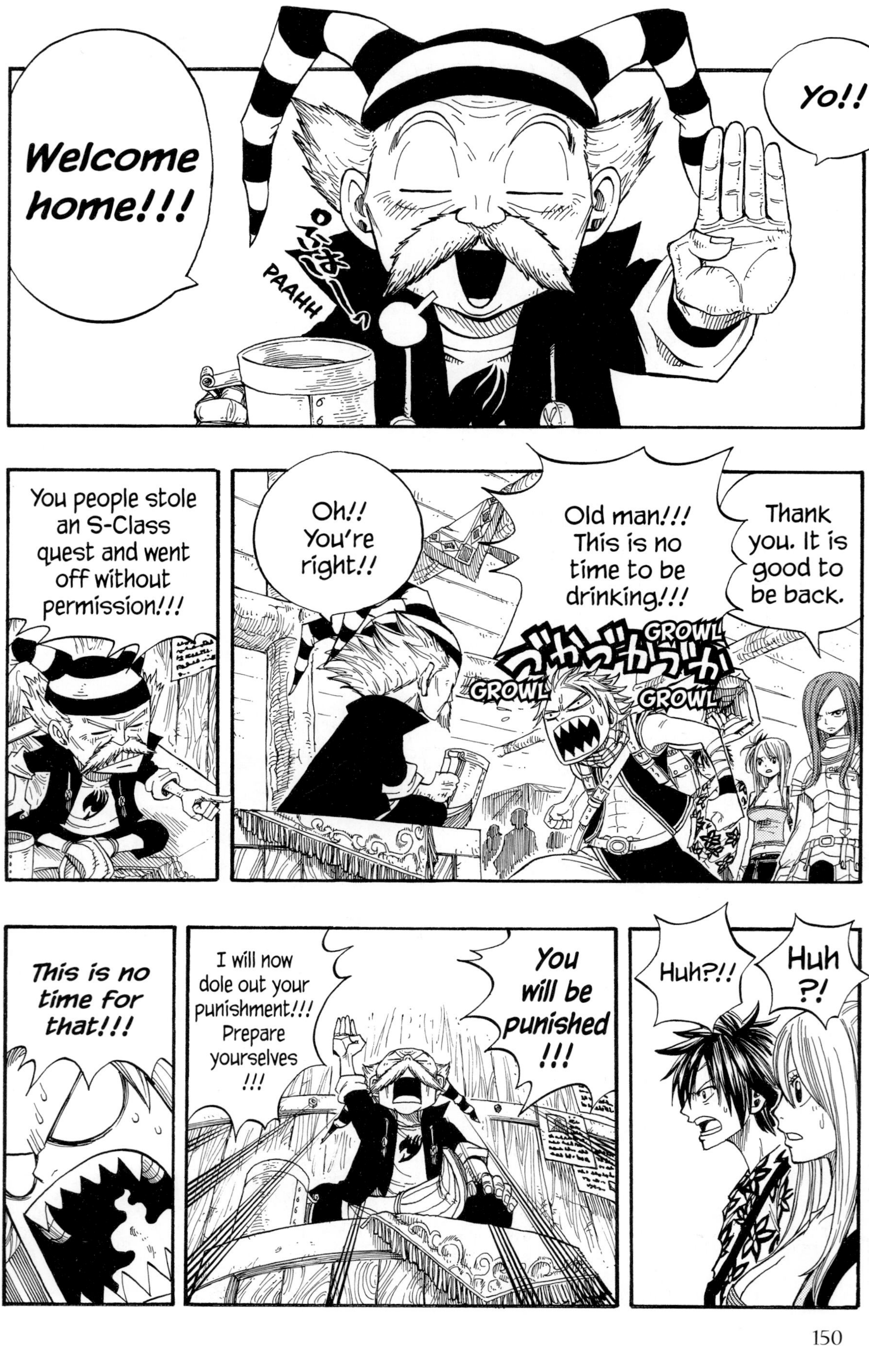
Yo!!
Welcome home!!!
PAAHH
Thank you. It is good to be back.
Old man!!! This is no time to be drinking!!!
Oh!! You're right!!
GROWL GROWL GROWL
You people stole an S-Class quest and went off without permission!!!
Huh ?!
Huh?!!
You will be punished !!!
I will now dole out your punishment!!! Prepare yourselves !!!
This is no time for that!!!

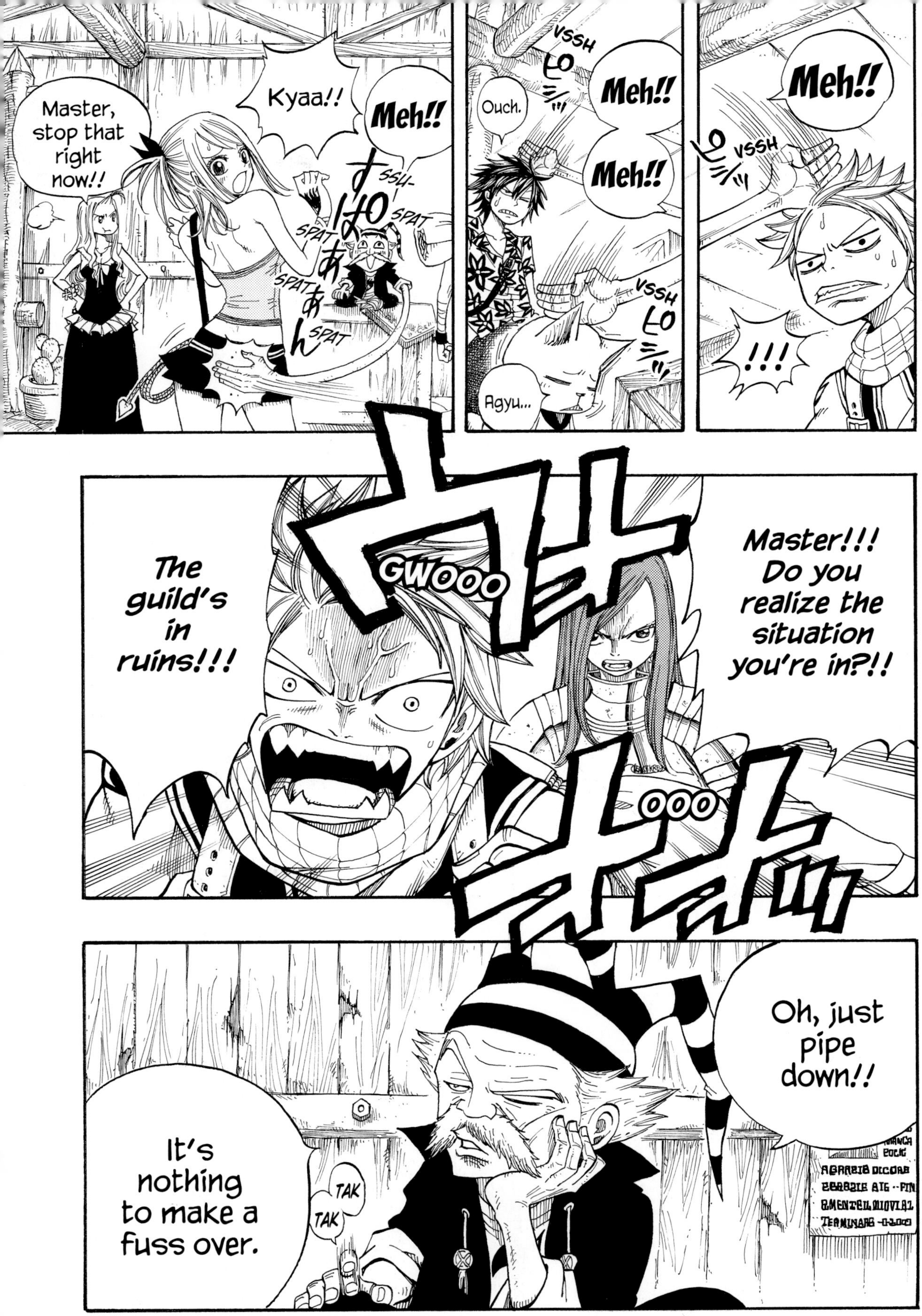
Meh!!
VSSH
!!!
VSSH
Meh!!
Meh!!
Ouch.
VSSH
Agyu...
Meh!!
SSU-
SPAT
SPAT
SPAT
SPAT
SPAT
Kyaa!!
Master, stop that right now!!
Master!!! Do you realize the situation you're in?!!
GWOOO
OOO
The guild's in ruins!!!
Oh, just pipe down!!
It's nothing to make a fuss over.
TAK
TAK

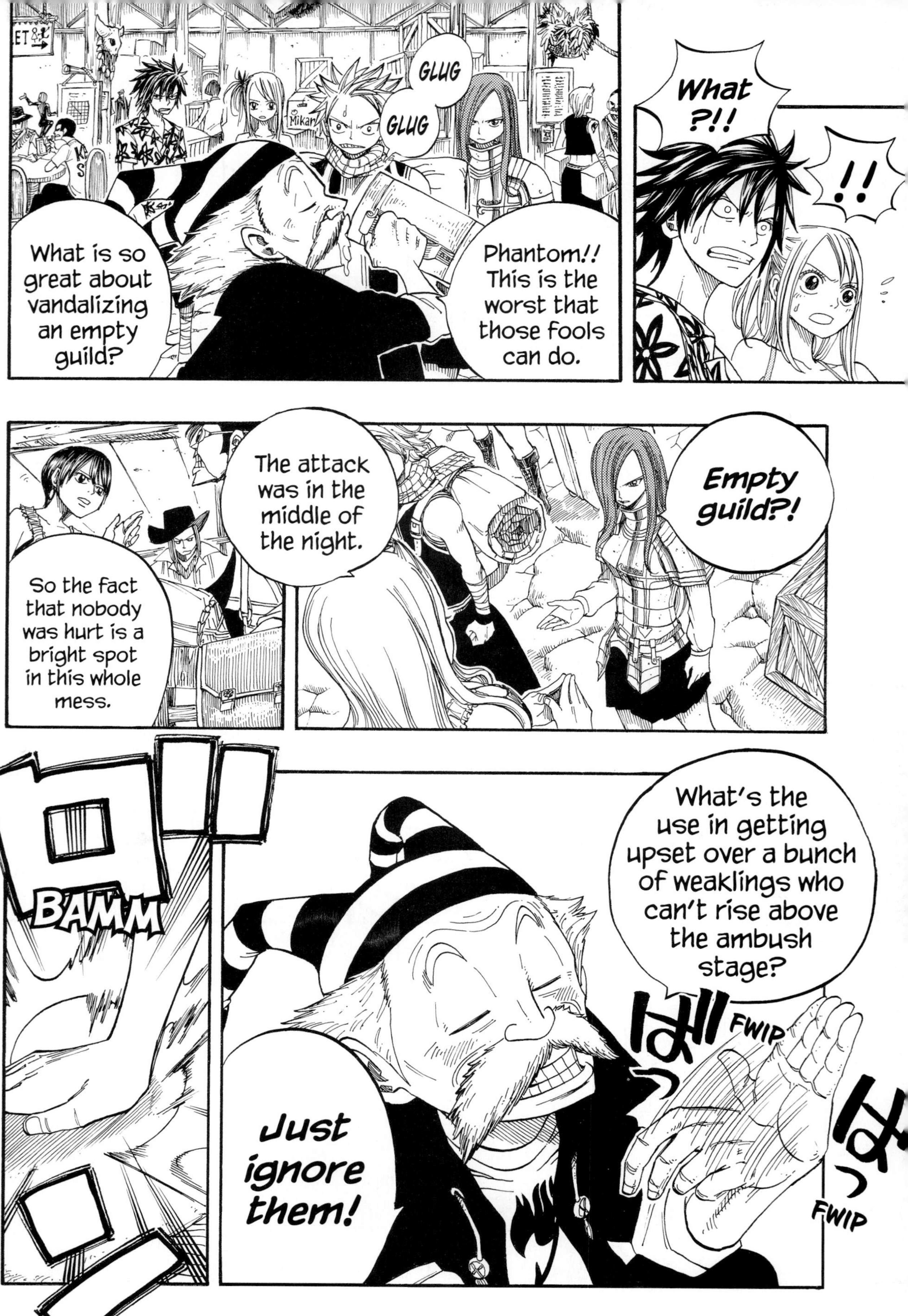
What ?!!
!!
GLUG
GLUG
Phantom!! This is the worst that those fools can do.
What is so great about vandalizing an empty guild?
Empty guild?!
The attack was in the middle of the night.
So the fact that nobody was hurt is a bright spot in this whole mess.
What's the use in getting upset over a bunch of weaklings who can't rise above the ambush stage?
FWIP
FWIP
Just ignore them!
BAMM

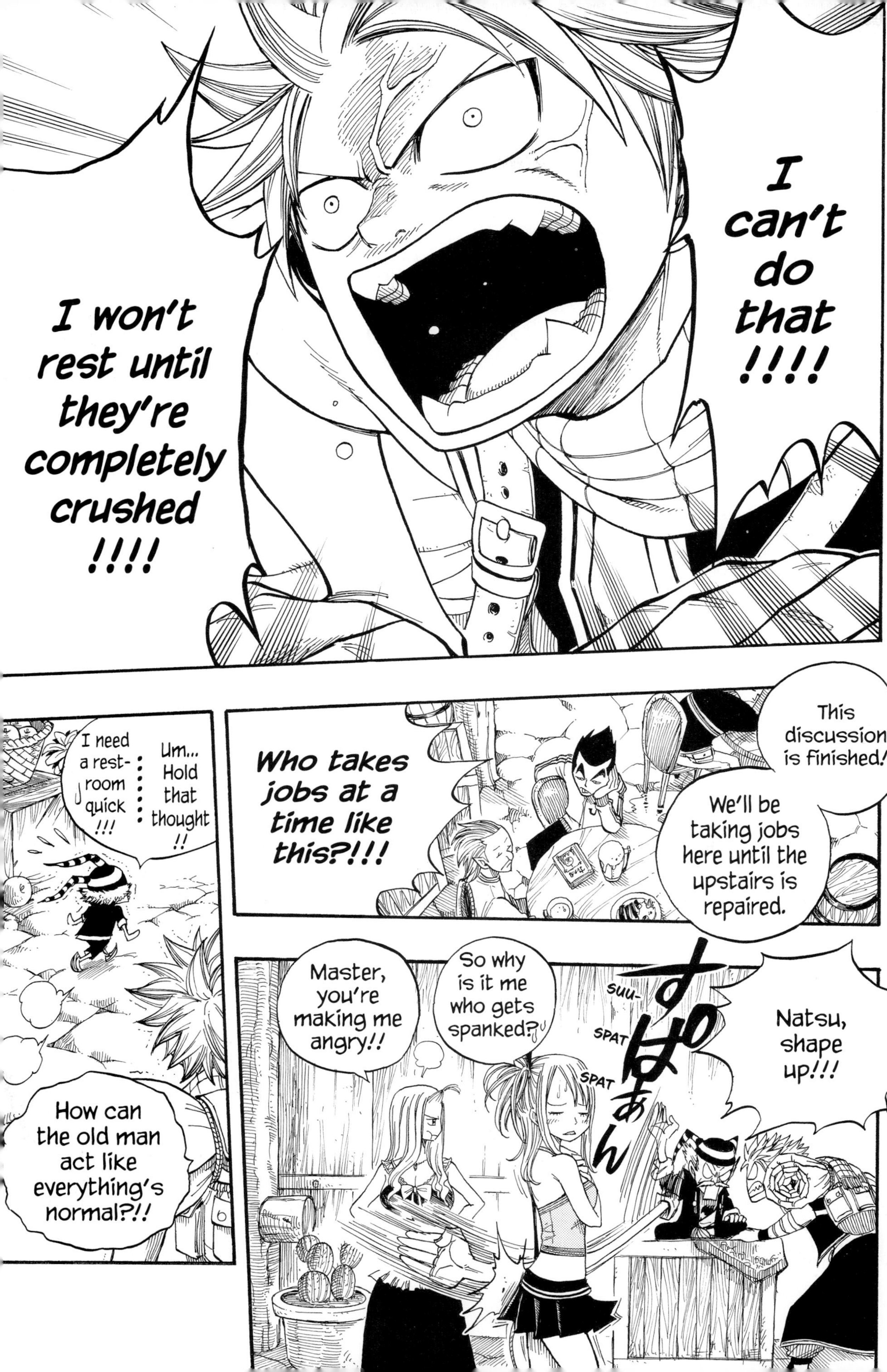
I can't do that!!!!
I won't rest until they're completely crushed!!!!
This discussion is finished!
We'll be taking jobs here until the upstairs is repaired.
Who takes jobs at a time like this?!!!
Natsu, shape up!!!
すぱあん
SUU-
SPAT
SPAT
So why is it me who gets spanked?
Master, you're making me angry!!
Um... Hold that thought!!
I need a rest-room quick!!!
How can the old man act like everything's normal?!!

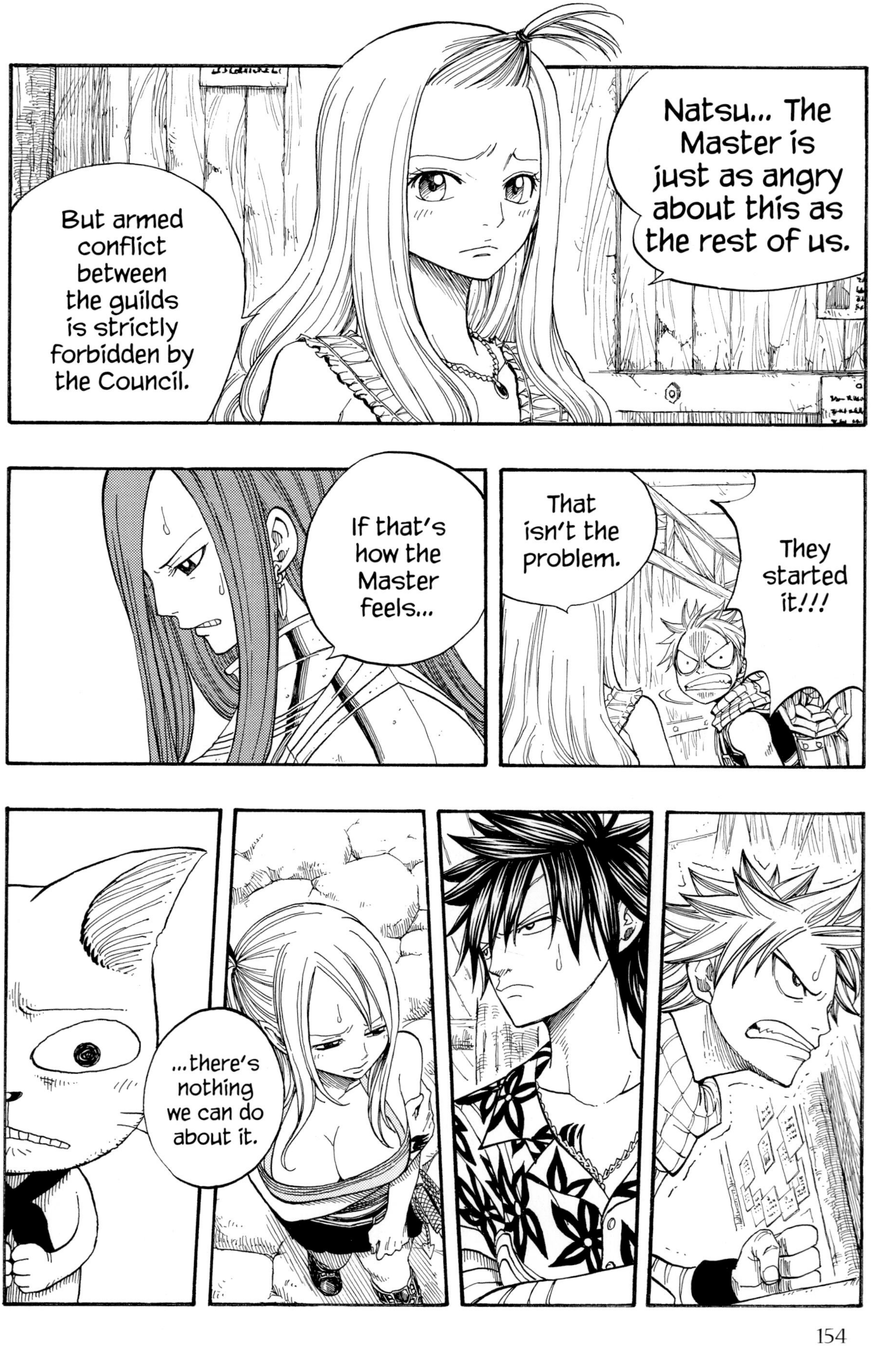
Natsu... The Master is just as angry about this as the rest of us.
But armed conflict between the guilds is strictly forbidden by the Council.
They started it!!!
That isn't the problem.
If that's how the Master feels...
...there's nothing we can do about it.

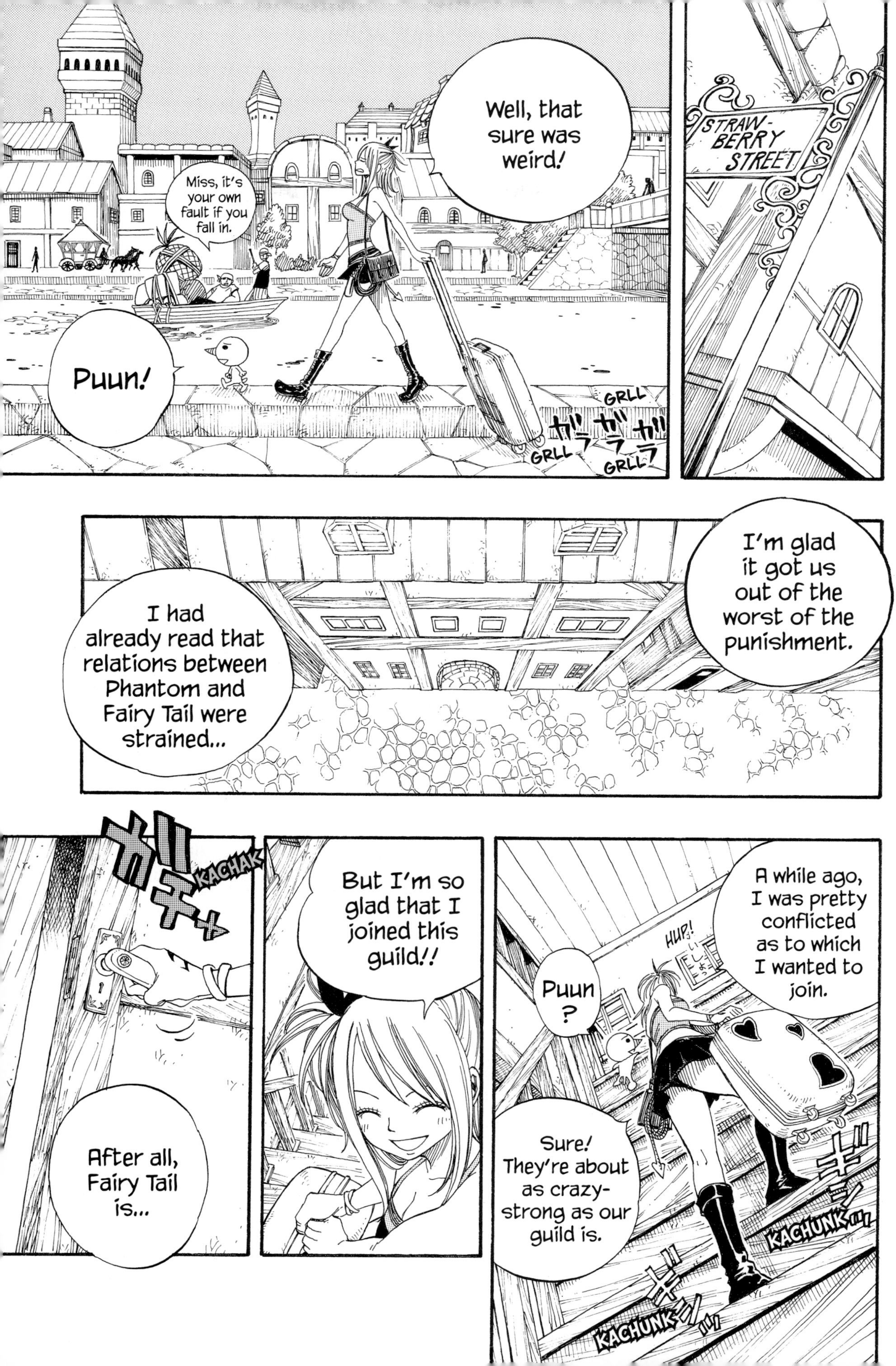
STRAW-BERRY STREET
Well, that sure was weird!
Miss, it's your own fault if you fall in.
Puun!
GRLL
GRLL
GRLL
I'm glad it got us out of the worst of the punishment.
I had already read that relations between Phantom and Fairy Tail were strained...
A while ago, I was pretty conflicted as to which I wanted to join.
HUP!
Puun ?
Sure! They're about as crazy-strong as our guild is.
KACHUNK
KACHUNK
But I'm so glad that I joined this guild!!
KACHAK
After all, Fairy Tail is...

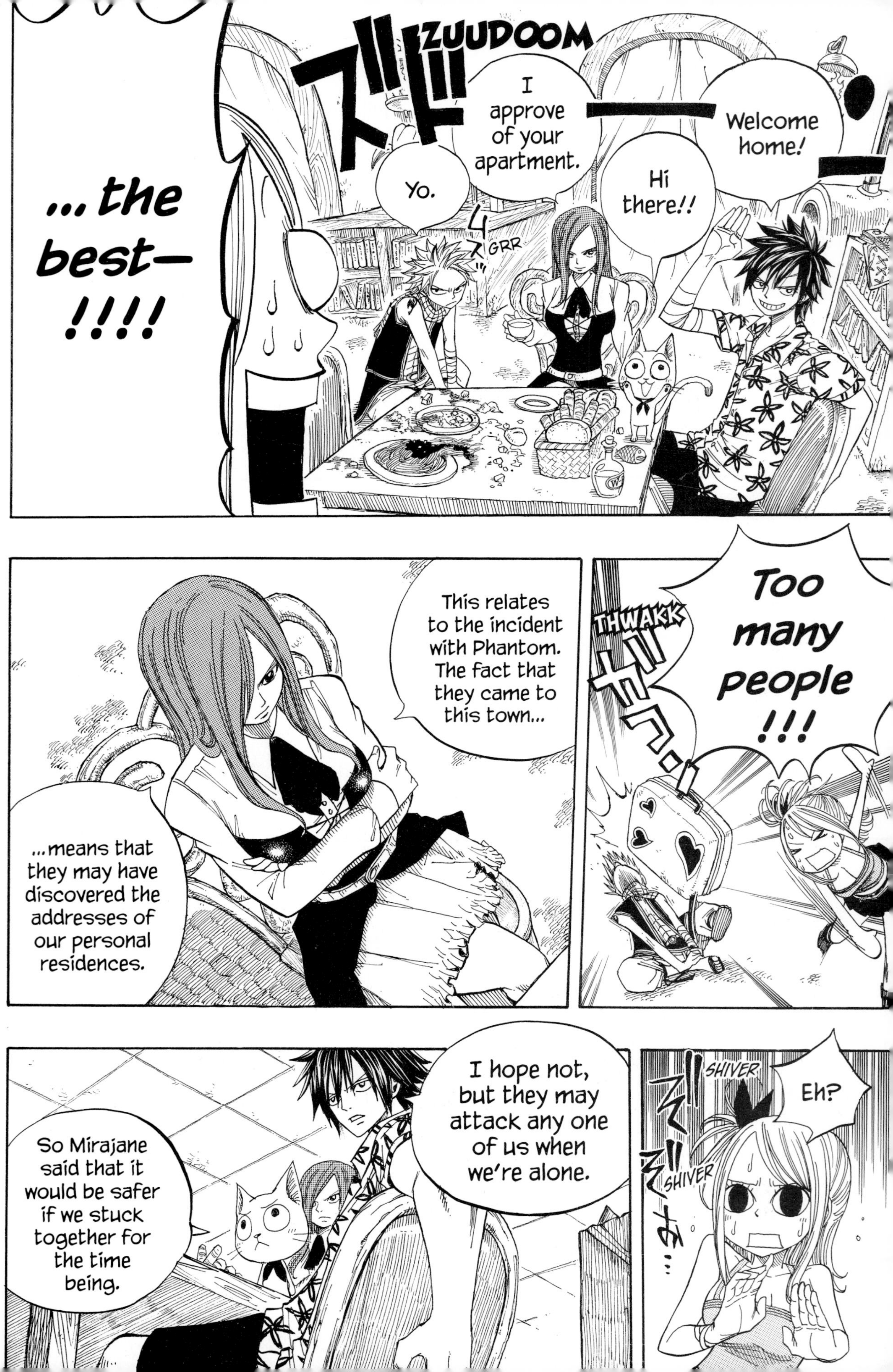
ZUUDOOM
Welcome home!
Hi there!!
I approve of your apartment.
Yo.
GRR
...the best—!!!!
THWAKK
Too many people!!!
This relates to the incident with Phantom. The fact that they came to this town...
...means that they may have discovered the addresses of our personal residences.
SHIVER
Eh?
SHIVER
I hope not, but they may attack any one of us when we're alone.
So Mirajane said that it would be safer if we stuck together for the time being.

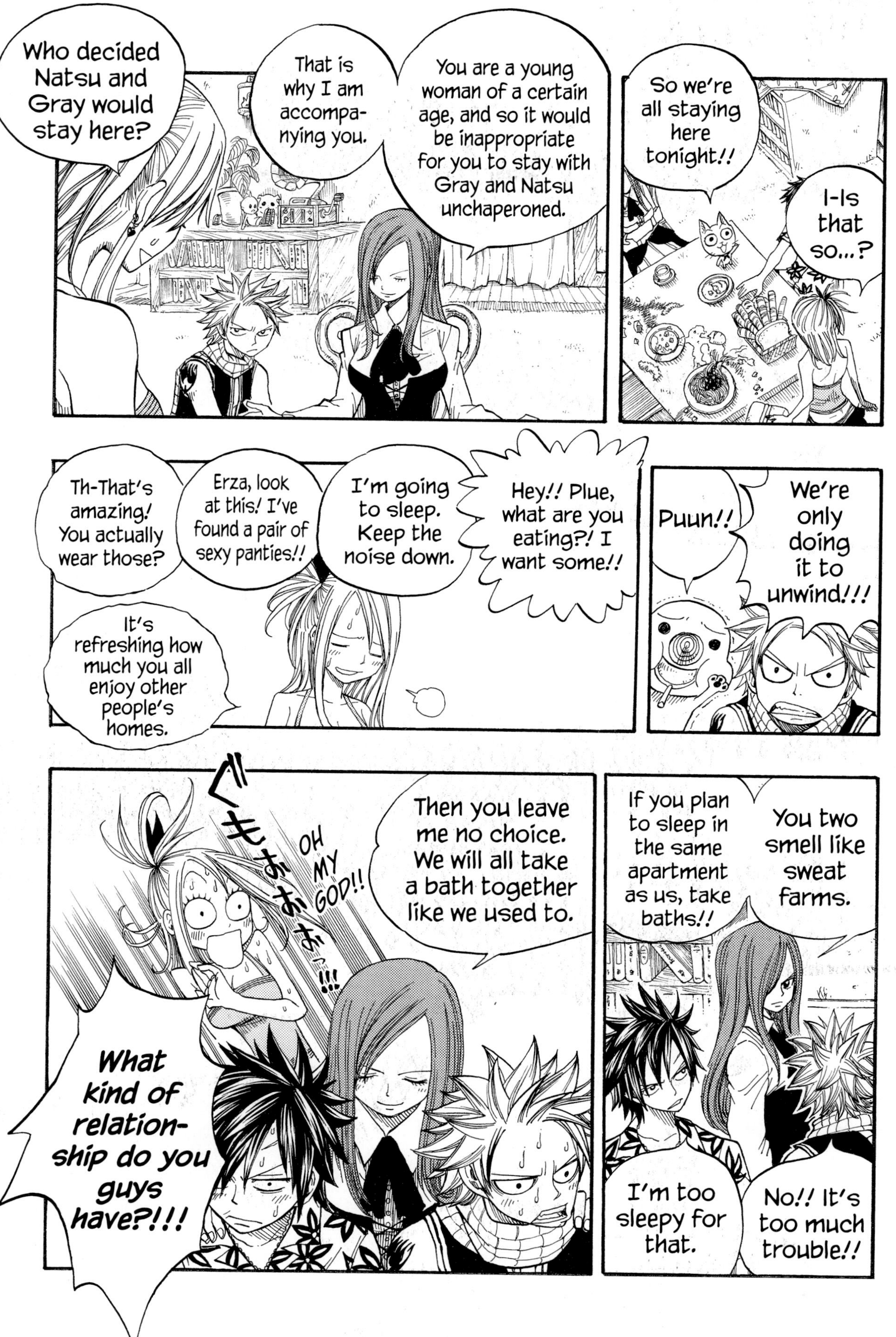
So we're all staying here tonight!!
I-Is that so...?
You are a young woman of a certain age, and so it would be inappropriate for you to stay with Gray and Natsu unchaperoned.
That is why I am accompanying you.
Who decided Natsu and Gray would stay here?
We're only doing it to unwind!!!
Puun!!
Hey!! Plue, what are you eating?! I want some!!
I'm going to sleep. Keep the noise down.
Erza, look at this! I've found a pair of sexy panties!!
Th-That's amazing! You actually wear those?
It's refreshing how much you all enjoy other people's homes.
You two smell like sweat farms.
If you plan to sleep in the same apartment as us, take baths!!
No!! It's too much trouble!!
I'm too sleepy for that.
Then you leave me no choice. We will all take a bath together like we used to.
OH MY GOD!!
ぐもおおおっ!!!
What kind of relationship do you guys have?!!!

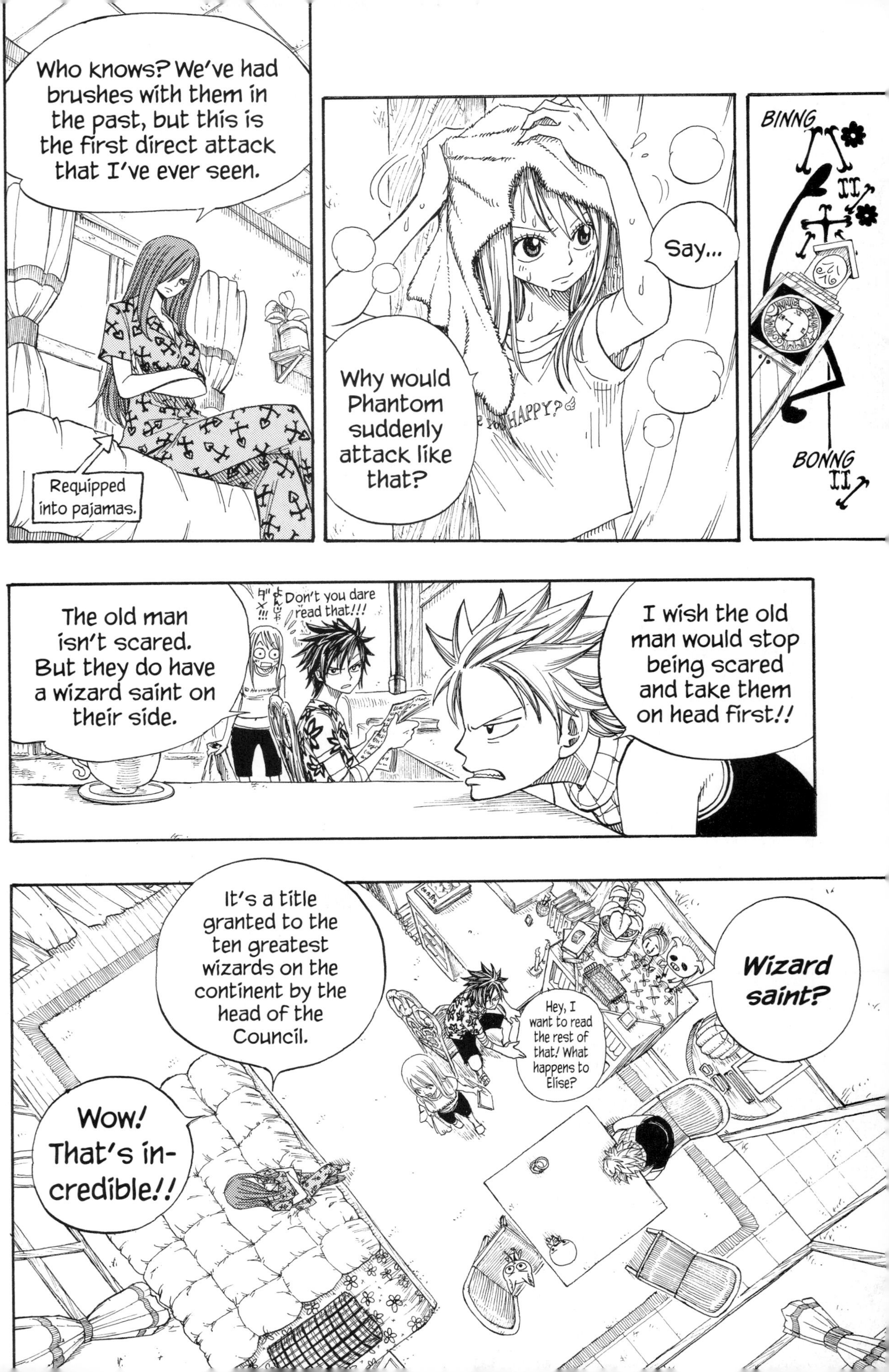
BINNG
BONNG
Say...
Why would Phantom suddenly attack like that?
Who knows? We've had brushes with them in the past, but this is the first direct attack that I've ever seen.
Requipped into pajamas.
I wish the old man would stop being scared and take them on head first!!
Don't you dare read that!!!
The old man isn't scared. But they do have a wizard saint on their side.
Wizard saint?
Hey, I want to read the rest of that! What happens to Elise?
It's a title granted to the ten greatest wizards on the continent by the head of the Council.
Wow! That's in-credible!!

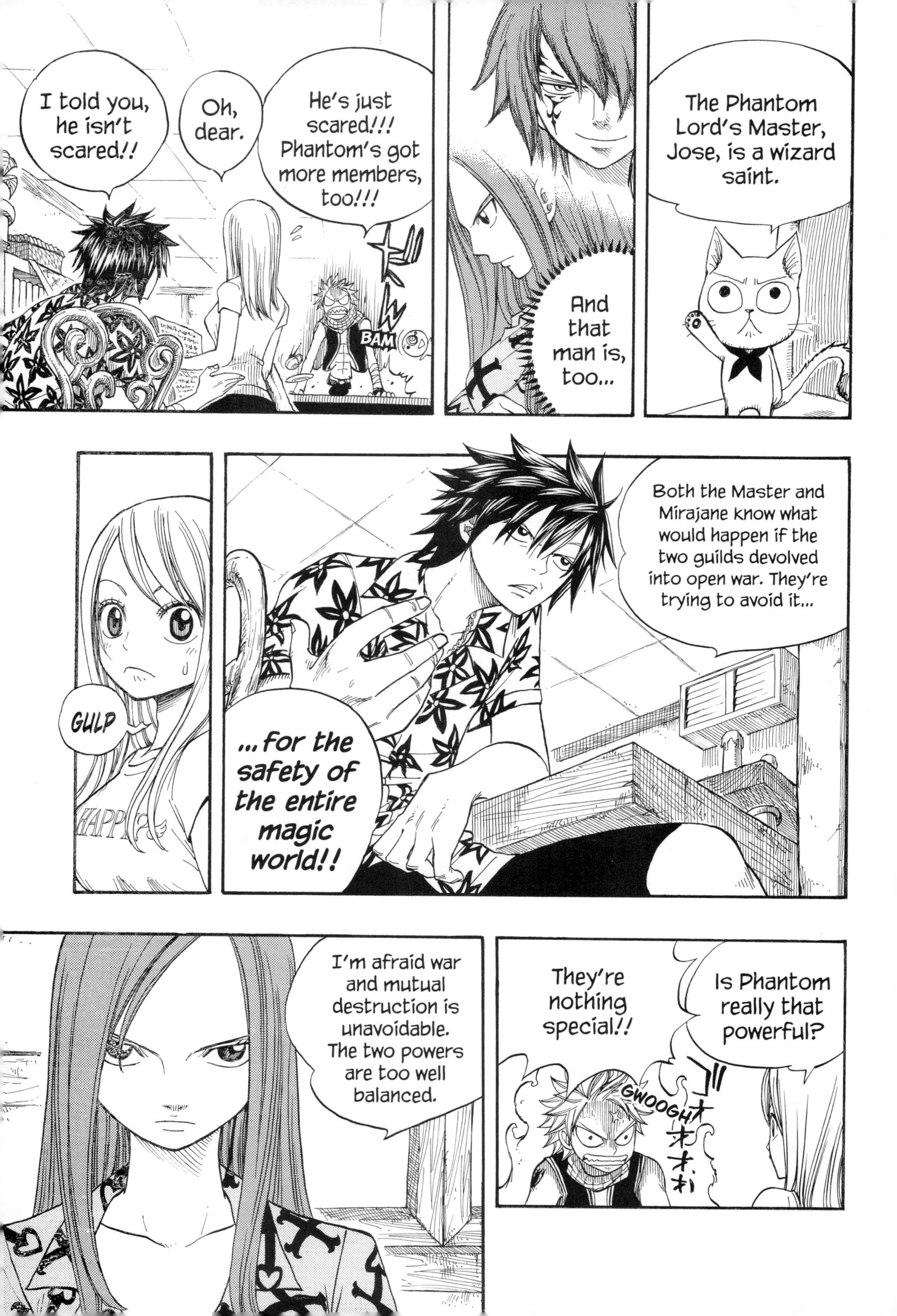
The Phantom Lord's Master, Jose, is a wizard saint.
And that man is, too...
He's just scared!!! Phantom's got more members, too!!!
BAM
Oh, dear.
I told you, he isn't scared!!
Both the Master and Mirajane know what would happen if the two guilds devolved into open war. They're trying to avoid it...
...for the safety of the entire magic world!!
GULP
Is Phantom really that powerful?
They're nothing special!!
GWOOGH
I'm afraid war and mutual destruction is unavoidable. The two powers are too well balanced.

Master Makarov versus the Wizard Saint Master Jose, who is said to be his match in magical power.

Also, they have four S-Class members, the Element 4.

And the one that will cause the most trouble is Kurogane Gajeel...

...the man who probably instigated the attack on our guild...

...the iron dragon slayer.

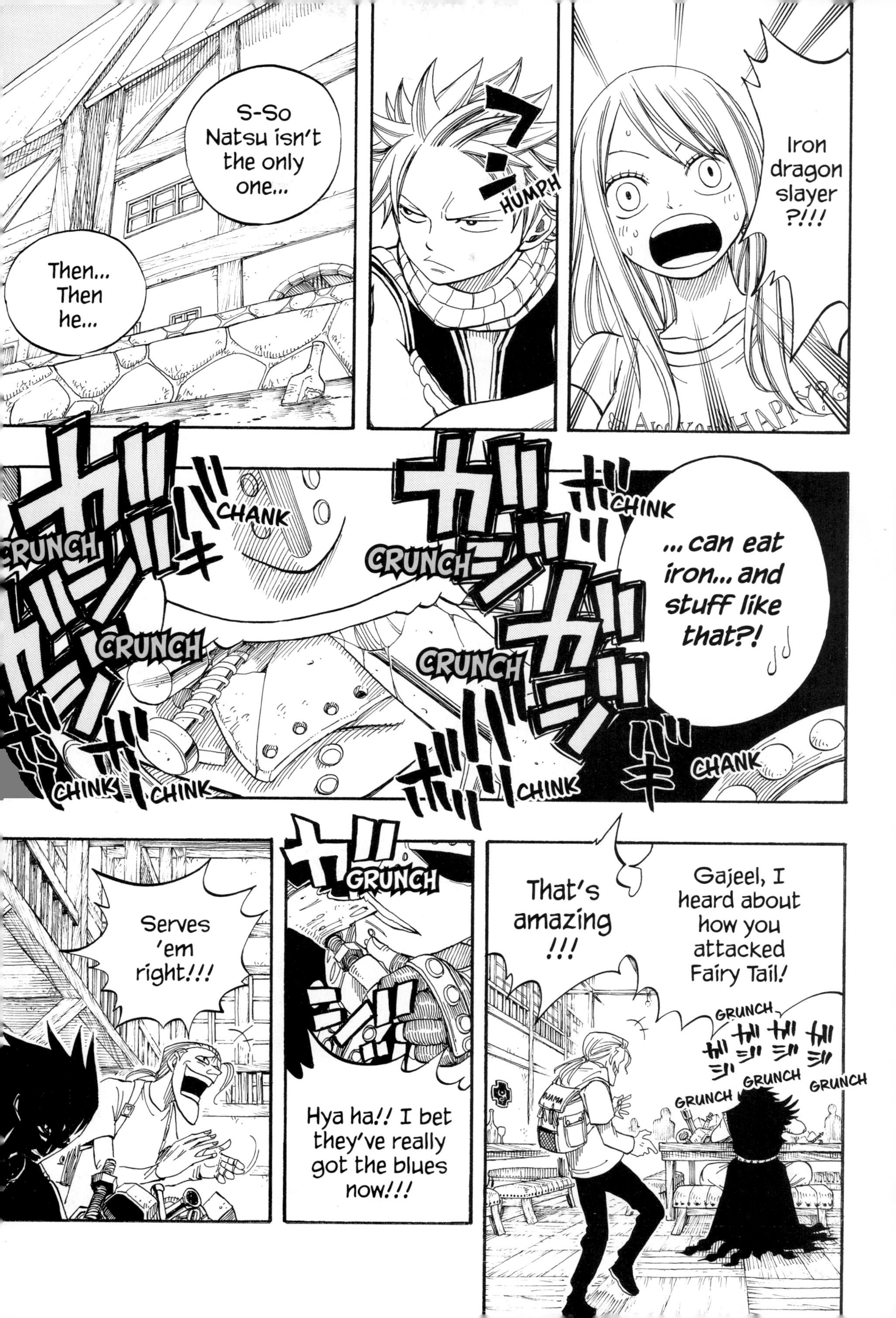
Iron dragon slayer ?!!!
HUMPH
S-So Natsu isn't the only one...
Then... Then he...
CHINK
...can eat iron... and stuff like that?!
CRUNCH
CRUNCH
CHANK
CHINK
CHANK
CRUNCH
CRUNCH
CHINK
CHINK
Gajeel, I heard about how you attacked Fairy Tail!
That's amazing !!!
GRUNCH
GRUNCH
GRUNCH
GRUNCH
GRUNCH
Hya ha!! I bet they've really got the blues now!!!
Serves 'em right!!!

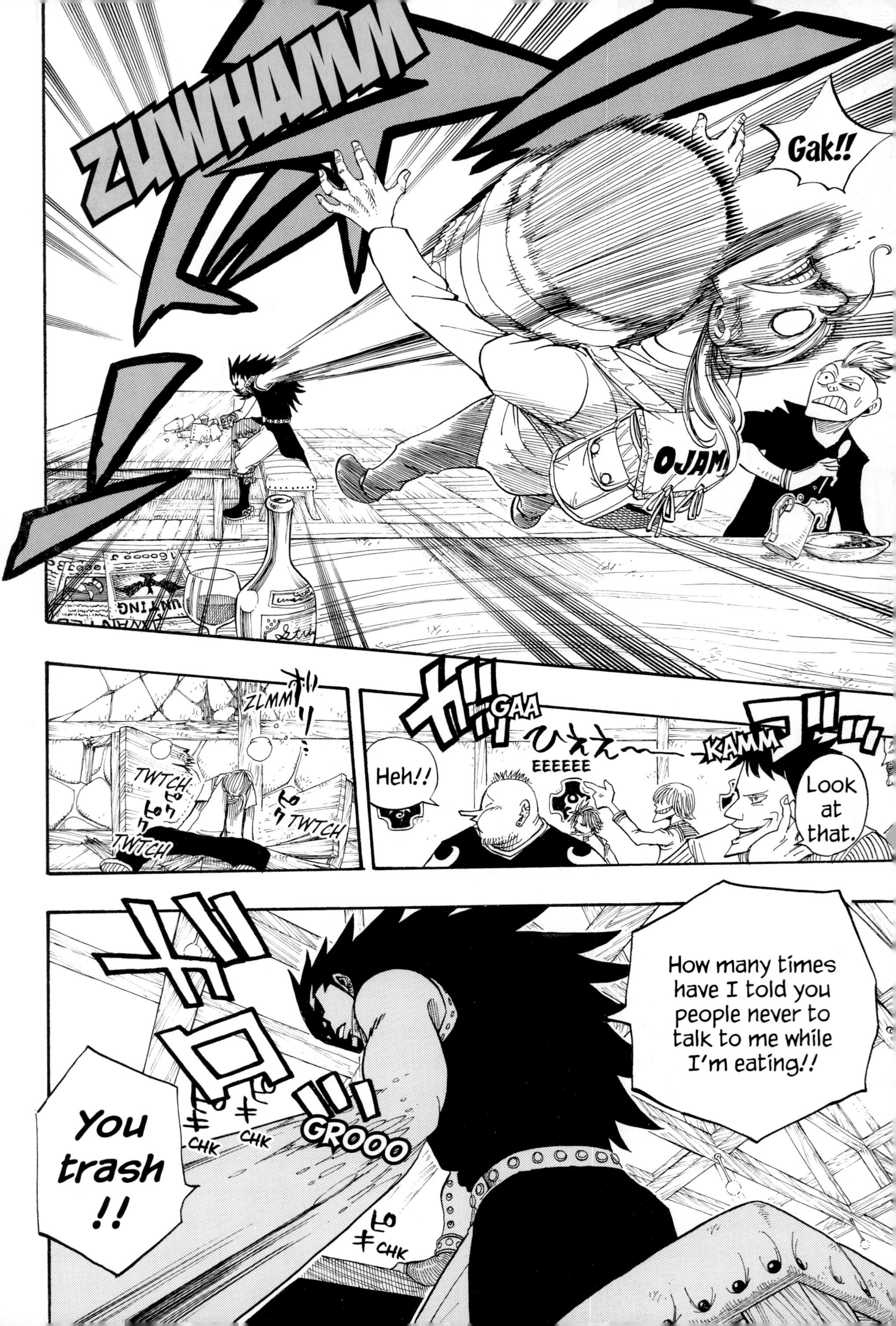
ZUWHAMM
Gak!!
OJAM
KAMM
Look at that.
ひえぇ~
EEEEEE
GAA
Heh!!
ZLMM
TWTCH
TWTCH
TWTCH
How many times have I told you people never to talk to me while I'm eating!!
GROOO
CHK
CHK
CHK
You trash!!

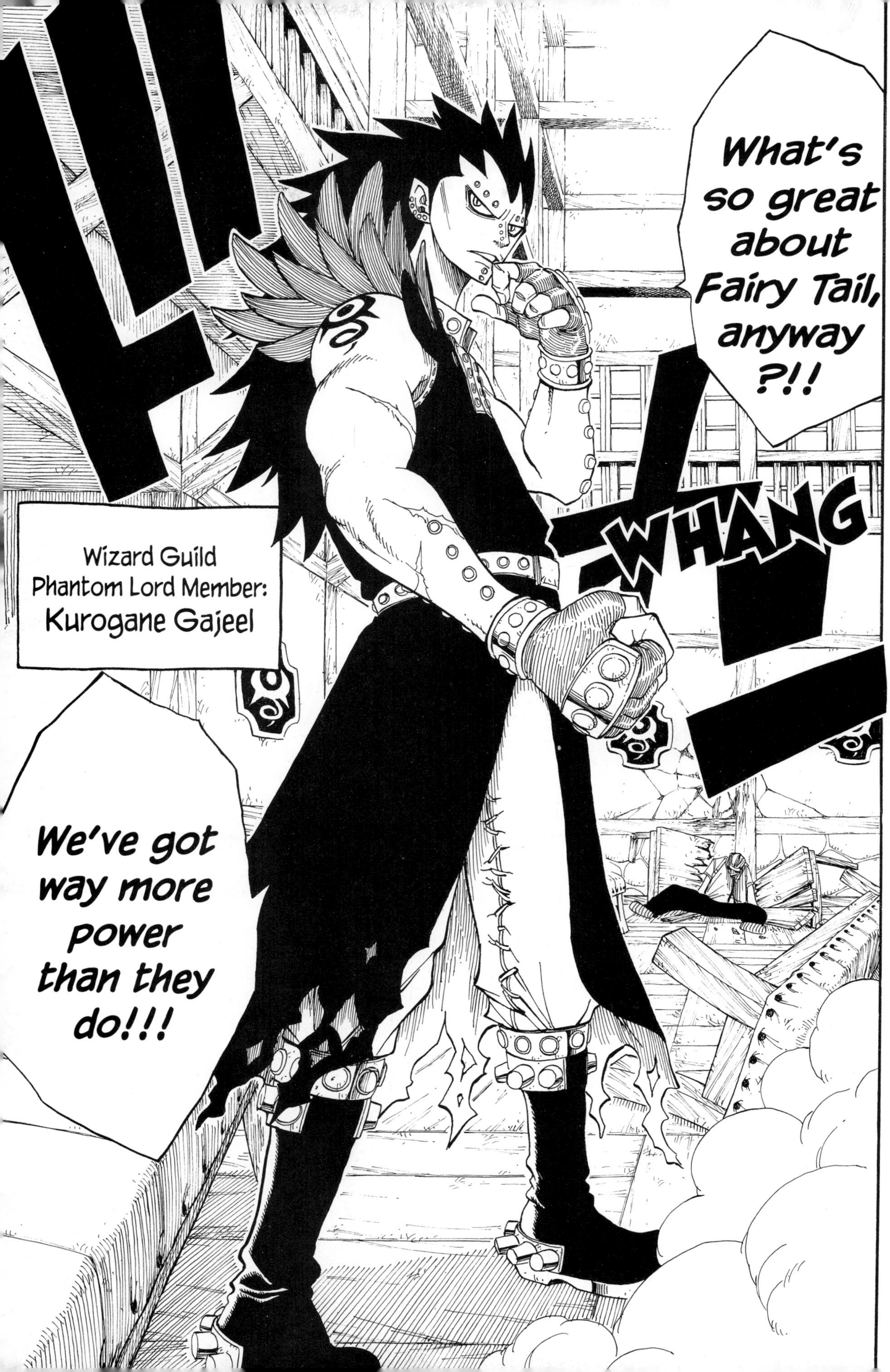
What's so great about Fairy Tail, anyway ?!!
WHANG
Wizard Guild Phantom Lord Member: Kurogane Gajeel
We've got way more power than they do!!!

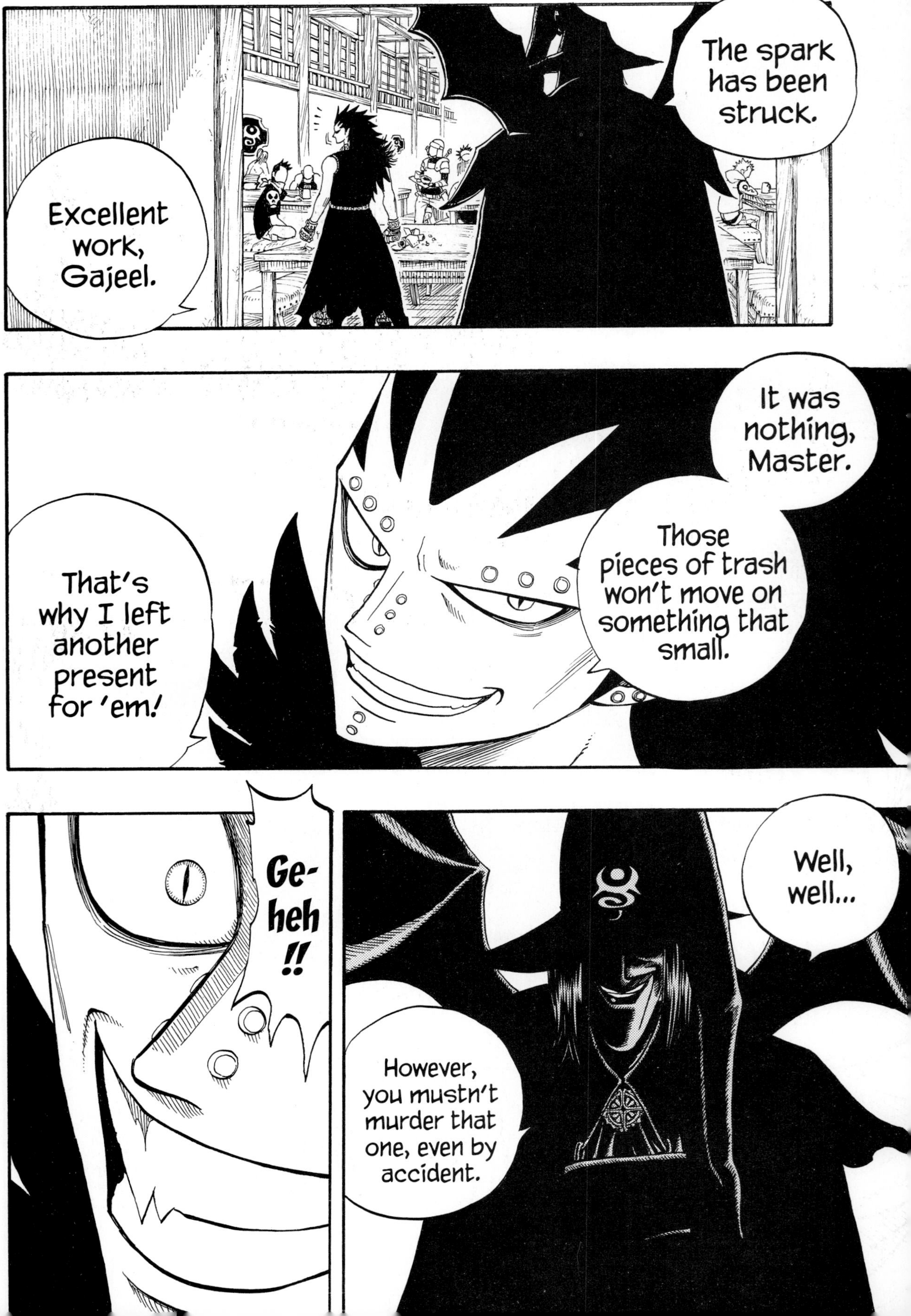
The spark has been struck.
Excellent work, Gajeel.
It was nothing, Master.
Those pieces of trash won't move on something that small.
That's why I left another present for 'em!
Well, well...
However, you mustn't murder that one, even by accident.
Ge-heh!!

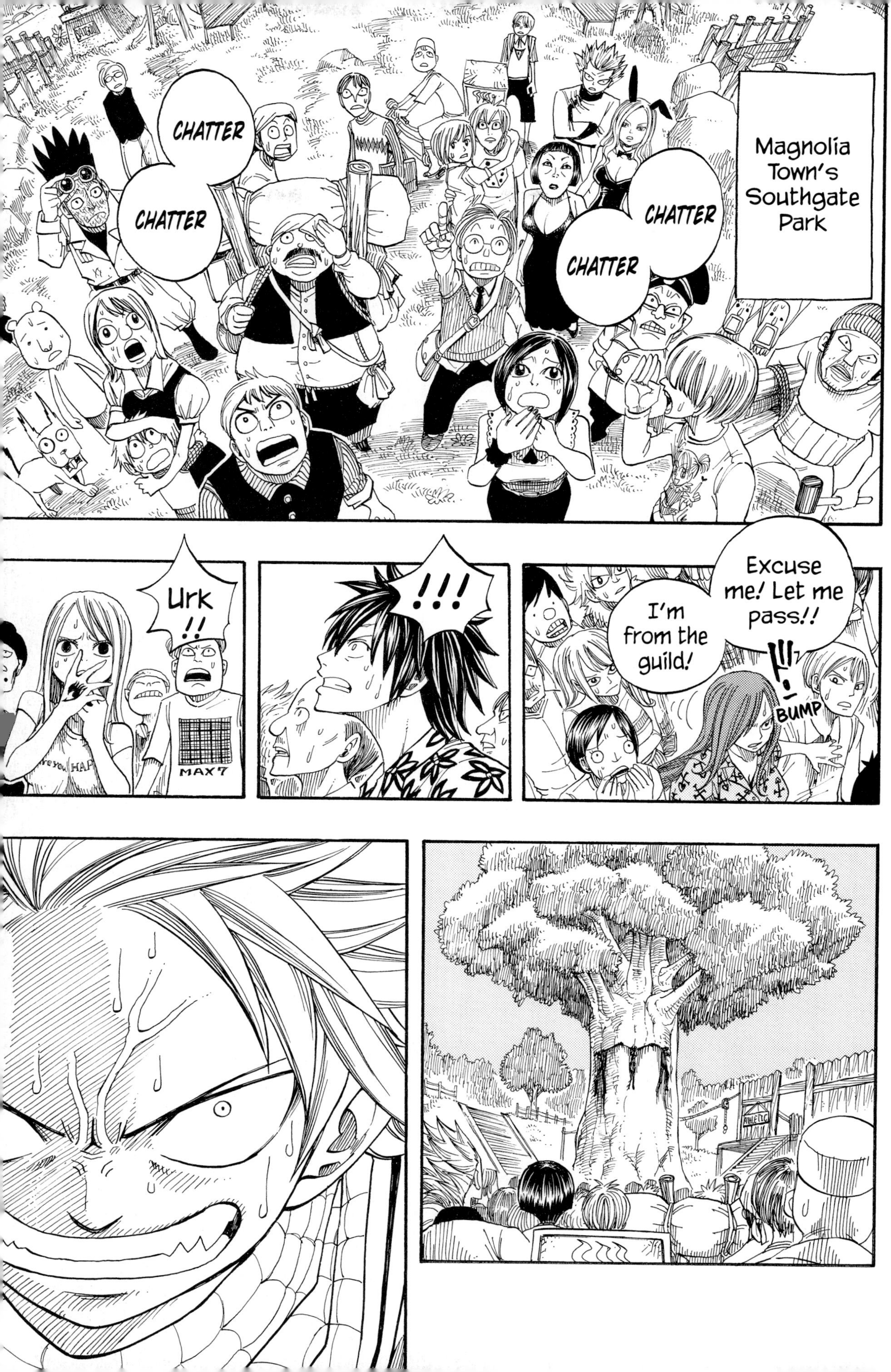
Magnolia Town's Southgate Park
CHATTER
CHATTER
CHATTER
CHATTER
Excuse me! Let me pass!!
I'm from the guild!
BUMP
!!!
Urk !!

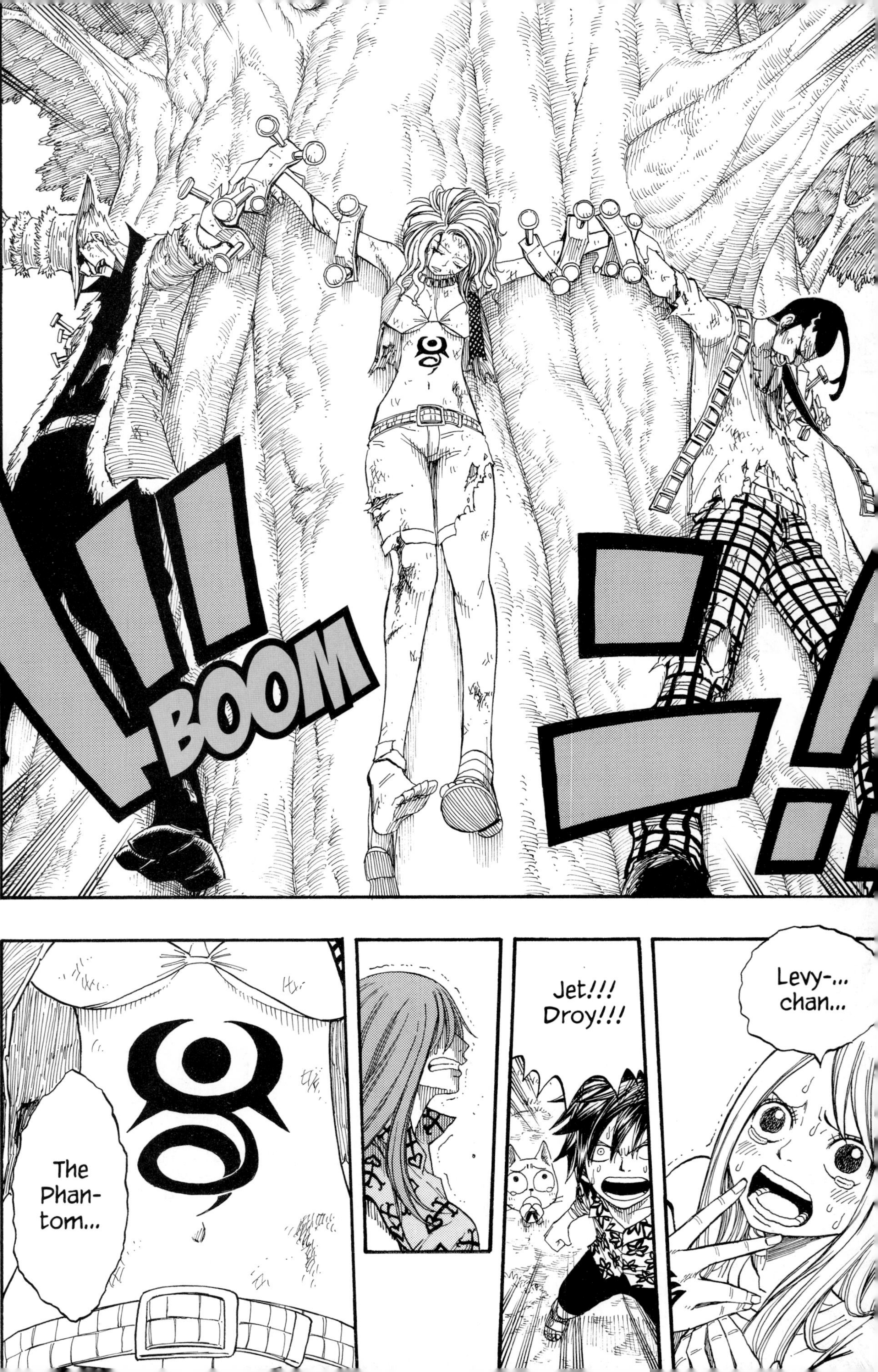
BOOM
Levy-... chan...
Jet!!! Droy!!!
The Phan-
tom...

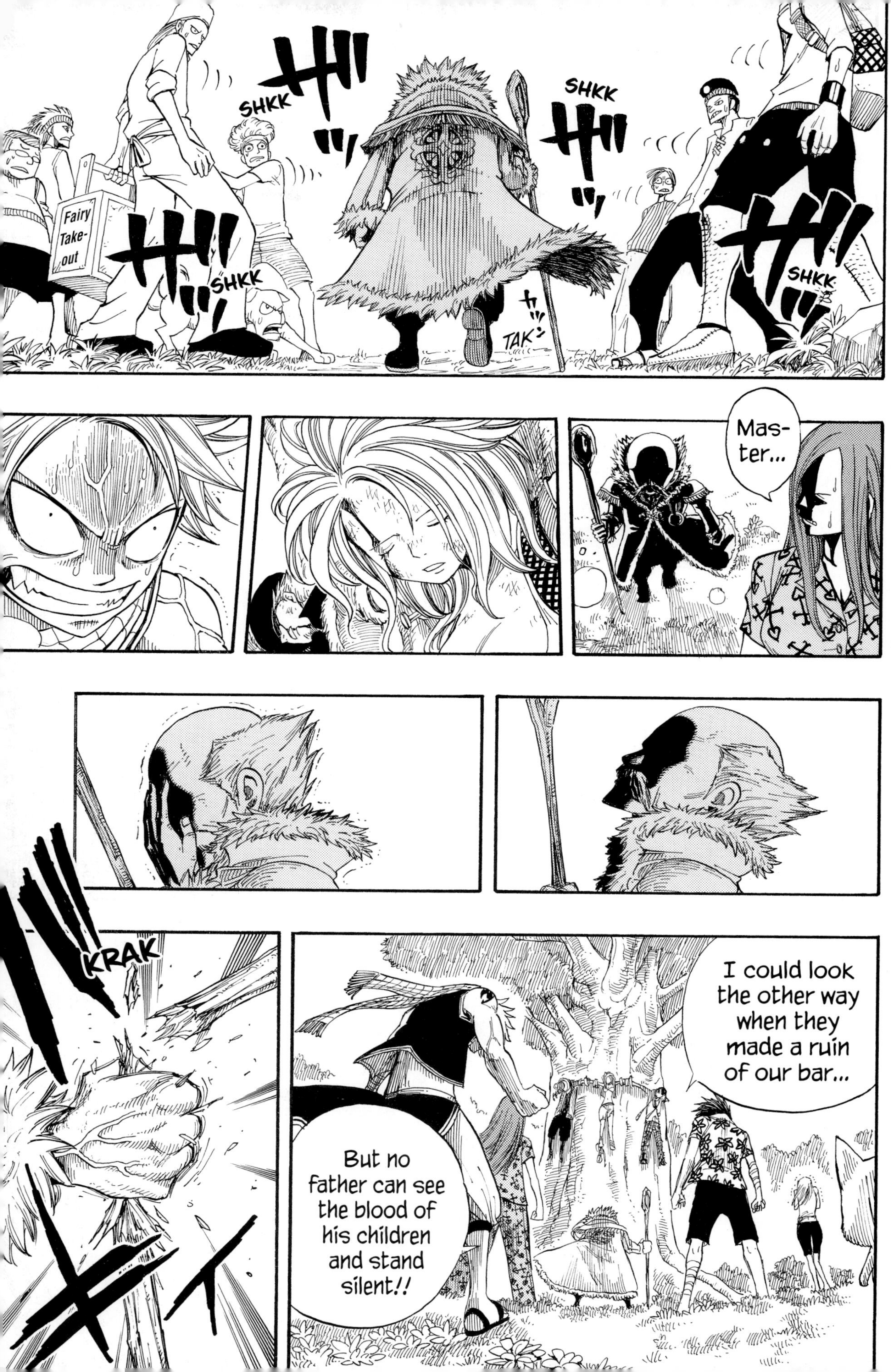
SHKK
SHKK
TAK
Fairy Take-out
SHKK
SHKK
Mas-ter...
I could look the other way when they made a ruin of our bar...
But no father can see the blood of his children and stand silent!!
KRAK

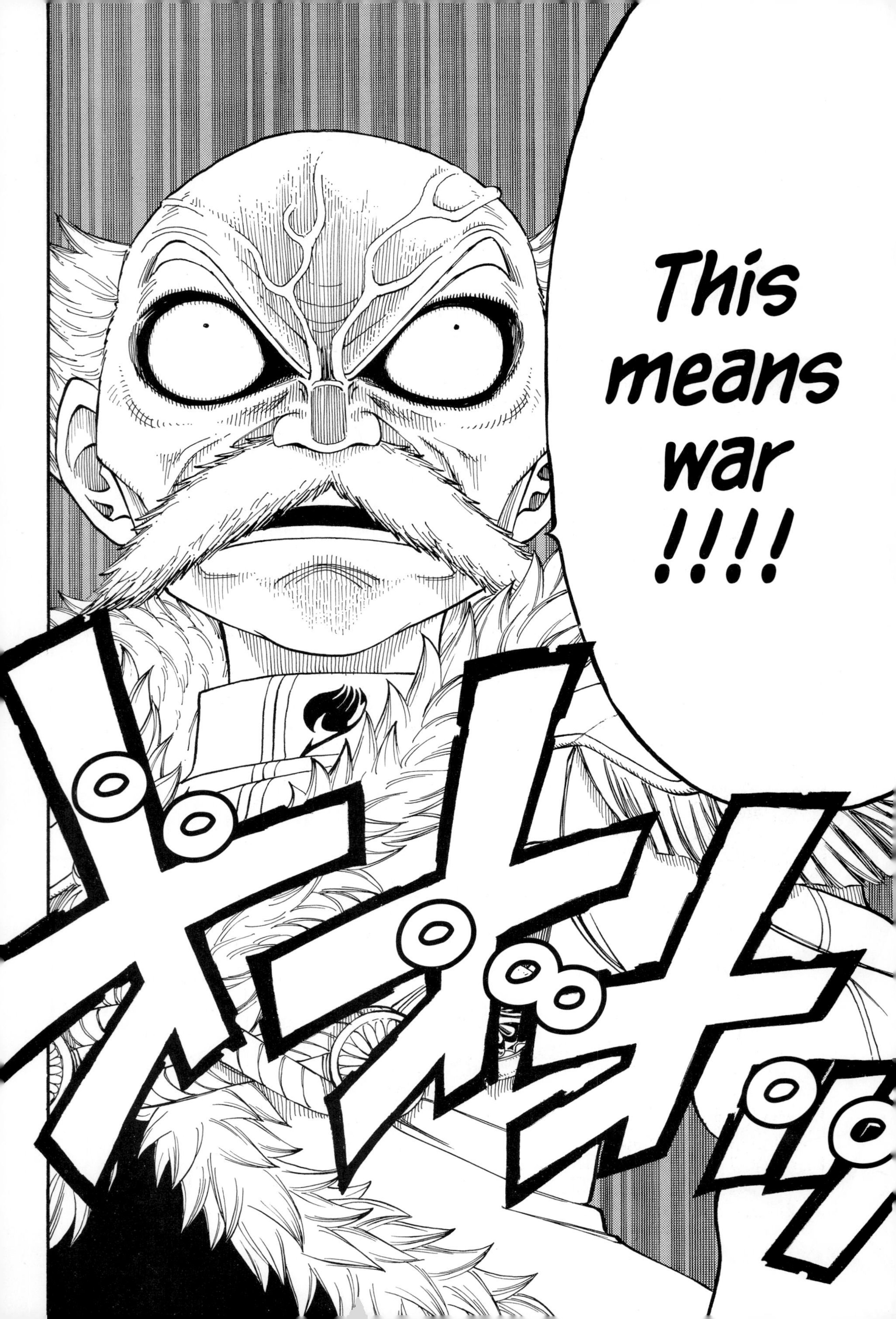
This means war !!!!
ドパーン

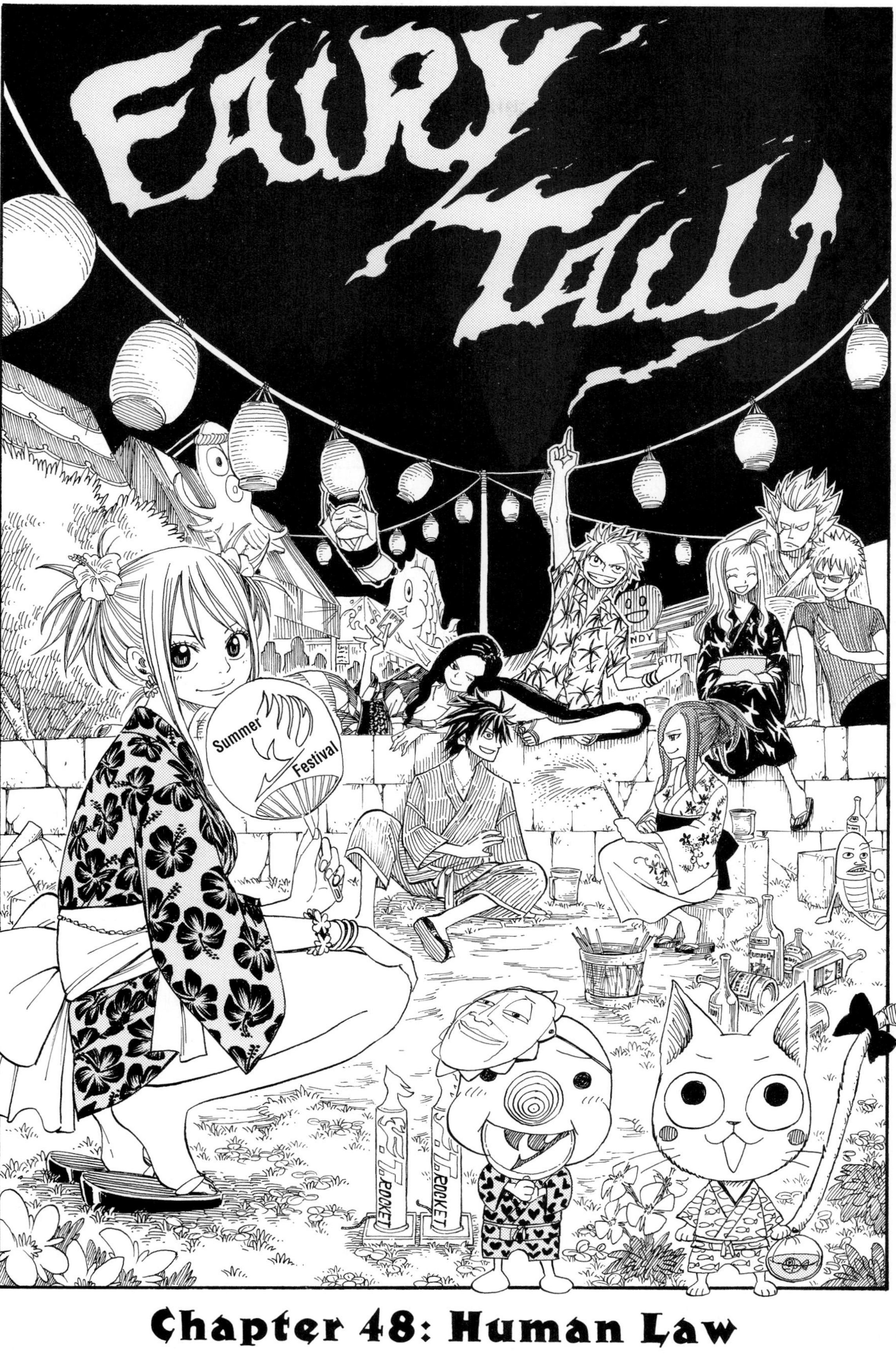
FAIRY TAIL
Summer
Festival

Chapter 48: Human Law

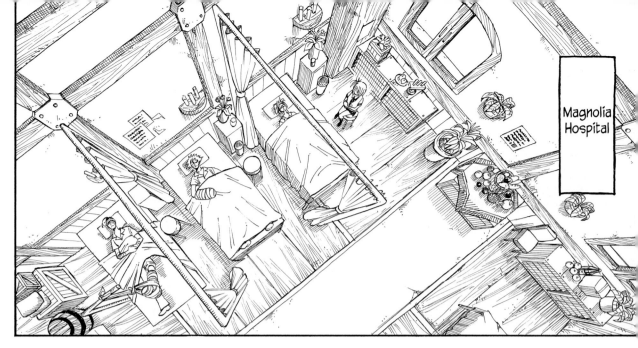

Magnolia Hospital

Droy...

Jet...

Levy-chan...

They sure can do some awful things...

These Phantom wizards...

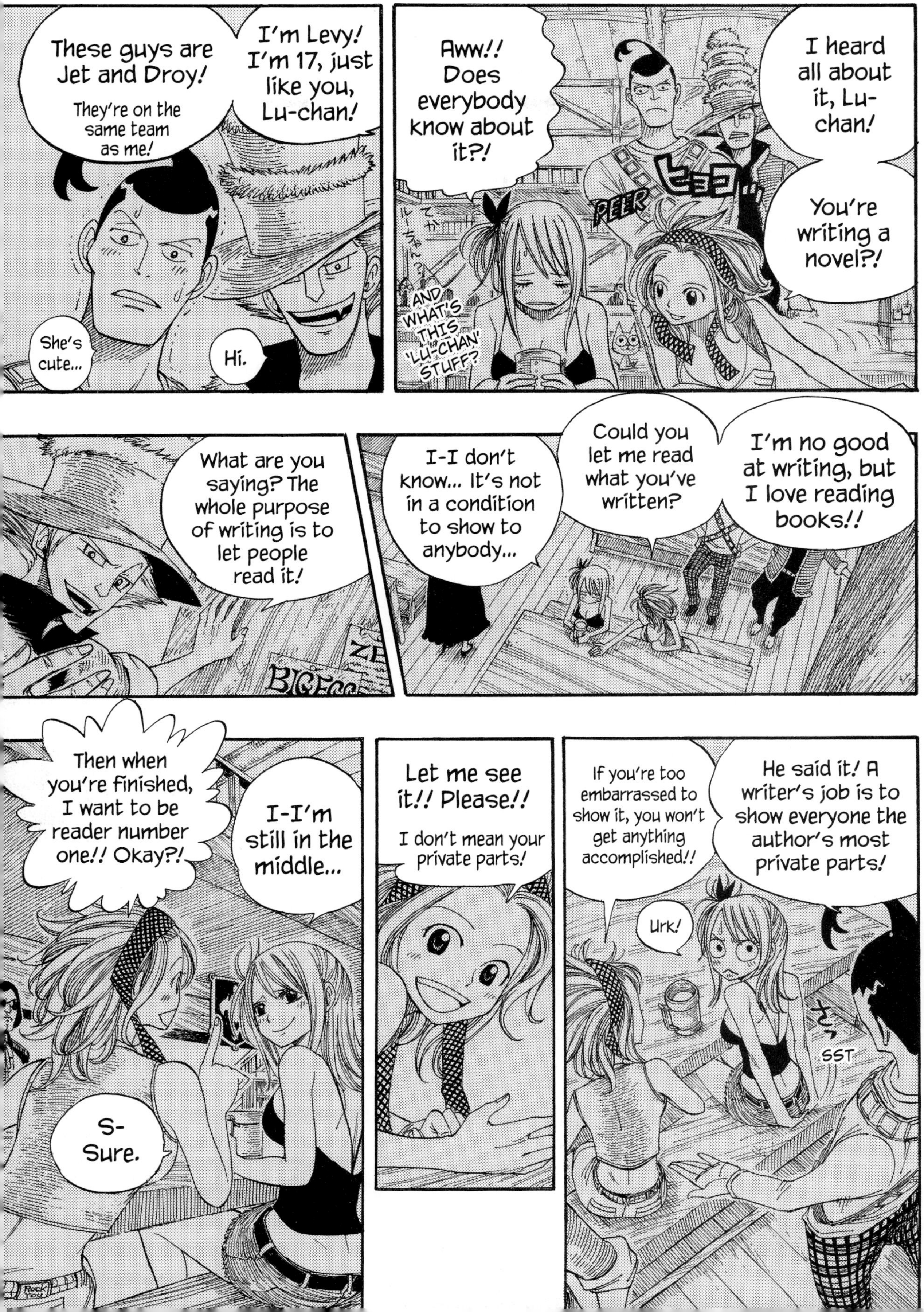
I heard all about it, Lu-chan!
You're writing a novel?!
PEER
Aww!! Does everybody know about it?!
AND WHAT'S THIS 'LU-CHAN' STUFF?
I'm Levy! I'm 17, just like you, Lu-chan!
These guys are Jet and Droy!
They're on the same team as me!
Hi.
She's cute...
I'm no good at writing, but I love reading books!!
Could you let me read what you've written?
I-I don't know... It's not in a condition to show to anybody...
What are you saying? The whole purpose of writing is to let people read it!
He said it! A writer's job is to show everyone the author's most private parts!
If you're too embarrassed to show it, you won't get anything accomplished!!
Urk!
SST
Let me see it!! Please!!
I don't mean your private parts!
Then when you're finished, I want to be reader number one!! Okay?!
I-I'm still in the middle...
S-Sure.

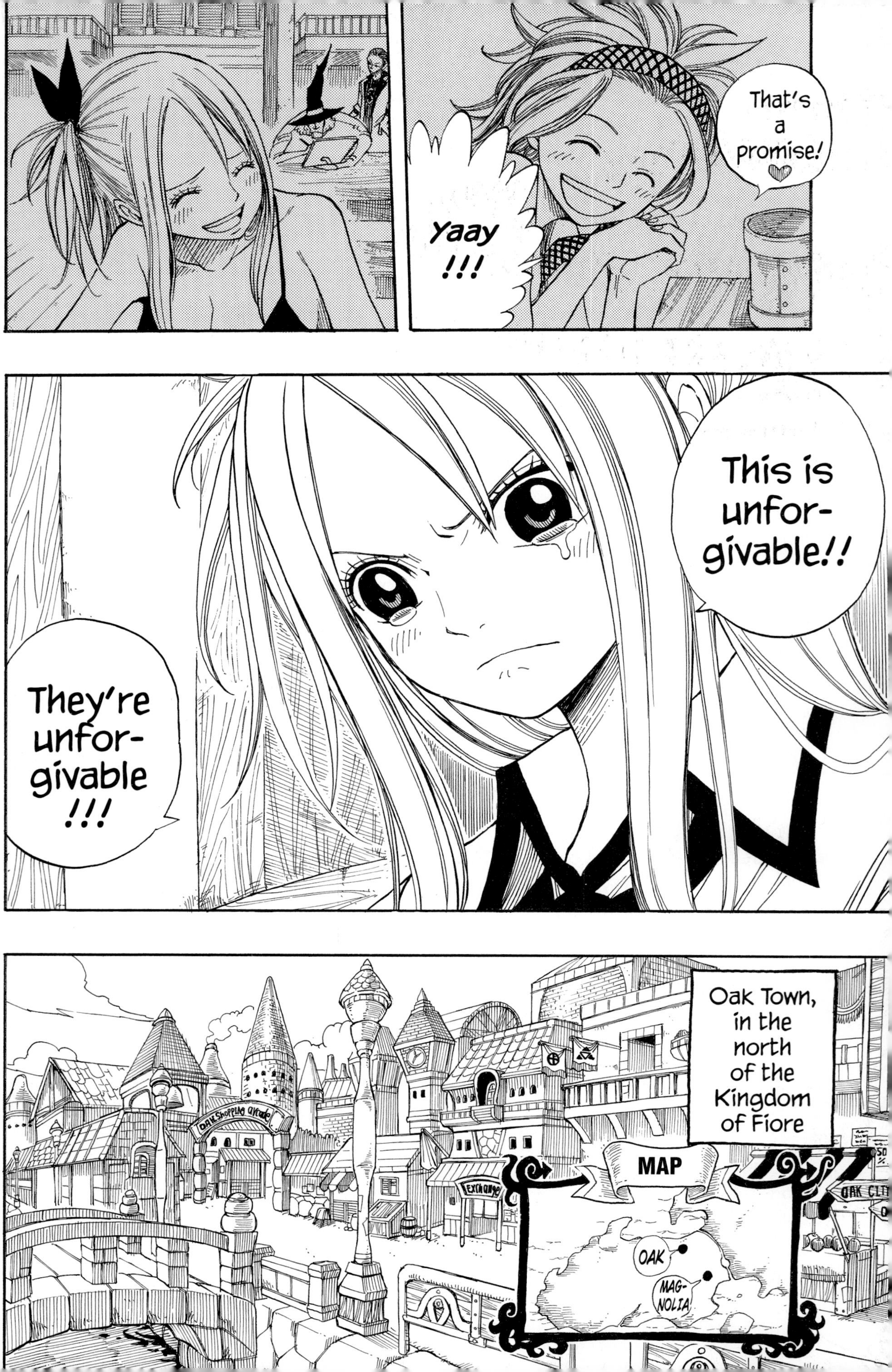
That's a promise!
Yaay!!!
This is unforgivable!!
They're unforgivable!!!
Oak Town, in the north of the Kingdom of Fiore
MAP
OAK
MAGNOLIA
OAK Shopping arcade
Exchange

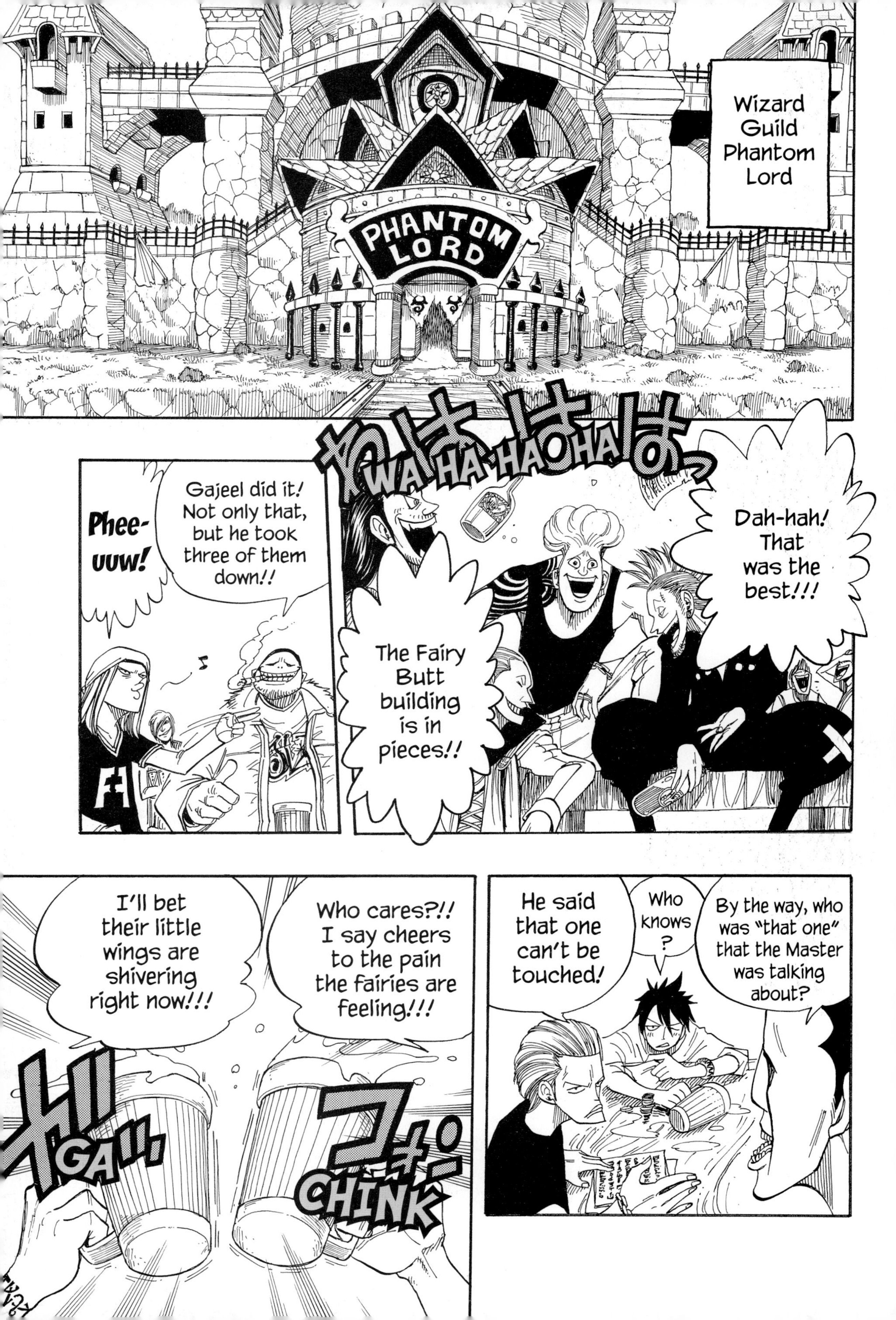
Wizard Guild Phantom Lord
PHANTOM LORD
WA HA HA HA HA
Dah-hah! That was the best!!!
The Fairy Butt building is in pieces!!
Gajeel did it! Not only that, but he took three of them down!!
Phee-uuw!
By the way, who was "that one" that the Master was talking about?
Who knows?
He said that one can't be touched!
Who cares?!! I say cheers to the pain the fairies are feeling!!!
I'll bet their little wings are shivering right now!!!
CHINK
GA

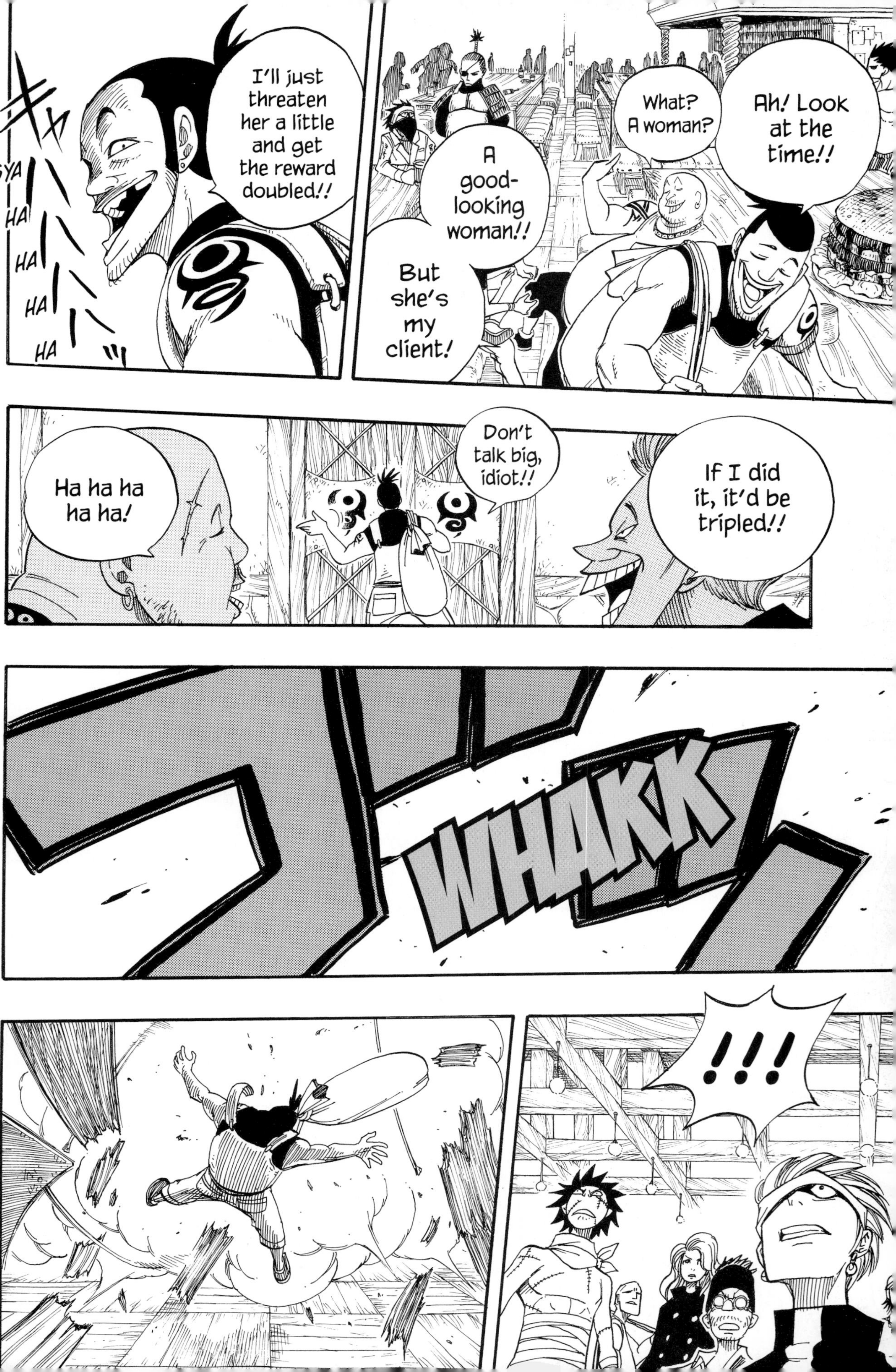
Ah! Look at the time!!
What? A woman?
A good-looking woman!!
But she's my client!
I'll just threaten her a little and get the reward doubled!!
GYA HA HA HA HA
If I did it, it'd be tripled!!
Don't talk big, idiot!!
Ha ha ha ha ha!
WHAKK
!!!

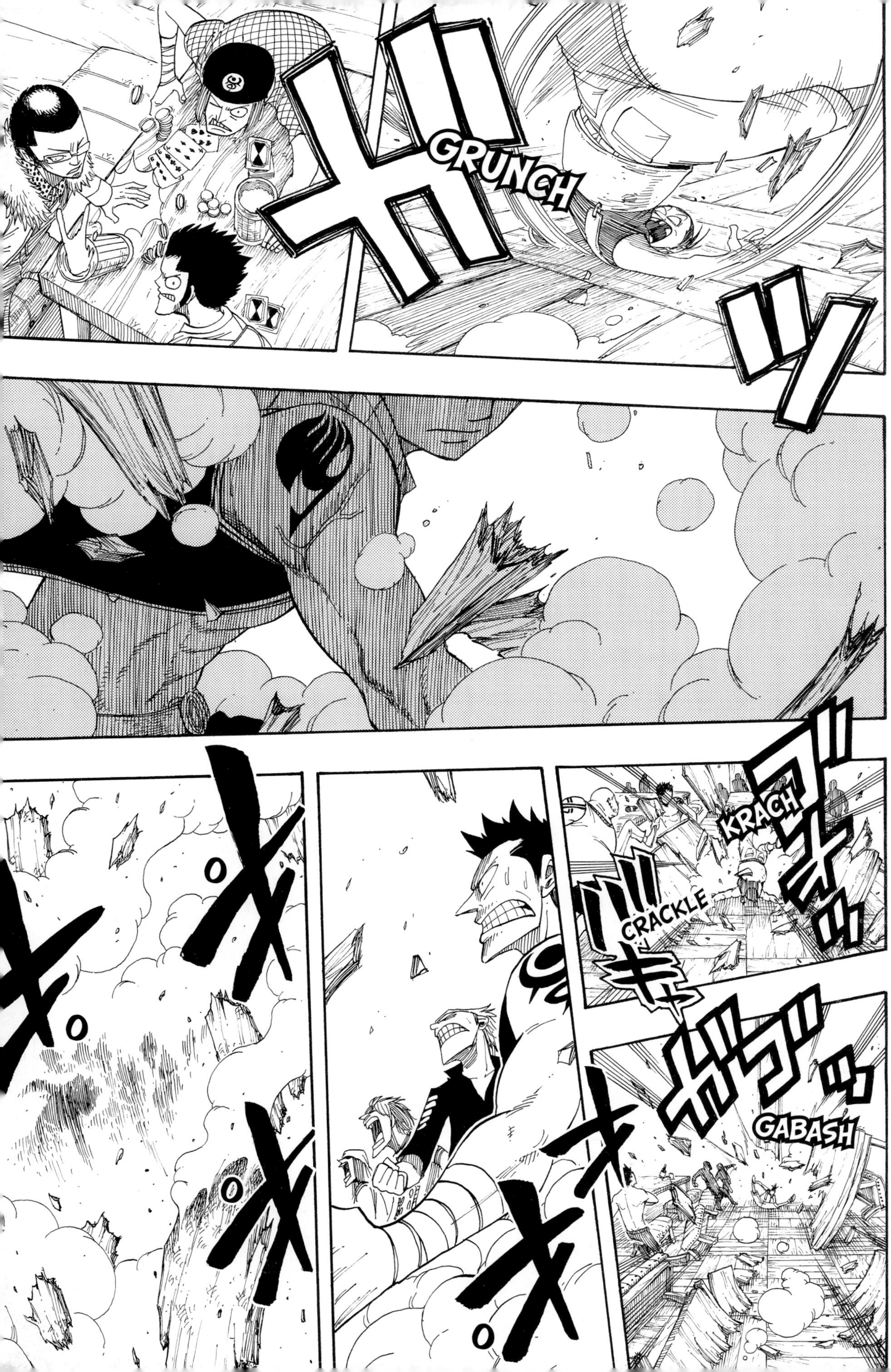
GRUNCH
KRACH
CRACKLE
GABASH

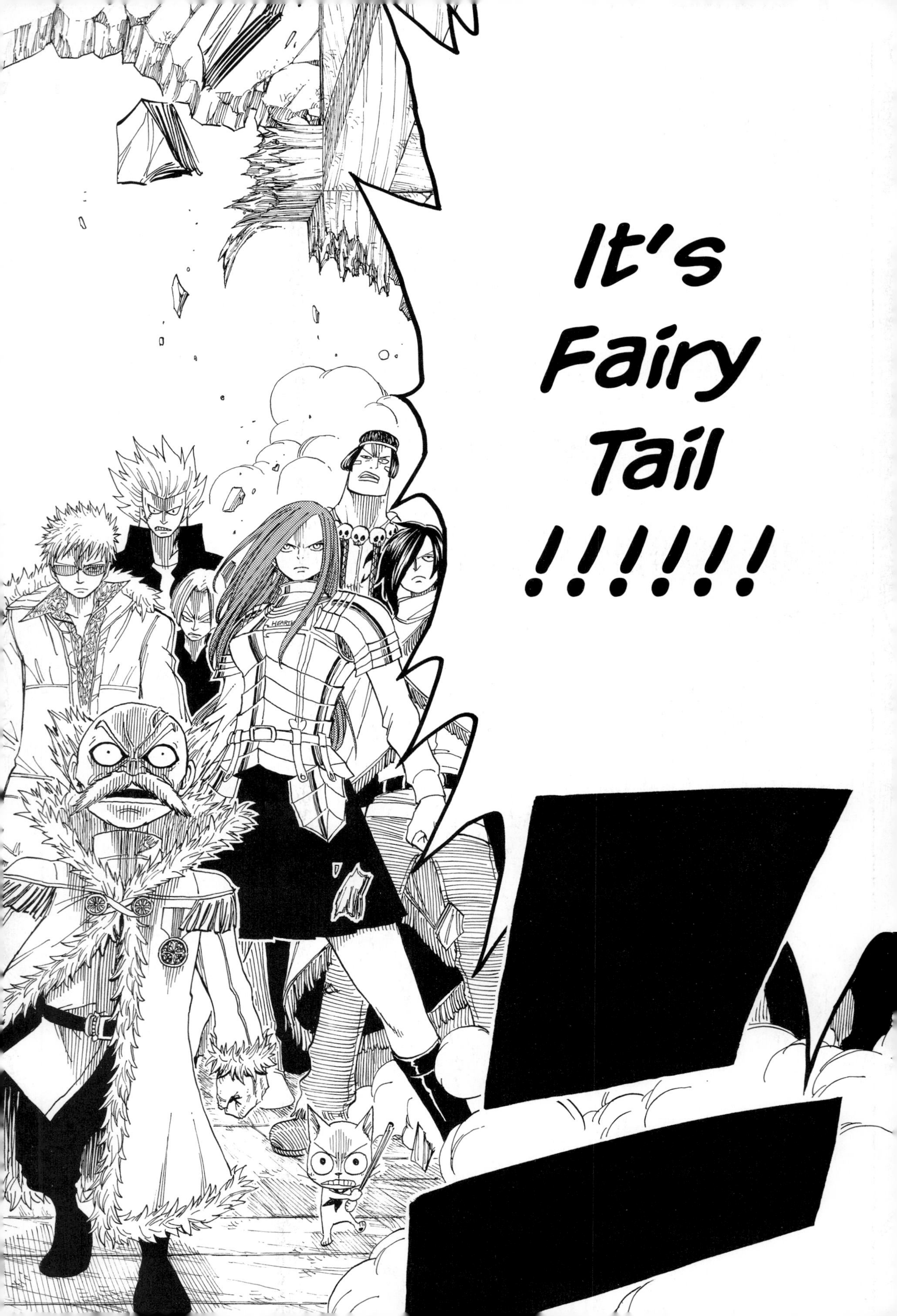
It's Fairy Tail !!!!!!

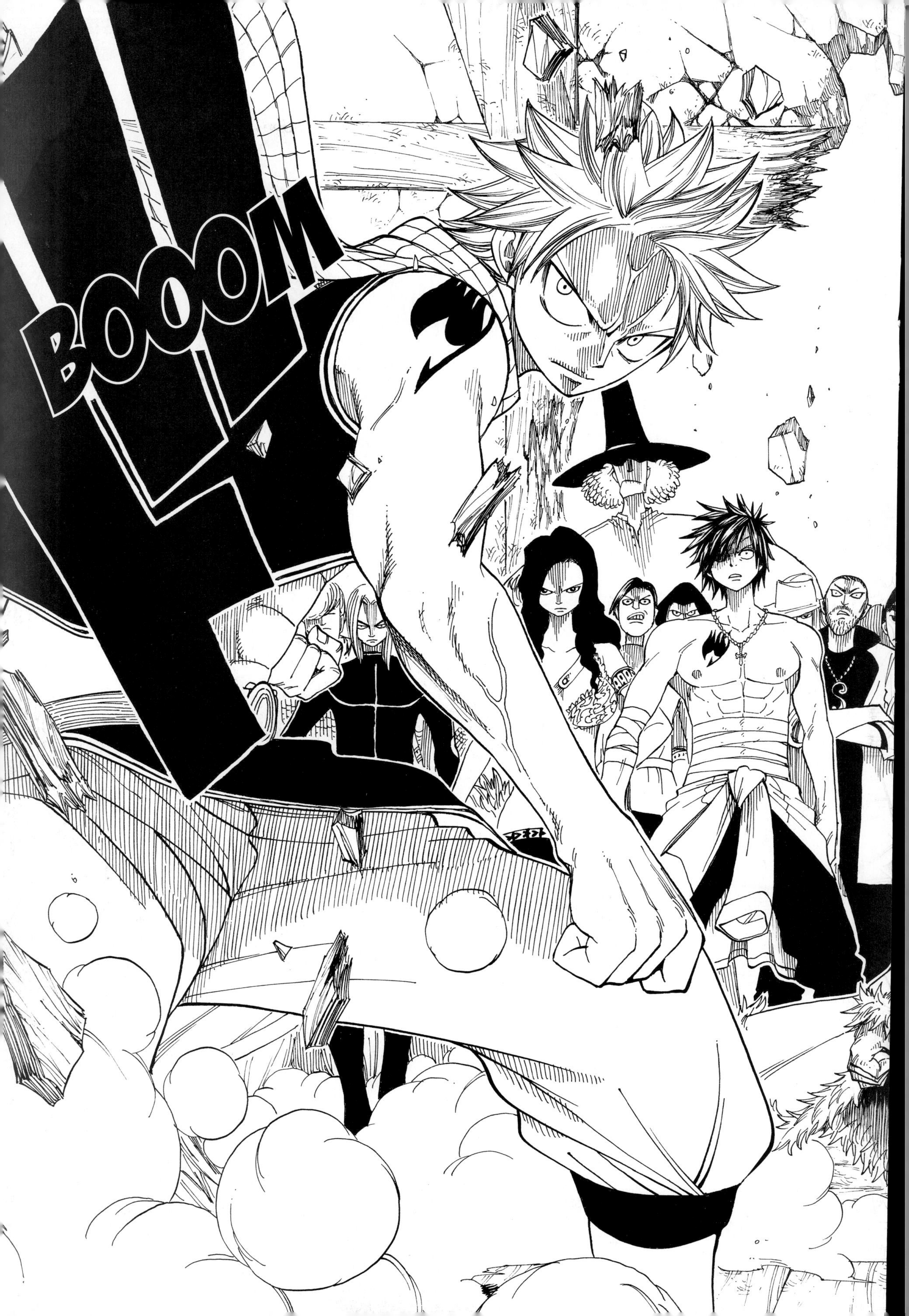
BOOOM

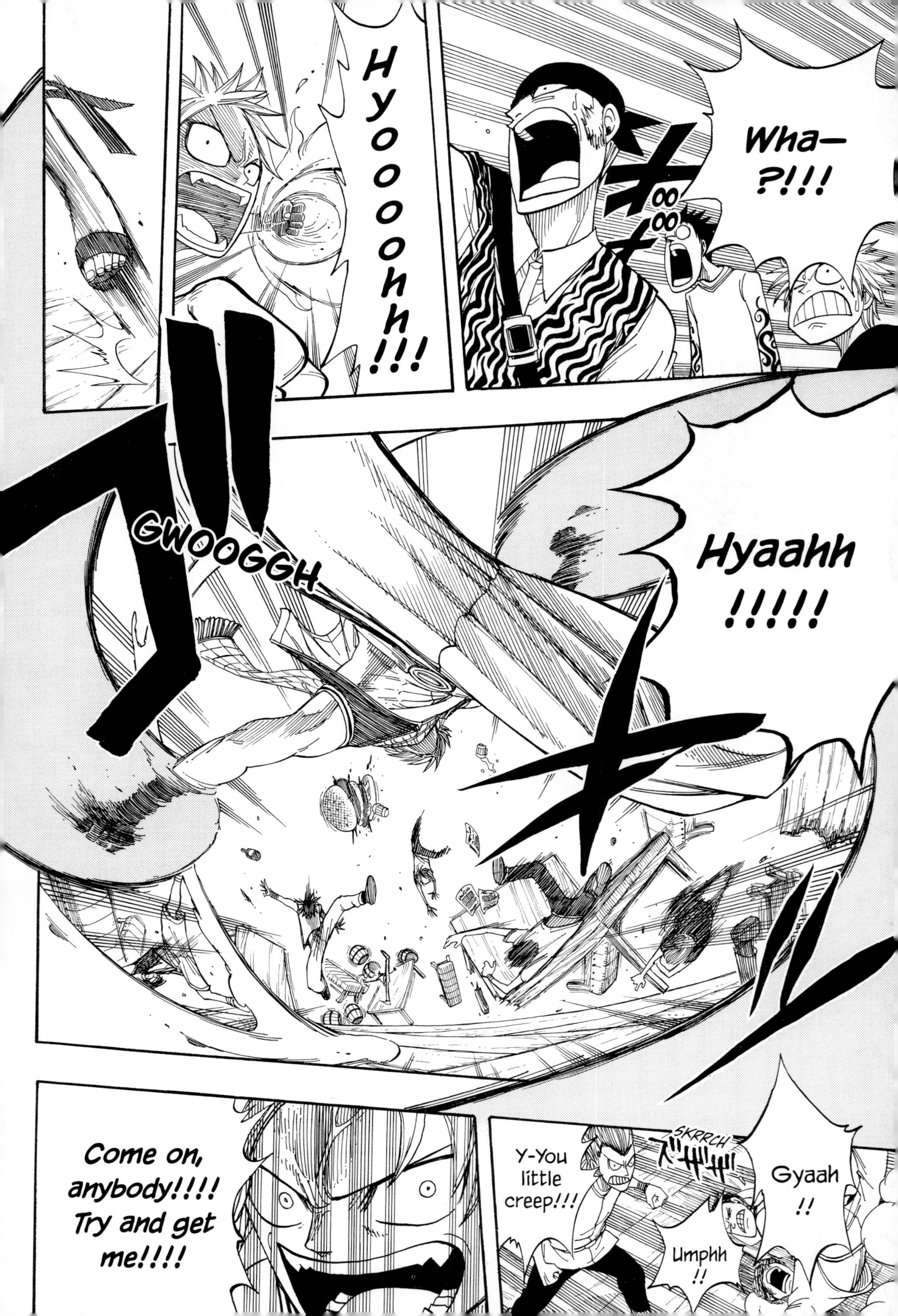
Wha—?!!!
Hyoooooohh!!!
Hyaahh!!!!!
GWOOGGH
Gyaah!!
SKRRCH
Y-You little creep!!!
Umphh!!
Come on, anybody!!!! Try and get me!!!!

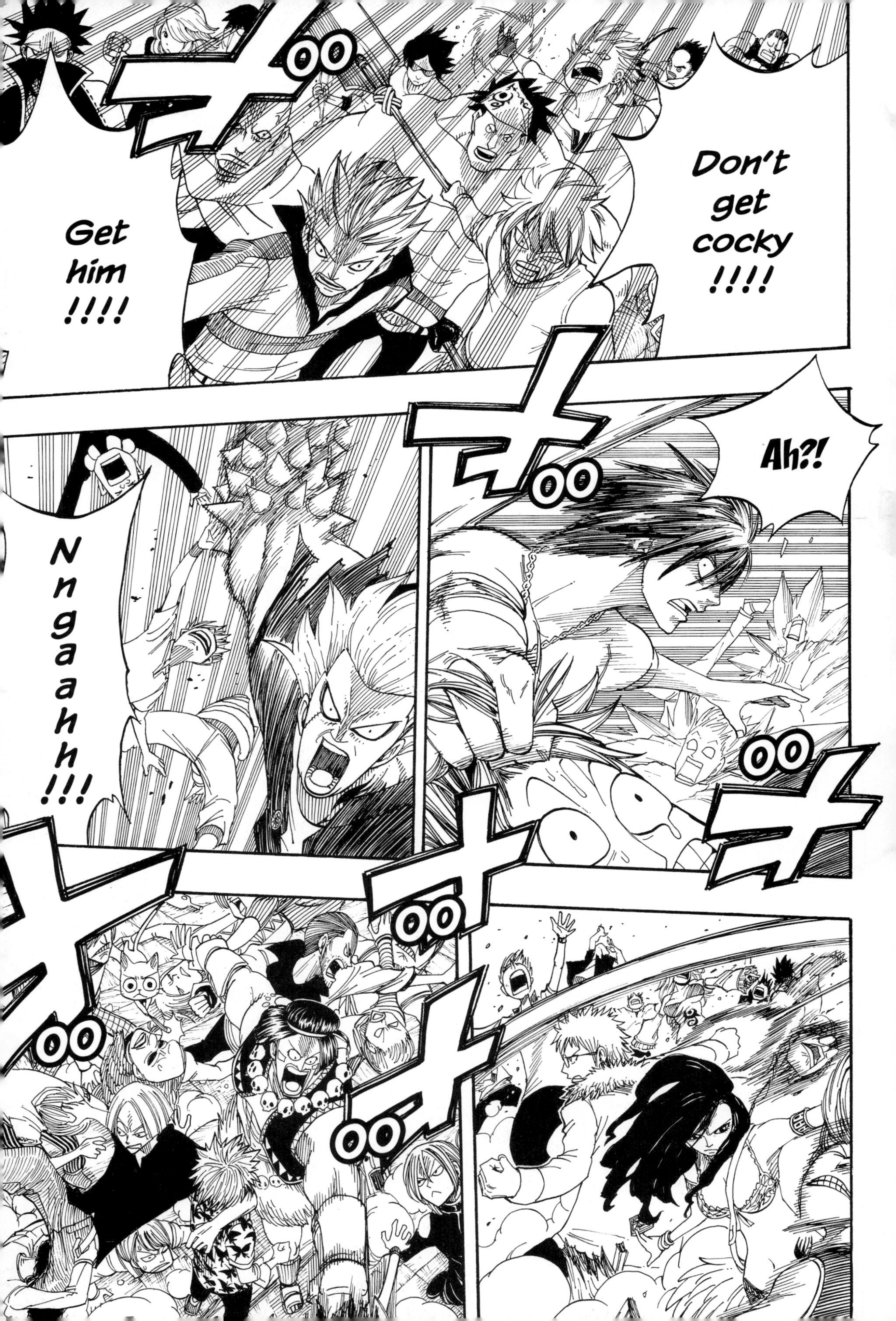
Don't get cocky!!!!
Get him!!!!
Ah?!
Nngaahh!!!

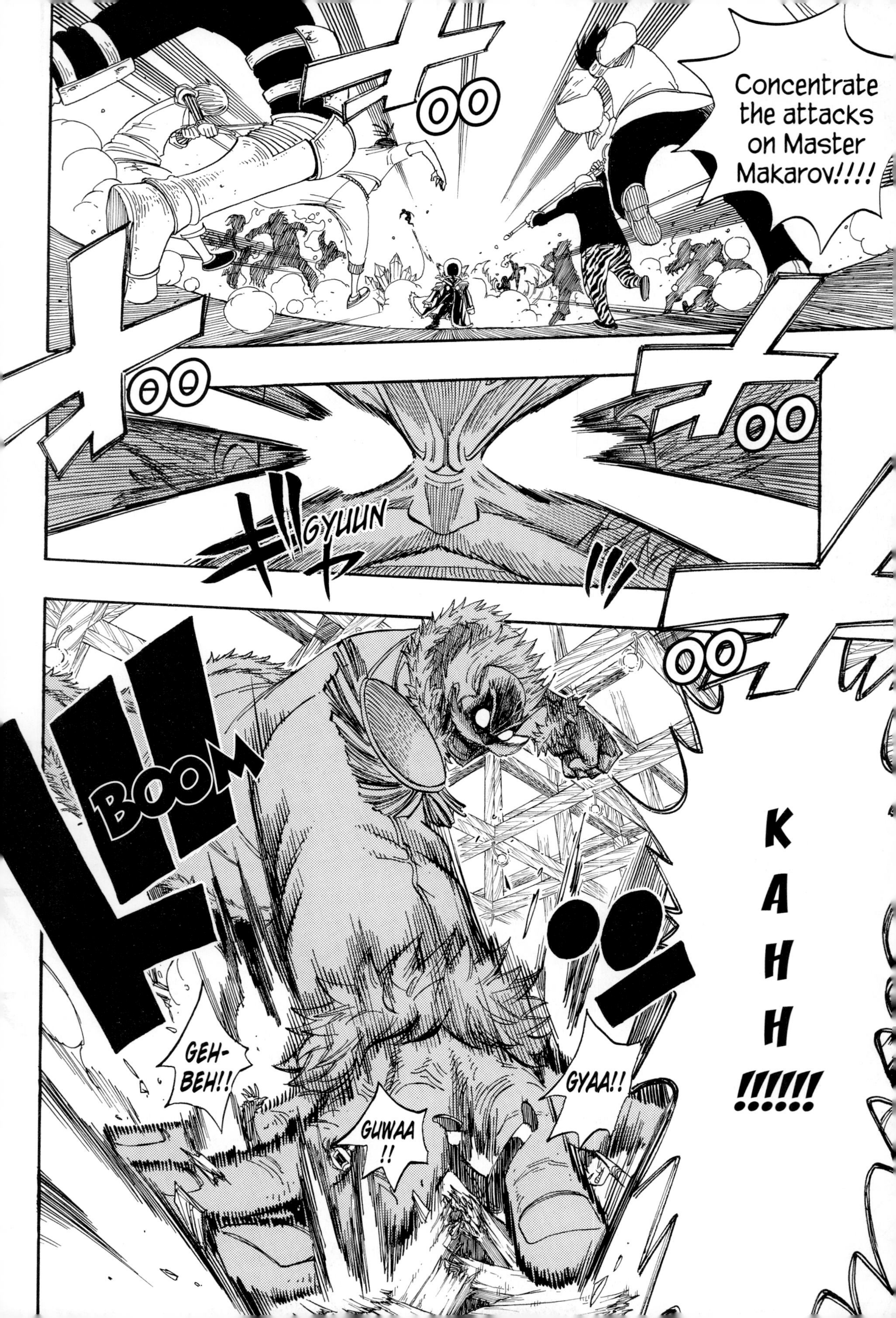
Concentrate the attacks on Master Makarov!!!!
GYUUN
BOOM
KAHH!!!!!!
GYAA!!
GEH-BEH!!
GUWAA!!

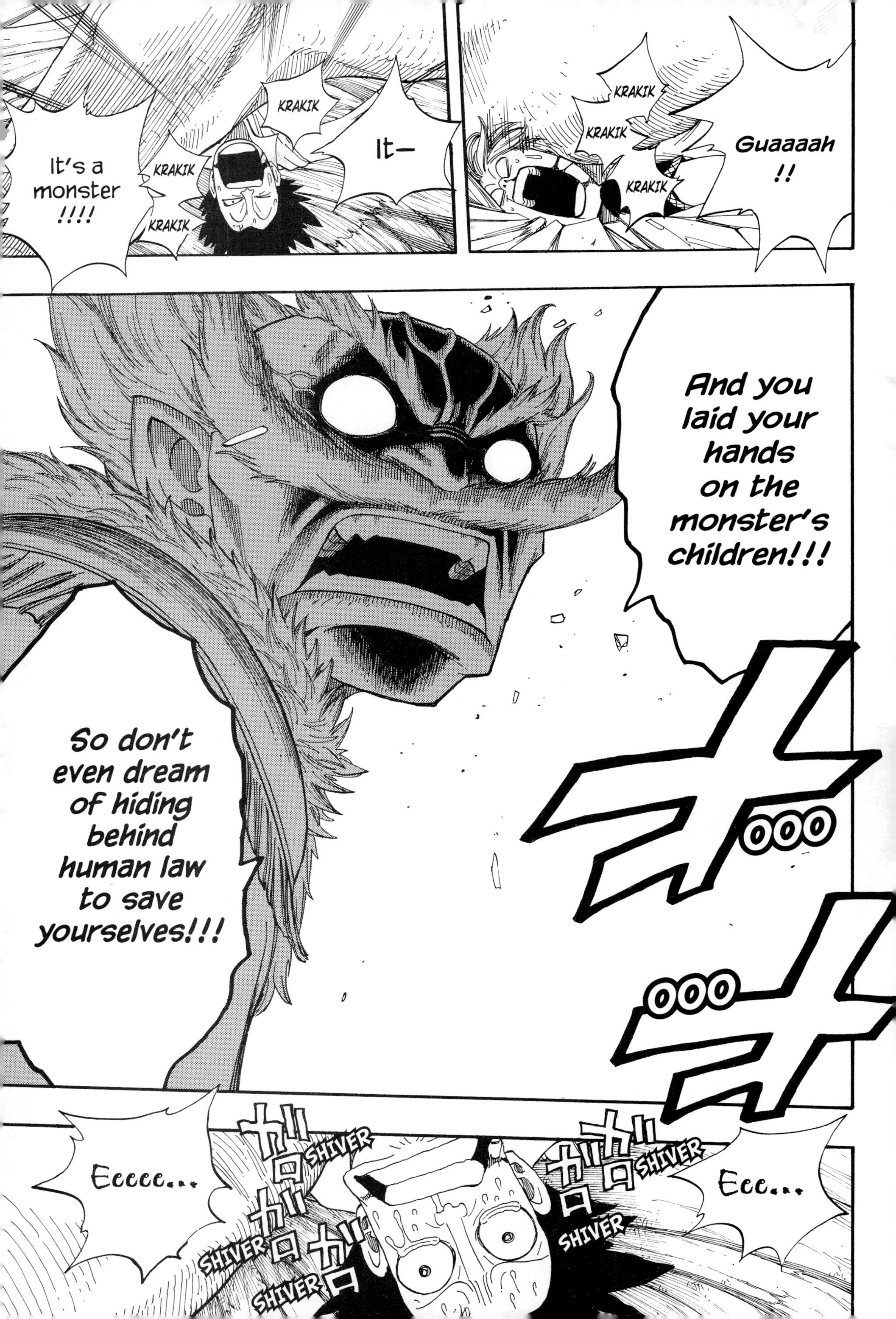
KRAKIK
KRAKIK
KRAKIK
Guaaaah!!
KRAKIK
It—
KRAKIK
It's a monster!!!!
KRAKIK
And you laid your hands on the monster's children!!!
ooo
ooo
So don't even dream of hiding behind human law to save yourselves!!!
Ecc...
SHIVER
SHIVER
SHIVER
Eeeee...
SHIVER
SHIVER
SHIVER

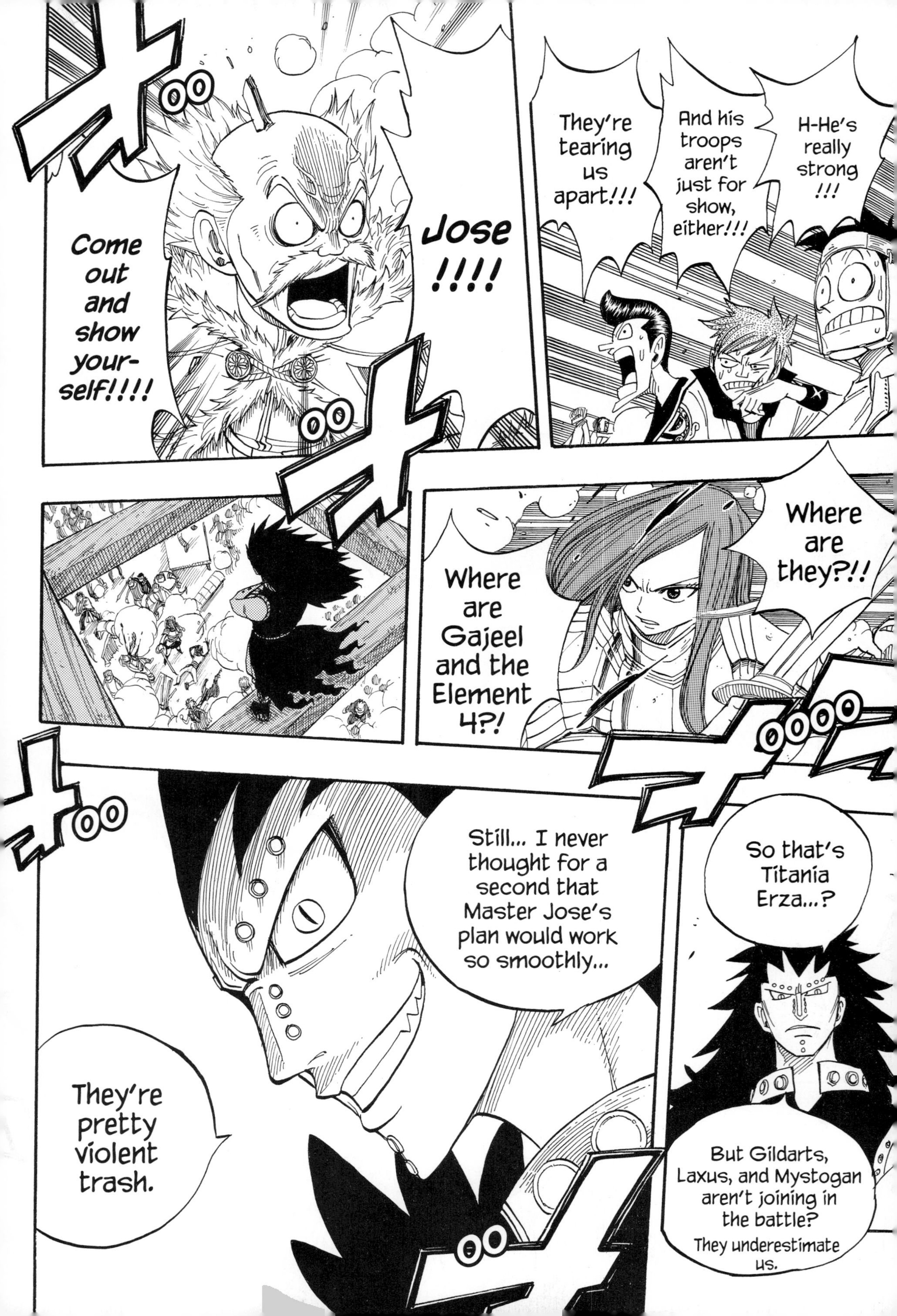
H-He's really strong!!!
And his troops aren't just for show, either!!!
They're tearing us apart!!!
Jose!!!!
Come out and show your-self!!!!
Where are they?!!
Where are Gajeel and the Element 4?!
So that's Titania Erza...?
But Gildarts, Laxus, and Mystogan aren't joining in the battle?
They underestimate us.
Still... I never thought for a second that Master Jose's plan would work so smoothly...
They're pretty violent trash.

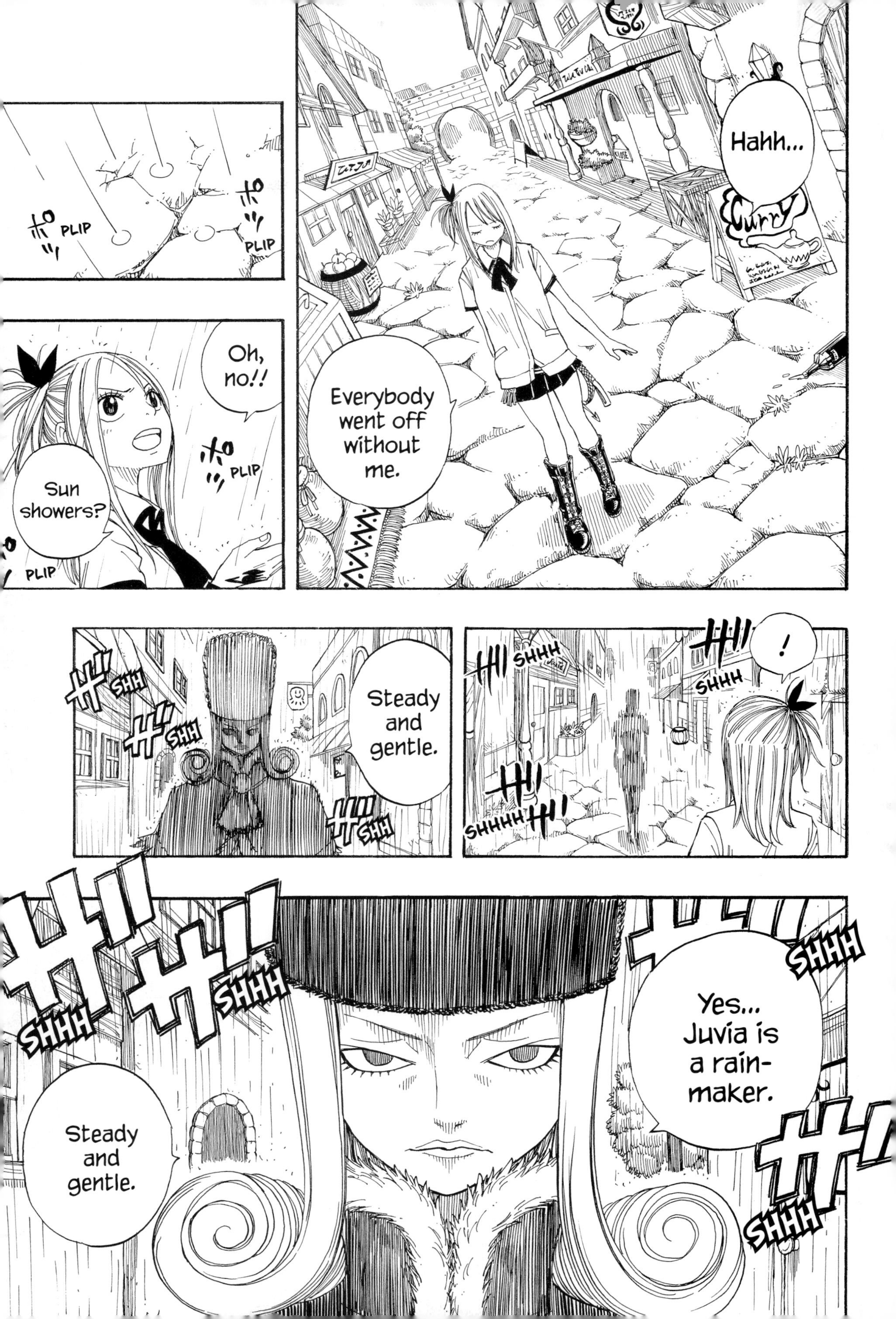

Hahh...
Everybody went off without me.
PLIP
PLIP
Oh, no!!
PLIP
Sun showers?
PLIP
!
SHHH
SHHH
SHHHH
Steady and gentle.
SHH
SHH
SHH
SHHH
Yes... Juvia is a rain-maker.
SHHH
SHHH
Steady and gentle.
SHHH

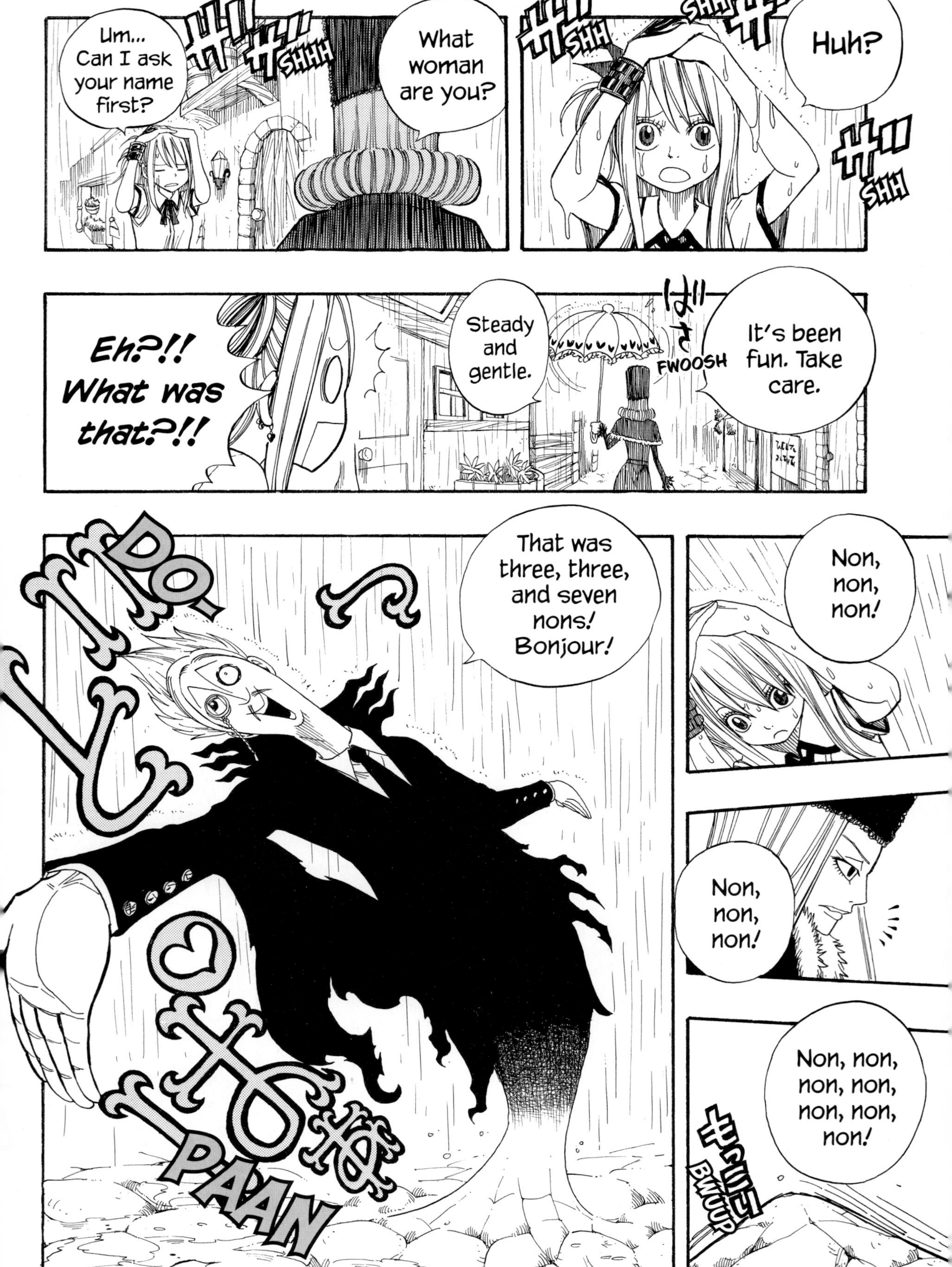
SHH
SHH
Huh?
SHH
What woman are you?
SHHH
Um... Can I ask your name first?
It's been fun. Take care.
FWOOSH
Steady and gentle.
Eh?!! What was that?!!
Non, non, non!
Non, non, non!
Non, non, non, non, non, non, non!
BWUUP
That was three, three, and seven nons! Bonjour!
DO-
PAAN

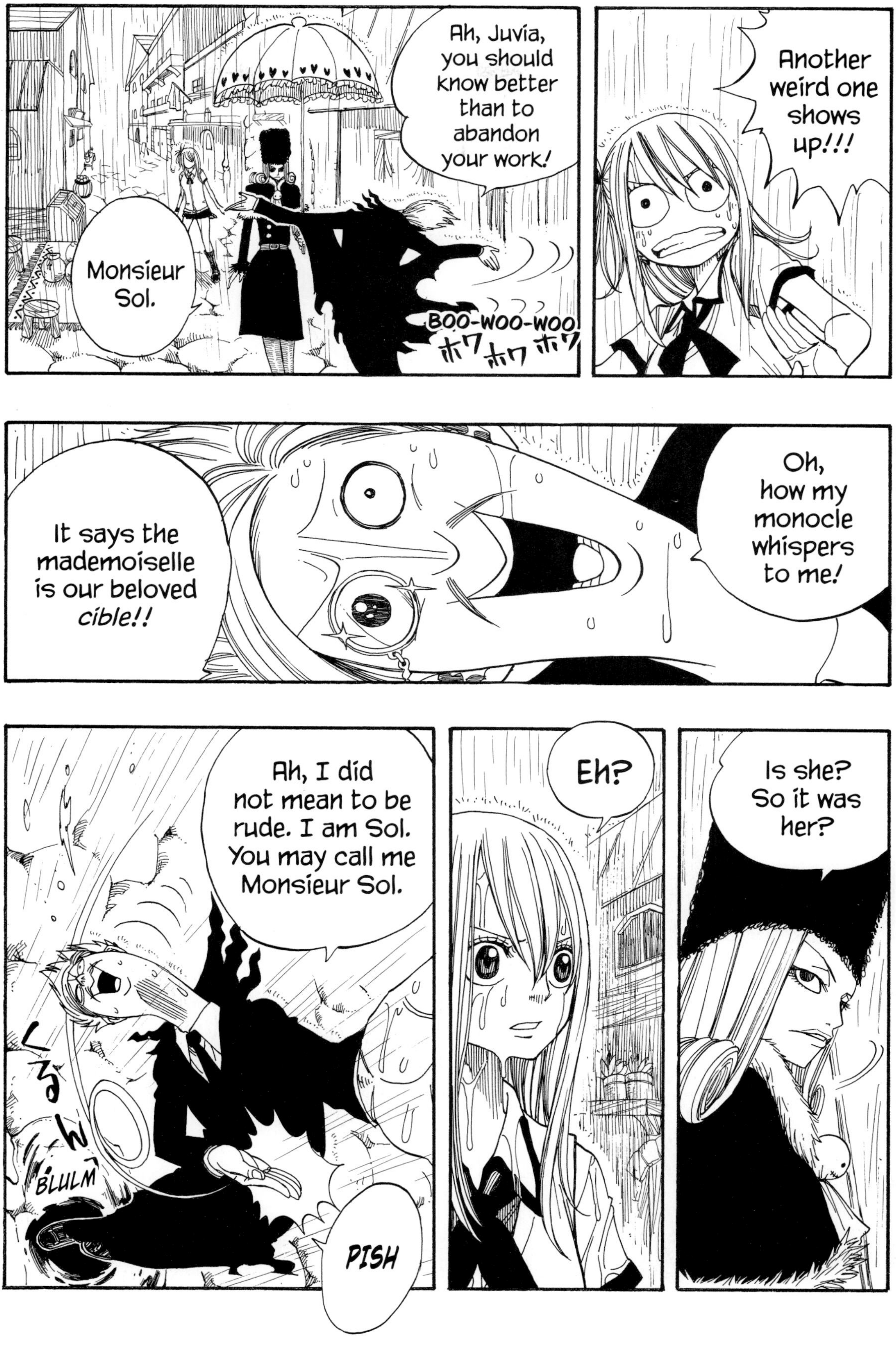
Another weird one shows up!!!
Ah, Juvia, you should know better than to abandon your work!
BOO-WOO-WOO
ホワホワホワ
Monsieur Sol.
Oh, how my monocle whispers to me!
It says the mademoiselle is our beloved *cible*!!
Is she? So it was her?
Eh?
Ah, I did not mean to be rude. I am Sol. You may call me Monsieur Sol.
PISH
くるん
BLULM

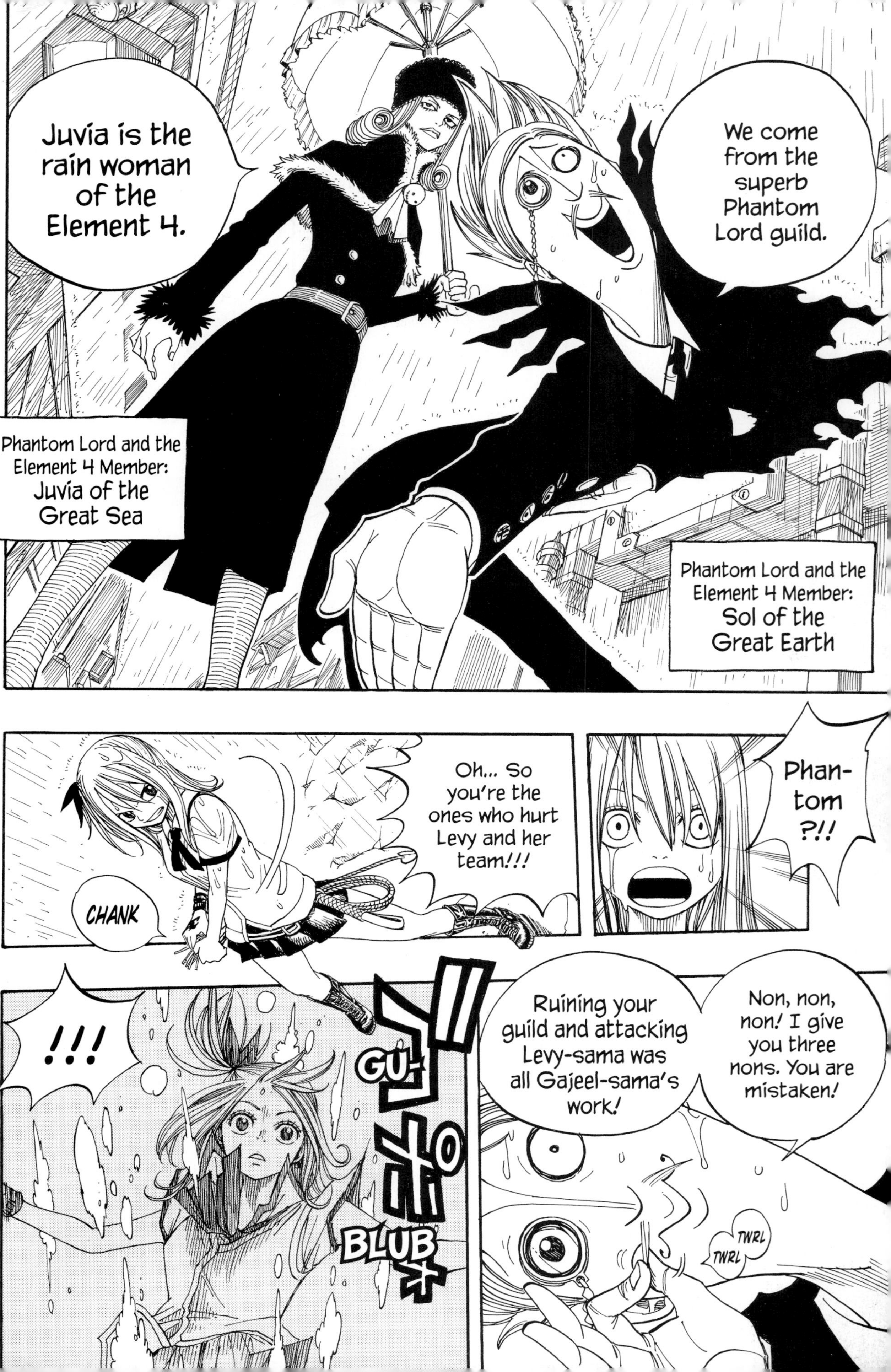
We come from the superb Phantom Lord guild.
Juvia is the rain woman of the Element 4.
Phantom Lord and the Element 4 Member: Juvia of the Great Sea
Phantom Lord and the Element 4 Member: Sol of the Great Earth
Phan-tom?!!
Oh... So you're the ones who hurt Levy and her team!!!
CHANK
Non, non, non! I give you three nons. You are mistaken!
Ruining your guild and attacking Levy-sama was all Gajeel-sama's work!
TWRL TWRL
GU-
BLUB
!!!

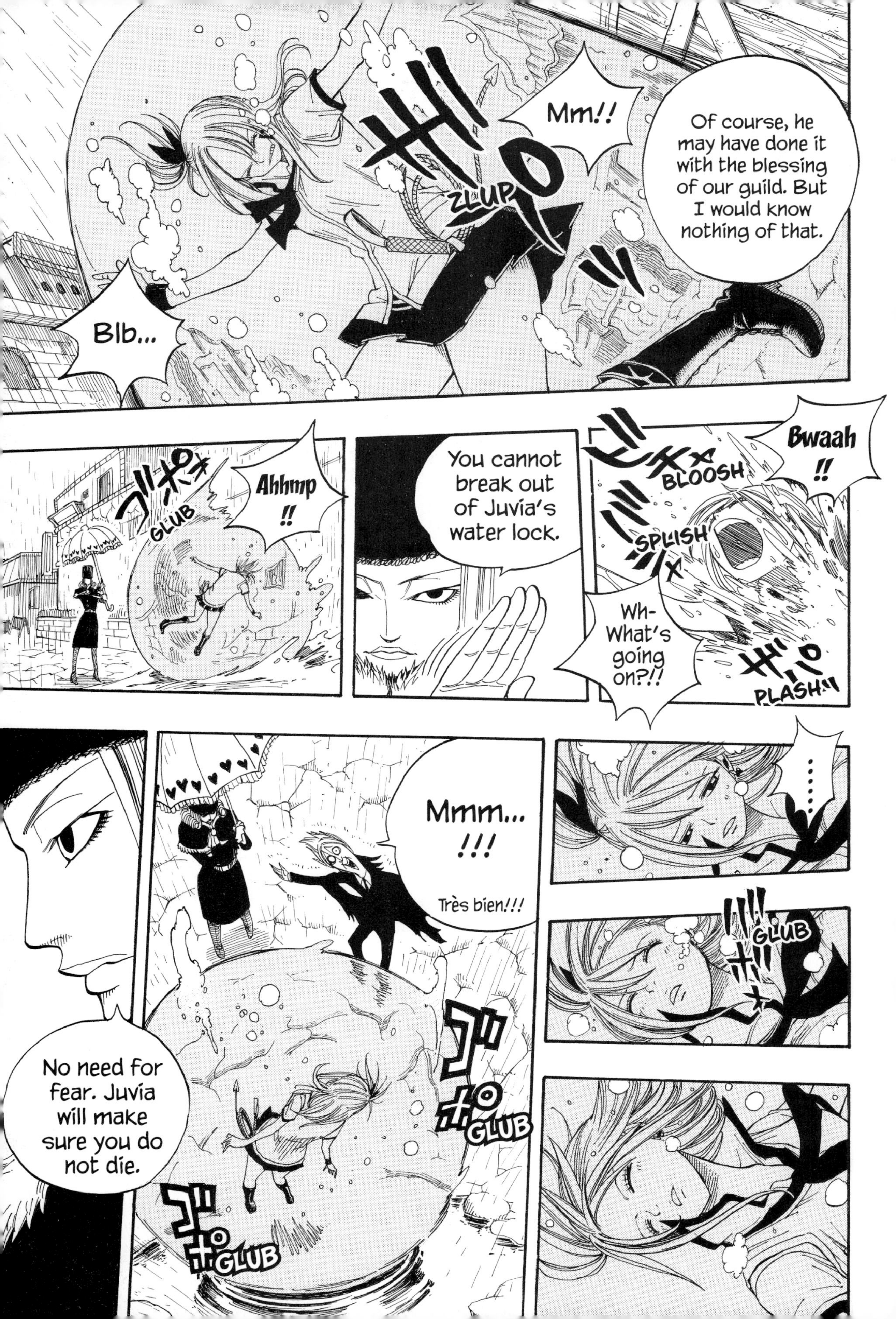
Of course, he may have done it with the blessing of our guild. But I would know nothing of that.
Mm!!
ZLUP
Blb...
Bwaah!!
BLOOSH
SPLISH
Wh- What's going on?!!
PLASH!!
You cannot break out of Juvia's water lock.
Ahhmp!!
GLUB
......
GLUB
Mmm...!!!
Très bien!!!
GLUB
GLUB
No need for fear. Juvia will make sure you do not die.

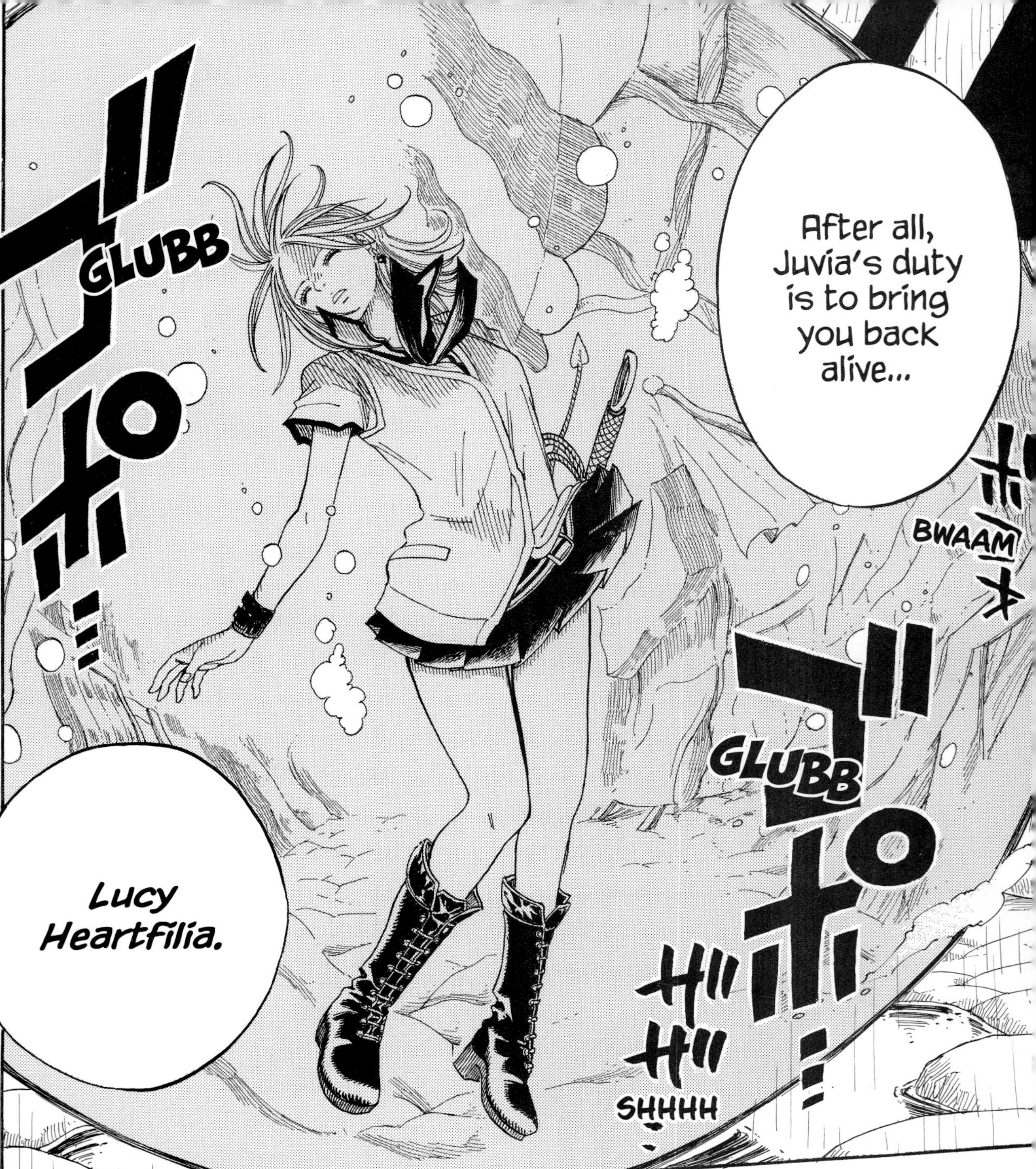
After all, Juvia's duty is to bring you back alive...
BWAAM
GLUBB
GLUBB
SHHHH
Lucy Heartfilia.
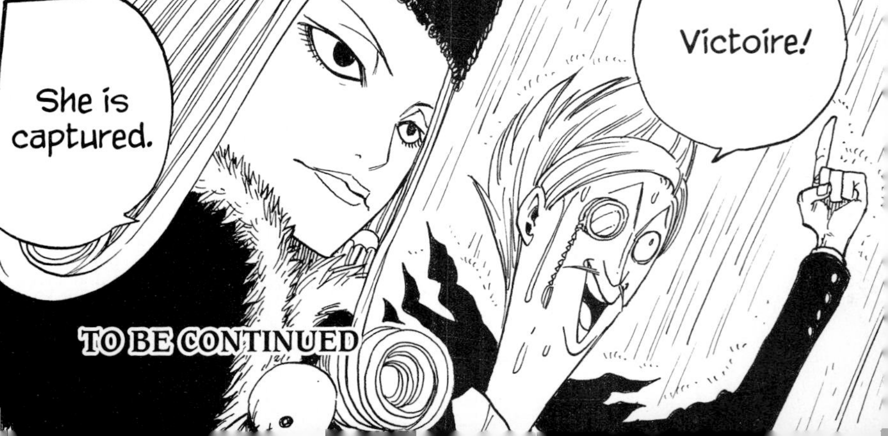
Victoire!
She is captured.
TO BE CONTINUED
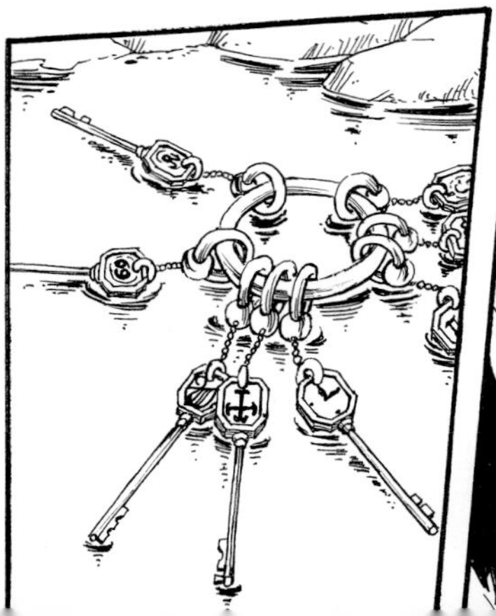

Dictionary of Unnecessary Characters

Name: Tablin   **Age:** 17 yrs.

Magic: Um...Doesn't have any magic.

Likes: Levy-chan   **Dislikes:** Pop Music

WIZARD GUILD×633

Remarks

A citizen of Magnolia who is, at times, seen in Fairy Tail. (By the way, anyone can enter the guild building to deliver food or liquor.)

Tablin wanted to join Levy's team, Shadow Gear, but he was refused because he isn't a wizard.

Recently he tried to learn some magic but it turned out to be more difficult than he counted on and he gave up.

Even so, he always seems to be hanging around in an effort to get closer to Levy.

TAIL D'ART

The *Fairy Tail* Guild d' Art is an explosion of fan art! Please send in your black-and-white art on large postcard stock!! Those chosen to be published will get a signed mini poster! ♪ Make sure you write your real name and address on the back of your postcard!

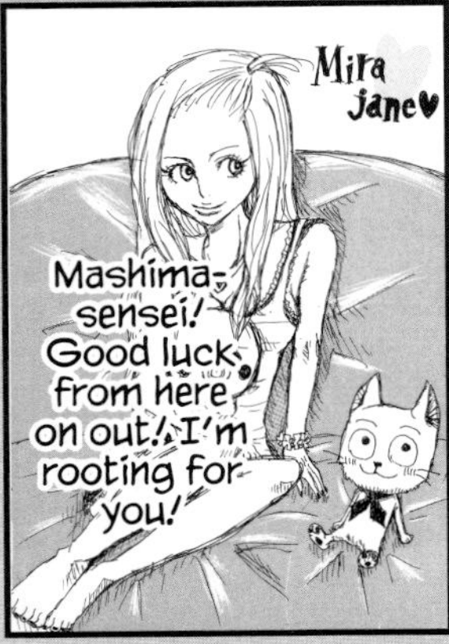
Mira jane♥
Mashima-sensei! Good luck from here on out! I'm rooting for you!

Mie Prefecture, Cherry

▼ If she looked at me like that, I'd be lost!

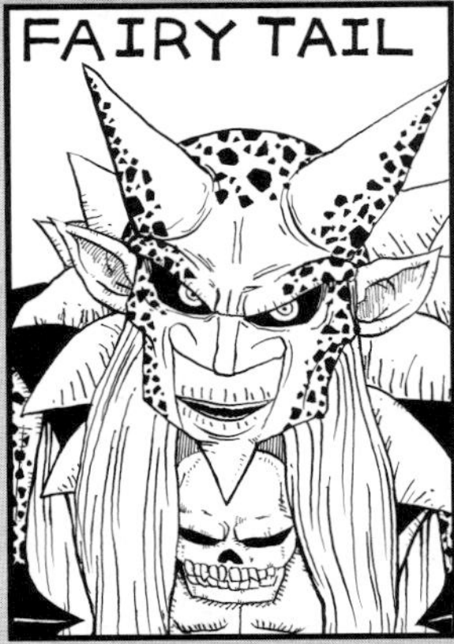
FAIRY TAIL

Miyagi Prefecture, Akihiro Satô

▼ The headman of the village on Galuna Island. This is his true form.

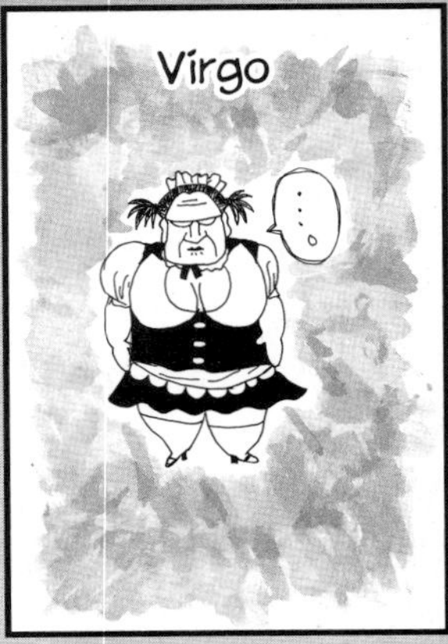
Virgo
…

Yamagata Prefecture, Misaki

▼ It's unusual to see the old version of Virgo. Maybe the artist is a fan of this version. (laughs)

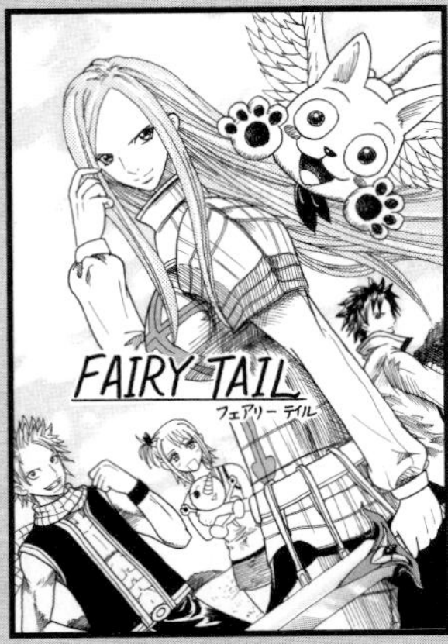
FAIRY TAIL
フェアリーテイル

Tokyo, Naya Shôta

▼ Erza is so intense and cool!! Her work is just beginning!

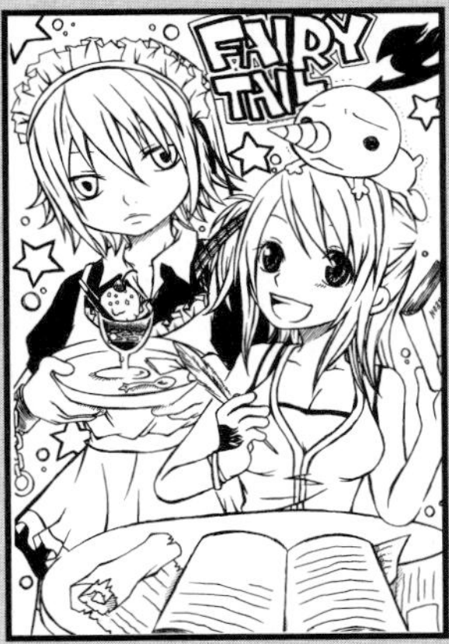
FAIRY TAIL

Hyogo Prefecture, Neko

▼ If Virgo existed in real life, she'd be very handy to have around. I need somebody to clean my place!

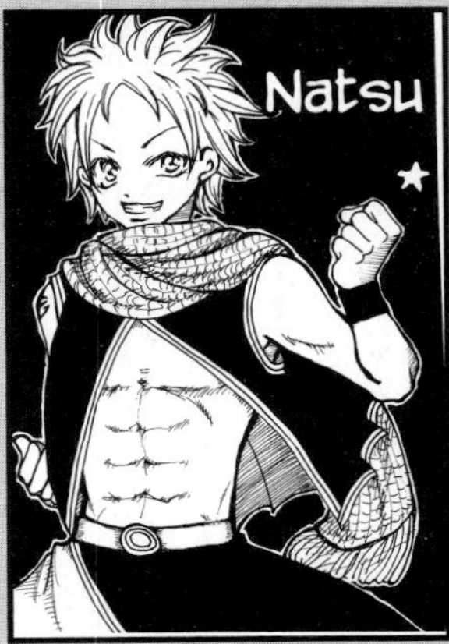
Natsu

Toyama Prefecture, Anzu

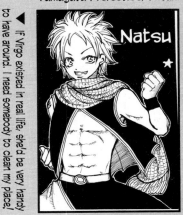

▼ The black space really makes the image stand out! A very manly Natsu, huh?

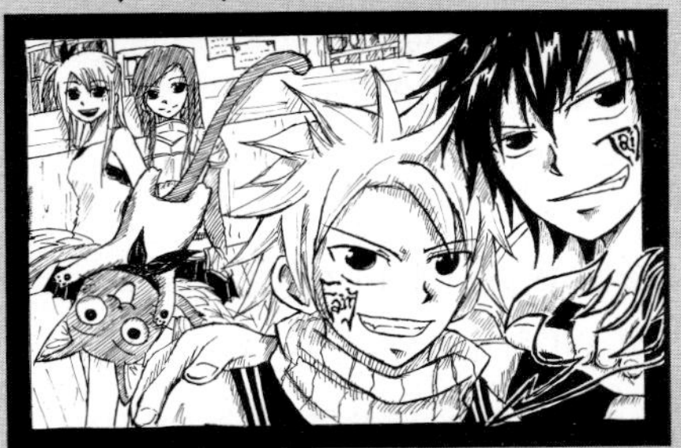

Mie Prefecture, Fujinami Wataru

▼ They're looking cool and tough! Happy's upside down though.

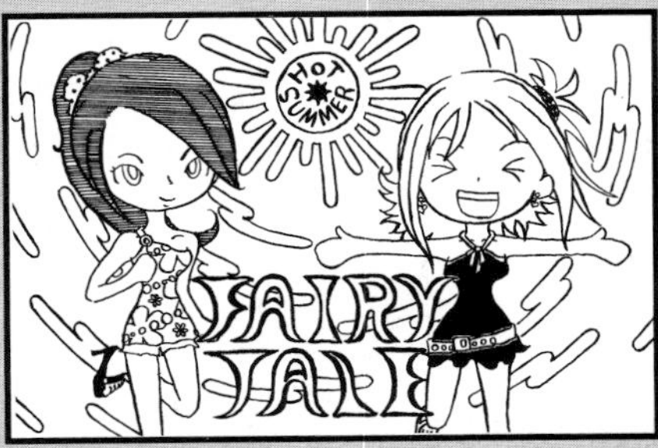
HOT SUMMER
FAIRY TAIL

Chiba Prefecture, Meesuke

▼ Wow!! So cute!! I just love this kind of picture!

Send to Hiro Mashima, Kodansha Comics
451 Park Ave. South, 7th Floor New York, NY 10016

FAIRY GUILD

Any letters and postcards you send with your personal information, such as your name, address, postal code, and other information, will be handed over, as is, to the author. When you send mail, please keep that in mind.

▼ Reedus-kun! You went and drew a picture of a lollipop!

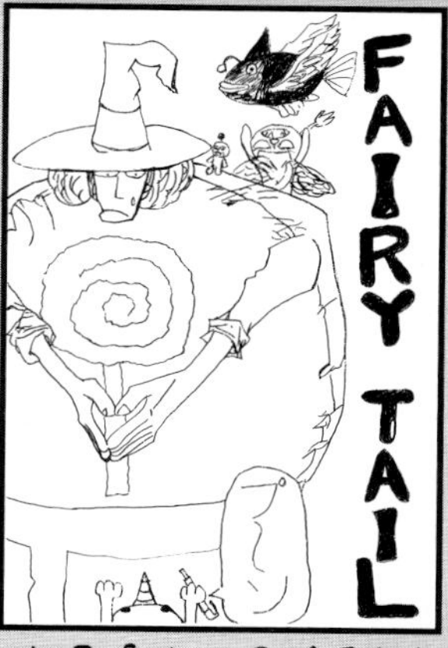
FAIRY TAIL

Iwate Prefecture, Satô Daisuke

▼ It's like a picture taken from the characters' memories!

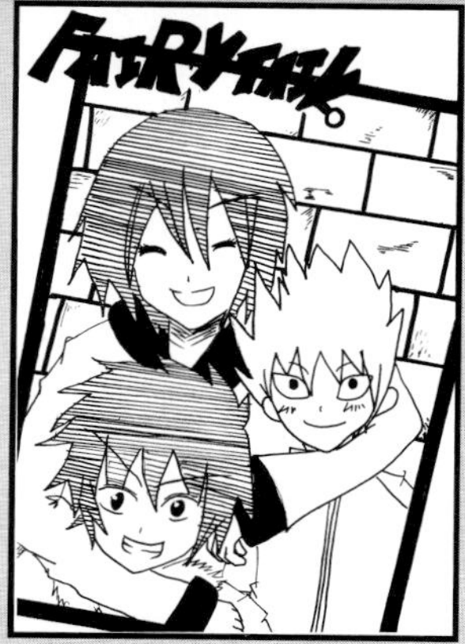

Toyama Prefecture, Naruya

▼ Ooh!! All of the celestial spirits together!!! The lines are so clearly drawn!

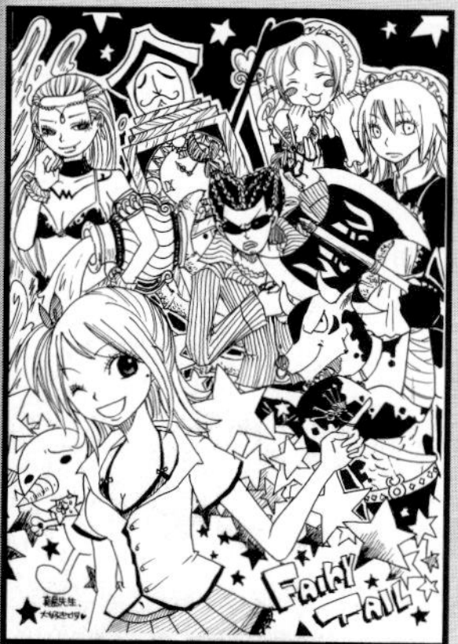

Nara Prefecture, Hasshii

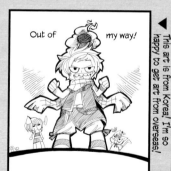

▼ This art is from Korea! I'm so happy to get art from overseas!

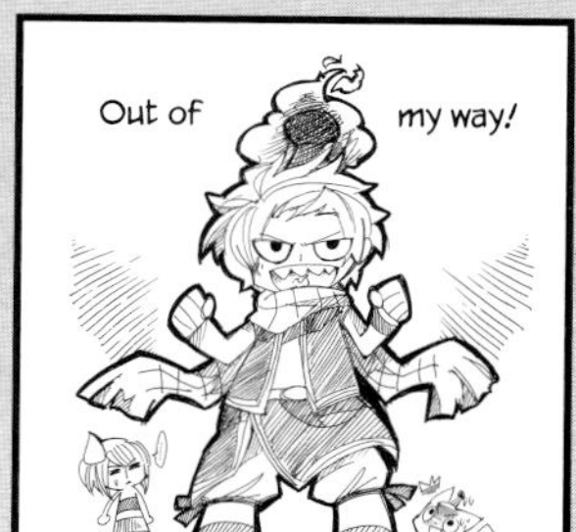
Out of
my way!

Korea, Sengkong

▼ Whoa!! Everyone's so cute!! Happy, especially, got the cute treatment!!

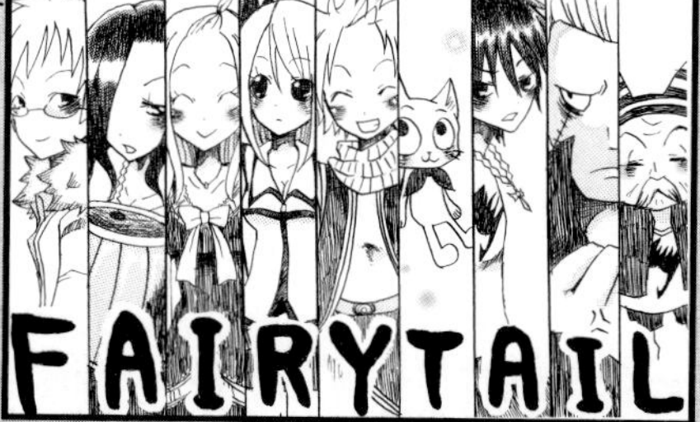
FAIRYTAIL

Mie Prefecture, Rangetsu Gekka

▼ Lucy, drawn a little closer to reality than normal. Extremely well done!

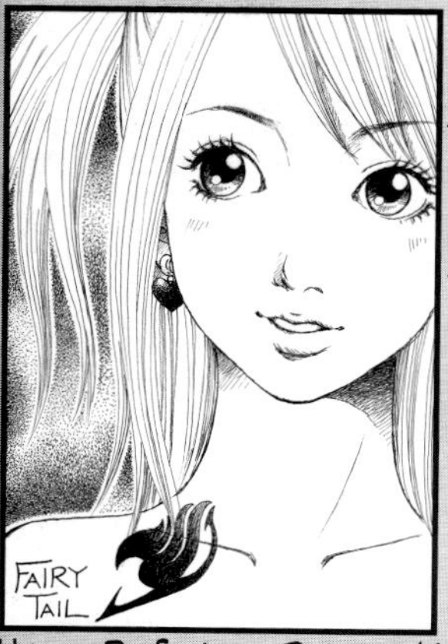
FAIRY TAIL

Hyogo Prefecture, Botamochi

Rejection Corner

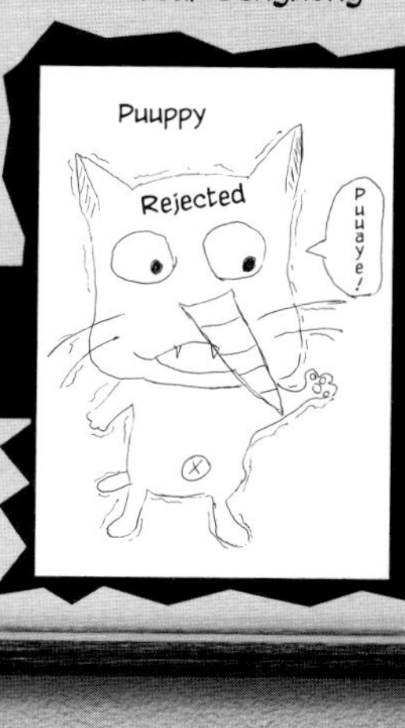
Puuppy
Rejected

▲ I guess it's easy to play fast and loose with Happy...

Nagano Prefecture, Some Creep Rejected by Life

Special Request: "Explain the Mysteries of Fairy Tail!"

From the Fairy Tail Bar

Lucy: Mira-san!! There are loads of letters this time!!

Mira: Really! You're so popular, Lucy! ♡

Lucy: Didn't you say something really similar last time...? They're letters with questions!! Questions!!

Mira: They like pointing out the author's faults, huh?

Lucy: No!! It's just that there are so many mysteries in this story!! Even I couldn't write something like this!!

Mira: Now that you mention it, here's a question about you, Lucy!

Lucy: Eh?! I don't feel like telling anybody my measurements. I understand how people would be curious, though...

Mira: Nope. Not even one letter has asked that question.

Lucy: ...

Lucy hardly ever locks her door when she goes out, does she? And her entire magic is rooted in keys...ha ha!

Lucy: I lock it all the time!!!

Mira: Everybody loves your apartment, huh, Lucy?

Lucy: That's something I'd like to know!! How do they always get in?!!

Mira: Let's go to the next question.

Why does Lucy always carry a whip? I mean...a whip?

↗

Lucy: It's for self-defense!! A weapon!! Nothing else!!

Mira: You mean it isn't meant for keeping those naughty celestial spirits in line?

Lucy: I'd never do something awful like that to my spirits!!

Mira: Okay, but what if they happen to like it?

Lucy: Th-That isn't one of my hobbies.

Mira: And this will be the last one.

I think that Lucy is the weakest member of Fairy Tail.

Lucy: That isn't a question!! Hey!!!

Mira: But you're always with Natsu and Erza. I think you'll get a lot stronger with time.

Lucy: Y-You think so? You're making my head spin!!

Mira: Ah! Speak of the devil!

Natsu: Mira!! Loan me the key to Lucy's place, okay?!

Lucy: Eh?

Mira: Sure!! Here you go!!

Natsu: Oh!! So you're here, Lucy! I'm heading over to your place to take a nap.

Lucy: W-Wait a second, Mira-san!! It was you all along?!! You've been handing out my key without my permission?!

Mira: Well, we're friends, right?

Lucy: Yeah, but... Why do you have a key to my apartment anyway?!

Mira: Heh heh heh... It's a secret. ♡

Lucy: Aw... This is the question corner!! A place for answers!! Why are there suddenly more mysteries?!!

AFTERWORD

"With this volume, the story is really getting fun!!!" I said to myself. I always wanted to do a war between two guilds. I thought I'd be doing it later in the series, but I decided to get it done while I was still excited about it! (laughs) I know that I already did a fight with a dark guild, but that was just Natsu and his friends. This time it's two entire guilds colliding head on!!! "Yeah!!! I'm on fire!!!" was the feeling I had while I was drawing it, and I felt that I really loved my job. I sometimes wonder about how I make my living. Once this series is over, maybe I should get a real job.

I mentioned this before, but I really haven't thought about what's going to happen in the future of this series. (sweat-sweat) There are plot elements that I want to draw, and scenes that I envision and other fragmentary plans, but there isn't even a hint of "first I want to do this, and then that" style of planning. And so, with every story, I find myself wondering, "What am I going to do next?" For example, since the enemy guild captured Lucy, the battle between the two guilds must have something to do with her. So what's going to happen…? I've been drawing manga in this kind of style for a long time now, but once in a while, I feel like I should decide what's going to happen before I write it. Well, I've gotten this far! And I'm sure the next volume will be even more fun!! I hope you read it! Oh, and please take a look at *Monster Soul 2nd,* which is coming out (in Japan) at the same time as this book!

Translation Notes

Japanese is a tricky language for most Westerners, and translation is often more art than science. For your edification and reading pleasure, here are notes on some of the places where we could have gone in a different direction in our translation of the work, or where a Japanese cultural reference is used.

General Notes:
Wizard

In the original Japanese version of *Fairy Tail*, you'll find panels in which the English word "wizard" is part of the original illustration. So this translation has taken that as its inspiration and translated the word *madôshi* as "wizard." But *madôshi*'s meaning is similar to certain Japanese words that have been borrowed by the English language, such as judo (the soft way) and kendo (the way of the sword). *Madô* is the way of magic, and *madôshi* are those who follow the way of magic. So although the word "wizard" is used in the original dialogue, a Japanese reader would be likely to think not of traditional Western wizards such as Merlin or Gandalf, but of martial artists.

Names

Hiro Mashima has graciously agreed to provide official English spellings for just about all of the characters in *Fairy Tail*. Because this version of *Fairy Tail* is the first publication of most of these spellings, there will inevitably be differences between these spellings and some of the fan interpretations that may have spread throughout the Web or in other fan circles. Rest assured that the spellings contained in this book are the spellings that Mashima-sensei wanted for *Fairy Tail*.

Hidane, page 85

The word for Droy's seeds is *hidane*. The character used for *hi* means "needed" or "necessary." The character for *dane* means "seed." So this word could be translated as "vital seeds."

De-Malevo-Lance, page 107

It wasn't a pun in the original, but the name was extremely hard to translate. The Japanese version named the weapon the *Haja no Yari*, which translates to the "Javelin of the Destruction of Evil." I searched for a word that meant "destruction of evil," and couldn't come up with a good one. (Now that the book is published, I'll probably come up with the perfect word...) So I wracked my brain for a day and decided on the De-malevolence Javelin. And while I was looking at the script a couple of days later, it struck me that "javelin" and "lance" had similar meanings. Thus, the pun. I apologize to anyone (everyone?) who doesn't find it humorous.

Baths at night, page 157

It's a Japanese custom to take a bath before going to bed (sometimes even before dinner). Since Japanese baths are deep and filled with very hot water, it becomes something like a nighttime hot tub. The evening soak is thought to help wash away not only dirt and grime, but also one's exhaustion from work.

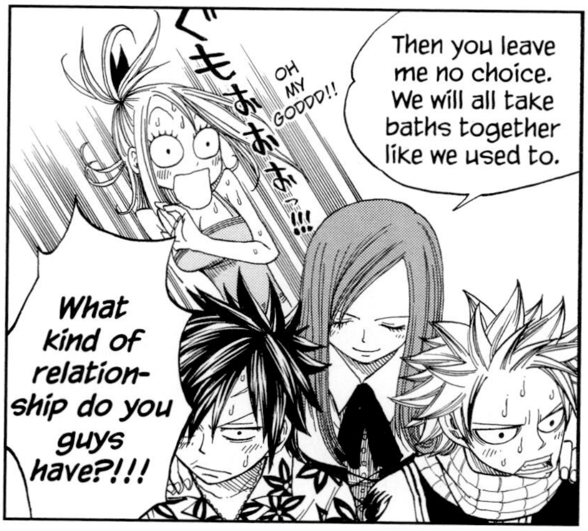
Then you leave me no choice. We will all take baths together like we used to.
OH MY GODDD!!
What kind of relation-ship do you guys have?!!!

Baths together, page 157

In Japan it is perfectly natural for a supervising adult to take a bath with a preschool-age child. A supervising adult may include aunts, uncles, other family or family friends. However, an adult woman, such as Erza, would not normally bathe with teenagers of the opposite sex.

Summer Festival, page 169

This scene represents many of the traditions found in the Obon festivals of August or other festivals held throughout the summer. Women often go dressed in the cool, cotton *yukata* kimonos, such as Lucy, Mirajane, and Erza are wearing. Men may also wear *yukata* or *jinbei*, such as Gray is wearing, but casual Western dress is more common. Paper lanterns normally festoon the festival area, and beneath them, vendors run games and sell food or toys. The fan that Lucy is holding and the mask on Plue are examples of the things one can buy from these vendors. Happy has been busy capturing fish at the *kingyô-sukui* game in which one captures goldfish with a flimsy net. Fireworks are a long-held custom from the time of Obon, and although large fireworks displays are held during or in conjunction with festivals, it is also customary for groups of family and friends to light sparklers and other small fireworks in private.

Lu-chan, page 171

Levy wants to be friends with Lucy, and so she calls Lucy with the cute honorific of *-chan*. Such an endearment can help create a friendship, or it can cool relations considerably if the honorific is misused. Of course Levy knows how to use her honorifics well.

Cible, page 185

Cible means "target" in French. Monsieur Sol mixes in French words with his Japanese in his dialogue. However, it did not have any other accent markers aside from the occasional French word, so this translation did the same. I admit, I was tempted to add "zis" and "zat" to the dialogue to highlight Monsieur Sol's Frenchness, but I realized that Mashima-sensei's visuals told most of the story anyway.

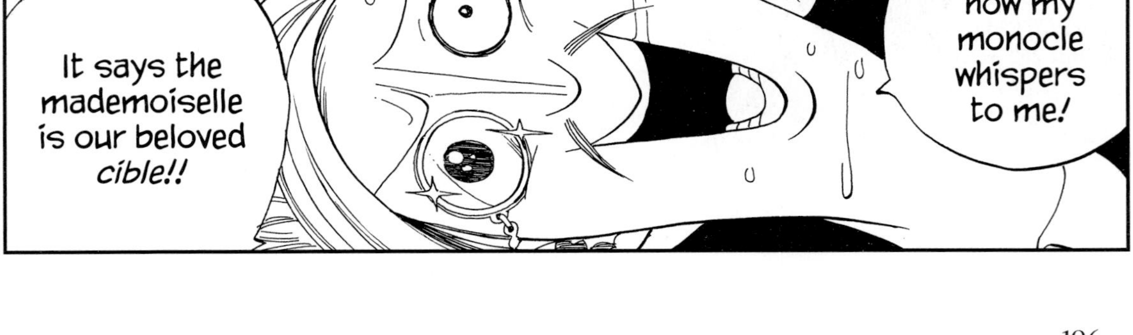
Oh, how my monocle whispers to me!
It says the mademoiselle is our beloved cible!!

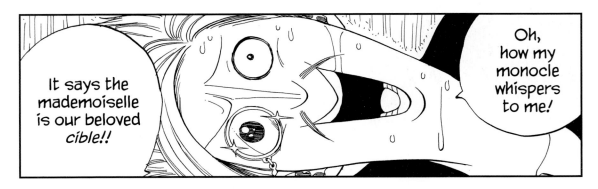

FAIRY TAIL

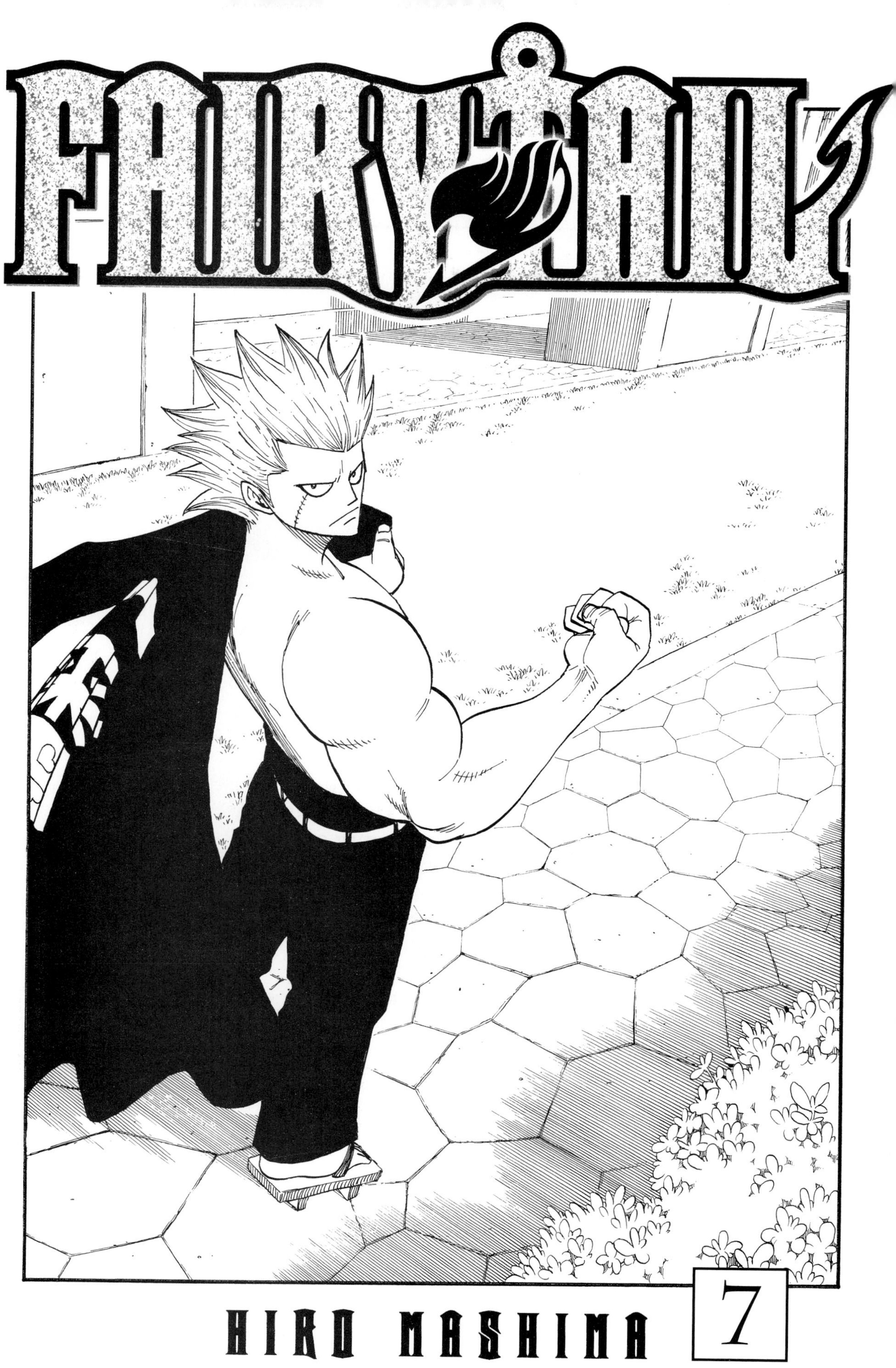

HIRO MASHIMA

7

I went to a signing in Taiwan!!
They gave me such a warm
and passionate welcome!
Some of the fans even brought
me bouquets of flowers!
Really! I was so happy to
be able to have such close
contact with the fans!
I got carried away and
shouted, "Everybody!! I love
you all!" For some reason,
that got printed in the local
newspapers.

—Hiro Mashima

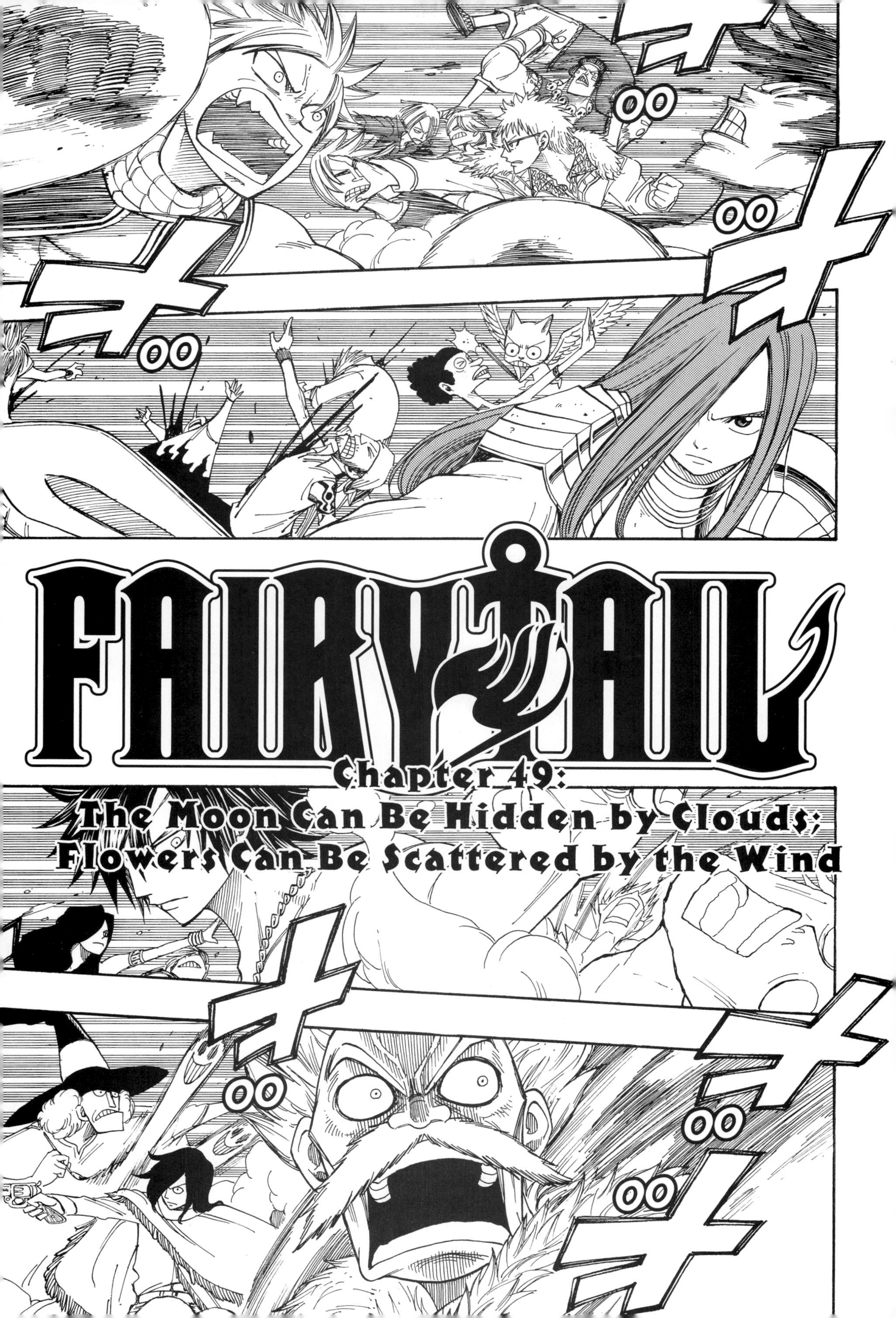
FAIRY TAIL
Chapter 49:
The Moon Can Be Hidden by Clouds;
Flowers Can Be Scattered by the Wind

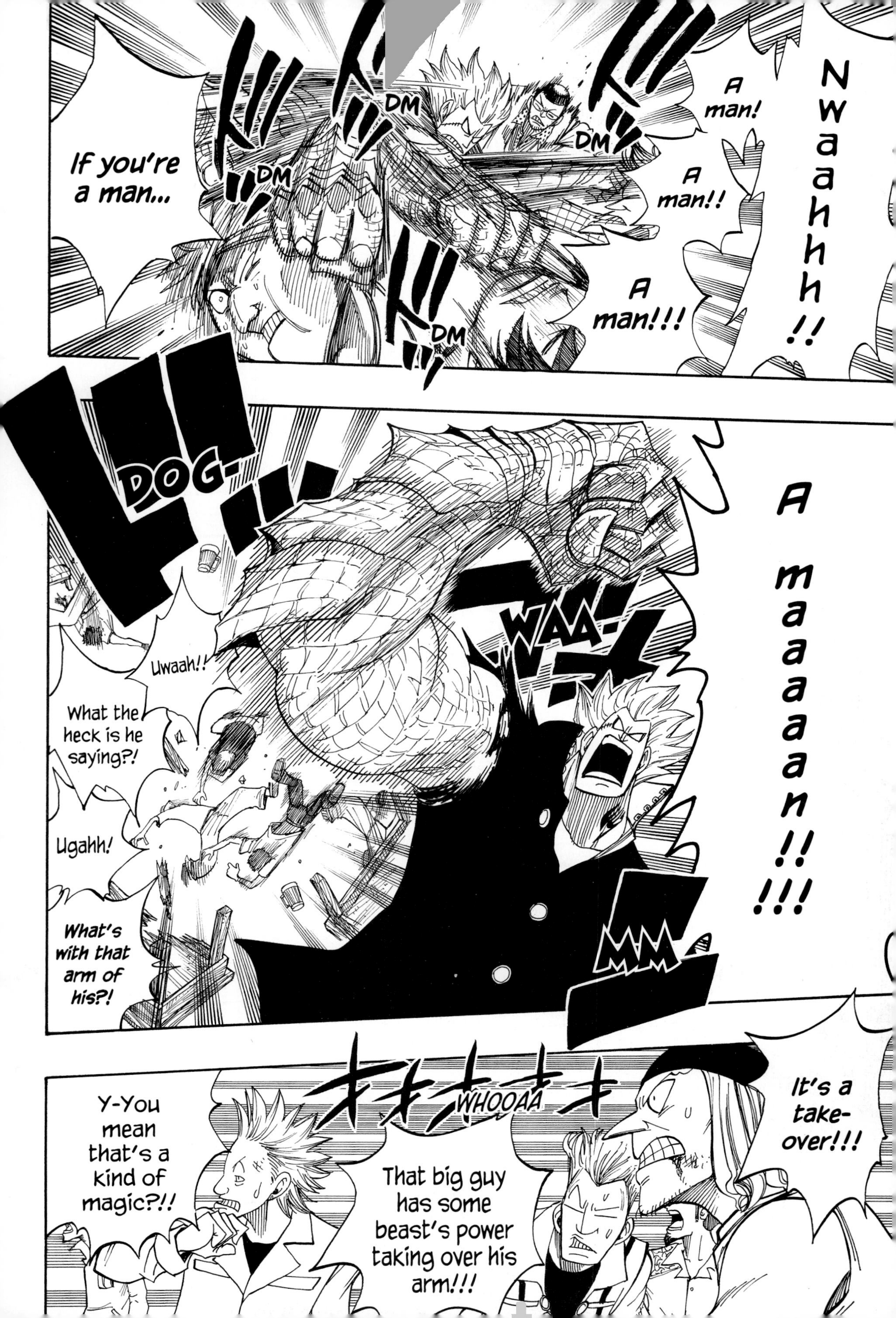
Nwaahhh!!
A man!
A man!!
A man!!!
DM
DM
DM
DM
If you're a man...
A maaaaaan!!!!!
WAA-
MM
DOG-
Uwaah!!
What the heck is he saying?!
Ugahh!
What's with that arm of his?!
It's a take-over!!!
WHOOAA
That big guy has some beast's power taking over his arm!!!
Y-You mean that's a kind of magic?!!

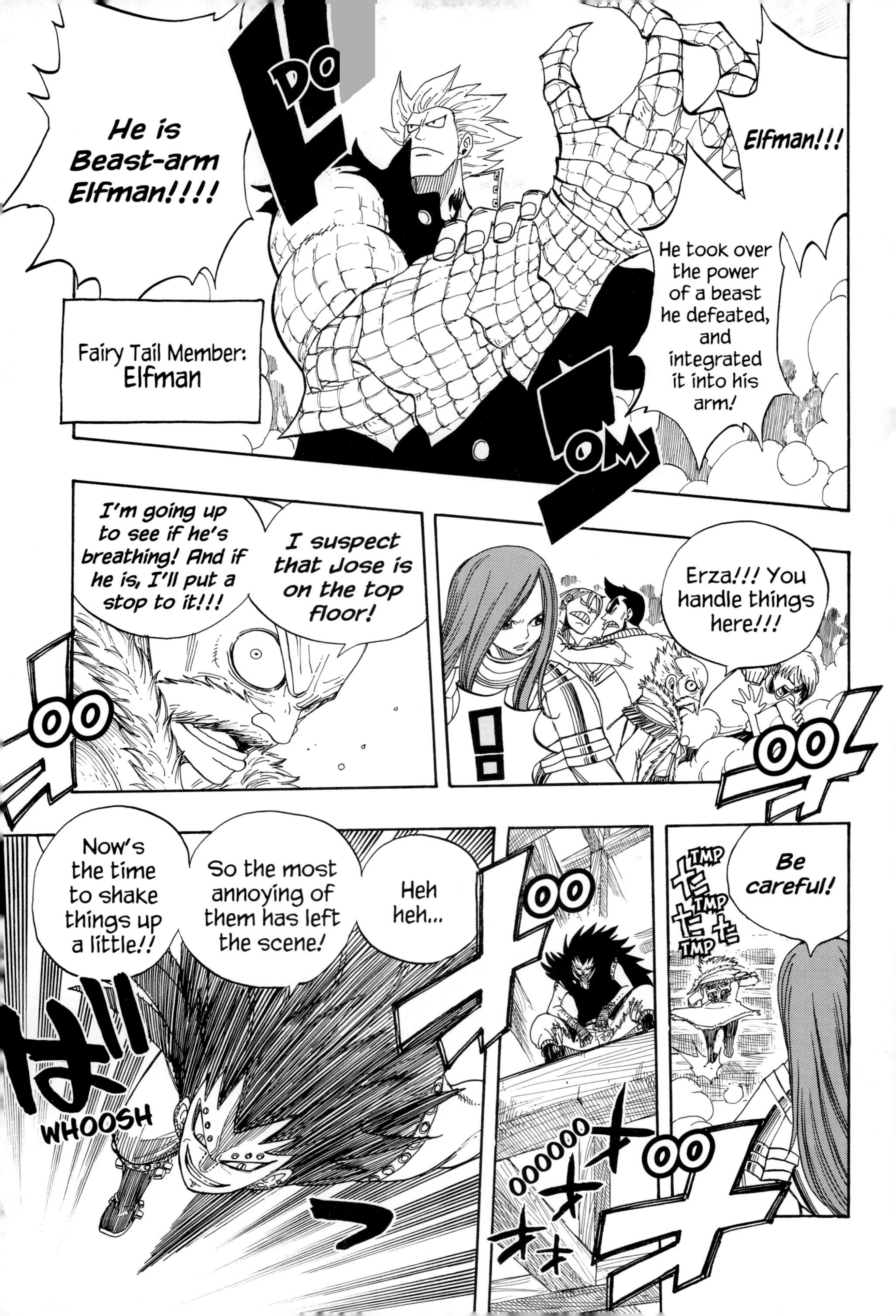
Elfman!!!
He took over the power of a beast he defeated, and integrated it into his arm!
He is Beast-arm Elfman!!!!
DO
OM
Fairy Tail Member: Elfman
Erza!!! You handle things here!!!
I suspect that Jose is on the top floor!
I'm going up to see if he's breathing! And if he is, I'll put a stop to it!!!
Be careful!
TMP
TMP
TMP
Heh heh...
So the most annoying of them has left the scene!
Now's the time to shake things up a little!!
WHOOSH

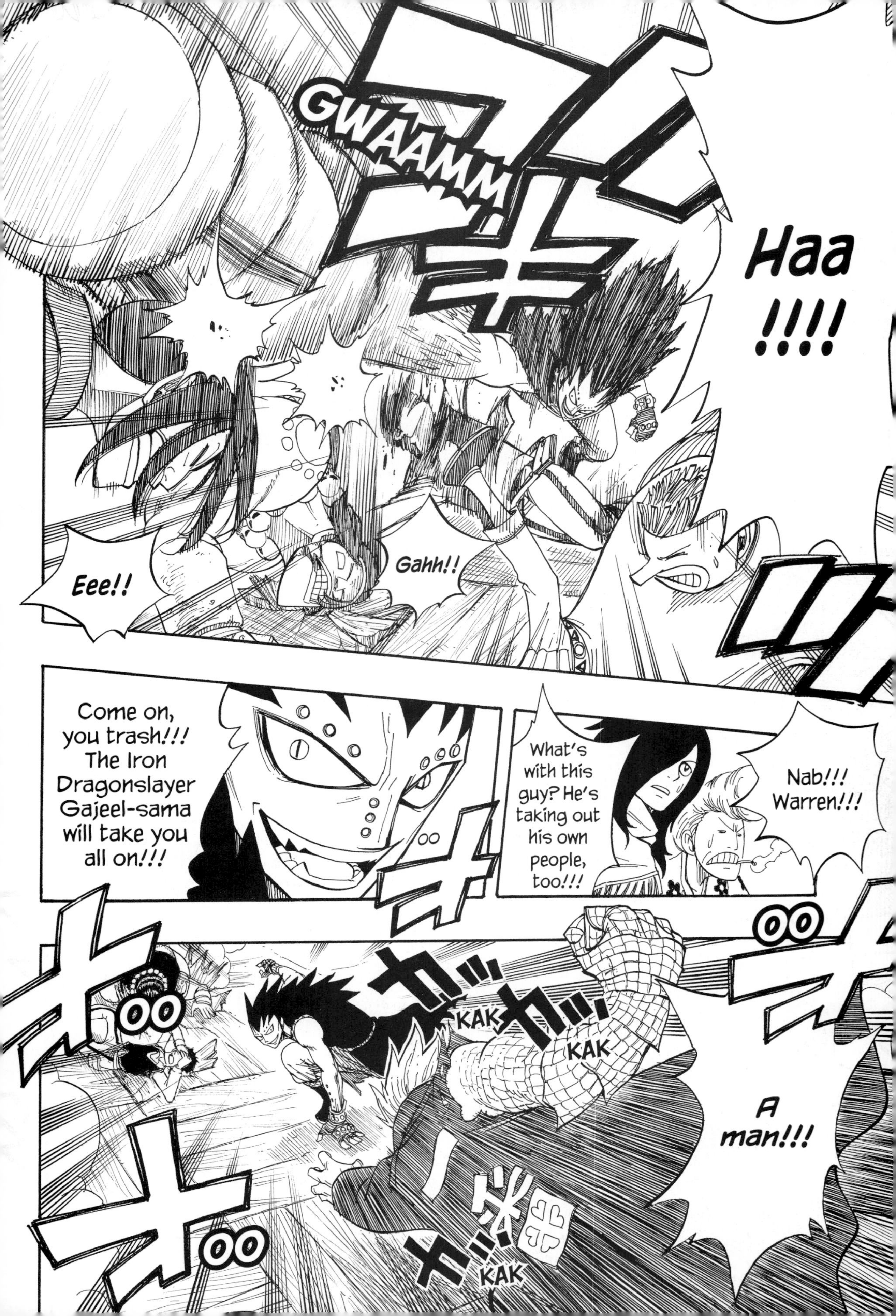
GWAAMM
Haa !!!!
Gahh!!
Eee!!
Nab!!! Warren!!!
What's with this guy? He's taking out his own people, too!!!
Come on, you trash!!! The Iron Dragonslayer Gajeel-sama will take you all on!!!
KAK
KAK
A man!!!
KAK

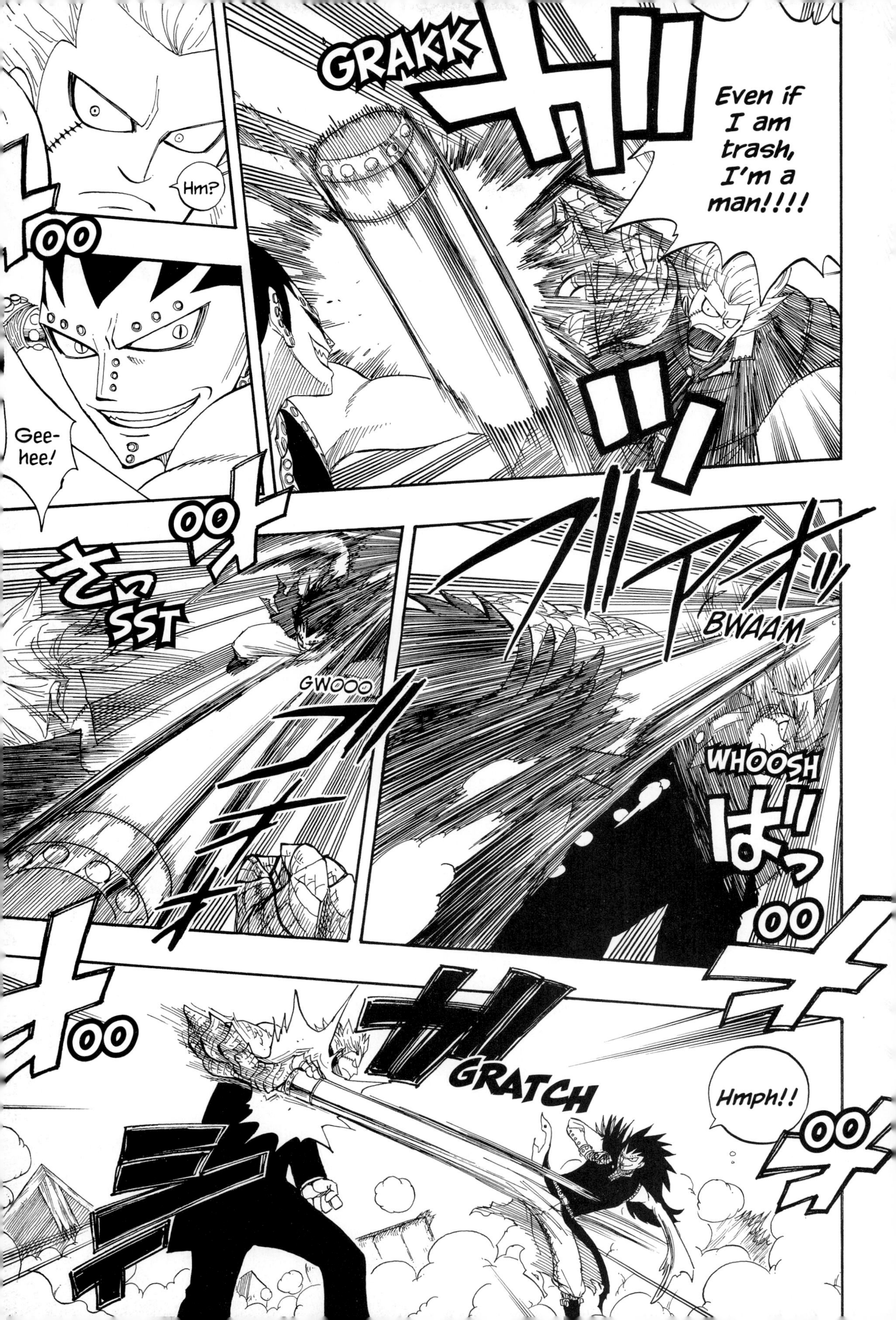
GRAKK
Even if I am trash, I'm a man!!!!
Hm?
Gee-hee!
BWAAM
WHOOSH
SST
GWOOO
Hmph!!
GRATCH

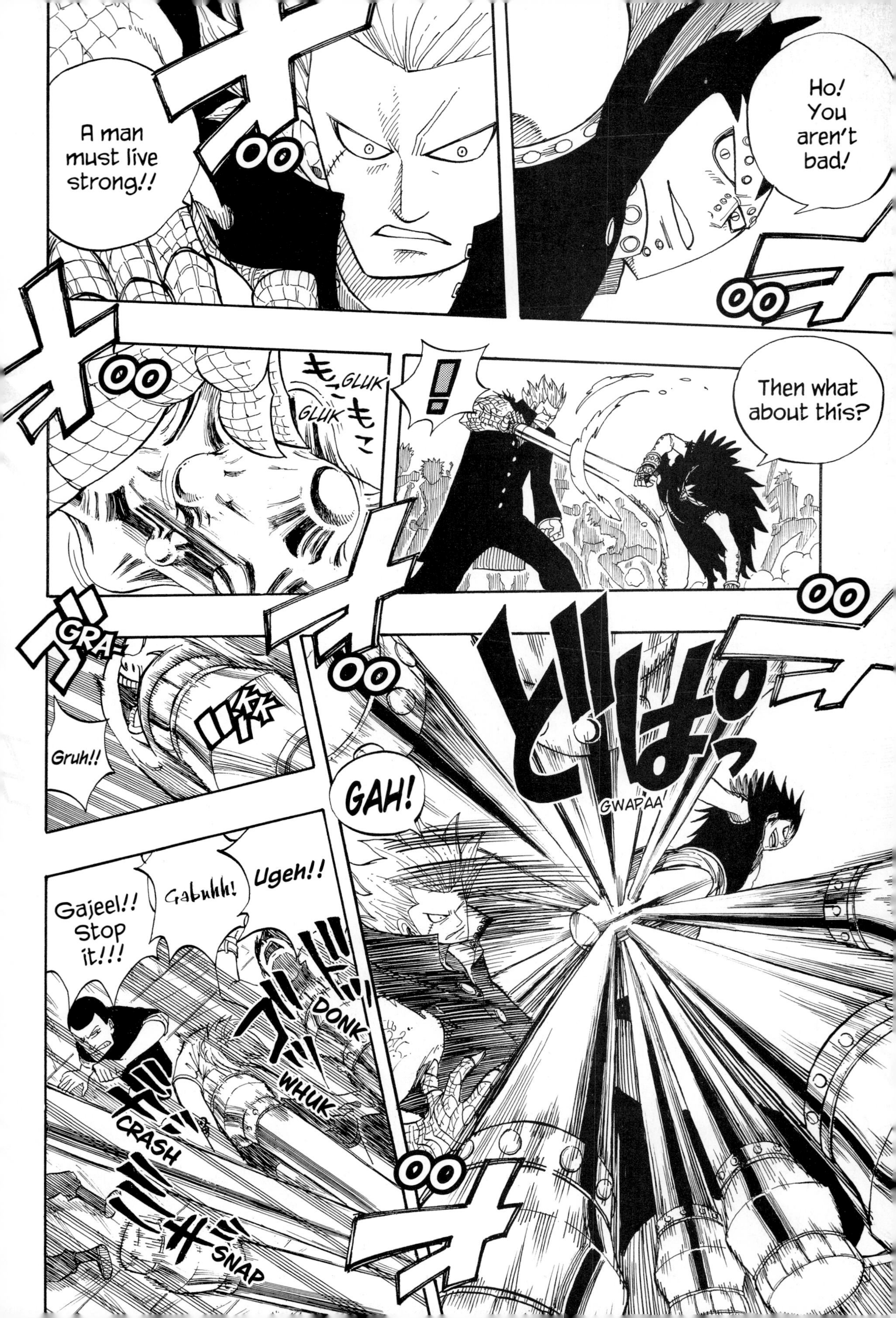
Ho! You aren't bad!
A man must live strong!!
Then what about this?
!
GLUK GLUK
GWAPAA
GAH!
GRA-
Gruh!!
Ugeh!!
Gabuhh!
Gajeel!! Stop it!!!
DONK
WHUK
CRASH
SNAP

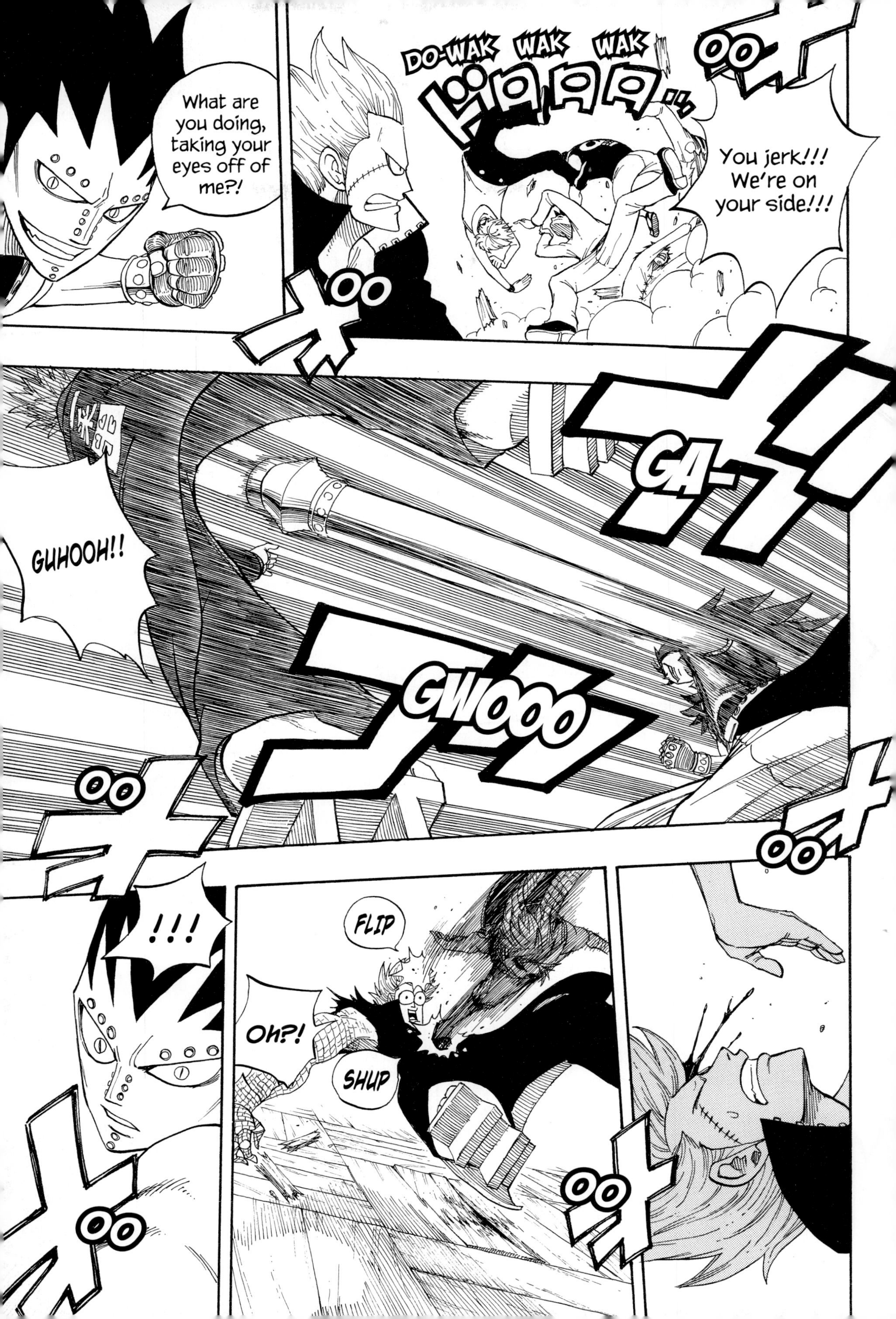
DO-WAK WAK WAK
OO
You jerk!!! We're on your side!!!
What are you doing, taking your eyes off of me?!
OO
GA-
GUHOOH!!
GWOOO
OO
OO
FLIP
Oh?!
SHUP
OO
!!!
OO

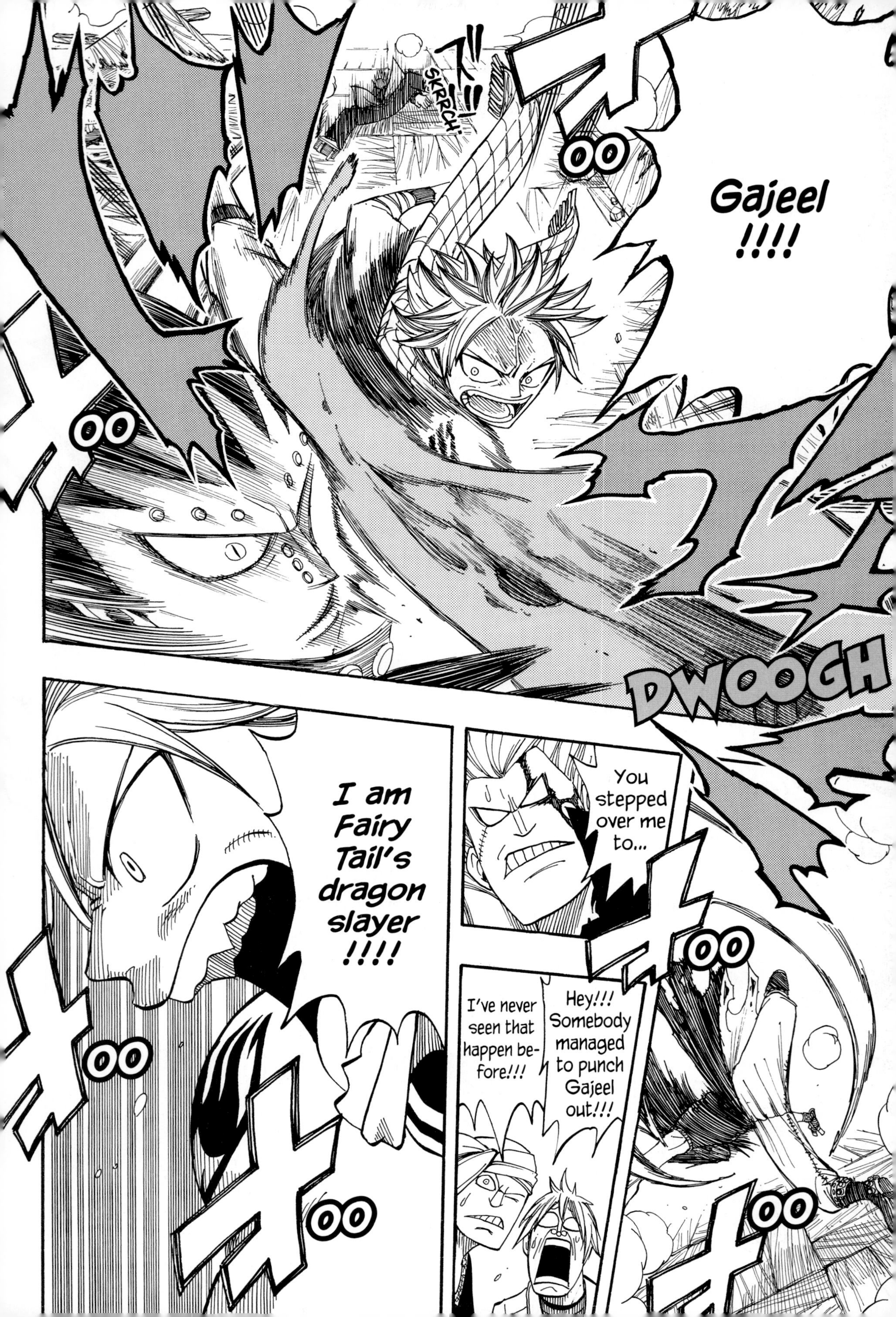
SKRRCH
Gajeel !!!!
DWOOGH
You stepped over me to...
Hey!!! Somebody managed to punch Gajeel out!!!
I've never seen that happen be-fore!!!
I am Fairy Tail's dragon slayer !!!!

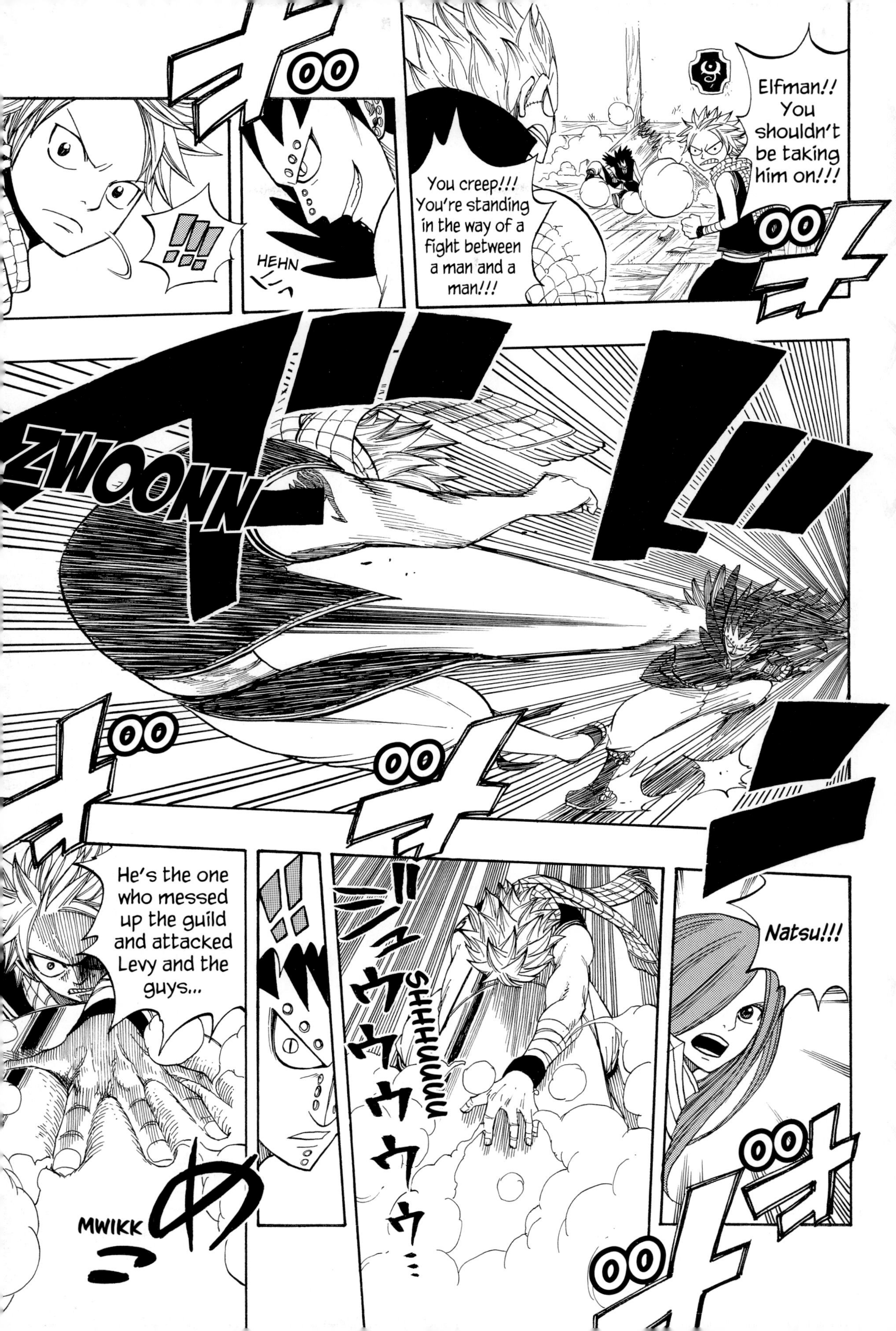
Elfman!! You shouldn't be taking him on!!!
You creep!!! You're standing in the way of a fight between a man and a man!!!
HEHN
ZWOONN
Natsu!!!
SHHUUUUU
He's the one who messed up the guild and attacked Levy and the guys...
MWIKK

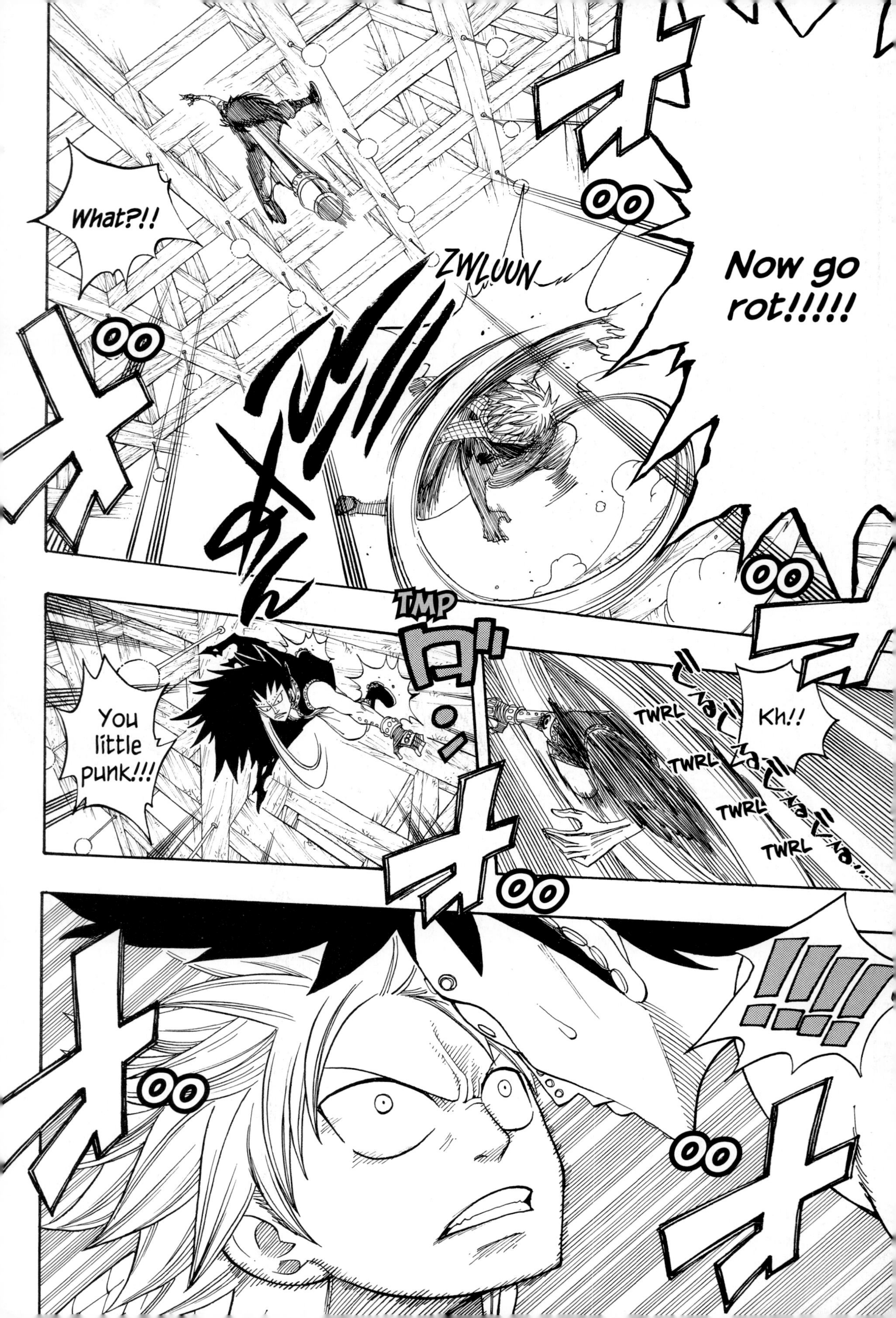

Now go rot!!!!!
ZWLUUN
What?!!
TMP
Kh!!
TWRL
TWRL
TWRL
TWRL
You little punk!!!

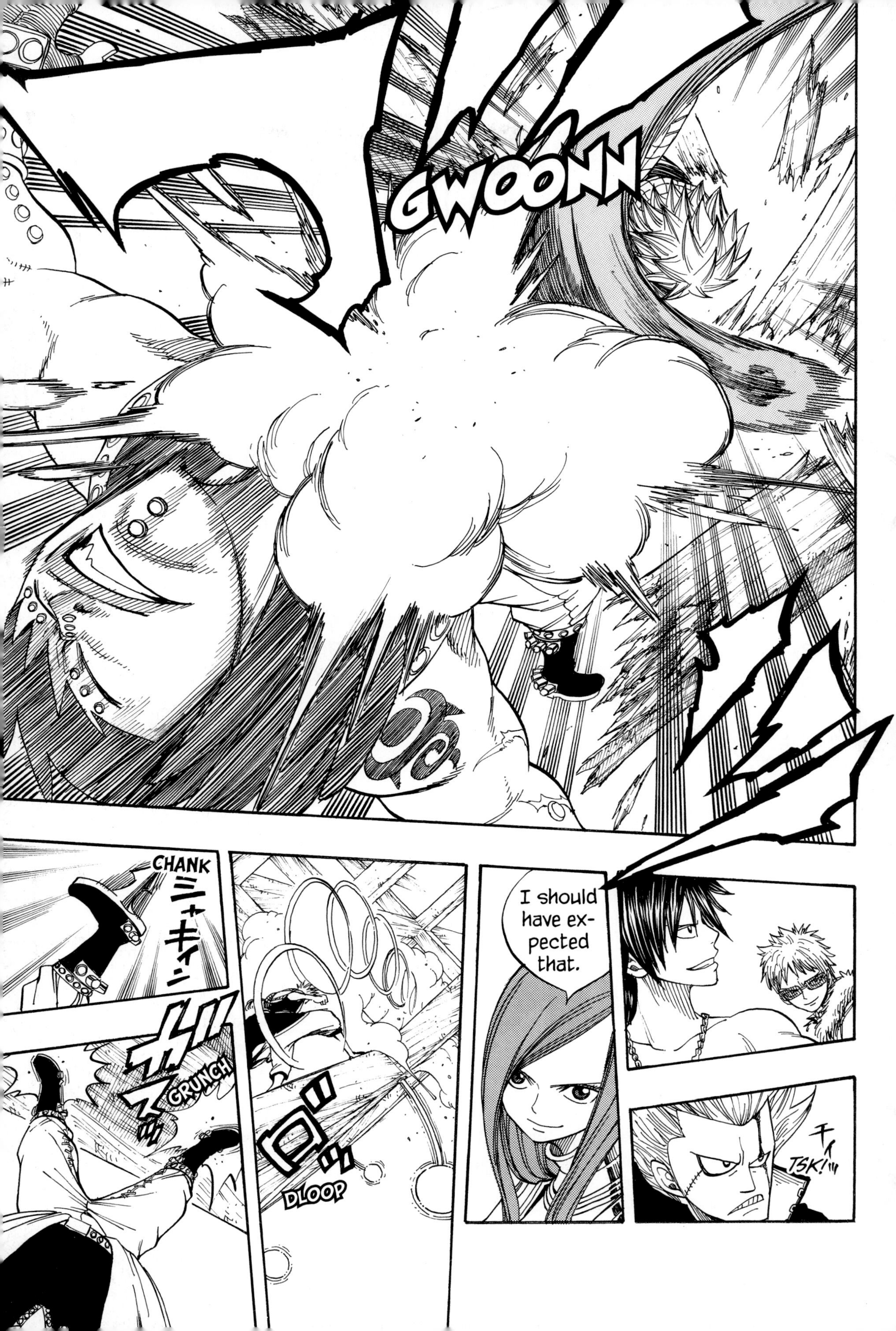
GWOONN
TSK!
I should have expected that.
DLOOP
CHANK
シャキィン
GRUNCH

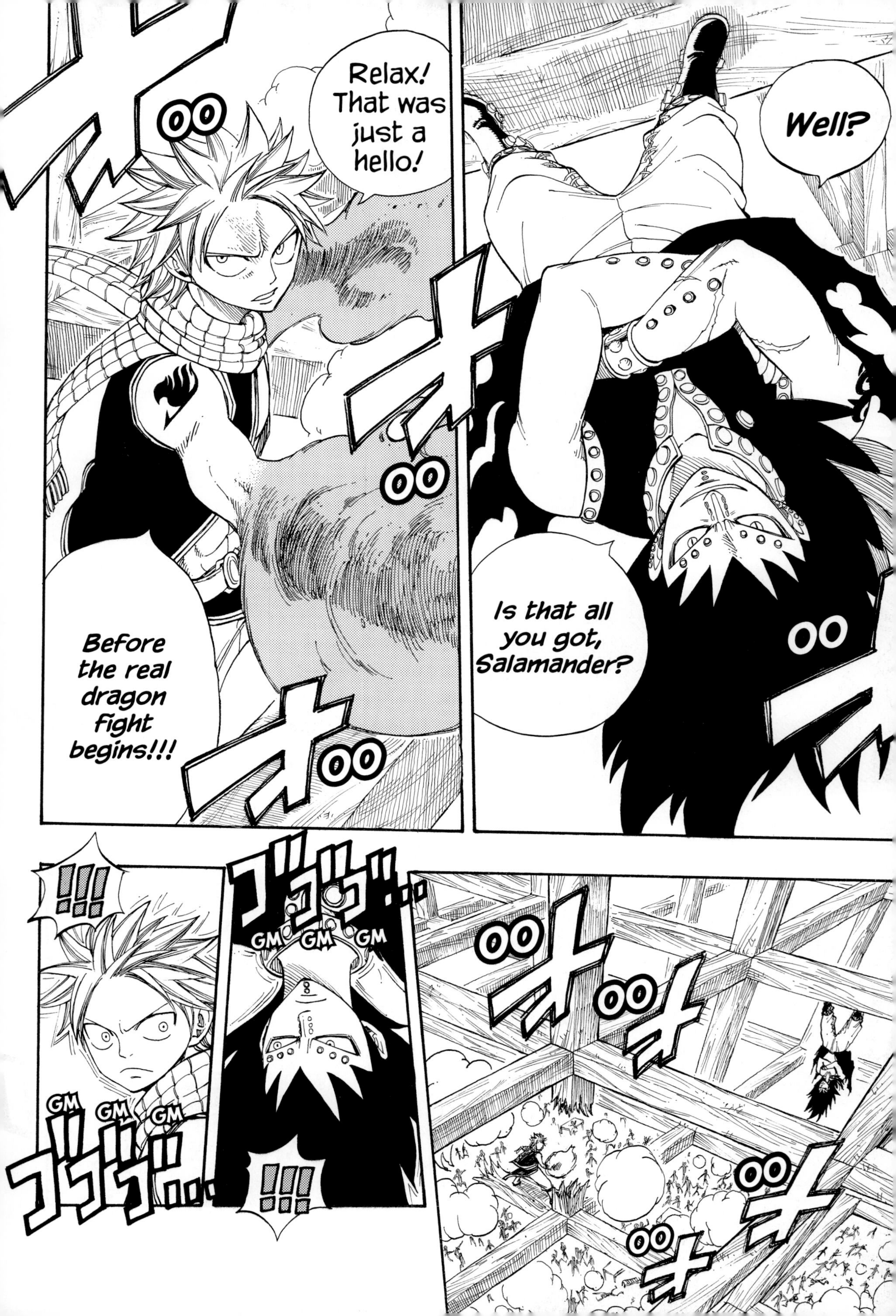
Well?
Is that all you got, Salamander?
OO
Relax! That was just a hello!
OO
OO
Before the real dragon fight begins!!!
OO
OO
OO
OO
OO
GM GM GM
!!!
!!!
GM GM GM

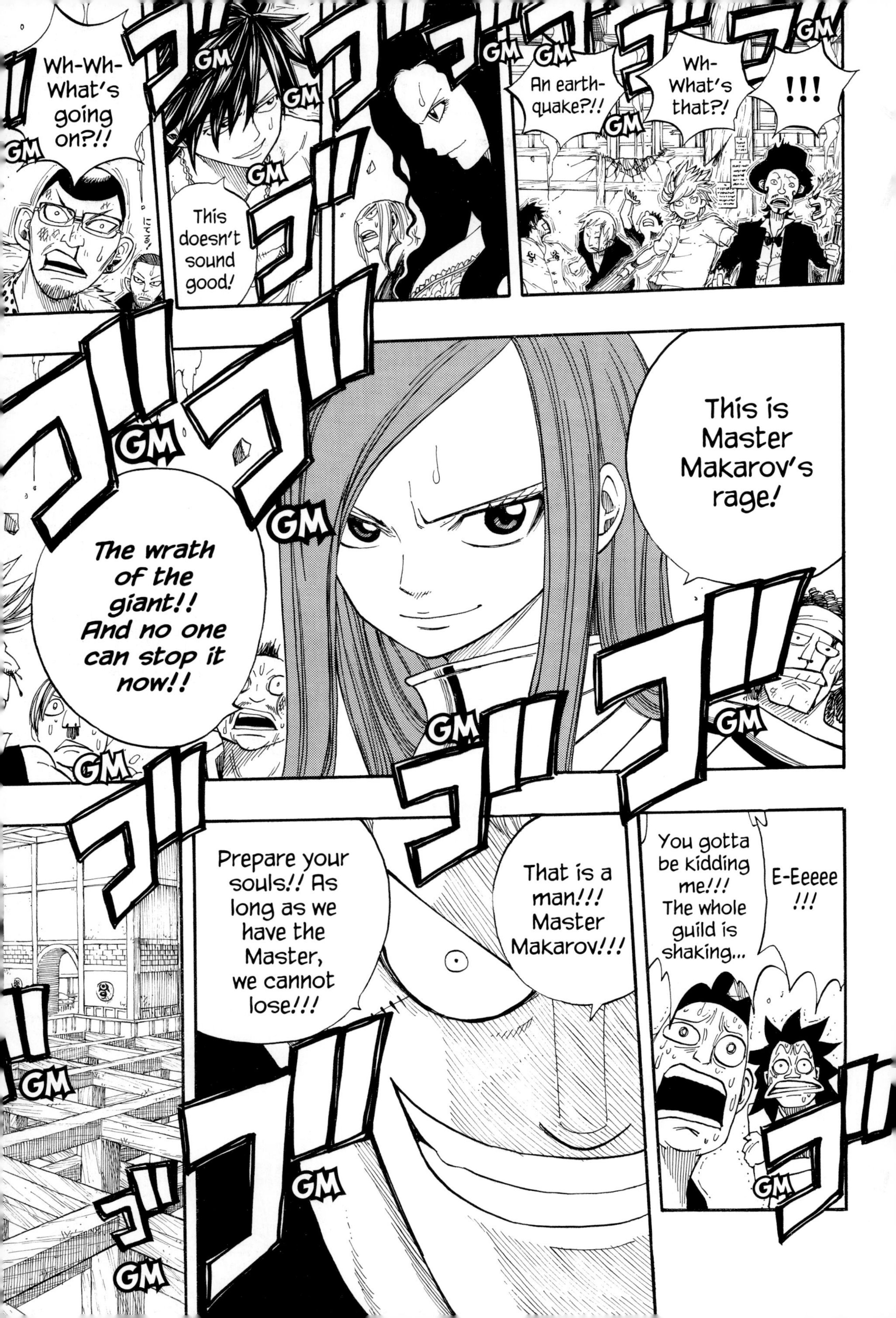
GM
!!!
Wh-What's that?!
An earthquake?!!
GM
GM
This doesn't sound good!
GM
GM
Wh-Wh-What's going on?!!
GM
This is Master Makarov's rage!
GM
GM
GM
The wrath of the giant!! And no one can stop it now!!
GM
GM
E-Eeeee!!!
You gotta be kidding me!!! The whole guild is shaking...
GM
That is a man!!! Master Makarov!!!
Prepare your souls!! As long as we have the Master, we cannot lose!!!
GM
GM
GM

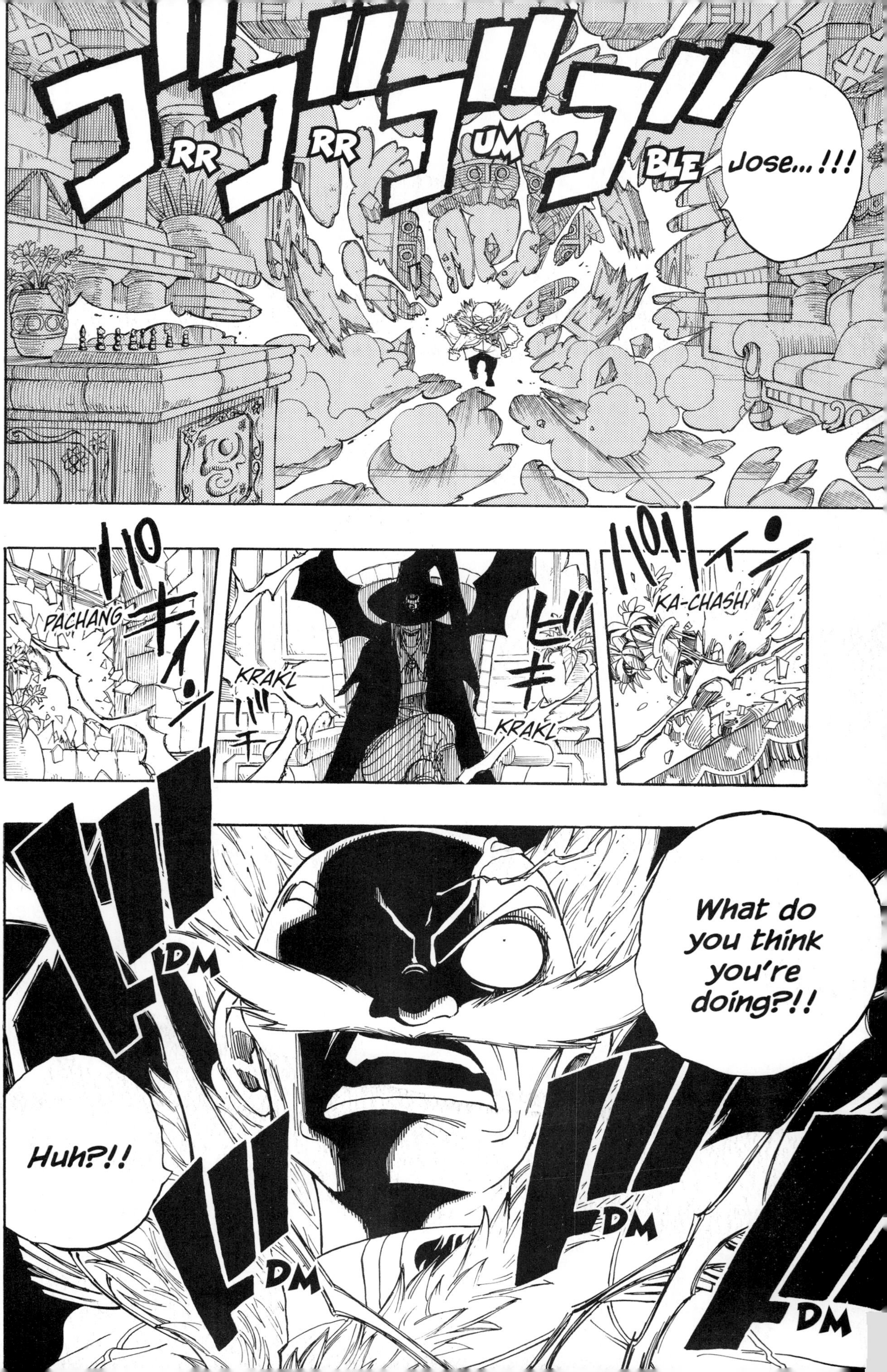
Jose...!!!
RRRRUMBLE
KA-CHASH
KRAKL
KRAKL
PACHANG
What do you think you're doing?!!
Huh?!!
DM
DM
DM
DM

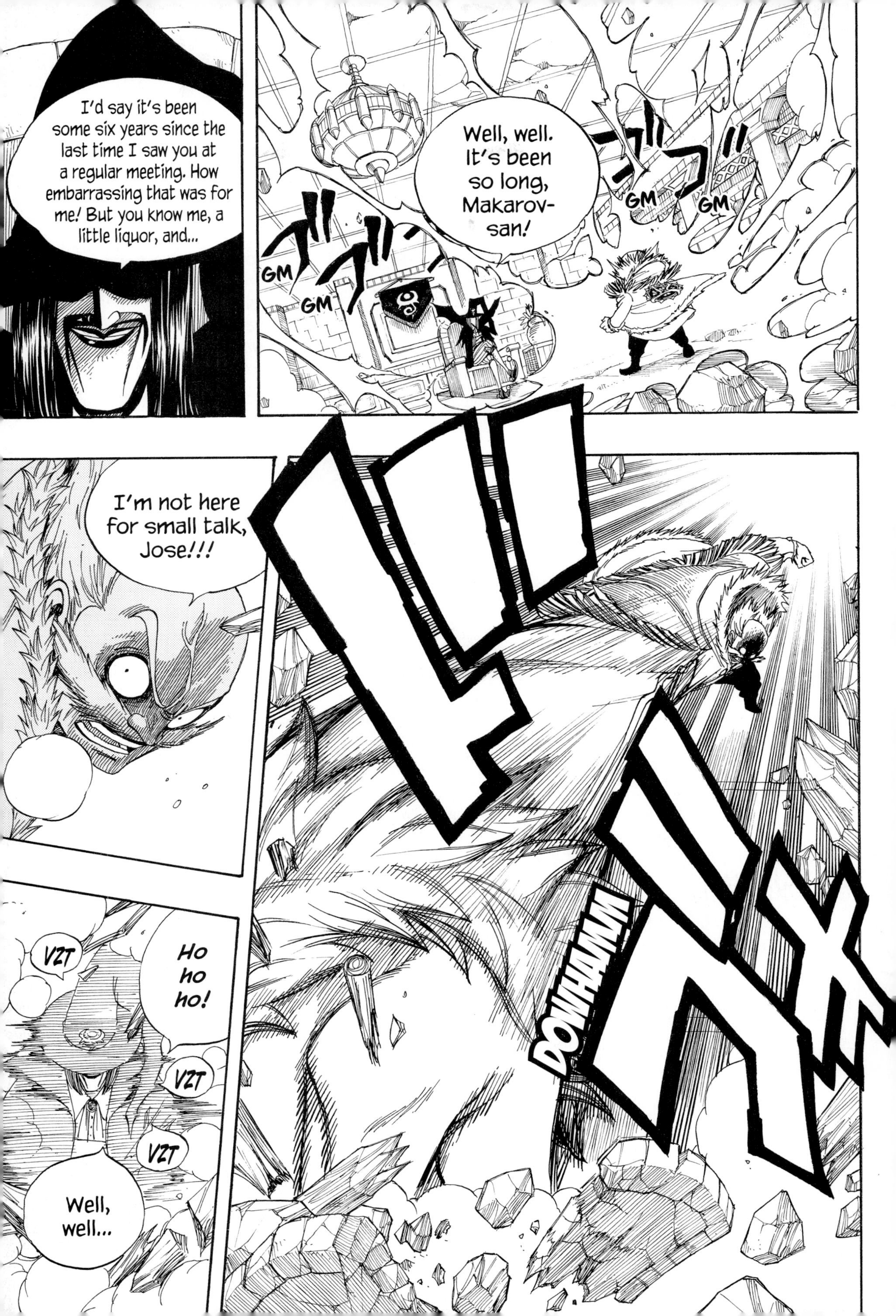
GM
GM
Well, well. It's been so long, Makarov-san!
GM
GM
I'd say it's been some six years since the last time I saw you at a regular meeting. How embarrassing that was for me! But you know me, a little liquor, and...
DOWHAMM
I'm not here for small talk, Jose!!!
Ho ho ho!
VZT
VZT
VZT
Well, well...

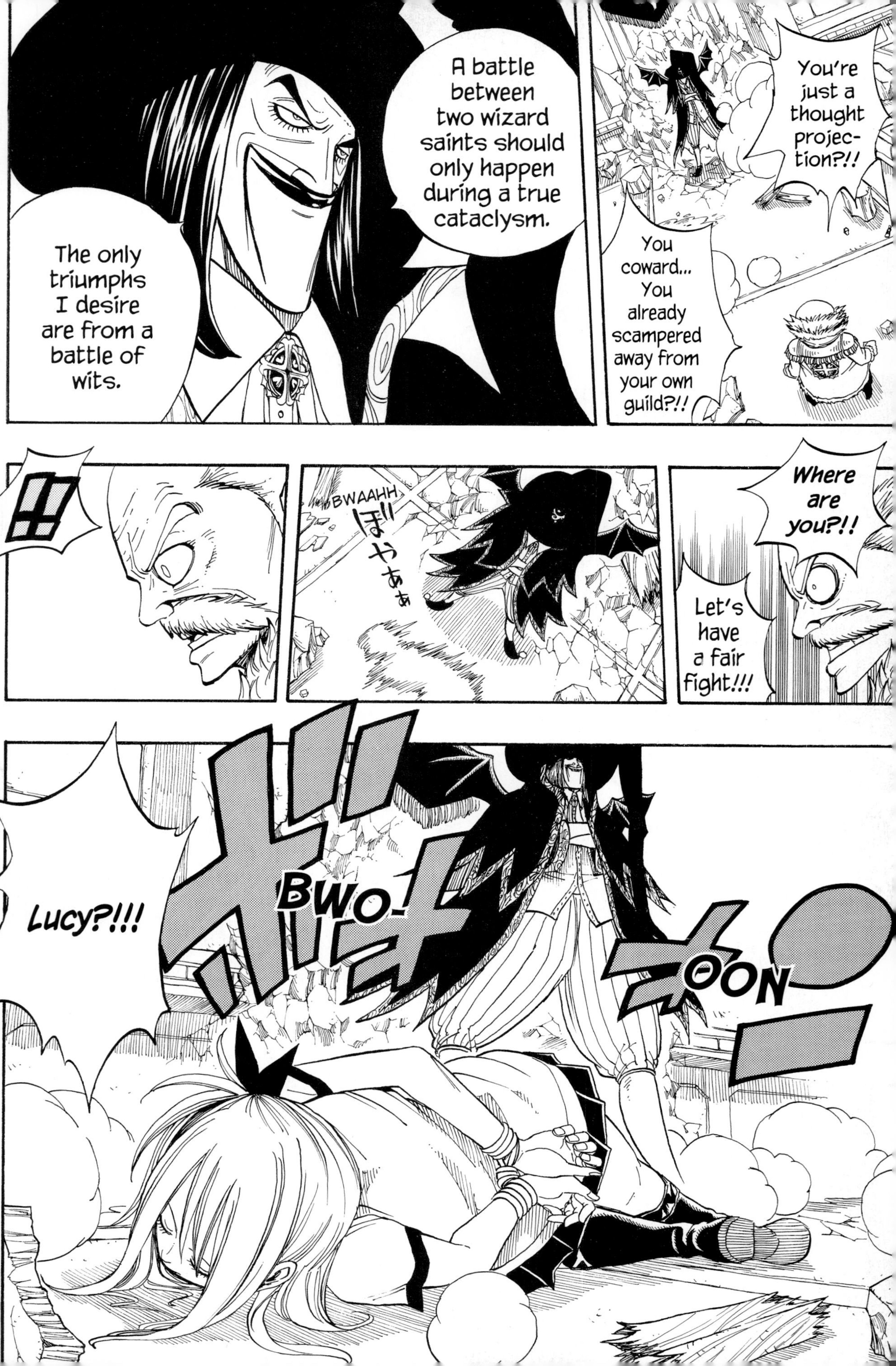
You're just a thought projection?!!
You coward... You already scampered away from your own guild?!!
A battle between two wizard saints should only happen during a true cataclysm.
The only triumphs I desire are from a battle of wits.
Where are you?!!
Let's have a fair fight!!!
BWAAHH
ぼやぁぁ
!!
BWO-
OON
Lucy?!!!

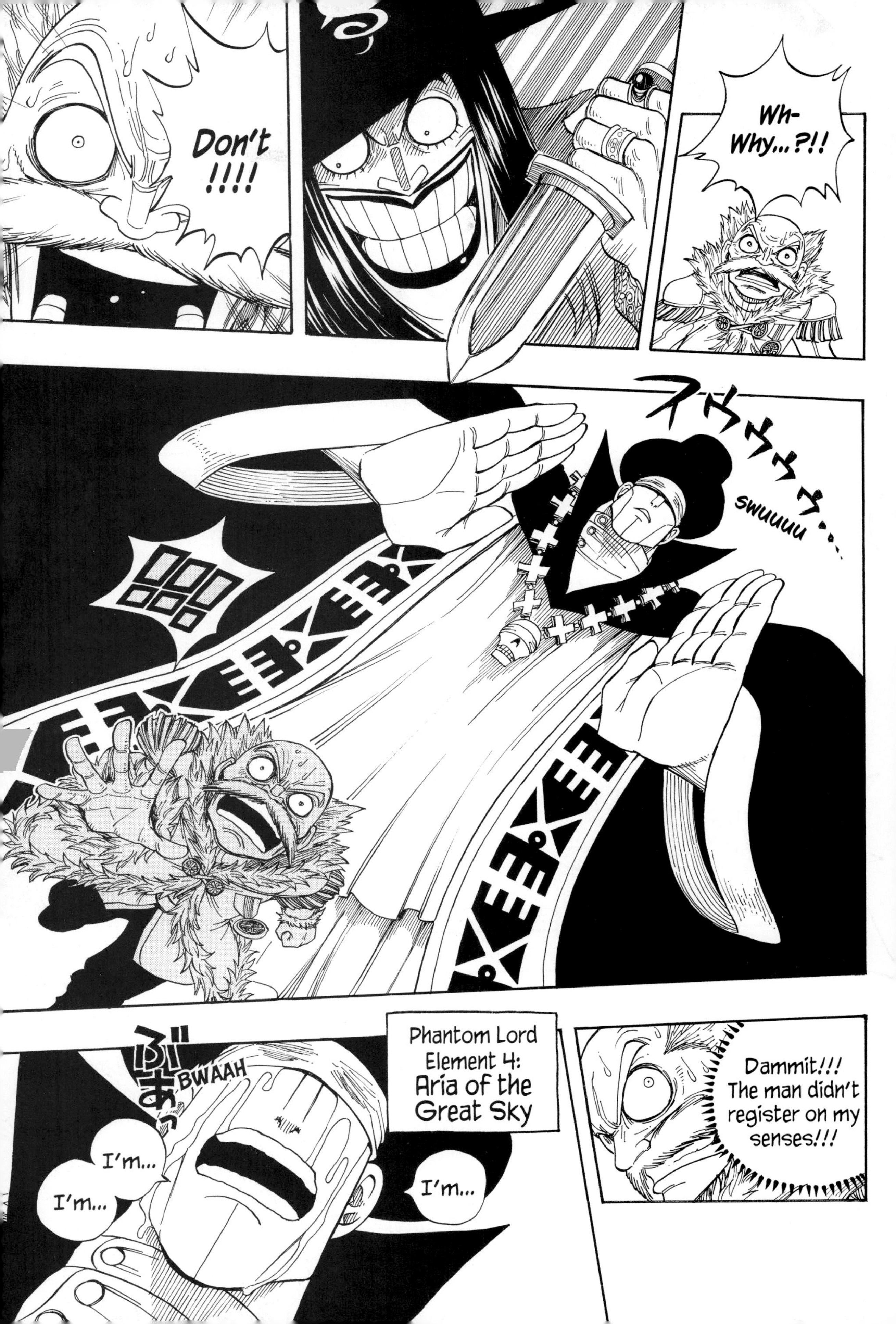
Wh- Why...?!!
Don't !!!!
swuuuu...
Dammit!!! The man didn't register on my senses!!!
Phantom Lord Element 4: Aria of the Great Sky
ぶあっ
BWAAH
I'm...
I'm...
I'm...

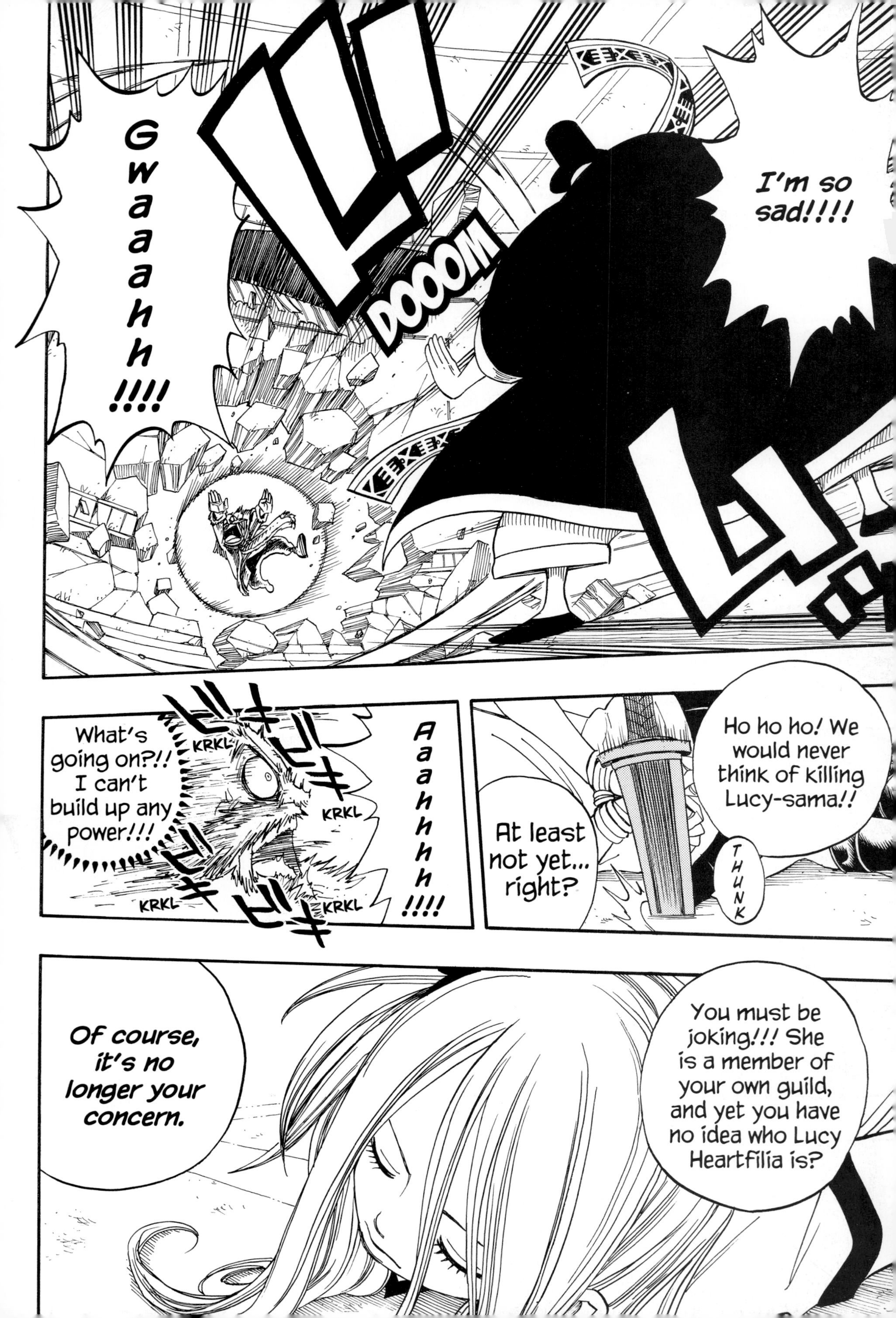
I'm so sad!!!!
DOOOM
Gwaaahh!!!!
Ho ho ho! We would never think of killing Lucy-sama!!
THUNK
At least not yet... right?
Aaahhhh!!!!
What's going on?!! I can't build up any power!!!
KRKL
KRKL
KRKL
KRKL
You must be joking!!! She is a member of your own guild, and yet you have no idea who Lucy Heartfilia is?
Of course, it's no longer your concern.

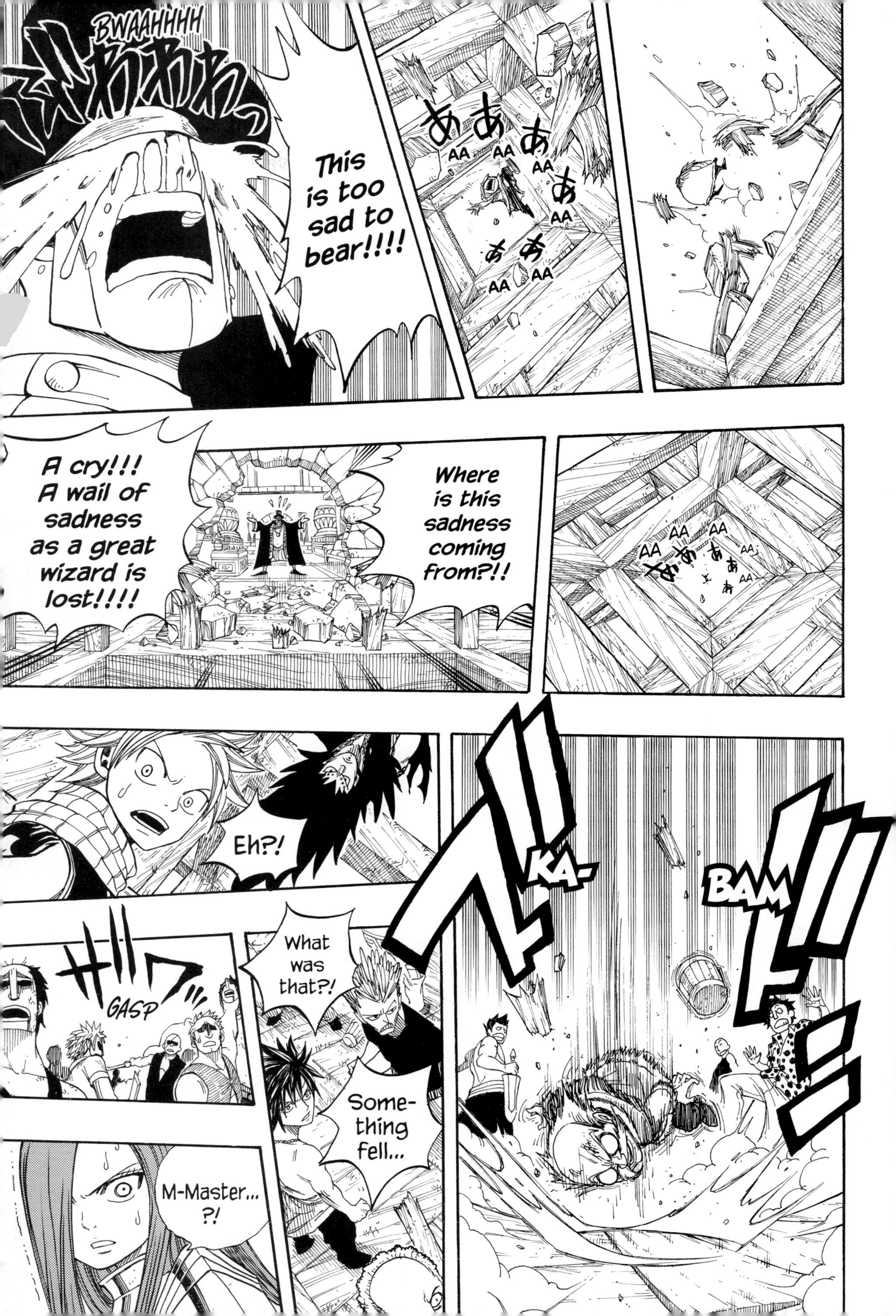
AA AA AA AA AA AA
BWAAHHHH
This is too sad to bear!!!!
AA AA AA AA AA
Where is this sadness coming from?!!
A cry!!! A wail of sadness as a great wizard is lost!!!!
KA-
BAM
Eh?!
What was that?!
GASP
Some-thing fell...
M-Master...?!

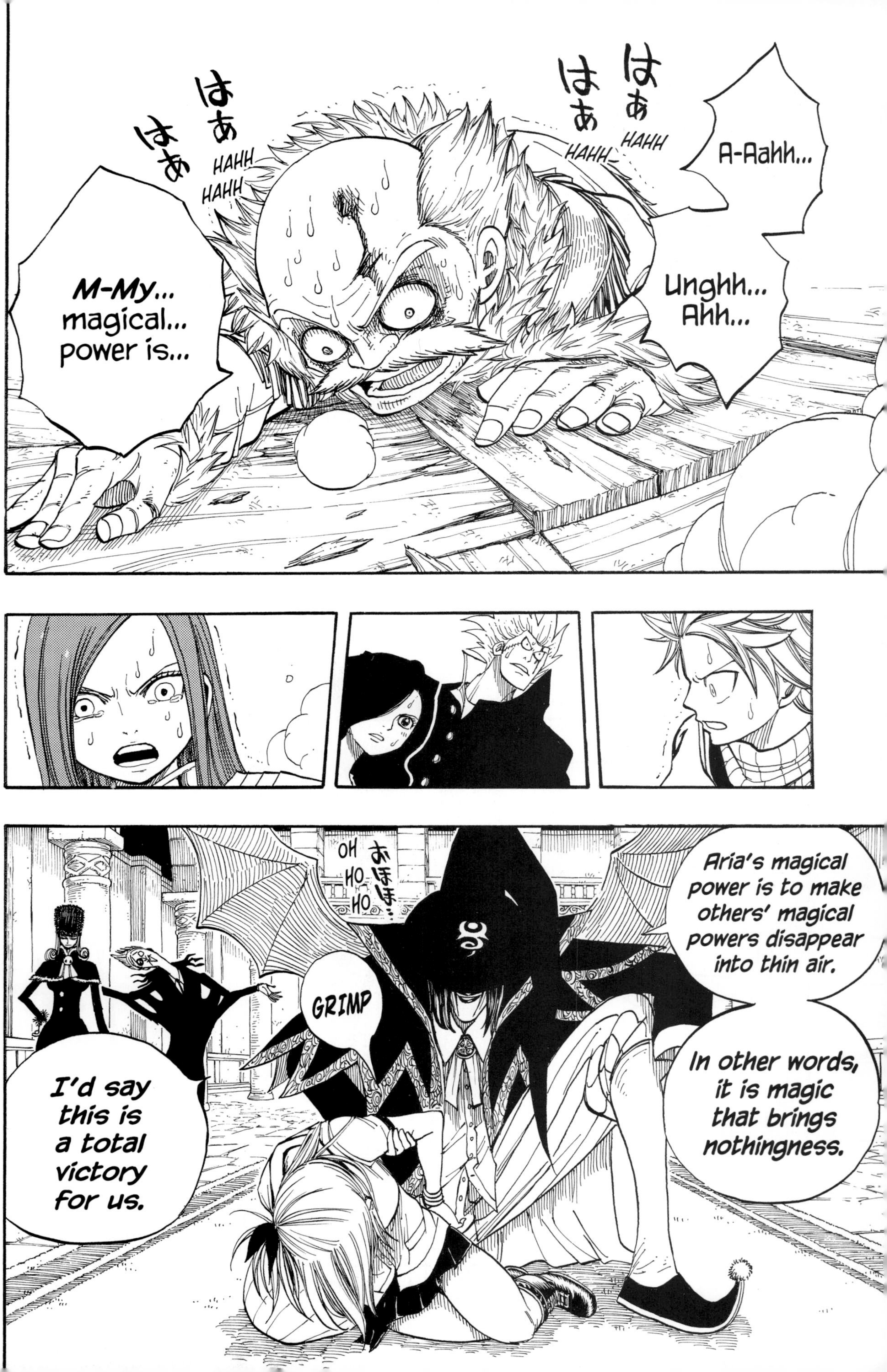
A-Aahh...
はぁ
はぁ
HAHH
HAHH
Unghh... Ahh...
はぁ
はぁ
HAHH
HAHH
M-My... magical... power is...
Aria's magical power is to make others' magical powers disappear into thin air.
In other words, it is magic that brings nothingness.
おほほ
OH HO HO
GRIMP
I'd say this is a total victory for us.

FAIRY TAIL

50

Chapter 50: Lucy Heartfilia

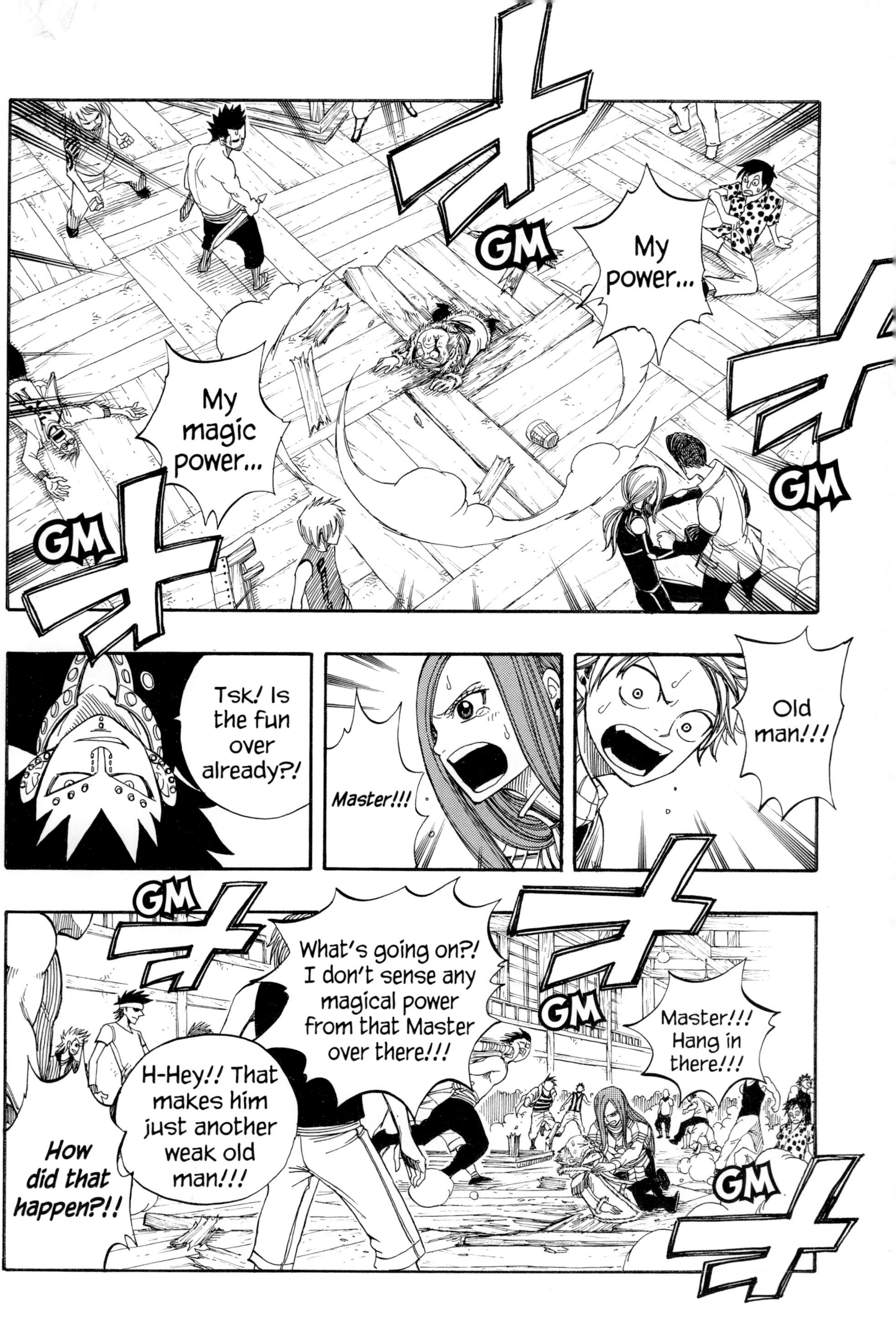
GM
My power...
GM
GM
My magic power...
Old man!!!
Master!!!
Tsk! Is the fun over already?!
GM
Master!!! Hang in there!!!
GM
What's going on?! I don't sense any magical power from that Master over there!!!
GM
H-Hey!! That makes him just another weak old man!!!
How did that happen?!!

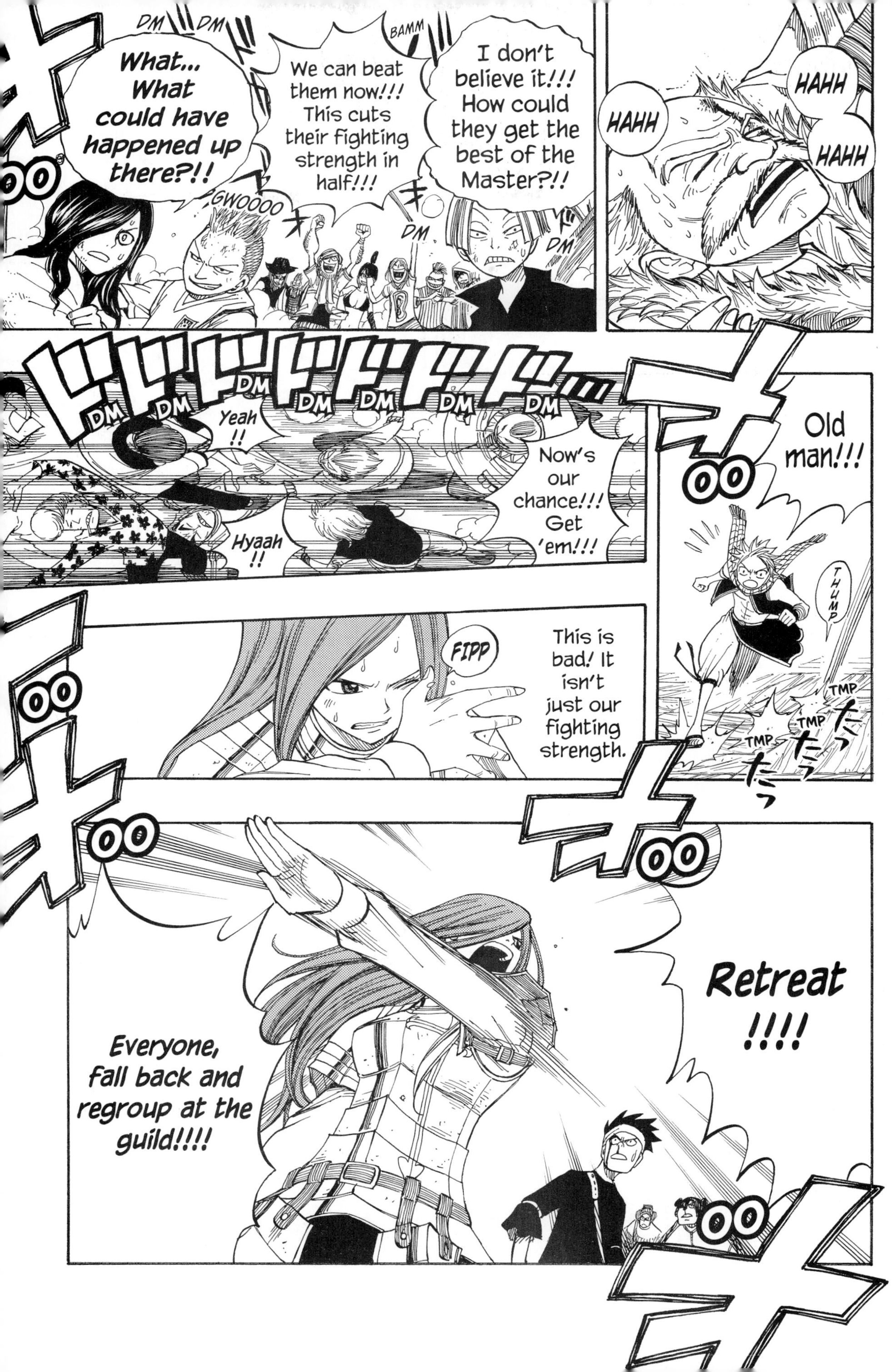
HAHH
HAHH
HAHH
I don't believe it!!! How could they get the best of the Master?!!
BAMM
We can beat them now!!! This cuts their fighting strength in half!!!
DM DM
What... What could have happened up there?!!
GWOOOO
DM
DM
Old man!!!
THUMP
TMP
TMP
TMP
DM DM DM DM DM DM DM
Now's our chance!!! Get 'em!!!
Yeah!!
Hyaah!!
This is bad! It isn't just our fighting strength.
FIPP
Retreat!!!!
Everyone, fall back and regroup at the guild!!!!

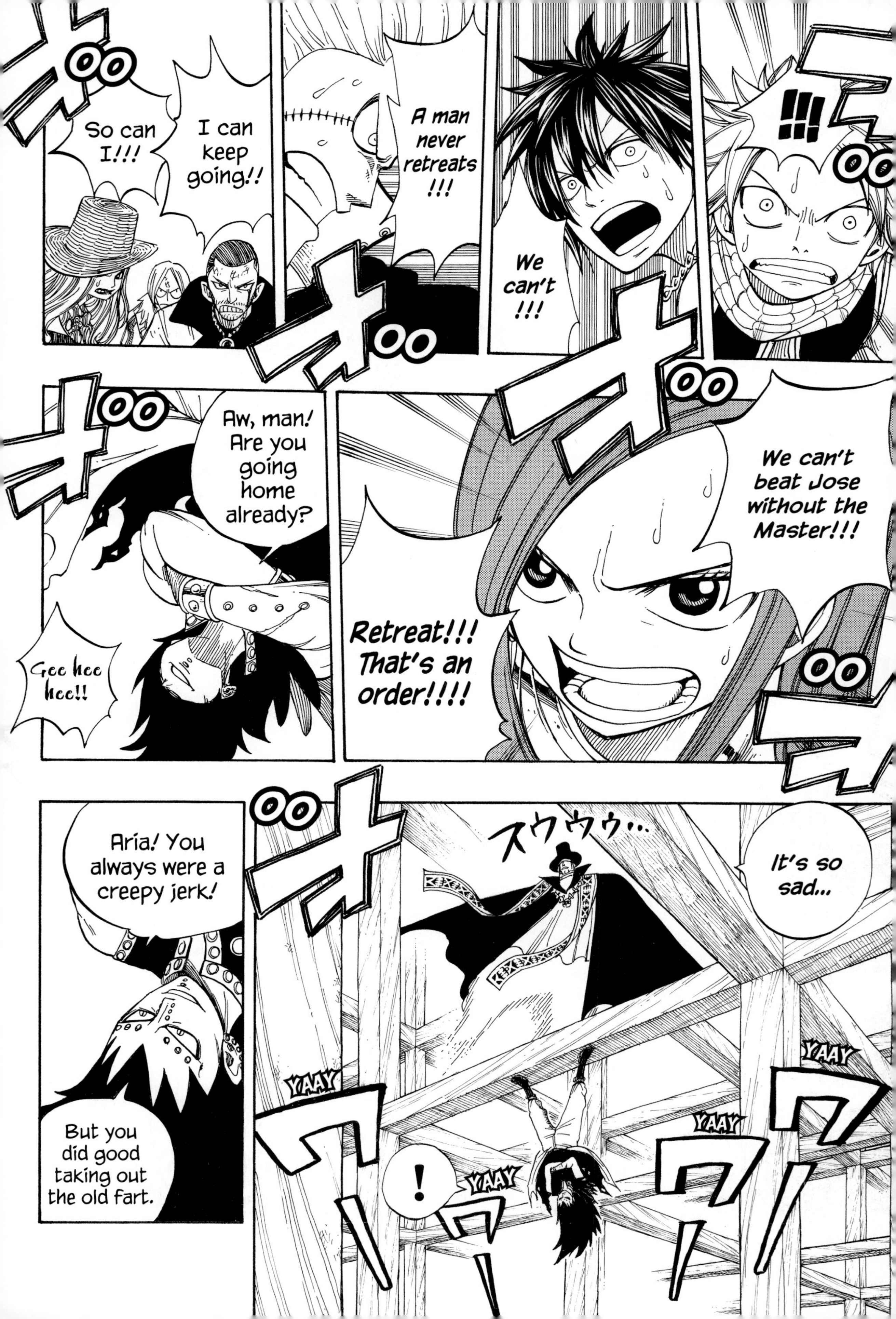
!!!
We can't!!!
A man never retreats!!!
I can keep going!!
So can I!!!
We can't beat Jose without the Master!!!
Retreat!!! That's an order!!!!
Aw, man! Are you going home already?
Gee hee hee!!
It's so sad...
スウウウ…
YAAY
YAAY
!
YAAY
YAAY
Aria! You always were a creepy jerk!
But you did good taking out the old fart.

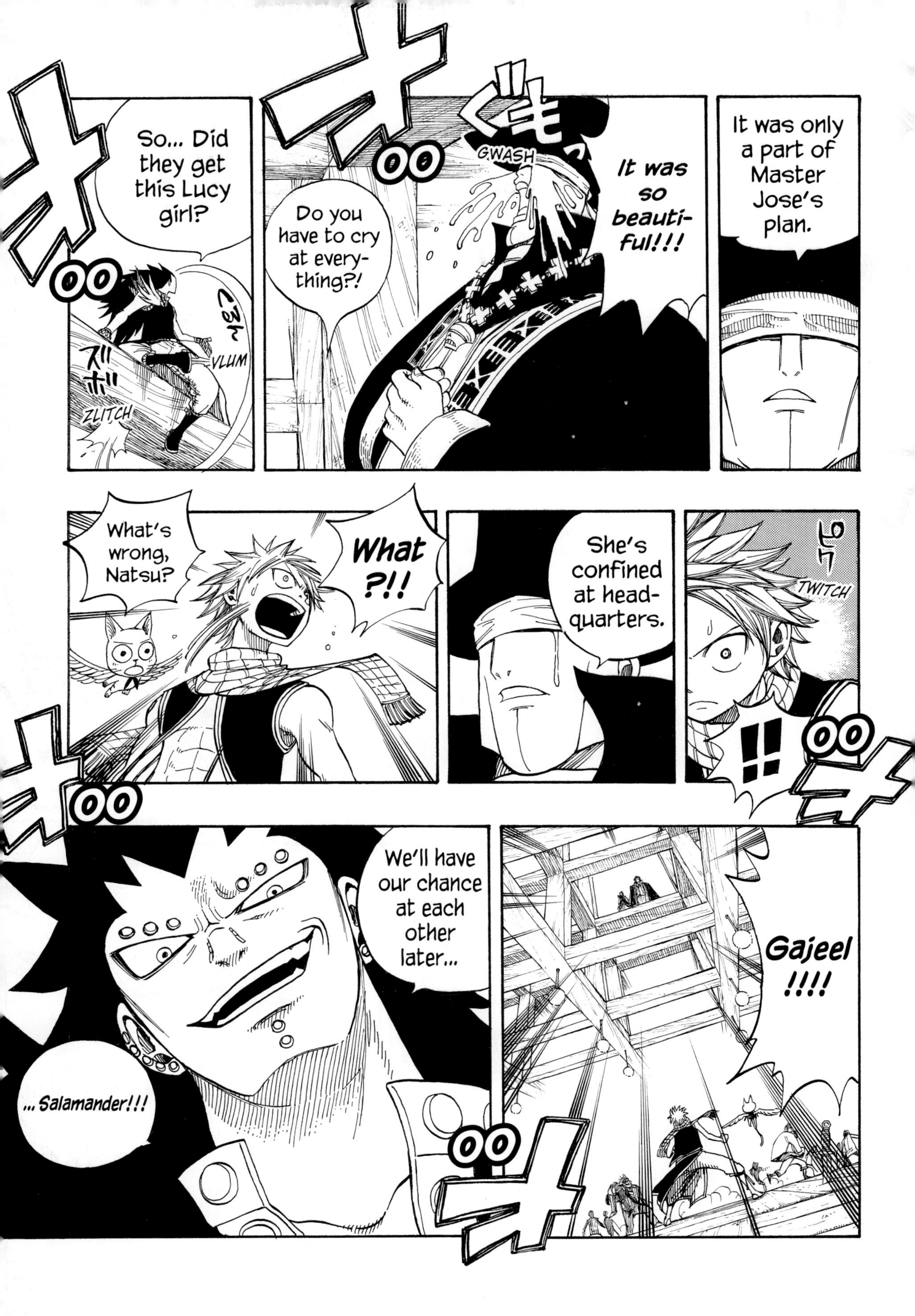
It was only a part of Master Jose's plan.
It was so beautiful!!!
GWASH
Do you have to cry at everything?!
So... Did they get this Lucy girl?
VLUM
ZLITCH
TWITCH
She's confined at headquarters.
What?!!
What's wrong, Natsu?
Gajeel!!!!
We'll have our chance at each other later...
...Salamander!!!

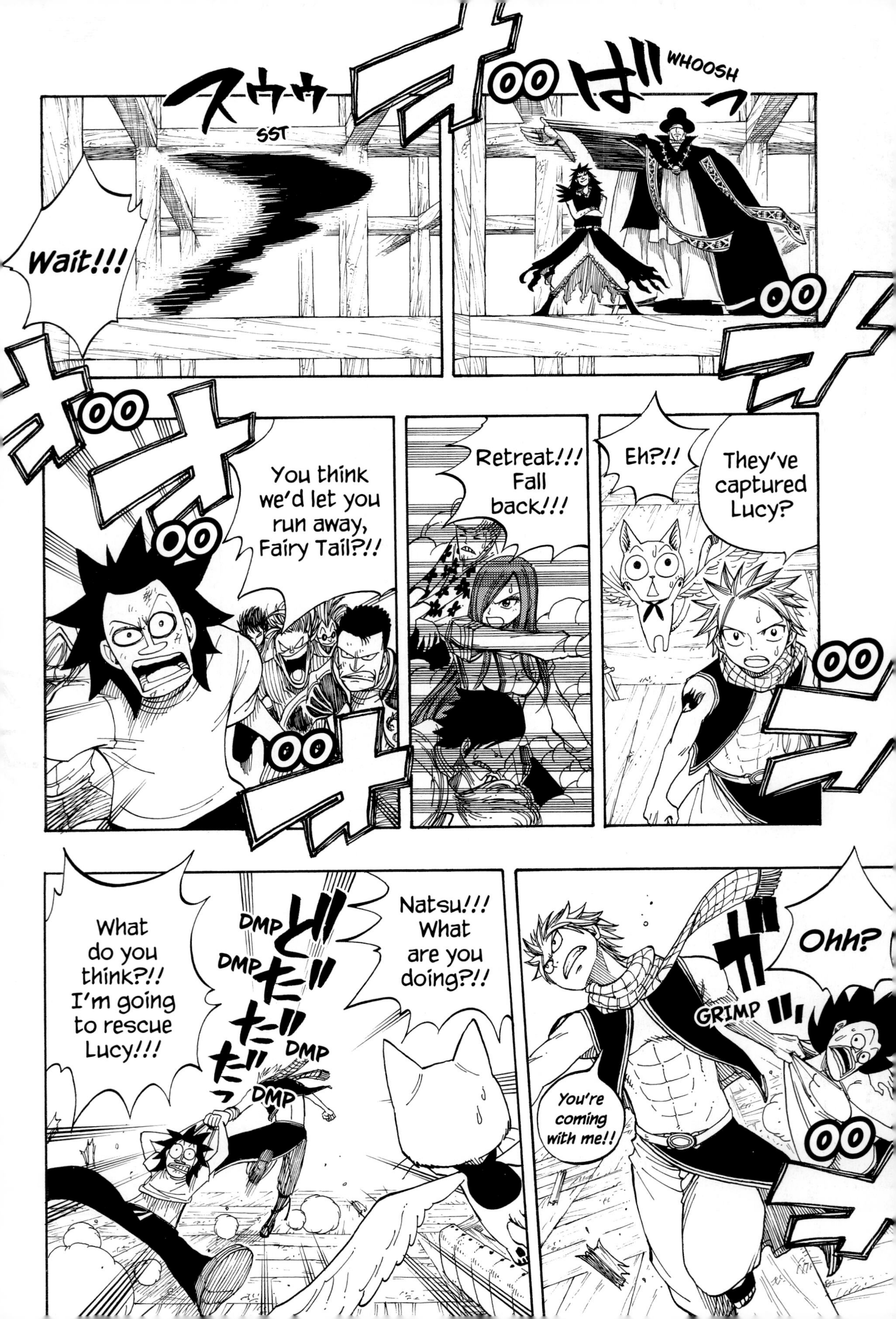
ばっ
WHOOSH
スゥゥ
SST
Wait!!!
They've captured Lucy?
Eh?!!
Retreat!!! Fall back!!!
You think we'd let you run away, Fairy Tail?!!
Ohh?
ガッ
GRIMP
You're coming with me!!
Natsu!!! What are you doing?!!
What do you think?!! I'm going to rescue Lucy!!!
どたたたっ
DMP
DMP
DMP
DMP

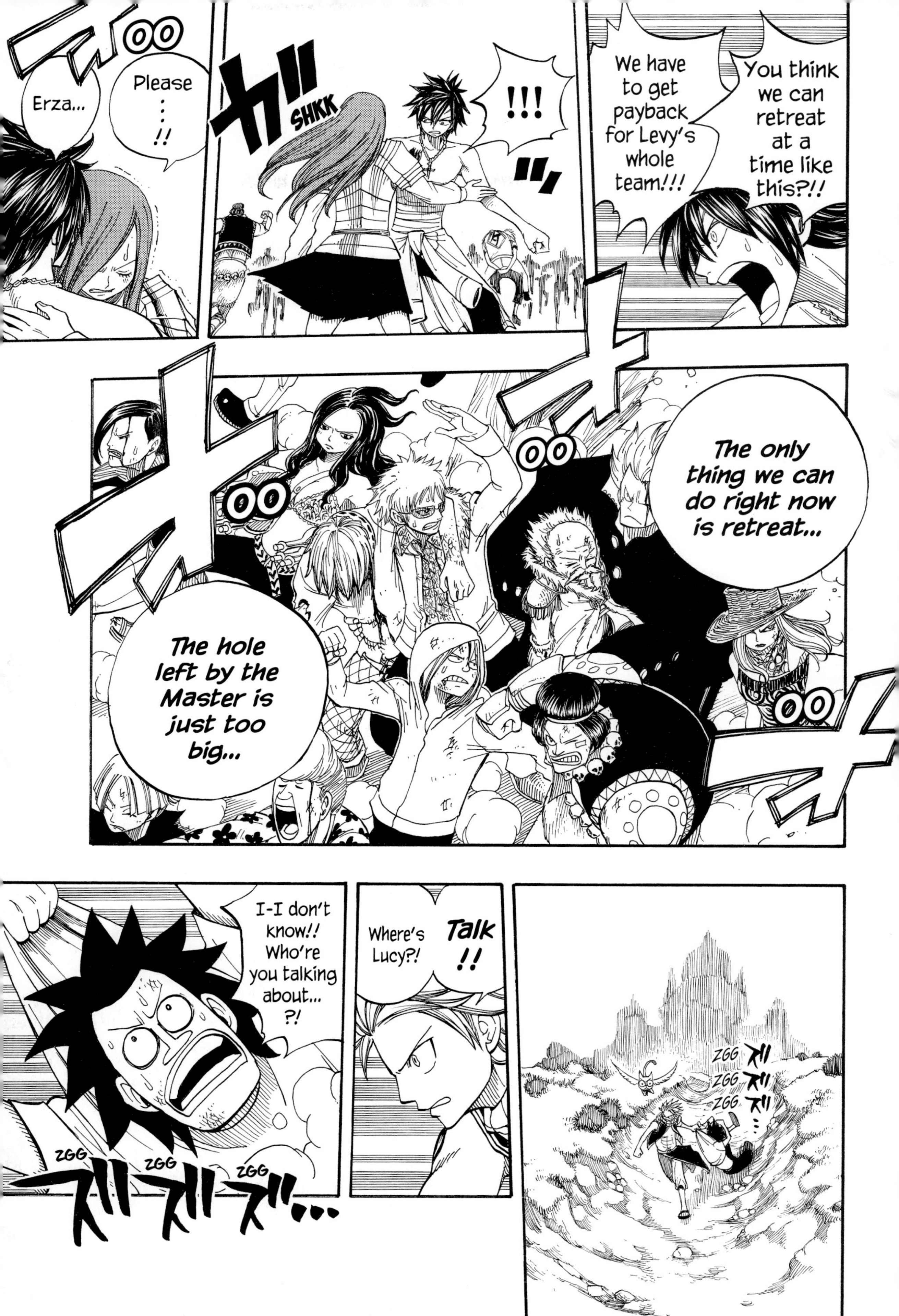
You think we can retreat at a time like this?!!
We have to get payback for Levy's whole team!!!
SHKK
!!!
Please ...!!
Erza...
The only thing we can do right now is retreat...
The hole left by the Master is just too big...
ZGG
ZGG
ZGG
Talk !!
Where's Lucy?!
I-I don't know!! Who're you talking about...?!
ZGG
ZGG
ZGG

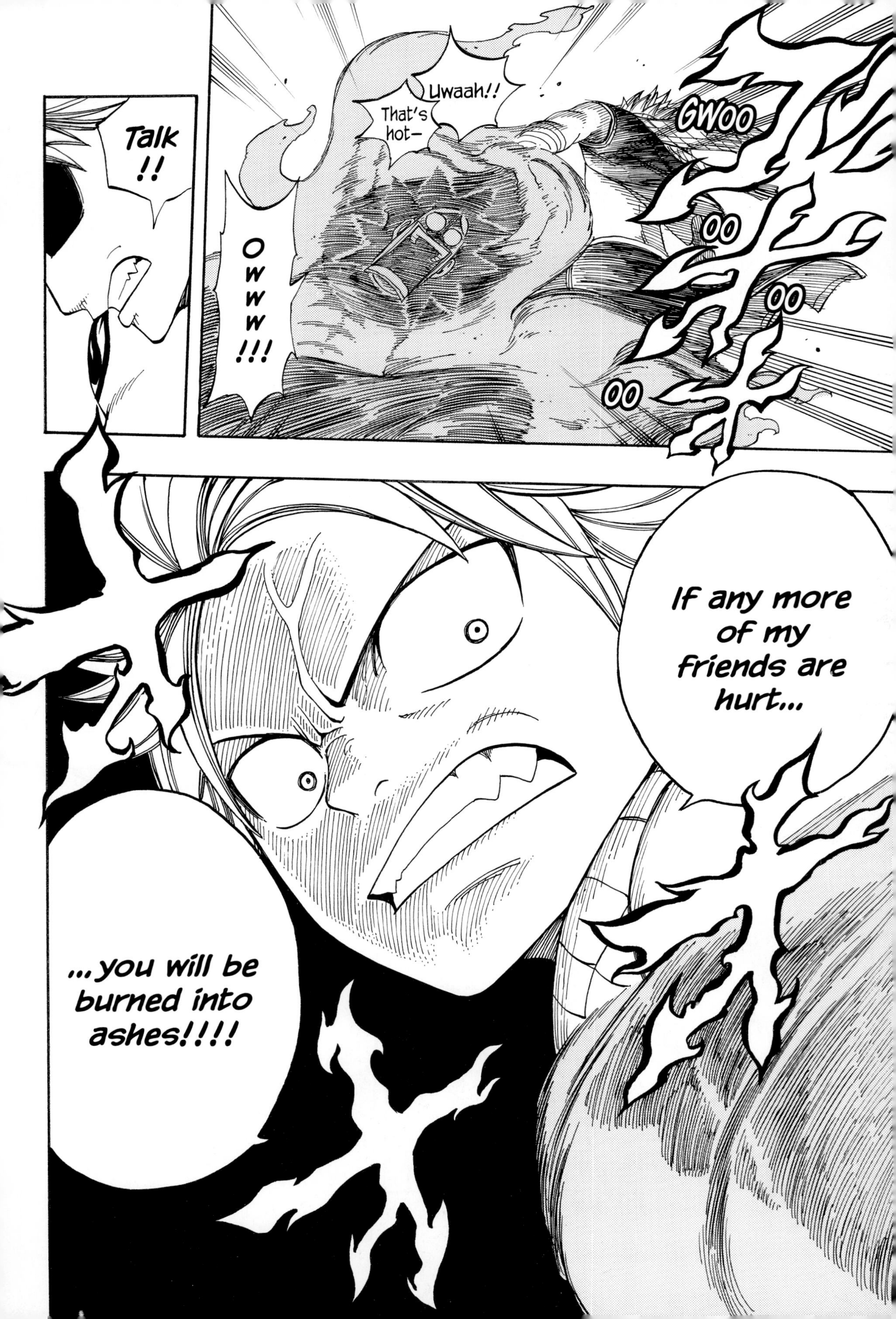
GWOO OO OO OO
Uwaah!!
That's hot-
Owwww!!!
Talk!!
If any more of my friends are hurt...
...you will be burned into ashes!!!!

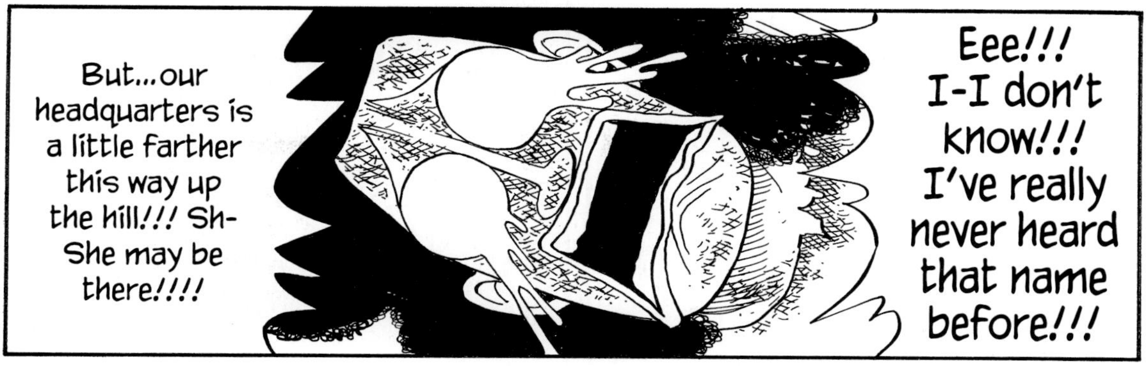
Eee!!! I-I don't know!!! I've really never heard that name before!!!
But...our headquarters is a little farther this way up the hill!!! Sh-She may be there!!!!

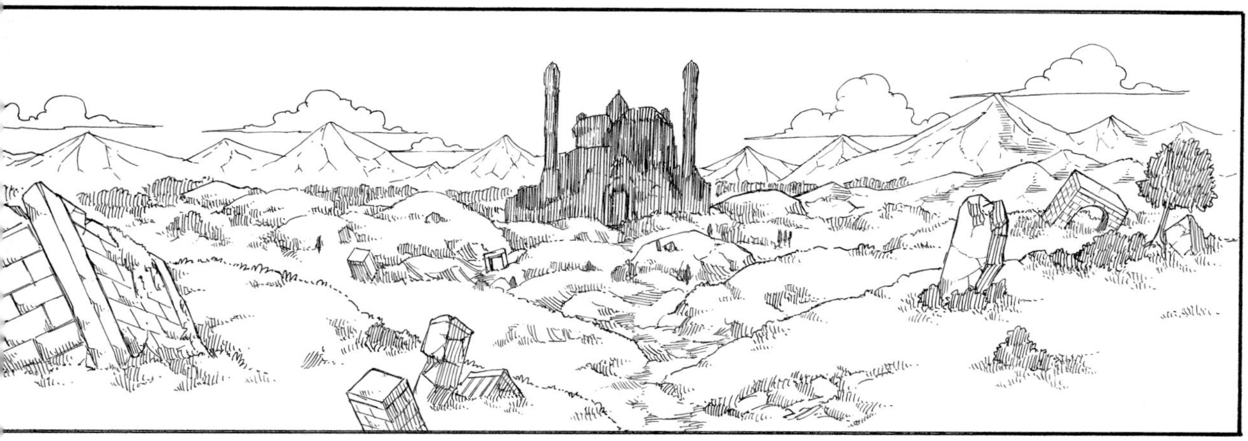

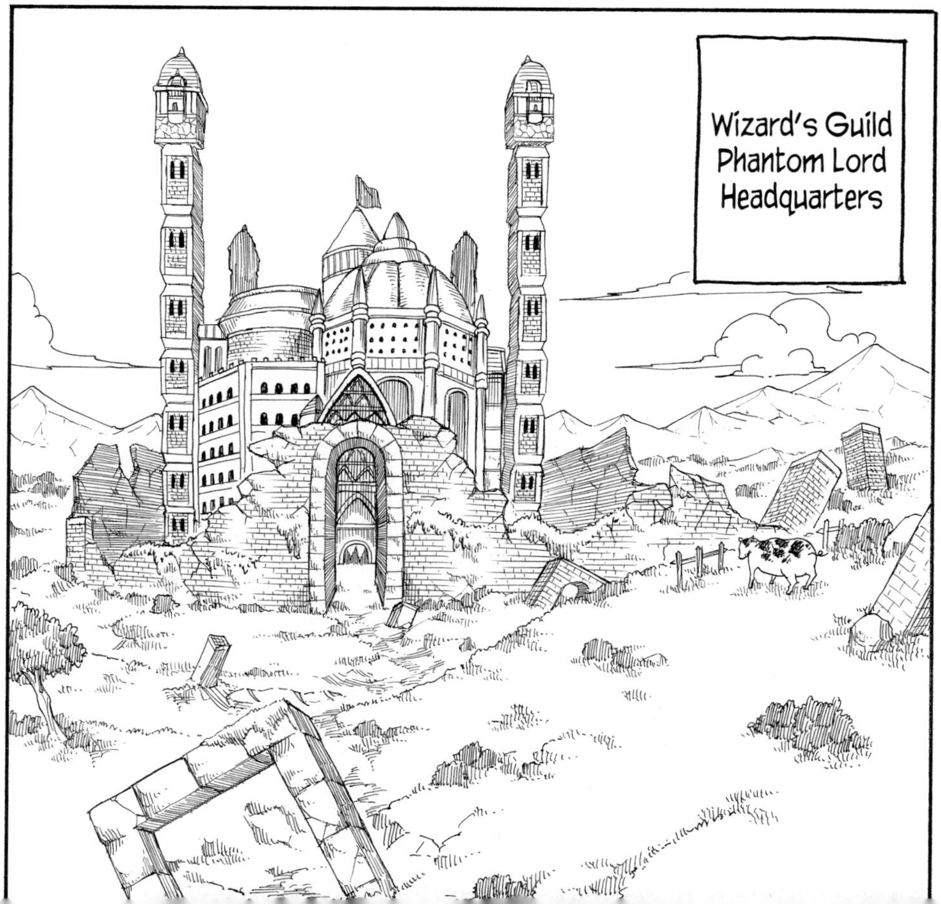
Wizard's Guild Phantom Lord Headquarters

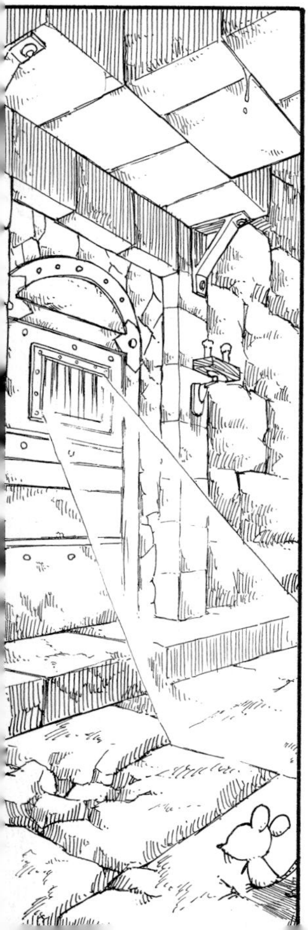

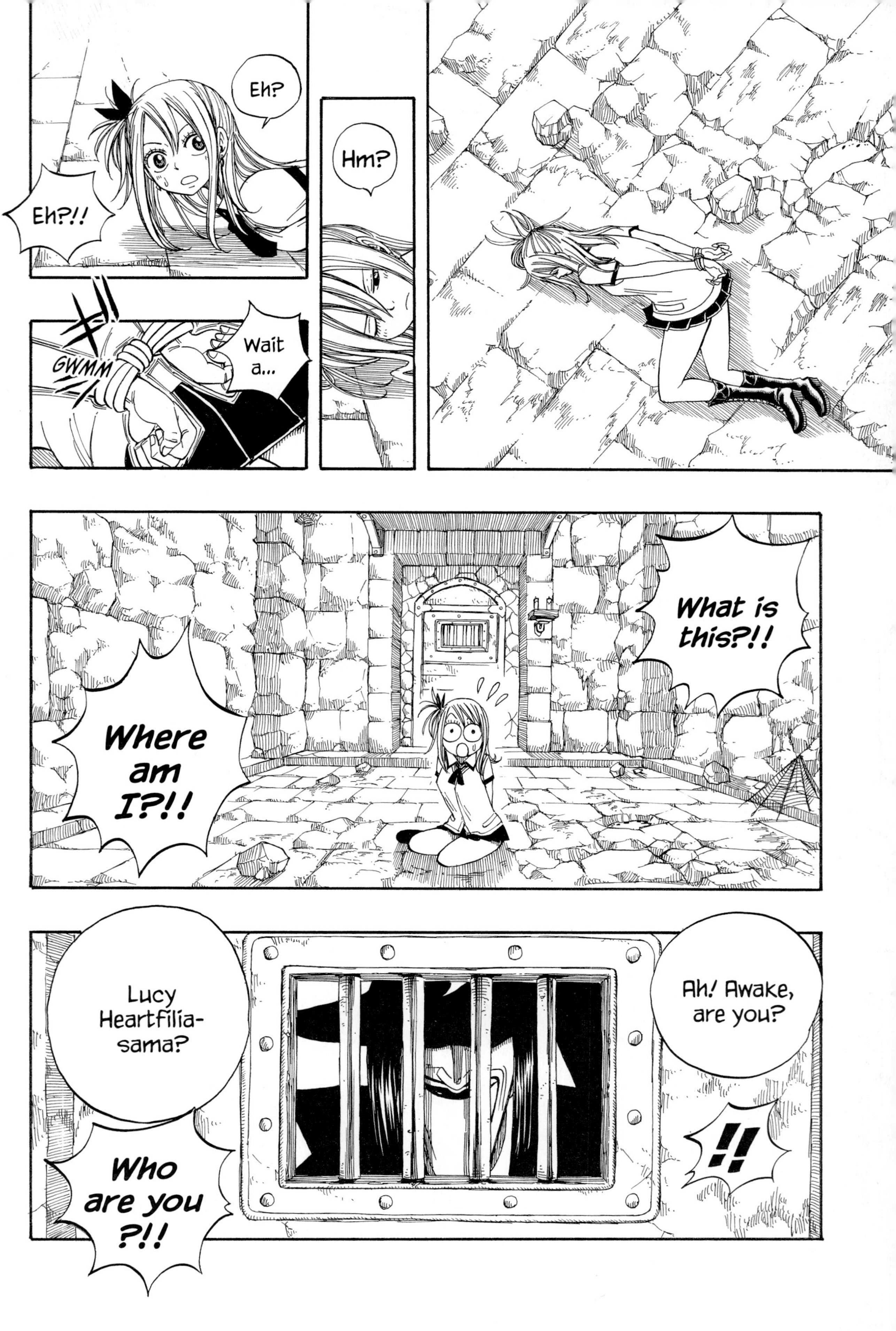
Hm?
Eh?
Eh?!!
GWMM
Wait a...
What is this?!!
Where am I?!!
Ah! Awake, are you?
!!
Lucy Heartfilia-sama?
Who are you ?!!

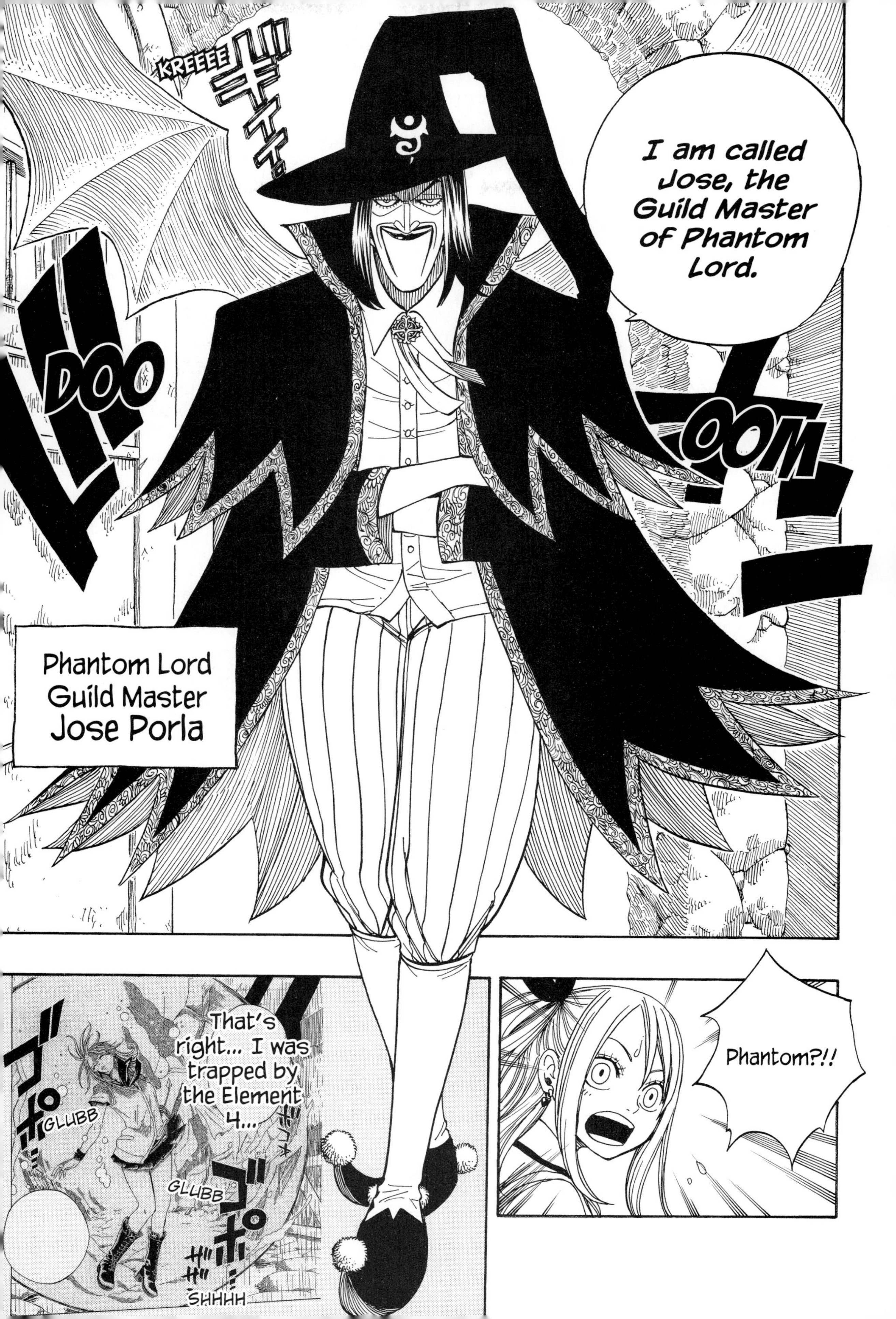
KREEEE
I am called Jose, the Guild Master of Phantom Lord.
DOOOOM
Phantom Lord Guild Master Jose Porla
Phantom?!!
That's right... I was trapped by the Element 4...
GLUBB
GLUBB
SHHHH

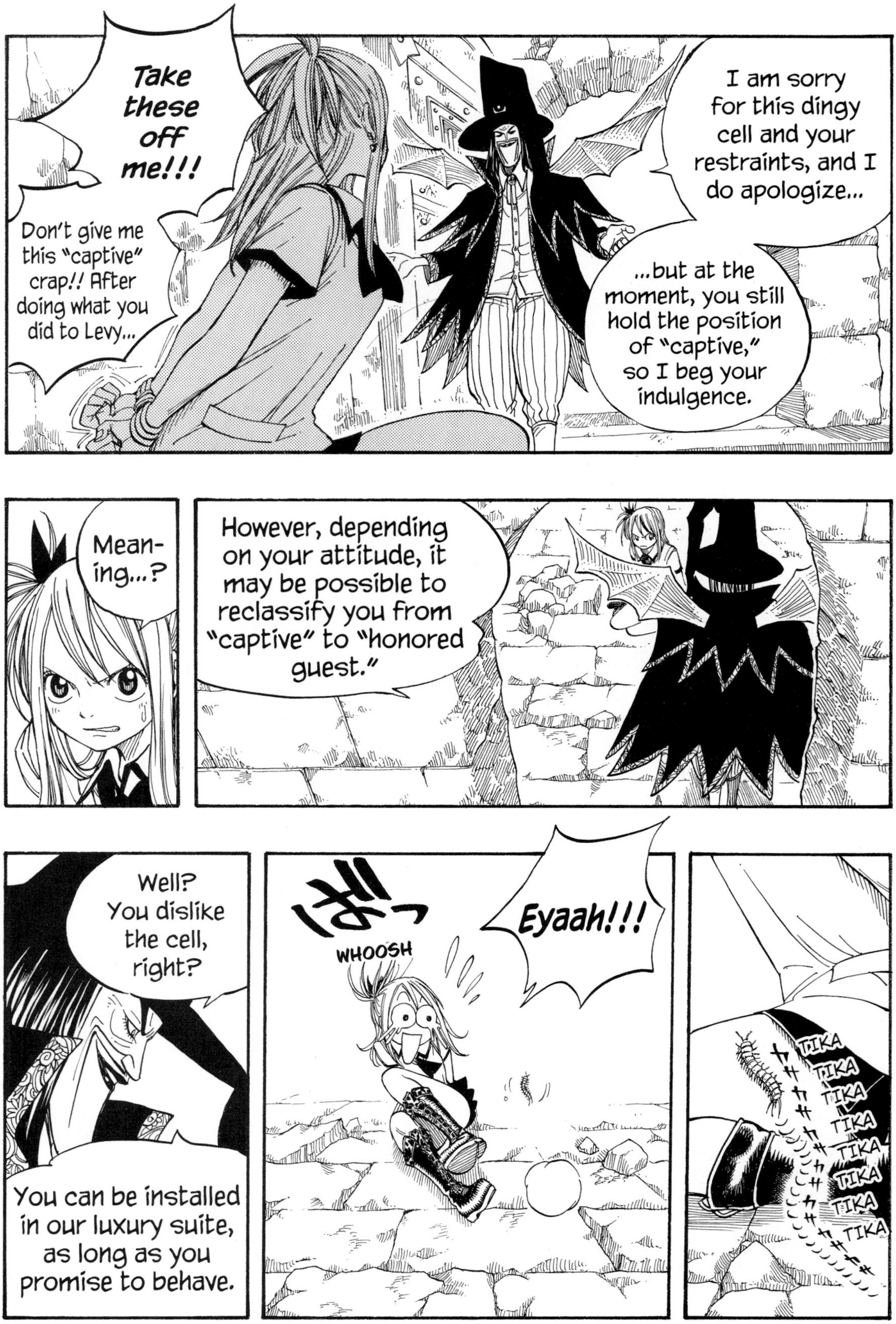
Take these off me!!!
I am sorry for this dingy cell and your restraints, and I do apologize...
...but at the moment, you still hold the position of "captive," so I beg your indulgence.
Don't give me this "captive" crap!! After doing what you did to Levy...
However, depending on your attitude, it may be possible to reclassify you from "captive" to "honored guest."
Mean-ing...?
TIKA TIKA TIKA TIKA TIKA TIKA TIKA TIKA
WHOOSH
Eyaah!!!
Well? You dislike the cell, right?
You can be installed in our luxury suite, as long as you promise to behave.

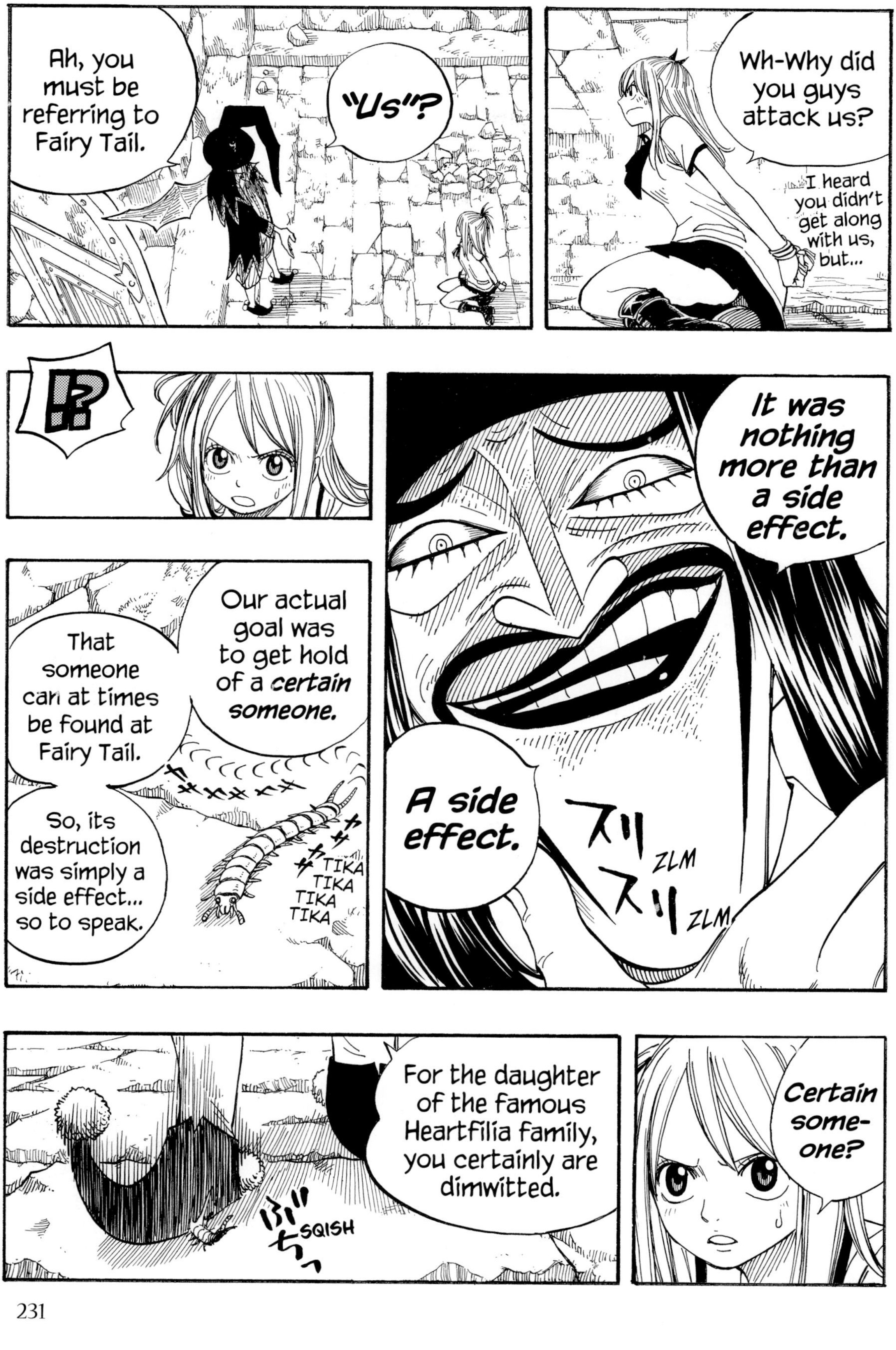
Wh-Why did you guys attack us?
I heard you didn't get along with us, but...
"Us"?
Ah, you must be referring to Fairy Tail.
It was nothing more than a side effect.
A side effect.
ZLM
ZLM
!?
Our actual goal was to get hold of a certain someone.
That someone can at times be found at Fairy Tail.
So, its destruction was simply a side effect... so to speak.
TIKA TIKA TIKA TIKA
Certain some-one?
For the daughter of the famous Heartfilia family, you certainly are dimwitted.
SQISH

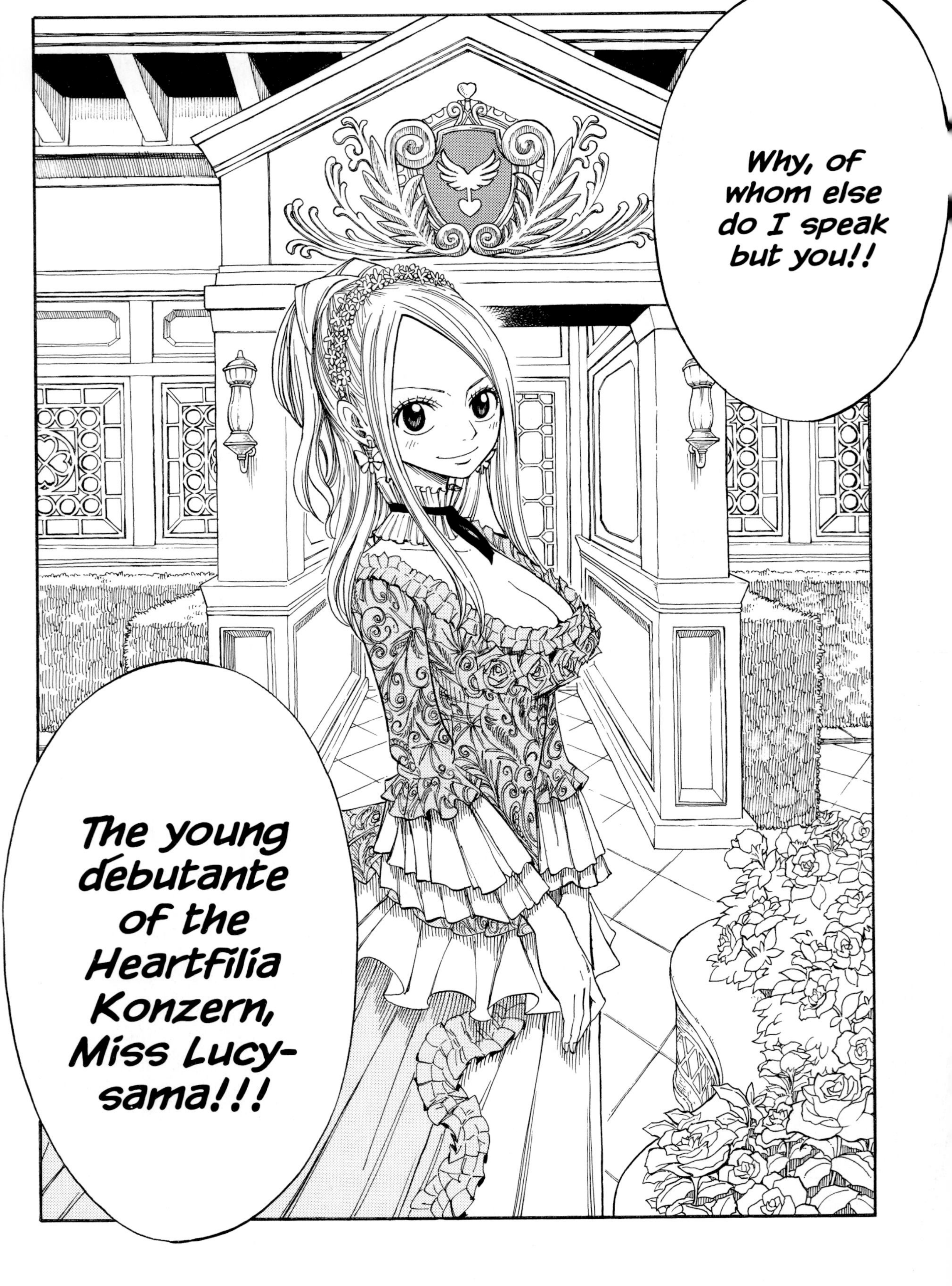
Why, of whom else do I speak but you!!
The young debutante of the Heartfilia Konzern, Miss Lucy-sama!!!

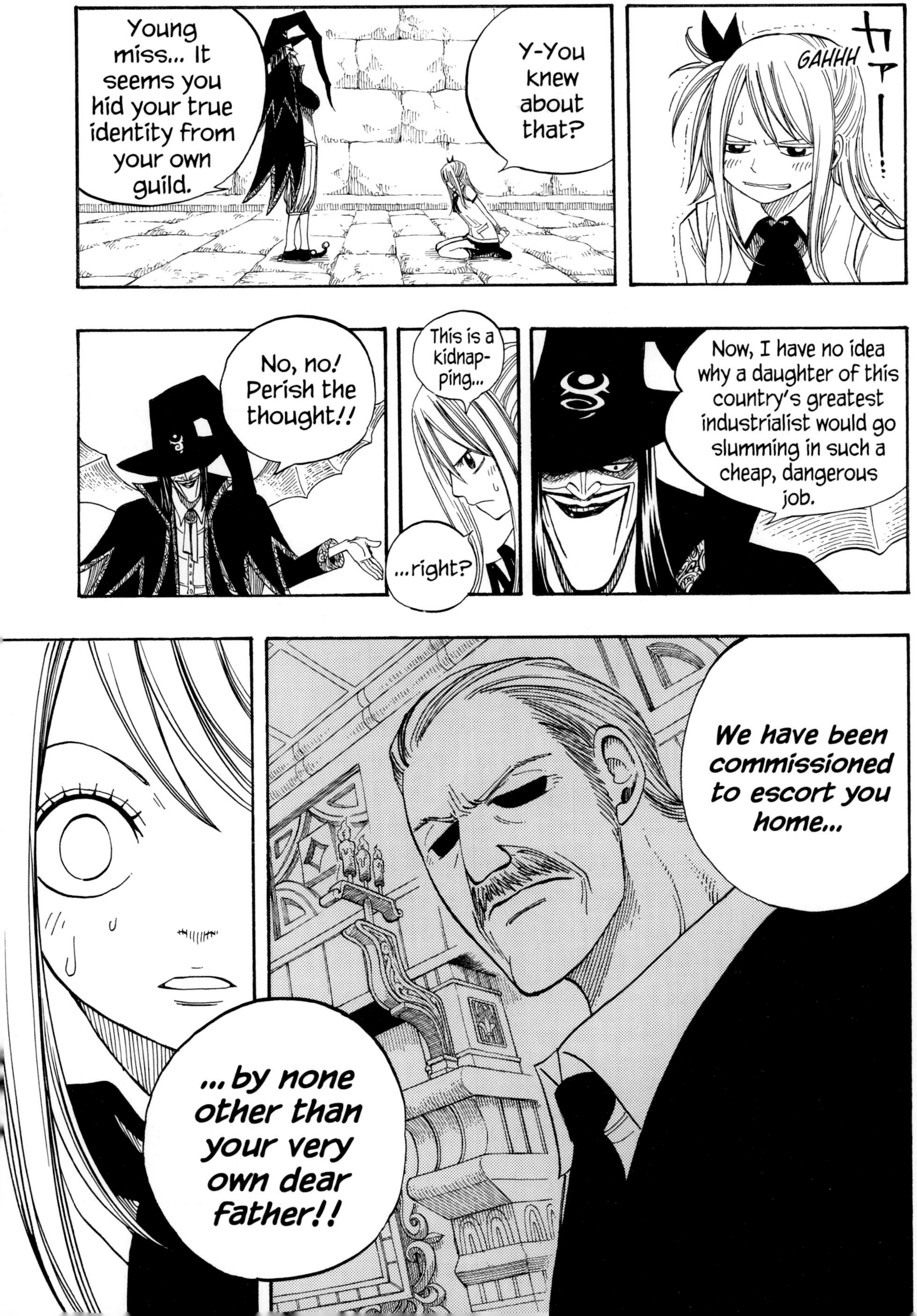
Young miss... It seems you hid your true identity from your own guild.
Y-You knew about that?
GAHHH
カァー!!
Now, I have no idea why a daughter of this country's greatest industrialist would go slumming in such a cheap, dangerous job.
This is a kidnap-ping...
...right?
No, no! Perish the thought!!
We have been commissioned to escort you home...
...by none other than your very own dear father!!

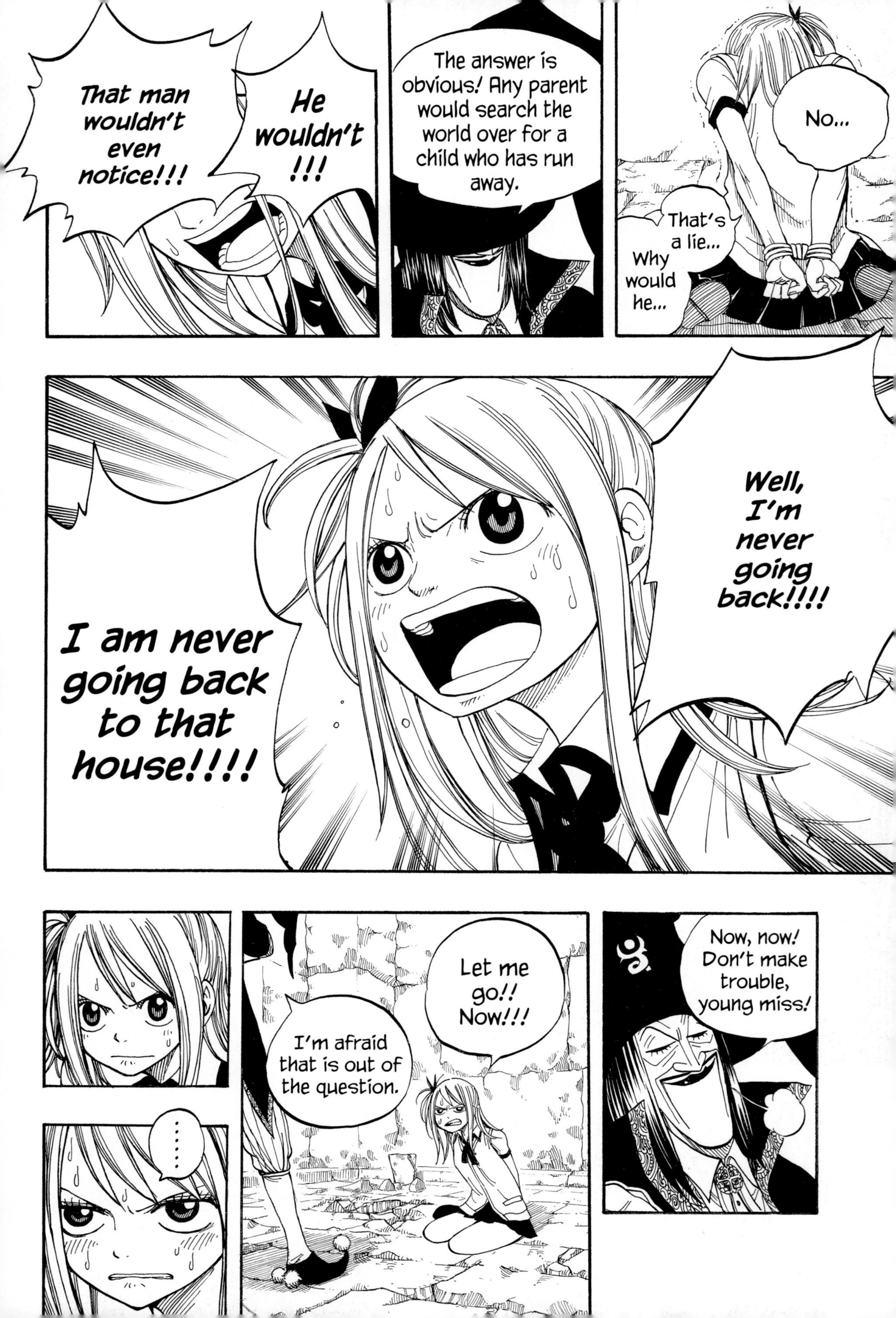
No...
That's a lie...
Why would he...
The answer is obvious! Any parent would search the world over for a child who has run away.
He wouldn't !!!
That man wouldn't even notice!!!
Well, I'm never going back!!!!
I am never going back to that house!!!!
Now, now! Don't make trouble, young miss!
Let me go!! Now!!!
I'm afraid that is out of the question.
......

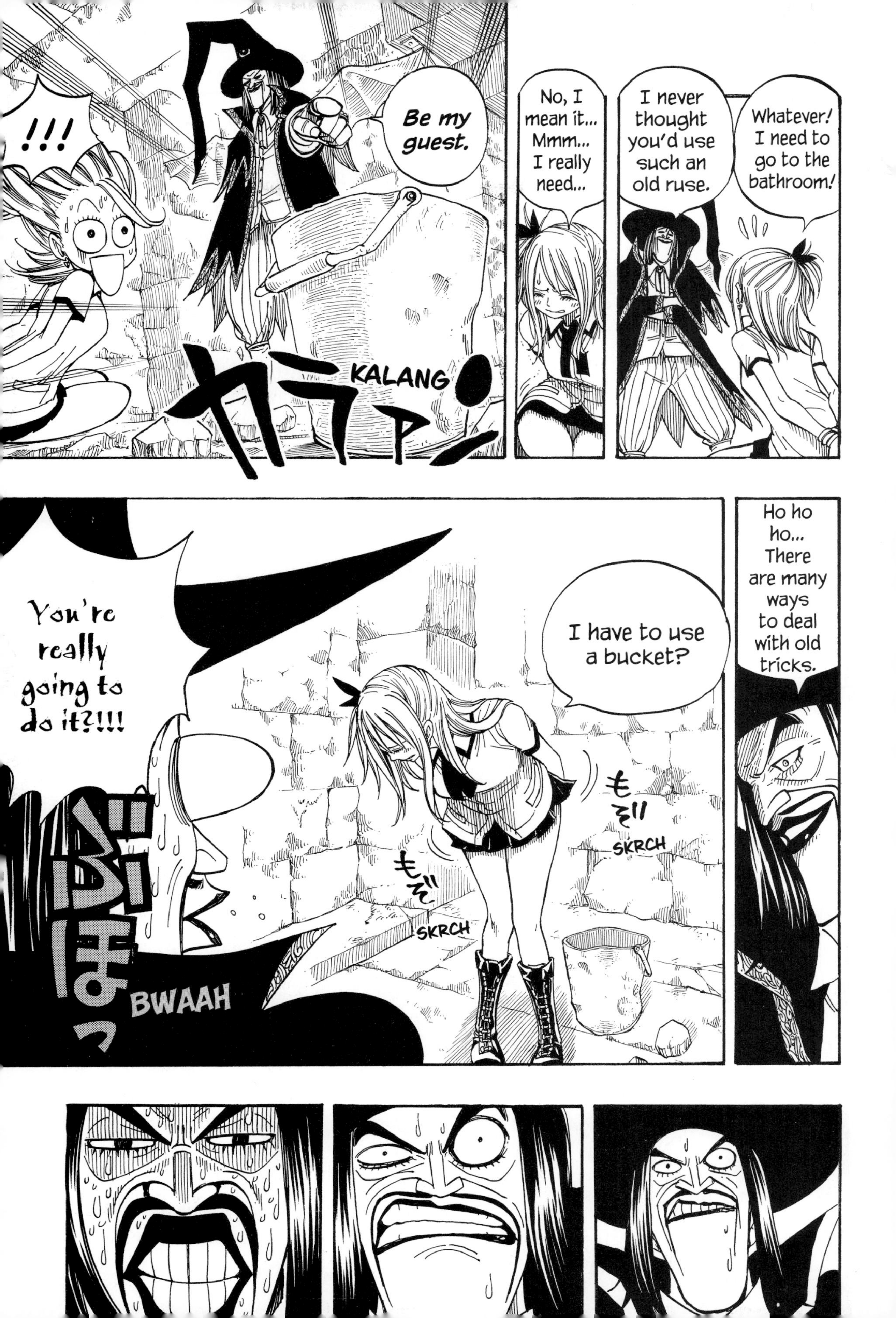
Whatever! I need to go to the bathroom!
I never thought you'd use such an old ruse.
No, I mean it... Mmm... I really need...
Be my guest.
!!!
KALANG
Ho ho ho... There are many ways to deal with old tricks.
I have to use a bucket?
SKRCH
SKRCH
You're really going to do it?!!!
BWAAH

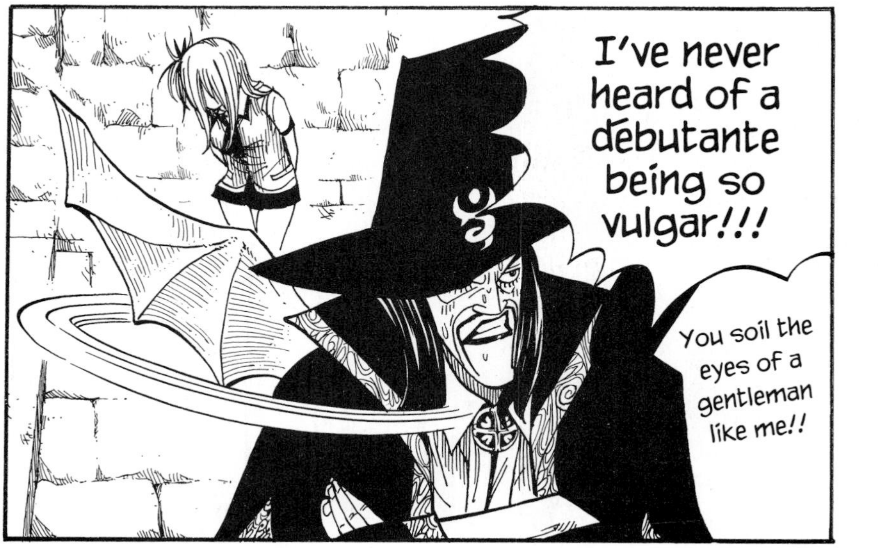
I've never heard of a debutante being so vulgar!!!
You soil the eyes of a gentleman like me!!
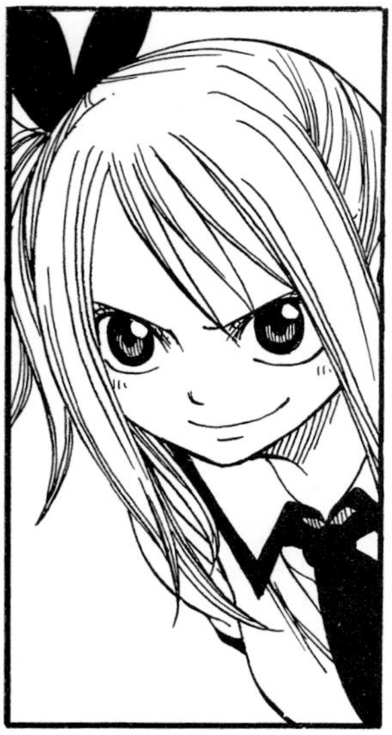
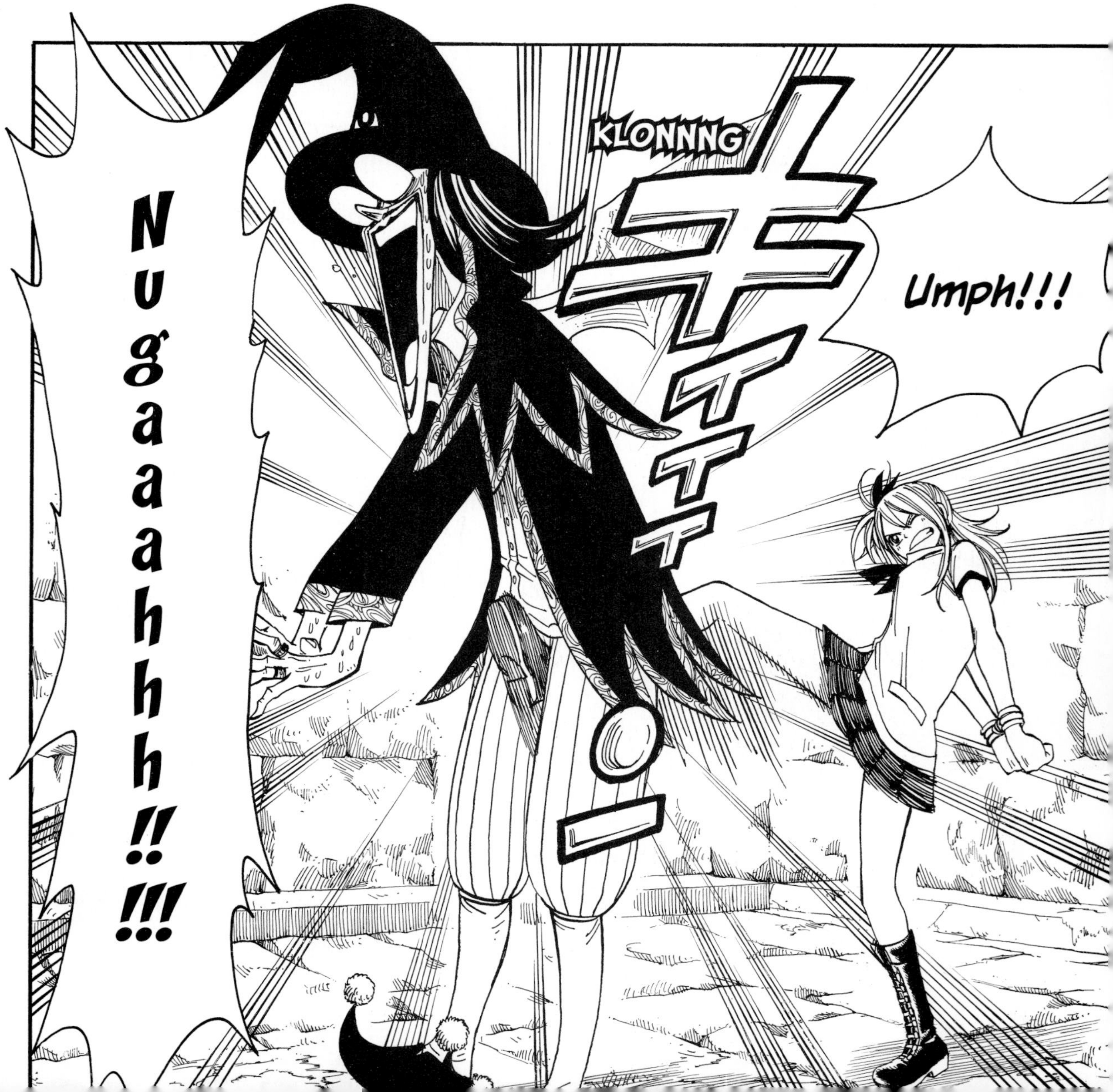
KLONNNG
Umph!!!
Nugaaahhh!!!!!

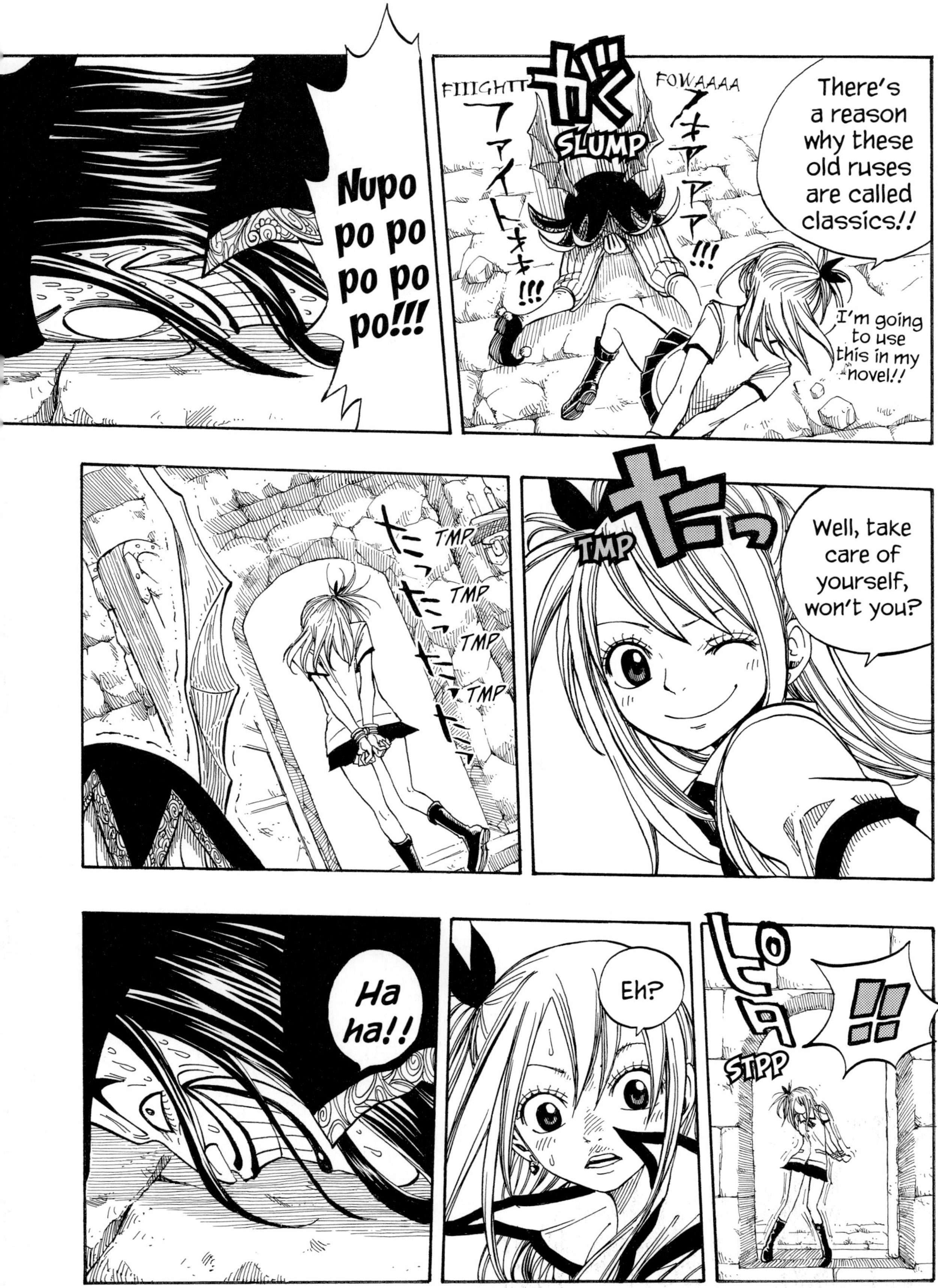
There's a reason why these old ruses are called classics!!
FOWAAAA
SLUMP
FIIIGHTT
I'm going to use this in my novel!!
Nupo po po po po po po!!!
TMP
Well, take care of yourself, won't you?
TMP
TMP
TMP
TMP
STPP
!!
Eh?
Ha ha!!

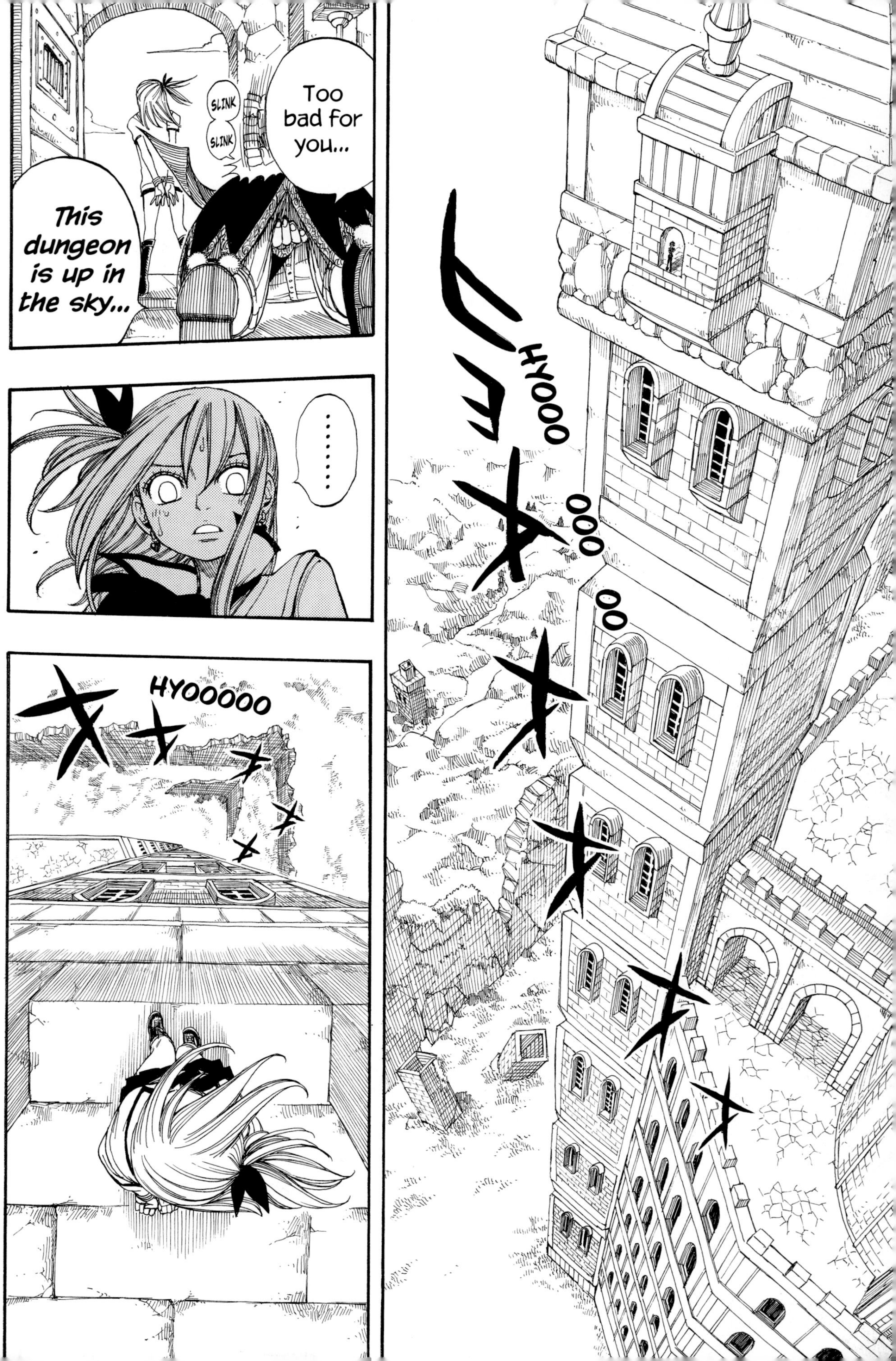
HYOOOOOOOO
Too bad for you...
SLINK
SLINK
This dungeon is up in the sky...
......
HYOOOOOO

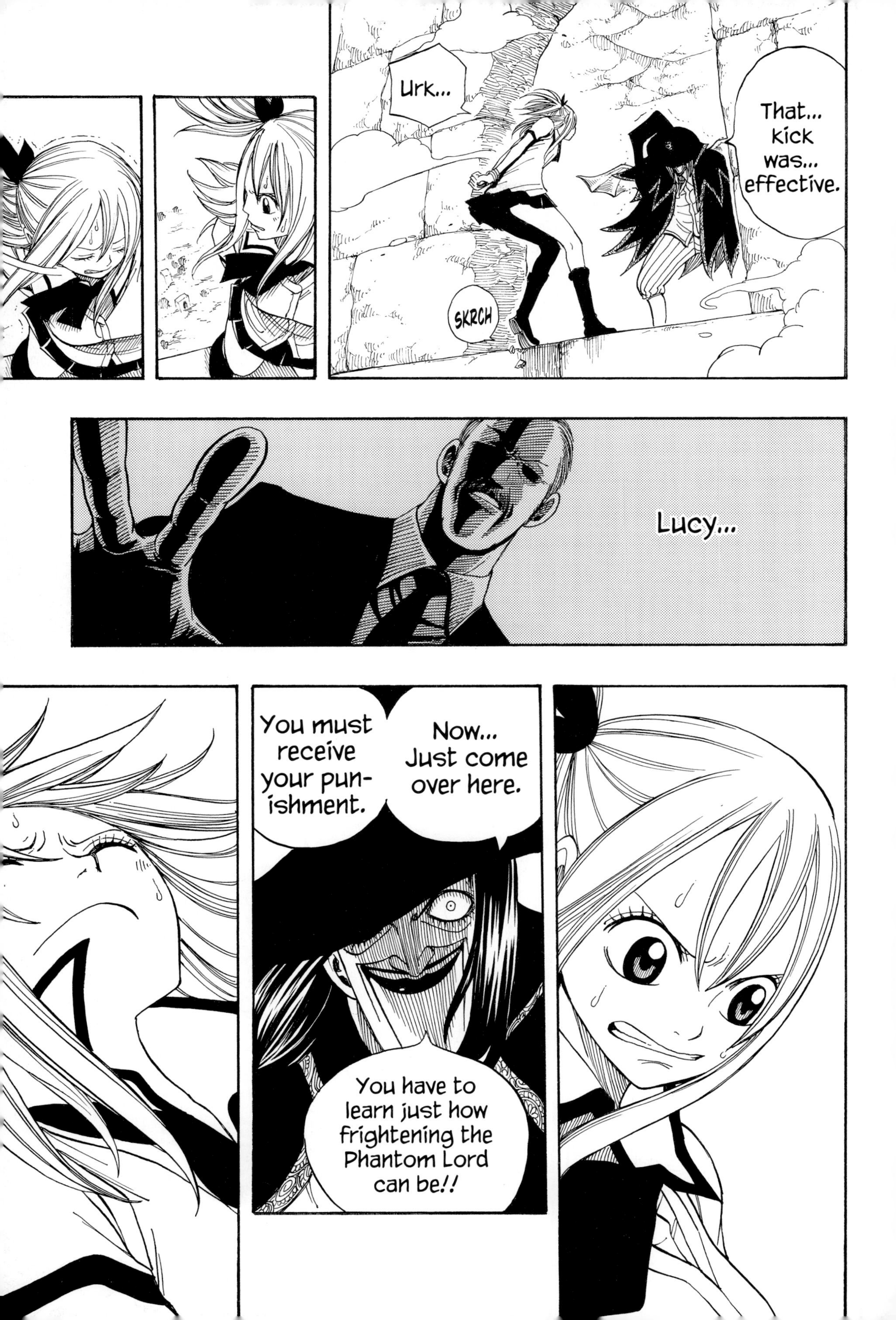
That... kick was... effective.
Urk...
SKRCH
Lucy...
Now... Just come over here.
You must receive your pun-ishment.
You have to learn just how frightening the Phantom Lord can be!!

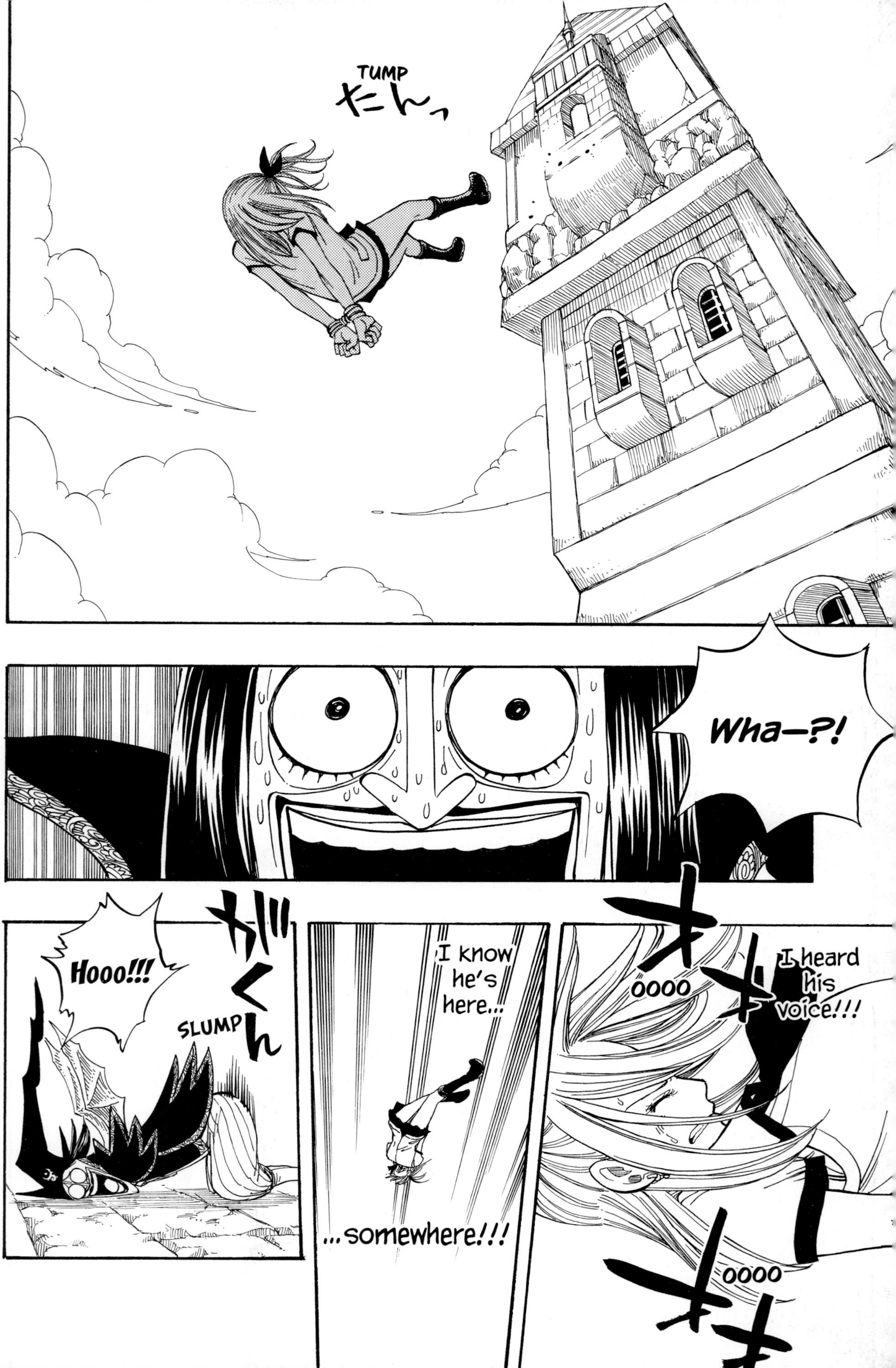
TUMP
たんっ
Wha–?!
I heard his voice!!!
oooo
oooo
I know he's here...
...somewhere!!!
Hooo!!!
SLUMP
がくん

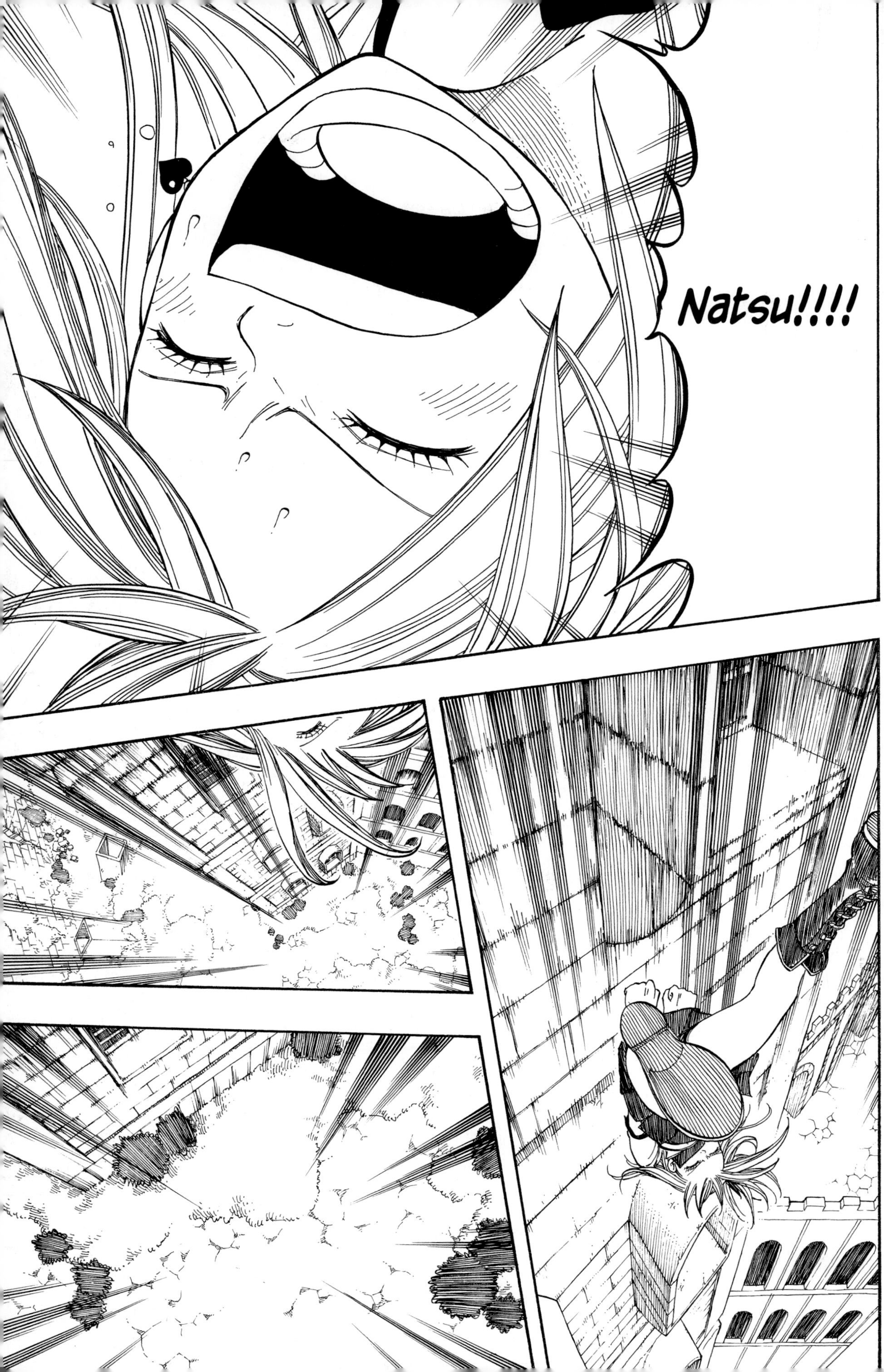
Natsu!!!!

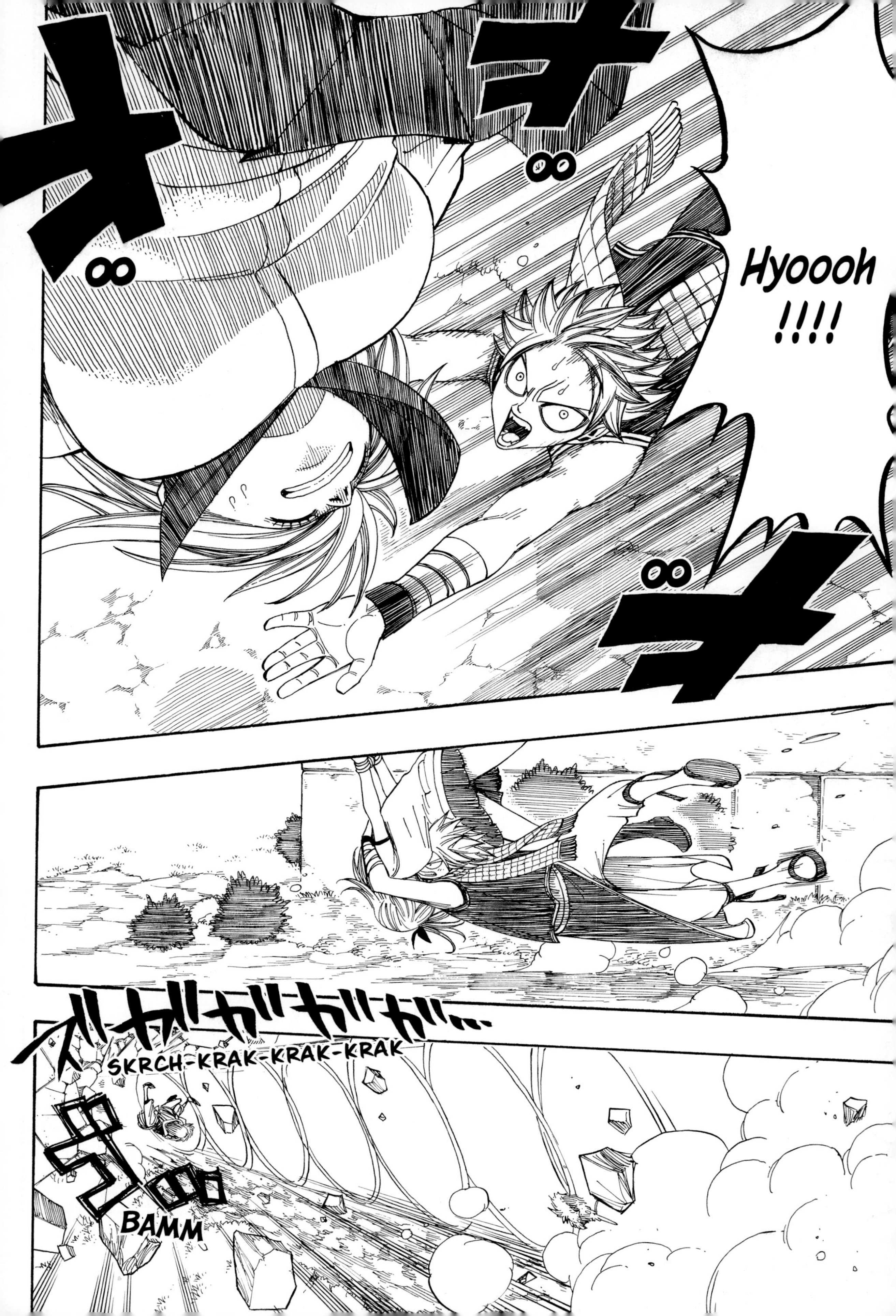
Hyoooh
!!!!
SKRCH-KRAK-KRAK-KRAK
BAMM

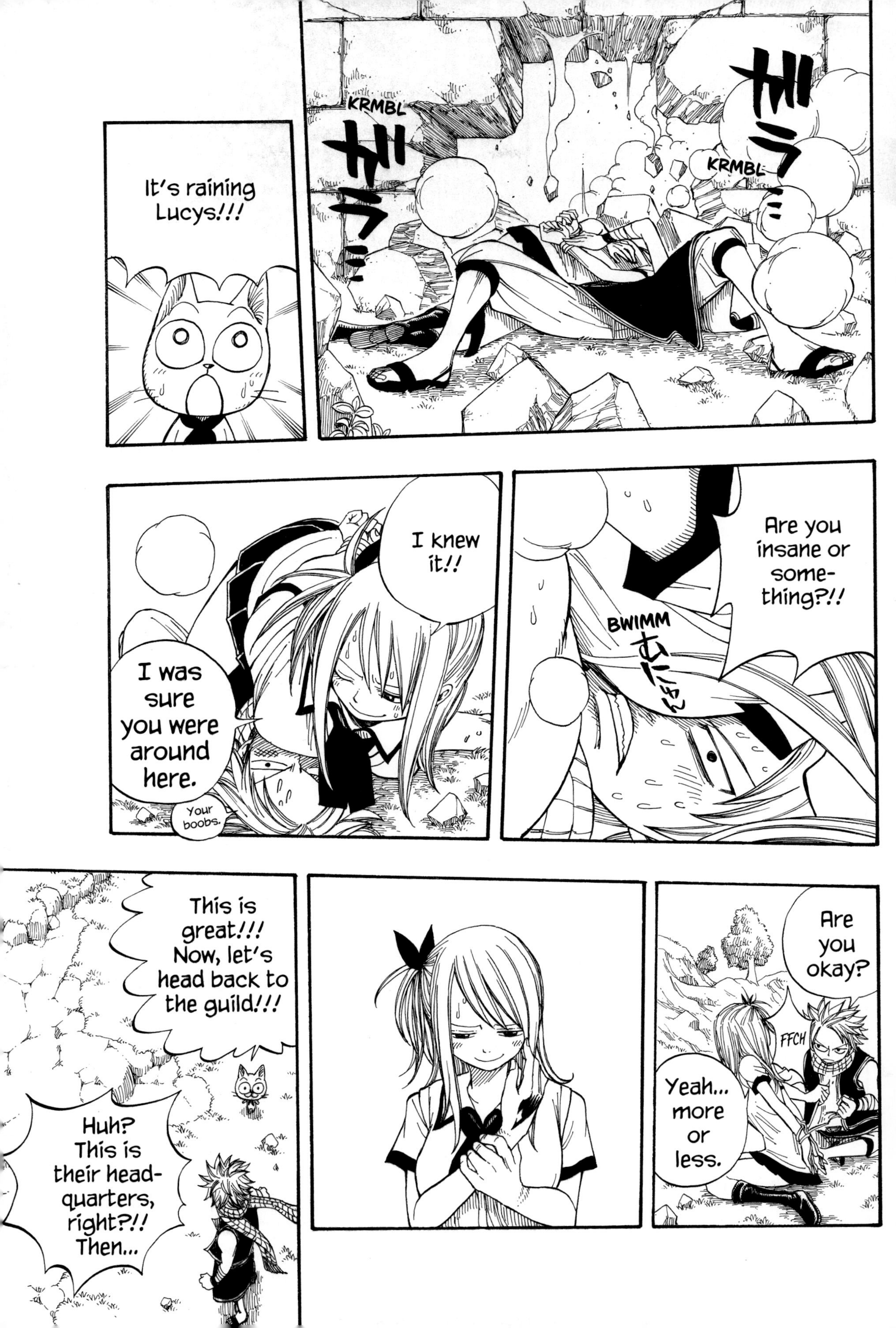
KRMBL
KRMBL
It's raining Lucys!!!
Are you insane or some-thing?!!
BWIMM
I knew it!!
I was sure you were around here.
Your boobs.
Are you okay?
FFCH
Yeah... more or less.
This is great!!! Now, let's head back to the guild!!!
Huh? This is their head-quarters, right?!! Then...

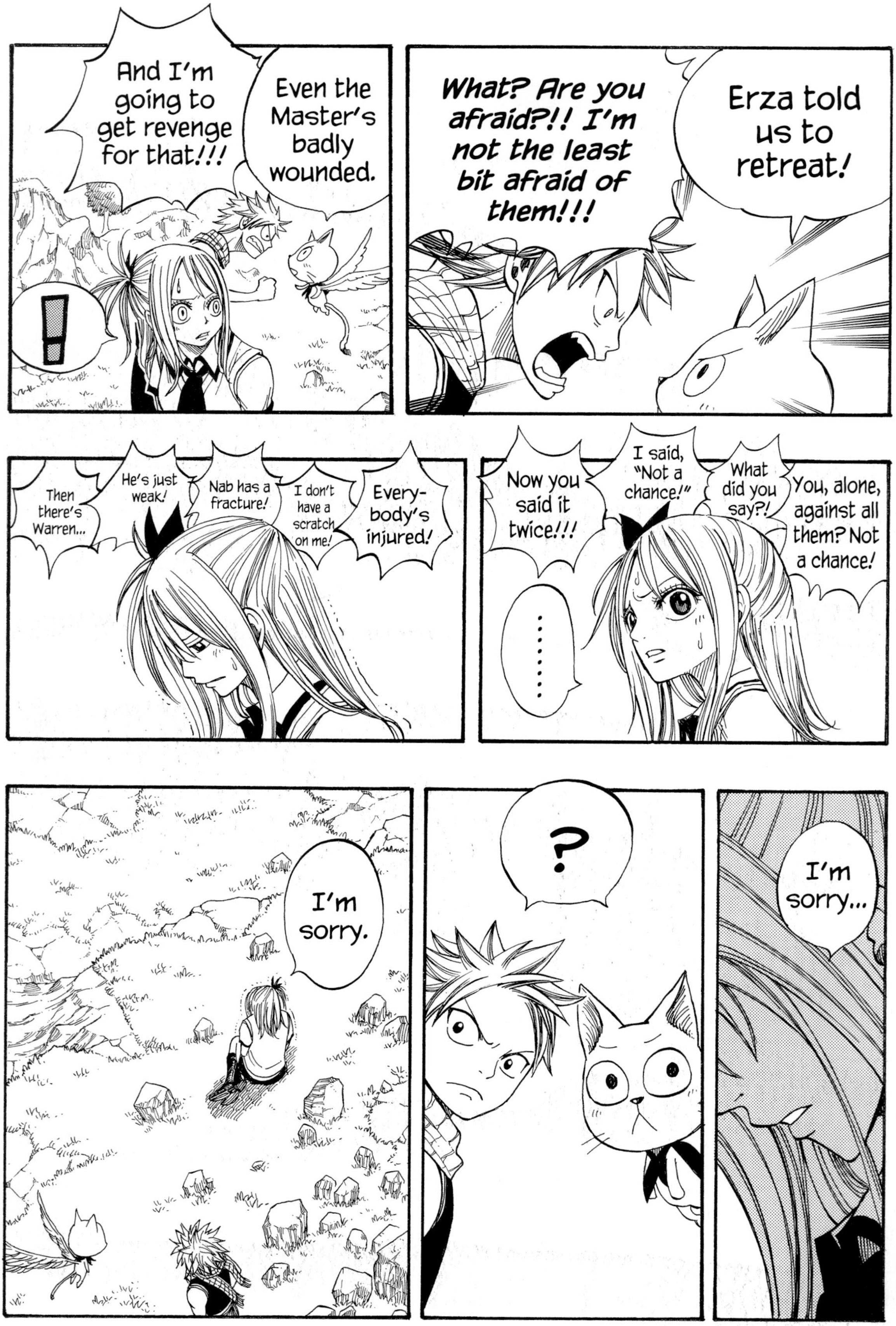
Erza told us to retreat!
What? Are you afraid?!! I'm not the least bit afraid of them!!!
Even the Master's badly wounded.
And I'm going to get revenge for that!!!
!
You, alone, against all them? Not a chance!
What did you say?!
I said, "Not a chance!"
Now you said it twice!!!
......
Every-body's injured!
I don't have a scratch on me!
Nab has a fracture!
He's just weak!
Then there's Warren...
I'm sorry...
?
I'm sorry.

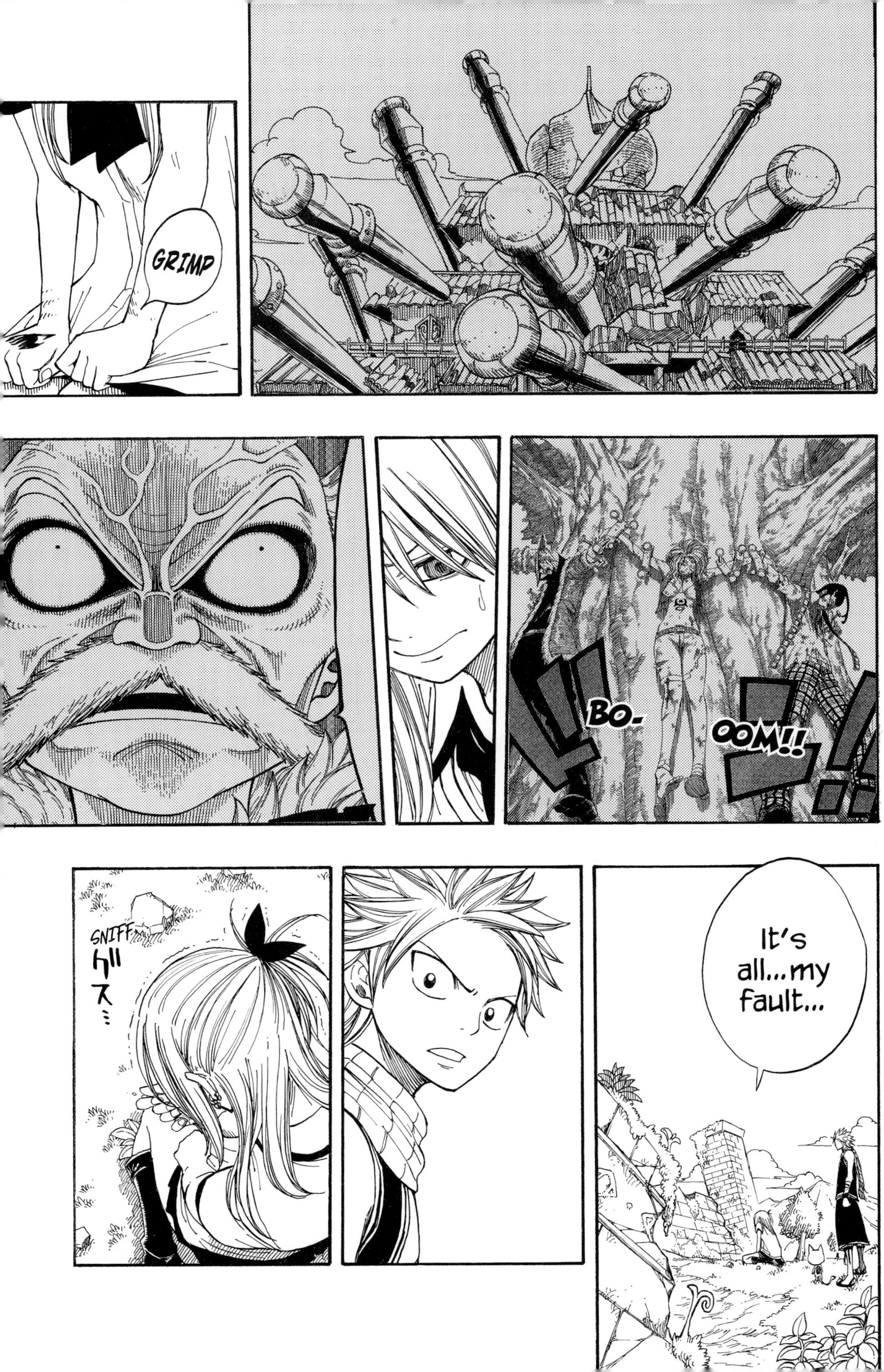
GRIMP
BO- OOM!!
It's all...my fault...
SNIFF
グス…

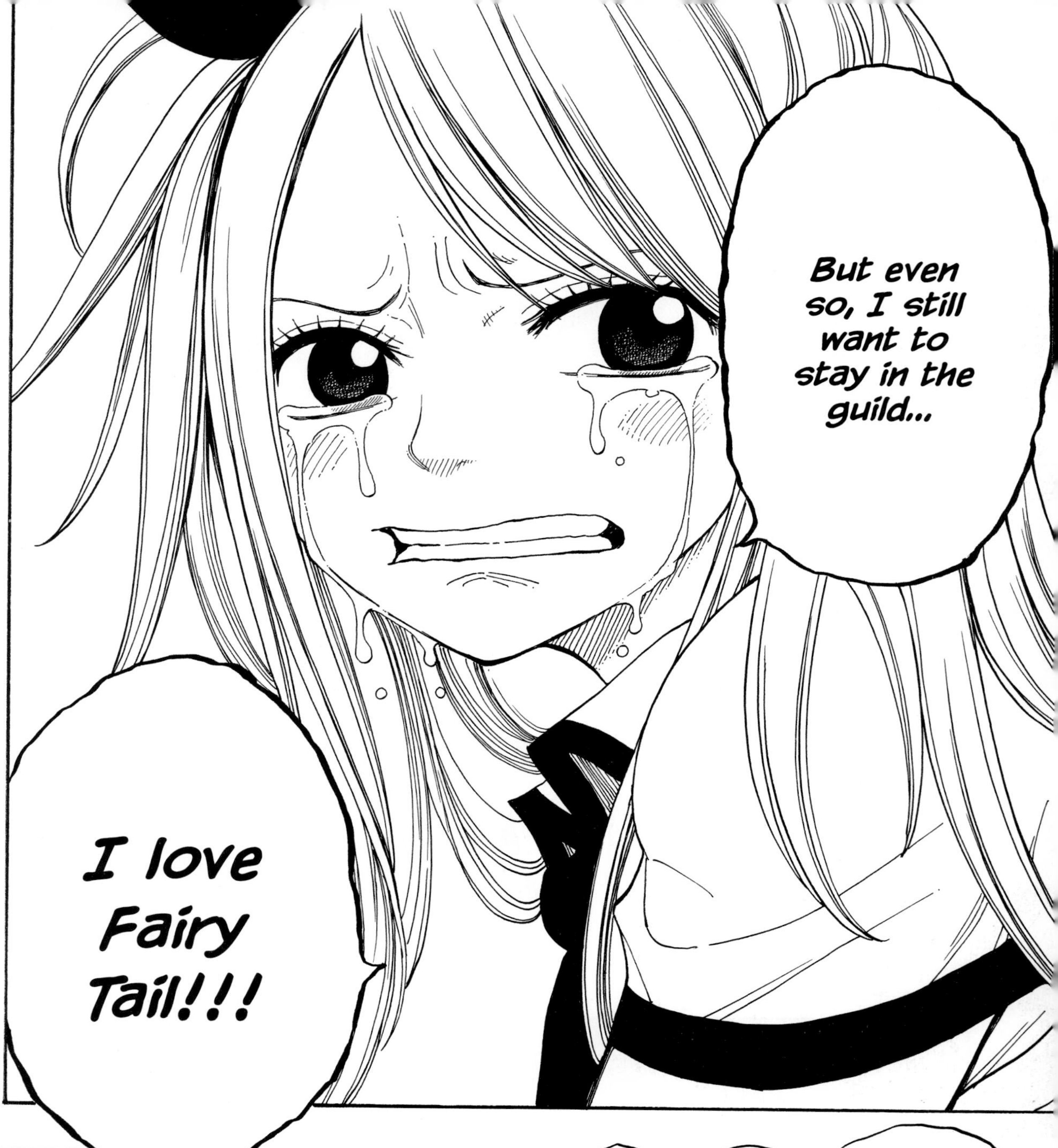
But even so, I still want to stay in the guild...
I love Fairy Tail!!!
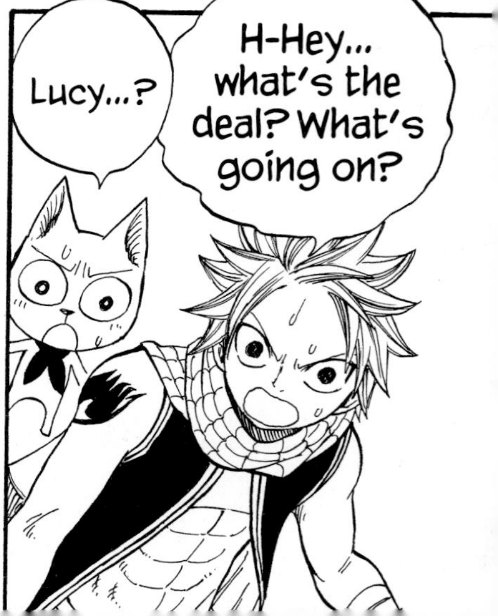
H-Hey... what's the deal? What's going on?
Lucy...?
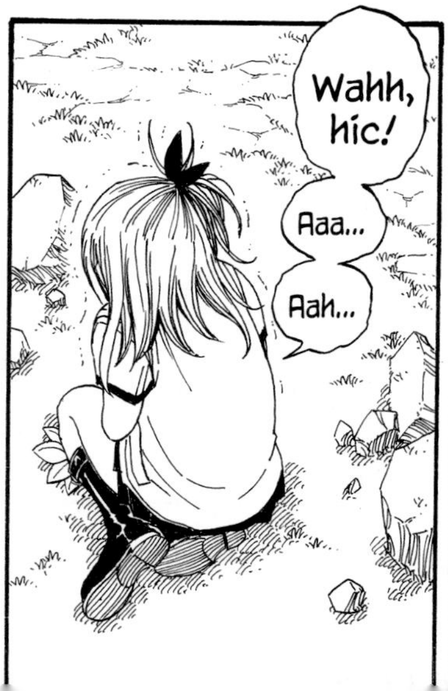
Wahh, hic!
Aaa...
Aah...
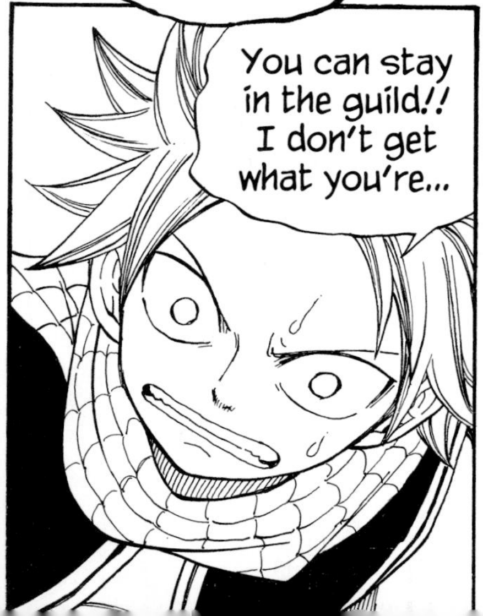
You can stay in the guild!! I don't get what you're...

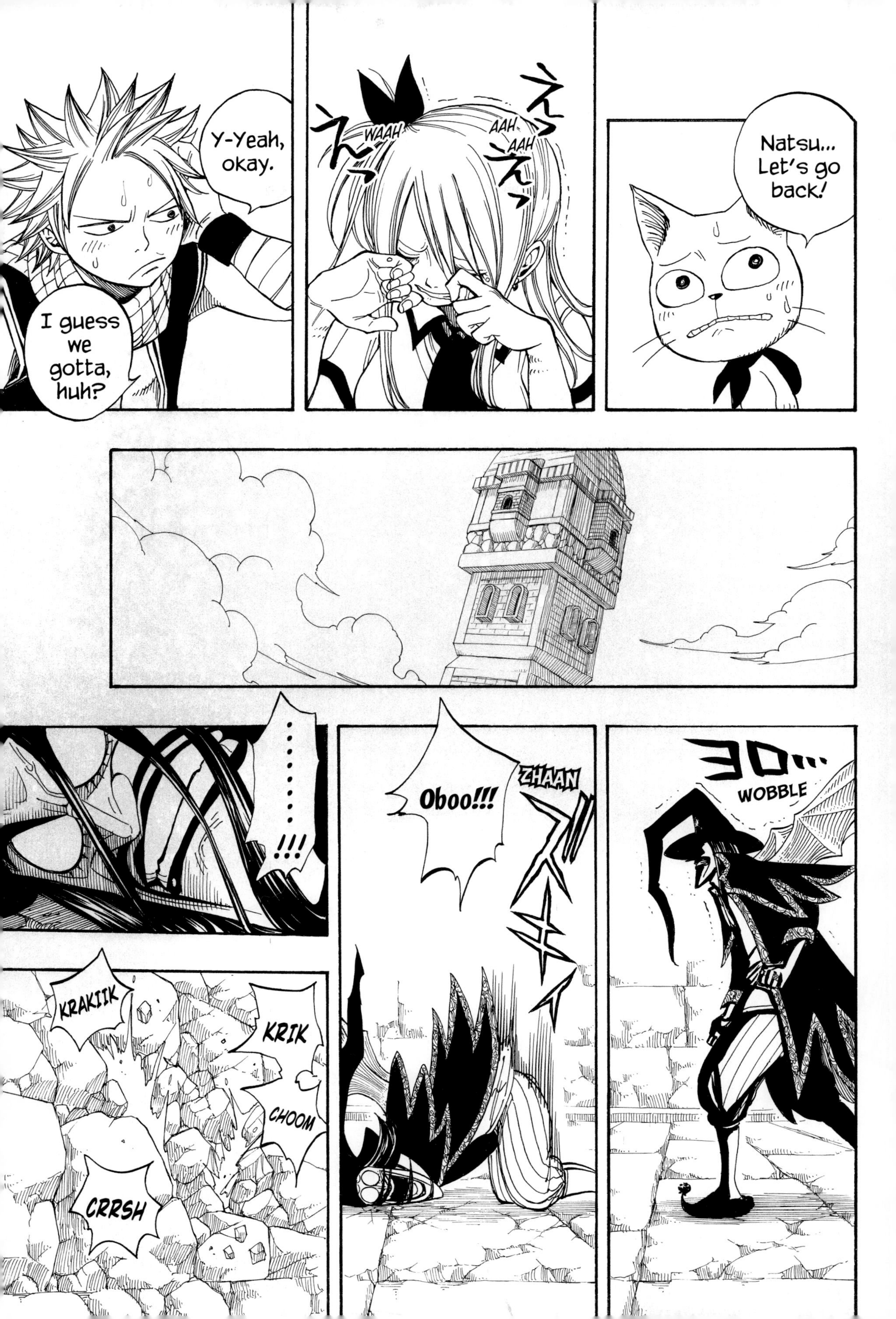

Natsu... Let's go back!
AAH AAH
WAAH
Y-Yeah, okay.
I guess we gotta, huh?
WOBBLE
Oboo!!!
ZHAAN
......!!!
KRAKIIK
KRIK
CHOOM
CRRSH

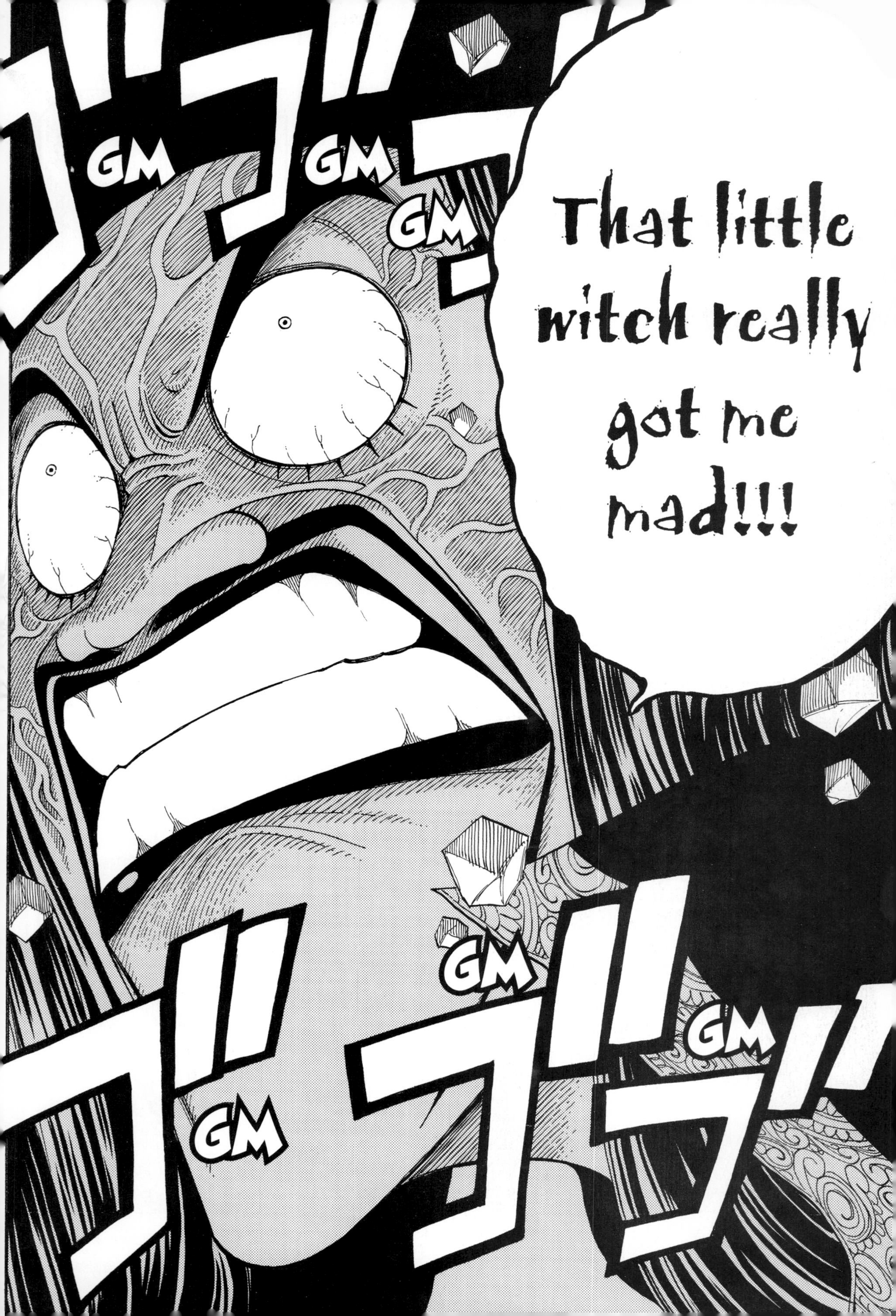
GM GM GM
That little witch really got me mad!!!
GM GM GM

FAIRY TAIL

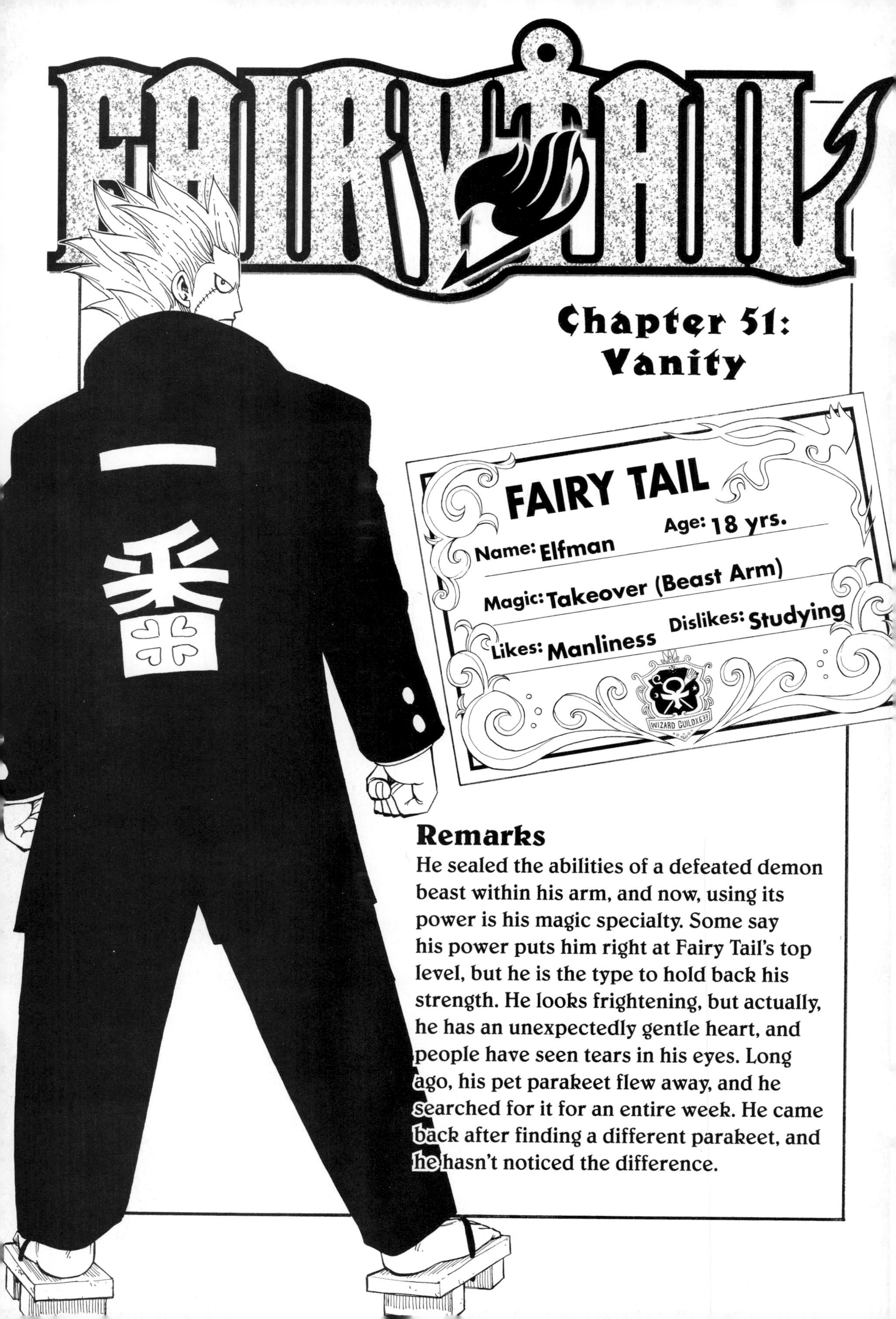

Chapter 51: Vanity

FAIRY TAIL

Name: Elfman

Age: 18 yrs.

Magic: Takeover (Beast Arm)

Likes: Manliness

Dislikes: Studying

WIZARD GUILDX633

Remarks

He sealed the abilities of a defeated demon beast within his arm, and now, using its power is his magic specialty. Some say his power puts him right at Fairy Tail's top level, but he is the type to hold back his strength. He looks frightening, but actually, he has an unexpectedly gentle heart, and people have seen tears in his eyes. Long ago, his pet parakeet flew away, and he searched for it for an entire week. He came back after finding a different parakeet, and he hasn't noticed the difference.

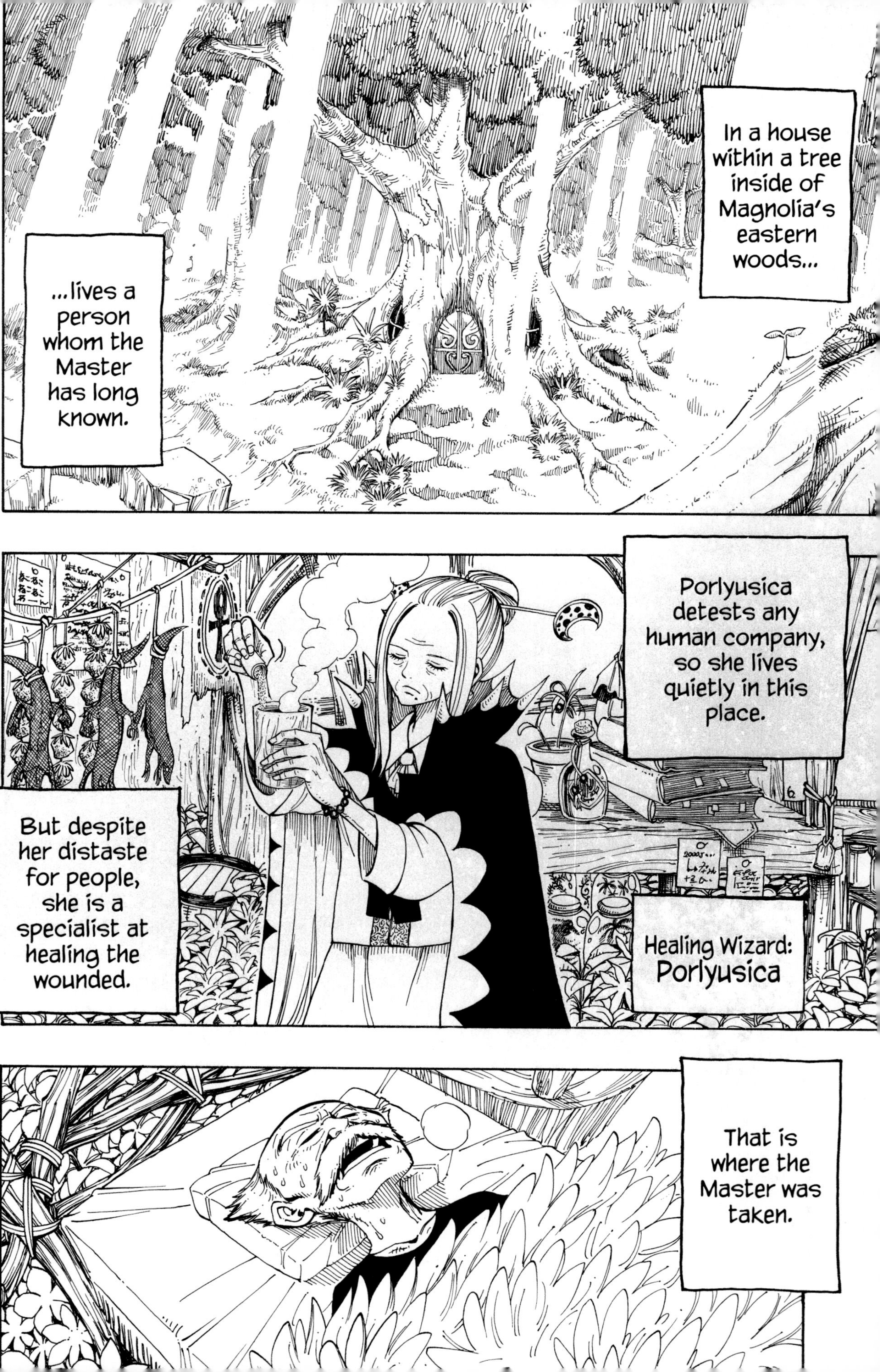
In a house within a tree inside of Magnolia's eastern woods...
...lives a person whom the Master has long known.
Porlyusica detests any human company, so she lives quietly in this place.
But despite her distaste for people, she is a specialist at healing the wounded.
Healing Wizard: Porlyusica
That is where the Master was taken.

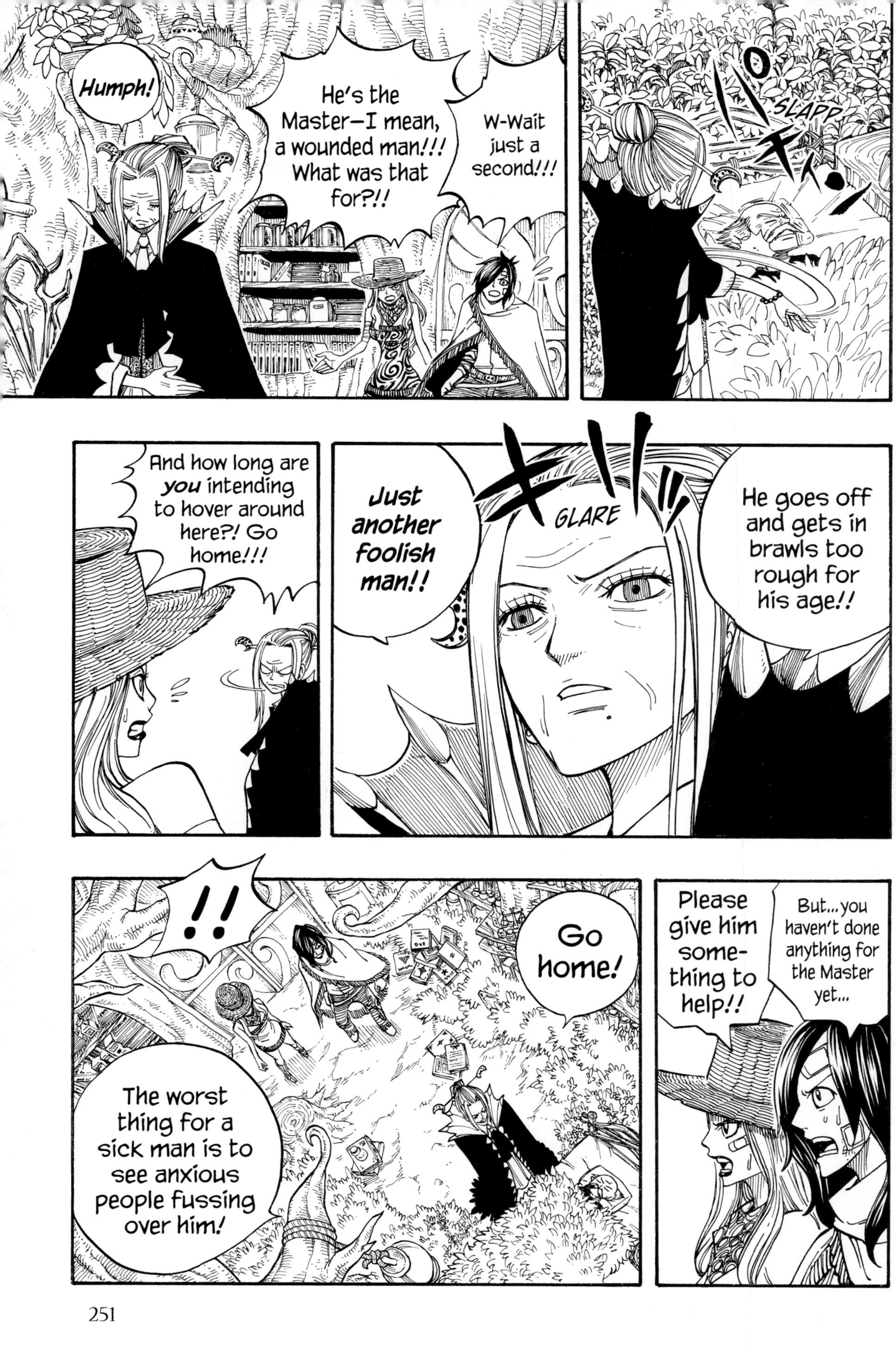
SLAPP
W-Wait just a second!!!
He's the Master—I mean, a wounded man!!! What was that for?!!
Humph!
He goes off and gets in brawls too rough for his age!!
GLARE
Just another foolish man!!
And how long are you intending to hover around here?! Go home!!!
But...you haven't done anything for the Master yet...
Please give him some-thing to help!!
Go home!
!!
The worst thing for a sick man is to see anxious people fussing over him!

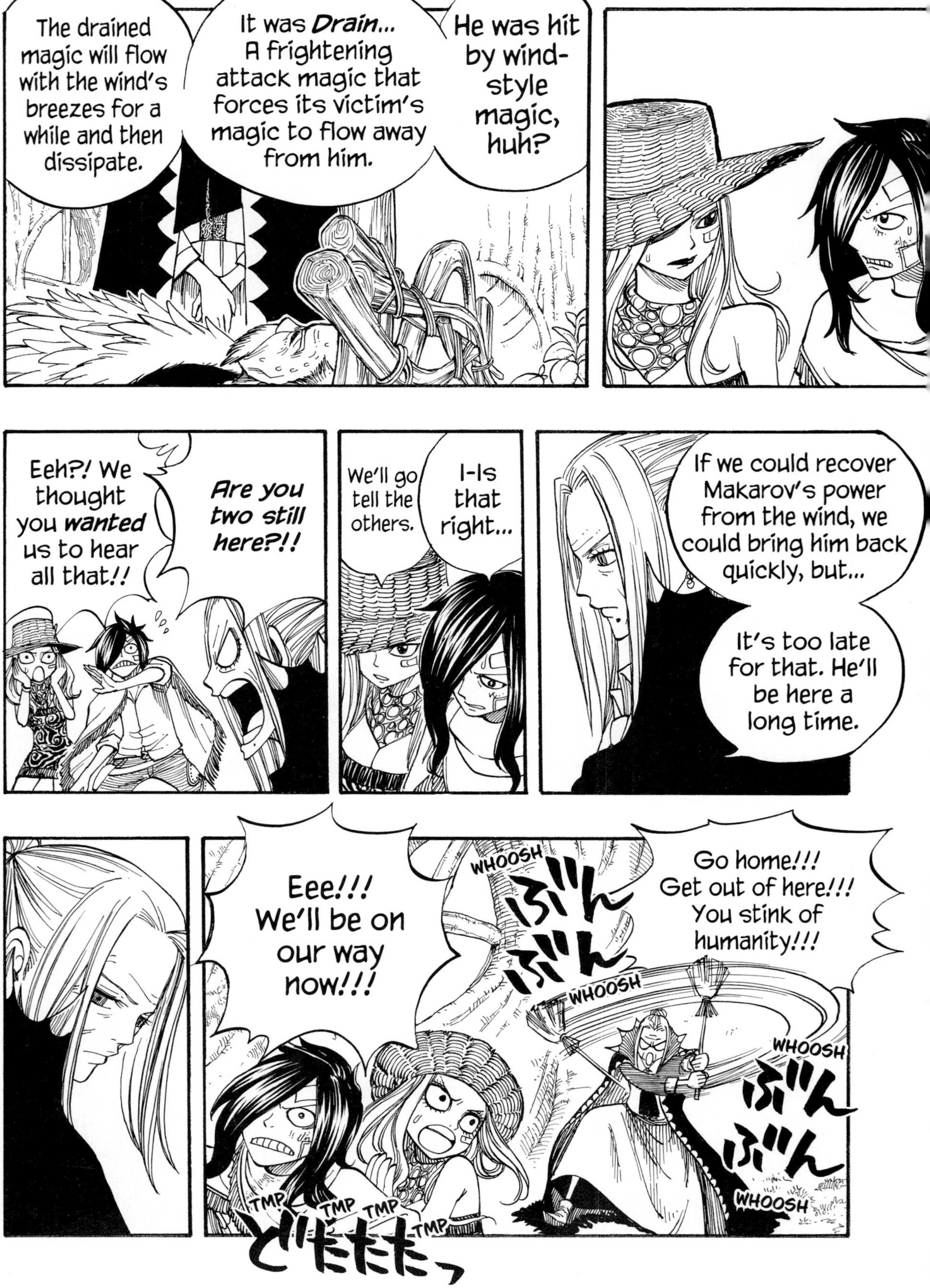
He was hit by wind-style magic, huh?
It was *Drain*... A frightening attack magic that forces its victim's magic to flow away from him.
The drained magic will flow with the wind's breezes for a while and then dissipate.
If we could recover Makarov's power from the wind, we could bring him back quickly, but...
It's too late for that. He'll be here a long time.
I-Is that right...
We'll go tell the others.
Are you two still here?!!
Eeh?! We thought you *wanted* us to hear all that!!
Go home!!! Get out of here!!! You stink of humanity!!!
WHOOSH
ぶんぶん
WHOOSH
WHOOSH
ぶんぶん
WHOOSH
Eee!!! We'll be on our way now!!!
TMP TMP TMP TMP
どたたたっ

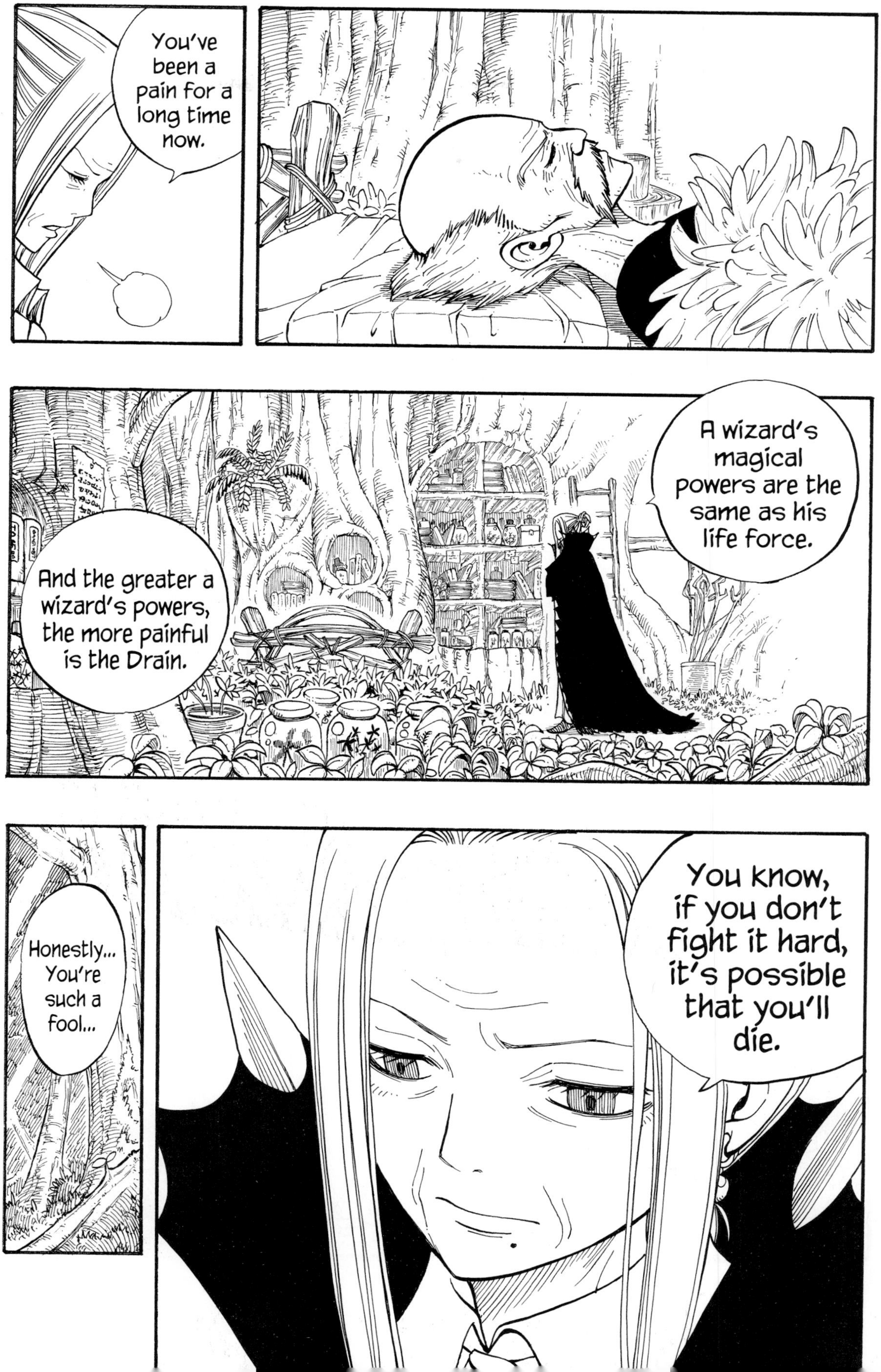
You've been a pain for a long time now.
A wizard's magical powers are the same as his life force.
And the greater a wizard's powers, the more painful is the Drain.
You know, if you don't fight it hard, it's possible that you'll die.
Honestly... You're such a fool...

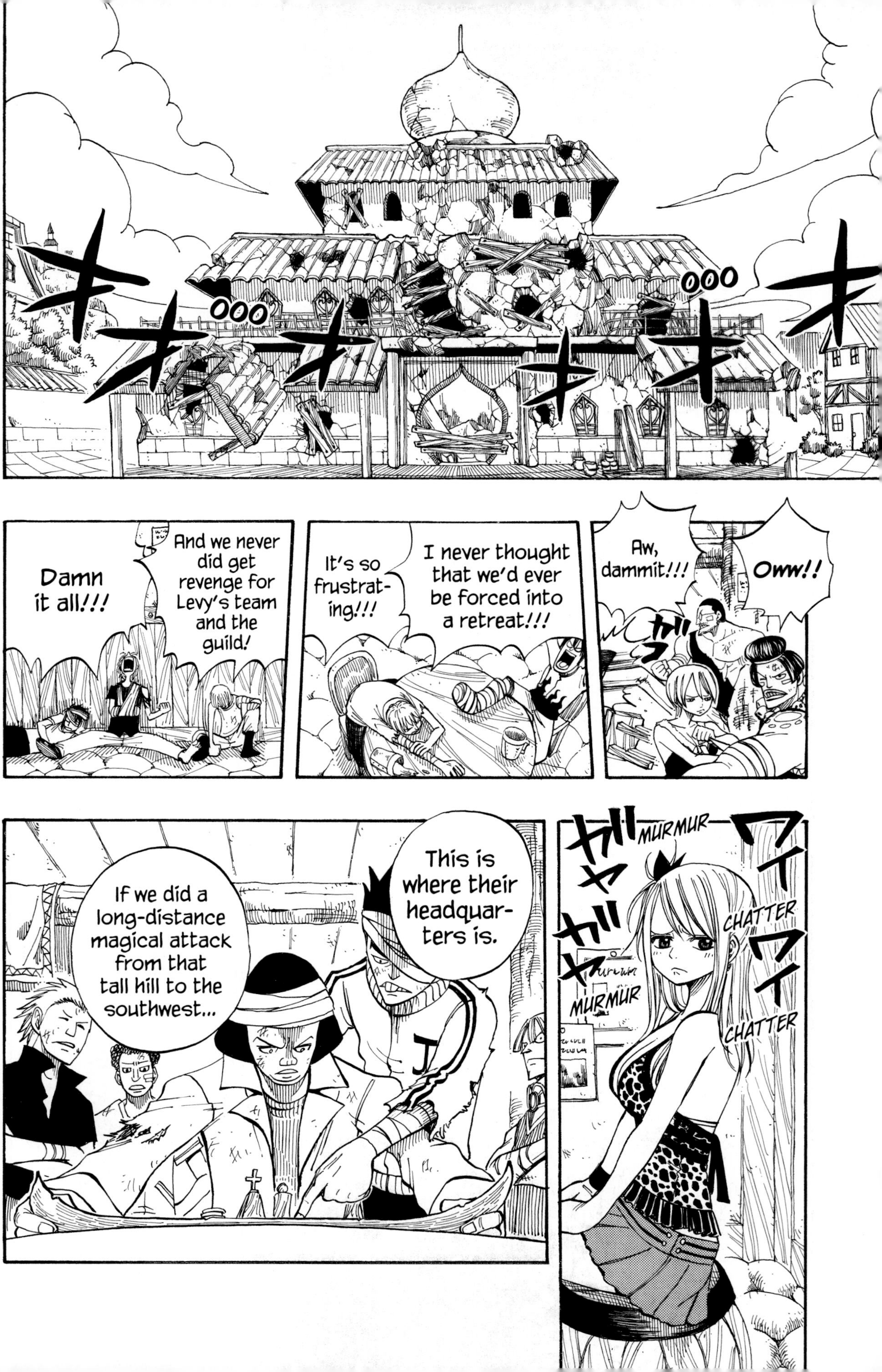
Ooo
Ooo
Oww!!
Aw, dammit!!!
I never thought that we'd ever be forced into a retreat!!!
It's so frustrat-ing!!!
And we never did get revenge for Levy's team and the guild!
Damn it all!!!
MURMUR
CHATTER
MURMUR
CHATTER
This is where their headquar-ters is.
If we did a long-distance magical attack from that tall hill to the southwest...

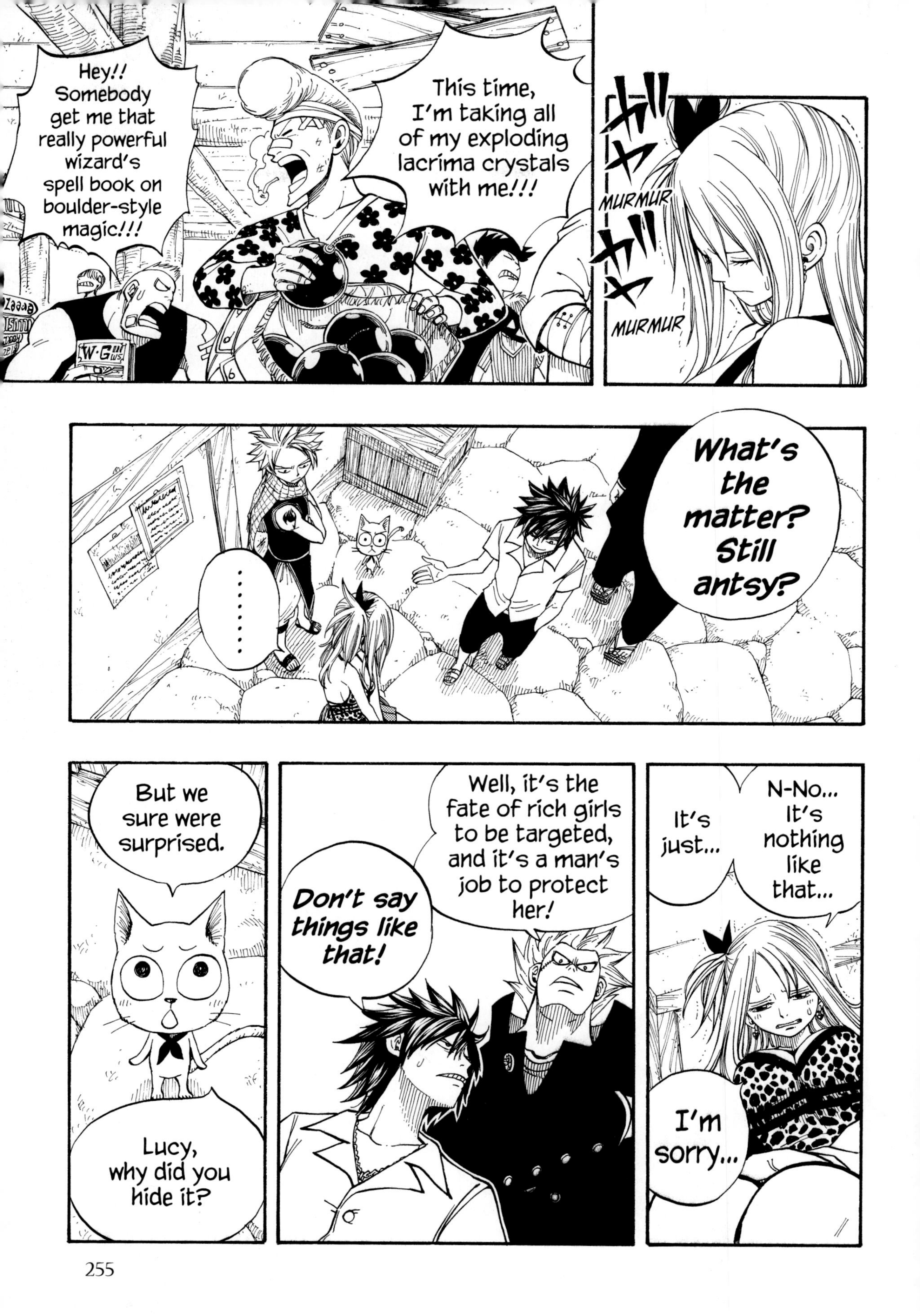
MURMUR
MURMUR
This time, I'm taking all of my exploding lacrima crystals with me!!!
Hey!! Somebody get me that really powerful wizard's spell book on boulder-style magic!!!
What's the matter? Still antsy?
......
N-No... It's nothing like that...
It's just...
I'm sorry...
Well, it's the fate of rich girls to be targeted, and it's a man's job to protect her!
Don't say things like that!
But we sure were surprised.
Lucy, why did you hide it?

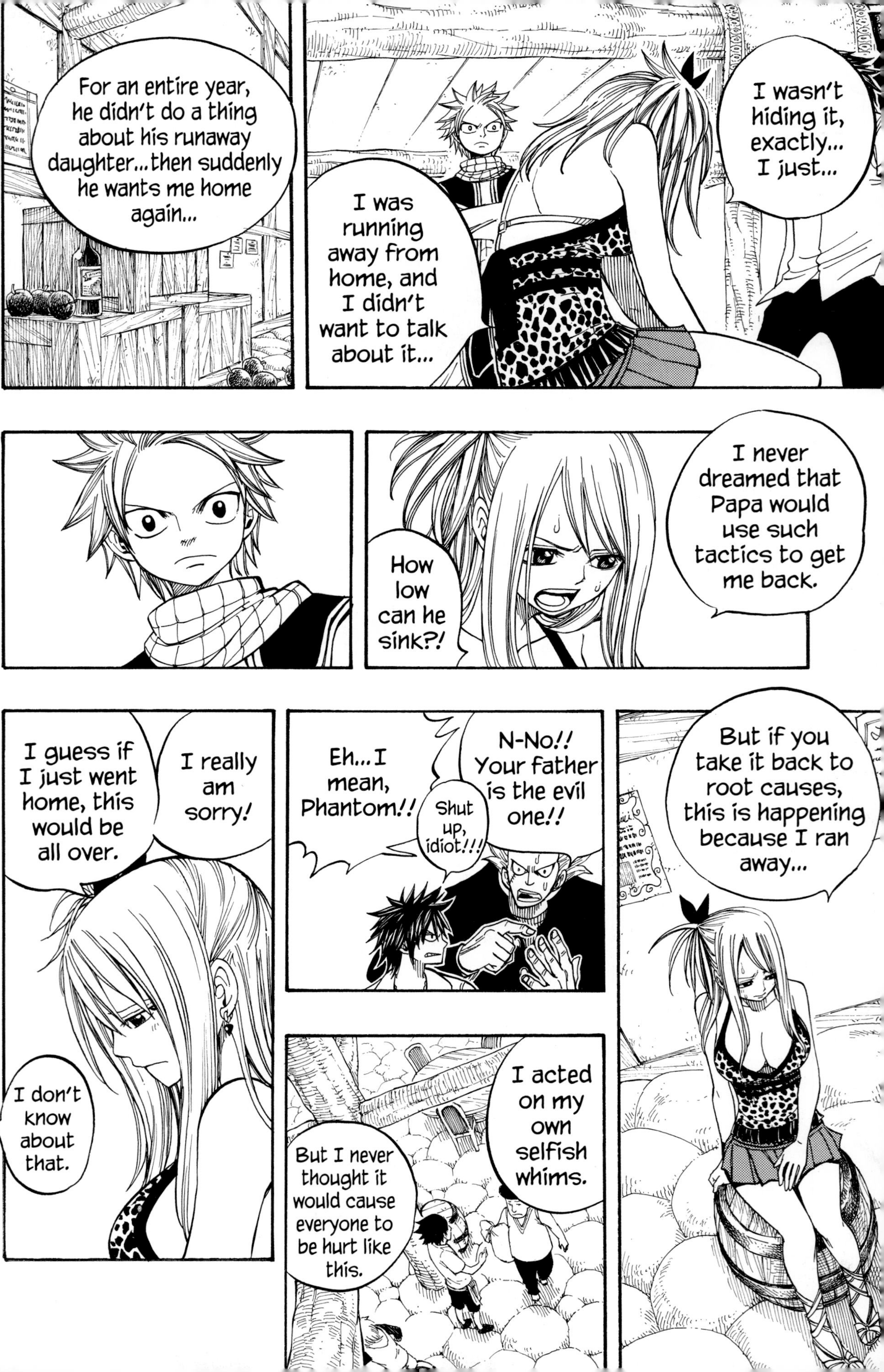
I wasn't hiding it, exactly... I just...
I was running away from home, and I didn't want to talk about it...
For an entire year, he didn't do a thing about his runaway daughter...then suddenly he wants me home again...
I never dreamed that Papa would use such tactics to get me back.
How low can he sink?!
But if you take it back to root causes, this is happening because I ran away...
N-No!! Your father is the evil one!!
Eh...I mean, Phantom!!
Shut up, idiot!!!
I acted on my own selfish whims.
But I never thought it would cause everyone to be hurt like this.
I really am sorry!
I guess if I just went home, this would be all over.
I don't know about that.

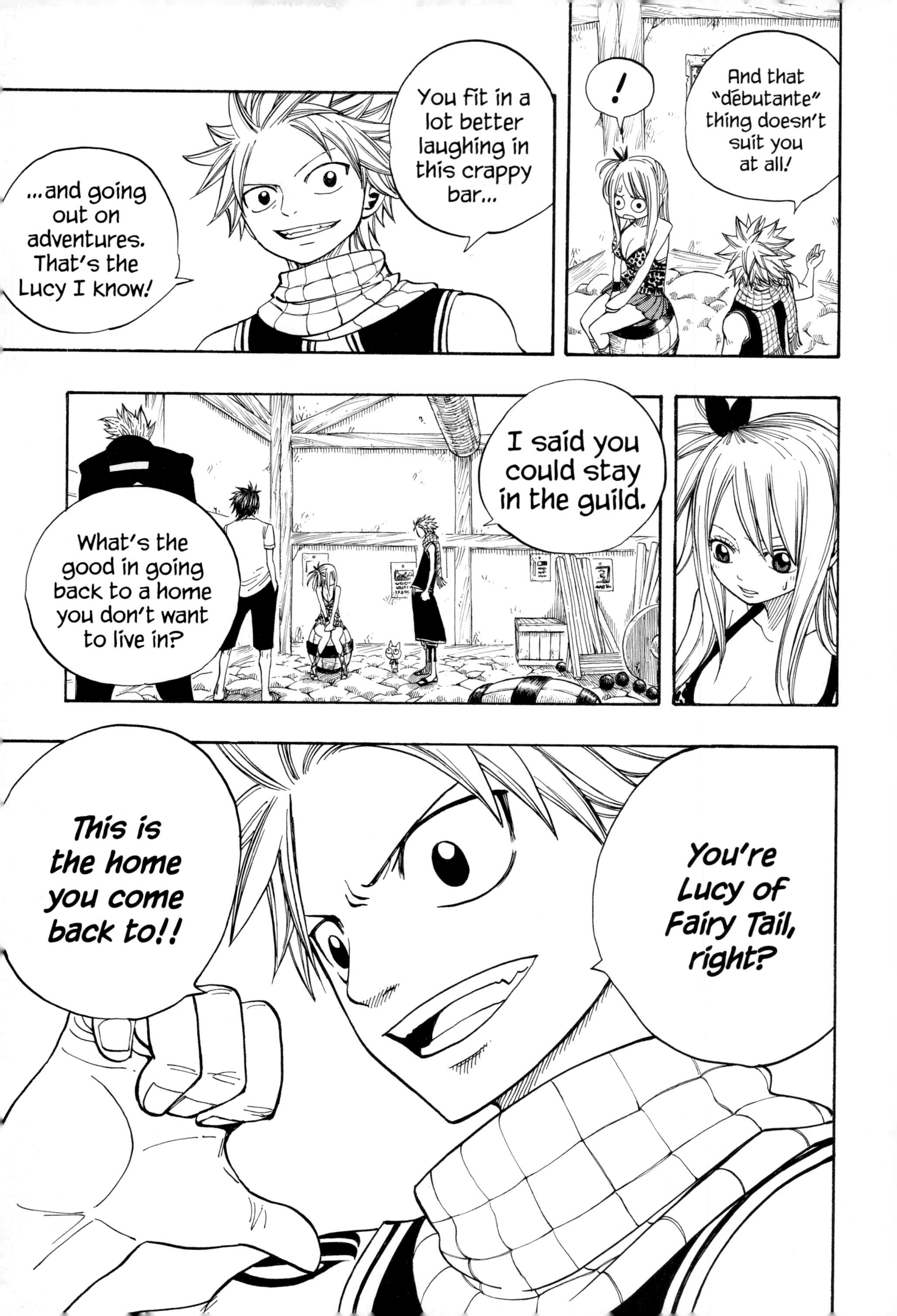
!
And that "débutante" thing doesn't suit you at all!
You fit in a lot better laughing in this crappy bar...
...and going out on adventures. That's the Lucy I know!
I said you could stay in the guild.
What's the good in going back to a home you don't want to live in?
You're Lucy of Fairy Tail, right?
This is the home you come back to!!

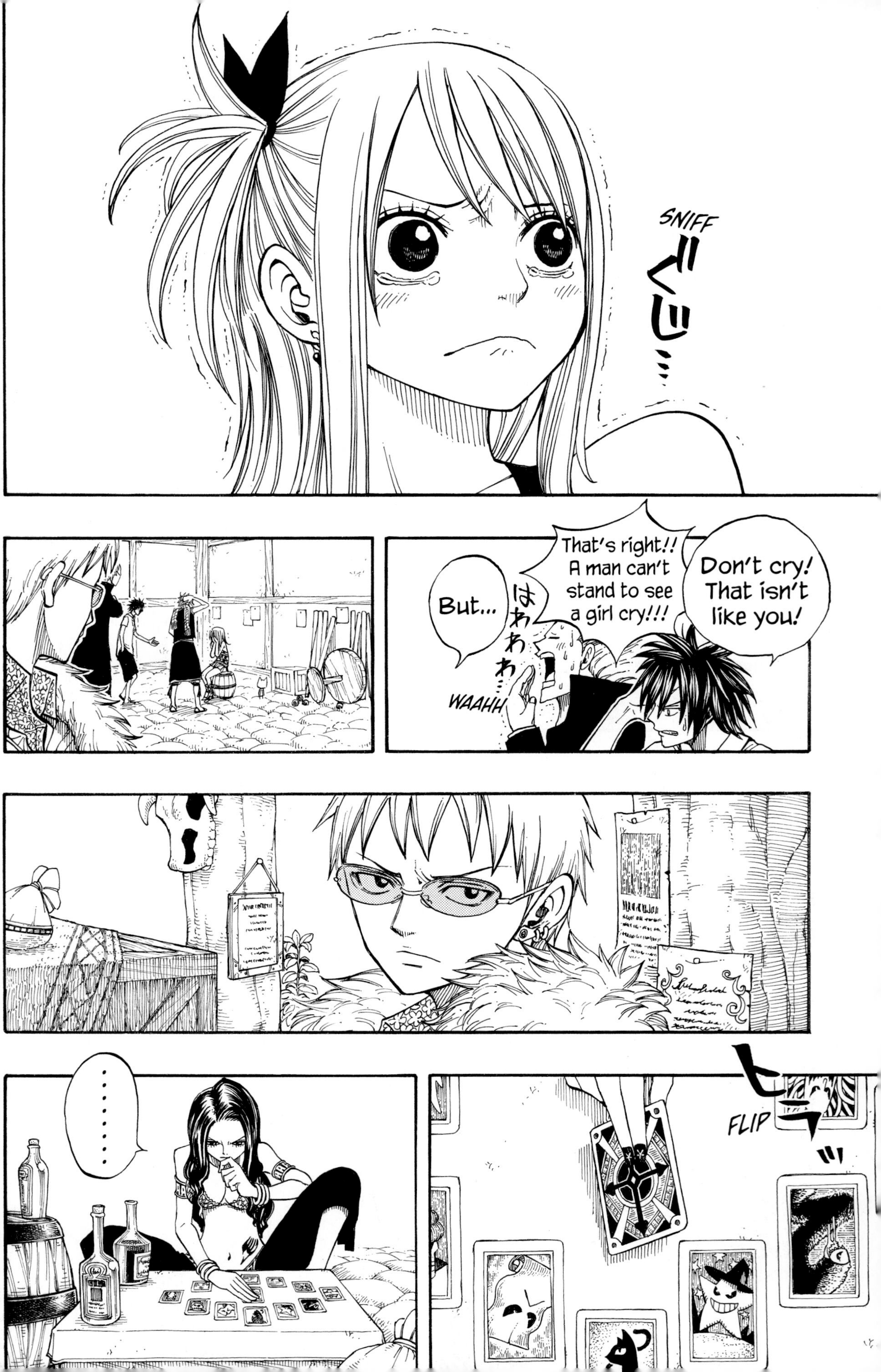
SNIFF
Don't cry! That isn't like you!
That's right!! A man can't stand to see a girl cry!!!
はわわわ…
WAAHH
But...
FLIP
....

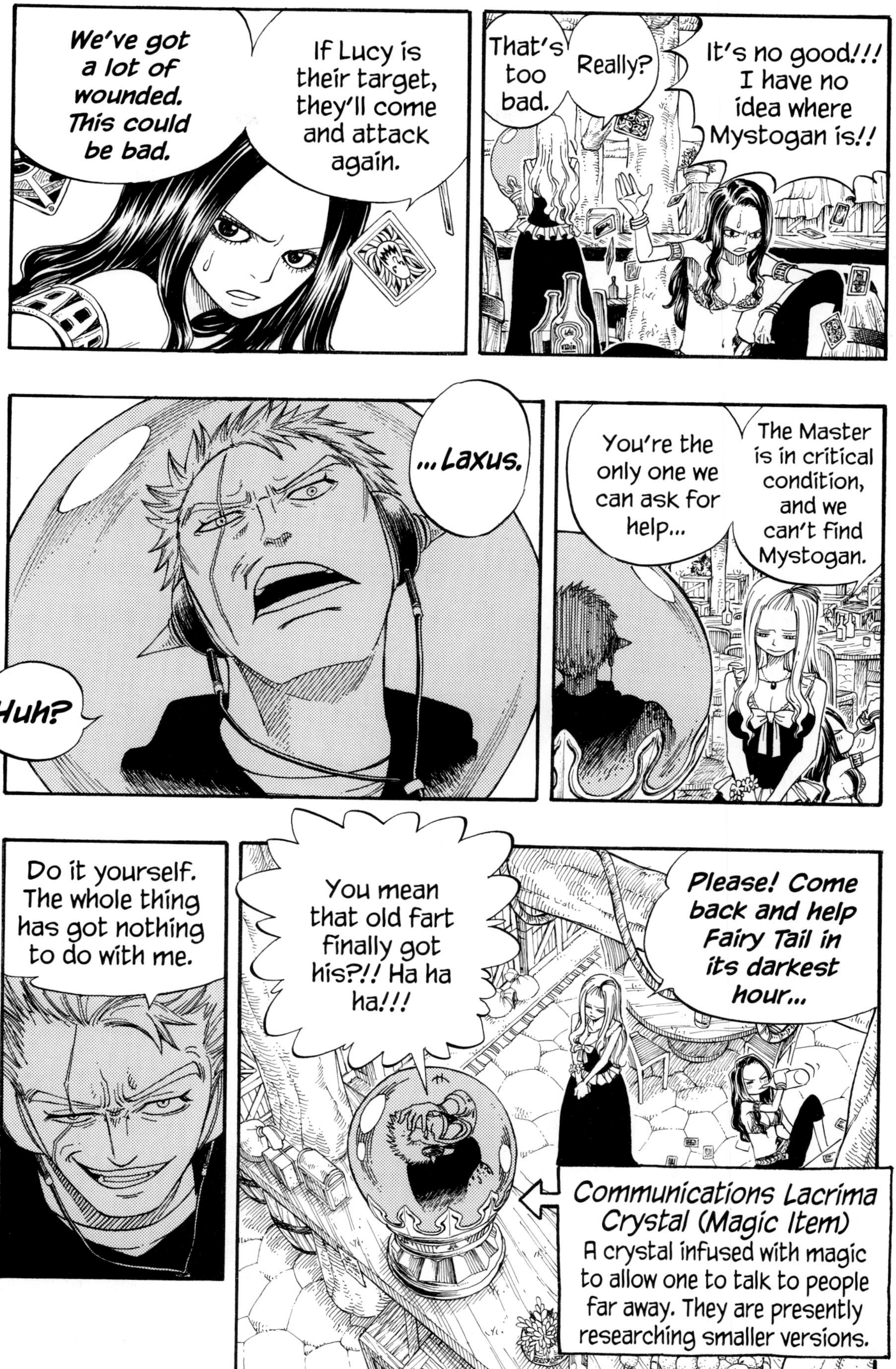
It's no good!!! I have no idea where Mystogan is!!
Really?
That's too bad.
If Lucy is their target, they'll come and attack again.
We've got a lot of wounded. This could be bad.
The Master is in critical condition, and we can't find Mystogan.
You're the only one we can ask for help...
...Laxus.
Huh?
Please! Come back and help Fairy Tail in its darkest hour...
You mean that old fart finally got his?!! Ha ha ha!!!
Communications Lacrima Crystal (Magic Item)
A crystal infused with magic to allow one to talk to people far away. They are presently researching smaller versions.
Do it yourself. The whole thing has got nothing to do with me.

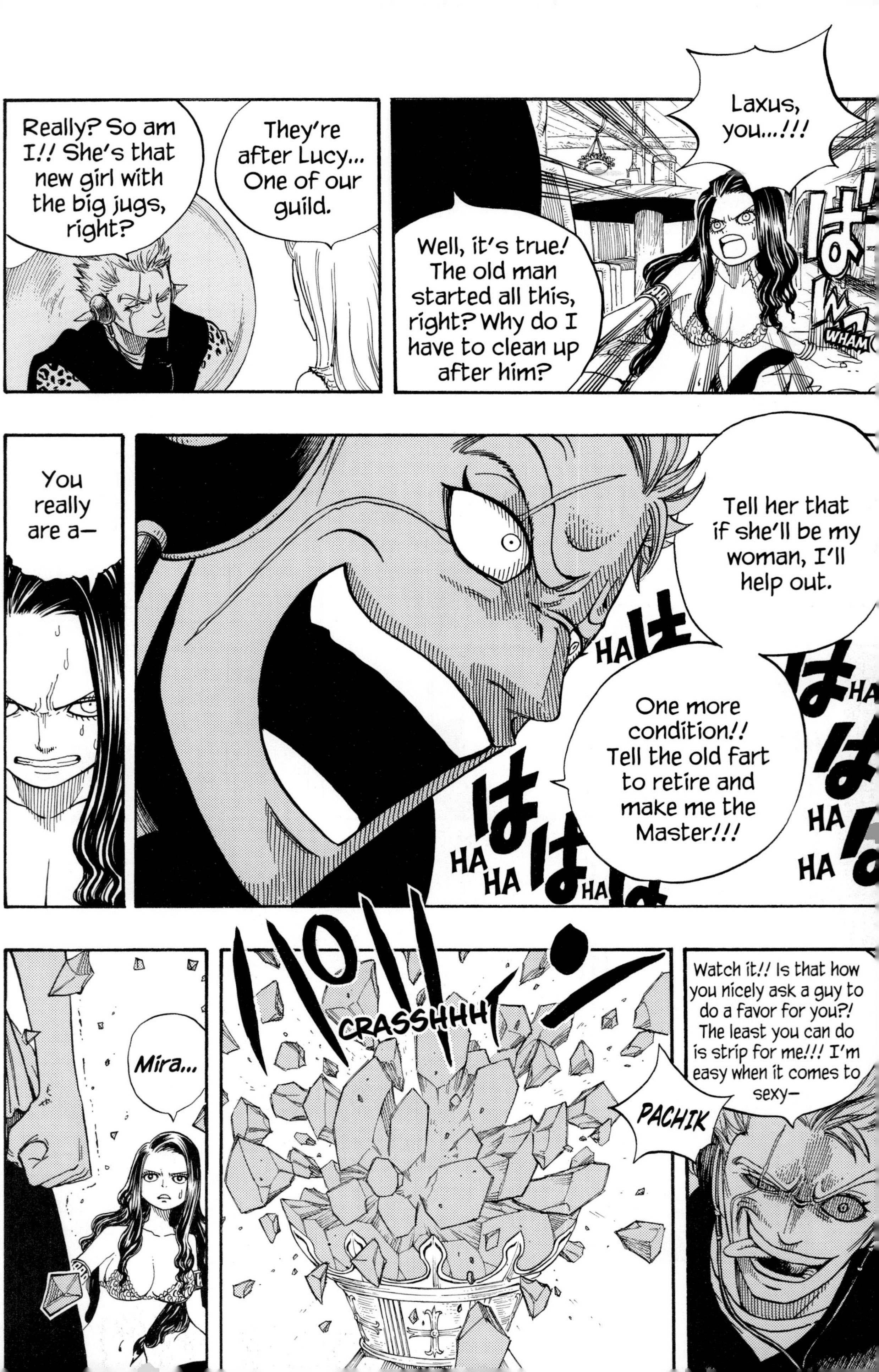
Laxus, you...!!!
WHAM
Well, it's true! The old man started all this, right? Why do I have to clean up after him?
They're after Lucy... One of our guild.
Really? So am I!! She's that new girl with the big jugs, right?
Tell her that if she'll be my woman, I'll help out.
One more condition!! Tell the old fart to retire and make me the Master!!!
HA HA HA HA HA HA HA
You really are a—
Watch it!! Is that how you nicely ask a guy to do a favor for you?! The least you can do is strip for me!!! I'm easy when it comes to sexy—
PACHIK
CRASSHHH
Mira...

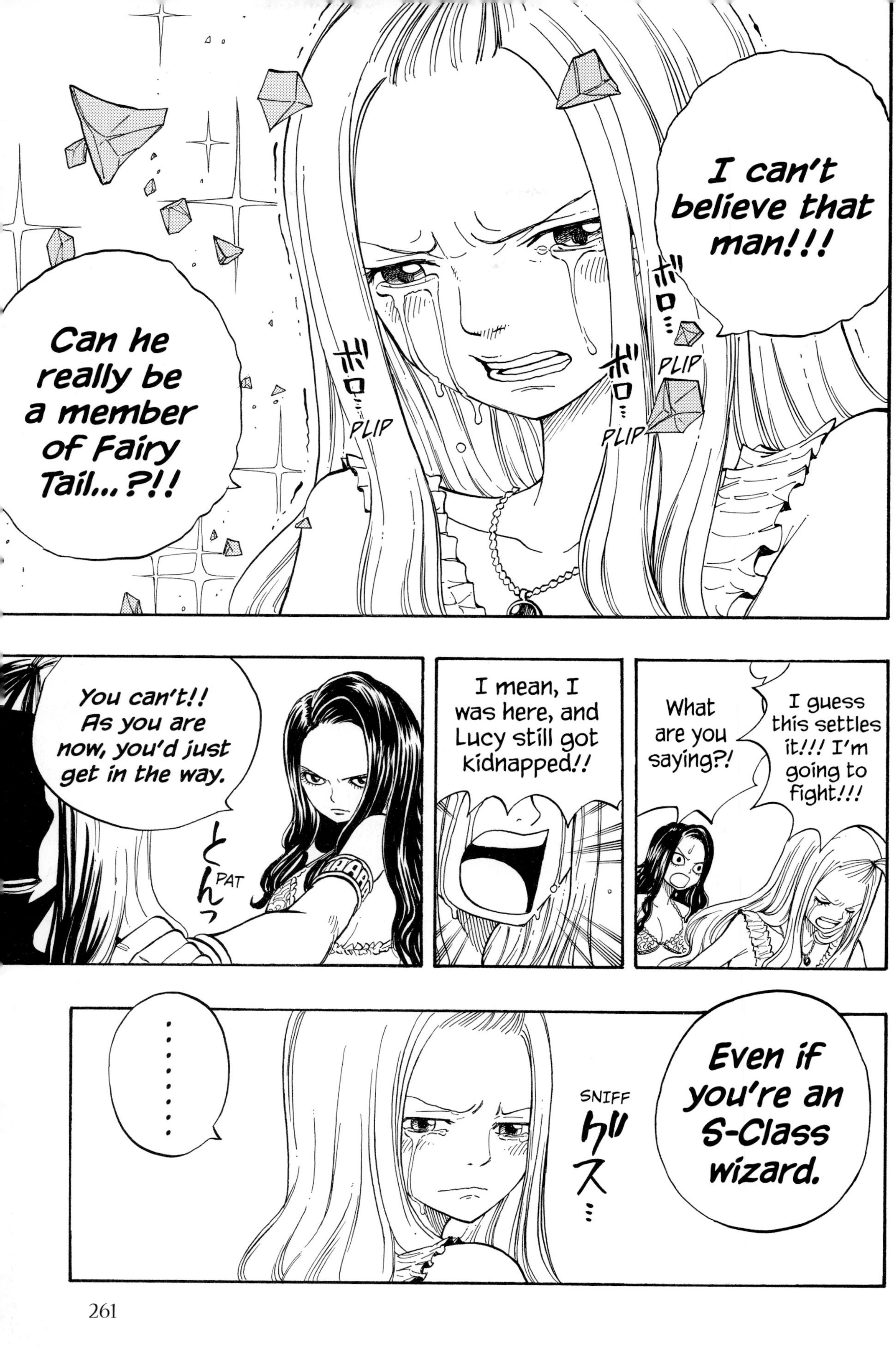
I can't believe that man!!!
ボロ
PLIP
ボロ
PLIP
Can he really be a member of Fairy Tail...?!!
ボロ
PLIP
I guess this settles it!!! I'm going to fight!!!
What are you saying?!
I mean, I was here, and Lucy still got kidnapped!!
You can't!! As you are now, you'd just get in the way.
とんっ
PAT
Even if you're an S-Class wizard.
SNIFF
グス
....

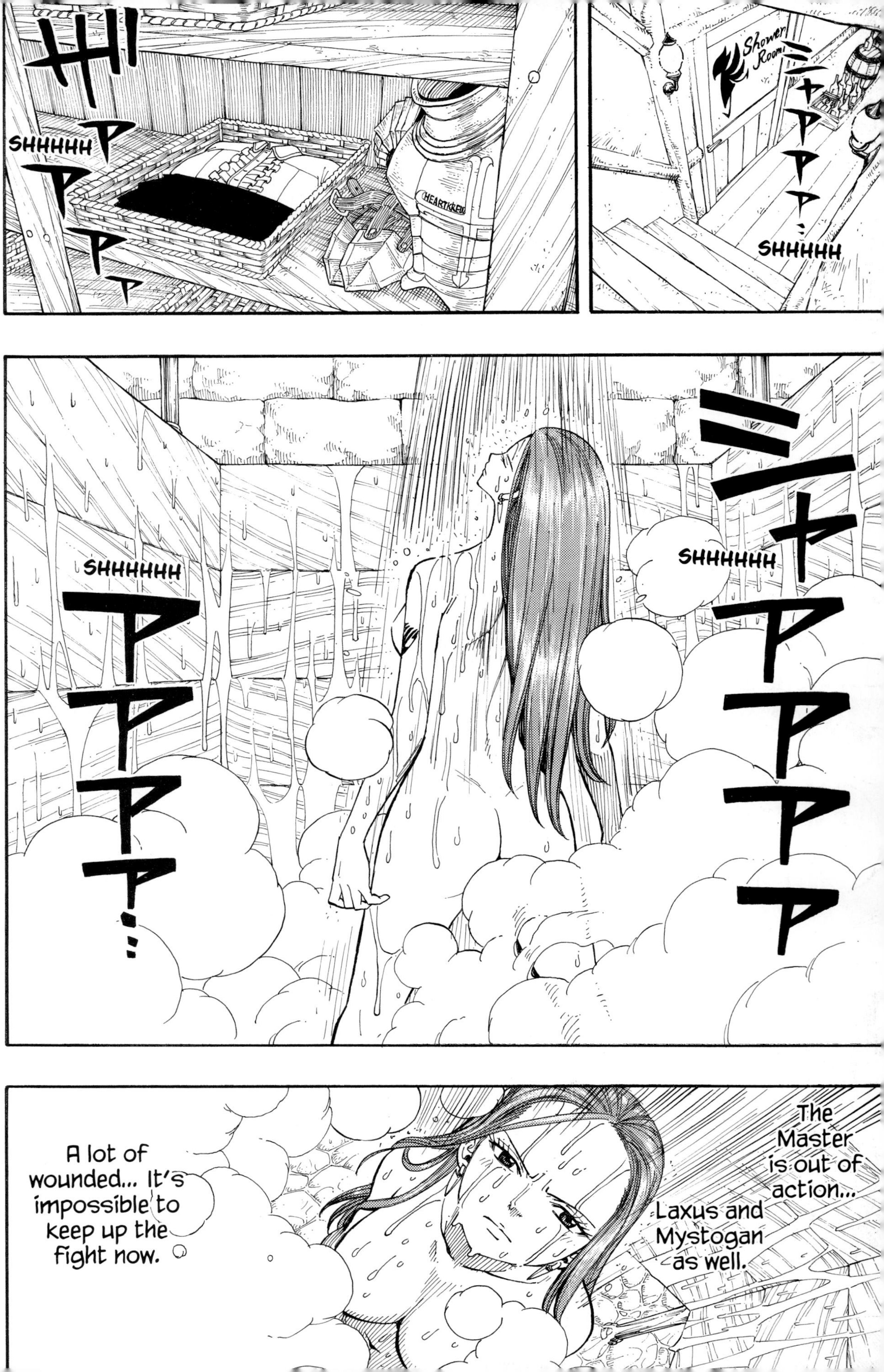
Shower Room
SHHHHH
SHHHHH
SHHHHHH
SHHHHHH
The Master is out of action...
Laxus and Mystogan as well.
A lot of wounded... It's impossible to keep up the fight now.

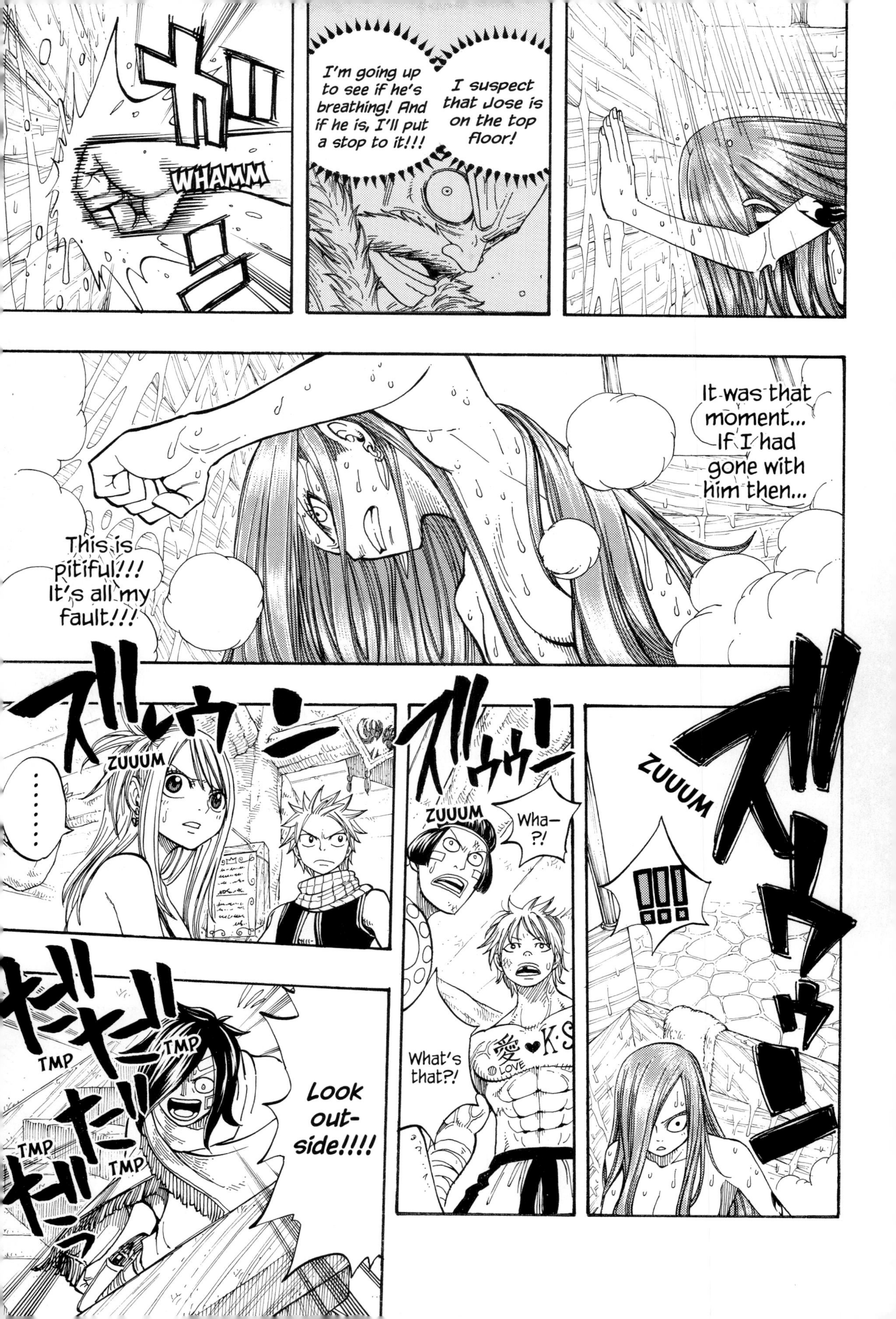
I suspect that Jose is on the top floor!
I'm going up to see if he's breathing! And if he is, I'll put a stop to it!!!
WHAMM
It was that moment... If I had gone with him then...
This is pitiful!!! It's all my fault!!!
ZUUUM
!!!!
ZUUUM
Wha-?!
What's that?!
ZUUUM
......
TMP
TMP
TMP
TMP
Look out-side!!!!

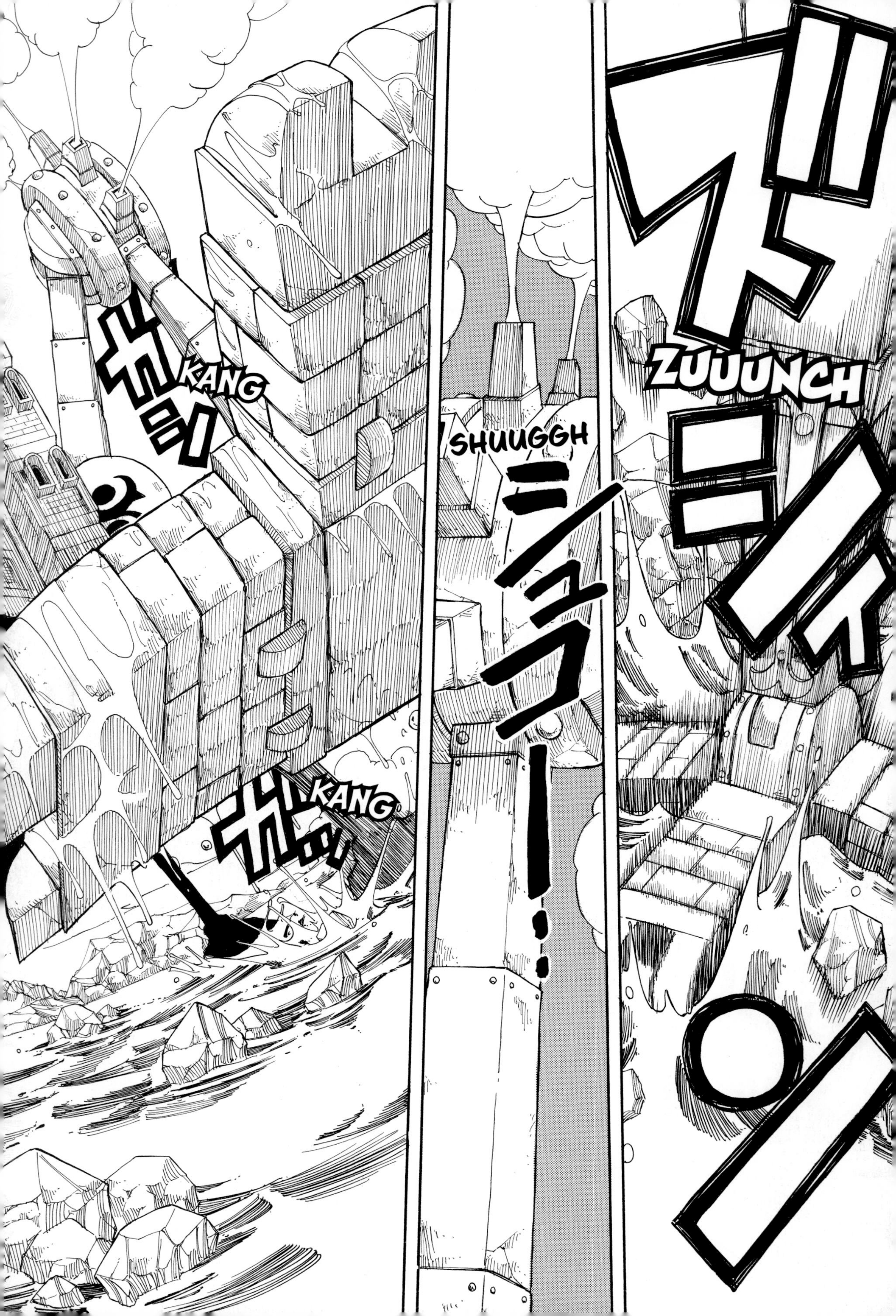
ZUUUNCH
SHUUGGH
KANG
KANG

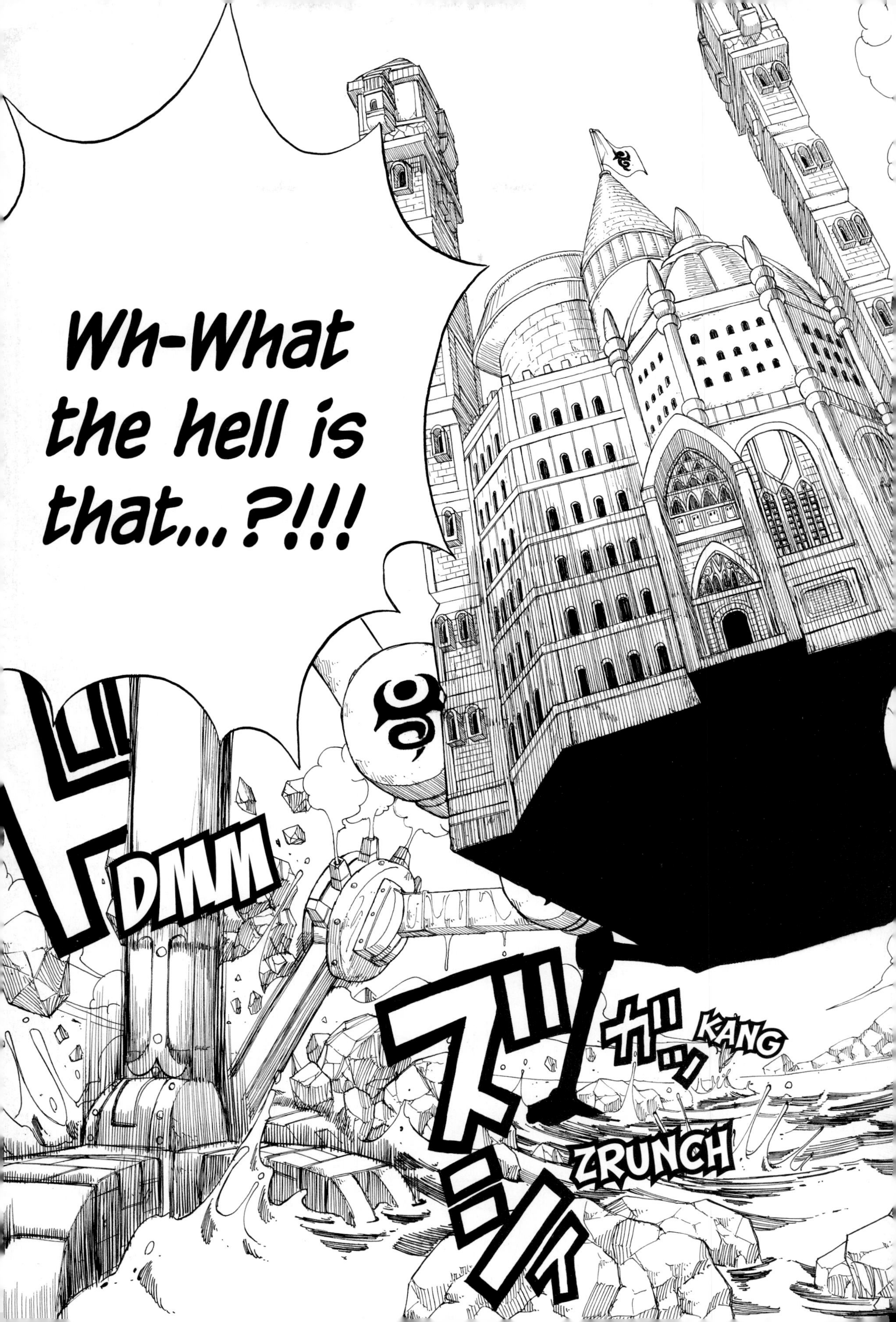
Wh-What the hell is that...?!!!
DMM
ズ
ガッ
KANG
ZRUNCH

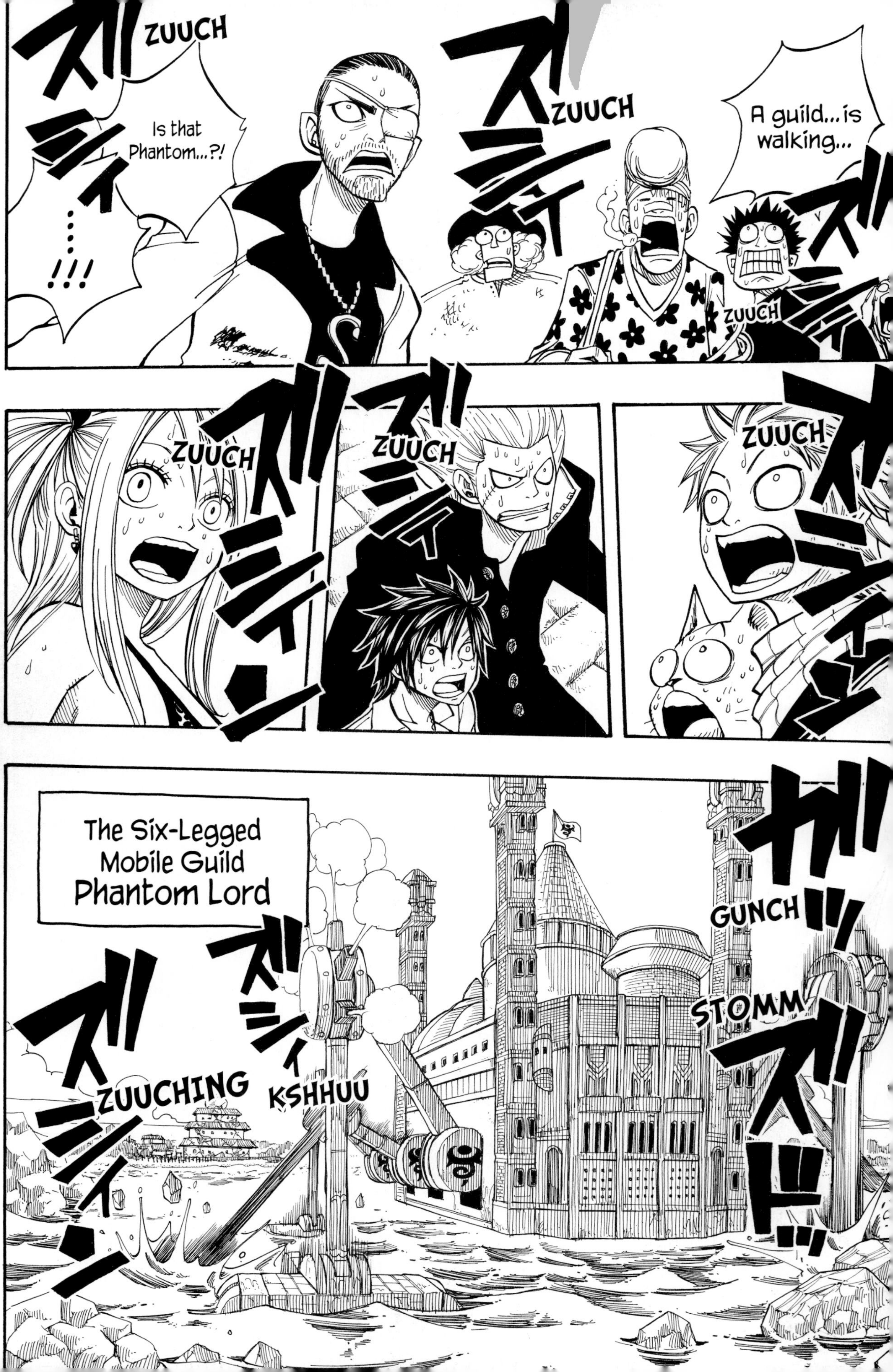
A guild...is walking...
ZUUCH
ZUUCH
ZUUCH
Is that Phantom...?!
...!!!
ZUUCH
ZUUCH
ZUUCH
GUNCH
STOMM
The Six-Legged Mobile Guild Phantom Lord
KSHHUU
ZUUCHING

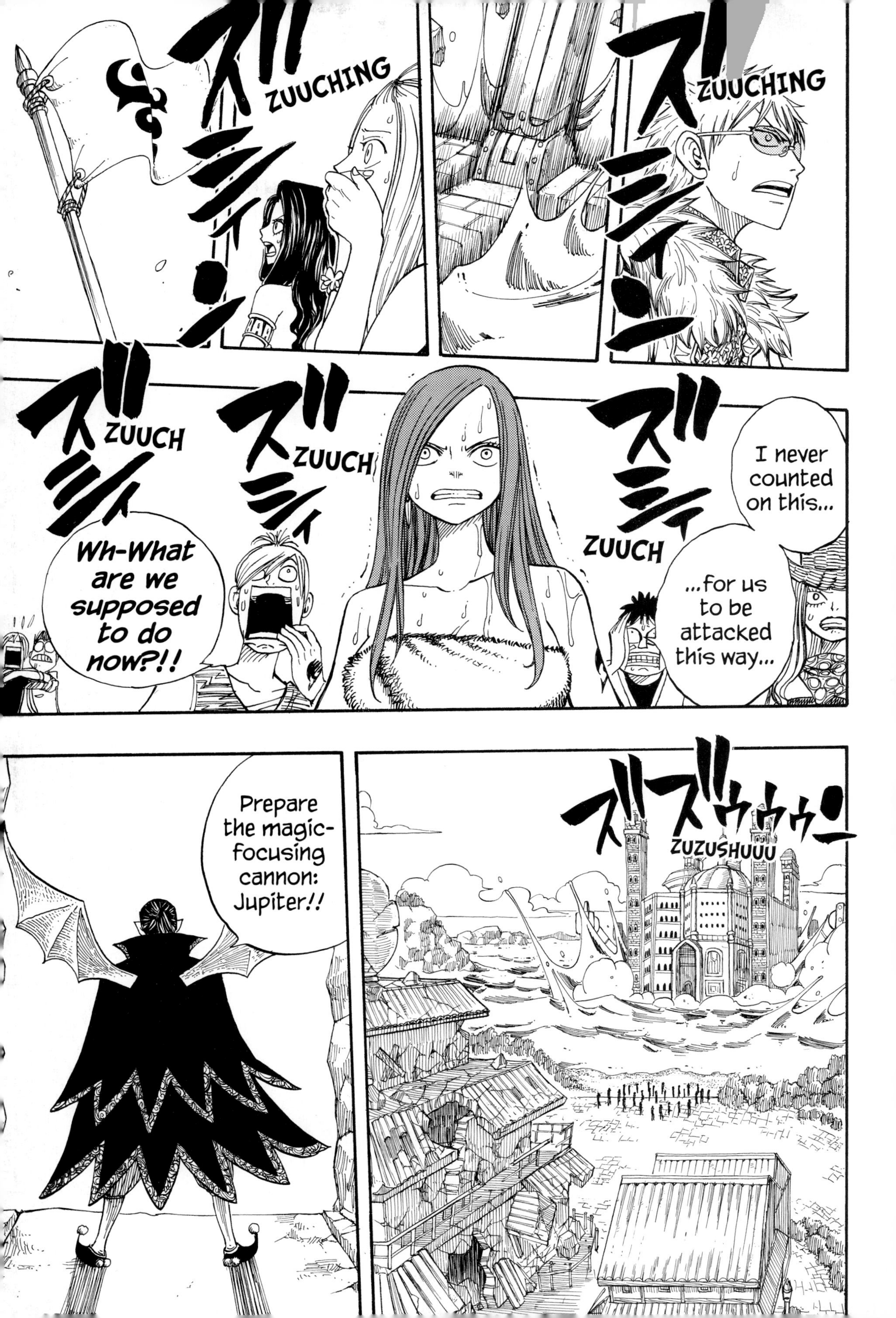
ZUUCHING
ZUUCHING
ZUUCH
I never counted on this...
...for us to be attacked this way...
ZUUCH
ZUUCH
Wh-What are we supposed to do now?!!
ZUZUSHUUU
Prepare the magic-focusing cannon: Jupiter!!

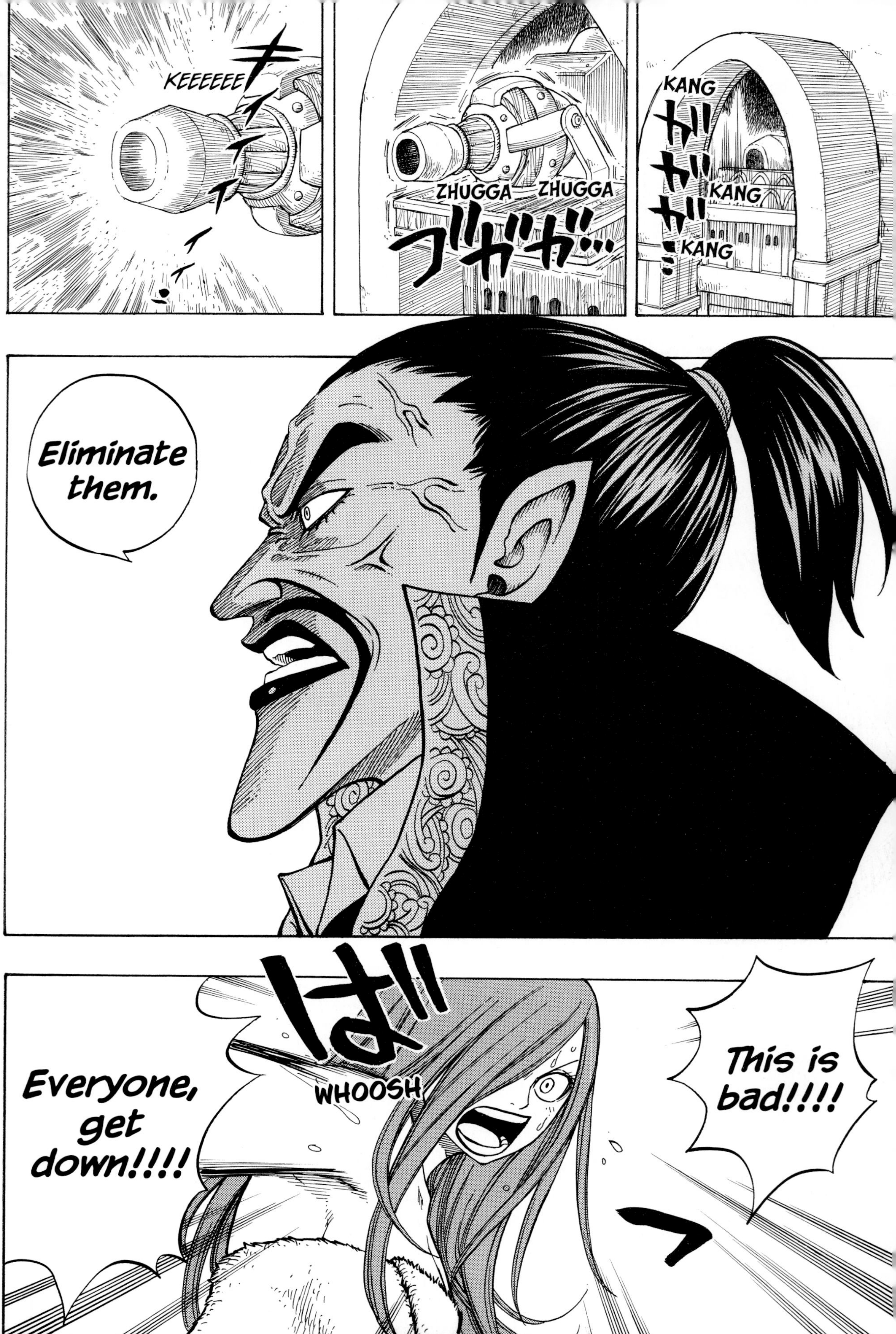
KANG
KANG
KANG
ZHUGGA ZHUGGA
KEEEEEE
Eliminate them.
This is bad!!!!
WHOOSH
Everyone, get down!!!!

FAIRY TAIL

Chapter 52: 15 Minutes

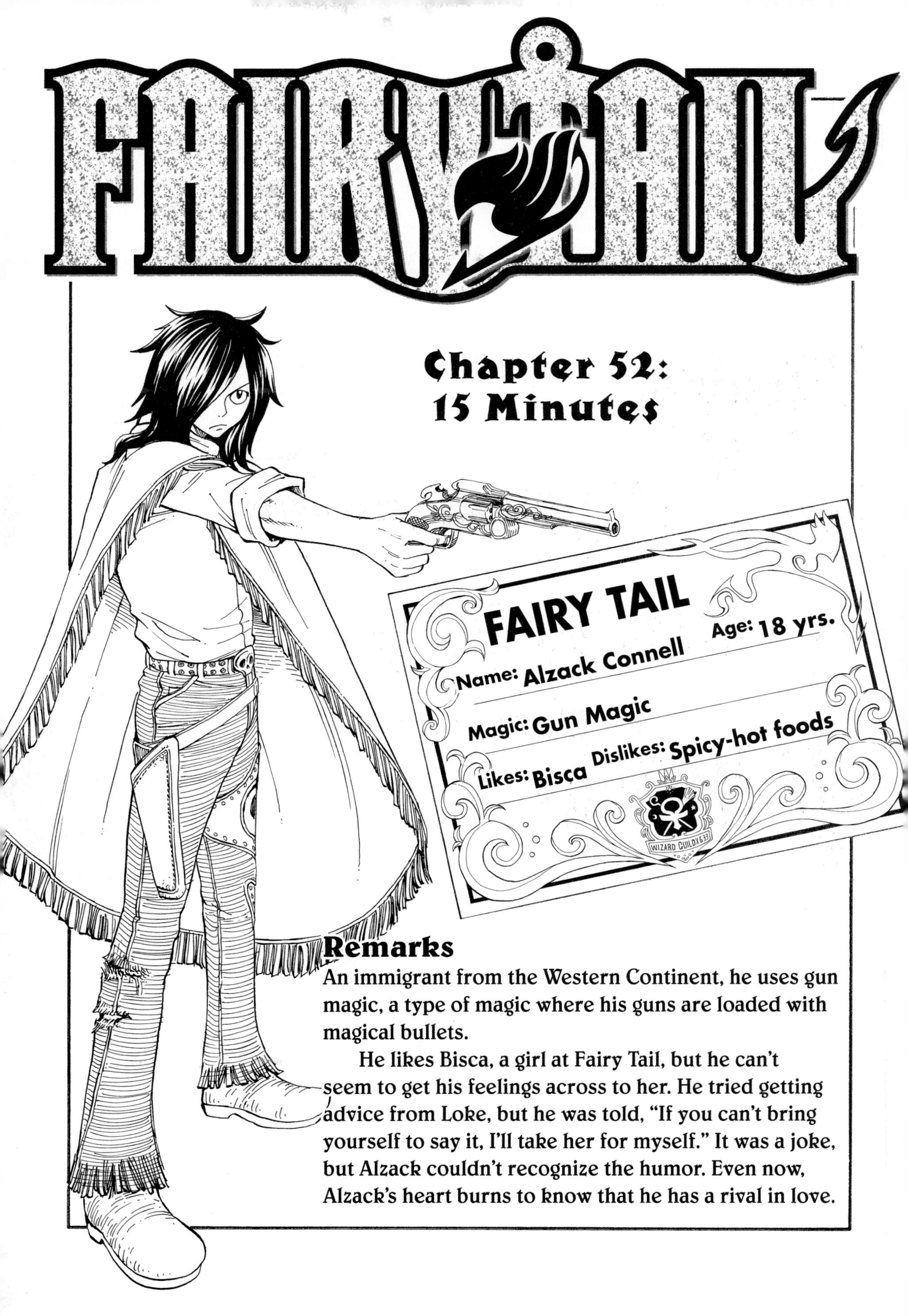
FAIRY TAIL
Name: Alzack Connell
Age: 18 yrs.
Magic: Gun Magic
Likes: Bisca
Dislikes: Spicy-hot foods
WIZARD GUILD×633

Remarks

An immigrant from the Western Continent, he uses gun magic, a type of magic where his guns are loaded with magical bullets.

He likes Bisca, a girl at Fairy Tail, but he can't seem to get his feelings across to her. He tried getting advice from Loke, but he was told, "If you can't bring yourself to say it, I'll take her for myself." It was a joke, but Alzack couldn't recognize the humor. Even now, Alzack's heart burns to know that he has a rival in love.

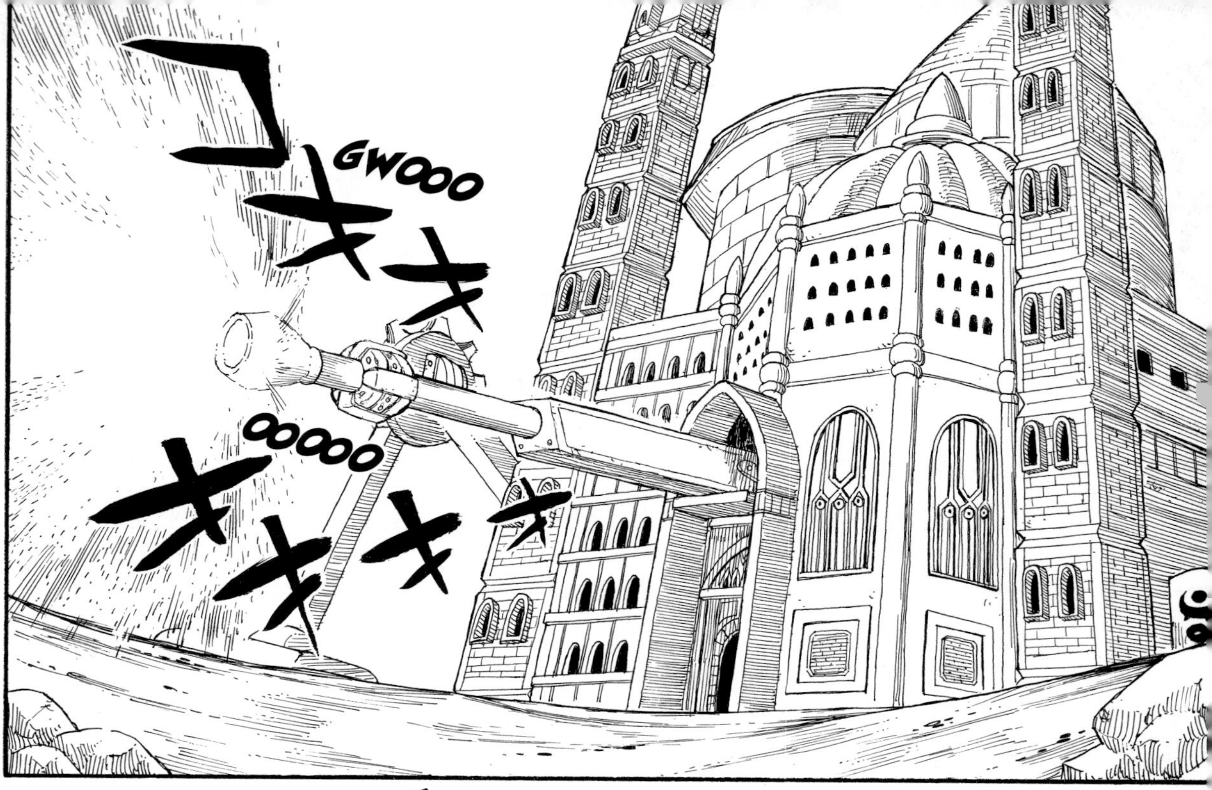
GWOOO
OOOOO

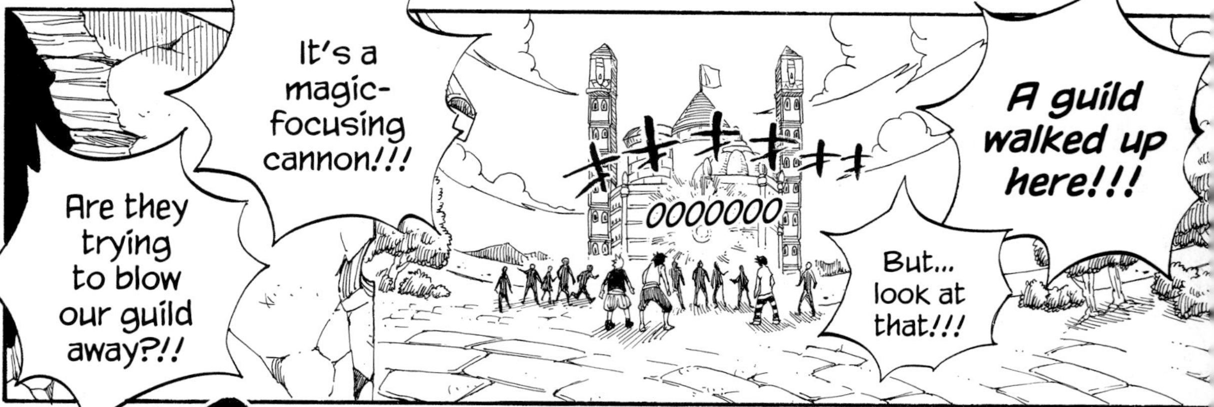
A guild walked up here!!!
But... look at that!!!
OOOOOOO
It's a magic-focusing cannon!!!
Are they trying to blow our guild away?!!

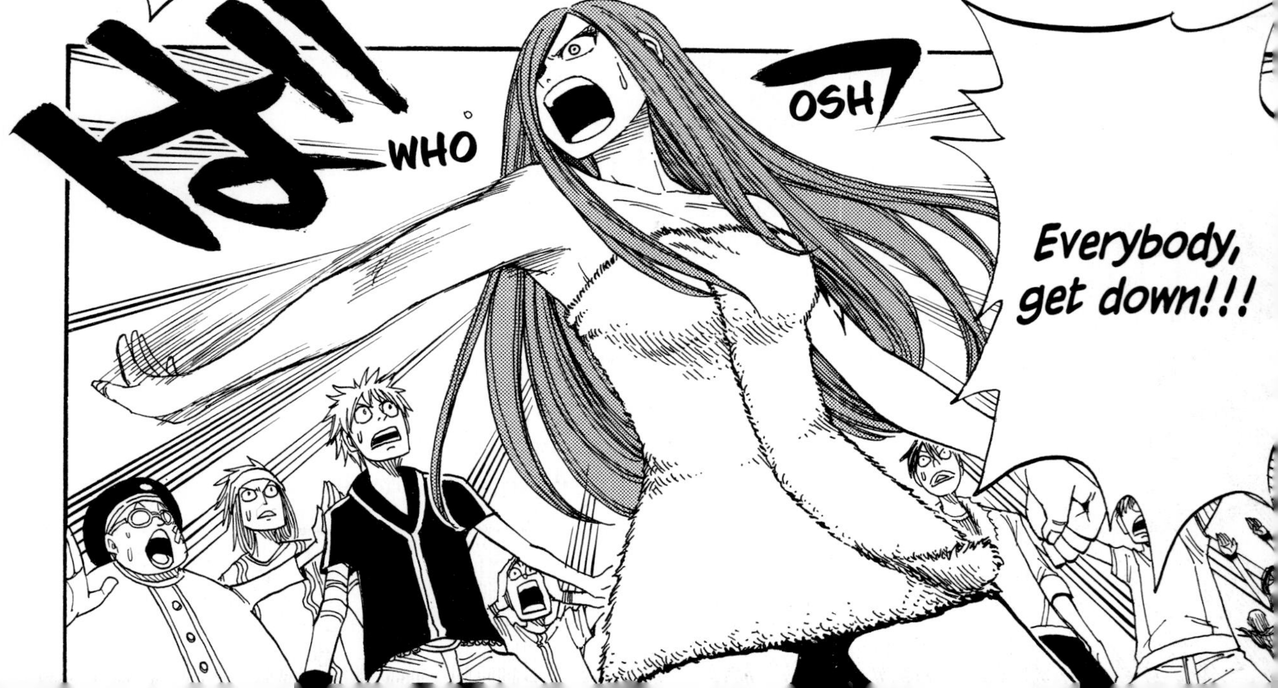
Everybody, get down!!!
WHO
OSH

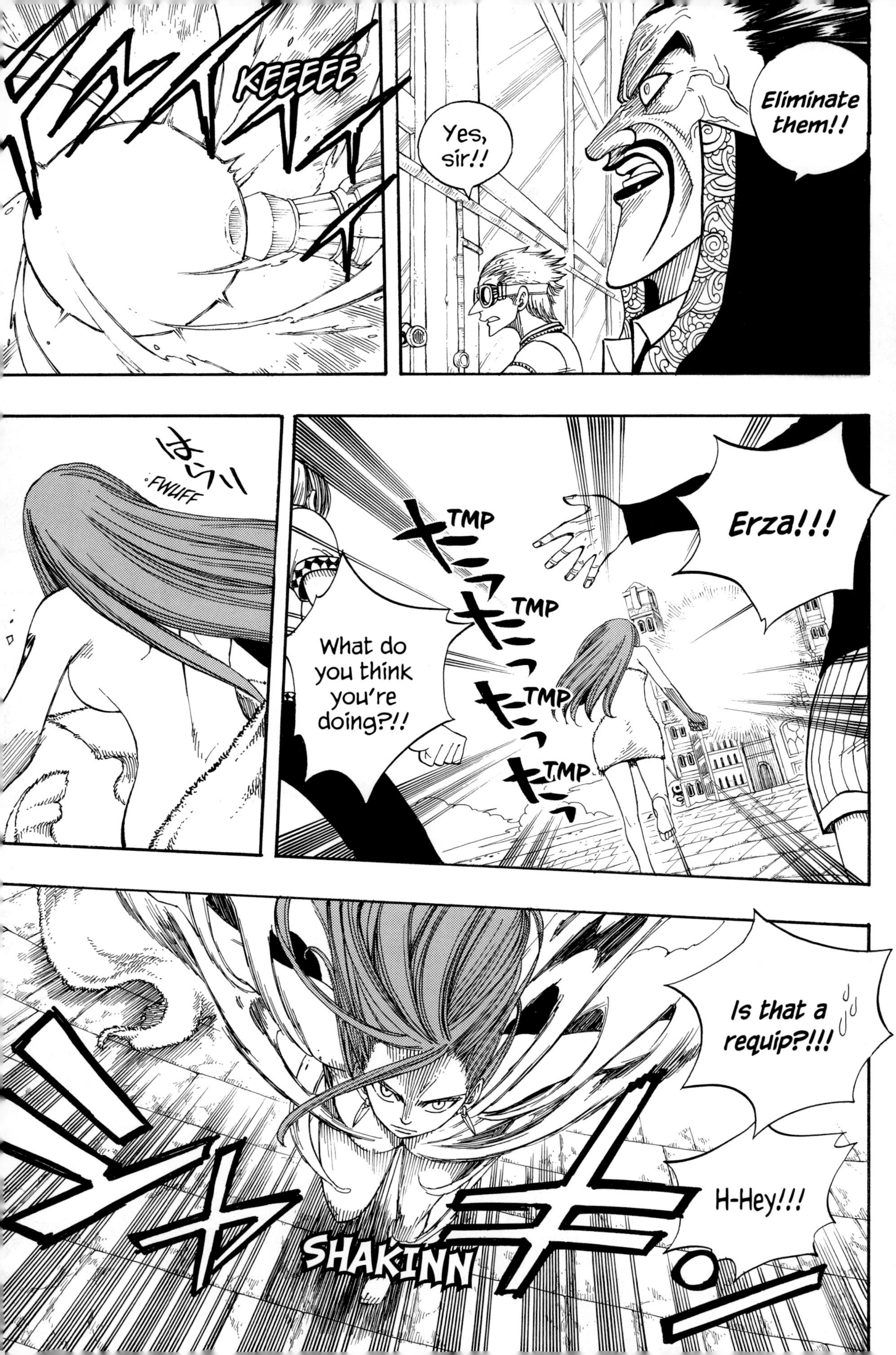
Eliminate them!!
Yes, sir!!
KEEEEEE
Erza!!!
What do you think you're doing?!!
TMP
TMP
TMP
TMP
FWUFF
Is that a requip?!!!
H-Hey!!!
SHAKINN

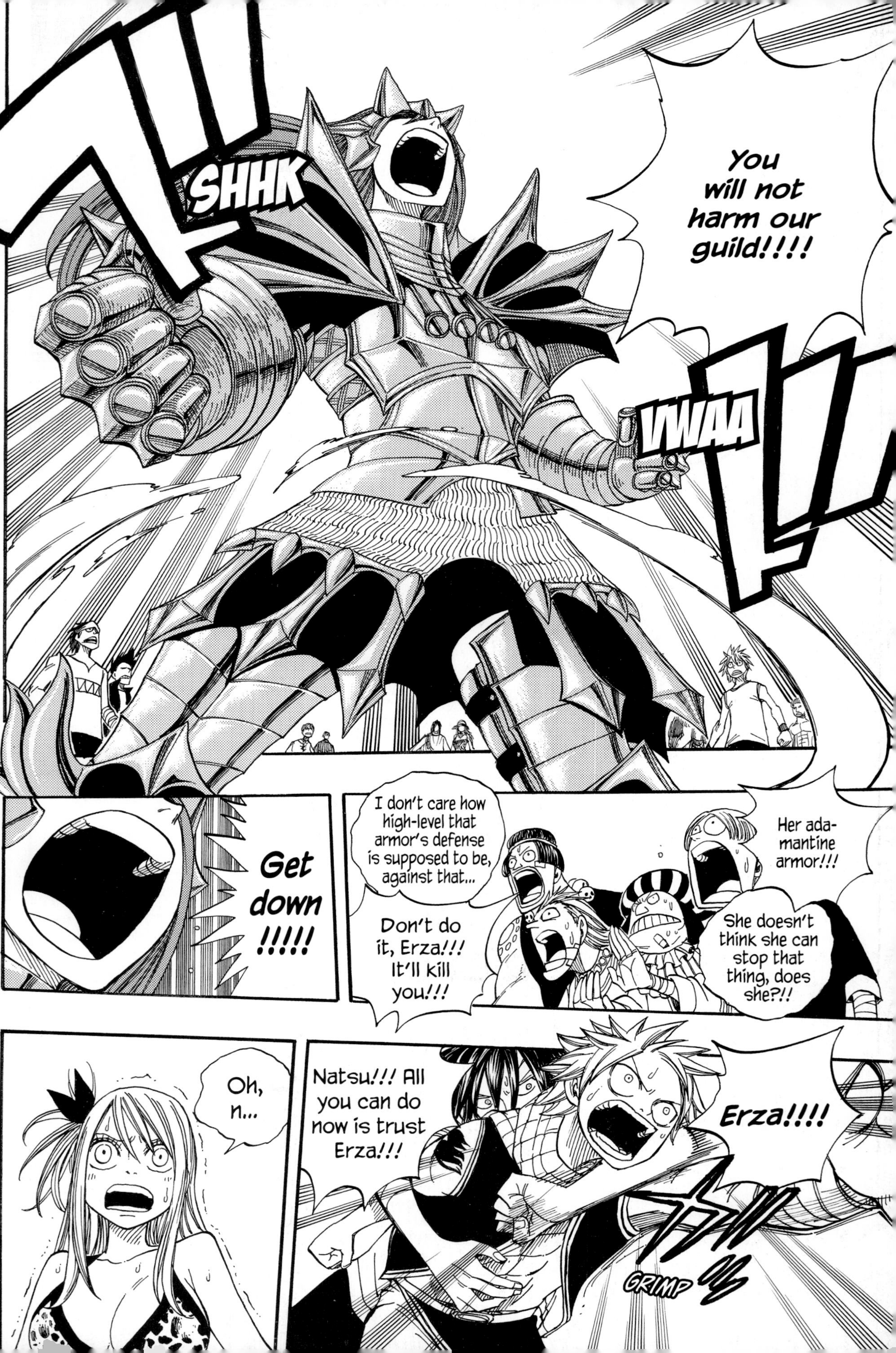
You will not harm our guild!!!!
SHHK
VWAA
Her ada-mantine armor!!!
I don't care how high-level that armor's defense is supposed to be, against that...
She doesn't think she can stop that thing, does she?!!
Don't do it, Erza!!! It'll kill you!!!
Get down !!!!!
Erza!!!!
Natsu!!! All you can do now is trust Erza!!!
GRIMP
Oh, n...

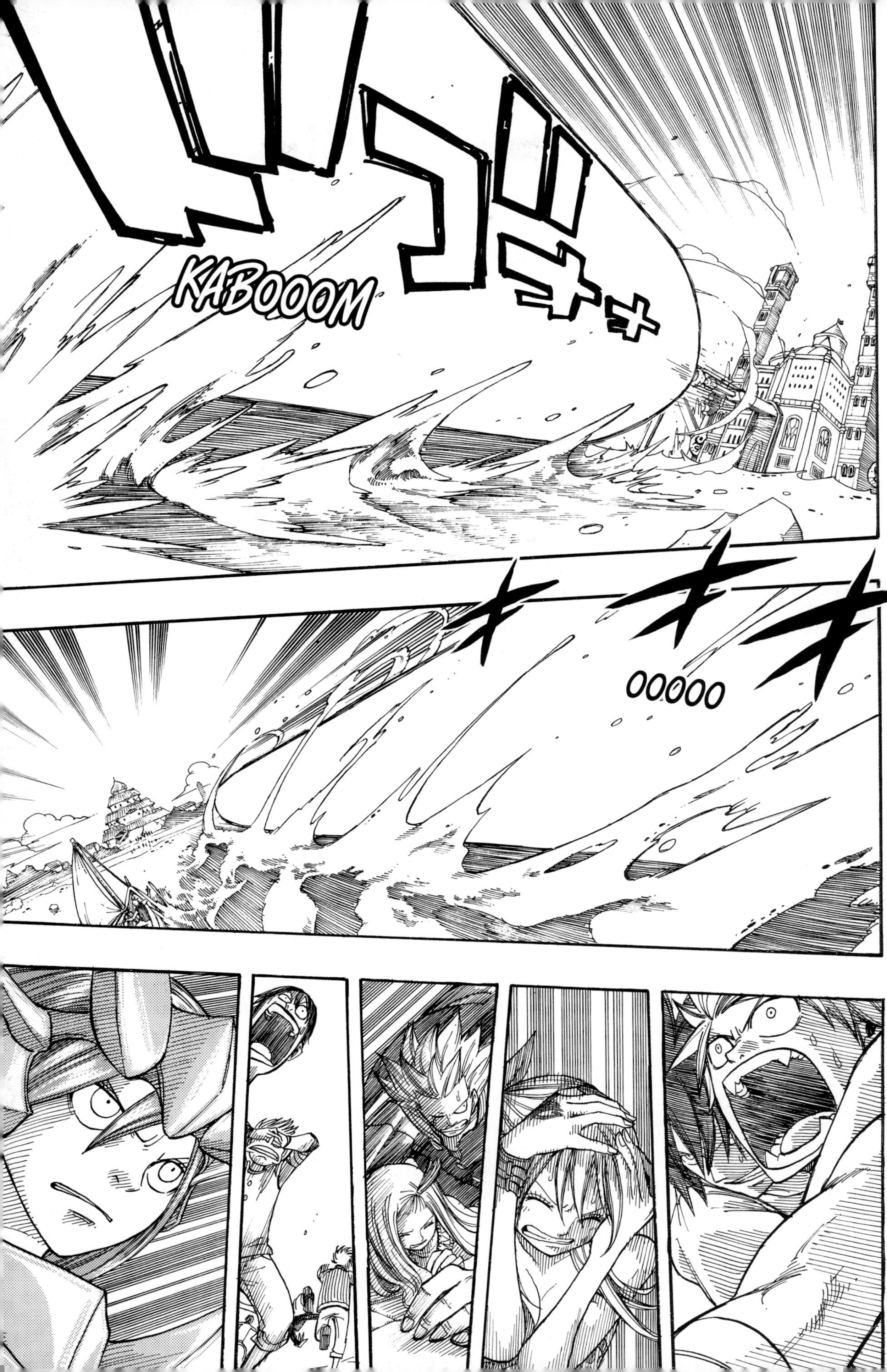
KABOOOM
OOOOO

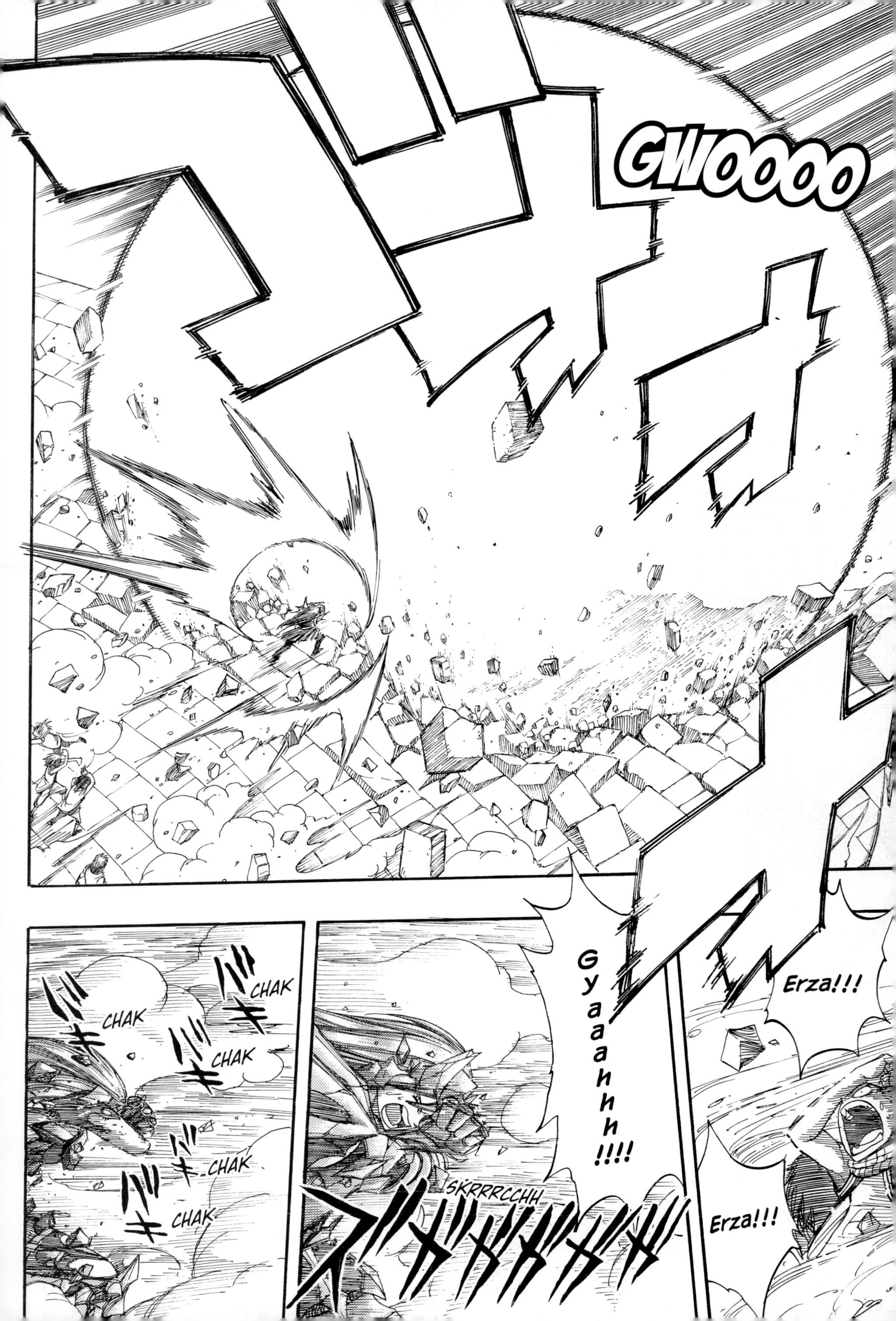
GWOOOO
Erza!!!
Erza!!!
Gyaaahhh!!!!
SKRRRCCHH
CHAK
CHAK
CHAK
CHAK
CHAK

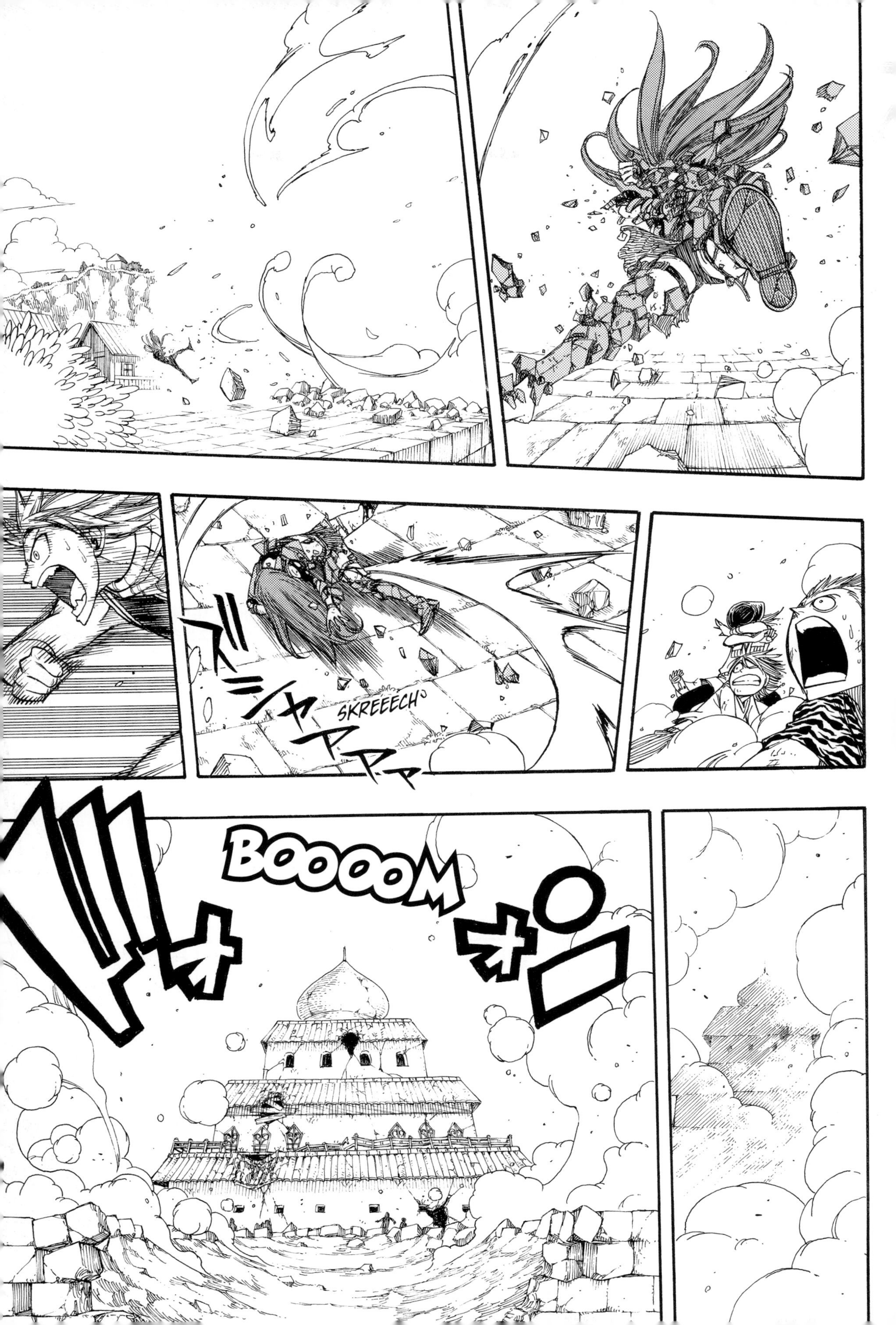
SKREEECH
BOOOOOM

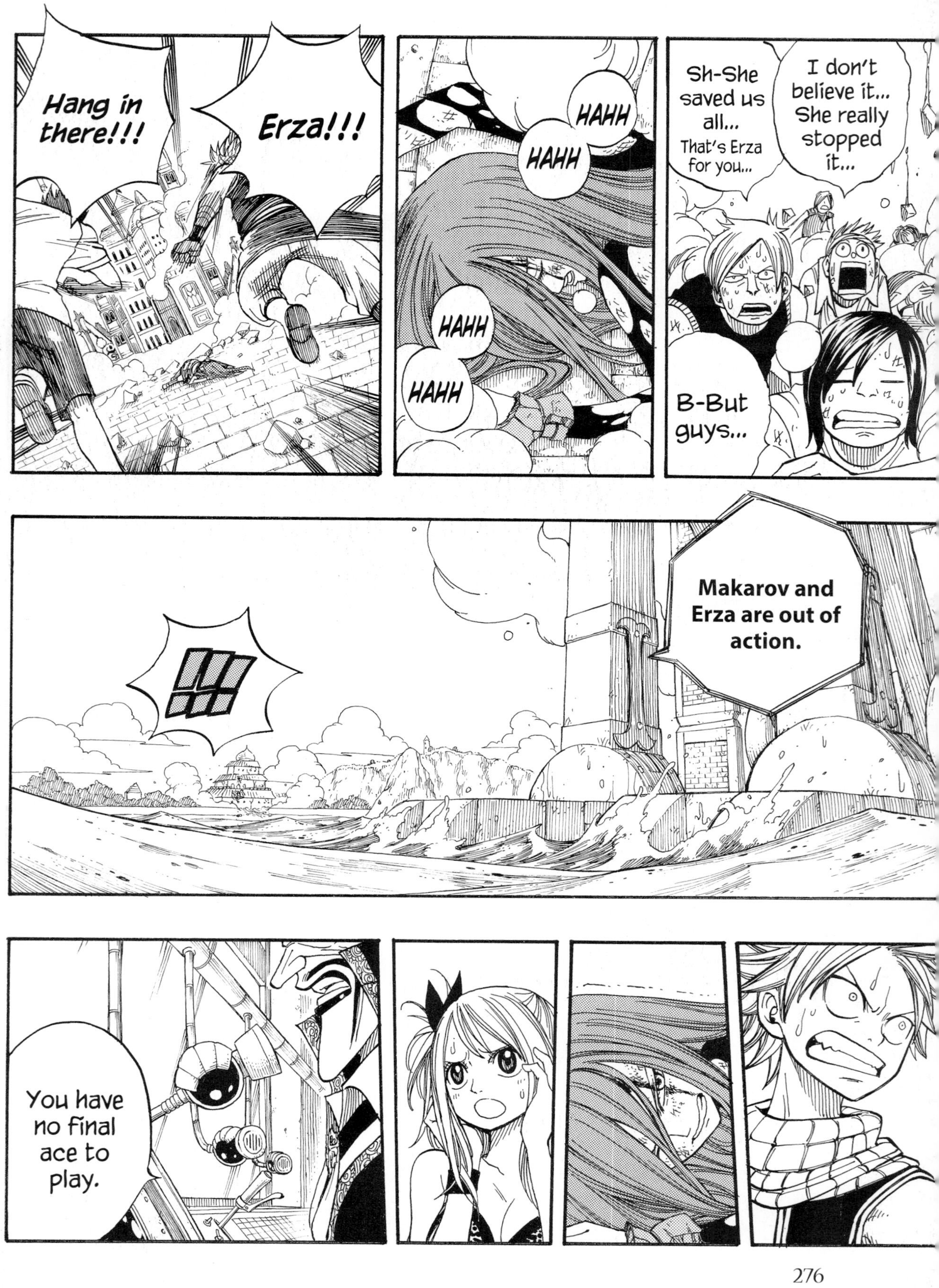
I don't believe it... She really stopped it...
Sh-She saved us all... That's Erza for you...
B-But guys...
HAHH
HAHH
HAHH
HAHH
Erza!!!
Hang in there!!!
Makarov and Erza are out of action.
!!
You have no final ace to play.

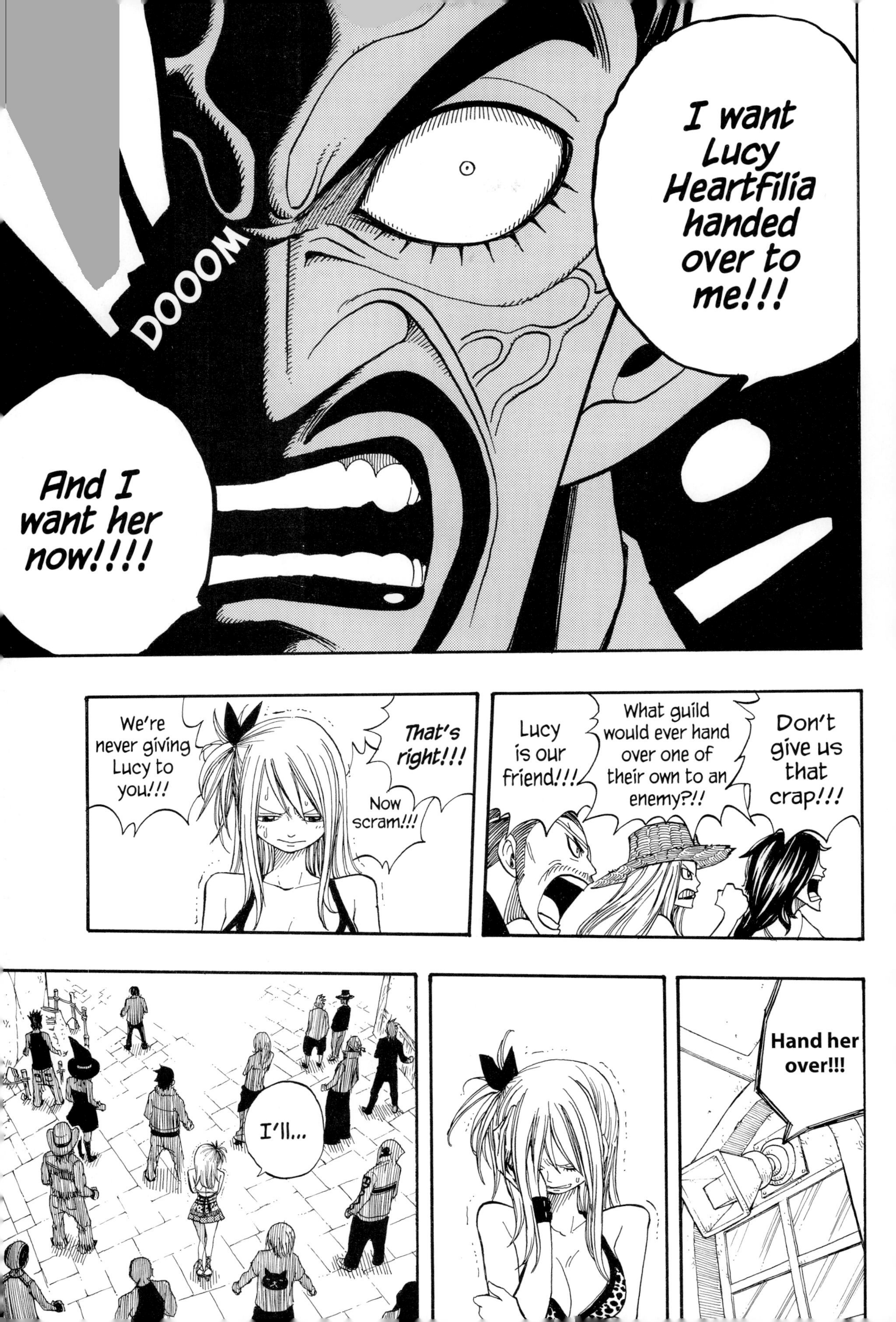
I want Lucy Heartfilia handed over to me!!!
DOOOM
And I want her now!!!!
Don't give us that crap!!!
What guild would ever hand over one of their own to an enemy?!!
Lucy is our friend!!!
That's right!!!
Now scram!!!
We're never giving Lucy to you!!!
Hand her over!!!
I'll...

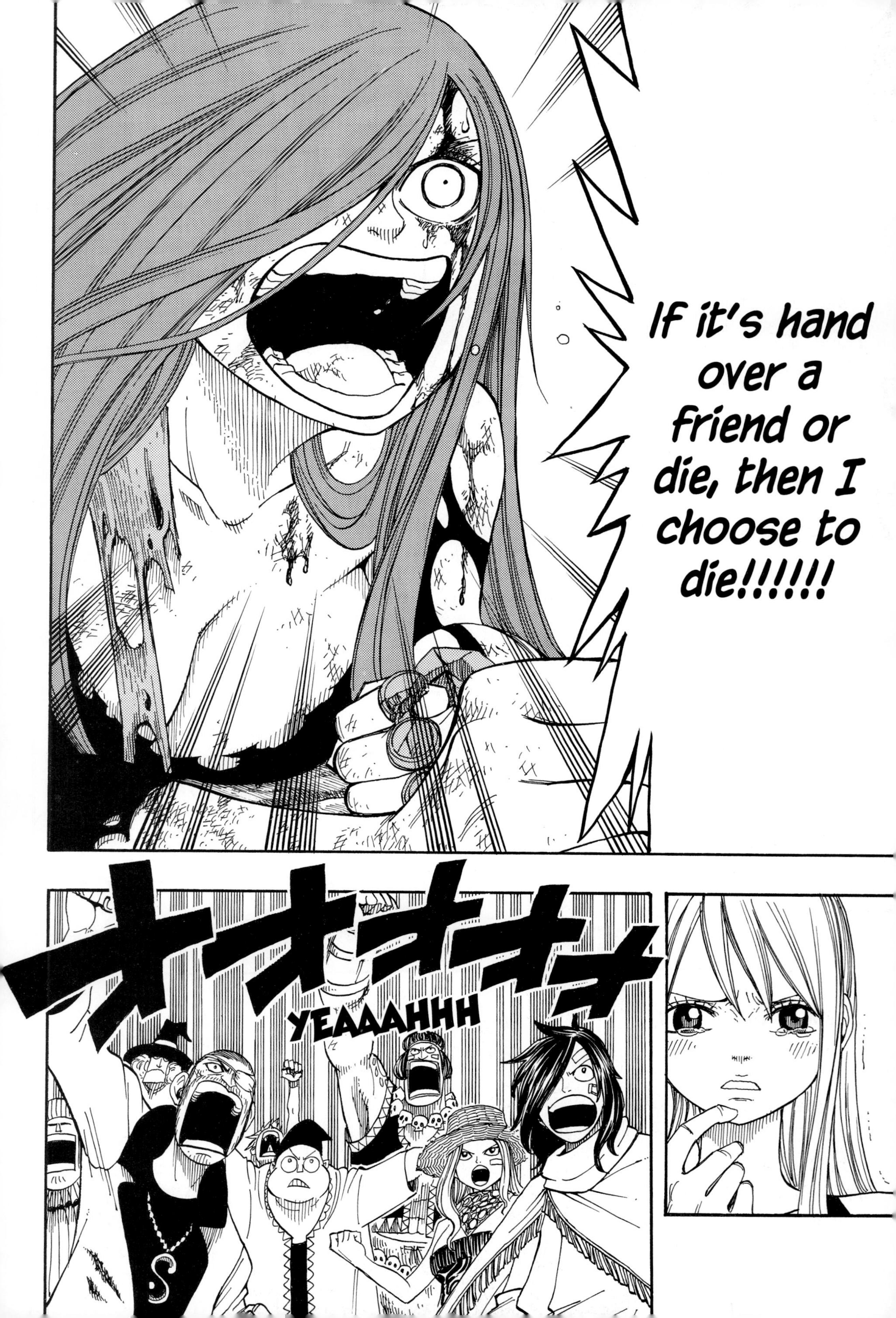
If it's hand over a friend or die, then I choose to die!!!!!!
オオオオオ
YEAAAHHH

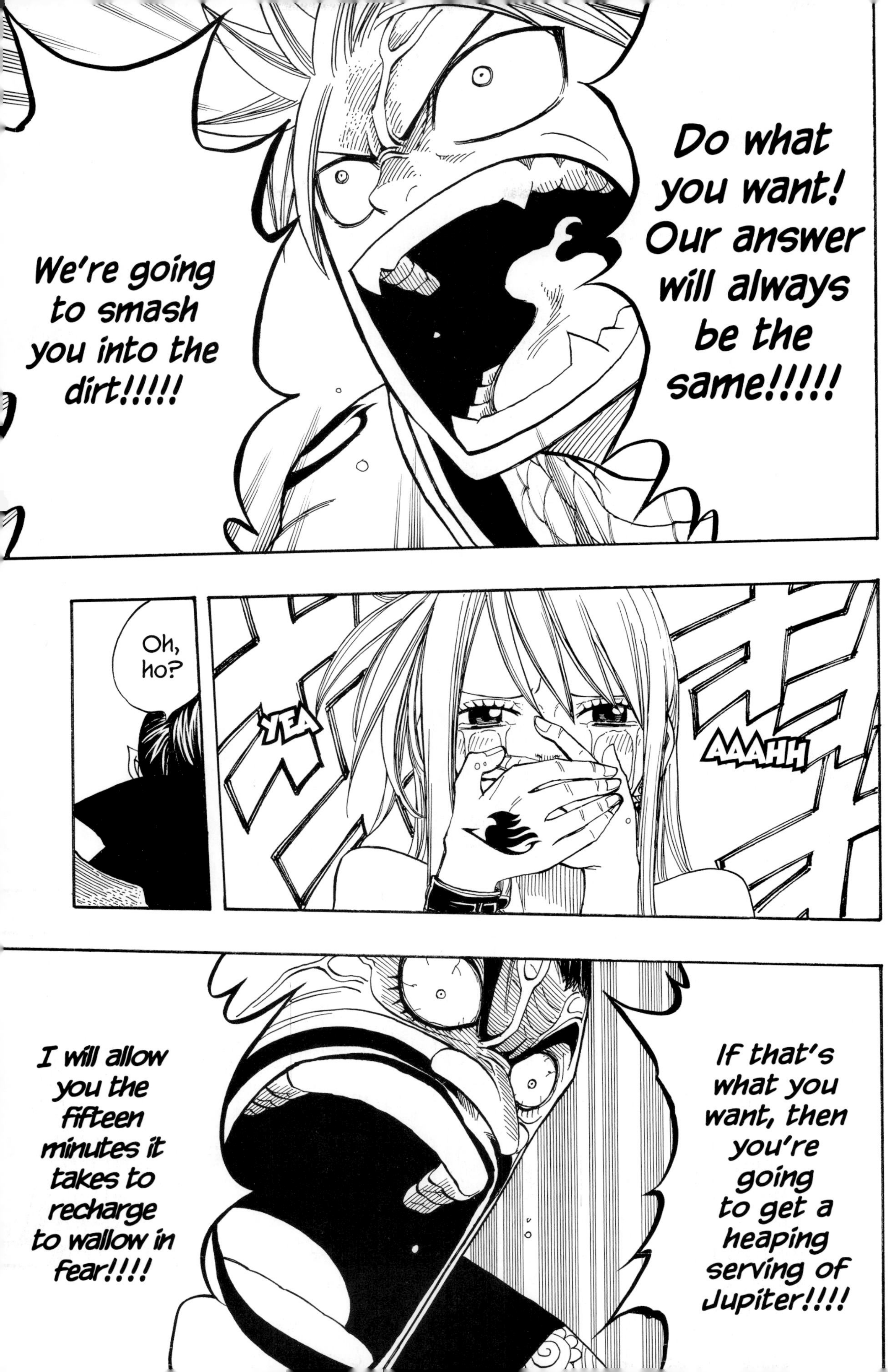
Do what you want! Our answer will always be the same!!!!!
We're going to smash you into the dirt!!!!!
YEA
AAAHH
Oh, ho?
If that's what you want, then you're going to get a heaping serving of Jupiter!!!!
I will allow you the fifteen minutes it takes to recharge to wallow in fear!!!!

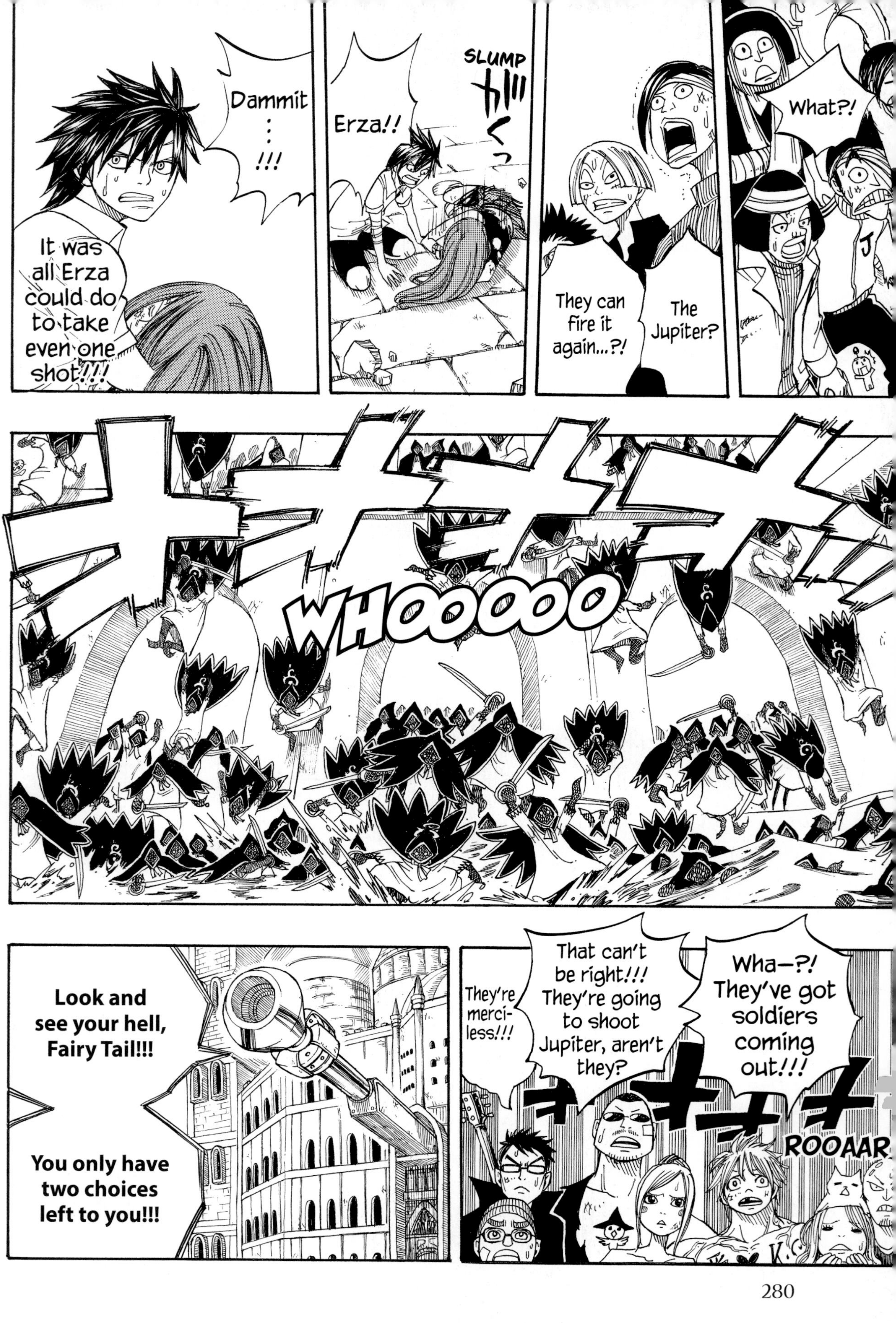
What?!
The Jupiter?
They can fire it again...?!
SLUMP
Erza!!
Dammit...!!!
It was all Erza could do to take even one shot!!!
WHOOOOO
Wha–?! They've got soldiers coming out!!!
That can't be right!!! They're going to shoot Jupiter, aren't they?
They're merciless!!!
ROOAAR
Look and see your hell, Fairy Tail!!!
You only have two choices left to you!!!

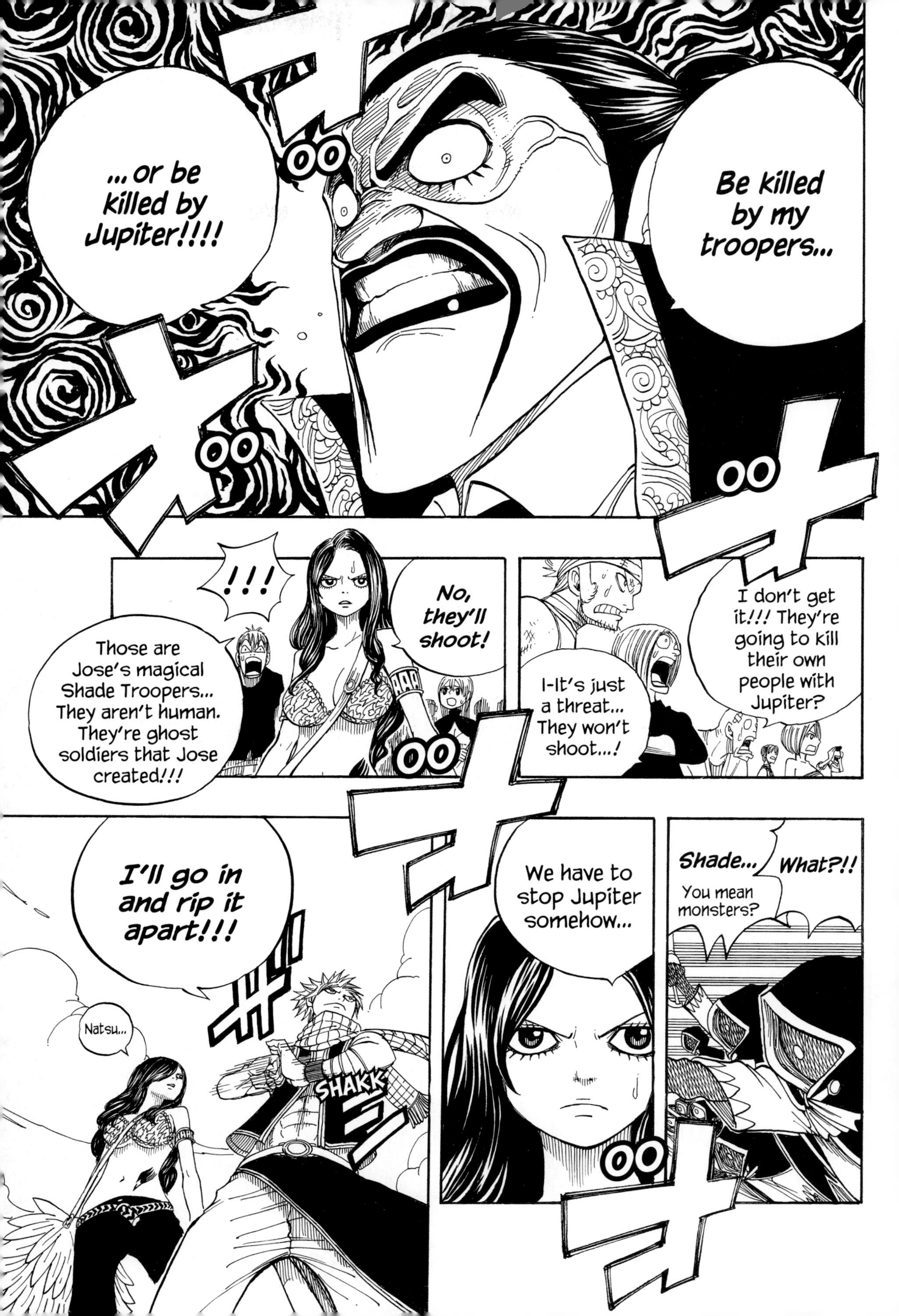
Be killed by my troopers...
...or be killed by Jupiter!!!!
I don't get it!!! They're going to kill their own people with Jupiter?
I-It's just a threat... They won't shoot...!
No, they'll shoot!
!!!
Those are Jose's magical Shade Troopers... They aren't human. They're ghost soldiers that Jose created!!!
What?!!
Shade...
You mean monsters?
We have to stop Jupiter somehow...
I'll go in and rip it apart!!!
Natsu...
SHAKK

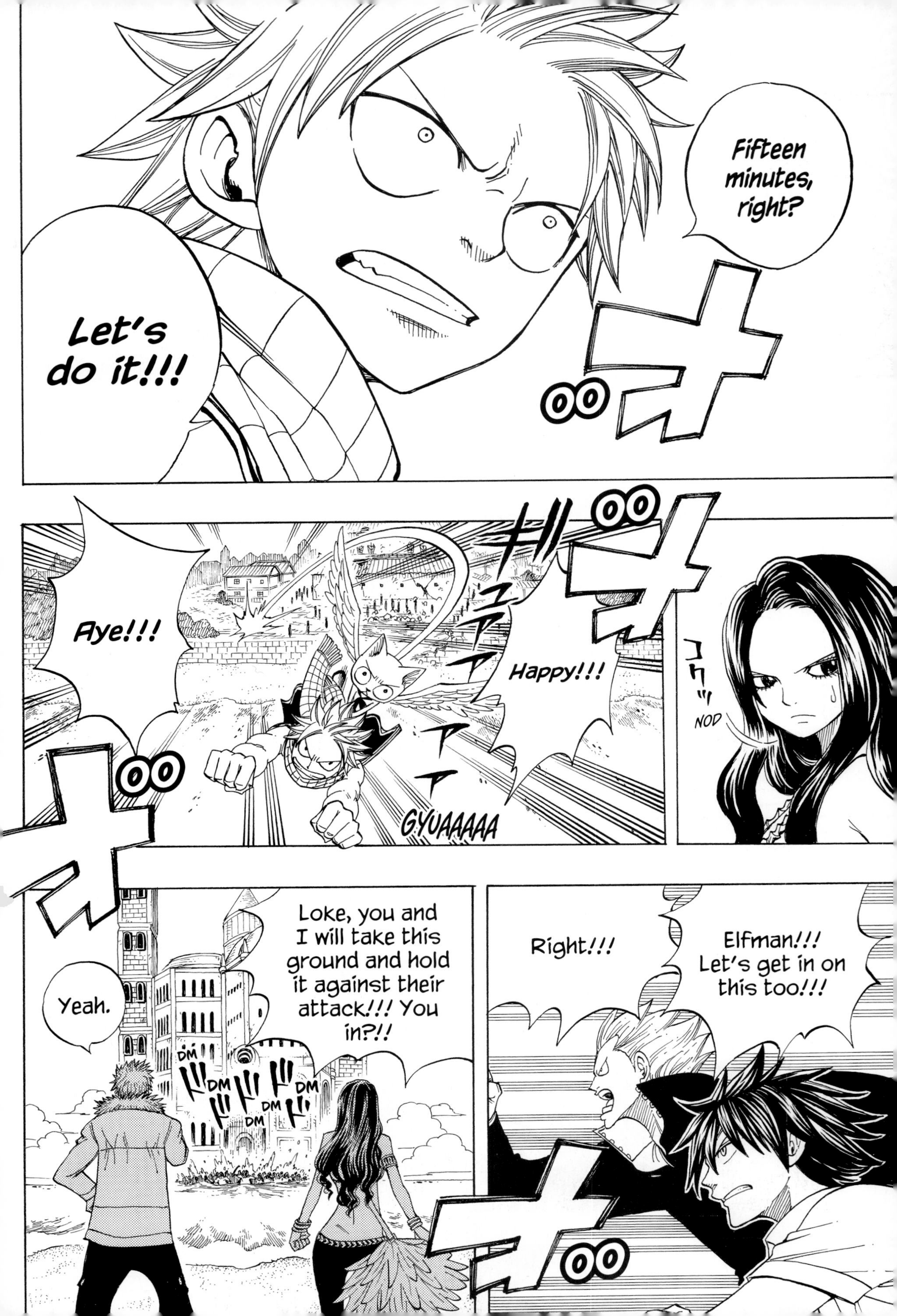
Fifteen minutes, right?
Let's do it!!!
OO
NOD
OO
Happy!!!
GYUAAAAA
Aye!!!
OO
Elfman!!! Let's get in on this too!!!
Right!!!
OO
Loke, you and I will take this ground and hold it against their attack!!! You in?!!
DM DM DM DM DM
Yeah.

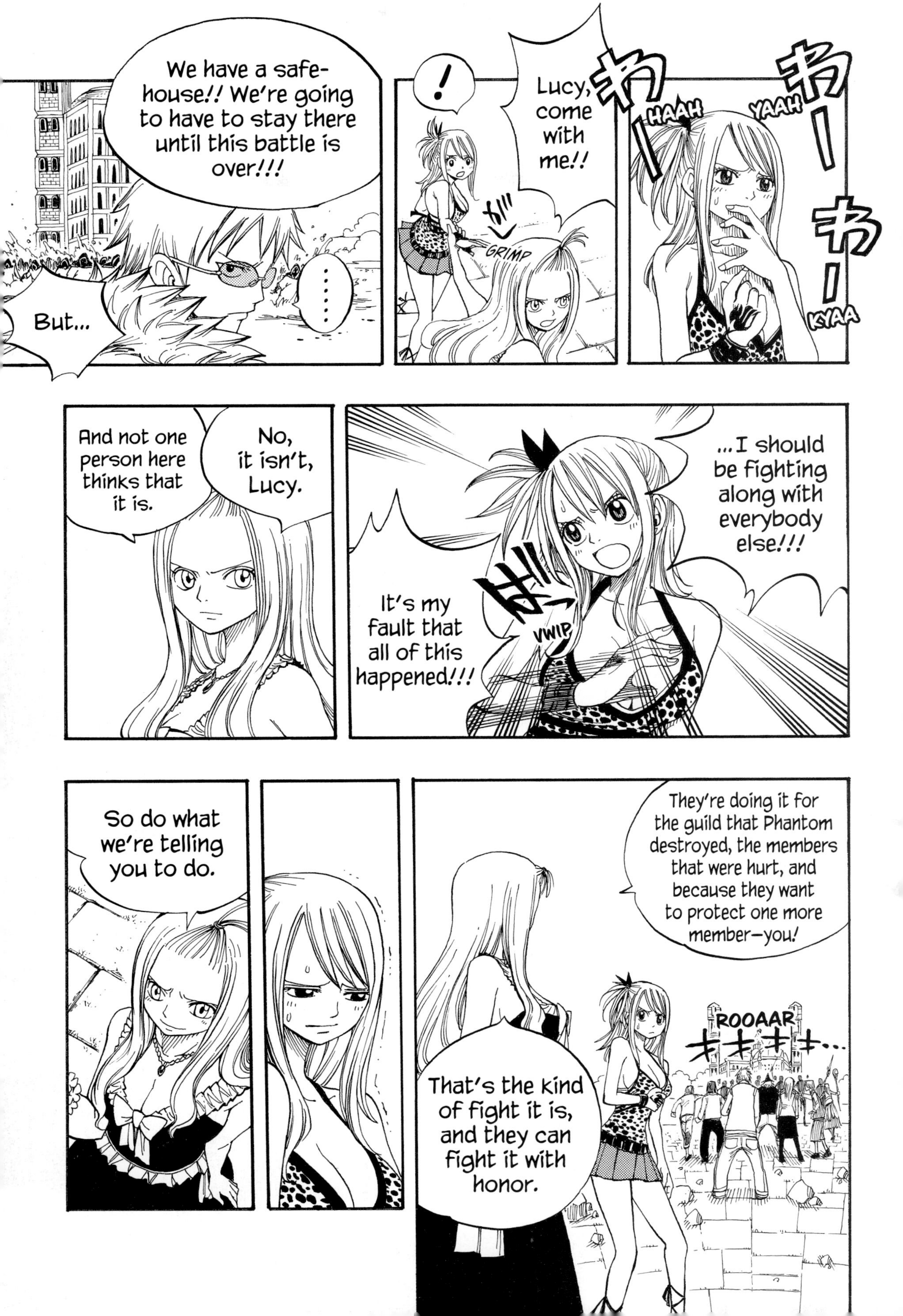
HAAH
YAAH
KYAA
!
Lucy, come with me!!
GRIMP
We have a safe-house!! We're going to have to stay there until this battle is over!!!
......
But...
...I should be fighting along with everybody else!!!
VWIP
It's my fault that all of this happened!!!
No, it isn't, Lucy.
And not one person here thinks that it is.
They're doing it for the guild that Phantom destroyed, the members that were hurt, and because they want to protect one more member—you!
ROOAAR
That's the kind of fight it is, and they can fight it with honor.
So do what we're telling you to do.

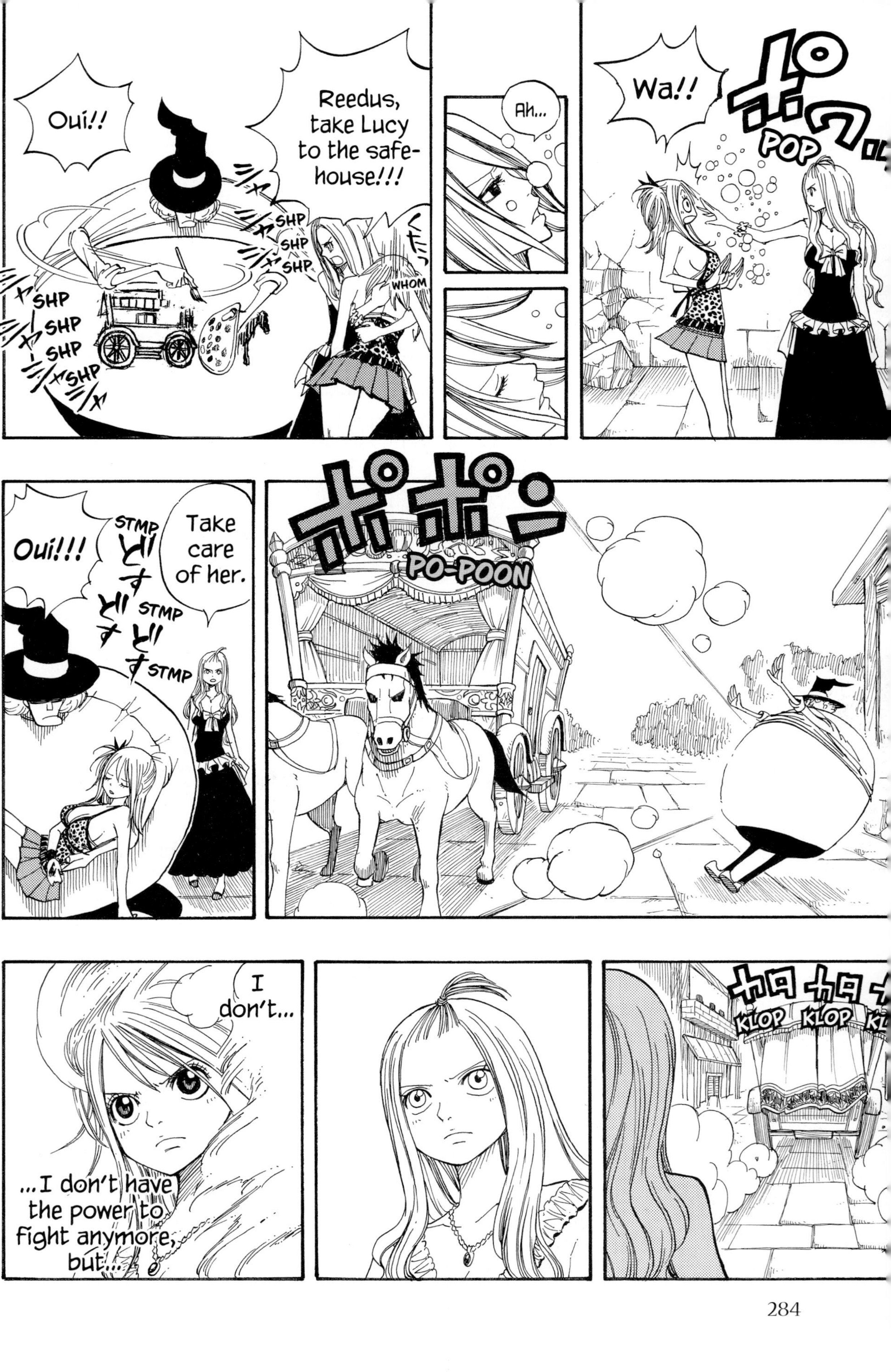
Wa!!
ポワ
POP
Ah...
Reedus, take Lucy to the safe-house!!!
Oui!!
SHP SHP SHP
SHP SHP SHP SHP
WHOM
ポポン
PO-POON
Take care of her.
Oui!!!
STMP STMP STMP
KLOP KLOP
I don't...
...I don't have the power to fight anymore, but...

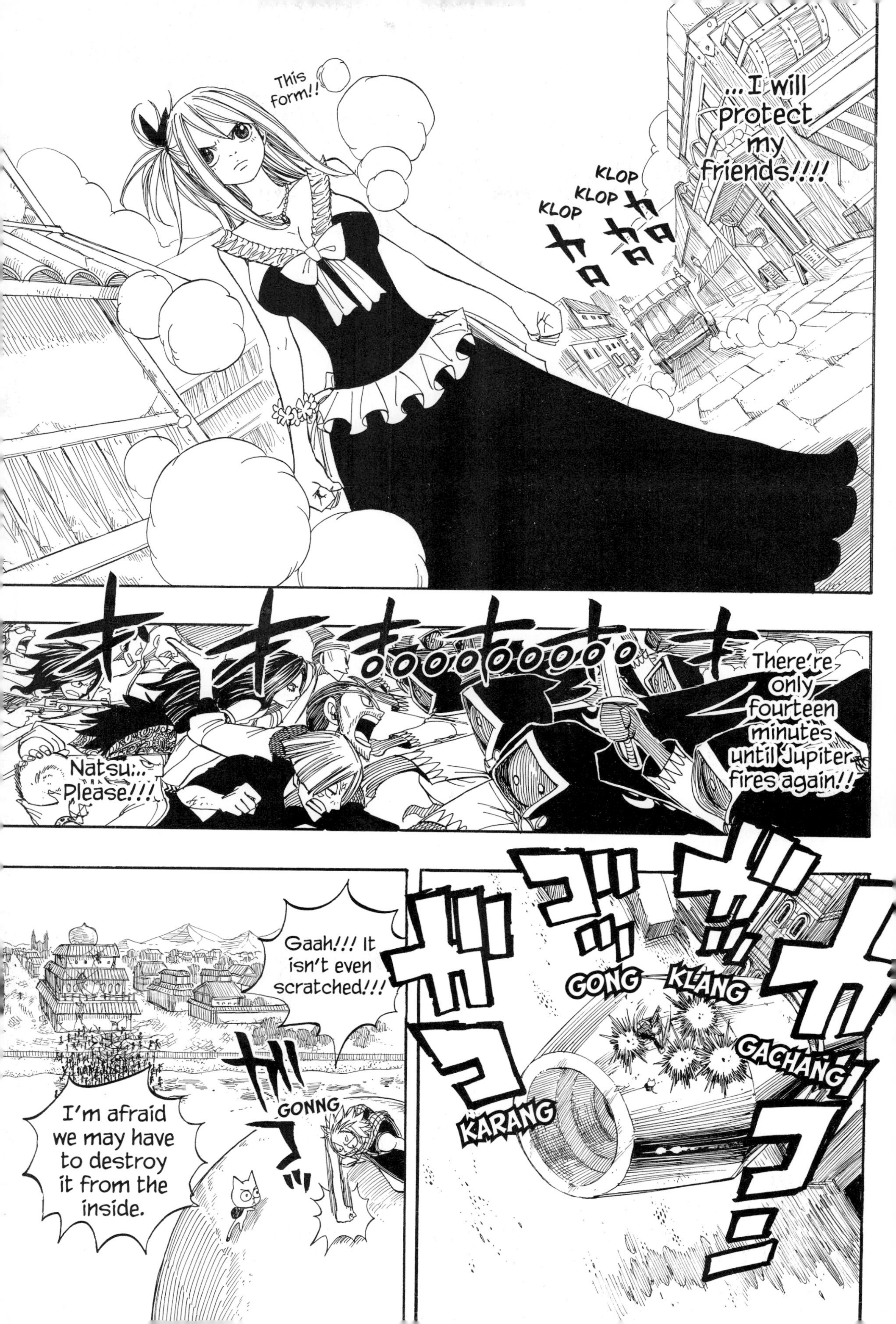
...I will protect my friends!!!!
KLOP
KLOP
KLOP
This form!!
There're only fourteen minutes until Jupiter fires again!!
Natsu... Please!!!
GONG
KLANG
GACHANG
KARANG
Gaah!!! It isn't even scratched!!!
GONNG
I'm afraid we may have to destroy it from the inside.

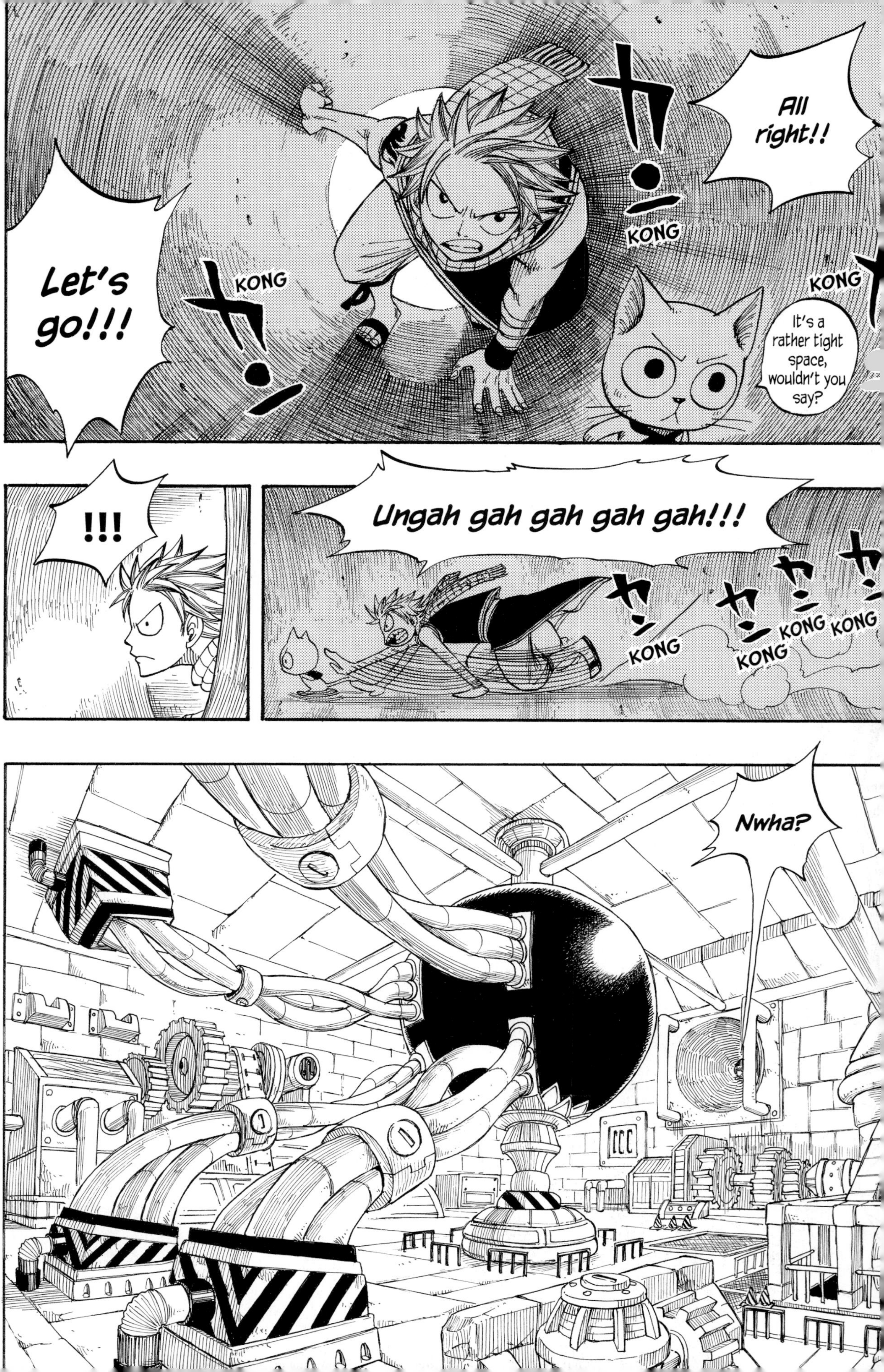
All right!!
KONG
KONG
It's a rather tight space, wouldn't you say?
Let's go!!!
KONG
Ungah gah gah gah gah!!!
KONG
KONG
KONG
KONG
!!!
Nwha?

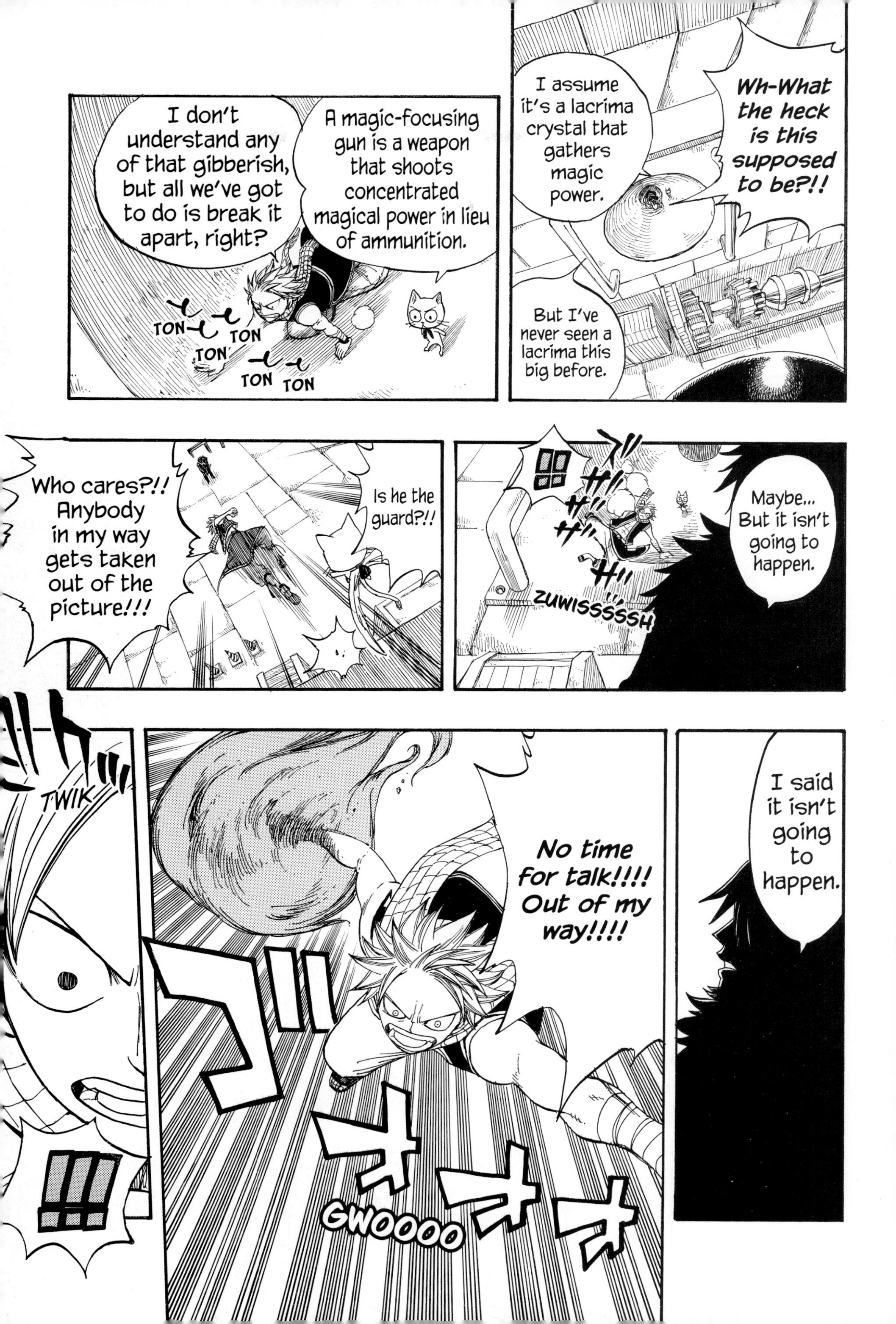
Wh-What the heck is this supposed to be?!!
I assume it's a lacrima crystal that gathers magic power.
But I've never seen a lacrima this big before.
A magic-focusing gun is a weapon that shoots concentrated magical power in lieu of ammunition.
I don't understand any of that gibberish, but all we've got to do is break it apart, right?
TON TON TON TON TON
ZUWISSSSSSH
Maybe... But it isn't going to happen.
Is he the guard?!!
Who cares?!! Anybody in my way gets taken out of the picture!!!
I said it isn't going to happen.
No time for talk!!!! Out of my way!!!!
GWOOOOO
TWIK

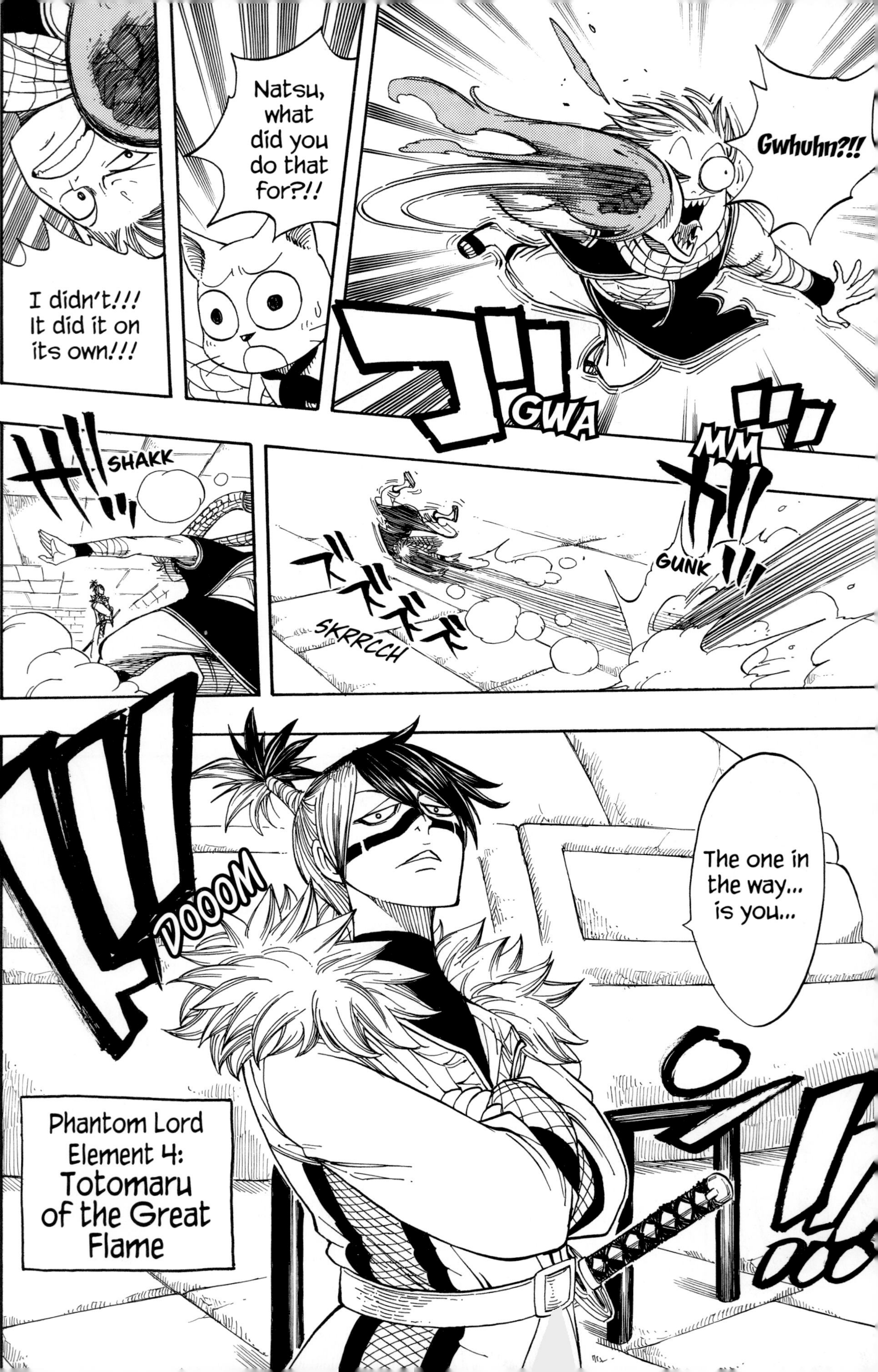
Gwhuhn?!!
GWA
Natsu, what did you do that for?!!
I didn't!!! It did it on its own!!!
MM
GUNK
SKRRCCH
SHAKK
The one in the way... is you...
DOOOM
Phantom Lord Element 4: Totomaru of the Great Flame

FAIRY TAIL

Chapter 53: The Heat of Battle

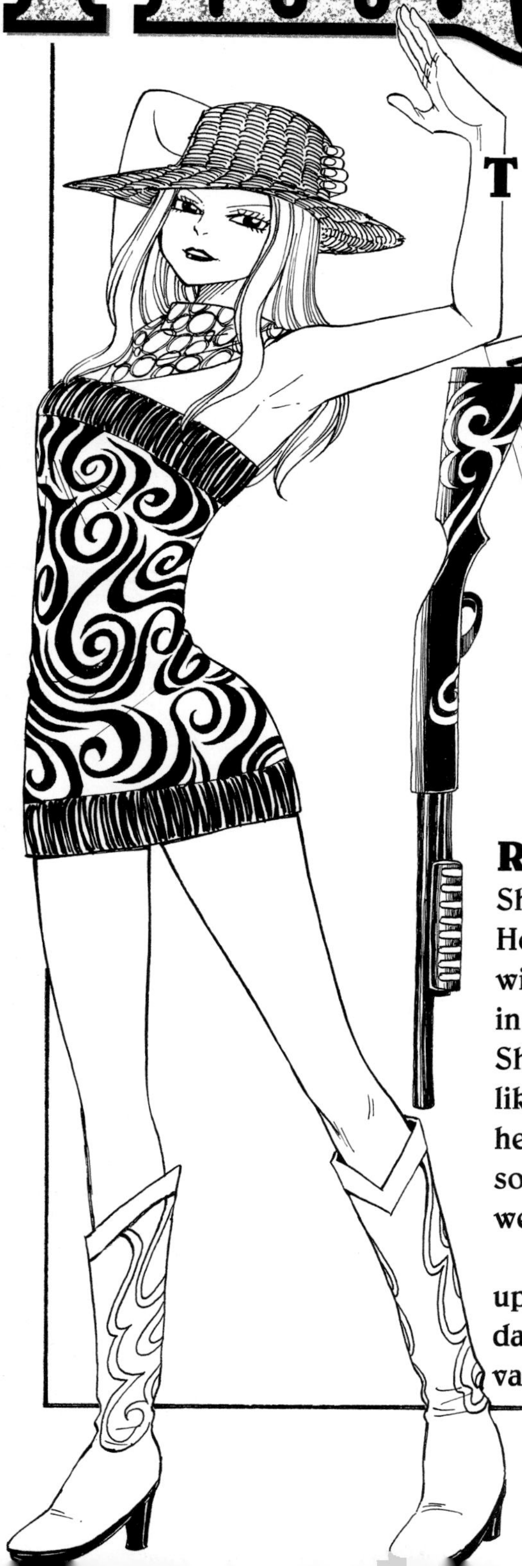

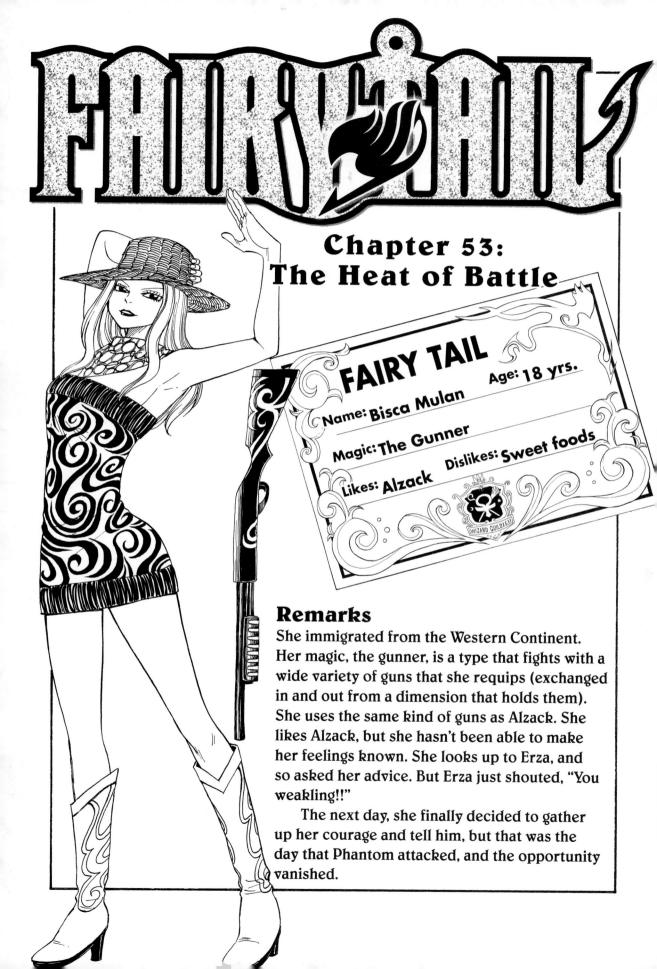

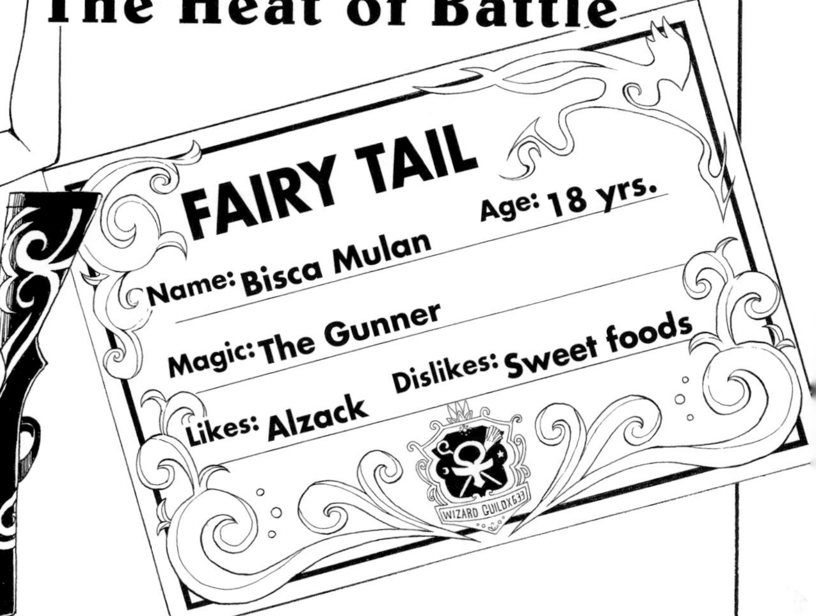
FAIRY TAIL
FAIRY TAIL
Age: 18 yrs.
Name: Bisca Mulan
Magic: The Gunner
Likes: Alzack
Dislikes: Sweet foods
WIZARD GUILD×633

Remarks

She immigrated from the Western Continent. Her magic, the gunner, is a type that fights with a wide variety of guns that she requips (exchanged in and out from a dimension that holds them). She uses the same kind of guns as Alzack. She likes Alzack, but she hasn't been able to make her feelings known. She looks up to Erza, and so asked her advice. But Erza just shouted, "You weakling!!"

The next day, she finally decided to gather up her courage and tell him, but that was the day that Phantom attacked, and the opportunity vanished.

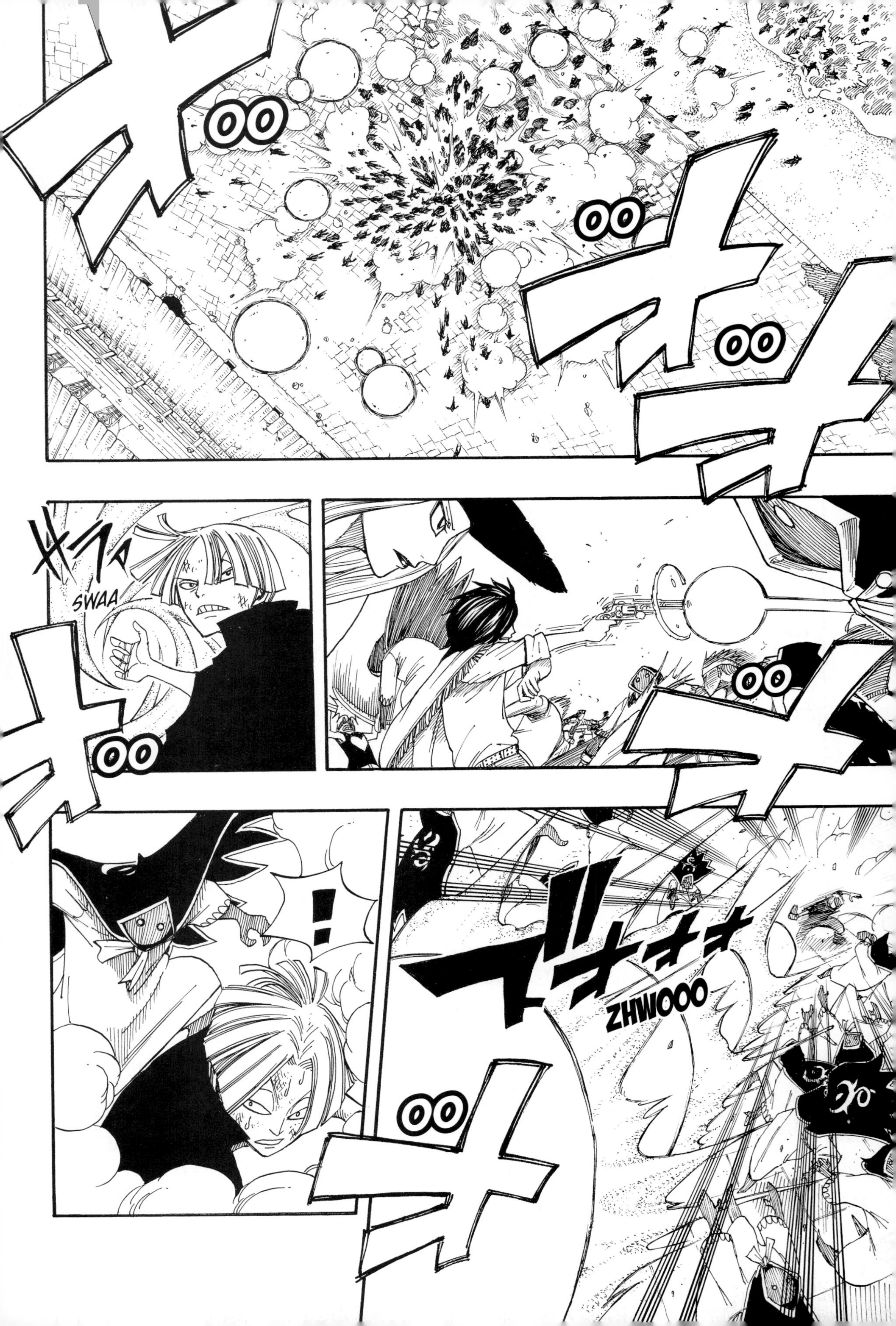
OO
OO
OO
OO
SWAA
OO
!
ZHWOOO
OO

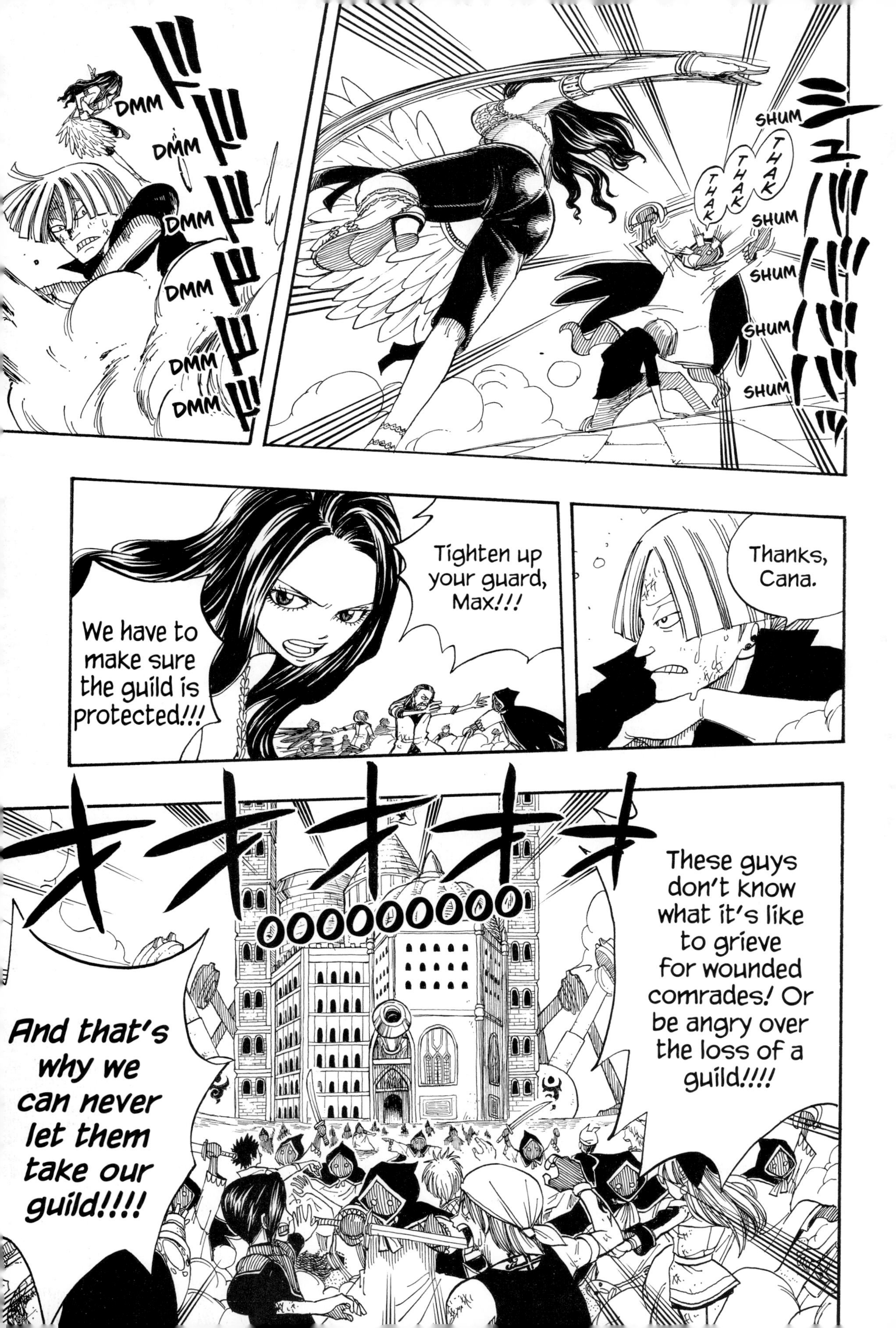
SHUM
THAK
THAK
THAK
SHUM
SHUM
SHUM
SHUM
DMM
DMM
DMM
DMM
DMM
DMM
Thanks, Cana.
Tighten up your guard, Max!!!
We have to make sure the guild is protected!!!
OOOOOOOOO
These guys don't know what it's like to grieve for wounded comrades! Or be angry over the loss of a guild!!!!
And that's why we can never let them take our guild!!!!

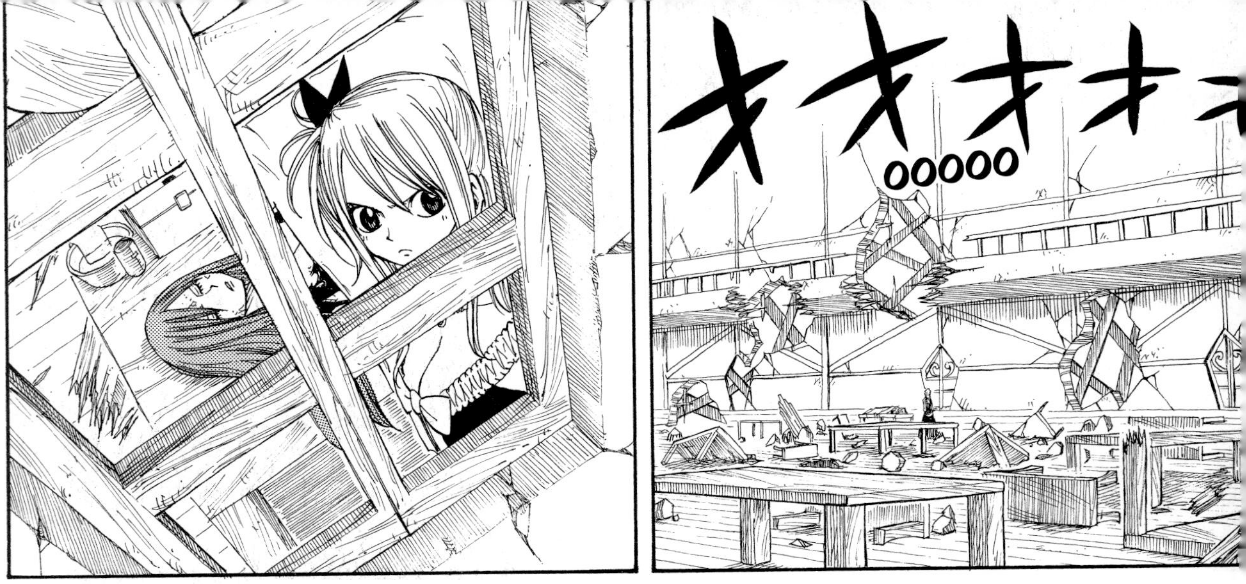
OOOOO

↑ Mirajane transformed into Lucy's likeness.

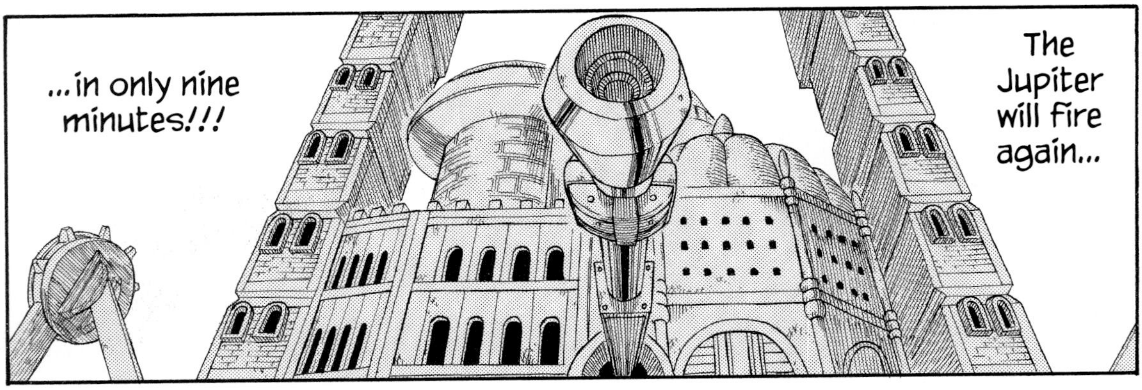
The Jupiter will fire again...
...in only nine minutes!!!

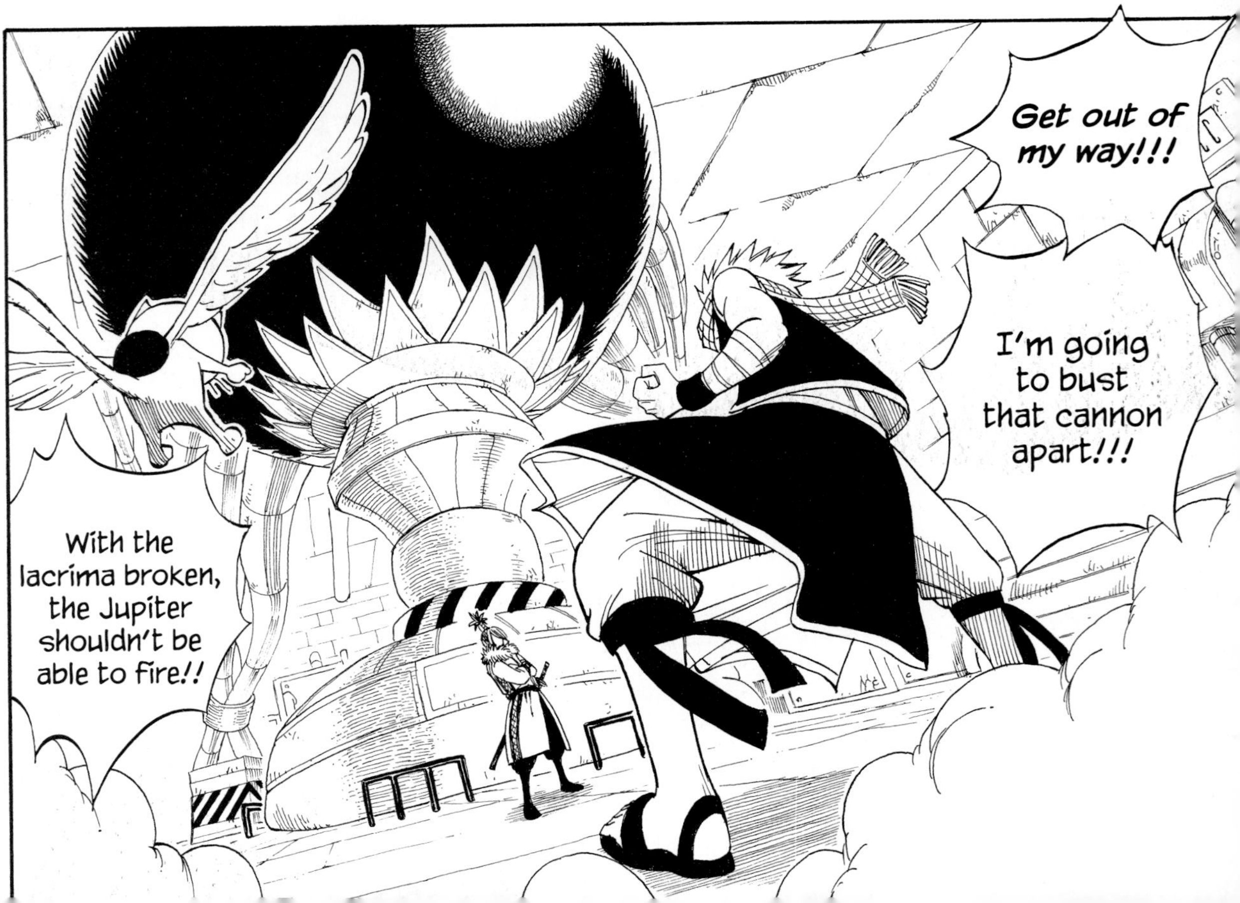
Get out of my way!!!
I'm going to bust that cannon apart!!!
With the lacrima broken, the Jupiter shouldn't be able to fire!!

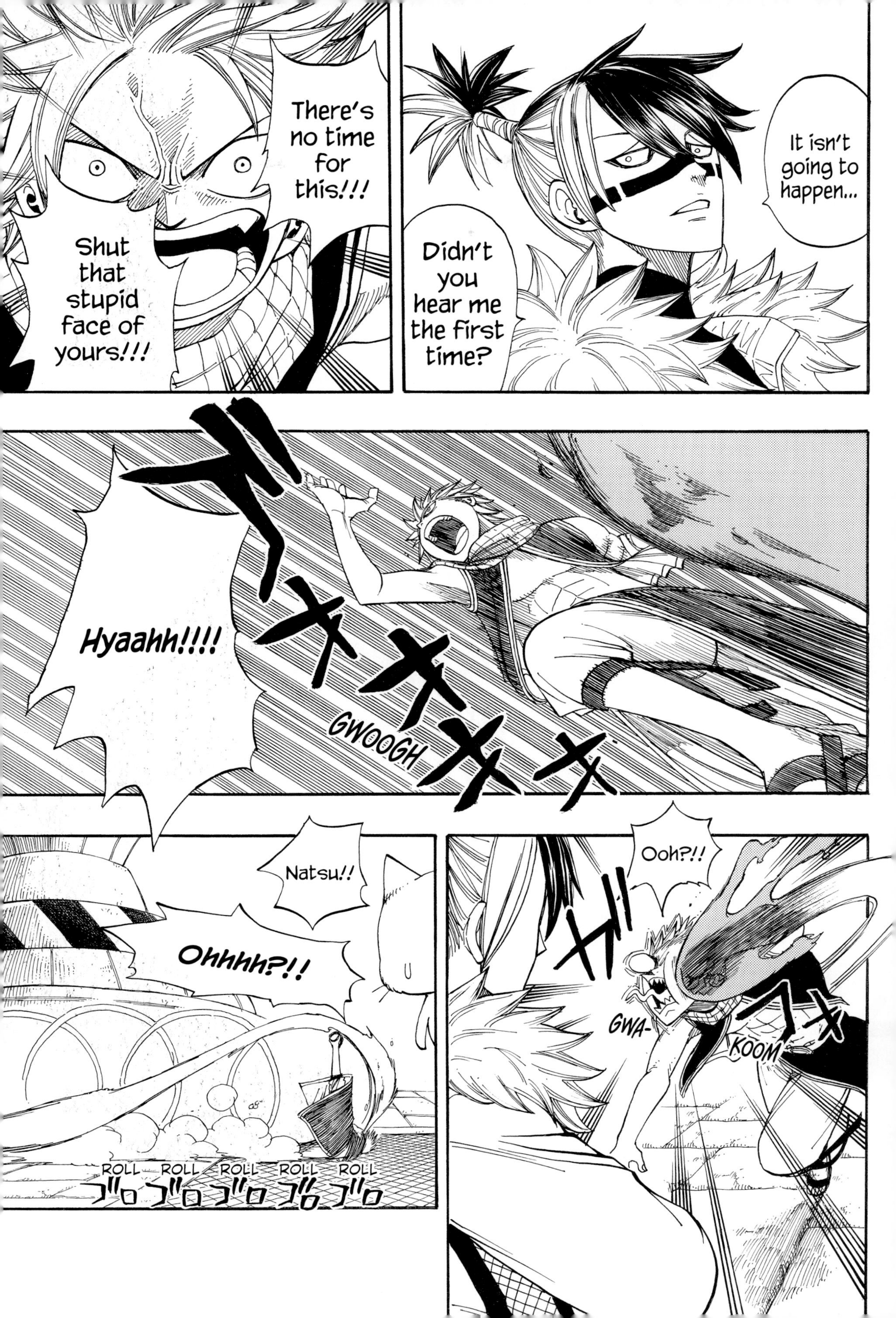
It isn't going to happen...
Didn't you hear me the first time?
There's no time for this!!!
Shut that stupid face of yours!!!
Hyaahh!!!!
GWOOGH
Ooh?!!
GWA-KOOM
Natsu!!
Ohhhh?!!
ROLL ROLL ROLL ROLL ROLL
ゴロゴロゴロゴロゴロ

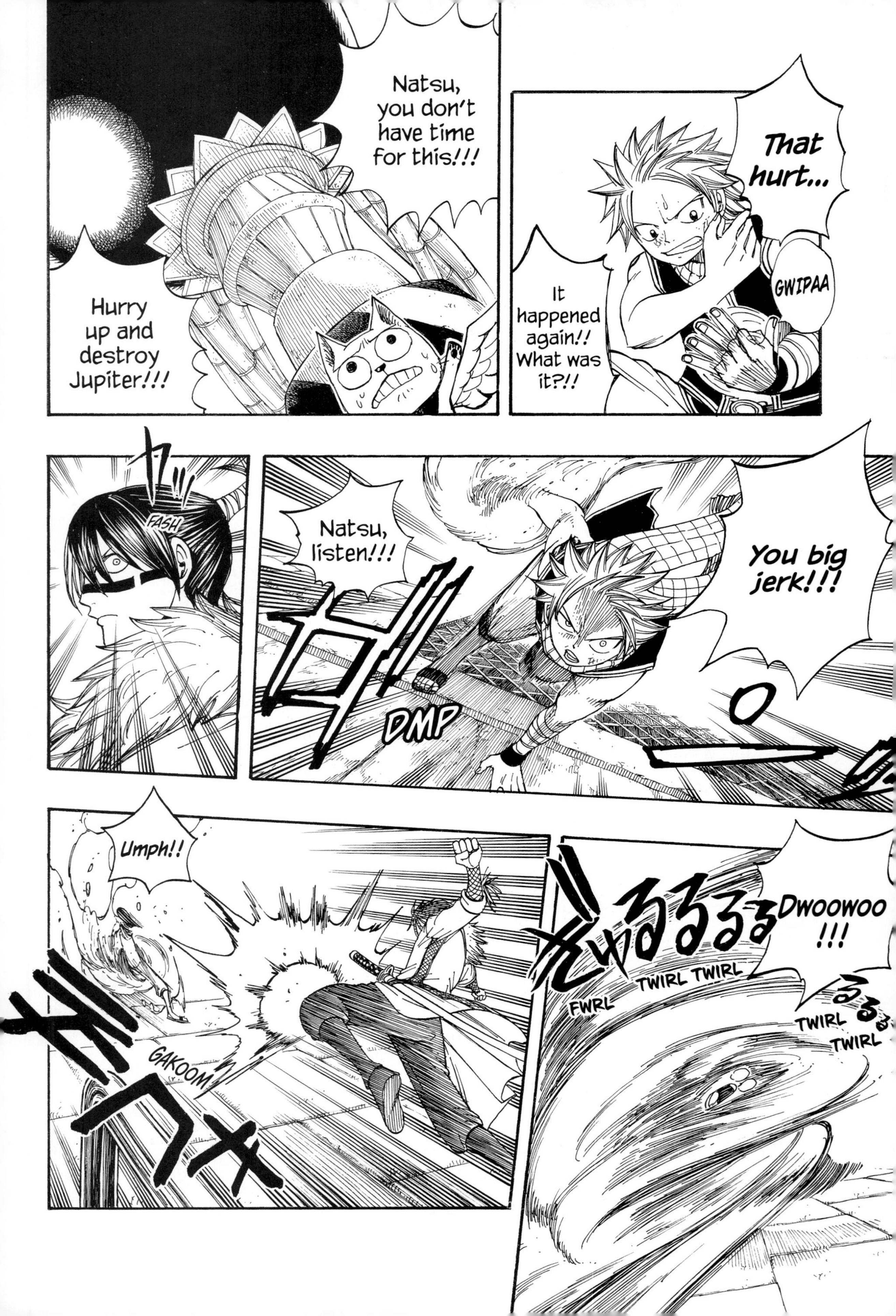
That hurt...
GWIPAA
It happened again!! What was it?!!
Natsu, you don't have time for this!!!
Hurry up and destroy Jupiter!!!
You big jerk!!!
Natsu, listen!!!
DMP
FASH
Dwoowoo !!!
TWIRL TWIRL
FWRL
TWIRL TWIRL
Umph!!
GAKOOM

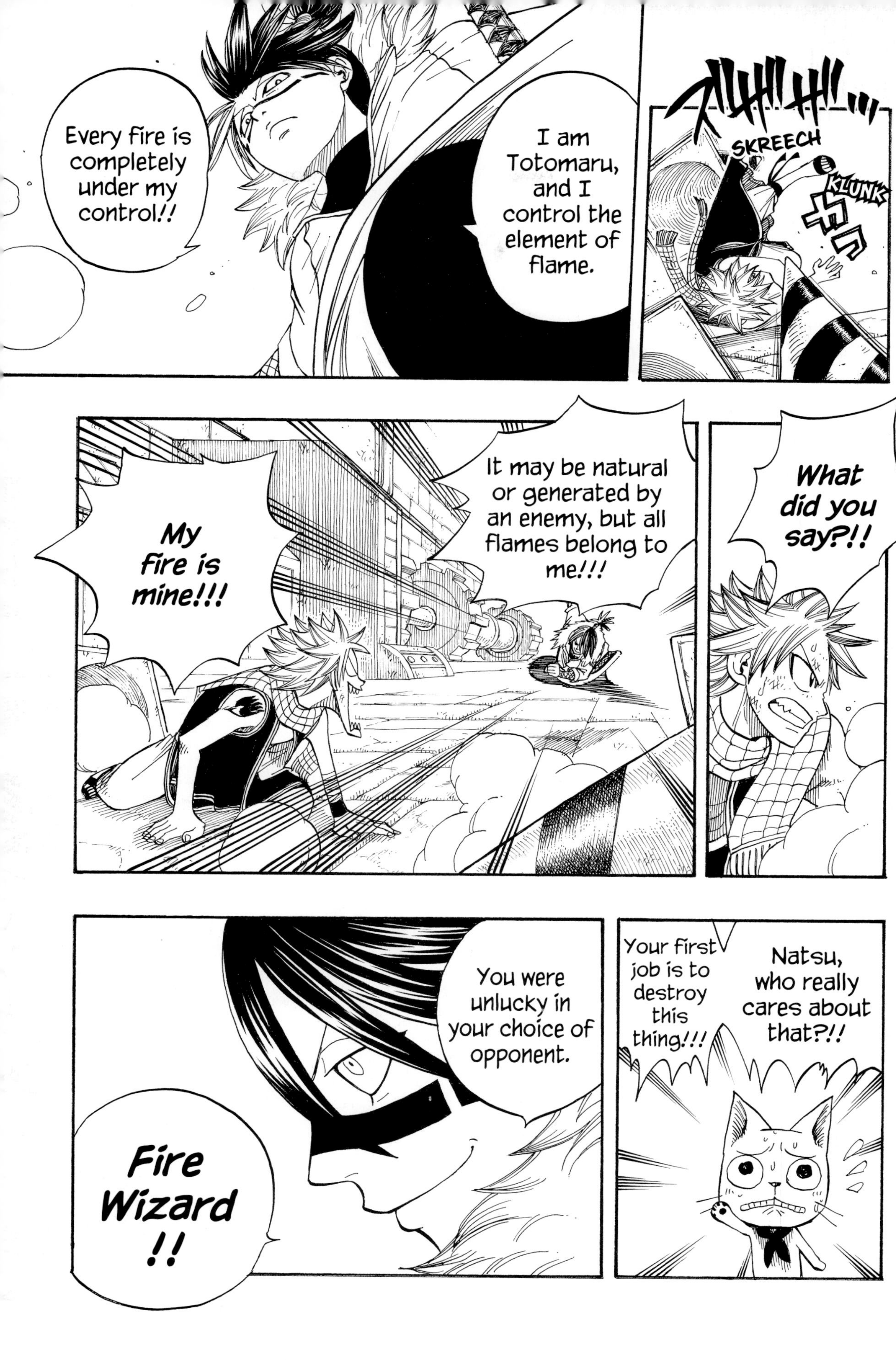
SKREECH
KLUNK
I am Totomaru, and I control the element of flame.
Every fire is completely under my control!!
What did you say?!!
It may be natural or generated by an enemy, but all flames belong to me!!!
My fire is mine!!!
Natsu, who really cares about that?!!
Your first job is to destroy this thing!!!
You were unlucky in your choice of opponent.
Fire Wizard!!

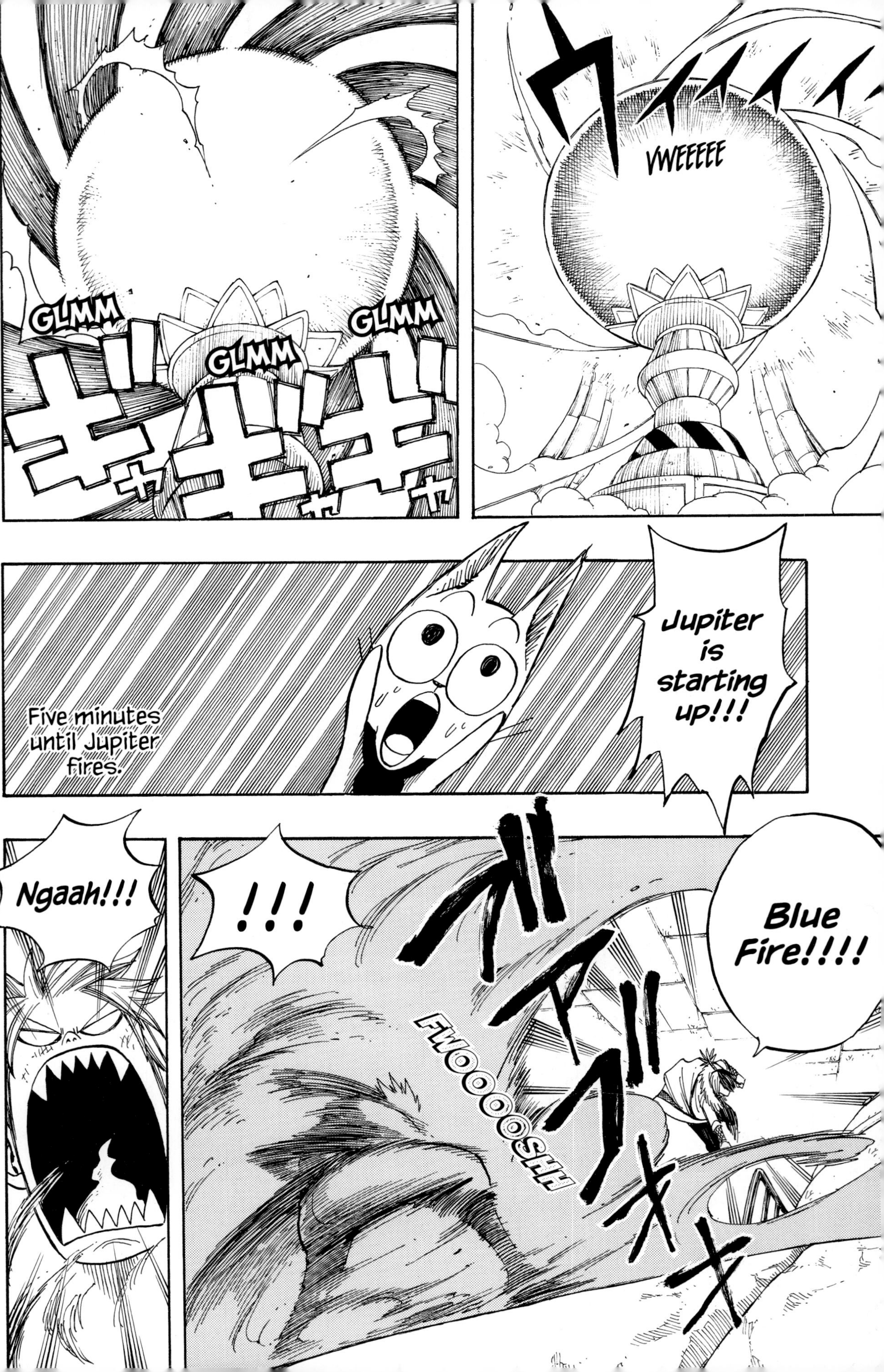
VWEEEEE
GLMM
GLMM
GLMM
Jupiter is starting up!!!
Five minutes until Jupiter fires.
Blue Fire!!!!
FWOOOOOSHH
!!!
Ngaah!!!

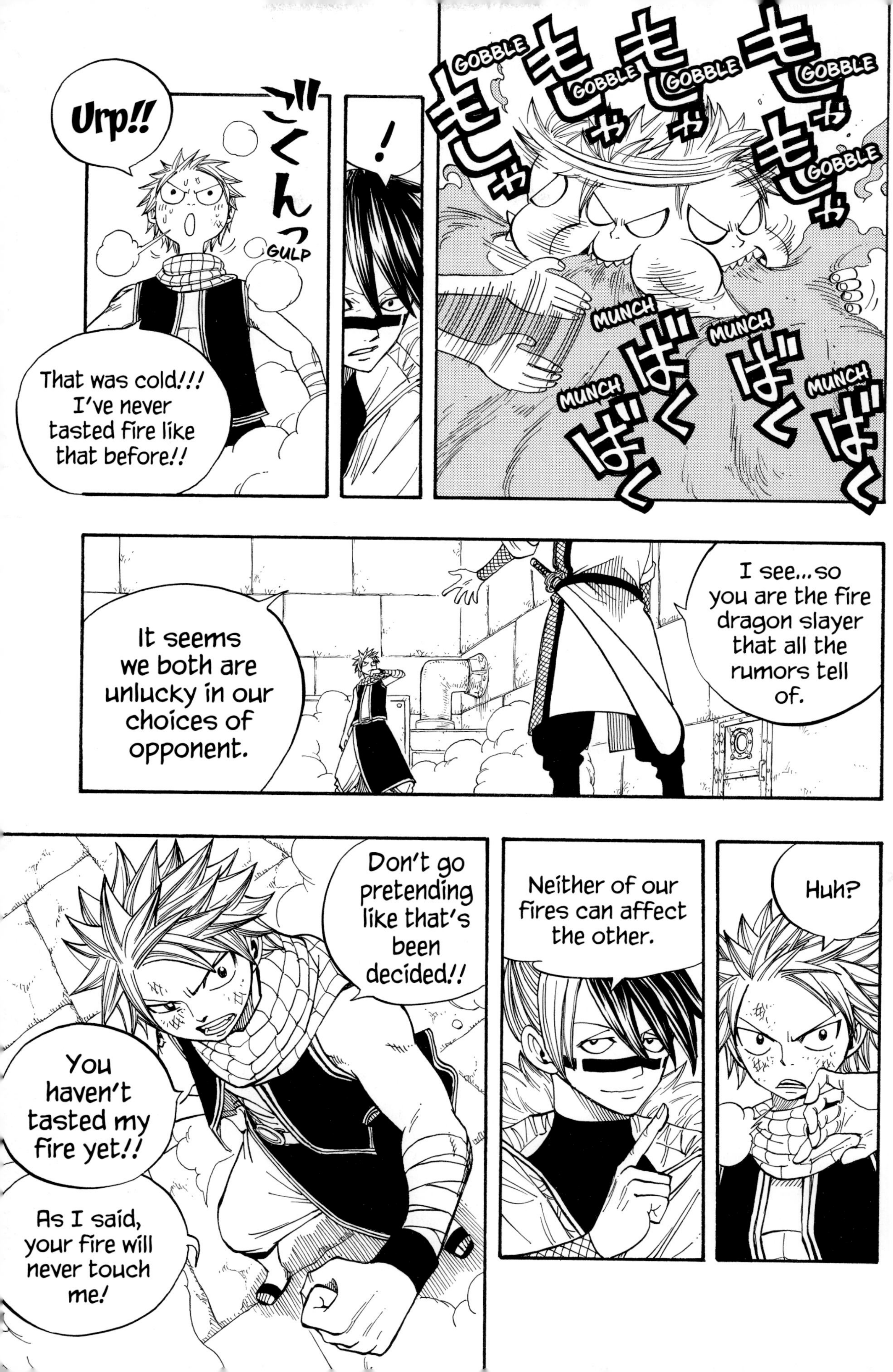

もしゃもしゃもしゃもしゃもしゃ
GOBBLE GOBBLE GOBBLE GOBBLE GOBBLE
ばくばくばくばく
MUNCH MUNCH MUNCH MUNCH
!
ごくんっ
GULP
Urp!!
That was cold!!! I've never tasted fire like that before!!
I see...so you are the fire dragon slayer that all the rumors tell of.
It seems we both are unlucky in our choices of opponent.
Huh?
Neither of our fires can affect the other.
Don't go pretending like that's been decided!!
You haven't tasted my fire yet!!
As I said, your fire will never touch me!

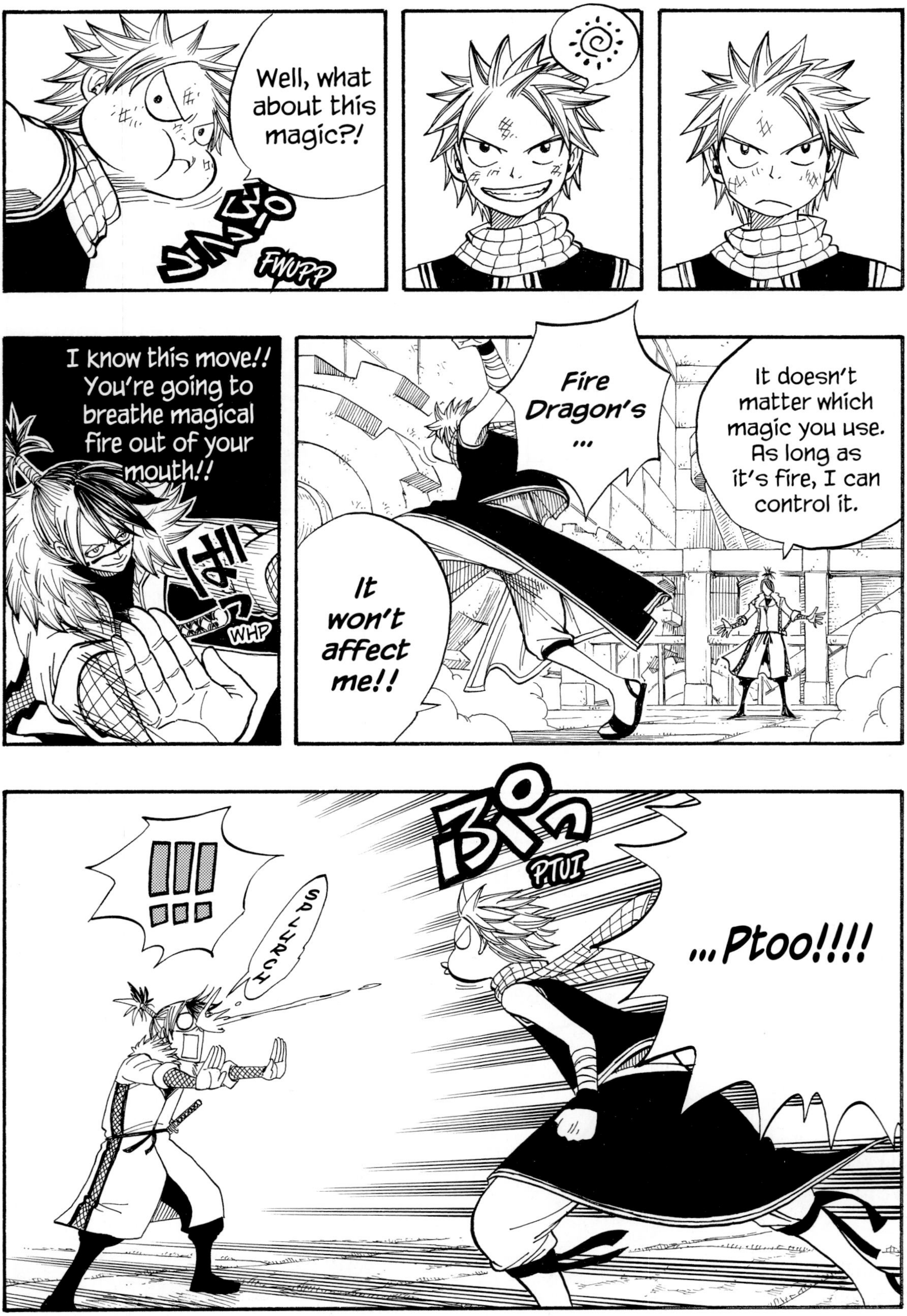
Well, what about this magic?!
FWUPP
It doesn't matter which magic you use. As long as it's fire, I can control it.
Fire Dragon's ...
It won't affect me!!
I know this move!! You're going to breathe magical fire out of your mouth!!
WHP
PTUI
...Ptoo!!!!
!!!!
SPLURCH

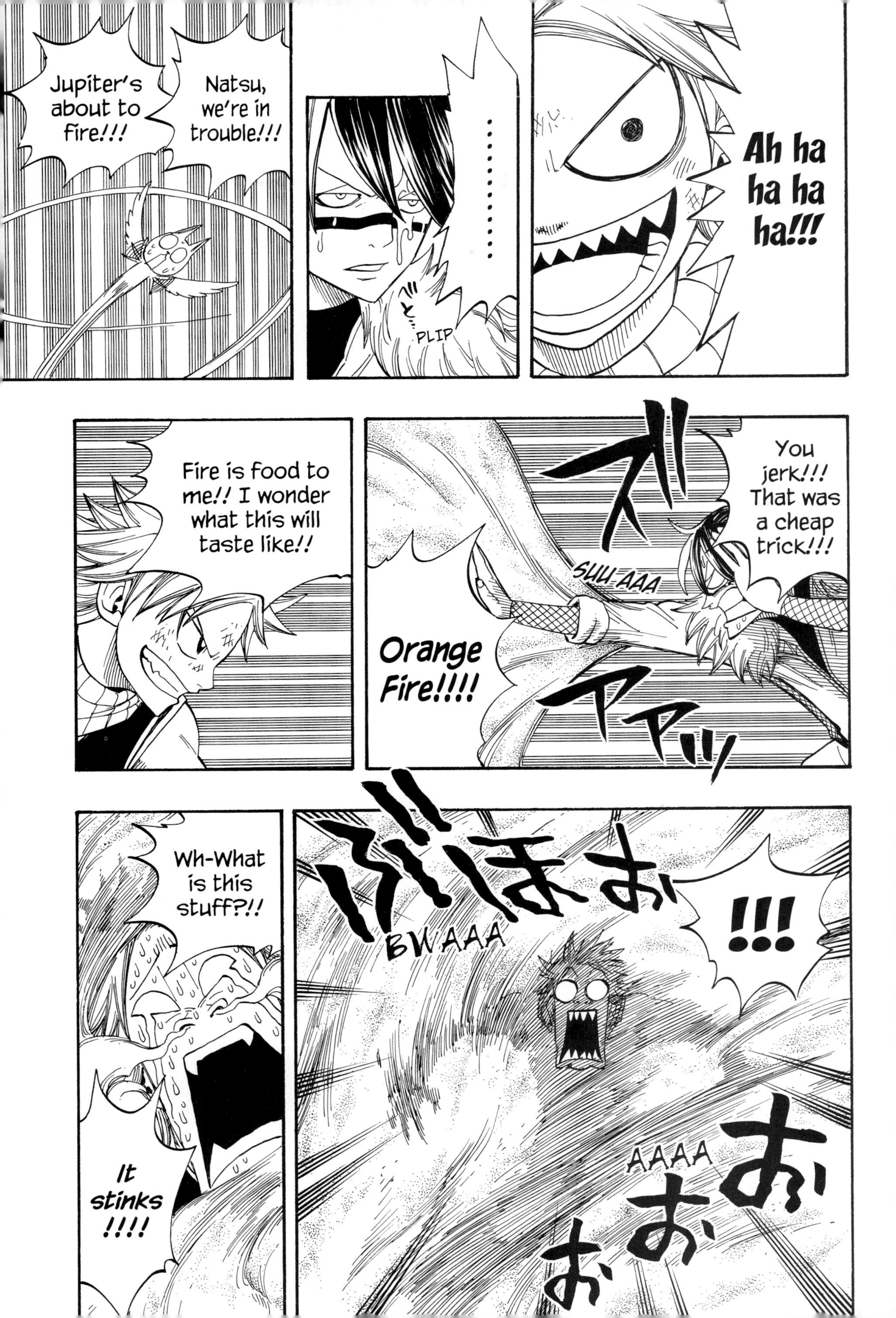
Ah ha ha ha ha!!!
......
PLIP
Natsu, we're in trouble!!!
Jupiter's about to fire!!!
You jerk!!! That was a cheap trick!!!
SUU AAA
Orange Fire!!!!
Fire is food to me!! I wonder what this will taste like!!
!!!
BWAAA
AAAA
Wh-What is this stuff?!!
It stinks!!!!

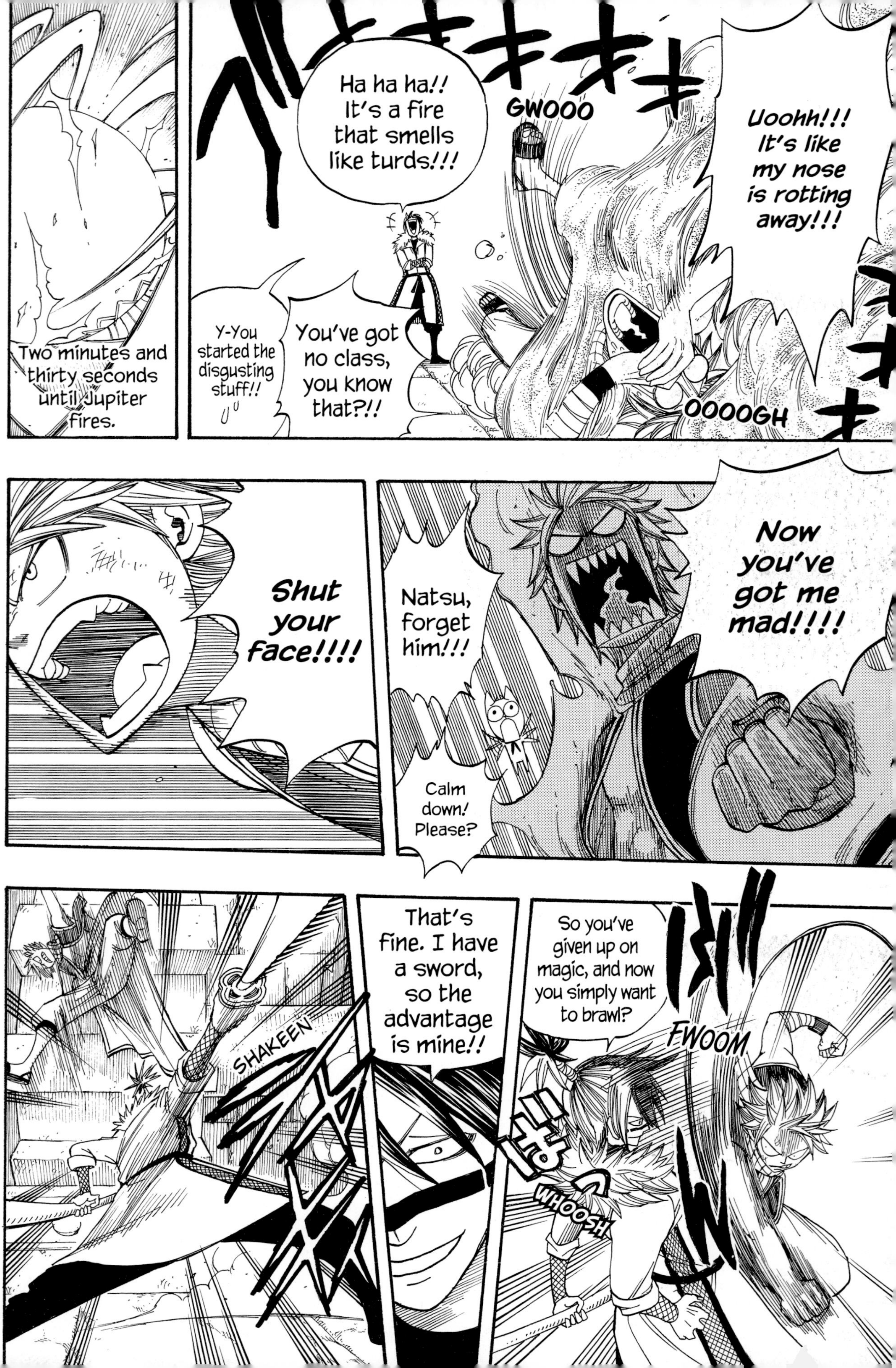
Uoohh!!! It's like my nose is rotting away!!!
GWOOO
OOOOGH
Ha ha ha!! It's a fire that smells like turds!!!
You've got no class, you know that?!!
Y-You started the disgusting stuff!!
Two minutes and thirty seconds until Jupiter fires.
Now you've got me mad!!!!
Natsu, forget him!!!
Calm down! Please?
Shut your face!!!!
So you've given up on magic, and now you simply want to brawl?
FWOOM
WHOOSH
That's fine. I have a sword, so the advantage is mine!!
SHAKEEN

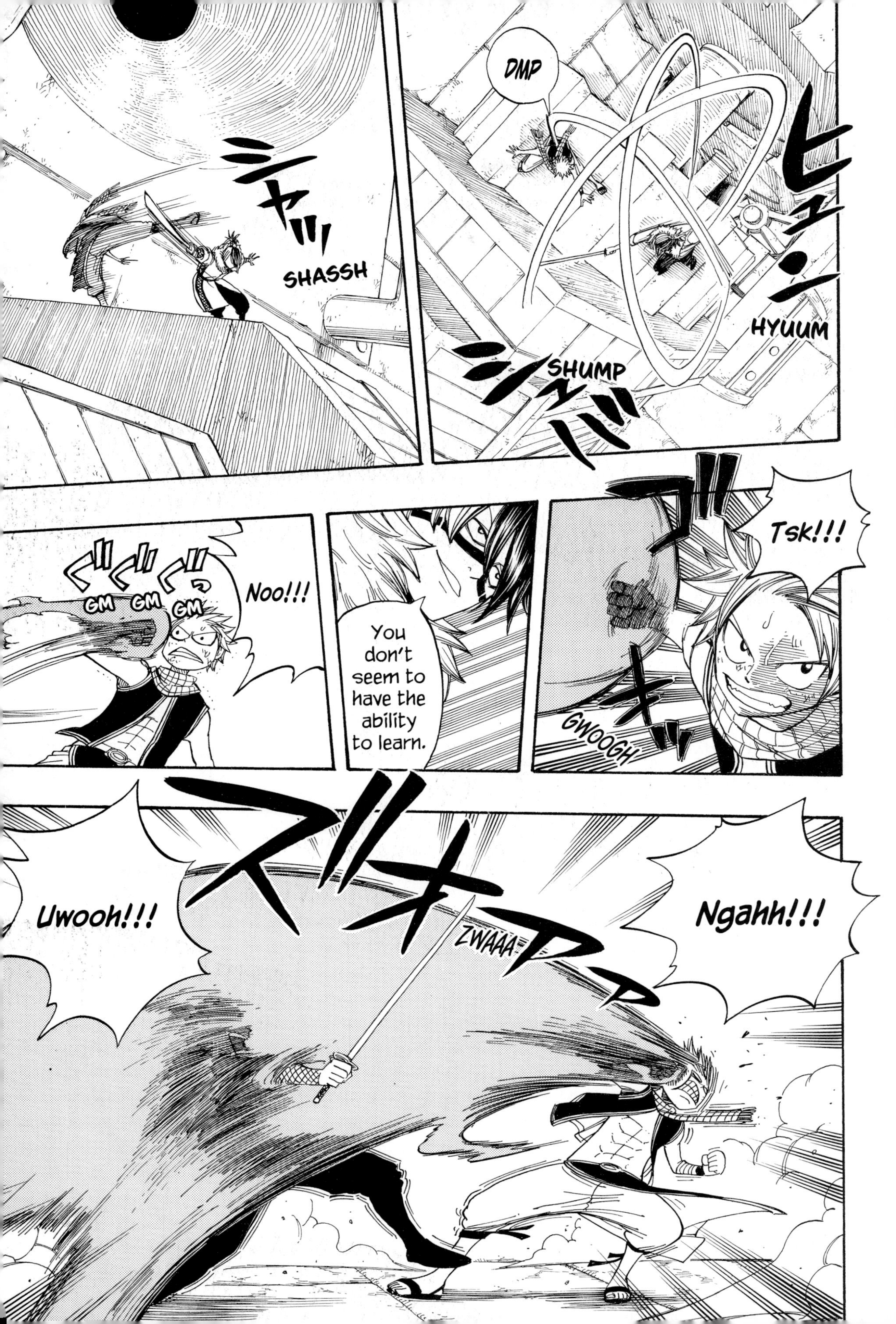
DMP
HYUUM
SHUMP
SHASSH
Tsk!!!
GWOOGH
You don't seem to have the ability to learn.
Noo!!!
GM GM GM
Ngahh!!!
ZWAAA
Uwooh!!!

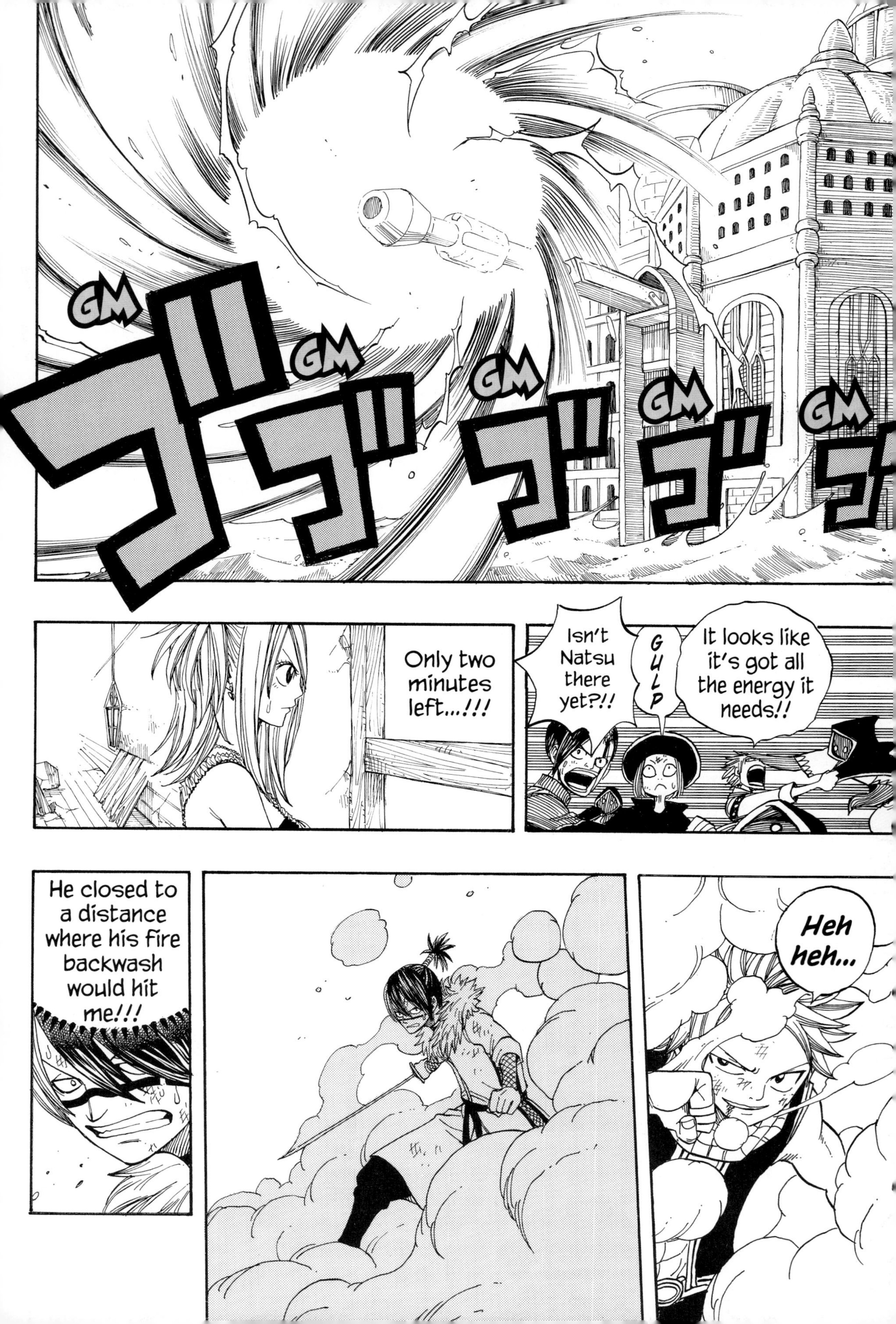
GM
GM
GM
GM
GM
It looks like it's got all the energy it needs!!
GULP
Isn't Natsu there yet?!!
Only two minutes left...!!!
Heh heh...
He closed to a distance where his fire backwash would hit me!!!

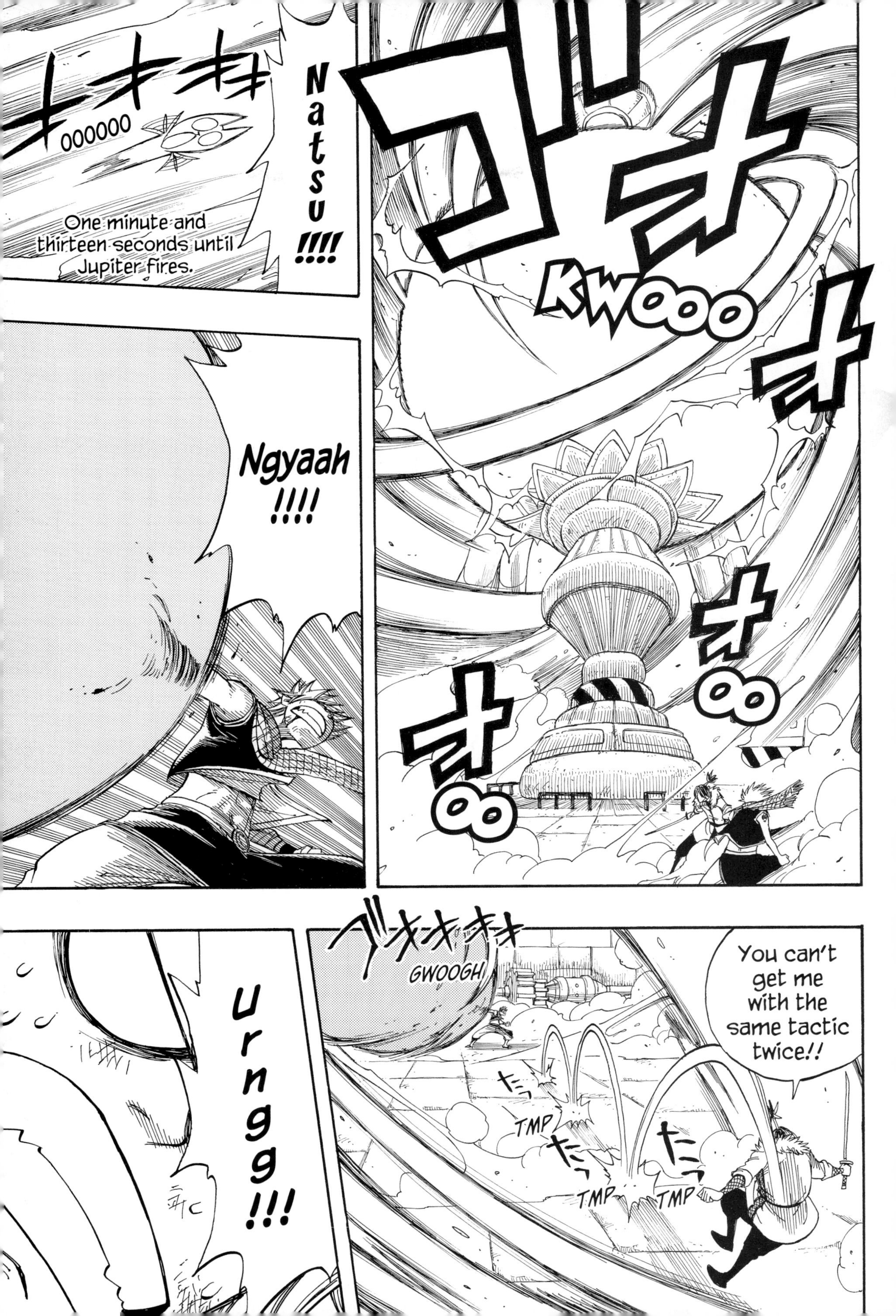
KWOOOO
Natsu!!!!
OOOOOO
One minute and thirteen seconds until Jupiter fires.
Ngyaah!!!!
GWOOGH
You can't get me with the same tactic twice!!
TMP
TMP
TMP
Urnggg!!!

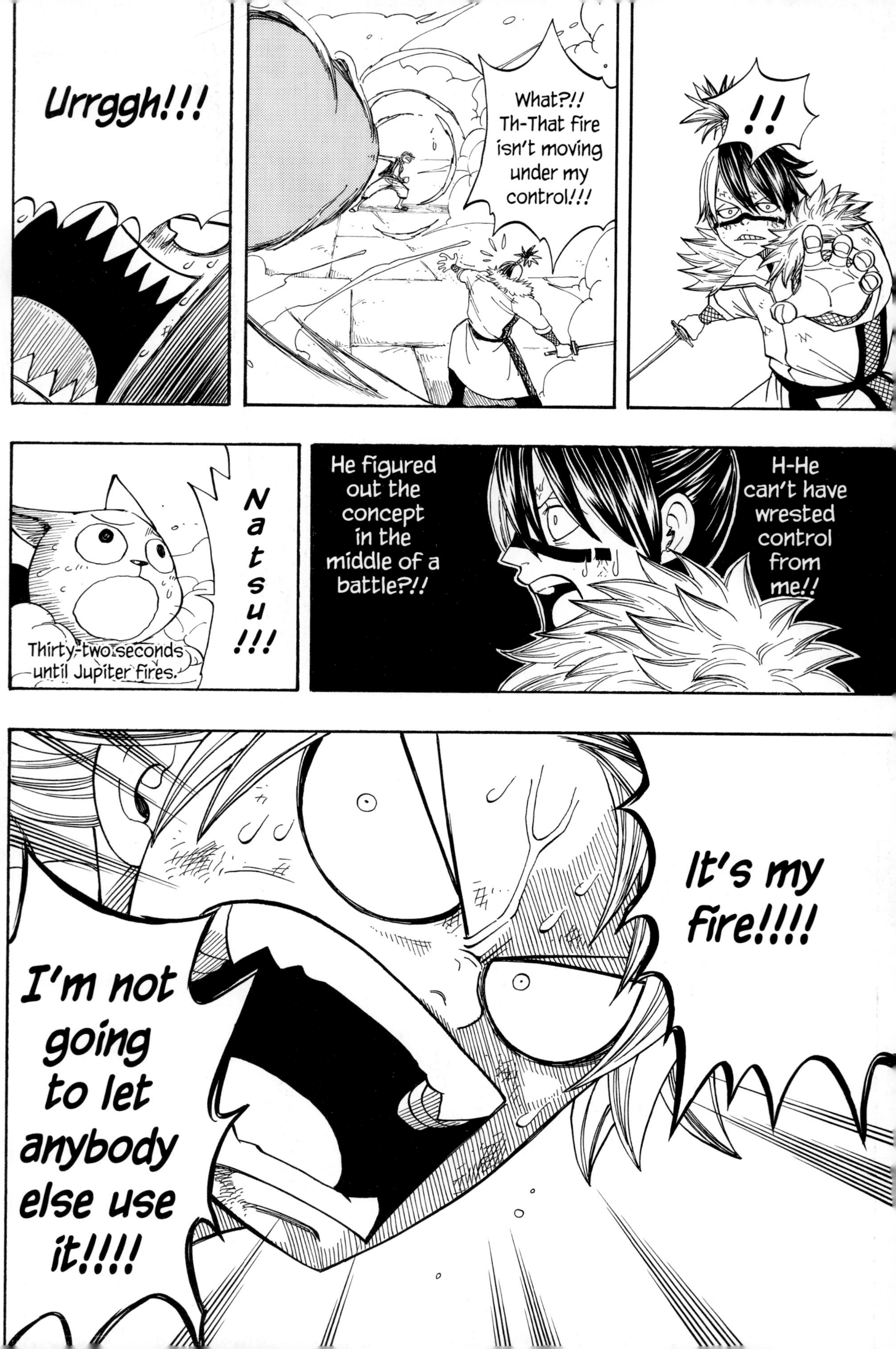
!!
What?!! Th-That fire isn't moving under my control!!!
Urrggh!!!
H-He can't have wrested control from me!!
He figured out the concept in the middle of a battle?!!
Natsu!!!
Thirty-two seconds until Jupiter fires.
It's my fire!!!!
I'm not going to let anybody else use it!!!!

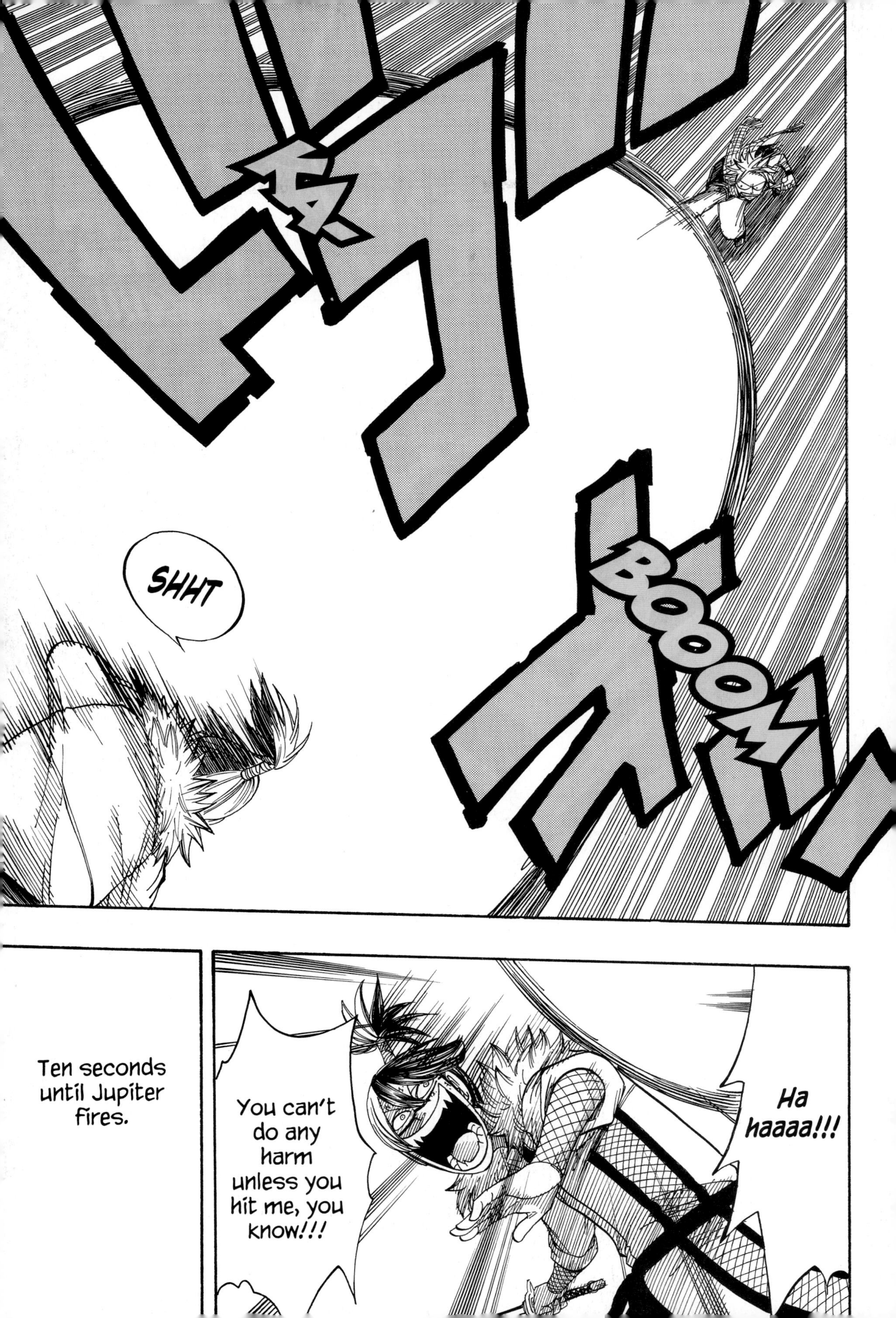
KA
BOOOM!!
SHHT
Ha haaaa!!!
You can't do any harm unless you hit me, you know!!!
Ten seconds until Jupiter fires.

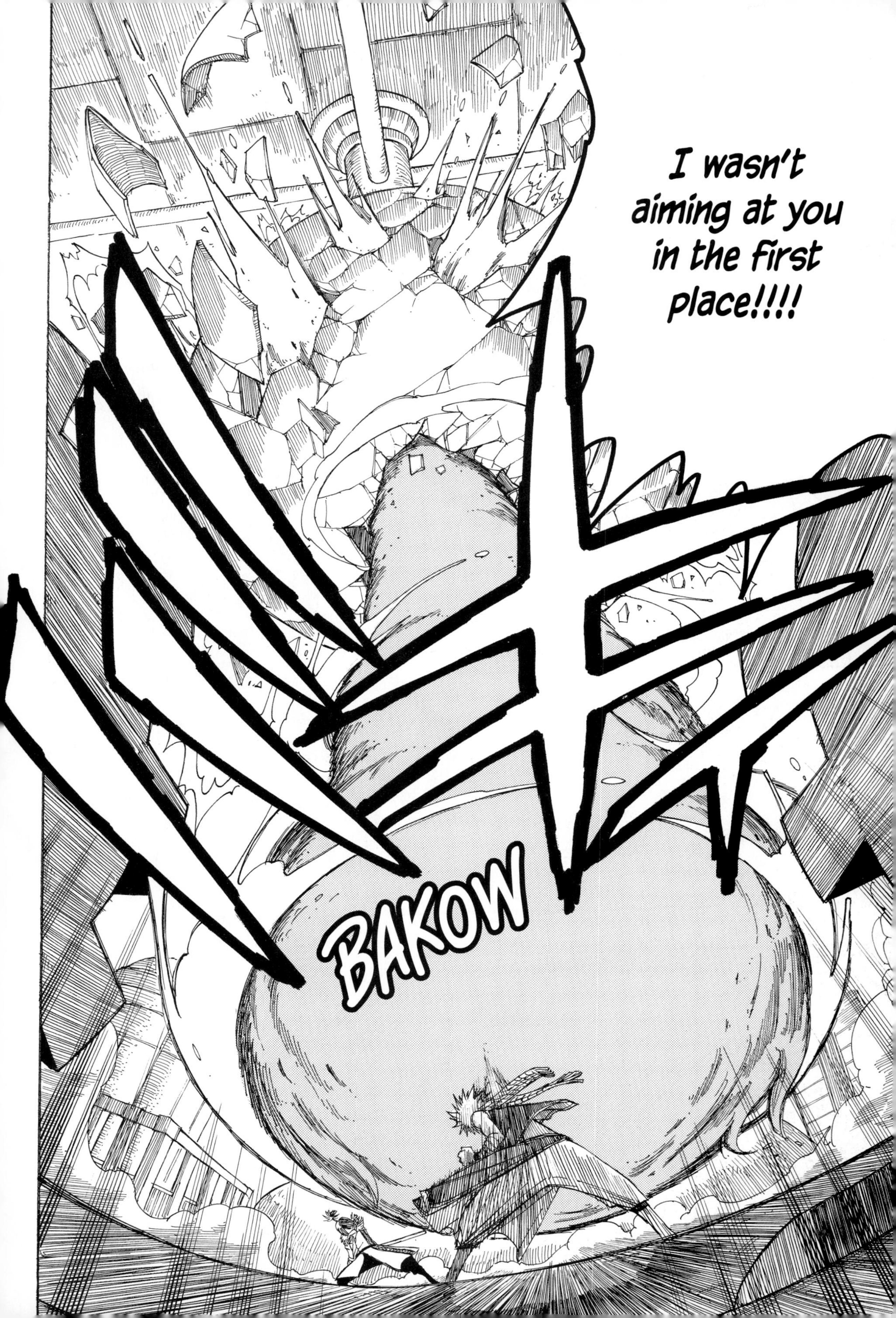
I wasn't aiming at you in the first place!!!!
BAKOW

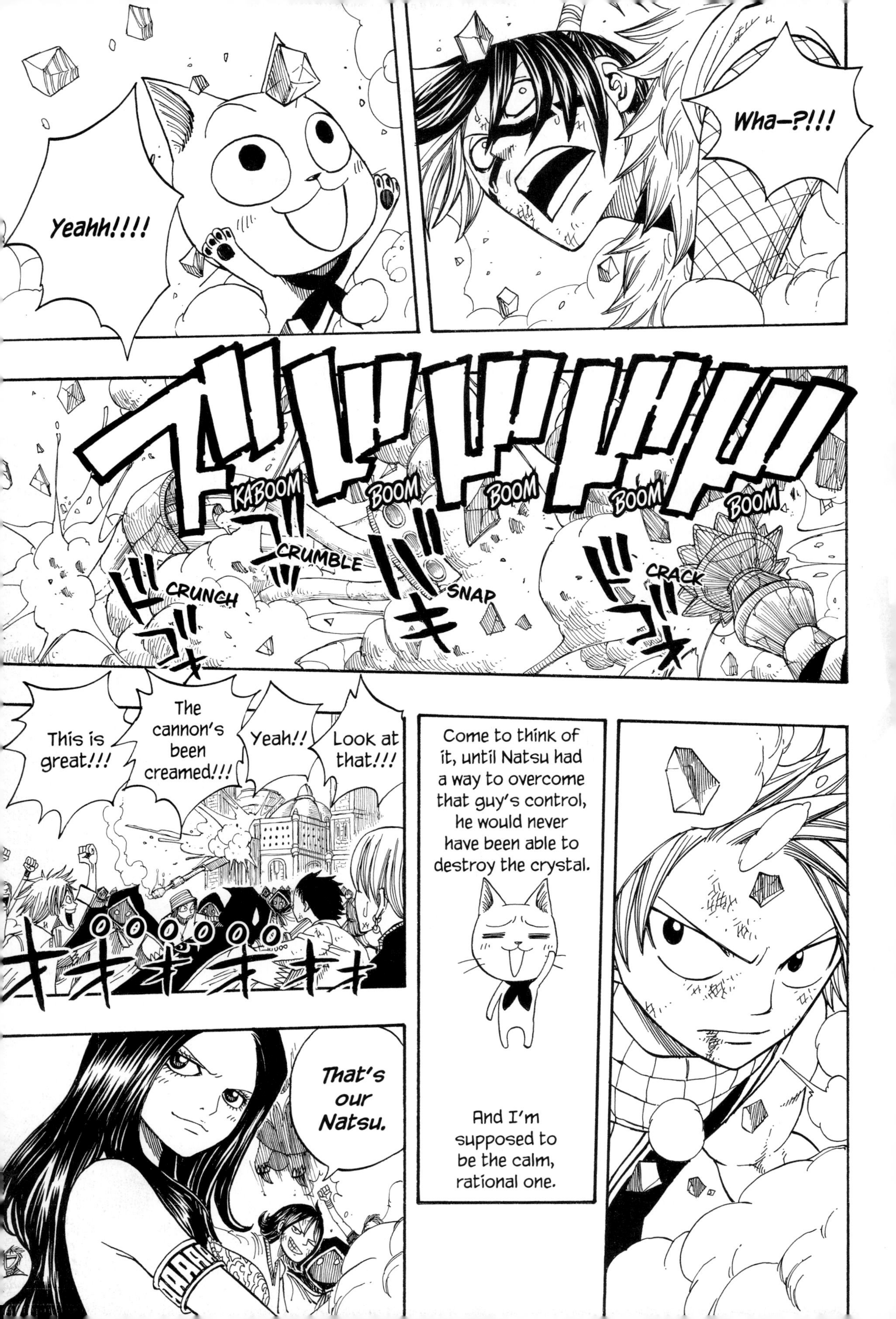
Wha–?!!!
Yeahh!!!!
KABOOM
BOOM
BOOM
BOOM
BOOM
CRUNCH
CRUMBLE
SNAP
CRACK
Come to think of it, until Natsu had a way to overcome that guy's control, he would never have been able to destroy the crystal.
And I'm supposed to be the calm, rational one.
Look at that!!!
Yeah!!
The cannon's been creamed!!!
This is great!!!
That's our Natsu.

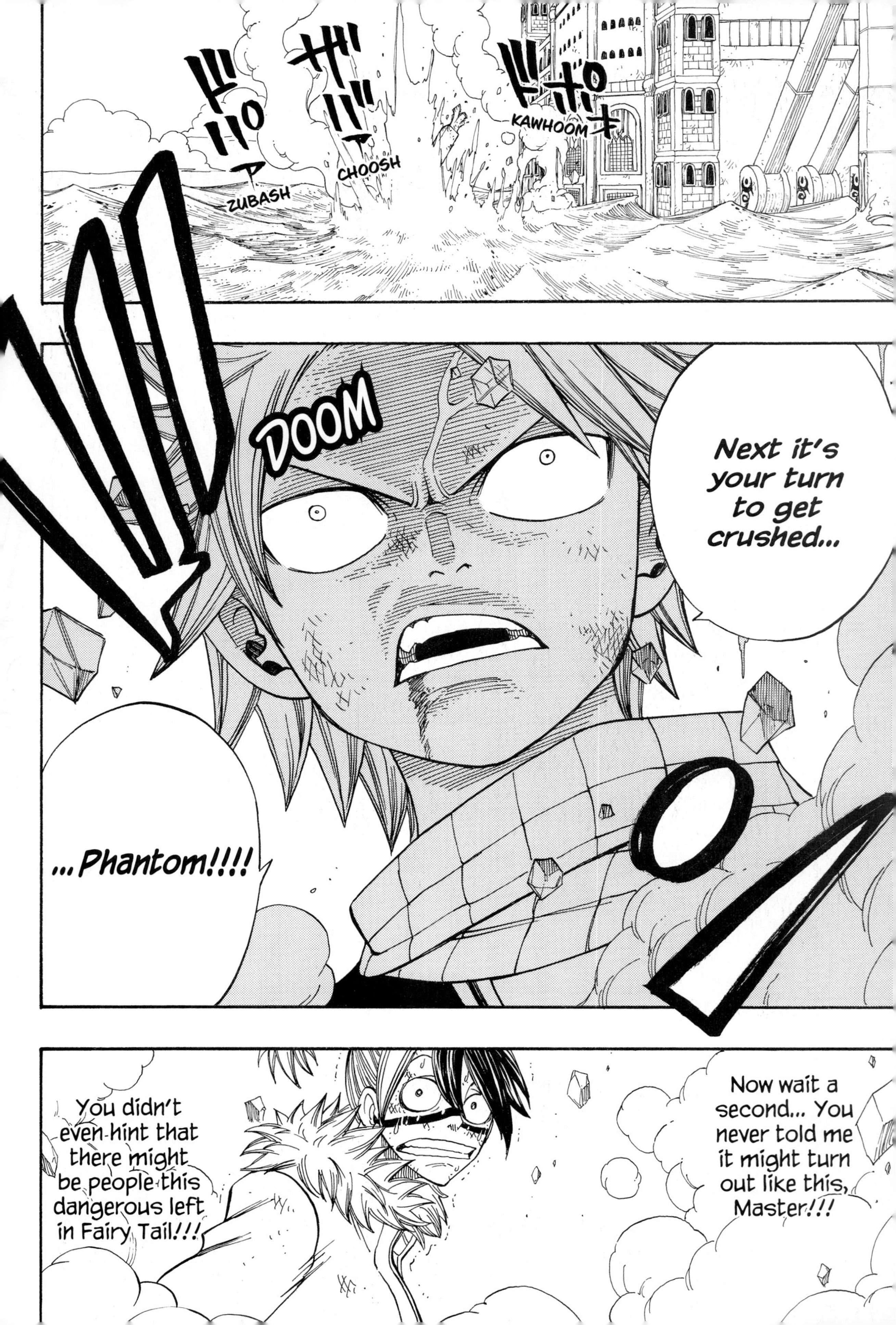
KAWHOOM
CHOOSH
ZUBASH
Next it's your turn to get crushed...
DOOM
...Phantom!!!!
Now wait a second... You never told me it might turn out like this, Master!!!
You didn't even hint that there might be people this dangerous left in Fairy Tail!!!

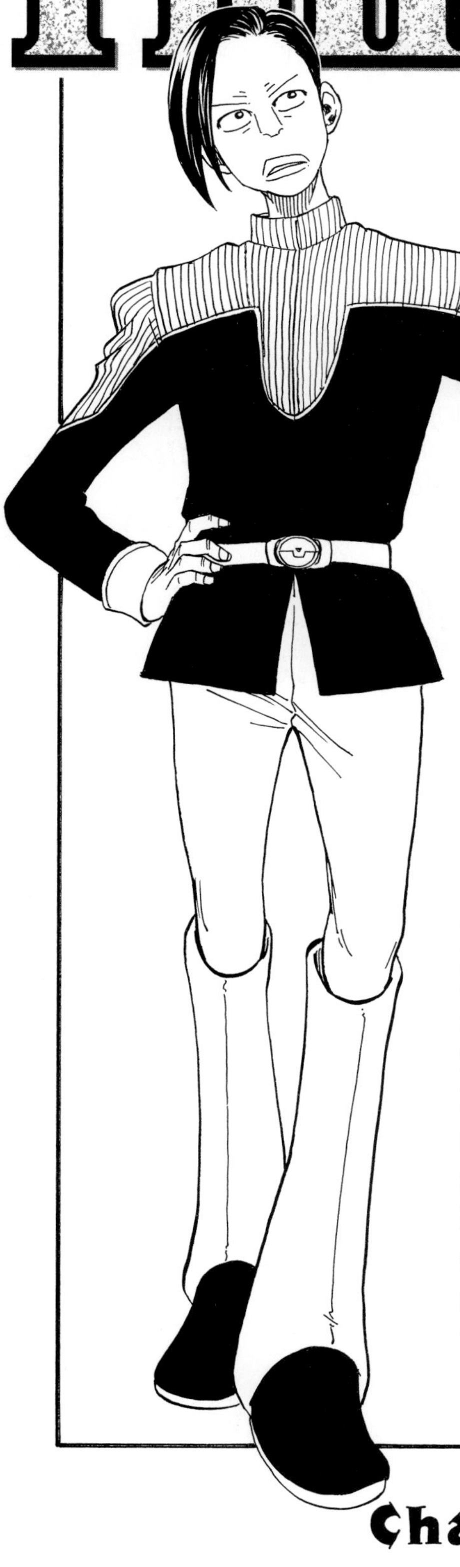

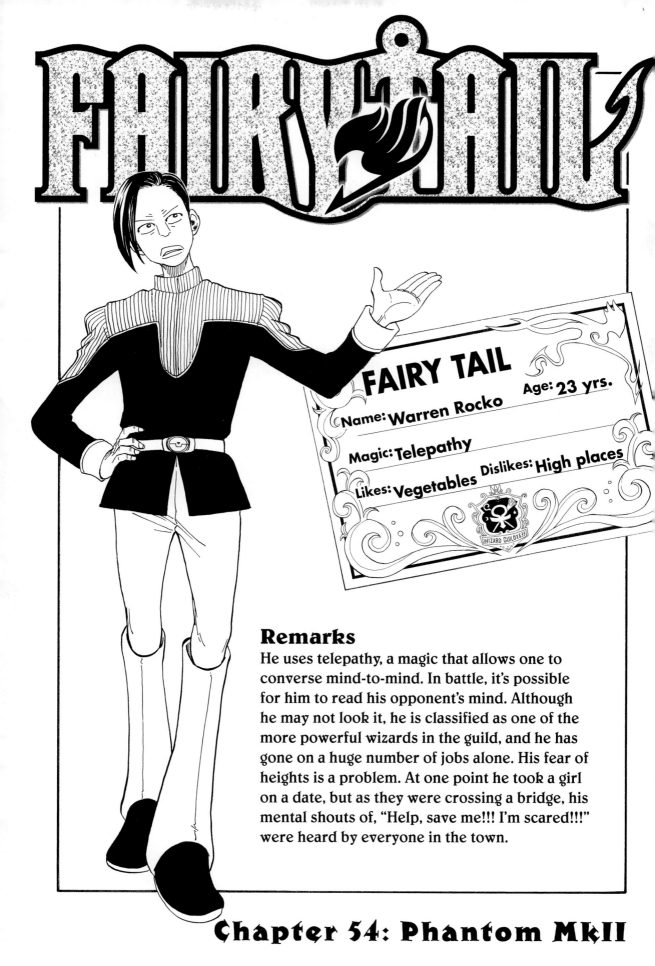

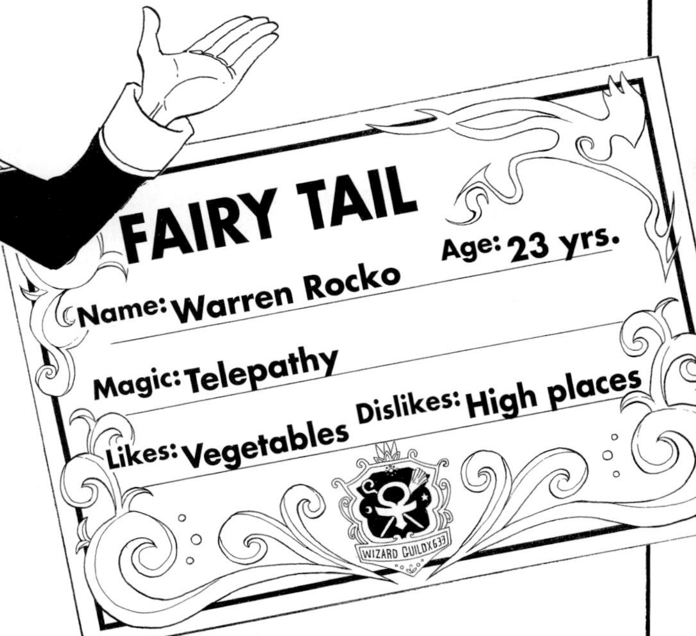
FAIRY TAIL
Name: Warren Rocko
Age: 23 yrs.
Magic: Telepathy
Likes: Vegetables
Dislikes: High places
WIZARD GUILD X633

Remarks

He uses telepathy, a magic that allows one to converse mind-to-mind. In battle, it's possible for him to read his opponent's mind. Although he may not look it, he is classified as one of the more powerful wizards in the guild, and he has gone on a huge number of jobs alone. His fear of heights is a problem. At one point he took a girl on a date, but as they were crossing a bridge, his mental shouts of, "Help, save me!!! I'm scared!!!" were heard by everyone in the town.

Chapter 54: Phantom MkII

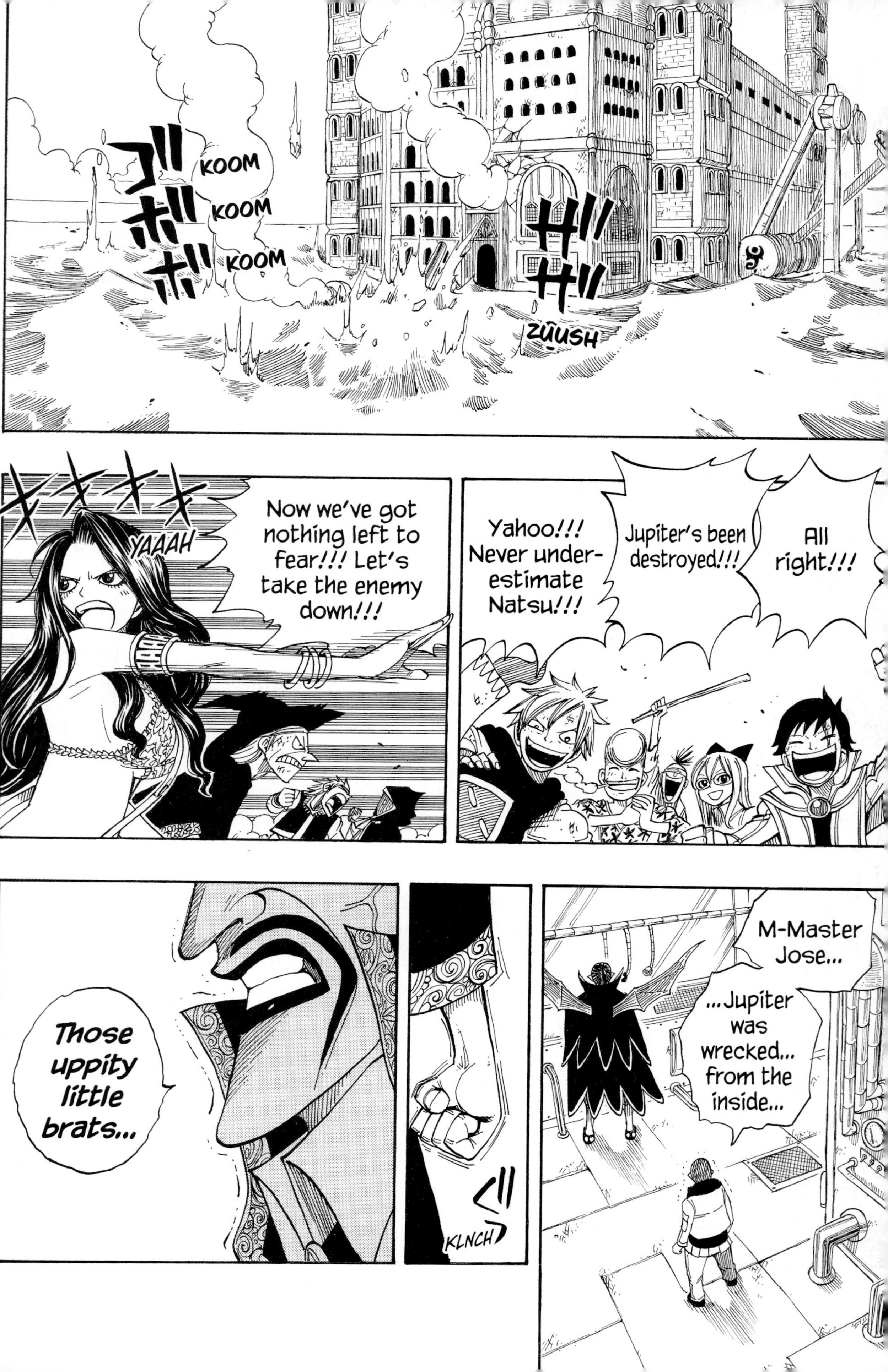
ZŪUSH
KOOM
KOOM
KOOM
All right!!!
Jupiter's been destroyed!!!
Yahoo!!! Never under-estimate Natsu!!!
Now we've got nothing left to fear!!! Let's take the enemy down!!!
YAAAH
M-Master Jose...
...Jupiter was wrecked... from the inside...
KLNCH
Those uppity little brats...

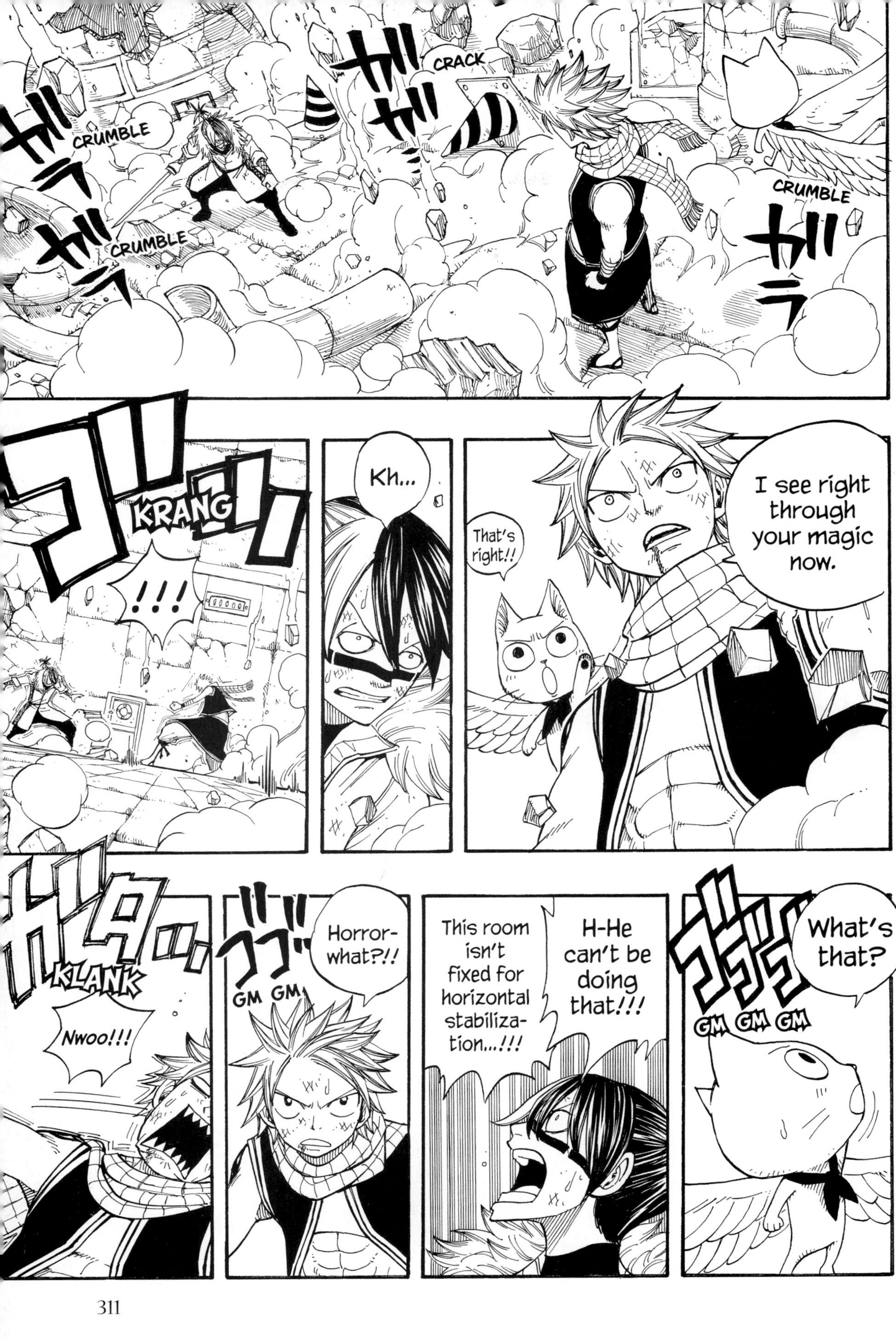
CRUMBLE
CRACK
CRUMBLE
CRUMBLE
I see right through your magic now.
That's right!!
Kh...
KRANG
!!!
What's that?
GM GM GM
H-He can't be doing that!!!
This room isn't fixed for horizontal stabiliza-tion...!!!
Horror-what?!!
GM GM
KLANK
Nwoo!!!

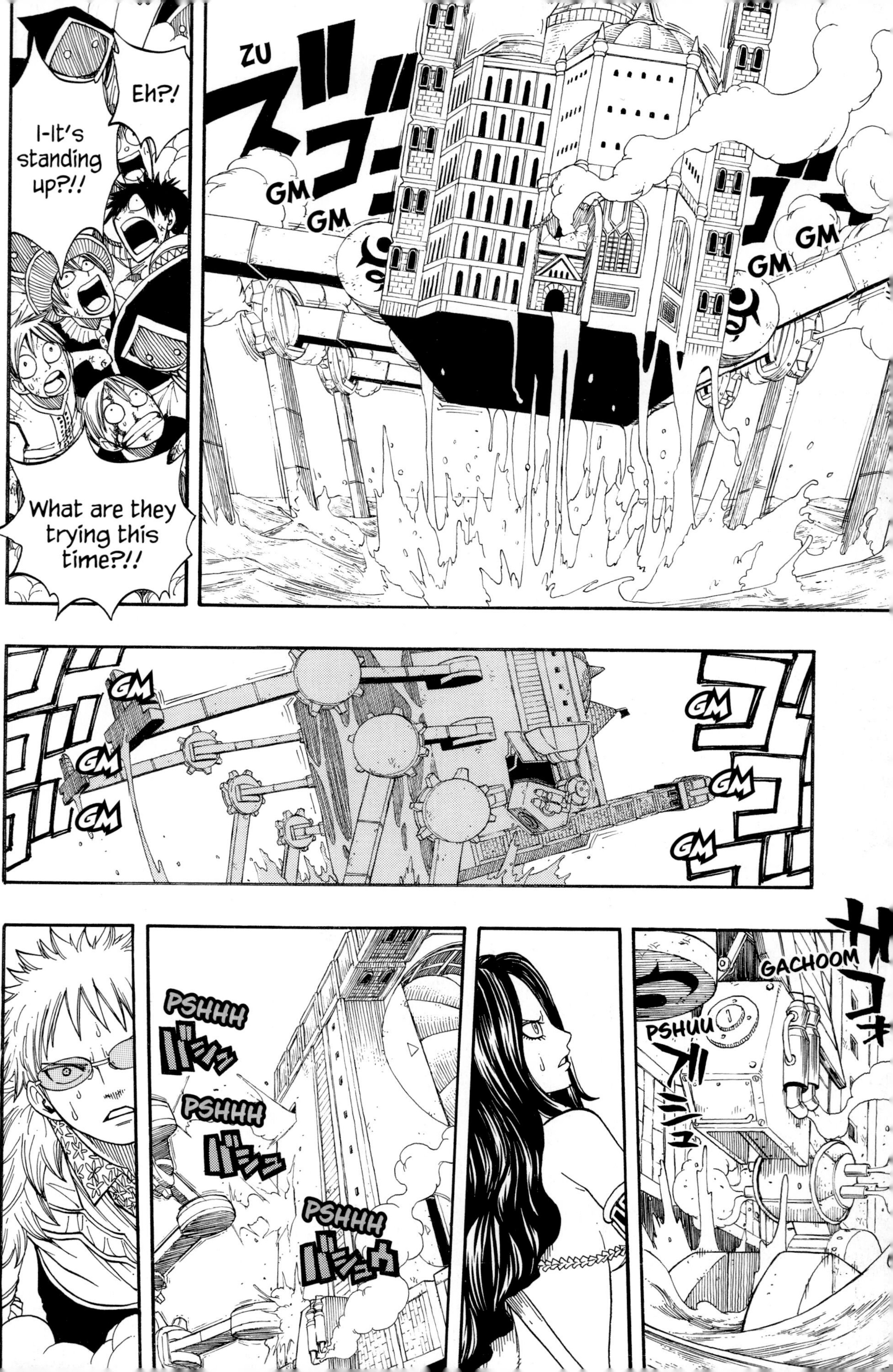
ZU
GM
GM
GM
GM
Eh?!
I-It's standing up?!!
What are they trying this time?!!
GM
GM
GM
GM
GM
GM
GACHOOM
PSHUU
PSHHH
PSHHH
PSHHH

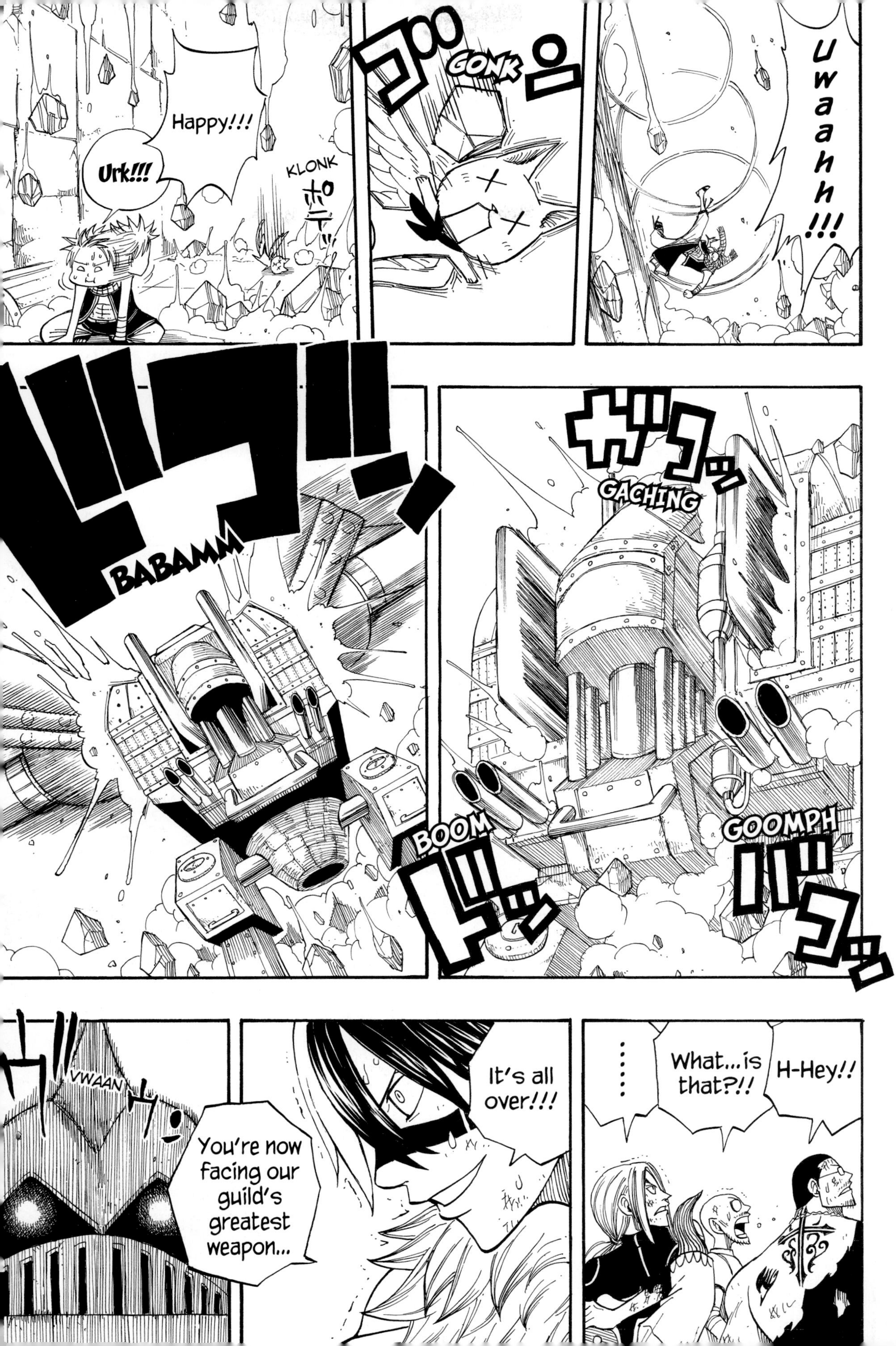
Uwaahh!!!
GONK
Happy!!!
Urk!!!
KLONK
GACHING
GOOMPH
BOOM
BABAMM
H-Hey!!
What...is that?!!
......
It's all over!!!
You're now facing our guild's greatest weapon...
VWAAN

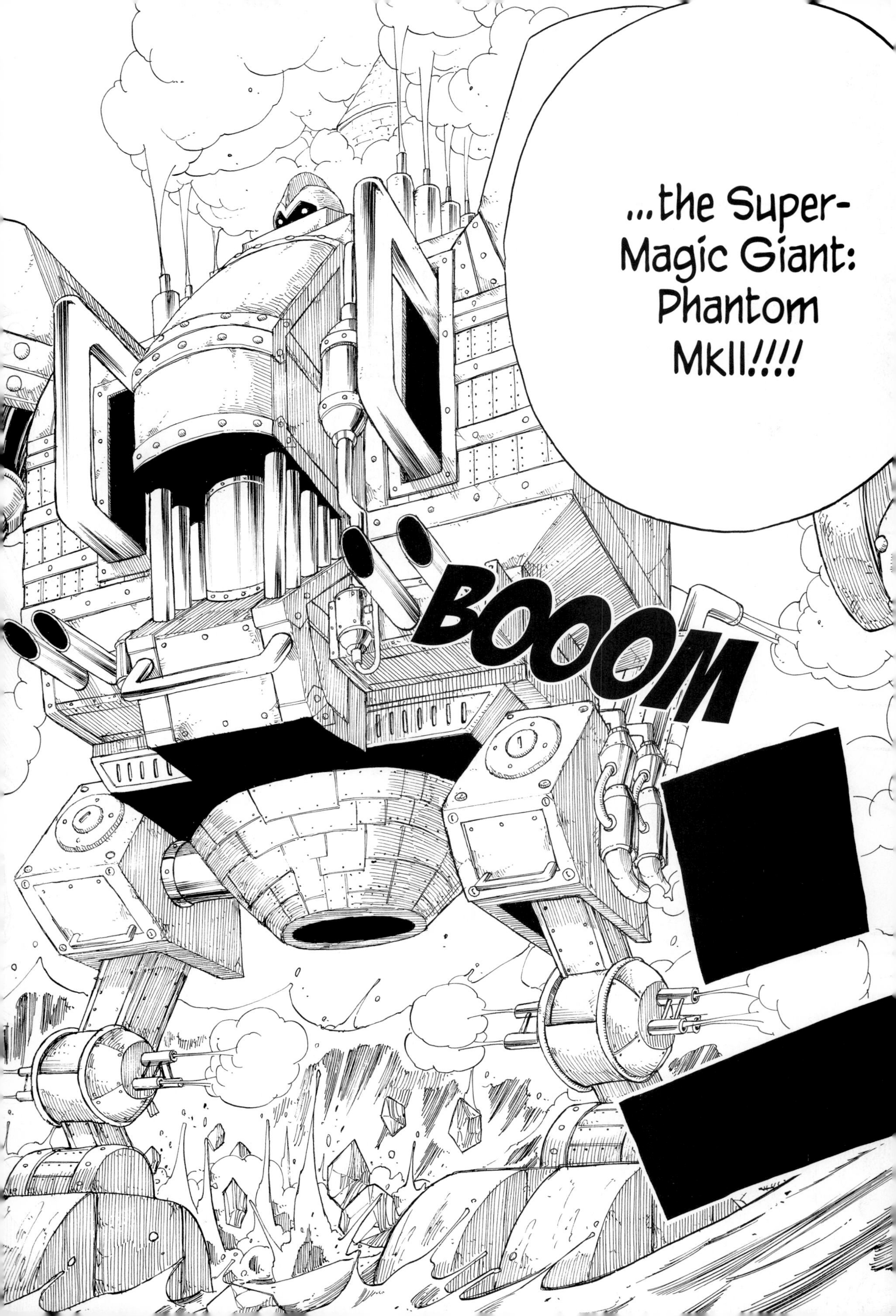
...the Super-Magic Giant: Phantom MkII!!!!
BOOOM

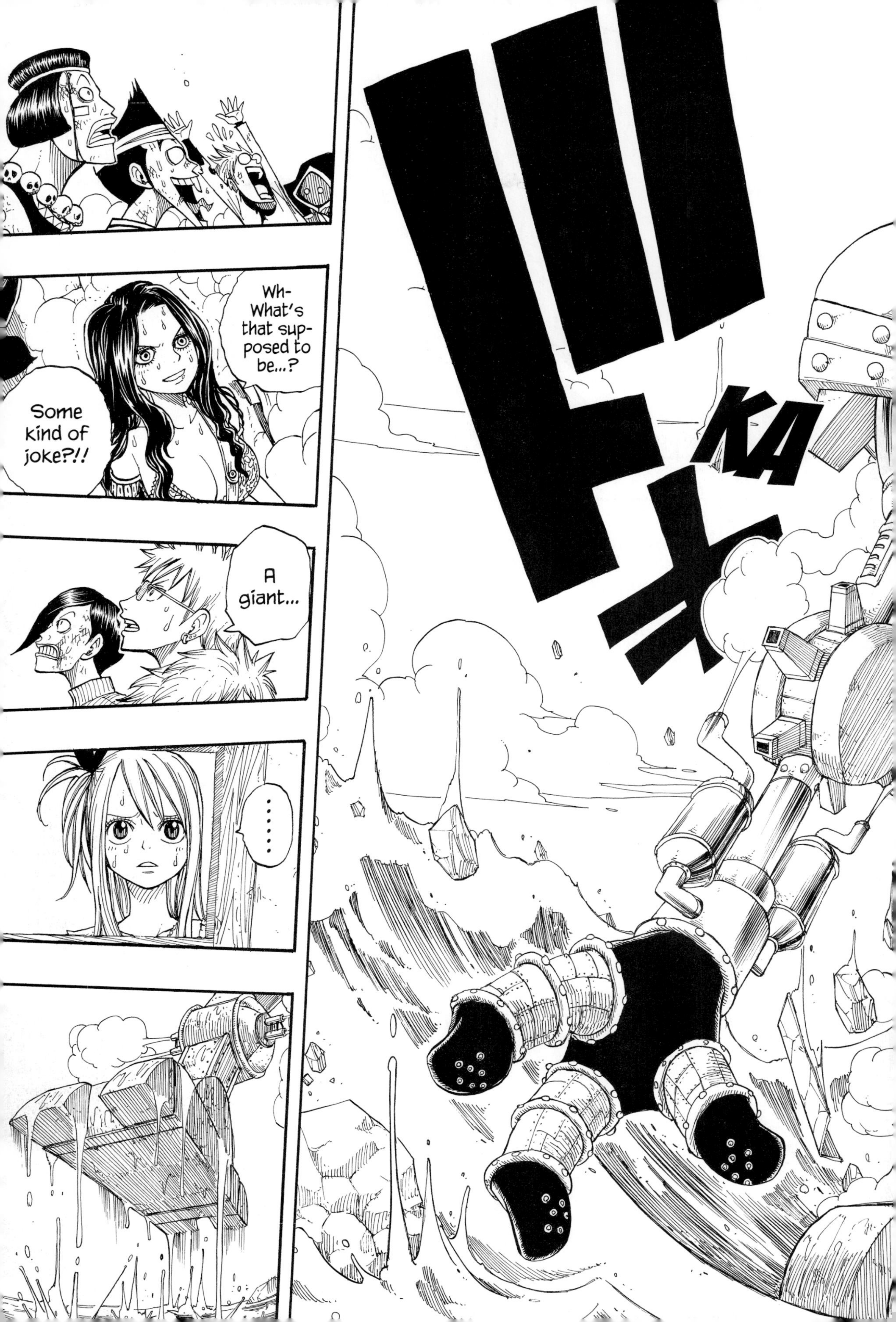
KA
Wh- What's that supposed to be...?
Some kind of joke?!!
A giant...
......

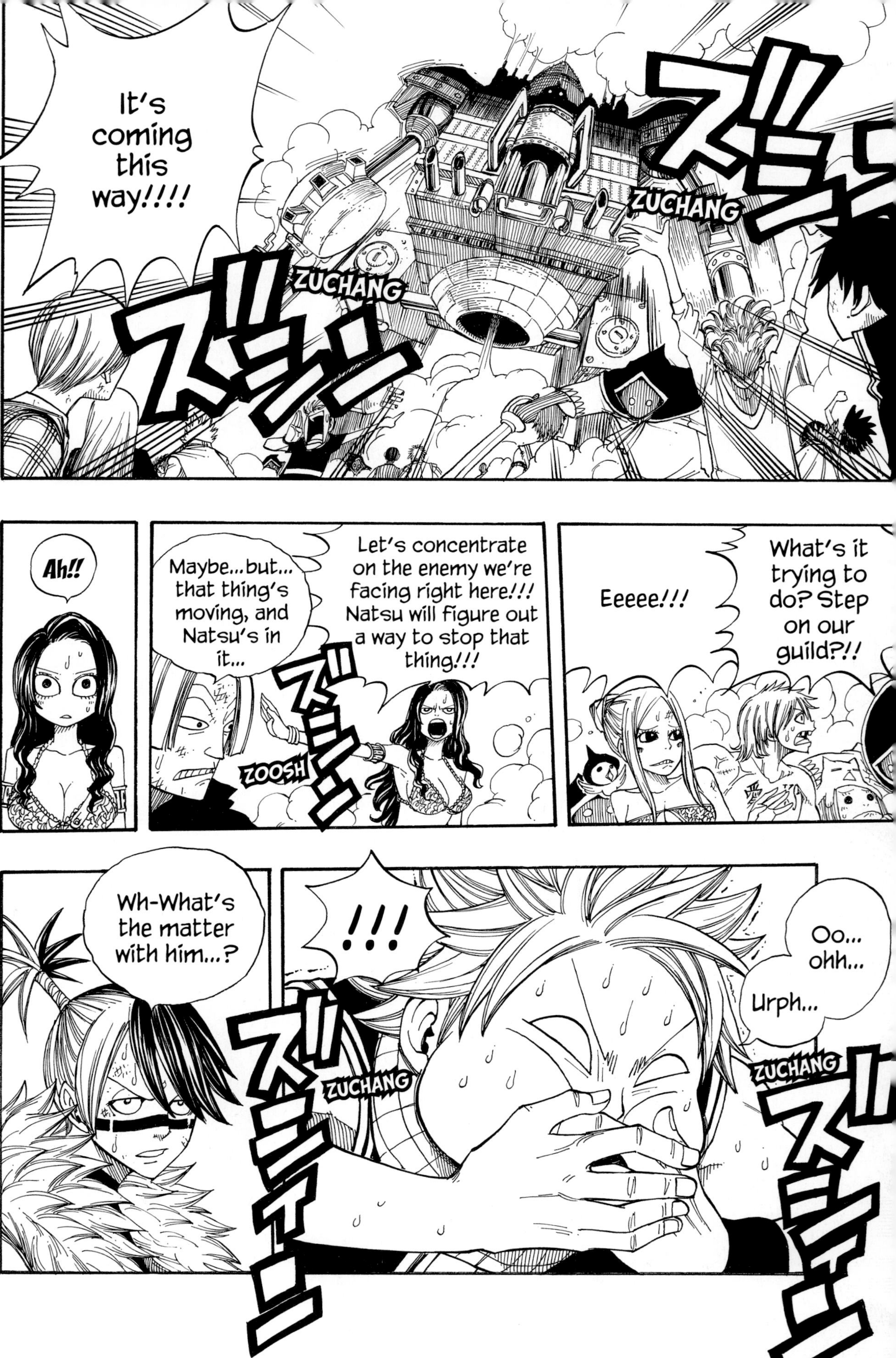
It's coming this way!!!!
ZUCHANG
ZUCHANG
What's it trying to do? Step on our guild?!!
Eeeee!!!
Let's concentrate on the enemy we're facing right here!!! Natsu will figure out a way to stop that thing!!!
Maybe...but... that thing's moving, and Natsu's in it...
ZOOSH
Ah!!
Oo... ohh...
Urph...
!!!
ZUCHANG
ZUCHANG
Wh-What's the matter with him...?

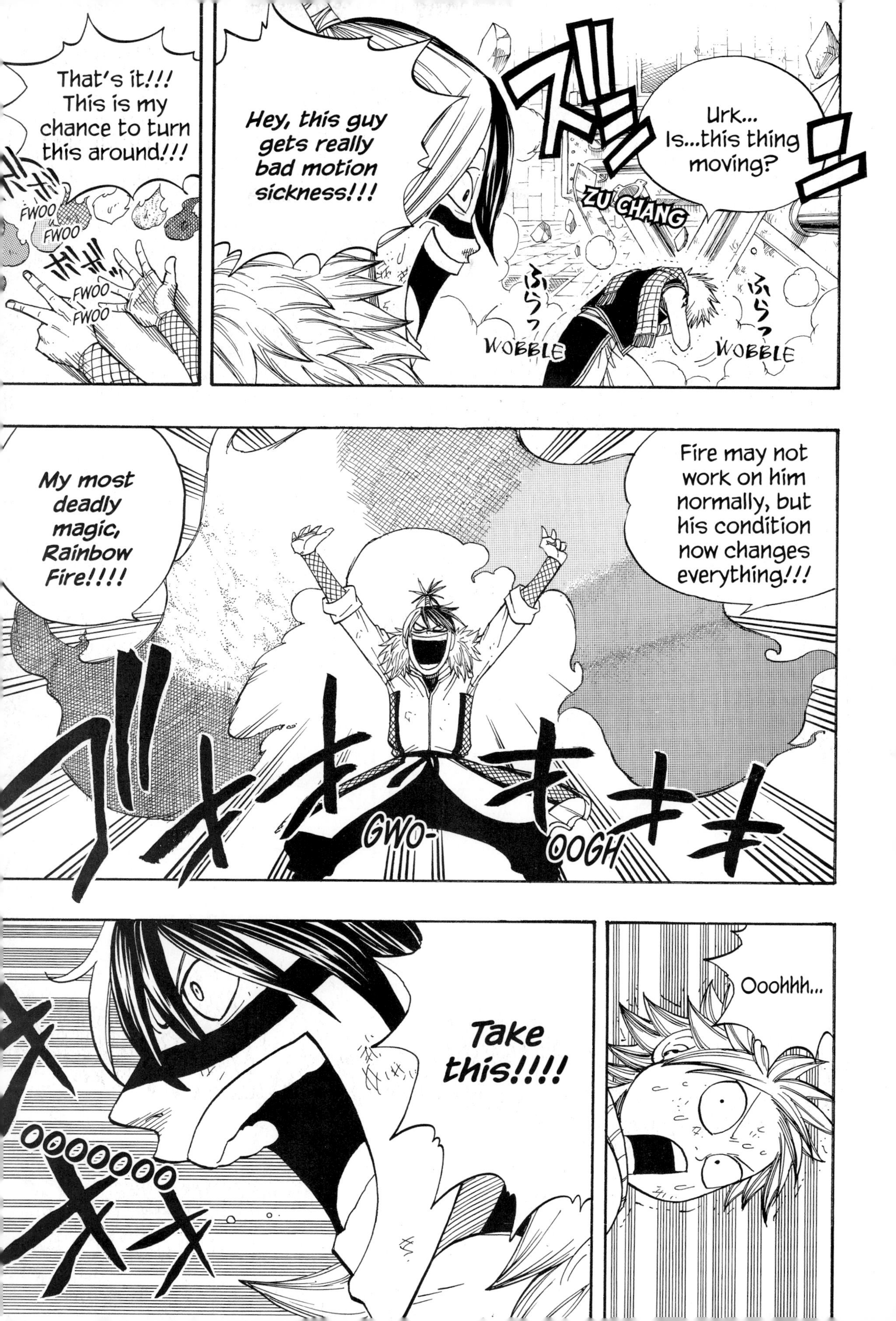
Urk... Is...this thing moving?
ZU CHANG
ふらっ
WOBBLE
ふらっ
WOBBLE
Hey, this guy gets really bad motion sickness!!!
That's it!!! This is my chance to turn this around!!!
FWOO
FWOO
FWOO
FWOO
Fire may not work on him normally, but his condition now changes everything!!!
My most deadly magic, Rainbow Fire!!!!
GWO-
OOGH
Ooohhh...
Take this!!!!

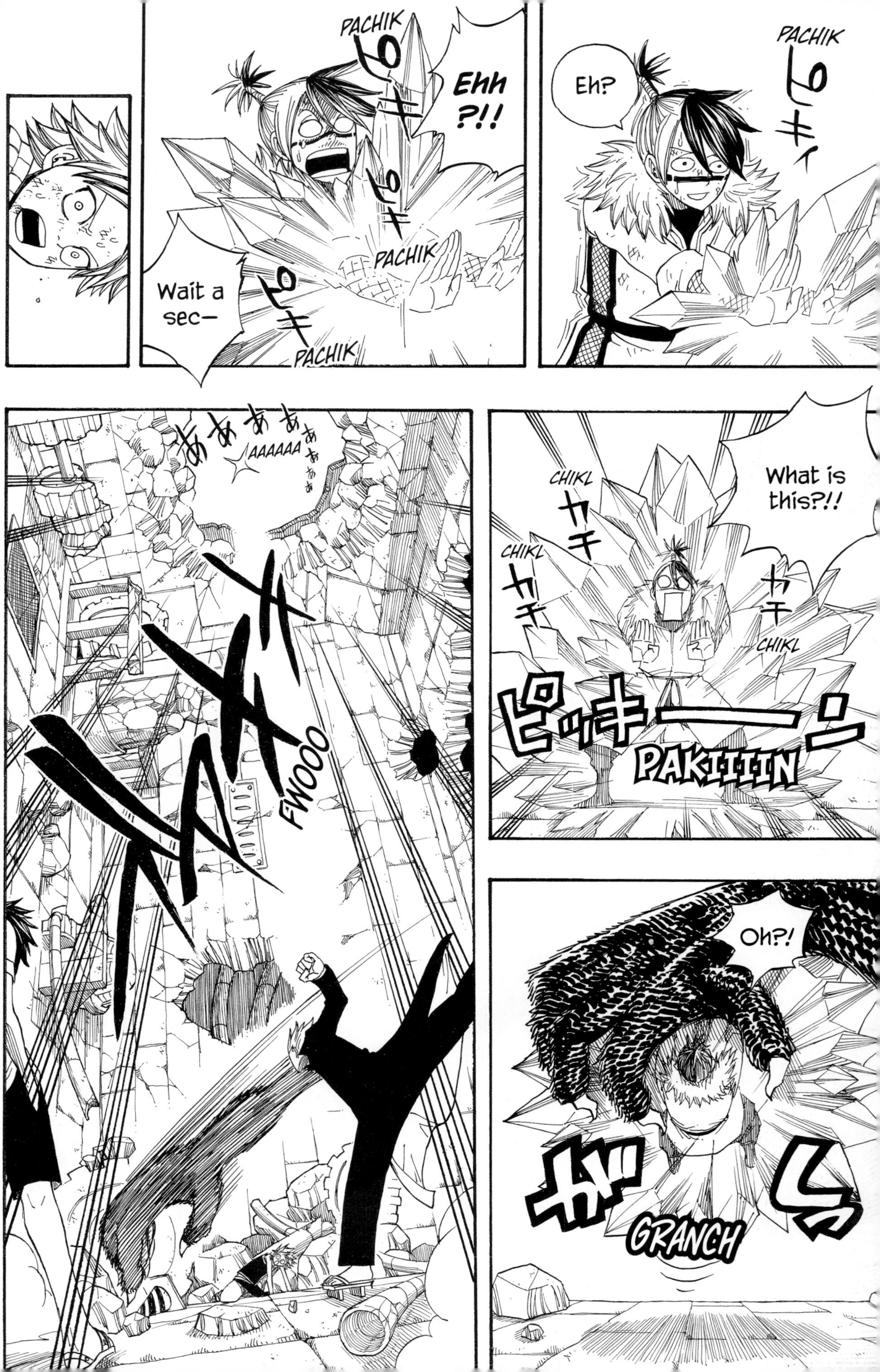

Eh?
PACHIK
ピキィ
Ehh?!!
PACHIK
PACHIK
PACHIK
Wait a sec—
What is this?!!
CHIKL
CHIKL
CHIKL
PAKIIIN
AAAAAA
FWOOO
Oh?!
GRANCH

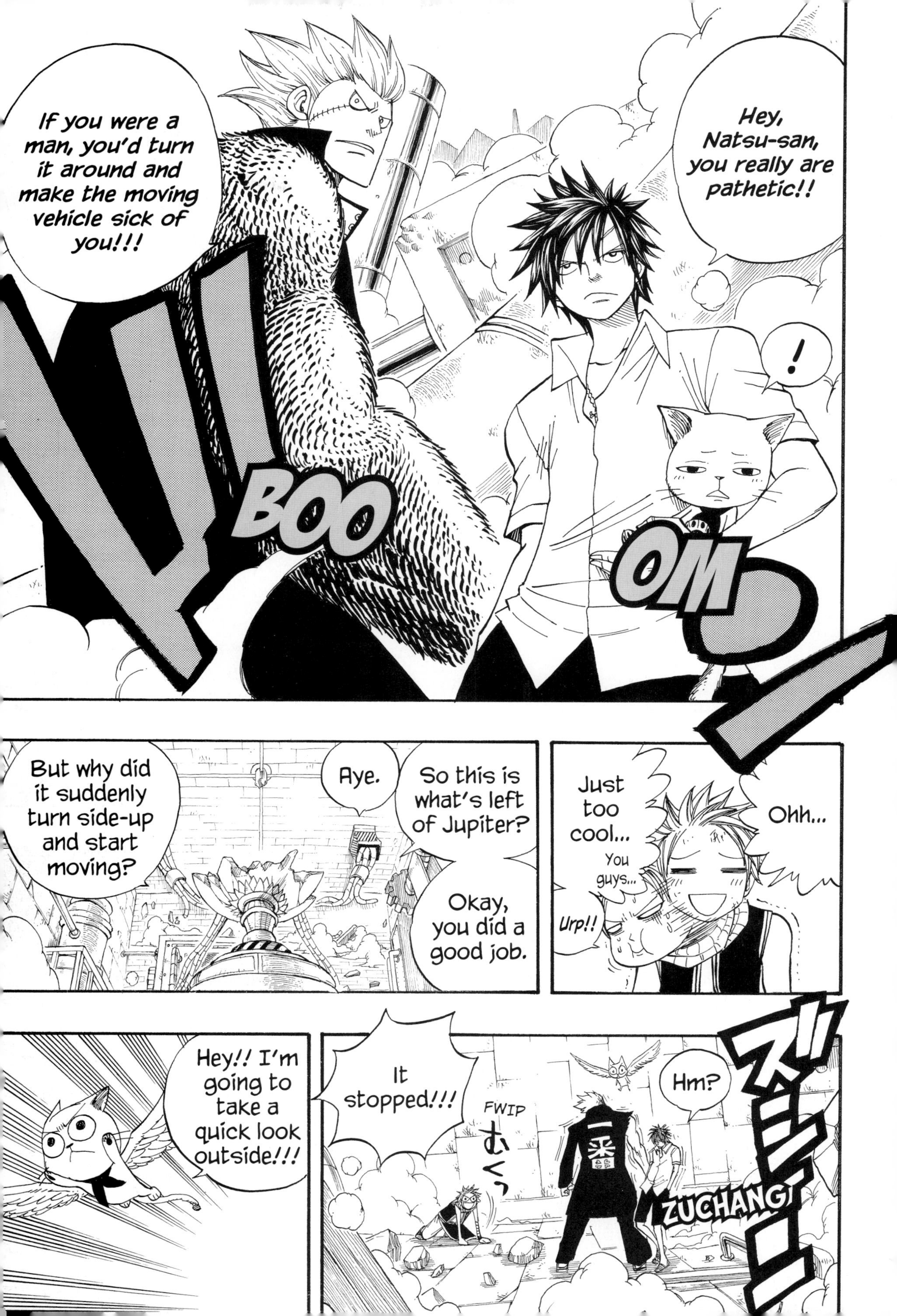
Hey, Natsu-san, you really are pathetic!!
!
If you were a man, you'd turn it around and make the moving vehicle sick of you!!!
BOOOM
Ohh...
Just too cool...
You guys...
Urp!!
So this is what's left of Jupiter?
Aye.
But why did it suddenly turn side-up and start moving?
Okay, you did a good job.
ZUCHANG
Hm?
It stopped!!!
FWIP
むくっ
Hey!! I'm going to take a quick look outside!!!

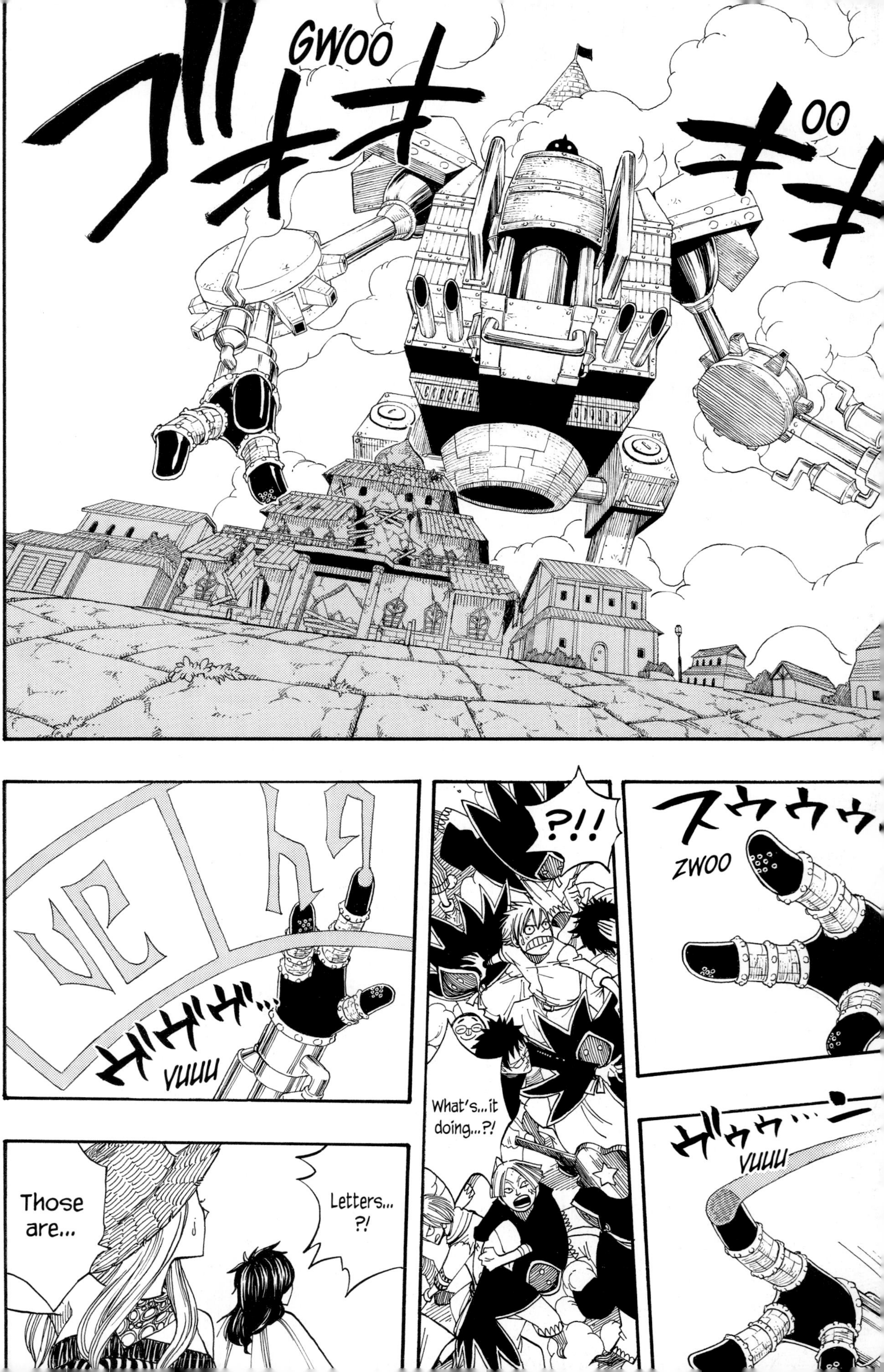
GWOO
OO
ZWOO
VUUU
?!!
What's...it doing...?!
VUUU
Letters... ?!
Those are...

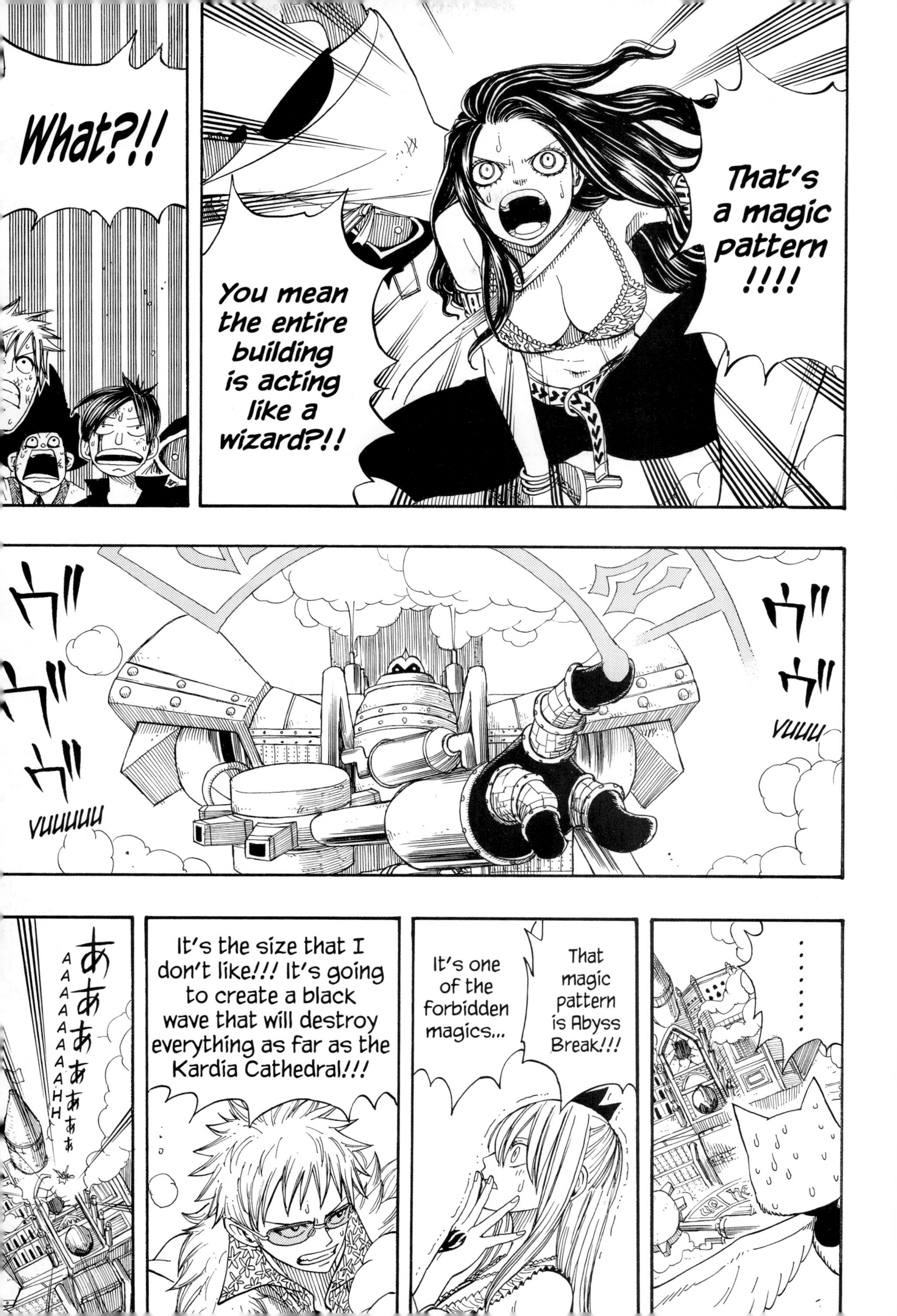
That's a magic pattern!!!!
You mean the entire building is acting like a wizard?!!
What?!!
ヴヴヴ
VUUU
ヴヴヴ
VUUUUU
......
That magic pattern is Abyss Break!!!
It's one of the forbidden magics...
It's the size that I don't like!!! It's going to create a black wave that will destroy everything as far as the Kardia Cathedral!!!
ああああああ
AAAAAAAAAHH

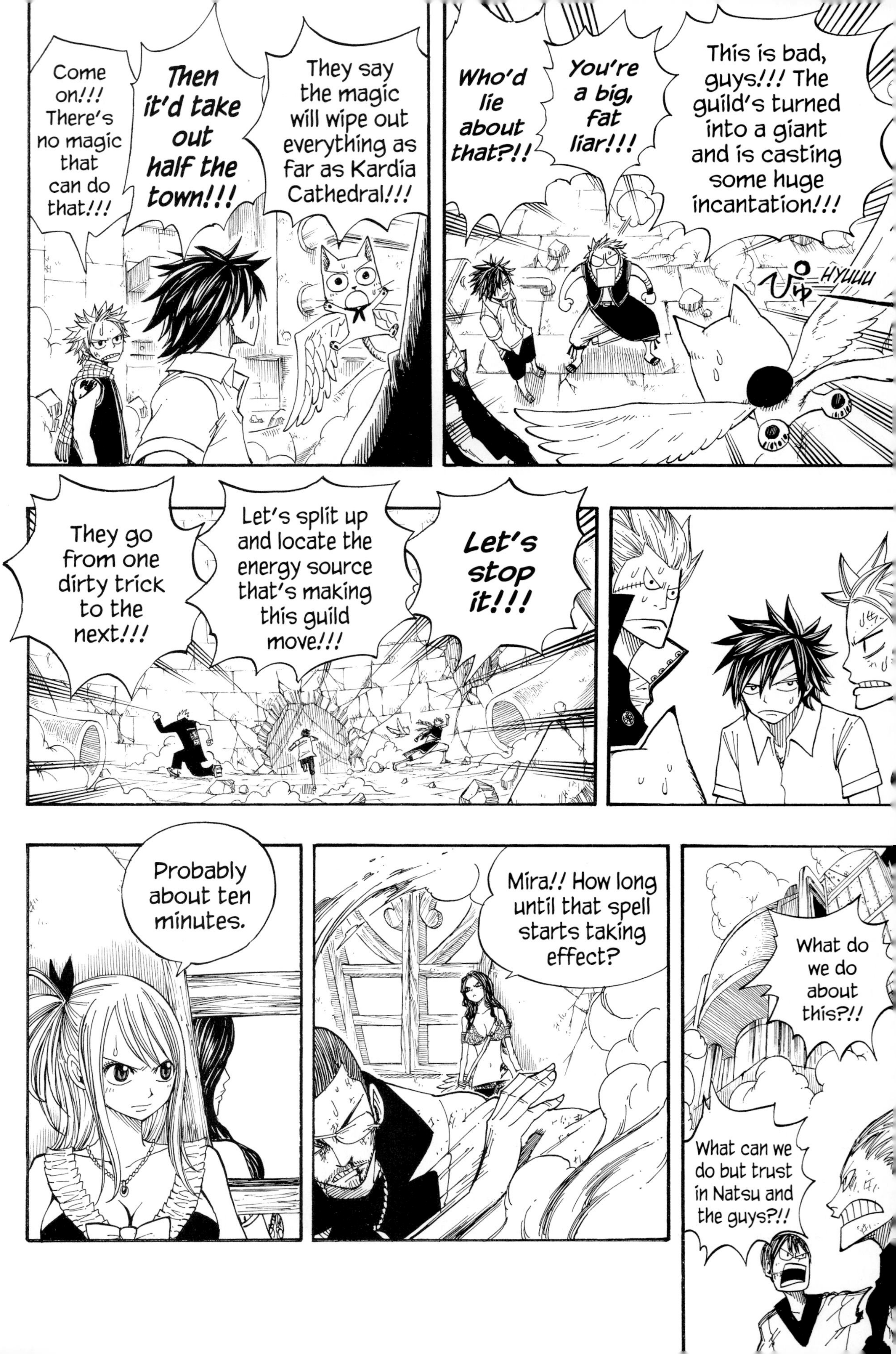
This is bad, guys!!! The guild's turned into a giant and is casting some huge incantation!!!
You're a big, fat liar!!!
Who'd lie about that?!!
HYUUU
They say the magic will wipe out everything as far as Kardia Cathedral!!!
Then it'd take out half the town!!!
Come on!!! There's no magic that can do that!!!
Let's stop it!!!
Let's split up and locate the energy source that's making this guild move!!!
They go from one dirty trick to the next!!!
What do we do about this?!!
What can we do but trust in Natsu and the guys?!!
Mira!! How long until that spell starts taking effect?
Probably about ten minutes.

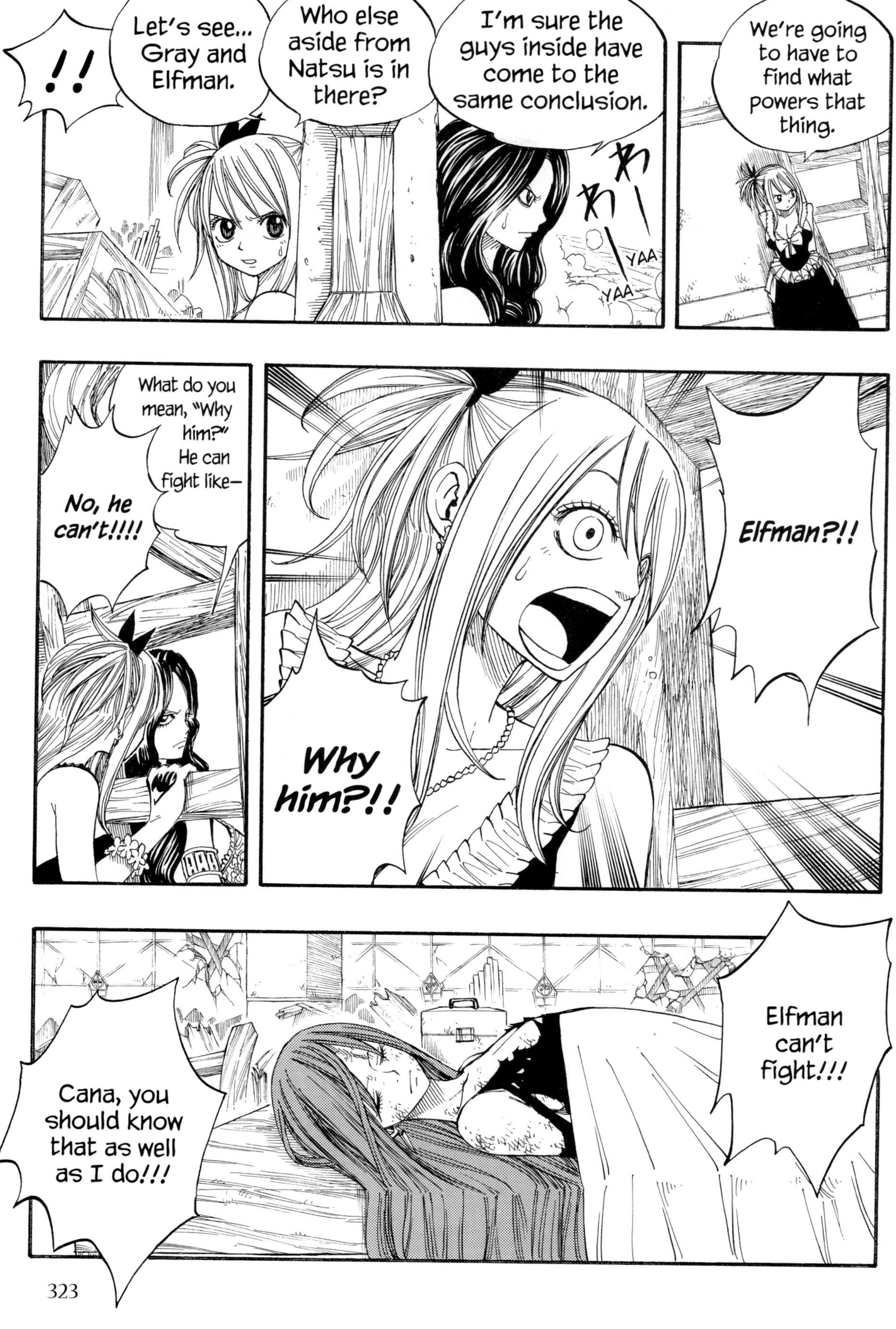
We're going to have to find what powers that thing.
I'm sure the guys inside have come to the same conclusion.
わ わ
YAA YAA
Who else aside from Natsu is in there?
Let's see... Gray and Elfman.
!!
Elfman?!!
Why him?!!
What do you mean, "Why him?" He can fight like—
No, he can't!!!!
Elfman can't fight!!!
Cana, you should know that as well as I do!!!

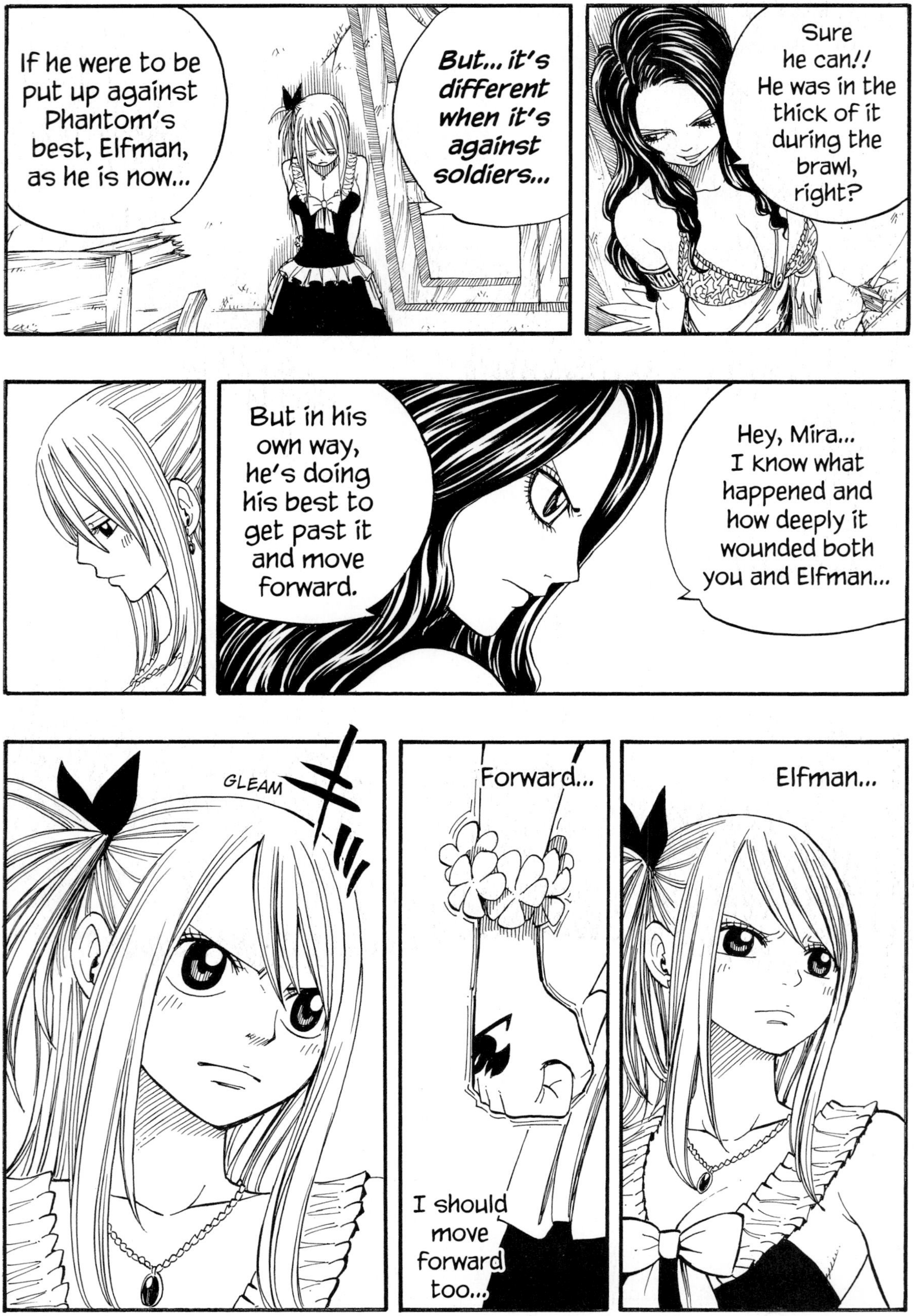
Sure he can!! He was in the thick of it during the brawl, right?
But... it's different when it's against soldiers...
If he were to be put up against Phantom's best, Elfman, as he is now...
Hey, Mira... I know what happened and how deeply it wounded both you and Elfman...
But in his own way, he's doing his best to get past it and move forward.
Elfman...
Forward...
I should move forward too...
GLEAM

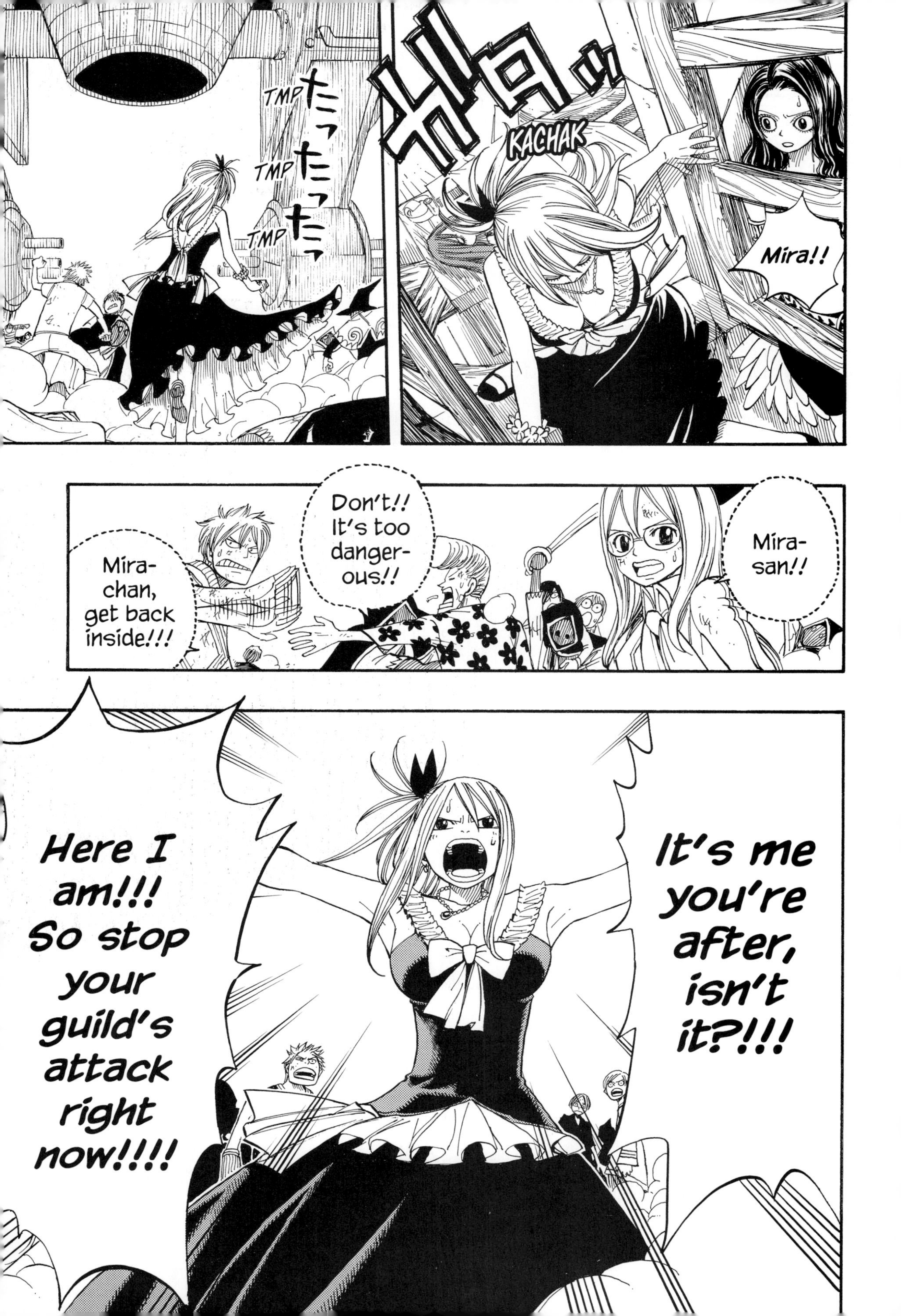

Mira!!
KACHAK
TMP
TMP
TMP
Mira-san!!
Don't!! It's too danger-ous!!
Mira-chan, get back inside!!!
It's me you're after, isn't it?!!!
Here I am!!! So stop your guild's attack right now!!!!

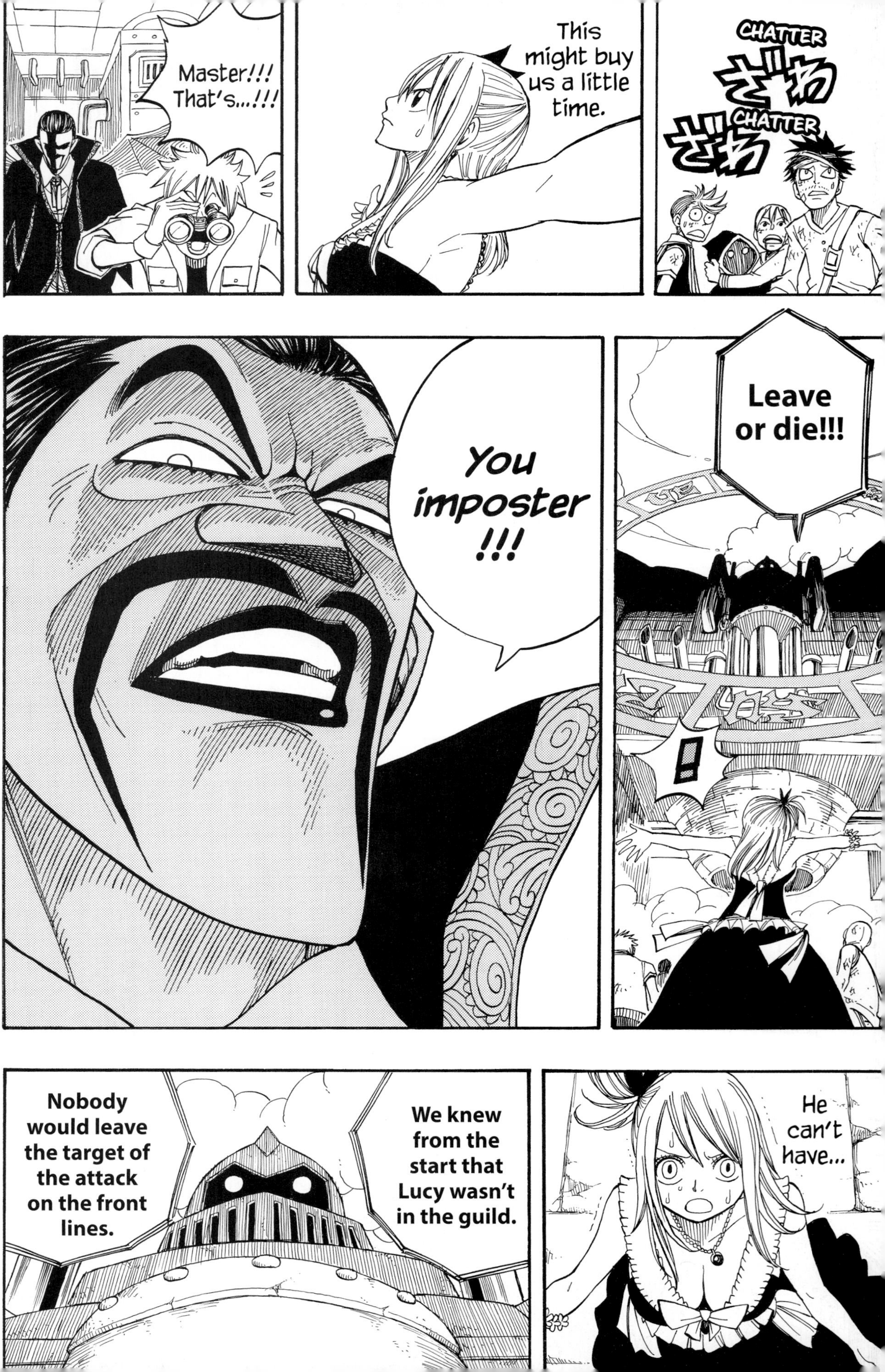
CHATTER
ざわ
CHATTER
ざわ
This might buy us a little time.
Master!!! That's...!!!
Leave or die!!!
!
You imposter!!!
He can't have...
We knew from the start that Lucy wasn't in the guild.
Nobody would leave the target of the attack on the front lines.

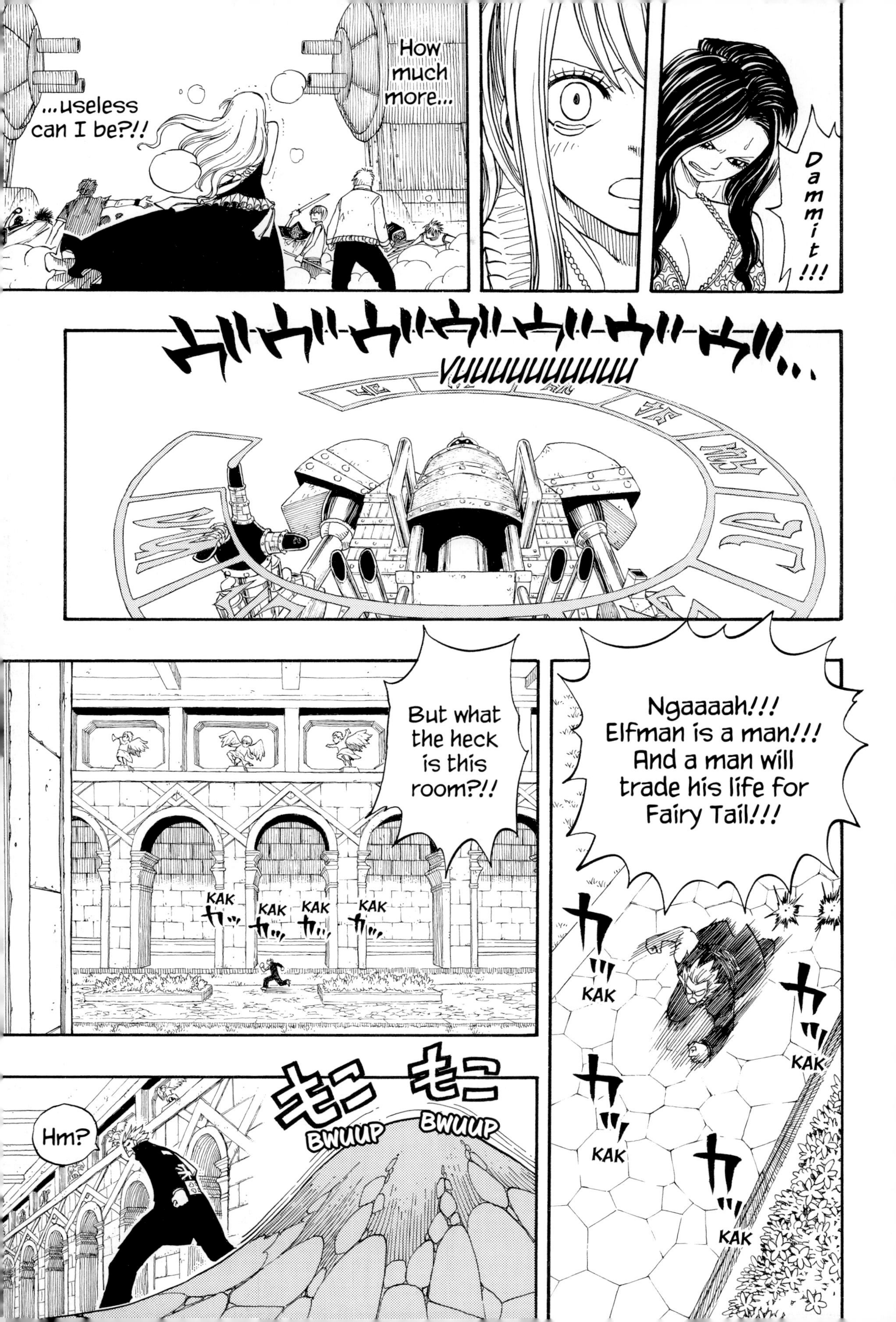
Dammit!!!
How much more...
...useless can I be?!!
VUUUUUUUUUUU
Ngaaaah!!! Elfman is a man!!! And a man will trade his life for Fairy Tail!!!
KAK
KAK
KAK
KAK
But what the heck is this room?!!
KAK
KAK
KAK
KAK
BWUUP
BWUUP
Hm?

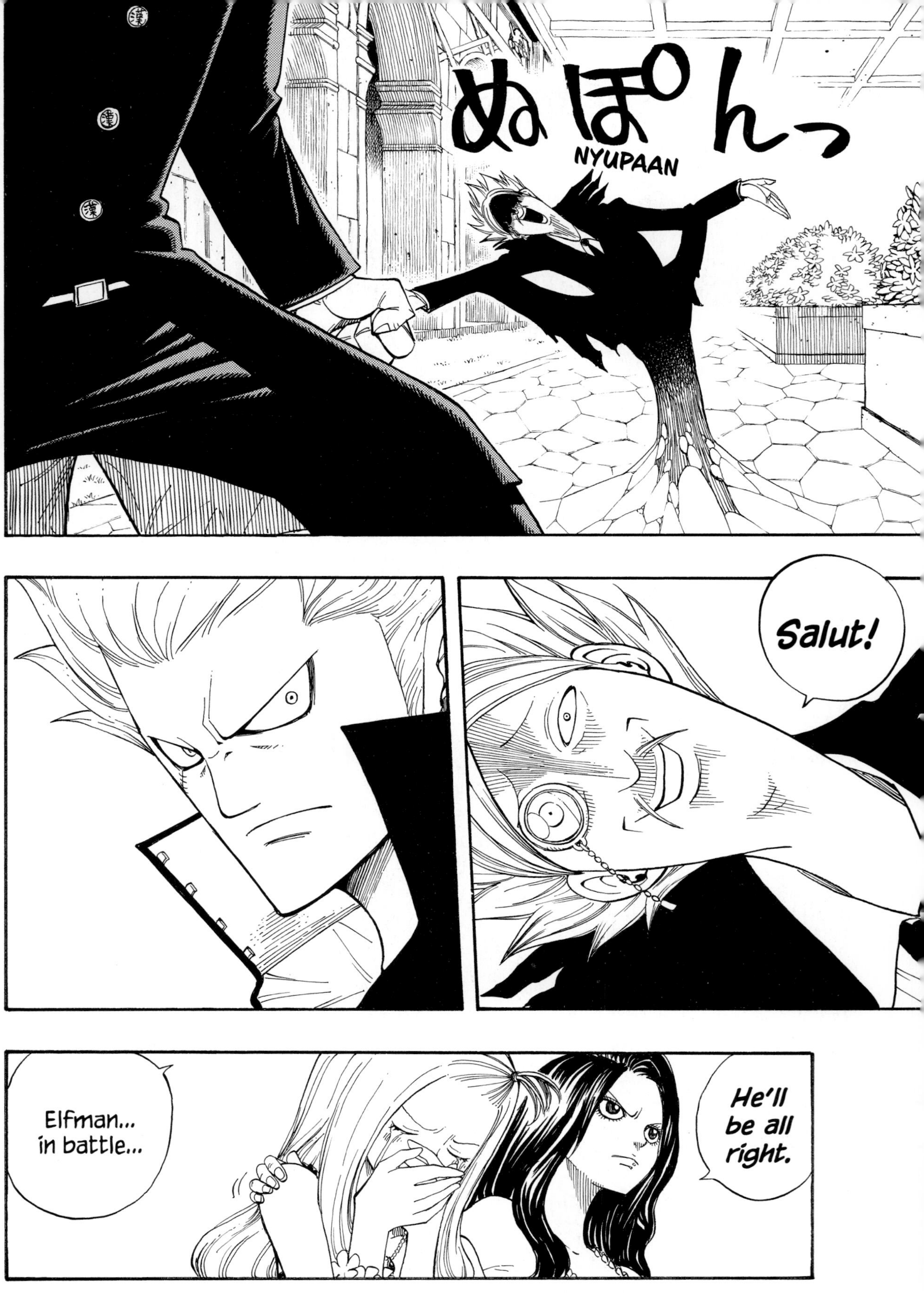
ぬぽんっ
NYUPAAN
Salut!
Elfman... in battle...
He'll be all right.

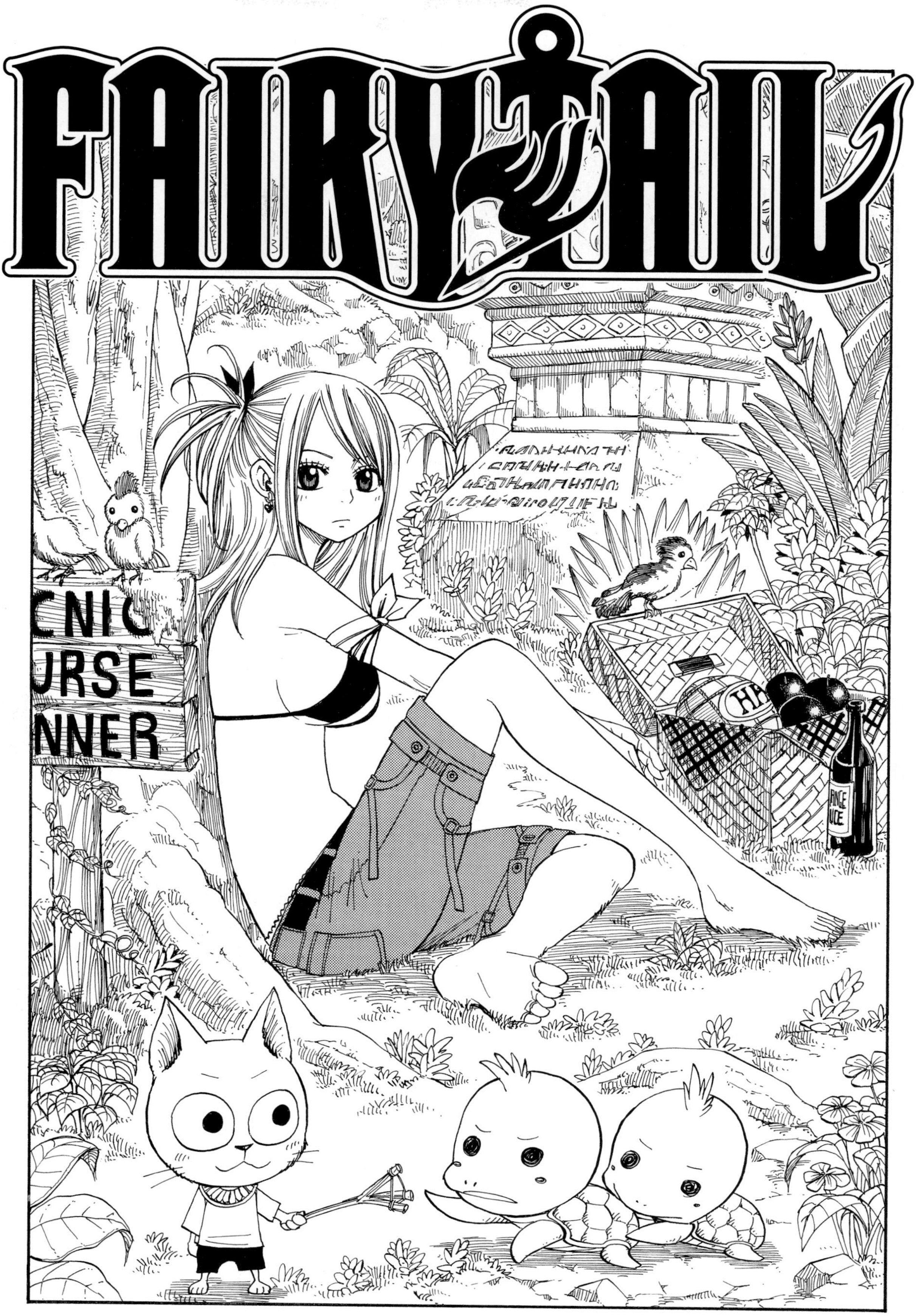
FAIRY TAIL
CNIC
URSE
NNER

Chapter 55: So No One Sees the Tears

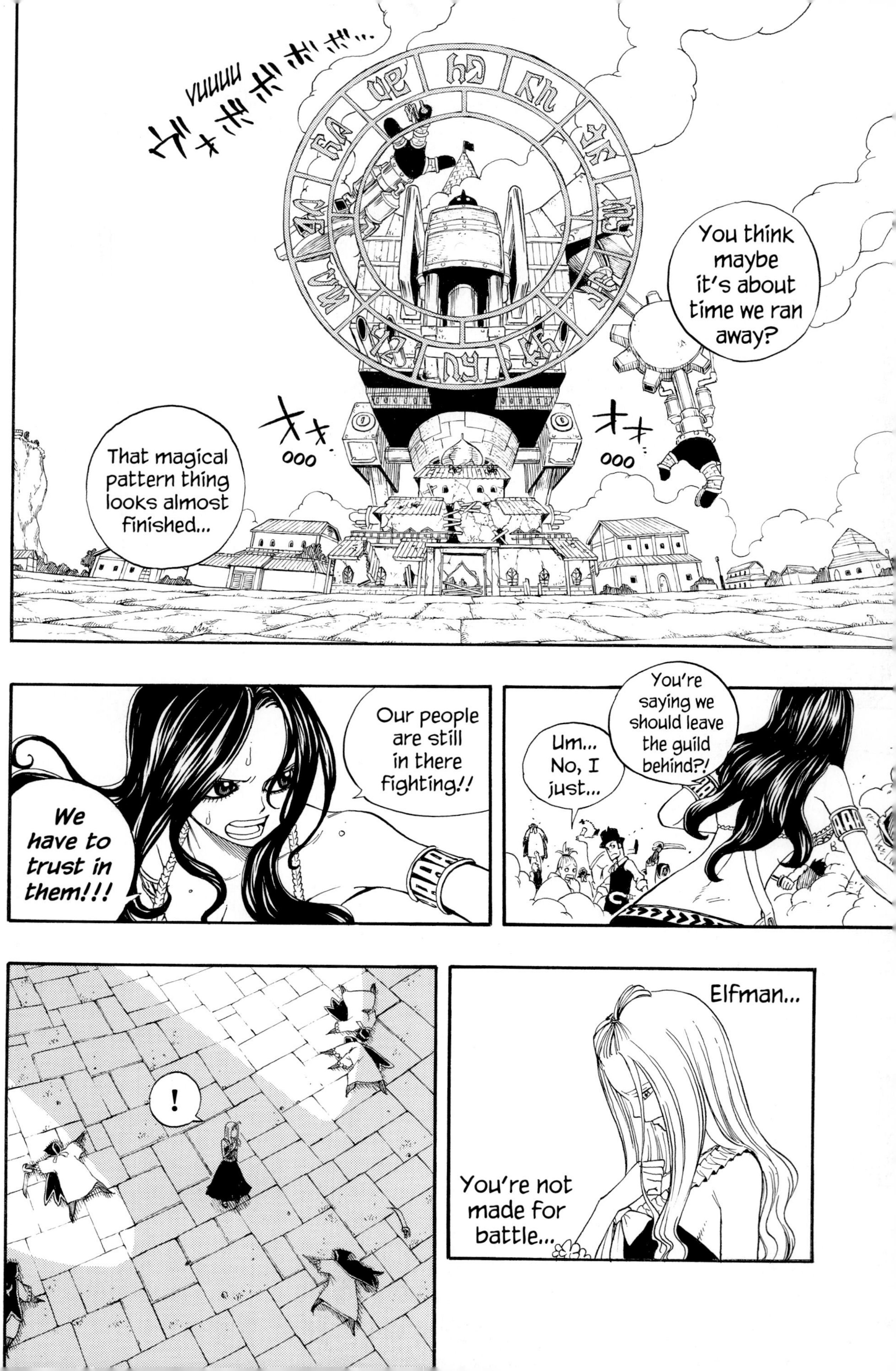
VUUUU
You think maybe it's about time we ran away?
OOO
OOO
That magical pattern thing looks almost finished...
You're saying we should leave the guild behind?!
Um... No, I just...
Our people are still in there fighting!!
We have to trust in them!!!
Elfman...
You're not made for battle...
!

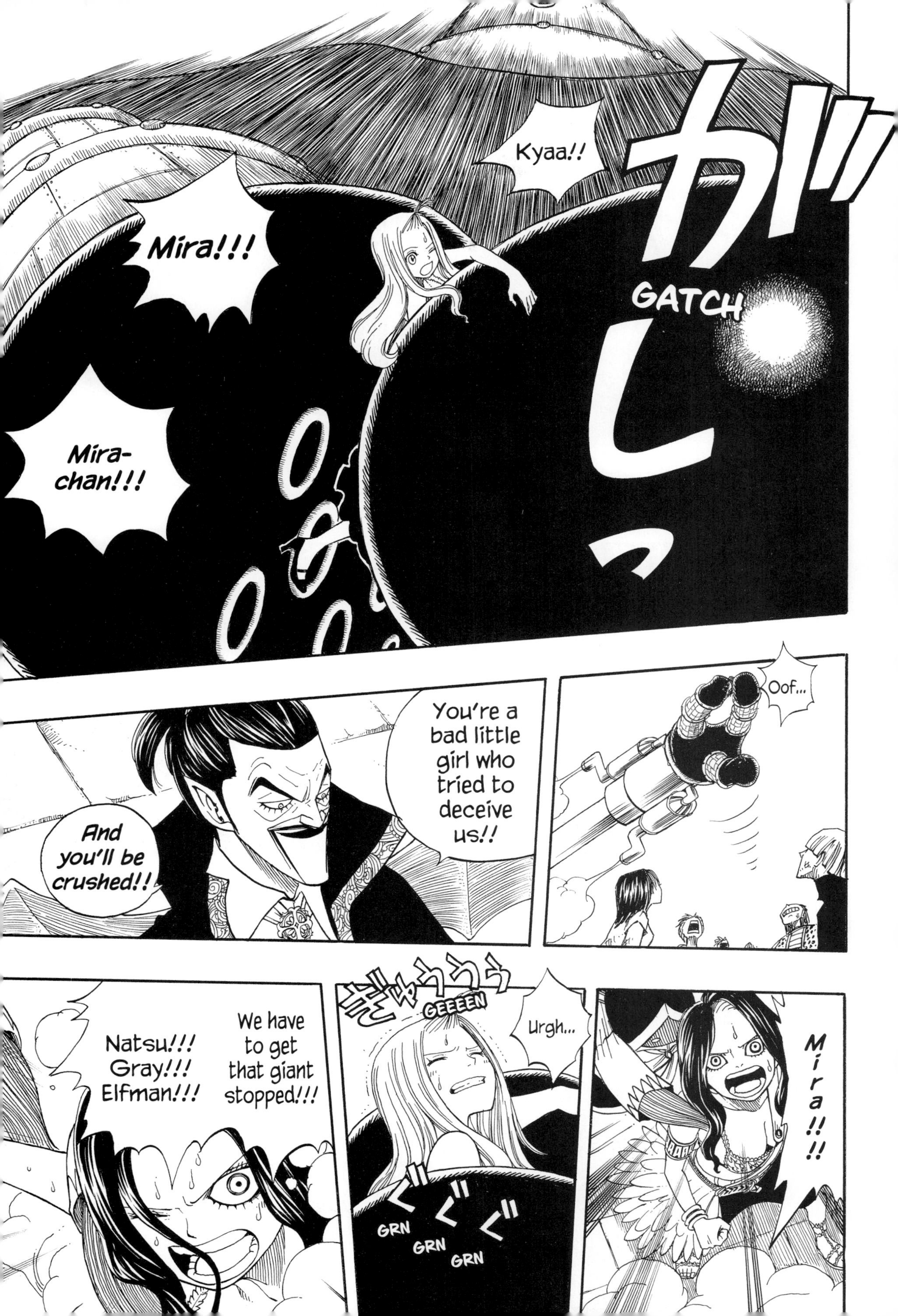

ガしっ
GATCH
Kyaa!!
Mira!!!
Mira-chan!!!
Oof...
You're a bad little girl who tried to deceive us!!
And you'll be crushed!!
Mira!!!!
ぎゅううう
GEEEEN
Urgh...
ぐぐぐ
GRN GRN GRN
We have to get that giant stopped!!!
Natsu!!! Gray!!! Elfman!!!

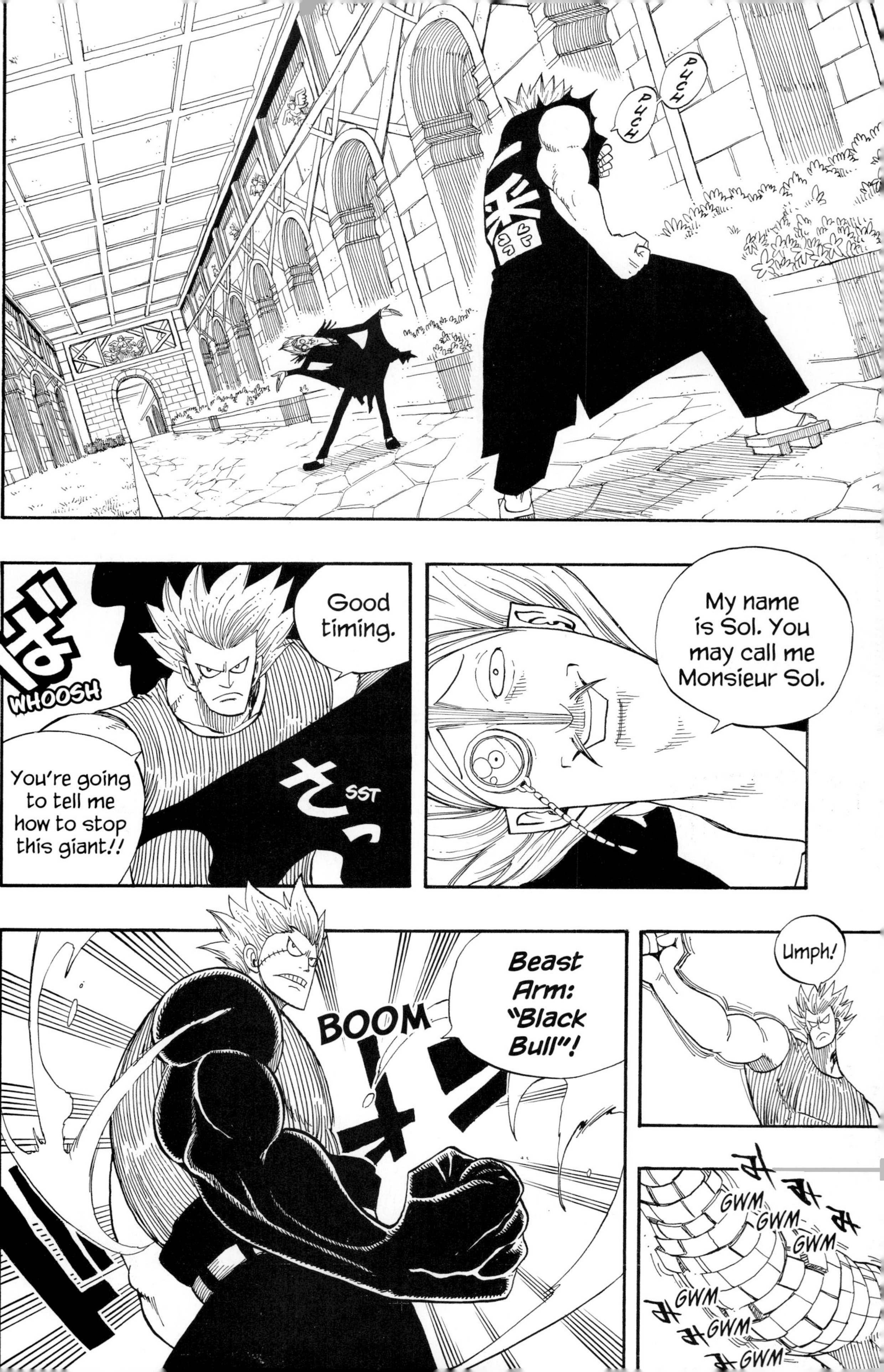
PUCH
PUCH
My name is Sol. You may call me Monsieur Sol.
Good timing.
WHOOSH
You're going to tell me how to stop this giant!!
SST
Umph!
GWM
GWM
GWM
GWM
GWM
GWM
Beast Arm: "Black Bull"!
BOOM

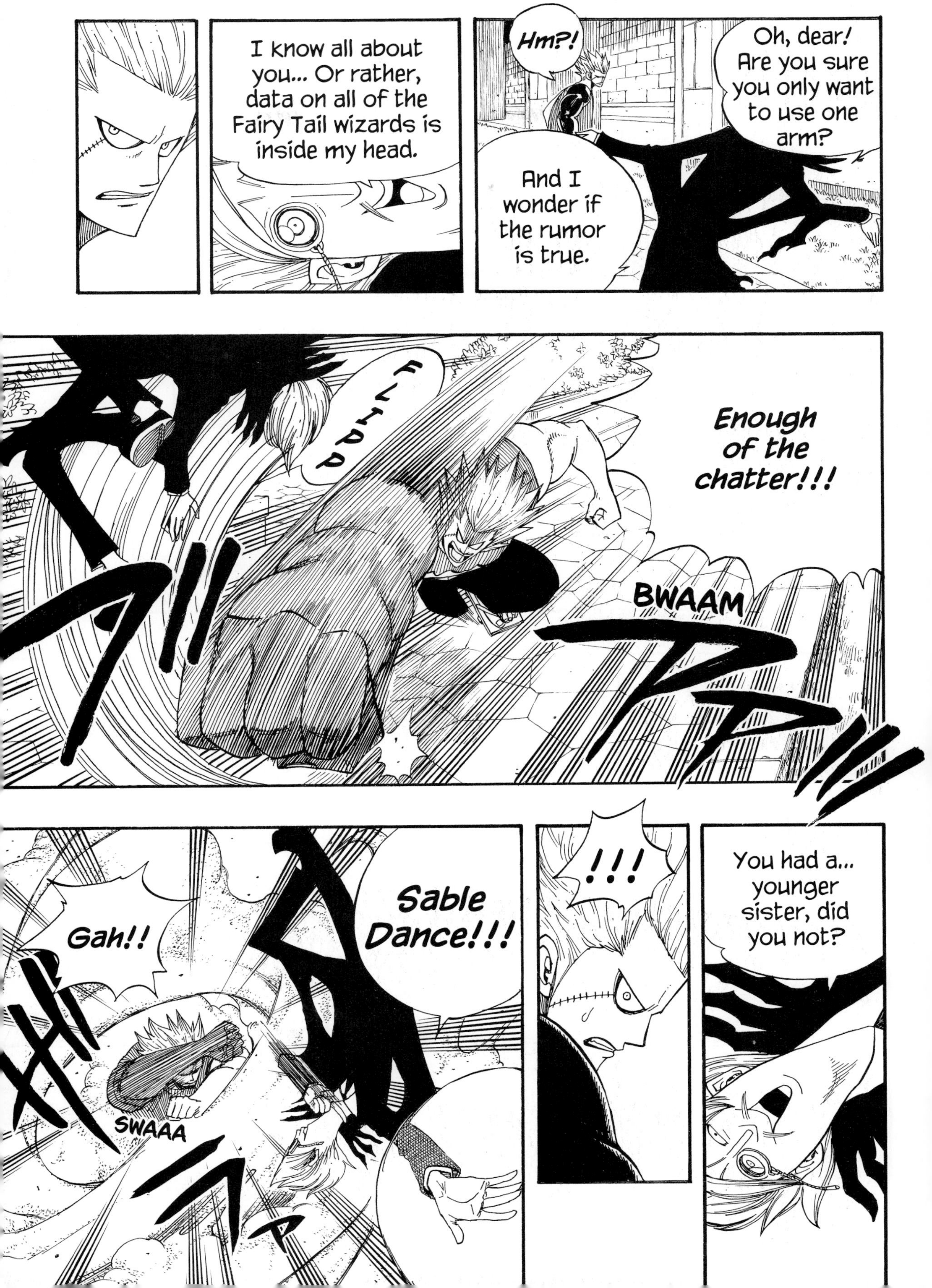
Oh, dear! Are you sure you only want to use one arm?
Hm?!
And I wonder if the rumor is true.
I know all about you... Or rather, data on all of the Fairy Tail wizards is inside my head.
Enough of the chatter!!!
BWAAM
FLIPP
You had a... younger sister, did you not?
!!!
Sable Dance!!!
Gah!!
SWAAA

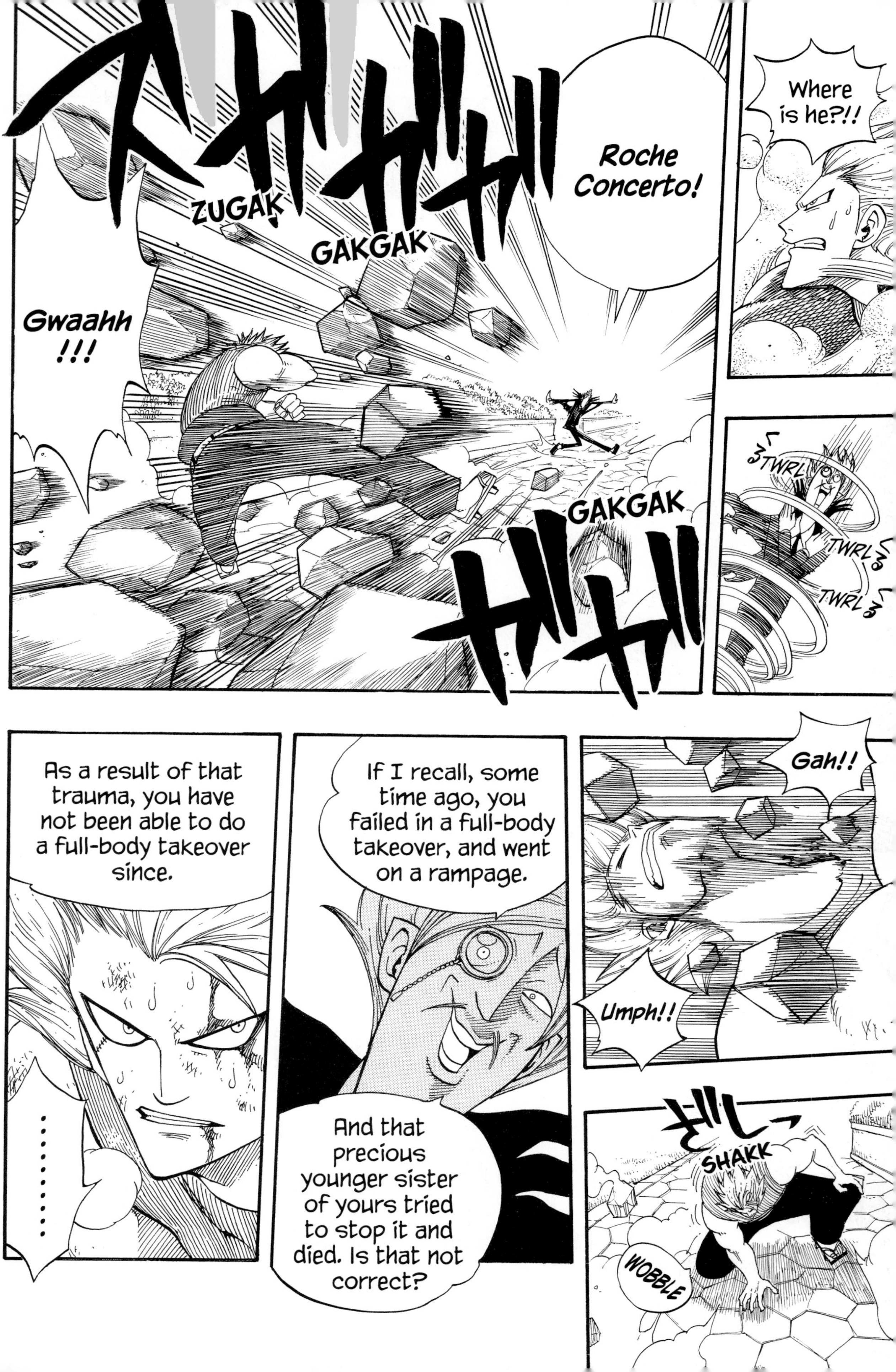

Where is he?!!
TWRL
TWRL
TWRL
Roche Concerto!
ZUGAK
GAKGAK
Gwaahh!!!
GAKGAK
Gah!!
Umph!!
SHAKK
WOBBLE
If I recall, some time ago, you failed in a full-body takeover, and went on a rampage.
And that precious younger sister of yours tried to stop it and died. Is that not correct?
As a result of that trauma, you have not been able to do a full-body takeover since.
....

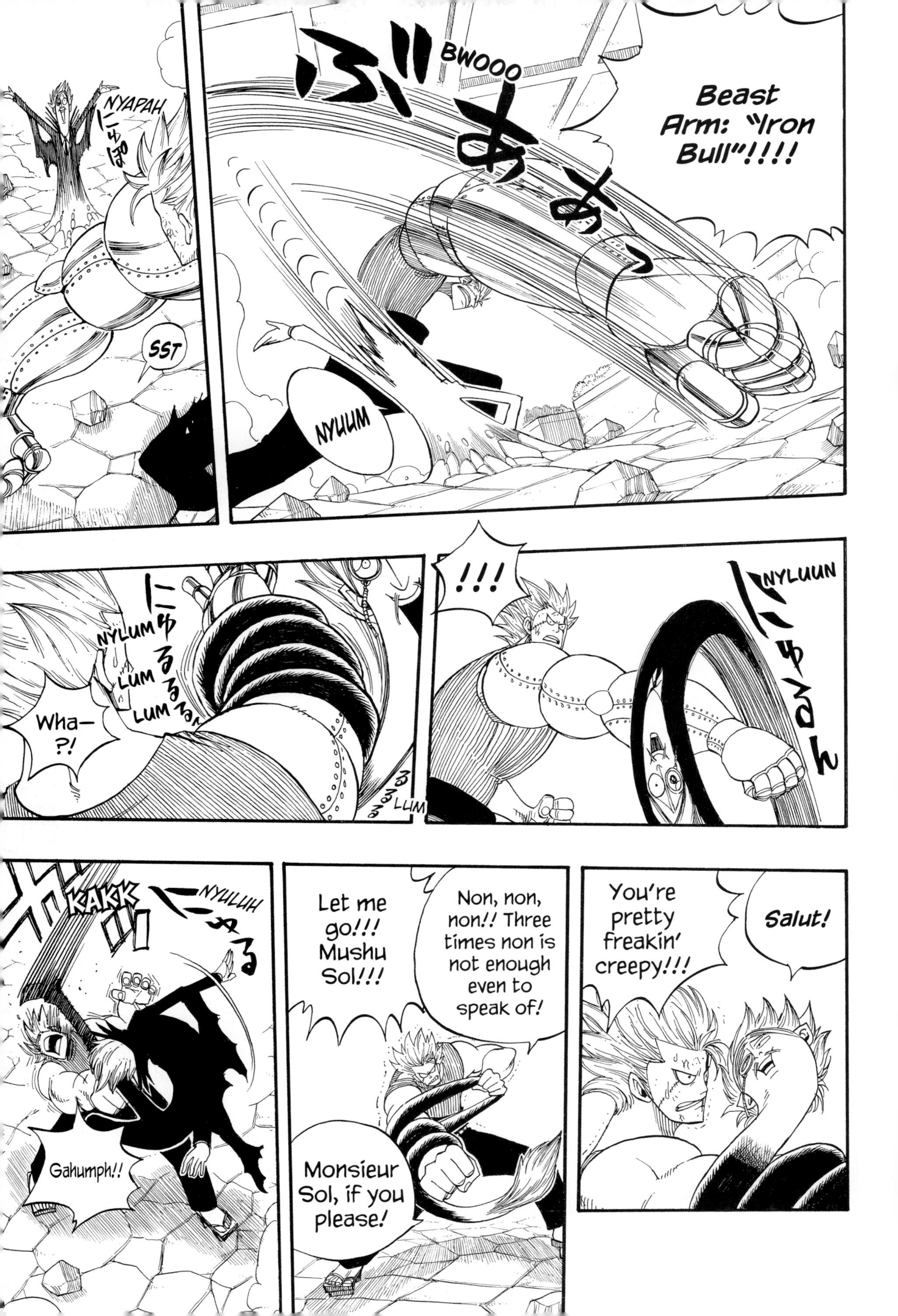
BWOOO
Beast Arm: "Iron Bull"!!!!
NYAPAH
SST
NYUUM
!!!
NYLUUN
NYLUM LUM LUM
Wha-?!
LUM
Salut!
You're pretty freakin' creepy!!!
Non, non, non!! Three times non is not enough even to speak of!
Let me go!!! Mushu Sol!!!
Monsieur Sol, if you please!
NYULUH
KAKK
Gahumph!!

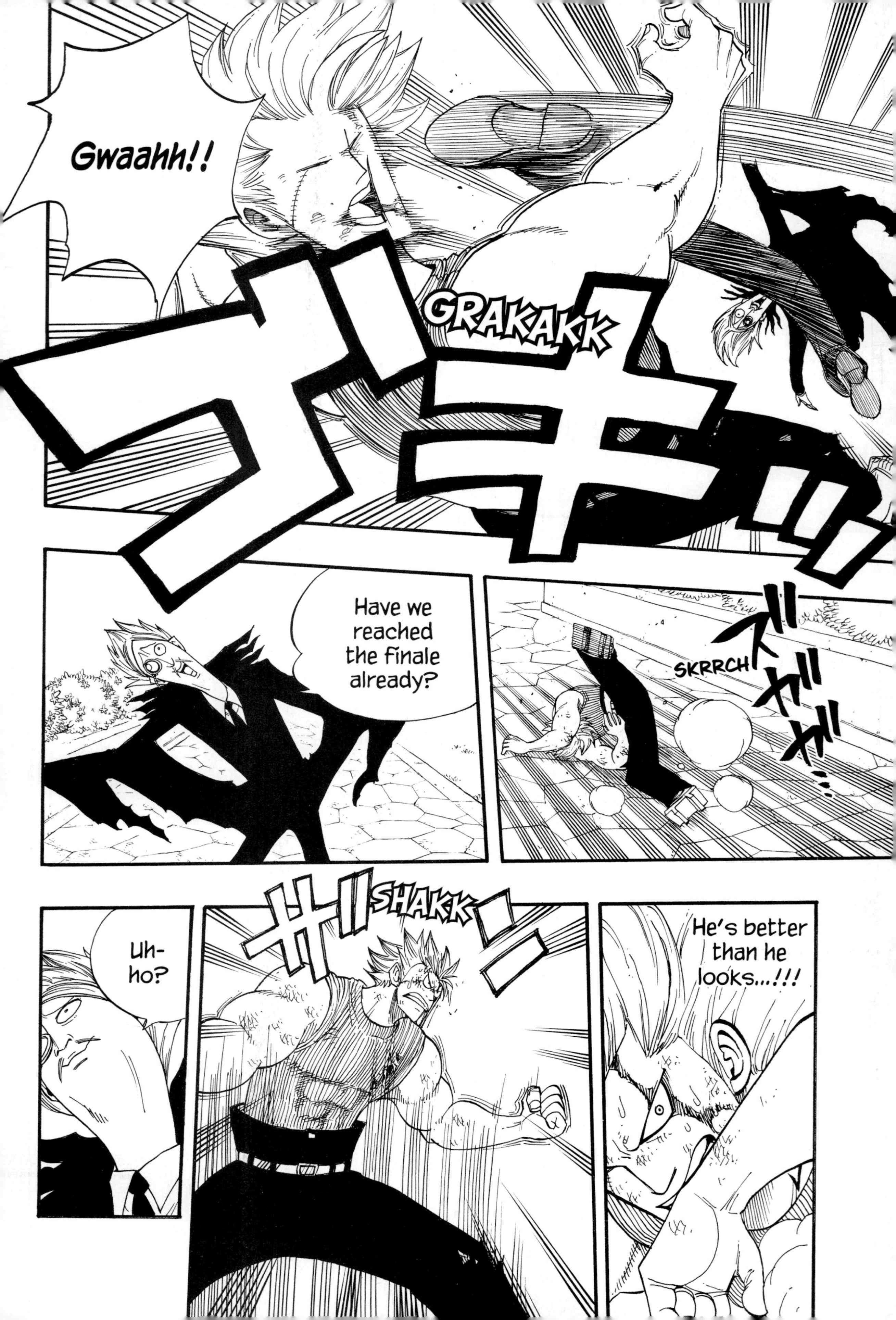
Gwaahh!!
GRAKAKK
SKRRCH
Have we reached the finale already?
He's better than he looks...!!!
SHAKK
Uh-ho?

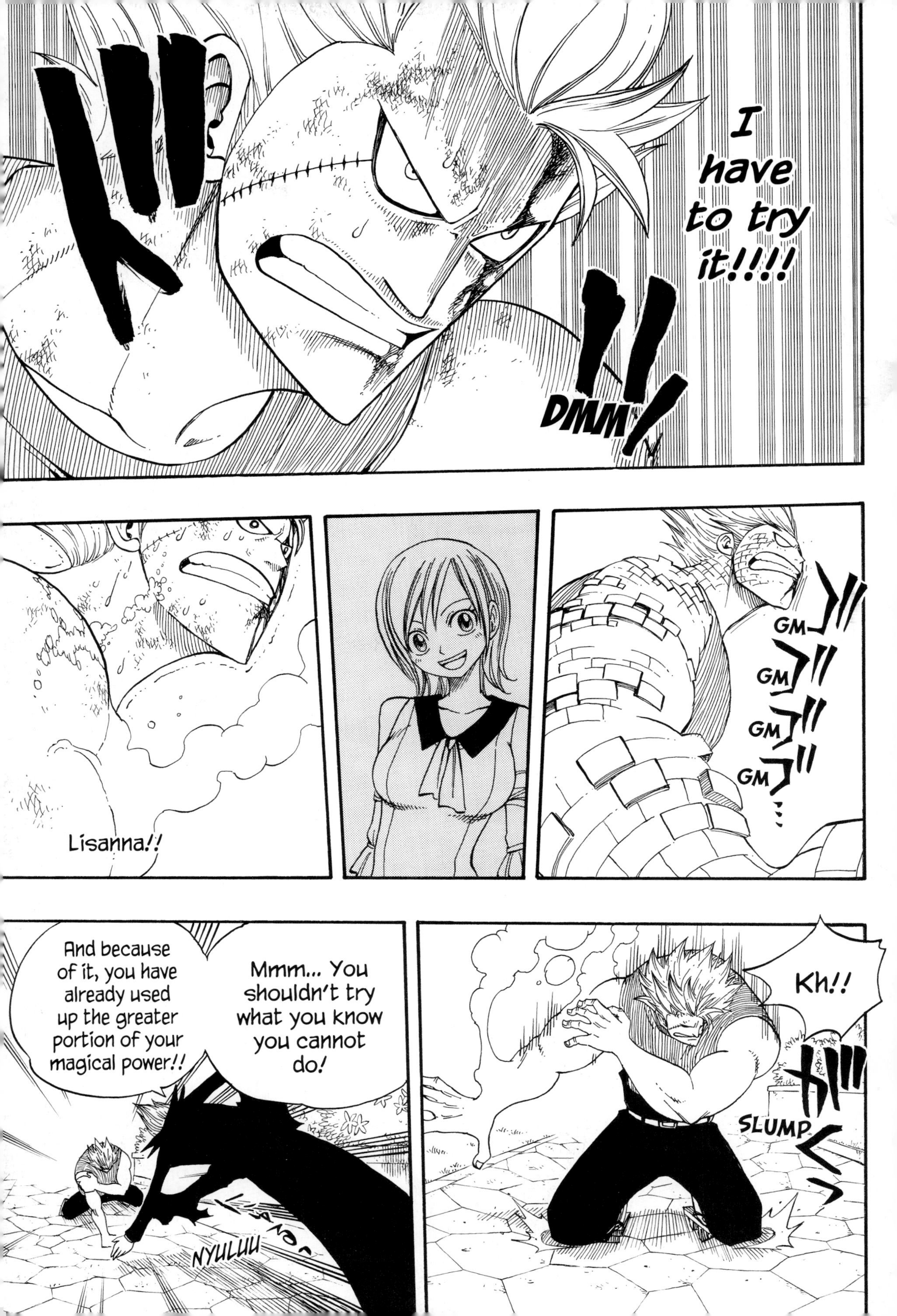
I have to try it!!!!
DMM
GM
GM
GM
GM
Lisanna!!
Kh!!
SLUMP
Mmm... You shouldn't try what you know you cannot do!
And because of it, you have already used up the greater portion of your magical power!!
NYULUU

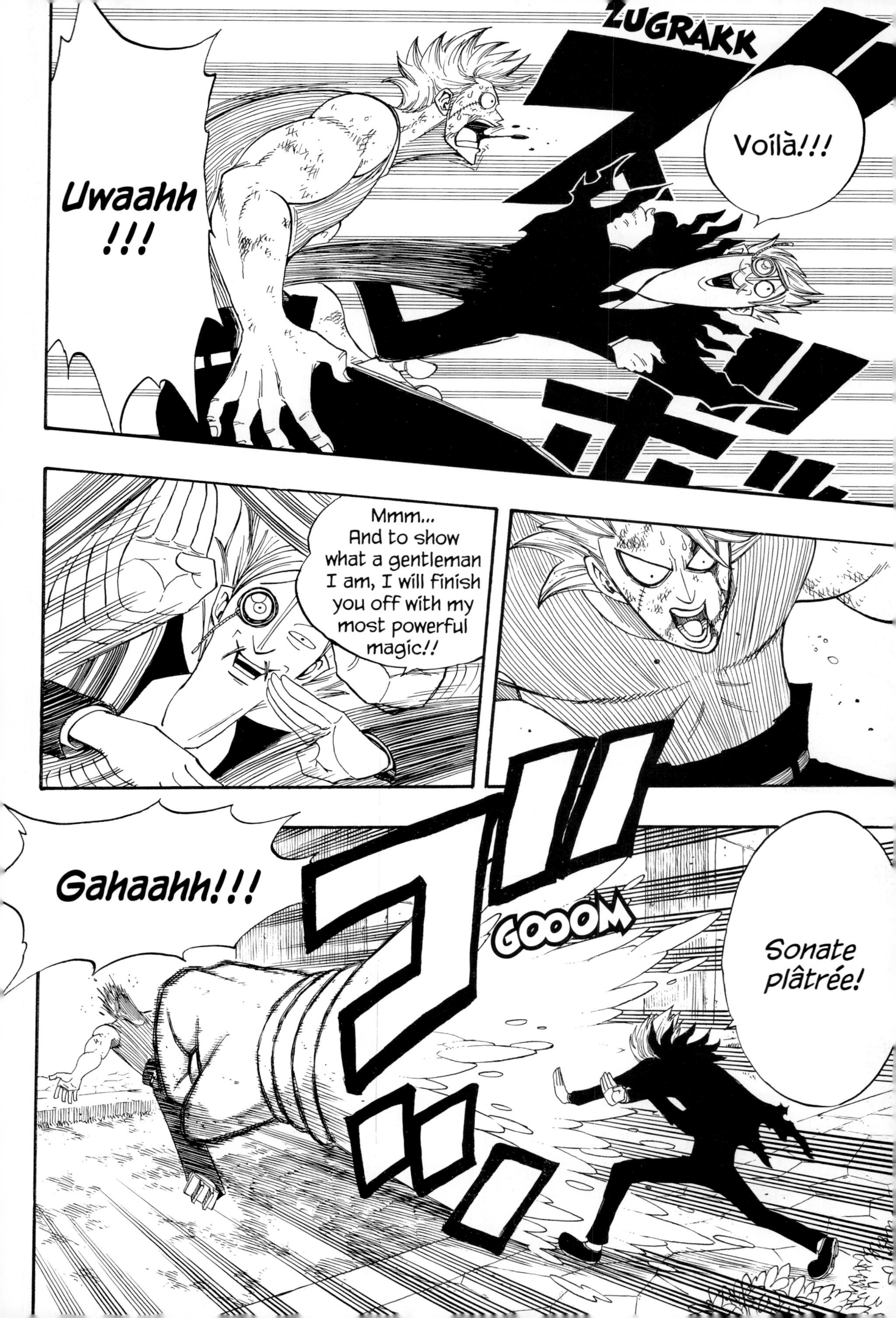
ZUGRAKK
Voilà!!!
Uwaahh!!!
Mmm... And to show what a gentleman I am, I will finish you off with my most powerful magic!!
Sonate plâtrée!
GOOOM
Gahaahh!!!

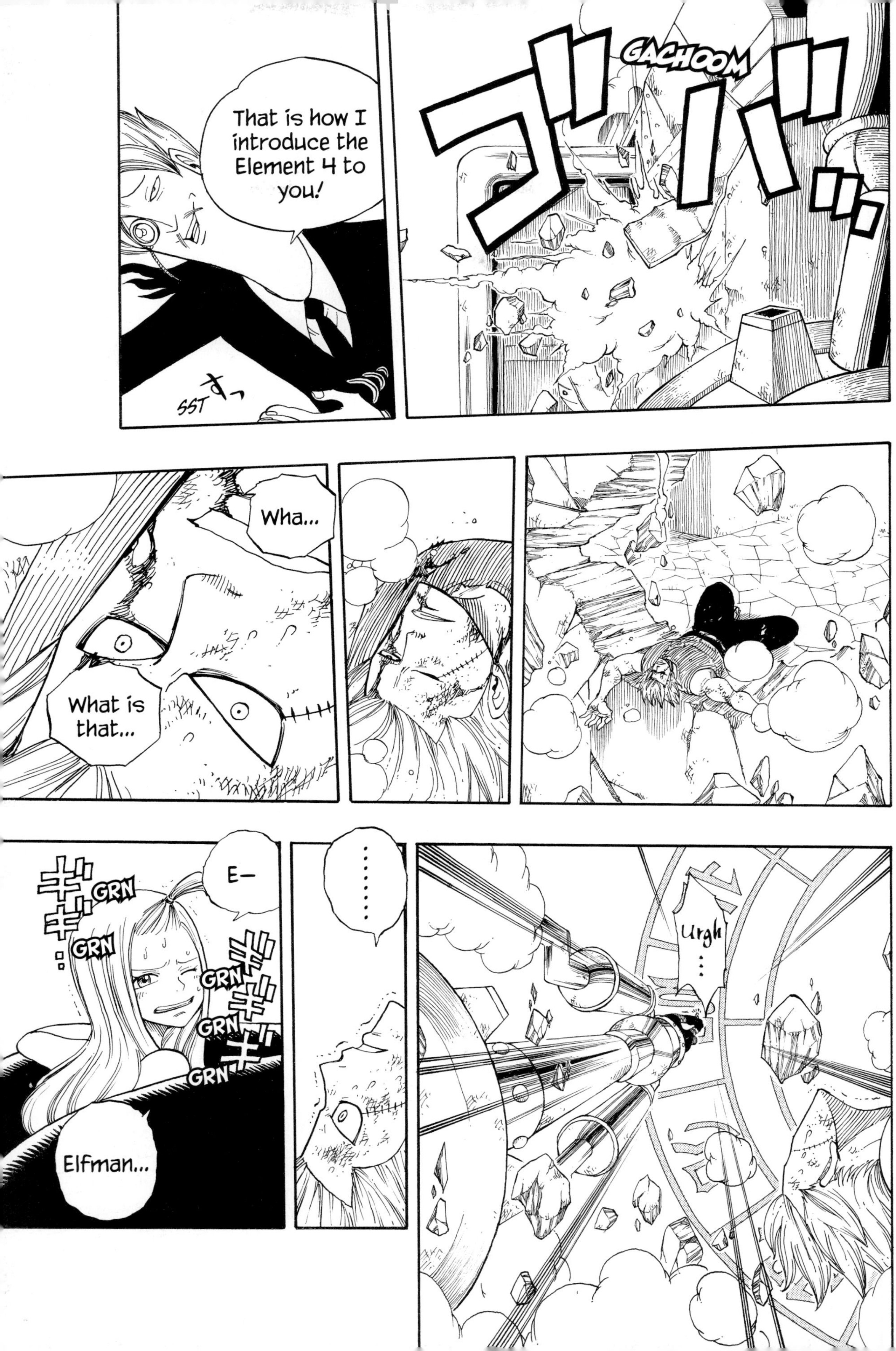
GACHOOM
That is how I introduce the Element 4 to you!
SST
Wha...
What is that...
Urgh...
....
E—
GRN
GRN
GRN
GRN
GRN
Elfman...

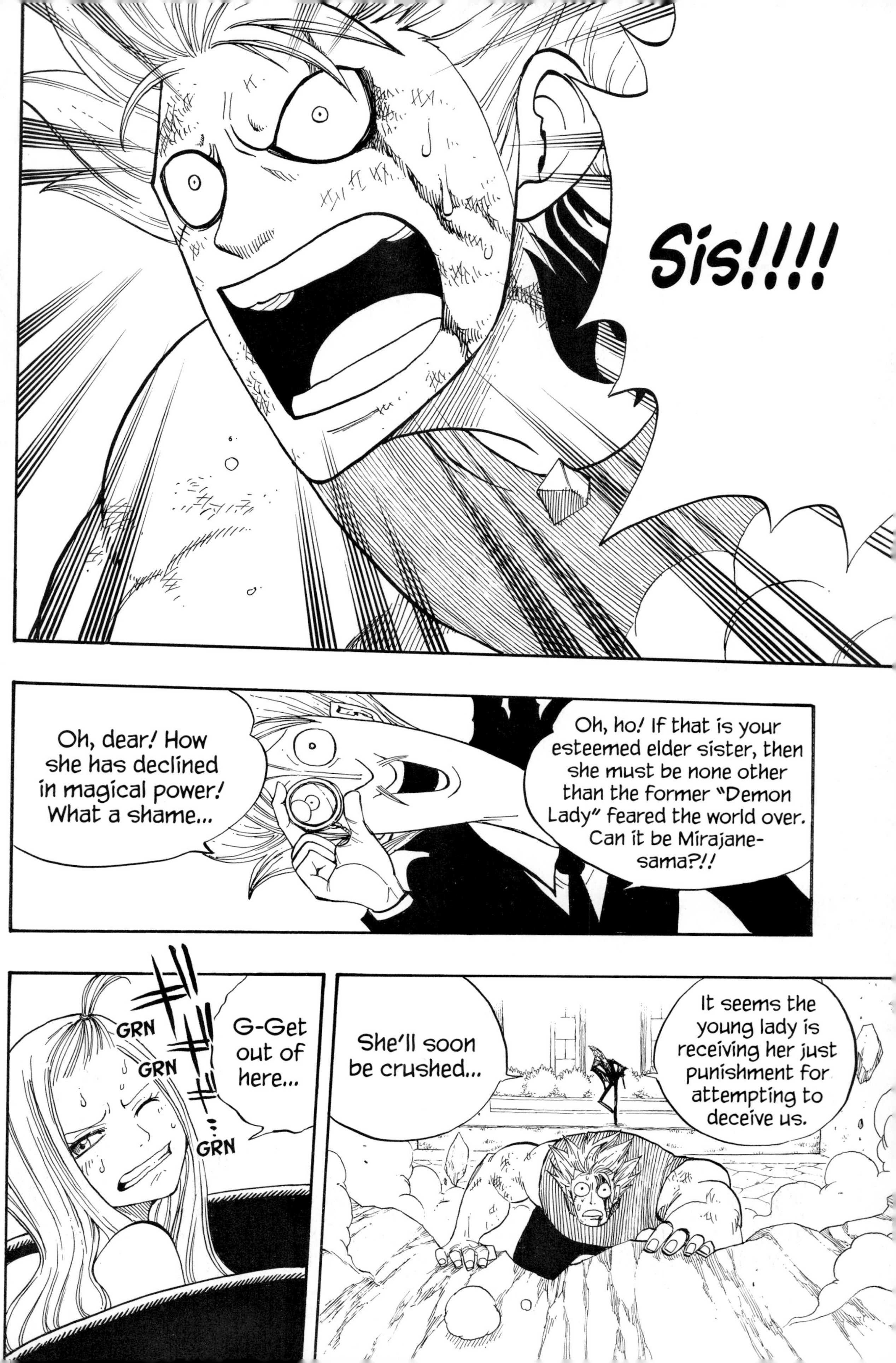
Sis!!!!
Oh, ho! If that is your esteemed elder sister, then she must be none other than the former "Demon Lady" feared the world over. Can it be Mirajane-sama?!!
Oh, dear! How she has declined in magical power! What a shame...
It seems the young lady is receiving her just punishment for attempting to deceive us.
She'll soon be crushed...
G-Get out of here...
GRN
GRN
GRN

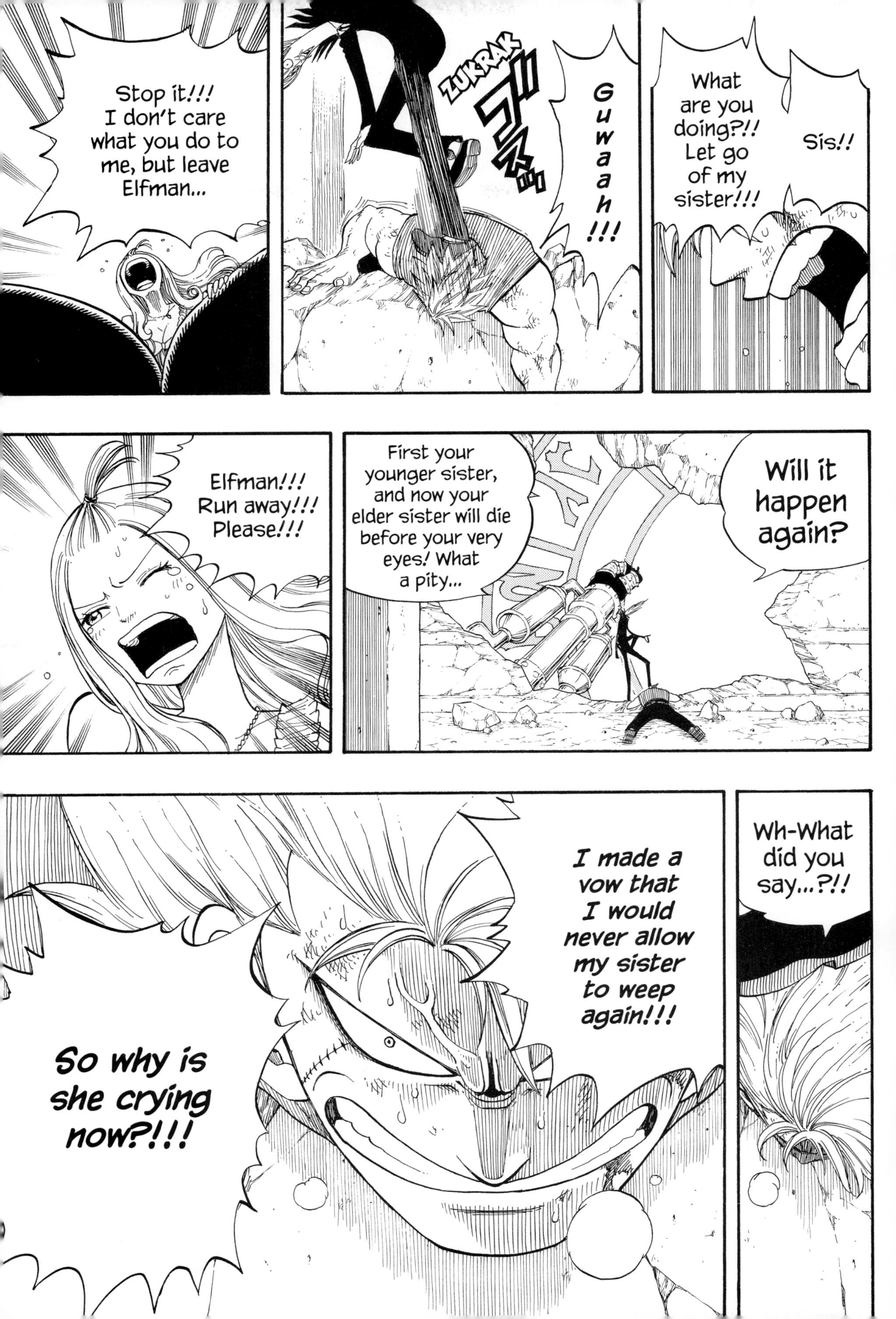
Sis!!
What are you doing?!! Let go of my sister!!!
ZUKRAK
Guwaah!!!
Stop it!!! I don't care what you do to me, but leave Elfman...
Will it happen again?
First your younger sister, and now your elder sister will die before your very eyes! What a pity...
Elfman!!! Run away!!! Please!!!
Wh-What did you say...?!!
I made a vow that I would never allow my sister to weep again!!!
So why is she crying now?!!!

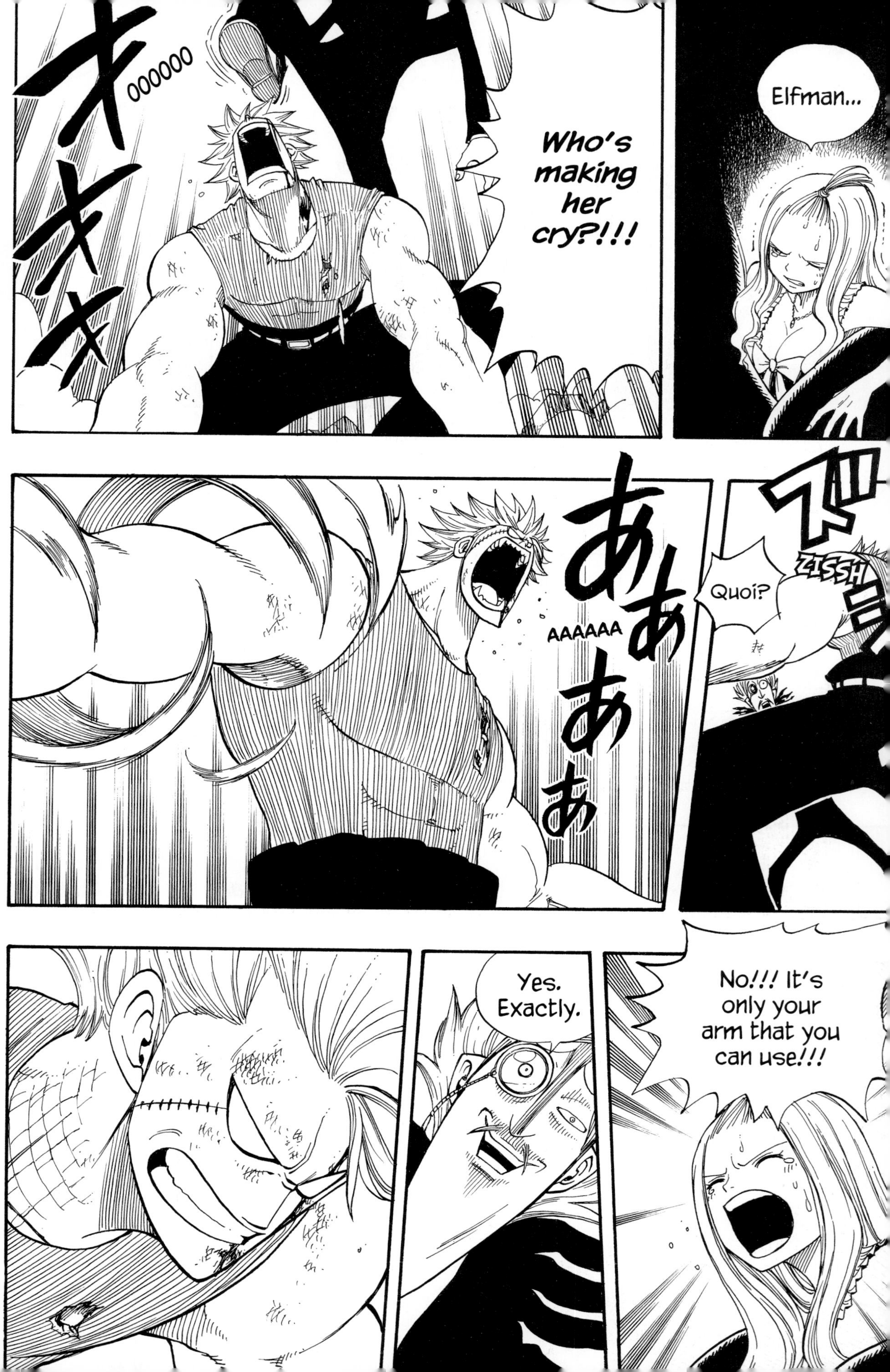
Elfman...
OOOOOO
Who's making her cry?!!!
ZISSH
Quoi?
AAAAAA
No!!! It's only your arm that you can use!!!
Yes. Exactly.

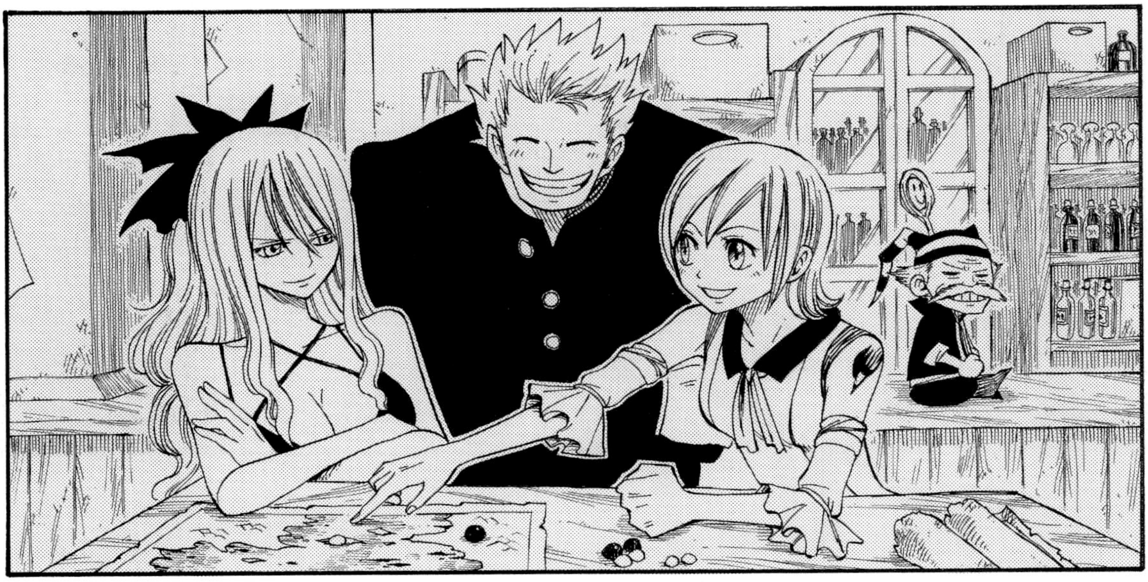

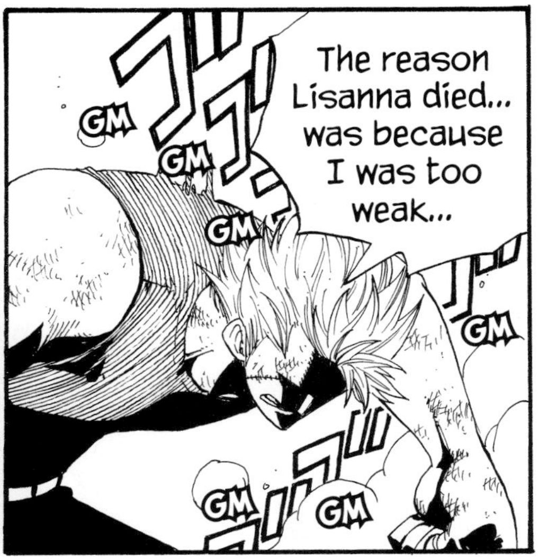
The reason Lisanna died... was because I was too weak...
GM GM GM GM GM GM

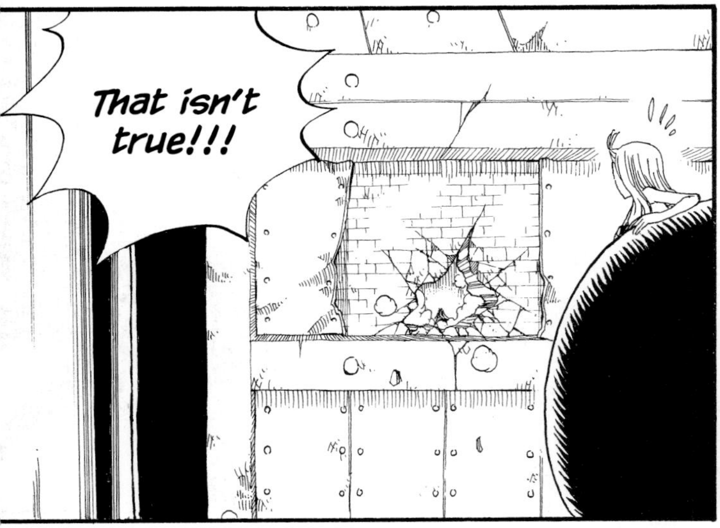
That isn't true!!!

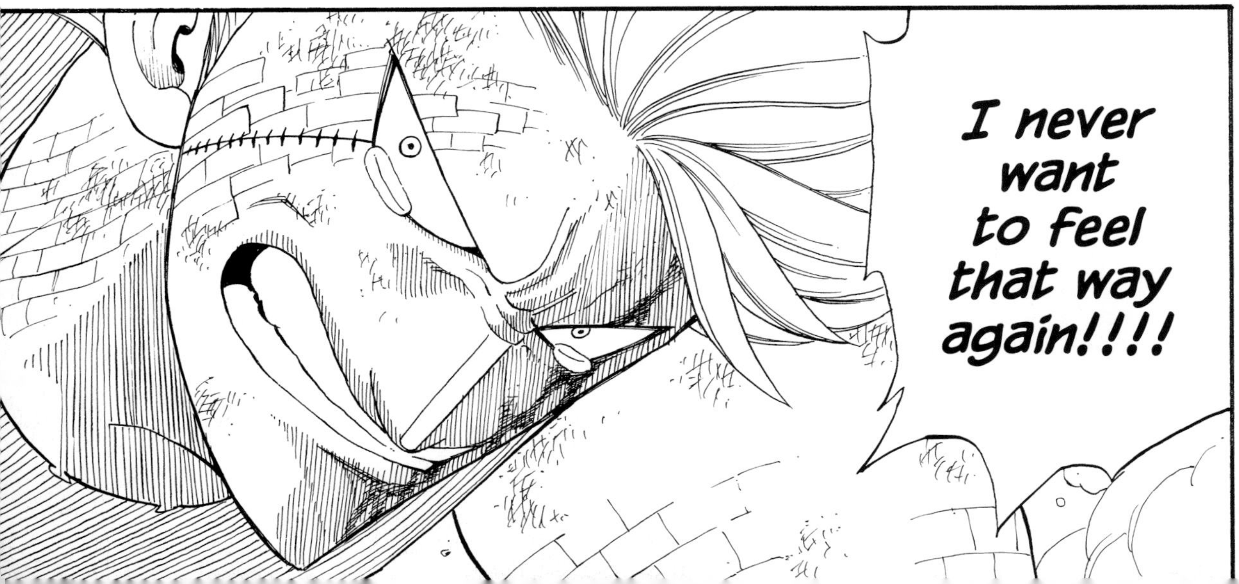
I never want to feel that way again!!!!

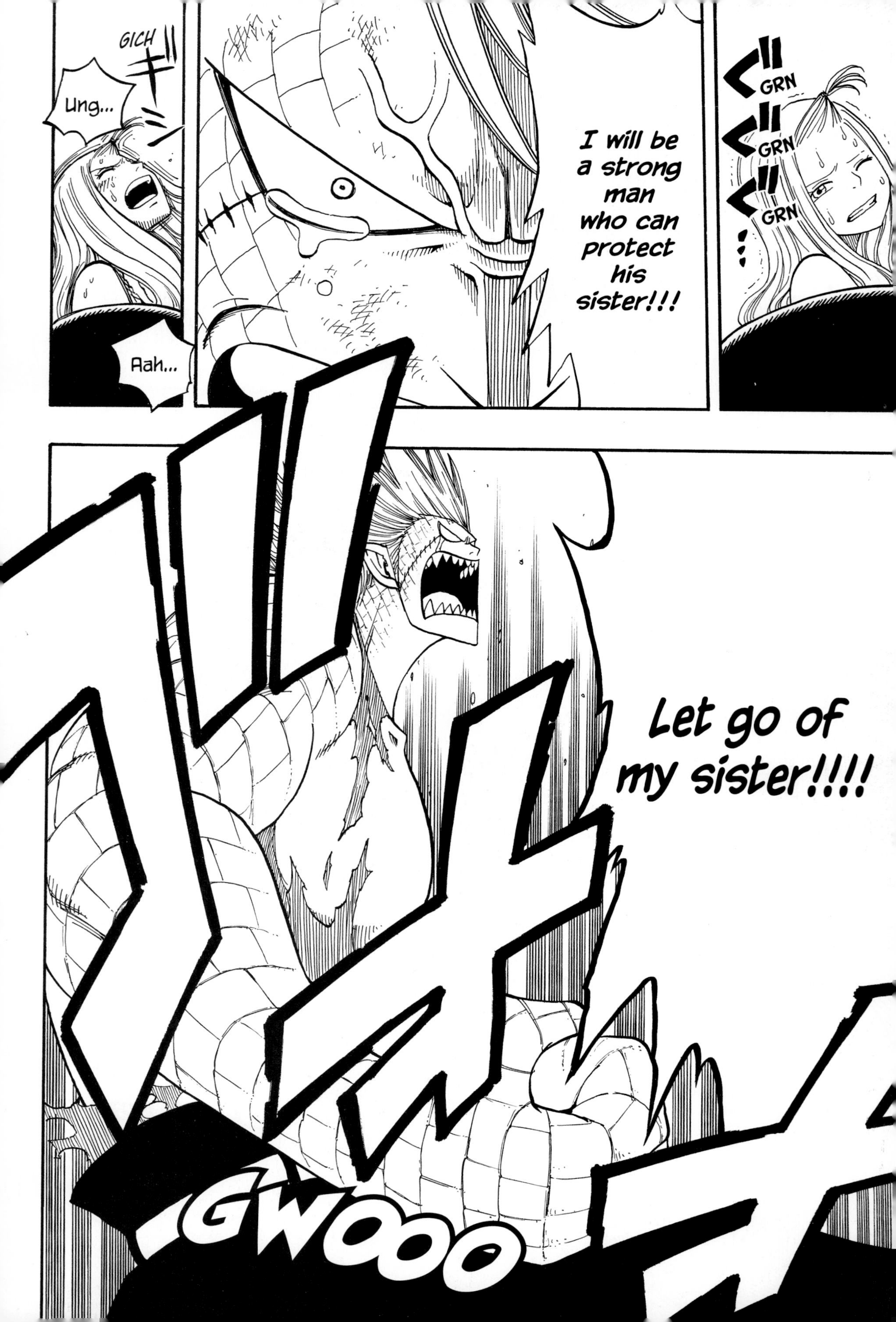
GRN
GRN
GRN
I will be a strong man who can protect his sister!!!
GICH
Ung...
Aah...
Let go of my sister!!!!
GWOOO

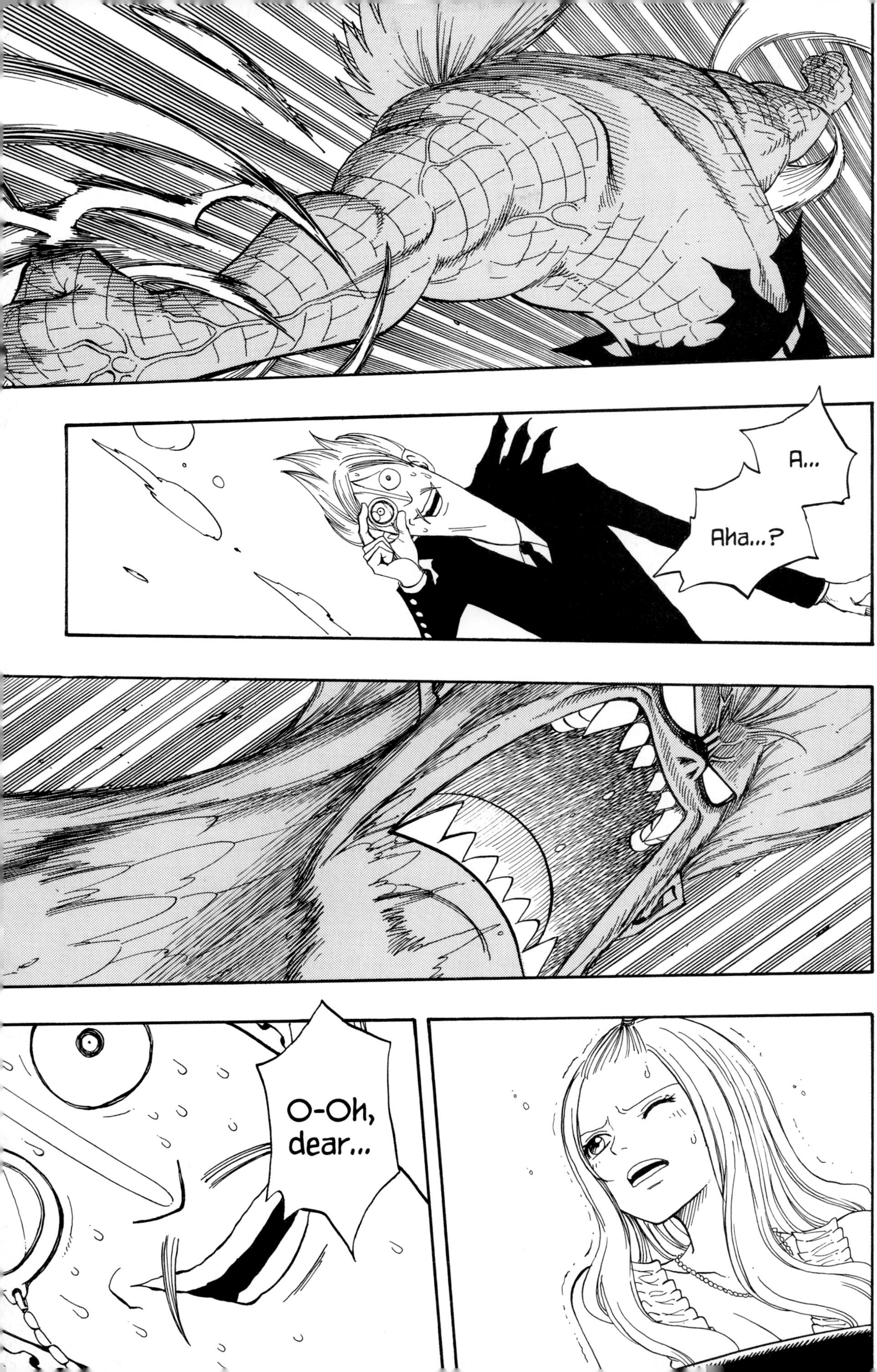
A...
Aha...?
O-Oh, dear...

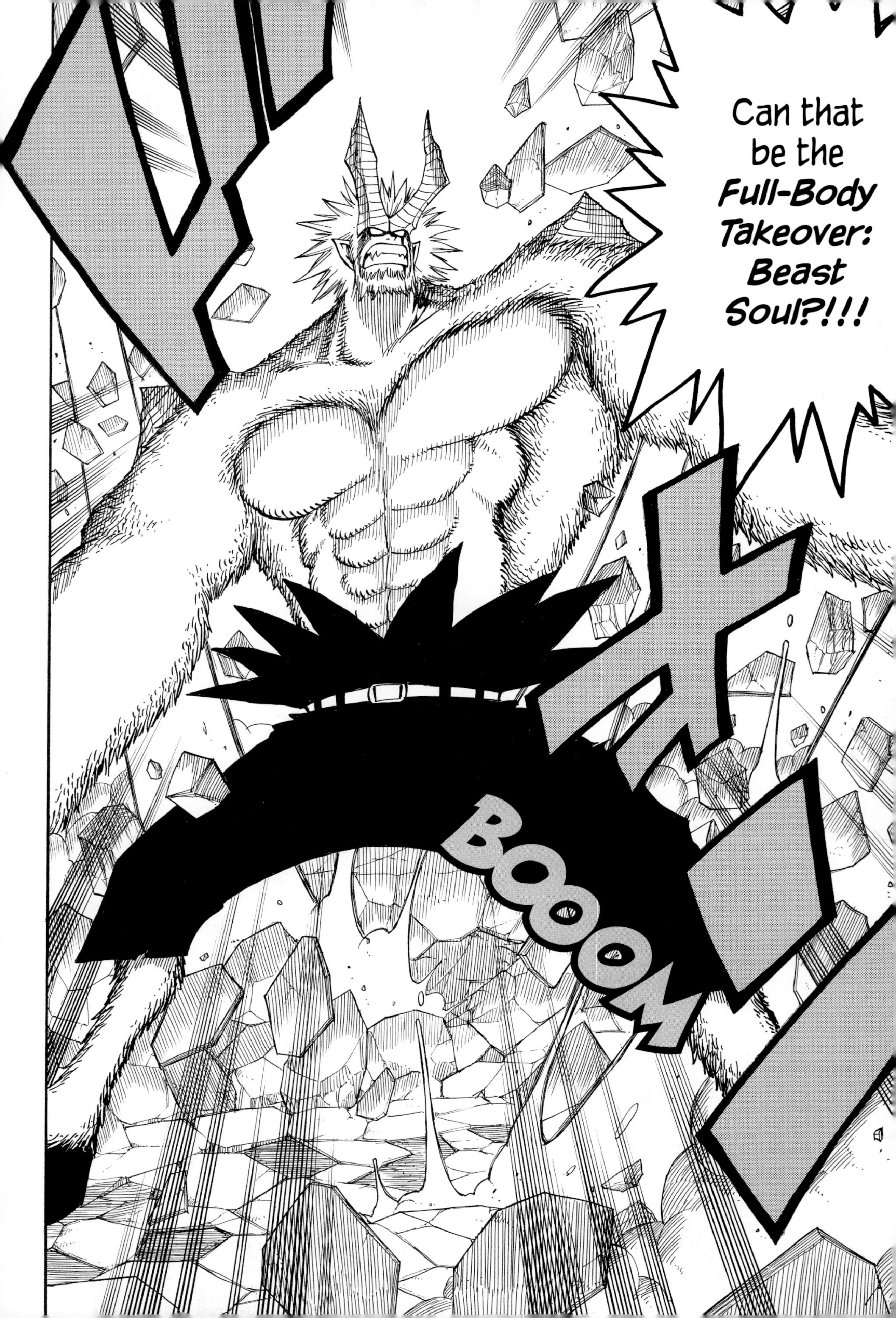
Can that be the *Full-Body Takeover: Beast Soul?!!!*
BOOOM

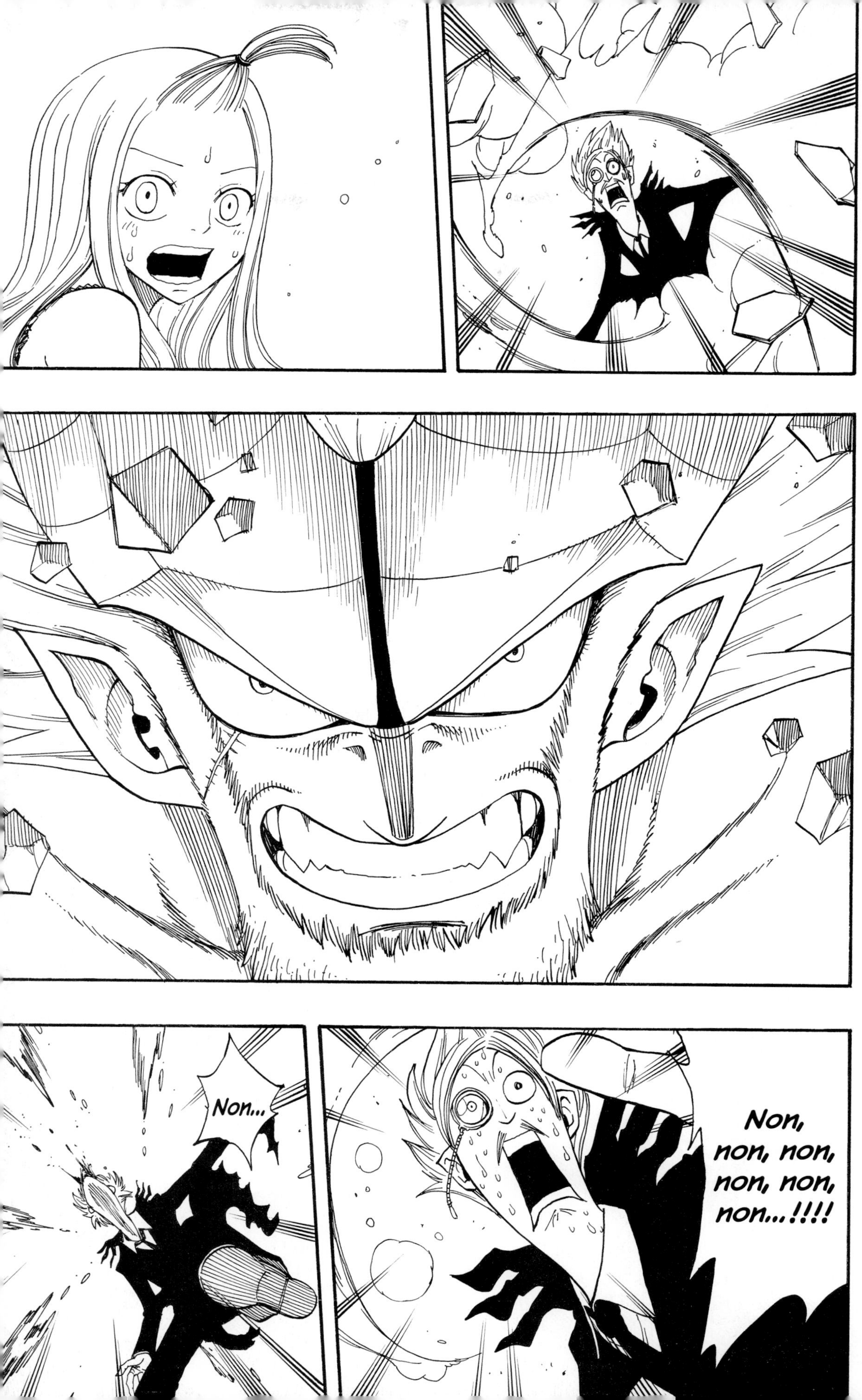
Non, non, non, non, non, non...!!!!
Non...

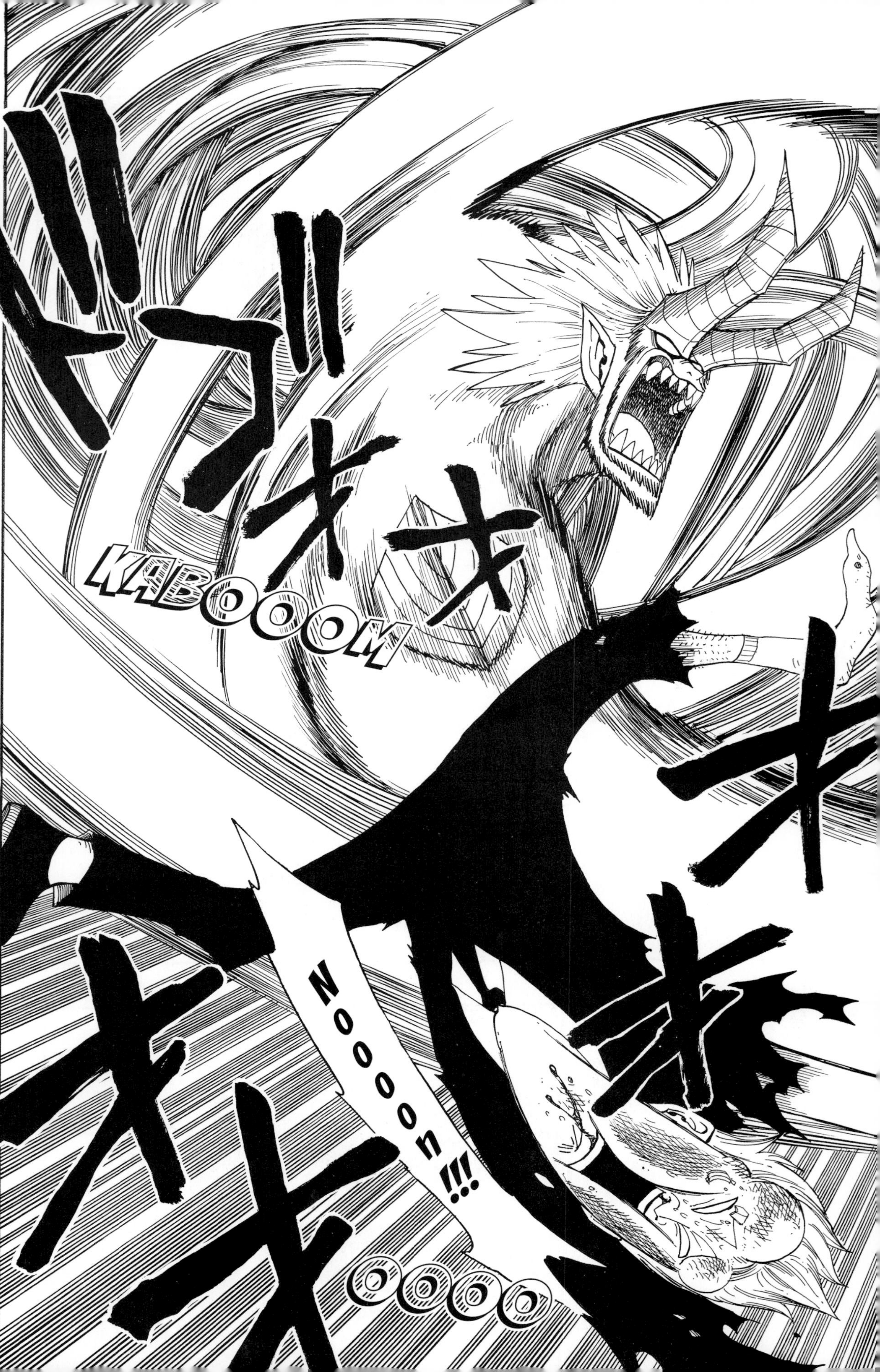
KABOOOM
Noooon!!!
OOOOO

FAIRY TAIL

Chapter 56: A Flower Blooms in the Rain

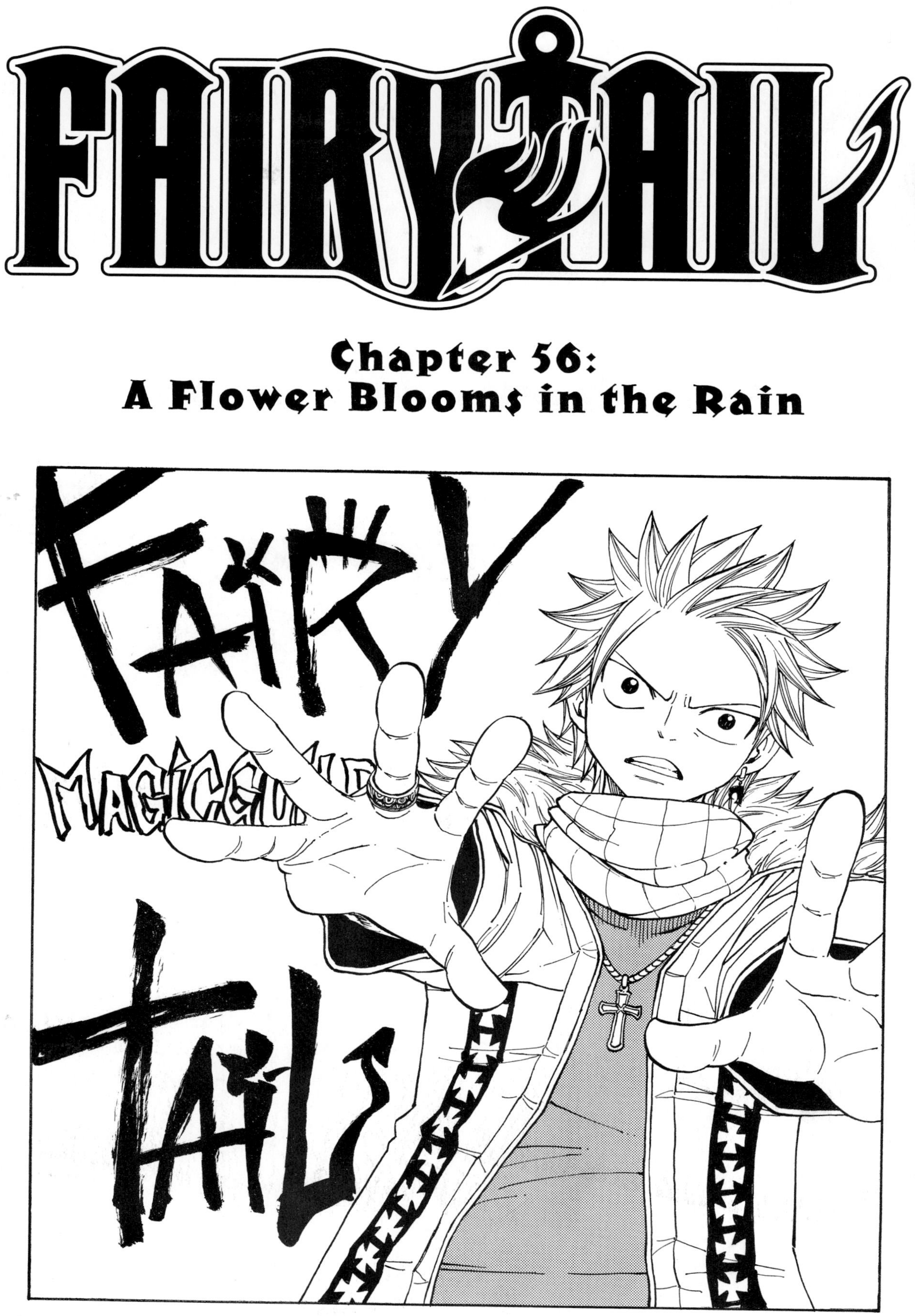
FAIRY
TAIL

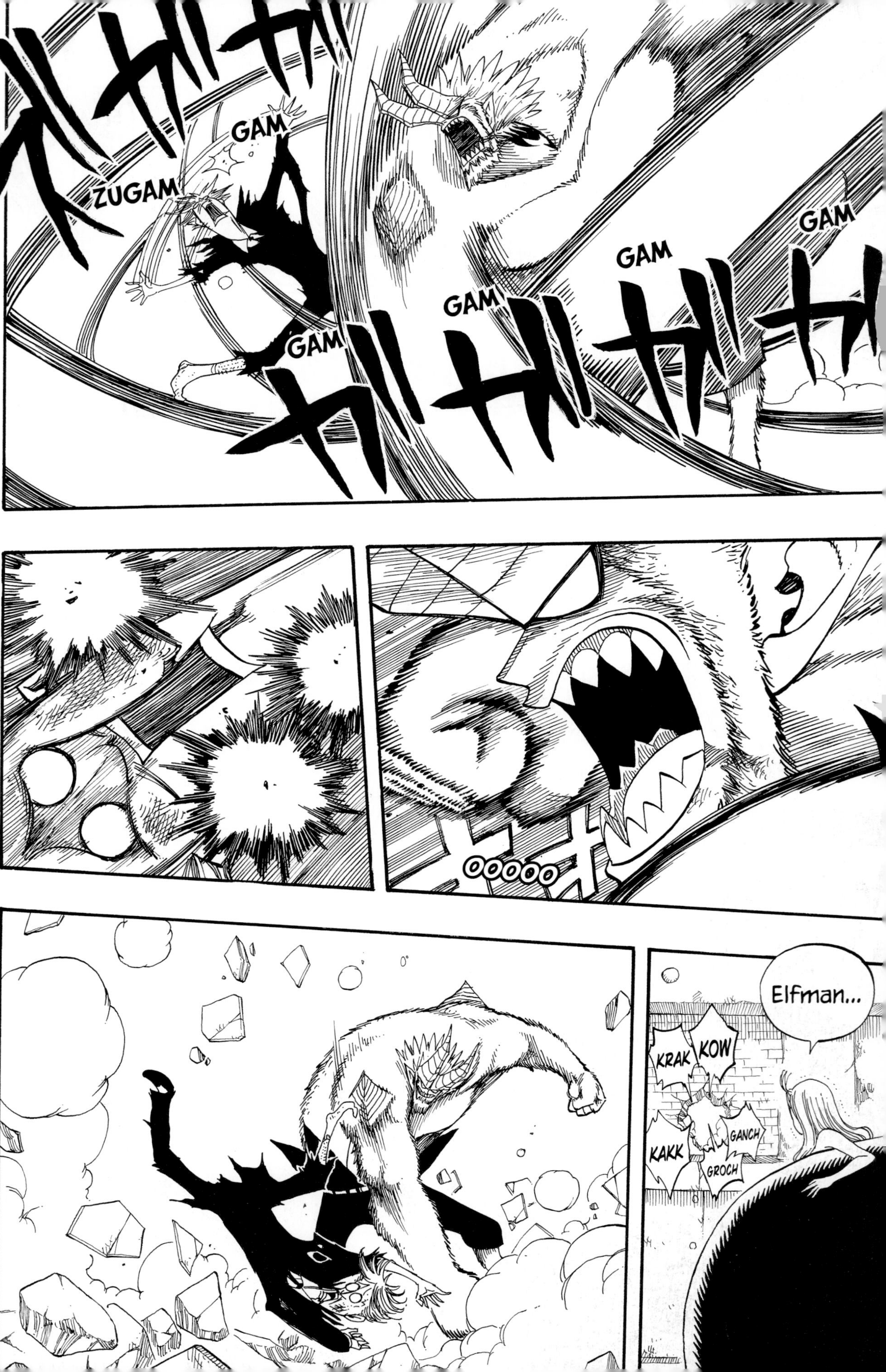
GAM
GAM
GAM
GAM
GAM
ZUGAM
OOOOO
Elfman...
KOW
KRAK
GANCH
GROCH
KAKK

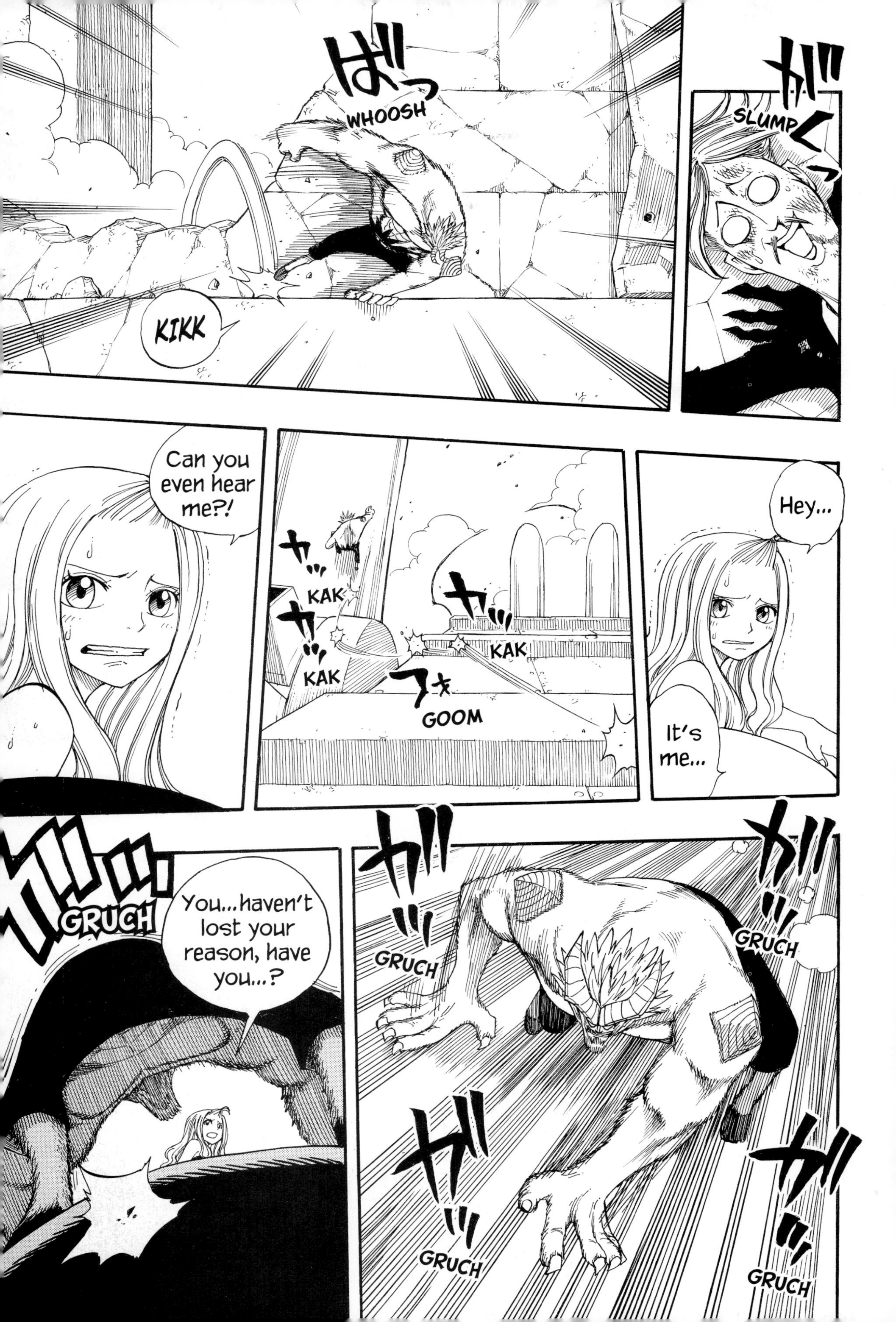

WHOOSH
KIKK
SLUMP
Hey...
It's me...
KAK
KAK
KAK
GOOM
Can you even hear me?!
GRUCH
GRUCH
GRUCH
GRUCH
GRUCH
You...haven't lost your reason, have you...?

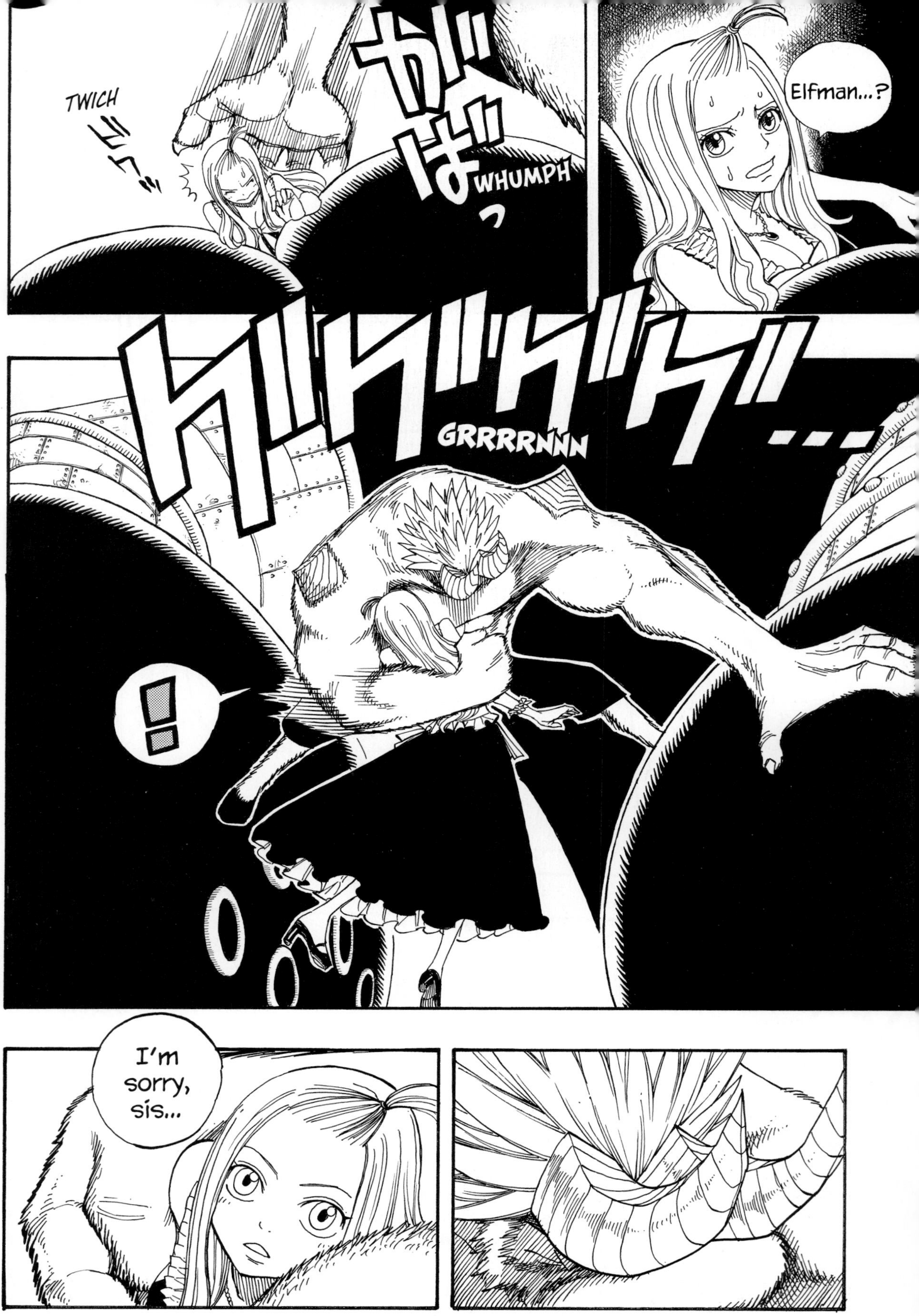
Elfman...?
TWICH
WHUMPH
GRRRRNNN
!
I'm sorry, sis...

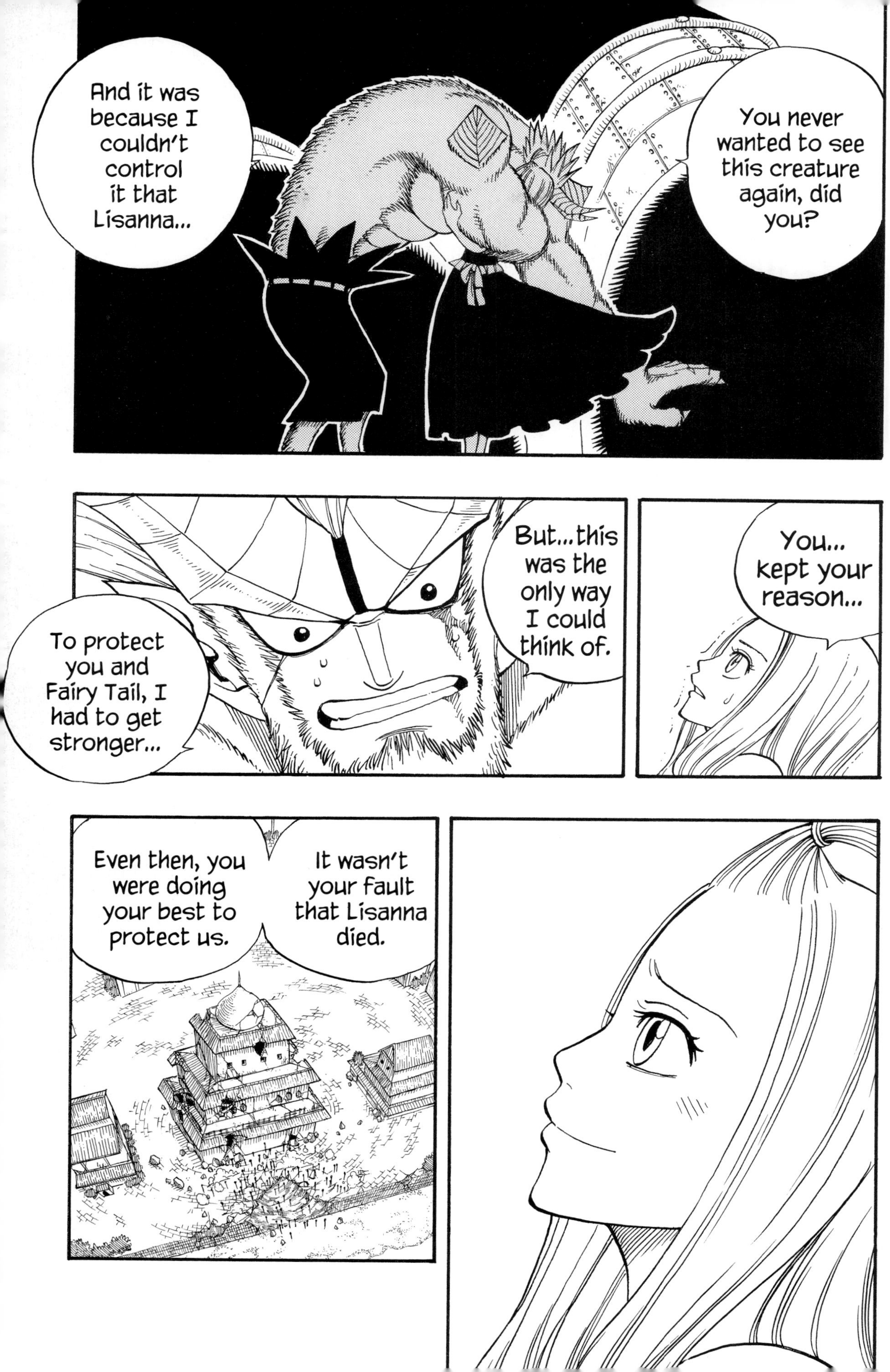
You never wanted to see this creature again, did you?
And it was because I couldn't control it that Lisanna...
You... kept your reason...
But...this was the only way I could think of.
To protect you and Fairy Tail, I had to get stronger...
It wasn't your fault that Lisanna died.
Even then, you were doing your best to protect us.

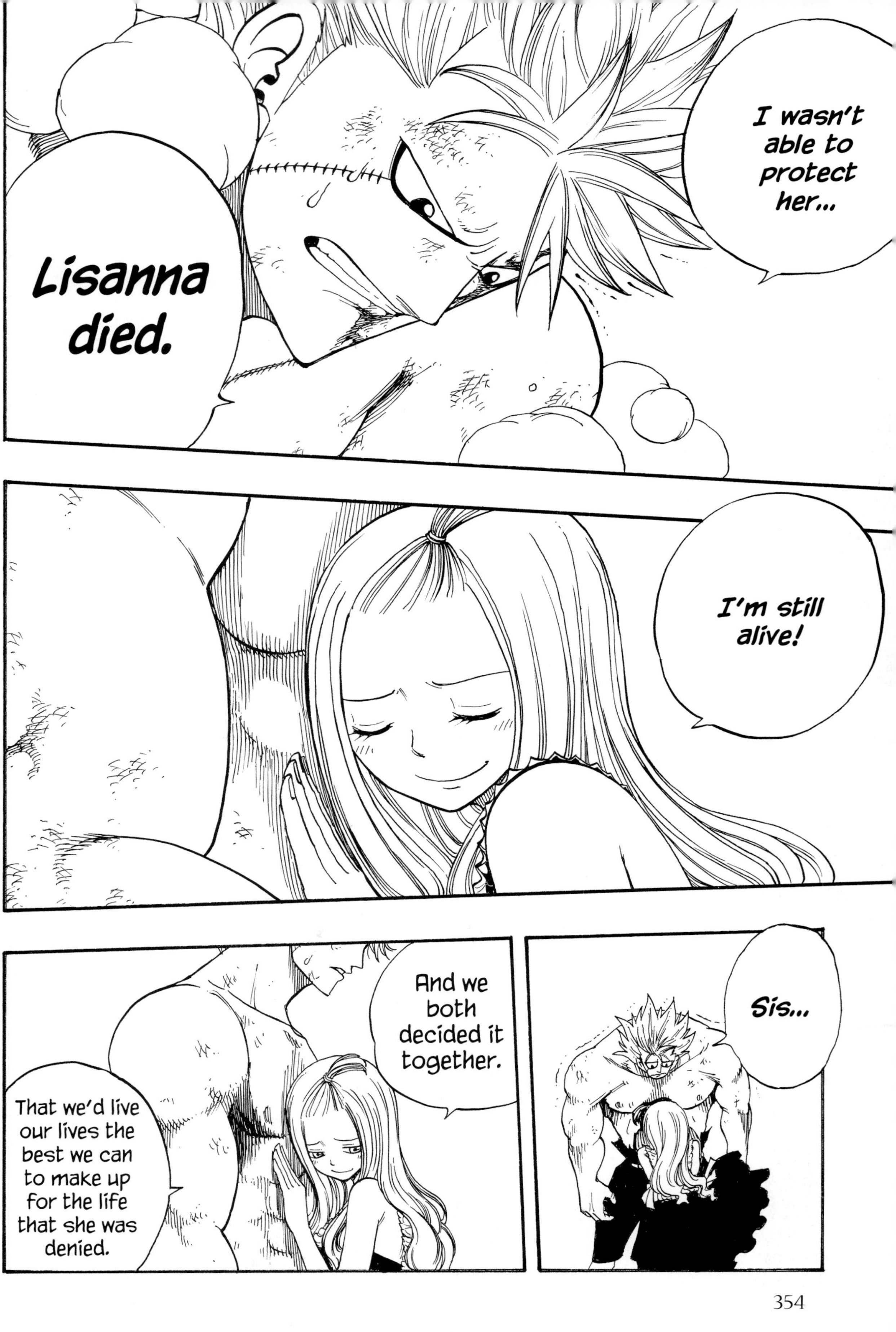
I wasn't able to protect her...
Lisanna died.
I'm still alive!
Sis...
And we both decided it together.
That we'd live our lives the best we can to make up for the life that she was denied.

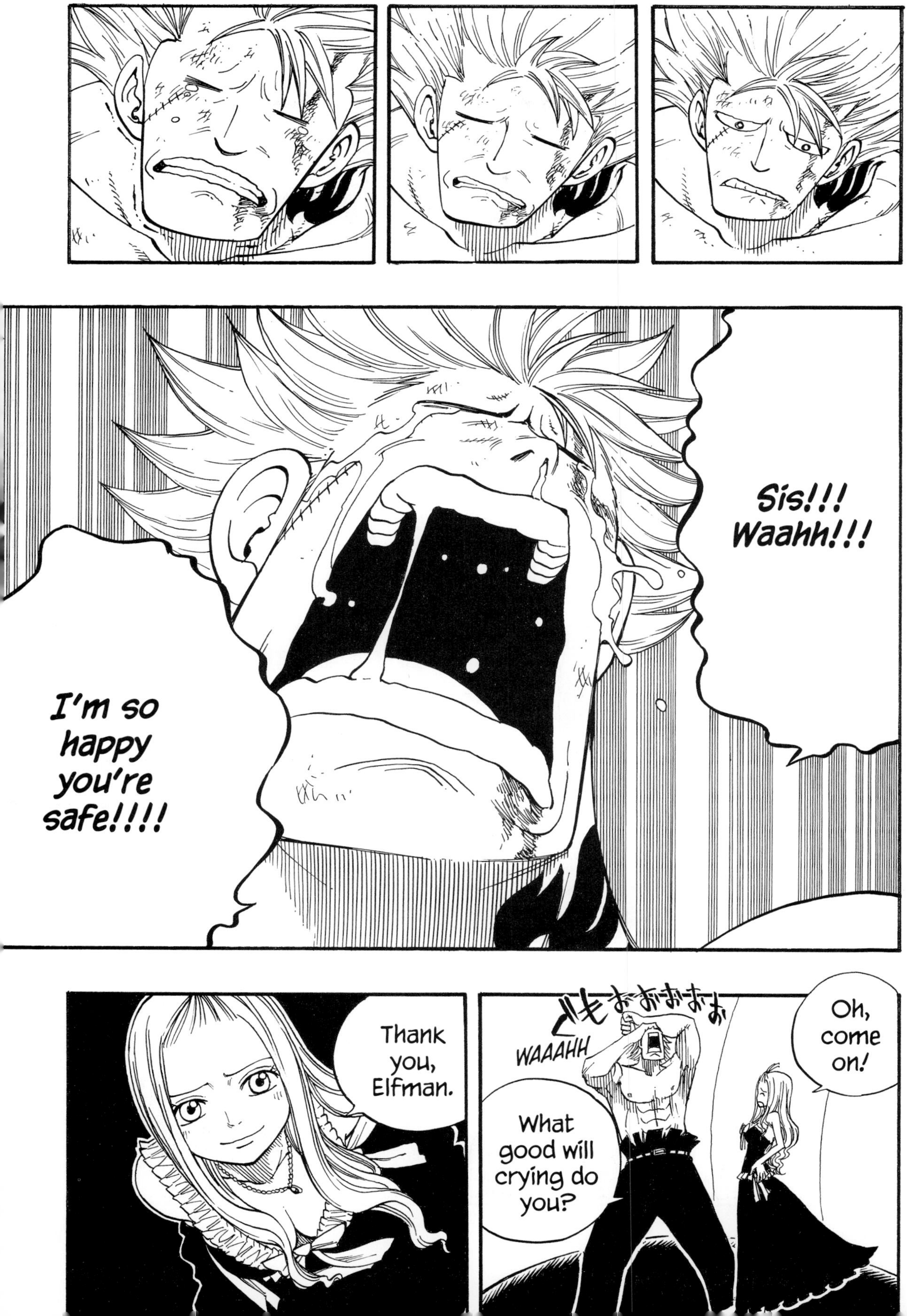
Sis!!! Waahh!!!
I'm so happy you're safe!!!!
Oh, come on!
WAAAHH
What good will crying do you?
Thank you, Elfman.

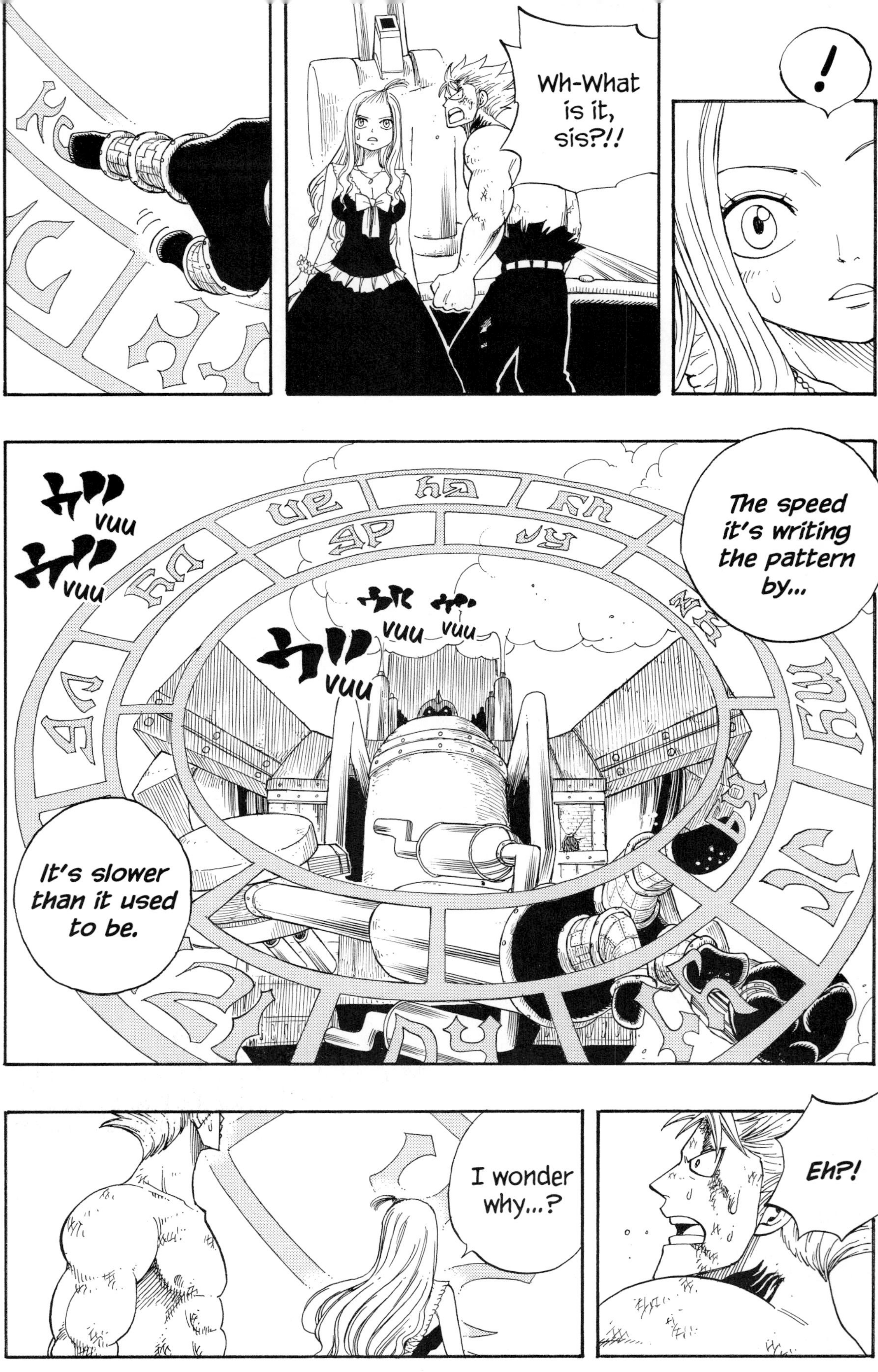
!
Wh-What is it, sis?!!
The speed it's writing the pattern by...
vuu
vuu
vuu
vuu
vuu
It's slower than it used to be.
Eh?!
I wonder why...?

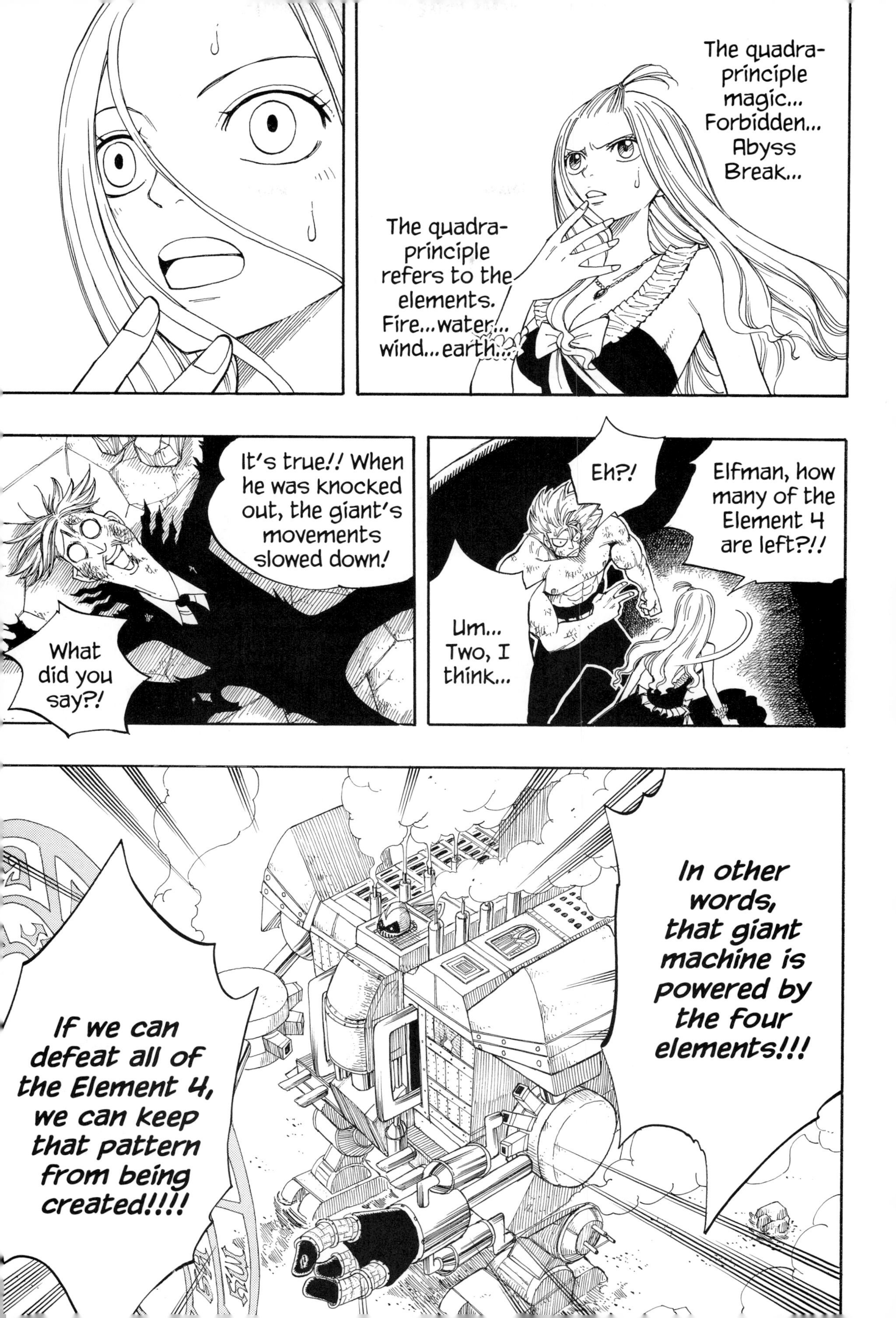
The quadra-principle magic... Forbidden... Abyss Break...
The quadra-principle refers to the elements. Fire...water... wind...earth...
Elfman, how many of the Element 4 are left?!!
Eh?!
Um... Two, I think...
It's true!! When he was knocked out, the giant's movements slowed down!
What did you say?!
In other words, that giant machine is powered by the four elements!!!
If we can defeat all of the Element 4, we can keep that pattern from being created!!!!

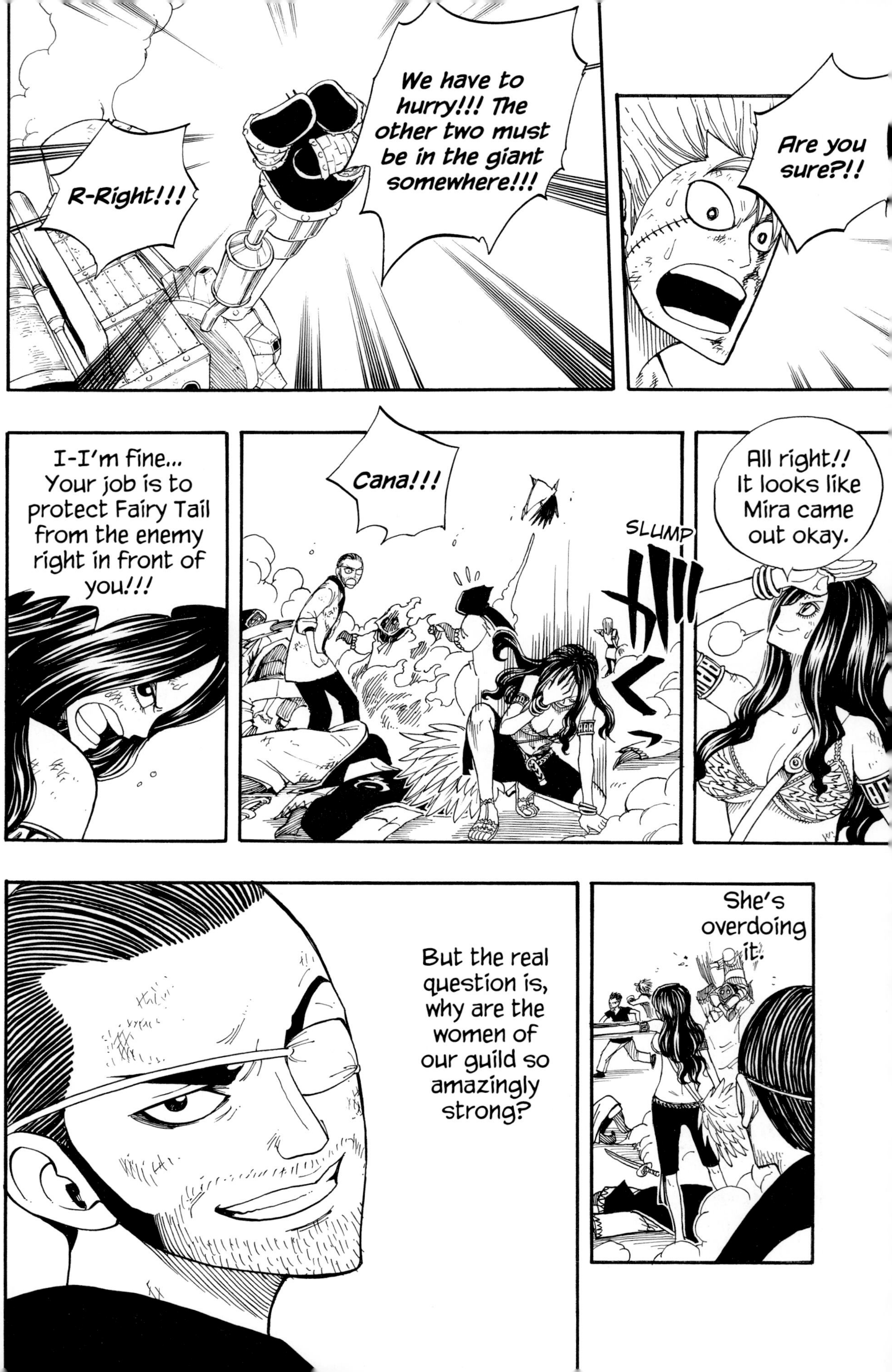
Are you sure?!!
We have to hurry!!! The other two must be in the giant somewhere!!!
R-Right!!!
All right!! It looks like Mira came out okay.
Cana!!!
SLUMP
I-I'm fine... Your job is to protect Fairy Tail from the enemy right in front of you!!!
She's overdoing it.
But the real question is, why are the women of our guild so amazingly strong?

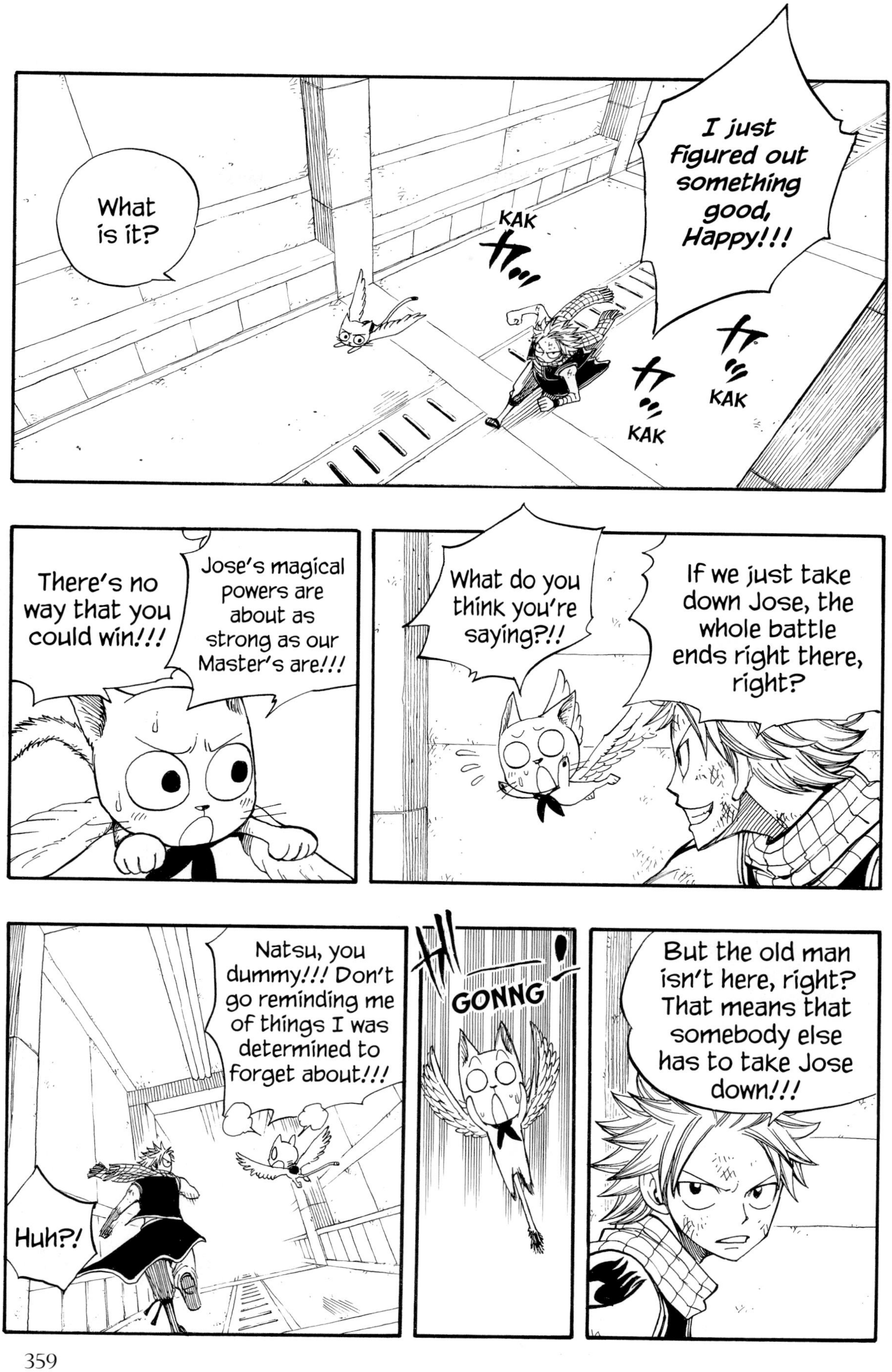
I just figured out something good, Happy!!!
KAK
KAK
KAK
What is it?
If we just take down Jose, the whole battle ends right there, right?
What do you think you're saying?!!
Jose's magical powers are about as strong as our Master's are!!!
There's no way that you could win!!!
But the old man isn't here, right? That means that somebody else has to take Jose down!!!
GONNG
Natsu, you dummy!!! Don't go reminding me of things I was determined to forget about!!!
Huh?!

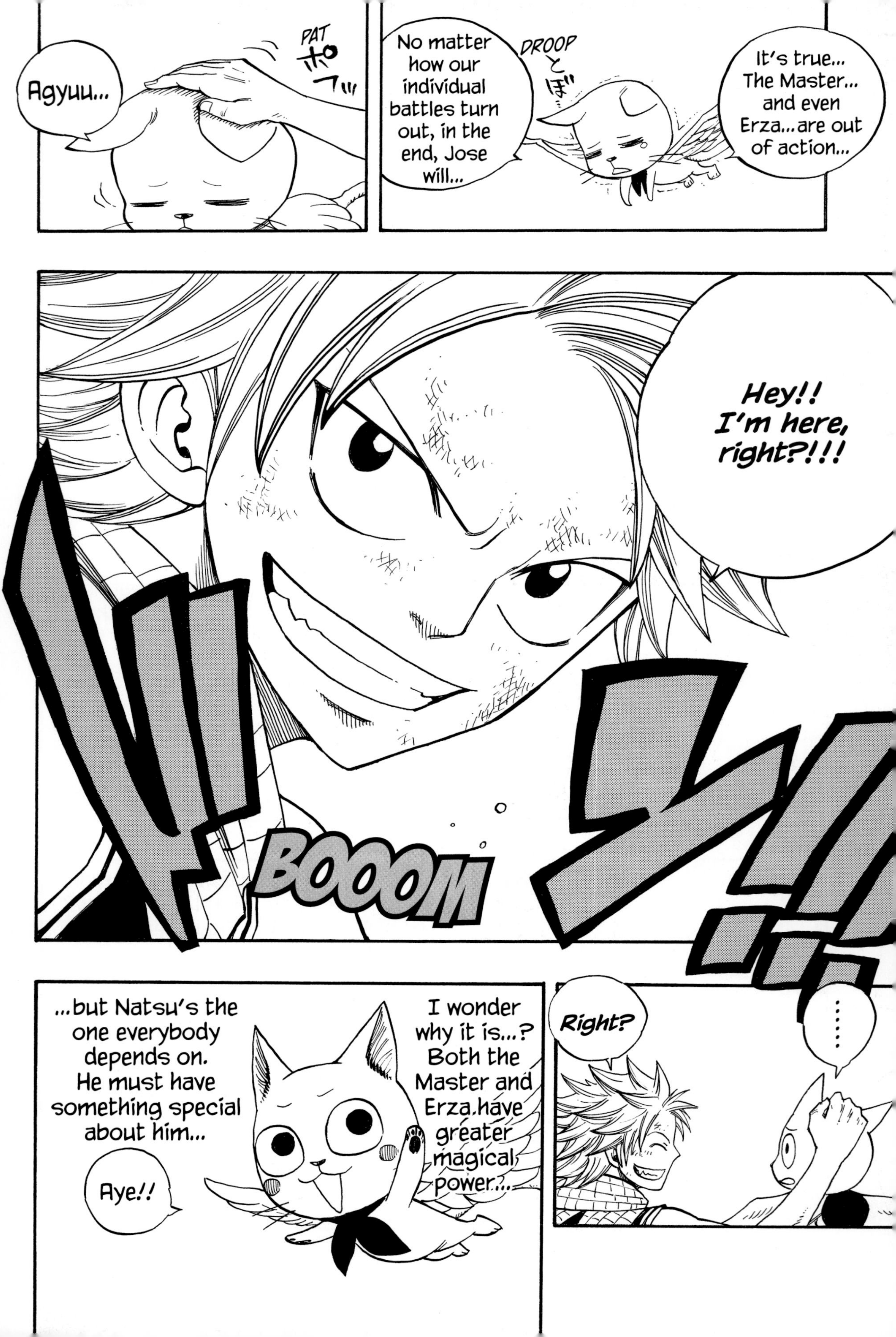
It's true... The Master... and even Erza...are out of action...
DROOP
とぼ
No matter how our individual battles turn out, in the end, Jose will...
PAT
ポフッ
Agyuu...
Hey!! I'm here, right?!!!
BOOOM
......
Right?
I wonder why it is...? Both the Master and Erza have greater magical power...
...but Natsu's the one everybody depends on. He must have something special about him...
Aye!!

It's so sad...

Wha-?!!

!!

HYUOOO

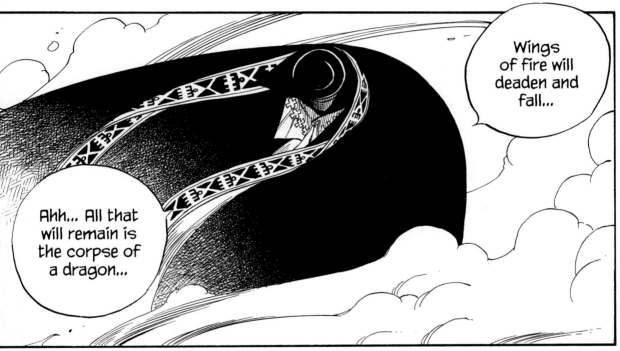

Wings of fire will deaden and fall...

Ahh... All that will remain is the corpse of a dragon...

Natsu... That guy's one of the Element 4!!!

Huh?

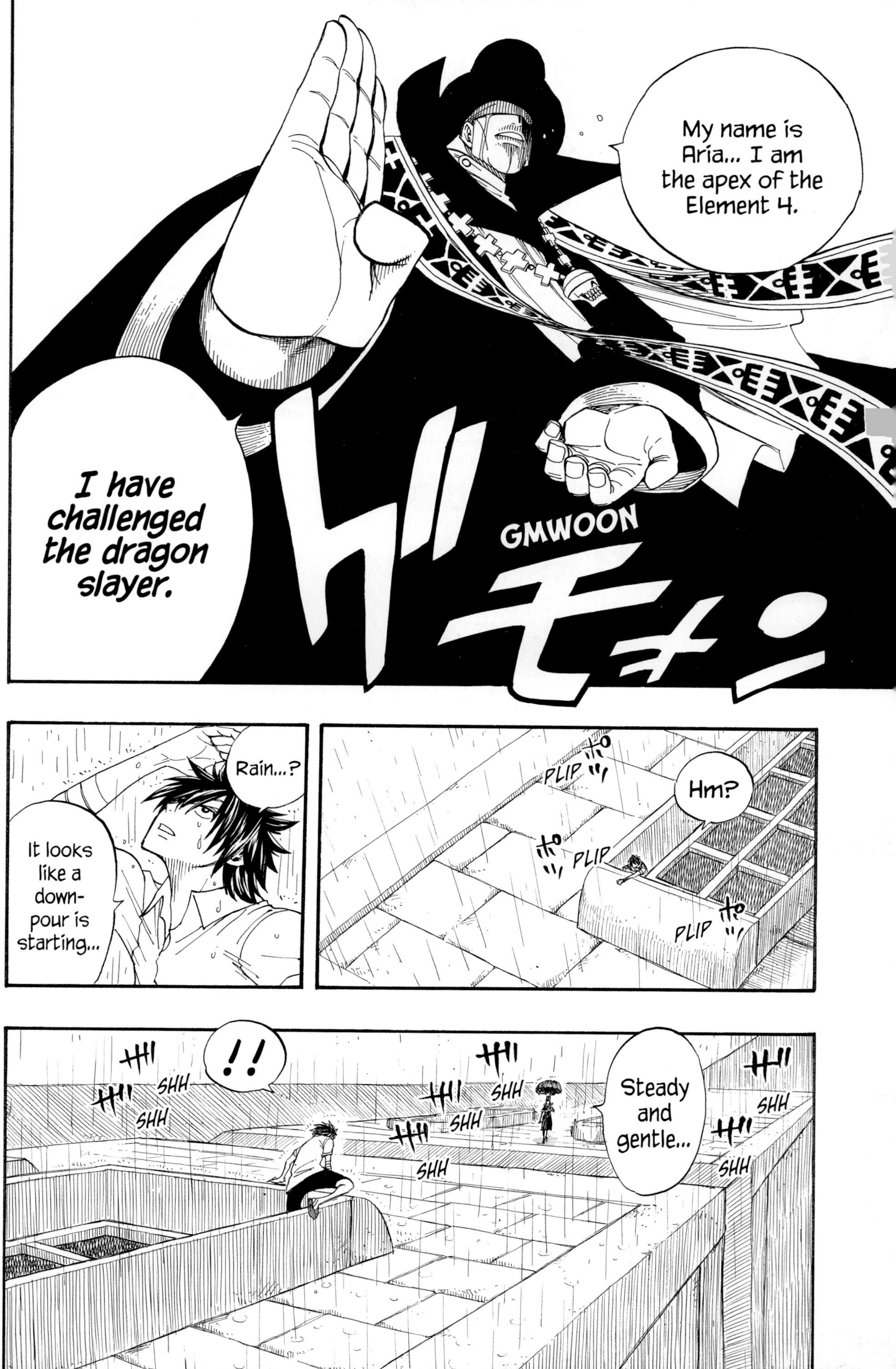
My name is Aria... I am the apex of the Element 4.
I have challenged the dragon slayer.
GMWOON
PLIP
Hm?
PLIP
PLIP
Rain...?
It looks like a down-pour is starting...
SHH
Steady and gentle...
SHH
SHH
SHH
SHH
!!
SHH
SHH

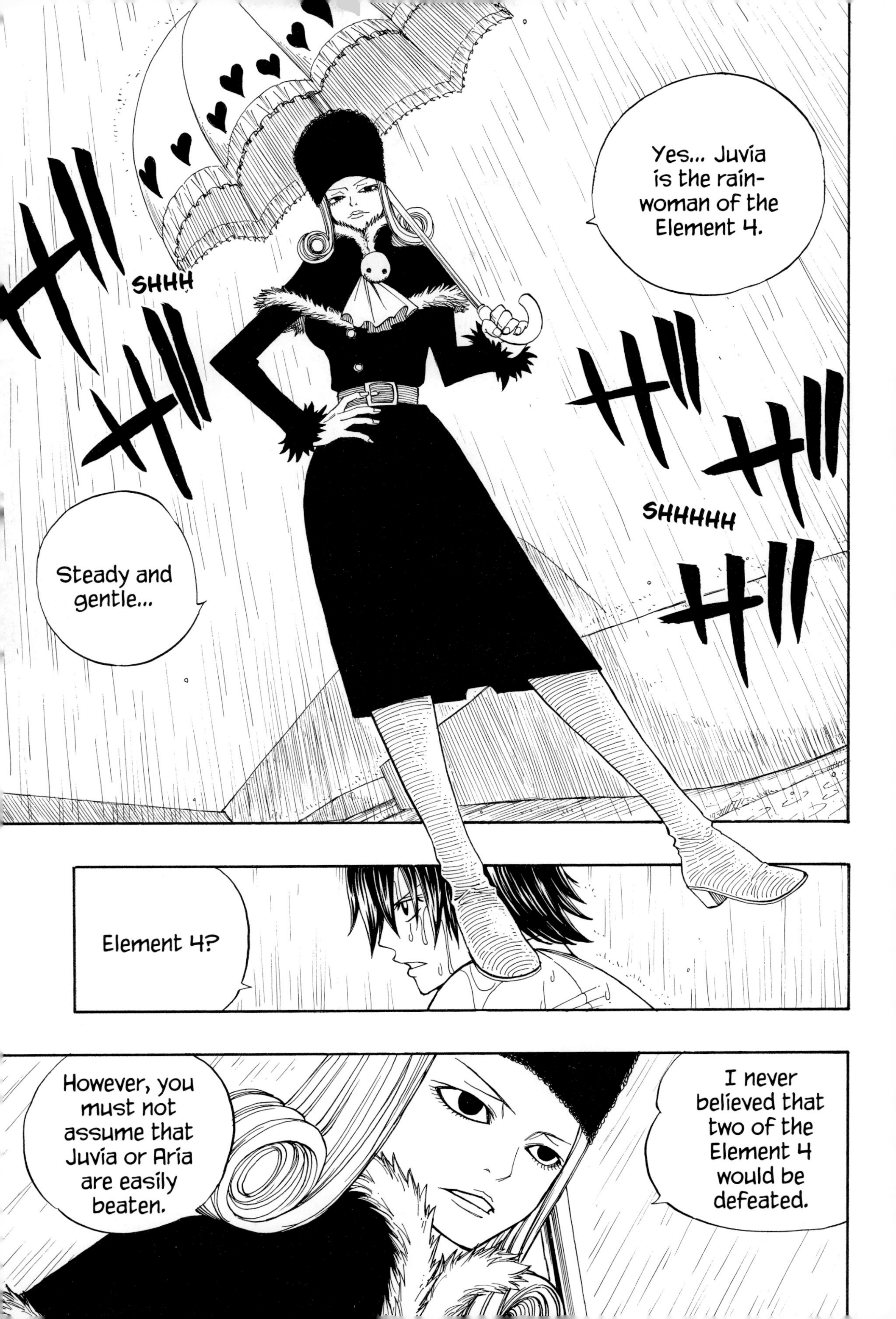
Yes... Juvia is the rain-woman of the Element 4.
SHHH
SHHHHH
Steady and gentle...
Element 4?
I never believed that two of the Element 4 would be defeated.
However, you must not assume that Juvia or Aria are easily beaten.

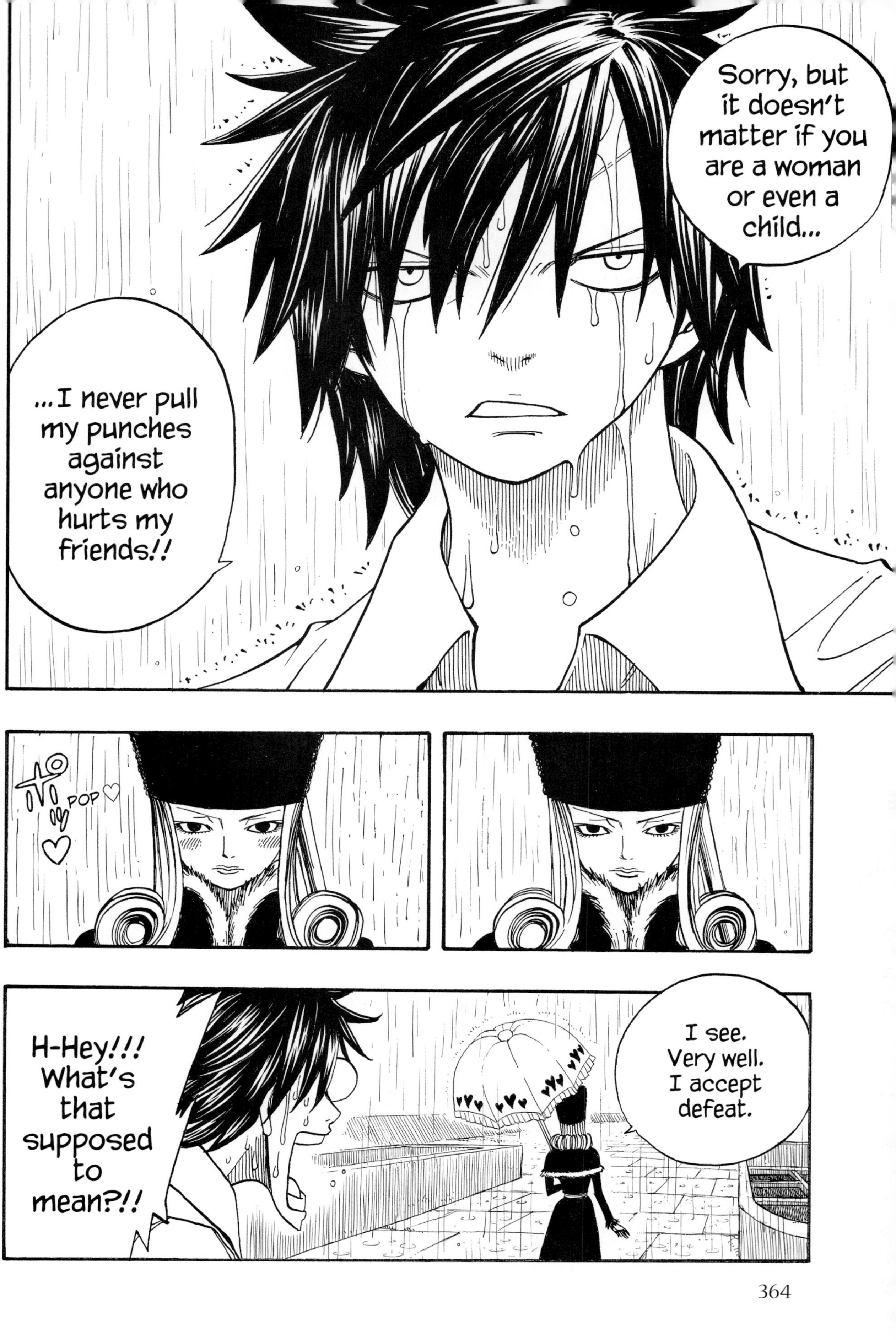
Sorry, but it doesn't matter if you are a woman or even a child...
...I never pull my punches against anyone who hurts my friends!!
POP
I see. Very well. I accept defeat.
H-Hey!!! What's that supposed to mean?!!

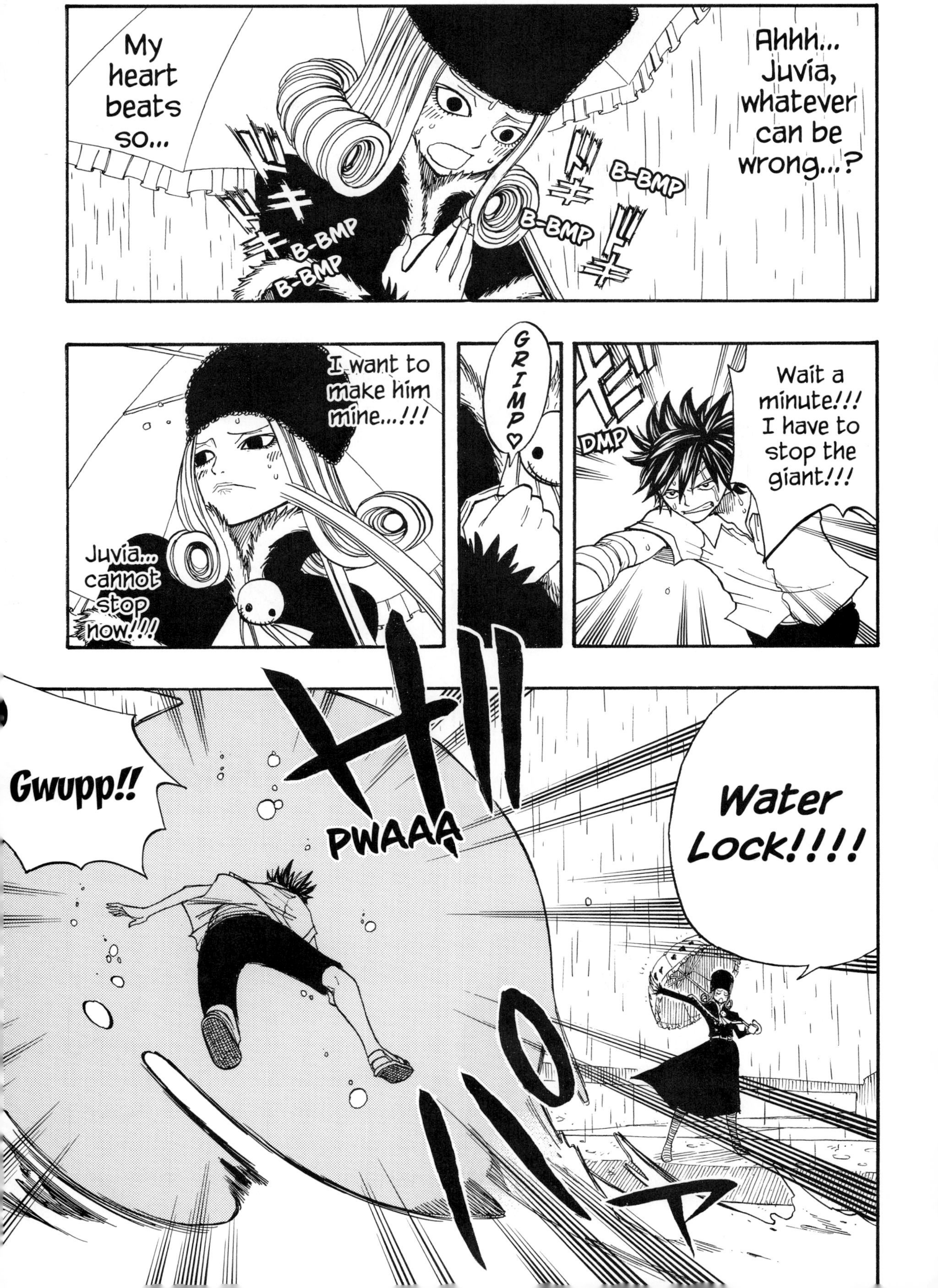
Ahhh... Juvia, whatever can be wrong...?
B-BMP
B-BMP
My heart beats so...
B-BMP
B-BMP
Wait a minute!!! I have to stop the giant!!!
DMP
GRIMP♡
I want to make him mine...!!!
Juvia... cannot stop now!!!
Water Lock!!!!
PWAAA
Gwupp!!

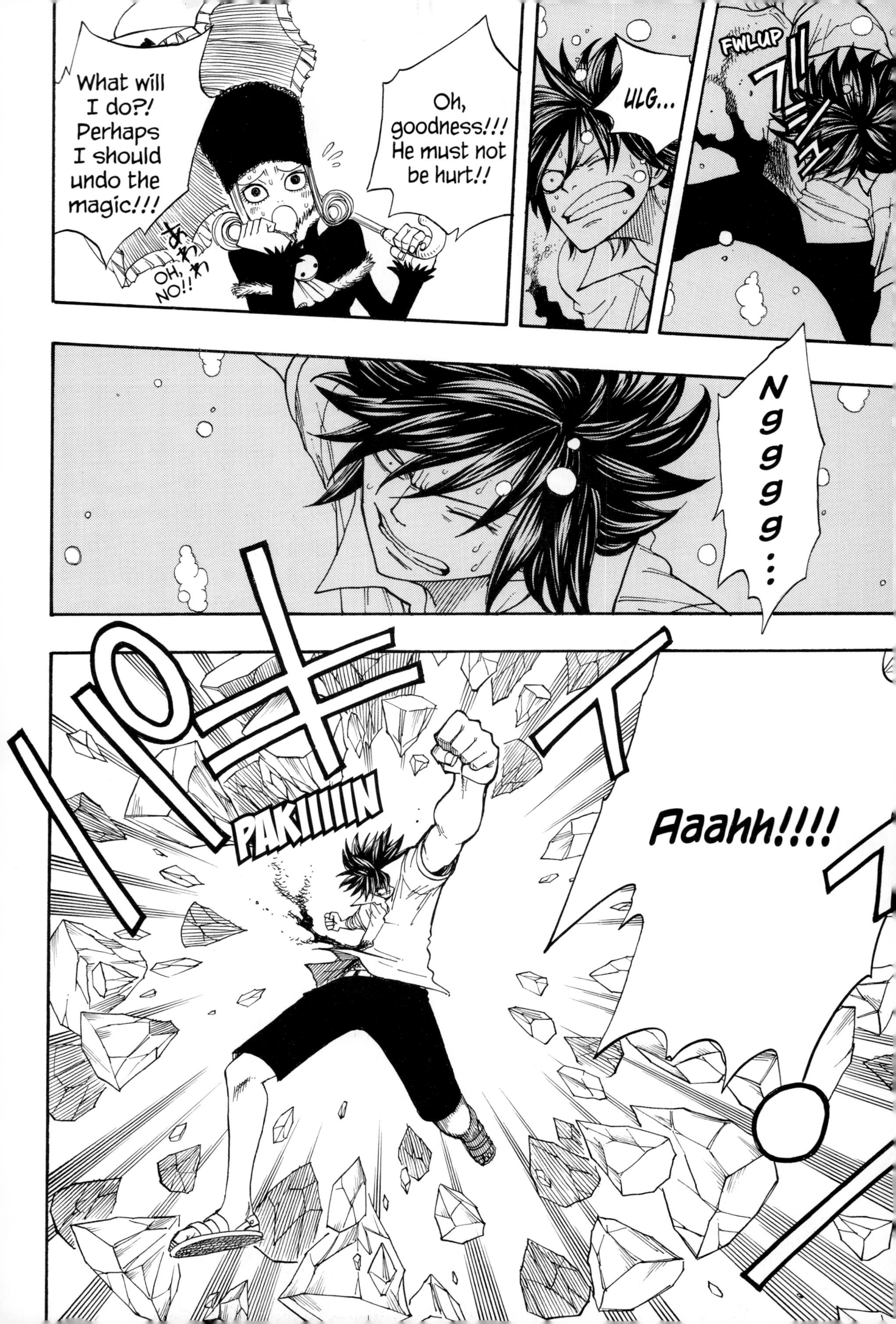
FWLUP
ULG...
Oh, goodness!!! He must not be hurt!!
What will I do?! Perhaps I should undo the magic!!!
あわわ
OH, NO!!
Ngggg...
PAKIIIIIN
Aaahh!!!!

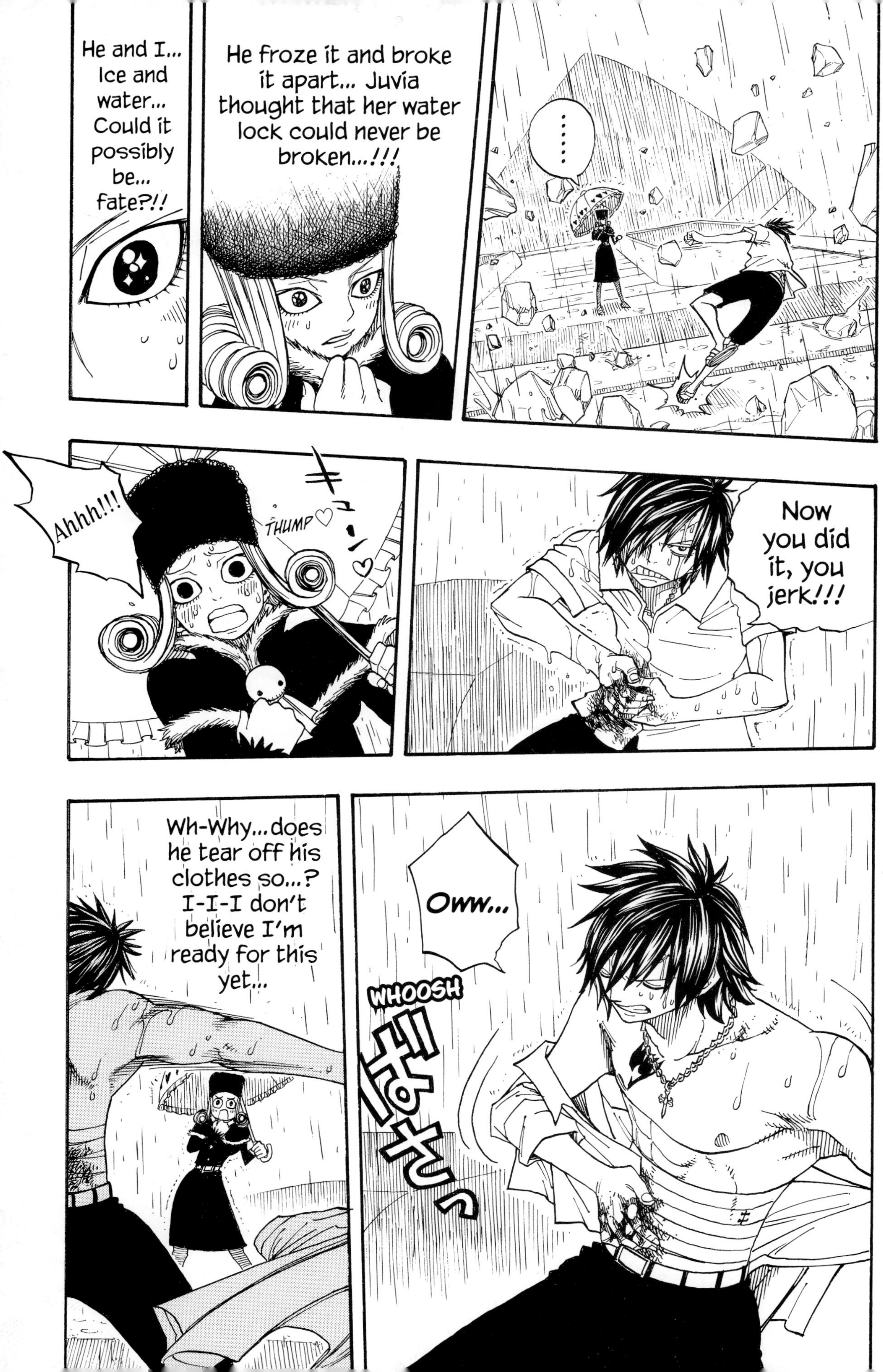
......
He froze it and broke it apart... Juvia thought that her water lock could never be broken...!!!
He and I... Ice and water... Could it possibly be... fate?!!
Now you did it, you jerk!!!
THUMP♡
Ahhh!!!
Oww...
WHOOSH
Wh-Why...does he tear off his clothes so...? I-I-I don't believe I'm ready for this yet...

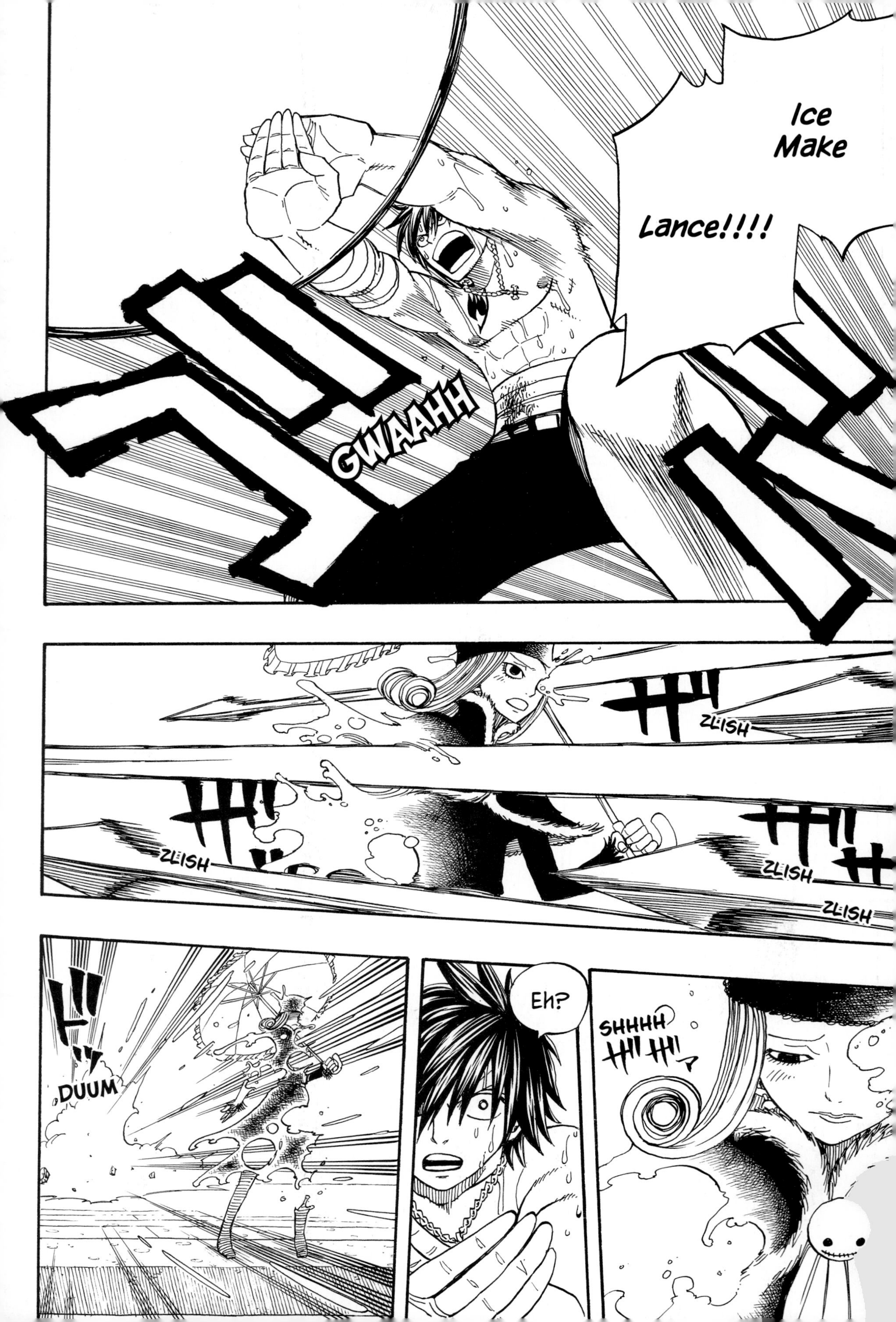
Ice Make Lance!!!!
GWAAHH
ZLISH
ZLISH
ZLISH
ZLISH
SHHHH
Eh?
DUUM

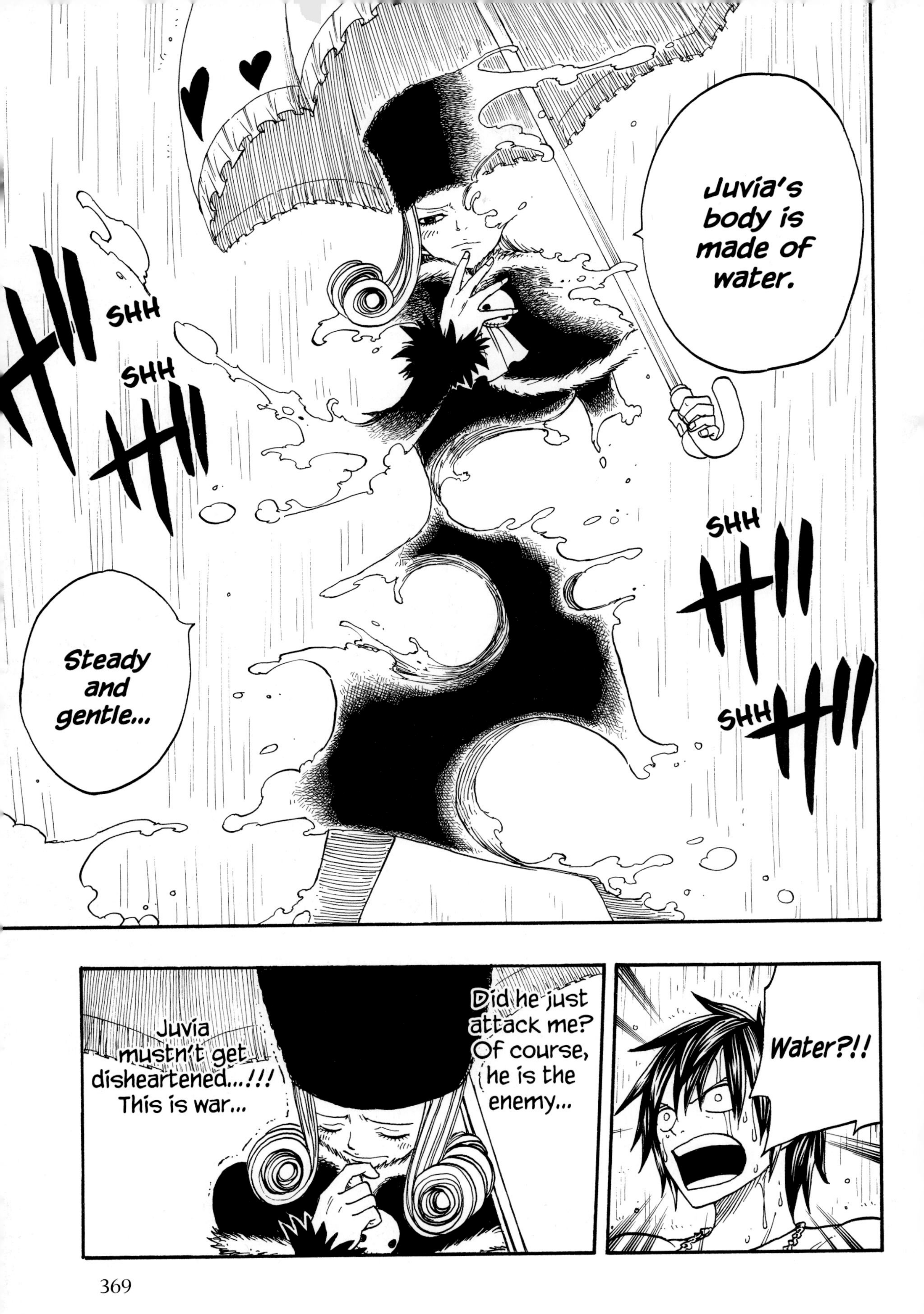
SHH
SHH
Juvia's body is made of water.
SHH
SHH
Steady and gentle...
Water?!!
Did he just attack me? Of course, he is the enemy...
Juvia mustn't get disheartened...!!! This is war...

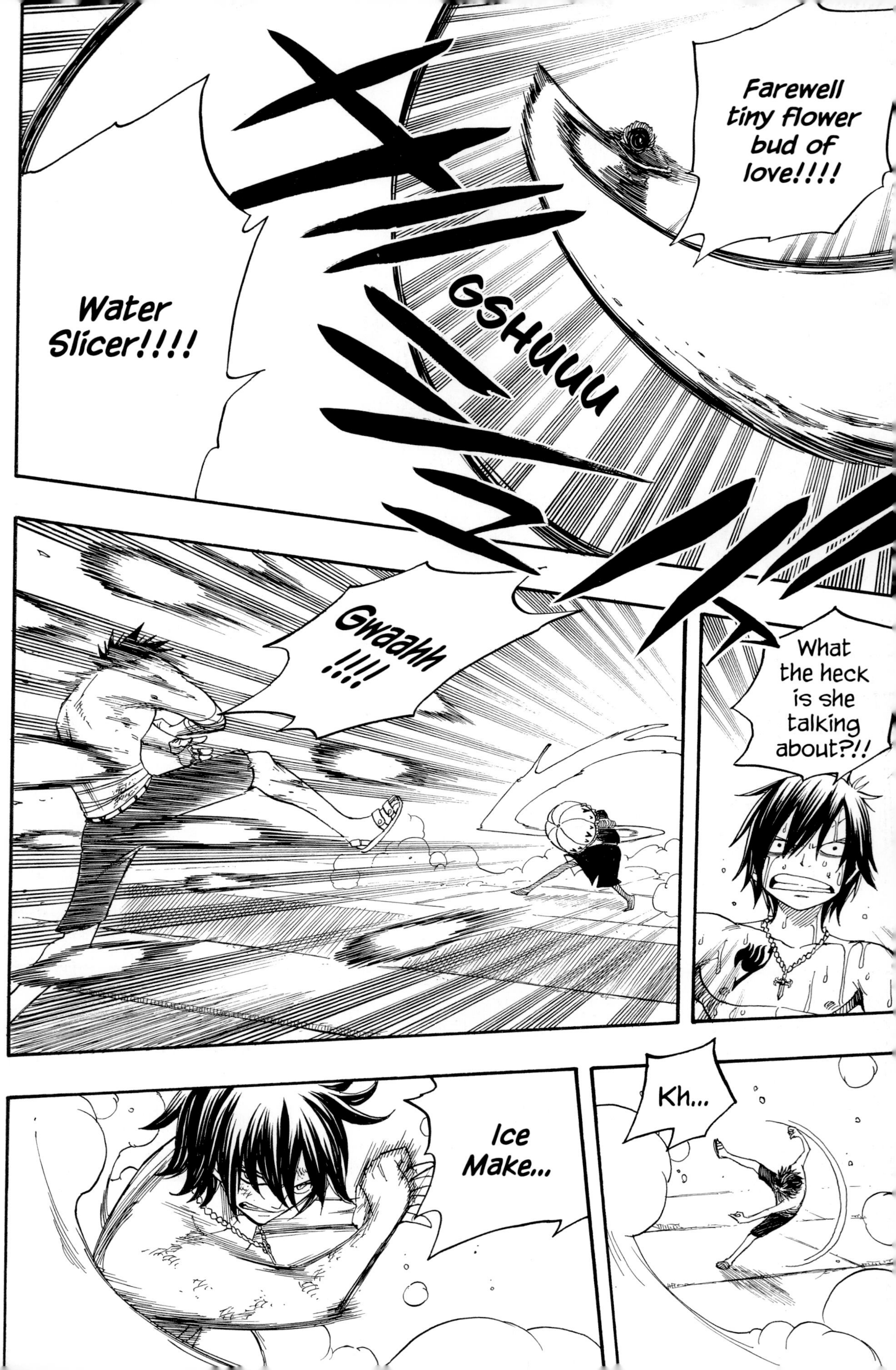
Farewell tiny flower bud of love!!!!
GSHUUUU
Water Slicer!!!!
What the heck is she talking about?!!
Gwaahh!!!!
Kh...
Ice Make...

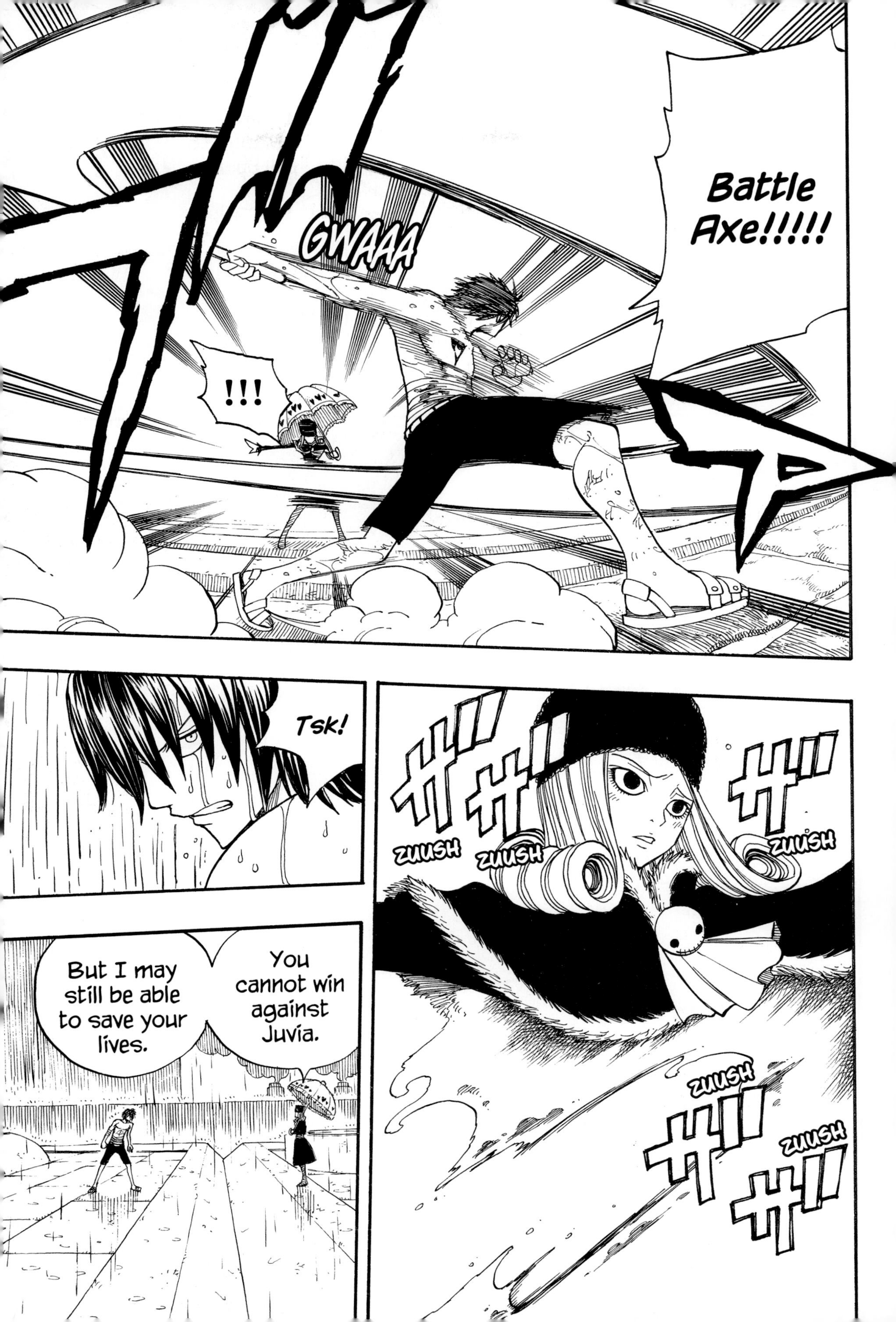
Battle Axe!!!!!
GWAAA
!!!
ZUUSH
ZUUSH
ZUUSH
ZUUSH
ZUUSH
Tsk!
You cannot win against Juvia.
But I may still be able to save your lives.

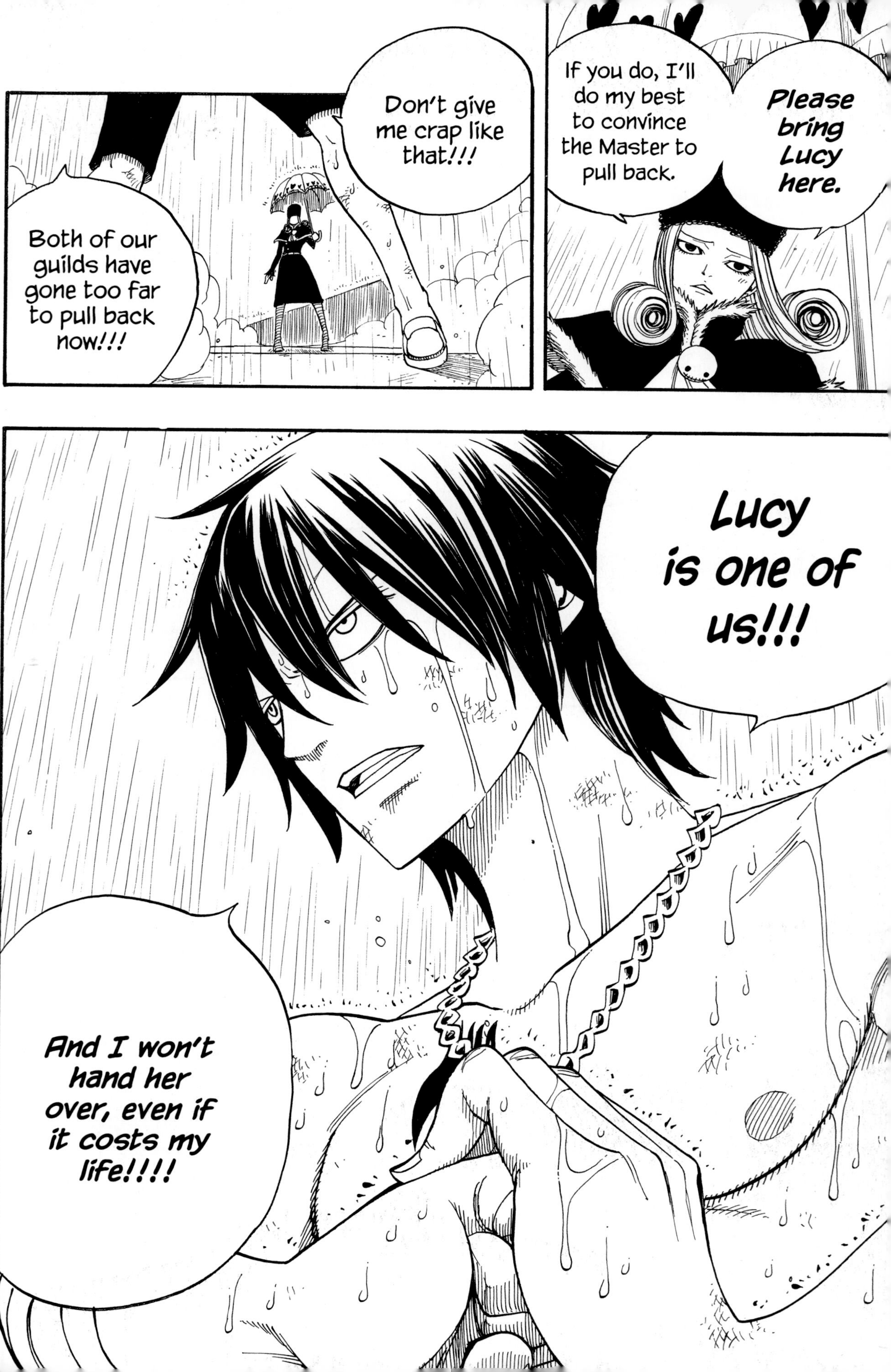
Please bring Lucy here.
If you do, I'll do my best to convince the Master to pull back.
Don't give me crap like that!!!
Both of our guilds have gone too far to pull back now!!!
Lucy is one of us!!!
And I won't hand her over, even if it costs my life!!!!

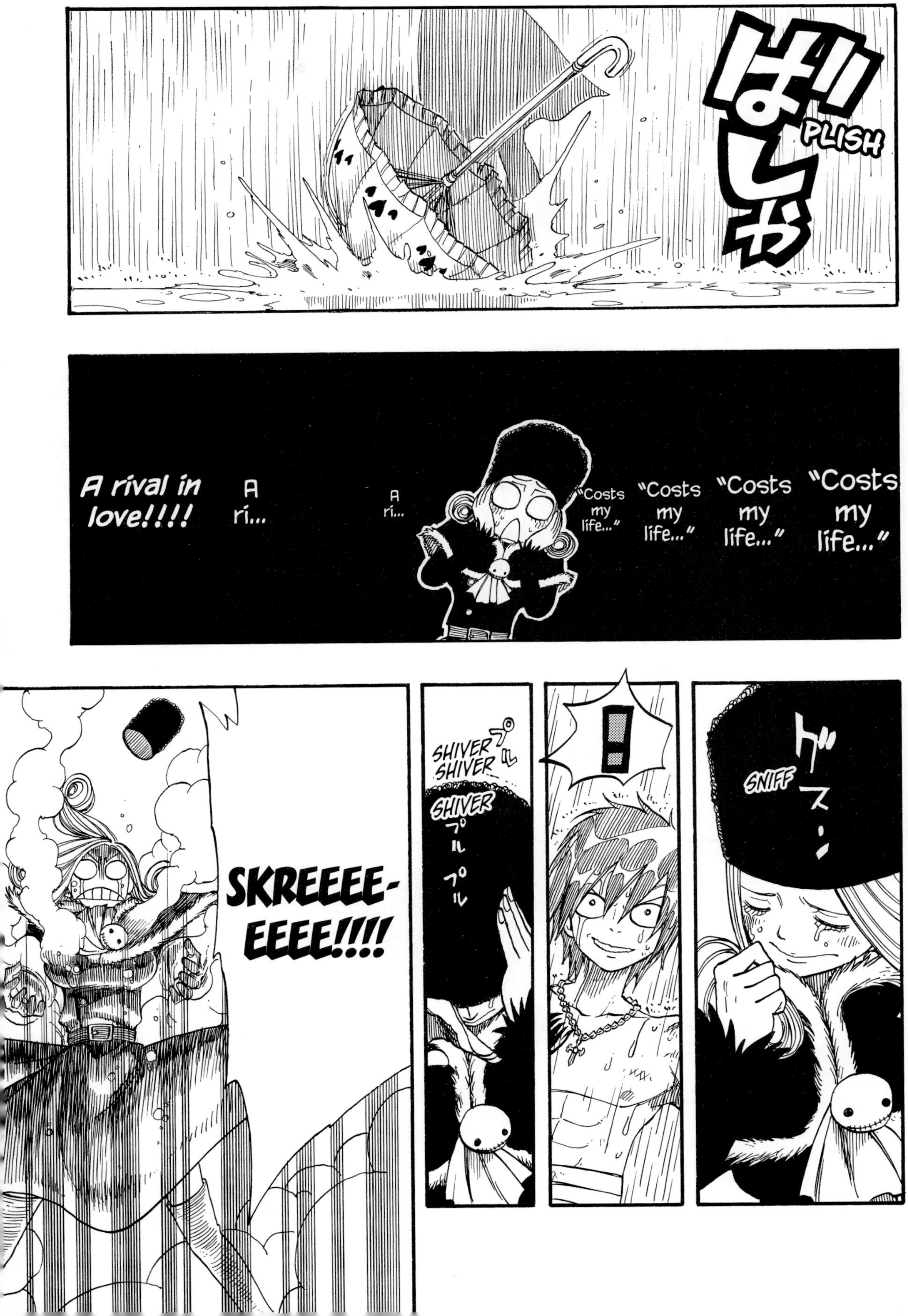
ばしゃ
PLISH
"Costs my life..."
"Costs my life..."
"Costs my life..."
"Costs my life..."
A ri...
A ri...
A rival in love!!!!
グズ…
SNIFF
!
SHIVER SHIVER
SHIVER
プルプルプル
SKREEEEE-EEEE!!!!

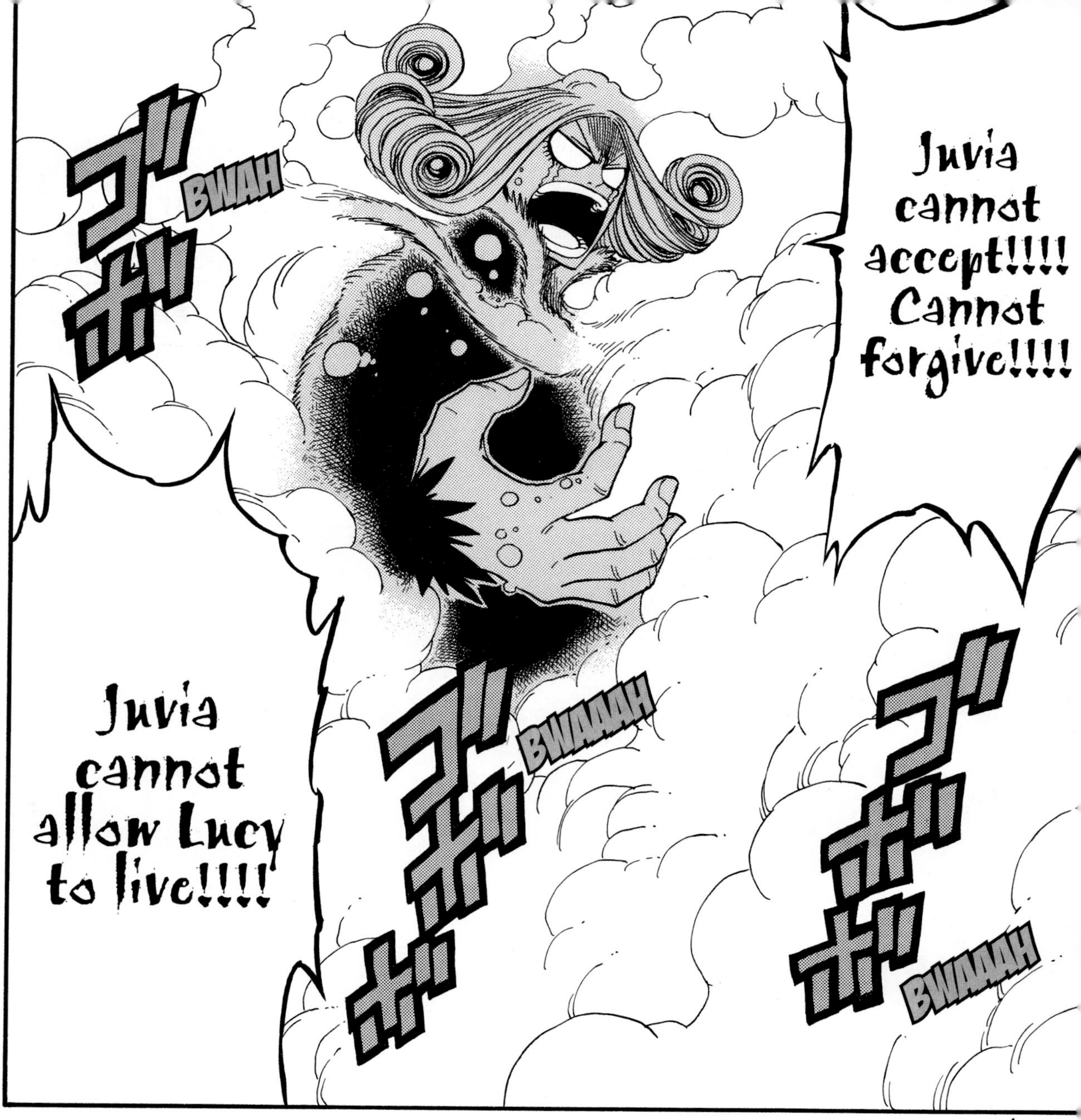
Juvia cannot accept!!!! Cannot forgive!!!!
BWAH
BWAAAH
BWAAAH
Juvia cannot allow Lucy to live!!!!

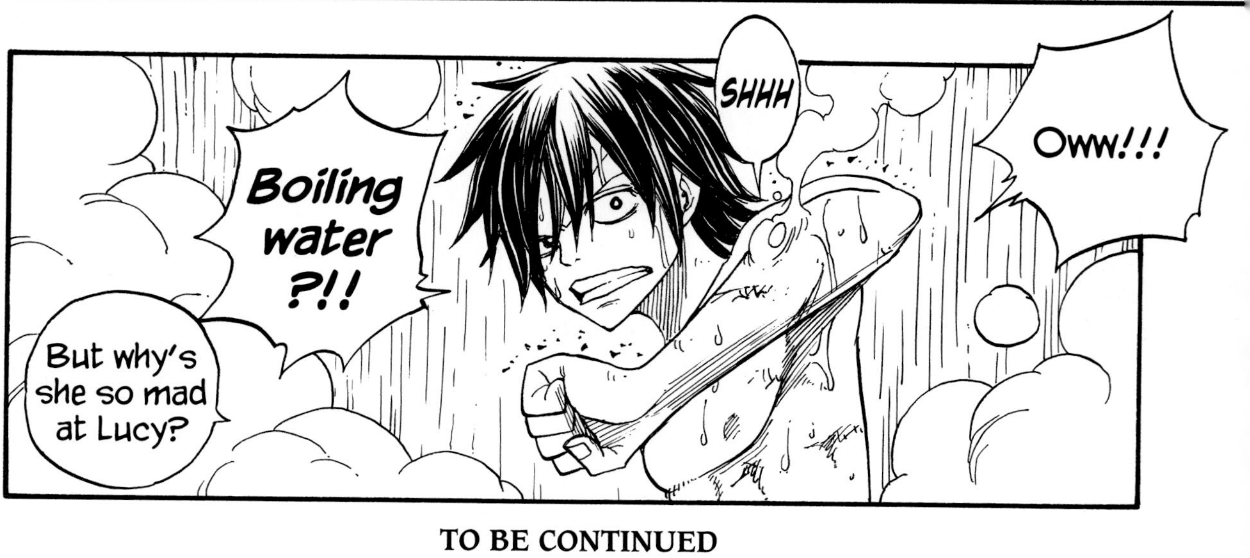
Oww!!!
SHHH
Boiling water?!!
But why's she so mad at Lucy?

TO BE CONTINUED

FAIRY TAIL

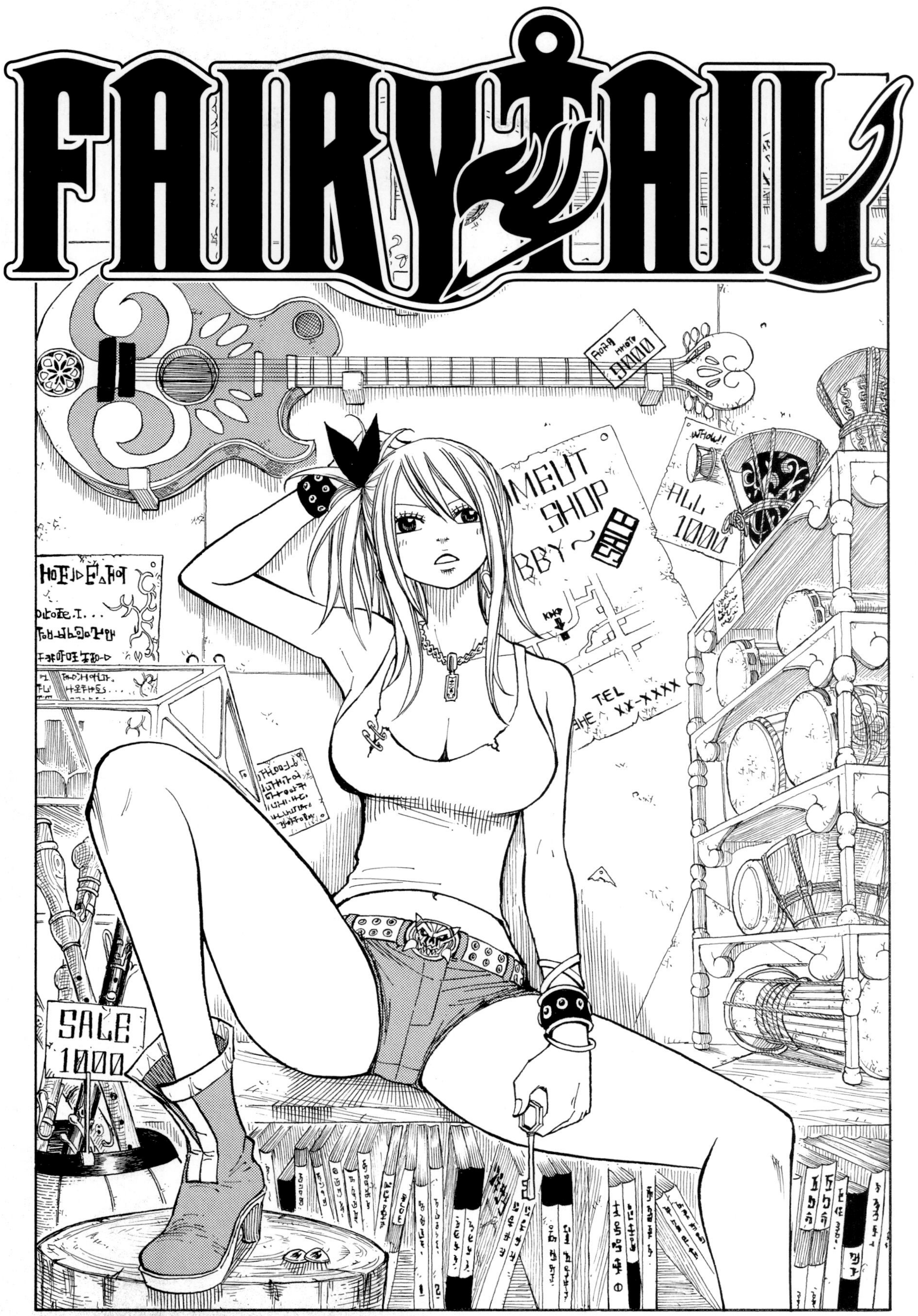

SHOP
SALE
ALL
1000
TEL XX-XXXX
SALE
1000

BONUS PAGES

TAIL D'ART

The *Fairy Tail* Guild d'Art is an explosion of fan art! Please send in your black-and-white art on large postcard stock!! Those chosen to be published will get a signed mini poster!♪ Make sure you write your real name and address on the back of your postcard!

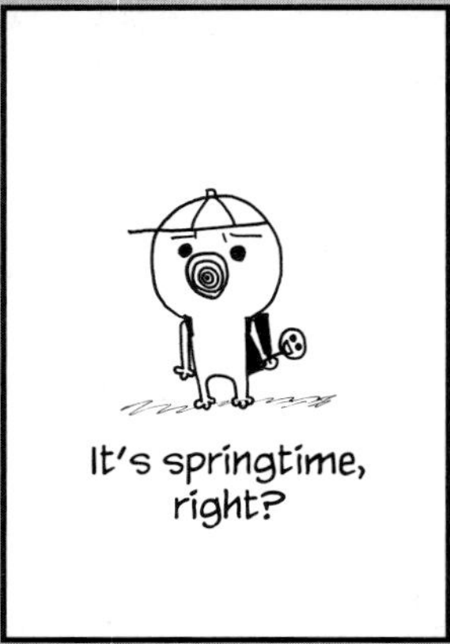
It's springtime, right?

Fukushima Prefecture, Kai

▼ Well... Let's just leave it at that. (laughs)

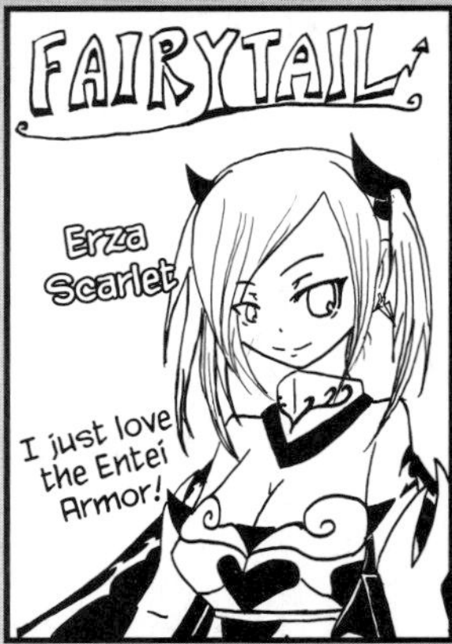
FAIRYTAIL
Erza Scarlet
I just love the Entei Armor!

Chiba Prefecture, Jelly

▼ Maybe the "Entei" (Fire Empress) armor will come some time later in the manga... (sweat, sweat)

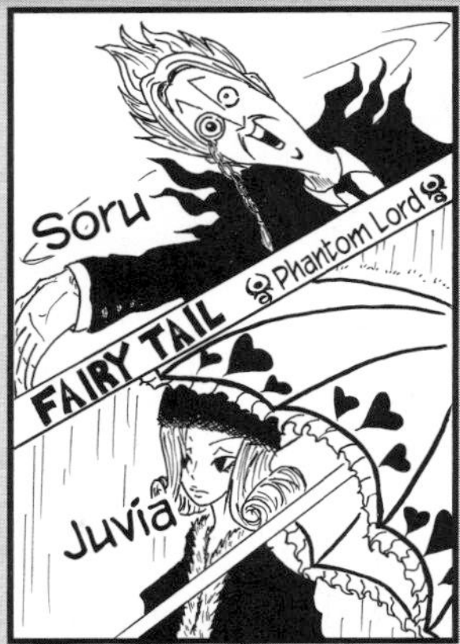
Soru
Phantom Lord
FAIRY TAIL
Juvia

Fukushima Prefecture, Narumi

▼ Non, non, non!! It is not Soru! It is Monsieur Sol!!

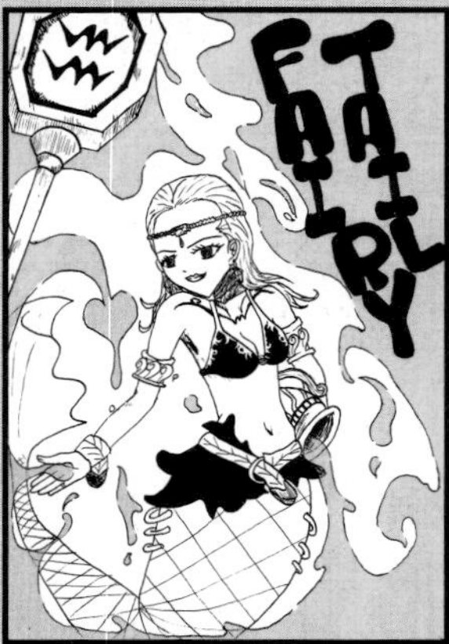
FAIRY
TAIL

Kanagawa Prefecture, Kaoringo

▼ Everybody knows that the Palace of the Water Bearer refers to the star sign Aquarius, right?

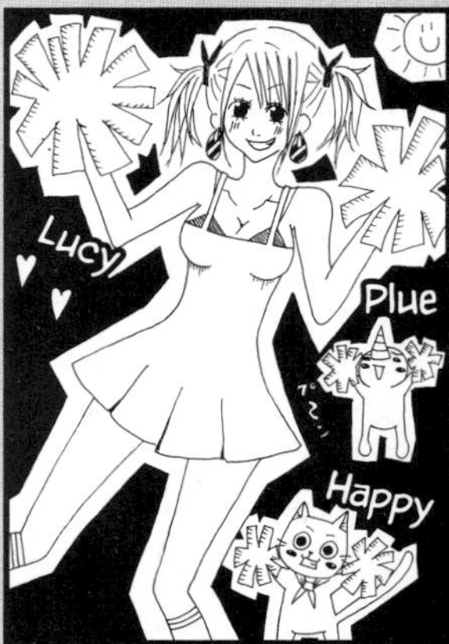
Lucy
Plue
Happy

Osaka, Haruna

▼ Everybody cheer!!! Hurray! Hurray! Ma-shi-ma!!

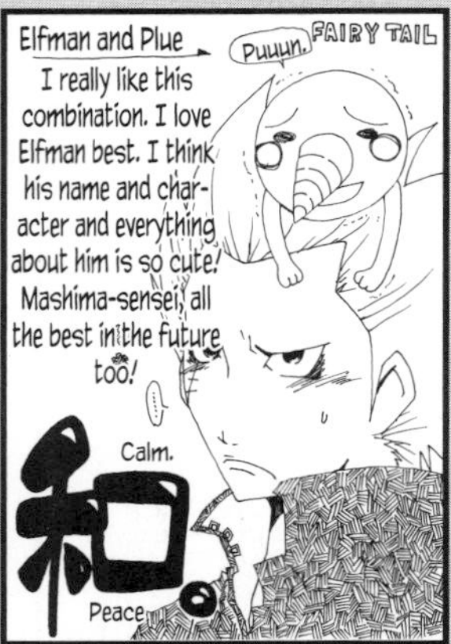
Elfman and Plue
FAIRY TAIL
Puuun.
I really like this combination. I love Elfman best. I think his name and character and everything about him is so cute! Mashima-sensei, all the best in the future too!
Calm.
和
Peace

Okayama Prefecture, Ikuma

▼ Elfman's popularity is really on the rise!! What did you think of his part in this volume?

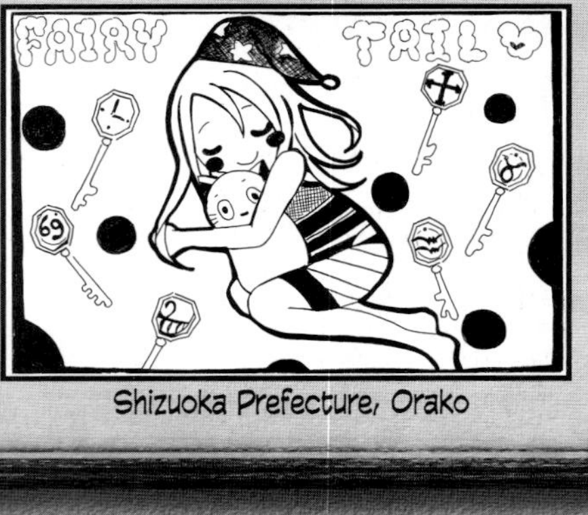
FAIRY
TAIL

Shizuoka Prefecture, Orako

▼ Wow!! So cute!! I wonder what kind of dream she's having!

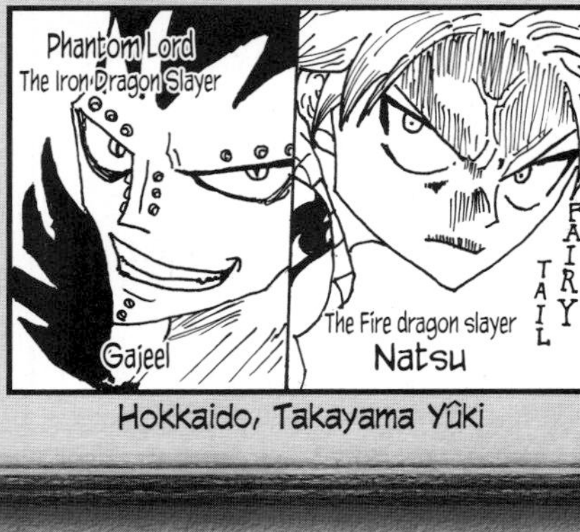
Phantom Lord
The Iron Dragon Slayer
Gajeel
The Fire dragon slayer
Natsu
FAIRY
TAIL

Hokkaido, Takayama Yûki

▼ Will these two fight out their ultimate battle?!! What will the outcome be?!!

Send to Hiro Mashima, Kodansha Comics
451 Park Ave. South, 7th Floor New York, NY 10016

FAIRY GUILD

Any letters and postcards you send with your personal information, such as your name, address, postal code, and other information, will be handed over, as is, to the author. When you send mail, please keep that in mind.

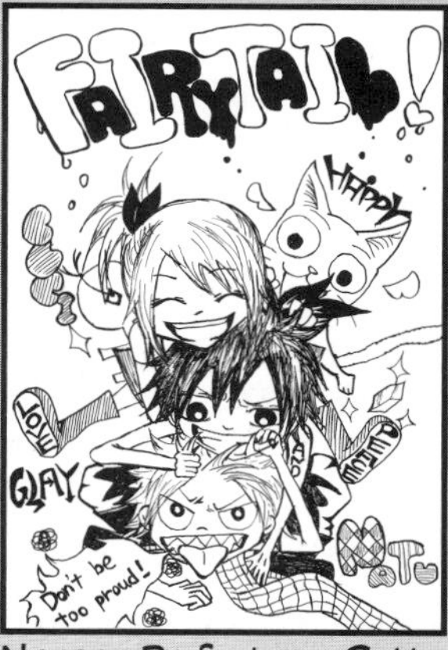
FAIRY TAIL!
Don't be too proud!

◀ Everyone looks like they're having so much fun!! Great facial expressions!

Nagano Prefecture, Getta

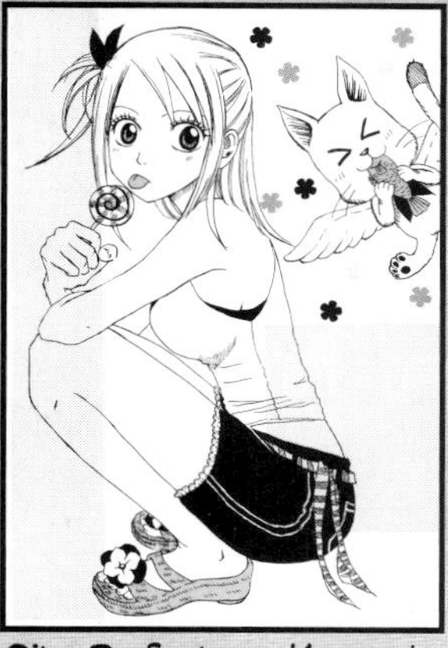

◀ So well drawn!!! This person must be experienced in drawing the human form.

Oita Prefecture, Kazaneko

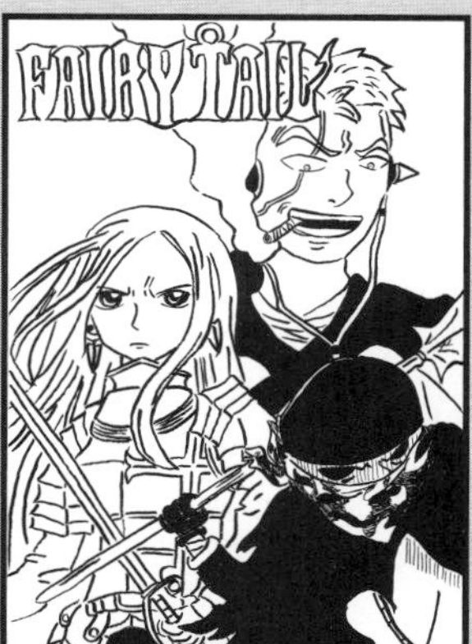
FAIRY TAIL

◀ The top three of Fairy Tail! (Probably.)

Shimane Prefecture, Iruka

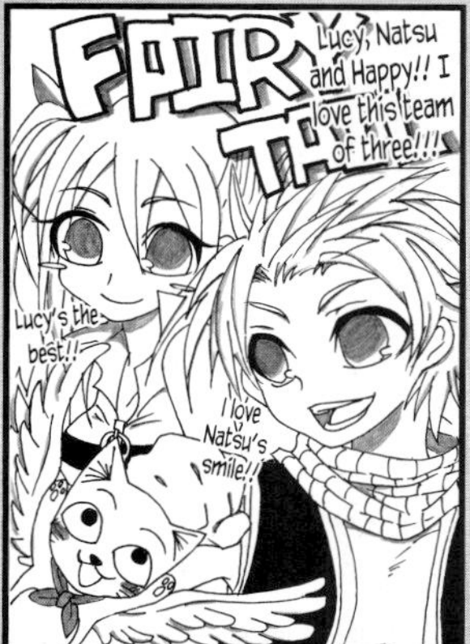
Lucy, Natsu and Happy!! I love this team of three!!!
Lucy's the best!!
I love Natsu's smile!!

◀ She says she loves this team of three!! Thank you!!!

Nara Prefecture, Sorano Yukimi

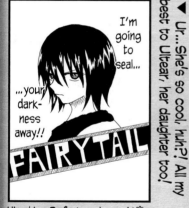

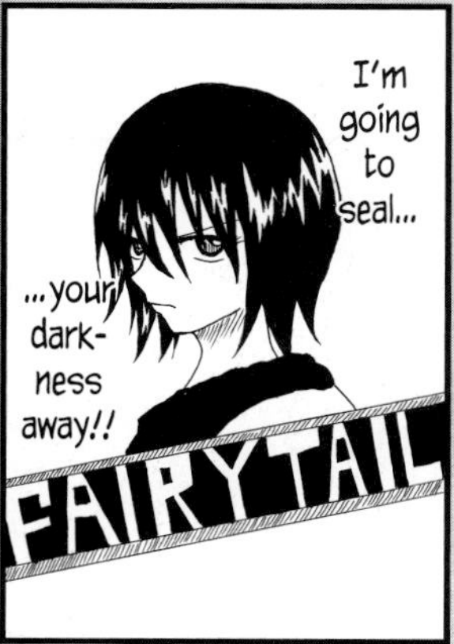
I'm going to seal...
...your darkness away!!
FAIRY TAIL

◀ Ur...She's so cool, huh?! All my best to Ultear, her daughter too!

Hiroshima Prefecture, Iwamori Yûka

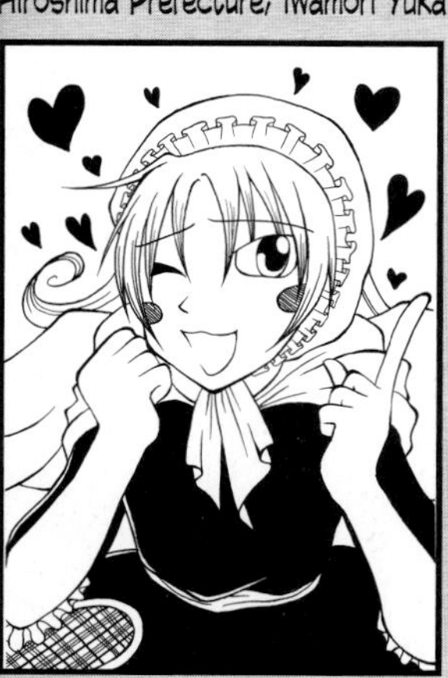

◀ Oh ho!! An unusual character makes her appearance!!

Fukushima Prefecture, Kasuga Hikari

Rejection Corner

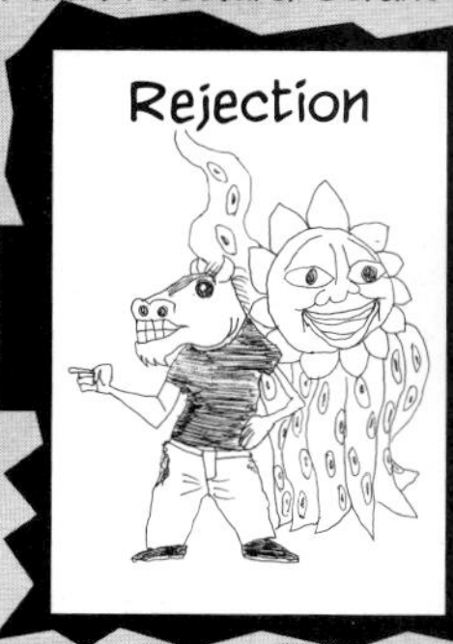
Rejection

◀ All right... Exactly as you wish...

Tôyama Prefecture, Impact Absorber

GUILD D'ART, STAFF EDITION!!

A bit of artwork that got caught up in the confusion.

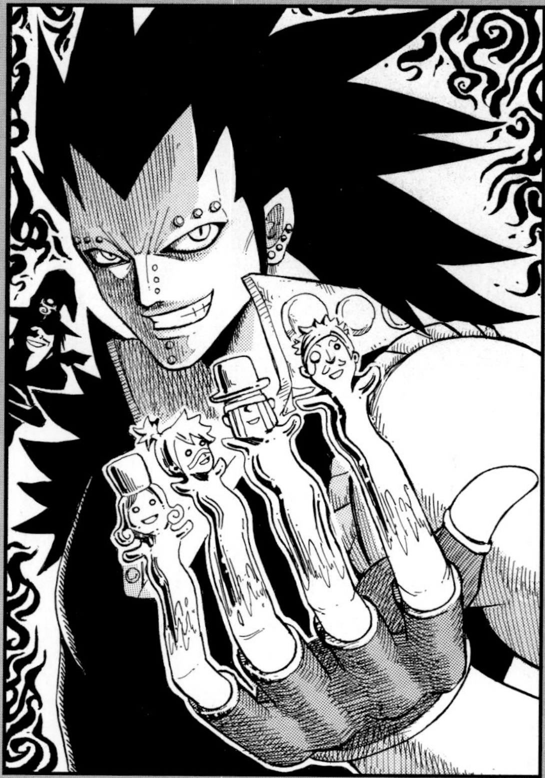

Bozu

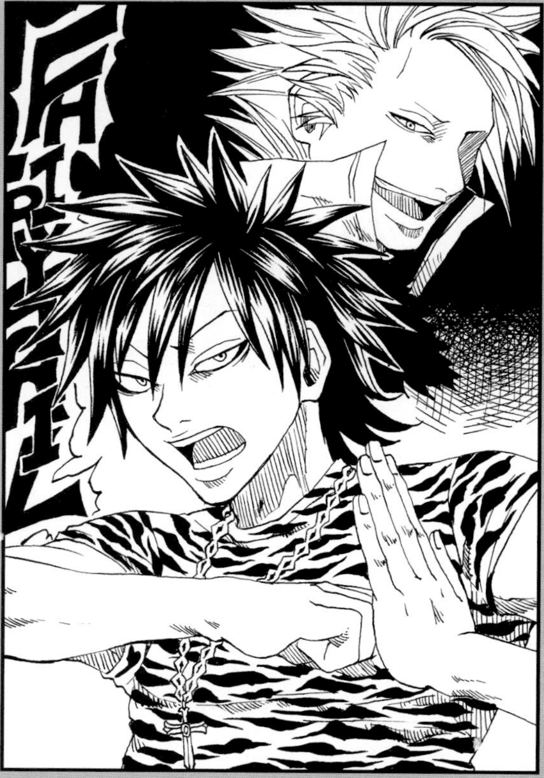

Nakamura Shô

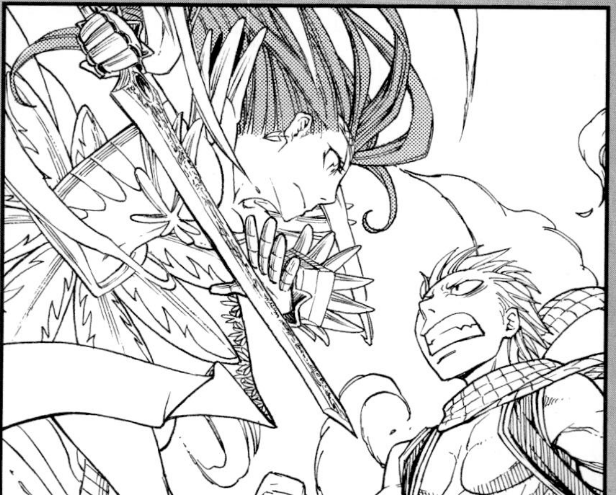

Bobby Ôsawa

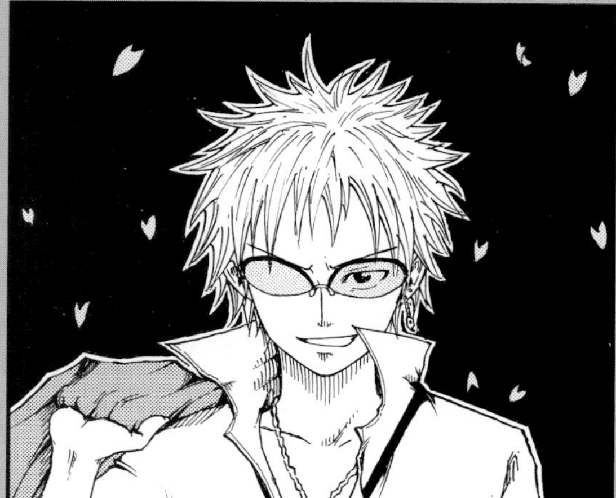

Ueda Yui

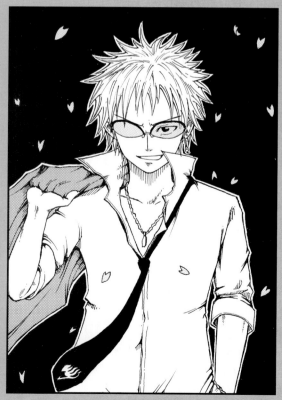

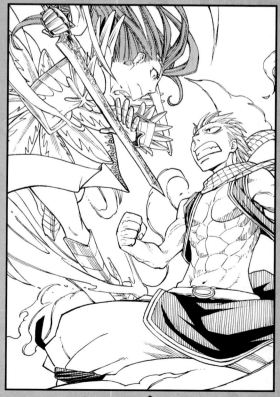

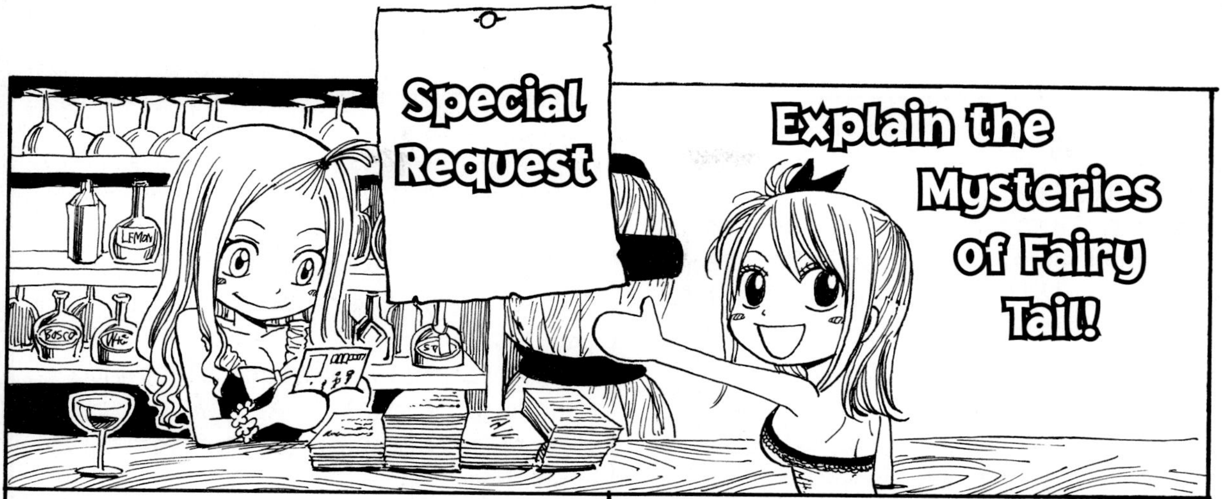
Special Request
Explain the Mysteries of Fairy Tail!

From the Fairy Tail Bar

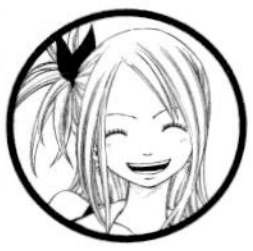: Hello there!! I'm Lucy, the cute and sexy manager of Fairy Tail!!

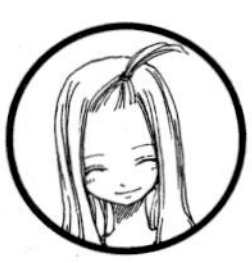: The author just loves to draw Lucy, doesn't he... Heh heh.

Lucy: Oh, he's just a lecher!! Really!! All he ever thinks about is sex!!
Mira: Let's get started. We've received a bunch of questions after people read volume 6.

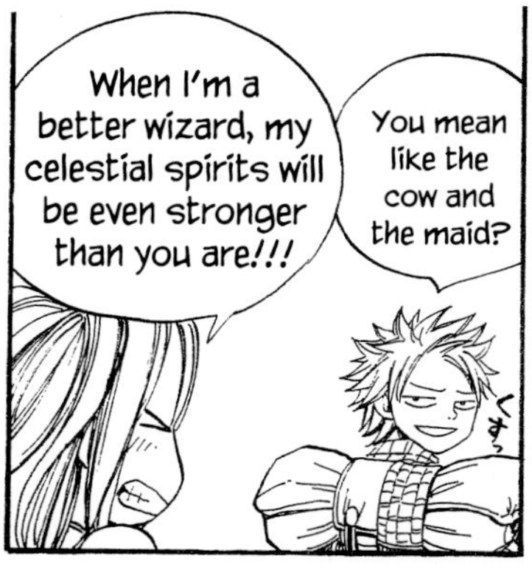
When I'm a better wizard, my celestial spirits will be even stronger than you are!!!
You mean like the cow and the maid?
くすっ

Does the strength of the celestial spirits change according to the magical power of the wizard using them?
Lucy: That's right.
Mira: ....
Lucy: ....
Mira: Is that all?

Lucy: I know what you want to say!! That the keys I have to the Twelve Golden Gates are wasted on me, right?
Mira: You knew exactly what I wanted to say.
Lucy: Ow!! That knife in my back hurts!! Sniff...
Mira: But we don't know what the future holds. When Lucy trains herself up to be a powerful wizard, I'd like to see what that bull looks like!
Lucy: Oh, Mira-san!! Sniff...
Mira: Just think of the T-bone barbecue we'll have then!!

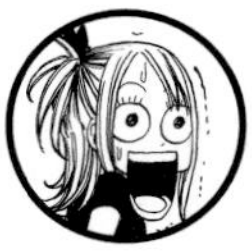: You can't eat him!!!!

Mira: Now on to the next question.

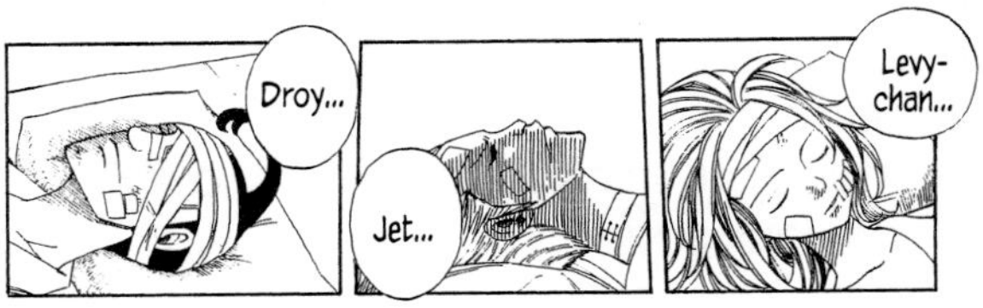
Levy-chan...
Jet...
Droy...

Is Levy-chan still alive?
Lucy: Of course she is!!
Mira: Don't worry. Jet and Droy are alive and kicking too.

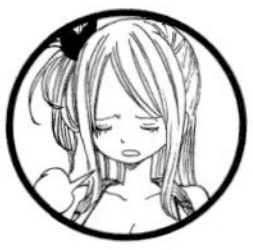: But with the author's previous work, leading characters died off, one after the other.

Continued on the next page

I can see why everyone would be nervous.

Mira: That's true. Sometimes the Master says, "I wonder if I'm the next to die!" and "It seems like a real possibility" and "I could just cry!" He seems really worried about it.

Lucy: Oh, dear... (sweat, sweat)

Mira: Let's go to the next question, shall we?

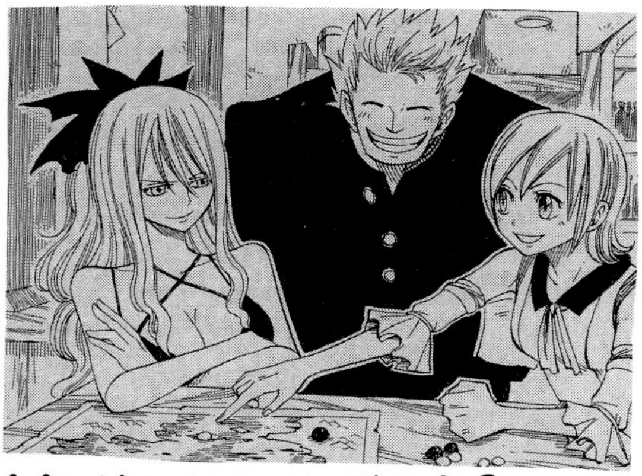

I-Is the one on the left... really...M-Mira-chan?

Shudder, shudder!

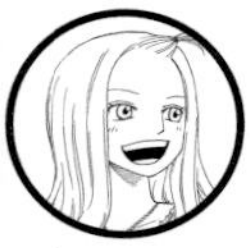 : Eh? Why would anyone bother to ask such an obvious question?

Lucy: B-But there's something about the girl in the picture that doesn't seem like you!

Mira: You think so? Well, I ***was*** quite young.♡

Lucy: A-And scary...

Mira: It was a fun time!! Elfman was a loose cannon who I always had to keep my eye on. But we'd go taking Lisanna with us...

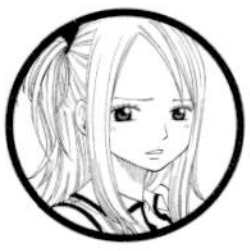 : Mira-san...

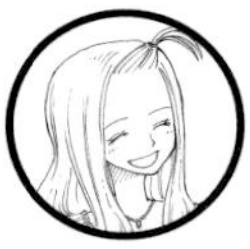 : And we'd get into all sorts of brawls with Erza or Natsu and the gang...

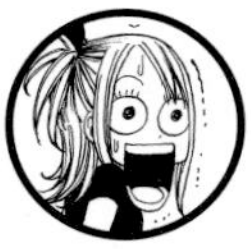 : ***Ehhhhh?!!!***

Mira: That's what it means to be young, Lucy! Everybody does it, don't they?

Lucy: Normally, girls don't get into that kind of stuff...

Mira: And now on to our last question.

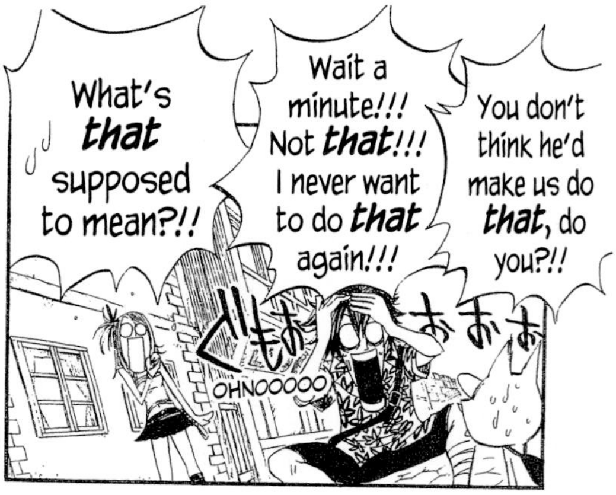
You don't think he'd make us do **that**, do you?!!
Wait a minute!!! Not **that**!!! I never want to do **that** again!!!
What's **that** supposed to mean?!!
OHNOOOOO

So what exactly is "that"?

Lucy: Urk! That's right!! I never did find out!!

Mira: Heh heh... Oh, of course, "that"!

Lucy: ?

Mira: We're still keeping it a secret.

***Lucy:* What the heck is "that"?!!**

We're collecting questions about *Fairy Tail!*
Send them to the address below!
↓
Hiro Mashima
Kodansha Comics
451 Park Ave. South, 7th Floor
New York, NY 10016

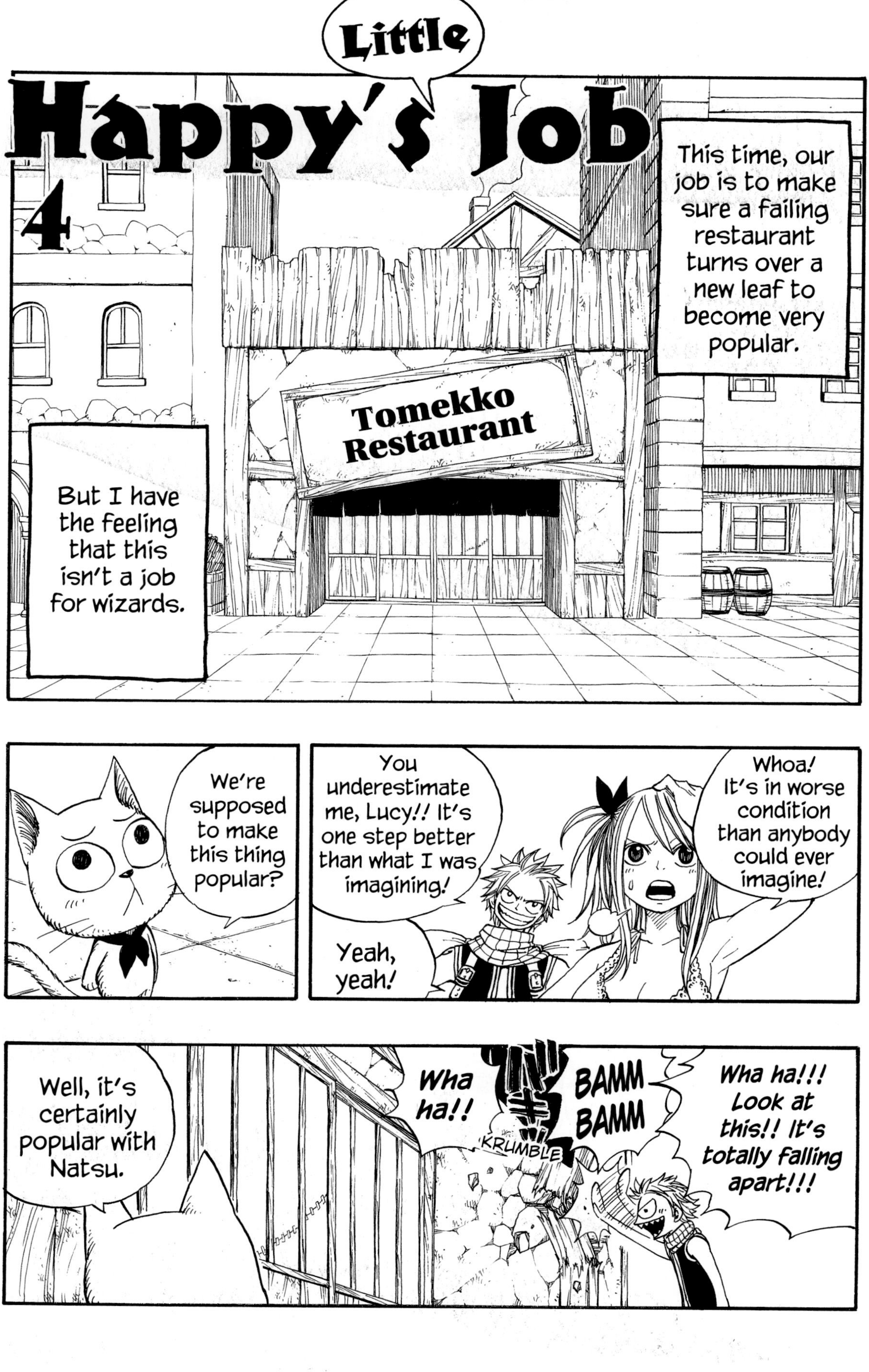
Happy's Little Job 4
Tomekko Restaurant
This time, our job is to make sure a failing restaurant turns over a new leaf to become very popular.
But I have the feeling that this isn't a job for wizards.
Whoa! It's in worse condition than anybody could ever imagine!
You underestimate me, Lucy!! It's one step better than what I was imagining!
Yeah, yeah!
We're supposed to make this thing popular?
Wha ha!!! Look at this!! It's totally falling apart!!!
BAMM BAMM
KRUMBLE
Wha ha!!
Well, it's certainly popular with Natsu.

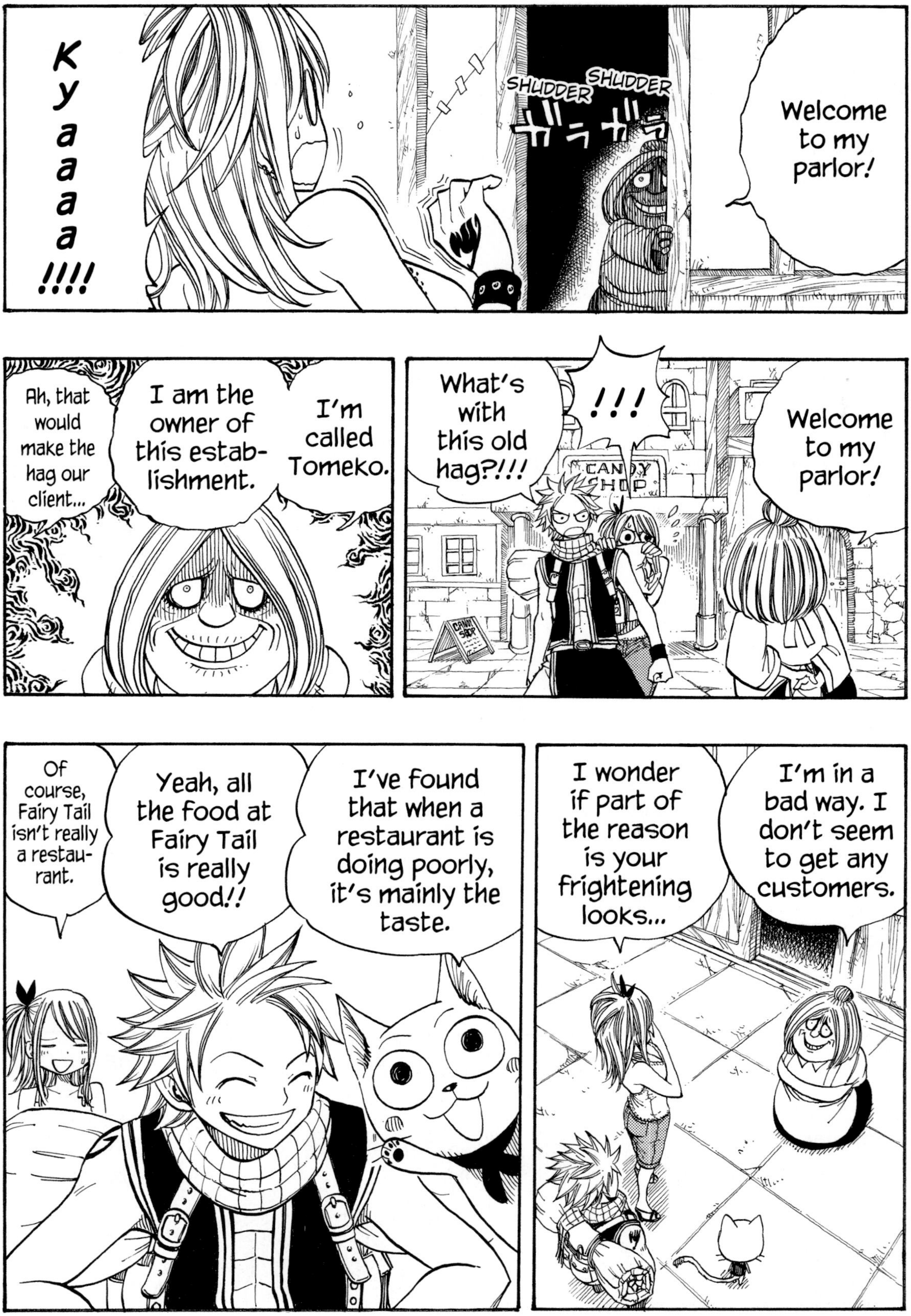
Welcome to my parlor!
SHUDDER SHUDDER
Kyaaaaa!!!!
Welcome to my parlor!
!!!
What's with this old hag?!!!
I'm called Tomeko.
I am the owner of this establishment.
Ah, that would make the hag our client...
I'm in a bad way. I don't seem to get any customers.
I wonder if part of the reason is your frightening looks...
I've found that when a restaurant is doing poorly, it's mainly the taste.
Yeah, all the food at Fairy Tail is really good!!
Of course, Fairy Tail isn't really a restaurant.

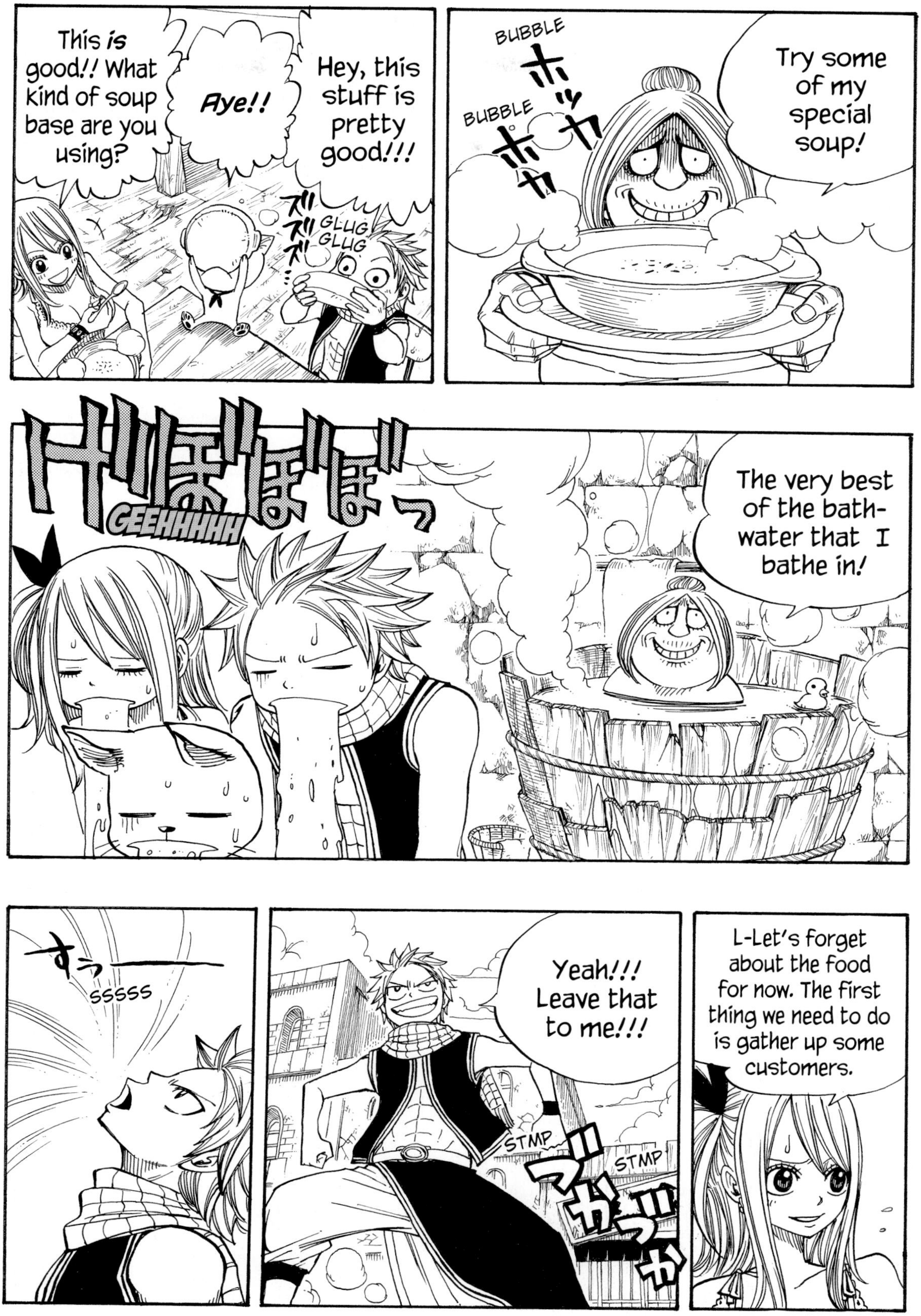
BUBBLE
BUBBLE
Try some of my special soup!
Hey, this stuff is pretty good!!!
Aye!!
This is good!! What kind of soup base are you using?
GLUG GLUG
GEEHHHHH
The very best of the bath-water that I bathe in!
L-Let's forget about the food for now. The first thing we need to do is gather up some customers.
Yeah!!! Leave that to me!!!
STMP
STMP
SSSSS

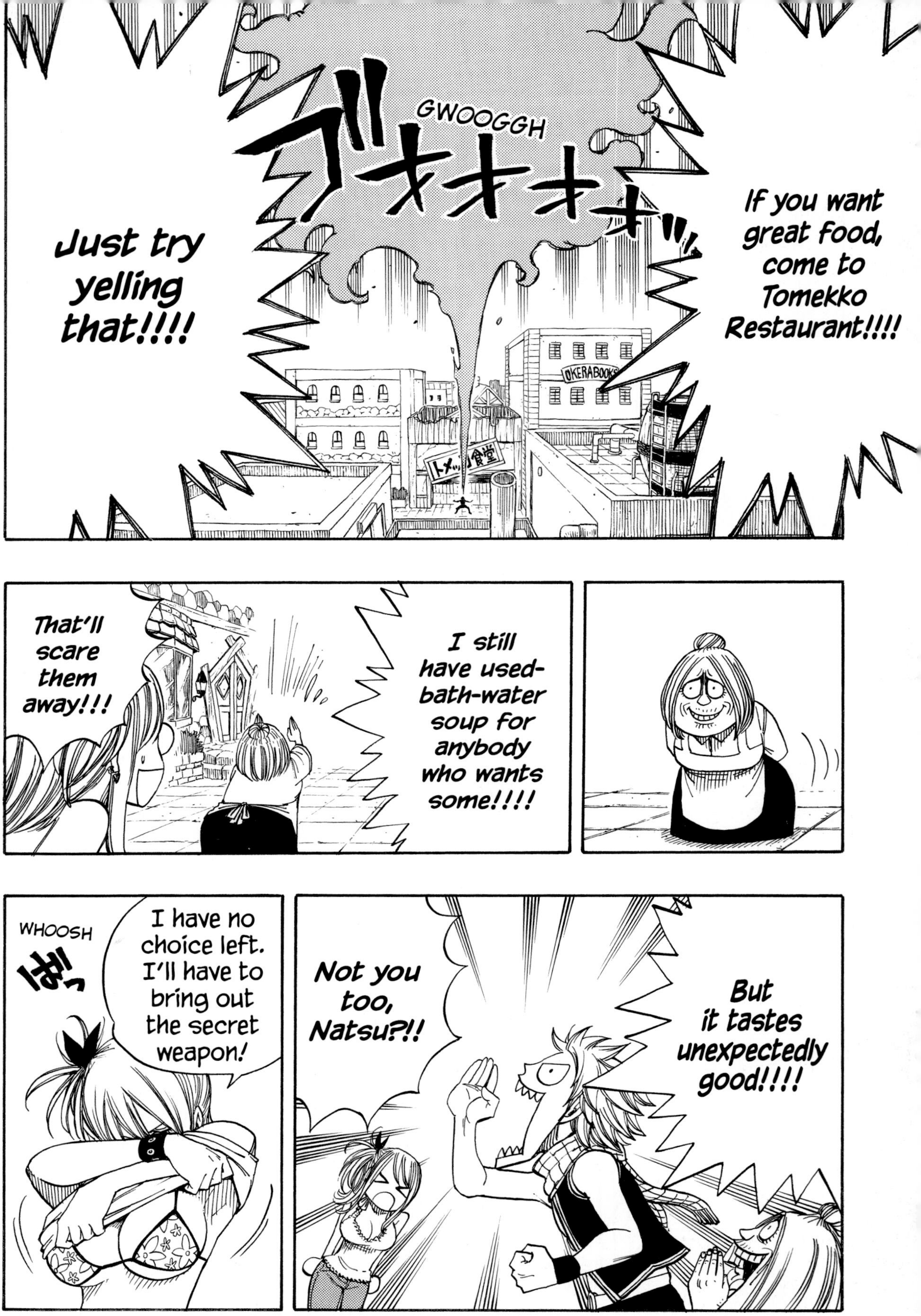
GWOOGGH
If you want great food, come to Tomekko Restaurant!!!!
Just try yelling that!!!!
OKERABOOKS
I still have used-bath-water soup for anybody who wants some!!!!
That'll scare them away!!!
But it tastes unexpectedly good!!!!
Not you too, Natsu?!!
I have no choice left. I'll have to bring out the secret weapon!
WHOOSH

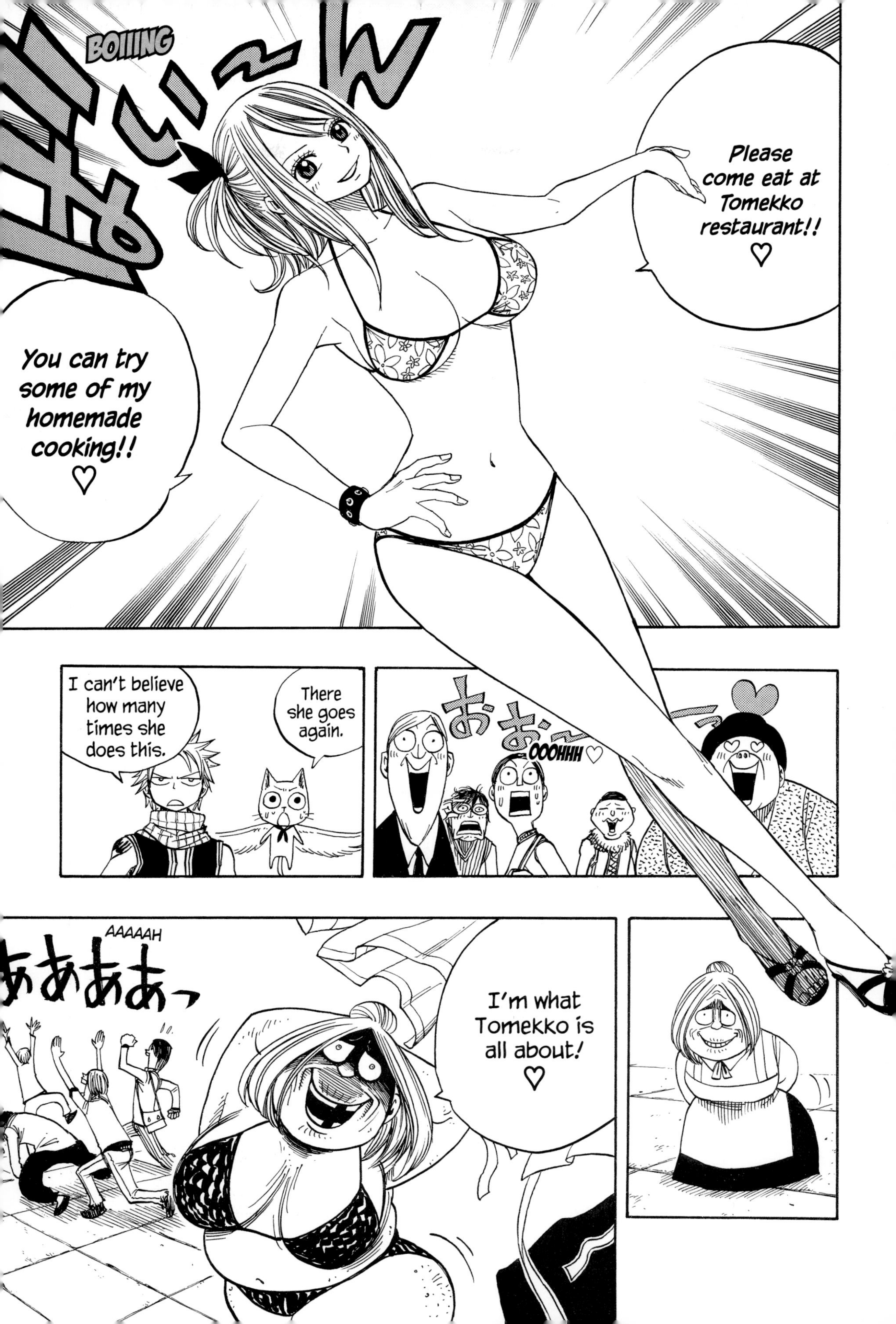
BOIIING
Please come eat at Tomekko restaurant!! ♡
You can try some of my homemade cooking!! ♡
OOOHHH♡
There she goes again.
I can't believe how many times she does this.
I'm what Tomekko is all about! ♡
AAAAAH
ああああっ

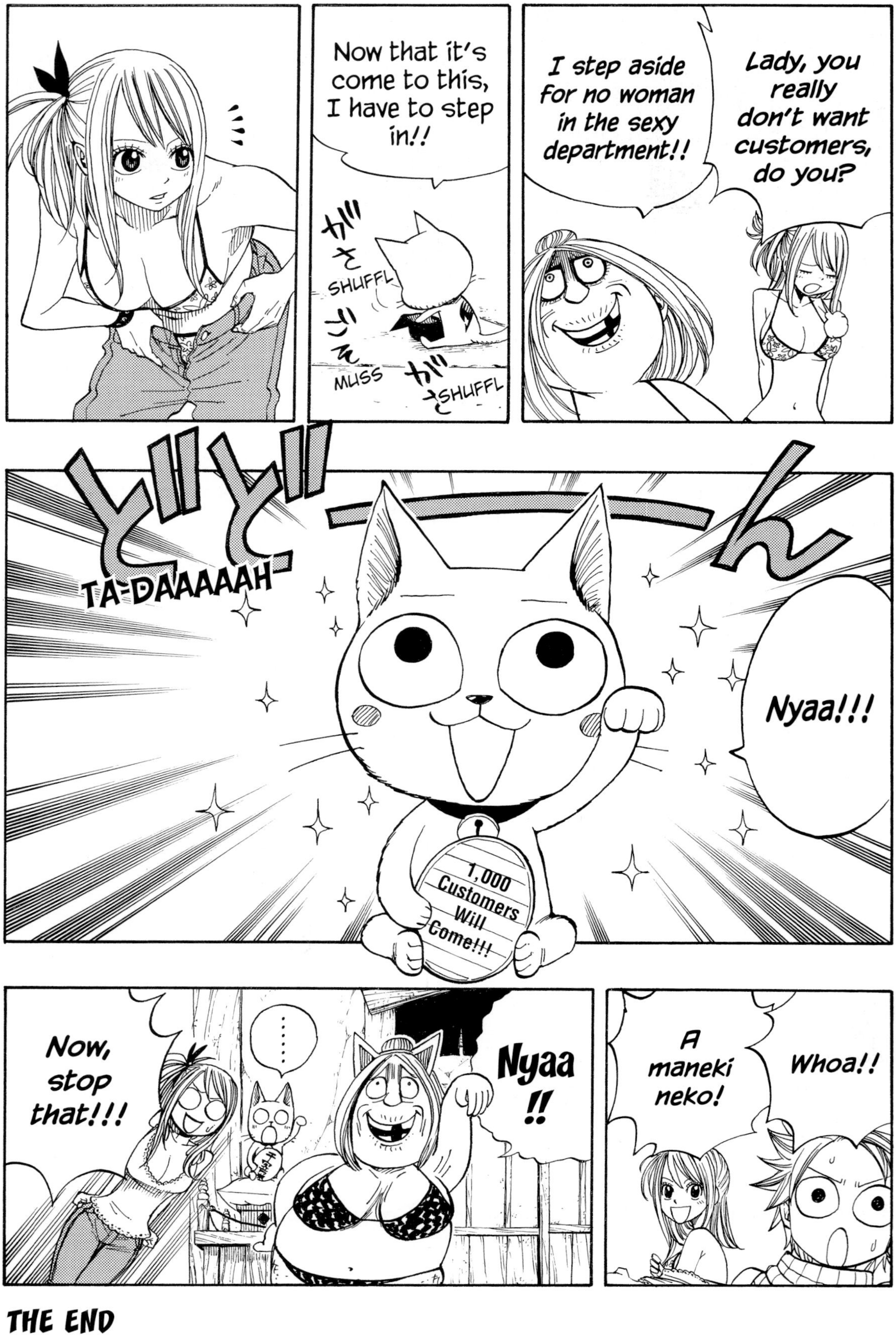
Lady, you really don't want customers, do you?
I step aside for no woman in the sexy department!!
Now that it's come to this, I have to step in!!
SHUFFL
MUSS
SHUFFL
TA-DAAAAH
Nyaa!!!
1,000 Customers Will Come!!!
Whoa!!
A maneki neko!
Nyaa!!
......
Now, stop that!!!

THE END

I'm sleepy!!! The seasons change, and I just can't keep my eyes open!! (Right now, the season is changing from summer to fall.) Long ago, I could get only a couple of hours sleep and still have lots of energy, but as I get older, that has slowly changed. Even so, I usually get about seven hours of sleep a night, and the other manga authors keep saying things like, "Wow, that's a lot!! I'm jealous!!" But even so, when I get sleepy, I get really sleepy. And with that, and the fact that I do work that takes long hours, I've figured out ways to deal with my sleepiness while I'm drawing my manga!

1 · I talk with the staff.
It depends on how much people are into the conversation, of course, but it can really charge my batteries back up! There are a lot of times when I even forget how sleepy I was! ◯

2 · Coffee and Cigarettes.
I go to the veranda and smoke one cigarette and come back to life! I have the feeling that coffee doesn't work on me anymore, so I use it more as a comfort drink. △

3 · Play.
I watch DVDs, play games, go outside for a bit, and come back refreshed!! But while I'm doing it, I can get absorbed, and the manga doesn't get drawn! △

4 · Sleep.
You know, just stop fighting it and get some sleep! And when you do, you don't just get rid of the sleepiness, you also get your strength back. ◎

Yeah, I know!! When you're sleepy, you should sleep! And to take my own advice...Good night, everybody!!

Translation Notes

Japanese is a tricky language for most Westerners, and translation is often more art than science. For your edification and reading pleasure, here are notes on some of the places where we could have gone in a different direction in our translation of the work, or where a Japanese cultural reference is used.

The Moon Can Be Hidden by Clouds, page 199

"The Moon Can Be Hidden by Clouds; Flowers Can Be Scattered by the Wind," is a Japanese proverb (*kotowaza*) that means that nothing in this world is certain.

The young debutant of the Heartfilia Konzern, Miss Lucy-sama!!!

Konzern, page 232

Konzern is a German word that Japanese sometimes borrows to refer to a business empire.

Lacrima, page 255

Lacrima is Latin for "tear," and the word has been used in Japanese to describe certain types of crystals and beads. The Fairy Tail universe seems to use the word for magical crystals.

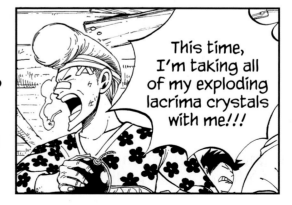

This time, I'm taking all of my exploding lacrima crystals with me!!!

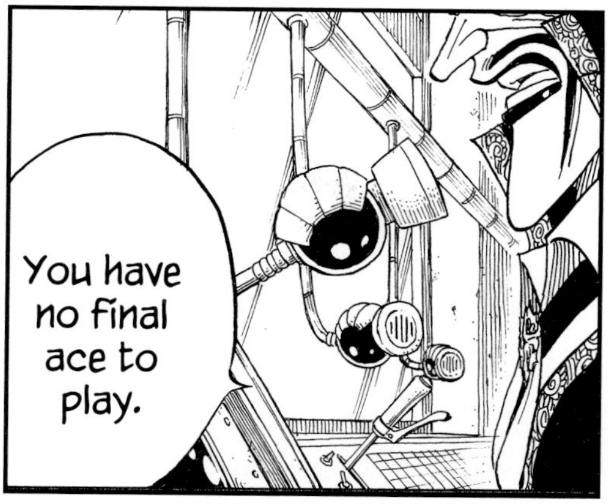
You have no final ace to play.

Final ace, page 80

This is an approximate translation. In Japanese, Jose said, "You will never have your triumphal song." That doesn't really come across in English as well as I wanted it to, so I changed the reference to playing aces in cards, which conveyed the same feeling without the unusual concept.

***Salut*, page 132**

Salut is French for "greetings."

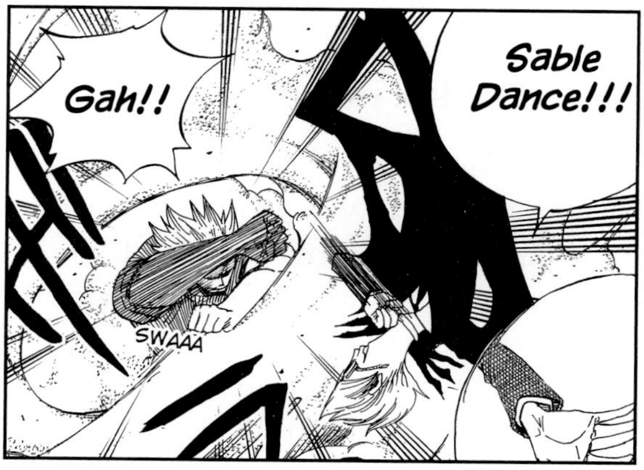
Sable Dance!!!
Gah!!
SWAAA

***Sable* Dance, page 137**

Sable is French for "sand."

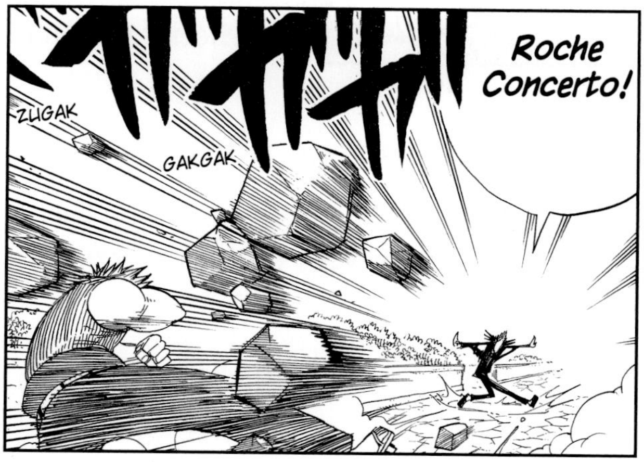
Roche Concerto!
ZUGAK
GAKGAK

***Roche* Concerto, page 138**

Roche is French for "rock."

Sonate plâtrée, page 142

Sonate plâtrée is French for "Plaster sonata."

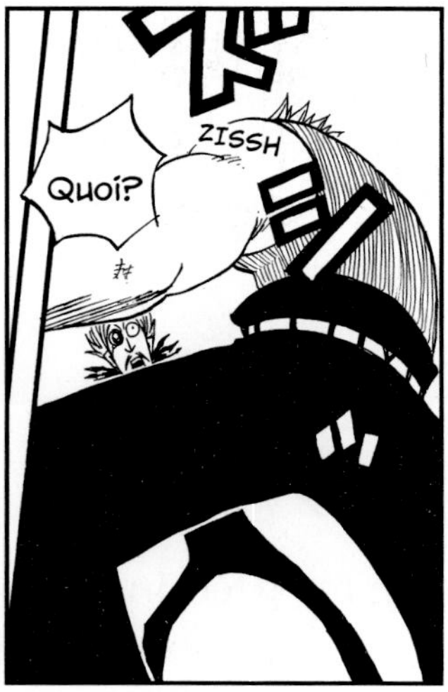
ZISSH
Quoi?

Quoi?, page 146

Of course, *quoi* means "what" in French.

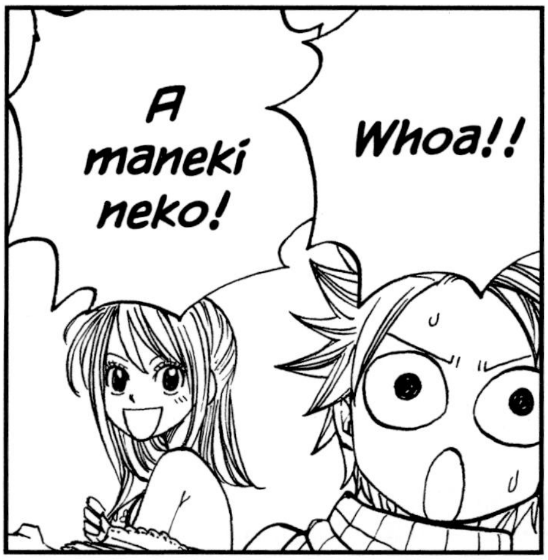
Whoa!!
A maneki neko!

maneki neko, page 190

Most Japanese businesses have a ceramic cat figure with one paw raised in a "come here"-like invitation and a traditional-style gold coin held close to its body. It is a good-luck charm made especially for businesses (but other establishments may also use it). The raised paw is an invitation for customers to come and the gold coin represents financial success.

Circles/triangles/X-marks, page 191

After Mashima-sensei describes his methods for staying awake, he gives them a rating. This rating is very common among Japanese. The circle ◎ represents a yes vote, or a stamp of approval. The triangle △ represents a flawed answer that may have good points, but doesn't really cut it. The no vote, or an answer that is completely wrong, is represented by an X-mark, X.

FAIRY TAIL

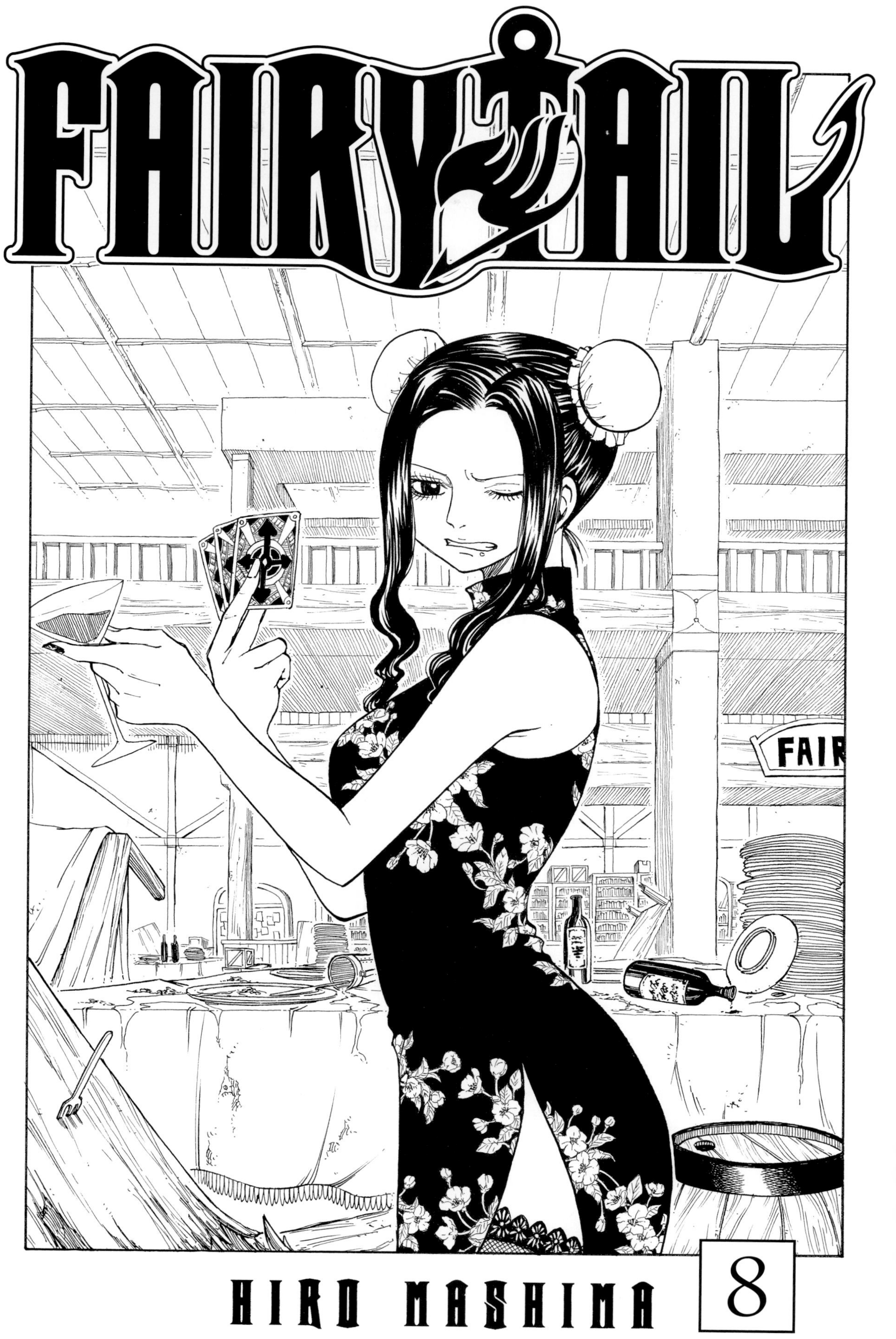
FAIR

HIRO MASHIMA

8

It happened so fast! My original goal of ten volumes is already in sight. Before I started, I thought that my previous work was so long (thirty-five volumes) that this time, I'd limit it to only about ten volumes. But it turned out to be much more fun drawing *FT* than I originally thought it would be. It looks like I can make this story a lot longer than planned! So root for me as I continue on…at least to volume 11!!

—Hiro Mashima

FAIRY TAIL

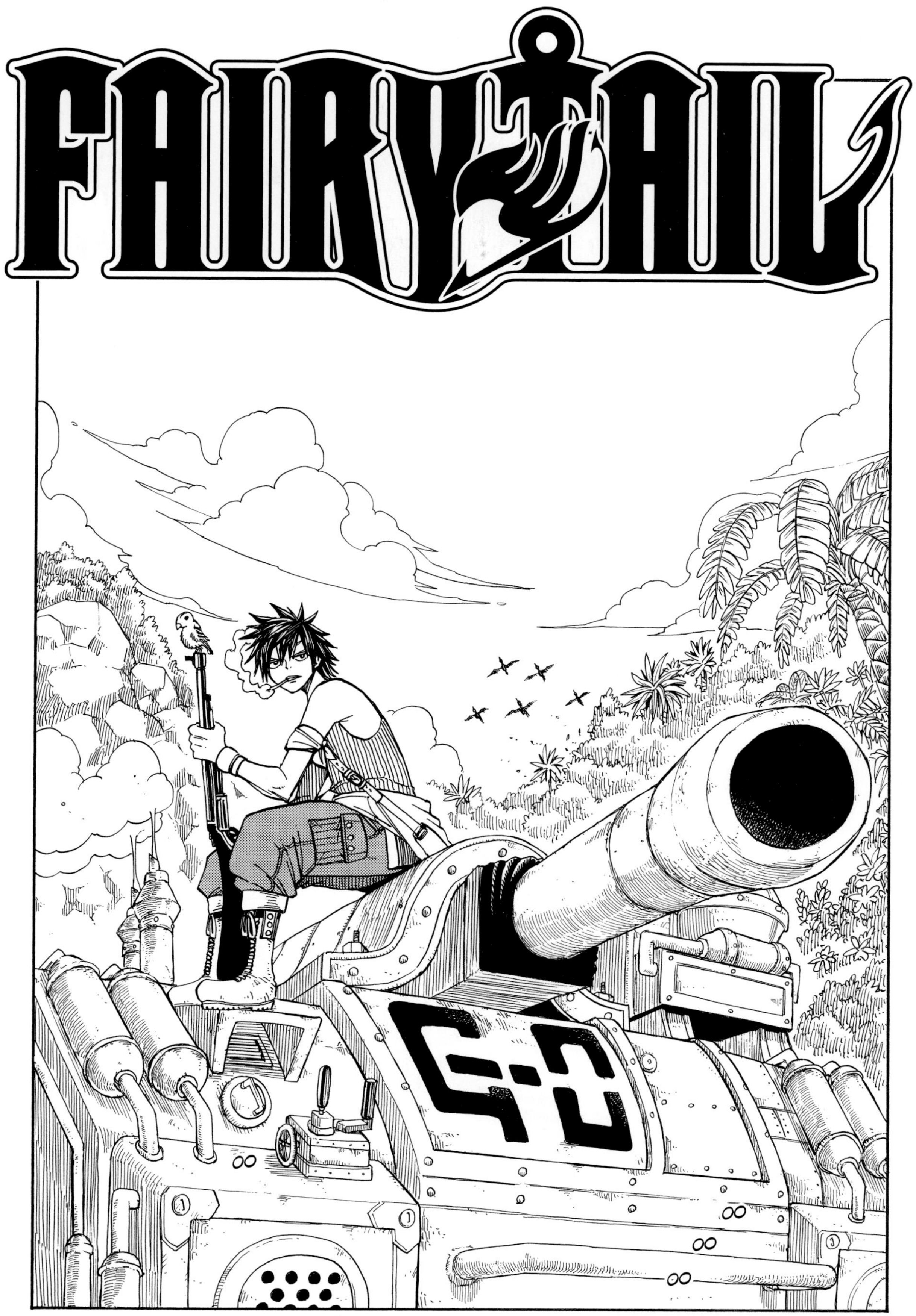

Chapter 57: Fair-Weather Charm

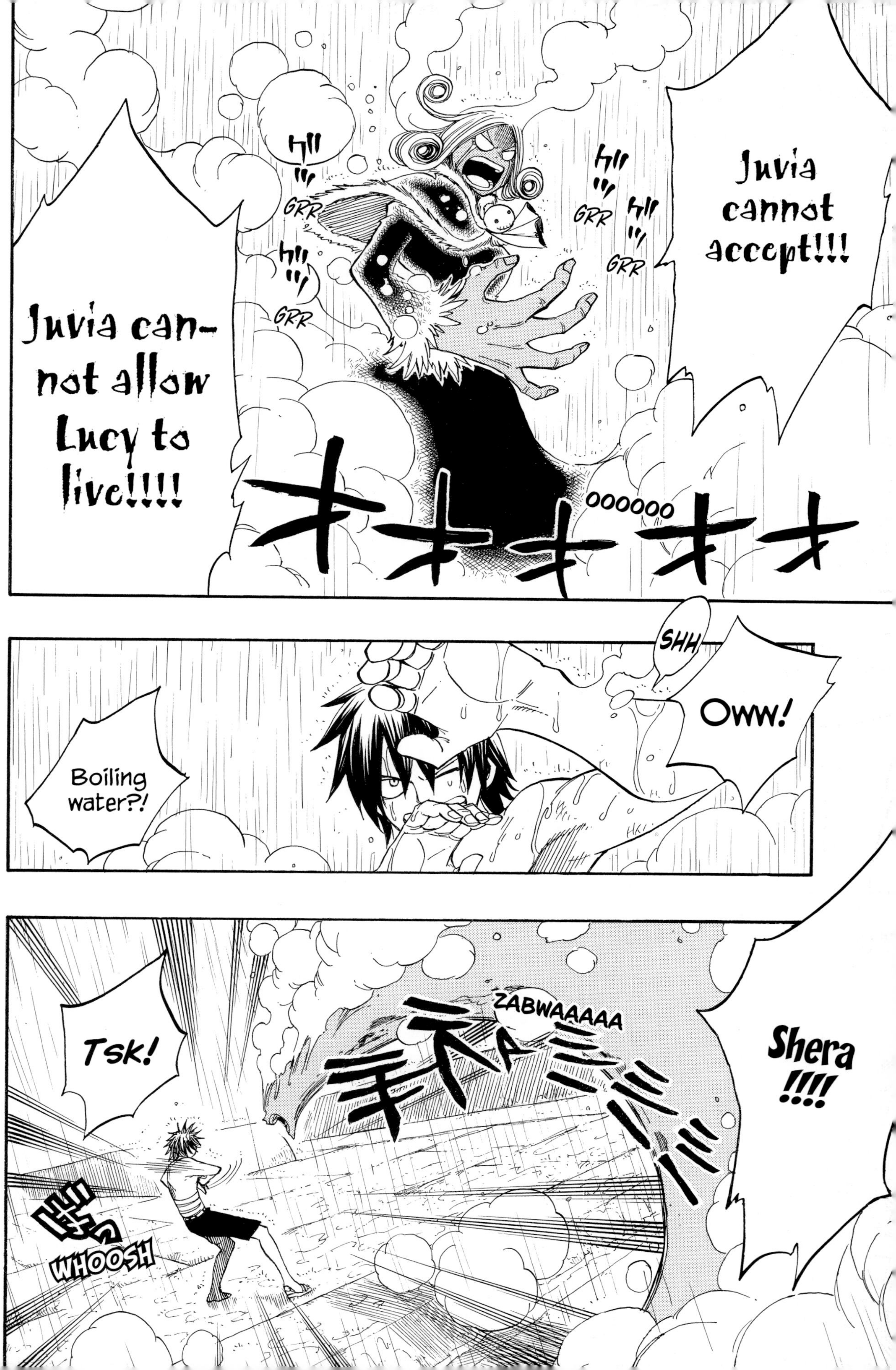
Juvia cannot accept!!!
GRR
GRR
GRR
GRR
GRR
Juvia cannot allow Lucy to live!!!!
OOOOOO
SHH
Oww!
Boiling water?!
Shera !!!!
ZABWAAAAA
Tsk!
WHOOSH

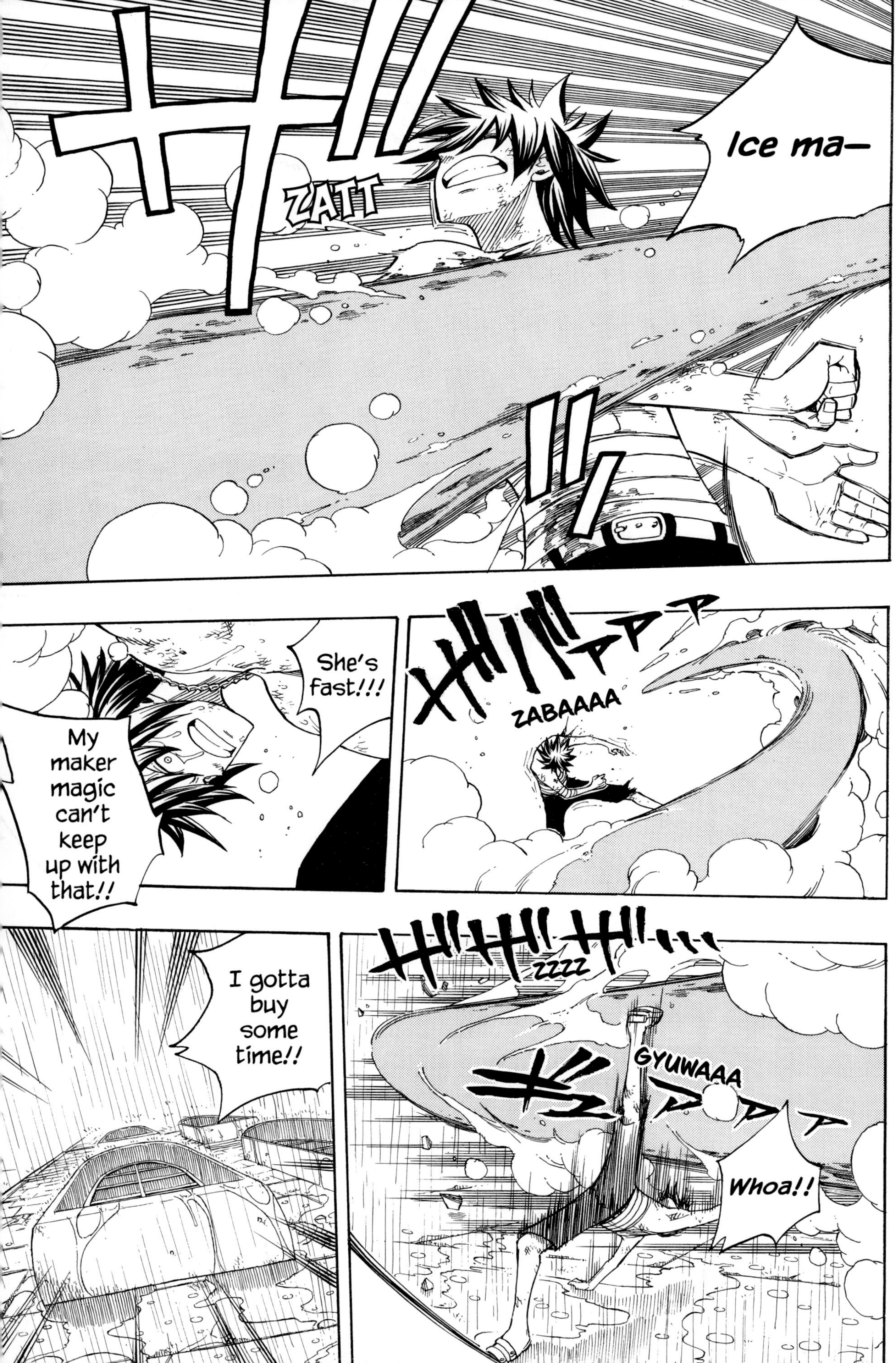
Ice ma—
ZATT
ZABAAAA
She's fast!!!
My maker magic can't keep up with that!!
ZZZZ
GYUWAAA
Whoa!!
I gotta buy some time!!

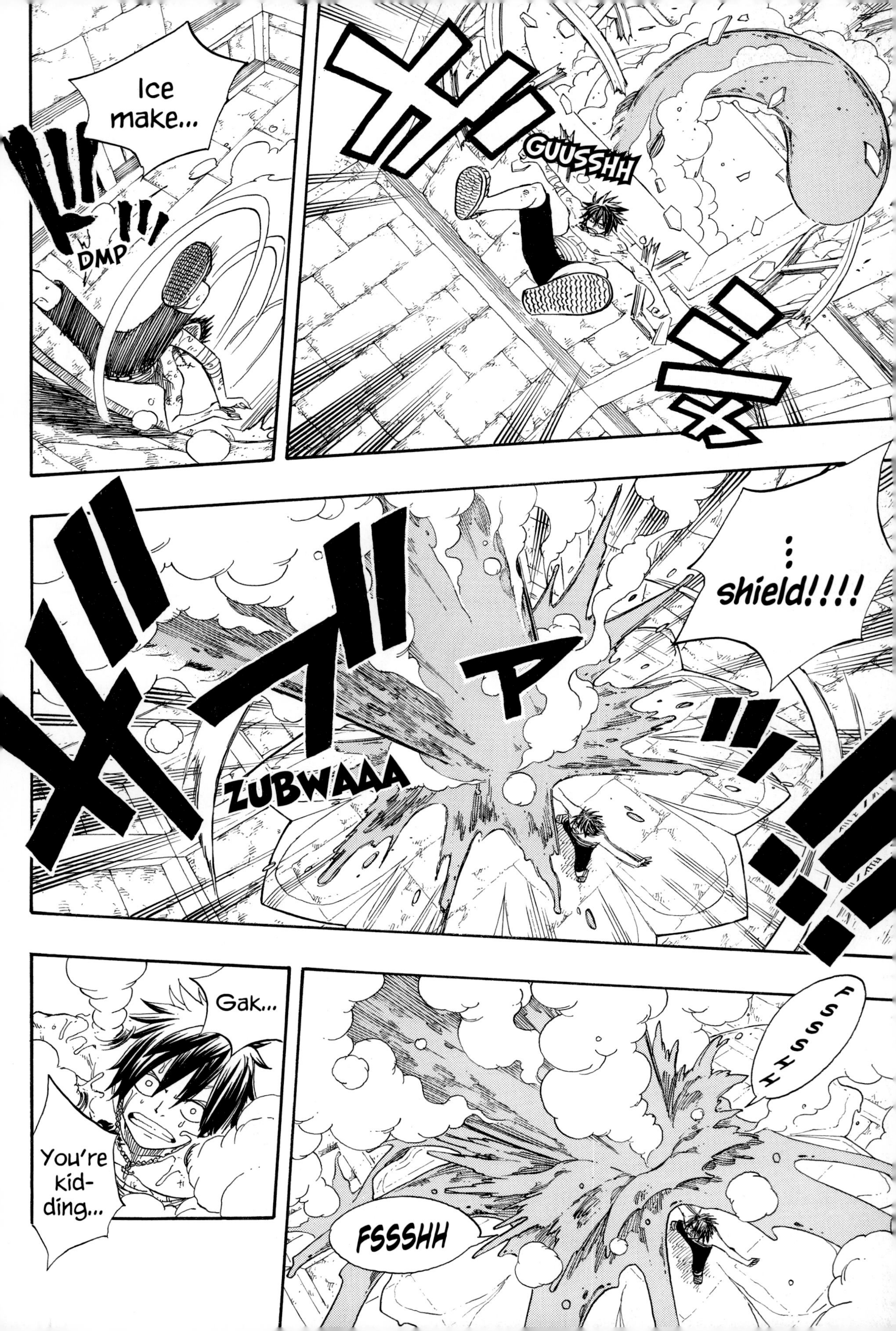
GUUSHH
Ice make...
DMP
: shield!!!!
ZUBWAAA
FSSSHH
FSSSHH
Gak...
You're kid-ding...

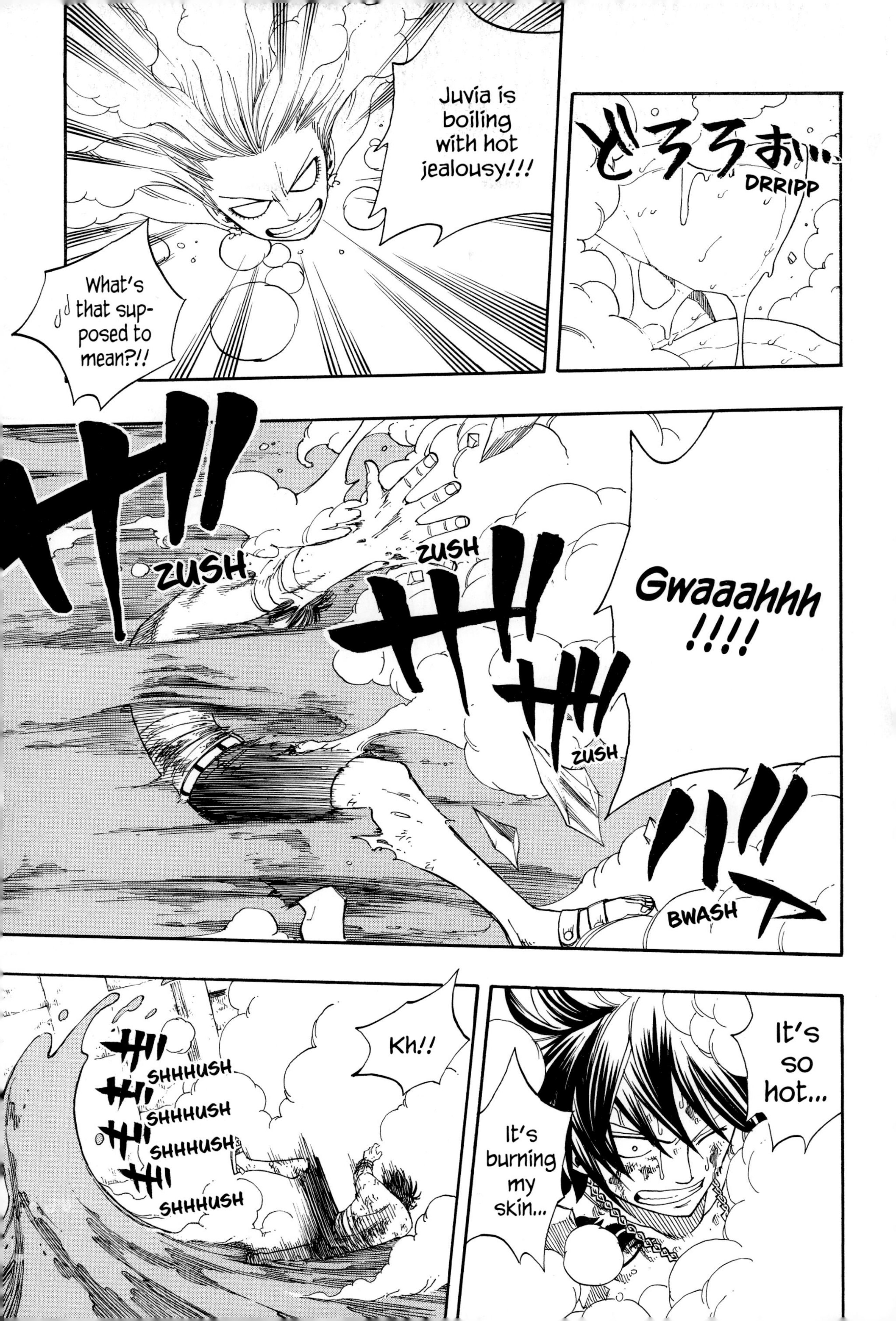
DRRIPP
Juvia is boiling with hot jealousy!!!
What's that supposed to mean?!!
Gwaaahhh!!!!
ZUSH
ZUSH
ZUSH
BWASH
It's so hot...
It's burning my skin...
Kh!!
SHHHUSH
SHHHUSH
SHHHUSH
SHHHUSH

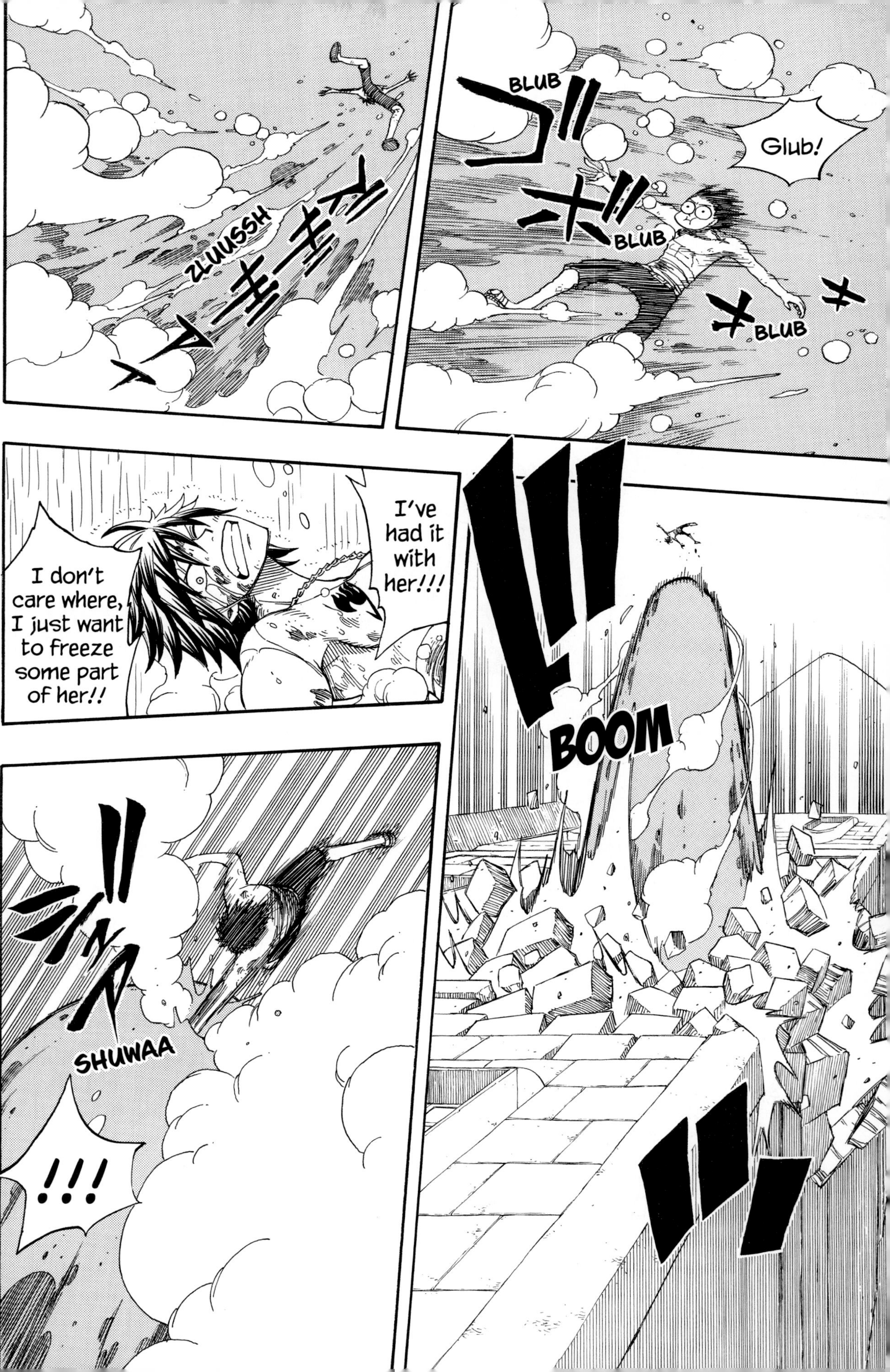
BLUB
Glub!
BLUB
BLUB
ZLUUSSH
BOOM
I've had it with her!!!
I don't care where, I just want to freeze some part of her!!
SHUWAA
!!!

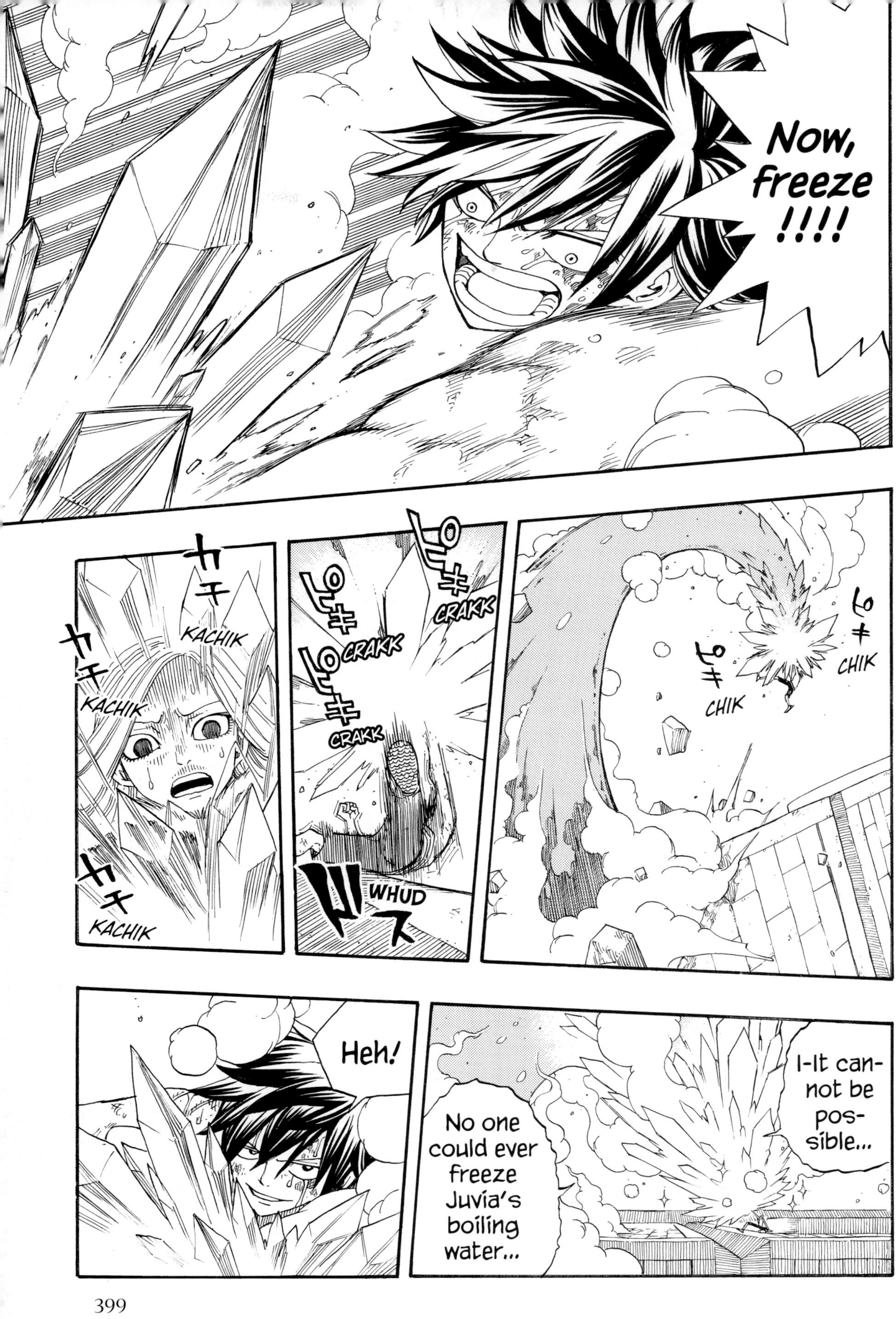
Now, freeze !!!!
ピキ
CHIK
ピキ
CHIK
ピキ
CRAKK
ピキ
CRAKK
ピキ
CRAKK
ドス
WHUD
カチ
KACHIK
カチ
KACHIK
カチ
KACHIK
I-It cannot be possible...
No one could ever freeze Juvia's boiling water...
Heh!

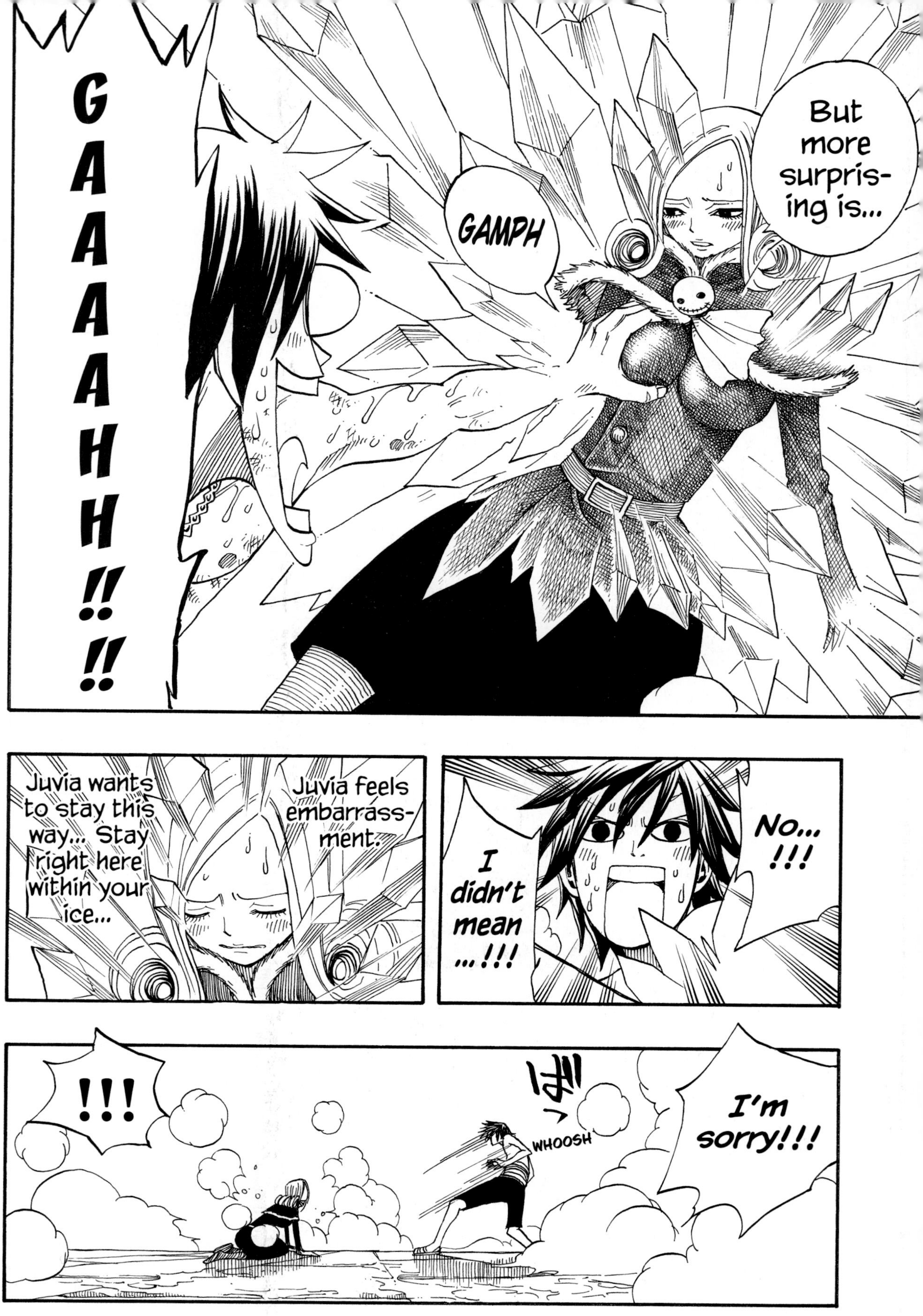
But more surprising is...
GAMPH
GAAAAHH!!!!
No...!!!
I didn't mean...!!!
Juvia feels embarrassment.
Juvia wants to stay this way... Stay right here within your ice...
I'm sorry!!!
WHOOSH
!!!

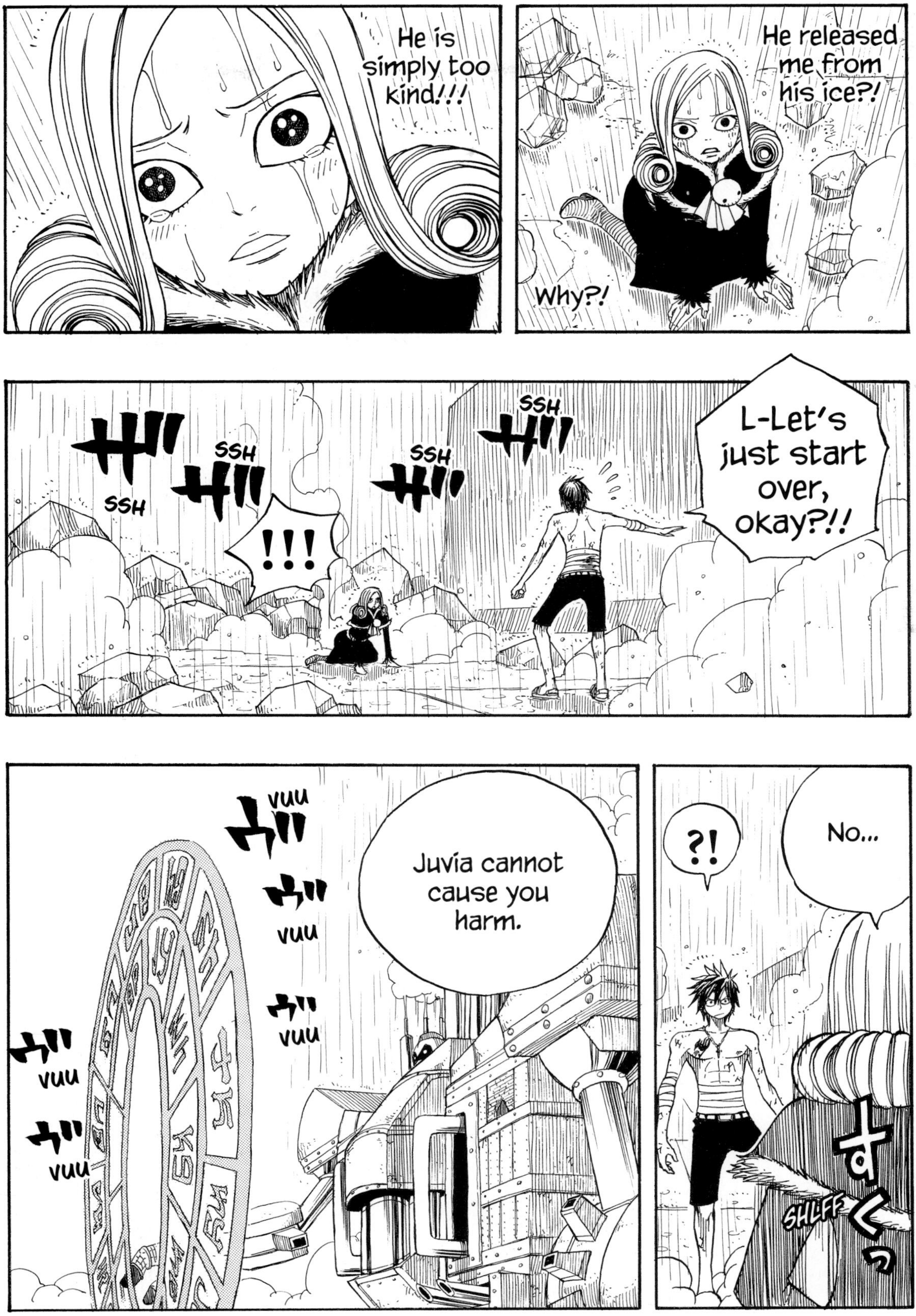
He released me from his ice?!
Why?!
He is simply too kind!!!
SSH
L-Let's just start over, okay?!!
SSH
!!!
SSH
SSH
No...
?!
SHLFF
VUU
Juvia cannot cause you harm.
VUU
VUU
VUU
VUU

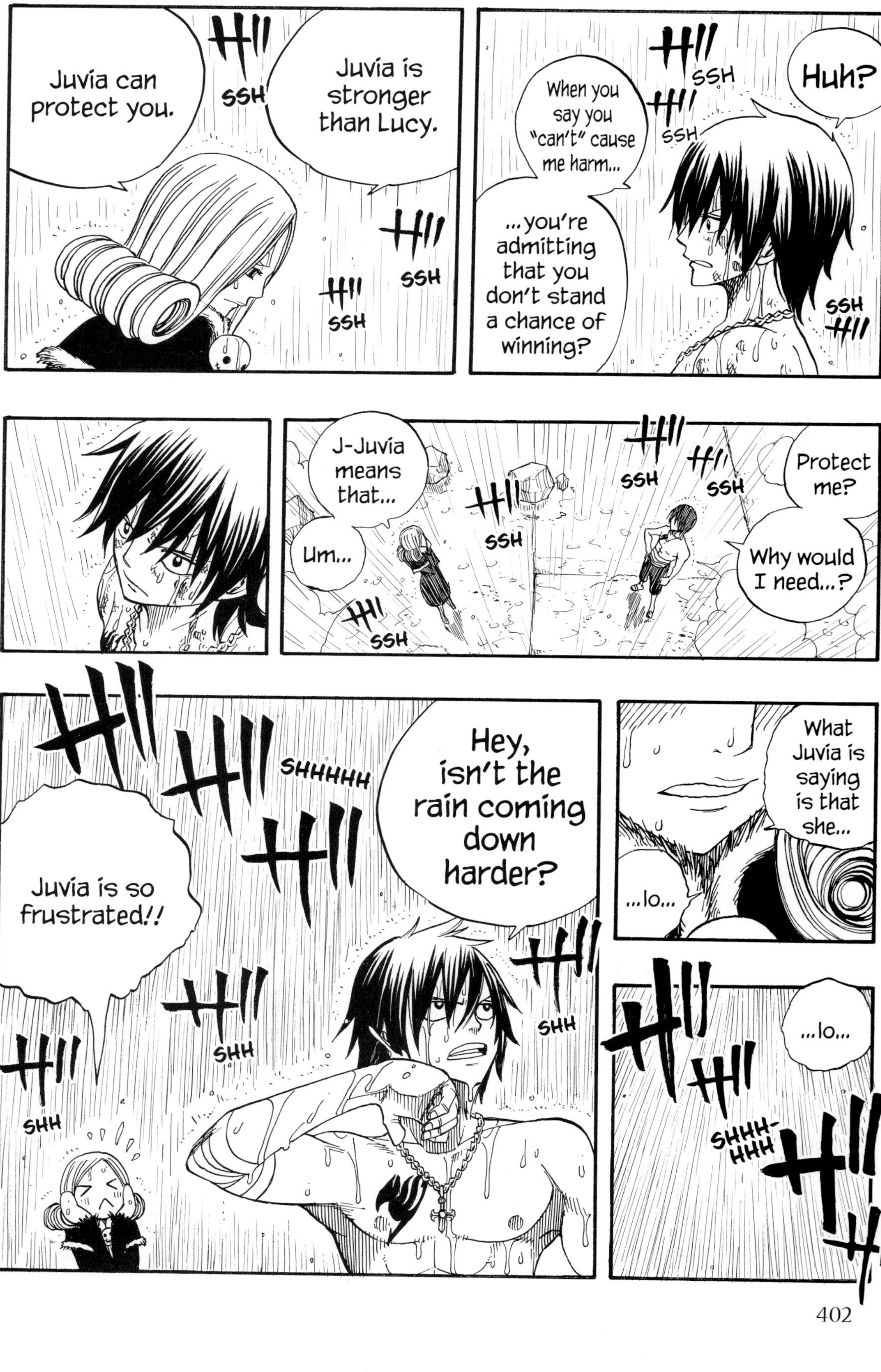
Huh?
When you say you "can't" cause me harm...
...you're admitting that you don't stand a chance of winning?
SSH
SSH
SSH
Juvia is stronger than Lucy.
Juvia can protect you.
SSH
SSH
SSH
Protect me?
Why would I need...?
SSH
SSH
J-Juvia means that...
Um...
SSH
SSH
What Juvia is saying is that she...
...lo...
...lo...
SHHH-HHH
Hey, isn't the rain coming down harder?
SHHHHH
Juvia is so frustrated!!
SHH
SHH
SHH

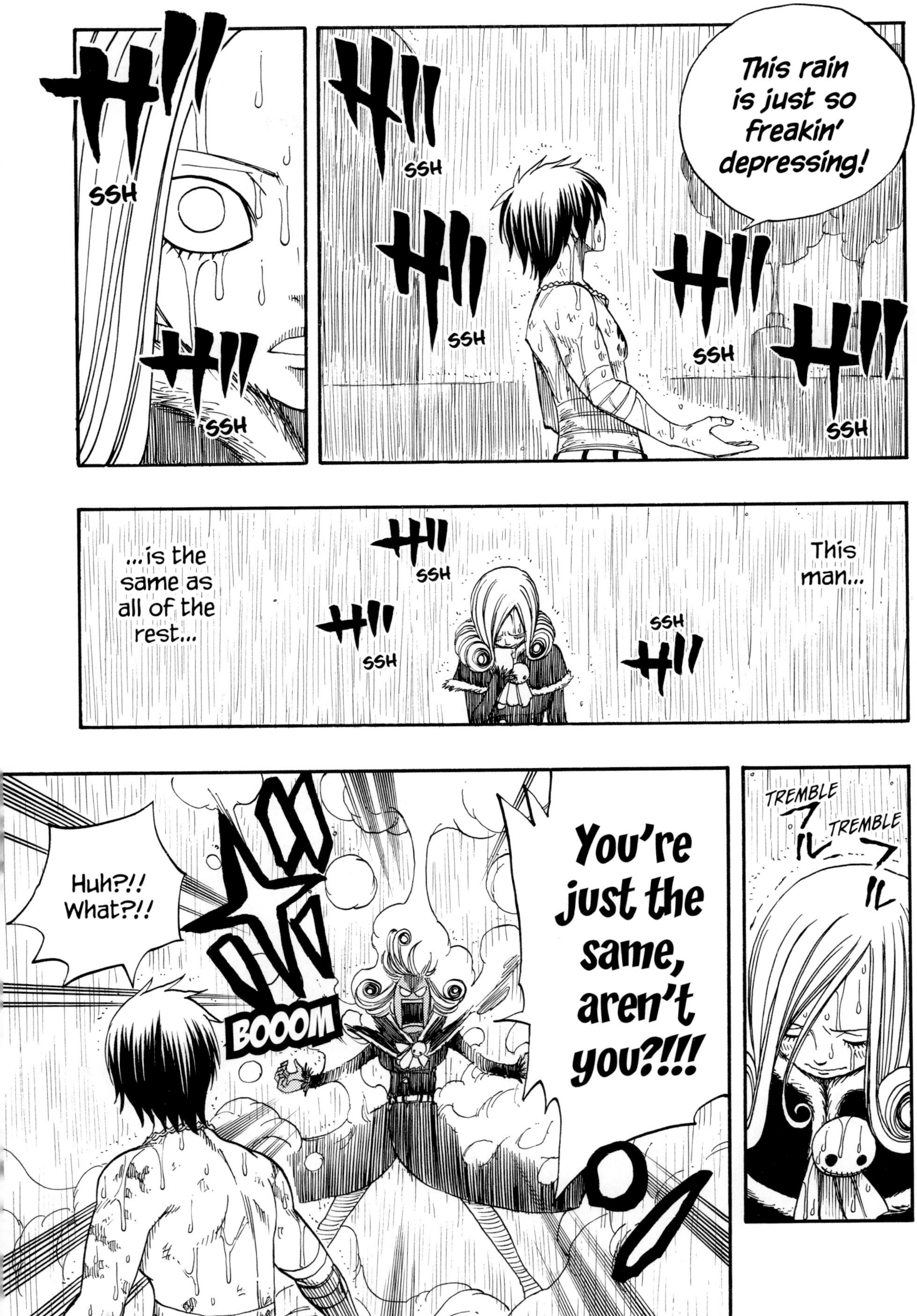
This rain is just so freakin' depressing!
SSH
SSH
SSH
SSH
SSH
SSH
This man...
...is the same as all of the rest...
SSH
SSH
SSH
TREMBLE
TREMBLE
You're just the same, aren't you?!!!
BOOOM
Huh?!! What?!!

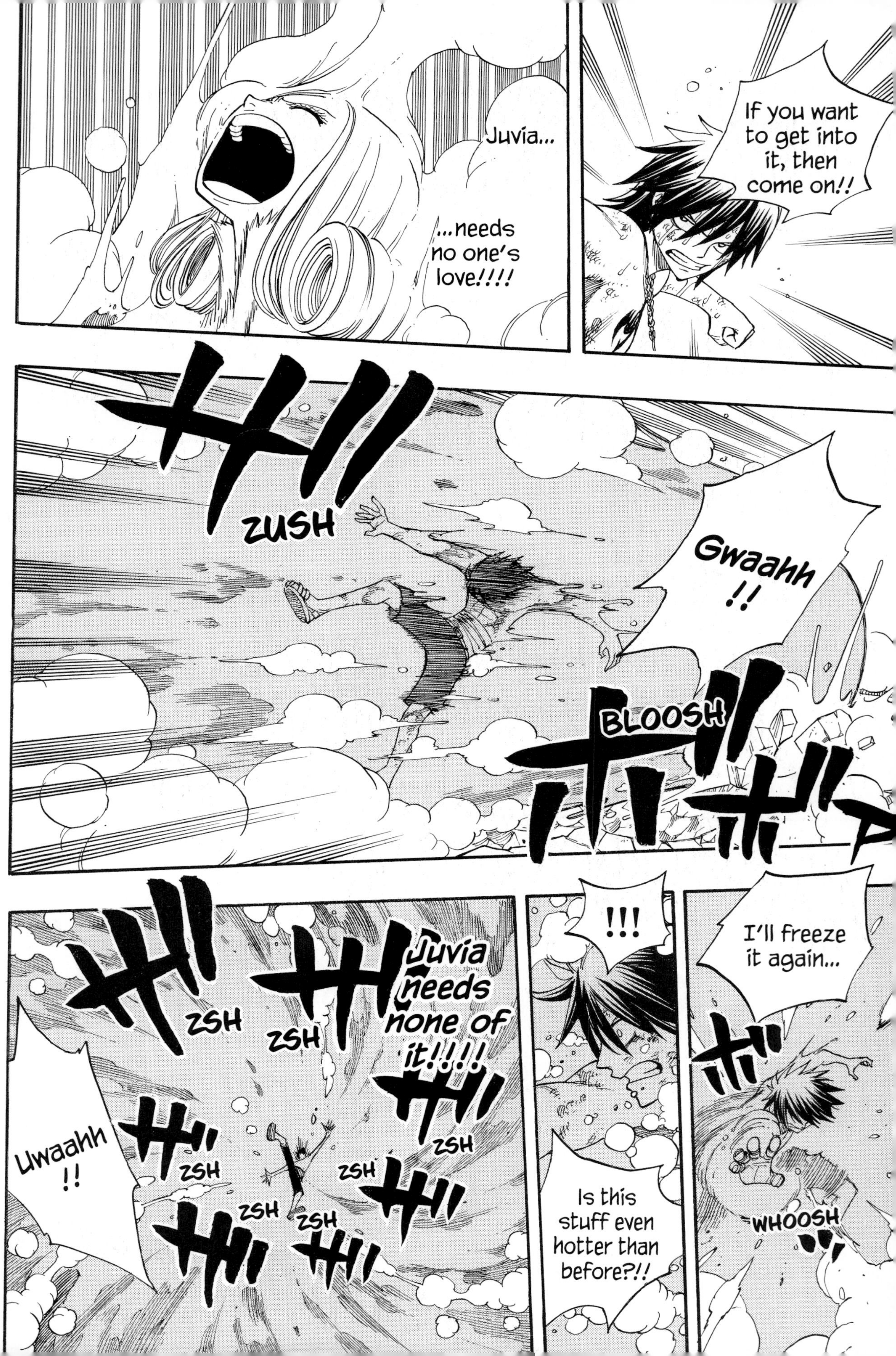
If you want to get into it, then come on!!
Juvia...
...needs no one's love!!!!
Gwaahh!!
BLOOSH
ZUSH
I'll freeze it again...
WHOOSH
!!!
Is this stuff even hotter than before?!!
Juvia needs none of it!!!!!
ZSH
ZSH
ZSH
ZSH
ZSH
ZSH
ZSH
Uwaahh!!

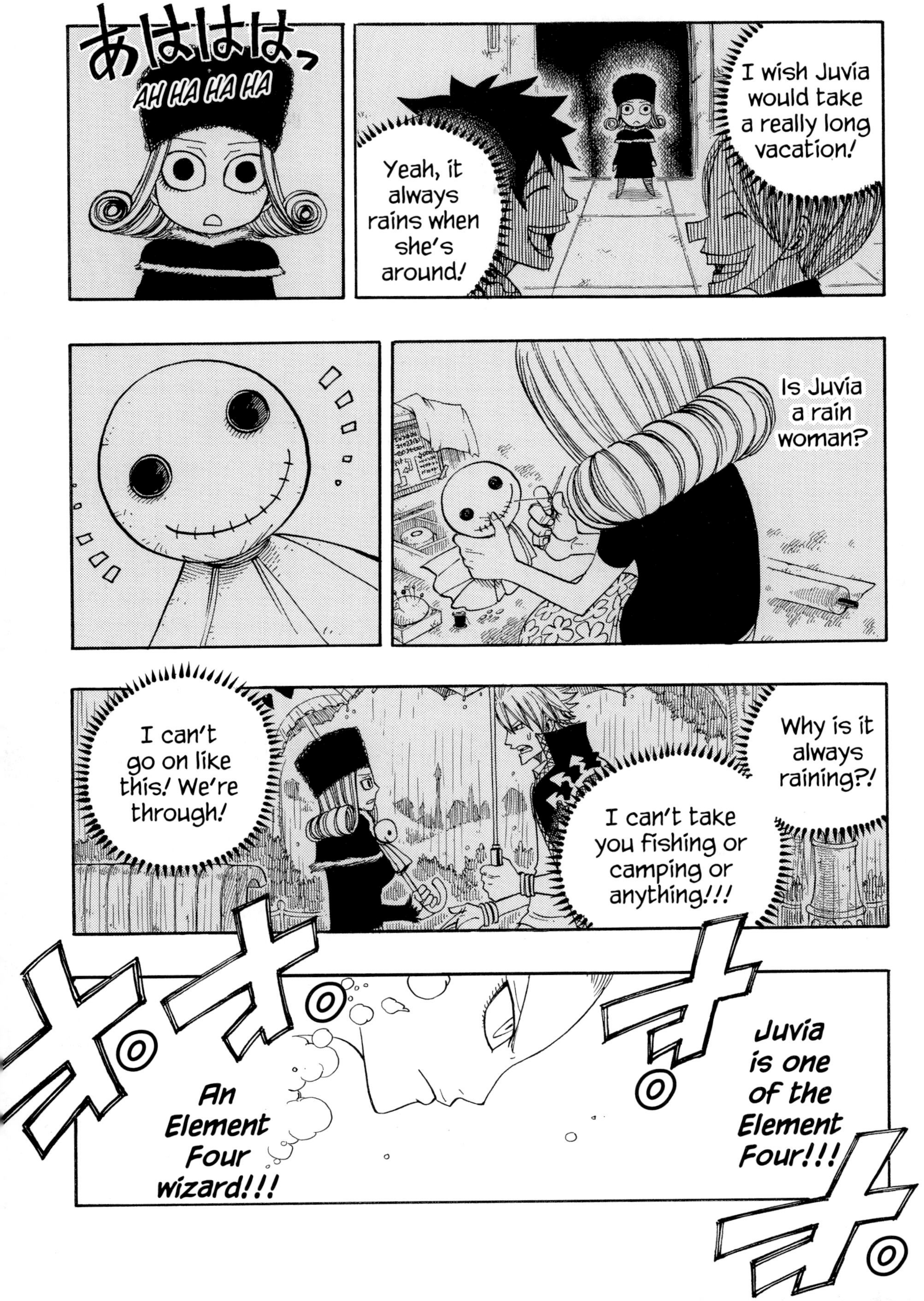
I wish Juvia would take a really long vacation!
Yeah, it always rains when she's around!
あははは
AH HA HA HA
Is Juvia a rain woman?
Why is it always raining?!
I can't take you fishing or camping or anything!!!
I can't go on like this! We're through!
Juvia is one of the Element Four!!!
An Element Four wizard!!!

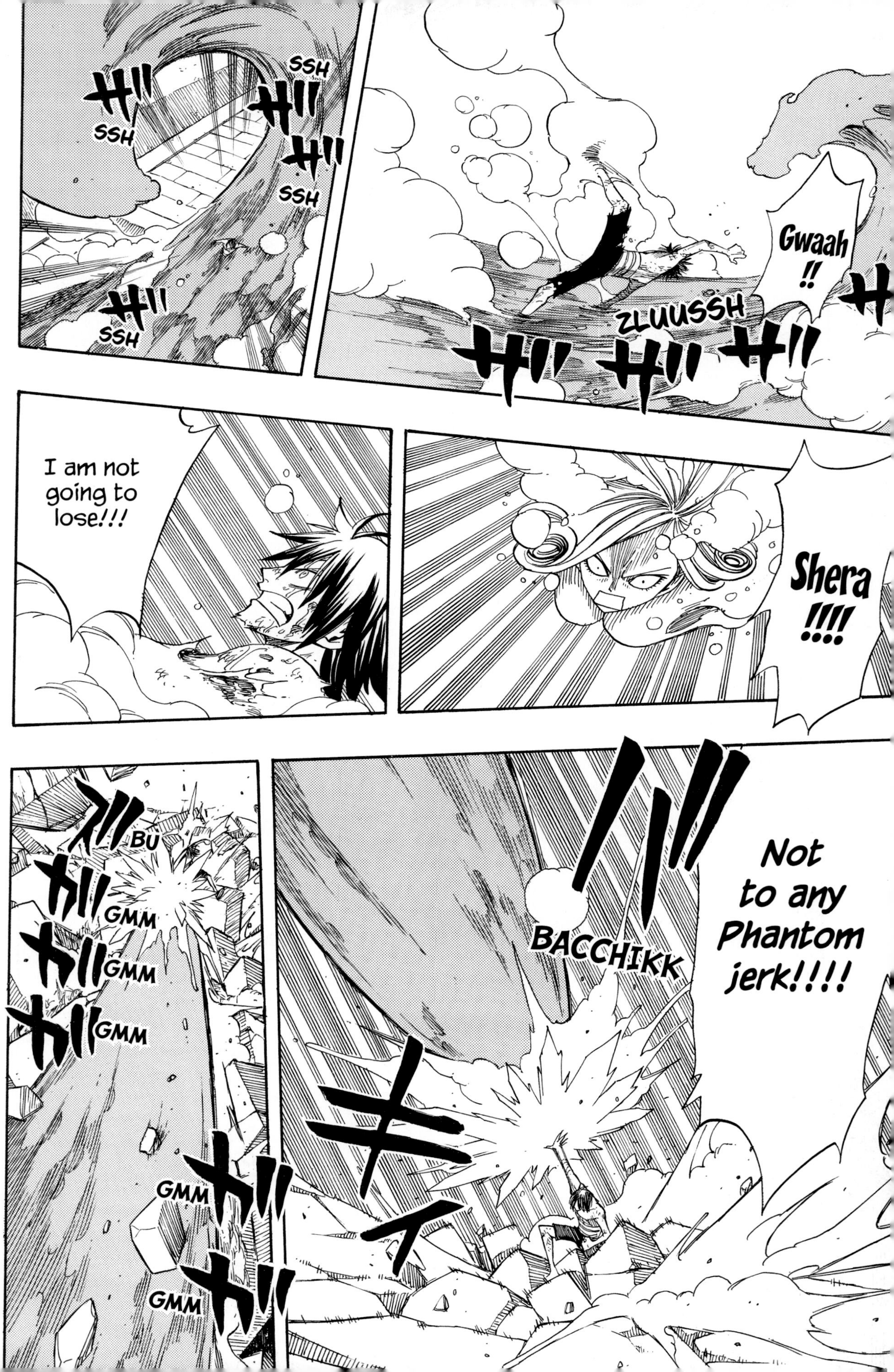
Gwaah!!
ZLUUSSH
SSH
SSH
SSH
SSH
Shera!!!!
I am not going to lose!!!
BACCHIKK
Not to any Phantom jerk!!!!
BU
GMM
GMM
GMM
GMM
GMM

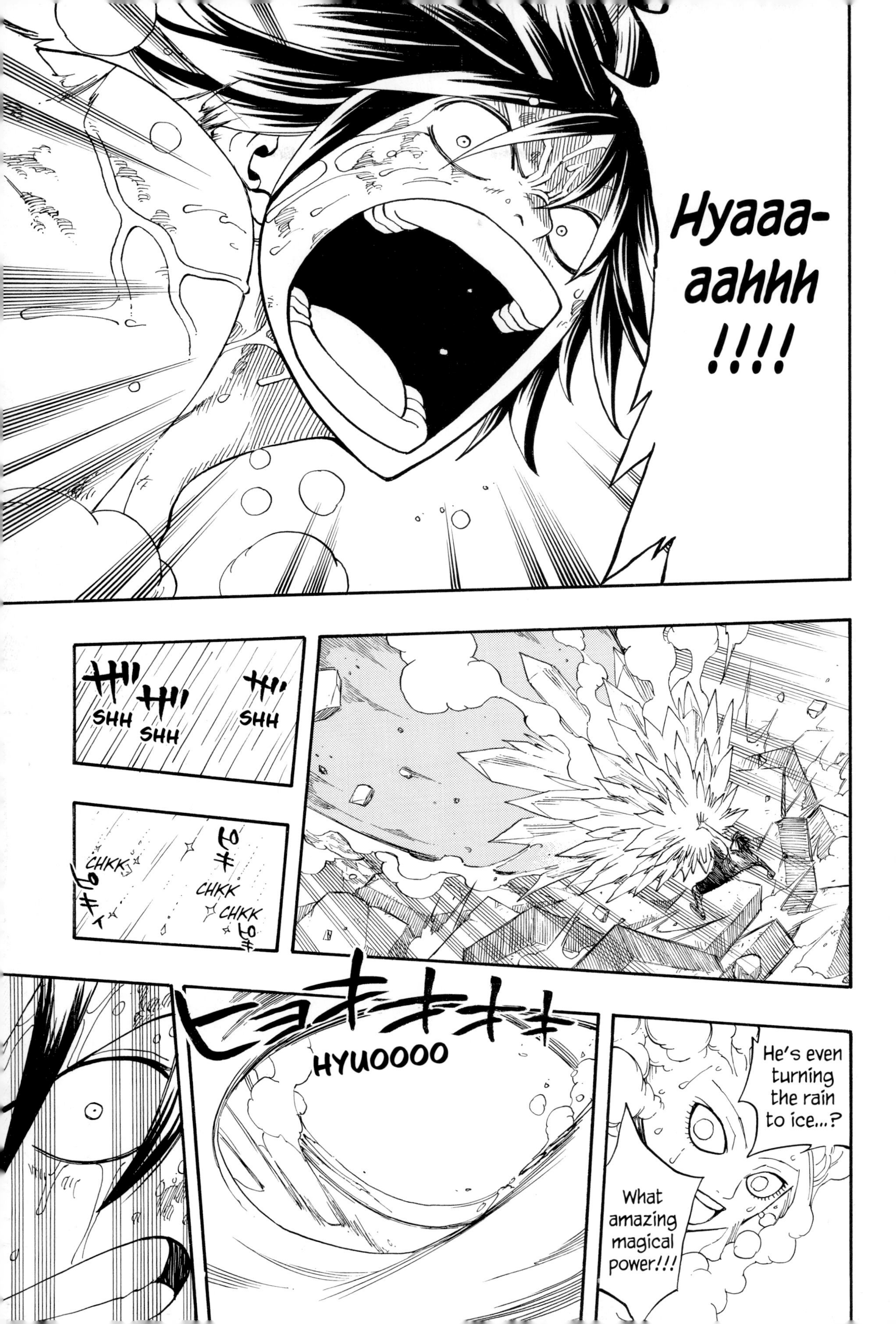
Hyaaa-aahhh!!!!
ザザ SHH
ザザ SHH
ザザ SHH
ピキ CHKK
ピキ CHKK
ピキィ CHKK
He's even turning the rain to ice...?
What amazing magical power!!!
ヒョオオオオ HYUOOOO

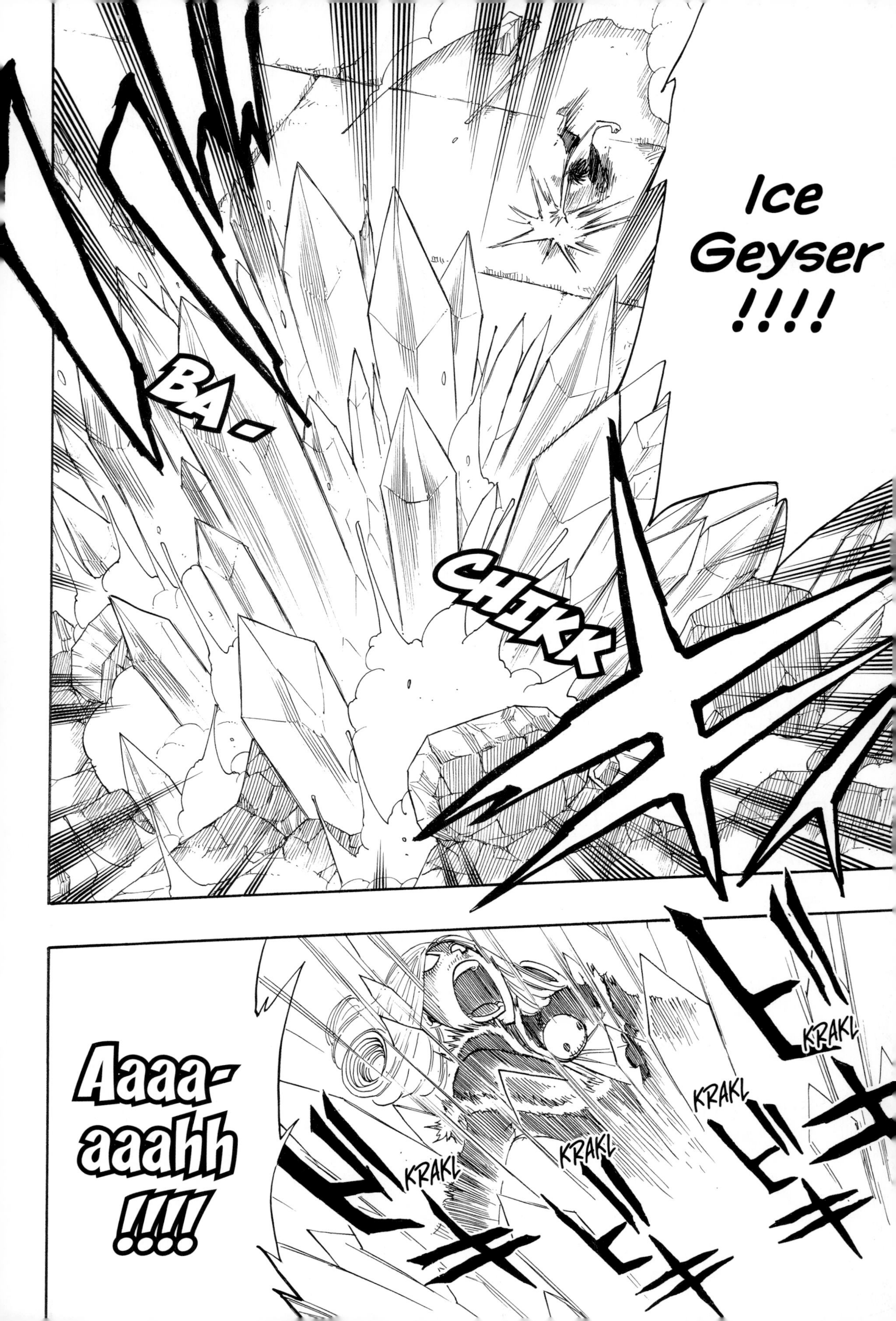
Ice Geyser !!!!
BA-
CHIKK
KRAKL
KRAKL
KRAKL
KRAKL
Aaaa-aaaahh !!!!

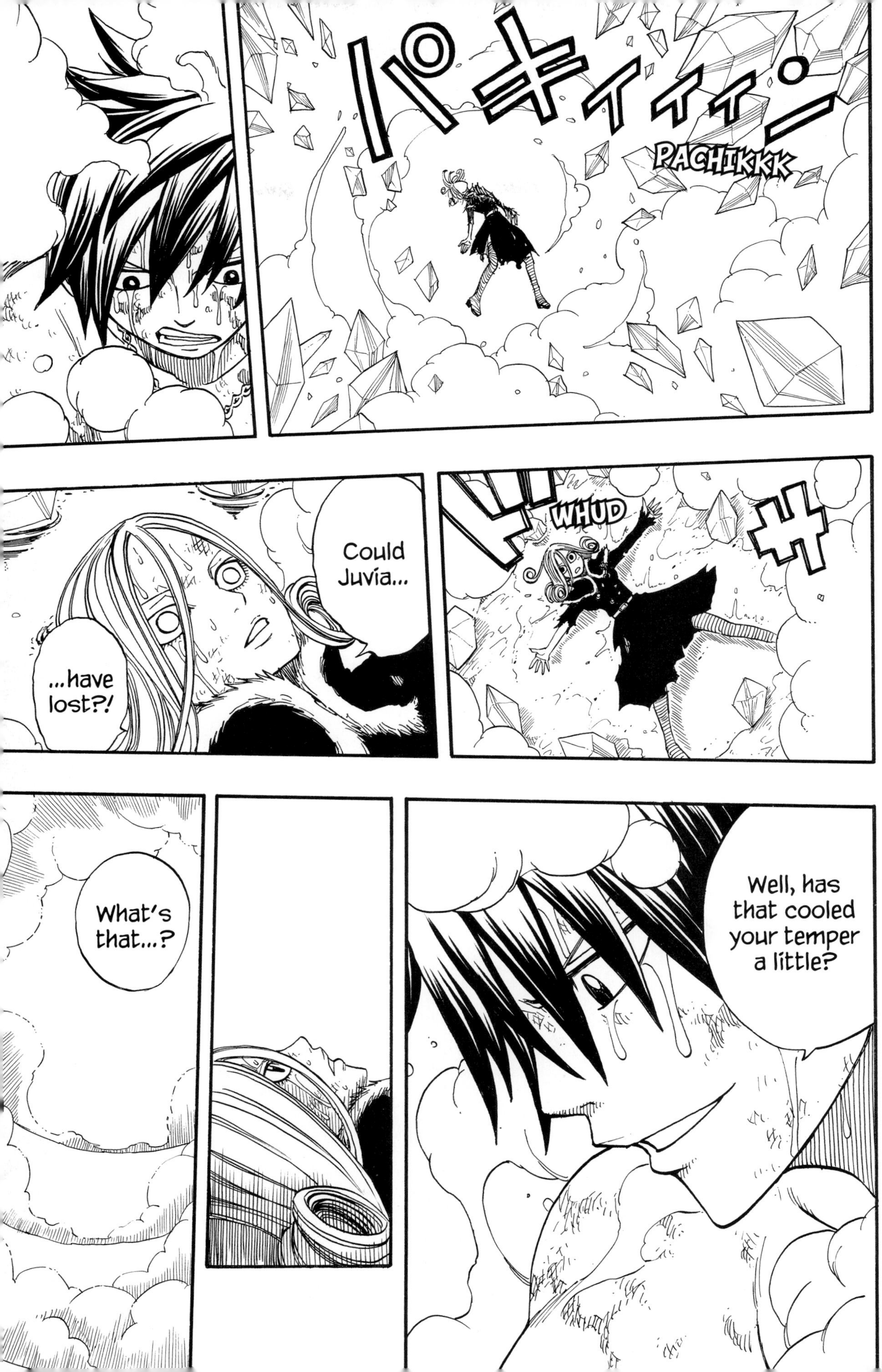
パキィィーン
PACHIKKK
WHUD
Could Juvia...
...have lost?!
Well, has that cooled your temper a little?
What's that...?

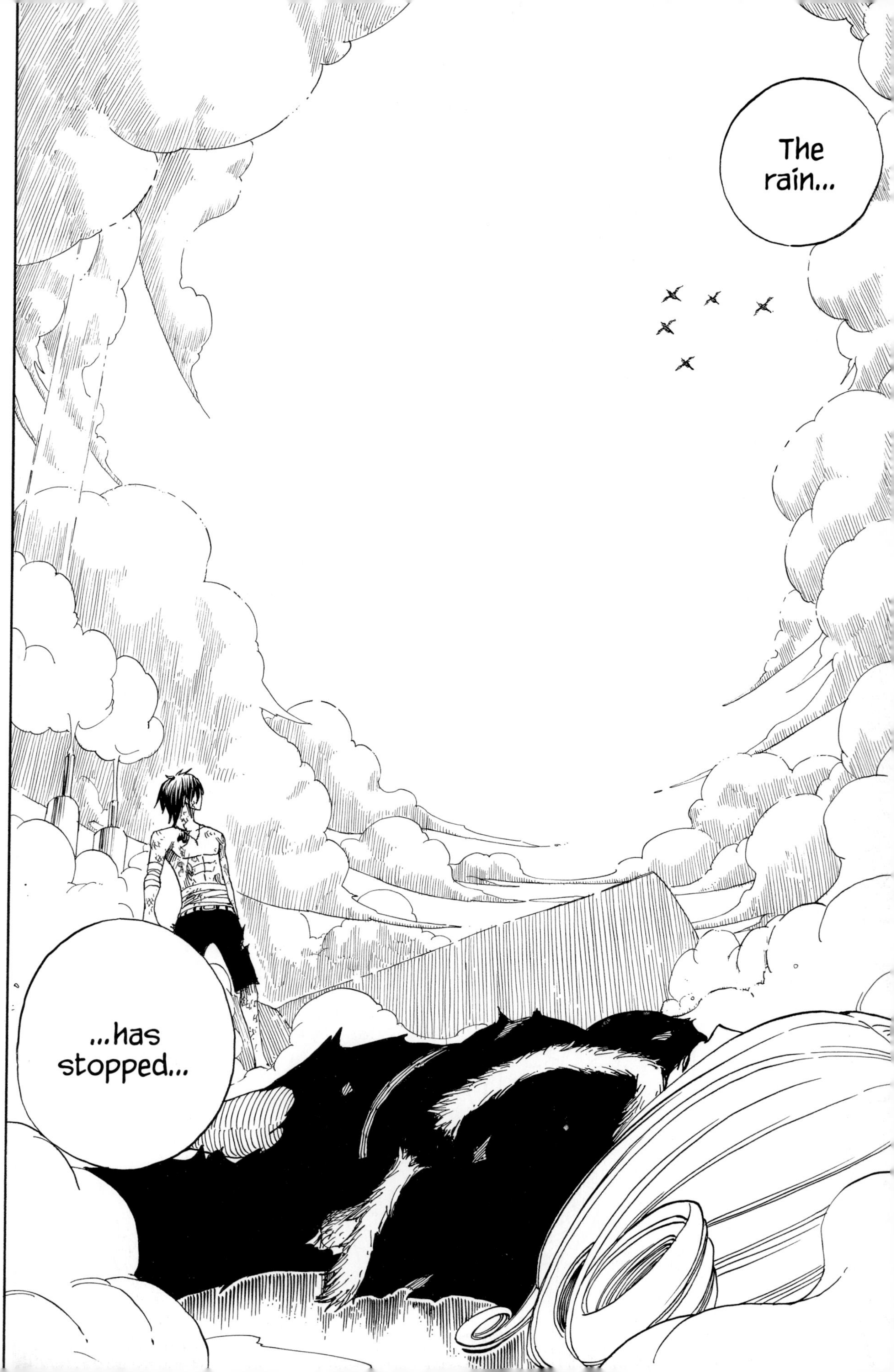
The rain...
...has stopped...

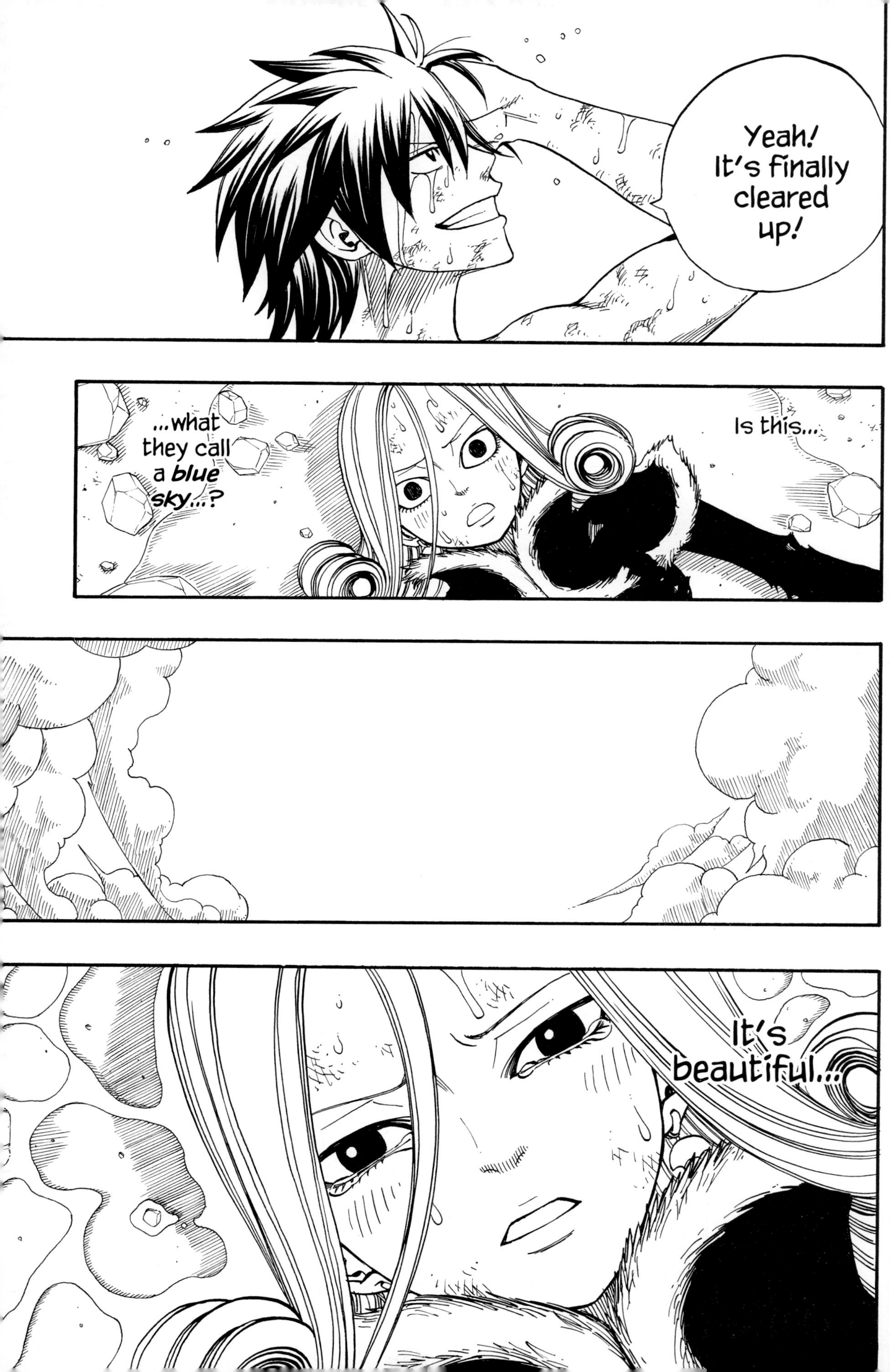
Yeah! It's finally cleared up!
Is this...
...what they call a *blue sky*...?
It's beautiful...

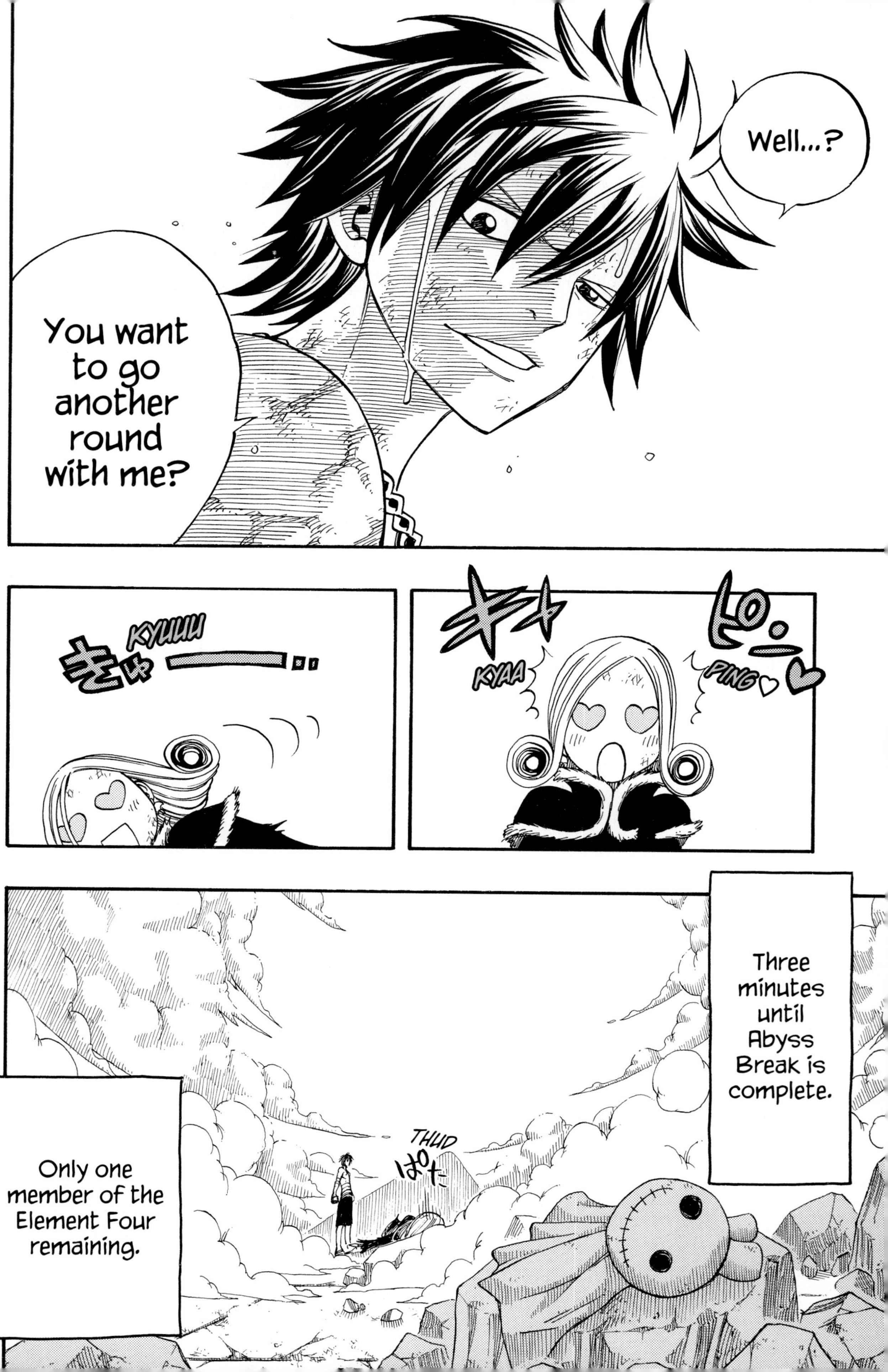
Well...?
You want to go another round with me?
KYAA
PING♡
KYUUU
Three minutes until Abyss Break is complete.
THUD
Only one member of the Element Four remaining.

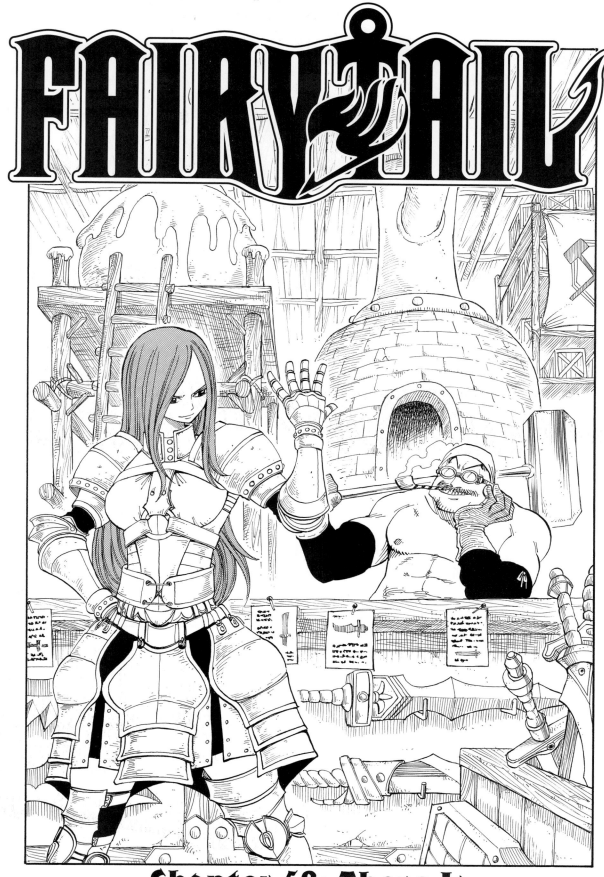

Chapter 58: There Is
Always Someone Better

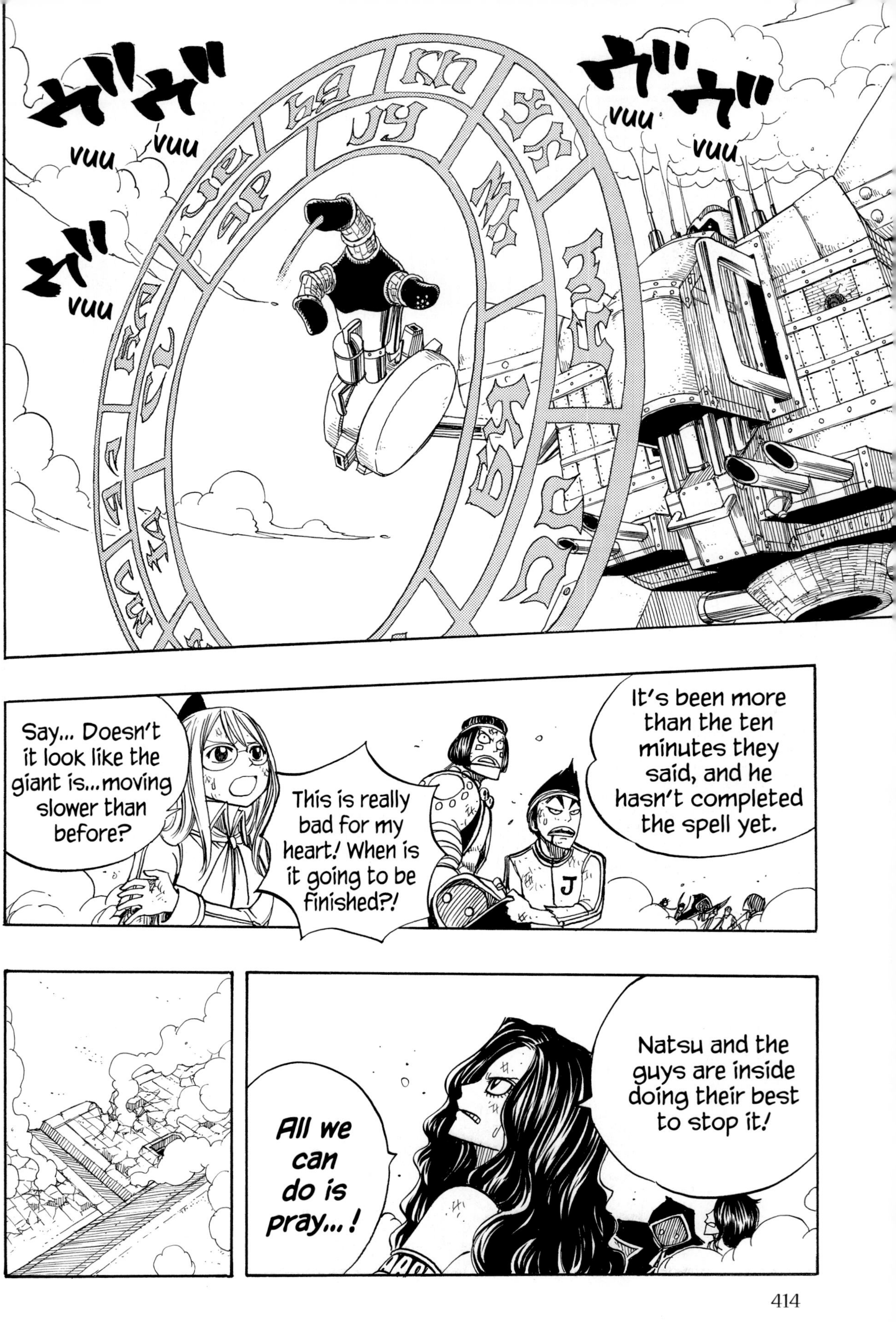
vuu
vuu
vuu
vuu
vuu
It's been more than the ten minutes they said, and he hasn't completed the spell yet.
This is really bad for my heart! When is it going to be finished?!
Say... Doesn't it look like the giant is...moving slower than before?
Natsu and the guys are inside doing their best to stop it!
All we can do is pray...!

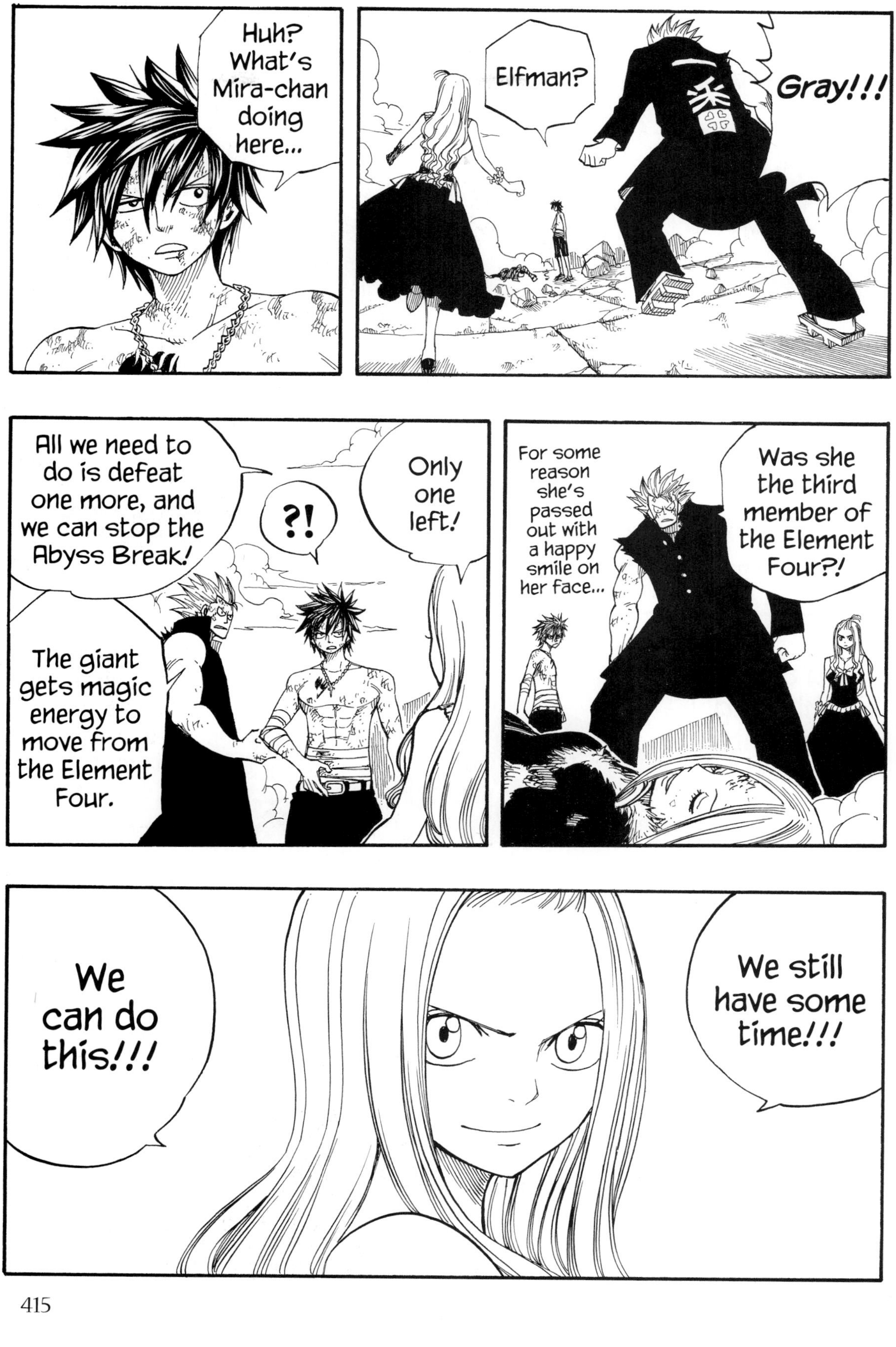
Gray!!!
Elfman?
Huh? What's Mira-chan doing here...
Was she the third member of the Element Four?!
For some reason she's passed out with a happy smile on her face...
Only one left!
?!
All we need to do is defeat one more, and we can stop the Abyss Break!
The giant gets magic energy to move from the Element Four.
We still have some time!!!
We can do this!!!

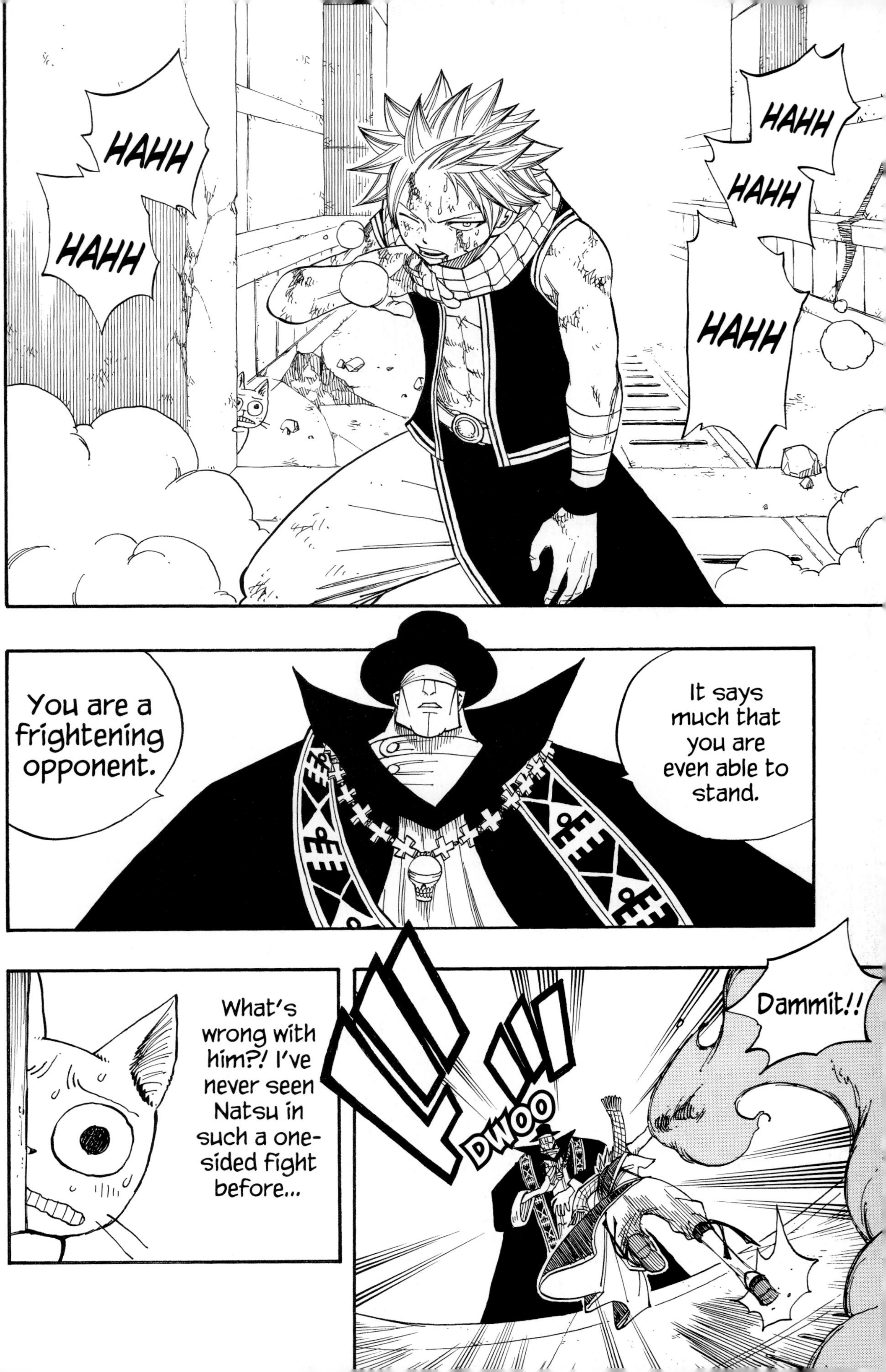
HAHH
HAHH
HAHH
HAHH
HAHH
It says much that you are even able to stand.
You are a frightening opponent.
Dammit!!
DWOO
What's wrong with him?! I've never seen Natsu in such a one-sided fight before...

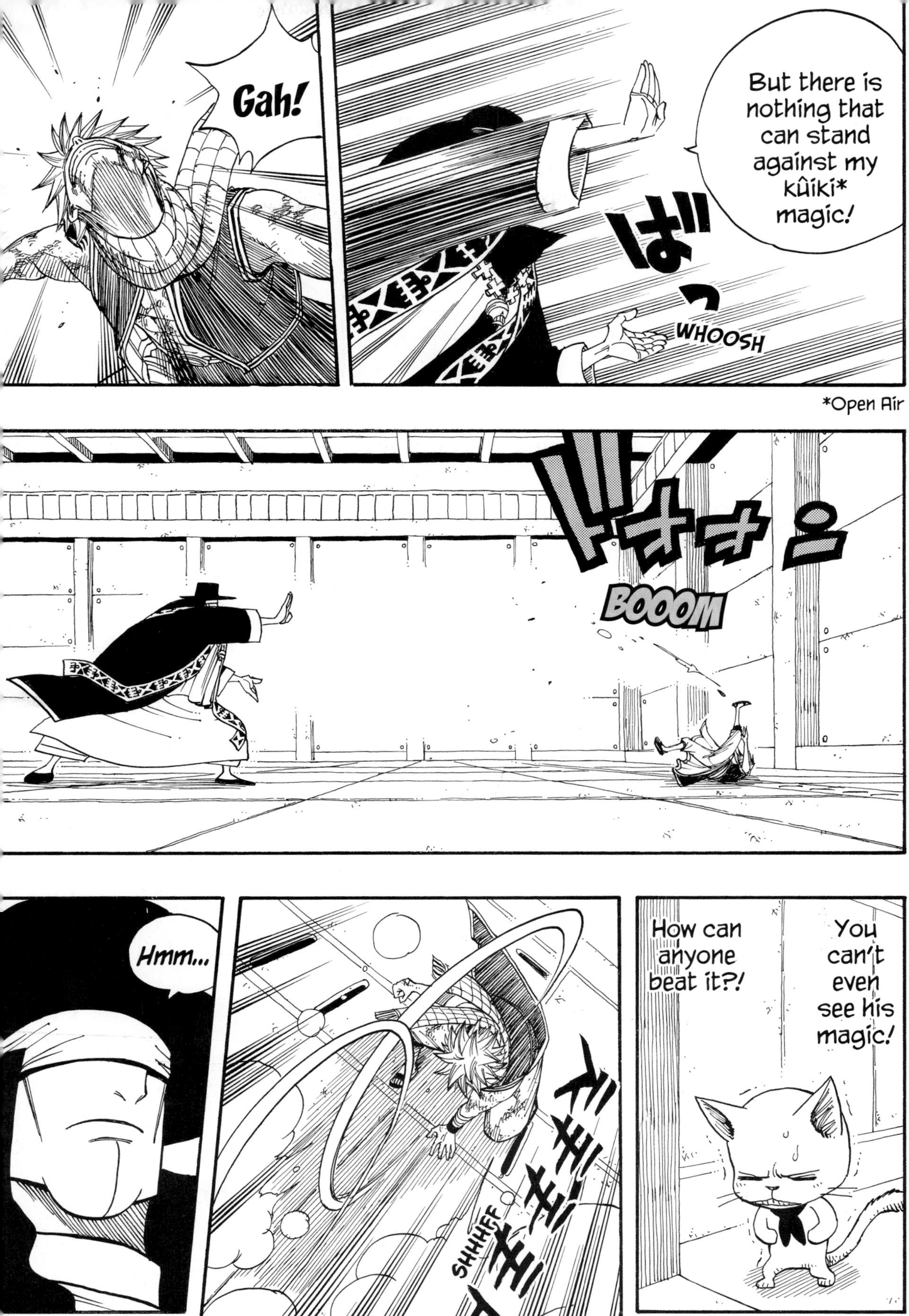
But there is nothing that can stand against my kûiki* magic!
ばっ
WHOOSH
Gah!
*Open Air
BOOOM
You can't even see his magic!
How can anyone beat it?!
SHHHFF
Hmm...

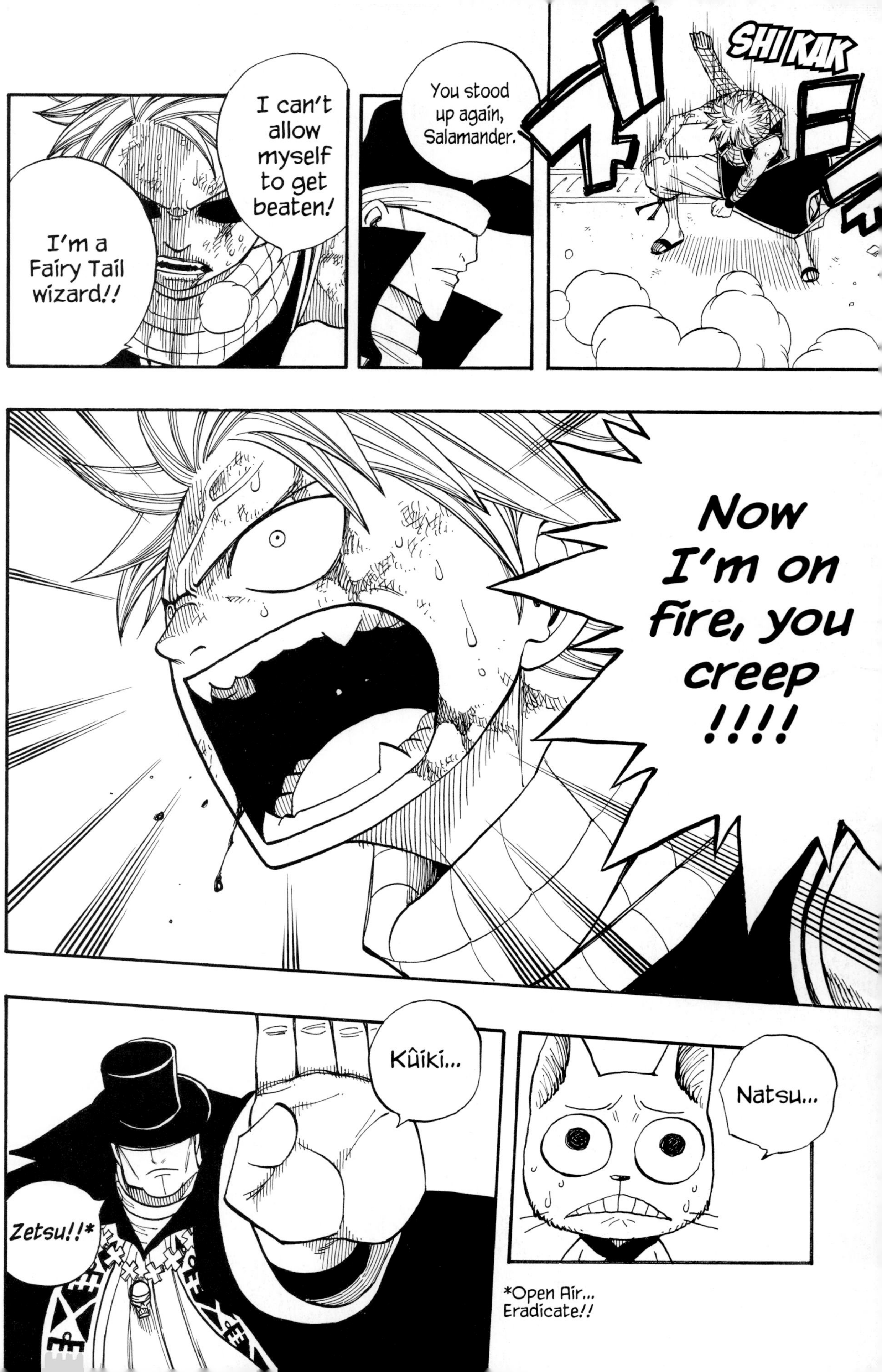
SHI KAK
You stood up again, Salamander.
I can't allow myself to get beaten!
I'm a Fairy Tail wizard!!
Now I'm on fire, you creep!!!!
Natsu...
Kûiki...
Zetsu!!*
*Open Air... Eradicate!!

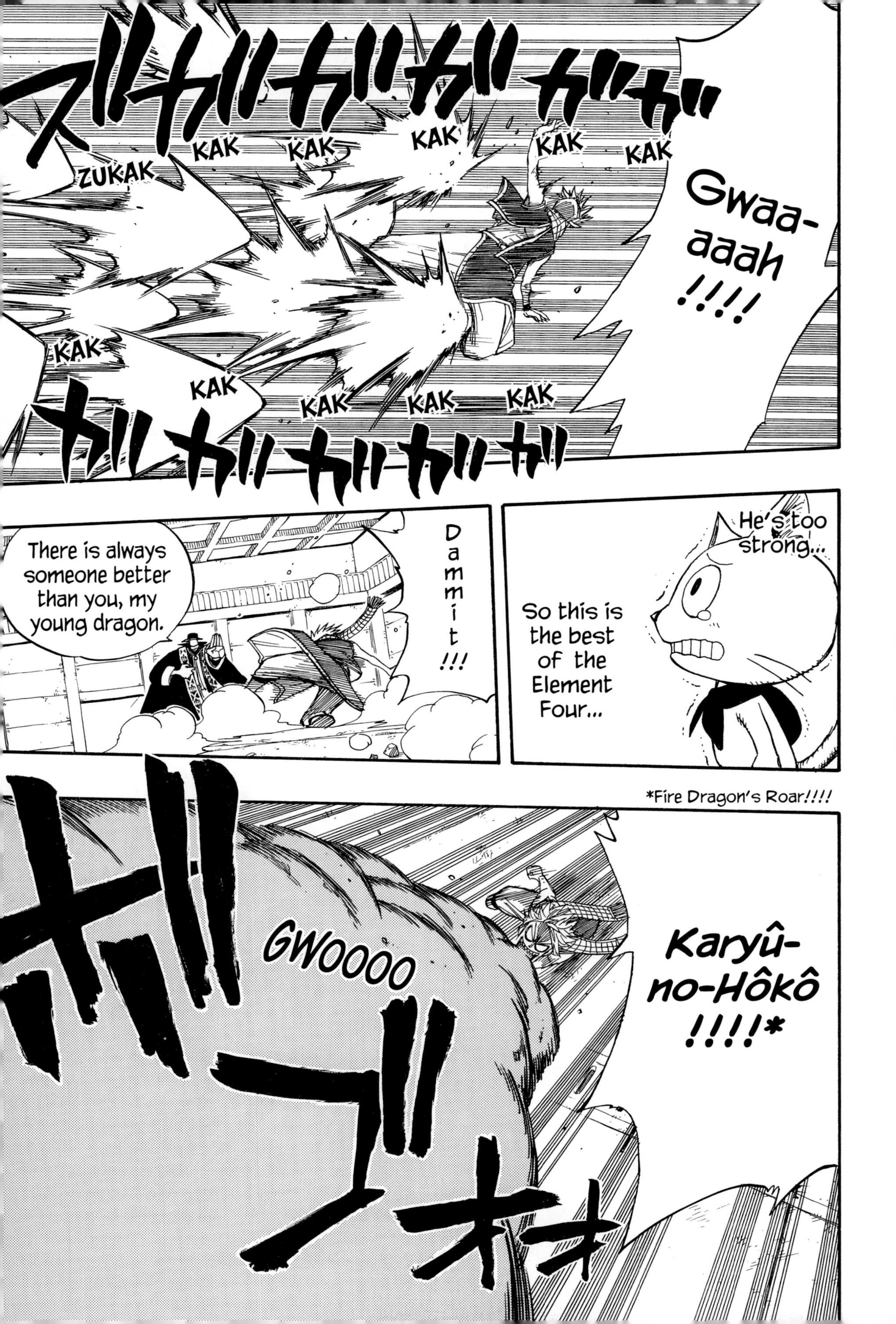
Gwaa-aaah!!!!
KAK
KAK
KAK
KAK
KAK
ZUKAK
KAK
KAK
KAK
KAK
KAK
He's too strong...
So this is the best of the Element Four...
Dammit!!!
There is always someone better than you, my young dragon.
Karyû-no-Hôkô!!!!*
GWOOOO

*Fire Dragon's Roar!!!!

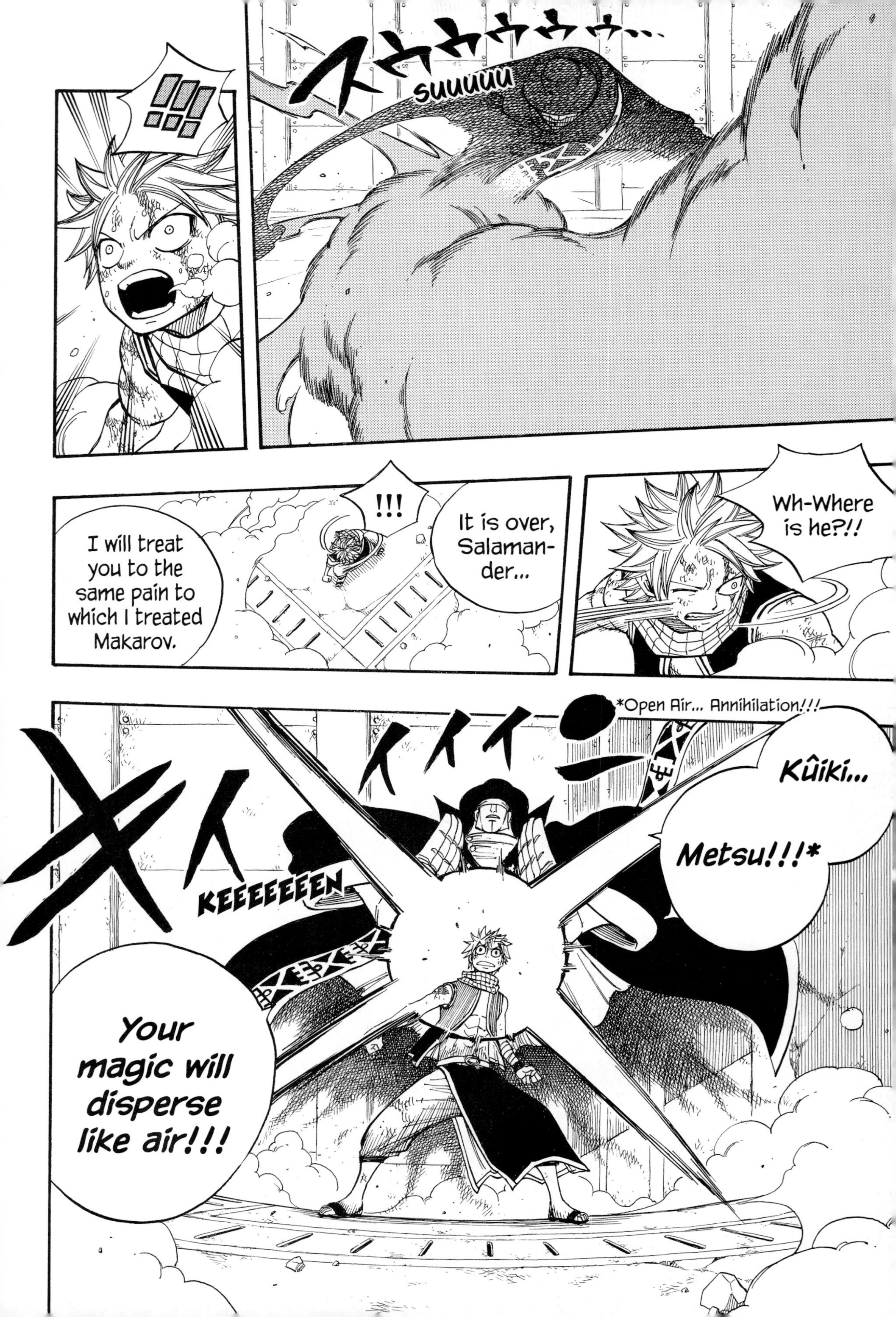
SUUUUUU
!!!
Wh-Where is he?!!
It is over, Salamander...
!!!
I will treat you to the same pain to which I treated Makarov.
*Open Air... Annihilation!!!
Kûiki...
Metsu!!!*
KEEEEEEEN
Your magic will disperse like air!!!

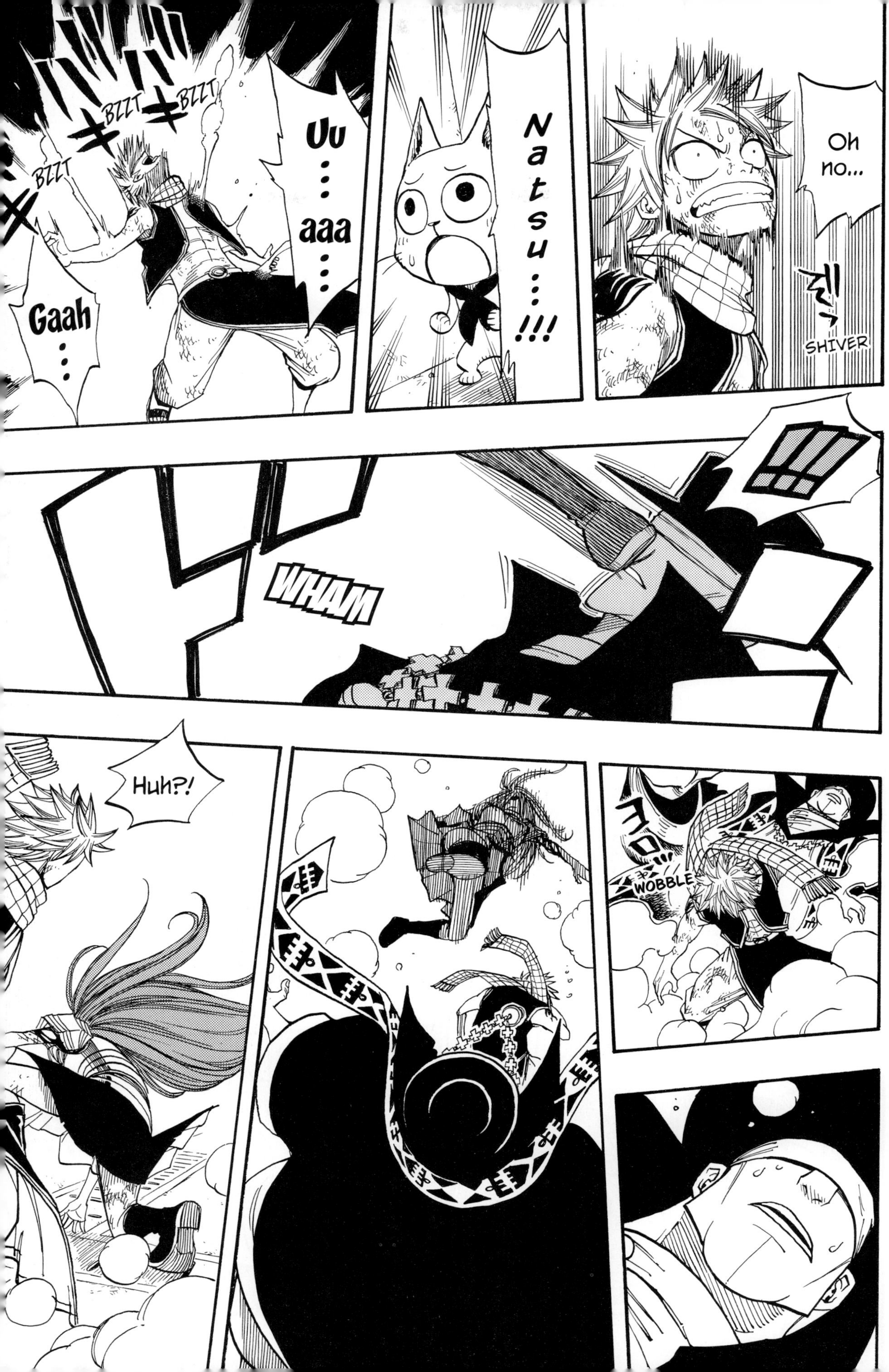

Oh no...
SHIVER
Natsu...!!!
Uu... aaa...
BZZT
BZZT
BZZT
Gaah...
WHAM
WOBBLE
Huh?!

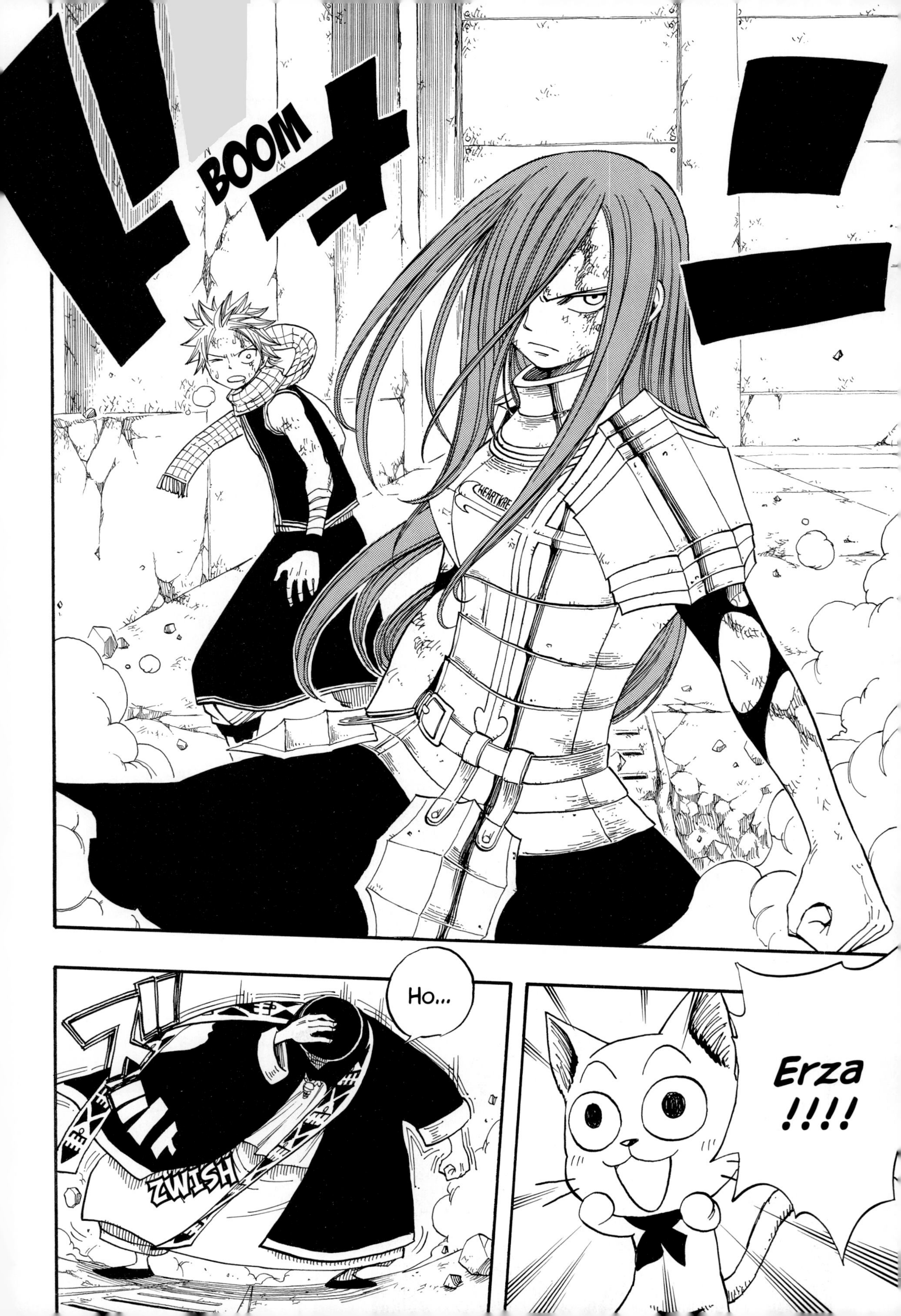
BOOM
HEARTKRE
Erza
!!!!
Ho...
ZWISH

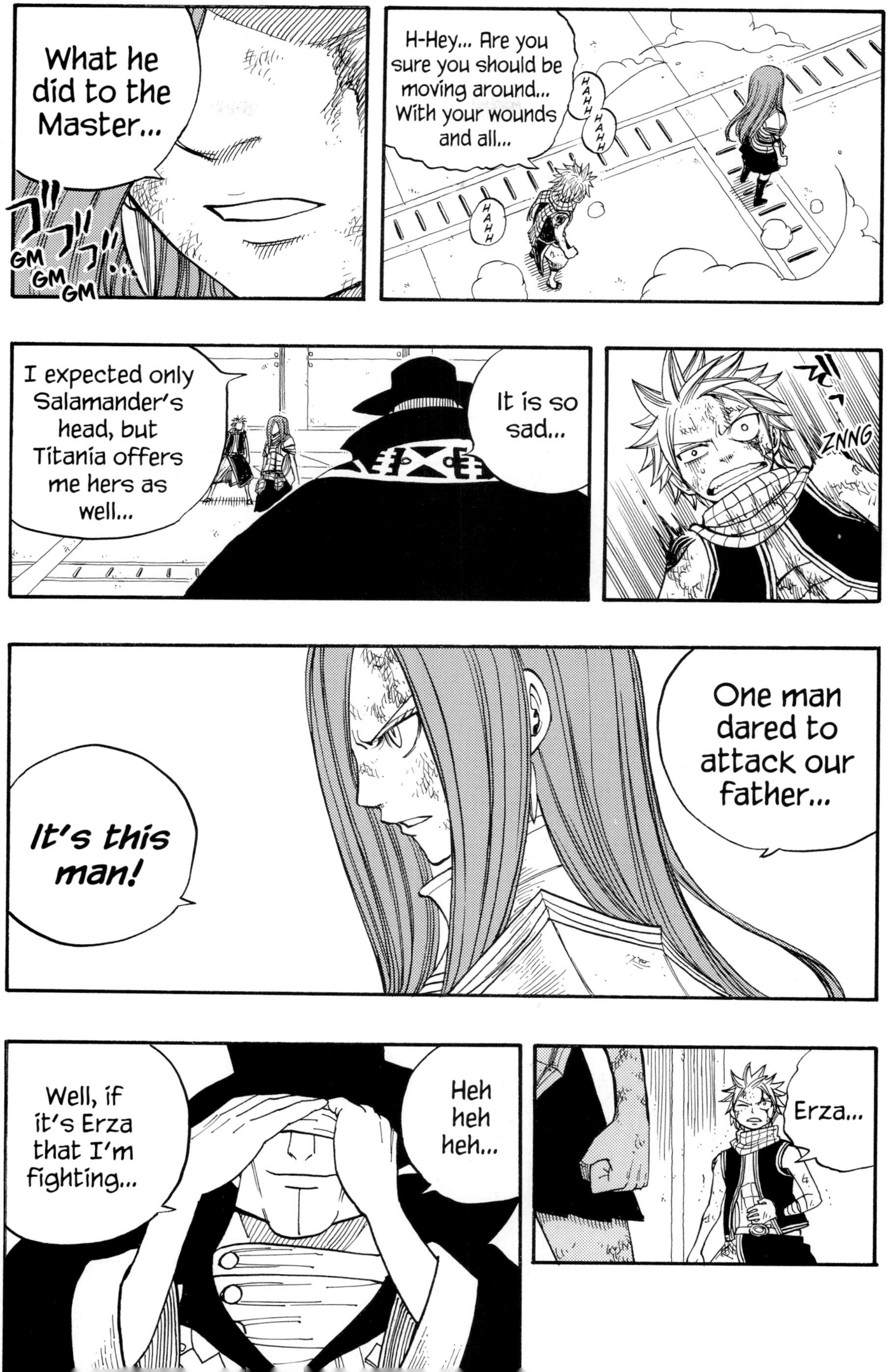
H-Hey... Are you sure you should be moving around... With your wounds and all...
HAHH
HAHH
HAHH
What he did to the Master...
GM GM GM
ZNNG
It is so sad...
I expected only Salamander's head, but Titania offers me hers as well...
One man dared to attack our father...
It's this man!
Erza...
Heh heh heh...
Well, if it's Erza that I'm fighting...

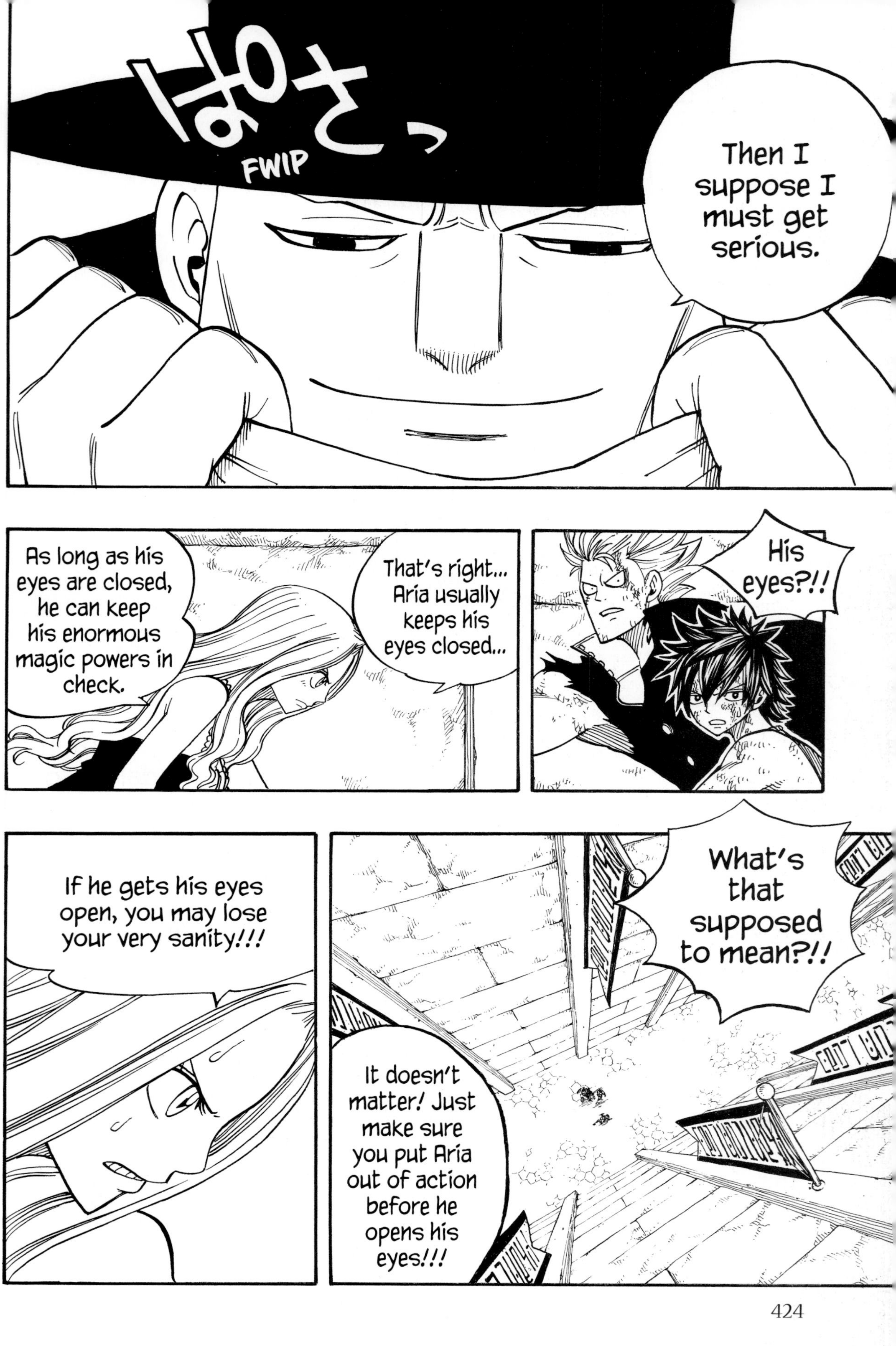
ぱさっ
FWIP
Then I suppose I must get serious.
His eyes?!!
That's right... Aria usually keeps his eyes closed...
As long as his eyes are closed, he can keep his enormous magic powers in check.
What's that supposed to mean?!!
It doesn't matter! Just make sure you put Aria out of action before he opens his eyes!!!
If he gets his eyes open, you may lose your very sanity!!!

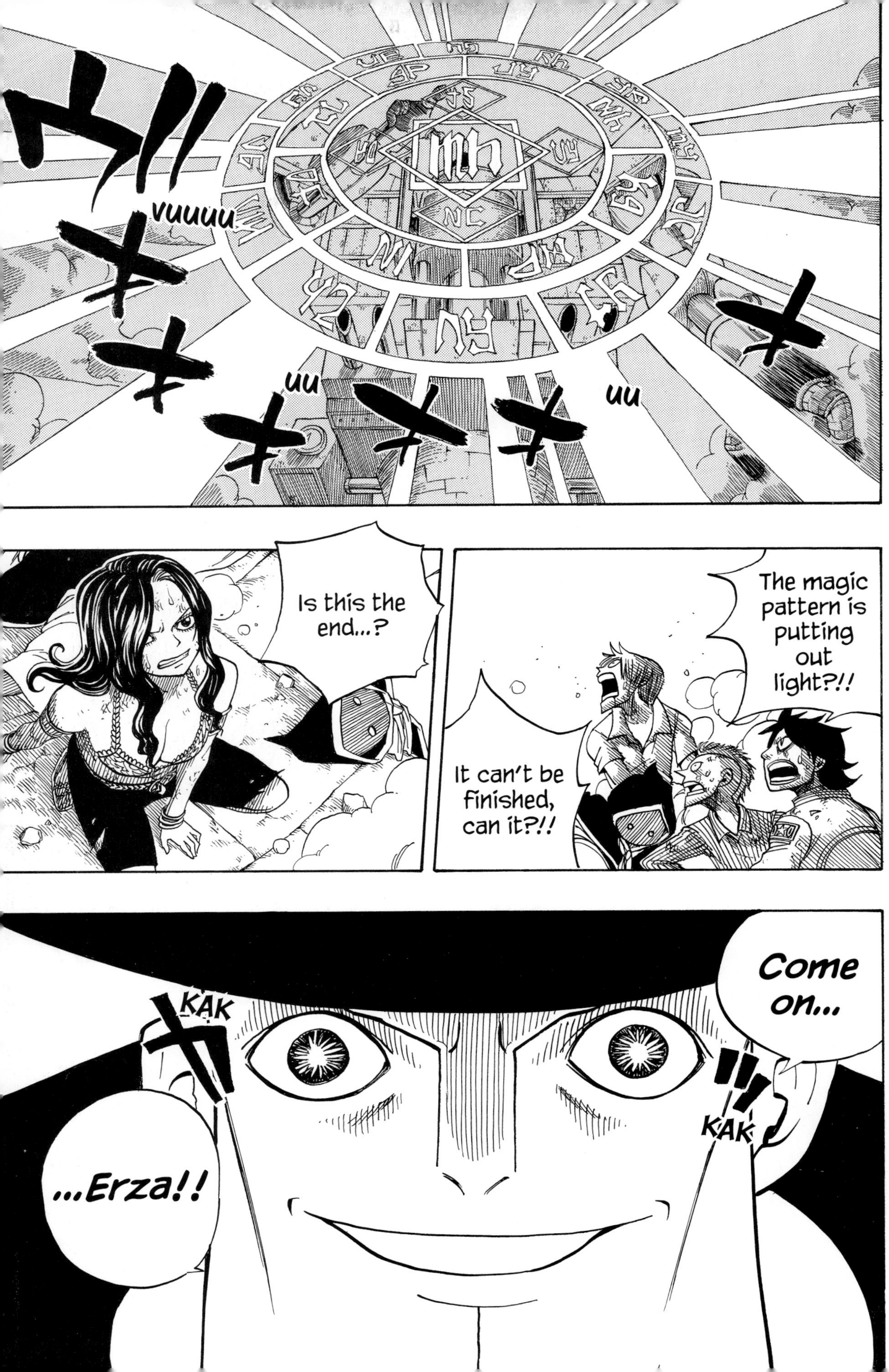
vuuuu
uu
uu
The magic pattern is putting out light?!!
It can't be finished, can it?!!
Is this the end...?
Come on...
KAK
KAK
...Erza!!

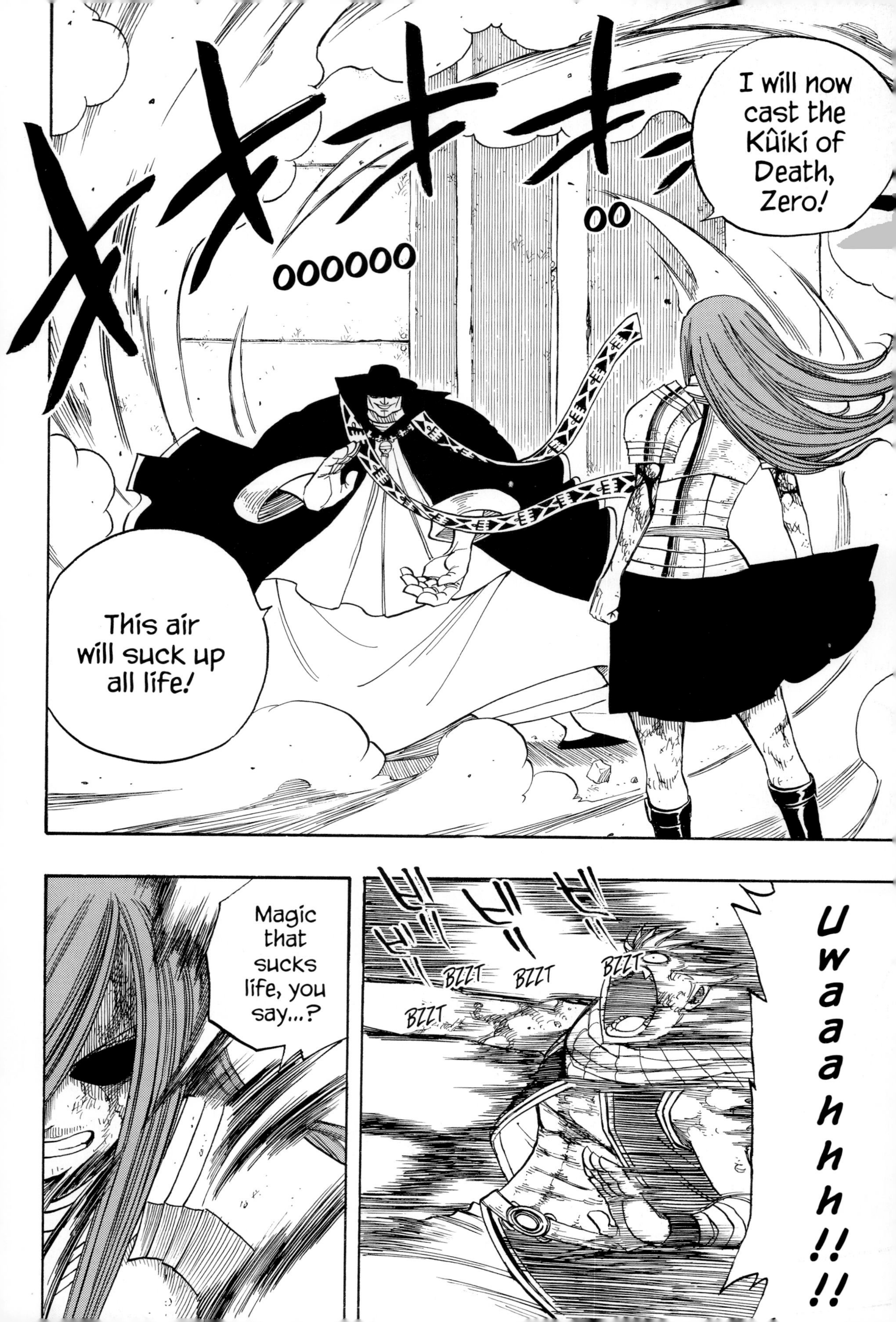
I will now cast the Kûiki of Death, Zero!
OOOOOO OO
This air will suck up all life!
BZZT
BZZT
BZZT
BZZT
Uwaaahhhh!!!!
Magic that sucks life, you say...?

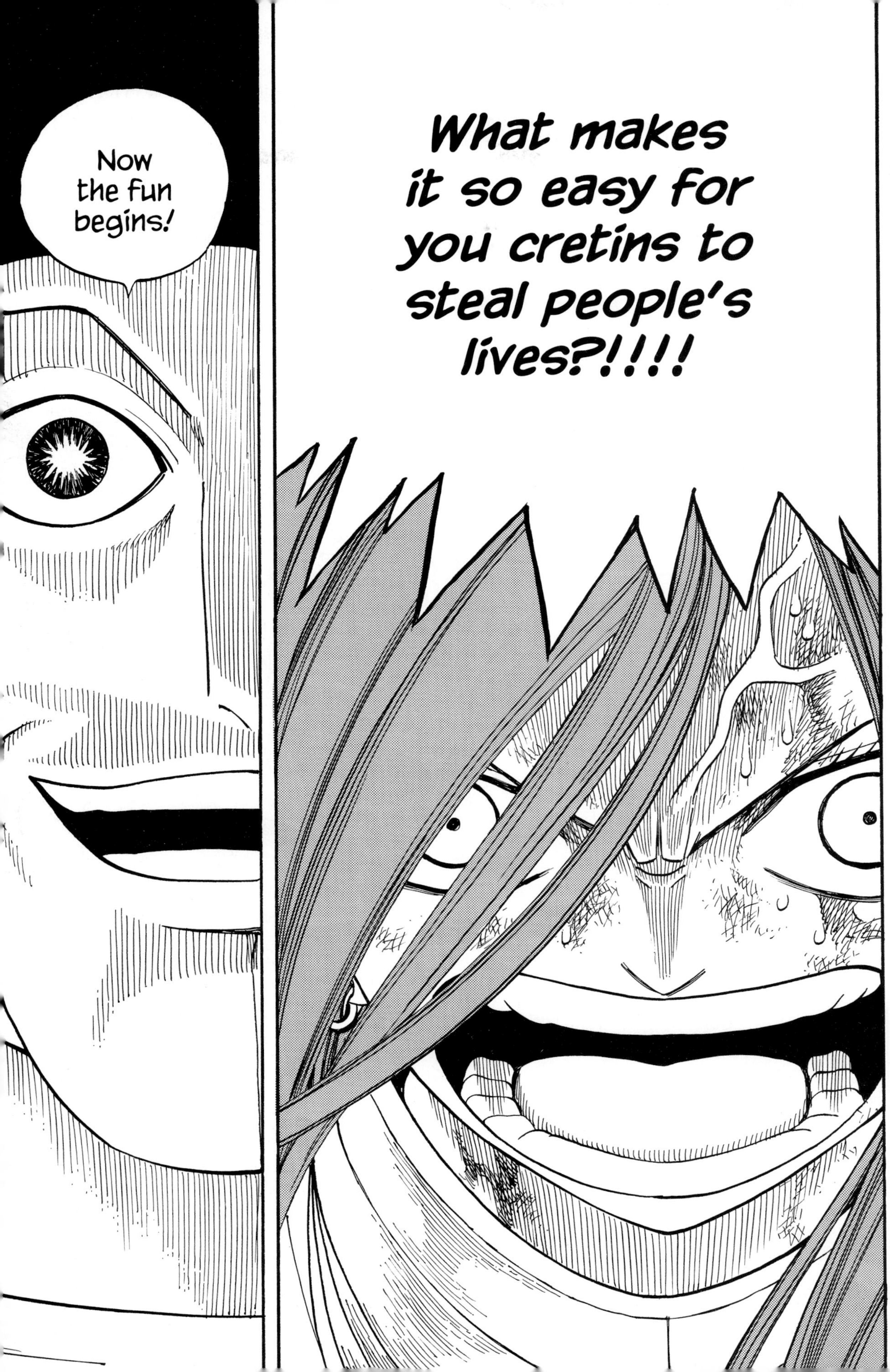
What makes it so easy for you cretins to steal people's lives?!!!!
Now the fun begins!

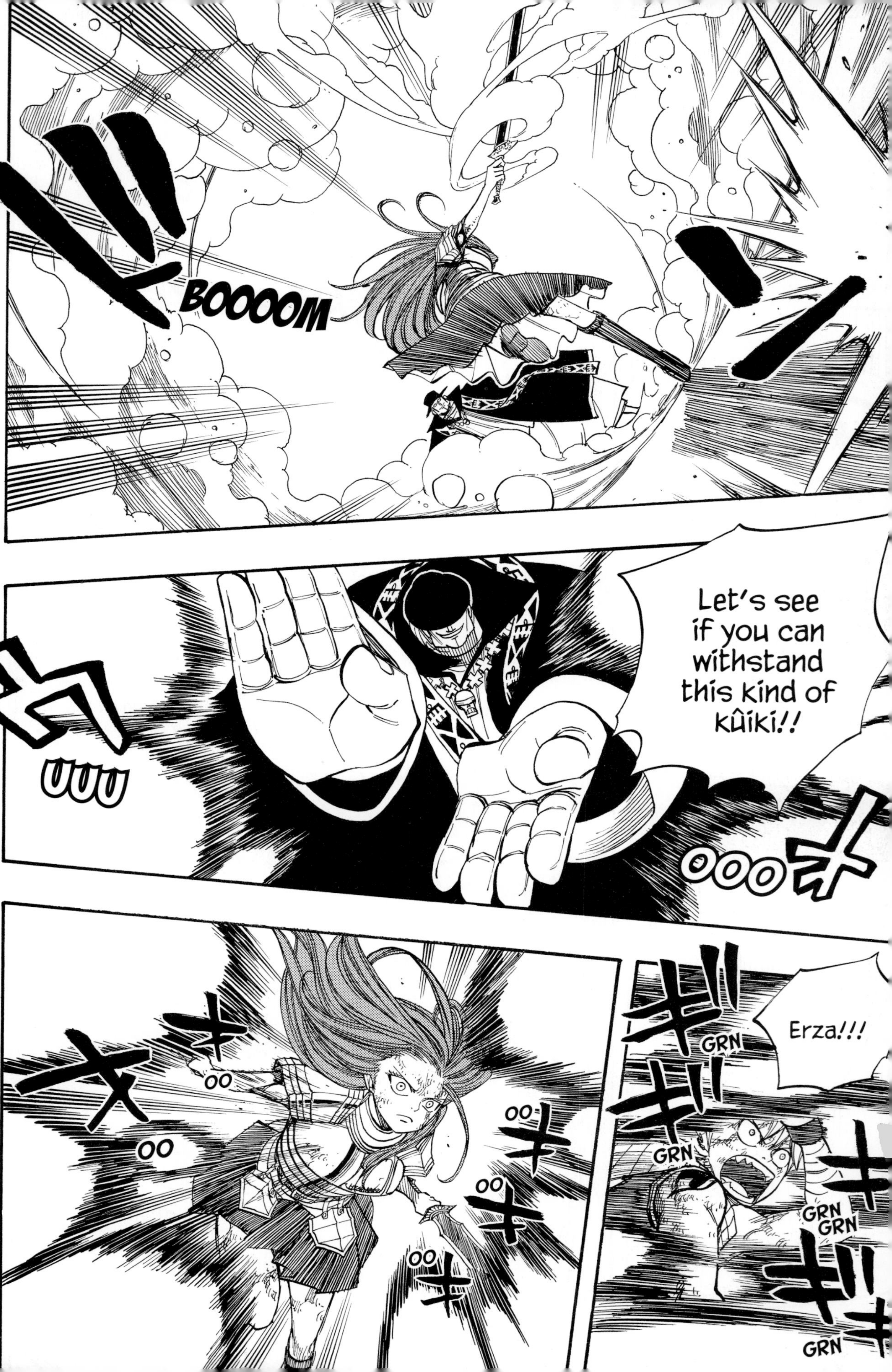
BOOOOM
Let's see if you can withstand this kind of kûiki!!
OOO
UUU
Erza!!!
GRN
GRN
GRN GRN
GRN
OO
OO
OO
OO
OO

Huh?!

ZUGYAAA

GYAAA

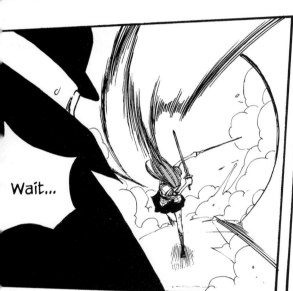

Wait...

That's impossible!!!

She's cutting through the very air itself...

VWSH VWSH VWSH VWSH

VWSH VWSH VWSH VWSH

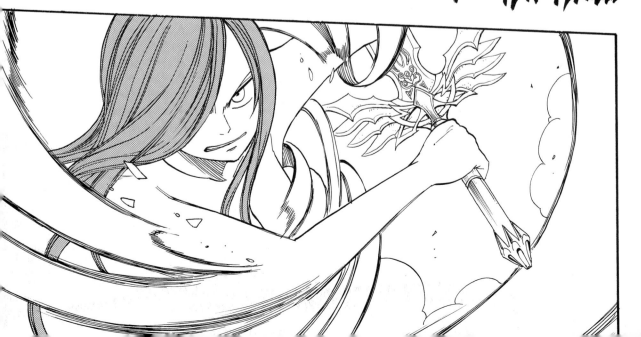

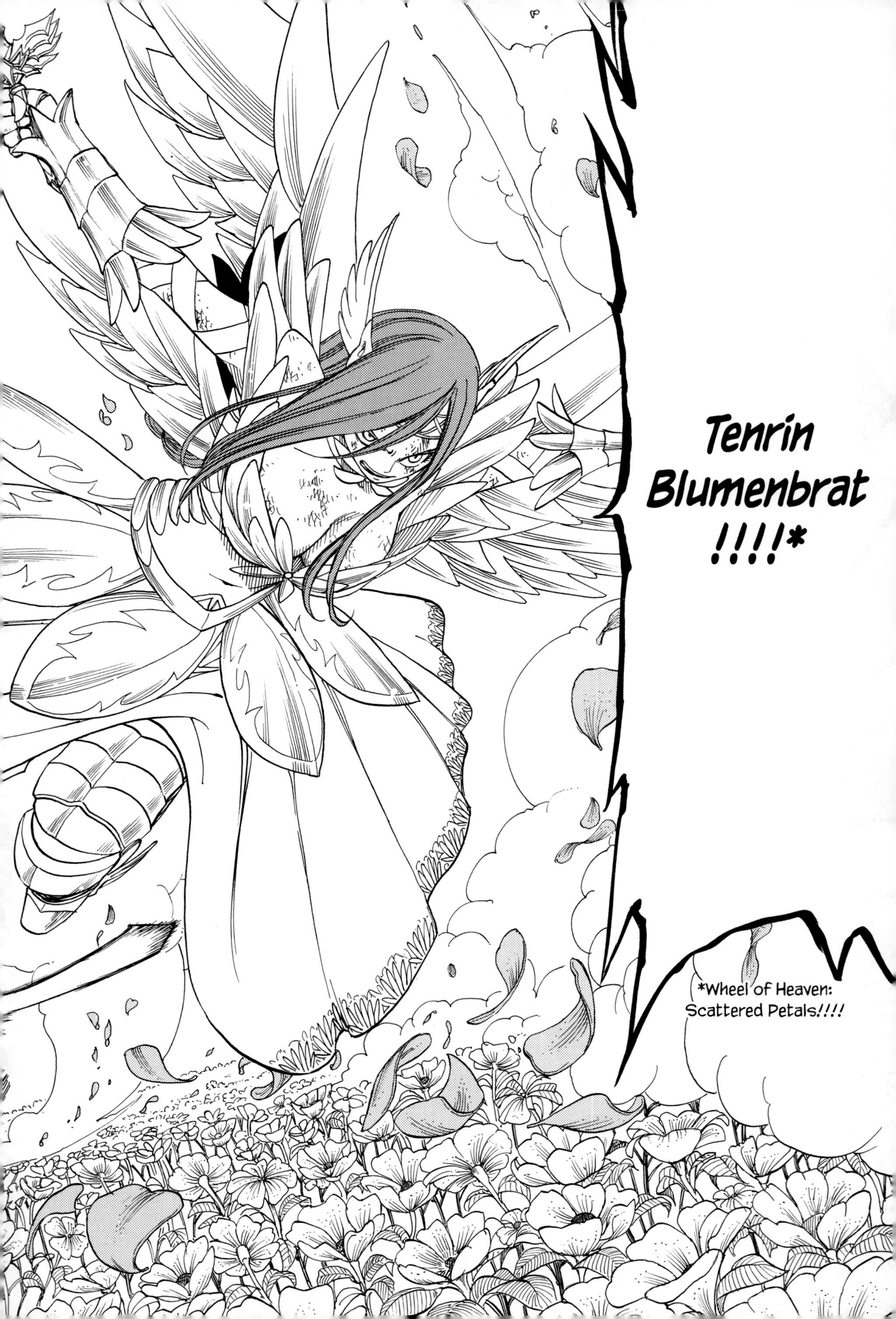
Tenrin Blumenbrat !!!!*
*Wheel of Heaven: Scattered Petals!!!!

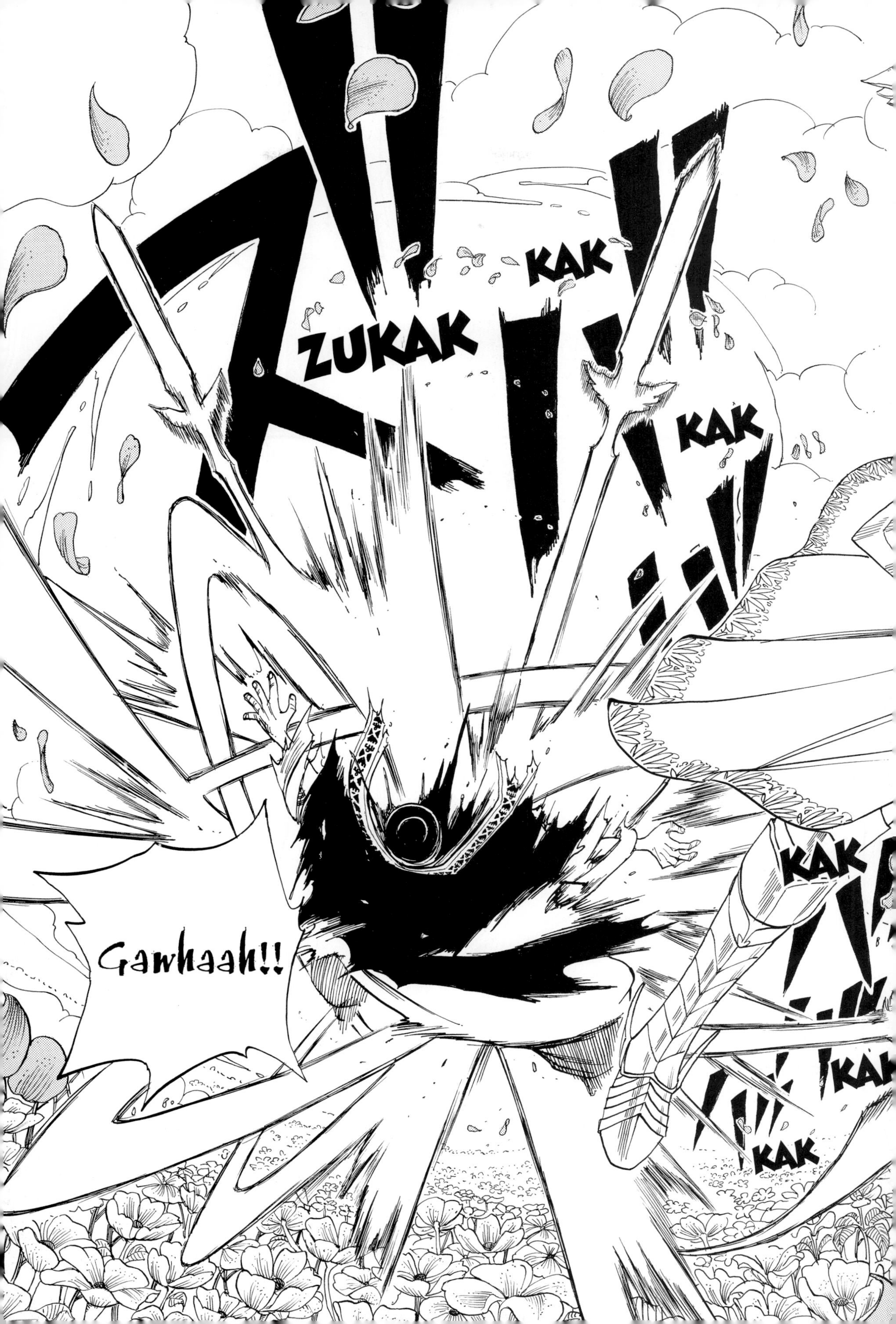
KAK
KAK
ZUKAK
KAK
KAK
KAK
Gawhaah!!

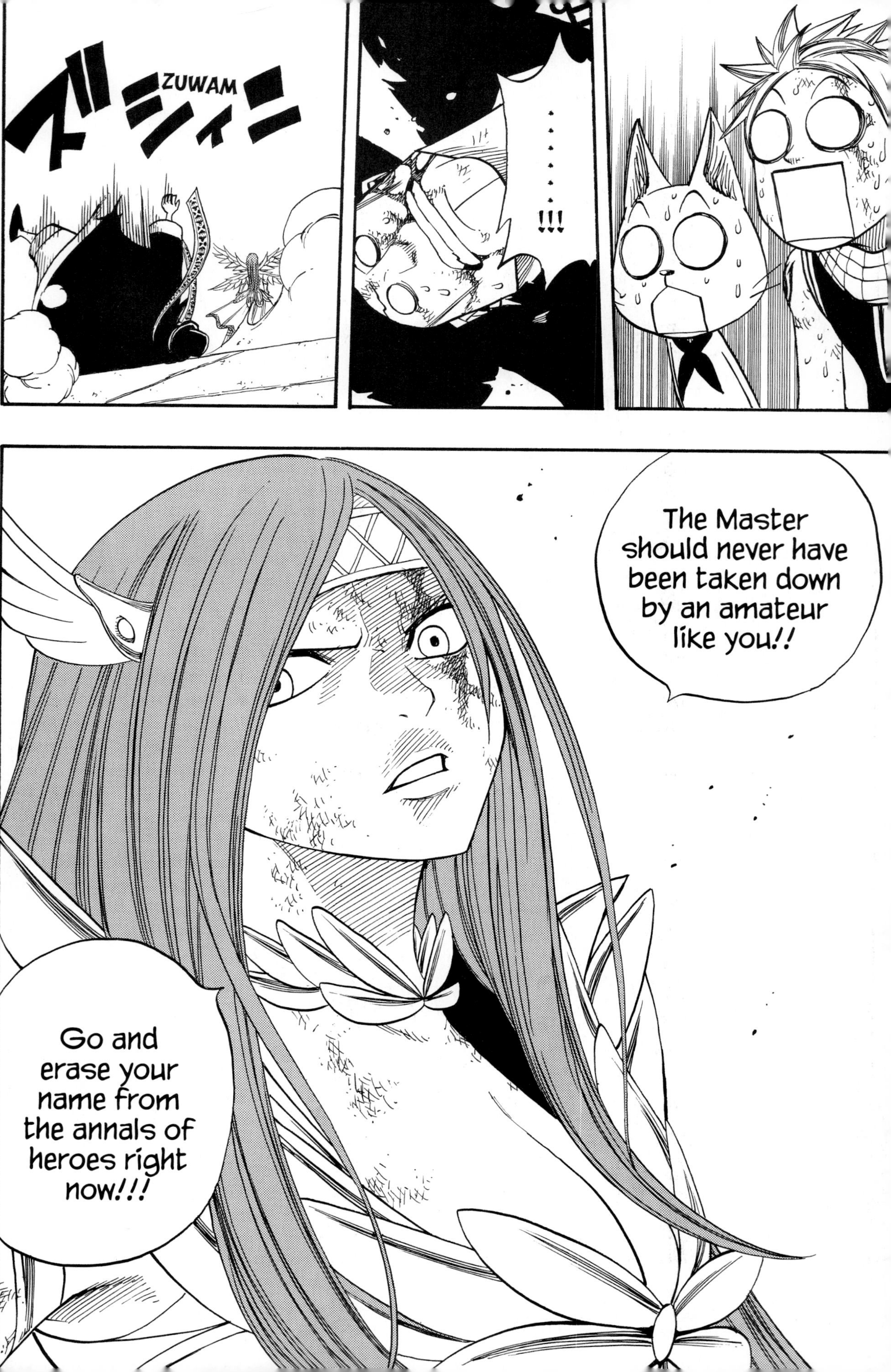
....!!!
ZUWAM
The Master should never have been taken down by an amateur like you!!
Go and erase your name from the annals of heroes right now!!!

FAIRY TAIL

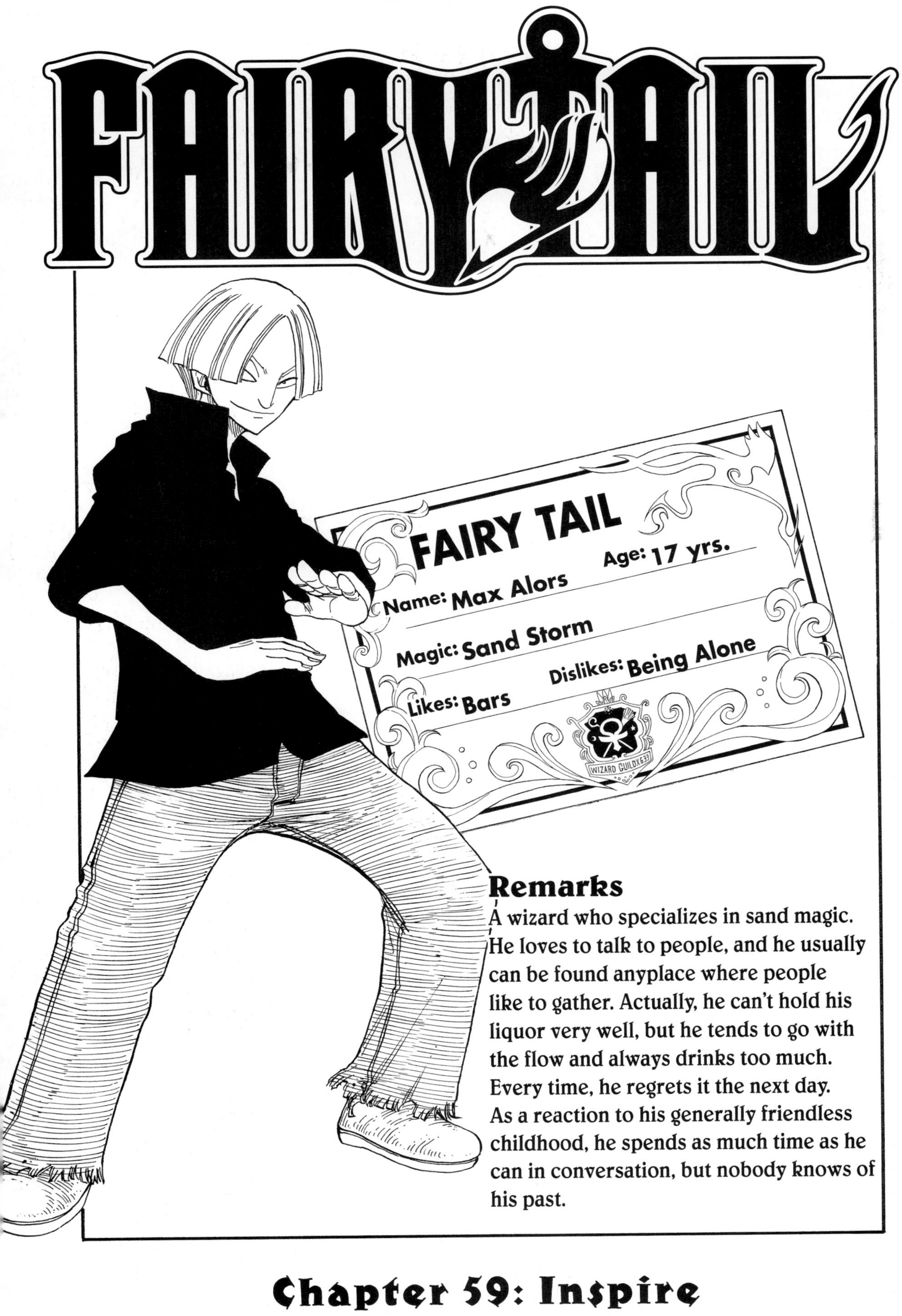
FAIRY TAIL
Age: 17 yrs.
Name: Max Alors
Magic: Sand Storm
Dislikes: Being Alone
Likes: Bars
WIZARD GUILD X633

Remarks

A wizard who specializes in sand magic. He loves to talk to people, and he usually can be found anyplace where people like to gather. Actually, he can't hold his liquor very well, but he tends to go with the flow and always drinks too much. Every time, he regrets it the next day. As a reaction to his generally friendless childhood, he spends as much time as he can in conversation, but nobody knows of his past.

Chapter 59: Inspire

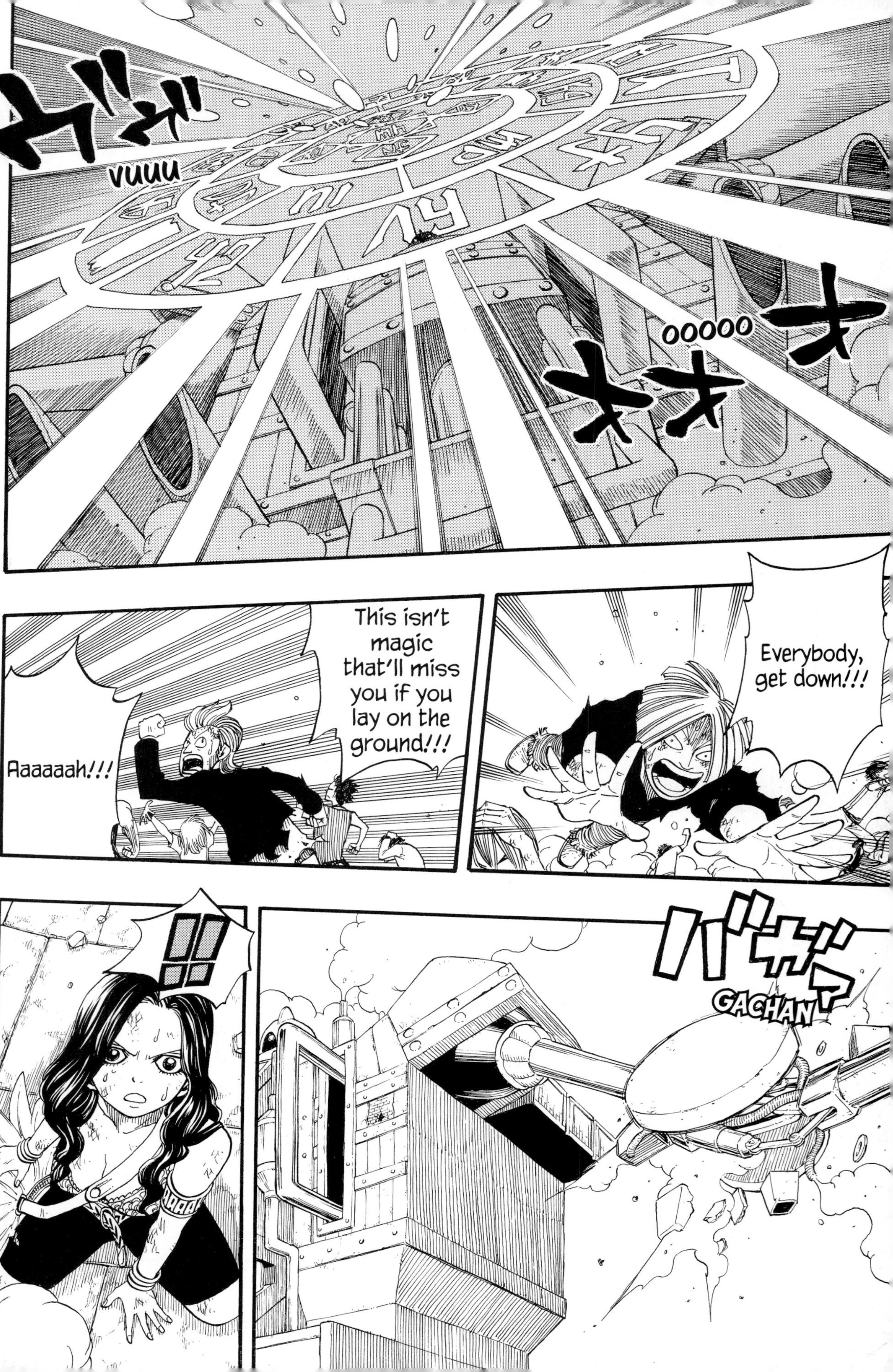
VUUU
OOOOO
Everybody, get down!!!
This isn't magic that'll miss you if you lay on the ground!!!
Aaaaaah!!!
GACHAN

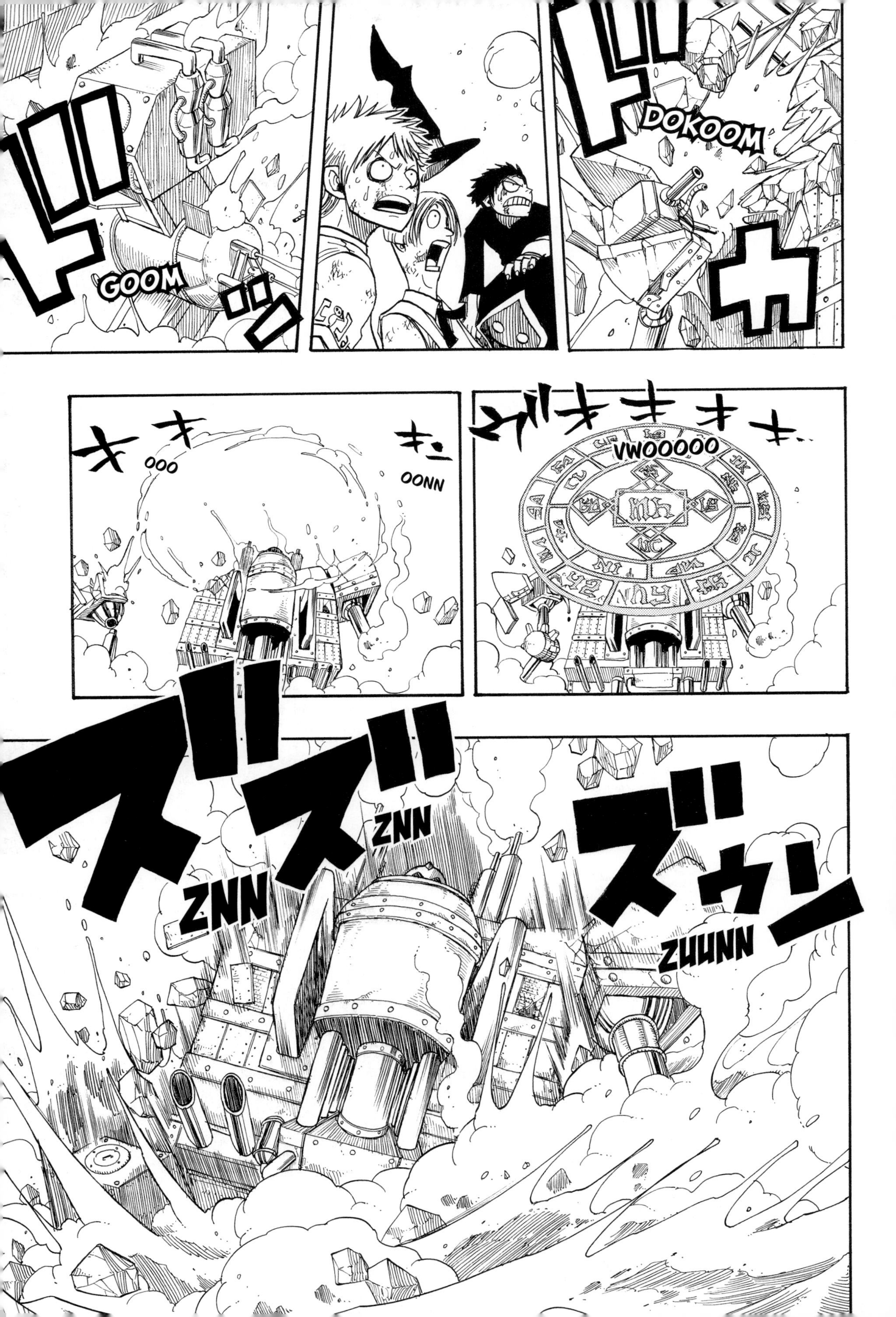
DOKOOM
GOOM
VWOOOOO
OOO
OONN
ZNN
ZNN
ZUUNN

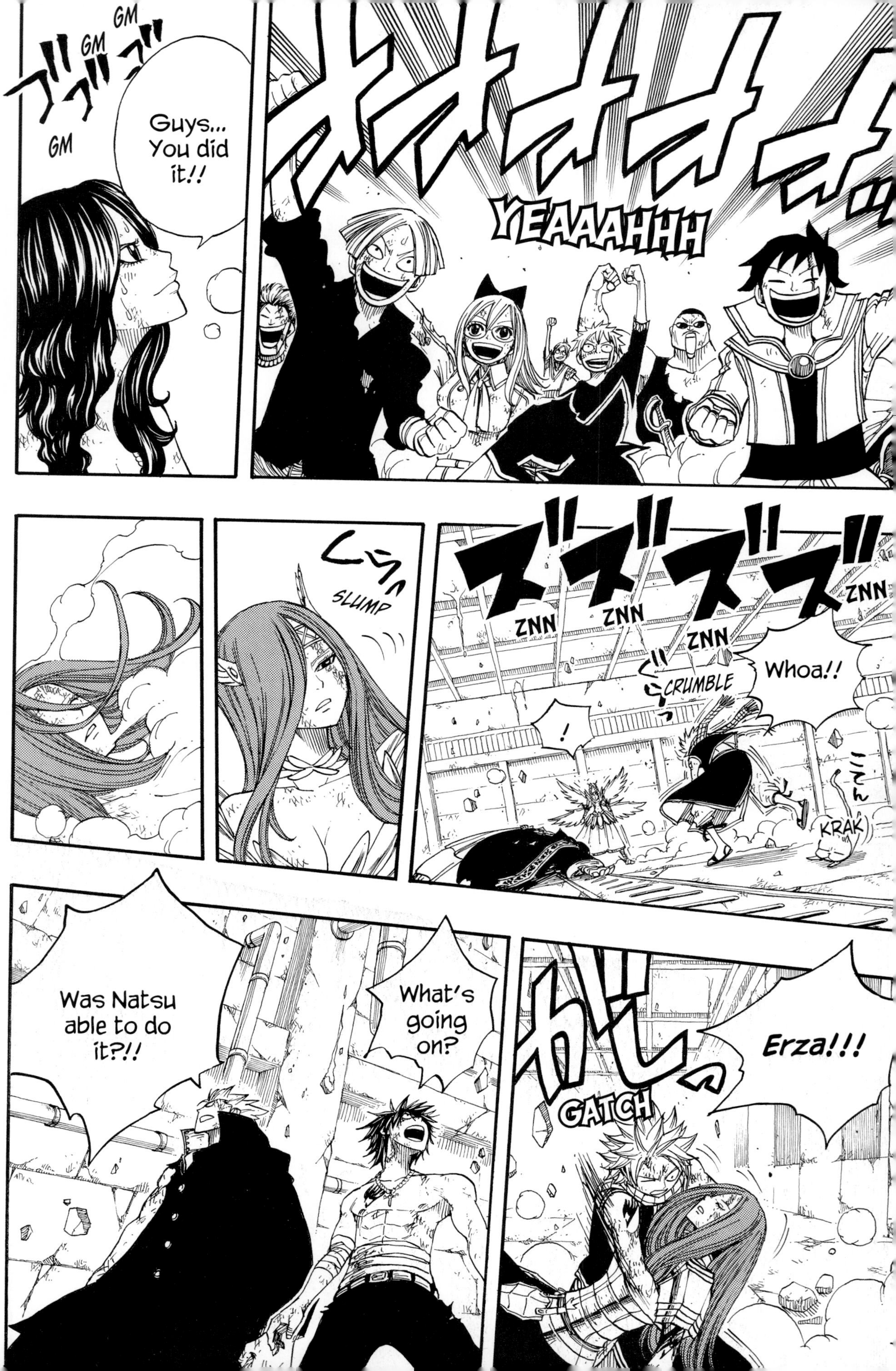

YEAAAHHH
GM GM GM
Guys... You did it!!
ZNN ZNN ZNN ZNN
CRUMBLE
Whoa!!
!
KRAK
SLUMP
Erza!!!
GATCH
What's going on?
Was Natsu able to do it?!!

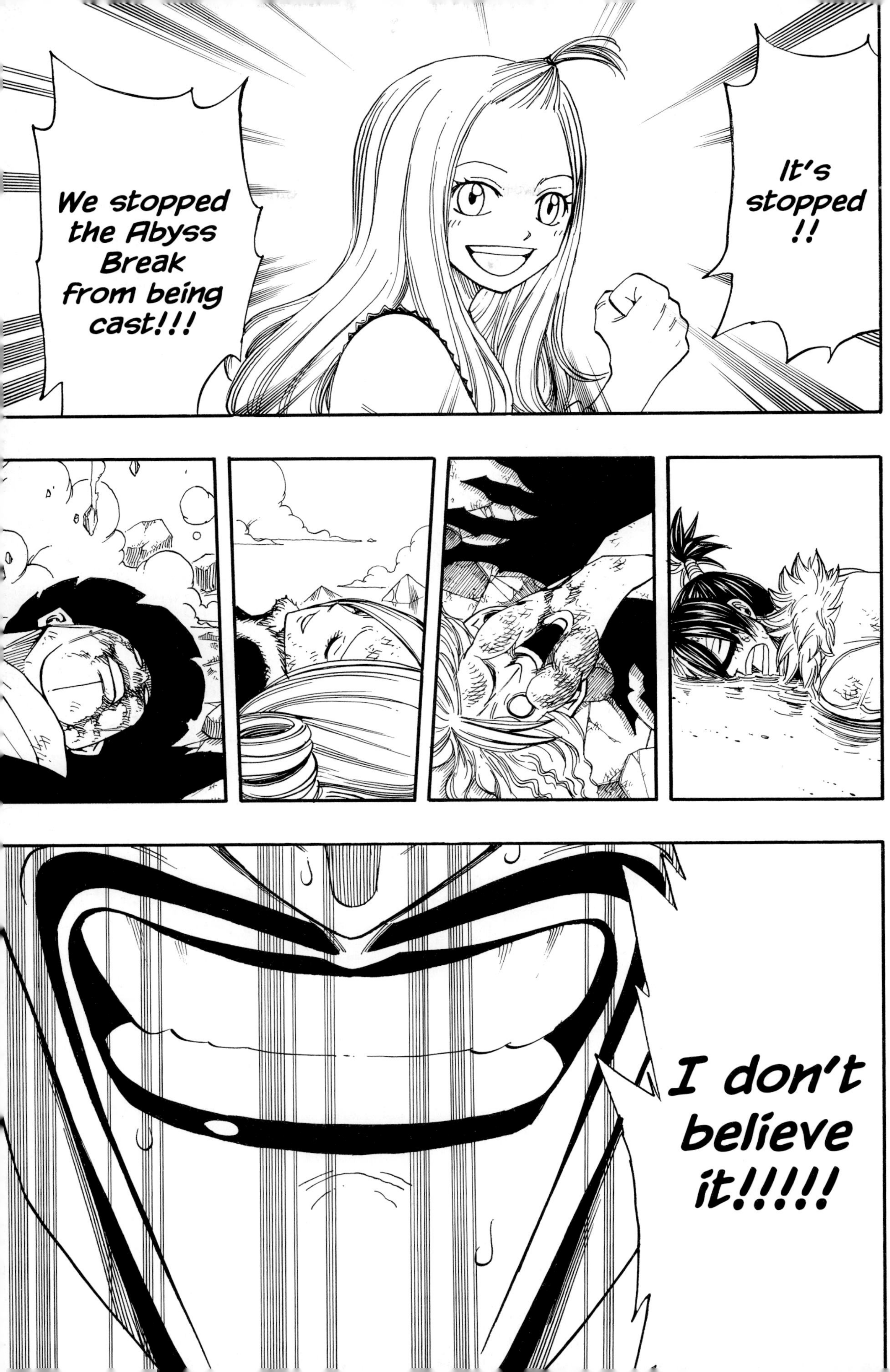
It's stopped!!
We stopped the Abyss Break from being cast!!!
I don't believe it!!!!!

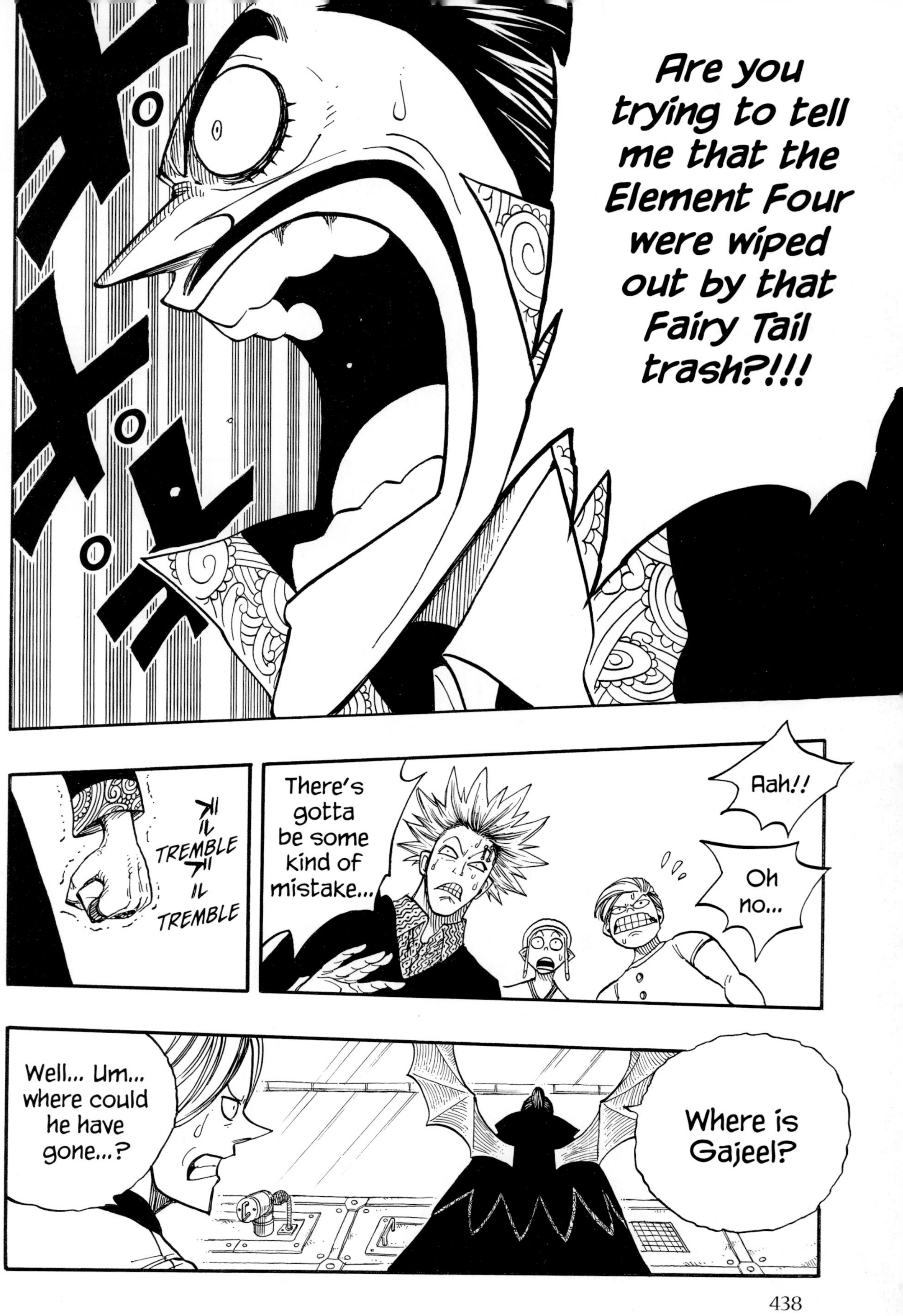
Are you trying to tell me that the Element Four were wiped out by that Fairy Tail trash?!!!
Aah!!
Oh no...
There's gotta be some kind of mistake...
TREMBLE
TREMBLE
Where is Gajeel?
Well... Um... where could he have gone...?

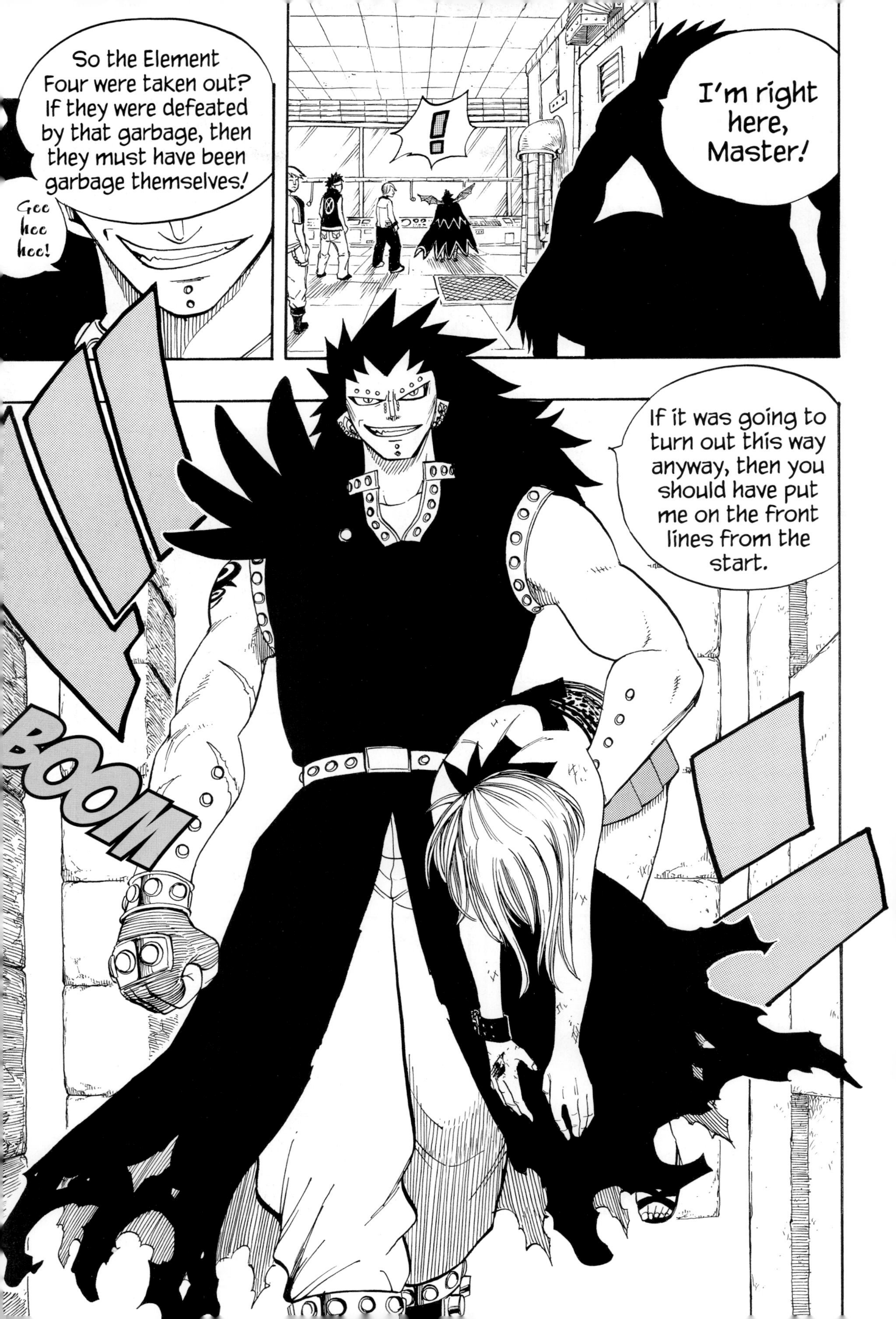
I'm right here, Master!
!
So the Element Four were taken out? If they were defeated by that garbage, then they must have been garbage themselves!
Gee hee hee!
If it was going to turn out this way anyway, then you should have put me on the front lines from the start.
BOOM

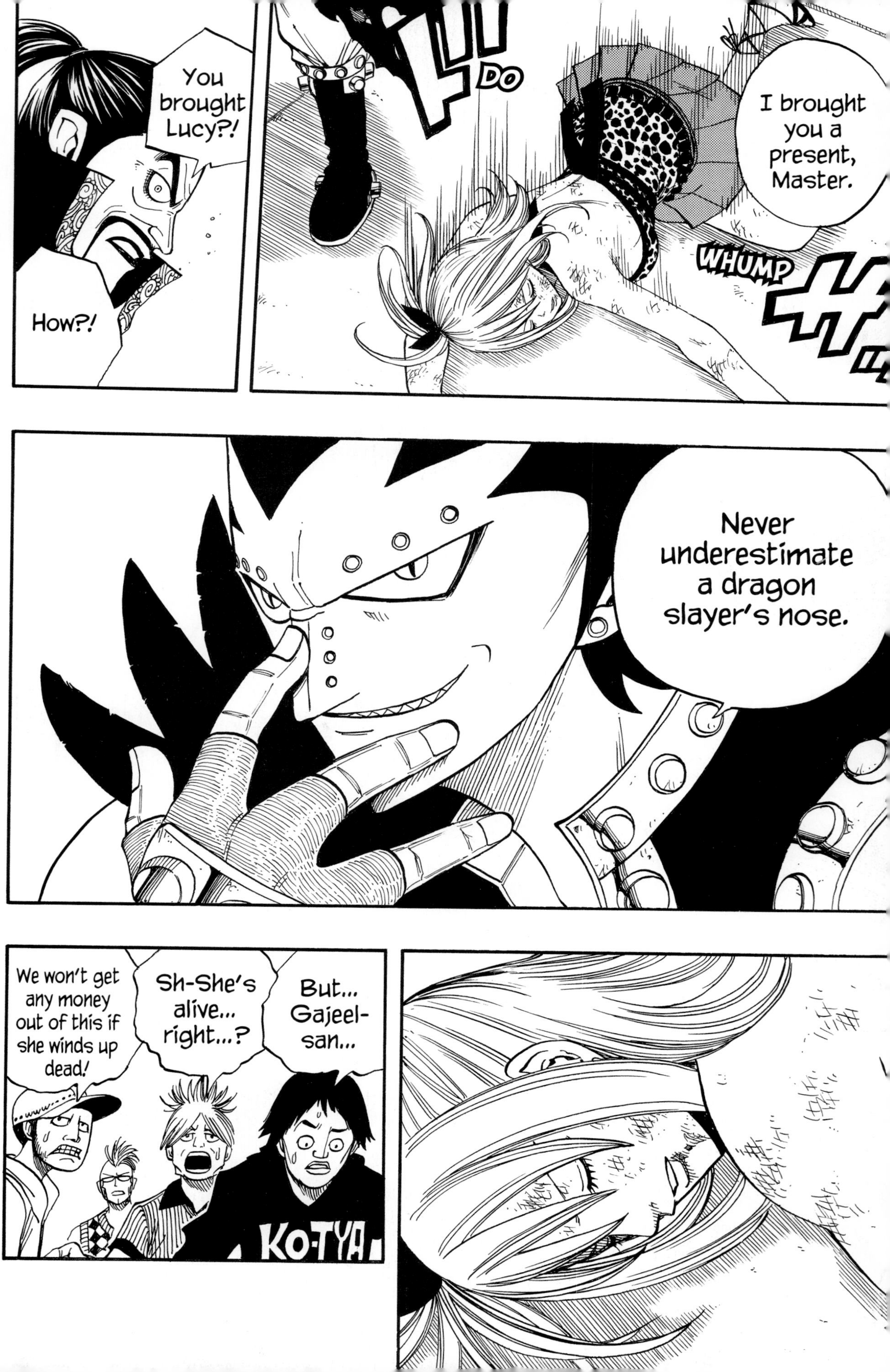
DO
I brought you a present, Master.
WHUMP
You brought Lucy?!
How?!
Never underestimate a dragon slayer's nose.
But... Gajeel-san...
Sh-She's alive... right...?
We won't get any money out of this if she winds up dead!
KO-TYA

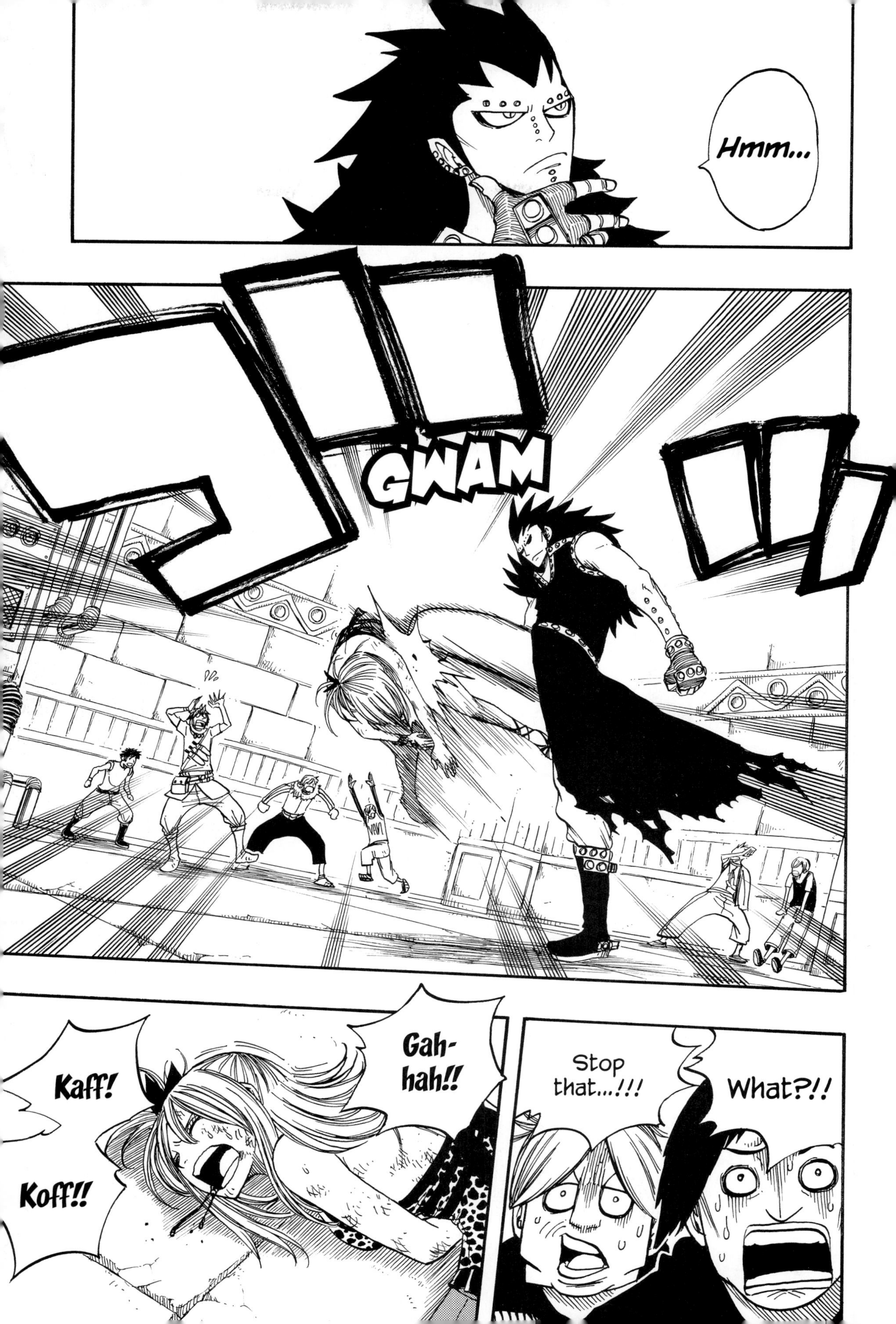
Hmm...
GWAM
What?!!
Stop that...!!!
Gah-hah!!
Kaff!
Koff!!

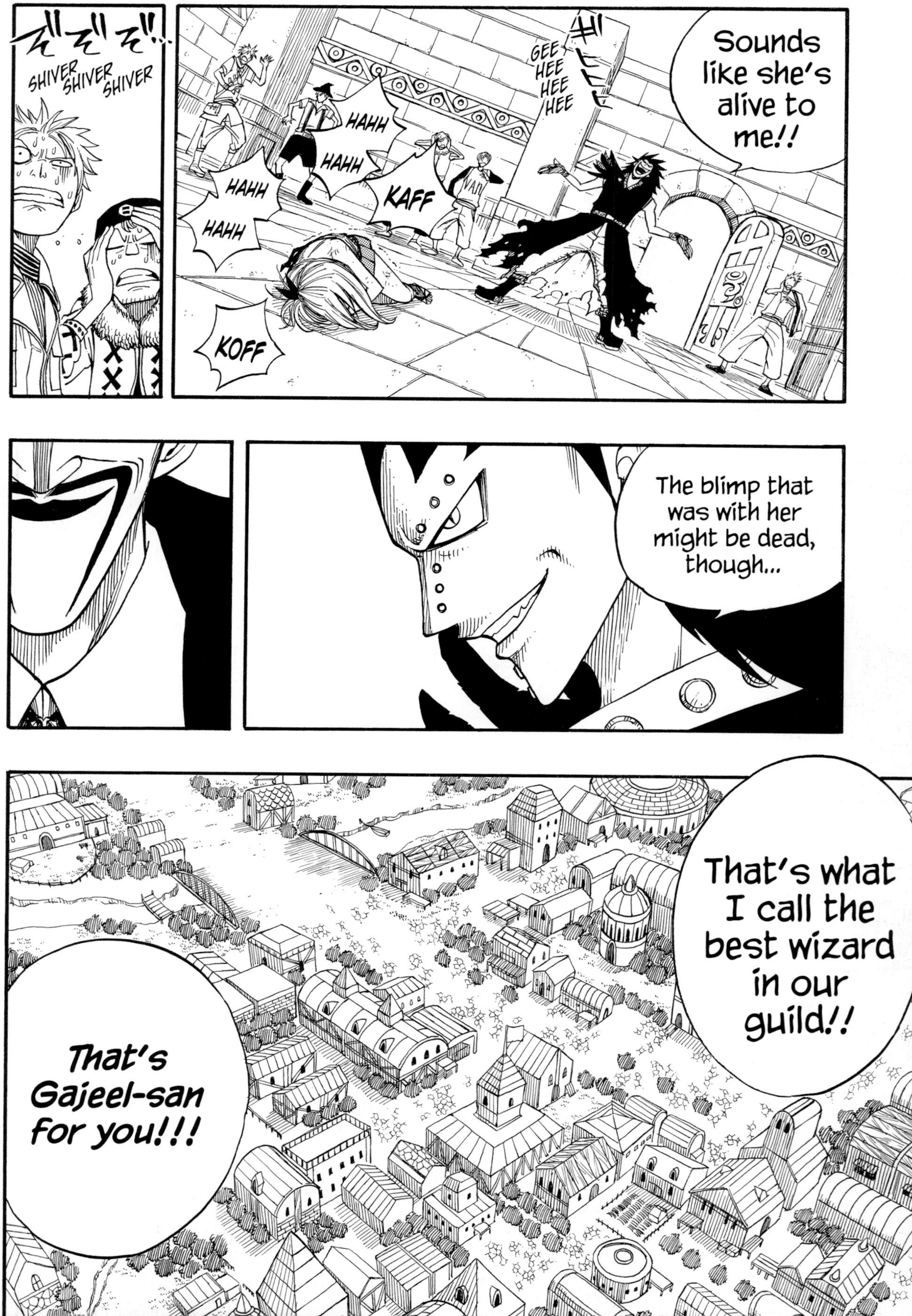
Sounds like she's alive to me!!
ギヒヒ
GEE HEE HEE HEE
HAHH
HAHH
KAFF
HAHH
HAHH
KOFF
ぞぞぞ
SHIVER SHIVER SHIVER
The blimp that was with her might be dead, though...
That's what I call the best wizard in our guild!!
That's Gajeel-san for you!!!

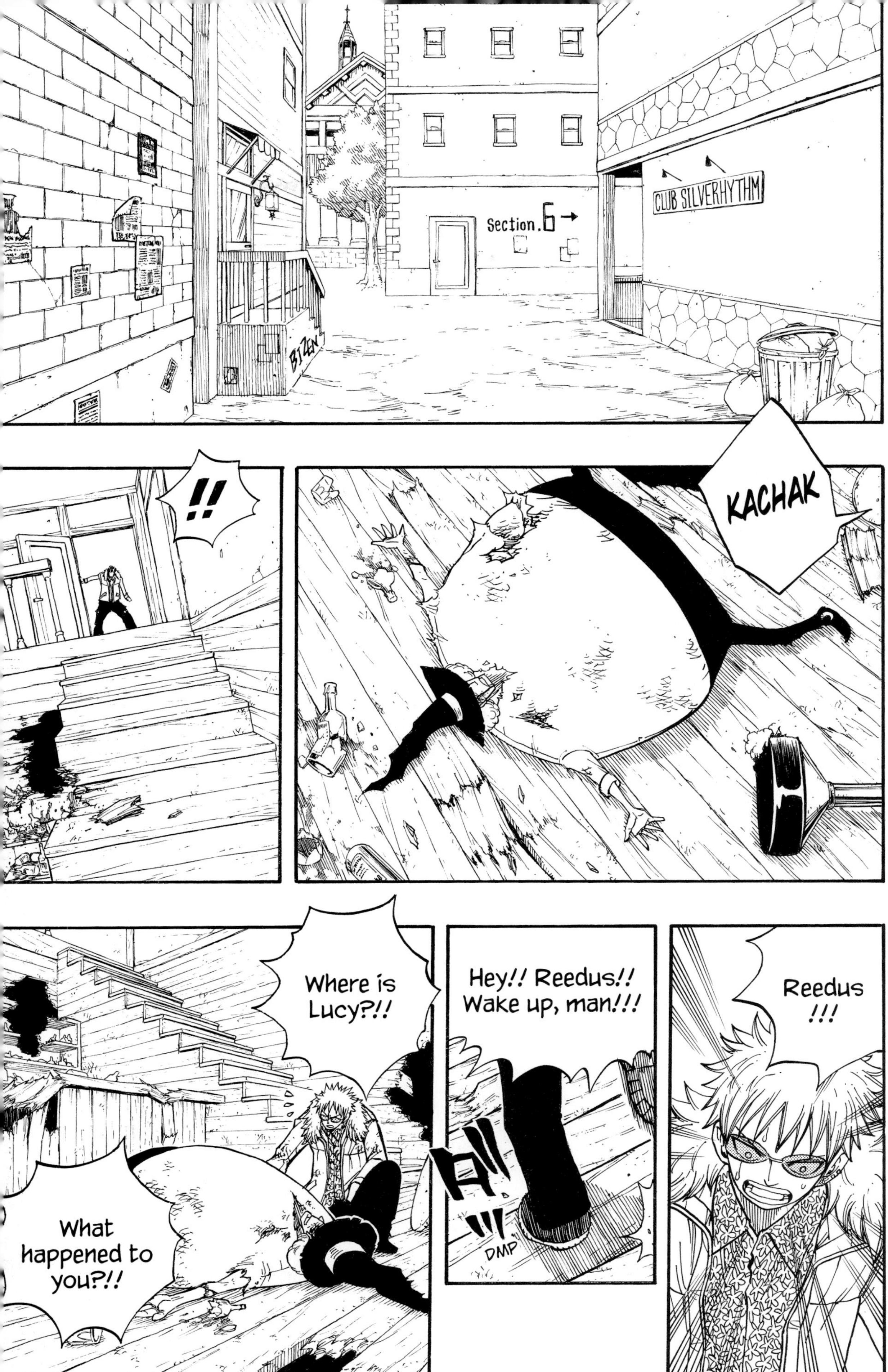
CLUB SILVERHYTHM
Section.6 →
BIZEN
KACHAK
!!
Reedus !!!
Hey!! Reedus!! Wake up, man!!!
DMP
Where is Lucy?!!
What happened to you?!!

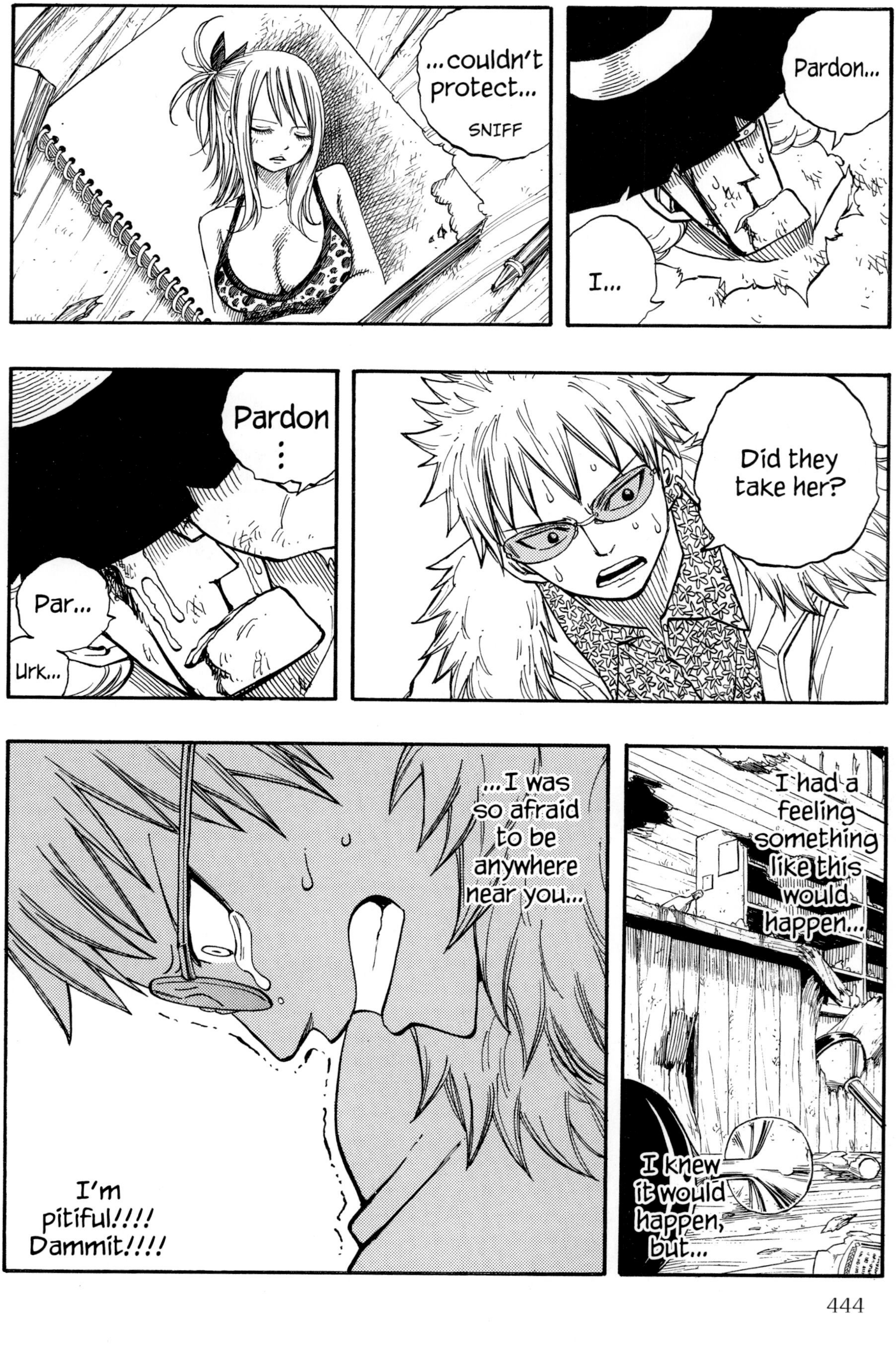
Pardon...
I...
...couldn't protect...
SNIFF
Did they take her?
Pardon...
Par...
Urk...
I had a feeling something like this would happen...
I knew it would happen, but...
...I was so afraid to be anywhere near you...
I'm pitiful!!!! Dammit!!!!

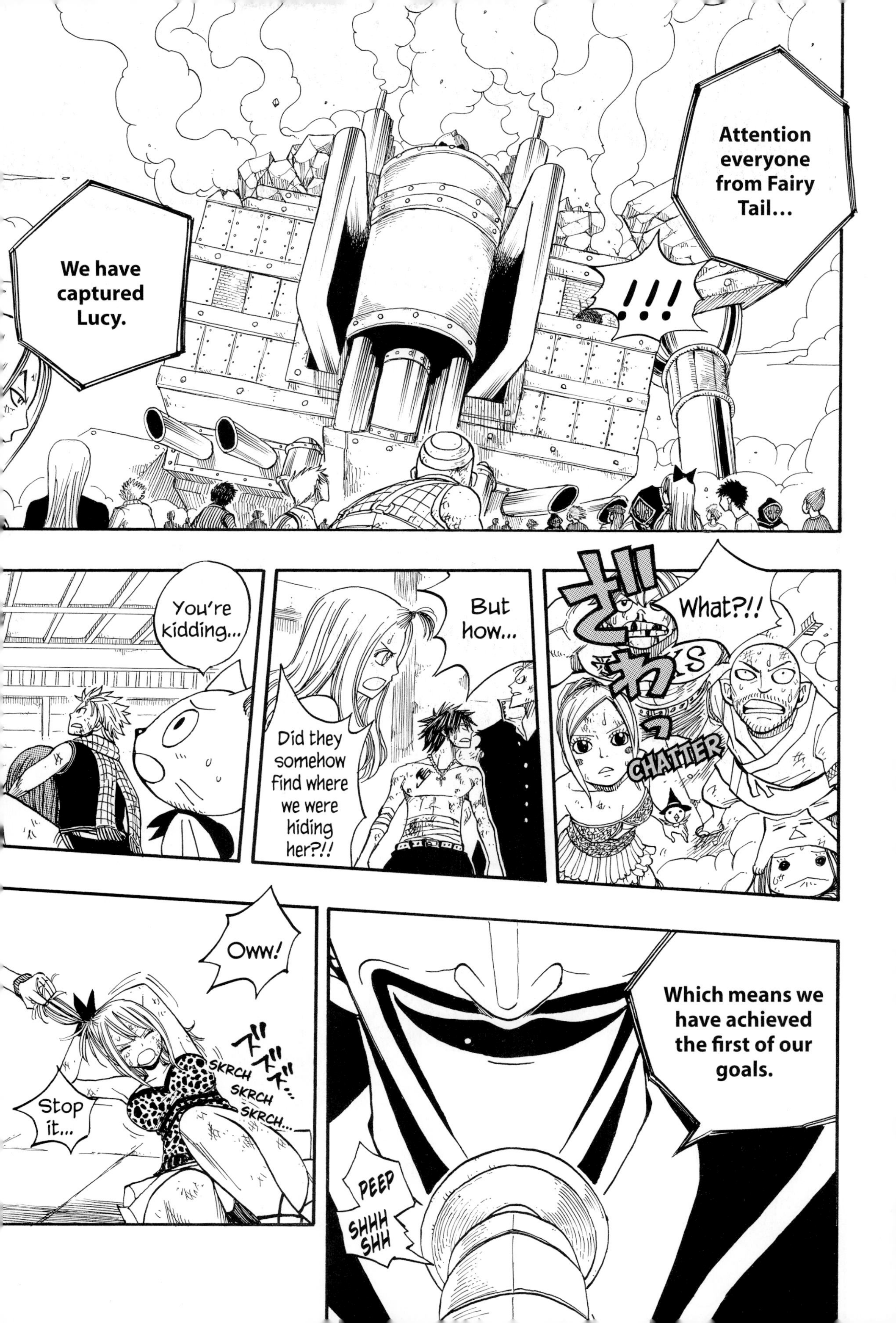
Attention everyone from Fairy Tail…
!!!
We have captured Lucy.
What?!!
CHATTER
But how...
Did they somehow find where we were hiding her?!!
You're kidding...
Which means we have achieved the first of our goals.
PEEP
SHHH SHH
Oww!
SKRCH SKRCH SKRCH...
Stop it...

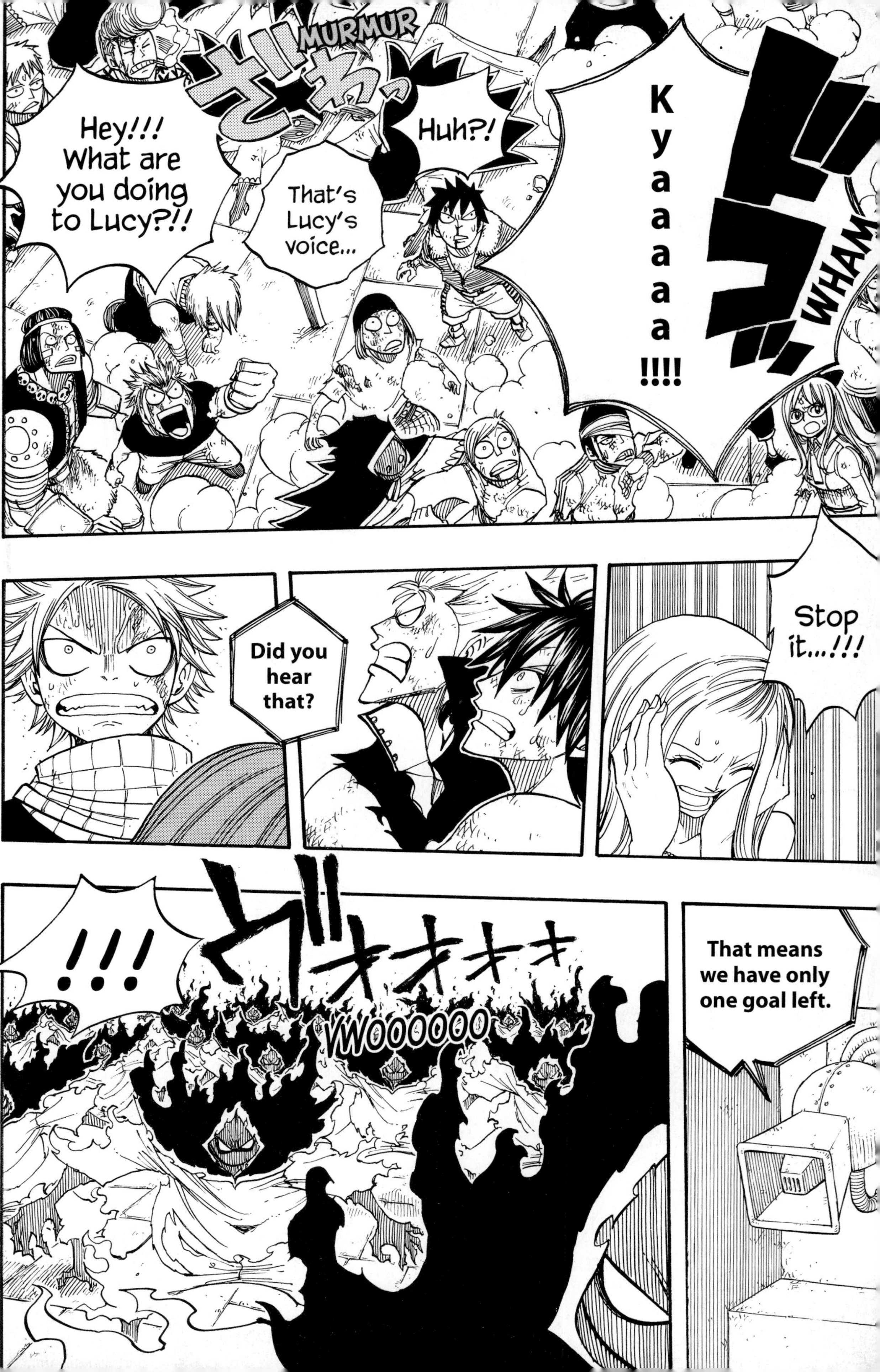
Kyaaaaa!!!!
WHAM
Huh?!
That's Lucy's voice...
MURMUR
Hey!!! What are you doing to Lucy?!!
Stop it...!!!
Did you hear that?
That means we have only one goal left.
!!!
VWOOOOOO

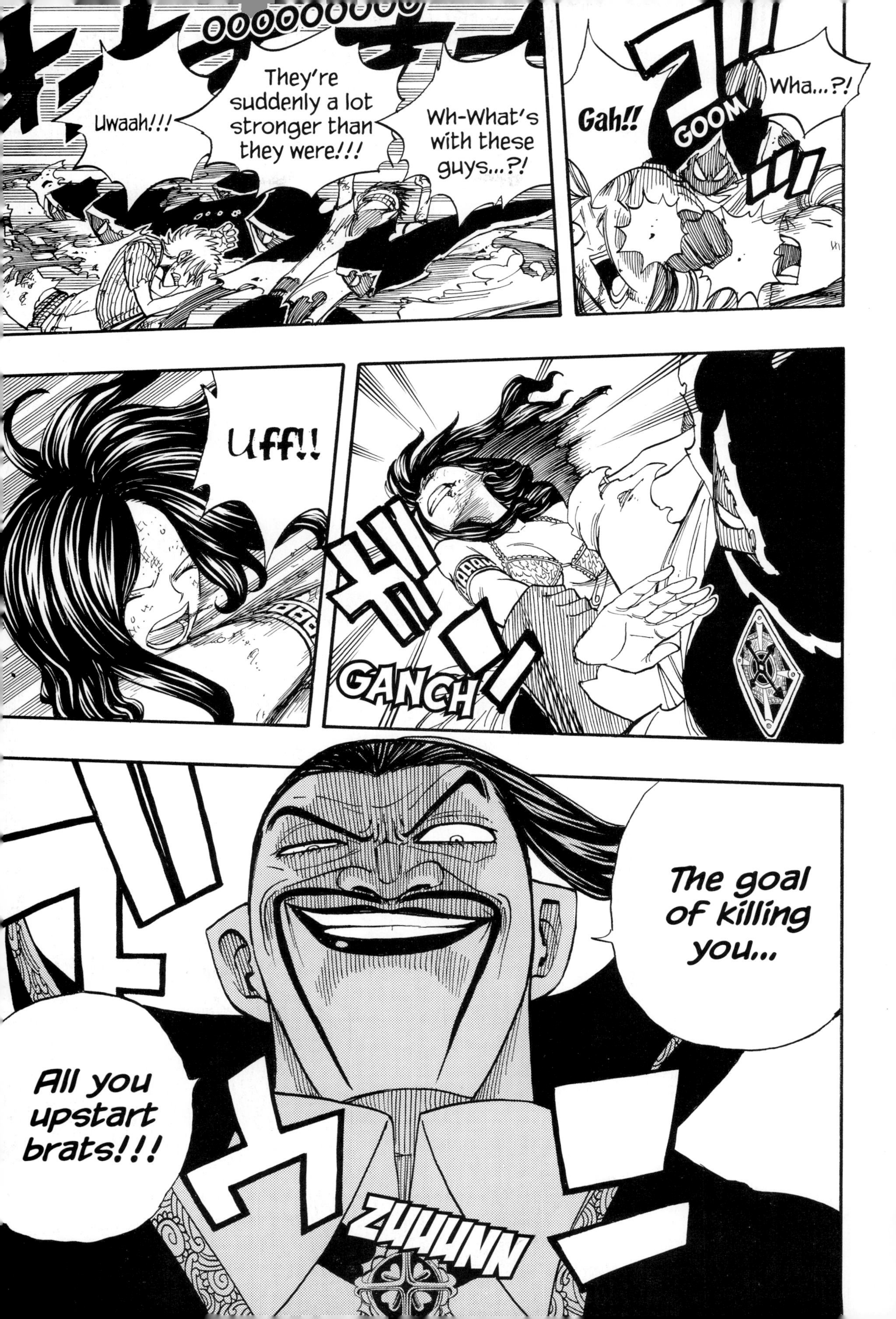
Wha...?!
Gah!!
GOOM
Wh-What's with these guys...?!
They're suddenly a lot stronger than they were!!!
Uwaah!!!
GANCH
Uff!!
The goal of killing you...
All you upstart brats!!!
ZHHUNN

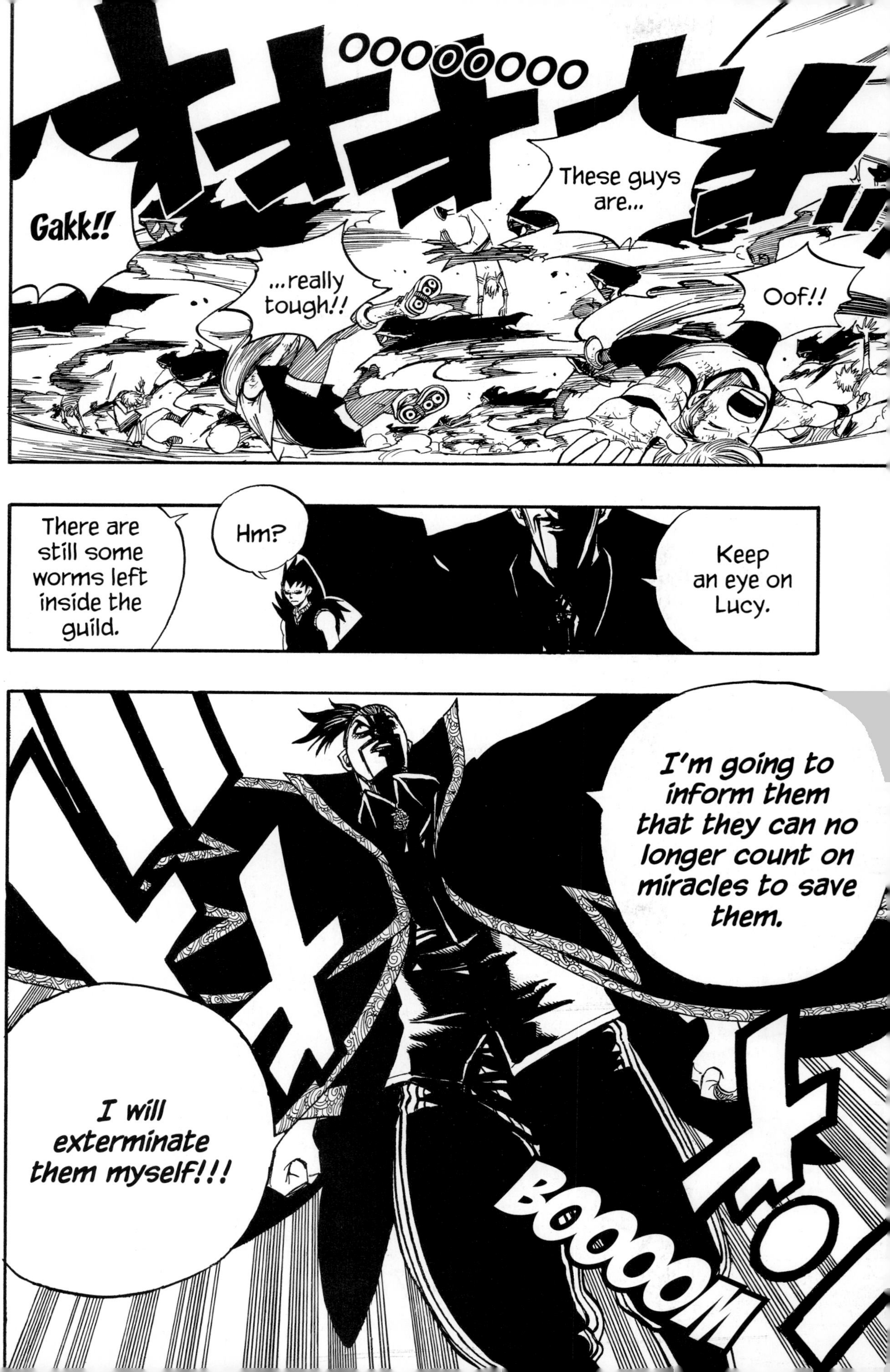
OOOOOOOO
Oof!!
These guys are...
...really tough!!
Gakk!!
Keep an eye on Lucy.
Hm?
There are still some worms left inside the guild.
I'm going to inform them that they can no longer count on miracles to save them.
I will exterminate them myself!!!
BOOOOM

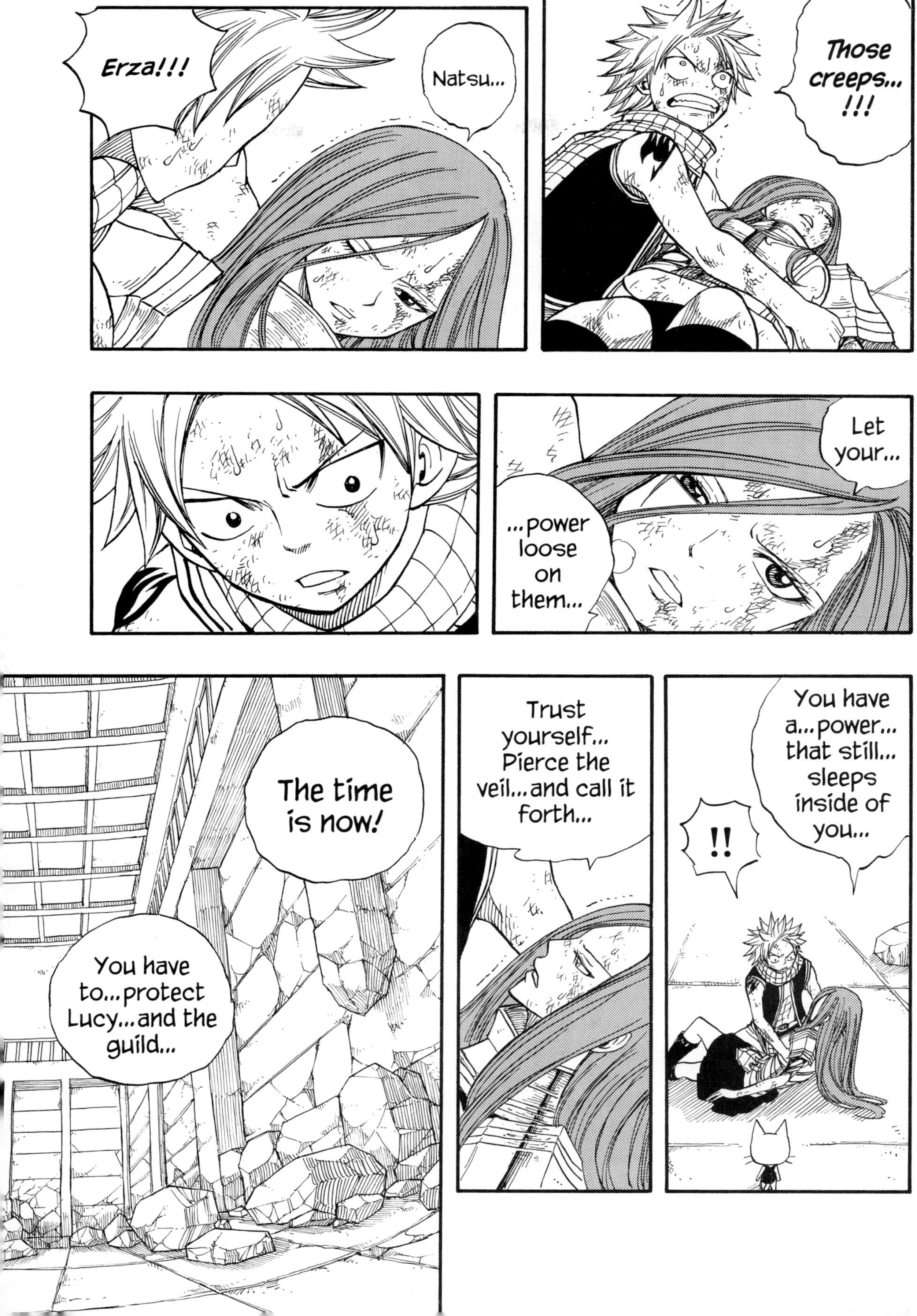

Those creeps...!!!
Erza!!!
Natsu...
Let your...
...power loose on them...
!!
You have a...power...that still...sleeps inside of you...
Trust yourself... Pierce the veil...and call it forth...
The time is now!
You have to...protect Lucy...and the guild...

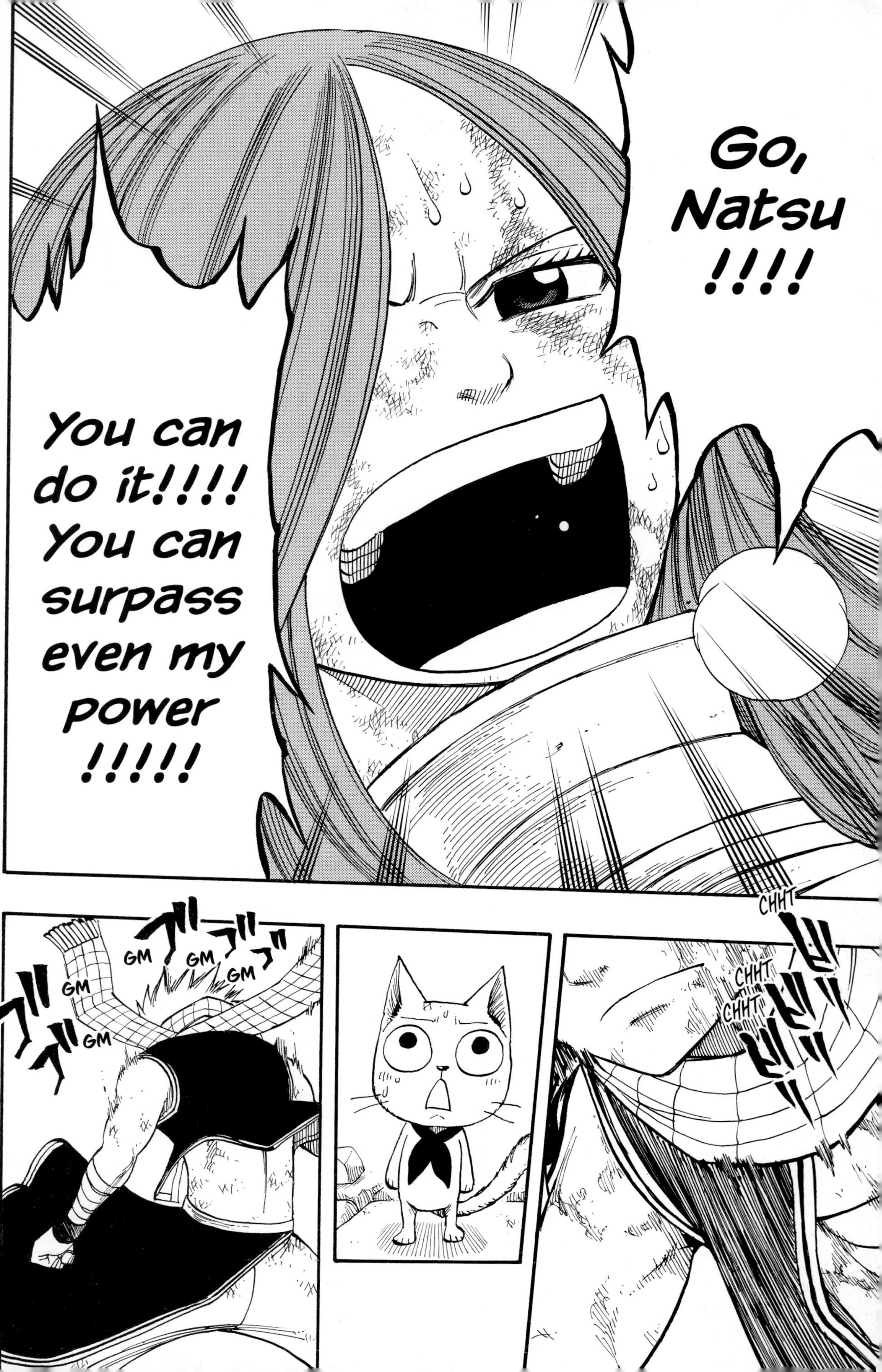
Go, Natsu!!!!
You can do it!!!! You can surpass even my power!!!!!
CHHT
CHHT
CHHT
GM
GM
GM
GM
GM

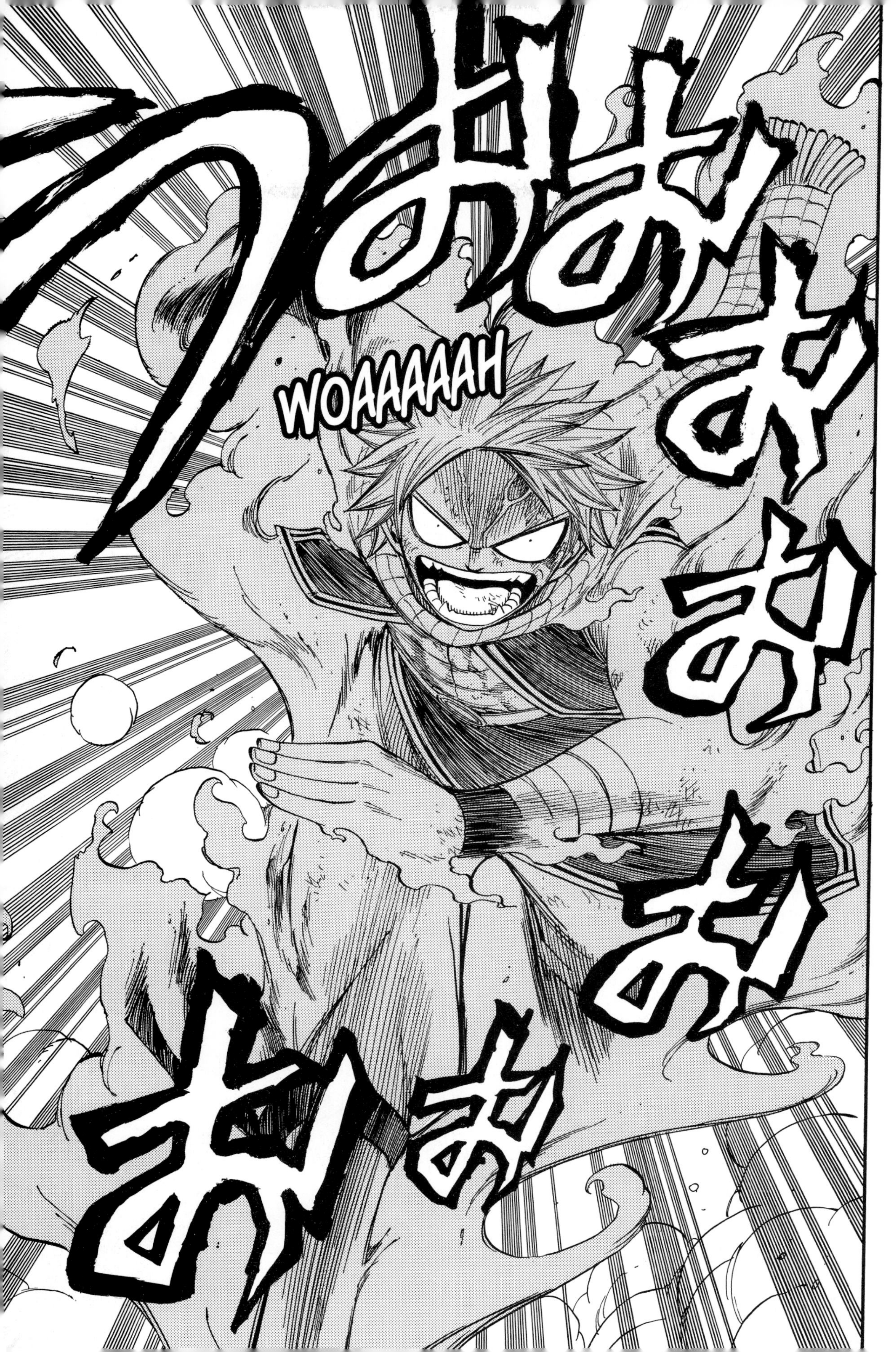
WOAAAAAH
つおおおおおおお

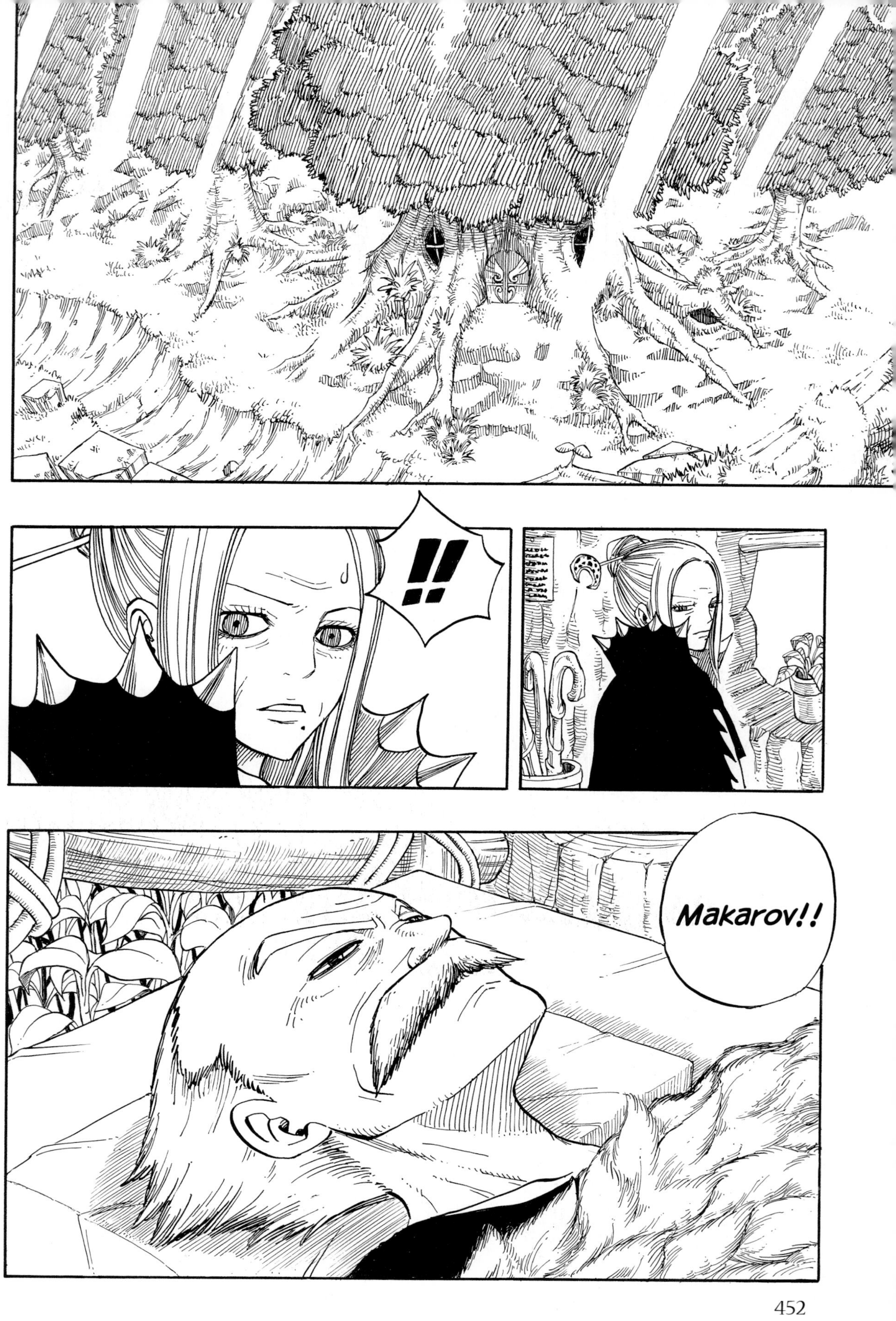
!!
Makarov!!

Chapter 60: Wings of Fire

FAIRY TAIL

Name: Vijeeter Ecor   **Age:** 16 yrs.

Magic: Dance

Likes: Dance   **Dislikes:** Fermented soybeans

WIZARD GUILD×633

Remarks

By dancing particular dances, he can do things such as boost the fighting power of all of his friends within a ten-meter radius or, similarly, reduce the fighting power of enemies with his dance magic. He's always loved dance, and can regularly be seen dancing within the guild. His plan for the future seems to be to save up his cash and go study at Minstrel, the cultural capital of dance. But he never can seem to save any money. As a side note, he has a hundred suits that all look alike.

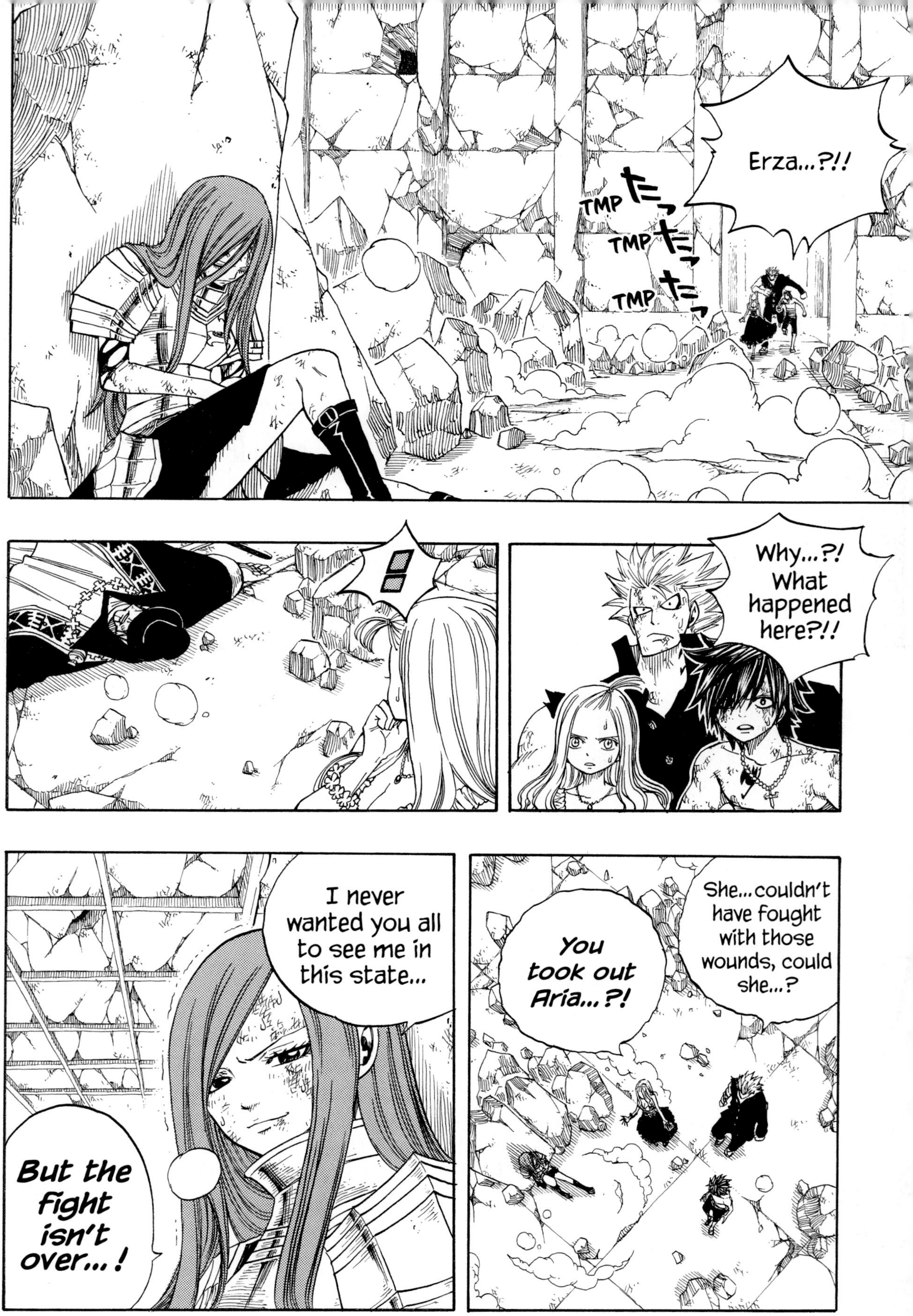
Erza...?!!
TMP
TMP
TMP
Why...?! What happened here?!!
!!
She...couldn't have fought with those wounds, could she...?
You took out Aria...?!
I never wanted you all to see me in this state...
But the fight isn't over...!

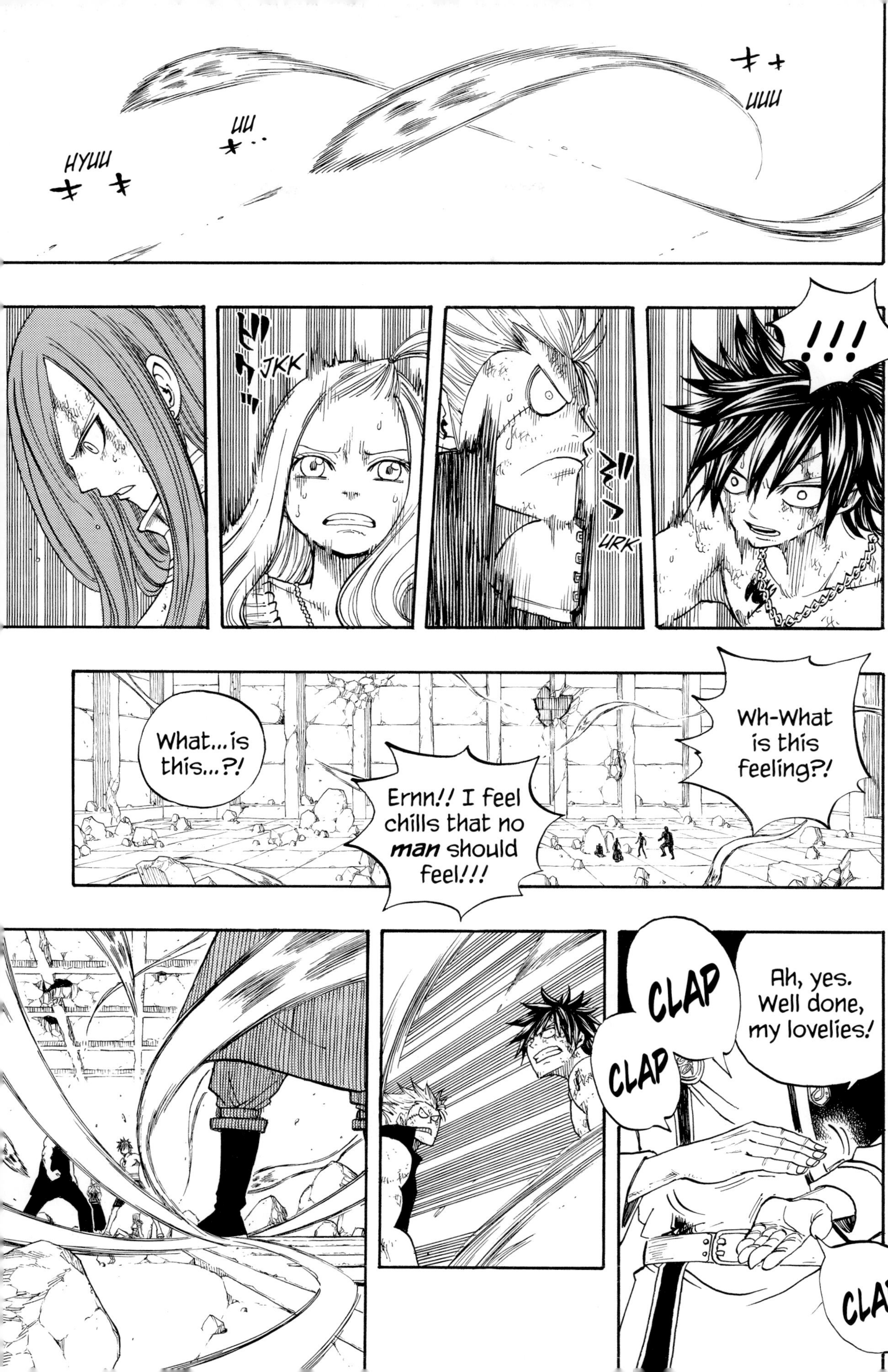
UUU
UU
HYUU
!!!
URK
JKK
Wh-What is this feeling?!
Ernn!! I feel chills that no *man* should feel!!!
What...is this...?!
CLAP
Ah, yes. Well done, my lovelies!
CLAP
CLAP

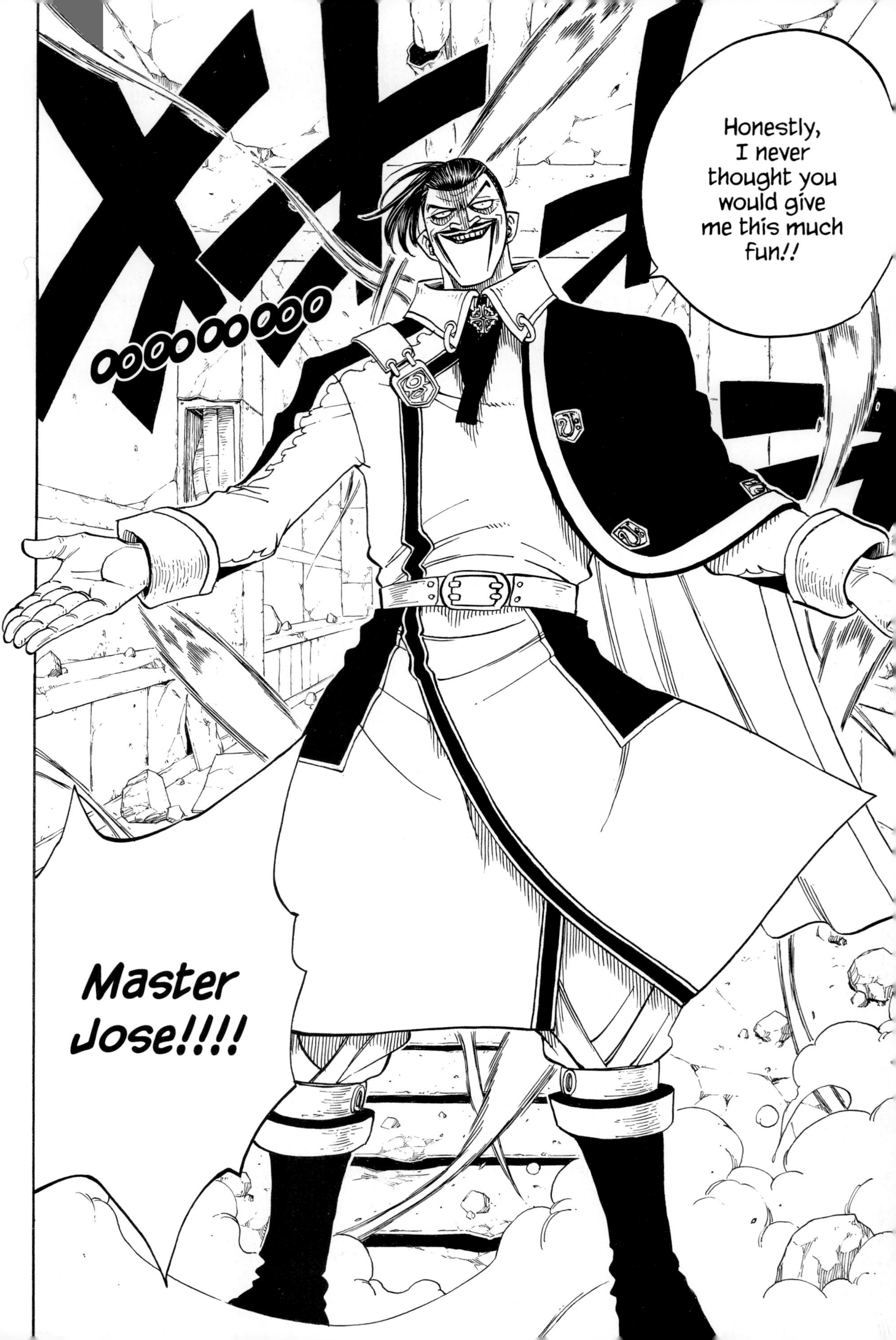
Honestly, I never thought you would give me this much fun!!
ooooooooo
Master Jose!!!!

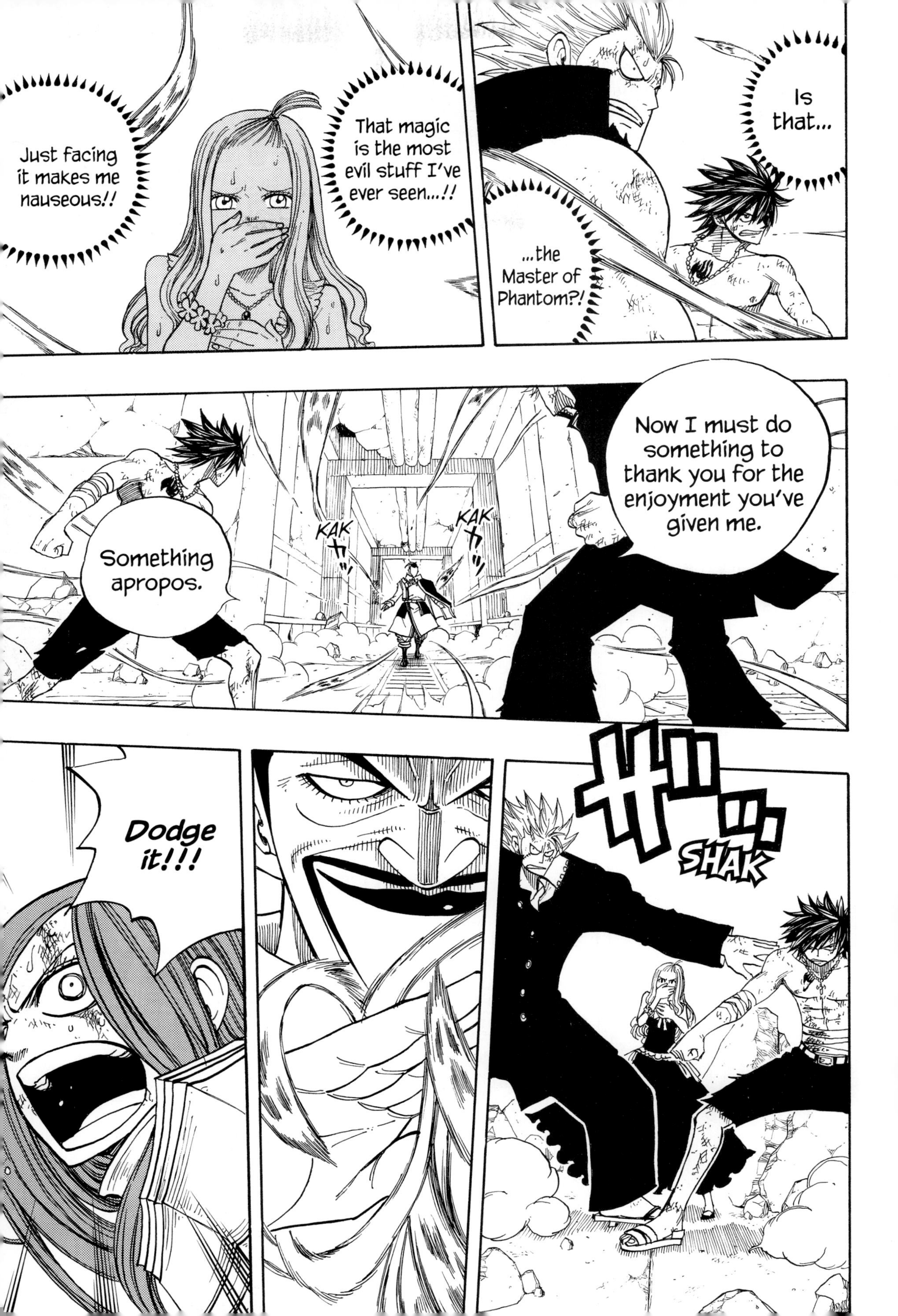
Is that...
...the Master of Phantom?!
That magic is the most evil stuff I've ever seen...!!
Just facing it makes me nauseous!!
Now I must do something to thank you for the enjoyment you've given me.
KAK
KAK
Something apropos.
SHAK
Dodge it!!!

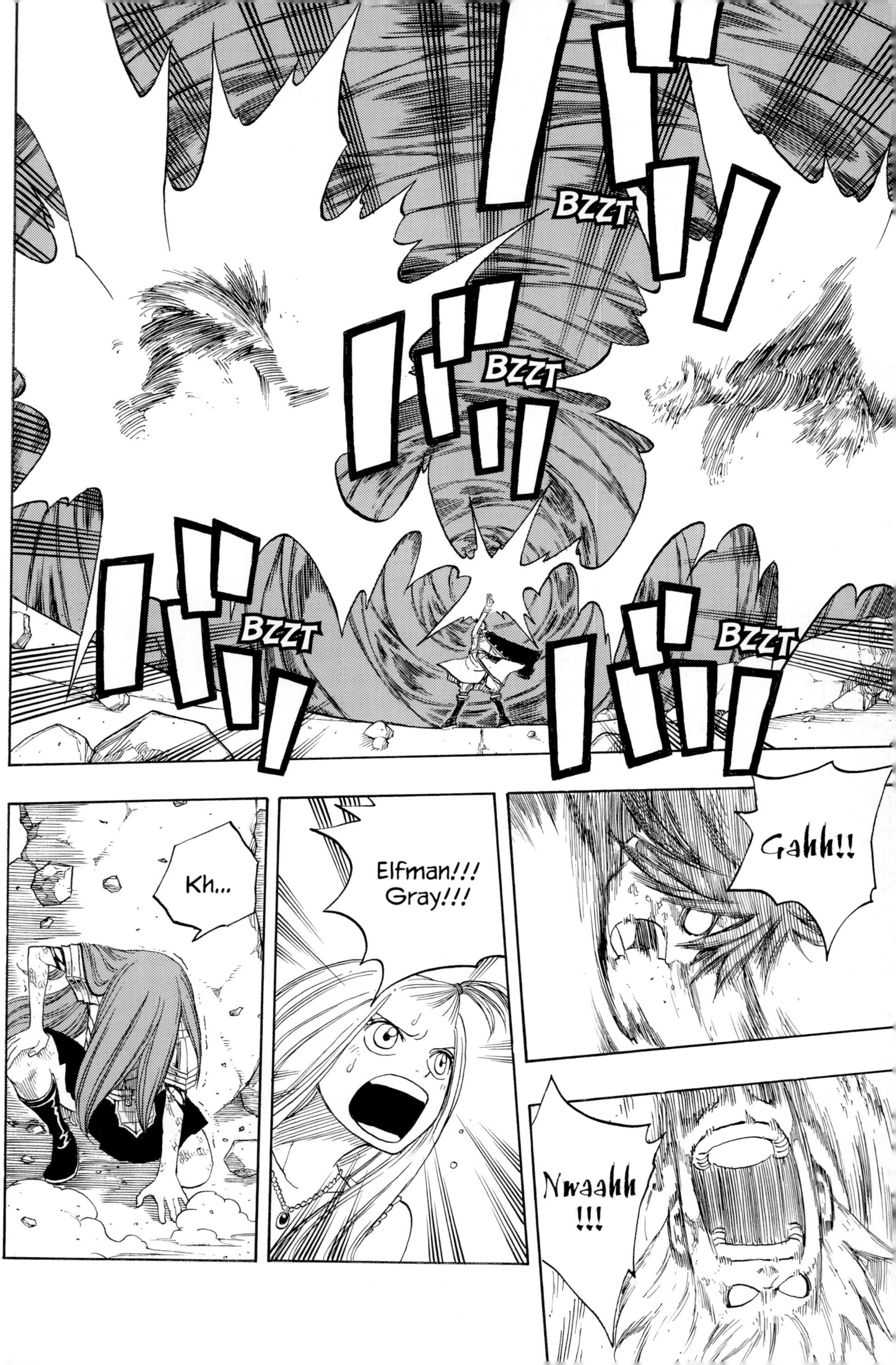
BZZT
BZZT
BZZT
BZZT
Gahh!!
Nwaahh !!!
Elfman!!! Gray!!!
Kh...

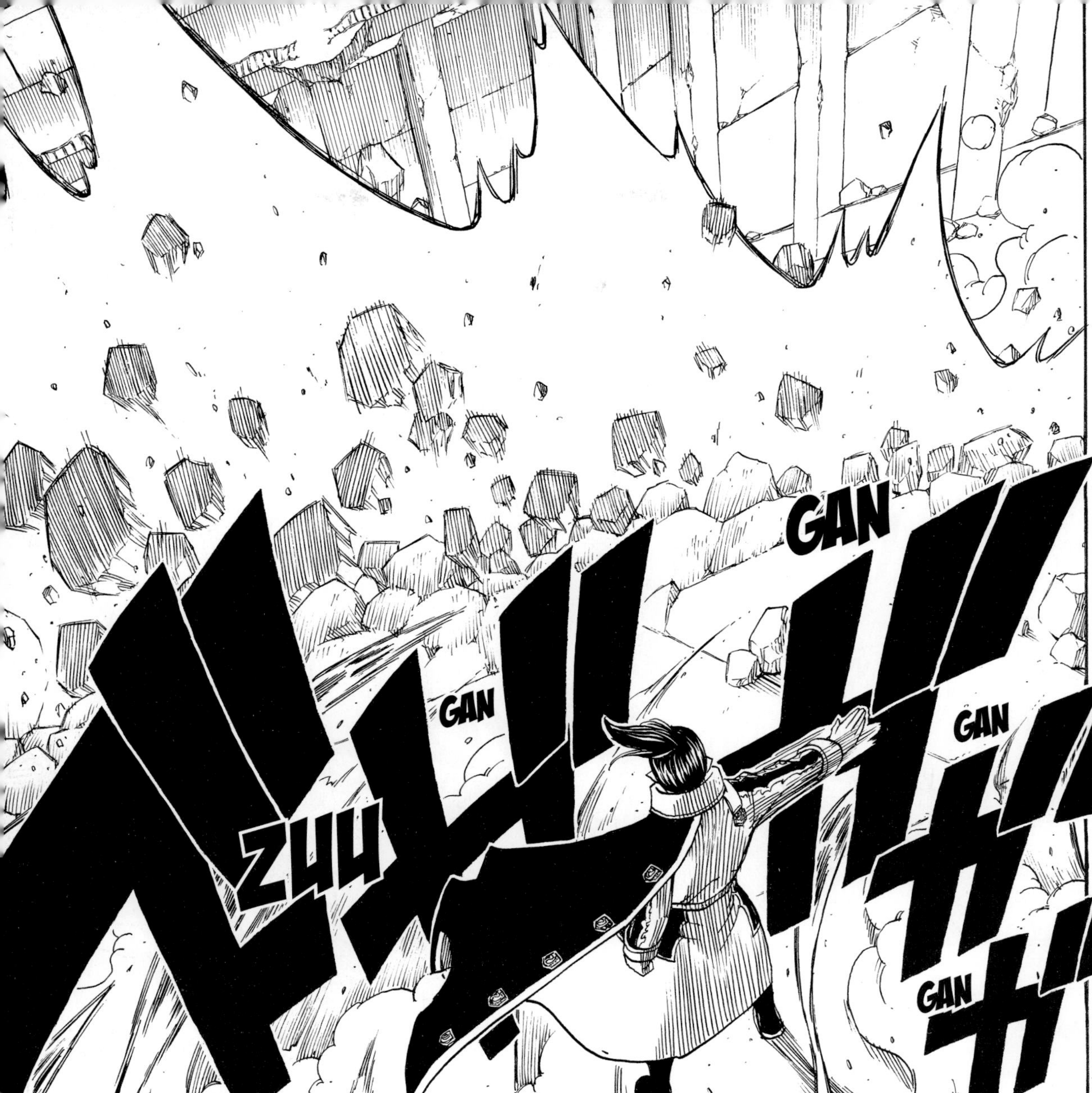
GAN
GAN
GAN
GAN
ZUU
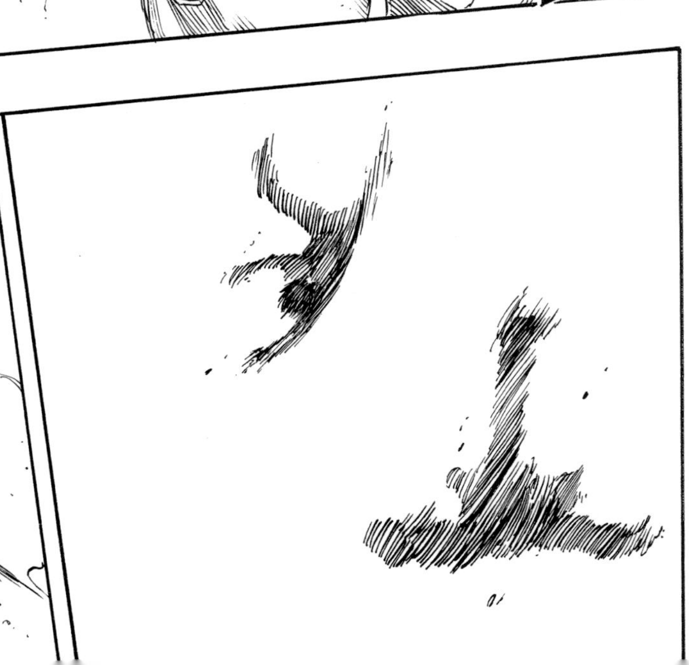
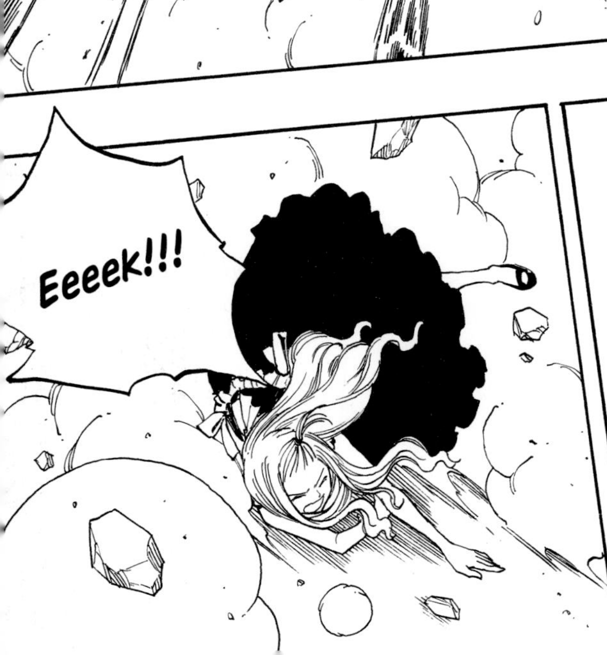
Eeeek!!!

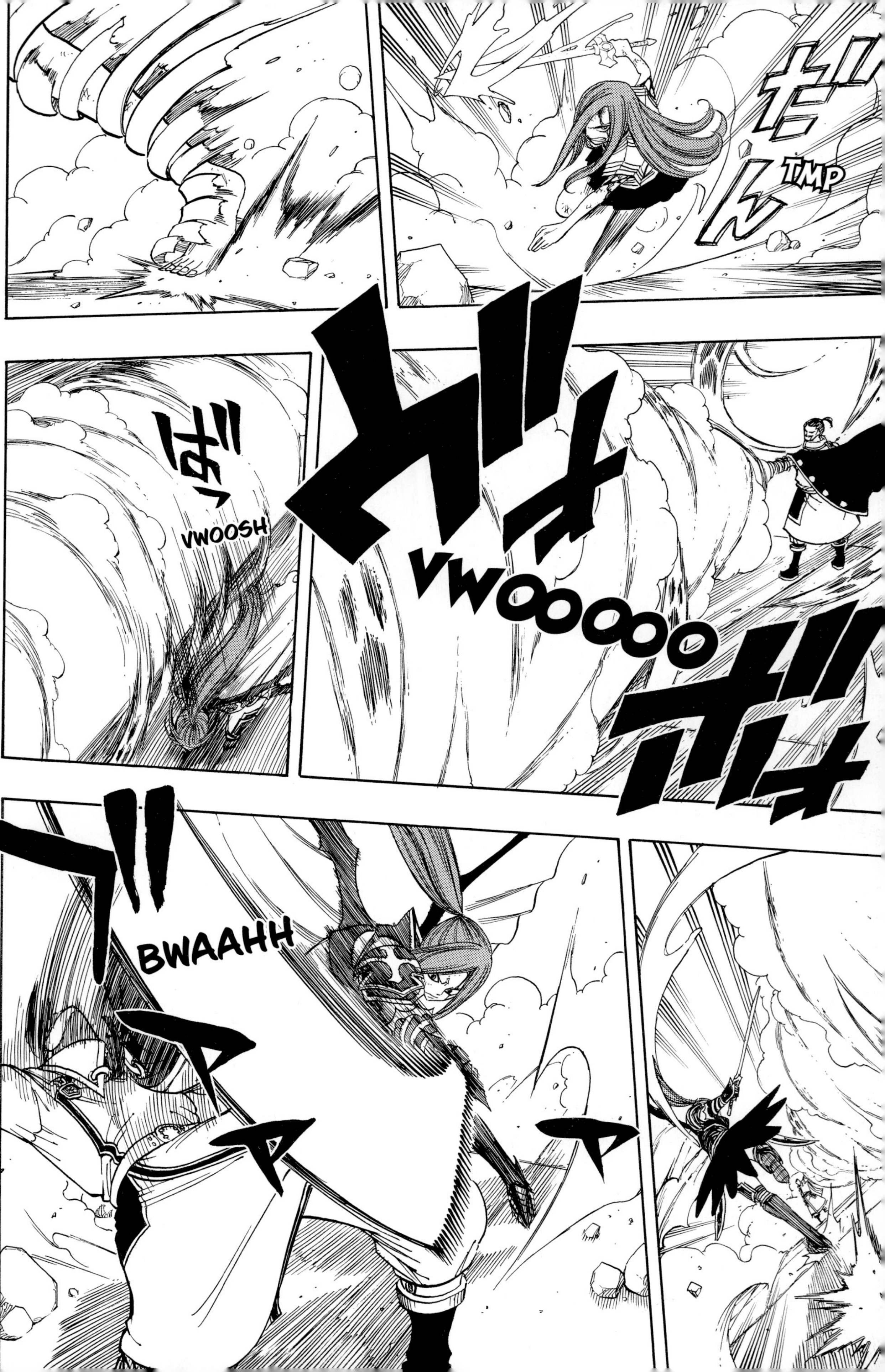
だん
TMP
VWOOOOOO
ばっ
VWOOSH
BWAAHH

GANCH

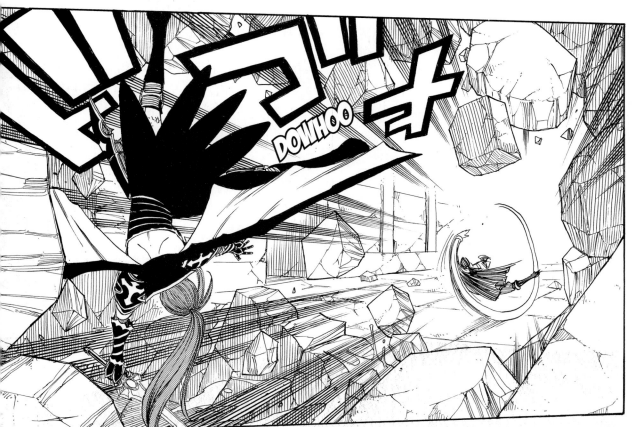

DOWHOO

DMPP

GRACH

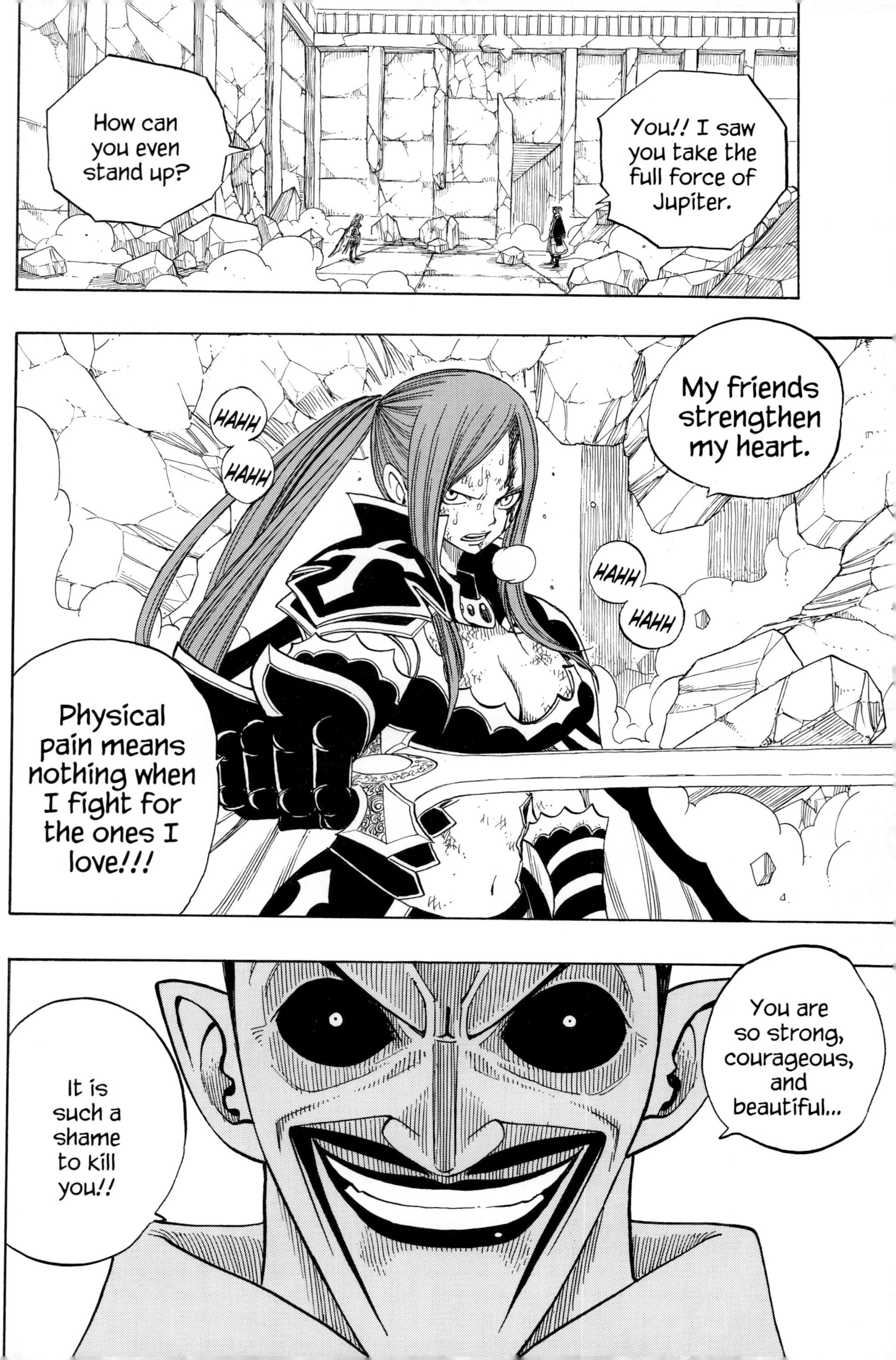
You!! I saw you take the full force of Jupiter.
How can you even stand up?
My friends strengthen my heart.
HAHH
HAHH
HAHH
HAHH
Physical pain means nothing when I fight for the ones I love!!!
You are so strong, courageous, and beautiful...
It is such a shame to kill you!!

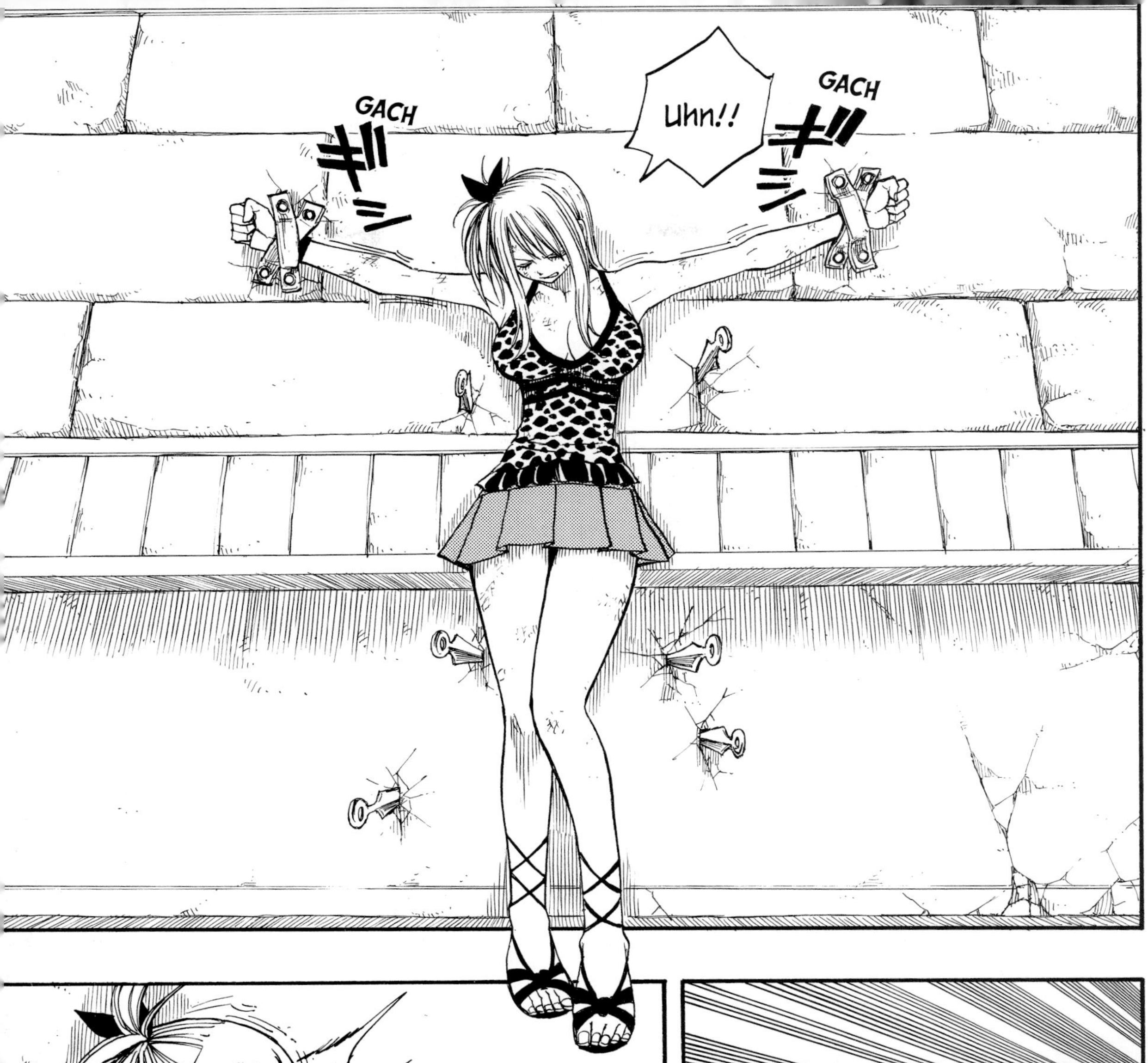
GACH
Uhn!!
GACH

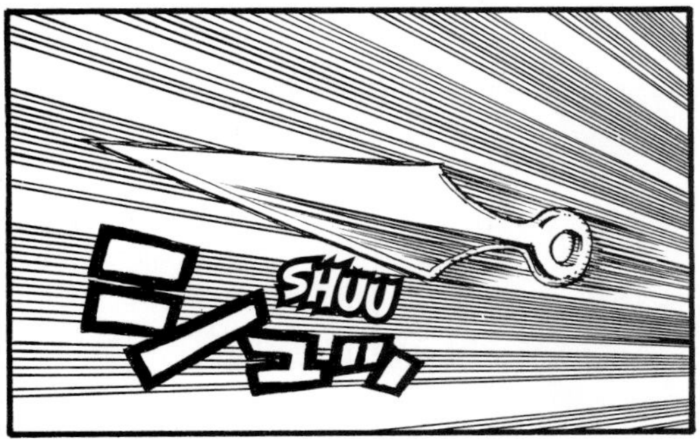
SHUU

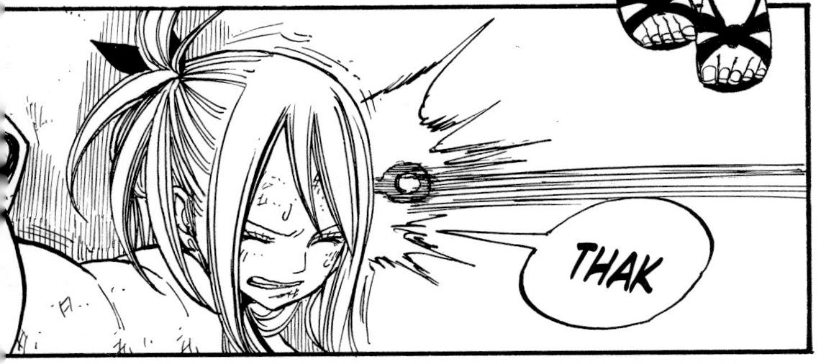
THAK

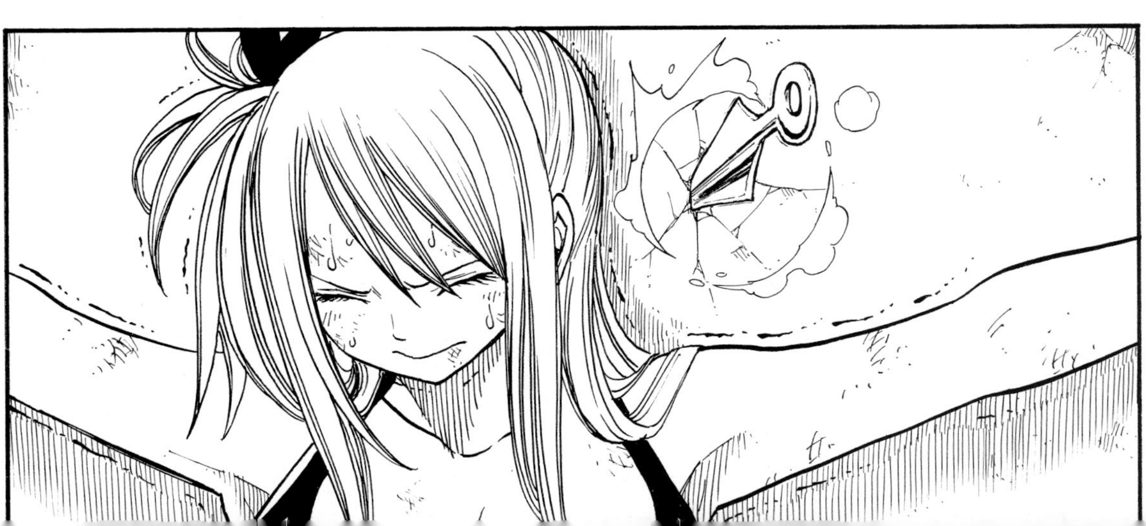

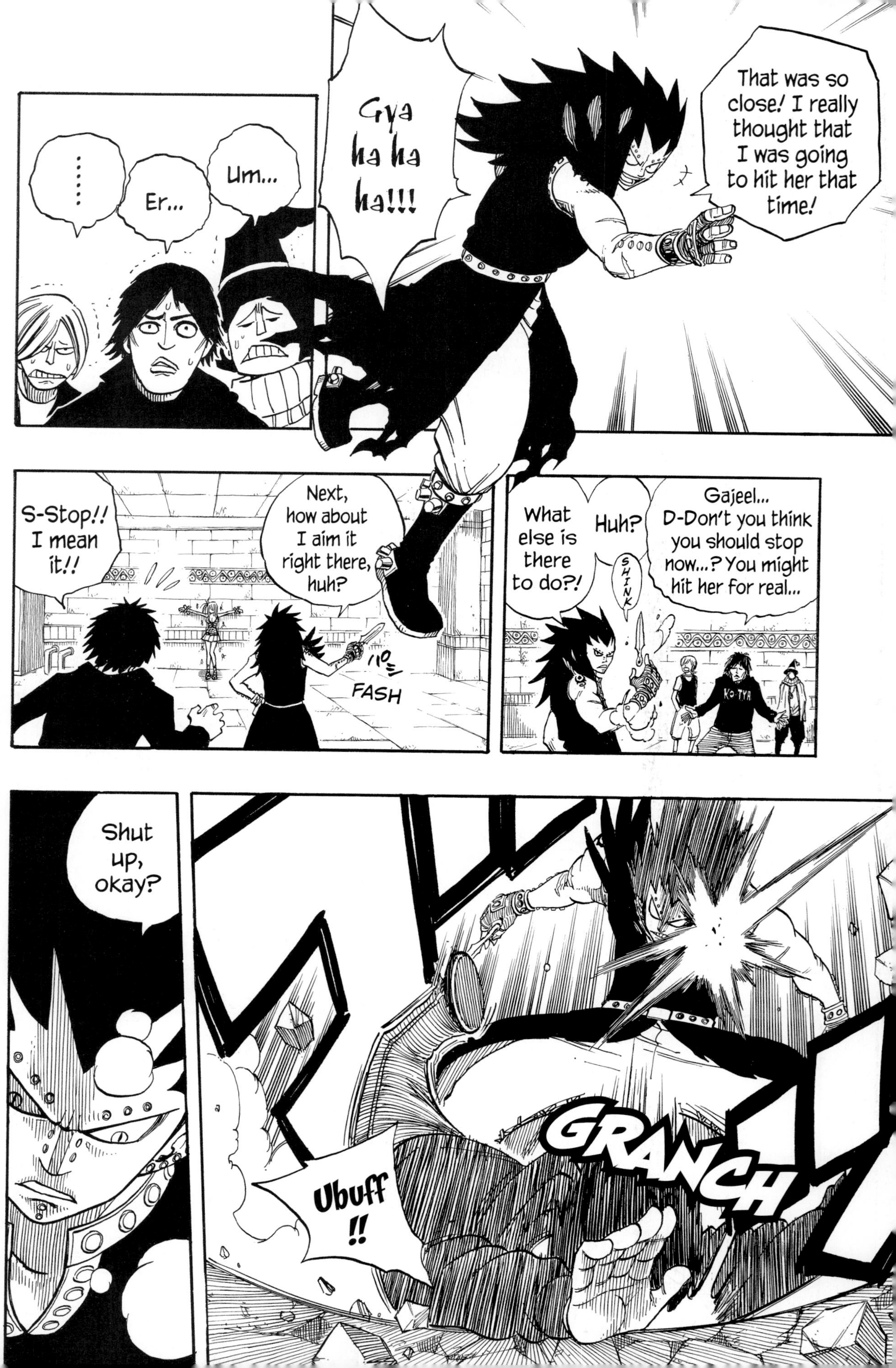
That was so close! I really thought that I was going to hit her that time!
Gya ha ha ha!!!
Um...
Er...
......
Gajeel... D-Don't you think you should stop now...? You might hit her for real...
Huh?
SHINK
What else is there to do?!
Next, how about I aim it right there, huh?
FASH
S-Stop!! I mean it!!
GRANCH
Ubuff !!
Shut up, okay?

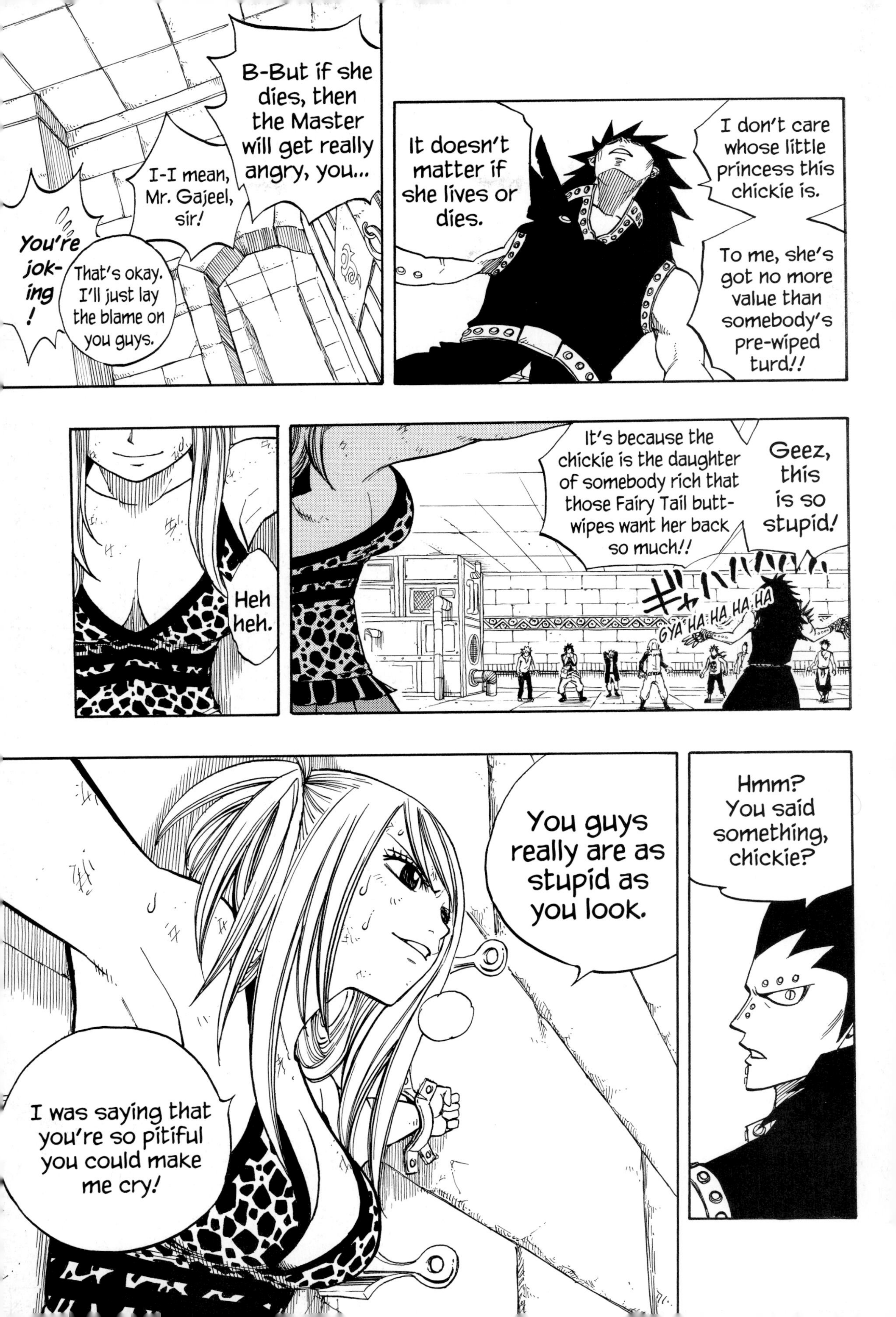
I don't care whose little princess this chickie is.
It doesn't matter if she lives or dies.
To me, she's got no more value than somebody's pre-wiped turd!!
B-But if she dies, then the Master will get really angry, you...
I-I mean, Mr. Gajeel, sir!
That's okay. I'll just lay the blame on you guys.
You're jok-ing!
Geez, this is so stupid!
It's because the chickie is the daughter of somebody rich that those Fairy Tail butt-wipes want her back so much!!
ギャハハハハ
GYA HA HA HA HA
Heh heh.
Hmm? You said something, chickie?
You guys really are as stupid as you look.
I was saying that you're so pitiful you could make me cry!

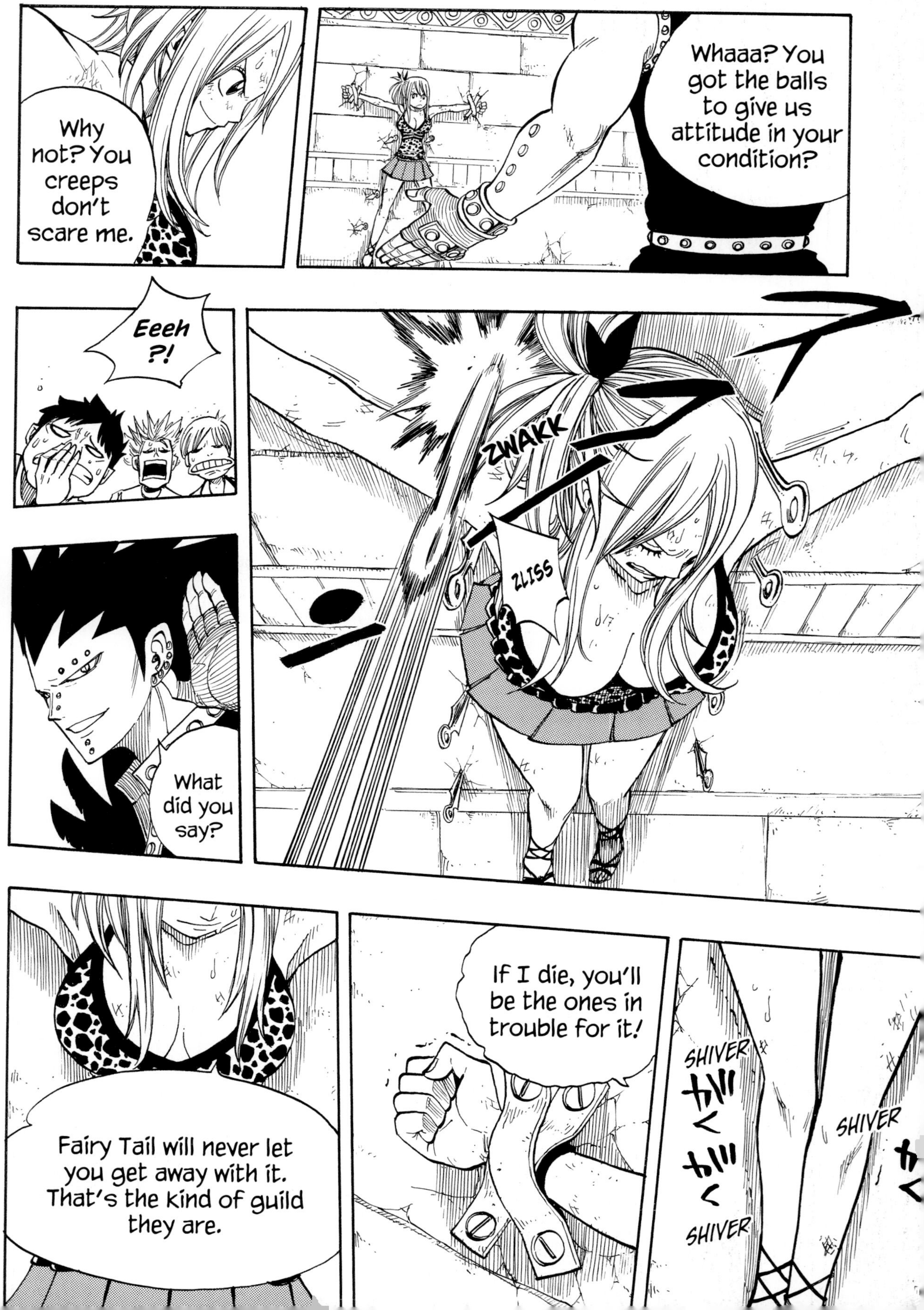
Whaaa? You got the balls to give us attitude in your condition?
Why not? You creeps don't scare me.
ZWAKK
ZLISS
Eeeh ?!
What did you say?
SHIVER
SHIVER
SHIVER
If I die, you'll be the ones in trouble for it!
Fairy Tail will never let you get away with it. That's the kind of guild they are.

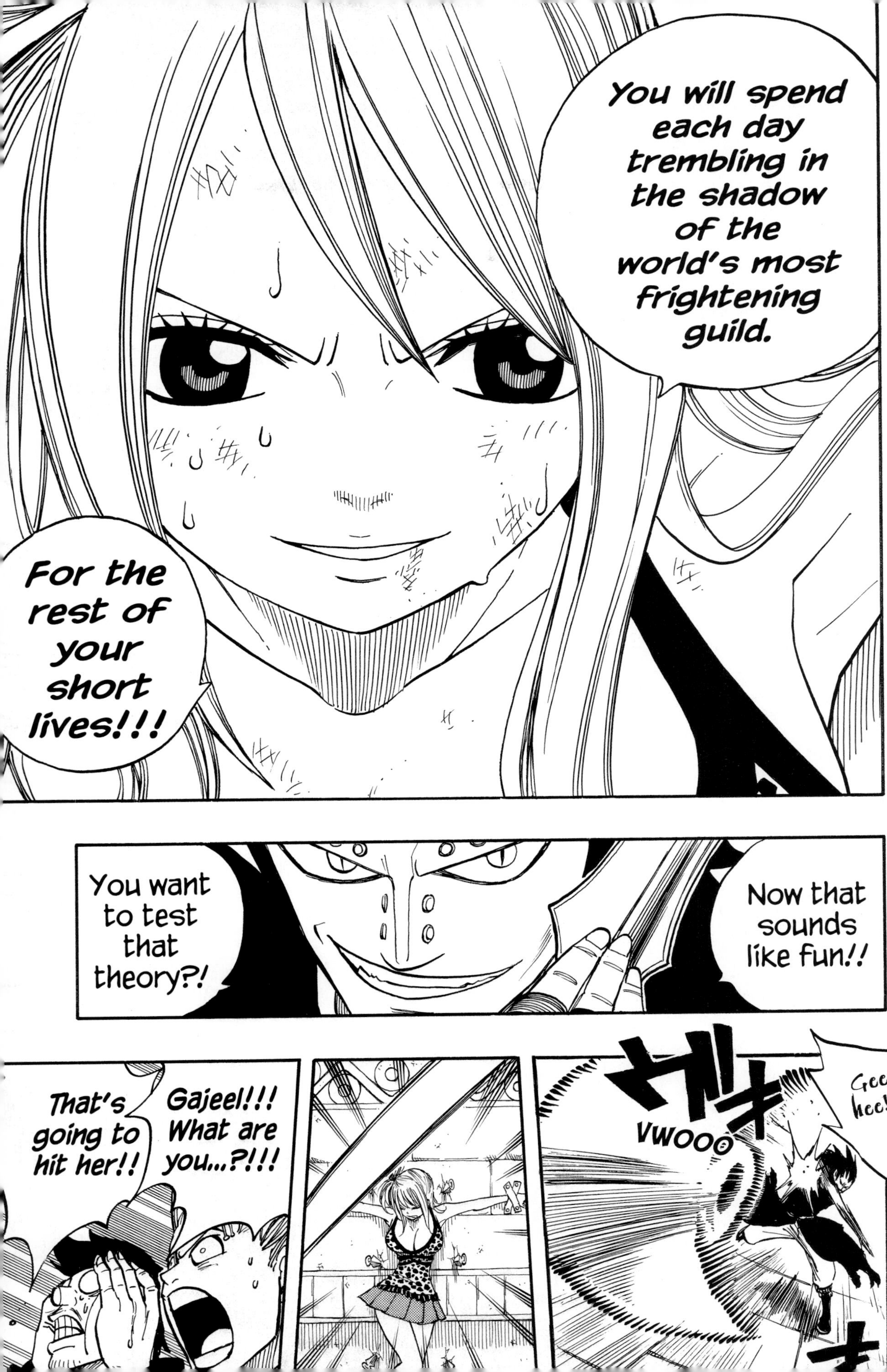
You will spend each day trembling in the shadow of the world's most frightening guild.
For the rest of your short lives!!!
Now that sounds like fun!!
You want to test that theory?!
Gee hee!!
VWOOO
Gajeel!!! What are you...?!!!
That's going to hit her!!

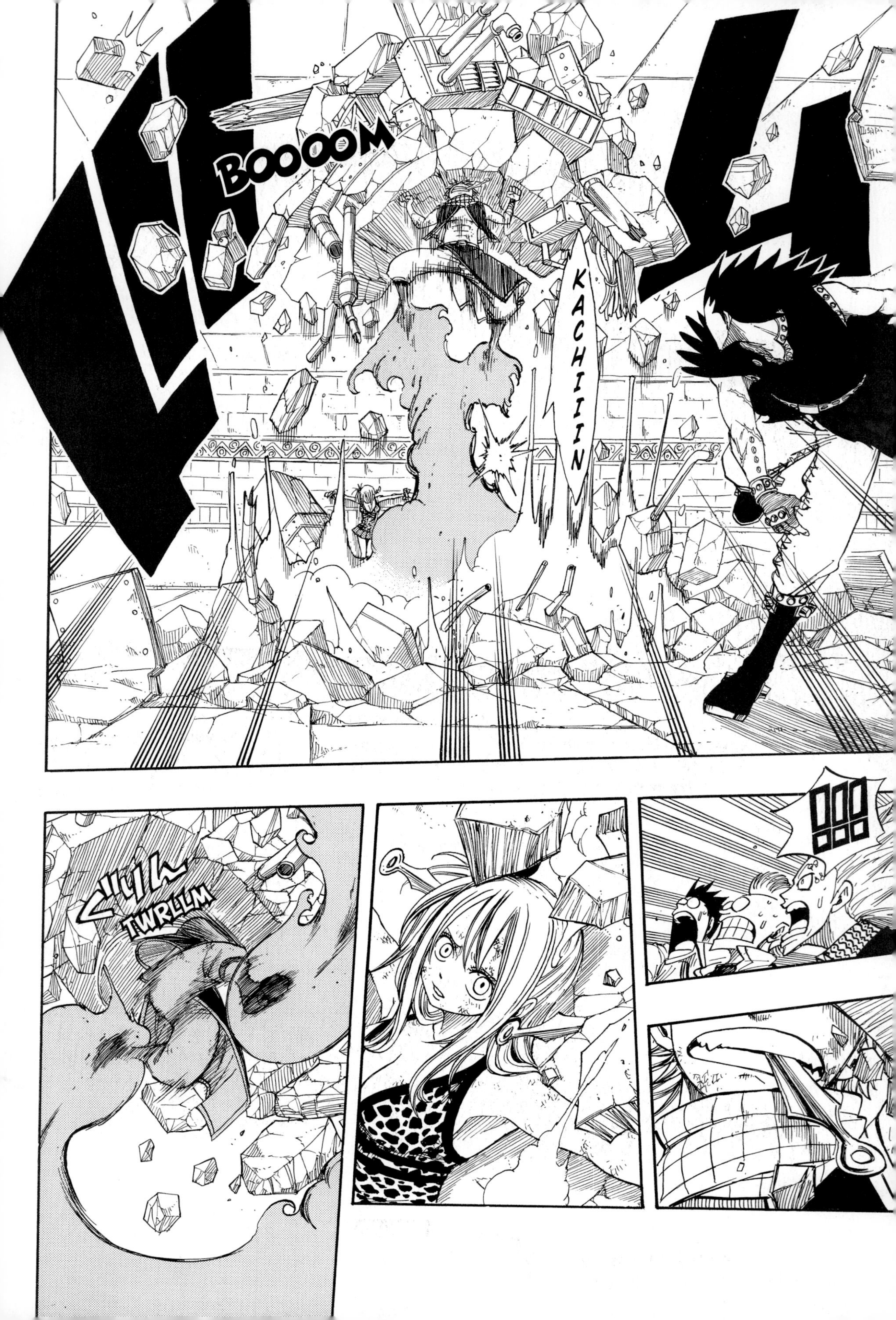
BOOOOM
KACHIIIN
TWRLLM

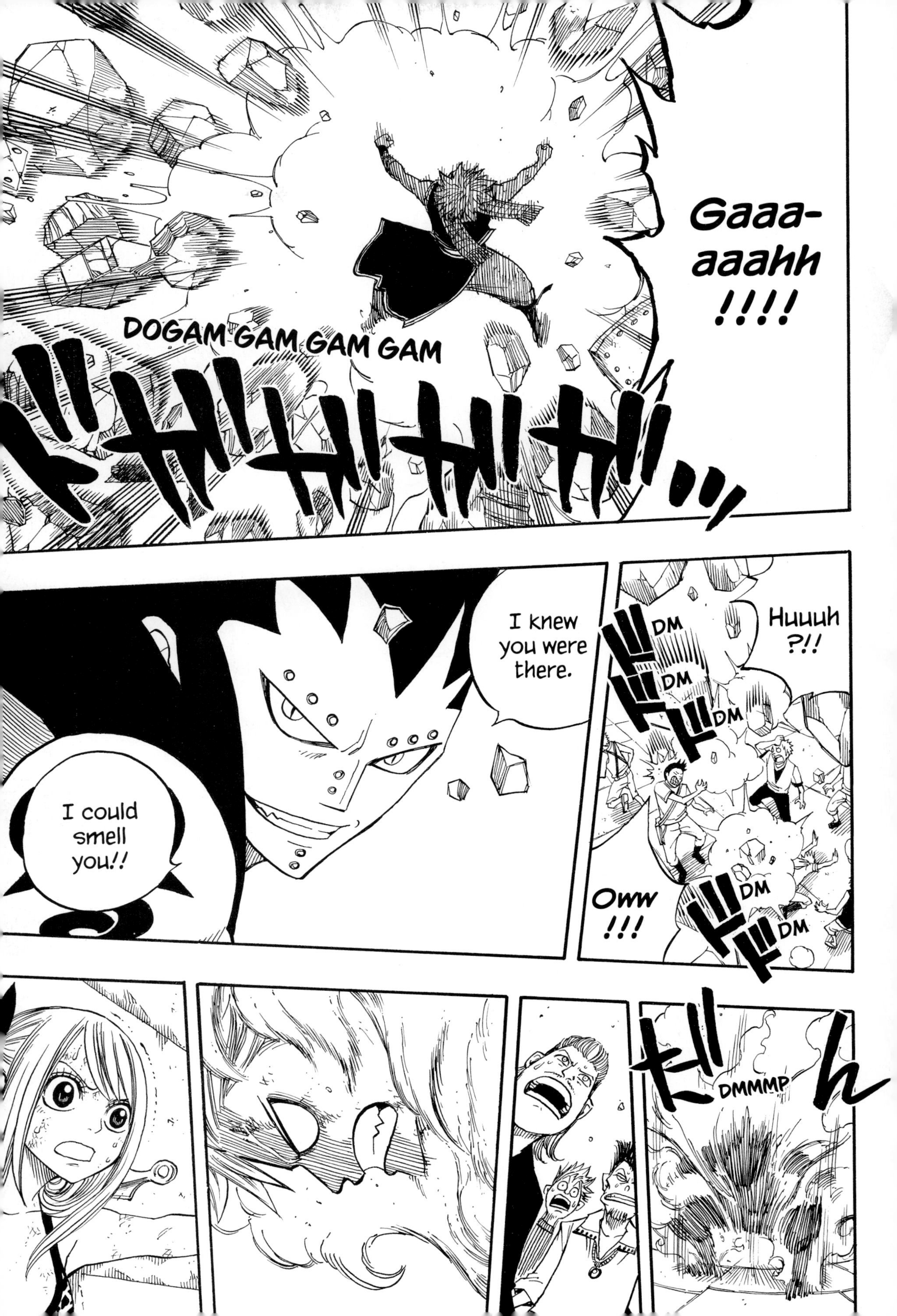
Gaaa-aaahh!!!!
DOGAM GAM GAM GAM
Huuuh?!!
DM
DM
DM
Oww!!!
DM
DM
I knew you were there.
I could smell you!!
DMMMP

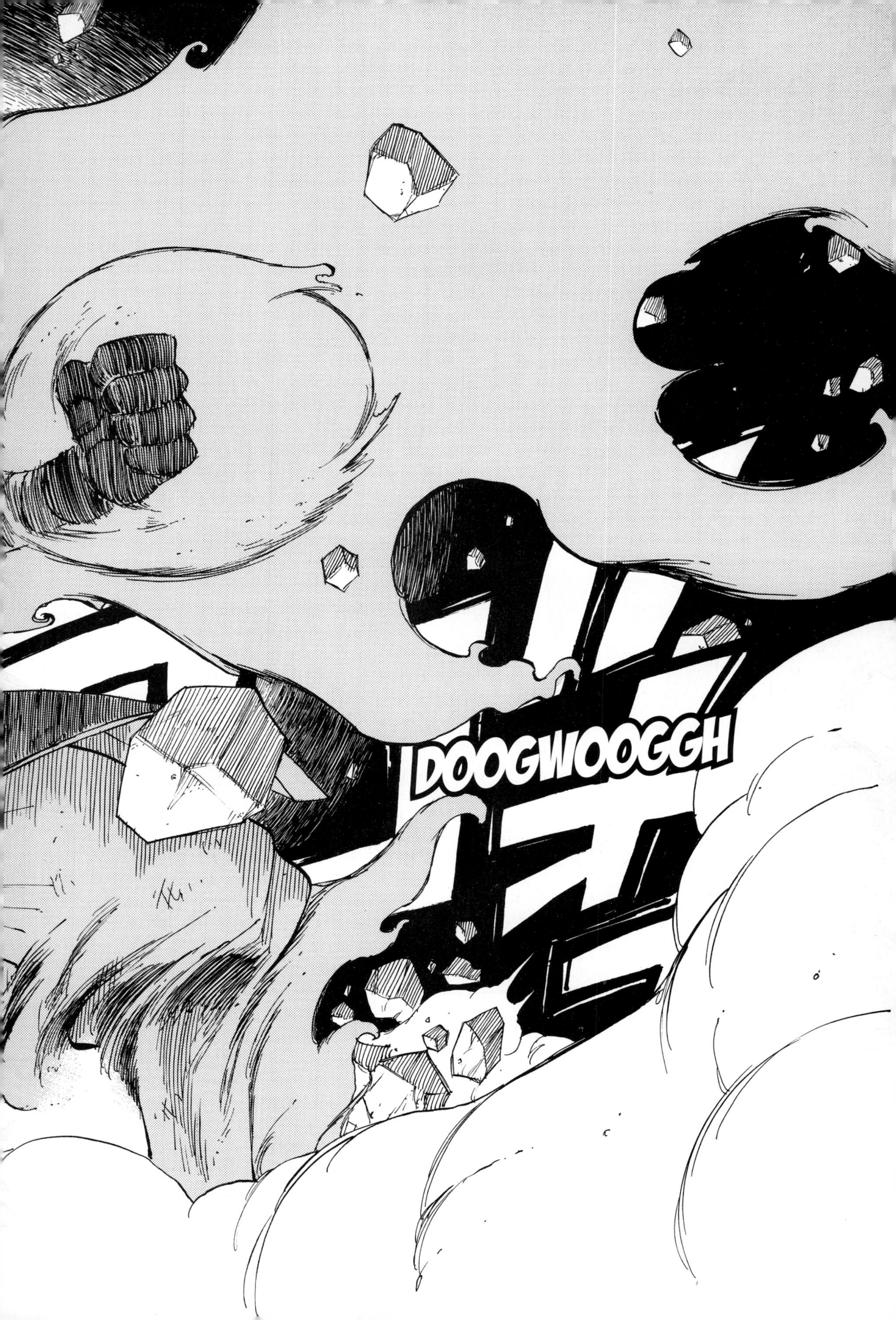
DOOGWOOGGH

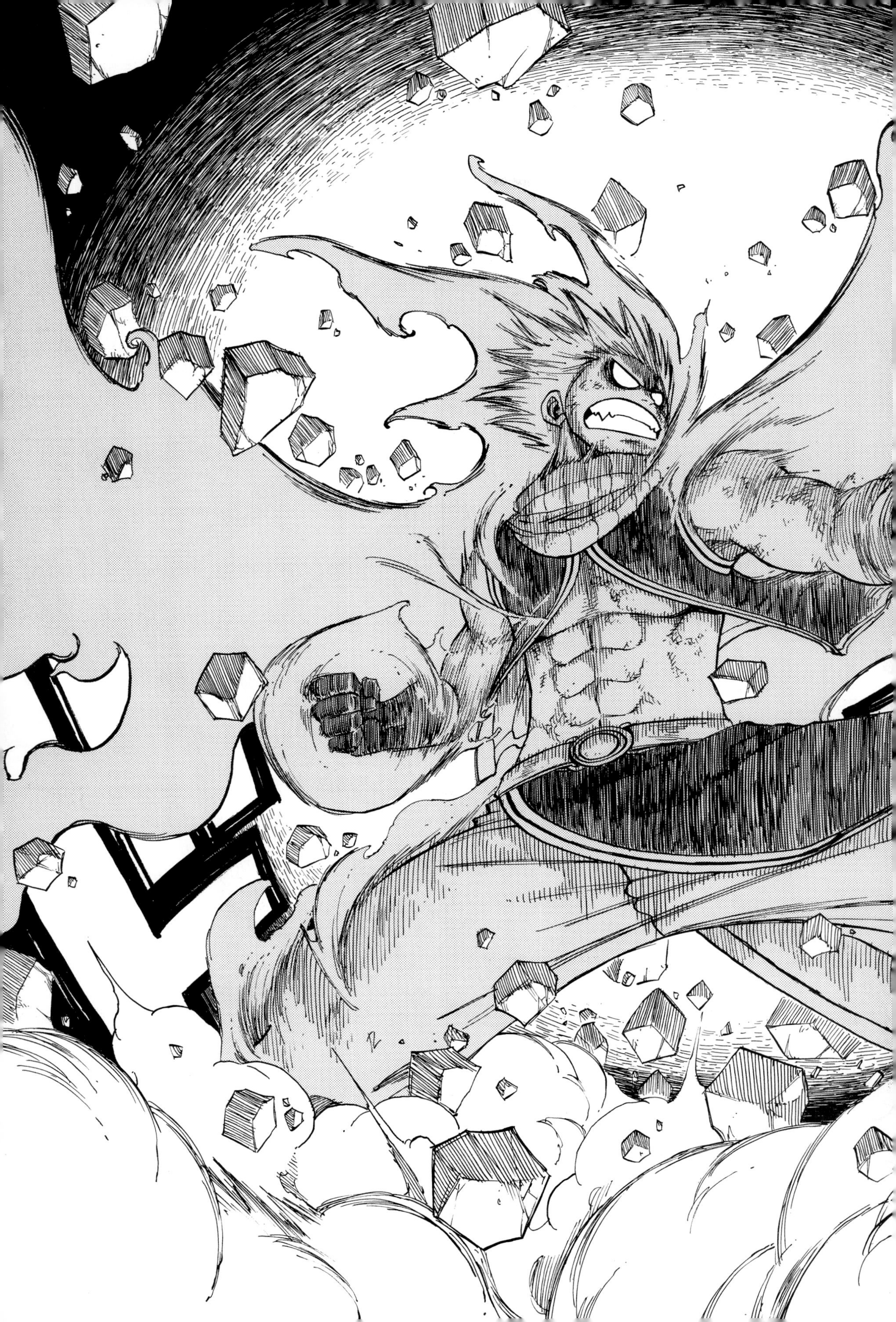

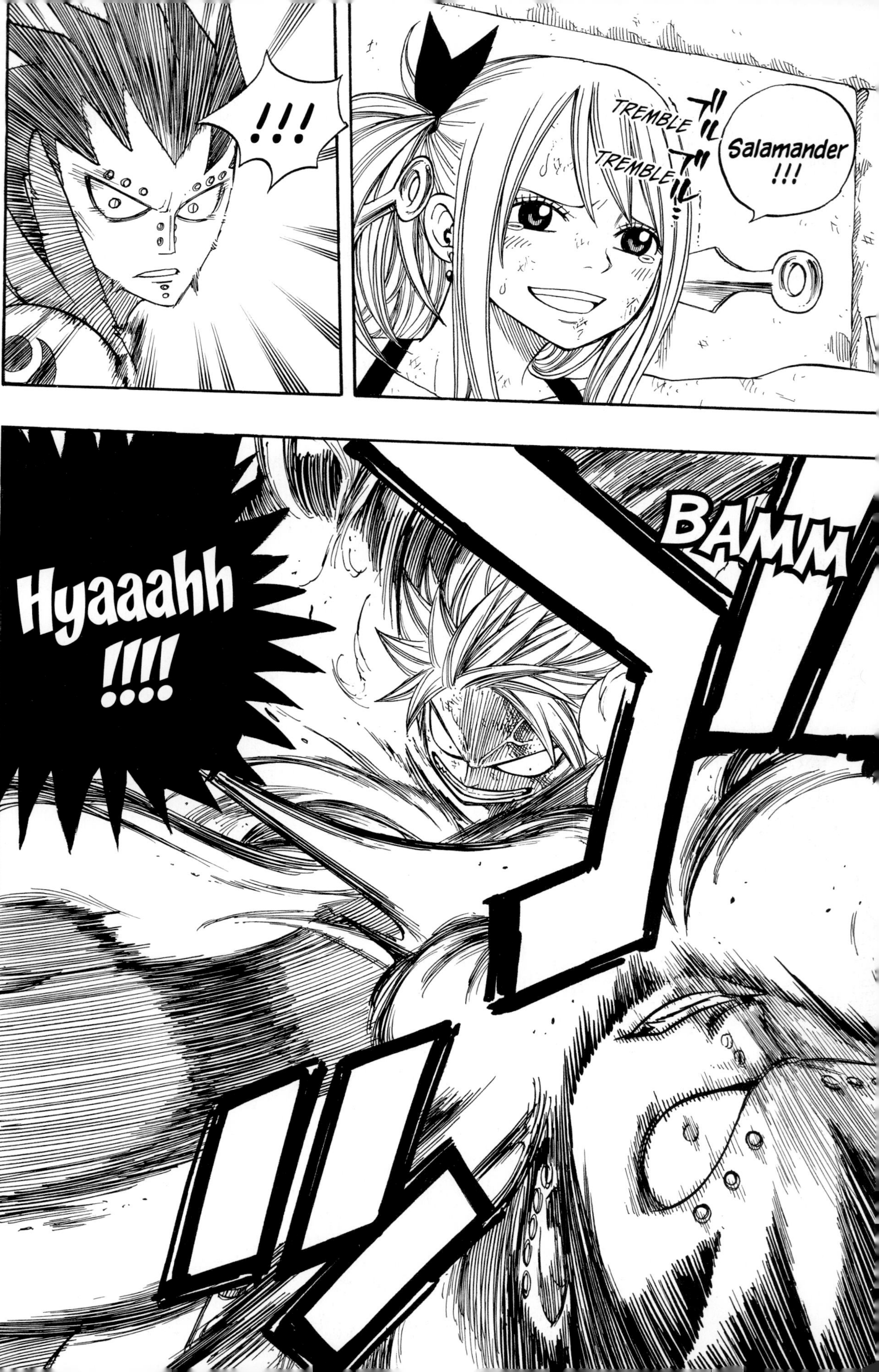
TREMBLE
TREMBLE
Salamander !!!
!!!
BAMM
Hyaaahh !!!!

FAIRY TAIL

FAIRY TAIL

Name: **Wakaba Mine**   Age: **36 yrs.**

Magic: **Smoke**

Likes: **Liquor, Tobacco, Women**   Dislikes: **His wife**

WIZARD GUILD X633

Remarks

A veteran wizard who can fight by shaping smoke into various forms. He has much the same history and is the same age as Macao, so at times they are drinking buddies, and at other times, rivals. He is henpecked by his wife, so even when he doesn't have work, you can find him at the guild trying to chat up the pretty young guild employees. His most recent target was Mirajane, saying that if she would agree to go out with him, he would break it off with his wife. She turned him down flat. He's well on the path to mastering the art of being a creepy old guy.

Chapter 61: The Two Dragon Slayers

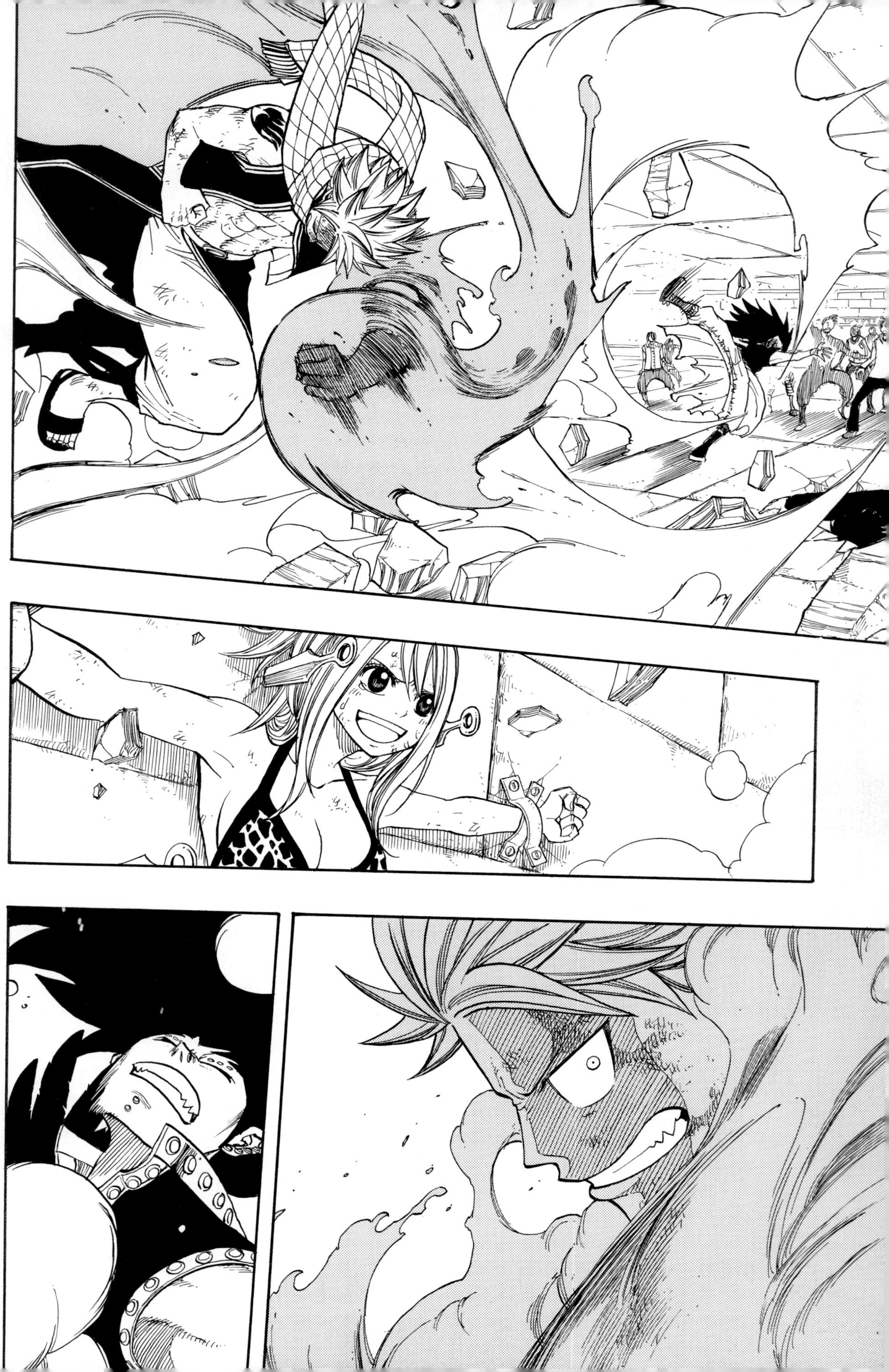

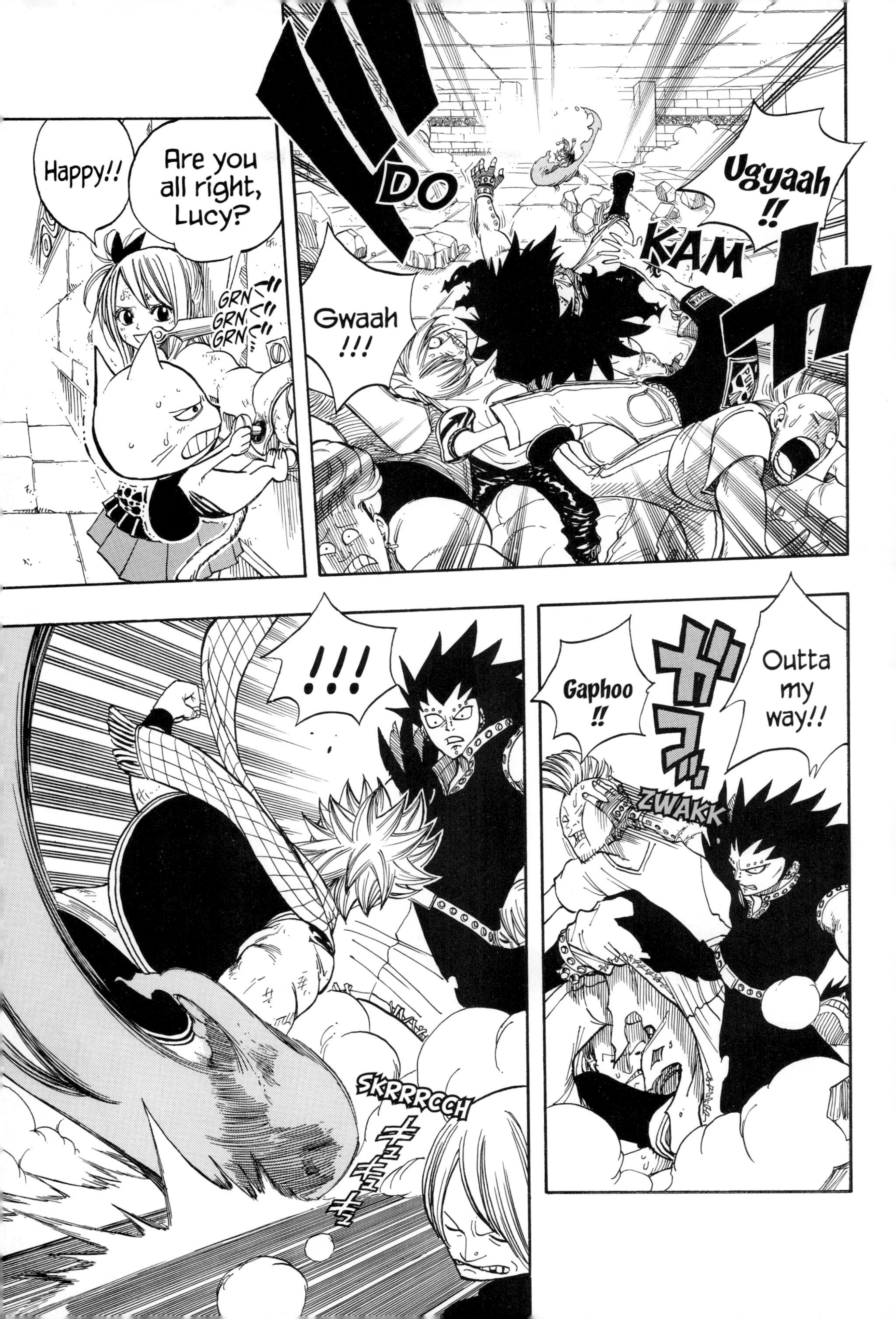
Ugyaah !!
DO
KAM
Gwaah !!!
Are you all right, Lucy?
Happy!!
GRN GRN GRN
Outta my way!!
Gaphoo !!
ZWAKK
!!!
SKRRRCCH

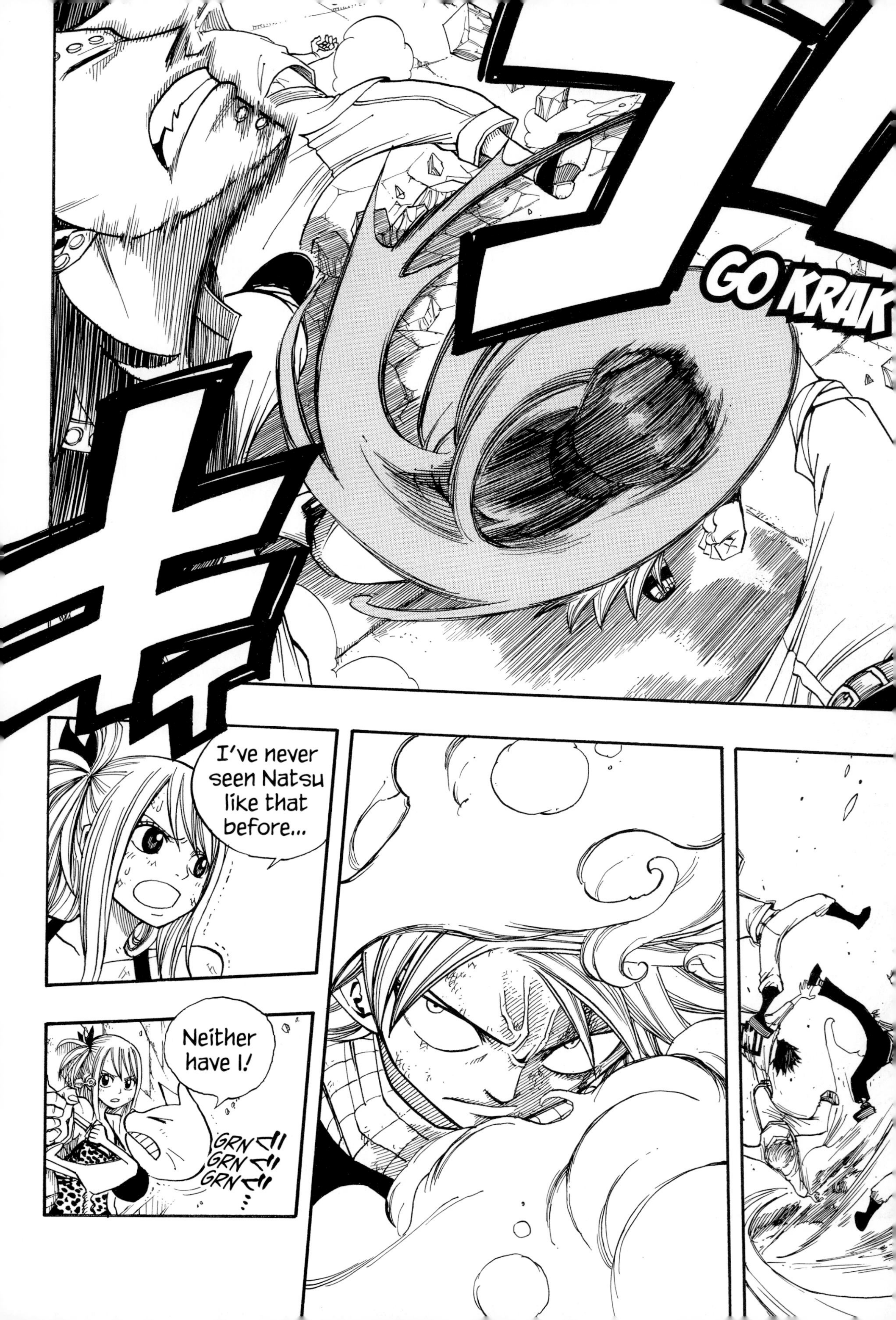
GO KRAK
I've never seen Natsu like that before...
Neither have I!
GRN GRN GRN

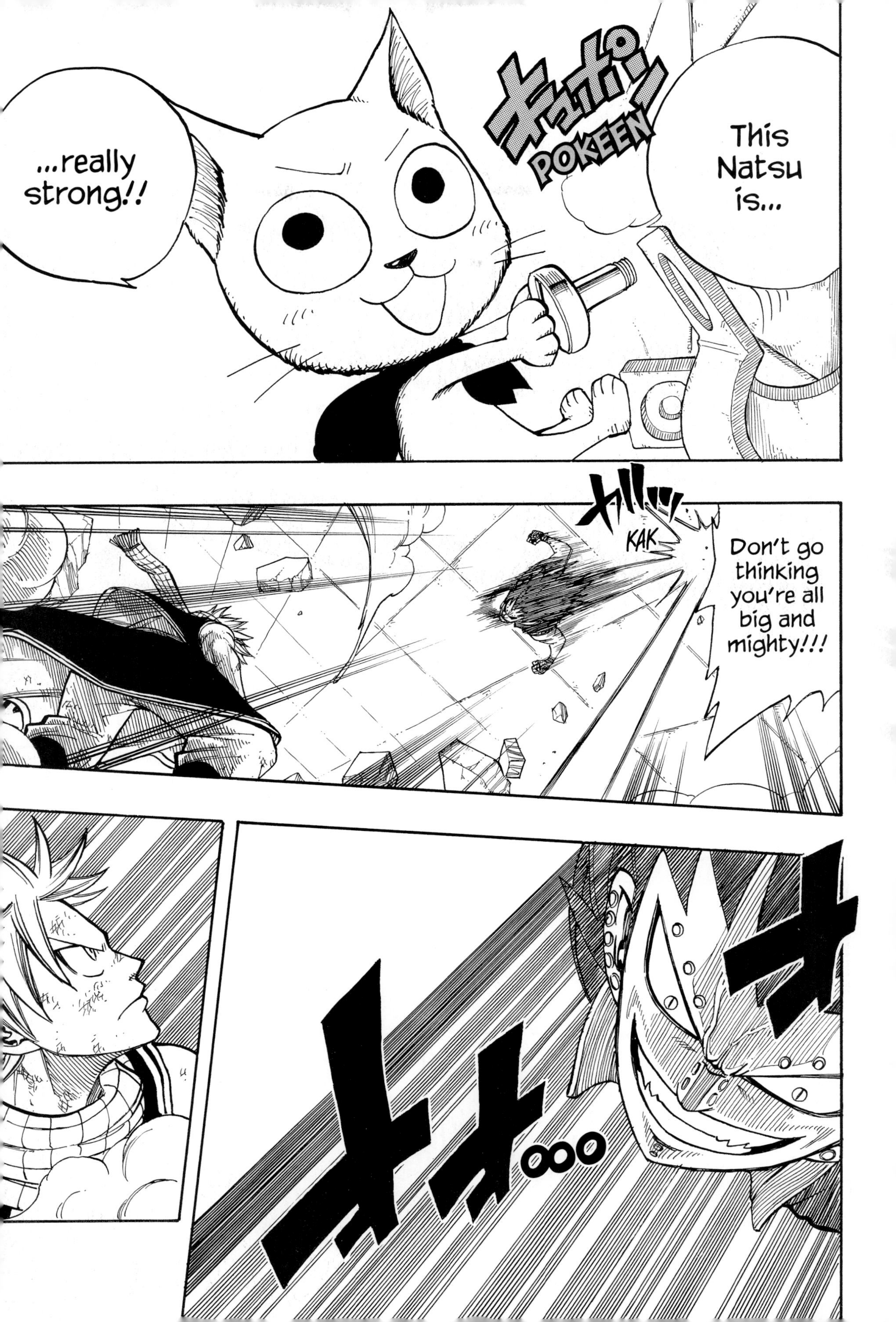

This Natsu is...
POKEEN
...really strong!!
KAK
Don't go thinking you're all big and mighty!!!

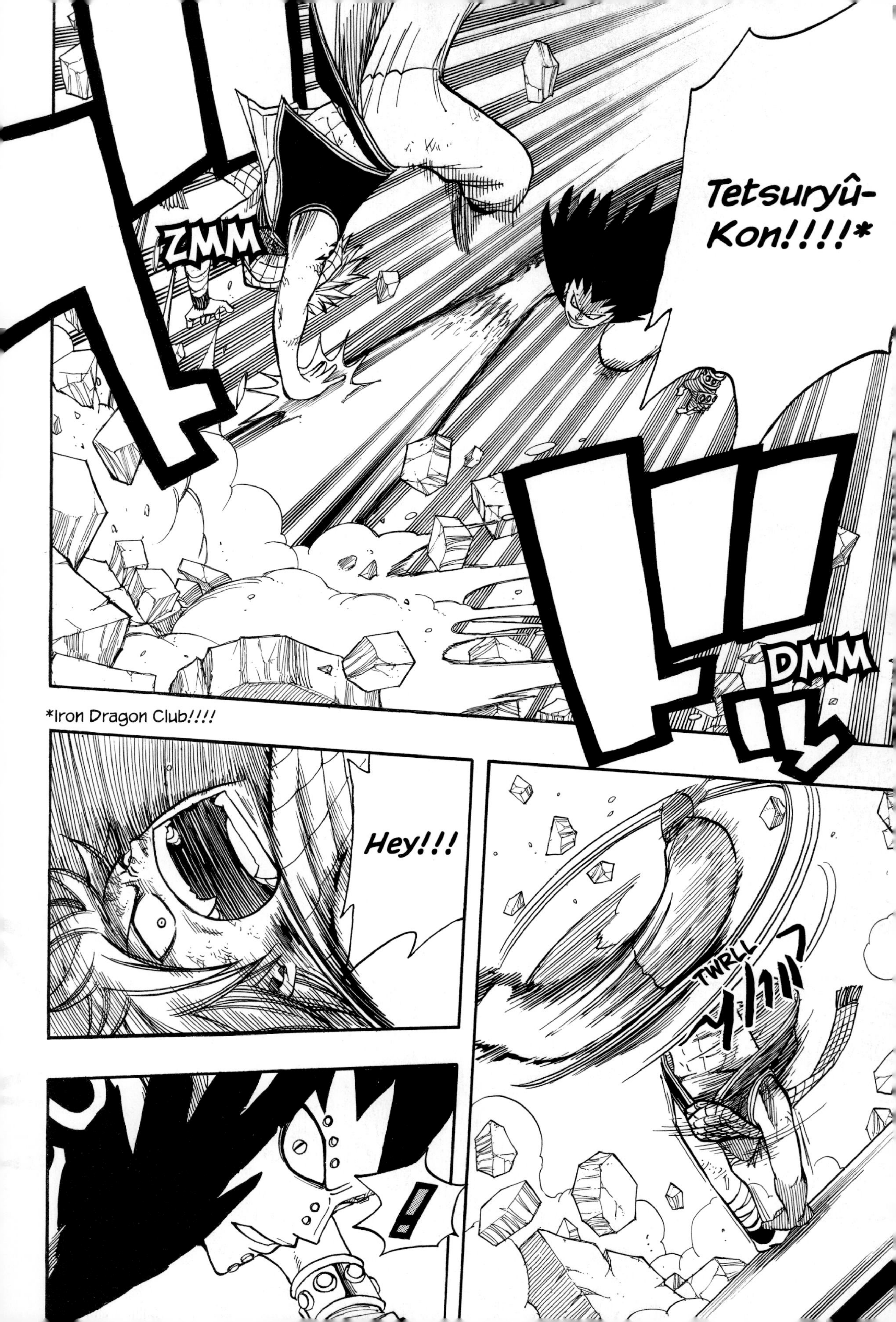
Tetsuryû-Kon!!!!*
ZMM
DMM
TWRLL
Hey!!!
*Iron Dragon Club!!!!

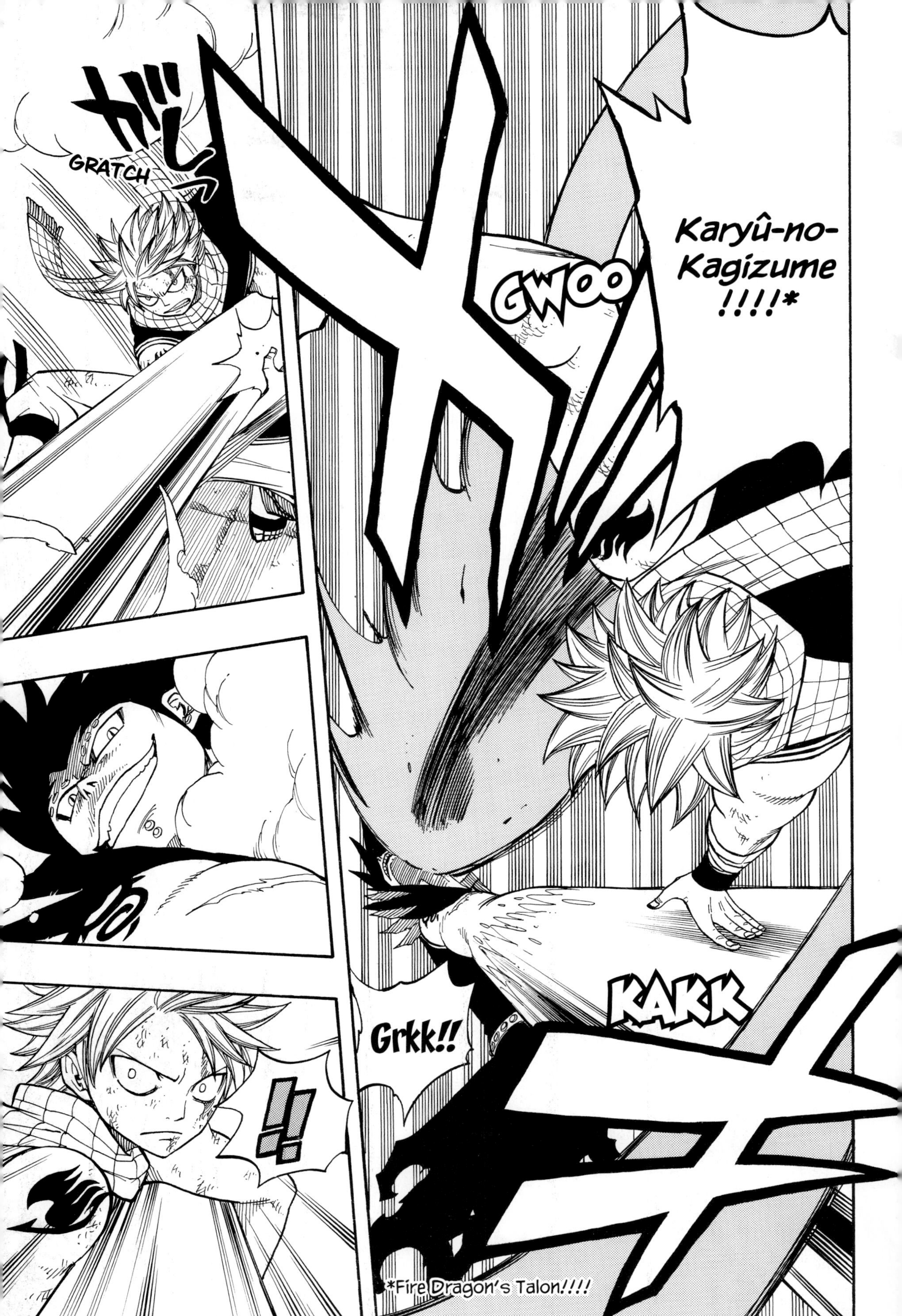
Karyû-no-Kagizume !!!!*
GWOO
KAKK
Grkk!!
GRATCH
!!

*Fire Dragon's Talon!!!!

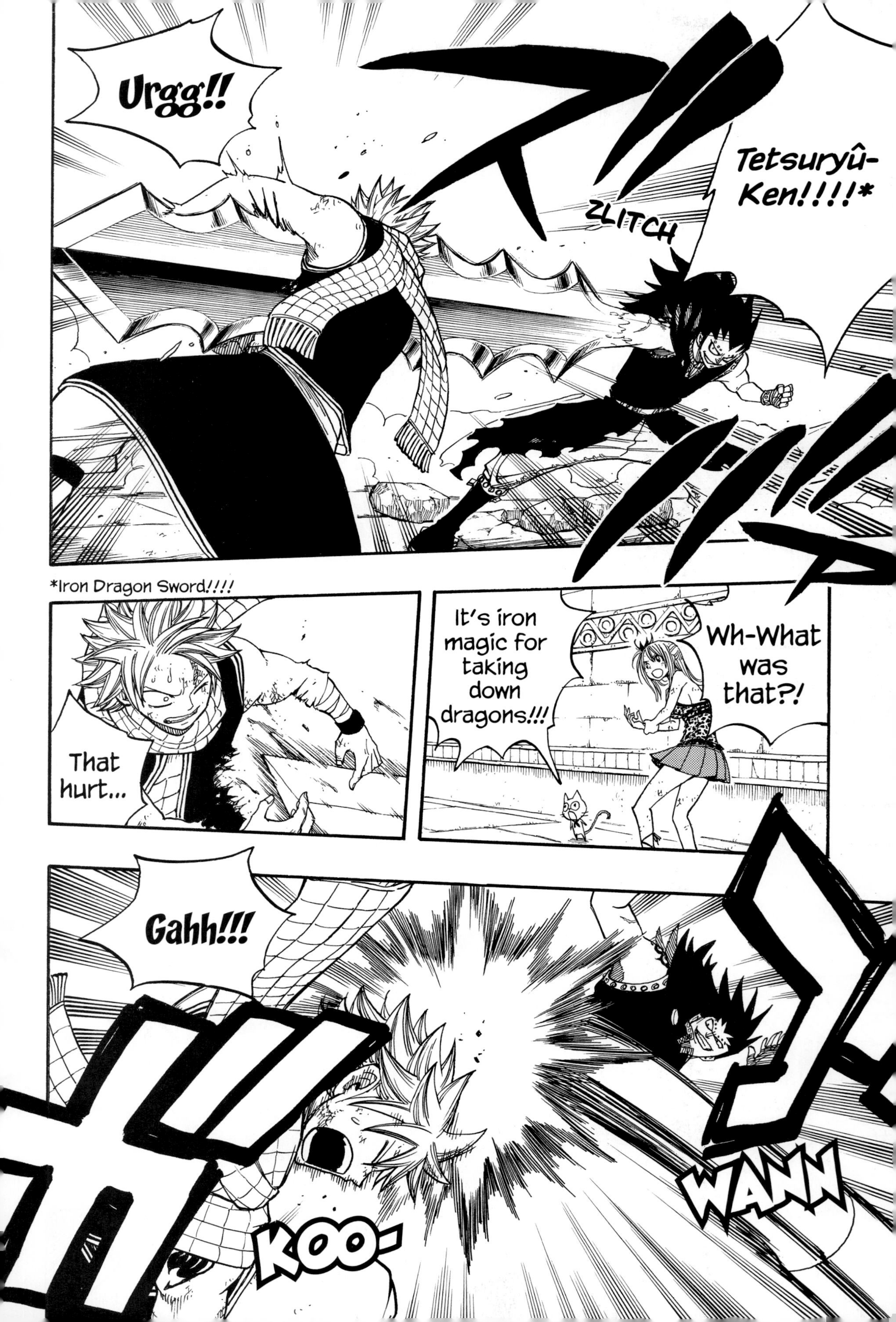
Tetsuryû-Ken!!!!*
ZLITCH
Urgg!!
Wh-What was that?!
It's iron magic for taking down dragons!!!
That hurt...
Gahh!!!
WANN
KOO-
*Iron Dragon Sword!!!!

SKRRCH

Natsu !!!

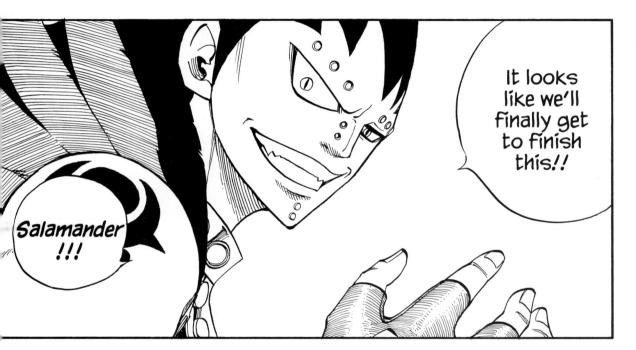

It looks like we'll finally get to finish this!!

Salamander !!!

It's got me all fired up!!

You scrap-iron creep!!!

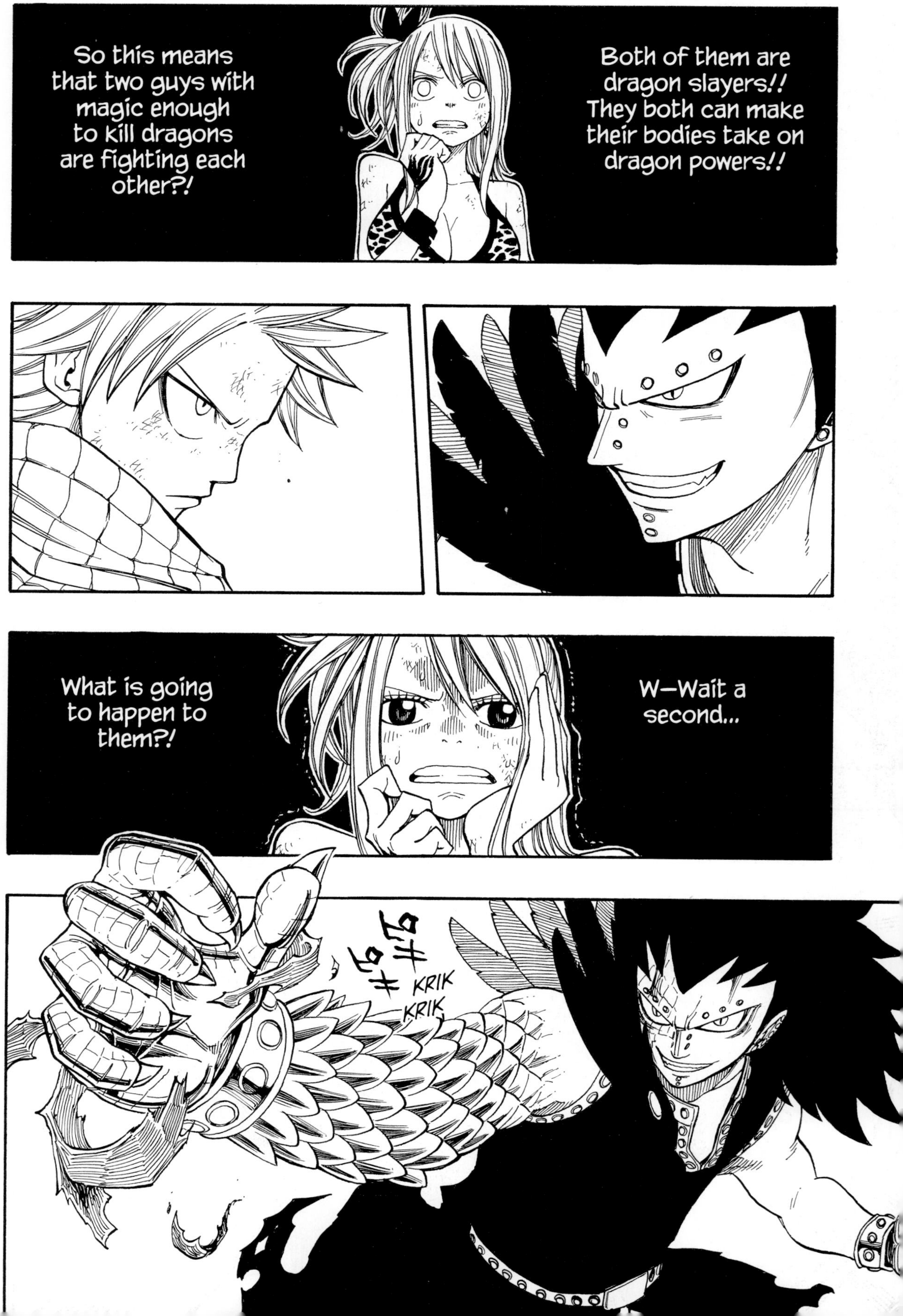
Both of them are dragon slayers!! They both can make their bodies take on dragon powers!!
So this means that two guys with magic enough to kill dragons are fighting each other?!
W—Wait a second...
What is going to happen to them?!
KRIK KRIK

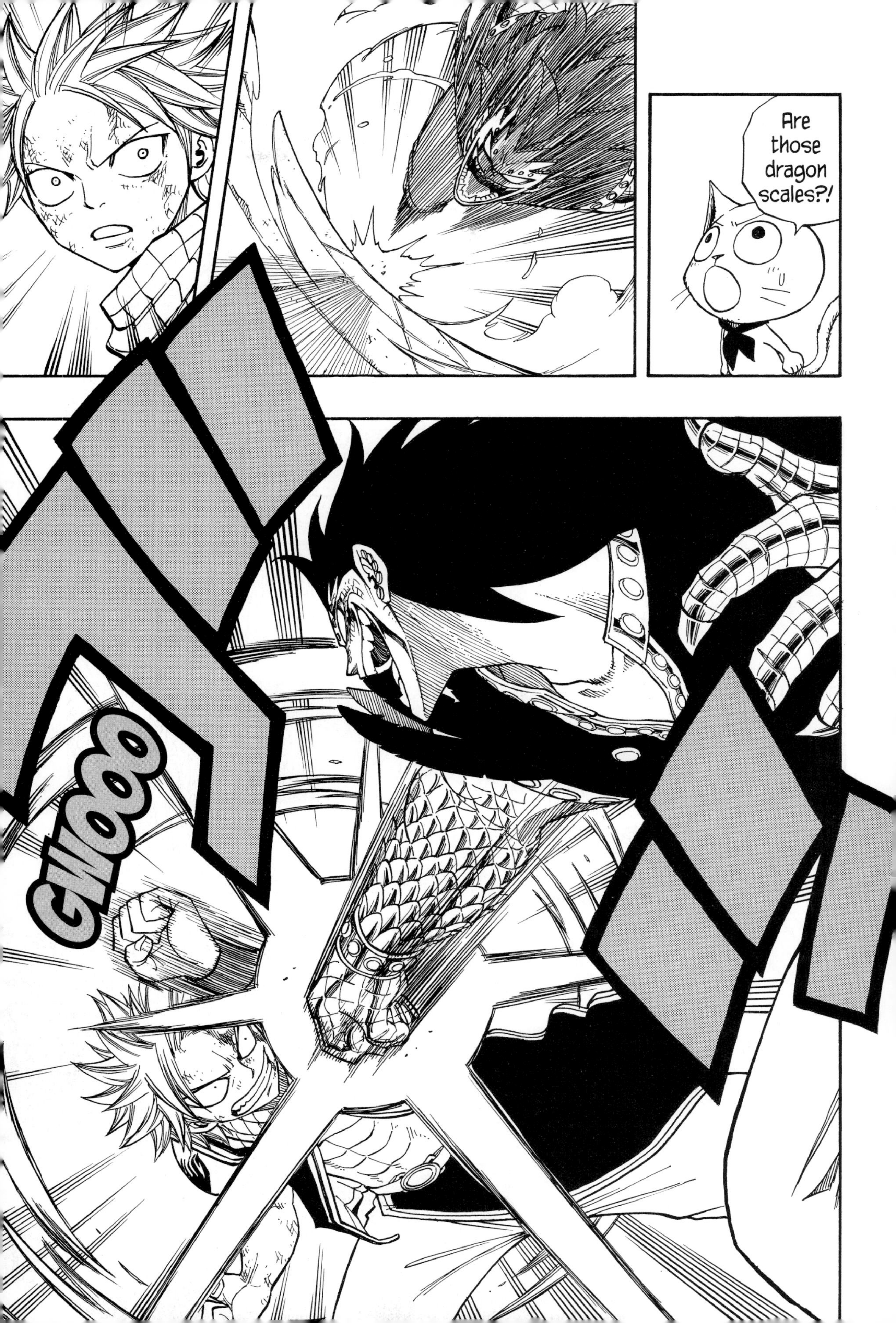
Are those dragon scales?!
GWOOO

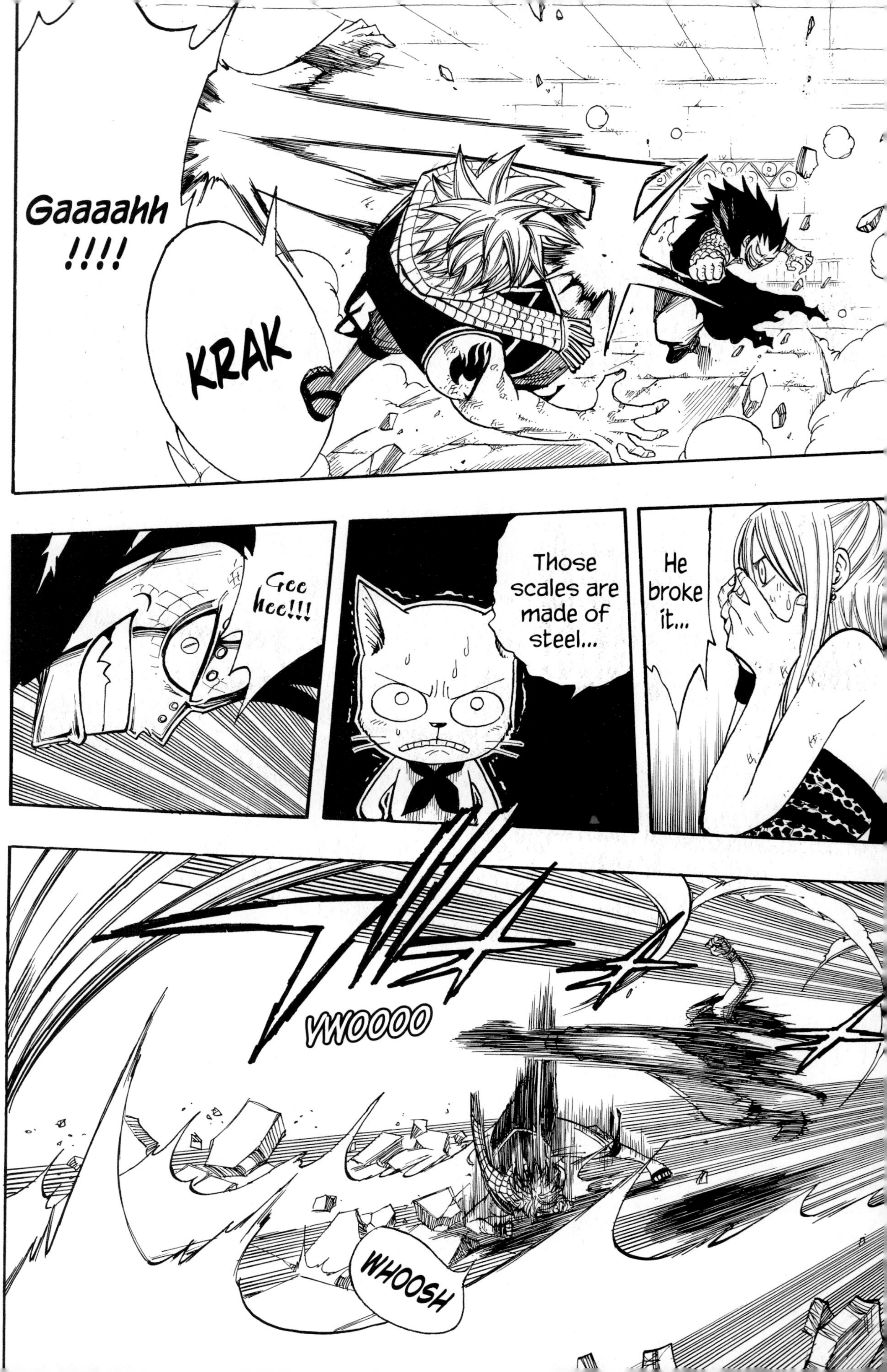
Gaaaahh !!!!
KRAK
He broke it...
Those scales are made of steel...
Gee hee!!!
VWOOOO
WHOOSH

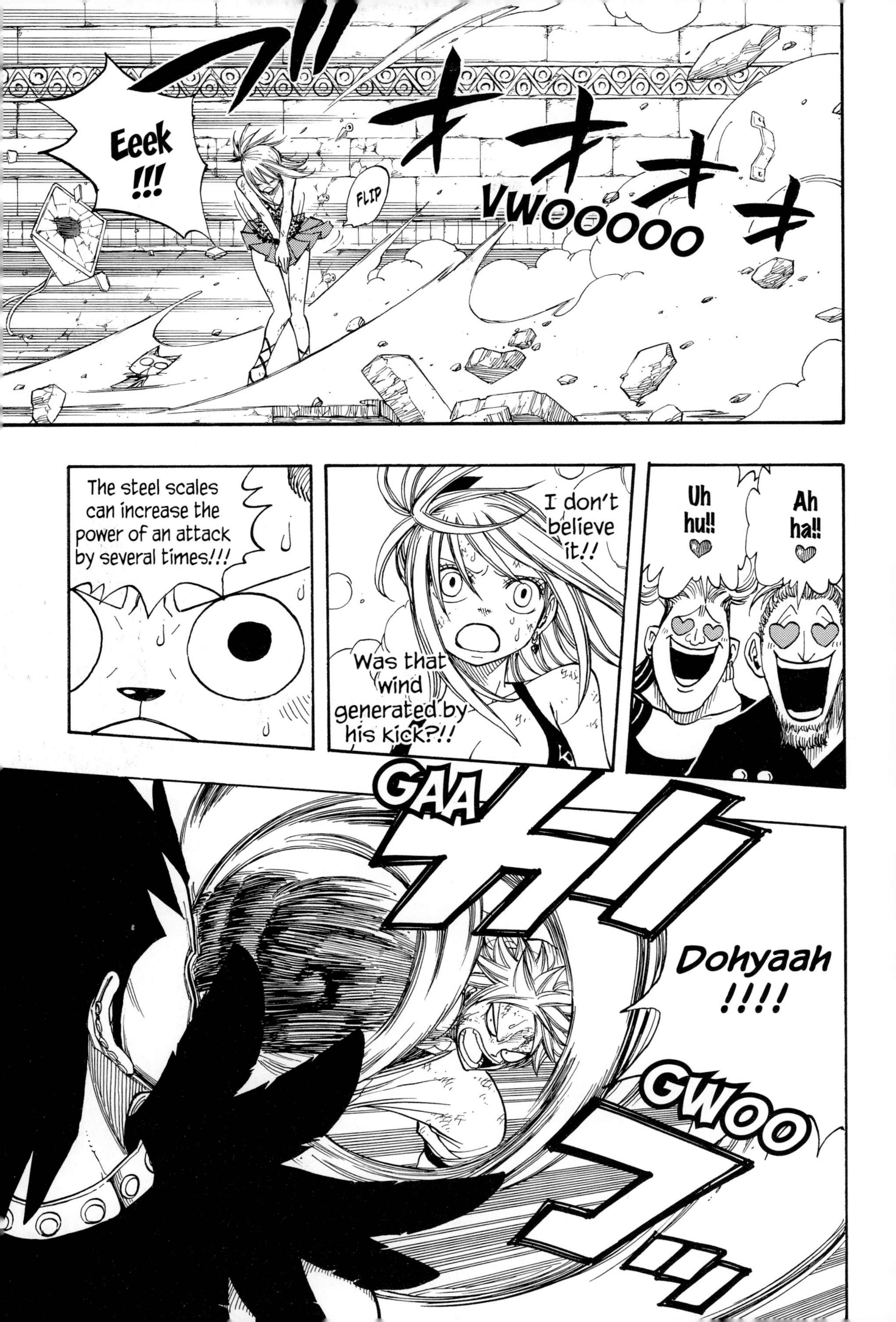
VWOOOOO
FLIP
Eeek!!!
Ah ha!! ♥
Uh hu!! ♥
I don't believe it!!
Was that wind generated by his kick?!!
The steel scales can increase the power of an attack by several times!!!
GAA
Dohyaah!!!!
GWOO

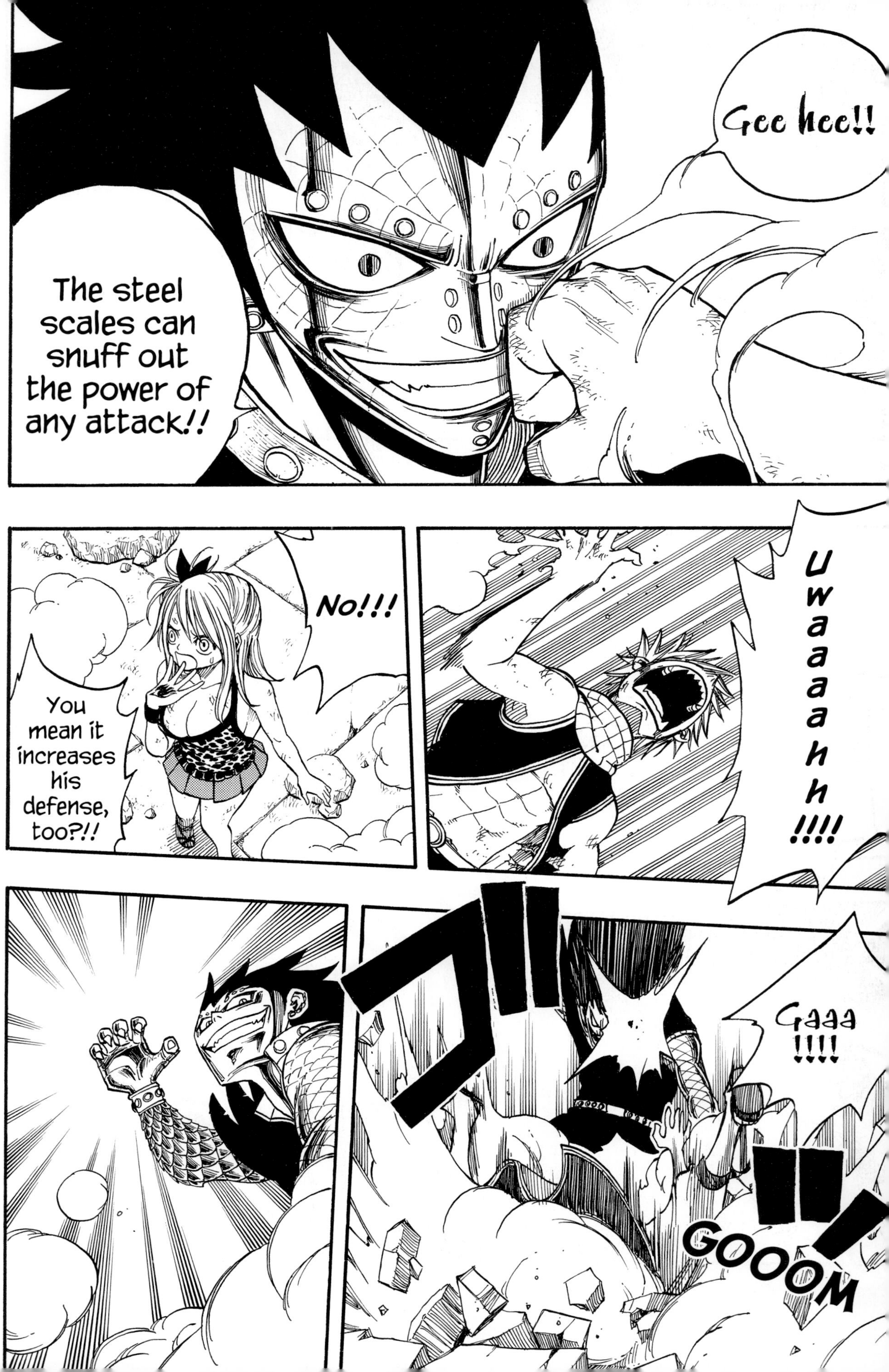
Gee hee!!
The steel scales can snuff out the power of any attack!!
Uwaaaaahh!!!!
No!!!
You mean it increases his defense, too?!!
Gaaa!!!!
GOOOM

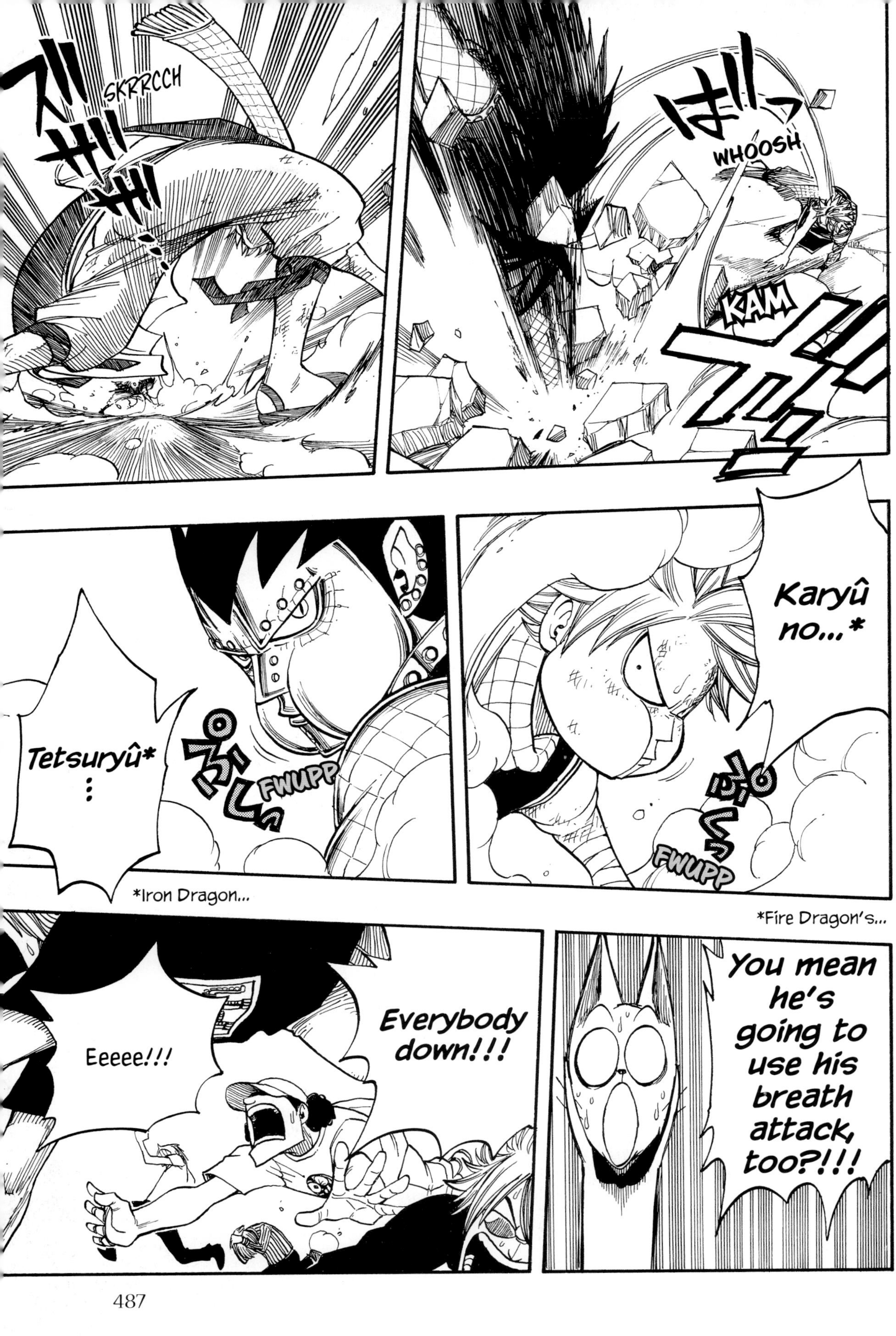
WHOOSH
KAM
SKRRCCH
Karyû no...*
FWUPP
Tetsuryû* ...
FWUPP
*Fire Dragon's...
*Iron Dragon...
You mean he's going to use his breath attack, too?!!!
Everybody down!!!
Eeeee!!!

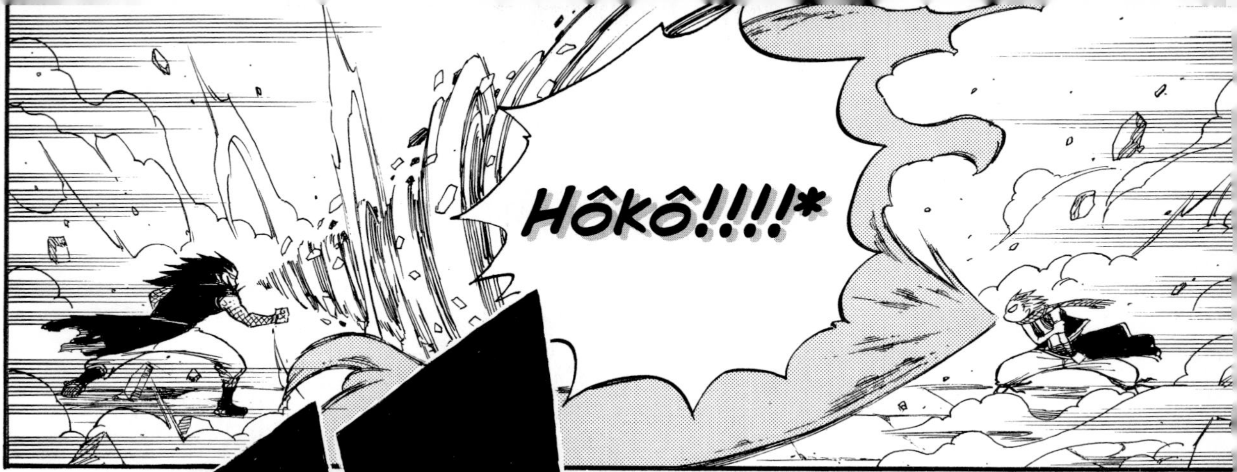
Hôkô!!!!*

*Roar!!!!

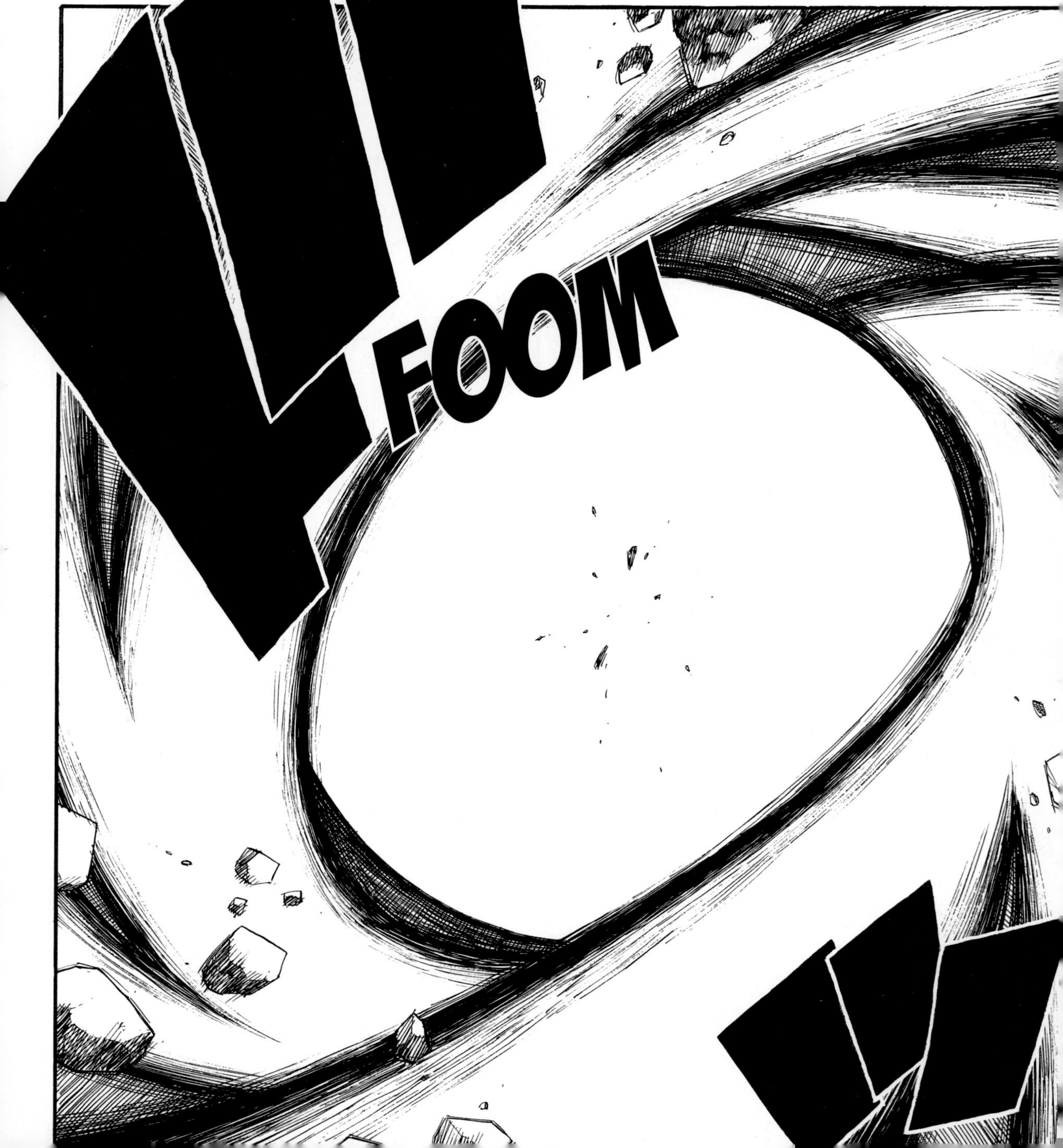
FOOM

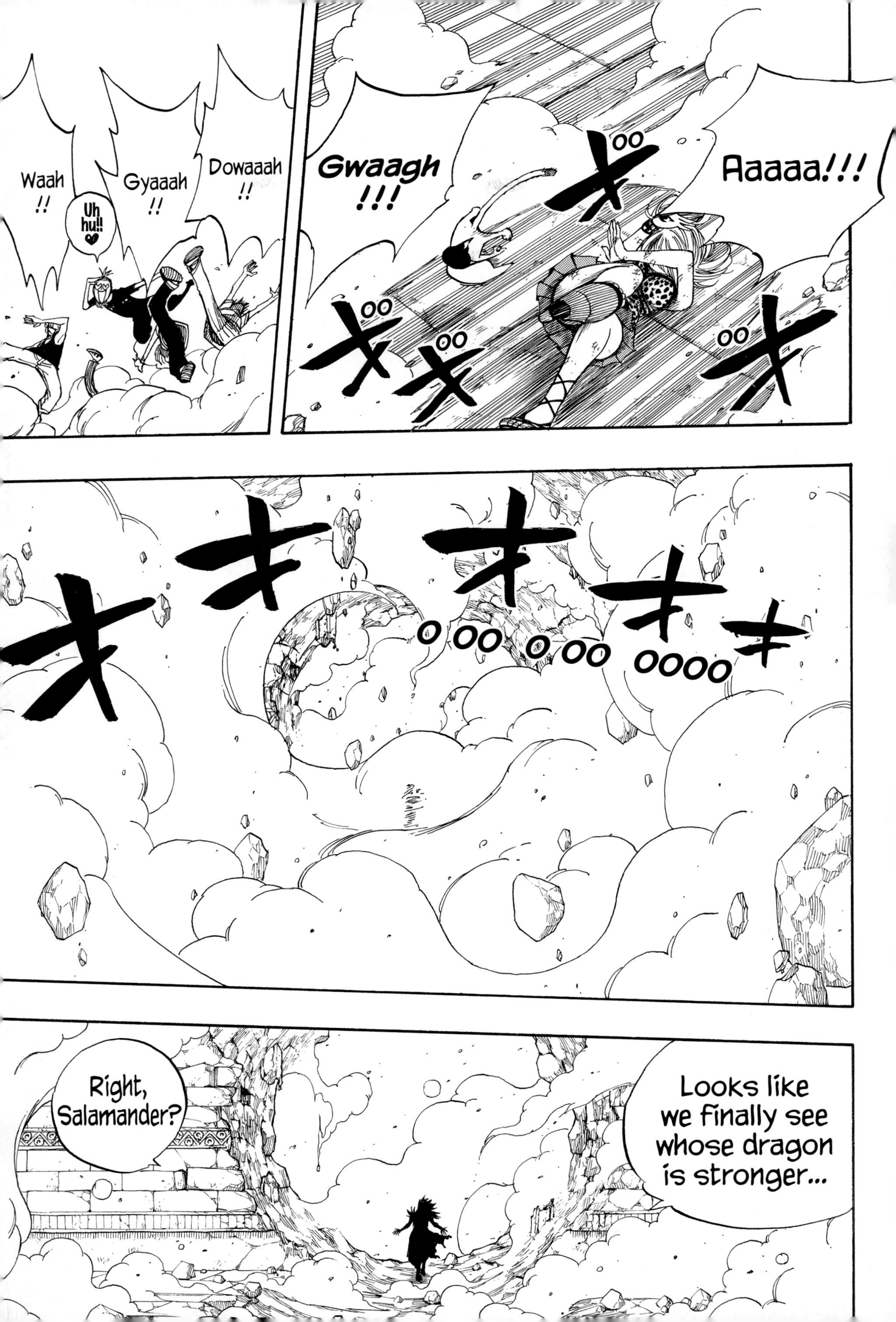
Aaaaa!!!
Gwaagh!!!
Dowaaah!!
Gyaaah!!
Uh hu!!
Waah!!
o oo o oo oooo
Looks like we finally see whose dragon is stronger...
Right, Salamander?

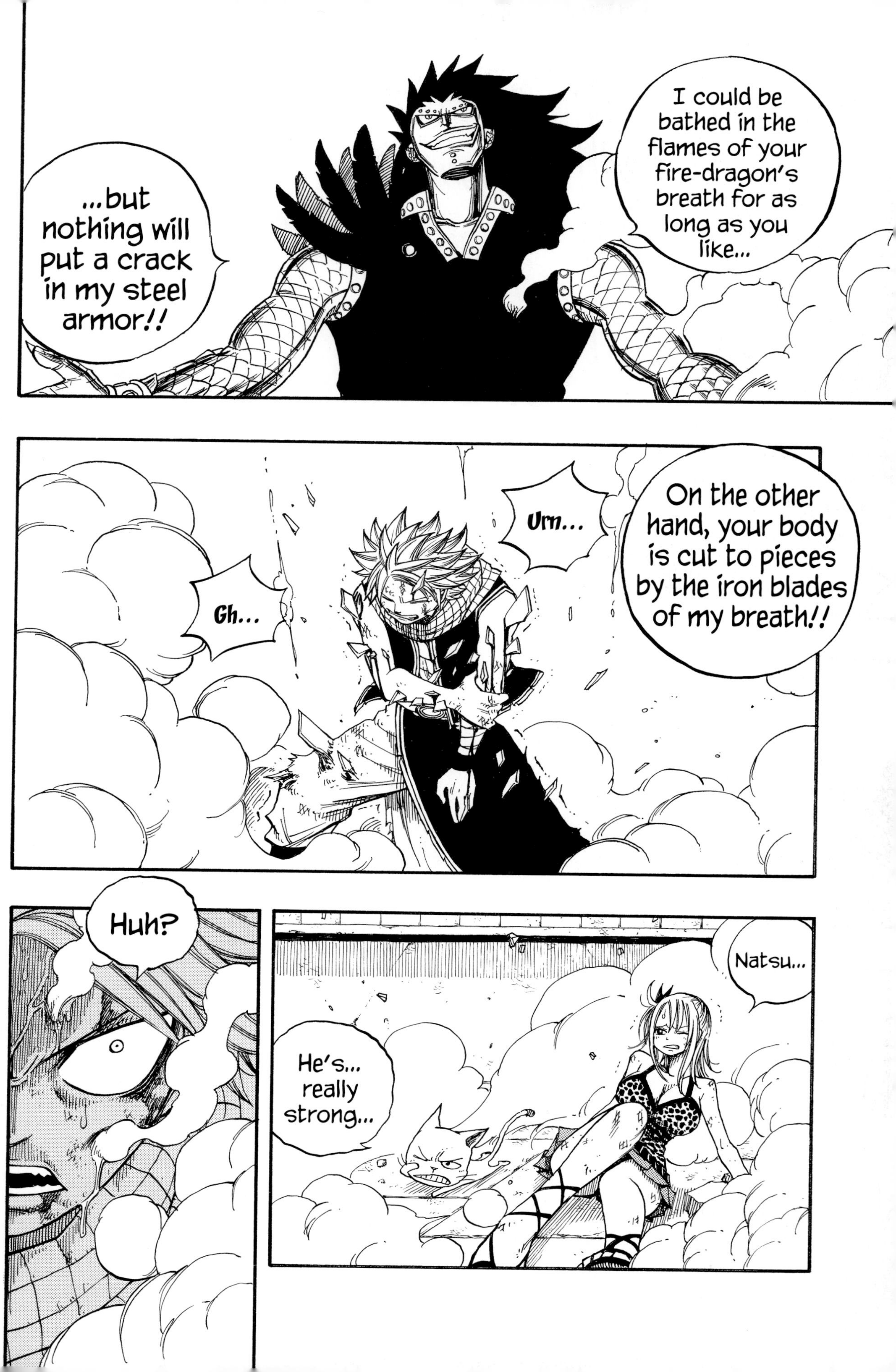
I could be bathed in the flames of your fire-dragon's breath for as long as you like...
...but nothing will put a crack in my steel armor!!
On the other hand, your body is cut to pieces by the iron blades of my breath!!
Urn...
Gh...
Natsu...
He's... really strong...
Huh?

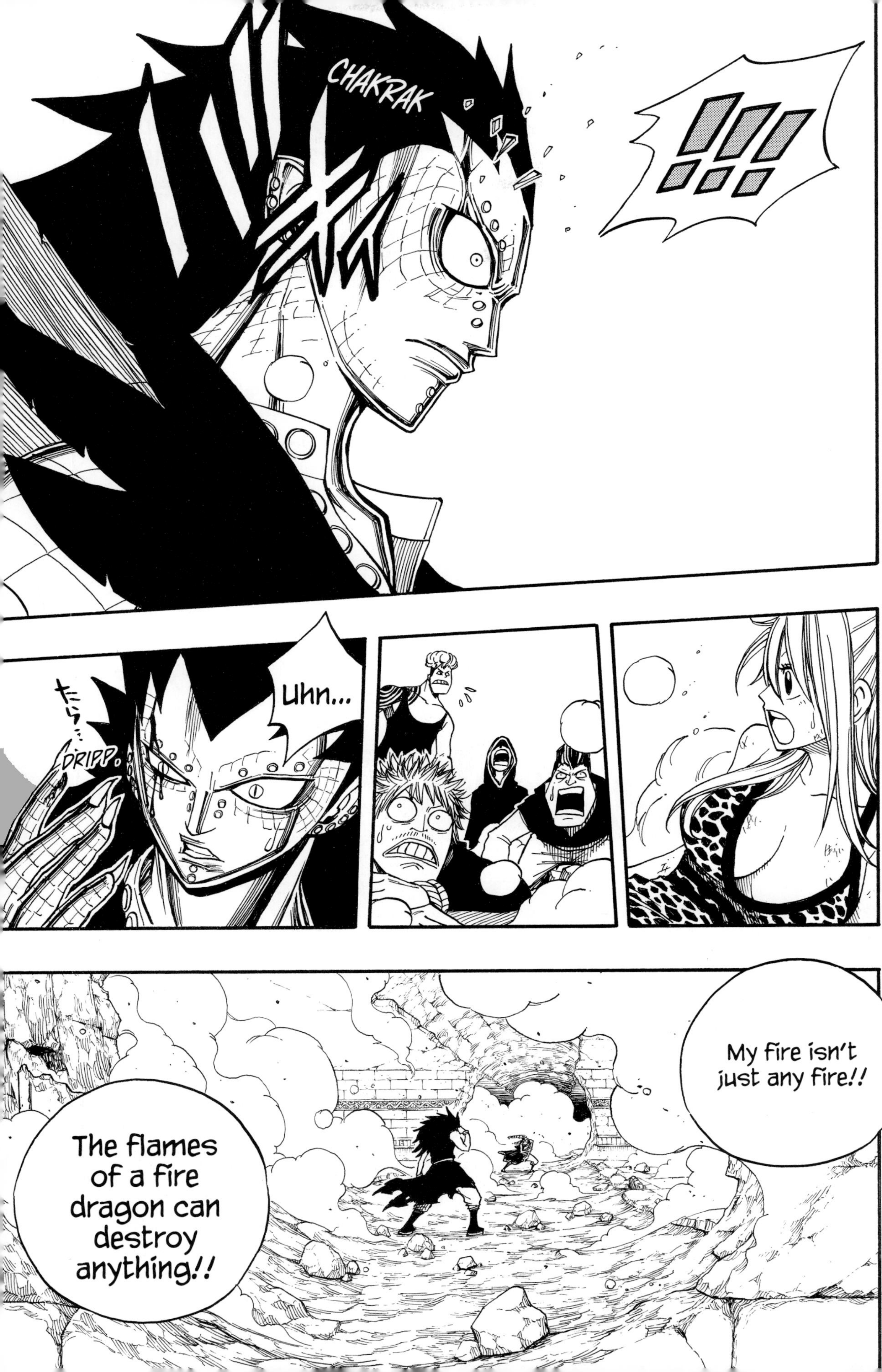
CHAKRAK
!!!
Uhn...
DRIPP
My fire isn't just any fire!!
The flames of a fire dragon can destroy anything!!

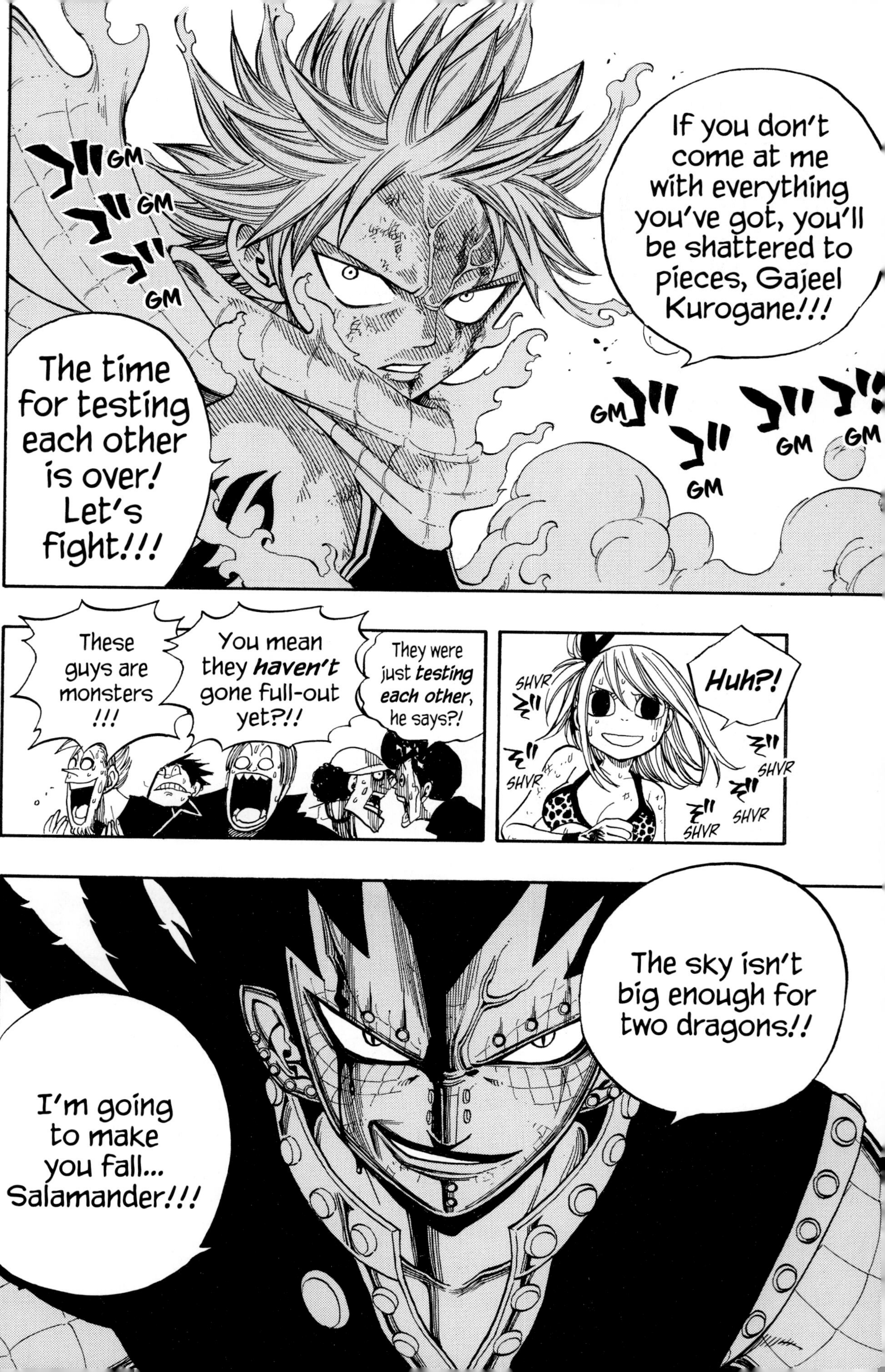
If you don't come at me with everything you've got, you'll be shattered to pieces, Gajeel Kurogane!!!
GM GM GM GM
GM GM GM
The time for testing each other is over! Let's fight!!!
Huh?!
SHVR SHVR SHVR SHVR SHVR
They were just *testing each other*, he says?!
You mean they ***haven't*** gone full-out yet?!!
These guys are monsters !!!
The sky isn't big enough for two dragons!!
I'm going to make you fall... Salamander!!!

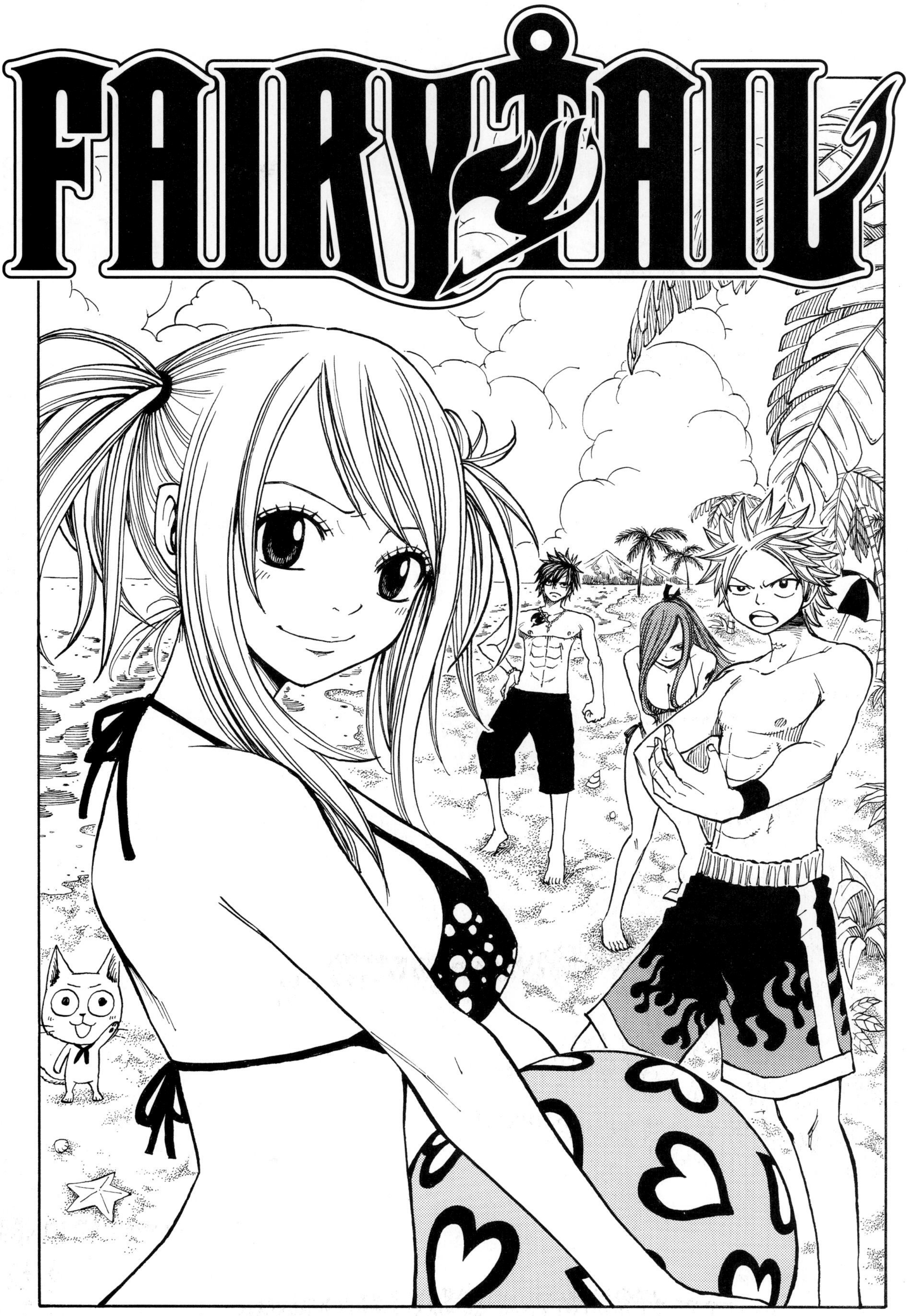
FAIRY TAIL

Chapter 62: When the Fairy Fell

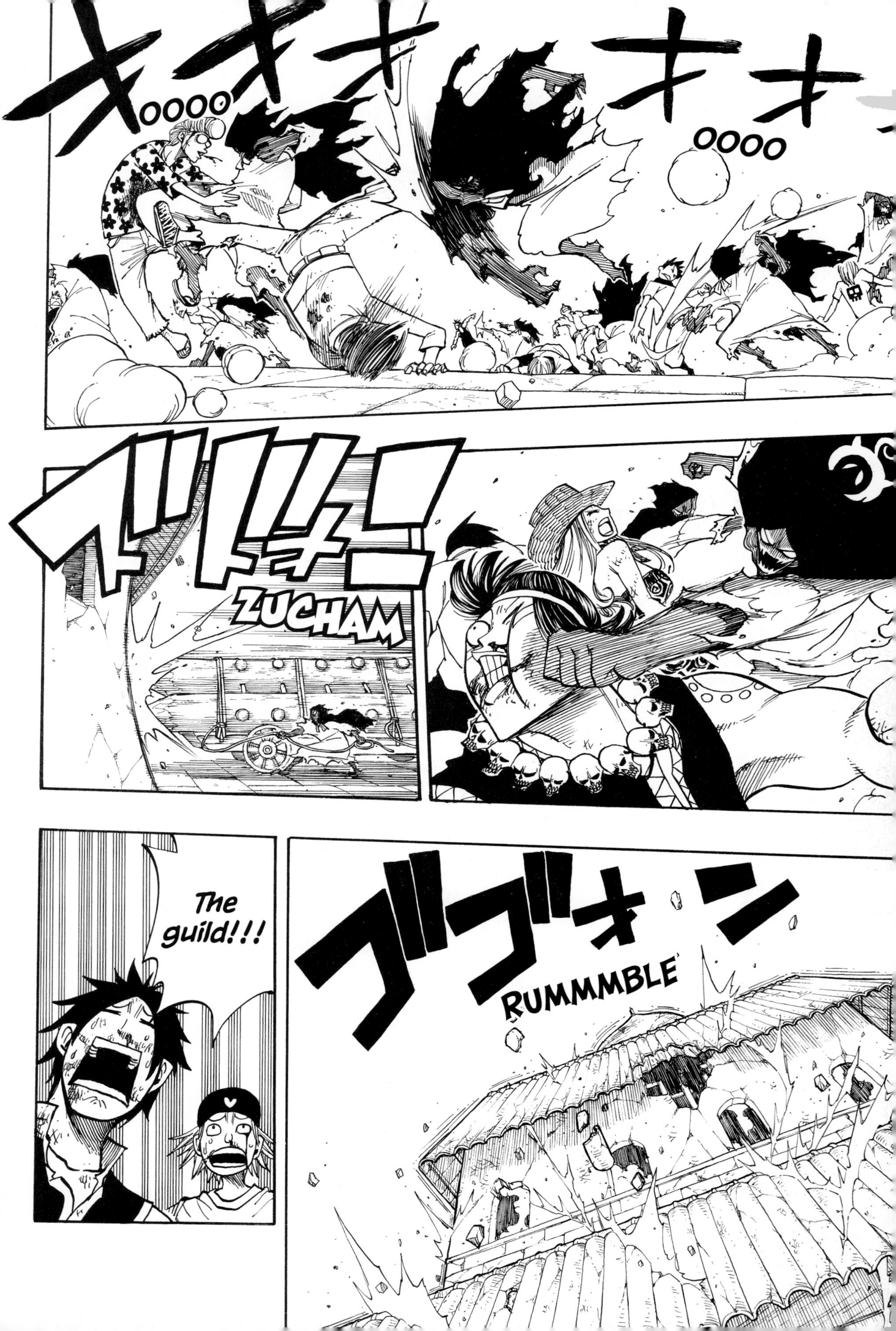
OOOO
OOOO
ZUCHAM
RUMMMBLE
The guild!!!

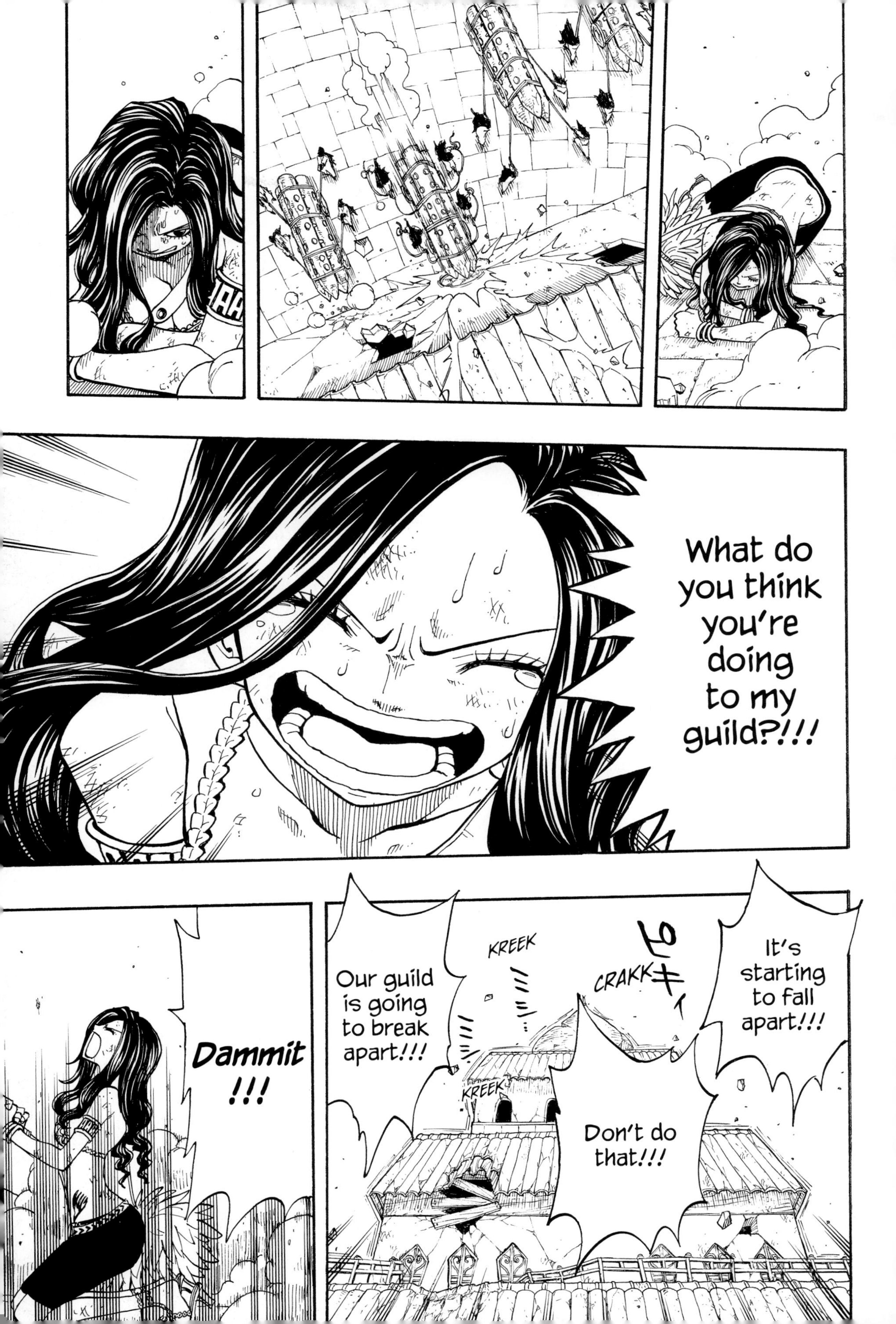
What do you think you're doing to my guild?!!!
It's starting to fall apart!!!
CRAKK
KREEK
Our guild is going to break apart!!!
KREEK
Don't do that!!!
Dammit!!!

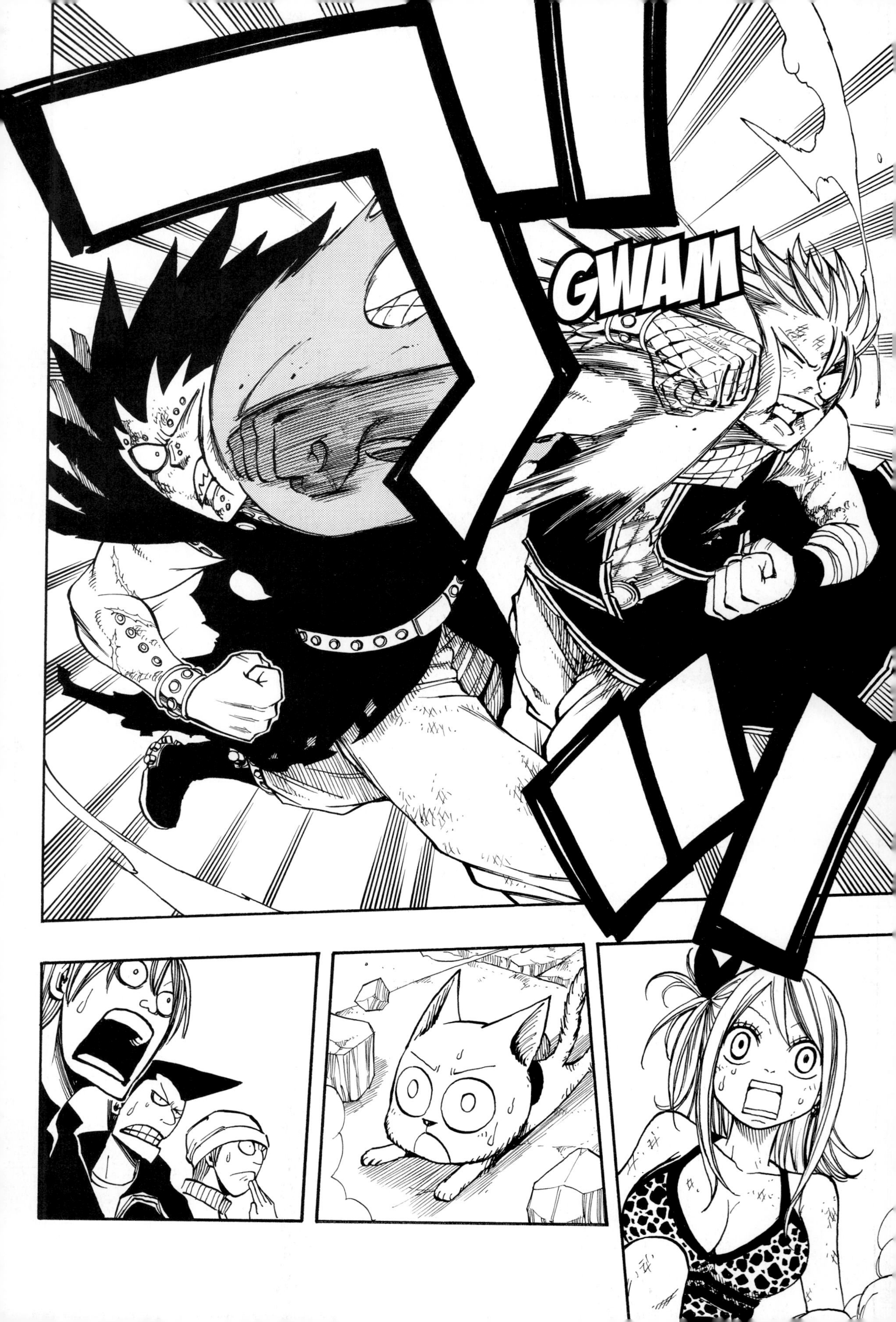
GWAM

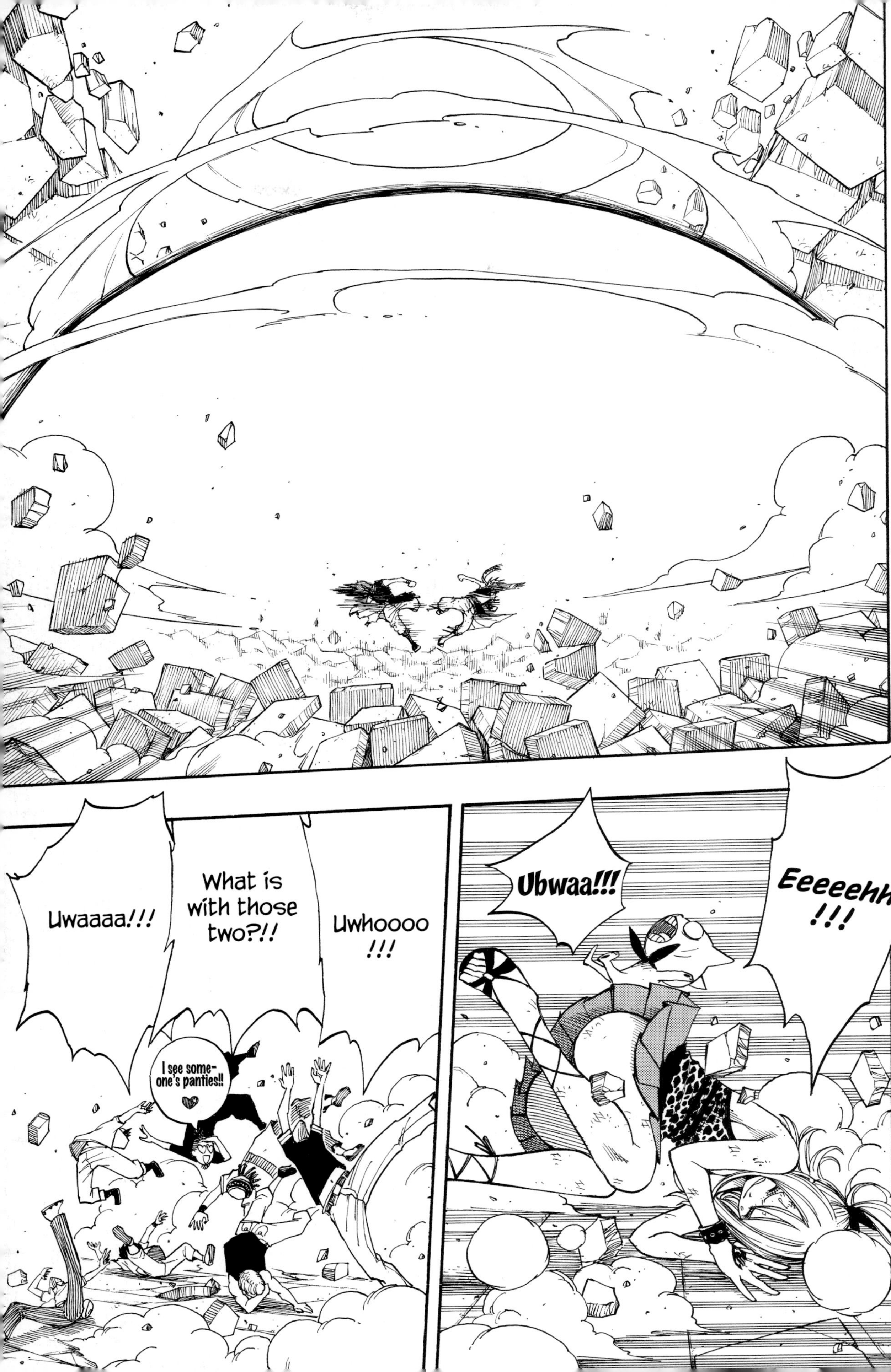
Eeeeehh !!!
Ubwaa!!!
Uwhoooo !!!
What is with those two?!!
Uwaaaa!!!
I see some-one's panties!!

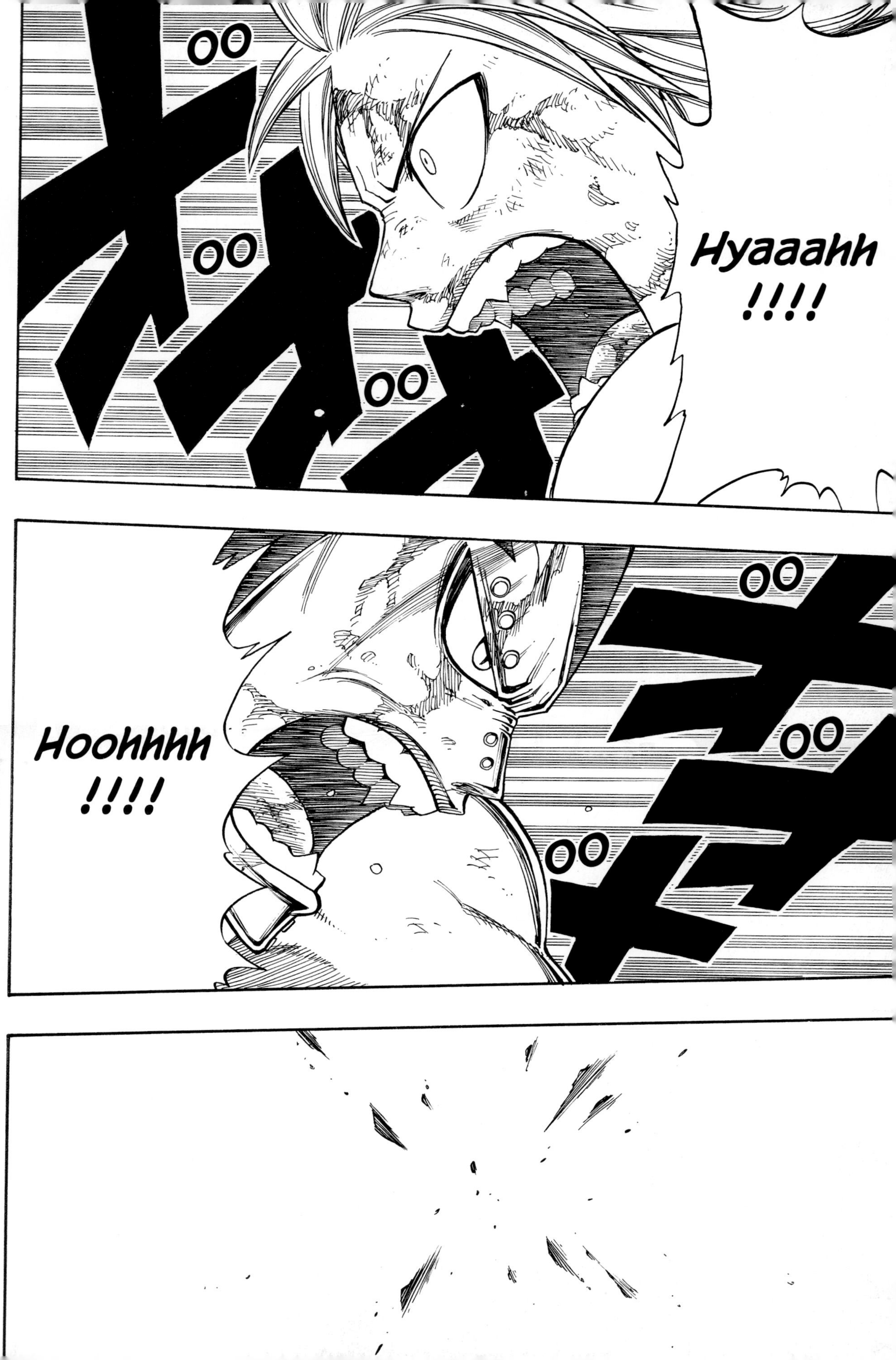
Hyaaahh !!!!
OO
OO
OO
OO
OO
OO
Hoohhhh !!!!

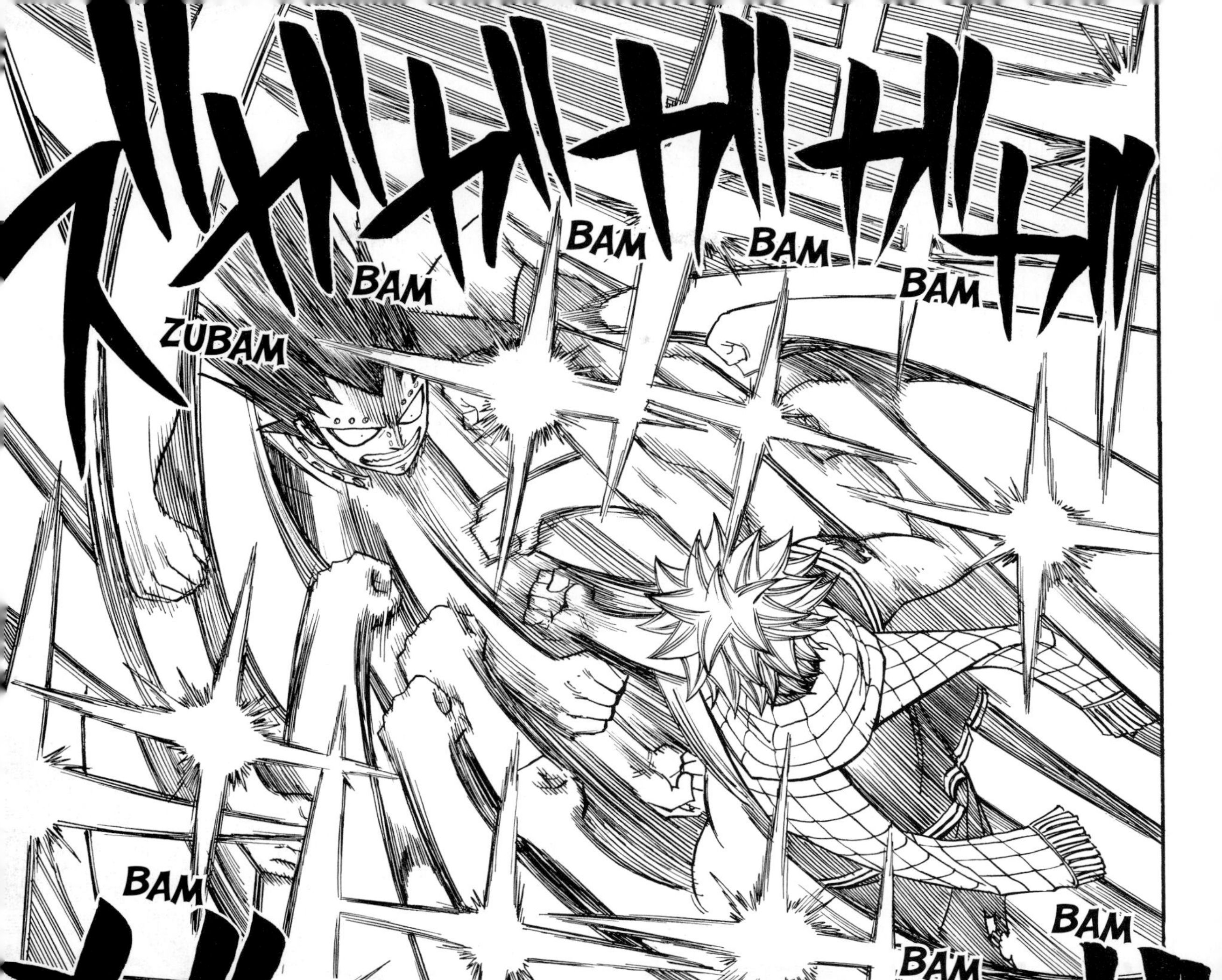
BAM
BAM
BAM
BAM
ZUBAM
BAM
BAM
BAM
BAM
BAM
BAM
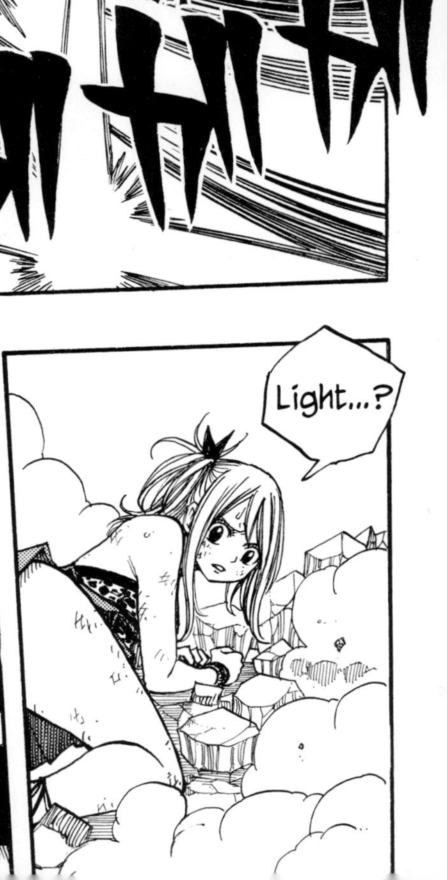
Light...?
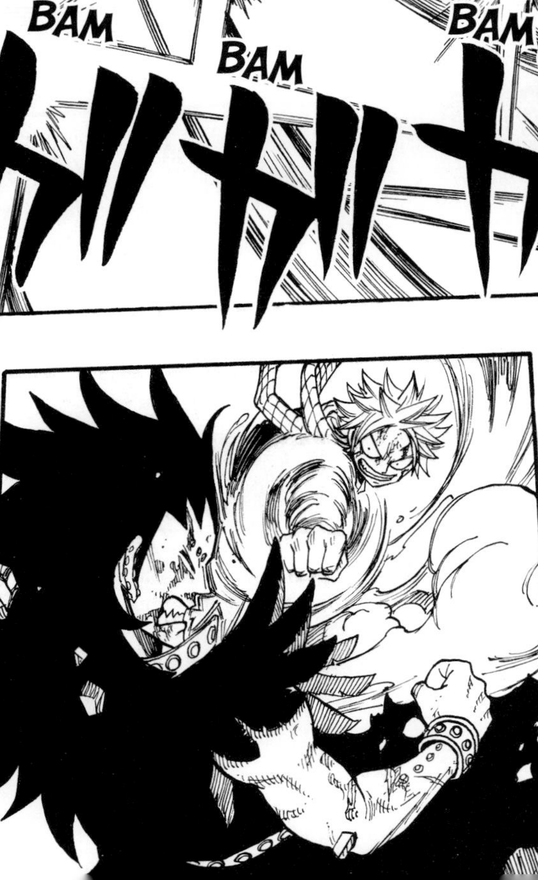
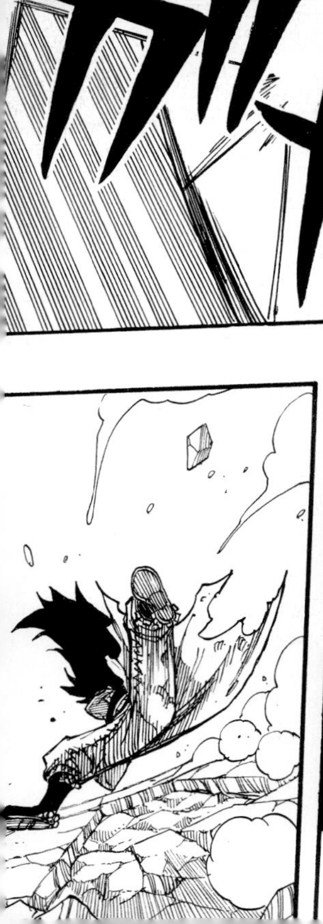

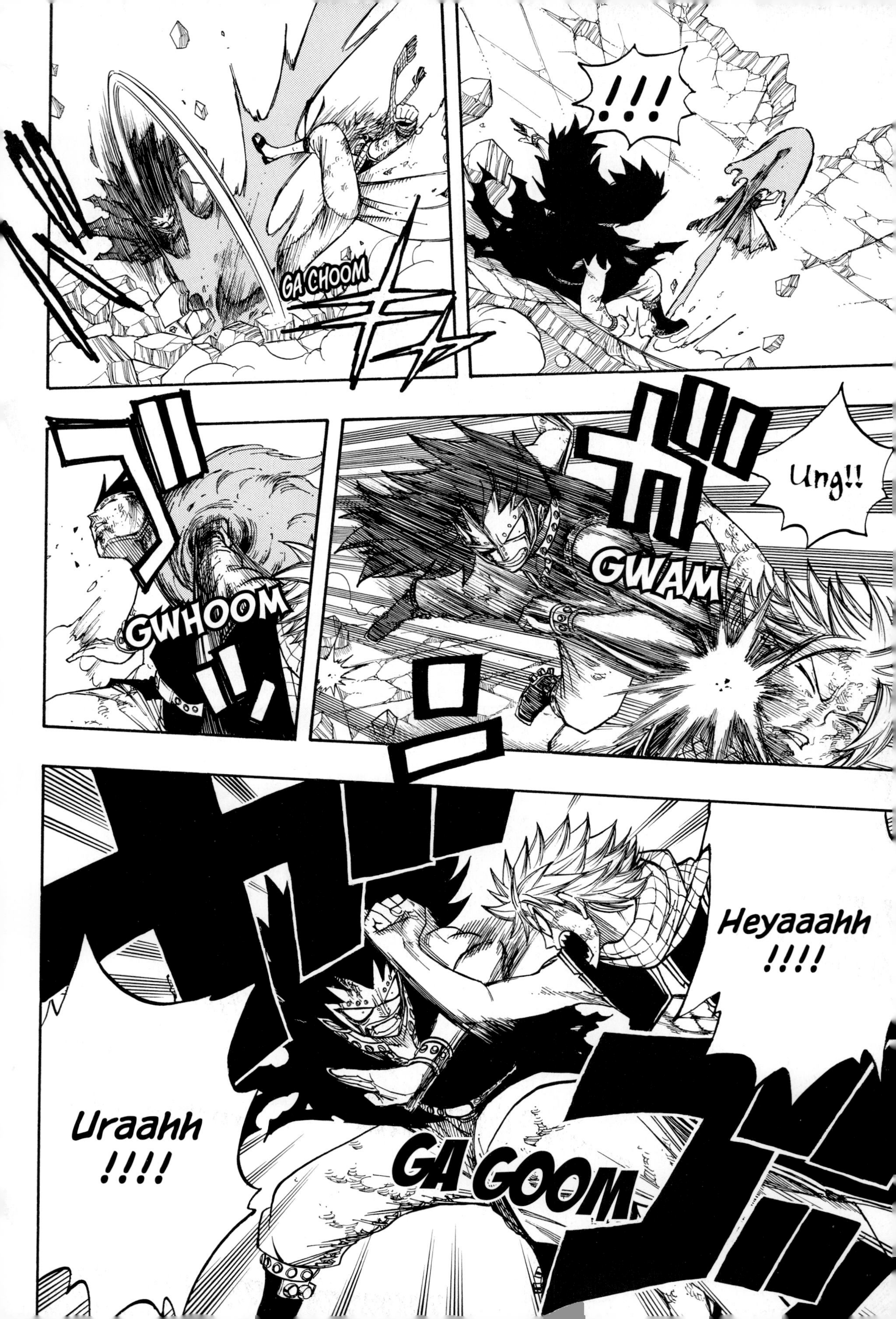
!!!
GA CHOOM
Ung!!
GWAM
GWHOOM
Heyaaahh !!!!
Uraahh !!!!
GA GOOM

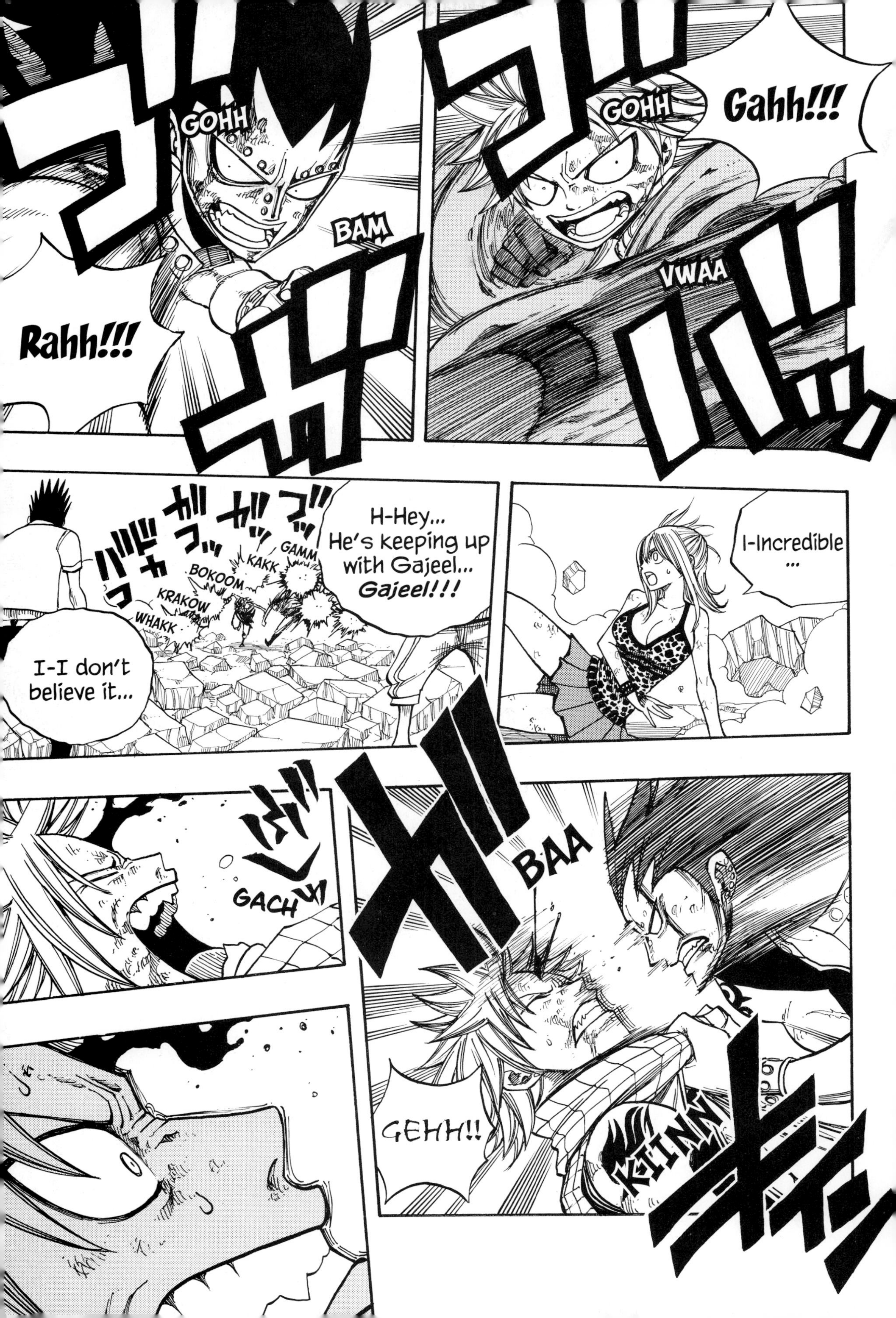
GOHH
Gahh!!!
VWAA
GOHH
BAM
Rahh!!!
I-Incredible ...
H-Hey... He's keeping up with Gajeel... *Gajeel!!!*
GAMM
KAKK
BOKOOM
KRAKOW
WHAKK
I-I don't believe it...
BAA
GEHH!!
KIINN
GACH

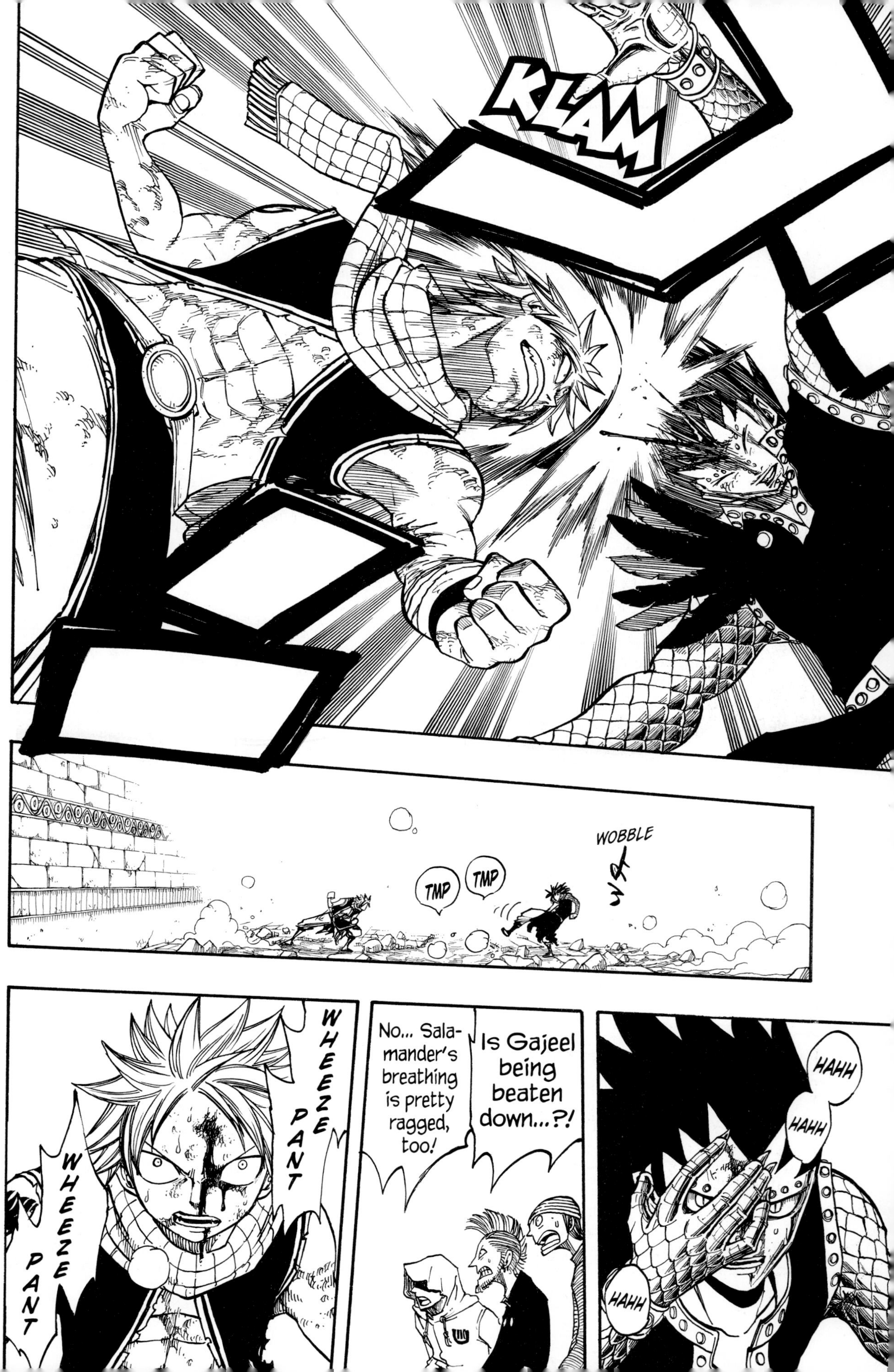
KLAM
WOBBLE
TMP
TMP
HAHH
HAHH
HAHH
Is Gajeel being beaten down...?!
No... Salamander's breathing is pretty ragged, too!
WHEEZE
PANT
WHEEZE
PANT

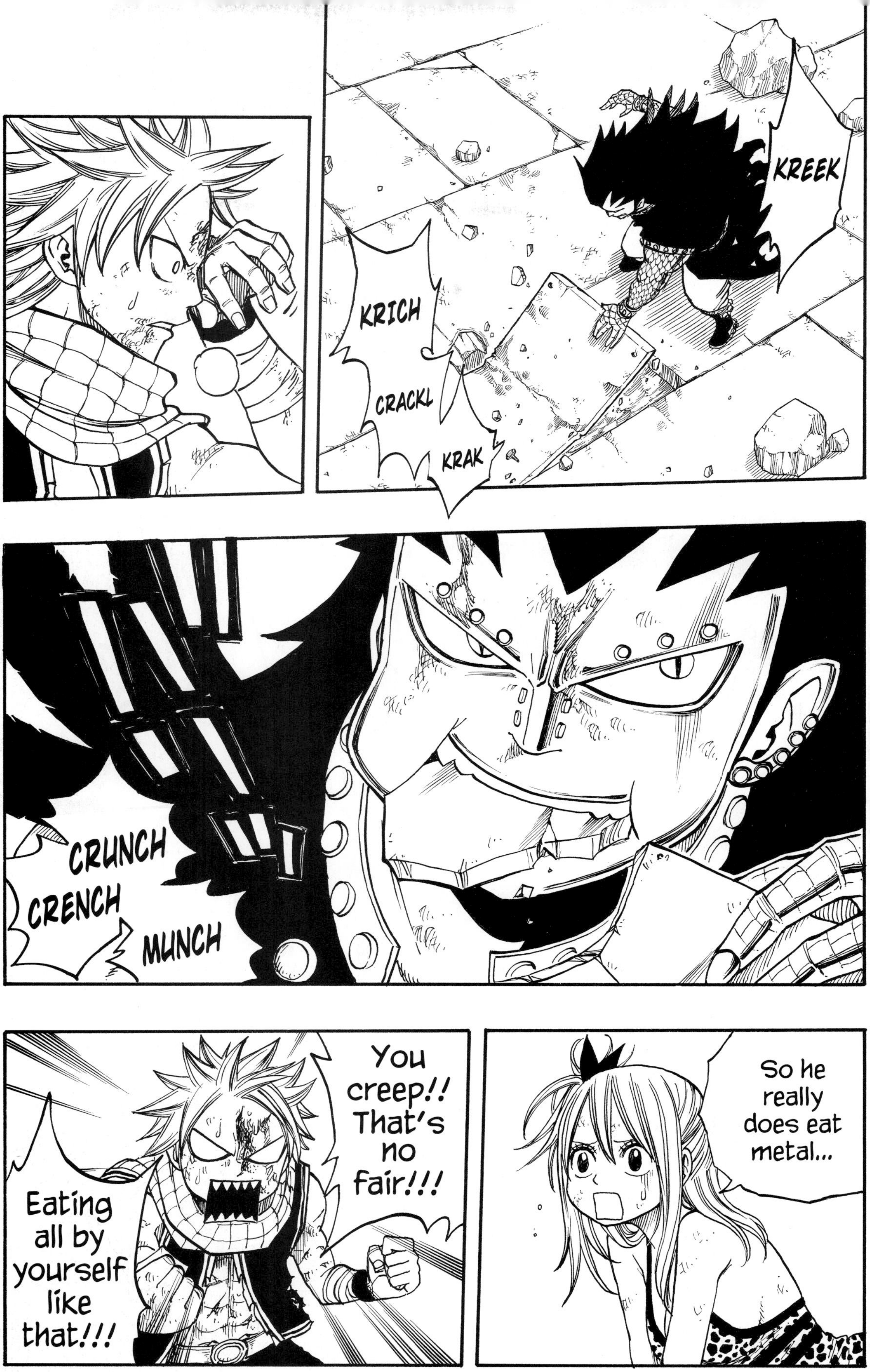
KREEK
KRICH
CRACKL
KRAK
CRUNCH
CRENCH
MUNCH
So he really does eat metal...
You creep!! That's no fair!!!
Eating all by yourself like that!!!

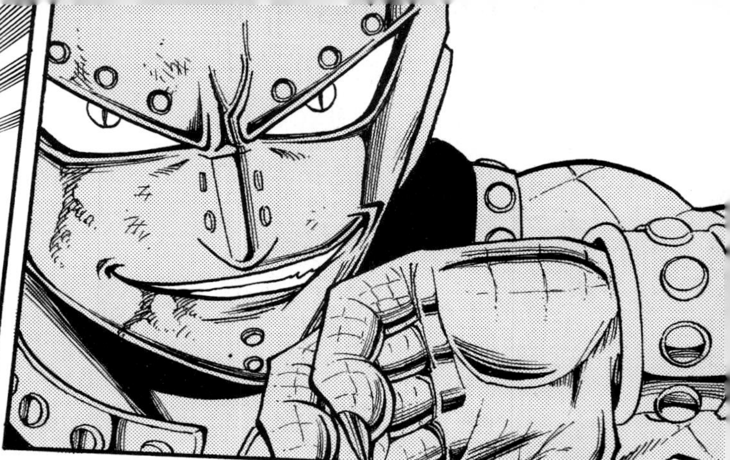

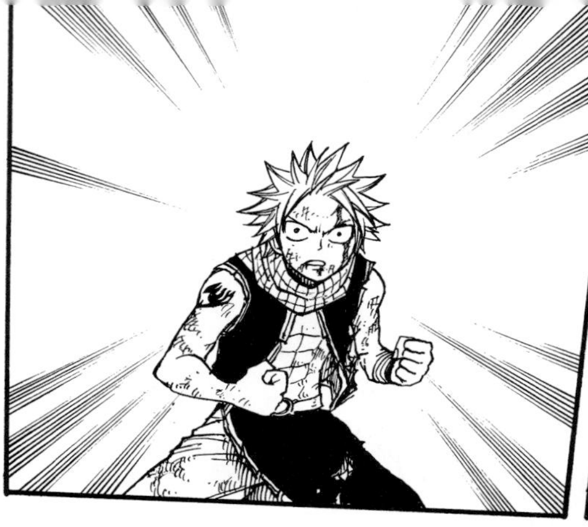

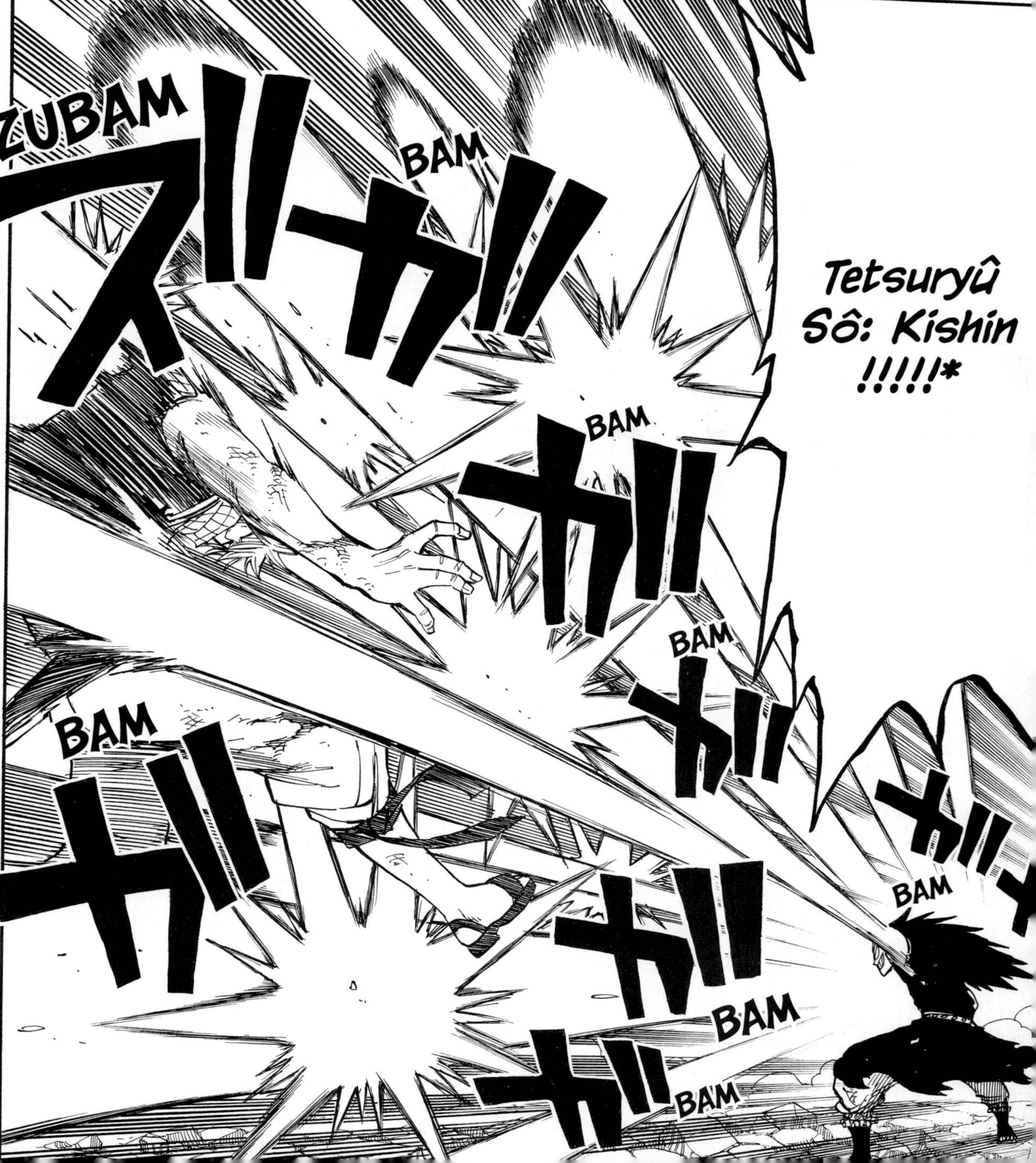
Tetsuryû Sô: Kishin !!!!!*
ZUBAM
BAM
BAM
BAM
BAM
BAM
BAM
BAM

*Iron Dragon Lance: Demon Logs

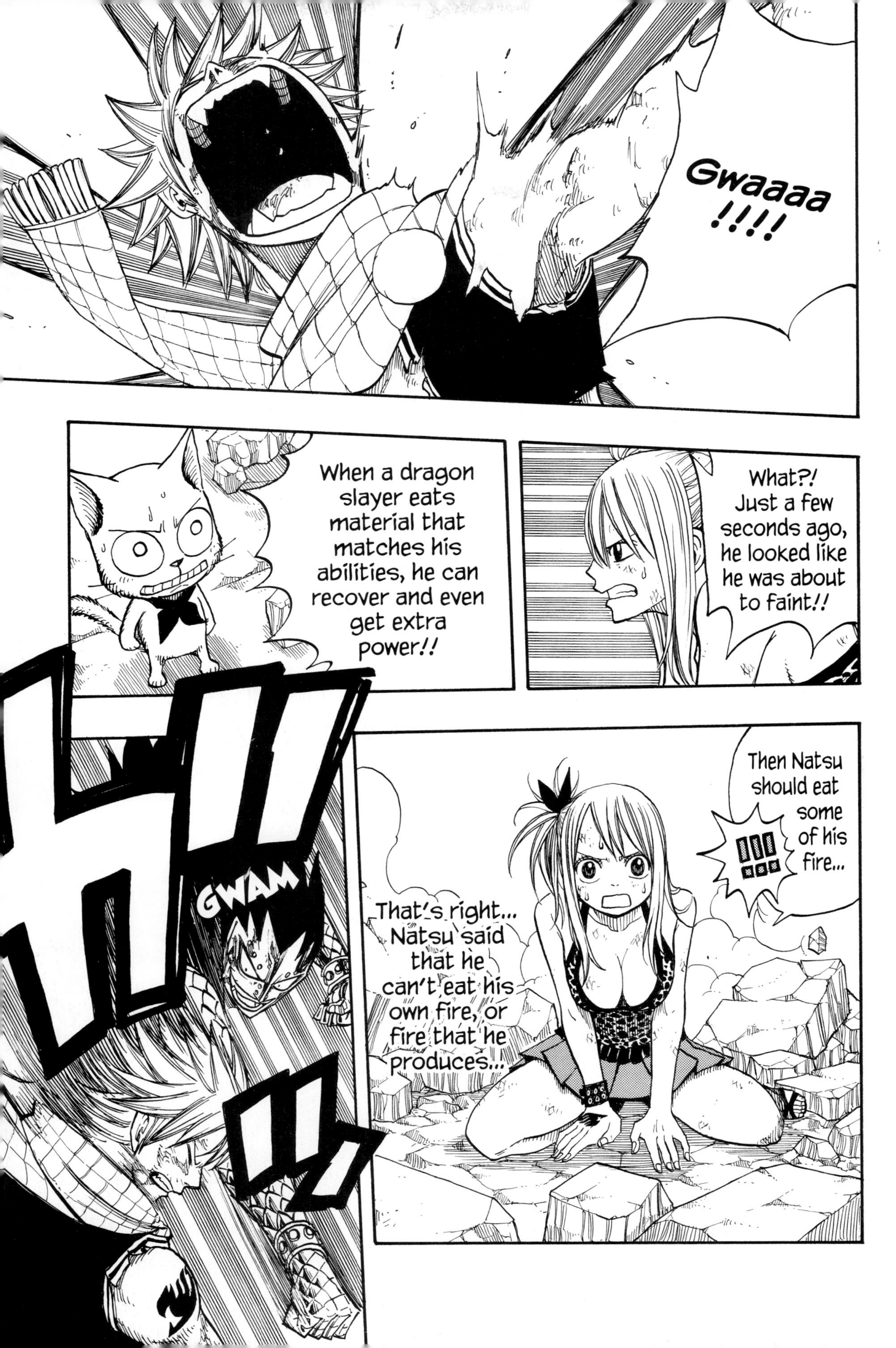
Gwaaaa!!!!
What?! Just a few seconds ago, he looked like he was about to faint!!
When a dragon slayer eats material that matches his abilities, he can recover and even get extra power!!
Then Natsu should eat some of his fire...
That's right... Natsu said that he can't eat his own fire, or fire that he produces...
GWAM

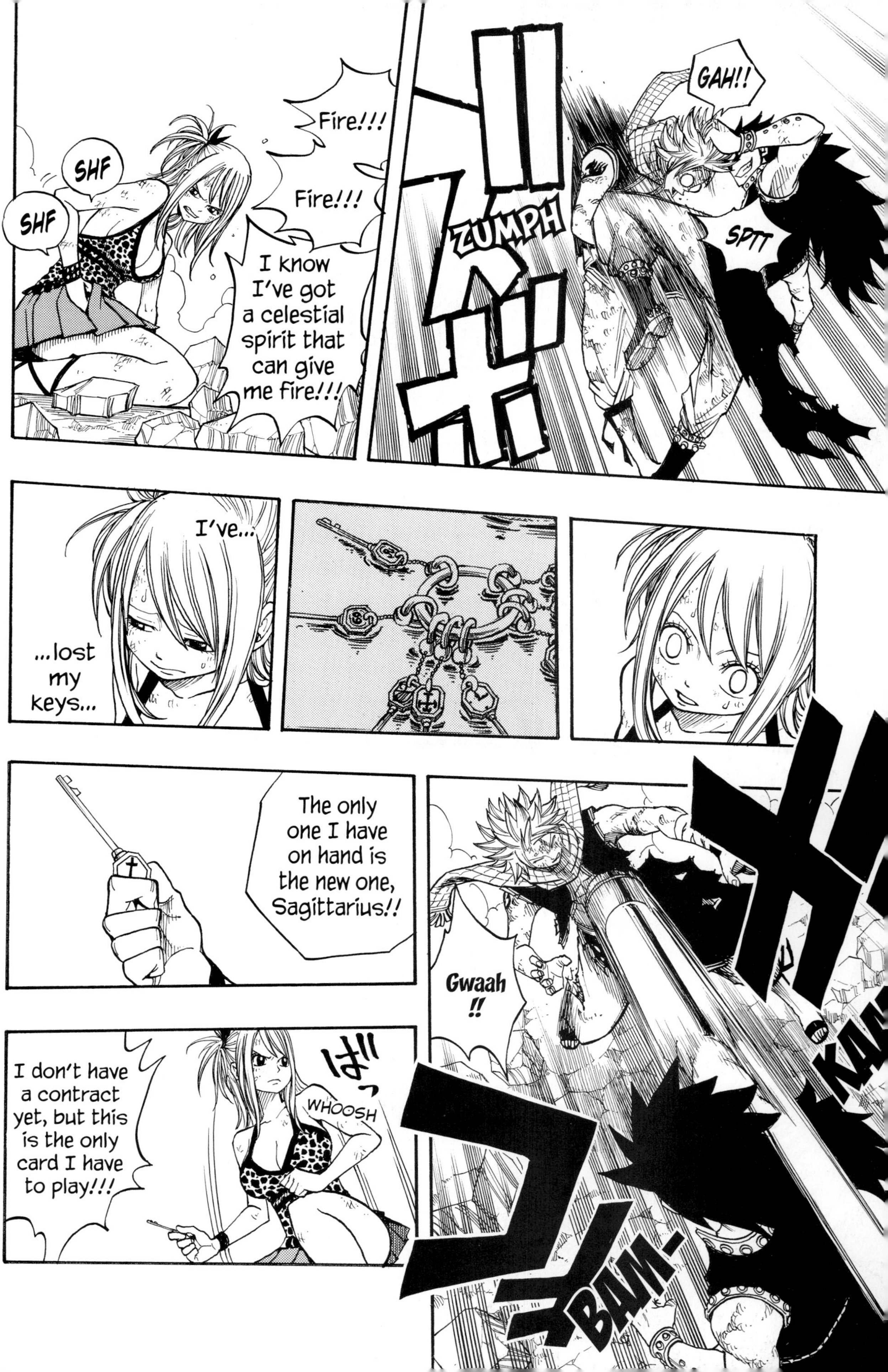
GAH!!
ZUMPH
SPTT
Fire!!!
Fire!!!
I know I've got a celestial spirit that can give me fire!!!
SHF
SHF
I've...
...lost my keys...
Gwaah!!
BAM-
The only one I have on hand is the new one, Sagittarius!!
I don't have a contract yet, but this is the only card I have to play!!!
ばっ
WHOOSH

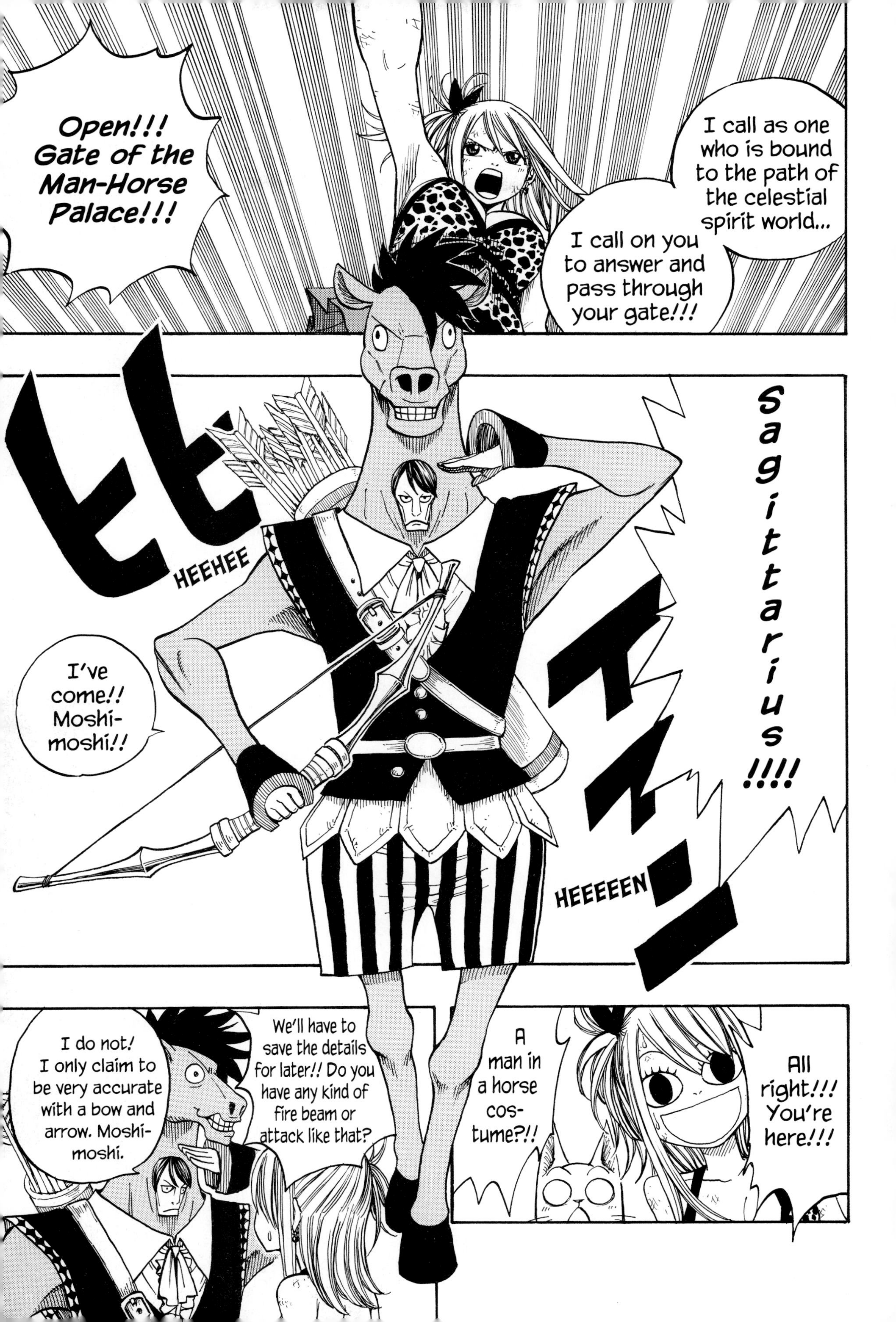
I call as one who is bound to the path of the celestial spirit world...
I call on you to answer and pass through your gate!!!
Open!!! Gate of the Man-Horse Palace!!!
Sagittarius!!!!
HEEHEE
HEEEEEN
I've come!! Moshi-moshi!!
All right!!! You're here!!!
A man in a horse costume?!!
We'll have to save the details for later!! Do you have any kind of fire beam or attack like that?
I do not! I only claim to be very accurate with a bow and arrow. Moshi-moshi.

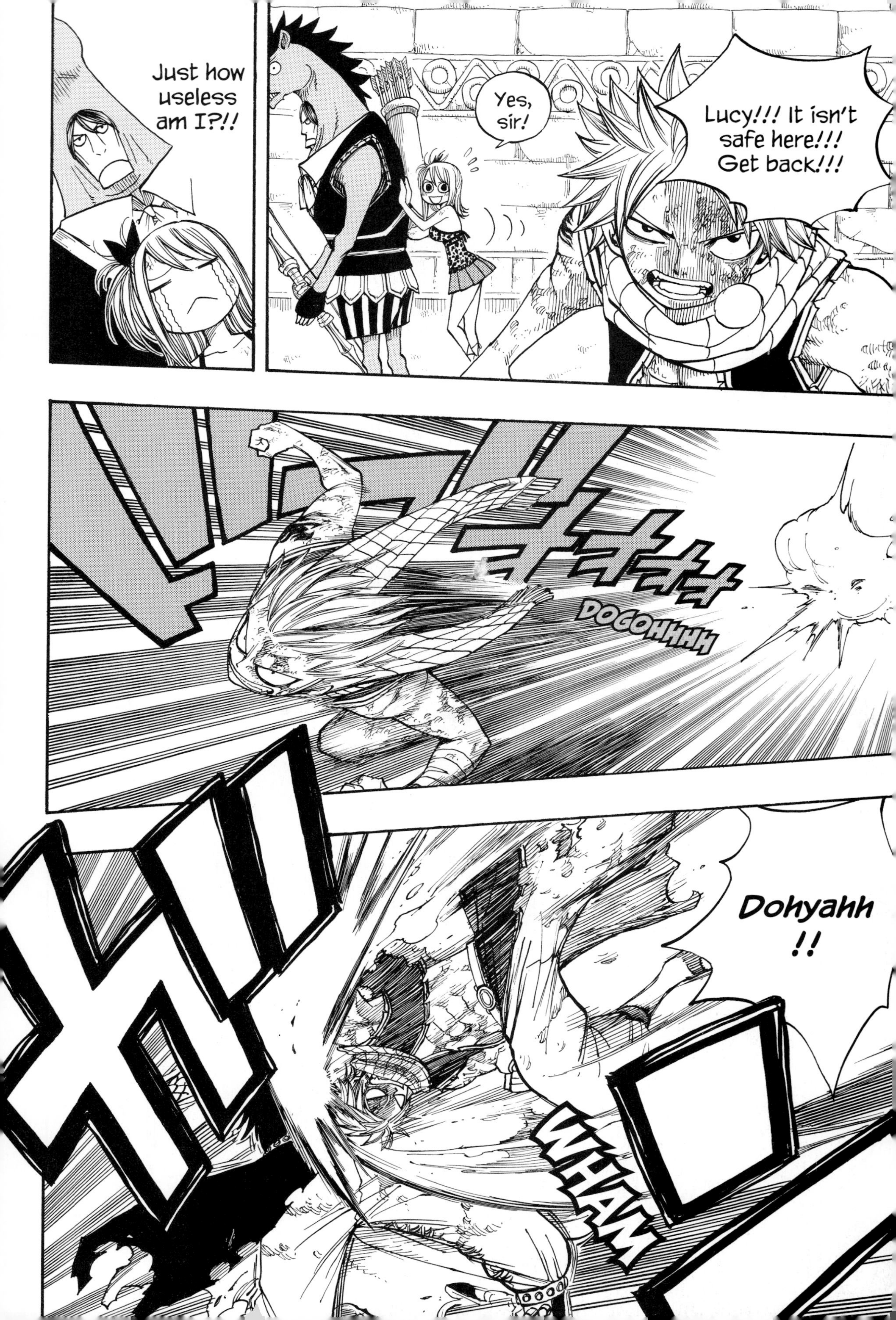
Lucy!!! It isn't safe here!!! Get back!!!
Yes, sir!
Just how useless am I?!!
DOGOHHHH
Dohyahh !!
WHAM

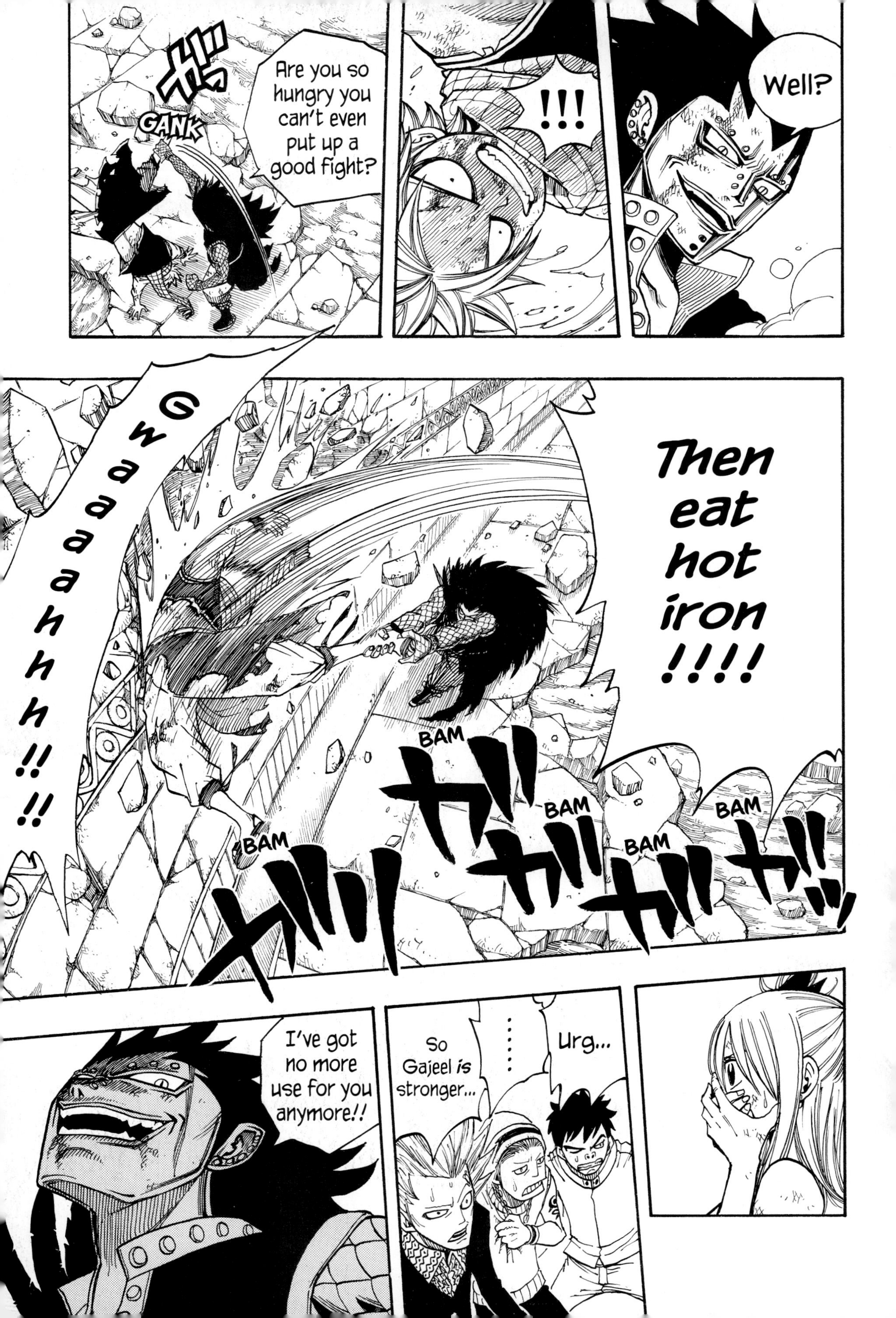
Well?
!!!
GANK
Are you so hungry you can't even put up a good fight?
Then eat hot iron!!!!
Gwaaaaaahhhh!!!!
BAM
BAM
BAM
BAM
BAM
Urg...
......
So Gajeel *is* stronger...
I've got no more use for you anymore!!

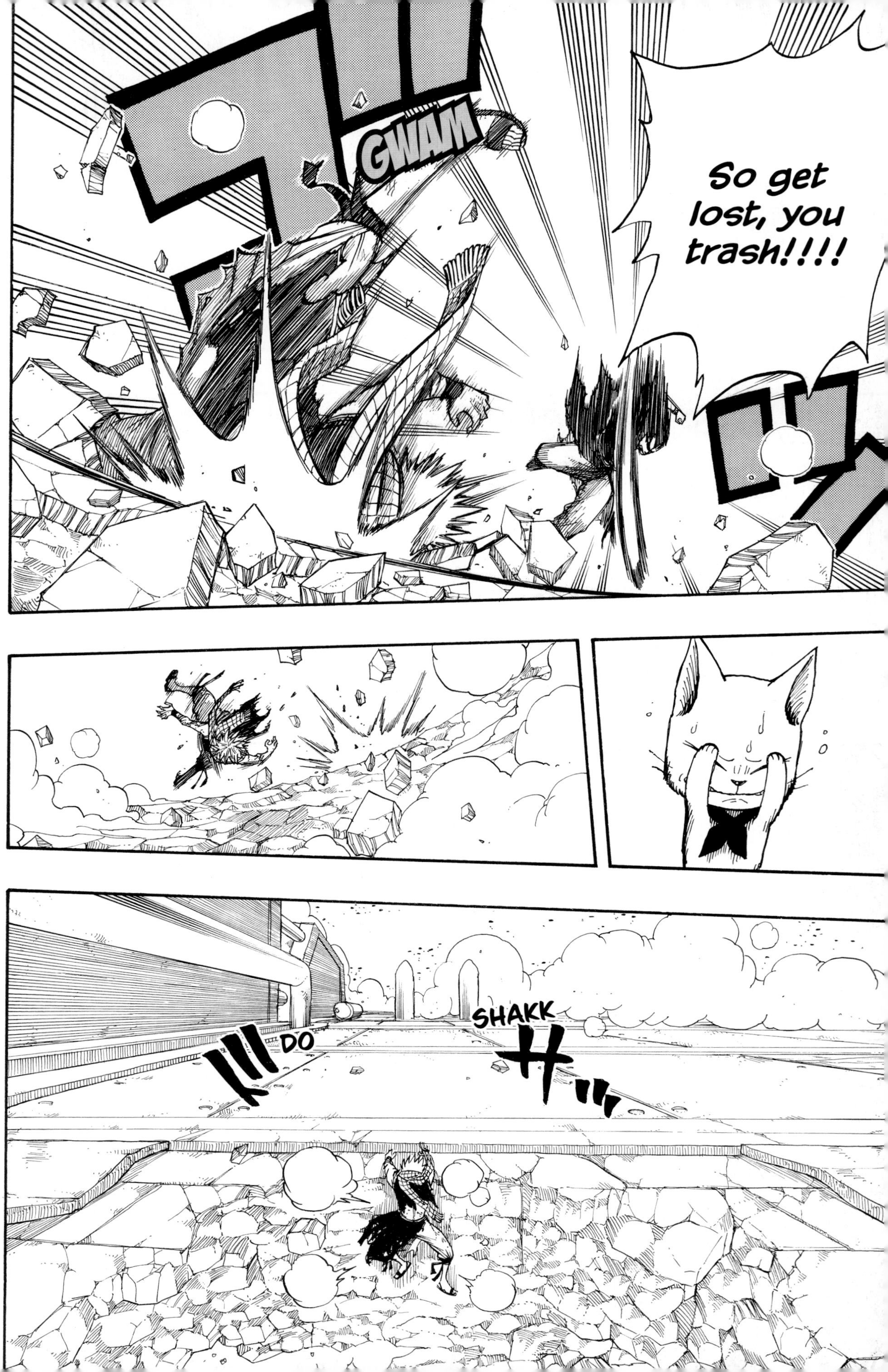
So get lost, you trash!!!!
GWAM
SHAKK
DO

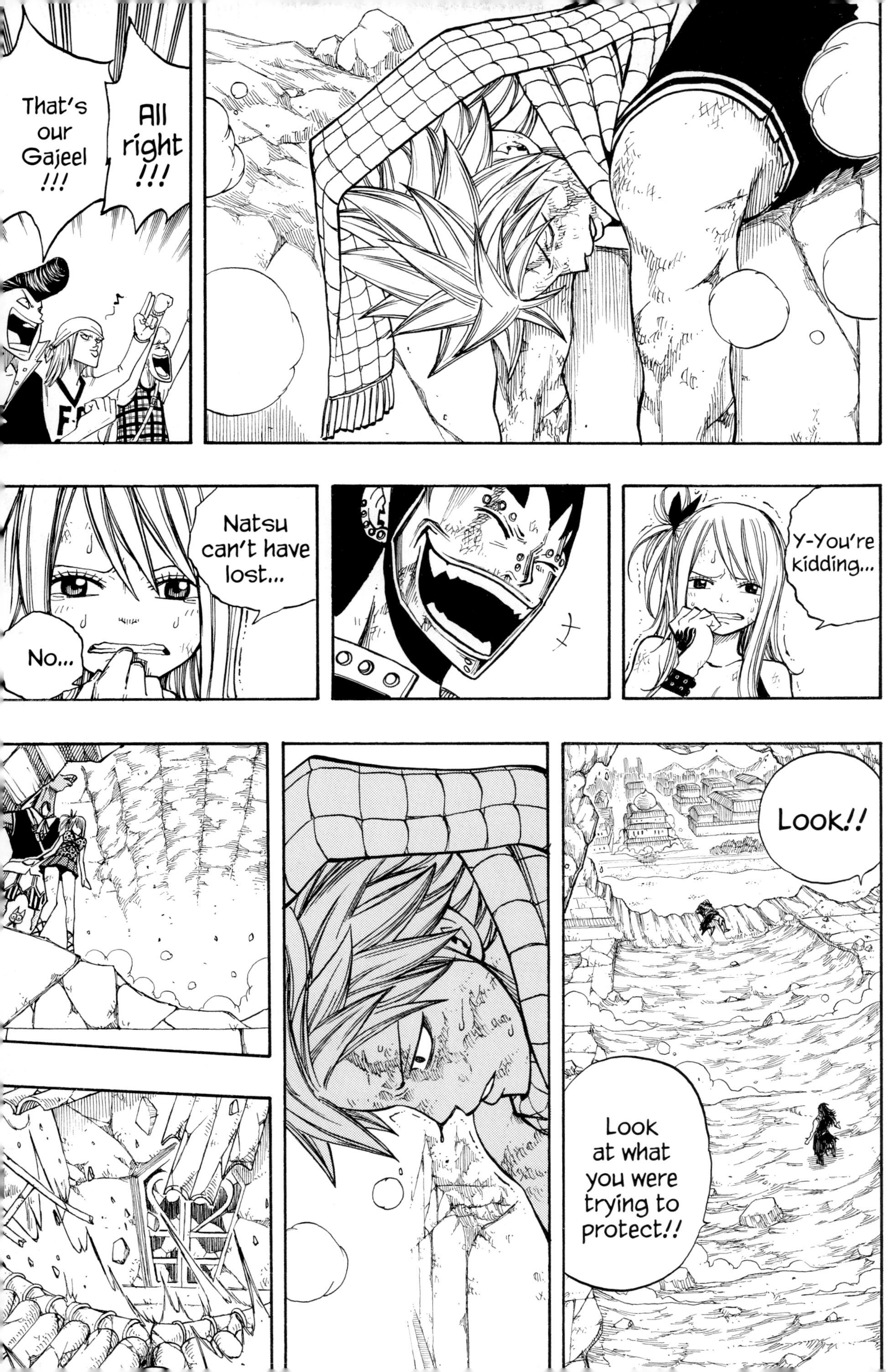
All right!!!
That's our Gajeel!!!
Y-You're kidding...
Natsu can't have lost...
No...
Look!!
Look at what you were trying to protect!!

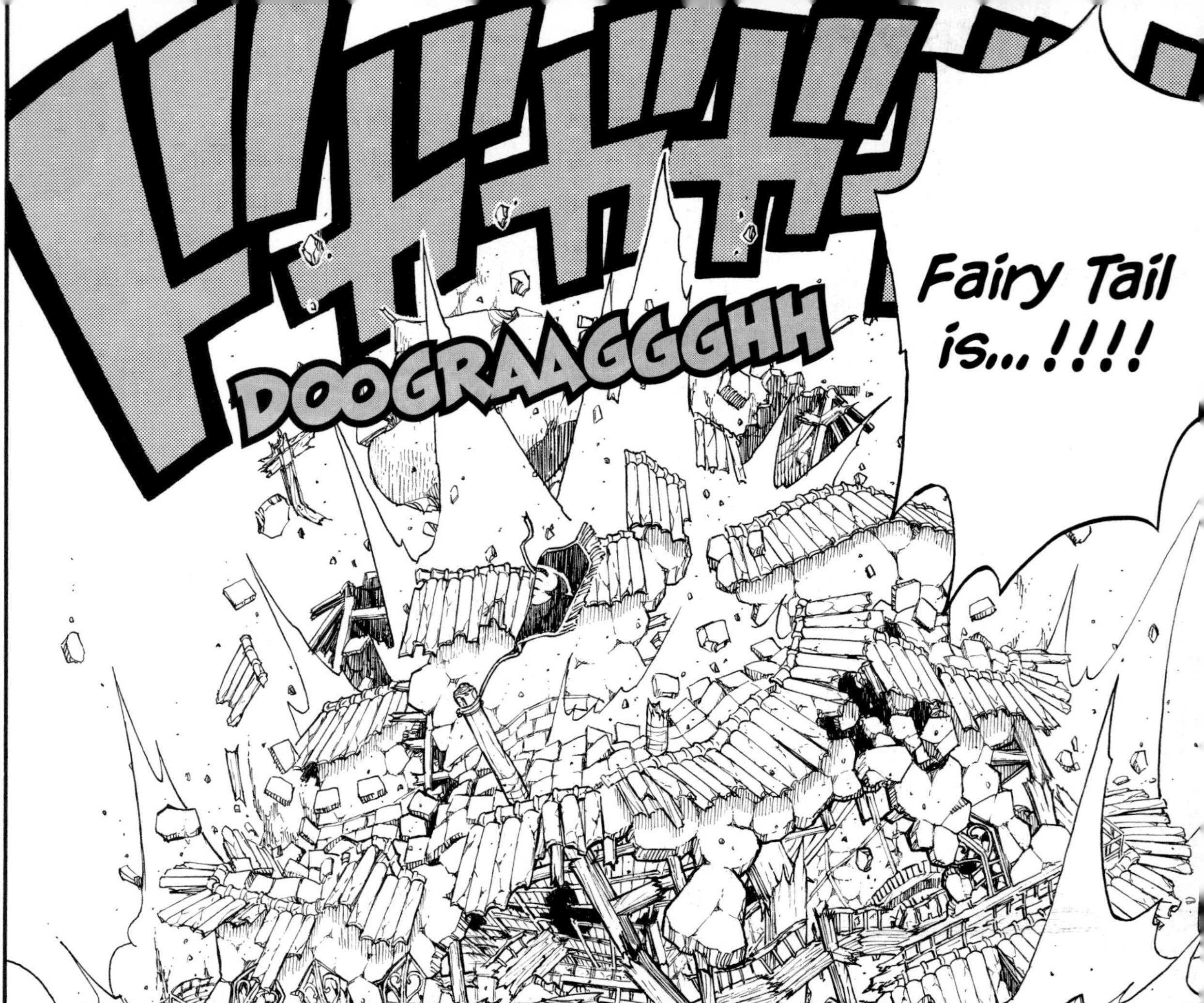
DOOGRAAGGGHH
Fairy Tail is...!!!!

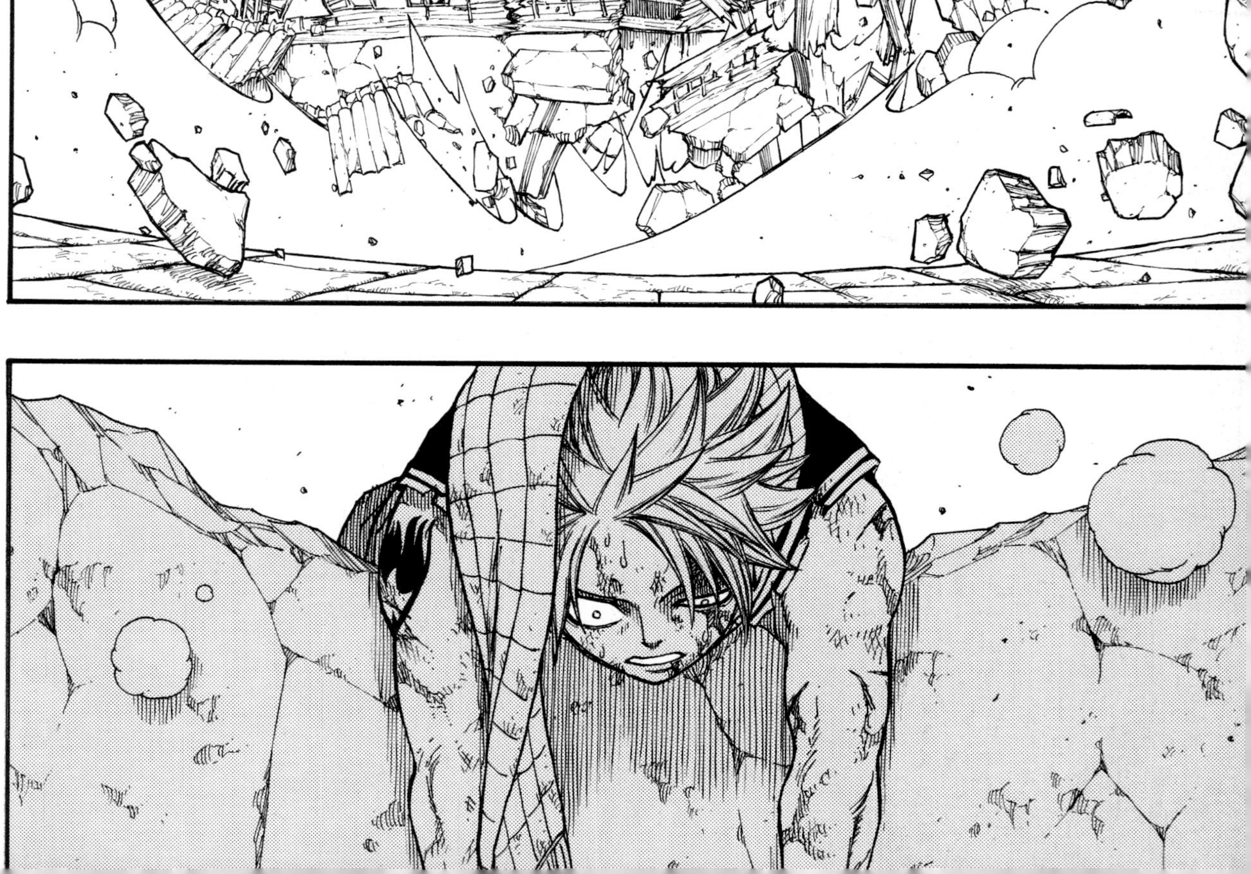

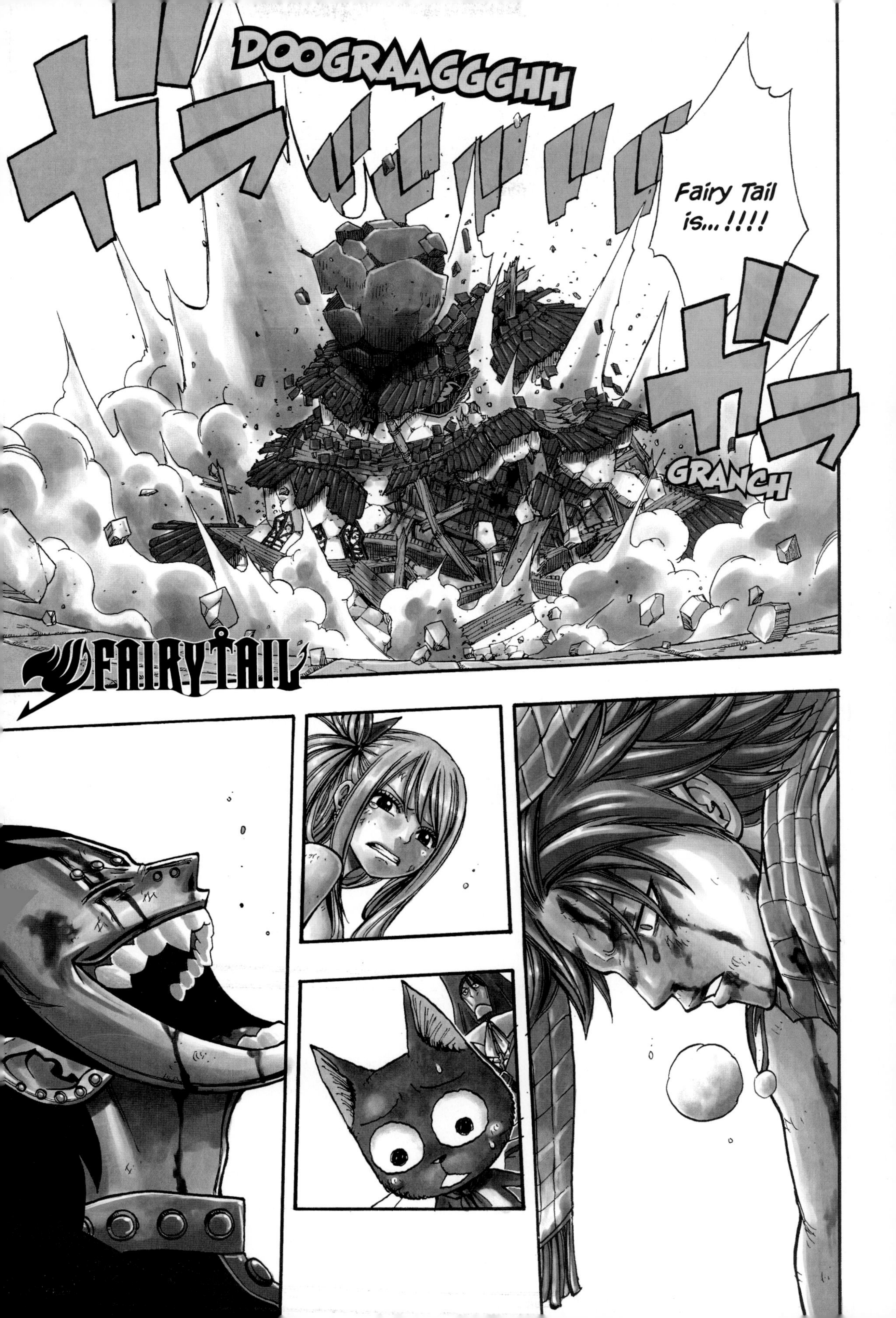
DOOGRAAGGGHH
Fairy Tail is...!!!!
GRANCH
FAIRY TAIL

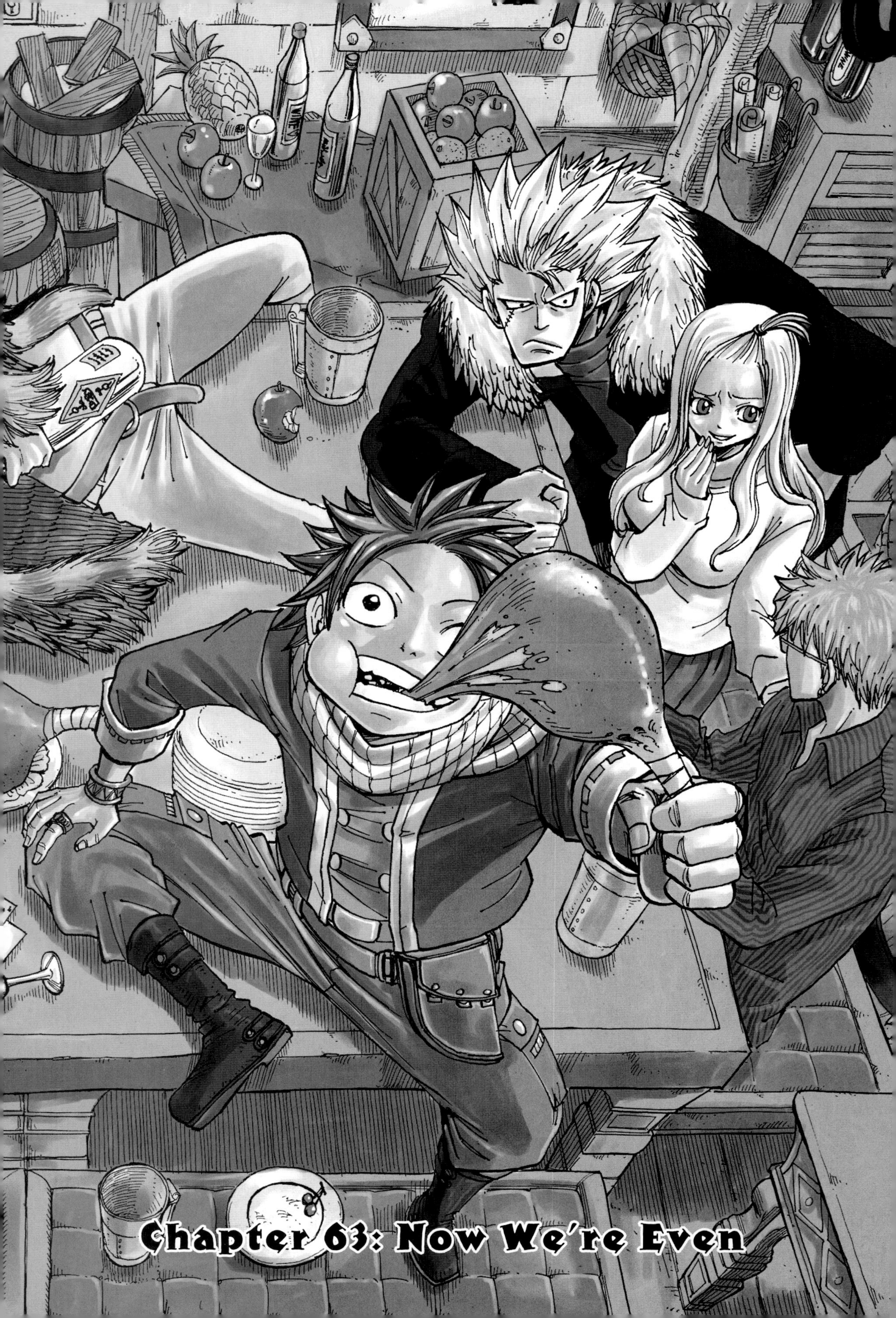
Chapter 63: Now We're Even

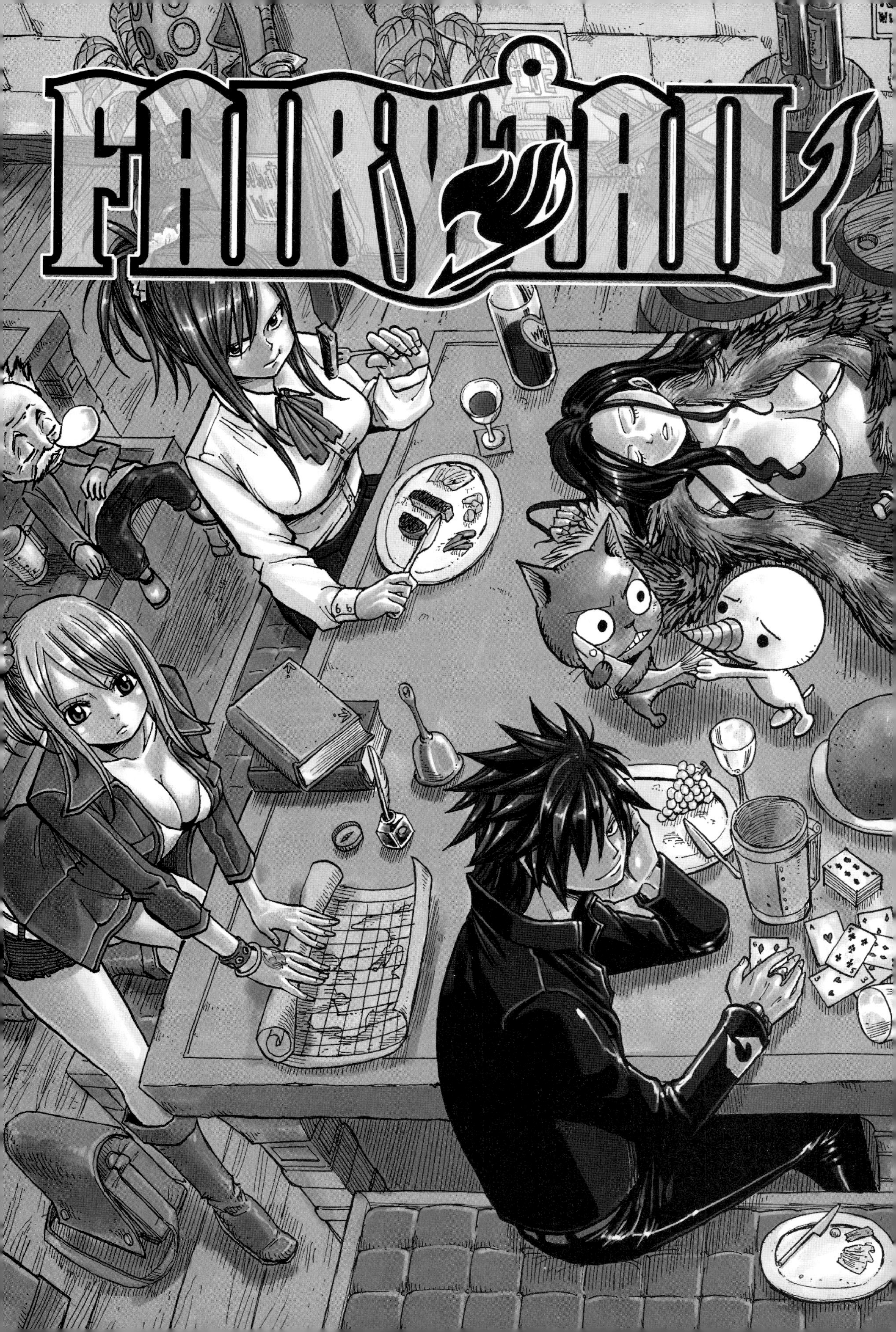
FAIRY TAIL

FAIRY TAIL

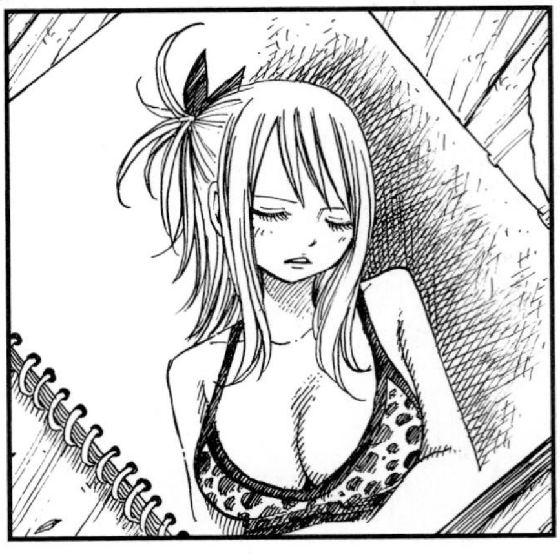

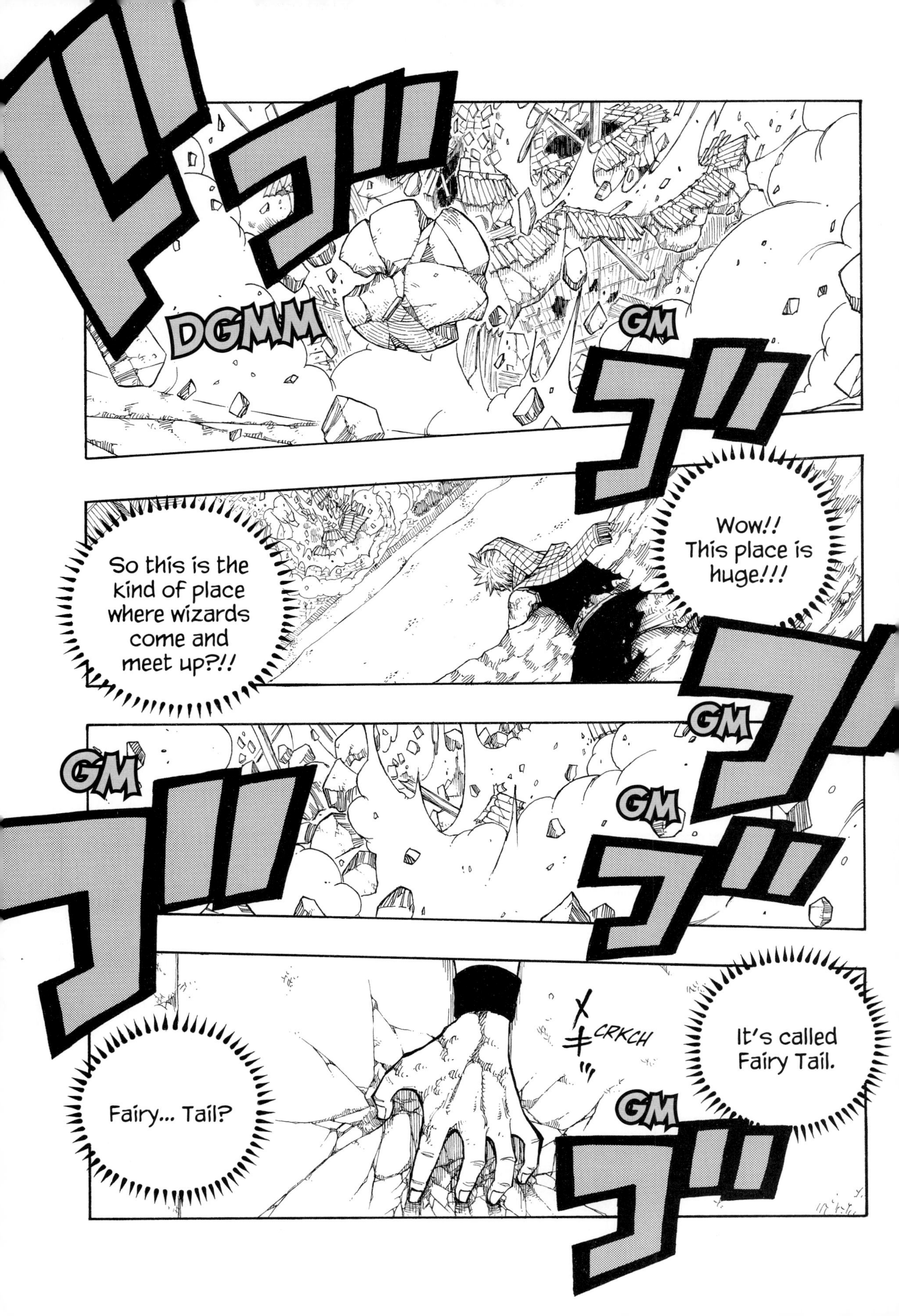
GM
DGMM
Wow!! This place is huge!!!
So this is the kind of place where wizards come and meet up?!!
GM
GM
GM
It's called Fairy Tail.
CRKCH
GM
Fairy... Tail?

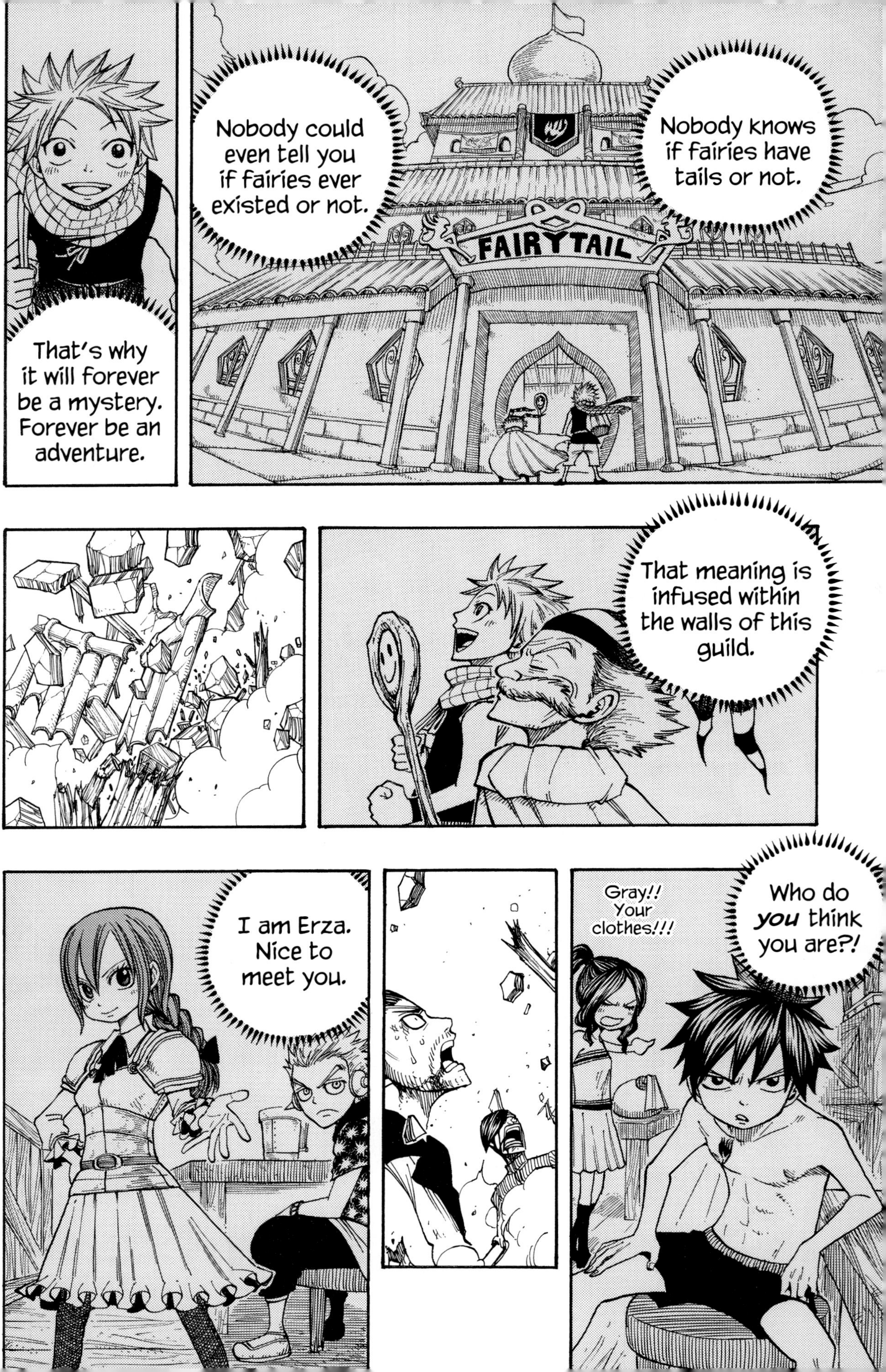
Nobody knows if fairies have tails or not.
Nobody could even tell you if fairies ever existed or not.
FAIRY TAIL
That's why it will forever be a mystery. Forever be an adventure.
That meaning is infused within the walls of this guild.
Who do *you* think you are?!
Gray!! Your clothes!!!
I am Erza. Nice to meet you.

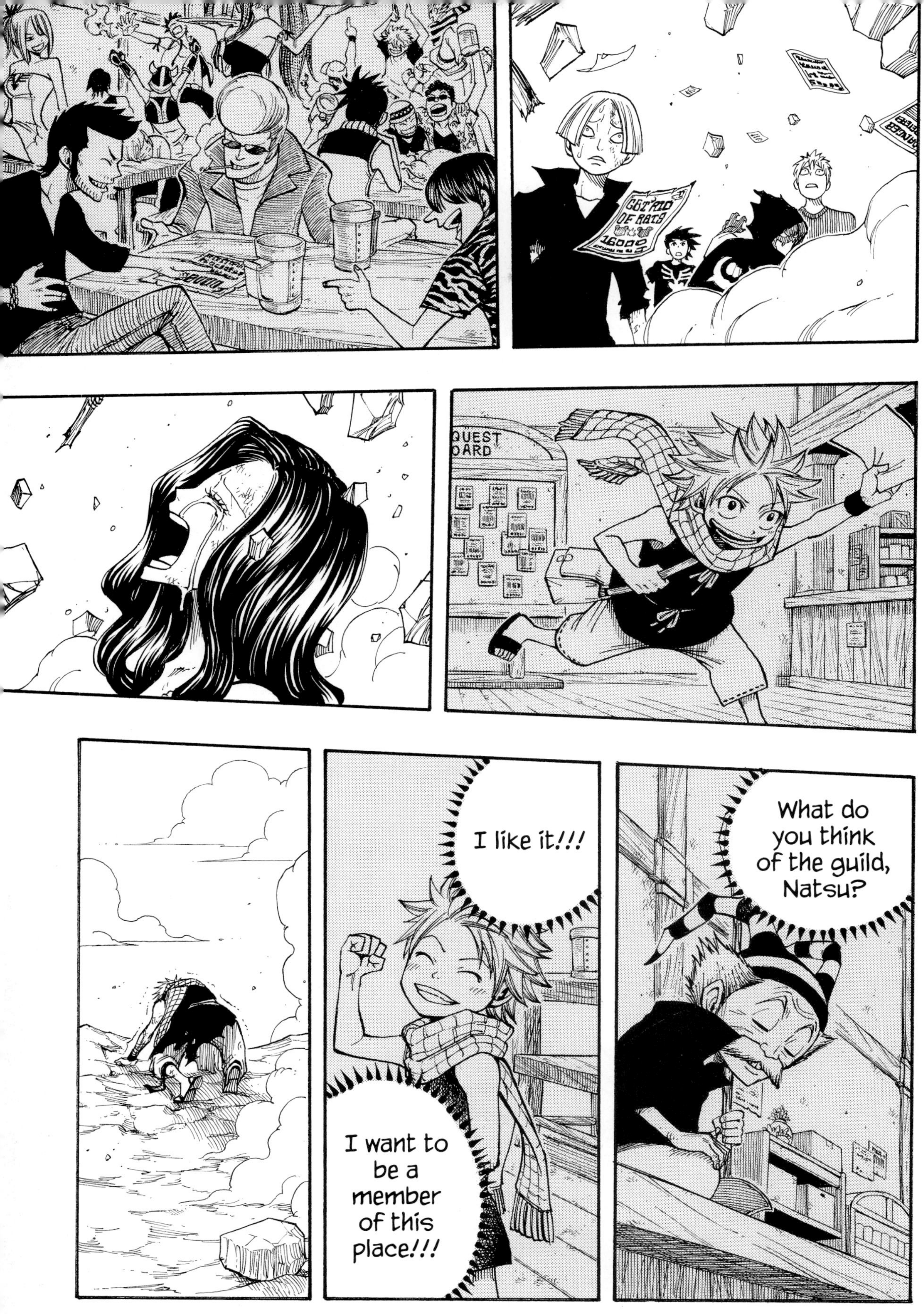
GET RID OF RATS
16000
QUEST
What do you think of the guild, Natsu?
I like it!!!
I want to be a member of this place!!!

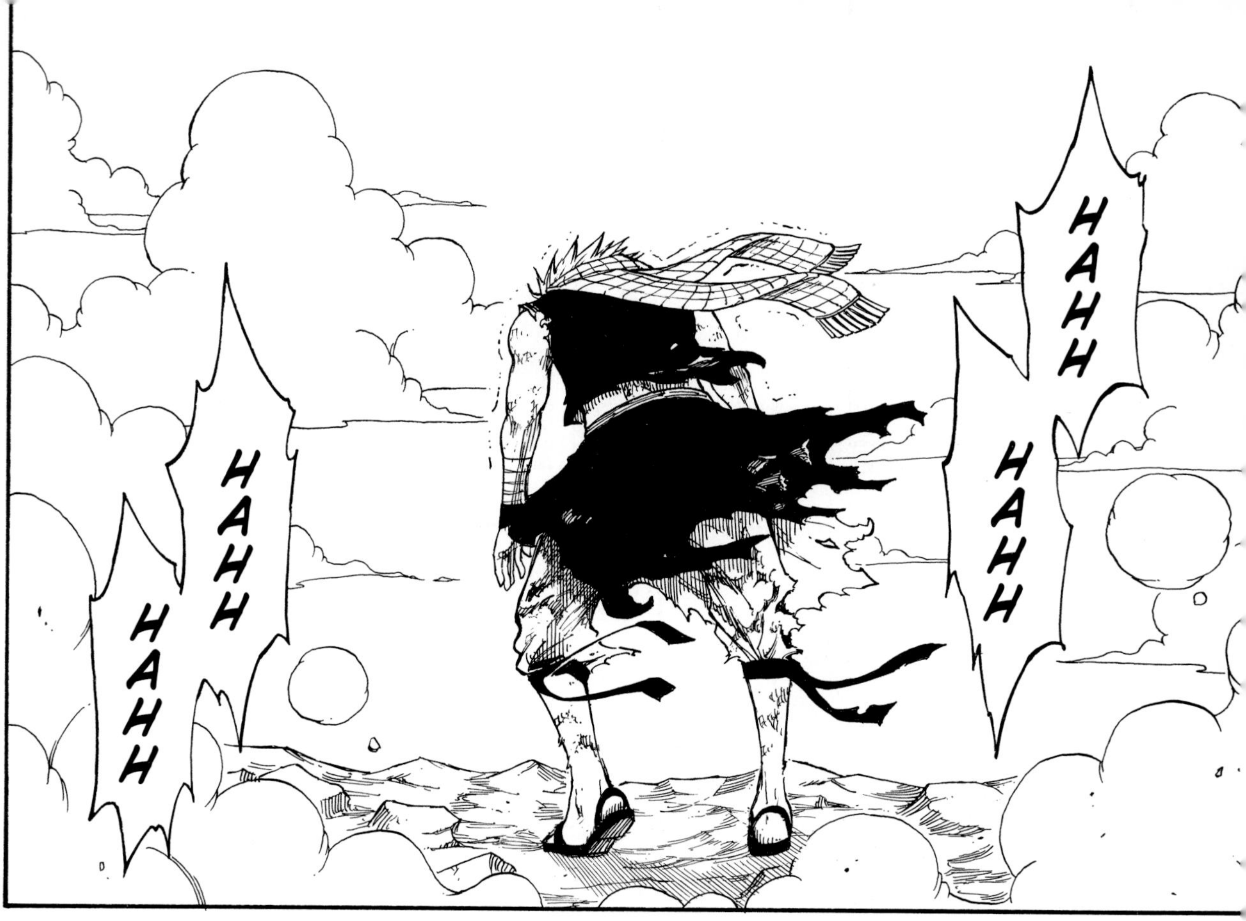
HAHH
HAHH
HAHH
HAHH
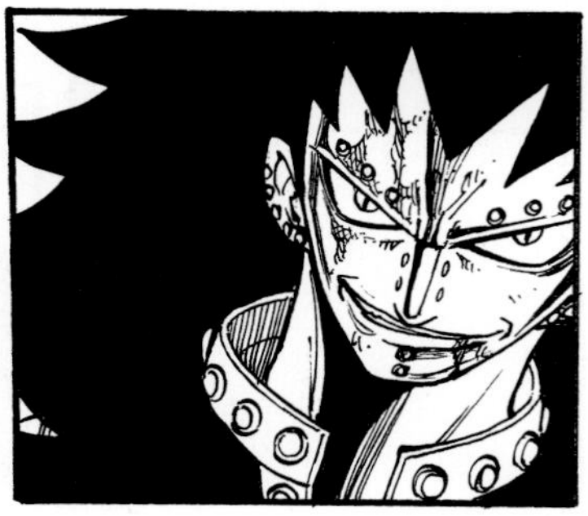
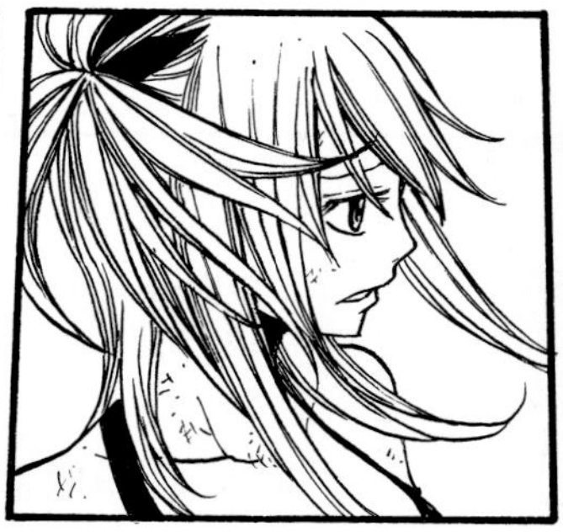
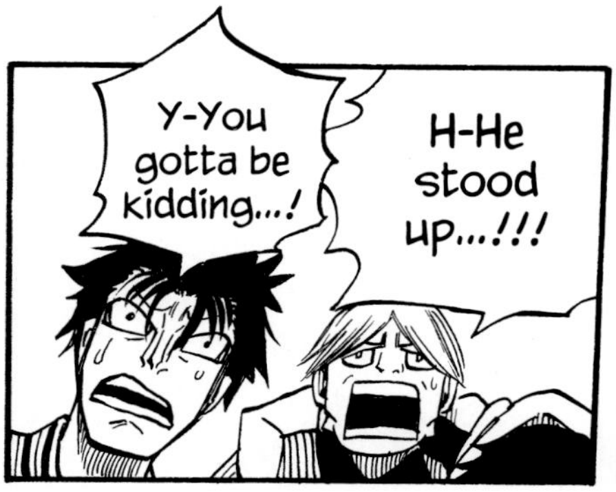
H-He stood up...!!!
Y-You gotta be kidding...!
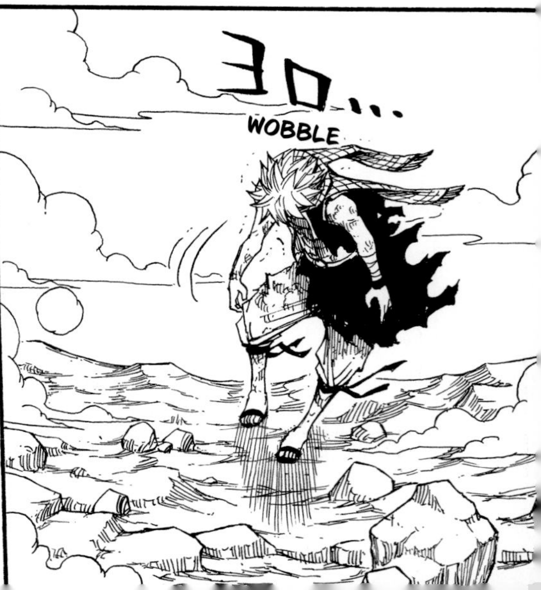
ヨロ...
WOBBLE
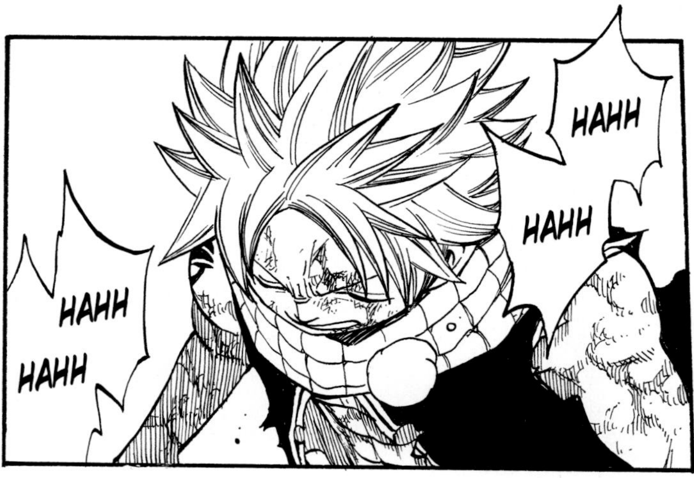
HAHH
HAHH
HAHH
HAHH

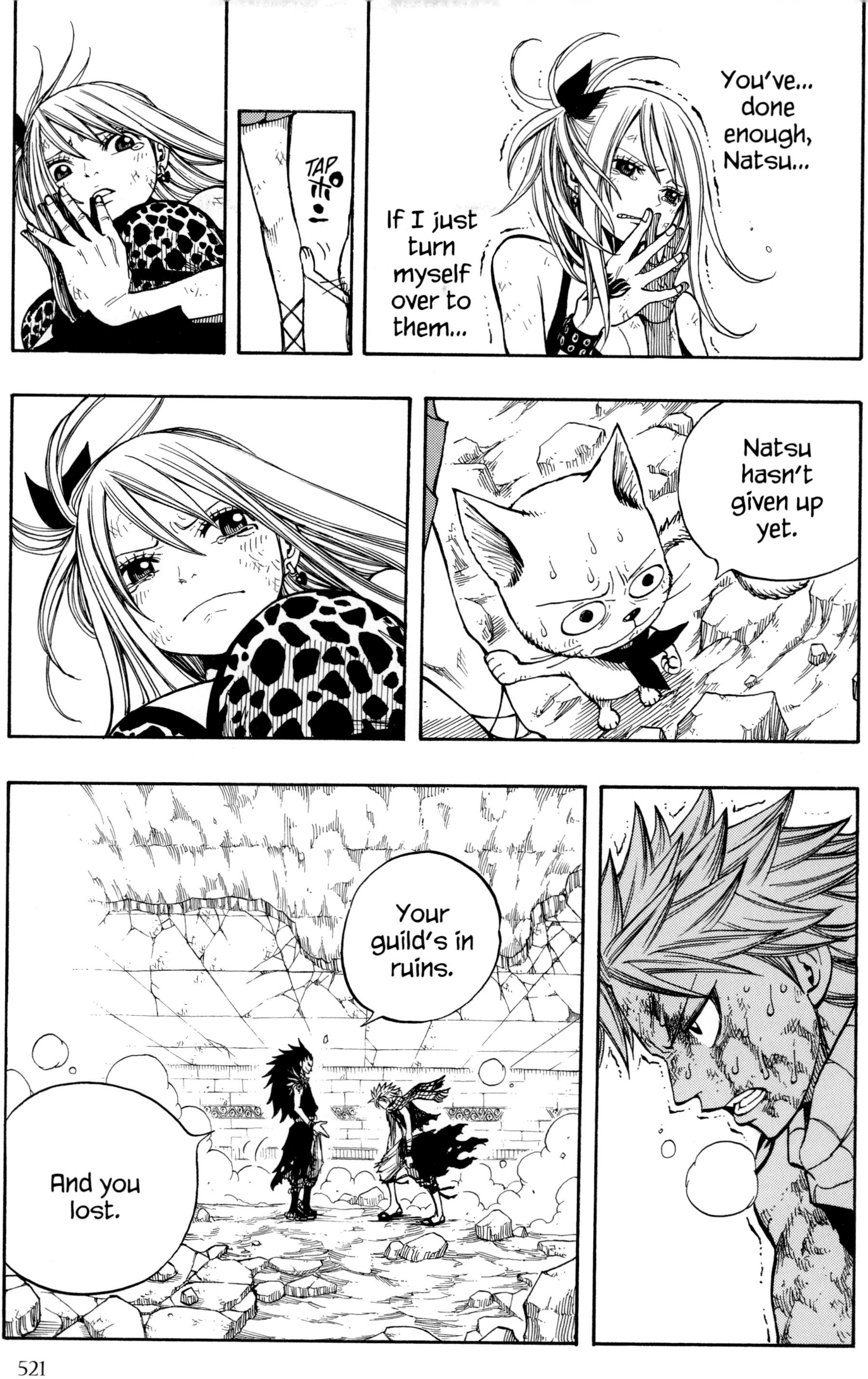
You've... done enough, Natsu...
If I just turn myself over to them...
TAP
Natsu hasn't given up yet.
Your guild's in ruins.
And you lost.

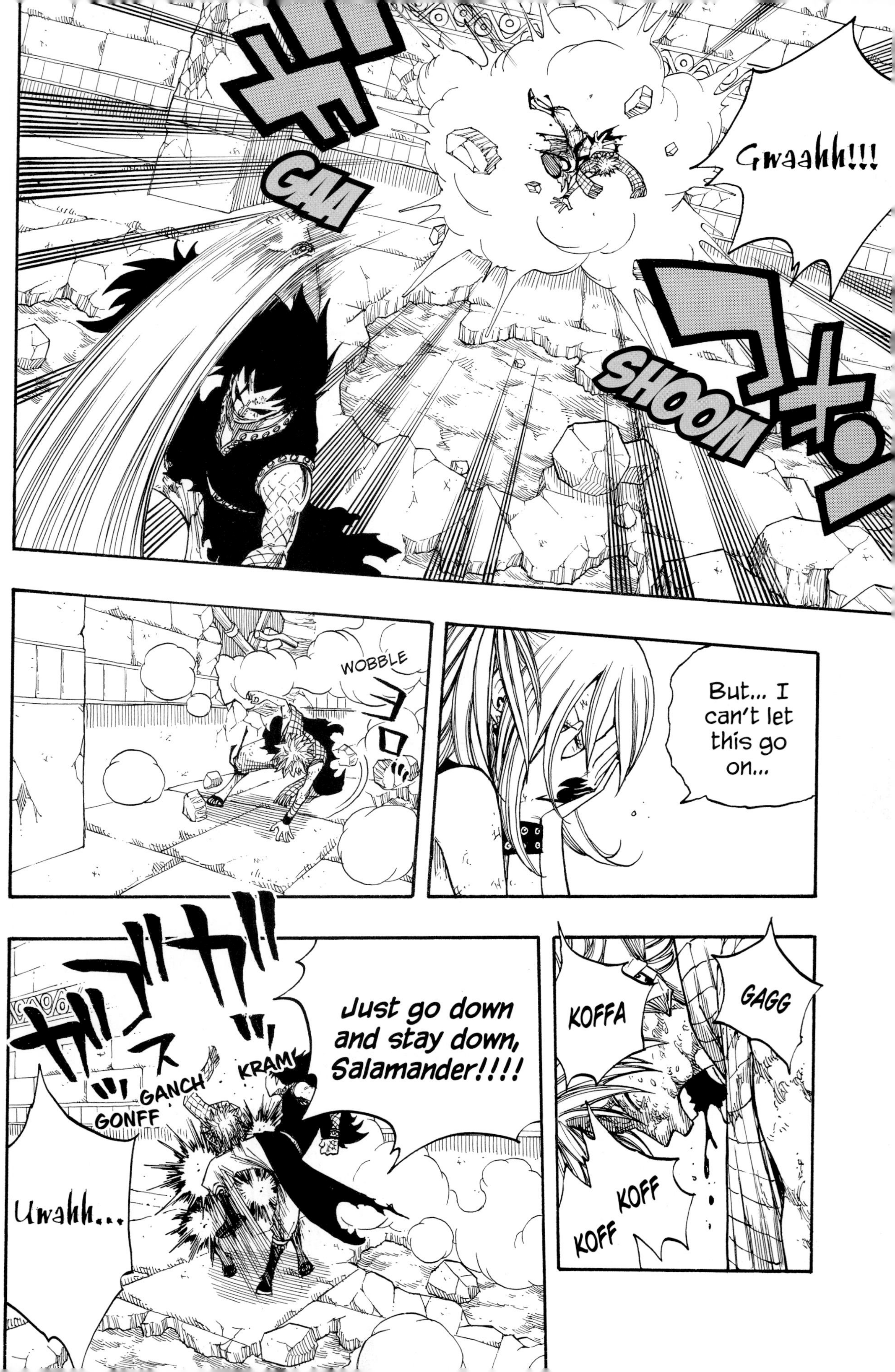
Gwaahh!!!
SHOOM
GAA
But... I can't let this go on...
WOBBLE
GAGG
KOFFA
KOFF
KOFF
Just go down and stay down, Salamander!!!!
KRAM
GANCH
GONFF
Uwahh...

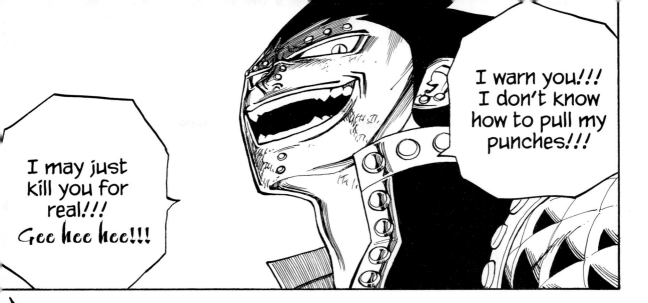

I warn you!!! I don't know how to pull my punches!!!
I may just kill you for real!!! Gee hee hee!!!
He destroyed Jupiter, and he took on your Element Four!!!
He's used up his magical powers!!!
If he could only eat some fire, Natsu would never lose!!!
……
!
Now I see...
SST
It seems we've had a bit of a miscommunication between us. Moshi-moshi.
GRN GRN

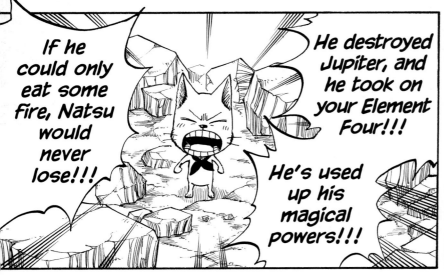

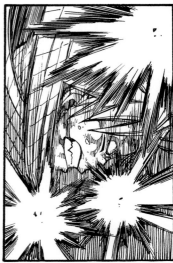

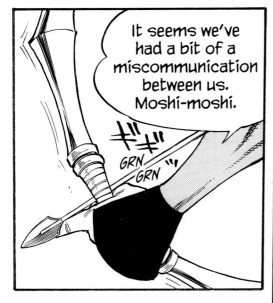

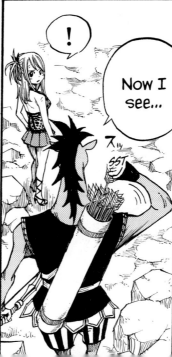

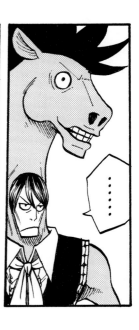

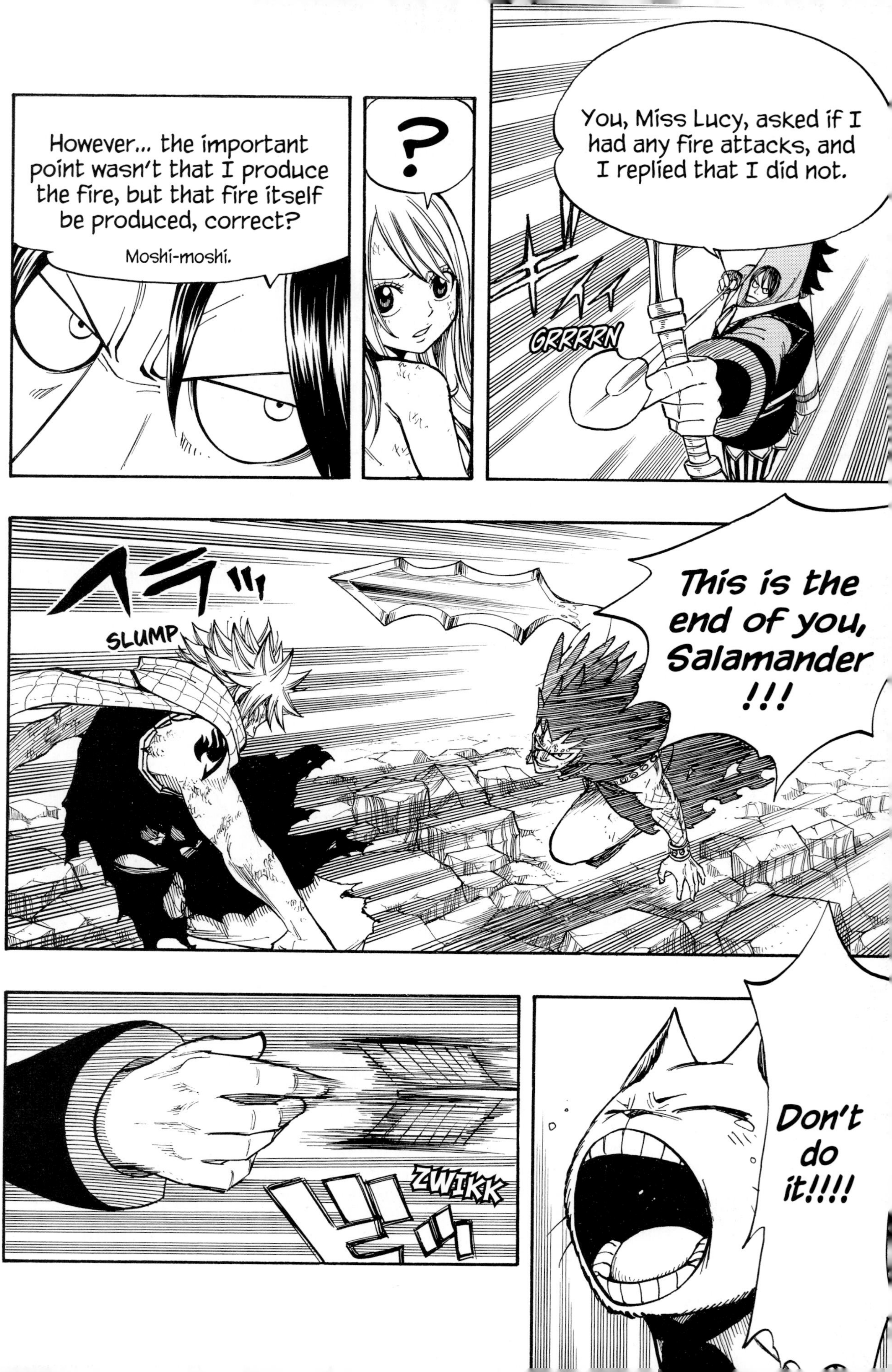
You, Miss Lucy, asked if I had any fire attacks, and I replied that I did not.
GRRRRN
?
However... the important point wasn't that I produce the fire, but that fire itself be produced, correct?
Moshi-moshi.
This is the end of you, Salamander !!!
SLUMP
Don't do it!!!!
ZWIKK

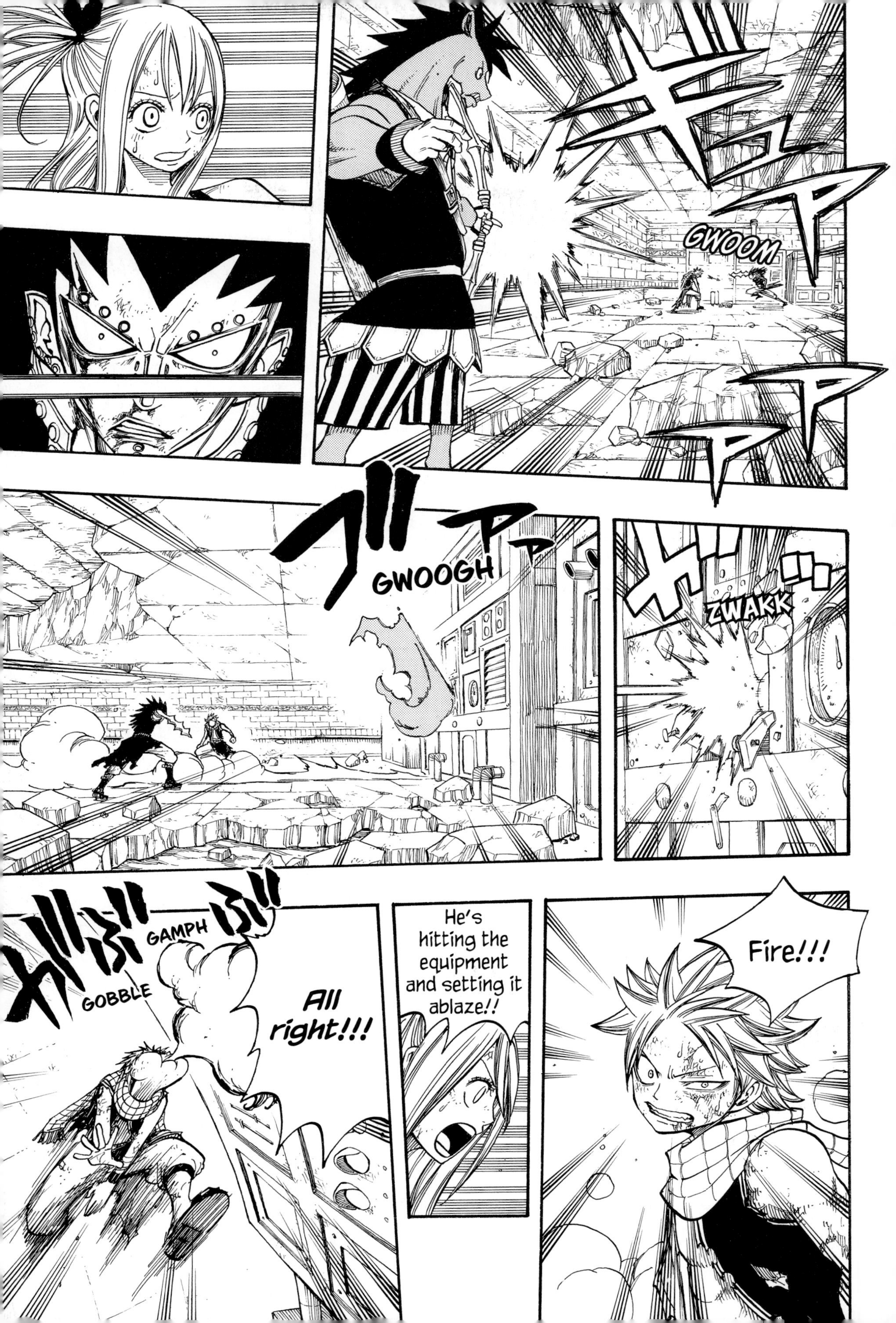
GWOOM
ZWAKK
GWOOGH
Fire!!!
He's hitting the equipment and setting it ablaze!!
All right!!!
GAMPH
GOBBLE

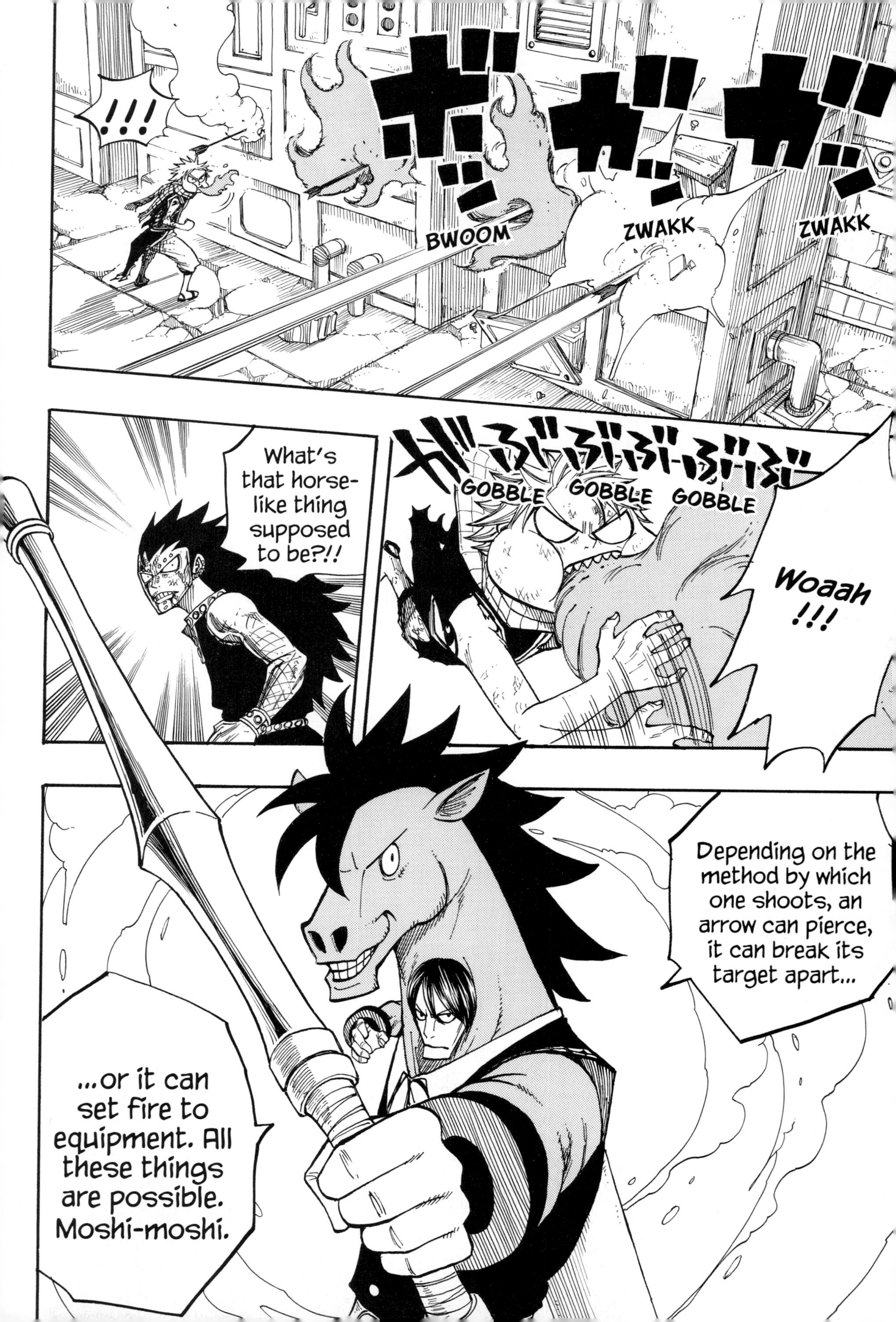
ZWAKK
ZWAKK
BWOOM
!!!
GOBBLE GOBBLE GOBBLE
Woaah !!!
What's that horse-like thing supposed to be?!!
Depending on the method by which one shoots, an arrow can pierce, it can break its target apart...
...or it can set fire to equipment. All these things are possible. Moshi-moshi.

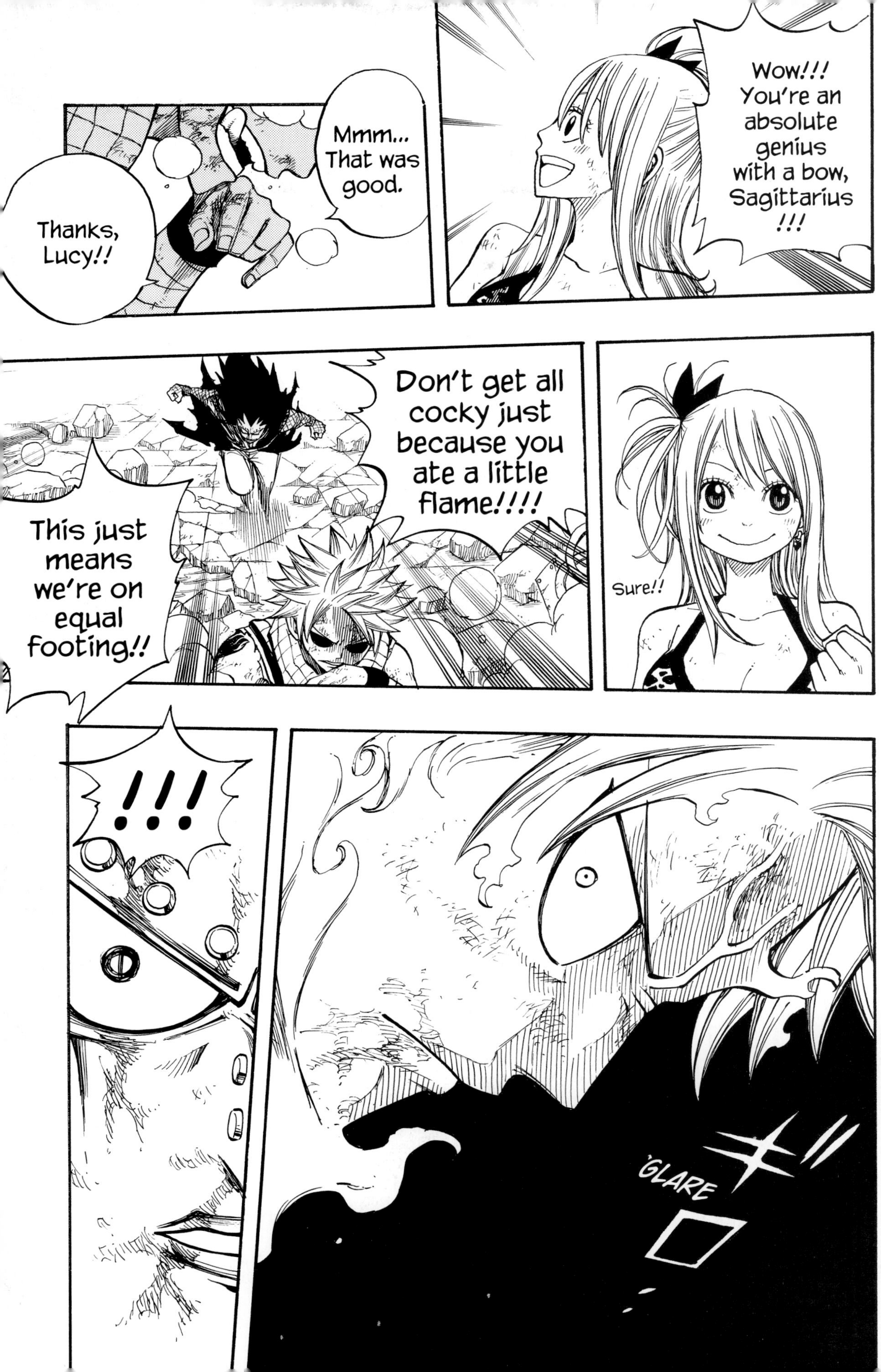
Wow!!! You're an absolute genius with a bow, Sagittarius !!!
Mmm... That was good.
Thanks, Lucy!!
Sure!!
Don't get all cocky just because you ate a little flame!!!!
This just means we're on equal footing!!
GLARE
!!!

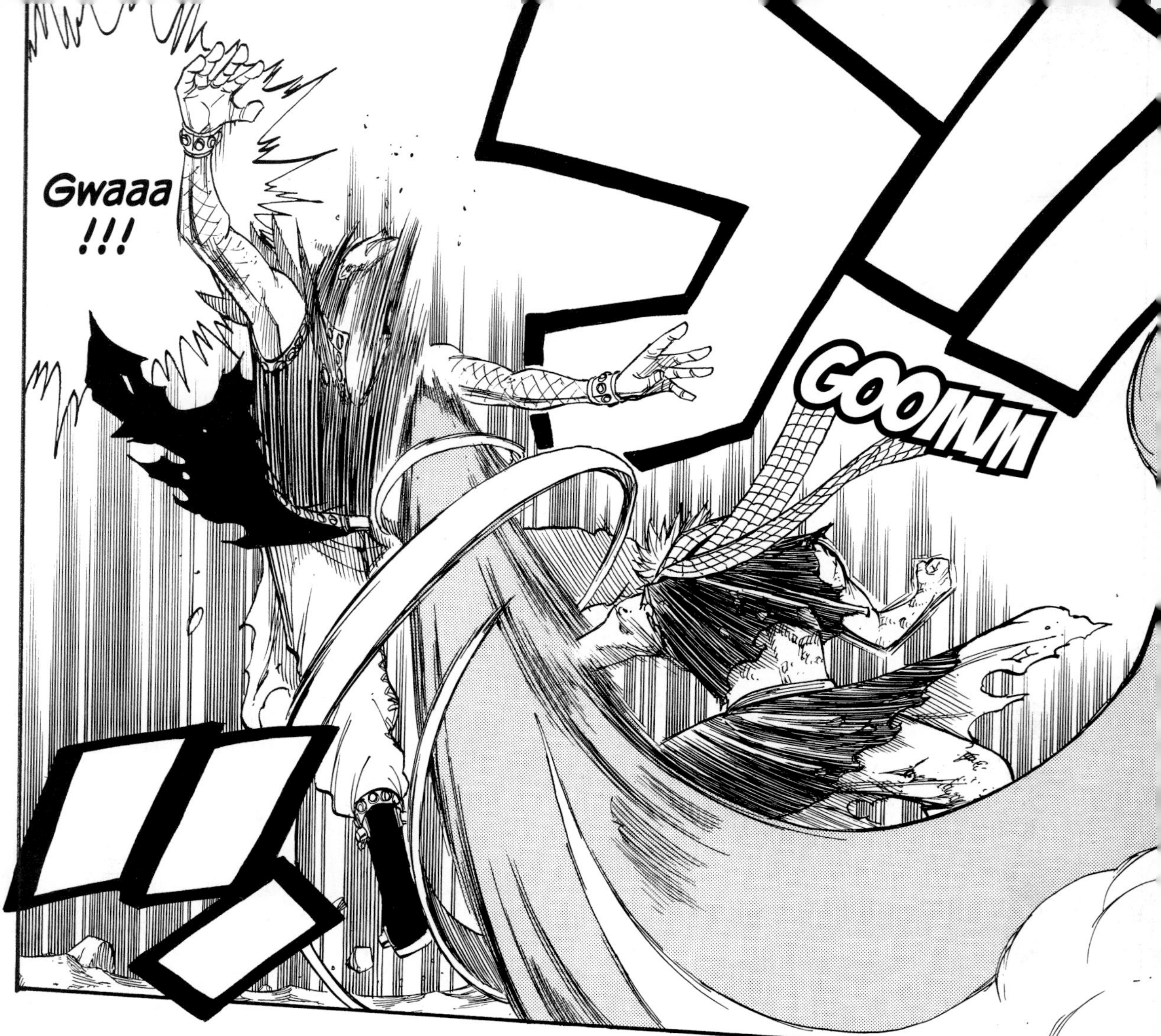
Gwaaa !!!
GOOMM
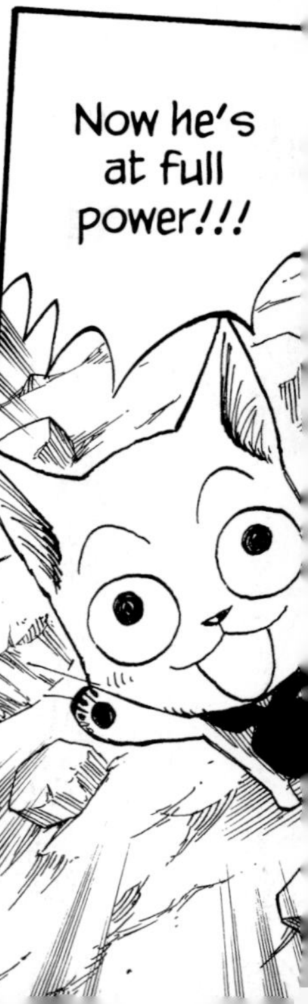
Now he's at full power!!!
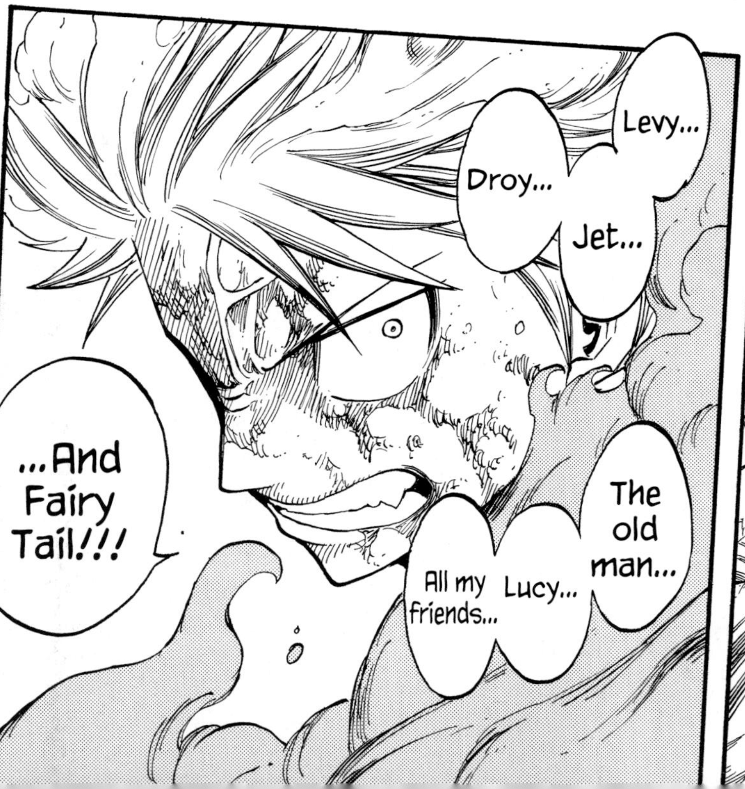
Levy...
Droy...
Jet...
The old man...
Lucy...
All my friends...
...And Fairy Tail!!!
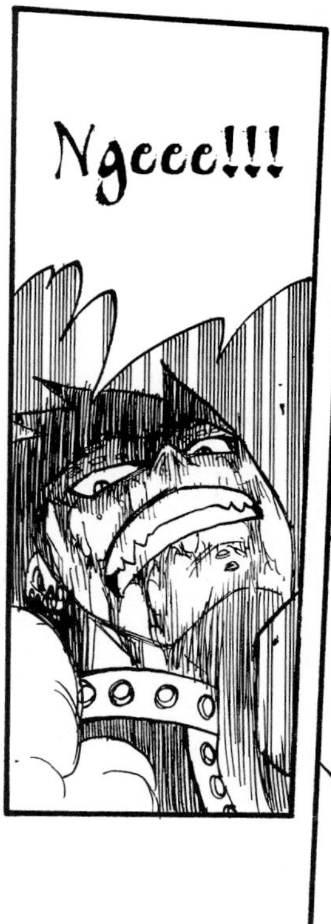
Ngeee!!!

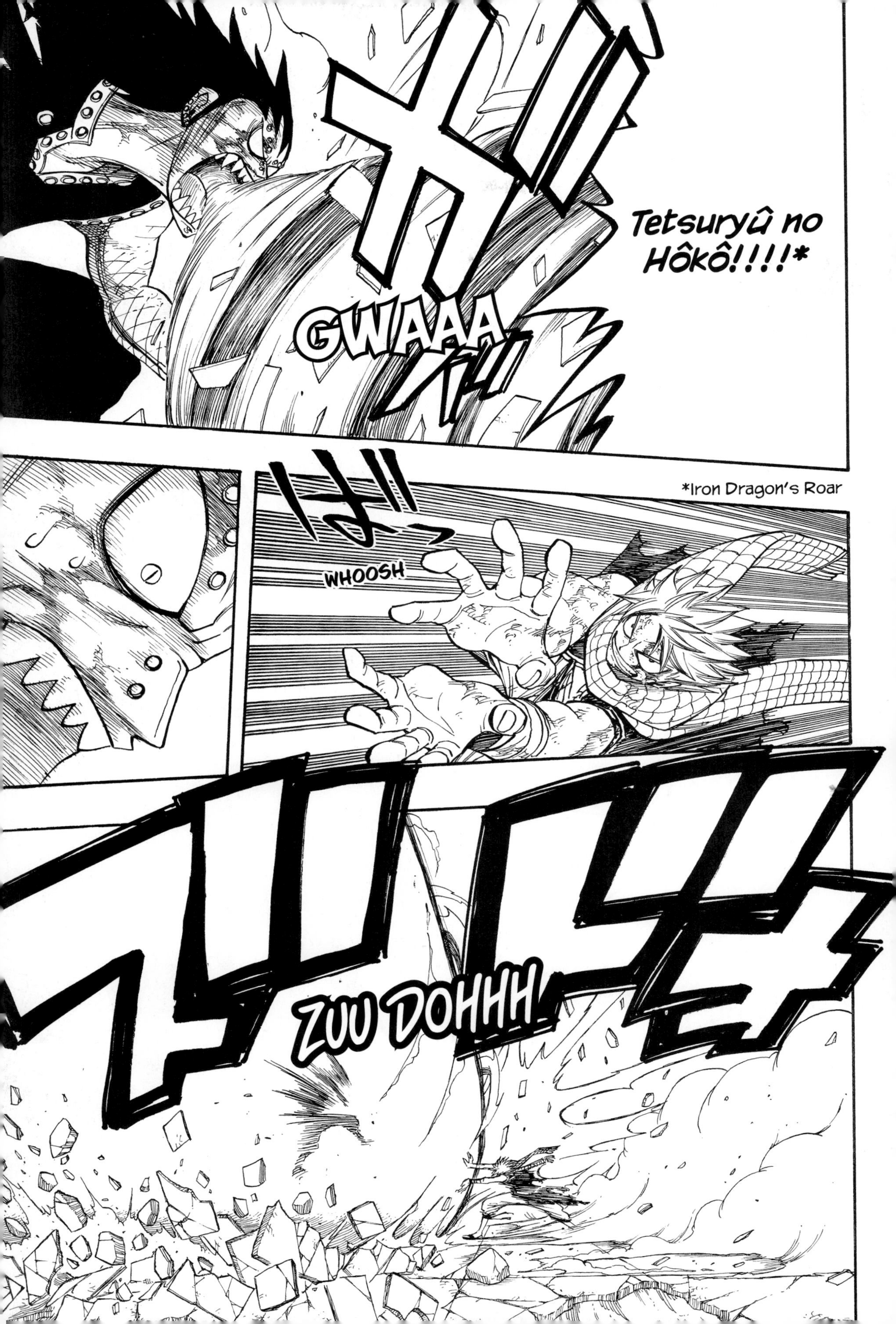
Tetsuryû no Hôkô!!!!*
GWAAA
*Iron Dragon's Roar
WHOOSH
ZUU DOHHH

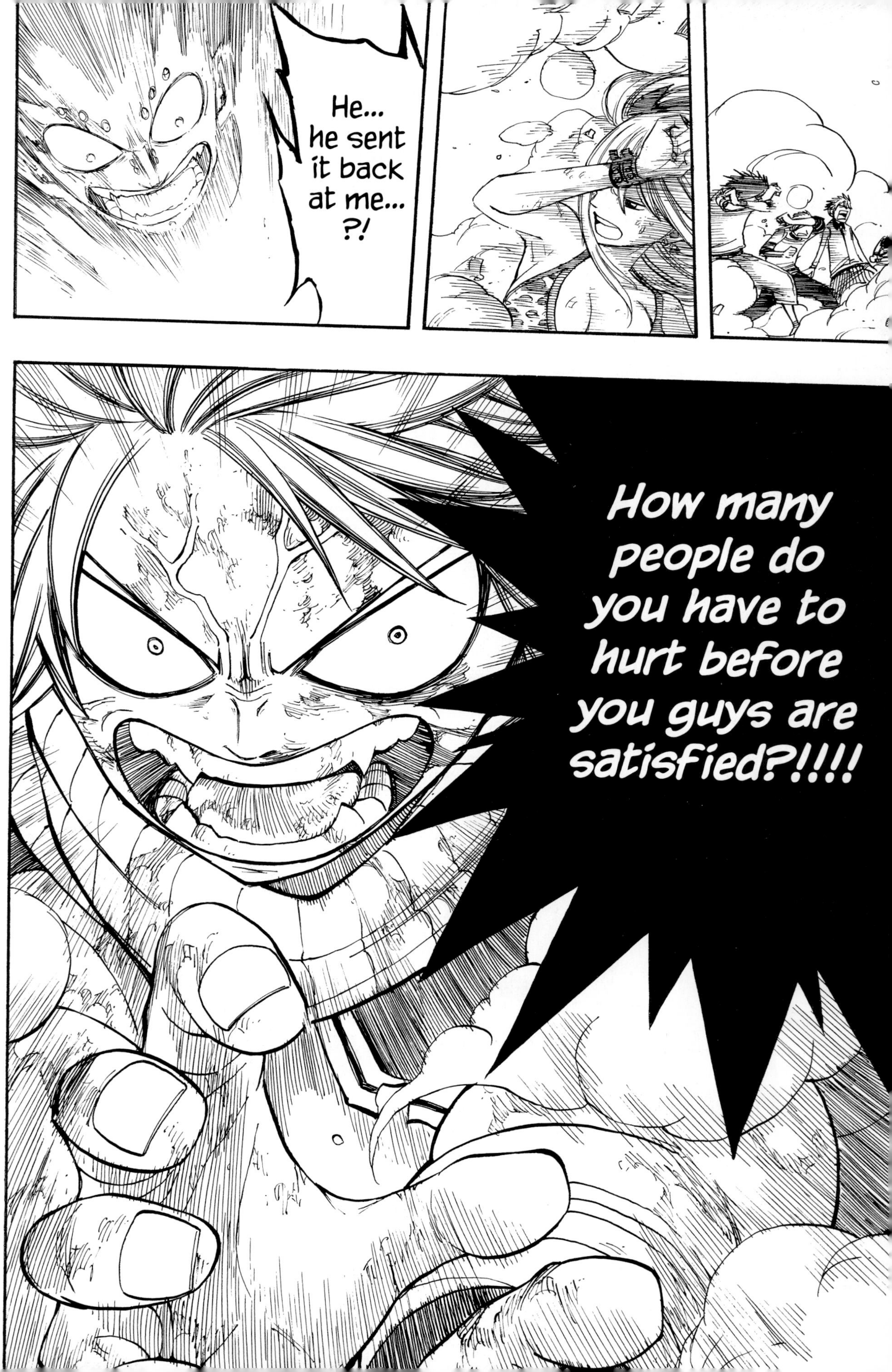
He... he sent it back at me...?!
How many people do you have to hurt before you guys are satisfied?!!!!

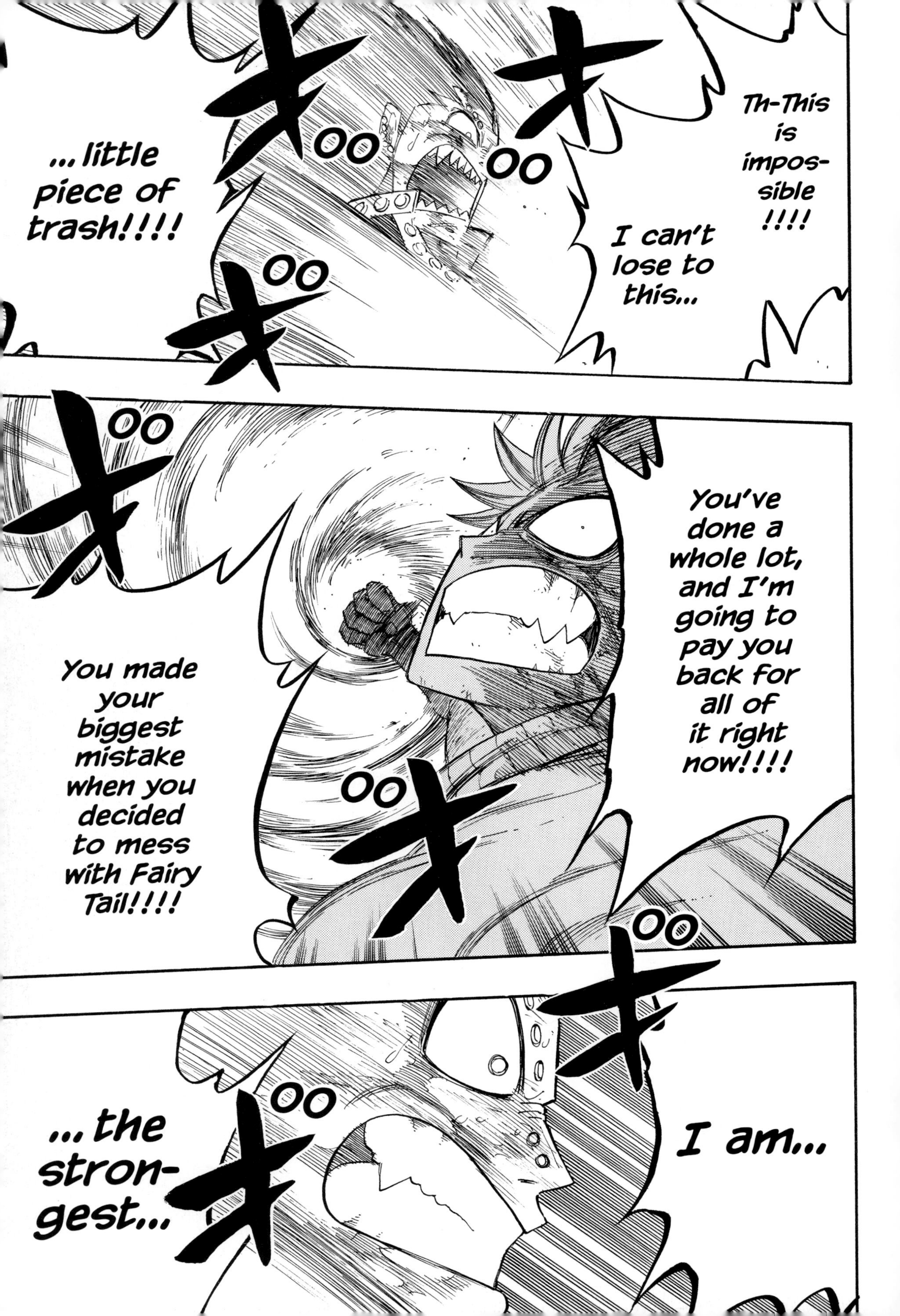
Th-This is impossible!!!!
I can't lose to this...
OO
OO
...little piece of trash!!!!
OO
OO
You've done a whole lot, and I'm going to pay you back for all of it right now!!!!
OO
You made your biggest mistake when you decided to mess with Fairy Tail!!!!
OO
I am...
OO
...the strongest...

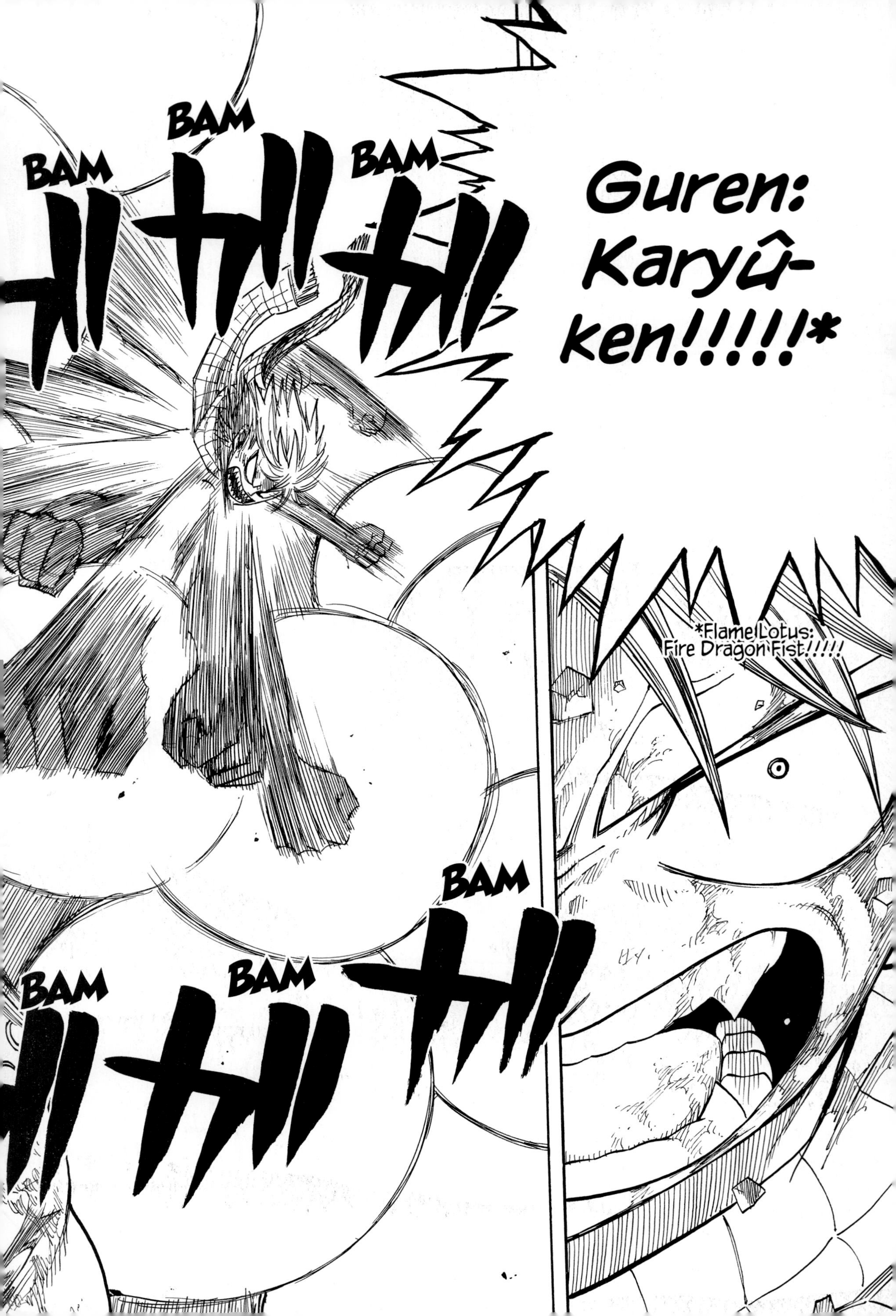
Guren: Karyû-ken!!!!!!*
*Flame Lotus: Fire Dragon Fist!!!!!!
BAM
BAM
BAM
BAM
BAM
BAM

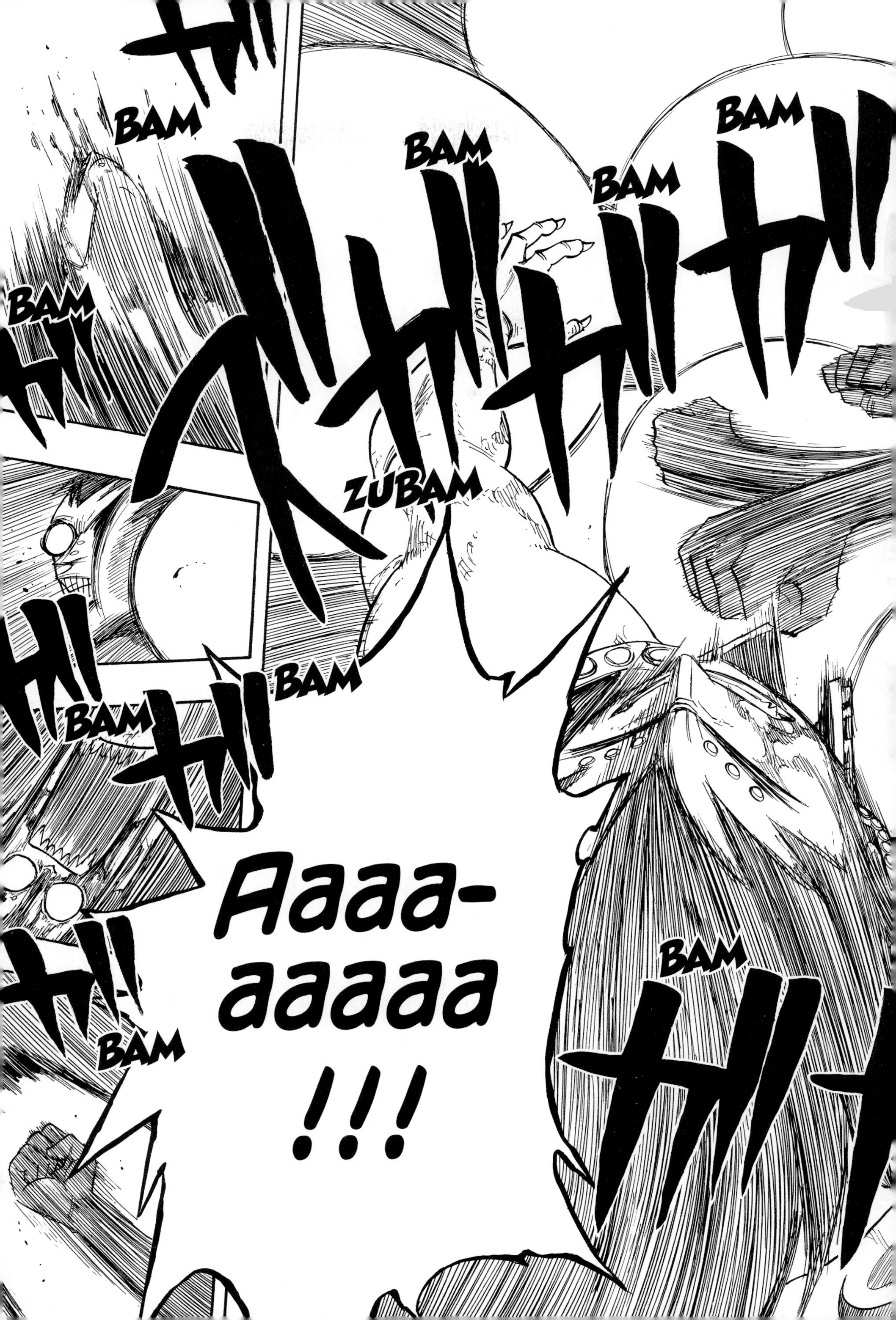
BAM
BAM
BAM
BAM
BAM
ZUBAM
BAM
BAM
BAM
Aaaa-aaaaaa!!!
BAM
BAM

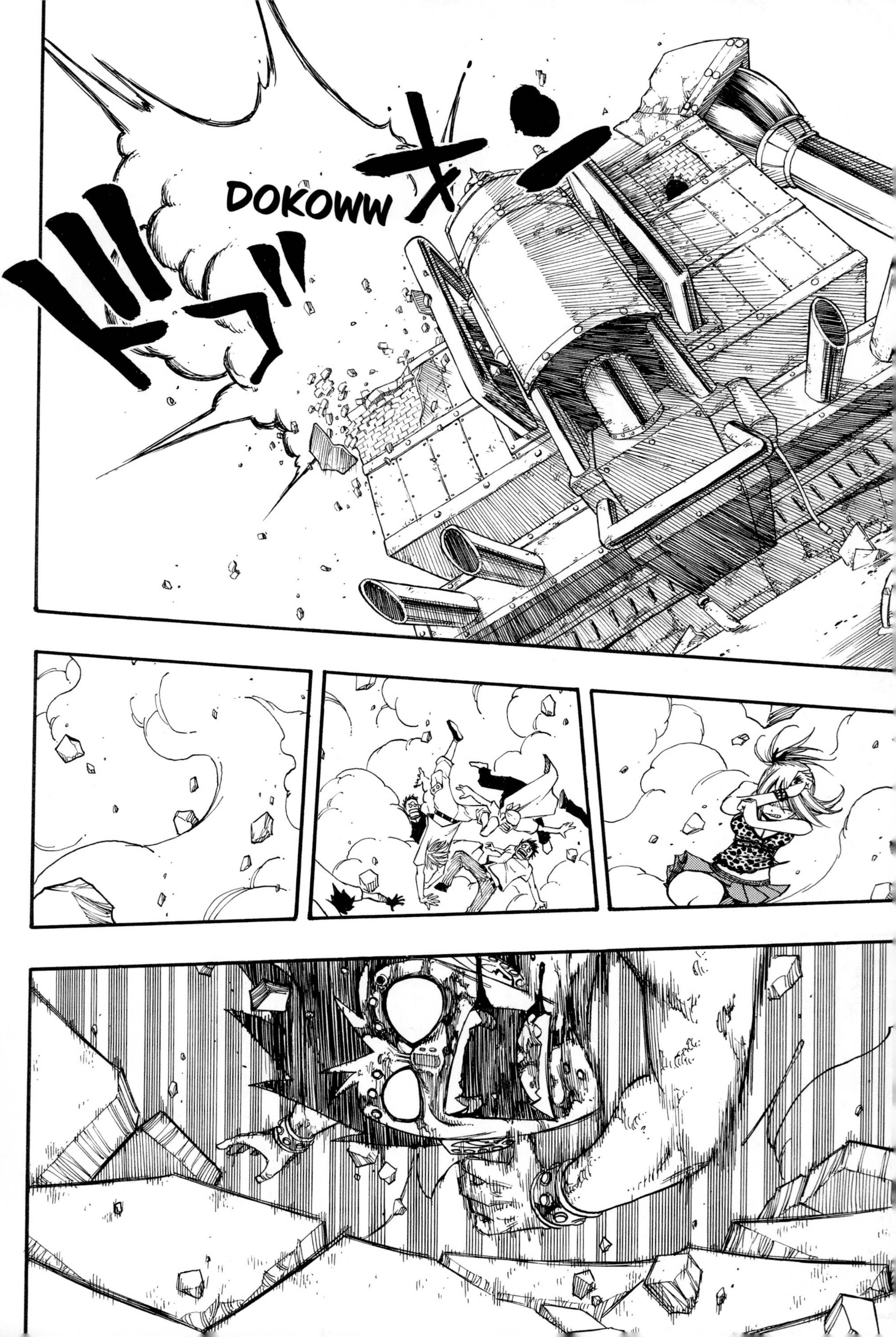
ドゴォ
DOKOWW

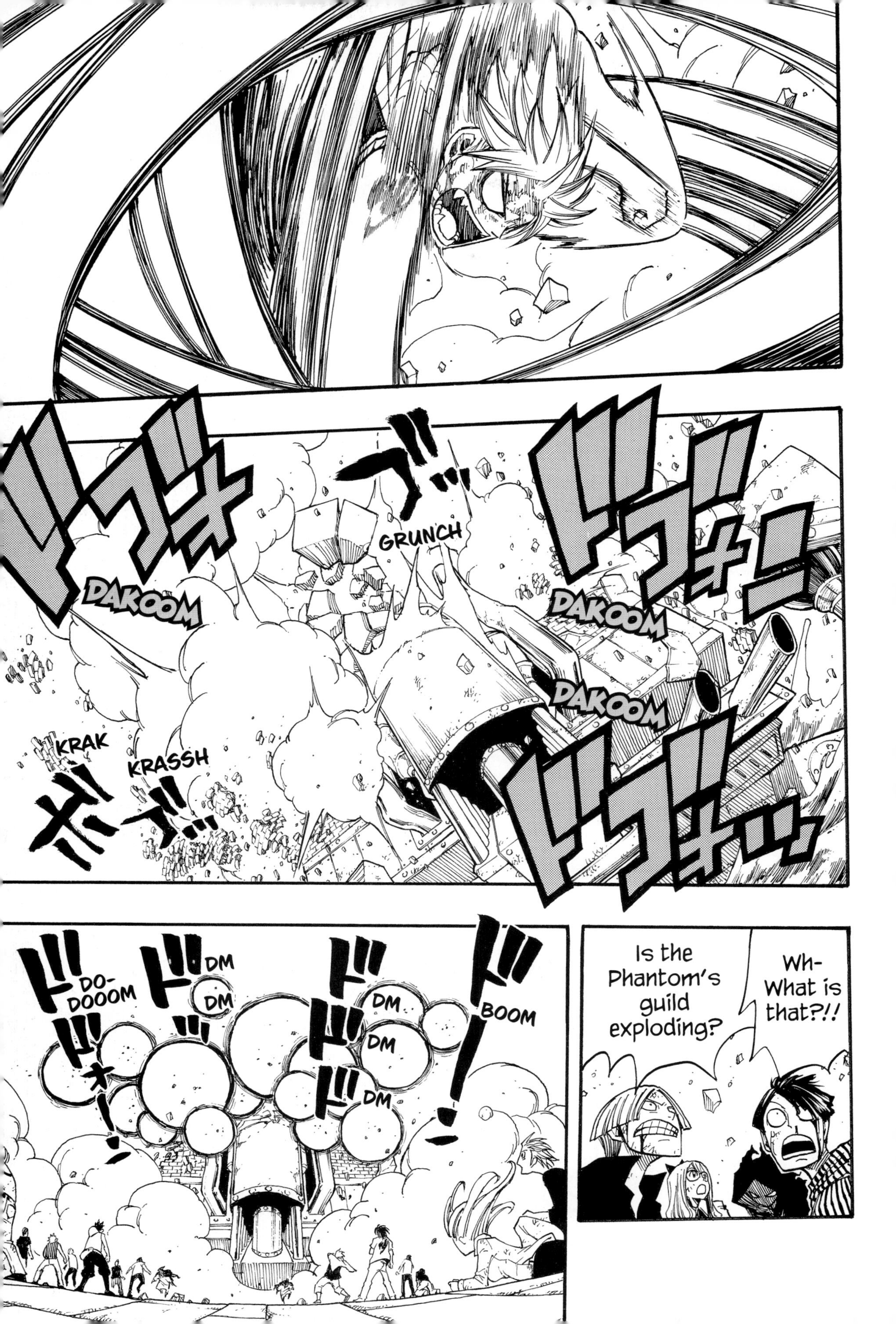
DAKOOM
DAKOOM
GRUNCH
DAKOOM
KRASSH
KRAK
Wh- What is that?!!
Is the Phantom's guild exploding?
BOOM
DM
DM
DM
DM
DM
DO-DOOOM

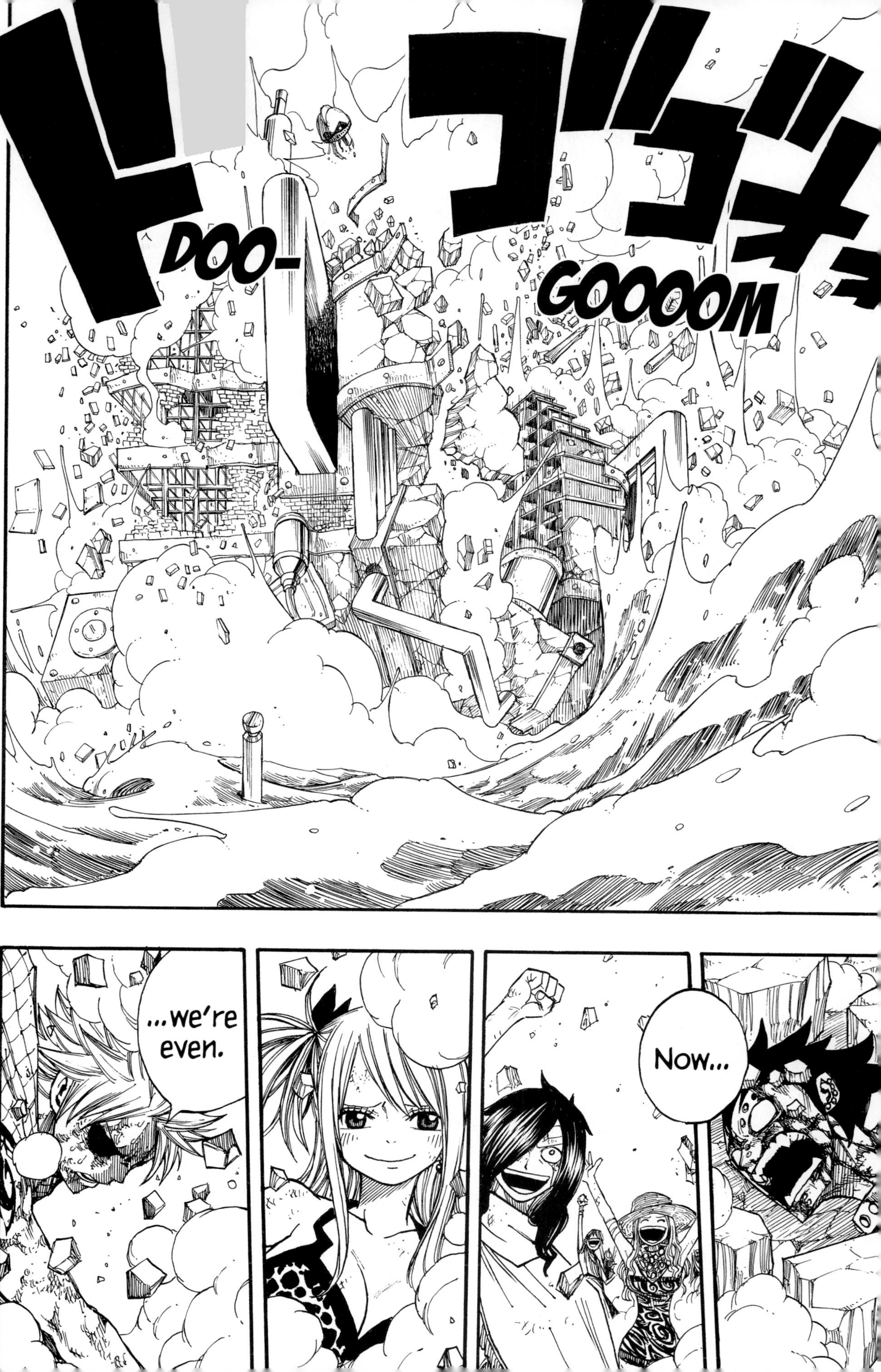
DOO-
GOOOOM
Now...
...we're
even.

FAIRY TAIL

Chapter 64:
The Best Guild

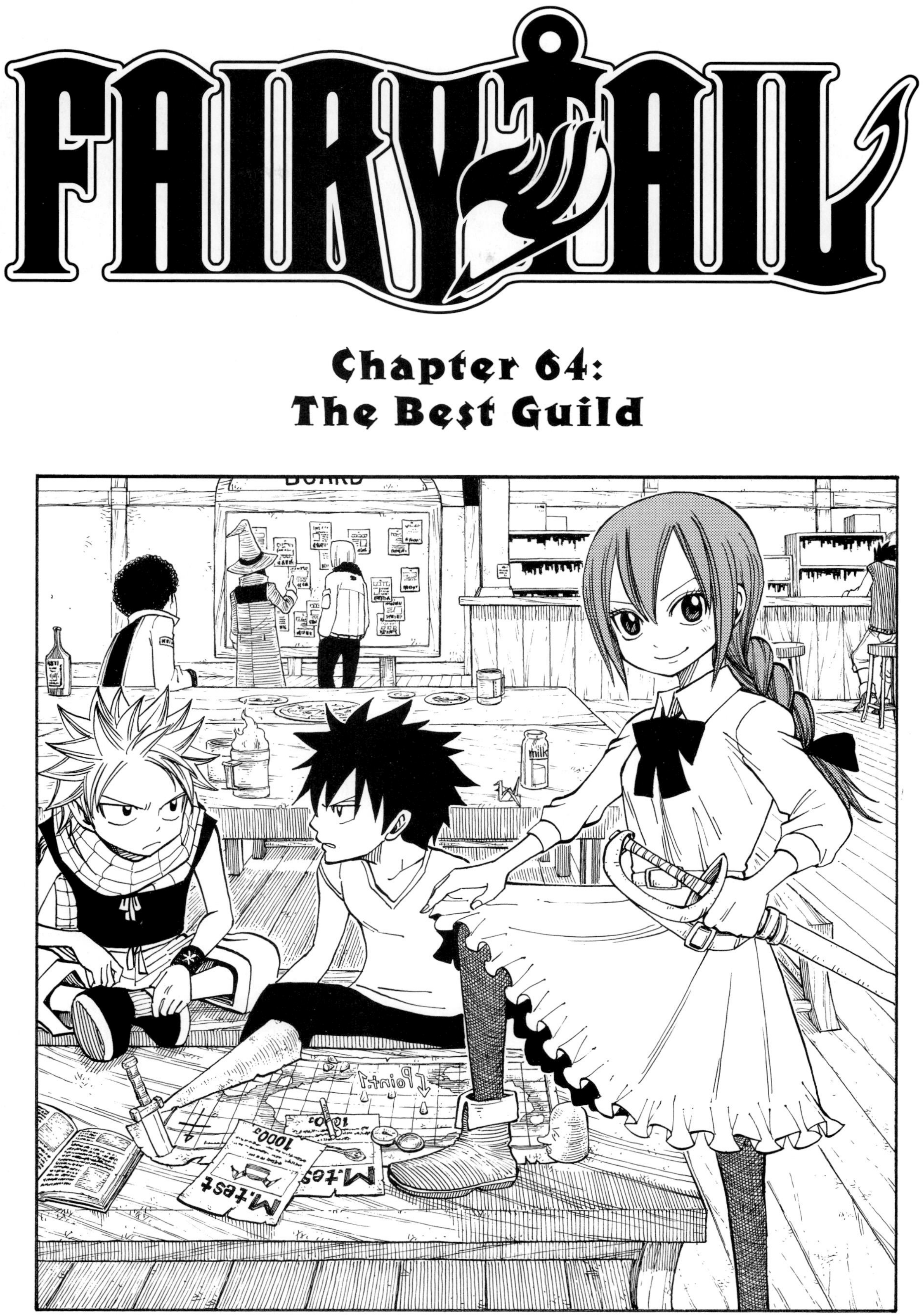

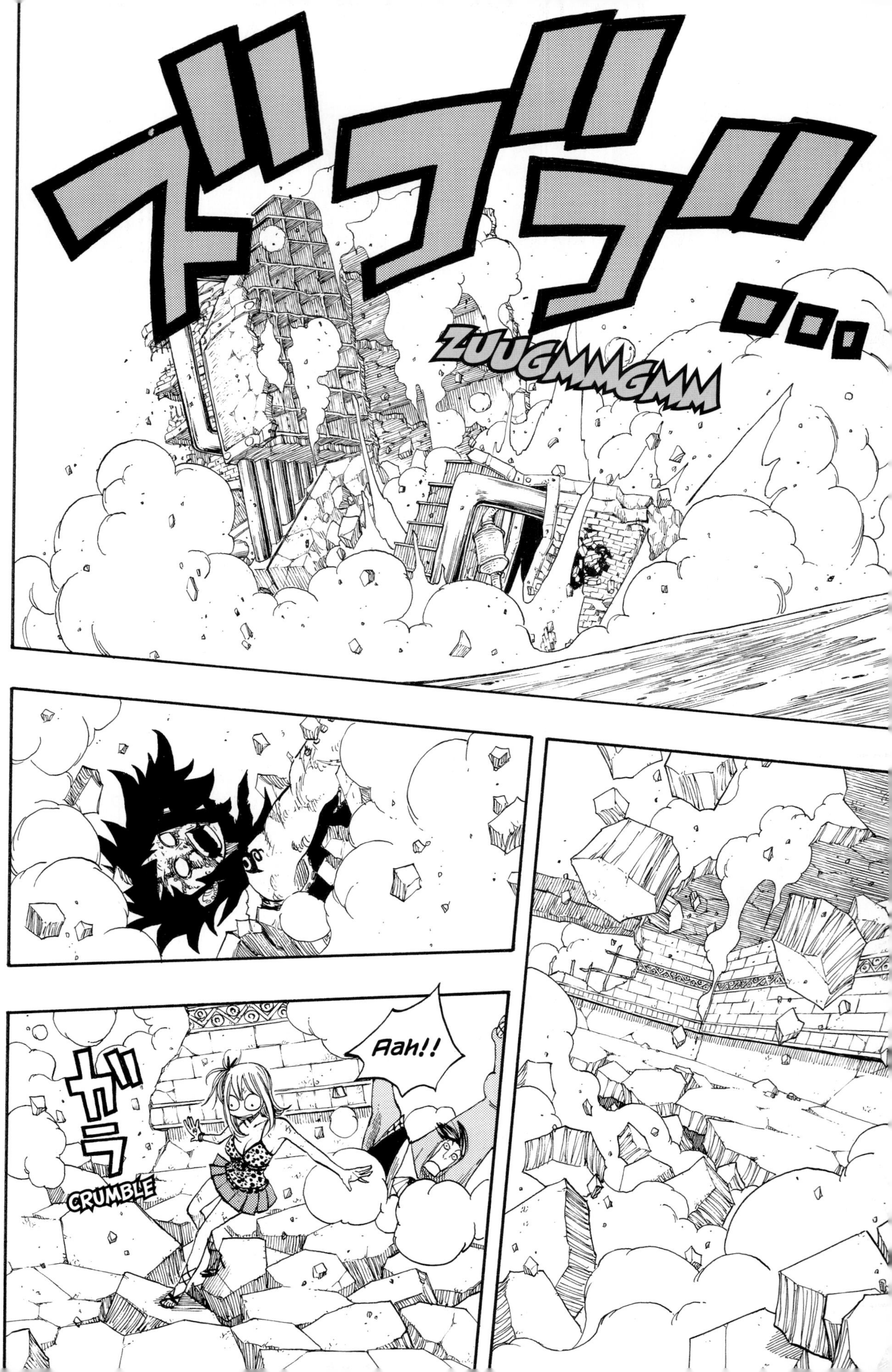
ズゴゴゴ…
ZUUGMMGMM
Aah!!
ガラ
CRUMBLE

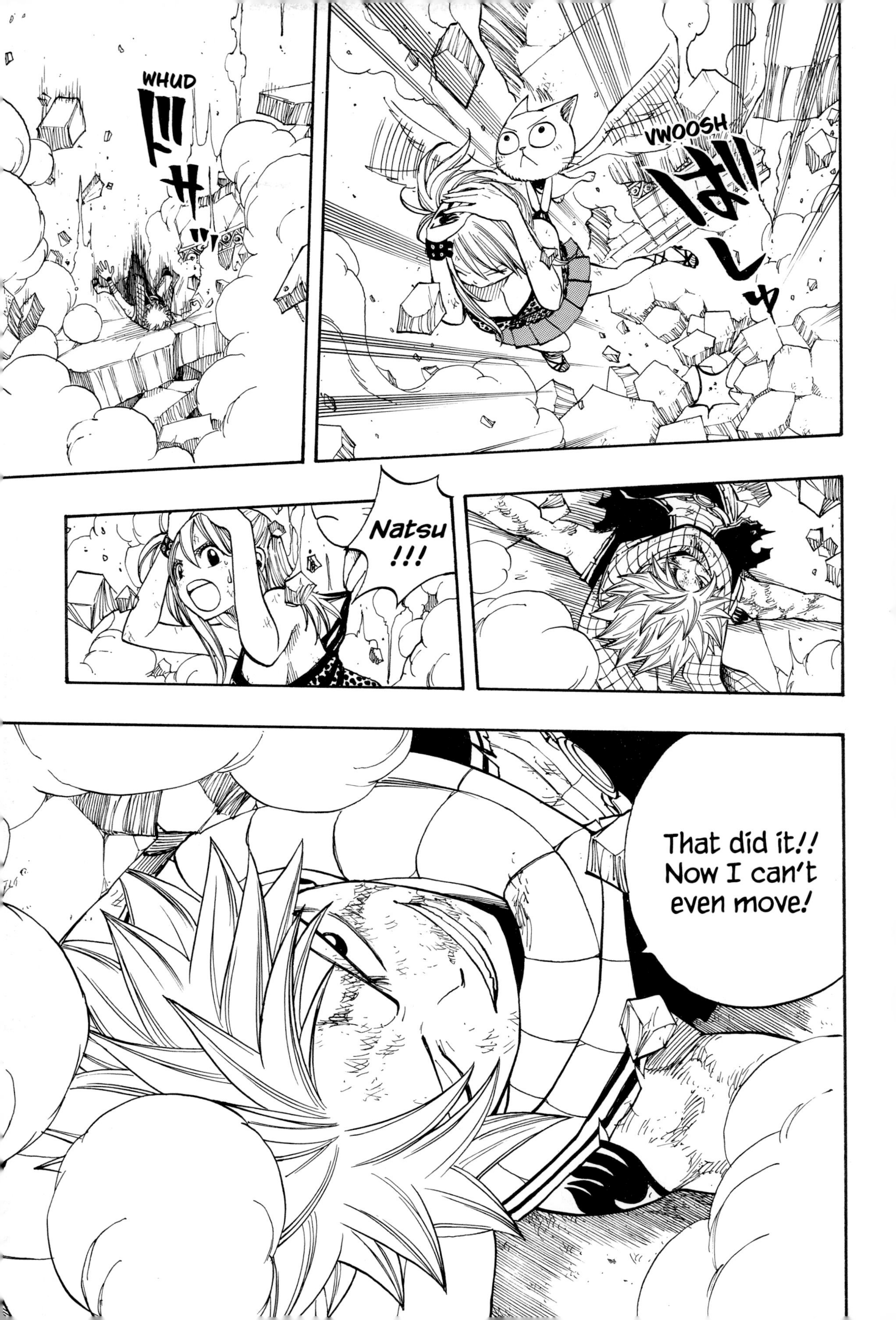
VWOOSH
ばしゅ
WHUD
ドサッ
Natsu!!!
That did it!! Now I can't even move!

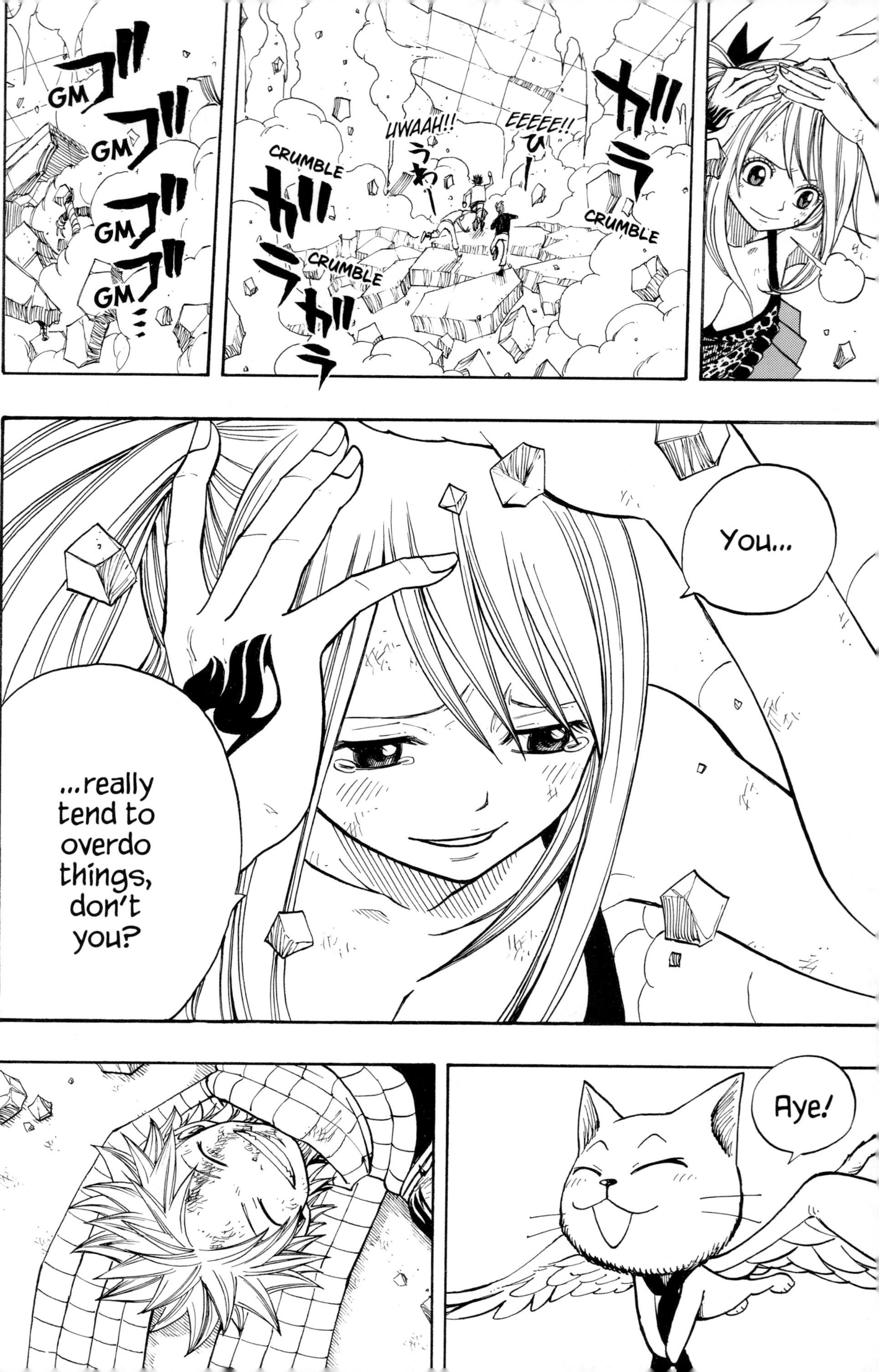
ガラ
CRUMBLE
EEEEE!!
ひー
UWAAH!!
うわー
CRUMBLE
ガラ
CRUMBLE
ガラ
GM
ゴ
GM
ゴ
GM
ゴ
GM
ゴ
You...
...really tend to overdo things, don't you?
Aye!

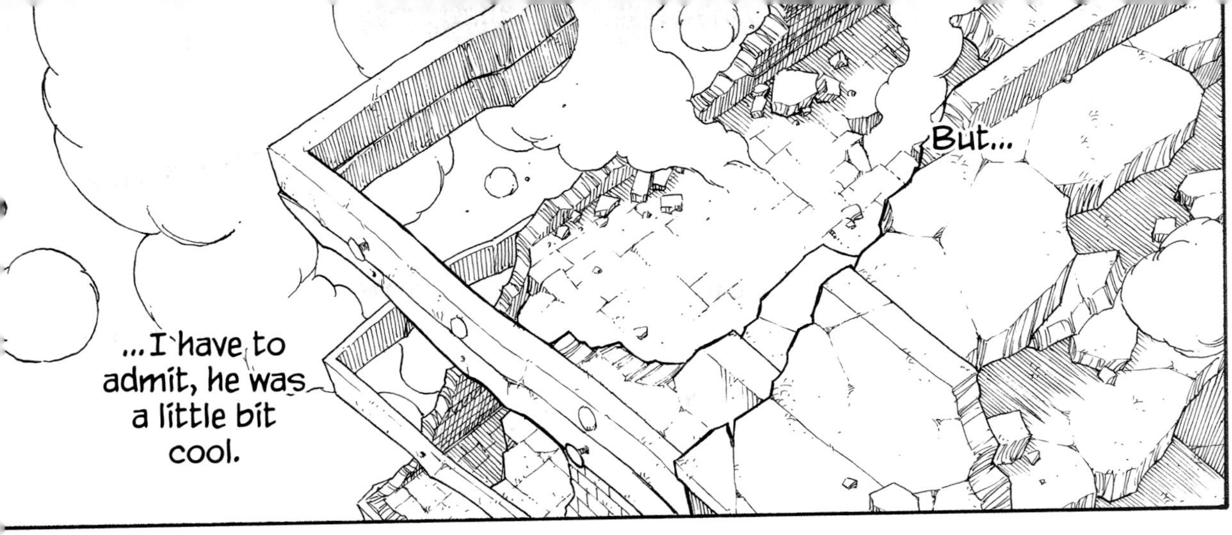
But...
...I have to admit, he was a little bit cool.

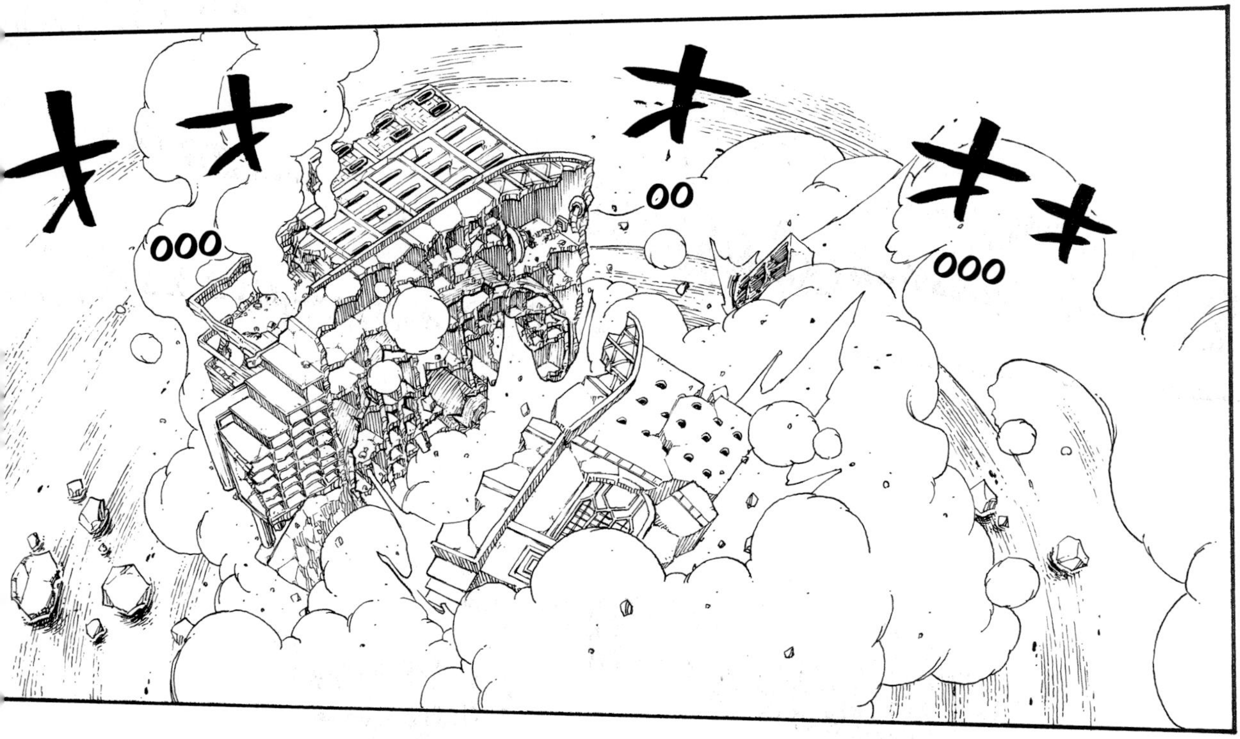
ooo
oo
ooo

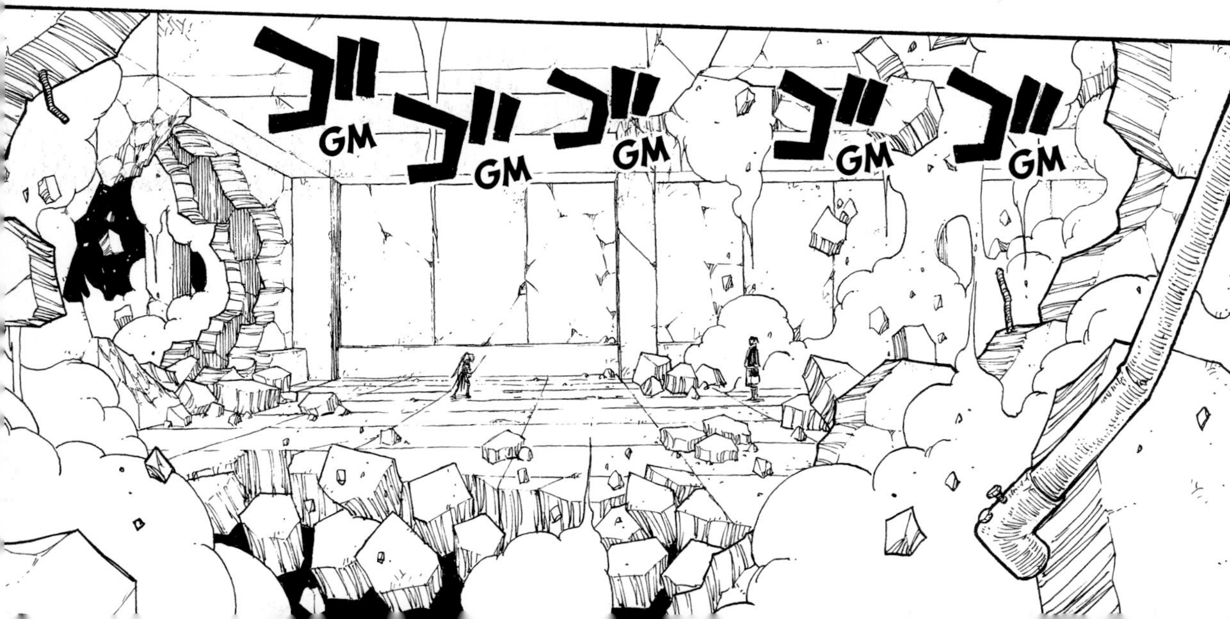
GM
GM
GM
GM
GM

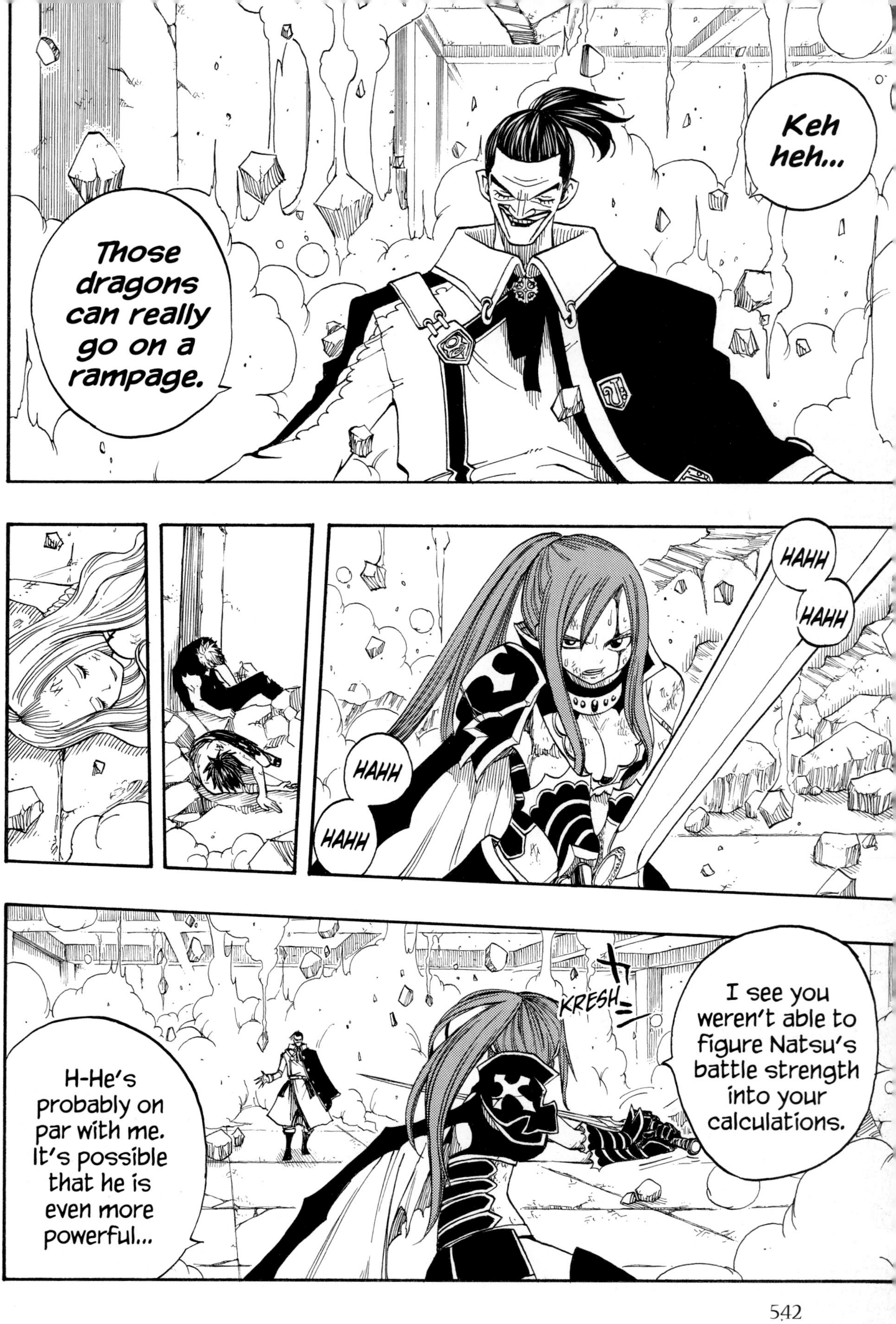
Keh heh...
Those dragons can really go on a rampage.
HAHH
HAHH
HAHH
HAHH
I see you weren't able to figure Natsu's battle strength into your calculations.
KRESH
H-He's probably on par with me. It's possible that he is even more powerful...

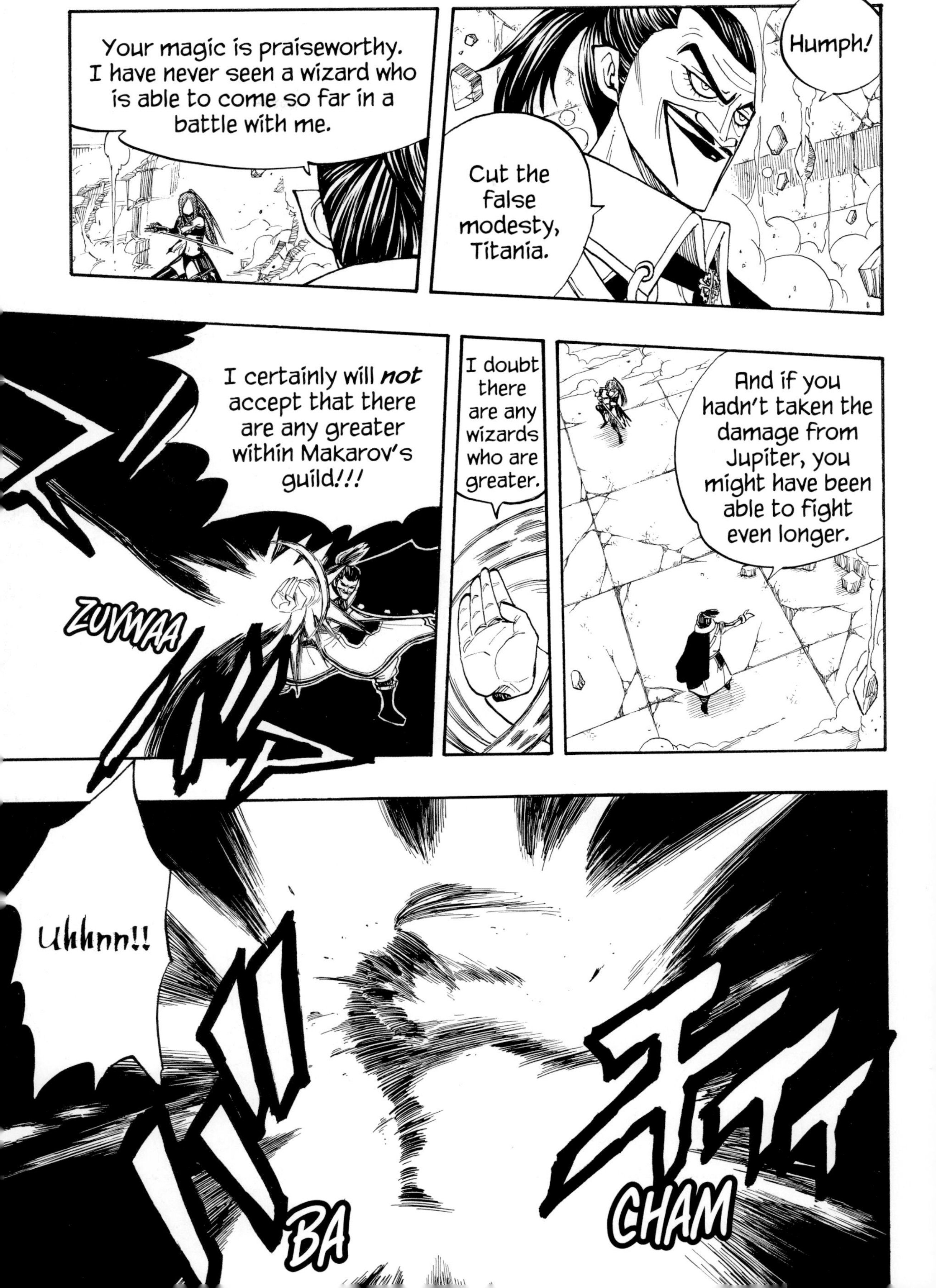
Humph!
Cut the false modesty, Titania.
Your magic is praiseworthy. I have never seen a wizard who is able to come so far in a battle with me.
And if you hadn't taken the damage from Jupiter, you might have been able to fight even longer.
I doubt there are any wizards who are greater.
I certainly will *not* accept that there are any greater within Makarov's guild!!!
ZUVWAA
Uhhnn!!
CHAM
BA

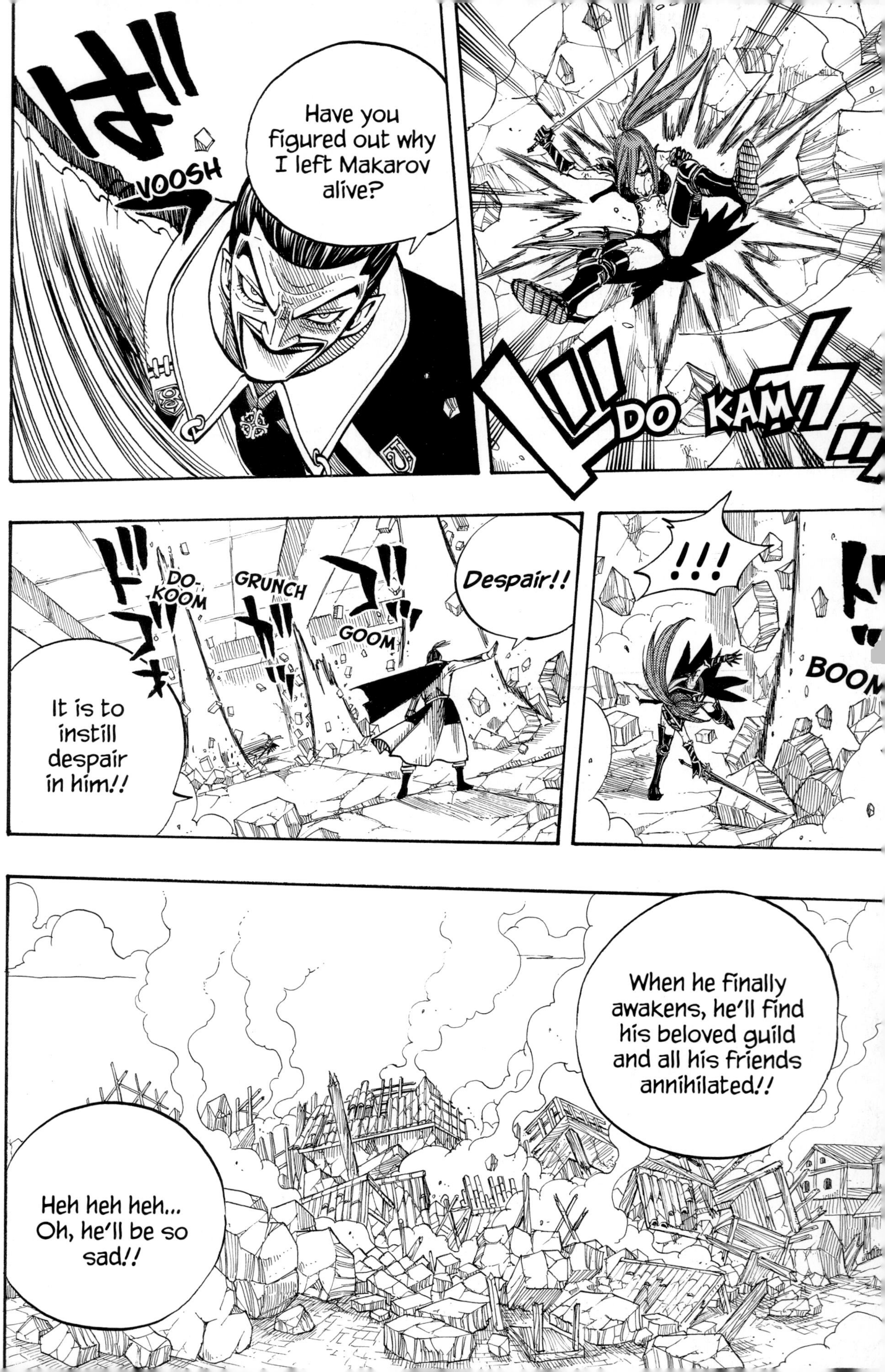
DO KAM
VOOSH
Have you figured out why I left Makarov alive?
!!!
BOOM
Despair!!
GOOM
GRUNCH
DO-KOOM
It is to instill despair in him!!
When he finally awakens, he'll find his beloved guild and all his friends annihilated!!
Heh heh heh... Oh, he'll be so sad!!

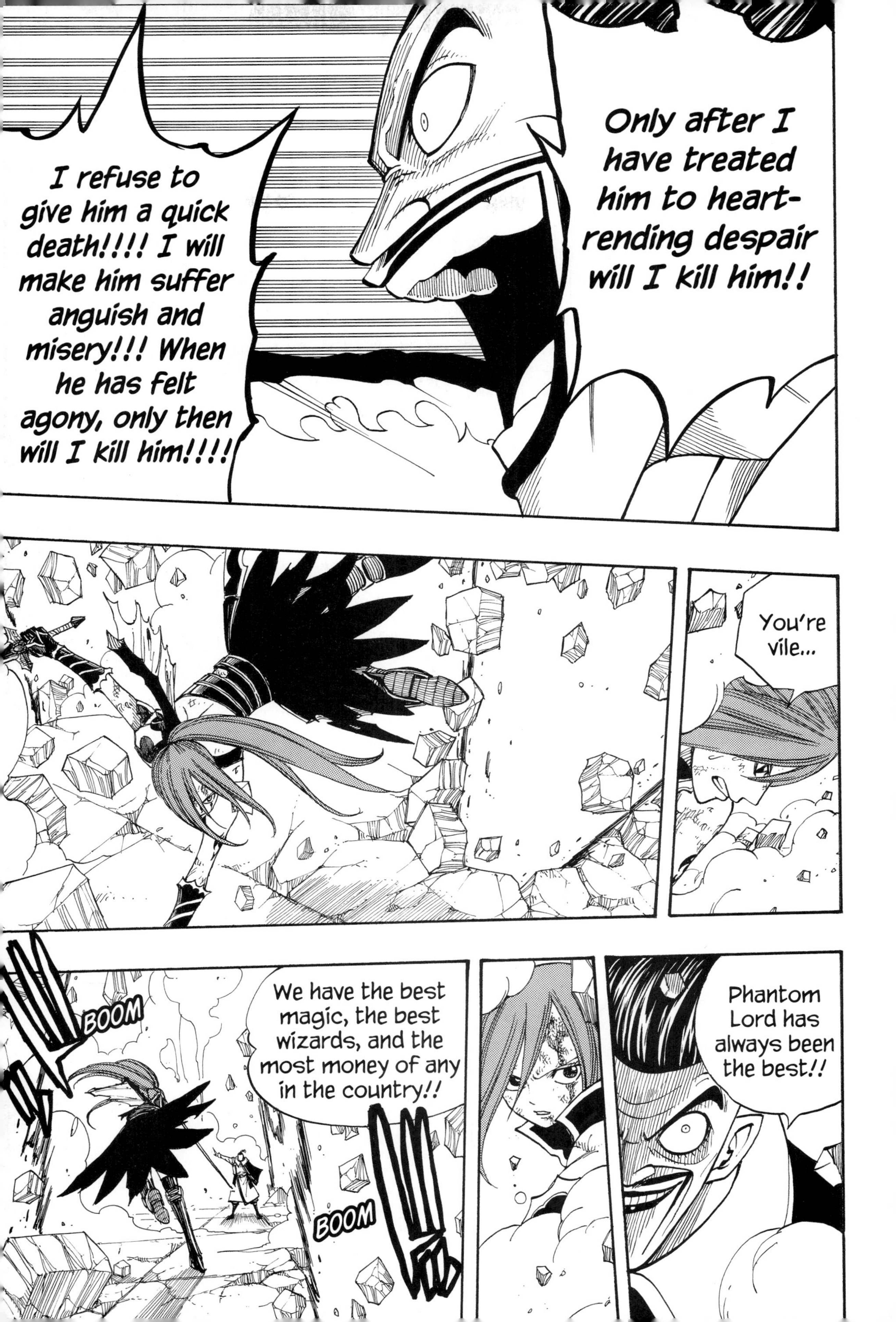
Only after I have treated him to heart-rending despair will I kill him!!
I refuse to give him a quick death!!!! I will make him suffer anguish and misery!!! When he has felt agony, only then will I kill him!!!!
You're vile...
Phantom Lord has always been the best!!
We have the best magic, the best wizards, and the most money of any in the country!!
BOOM
BOOM

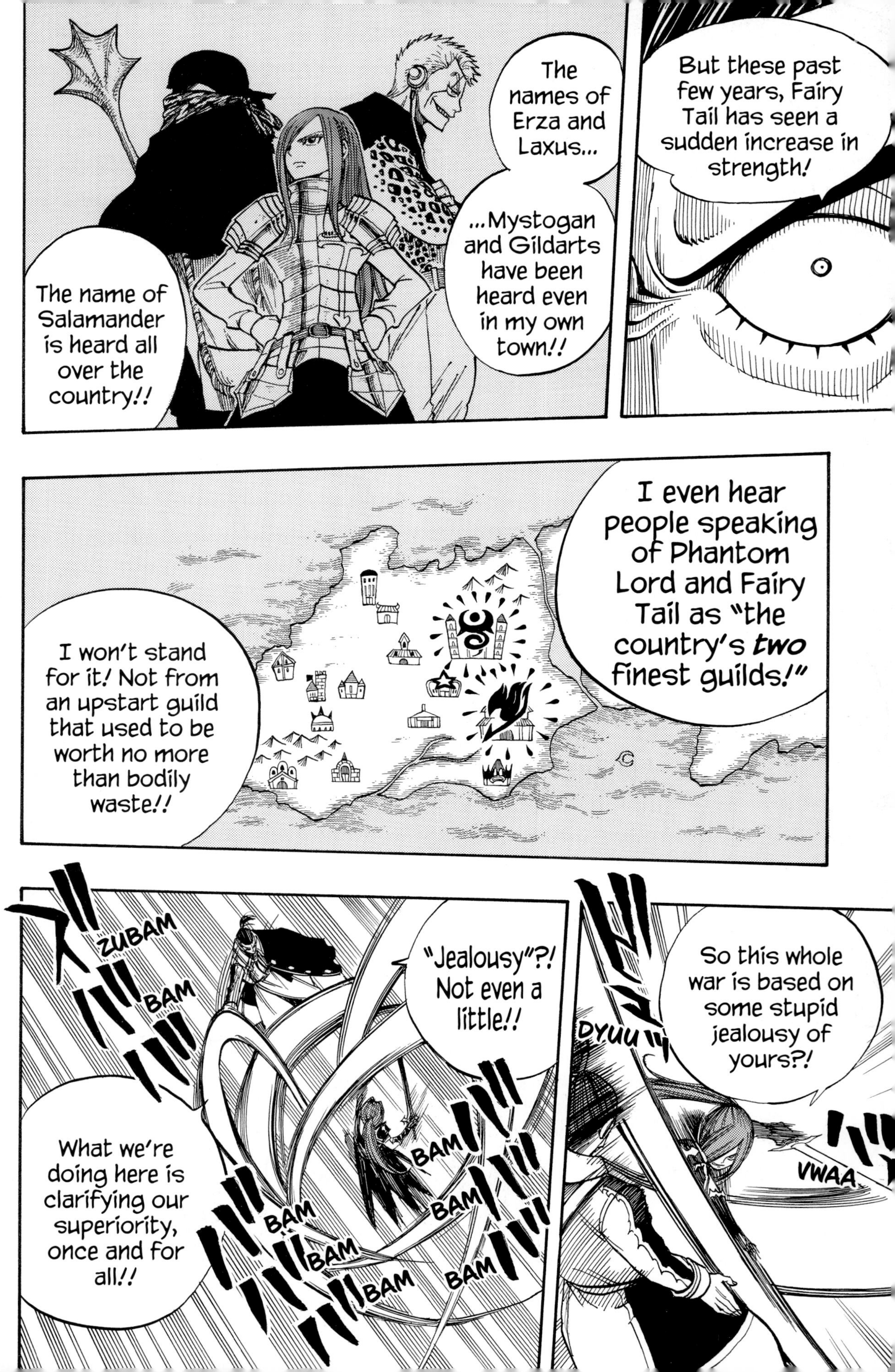
But these past few years, Fairy Tail has seen a sudden increase in strength!
The names of Erza and Laxus...
...Mystogan and Gildarts have been heard even in my own town!!
The name of Salamander is heard all over the country!!
I even hear people speaking of Phantom Lord and Fairy Tail as "the country's *two* finest guilds!"
I won't stand for it! Not from an upstart guild that used to be worth no more than bodily waste!!
DYUU
So this whole war is based on some stupid jealousy of yours?!
VWAA
ZUBAM
BAM
"Jealousy"?! Not even a little!!
BAM
BAM
BAM
BAM
BAM
BAM
What we're doing here is clarifying our superiority, once and for all!!

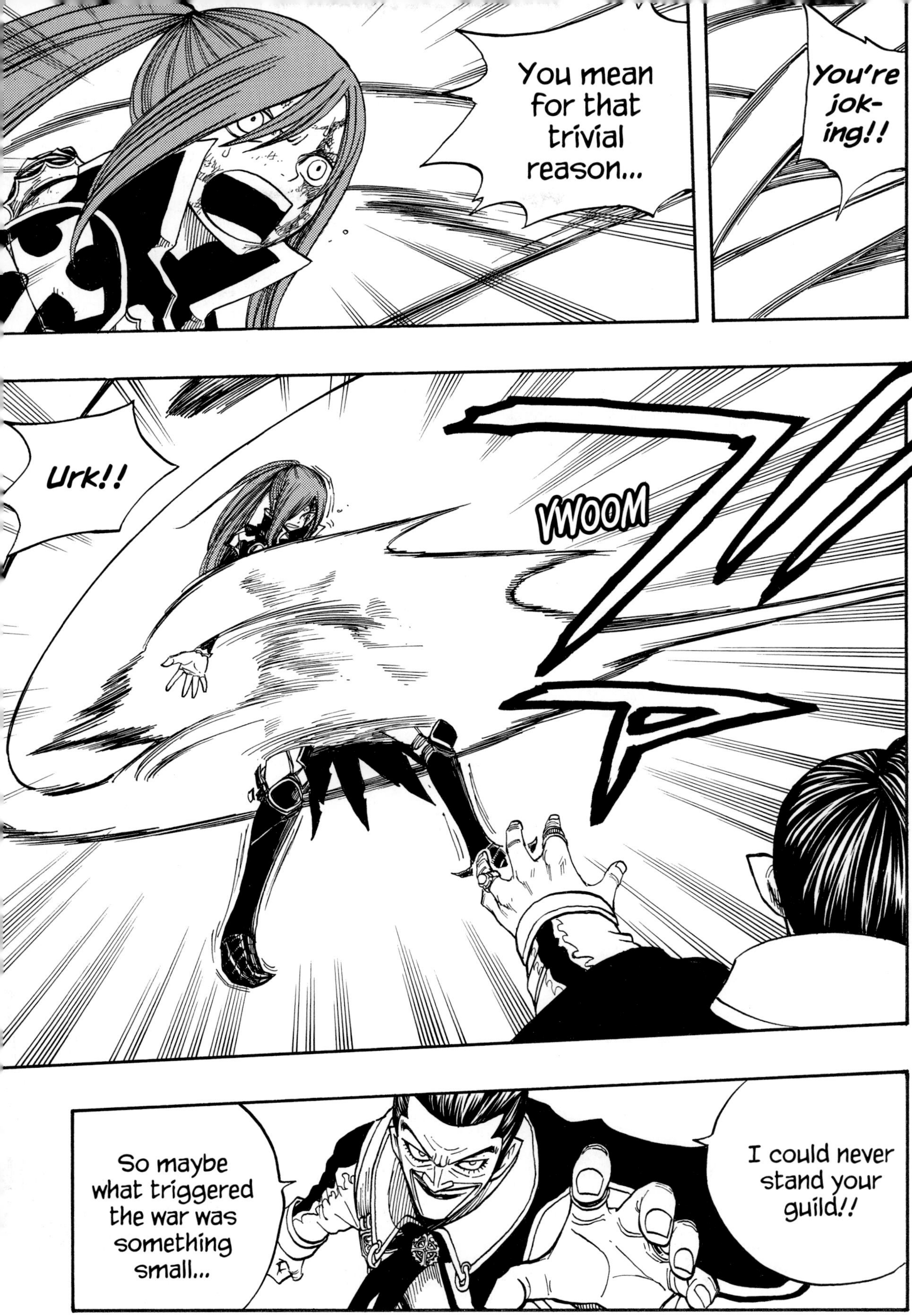
You're jok-ing!!
You mean for that trivial reason...
Urk!!
VWOOM
I could never stand your guild!!
So maybe what triggered the war was something small...

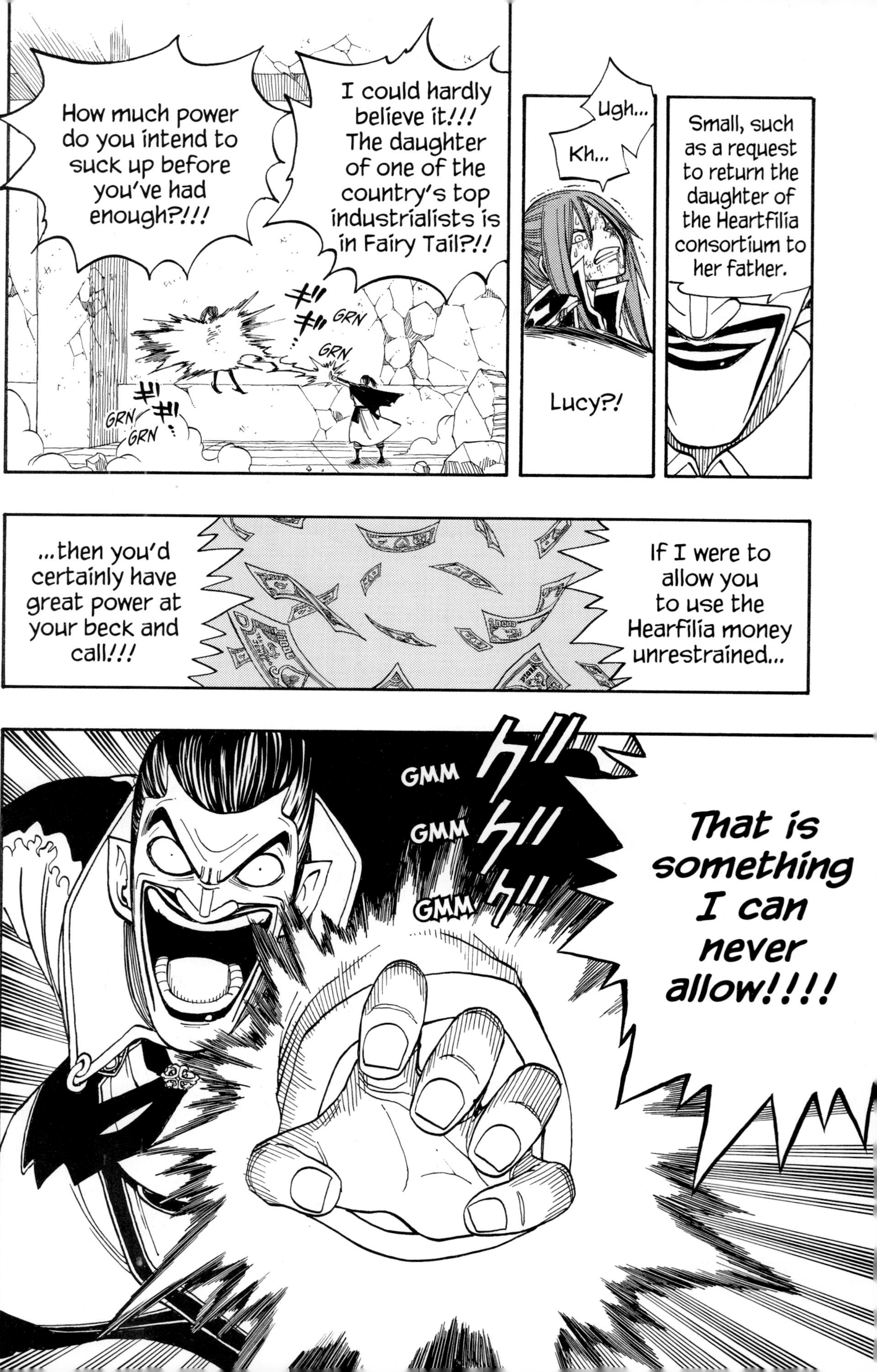
Small, such as a request to return the daughter of the Heartfilia consortium to her father.
Ugh...
Kh...
Lucy?!
I could hardly believe it!!! The daughter of one of the country's top industrialists is in Fairy Tail?!!
How much power do you intend to suck up before you've had enough?!!!
GRN
GRN
GRN
GRN
If I were to allow you to use the Hearfilia money unrestrained...
...then you'd certainly have great power at your beck and call!!!
GMM
GMM
GMM
That is something I can never allow!!!!

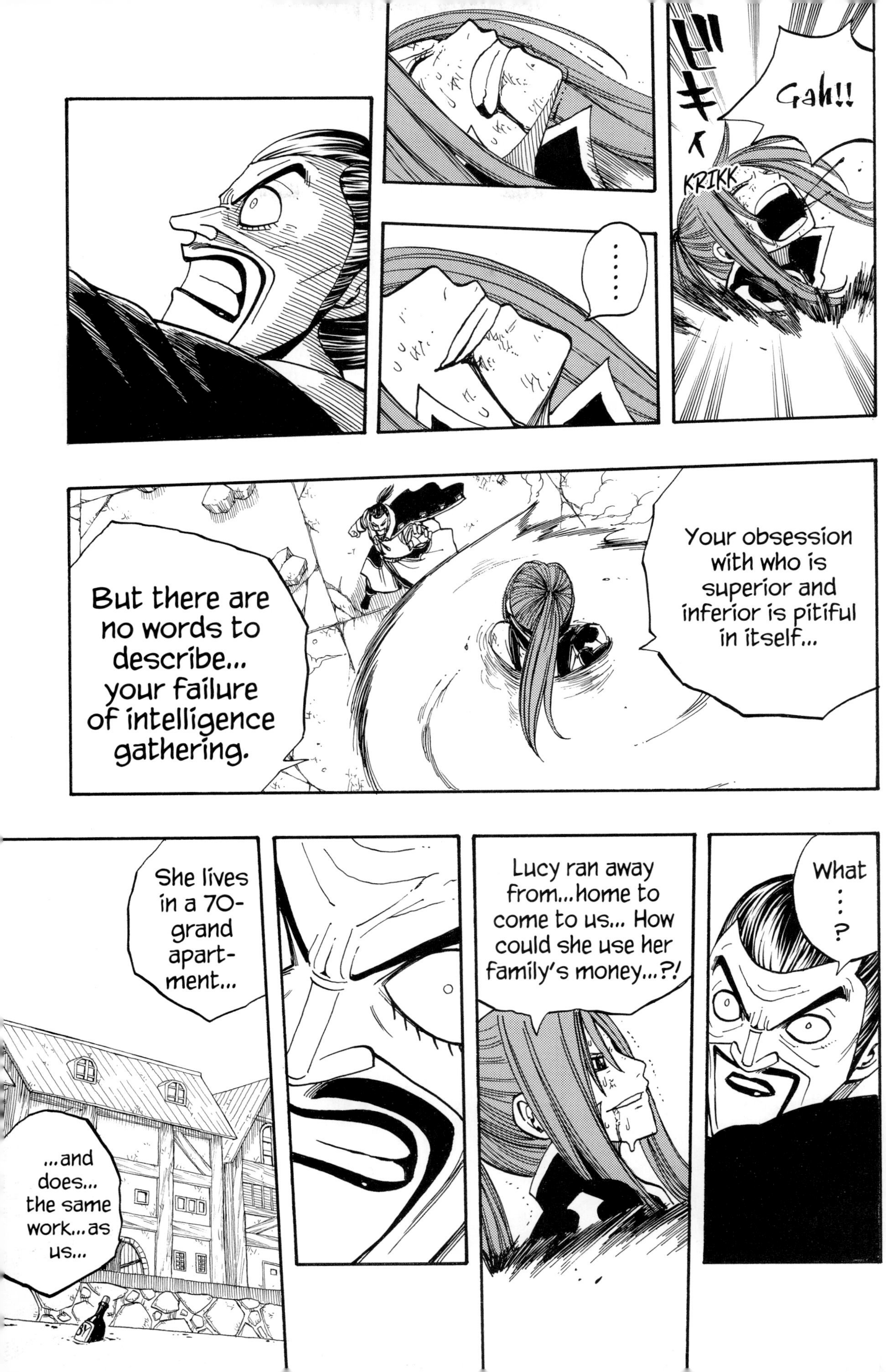
ビキィ
KRIKK
Gah!!
......
Your obsession with who is superior and inferior is pitiful in itself...
But there are no words to describe... your failure of intelligence gathering.
What...?
Lucy ran away from...home to come to us... How could she use her family's money...?!
She lives in a 70-grand apartment...
...and does... the same work...as us...

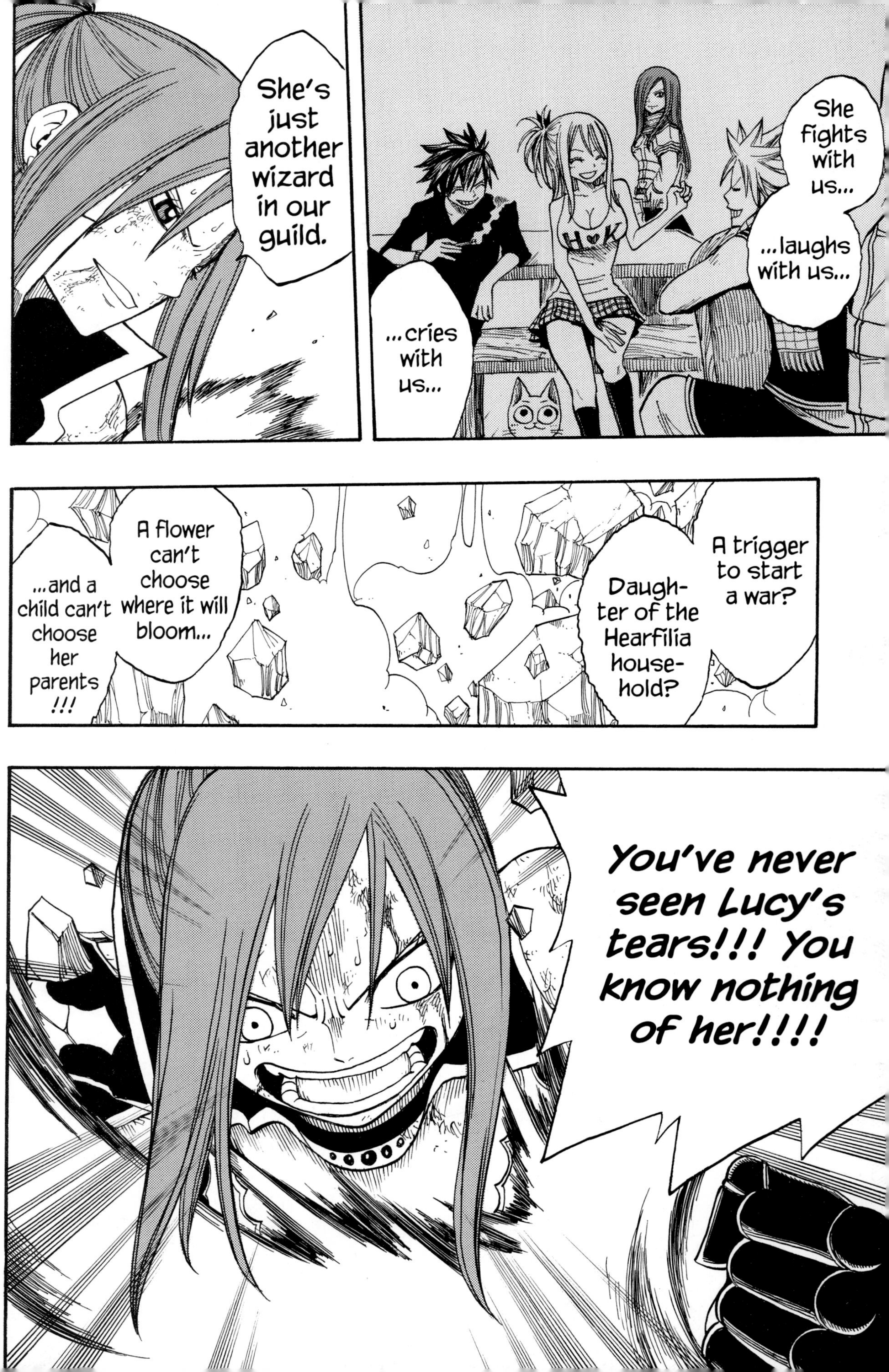
She fights with us...
...laughs with us...
...cries with us...
She's just another wizard in our guild.
A trigger to start a war?
Daughter of the Hearfilia household?
A flower can't choose where it will bloom...
...and a child can't choose her parents!!!
You've never seen Lucy's tears!!! You know nothing of her!!!!

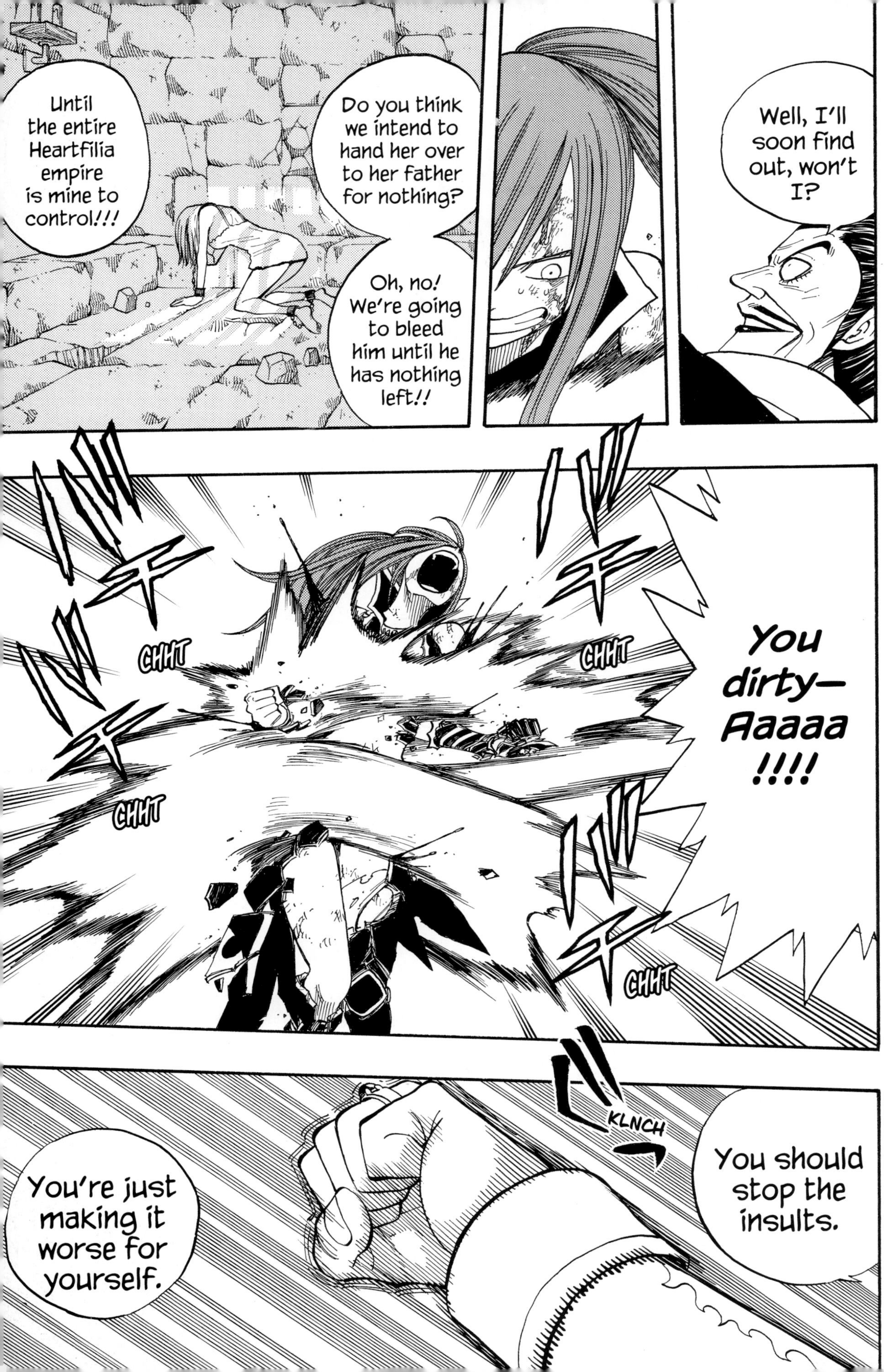
Well, I'll soon find out, won't I?
Do you think we intend to hand her over to her father for nothing?
Oh, no! We're going to bleed him until he has nothing left!!
Until the entire Heartfilia empire is mine to control!!!
CHHT
CHHT
You dirty— Aaaaa!!!!
CHHT
CHHT
KLNCH
You should stop the insults.
You're just making it worse for yourself.

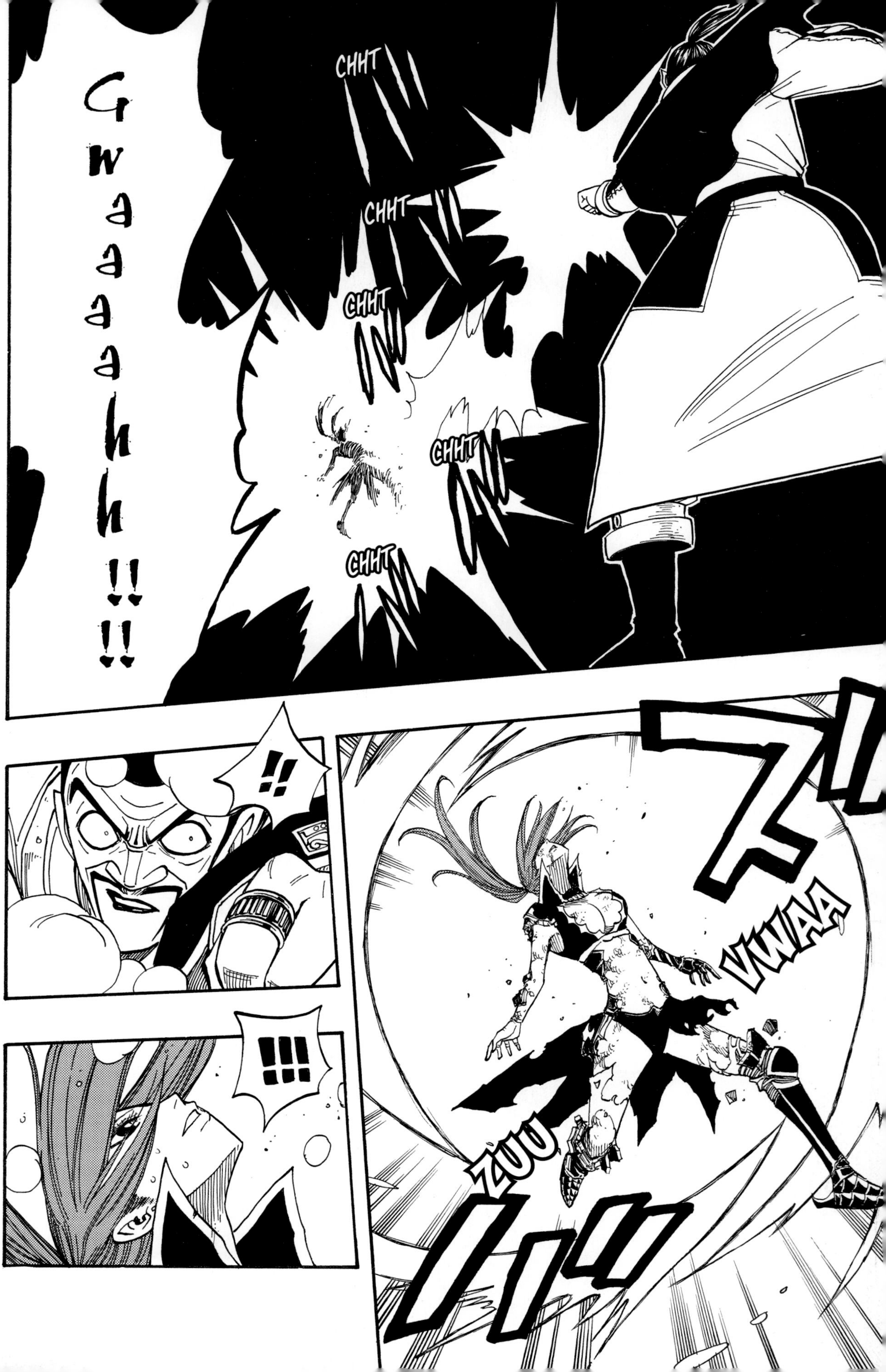
CHHT
CHHT
CHHT
CHHT
CHHT
Gwaaaaahh!!!!
VWAA
ZUU
!!
!!!!

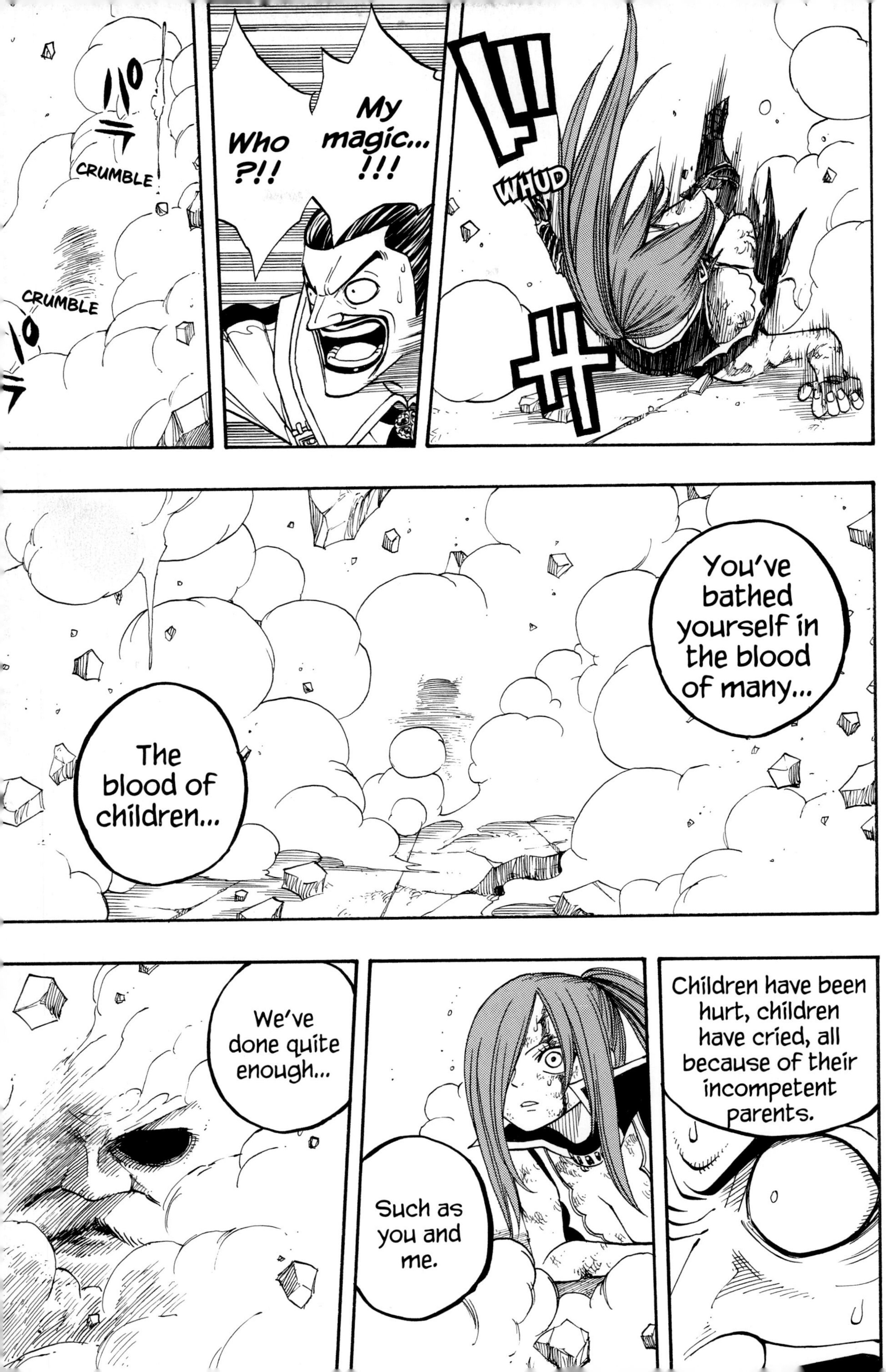
WHUD
My magic...!!!
Who?!!
CRUMBLE
CRUMBLE
You've bathed yourself in the blood of many...
The blood of children...
Children have been hurt, children have cried, all because of their incompetent parents.
Such as you and me.
We've done quite enough...

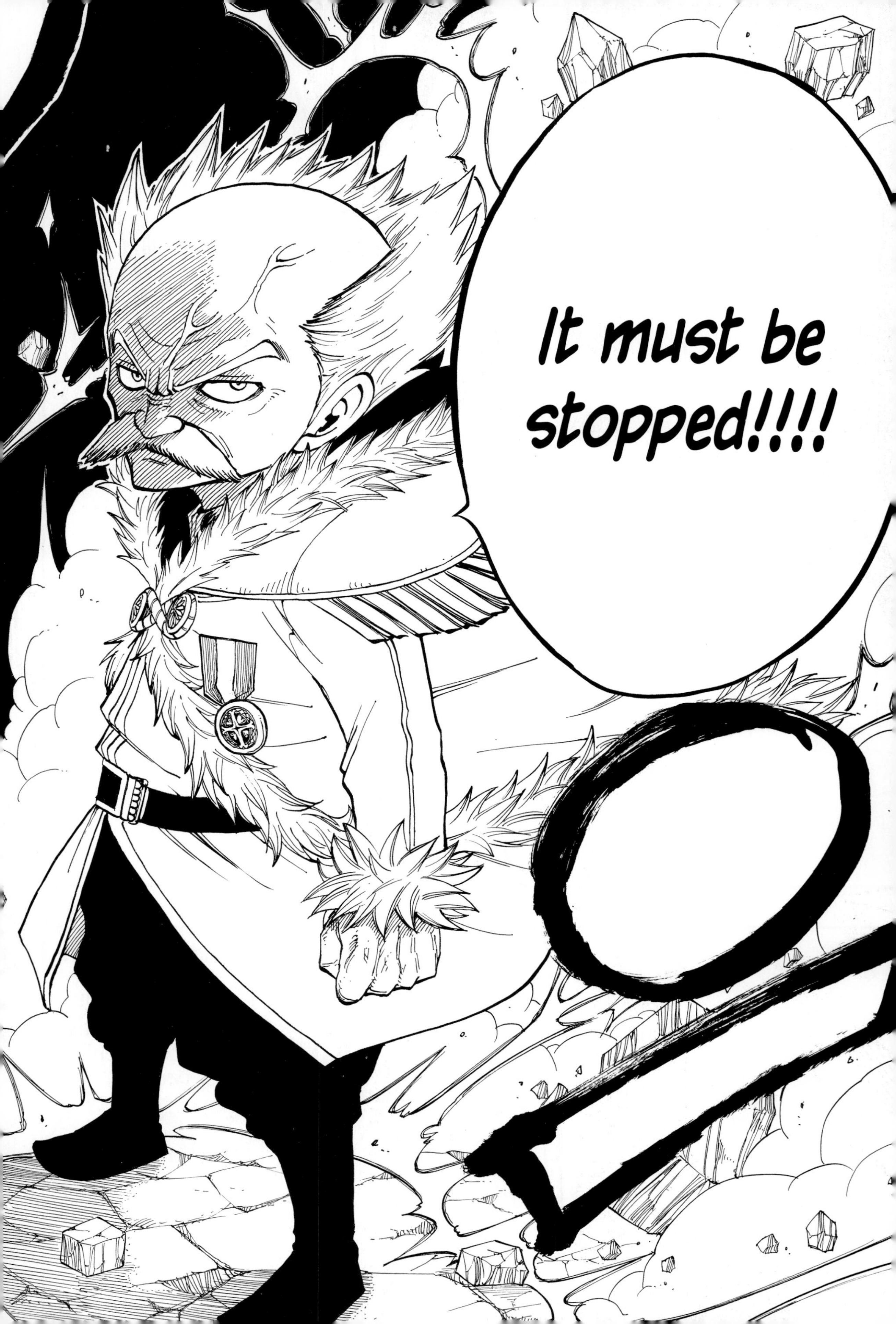
It must be stopped!!!!

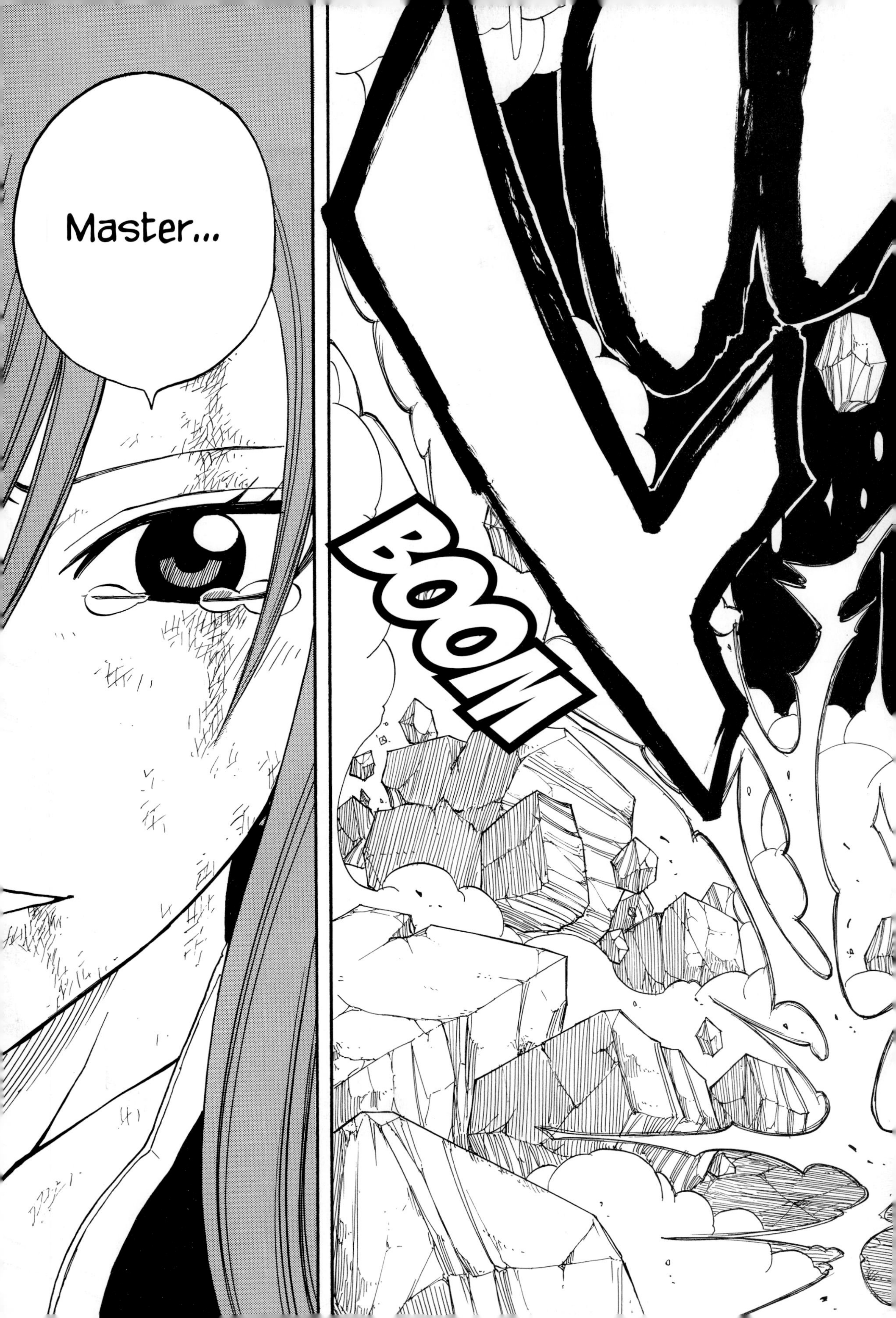
BOOM
Master...

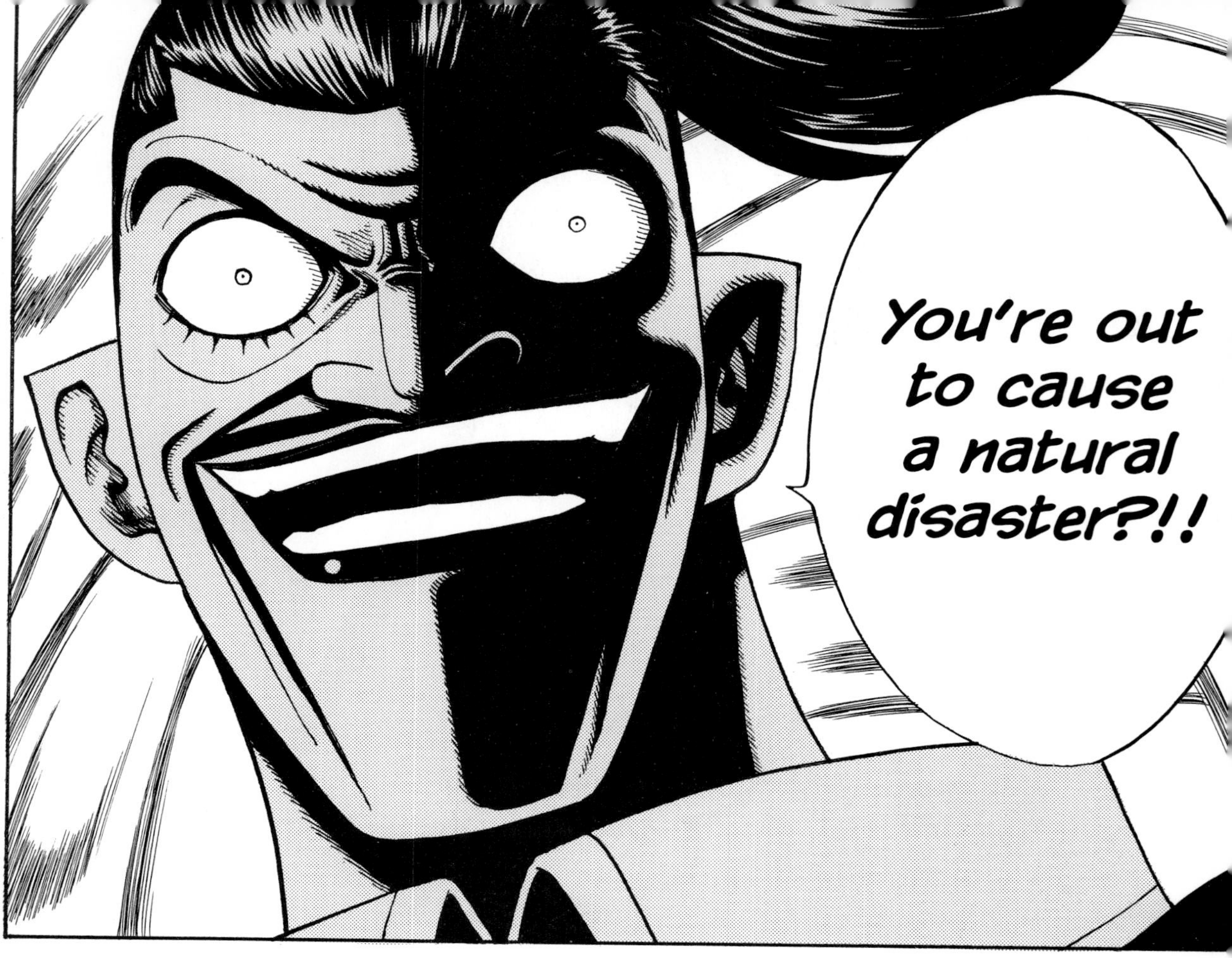
You're out to cause a natural disaster?!!
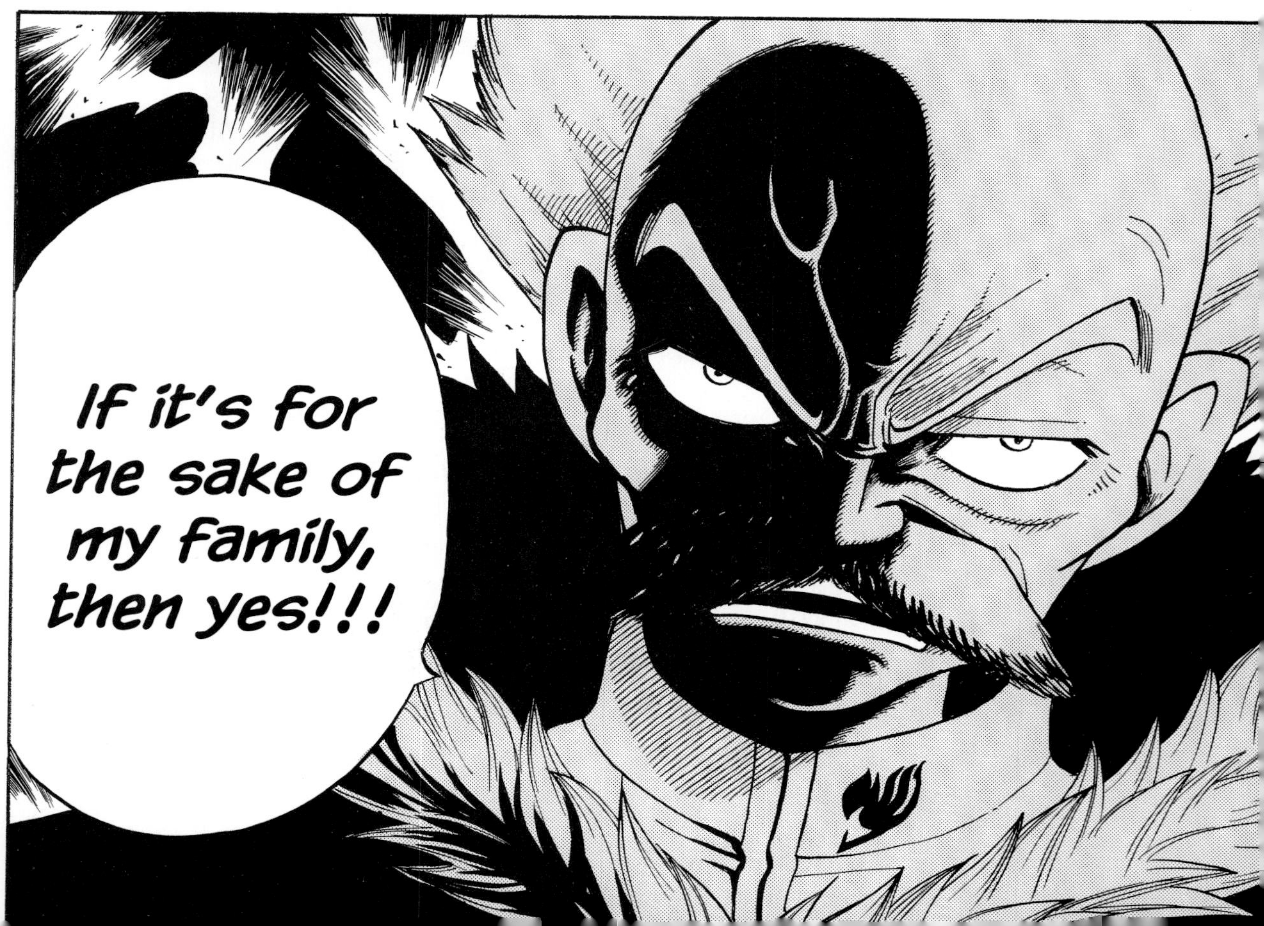
If it's for the sake of my family, then yes!!!

FAIRY TAIL

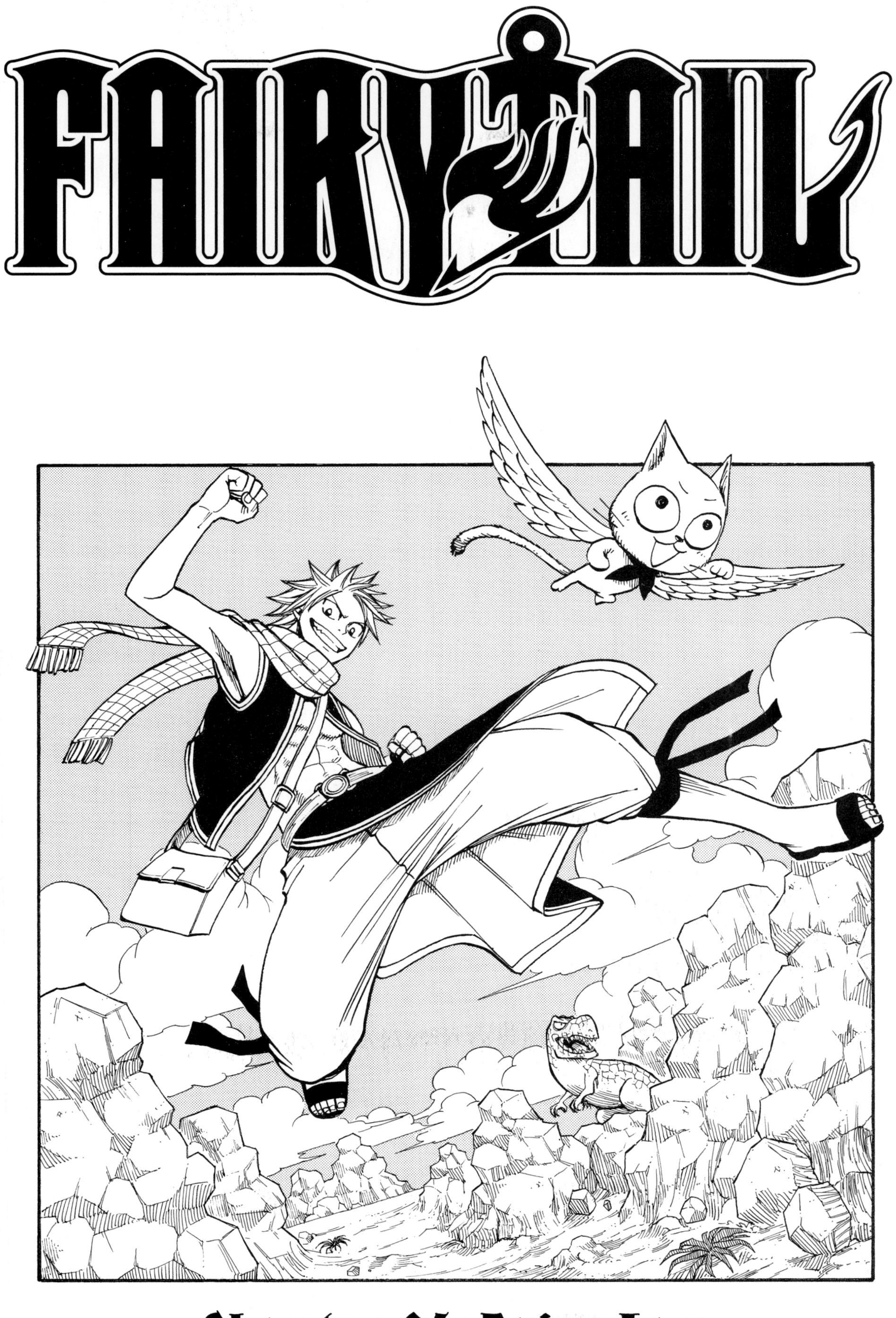

Chapter 65: Fairy Law

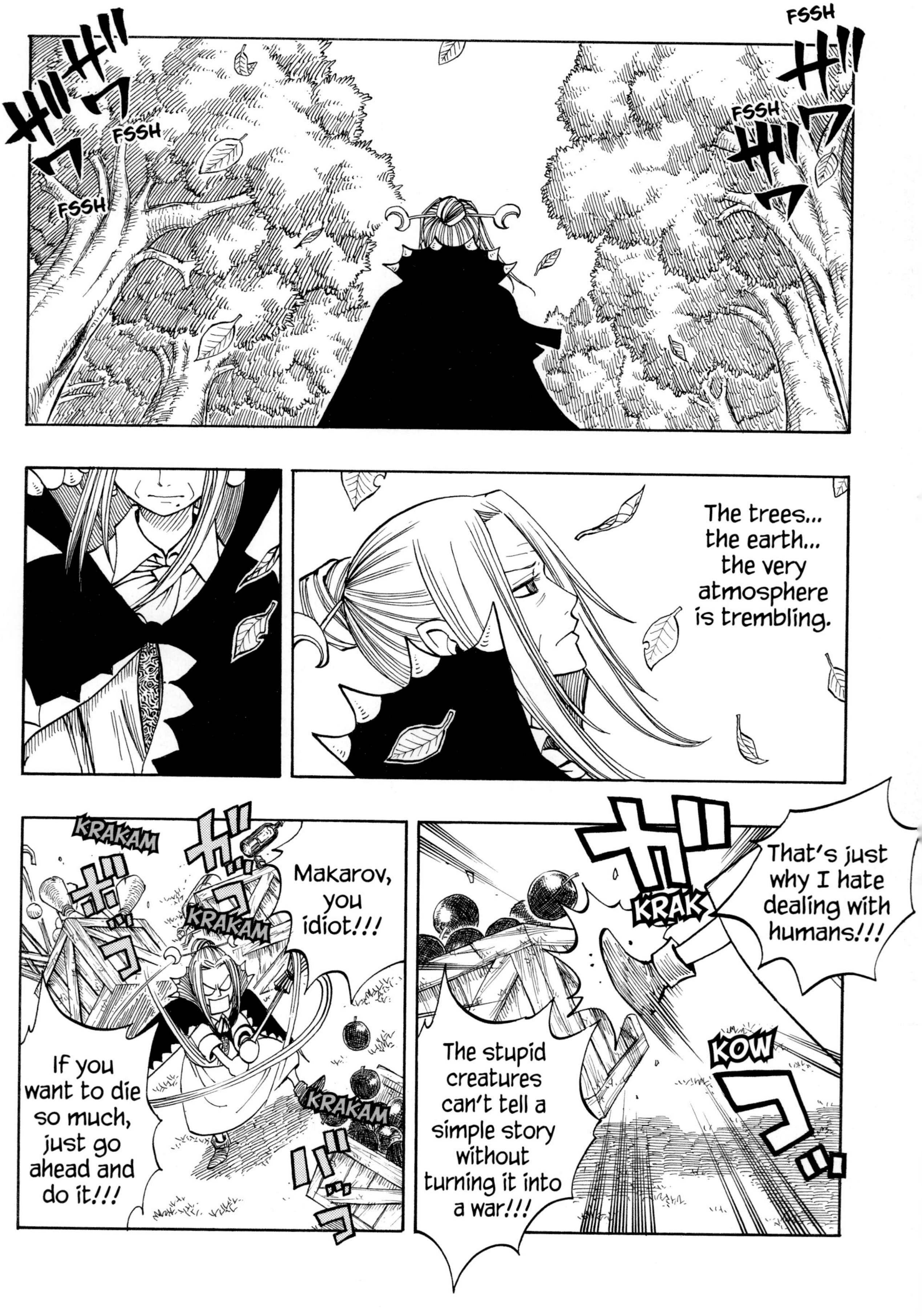
FSSH
FSSH
FSSH
FSSH
The trees... the earth... the very atmosphere is trembling.
KRAK
That's just why I hate dealing with humans!!!
The stupid creatures can't tell a simple story without turning it into a war!!!
KOW
KRAKAM
KRAKAM
Makarov, you idiot!!!
If you want to die so much, just go ahead and do it!!!
KRAKAM

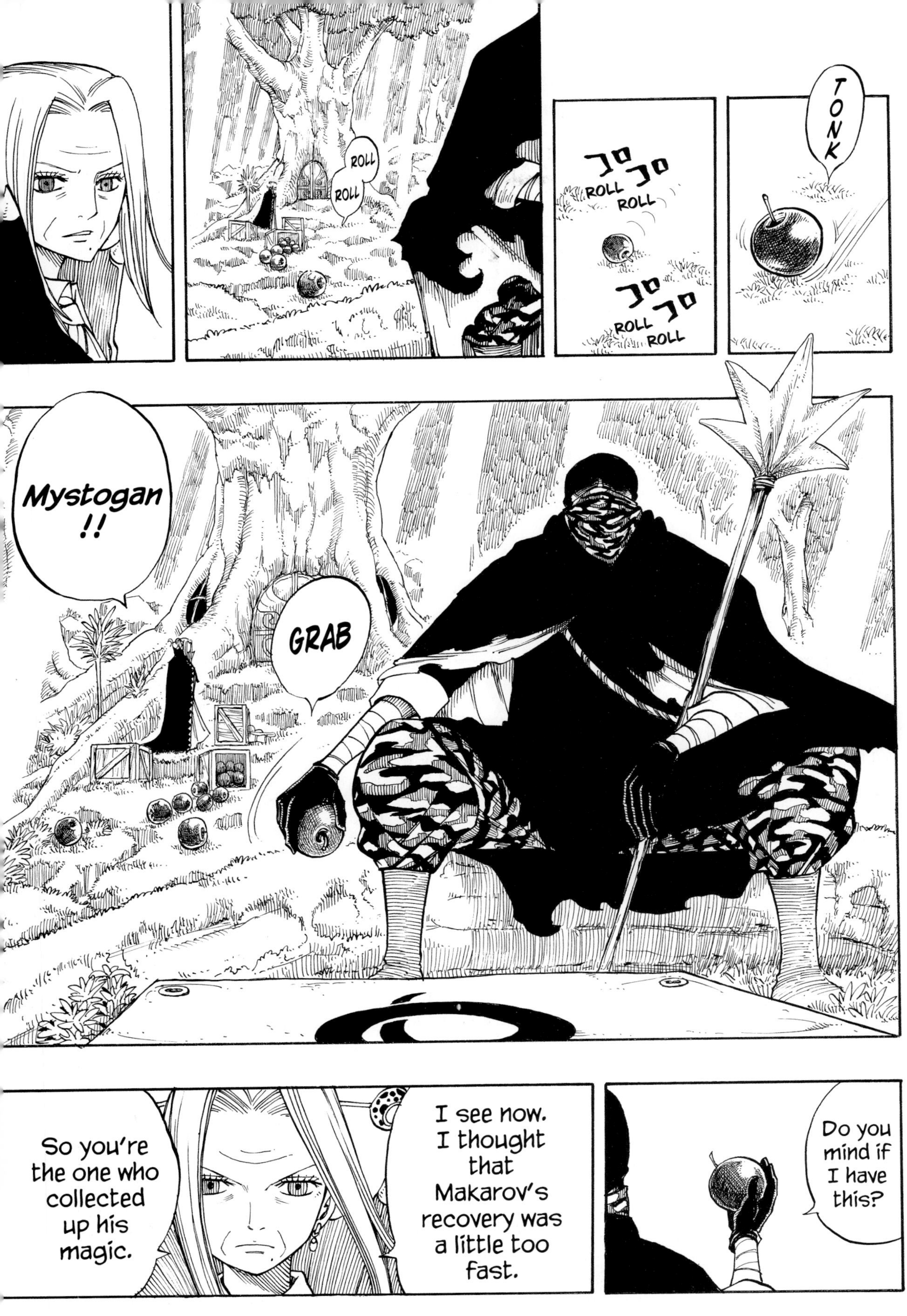
TONK
コロコロ
ROLL ROLL
コロコロ
ROLL ROLL
ROLL ROLL
Mystogan !!
GRAB
Do you mind if I have this?
I see now. I thought that Makarov's recovery was a little too fast.
So you're the one who collected up his magic.

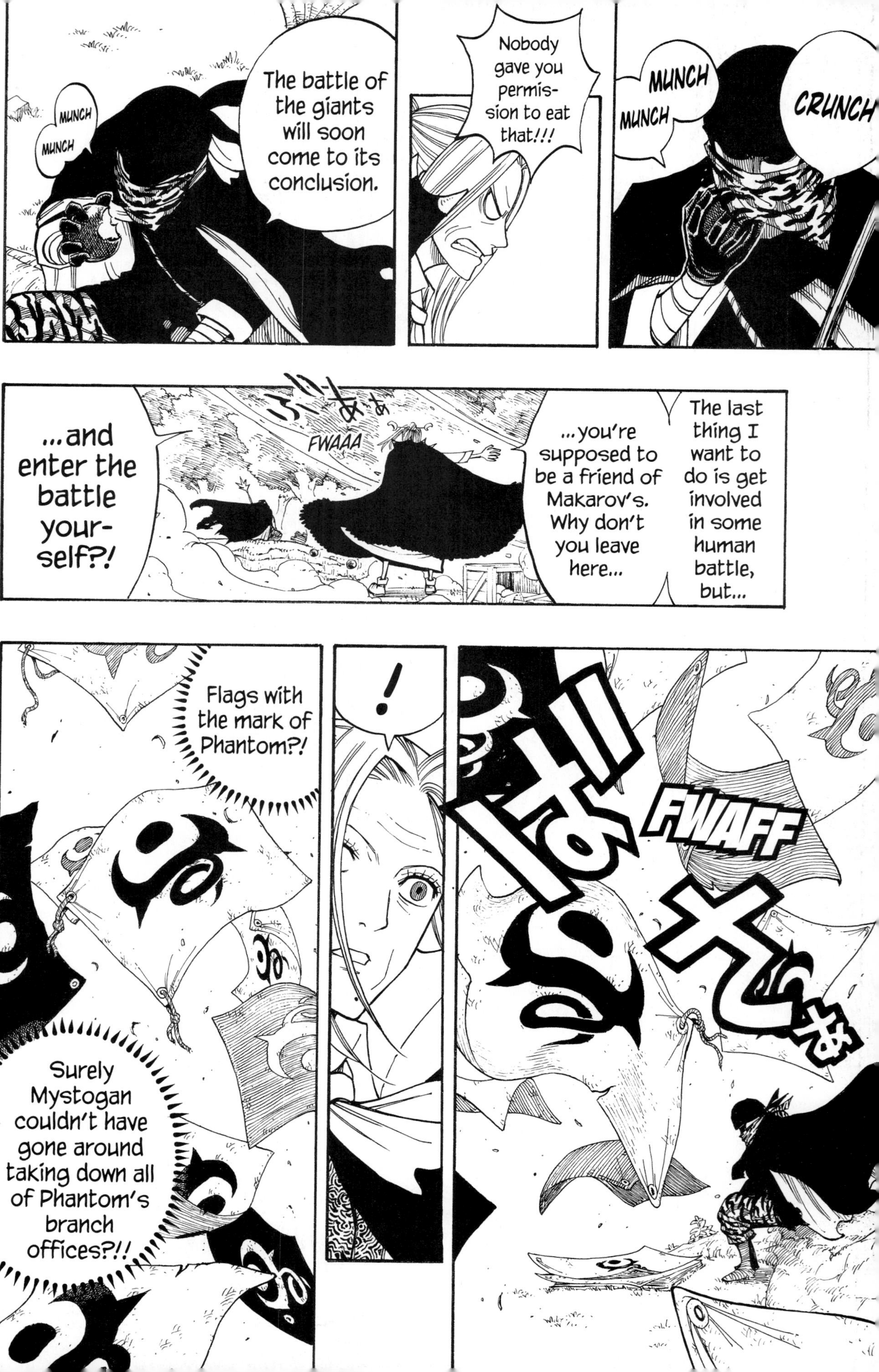
MUNCH
MUNCH
CRUNCH
Nobody gave you permis-sion to eat that!!!
MUNCH
MUNCH
The battle of the giants will soon come to its conclusion.
The last thing I want to do is get involved in some human battle, but...
...you're supposed to be a friend of Makarov's. Why don't you leave here...
FWAAA
...and enter the battle your-self?!
FWAFF
!
Flags with the mark of Phantom?!
Surely Mystogan couldn't have gone around taking down all of Phantom's branch offices?!!

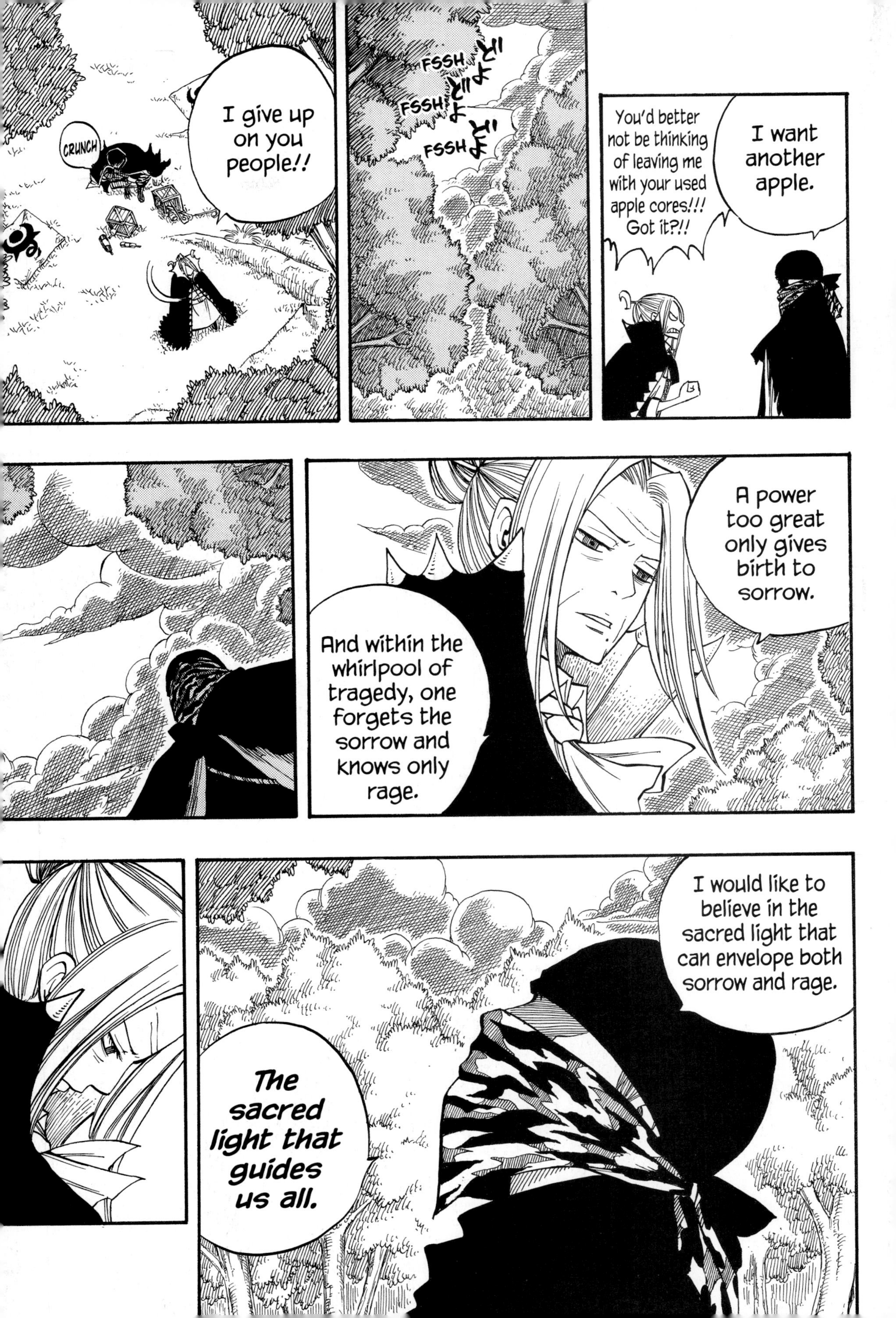
I want another apple.
You'd better not be thinking of leaving me with your used apple cores!!! Got it?!!
FSSH
FSSH
FSSH
I give up on you people!!
CRUNCH
A power too great only gives birth to sorrow.
And within the whirlpool of tragedy, one forgets the sorrow and knows only rage.
I would like to believe in the sacred light that can envelope both sorrow and rage.
The sacred light that guides us all.

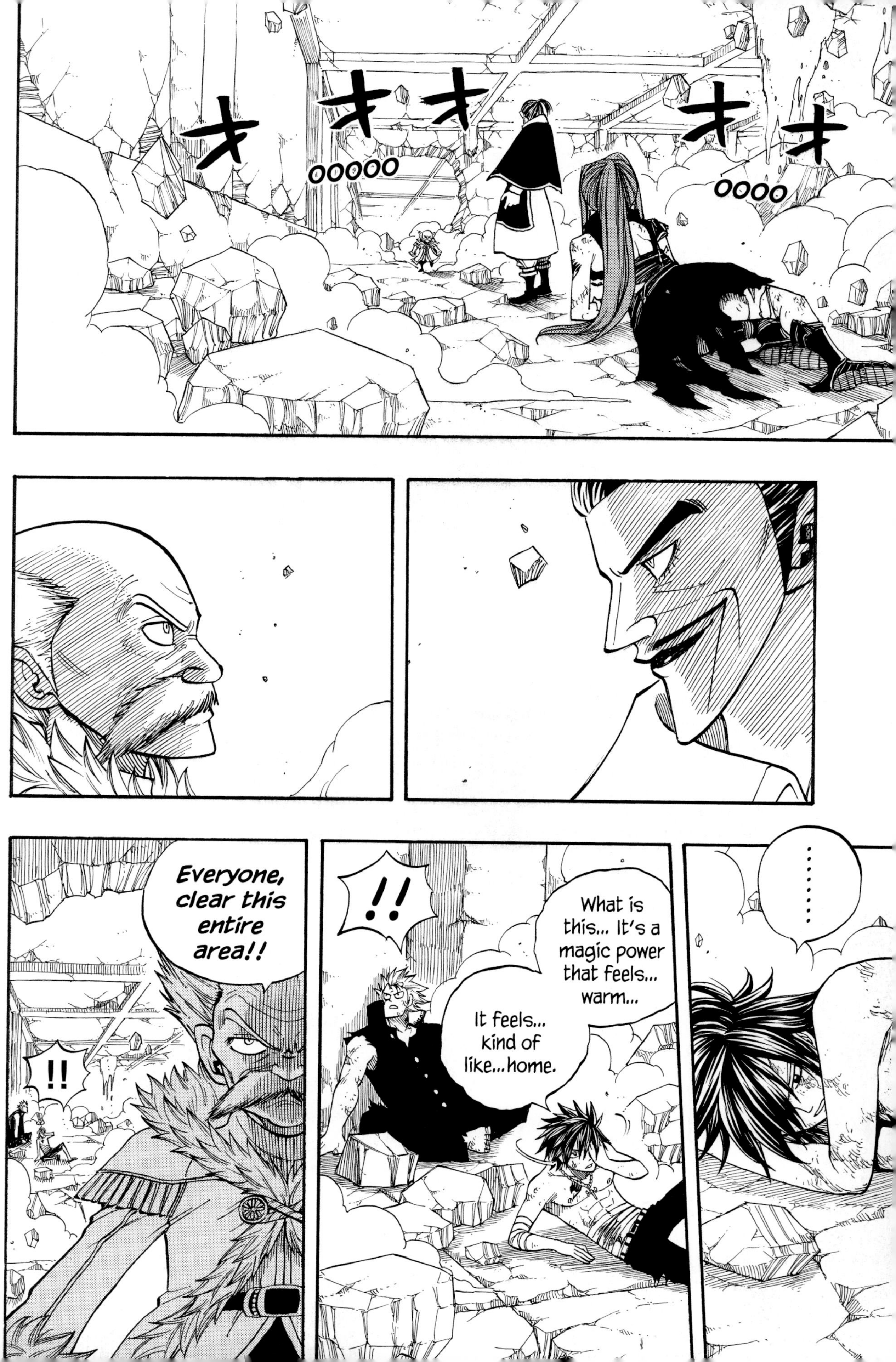
オオ
OOOO
オオオ
OOOOO
....
!!
What is this... It's a magic power that feels... warm...
It feels... kind of like...home.
Everyone, clear this entire area!!
!!

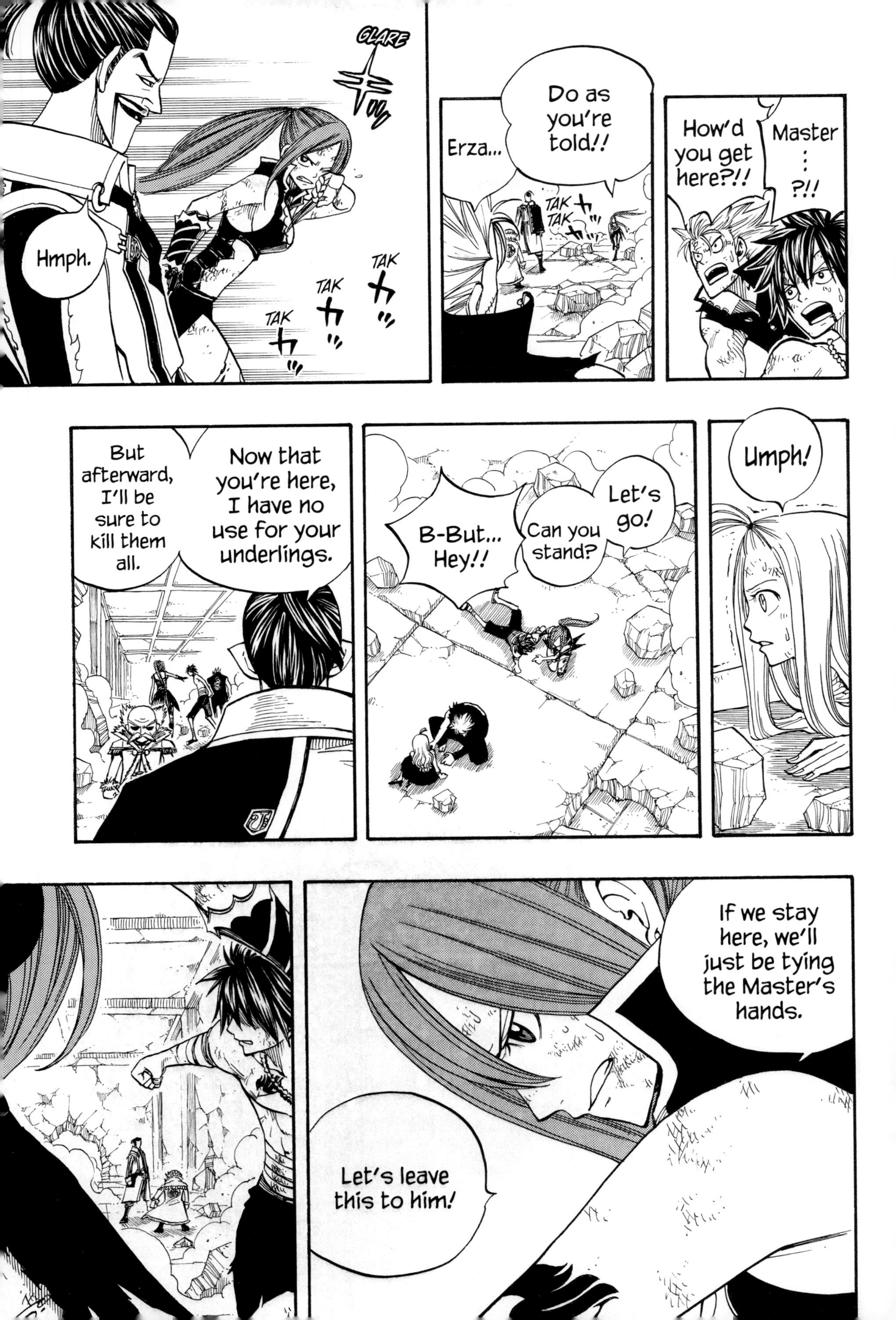
Master : : ?!!
How'd you get here?!!
Do as you're told!!
Erza...
TAK TAK
GLARE
Hmph.
TAK TAK TAK
Umph!
Let's go!
Can you stand?
B-But... Hey!!
Now that you're here, I have no use for your underlings.
But afterward, I'll be sure to kill them all.
If we stay here, we'll just be tying the Master's hands.
Let's leave this to him!

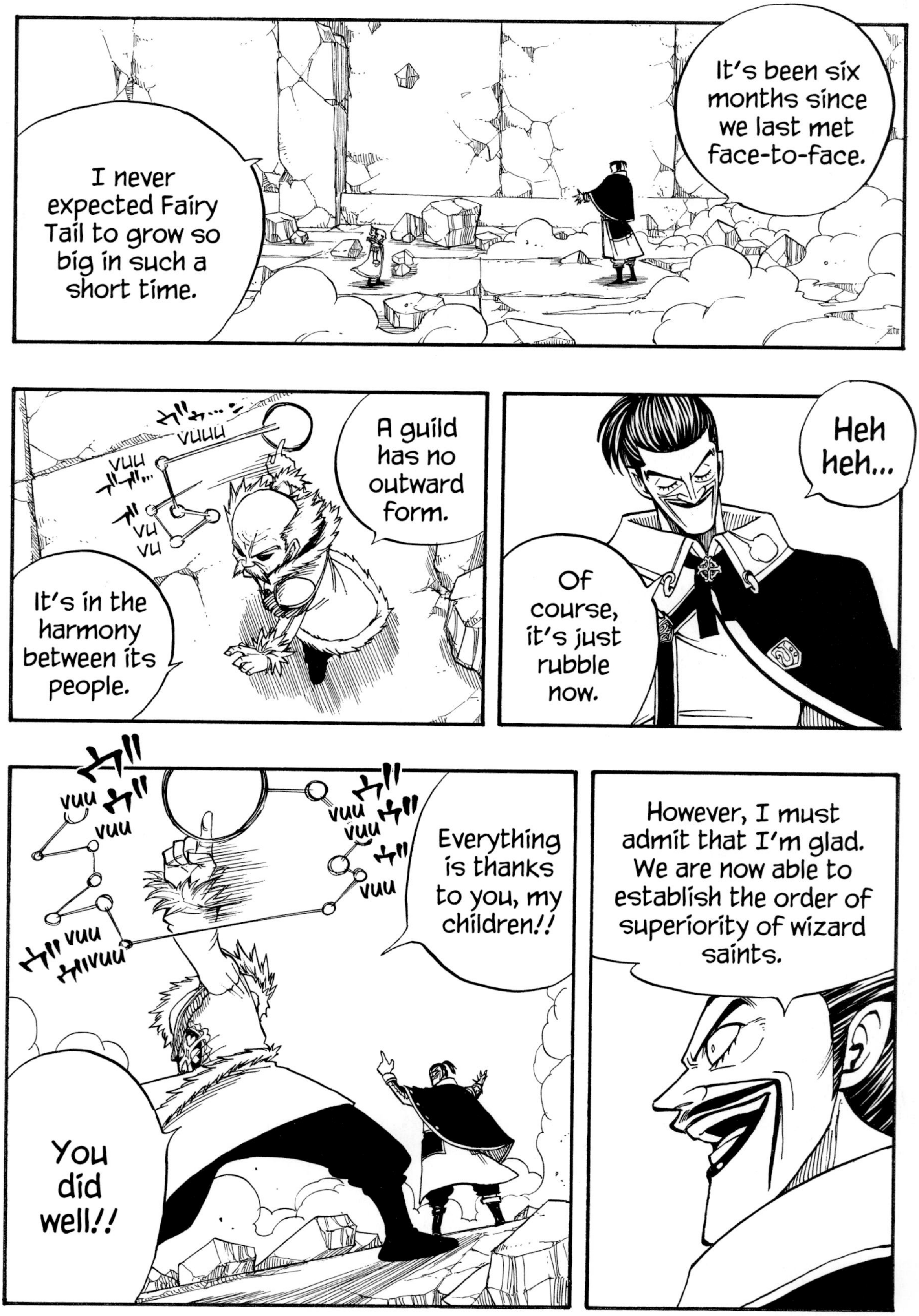
It's been six months since we last met face-to-face.
I never expected Fairy Tail to grow so big in such a short time.
Heh heh...
Of course, it's just rubble now.
vuuu
vuu
vu vu
A guild has no outward form.
It's in the harmony between its people.
However, I must admit that I'm glad. We are now able to establish the order of superiority of wizard saints.
vuu vuu vuu
vuu vuu vuu
Everything is thanks to you, my children!!
You did well!!

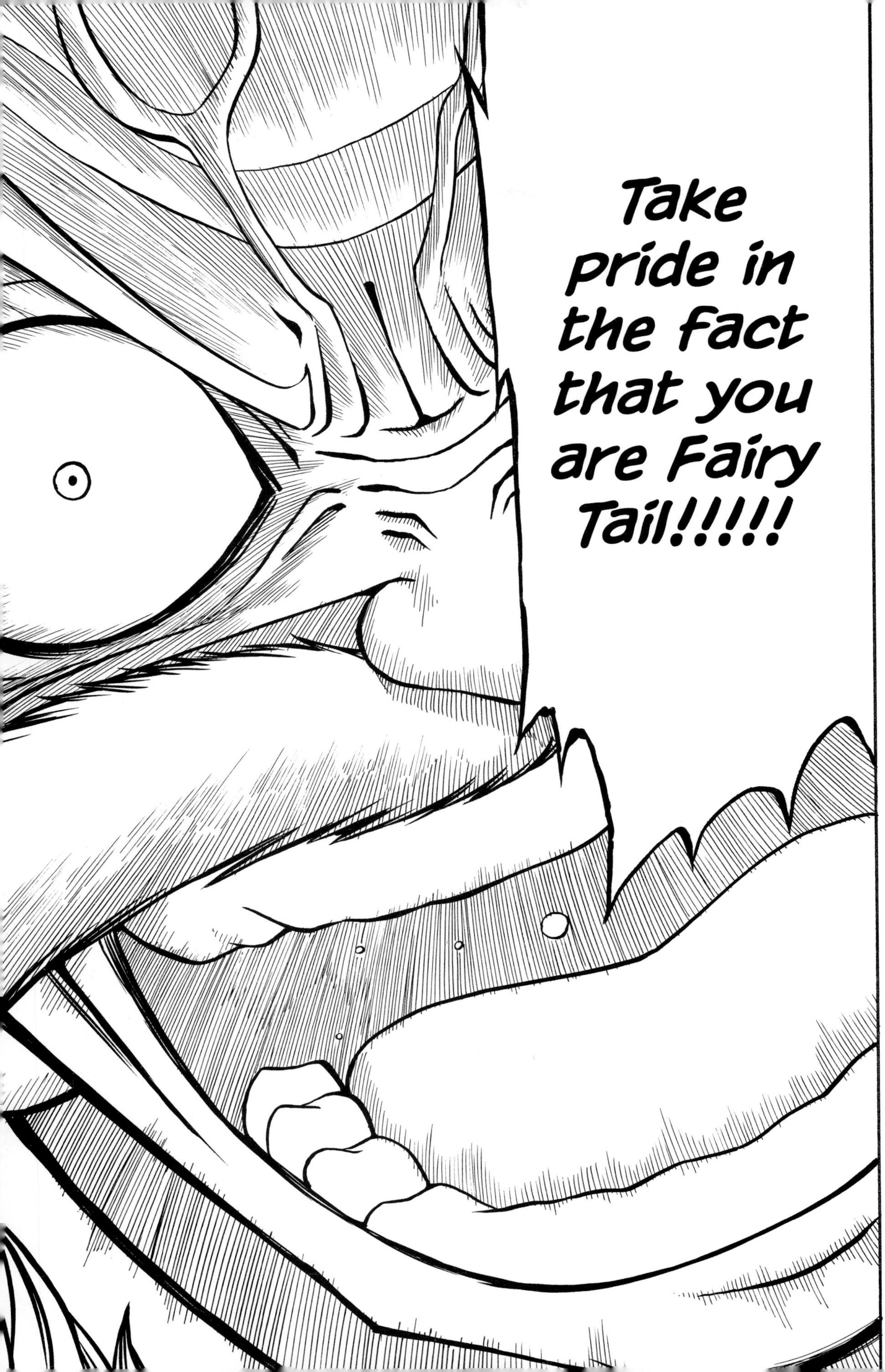
Take pride in the fact that you are Fairy Tail!!!!!

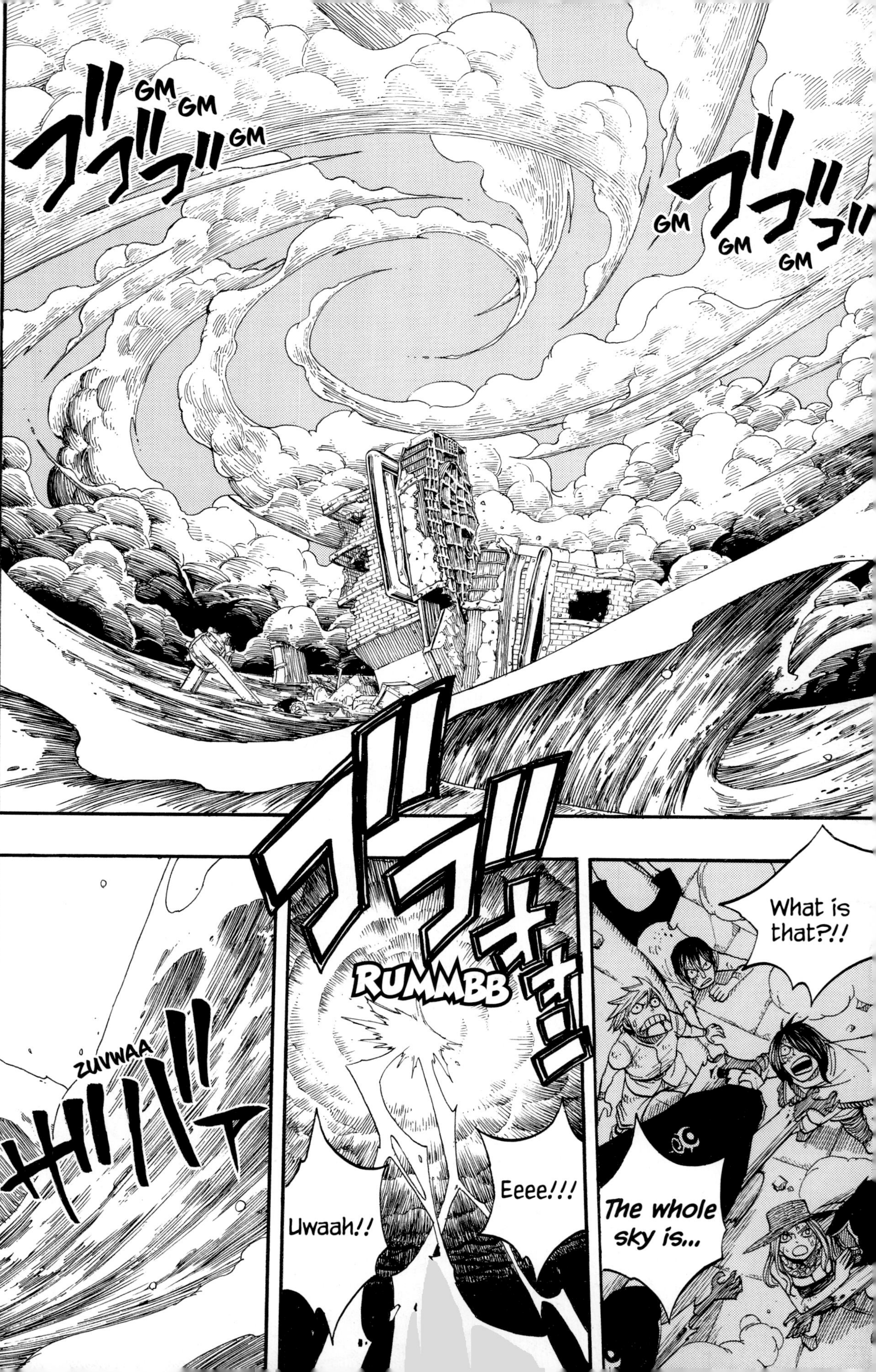
GM GM GM
GM GM GM
What is that?!!
The whole sky is...
RUMMBB
Eeee!!!
Uwaah!!
ZUVWAA

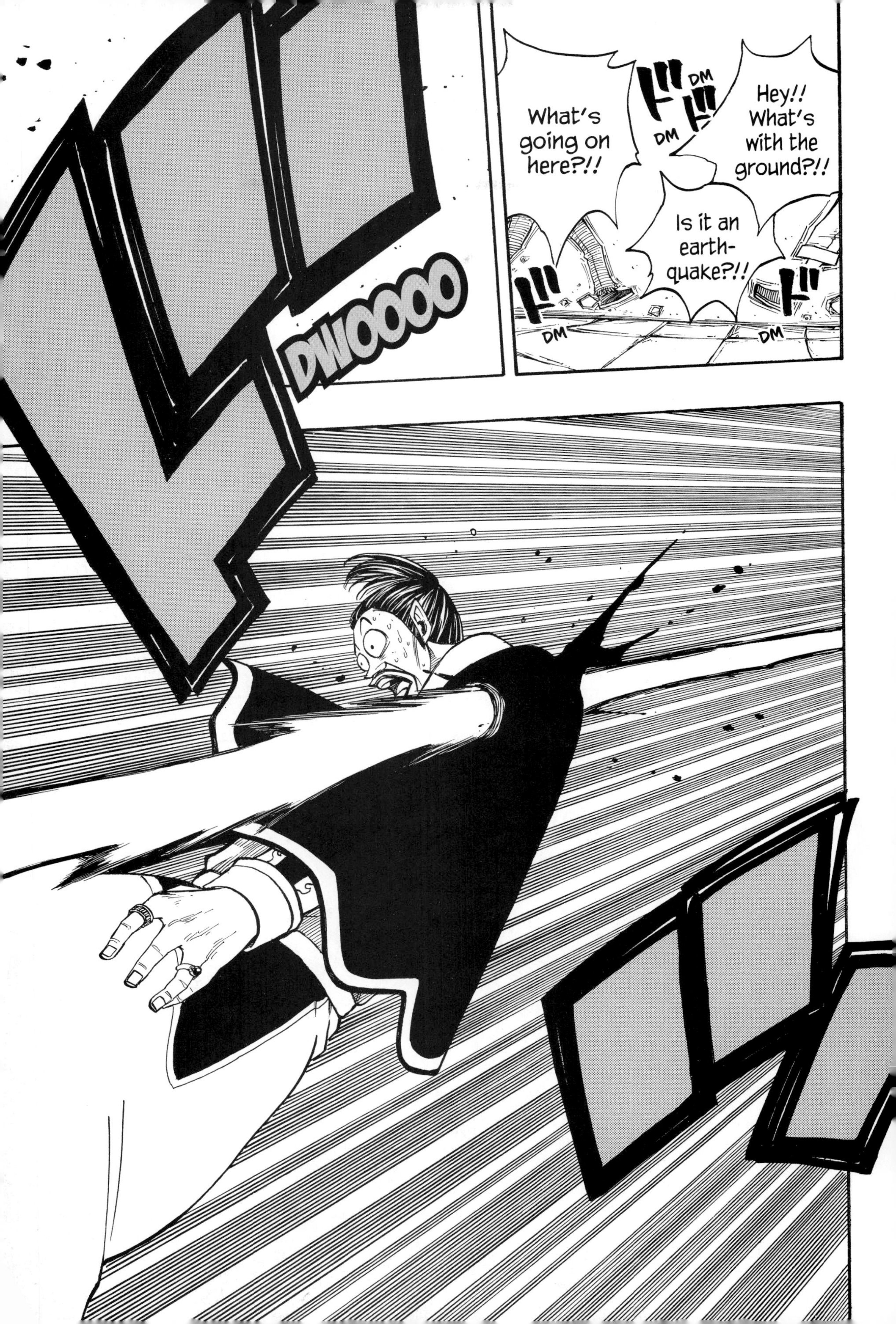
Hey!! What's with the ground?!!
ドド DM DM
What's going on here?!!
Is it an earth-quake?!!
ド DM
ド DM
DWOOOO

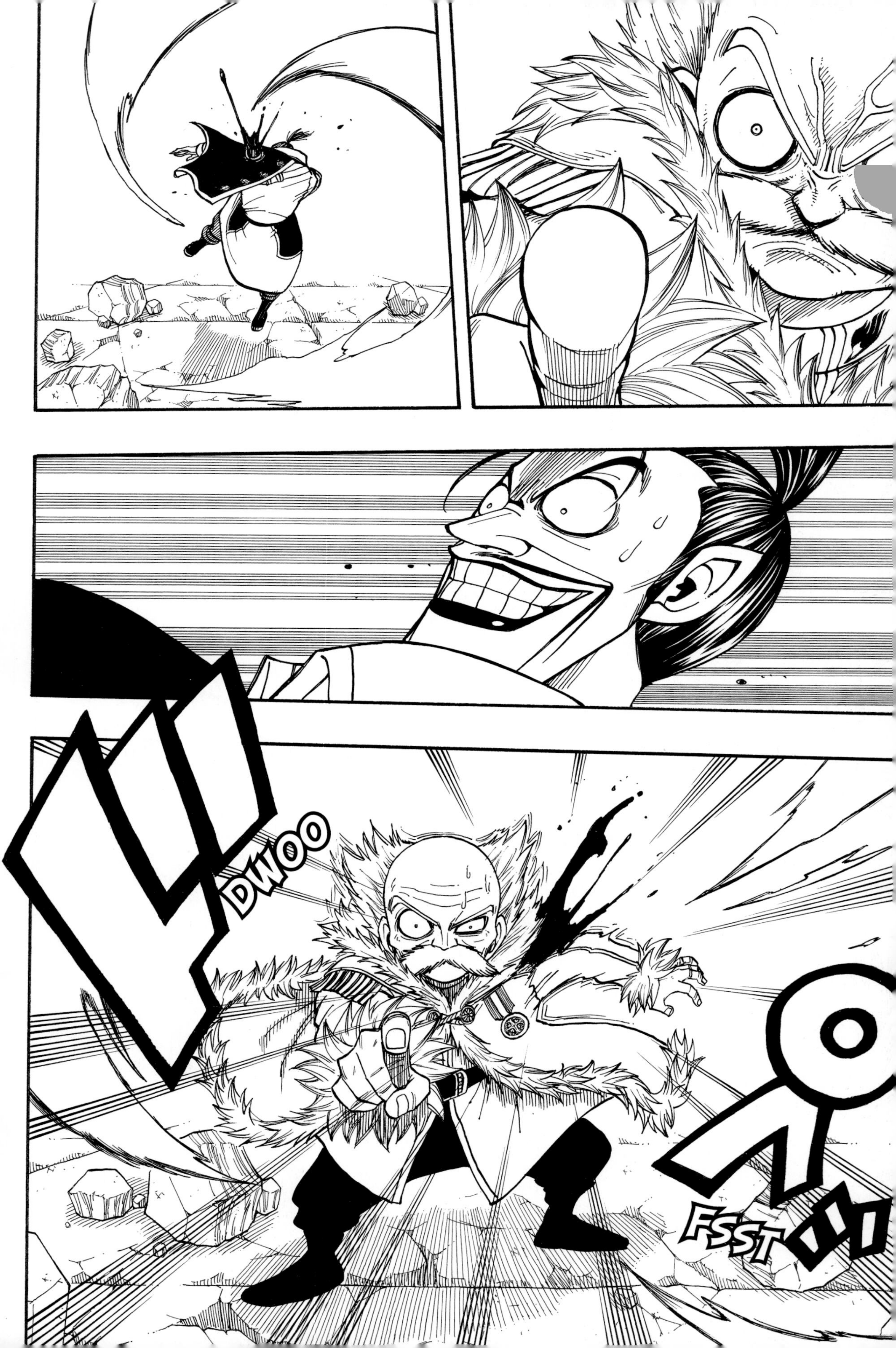
DWOO
FSST

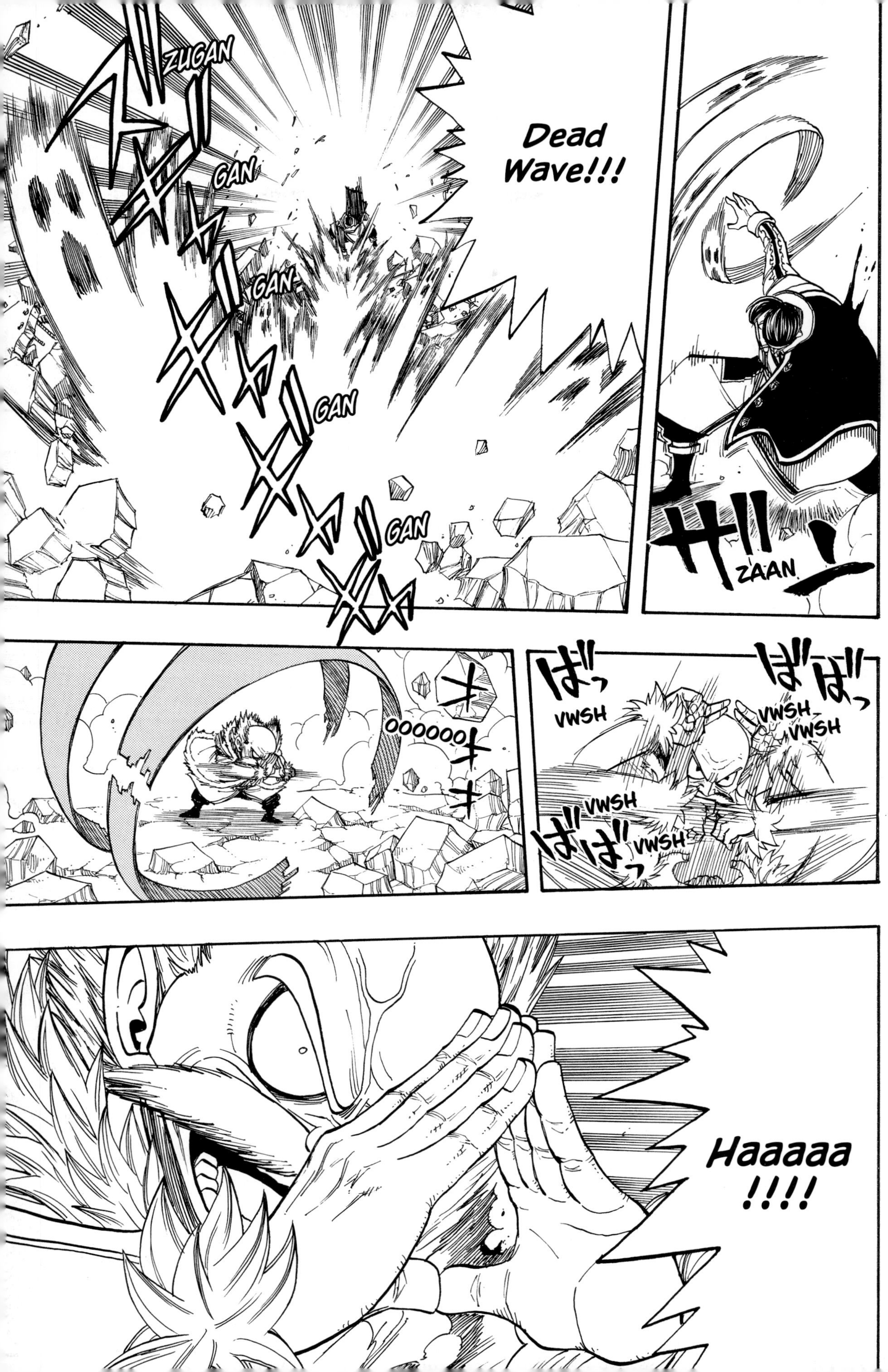
ZAAN
Dead Wave!!!
ZUGAN
GAN
GAN
GAN
GAN
VWSH
VWSH
VWSH
VWSH
VWSH
OOOOOO
Haaaaa !!!!

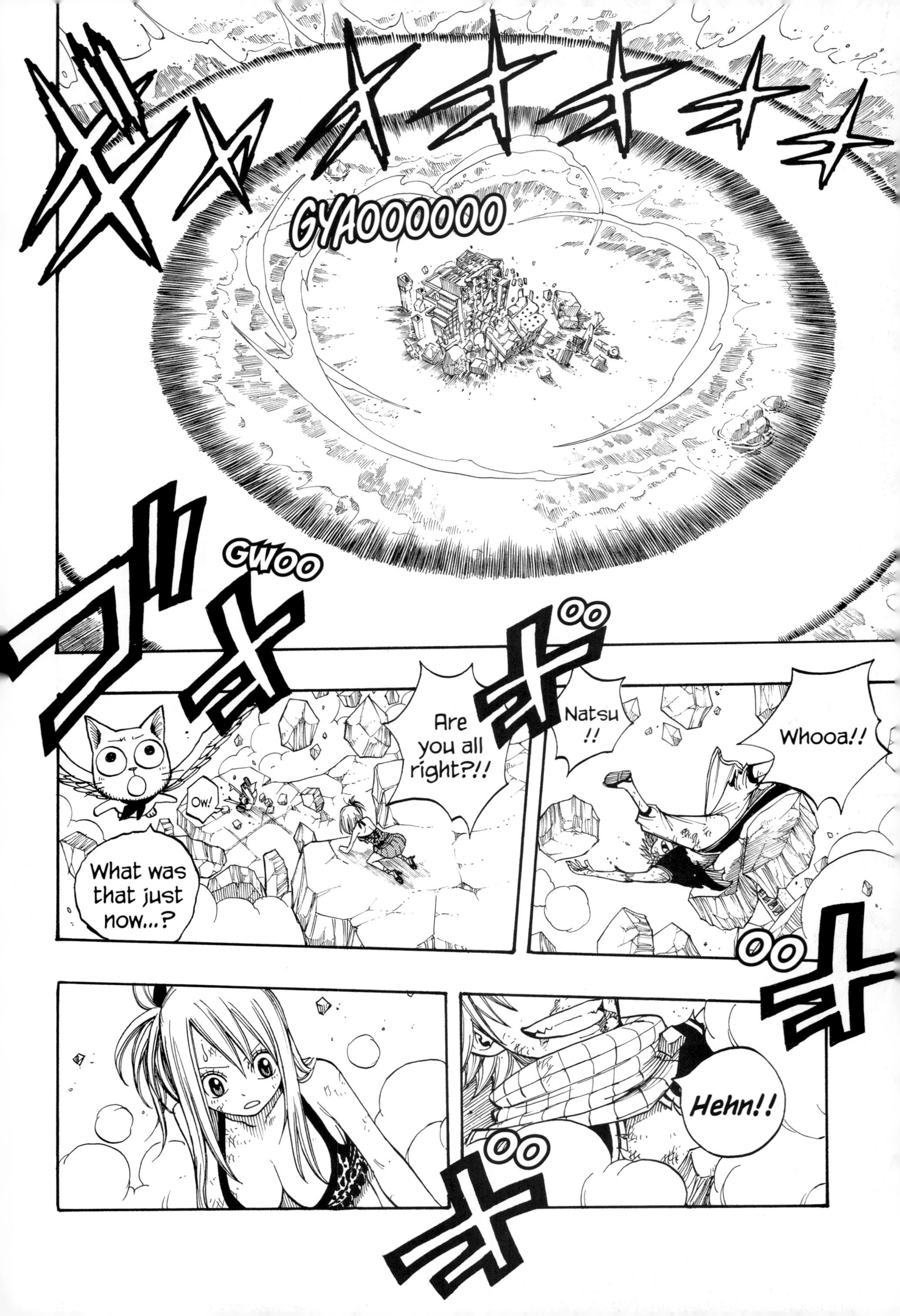
GYAOOOOOO
GWOO
Whooa!!
Natsu!!
Are you all right?!!
Ow!
What was that just now...?
Hehn!!

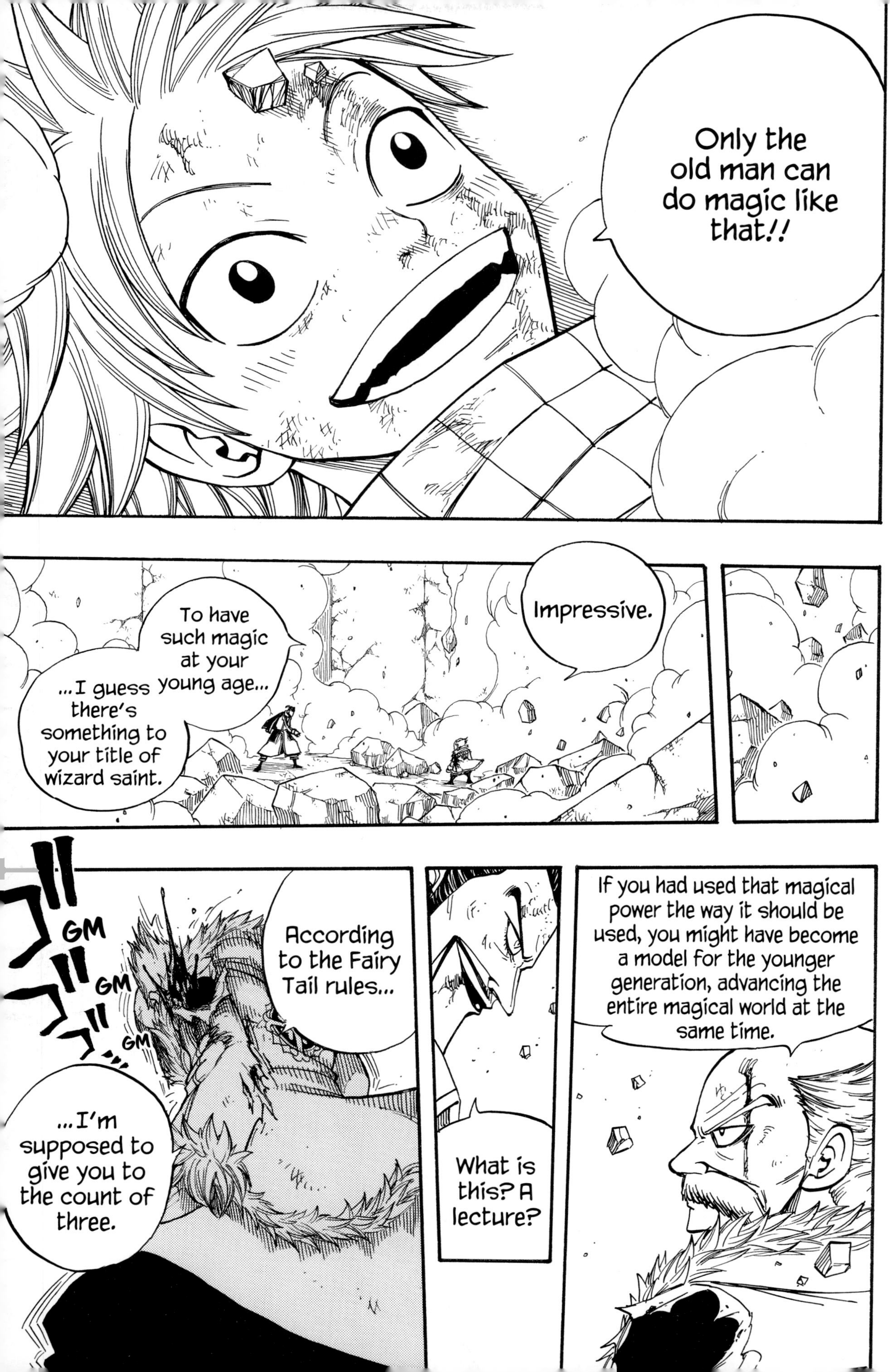
Only the old man can do magic like that!!
Impressive.
To have such magic at your young age...
...I guess there's something to your title of wizard saint.
If you had used that magical power the way it should be used, you might have become a model for the younger generation, advancing the entire magical world at the same time.
What is this? A lecture?
According to the Fairy Tail rules...
GM
GM
GM
...I'm supposed to give you to the count of three.

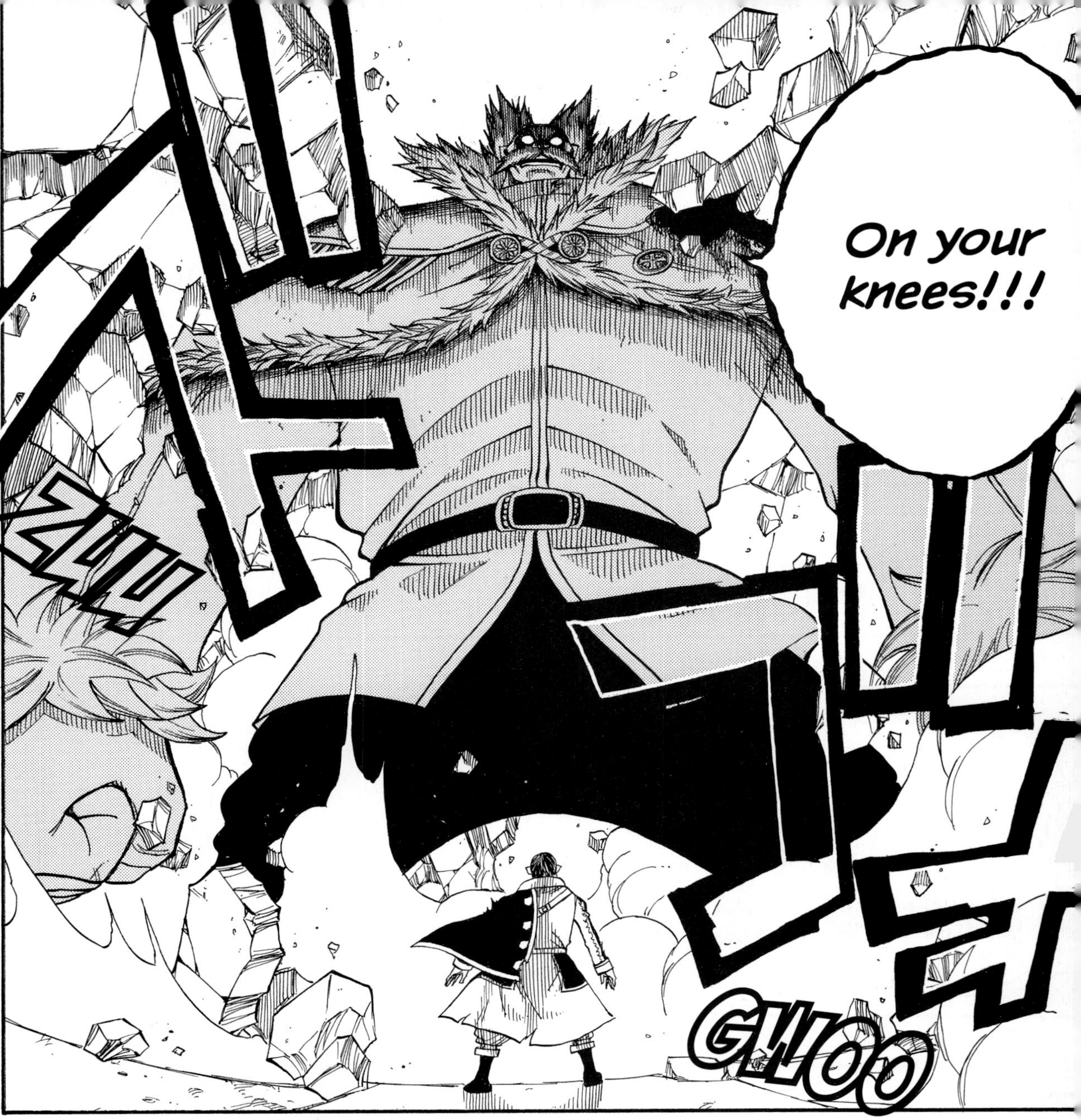
On your knees!!!
GWOO

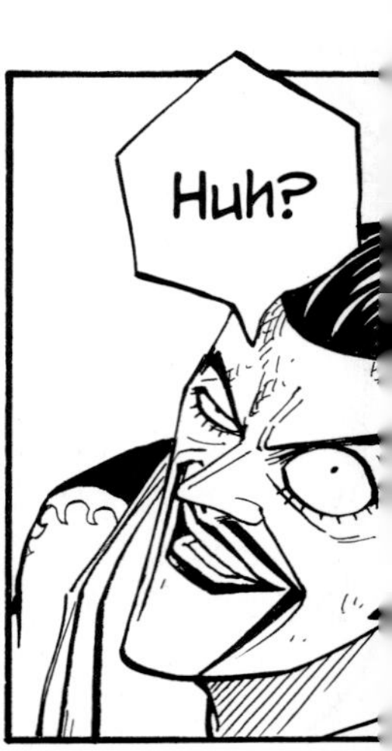
Huh?

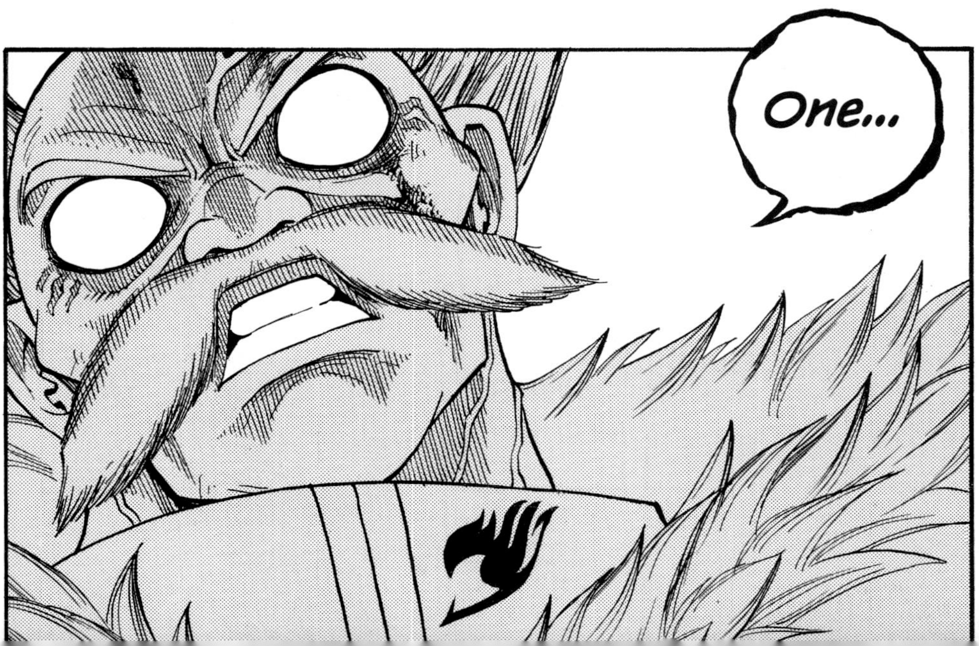
One...

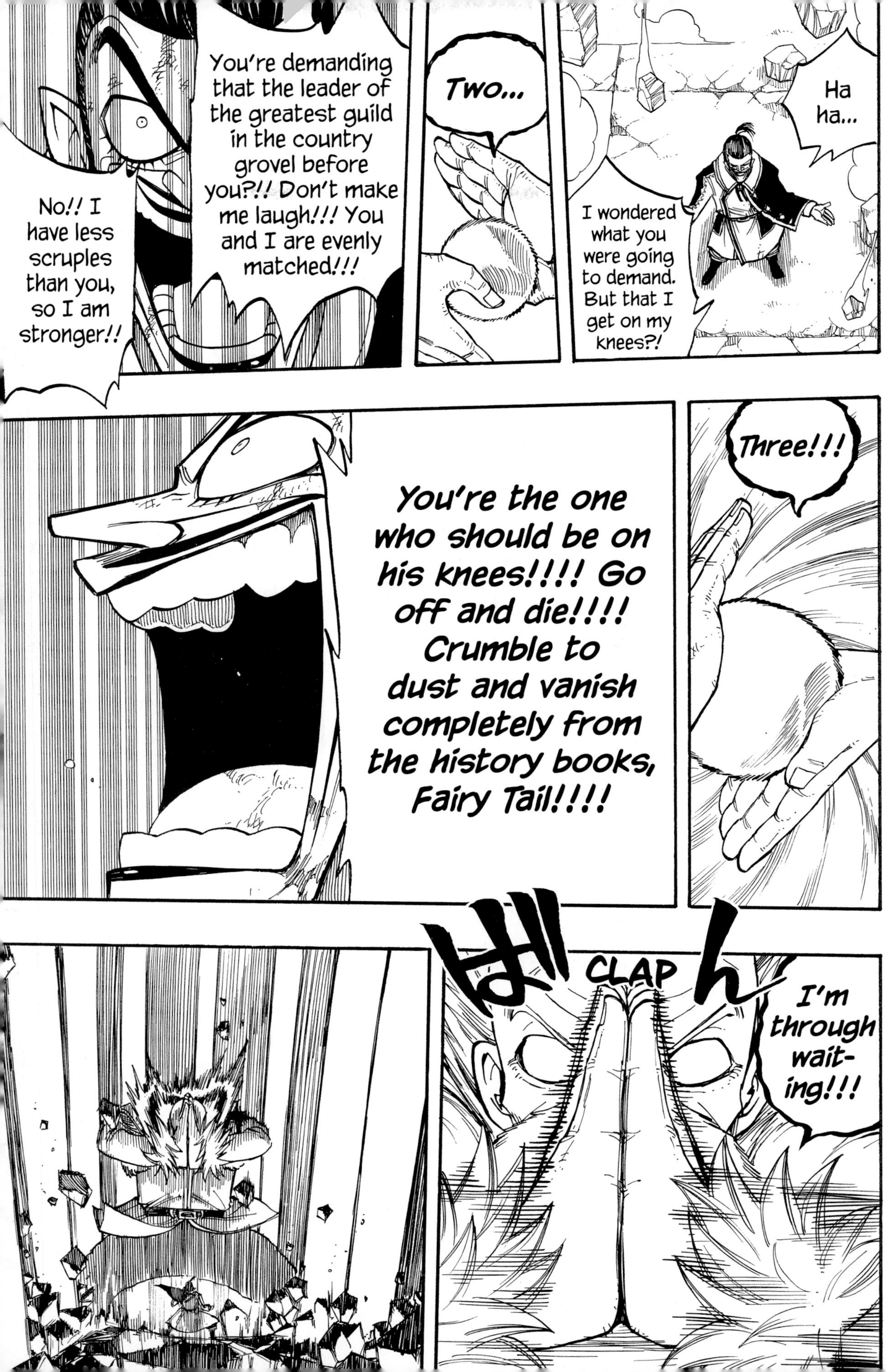
Ha ha...
I wondered what you were going to demand. But that I get on my knees?!
Two...
You're demanding that the leader of the greatest guild in the country grovel before you?!! Don't make me laugh!!! You and I are evenly matched!!!
No!! I have less scruples than you, so I am stronger!!
Three!!!
You're the one who should be on his knees!!!! Go off and die!!!! Crumble to dust and vanish completely from the history books, Fairy Tail!!!!
CLAP
I'm through wait-ing!!!

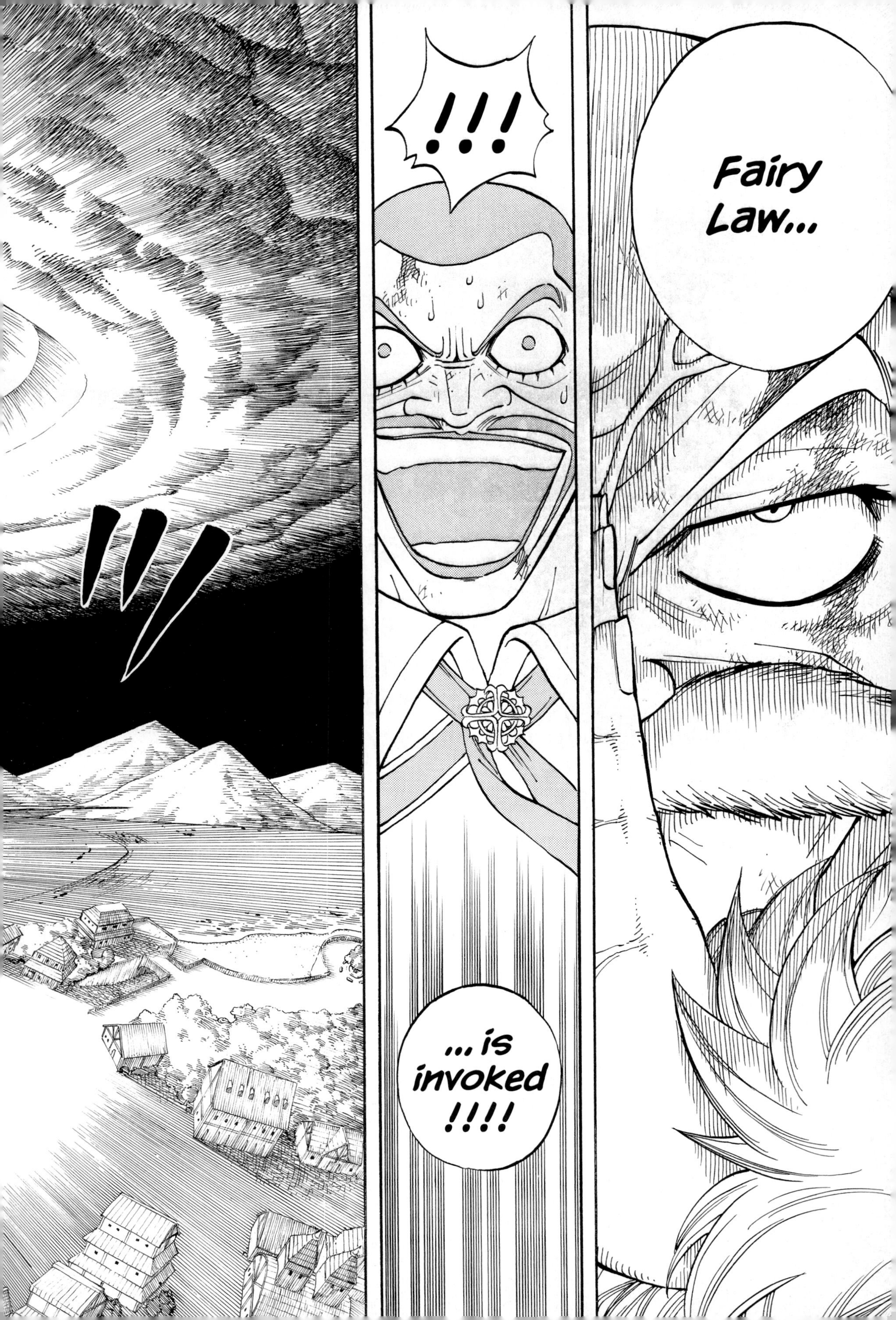
Fairy Law...
!!!
...is invoked !!!!

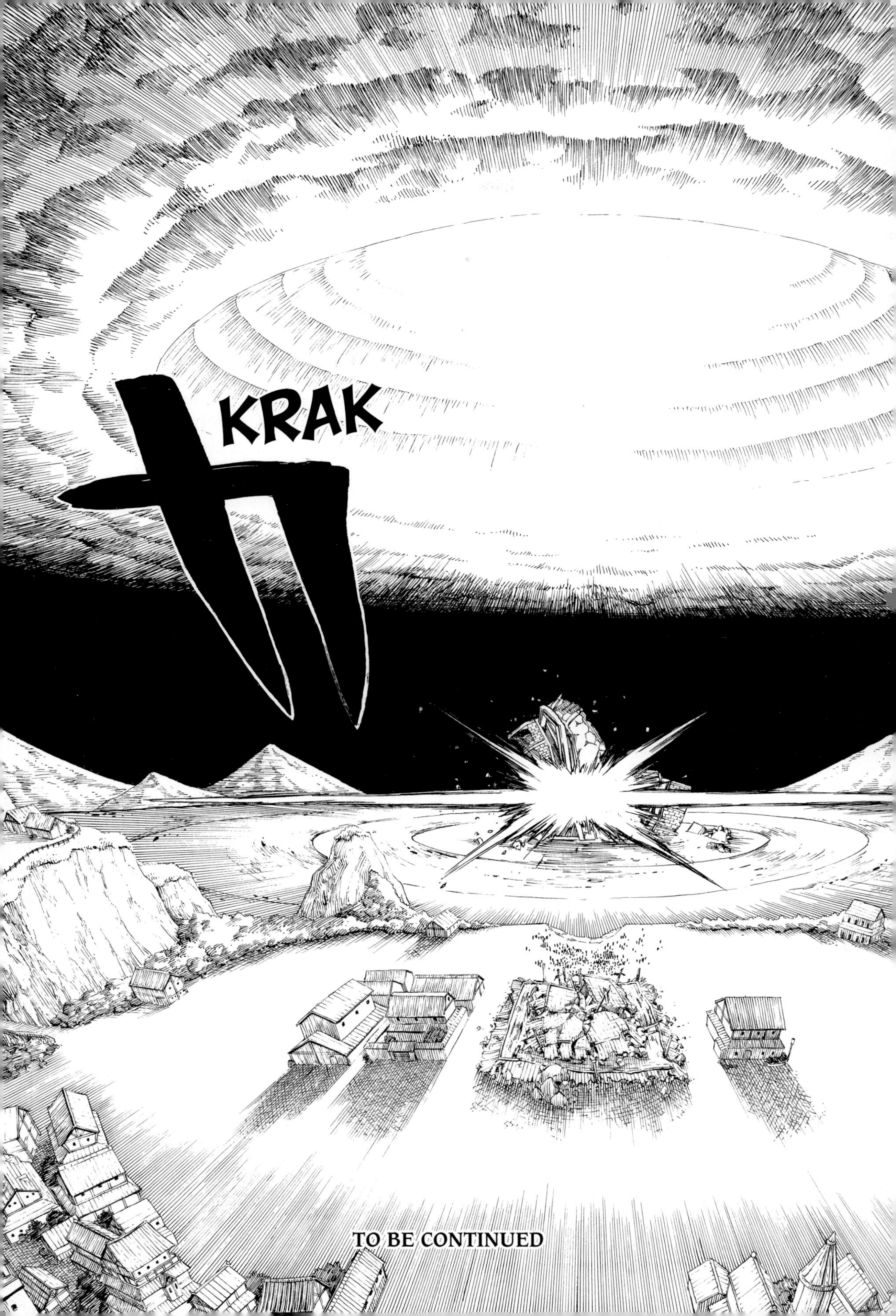
KRAK
TO BE CONTINUED

Continued from the left-hand page

Mira: Shall we read the next question?

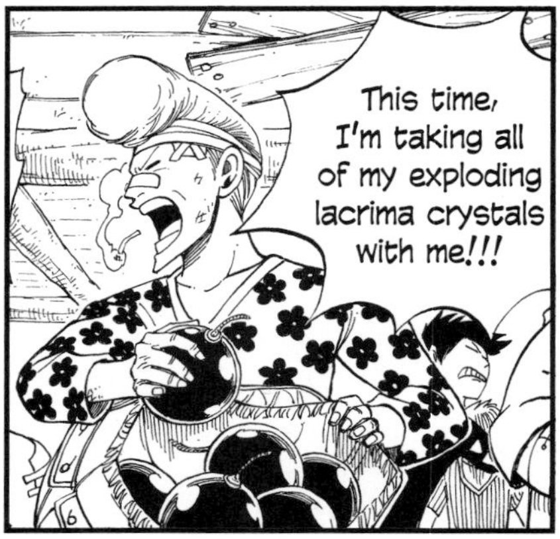
This time, I'm taking all of my exploding lacrima crystals with me!!!

What's a lacrima?

Lucy: It's a magical crystal. A magic item that even normal humans can use.
Mira: That's right. I think for people living in the world these questions are coming from, you should picture a lighter in your minds. Even if you can't do magic, you can make fire with a lighter, right? In the same way, there are magical items in our world that have made their way into people's everyday lives.
Lucy: "Lacrima"...that means "tear," right?
Mira: Yep! But if lacrima are distributed too widely, then our work as wizards might dry up! I think that's why the creator gave it such a masochistic-sounding name.

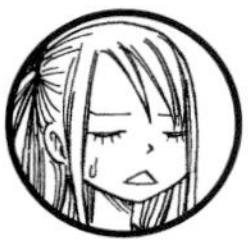
: Is...that...right...?

Mira: And now, our final question.
Lucy: All right!! Now we hit the sea!!
Mira: It's a question ***about*** the sea.
Lucy: Huh?

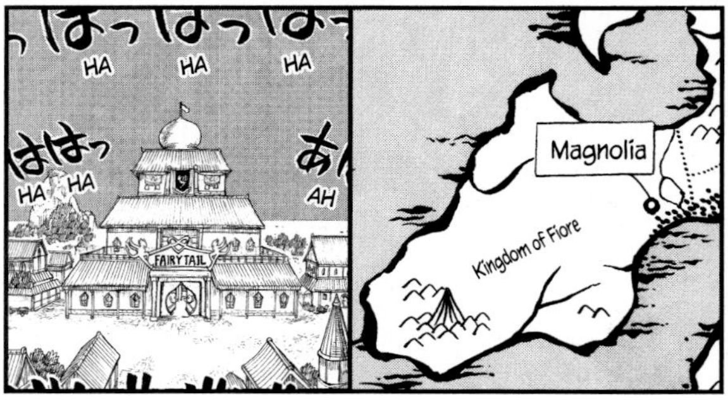
HA
HA
HA
HA HA
AH
FAIRY TAIL
Magnolia
Kingdom of Fiore

In some scenes, the Fairy Tail guild is shown right in front of a huge sea, but on the map, the guild seems to be pretty far inland...?

Mira: ....
Lucy: ....

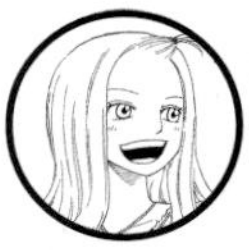
:Why don't we go swimming, Lucy?

Lucy: Sure! But what is the meaning of this?!
Mira: You've got to give the reader credit. He's pretty sharp.
Lucy: I'm sure the author is putting on a face that says, "Oops!" right now.
Mira: Actually, that's a lake.
Lucy: Don't you think it might be a little too big for a lake?

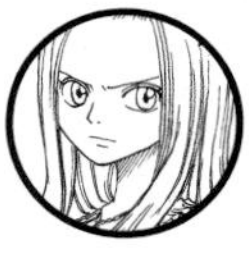
: Let's just say it's a lake and let it go at that, okay?
Lucy: I-I...guess...it's okay...
Mira: Fine! Now, let's go swimming.

: With a lake that close, I don't have any idea why we came all the way to the seaside to swim, though.

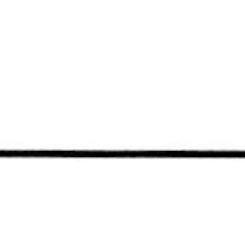

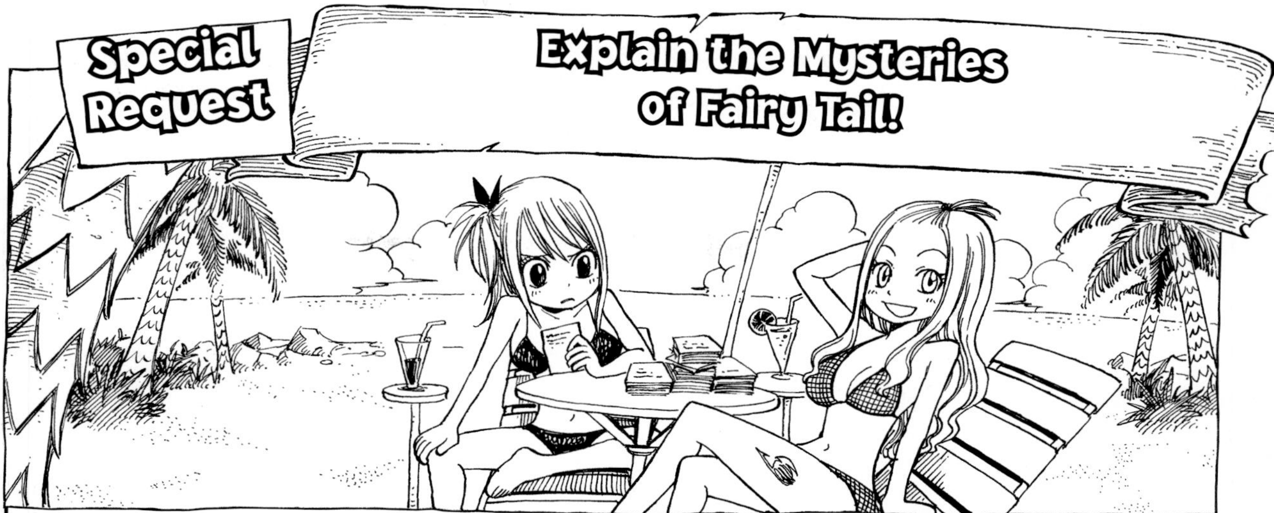
Special Request
Explain the Mysteries of Fairy Tail!

From the Beach at Hargeon

: This time, we bring you this corner, not from the guild, but from the seaside!

: We're at the beach! We should be having fun!! Why do we have to do this?!!

Mira: Because the artist doesn't really think his stories through, so there are a lot of postcards from the readers with questions.
Lucy: Then let's get this over with fast, so we can go swimming!! Come on, Mira-san!!
Mira: Okay, here's our first question.

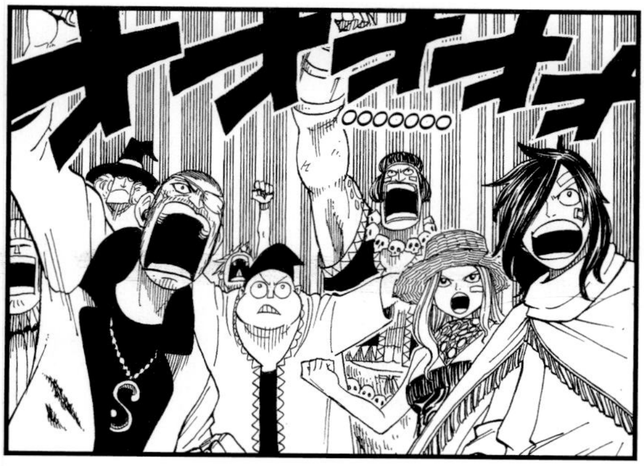
OOOOOOO

Does every member of Fairy Tail have the symbol somewhere on their bodies?
Lucy: Normally, it's in a place you can't see.
Mira: Yes, of course everybody does.
Lucy: I have mine on the back of my hand. It's on Natsu's right shoulder. It's on Erza's left arm.
Mira: As you can see ↑, it's on my left thigh.

: Wow!! So that's where you have it?

: Loke has it on his **ck.

: **His **ck?!!!!**

Mira: That's right. His **ck.

Lucy: Mira-san...Um...Uh...Is that...okay?

Mira: Of course! It's a magic stamp! Not a tattoo!!

Lucy: No, I don't mean that. I mean...is it okay to talk about things like that here...?

Mira: Huh? Why would talking about his B-A-C-K not be okay?

Lucy: His... b... ack...?

Mira: Of course. His **ck.

Lucy: Y-You know, in my opinion, there's no reason to censor that.

Continued on the right-hand page ↗

TAIL d'ART

The *Fairy Tail* Guild d'Art is an explosion of fan art! Please send in your black-and-white art on large postcard stock!! Those chosen to be published will get a signed mini poster!♪ Make sure you write your real name and address on the back of your postcard!

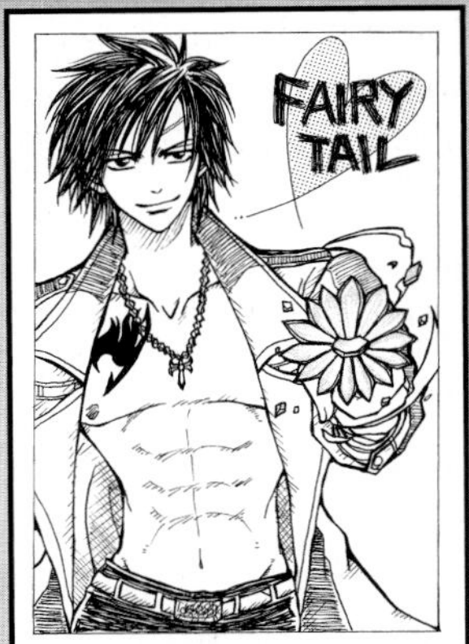
FAIRY TAIL

▼ Whoa! He's cool!! It looks like Gray's popularity isn't slipping in the slightest! (How does a guy that shy and retiring do it?)

Kagawa Prefecture, Tôjûrô

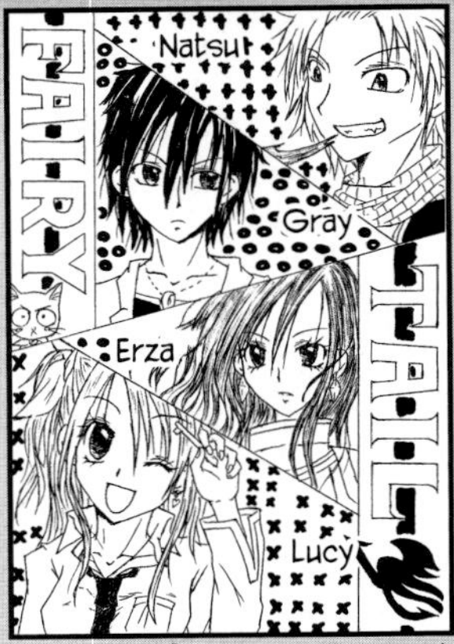
Natsu
Gray
Erza
Lucy
FAIRY
TAIL

▼ I especially like Erza and the odd way that she shines.

Akita Prefecture, Mikan-bako

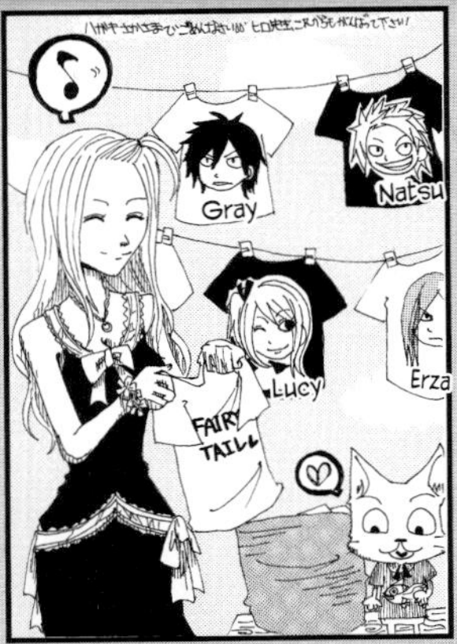
Gray
Natsu
Lucy
Erza
FAIRY TAIL

▼ I think that Mira-chan actually does everybody's laundry, too!

Shizuoka Prefecture, Chawanmushi

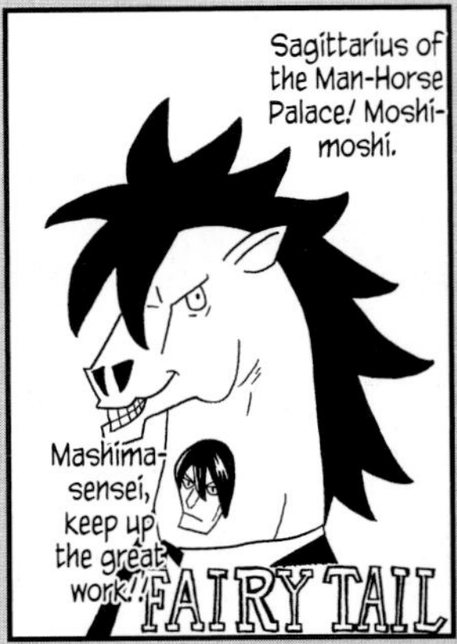
Sagittarius of the Man-Horse Palace! Moshi-moshi.
Mashima-sensei, keep up the great work!!
FAIRY TAIL

▼ Here's our "rare-character" fan art for this time. I never expected it to be *this* character!!

Saitama Prefecture, Ishii Jun

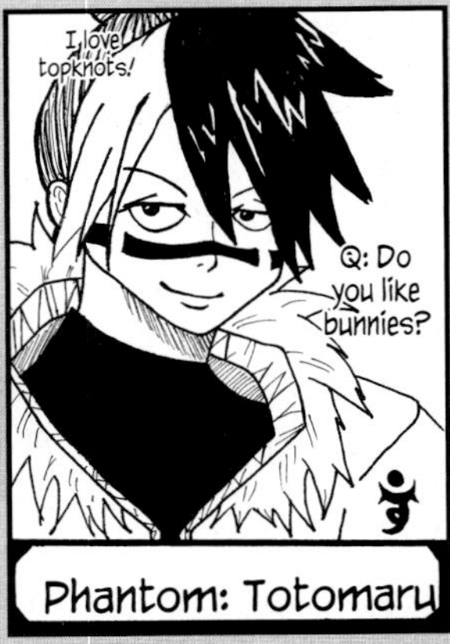
I love topknots!
Q: Do you like bunnies?
Phantom: Totomaru

▼ So you like bunnies? I have to say that is...pretty normal.

Niigata Prefecture, Neko-Punch

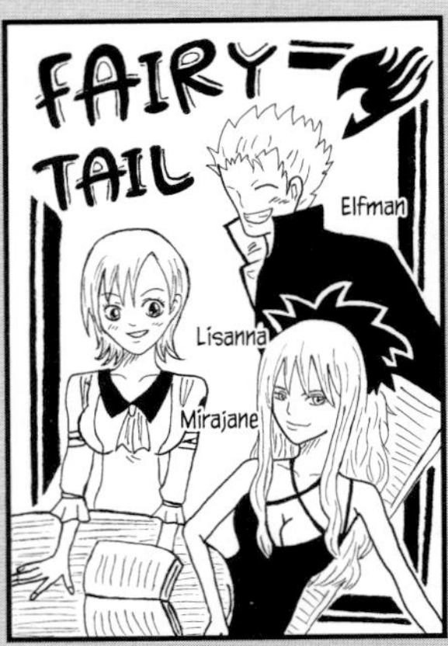
FAIRY TAIL
Elfman
Lisanna
Mirajane

▼ The story of these three isn't over yet! I'm going to draw the next chapter someday!

Tokushima Prefecture, Black

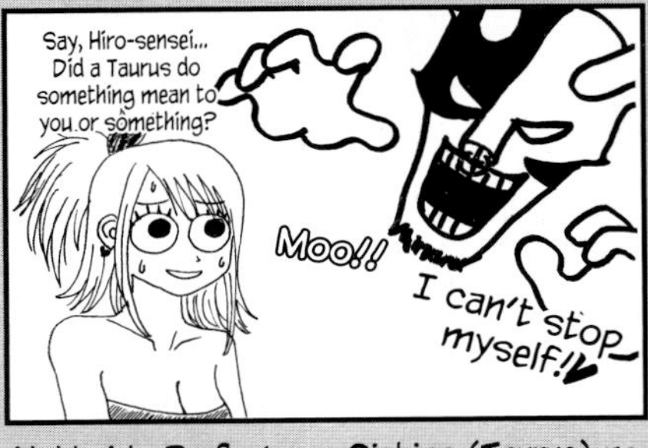
Say, Hiro-sensei... Did a Taurus do something mean to you or something?
Moo!!
I can't stop myself!!♥

▼ Actually, I'm a Taurus myself! So I draw him with the utmost loving attention!

Hokkaido Prefecture, Oishiza (Taurus) no-i

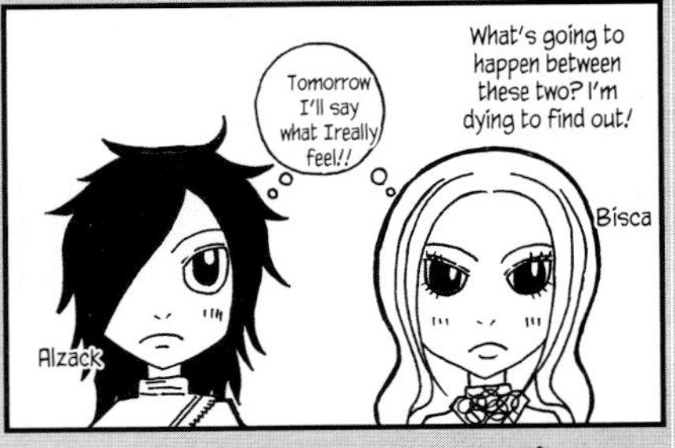
What's going to happen between these two? I'm dying to find out!
Tomorrow I'll say what I really feel!!
Bisca
Alzack

▼ Thanks for rooting for the simple love story! Now, what will happen between them?

Kôchi Prefecture, Karyû

Send to Hiro Mashima, Kodansha Comics
451 Park Ave. South, 7th Floor New York, NY 10016

FAIRY GUILD

Any letters and postcards you send with your personal information, such as your name, address, postal code, and other information, will be handed over, as is, to the author. When you send mail, please keep that in mind.

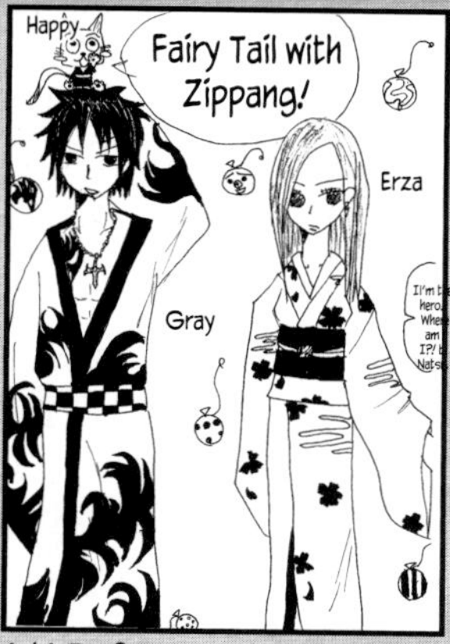
Happy
Fairy Tail with Zippang!
Erza
Gray
Aichi Prefecture, Nakane Chisato

◀ Hey, I like this kind of picture, too! I really like the slender Erza!!

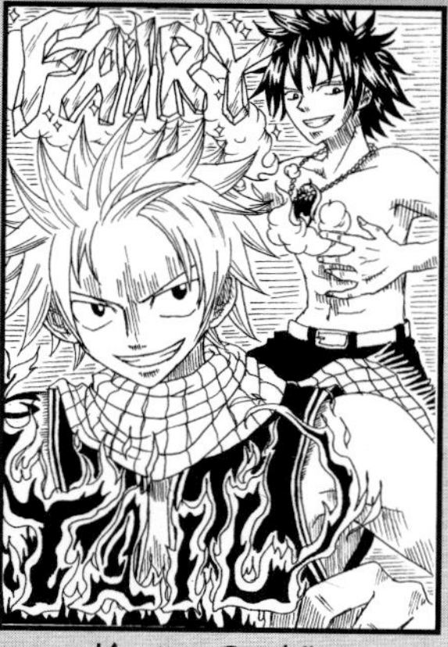
FAIRY TAIL
Kyoto, Sachiko

◀ This artist did the logo as fire and ice!! I never thought of that!

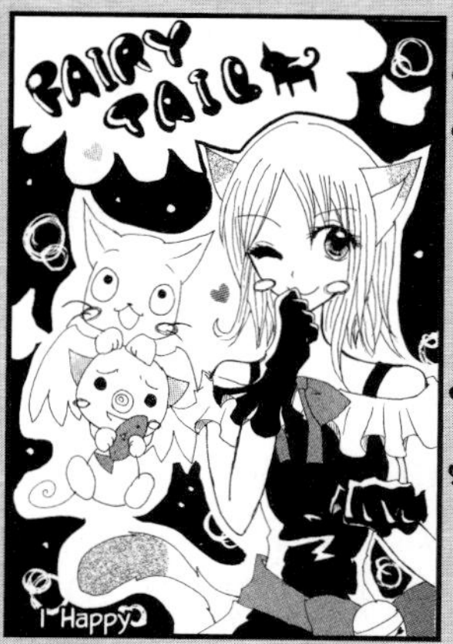
FAIRY TAIL
I Happy
Aichi Prefecture, Happy Love2

◀ These are what people call "nekomimi" (cat's ears). I think *zōmimi* (elephant ears) are going to be the next big thing!

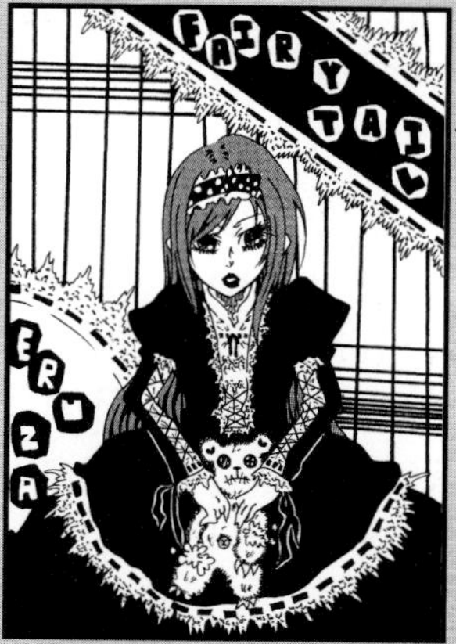
FAIRY TAIL
ERZA
Gunma Prefecture, Ishijima Tomoka

◀ Goth Erza, and so well done!! I'm really bad at drawing clothes like that!! (Just look at Sherry!)

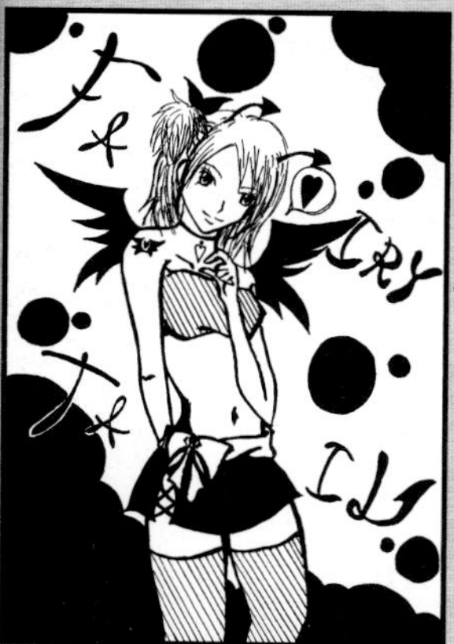
Ibaragi Prefecture, Namikaze

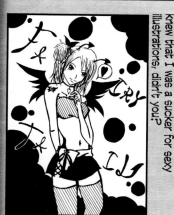

◀ A little devil Lucy. Hm... You already knew that I was a sucker for sexy illustrations, didn't you?

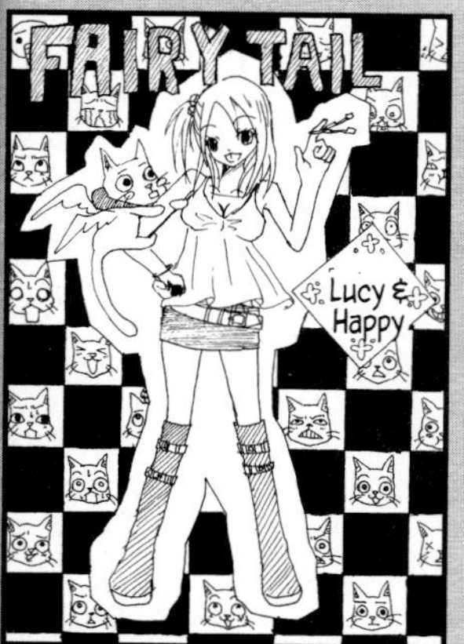
FAIRY TAIL
Lucy & Happy
Saitama Prefecture, Ajisai

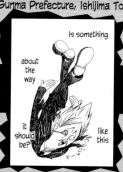

◀ There are a ton of Happys in the background all making great faces!!

Rejection Corner

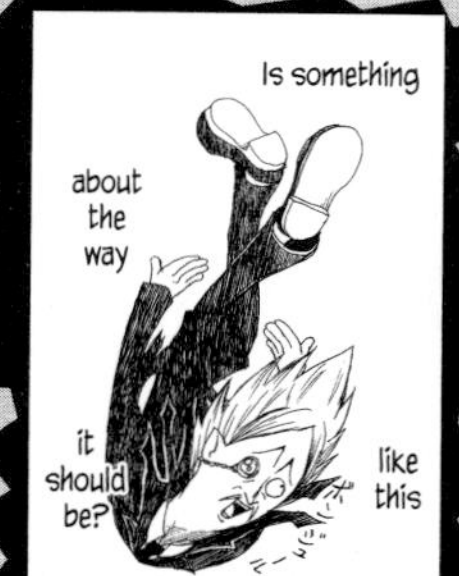
Is something
about the way
like this
it should be?

◀ Well... Sure, why wouldn't it be? Whatever that means.

Kyoto, Hirorin Sumiyabazaru

AFTERWORD

Once I set on the idea of doing a dragon slayer, I knew that other dragon slayers would show up. And after a long wait, the one who showed up was Gajeel-kun (at work, we all call him Gajeel-kun (♦♦)). As Natsu's rival, he was extremely scary right from the start. Actually, there was a fight scene planned between Gajeel-kun on one side and Loke (guy with glasses) and Reedus (big guy) on the other, but with the way the episode shaped up, it had to be cut. Still, instead we got a pretty hot fight between him and Natsu, so we'll call it a good thing. Right at the very beginning, some characters called the dragon-slaying magic "Dragon Slayer," but in point of fact, dragon slayers are the people who use dragon-slaying magic. Sorry for all the confusion. This wasn't a mistake. It's just such an old form of magic that the characters don't understand the term anymore. As time went on, people had trouble differentiating between the magic and the users of that magic. But I didn't get that across to the readers very well, huh?(♦)

By the way, there are even more dragon slayers in this world. They may appear over the course of the story, but then again, they may not. The dragon Igneel passed on the techniques for slaying dragons and then disappeared. Hmm…A weird story. But I have my reasons for it, and those reasons may become key information later on. But then again, they may not. Hmm…I sort of forgot what I was trying to say, so I'm just going to end this here.

Translation Notes

Japanese is a tricky language for most Westerners, and translation is often more art than science. For your edification and reading pleasure, here are notes on some of the places where we could have gone in a different direction in our translation of the work, or where a Japanese cultural reference is used.

Fair-Weather Charm, page 393

The Japanese have a popular charm that is supposed to avert rain: the *teru-teru bôzu*, where *teru* means "to shine" as in sunshine, and *bôzu* means a Buddhist priest or monk. To make one, a white tissue, napkin, or cloth is wrapped around a ball and tied off at the "neck" making a head with the rest of the cloth or paper trailing off as robes. Usually a smiley face is drawn on it (see page 15 for a slightly clumsy example). It is called a *"bôzu"* because it has a round, bald head much like Buddhist monks or priests do. Once the charm is made, it is usually hung under the roof's rafters as a charm to stop the rain. If it is hung upside down, it is supposed to encourage the rain to fall.

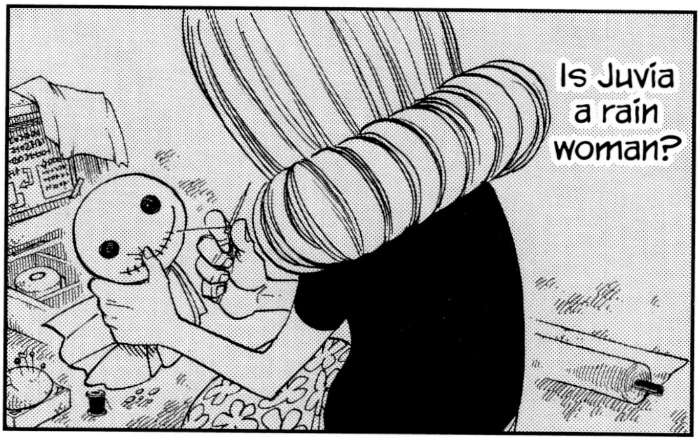
Is Juvia a rain woman?

Rain Woman, page 405

Rain Women (*Ame onna* in Japanese) are a recurrent theme in Japanese folklore, and later, much used in manga and anime. In ancient Japan's agrarian culture, the rain women were called upon to help rain fall on the crops, and some worshipped *Ame onna* as deities. In more recent depictions they tend to be tragic figures who bring nonstop rain wherever they go, shunned and ostracized for something they cannot control.

Nattô, page 453

There are foods in nearly every culture that are generally loved by those within the culture and abhorred by almost anyone coming to the culture from the outside. Hawaii has *poi*, the Inuit have *muqtuq* blubber, and the Japanese have *nattô*. *Nattô* is a strong-smelling fermented soybean dish in which beans are connected by a viscous, stringy, slimy fluid. The dish is very nutritious, containing *nattokinase*, a fibrinolytic enzyme that is said to prevent clotting in the arteries. However, despite the benefits, most non-Japanese can't palate it. Of course, there are some Western lovers of *nattô*, and a large number of Japanese who do not eat it—in other words, there are always exceptions—but the rule is, Japanese love *nattô* and foreigners can't stand the stuff.

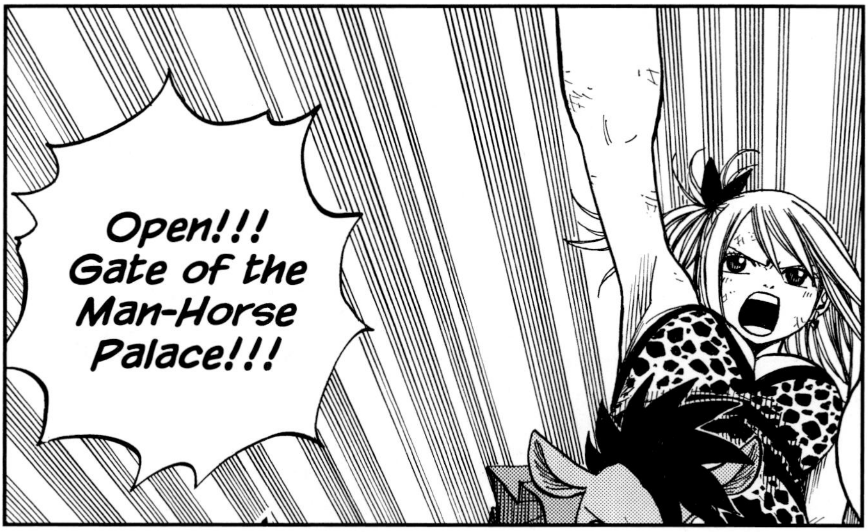
Open!!! Gate of the Man-Horse Palace!!!

Man-Horse Palace, page 507

Sagittarius is Latin for "Archer," and that is how it is referred to in astrology, but in Greek mythology, Sagittarius is Chiron, the Centaur. Chiron was unlike the other, bestial centaurs, and instead was a wise and learned hunter and healer. In this version, Mashima-sensei makes a joke of the man-horse by presenting it in an unusual way. However, if I had translated the palace as the "Centaur Palace," Mashima's version of the man-horse wouldn't follow logically as it does with the more literal translation of "Man-Horse Palace."

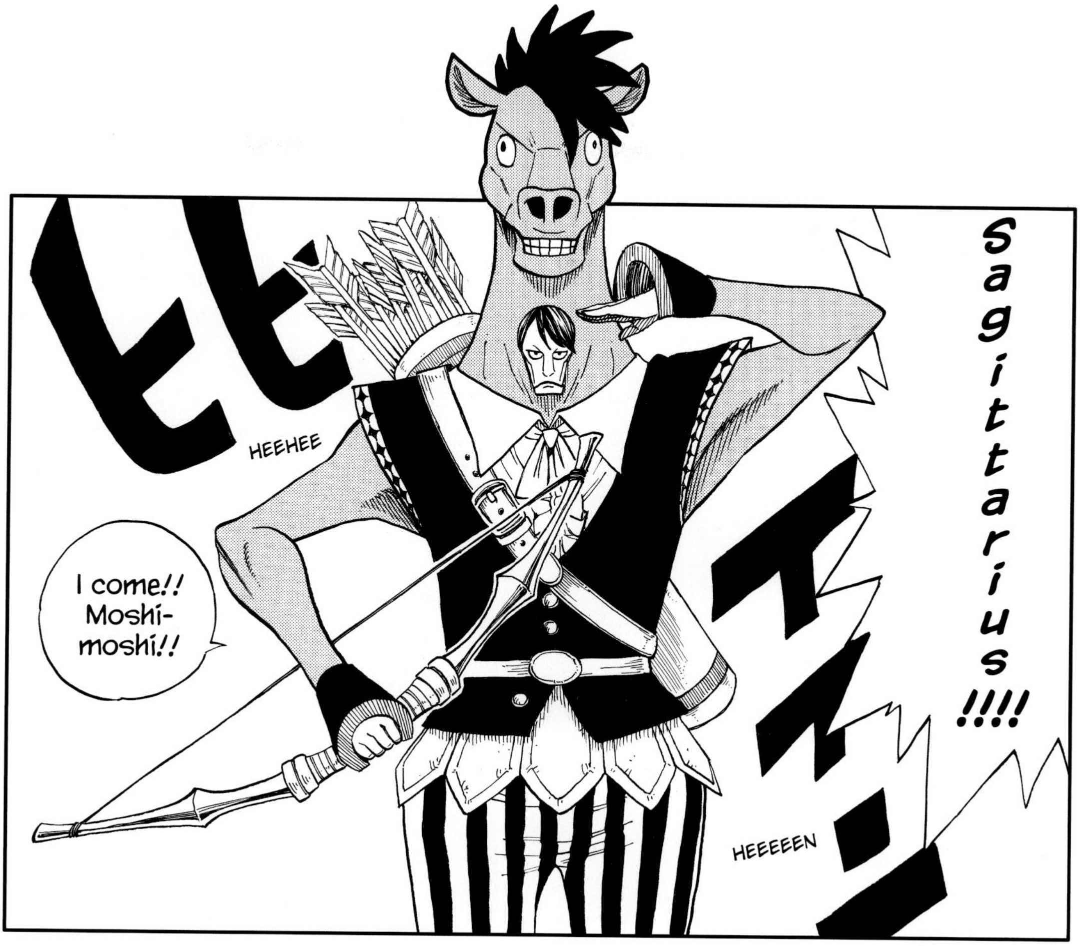
Sagittarius!!!!
HEEHEE
I come!! Moshi-moshi!!
HEEEEEN

Moshi-moshi, page 507

At first, I thought Sagittarius's "moshi-moshi," was a Japanese horse sound, but I could find no incidents of horses using that sound in my research. (If you know of examples, let me know!) I just have to assume that it is a cute sentence-ending sound much like Cancer's "-ebi" at the end of his sentences (see the note in volume 2). By the way, the phrase, "moshi-moshi" is generally used as the English "hello" is used when answering the phone or when tentatively trying to get someone's attention. That doesn't seem to be Sagittarius's meaning when using the phrase here, though.

Topknots, page 578

Most samurai-movie fans recognize the classic samurai hairstyle of a shaved forehead and a topknot (an oiled ponytail that comes forward over the top of the head). It is called in Japanese a *chonmage.* Totomaru doesn't have the samurai style of topknot, but he does have a rather punk-style topknot.

FAIRY TAIL

9

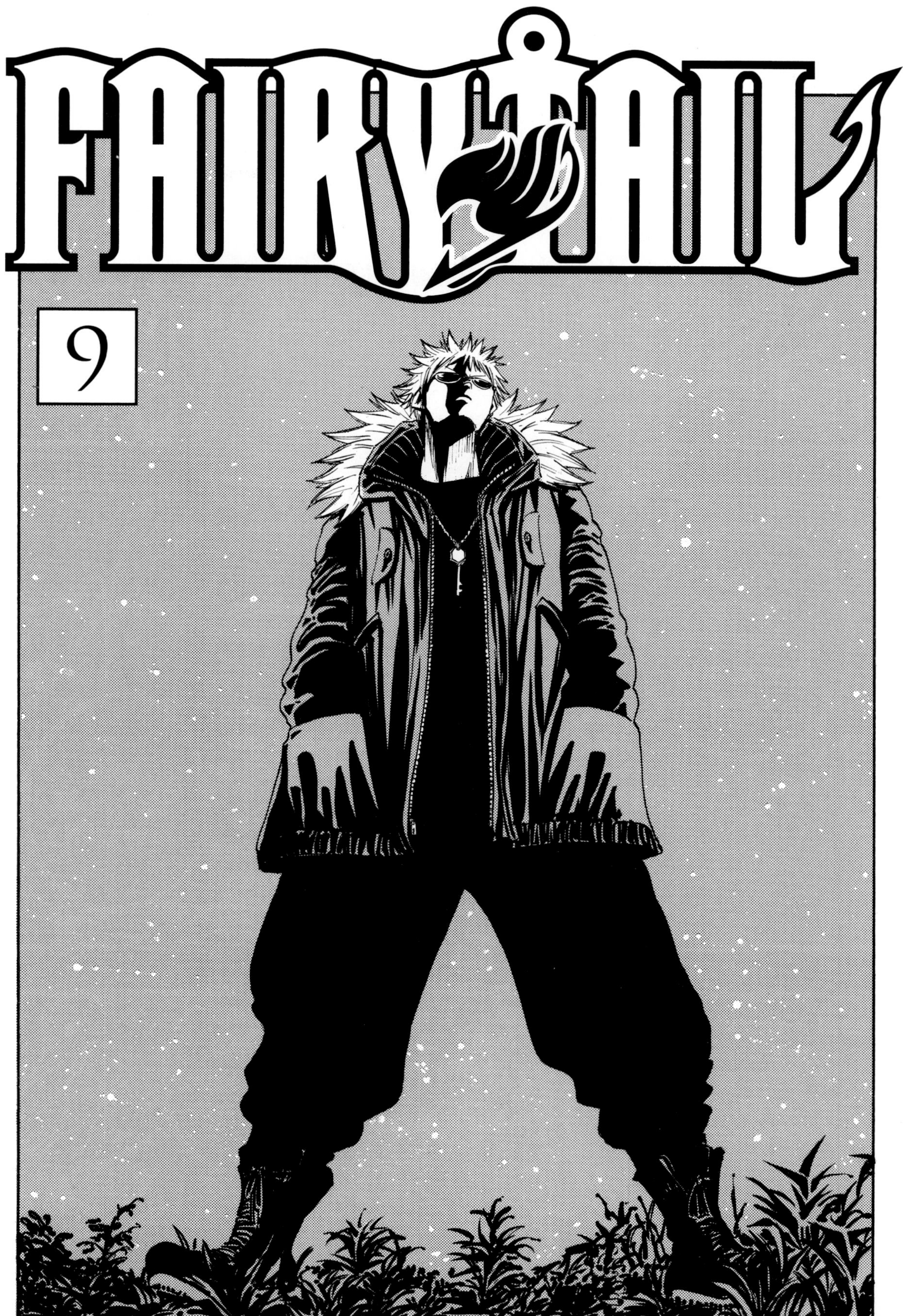

HIRO MASHIMA

Photo of the Mashima Group and
Yoshikawa Group combined.

I've been hanging out with Miki
Yoshikawa-sensei (I usually follow
her name with "-chan" but...) for
more than five years. She has been
a good friend at times, and at other
times a good rival. Although she
started in manga after me, she's a
well-respected member of my circle
of friends. Since we're both so
busy, we are only able to hang out
together once or twice a year, but
during the times we can get both
of our groups together, it's really
fun! On the day of this picture, we
were playing video games from the
morning on....What a great group
of adults, huh? Ah ha ha ha!! They
were really fun people!

—Hiro Mashima

FAIRY TAIL

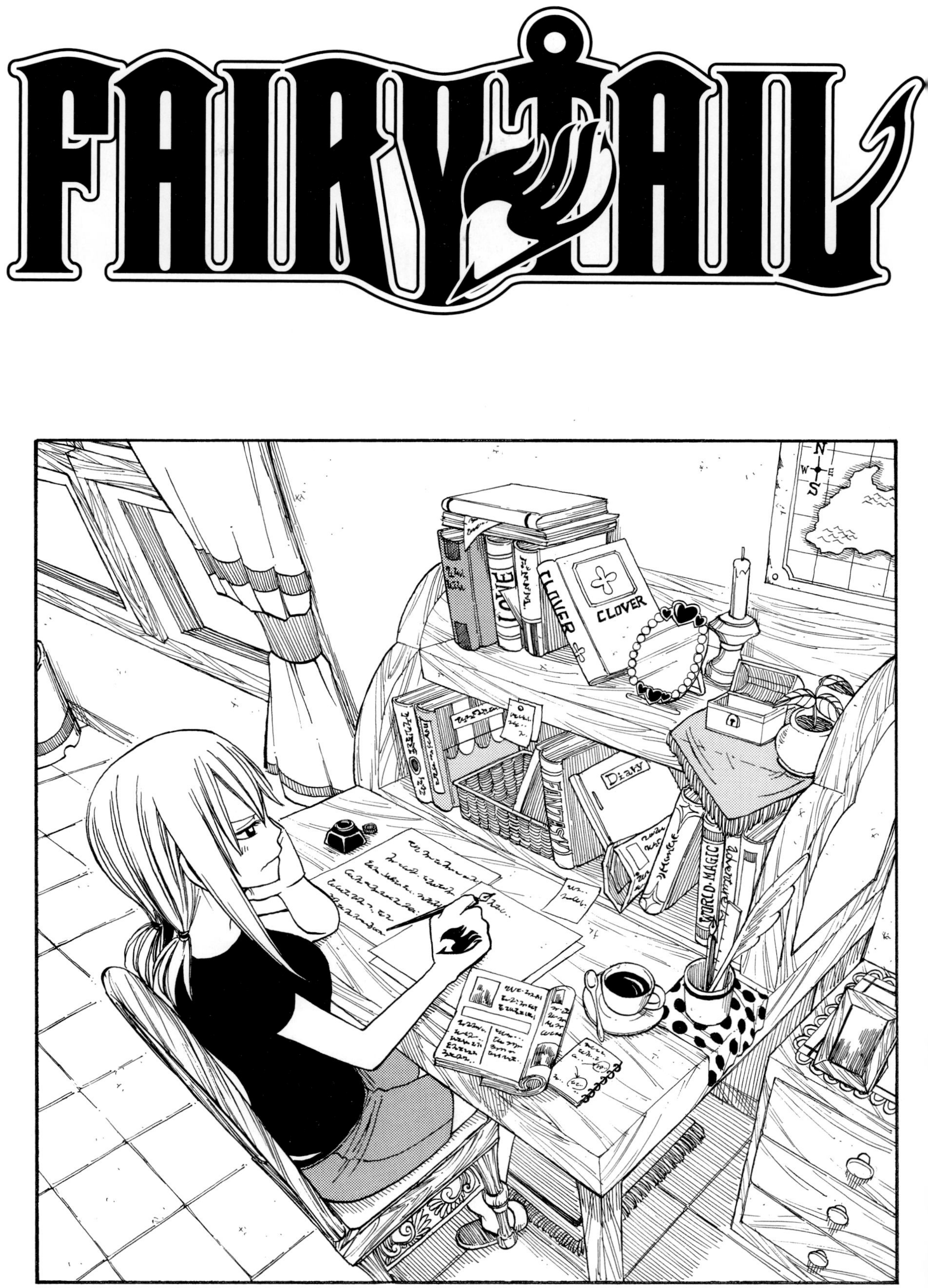
CLOVER
CLOVER
Diary
WORLD-MAGIC

Chapter 66: Like-Minded

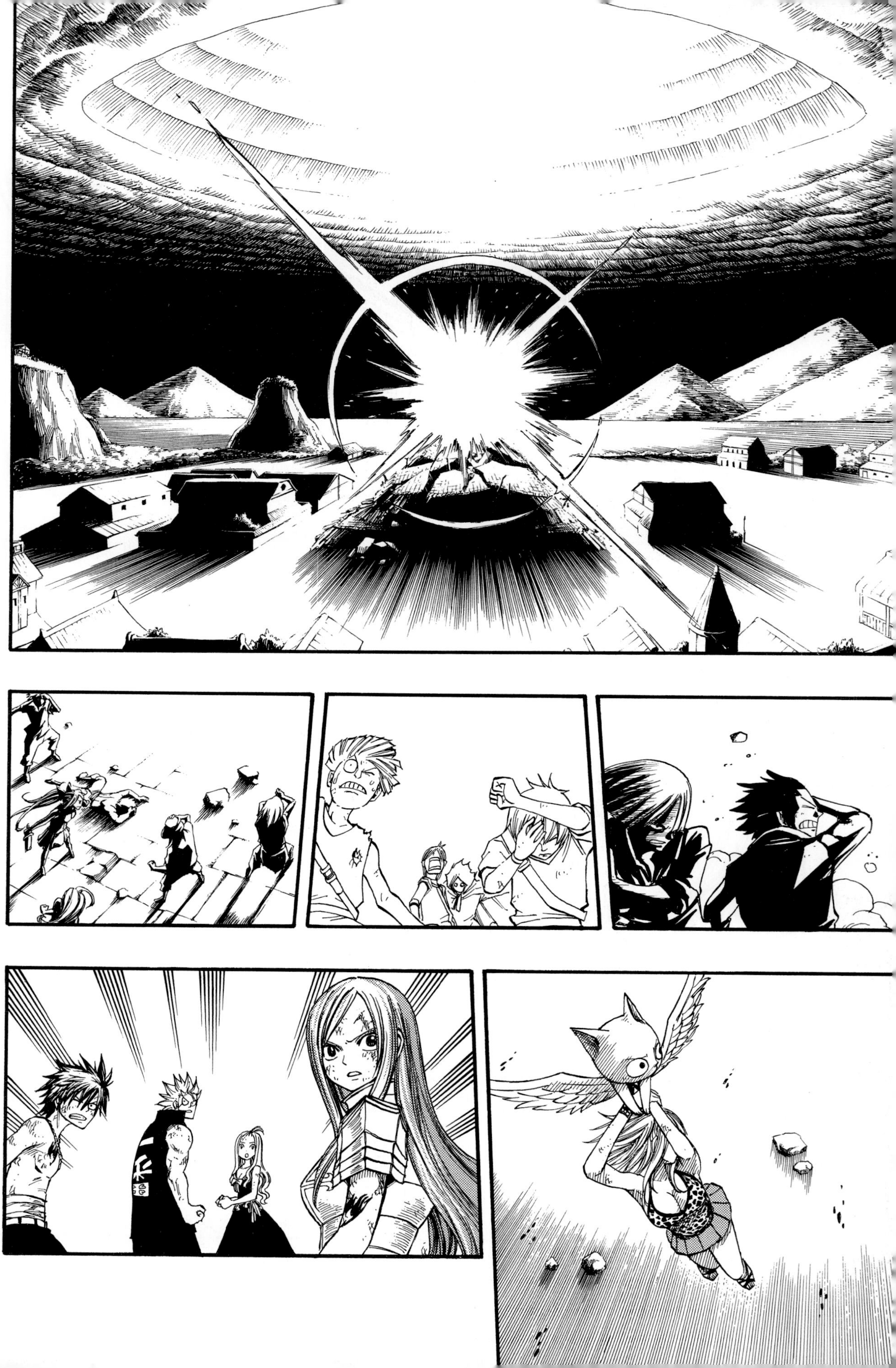

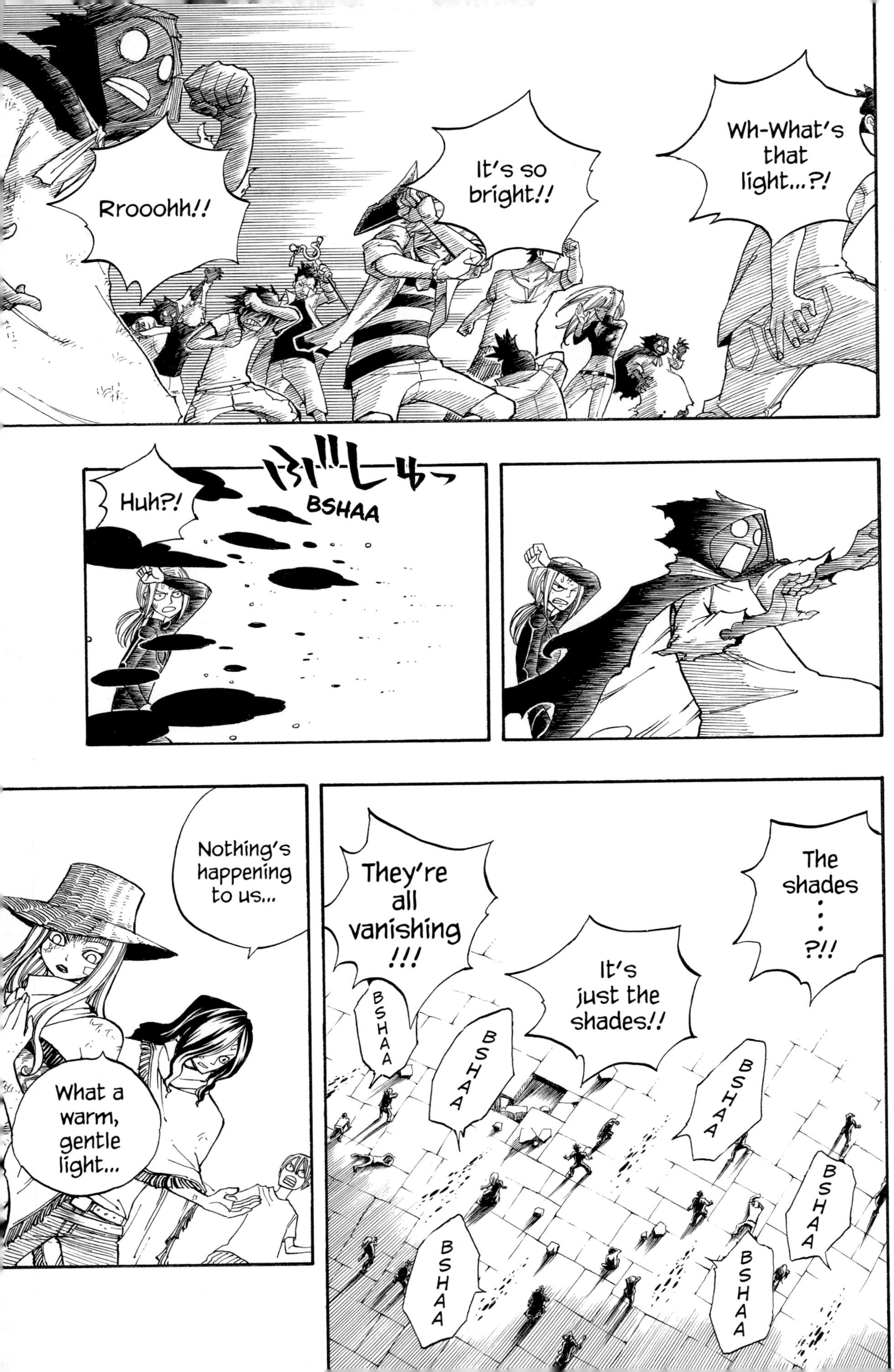
Wh-What's that light...?!
It's so bright!!
Rroooh!!
BSHAA
Huh?!
The shades...?!!
They're all vanishing!!!
It's just the shades!!
BSHAA
BSHAA
BSHAA
BSHAA
BSHAA
BSHAA
Nothing's happening to us...
What a warm, gentle light...

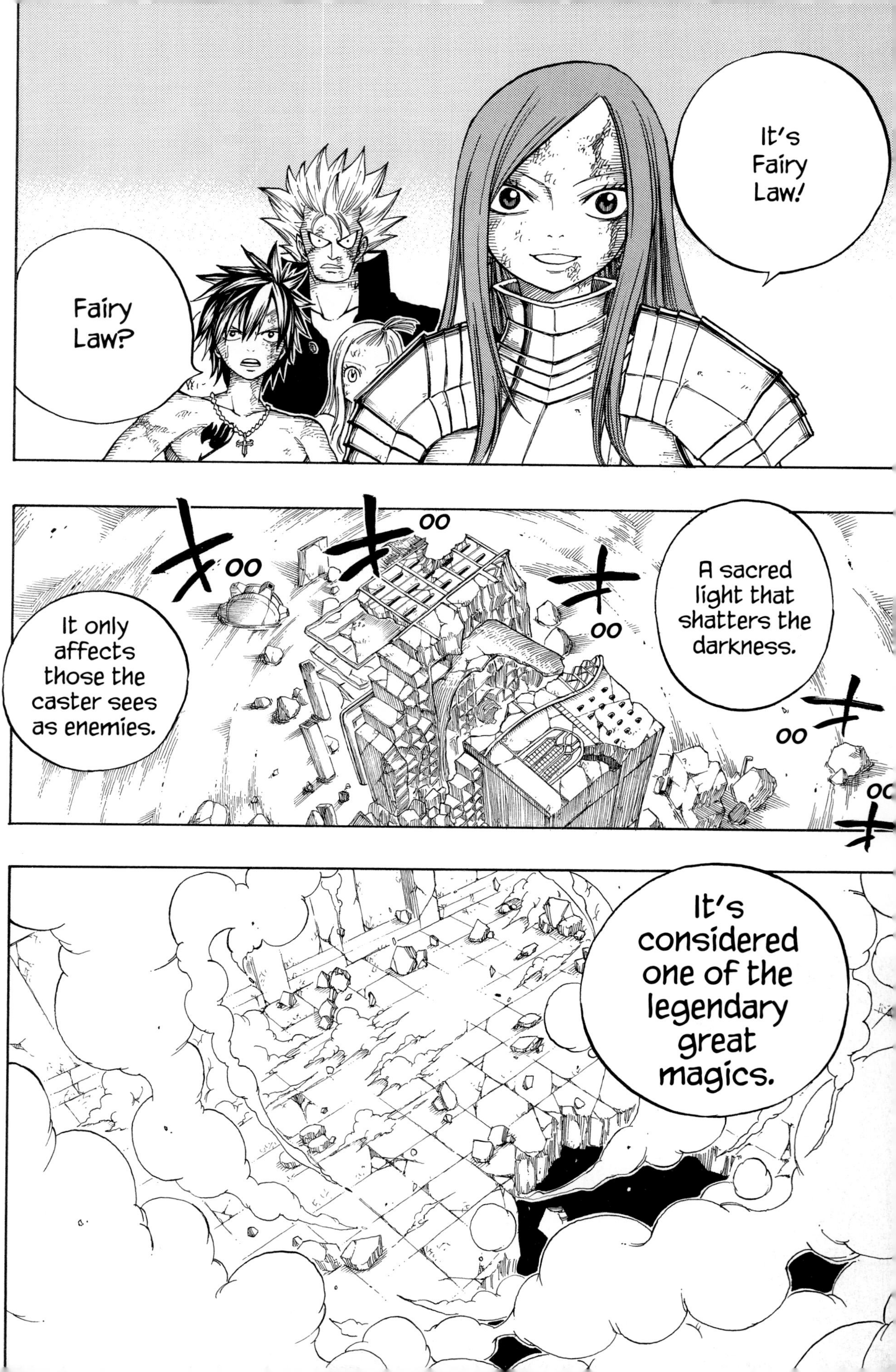
It's Fairy Law!
Fairy Law?
A sacred light that shatters the darkness.
It only affects those the caster sees as enemies.
It's considered one of the legendary great magics.

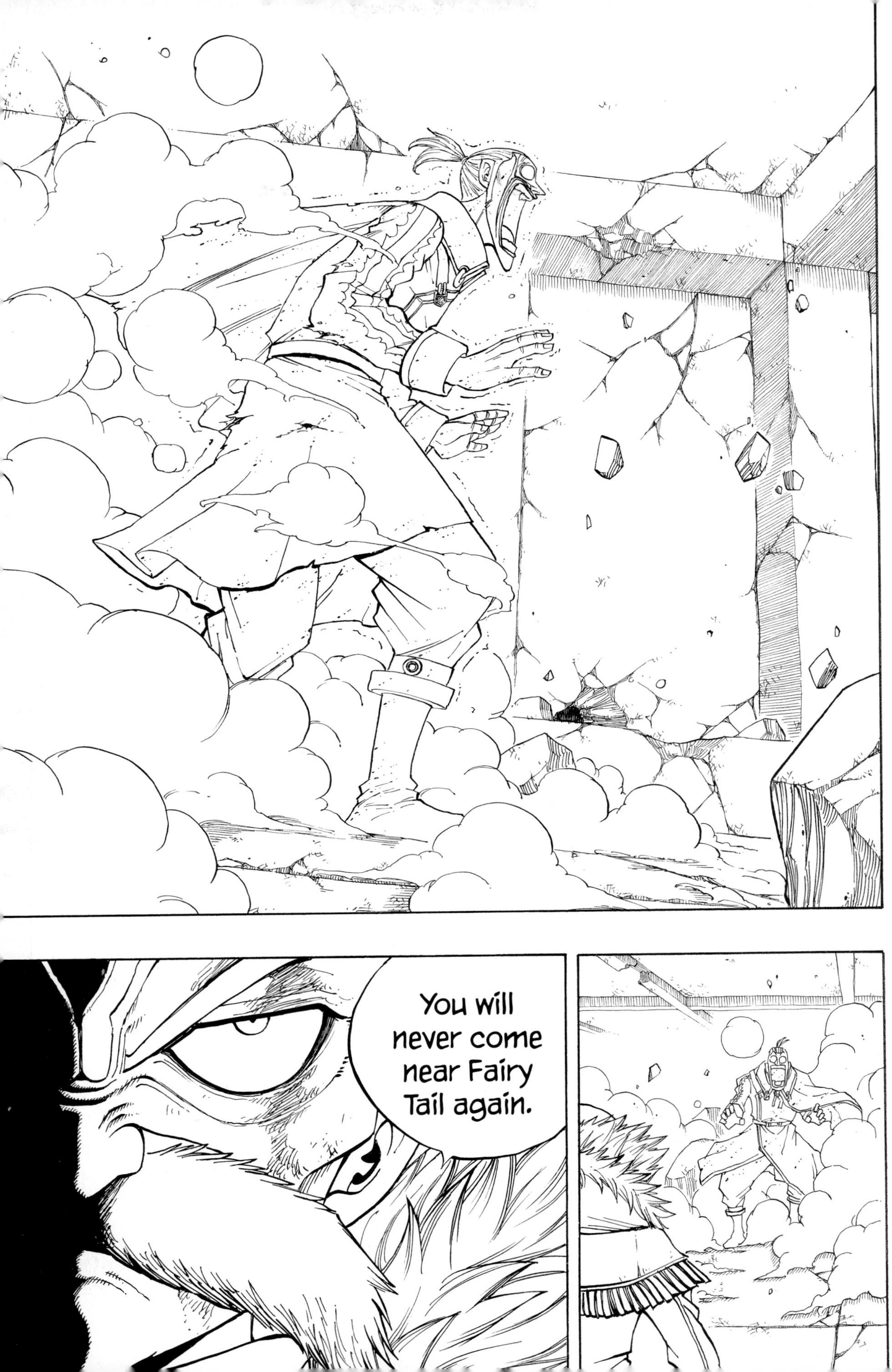
You will never come near Fairy Tail again.

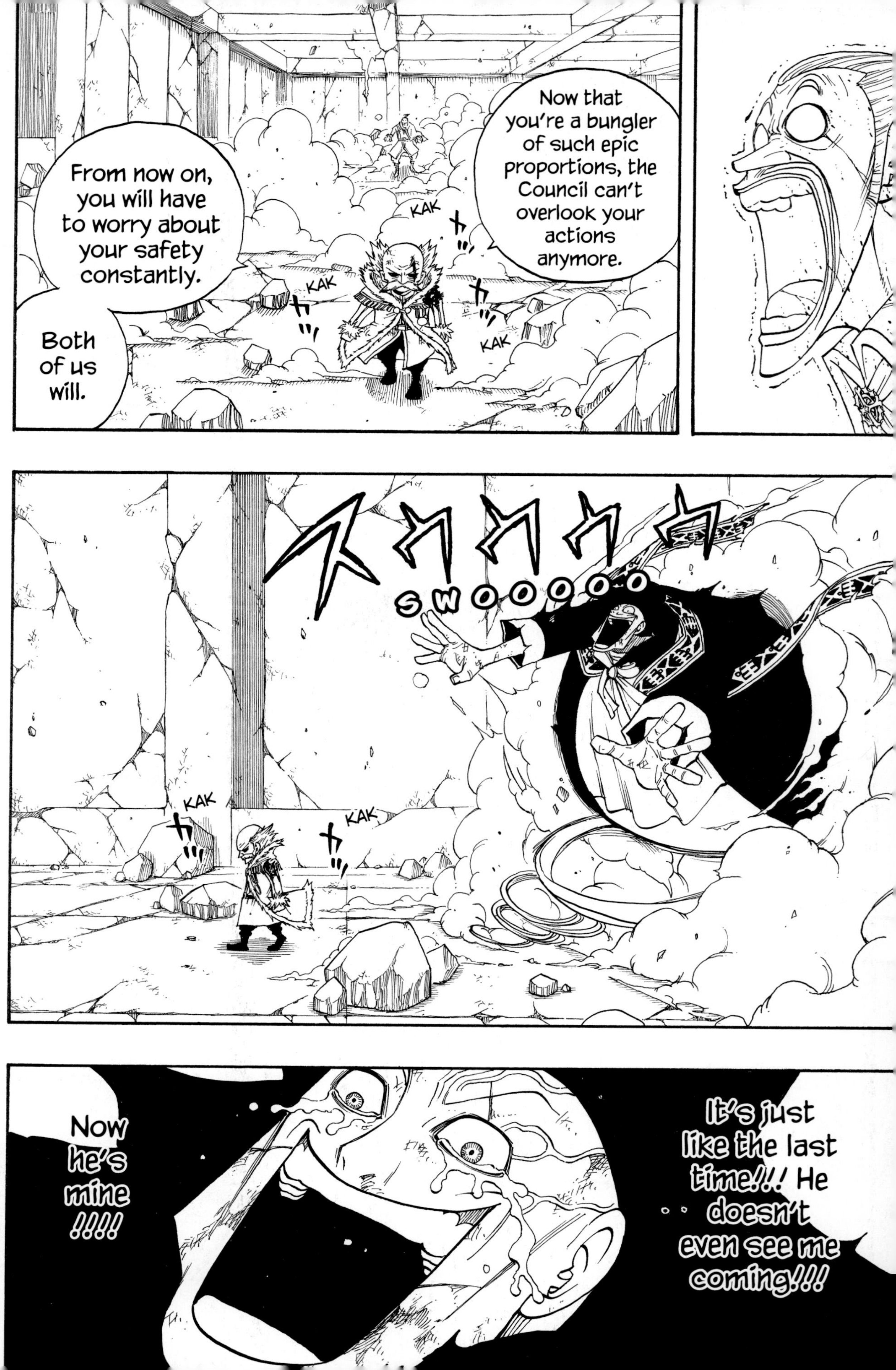
Now that you're a bungler of such epic proportions, the Council can't overlook your actions anymore.
From now on, you will have to worry about your safety constantly.
KAK
KAK
KAK
Both of us will.
スウウウウ
SWOOOOO
KAK
KAK
It's just like the last time!!! He doesn't even see me coming!!!
Now he's mine!!!!

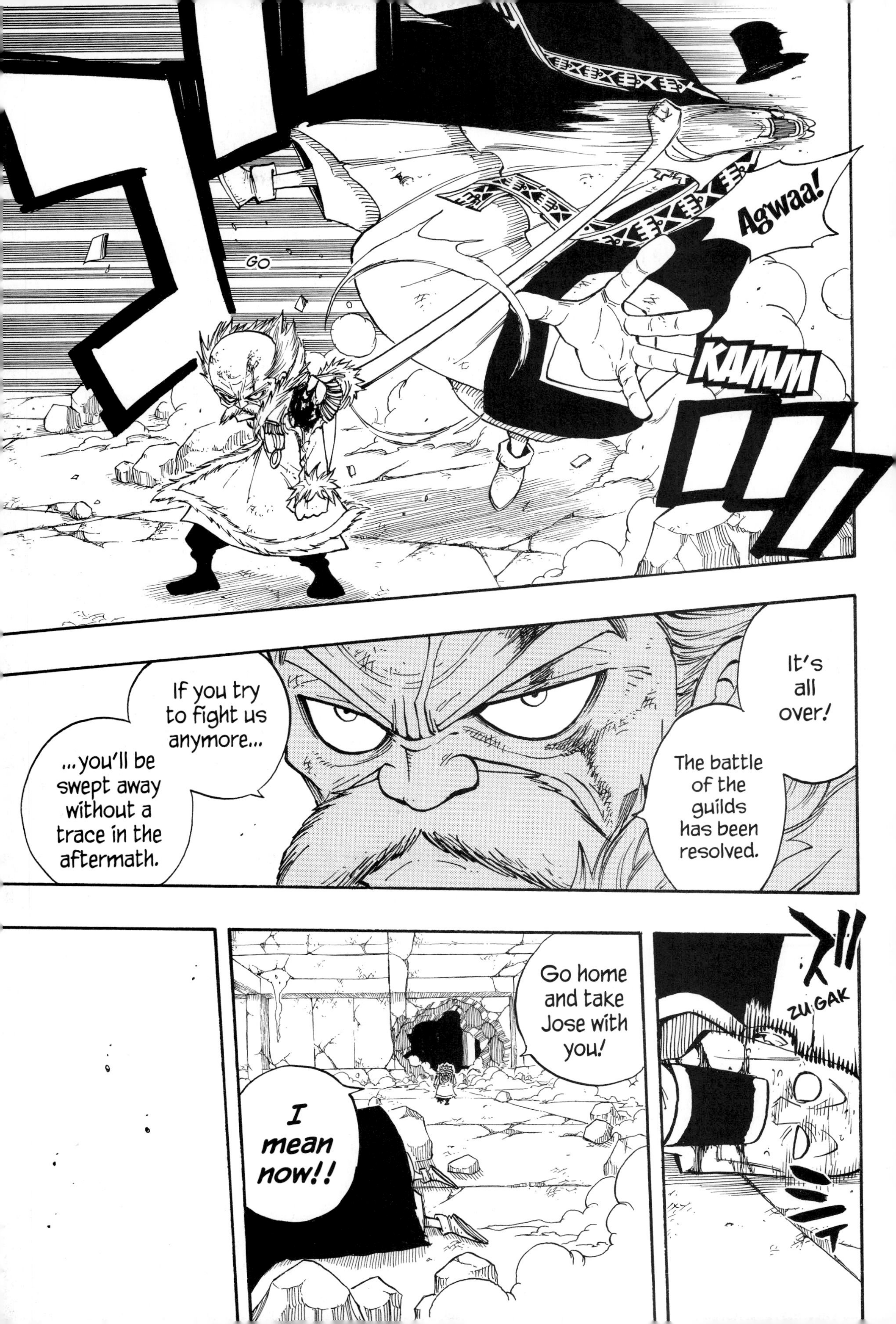
Agwaa!
KAMM
GO
It's all over!
The battle of the guilds has been resolved.
If you try to fight us anymore...
...you'll be swept away without a trace in the aftermath.
ZUGAK
Go home and take Jose with you!
I mean now!!

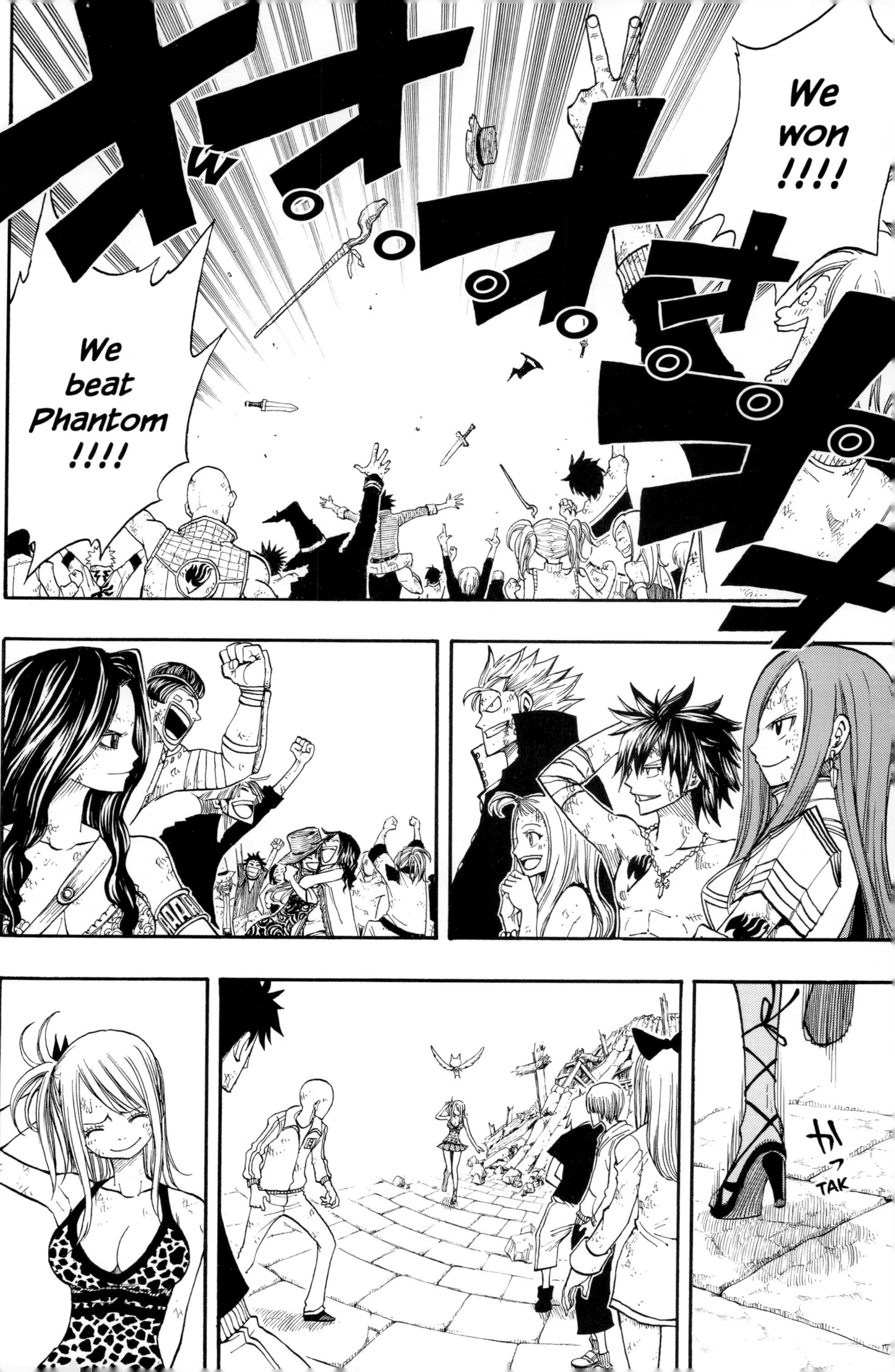
We won !!!!
We beat Phantom !!!!
TAK

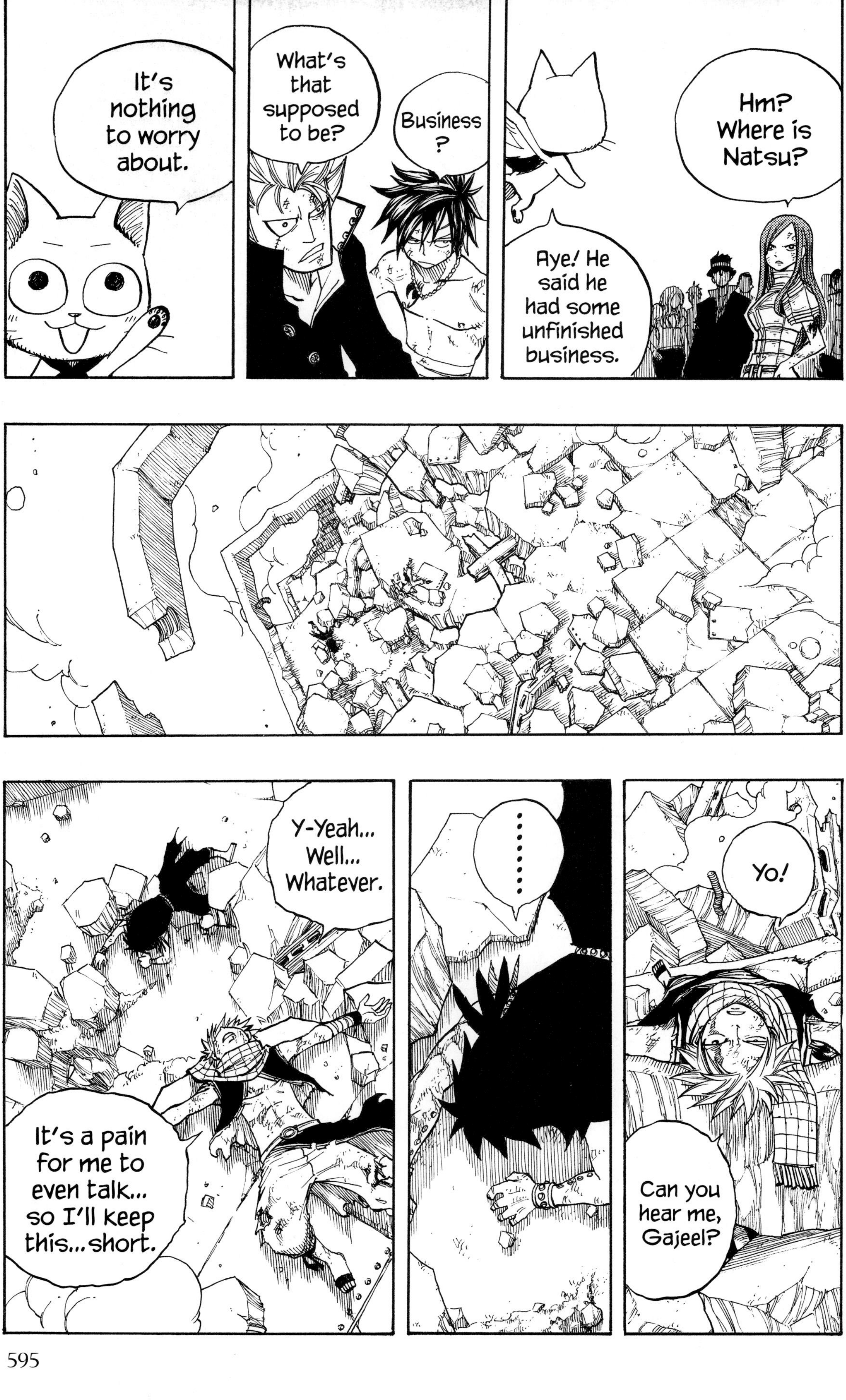
Hm? Where is Natsu?
Aye! He said he had some unfinished business.
Business ?
What's that supposed to be?
It's nothing to worry about.
Yo!
Can you hear me, Gajeel?
......
Y-Yeah... Well... Whatever.
It's a pain for me to even talk... so I'll keep this... short.

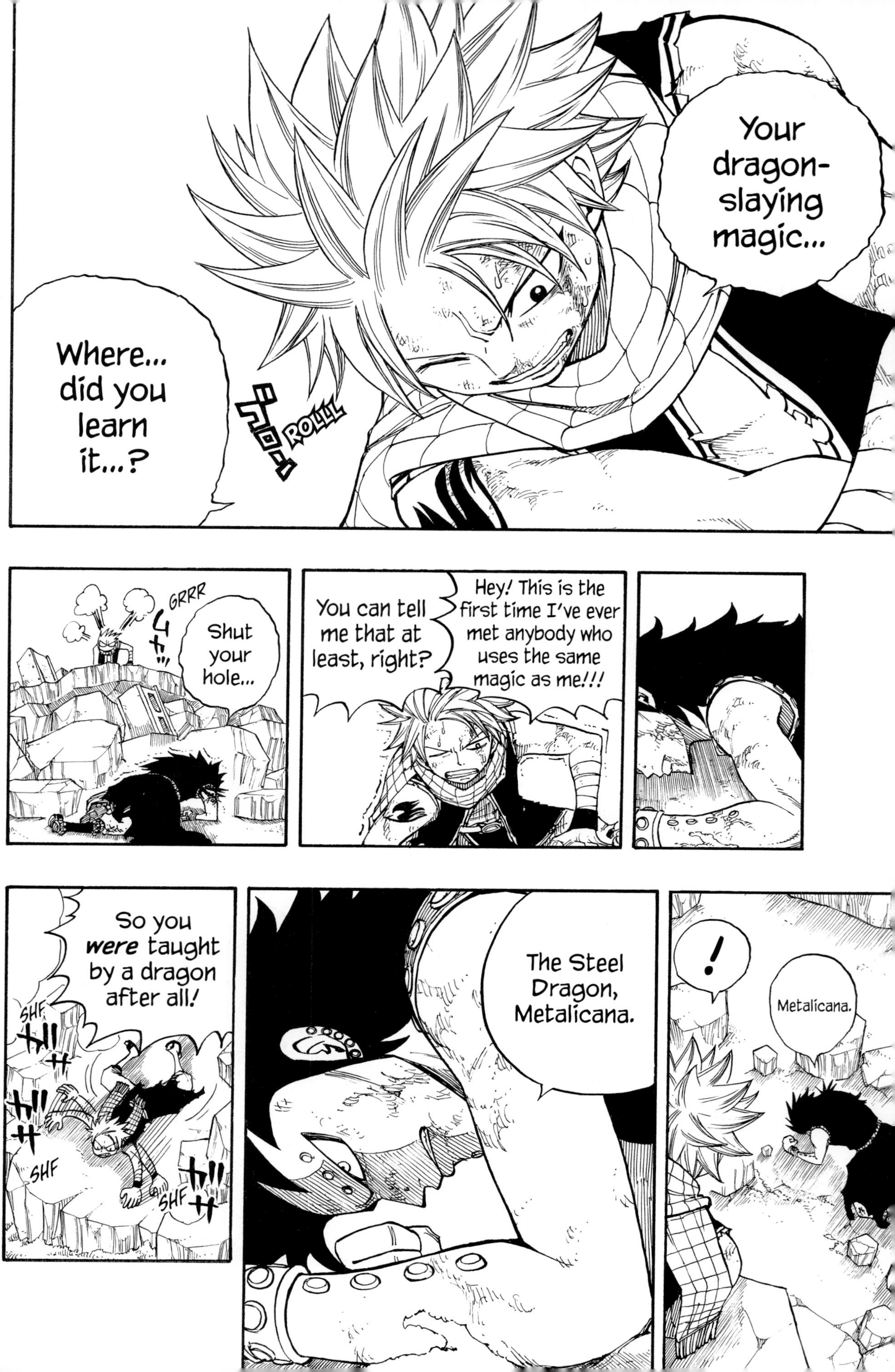
Your dragon-slaying magic...
ROLLL
Where... did you learn it...?
Hey! This is the first time I've ever met anybody who uses the same magic as me!!!
You can tell me that at least, right?
GRRR
Shut your hole...
!
Metalicana.
The Steel Dragon, Metalicana.
So you *were* taught by a dragon after all!
SHF
SHF
SHF

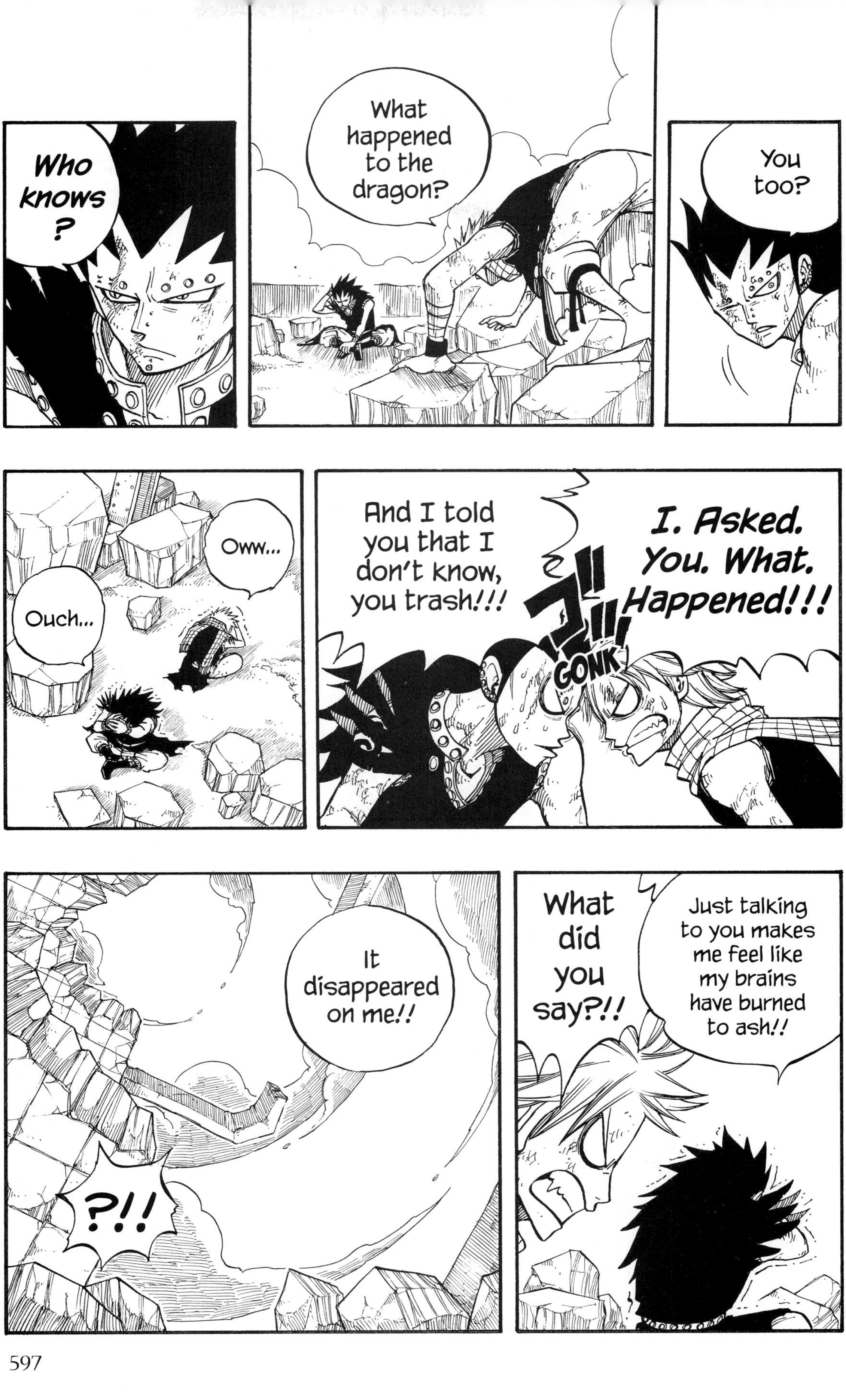

You too?
What happened to the dragon?
Who knows?
I. Asked. You. What. Happened!!!
And I told you that I don't know, you trash!!!
GONK
Oww...
Ouch...
Just talking to you makes me feel like my brains have burned to ash!!
What did you say?!!
It disappeared on me!!
?!!

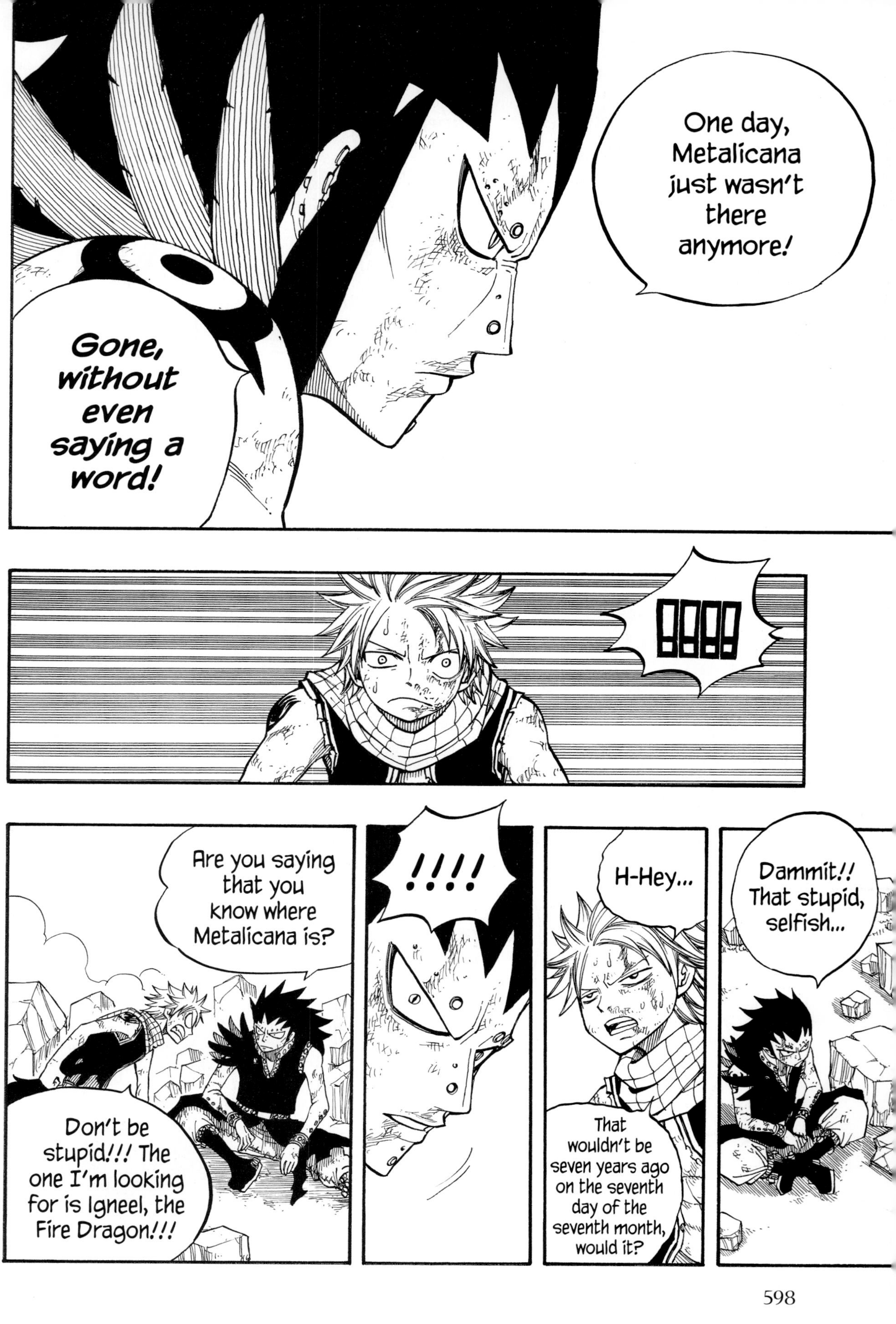
One day, Metalicana just wasn't there anymore!
Gone, without even saying a word!
!!!!
Dammit!! That stupid, selfish...
H-Hey...
That wouldn't be seven years ago on the seventh day of the seventh month, would it?
!!!!
Are you saying that you know where Metalicana is?
Don't be stupid!!! The one I'm looking for is Igneel, the Fire Dragon!!!

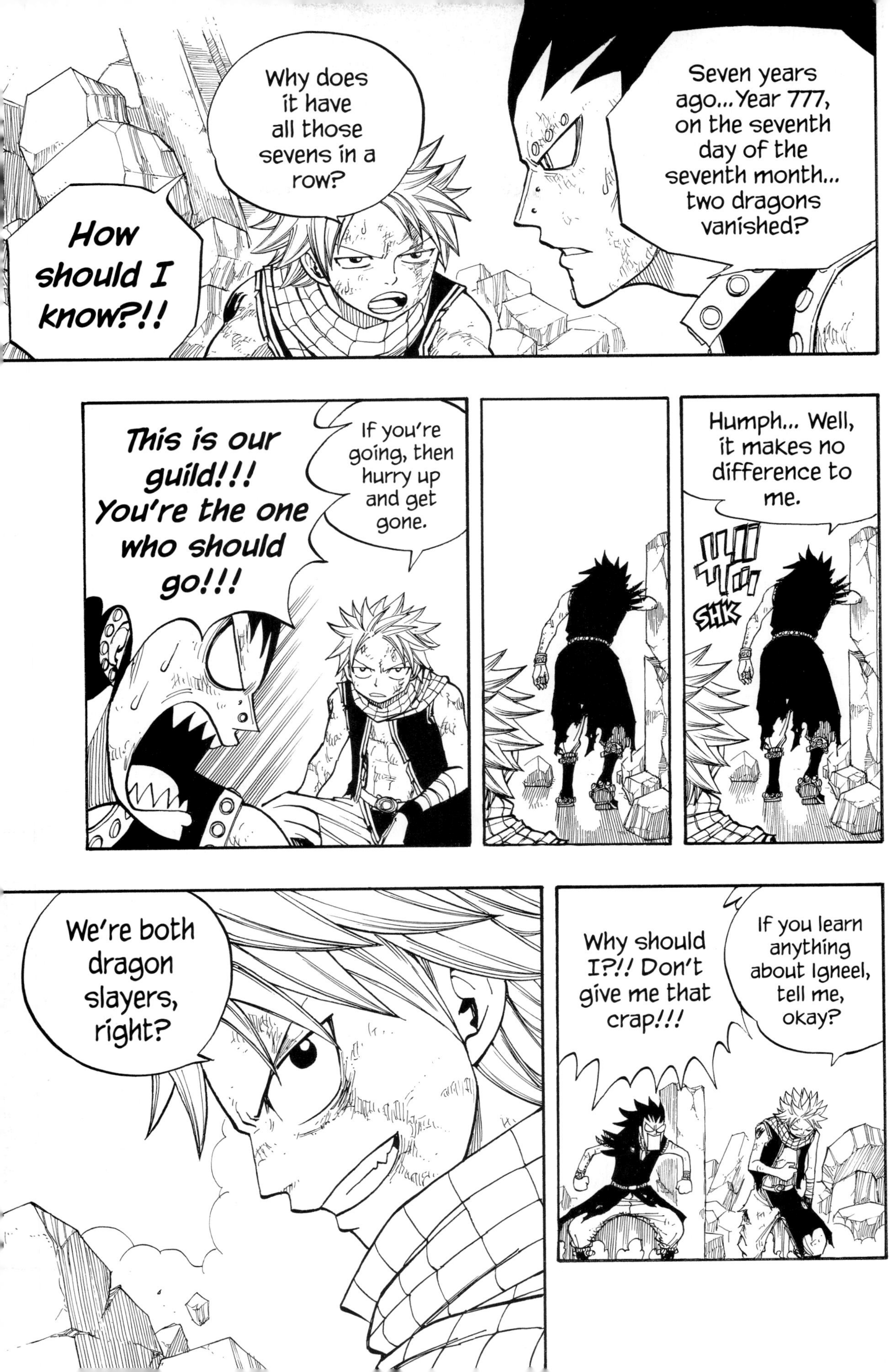
Seven years ago...Year 777, on the seventh day of the seventh month... two dragons vanished?
Why does it have all those sevens in a row?
How should I know?!!
Humph... Well, it makes no difference to me.
SHK
If you're going, then hurry up and get gone.
This is our guild!!! You're the one who should go!!!
If you learn anything about Igneel, tell me, okay?
Why should I?!! Don't give me that crap!!!
We're both dragon slayers, right?

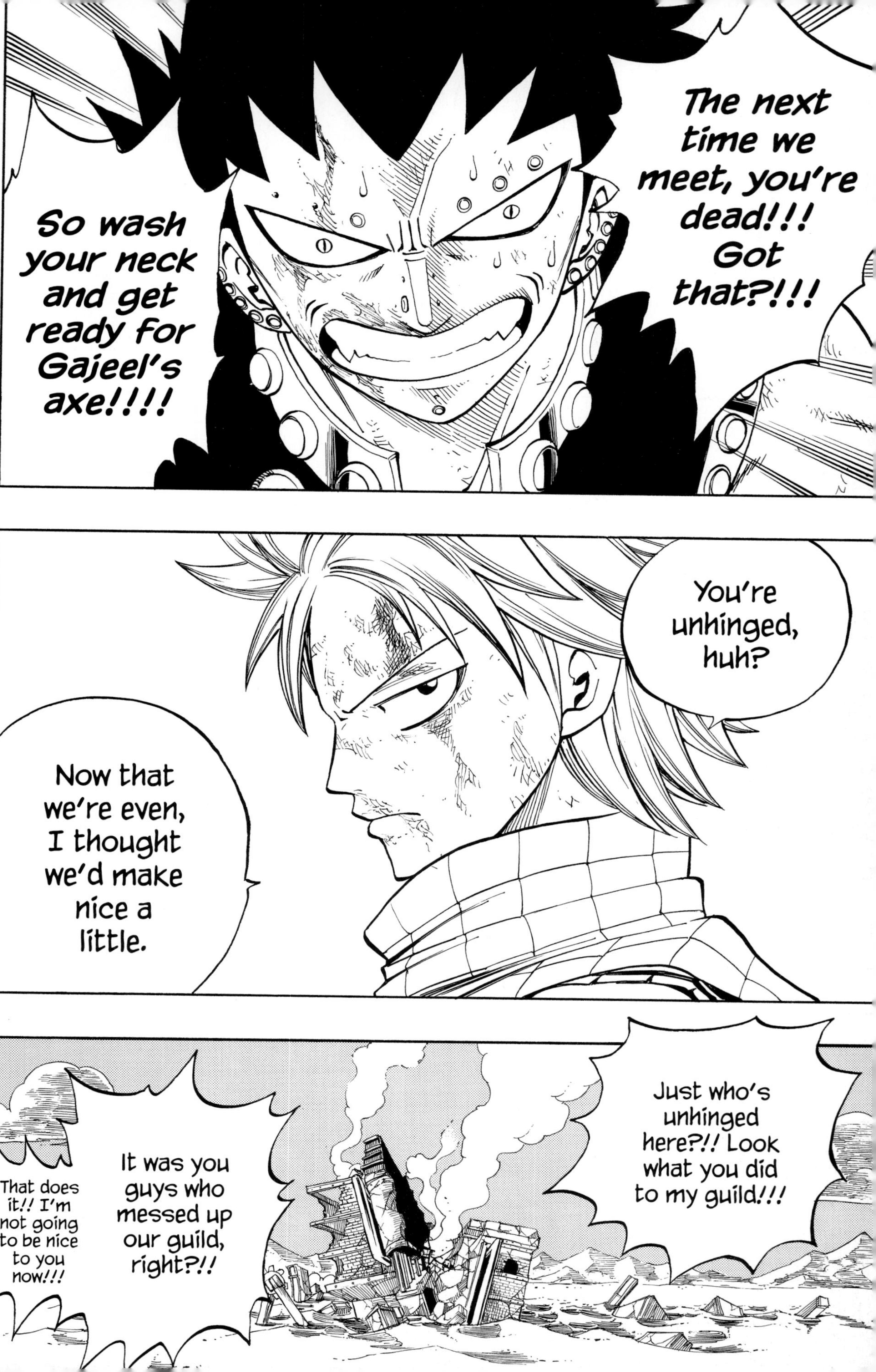
The next time we meet, you're dead!!! Got that?!!!
So wash your neck and get ready for Gajeel's axe!!!!
You're unhinged, huh?
Now that we're even, I thought we'd make nice a little.
Just who's unhinged here?!! Look what you did to my guild!!!
It was you guys who messed up our guild, right?!!
That does it!! I'm not going to be nice to you now!!!

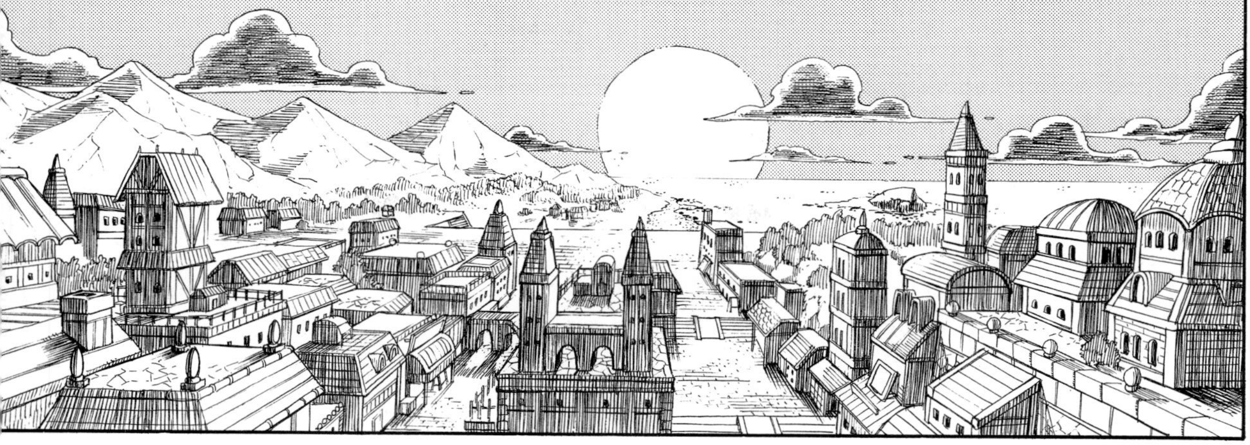
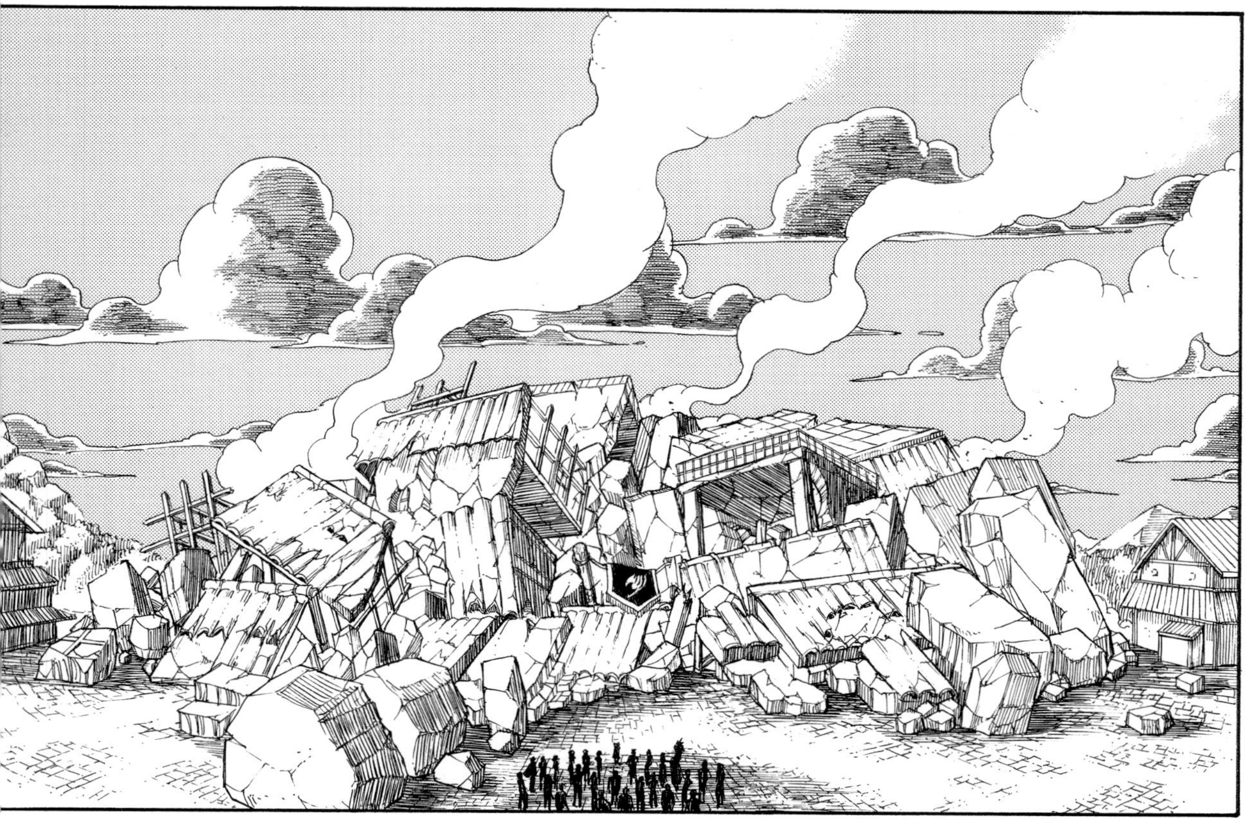
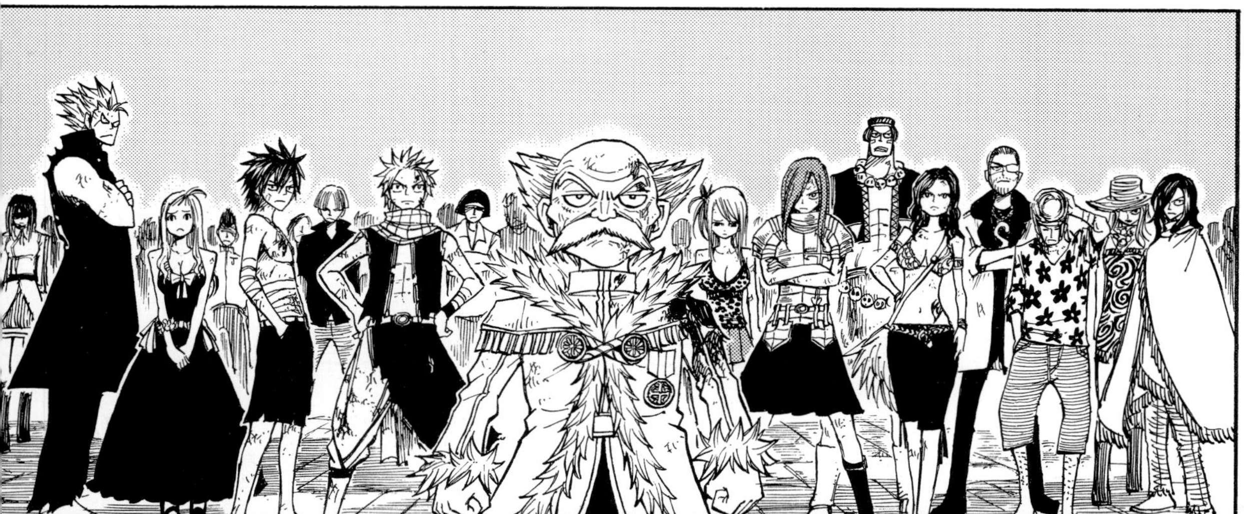

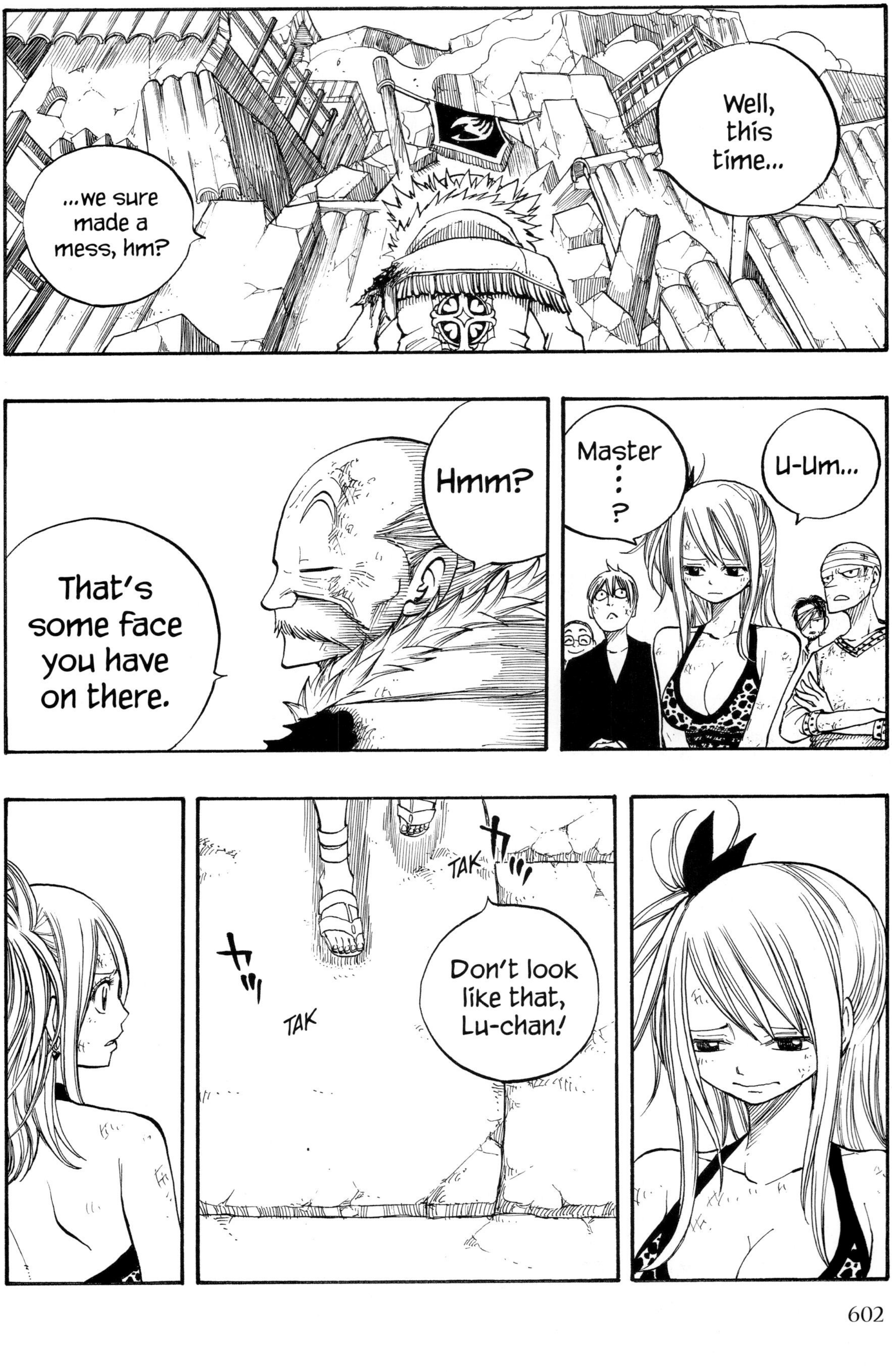
Well, this time...
...we sure made a mess, hm?
U-Um...
Master...?
Hmm?
That's some face you have on there.
TAK
Don't look like that, Lu-chan!
TAK

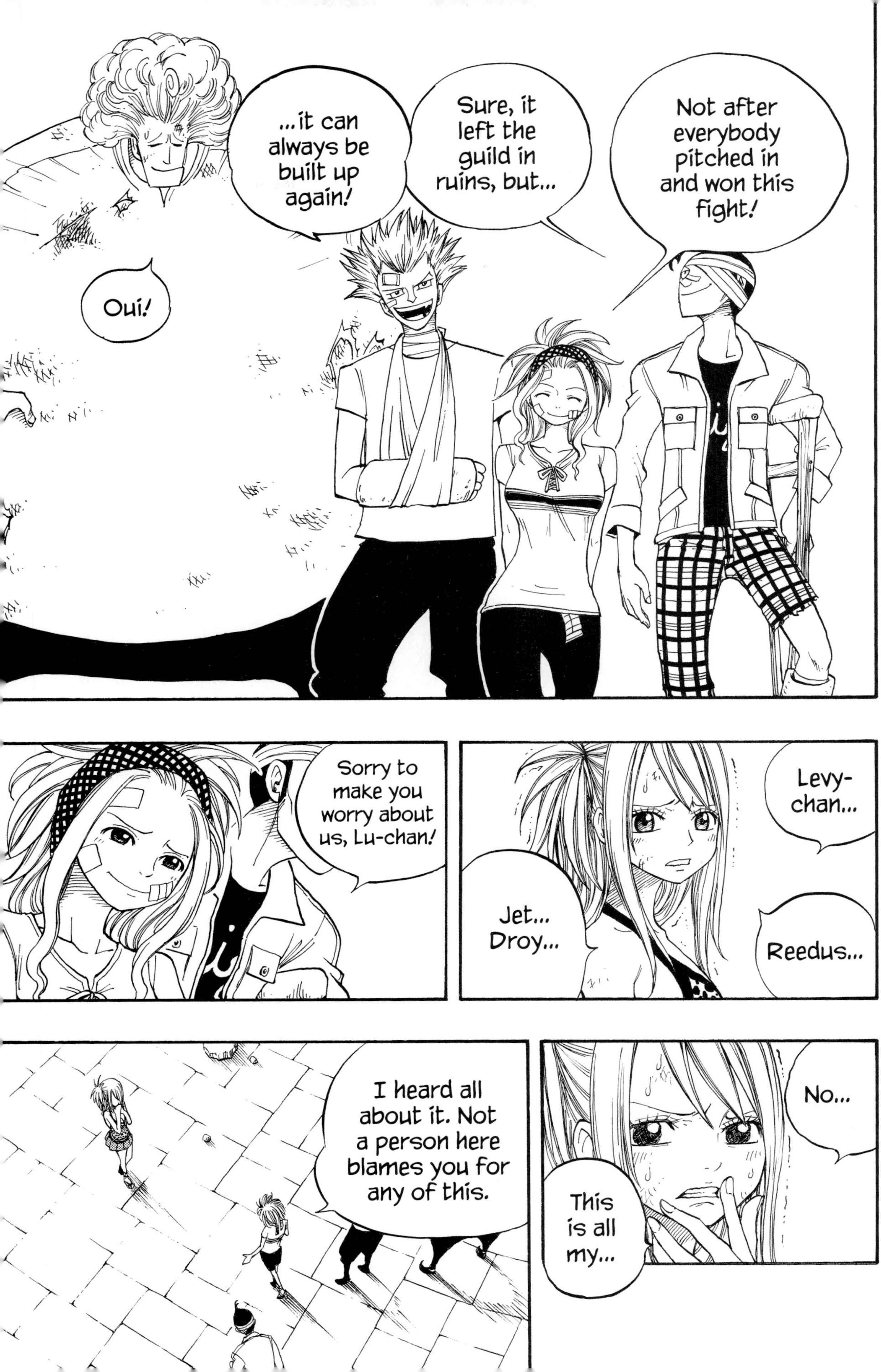
Not after everybody pitched in and won this fight!
Sure, it left the guild in ruins, but...
...it can always be built up again!
Oui!
Levy-chan...
Reedus...
Jet... Droy...
Sorry to make you worry about us, Lu-chan!
No...
This is all my...
I heard all about it. Not a person here blames you for any of this.

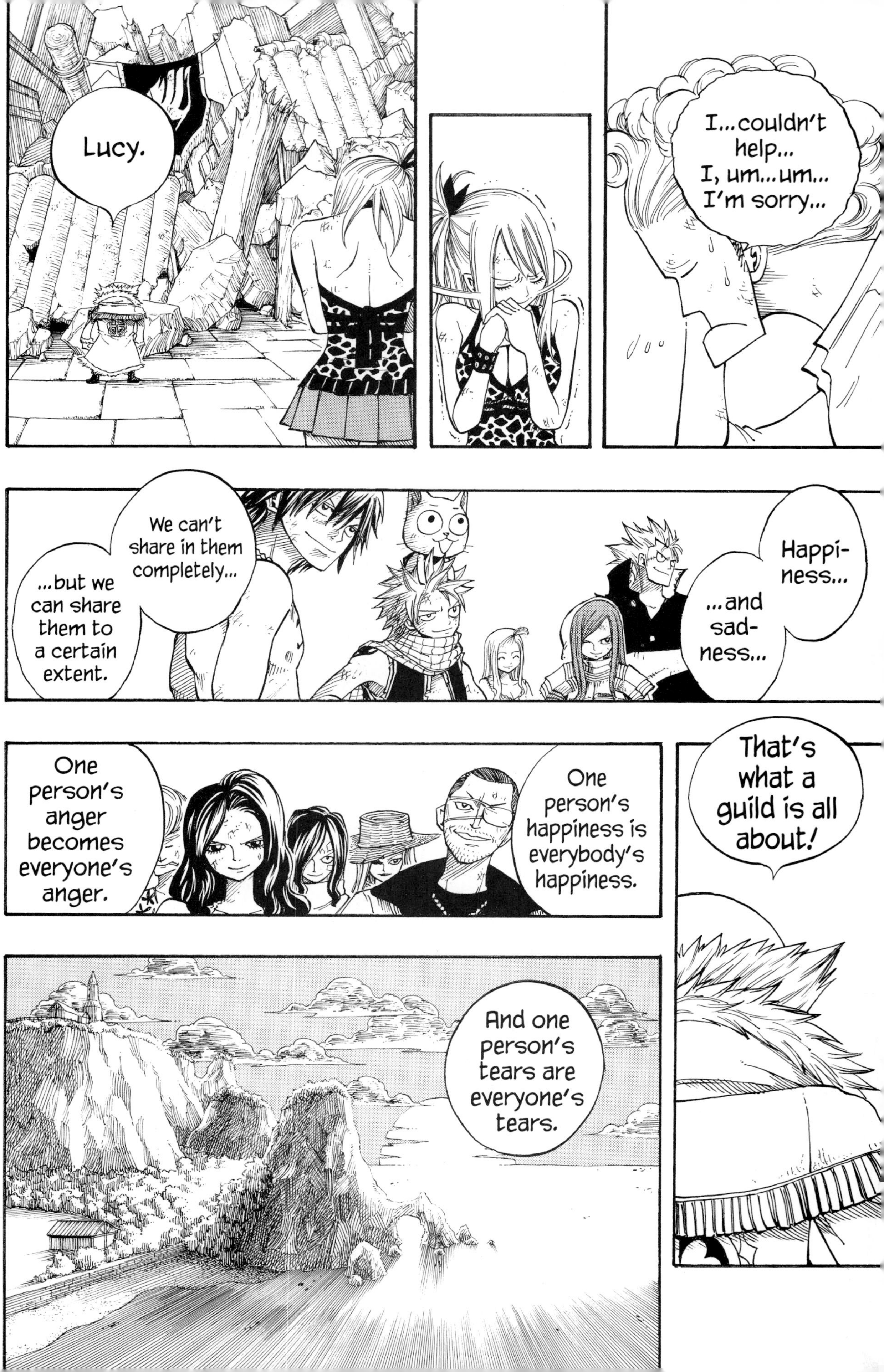
I...couldn't help... I, um...um... I'm sorry...
Lucy.
Happiness...
...and sadness...
We can't share in them completely...
...but we can share them to a certain extent.
One person's happiness is everybody's happiness.
One person's anger becomes everyone's anger.
And one person's tears are everyone's tears.
That's what a guild is all about!

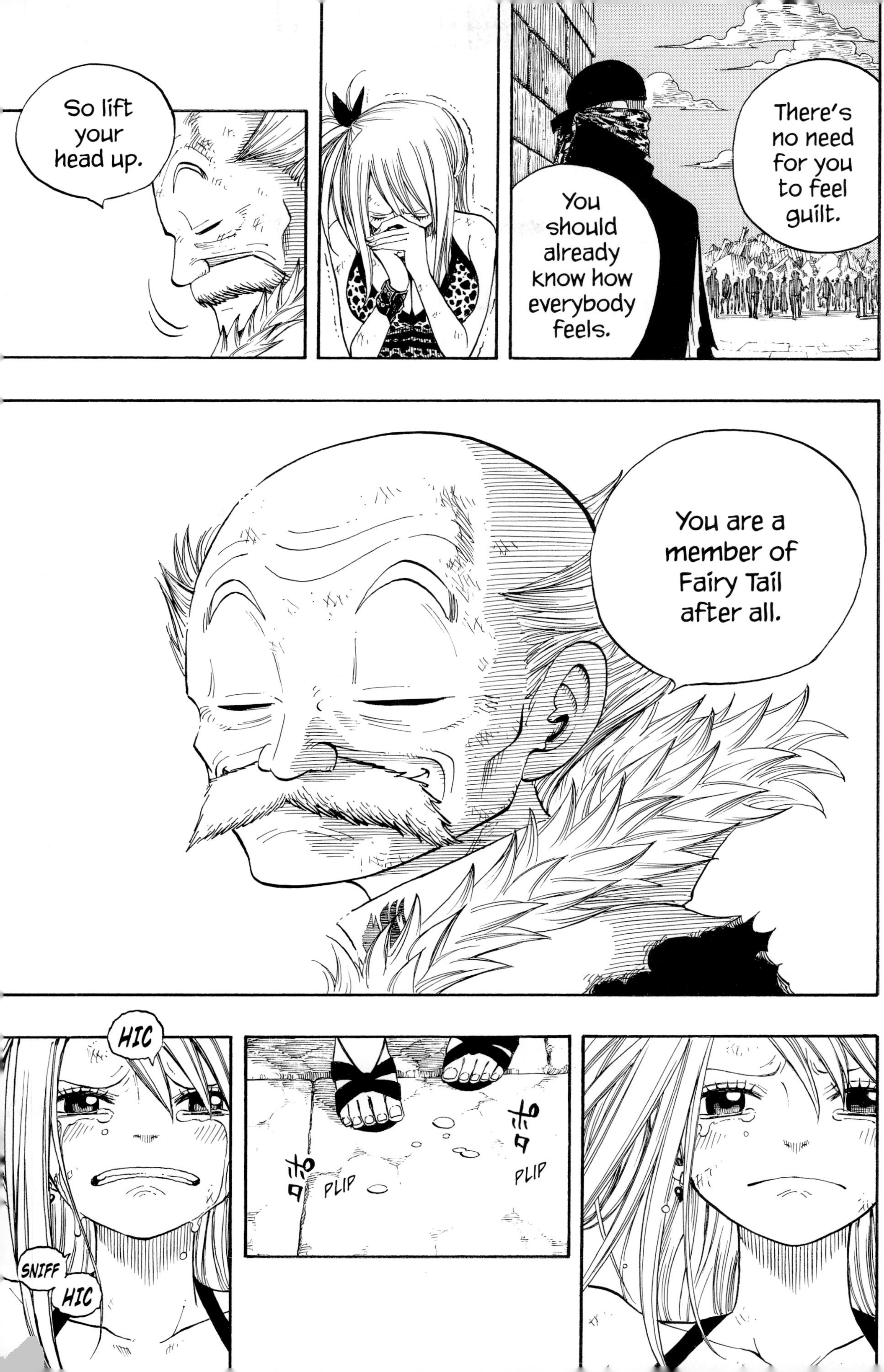
There's no need for you to feel guilt.
You should already know how everybody feels.
So lift your head up.
You are a member of Fairy Tail after all.
ポロ
PLIP
ポロ
PLIP
HIC
SNIFF
HIC

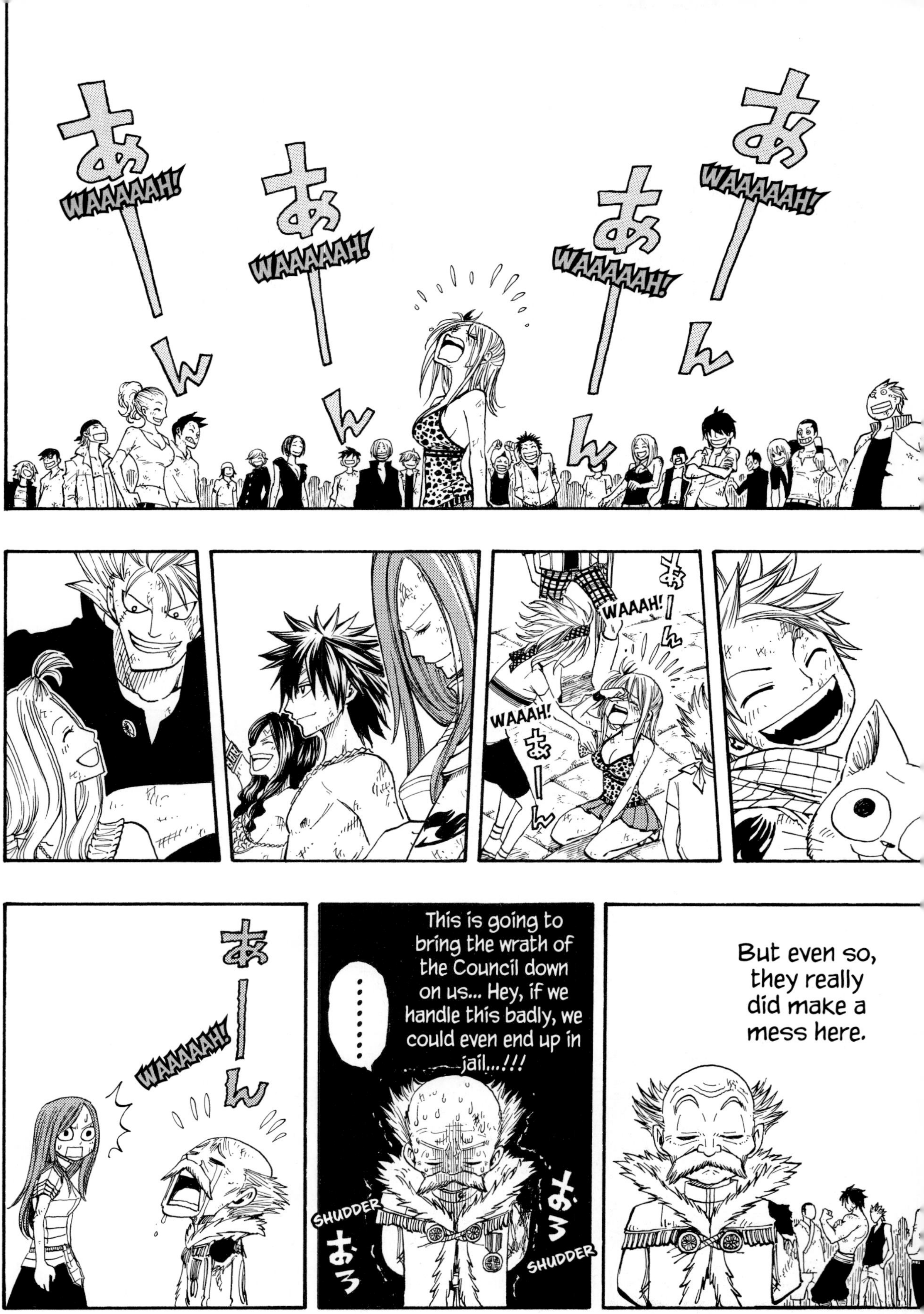
あーん
WAAAAAH!
あーん
WAAAAAH!
あーん
WAAAAAH!
あーん
WAAAAAH!
あーん
WAAAH!
あーん
WAAAH!
But even so, they really did make a mess here.
This is going to bring the wrath of the Council down on us... Hey, if we handle this badly, we could even end up in jail...!!!
......
おろ
SHUDDER
おろ
SHUDDER
あーん
WAAAAAH!

FAIRY TAIL

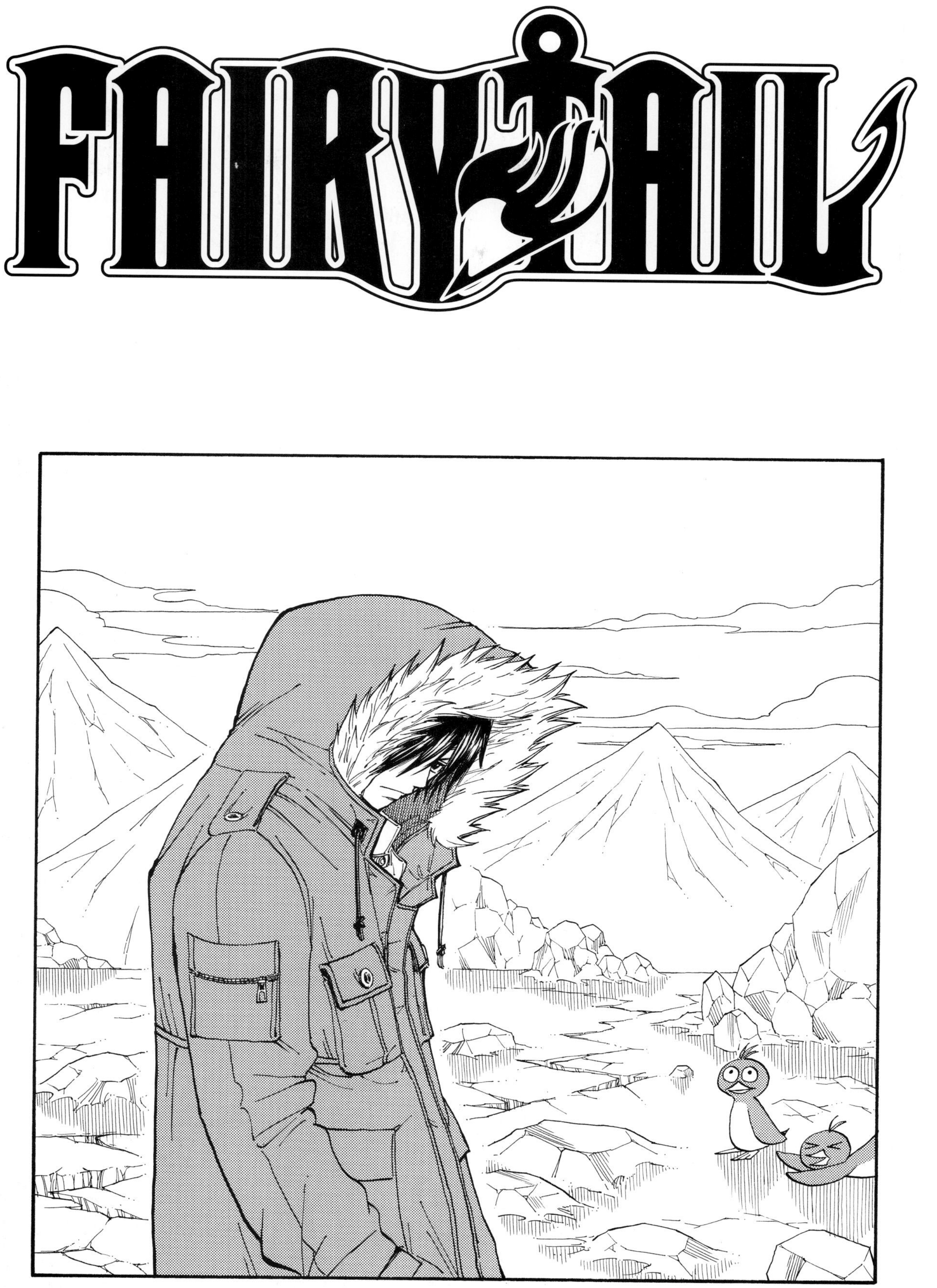

Chapter 67: My Decision

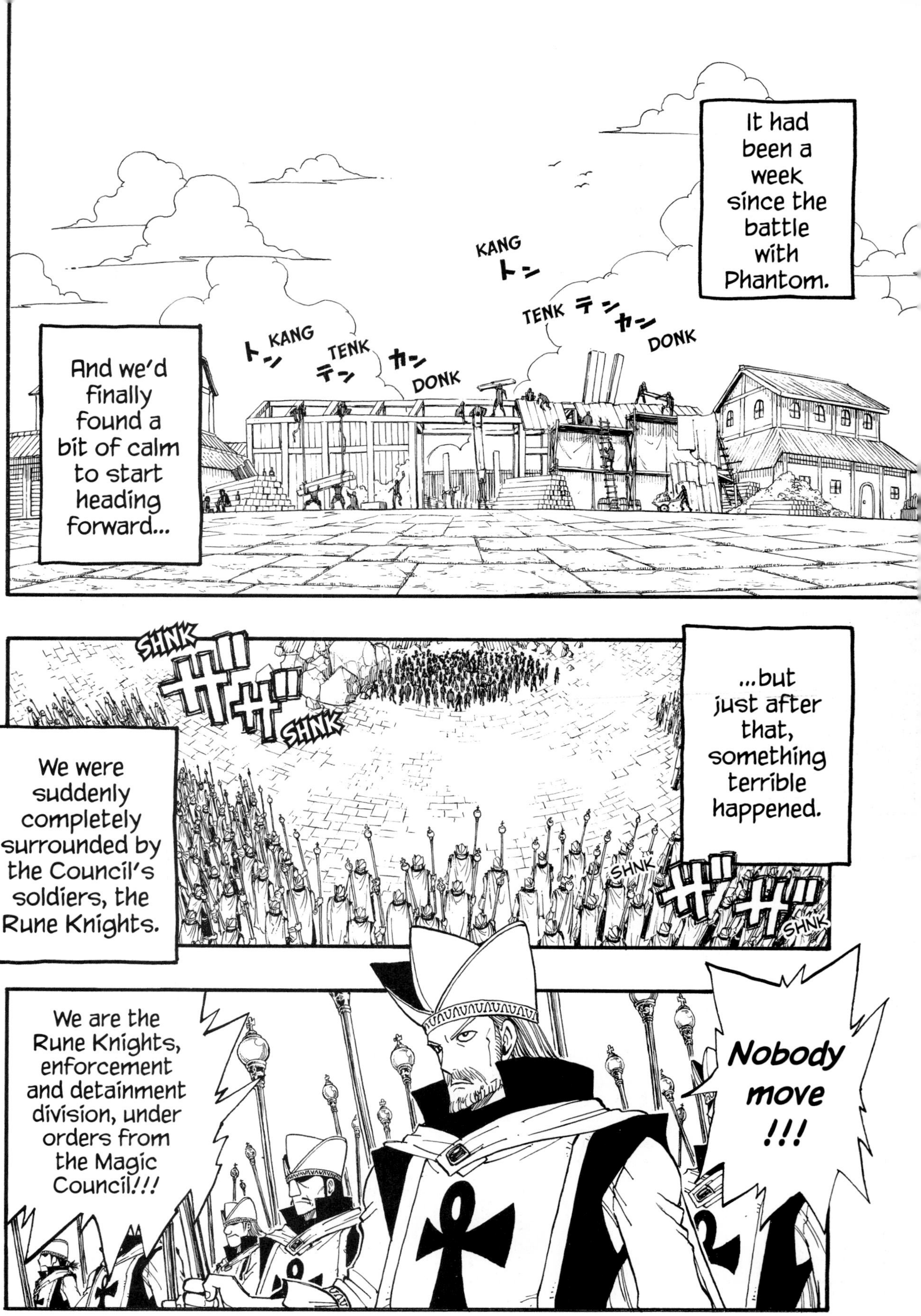

It had been a week since the battle with Phantom.
KANG トン
TENK テン カン
DONK
And we'd finally found a bit of calm to start heading forward...
KANG トン
TENK テン
カン
DONK
...but just after that, something terrible happened.
We were suddenly completely surrounded by the Council's soldiers, the Rune Knights.
SHNK
SHNK
SHNK
SHNK
Nobody move!!!
We are the Rune Knights, enforcement and detainment division, under orders from the Magic Council!!!

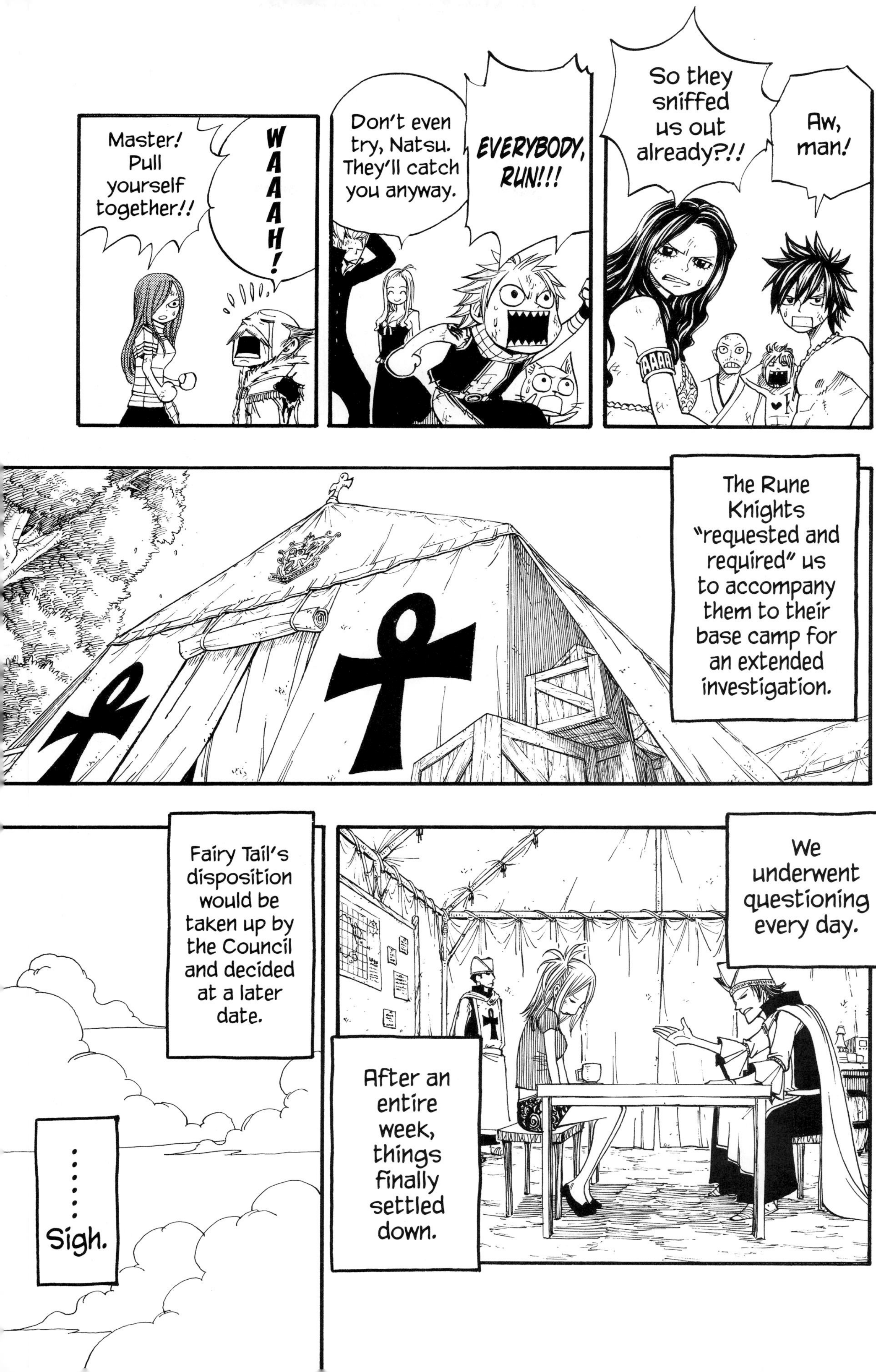
Aw, man!
So they sniffed us out already?!!
EVERYBODY, RUN!!!
Don't even try, Natsu. They'll catch you anyway.
WAAAAH!
Master! Pull yourself together!!
The Rune Knights "requested and required" us to accompany them to their base camp for an extended investigation.
We underwent questioning every day.
After an entire week, things finally settled down.
Fairy Tail's disposition would be taken up by the Council and decided at a later date.
......Sigh.

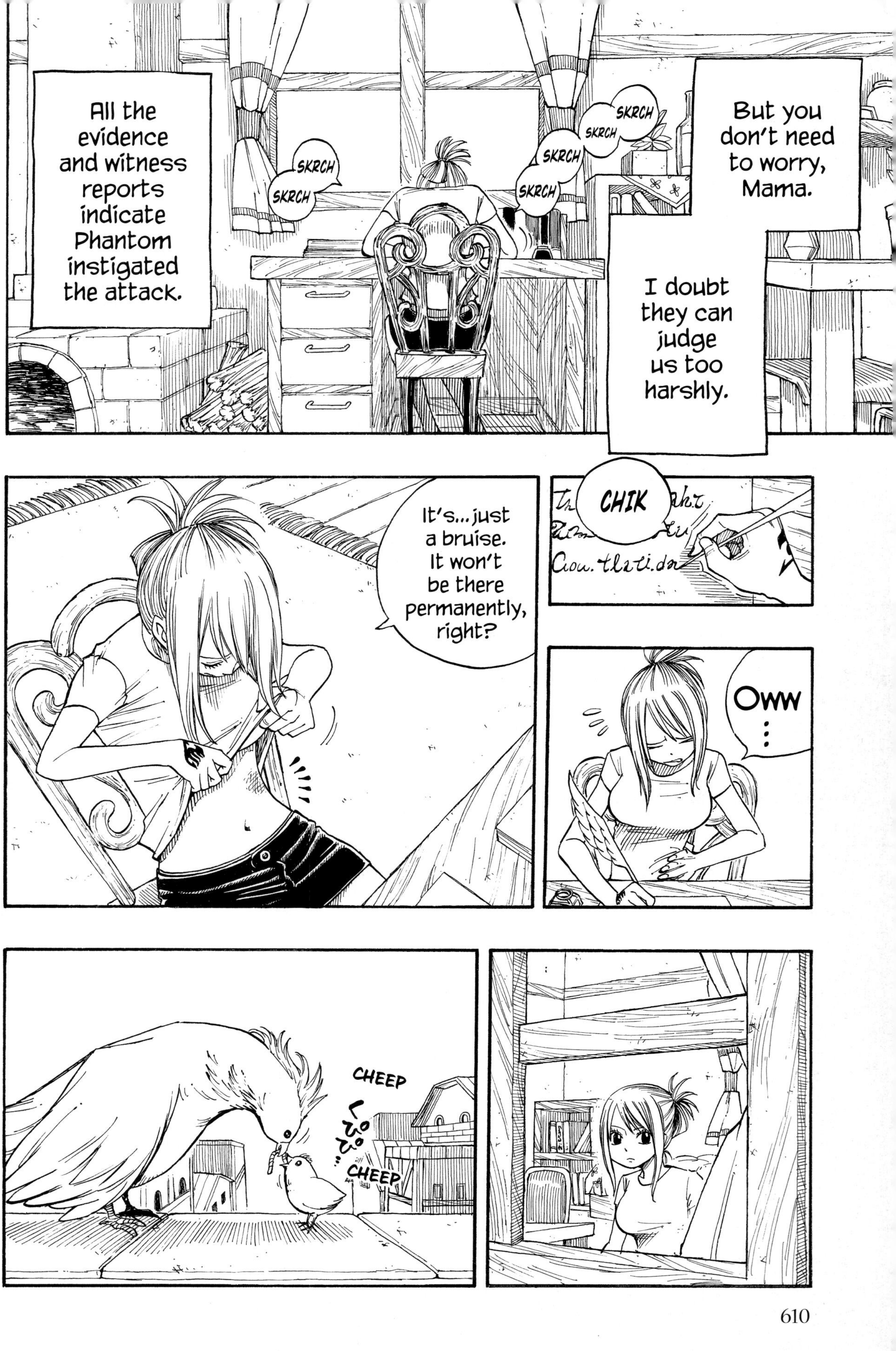
All the evidence and witness reports indicate Phantom instigated the attack.
SKRCH
SKRCH
SKRCH
SKRCH
SKRCH
SKRCH
But you don't need to worry, Mama.
I doubt they can judge us too harshly.
CHIK
Oww…
It's…just a bruise. It won't be there permanently, right?
CHEEP
CHEEP

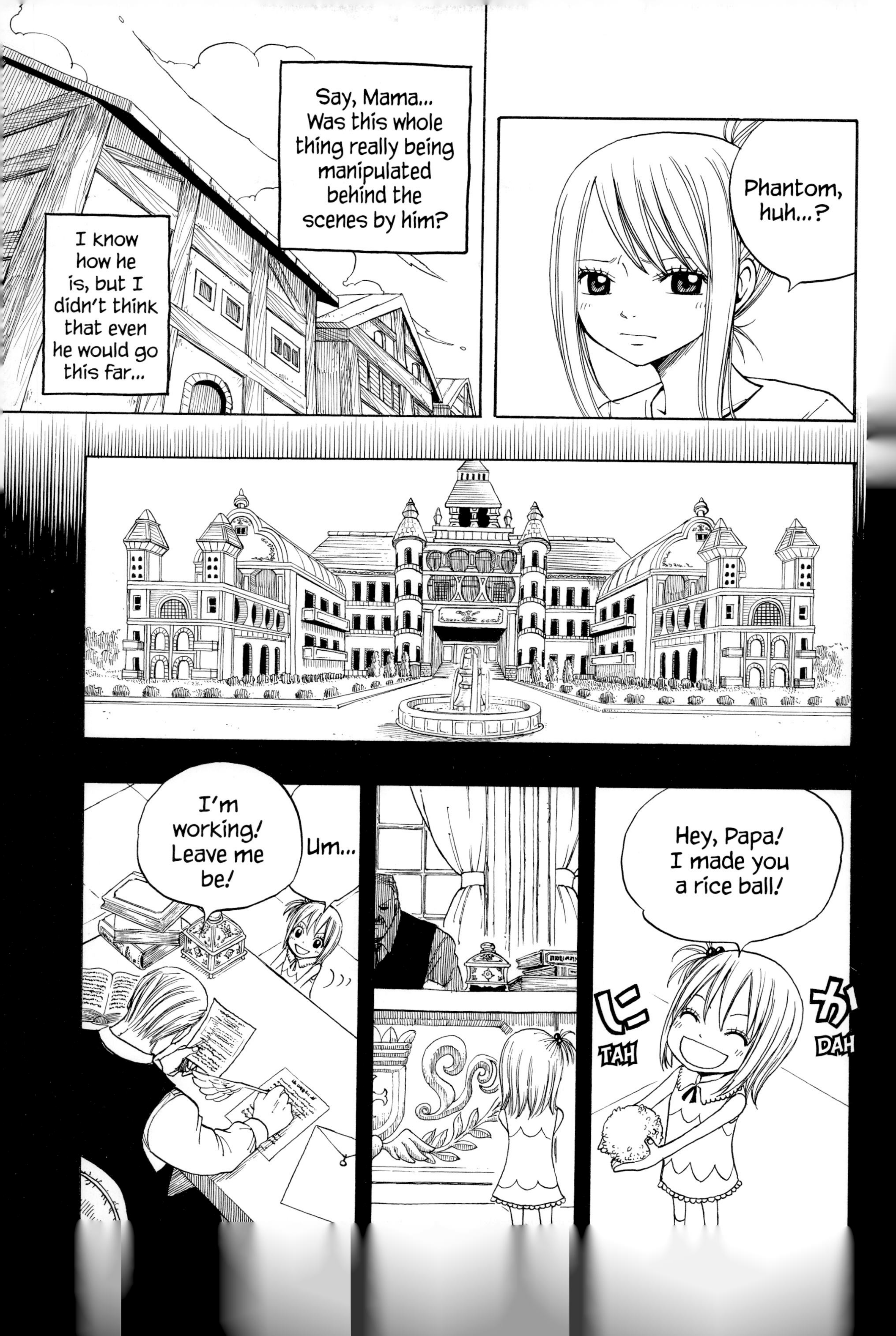
Phantom, huh...?
Say, Mama... Was this whole thing really being manipulated behind the scenes by him?
I know how he is, but I didn't think that even he would go this far...
Hey, Papa! I made you a rice ball!
に TAH
か DAH
Um...
I'm working! Leave me be!

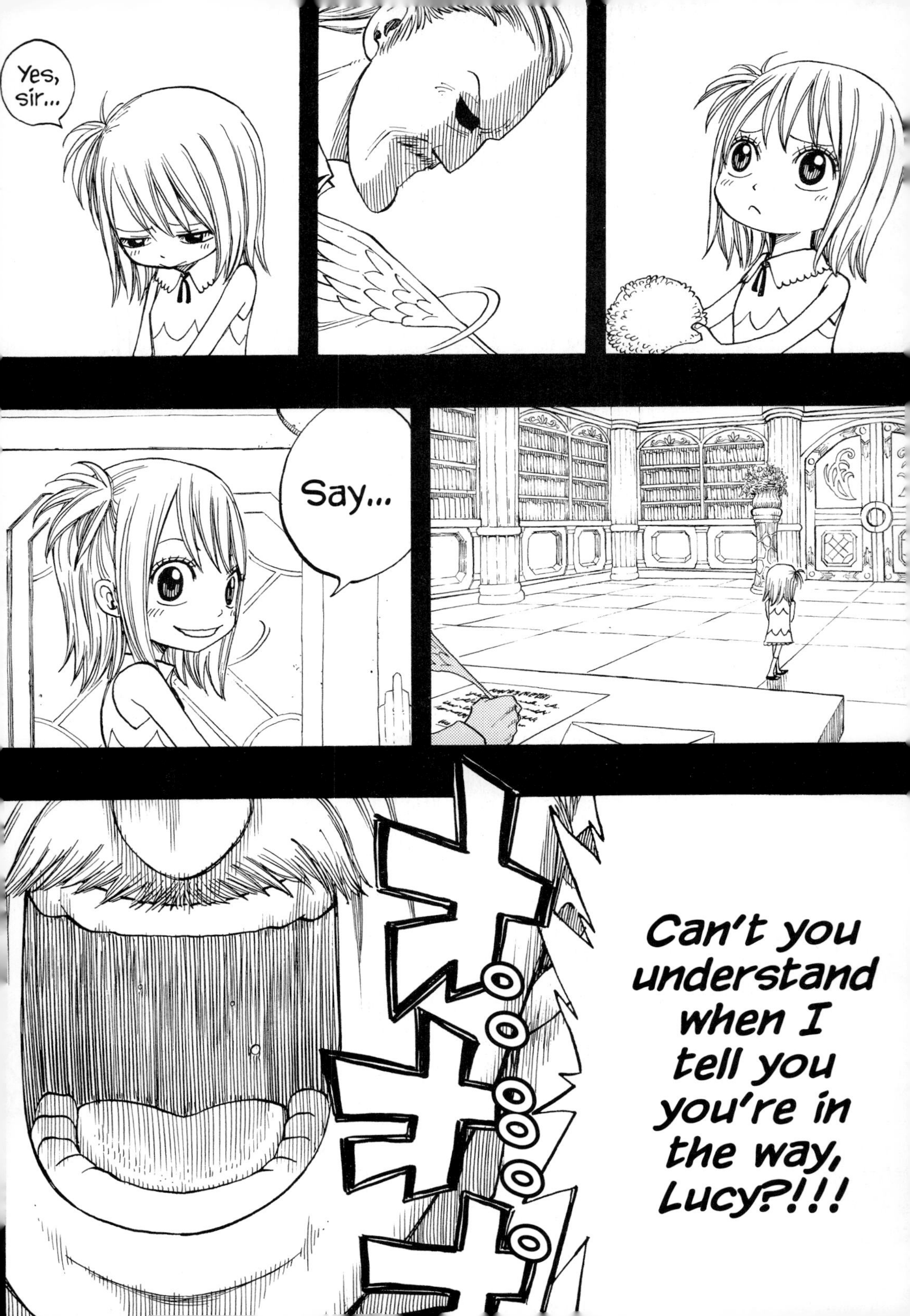
Yes, sir...
Say...
Can't you understand when I tell you you're in the way, Lucy?!!!

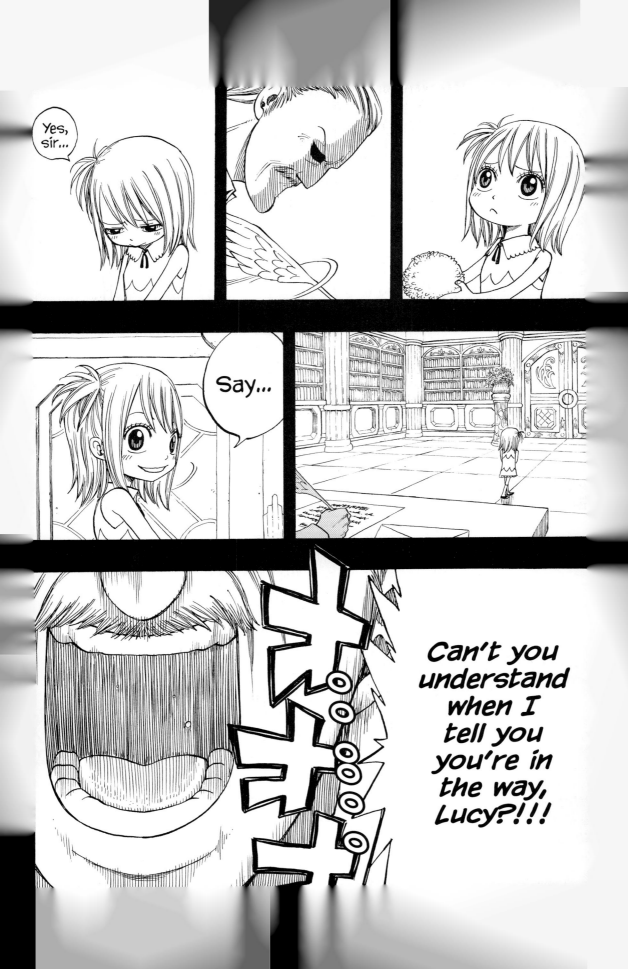

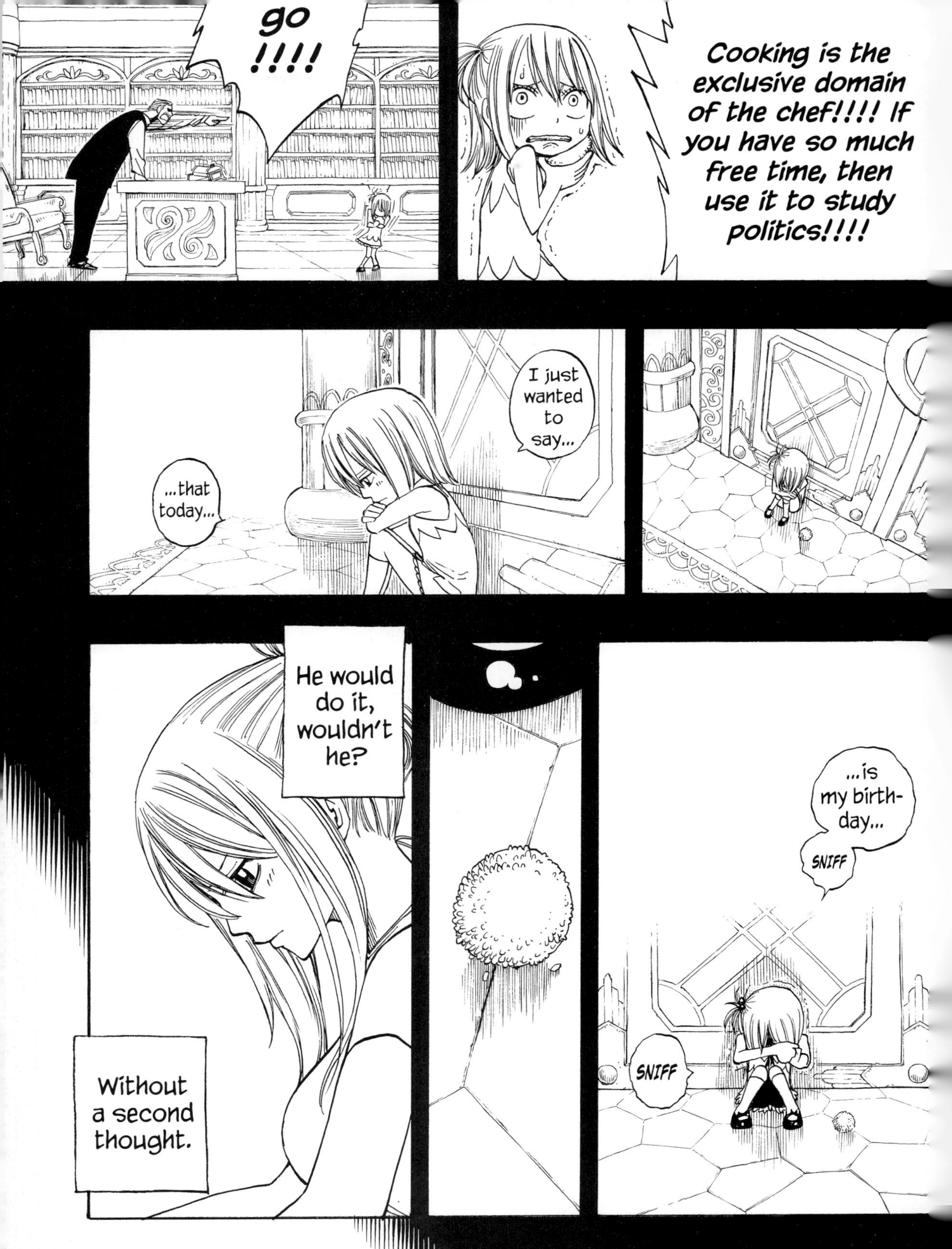
Cooking is the exclusive domain of the chef!!!! If you have so much free time, then use it to study politics!!!!
go !!!!
I just wanted to say...
...that today...
...is my birth-day...
SNIFF
SNIFF
He would do it, wouldn't he?
Without a second thought.

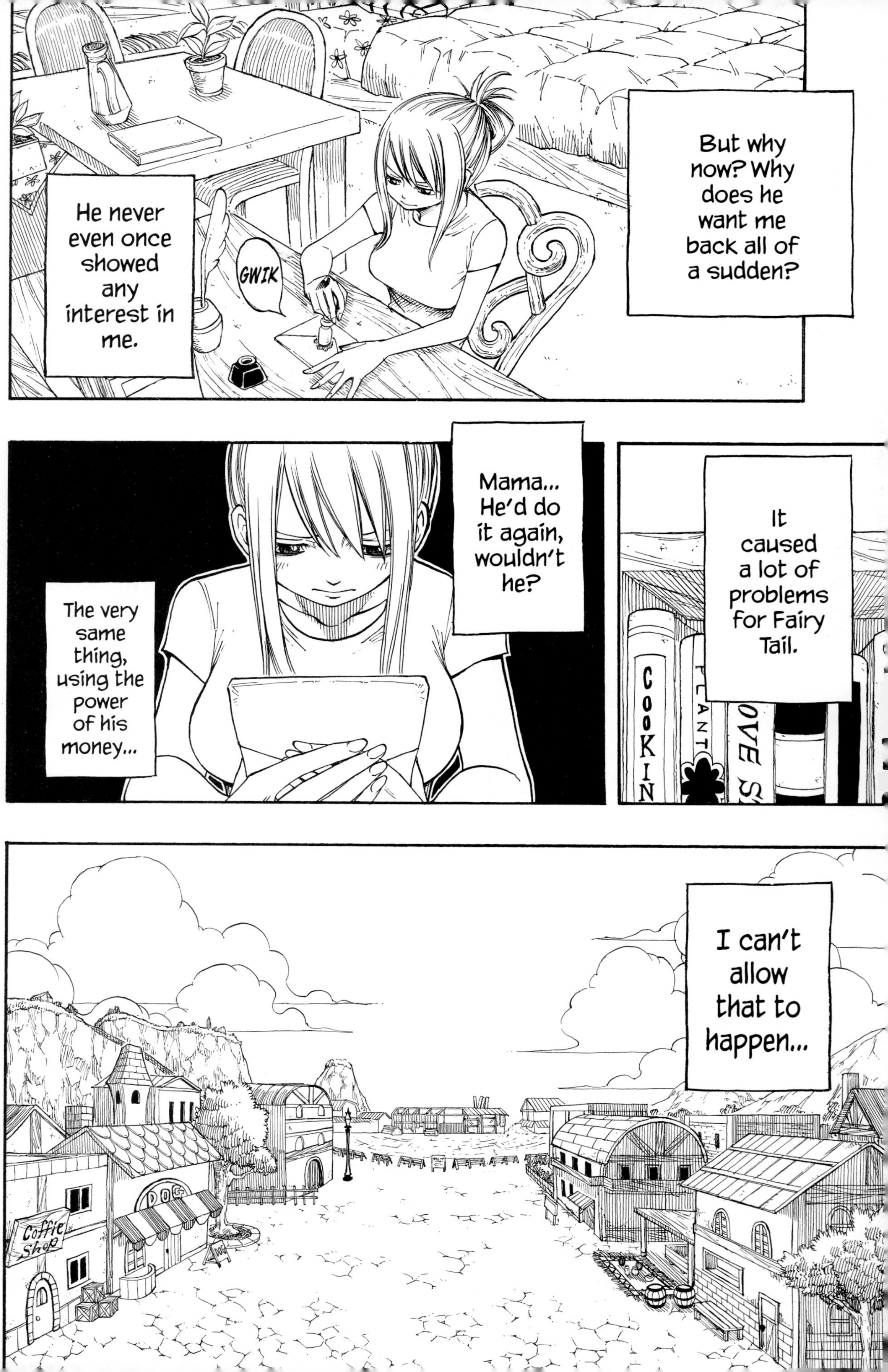
But why now? Why does he want me back all of a sudden?
He never even once showed any interest in me.
GWIK
It caused a lot of problems for Fairy Tail.
Mama... He'd do it again, wouldn't he?
The very same thing, using the power of his money...
I can't allow that to happen...
DOG
Coffie Shop

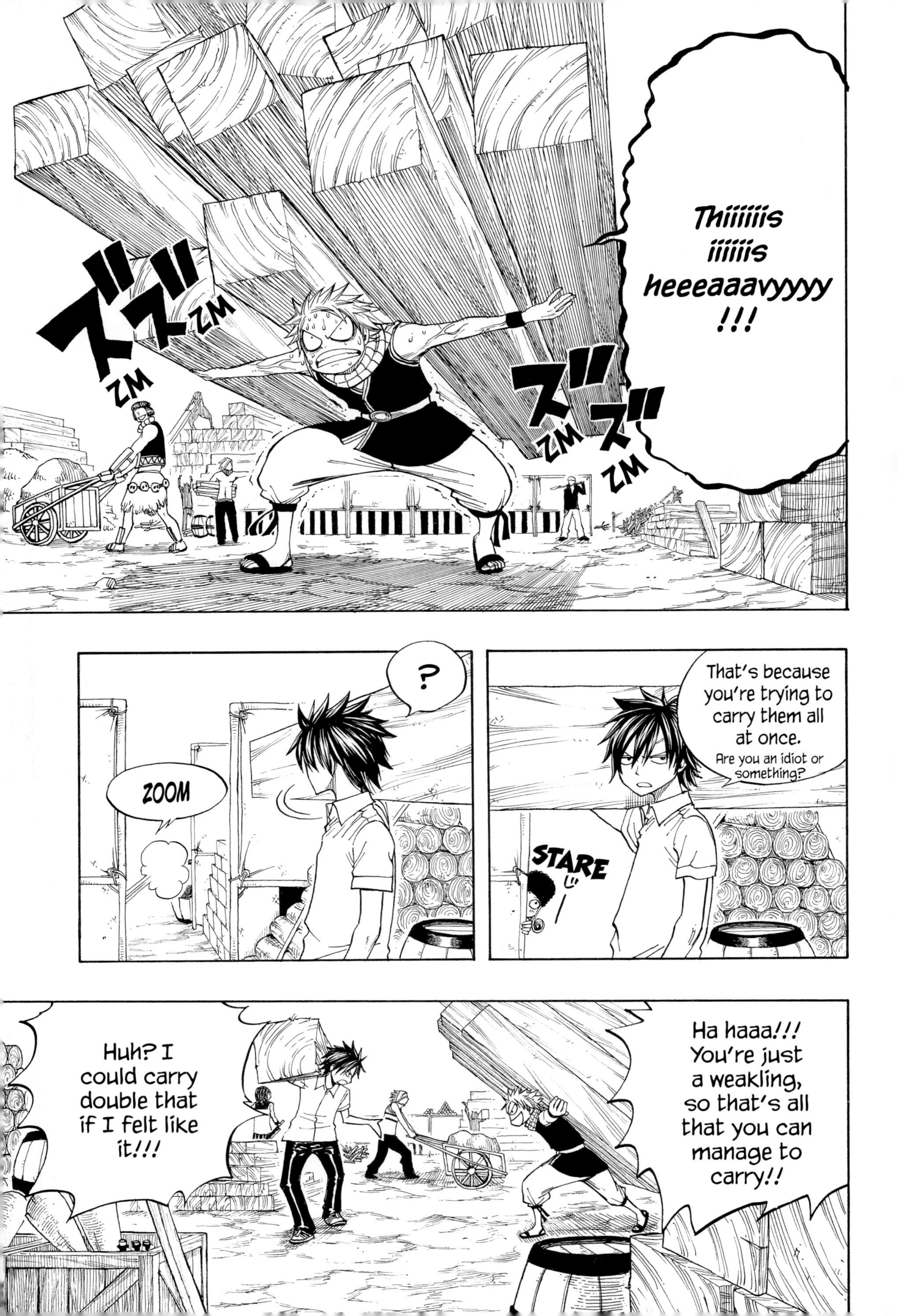
ズズ
ZM
ZM
ズズ
ZM
ズズ
ZM
Thiiiiiis iiiiiis heeeaaavyyyy!!!
That's because you're trying to carry them all at once.
Are you an idiot or something?
STARE
?
ZOOM
Ha haaa!!! You're just a weakling, so that's all that you can manage to carry!!
Huh? I could carry double that if I felt like it!!!

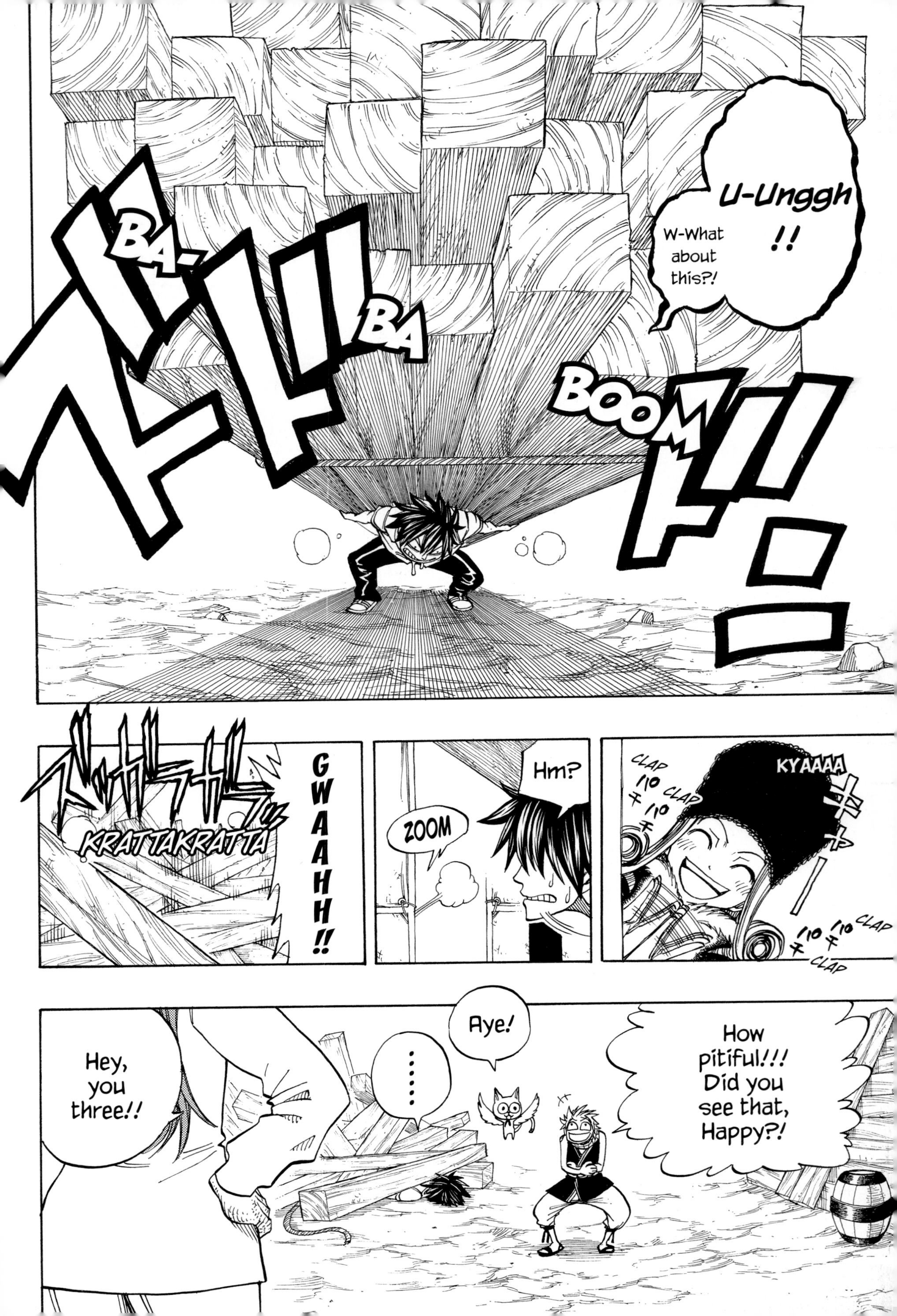
U-Unggh!!
W-What about this?!
BOOM!!
BA-BA
KYAAAA
CLAP CLAP
CLAP CLAP
Hm?
ZOOM
GWAAHH!!
KRATTAKRATTA
How pitiful!!! Did you see that, Happy?!
Aye!
......
Hey, you three!!

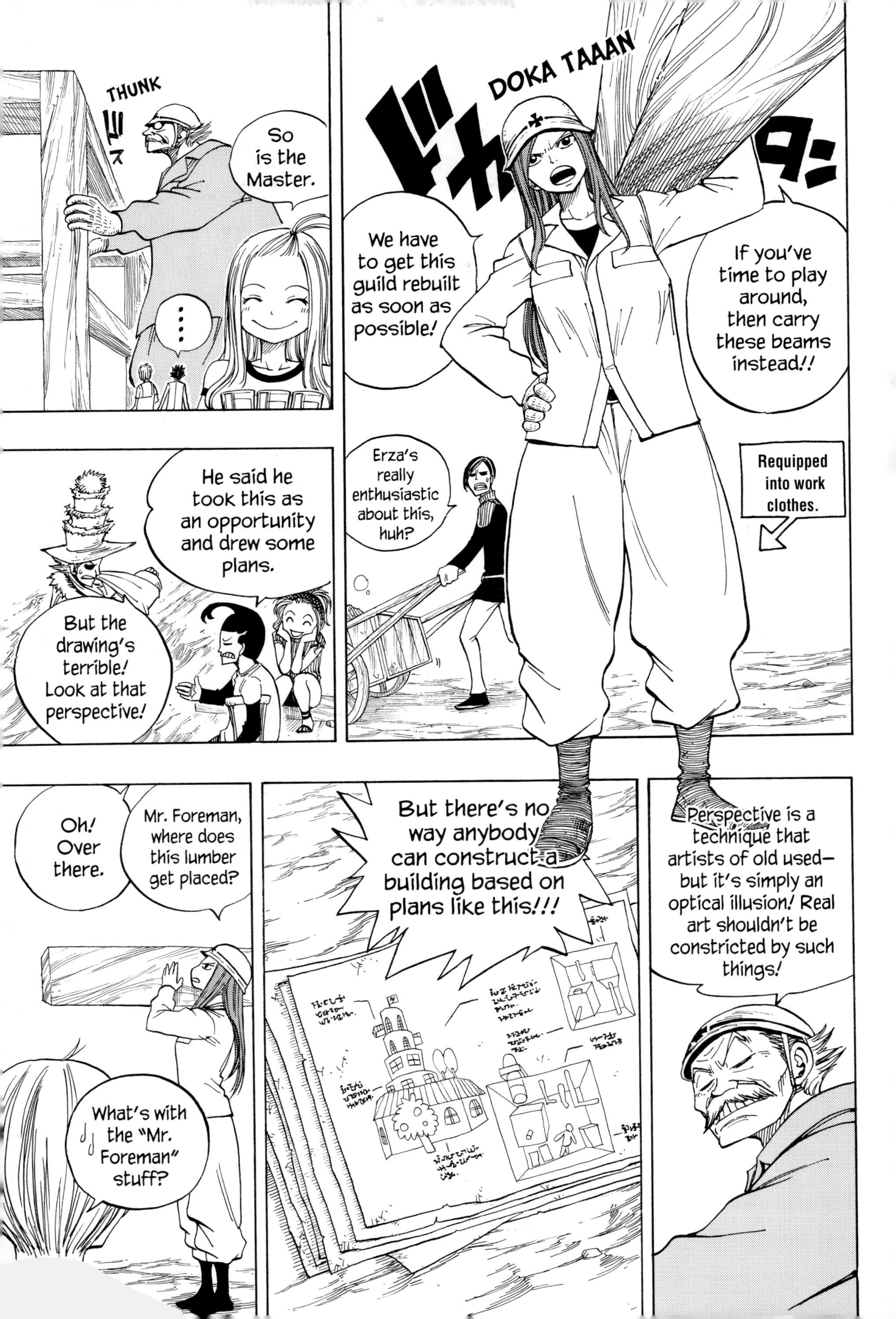
DOKA TAAAN
We have to get this guild rebuilt as soon as possible!
If you've time to play around, then carry these beams instead!!
THUNK
So is the Master.
....
Erza's really enthusiastic about this, huh?
Requipped into work clothes.
He said he took this as an opportunity and drew some plans.
But the drawing's terrible! Look at that perspective!
Perspective is a technique that artists of old used— but it's simply an optical illusion! Real art shouldn't be constricted by such things!
But there's no way anybody can construct a building based on plans like this!!!
Mr. Foreman, where does this lumber get placed?
Oh! Over there.
What's with the "Mr. Foreman" stuff?

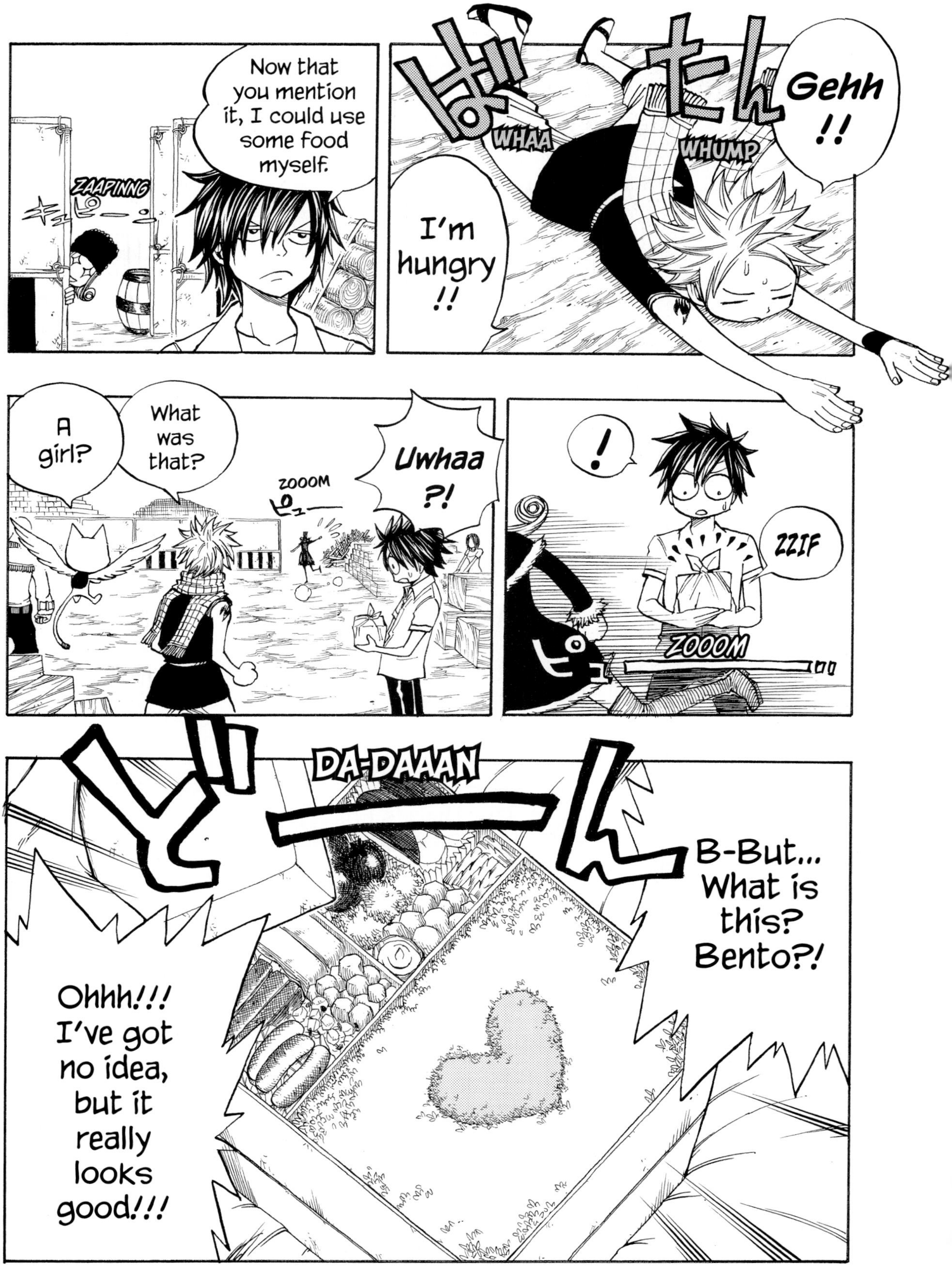
WHAA
WHUMP
Gehh!!
I'm hungry!!
ZAAPINNG
Now that you mention it, I could use some food myself.
!
ZZIF
ZOOOM
Uwhaa?!
ZOOOM
What was that?
A girl?
DA-DAAN
B-But... What is this? Bento?!
Ohhh!!! I've got no idea, but it really looks good!!!

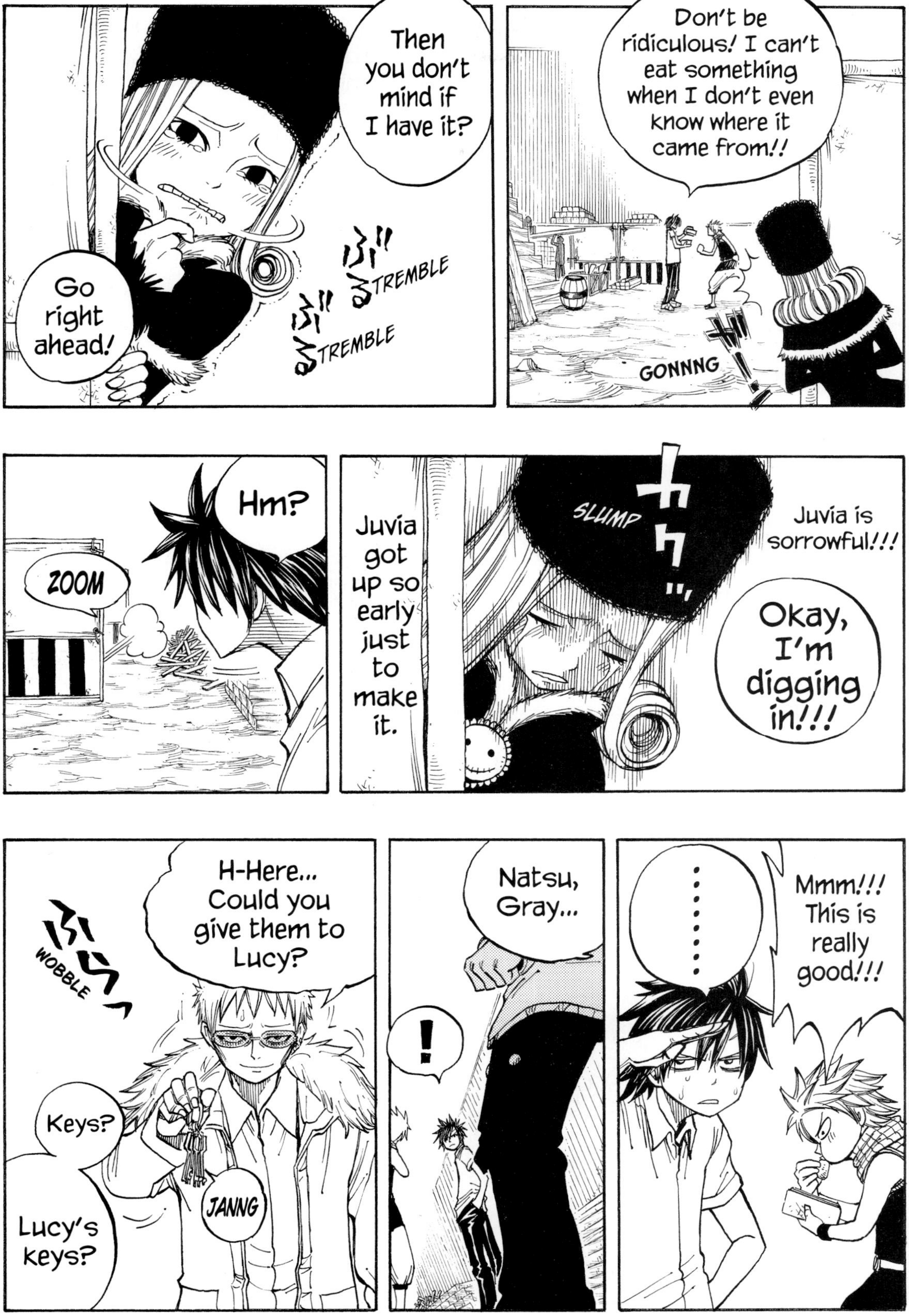
Don't be ridiculous! I can't eat something when I don't even know where it came from!!
GONNNG
Then you don't mind if I have it?
Go right ahead!
TREMBLE
TREMBLE
Juvia is sorrowful!!!
SLUMP
Juvia got up so early just to make it.
Okay, I'm digging in!!!
Hm?
ZOOM
Mmm!!! This is really good!!!
....
Natsu, Gray...
!
H-Here... Could you give them to Lucy?
WOBBLE
JANNG
Keys?
Lucy's keys?

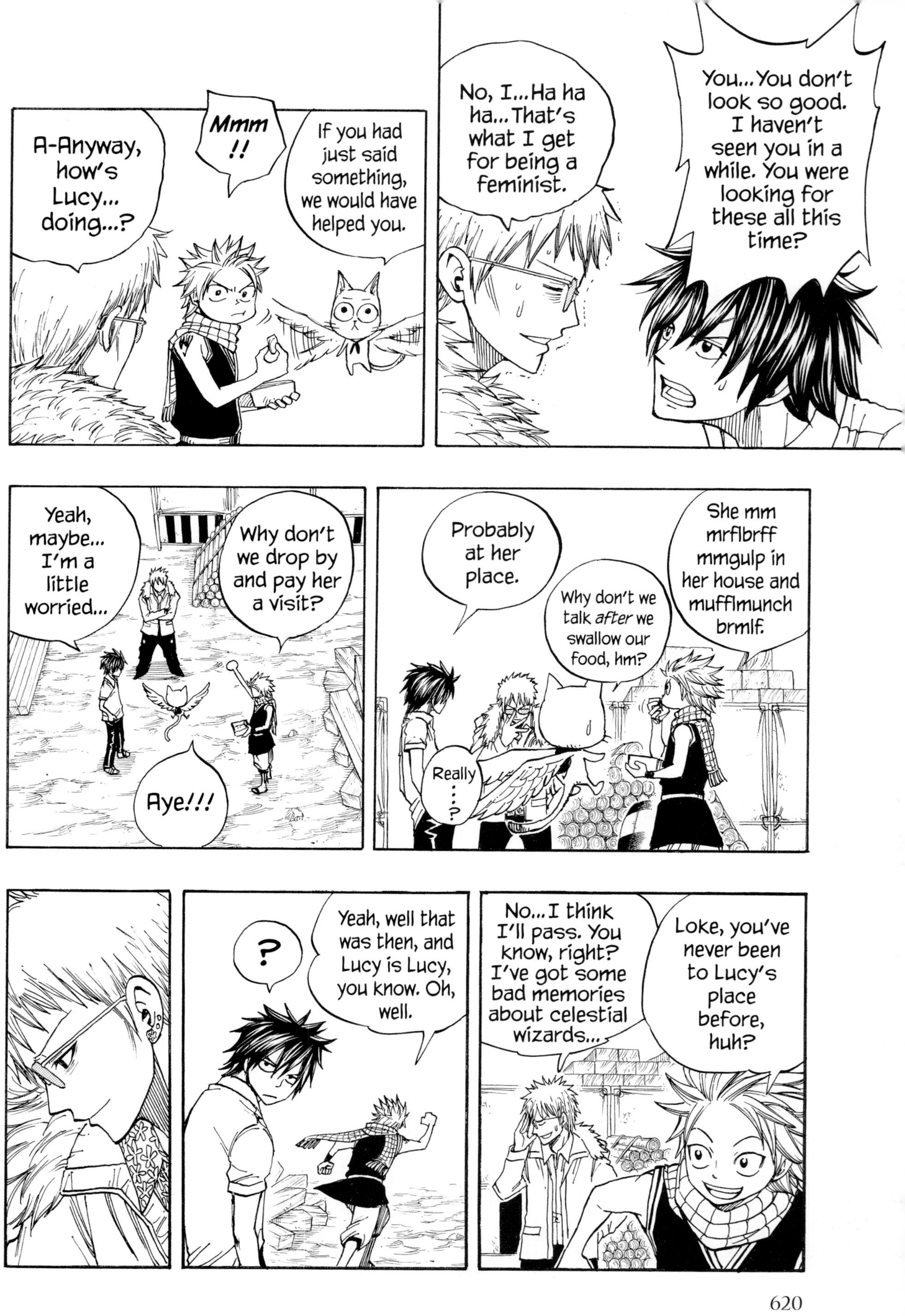
You... You don't look so good. I haven't seen you in a while. You were looking for these all this time?
No, I... Ha ha ha... That's what I get for being a feminist.
If you had just said something, we would have helped you.
Mmm!!
A-Anyway, how's Lucy... doing...?
She mm mrflbrff mmgulp in her house and mufflmunch brmlf.
Why don't we talk *after* we swallow our food, hm?
Probably at her place.
Really...?
Why don't we drop by and pay her a visit?
Yeah, maybe... I'm a little worried...
Aye!!!
Loke, you've never been to Lucy's place before, huh?
No... I think I'll pass. You know, right? I've got some bad memories about celestial wizards...
Yeah, well that was then, and Lucy is Lucy, you know. Oh, well.
?

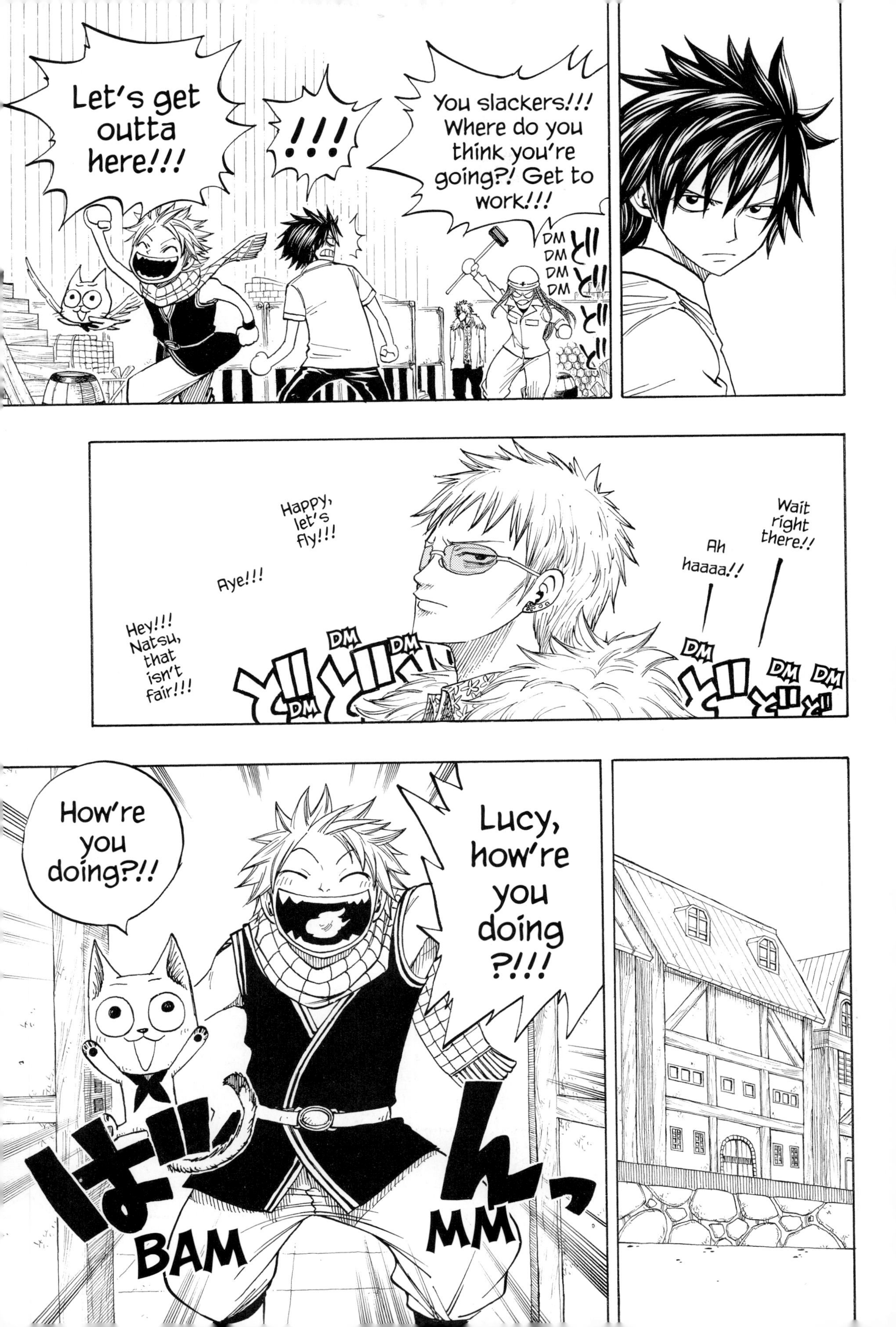
You slackers!!! Where do you think you're going?! Get to work!!!
!!!
Let's get outta here!!!
DM DM DM DM
Wait right there!!
Ah haaaa!!
Happy, let's fly!!!
Aye!!!
Hey!!! Natsu, that isn't fair!!!
DM DM DM DM DM DM
Lucy, how're you doing?!!!
How're you doing?!!
MM
BAM

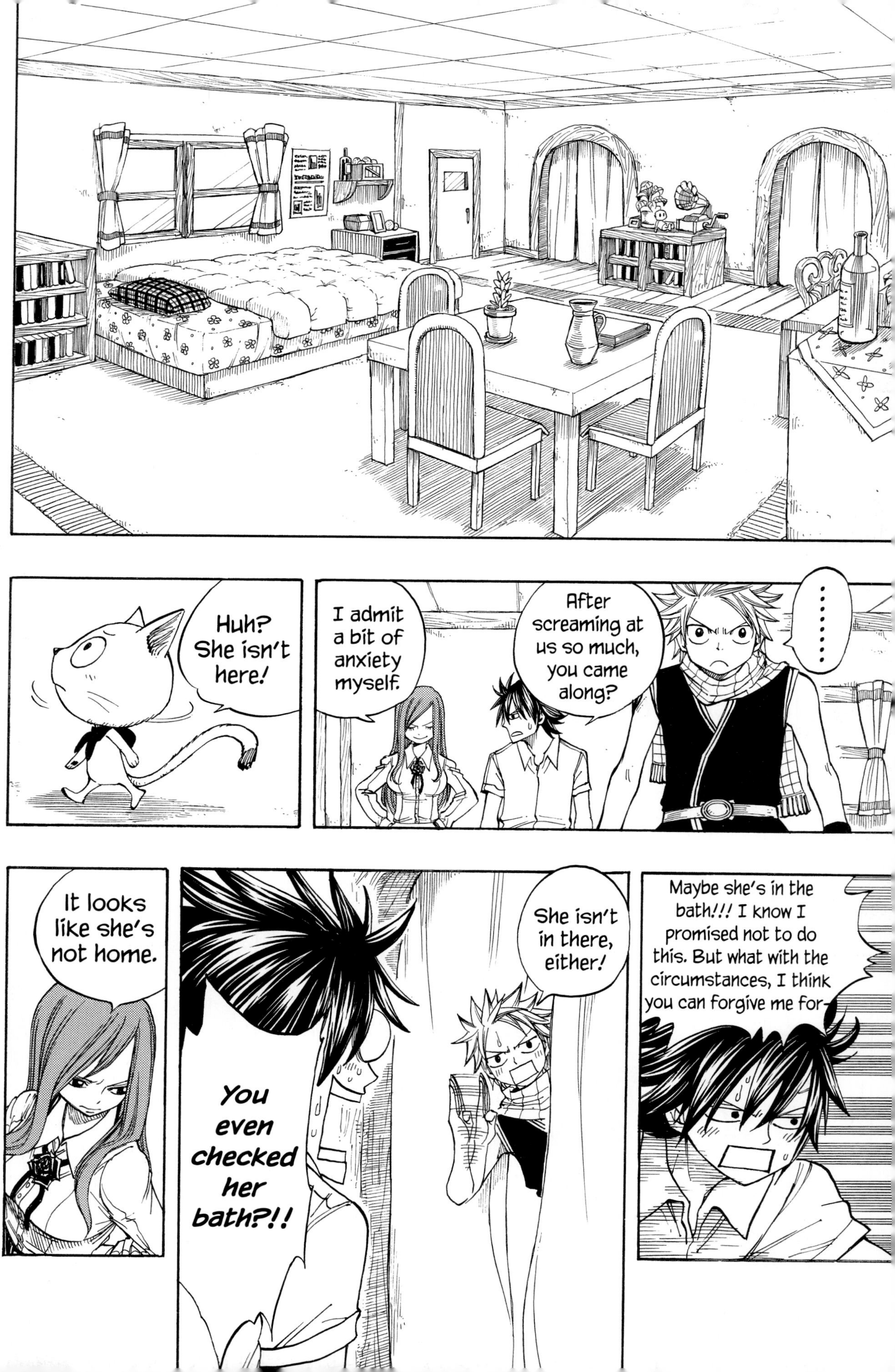
......
After screaming at us so much, you came along?
I admit a bit of anxiety myself.
Huh? She isn't here!
Maybe she's in the bath!!! I know I promised not to do this. But what with the circumstances, I think you can forgive me for-
She isn't in there, either!
You even checked her bath?!!
It looks like she's not home.

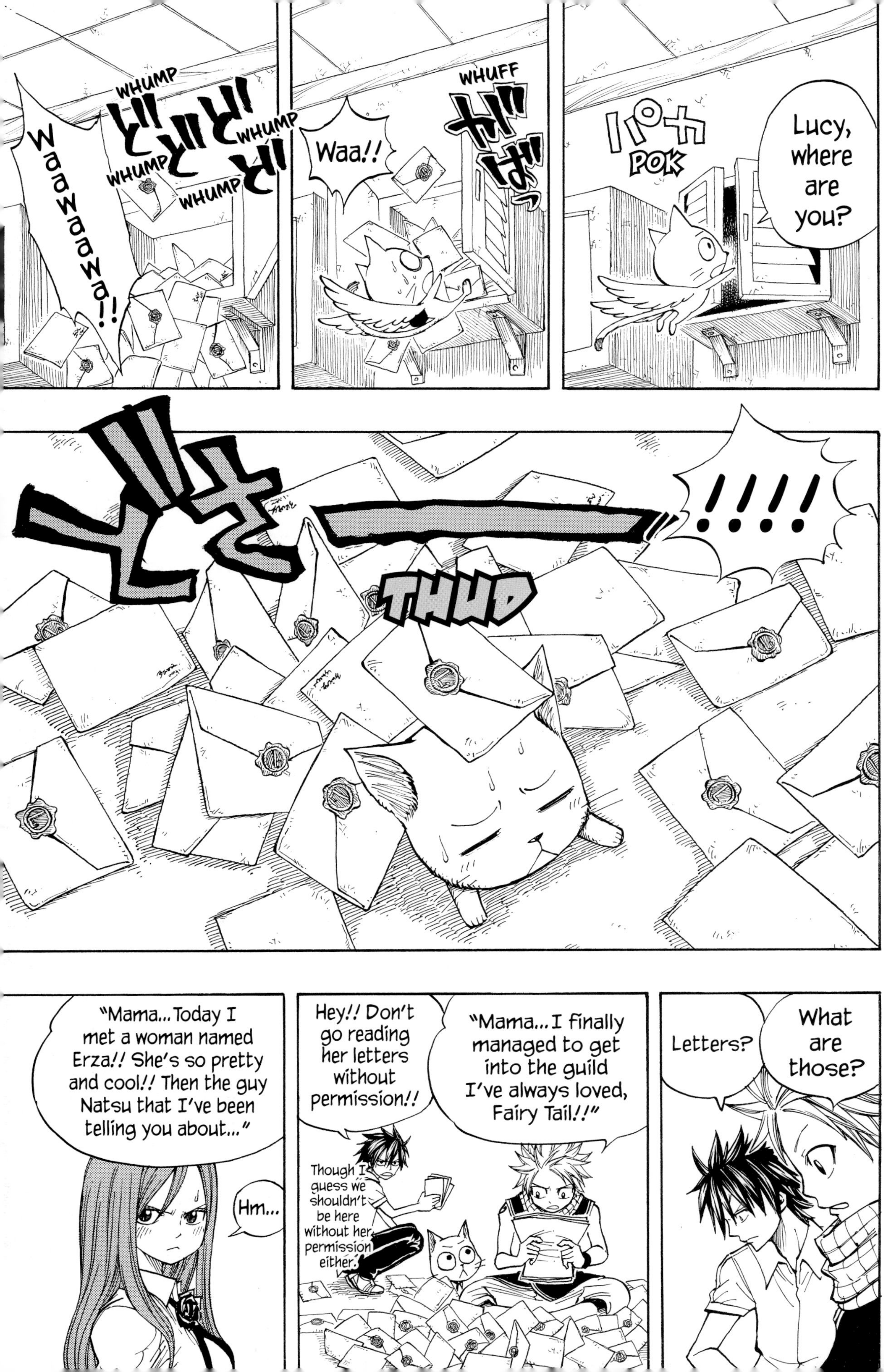

パカ
POK
Lucy, where are you?
WHUFF
Waa!!
WHUMP
WHUMP
WHUMP
WHUMP
Waawaawaa!!
THUD
!!!!
What are those?
Letters?
"Mama...I finally managed to get into the guild I've always loved, Fairy Tail!!"
Hey!! Don't go reading her letters without permission!!
Though I guess we shouldn't be here without her permission either.
"Mama...Today I met a woman named Erza!! She's so pretty and cool!! Then the guy Natsu that I've been telling you about..."
Hm...

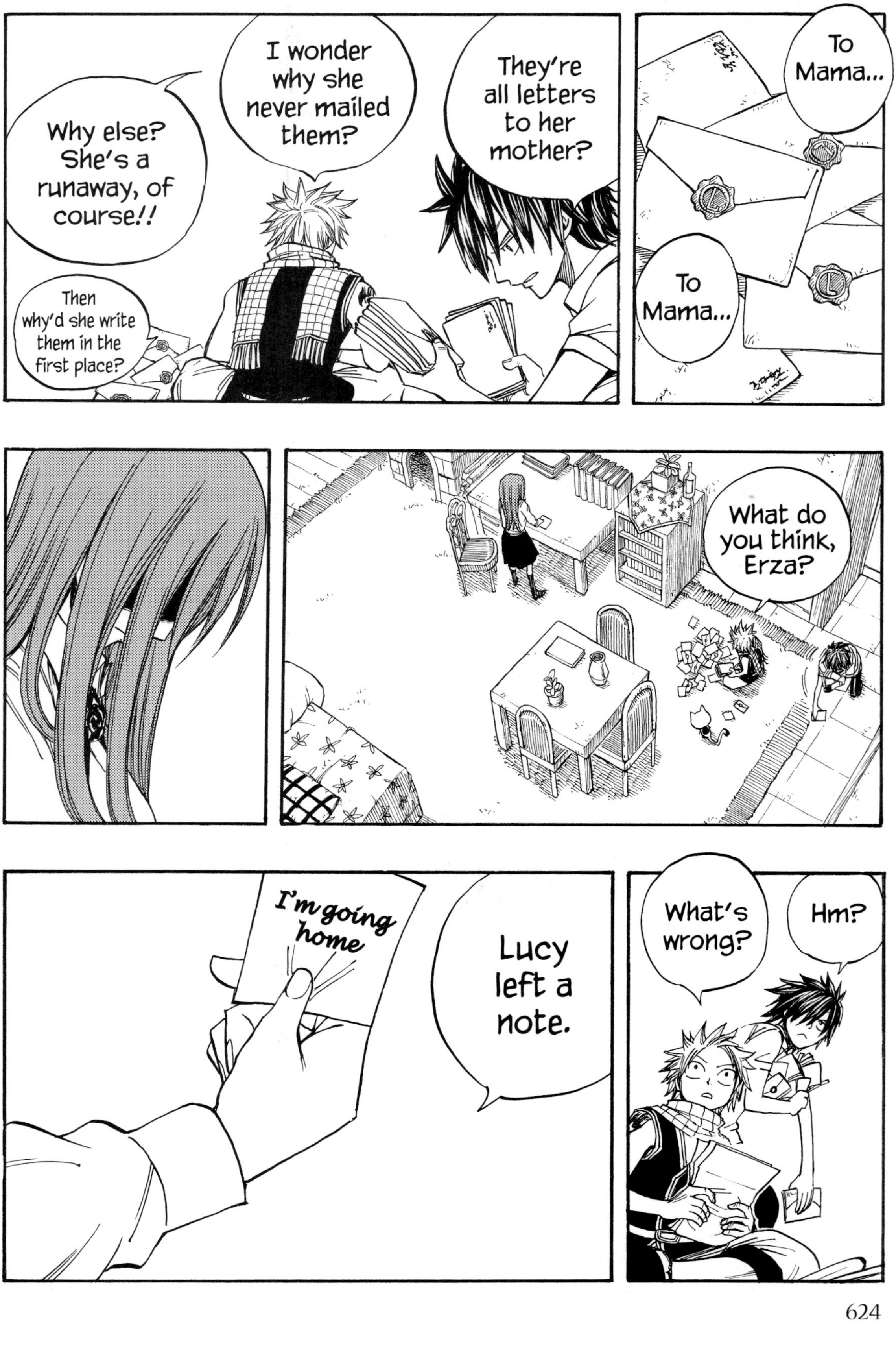
To Mama...
To Mama...
They're all letters to her mother?
I wonder why she never mailed them?
Why else? She's a runaway, of course!!
Then why'd she write them in the first place?
What do you think, Erza?
Hm?
What's wrong?
Lucy left a note.
I'm going home

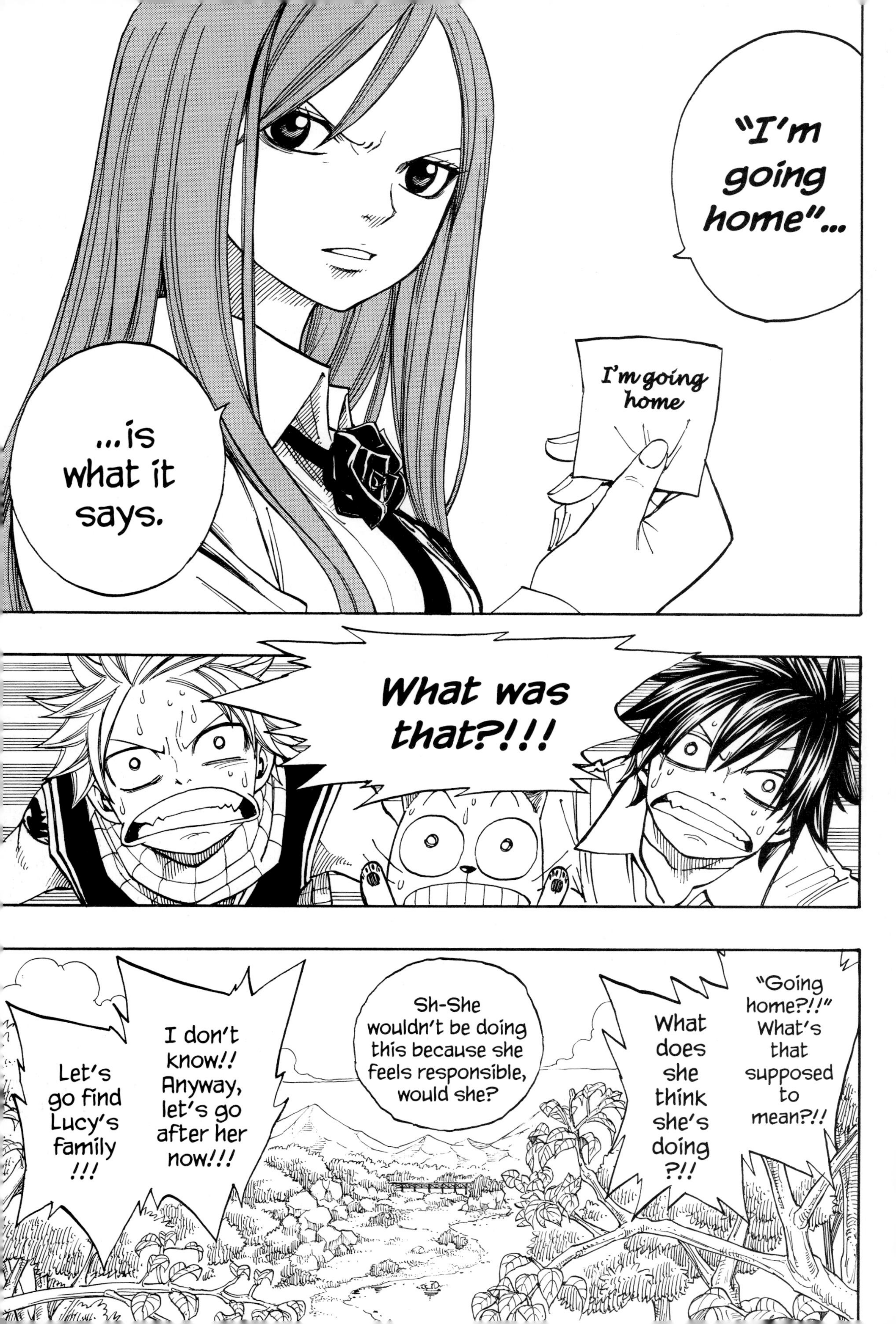
"I'm going home"...
I'm going home
...is what it says.
What was that?!!!
"Going home?!!" What's that supposed to mean?!!
What does she think she's doing?!!
Sh-She wouldn't be doing this because she feels responsible, would she?
I don't know!! Anyway, let's go after her now!!!
Let's go find Lucy's family!!!

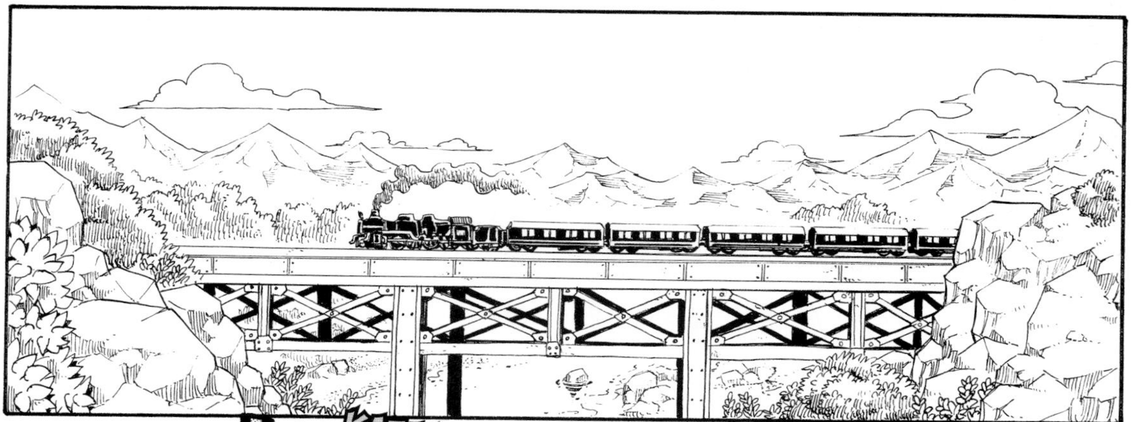

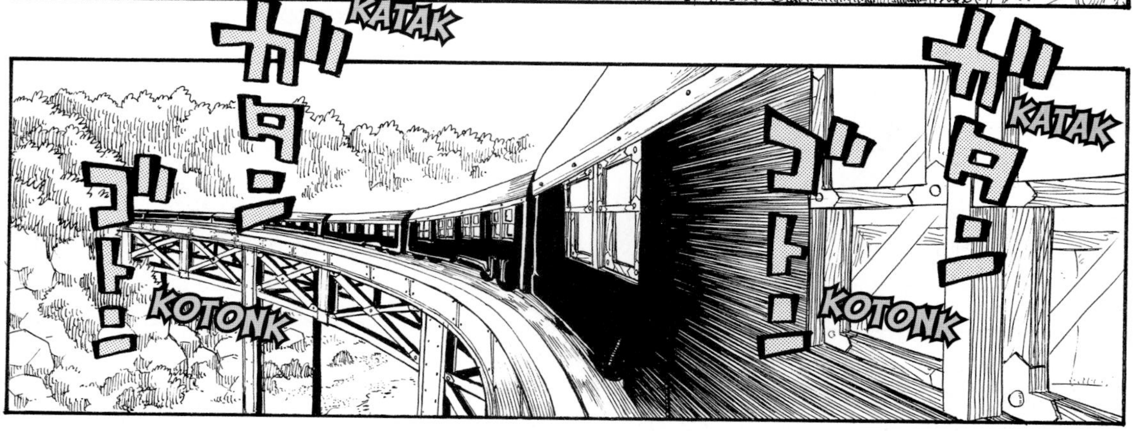
ガタン
KATAK
ゴトン!!
KOTONK
ガタン
KATAK
ゴトン!!
KOTONK

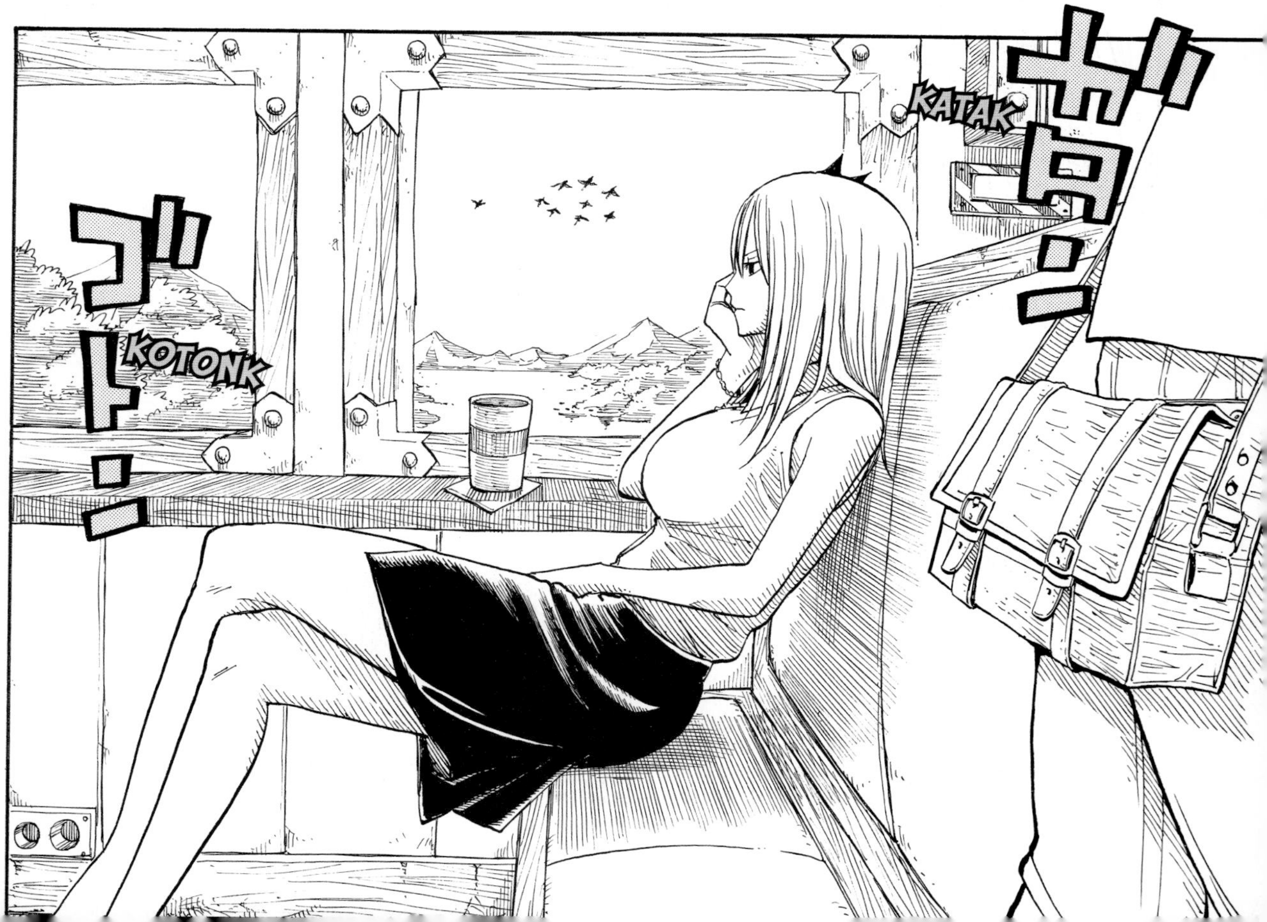
ガタン
KATAK
ゴトン!!
KOTONK

FAIRY TAIL

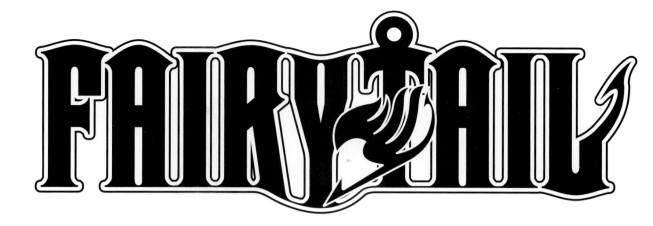

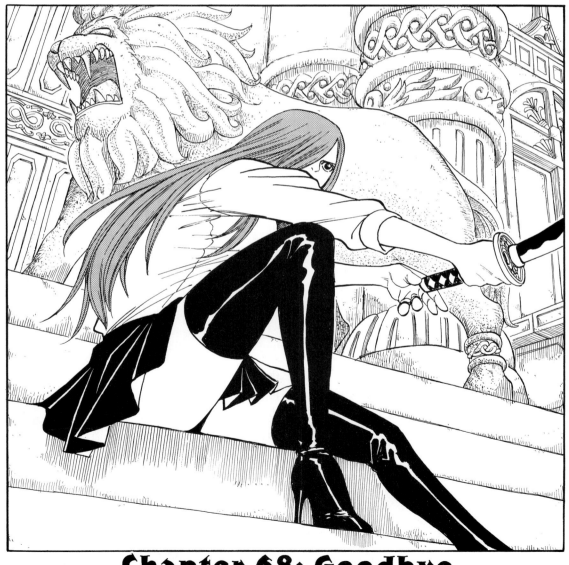

Chapter 68: Goodbye

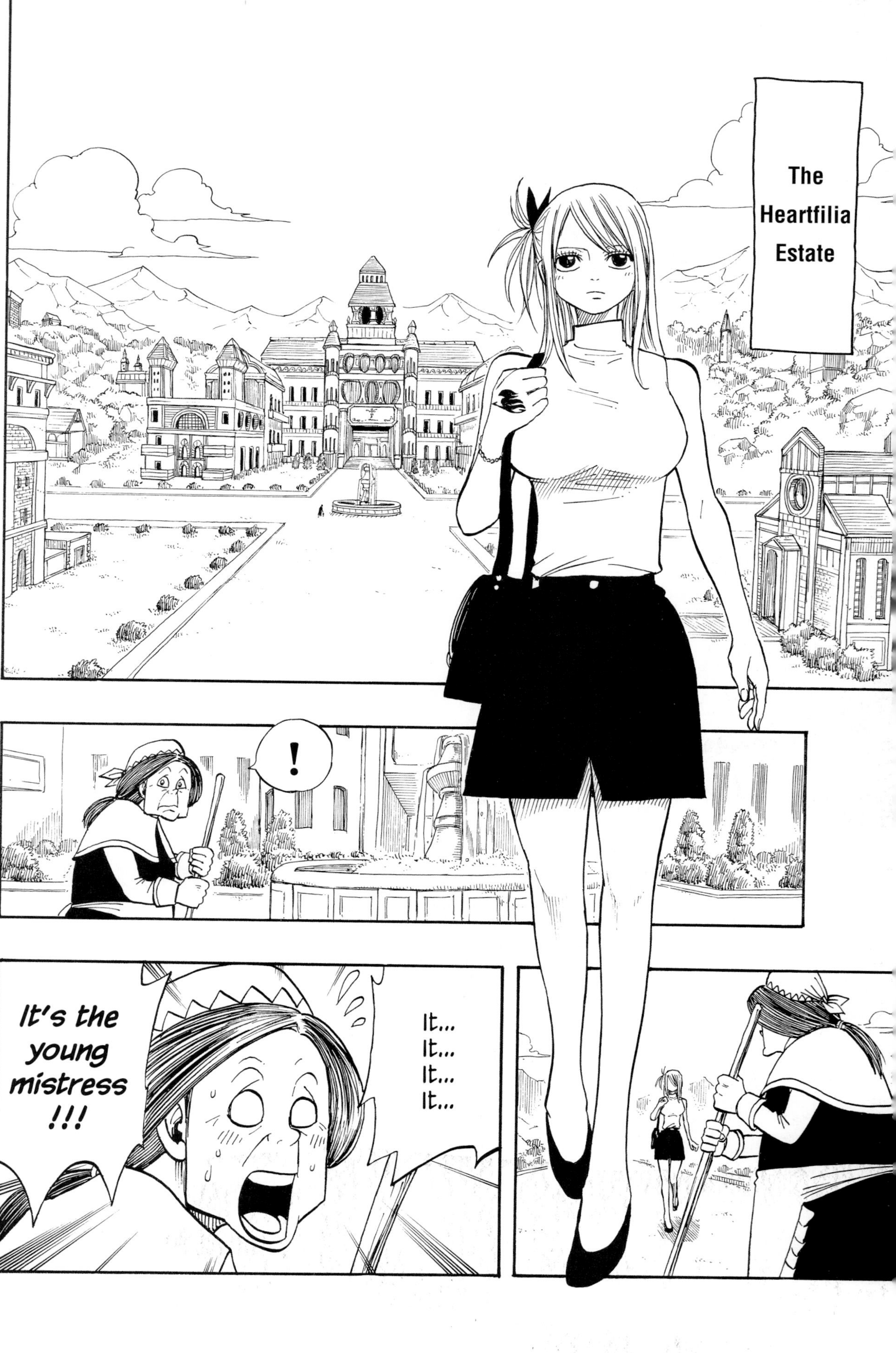
The Heartfilia Estate
!
It... It... It... It...
It's the young mistress!!!

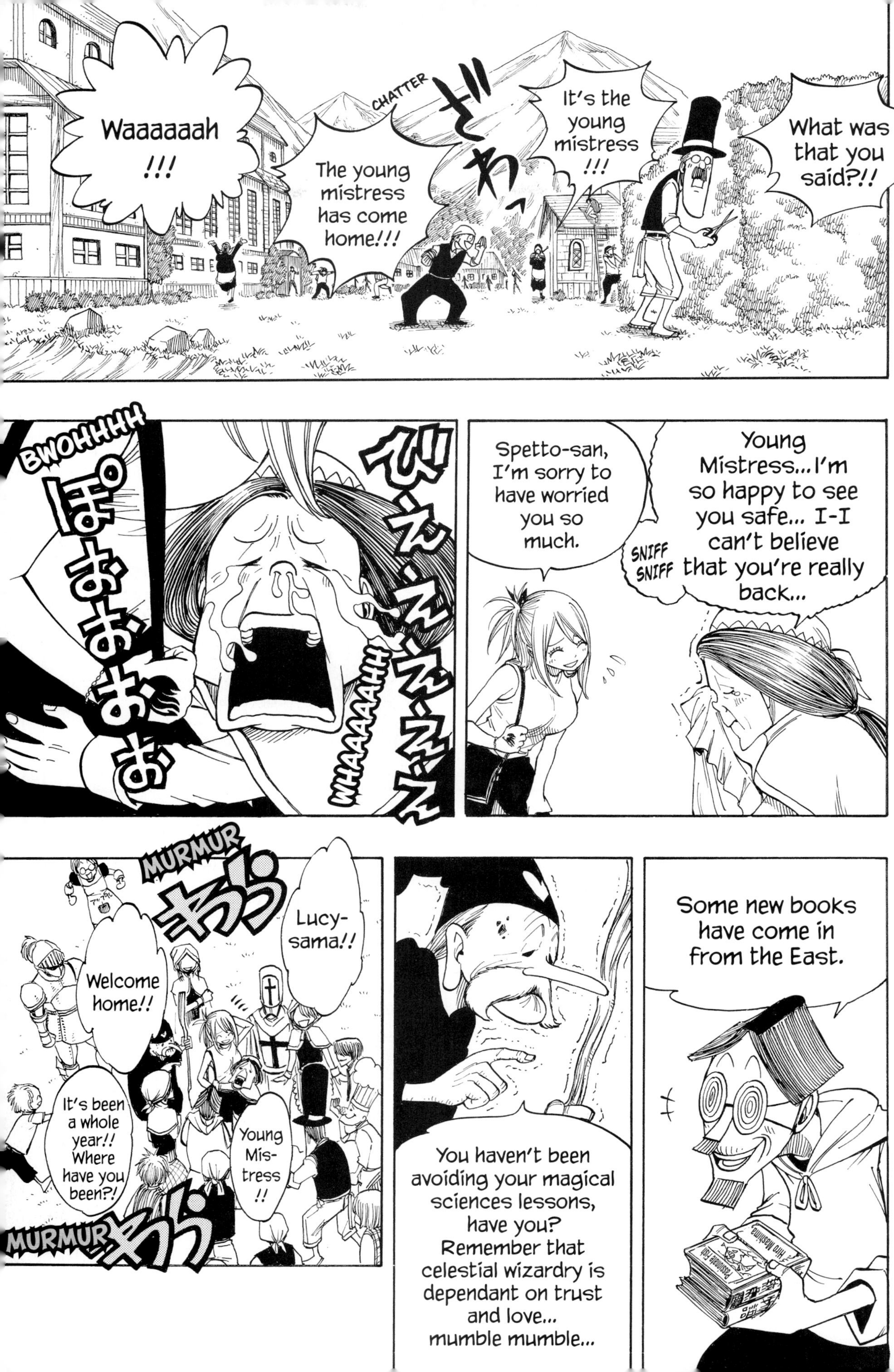
What was that you said?!!
It's the young mistress!!!
CHATTER
The young mistress has come home!!!
Waaaaaah!!!
Young Mistress...I'm so happy to see you safe... I-I can't believe that you're really back...
SNIFF SNIFF
Spetto-san, I'm sorry to have worried you so much.
WHAAAAAHH
BWOHHHH
Some new books have come in from the East.
You haven't been avoiding your magical sciences lessons, have you? Remember that celestial wizardry is dependant on trust and love... mumble mumble...
Lucy-sama!!
MURMUR
Welcome home!!
Young Mis-tress!!
It's been a whole year!! Where have you been?!
MURMUR

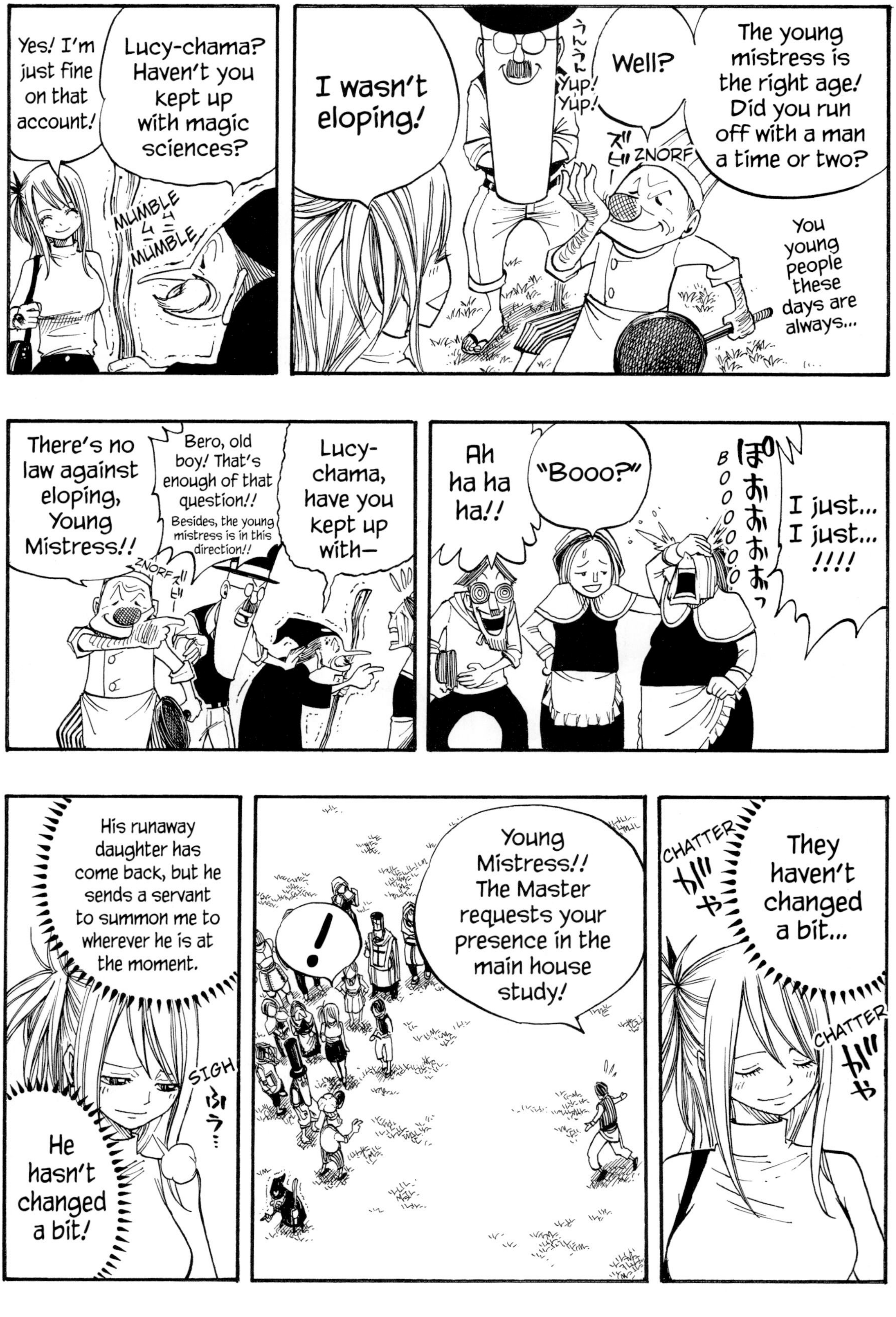
The young mistress is the right age! Did you run off with a man a time or two?
You young people these days are always...
ZNORF
ズビー
うんうん
Yup! Yup!
Well?
I wasn't eloping!
Lucy-chama? Haven't you kept up with magic sciences?
MUMBLE ムニ MUMBLE
Yes! I'm just fine on that account!
I just... I just... !!!!
ぼおおおおおっ
BOOOOOOO
"Booo?"
Ah ha ha!!
Lucy-chama, have you kept up with—
Bero, old boy! That's enough of that question!! Besides, the young mistress is in this direction!!
ズビー
ZNORF
There's no law against eloping, Young Mistress!!
They haven't changed a bit...
CHATTER
ガヤ
CHATTER
ガヤ
Young Mistress!! The Master requests your presence in the main house study!
!
His runaway daughter has come back, but he sends a servant to summon me to wherever he is at the moment.
SIGH
ふう...
He hasn't changed a bit!

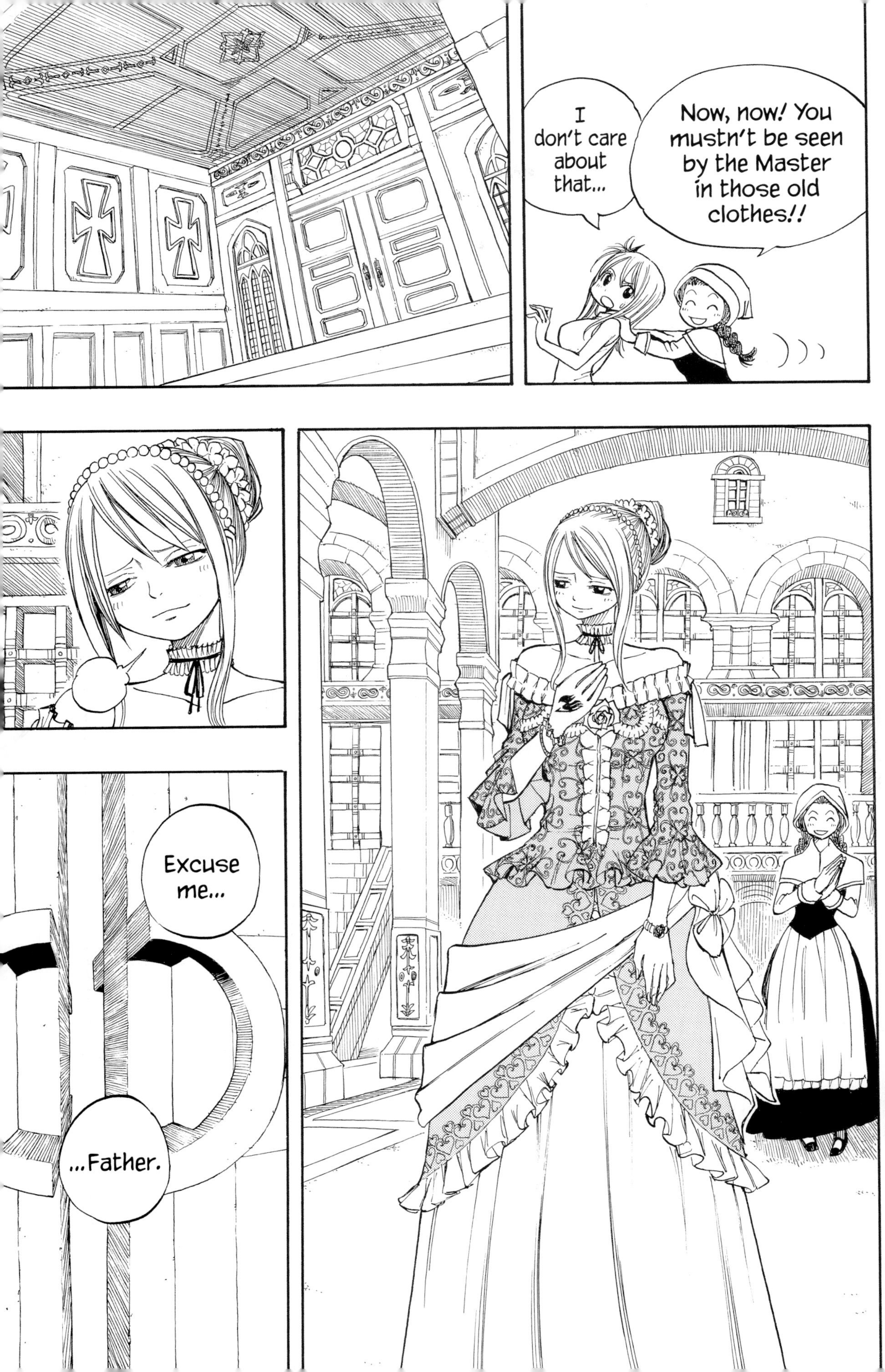
Now, now! You mustn't be seen by the Master in those old clothes!!
I don't care about that...
Excuse me...
...Father.

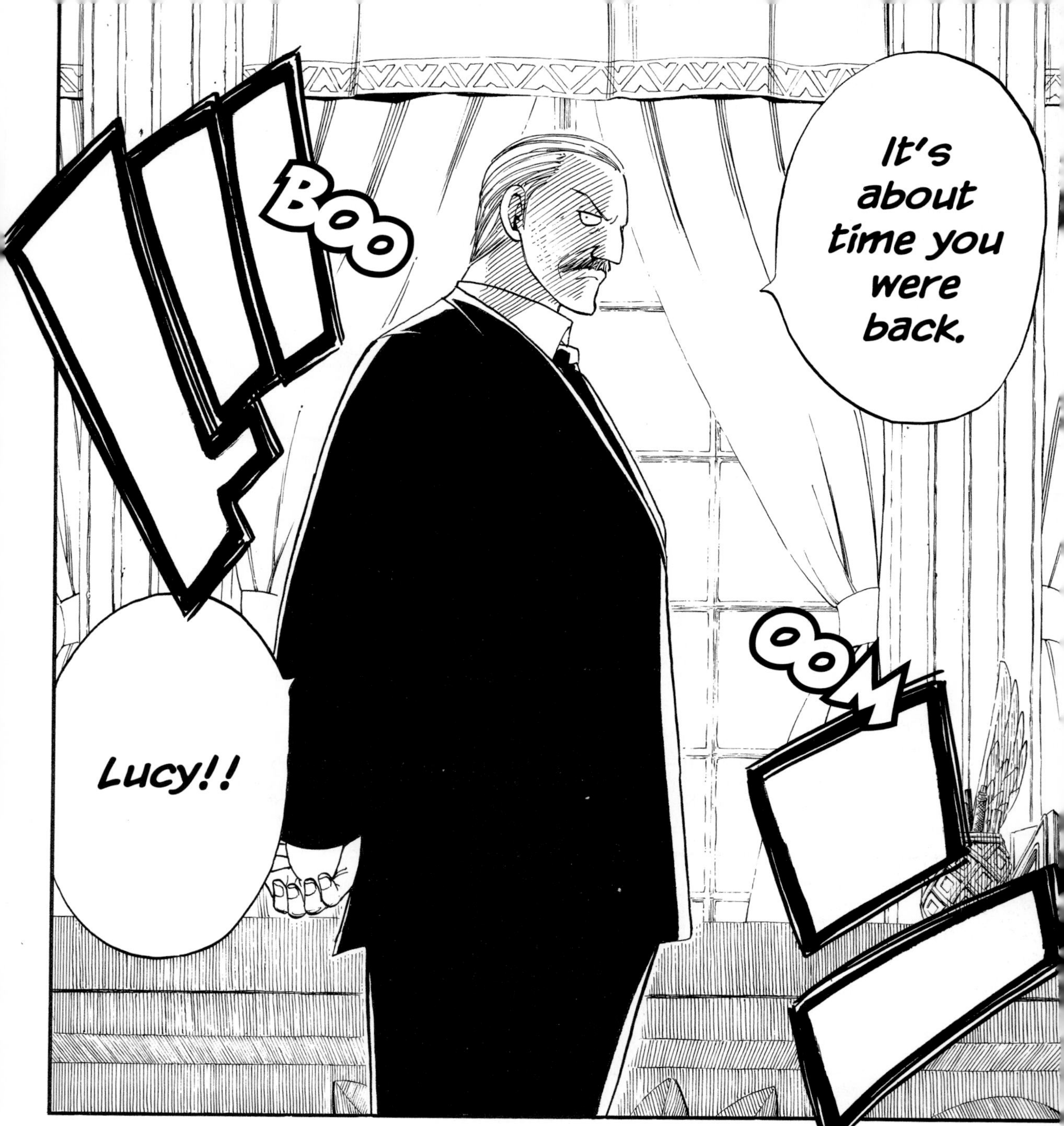
It's about time you were back.
BOOOOM
Lucy!!

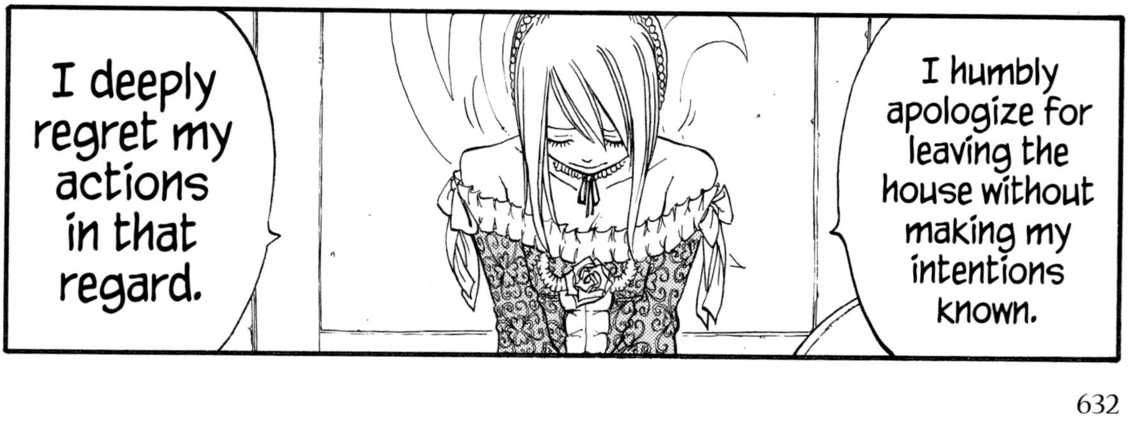
I humbly apologize for leaving the house without making my intentions known.
I deeply regret my actions in that regard.

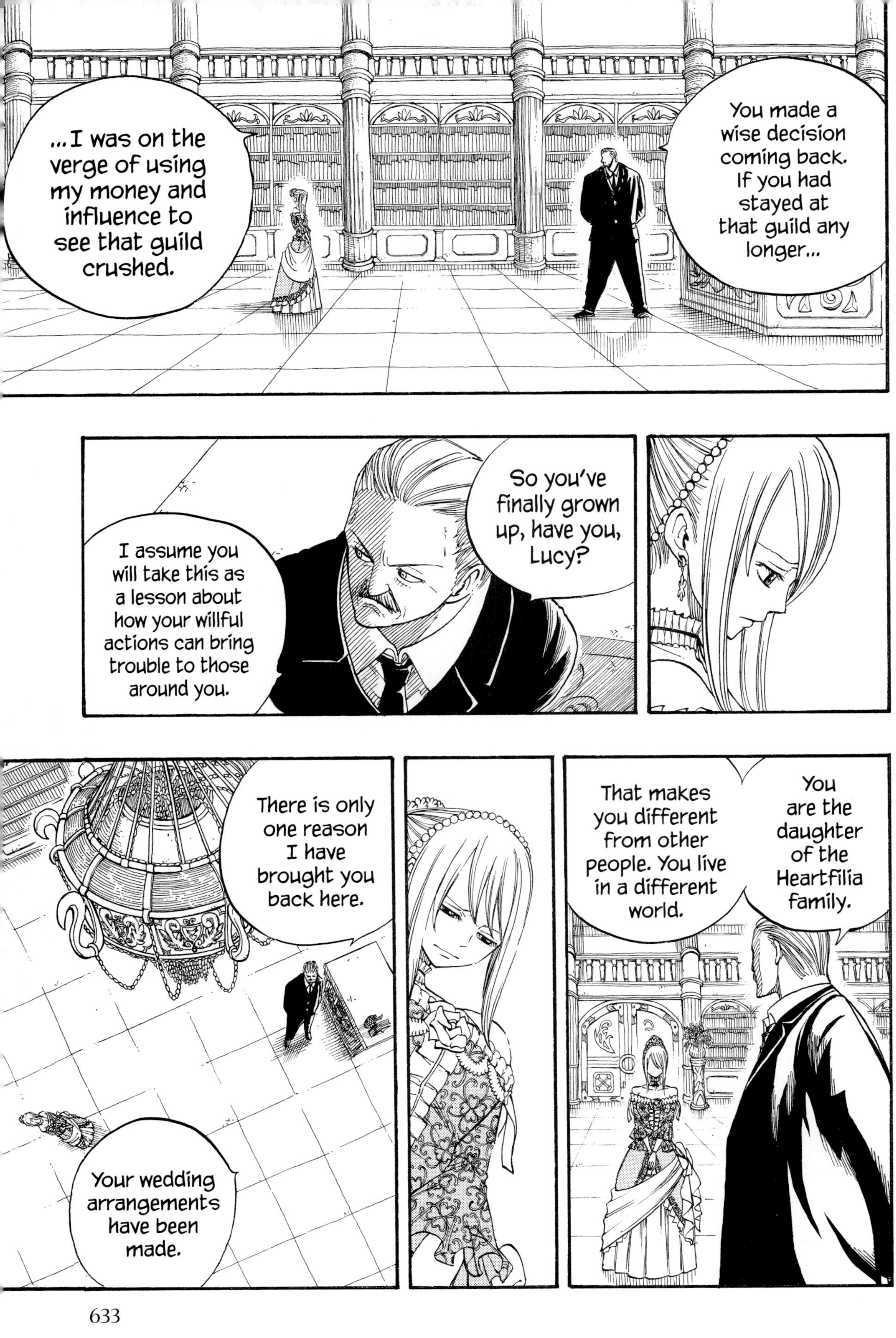
You made a wise decision coming back. If you had stayed at that guild any longer...
...I was on the verge of using my money and influence to see that guild crushed.
So you've finally grown up, have you, Lucy?
I assume you will take this as a lesson about how your willful actions can bring trouble to those around you.
You are the daughter of the Heartfilia family.
That makes you different from other people. You live in a different world.
There is only one reason I have brought you back here.
Your wedding arrangements have been made.

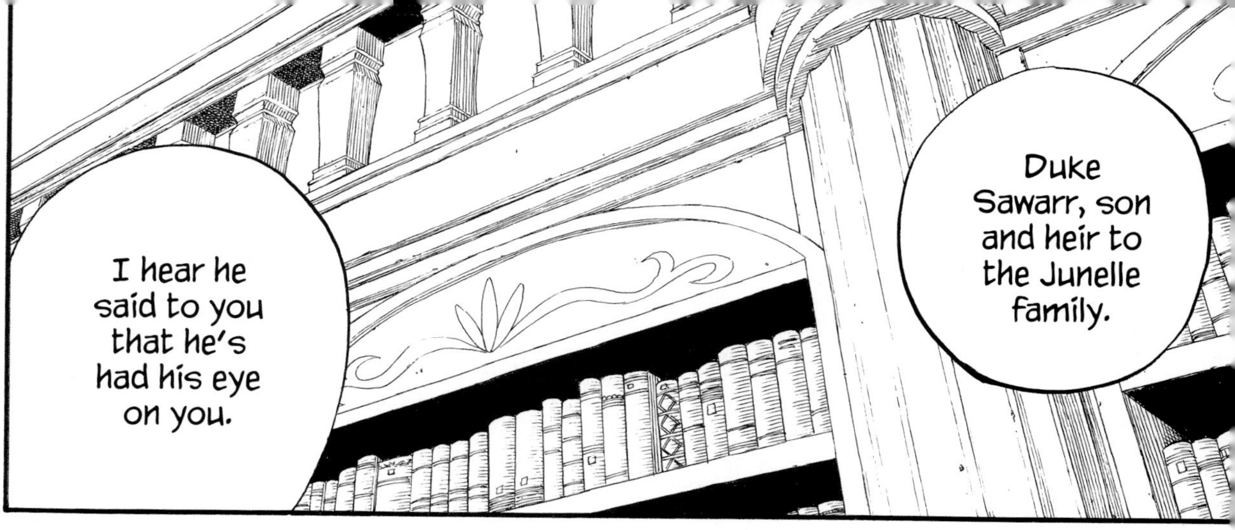
Duke Sawarr, son and heir to the Junelle family.
I hear he said to you that he's had his eye on you.

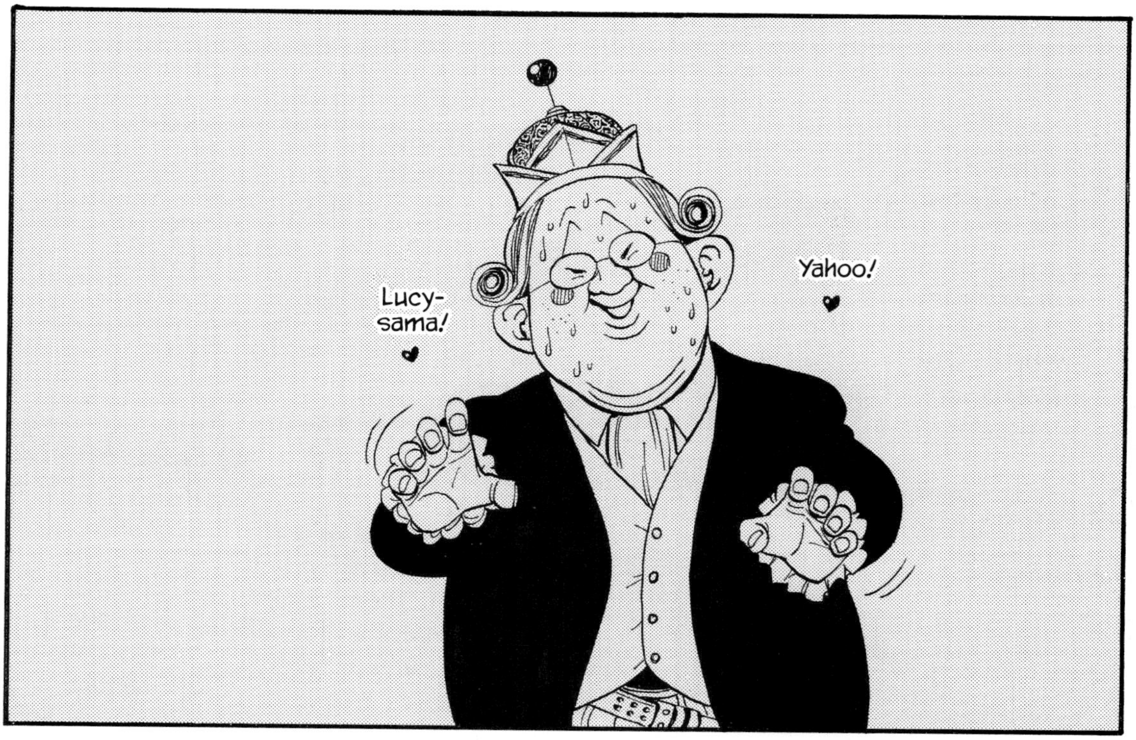
Yahoo!
Lucy-sama!

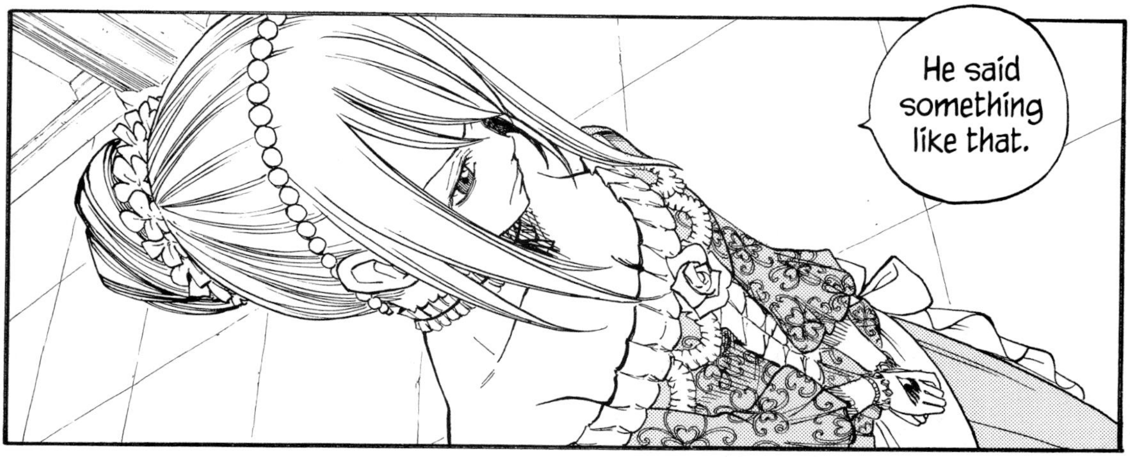
He said something like that.

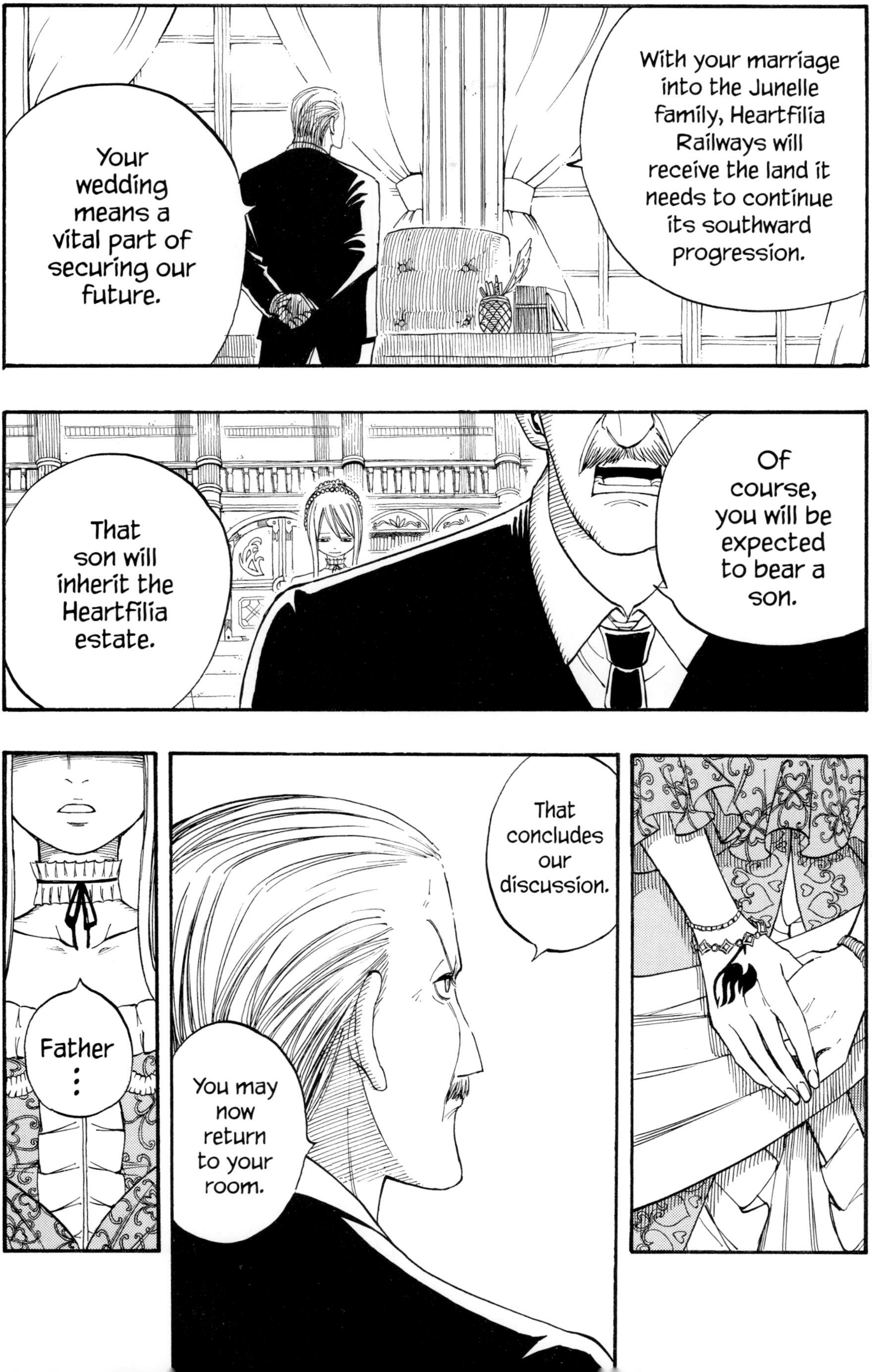
With your marriage into the Junelle family, Heartfilia Railways will receive the land it needs to continue its southward progression.
Your wedding means a vital part of securing our future.
Of course, you will be expected to bear a son.
That son will inherit the Heartfilia estate.
That concludes our discussion.
You may now return to your room.
Father...

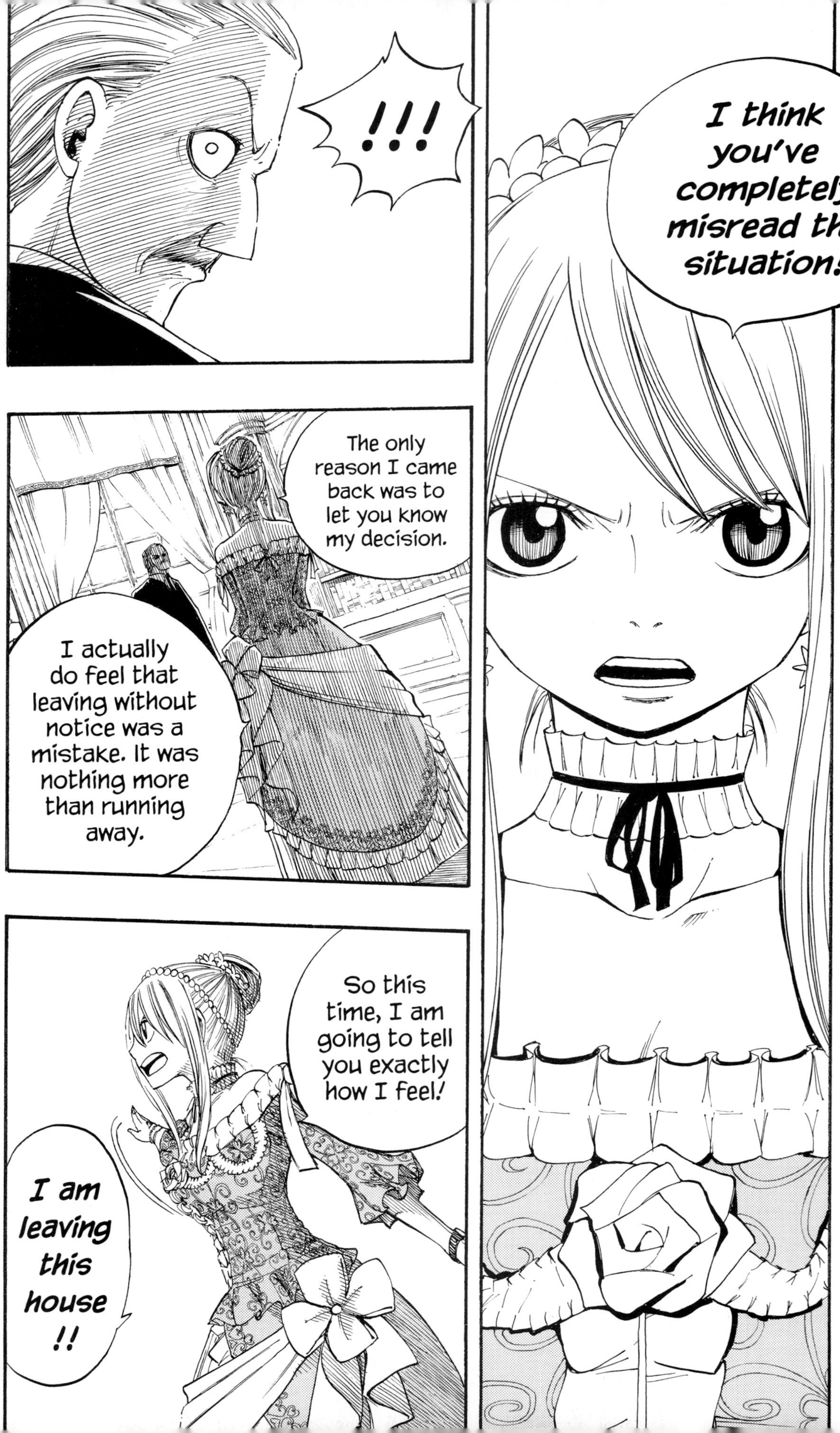
I think you've completely misread the situation!
!!!
The only reason I came back was to let you know my decision.
I actually do feel that leaving without notice was a mistake. It was nothing more than running away.
So this time, I am going to tell you exactly how I feel!
I am leaving this house !!

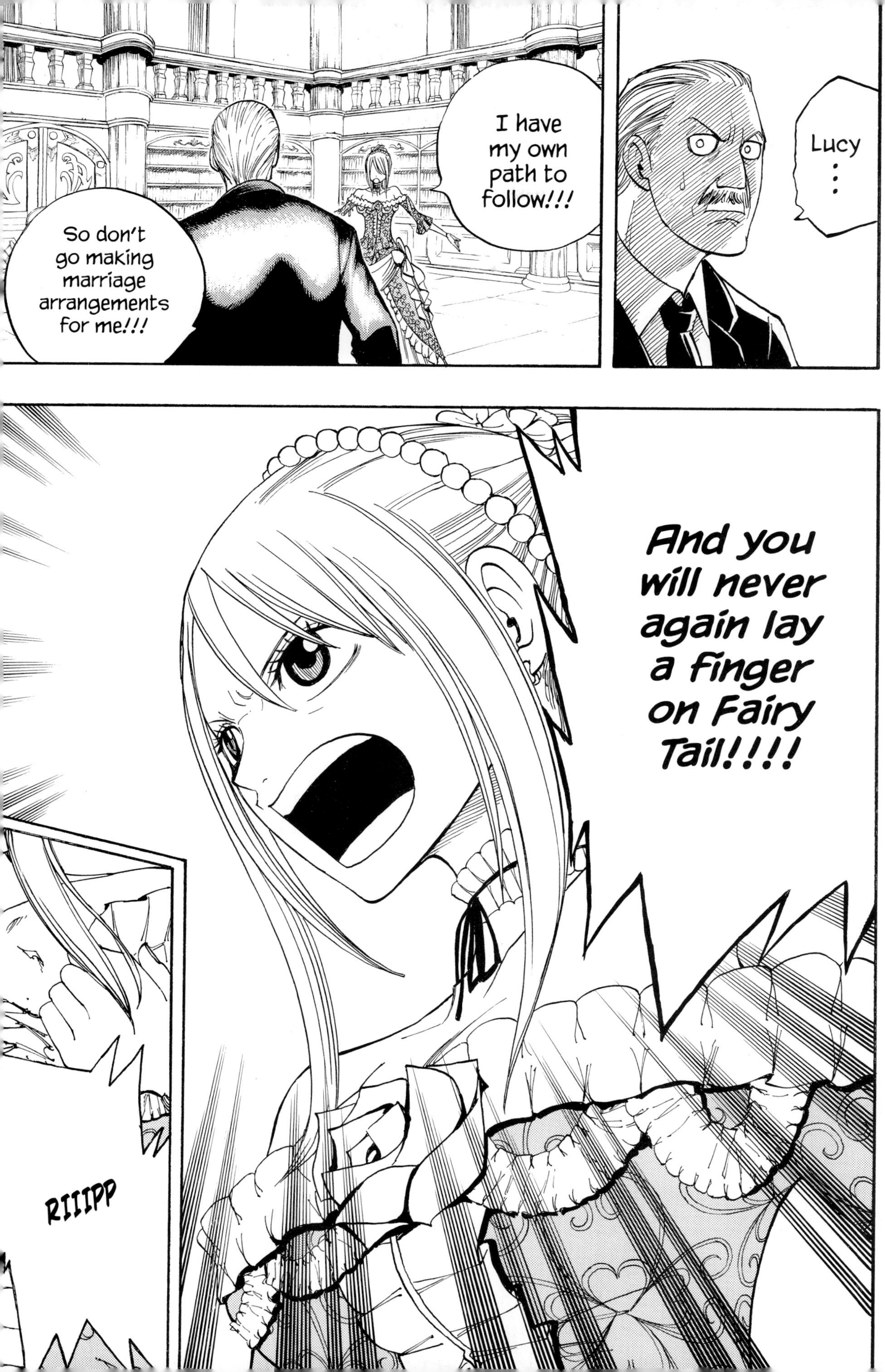
Lucy ...
I have my own path to follow!!!
So don't go making marriage arrangements for me!!!
And you will never again lay a finger on Fairy Tail!!!!
RIIIPP

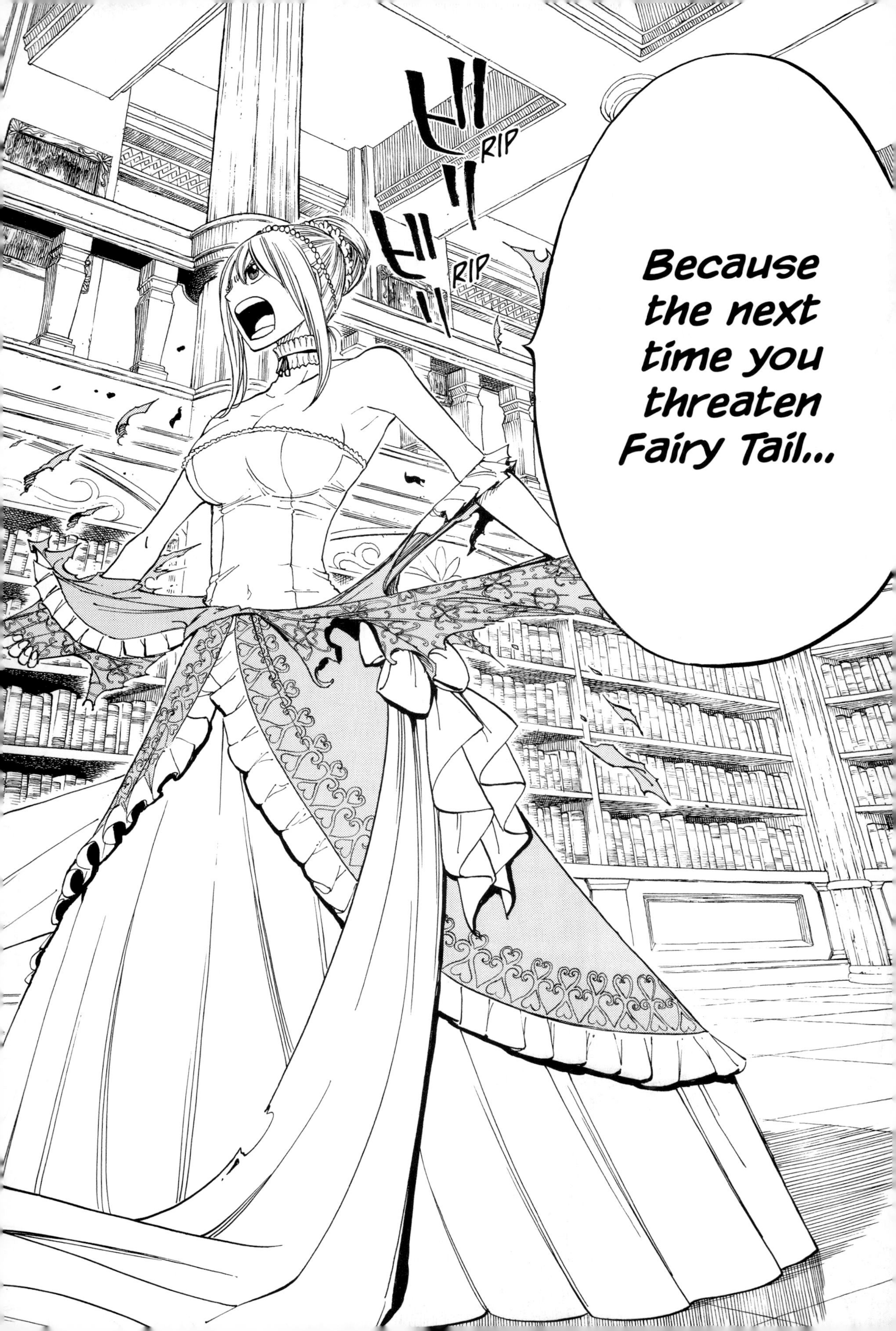
RIP
RIP
Because the next time you threaten Fairy Tail...

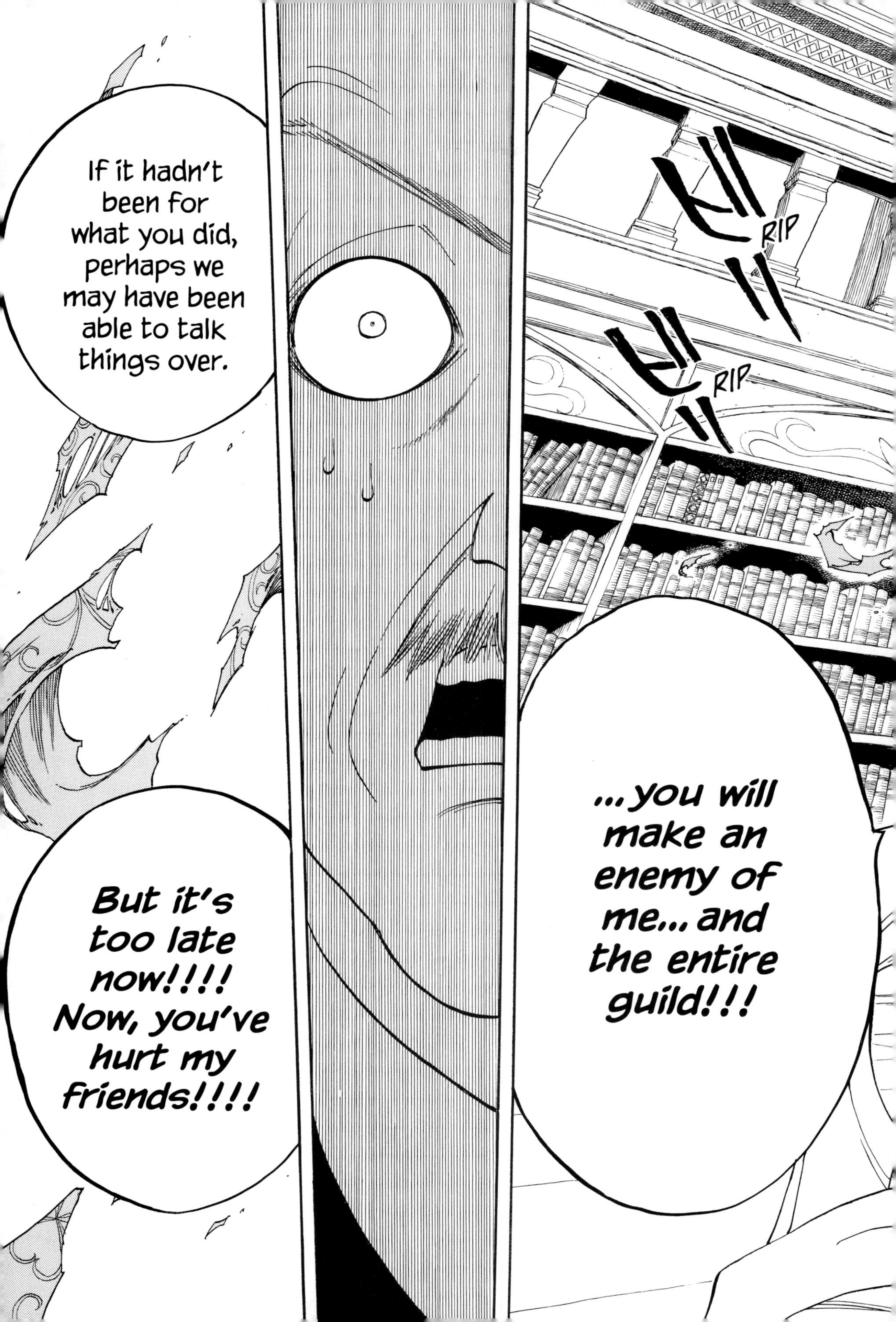
If it hadn't been for what you did, perhaps we may have been able to talk things over.
But it's too late now!!!! Now, you've hurt my friends!!!!
RIP
RIP
...you will make an enemy of me...and the entire guild!!!

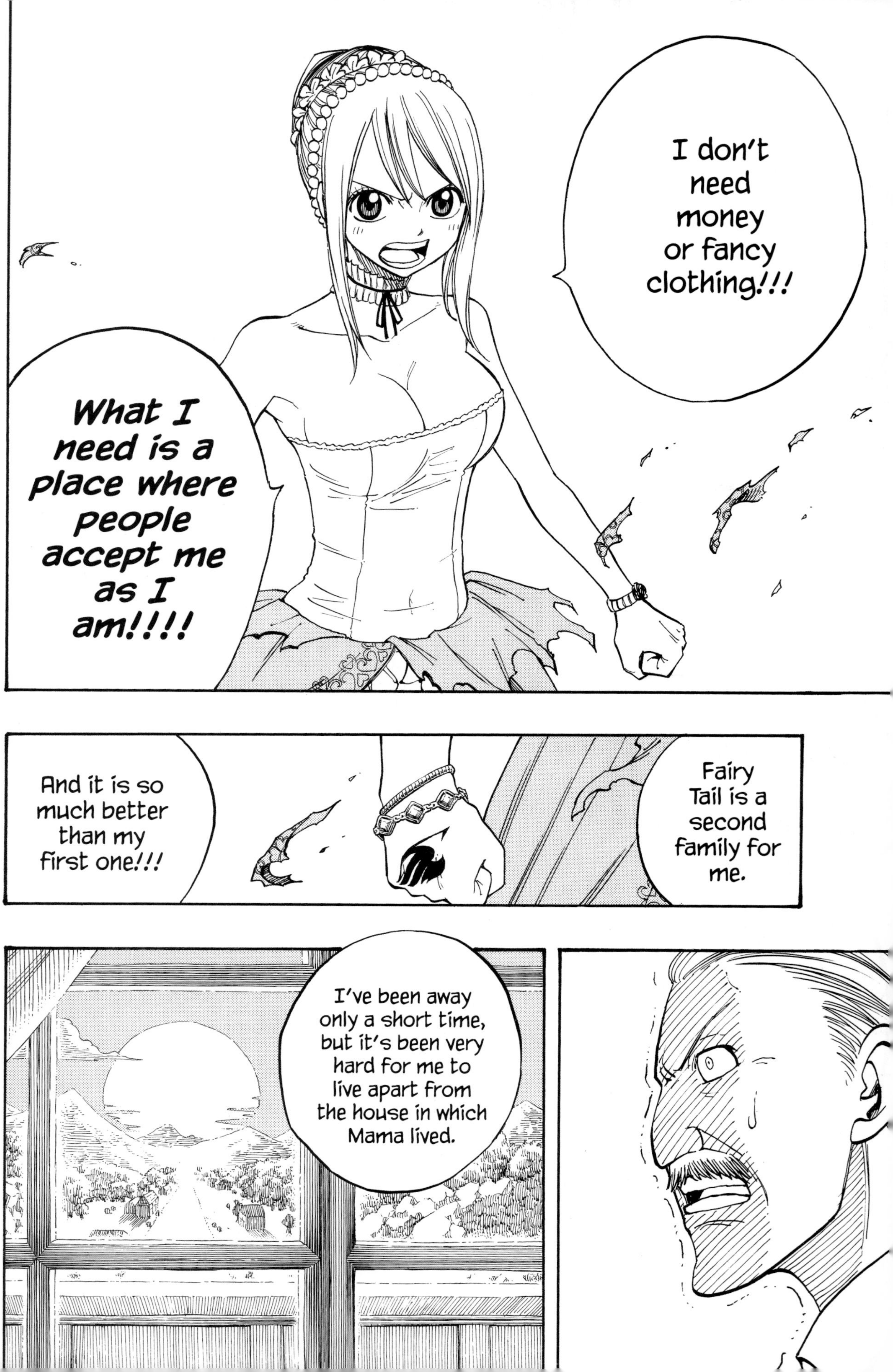
I don't need money or fancy clothing!!!
What I need is a place where people accept me as I am!!!!
Fairy Tail is a second family for me.
And it is so much better than my first one!!!
I've been away only a short time, but it's been very hard for me to live apart from the house in which Mama lived.

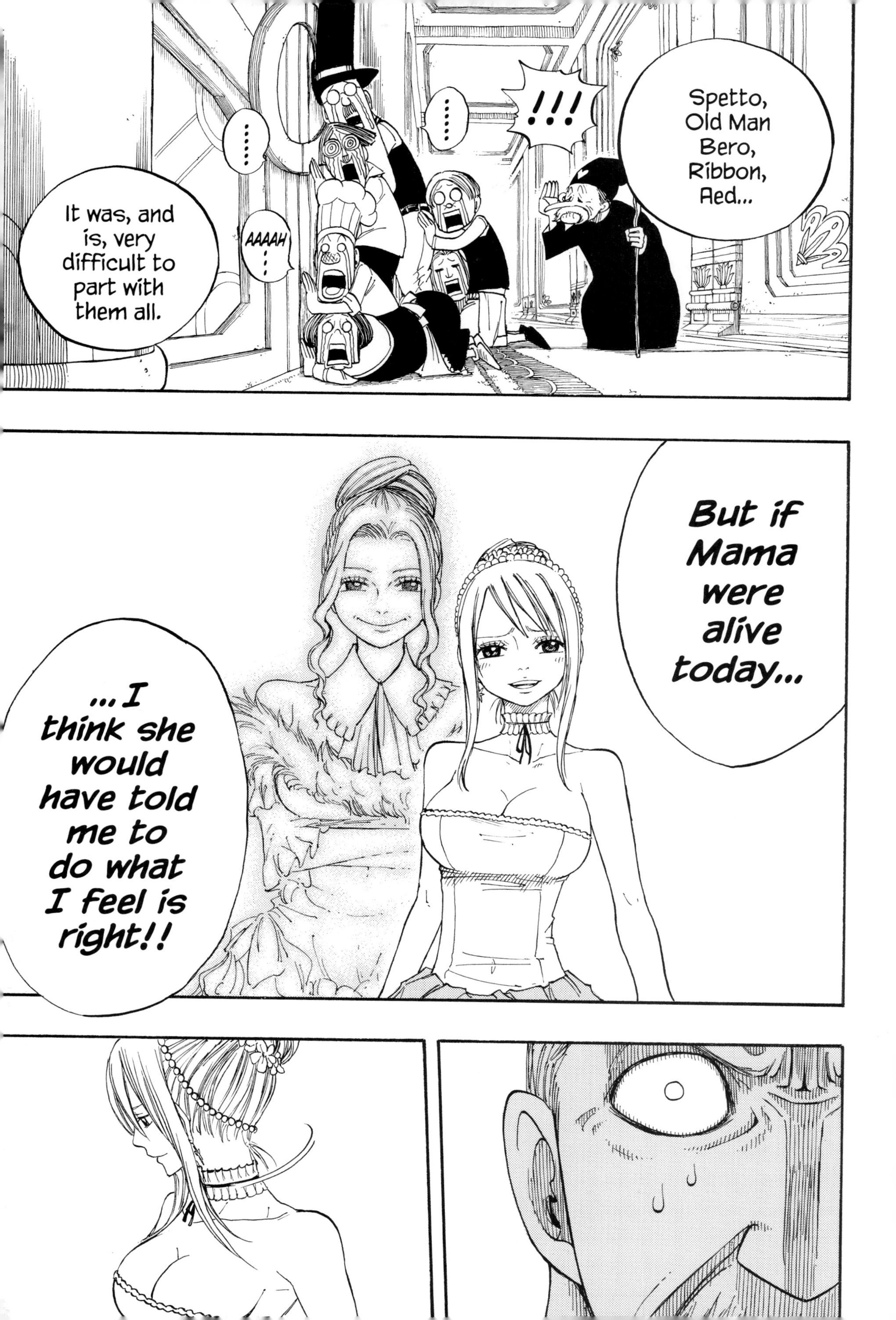
Spetto, Old Man Bero, Ribbon, Aed...
!!!
......
......
AAAAH ...
It was, and is, very difficult to part with them all.
But if Mama were alive today...
...I think she would have told me to do what I feel is right!!

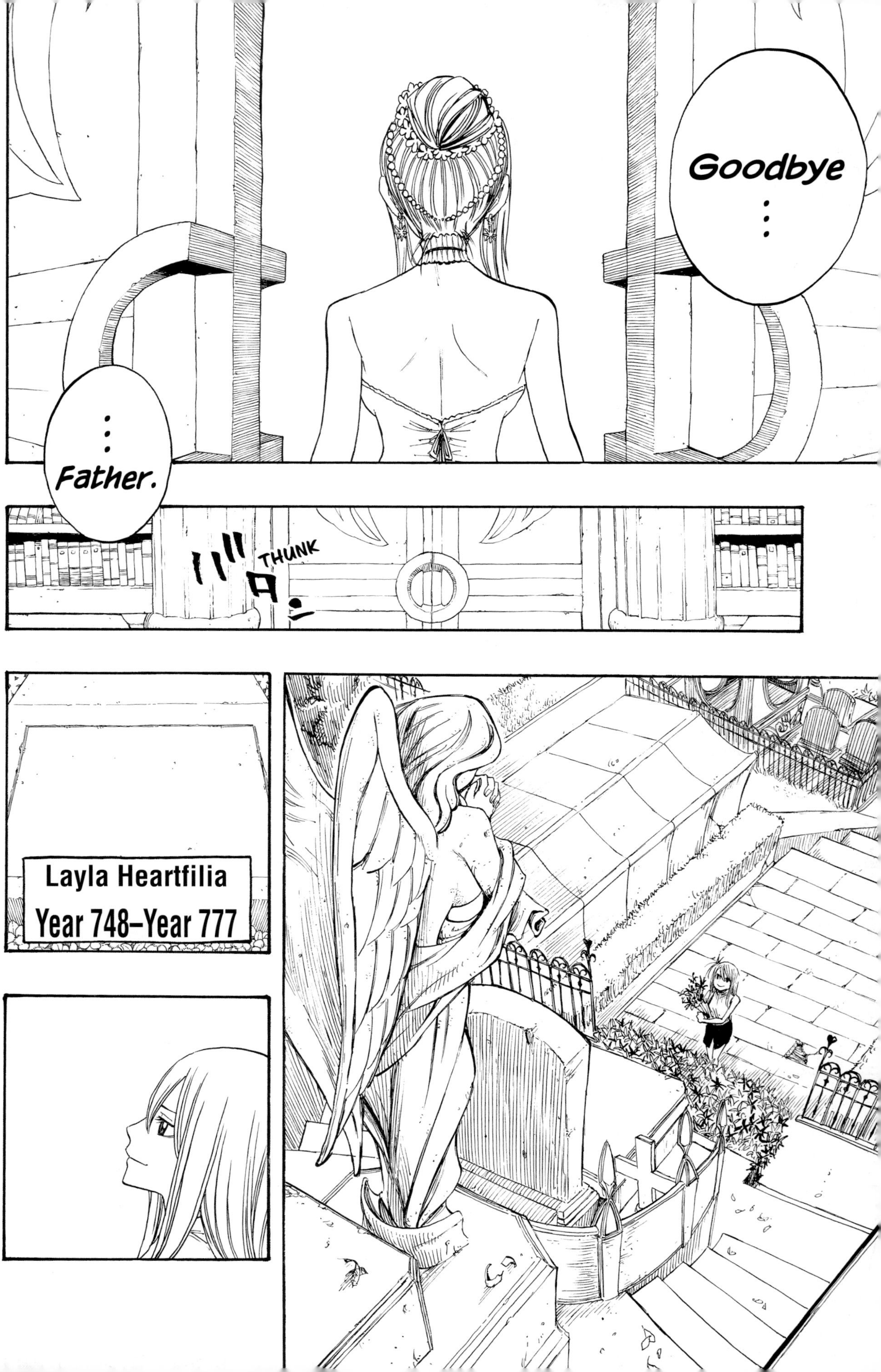
Goodbye
...
...
Father.
THUNK
Layla Heartfilia
Year 748–Year 777

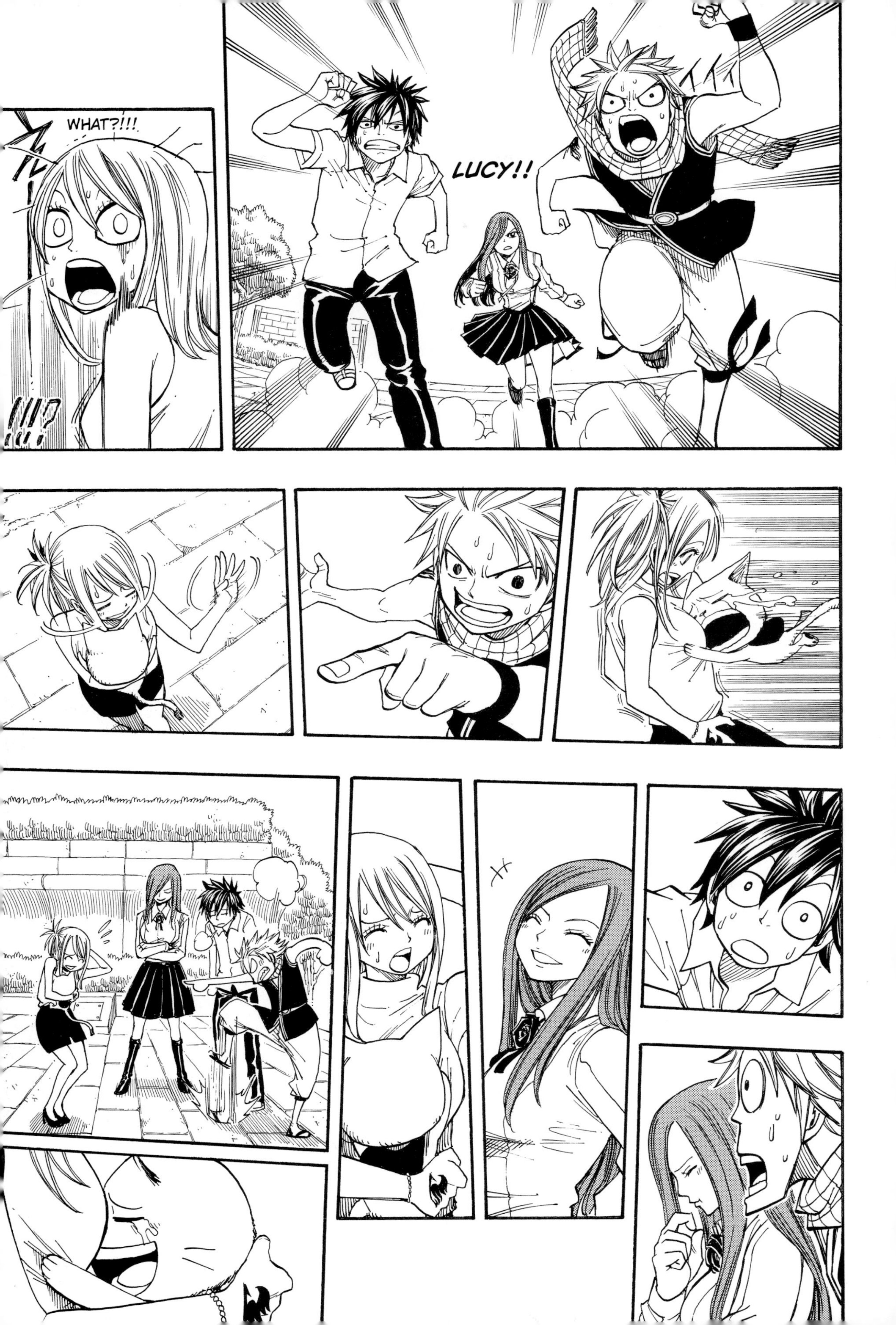
LUCY!!
WHAT?!!!

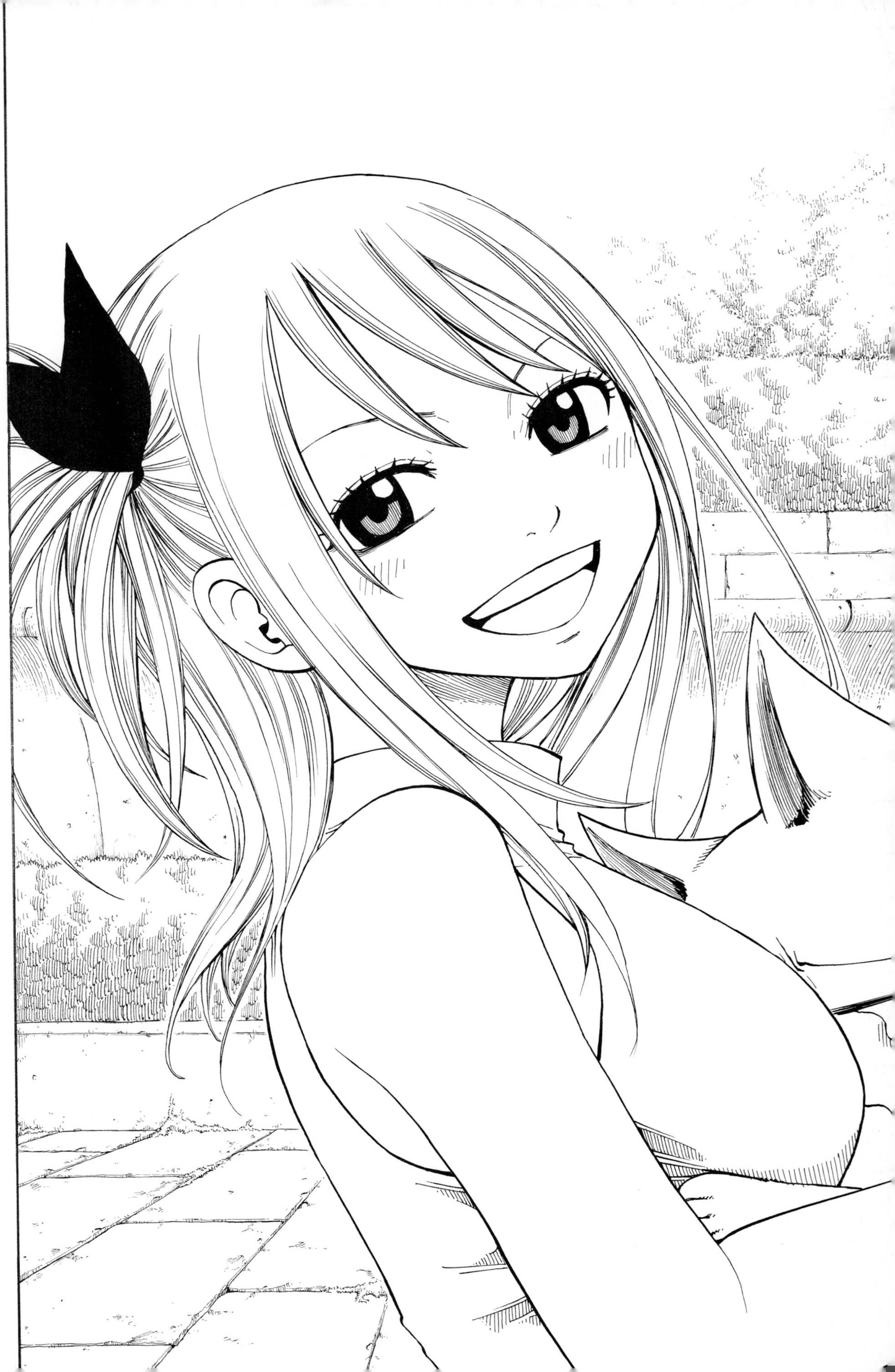

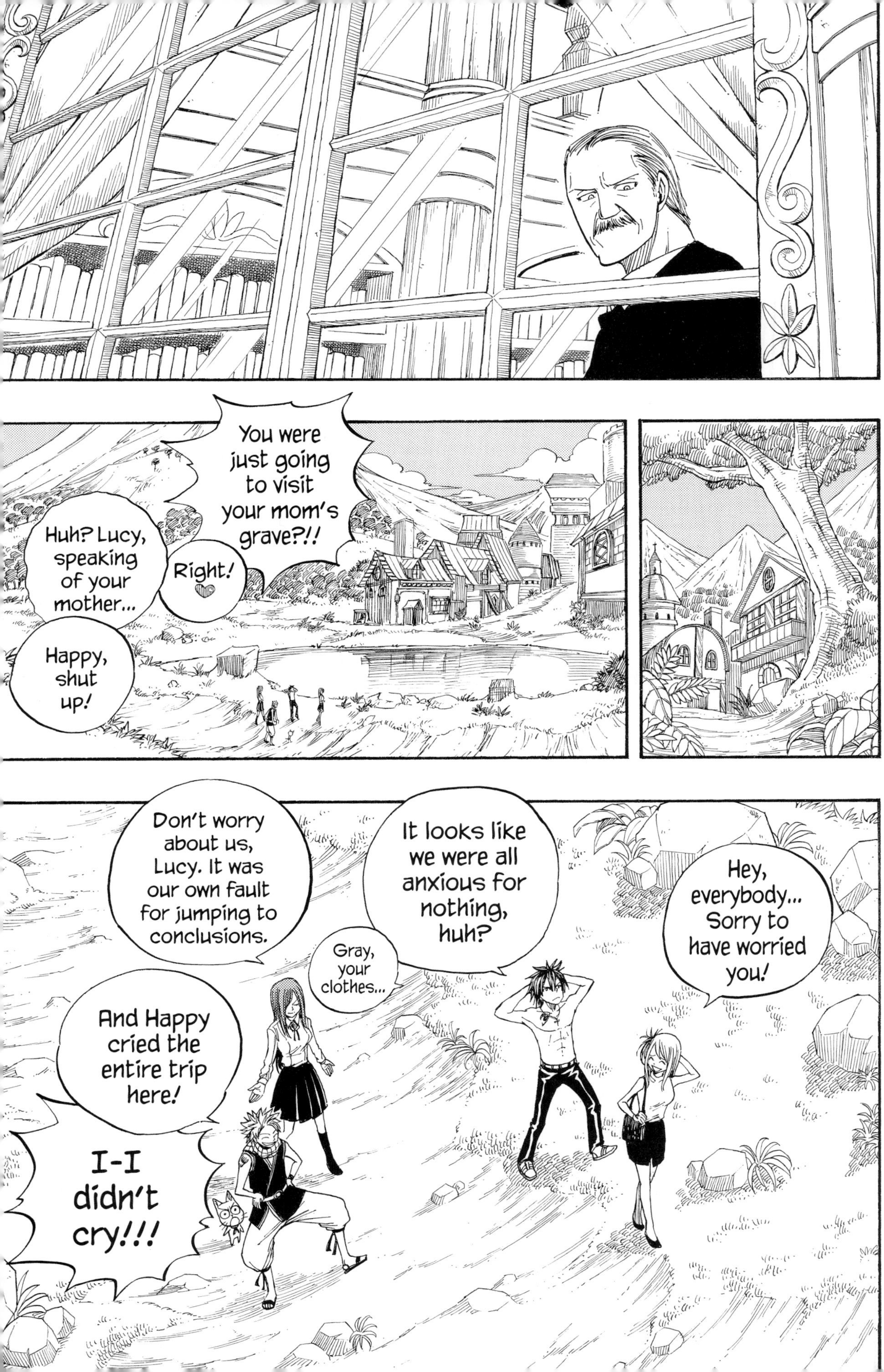
You were just going to visit your mom's grave?!!
Right!
Huh? Lucy, speaking of your mother...
Happy, shut up!
Hey, everybody... Sorry to have worried you!
It looks like we were all anxious for nothing, huh?
Gray, your clothes...
Don't worry about us, Lucy. It was our own fault for jumping to conclusions.
And Happy cried the entire trip here!
I-I didn't cry!!!

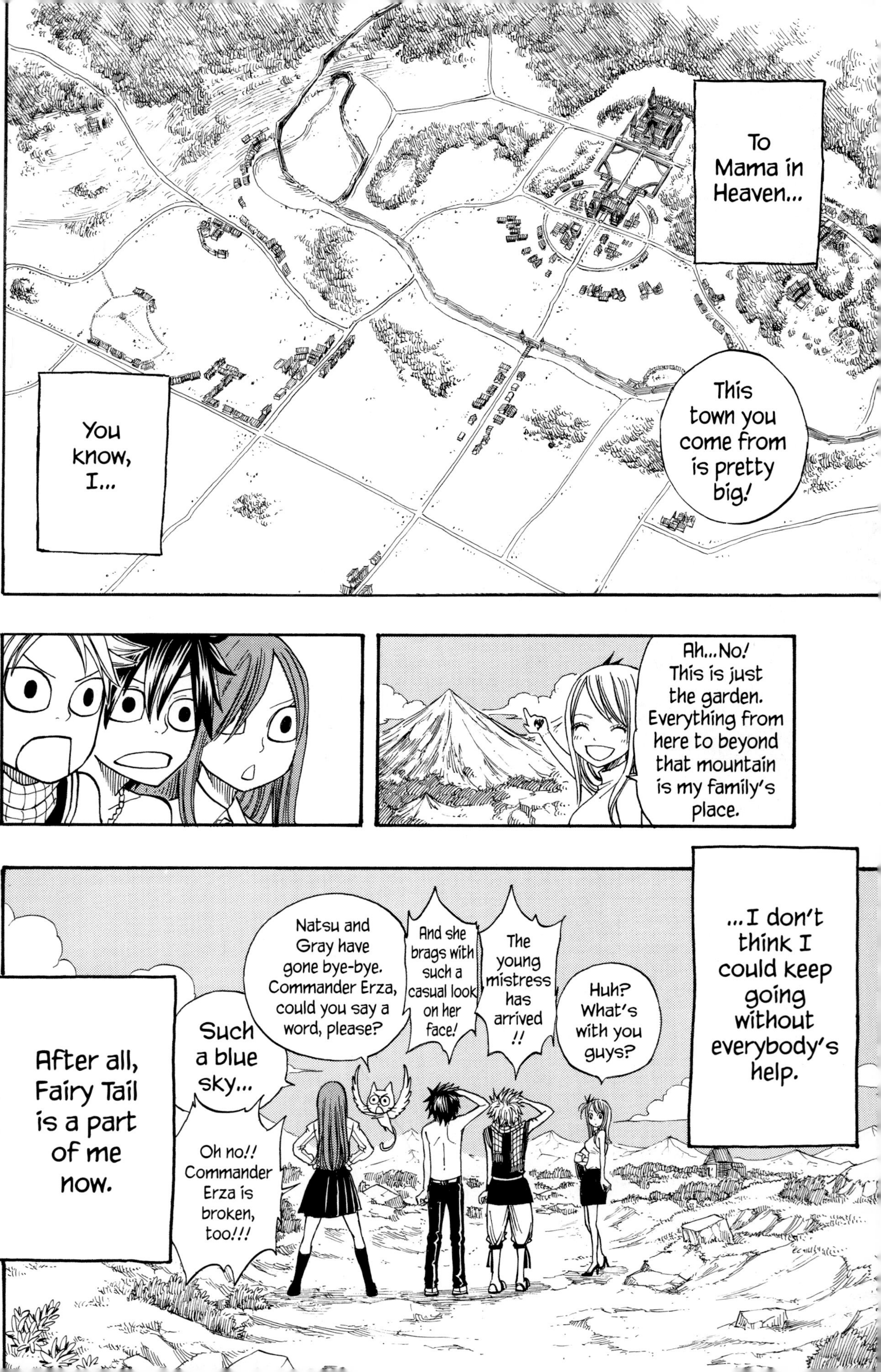
To Mama in Heaven...
This town you come from is pretty big!
You know, I...
Ah...No! This is just the garden. Everything from here to beyond that mountain is my family's place.
...I don't think I could keep going without everybody's help.
Huh? What's with you guys?
The young mistress has arrived!!
And she brags with such a casual look on her face!
Natsu and Gray have gone bye-bye. Commander Erza, could you say a word, please?
Such a blue sky...
Oh no!! Commander Erza is broken, too!!!
After all, Fairy Tail is a part of me now.

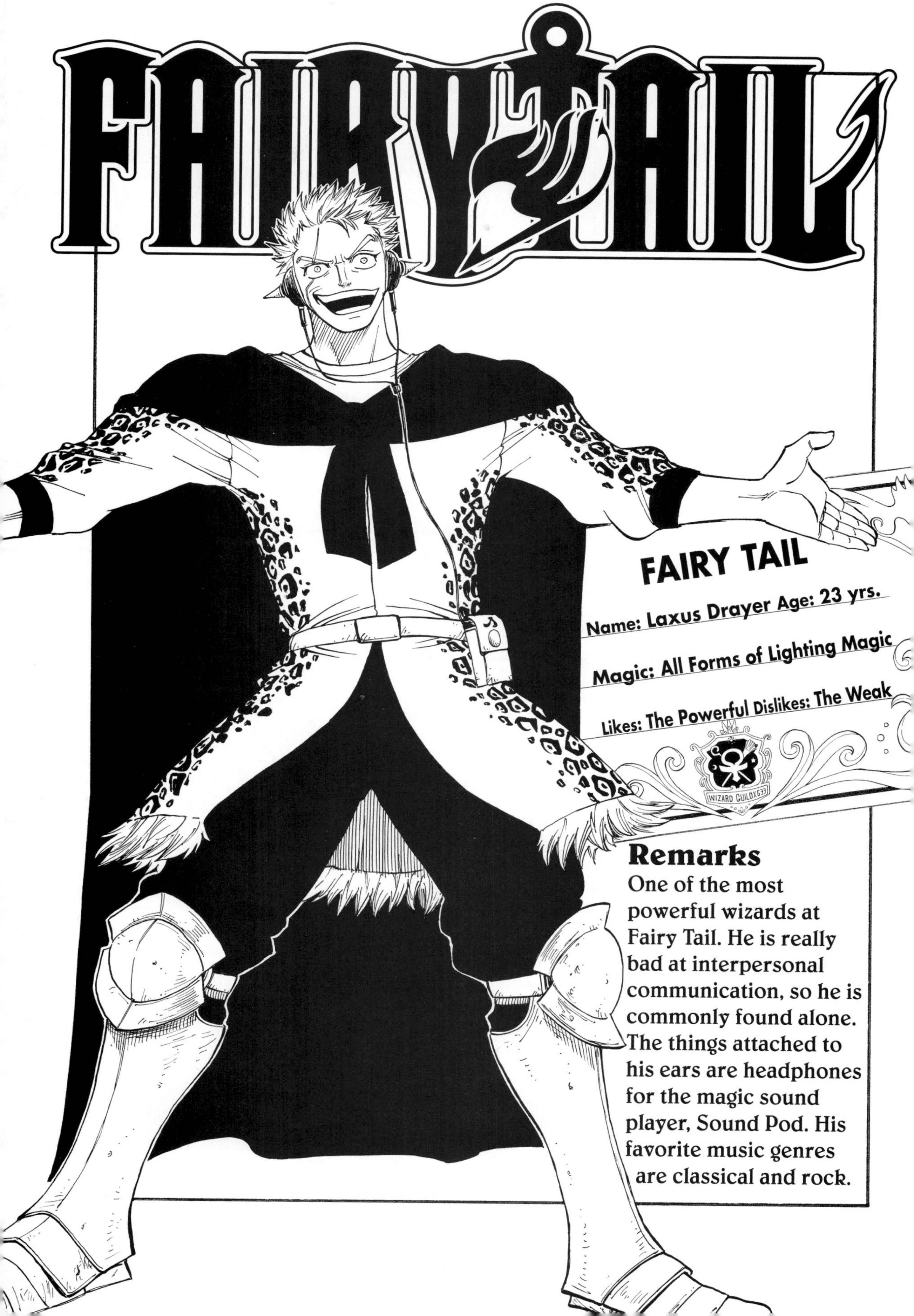
FAIRY TAIL
FAIRY TAIL
Name: Laxus Drayer Age: 23 yrs.
Magic: All Forms of Lighting Magic
Likes: The Powerful Dislikes: The Weak
WIZARD GUILDX633
Remarks
One of the most powerful wizards at Fairy Tail. He is really bad at interpersonal communication, so he is commonly found alone. The things attached to his ears are headphones for the magic sound player, Sound Pod. His favorite music genres are classical and rock.

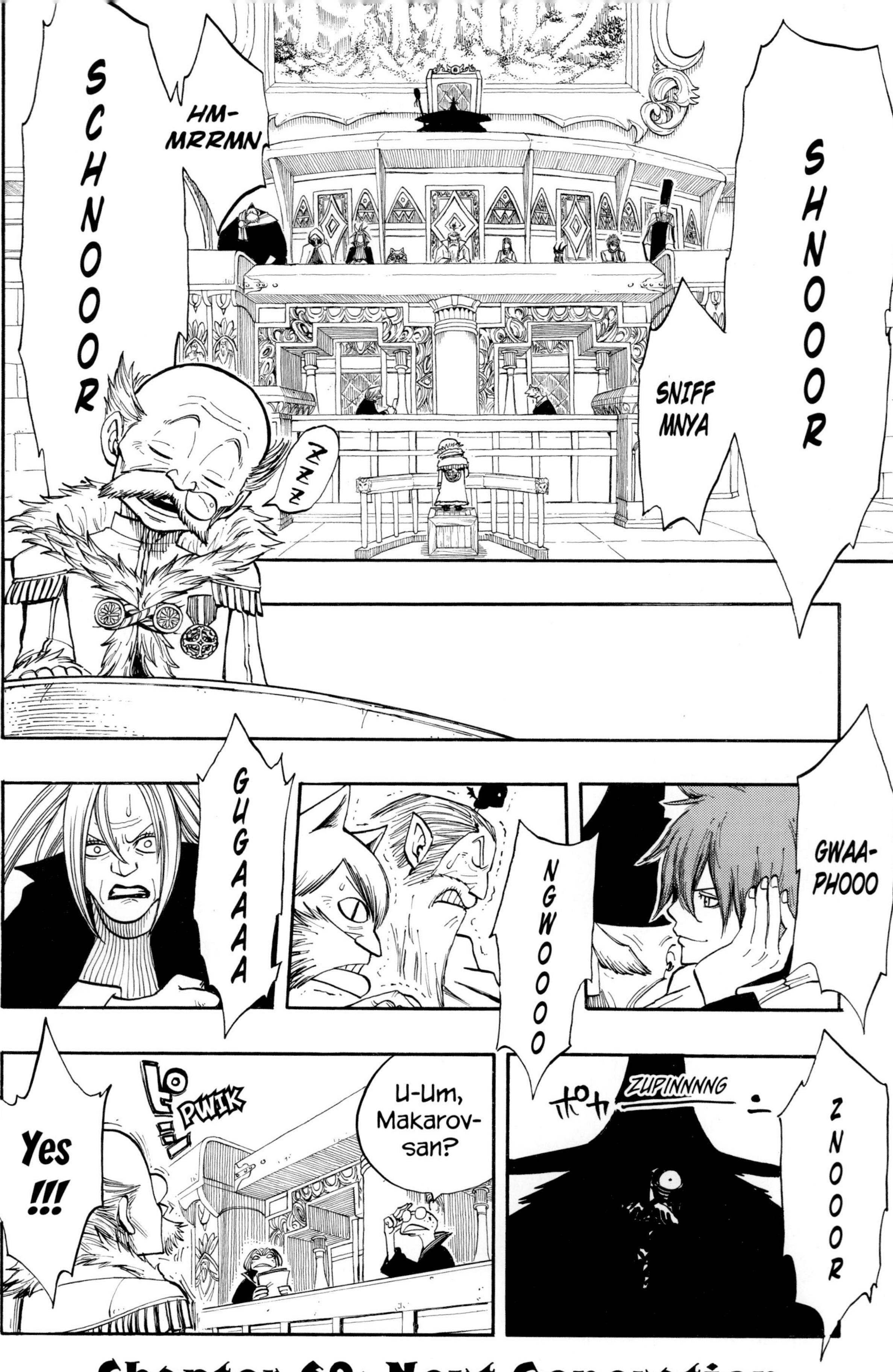
SHNOOOOR
HM-MRRMN
SCHNOOOOR
SNIFF MNYA
ZZZ
GWAA-PHOOO
NGWOOOOO
GUGAAAA
ZUPINNNNG
ZNOOOOR
U-Um, Makarov-san?
PWIK
Yes !!!

Chapter 69: Next Generation

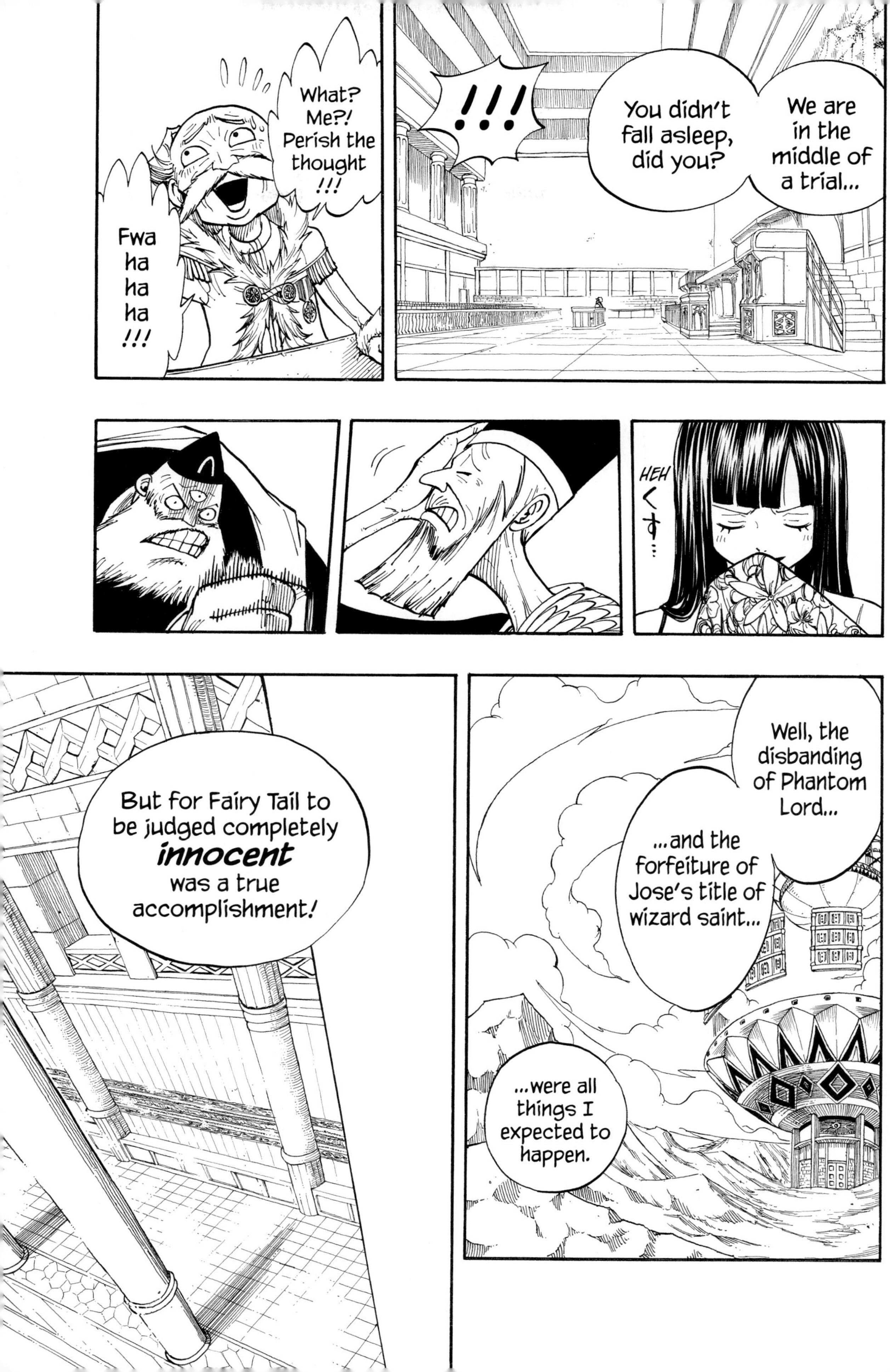
!!!
You didn't fall asleep, did you?
We are in the middle of a trial...
What? Me?! Perish the thought!!!
Fwa ha ha ha!!!
HEH
くす…
Well, the disbanding of Phantom Lord...
...and the forfeiture of Jose's title of wizard saint...
...were all things I expected to happen.
But for Fairy Tail to be judged completely *innocent* was a true accomplishment!

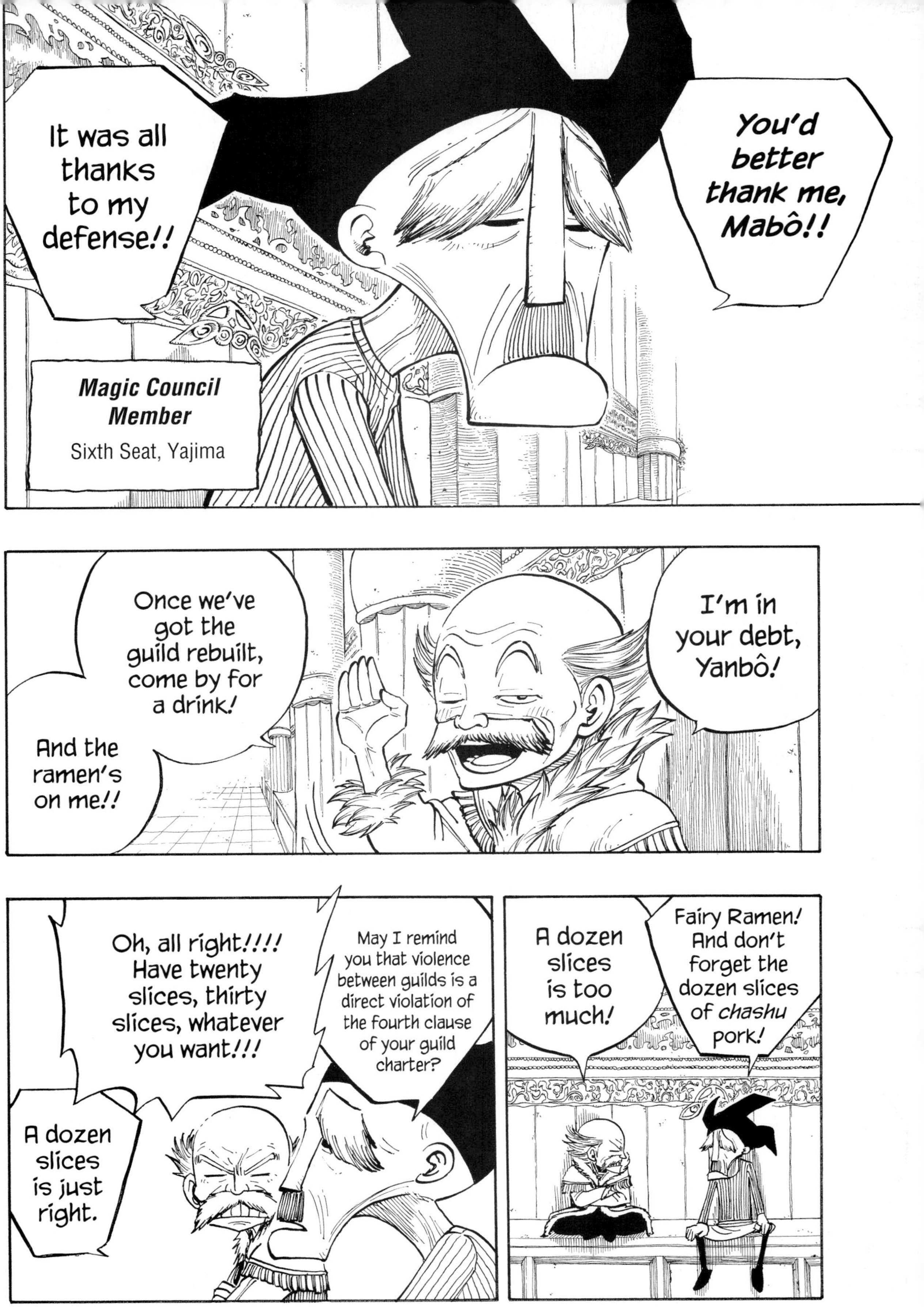
You'd better thank me, Mabô!!
It was all thanks to my defense!!
Magic Council Member
Sixth Seat, Yajima
I'm in your debt, Yanbô!
Once we've got the guild rebuilt, come by for a drink!
And the ramen's on me!!
Fairy Ramen! And don't forget the dozen slices of *chashu* pork!
A dozen slices is too much!
May I remind you that violence between guilds is a direct violation of the fourth clause of your guild charter?
Oh, all right!!!! Have twenty slices, thirty slices, whatever you want!!!
A dozen slices is just right.

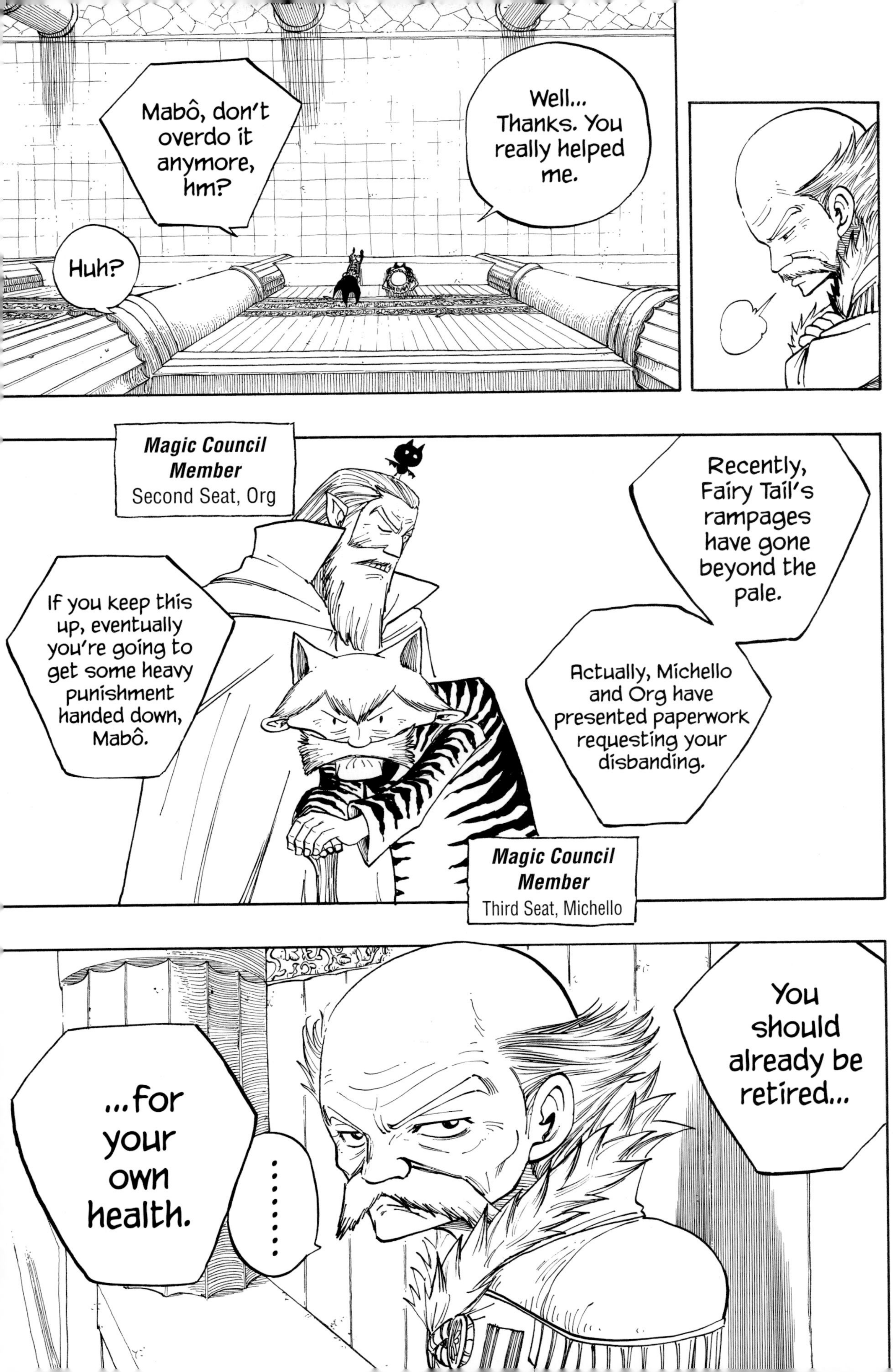
Well... Thanks. You really helped me.
Mabô, don't overdo it anymore, hm?
Huh?
Recently, Fairy Tail's rampages have gone beyond the pale.
Actually, Michello and Org have presented paperwork requesting your disbanding.
Magic Council Member
Second Seat, Org
If you keep this up, eventually you're going to get some heavy punishment handed down, Mabô.
Magic Council Member
Third Seat, Michello
You should already be retired...
......
...for your own health.

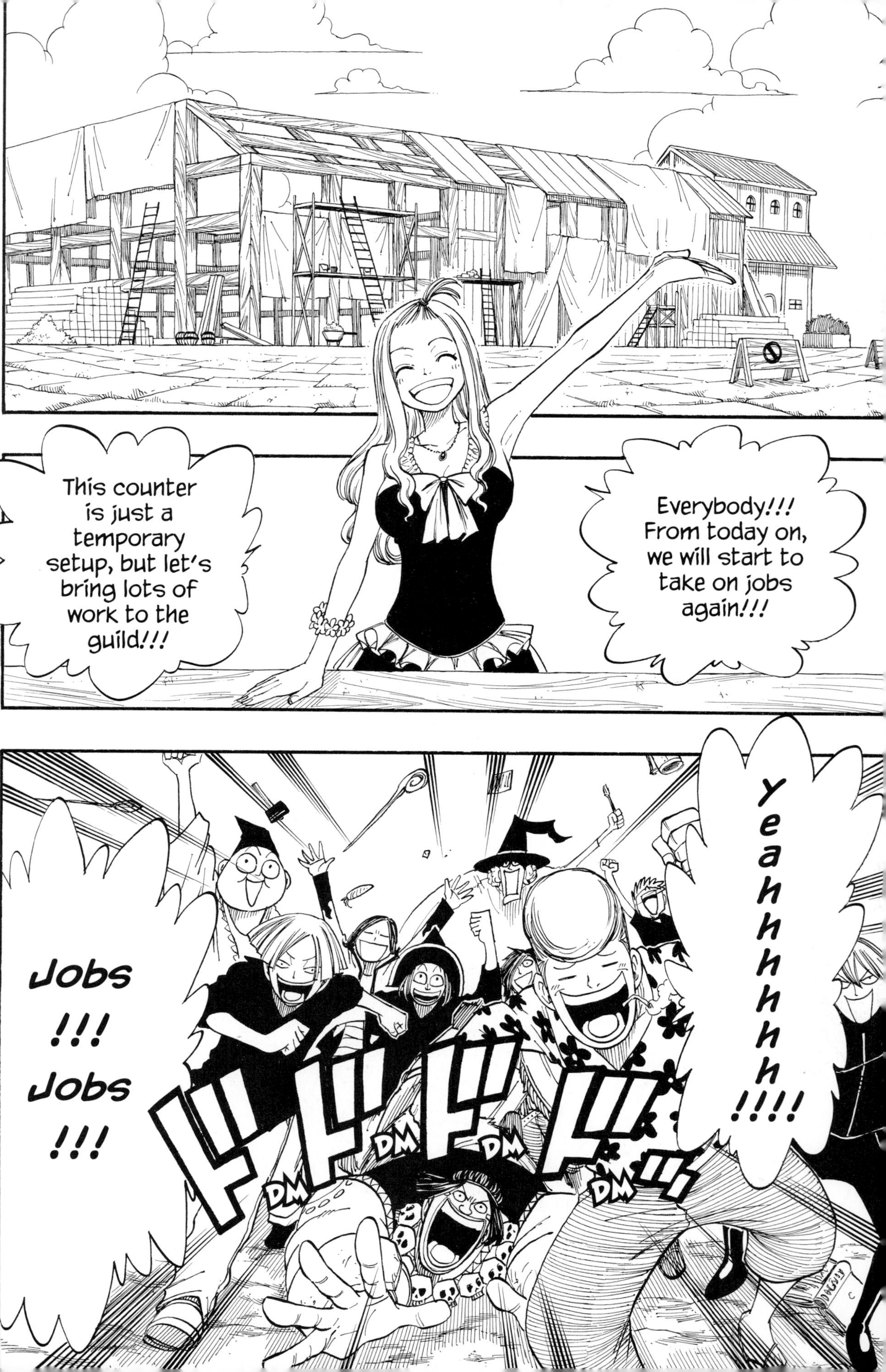
Everybody!!! From today on, we will start to take on jobs again!!!
This counter is just a temporary setup, but let's bring lots of work to the guild!!!
Yeahhhhhhh!!!!
DM DM DM DM
Jobs!!! Jobs!!!

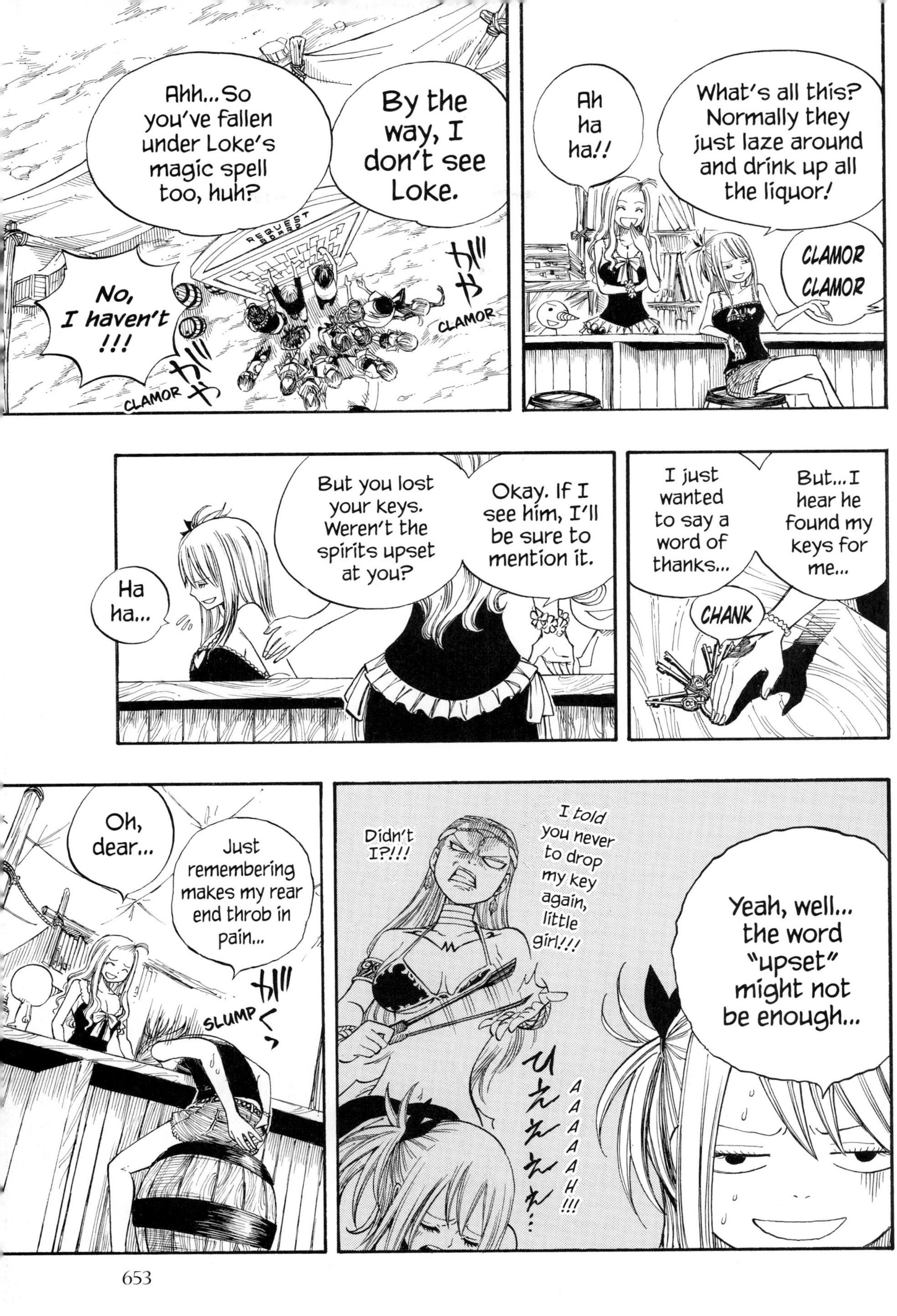
What's all this? Normally they just laze around and drink up all the liquor!
Ah ha ha!!
CLAMOR CLAMOR
By the way, I don't see Loke.
Ahh...So you've fallen under Loke's magic spell too, huh?
REQUEST BOARD
CLAMOR
No, I haven't!!!
CLAMOR
But...I hear he found my keys for me...
I just wanted to say a word of thanks...
CHANK
Okay. If I see him, I'll be sure to mention it.
But you lost your keys. Weren't the spirits upset at you?
Ha ha...
Yeah, well... the word "upset" might not be enough...
I told you never to drop my key again, little girl!!!
Didn't I?!!!
AAAAAAH!!!
Oh, dear...
Just remembering makes my rear end throb in pain...
SLUMP

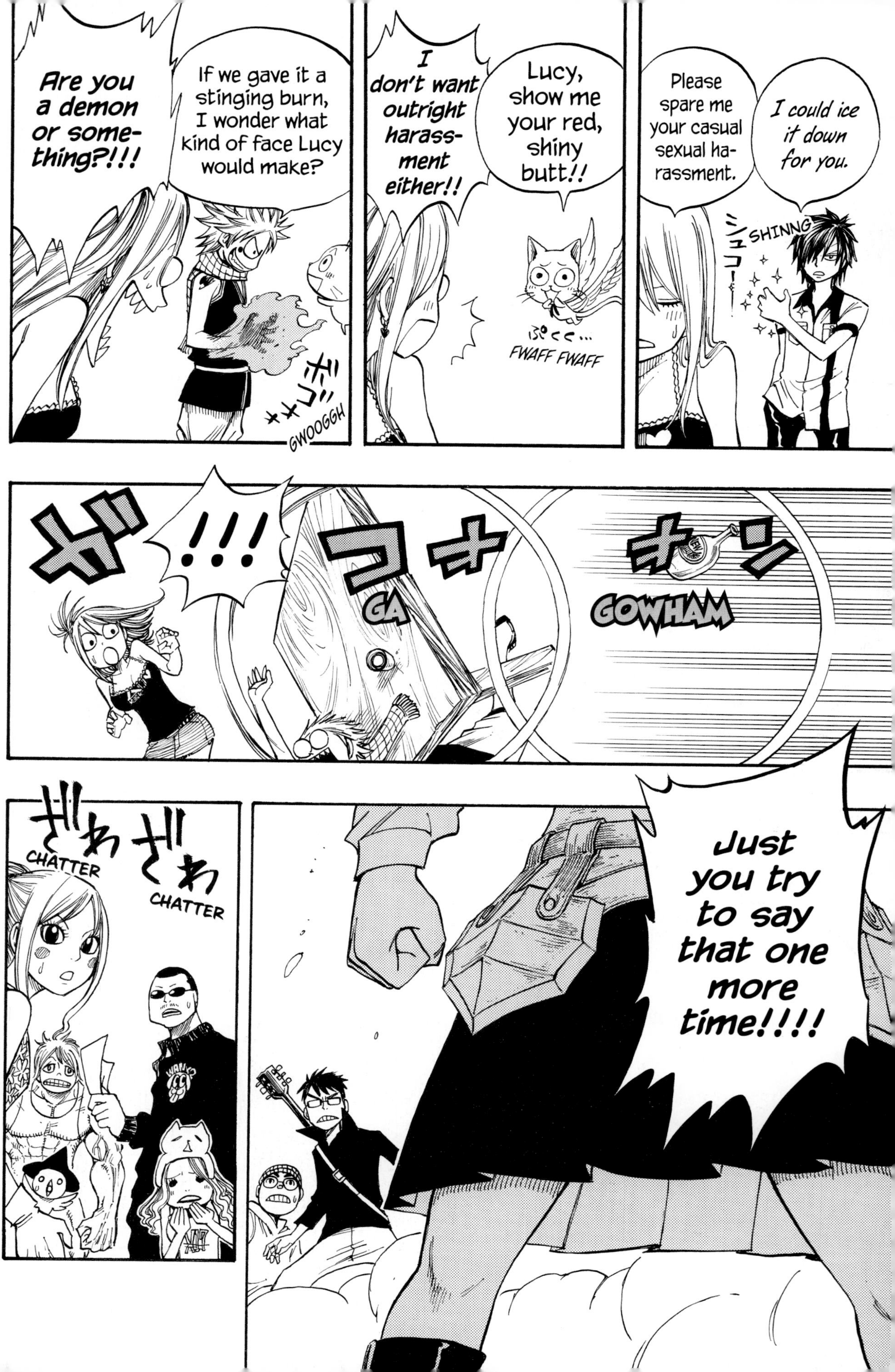
I could ice it down for you.
Please spare me your casual sexual harassment.
シュコー!
SHINNG
Lucy, show me your red, shiny butt!!
ぷくく…
FWAFF FWAFF
I don't want outright harassment either!!
If we gave it a stinging burn, I wonder what kind of face Lucy would make?
GWOOGGH
Are you a demon or something?!!!
!!!!
GA
GOWHAM
Just you try to say that one more time!!!!
ざわざわ
CHATTER
CHATTER

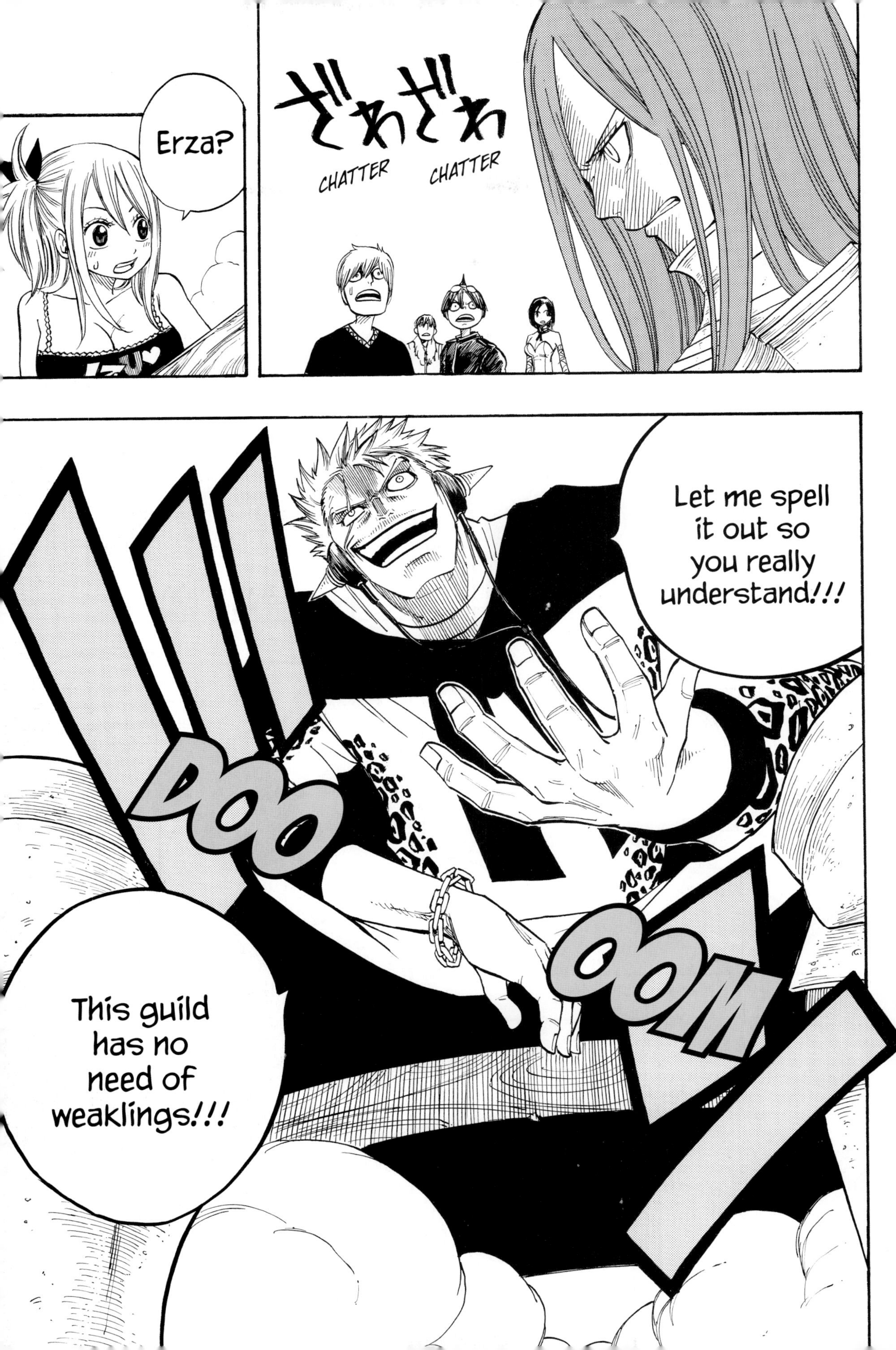
ざわざわ
CHATTER CHATTER
Erza?
Let me spell it out so you really understand!!!
DOOOOM
This guild has no need of weaklings!!!

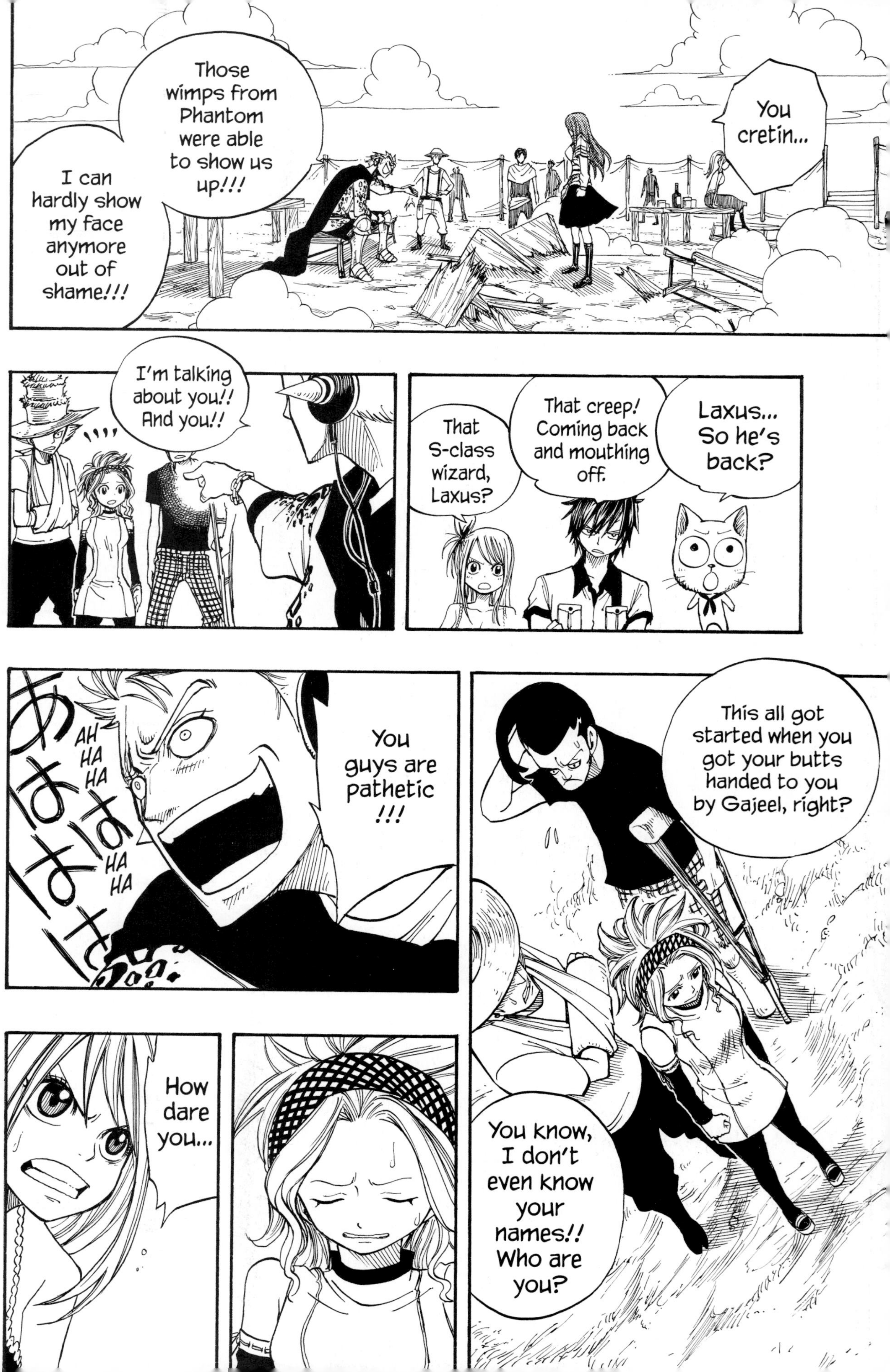
Those wimps from Phantom were able to show us up!!!
I can hardly show my face anymore out of shame!!!
You cretin...
Laxus... So he's back?
That creep! Coming back and mouthing off.
That S-class wizard, Laxus?
I'm talking about you!! And you!!
This all got started when you got your butts handed to you by Gajeel, right?
You know, I don't even know your names!! Who are you?
You guys are pathetic!!!
AH HA HA HA HA
あははは
How dare you...

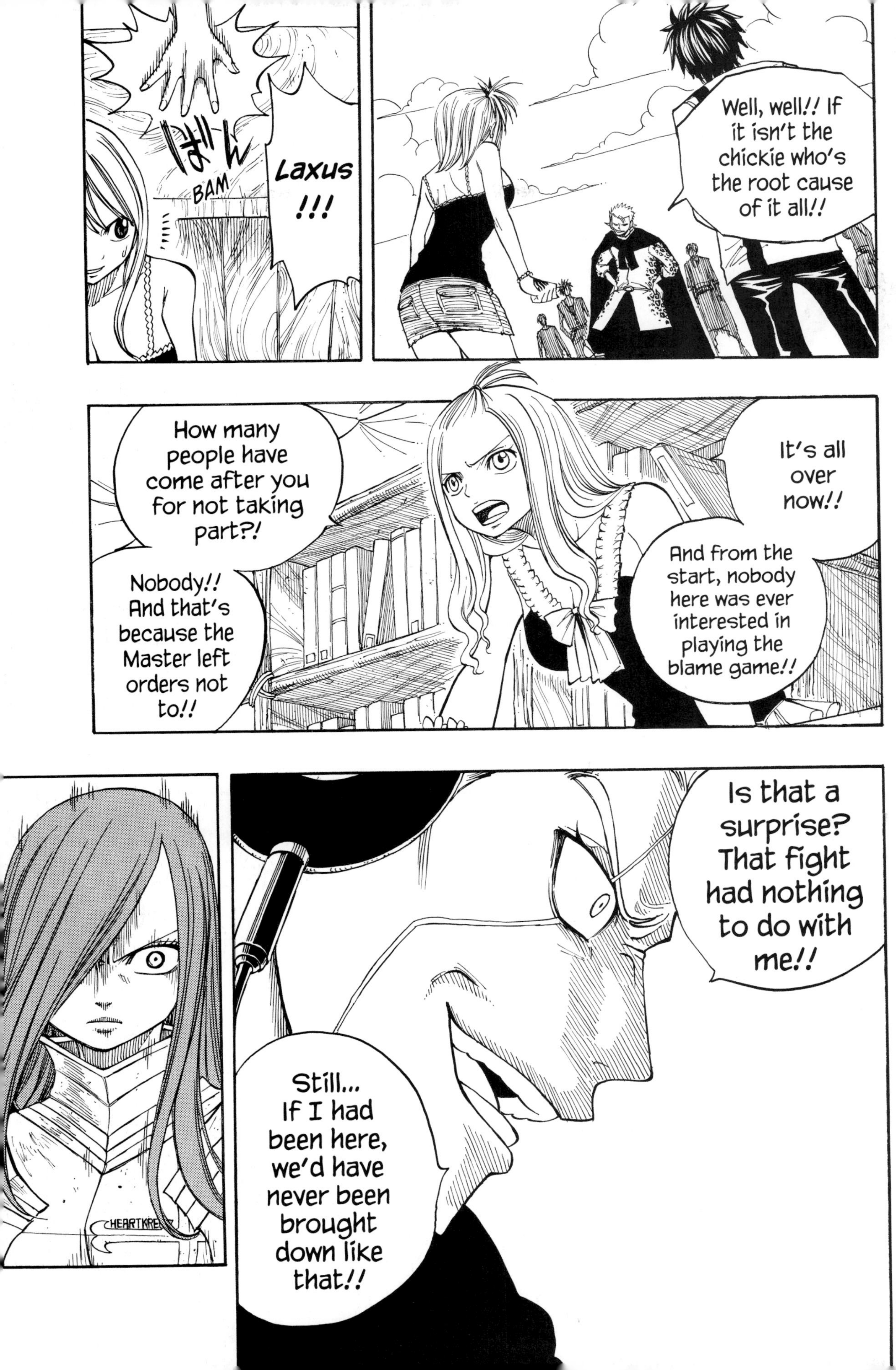
Well, well!! If it isn't the chickie who's the root cause of it all!!
ばん
BAM
Laxus!!!
It's all over now!!
And from the start, nobody here was ever interested in playing the blame game!!
How many people have come after you for not taking part?!
Nobody!! And that's because the Master left orders not to!!
Is that a surprise? That fight had nothing to do with me!!
Still... If I had been here, we'd have never been brought down like that!!
HEARTKREUZ

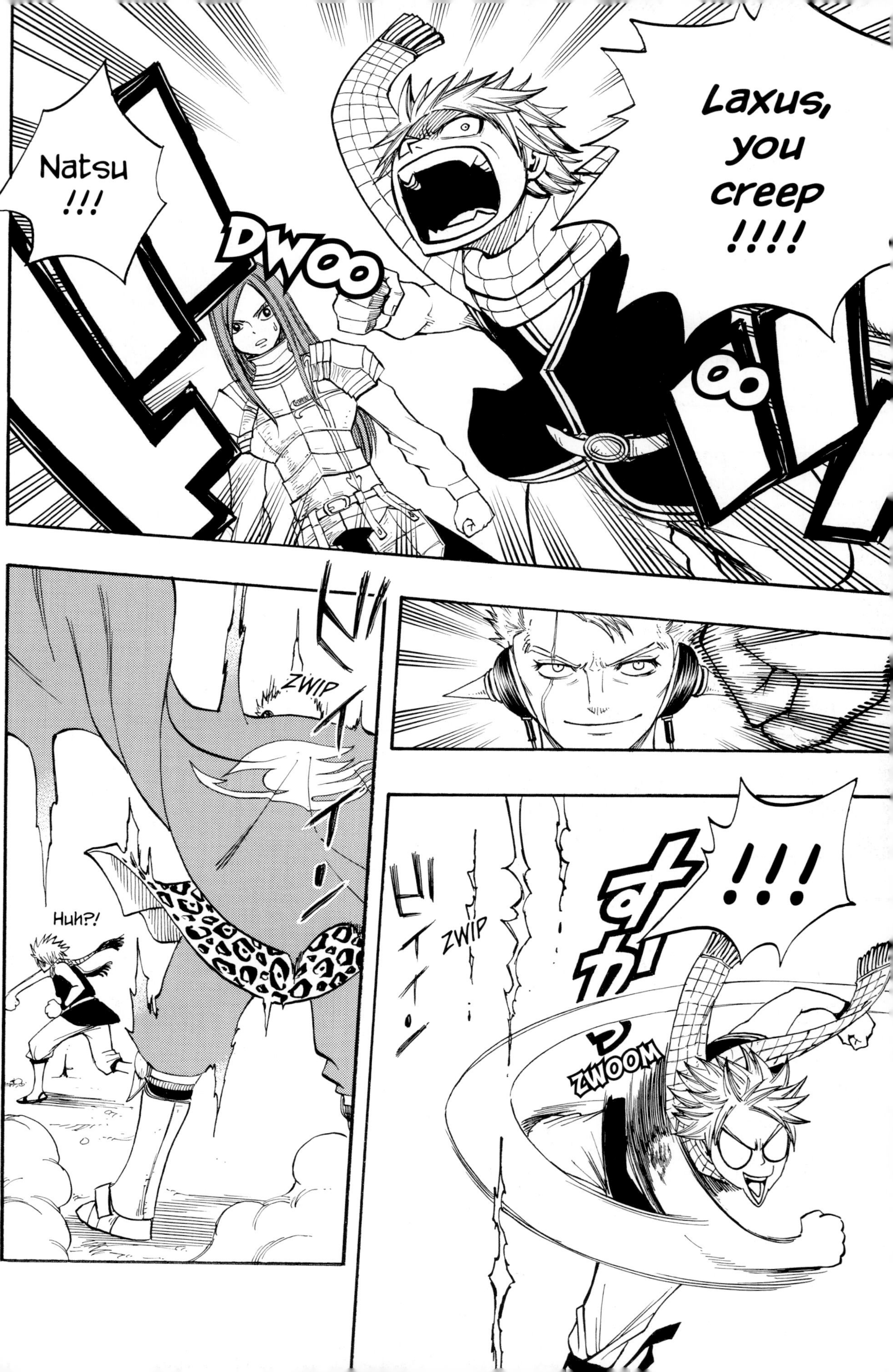
Laxus, you creep!!!!
DWOO
Natsu!!!
!!!
ZWIP
ZWOOM
ZWIP
Huh?!

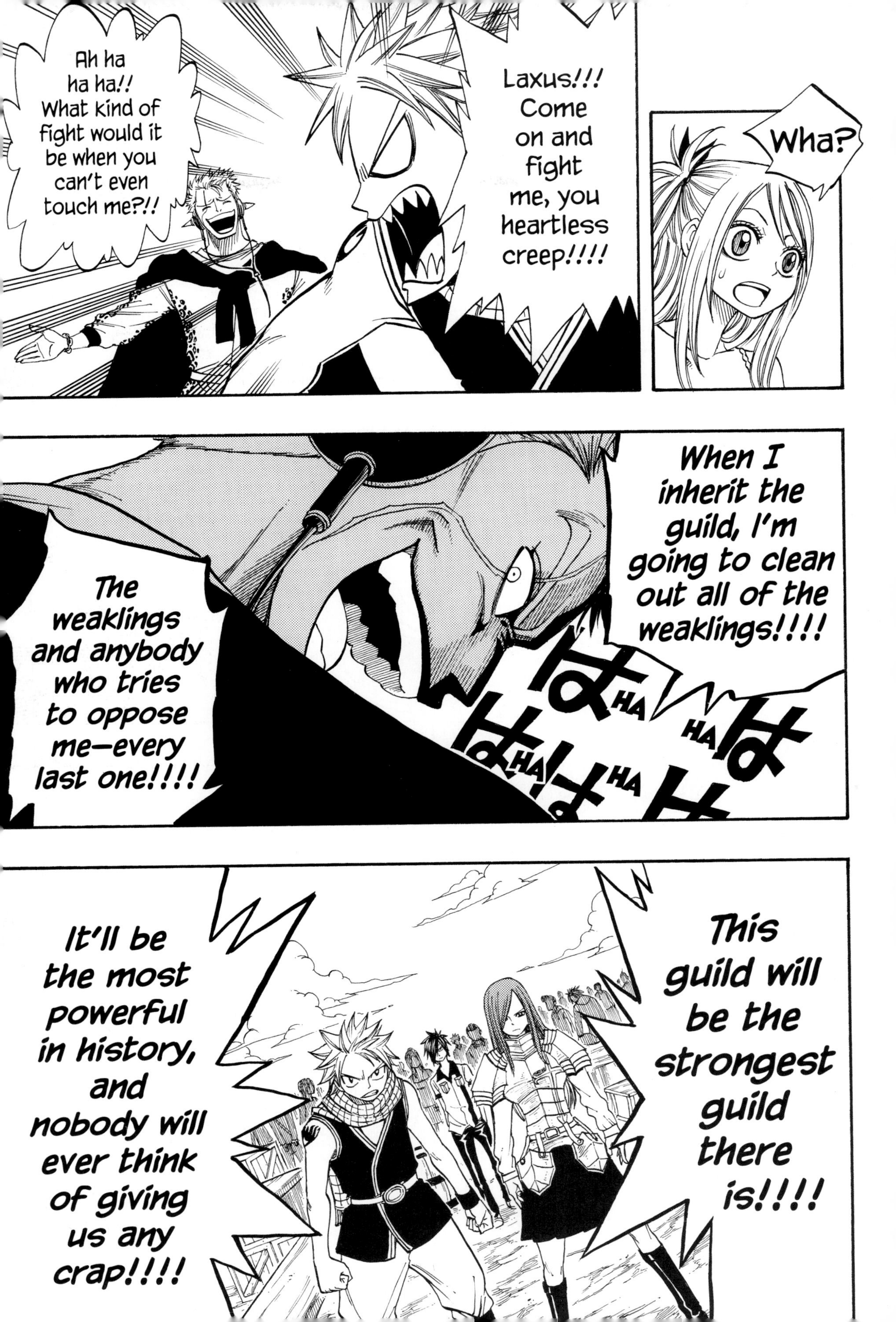
Wha?
Laxus!!! Come on and fight me, you heartless creep!!!!
Ah ha ha ha!! What kind of fight would it be when you can't even touch me?!!
When I inherit the guild, I'm going to clean out all of the weaklings!!!!
The weaklings and anybody who tries to oppose me—every last one!!!!
はHA はHA はHA はHA
This guild will be the strongest guild there is!!!!
It'll be the most powerful in history, and nobody will ever think of giving us any crap!!!!

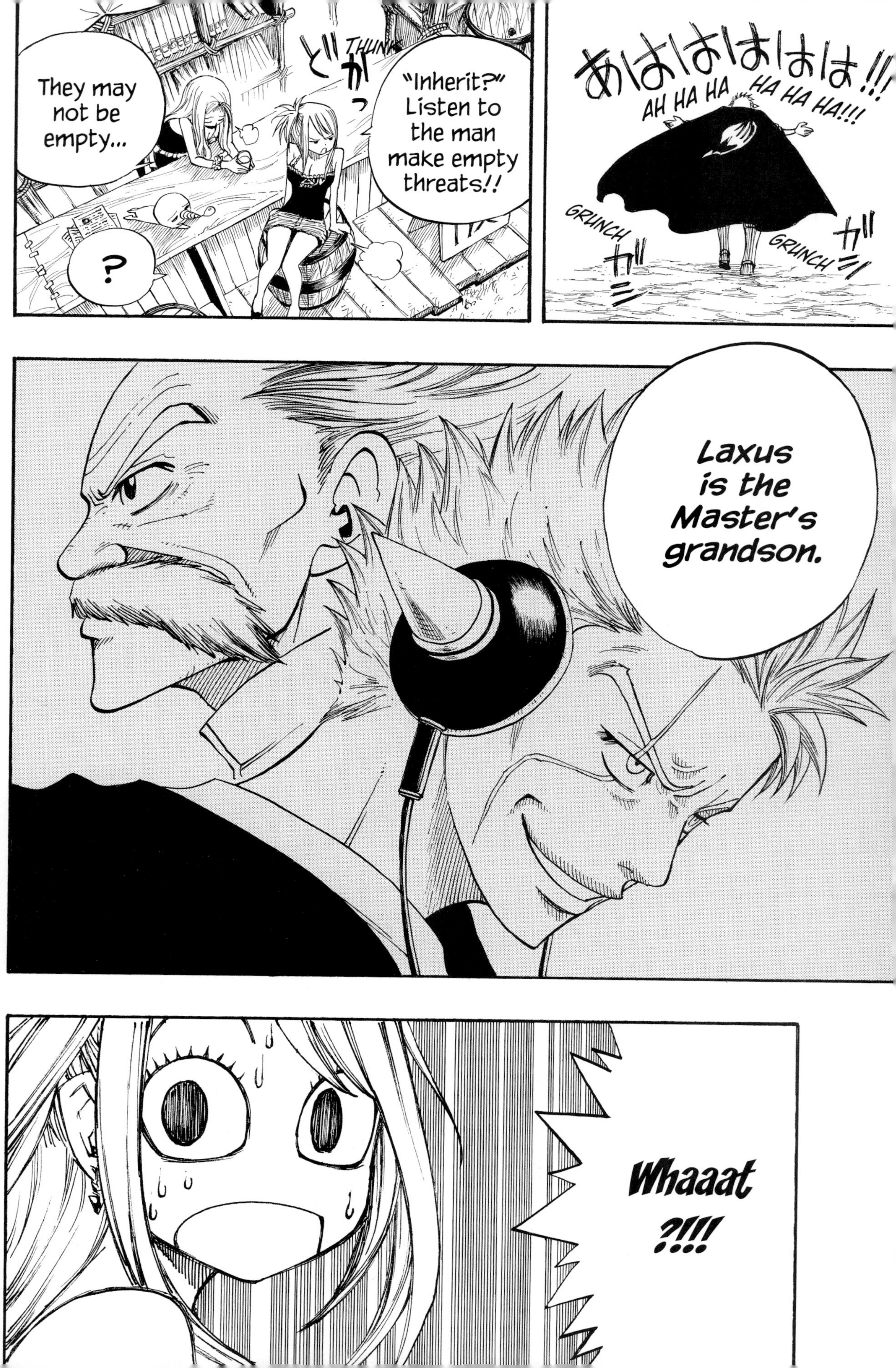
あははははは!!!
AH HA HA HA HA HA!!!
GRUNCH
ガ
GRUNCH
ガ
"Inherit?" Listen to the man make empty threats!!
どがっ
THUNK
They may not be empty...
?
Laxus is the Master's grandson.
Whaaat ?!!!

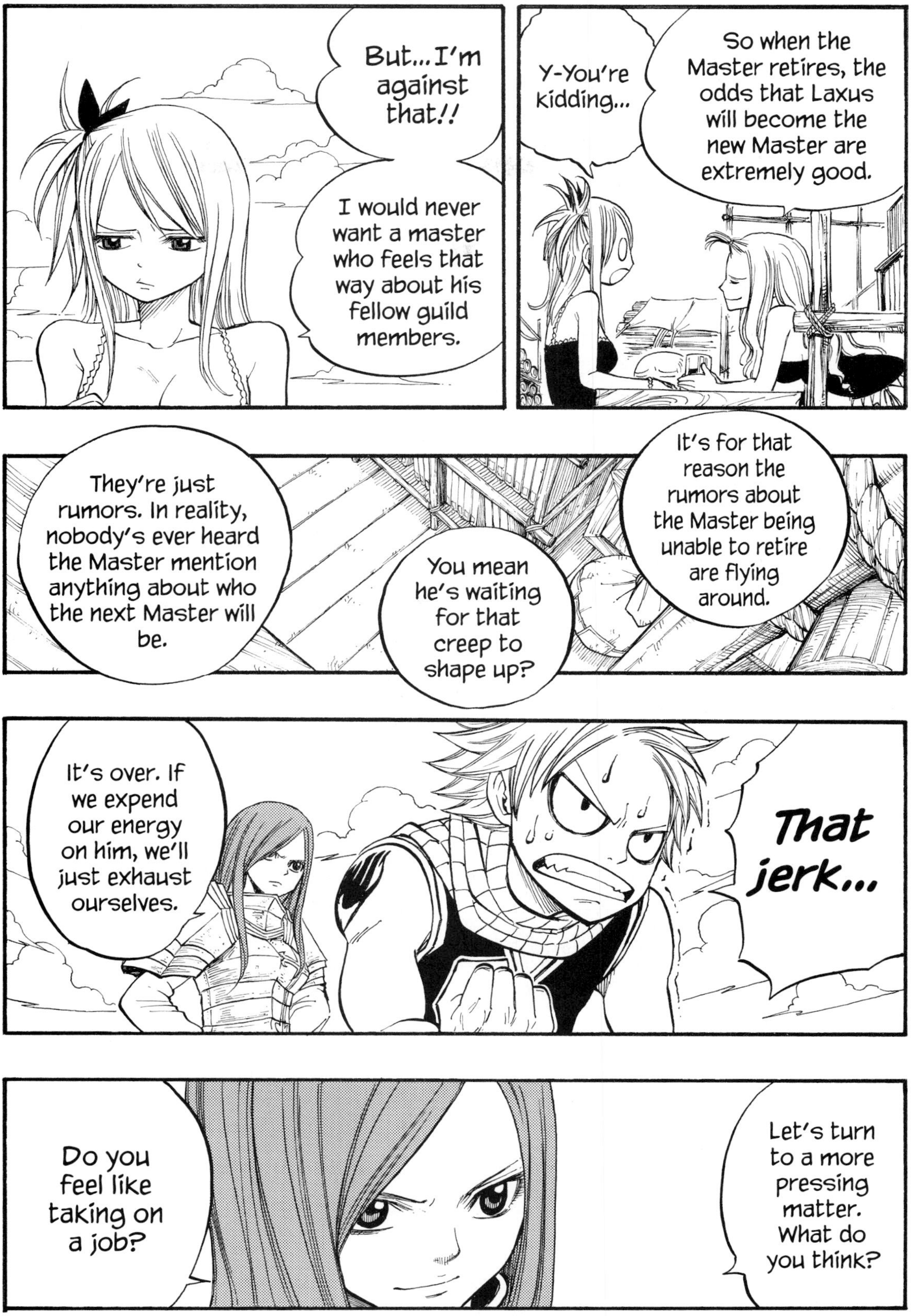
So when the Master retires, the odds that Laxus will become the new Master are extremely good.
Y-You're kidding...
But...I'm against that!!
I would never want a master who feels that way about his fellow guild members.
It's for that reason the rumors about the Master being unable to retire are flying around.
You mean he's waiting for that creep to shape up?
They're just rumors. In reality, nobody's ever heard the Master mention anything about who the next Master will be.
That jerk...
It's over. If we expend our energy on him, we'll just exhaust ourselves.
Let's turn to a more pressing matter. What do you think?
Do you feel like taking on a job?

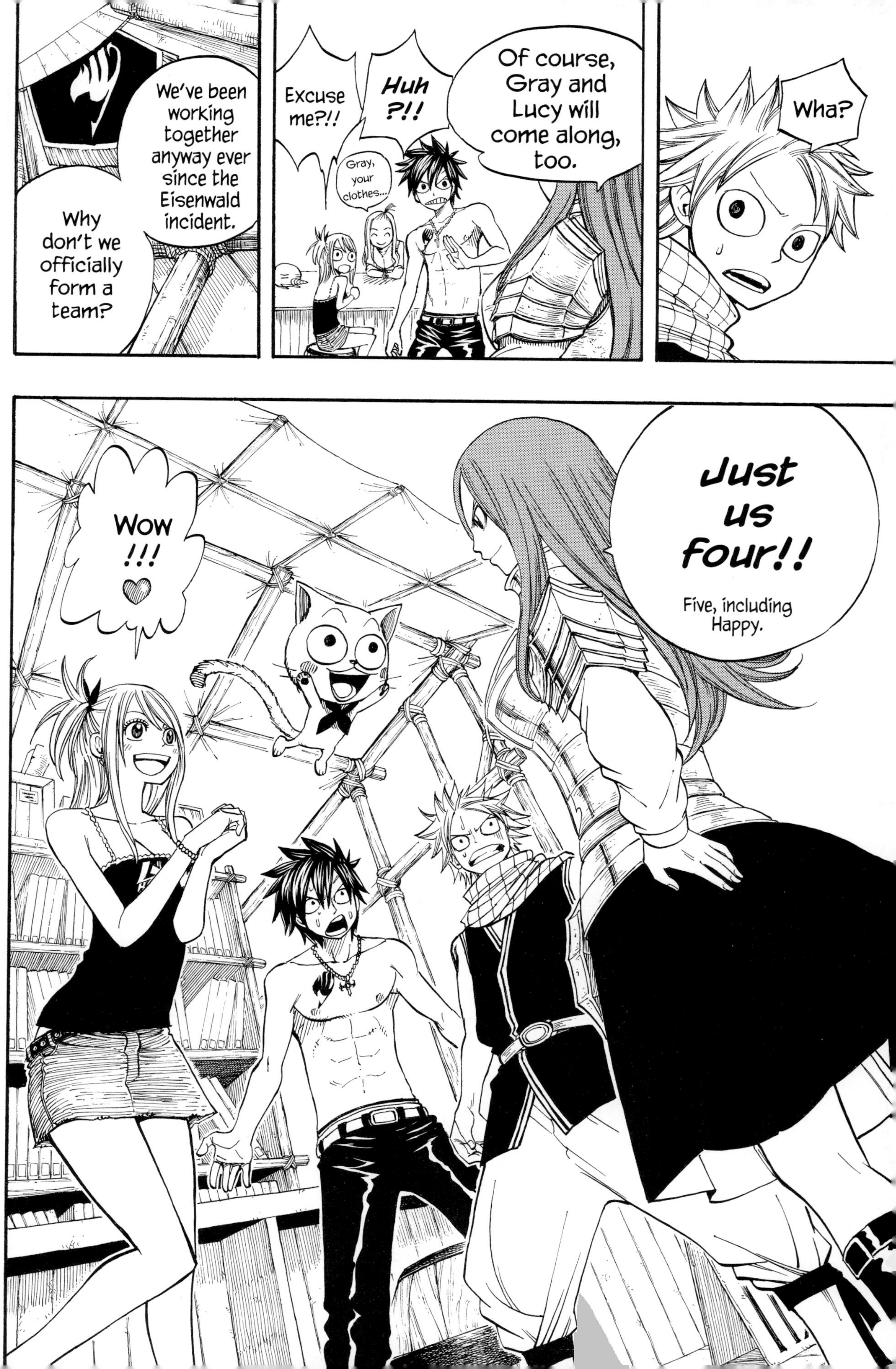
Wha?
Of course, Gray and Lucy will come along, too.
Huh ?!!
Excuse me?!!
Gray, your clothes...
We've been working together anyway ever since the Eisenwald incident.
Why don't we officially form a team?
Just us four!!
Five, including Happy.
Wow !!! ♥

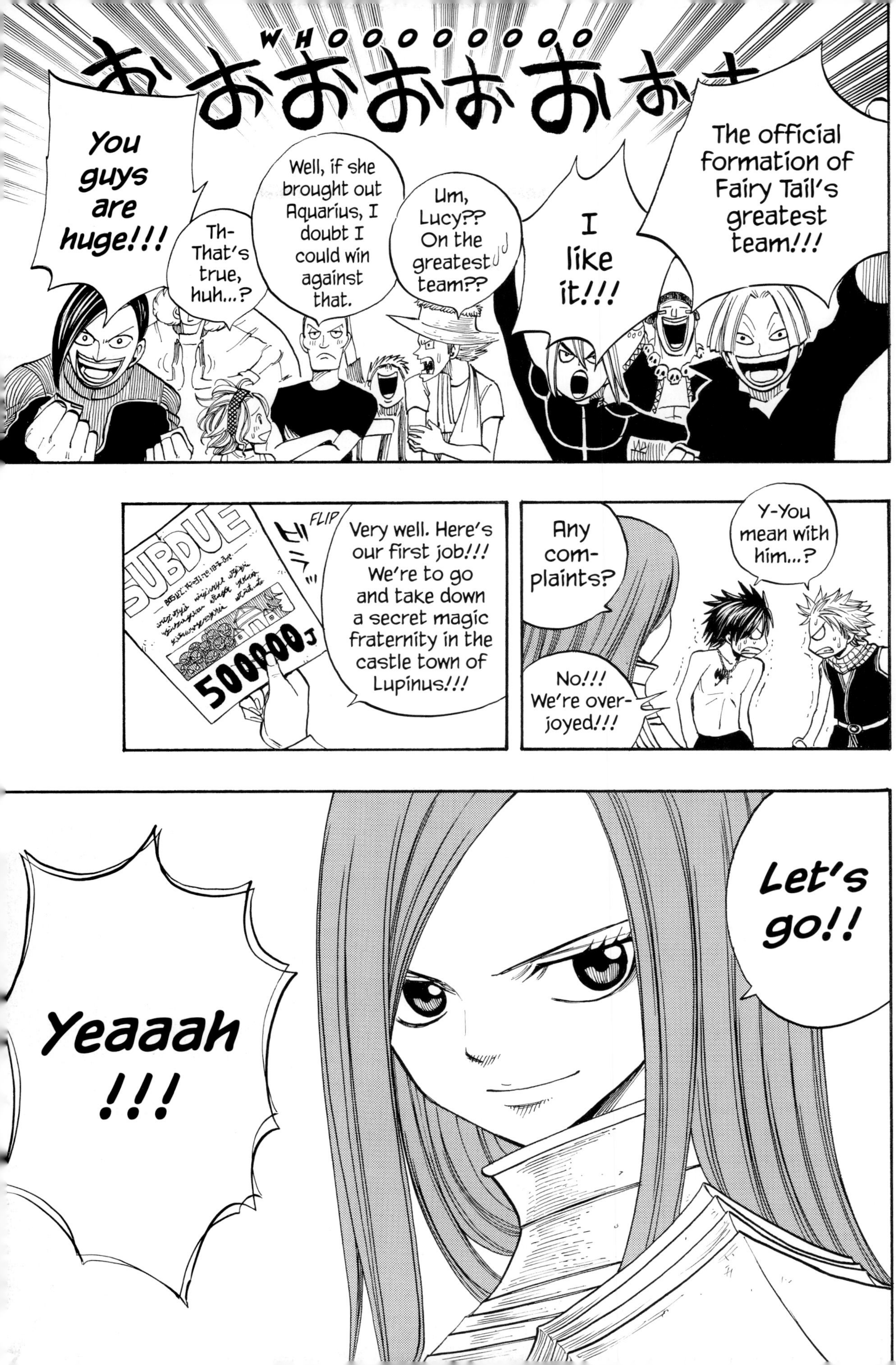
WHOOOOOOOO
The official formation of Fairy Tail's greatest team!!!
I like it!!!
Um, Lucy?? On the greatest team??
Well, if she brought out Aquarius, I doubt I could win against that.
Th- That's true, huh...?
You guys are huge!!!
Y-You mean with him...?
Any com-plaints?
No!!! We're over-joyed!!!
FLIP
Very well. Here's our first job!!! We're to go and take down a secret magic fraternity in the castle town of Lupinus!!!
SUBDUE
500000J
Let's go!!
Yeaaah!!!

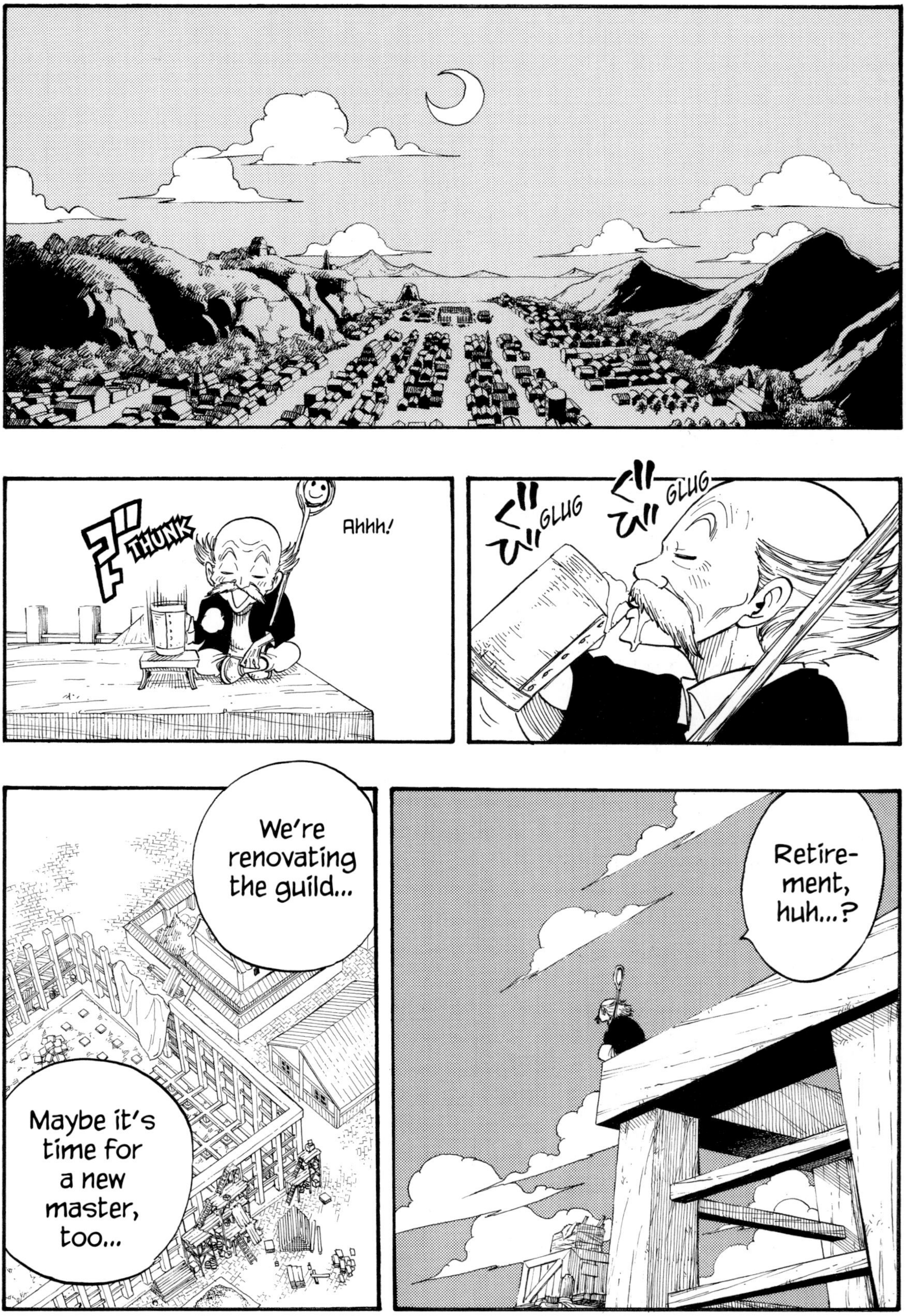
GLUG
GLUG
THUNK
Ahhh!
Retire-ment, huh...?
We're renovating the guild...
Maybe it's time for a new master, too...

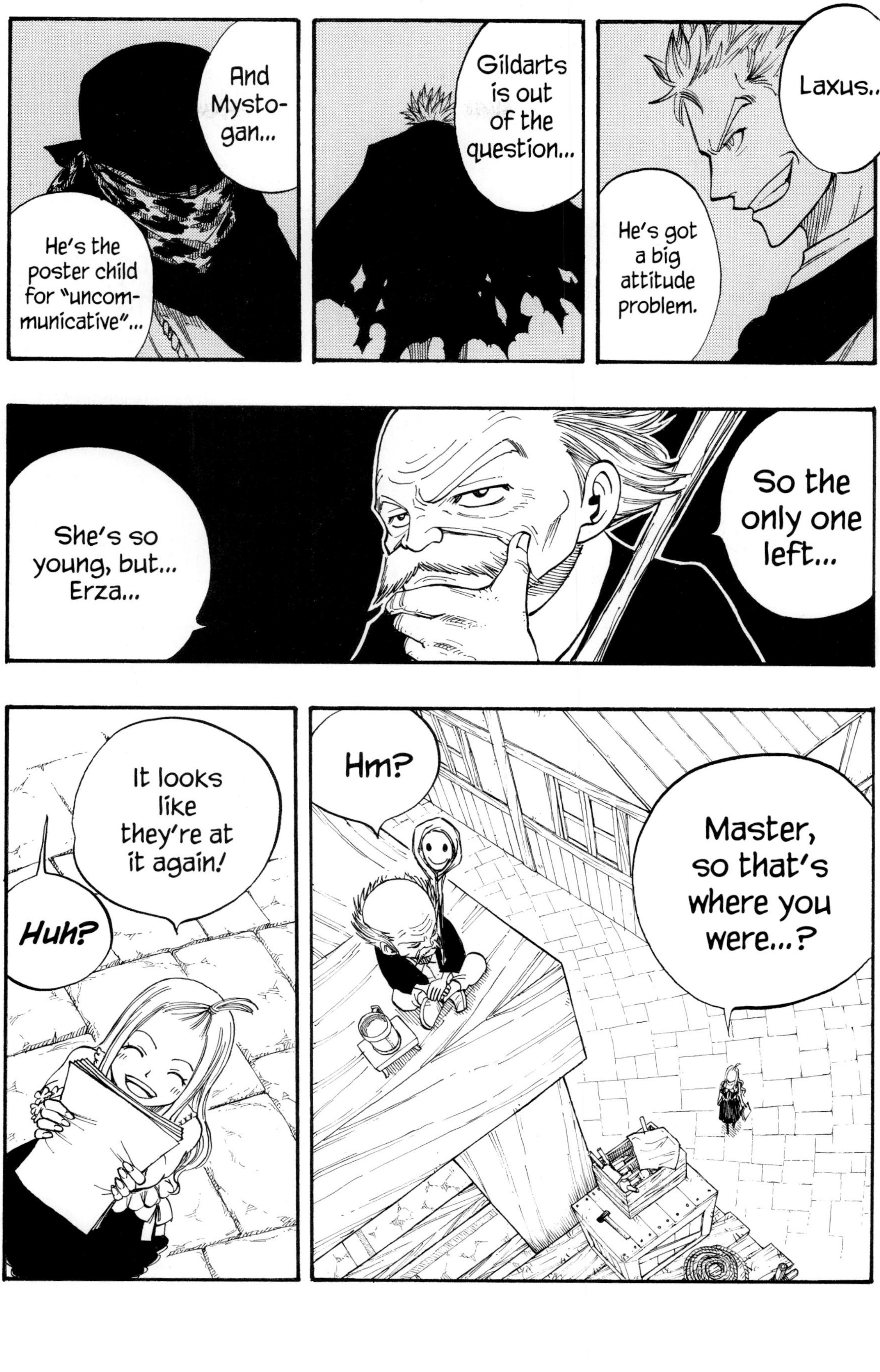
Laxus...
He's got a big attitude problem.
Gildarts is out of the question...
And Mysto-gan...
He's the poster child for "uncom-municative"...
So the only one left...
She's so young, but... Erza...
Master, so that's where you were...?
Hm?
It looks like they're at it again!
Huh?

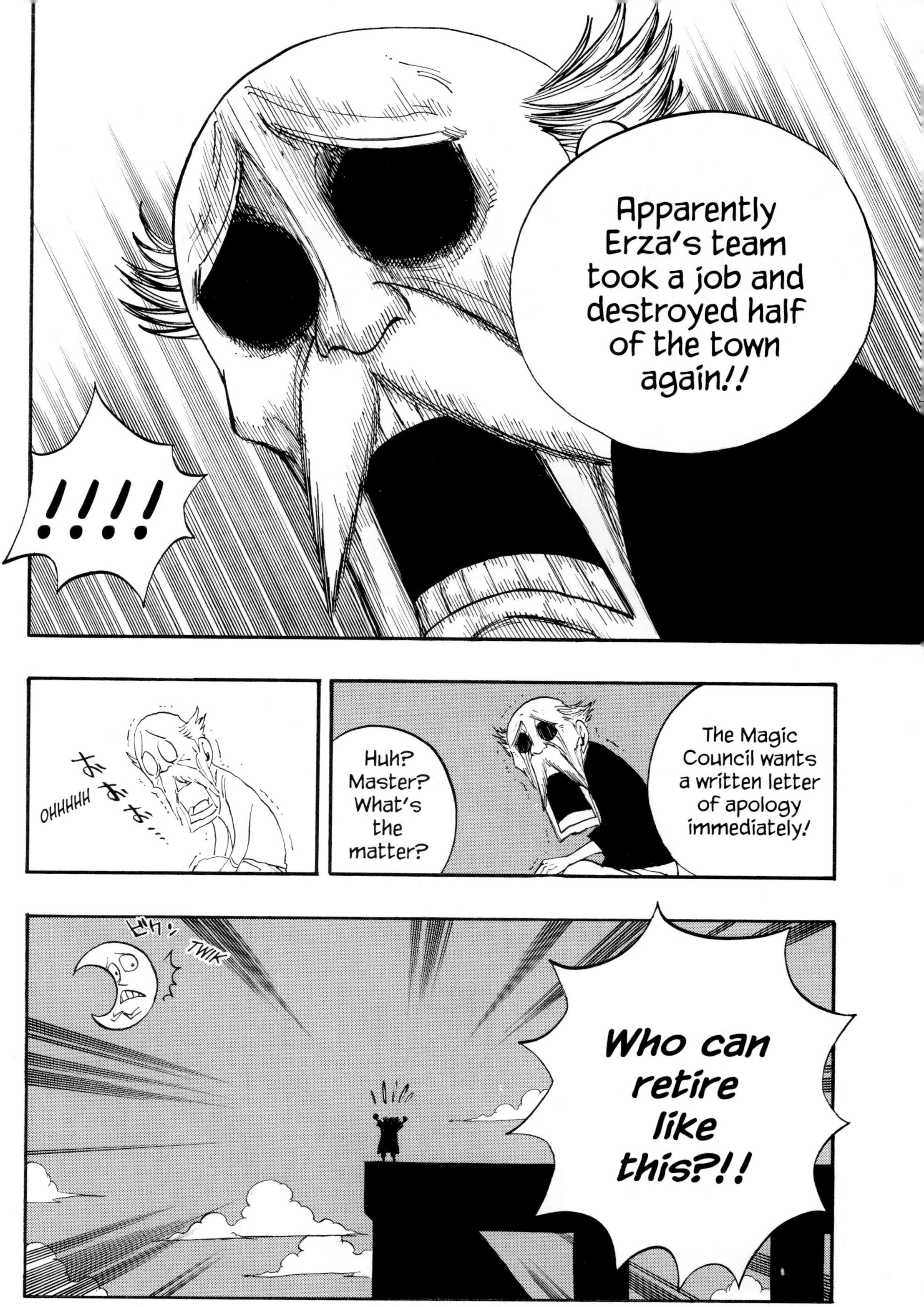

Apparently Erza's team took a job and destroyed half of the town again!!
!!!!
The Magic Council wants a written letter of apology immediately!
Huh? Master? What's the matter?
おおお…
OHHHHH
Who can retire like this?!!
ピクッ
TWIK

Chapter 70: Frederick & Yanderica

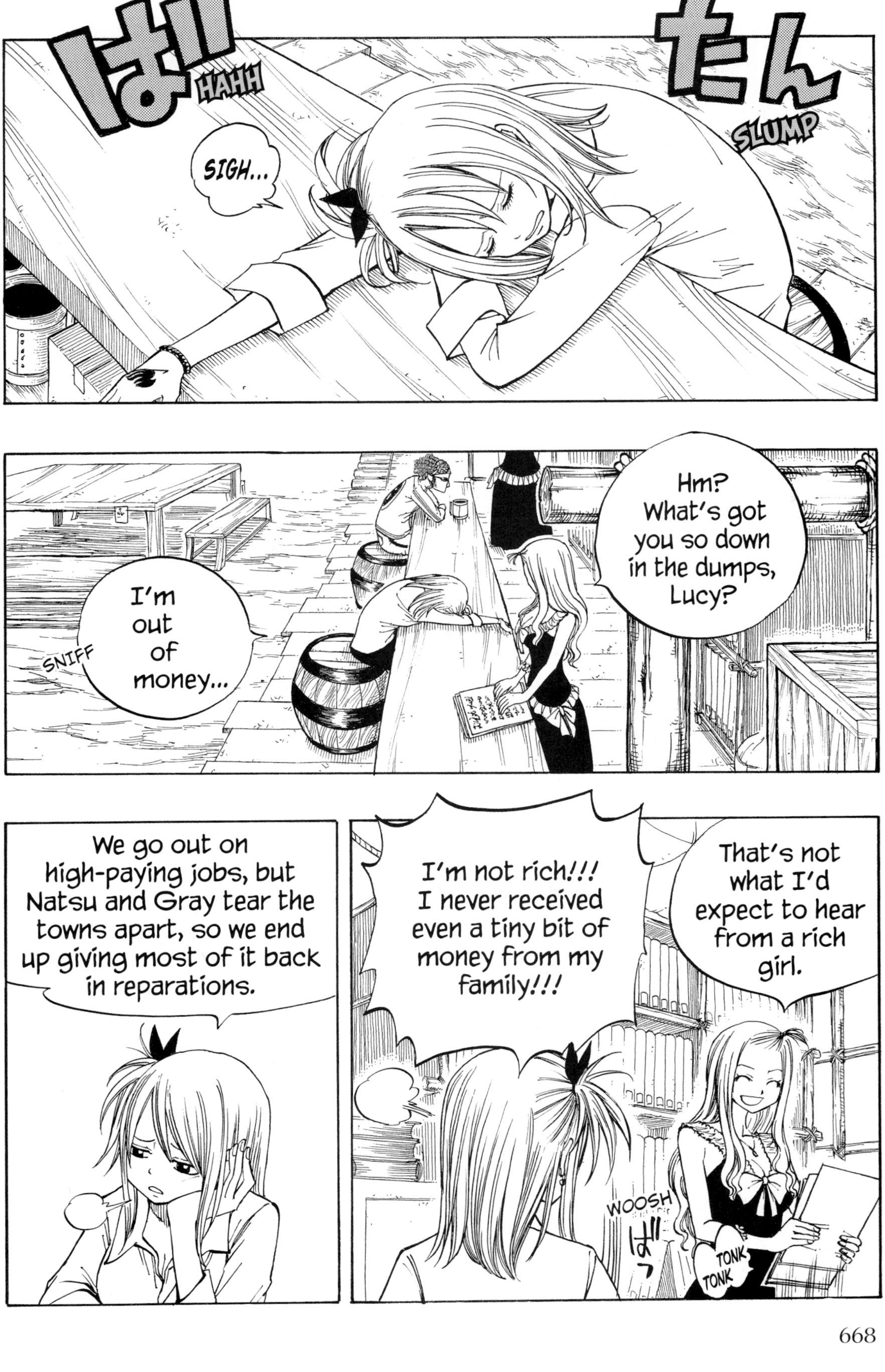
はぁ
HAHH
たん
SLUMP
SIGH...
Hm? What's got you so down in the dumps, Lucy?
I'm out of money...
SNIFF
That's not what I'd expect to hear from a rich girl.
I'm not rich!!! I never received even a tiny bit of money from my family!!!
WOOSH
ばっ
TONK TONK
We go out on high-paying jobs, but Natsu and Gray tear the towns apart, so we end up giving most of it back in reparations.

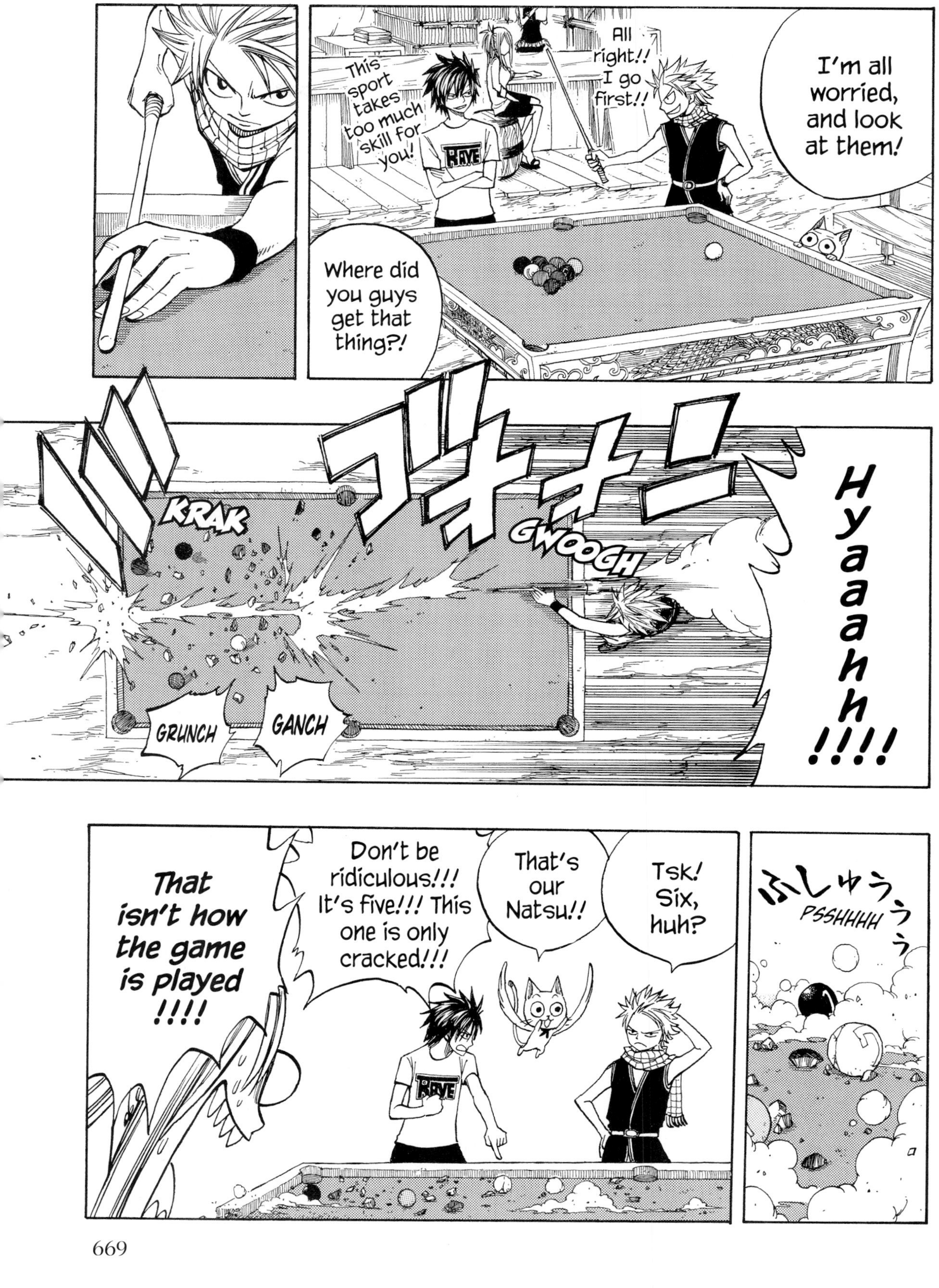
I'm all worried, and look at them!
All right!! I go first!!
This sport takes too much skill for you!
Where did you guys get that thing?!
Hyaaaahh!!!!
GWOOGH
KRAK
GANCH
GRUNCH
ふしゅううう
PSSHHHH
Tsk! Six, huh?
That's our Natsu!!
Don't be ridiculous!!! It's five!!! This one is only cracked!!!
That isn't how the game is played!!!!

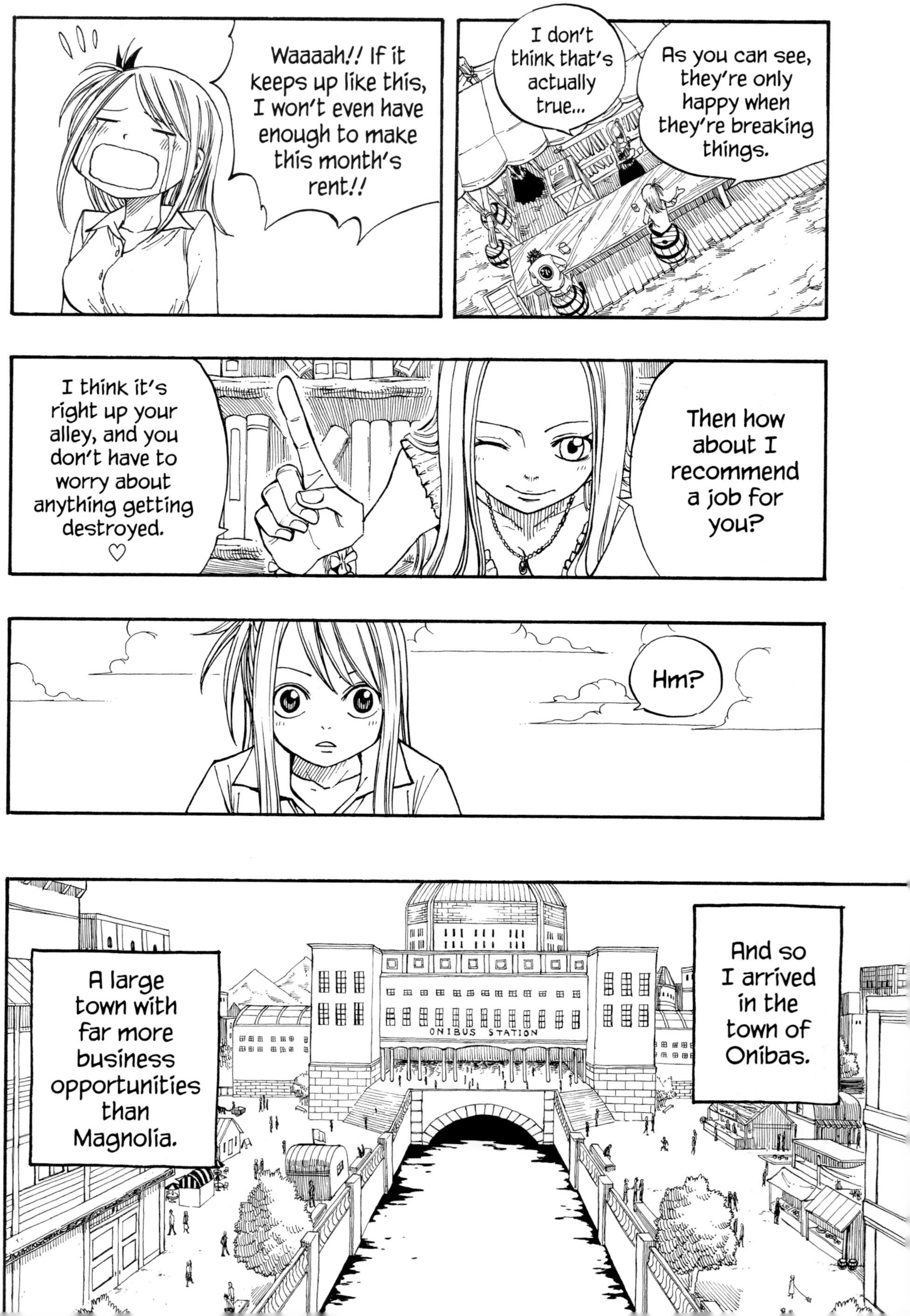
As you can see, they're only happy when they're breaking things.
I don't think that's actually true...
Waaaah!! If it keeps up like this, I won't even have enough to make this month's rent!!
Then how about I recommend a job for you?
I think it's right up your alley, and you don't have to worry about anything getting destroyed. ♡
Hm?
And so I arrived in the town of Onibas.
ONIBUS STATION
A large town with far more business opportunities than Magnolia.

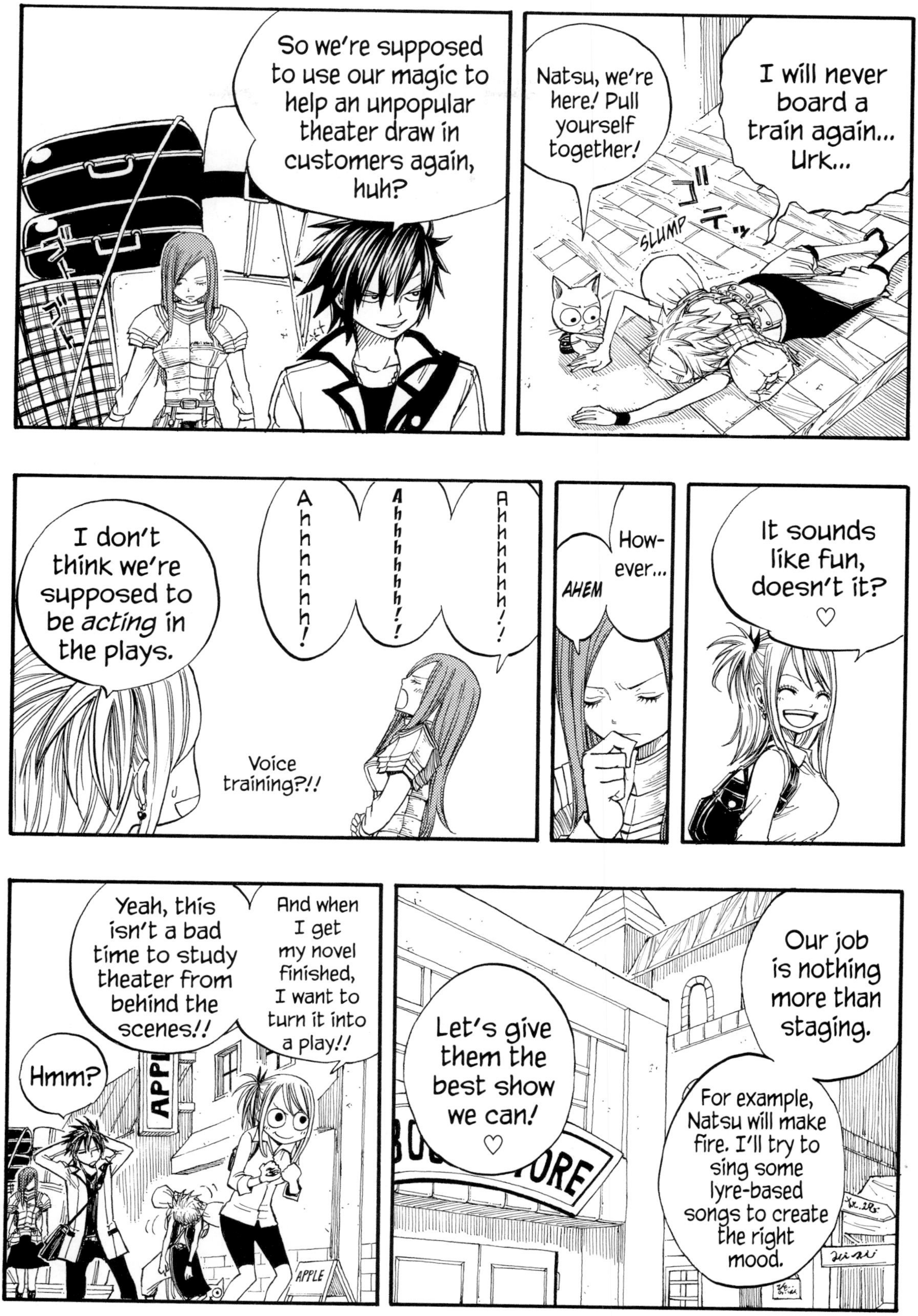
I will never board a train again... Urk...
Natsu, we're here! Pull yourself together!
SLUMP
So we're supposed to use our magic to help an unpopular theater draw in customers again, huh?
It sounds like fun, doesn't it? ♡
However...
AHEM
Ahhhhhhh!!
Ahhhhhhh!!
Ahhhhhh!
I don't think we're supposed to be *acting* in the plays.
Voice training?!!
Our job is nothing more than staging.
Let's give them the best show we can! ♡
For example, Natsu will make fire. I'll try to sing some lyre-based songs to create the right mood.
And when I get my novel finished, I want to turn it into a play!!
Yeah, this isn't a bad time to study theater from behind the scenes!!
Hmm?
APPLE

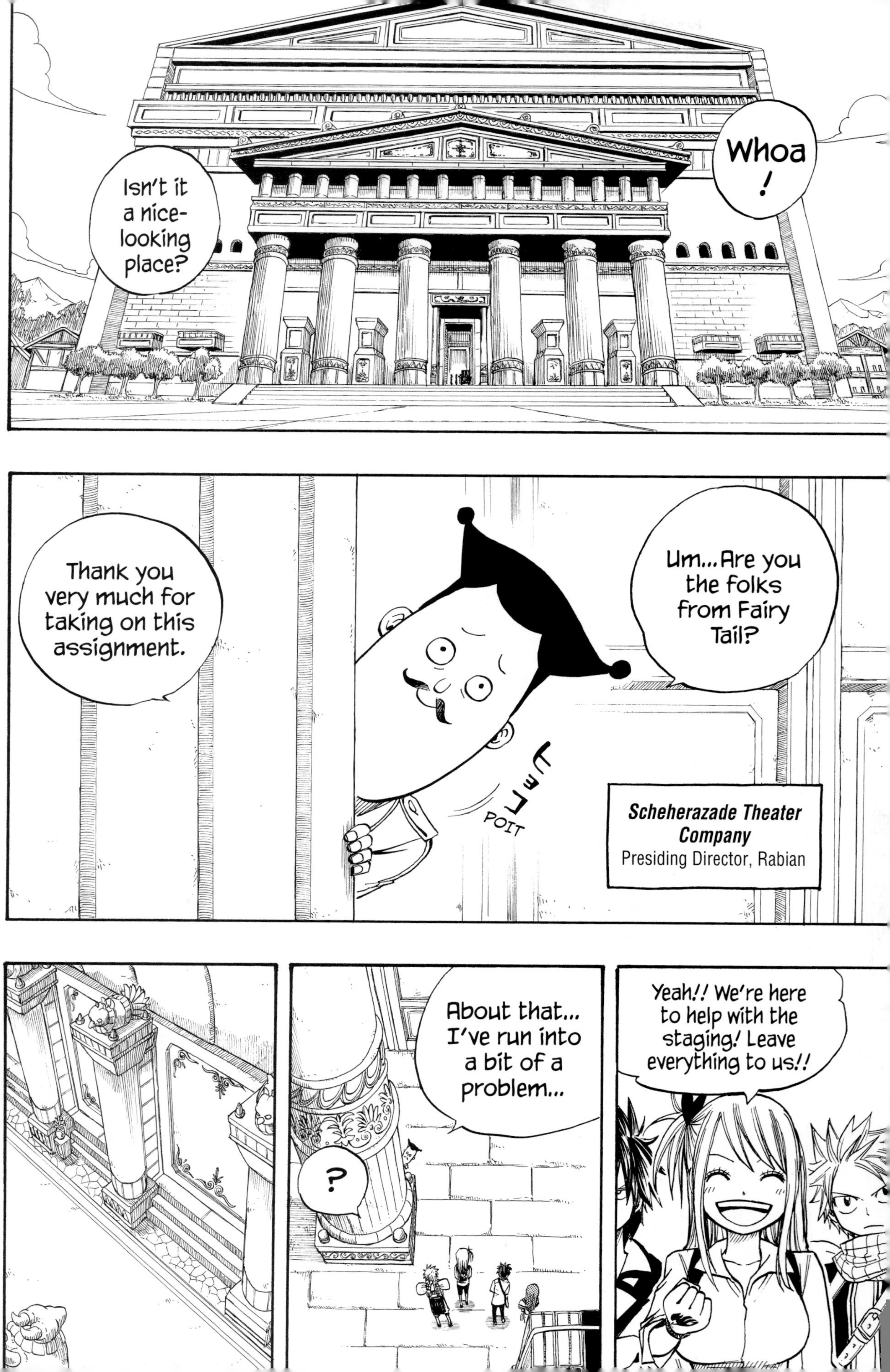
Whoa!
Isn't it a nice-looking place?
Um...Are you the folks from Fairy Tail?
POIT
Scheherazade Theater Company
Presiding Director, Rabian
Thank you very much for taking on this assignment.
Yeah!! We're here to help with the staging! Leave everything to us!!
About that... I've run into a bit of a problem...
?

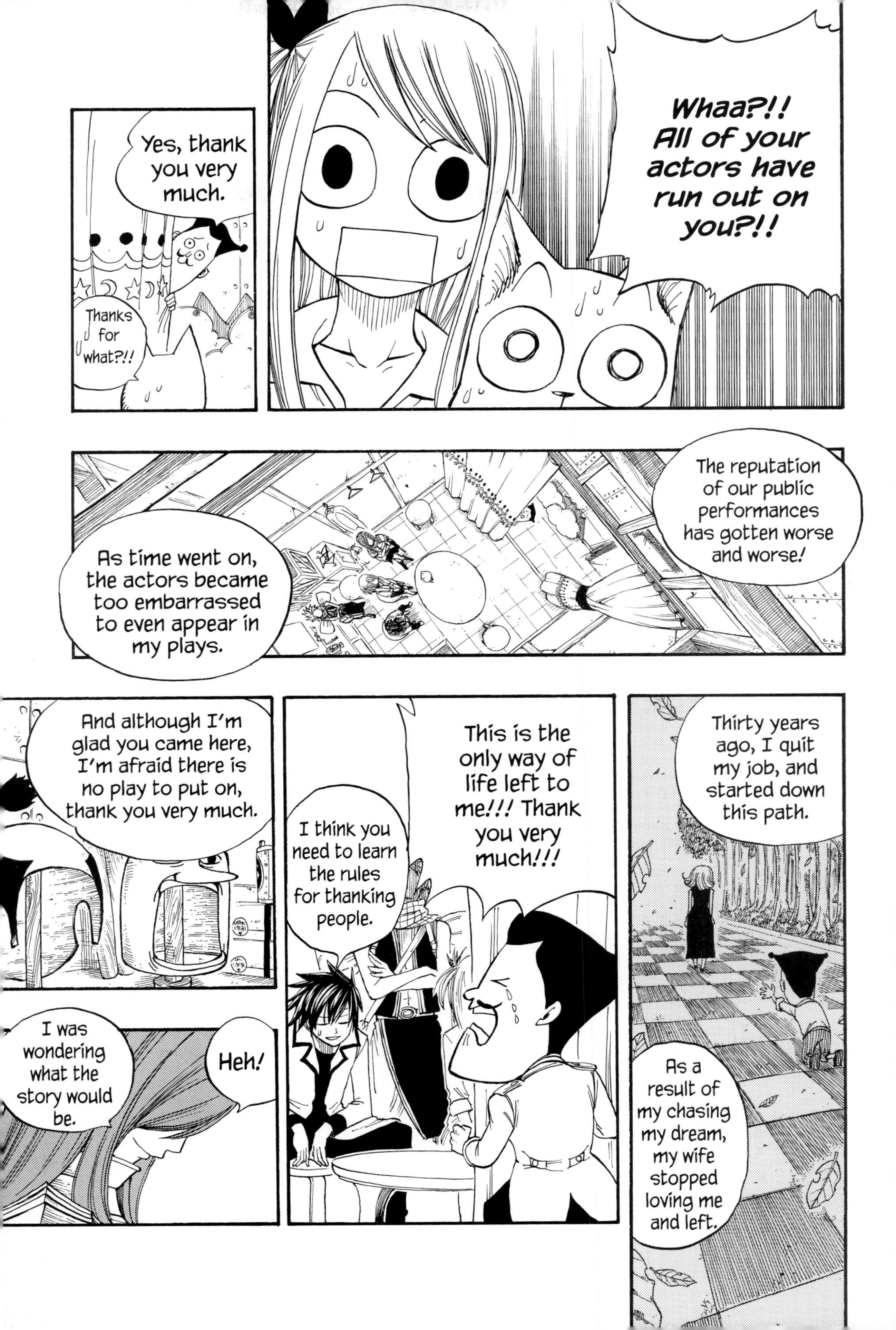
Whaa?!! All of your actors have run out on you?!!
Yes, thank you very much.
Thanks for what?!!
The reputation of our public performances has gotten worse and worse!
As time went on, the actors became too embarrassed to even appear in my plays.
Thirty years ago, I quit my job, and started down this path.
As a result of my chasing my dream, my wife stopped loving me and left.
This is the only way of life left to me!!! Thank you very much!!!
I think you need to learn the rules for thanking people.
And although I'm glad you came here, I'm afraid there is no play to put on, thank you very much.
I was wondering what the story would be.
Heh!

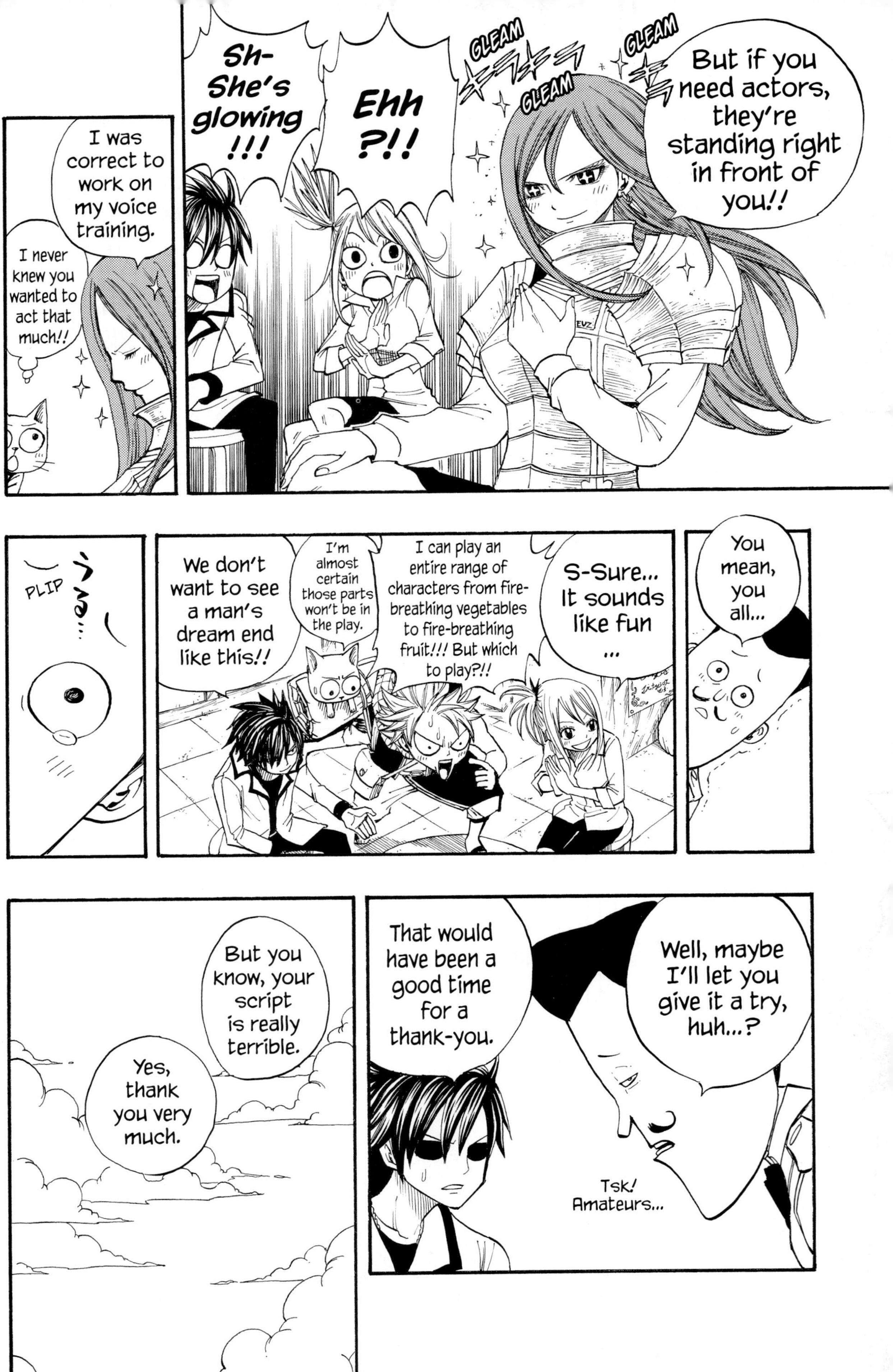
GLEAM
GLEAM
GLEAM
But if you need actors, they're standing right in front of you!!
Ehh ?!!
Sh- She's glowing !!!
I was correct to work on my voice training.
I never knew you wanted to act that much!!
You mean, you all...
S-Sure... It sounds like fun ...
I can play an entire range of characters from fire-breathing vegetables to fire-breathing fruit!!! But which to play?!!
I'm almost certain those parts won't be in the play.
We don't want to see a man's dream end like this!!
うる…
PLIP
Well, maybe I'll let you give it a try, huh...?
That would have been a good time for a thank-you.
Tsk! Amateurs...
But you know, your script is really terrible.
Yes, thank you very much.

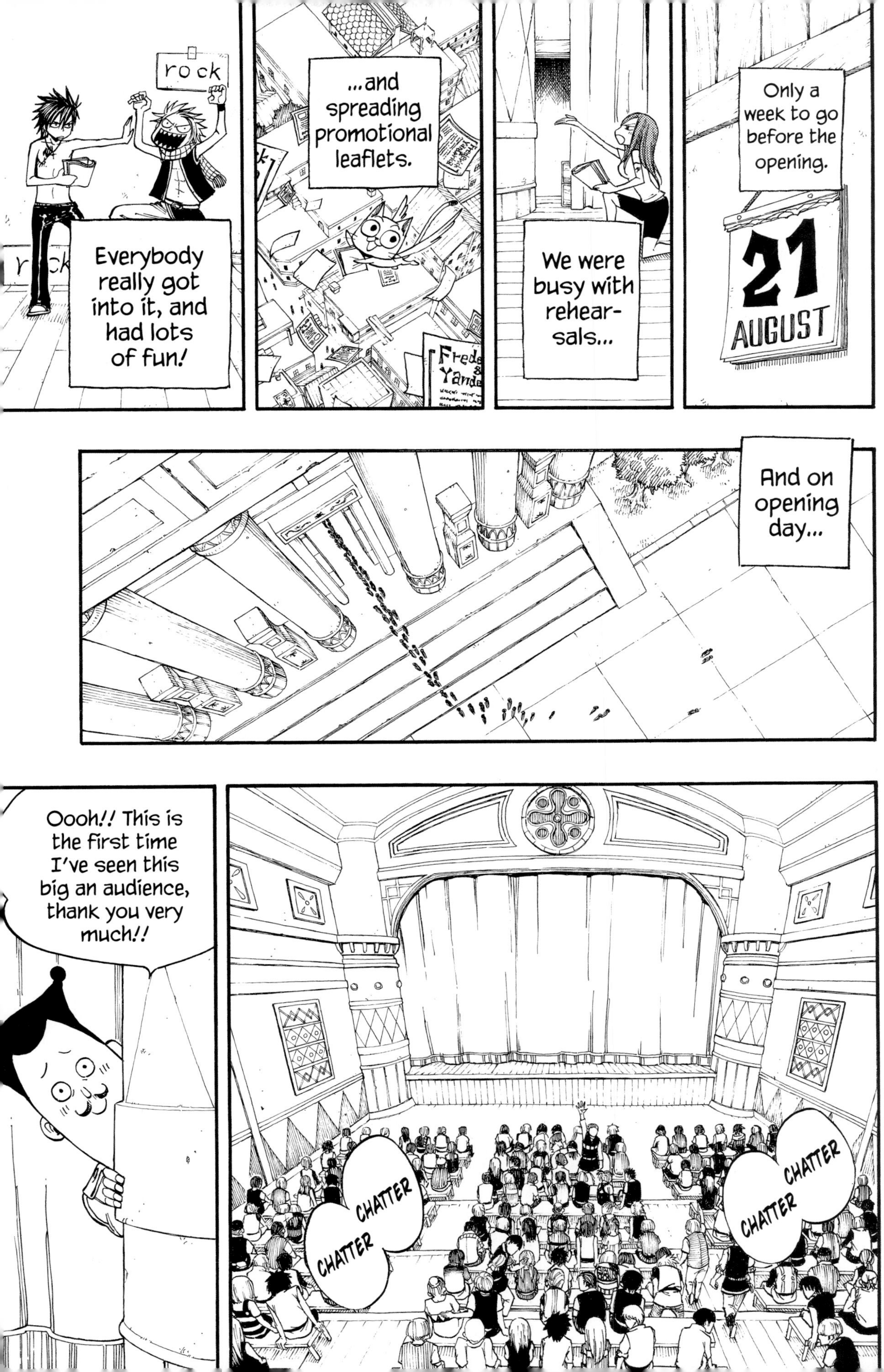
Only a week to go before the opening.
21
AUGUST
We were busy with rehearsals...
...and spreading promotional leaflets.
Everybody really got into it, and had lots of fun!
rock
rock
And on opening day...
CHATTER CHATTER
CHATTER CHATTER
Oooh!! This is the first time I've seen this big an audience, thank you very much!!

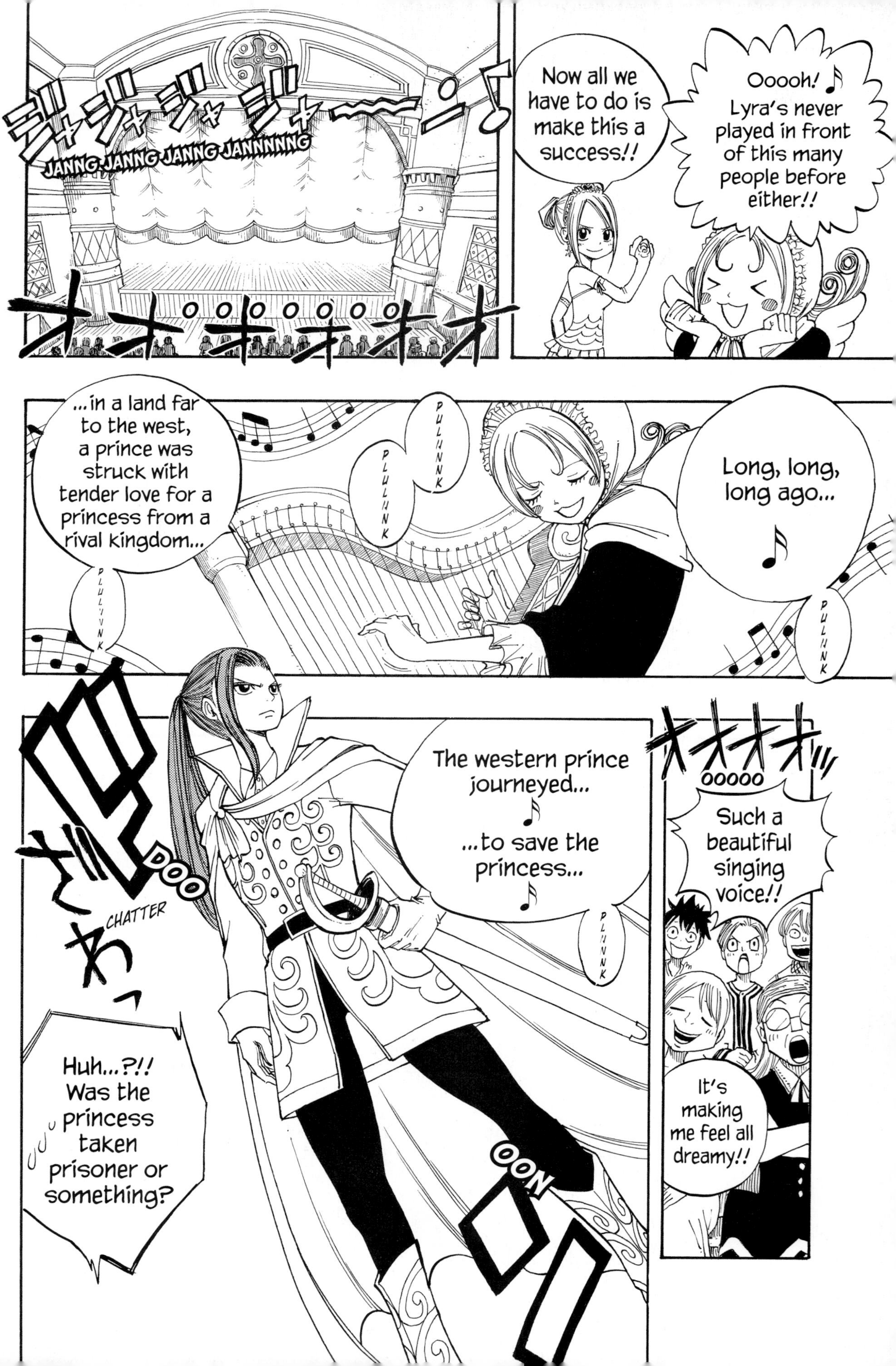
Now all we have to do is make this a success!!
Ooooh! ♪ Lyra's never played in front of this many people before either!!
JANNG JANNG JANNG JANNNNNG
OOOOOOOO
Long, long, long ago... ♪
PULINNK
PLULINNK
...in a land far to the west, a prince was struck with tender love for a princess from a rival kingdom...
PLULINNK
PULINNK
OOOOO
Such a beautiful singing voice!!
It's making me feel all dreamy!!
The western prince journeyed... ♪ ...to save the princess... ♪
PLINNK
DOO
CHATTER
Huh...?!! Was the princess taken prisoner or something?
OON

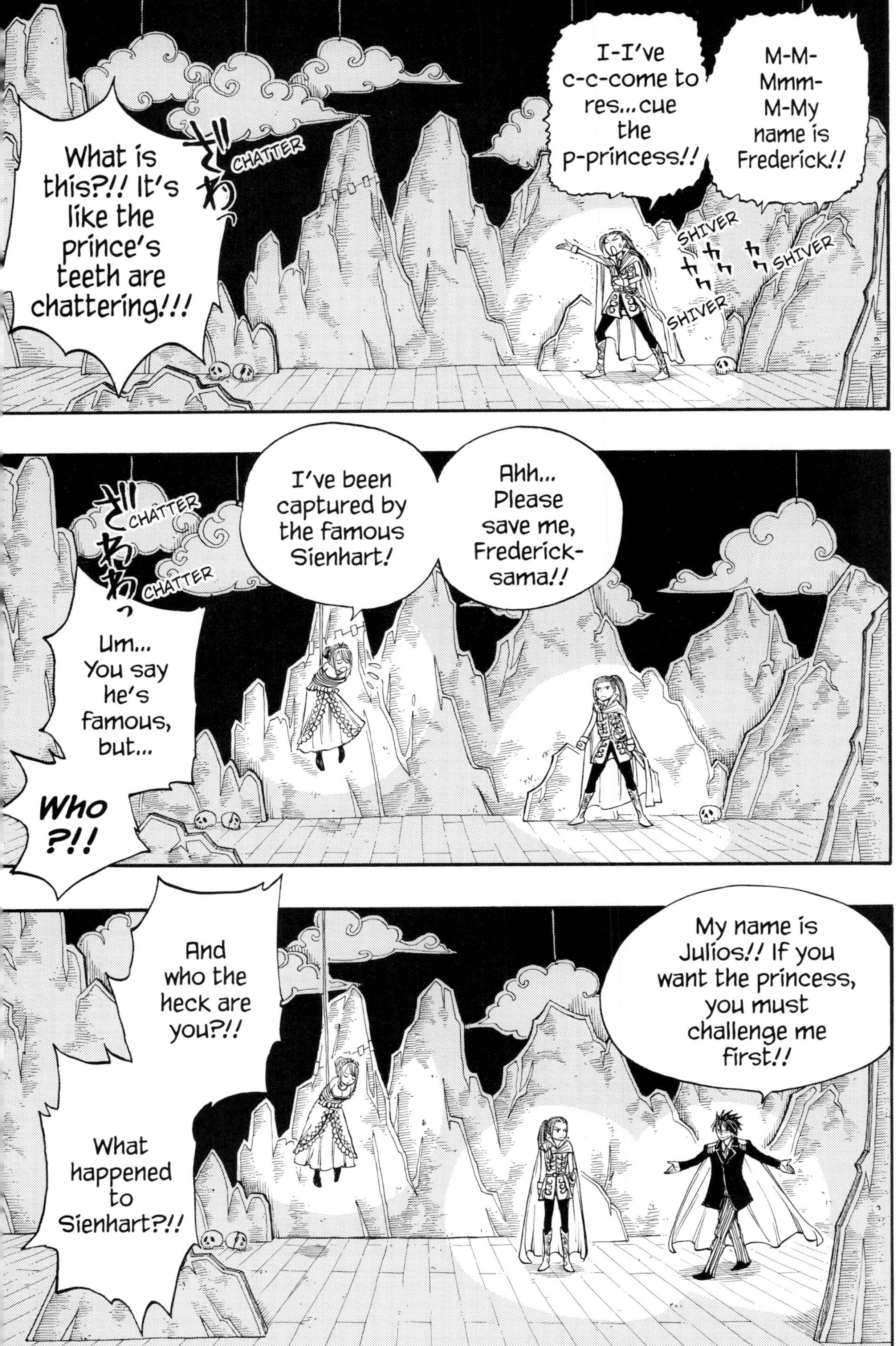
M-M-Mmm-M-My name is Frederick!!
I-I've c-c-come to res...cue the p-princess!!
SHIVER
SHIVER
SHIVER
CHATTER
What is this?!! It's like the prince's teeth are chattering!!!
Ahh... Please save me, Frederick-sama!!
I've been captured by the famous Sienhart!
CHATTER
CHATTER
Um... You say he's famous, but...
Who?!!
My name is Julios!! If you want the princess, you must challenge me first!!
And who the heck are you?!!
What happened to Sienhart?!!

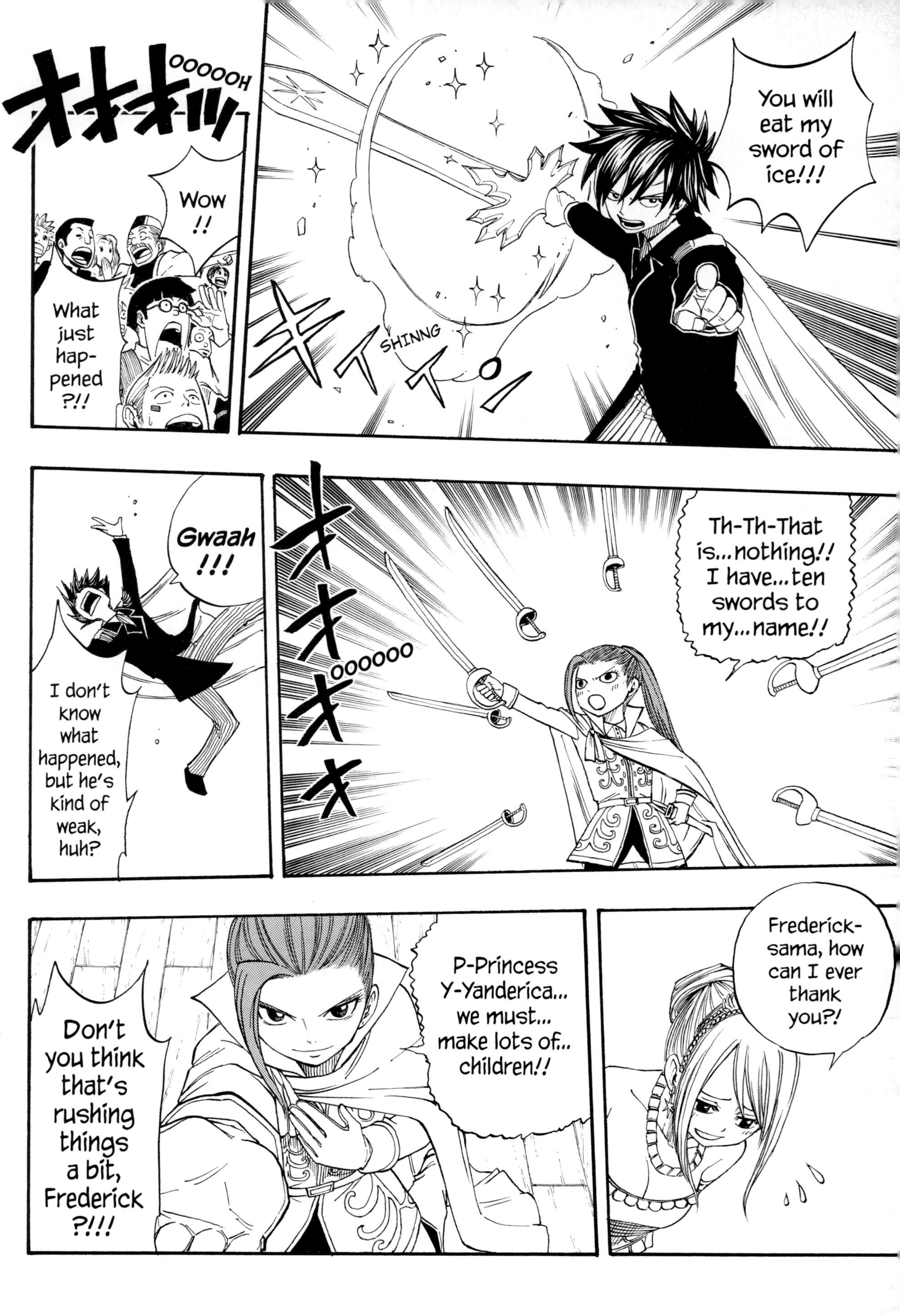
You will eat my sword of ice!!!
SHINNG
OOOOOH
Wow!!
What just hap-pened?!!
Th-Th-That is...nothing!! I have...ten swords to my...name!!
OOOOOO
Gwaah!!!
I don't know what happened, but he's kind of weak, huh?
Frederick-sama, how can I ever thank you?!
P-Princess Y-Yanderica... we must... make lots of.. children!!
Don't you think that's rushing things a bit, Frederick?!!!

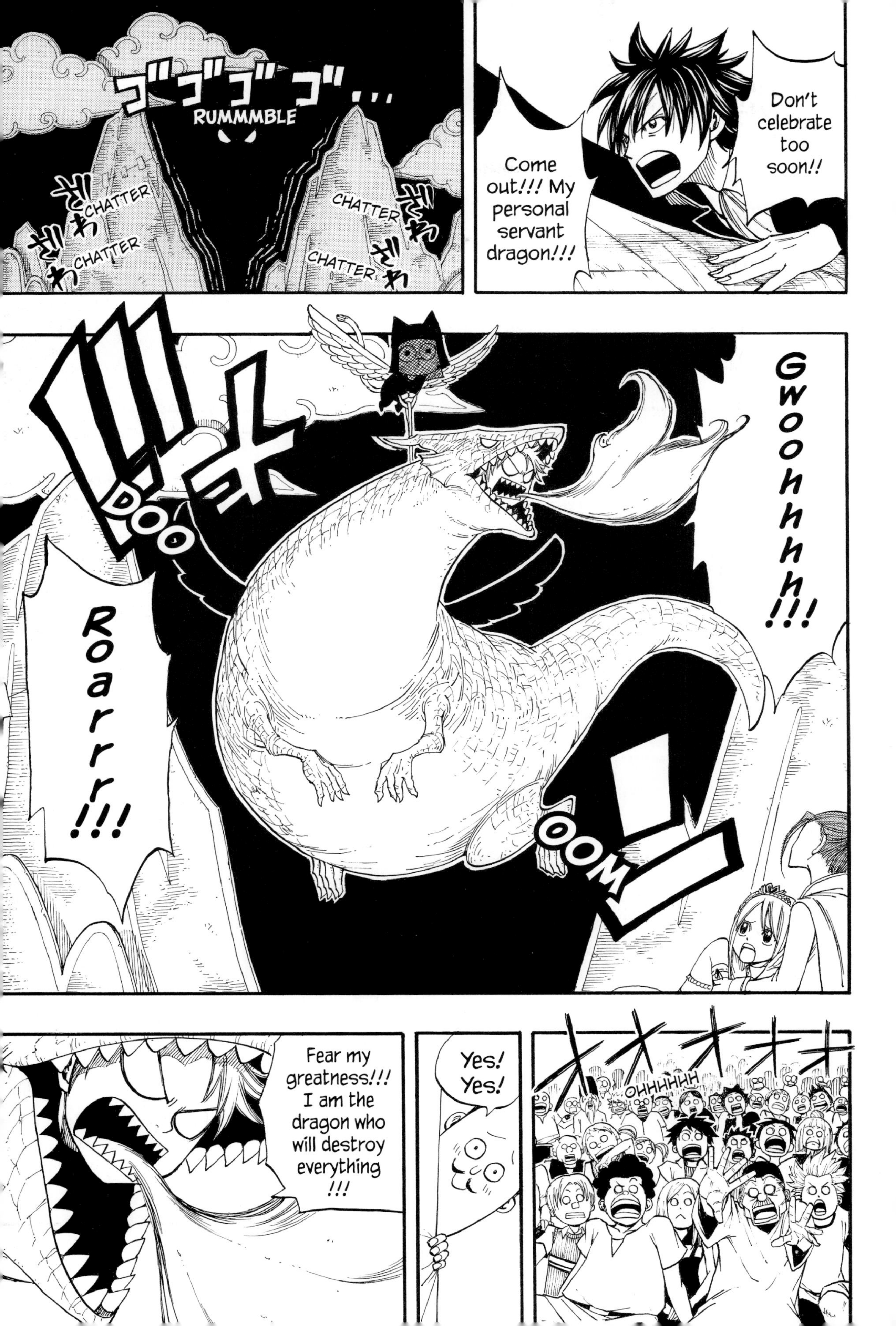
Don't celebrate too soon!!
Come out!!! My personal servant dragon!!!
ゴゴゴゴ...
RUMMMBLE
ざわ CHATTER
ざわ CHATTER
ざわ CHATTER
ざわ CHATTER
Gwoohhhhh!!!
ドオ
DOO
OOM!
Roarrrr!!!
オオオオ
OHHHHHH
Yes! Yes!
Fear my greatness!!! I am the dragon who will destroy everything!!!

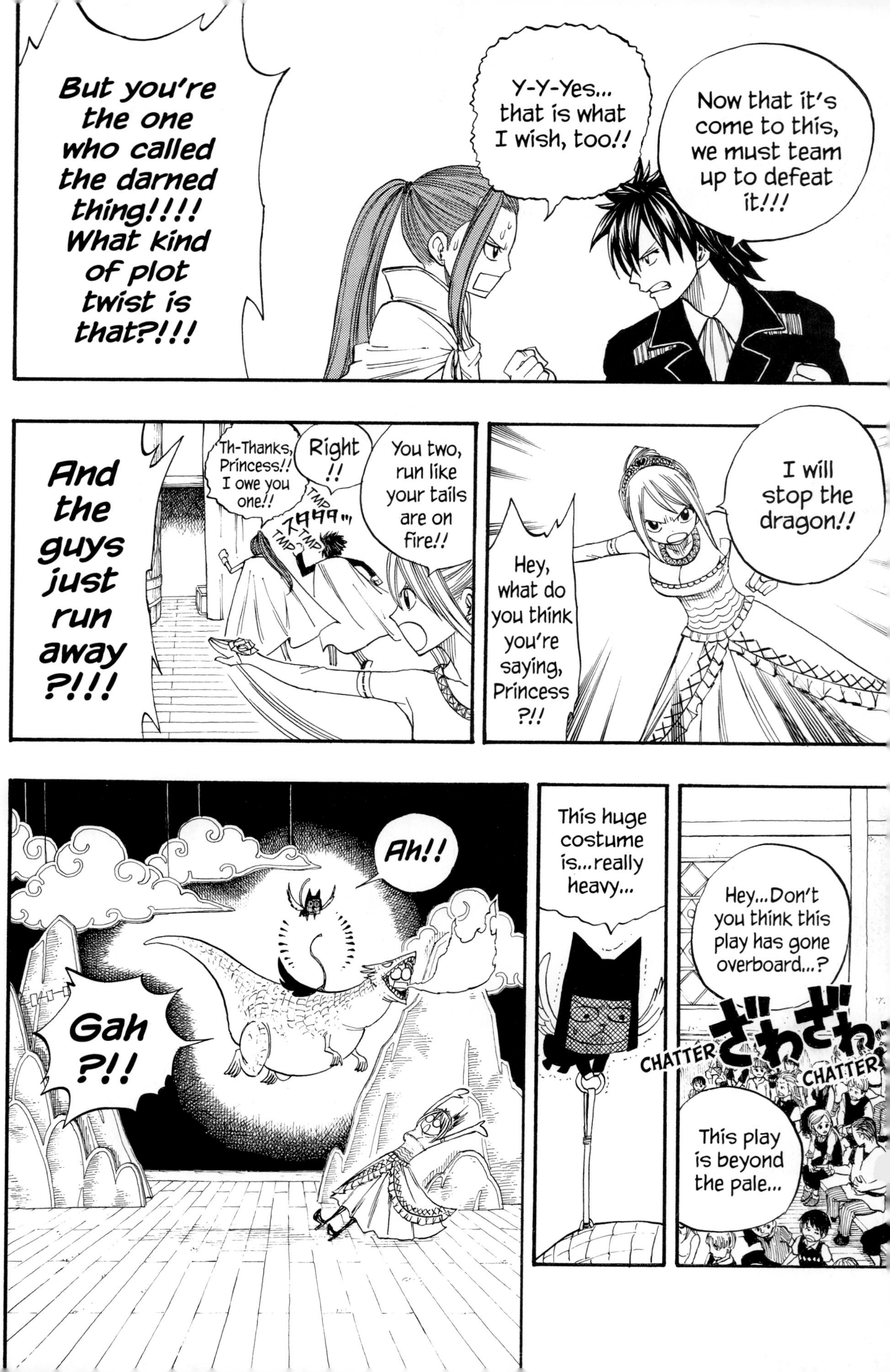

Now that it's come to this, we must team up to defeat it!!!
Y-Y-Yes... that is what I wish, too!!
But you're the one who called the darned thing!!!! What kind of plot twist is that?!!!
I will stop the dragon!!
Hey, what do you think you're saying, Princess?!!
You two, run like your tails are on fire!!
Right !!
Th-Thanks, Princess!! I owe you one!!
TMP TMP TMP
And the guys just run away?!!!
Hey...Don't you think this play has gone overboard...?
ざわざわ
CHATTER CHATTER
This play is beyond the pale...
This huge costume is...really heavy...
Ah!!
Gah ?!!

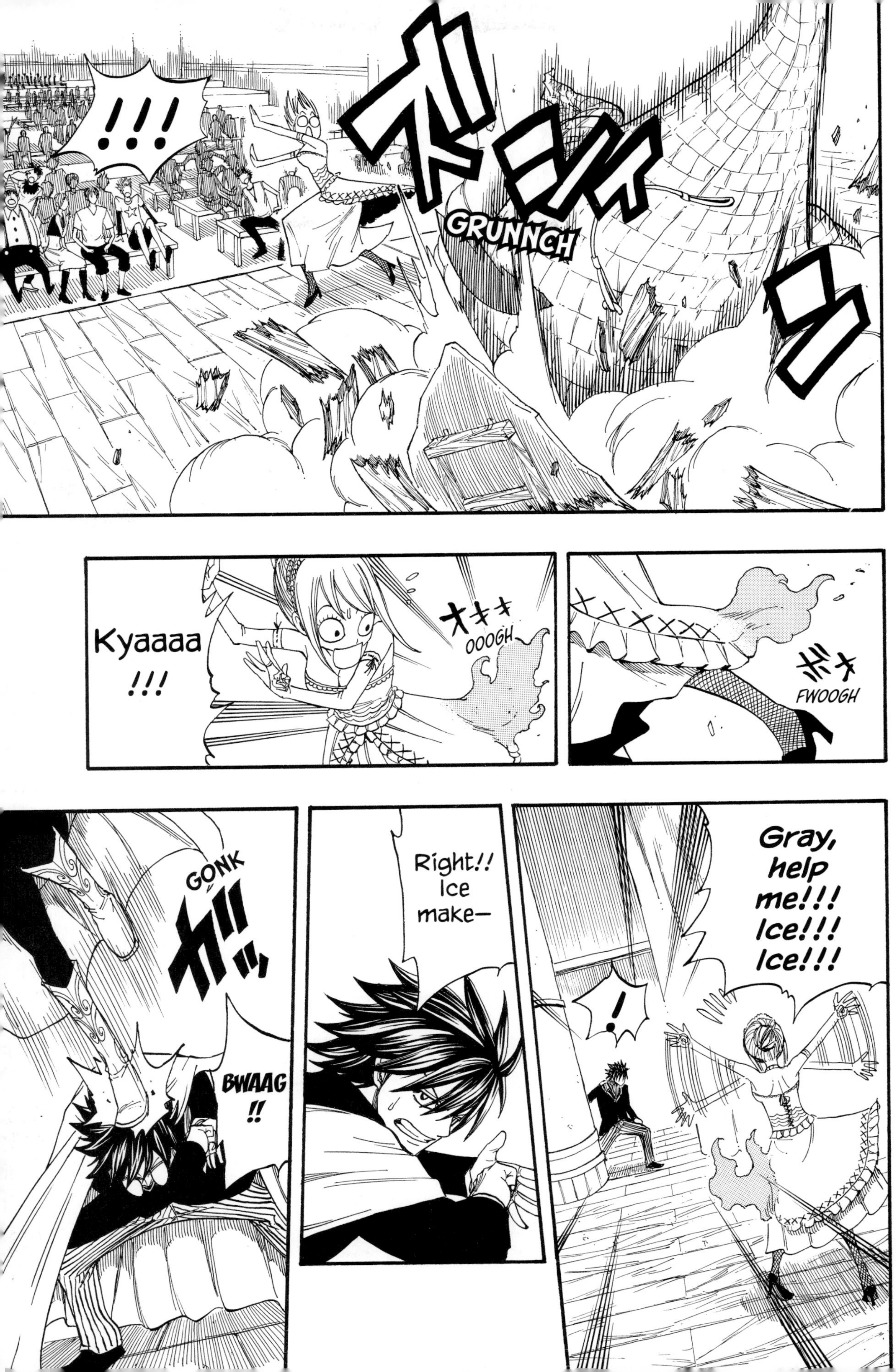
!!!
GRUNNCH
FWOOGH
Kyaaaa !!!
OOOGH
Gray, help me!!! Ice!!! Ice!!!
!
Right!! Ice make—
GONK
BWAAG !!

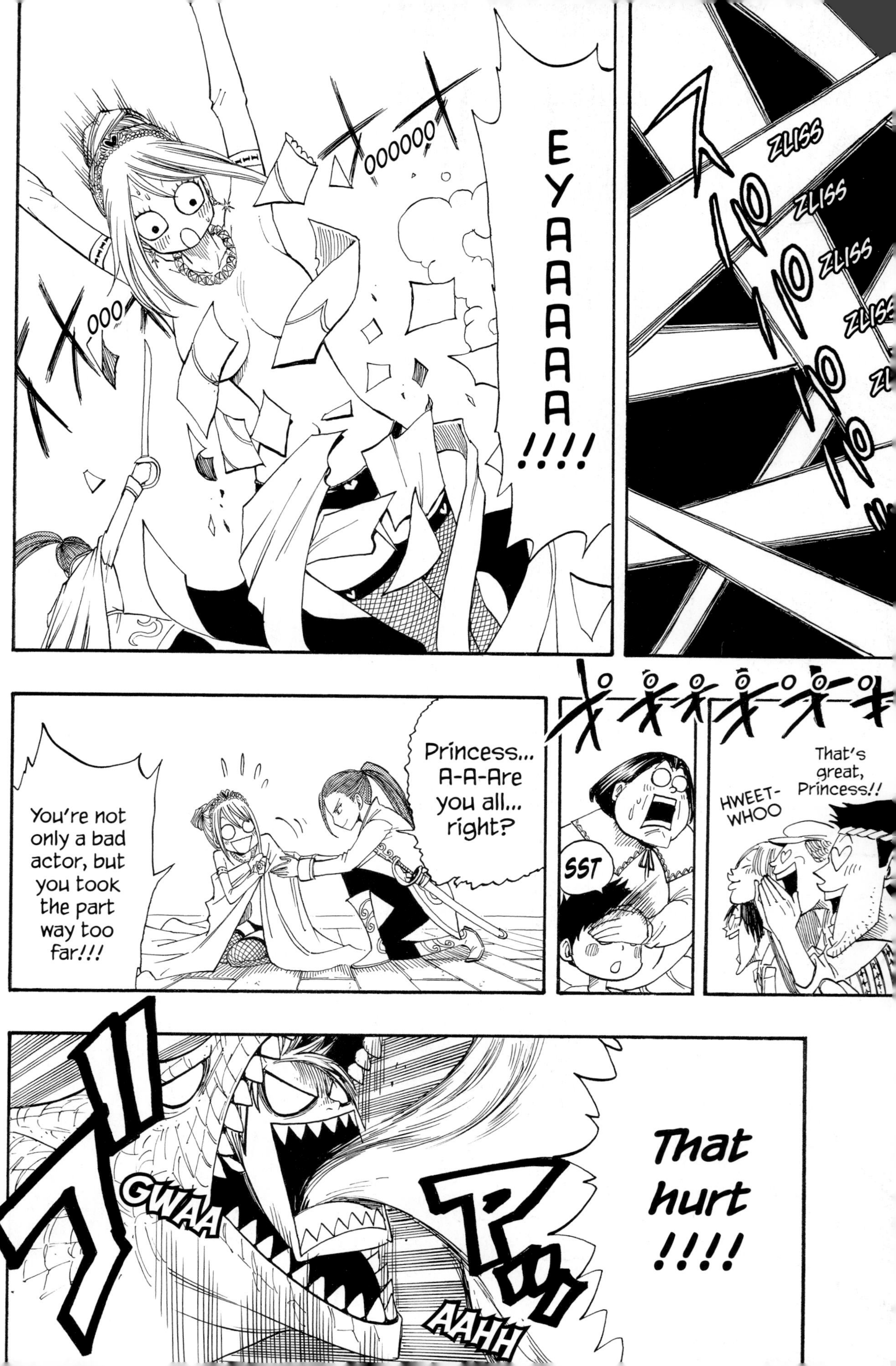
ZLISS
ZLISS
ZLISS
ZLISS
EYAAAAAA!!!!
oooooo
ooo
That's great, Princess!!
HWEET-WHOO
SST
Princess... A-A-Are you all... right?
You're not only a bad actor, but you took the part way too far!!!
That hurt!!!!
GWAA
AAHH

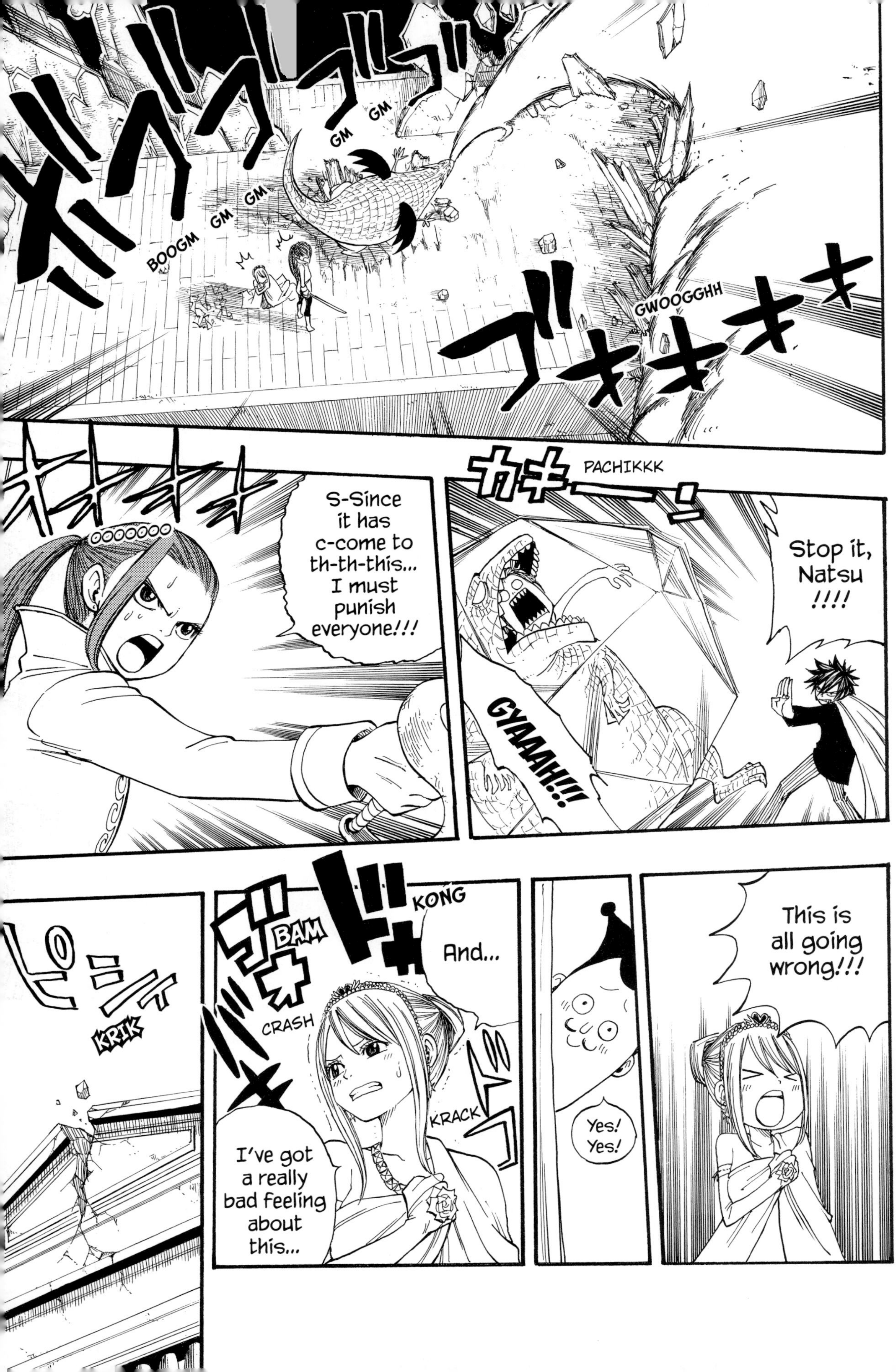
GM GM
BOOGM GM GM
GWOOGGHH
PACHIKKK
Stop it, Natsu!!!!
GYAAAH!!!!
S-Since it has c-come to th-th-this... I must punish everyone!!!
This is all going wrong!!!
Yes! Yes!
KONG
BAM
And...
CRASH
KRACK
I've got a really bad feeling about this...
KRIK

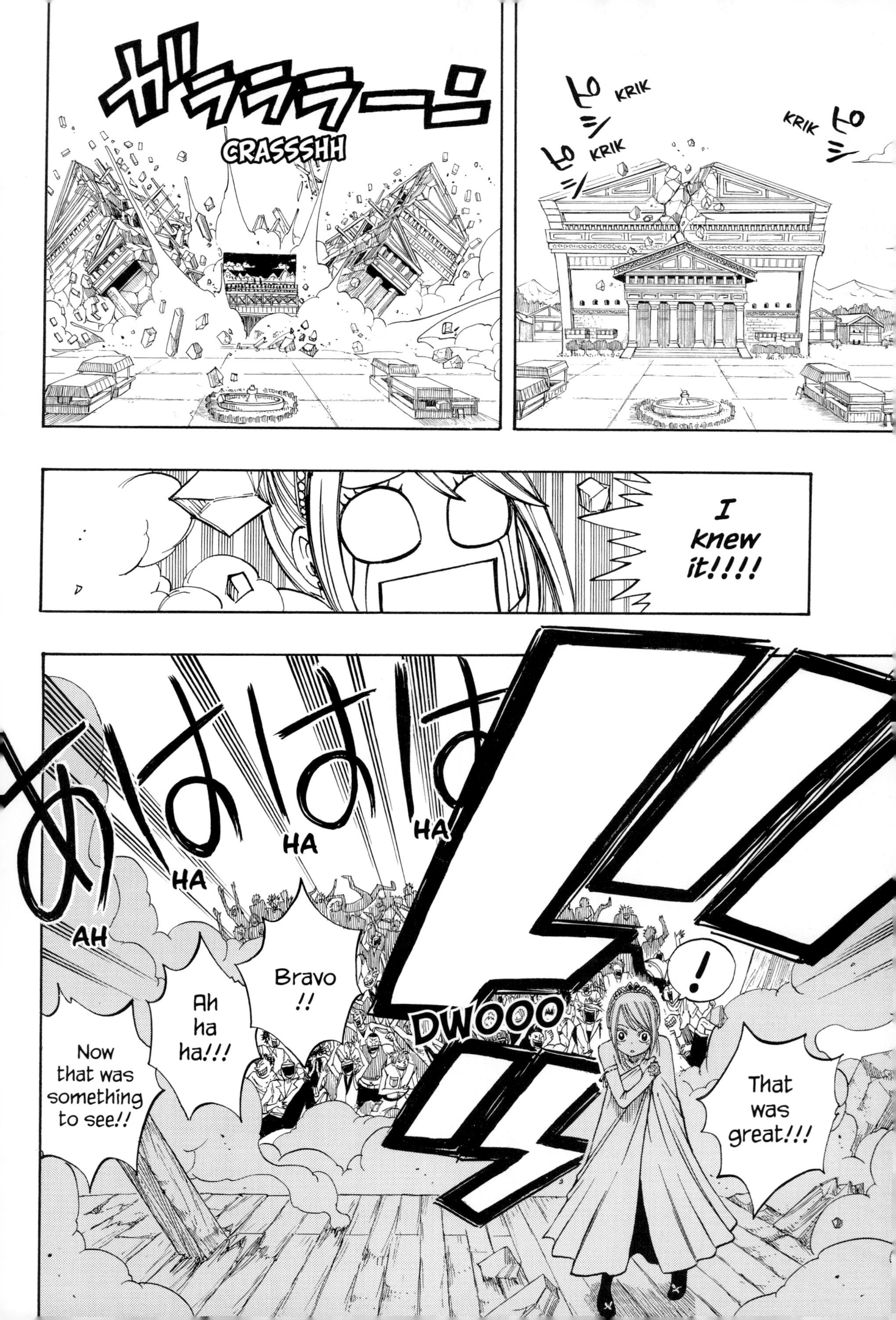
ピシ
KRIK
ピシ
KRIK
ピシ
KRIK
CRASSSHH
I knew it!!!!
HA
HA
HA
AH
That was great!!!
!
DWOOO
Bravo!!
Ah ha ha!!!
Now that was something to see!!

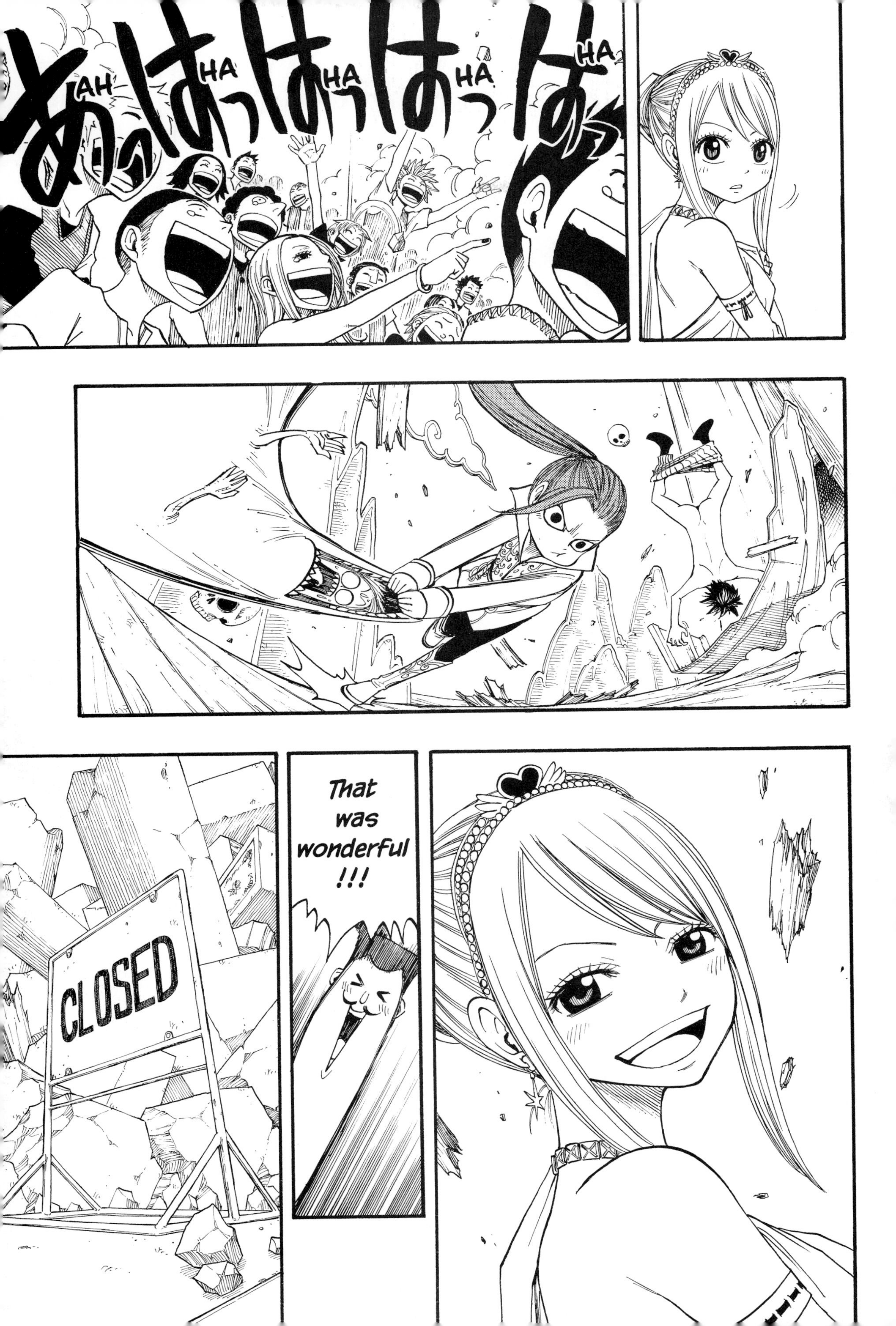
あっはっはっはっはっ
AH HA HA HA HA
That was wonderful !!!
CLOSED

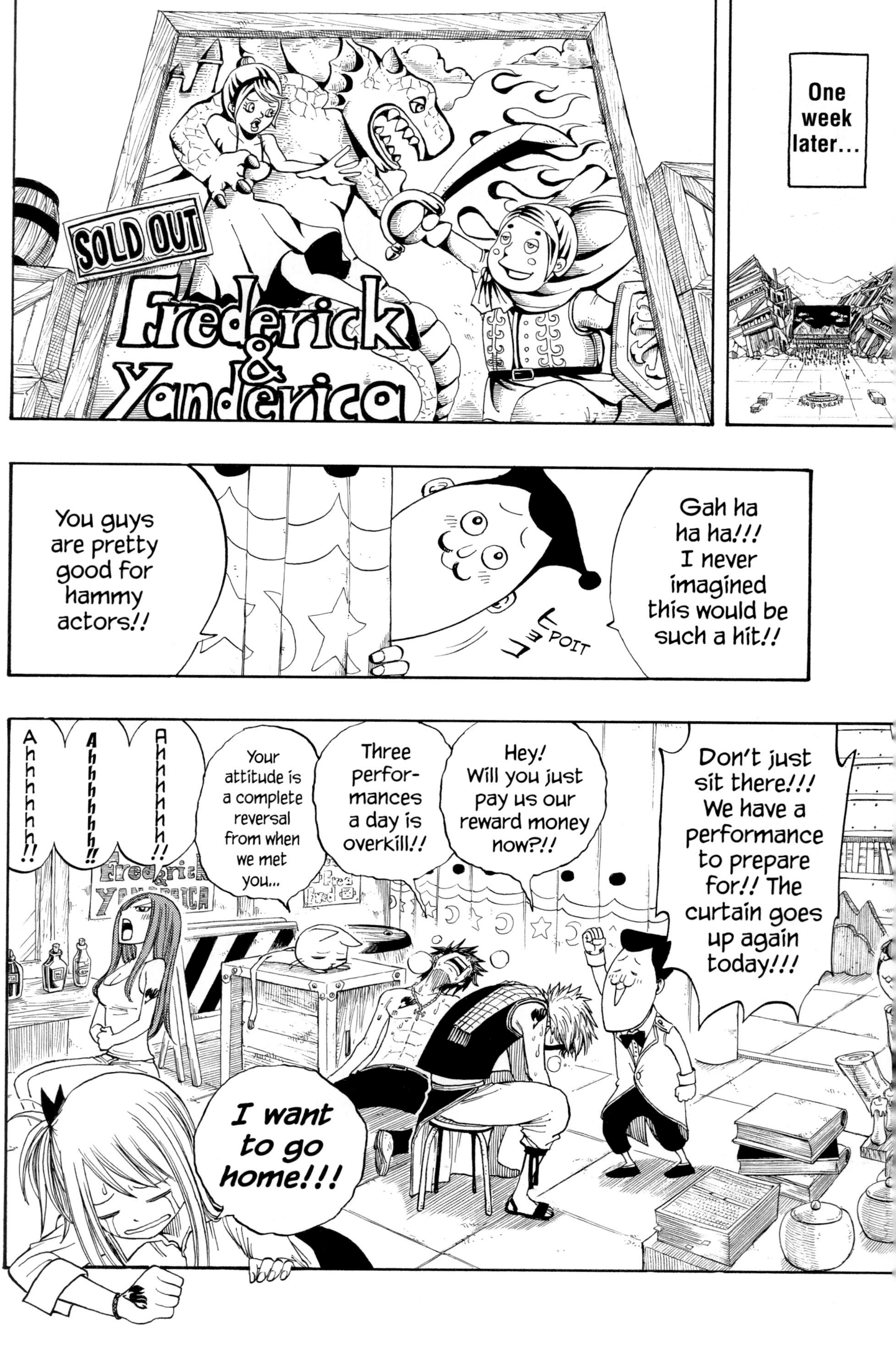
One week later...
SOLD OUT
Frederick & Yanderica
Gah ha ha ha!!! I never imagined this would be such a hit!!
POIT
You guys are pretty good for hammy actors!!
Don't just sit there!!! We have a performance to prepare for!! The curtain goes up again today!!!
Hey! Will you just pay us our reward money now?!!
Three perfor-mances a day is overkill!!
Your attitude is a complete reversal from when we met you...
Ahhhhhh!!
Ahhhhhhh!!
Ahhhhhhh!!
I want to go home!!!

Chapter 71: A Night in Impatiens

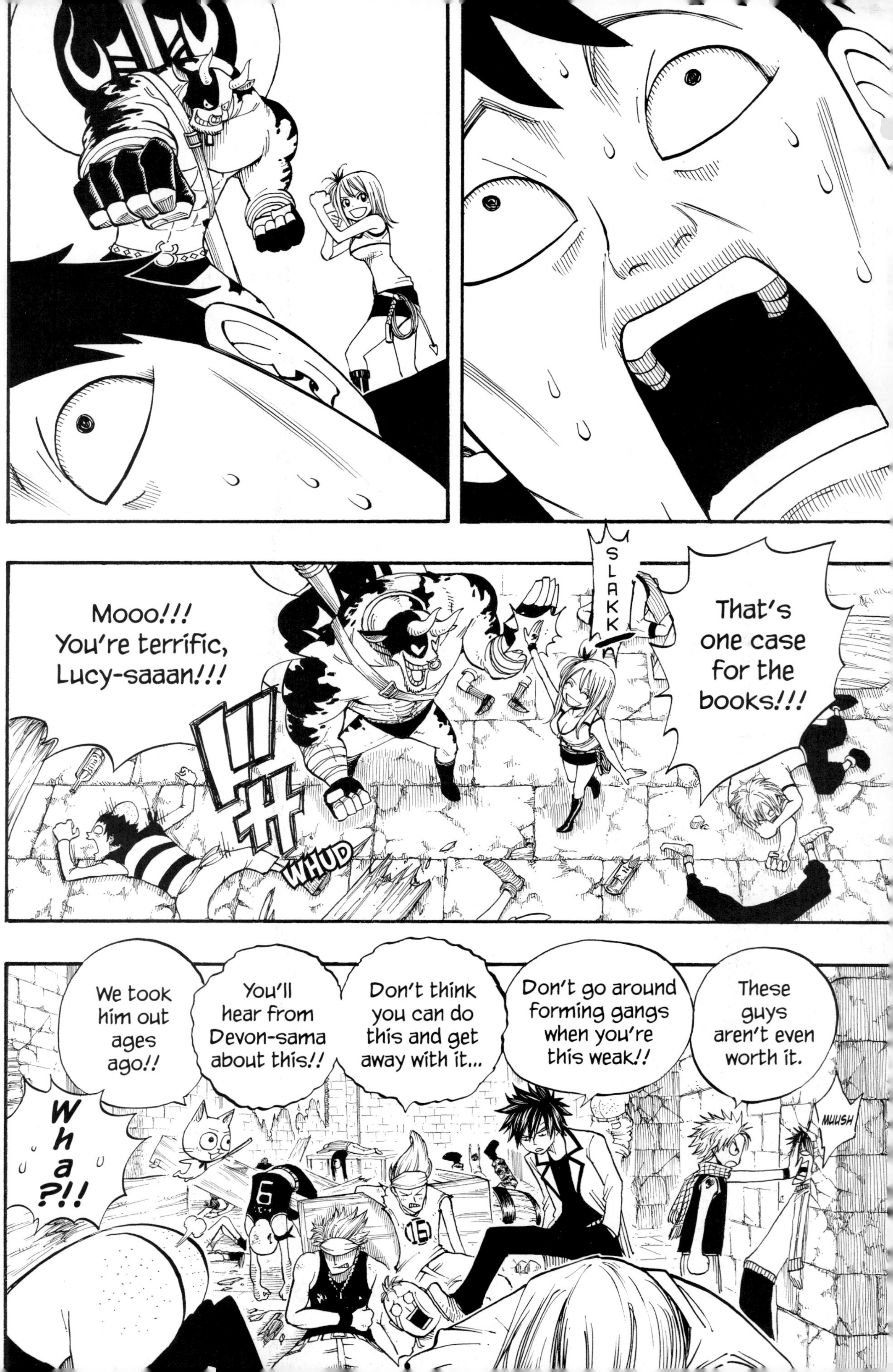
That's one case for the books!!!
SLAKK
Mooo!!! You're terrific, Lucy-saaan!!!
WHUD
MUUSH
These guys aren't even worth it.
Don't go around forming gangs when you're this weak!!
Don't think you can do this and get away with it...
You'll hear from Devon-sama about this!!
We took him out ages ago!!
Wha?!!

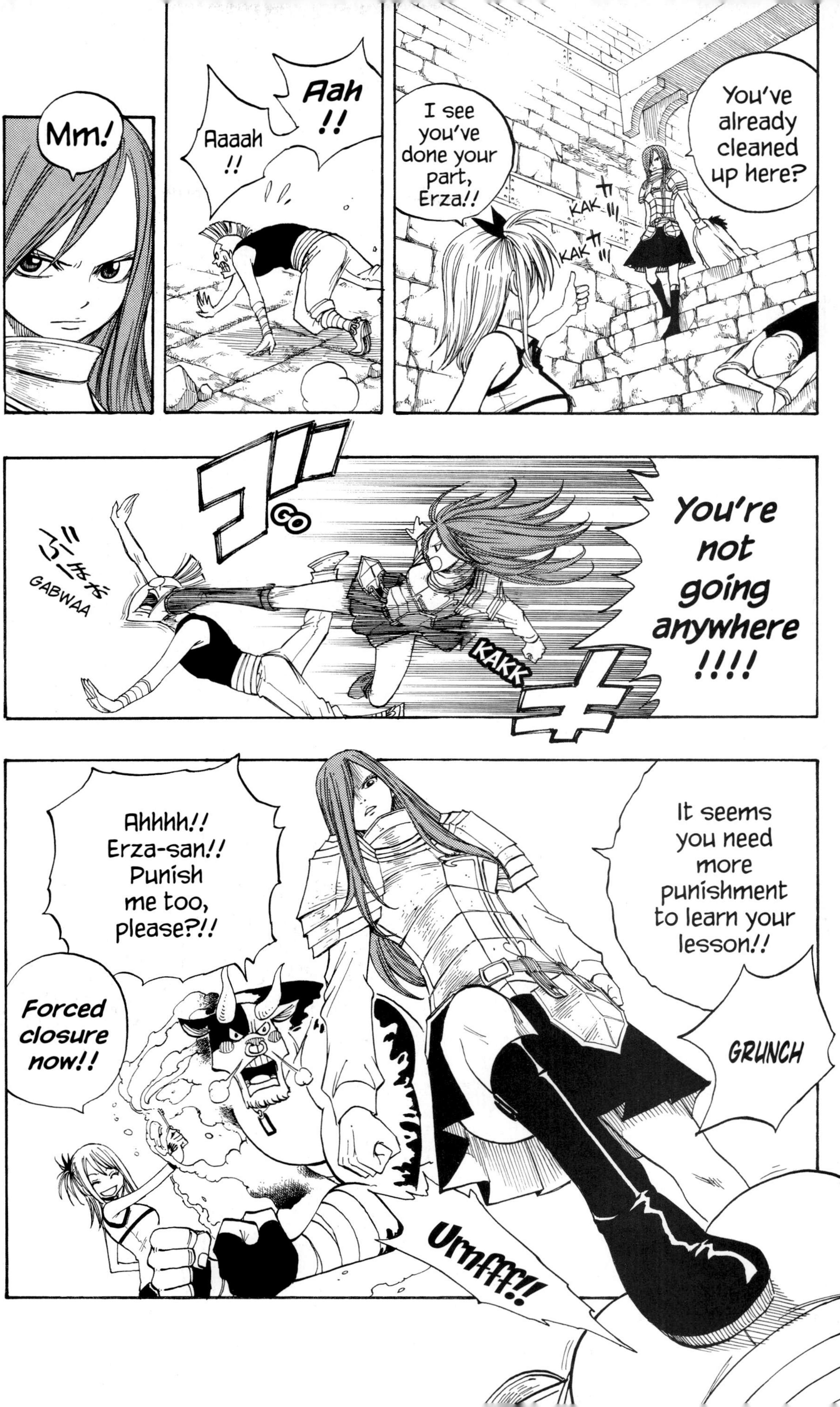
You've already cleaned up here?
I see you've done your part, Erza!!
KAK
KAK
Aah!!
Aaaah!!
Mm!
You're not going anywhere!!!!
GO
KAKK
GABWAA
It seems you need more punishment to learn your lesson!!
GRUNCH
Ahhhh!! Erza-san!! Punish me too, please?!!
Forced closure now!!
Umfff!!

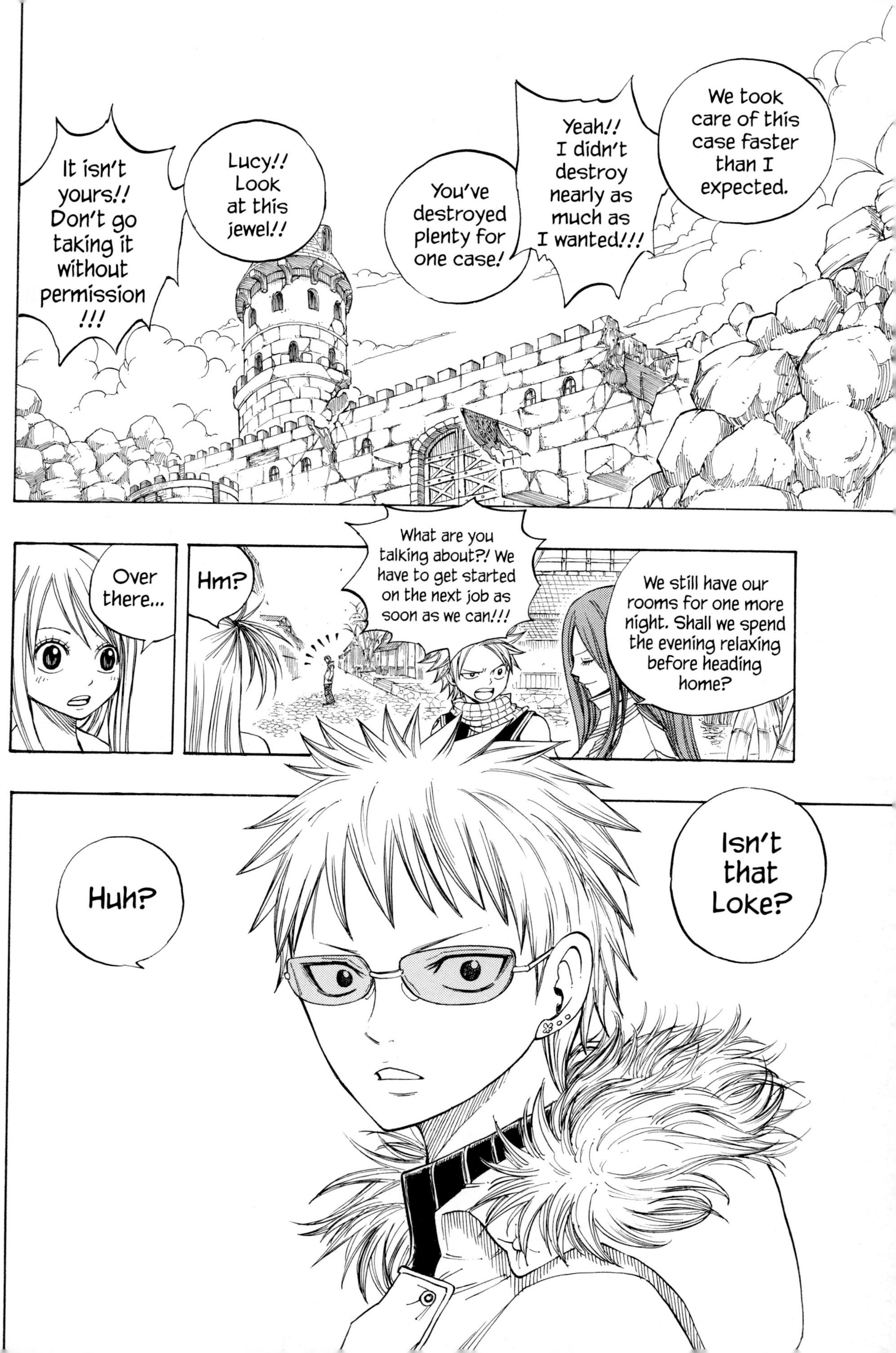
We took care of this case faster than I expected.
Yeah!! I didn't destroy nearly as much as I wanted!!!
You've destroyed plenty for one case!
Lucy!! Look at this jewel!!
It isn't yours!! Don't go taking it without permission!!!
We still have our rooms for one more night. Shall we spend the evening relaxing before heading home?
What are you talking about?! We have to get started on the next job as soon as we can!!!
Hm?
Over there...
Isn't that Loke?
Huh?

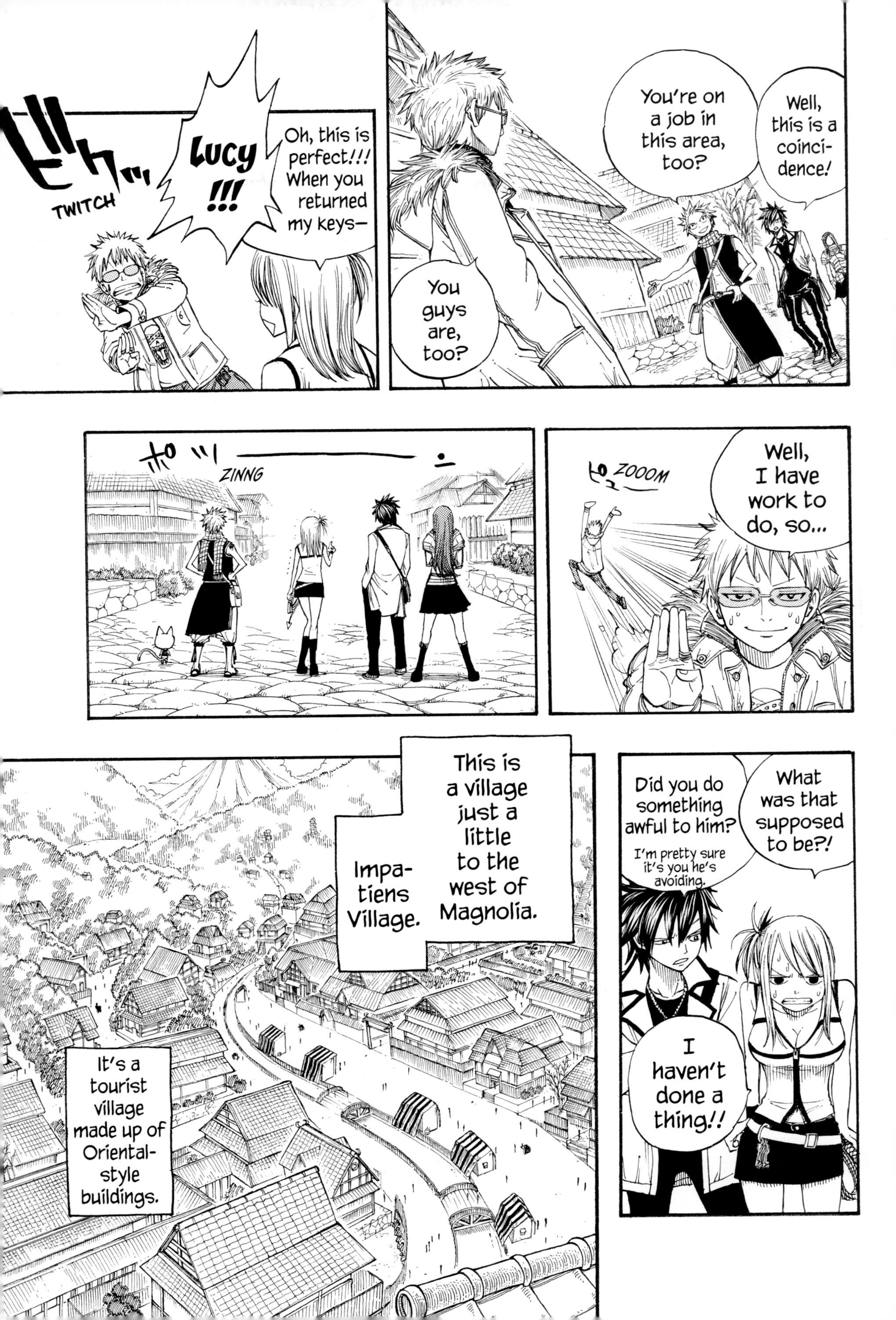
Well, this is a coinci-dence!
You're on a job in this area, too?
You guys are, too?
Oh, this is perfect!!! When you returned my keys—
Lucy!!!
TWITCH
ZOOOM
Well, I have work to do, so...
ZINNG
What was that supposed to be?!
Did you do something awful to him?
I'm pretty sure it's you he's avoiding.
I haven't done a thing!!
This is a village just a little to the west of Magnolia.
Impa-tiens Village.
It's a tourist village made up of Oriental-style buildings.

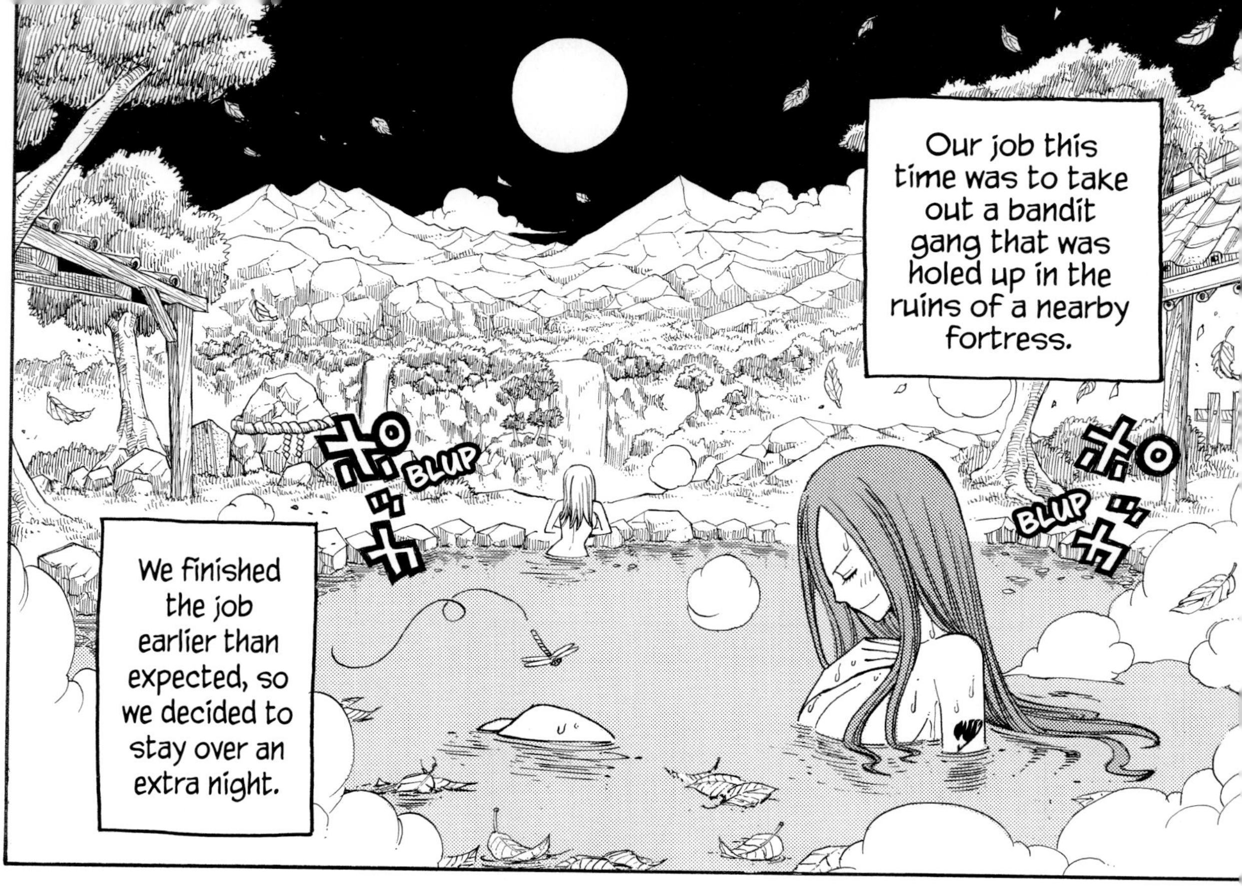
Our job this time was to take out a bandit gang that was holed up in the ruins of a nearby fortress.
BLUP
BLUP
We finished the job earlier than expected, so we decided to stay over an extra night.

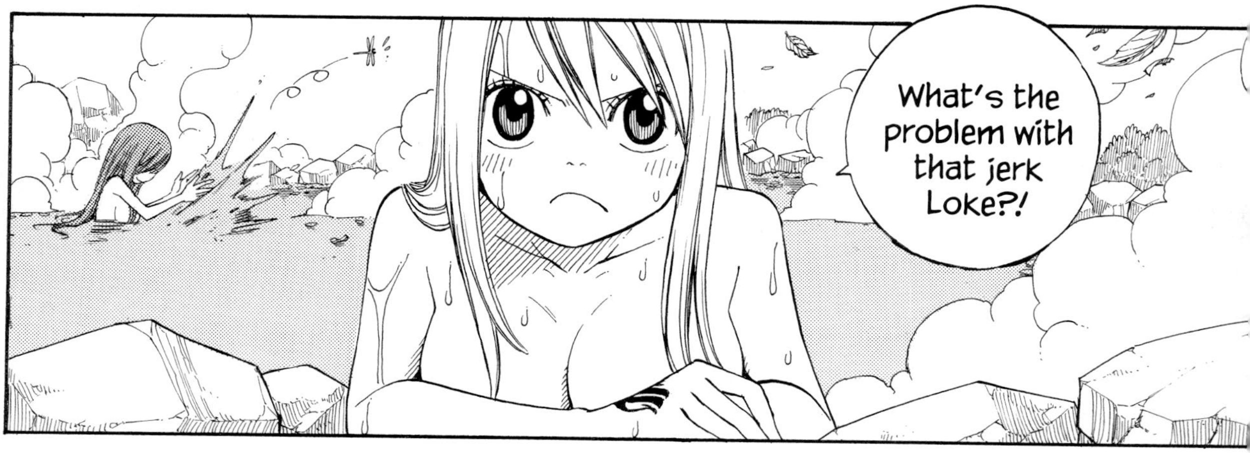
What's the problem with that jerk Loke?!

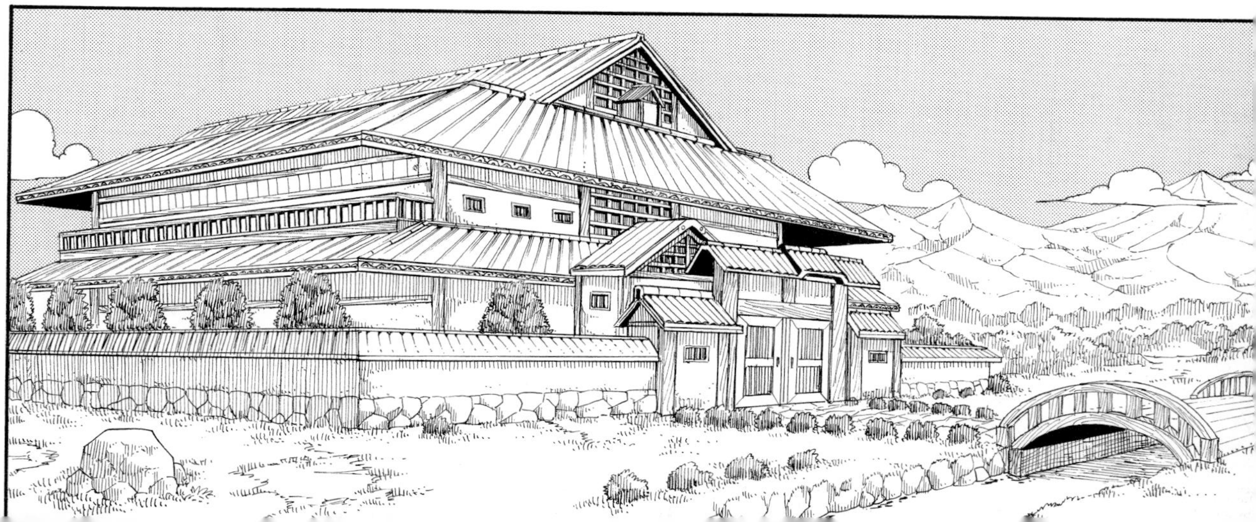

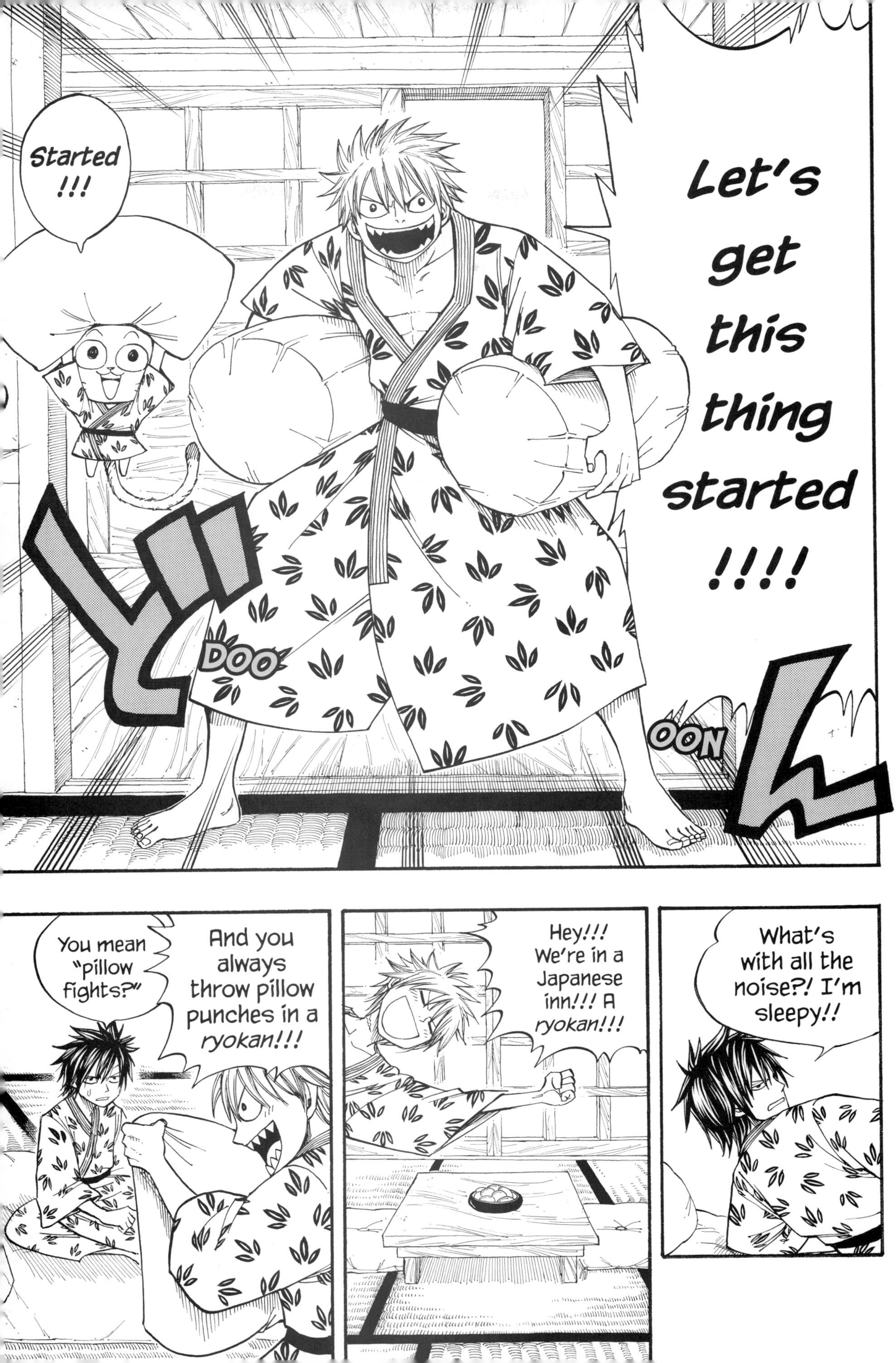
Let's get this thing started!!!!
Started!!!
DOO
OON
What's with all the noise?! I'm sleepy!!
Hey!!! We're in a Japanese inn!!! A ryokan!!!
And you always throw pillow punches in a ryokan!!!
You mean "pillow fights?"

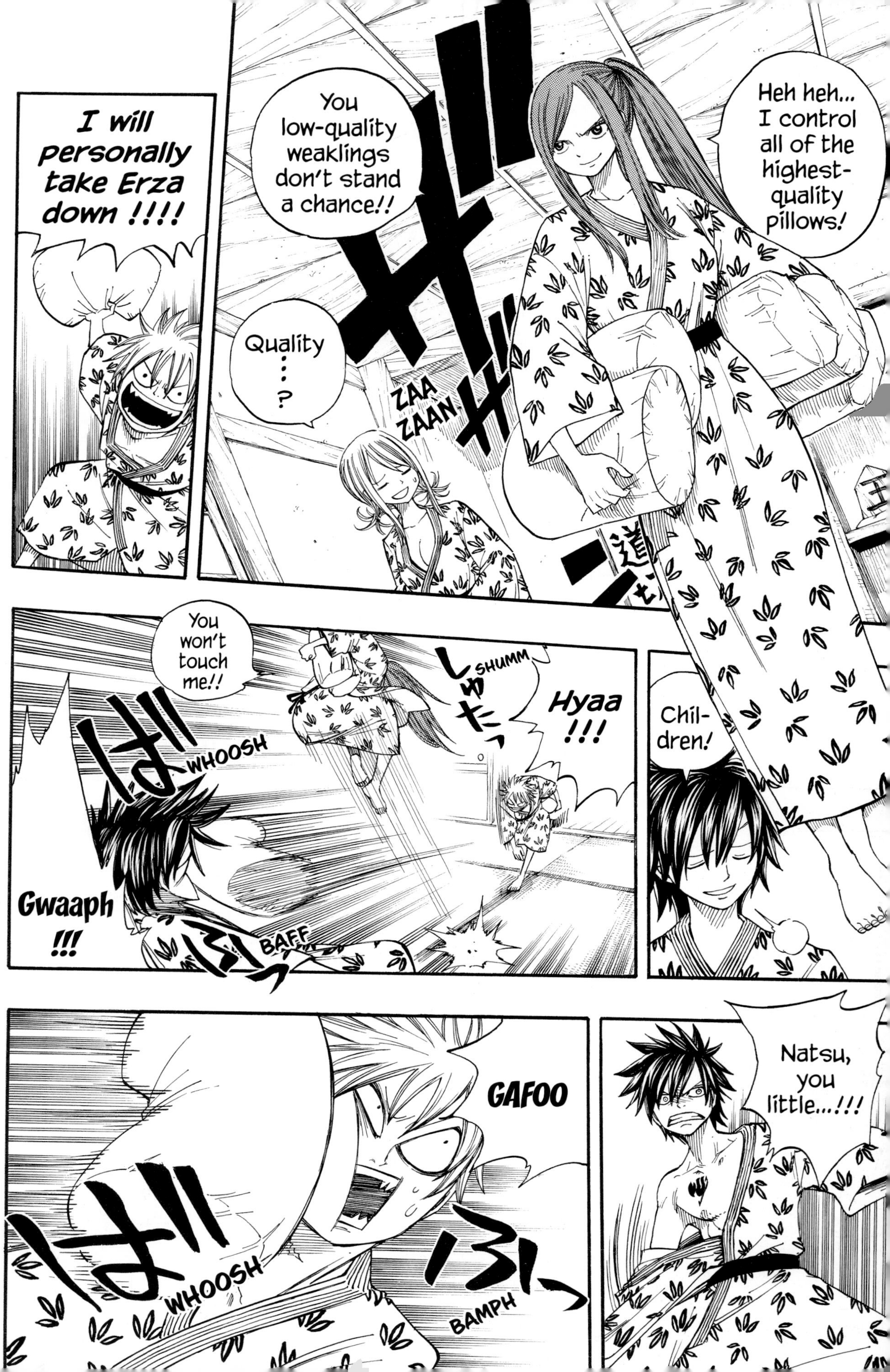
Heh heh... I control all of the highest-quality pillows!
You low-quality weaklings don't stand a chance!!
ZAA ZAAN
Quality...?
I will personally take Erza down!!!!
Children!
Hyaa!!!
SHUMM
You won't touch me!!
WHOOSH
Gwaaph!!!
BAFF
Natsu, you little...!!!
GAFOO
WHOOSH
BAMPH

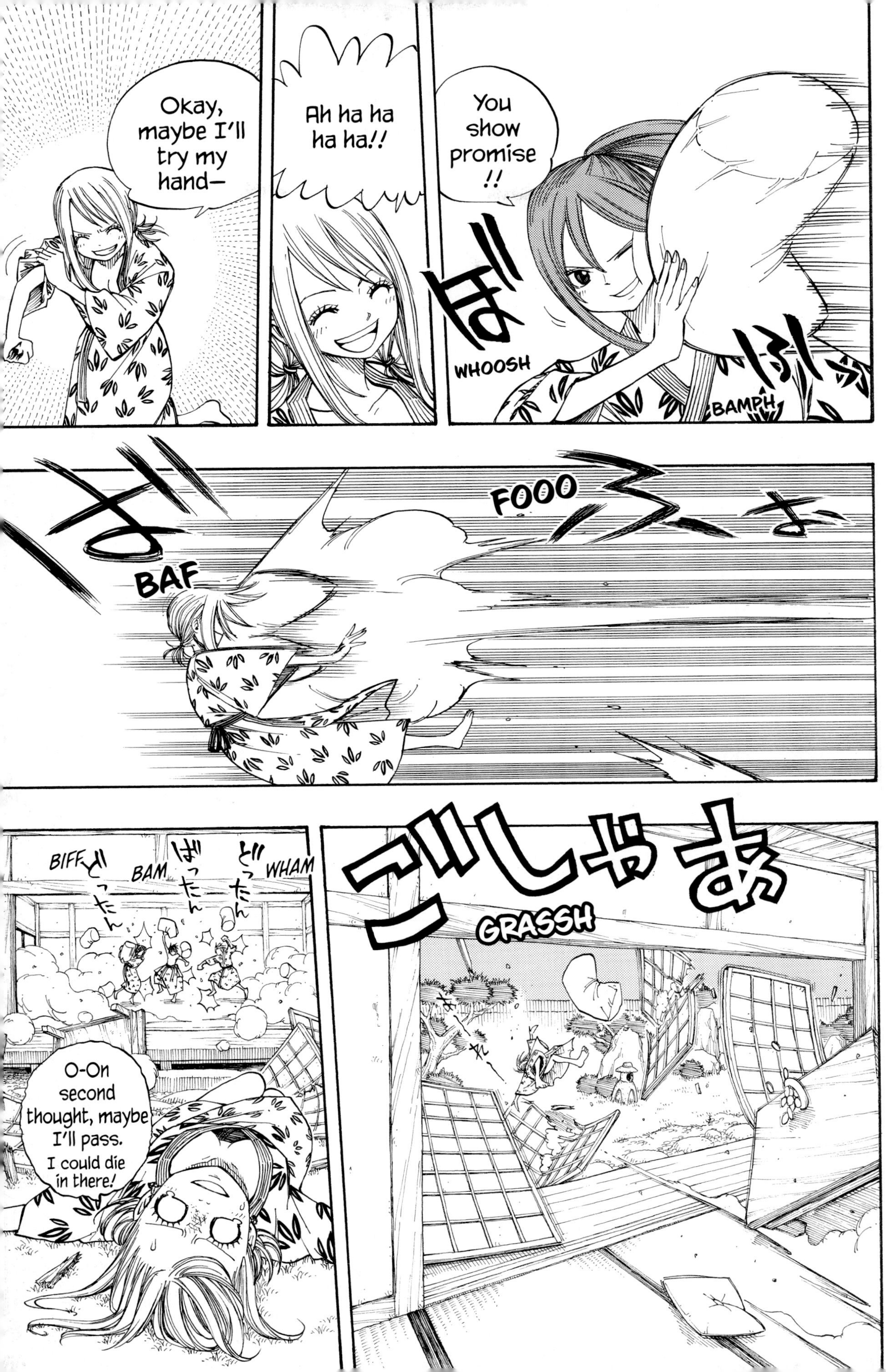
You show promise!!
WHOOSH
BAMPH
Ah ha ha ha ha!!
Okay, maybe I'll try my hand–
FOOO
BAF
ごしゃあ
GRASSH
WHAM
どったん
BAM
ばったん
BIFF
どったん
O-On second thought, maybe I'll pass. I could die in there!

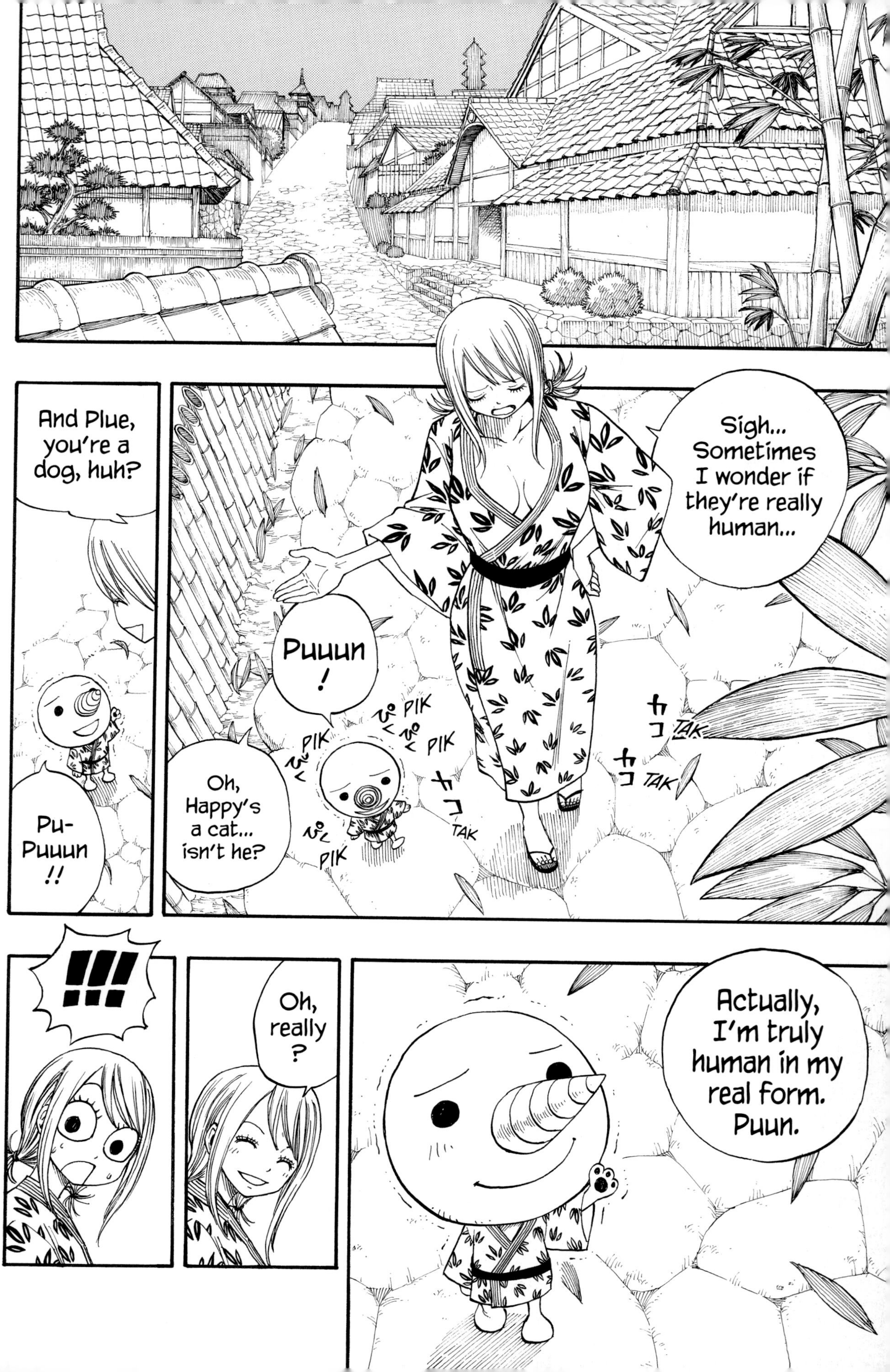
Sigh... Sometimes I wonder if they're really human...
TAK TAK
TAK
Puuun!
PIK PIK PIK PIK
Oh, Happy's a cat... isn't he?
And Plue, you're a dog, huh?
Pu-Puuun!!
Actually, I'm truly human in my real form. Puun.
Oh, really?
!!!

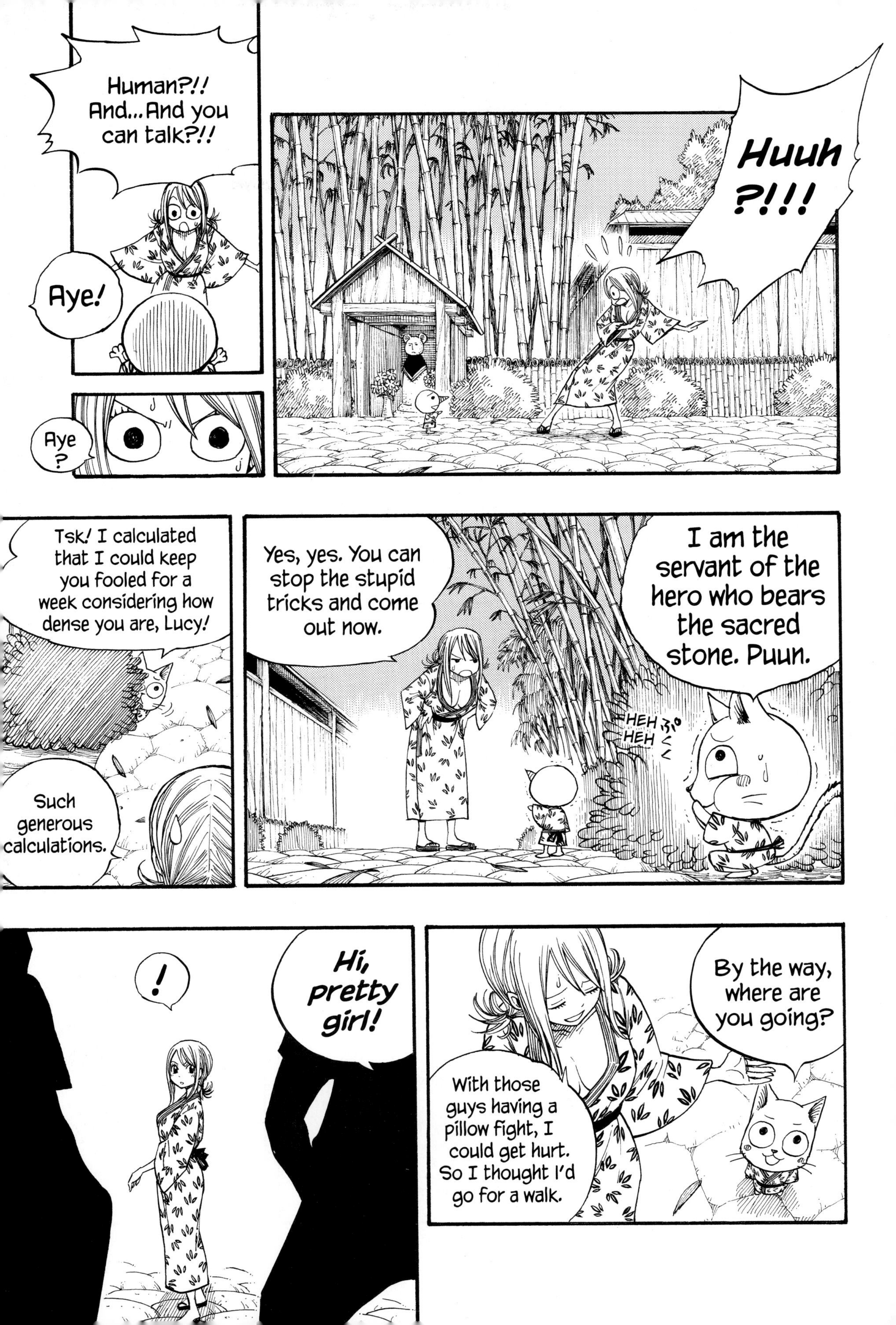
Huuh ?!!!
Human?!! And...And you can talk?!!
Aye!
Aye ?
I am the servant of the hero who bears the sacred stone. Puun.
HEH HEH
Yes, yes. You can stop the stupid tricks and come out now.
Tsk! I calculated that I could keep you fooled for a week considering how dense you are, Lucy!
Such generous calculations.
By the way, where are you going?
With those guys having a pillow fight, I could get hurt. So I thought I'd go for a walk.
Hi, pretty girl!
!

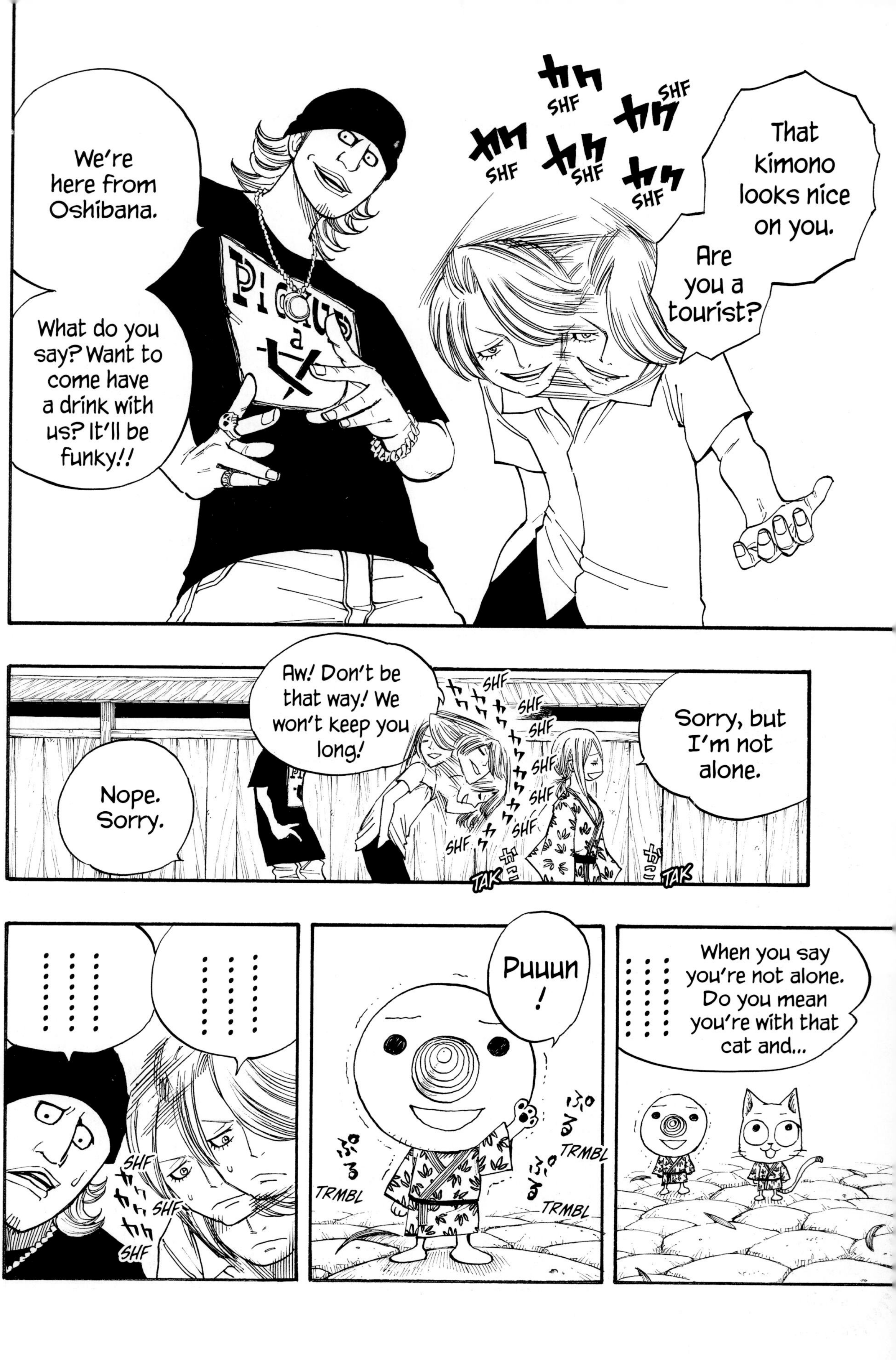
SHF
That kimono looks nice on you.
Are you a tourist?
We're here from Oshibana.
What do you say? Want to come have a drink with us? It'll be funky!!
Sorry, but I'm not alone.
SHF
Aw! Don't be that way! We won't keep you long!
TAK
Nope. Sorry.
......
When you say you're not alone. Do you mean you're with that cat and...
Puuun!
TRMBL
......
......
SHF

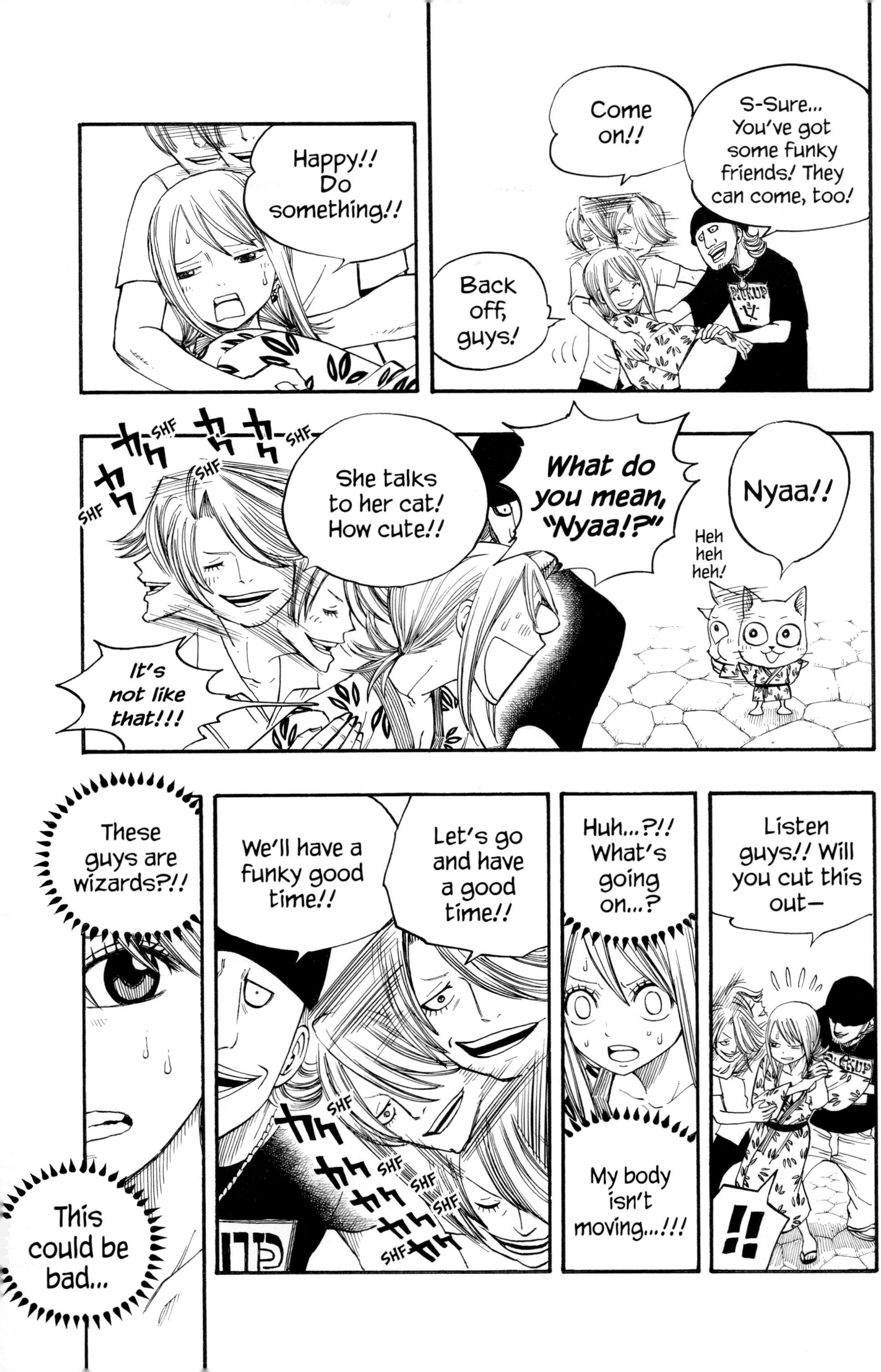
S-Sure... You've got some funky friends! They can come, too!
Come on!!
Back off, guys!
Happy!! Do something!!
Nyaa!!
Heh heh heh!
What do you mean, "Nyaa!?"
She talks to her cat! How cute!!
SHF
SHF
SHF
SHF
It's not like that!!!
Listen guys!! Will you cut this out—
!!
Huh...?!! What's going on...?
My body isn't moving...!!!
Let's go and have a good time!!
We'll have a funky good time!!
SHF
SHF
SHF
SHF
SHF
These guys are wizards?!!
This could be bad...

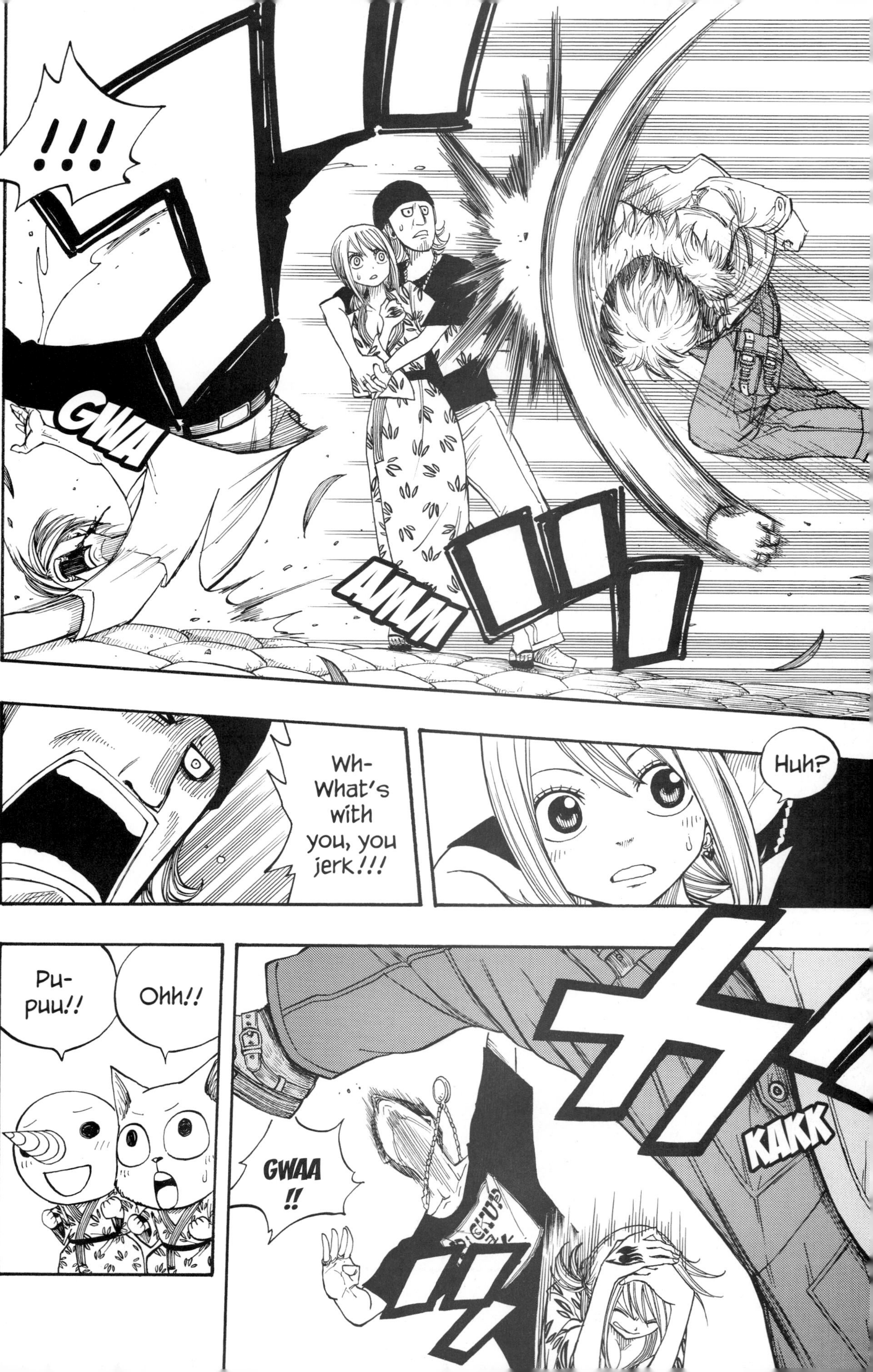
!!!
GWA
AWW
Huh?
Wh- What's with you, you jerk!!!
KAKK
GWAA !!
Ohh!!
Pu-puu!!

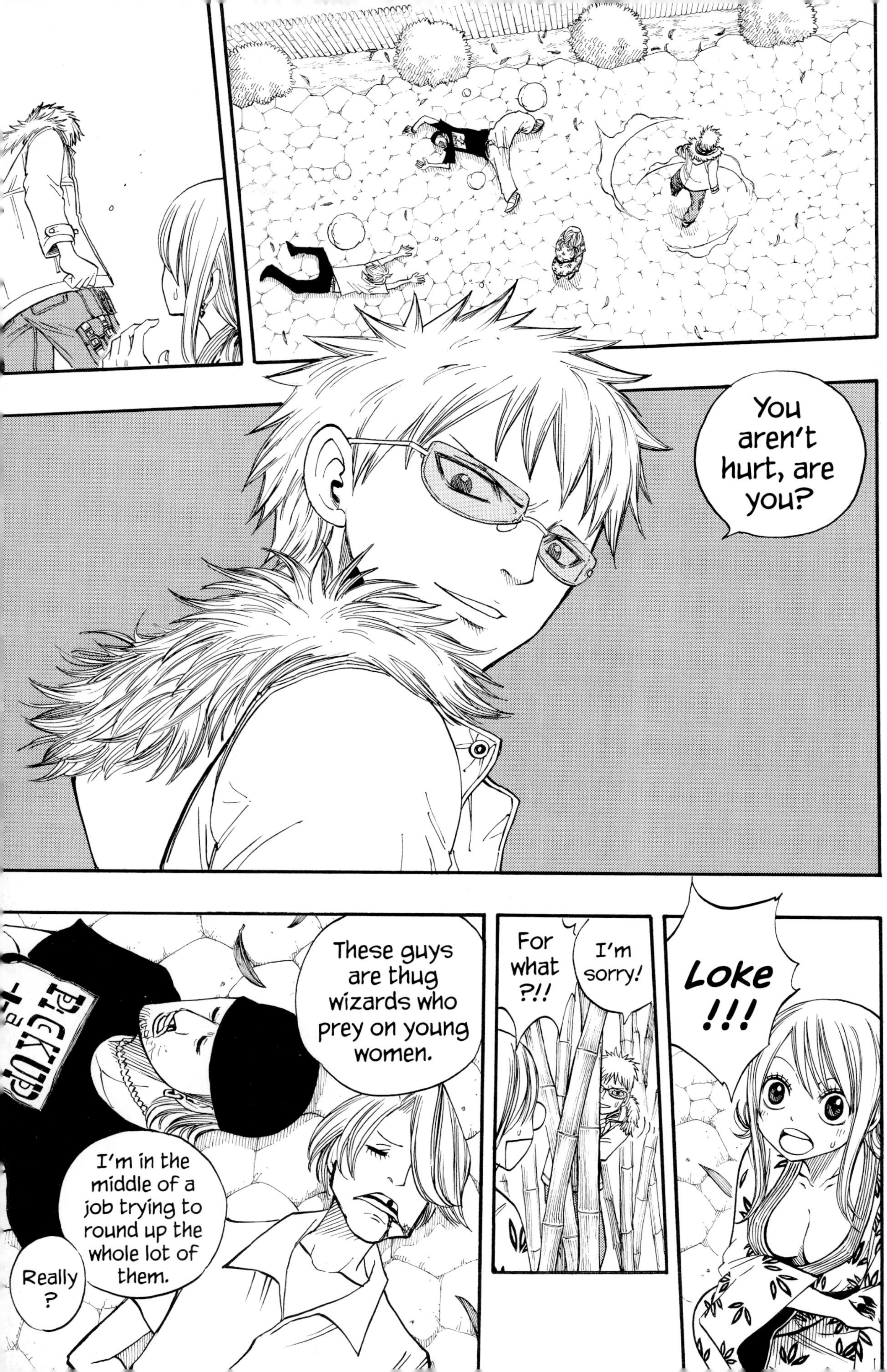
You aren't hurt, are you?
Loke!!!
I'm sorry!
For what?!!
These guys are thug wizards who prey on young women.
I'm in the middle of a job trying to round up the whole lot of them.
Really?

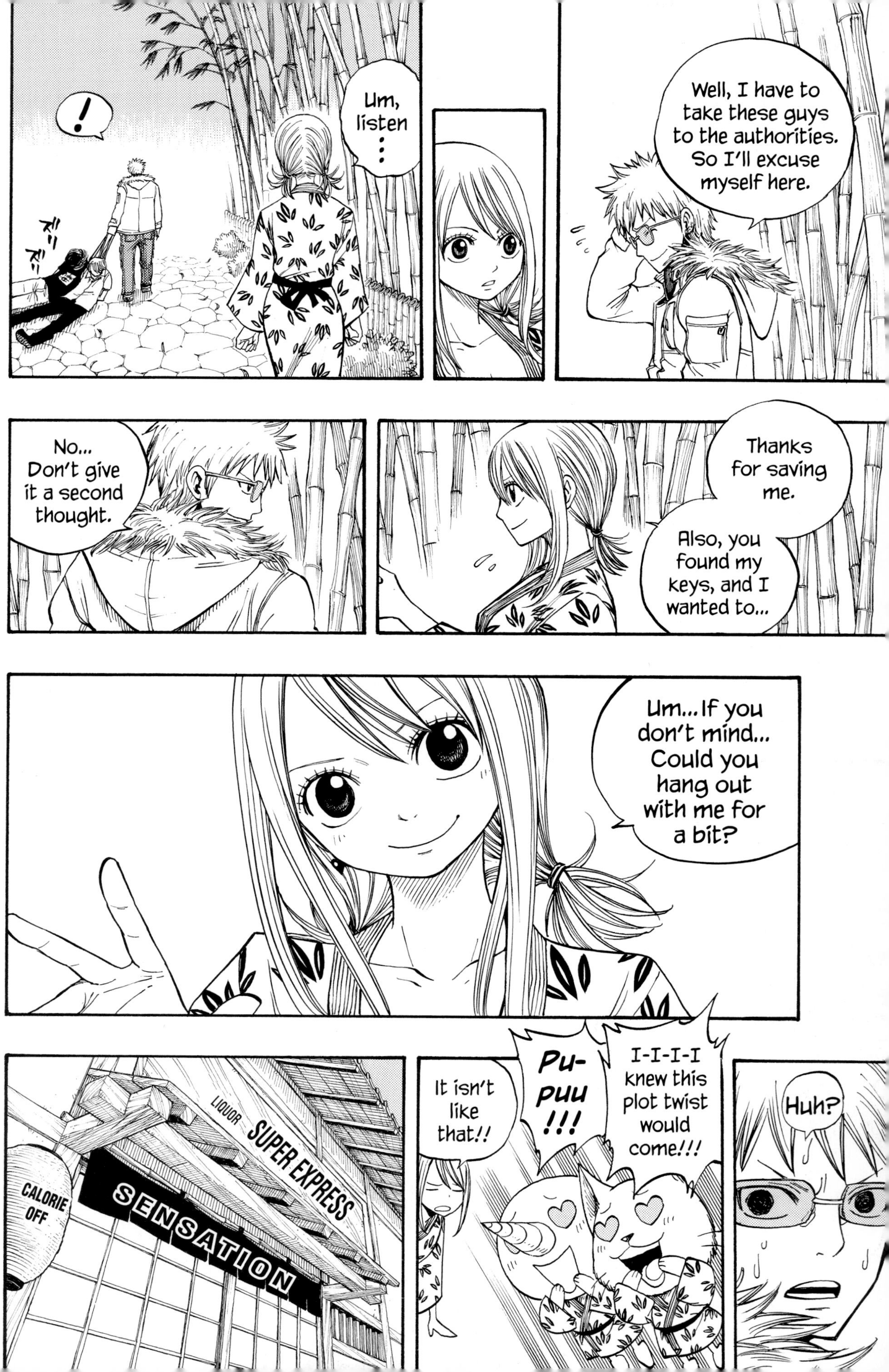
Well, I have to take these guys to the authorities. So I'll excuse myself here.
Um, listen...
!
Thanks for saving me.
Also, you found my keys, and I wanted to...
No... Don't give it a second thought.
Um...If you don't mind... Could you hang out with me for a bit?
Huh?
I-I-I-I knew this plot twist would come!!!
Pu-puu!!!
It isn't like that!!
LIQUOR
SUPER EXPRESS
SENSATION
CALORIE OFF

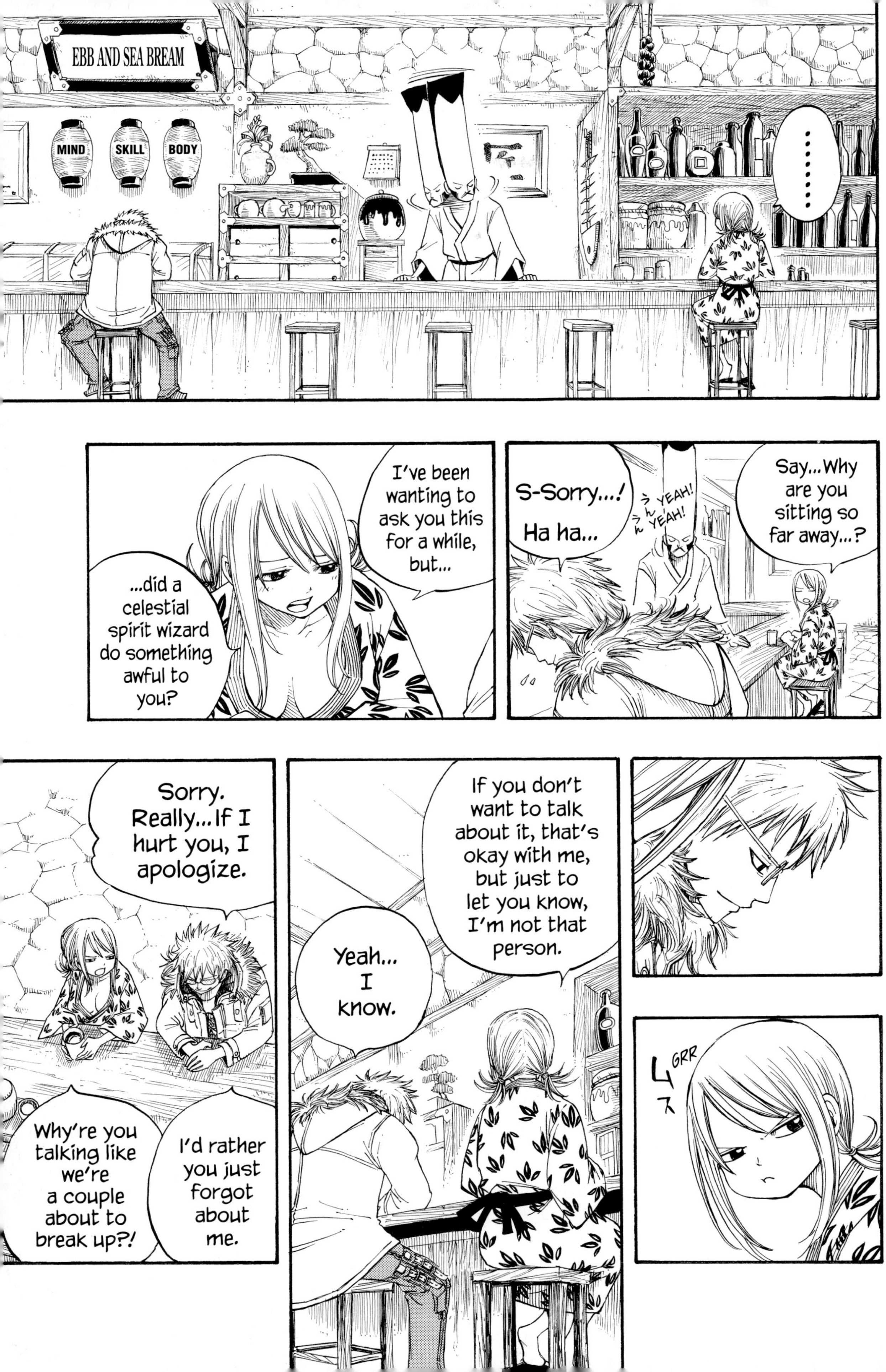
EBB AND SEA BREAM
MIND
SKILL
BODY
......
Say...Why are you sitting so far away...?
S-Sorry...! Ha ha...
YEAH! YEAH!
I've been wanting to ask you this for a while, but...
...did a celestial spirit wizard do something awful to you?
GRR
If you don't want to talk about it, that's okay with me, but just to let you know, I'm not that person.
Yeah... I know.
Sorry. Really...If I hurt you, I apologize.
I'd rather you just forgot about me.
Why're you talking like we're a couple about to break up?!

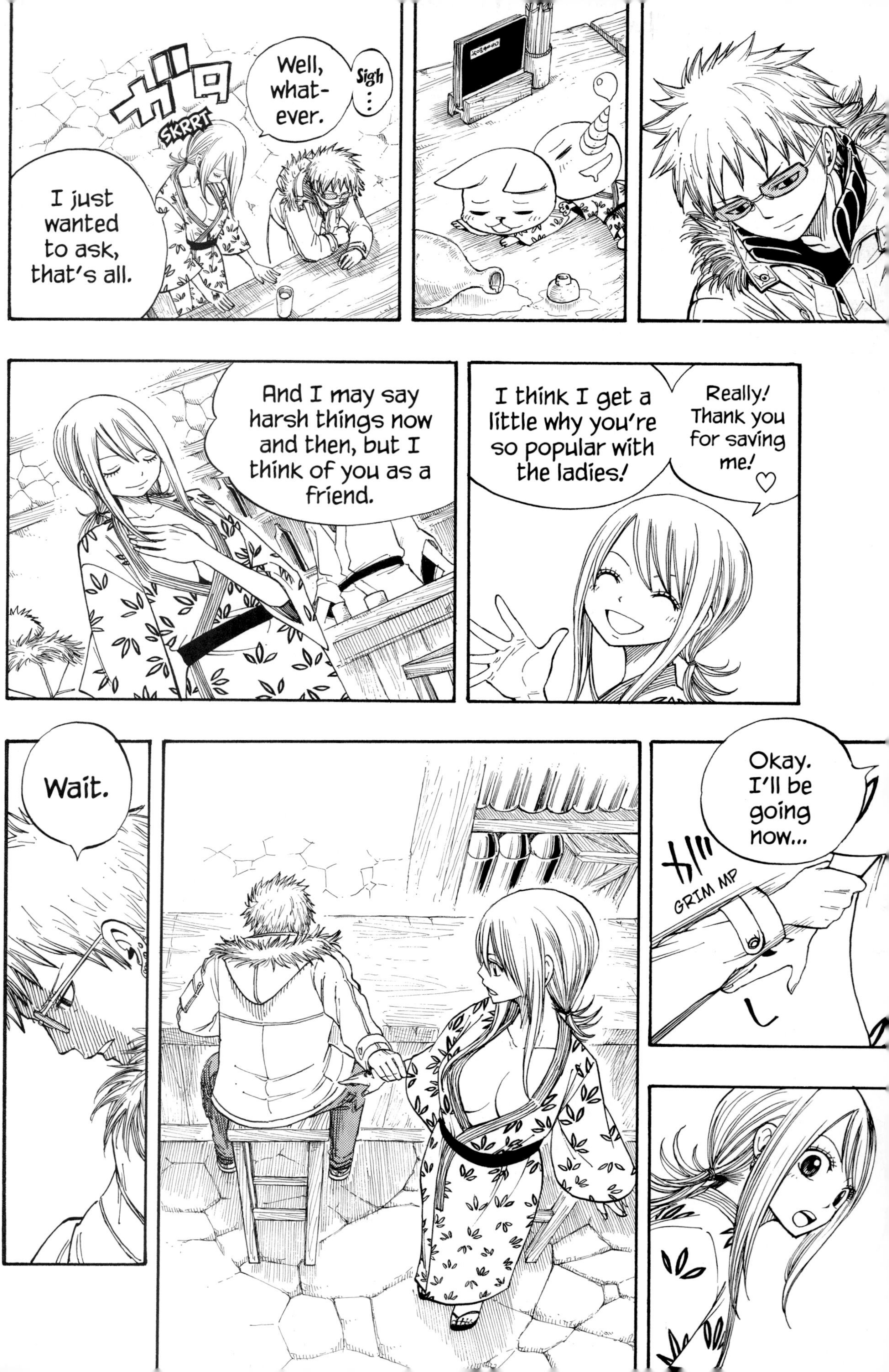
Sigh...
Well, whatever.
SKRRT
I just wanted to ask, that's all.
Really! Thank you for saving me! ♡
I think I get a little why you're so popular with the ladies!
And I may say harsh things now and then, but I think of you as a friend.
Okay. I'll be going now...
GRIM MP
Wait.

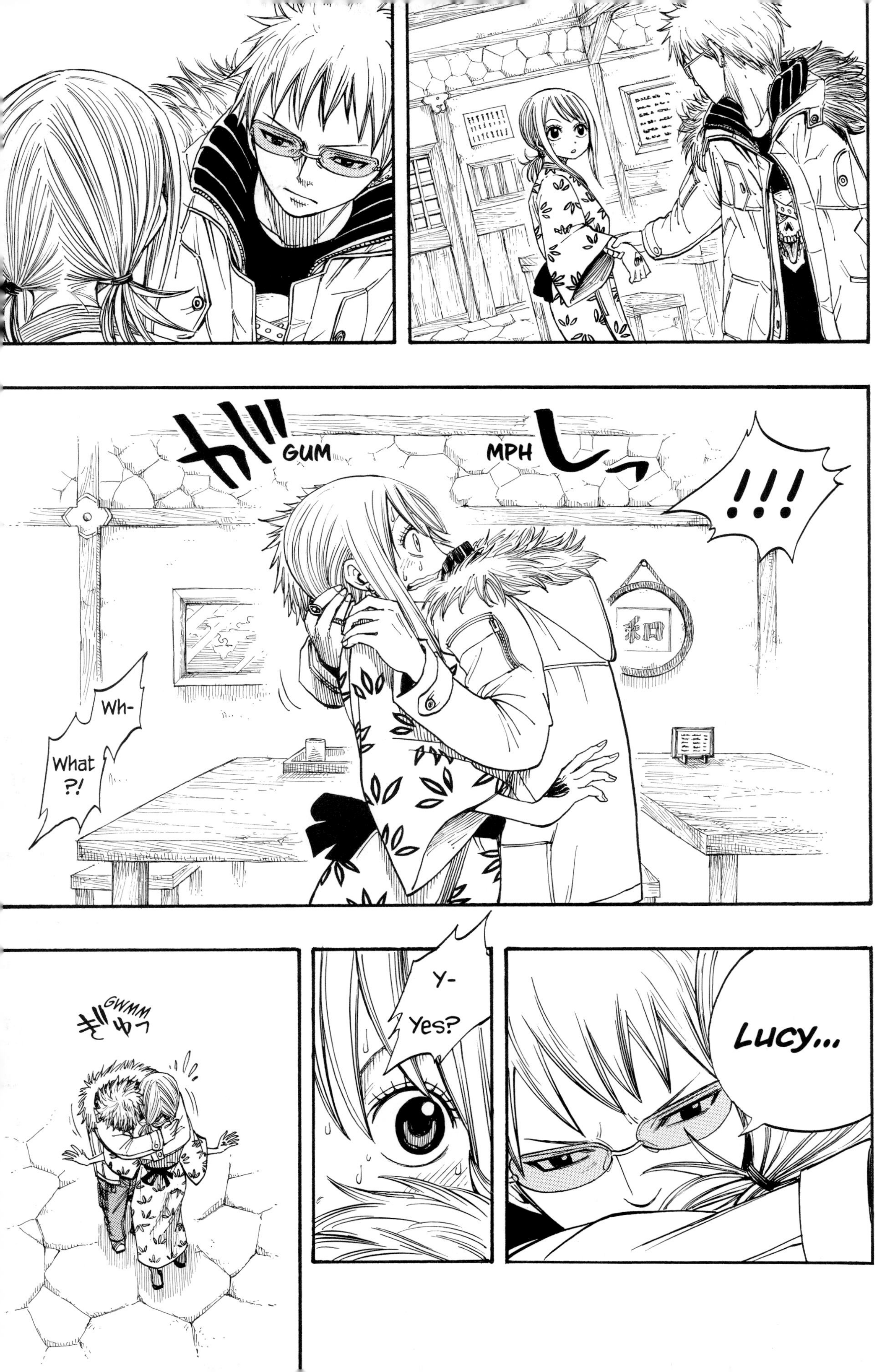

MPH しっ
!!!
ガバ GUM
Wh-
What ?!
Lucy...
Y- Yes?
ぎゅっ GWMM

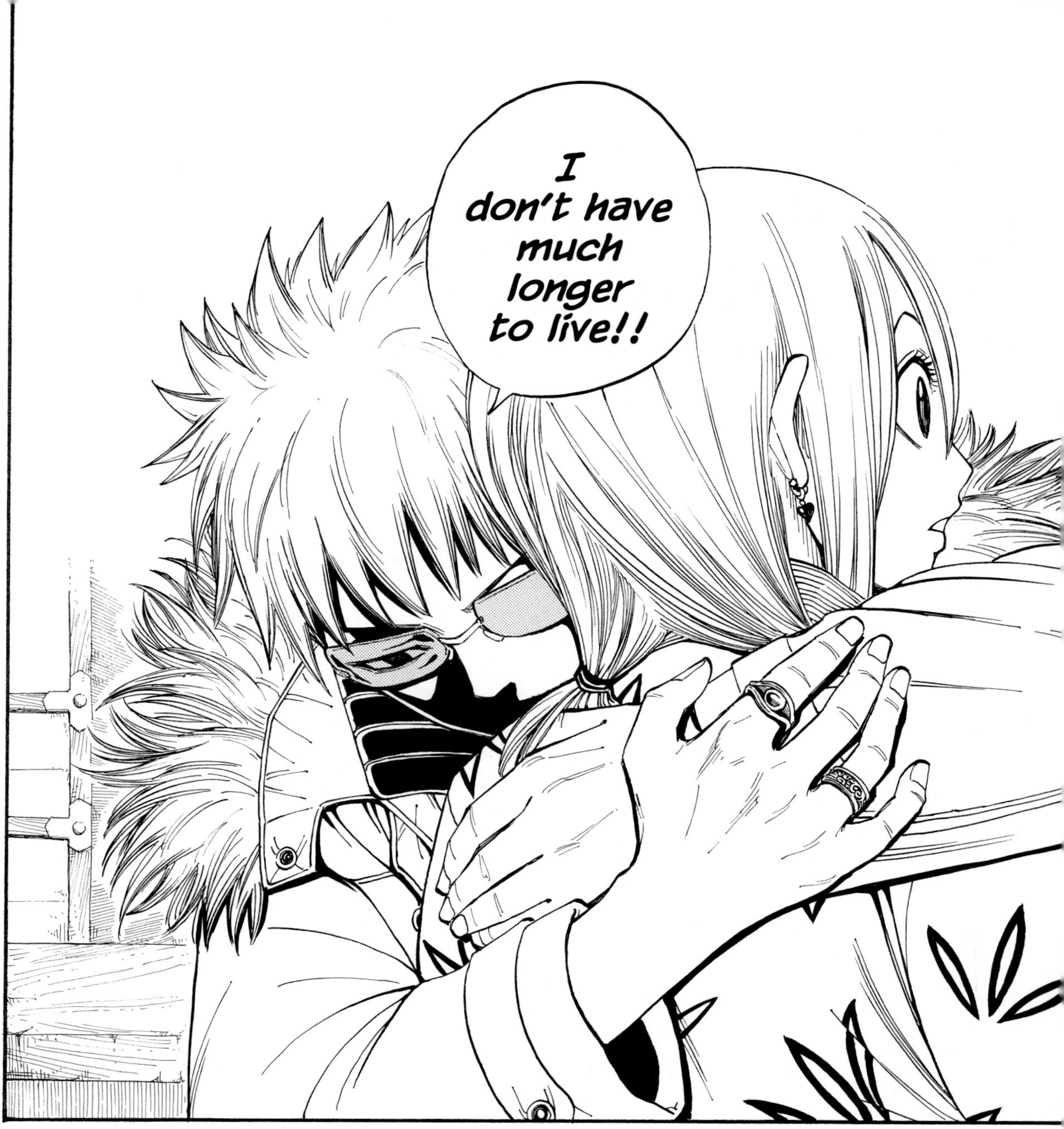
I don't have much longer to live!!
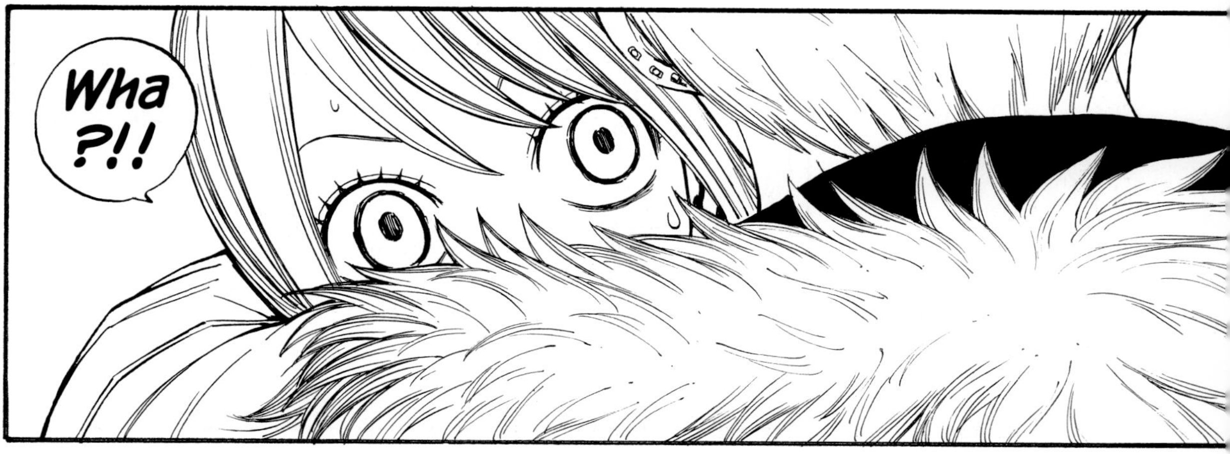
Wha ?!!

Chapter 72: The Star That Will Never Return to the Sky

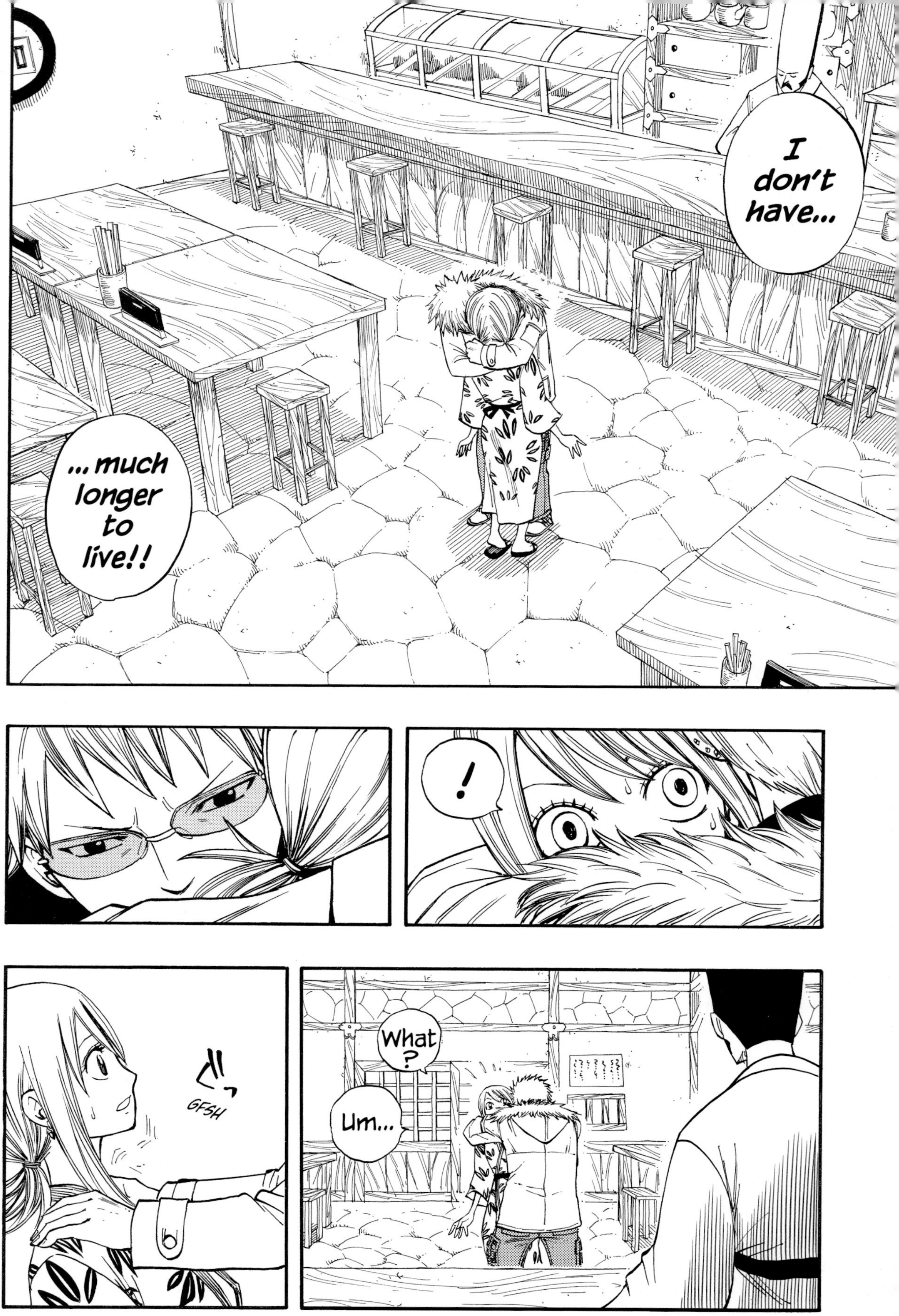
I don't have...
...much longer to live!!
!
What?
Um...
GFSH

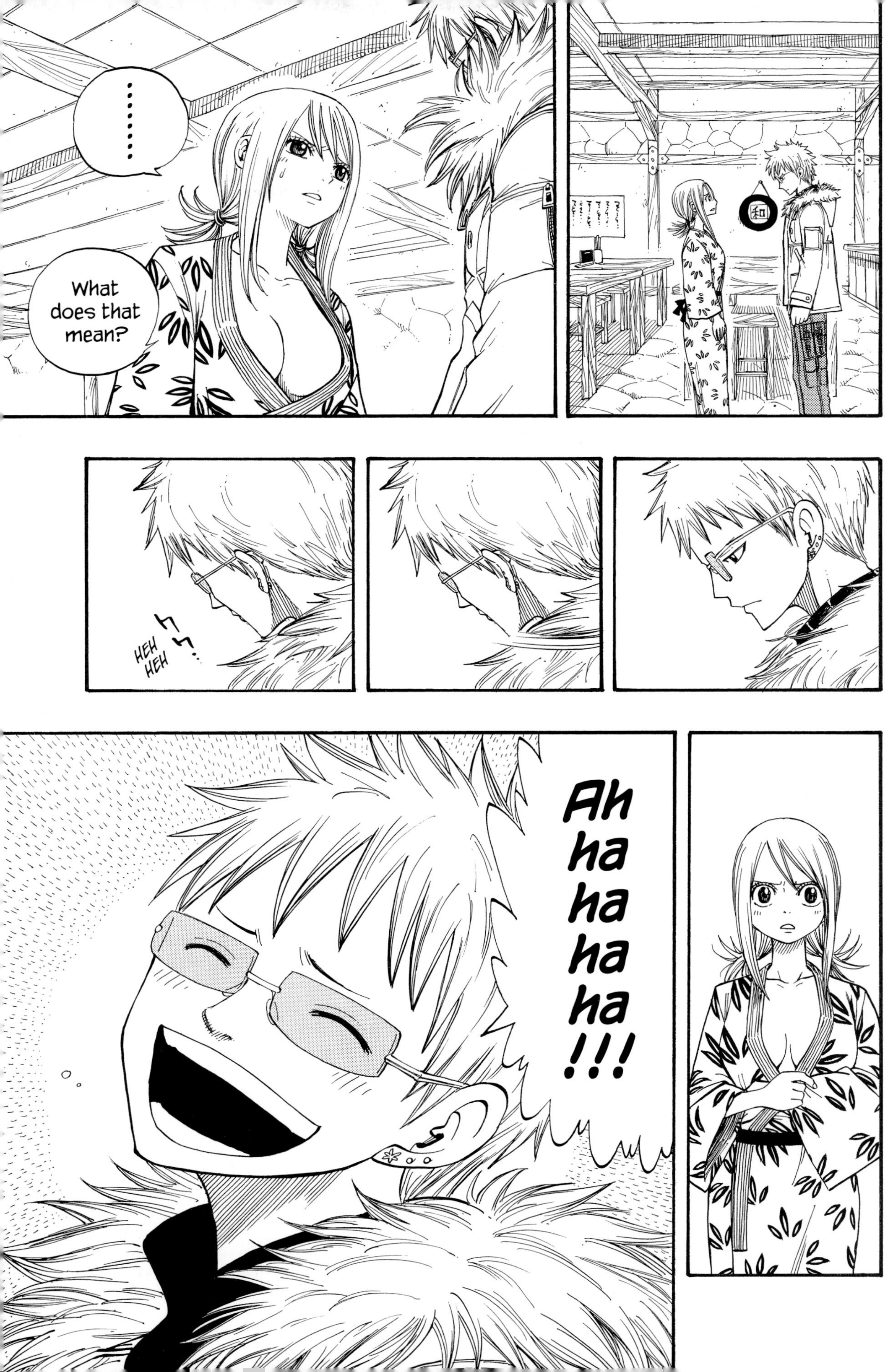
......
What does that mean?
HEH HEH
Ah ha ha ha ha ha!!!

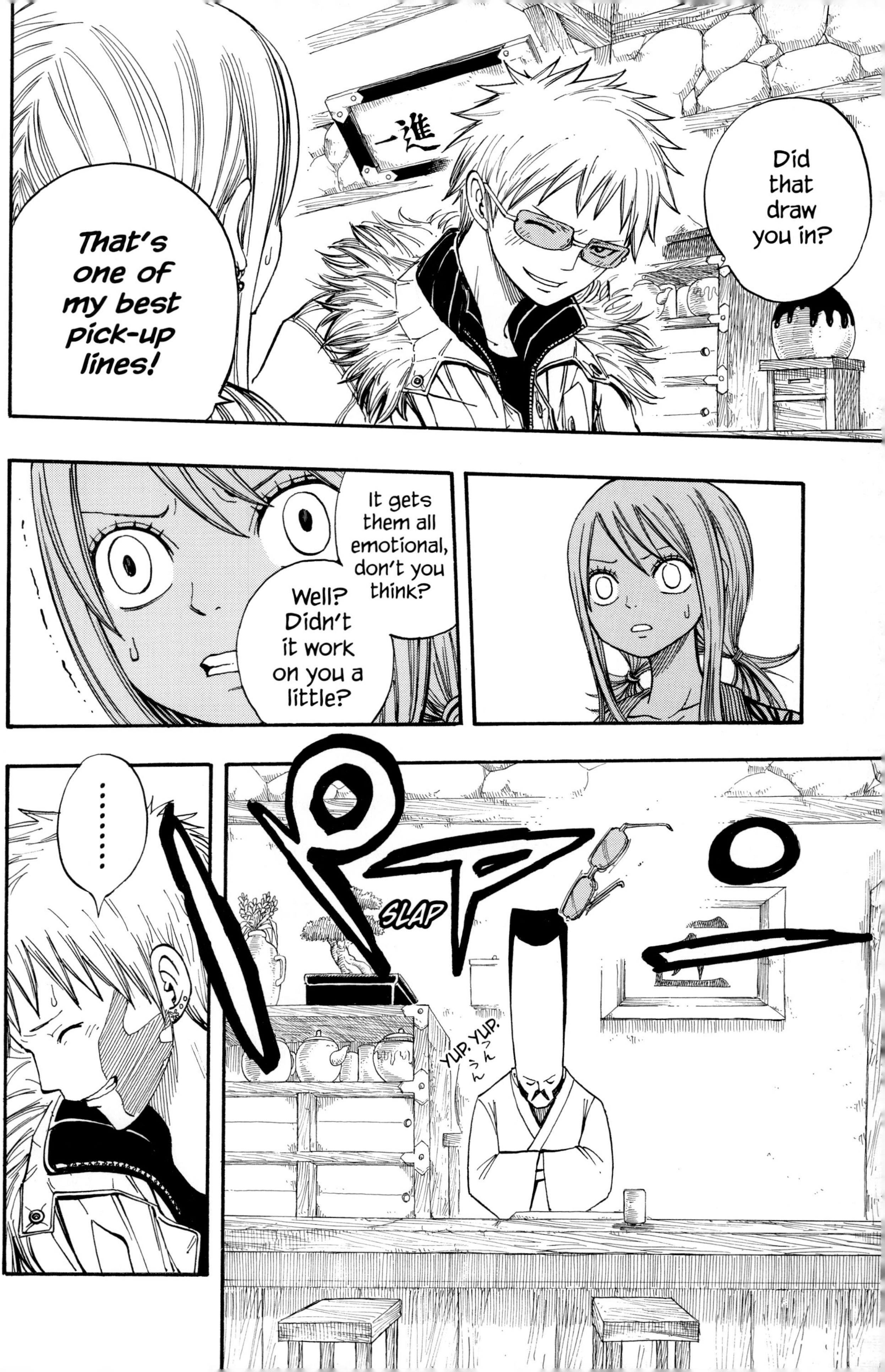
一進
Did that draw you in?
That's one of my best pick-up lines!
It gets them all emotional, don't you think?
Well? Didn't it work on you a little?
SLAP
YUP. YUP.
うん うん
......

...I really hate jokes like that!!!

I really...

Come on, Happy!! Plue!! We're going!!!

AGNAA!!

PU-PUU!!

STMP STMP STMP STMP

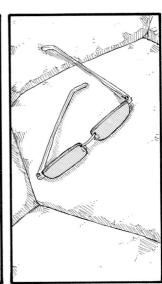

SLAM

Puuun?

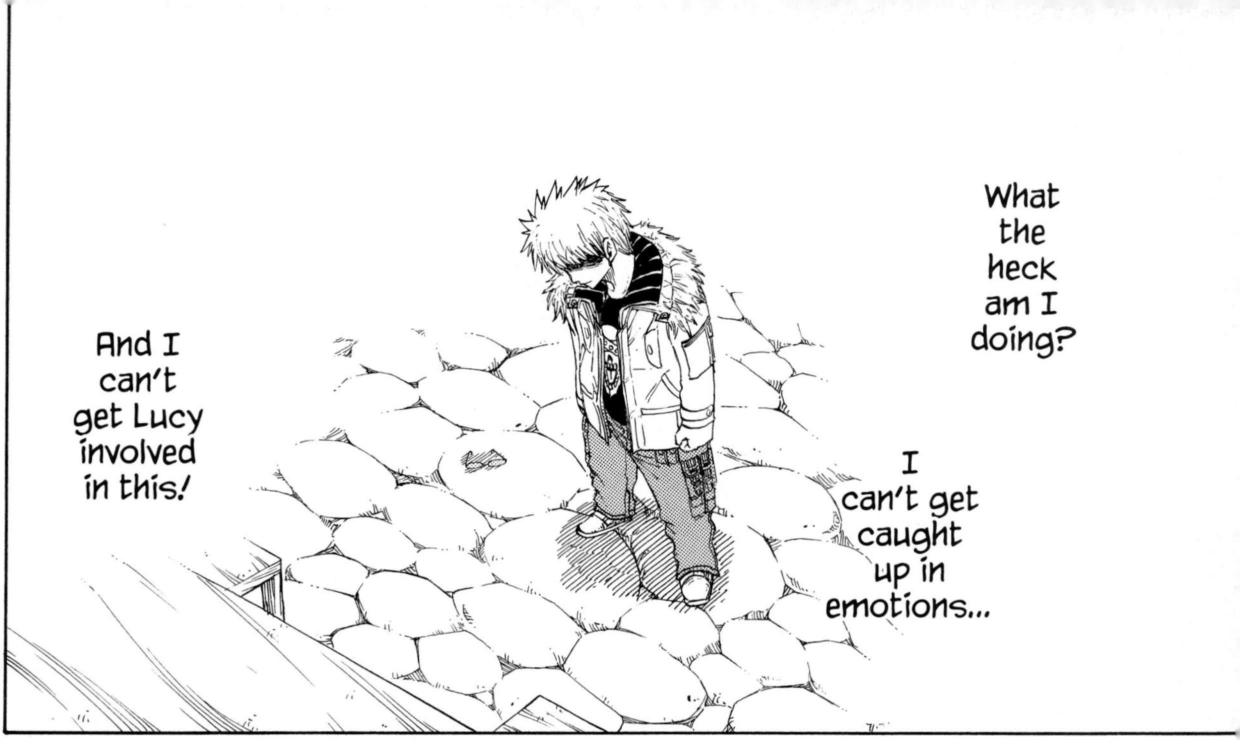
What the heck am I doing?
I can't get caught up in emotions...
And I can't get Lucy involved in this!

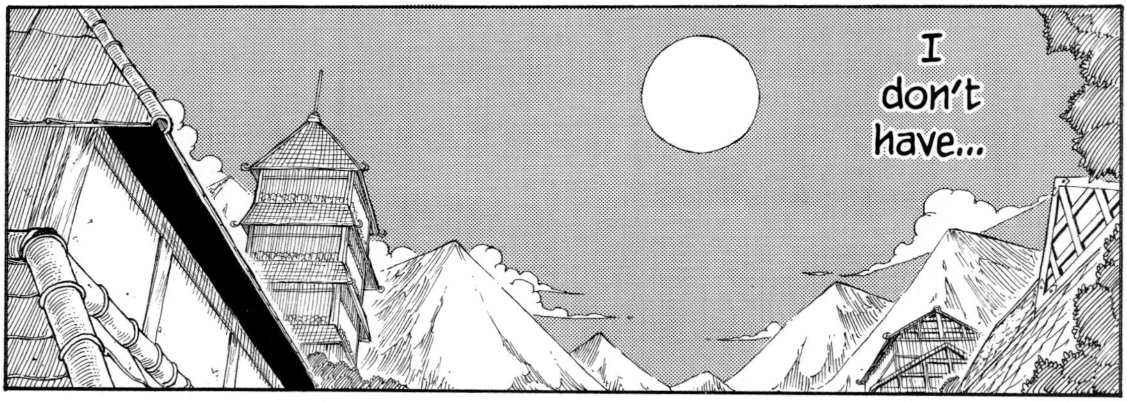
I don't have...

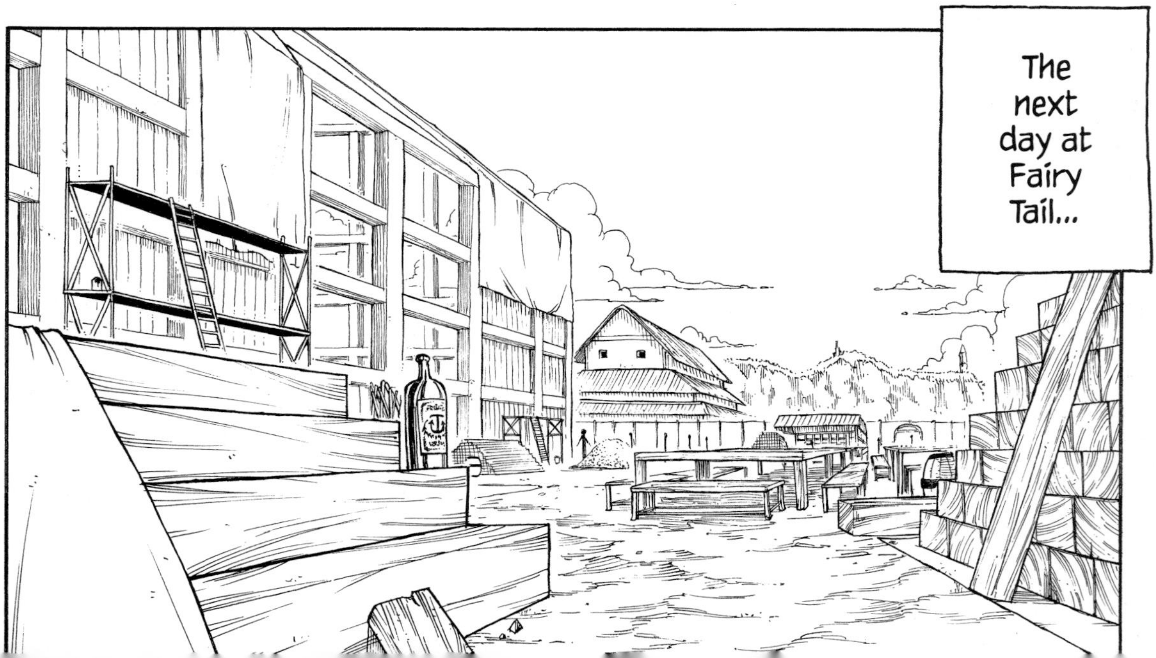
The next day at Fairy Tail...

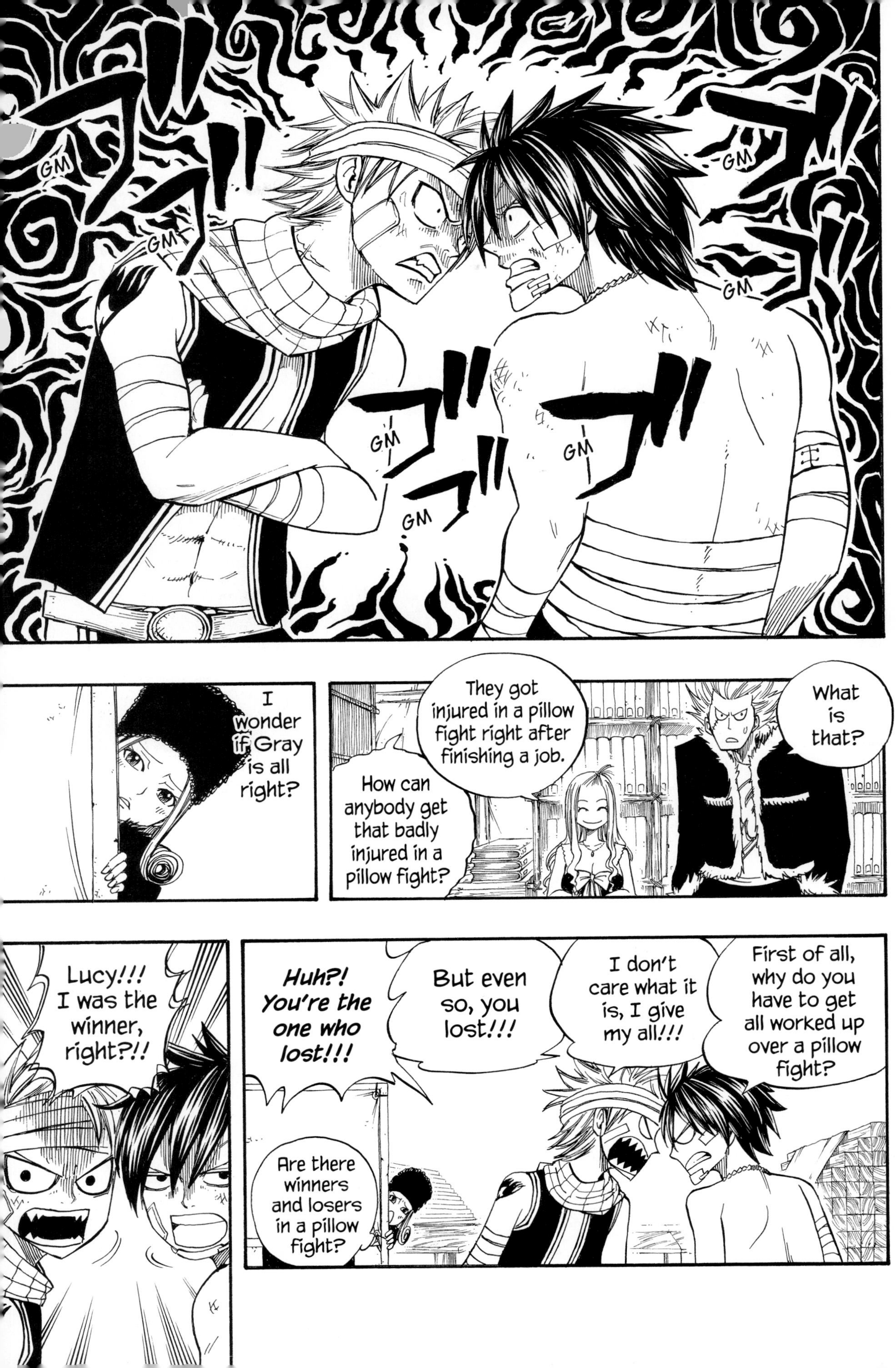
GM
GM
GM
GM
GM
GM
GM
What is that?
They got injured in a pillow fight right after finishing a job.
How can anybody get that badly injured in a pillow fight?
I wonder if Gray is all right?
First of all, why do you have to get all worked up over a pillow fight?
I don't care what it is, I give my all!!!
But even so, you lost!!!
Huh?! You're the one who lost!!!
Are there winners and losers in a pillow fight?
Lucy!!! I was the winner, right?!!

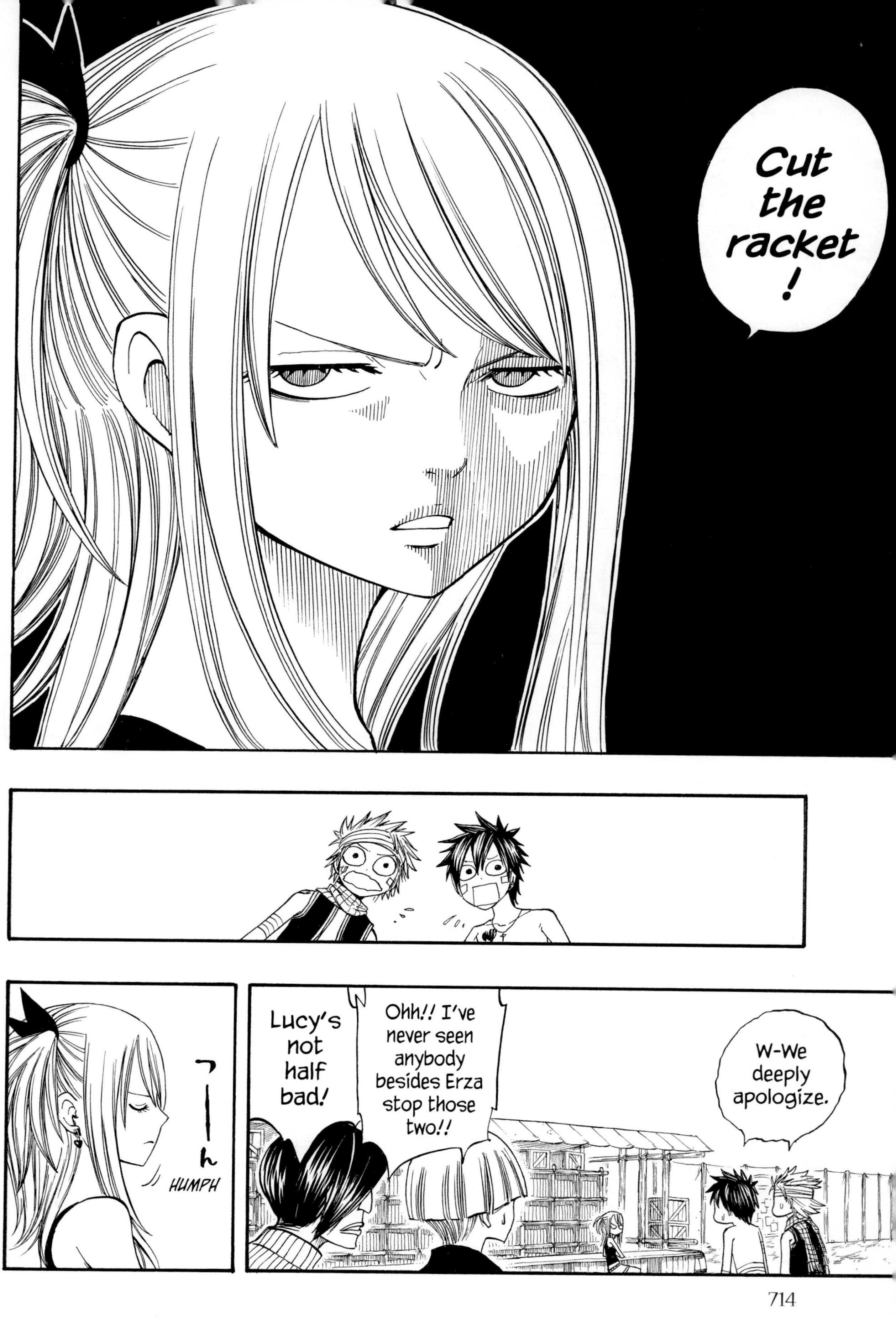
Cut the racket!
W-We deeply apologize.
Ohh!! I've never seen anybody besides Erza stop those two!!
Lucy's not half bad!
HUMPH

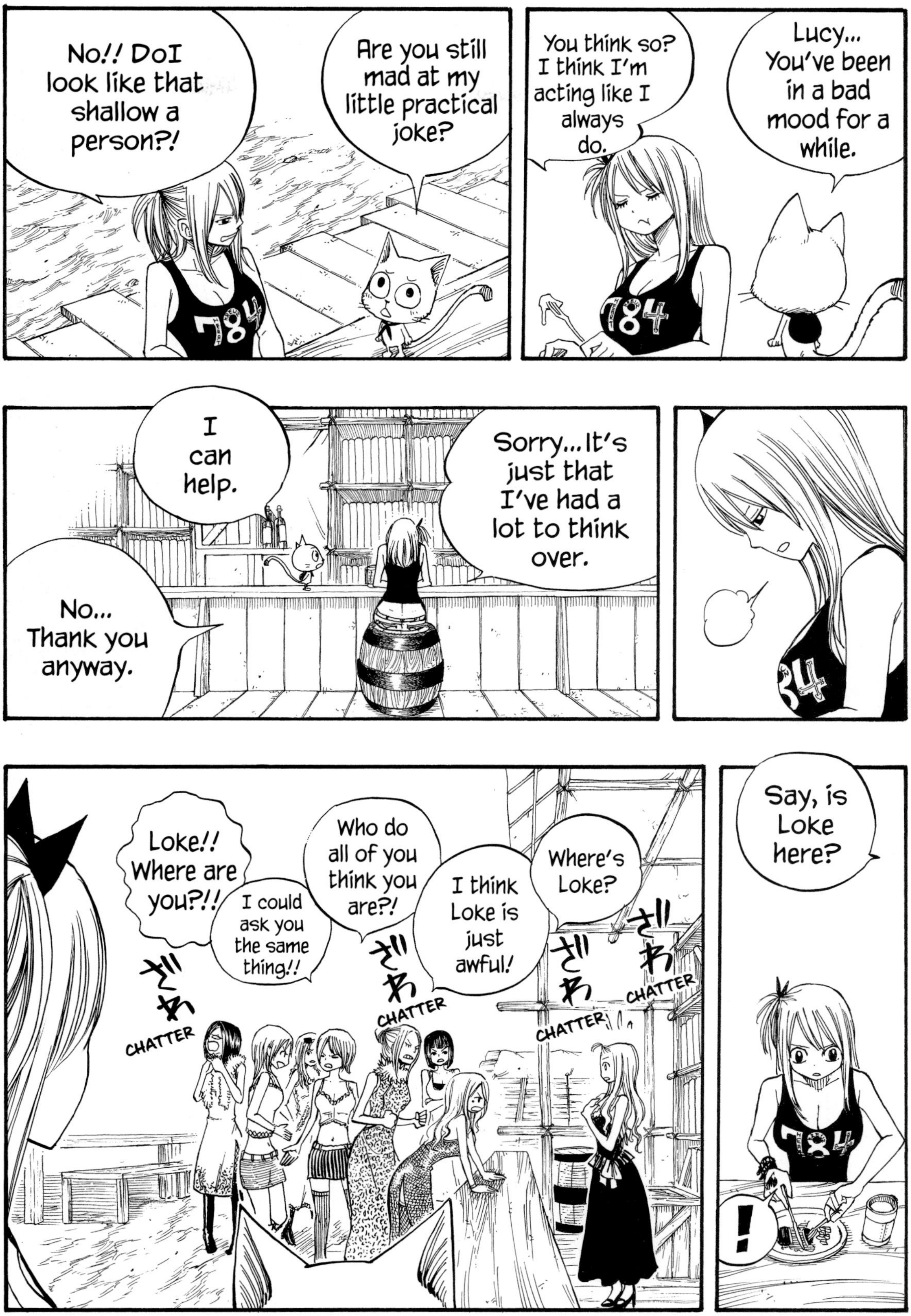
Lucy... You've been in a bad mood for a while.
You think so? I think I'm acting like I always do.
Are you still mad at my little practical joke?
No!! Do I look like that shallow a person?!
Sorry...It's just that I've had a lot to think over.
I can help.
No... Thank you anyway.
Say, is Loke here?
!
ざわ
CHATTER
ざわ
CHATTER
Where's Loke?
I think Loke is just awful!
ざわ
CHATTER
Who do all of you think you are?!
I could ask you the same thing!!
Loke!! Where are you?!!
ざわ
CHATTER

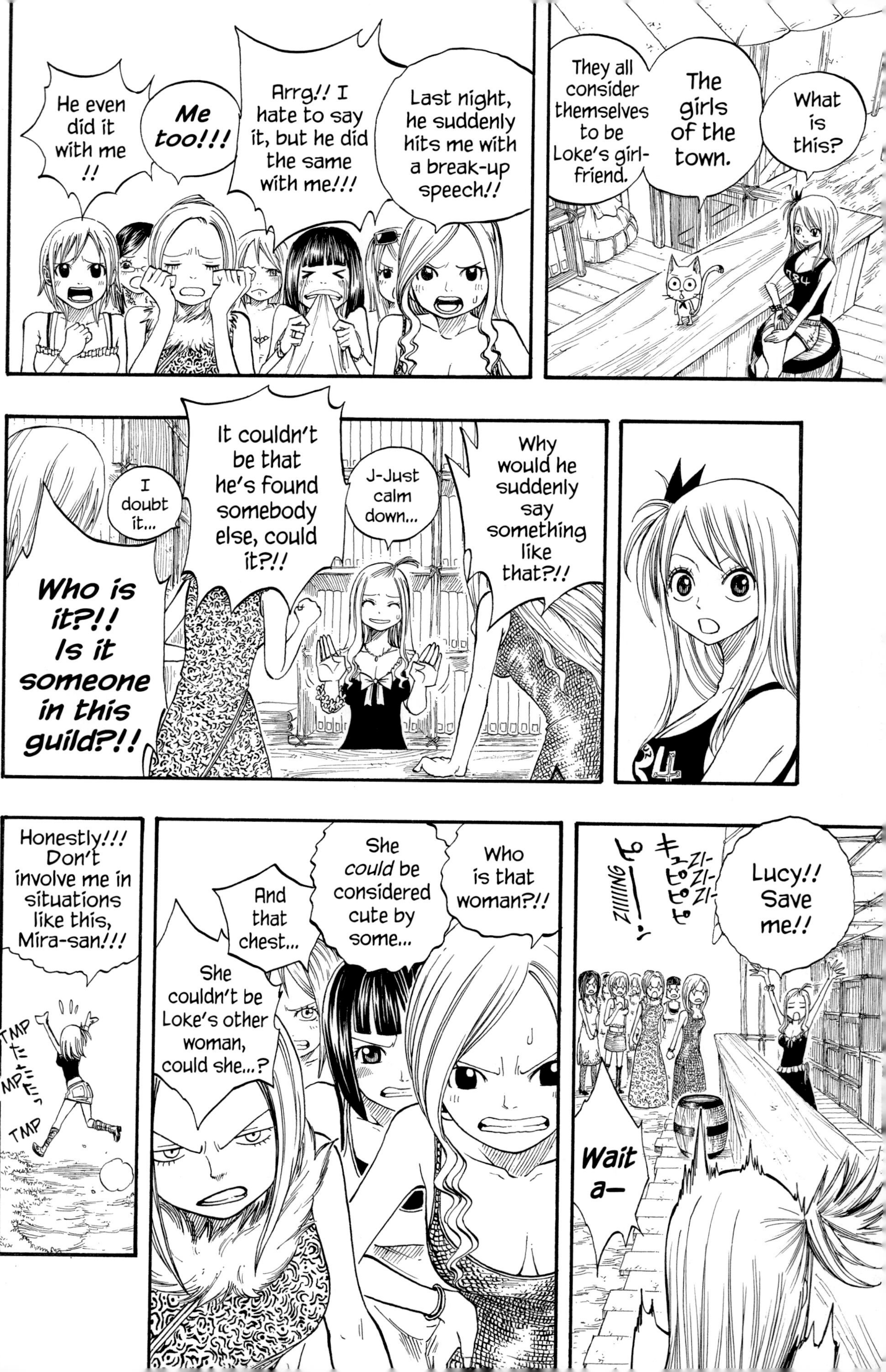
What is this?
The girls of the town.
They all consider themselves to be Loke's girl-friend.
Last night, he suddenly hits me with a break-up speech!!
Arrg!! I hate to say it, but he did the same with me!!!
Me too!!!
He even did it with me !!
Why would he suddenly say something like that?!!
J-Just calm down...
It couldn't be that he's found somebody else, could it?!!
I doubt it...
Who is it?!! Is it someone in this guild?!!
Lucy!! Save me!!
キュピピピ
ZII- ZII- ZII-
ピ——!!
ZIIIIING
Wait a—
Who is that woman?!!
She could be considered cute by some...
And that chest...
She couldn't be Loke's other woman, could she...?
Honestly!!! Don't involve me in situations like this, Mira-san!!!
TMP
TMP
TMP

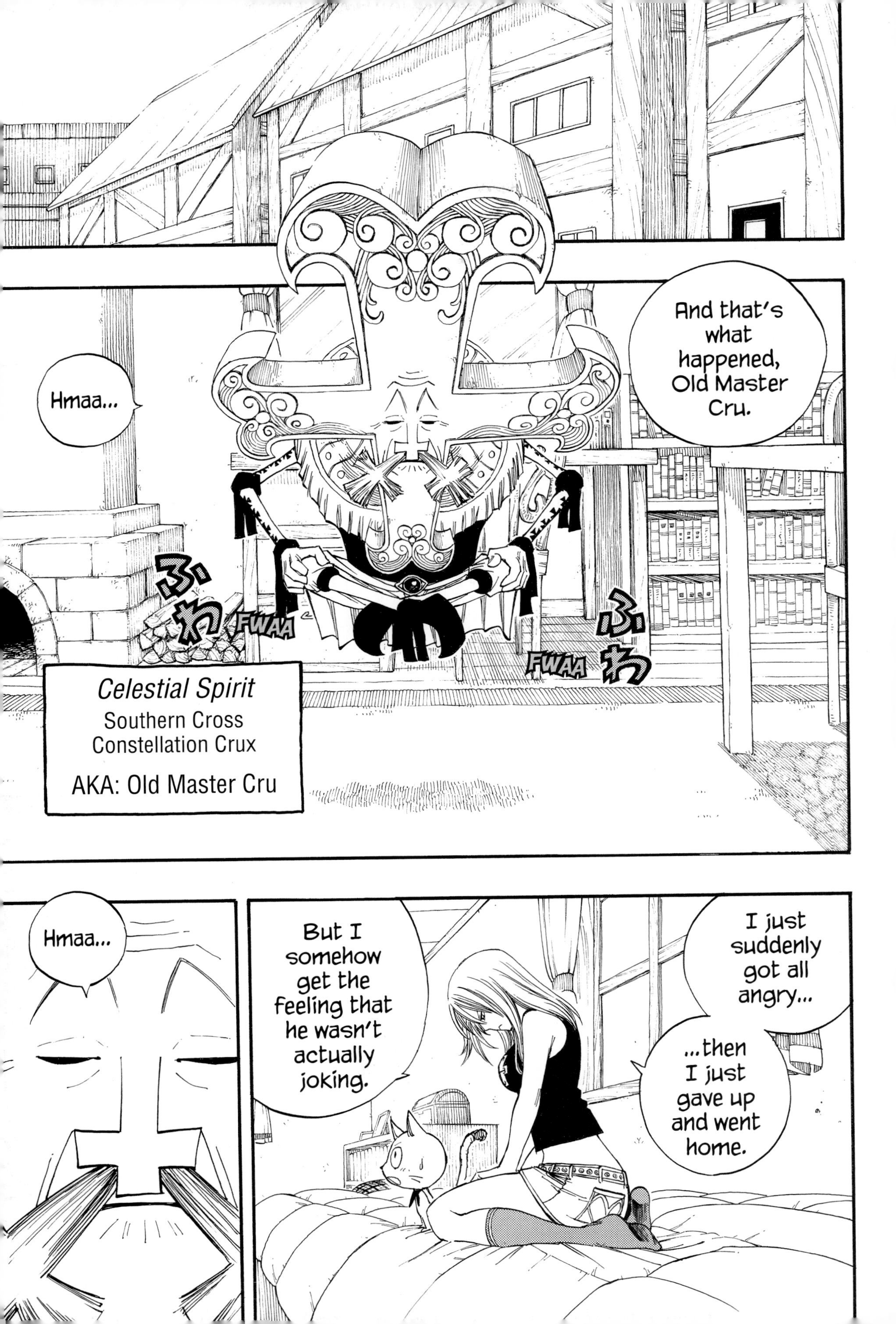
And that's what happened, Old Master Cru.
Hmaa...
ふわ FWAA
ふわ FWAA
Celestial Spirit
Southern Cross Constellation Crux
AKA: Old Master Cru
I just suddenly got all angry...
...then I just gave up and went home.
But I somehow get the feeling that he wasn't actually joking.
Hmaa...

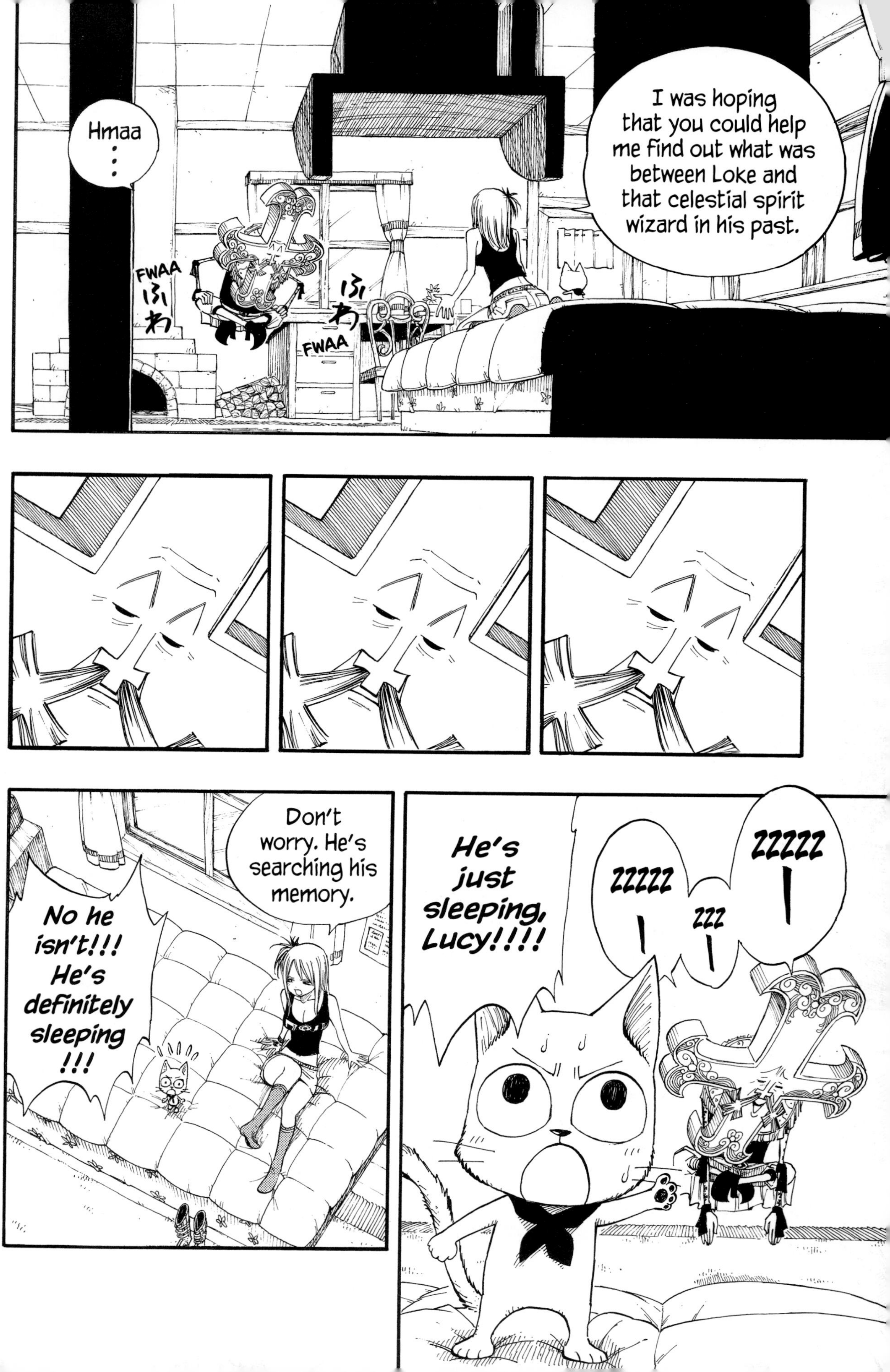
Hmaa...
FWAA ふわ
ふわ FWAA
I was hoping that you could help me find out what was between Loke and that celestial spirit wizard in his past.
Don't worry. He's searching his memory.
No he isn't!!! He's definitely sleeping!!!
He's just sleeping, Lucy!!!!
ZZZZZ
zzz
ZZZZZ

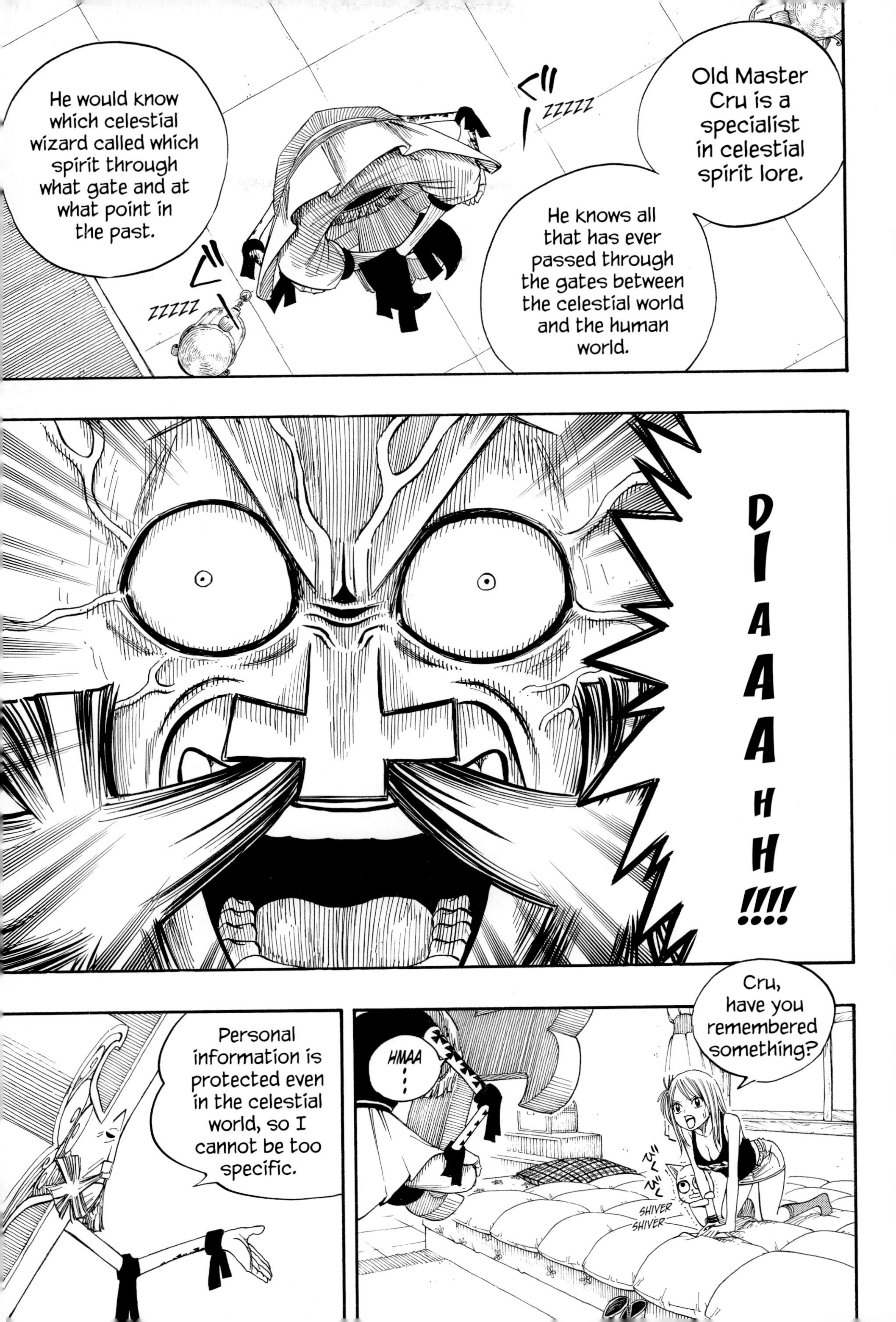

Old Master Cru is a specialist in celestial spirit lore.
He knows all that has ever passed through the gates between the celestial world and the human world.
ZZZZZ
He would know which celestial wizard called which spirit through what gate and at what point in the past.
ZZZZZ
DIAAAAHH!!!!
Cru, have you remembered something?
HMAA...
SHIVER SHIVER
Personal information is protected even in the celestial world, so I cannot be too specific.

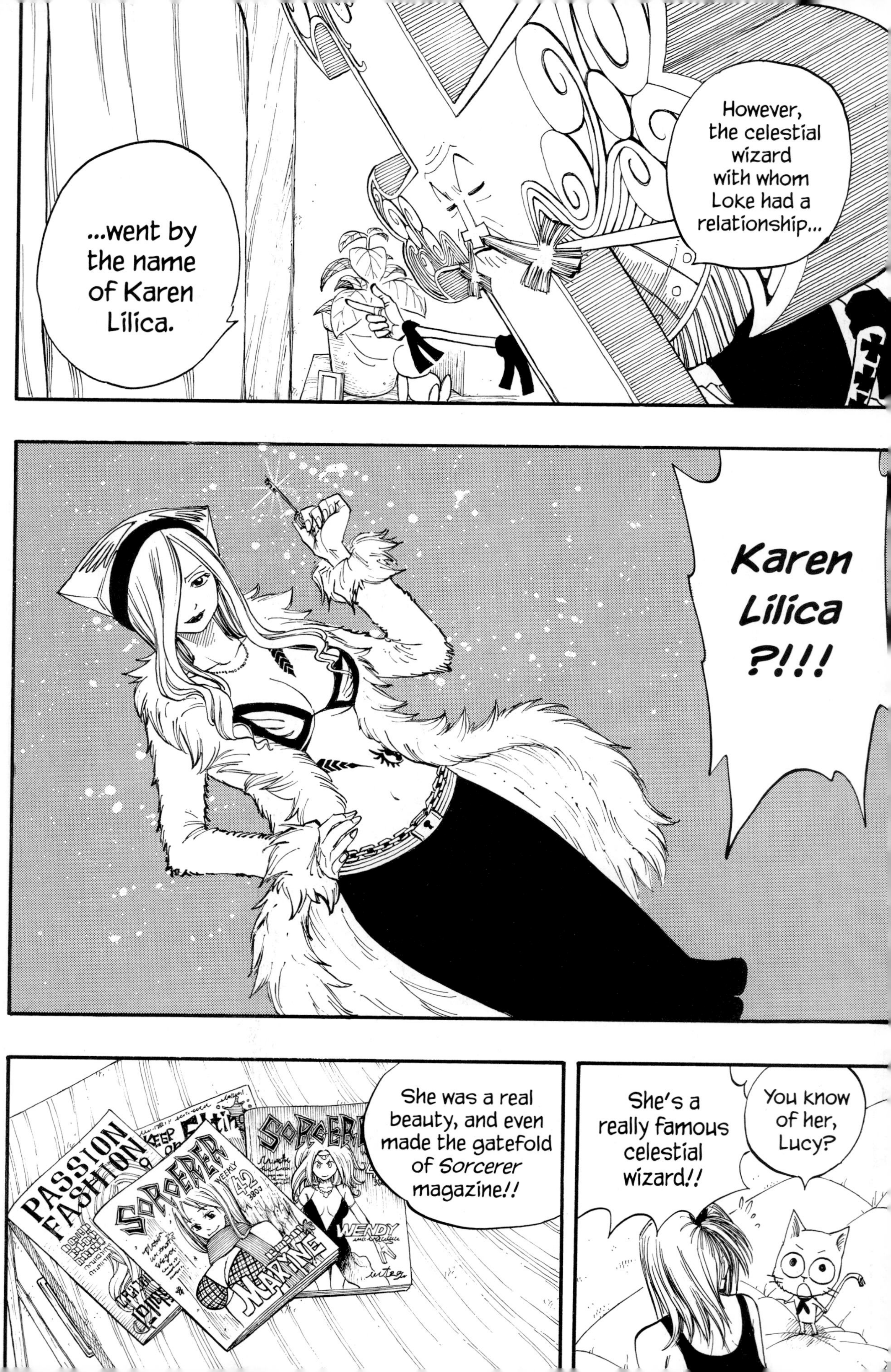
However, the celestial wizard with whom Loke had a relationship...
...went by the name of Karen Lilica.
Karen Lilica ?!!!
You know of her, Lucy?
She's a really famous celestial wizard!!
She was a real beauty, and even made the gatefold of *Sorcerer* magazine!!
PASSION FASHION
SORCERER
WEEKLY 42
MARINE
WENDY

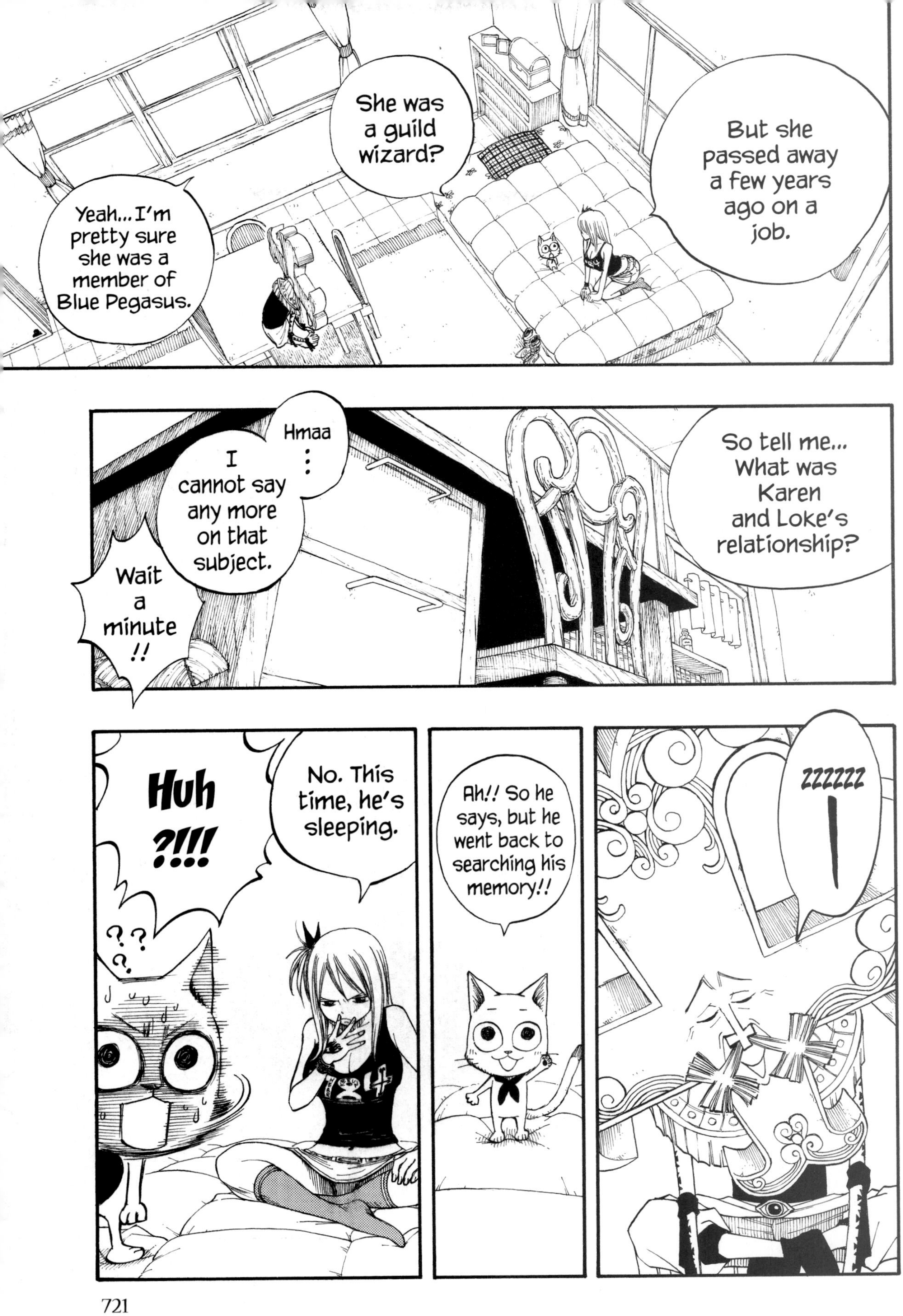
But she passed away a few years ago on a job.
She was a guild wizard?
Yeah...I'm pretty sure she was a member of Blue Pegasus.
So tell me... What was Karen and Loke's relationship?
Hmaa...
I cannot say any more on that subject.
Wait a minute!!
ZZZZZZ
Ah!! So he says, but he went back to searching his memory!!
No. This time, he's sleeping.
Huh?!!!
???

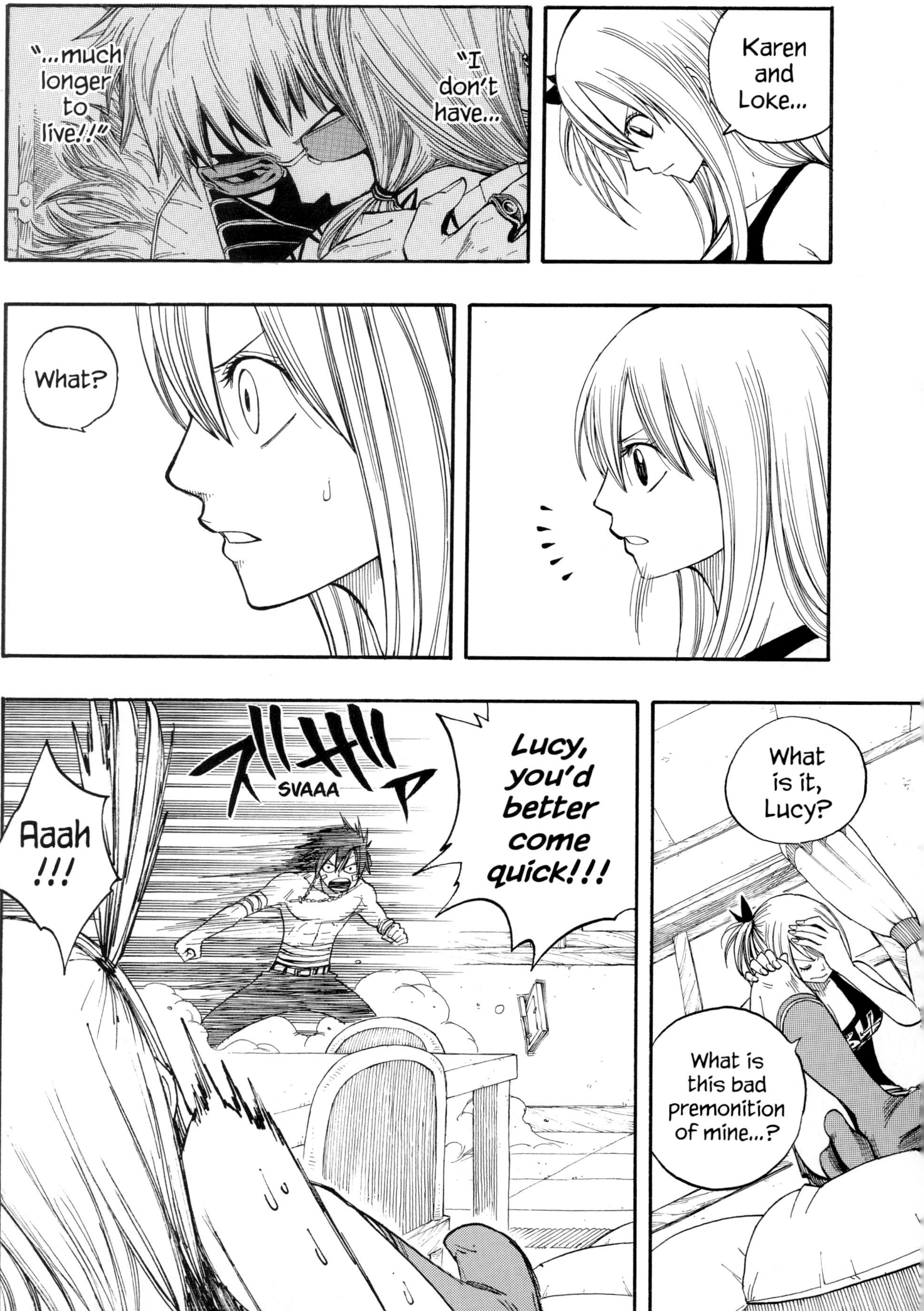
Karen and Loke...
"I don't have...
"...much longer to live!!"
What?
What is it, Lucy?
What is this bad premonition of mine...?
Lucy, you'd better come quick!!!
SVAAA
Aaah!!!

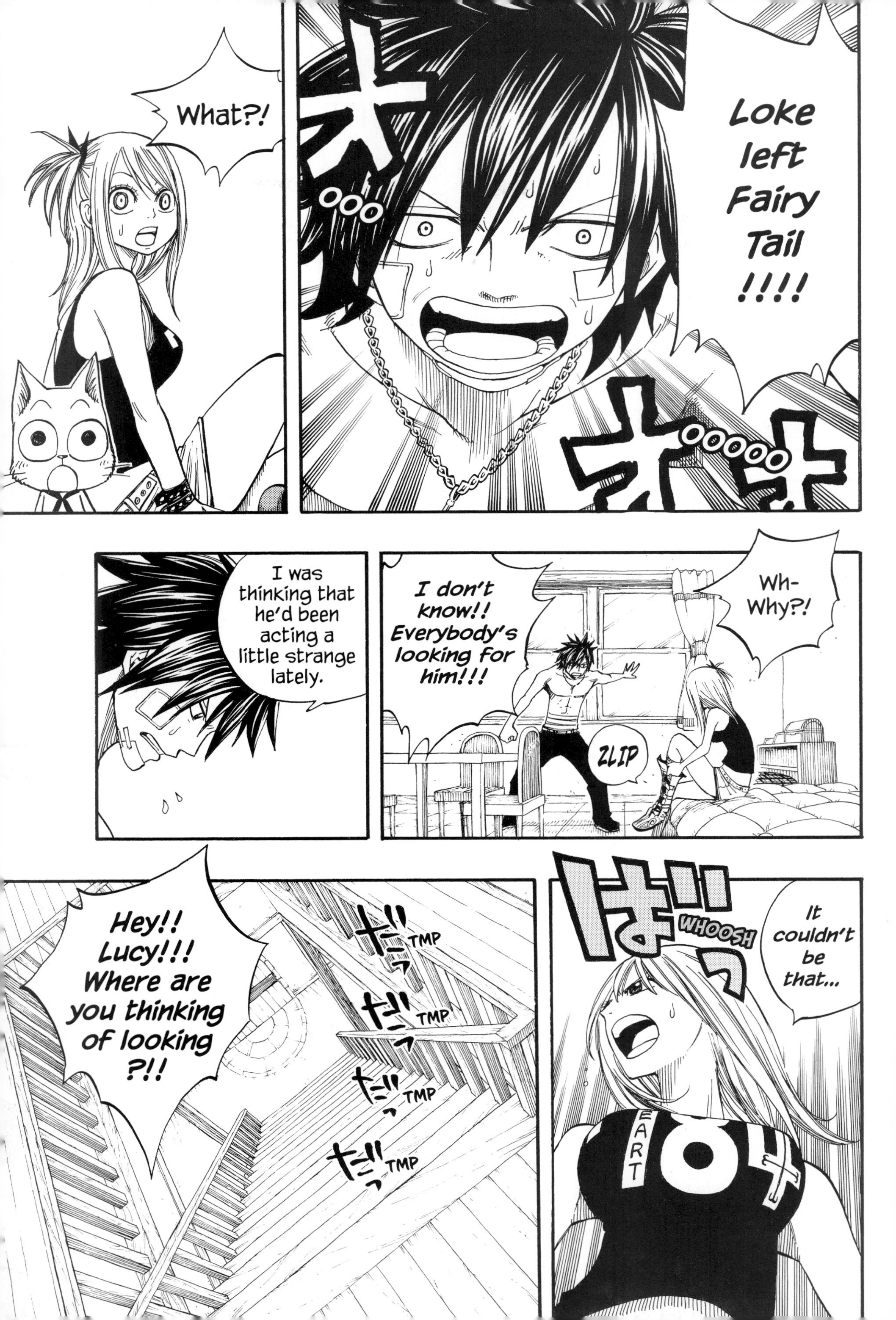
Loke left Fairy Tail !!!!
OOO
OOOOO
What?!
Wh- Why?!
I don't know!! Everybody's looking for him!!!
ZLIP
I was thinking that he'd been acting a little strange lately.
WHOOSH
It couldn't be that...
Hey!! Lucy!!! Where are you thinking of looking ?!!
TMP
TMP
TMP
TMP

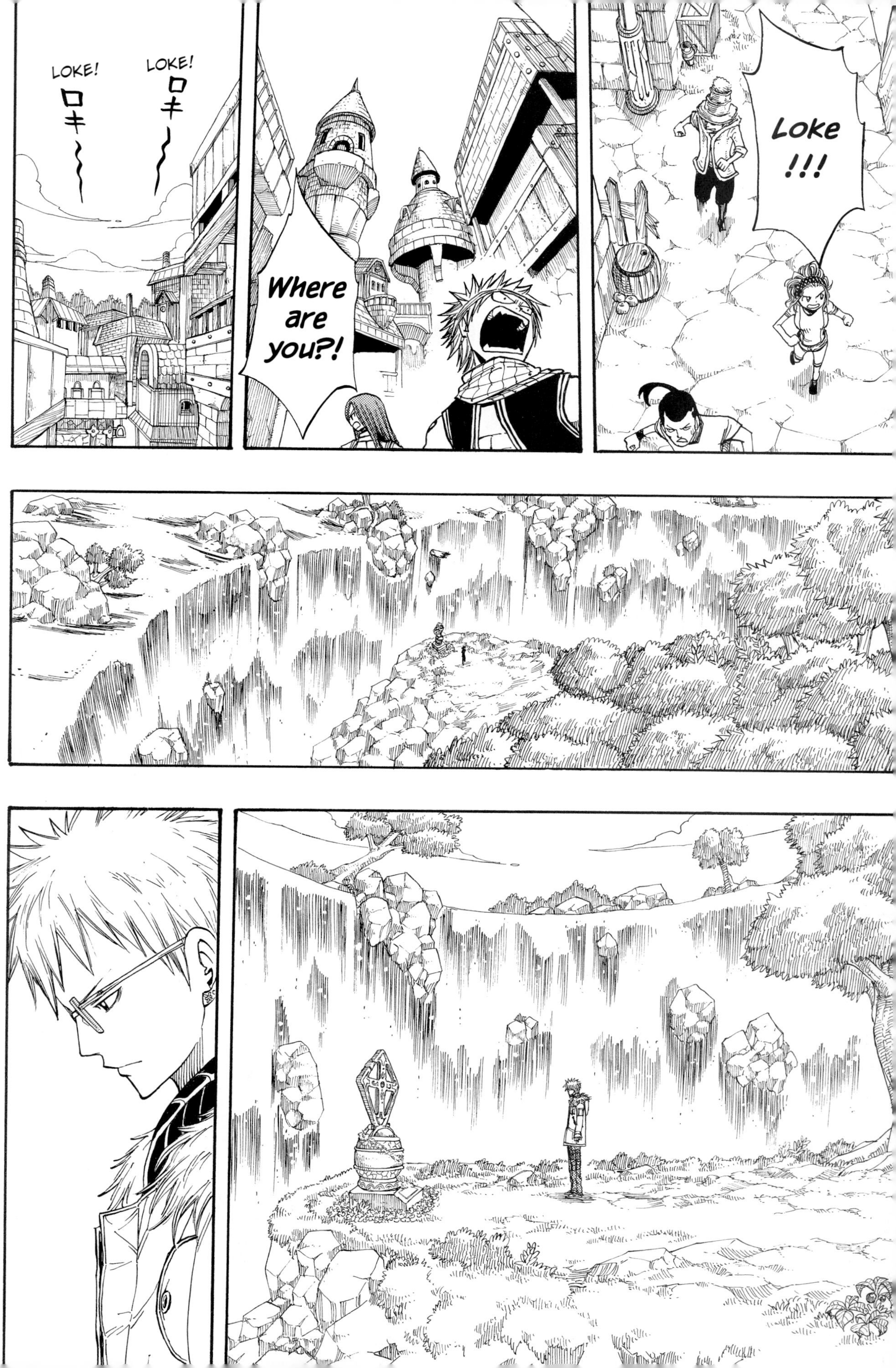
Loke !!!
Where are you?!
LOKE! ロキ〜
LOKE! ロキ〜

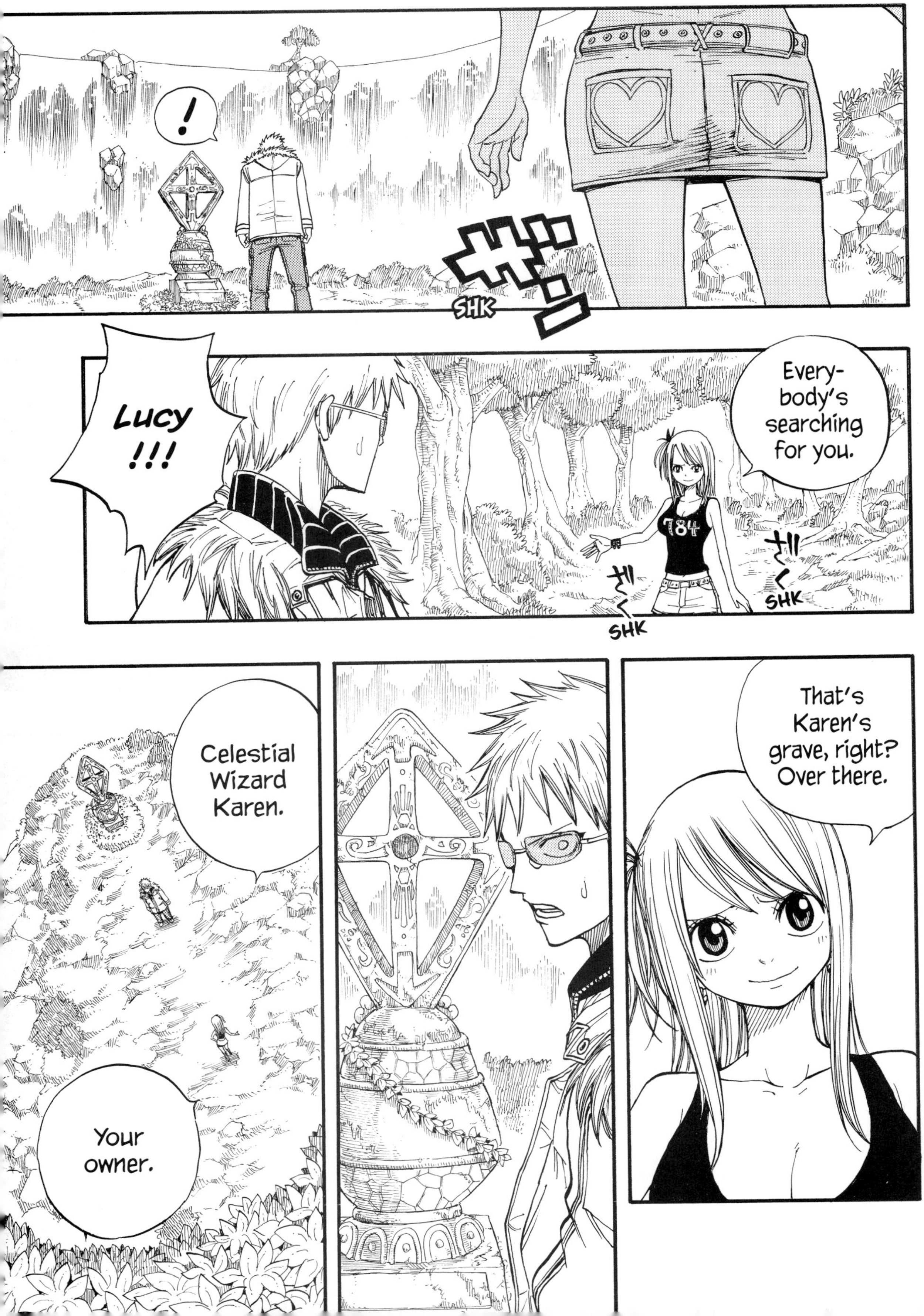
!
SHK
Every-body's searching for you.
Lucy!!!
SHK
SHK
That's Karen's grave, right? Over there.
Celestial Wizard Karen.
Your owner.

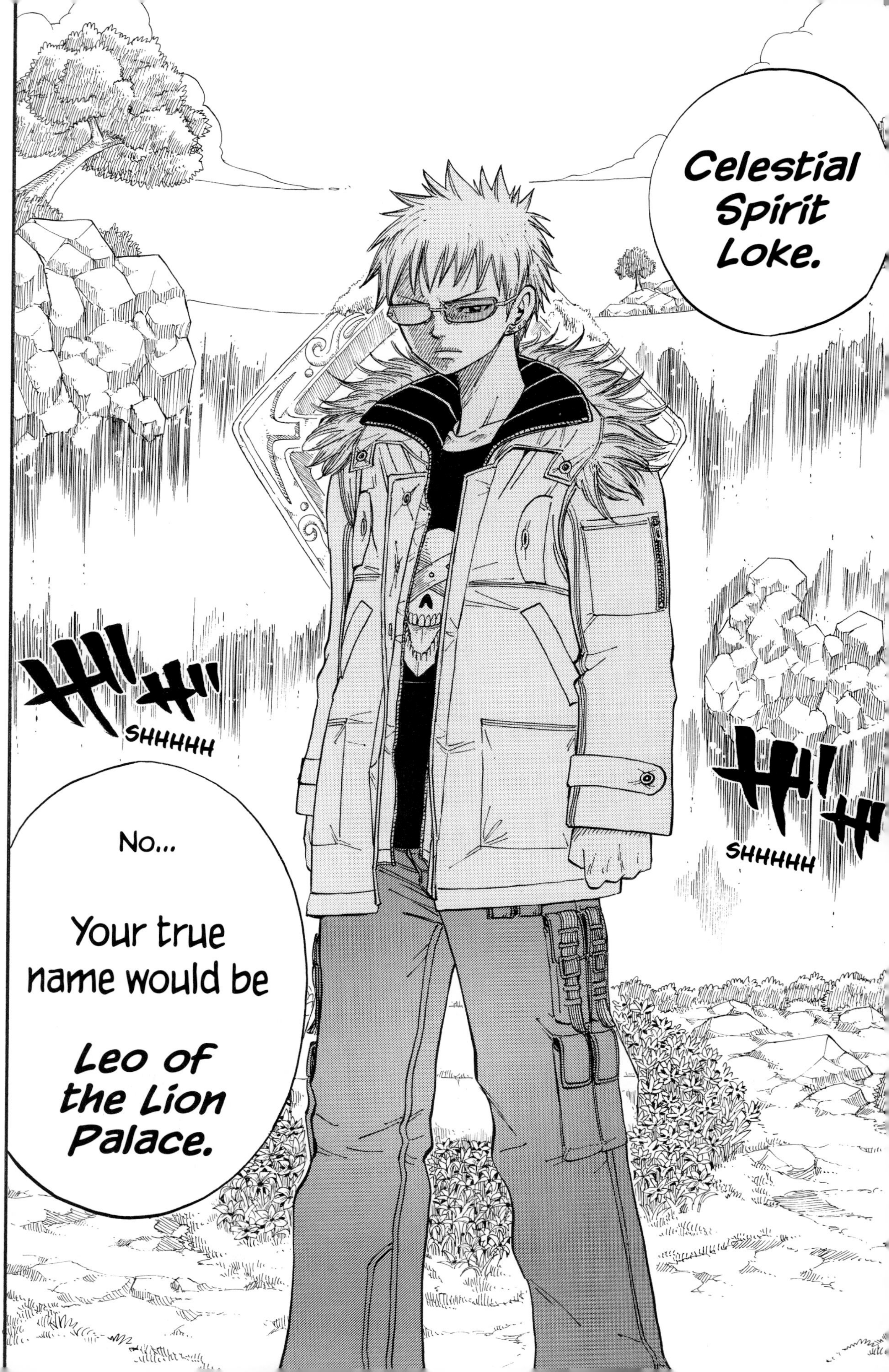
Celestial Spirit Loke.
No... Your true name would be Leo of the Lion Palace.
SHHHHH
SHHHHH

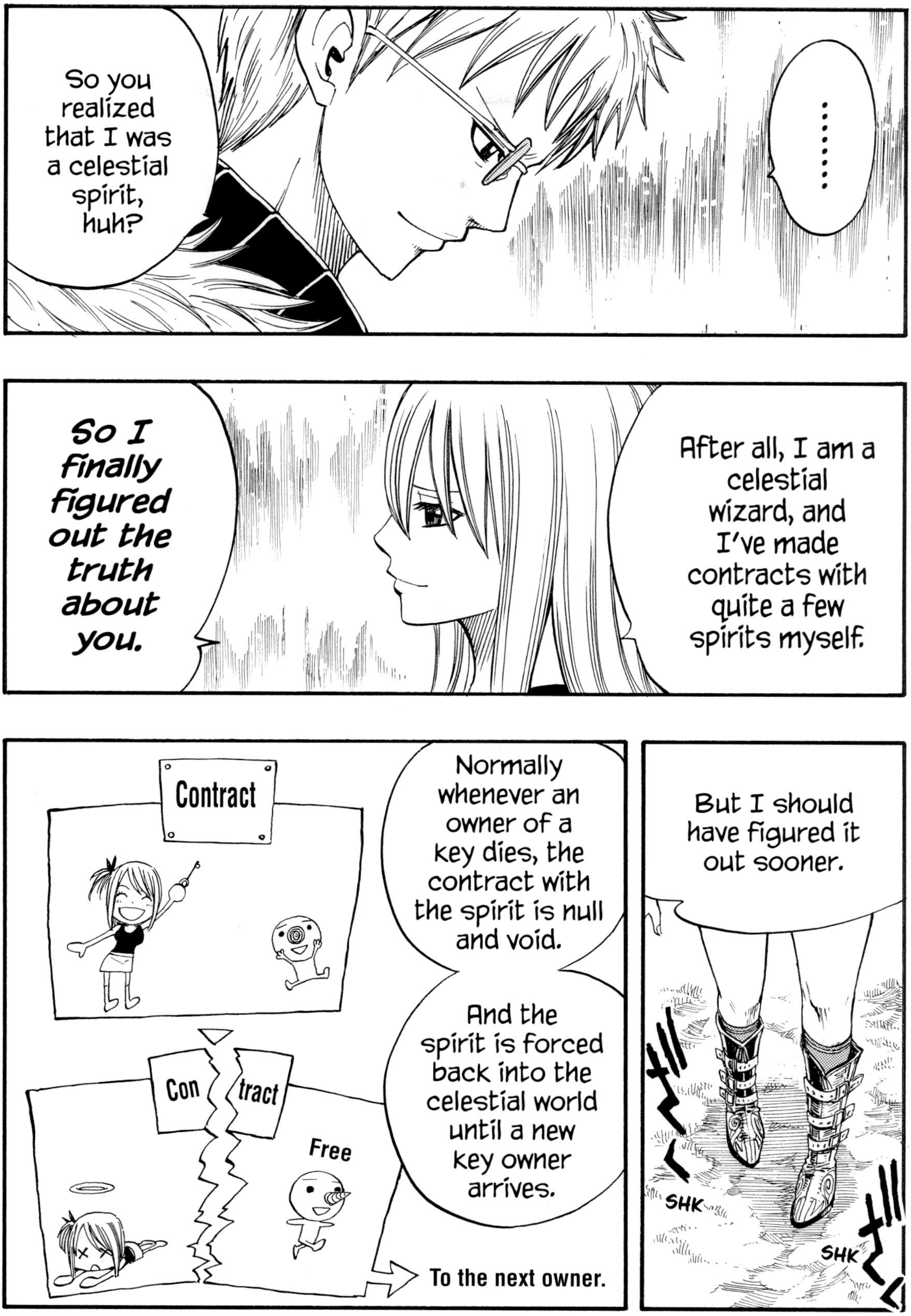

......
So you realized that I was a celestial spirit, huh?
After all, I am a celestial wizard, and I've made contracts with quite a few spirits myself.
So I finally figured out the truth about you.
But I should have figured it out sooner.
SHK
SHK
Normally whenever an owner of a key dies, the contract with the spirit is null and void.
And the spirit is forced back into the celestial world until a new key owner arrives.
Contract
Con tract
Free
To the next owner.

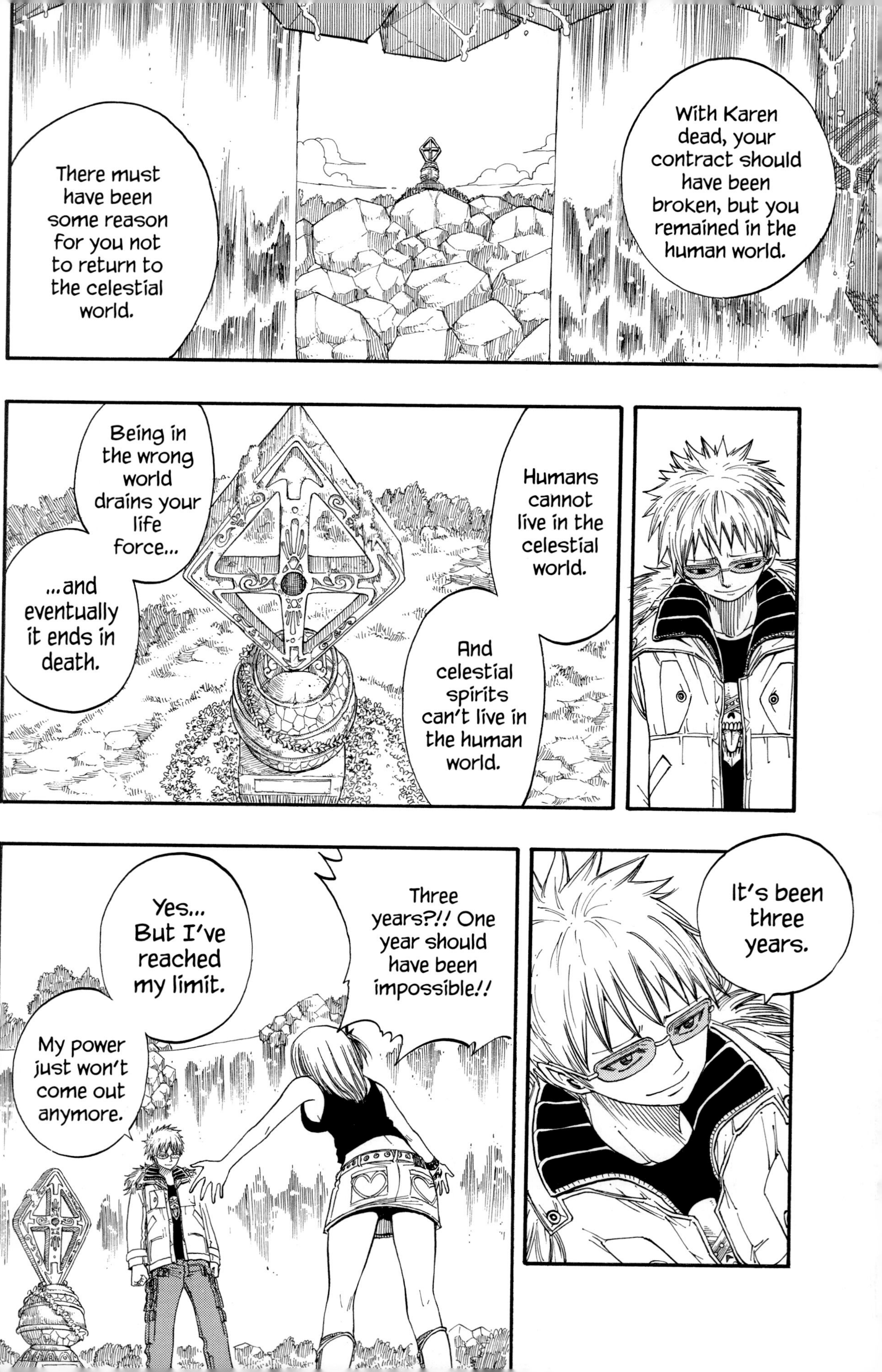
With Karen dead, your contract should have been broken, but you remained in the human world.
There must have been some reason for you not to return to the celestial world.
Humans cannot live in the celestial world.
And celestial spirits can't live in the human world.
Being in the wrong world drains your life force...
...and eventually it ends in death.
It's been three years.
Three years?!! One year should have been impossible!!
Yes... But I've reached my limit.
My power just won't come out anymore.

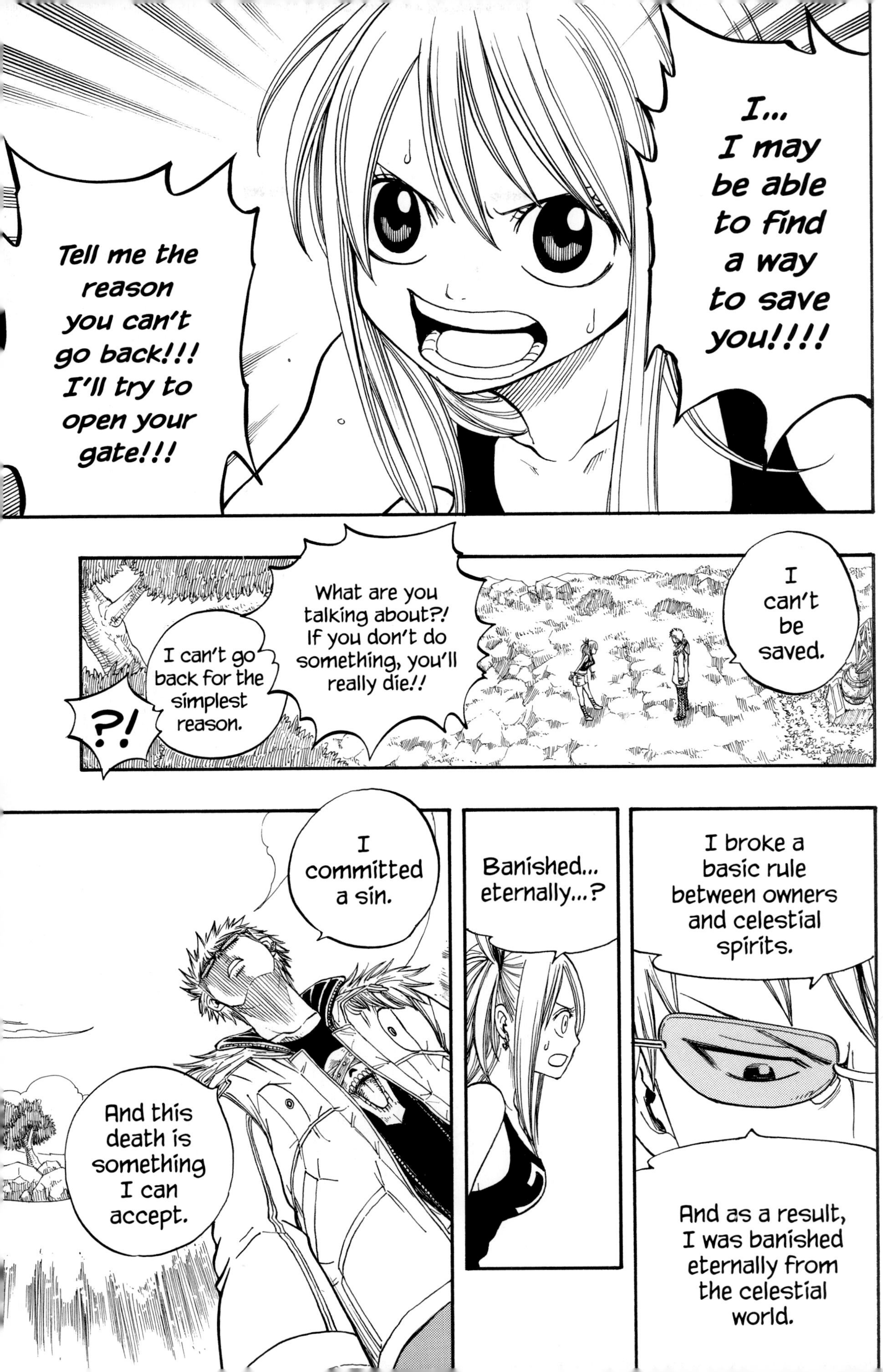
I... I may be able to find a way to save you!!!!
Tell me the reason you can't go back!!! I'll try to open your gate!!!
I can't be saved.
What are you talking about?! If you don't do something, you'll really die!!
I can't go back for the simplest reason.
?!
I broke a basic rule between owners and celestial spirits.
And as a result, I was banished eternally from the celestial world.
Banished... eternally...?
I committed a sin.
And this death is something I can accept.

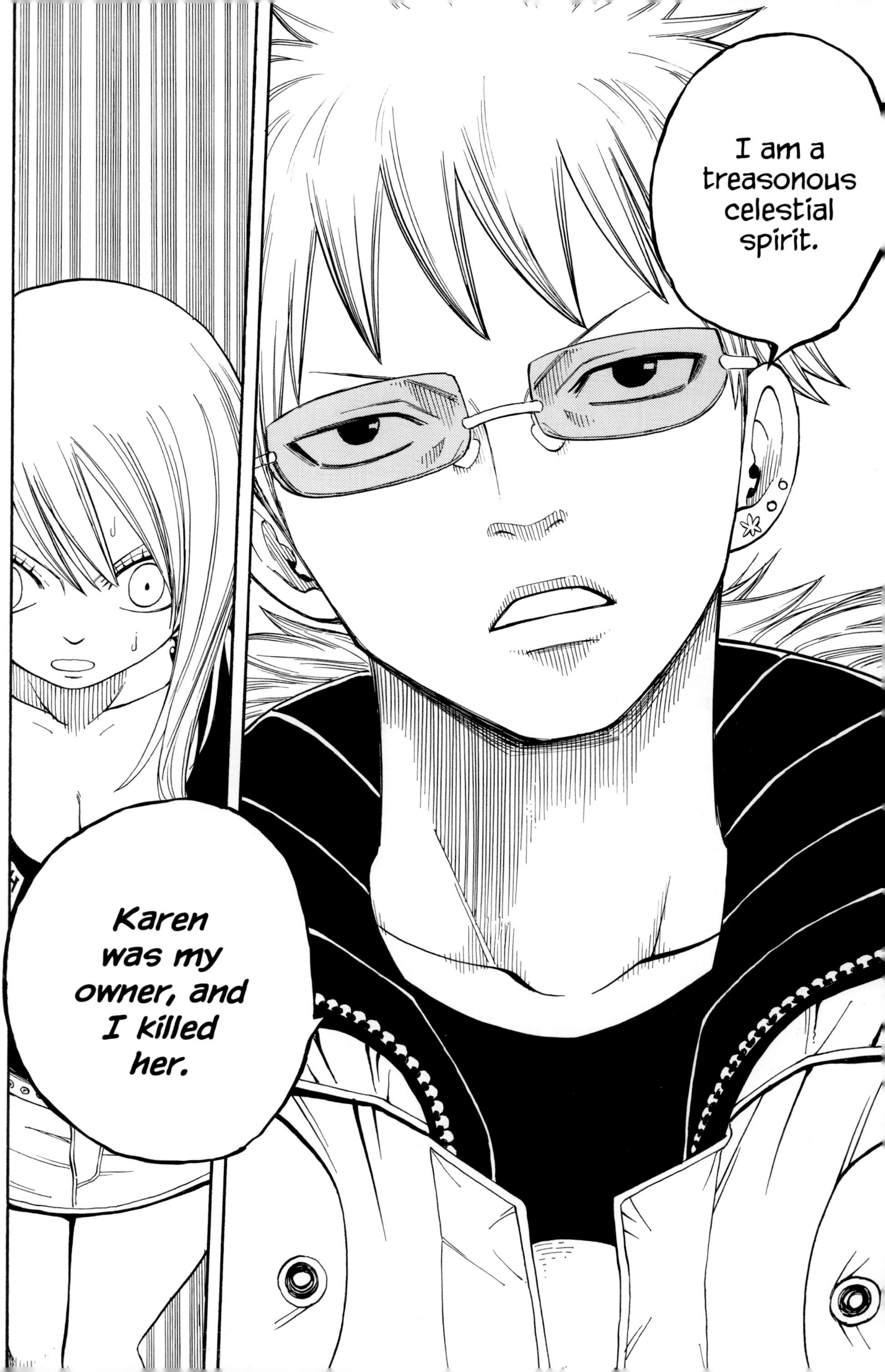
I am a treasonous celestial spirit.
Karen was my owner, and I killed her.

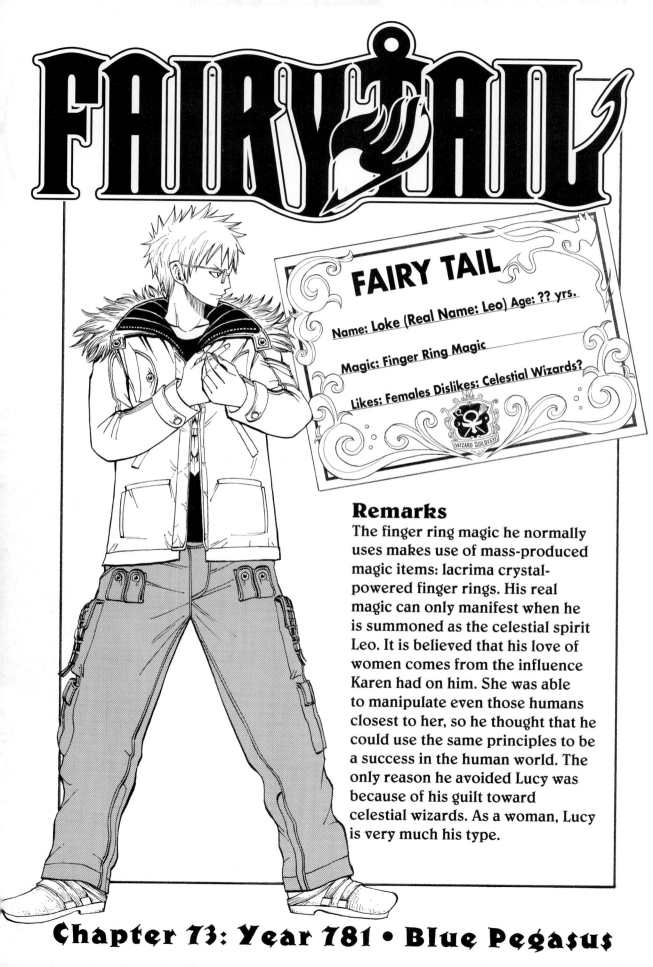

FAIRY TAIL

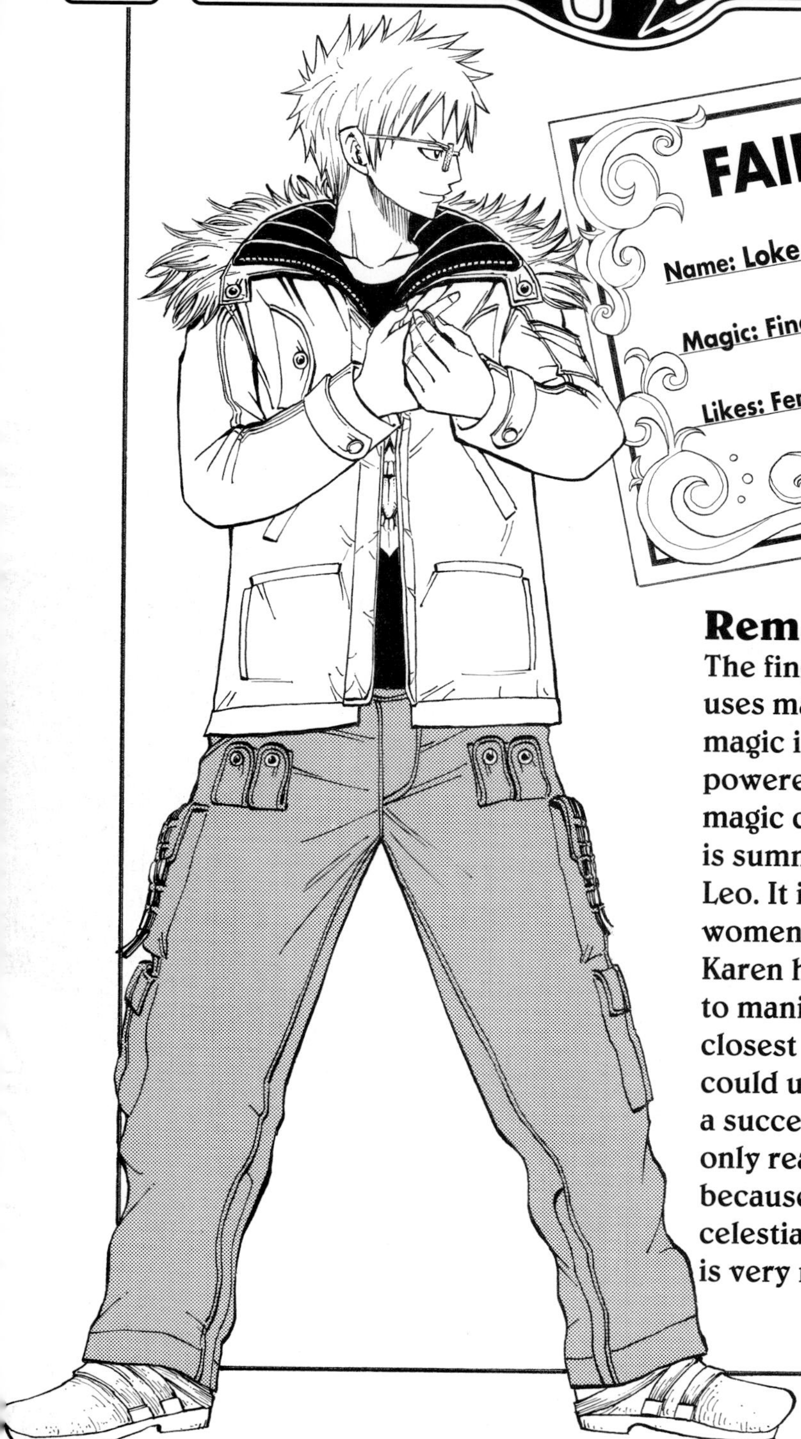

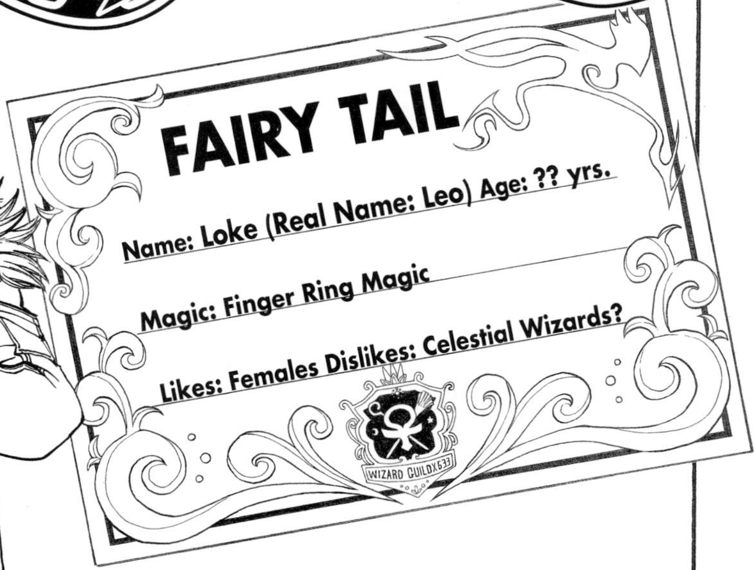

FAIRY TAIL
Name: Loke (Real Name: Leo) Age: ?? yrs.
Magic: Finger Ring Magic
Likes: Females Dislikes: Celestial Wizards?
WIZARD GUILD X633

Remarks

The finger ring magic he normally uses makes use of mass-produced magic items: lacrima crystal-powered finger rings. His real magic can only manifest when he is summoned as the celestial spirit Leo. It is believed that his love of women comes from the influence Karen had on him. She was able to manipulate even those humans closest to her, so he thought that he could use the same principles to be a success in the human world. The only reason he avoided Lucy was because of his guilt toward celestial wizards. As a woman, Lucy is very much his type.

Chapter 73: Year 781 • Blue Pegasus

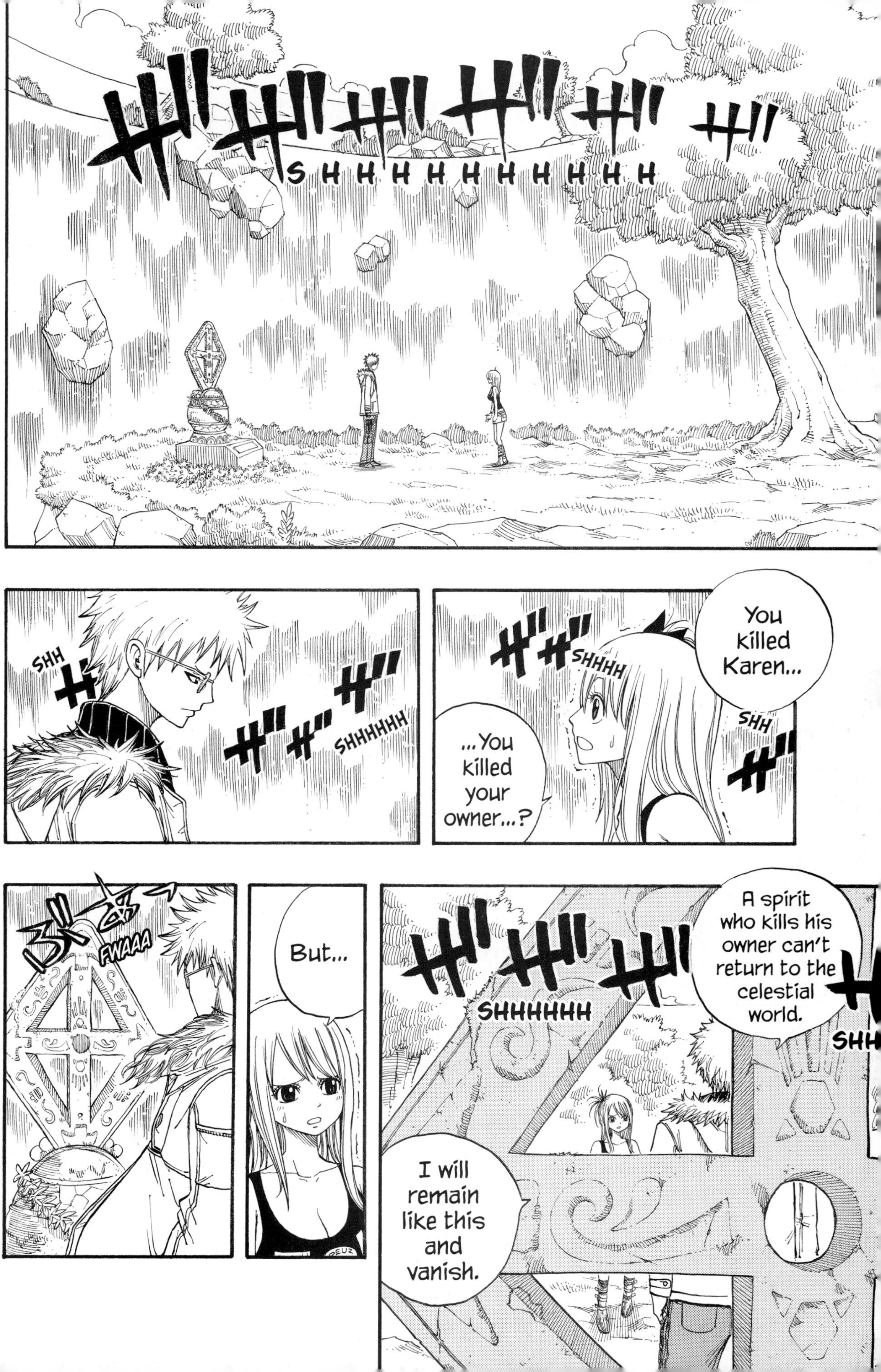
SHHHHHHHHH
You killed Karen...
SHHHH
SHH
...You killed your owner...?
SHH
SHHHHHH
A spirit who kills his owner can't return to the celestial world.
SHHHHHHH
SHH
I will remain like this and vanish.
But...
FWAAA

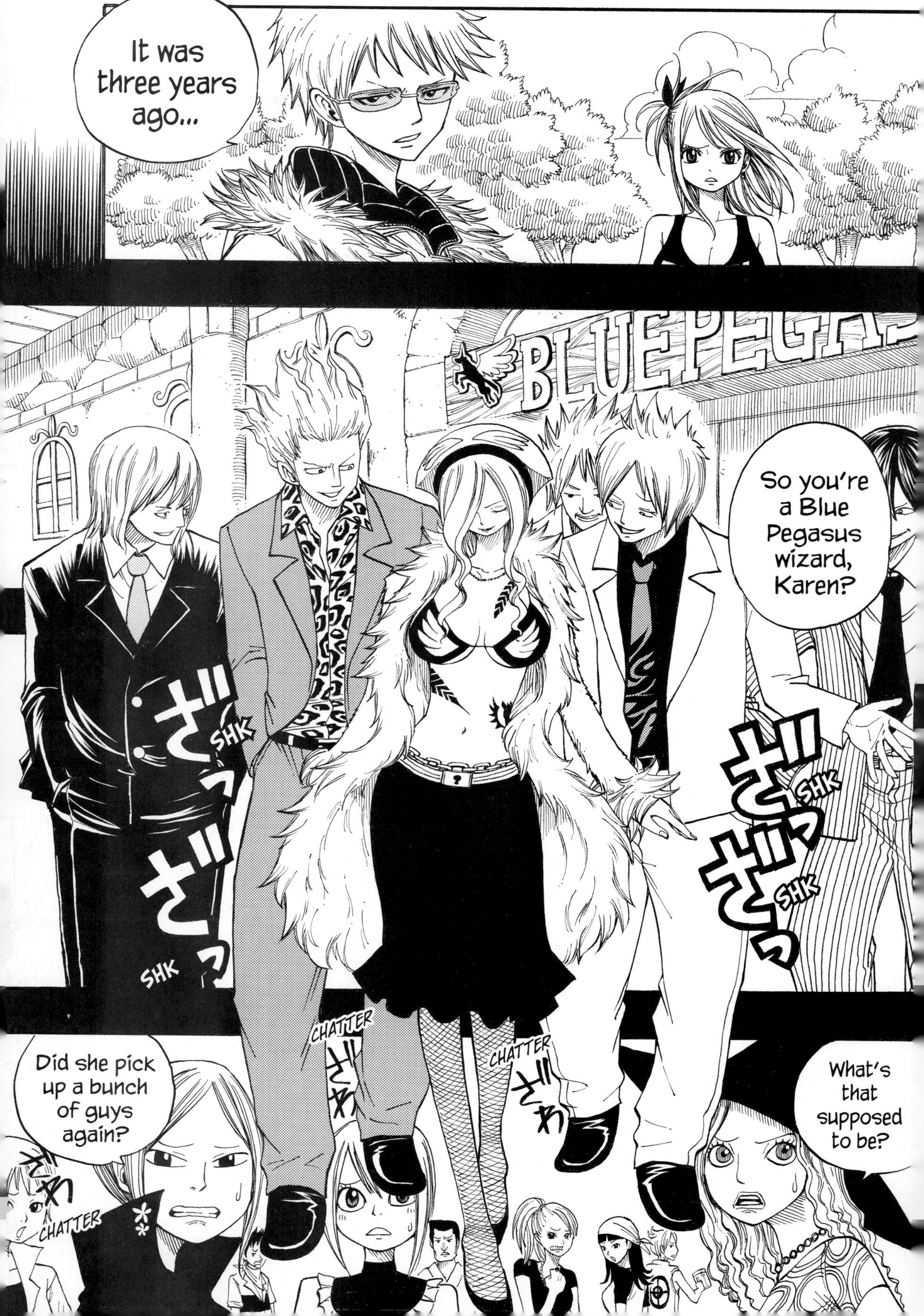
It was three years ago...
BLUEPEGA
So you're a Blue Pegasus wizard, Karen?
ざっ
SHK
ざっ
SHK
ざっ
SHK
ざっ
SHK
What's that supposed to be?
ざわ
CHATTER
ざわ
CHATTER
Did she pick up a bunch of guys again?
ざわ
CHATTER

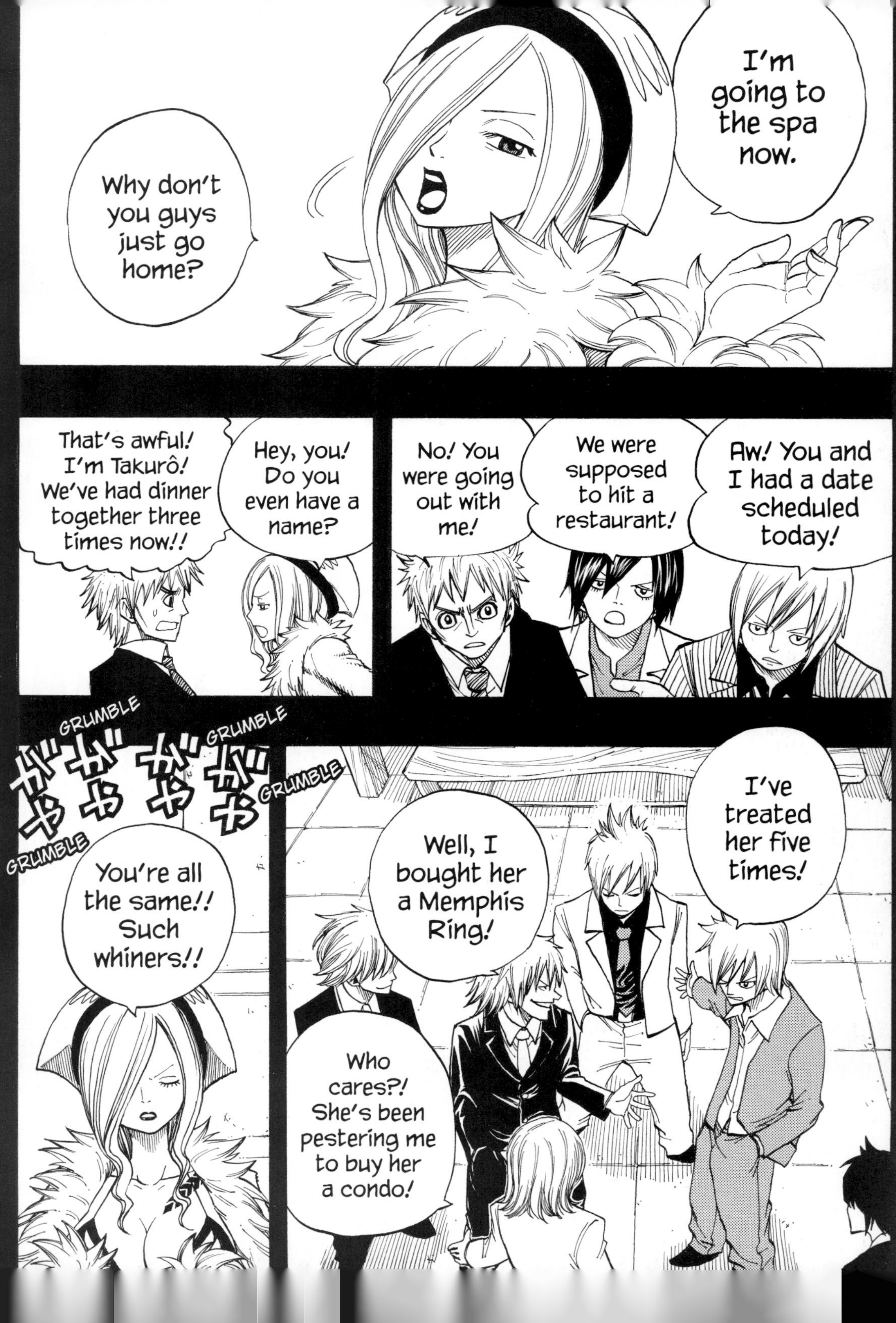
I'm going to the spa now.
Why don't you guys just go home?
Aw! You and I had a date scheduled today!
We were supposed to hit a restaurant!
No! You were going out with me!
Hey, you! Do you even have a name?
That's awful! I'm Takurô! We've had dinner together three times now!!
I've treated her five times!
Well, I bought her a Memphis Ring!
Who cares?! She's been pestering me to buy her a condo!
GRUMBLE GRUMBLE GRUMBLE GRUMBLE
You're all the same!! Such whiners!!

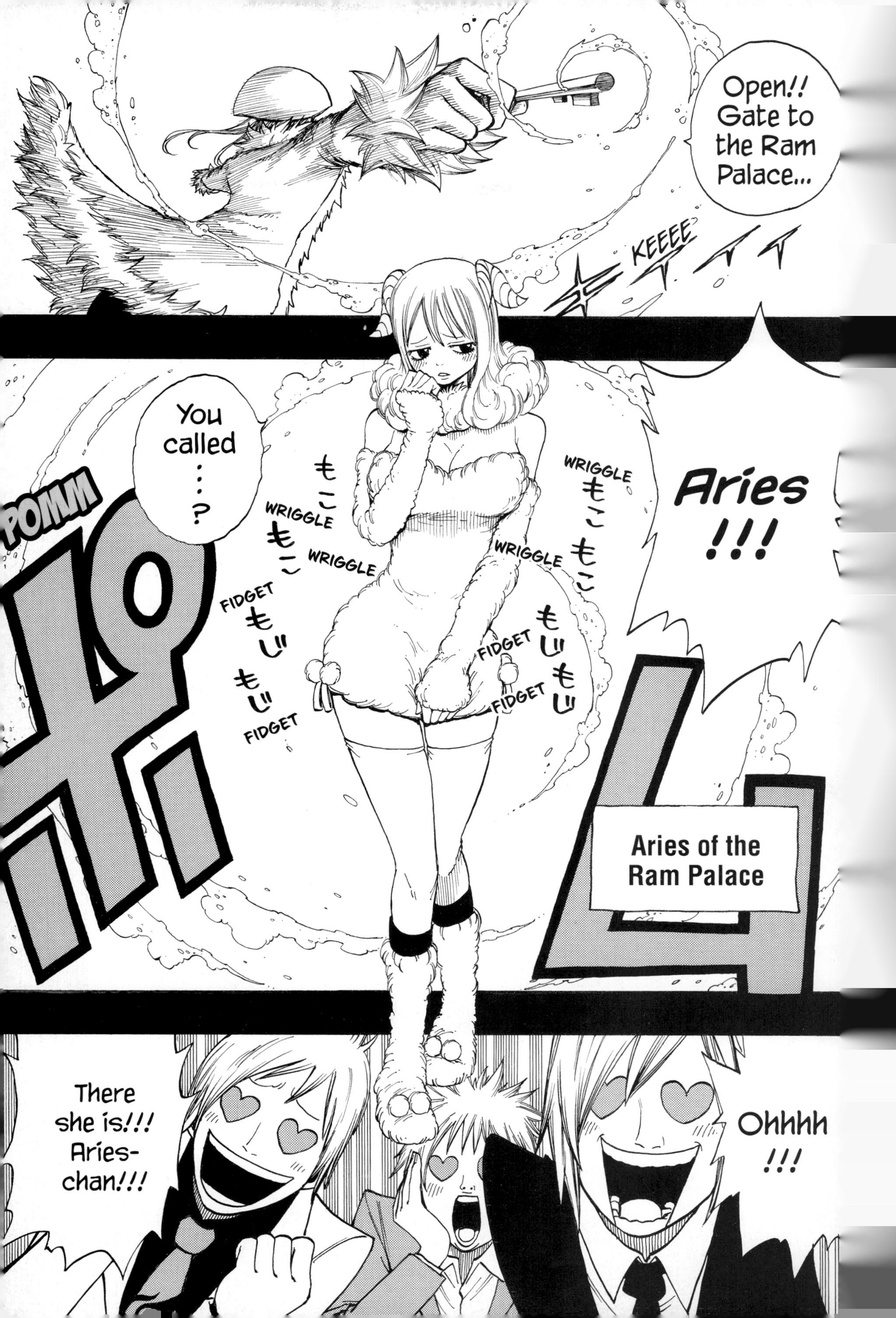
Open!! Gate to the Ram Palace...
KEEEE
Aries!!!
Aries of the Ram Palace
WRIGGLE もこ
WRIGGLE もこ
FIDGET もじ
FIDGET もじ
You called...?
WRIGGLE もこ
WRIGGLE もこ
FIDGET もじ
FIDGET もじ
POMM
Ohhhh!!!
There she is!!! Aries-chan!!!

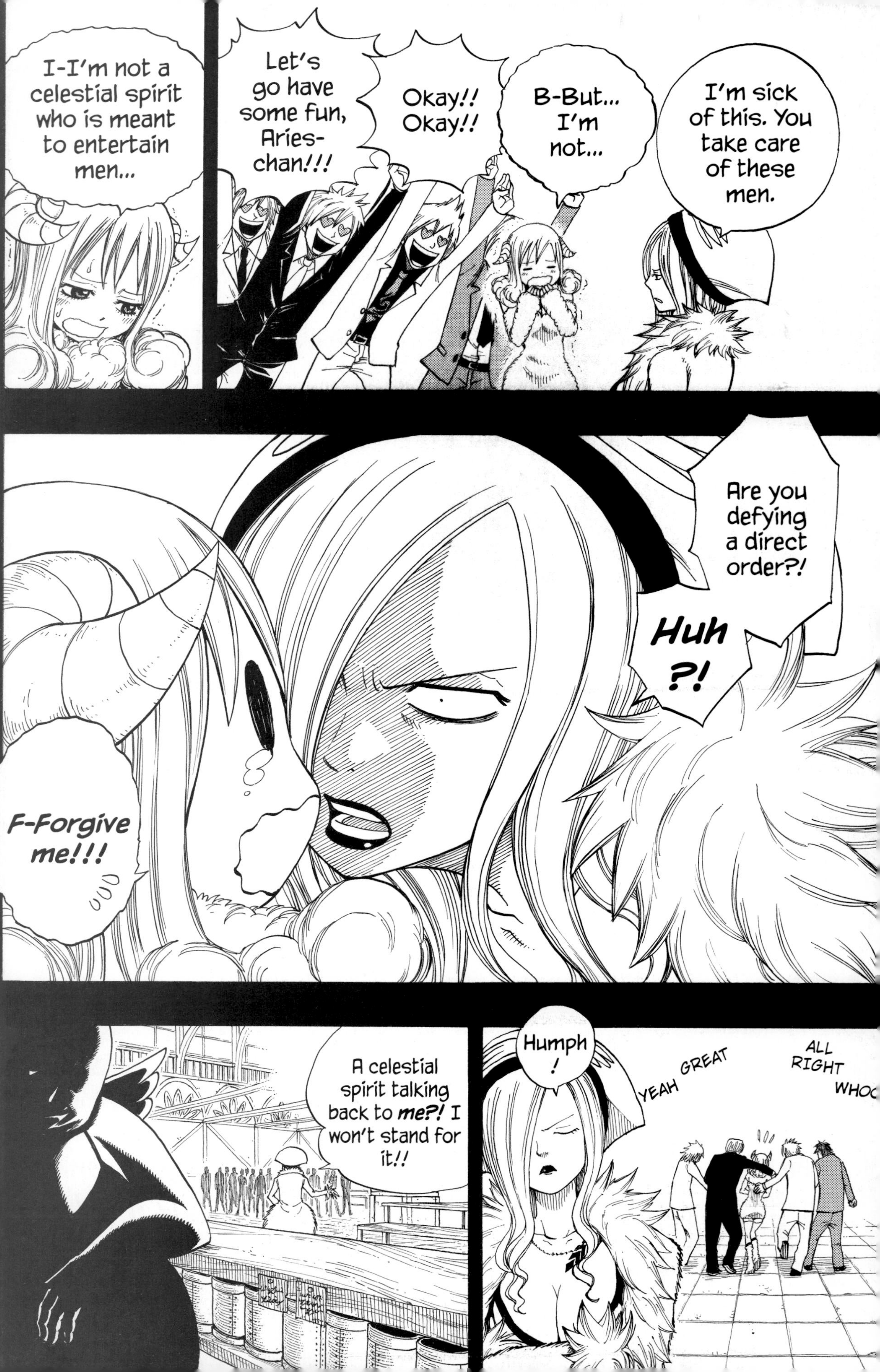
I'm sick of this. You take care of these men.
B-But... I'm not...
Okay!! Okay!!
Let's go have some fun, Aries-chan!!!
I-I'm not a celestial spirit who is meant to entertain men...
Are you defying a direct order?!
Huh ?!
F-Forgive me!!!
Humph !
ALL RIGHT
WHO
GREAT
YEAH
A celestial spirit talking back to ***me?!*** I won't stand for it!!

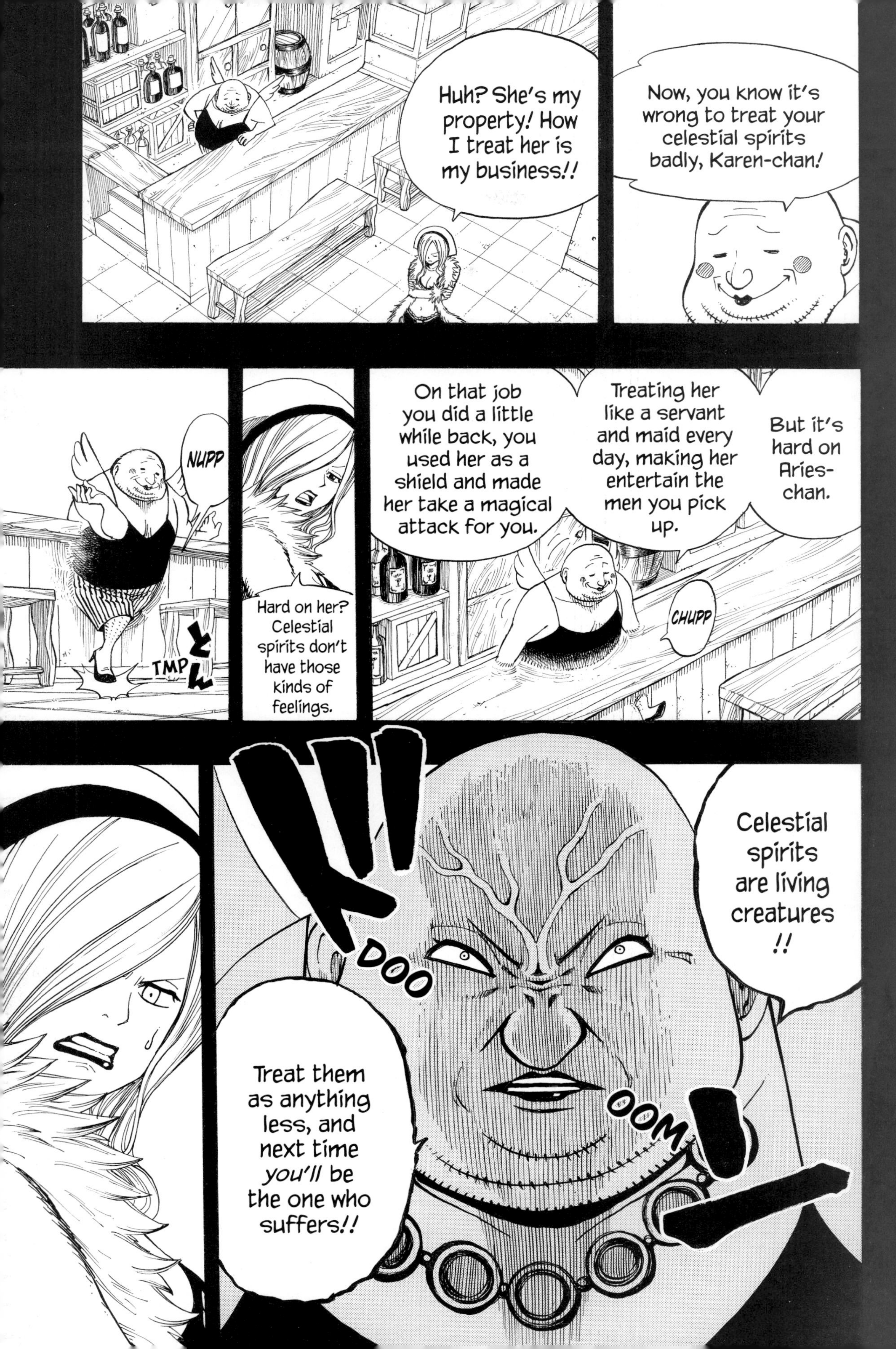
Now, you know it's wrong to treat your celestial spirits badly, Karen-chan!
Huh? She's my property! How I treat her is my business!!
But it's hard on Aries-chan.
Treating her like a servant and maid every day, making her entertain the men you pick up.
On that job you did a little while back, you used her as a shield and made her take a magical attack for you.
CHUPP
Hard on her? Celestial spirits don't have those kinds of feelings.
NUPP
TMP
Celestial spirits are living creatures!!
DOO
OOM
Treat them as anything less, and next time *you'll* be the one who suffers!!

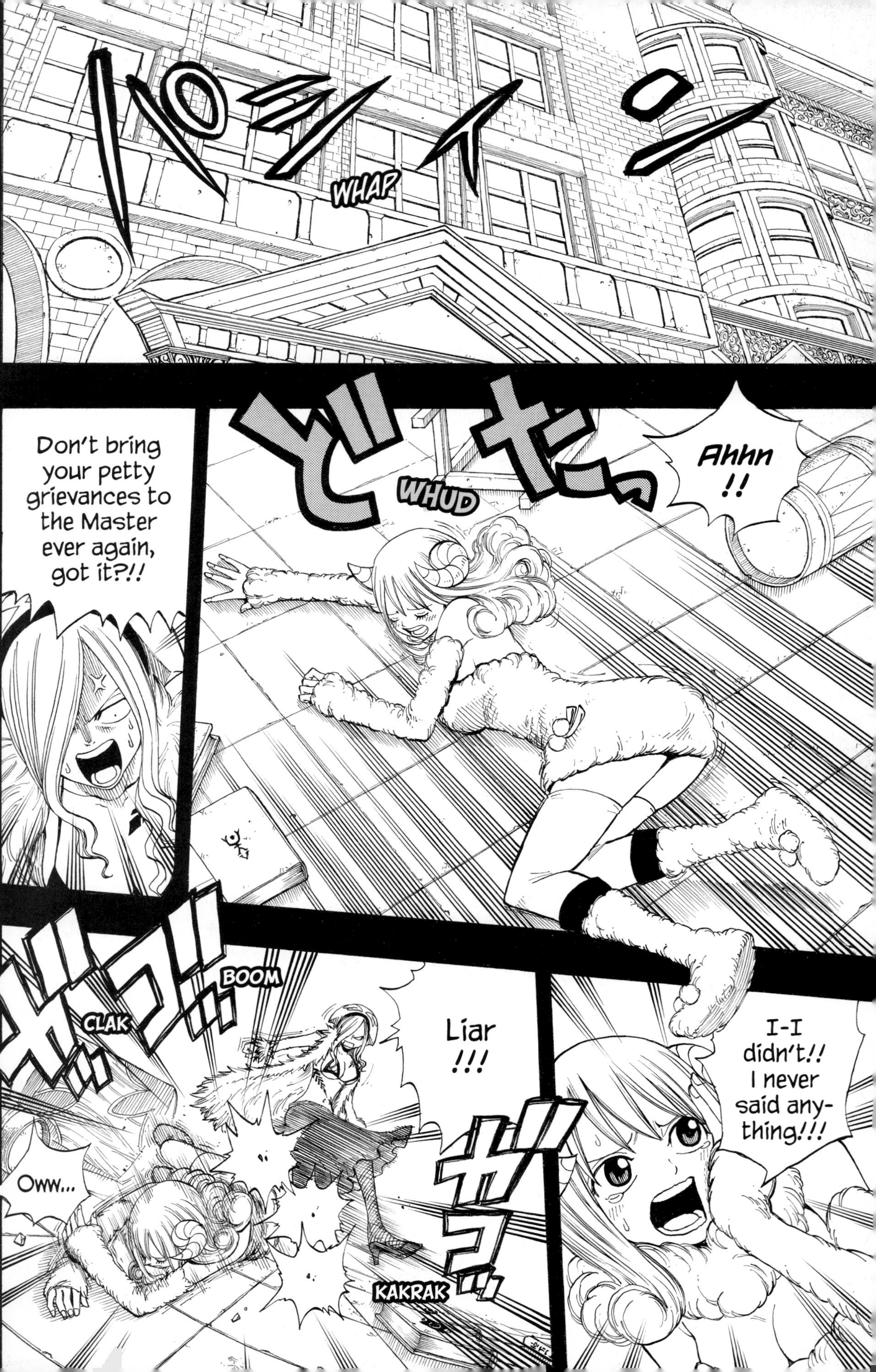
WHAP
WHUD
Ahhn !!
Don't bring your petty grievances to the Master ever again, got it?!!
I-I didn't!! I never said any-thing!!!
Liar !!!
BOOM
CLAK
KAKRAK
Oww...

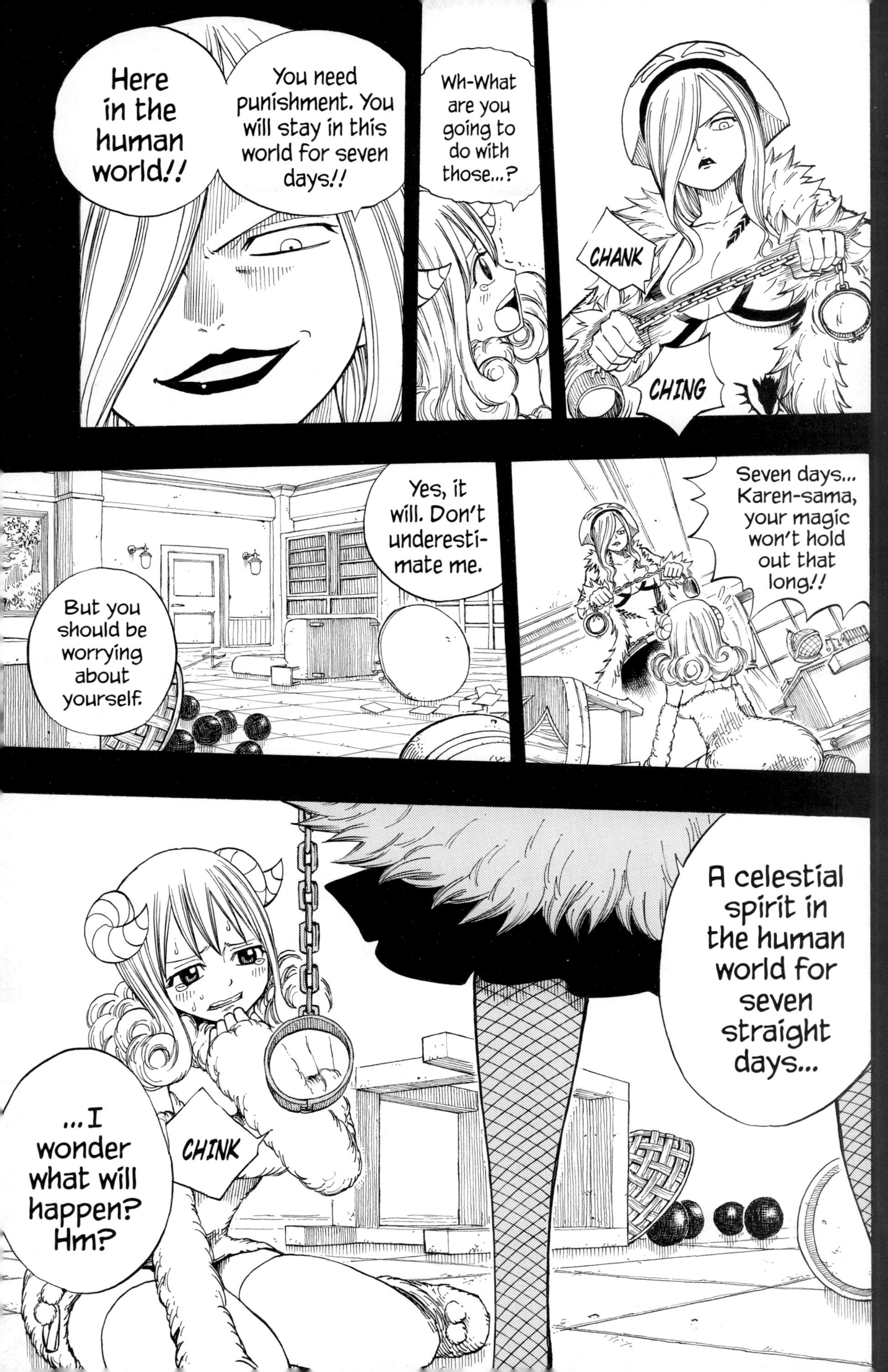
CHANK
CHING
Wh-What are you going to do with those...?
You need punishment. You will stay in this world for seven days!!
Here in the human world!!
Seven days... Karen-sama, your magic won't hold out that long!!
Yes, it will. Don't underestimate me.
But you should be worrying about yourself.
A celestial spirit in the human world for seven straight days...
CHINK
...I wonder what will happen? Hm?

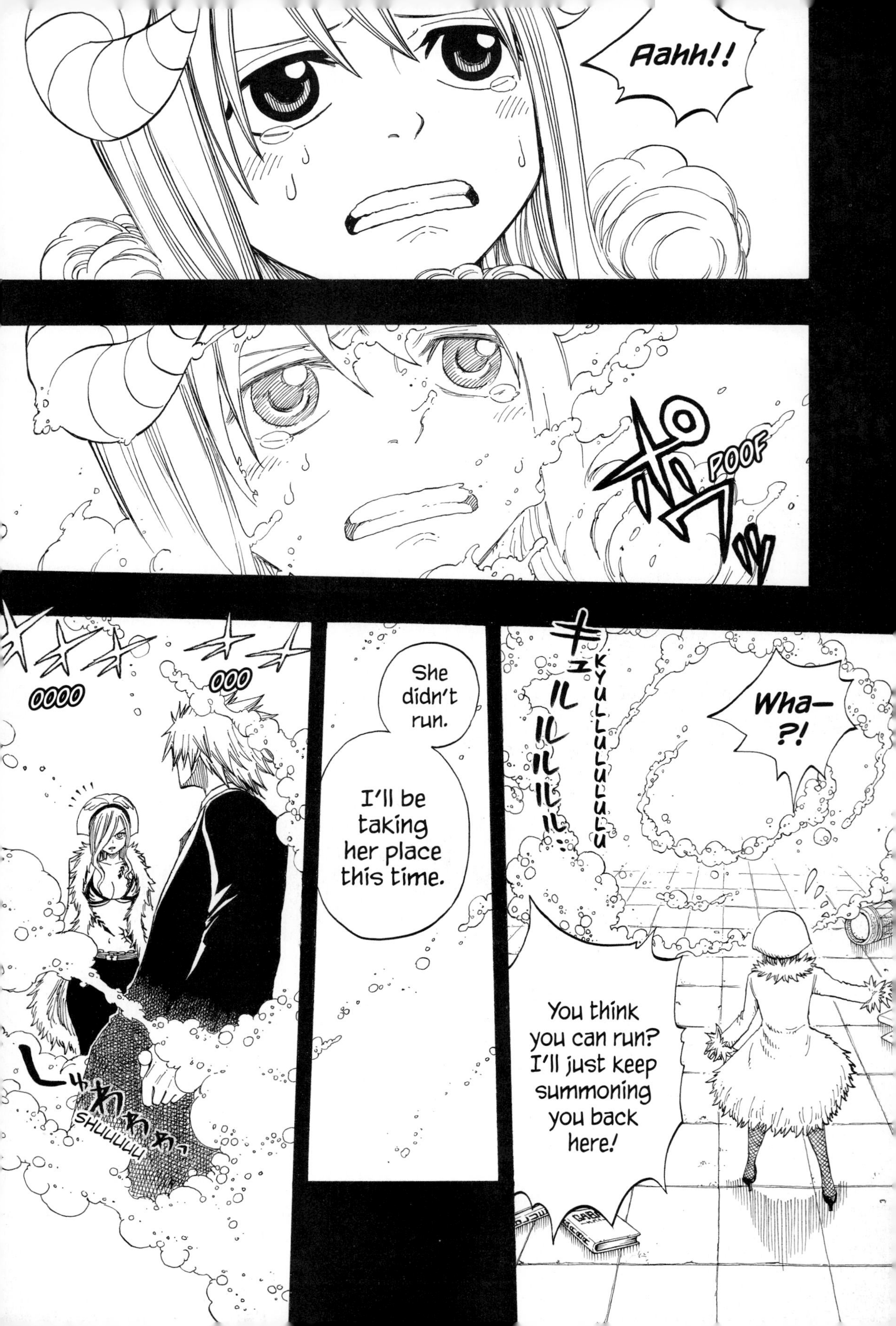
Aahh!!
POOF
Wha—?!
KYULLULULULU
You think you can run? I'll just keep summoning you back here!
She didn't run.
I'll be taking her place this time.
OOO
OOOO
SHUUUUU

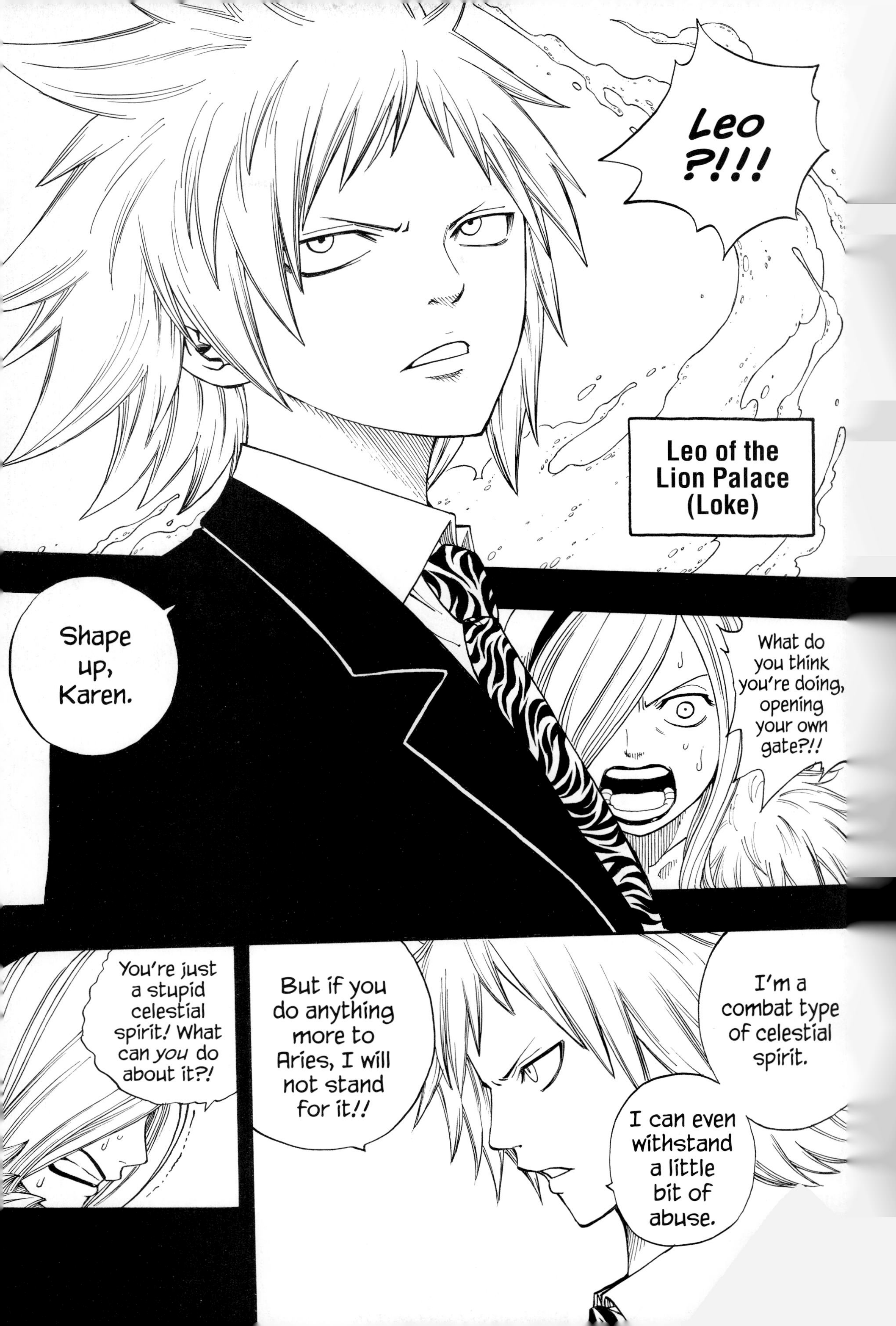
Leo ?!!!
Leo of the Lion Palace (Loke)
What do you think you're doing, opening your own gate?!!
Shape up, Karen.
I'm a combat type of celestial spirit.
I can even withstand a little bit of abuse.
But if you do anything more to Aries, I will not stand for it!!
You're just a stupid celestial spirit! What can *you* do about it?!

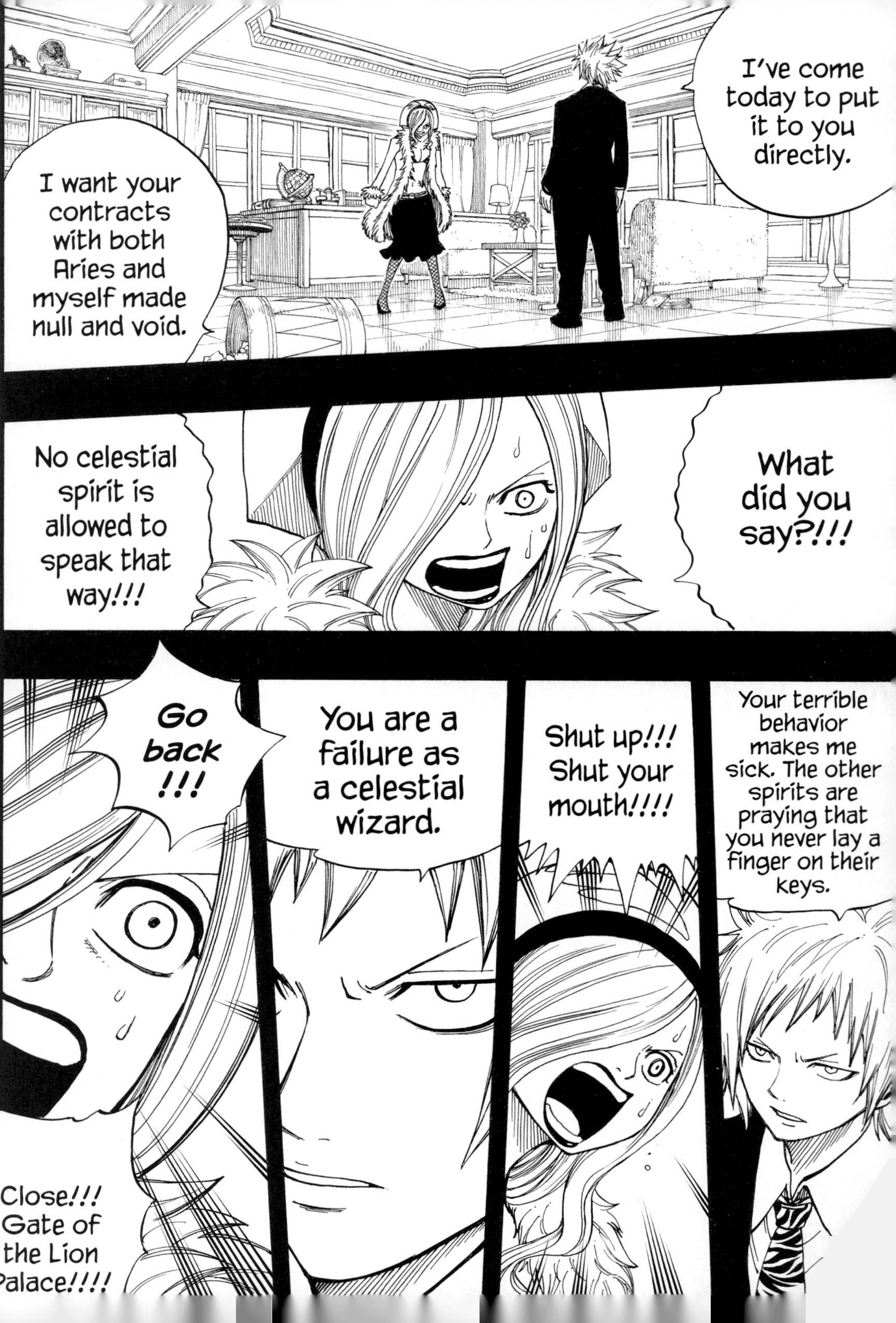
I've come today to put it to you directly.
I want your contracts with both Aries and myself made null and void.
What did you say?!!!
No celestial spirit is allowed to speak that way!!!
Your terrible behavior makes me sick. The other spirits are praying that you never lay a finger on their keys.
Shut up!!! Shut your mouth!!!!
You are a failure as a celestial wizard.
Go back!!!
Close!!! Gate of the Lion Palace!!!!

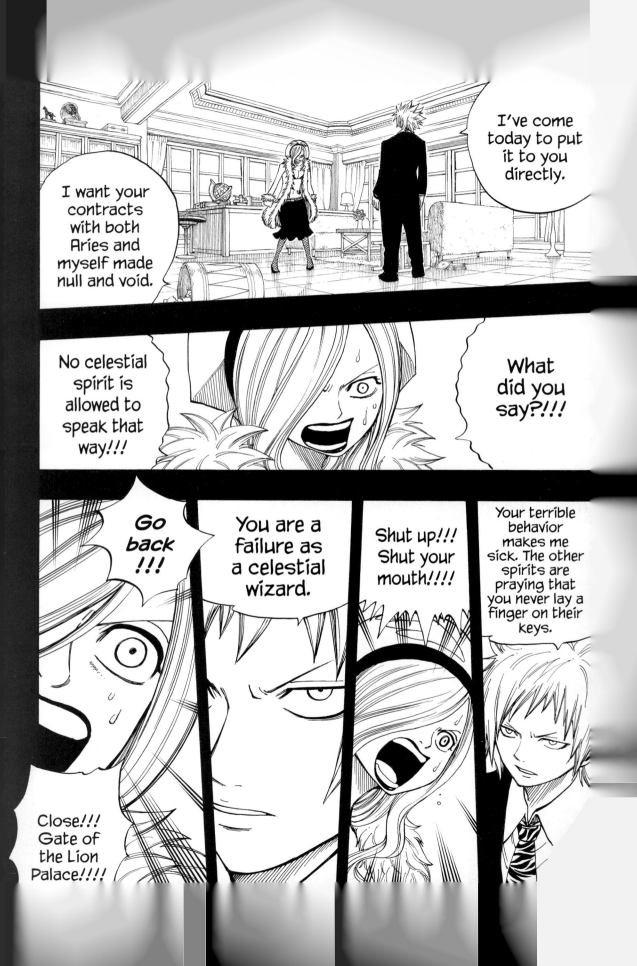

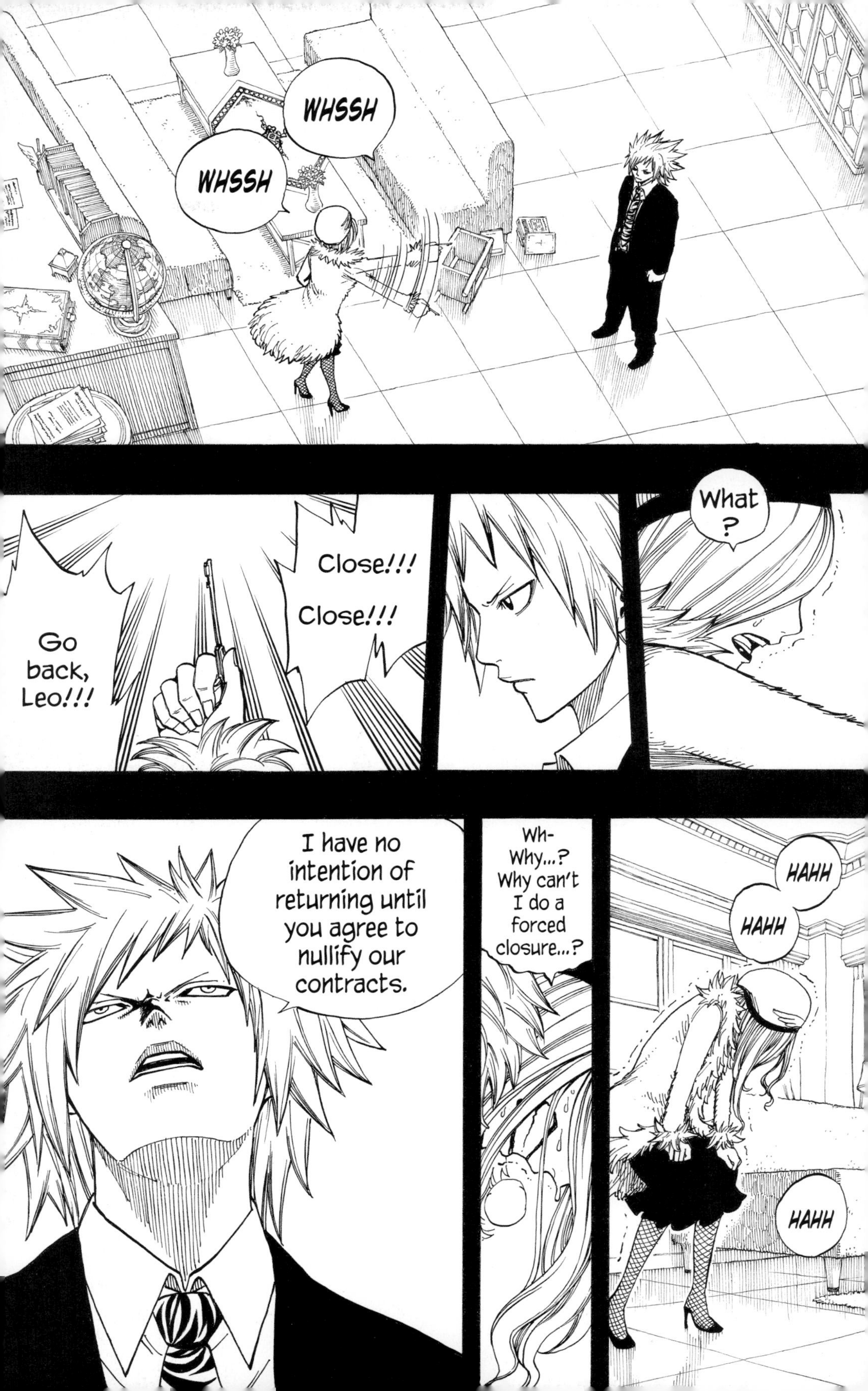
WHSSH
WHSSH
What ?
Close!!!
Close!!!
Go back, Leo!!!
HAHH
HAHH
HAHH
Wh- Why...? Why can't I do a forced closure...?
I have no intention of returning until you agree to nullify our contracts.

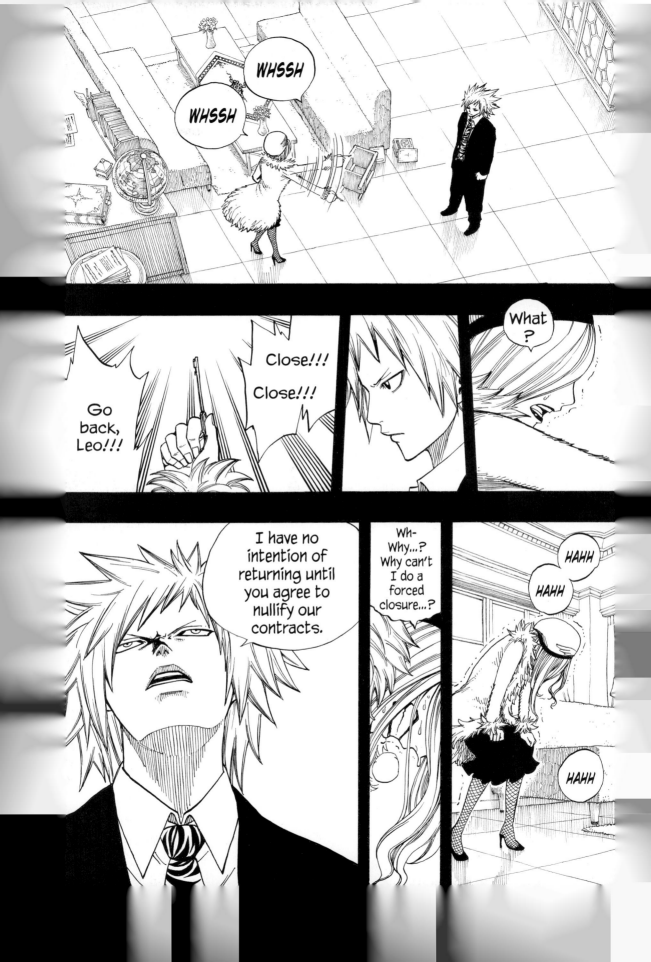

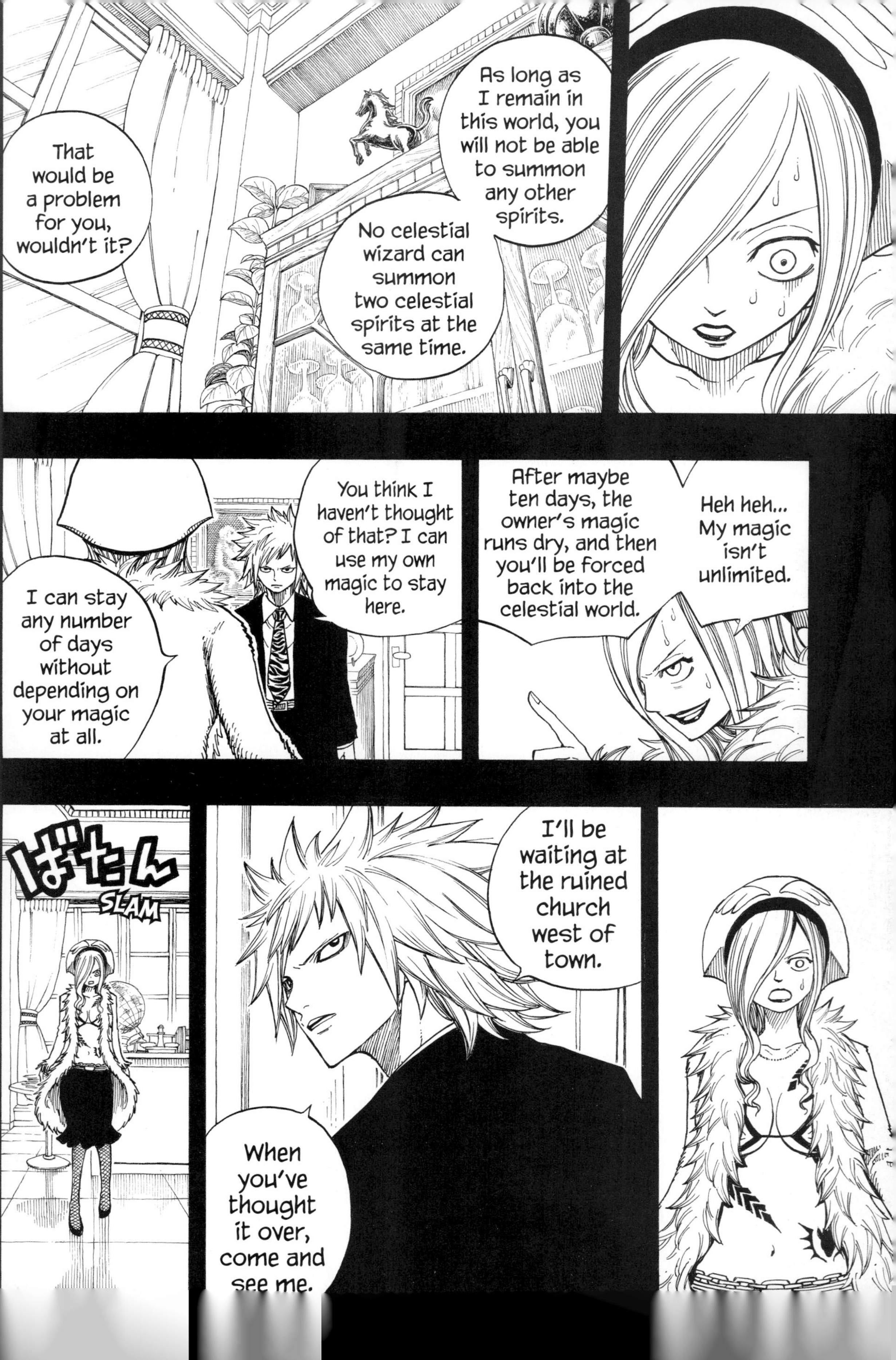
As long as I remain in this world, you will not be able to summon any other spirits.
No celestial wizard can summon two celestial spirits at the same time.
That would be a problem for you, wouldn't it?
Heh heh... My magic isn't unlimited.
After maybe ten days, the owner's magic runs dry, and then you'll be forced back into the celestial world.
You think I haven't thought of that? I can use my own magic to stay here.
I can stay any number of days without depending on your magic at all.
I'll be waiting at the ruined church west of town.
When you've thought it over, come and see me.
ばたん
SLAM

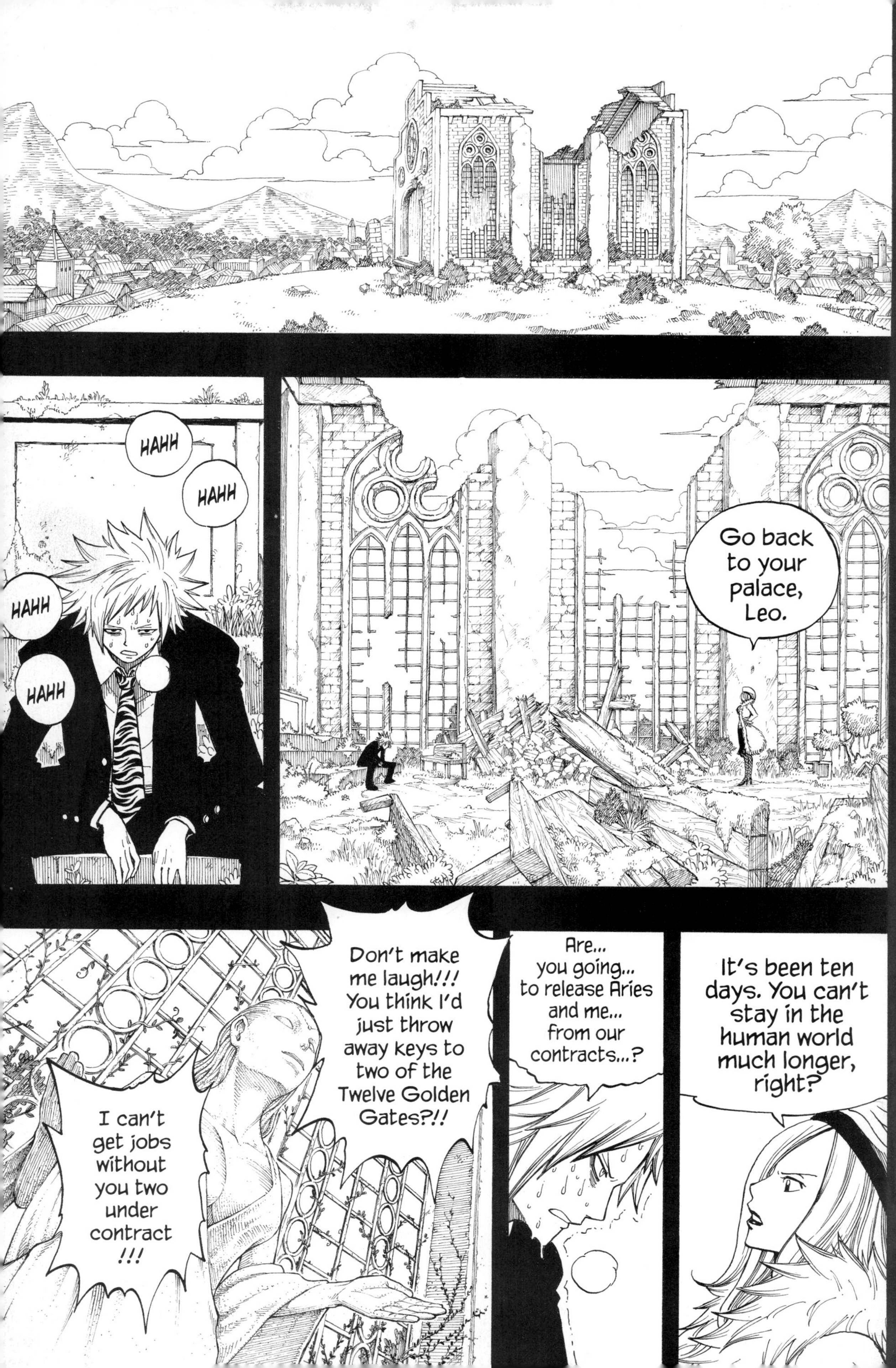
Go back to your palace, Leo.
HAHH
HAHH
HAHH
HAHH
It's been ten days. You can't stay in the human world much longer, right?
Are... you going... to release Aries and me... from our contracts...?
Don't make me laugh!!! You think I'd just throw away keys to two of the Twelve Golden Gates?!!
I can't get jobs without you two under contract!!!

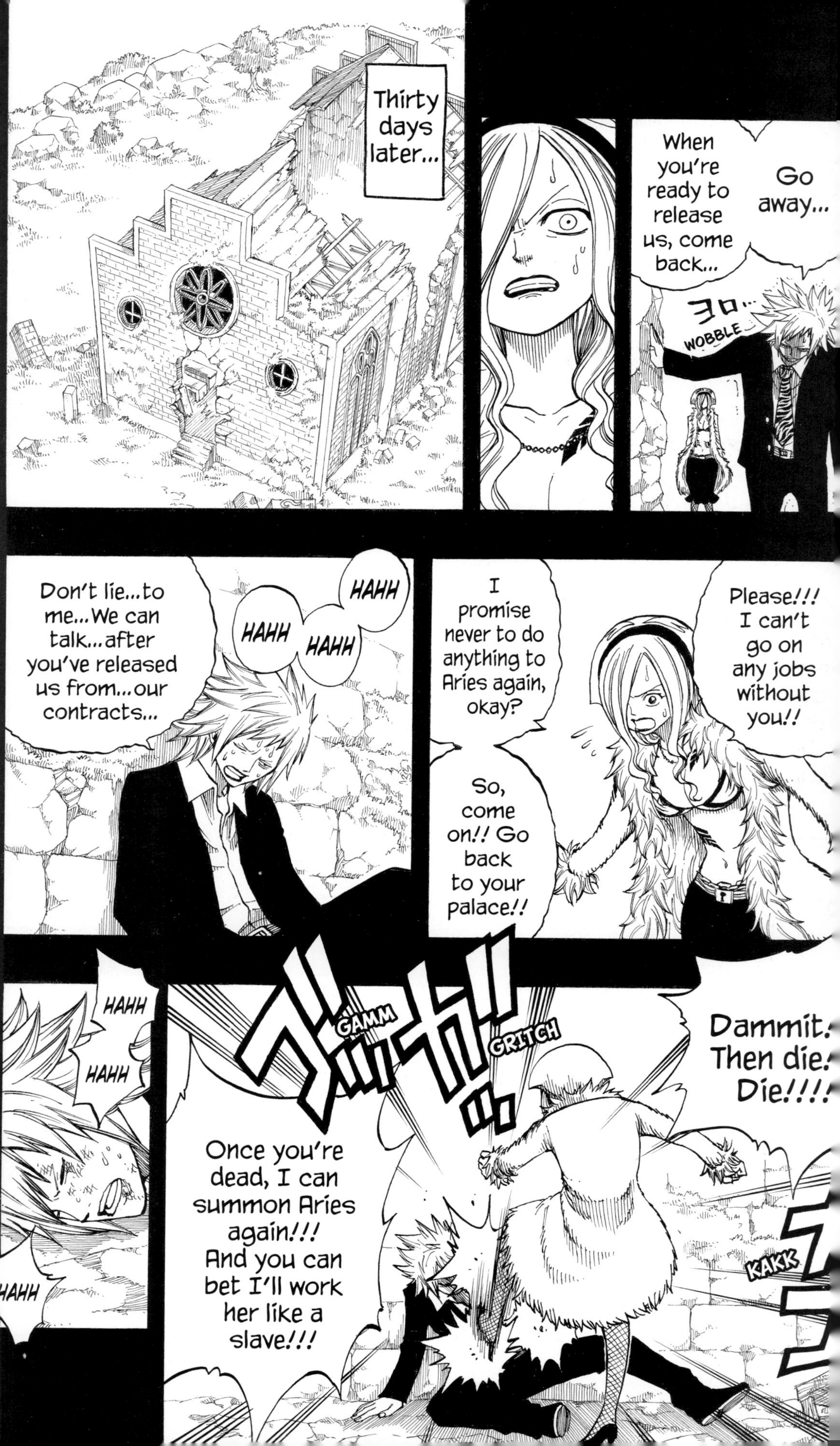
Go away...
When you're ready to release us, come back...
ヨロ… WOBBLE
Thirty days later...
Please!!! I can't go on any jobs without you!!
I promise never to do anything to Aries again, okay?
So, come on!! Go back to your palace!!
HAHH
HAHH
HAHH
Don't lie...to me...We can talk...after you've released us from...our contracts...
Dammit!! Then die!! Die!!!!
GAMM
GRITCH
KAKK
Once you're dead, I can summon Aries again!!! And you can bet I'll work her like a slave!!!
HAHH
HAHH
HAHH

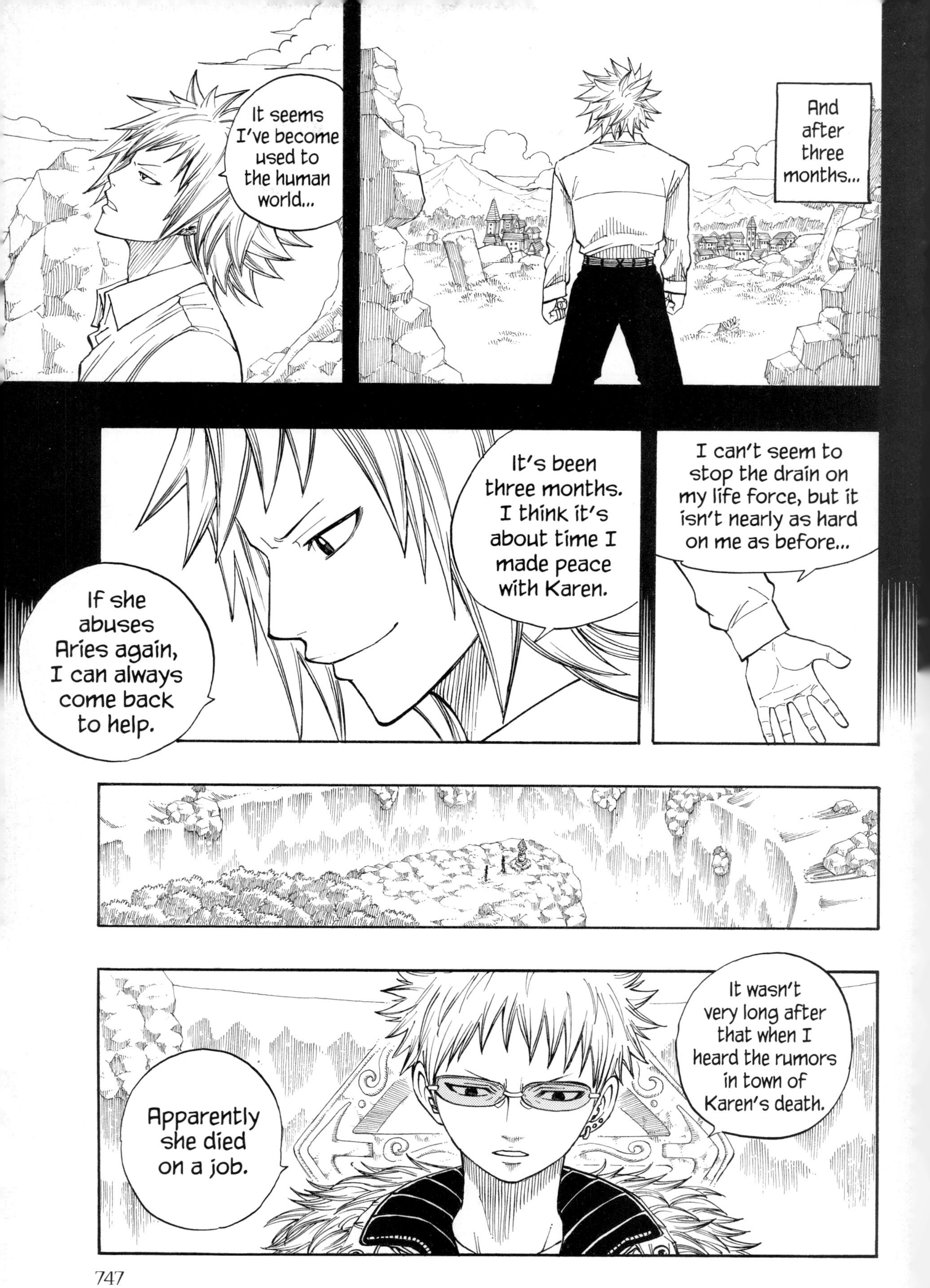
And after three months...
It seems I've become used to the human world...
I can't seem to stop the drain on my life force, but it isn't nearly as hard on me as before...
It's been three months. I think it's about time I made peace with Karen.
If she abuses Aries again, I can always come back to help.
It wasn't very long after that when I heard the rumors in town of Karen's death.
Apparently she died on a job.

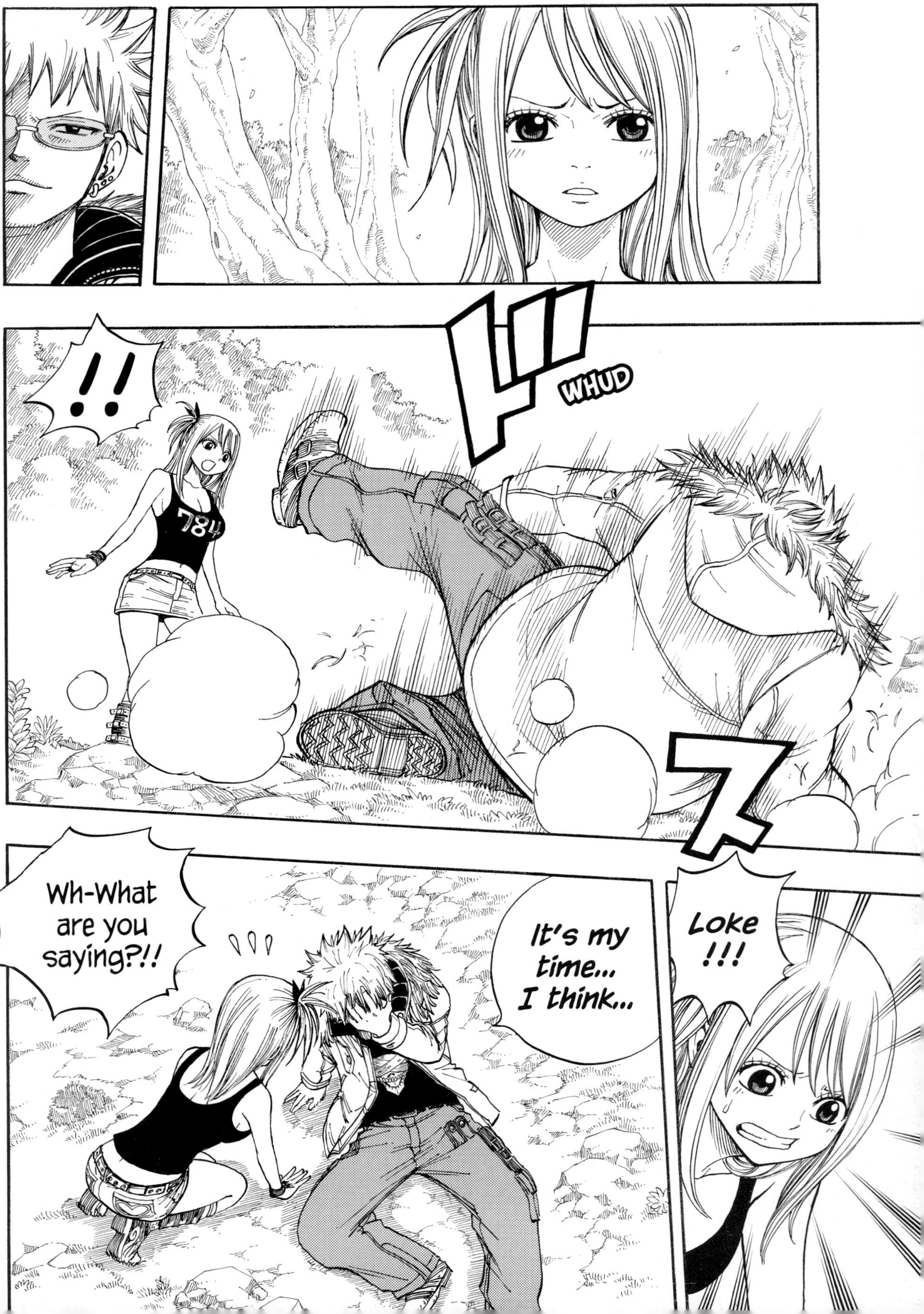

ドッ
WHUD
!!
ズ
Loke !!!
It's my time... I think...
Wh-What are you saying?!!

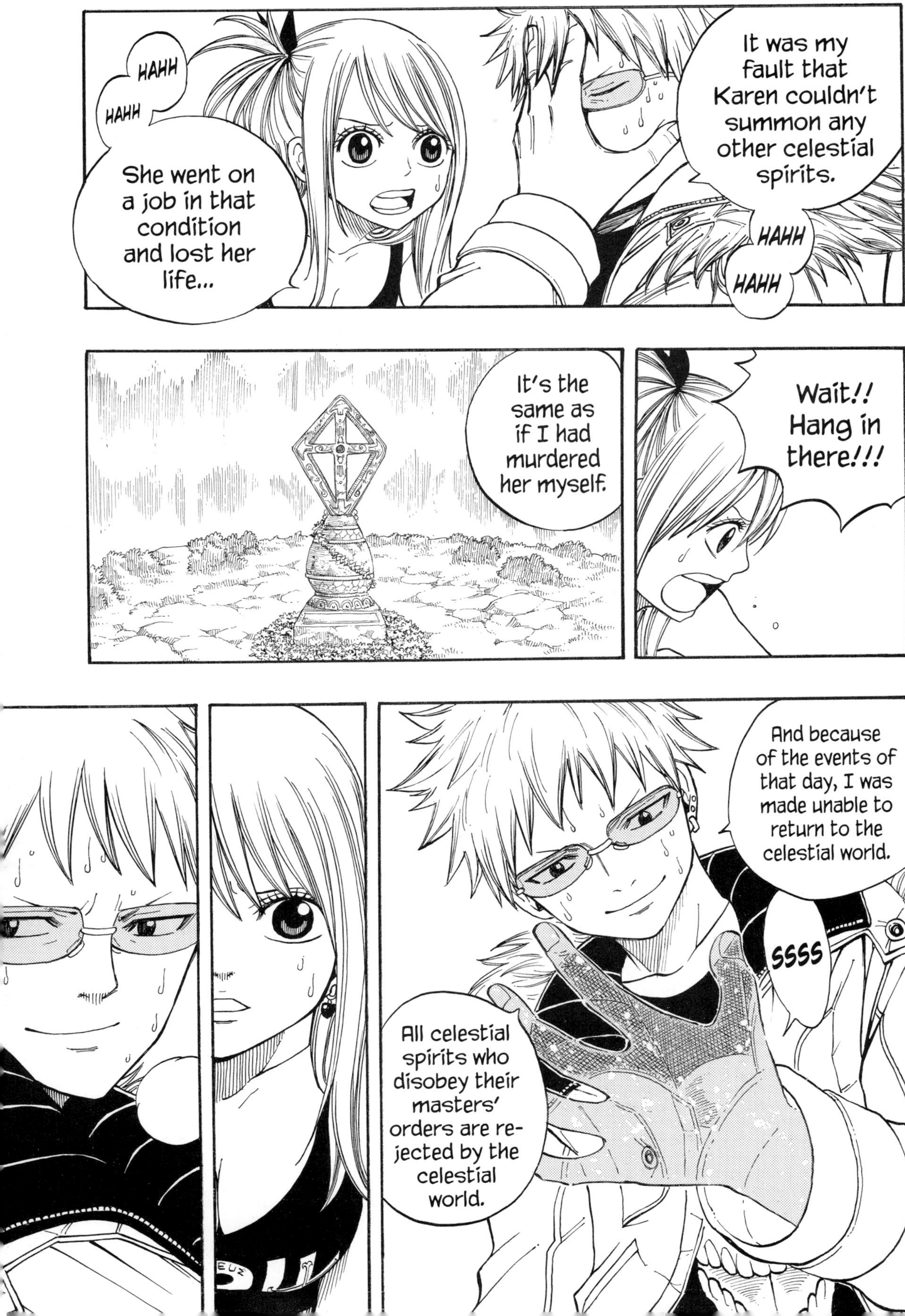
It was my fault that Karen couldn't summon any other celestial spirits.
HAHH
HAHH
HAHH
HAHH
She went on a job in that condition and lost her life...
Wait!! Hang in there!!!
It's the same as if I had murdered her myself.
And because of the events of that day, I was made unable to return to the celestial world.
SSSS
All celestial spirits who disobey their masters' orders are rejected by the celestial world.

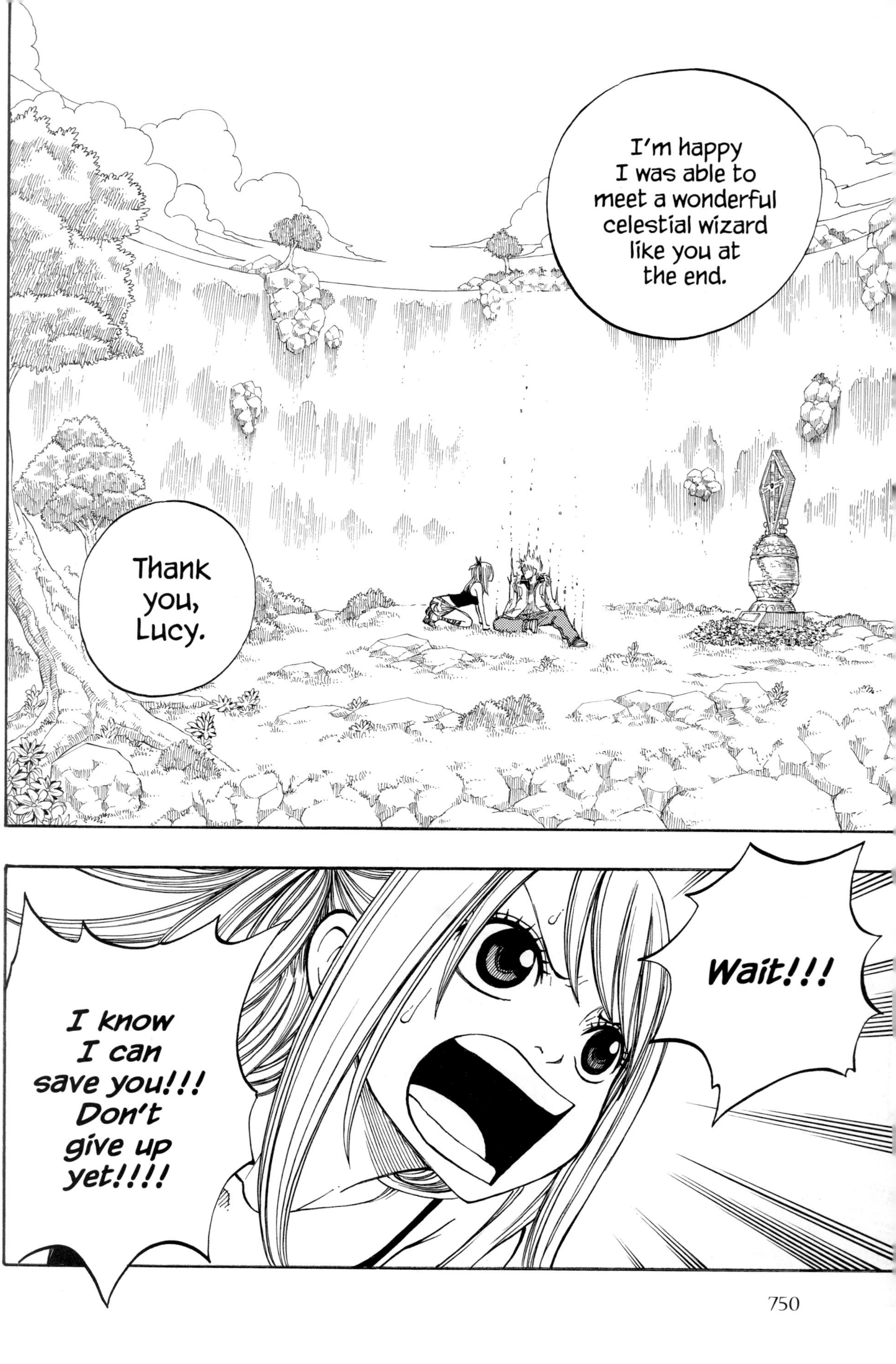
I'm happy I was able to meet a wonderful celestial wizard like you at the end.
Thank you, Lucy.
Wait!!!
I know I can save you!!! Don't give up yet!!!!

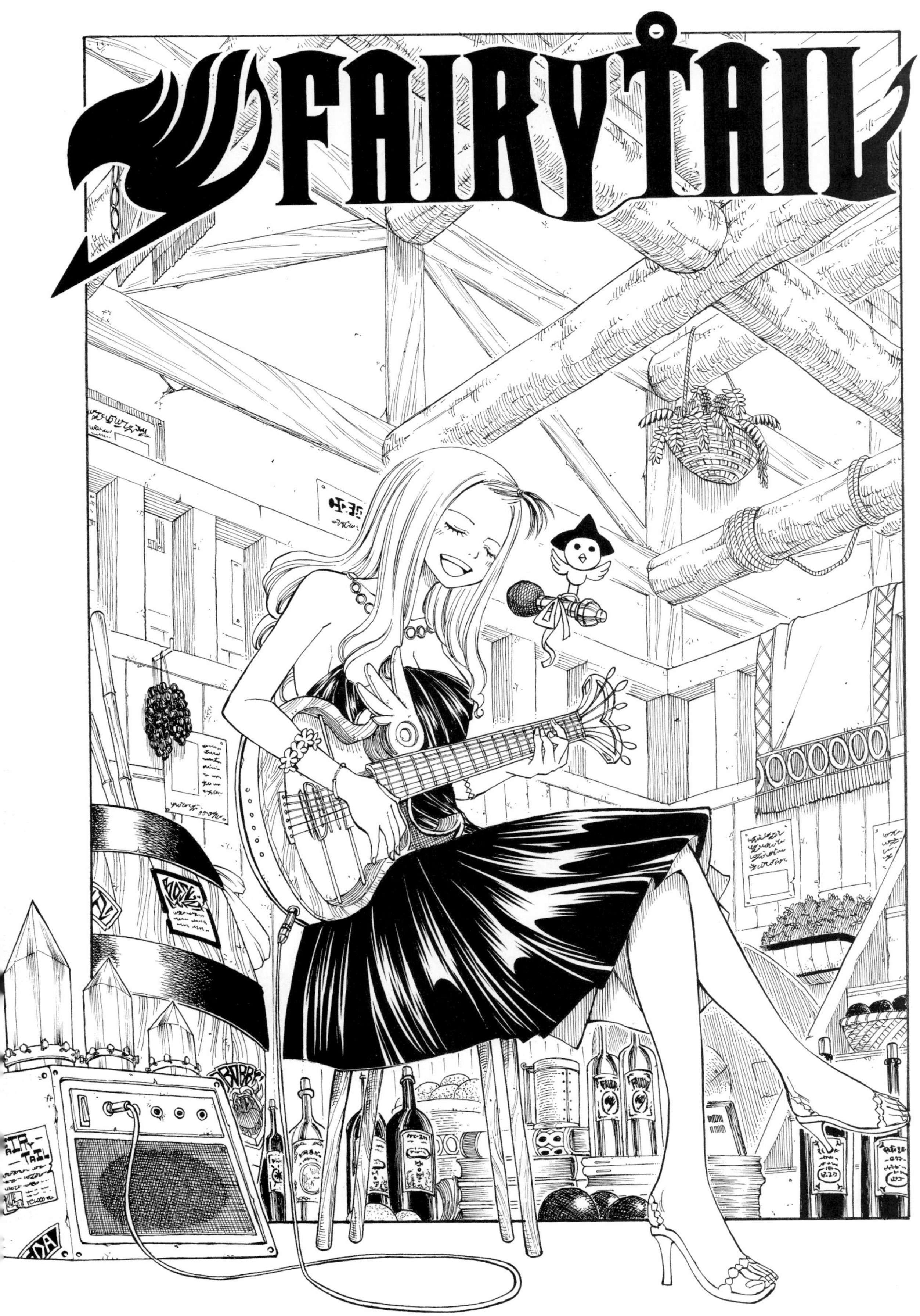
FAIRY TAIL

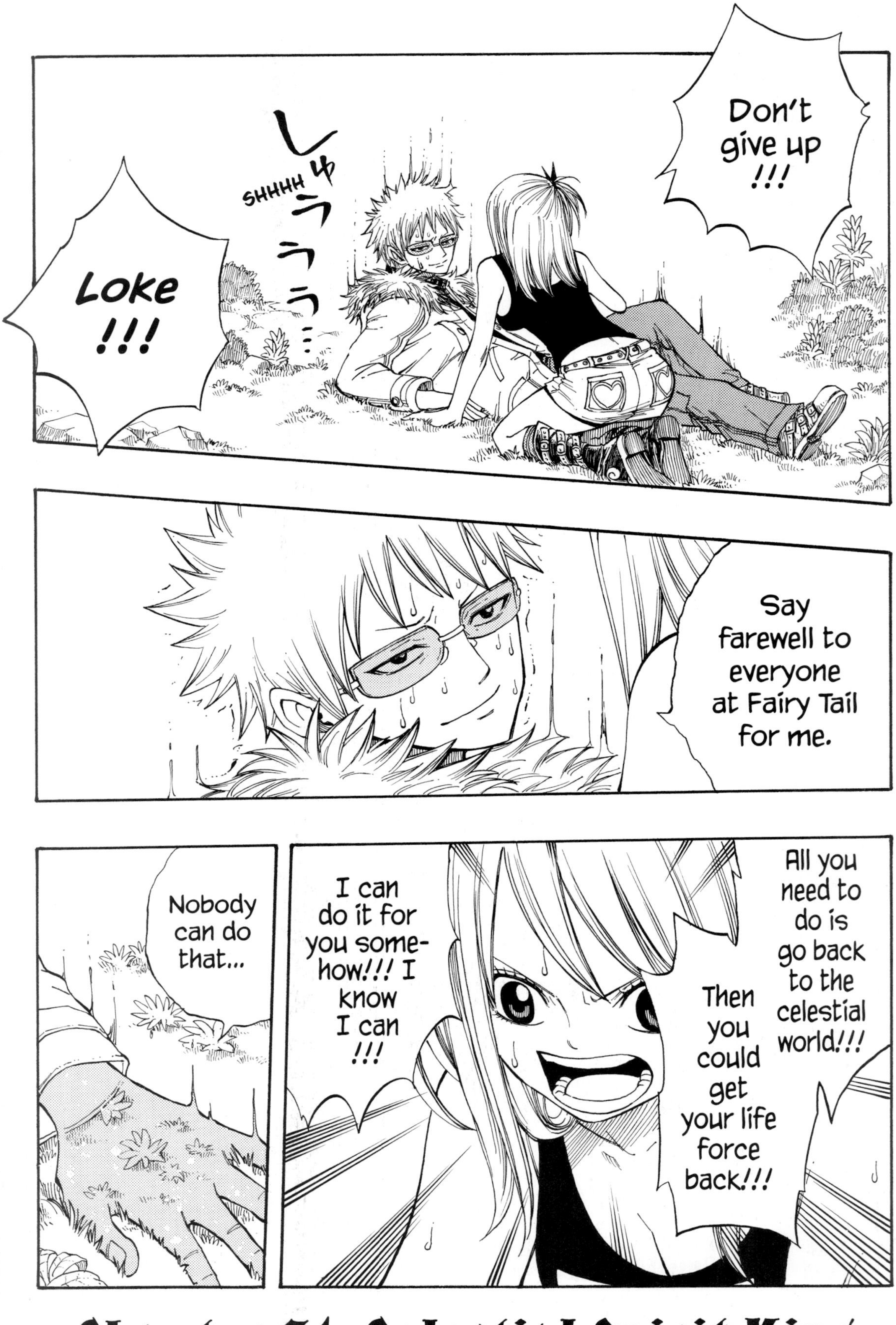
Don't give up !!!
しゅううう…
SHHHH
Loke !!!
Say farewell to everyone at Fairy Tail for me.
All you need to do is go back to the celestial world!!!
Then you could get your life force back!!!
I can do it for you some-how!!! I know I can !!!
Nobody can do that...

Chapter 74: Celestial Spirit King

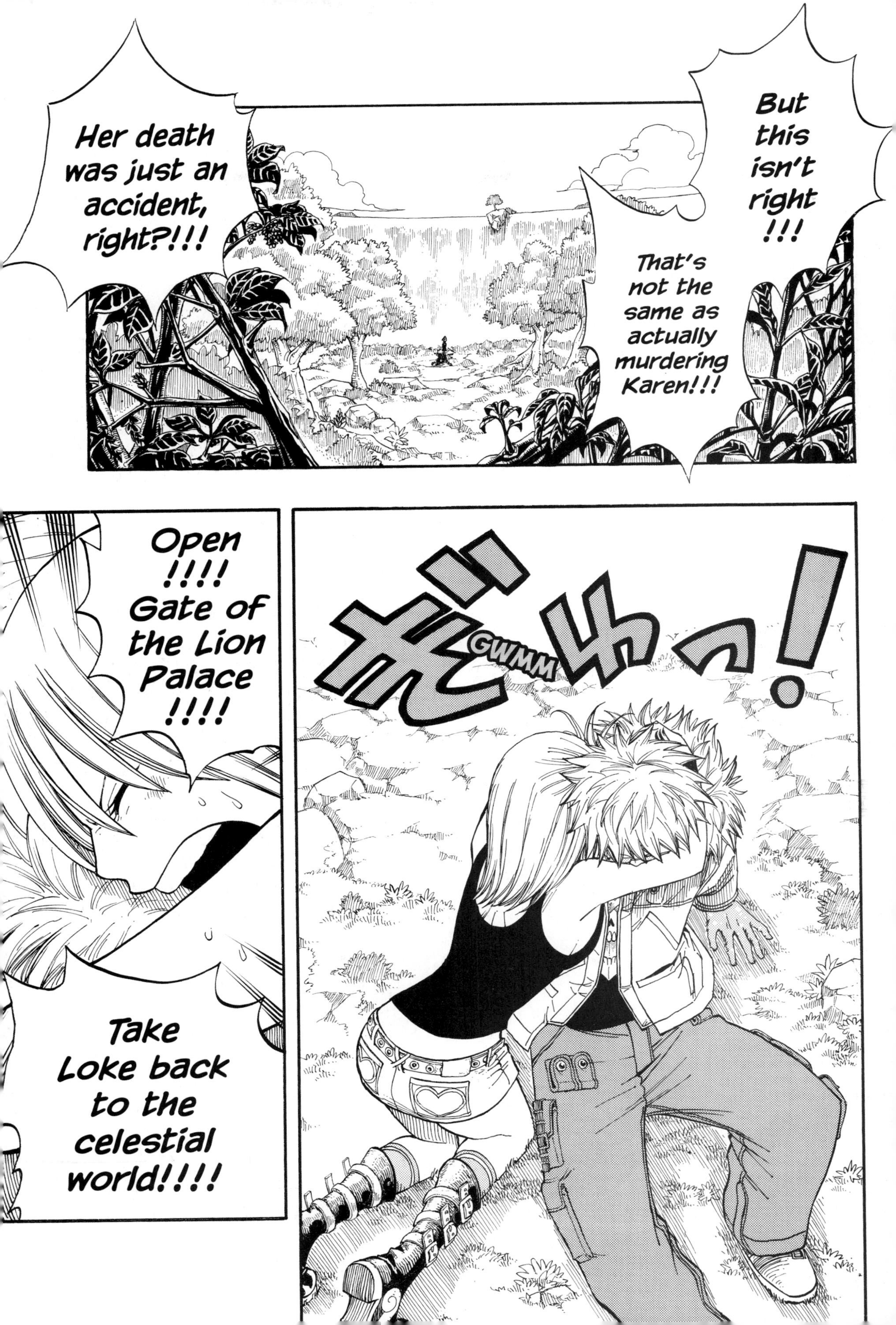

But this isn't right!!!
That's not the same as actually murdering Karen!!!
Her death was just an accident, right?!!!
GWMM
Open!!!! Gate of the Lion Palace!!!!
Take Loke back to the celestial world!!!!

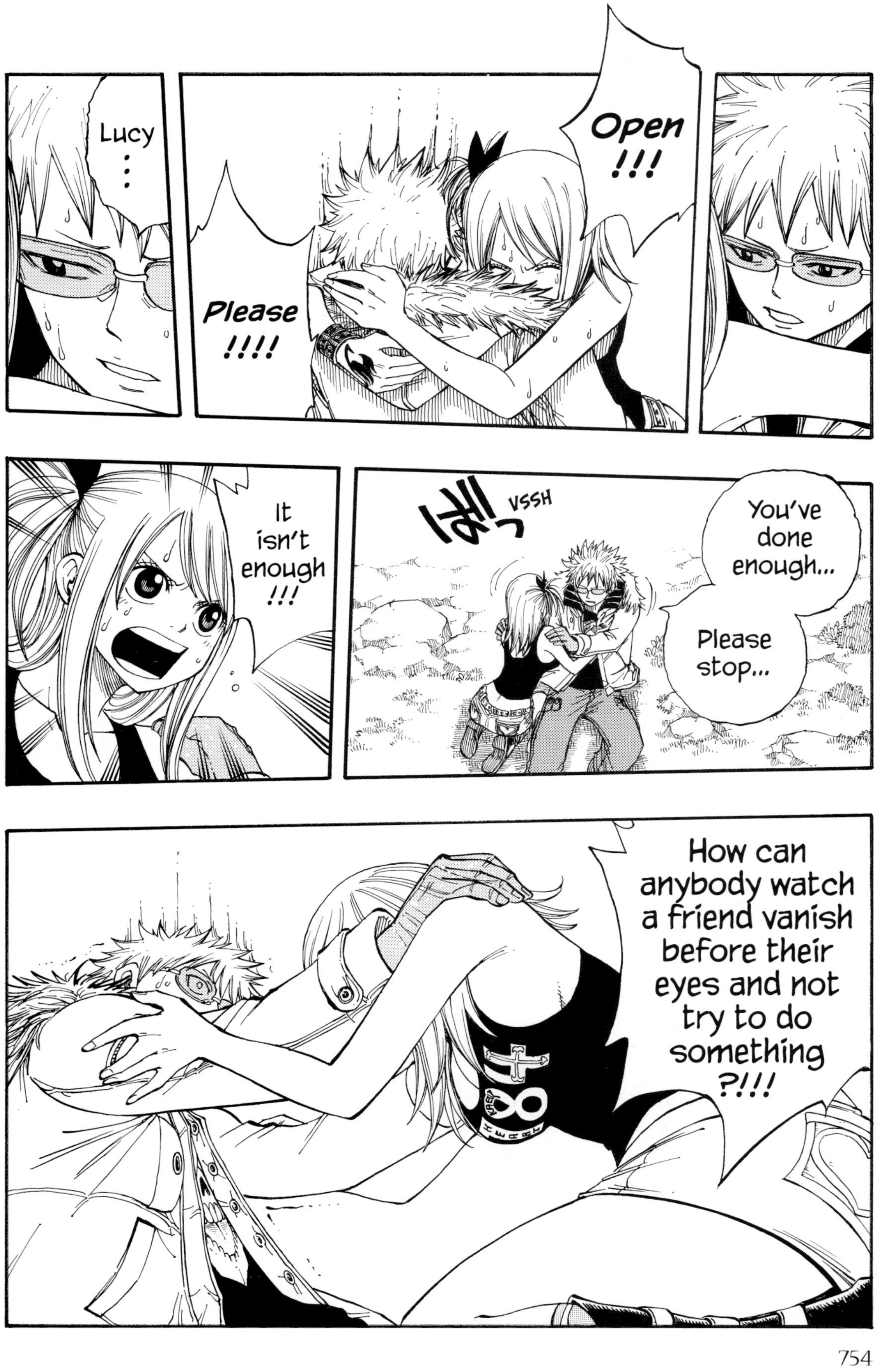
Open!!!
Please!!!!
Lucy...
VSSH
You've done enough...
Please stop...
It isn't enough!!!
How can anybody watch a friend vanish before their eyes and not try to do something?!!!

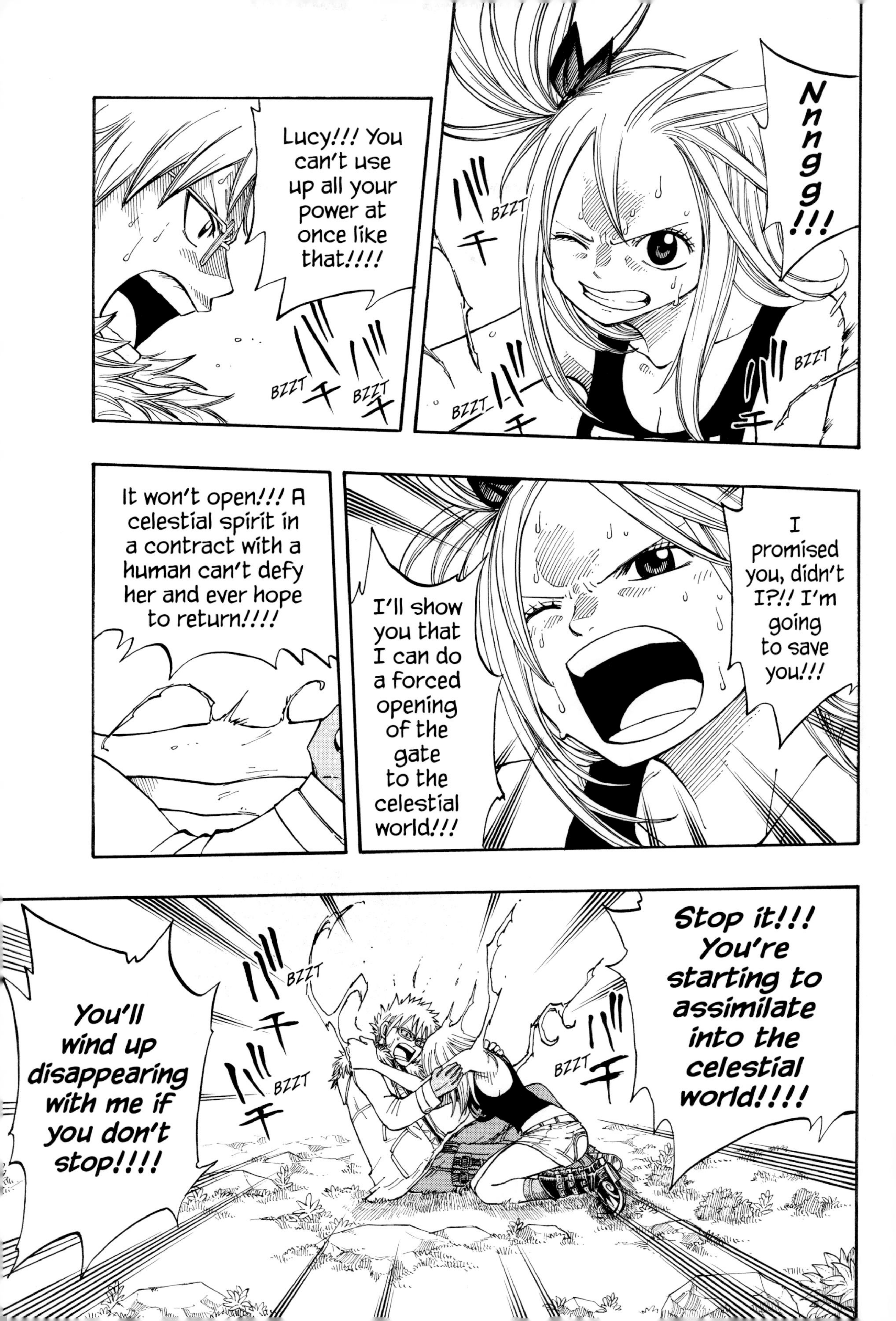

Nnngg!!!
BZZT
BZZT
BZZT
Lucy!!! You can't use up all your power at once like that!!!!
BZZT
BZZT
I promised you, didn't I?!! I'm going to save you!!!
I'll show you that I can do a forced opening of the gate to the celestial world!!!
It won't open!!! A celestial spirit in a contract with a human can't defy her and ever hope to return!!!!
Stop it!!! You're starting to assimilate into the celestial world!!!!
BZZT
BZZT
BZZT
You'll wind up disappearing with me if you don't stop!!!!

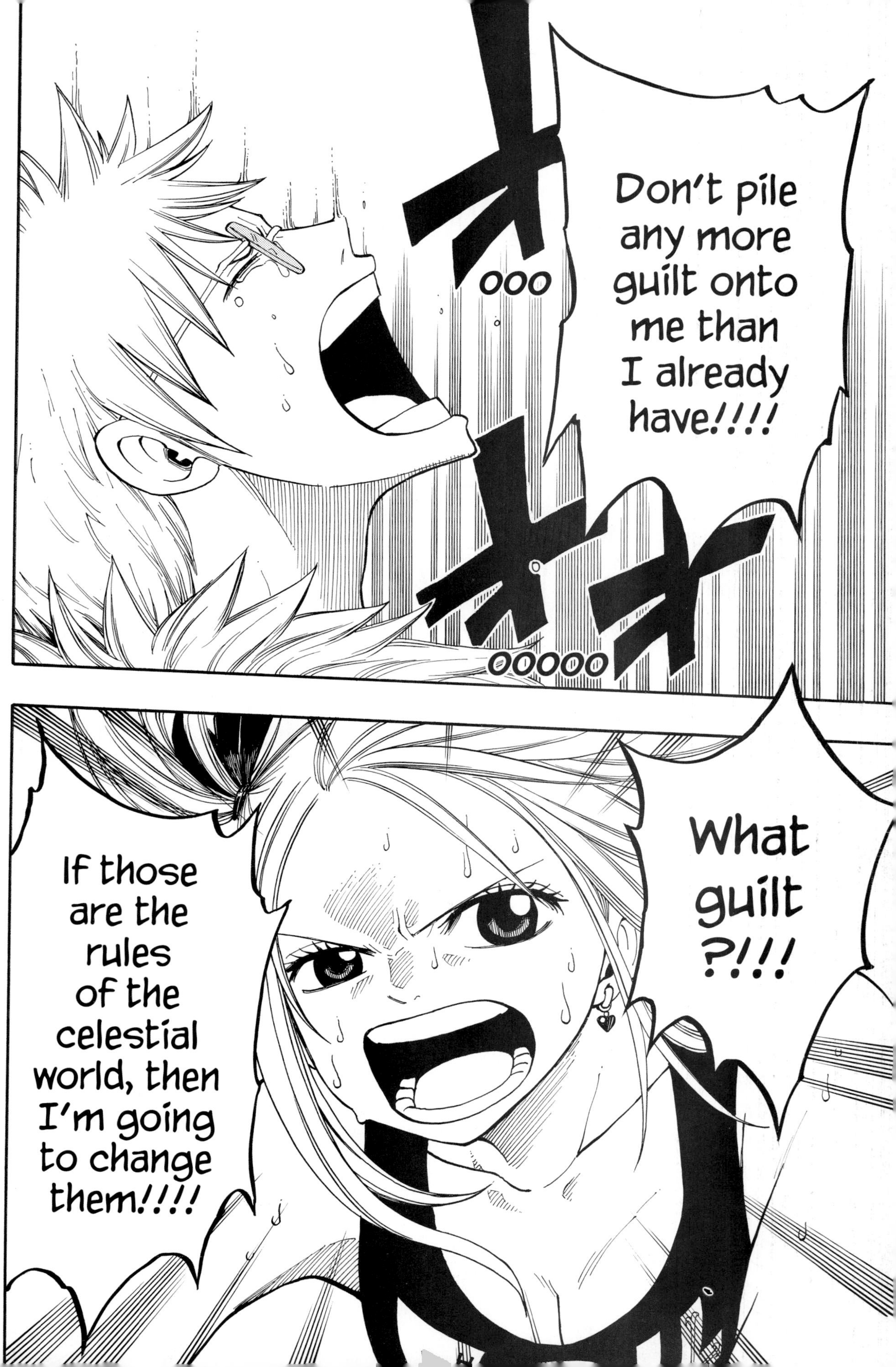
Don't pile any more guilt onto me than I already have!!!!
ooo
ooooo
What guilt?!!!
If those are the rules of the celestial world, then I'm going to change them!!!!

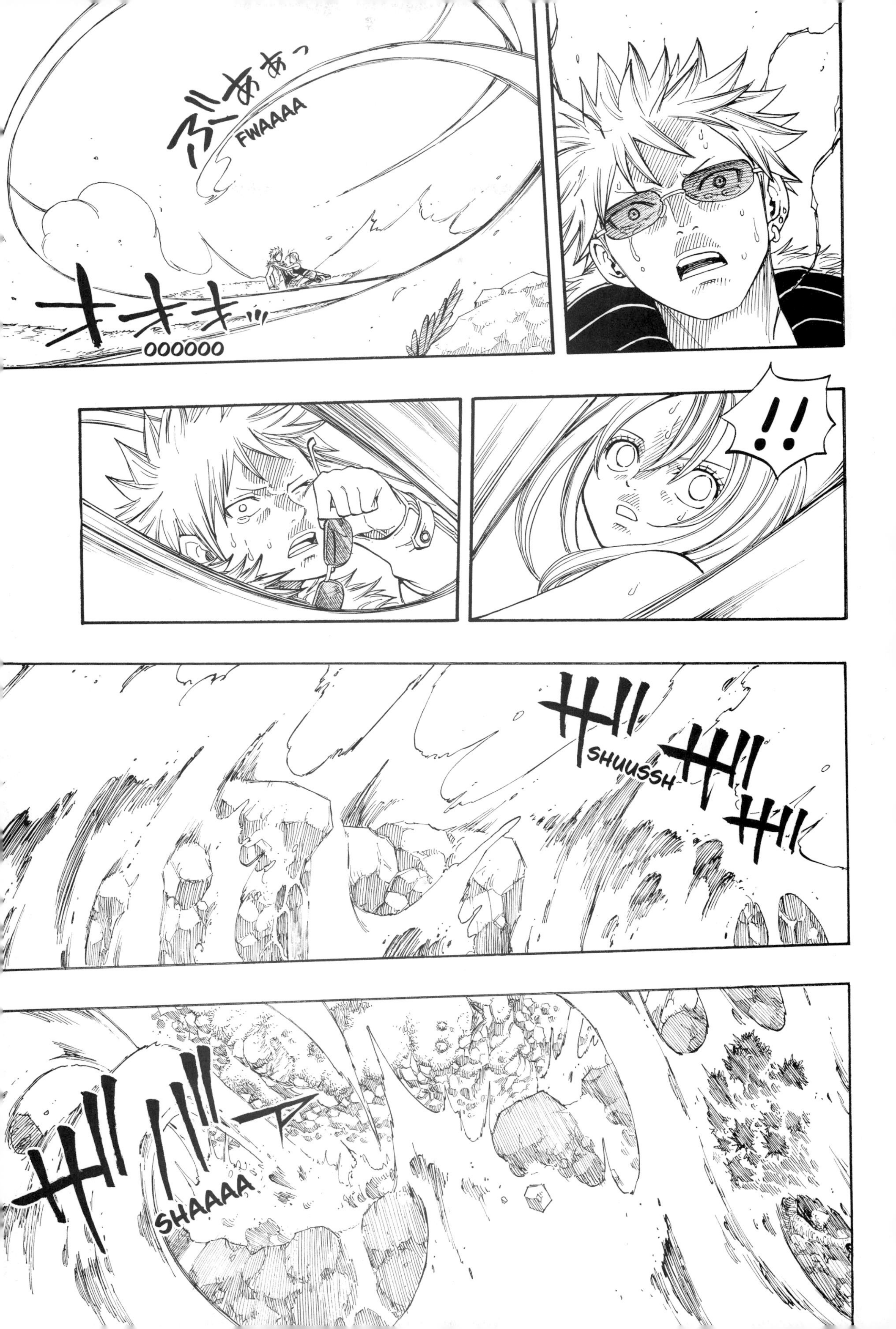
FWAAAA
OOOOOO
!!
SHUUSSH
SHAAAA

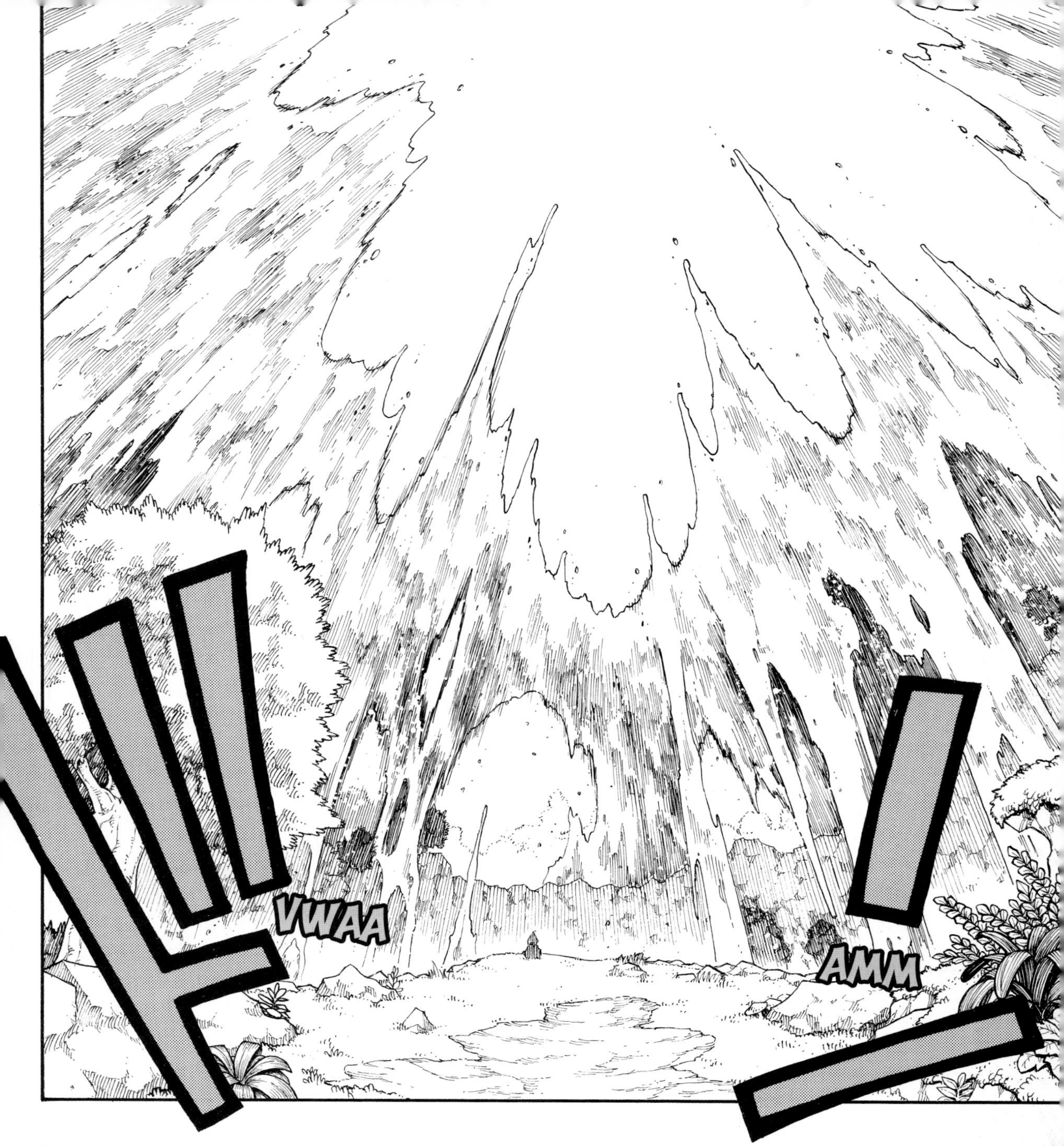
VWAA
AMM

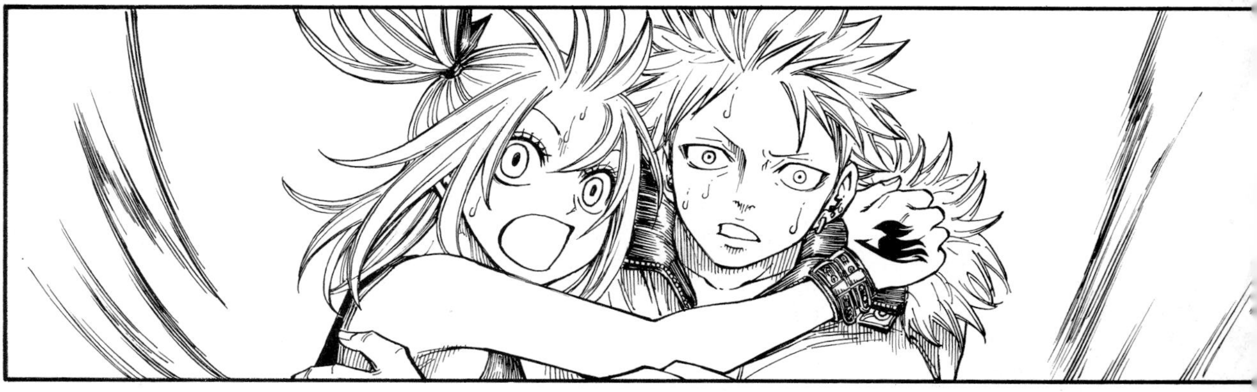

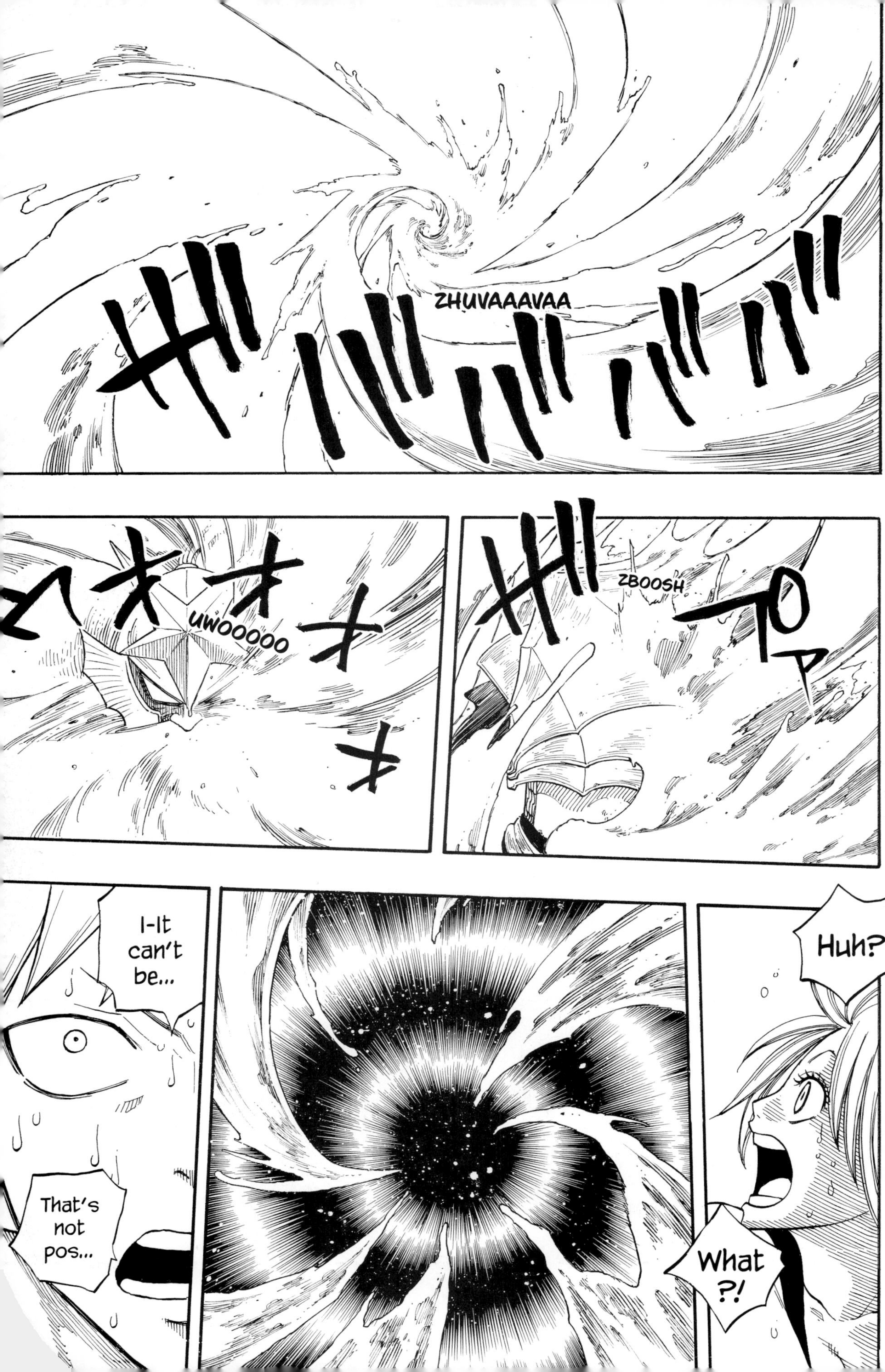
ZHUVAAAVAA
ZBOOSH
UWOOOOO
Huh?
What?!
I-It can't be...
That's not pos...

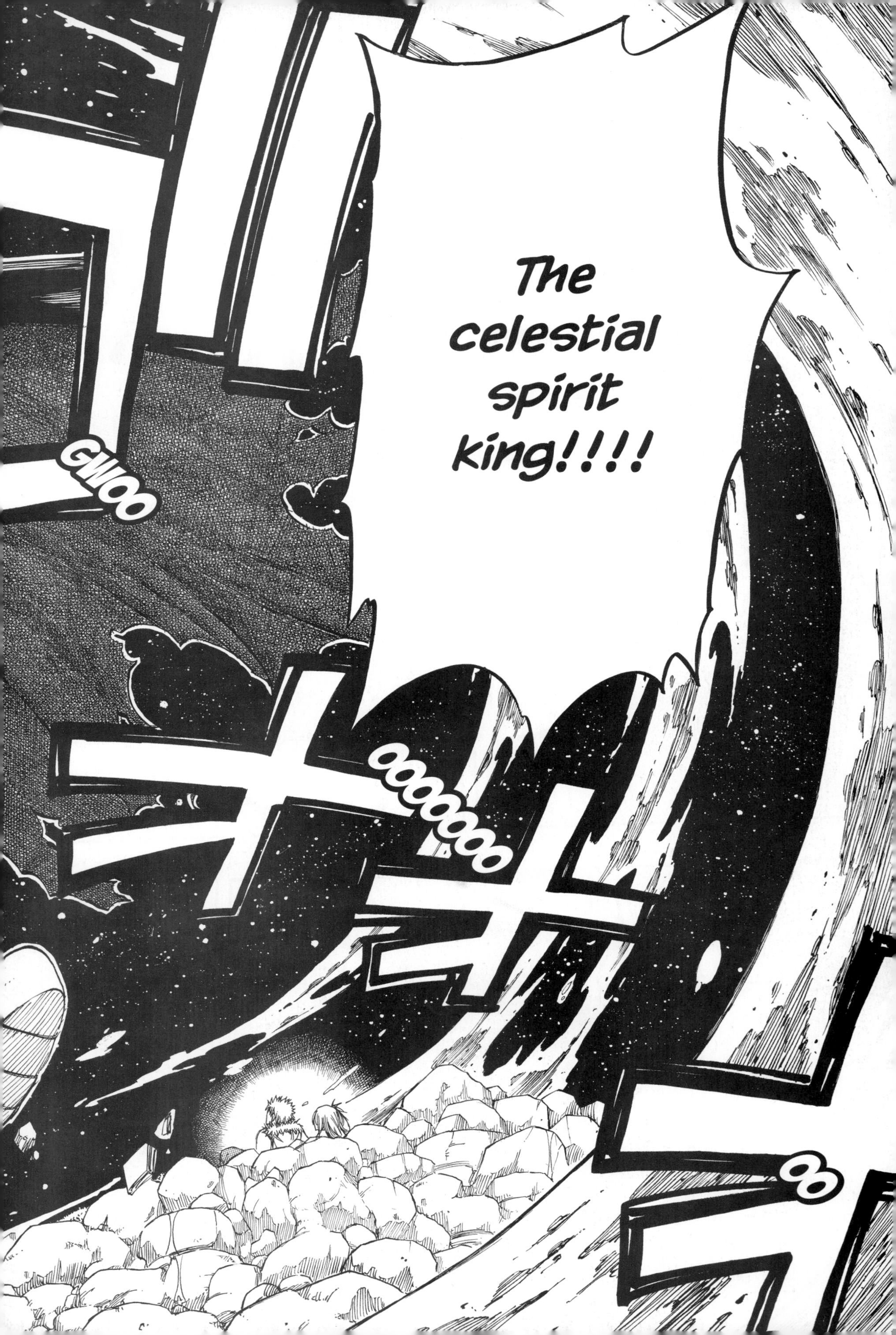
The celestial spirit king!!!!
GWOO
OOOOOOO
OO

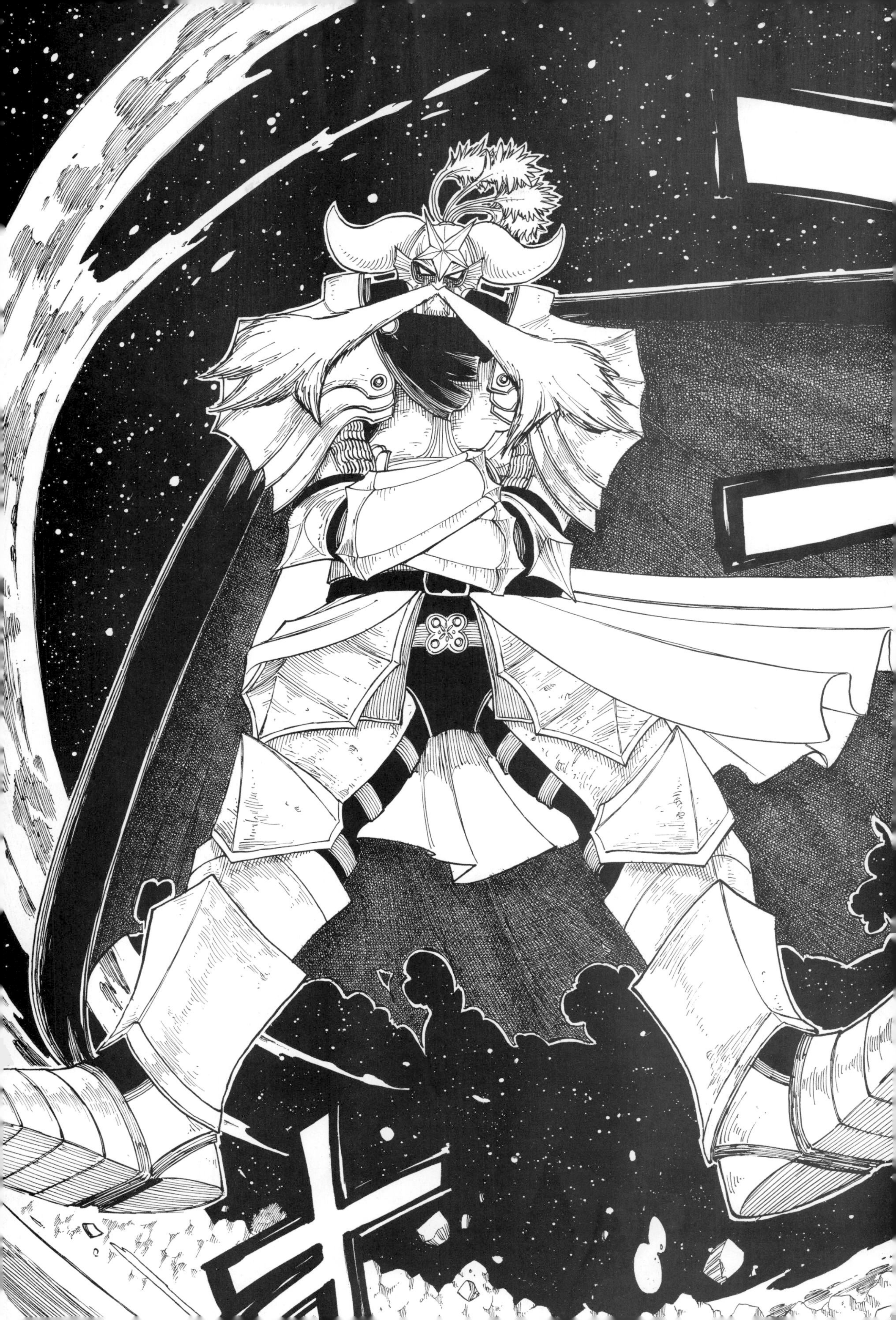

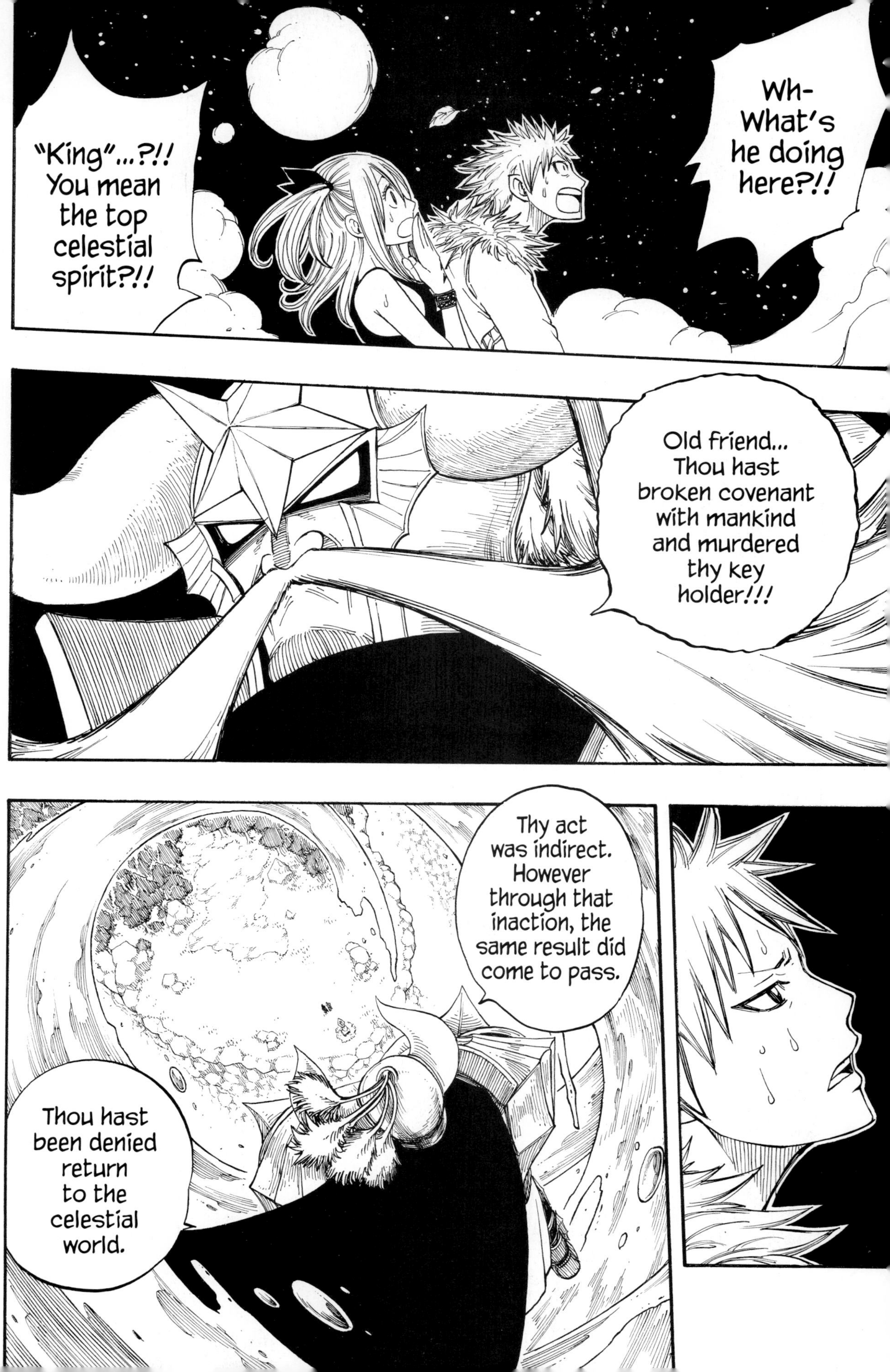
Wh- What's he doing here?!!
"King"...?!! You mean the top celestial spirit?!!
Old friend... Thou hast broken covenant with mankind and murdered thy key holder!!!
Thy act was indirect. However through that inaction, the same result did come to pass.
Thou hast been denied return to the celestial world.

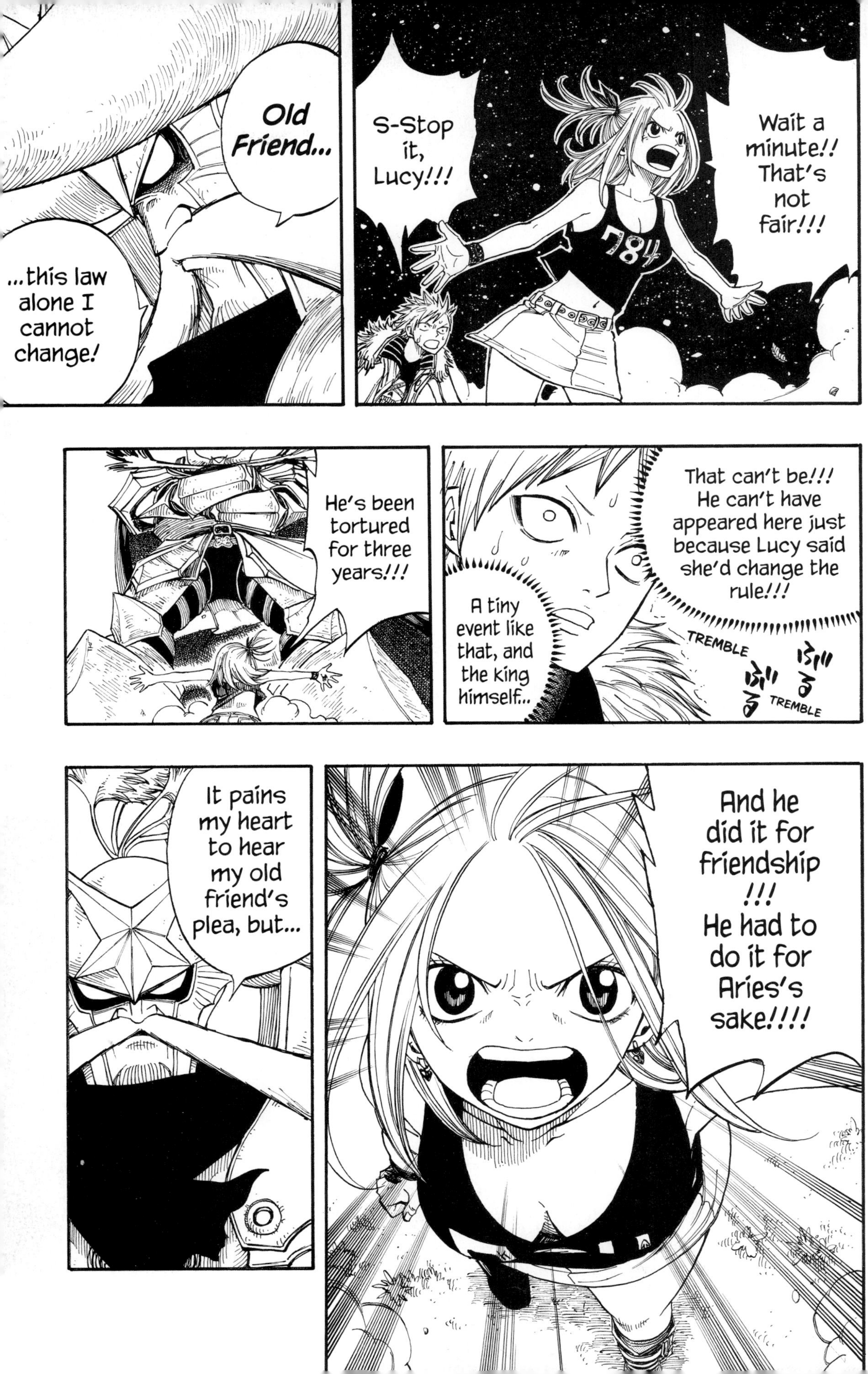
Wait a minute!! That's not fair!!!
S-Stop it, Lucy!!!
Old Friend...
...this law alone I cannot change!
That can't be!!! He can't have appeared here just because Lucy said she'd change the rule!!!
A tiny event like that, and the king himself...
TREMBLE
TREMBLE
He's been tortured for three years!!!
And he did it for friendship!!! He had to do it for Aries's sake!!!!
It pains my heart to hear my old friend's plea, but...

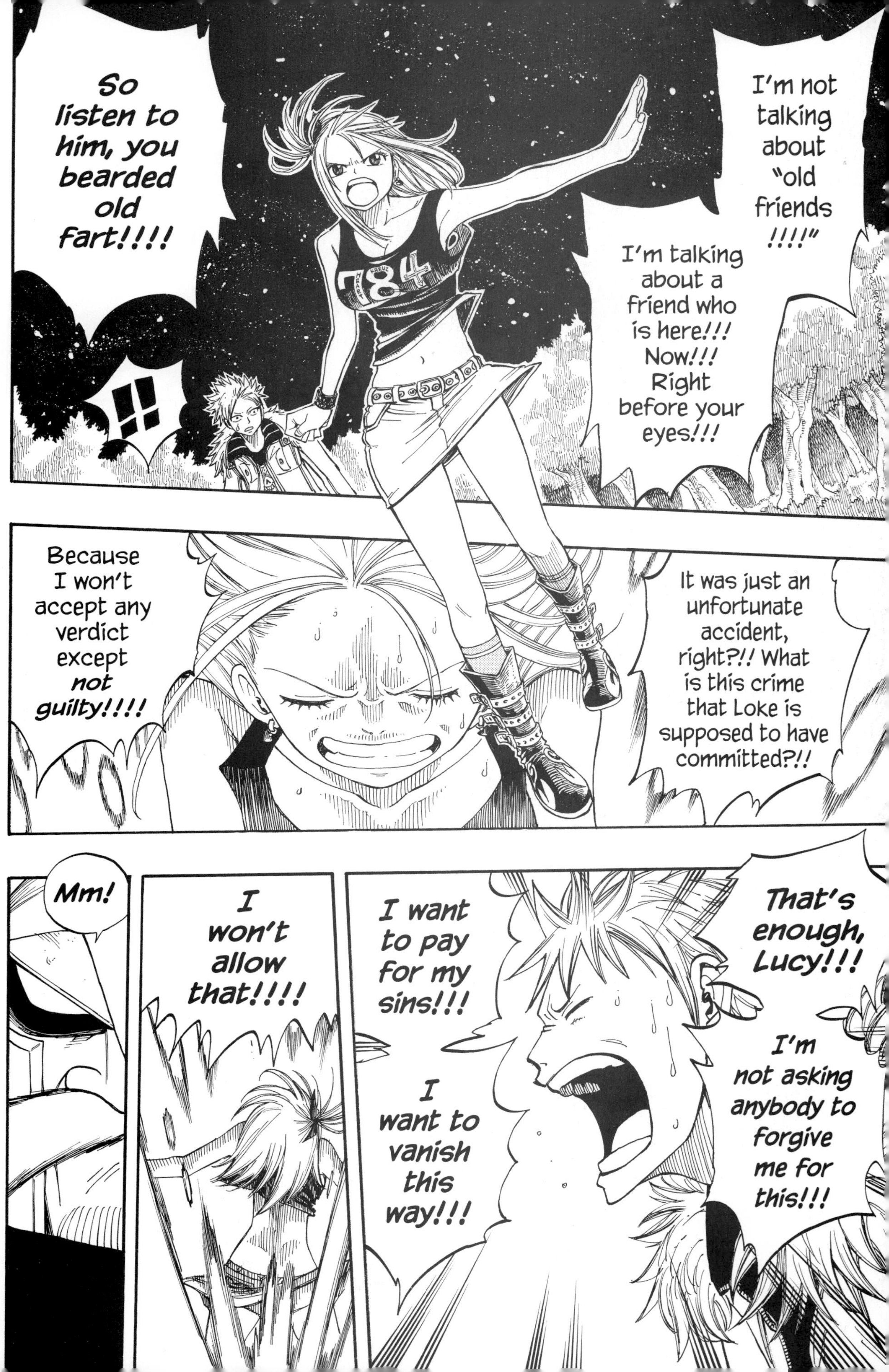
I'm not talking about "old friends!!!!"
I'm talking about a friend who is here!!! Now!!! Right before your eyes!!!
So listen to him, you bearded old fart!!!!
!!
It was just an unfortunate accident, right?!! What is this crime that Loke is supposed to have committed?!!
Because I won't accept any verdict except not guilty!!!!
That's enough, Lucy!!!
I'm not asking anybody to forgive me for this!!!
I want to pay for my sins!!!
I want to vanish this way!!!
I won't allow that!!!!
Mm!

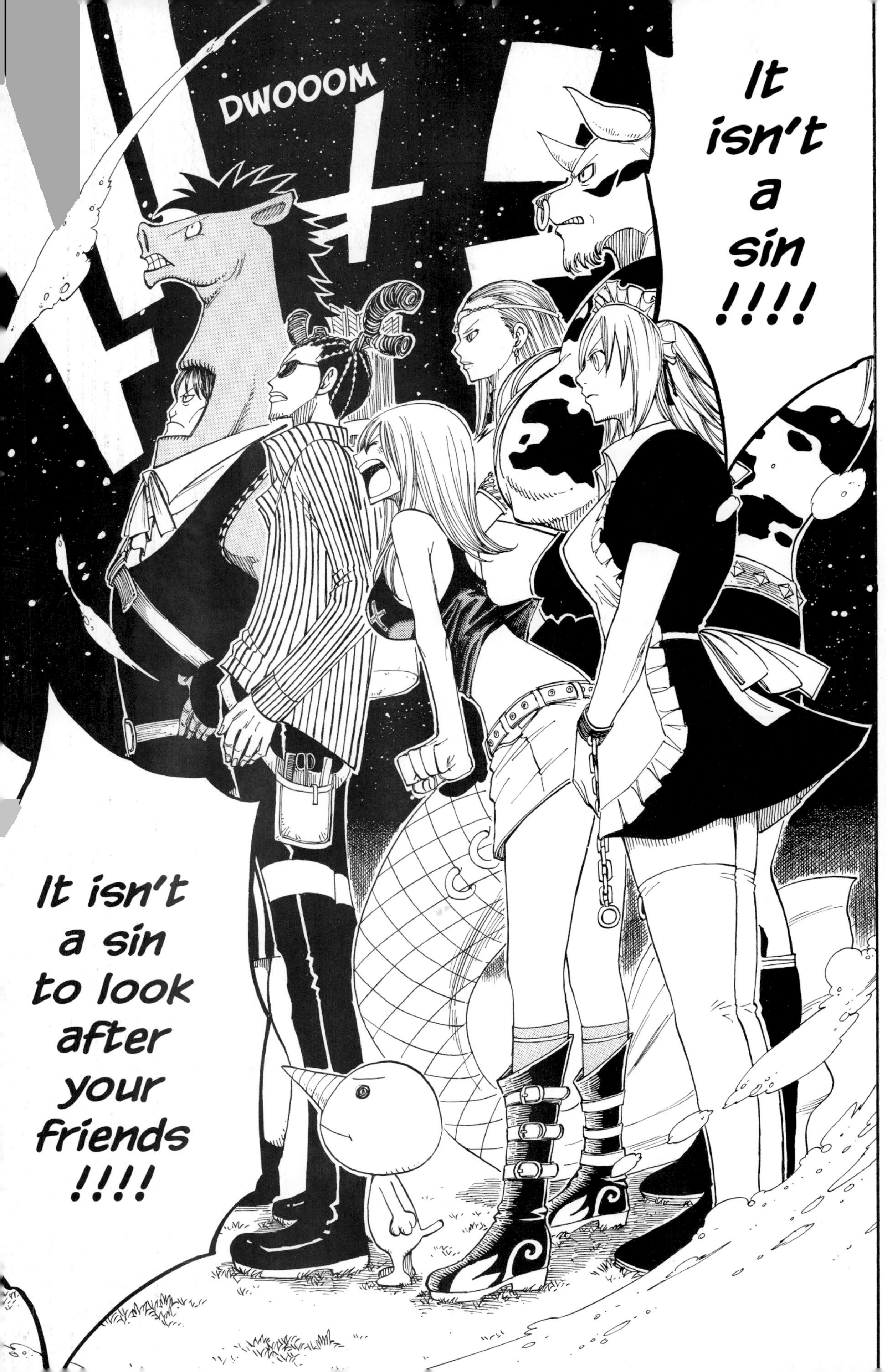
DWOOOM
It isn't a sin !!!!
It isn't a sin to look after your friends !!!!

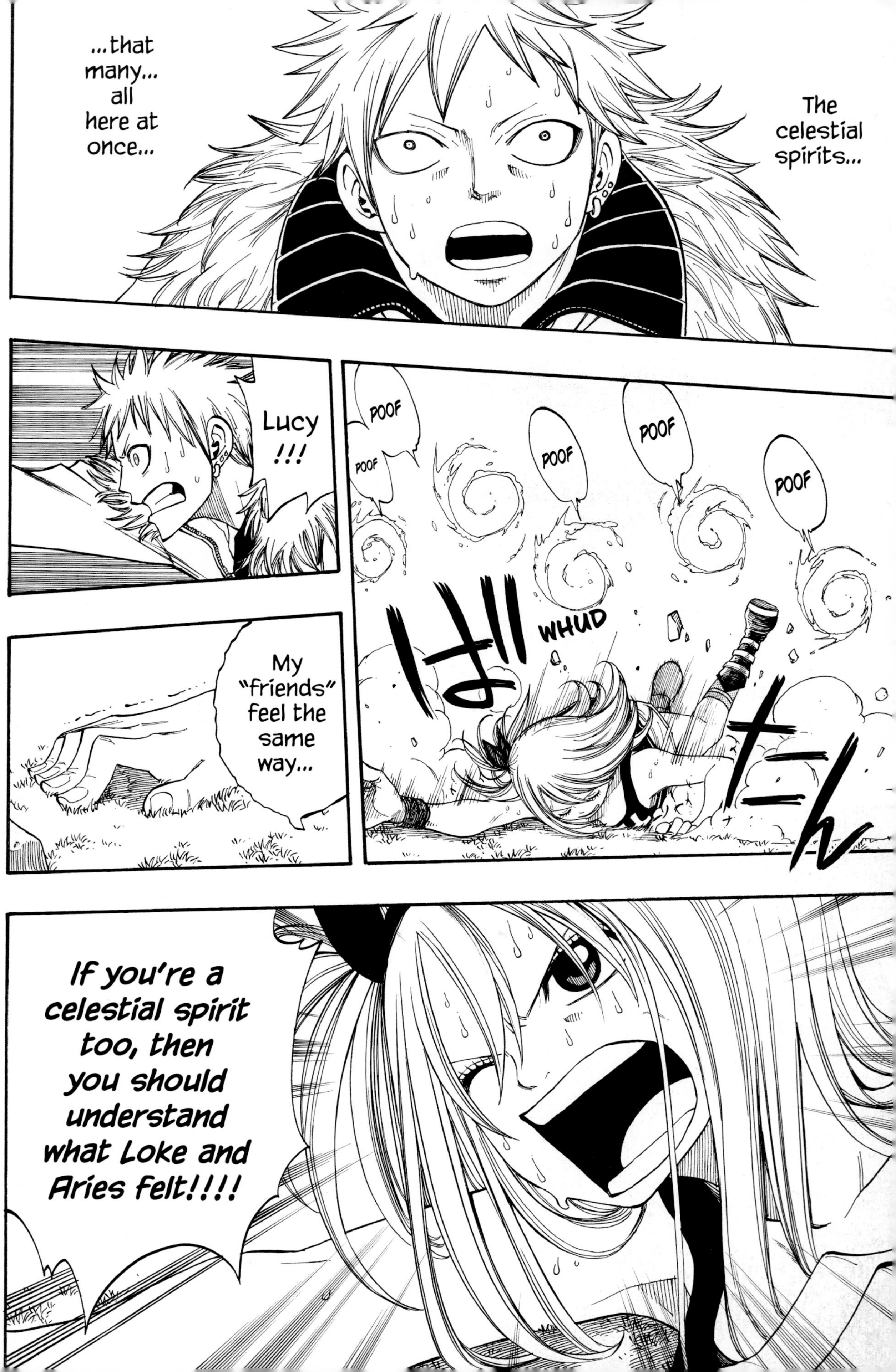
The celestial spirits...
...that many... all here at once...
POOF
POOF
POOF
POOF
POOF
WHUD
ばたーん
Lucy!!!
My "friends" feel the same way...
If you're a celestial spirit too, then you should understand what Loke and Aries felt!!!!

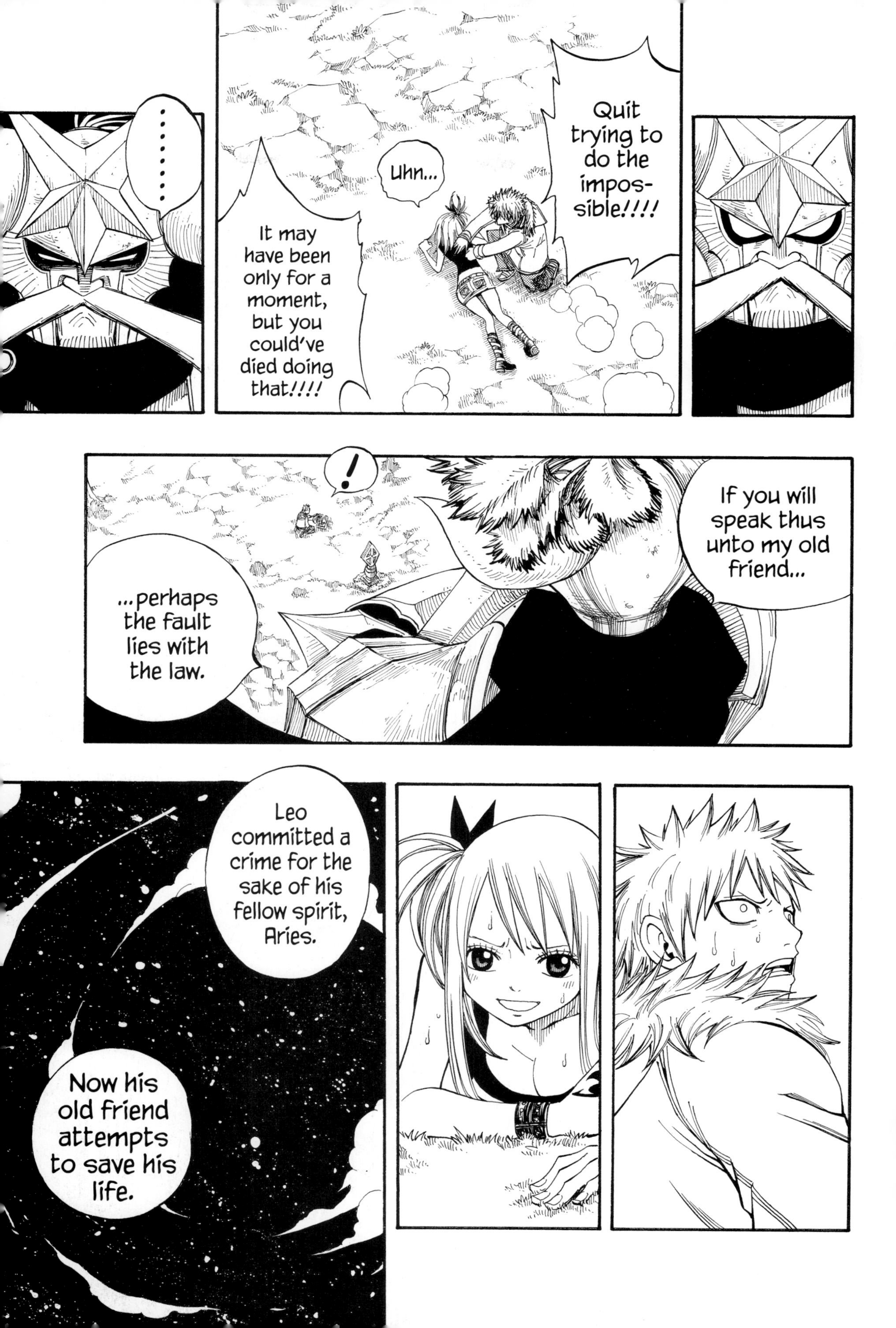
Quit trying to do the impossible!!!!
Uhn...
It may have been only for a moment, but you could've died doing that!!!!
......
If you will speak thus unto my old friend...
!
...perhaps the fault lies with the law.
Leo committed a crime for the sake of his fellow spirit, Aries.
Now his old friend attempts to save his life.

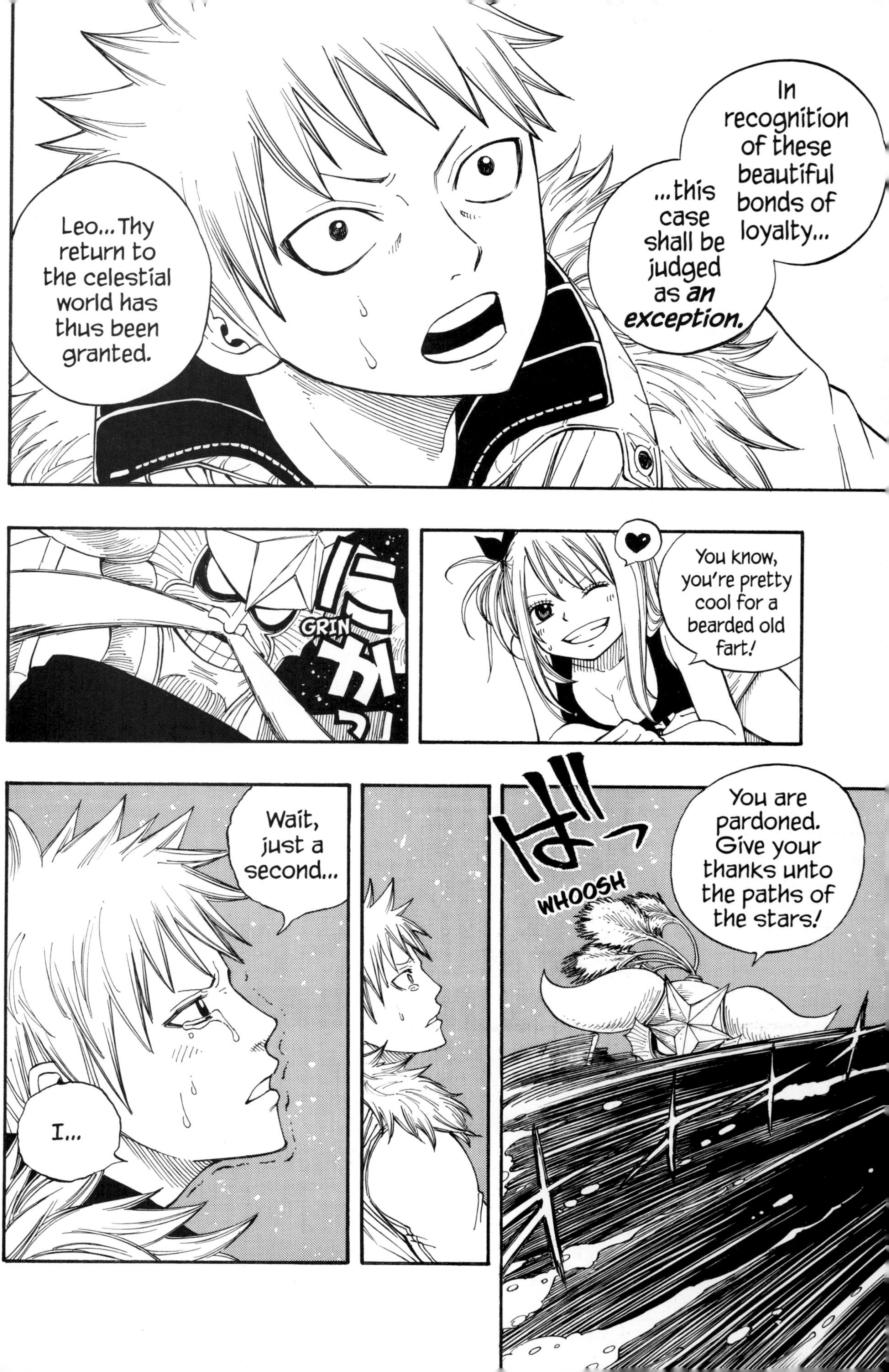
In recognition of these beautiful bonds of loyalty...
...this case shall be judged as *an exception.*
Leo...Thy return to the celestial world has thus been granted.
You know, you're pretty cool for a bearded old fart!
GRIN
WHOOSH
You are pardoned. Give your thanks unto the paths of the stars!
Wait, just a second...
I...

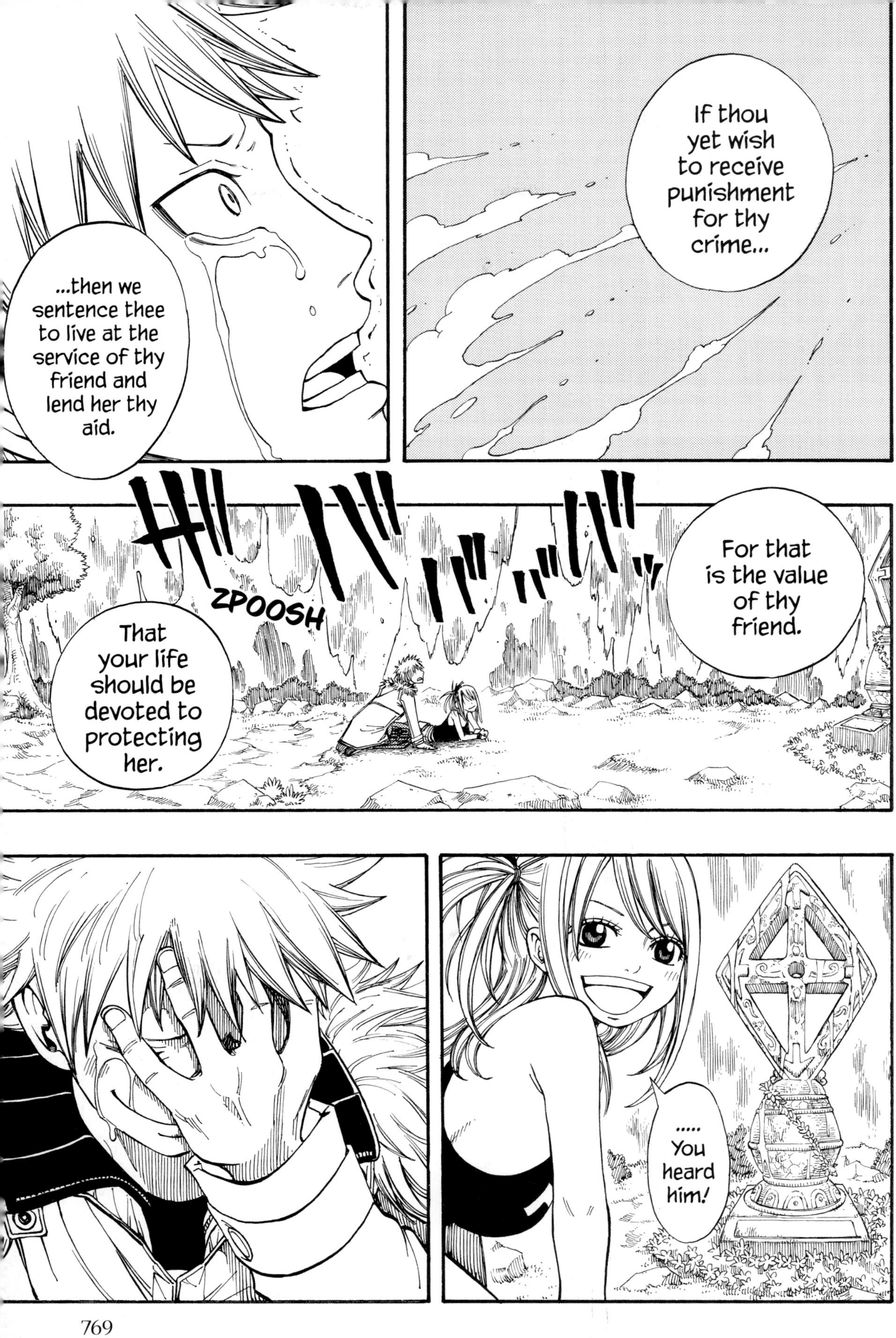
If thou yet wish to receive punishment for thy crime...
...then we sentence thee to live at the service of thy friend and lend her thy aid.
For that is the value of thy friend.
That your life should be devoted to protecting her.
ZPOOSH
..... You heard him!

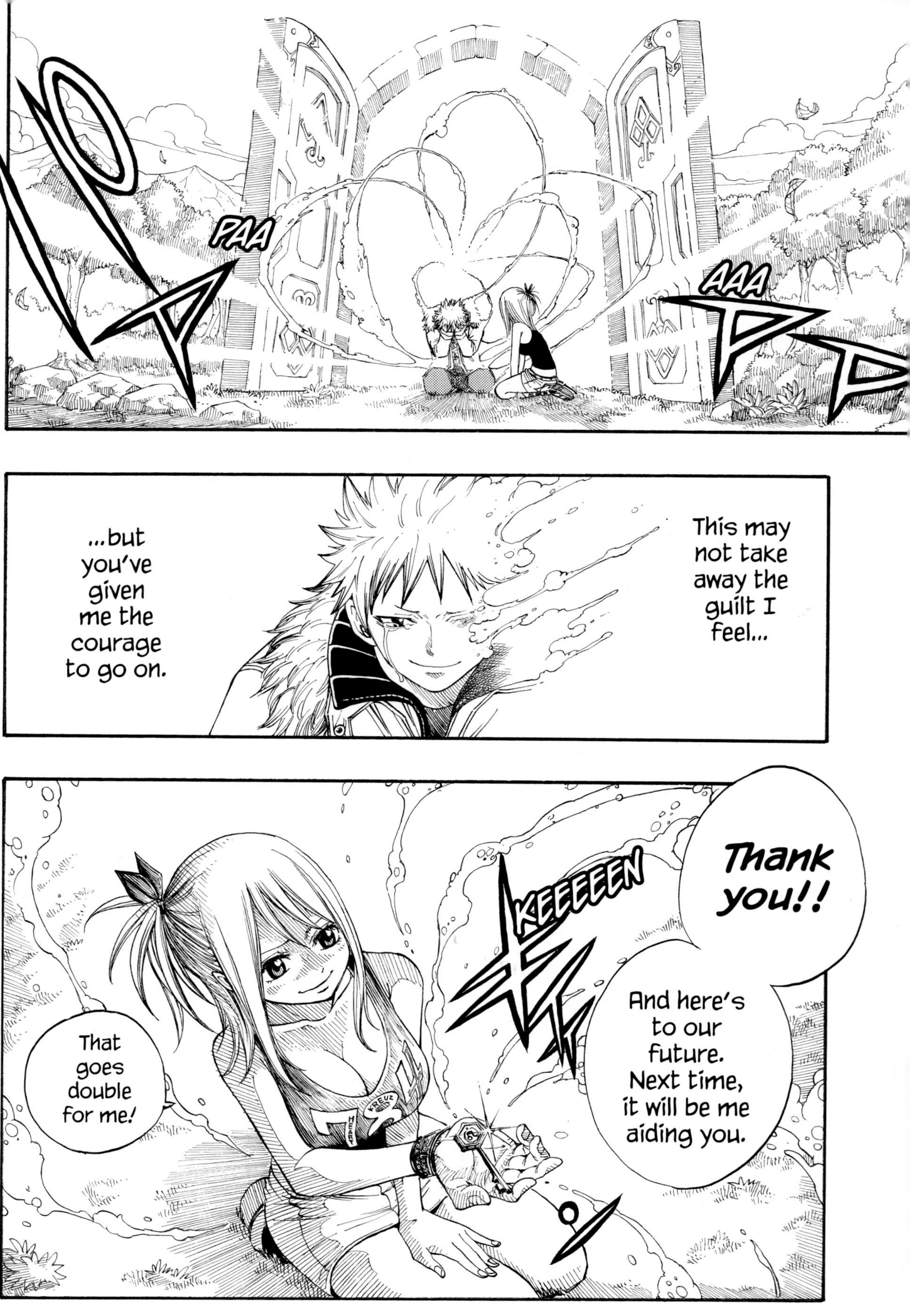
PAA
AAA
This may not take away the guilt I feel...
...but you've given me the courage to go on.
Thank you!!
KEEEEEN
And here's to our future. Next time, it will be me aiding you.
That goes double for me!

TO BE CONTINUED

Man, am I busy!! Yeah, for a manga-ka that's a great thing to be able to say, but I'm way too busy!! If you want to know why, it's because I have another manga series—this time a monthly series. I've done this in the past, doing a monthly and a weekly series at the same time, but this time there are so many more pages required than last time! So the pace is so much different than before. By the way, when I was only doing a weekly manga, the amount of work equaled twenty pages of manga, twenty pages of *name* (the Japanese term for a rough-sketched story and dialogue), plus a couple of color pieces and small odd jobs. But the quantity of work I had last week was forty-three manga pages, sixty-nine pages of *name,* four color pages, and tons of those small, odd jobs. What the heck was that week all about?!! The only thing I can do is laugh about it!! Yeah, it was an unusually heavy week that included a short story, so the page numbers were artificially high, but even so, my regular work week is about twice as busy as before. Man! It's unbelievable!!

Recently I met another creator, and was asked what my motivation is for doing all of that work. I don't know how to answer that question. I never even considered the concept of motivation. Of course, I love manga, and that's why I draw it. But that's the basic assumption for any manga-ka. In my case, maybe it includes journeyman-style training. That probably sums it up. I've been doing this work for over ten years, but I can't seem to get good at drawing. (Ha ha!) Is it true that if I draw a lot, I'll become better? Normally, you'd think so…Anyway, I'm busy! Really busy! And that's what comes out of my mouth when I'm talking to the people around me, but inside I'm having so much fun, I can hardly contain it! I can draw a whole lot of manga! My manga will be read by a whole lot of people! That's probably my motivation, huh?

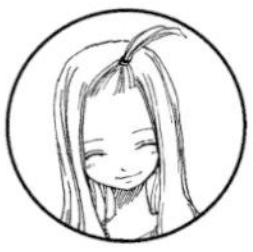
: By the way, I entered six years ago, bringing Elfman and Lisanna with me.

Erza: Natsu entered seven years ago, and Gray had entered even before I did.

Lucy: Huh? You guys have been in the guild a long time! It hasn't even been a year for me!

Erza: The story of my life before Fairy Tail is touched on in Volume 10.

Mira: I'm interested in learning about that!

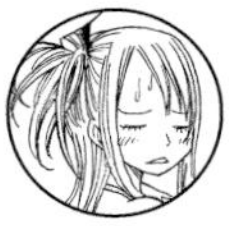
: What was that? You just casually throw a preview of the next volume into the conversation?

Mira: Okay, the final question.

Who is the heroine of Fairy Tail? Lucy or Erza?

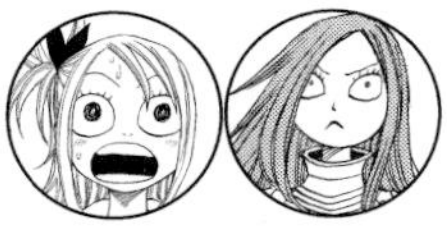
: ***!!!***

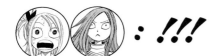

Mira: Nobody cares who the "heroine" is, right?

Lucy: What do you mean "nobody?!" I mean, people would automatically assume it's me, right?

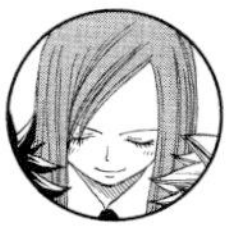
: Well...I feel a little embarrassed being addressed as the heroine, but...Am I truly being looked upon in that fashion?

Lucy: Wait a minute!! What are you blushing for?!!

Mira: Certainly at first glance, one would think it's Lucy, but I hear that Erza has more fans.

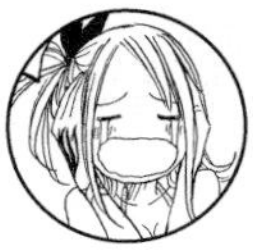
: ***You're kidding!!!***

Erza: Is that so?

Lucy: Wait!! Just look at the cover of Volume 9! It's me!! All me!! I carry the entire cover all by myself!!

Mira: If you look closely, you see an awful lot of celestial spirits there too.

Erza: Lucy, did you know? They included a poster of me in *Weekly Magazine*.

Lucy: Waaaaaah!!

Erza: And that was only me. Heh heh...

Lucy: Waaaaaaaaaahh!

Mira: Well, none of this bickering will settle the matter. So why don't we ask the author directly?

------- And so... -------

Mashima: You're asking who the heroine is?

Lucy: It's me, right?! You love drawing pictures of me, don't you?!!

Erza: Do not forget that you drew a poster that was me and me alone.

Mashima: I give up. I think it's okay for the readers to decide who they think the heroine is for themselves.

Mira: Exactly! Nobody cares who it is!

Mashima: Frankly, I think it's okay for the heroine to be Tomeko from Tokekko Restaurant.

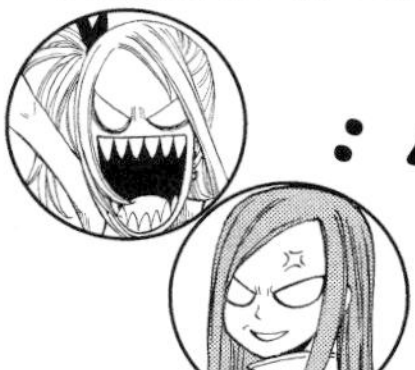
: ***It is not okay!!***

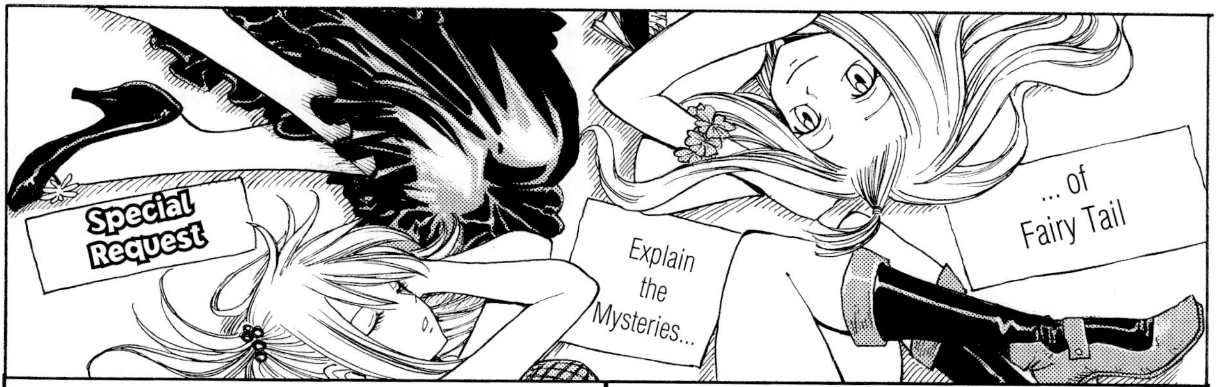
Special Request
Explain the Mysteries...
... of Fairy Tail

From the Counter at Fairy Tail...

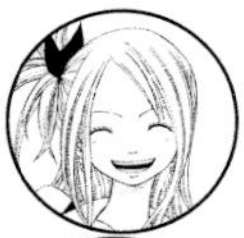 : All you readers out there, hello!

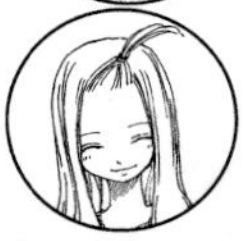 : Hello! You're in a good mood today, Lucy!

Lucy: Sure! It's the ninth volume, and the stories were all about me!! It's like Volume 9 was drawn especially for me!

Mira: That's what it means to be a heroine, I guess, huh? Well, while you're in such a good mood, let's get started on the questions.

How many sets of armor total can Erza requip into?

Lucy: That question is pretty painful...er...I mean sharp!

Mira: The two of us can't answer it, so let's call in the woman herself. Introducing our special guest, Erza!

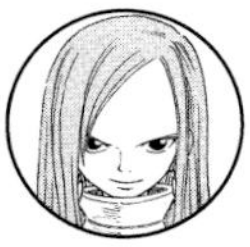 : Mm.

Lucy: Don't just say, "Mm"! If you don't come up with some greeting, you'll lose popularity points!

Erza: No...Well...I suppose I am not used to this...Uh...Hello.

Mira: So about the question we just heard. Erza, how many suits of armor do you have?

Erza: Many.

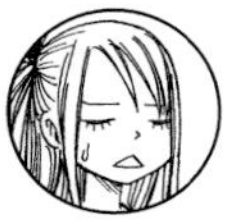 : Wait a second! None of the readers will really count that as an answer! You're going to have to do better than that to increase your point score!

Mira: What are popularity points exactly?

Erza: I have more than a hundred different types. I haven't counted them all myself, but I also count within their ranks dresses and kimono.

Lucy: Requipping is such a great concept! Dressing must be a breeze!

Mira: On to the next question.

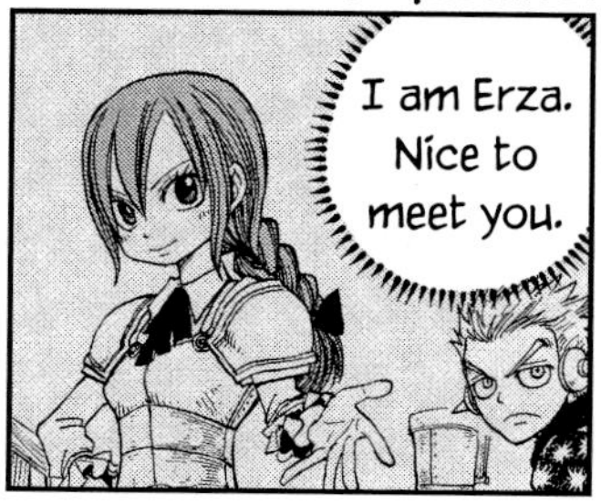
I am Erza. Nice to meet you.

How long has Erza been in the Fairy Tail guild?

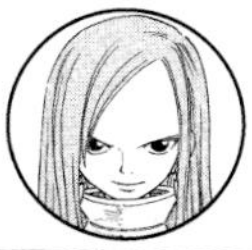 : Eight years. That brings back memories.

Continued on the right-hand page

The Fairy Tail Guild d'Art is an explosion of fan art! Please send in your black-and-white art on large postcard stock!! Those chosen to be published will get a signed mini poster! ♪ Make sure you write your real name and address on the back of your postcard!

d'ART

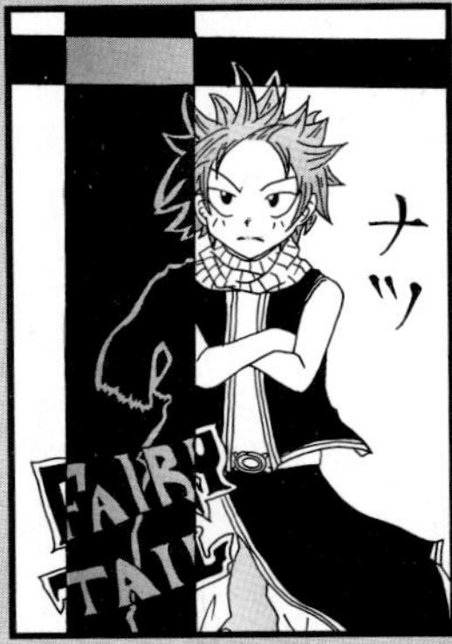

ナツ
FAIRY TAIL

Iwate Prefecture, Sena Minazuki

▼ Whoa! This one has some great artistic sense!

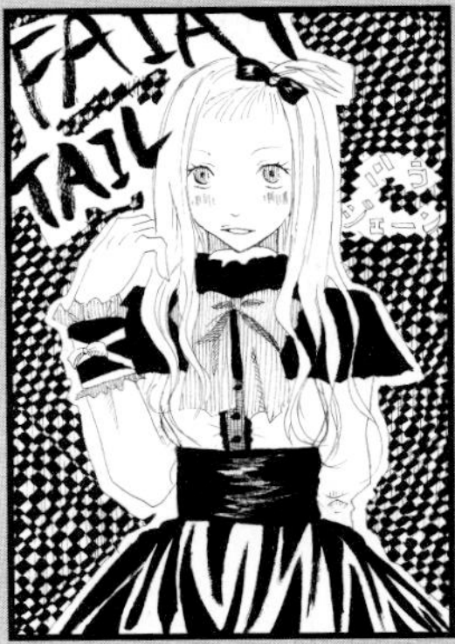

FAIRY TAIL

Iwate Prefecture, Kô Minamikaze

▼ This one's very cute!! And well done!

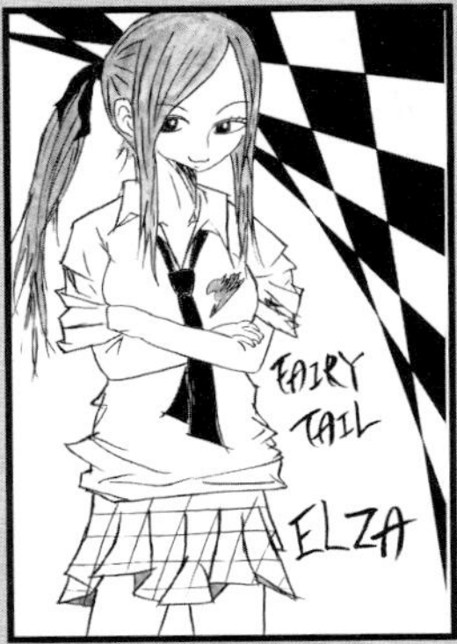

FAIRY TAIL
ELZA

Gunma Prefecture, Kayo

▼ An Erza in a school uniform, huh? Just a little while ago I drew a side story like that.

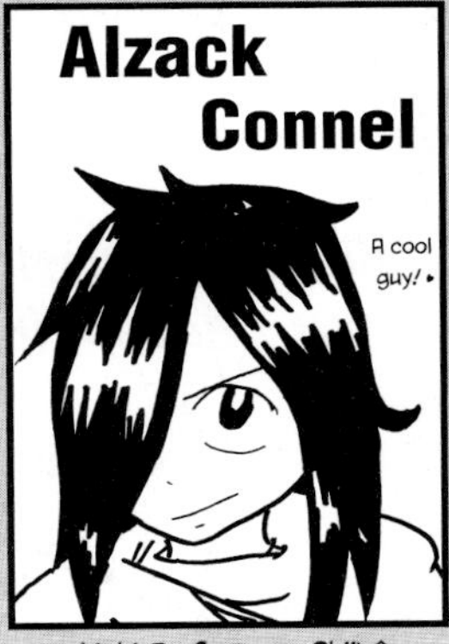

Alzack Connel
A cool guy!

Aichi Prefecture, Chiibô

▼ Are you a part of the Gloomy Character Fan Club? Maybe not, huh?

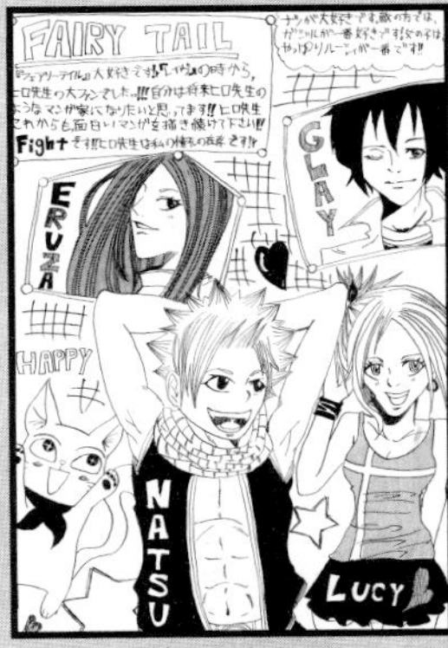

FAIRY TAIL
ERUZA
GLAY
HAPPY
NATSU
LUCY

Hokkaido, Seiryu Tanaka

▼ A fan from my previous work. I'm so happy I could cry!

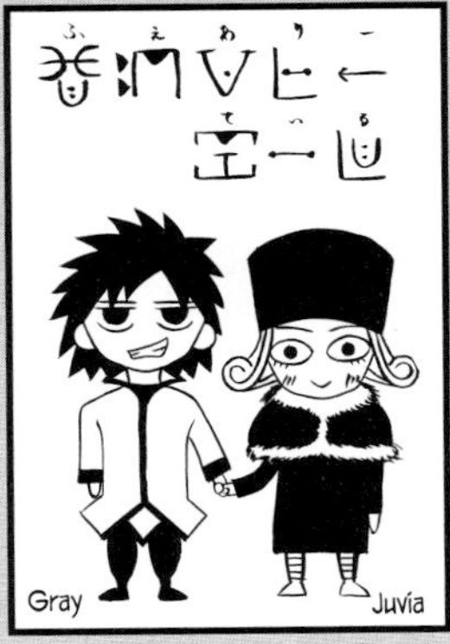

Gray
Juvia

Hyôgo Prefecture, Kôsuke Shimoda

▼ It seems that the battle between these two has gotten itself a good reputation.

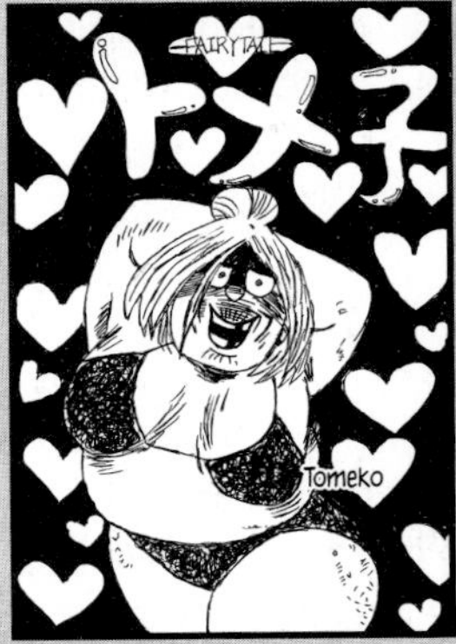

FAIRY TAIL
トメ子
Tomeko

Ishikawa Prefecture, Natsu vs. Haru

▼ And there's Tomeko!!! One came!!! Yeah, but actually there are about twenty other pictures of her! (Ha ha!)

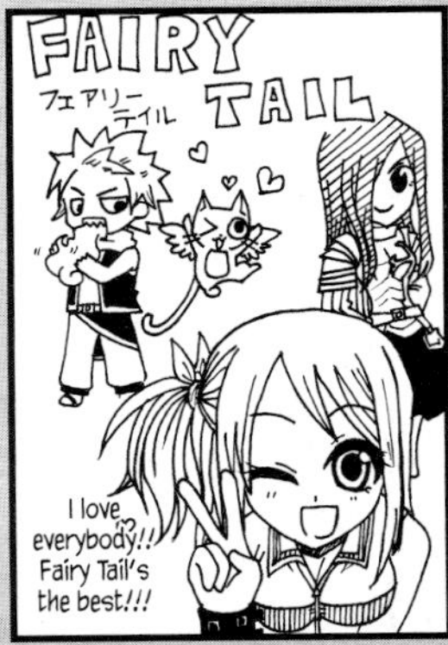

FAIRY TAIL
フェアリーテイル
I love everybody!!! Fairy Tail's the best!!!

Chiba Prefecture, Koharu

▼ Thank you!! Keep on rooting for me, please!

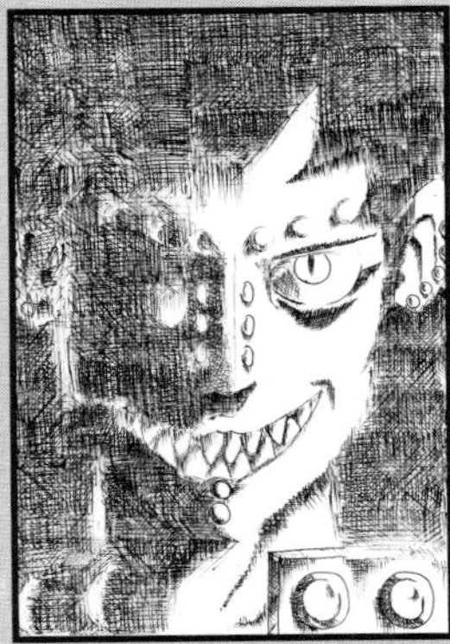

Niigata Prefecture, Tomohiko Enamoto

▼ Whoa! Gajeel's scary! This is one page that's got him pinned!

Send to Hiro Mashima, Kodansha Comics
451 Park Ave. South, 7th Floor, New York, NY 10016

GUILD

By sending in letters or postcards you give us permission to give your name, address, postal code and any other information you include to the author as is. Please keep that in mind.

Rejection Corner

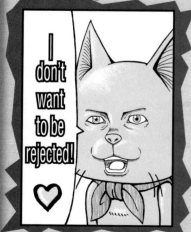

I don't want to be rejected!

Saitama Prefecture, Keisuke Gôtô

▲ You can't get everything you want!

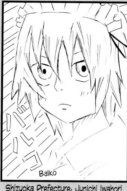

Balko

Shizuoka Prefecture, Junichi Iwahori

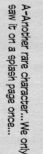

◀ Ehh? By the way, it's Balgo. Although Balko makes a nice girl's name.

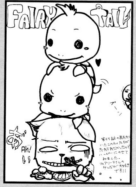

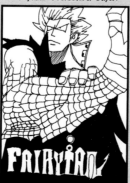

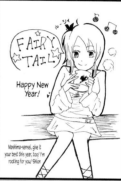

FAIRY TAIL
Happy New Year!
Mashima-sensei, give it your best this year, too! I'm rooting for you! Shion

Miyagi Prefecture, Shion

◀ Happy New Year's to you! And thanks for all of the New Year's cards!

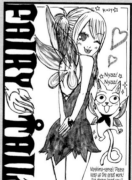

FAIRY TAIL
Ah!

Miyazaki Prefecture, Sayuri

◀ A-Another rare character...We only saw it on a splash page once...

FAIRY TAIL
Rusy
Nyaa! Nyaa!
Mashima-sensei! Please keep up the great work! I've always loved you!!

Shizuoka Prefecture, Kahori Matsushima

◀ Wow, that's cute! Is she doing cosplay as a fairy?

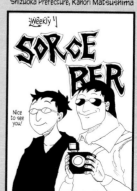

FAIRY TAIL

Ibaragi Prefecture, Masahiro Ishizaki

◀ I wonder when his next active appearance will be...?

Weekly
SORCERER
Nice to see you!

Hyôgo Prefecture, Puririn

◀ These appeared in a limited edition publication. Actually they're based on editors of mine.

Translation Notes

Japanese is a tricky language for most Westerners, and translation is often more art than science. For your edification and reading pleasure, here are notes on some of the places where we could have gone in a different direction in our translation of the work, or where a Japanese cultural reference is used.

Bento, page 618

The traditional boxed lunch of Japan usually features a main course on a bed of rice and includes pickled veggies, salad, cooked egg, and other foods along with sweet beans for dessert. Women are known for waking up early and fixing elaborate bento boxes. Single girls prepare them for themselves or their boyfriends, while mothers fix bento boxes for their children's school lunches.

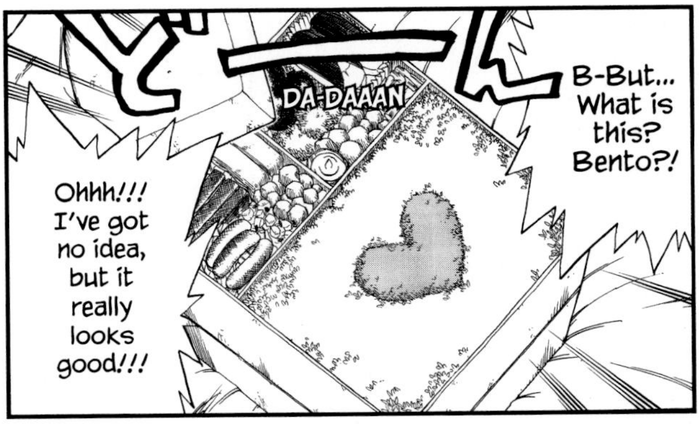
DA-DAAAN
B-But... What is this? Bento?!
Ohhh!!! I've got no idea, but it really looks good!!!

Feminist, page 620

In America, the word "feminist" has taken on nuances of a radical activist for women's rights. In Japan, the connotations are much broader, spanning the range from activist to someone who simply likes women.

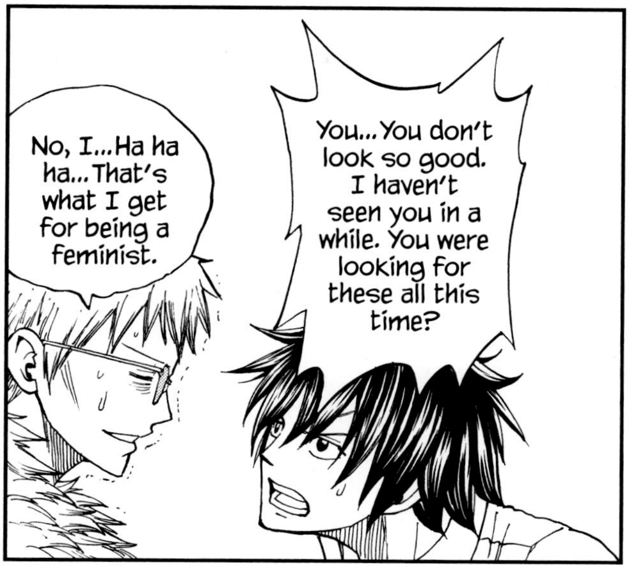
You...You don't look so good. I haven't seen you in a while. You were looking for these all this time?
No, I...Ha ha ha...That's what I get for being a feminist.

Passionate Fish, page 629

The title of the top book the librarian is holding was written in Japanese, *Jônetsu-gyo*, which means "Passionate Fish" or "Passion Fish." One might assume that, as translator, I would use the name of the movie, *Passion Fish*, for the translation, but it did not seem appropriate in this instance. When the movie came out, the Japanese title was not in Japanese, but instead used the English words in Japanese *katakana* characters, *Passhon Fisshu*. Since Mashima-sensei didn't use the proper name for the movie title, it seemed wrong for the translation to use the proper title of the movie either.

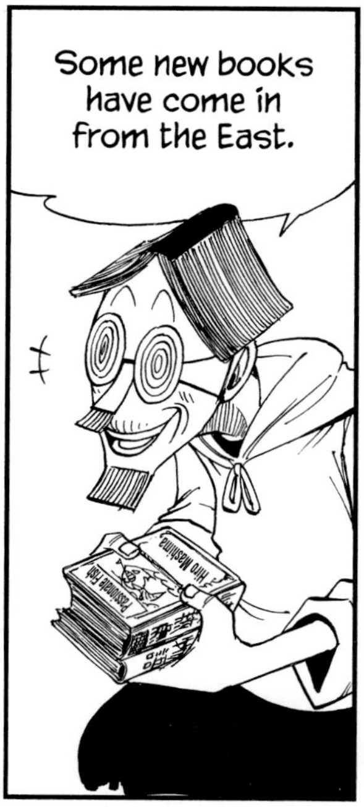
Some new books have come in from the East.

Mabô and Yanbô, page 650

There are many types of nicknames in Japanese, and this is one example. One takes the first syllable of the name and adds *bô* to the end (or *nbô* depending on phonics and the whim of the one assigning the nickname). This is generally a nickname used by men for male friends, and although it is still heard now and again, the popularity of that nickname declined decades ago. The use of the nicknames indicate that Master Makarov and Yajima are either old, very close friends, or former classmates.

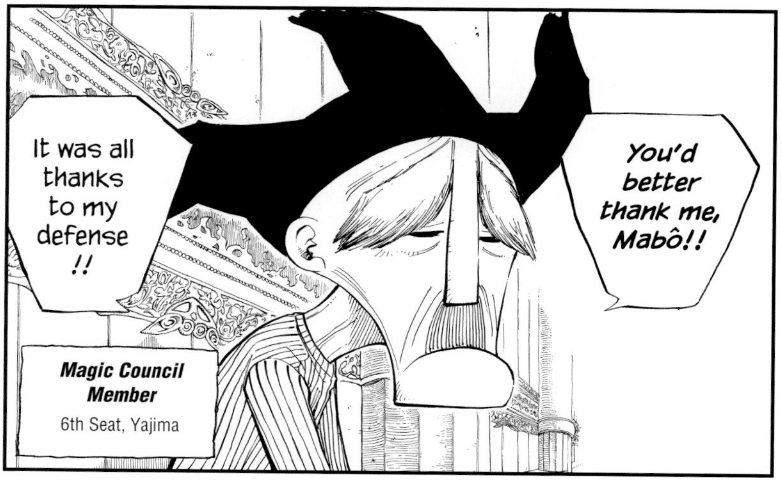
You'd better thank me, Mabô!!
It was all thanks to my defense!!
Magic Council Member
6th Seat, Yajima

Ramen, *chashu* pork, page 650

The Chinese barbecue pork, *char siu*, is pronounced *chashu* in Japan, and the most common dish associated with *chashu* is ramen. One can order *chashu* Ramen as a menu item in most ramen restaurants/Chinese restaurants in Japan, or one can order extra *chashu* to be added to other ramen dishes such as Miso Ramen. *Chashu* consists of thin slices of pork (usually pork shoulder), and one usually only receives two or three slices per ramen dish.

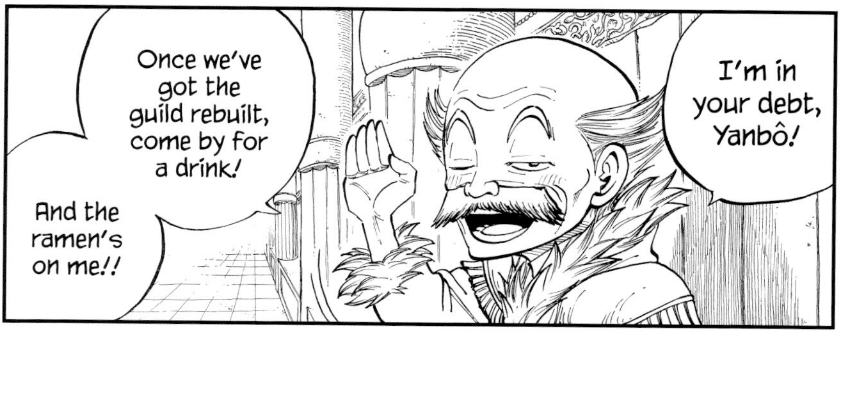
I'm in your debt, Yanbô!
Once we've got the guild rebuilt, come by for a drink!
And the ramen's on me!!

Ebb and Sea Bream, page 703

There is a phrase in Japanese, *isshin-ittai*, which means "ebb and flow." Of course it refers to the tides, but it also indicates the ups and downs of one's life. But in Japanese pun-loving fashion, here the normal *kanji* for *tai* has been replaced with a different *kanji*, also pronounced *tai*, but meaning "sea bream." Not the easiest pun to try to translate, but since English has few uses for the word "ebb" in any other context than "ebb and flow," juxtaposing "ebb and " with "sea bream" gives one the idea that someone is trying to make a joke—no matter how less-than-hilarious the pun was in this English translation.

EBB AND SEA BREAM
MIND
SKILL
BODY
....

Hmaa, page 717

This is simply one of those mumbling vocalizations that old men make in between sentences and phrases. I left the sound the same as in the Japanese.

And that's what happened, Old Master Cru.
Homaa...
ふわ
FWAA
ふわ
FWAA
Celestial Spirit
Southern Cross Constellation Crux
AKA: Old Master Cru

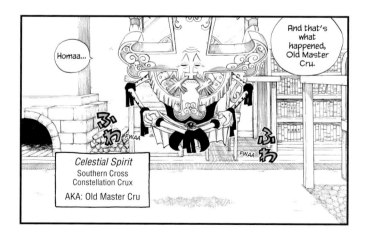

Memphis Ring, page 734

The Memphis Ring is a magic item that can be found in the Japanese massively multi-player role-playing game (MMRPG), Strugarden Neo. The item is a finger ring with enough power to defeat a boss in the game.

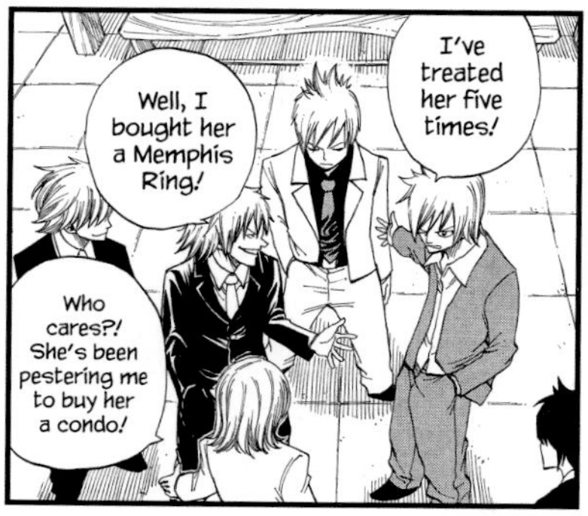
I've treated her five times!
Well, I bought her a Memphis Ring!
Who cares?! She's been pestering me to buy her a condo!

Old Friend, page 762

In Japanese, the celestial spirit king used the term *furuki tomo*, which is a rather archaic way of saying "old friend." I was unable to find any other instances where this phrase was used in Japanese history or literature, so I can't claim to be an expert in the nuances of this phrase. Only that he used it as a way of saying "you" in the Japanese—even to Lucy who he had just met. The rest of his speech was rather archaic as well, and so the translation used "thees," "thous," and similar language to convey that concept.

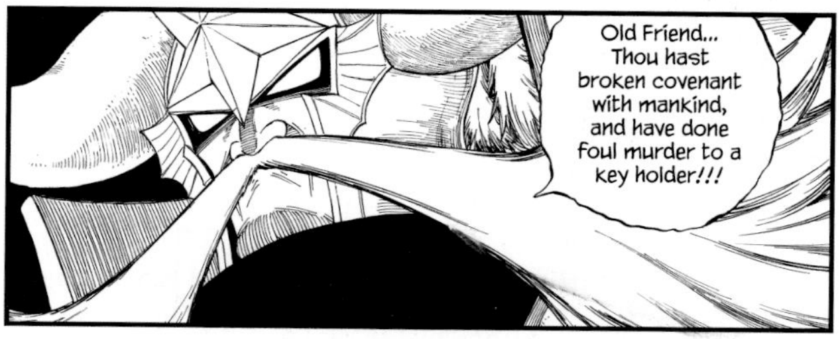
Old Friend... Thou hast broken covenant with mankind, and have done foul murder to a key holder!!!

FAIRY TAIL

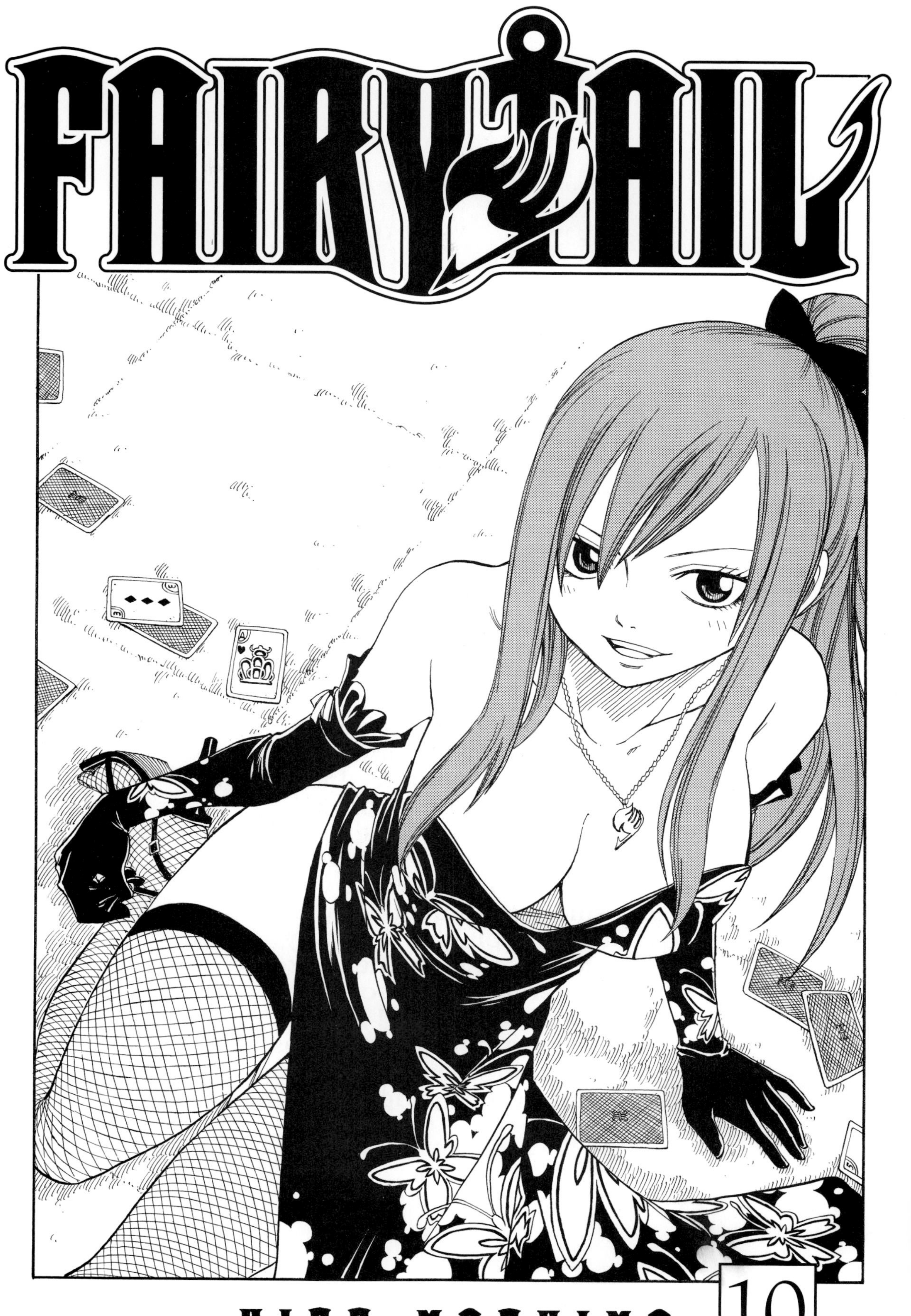

HIRO MASHIMA

10

With Kase-sensei!

Weekly Shônen Magazine
is celebrating its fiftieth
birthday!!! And as part of
the festivities, I get to draw
a manga that is a tribute
to Kase-sensei's manga,
Chameleon. This is a picture
of when I conferred with
him. I think it's pretty
incredible to be able to be in
the same photo as a manga-
ka that I've admired ever
since my student days! And
that thought was keenly
felt throughout the entire
interview. Even so, Kase-
sensei is a fun guy! But that's
only natural since the most
interesting manga come from
interesting people, huh?

—Hiro Mashima

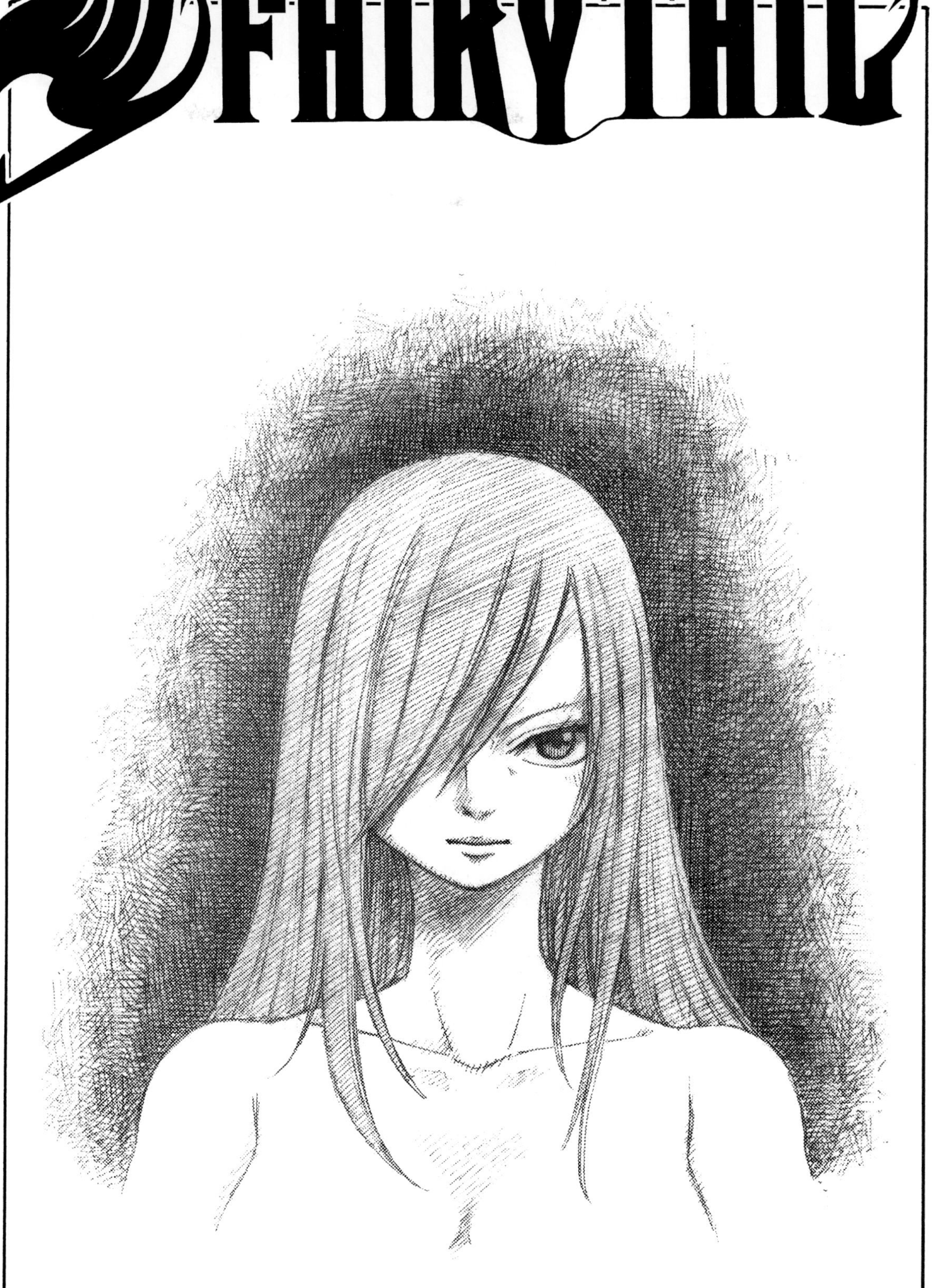

Chapter 75:
Dream of a Butterfly

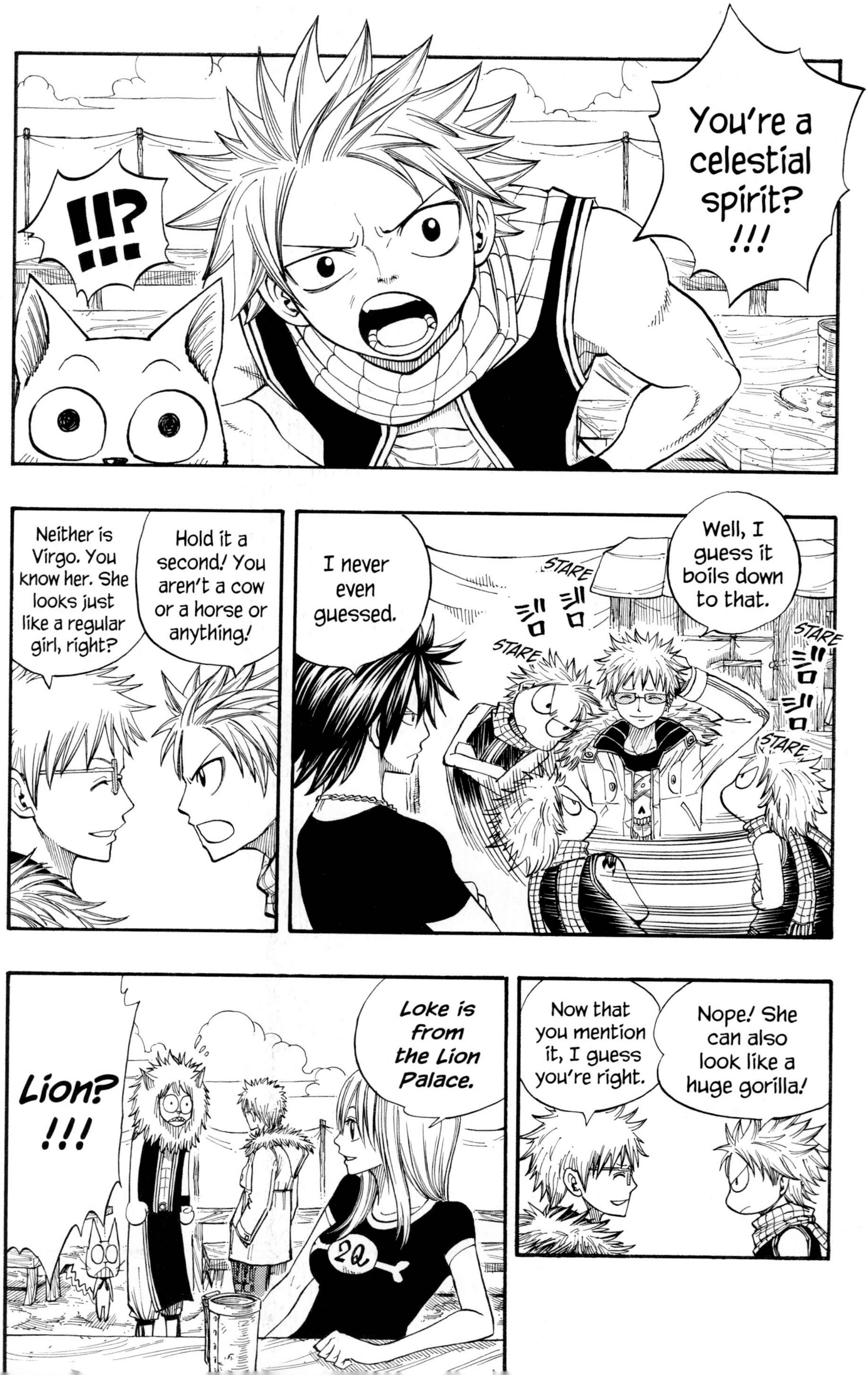
You're a celestial spirit? !!!
!!?
Well, I guess it boils down to that.
STARE
ジロ ジロ
STARE
ジロ ジロ
STARE
STARE
I never even guessed.
Hold it a second! You aren't a cow or a horse or anything!
Neither is Virgo. You know her. She looks just like a regular girl, right?
Nope! She can also look like a huge gorilla!
Now that you mention it, I guess you're right.
Loke is from the Lion Palace.
Lion? !!!

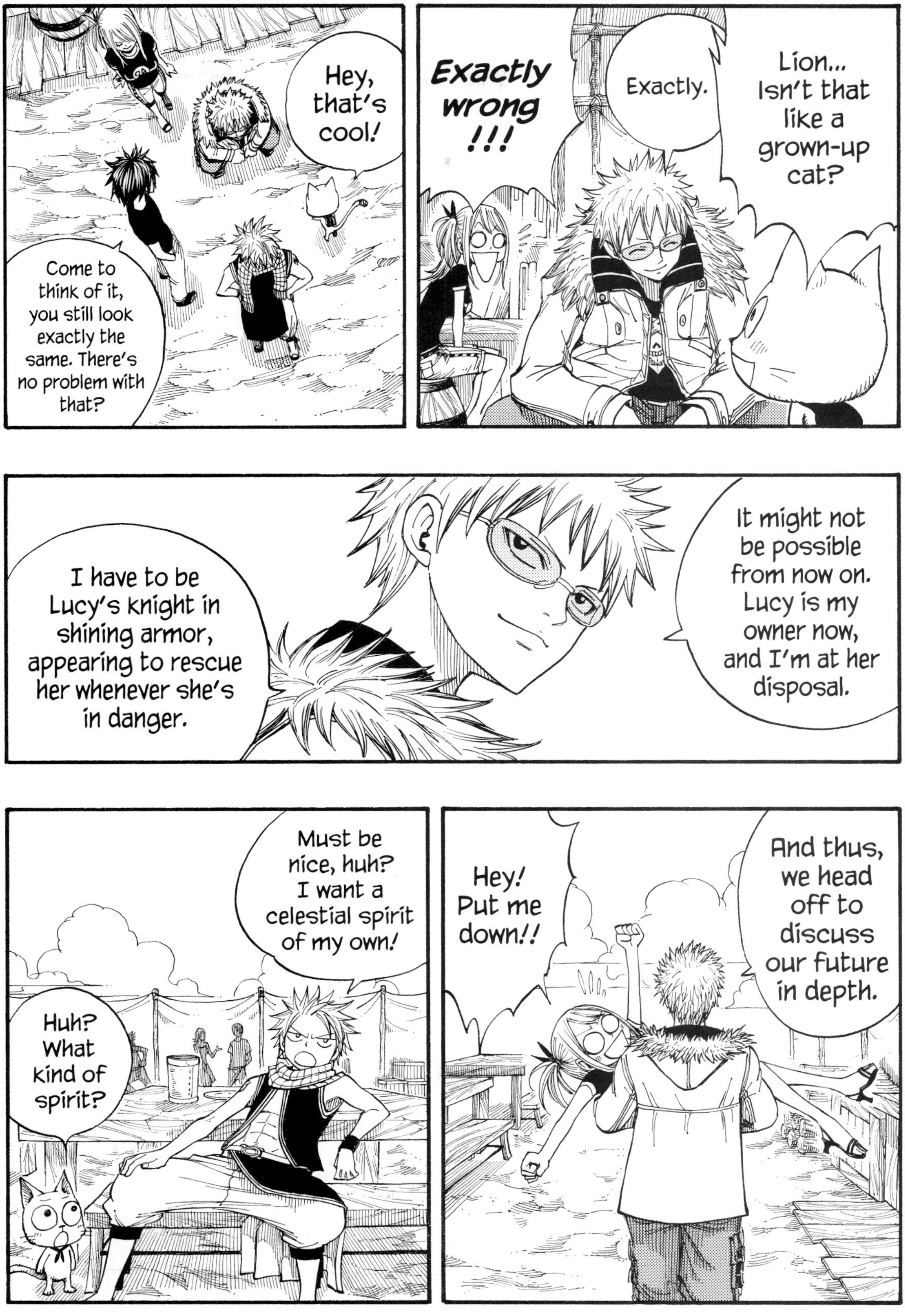
Lion... Isn't that like a grown-up cat?
Exactly.
Exactly wrong!!!
Hey, that's cool!
Come to think of it, you still look exactly the same. There's no problem with that?
It might not be possible from now on. Lucy is my owner now, and I'm at her disposal.
I have to be Lucy's knight in shining armor, appearing to rescue her whenever she's in danger.
And thus, we head off to discuss our future in depth.
Hey! Put me down!!
Must be nice, huh? I want a celestial spirit of my own!
Huh? What kind of spirit?

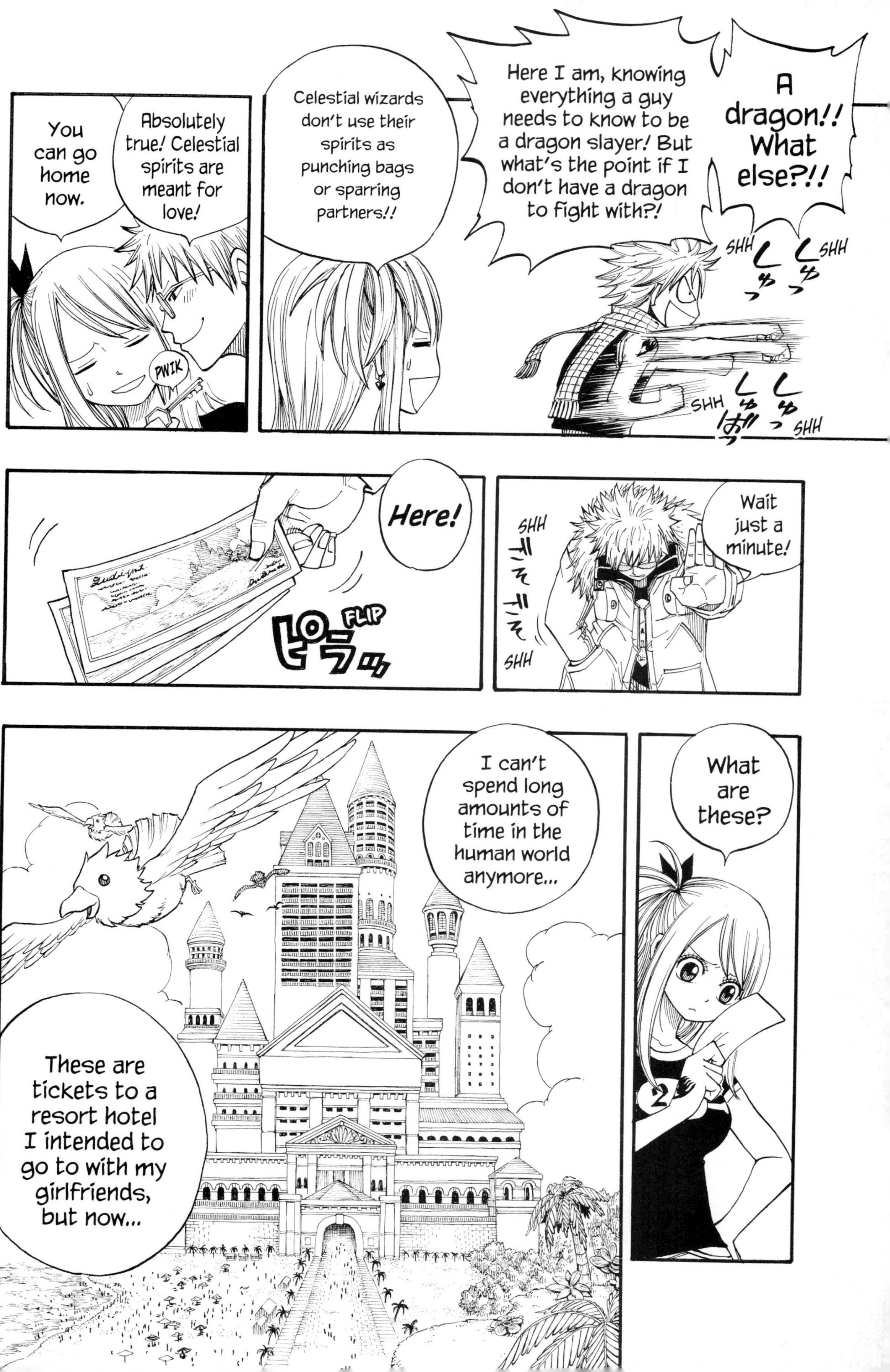
A dragon!! What else?!!
Here I am, knowing everything a guy needs to know to be a dragon slayer! But what's the point if I don't have a dragon to fight with?!
SHH
SHH
SHH
SHH
Celestial wizards don't use their spirits as punching bags or sparring partners!!
Absolutely true! Celestial spirits are meant for love!
You can go home now.
PWIK
Wait just a minute!
SHH
SHH
Here!
FLIP
What are these?
I can't spend long amounts of time in the human world anymore...
These are tickets to a resort hotel I intended to go to with my girlfriends, but now...

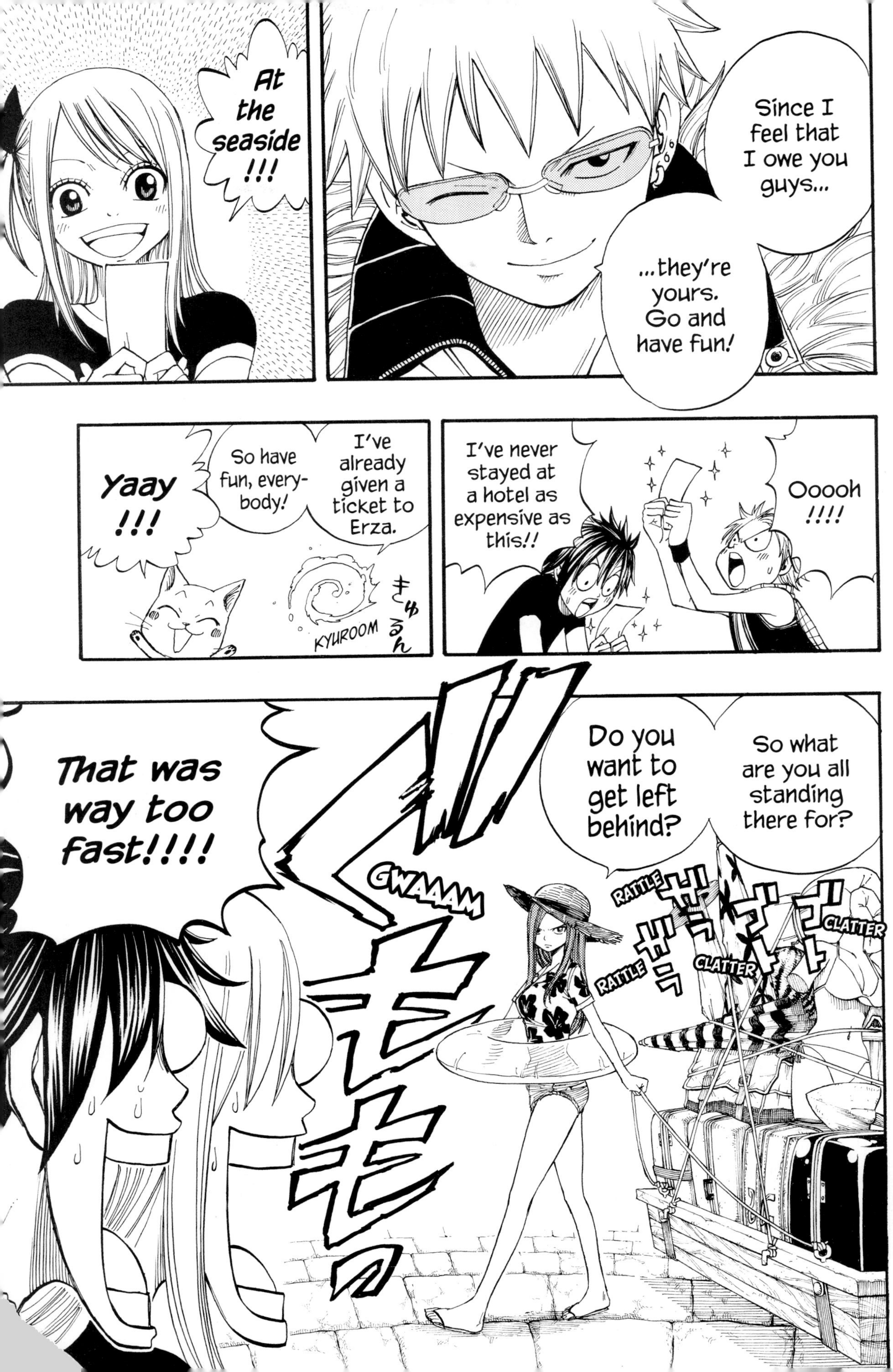
Since I feel that I owe you guys...
...they're yours. Go and have fun!
At the seaside!!!
Ooooh!!!!
I've never stayed at a hotel as expensive as this!!
I've already given a ticket to Erza.
So have fun, every-body!
Yaay!!!
KYUROOM
So what are you all standing there for?
Do you want to get left behind?
RATTLE
CLATTER
RATTLE
CLATTER
GWAAAM
That was way too fast!!!!

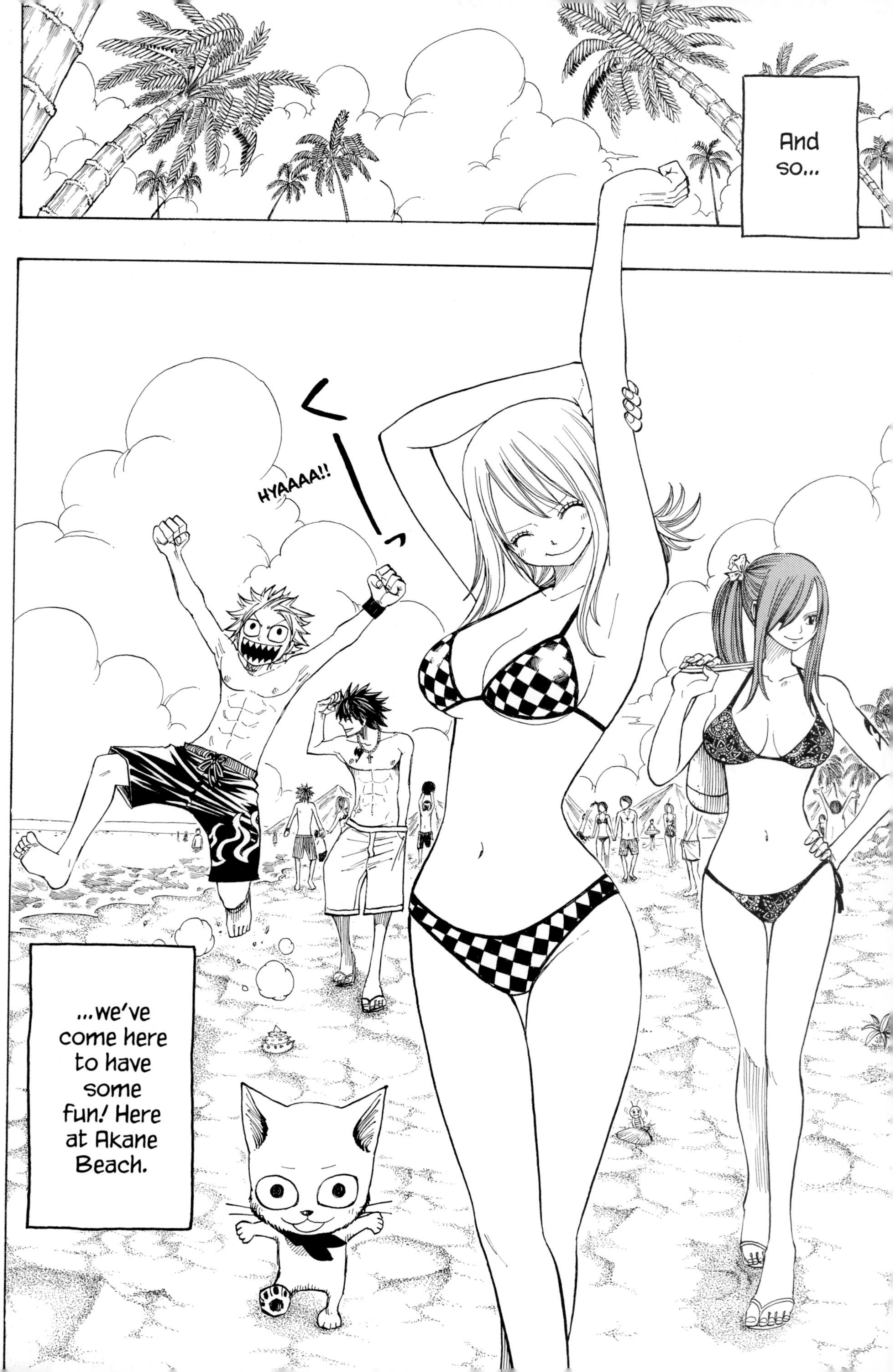
And so...
HYAAAA!!
...we've come here to have some fun! Here at Akane Beach.

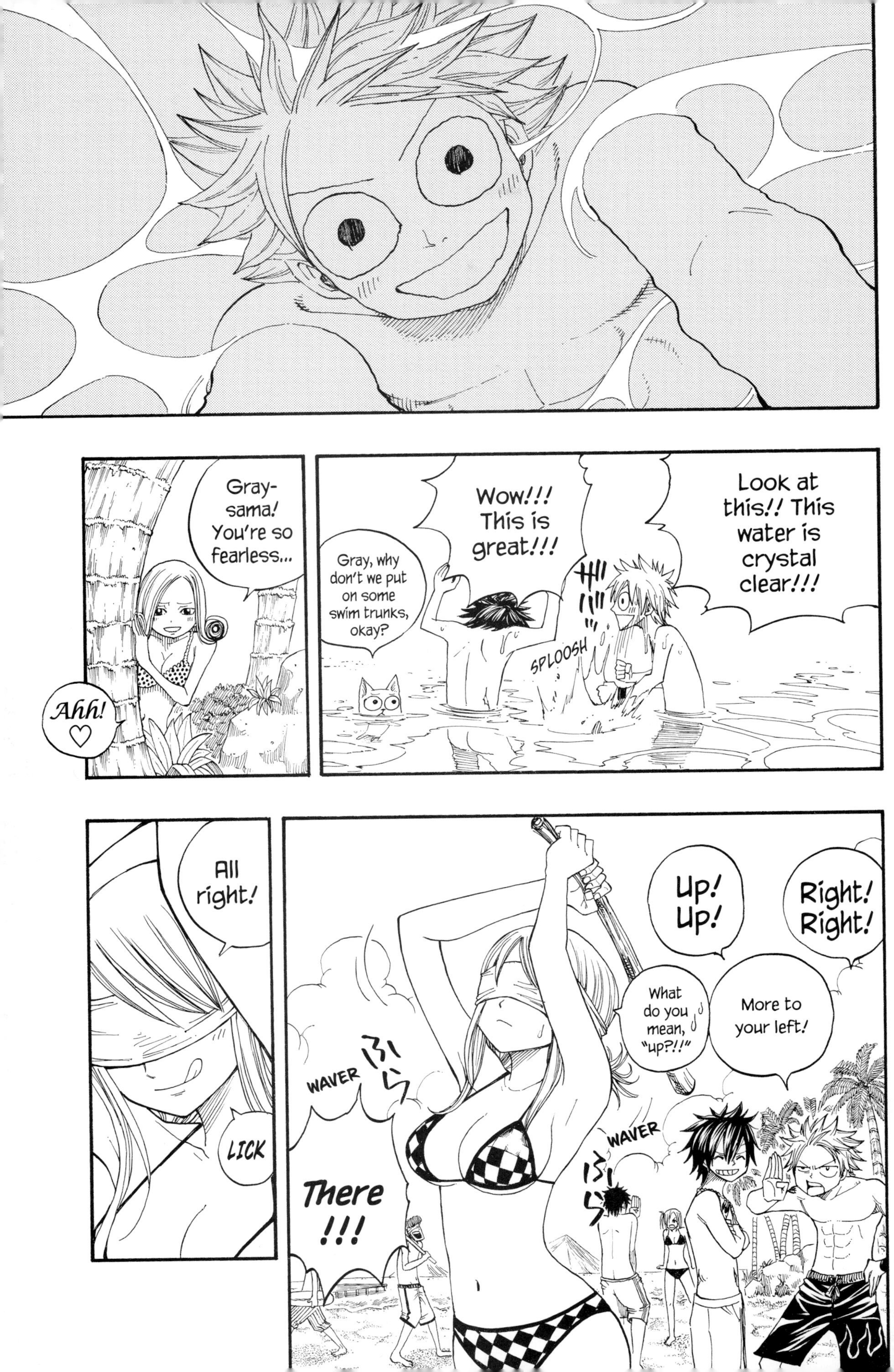

Look at this!! This water is crystal clear!!!
Wow!!! This is great!!!
Gray, why don't we put on some swim trunks, okay?
SPLOOSH
Gray-sama! You're so fearless...
Ahh! ♡
Right! Right!
Up! Up!
More to your left!
What do you mean, "up?!!"
WAVER
WAVER
There!!!
All right!
LICK

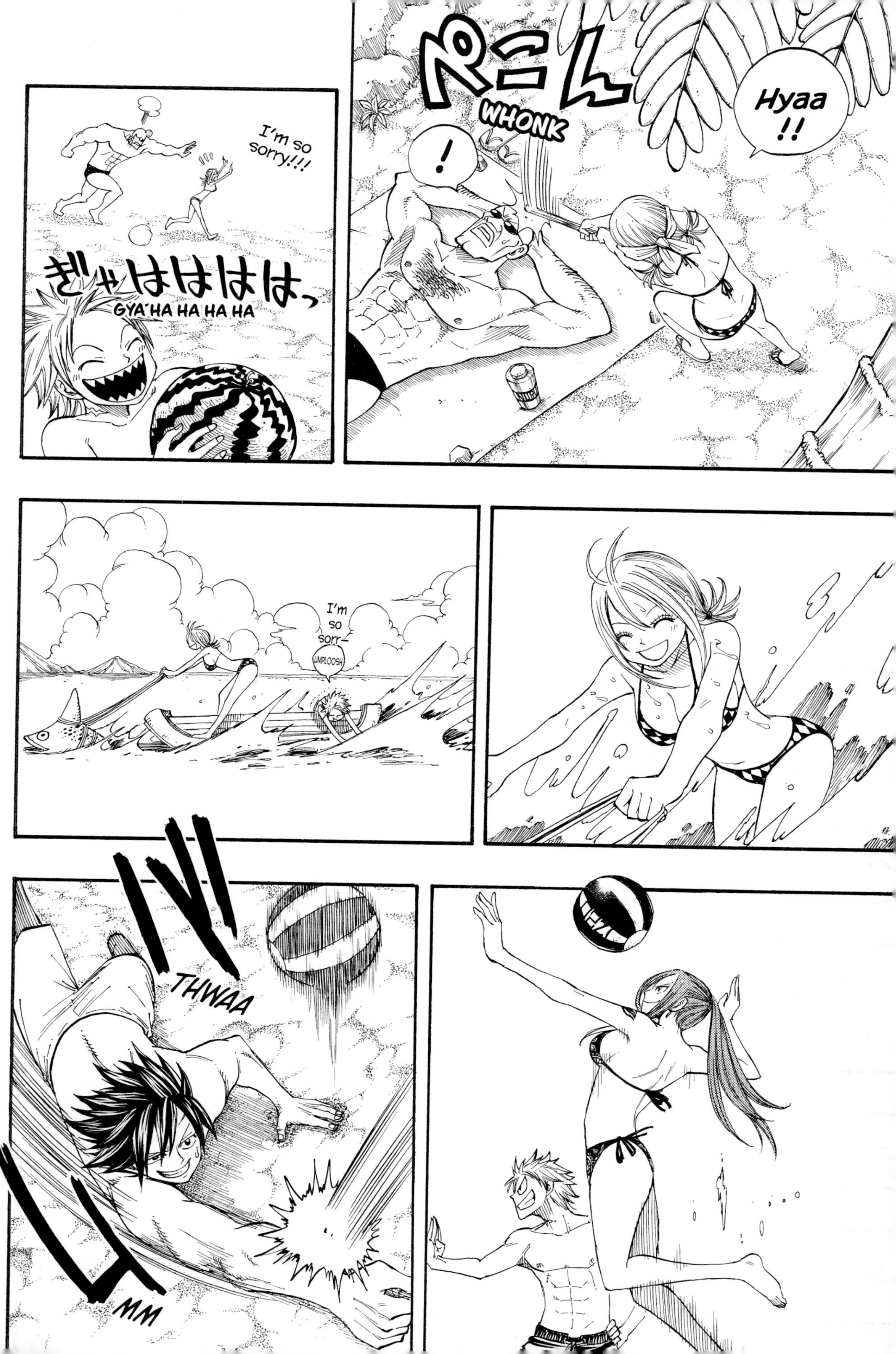
Hyaa!!
ぺこん
WHONK
!
I'm so sorry!!!
ぎゃははははっ
GYA HA HA HA HA
I'm so sorr—
UMPLOOSH
THWAA
MM

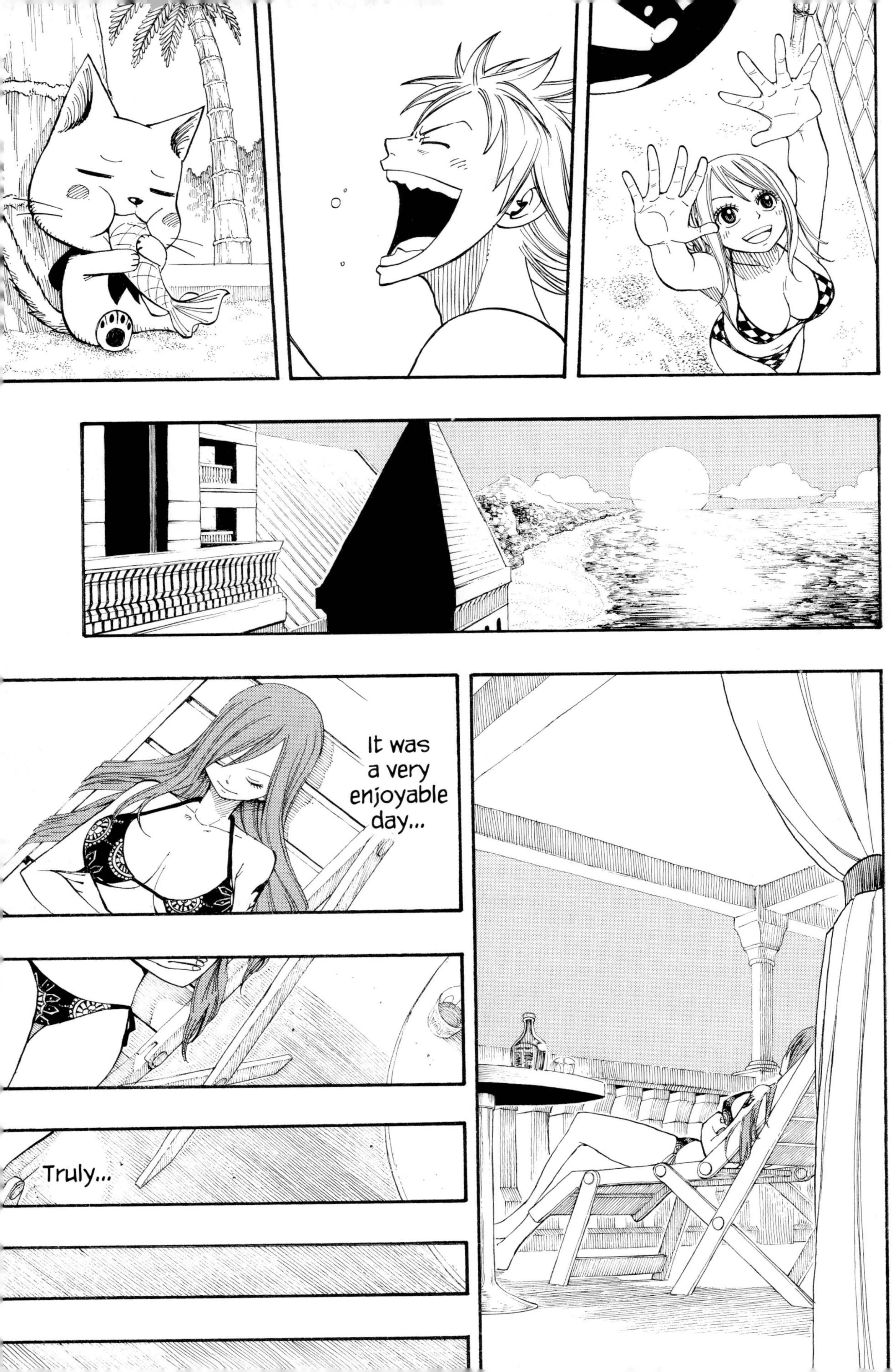
It was a very enjoyable day...
Truly...

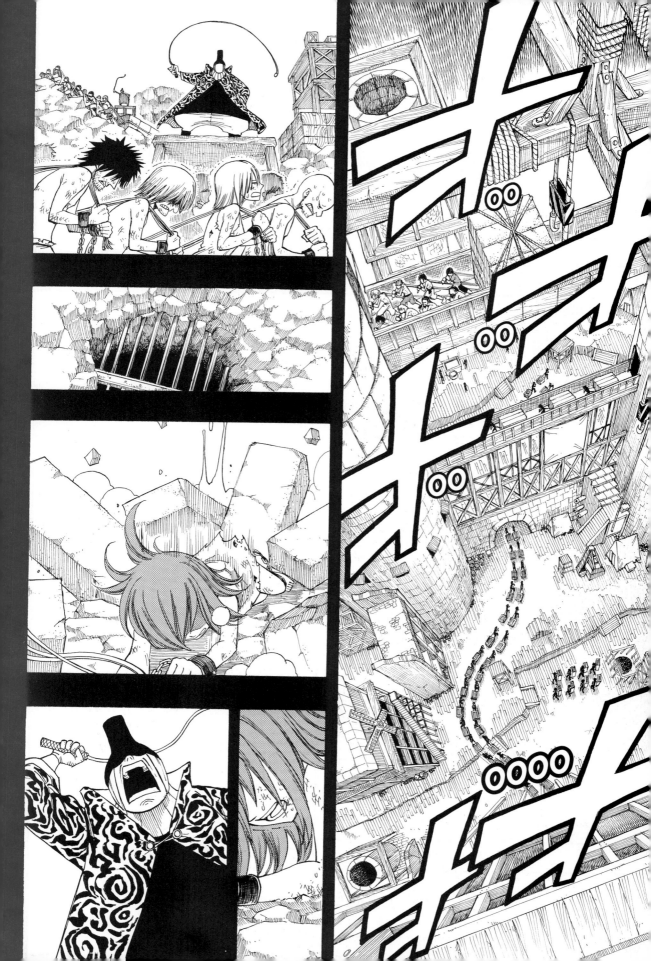

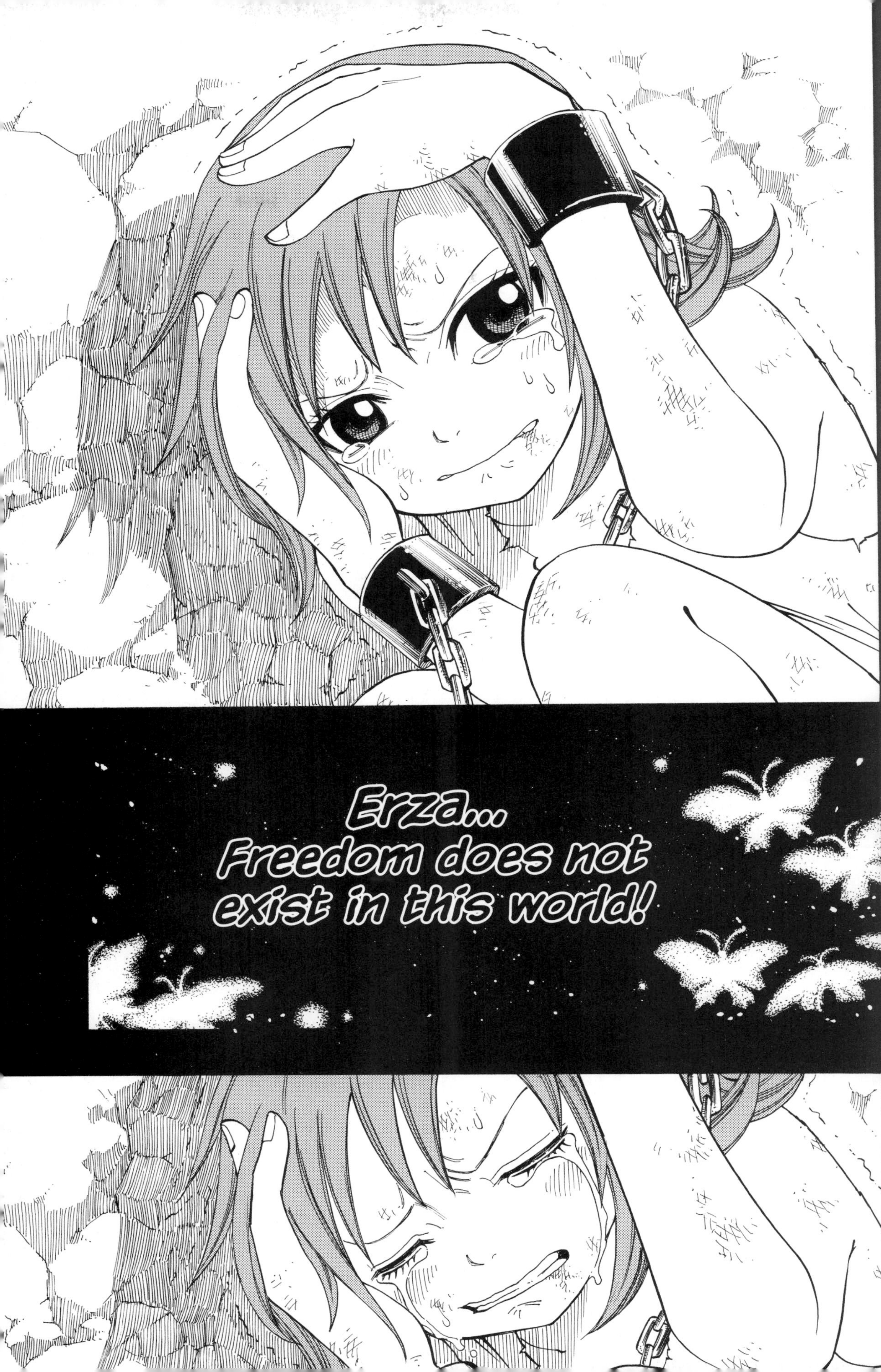
Erza...
Freedom does not exist in this world!

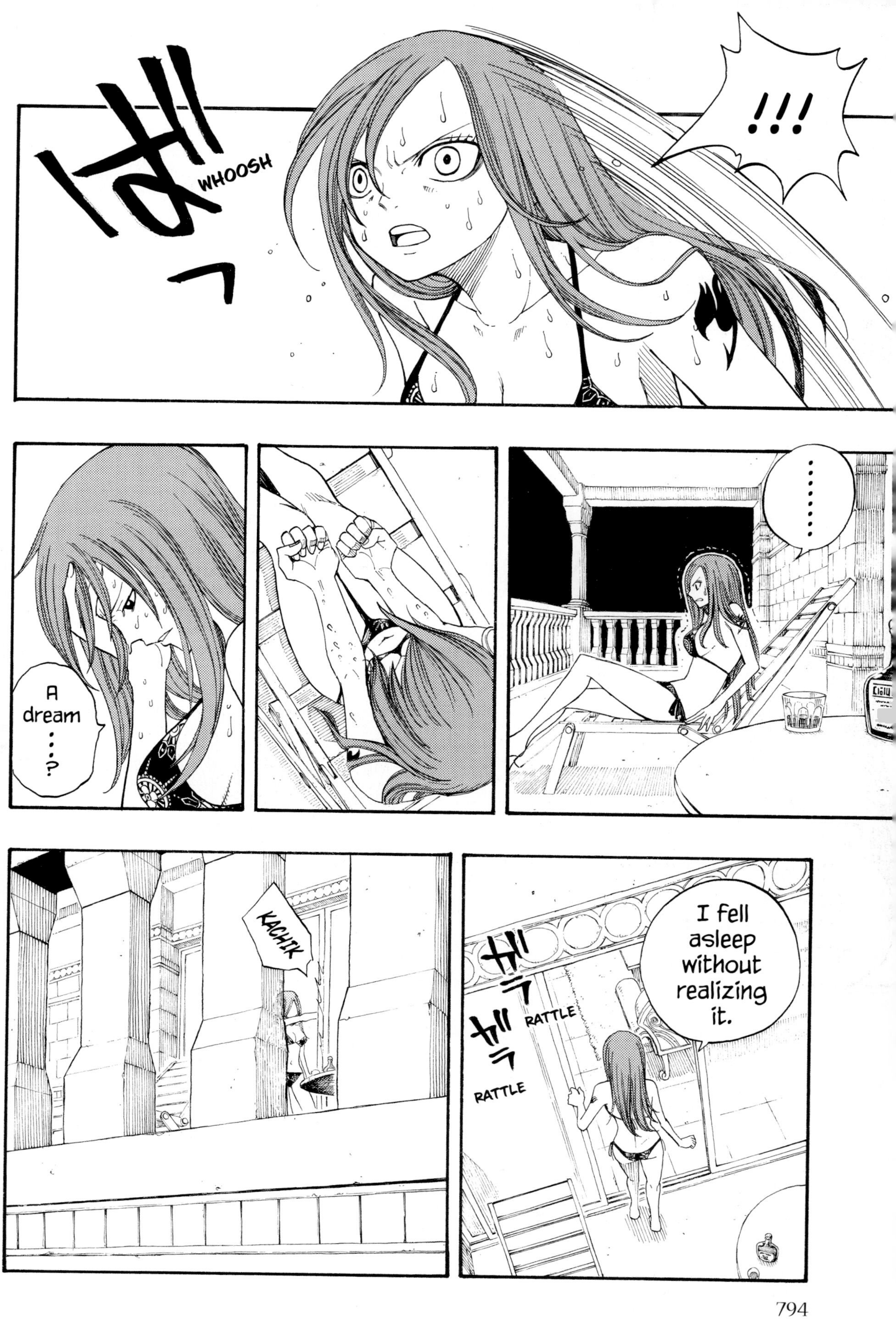
!!!
WHOOSH
......
A dream ...?
I fell asleep without realizing it.
RATTLE
RATTLE
KACHIK

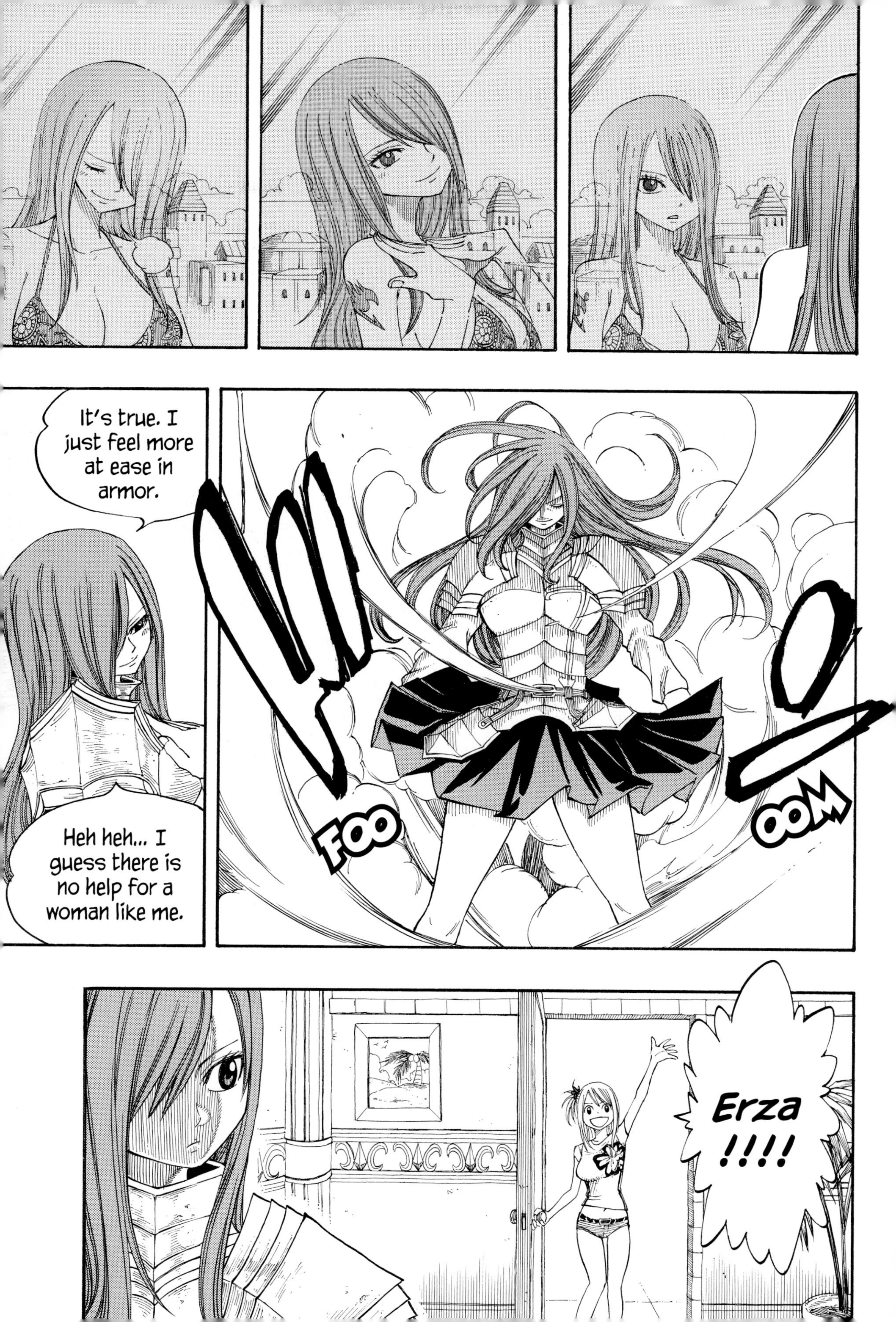
FOO
OOM
It's true. I just feel more at ease in armor.
Heh heh... I guess there is no help for a woman like me.
Erza !!!!

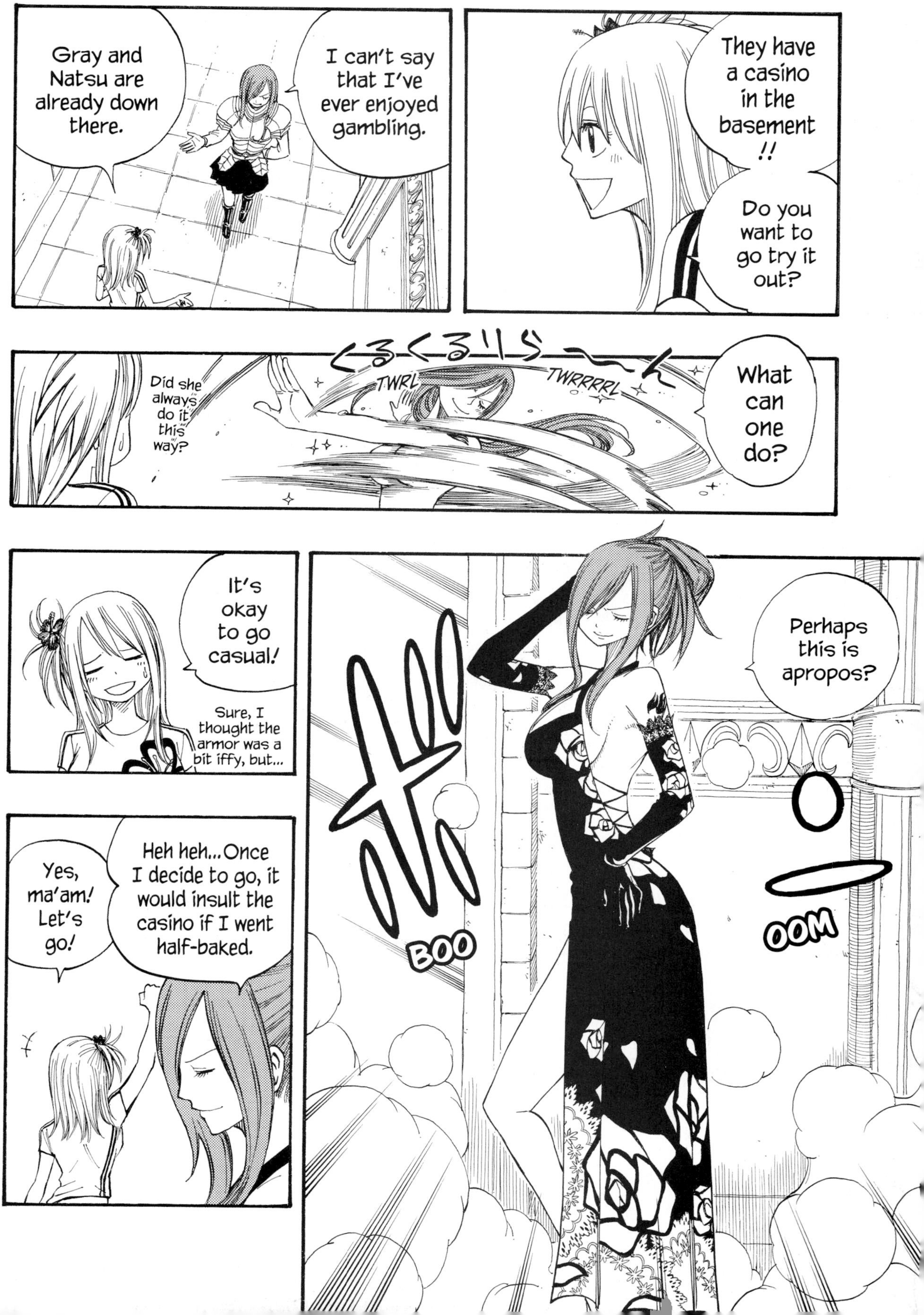
They have a casino in the basement!!
Do you want to go try it out?
I can't say that I've ever enjoyed gambling.
Gray and Natsu are already down there.
What can one do?
くるくるりらーーん
TWRL
TWRRRRL
Did she always do it this way?
Perhaps this is apropos?
BOO
OOM
It's okay to go casual!
Sure, I thought the armor was a bit iffy, but...
Heh heh...Once I decide to go, it would insult the casino if I went half-baked.
Yes, ma'am! Let's go!

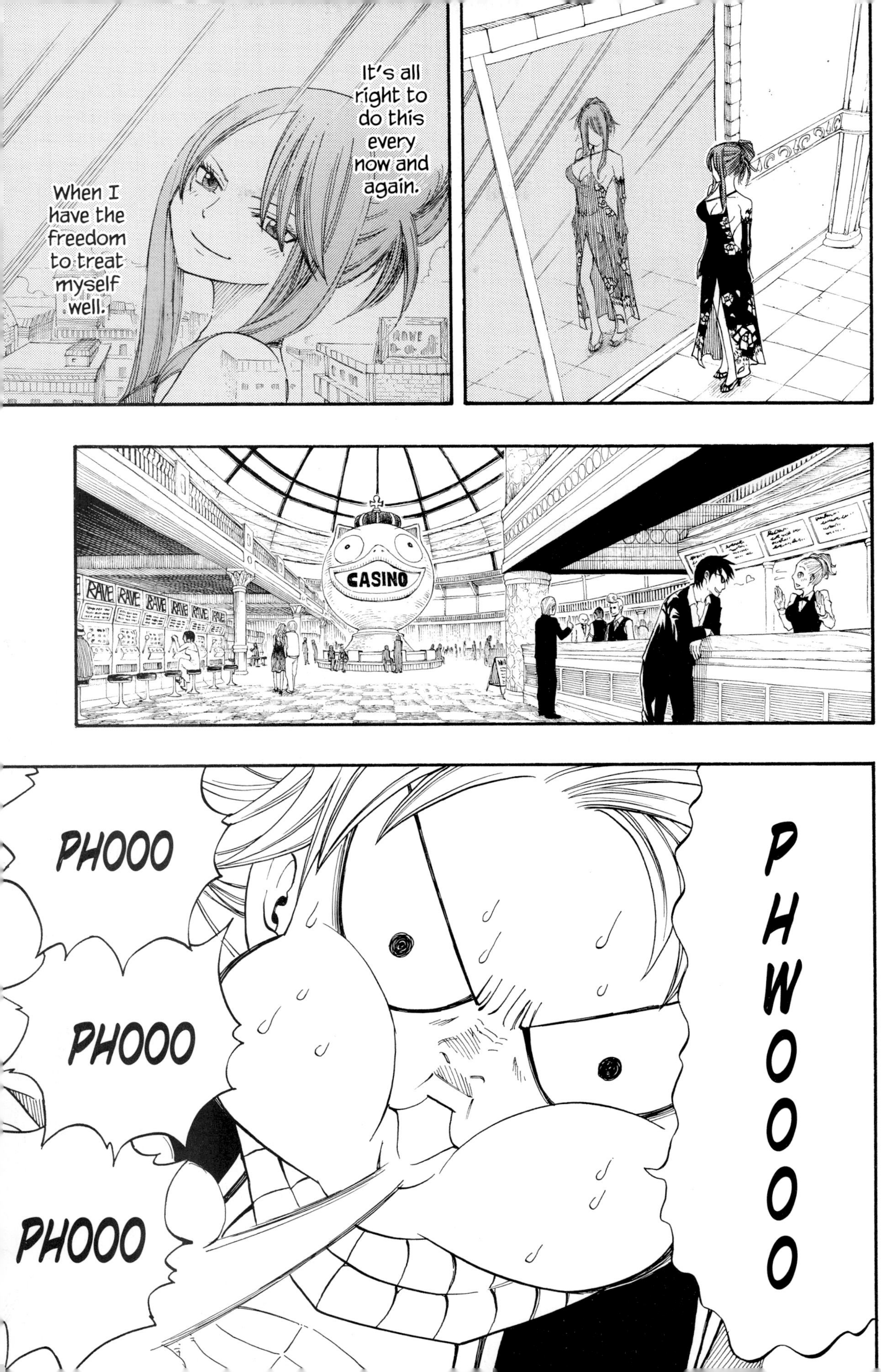
It's all right to do this every now and again.
When I have the freedom to treat myself well.
CASINO
RAVE
RAVE
RAVE
RAVE
RAVE
RAVE
PHWOOOOO
PHOOO
PHOOO
PHOOO

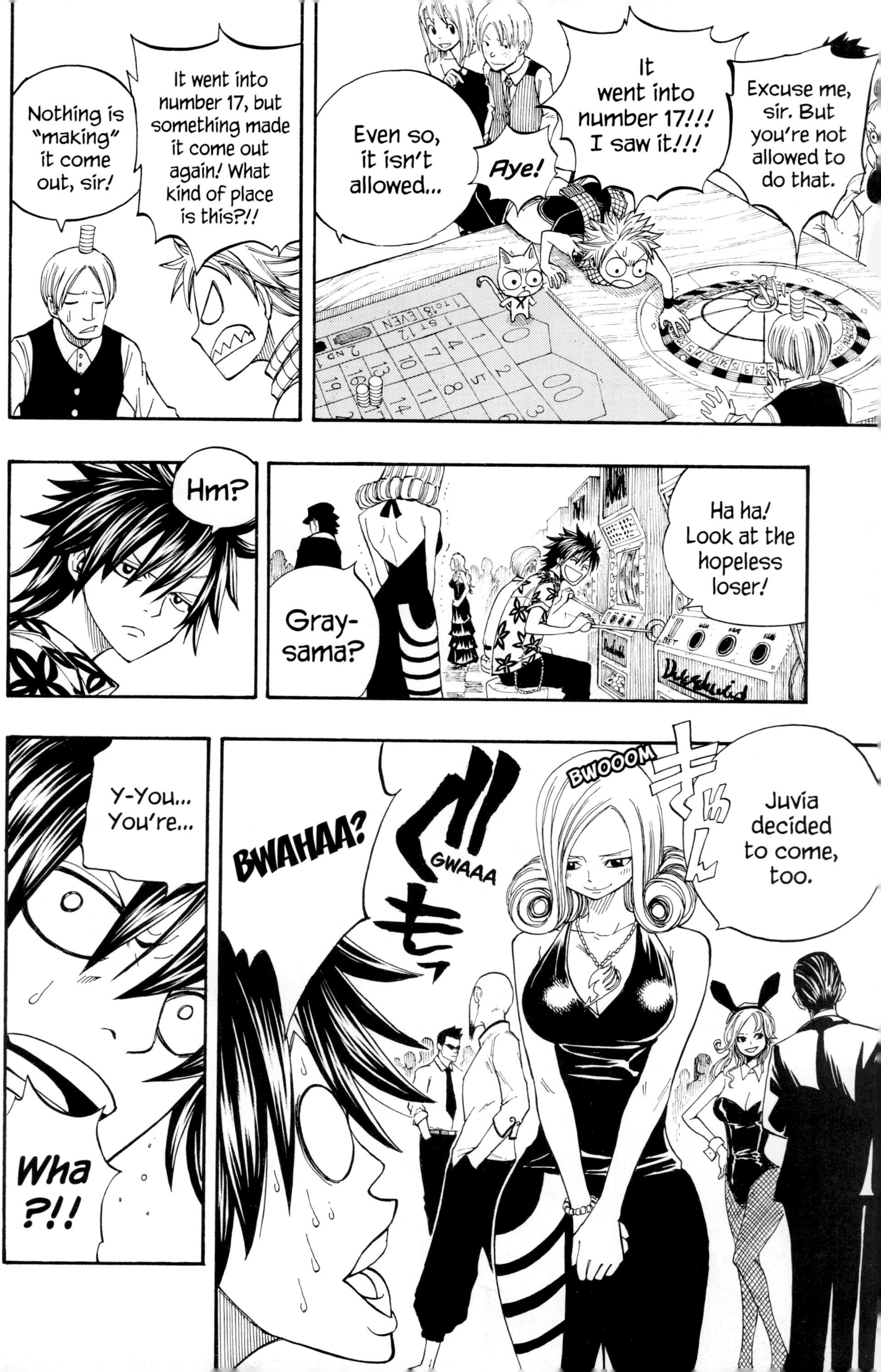
Excuse me, sir. But you're not allowed to do that.
It went into number 17!!! I saw it!!!
Aye!
Even so, it isn't allowed...
It went into number 17, but something made it come out again! What kind of place is this?!!
Nothing is "making" it come out, sir!
Ha ha! Look at the hopeless loser!
Gray-sama?
Hm?
Juvia decided to come, too.
BWOOOM
GWAAA
BWAHAA?
Y-You... You're...
Wha ?!!

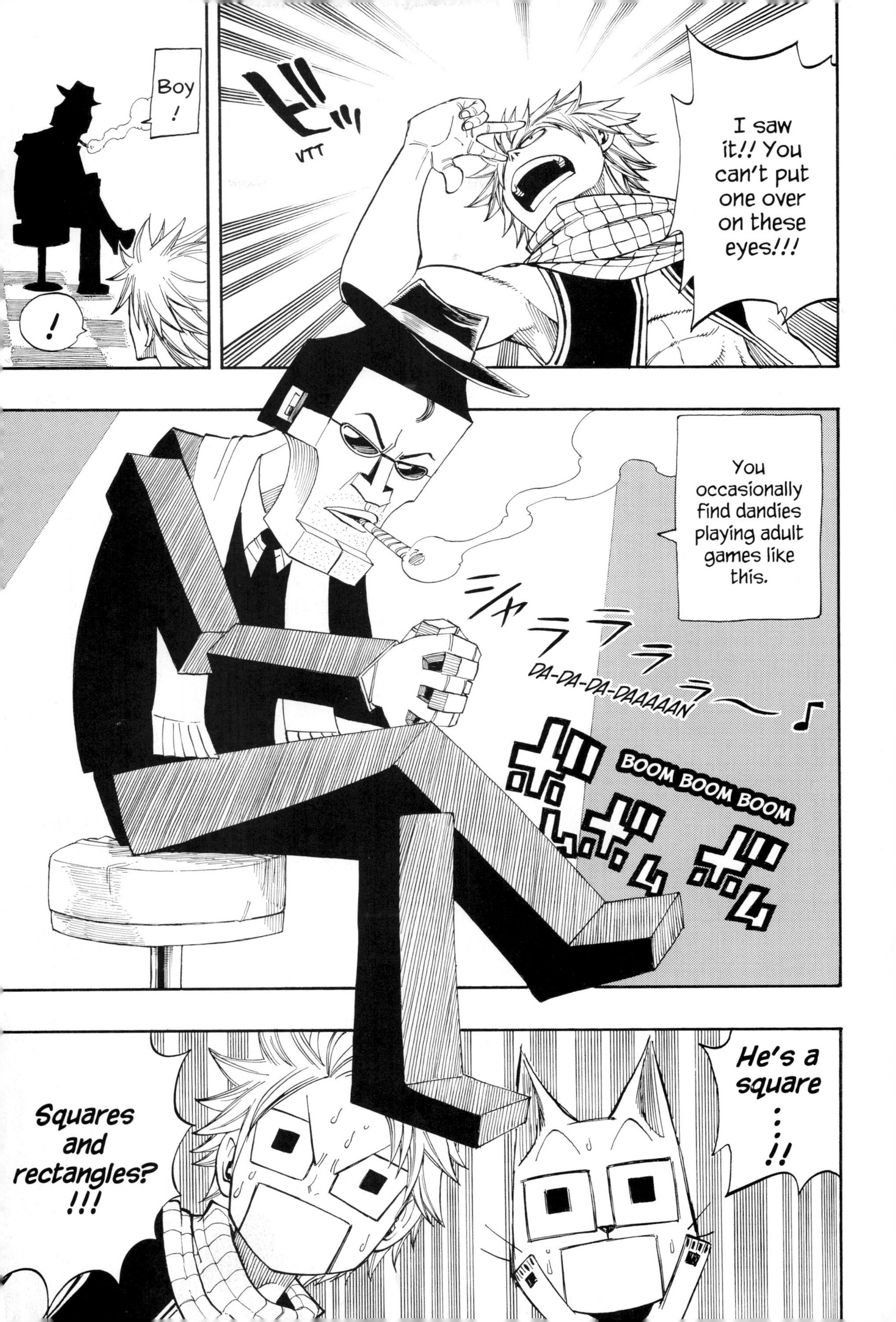
I saw it!! You can't put one over on these eyes!!!
VTT
Boy!
!
You occasionally find dandies playing adult games like this.
DA-DA-DA-DAAAAAN
BOOM BOOM BOOM
He's a square...!!
Squares and rectangles?!!!

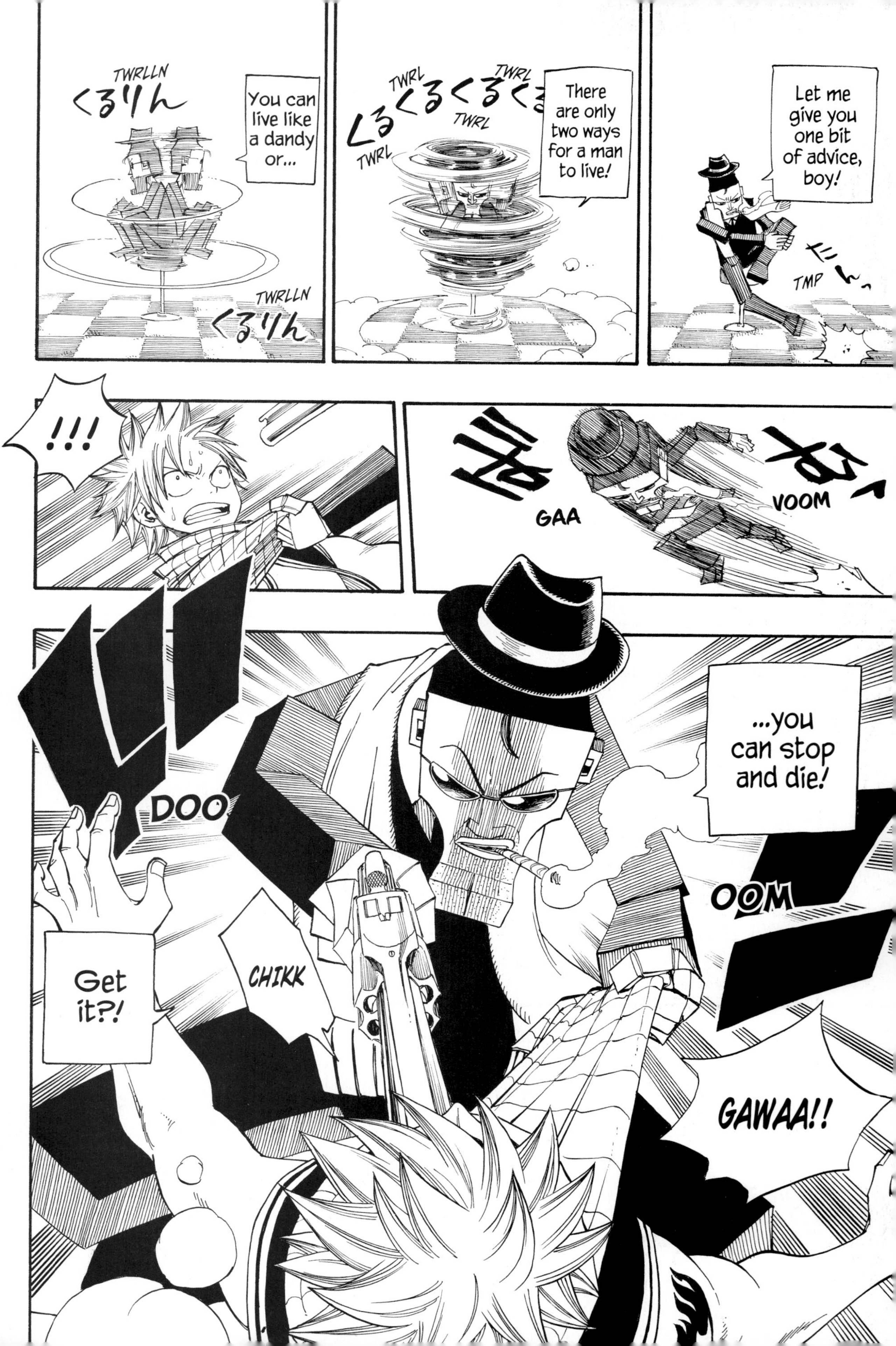
Let me give you one bit of advice, boy!
TMP
TWRL
TWRL
There are only two ways for a man to live!
TWRL
TWRL
TWRLLN
くるりん
You can live like a dandy or...
TWRLLN
くるりん
VOOM
GAA
!!!
...you can stop and die!
OOM
DOO
CHIKK
Get it?!
GAWAA!!

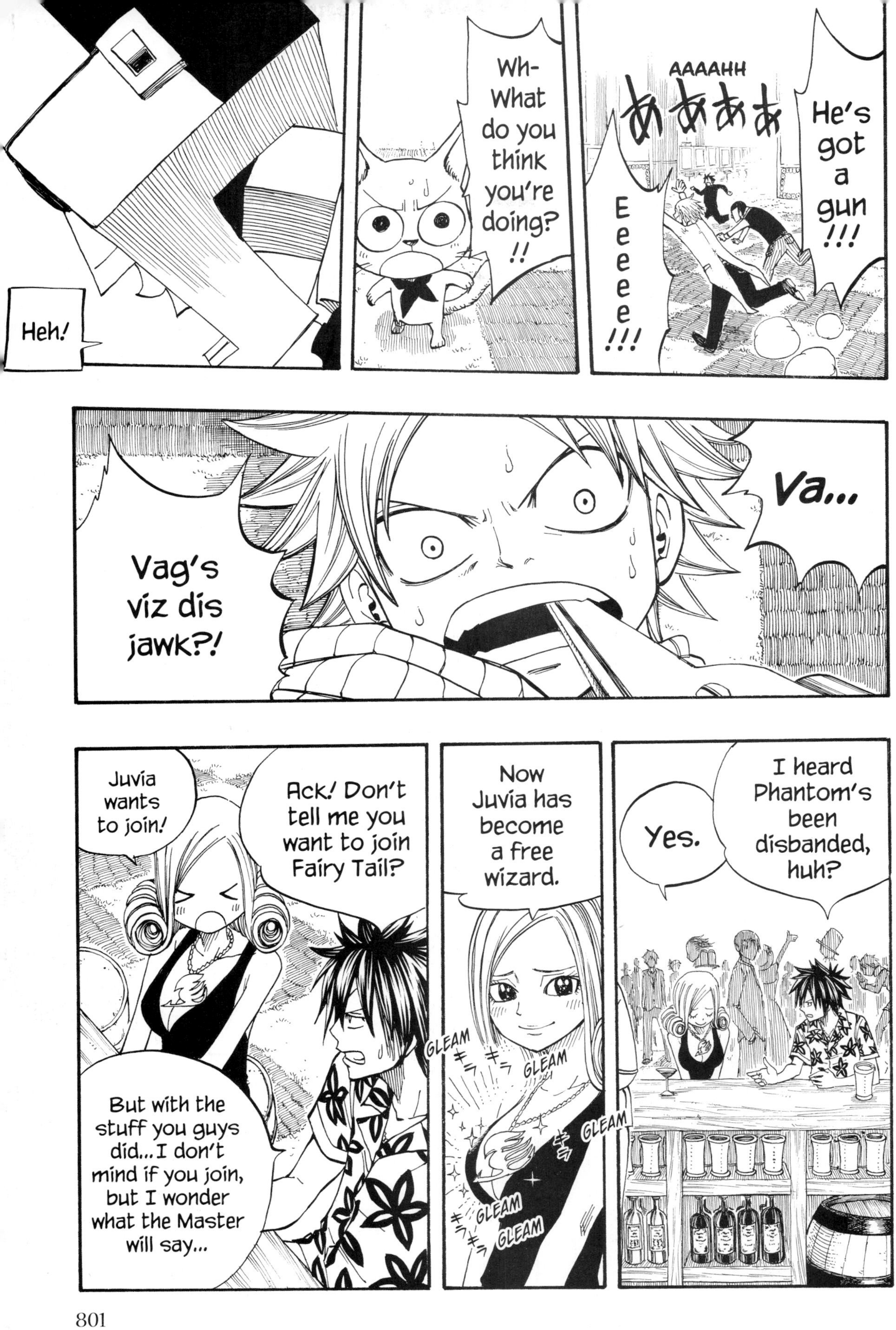
AAAAHH
あああぁ
He's got a gun!!!
Eeeee!!!
Wh-What do you think you're doing?!!
Heh!
Va...
Vag's viz dis jawk?!
I heard Phantom's been disbanded, huh?
Yes.
Now Juvia has become a free wizard.
GLEAM
GLEAM
GLEAM
GLEAM
GLEAM
Ack! Don't tell me you want to join Fairy Tail?
Juvia wants to join!
But with the stuff you guys did...I don't mind if you join, but I wonder what the Master will say...

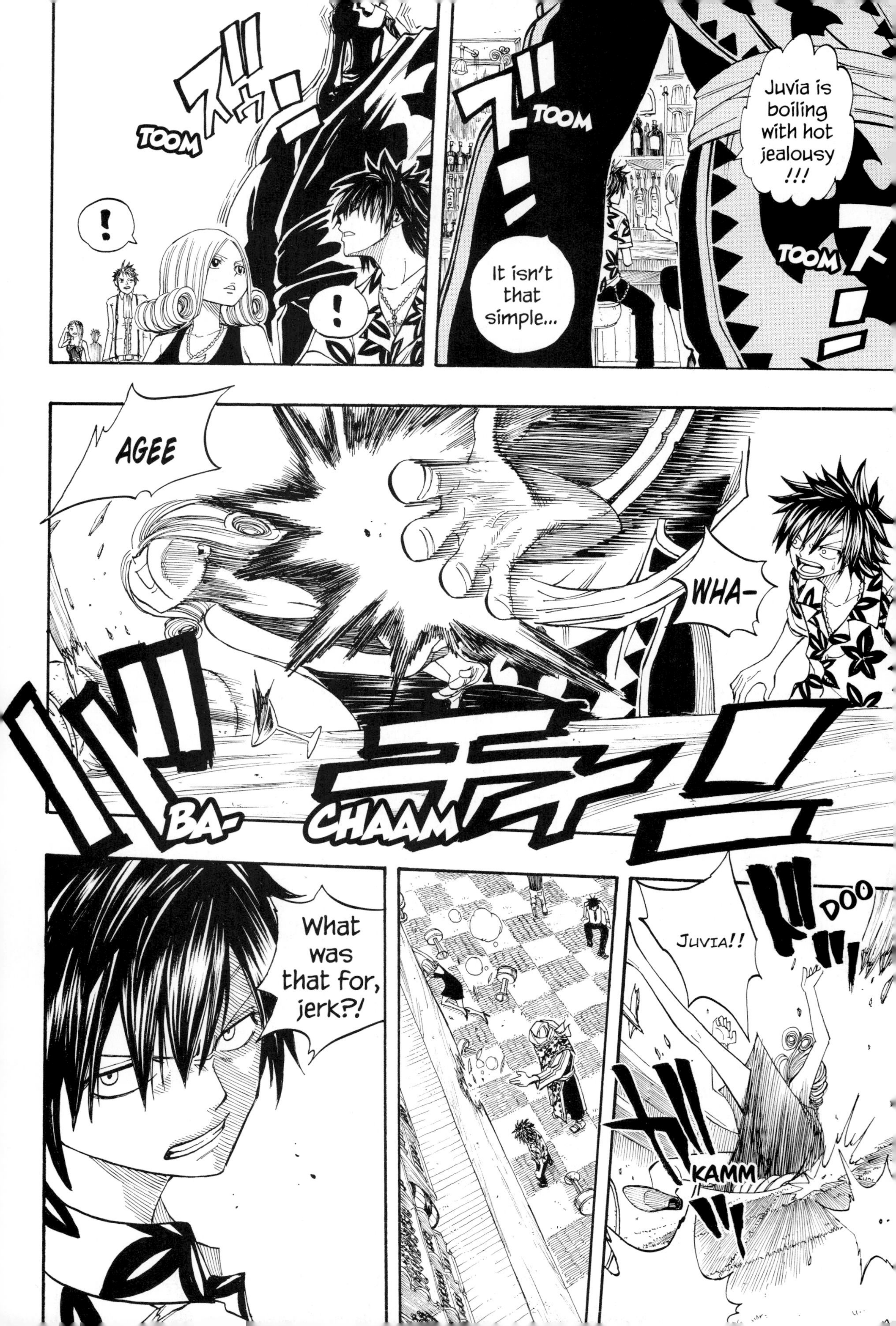

Juvia is boiling with hot jealousy!!!
TOOM
TOOM
It isn't that simple...
TOOM
!
!
AGEE
WHA-
BA- CHAAM
DOO
JUVIA!!
KAMM
What was that for, jerk?!

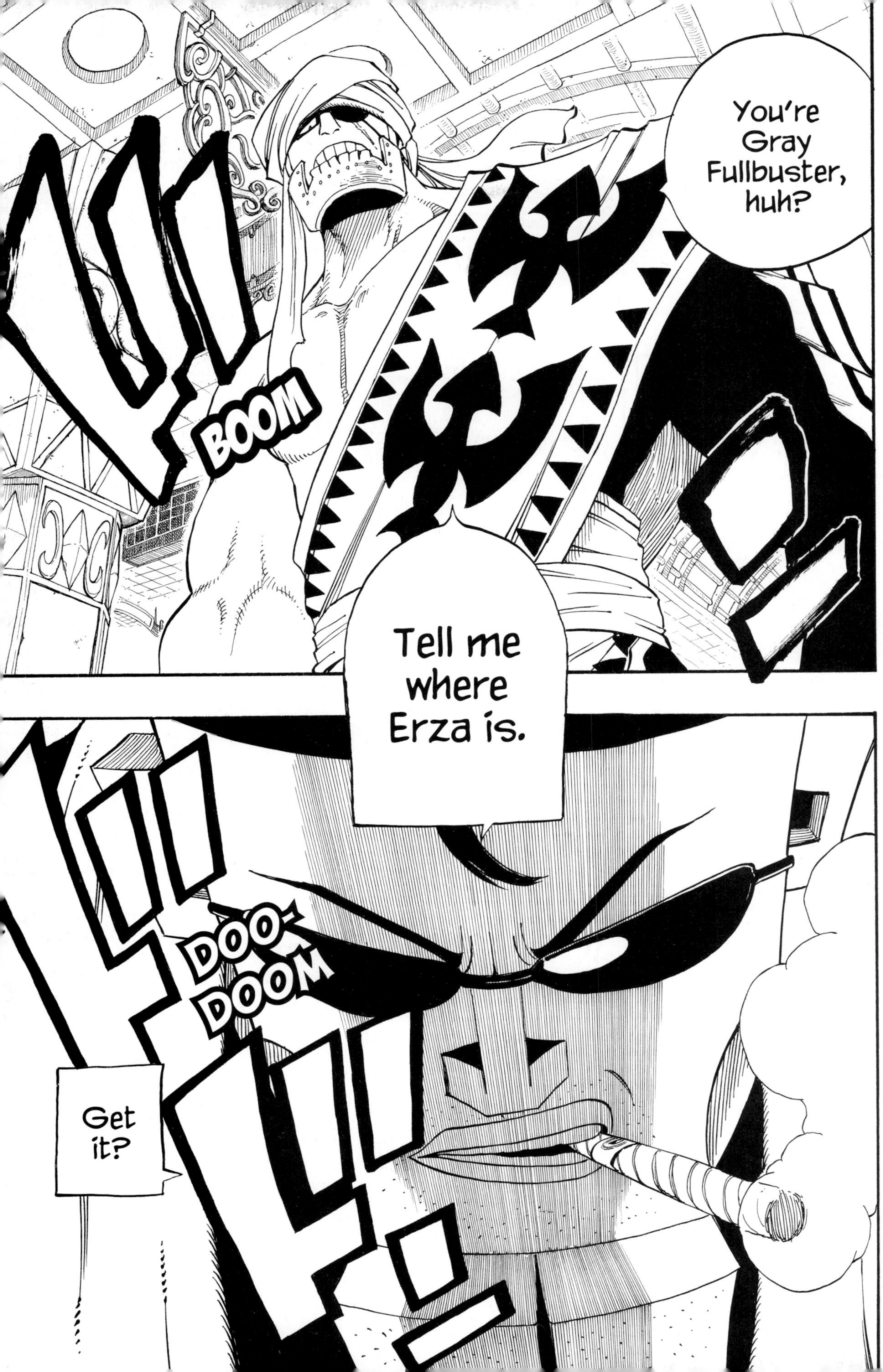
You're Gray Fullbuster, huh?
BOOM
Tell me where Erza is.
DOO-DOOM
Get it?

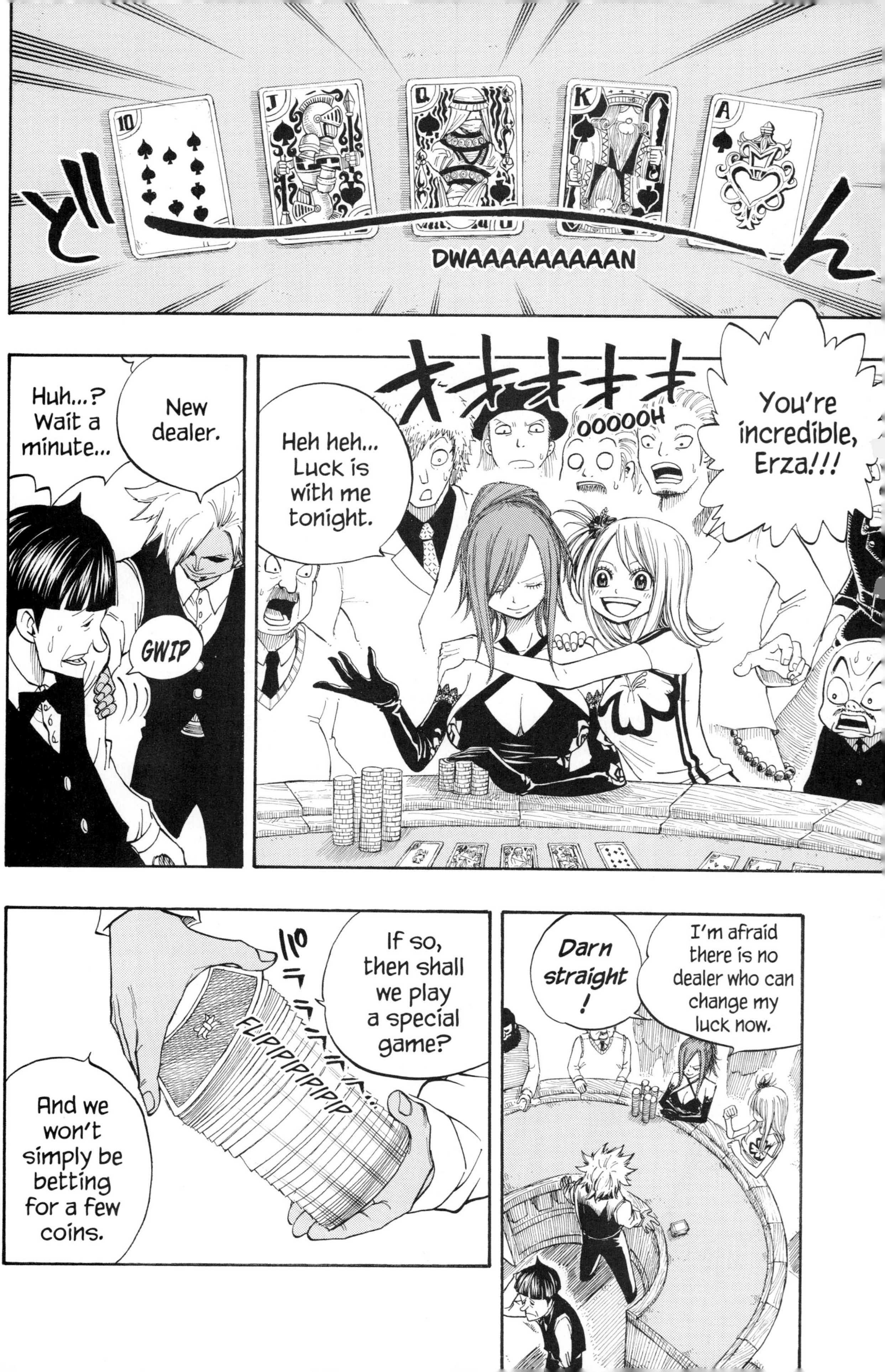
DWAAAAAAAAAN
You're incredible, Erza!!!
OOOOOH
Heh heh... Luck is with me tonight.
New dealer.
Huh...? Wait a minute...
GWIP
I'm afraid there is no dealer who can change my luck now.
Darn straight!
If so, then shall we play a special game?
FLIPIPIPIPIPIP
And we won't simply be betting for a few coins.

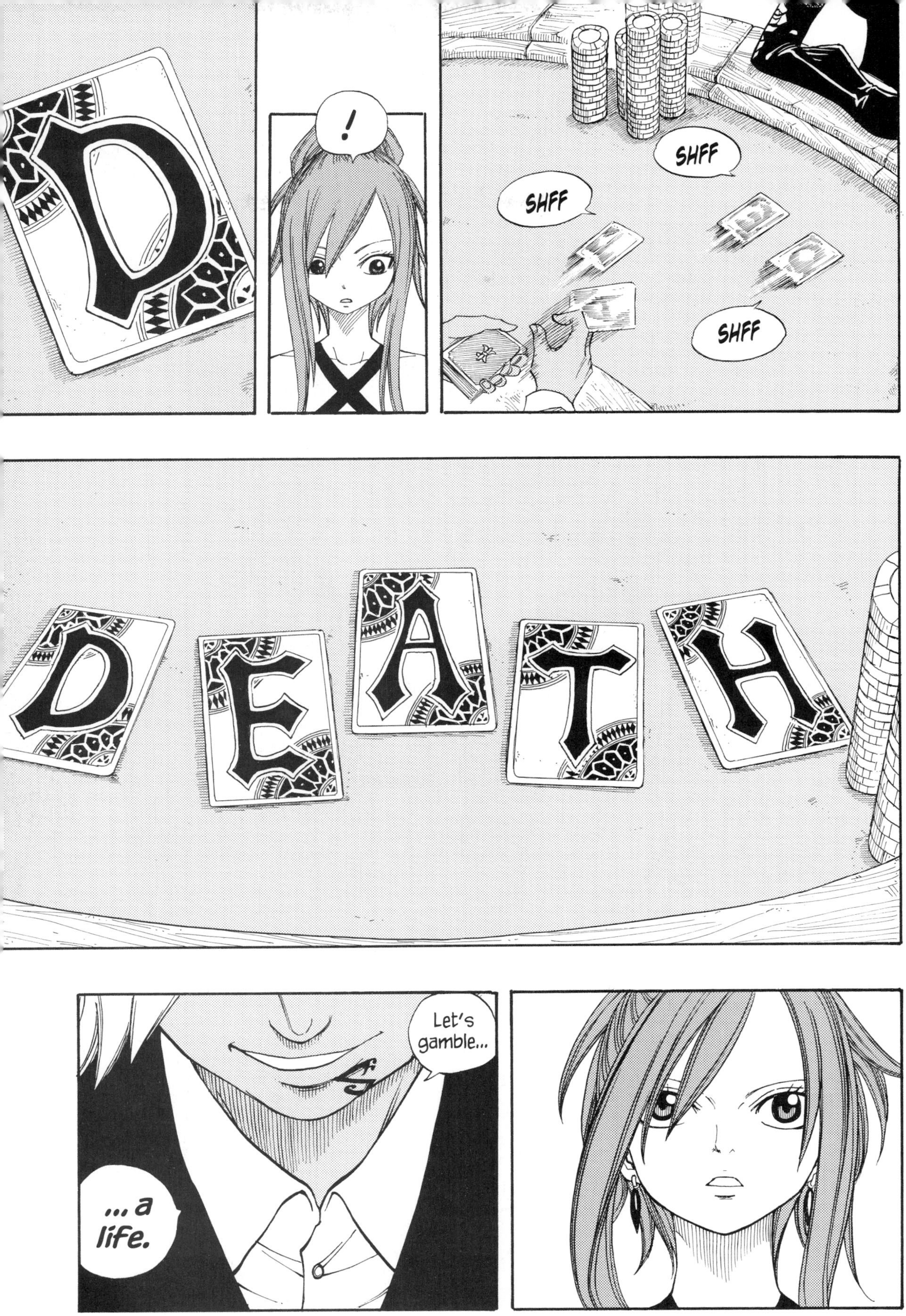
SHFF
SHFF
SHFF
!
D
D
E
A
T
H
Let's gamble...
...a life.

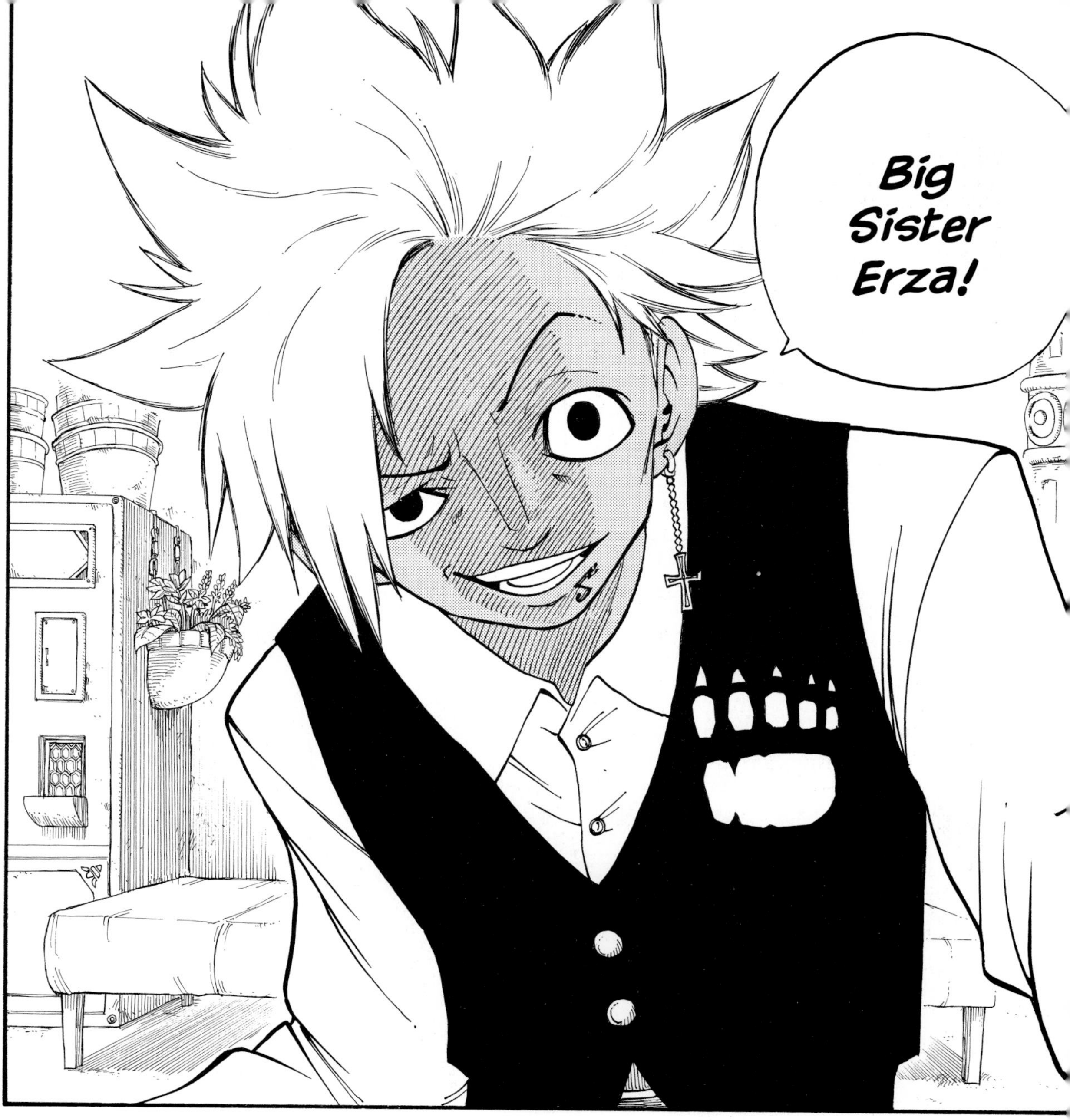
Big Sister Erza!
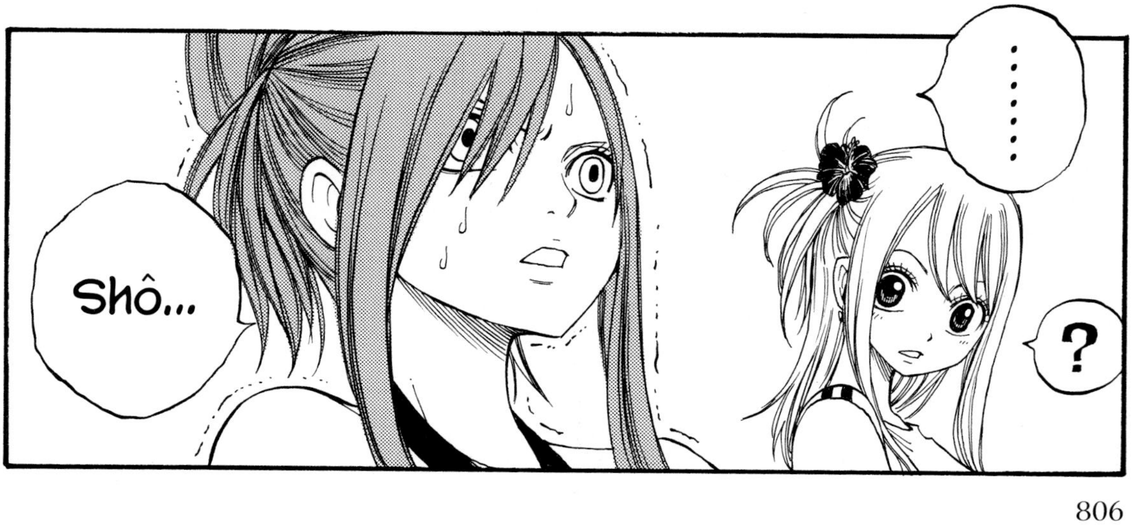
......
Shô...
?

Chapter 76:
The Tower of Heaven

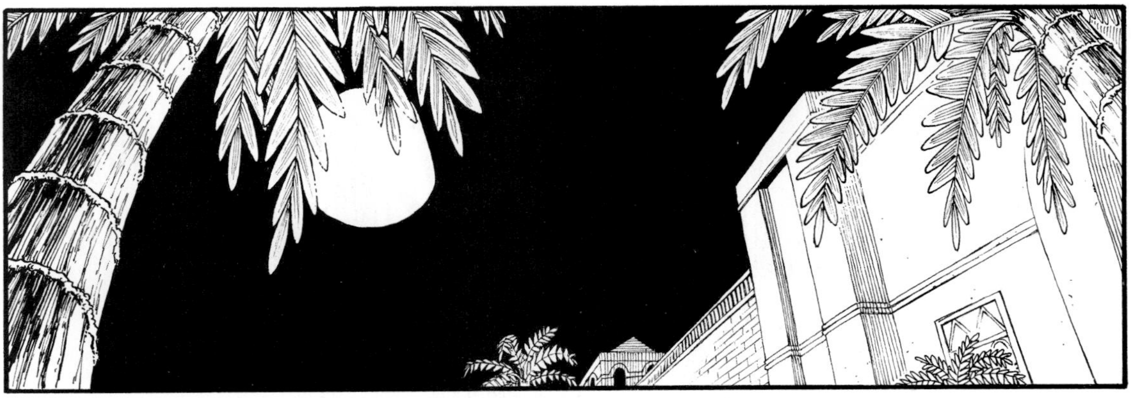

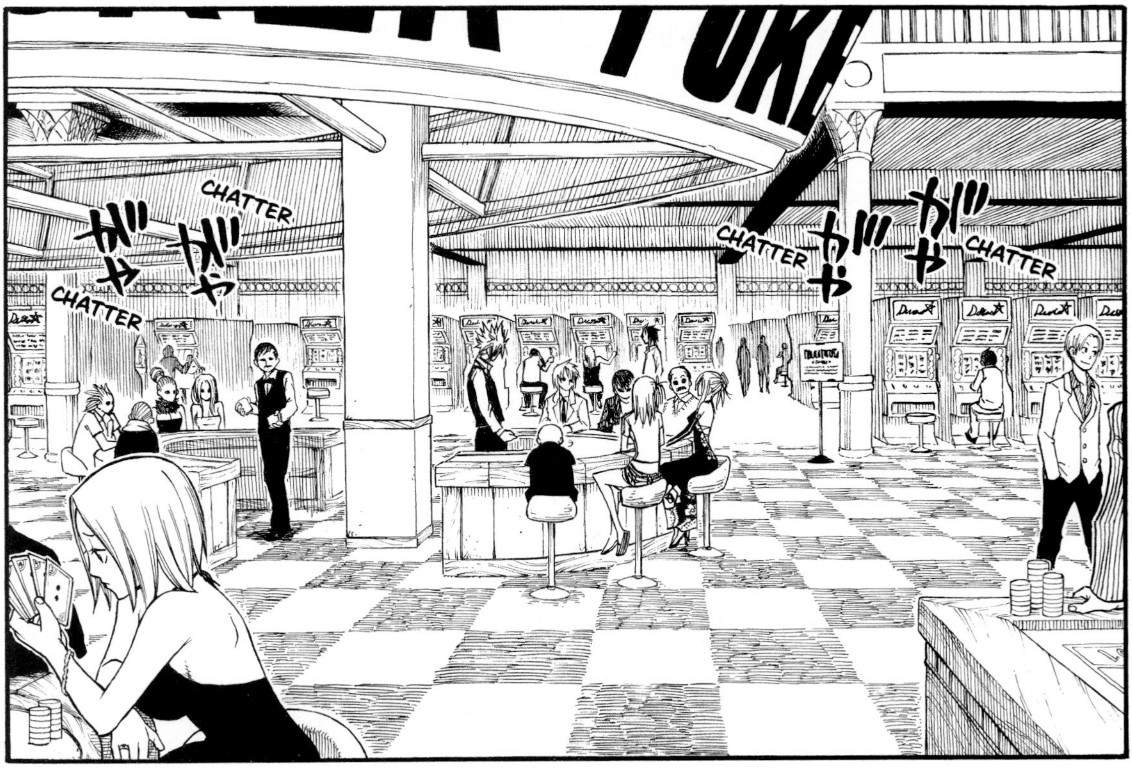
CHATTER
ガヤ
ガヤ
CHATTER
CHATTER
ガヤ
ガヤ
CHATTER

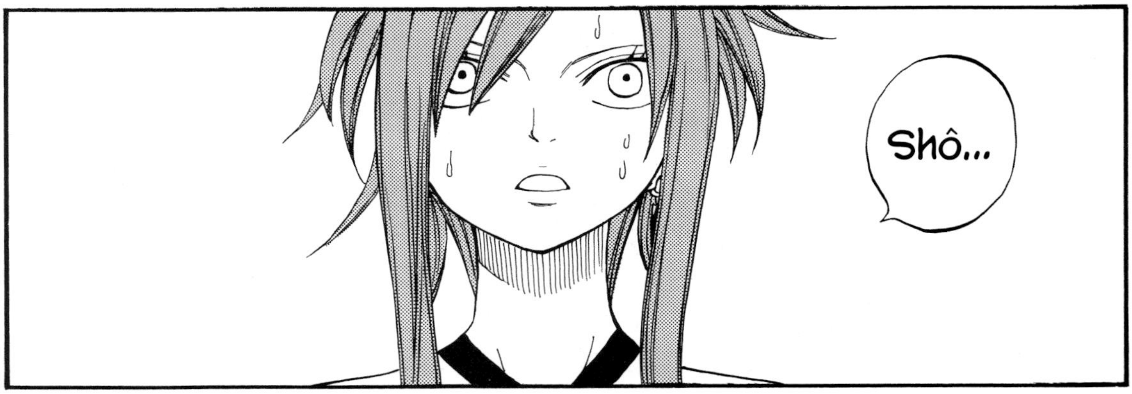
Shô...

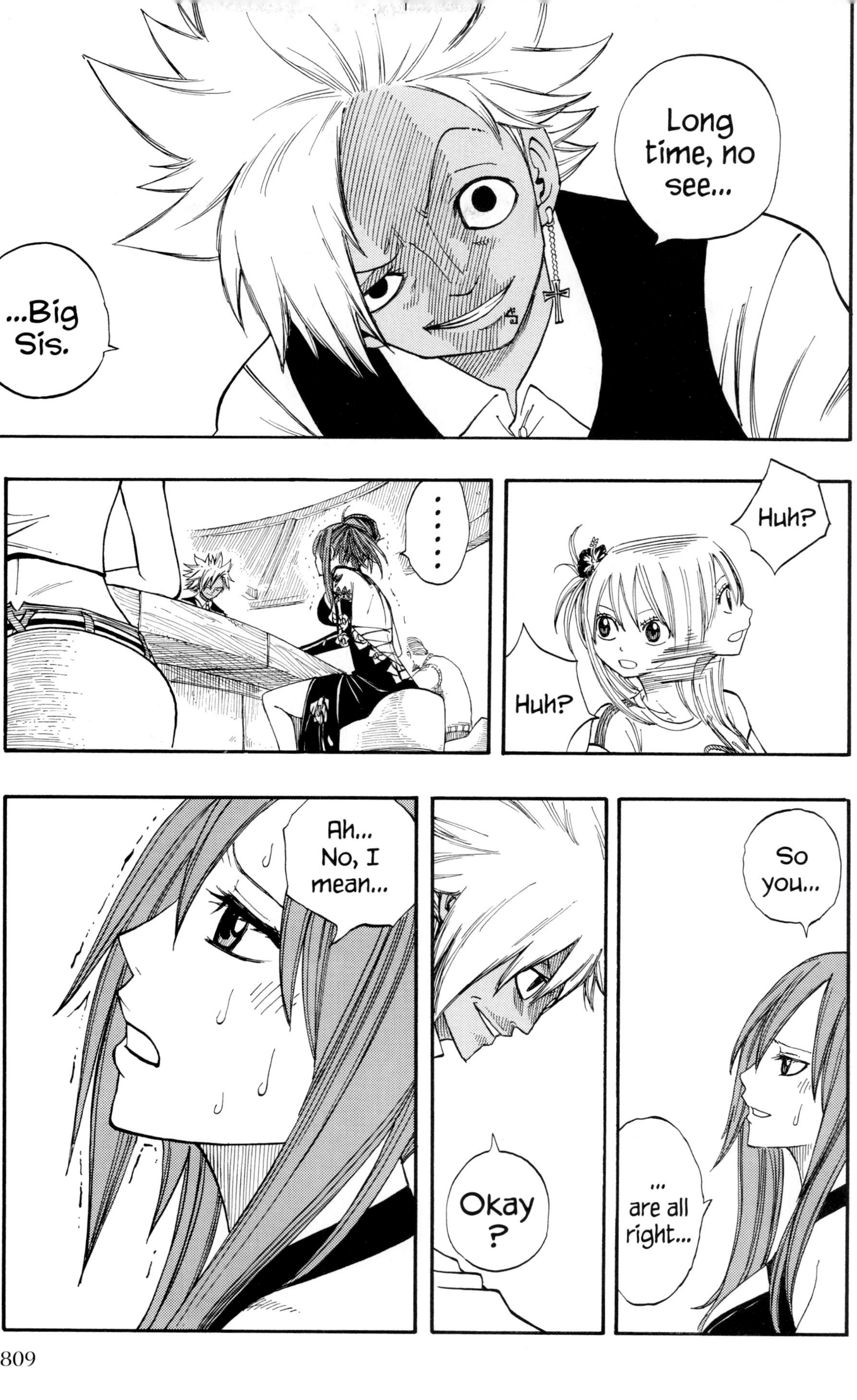
Long time, no see...
...Big Sis.
Huh?
Huh?
......
So you...
... are all right...
Okay?
Ah... No, I mean...

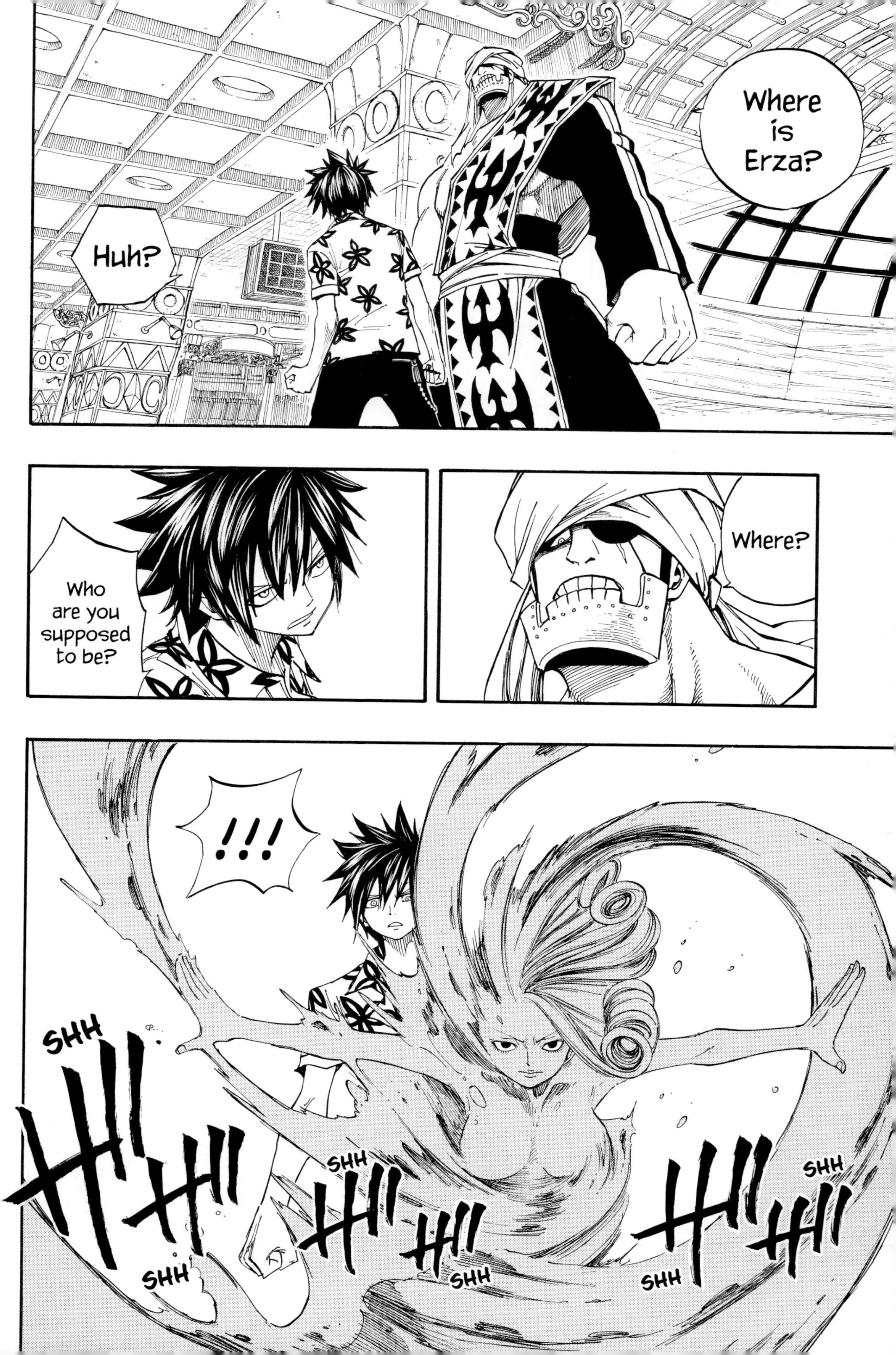
Where is Erza?
Huh?
Where?
Who are you supposed to be?
!!!
SHH
SHH
SHH
SHH
SHH
SHH

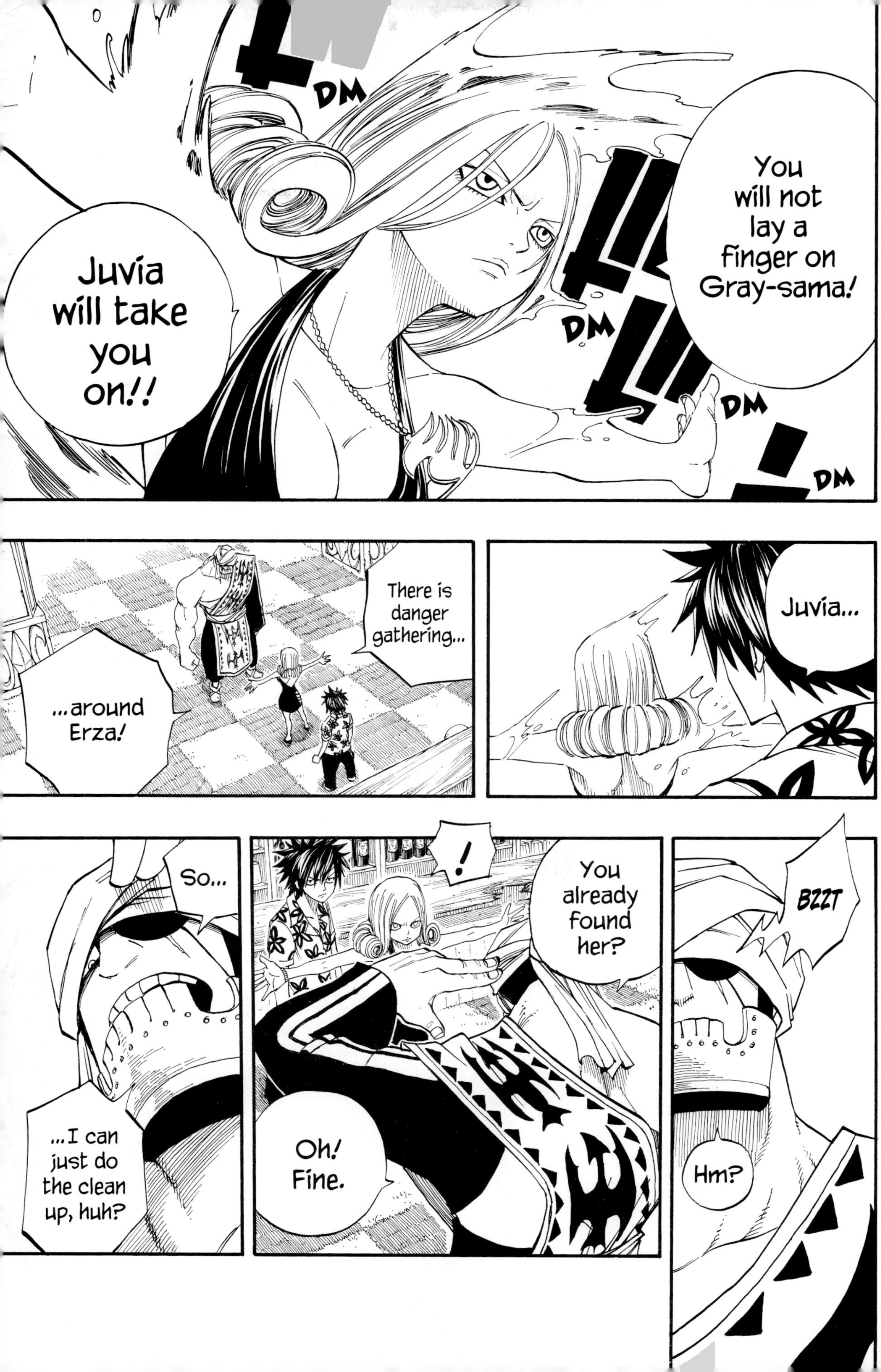
DM
You will not lay a finger on Gray-sama!
DM
DM
DM
Juvia will take you on!!
Juvia...
There is danger gathering...
...around Erza!
BZZT
Hm?
!
You already found her?
Oh! Fine.
So...
...I can just do the clean up, huh?

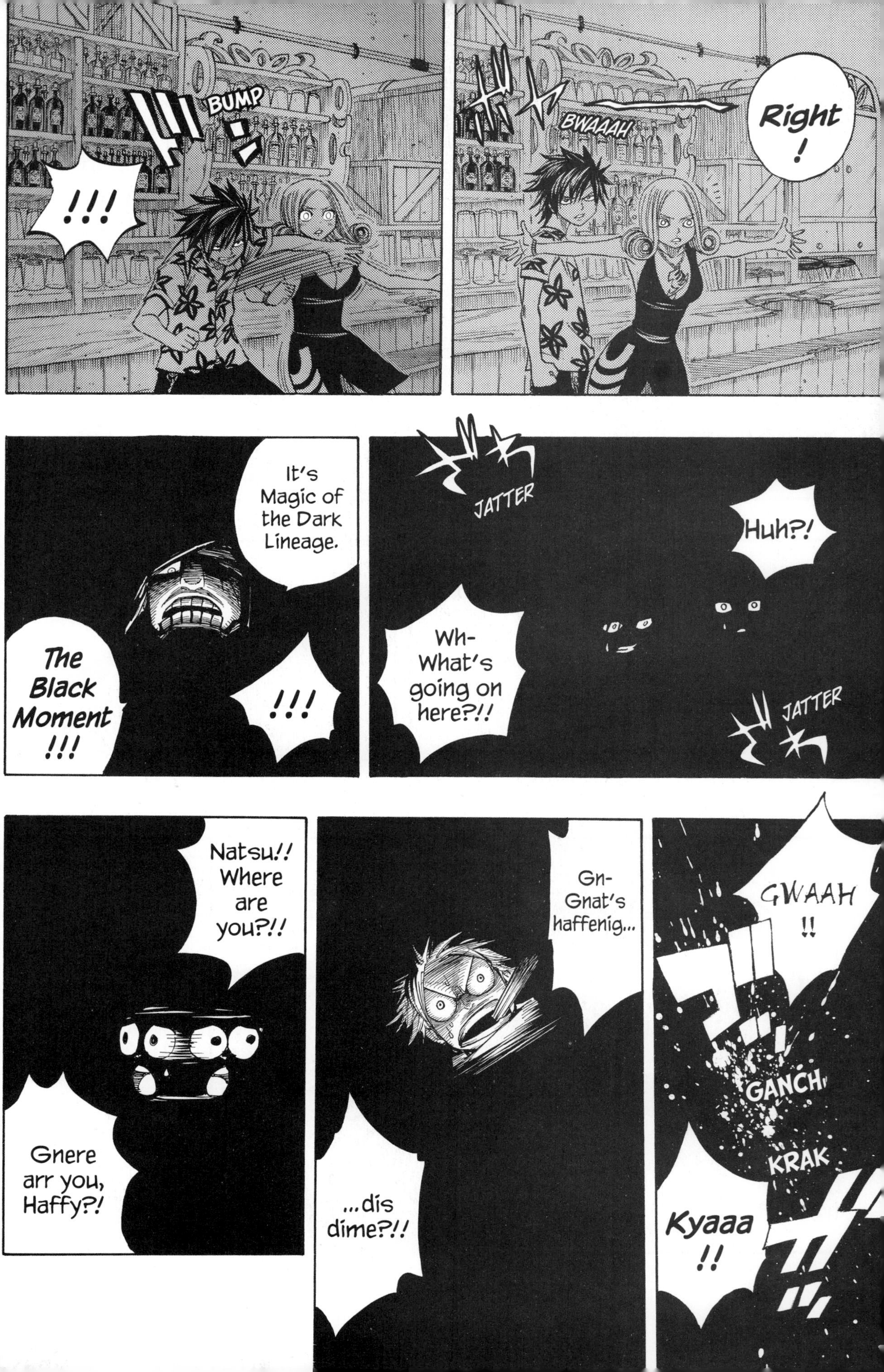
Right!
BWAAAH
BUMP
!!!
Huh?!
JATTER
Wh- What's going on here?!!
JATTER
It's Magic of the Dark Lineage.
!!!
The Black Moment!!!
GWAAH!!
GANCH
KRAK
Kyaaa!!
Gn- Gnat's haffenig...
...dis dime?!!
Natsu!! Where are you?!!
Gnere arr you, Haffy?!

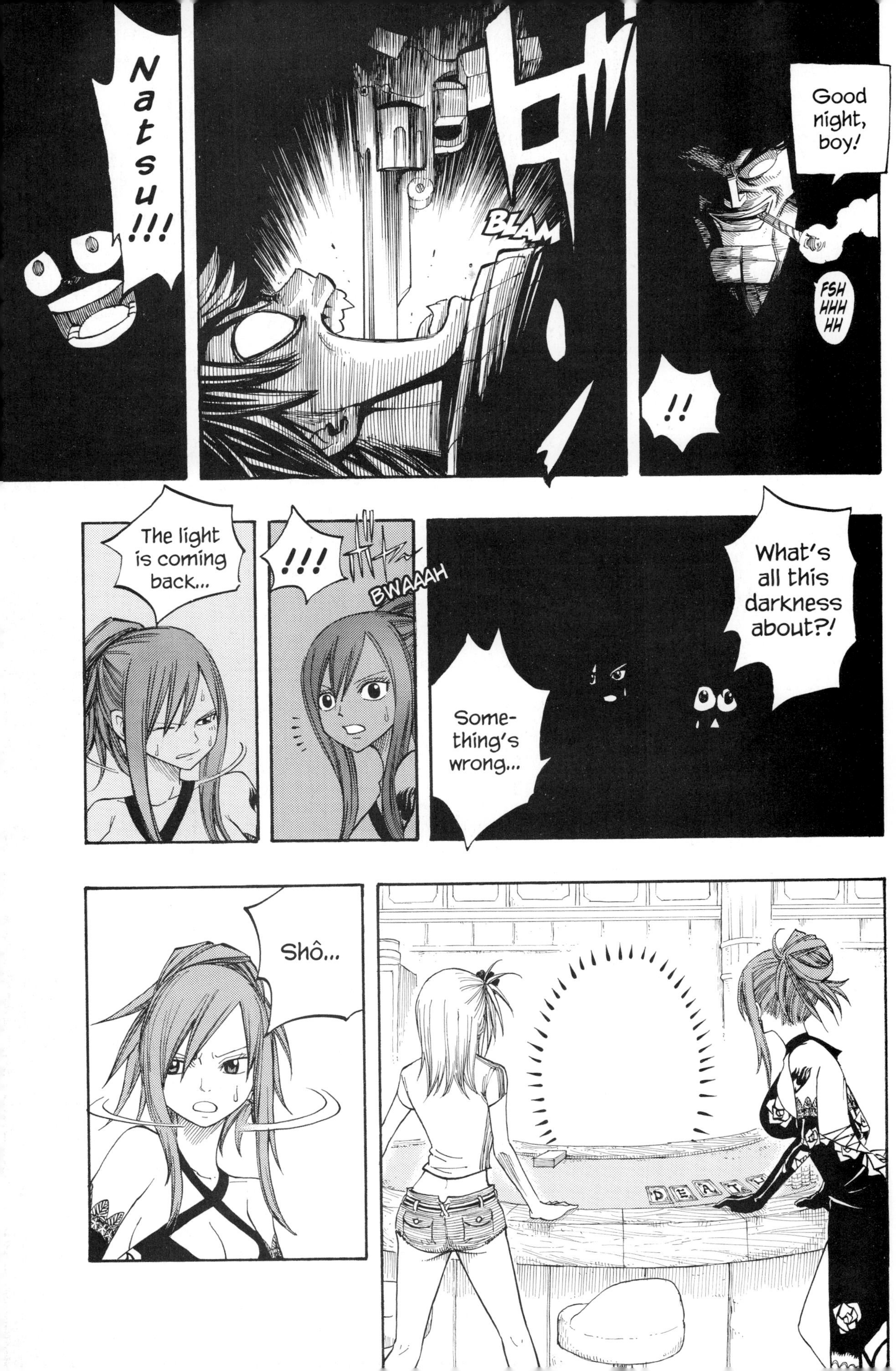
Good night, boy!
FSHHHHHH
!!
BLAM
Natsu!!!
What's all this darkness about?!
Some-thing's wrong...
!!!
BWAAAH
The light is coming back...
Shô...

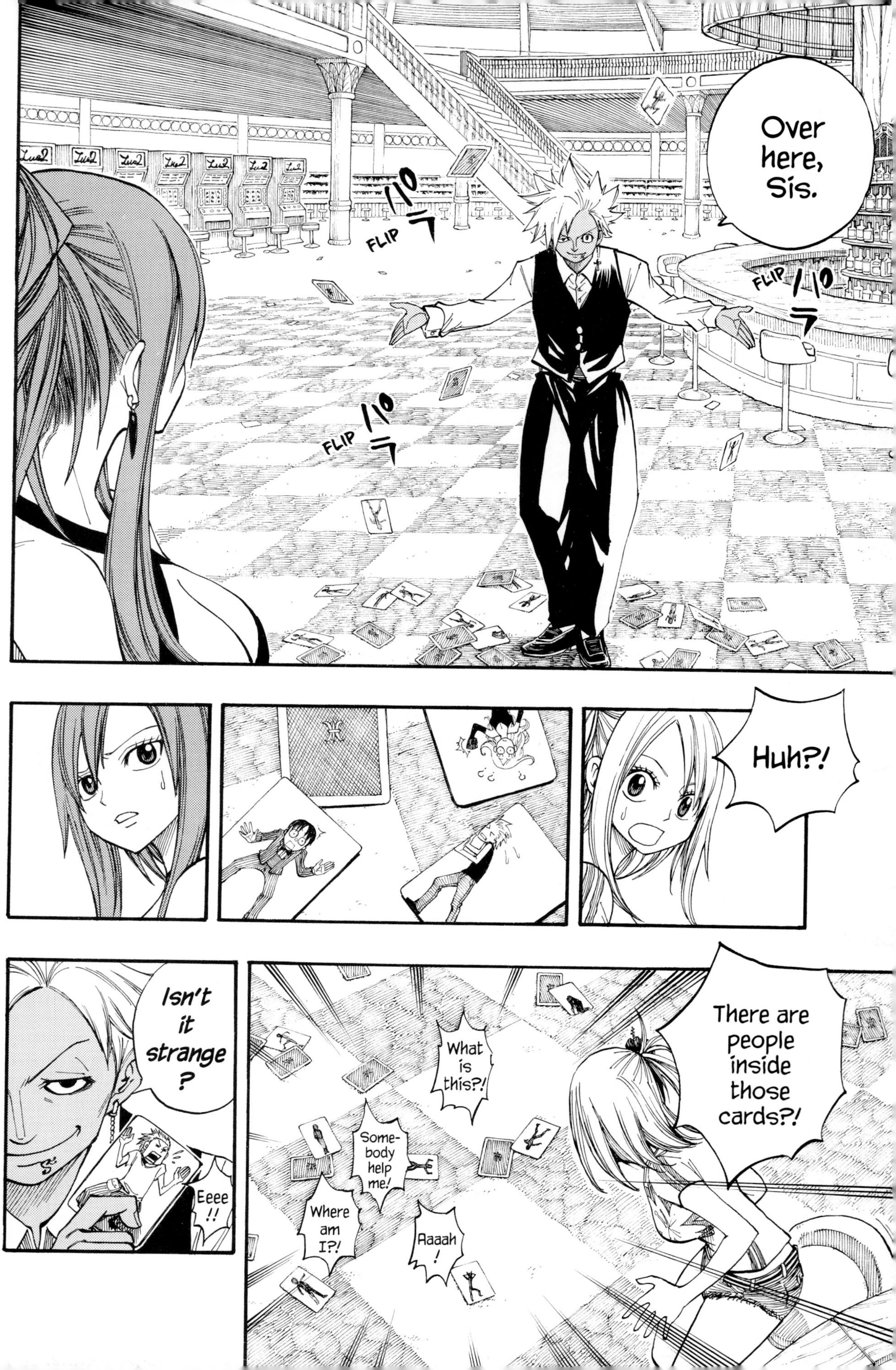
Over here, Sis.
FLIP
FLIP
FLIP
Huh?!
There are people inside those cards?!
What is this?!
Somebody help me!
Where am I?!
Aaaah!
Isn't it strange?
Eeee!!

Magic?!

I'm able to use magic now, too.

HEH HEH HEH...

You...? How...?

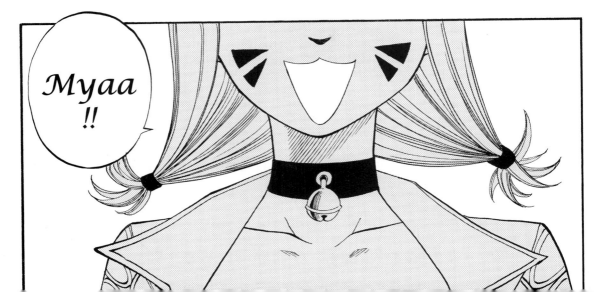

Myaa!!

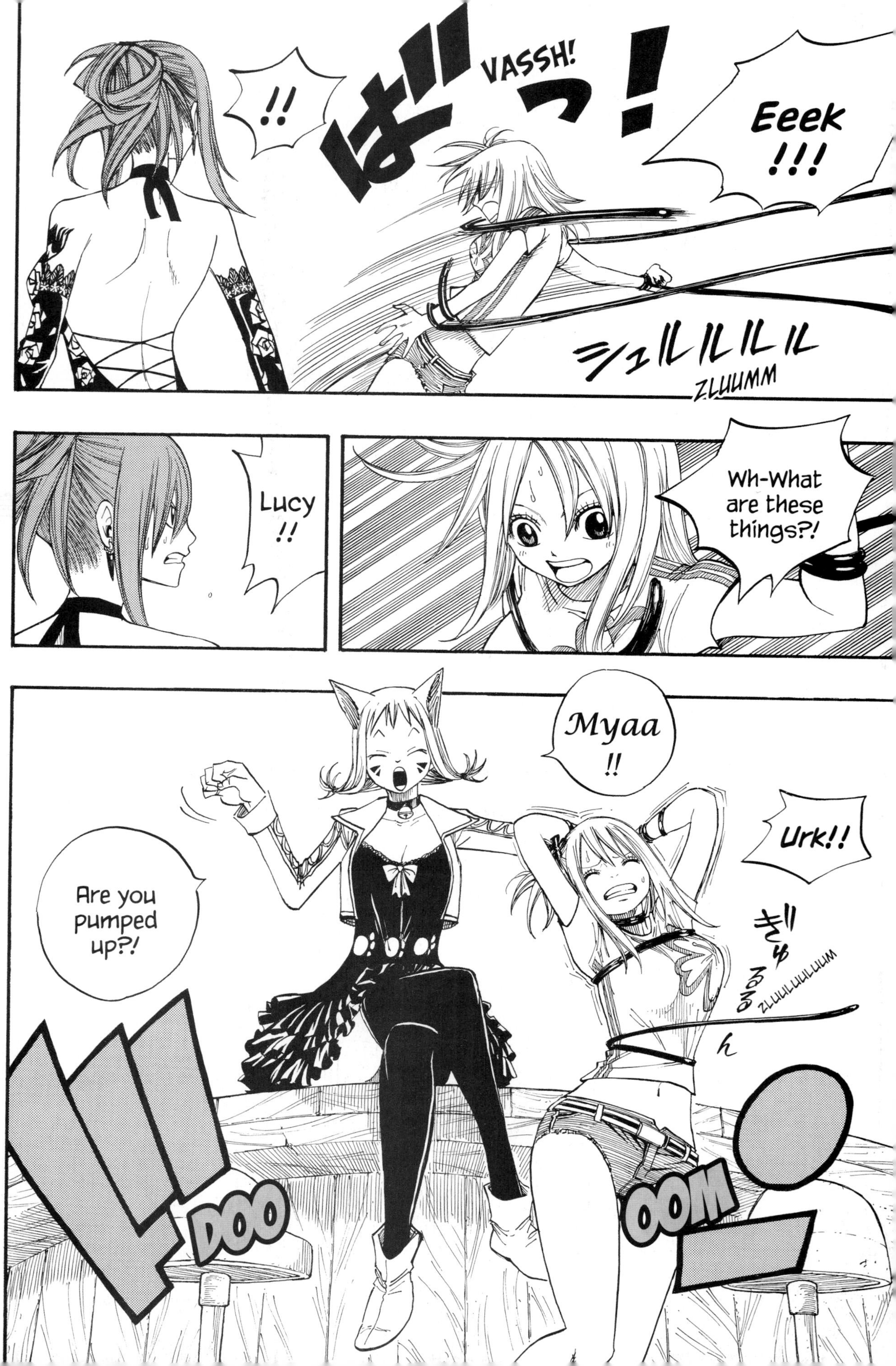

Eeek !!!
はっ!
VASSH!
!!
シュルルルル
ZLUUMM
Wh-What are these things?!
Lucy !!
Myaa !!
Urk!!
ぎゅるるん
ZLUULULUUM
Are you pumped up?!
DOO
OOM

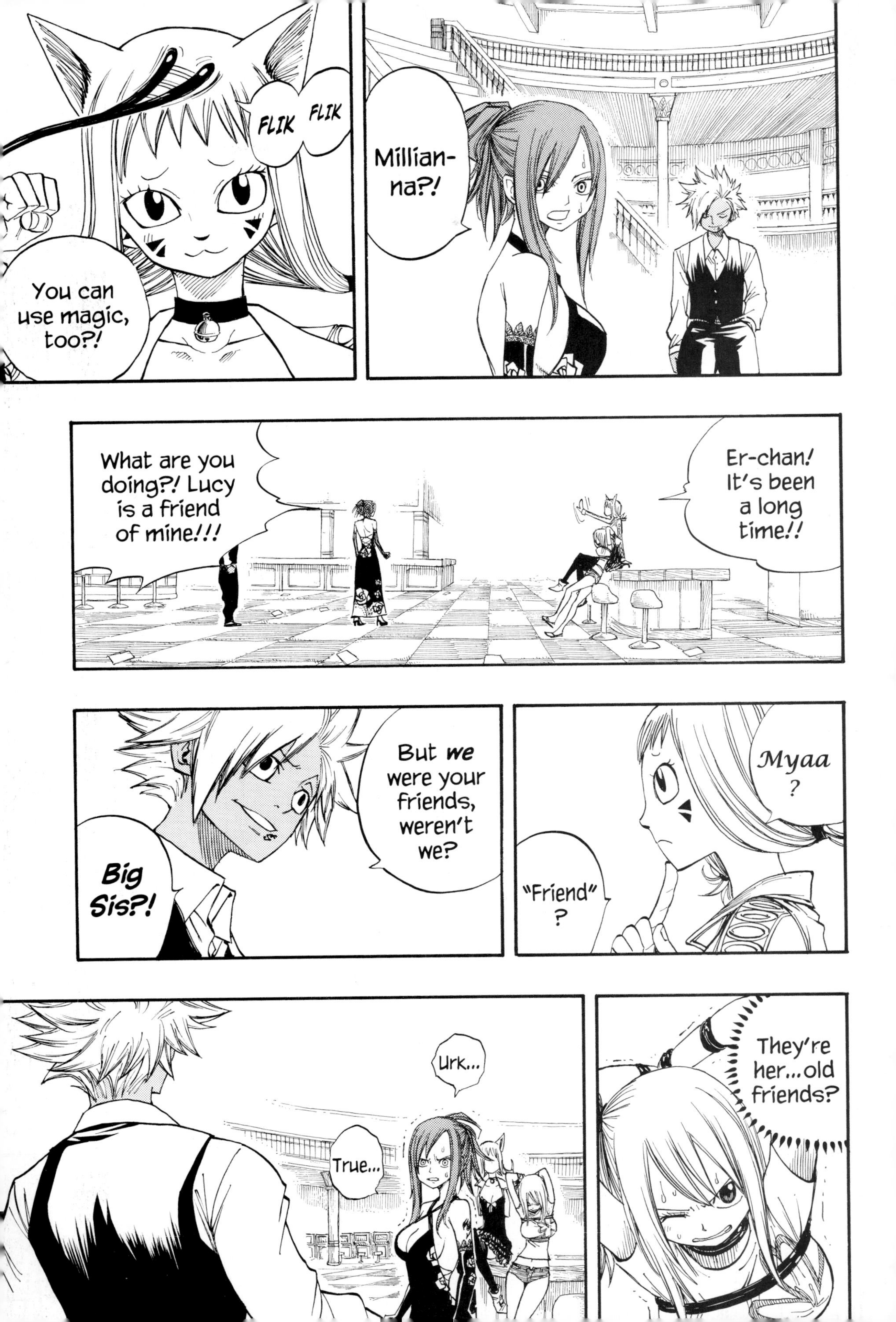
Millian-
na?!
FLIK FLIK
You can use magic, too?!
Er-chan! It's been a long time!!
What are you doing?! Lucy is a friend of mine!!!
Myaa?
"Friend"?
But we were your friends, weren't we?
Big Sis?!
They're her...old friends?
Urk...
True...

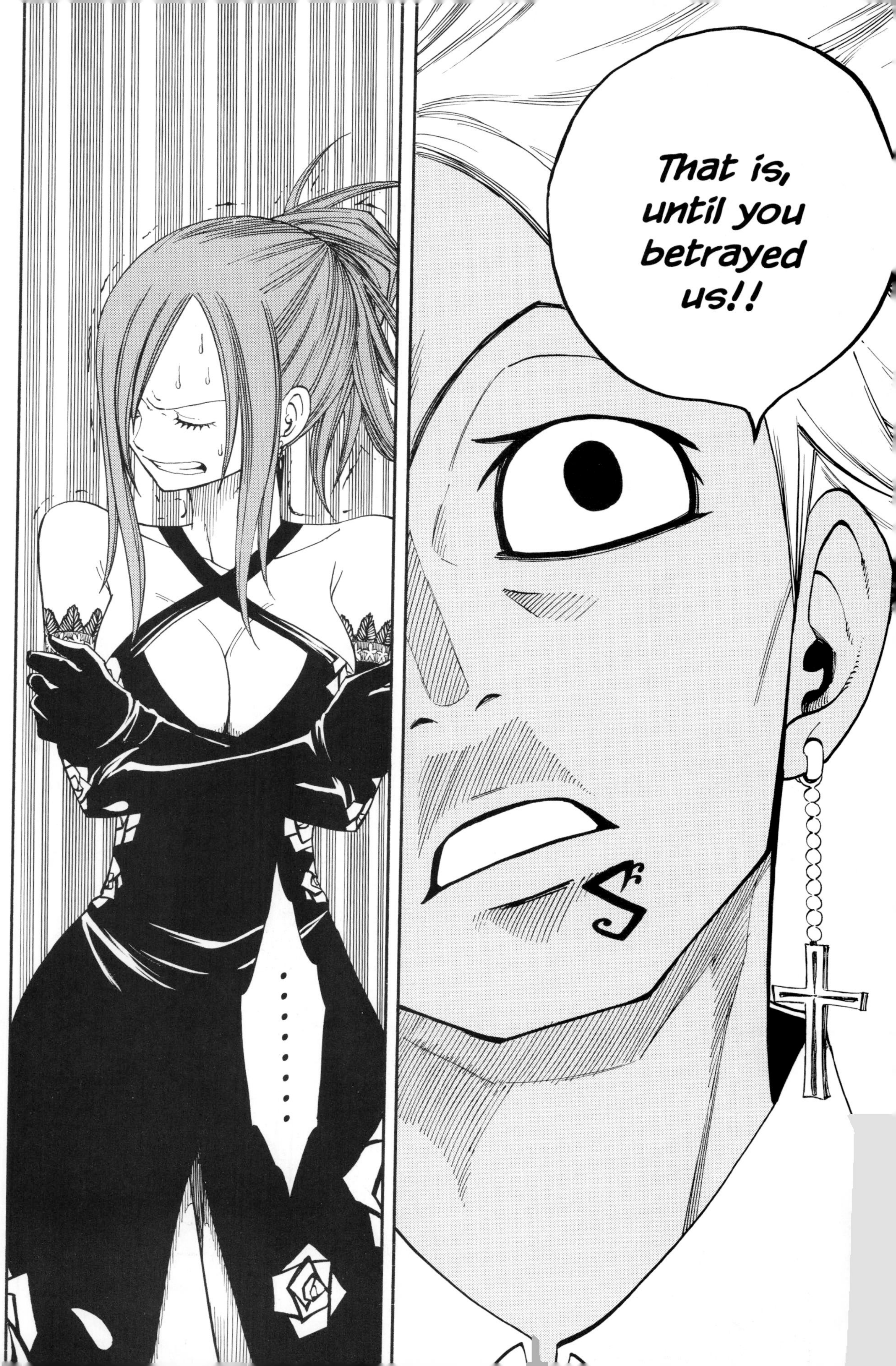
That is, until you betrayed us!!

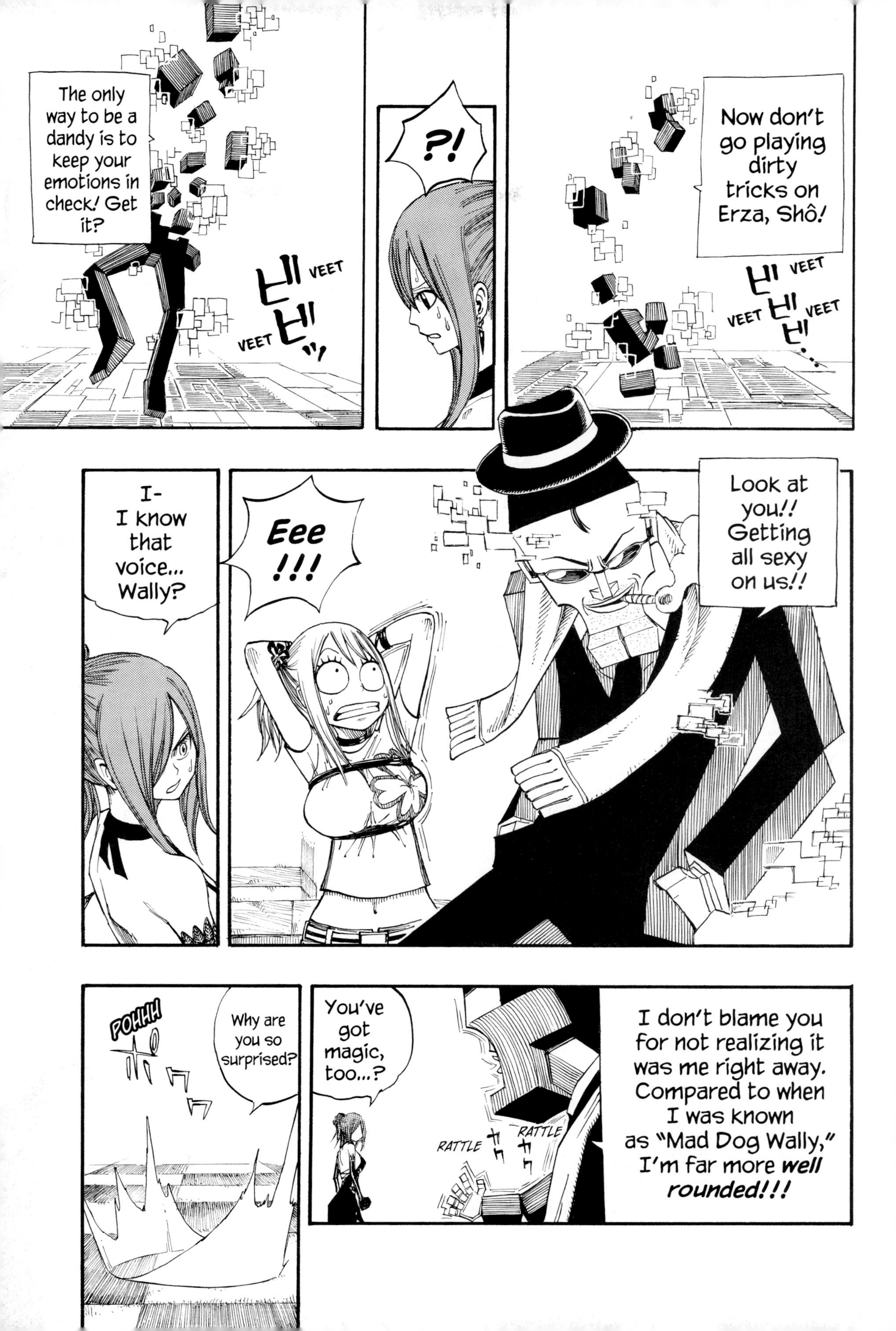
Now don't go playing dirty tricks on Erza, Shô!
VEET VEET VEET
?!
The only way to be a dandy is to keep your emotions in check! Get it?
VEET VEET
Look at you!! Getting all sexy on us!!
Eee!!!
I- I know that voice... Wally?
I don't blame you for not realizing it was me right away. Compared to when I was known as "Mad Dog Wally," I'm far more well rounded!!!
RATTLE RATTLE
You've got magic, too...?
Why are you so surprised?
POHHH

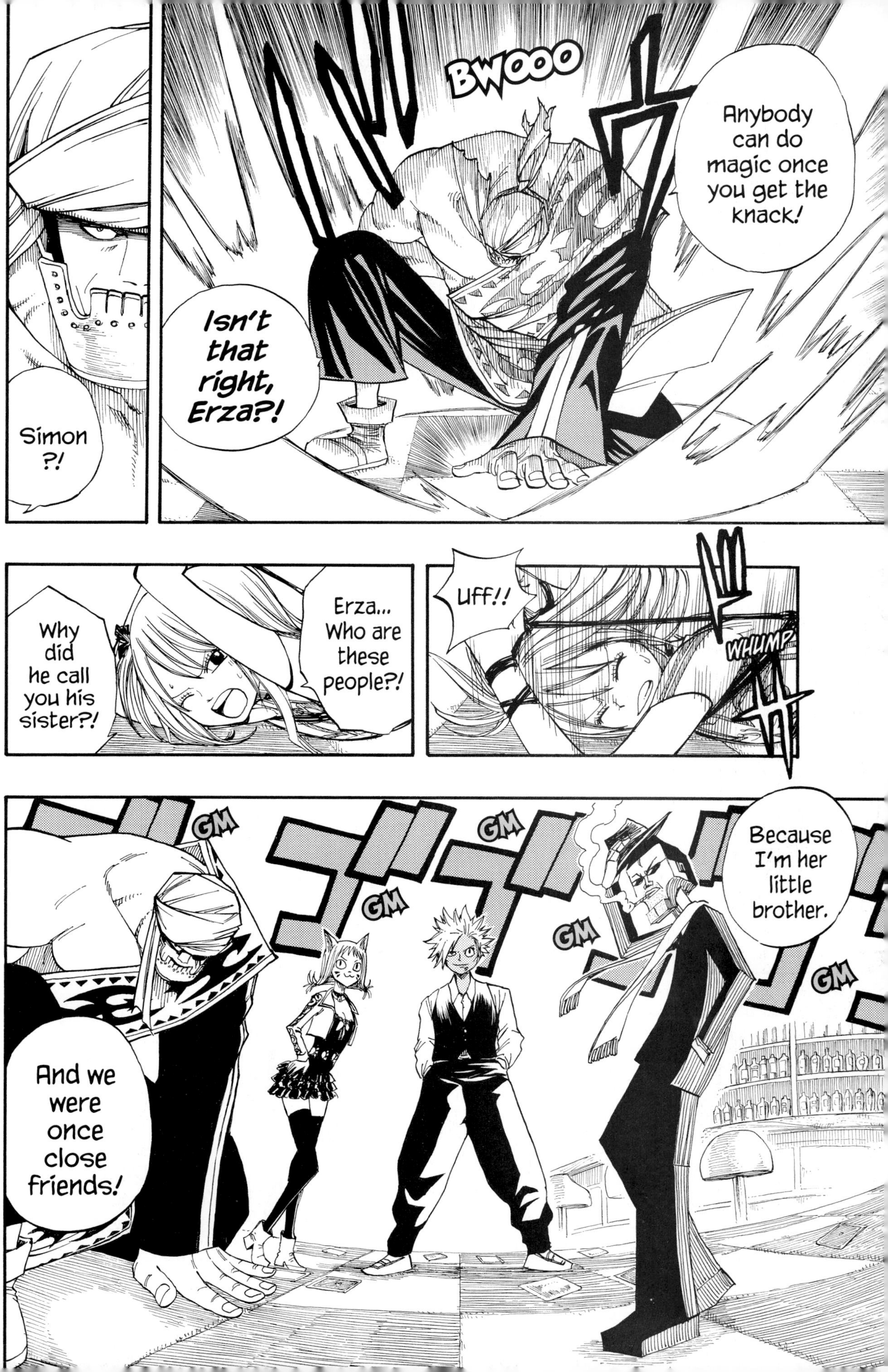
BWOOO
Anybody can do magic once you get the knack!
Isn't that right, Erza?!
Simon ?!
Uff!!
WHUMP
Erza... Who are these people?!
Why did he call you his sister?!
GM
Because I'm her little brother.
And we were once close friends!

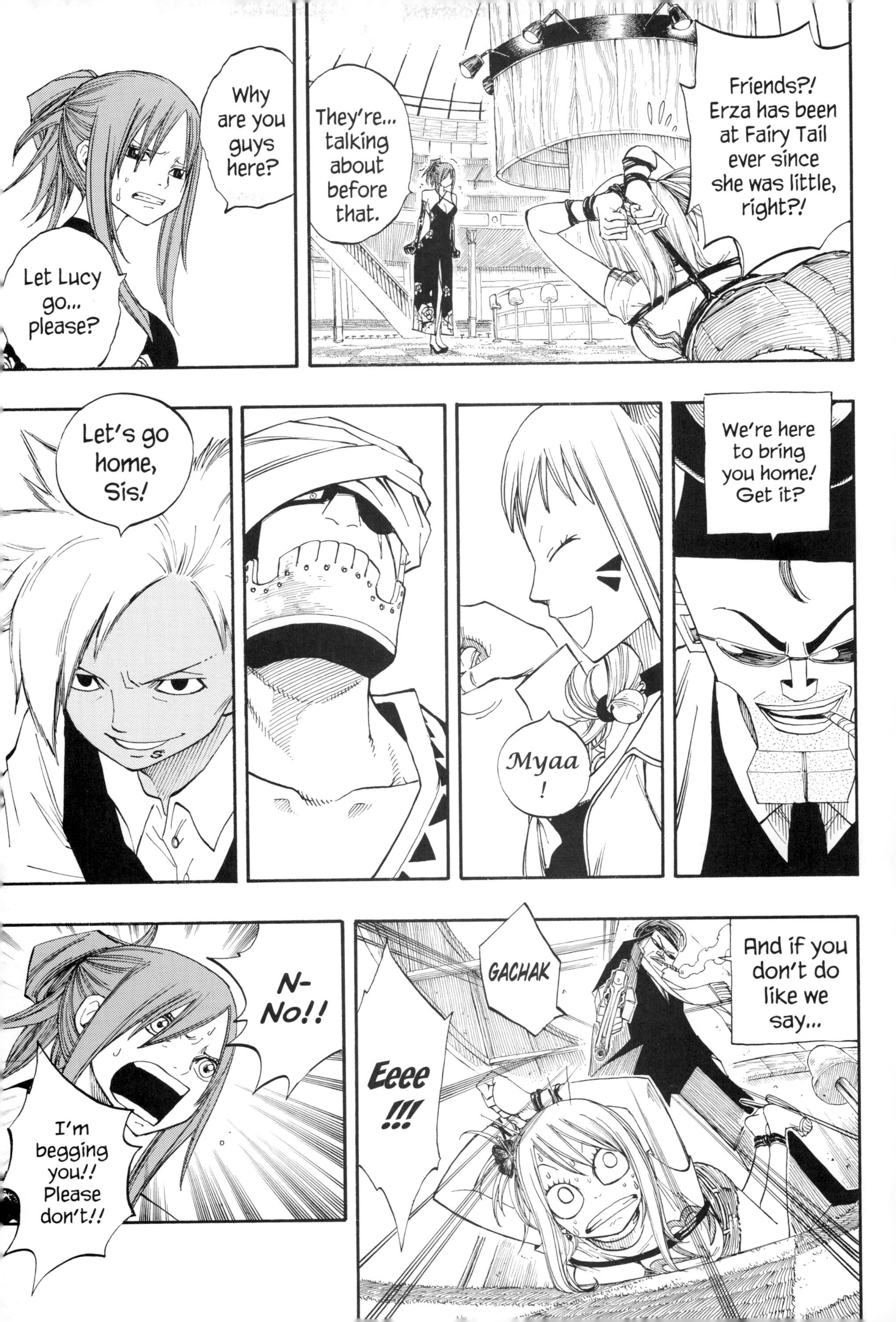
Friends?! Erza has been at Fairy Tail ever since she was little, right?!
They're... talking about before that.
Why are you guys here?
Let Lucy go... please?
We're here to bring you home! Get it?
Myaa!
Let's go home, Sis!
And if you don't do like we say...
GACHAK
Eeee!!!
N- No!!
I'm begging you!! Please don't!!

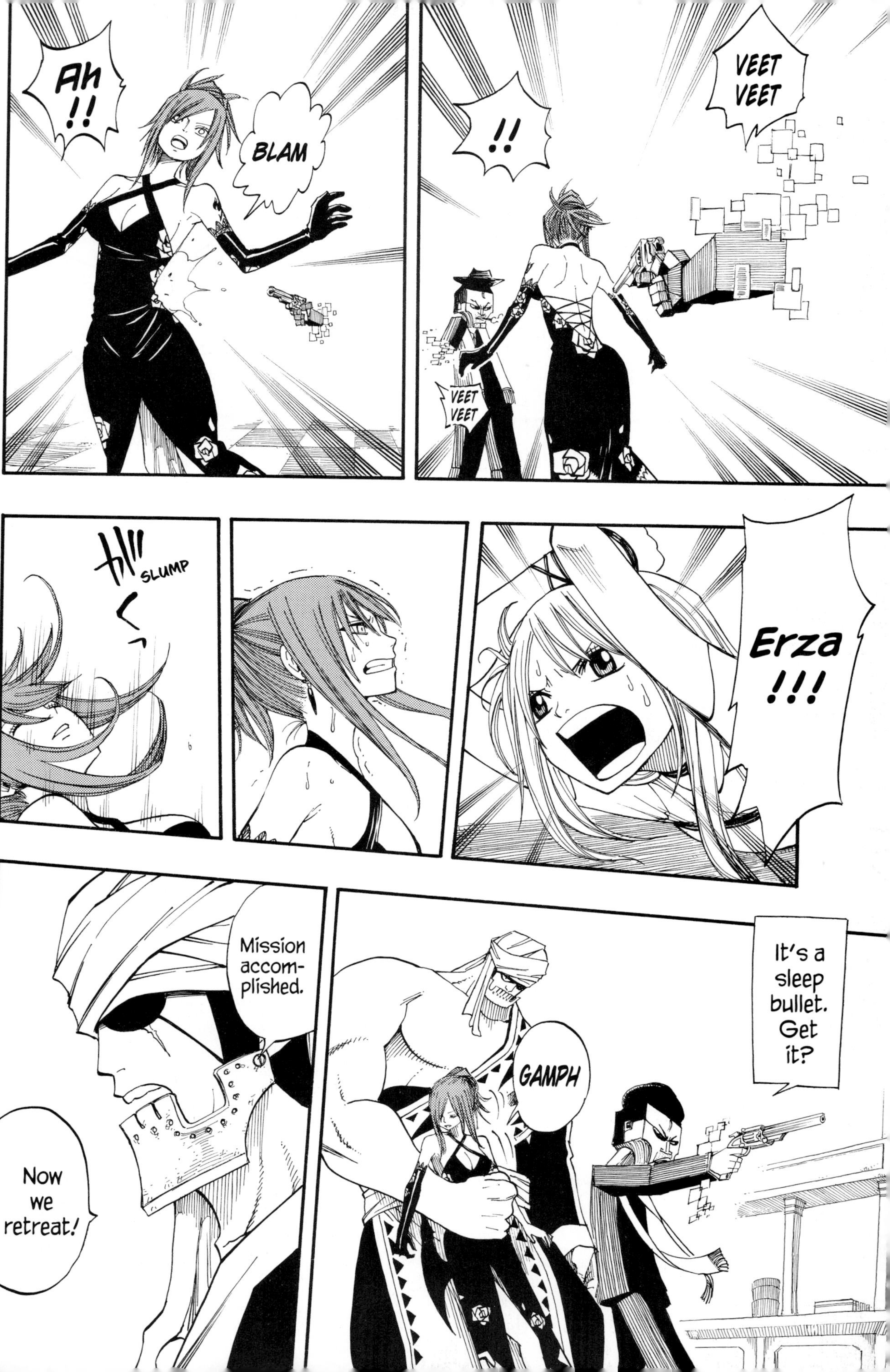
VEET VEET
!!
VEET VEET
Ah !!
BLAM
Erza !!!
SLUMP
It's a sleep bullet. Get it?
GAMPH
Mission accomplished.
Now we retreat!

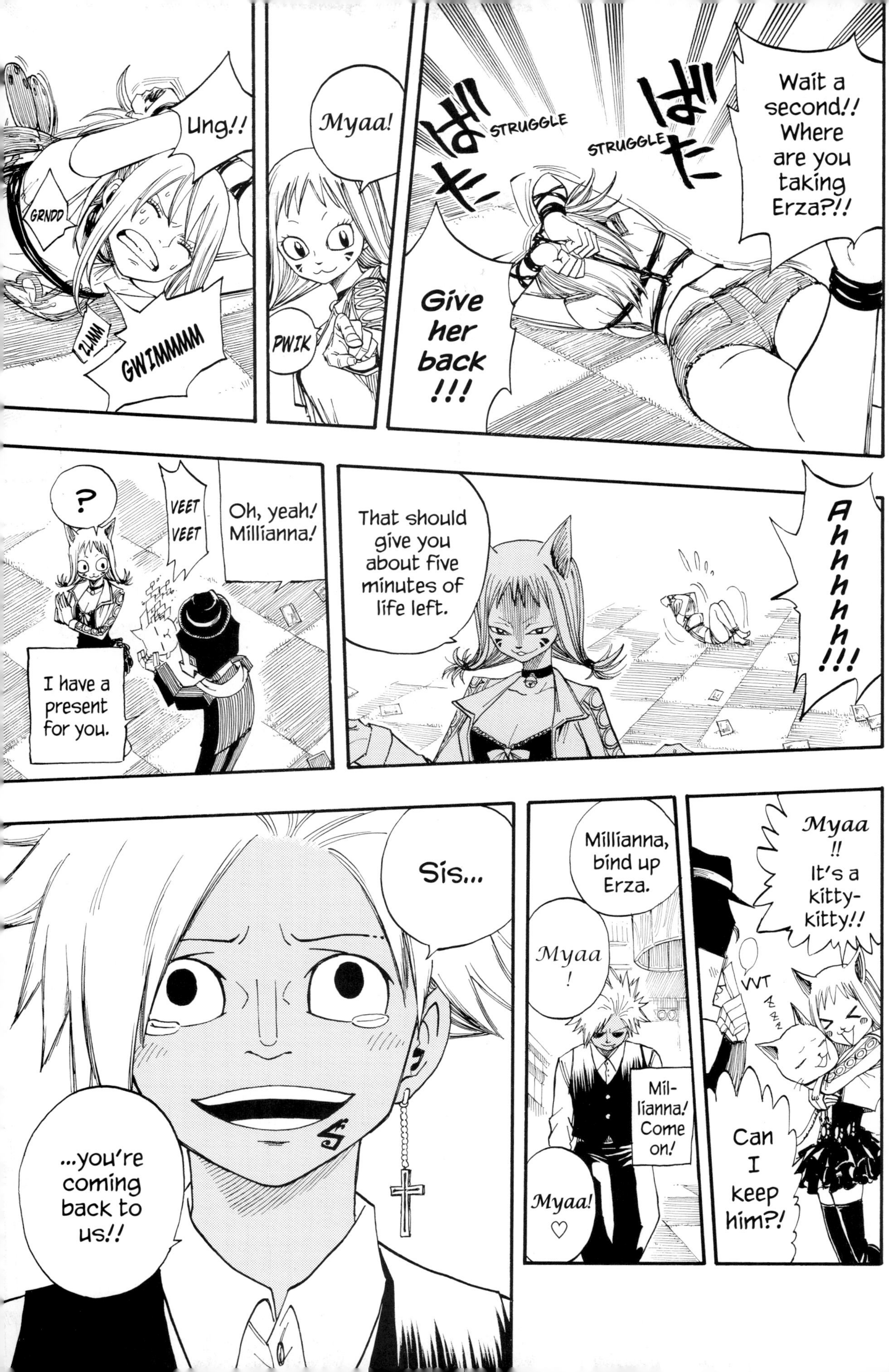

Wait a second!! Where are you taking Erza?!!
ばた
STRUGGLE
ばた
STRUGGLE
Give her back!!!
Myaa!
PWIK
Ung!!
GRNDD
GWIMMMM
Ahhhhhh!!!
That should give you about five minutes of life left.
Oh, yeah! Millianna!
VEET VEET
?
I have a present for you.
Myaa!! It's a kitty-kitty!!
VVT
Can I keep him?!
Millianna, bind up Erza.
Myaa!
Millianna! Come on!
Myaa! ♡
Sis...
...you're coming back to us!!

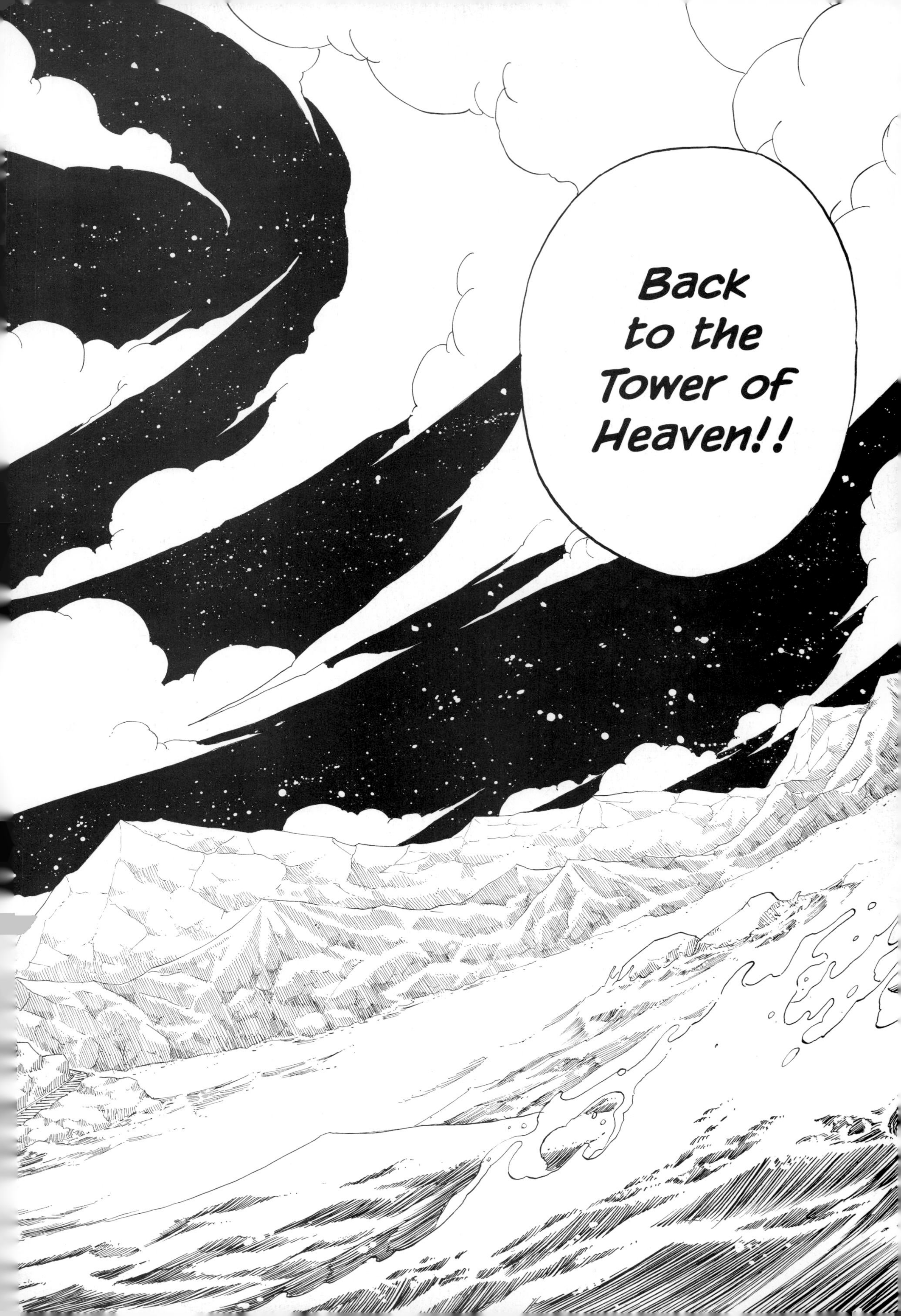
Back to the Tower of Heaven!!

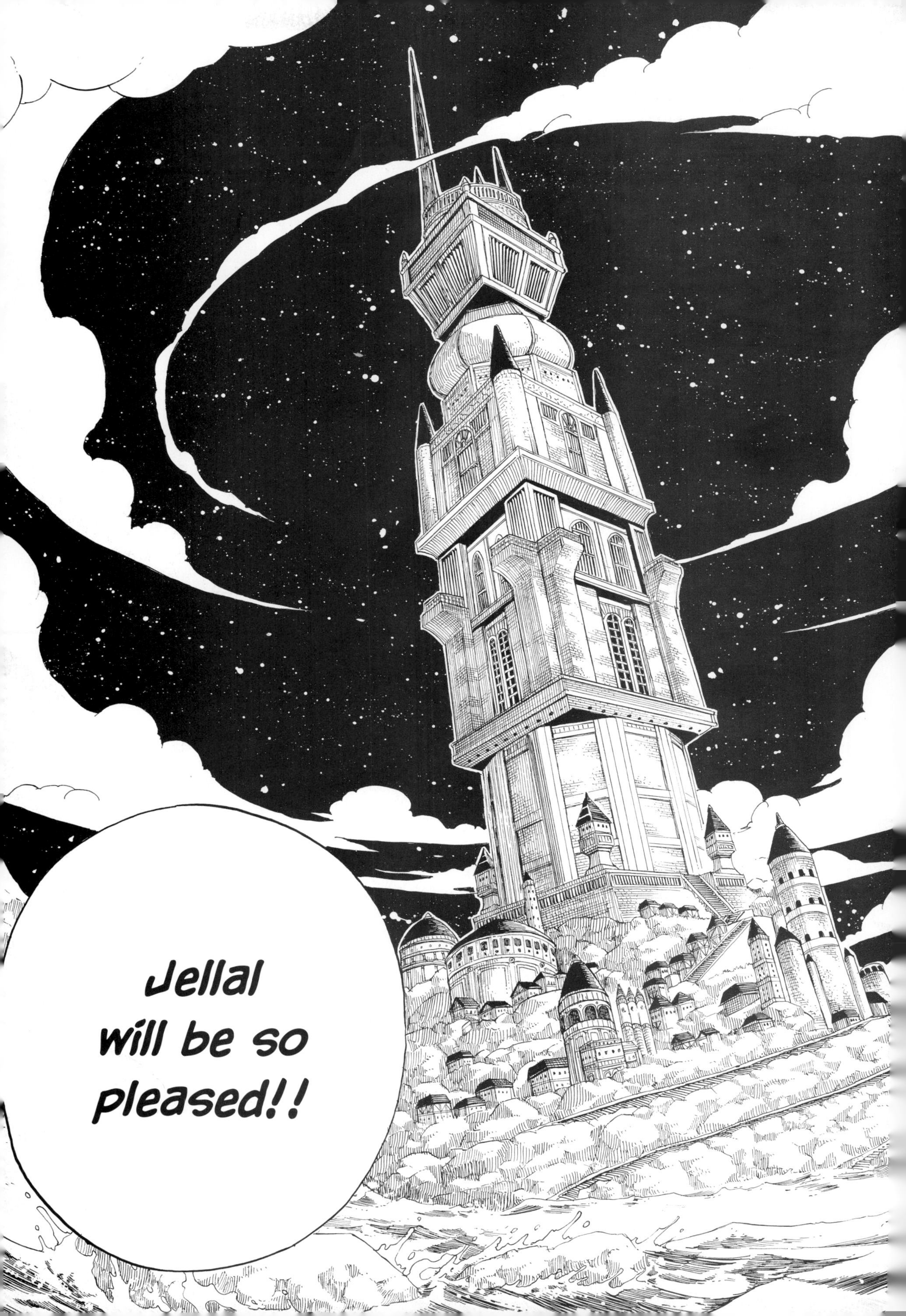
Jellal will be so pleased!!

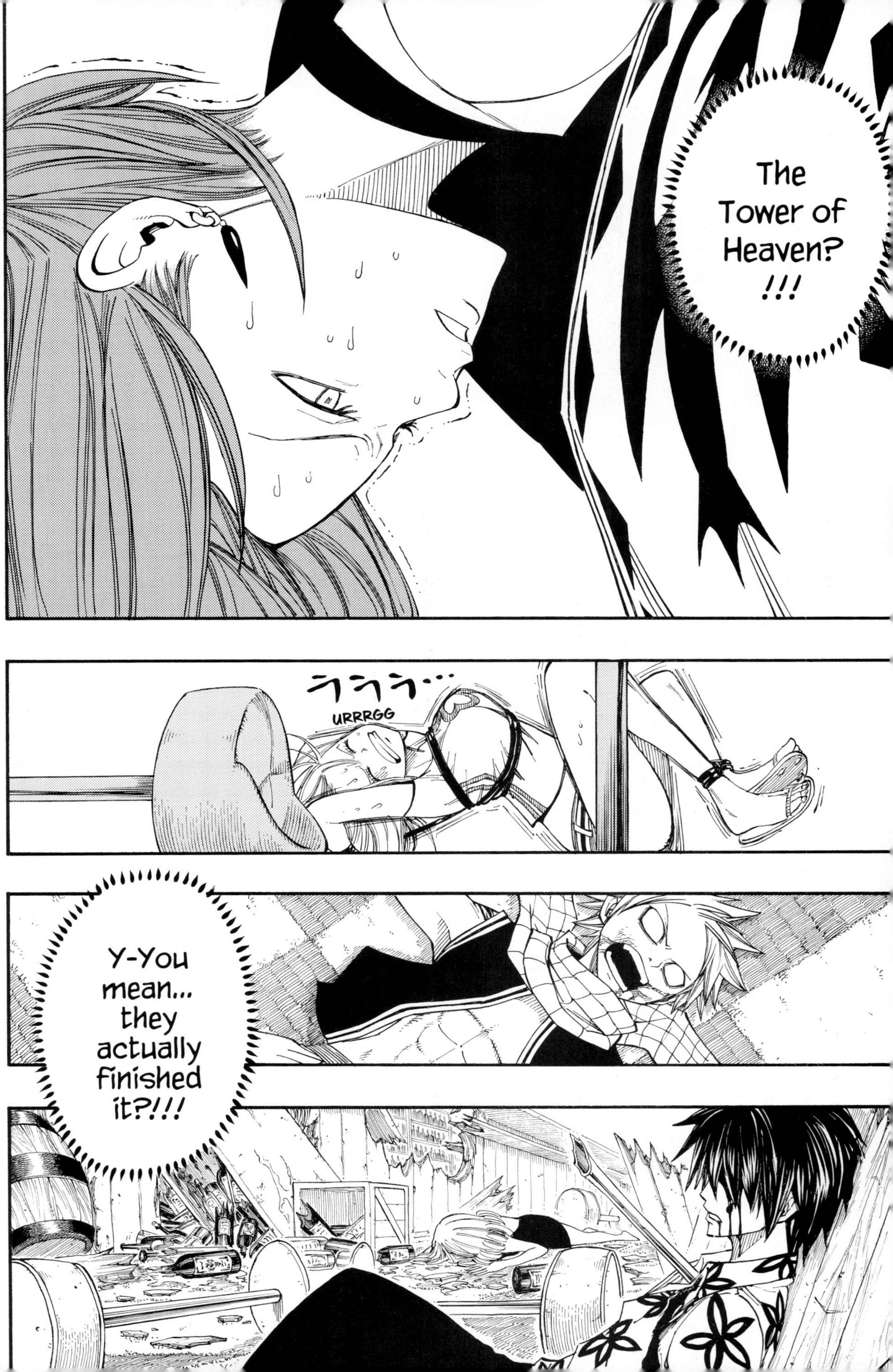
The Tower of Heaven? !!!
ラララ…
URRRGG
Y-You mean... they actually finished it?!!!

FAIRY TAIL

Chapter 77: Jellal

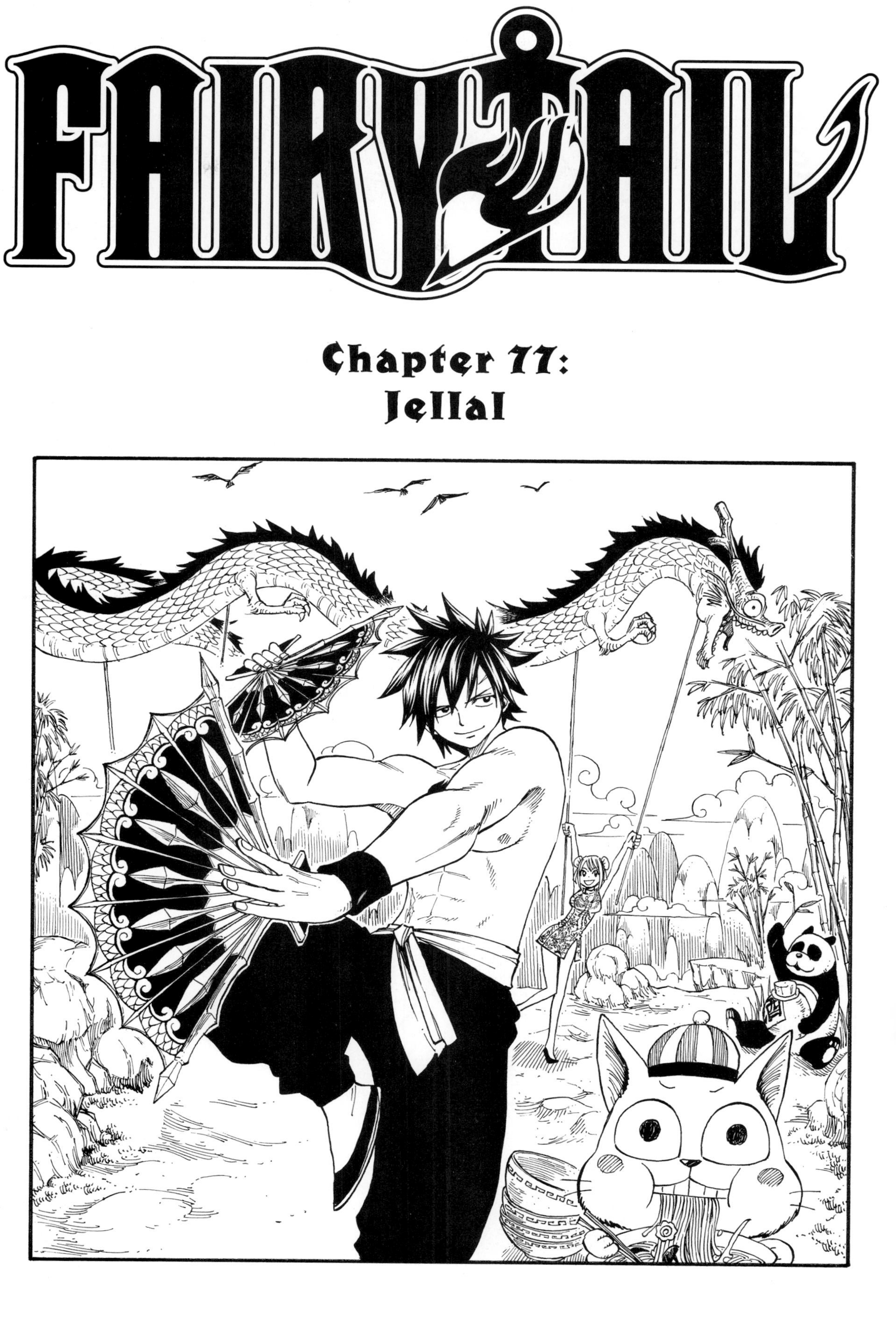

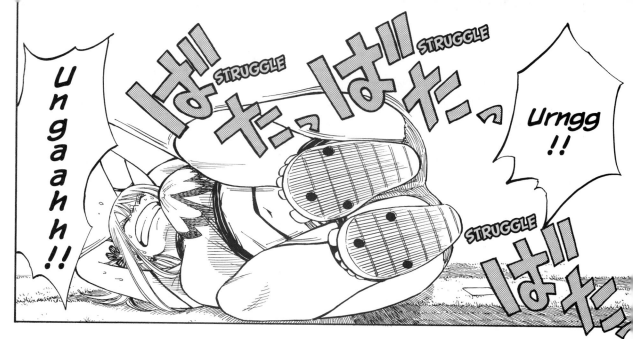

Urngg!!
ばたっ STRUGGLE
ばたっ STRUGGLE
ばたっ STRUGGLE
Ungaahhh!!
ごろん ROLL
ごろん ROLL
ばた WHUMP
ばた WHUMP
CHANK
O-Open... Door to the great...
Crab Palace...!
H-Huh?
Cancer!!!
Taurus!!! Loke!!! Come out!!!

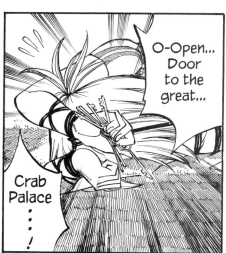

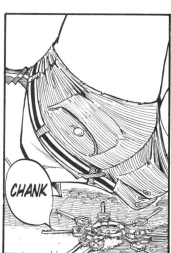

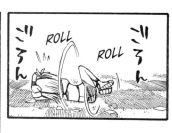

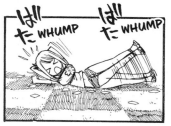

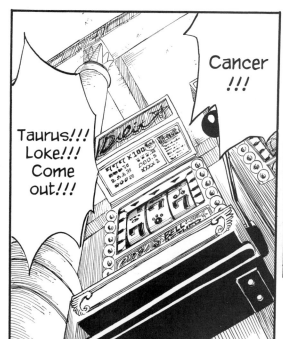

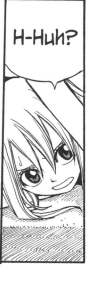

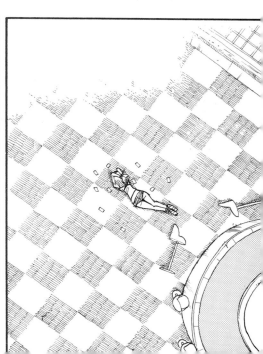

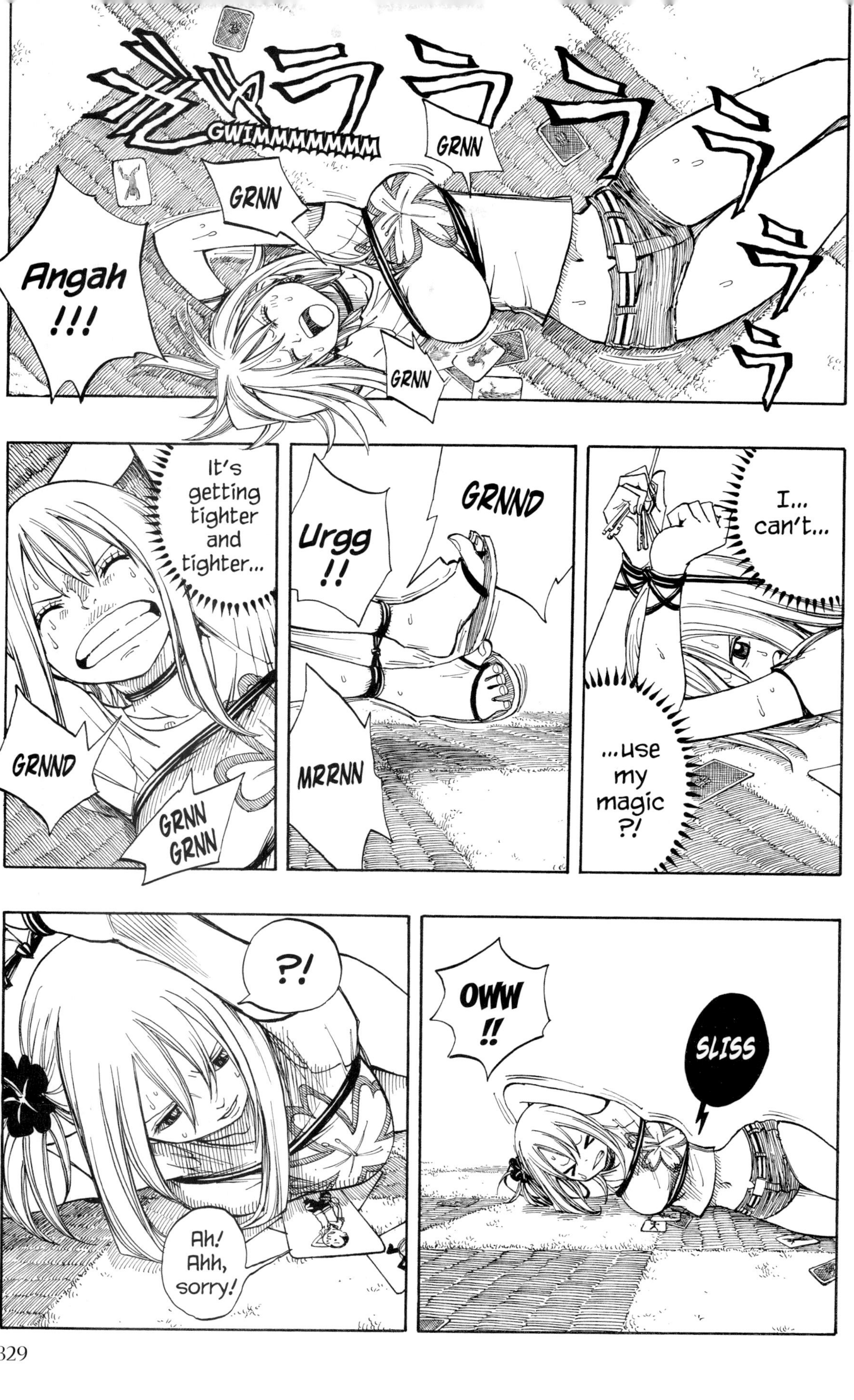

GWIMMMMMMMM
GRNN
GRNN
Angah!!!
GRNN
I... can't...
...use my magic?!
GRNND
Urgg!!
MRRNN
It's getting tighter and tighter...
GRNND
GRNN GRNN
OWW!!
SLISS
?!
Ah! Ahh, sorry!

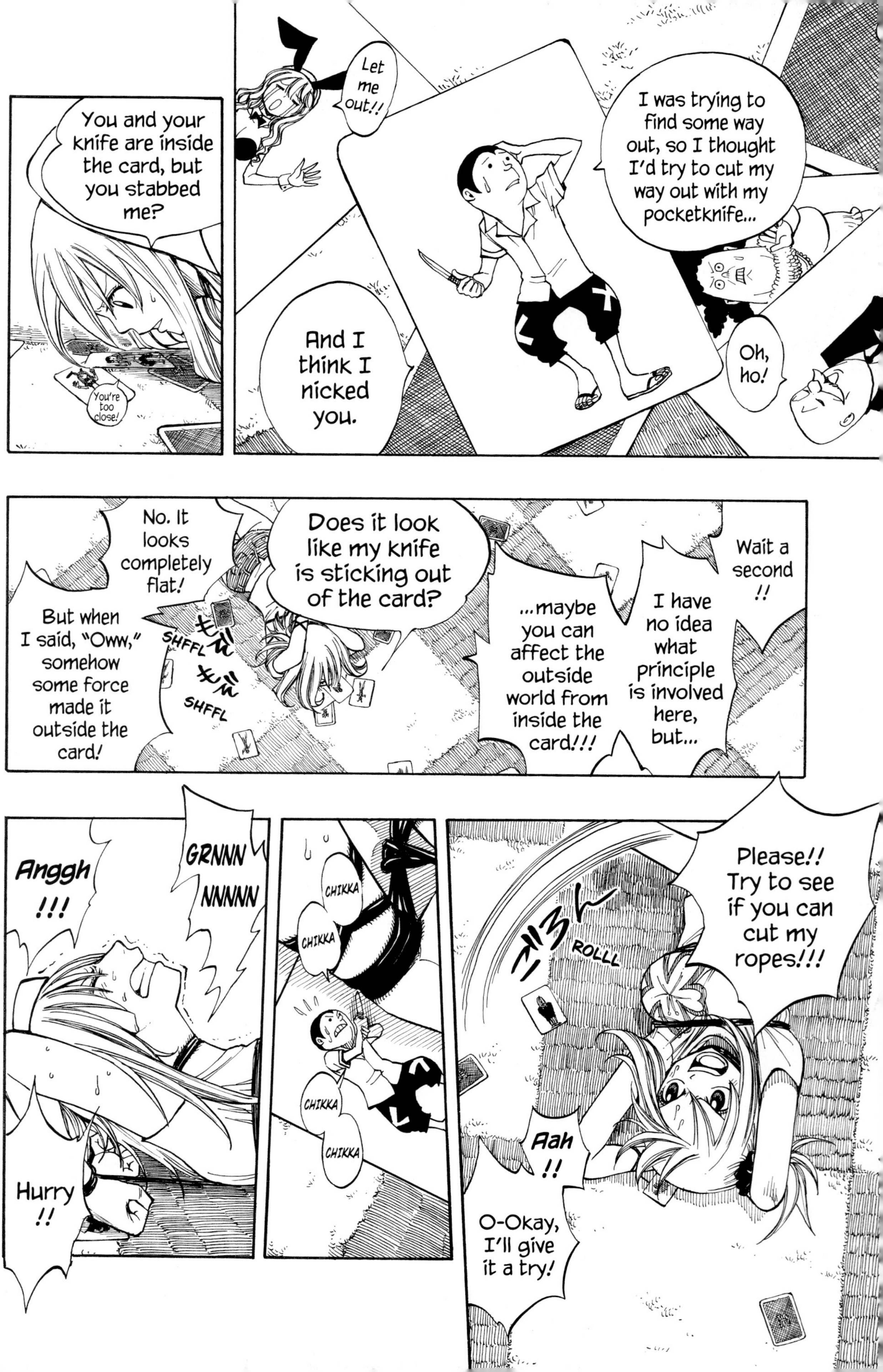
Let me out!!
I was trying to find some way out, so I thought I'd try to cut my way out with my pocketknife...
And I think I nicked you.
Oh, ho!
You and your knife are inside the card, but you stabbed me?
You're too close!
Wait a second!!
I have no idea what principle is involved here, but...
...maybe you can affect the outside world from inside the card!!!
Does it look like my knife is sticking out of the card?
No. It looks completely flat!
SHFFL
SHFFL
But when I said, "Oww," somehow some force made it outside the card!
Please!! Try to see if you can cut my ropes!!!
ROLLL
Aah!!
O-Okay, I'll give it a try!
CHIKKA
CHIKKA
CHIKKA
CHIKKA
GRNNN NNNNN
Anggh!!!
Hurry!!

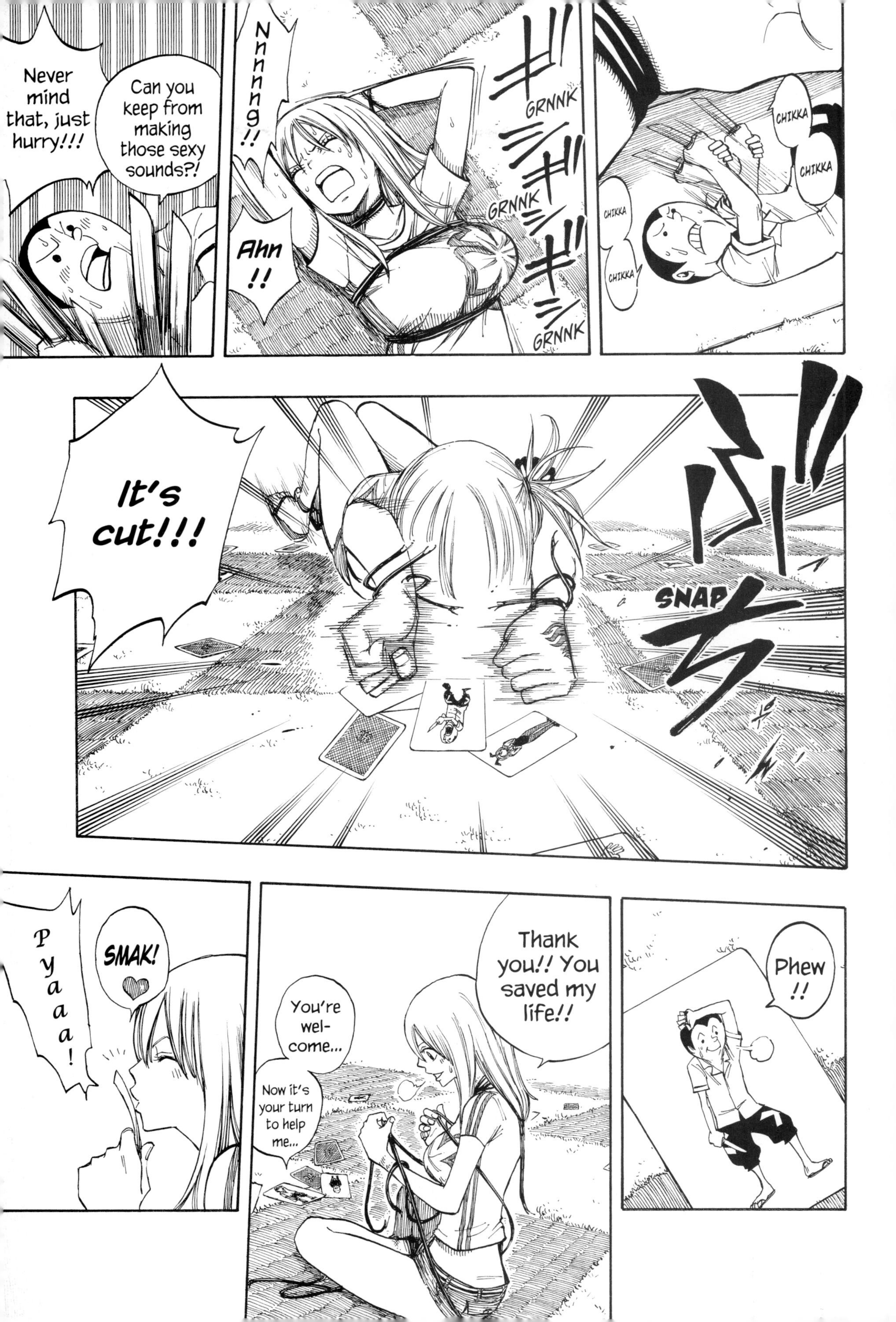
CHIKKA
CHIKKA
CHIKKA
CHIKKA
Nnnnng!!
GRNNK
GRNNK
GRNNK
Ahn!!
Can you keep from making those sexy sounds?!
Never mind that, just hurry!!!
SNAP
It's cut!!!
Phew!!
Thank you!! You saved my life!!
You're wel-come...
Now it's your turn to help me...
SMAK!
Pyaaa!

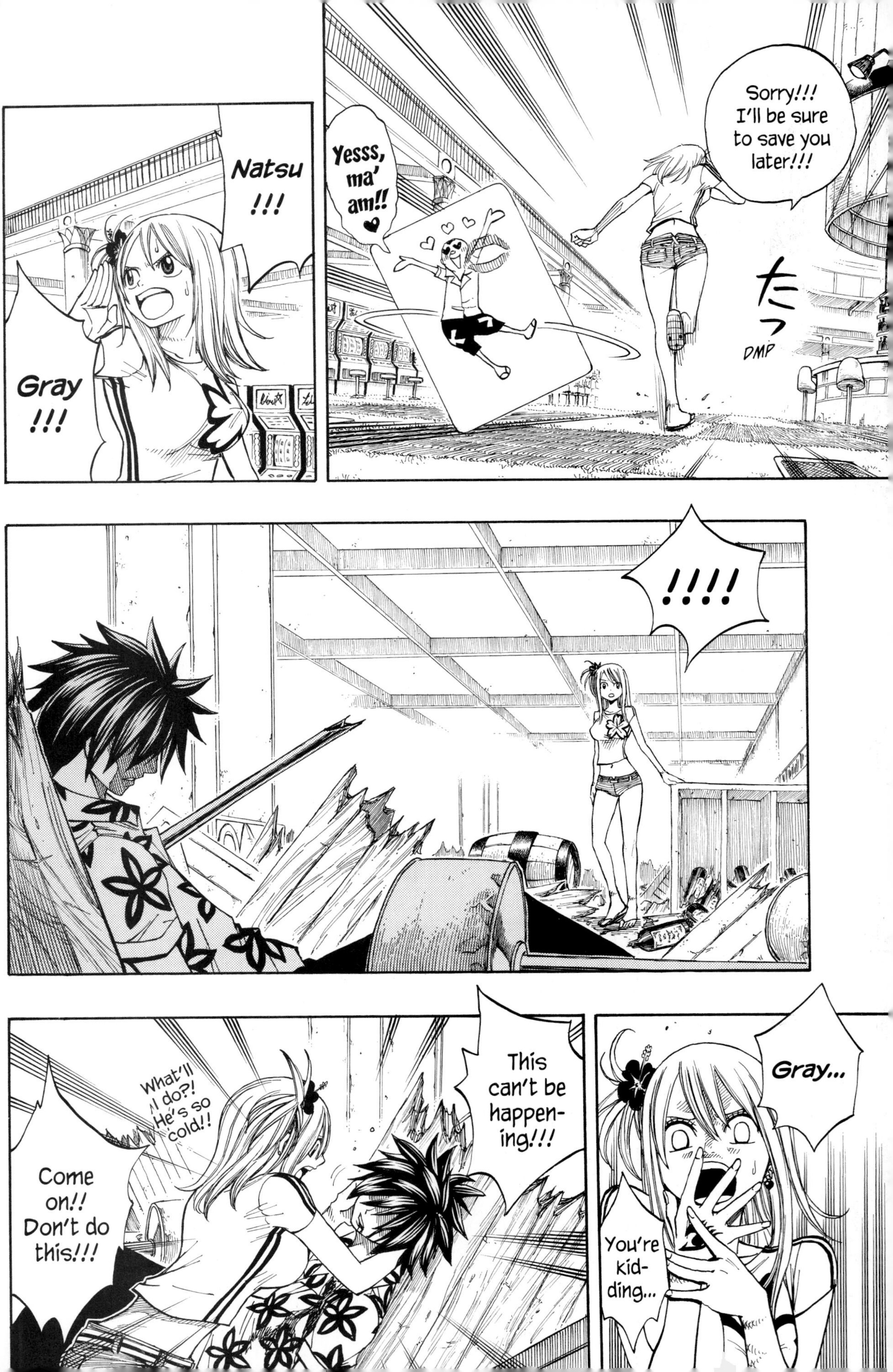
Sorry!!! I'll be sure to save you later!!!
Yesss, ma' am!! ♥
たっ
DMP
Natsu!!!
Gray!!!
!!!!
Gray...
You're kid-ding...
This can't be happen-ing!!!
What'll I do?! He's so cold!!
Come on!! Don't do this!!!

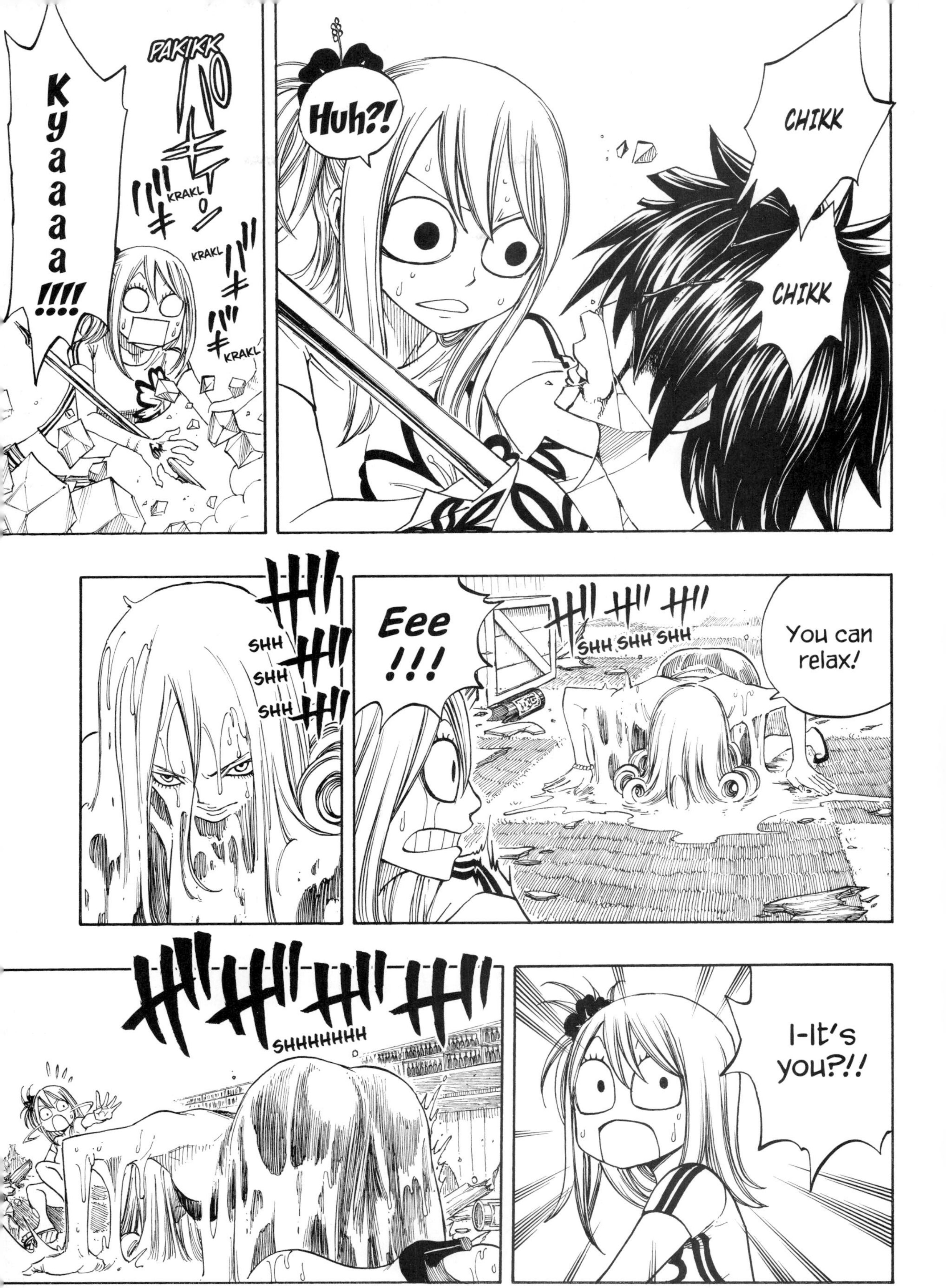
CHIKK
CHIKK
Huh?!
PAKIKK
Kyaaaaa!!!!
KRAKL
KRAKL
KRAKL
You can relax!
SHH SHH SHH
Eee!!!
SHH
SHH
SHH
I-It's you?!!
SHHHHHHH

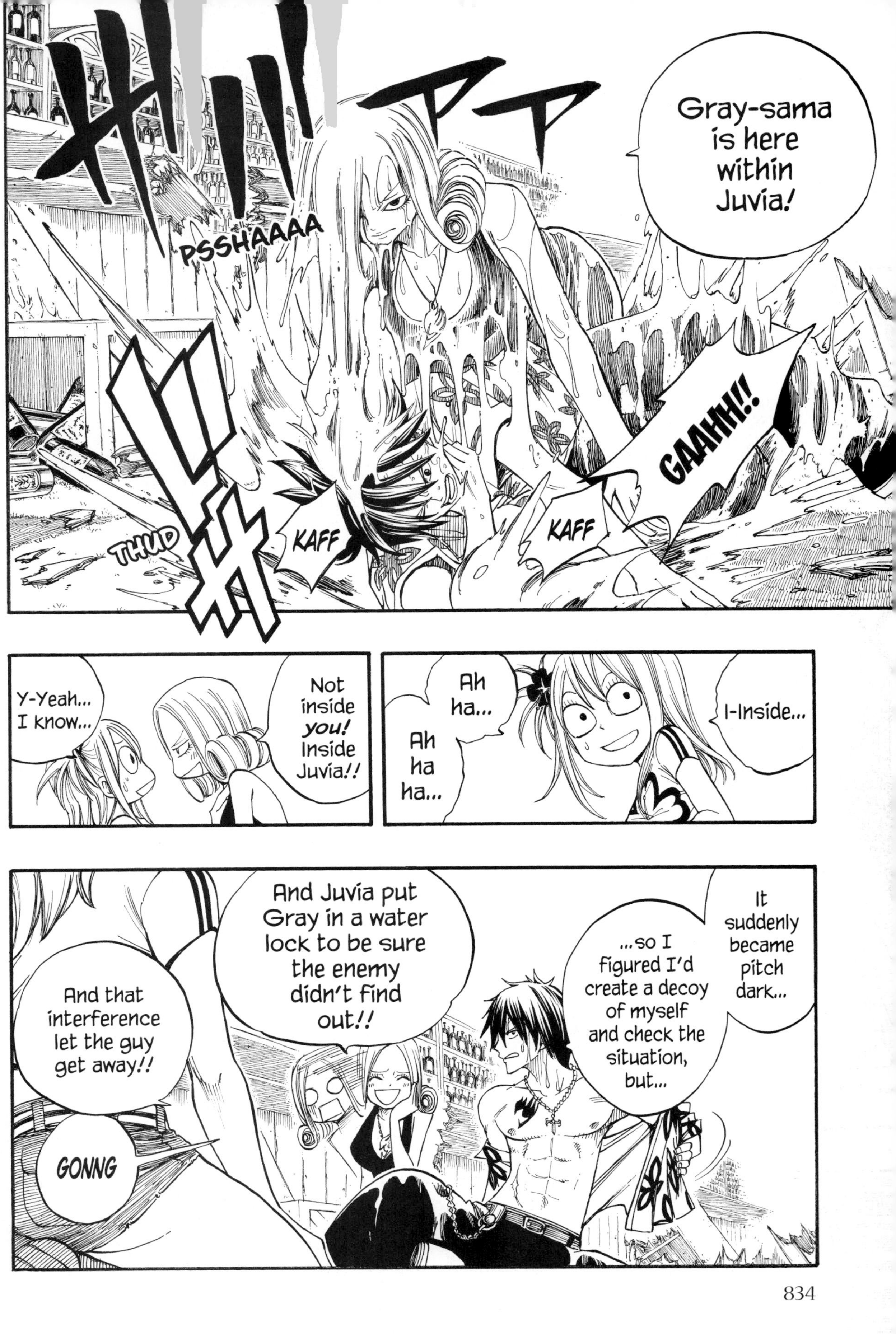
Gray-sama is here within Juvia!
PSSHAAAA
GAAHH!!
KAFF
KAFF
THUD
I-Inside...
Ah ha...
Ah ha ha...
Not inside *you!* Inside Juvia!!
Y-Yeah... I know...
It suddenly became pitch dark...
...so I figured I'd create a decoy of myself and check the situation, but...
And Juvia put Gray in a water lock to be sure the enemy didn't find out!!
And that interference let the guy get away!!
GONNG

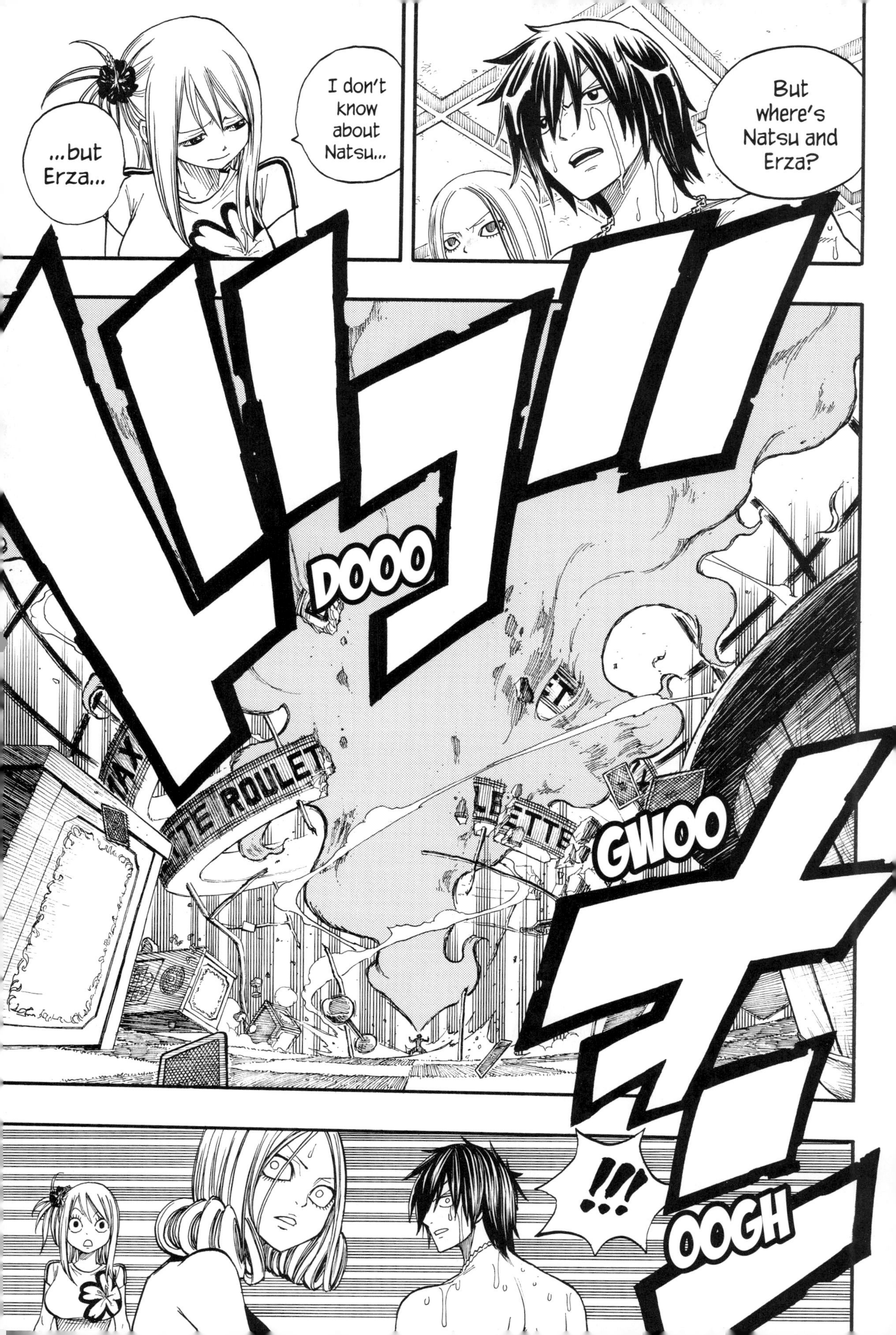
But where's Natsu and Erza?
I don't know about Natsu...
...but Erza...
DOOO
TE ROULET
GWOO
OOGH
!!!

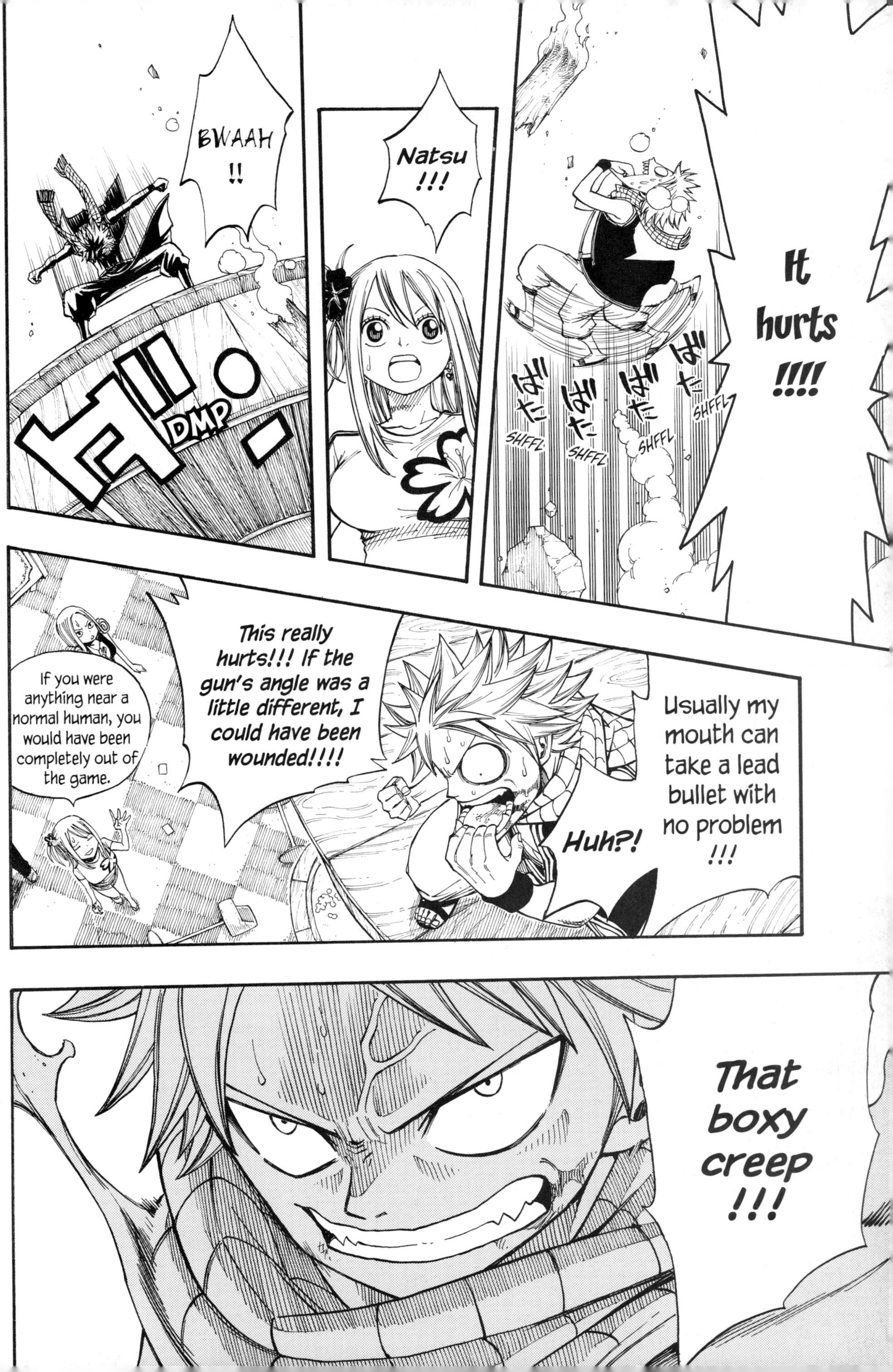
It hurts!!!!
ばた ばた ばた ばた
SHFFL SHFFL SHFFL SHFFL
Natsu!!!
BWAAH!!
DMP
Usually my mouth can take a lead bullet with no problem!!!
Huh?!
This really hurts!!! If the gun's angle was a little different, I could have been wounded!!!!
If you were anything near a normal human, you would have been completely out of the game.
That boxy creep!!!

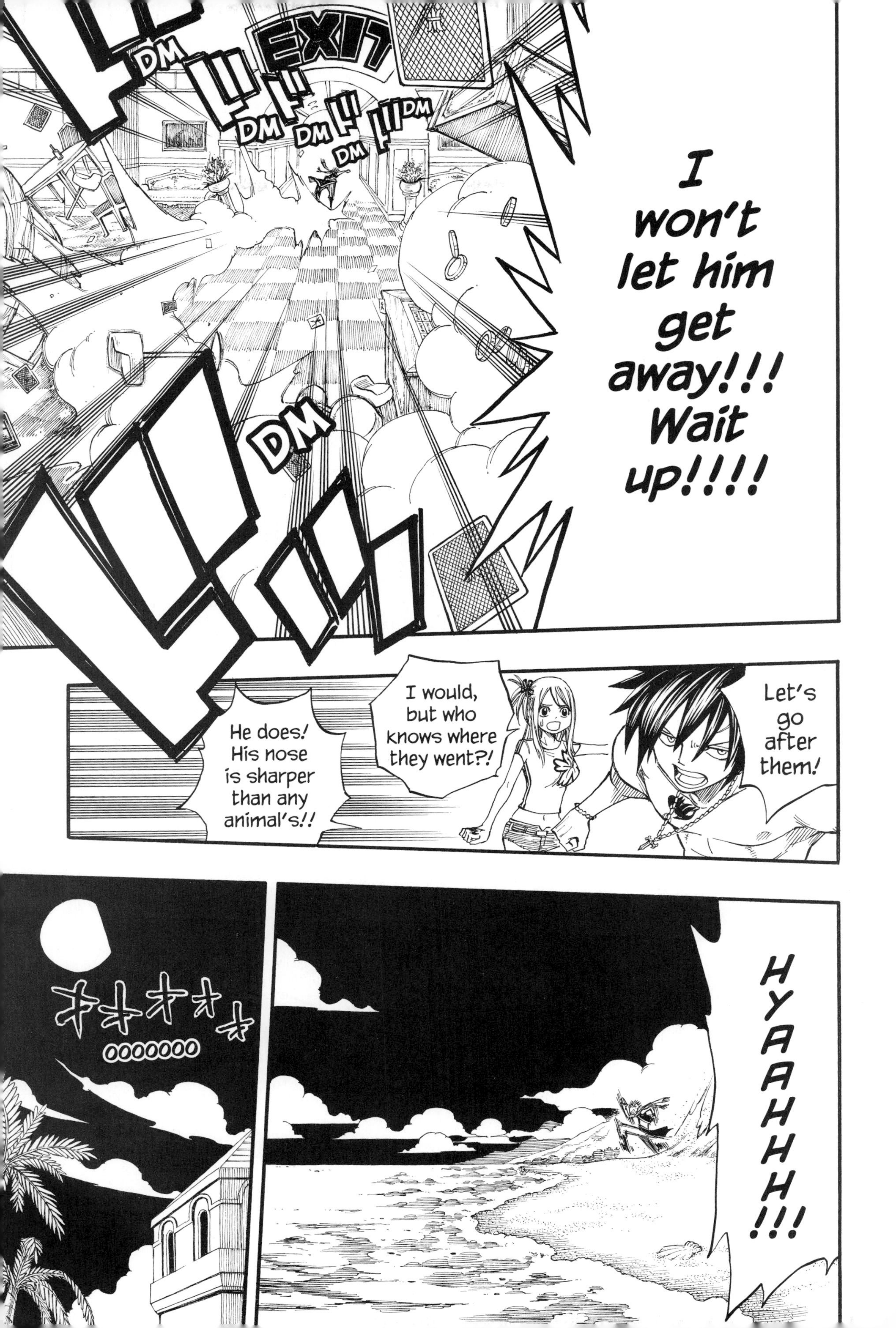
DM
EXIT
DM
DM
DM
DM
DM
I won't let him get away!!! Wait up!!!!
Let's go after them!
I would, but who knows where they went?!
He does! His nose is sharper than any animal's!!
HYAAAHHH!!!
オォォォォ
OOOOOOO

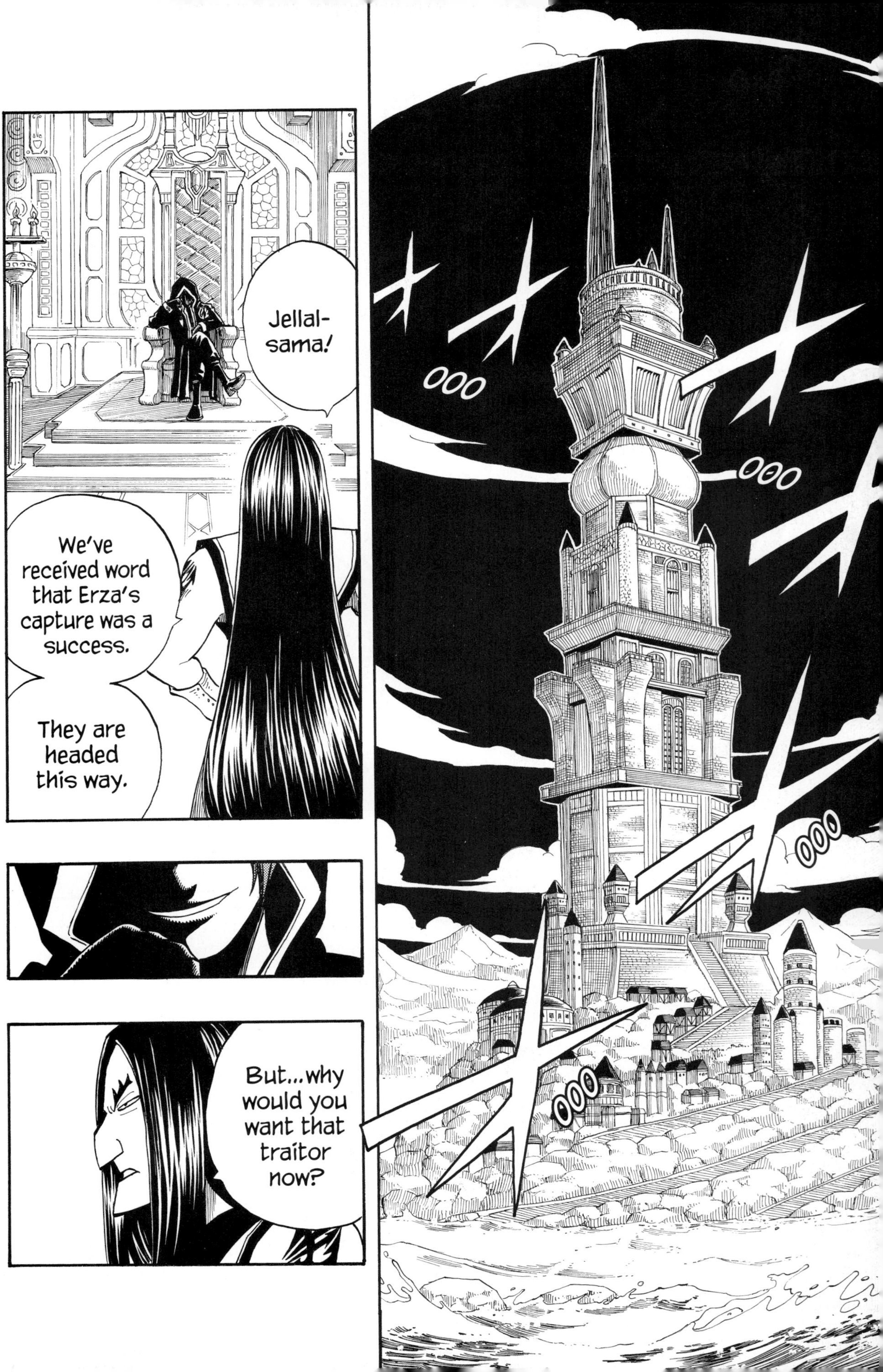

ooo
ooo
ooo
ooo
ooo
Jellal-sama!
We've received word that Erza's capture was a success.
They are headed this way.
But...why would you want that traitor now?

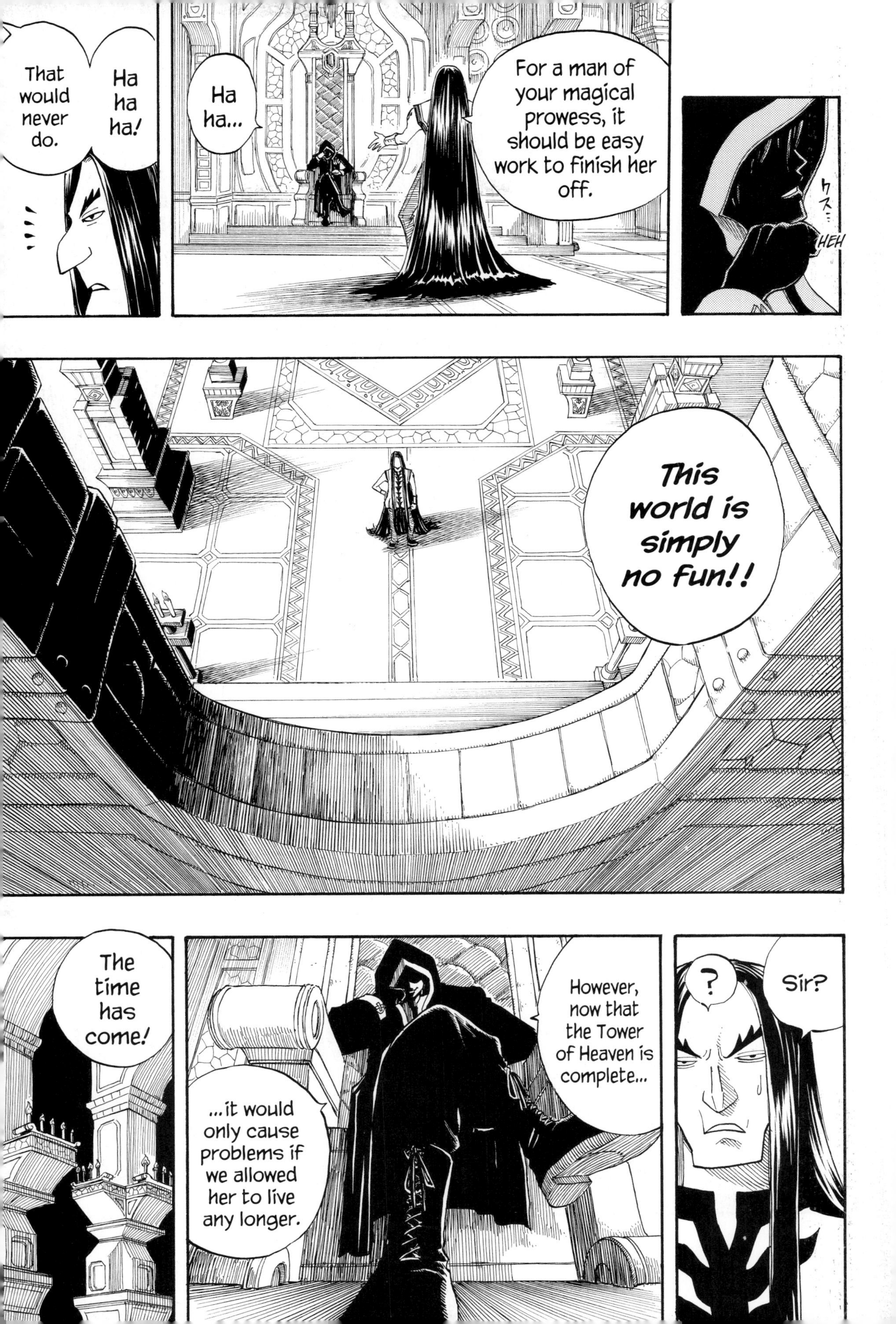
クス…
HEH
For a man of your magical prowess, it should be easy work to finish her off.
Ha ha...
Ha ha ha!
That would never do.
This world is simply no fun!!
Sir?
?
However, now that the Tower of Heaven is complete...
...it would only cause problems if we allowed her to live any longer.
The time has come!

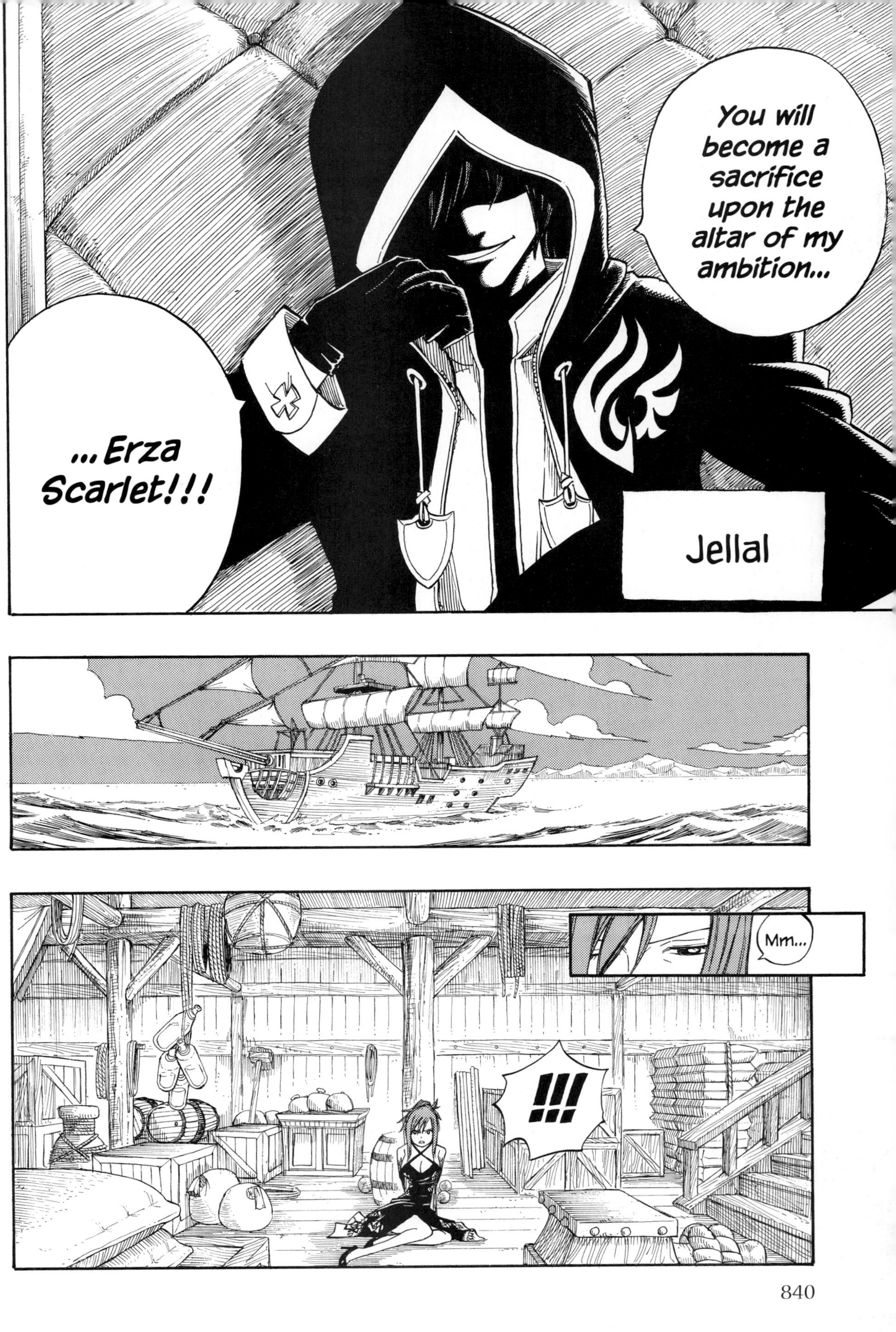
You will become a sacrifice upon the altar of my ambition...
...Erza Scarlet!!!
Jellal
Mm...
!!!

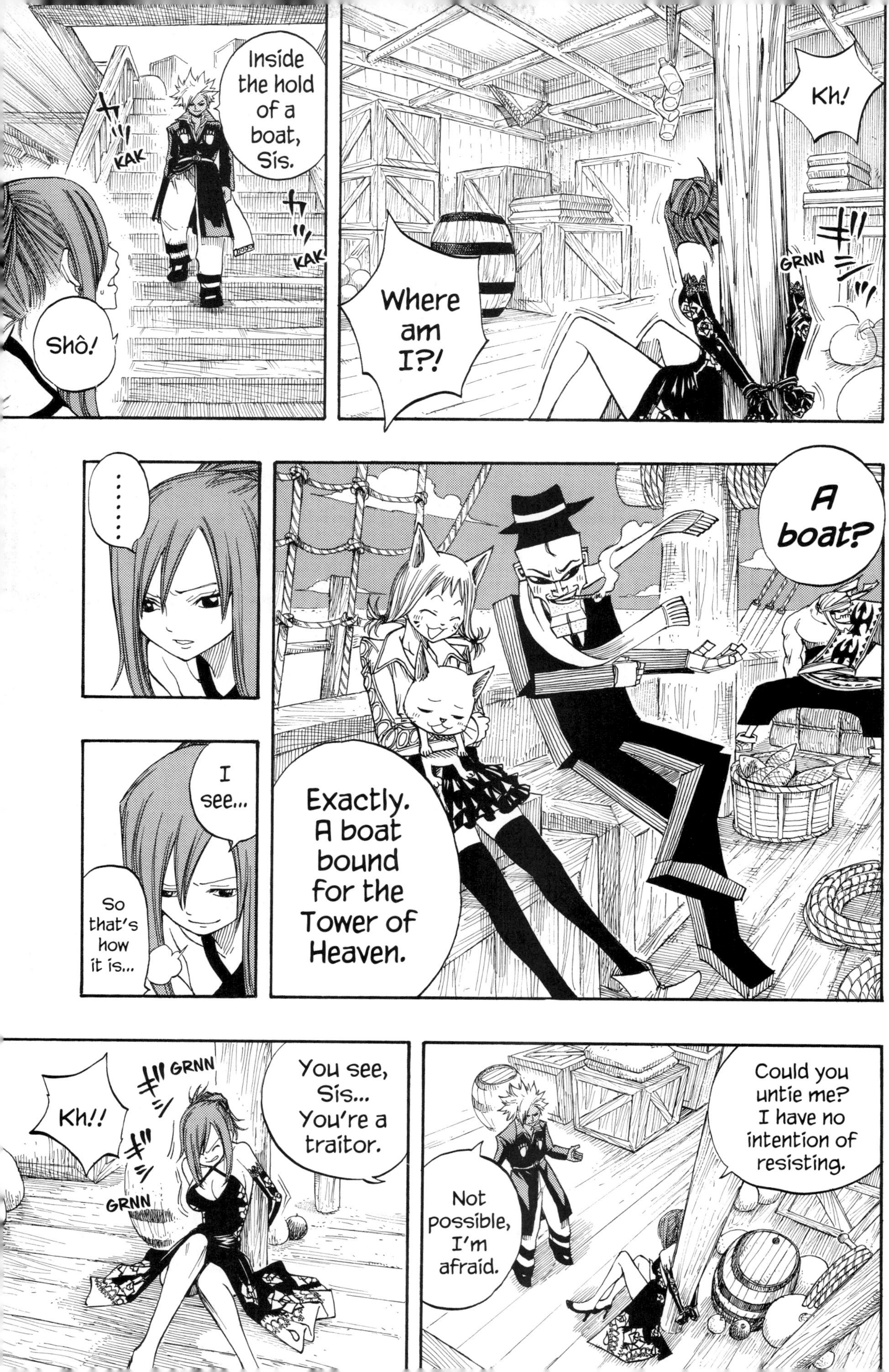

Kh!
GRNN
Where am I?!
Inside the hold of a boat, Sis.
KAK
KAK
Shô!
A boat?
Exactly. A boat bound for the Tower of Heaven.
......
I see...
So that's how it is...
Could you untie me? I have no intention of resisting.
Not possible, I'm afraid.
You see, Sis... You're a traitor.
GRNN
Kh!!
GRNN

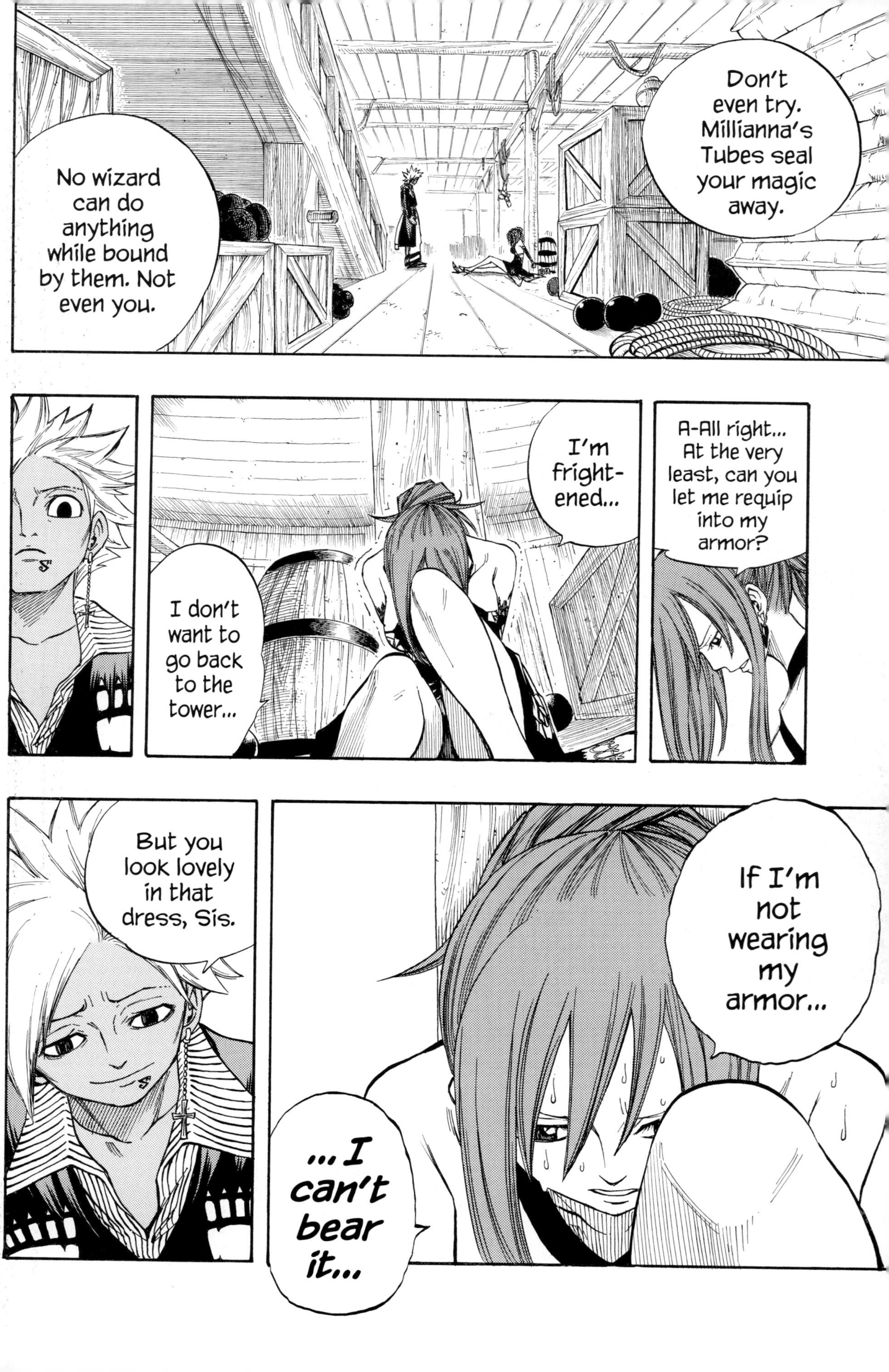
Don't even try. Millianna's Tubes seal your magic away.
No wizard can do anything while bound by them. Not even you.
A-All right... At the very least, can you let me requip into my armor?
I'm very fright-ened...
I don't want to go back to the tower...
If I'm not wearing my armor...
...I can't bear it...
But you look lovely in that dress, Sis.

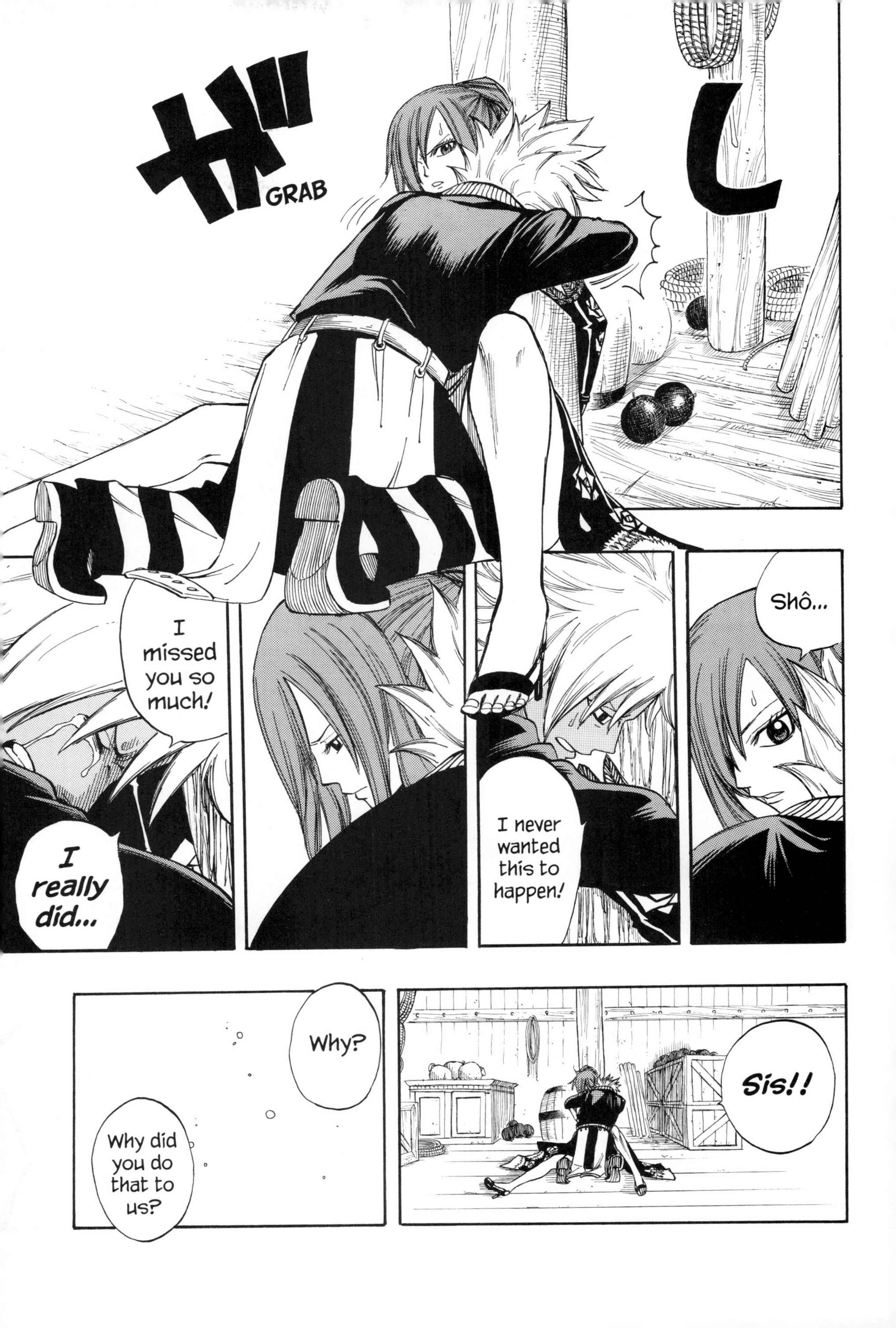
ガシ
GRAB
Shô...
I never wanted this to happen!
I missed you so much!
I really did...
Sis!!
Why?
Why did you do that to us?

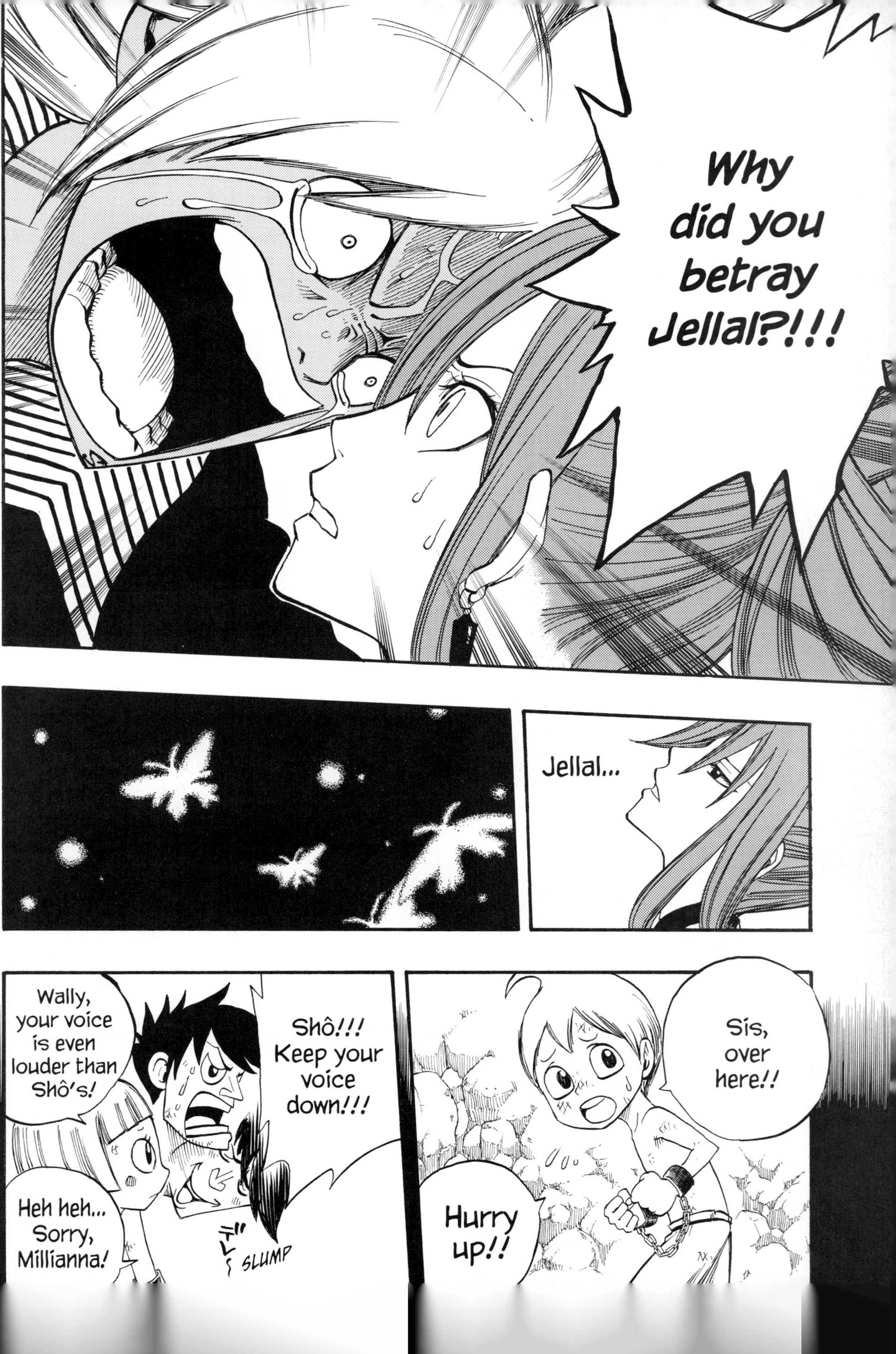
Why did you betray Jellal?!!!
Jellal...
Sis, over here!!
Hurry up!!
Shô!!! Keep your voice down!!!
Wally, your voice is even louder than Shô's!
Heh heh... Sorry, Millianna!
SLUMP

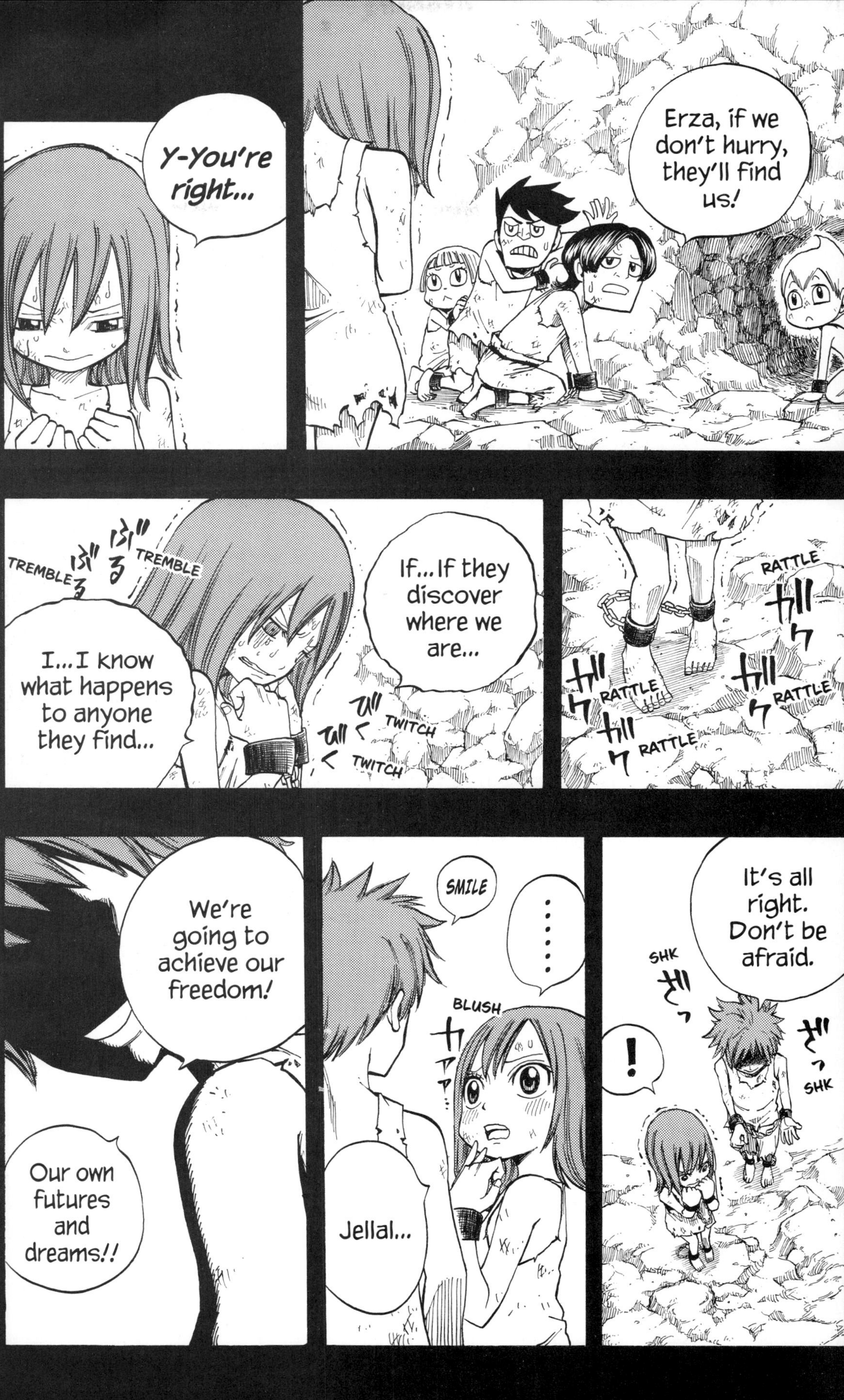
Erza, if we don't hurry, they'll find us!
Y-You're right...
RATTLE
RATTLE
RATTLE
RATTLE
If...If they discover where we are...
TREMBLE
TREMBLE
I...I know what happens to anyone they find...
TWITCH
TWITCH
It's all right. Don't be afraid.
SHK
SHK
!
SMILE
......
BLUSH
Jellal...
We're going to achieve our freedom!
Our own futures and dreams!!

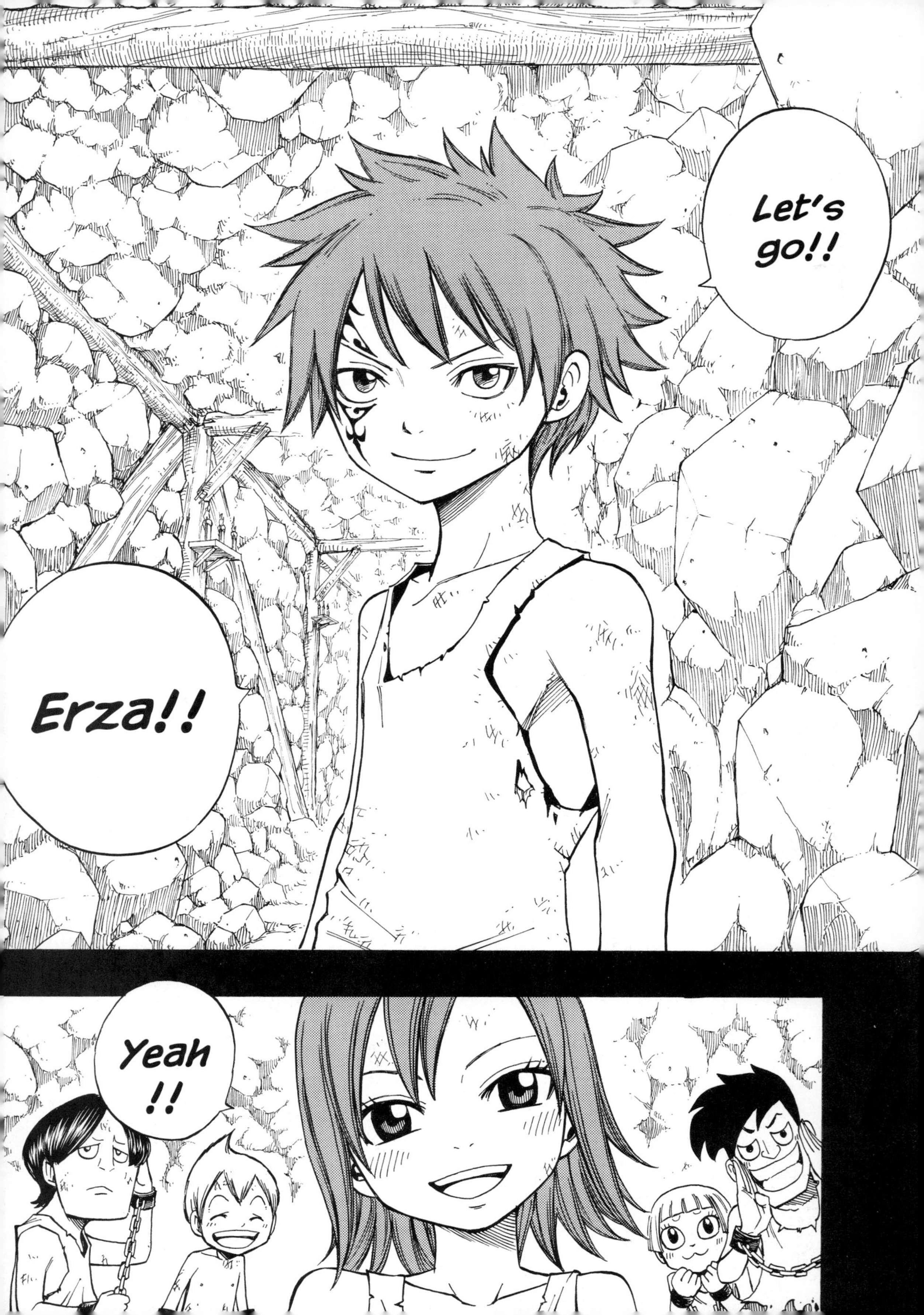
Let's go!!
Erza!!
Yeah !!

FAIRY TAIL

Chapter 78: Heaven Over There

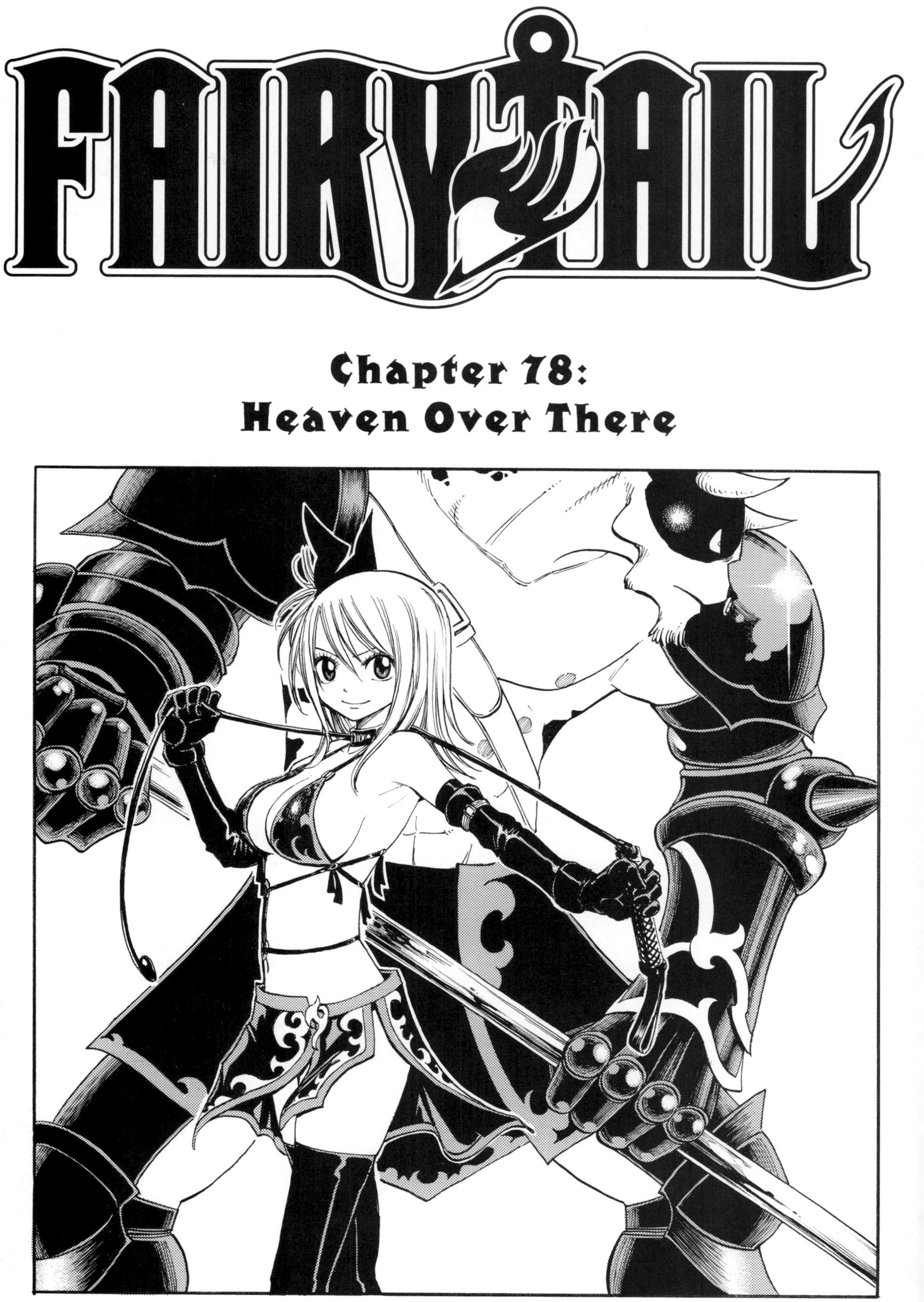

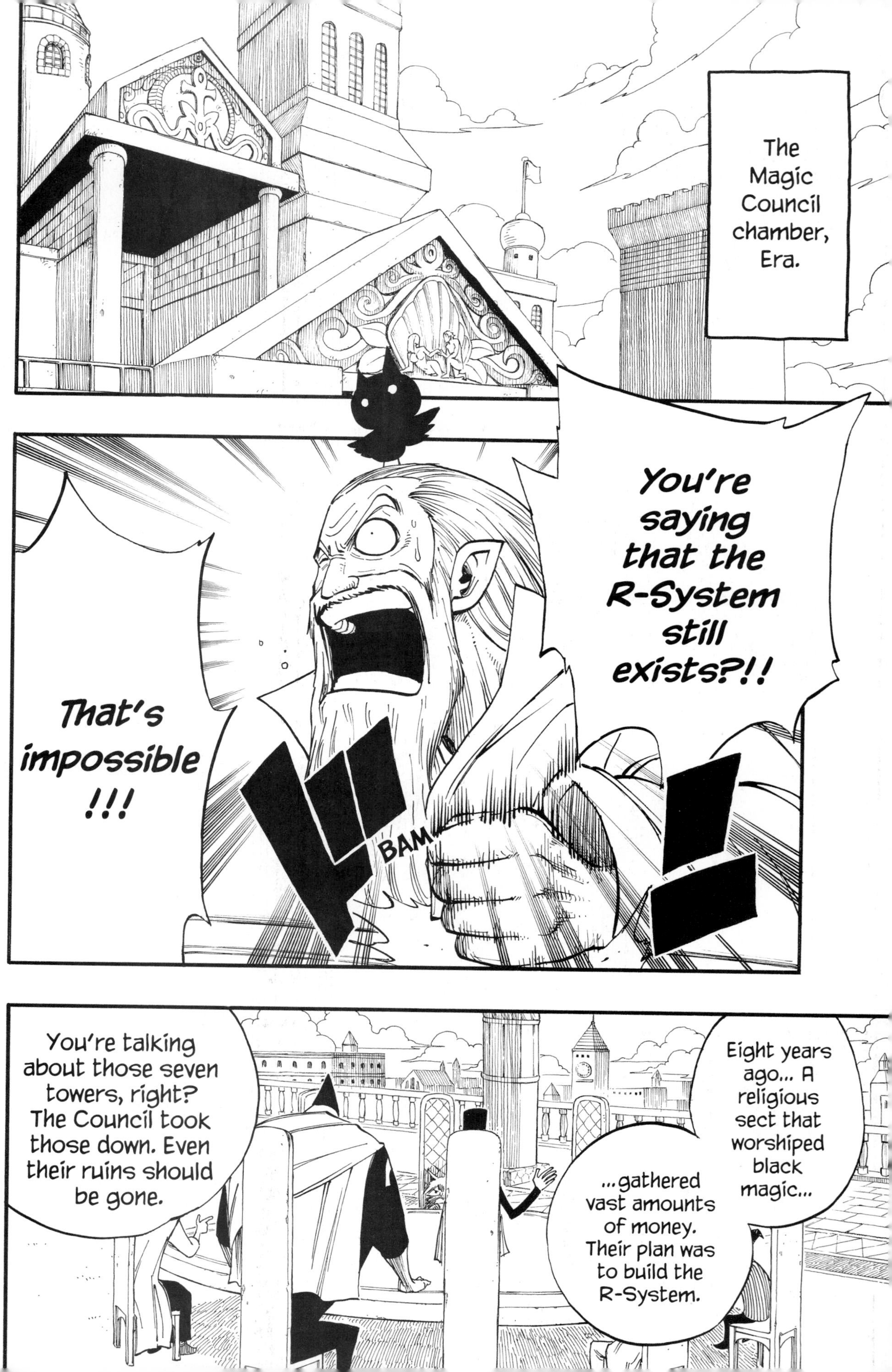
The Magic Council chamber, Era.
You're saying that the R-System still exists?!!
That's impossible!!!
BAM
Eight years ago... A religious sect that worshiped black magic...
...gathered vast amounts of money. Their plan was to build the R-System.
You're talking about those seven towers, right? The Council took those down. Even their ruins should be gone.

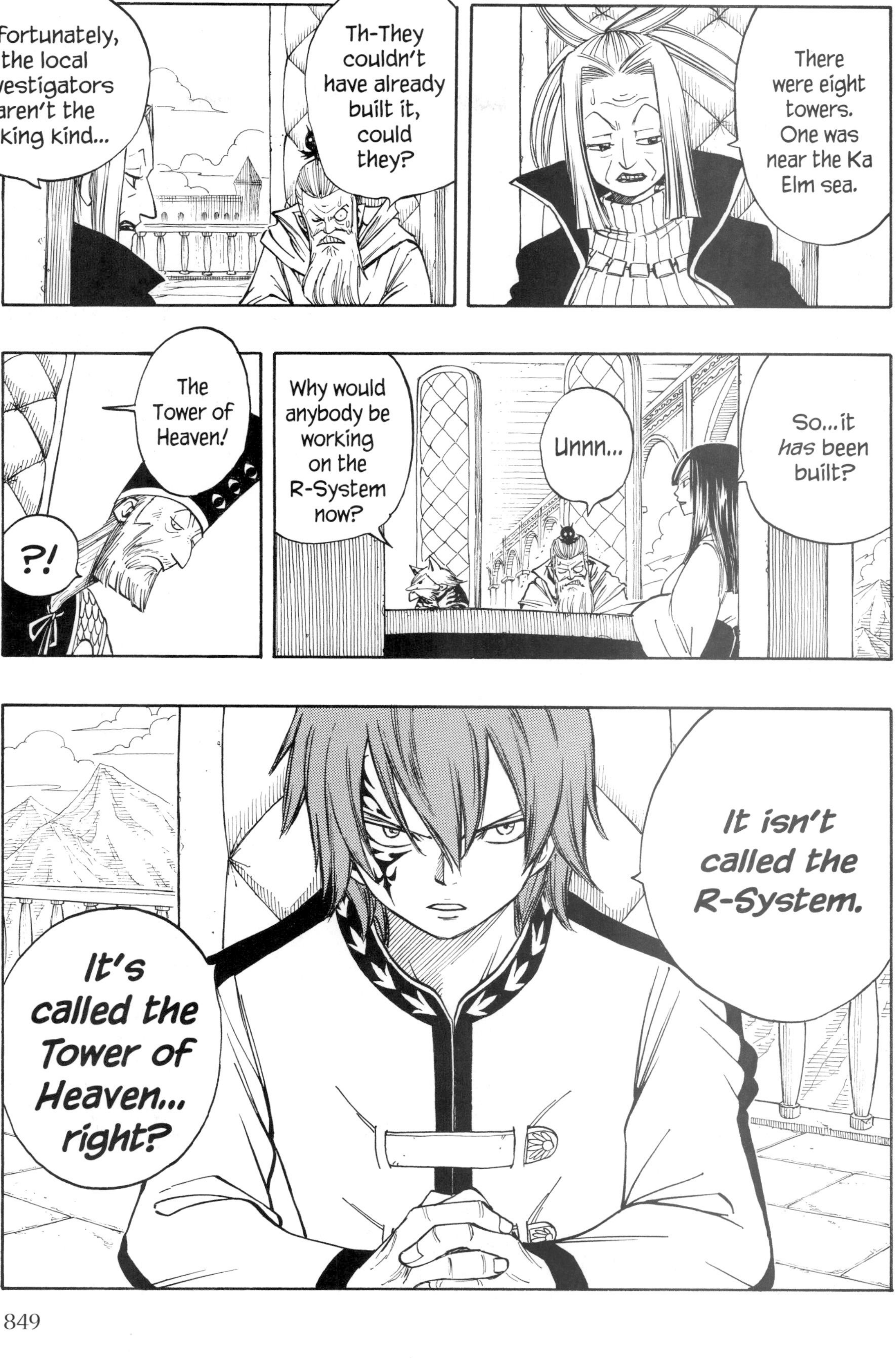
There were eight towers. One was near the Ka Elm sea.
Th-They couldn't have already built it, could they?
Unfortunately, the local investigators aren't the joking kind...
So...it *has* been built?
Unnn...
Why would anybody be working on the R-System now?
The Tower of Heaven!
?!
It isn't called the R-System.
It's called the Tower of Heaven... right?

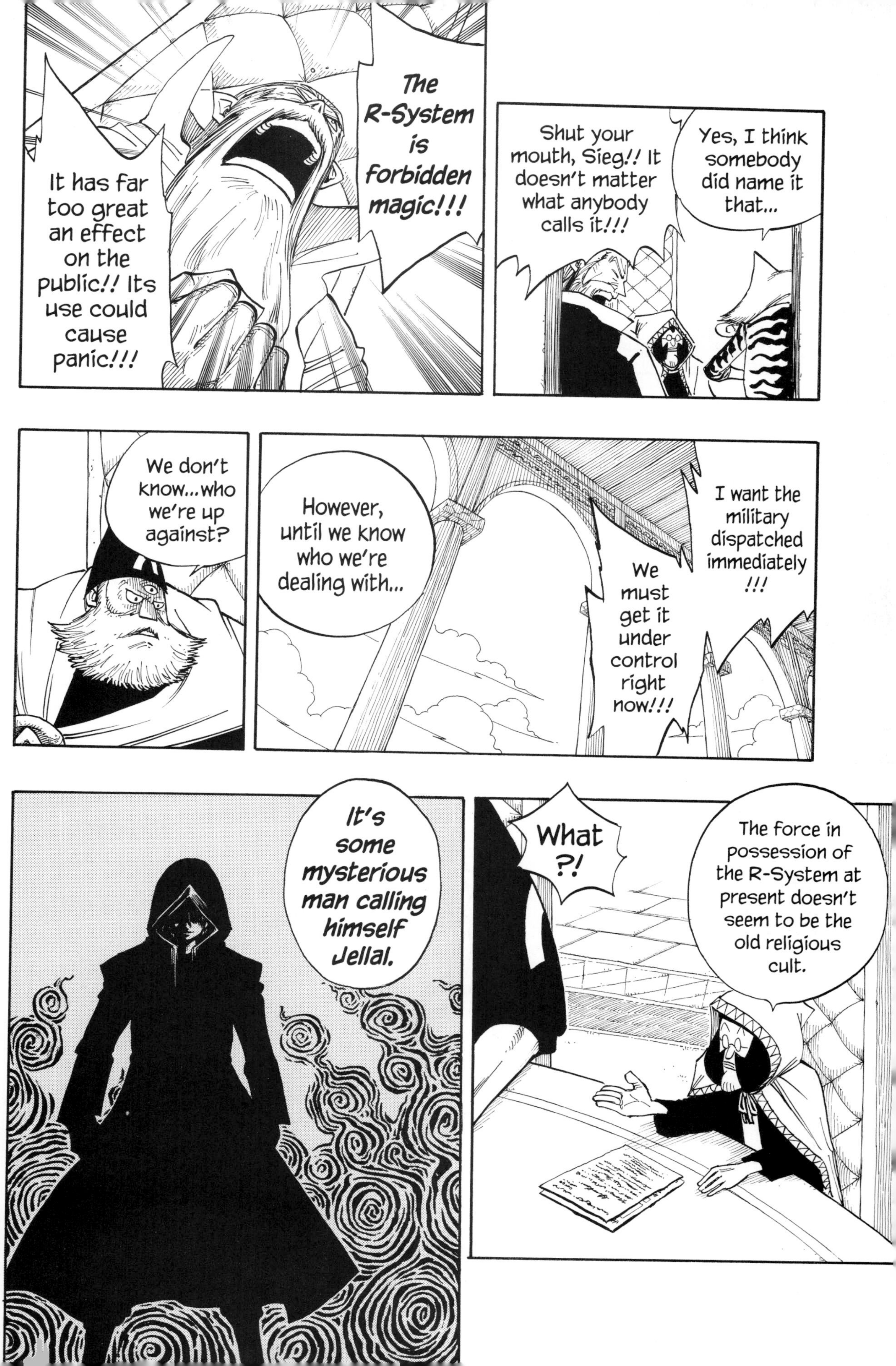

Yes, I think somebody did name it that...
Shut your mouth, Sieg!! It doesn't matter what anybody calls it!!!
The R-System is forbidden magic!!!
It has far too great an effect on the public!! Its use could cause panic!!!
I want the military dispatched immediately!!!
We must get it under control right now!!!
However, until we know who we're dealing with...
We don't know...who we're up against?
The force in possession of the R-System at present doesn't seem to be the old religious cult.
What?!
It's some mysterious man calling himself Jellal.

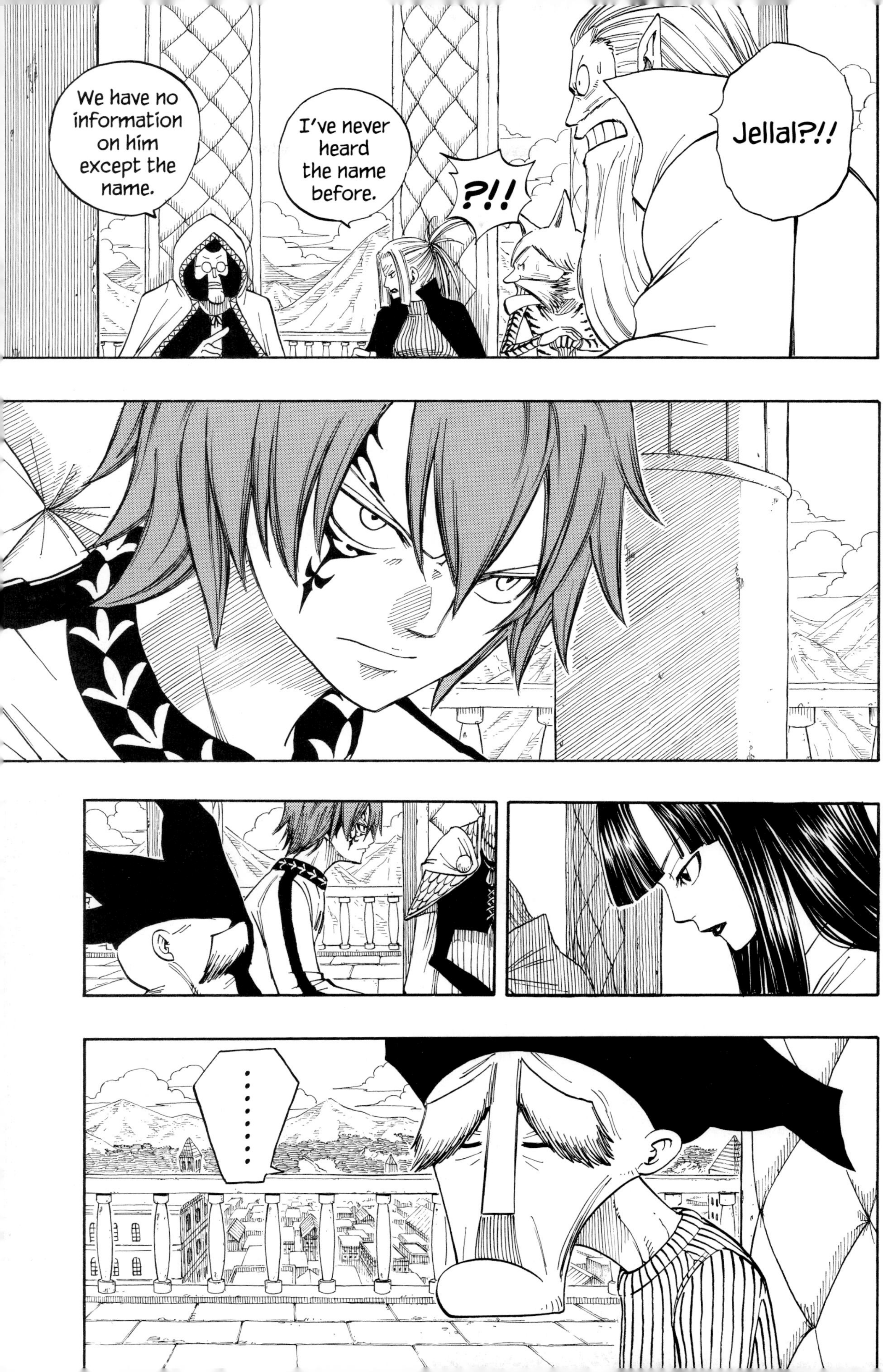
Jellal?!!
?!!
I've never heard the name before.
We have no information on him except the name.
....

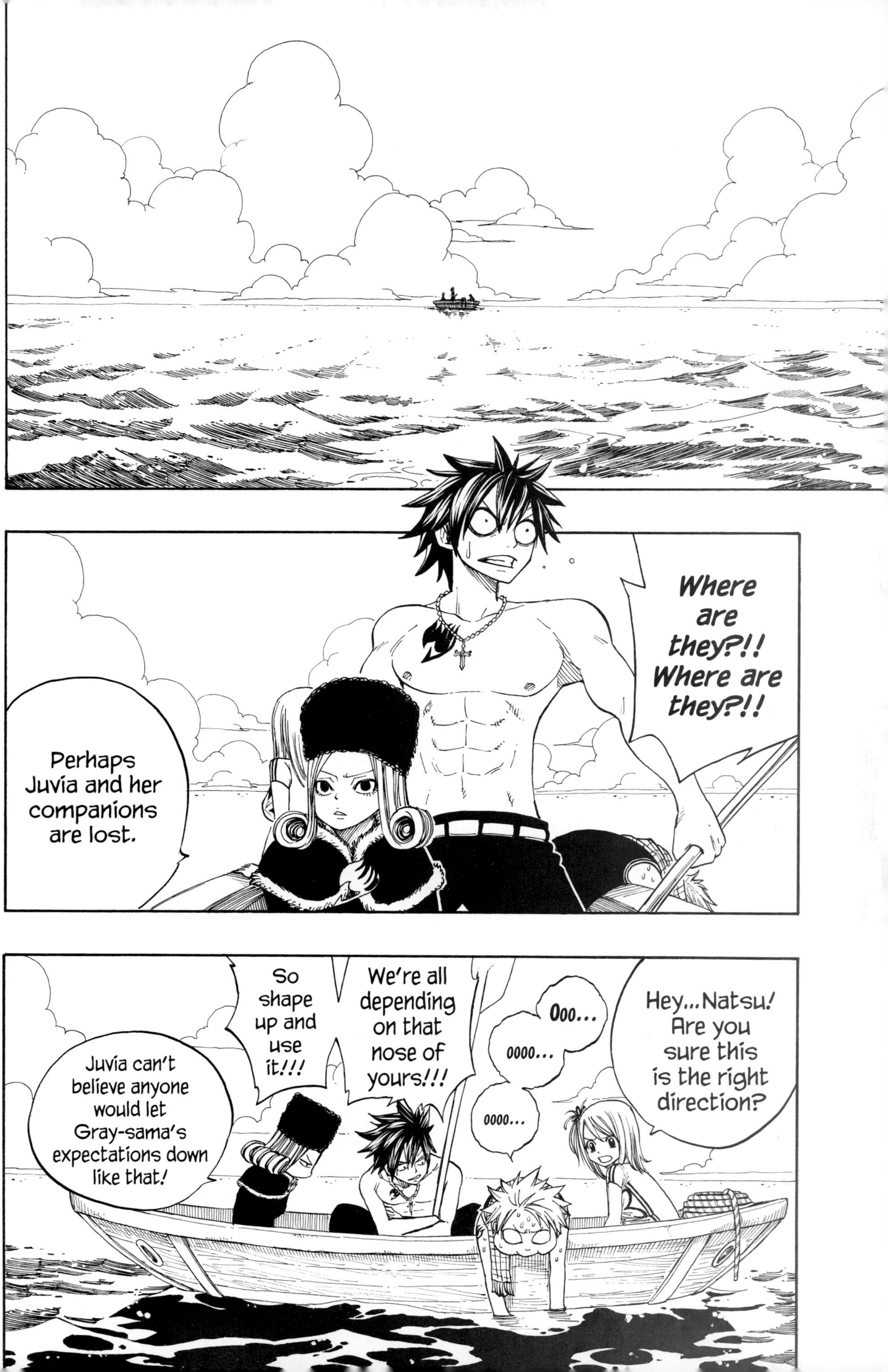
Where are they?!! Where are they?!!
Perhaps Juvia and her companions are lost.
Hey...Natsu! Are you sure this is the right direction?
Ooo...
oooo...
oooo...
We're all depending on that nose of yours!!!
So shape up and use it!!!
Juvia can't believe anyone would let Gray-sama's expectations down like that!

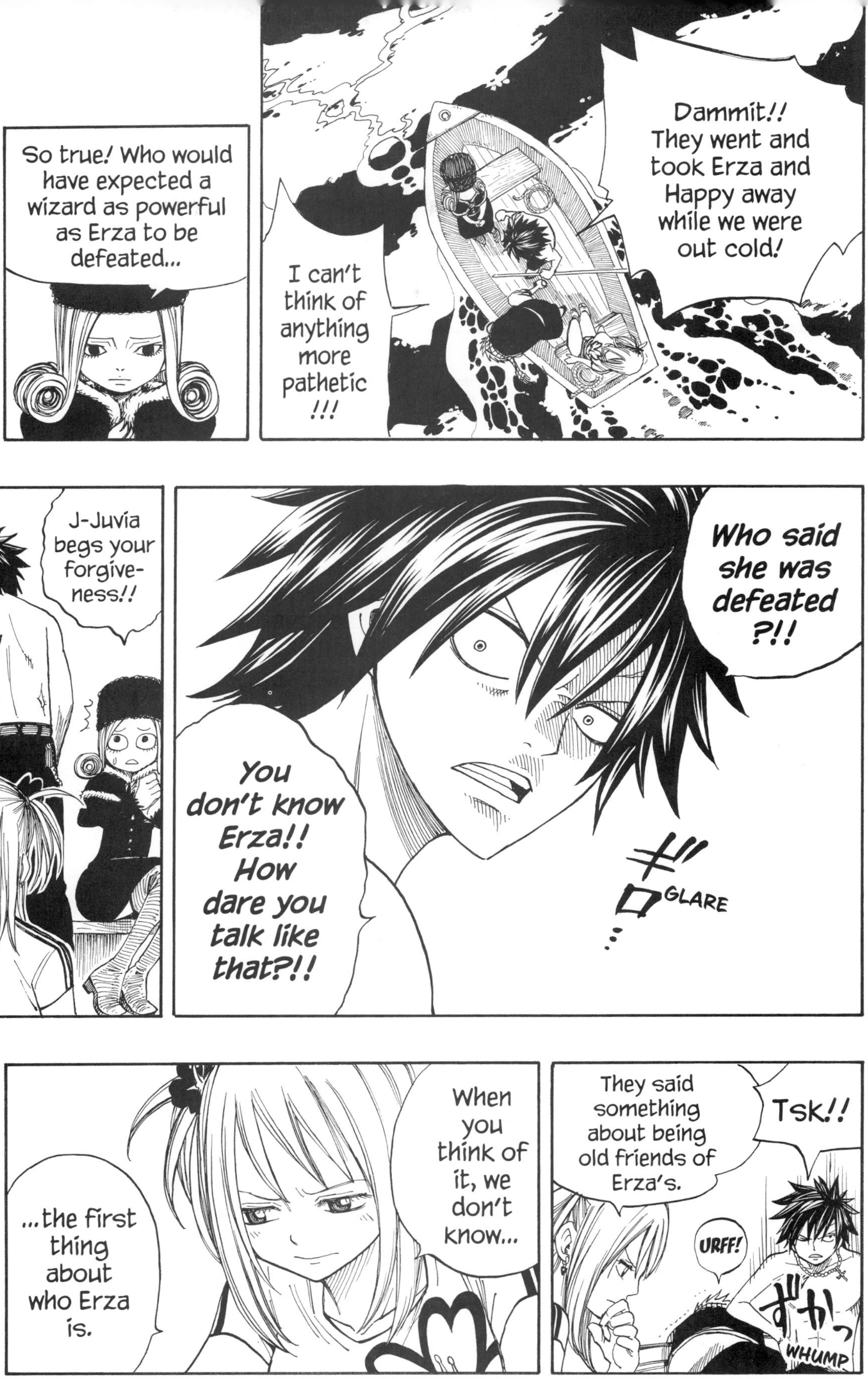
Dammit!! They went and took Erza and Happy away while we were out cold!
I can't think of anything more pathetic!!!
So true! Who would have expected a wizard as powerful as Erza to be defeated...
Who said she was defeated?!!
You don't know Erza!! How dare you talk like that?!!
ギロ
GLARE
J-Juvia begs your forgiveness!!
Gray, calm down!!
Tsk!!
They said something about being old friends of Erza's.
URFF!
ずかっ
WHUMP
When you think of it, we don't know...
...the first thing about who Erza is.

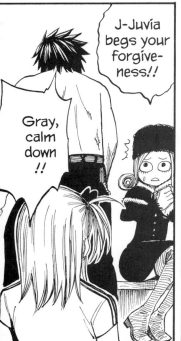

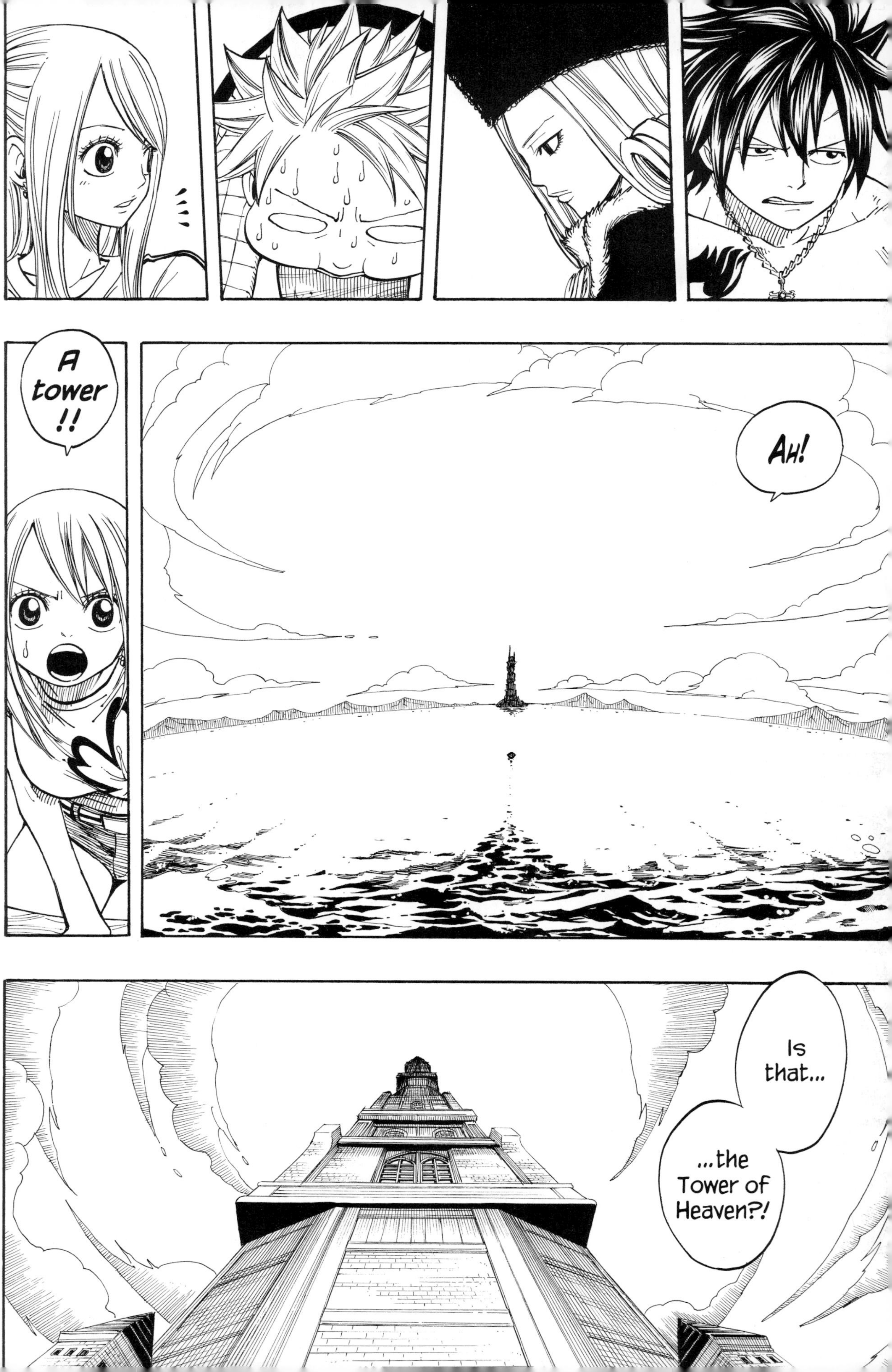

Ah!
A tower!!
Is that...
...the Tower of Heaven?!

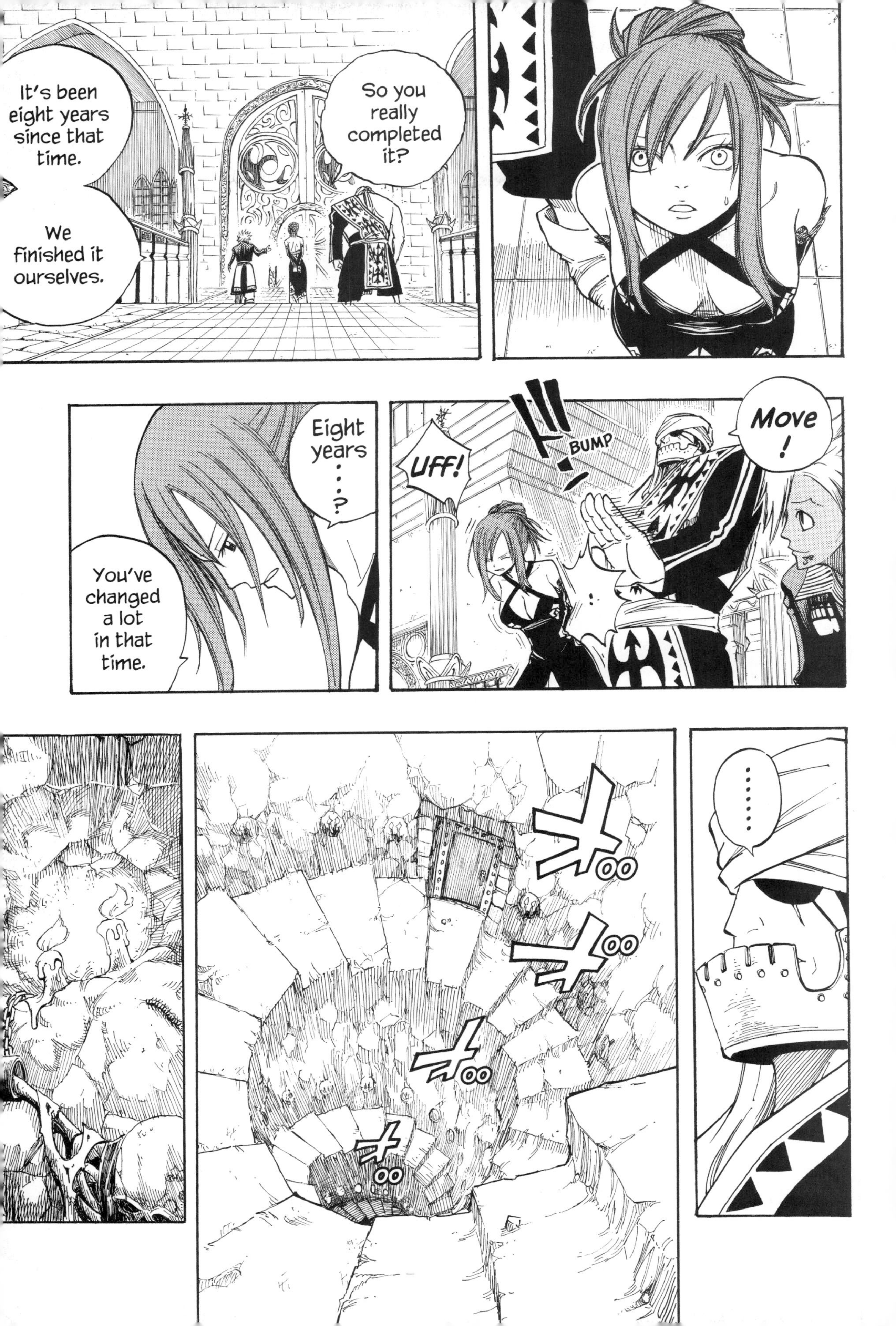
So you really completed it?
It's been eight years since that time.
We finished it ourselves.
Move!
BUMP
UFF!
Eight years...?
You've changed a lot in that time.
......

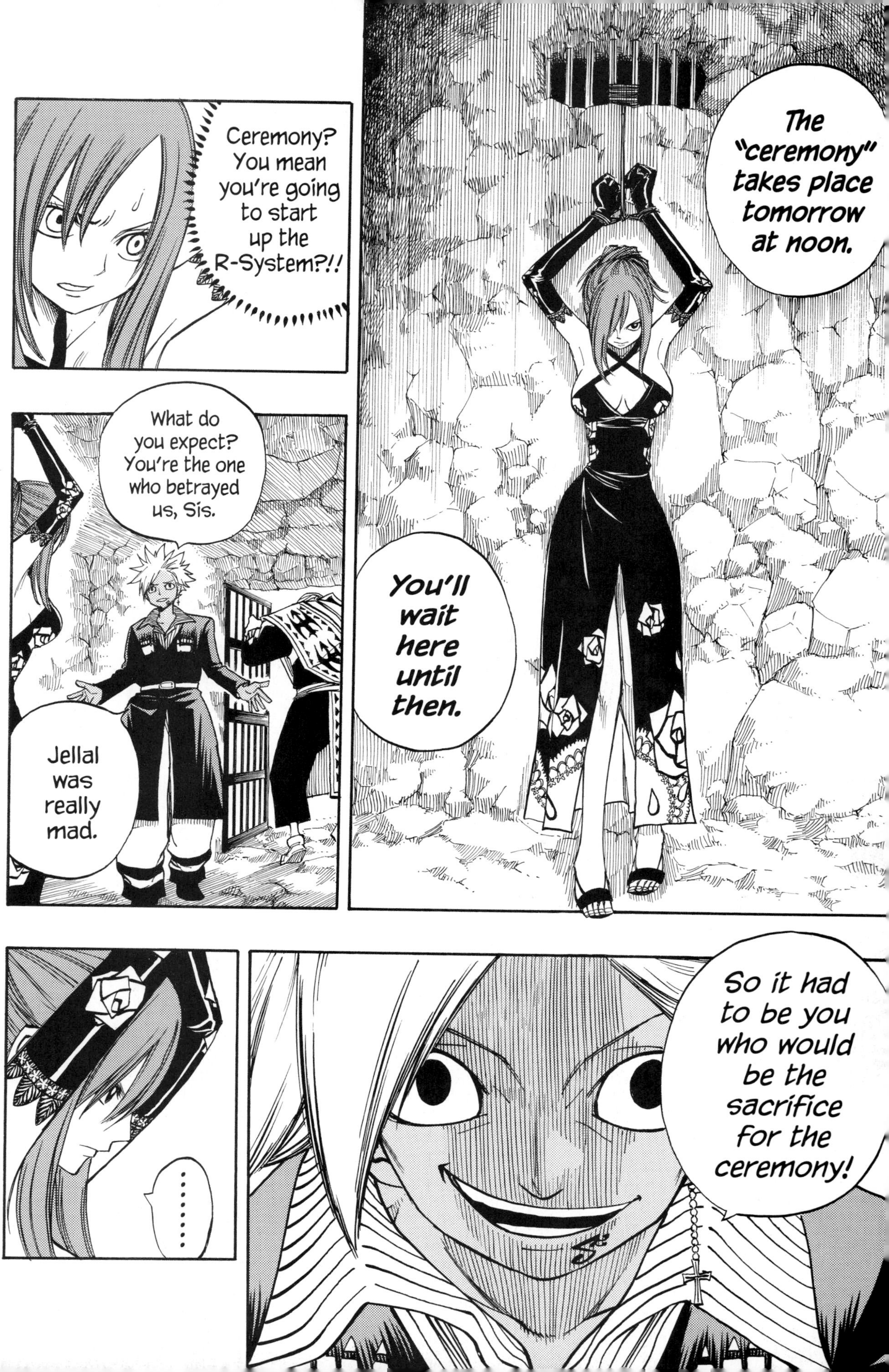
The "ceremony" takes place tomorrow at noon.
You'll wait here until then.
Ceremony? You mean you're going to start up the R-System?!!
What do you expect? You're the one who betrayed us, Sis.
Jellal was really mad.
So it had to be you who would be the sacrifice for the ceremony!
....

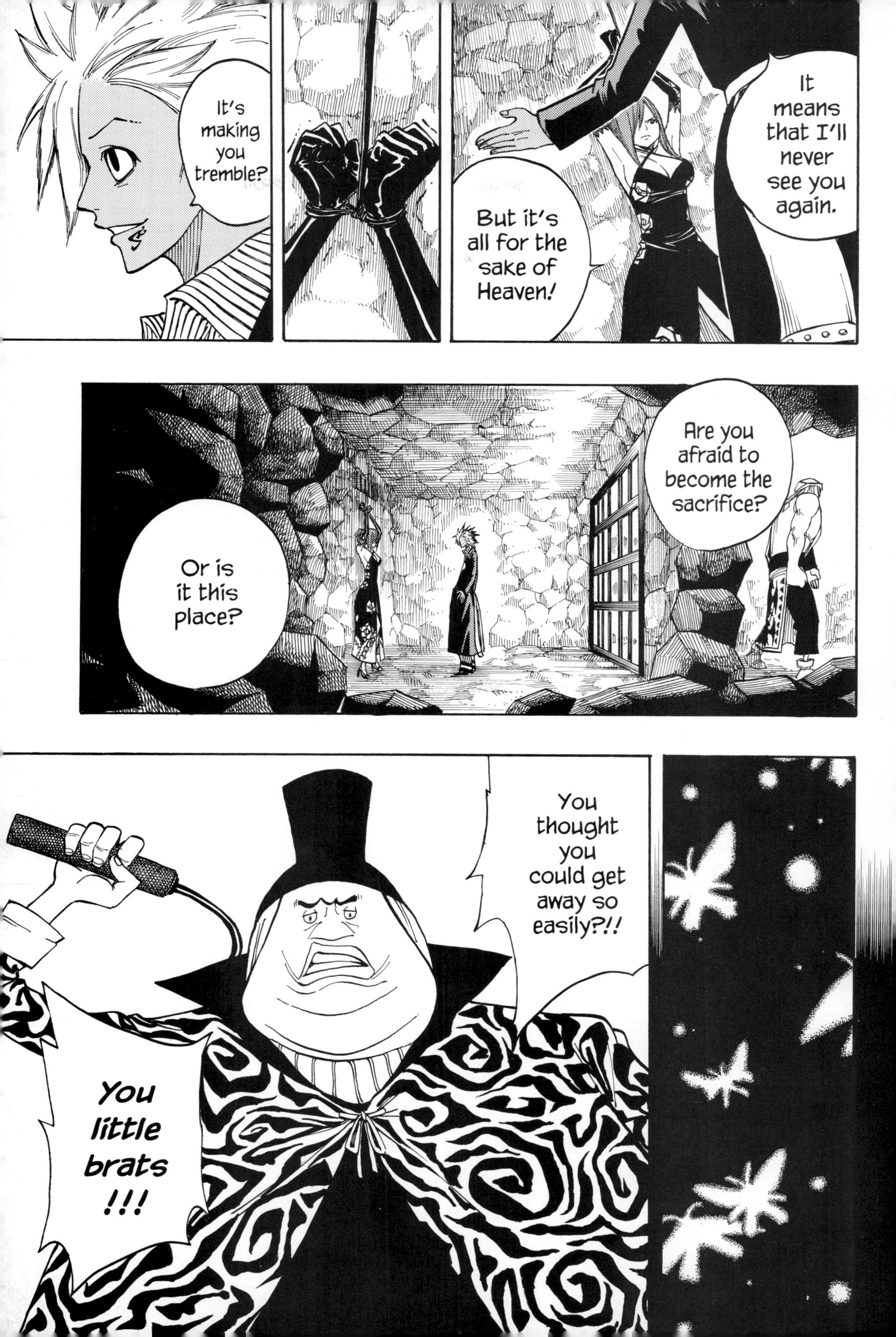
It means that I'll never see you again.
But it's all for the sake of Heaven!
It's making you tremble?
Are you afraid to become the sacrifice?
Or is it this place?
You thought you could get away so easily?!!
You little brats!!!

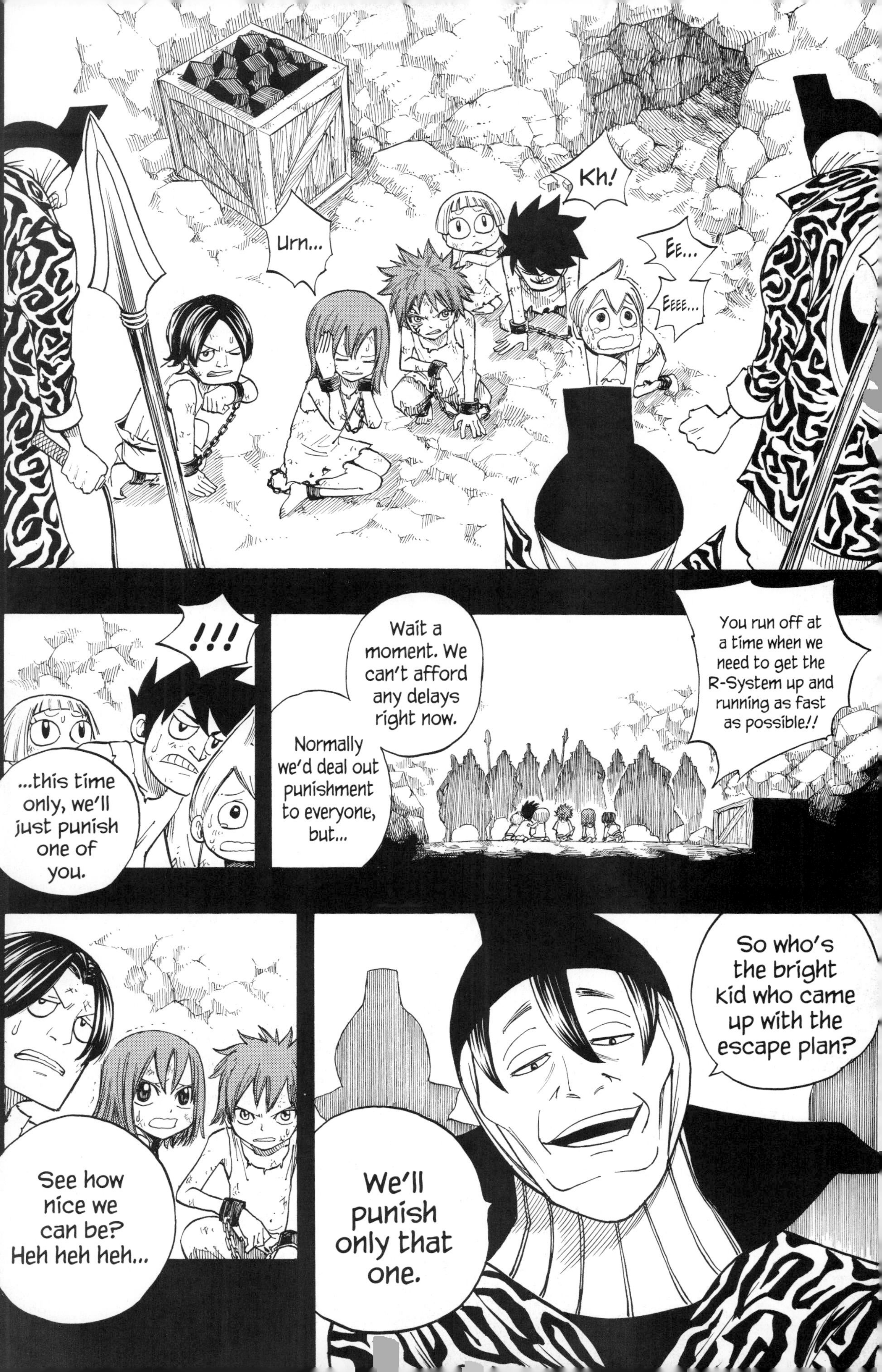
Kh!
Ee...
Eeee...
Urn...
You run off at a time when we need to get the R-System up and running as fast as possible!!
Wait a moment. We can't afford any delays right now.
Normally we'd deal out punishment to everyone, but...
!!!
...this time only, we'll just punish one of you.
So who's the bright kid who came up with the escape plan?
We'll punish only that one.
See how nice we can be? Heh heh heh...

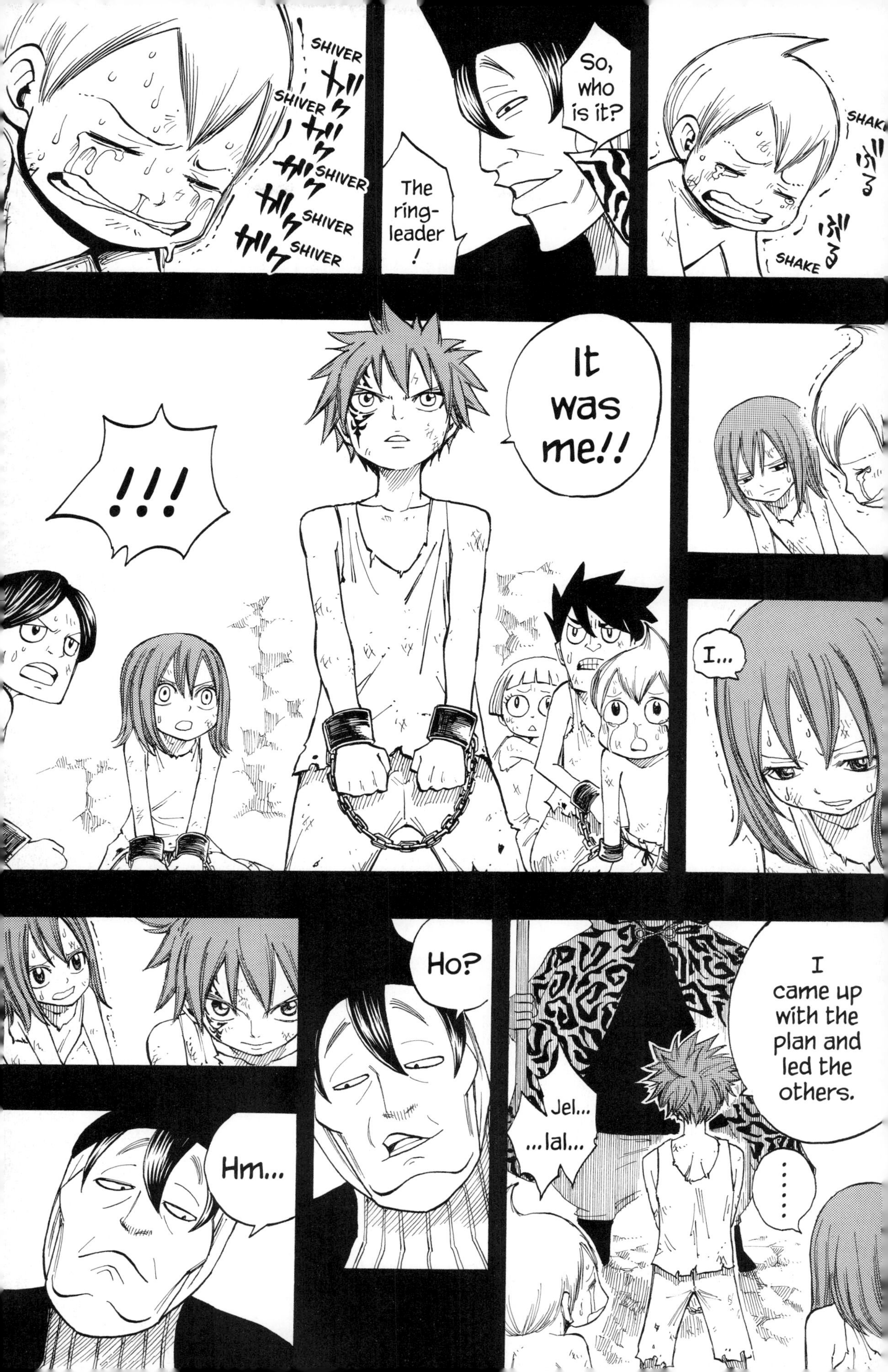
SHAKE
SHAKE
So, who is it?
The ring-leader!
SHIVER
SHIVER
SHIVER
SHIVER
SHIVER
I...
It was me!!
!!!
I came up with the plan and led the others.
......
Jel...
...lal...
Ho?
Hm...

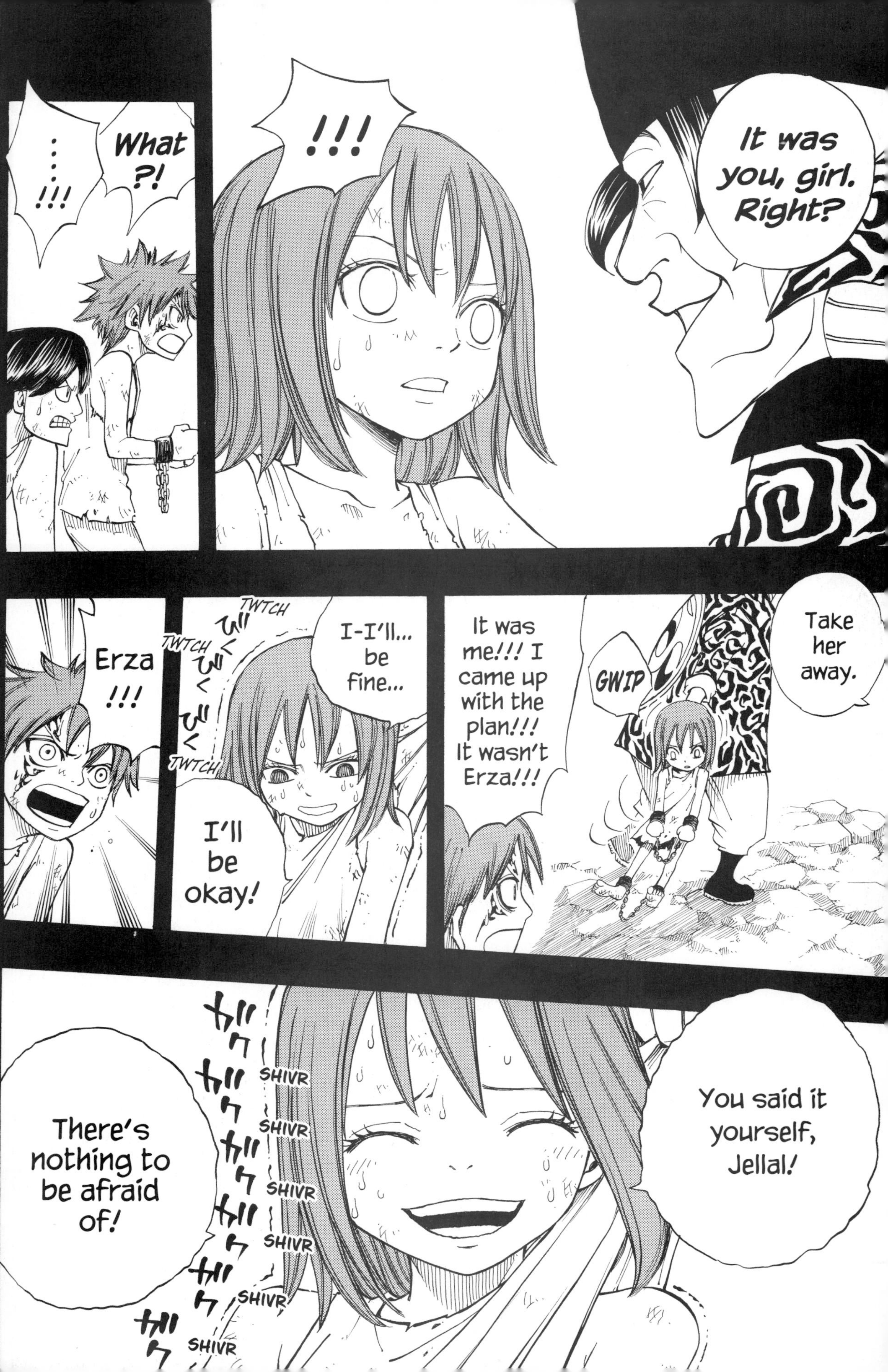
It was you, girl. Right?
!!!
What ?!
...!!!
Take her away.
GWIP
It was me!!! I came up with the plan!!! It wasn't Erza!!!
I-I'll... be fine...
TWTCH
TWTCH
TWTCH
I'll be okay!
Erza !!!
You said it yourself, Jellal!
There's nothing to be afraid of!
SHIVR
SHIVR
SHIVR
SHIVR
SHIVR
SHIVR

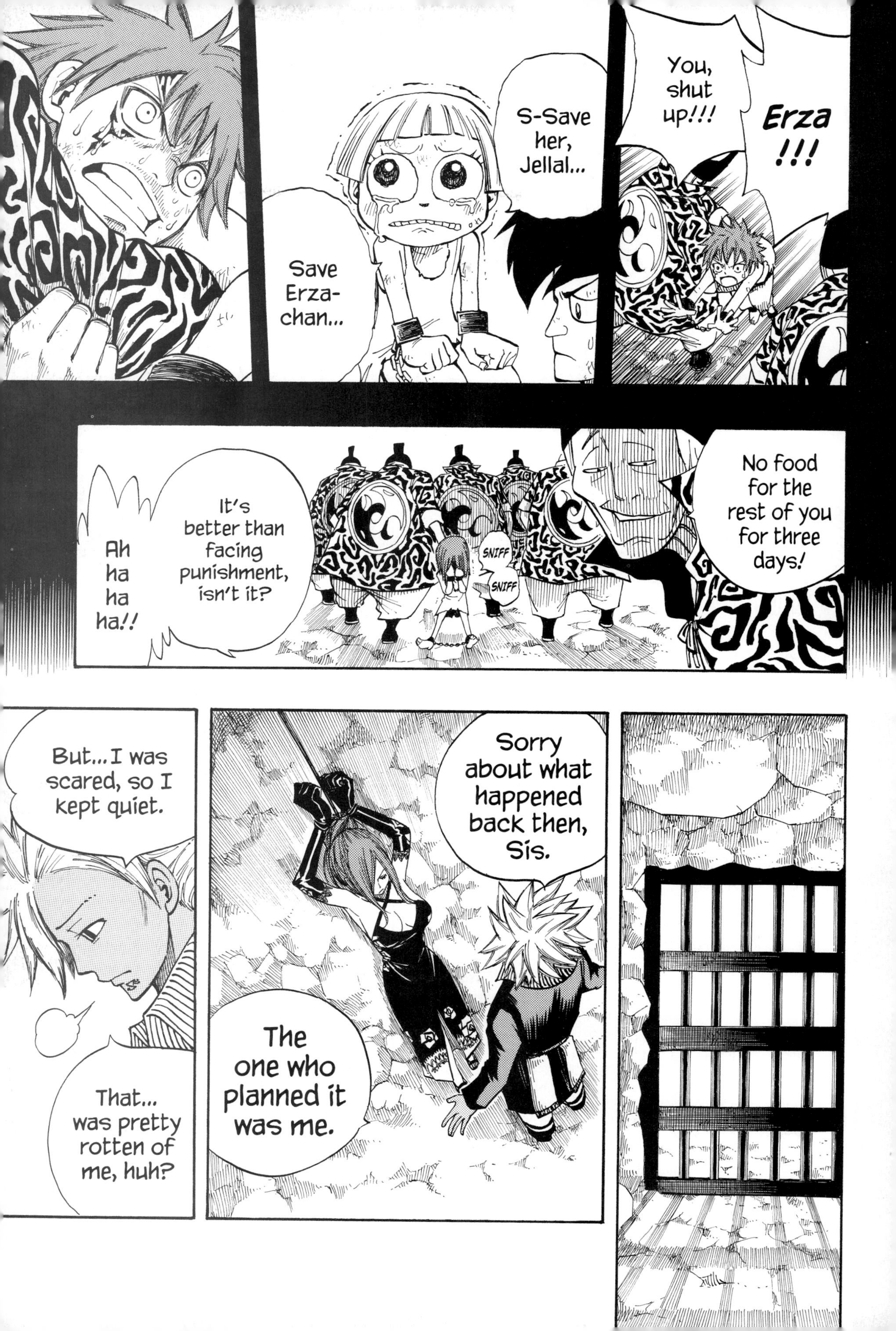
Erza!!!
You, shut up!!!
S-Save her, Jellal...
Save Erza-chan...
No food for the rest of you for three days!
SNIFF
SNIFF
It's better than facing punishment, isn't it?
Ah ha ha ha!!
Sorry about what happened back then, Sis.
The one who planned it was me.
But...I was scared, so I kept quiet.
That... was pretty rotten of me, huh?

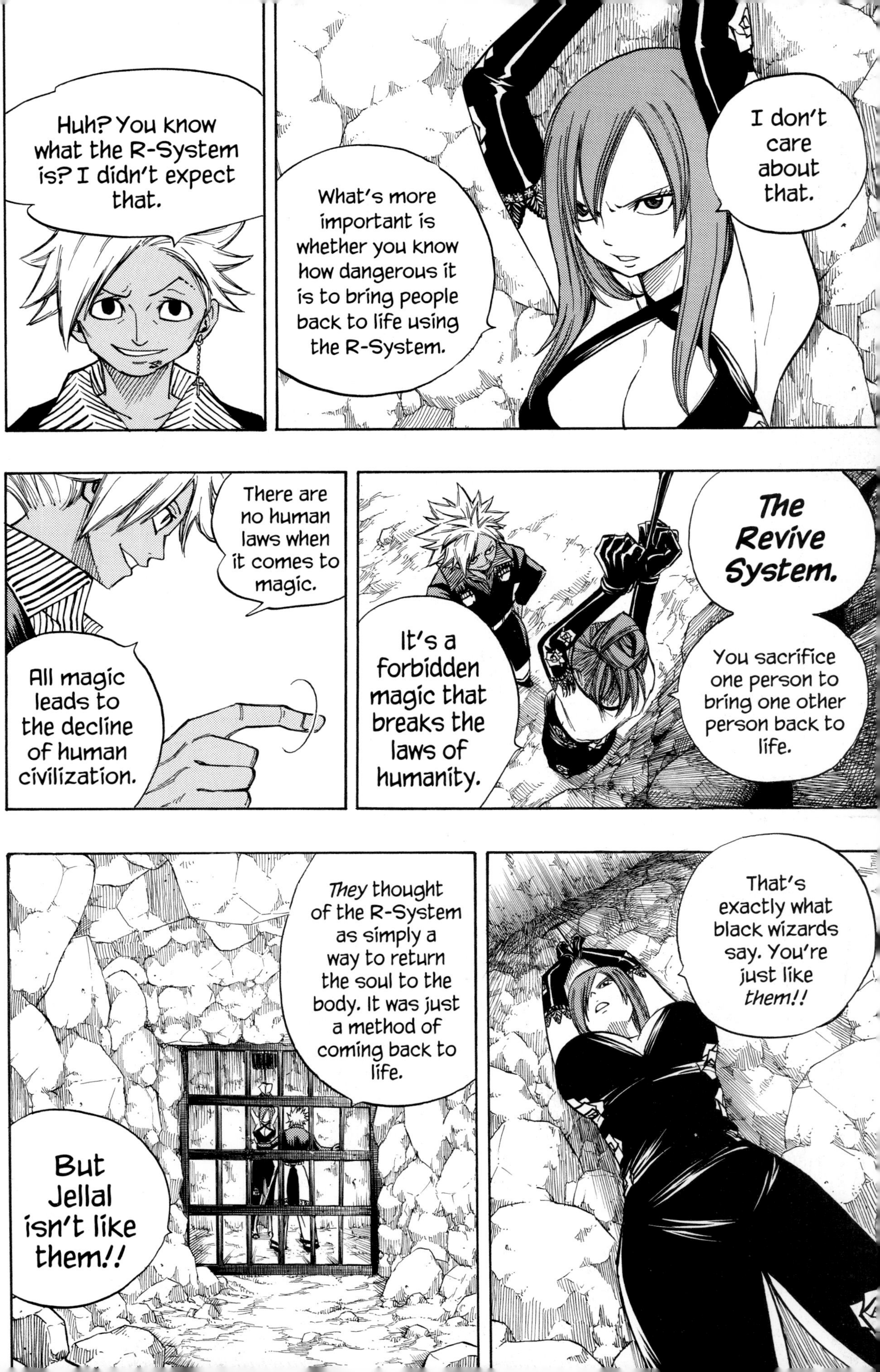
I don't care about that.
What's more important is whether you know how dangerous it is to bring people back to life using the R-System.
Huh? You know what the R-System is? I didn't expect that.
The Revive System.
You sacrifice one person to bring one other person back to life.
It's a forbidden magic that breaks the laws of humanity.
There are no human laws when it comes to magic.
All magic leads to the decline of human civilization.
That's exactly what black wizards say. You're just like *them*!!
They thought of the R-System as simply a way to return the soul to the body. It was just a method of coming back to life.
But Jellal isn't like them!!

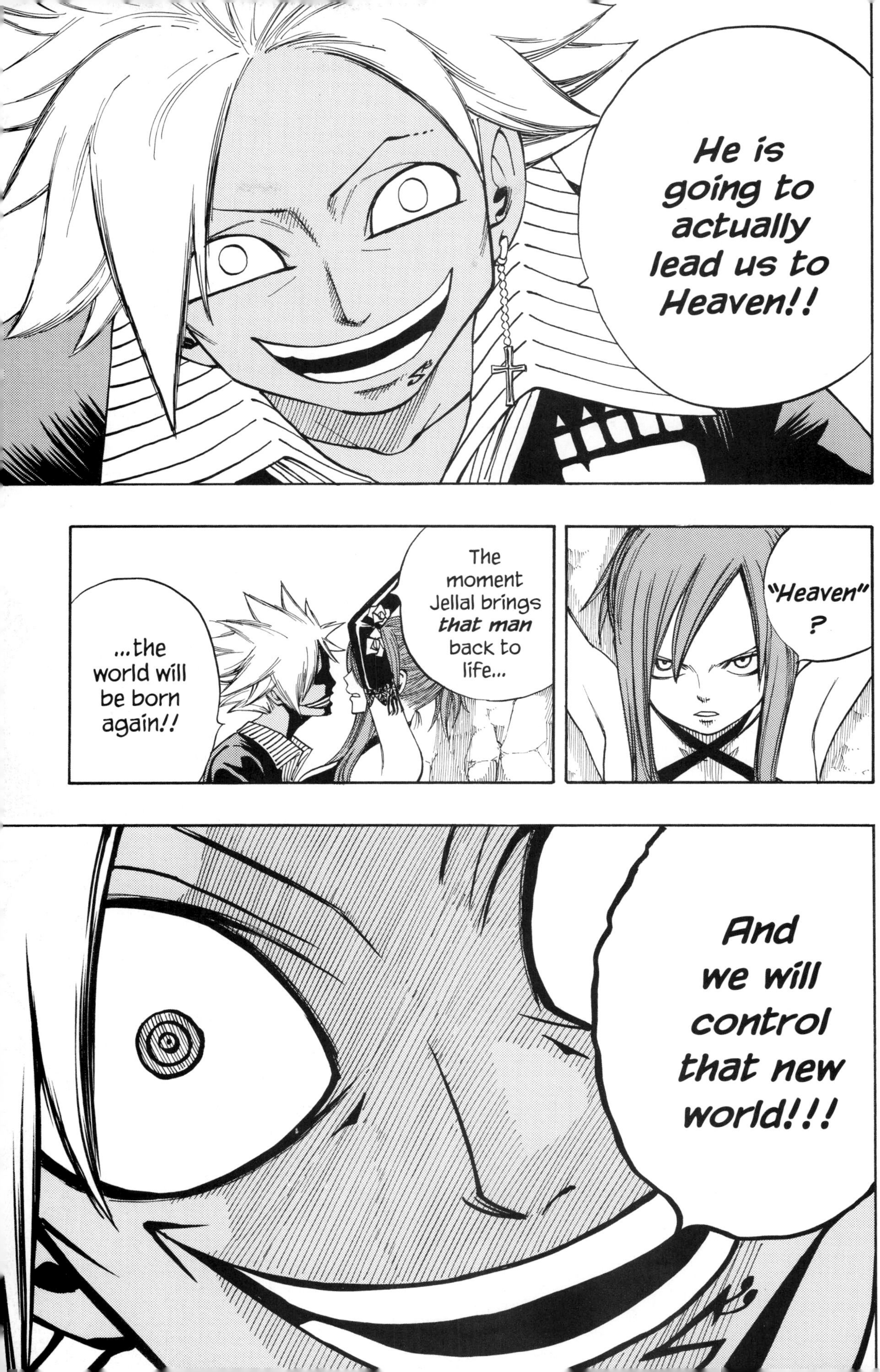
He is going to actually lead us to Heaven!!
"Heaven"?
The moment Jellal brings *that man* back to life...
...the world will be born again!!
And we will control that new world!!!

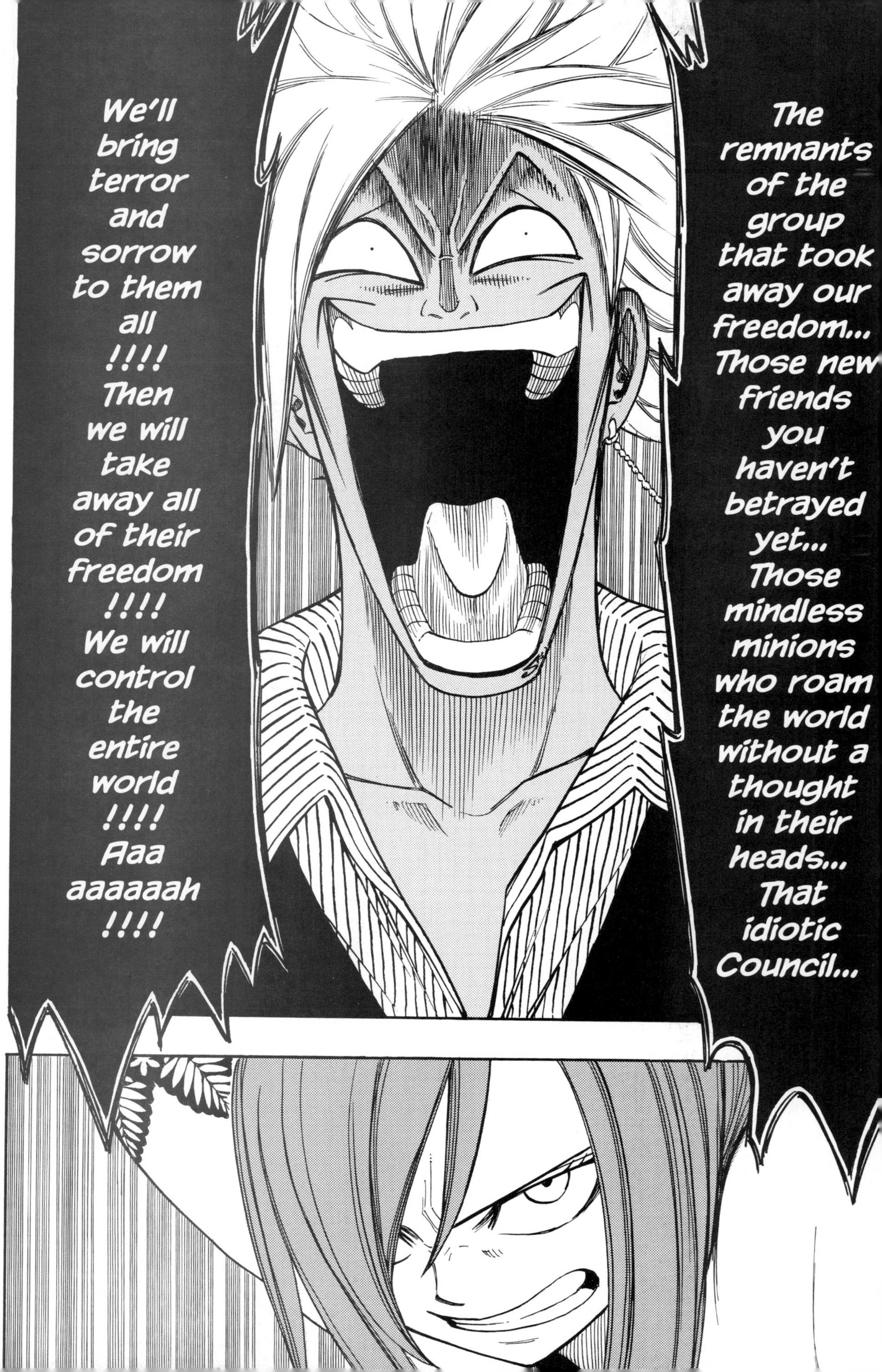
The remnants of the group that took away our freedom... Those new friends you haven't betrayed yet... Those mindless minions who roam the world without a thought in their heads... That idiotic Council...
We'll bring terror and sorrow to them all !!!! Then we will take away all of their freedom !!!! We will control the entire world !!!! Aaa aaaaaah !!!!

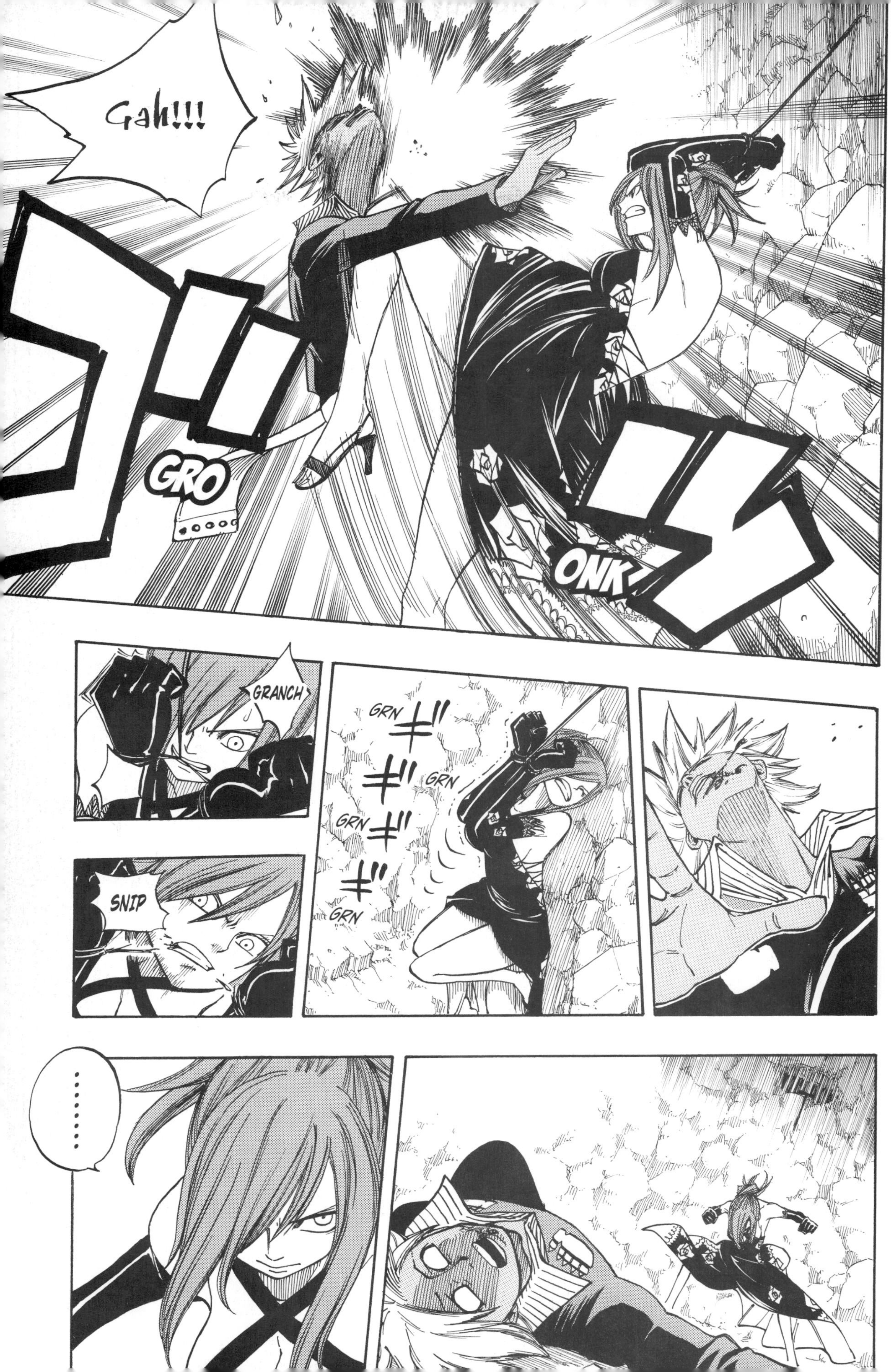
Gah!!!
GRO
ONK
GRN
GRN
GRN
GRN
GRANCH
SNIP
....

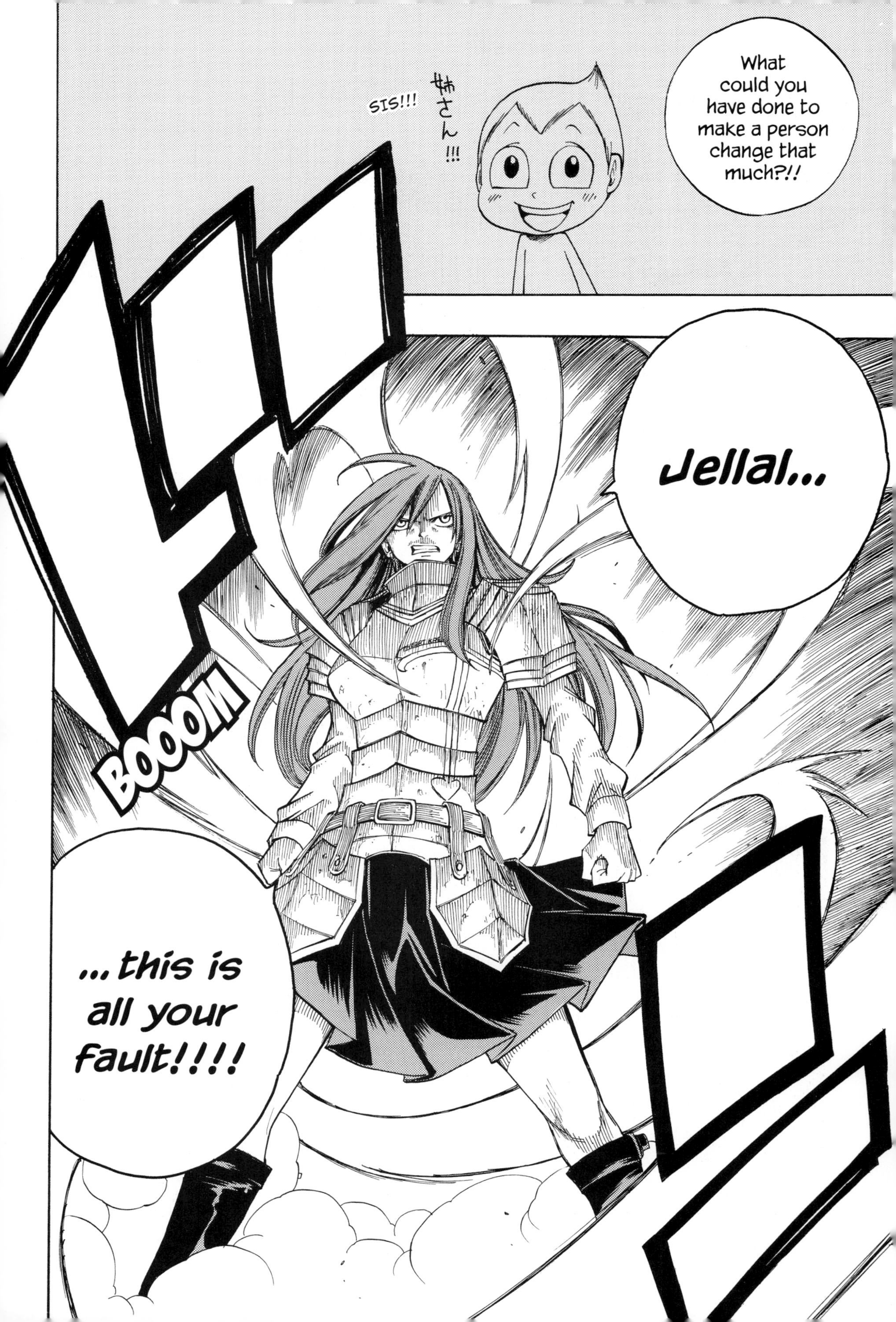
What could you have done to make a person change that much?!!
姉さん!!!
SIS!!!
Jellal...
...this is all your fault!!!!
BOOOM

FAIRY TAIL

Chapter 79:
Siegrain's Decision

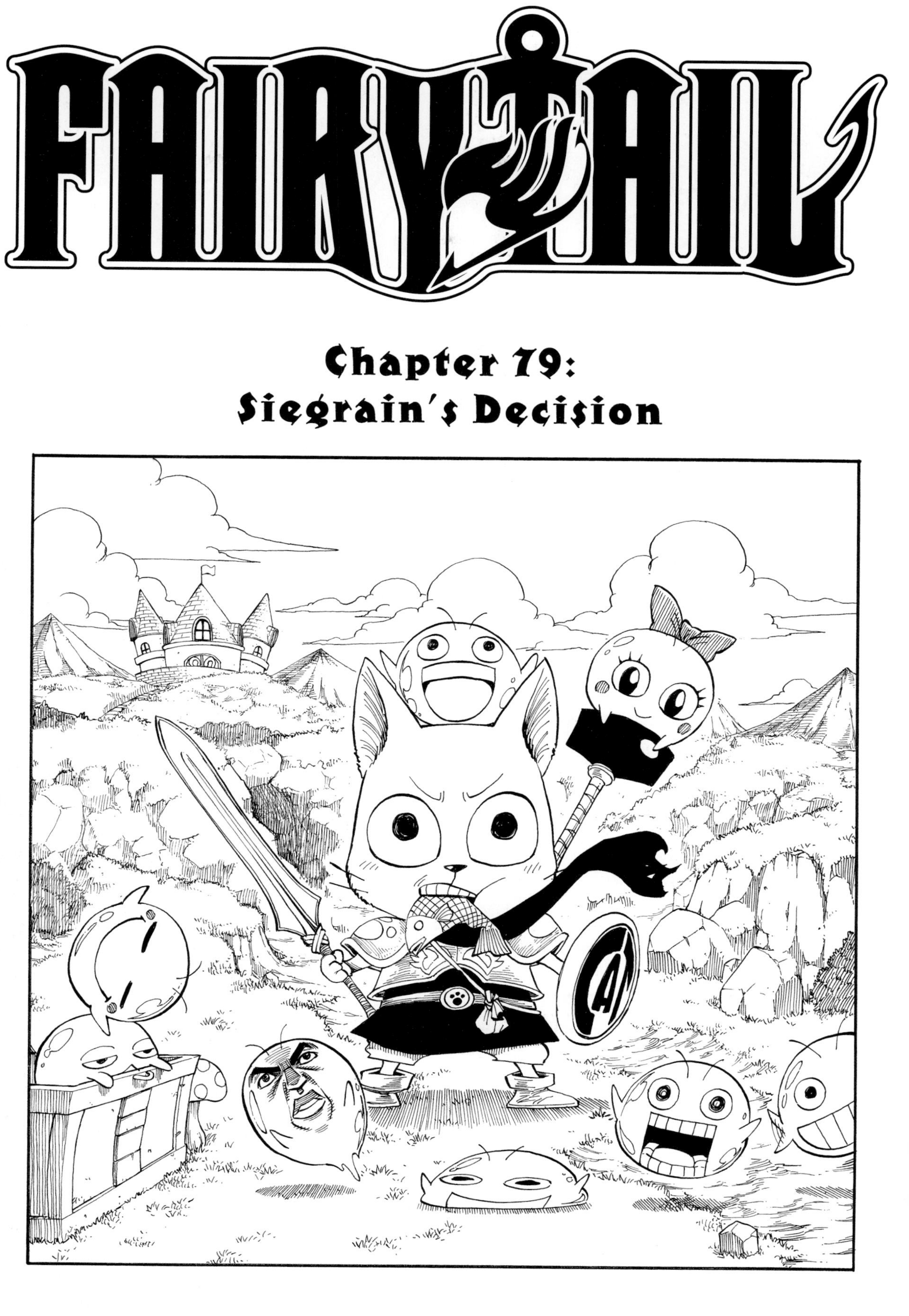

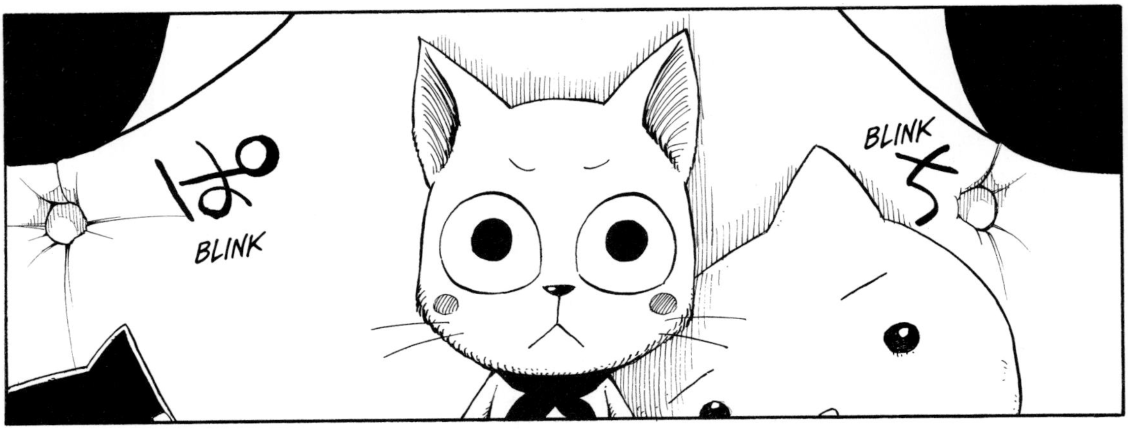
BLINK
ち
ぱ
BLINK

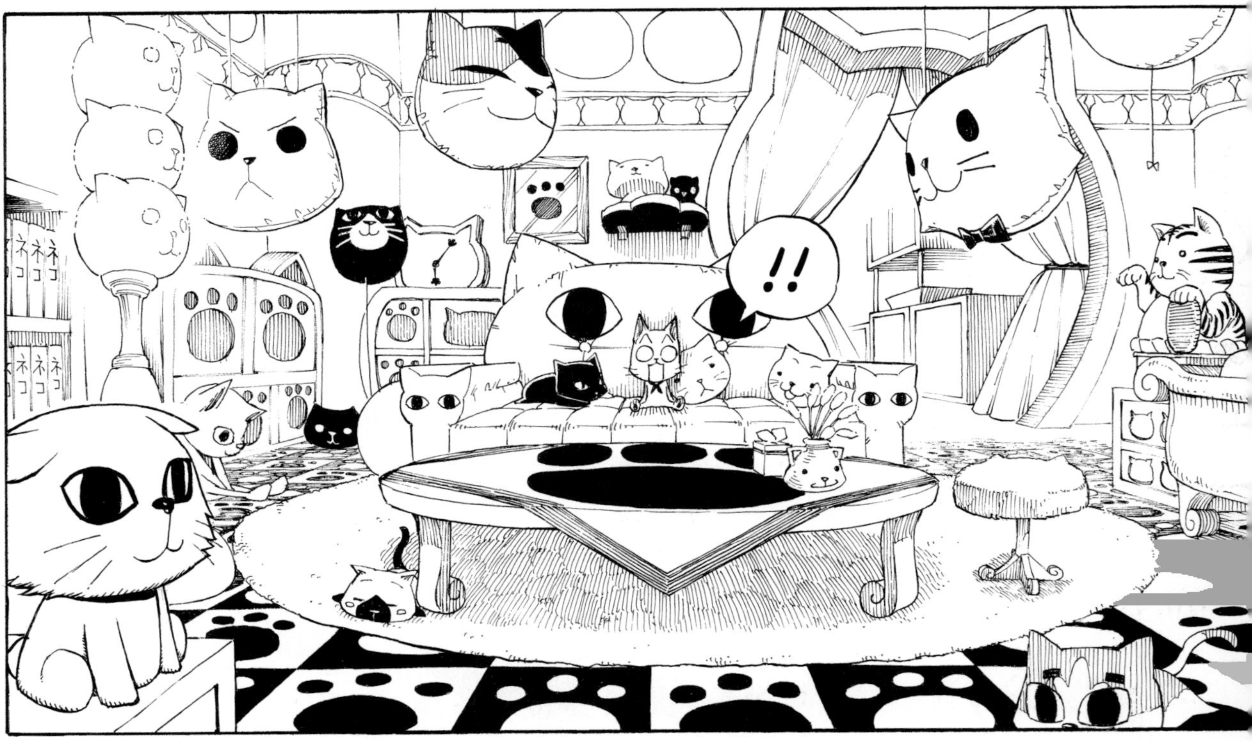
!!

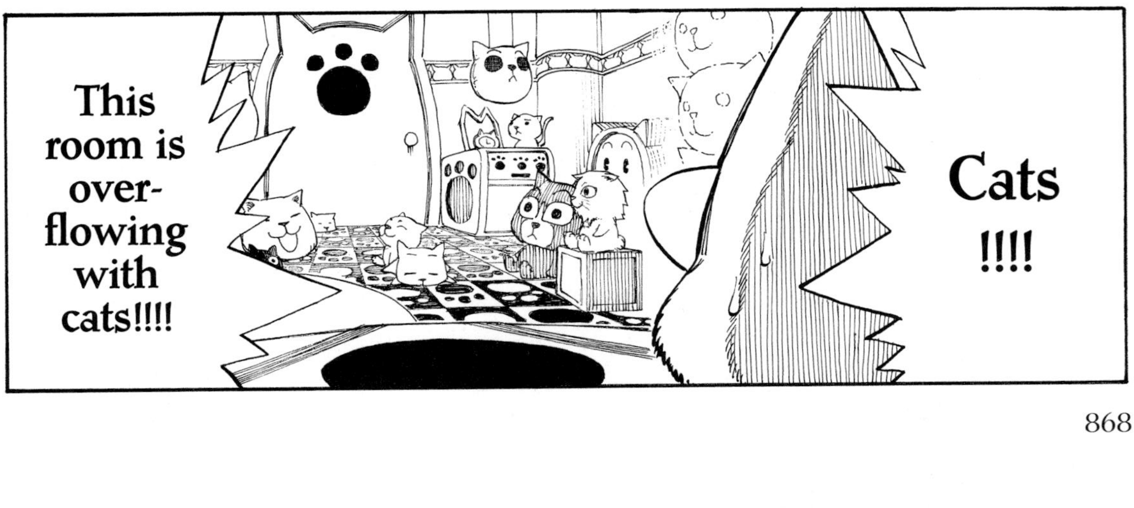
Cats !!!!
This room is over-flowing with cats!!!!

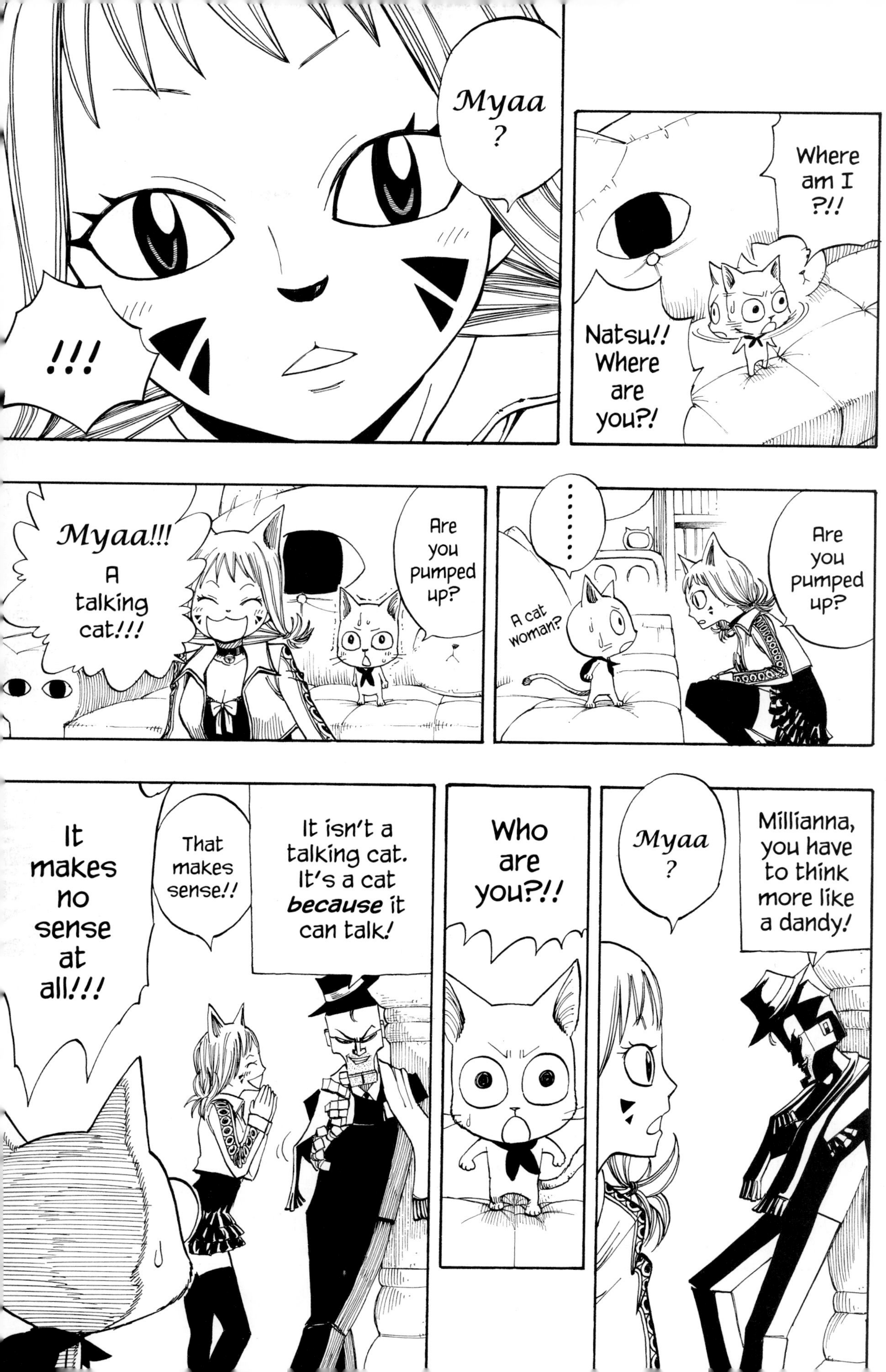
Where am I ?!!
Natsu!! Where are you?!
Myaa ?
!!!
Are you pumped up?
......
A cat woman?
Are you pumped up?
Myaa!!! A talking cat!!!
Millianna, you have to think more like a dandy!
Myaa ?
Who are you?!!
It isn't a talking cat. It's a cat *because* it can talk!
That makes sense!!
It makes no sense at all!!!

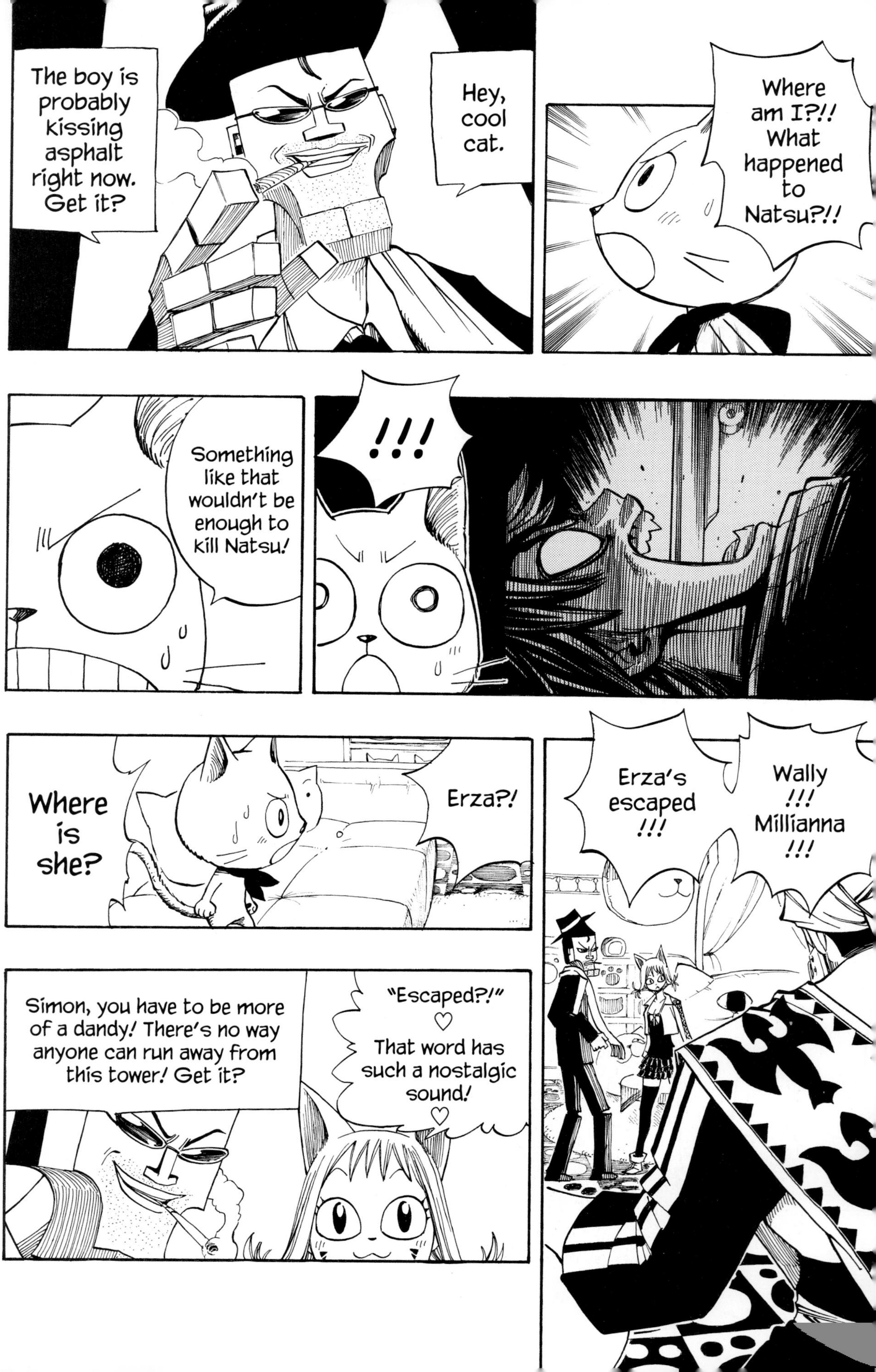
Where am I?!! What happened to Natsu?!!
Hey, cool cat.
The boy is probably kissing asphalt right now. Get it?
!!!
Something like that wouldn't be enough to kill Natsu!
Wally!!! Millianna!!!
Erza's escaped!!!
Erza?!
Where is she?
"Escaped?!" ♡ That word has such a nostalgic sound! ♡
Simon, you have to be more of a dandy! There's no way anyone can run away from this tower! Get it?

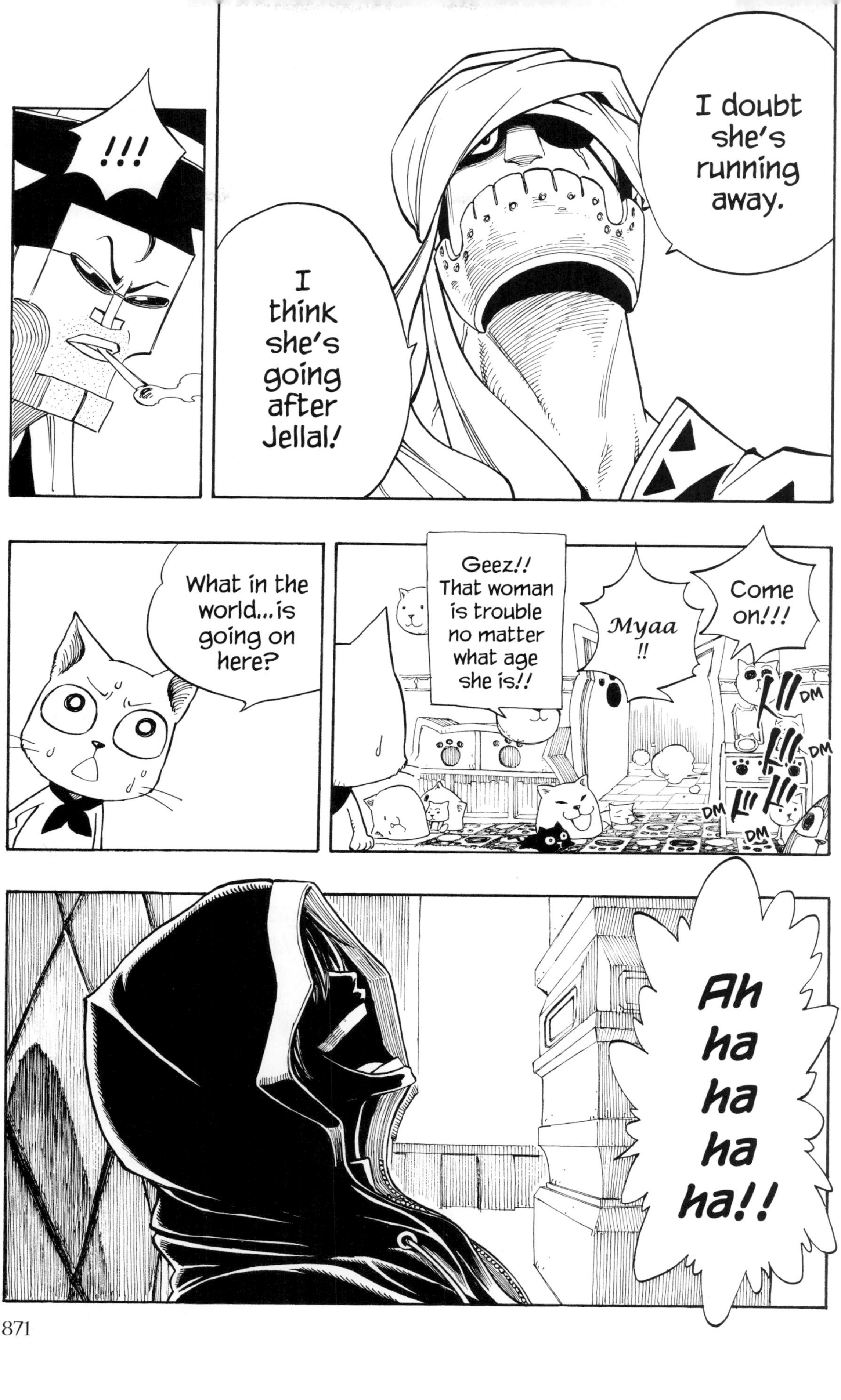

I doubt she's running away.
I think she's going after Jellal!
!!!
Come on!!!
DM
DM
DM
DM
Myaa!!
Geez!! That woman is trouble no matter what age she is!!
What in the world...is going on here?
Ah ha ha ha ha!!

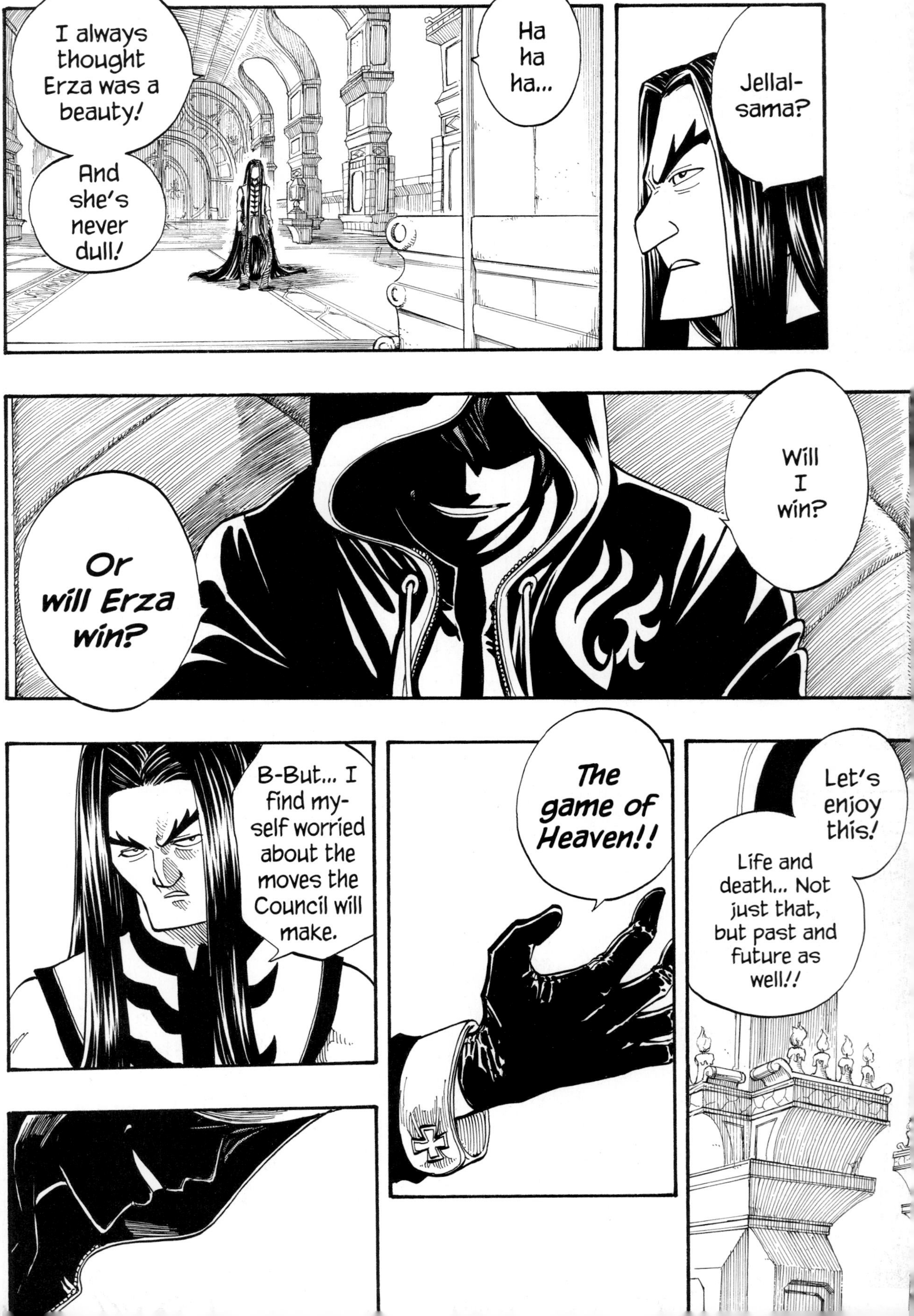
Jellal-sama?
Ha ha ha...
I always thought Erza was a beauty!
And she's never dull!
Will I win?
Or will Erza win?
Let's enjoy this!
Life and death... Not just that, but past and future as well!!
The game of Heaven!!
B-But... I find myself worried about the moves the Council will make.

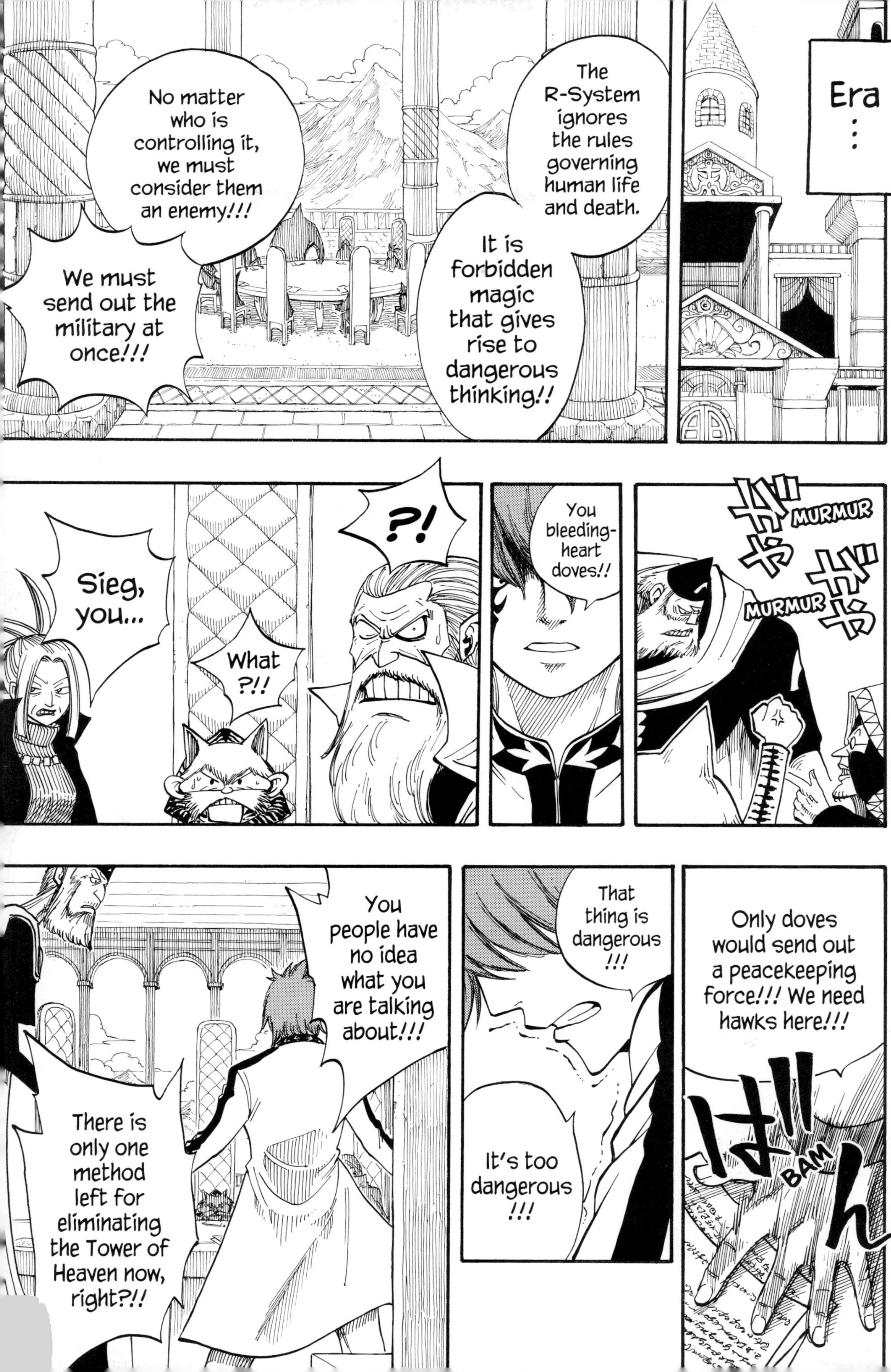
Era...
The R-System ignores the rules governing human life and death.
It is forbidden magic that gives rise to dangerous thinking!!
No matter who is controlling it, we must consider them an enemy!!!
We must send out the military at once!!!
MURMUR
MURMUR
You bleeding-heart doves!!
?!
Sieg, you...
What?!!
Only doves would send out a peacekeeping force!!! We need hawks here!!!
BAM
That thing is dangerous!!!
It's too dangerous!!!
You people have no idea what you are talking about!!!
There is only one method left for eliminating the Tower of Heaven now, right?!!

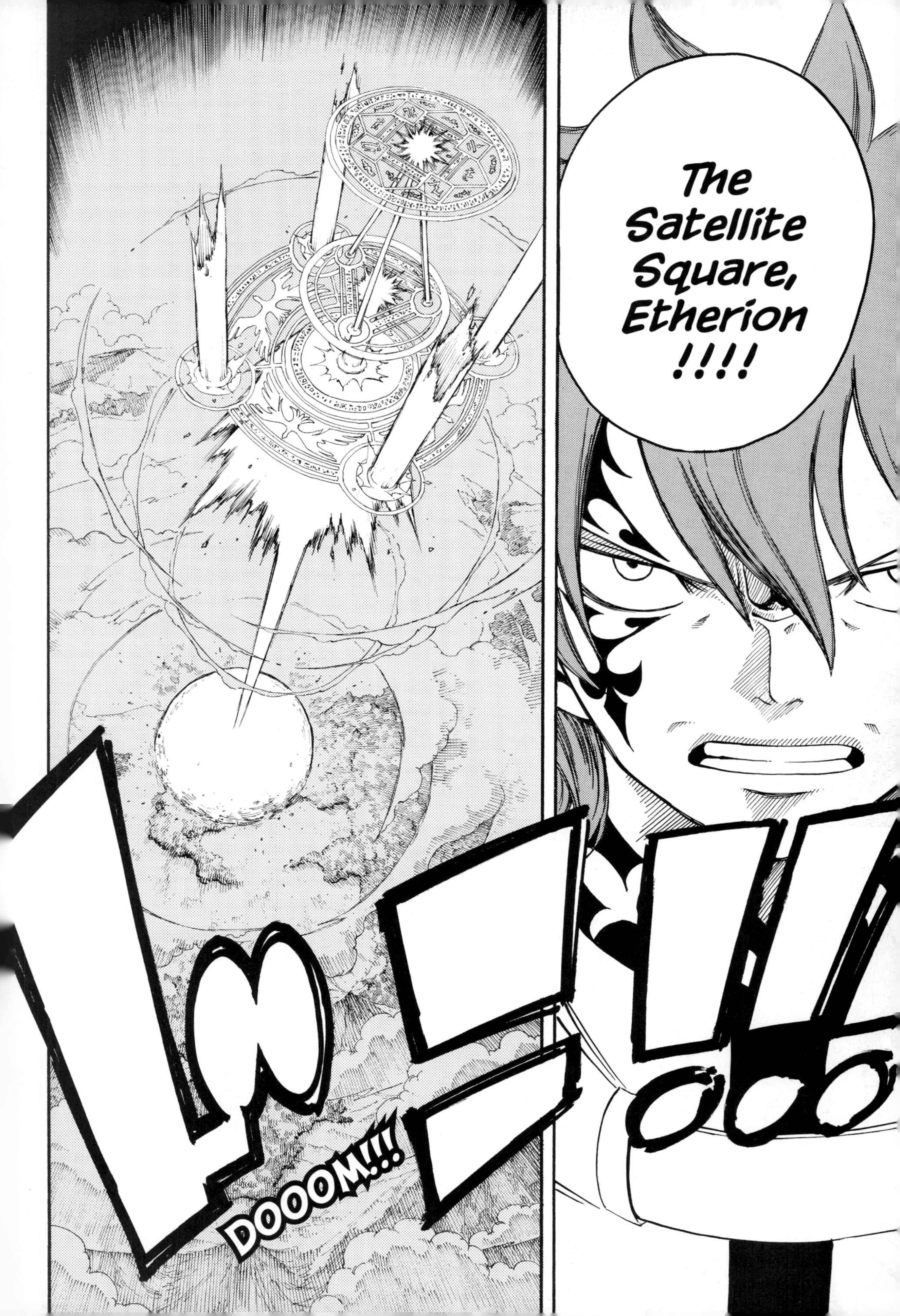
The Satellite Square, Etherion !!!!
DOOOM!!!

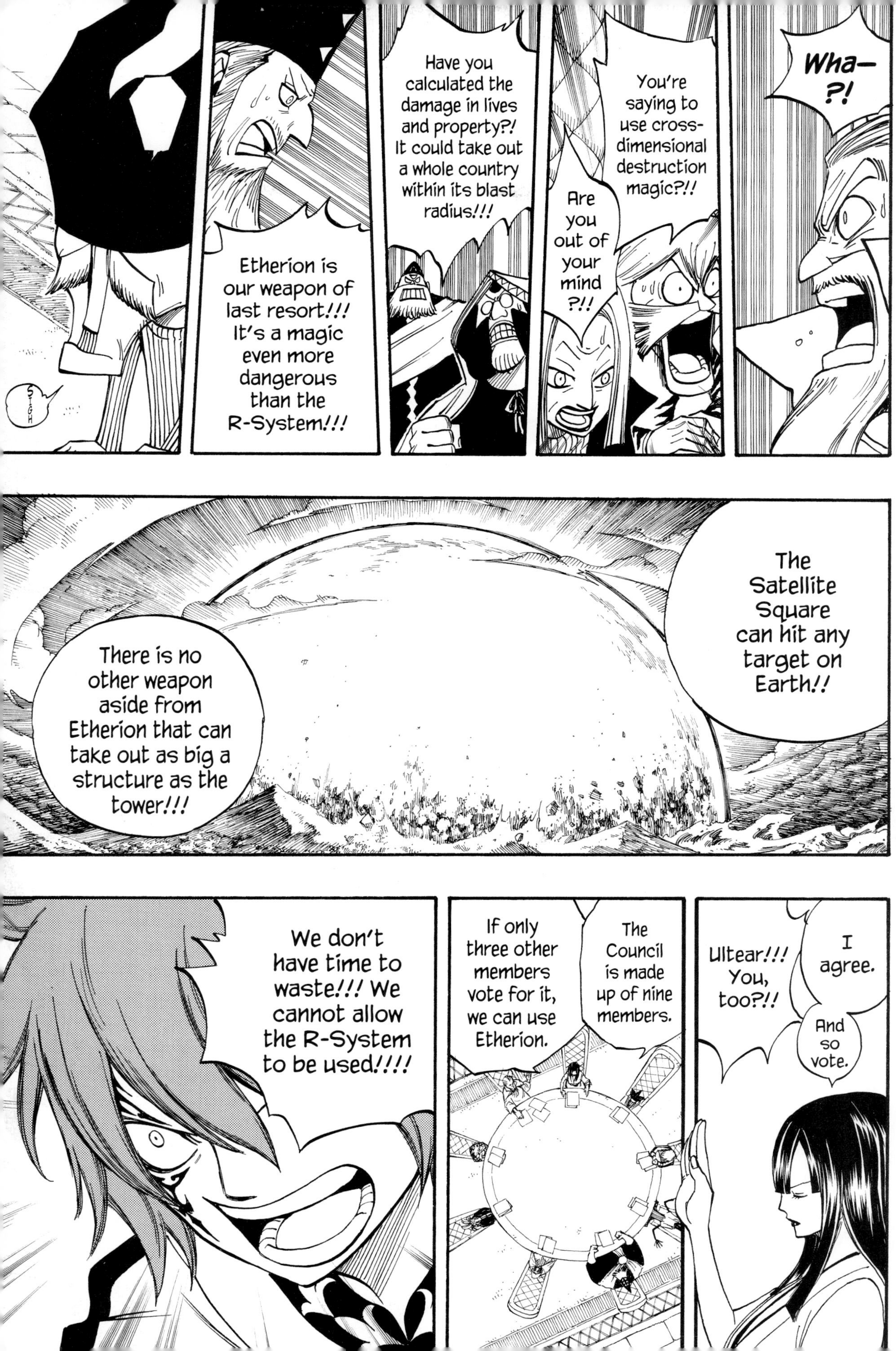
Wha—?!
You're saying to use cross-dimensional destruction magic?!!
Are you out of your mind?!!
Have you calculated the damage in lives and property?! It could take out a whole country within its blast radius!!!
Etherion is our weapon of last resort!!! It's a magic even more dangerous than the R-System!!!
SIGH
The Satellite Square can hit any target on Earth!!
There is no other weapon aside from Etherion that can take out as big a structure as the tower!!!
I agree.
Ultear!!! You, too?!!
And so vote.
The Council is made up of nine members.
If only three other members vote for it, we can use Etherion.
We don't have time to waste!!! We cannot allow the R-System to be used!!!!

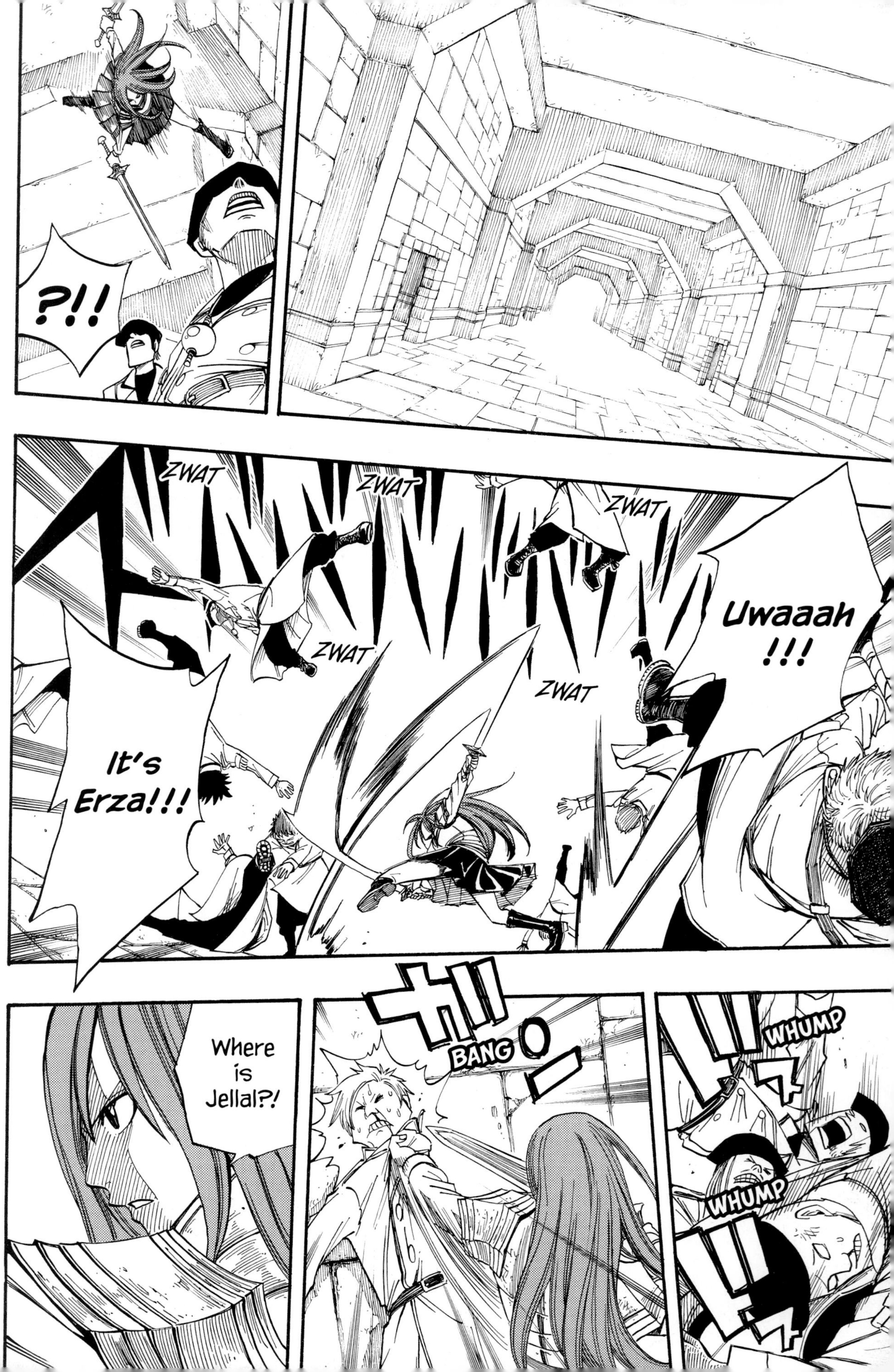
?!!
Uwaaah !!!
ZWAT
ZWAT
ZWAT
ZWAT
ZWAT
It's Erza!!!
WHUMP
WHUMP
BANG
Where is Jellal?!

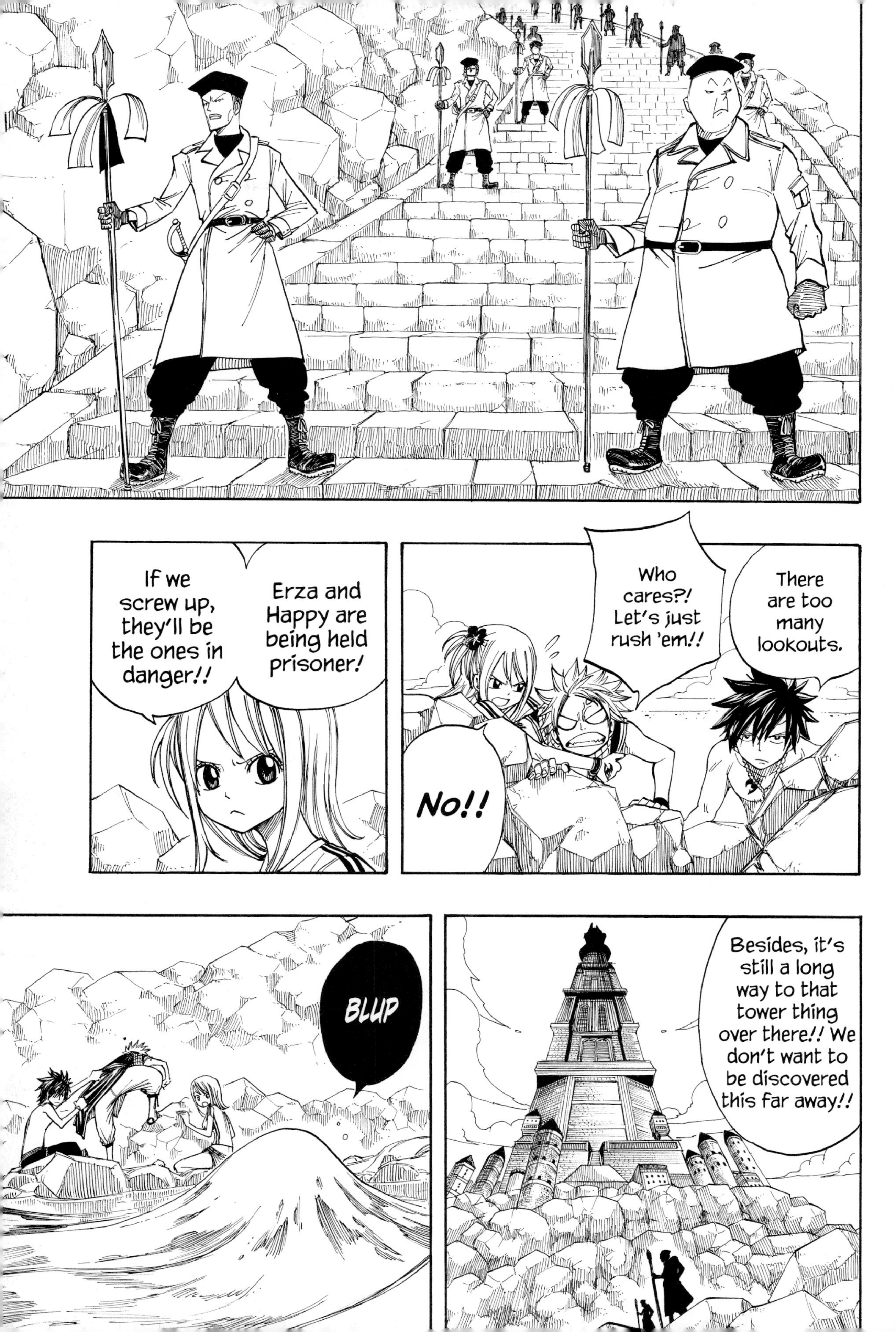
There are too many lookouts.
Who cares?! Let's just rush 'em!!
No!!
Erza and Happy are being held prisoner!
If we screw up, they'll be the ones in danger!!
Besides, it's still a long way to that tower thing over there!! We don't want to be discovered this far away!!
BLUP

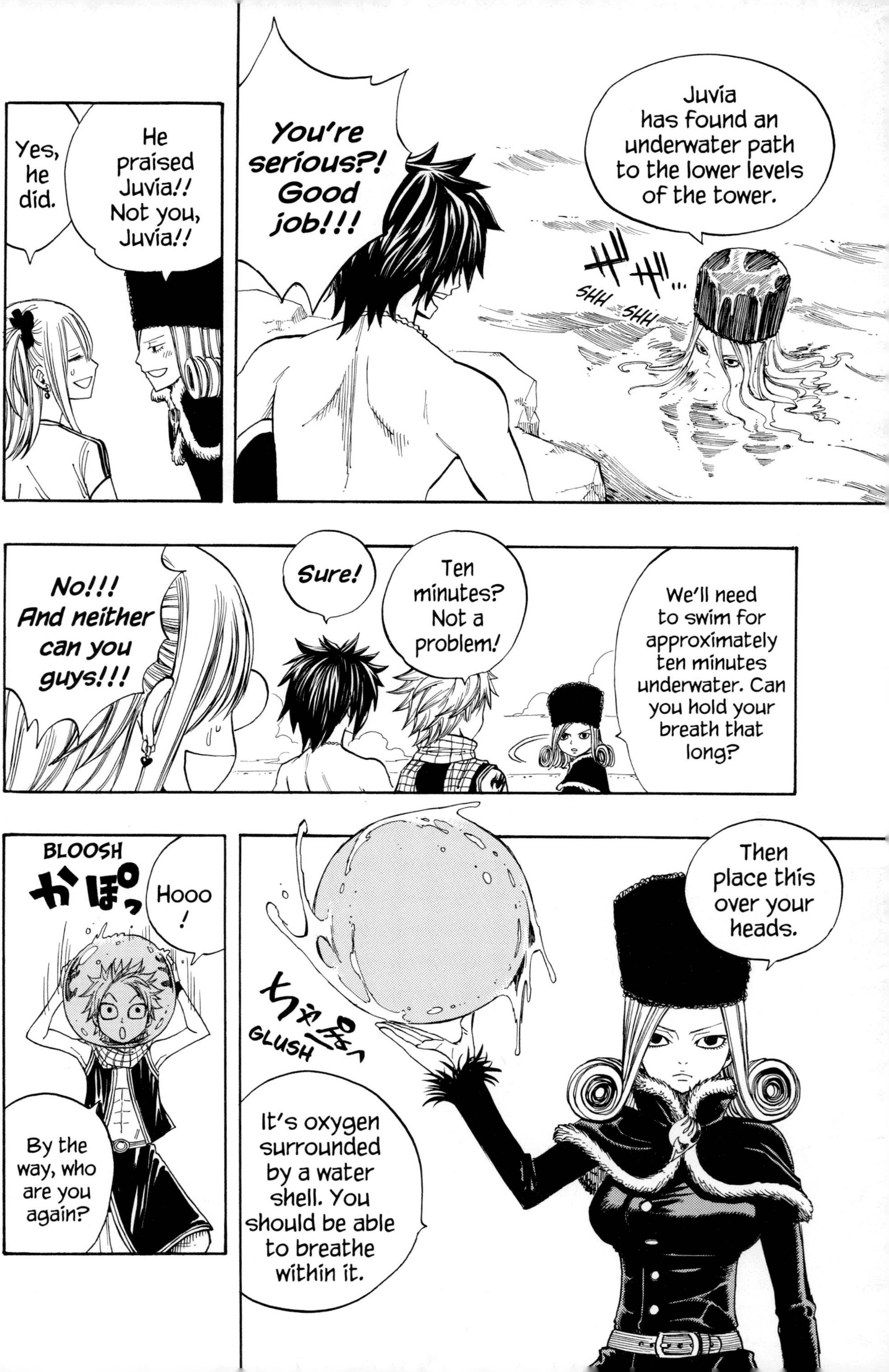
Juvia has found an underwater path to the lower levels of the tower.
SHH SHH
You're serious?! Good job!!!
He praised Juvia!! Not you, Juvia!!
Yes, he did.
We'll need to swim for approximately ten minutes underwater. Can you hold your breath that long?
Ten minutes? Not a problem!
Sure!
No!!! And neither can you guys!!!
Then place this over your heads.
GLUSH
It's oxygen surrounded by a water shell. You should be able to breathe within it.
BLOOSH
かぽっ
Hooo!
By the way, who are you again?

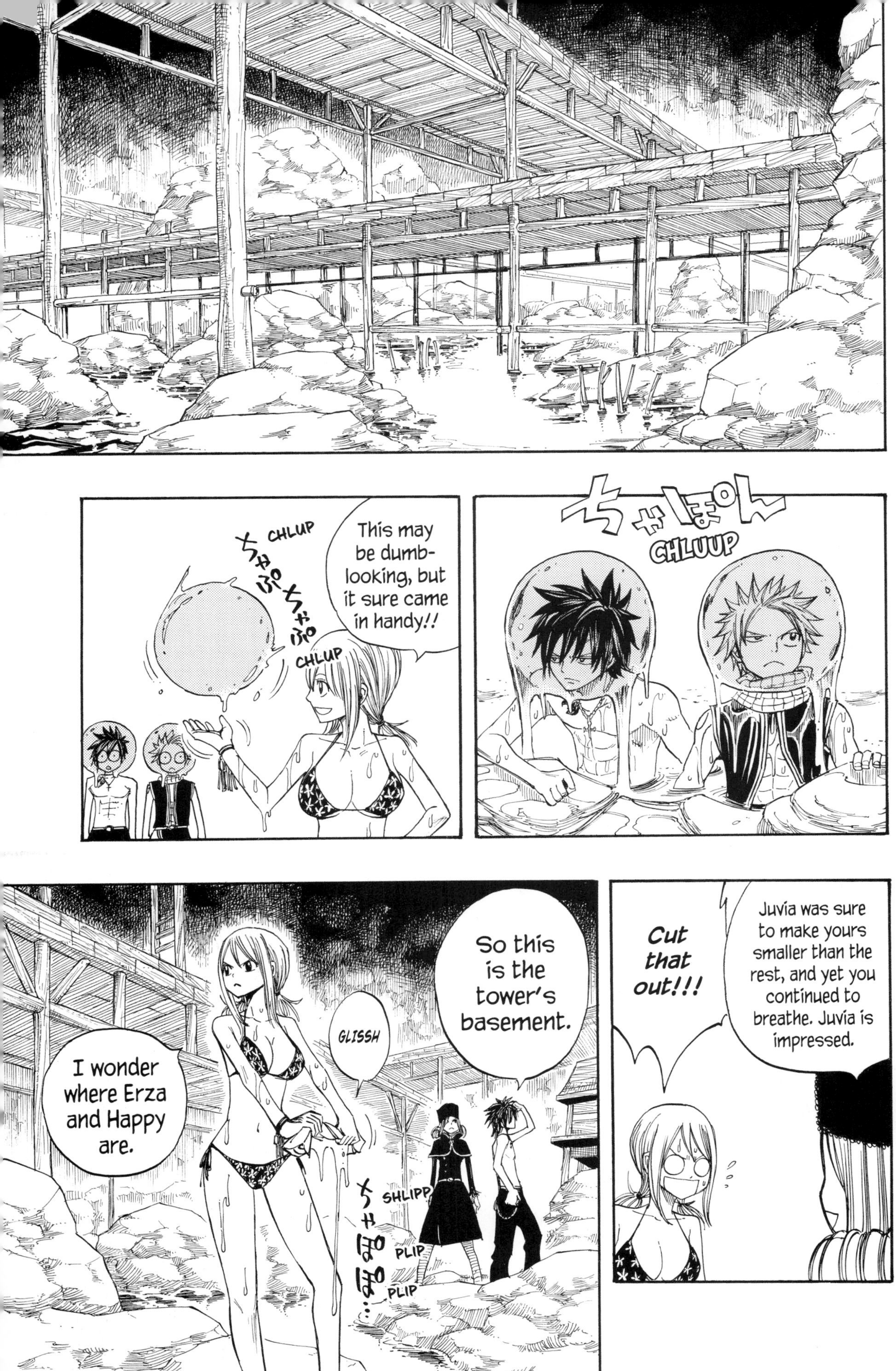

ちゃぽん
CHLUUP
CHLUP
This may be dumb-looking, but it sure came in handy!!
CHLUP
Juvia was sure to make yours smaller than the rest, and yet you continued to breathe. Juvia is impressed.
Cut that out!!!
So this is the tower's basement.
GLISSH
I wonder where Erza and Happy are.
SHLIPP
PLIP
PLIP

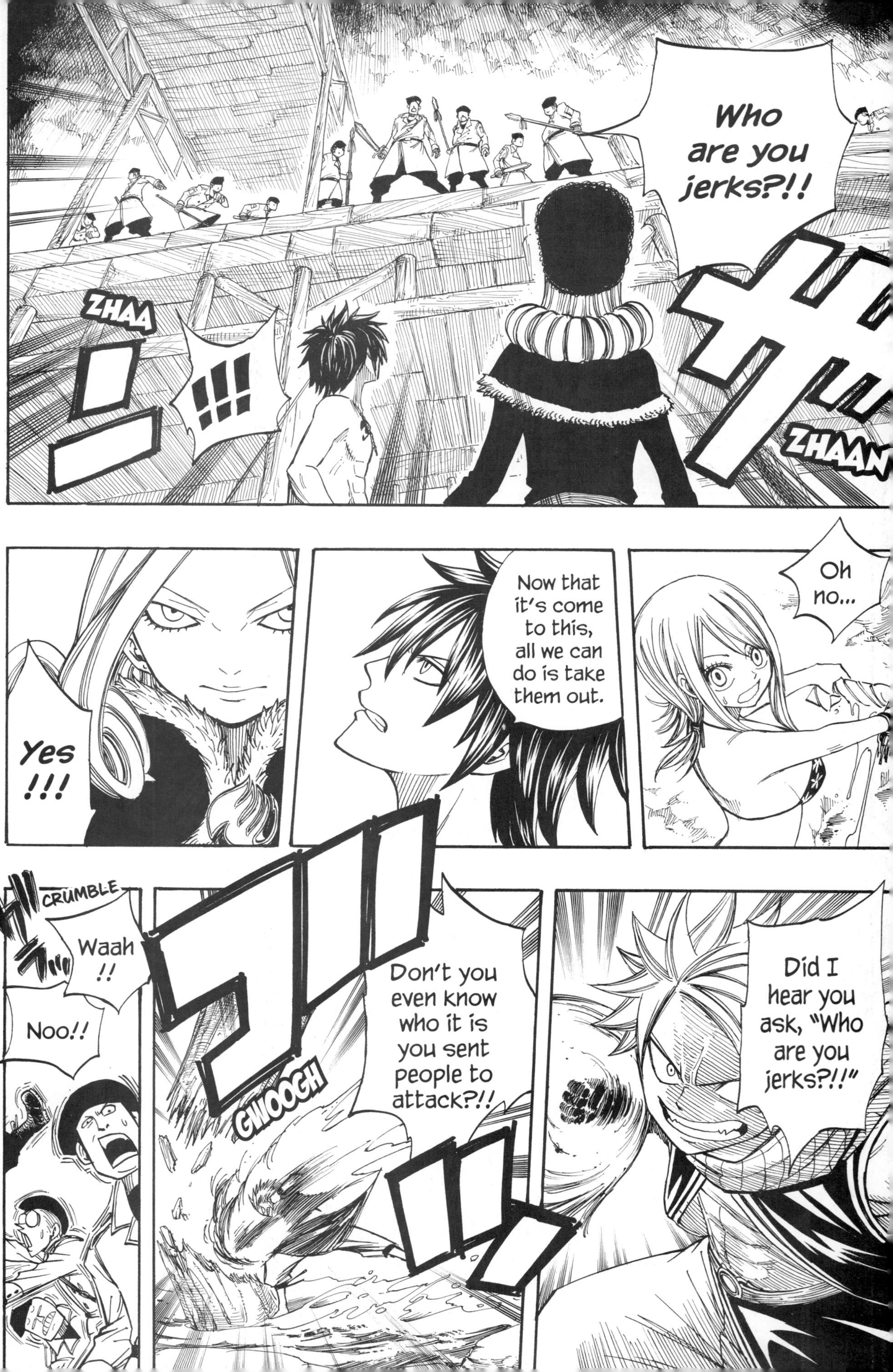
Who are you jerks?!!
ZHAAN
ZHAA
!!!
Oh no...
Now that it's come to this, all we can do is take them out.
Yes!!!
Did I hear you ask, "Who are you jerks?!!"
Don't you even know who it is you sent people to attack?!!
GWOOGH
CRUMBLE
Waah!!
Noo!!

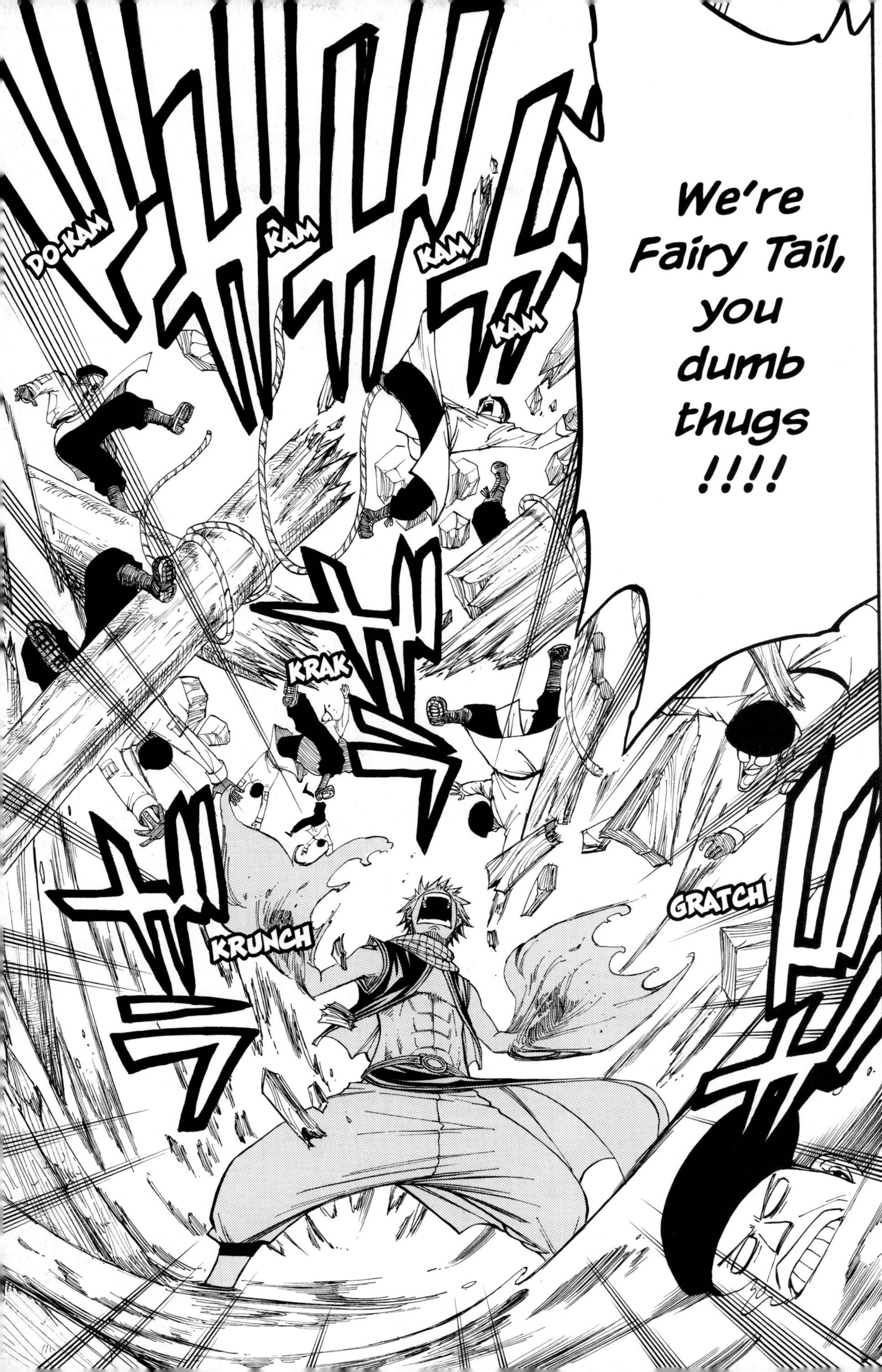
We're Fairy Tail, you dumb thugs!!!!
DO-KAM
KAM
KAM
KAM
KRAK
GRATCH
KRUNCH

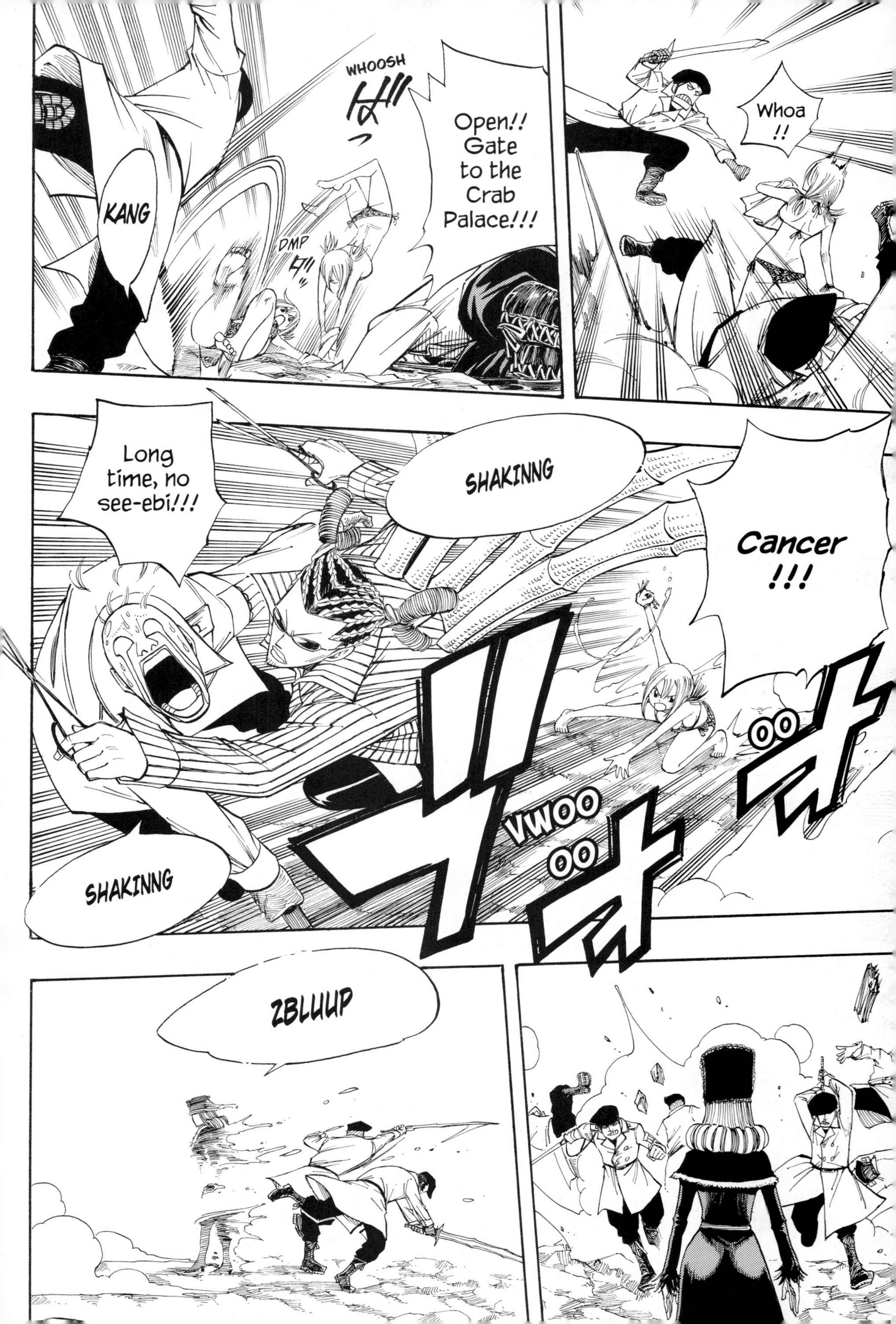
Whoa !!
Open!! Gate to the Crab Palace!!!
WHOOSH
DMP
KANG
Cancer !!!
SHAKINNG
Long time, no see-ebi!!!
VWOOOO
SHAKINNG
ZBLUUP

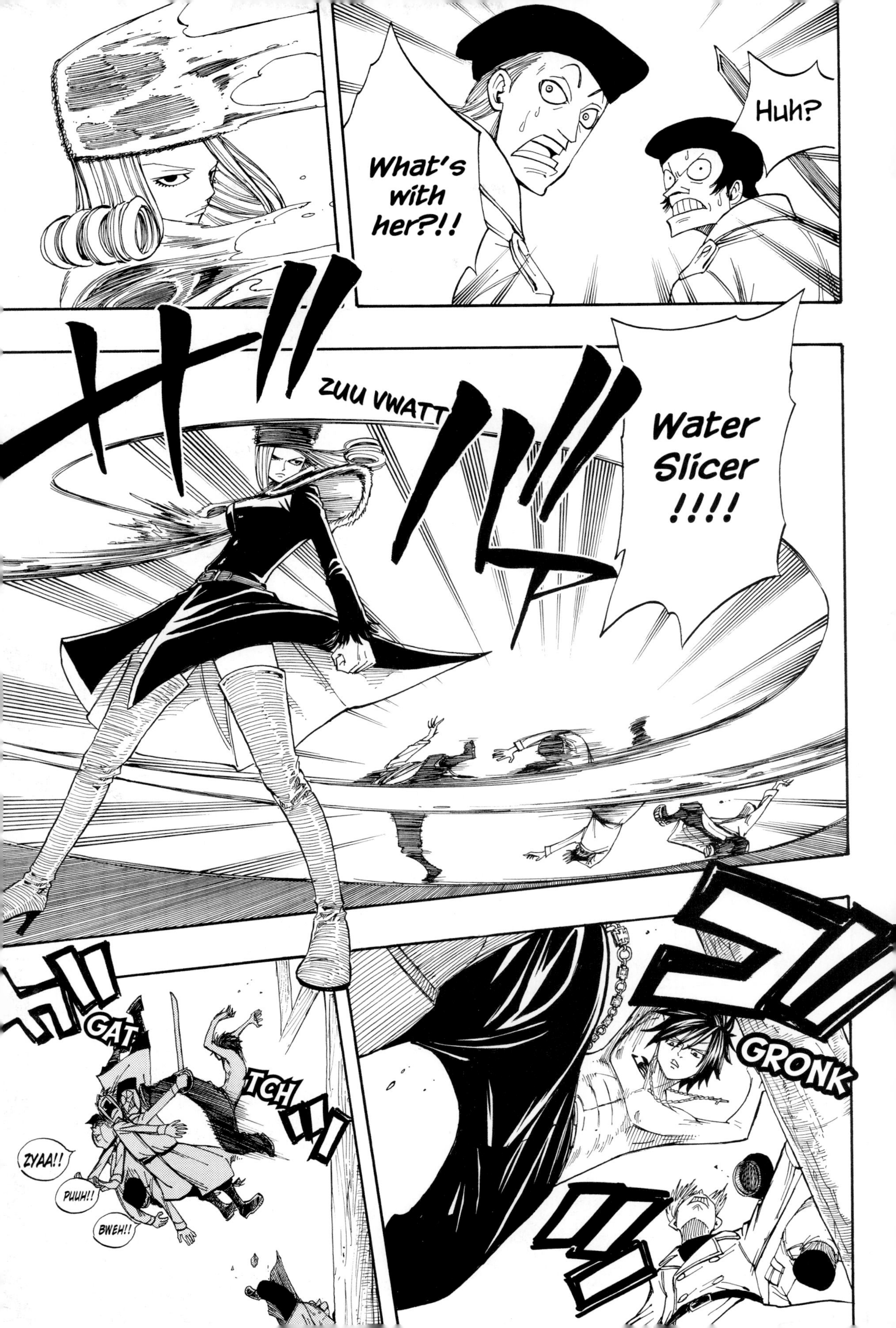
Huh?
What's with her?!!
Water Slicer !!!!
ZUU VWATT
GRONK
GAT TCH
ZYAA!!
PUUH!!
BWEH!!

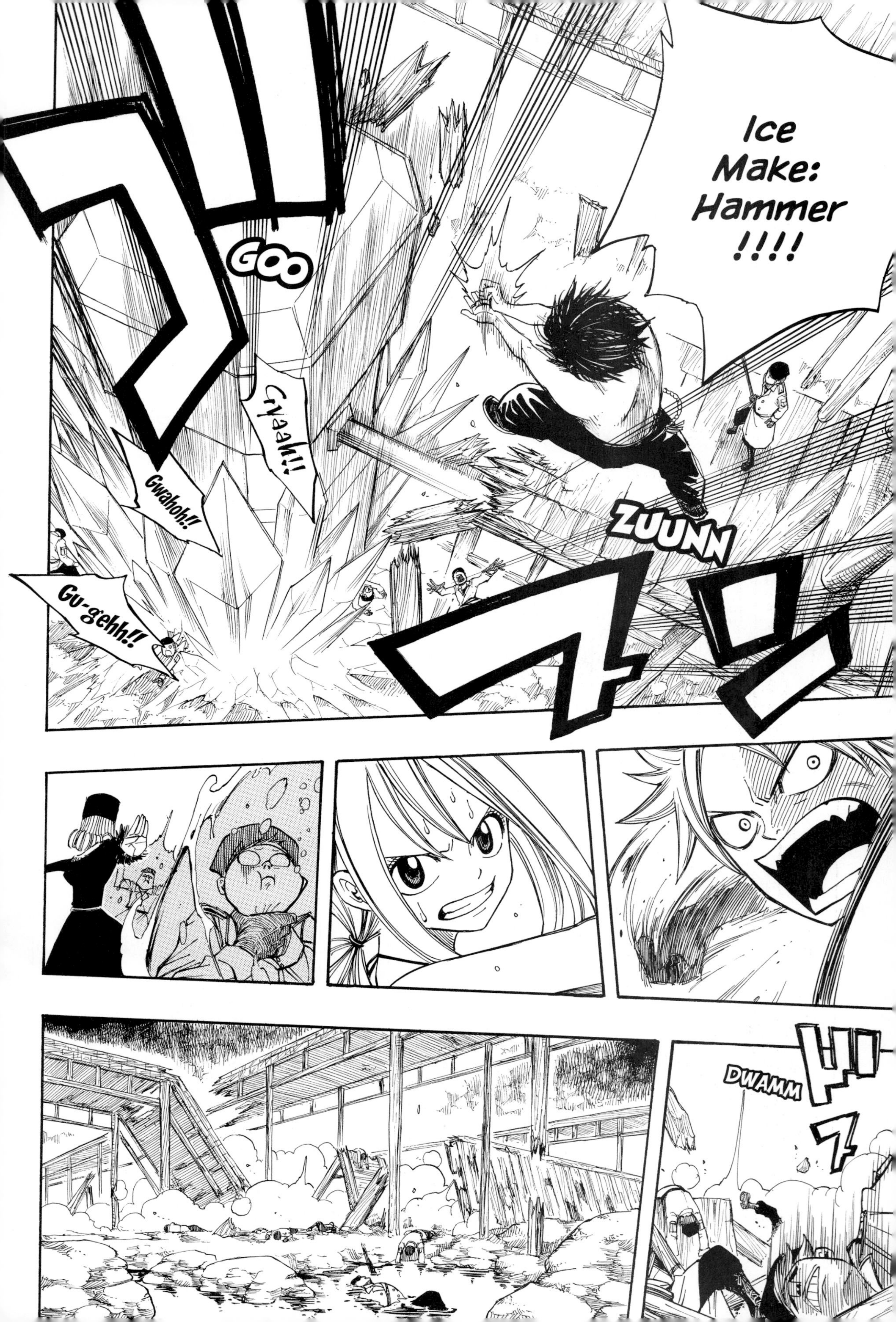
Ice Make: Hammer !!!!
GOO
Gwaah!!
ZUUNN
Gwahoh!!
Gu-gehh!!
DWAMM

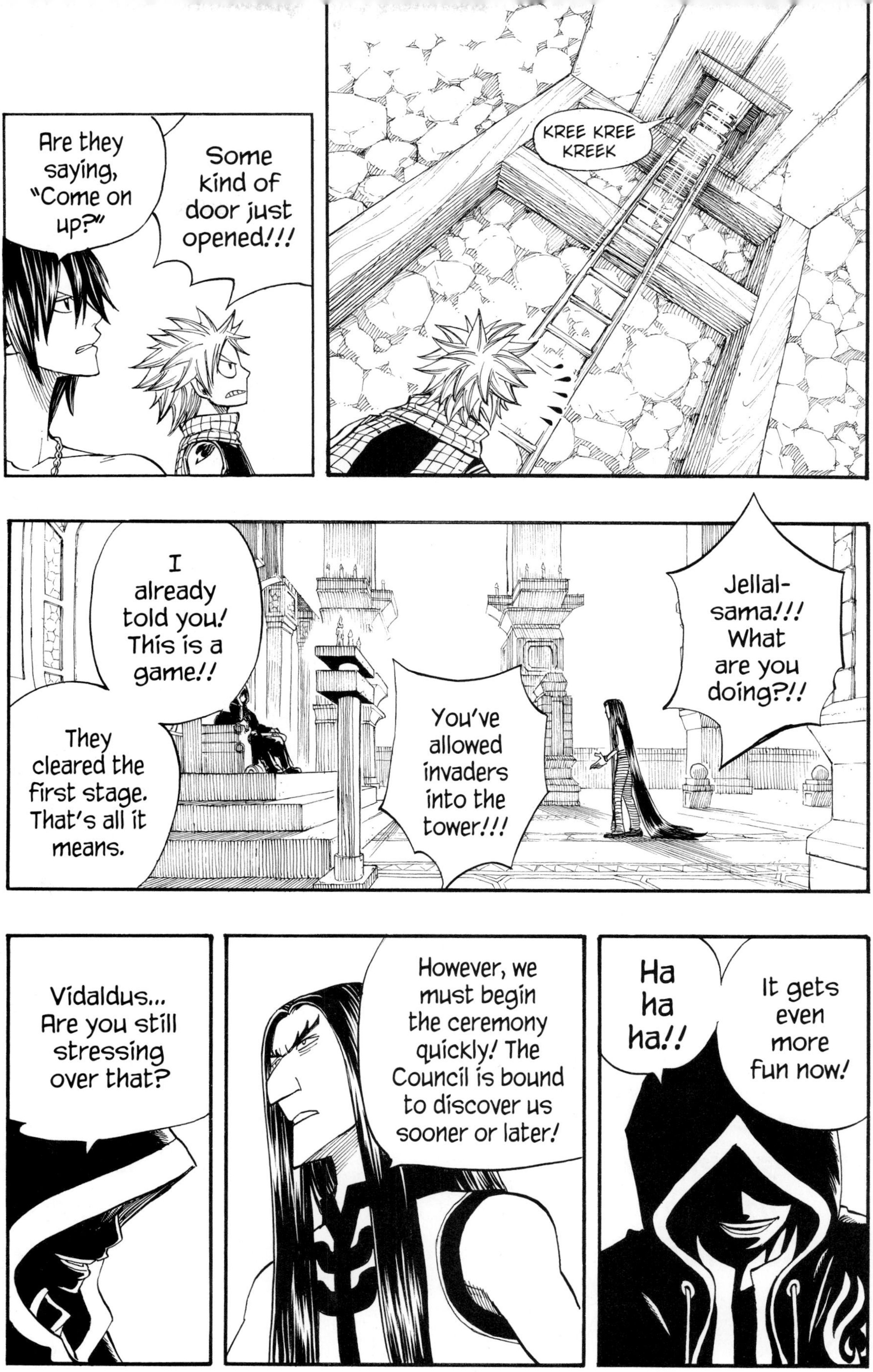
KREE KREE KREEK
Some kind of door just opened!!!
Are they saying, "Come on up?"
Jellal-sama!!! What are you doing?!!
You've allowed invaders into the tower!!!
I already told you! This is a game!!
They cleared the first stage. That's all it means.
Ha ha ha!!
It gets even more fun now!
However, we must begin the ceremony quickly! The Council is bound to discover us sooner or later!
Vidaldus... Are you still stressing over that?

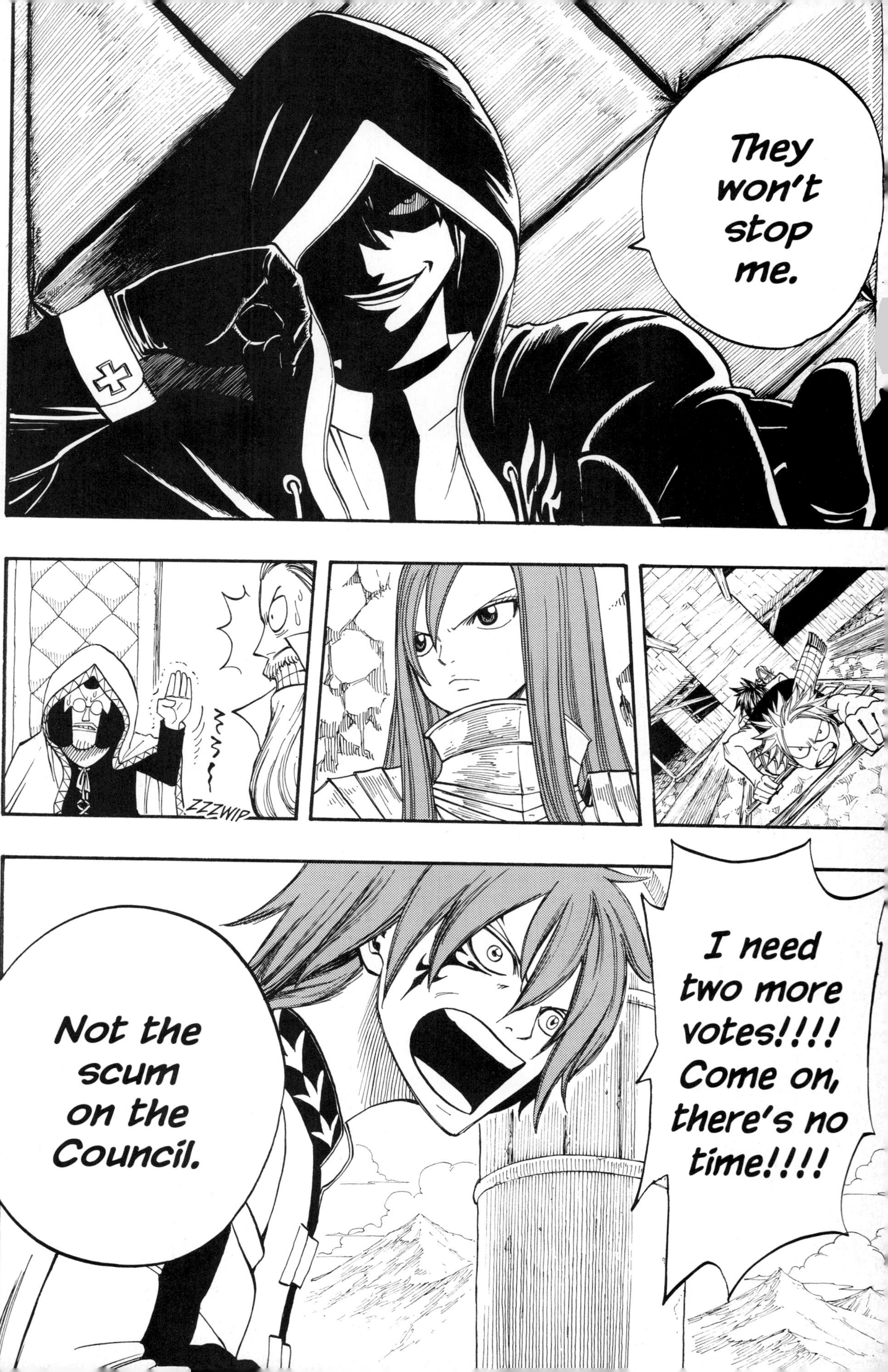
They won't stop me.
ZZZWIP
I need two more votes!!!! Come on, there's no time!!!!
Not the scum on the Council.

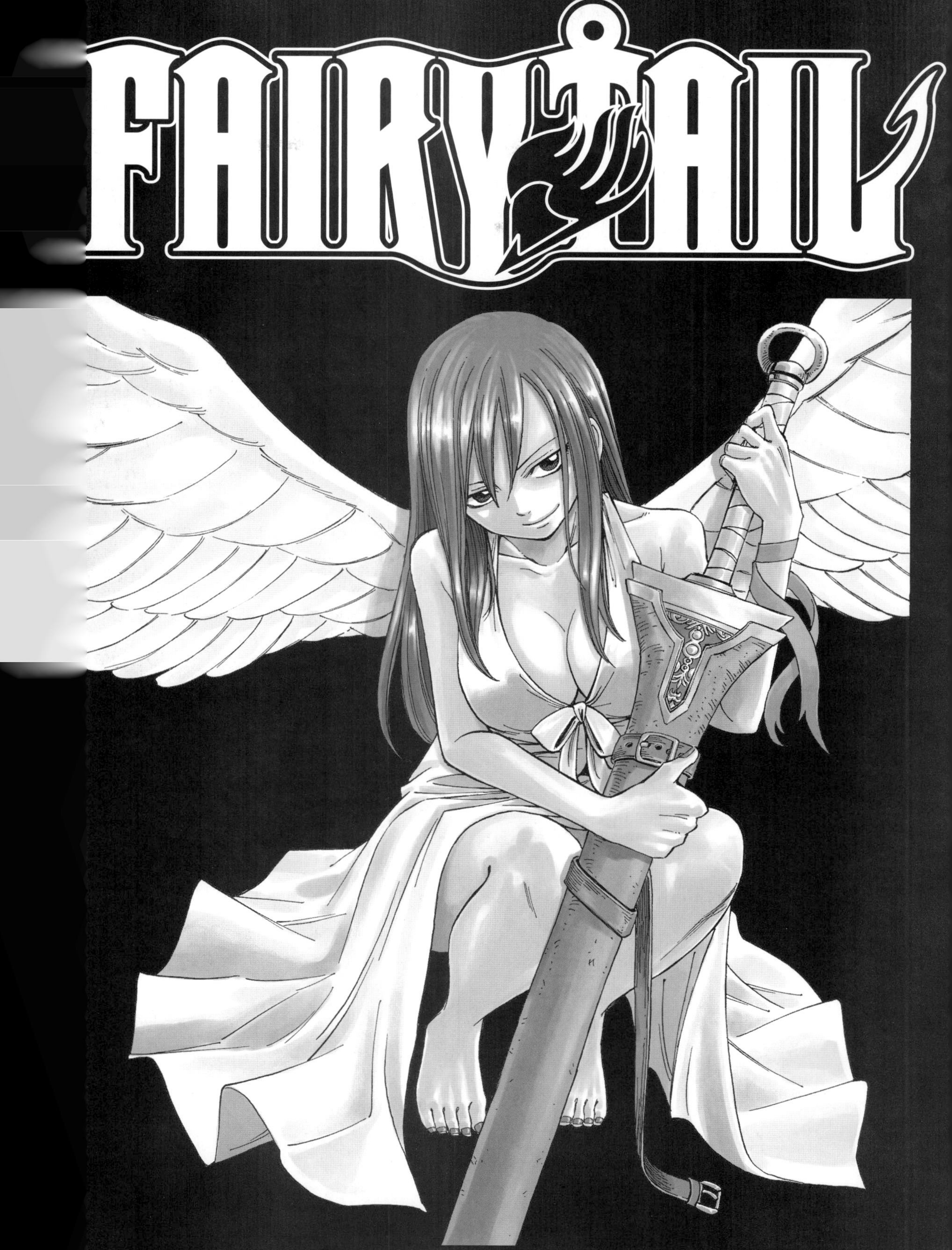
FAIRY TAIL

Chapter 80: Joan of Arc

FAIRY TAIL

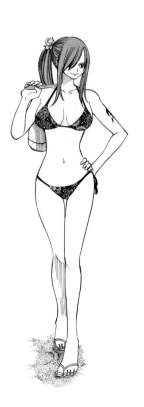

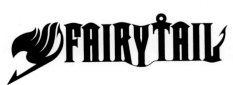

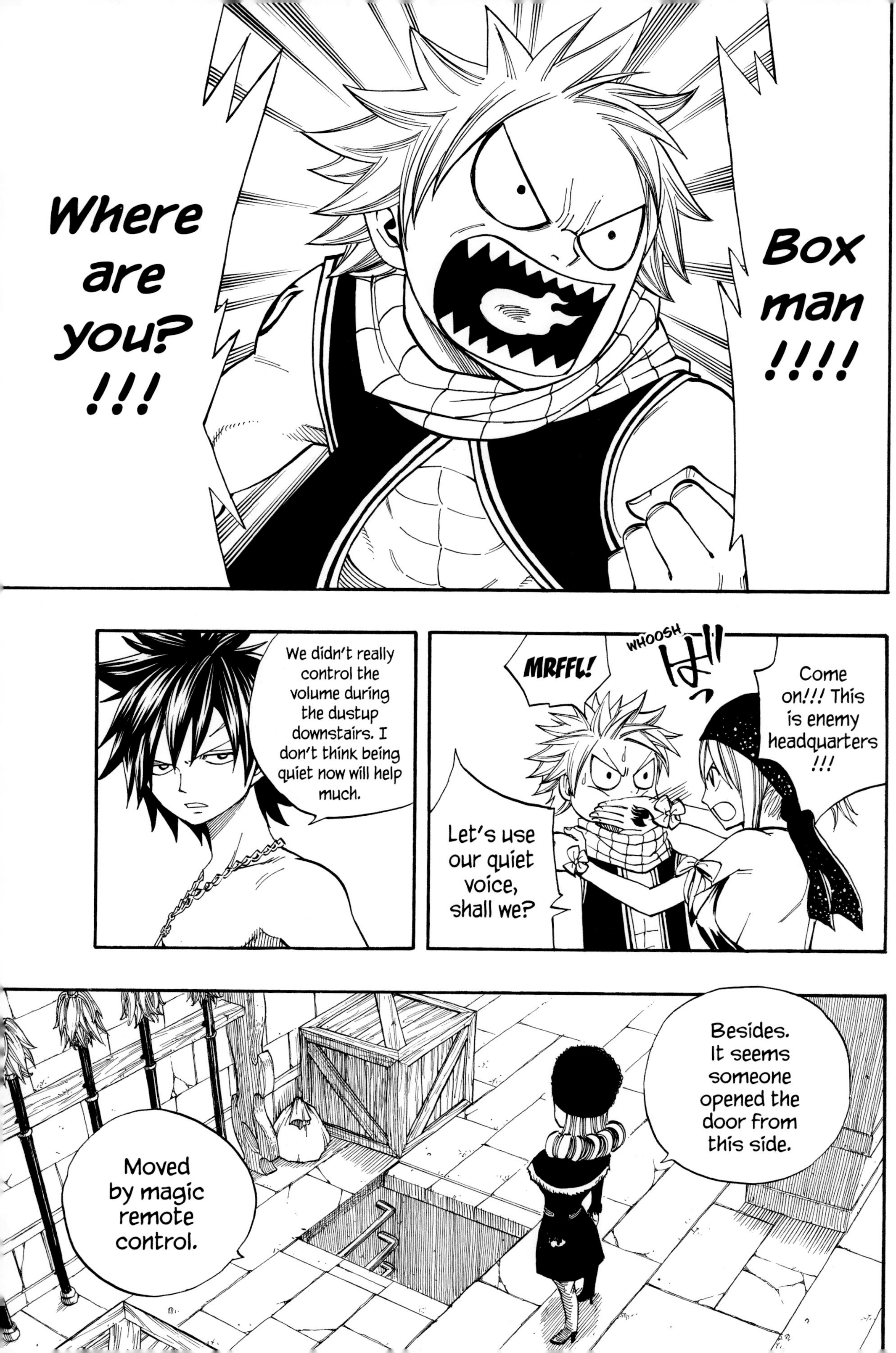
Box man!!!!
Where are you?!!!
Come on!!! This is enemy headquarters!!!
WHOOSH
MRFFL!
Let's use our quiet voice, shall we?
We didn't really control the volume during the dustup downstairs. I don't think being quiet now will help much.
Besides. It seems someone opened the door from this side.
Moved by magic remote control.

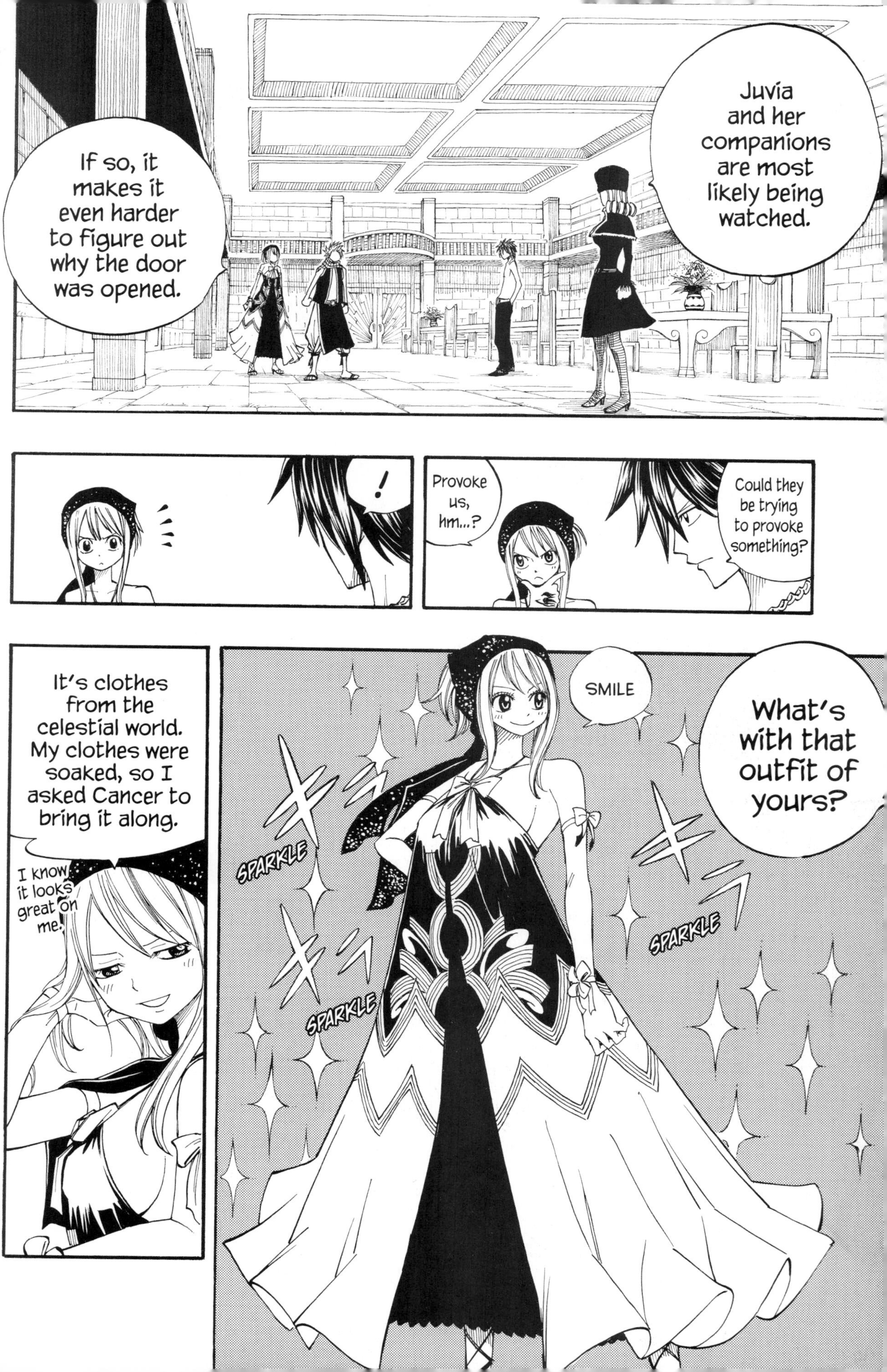
Juvia and her companions are most likely being watched.
If so, it makes it even harder to figure out why the door was opened.
Could they be trying to provoke something?
Provoke us, hm...?
!
What's with that outfit of yours?
SMILE
SPARKLE
SPARKLE
SPARKLE
It's clothes from the celestial world. My clothes were soaked, so I asked Cancer to bring it along.
I know it looks great on me.

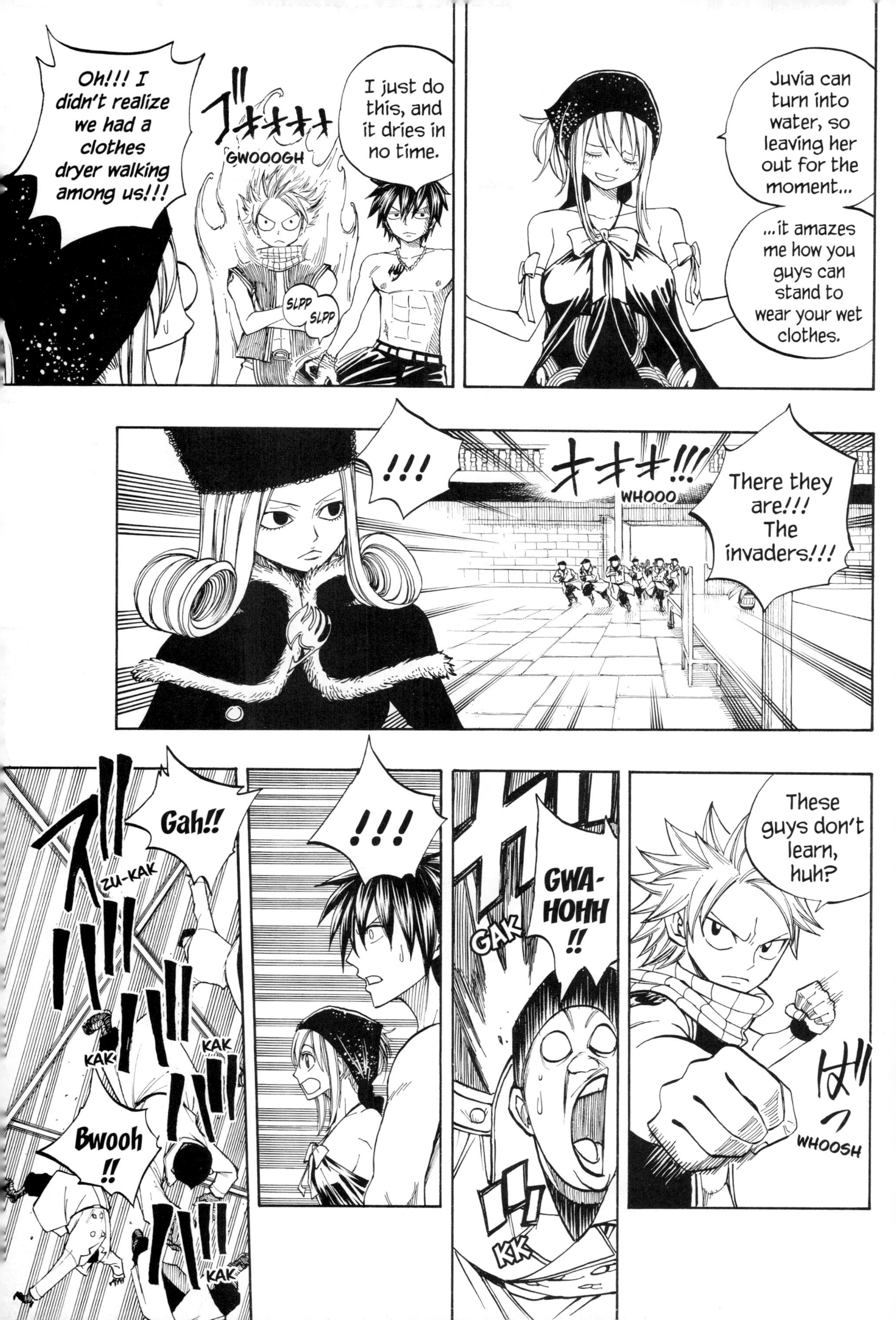
Juvia can turn into water, so leaving her out for the moment...
...it amazes me how you guys can stand to wear your wet clothes.
I just do this, and it dries in no time.
ゴオオオオ
GWOOOGH
SLPP
SLPP
Oh!!! I didn't realize we had a clothes dryer walking among us!!!
There they are!!! The invaders!!!
オオオ!!!
WHOOO
!!!
These guys don't learn, huh?
はっ
WHOOSH
GWA-HOHH!!
GAK
KK
!!!
Gah!!
ZU-KAK
KAK
KAK
Bwooh!!
KAK

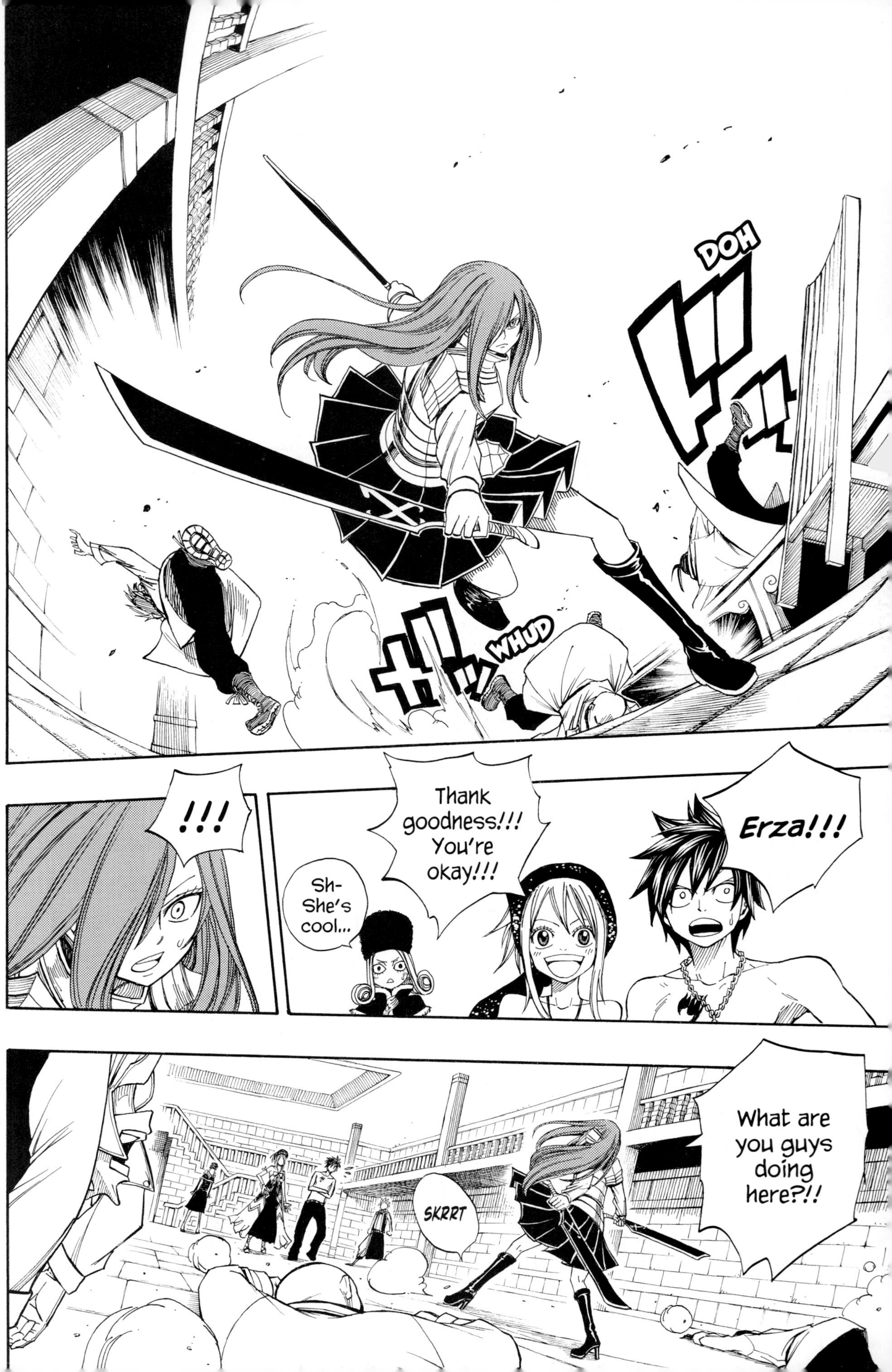
DOH
WHUD
Erza!!!
Thank goodness!!! You're okay!!!
Sh-She's cool...
!!!
What are you guys doing here?!!
SKRRT

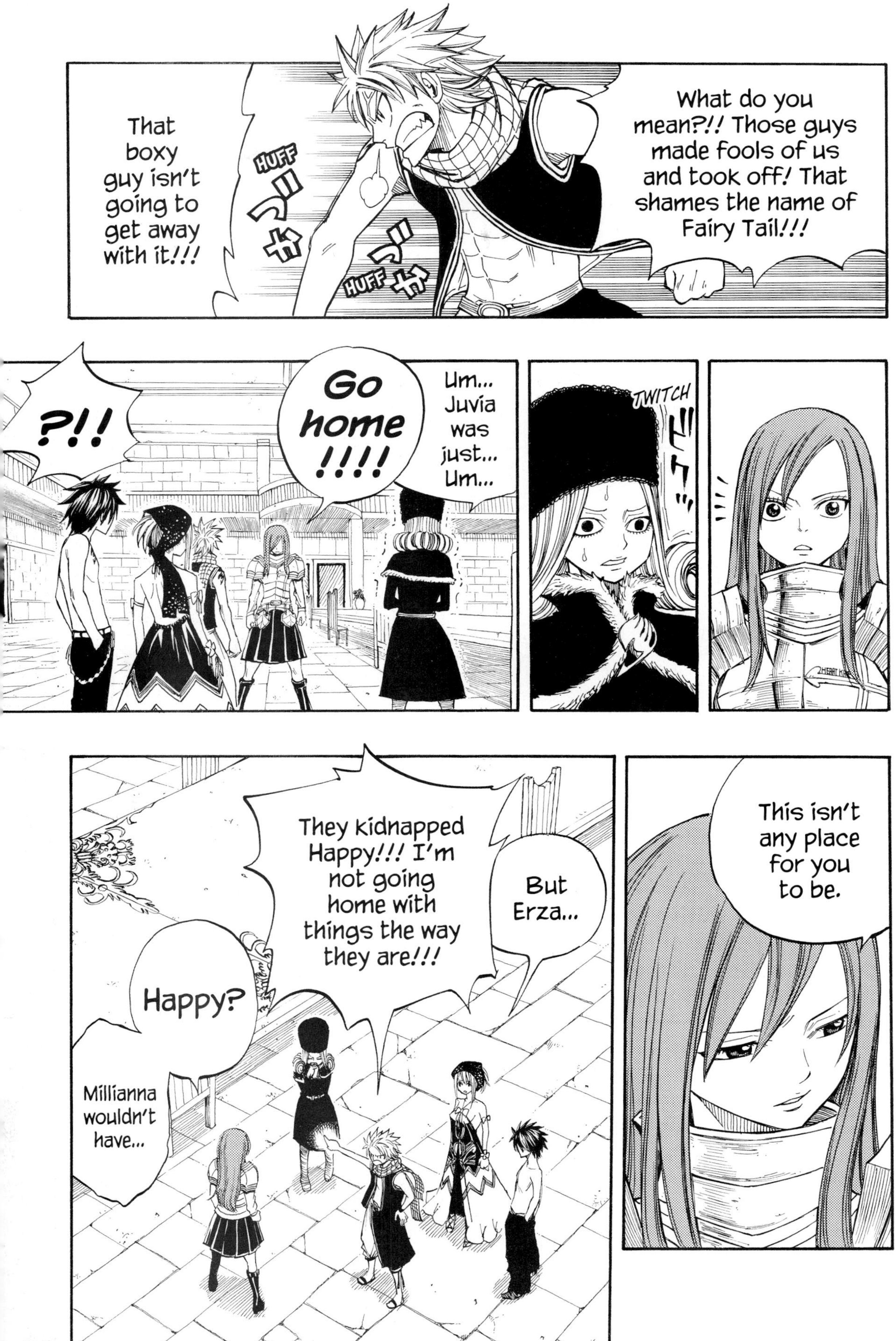

What do you mean?!! Those guys made fools of us and took off! That shames the name of Fairy Tail!!!
That boxy guy isn't going to get away with it!!!
HUFF
HUFF
TWITCH
Um... Juvia was just... Um...
Go home!!!!
?!!
This isn't any place for you to be.
But Erza...
They kidnapped Happy!!! I'm not going home with things the way they are!!!
Happy?
Millianna wouldn't have...

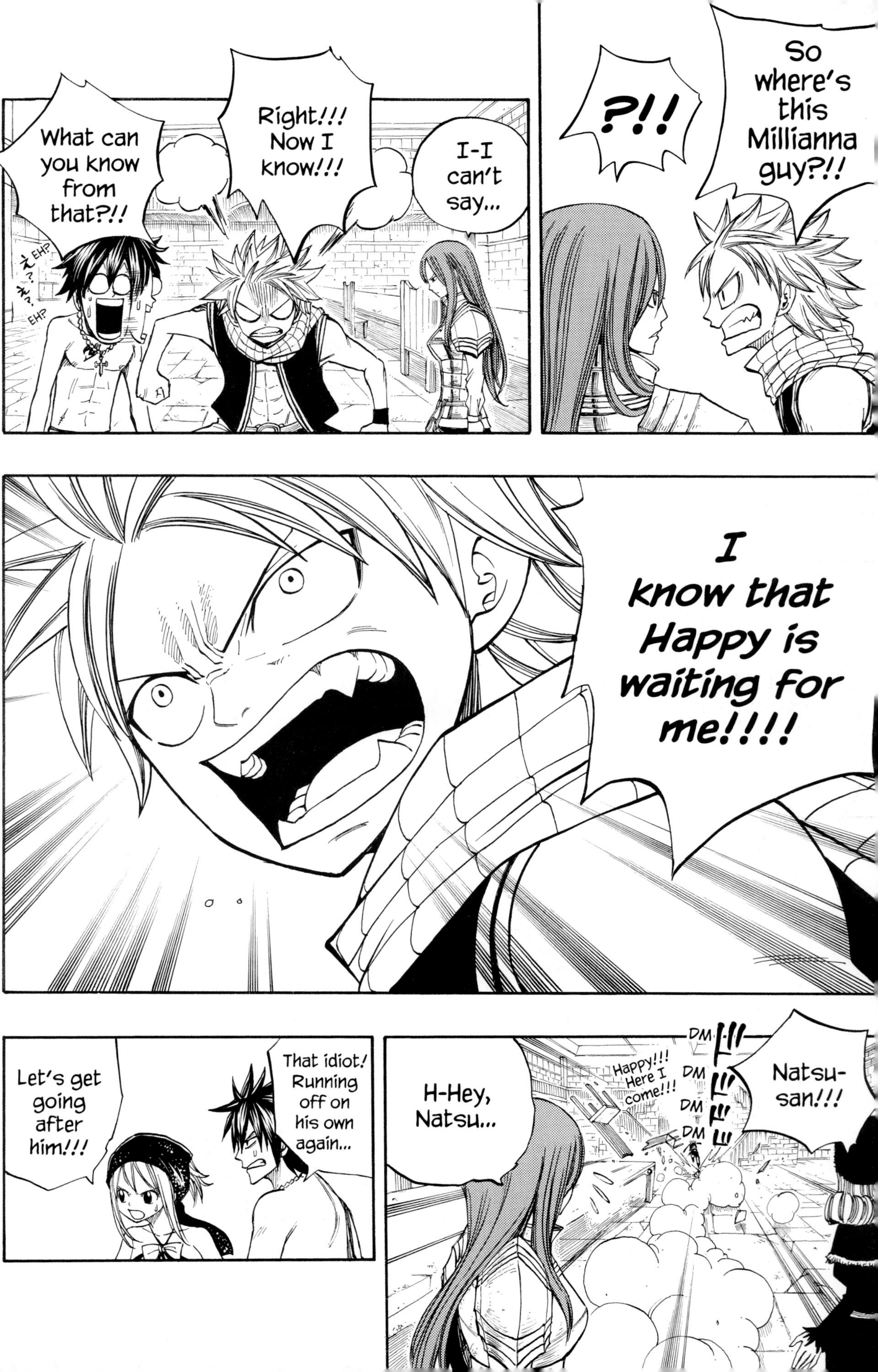
So where's this Millianna guy?!!
?!!
I-I can't say...
Right!!! Now I know!!!
What can you know from that?!!
え EH? え EH?
I know that Happy is waiting for me!!!!
Natsu-san!!!
DM DM DM DM
Happy!!! Here I come!!!
H-Hey, Natsu...
That idiot! Running off on his own again...
Let's get going after him!!!

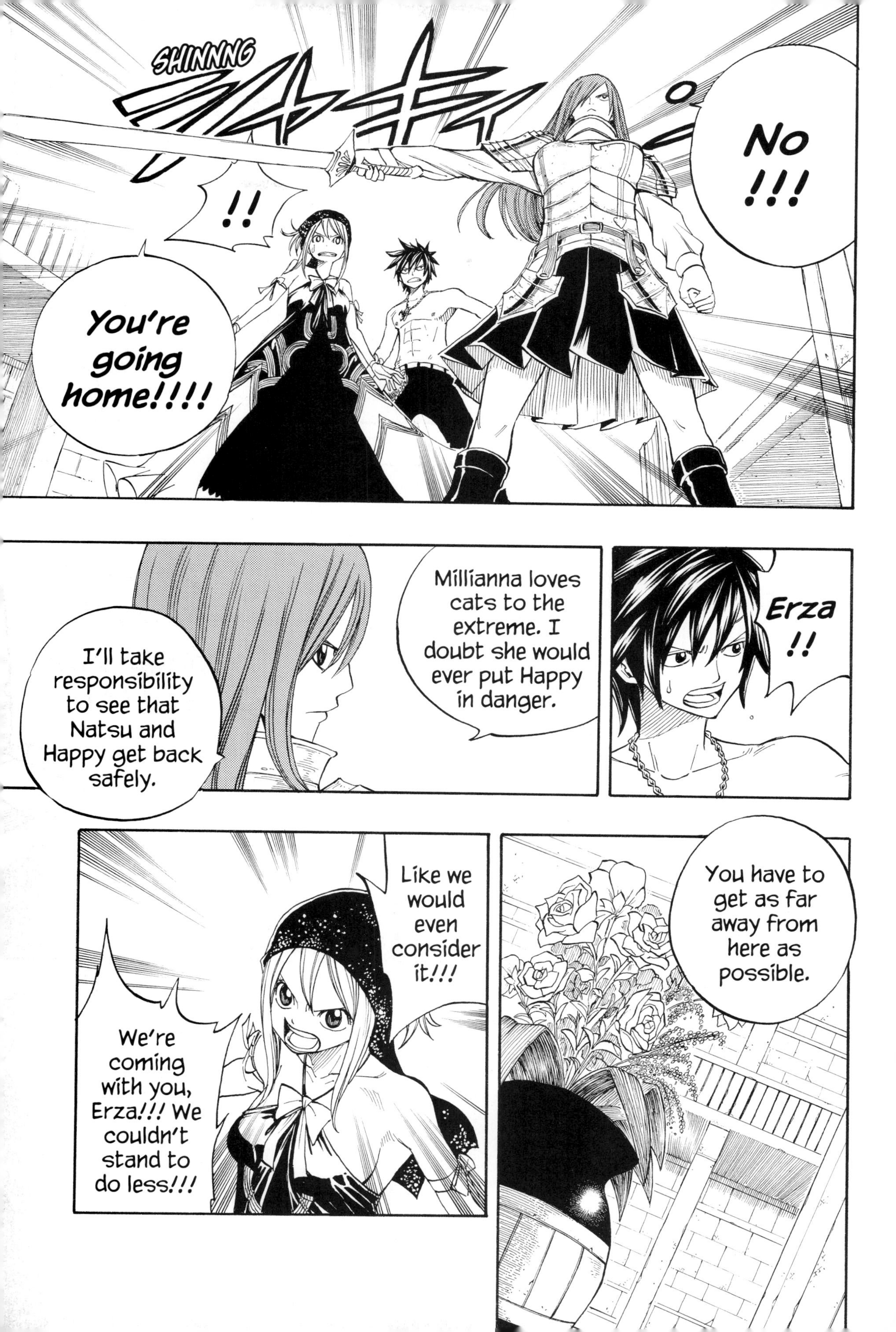
No!!!
SHINNNG
!!
You're going home!!!!
Erza!!
Millianna loves cats to the extreme. I doubt she would ever put Happy in danger.
I'll take responsibility to see that Natsu and Happy get back safely.
You have to get as far away from here as possible.
Like we would even consider it!!!
We're coming with you, Erza!!! We couldn't stand to do less!!!

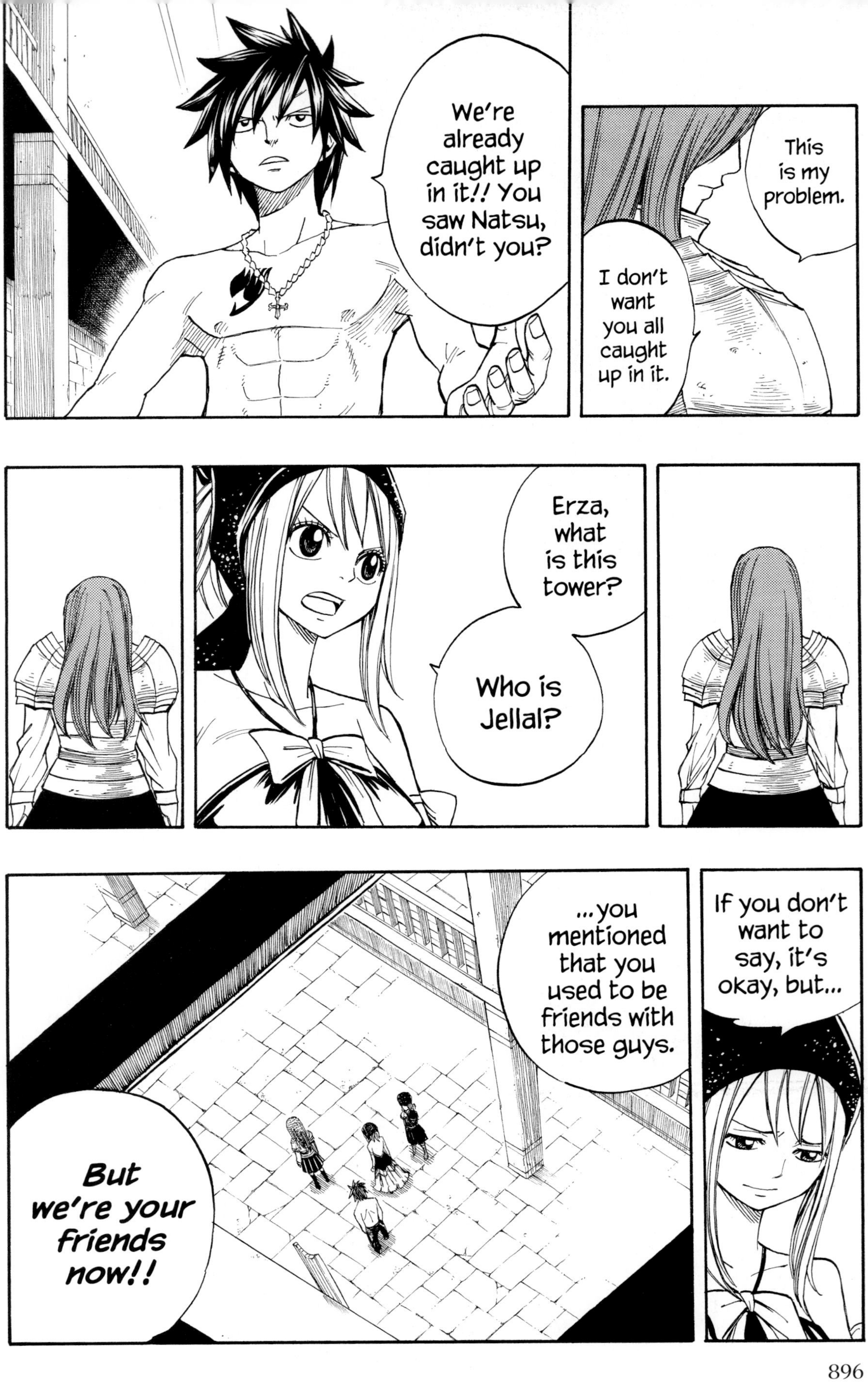
This is my problem.
I don't want you all caught up in it.
We're already caught up in it!! You saw Natsu, didn't you?
Erza, what is this tower?
Who is Jellal?
If you don't want to say, it's okay, but...
...you mentioned that you used to be friends with those guys.
But we're your friends now!!

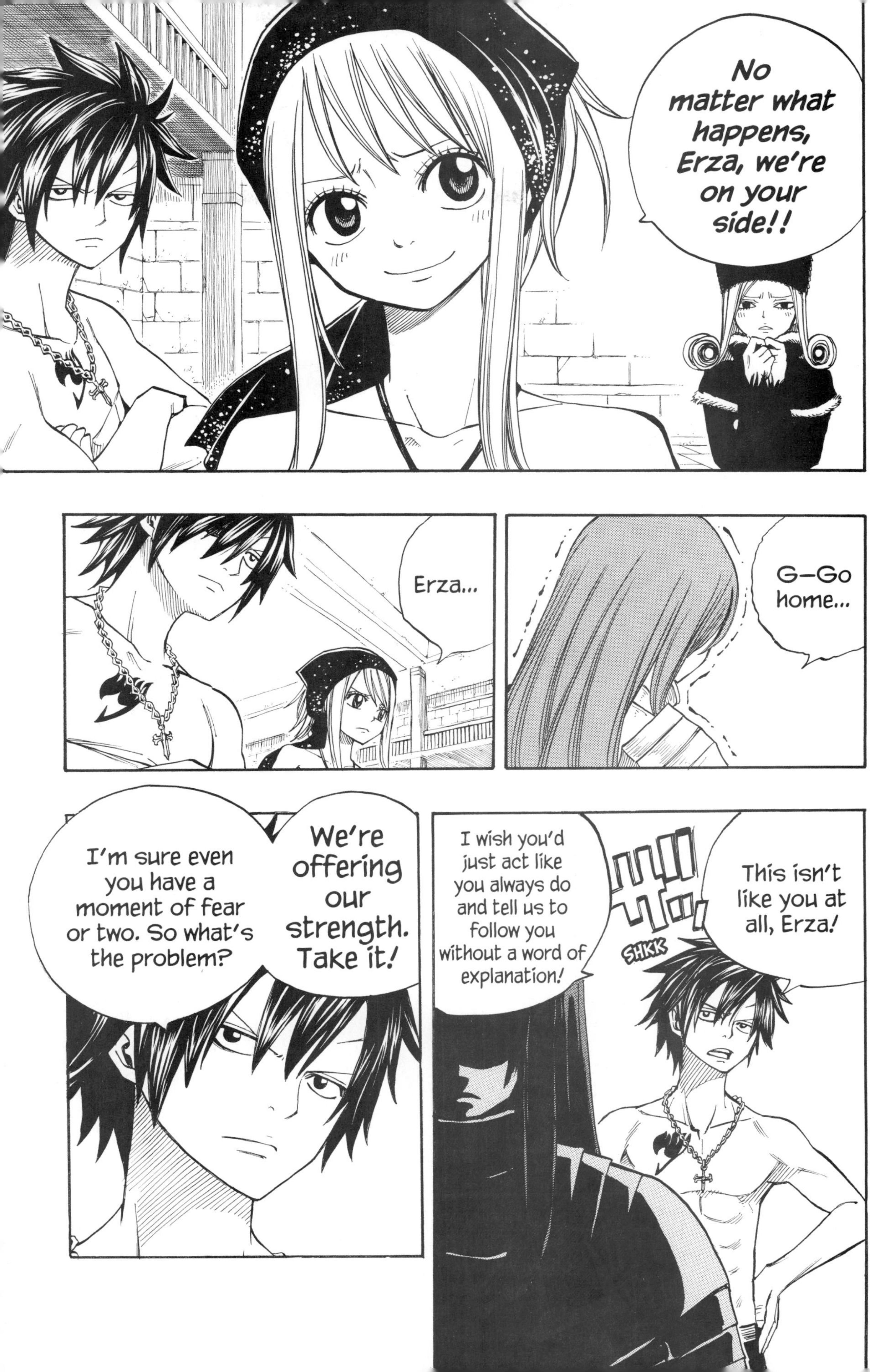
No matter what happens, Erza, we're on your side!!
G–Go home...
Erza...
This isn't like you at all, Erza!
I wish you'd just act like you always do and tell us to follow you without a word of explanation!
SHKK
We're offering our strength. Take it!
I'm sure even you have a moment of fear or two. So what's the problem?

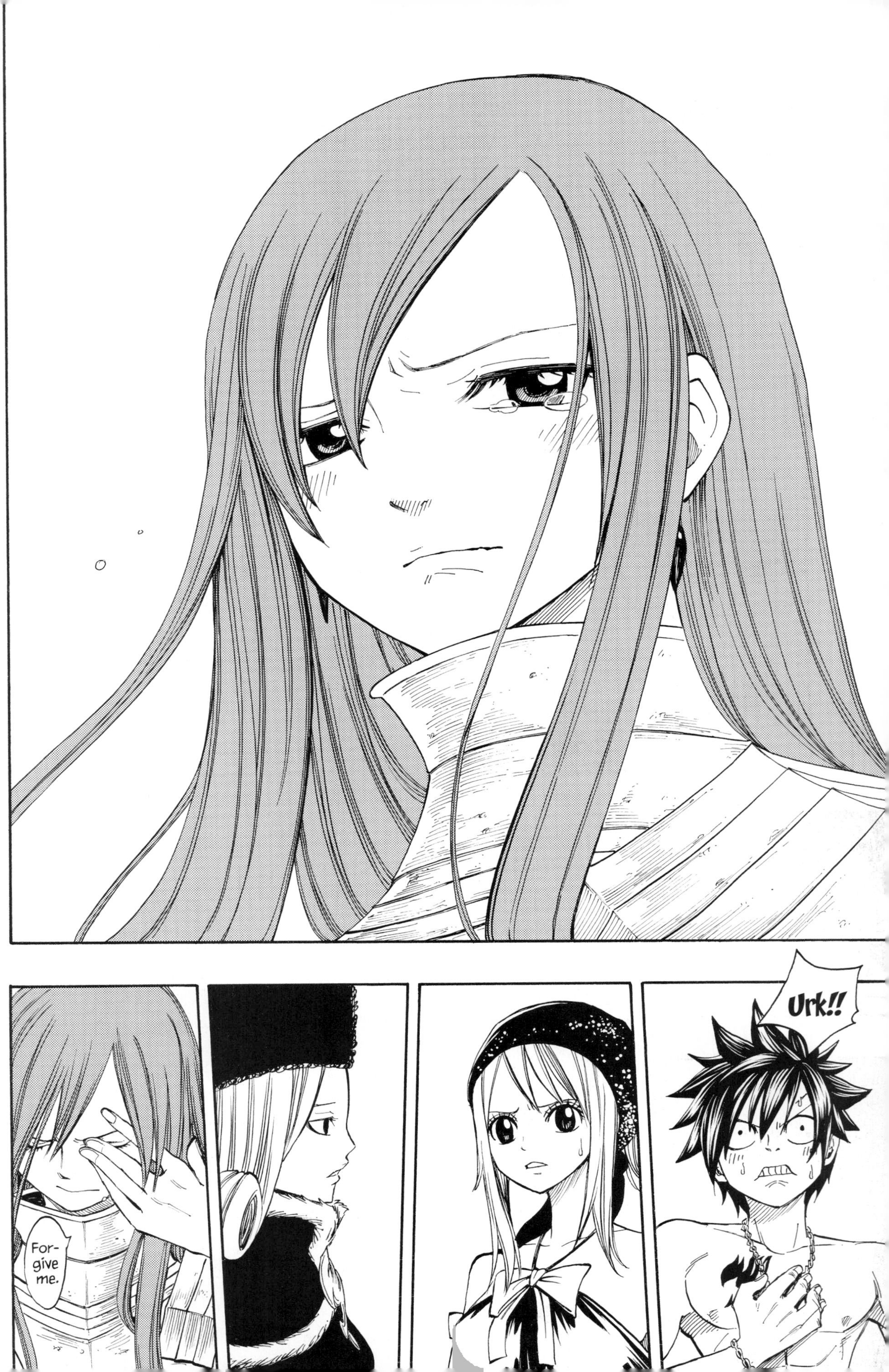
Urk!!
For-give me.

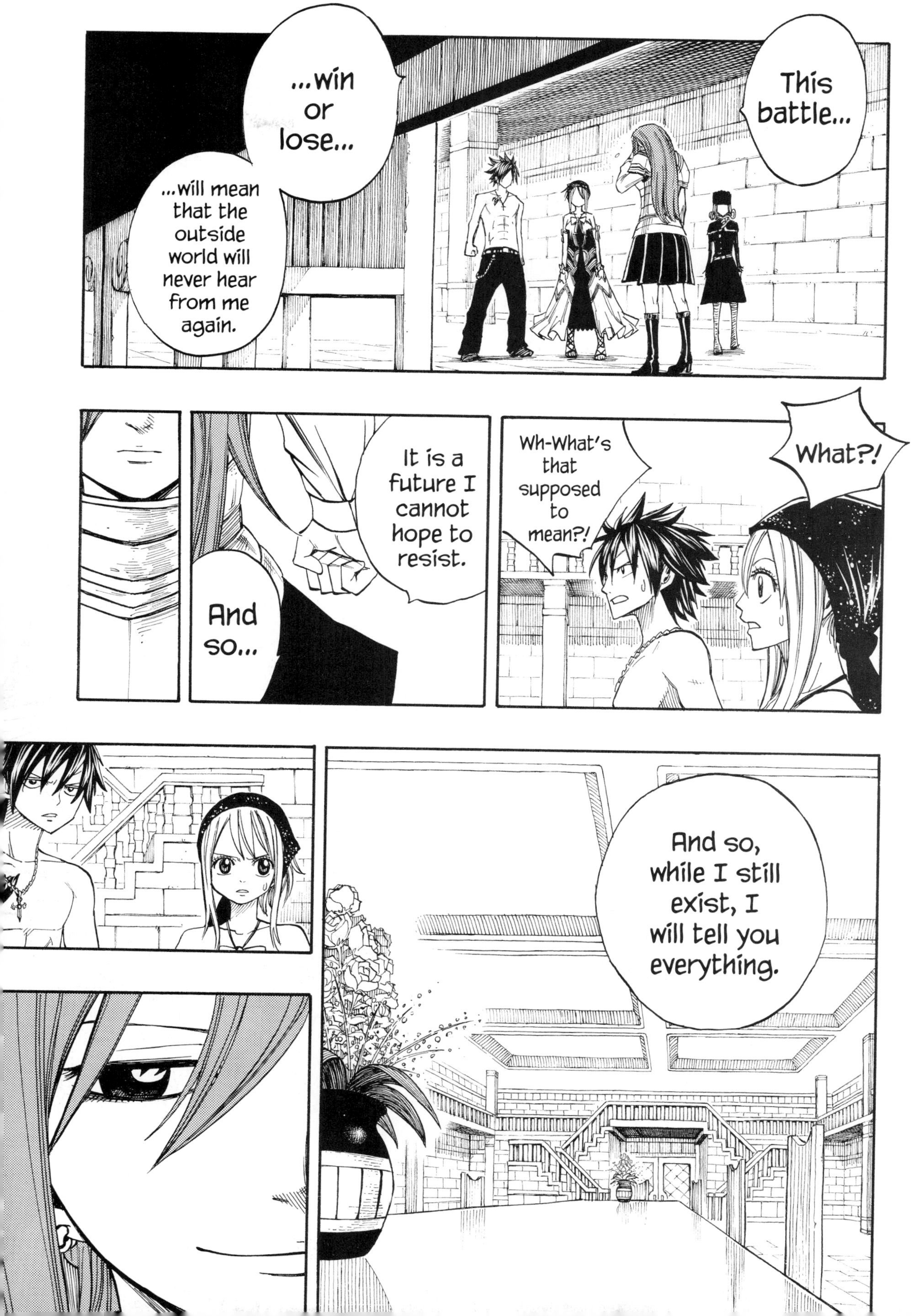

This battle...
...win or lose...
...will mean that the outside world will never hear from me again.
What?!
Wh-What's that supposed to mean?!
It is a future I cannot hope to resist.
And so...
And so, while I still exist, I will tell you everything.

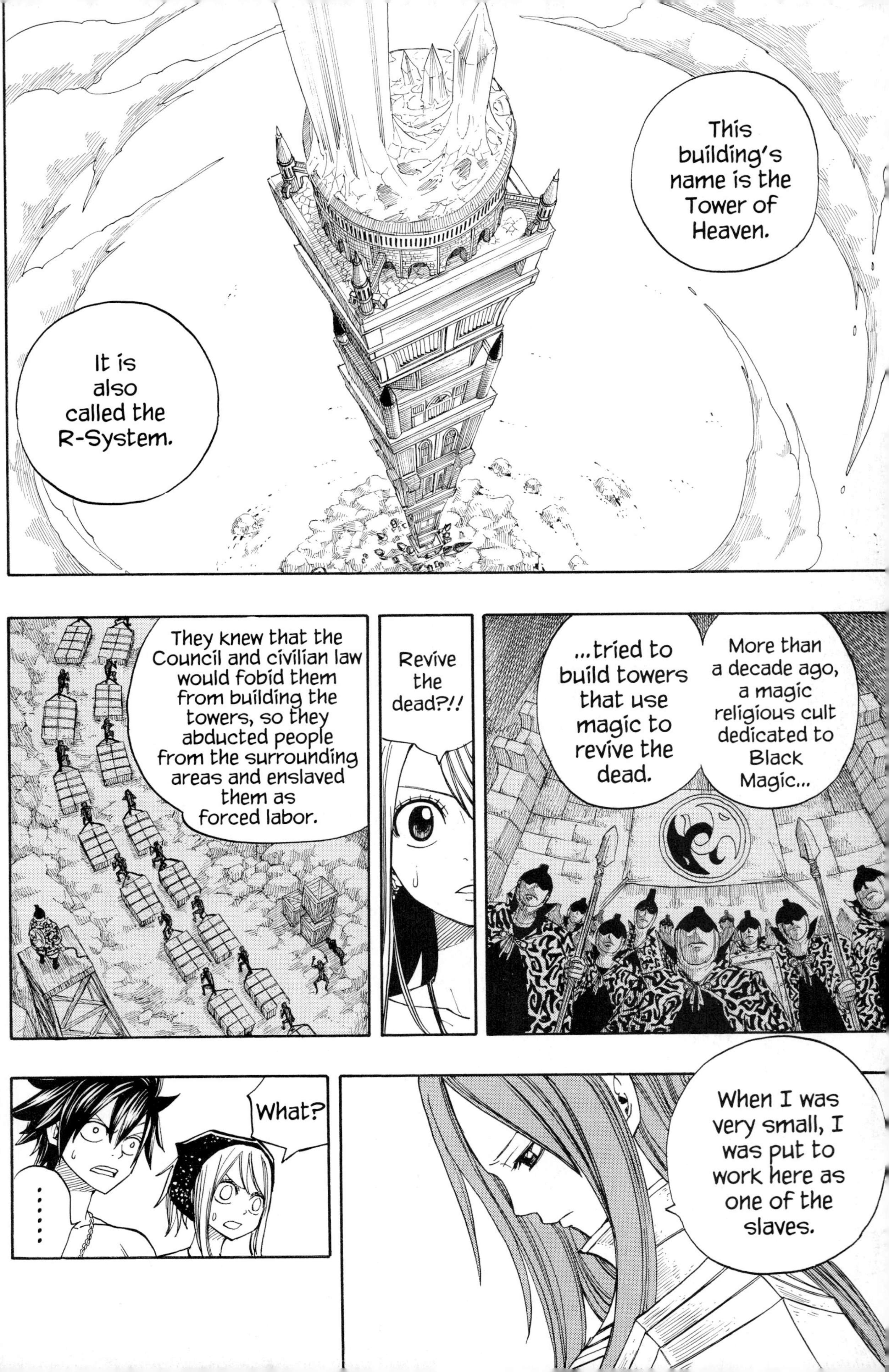
This building's name is the Tower of Heaven.
It is also called the R-System.
More than a decade ago, a magic religious cult dedicated to Black Magic...
...tried to build towers that use magic to revive the dead.
Revive the dead?!!
They knew that the Council and civilian law would fobid them from building the towers, so they abducted people from the surrounding areas and enslaved them as forced labor.
When I was very small, I was put to work here as one of the slaves.
What?
......

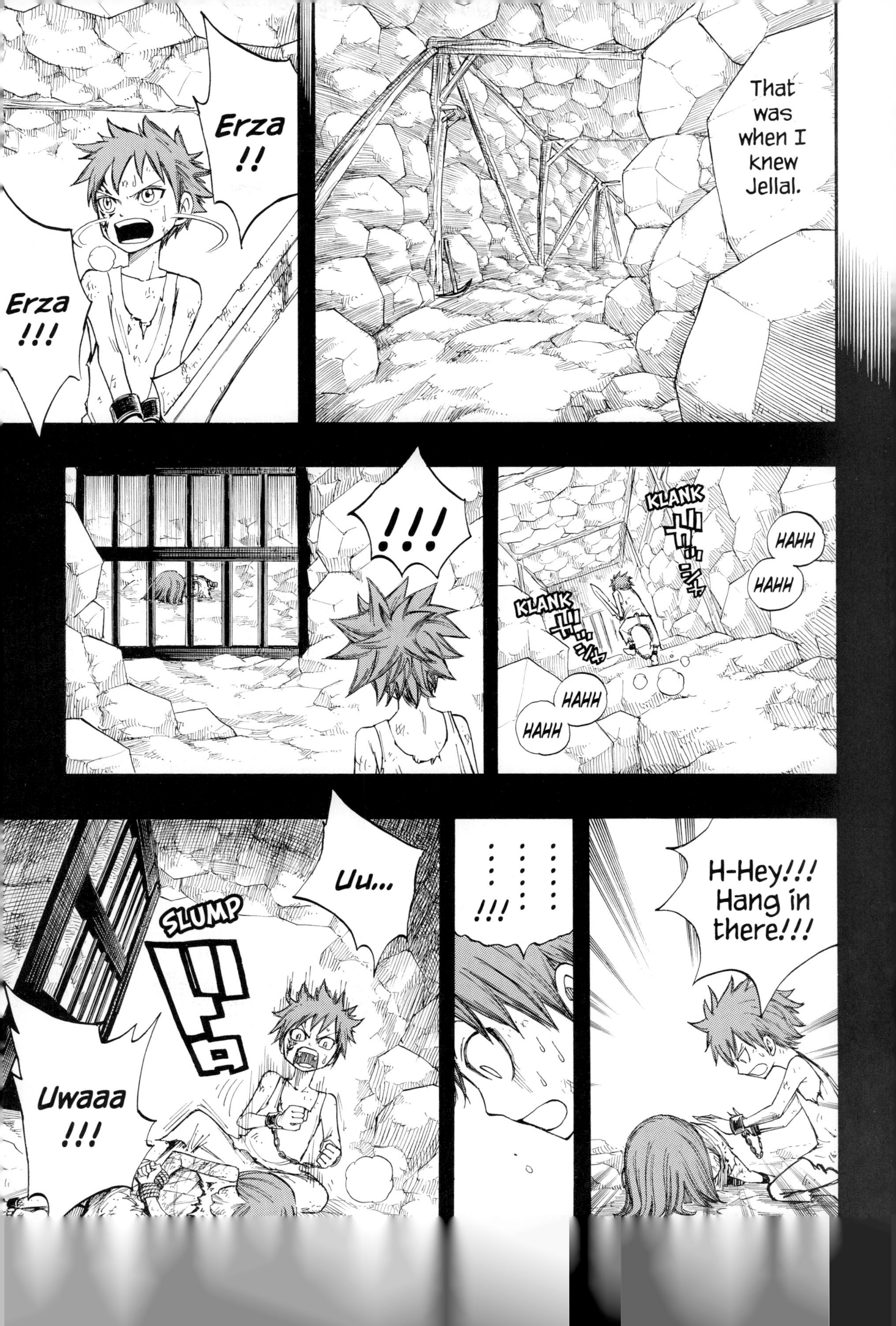

That was when I knew Jellal.
Erza!!
Erza!!!
KLANK
HAHH
HAHH
KLANK
HAHH
HAHH
!!!
H-Hey!!! Hang in there!!!
......!!!
Uu...
SLUMP
Uwaaa!!!

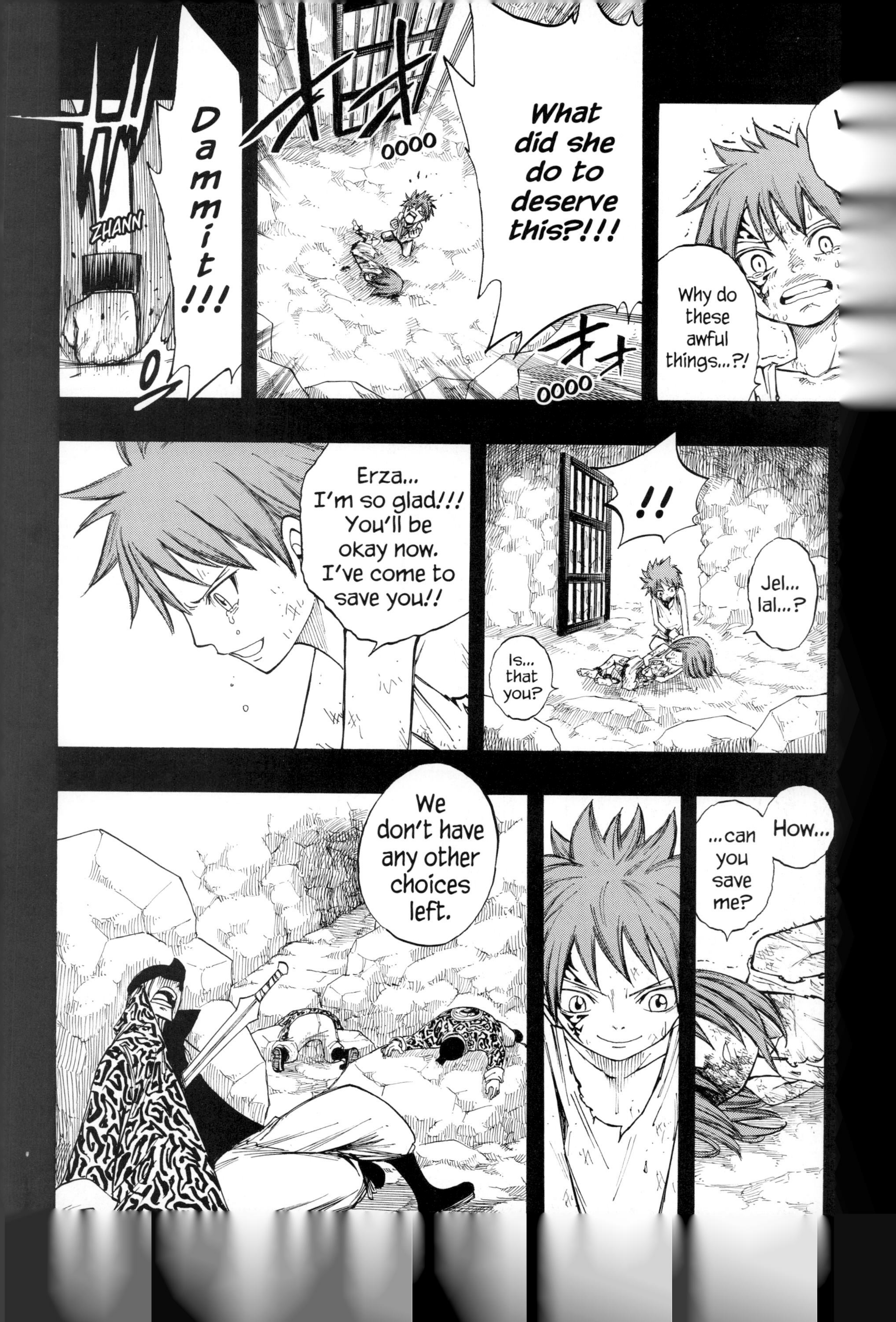
Why do these awful things...?!
What did she do to deserve this?!!!
OOOO
OOOO
Dammit!!!
ZHANN
!!
Jel... lal...?
Is... that you?
Erza... I'm so glad!!! You'll be okay now. I've come to save you!!
How...
...can you save me?
We don't have any other choices left.

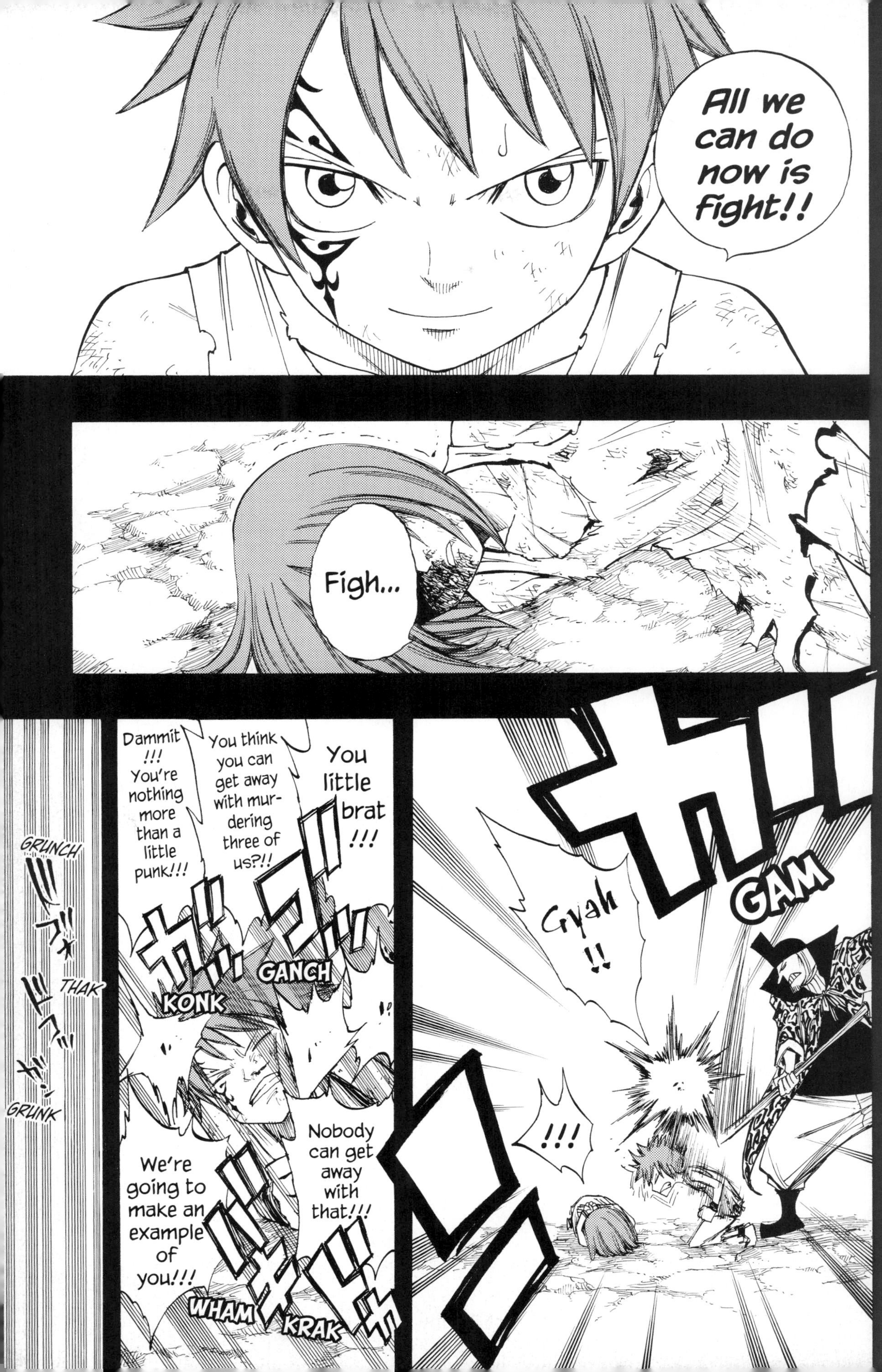
All we can do now is fight!!
Figh...
GAM
Gyah !!
!!!
You little brat !!!
You think you can get away with mur-dering three of us?!!
Dammit !!! You're nothing more than a little punk!!!
GANCH
KONK
GRUNCH
THAK
GRUNK
Nobody can get away with that!!!
We're going to make an example of you!!!
WHAM
KRAK

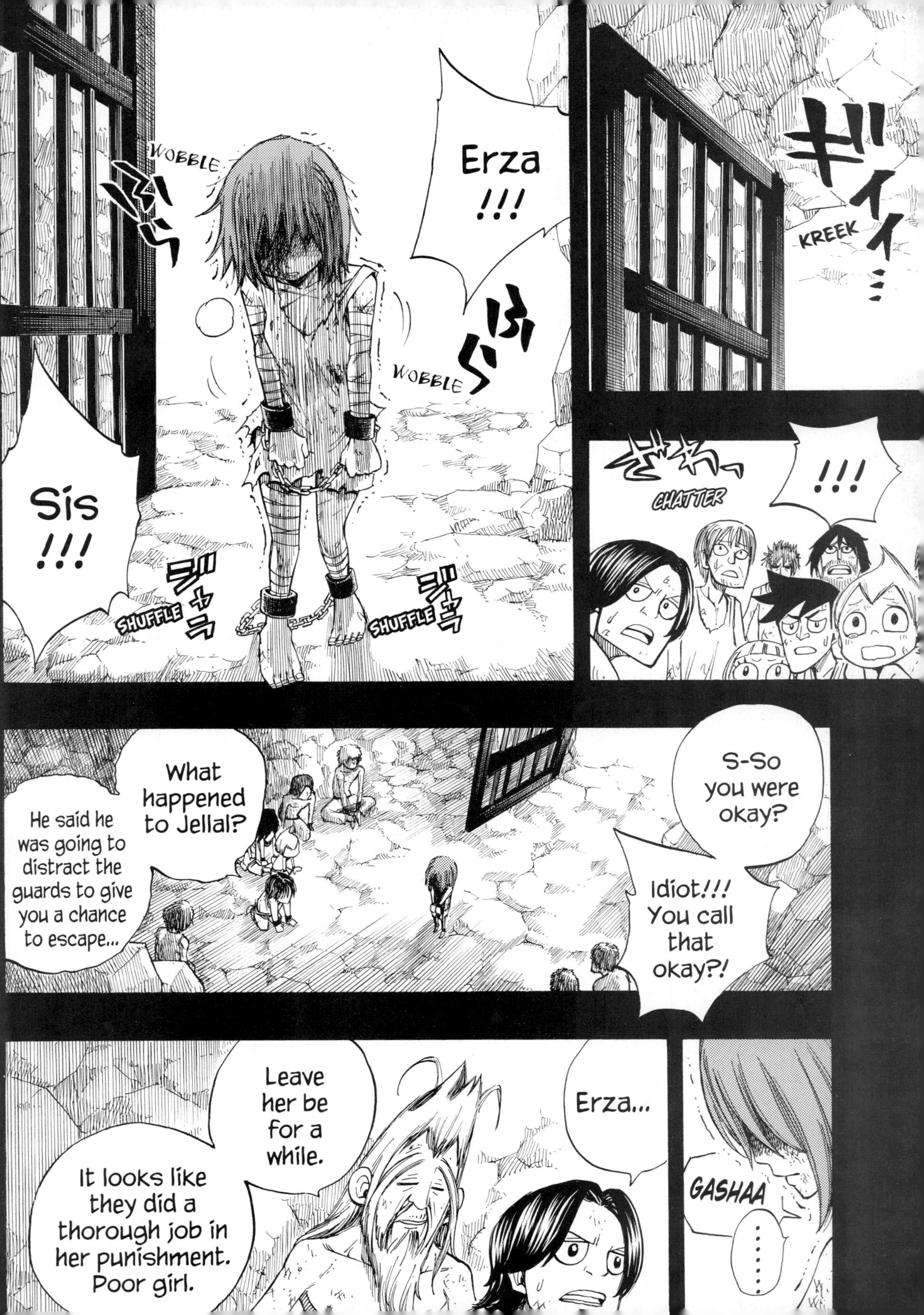

ギイィ
KREEK
!!!
ざわっ
CHATTER
Erza !!!
ふら
WOBBLE
ふら
WOBBLE
Sis !!!
ジャラ
SHUFFLE
ジャラ
SHUFFLE
S-So you were okay?
Idiot!!! You call that okay?!
What happened to Jellal?
He said he was going to distract the guards to give you a chance to escape...
......
GASHAA
Erza...
Leave her be for a while.
It looks like they did a thorough job in her punishment. Poor girl.

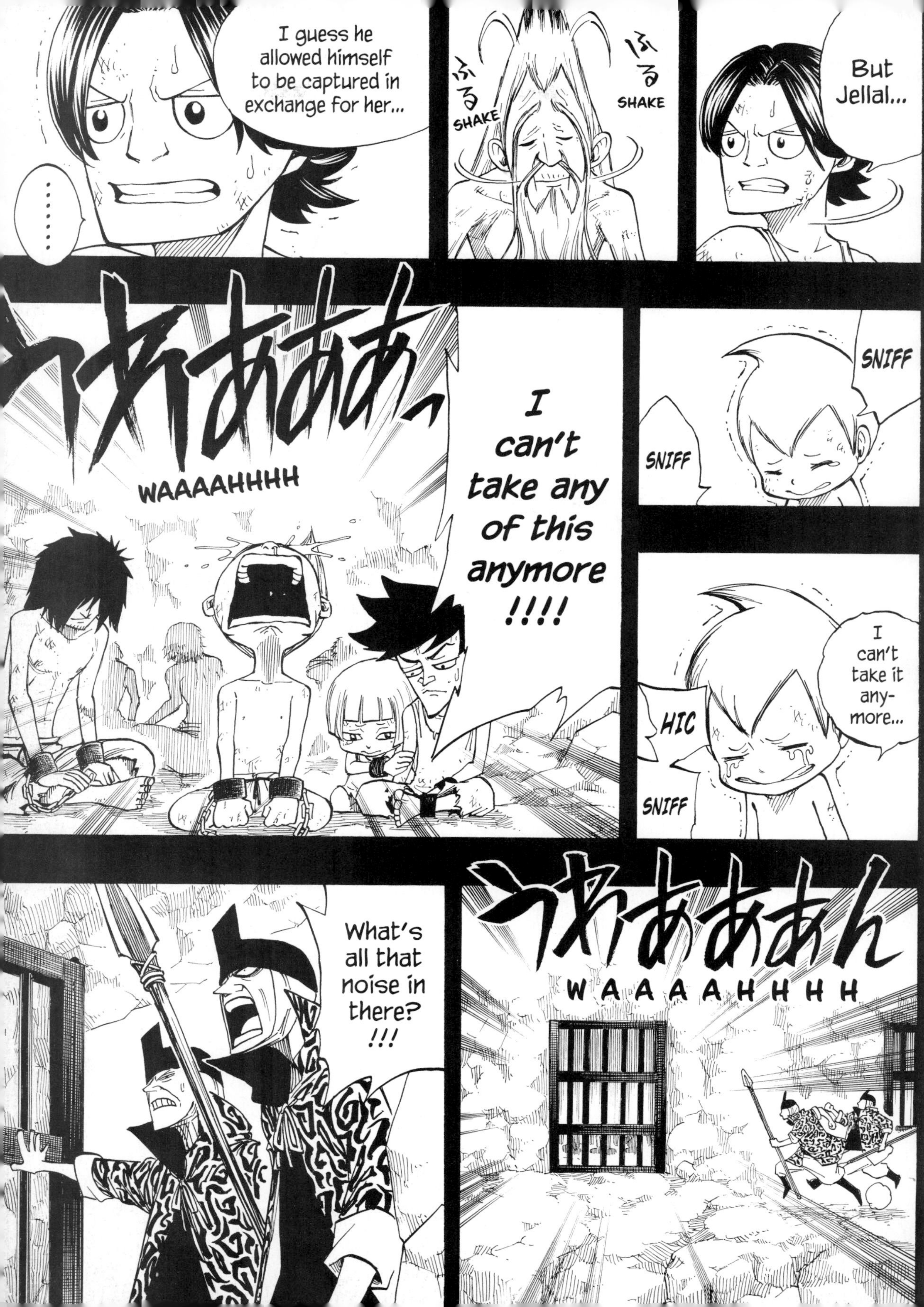
But Jellal...
ふる
SHAKE
ふる
SHAKE
I guess he allowed himself to be captured in exchange for her...
......
SNIFF
SNIFF
I can't take it any-more...
HIC
SNIFF
I can't take any of this anymore !!!!
うわあああ
WAAAAHHHH
うわあああん
WAAAAHHHH
What's all that noise in there? !!!

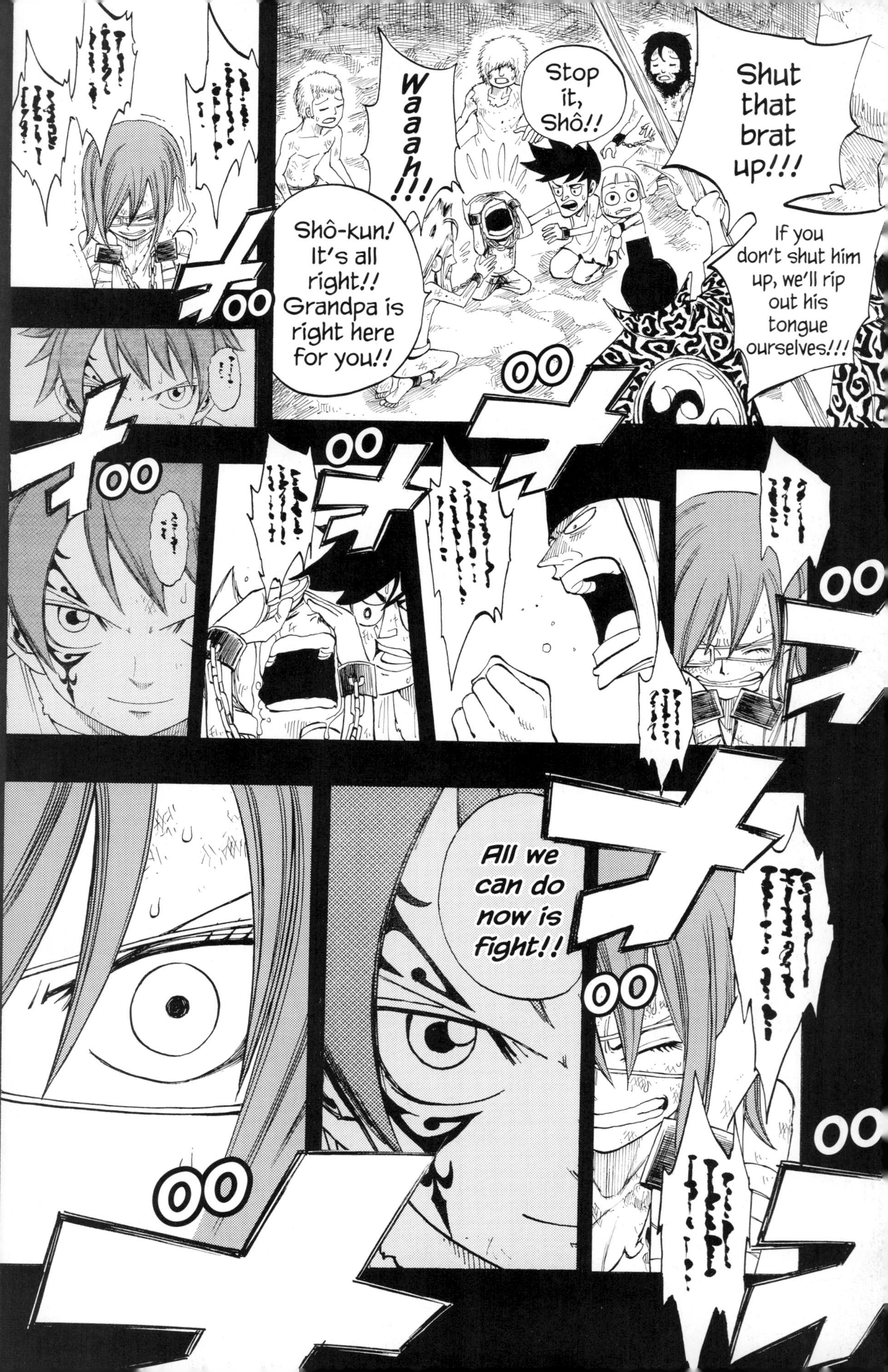
Shut that brat up!!!
If you don't shut him up, we'll rip out his tongue ourselves!!!
Stop it, Shô!!
Waaaah!!!
Shô-kun! It's all right!! Grandpa is right here for you!!
All we can do now is fight!!

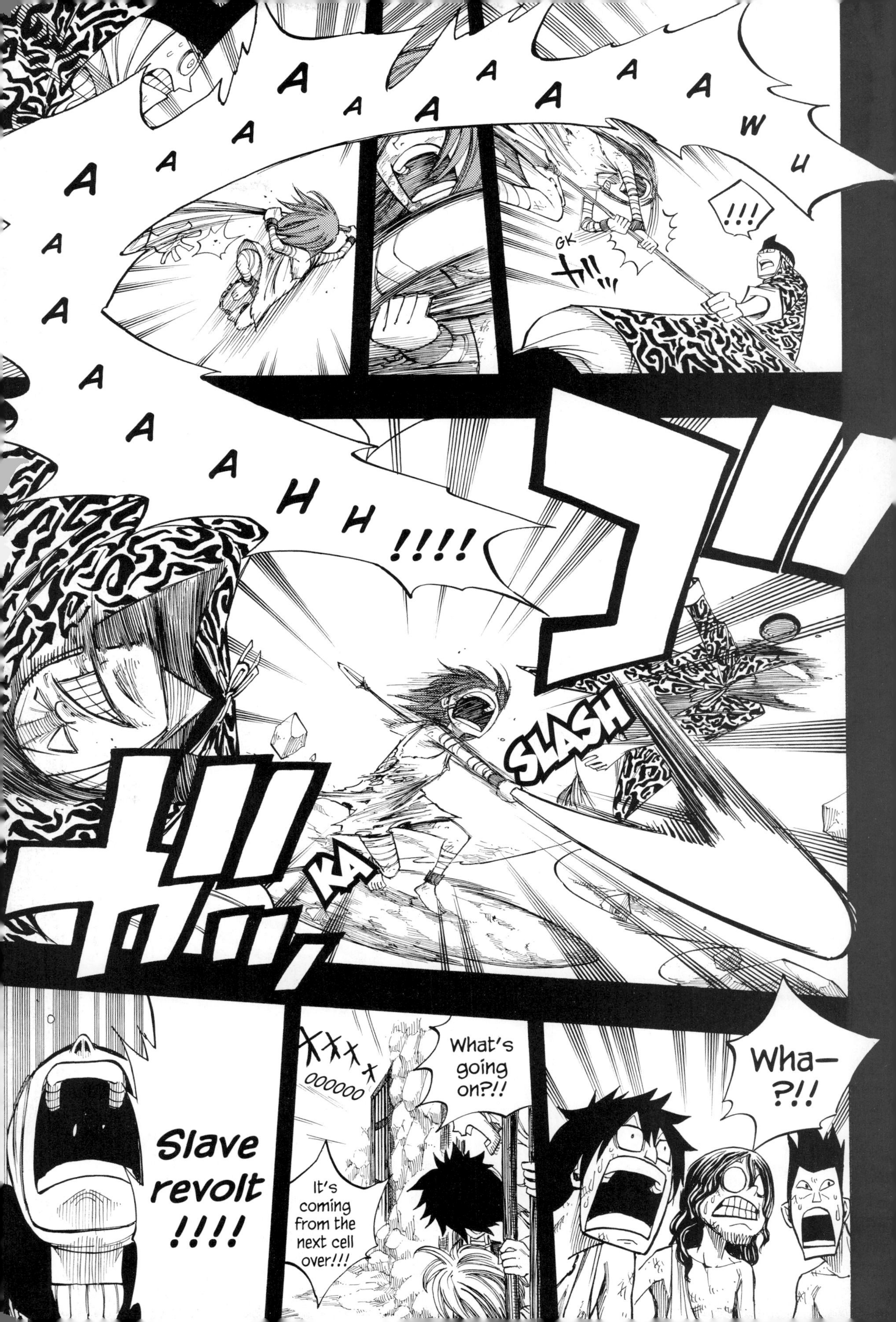

UWAAAAAAAAAAAAAAAHH!!!!
!!!
GK
SLASH
KA
Wha—?!!
What's going on?!!
OOOOOO
It's coming from the next cell over!!!
Slave revolt!!!!

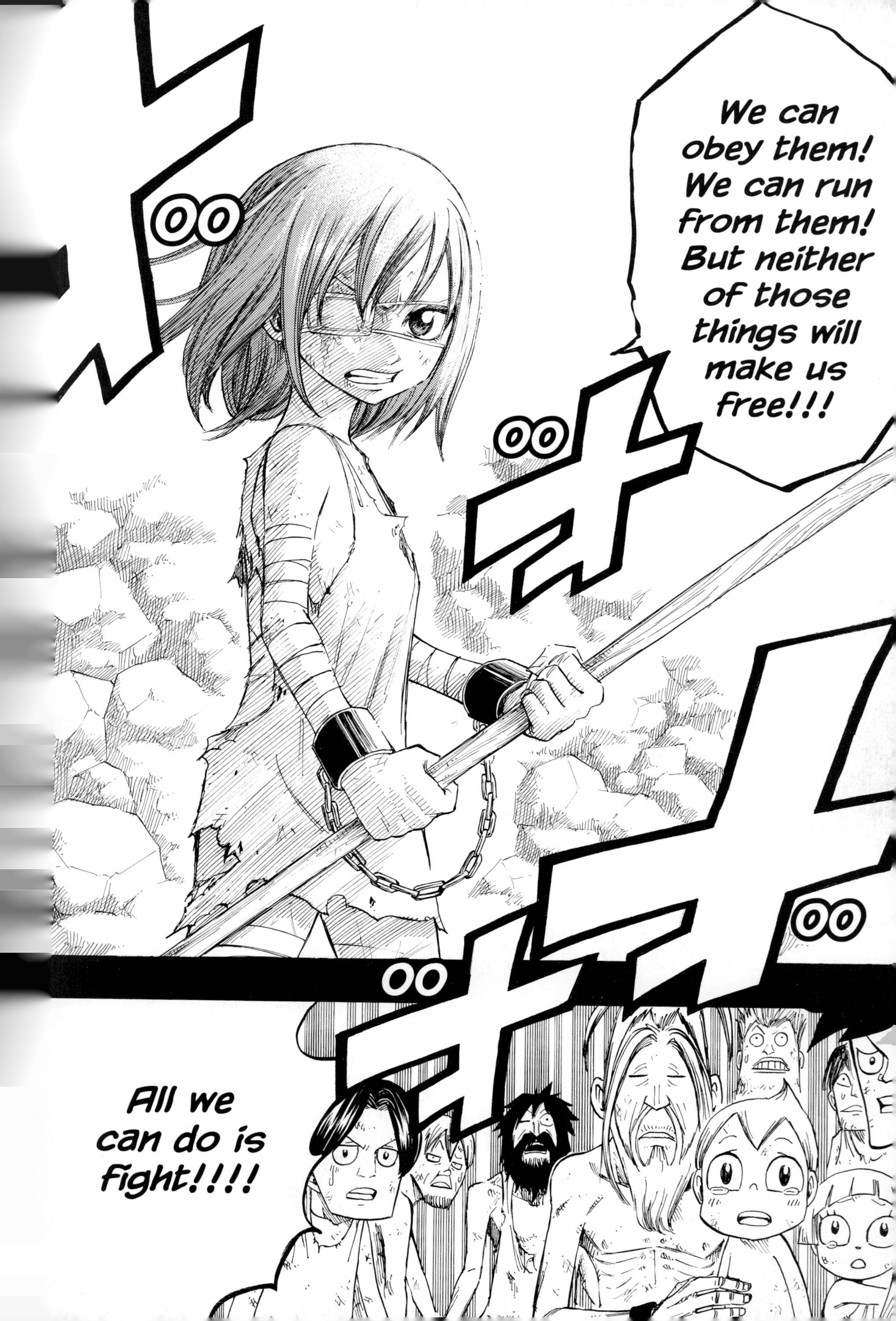
We can obey them! We can run from them! But neither of those things will make us free!!!
OO
OO
OO
OO
All we can do is fight!!!!

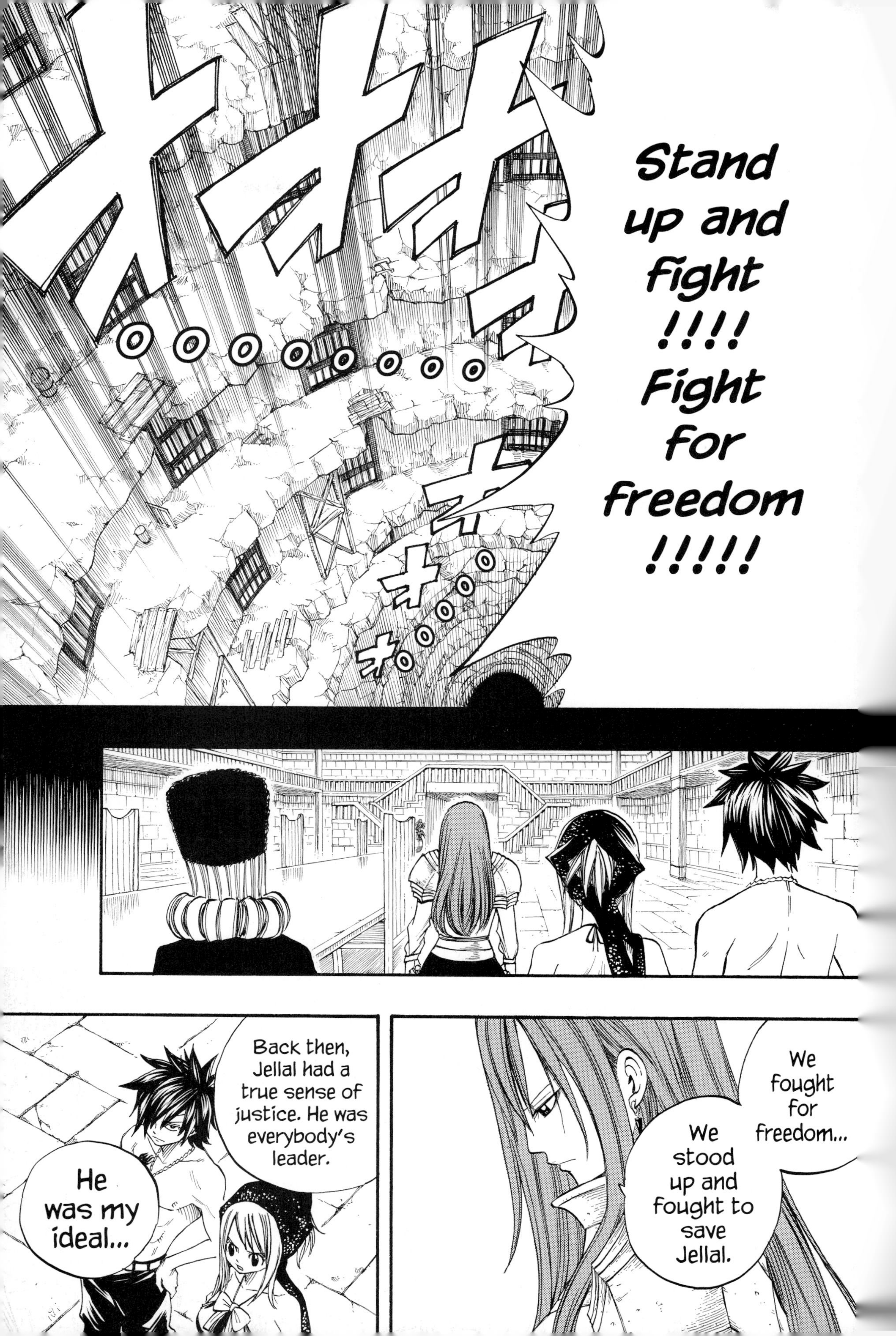
Stand up and fight !!!! Fight for freedom !!!!!
We fought for freedom...
We stood up and fought to save Jellal.
Back then, Jellal had a true sense of justice. He was everybody's leader.
He was my ideal...

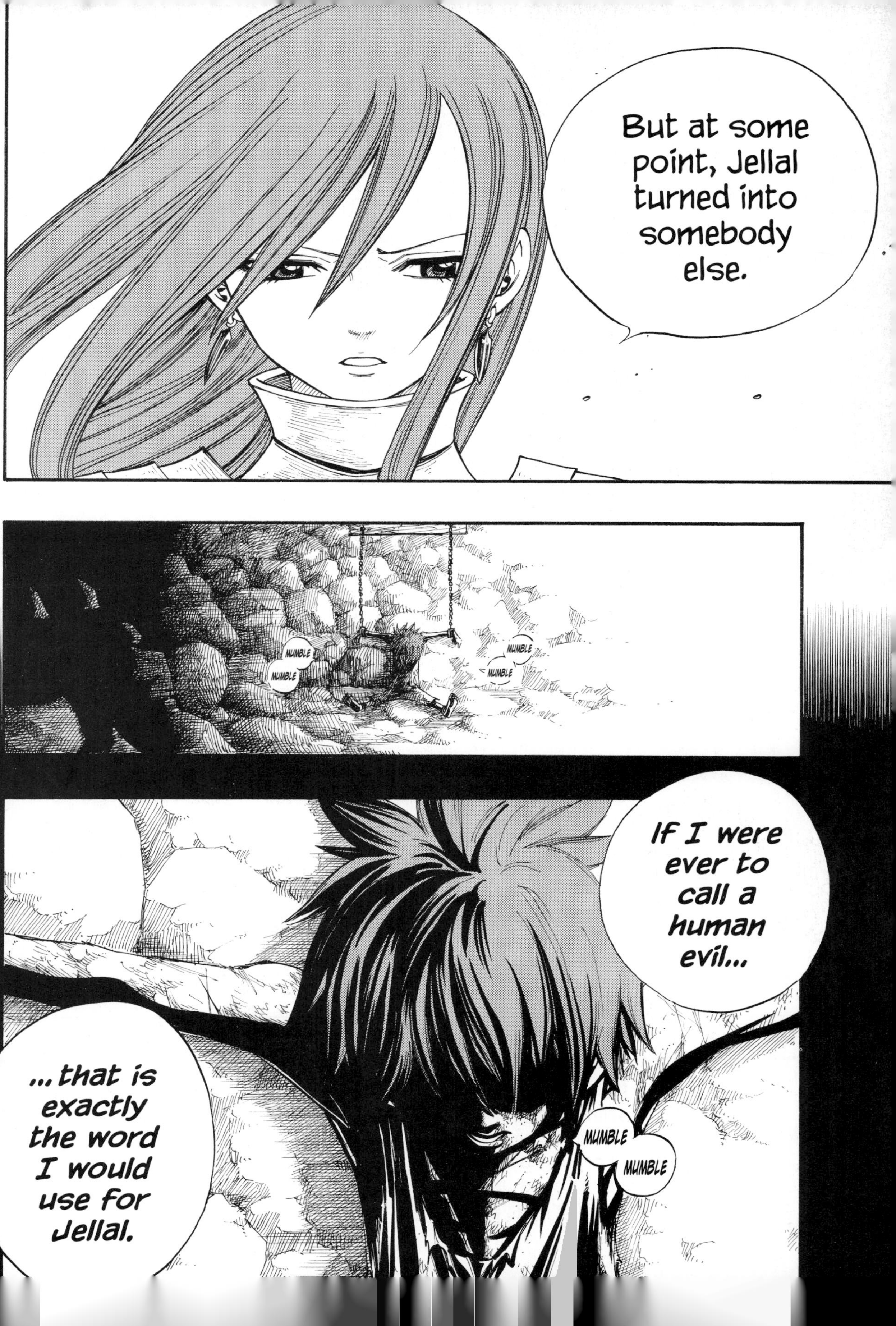
But at some point, Jellal turned into somebody else.
MUMBLE
MUMBLE
MUMBLE
MUMBLE
If I were ever to call a human evil...
...that is exactly the word I would use for Jellal.
MUMBLE
MUMBLE

FAIRY TAIL

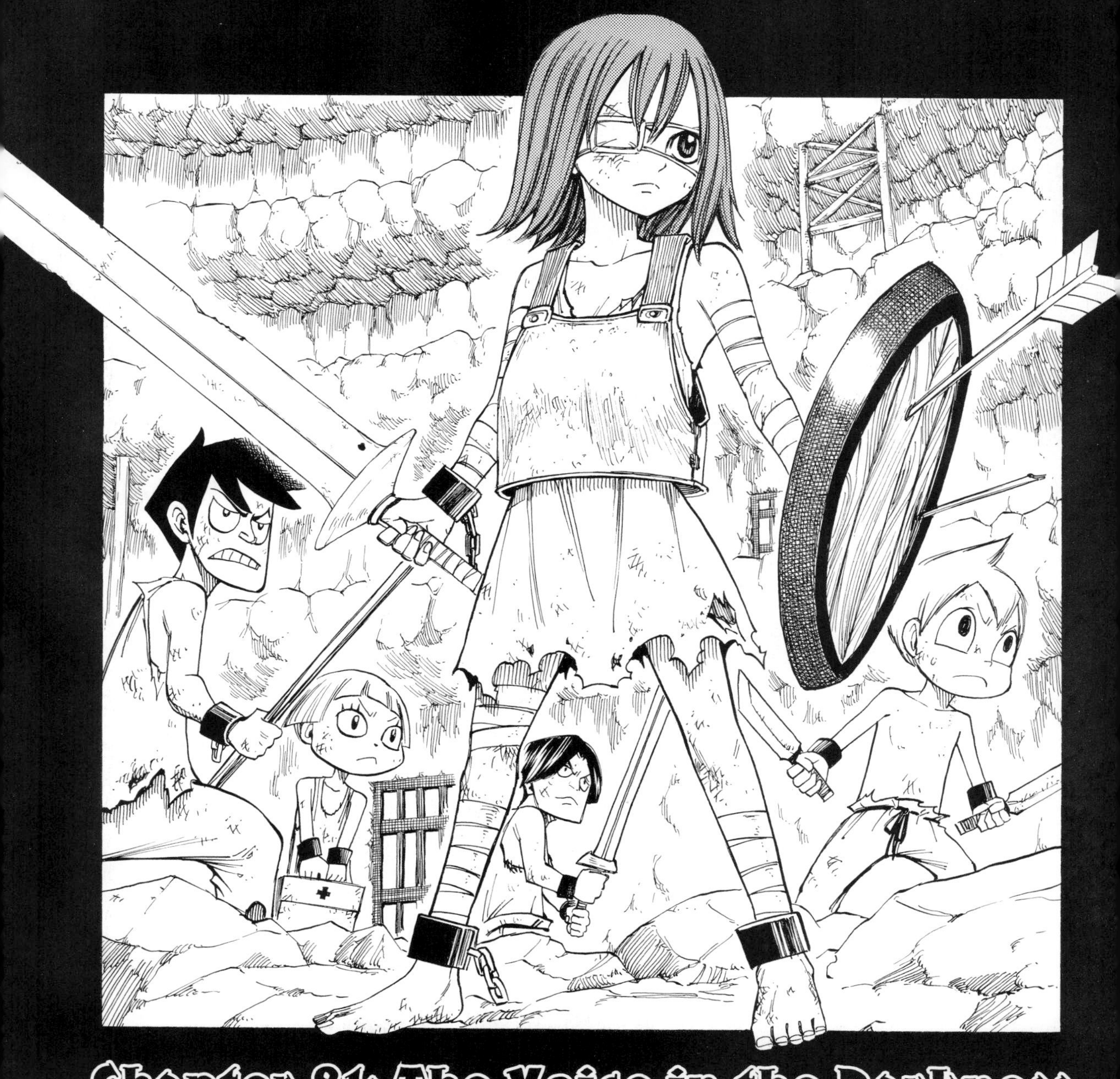

Chapter 81: The Voice in the Darkness

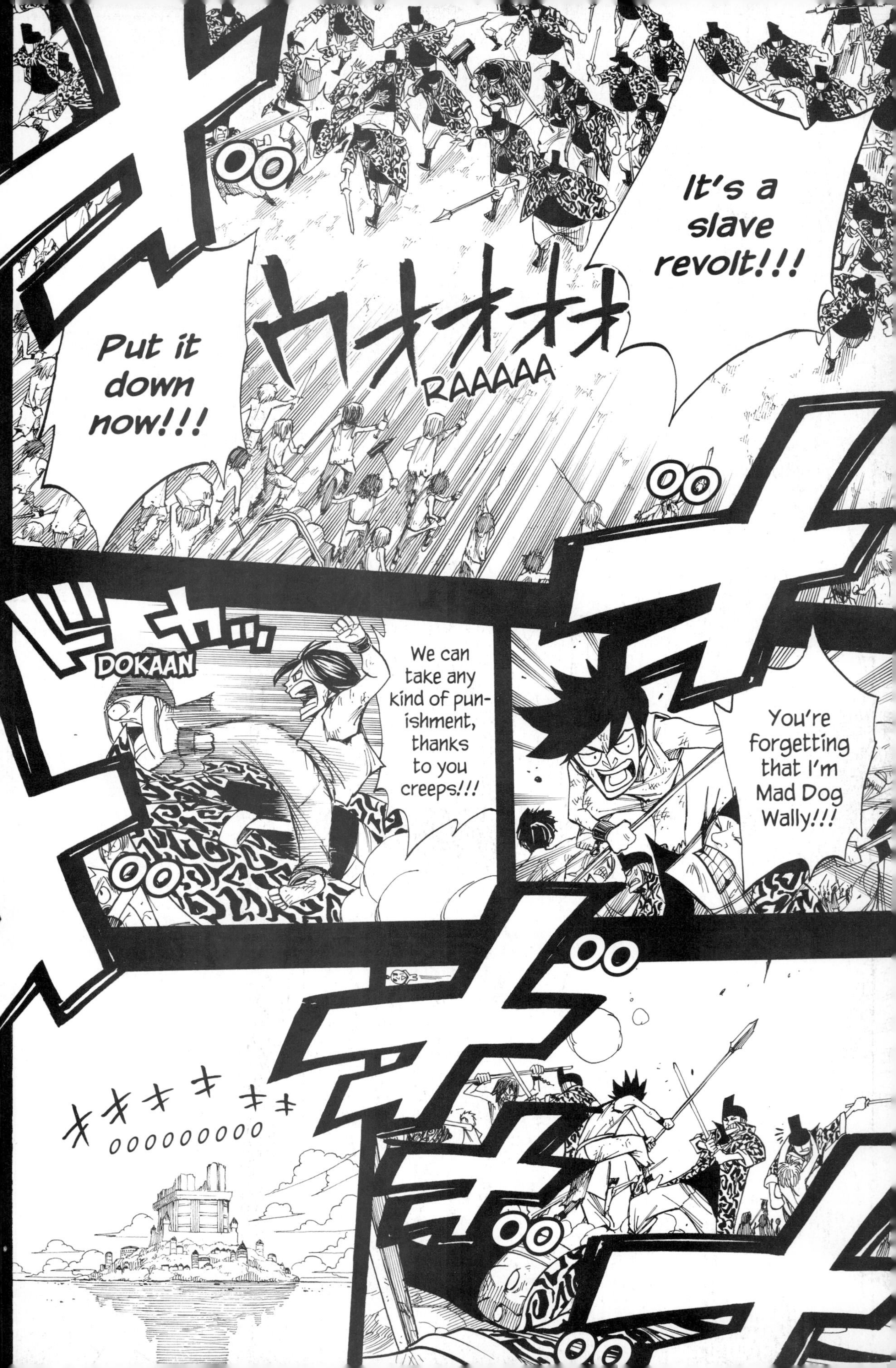
It's a slave revolt!!!
ウオオオオ
RAAAAA
Put it down now!!!
You're forgetting that I'm Mad Dog Wally!!!
DOKAAN
We can take any kind of pun-ishment, thanks to you creeps!!!
OOOOOOOOO

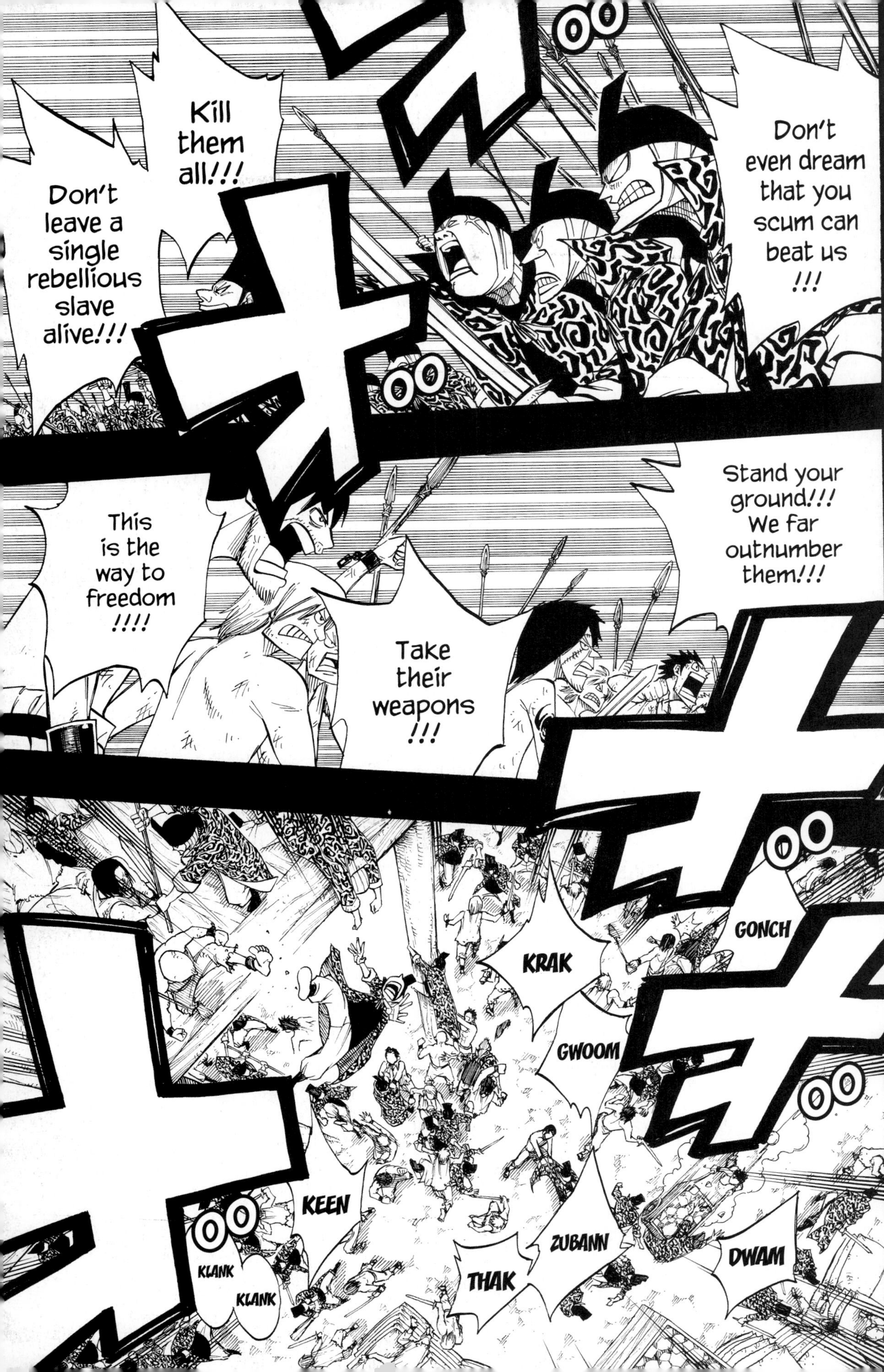
Don't even dream that you scum can beat us!!!
Kill them all!!!
Don't leave a single rebellious slave alive!!!
Stand your ground!!! We far outnumber them!!!
Take their weapons!!!
This is the way to freedom!!!!
GONCH
KRAK
GWOOM
DWAM
ZUBANN
THAK
KEEN
KLANK
KLANK

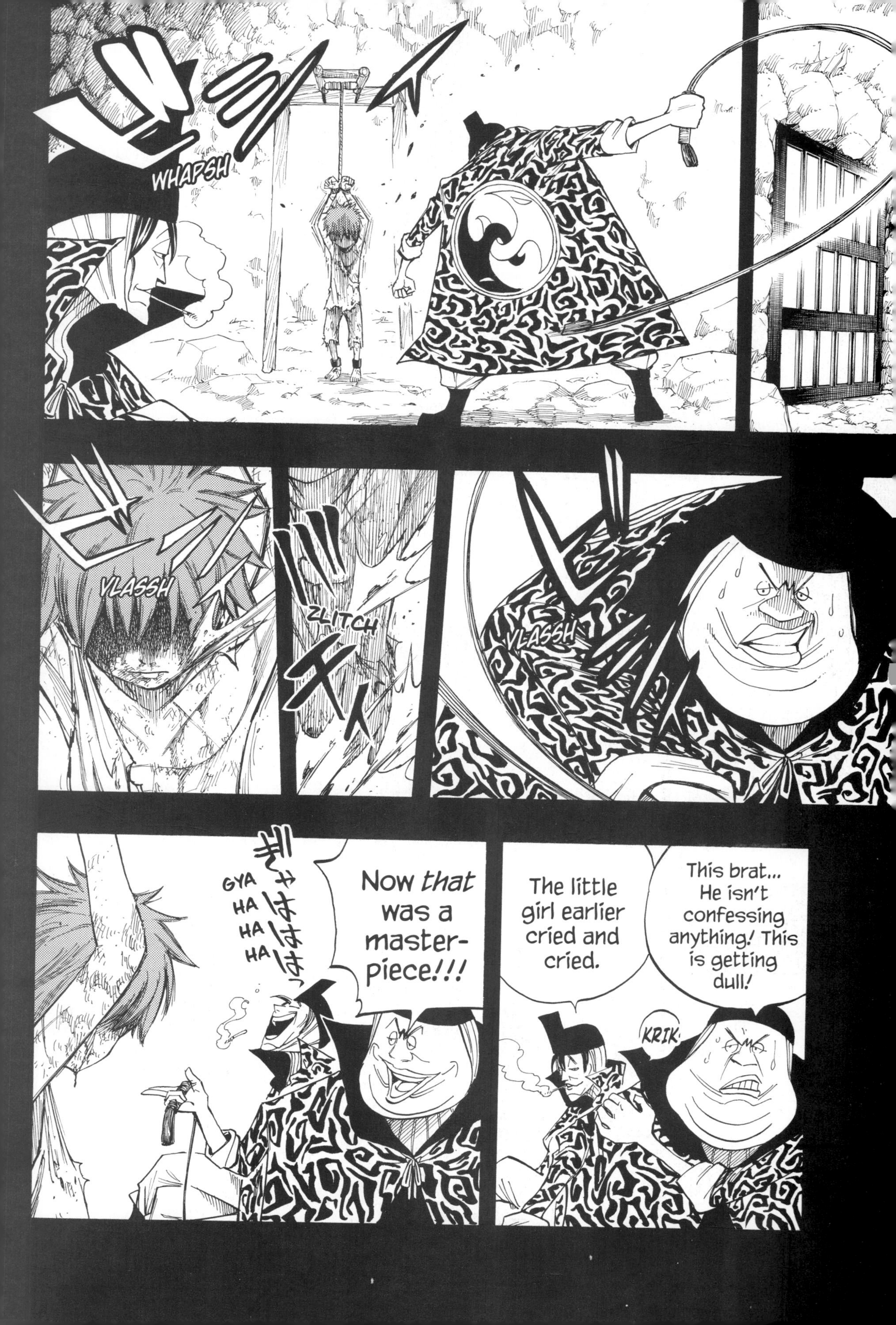
WHAPSH
VLASSH
ZLITCH
VLASSH
This brat... He isn't confessing anything! This is getting dull!
The little girl earlier cried and cried.
KRIK
Now *that* was a masterpiece!!!
GYA HA HA HA
ぎゃははは

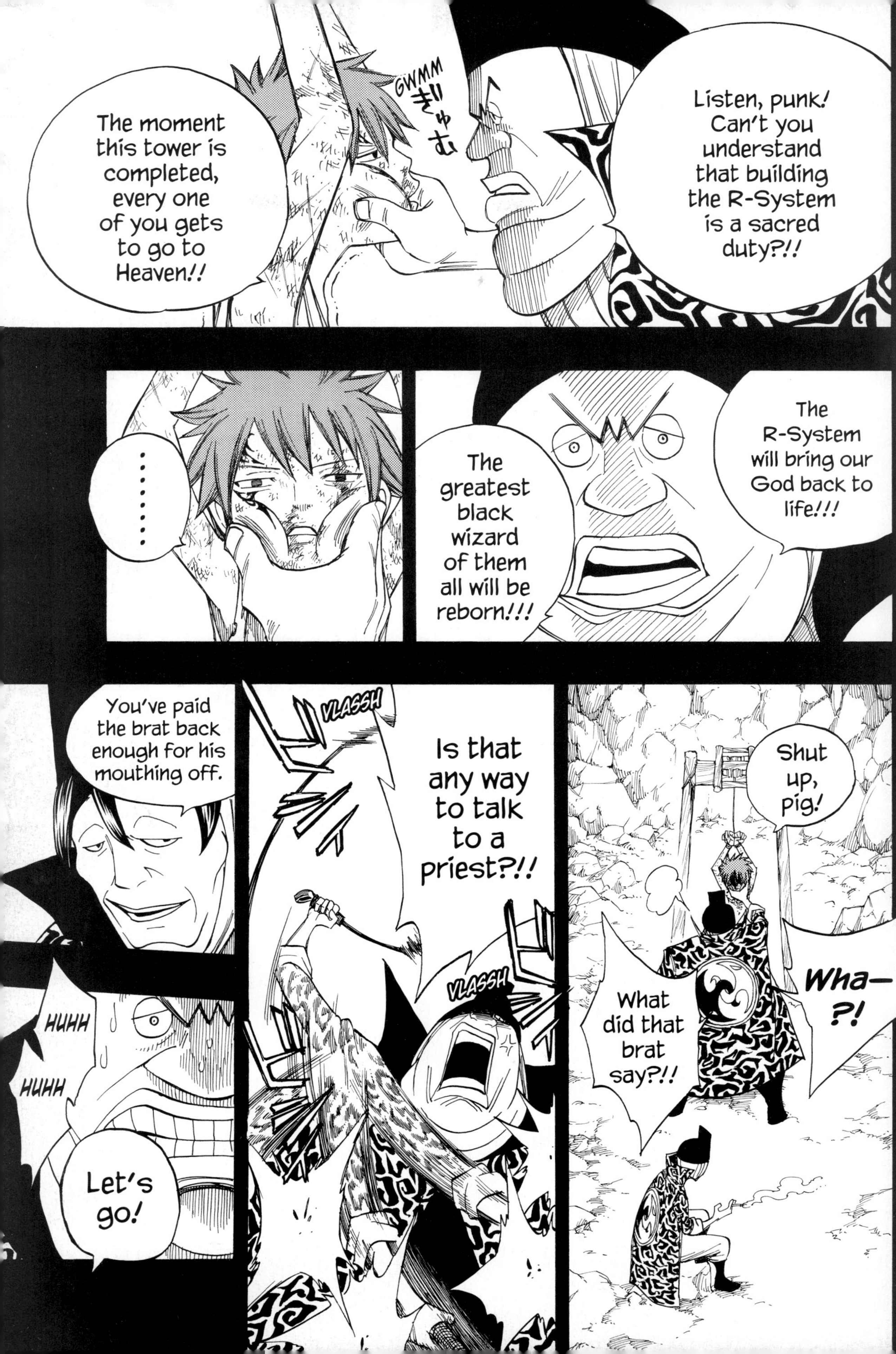
Listen, punk! Can't you understand that building the R-System is a sacred duty?!!
GWMM
きゅむ
The moment this tower is completed, every one of you gets to go to Heaven!!
The R-System will bring our God back to life!!!
The greatest black wizard of them all will be reborn!!!
....
Shut up, pig!
Wha—?!
What did that brat say?!!
Is that any way to talk to a priest?!!
VLASSH
VLASSH
You've paid the brat back enough for his mouthing off.
HUHH
HUHH
Let's go!

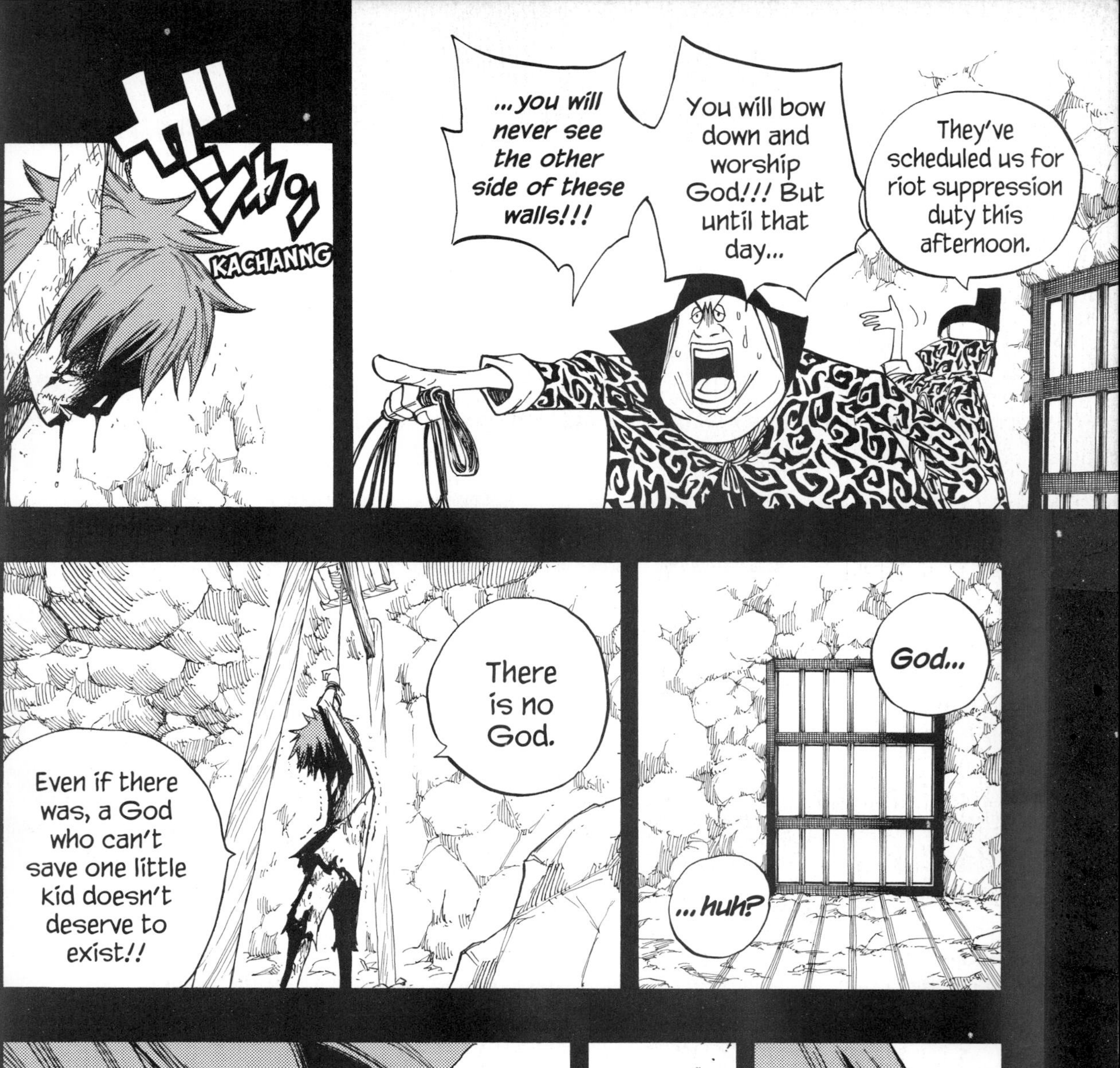

They've scheduled us for riot suppression duty this afternoon.
You will bow down and worship God!!! But until that day...
...you will never see the other side of these walls!!!
KACHANNG
God...
...huh?
There is no God.
Even if there was, a God who can't save one little kid doesn't deserve to exist!!
I hate them...
Hate...
I hate them all!!
I hate them!! I hate their God!! I hate everything in the whole lousy world!!!

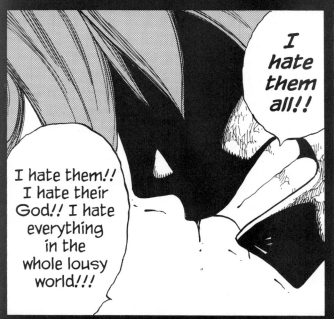

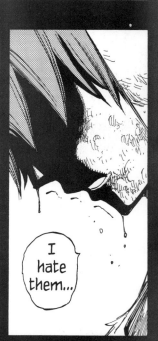

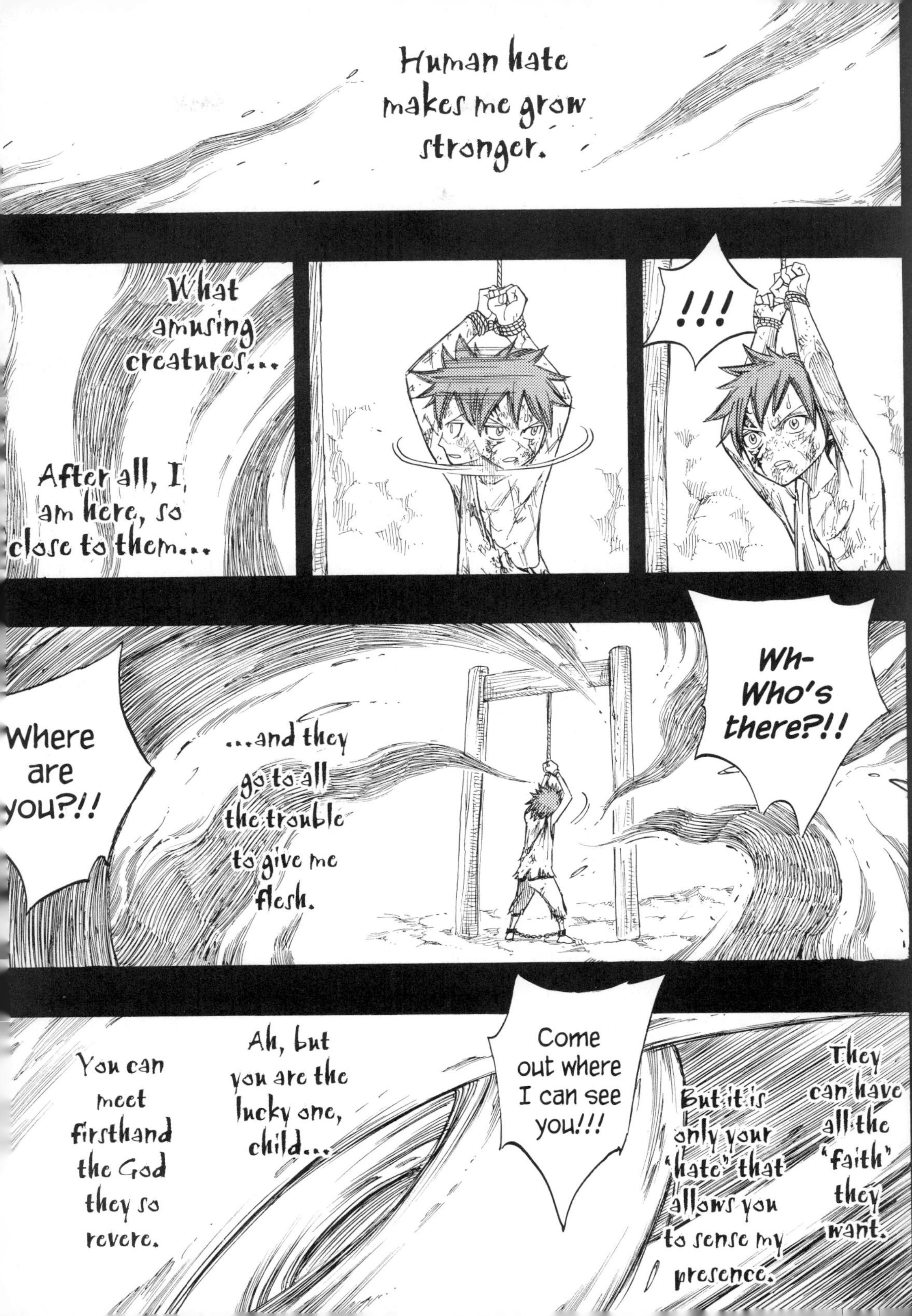
Human hate makes me grow stronger.
!!!
What amusing creatures...
After all, I, am here, so close to them...
Wh-Who's there?!!
...and they go to all the trouble to give me flesh.
Where are you?!!
They can have all the "faith" they want.
But it is only your "hate" that allows you to sense my presence.
Come out where I can see you!!!
Ah, but you are the lucky one, child...
You can meet firsthand the God they so revere.

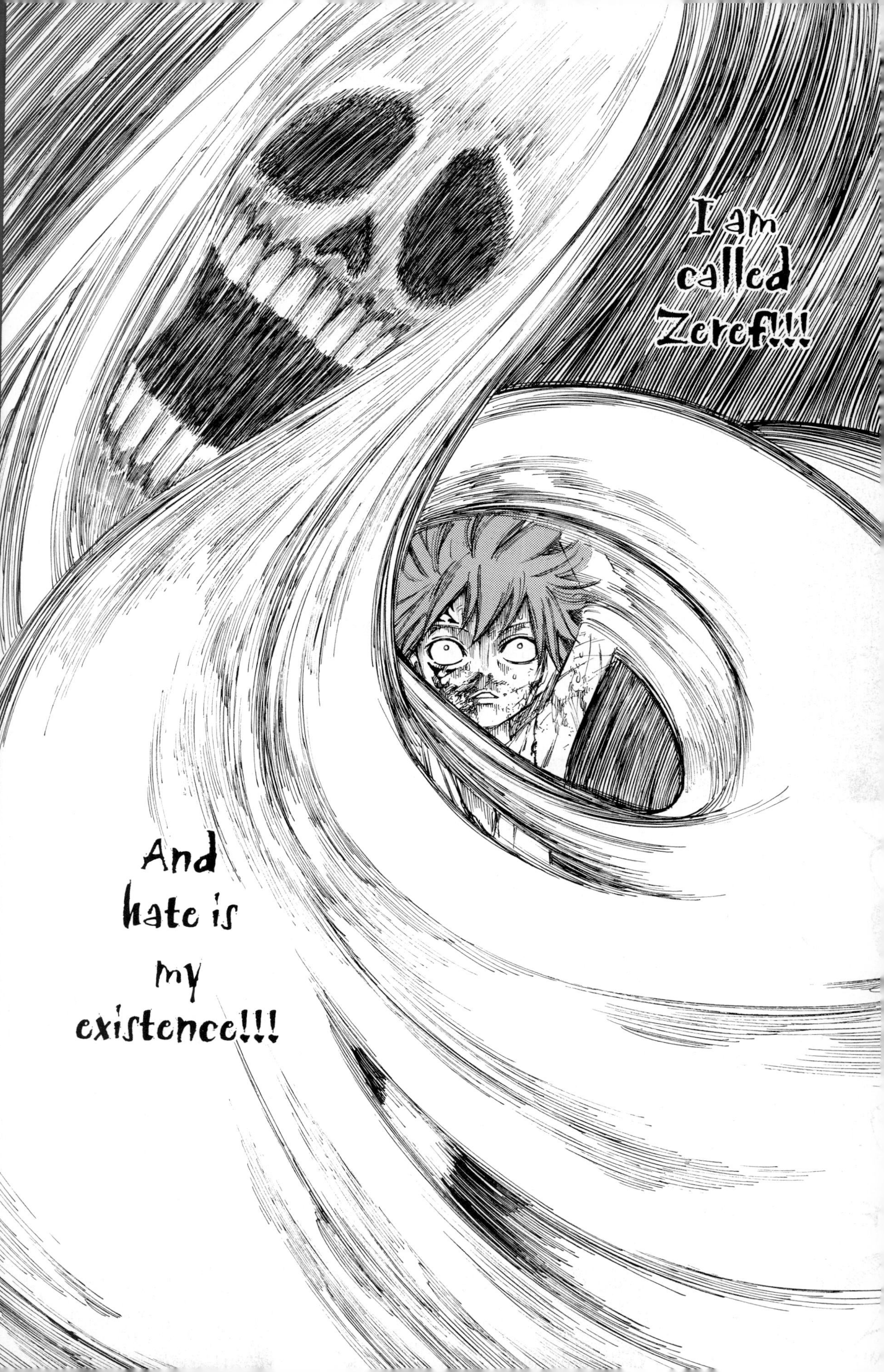
I am called Zeref!!!
And hate is my existence!!!

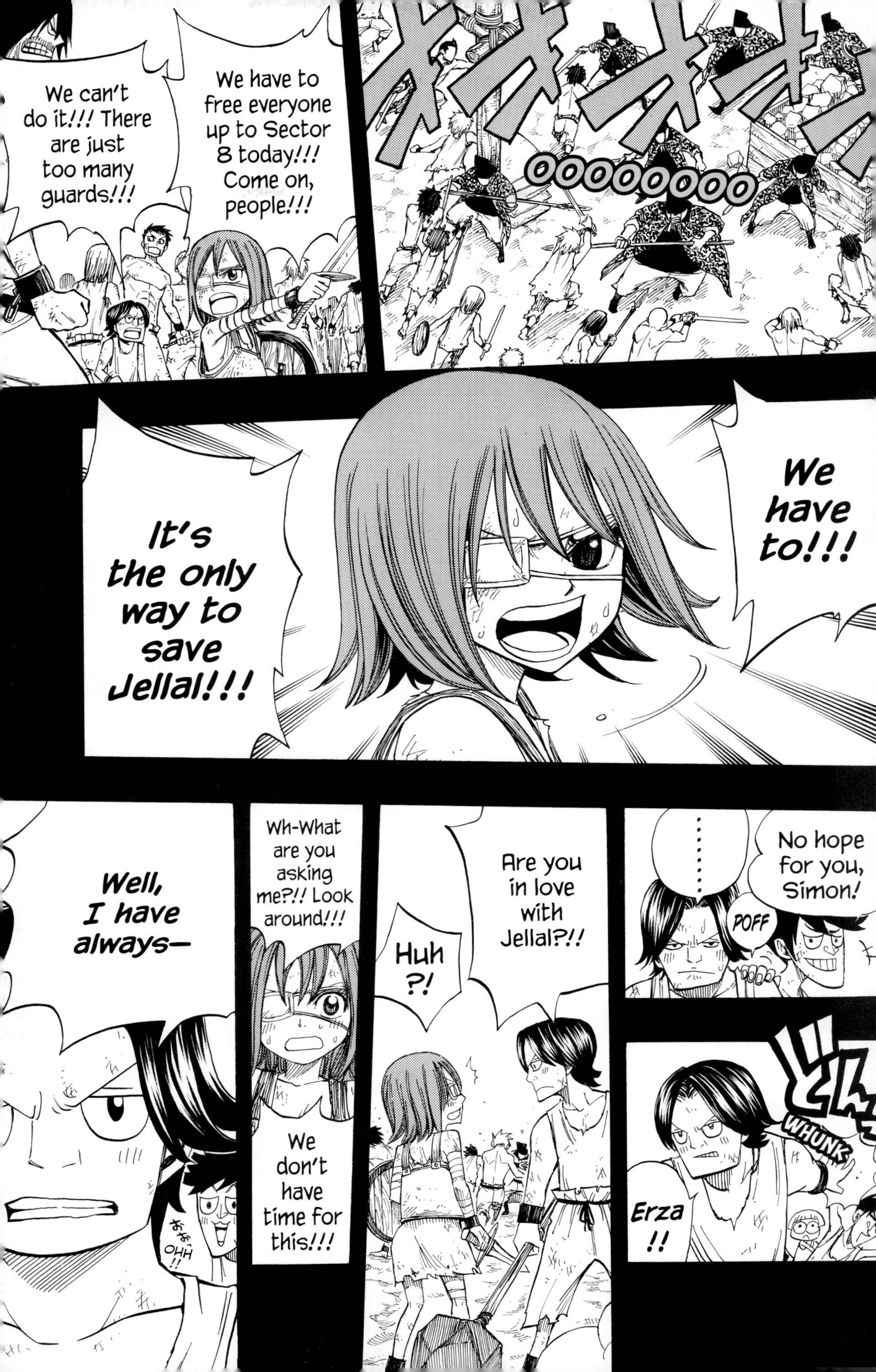
OOOOOOOO
We have to free everyone up to Sector 8 today!!! Come on, people!!!
We can't do it!!! There are just too many guards!!!
We have to!!!
It's the only way to save Jellal!!!
Erza!!
WHUNK
Are you in love with Jellal?!!
Huh?!
Wh-What are you asking me?!! Look around!!!
We don't have time for this!!!
Well, I have always—
OHH!!
......
POFF
No hope for you, Simon!

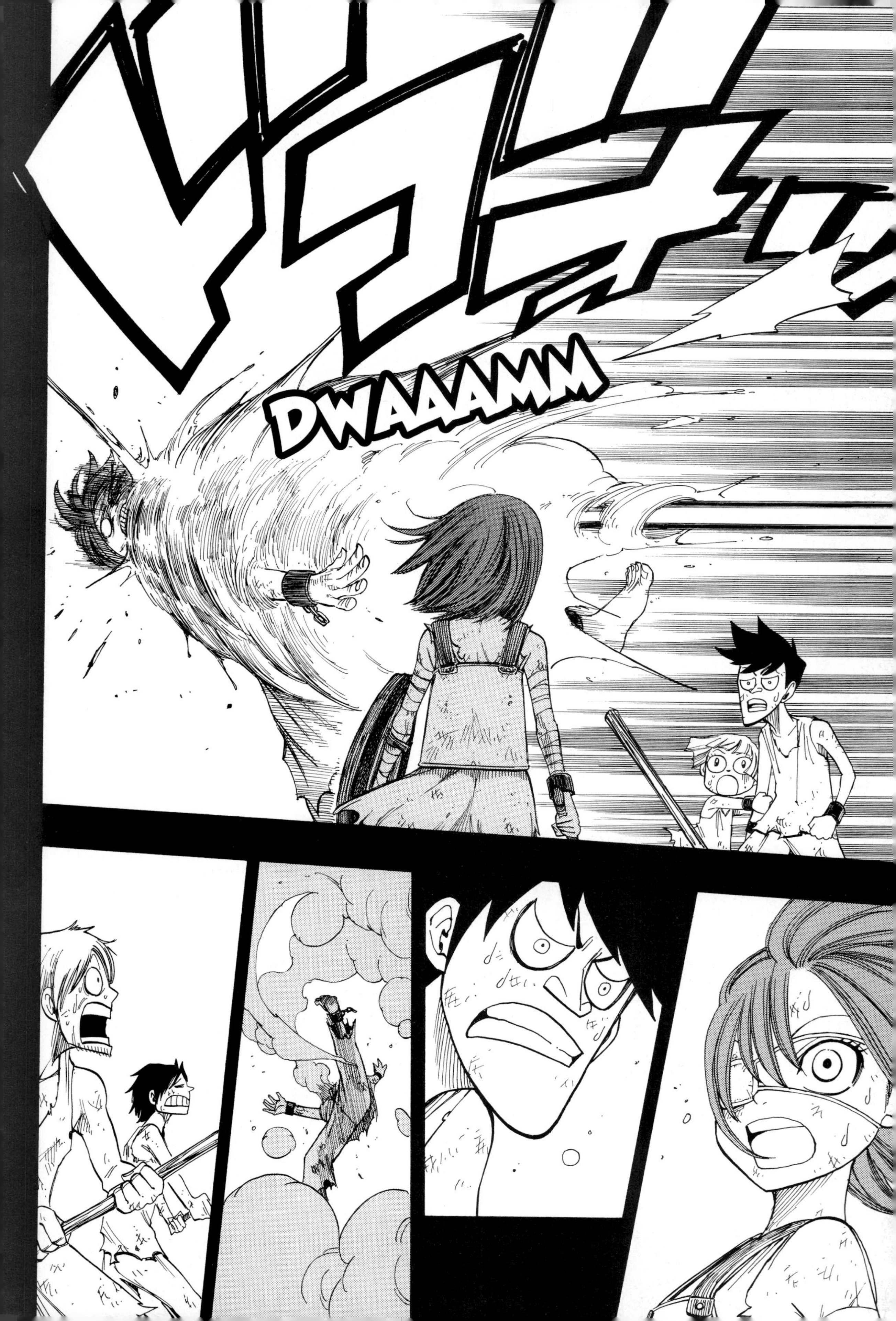
DWAAAMM

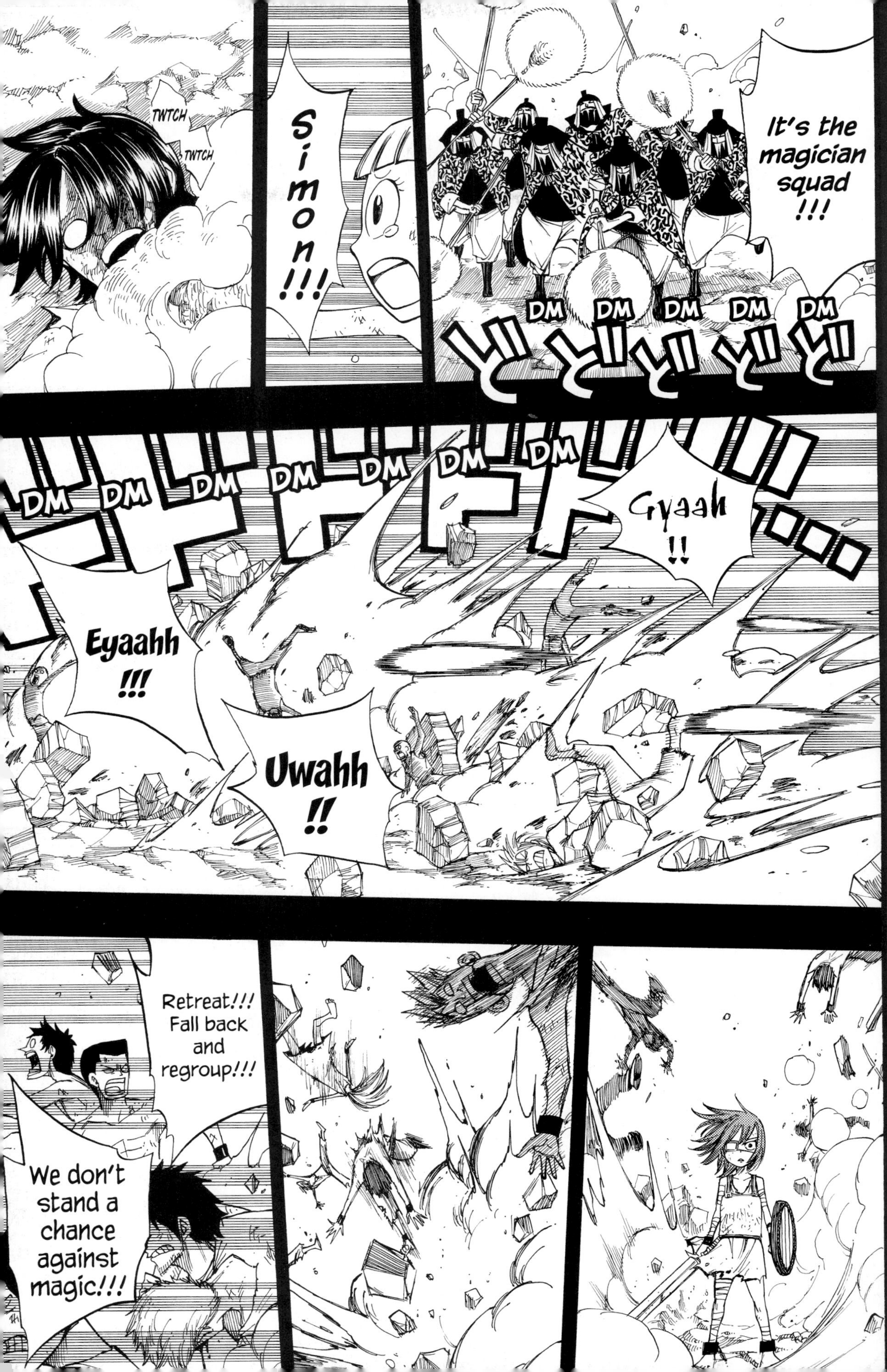
It's the magician squad !!!
DM DM DM DM DM
Simon!!!
TWTCH
TWTCH
DM DM DM DM DM DM DM
Gyaah !!
Uwahh !!
Eyaahh !!!
Retreat!!! Fall back and regroup!!!
We don't stand a chance against magic!!!

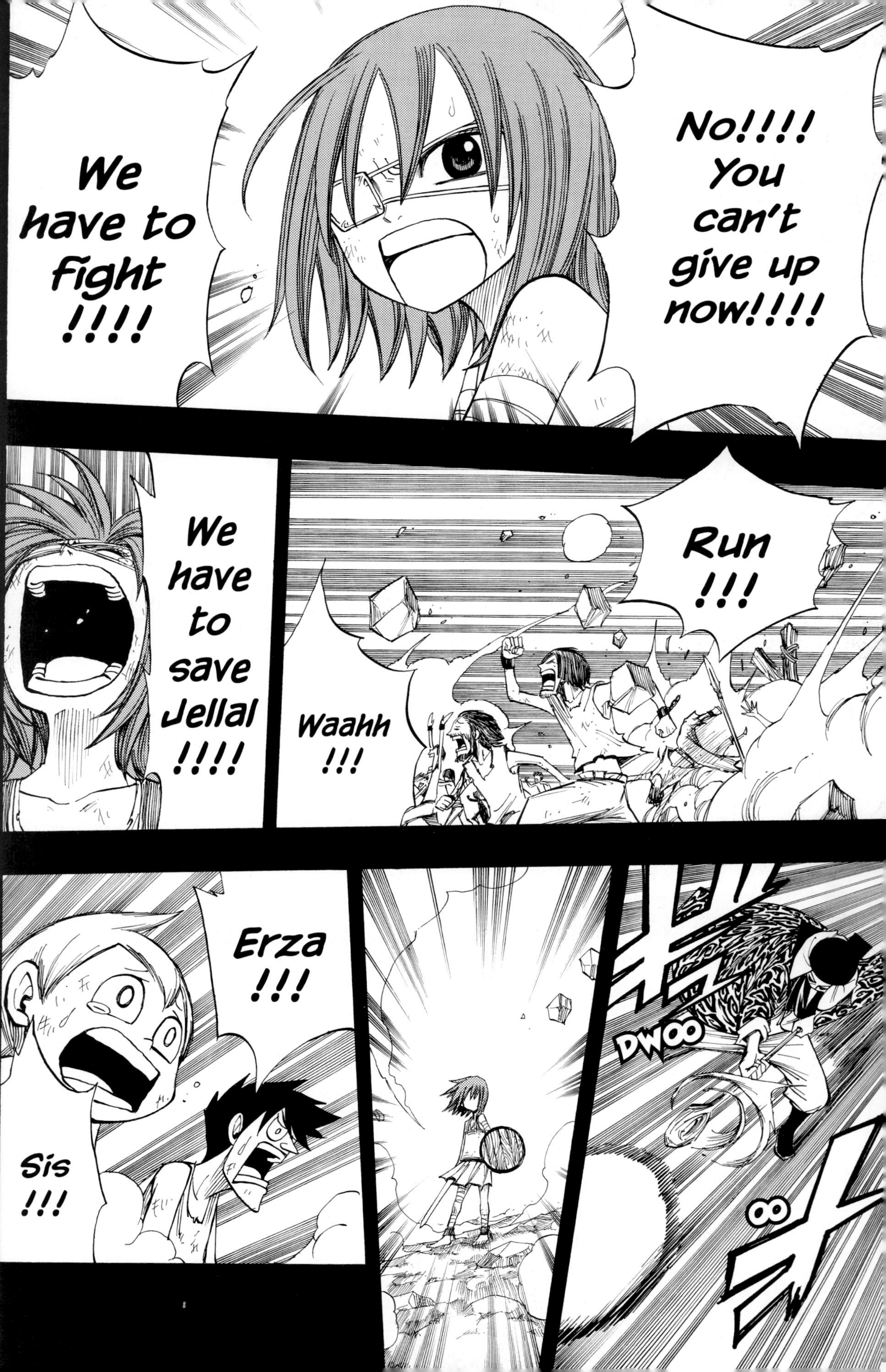
No!!!! You can't give up now!!!!
We have to fight!!!!
Run!!!
Waahh!!!
We have to save Jellal!!!!
DWOO
Erza!!!
Sis!!!

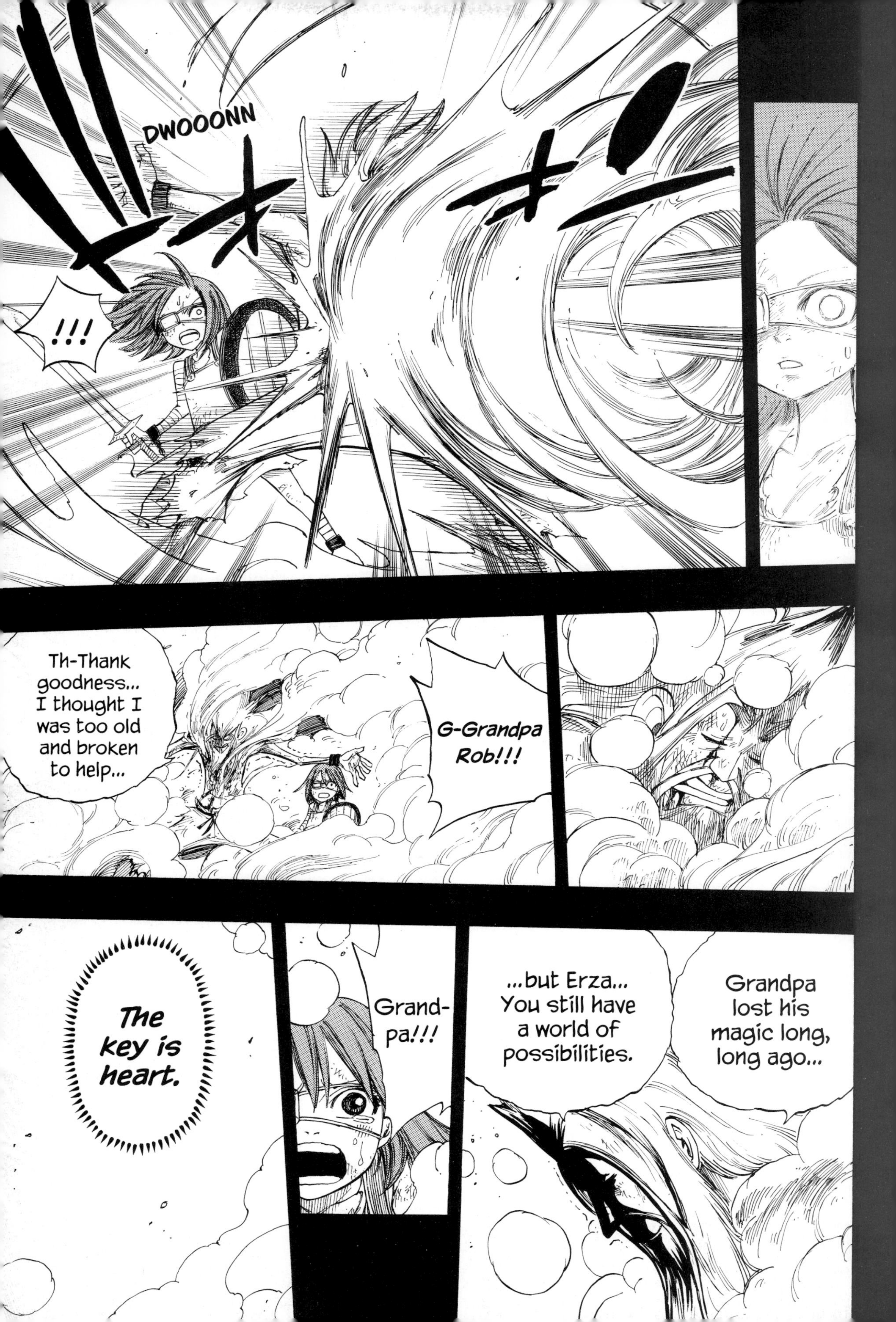
DWOOONN
!!!
G-Grandpa Rob!!!
Th-Thank goodness... I thought I was too old and broken to help...
Grandpa lost his magic long, long ago...
...but Erza... You still have a world of possibilities.
Grand-pa!!!
The key is heart.

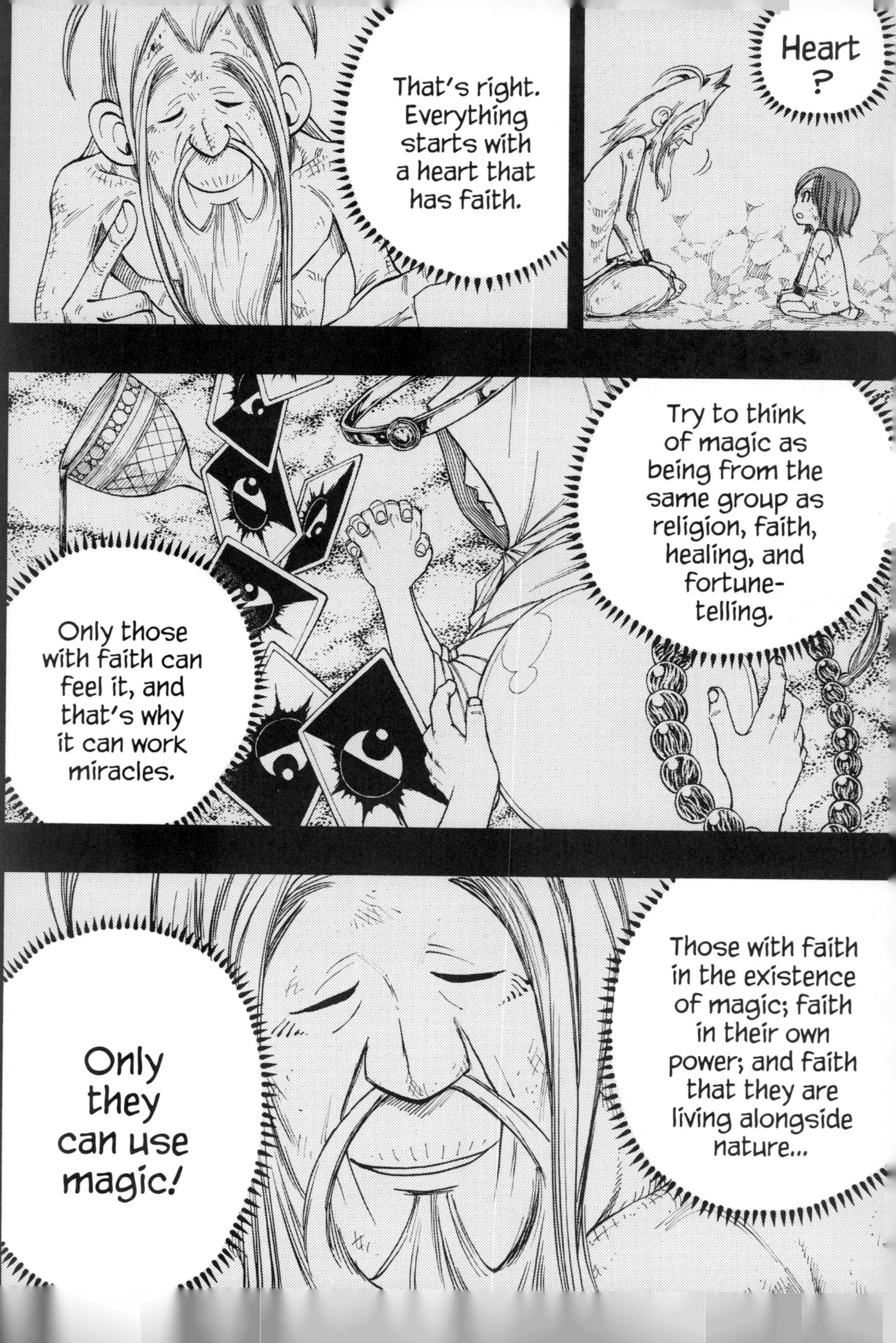
Heart?
That's right. Everything starts with a heart that has faith.
Try to think of magic as being from the same group as religion, faith, healing, and fortune-telling.
Only those with faith can feel it, and that's why it can work miracles.
Those with faith in the existence of magic; faith in their own power; and faith that they are living alongside nature...
Only they can use magic!

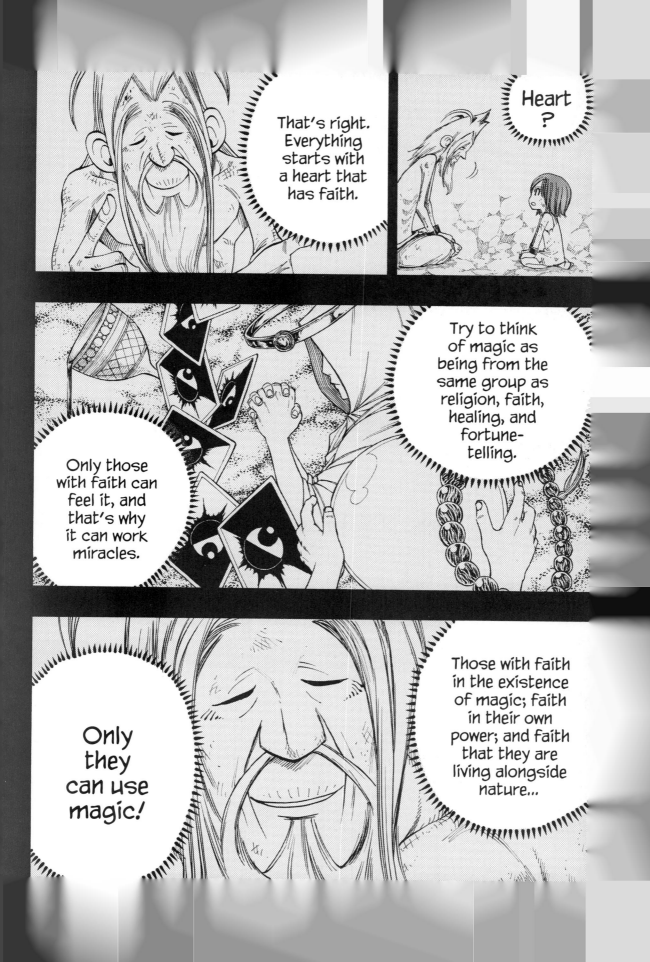

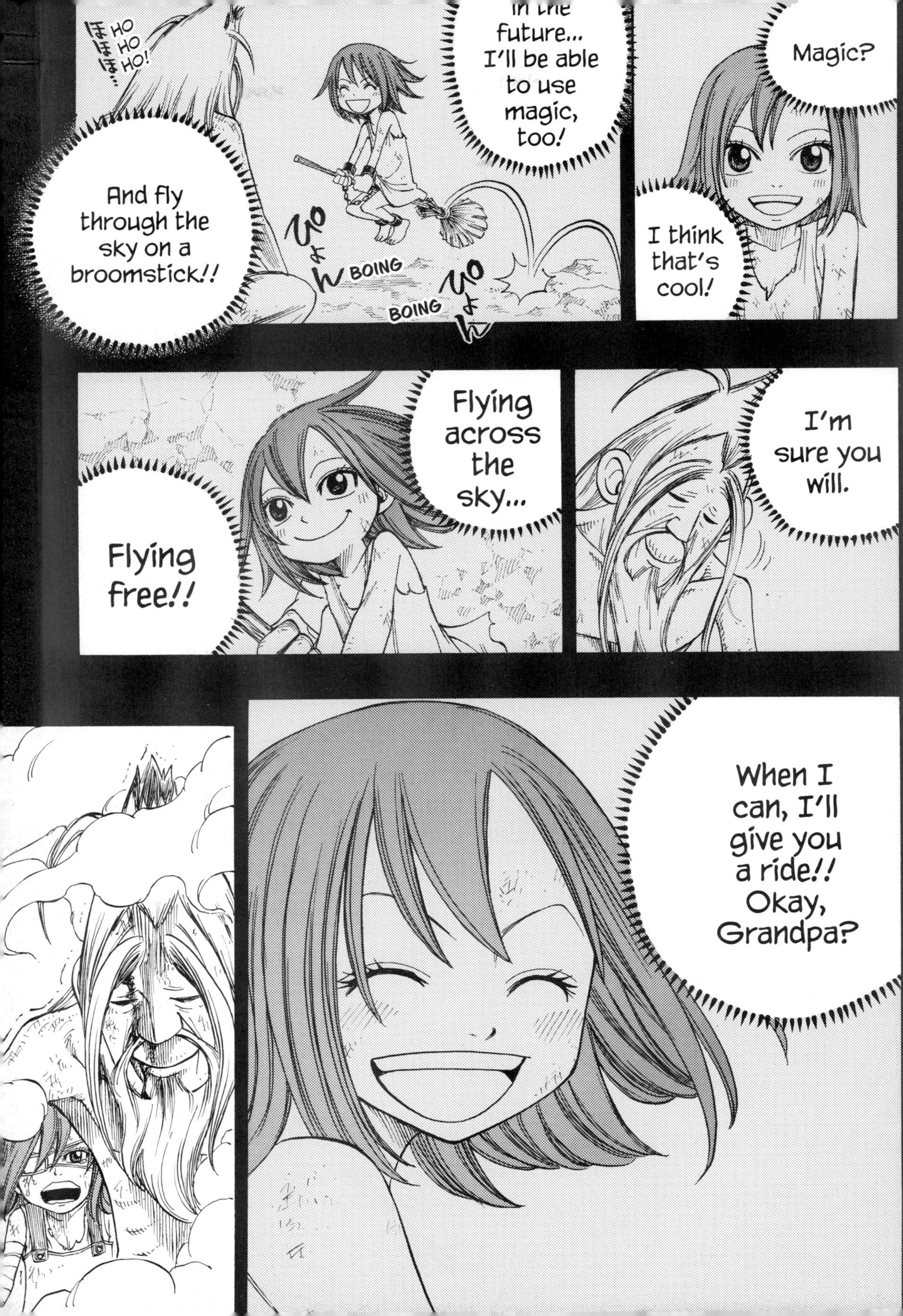
Magic?
I think that's cool!
future... I'll be able to use magic, too!
ほほほ
HO HO HO!
And fly through the sky on a broomstick!!
BOING
BOING
I'm sure you will.
Flying across the sky...
Flying free!!
When I can, I'll give you a ride!! Okay, Grandpa?

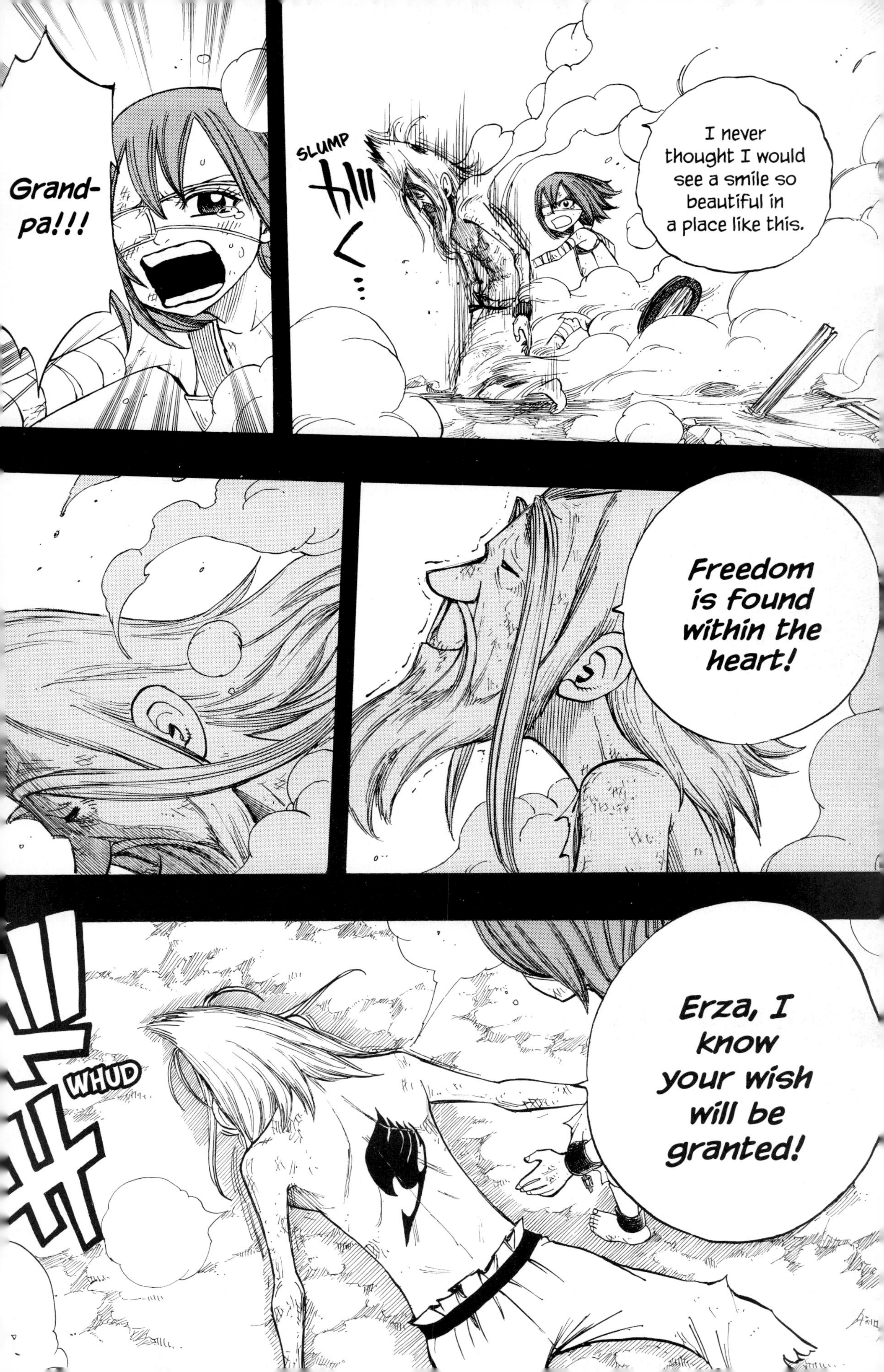
I never thought I would see a smile so beautiful in a place like this.
SLUMP
Grand-pa!!!
Freedom is found within the heart!
Erza, I know your wish will be granted!
WHUD

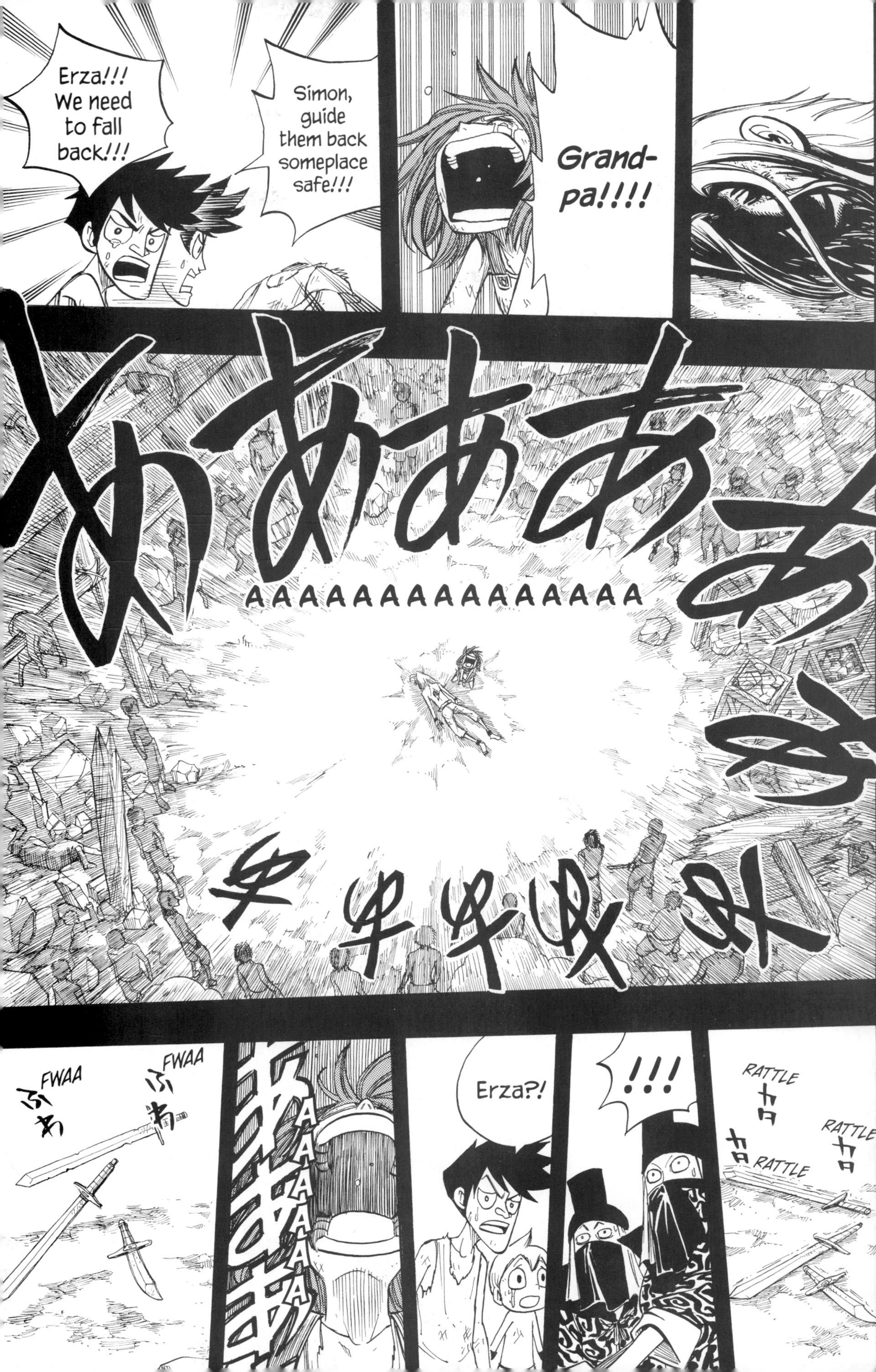
Grand-pa!!!!
Erza!!! We need to fall back!!!
Simon, guide them back someplace safe!!!
AAAAAAAAAAAAAAAAA
RATTLE
RATTLE
RATTLE
!!!
Erza?!
AAAAAAAA
FWAA
FWAA

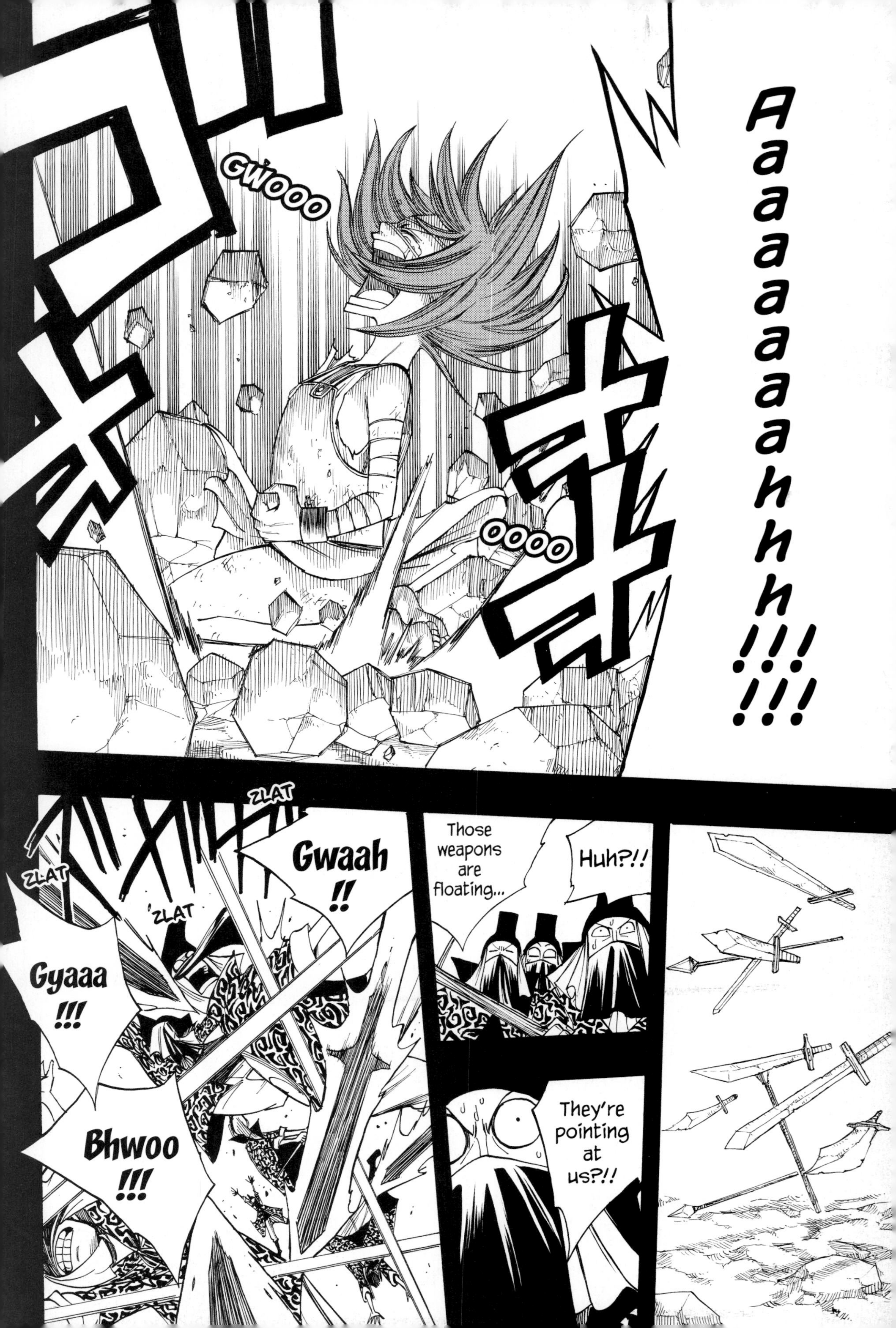
Aaaaaaaahhh!!!!!!
GWOOO
OOOO
Huh?!!
Those weapons are floating...
They're pointing at us?!!
ZLAT
ZLAT
Gwaah!!
ZLAT
Gyaaa!!!
Bhwoo!!!

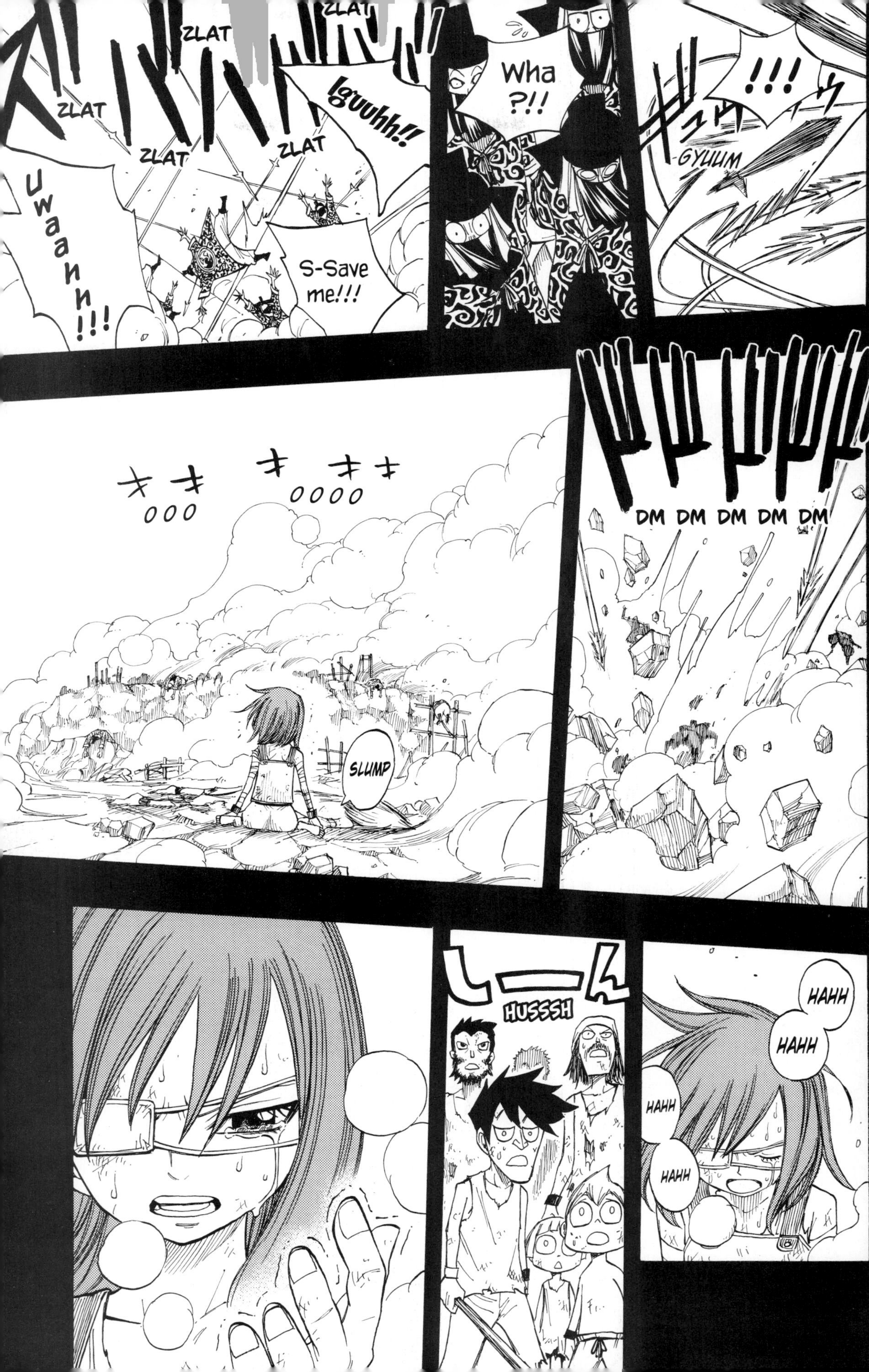
!!!
GYUUM
Wha ?!!
ZLAT
ZLAT
ZLAT
ZLAT
ZLAT
ZLAT
Iguuhh!!
S-Save me!!!
Uwaahh!!!
DM DM DM DM DM
SLUMP
HAHH
HAHH
HAHH
HAHH
HUSSSH

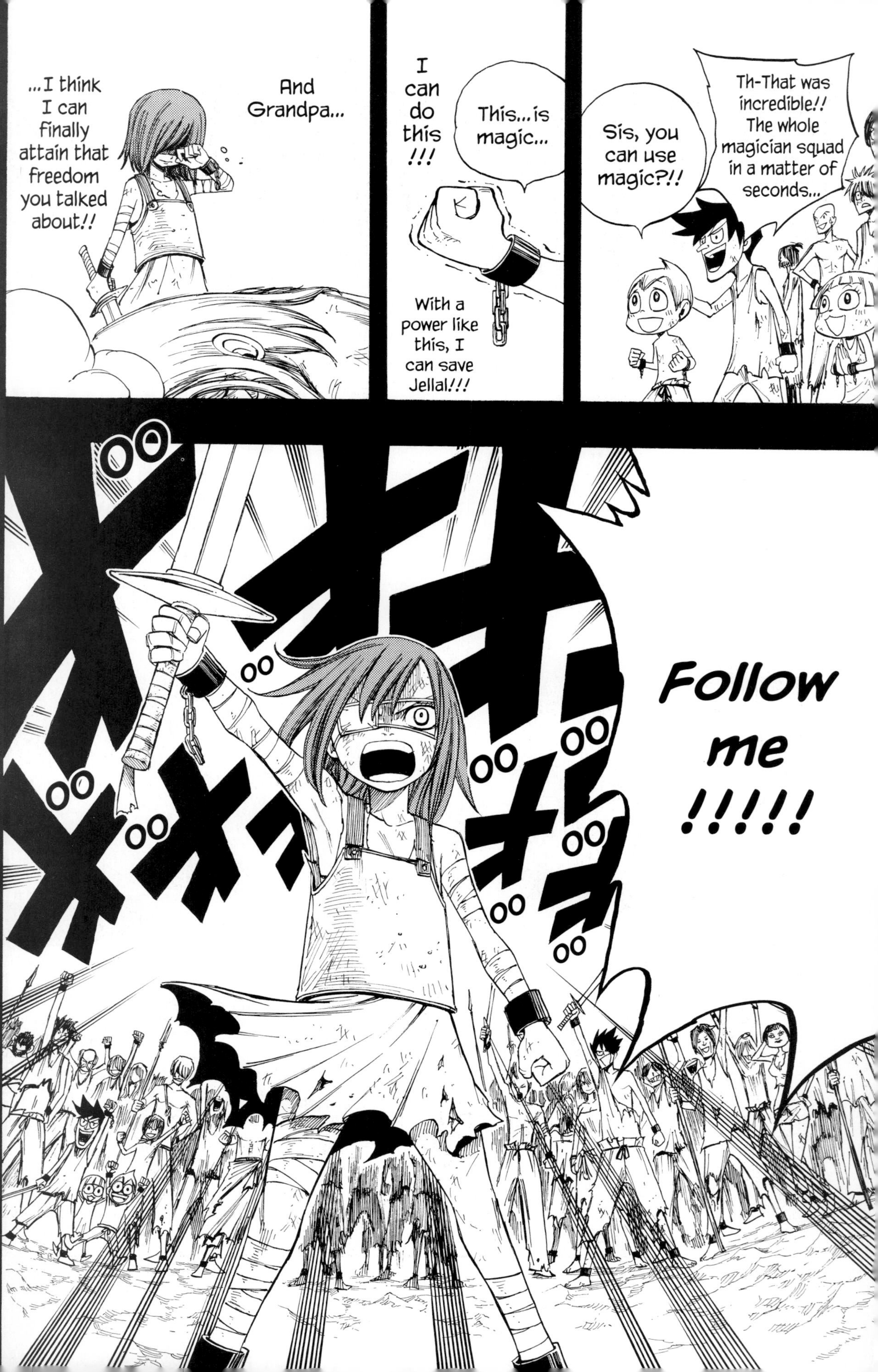
Th-That was incredible!! The whole magician squad in a matter of seconds...
Sis, you can use magic?!!
This...is magic...
I can do this!!!
With a power like this, I can save Jellal!!!
And Grandpa...
...I think I can finally attain that freedom you talked about!!
Follow me!!!!!!

Chapter 82:
Howling at the Moon

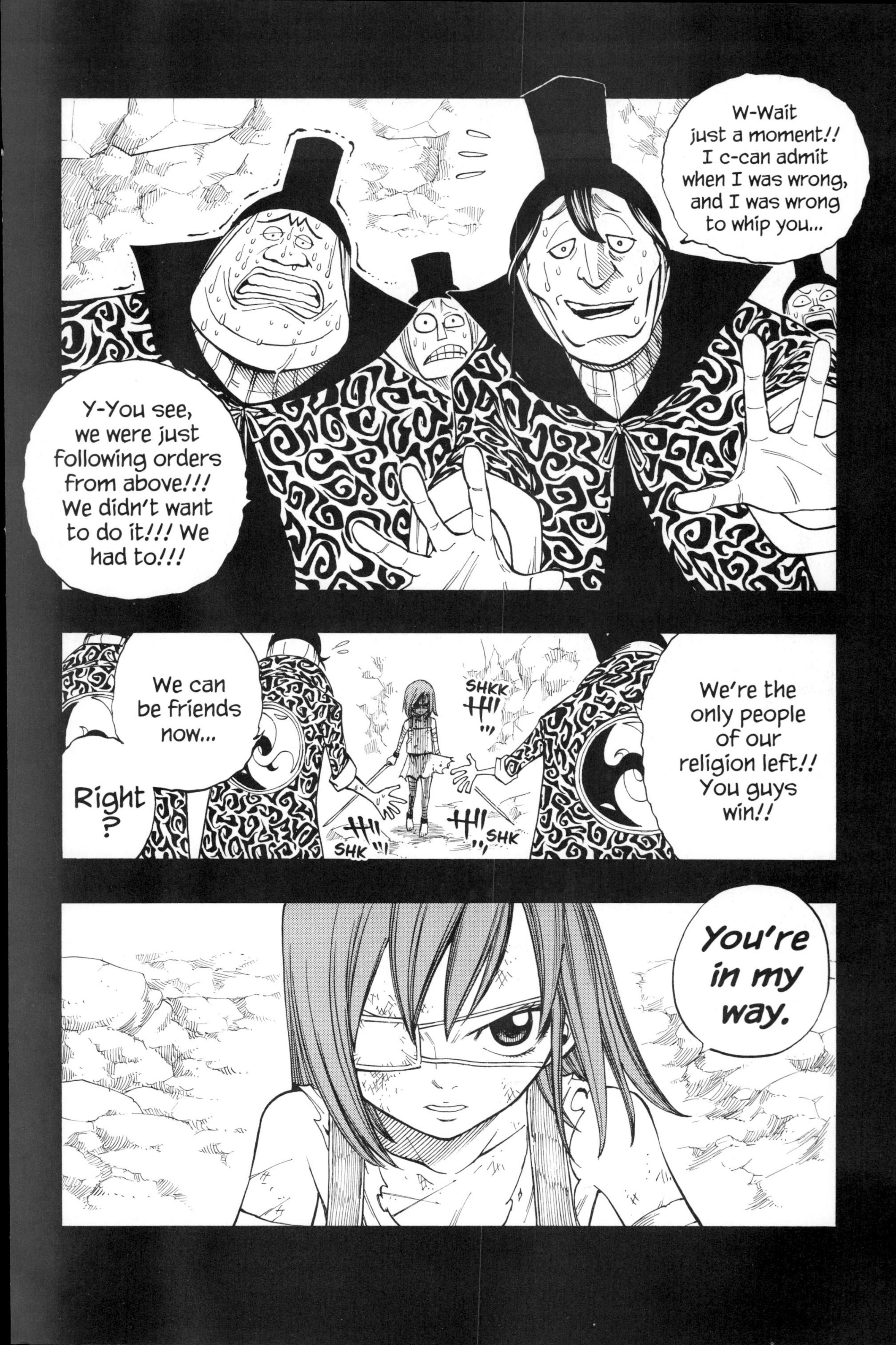
W-Wait just a moment!! I c-can admit when I was wrong, and I was wrong to whip you...
Y-You see, we were just following orders from above!!! We didn't want to do it!!! We had to!!!
We're the only people of our religion left!! You guys win!!
SHKK
SHK
SHK
We can be friends now...
Right?
You're in my way.

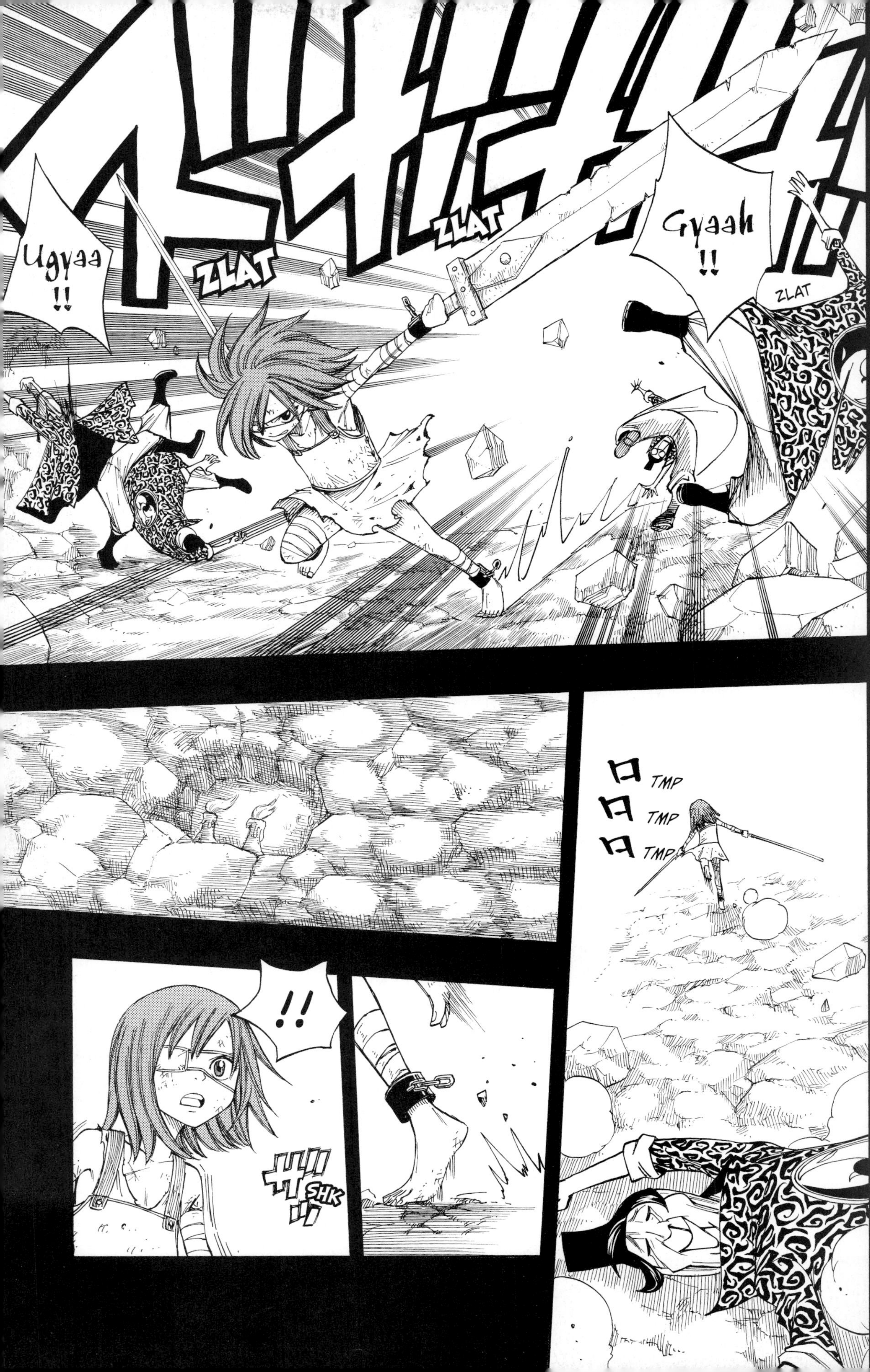
Gyaah !!
ZLAT
ZLAT
ZLAT
Ugyaa !!
TMP
TMP
TMP
!!
SHK

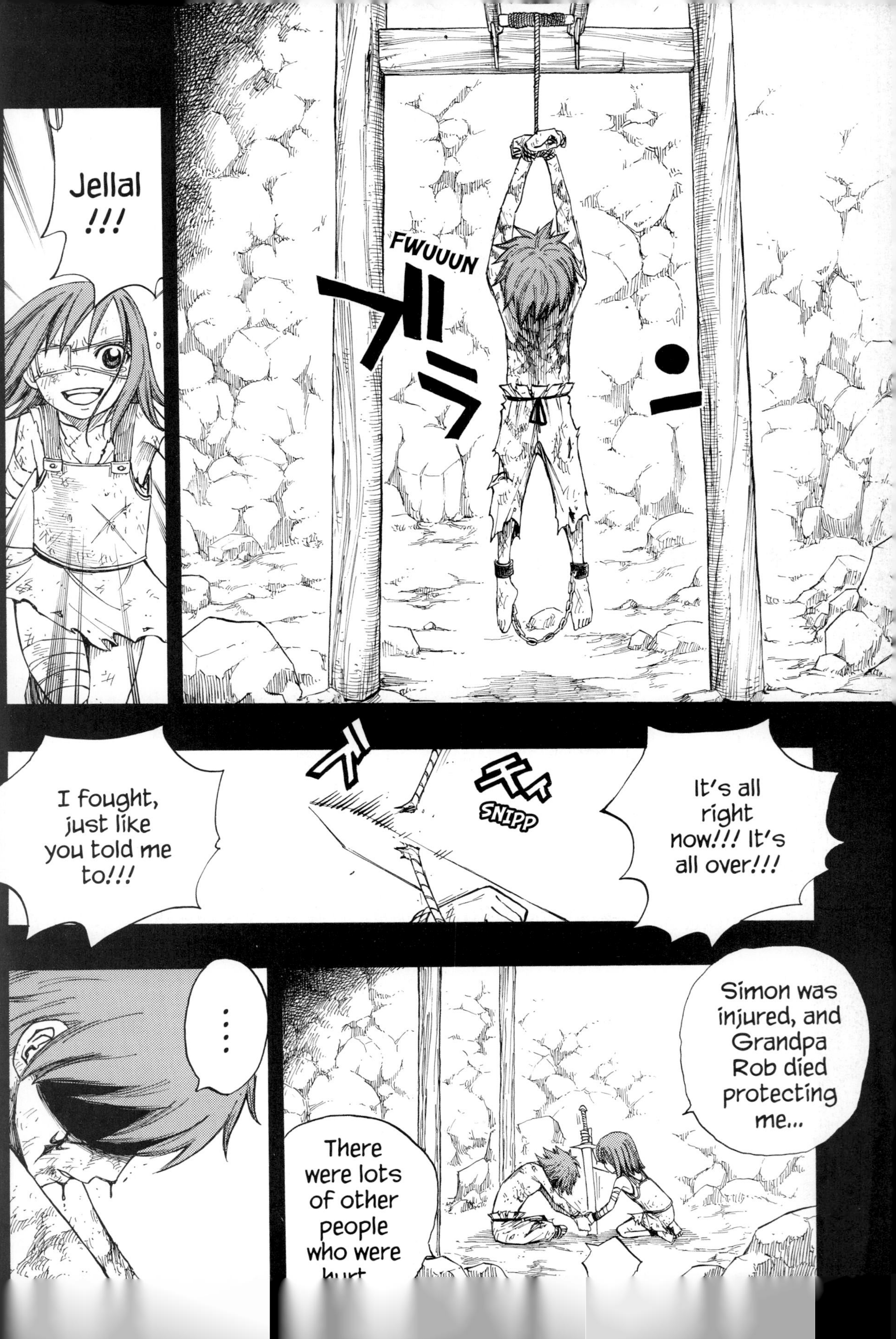
FWUUUN
Jellal !!!
It's all right now!!! It's all over!!!
SNIPP
I fought, just like you told me to!!!
Simon was injured, and Grandpa Rob died protecting me...
There were lots of other people who were
....

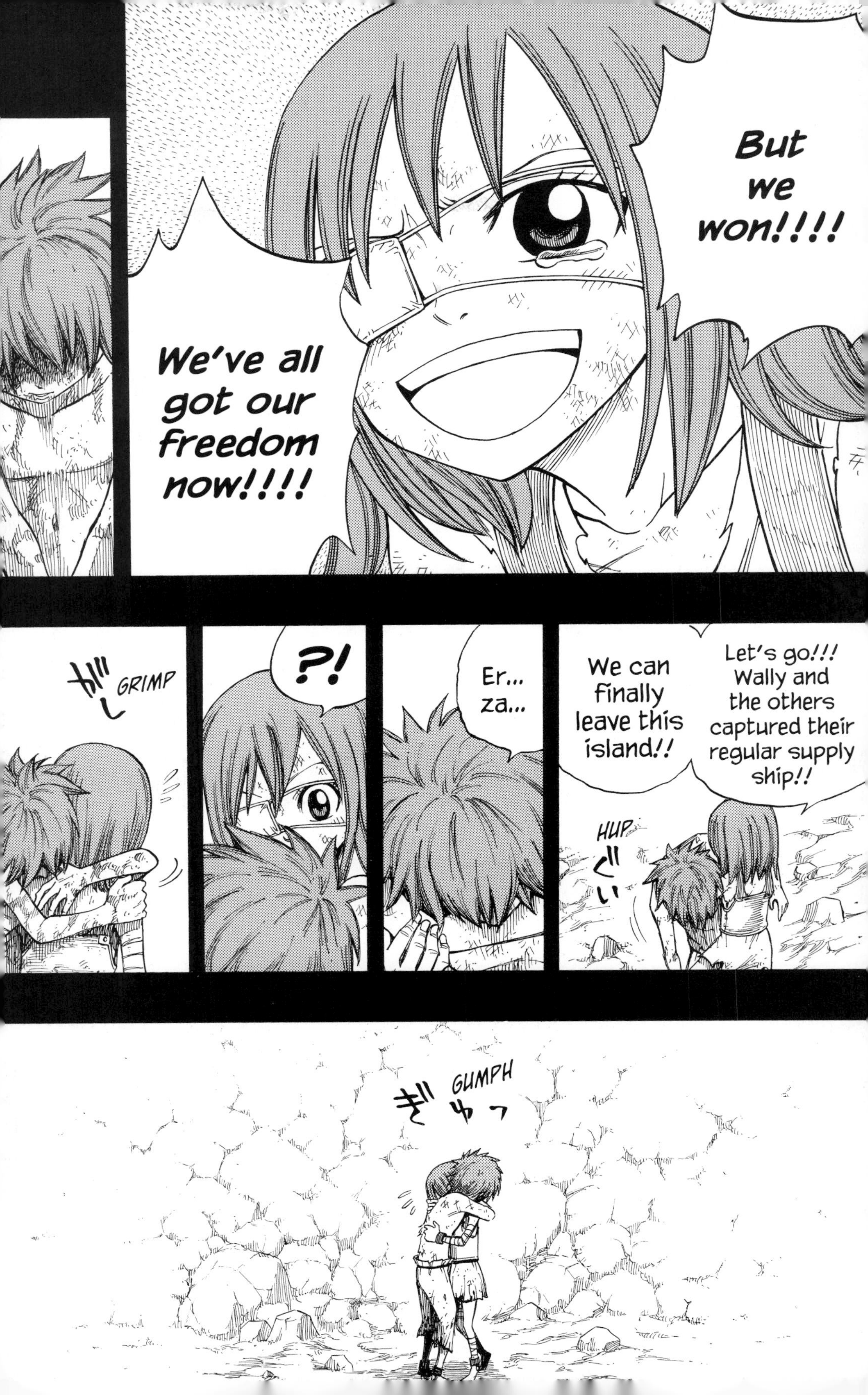
But we won!!!!
We've all got our freedom now!!!!
Let's go!!! Wally and the others captured their regular supply ship!!
We can finally leave this island!!
ぐい HUP
Er... za...
?!
がし GRIMP
ぎゅっ GUMPH

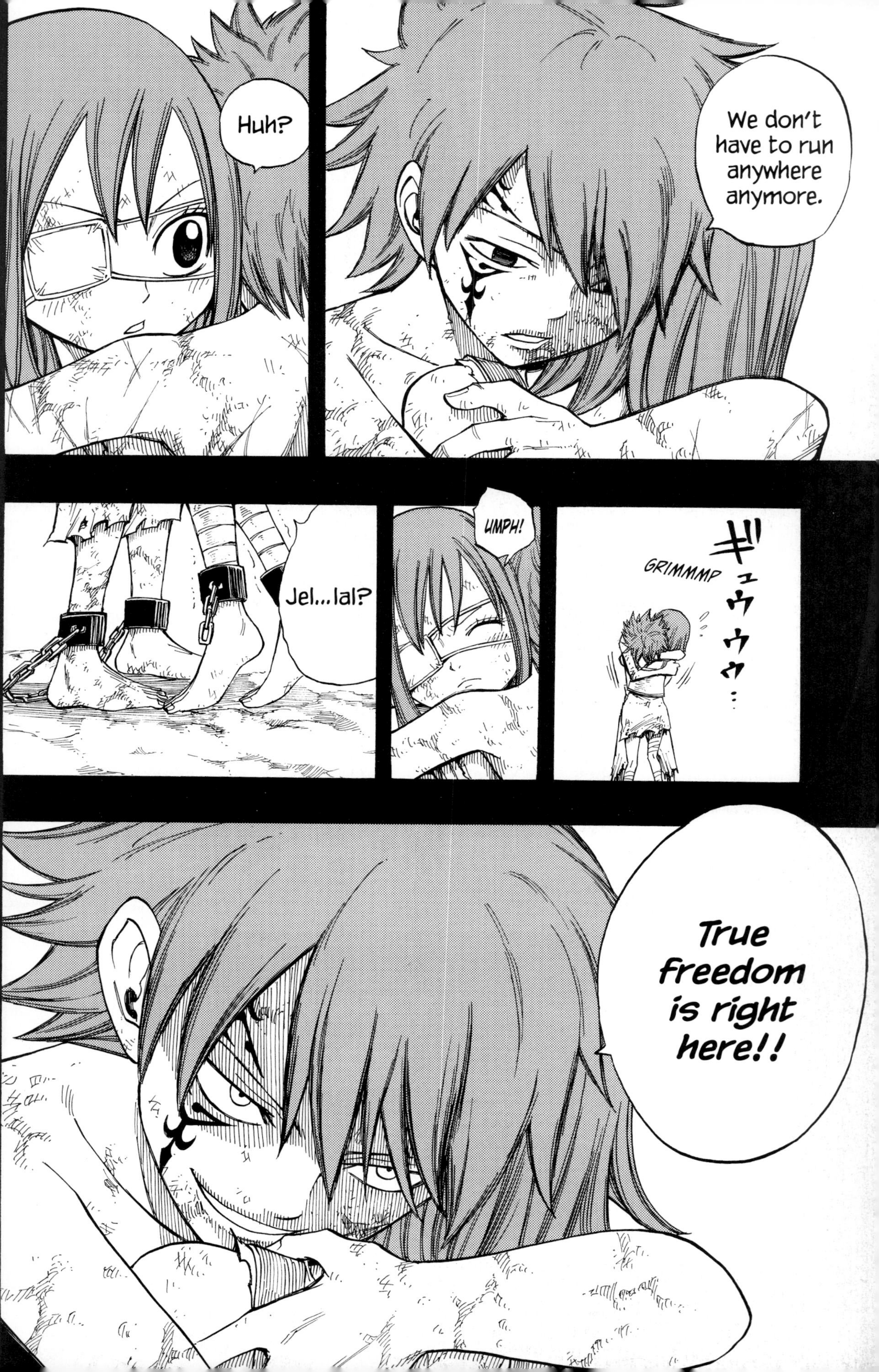
We don't have to run anywhere anymore.
Huh?
ギュウウウ…
GRIMMMP
UMPH!
Jel...lal?
True freedom is right here!!

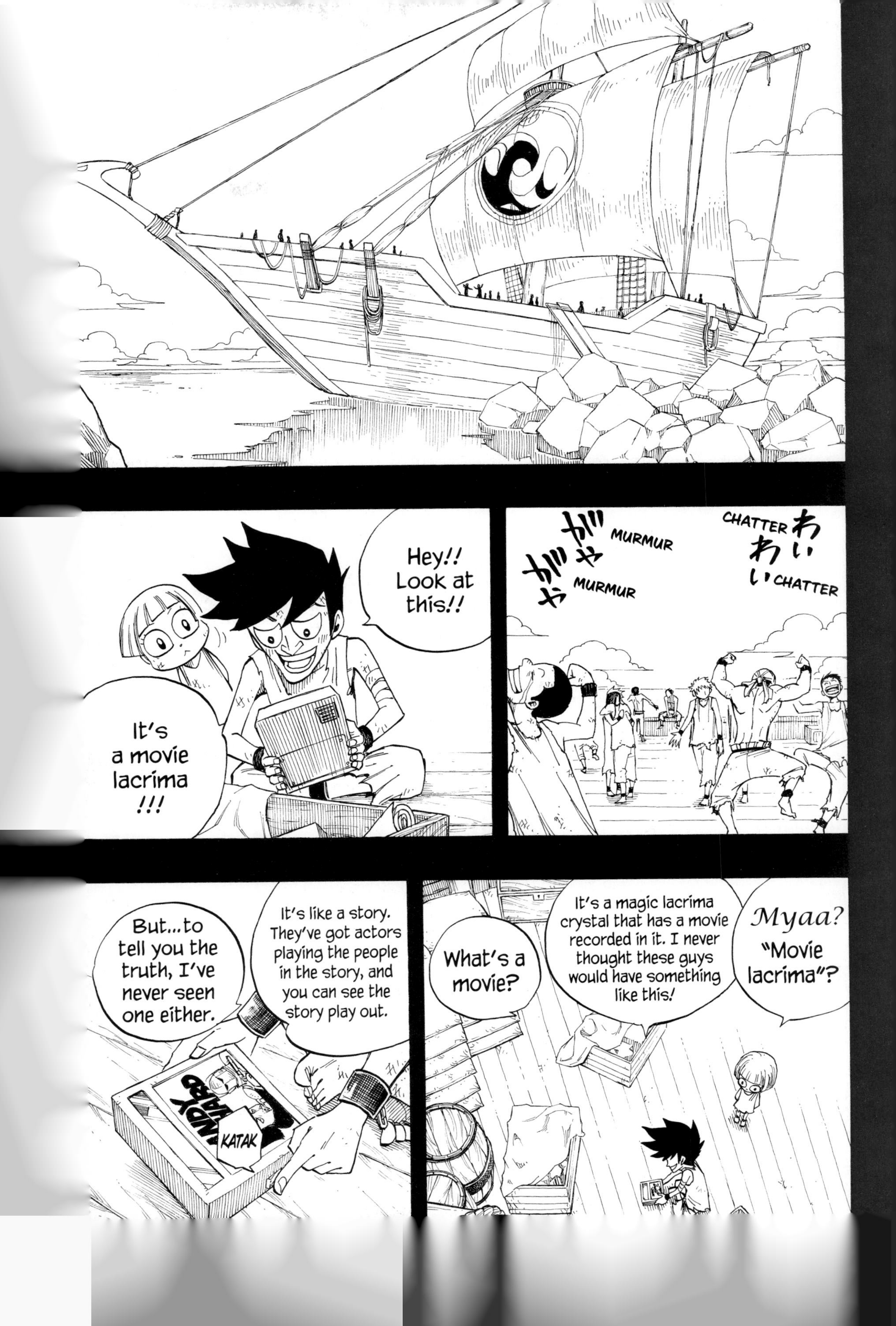

わい わい
CHATTER
CHATTER
がや がや
MURMUR
MURMUR
Hey!! Look at this!!
It's a movie lacrima !!!
Myaa? "Movie lacrima"?
It's a magic lacrima crystal that has a movie recorded in it. I never thought these guys would have something like this!
What's a movie?
It's like a story. They've got actors playing the people in the story, and you can see the story play out.
But...to tell you the truth, I've never seen one either.
KATAK

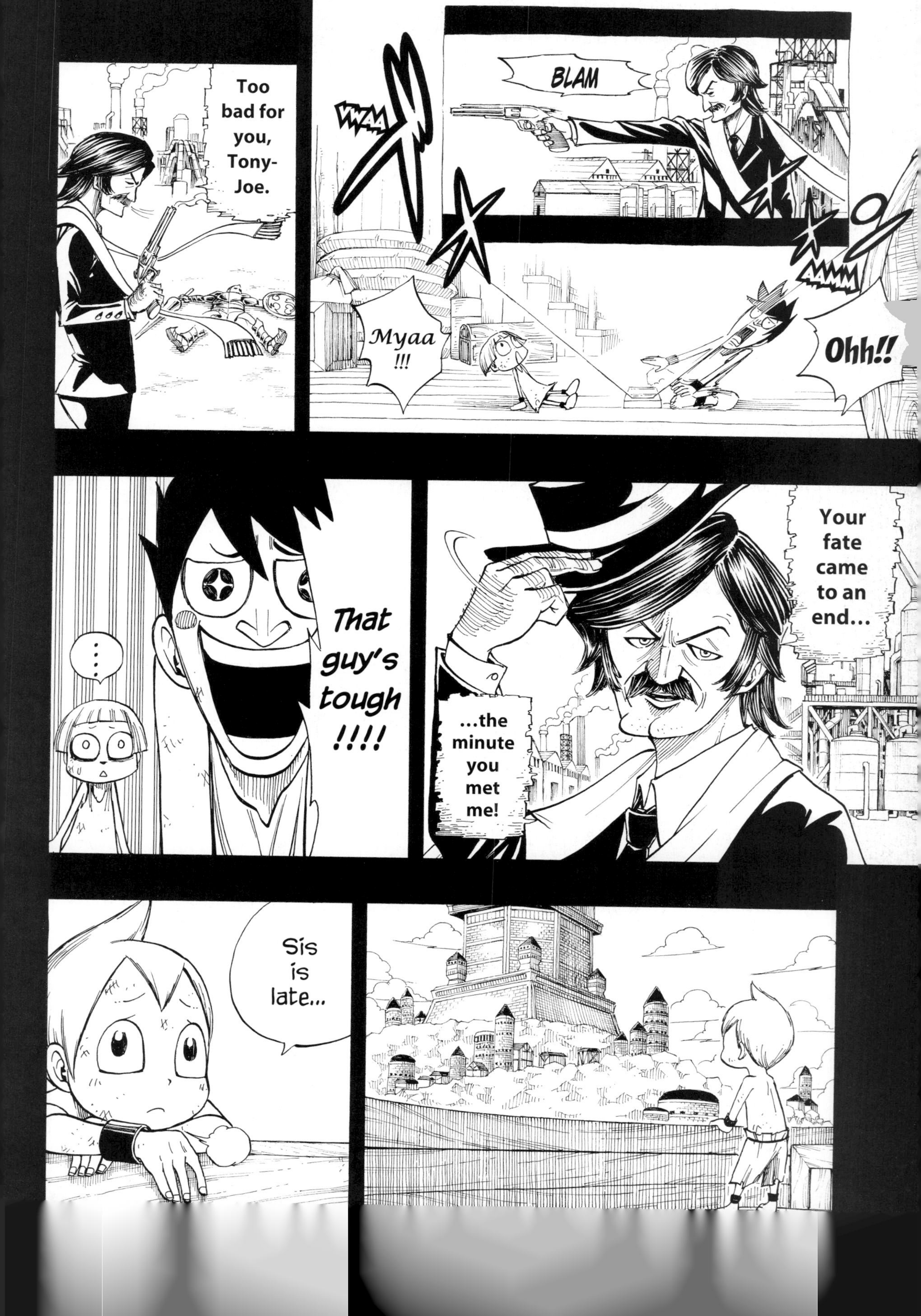
BLAM
VWAA
AAMM
Ohh!!
Myaa !!!
Too bad for you, Tony-Joe.
Your fate came to an end...
...the minute you met me!
That guy's tough !!!!
...
Sis is late...

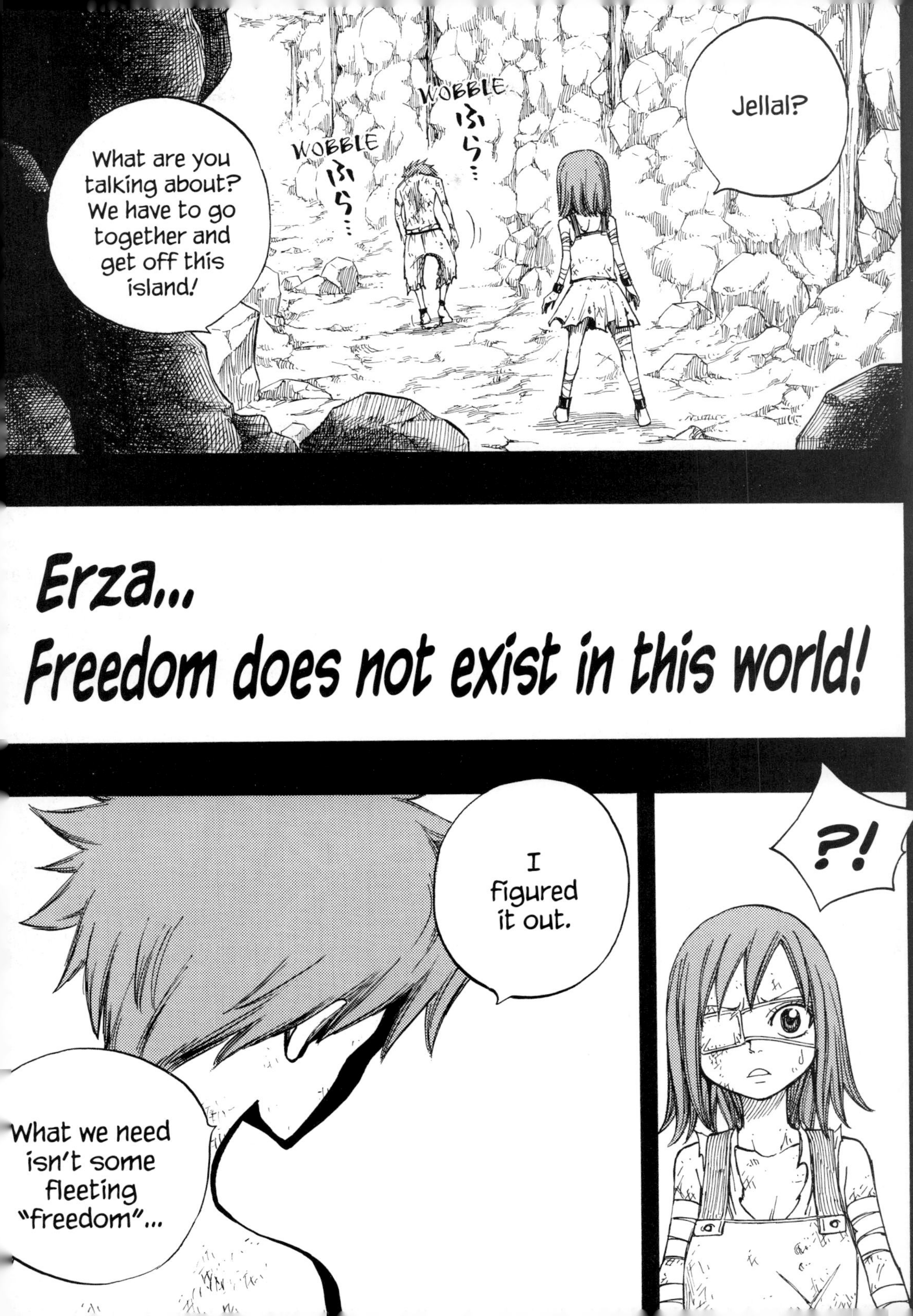
Jellal?
WOBBLE ふら…
WOBBLE ふら…
What are you talking about? We have to go together and get off this island!
Erza...
Freedom does not exist in this world!
?!
I figured it out.
What we need isn't some fleeting "freedom"...

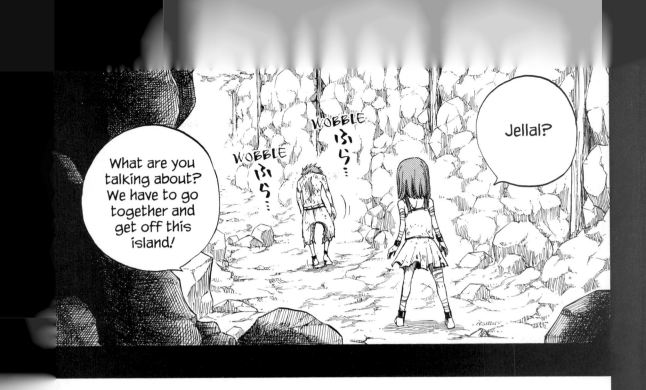

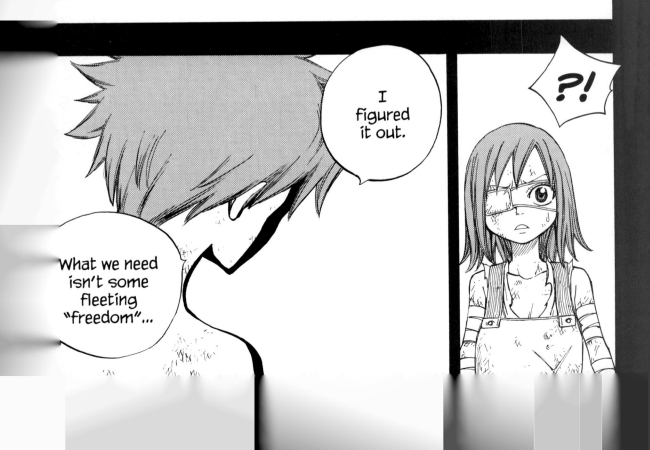

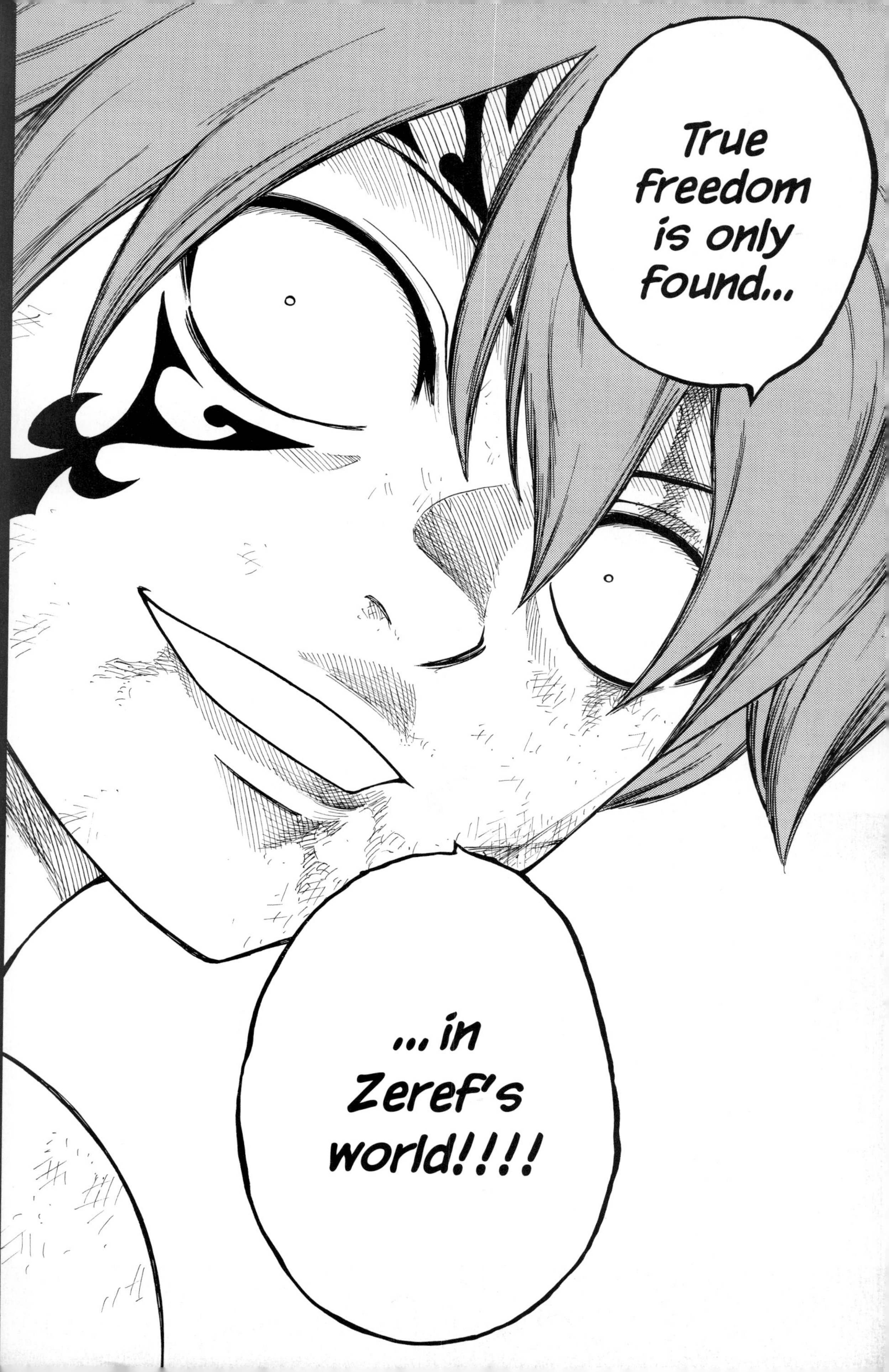
True freedom is only found...
...in Zeref's world!!!!

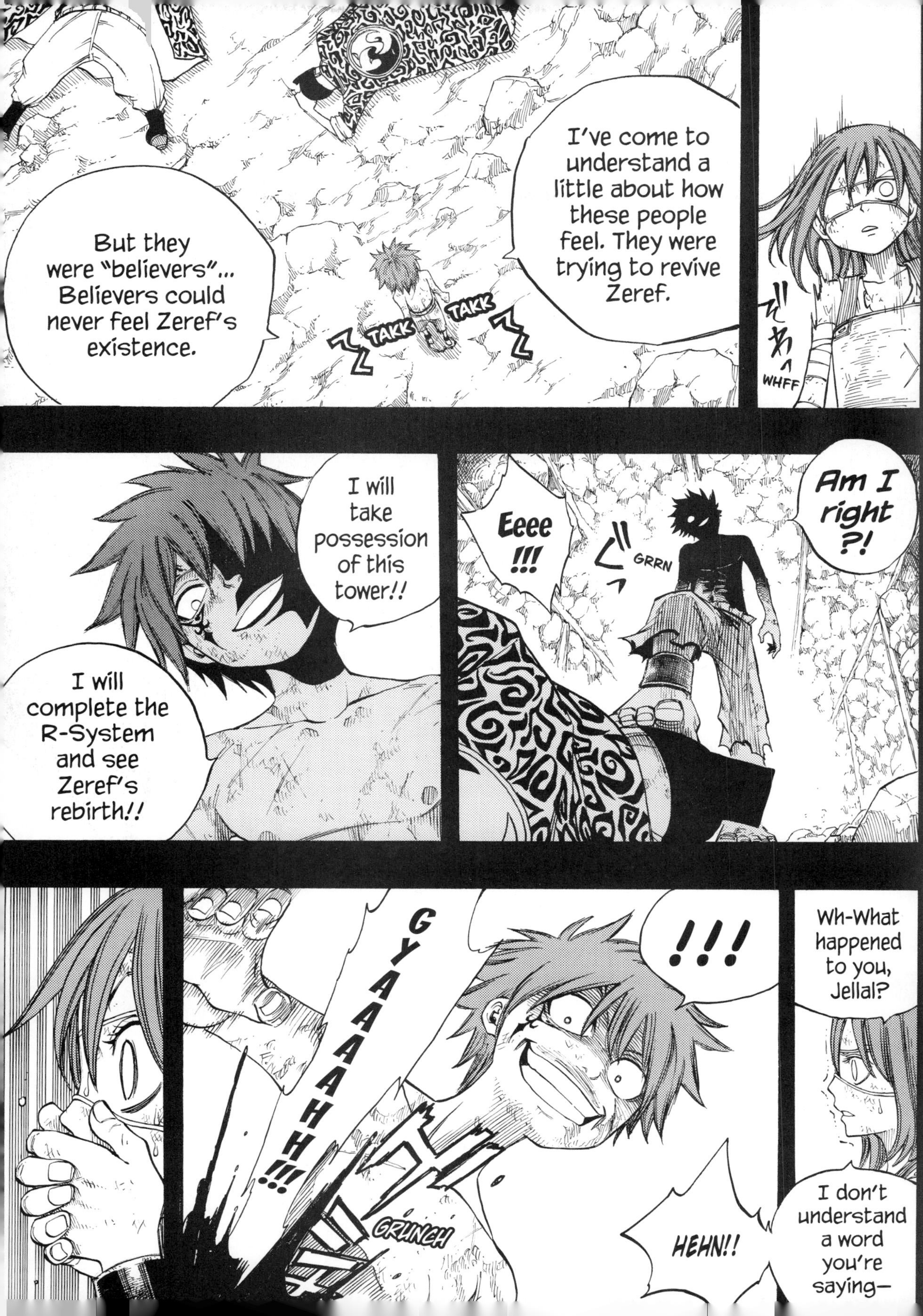
WHFF
I've come to understand a little about how these people feel. They were trying to revive Zeref.
But they were "believers"... Believers could never feel Zeref's existence.
TAKK
TAKK
Am I right?!
GRRN
Eeee!!!
I will take possession of this tower!!
I will complete the R-System and see Zeref's rebirth!!
Wh-What happened to you, Jellal?
I don't understand a word you're saying—
HEHN!!
!!!
GYAAAAAHHH!!!
GRUNCH

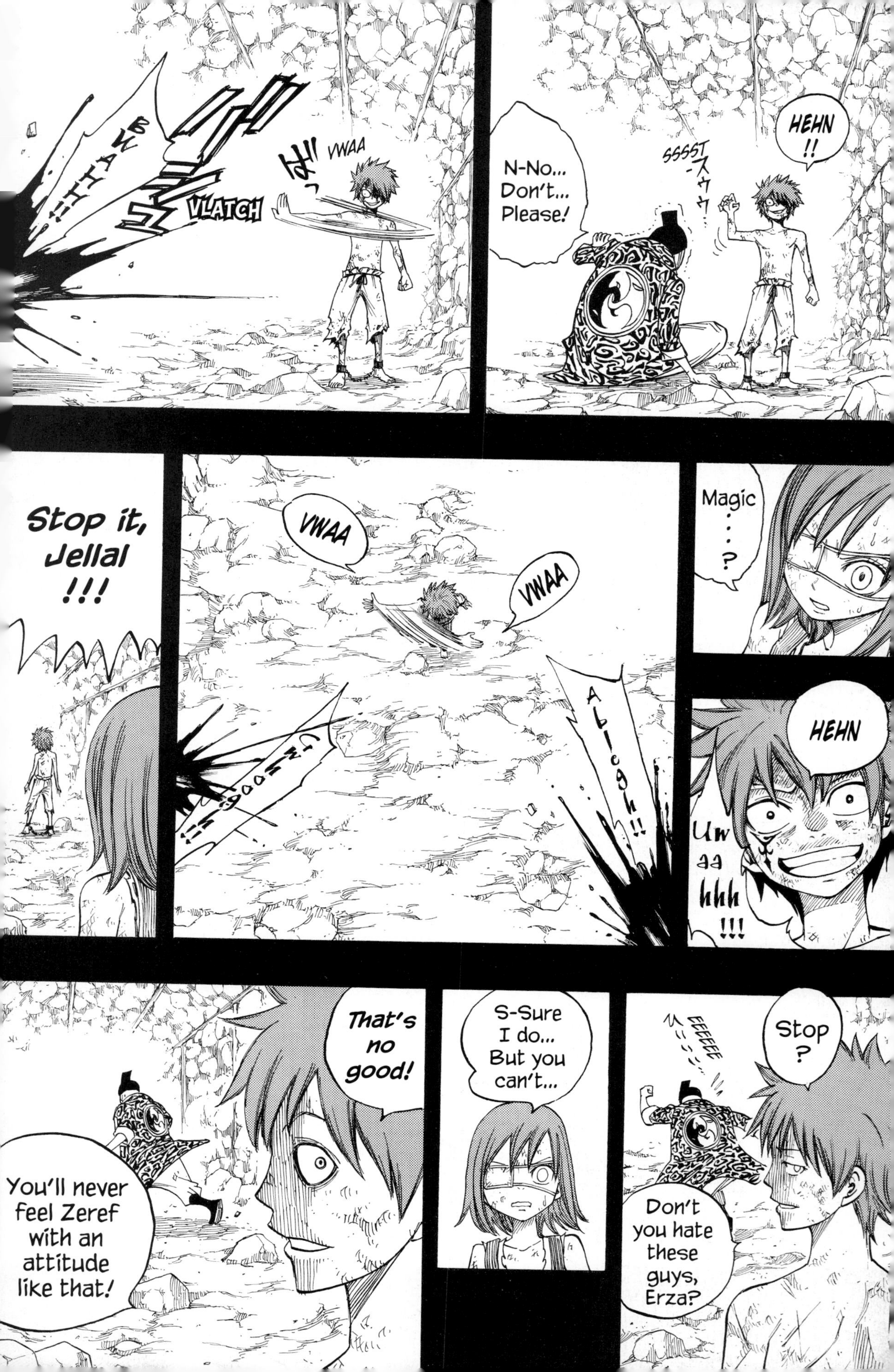
HEHN !!
SSSST
N-No... Don't... Please!
VWAA
VLATCH
Magic...?
HEHN
Uwaahhh!!!
VWAA
VWAA
Ablegh!!
Stop it, Jellal!!!
Stop?
EEEEEE
Don't you hate these guys, Erza?
S-Sure I do... But you can't...
That's no good!
You'll never feel Zeref with an attitude like that!

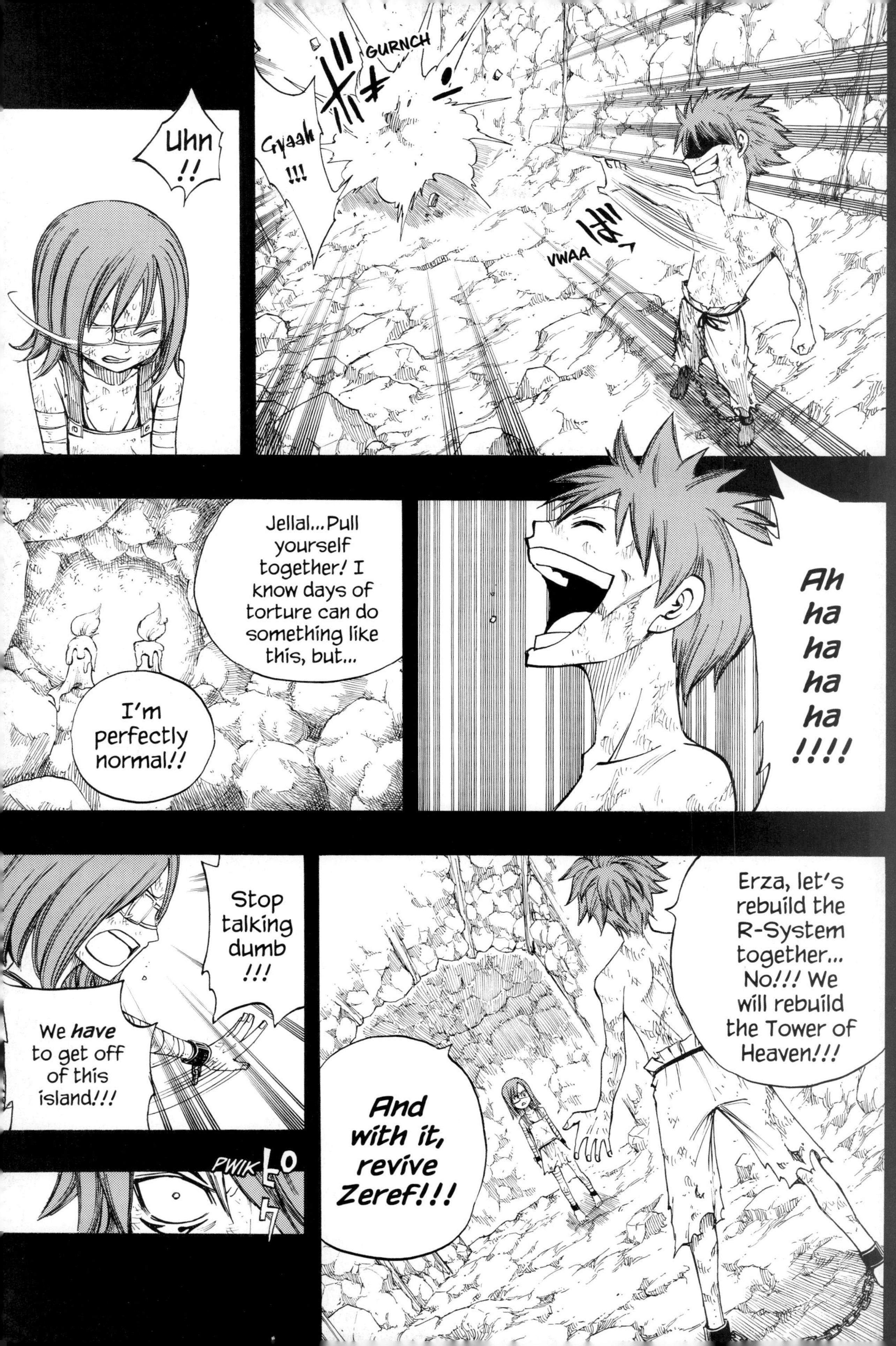
GURNCH
Gyaah!!!
VWAA
Uhn!!
Ah ha ha ha ha!!!!
Jellal...Pull yourself together! I know days of torture can do something like this, but...
I'm perfectly normal!!
Erza, let's rebuild the R-System together... No!!! We will rebuild the Tower of Heaven!!!
And with it, revive Zeref!!!
Stop talking dumb!!!
We *have* to get off of this island!!!
PWIK

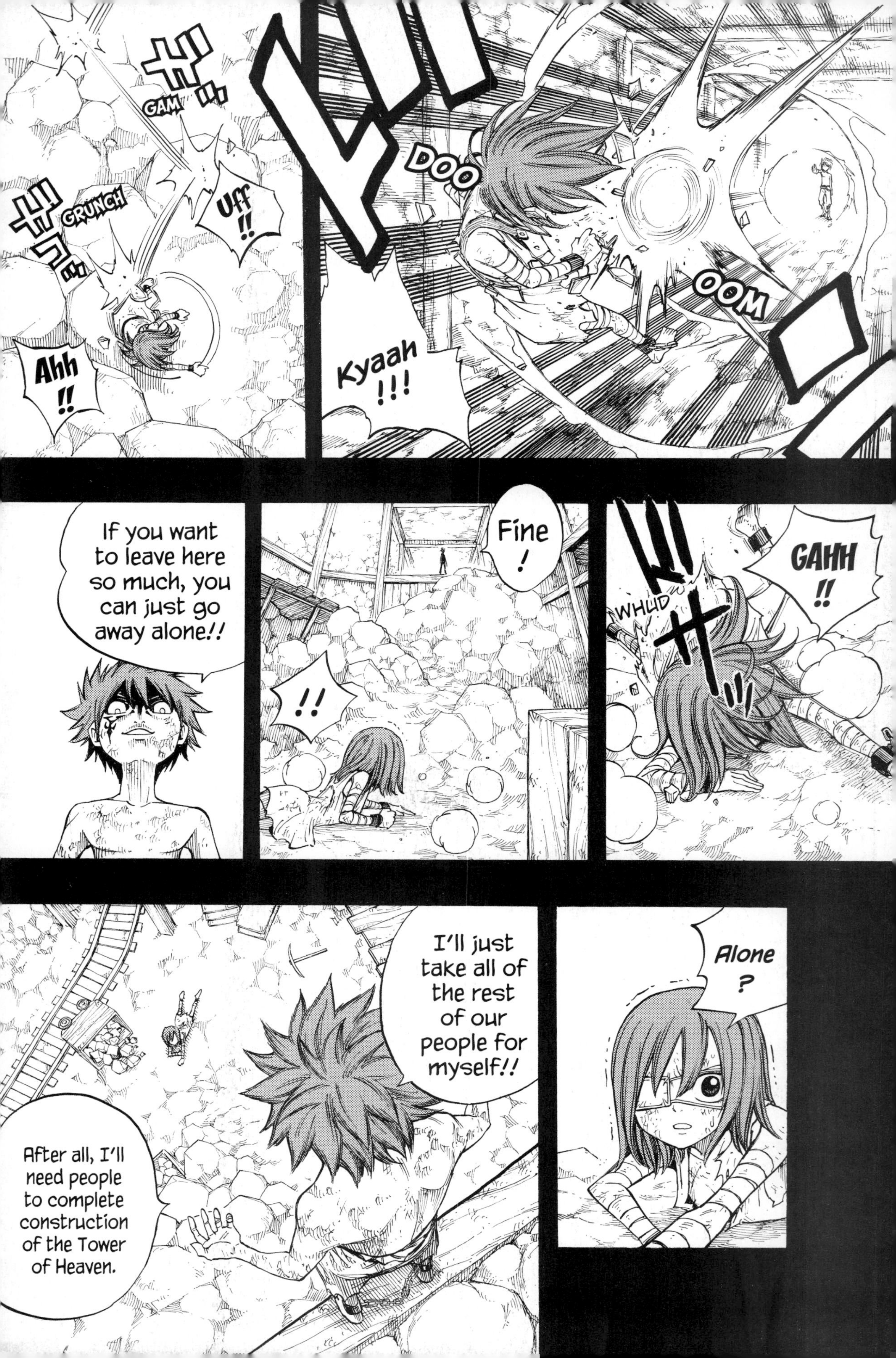
DOO
OOM
Kyaah!!!
GAM
Uff!!
GRUNCH
Ahh!!
GAHH!!
WHUD
Fine!
!!
If you want to leave here so much, you can just go away alone!!
Alone?
I'll just take all of the rest of our people for myself!!
After all, I'll need people to complete construction of the Tower of Heaven.

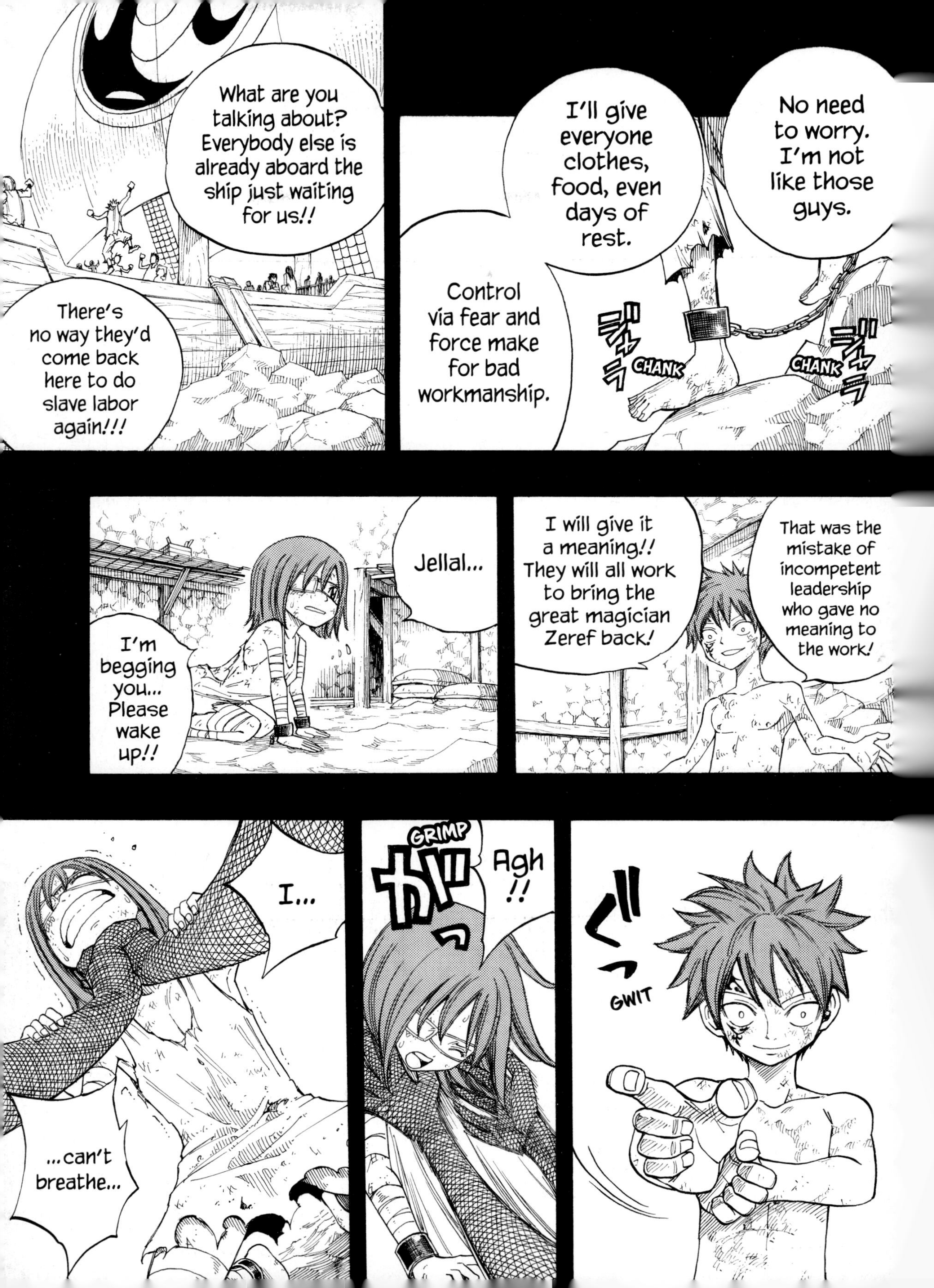
No need to worry. I'm not like those guys.
I'll give everyone clothes, food, even days of rest.
CHANK
CHANK
Control via fear and force make for bad workmanship.
What are you talking about? Everybody else is already aboard the ship just waiting for us!!
There's no way they'd come back here to do slave labor again!!!
That was the mistake of incompetent leadership who gave no meaning to the work!
I will give it a meaning!! They will all work to bring the great magician Zeref back!
Jellal...
I'm begging you... Please wake up!!
GWIT
GRIMP
Agh!!
I...
...can't breathe...

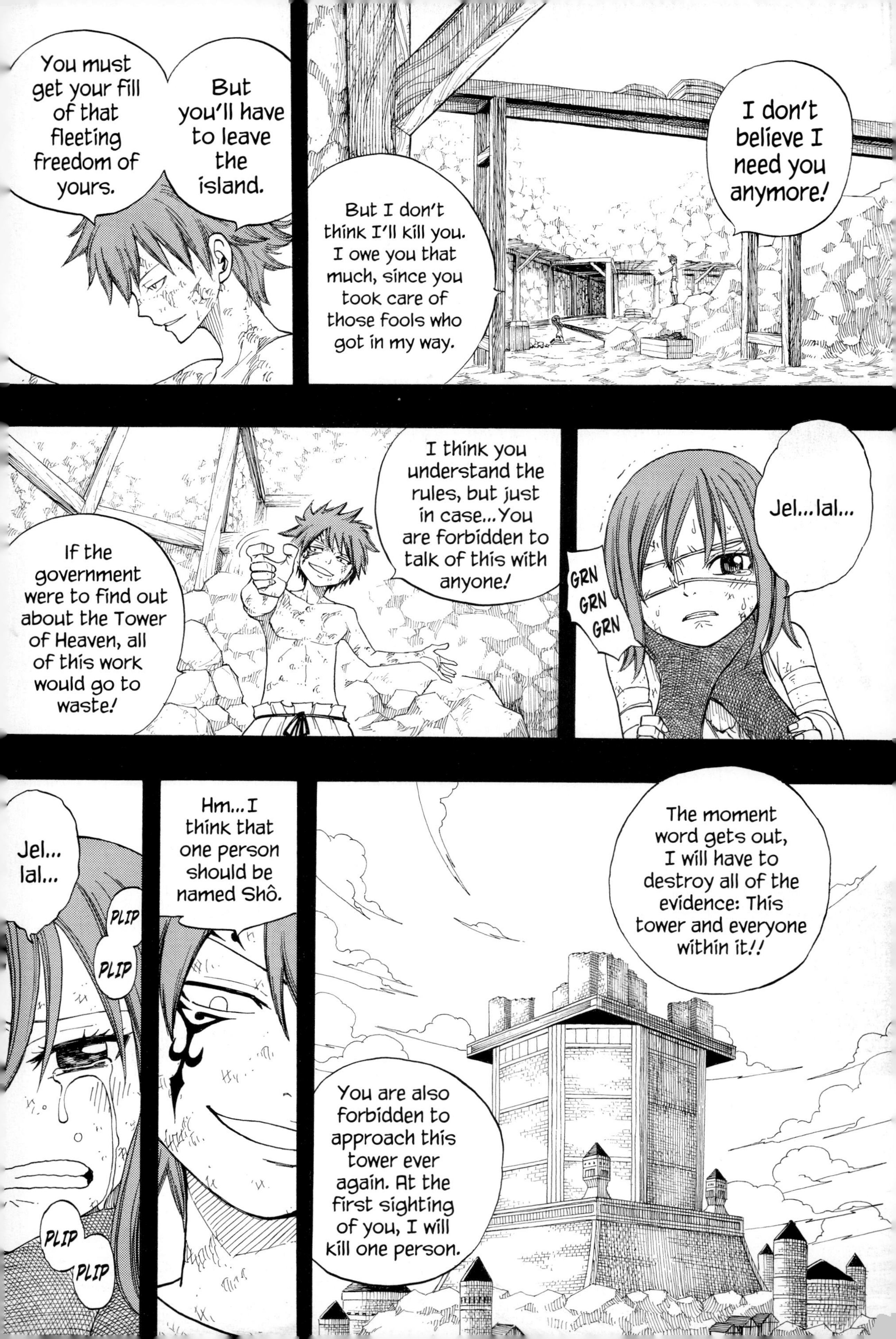
I don't believe I need you anymore!
But I don't think I'll kill you. I owe you that much, since you took care of those fools who got in my way.
But you'll have to leave the island.
You must get your fill of that fleeting freedom of yours.
Jel...lal...
GRN GRN GRN
I think you understand the rules, but just in case...You are forbidden to talk of this with anyone!
If the government were to find out about the Tower of Heaven, all of this work would go to waste!
The moment word gets out, I will have to destroy all of the evidence: This tower and everyone within it!!
You are also forbidden to approach this tower ever again. At the first sighting of you, I will kill one person.
Hm...I think that one person should be named Shô.
Jel... lal...
PLIP
PLIP
PLIP
PLIP

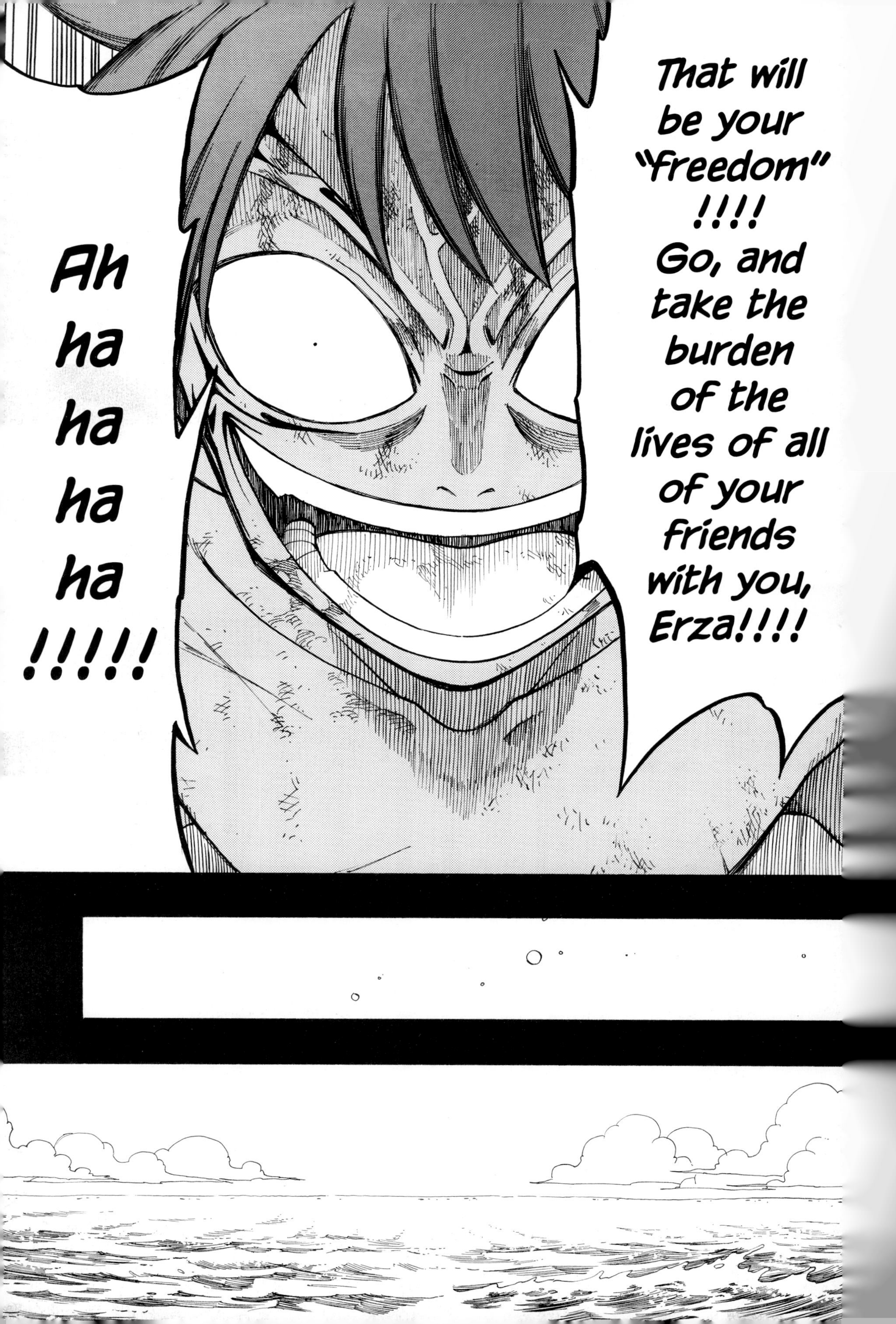
That will be your "freedom" !!!! Go, and take the burden of the lives of all of your friends with you, Erza!!!!
Ah ha ha ha ha !!!!!

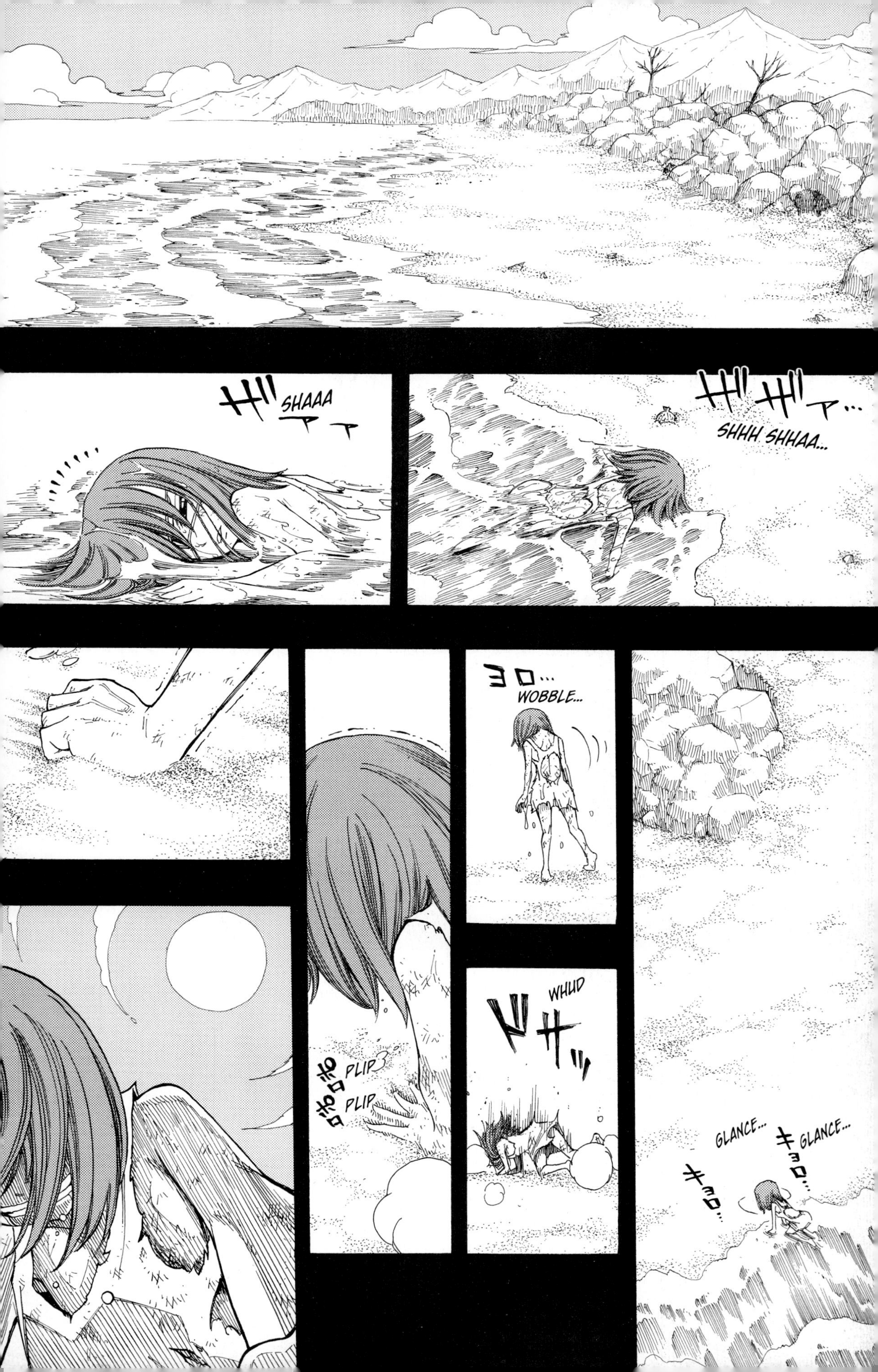
ザザァ…
SHHH SHHAA...
ザァァ
SHAAA
キョロ…
GLANCE...
キョロ…
GLANCE...
ヨロ…
WOBBLE...
ドサッ
WHUD
ポロポロ
PLIP
PLIP

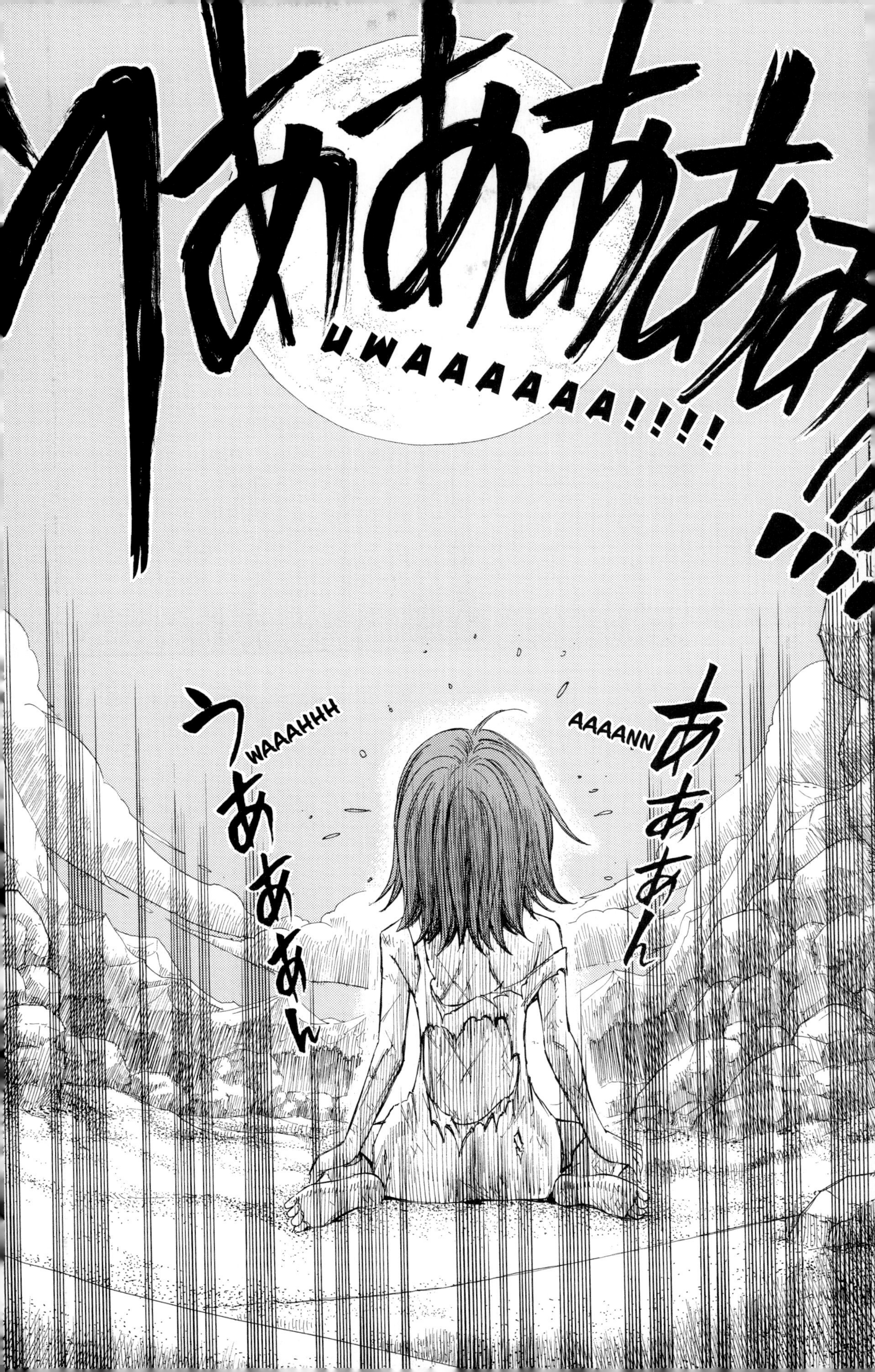

うあああああ…!!
UWAAAAAAAA!!!!
あああん
AAAANN
うあああん
WAAAHHH

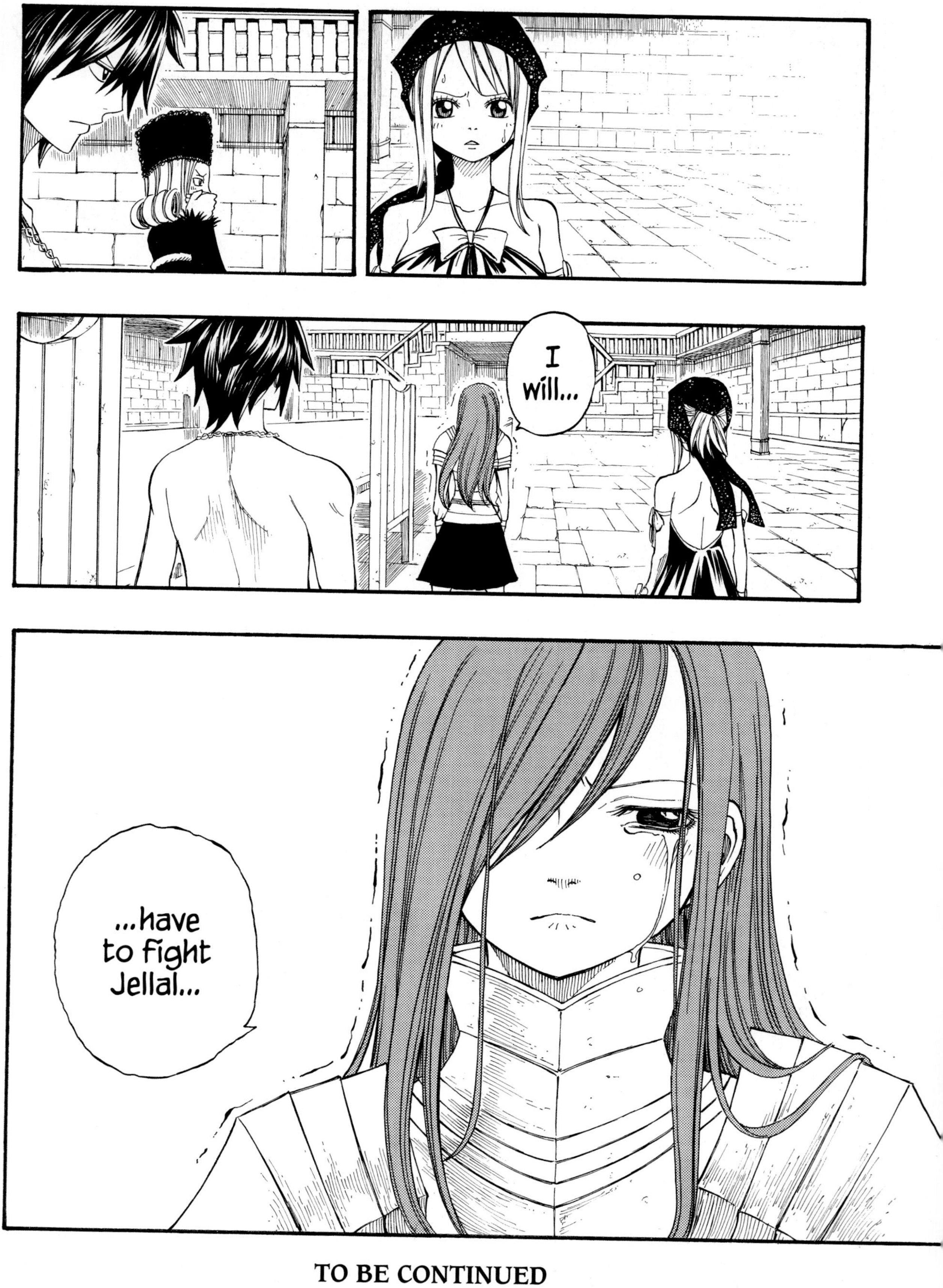
I will...
...have to fight Jellal...

TO BE CONTINUED

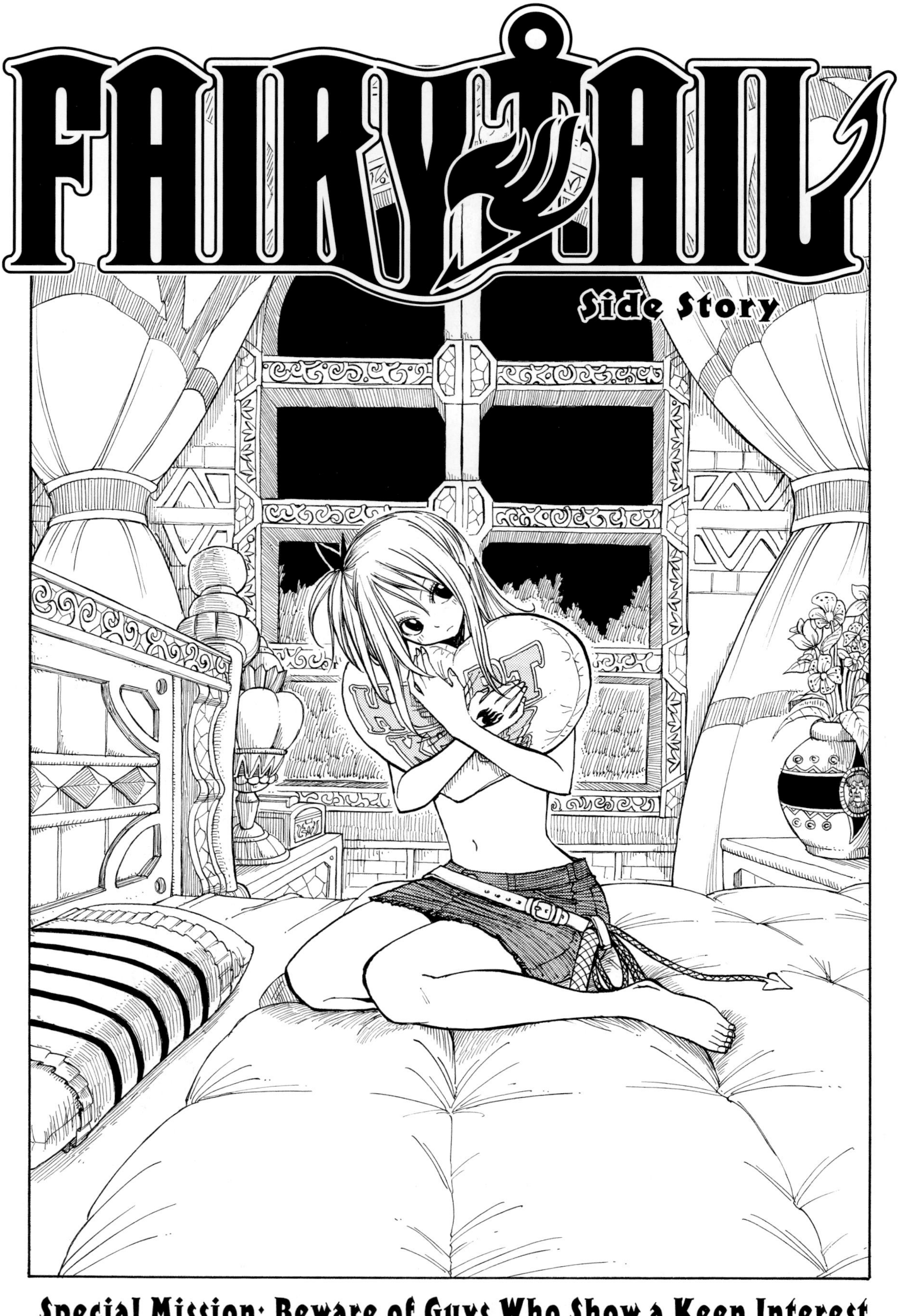
FAIRY TAIL
Side Story

Special Mission: Beware of Guys Who Show a Keen Interest

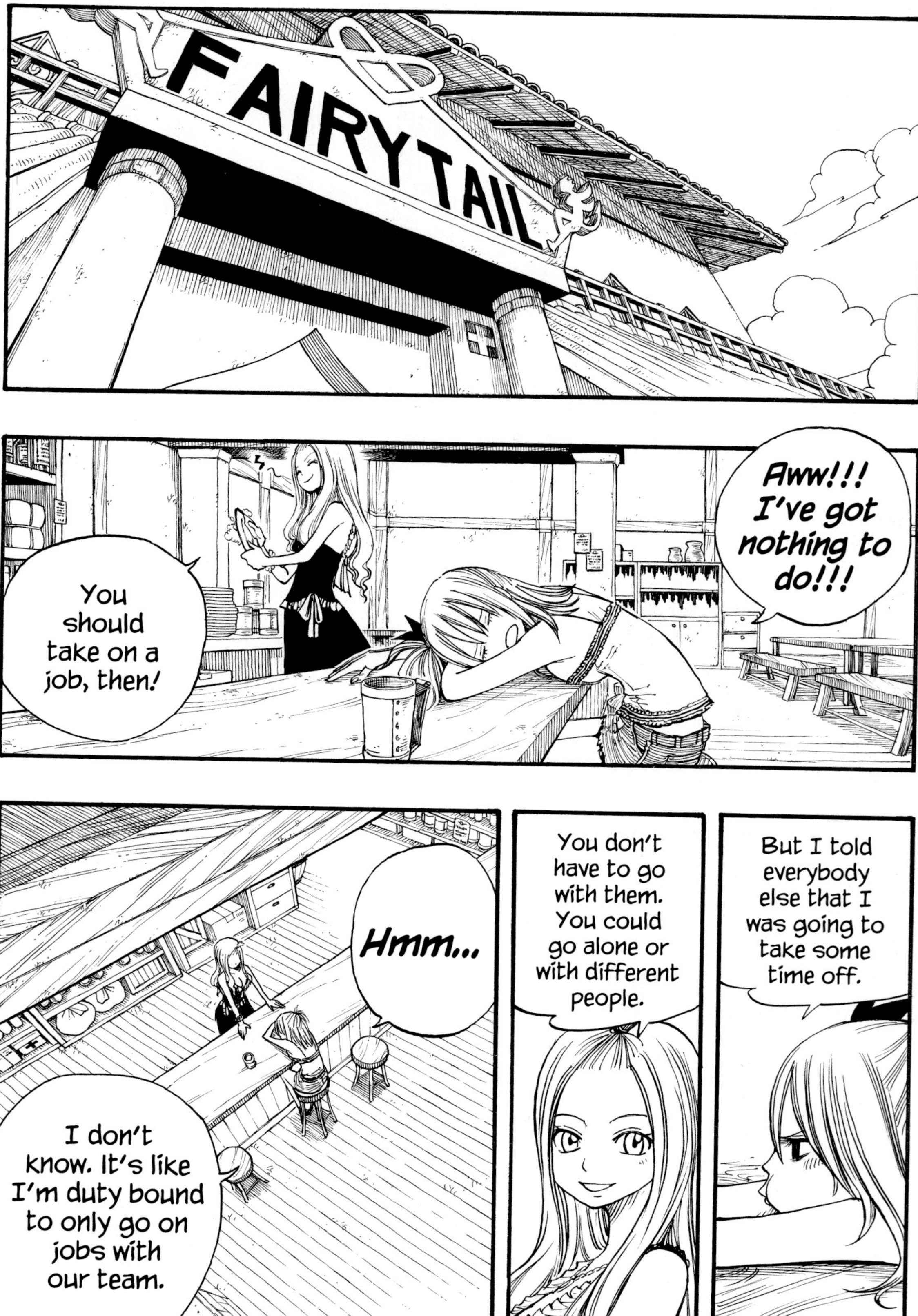
FAIRYTAIL
Aww!!! I've got nothing to do!!!
You should take on a job, then!
But I told everybody else that I was going to take some time off.
You don't have to go with them. You could go alone or with different people.
Hmm...
I don't know. It's like I'm duty bound to only go on jobs with our team.

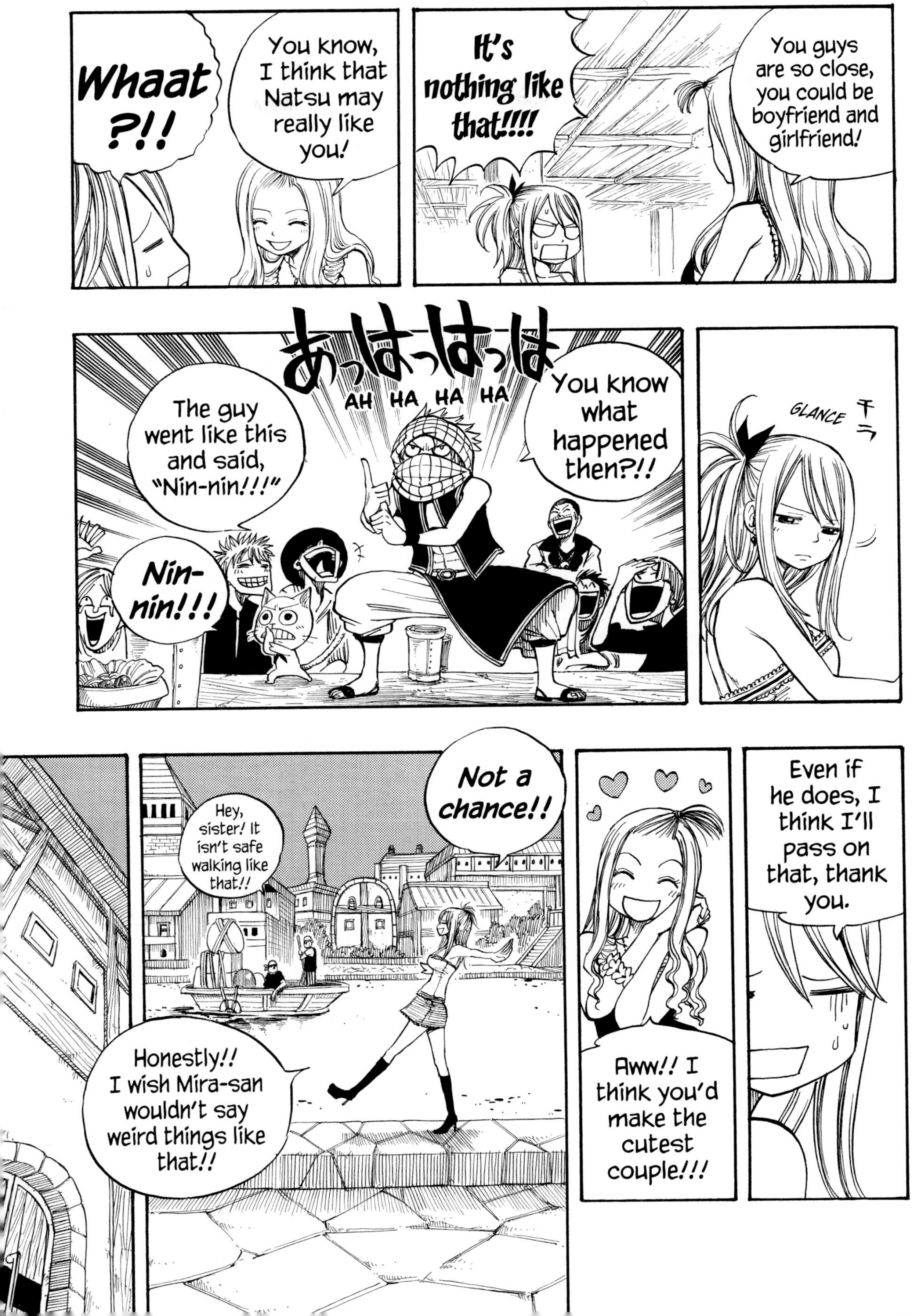

You guys are so close, you could be boyfriend and girlfriend!
It's nothing like that!!!!
You know, I think that Natsu may really like you!
Whaat?!!
GLANCE
チラ
あっはっはっは
AH HA HA HA
You know what happened then?!!
The guy went like this and said, "Nin-nin!!!"
Nin-nin!!!
Even if he does, I think I'll pass on that, thank you.
Aww!! I think you'd make the cutest couple!!!
Not a chance!!
Hey, sister! It isn't safe walking like that!!
Honestly!! I wish Mira-san wouldn't say weird things like that!!

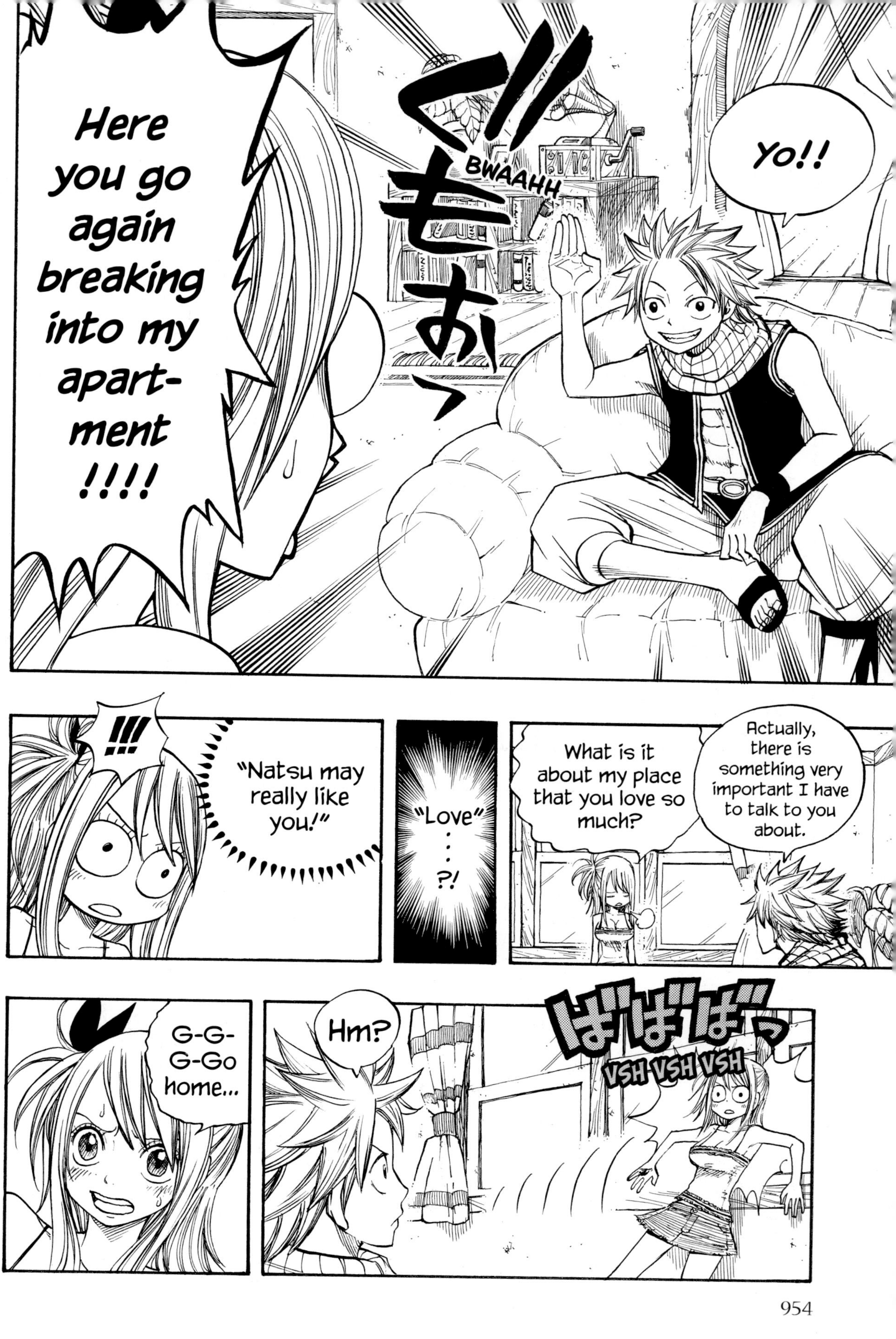

Yo!!
BWAAHH
Here you go again breaking into my apartment!!!!
What is it about my place that you love so much?
Actually, there is something very important I have to talk to you about.
"Love" . . . ?!
"Natsu may really like you!"
!!!
ばばばっ
VSH VSH VSH
Hm?
G-G-G-Go home...

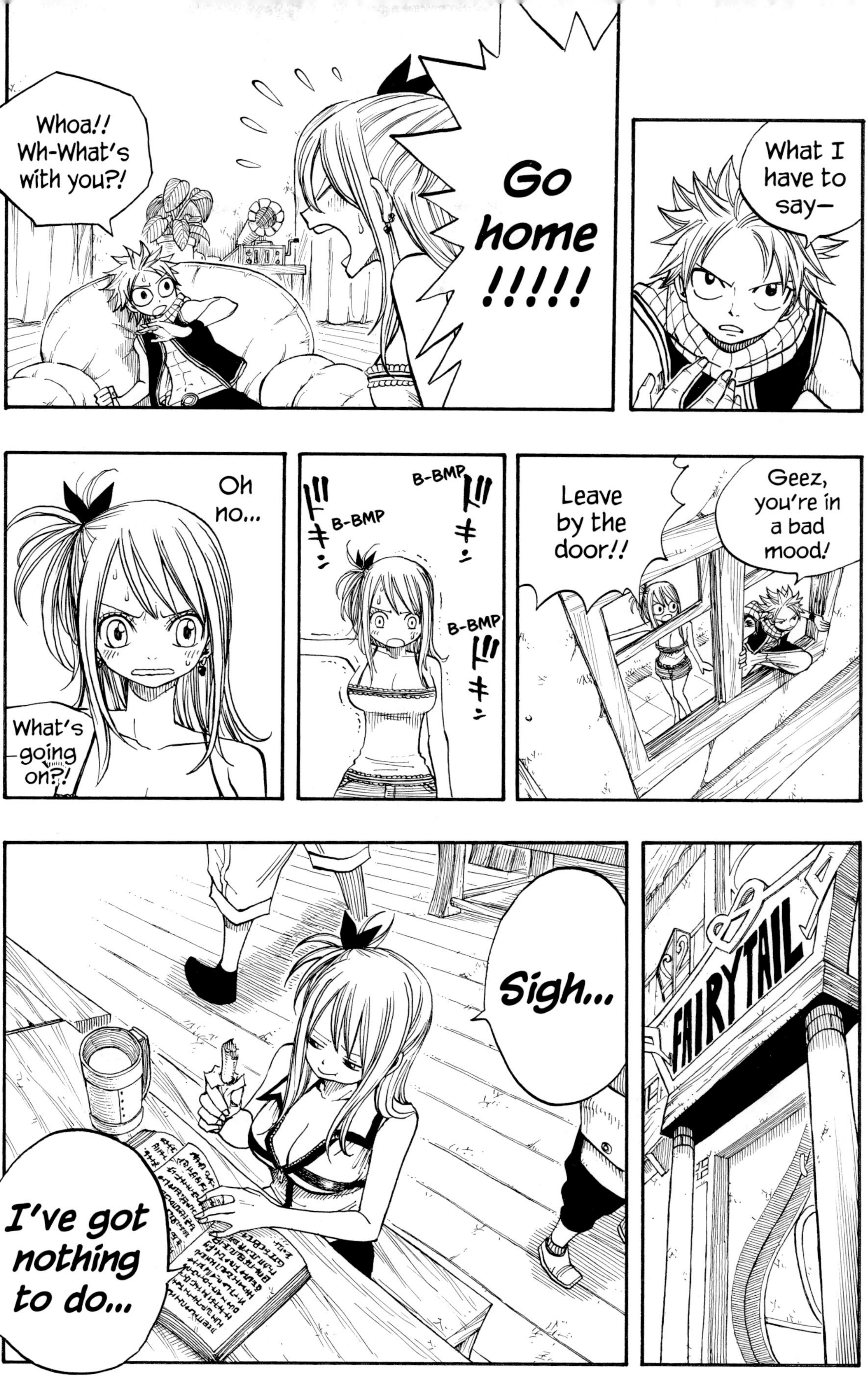
What I have to say—
Go home!!!!!
Whoa!! Wh-What's with you?!
Geez, you're in a bad mood!
Leave by the door!!
B-BMP
B-BMP
B-BMP
Oh no...
What's going on?!
FAIRY TAIL
Sigh...
I've got nothing to do...

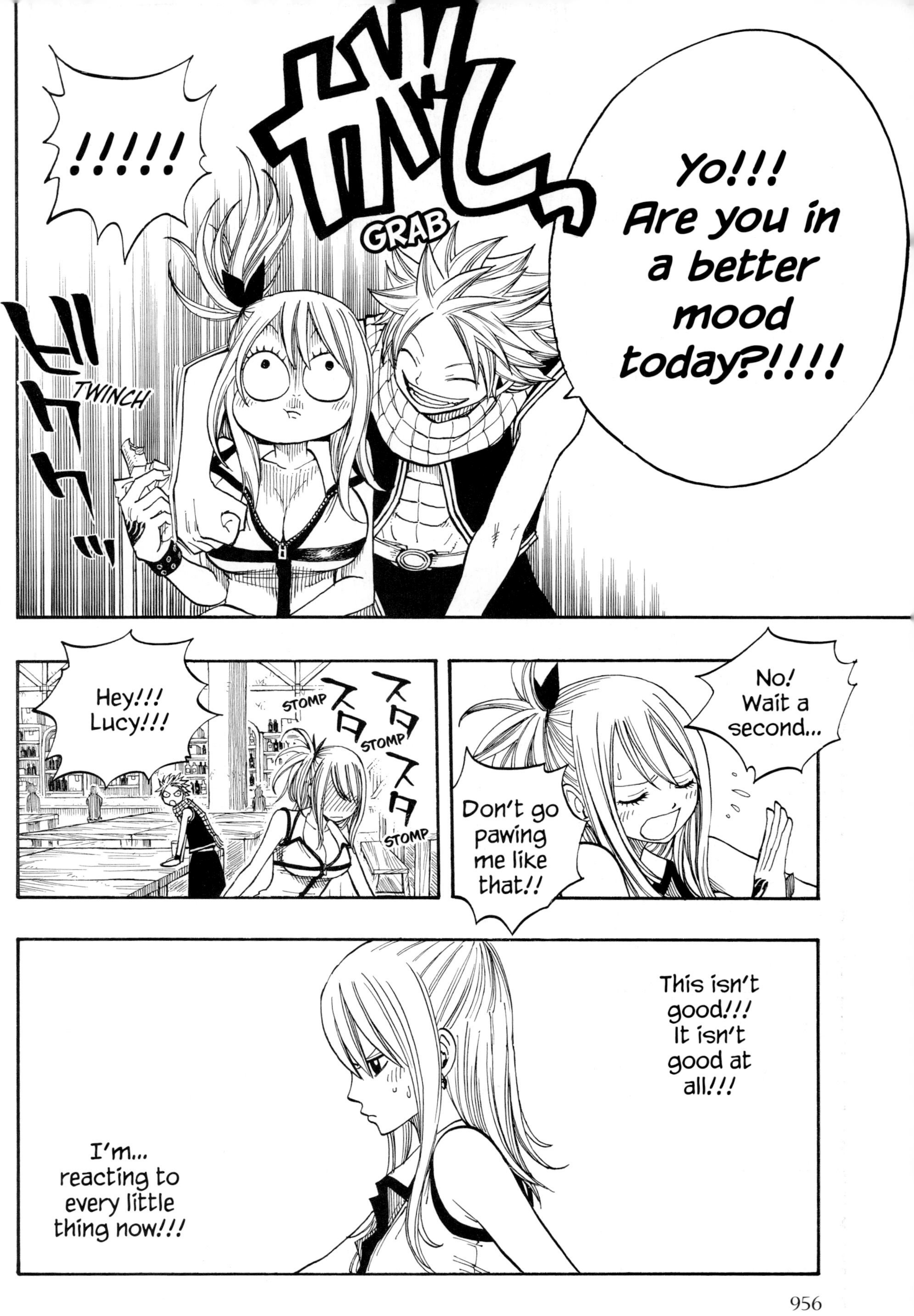
Yo!!! Are you in a better mood today?!!!!
GRAB
!!!!!
TWINCH
No! Wait a second...
Don't go pawing me like that!!
STOMP STOMP STOMP
Hey!!! Lucy!!!
This isn't good!!! It isn't good at all!!!
I'm... reacting to every little thing now!!!

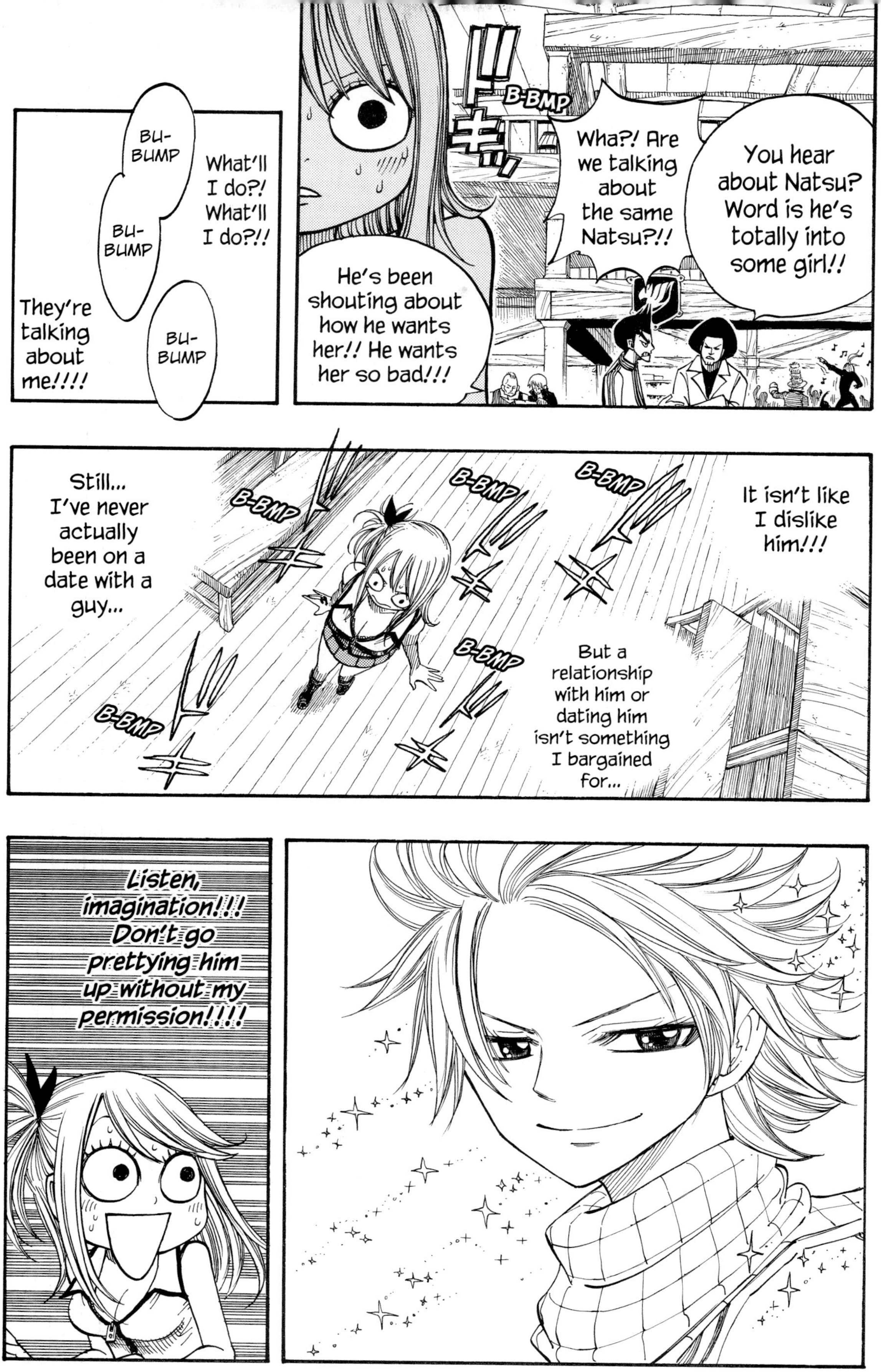
You hear about Natsu? Word is he's totally into some girl!!
Wha?! Are we talking about the same Natsu?!!
B-BMP
He's been shouting about how he wants her!! He wants her so bad!!!
What'll I do?! What'll I do?!!
BU-BUMP
BU-BUMP
BU-BUMP
They're talking about me!!!!
It isn't like I dislike him!!!
B-BMP
B-BMP
B-BMP
But a relationship with him or dating him isn't something I bargained for...
B-BMP
Still... I've never actually been on a date with a guy...
B-BMP
Listen, imagination!!! Don't go prettying him up without my permission!!!!

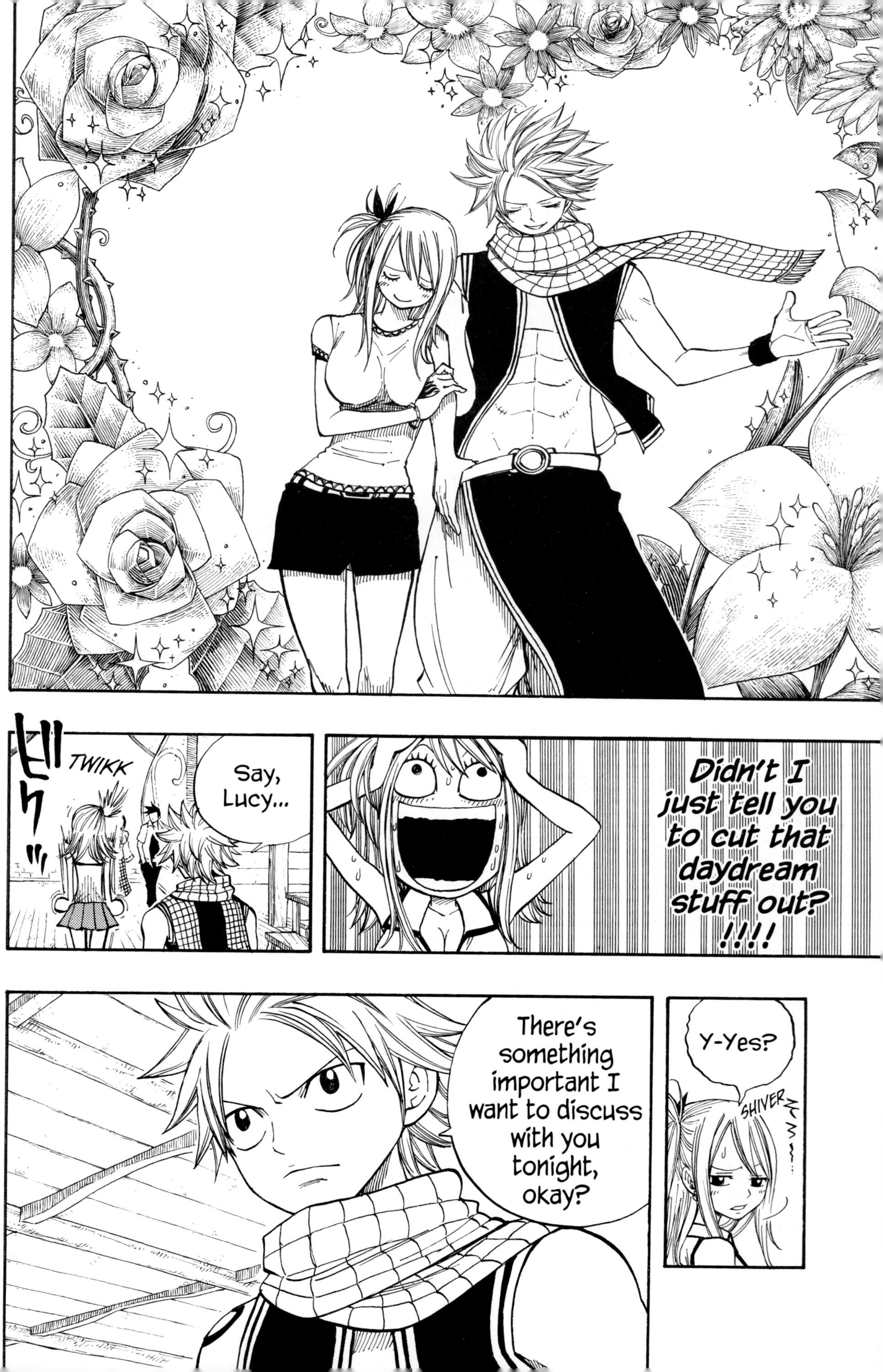
TWIKK
Say, Lucy...
Didn't I just tell you to cut that daydream stuff out? !!!!
There's something important I want to discuss with you tonight, okay?
Y-Yes?
SHIVER

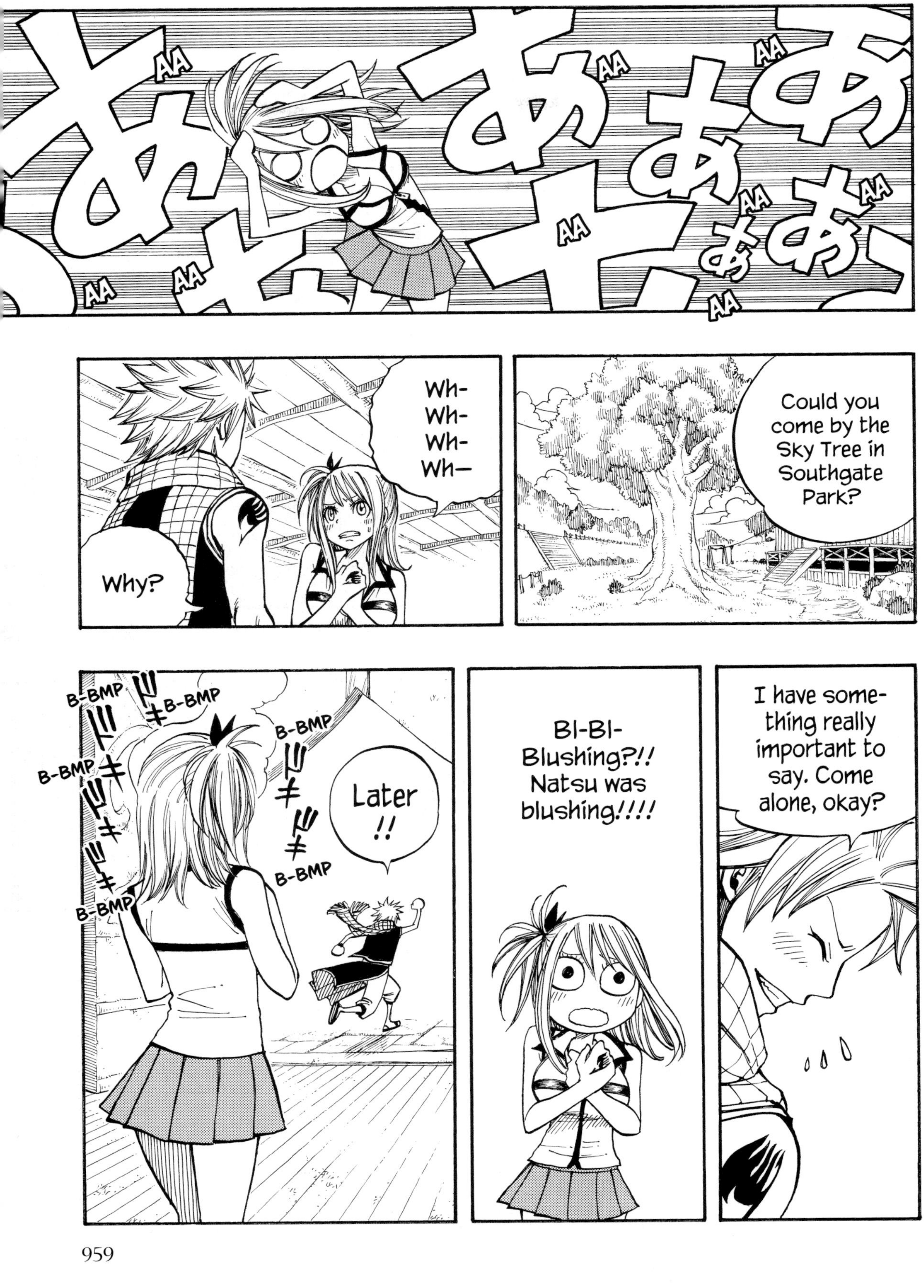
AA
AA
AA
AA
AA
AA
AA
AA
AA
Could you come by the Sky Tree in Southgate Park?
Wh- Wh- Wh- Wh—
Why?
I have some-thing really important to say. Come alone, okay?
Bl-Bl-Blushing?!! Natsu was blushing!!!!
Later !!
B-BMP
B-BMP
B-BMP
B-BMP
B-BMP
B-BMP

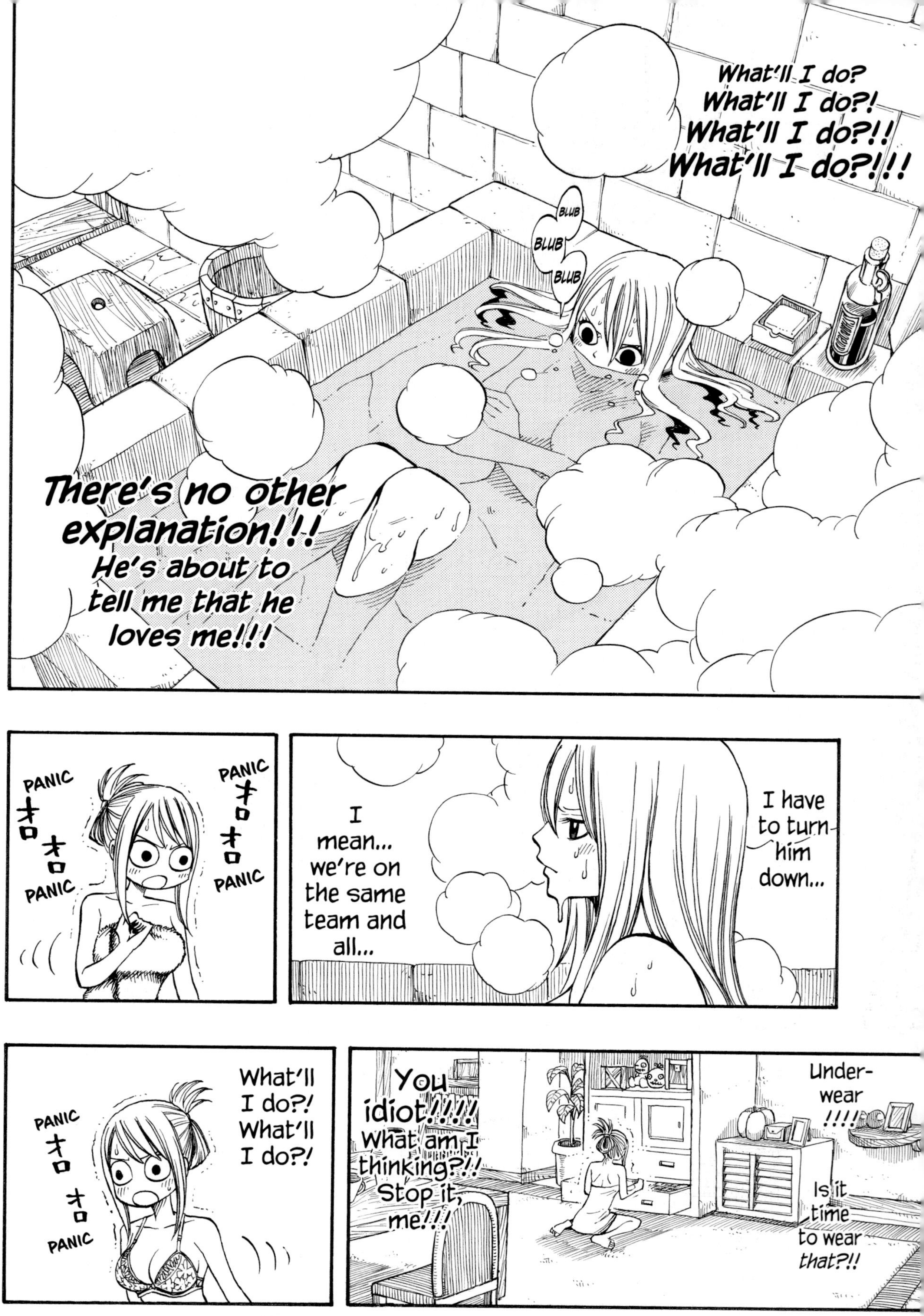
What'll I do?
What'll I do?!
What'll I do?!!
What'll I do?!!!
BLUB
BLUB
BLUB
There's no other explanation!!! He's about to tell me that he loves me!!!
I have to turn him down...
I mean... we're on the same team and all...
PANIC オロ
PANIC オロ
PANIC オロ
PANIC
Under-wear!!!!
Is it time to wear that?!!
You idiot!!!! What am I thinking?!! Stop it, me!!!
What'll I do?! What'll I do?!
PANIC オロ
オロ PANIC

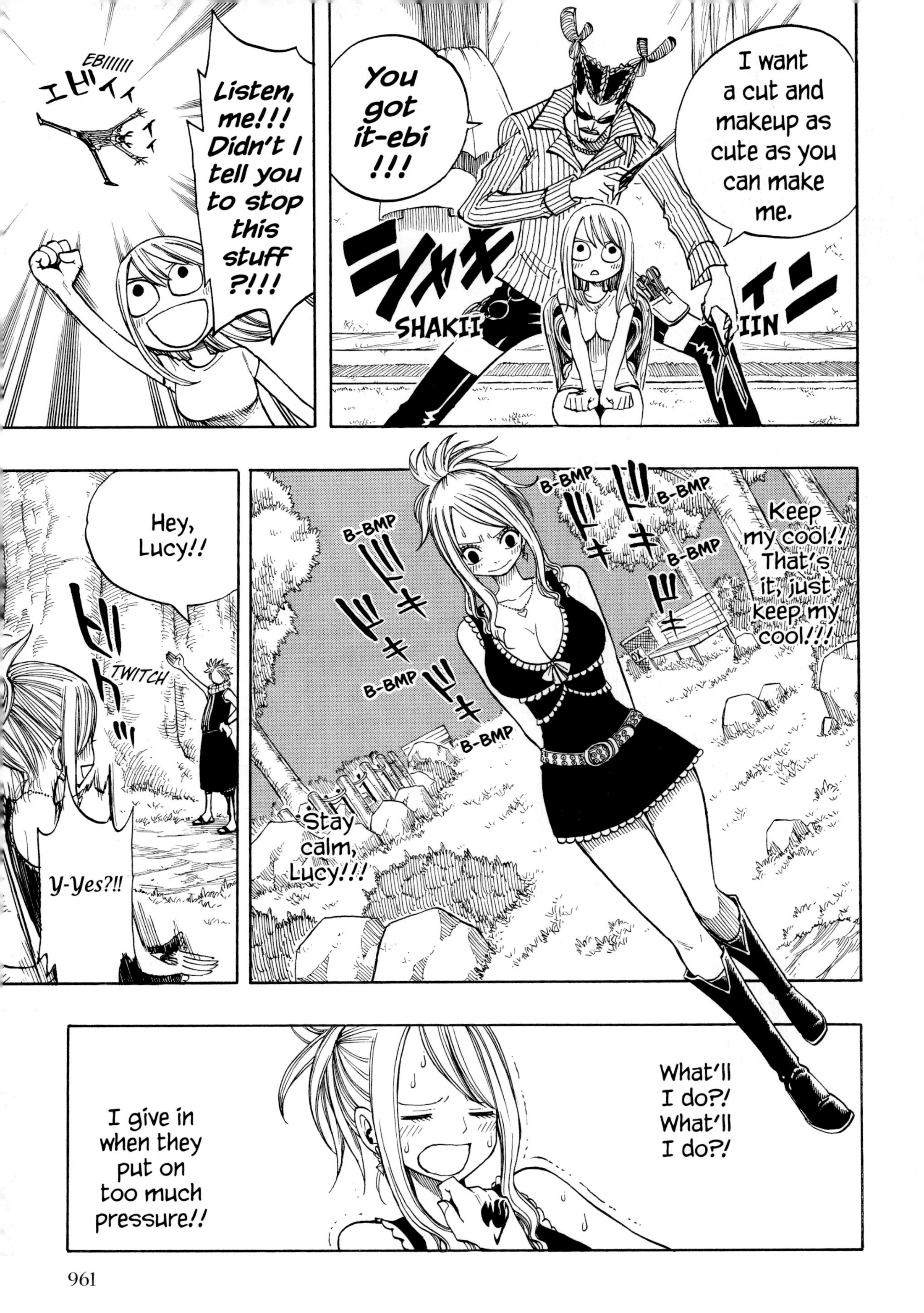
I want a cut and makeup as cute as you can make me.
You got it-ebi!!!
SHAKIIIN
EBIIIIII
Listen, me!!! Didn't I tell you to stop this stuff?!!!
B-BMP
B-BMP
B-BMP
B-BMP
B-BMP
B-BMP
Keep my cool!! That's it, just keep my cool!!!
Stay calm, Lucy!!!
Hey, Lucy!!
TWITCH
Y-Yes?!!
What'll I do?! What'll I do?!
I give in when they put on too much pressure!!

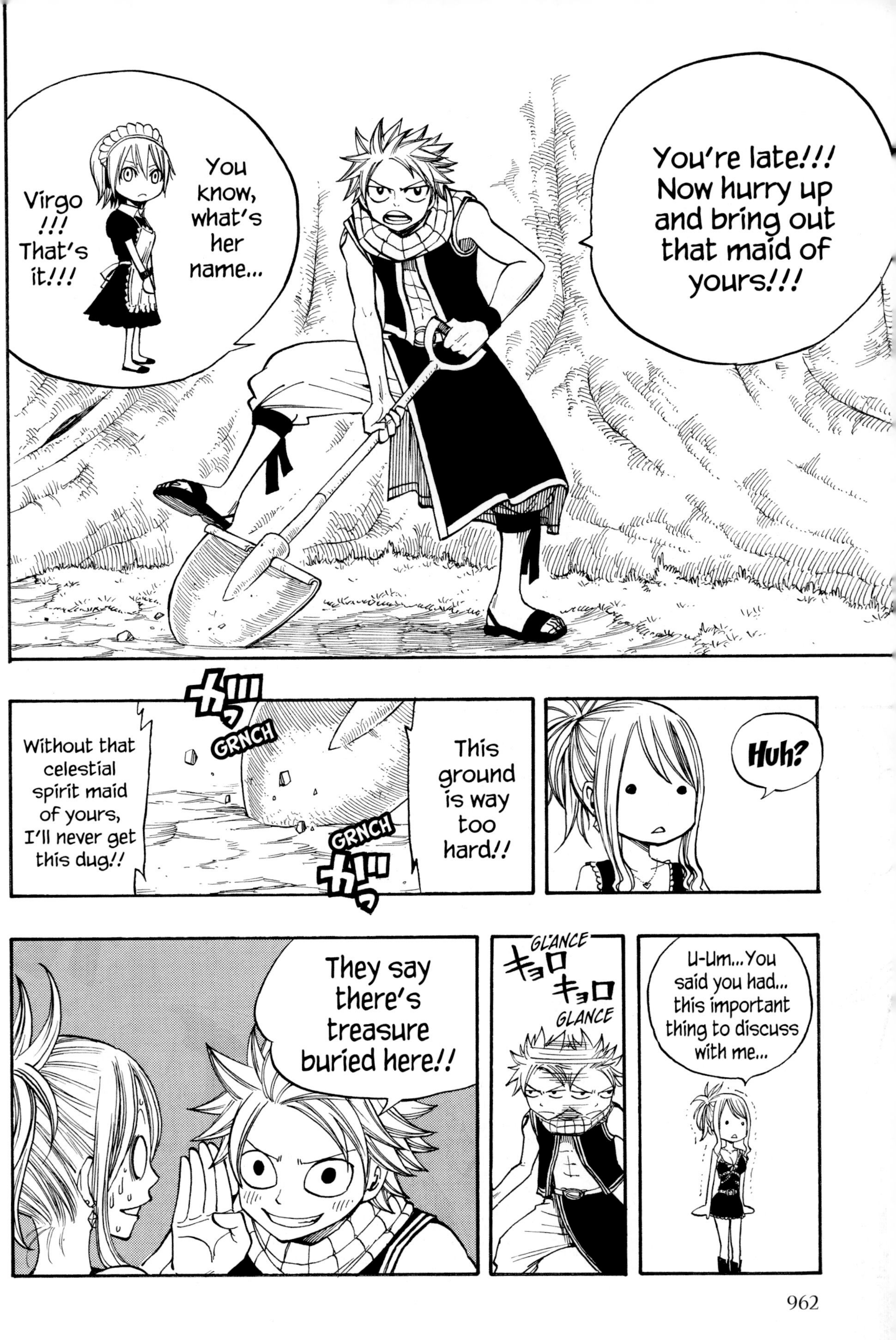
You're late!!! Now hurry up and bring out that maid of yours!!!
You know, what's her name...
Virgo!!! That's it!!!
Huh?
This ground is way too hard!!
ガッ
GRNCH
GRNCH
ガッ
Without that celestial spirit maid of yours, I'll never get this dug!!
U-Um...You said you had... this important thing to discuss with me...
GLANCE
キョロ
キョロ
GLANCE
They say there's treasure buried here!!

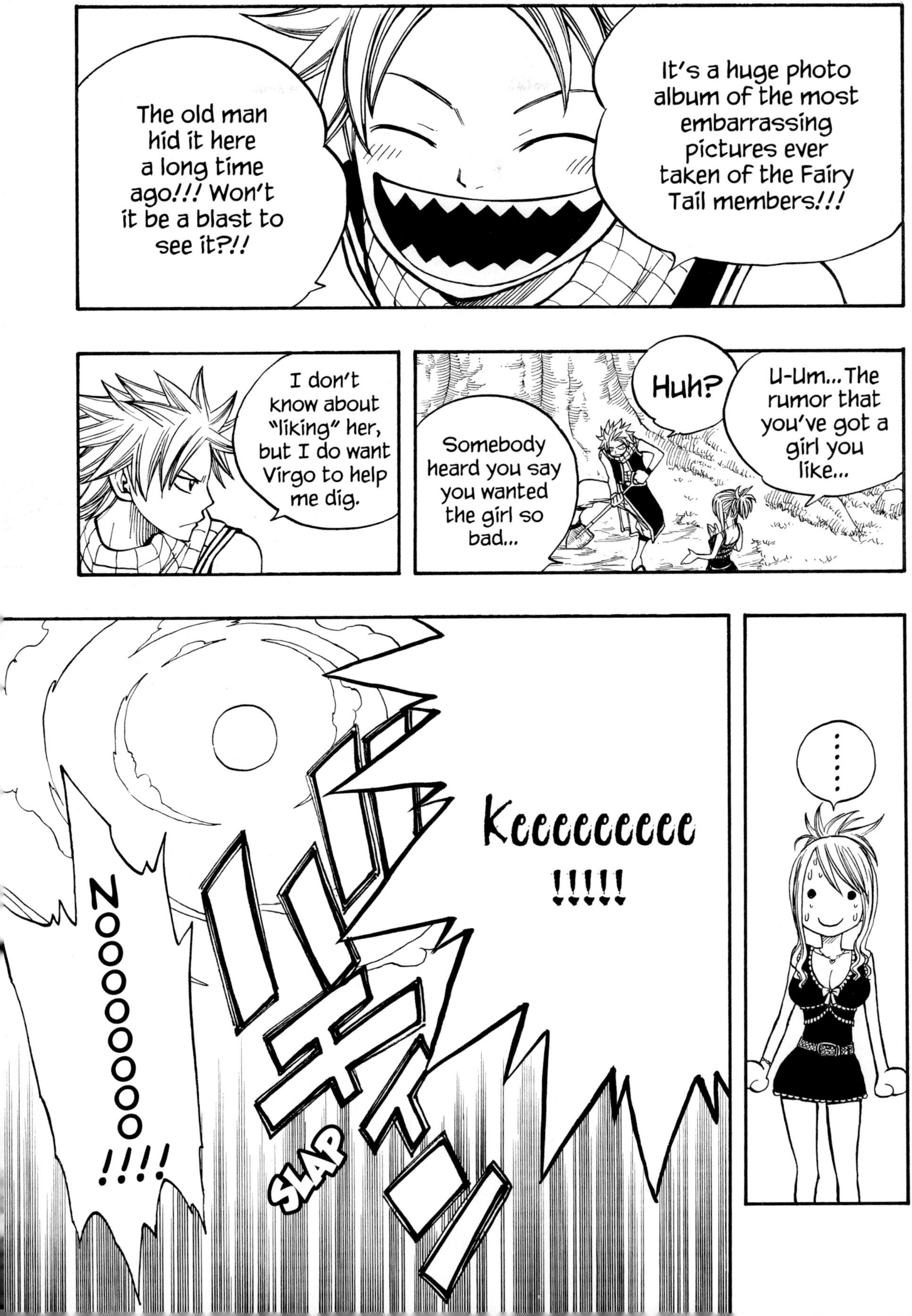
It's a huge photo album of the most embarrassing pictures ever taken of the Fairy Tail members!!!
The old man hid it here a long time ago!!! Won't it be a blast to see it?!!
U-Um...The rumor that you've got a girl you like...
Huh?
Somebody heard you say you wanted the girl so bad...
I don't know about "liking" her, but I do want Virgo to help me dig.
......
Keeeeeeeee !!!!!
SLAP
Nooooooooo !!!!

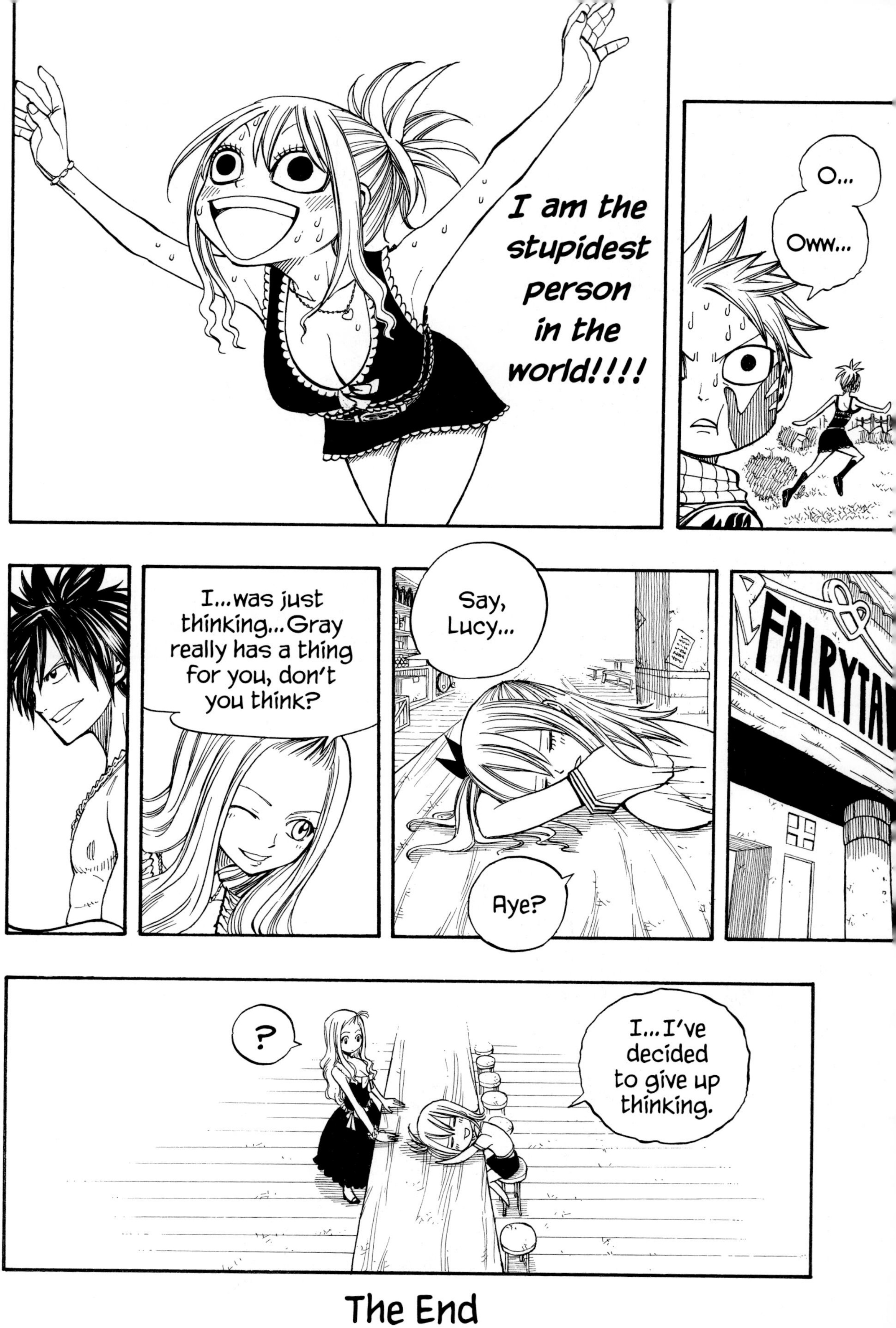
O...
Oww...
I am the stupidest person in the world!!!!
Say, Lucy...
Aye?
I...was just thinking...Gray really has a thing for you, don't you think?
I...I've decided to give up thinking.
?

The End

FAIRY TAIL

Bonus Pages

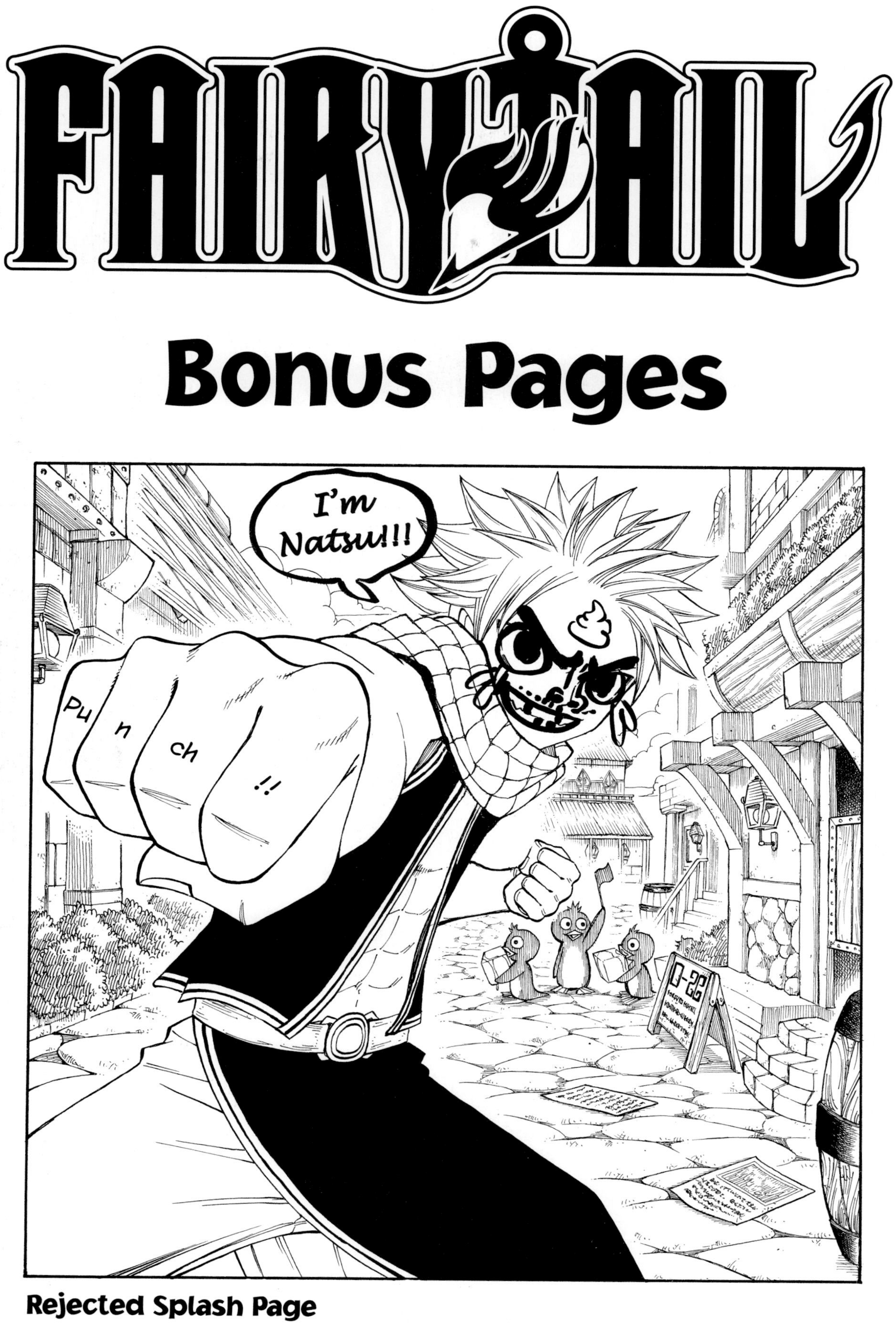
I'm Natsu!!!
Pu n ch !!

Rejected Splash Page

The pose wasn't very natural. After I noticed that, I quickly placed it in the rejected pile.

TAIL d'ART

The *Fairy Tail* Guild d'Art is an explosion of fan art! Please send in your black-and-white art on large postcard stock!! Those chosen to be published will get a signed mini poster! ♪ Make sure you write your real name and address on the back of your postcard!

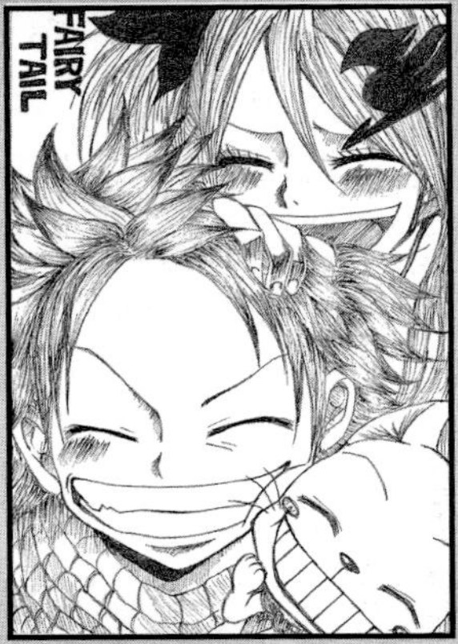
FAIRY TAIL

▼ What wonderful smiles!! One great piece of artwork!

Hiroshima Prefecture, MIE

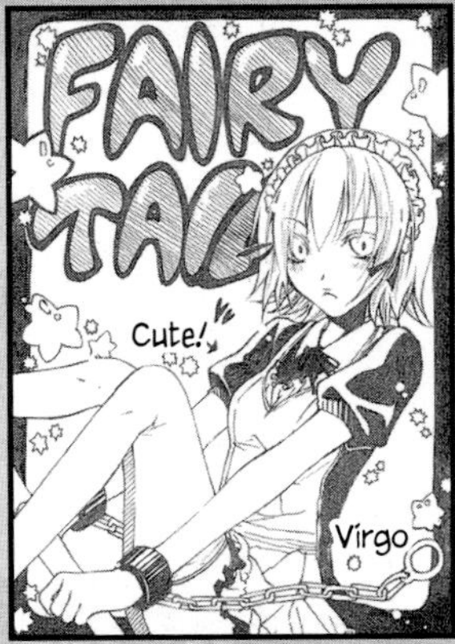
FAIRY TAIL
Cute!
Virgo

▼ This is extremely cute!! And so well drawn!

Aomori Prefecture, Kuro

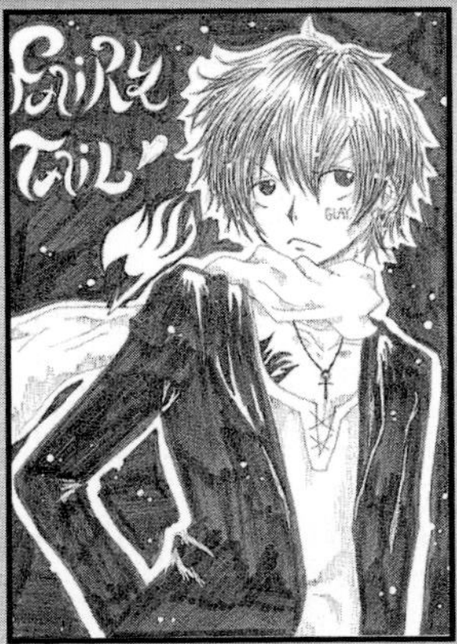
Fairy Tail

▼ That's so cool! You know, you're not supposed to draw better than I can!!

Niigata Prefecture, Ai

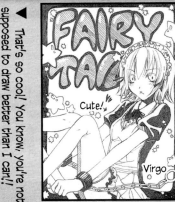

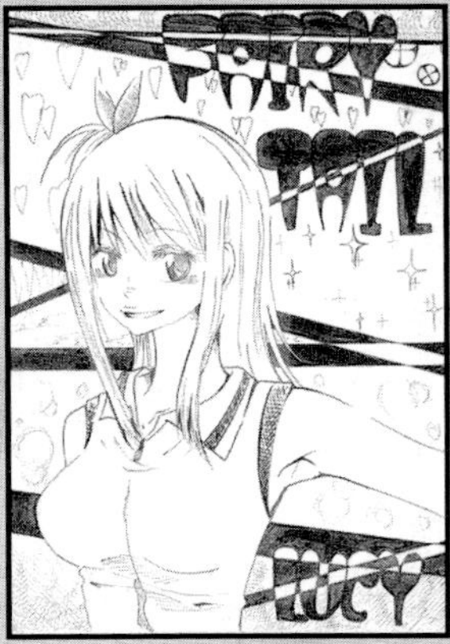
LUCY

▼ Well done!! You've got drawing experience, don't you?

Niigata Prefecture, Reina

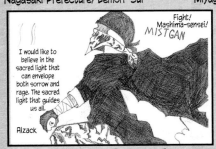

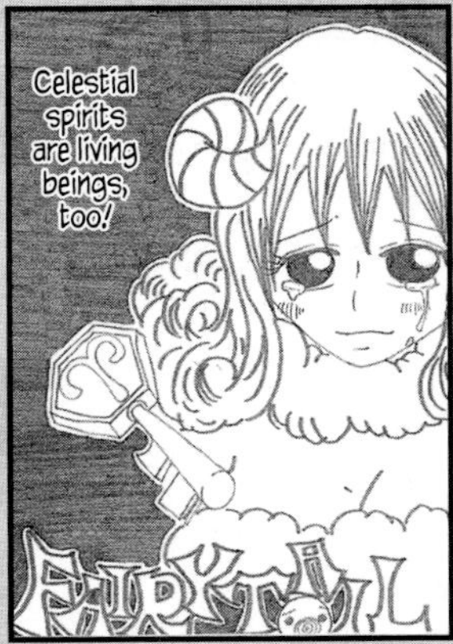
Celestial spirits are living beings, too!

▼ I get lots of letters asking what became of this girl!

Miyagi Prefecture, Ikkome-chan

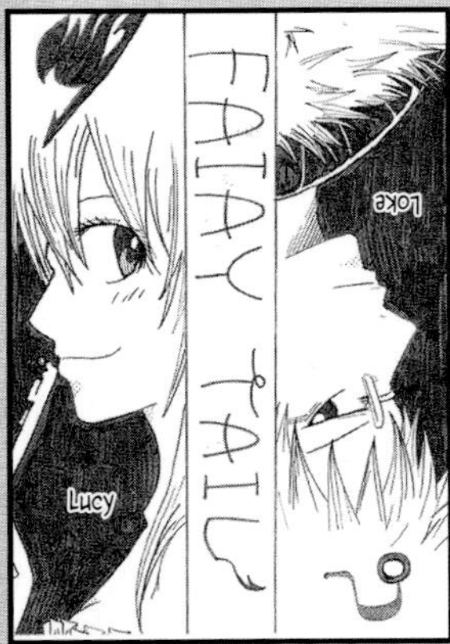
FAIAY TAIL
Loke
Lucy

▼ What did you think of the Loke story? Personally I liked it a lot.

Nagasaki Prefecture, Lemon-Sui

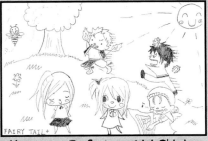

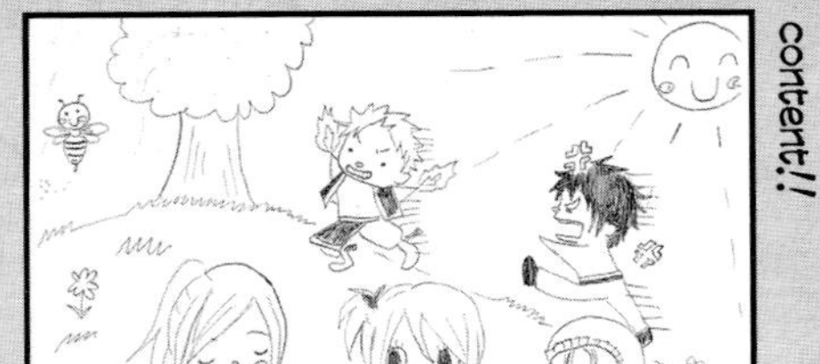
FAIRY TAIL

▼ This is so cute!! Oh no!! I'm feeling too content!!

Kanagawa Prefecture, Mei Shimizu

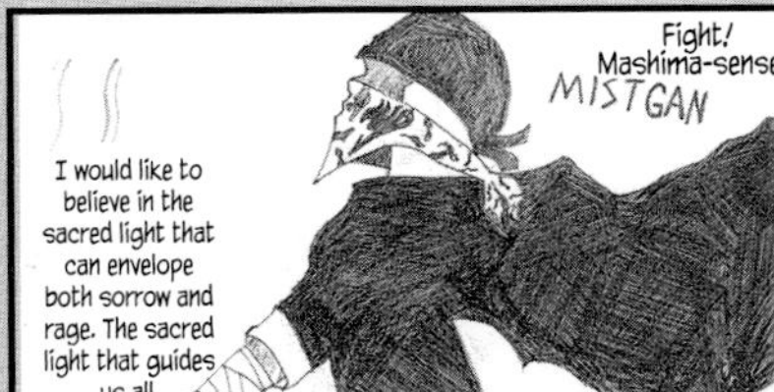
Fight! Mashima-sensei!
MISTGAN
I would like to believe in the sacred light that can envelope both sorrow and rage. The sacred light that guides us all.
Alzack

▼ I-I know his back-story!! R-Really! I've thought everything out!!

Yamagata Prefecture, Fuyu

Send to Hiro Mashima, Kodansha Comics
451 Park Ave. South, 7th Floor, New York, NY 10016

FAIRY GUILD

By sending in letters or postcards you give us permission to give your name, address, postal code and any other information you include to the author as is. Please keep that in mind.

▼ It's Mira-chan from long ago! I'm getting the itch to tell that story.

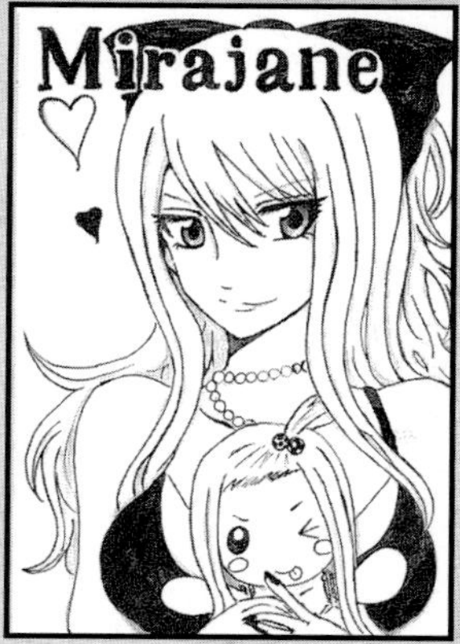
Mirajane

Miyagi Prefecture, Aoi

▼ I like her expression and pose! Petite and sexy!

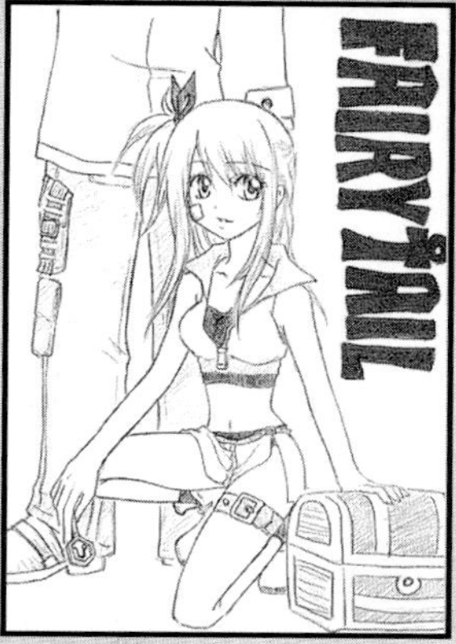
FAIRY TAIL

Gifu Prefecture, Yasuyo Hayasaka

▼ This picture has an interesting flavor. What's that in the bottom left...?

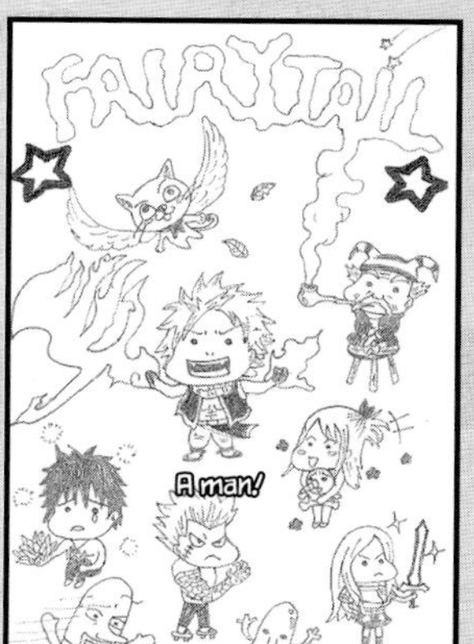
FAIRYTAIL
A man!

Wakayama Prefecture, Buguo

▼ This Natsu is pretty wild, huh?

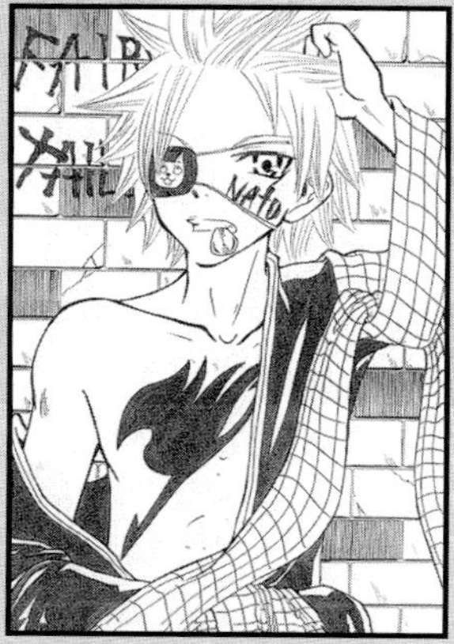

Hiroshima Prefecture, Tabinosuke

Rejection Corner

▼ His name is Alfred DeCorn. Be nice to him.

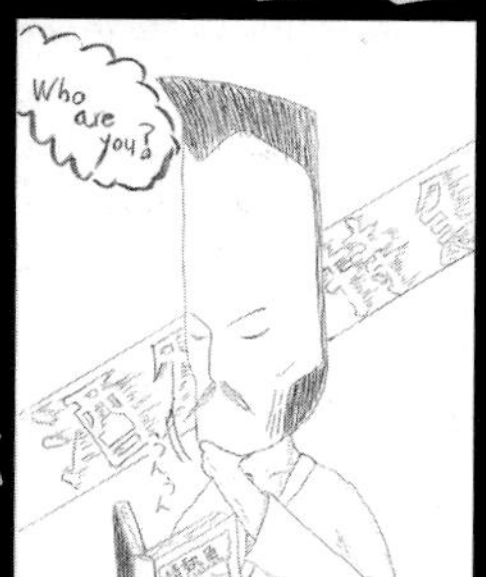
Who are you?

Osaka, Yûki Inoue

▼ Everybody's in animal costumes!! But Happy doesn't need a costume!

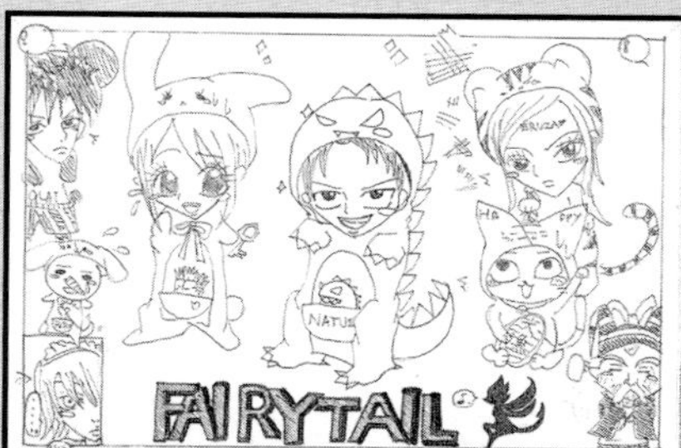
FAIRYTAIL

Shiga Prefecture, Ami Horii

▼ That's amazingly cute!! I love this kind of picture!!

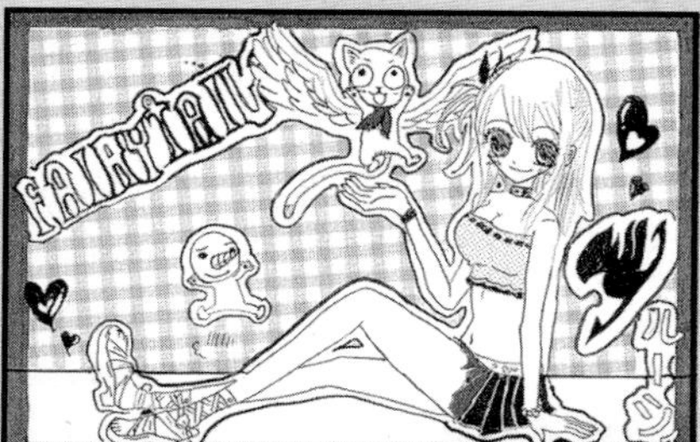
FAIRYTAIL

Okayama Prefecture, Arashi ♡

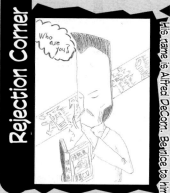

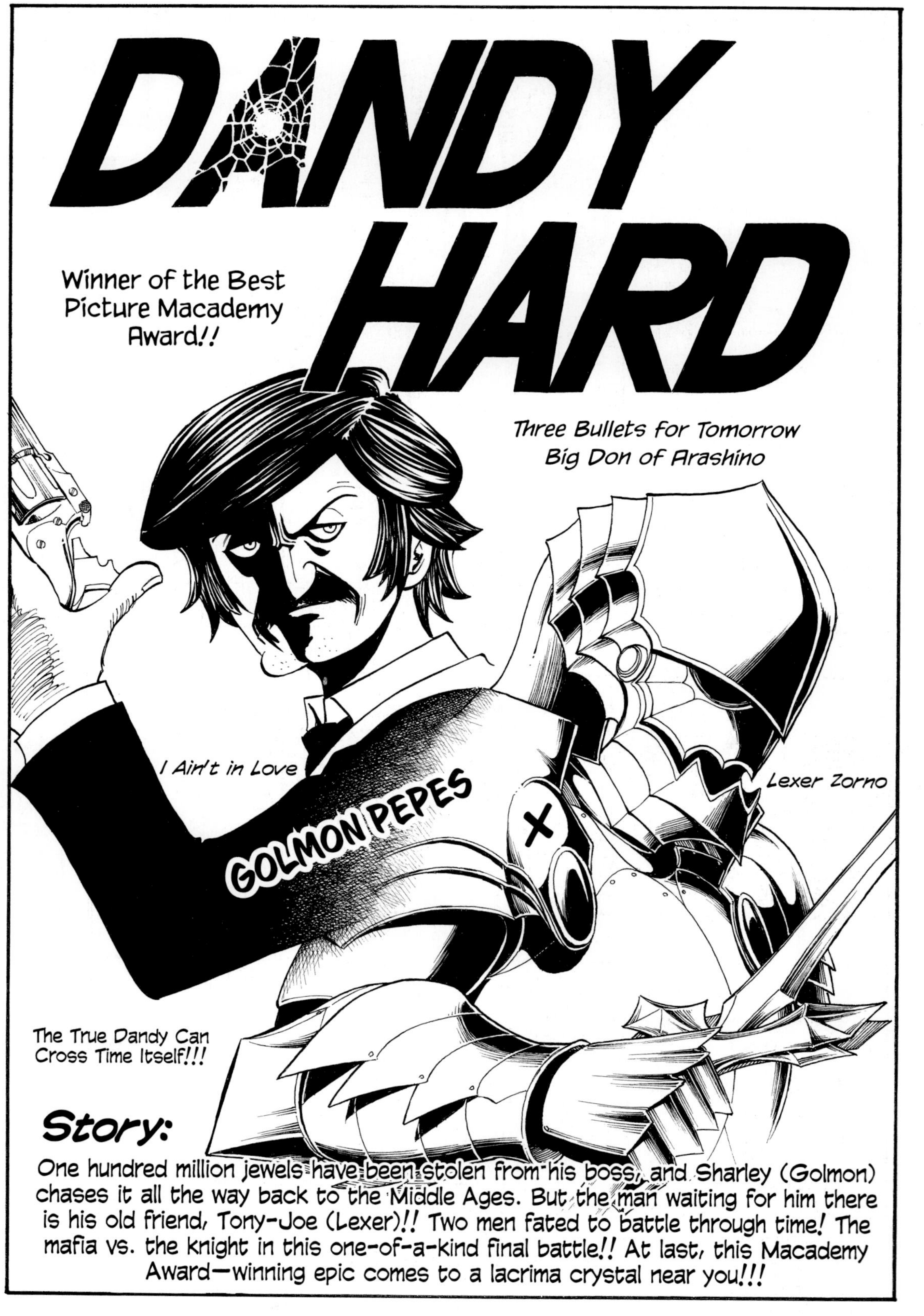
DANDY HARD
Winner of the Best Picture Macademy Award!!
Three Bullets for Tomorrow
Big Don of Arashino
I Ain't in Love
Lexer Zorno
GOLMON PEPES
×
The True Dandy Can Cross Time Itself!!!

Story:

One hundred million jewels have been stolen from his boss, and Sharley (Golmon) chases it all the way back to the Middle Ages. But the man waiting for him there is his old friend, Tony-Joe (Lexer)!! Two men fated to battle through time! The mafia vs. the knight in this one-of-a-kind final battle!! At last, this Macademy Award—winning epic comes to a lacrima crystal near you!!!

Happy's Little Job

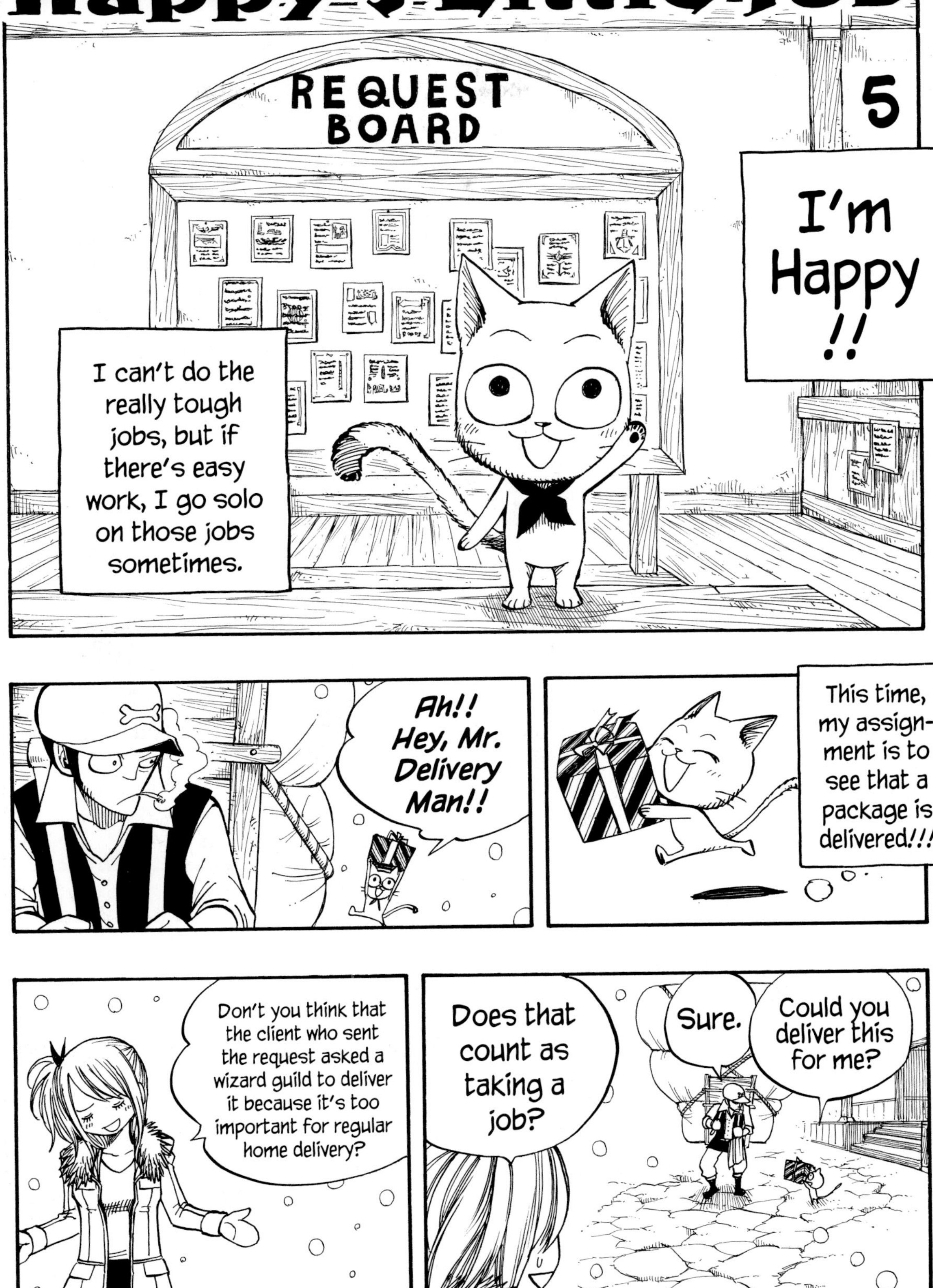
5
I'm Happy!!
I can't do the really tough jobs, but if there's easy work, I go solo on those jobs sometimes.
REQUEST BOARD
This time, my assignment is to see that a package is delivered!!!
Ah!! Hey, Mr. Delivery Man!!
Could you deliver this for me?
Sure.
Does that count as taking a job?
Don't you think that the client who sent the request asked a wizard guild to deliver it because it's too important for regular home delivery?

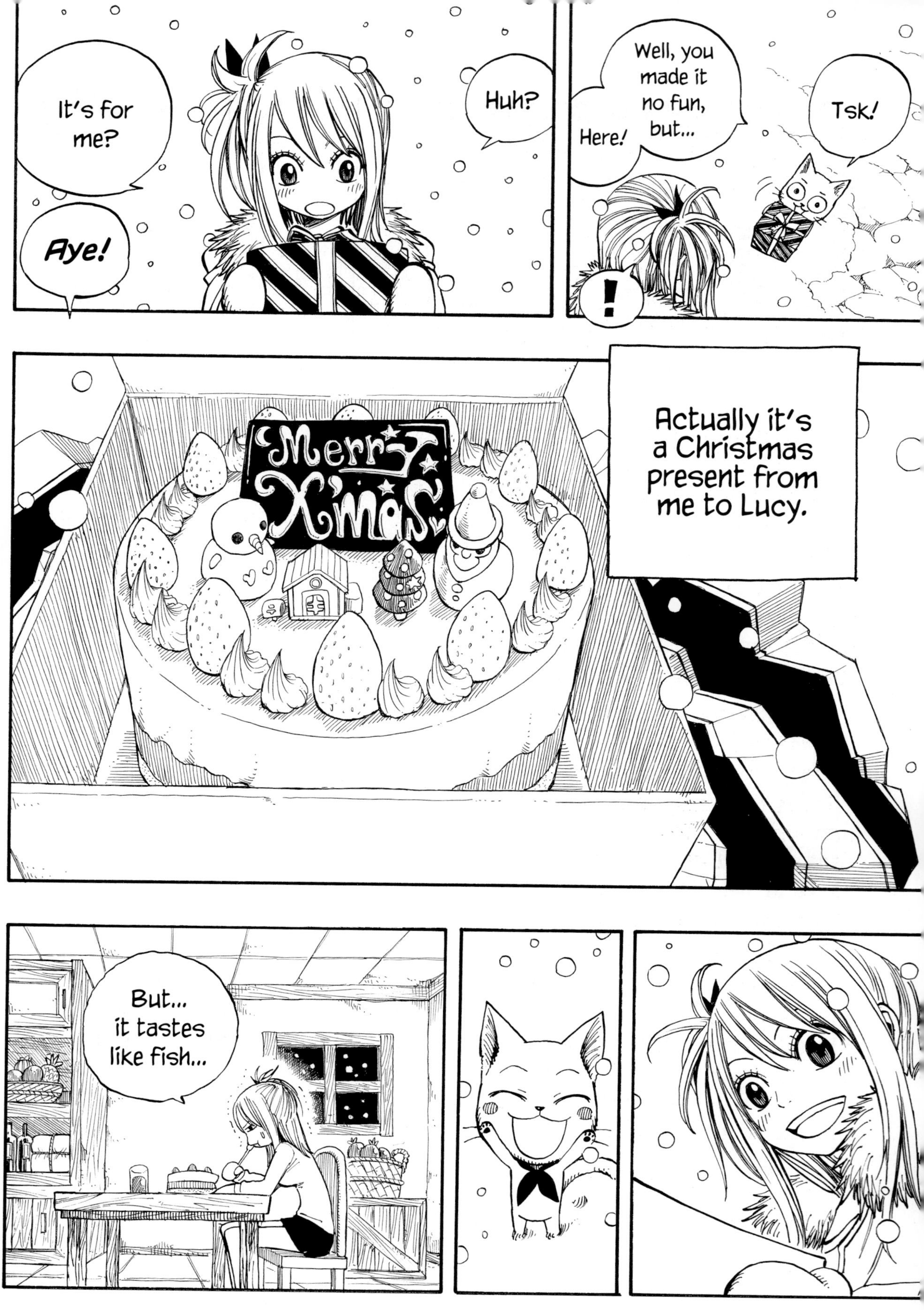

Tsk!
Well, you made it no fun, but...
Here!
!
Huh?
It's for me?
Aye!
Actually it's a Christmas present from me to Lucy.
Merry X'mas
But... it tastes like fish...

The End

AFTERWORD

In this volume, we plunge right into the Erza story!! You know, it's kind of hard to get the balance between the heavy dramatic stuff and the fun stuff! I try to get even a small laugh at least once into every chapter, but really, these dramatic scenes truly get in the way! This series of episodes is extremely heavy, but upon second reading, there were a lot more fun scenes than I expected (sweat sweat)!

By the way, does anybody have any guesses why there are butterflies when we first go into Erza's flashback scenes? Actually this was left over from an idea that was rejected. Does anybody out there know of the Chinese story, "The Dream of the Butterfly"?

> One day, there was a man who dreamed that he was a butterfly. When he awakened, an odd thought struck him. Could it be that my life as a butterfly was real? That I am not a man dreaming that I am a butterfly, but...

I was thinking of using a plot like that. That the present Erza is actually just the young Erza's dream of the future. Or something to that effect. But if I were to use that idea for real, what would happen to Natsu and Lucy and everybody else?! And I thought about it for a few weeks, and now the idea can only be found in those remnants. Keeping it would have made the story very complicated!

Also, there is a one other secret that's part of this episode. It's a very mean-spirited, evil plot (ha ha)! Those in the know will know what I'm talking about! And those who don't will have the enjoyment of watching the whole thing unfold. It will all become clear in volume 11...or maybe volume 12? Any of you who were fooled should scream out the words as follows:

"Mashima, you meanie!!!"

And I'll give you my answer in advance,

"I'm sorry!!"

About the Creator

HIRO MASHIMA was born May 3, 1977, in Nagano Prefecture. His series *Rave Master* has made him one of the most popular manga artists in America. *Fairy Tail*, currently being serialized in *Weekly Shonen Magazine*, is his latest creation.

Translation Notes

Japanese is a tricky language for most Westerners, and translation is often more art than science. For your edification and reading pleasure, here are notes on some of the places where we could have gone in a different direction in our translation of the work, or where a Japanese cultural reference is used.

Dream of a Butterfly, page 783

The story that Mashima-sensei notes in his Afterword is a retelling of a story told in a book by the ancient Chinese philosopher Zhuangzi (also known as Chuang Tzu, 369–286 BC), who is considered to be one of the two greatest philosophers of Daoism. While Confucianism was based on self-sacrifice and conformity, the Daoism of Zhuangzi was the opposite, based on individual freedoms and escape from society and its pressures. Zhuangzi encouraged spontaneous behavior and thought, since he believed that such was a reaction to reality as it truly is, rising above societal and linguistic limitations.

Smashing Watermelons on the Beach, page 790

This is a traditional summer game for children in Japan. Like piñata games, the player is blindfolded and given a stick. Unlike a piñata, the watermelon is left sitting on the sand (or on a blanket on the sand) so Natsu's direction of "up" would make no sense. Once the watermelon is smashed, all the children divide up the watermelon pieces and eat it.

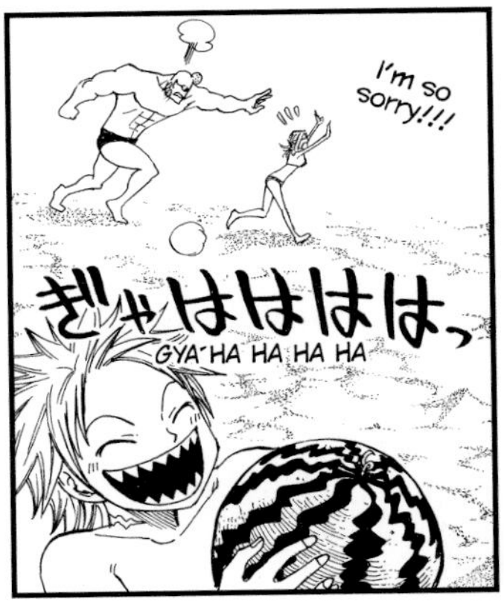
I'm so sorry!!!
ぎゃはははは
GYA-HA HA HA HA

Dandy, page 800

There are many words that make their way from English into Japanese and get their meanings changed along the way. The word "dandy" doesn't mean the same in Japanese as its present English definition of a fop or a shallow, fashion-obsessed man. One Japanese dictionary starts off its definition with "a real gentleman." That is probably what Mashima-sensei was thinking when he wrote Wally's character. Since Wally got the word from the lacrima crystal movie Dandy Hard, I couldn't use "gentleman" or any other English word that might more closely indicate the Japanese meaning.

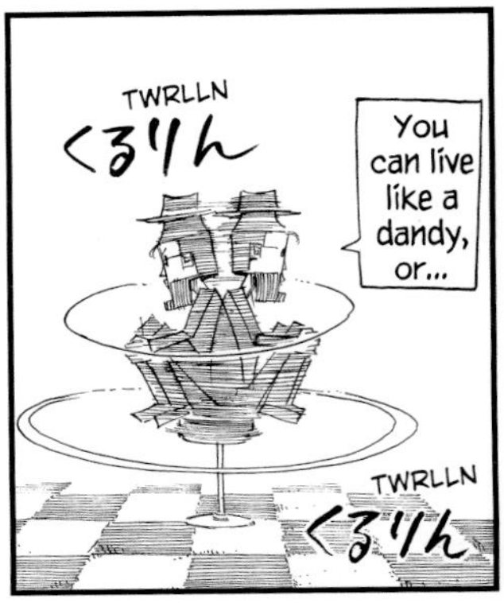
TWRLLN
くるりん
You can live like a dandy, or...
TWRLLN
くるりん

Get it?, page 803

This is an approximation rather than a translation. In Japanese, Wally uses the sentence ending particle ze at the end of most of his sentences. The way Wally uses the particle is the same way men use it when they are trying to act tough — like in the yakuza or in a street gang. The "get it" in English sounds a little like the tough character that Wally wants to be.

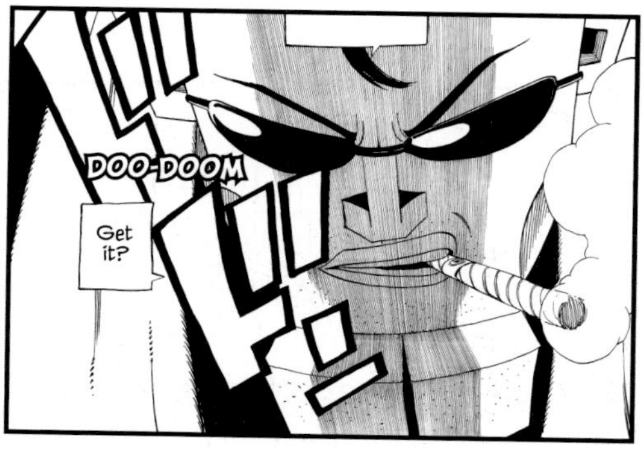
DOO-DOOM
Get it?

Big Sis, page 806

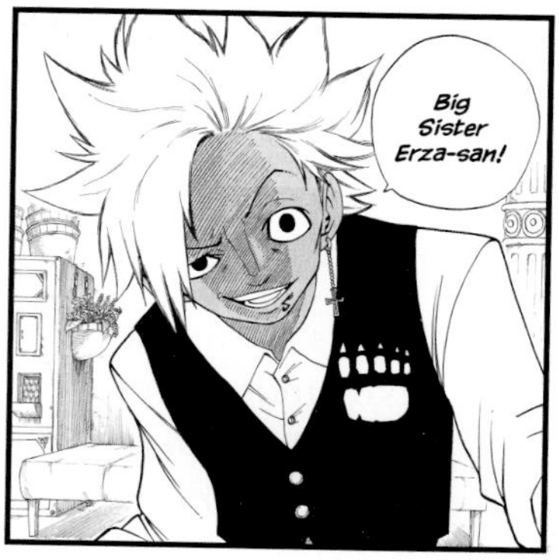
Big Sister Erza-san!

Readers of the manga *School Rumble* will be familiar with the Japanese honorific *nee-san* (or *Onee-san*), which is used by younger siblings when referring to their older sister. However, this honorific can also be used by people who are unrelated to the "big sister," such as children talking to an older girl or shop clerks who want to address a young lady but don't know her name. In *School Rumble*, the honorific appears all of the time. But here, only Shô uses it, so I decided to translate it rather than leave the honorific in Japanese.

Are you pumped up?, page 816

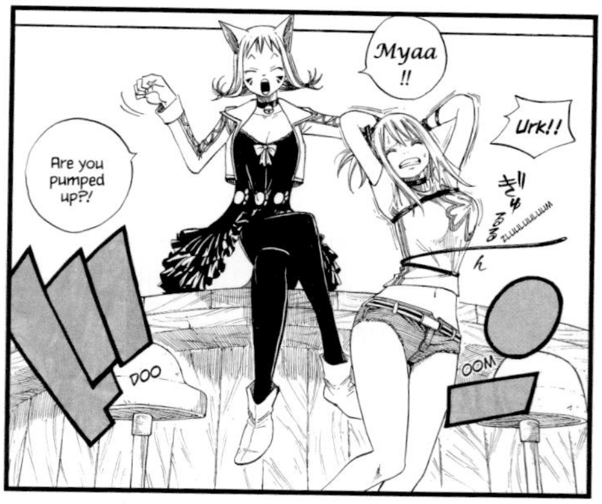
Myaa !!
Urk!!
Are you pumped up?!
DOO
OOM

This was kind of difficult to translate. This is a slightly unusual phrase in Japanese that Millianna used that means about the same thing as "Are you at top energy?" But it's also similar to the standard Japanese question, *O-genki desu ka*, which basically means, "How are you?" I had to come up with a distinctive phrase that could be Millianna's catchphrase without losing the meaning of the original. "Are you pumped up?" seemed like a good compromise.

-ebi, page 882

As explained in the notes for volume 2, some manga and anime characters end their sentences with small, meaningless syllables that are distinctive to the character. In Japanese children's stories, crabs usually end their sentences with *-kani* (*kani* means "crab" in Japanese). But although Cancer is a crab, he ends his sentences with *-ebi* (*ebi* means "shrimp" in Japanese). It was a little joke in volume 2, but it has also become a part of Cancer's character.

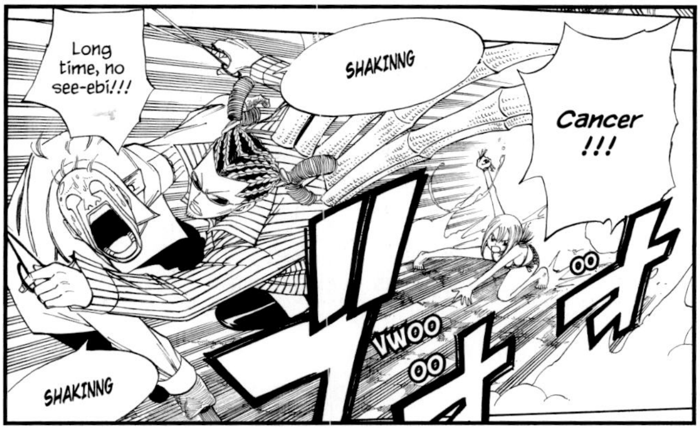
Cancer !!!
SHAKINNG
Long time, no see-ebi!!!
VWOOOOOO
SHAKINNG

Fairy Tail: Master's Edition 2 is a work of fiction. Names, characters, places, and incidents are the products of the author's imagination or are used fictitiously. Any resemblance to actual events, locales, or persons, living or dead, is entirely coincidental.

A Kodansha Comics Trade Paperback Original

Fairy Tail: Master's Edition 2 copyright © 2007-2008 Hiro Mashima
English translation copyright © 2009-2016 Hiro Mashima

All rights reserved.

Published in the United States by Kodansha Comics, an imprint of Kodansha USA Publishing, LLC, New York.

Publication rights for this English edition arranged through Kodansha Ltd., Tokyo.

First published in Japan in 2007-2008 by Kodansha Ltd., Tokyo as *Fairy Tail*, volumes 6-10.

ISBN 978-1-63236-277-3

Printed in the United States of America.

www.kodanshacomics.com

9 8 7 6 5 4 3 2 1
Translation and adaptation: William Flanagan
Lettering: North Market Street Graphics
Layout and additional lettering: Maggie Vicknair and Belynda Ungurath
Editing: David Yoo and Molly Brenan

Cover design by Phil Balsman